SUBSTANCE ABUSE

A Comprehensive Textbook

Third Edition

SUBSTANCE ABUSE
A Comprehensive Textbook

Third Edition

Editors

Joyce H. Lowinson, M.D.
Professor Emeritus of Psychiatry
Albert Einstein College of Medicine of Yeshiva University
Adjunct Faculty The Rockefeller University
New York, New York

Pedro Ruiz, M.D.
Professor and Vice Chair for Clinical Affairs
Department of Psychiatry and Behavioral Sciences
The University of Texas, Houston Health Science Center
Houston, Texas

Robert B. Millman, M.D.
Saul P. Steinberg Distinguished Professor of Psychiatry and Public Health
Cornell University Medical College
Director, Division of Substance Abuse Services
New York Hospital-Payne Whitney Psychiatry Clinic
New York, New York

John G. Langrod, Ph.D., A.C.S.W.
Director of Admissions and Evaluation
Division of Substance Abuse
Albert Einstein College of Medicine of Yeshiva University
Bronx, New York

Williams & Wilkins
A WAVERLY COMPANY

BALTIMORE • PHILADELPHIA • LONDON • PARIS • BANGKOK
BUENOS AIRES • HONG KONG • MUNICH • SYDNEY • TOKYO • WROCLAW

Managing Editor: Kathleen Courtney Millet
Production Coordinator: Carol Eckhart
Copy Editors: Bonnie Montgomery and Bill Cady
Illustration Planner: Ray Lowman
Cover Design: Silverchair Science & Communications, Inc.
Typesetter: Peirce Graphic Services
Printer and Binder: R. R. Donnelley

Copyright © 1997 Williams & Wilkins

351 West Camden Street
Baltimore, Maryland 21201–2436 USA

Rose Tree Corporate Center
1400 North Providence Road
Building II, Suite 5025
Media, Pennsylvania 19063–2043 USA

Accurate indications, adverse reactions and dosage schedules for drugs are provided in this book, but it is possible that they may change. The reader is urged to review the package information data of the manufacturers of the medications mentioned.

Printed in the United States of America

First Edition, 1981; Second Edition, 1992

Library of Congress Cataloging-in-Publication Data

Substance abuse : a comprehensive textbook / editors, Joyce H.
  Lowinson ... [et al.].—3rd ed.
        p. cm.
    Includes bibliographical references and index.
    ISBN 0–683–18179–3
    1. Substance abuse. 2. Substance abuse—Treatment. 3. Substance
  abuse—Social aspects. 4. Substance abuse—United States.
  I. Lowinson, Joyce H.
    [DNLM: 1. Substance Abuse. WM 270 S941 1997]
  RC564.S826 1997
  362.29—dc20
  DNLM/DLC
  for Library of Congress   96–43039
                                                   CIP

The publishers have made every effort to trace the copyright holders for borrowed material. If they have inadvertently overlooked any, they will be pleased to make the necessary arrangements at the first opportunity.

To purchase additional copies of this book, call our customer service department at **(800) 638-0672** or fax orders to **(800) 447-8438.** For other book services, including chapter reprints and large quantity sales, ask for the Special Sales department.

Canadian customers should call **(800) 268-4178** or fax **(905) 470-6780.** For all other calls originating outside of the United States, please call **(410) 528-4223** or fax us at **(410) 528-8550.**

Visit Williams & Wilkins on the Internet: **http://www.wwilkins.com** or contact our customer service department at **custserv@wwilkins.com.** Williams & Wilkins customer service representatives are available from 8:30 am to 6:00 pm, EST, Monday through Friday, for telephone access.

97 98 99 00 01
1 2 3 4 5 6 7 8 9 10

DEDICATION

We wish to dedicate this book to the memory of Dr. Marie Nyswander, whose contributions to the field of substance abuse are legendary, as well as to substance abusers themselves, who were the inspiration for Dr. Nyswander's work. We hope that they will benefit from the research, educational, and service advances offered by this book.

FOREWORD

When Dr. Joyce Lowinson asked me to contribute a foreword to the latest edition of *Substance Abuse: A Comprehensive Textbook,* I was pleased to accept. After all, this is a major resource for the substance abuse fields, covering, as it does, everything about alcohol and other drug abuse from history to politics, from biology to behavior, from research to practice. The editors and authors have done well in presenting a massive amount of material in a logical and readable format, and I welcome the opportunity to congratulate them.

While the information in *Substance Abuse: A Comprehensive Textbook* is valuable to the alcohol and other drug abuse fields, I believe that what this textbook *symbolizes* is equally valuable, and I will briefly touch on why here.

We in the National Institute on Alcohol Abuse and Alcoholism have just celebrated our 25th anniversary. As part of the year-long celebration, we have had time to reflect upon the changes in the alcohol field since our creation in 1970. From a field born of and existing outside science and medicine, we have progressed to one where researchers work at the cutting edge of science to produce new knowledge. From a time when counselors were credentialed by their own recovery experience, we have progressed to a time where standards of training for clinicians and for clinical care are the norm. We have progressed from a time when treatment staff worked by the "seat of their pants" to help their patients, where mainstream medicine could or would not, to a time where scientifically validated screening, assessment, and diagnostic tools are standard. We have made progress in training those who provide alcoholism services; the one- or two-hour-long lectures typically found in medical schools, schools of nursing, and other health professions training programs are giving way to the increasing availability of comprehensive training in the addictions. Most importantly, we have made progress toward erasing the stigma of alcoholism. What, then, does *Substance Abuse: A Comprehensive Textbook* symbolize? It symbolizes progress. It symbolizes the progress that the addictions fields have made toward becoming a part of science and medicine. It symbolizes the progress that has been made in prevention and in practice. And it symbolizes the very real progress that has been made toward acceptance of the addictions as legitimate health concerns.

This progress was made neither quickly nor easily. Twenty-five years ago, a textbook on addictions might have been met at best with skepticism, at worst with outright derision. In the alcohol field, this response was as prominent in the alcohol treatment community as it was in the scientific and medical communities. On the one hand, alcoholism and other alcohol-related problems were considered problems of character or of criminal behavior. Alcoholism could be "cured" by helping individuals to see the "error" of their ways or by punishing those who could not stop drinking. Alcoholism, thus, was deemed a problem for religion or law enforcement, not science and medicine. The irony, of course, is that medicine, at least, was dealing with the *consequences* of alcohol abuse and alcoholism, such as liver disease, all along. If a cause other than alcoholism of so major an illness had been identified, science would have embraced the challenge of finding a "cure," and medicine would have demanded more effective ways to help its patients. This is happening now, but it took a long time to get to this place where other major illnesses always have lived. National and international societies for alcohol-related research now exist, and there is a national medical society for addiction medicine. Within the ranks of these organizations are many outstanding scientists and clinicians recognized for their contributions to medical science whose research is reflected in this textbook.

Conversely, the early alcohol treatment community was composed mainly of individuals who had themselves recovered, for the most part, through Alcoholics Anonymous (AA). I have often said, and I think it is important enough to bear repeating, that it is as though when Bill W. wrote the AA Big Book in 1935, nothing new was needed, certainly not a textbook. The feeling was prominent that only those who had recovered could provide alcoholism treatment to active alcoholics. An individual's own recovery, thus, served as the "textbook" for alcohol treatment providers. Medicine had already failed to respond and was mistrusted. Because treatment was a "solved problem," science was unnecessary. The alcoholism treatment field was only concerned with how to get individuals into treatment and how to pay for it. Yet Bill W. himself understood that AA is a part of a larger whole aimed at helping alcoholics to recover; it was never intended to be all there ever was. In an address before the New York State Medical Society in 1958, he said:

> We also realize that the discoveries of the psychiatrists and the biochemists have vast implications for us alcoholics. Indeed these discoveries are today far more than implications. Your president and other pioneers in and outside your society have been achieving notable results for a long time, many of their patients have made good recoveries without any AA at all. It should here be noted that some of the recovery methods employed outside AA are quite in contradiction to AA principles and practice. Nevertheless, we of AA ought to applaud the fact that certain of these efforts are meeting with increasing success. . . . Therefore I would like to make a pledge to the whole medical fraternity that AA will always stand ready to cooperate, that AA will never trespass upon medicine, that our members who feel the call will increasingly help in those great enterprises of education, rehabilitation and research which are now going forward with such great promise.

Now, many years later, there has finally begun a willingness by the alcohol treatment community to examine the effectiveness of alcoholism treatment. A good example of this change comes from AA itself, which in the late 1980s began publishing triennial worldwide surveys showing, among other things, attrition in attendance at AA meetings after initial contact. Twenty years ago such self-analysis would have been unthinkable. I believe that the alcohol treatment field also is beginning to recognize the need for increased attention to research. This recognition stems, in part, from demands by managed care organizations, other third-party insurers, state funding agencies, and by the United States Congress for the same type of safety and efficacy evidence for alcoholism required for all other illnesses. We may believe we know what works, but it is the evidence of efficacy that will bring financial and patient support.

This is where we have been and to where we have progressed as a field. I believe that we are at the end of stigma within science, within medicine, and the stigma placed on one part of the alcoholism field by another. Even more important, we are at the beginning of an exciting period of discovery about the biological and behavioral origins of alcoholism, spurred in large part by several key conceptual advances in alcoholism research and practice.

One such advance has been the clear demonstration that some of the vulnerability to alcoholism is inherited. This conceptual advance has led to an explosion in human and animal genetic work that promises to lead to the development of new treatments and better focussed prevention efforts for those individuals identified as most vulnerable to developing alcohol dependence. A second conceptual advance is the application of neuroscience to understanding drinking and the phenomenon of addiction. This has led to the development, among other things, of new pharmacotherapies for alcoholism treatment. The acceptance of the study of "mental processes" in alcohol action may be considered a third advance in how we think about alcohol addiction. Certain experiences with alcohol, some of which can only be discovered by asking about mental processes, affect the reaction to alcohol. This understanding has led to two areas of science that are very important: the issue of expectancies, where some of the actions of alcohol are produced because they are expected, not because of the pharmacology of the drug itself; and the fundamental issue of craving, i.e., whether craving exists intrinsically or whether it is dependent on cues from the environment. Yet another advance has been in our understanding of how alcohol damages organs. This includes new understanding of the impact of repeated withdrawal on brain function, increased understanding of the mechanisms involved in alcoholic liver damage, and how alcohol damages the fetus. We also have a much better understanding of alcohol's protective effects with respect to coronary artery disease and osteoporosis in postmenopausal women.

A fifth advance, and one that I believe has done much to establish the credibility of alcoholism treatment within the medical establishment, has been the application of all the techniques of the classic clinical trial, i.e., randomization, appropriate controls, blinding, power calculations, defined and objectively measured outcomes, to alcoholism therapies. Related to this has been the development of effective research strategies to test the effectiveness of various patient/treatment matching strategies. A final but no less important advance has been the demonstration that doing scientifically rigorous research in alcohol prevention is possible. The findings from this type of research, which includes research on social and regulatory policies, has been useful in public policy formulation. For example, a federal law designed to raise the minimum drinking age to 21 in all states was based, in part, on research that demonstrated that this change would save lives.

Where do we go from here? Given these tremendous strides in understanding both the biology and behavior of alcoholism and other addictions, I believe that science will continue to produce new knowledge that will not only help us to understand alcohol and other drug abuse, but also how the brain and body work together to prevent or increase the risk for disease. With growing public advocacy of policies aimed at decreasing the consequences of alcohol and other drug abuse, I am hopeful that the tenuous links thus far made between science and public policy development will be strengthened. Our treatment programs, I believe, will survive the transition to managed care and other forms of health care reform. Why? Because we will have the same science-based evidentiary support for the efficacy of alcoholism and drug abuse treatment as all other fields of medicine, and because we will know much more about how to prevent alcohol and other drug-related problems—what works, with whom, under what circumstances, and at what cost. In this era of "downsizing," this type of prevention evidence will allow us to decide rationally about where to spend our resources most effectively.

Compiling an informative, science-based, and comprehensive text is a formidable undertaking in any subject and, given the many complex health, social, political, and economic interactions that exist in the addictions fields, makes the task much more difficult. The editors and authors of the third edition of *Substance Abuse: A Comprehensive Textbook* most certainly deserve our congratulations and our thanks for their efforts.

Enoch Gordis, M.D.
Director
National Institute on Alcohol Abuse and Alcoholism
National Institutes of Health

FOREWORD

Scientific advances over the past two decades have revolutionized our understanding of substance abuse and addiction. These advances have dramatic implications for how practitioners prevent and treat these disorders. Many of the contributors to the world's contemporary knowledge base in the substance abuse field are authors in this textbook. Nowhere else will you find such comprehensive and detailed coverage from the researchers, clinicians, policymakers, and administrators who are actually working in this evolving field. The reader is presented, from start to finish, with the most current and authoritative presentations of basic and applied knowledge in research, prevention, education, and treatment.

In part because of the work of many of these authors, we now know that drug abuse is a preventable behavior and that drug addiction is, fundamentally, a treatable, chronic, relapsing disease of the brain. We also now have tremendously detailed knowledge of what drugs actually do to an individual's brain and behavior. For example, scientists have identified and cloned receptors in the brain for every major drug of abuse. They have identified the cellular sites where drugs like cocaine, marihuana, and opiates bind to the brain. In the case of cocaine, they have recognized the dopamine reuptake transporter as a major site of action. Researchers have discovered not only specific brain circuits involved in drug experiences, like euphoria, but the processes of addiction and drug withdrawal as well. Research also shows that addiction occurs as a result of the prolonged effects of abusable drugs on the brain—and that addiction actually results in a changed brain.

As the research (and the book) attests, it is important that addiction not be seen simply as a brain disease. It is a special class of brain disease, one that is expressed in behavioral ways and within a social context. It is the quintessential biobehavioral disorder—a brain disease with embedded behavioral and social context aspects. For example, the environmental cues, or conditioning factors, discussed in Section II, that are associated with drug use actually become, in some sense, a part of the addiction. Even for successfully treated addicts, mere exposure to cues associated with drug use can trigger tremendous craving and relapse to drug use, even after long periods of abstinence. In fact, clinical research has actually "captured" drug craving or the "memory of drugs" in positron emission tomography (PET) scans of addicts while they are craving drugs. These findings have tremendous importance for developing treatment strategies, which must encompass mechanisms to enable the patient to deal with continued exposure to drug-related cues long after formal treatment is completed.

Prevention and treatment are two areas that are given significant attention in this textbook. Because of the vital strides made in understanding this disease, we are now able to increase the effectiveness of prevention and treatment strategies.

Understanding what determines an individual's vulnerability and susceptibility to substance abuse is crucial to effective preventive intervention. There is no single factor that determines whether a person might abuse a sub-

stance; instead, substance abuse develops from the interaction of complex biological, psychological, and social/environmental determinants. Researchers have identified many of the risk factors that are typically associated with those who develop substance abuse problems, including the community and environment, peer influences, lack of parental involvement, and drug availability. Although these risk factors are not necessarily predicative for a particular individual, they are useful in defining levels of risk for initial drug use. Researchers have also identified many of the protective or resilience factors, such as parental involvement in the life of a child, that typically reduce the chance of an individual becoming a substance abuser. By combining advances in understanding both risk and protective factors, we are now able to develop more effective prevention strategies. Prevention research has shown that comprehensive prevention programs that involve the family, schools, communities, and the media are effective in reducing drug abuse.

In addition to identifying risk and protective factors to be used in prevention strategies, we now have research that shows that addiction is eminently treatable. As the chapters in Section VI illustrate, a wide variety of efficacious treatment approaches exist. Appropriate treatment varies depending on the individual, but may be outpatient or inpatient; short-term or long-term; behavioral or pharmacological or a combination of both. Addiction treatment has been shown to be effective in reducing drug use and HIV infection, diminishing the health and social costs that result from addiction, and decreasing criminal behavior. The greatest difficulty in fully realizing the benefits of treatment research has been and continues to be a lack of public commitment to the treatment of addicted individuals. One of the objectives that I am personally committed to achieving, and am certain this book will be instrumental in helping to accomplish, is changing the public's perception of the nature of addiction and removing the stigma associated with this disease. A "great disconnect" exists between the public's perception of substance abuse and addiction and the scientific facts. When addiction is perceived as a treatable disease rather than only as a moral or legal problem, access to, and the effectiveness of, available treatments will improve, and new treatments will be incorporated quickly into the health care system.

Although scientific advances have brought us a long way in our understanding of and approaches to substance abuse and addiction, we still have a lengthy journey ahead in finding solutions to this complex problem. There will be no magic bullet that is going to make substance abuse and addiction go away, but as the information in this book conveys, there is great cause for hope that we will continue to make progress in dealing with this, the most complex and compelling issue facing modern day society.

Alan I. Leshner, Ph.D.
Director
National Institute on Drug Abuse
National Institutes of Health

Preface to the Third Edition

The third edition of *Substance Abuse: A Comprehensive Textbook* is a response to society's growing recognition of the prevalence of alcohol and drug use, abuse, and dependence and of their profound impact not only on people's health but on every aspect of life. This volume also draws on and makes available to workers the latest information resulting from the remarkable growth of basic and applied research and clinical care in the areas of epidemiology, pharmacology, treatment, policy, and other phenomena related to substance abuse. The exponential increase in knowledge and expertise required not only of health professionals, but of social service, law enforcement, judicial, legal, and correctional personnel, as well as of economists, ethicists, and government and private administrative staff has been a determining factor with the organization of this volume.

The principal objective for this edition is quite ambitious. As with the previous editions, our goal is to provide the most authoritative and comprehensive resource on the subject of substance abuse and related areas. The book can serve as the definitive text for students in all professional disciplines who are entering their chosen fields, as well as a source of information for scientists and clinicians working on drug, alcohol, and other addictions. The book is useful to other health care professionals, particularly those involved in primary care, and to workers in related fields who require an overview of particular areas or detailed discussions of specific scientific, clinical, or administrative subjects. Because scientists must know the questions that clinicians are asking and policymakers must understand how treatments work, this volume translates data across disciplines to facilitate research, clinical care, and policy development.

This textbook provides state-of-the-art presentations by experts in their respective areas. For instance, chapters on the clinical evaluation of patients with alcohol and substance abuse disorders in all their diversity offer guidelines for optimal patient care and for developing programs of excellence.

The section on treating the acute sequelae of various drugs, as well as the treatment of various withdrawal symptoms, has been much expanded. Discussions of basic scientific and clinical research developments (which become clinically relevant at an ever-increasing rate) are now integral parts of the sections on pharmacology and on treatment of the various substance abuse syndromes.

Because they continue to be unique and valuable, we have retained the sections on sociology, evaluation, and treatment of particular populations. We have added much new information on the relation of psychopathology to substance abuse as well as psychiatric diagnoses of, and most effective methods and programs for treating, these patients with dual diagnoses.

New chapters include studies of other addictive behaviors, such as gambling, sex, and cults. Because some characteristics of these behaviors are similar to behaviors of patients with substance abuse and dependency problems, addictive behaviors such as gambling may be associated with the use of drugs and alcohol.

In view of the increased use of cognitive therapies to treat substance abuse and related behaviors, we have added a chapter on the history, indications, and detailed methodologies of these therapies. Expanded sections have been developed on the subject of drug policy, a critical factor in the future of substance abuse research and treatment. Issues such as demand and supply reduction, legalization, decriminalization, and harm reduction are covered in considerable detail.

The complexion of the health care system has changed remarkably in recent years. In the name of cost containment, managed care companies using capitation payment methods and health maintenance organizations are forcing those involved in the substance abuse and psychiatric treatment system to accept significant change. We have included in this edition separate chapters on insurance and managed care, and much information in many other sections deals with the health care insurance system, its historical antecedents, and likely future developments and consequences. The health care system, in general, and behavioral health care, in particular, are facing serious restrictions in their funding and practices. How can workers in these systems continue to serve people of low and middle socioeconomic levels who have serious substance abuse problems and require long-term, highly intensive care?

Specific treatment approaches useful in detoxification, attainment and maintenance of abstinence, relapse-prevention techniques, and psychotherapeutic and pharmacotherapeutic regimens are again described in considerable detail in this volume. Many therapists and treatment programs have become more sophisticated, more effective, and perhaps more humane than in the past. Some programs zealously advance and protect their therapeutic regimens, but often disparage methods based on other etiological models. Important therapeutic modalities do not necessarily share identical objectives. For example, rehabilitation programs based on a 12-step system require abstinence as their main objective; what do proponents of these programs think about maintenance programs using methadone, LAAM, buprenorphine, or naltrexone, programs that value function over abstinence and that espouse harm reduction techniques and objectives of improved health and well-being? It is startling and humbling to recall that few of these programs are over 30 years old, and thus barely out of their adolescence.

Each patient or client develops problems in unique ways and forms a unique relation to the substance of choice. Common sense dictates that treatment must respond to the needs of each individual. Therapists must try to learn as much as possible about patients and their problems to match them to the most effective, least expensive treatments or to develop new, more effective treatments that integrate several strategies.

Whenever possible, chapters dealing with treatment modalities provide process and outcome data designed to improve workers' evaluative and referral capabilities. New and alternative programs, now developing, often combine elements of conventional modalities into interesting hybrids. These new programs need room to change and expand. Referral agents are often motivated to send patients to programs that reflect their own belief systems, and therapists often treat patients according to their own philosophies. We hope that this volume facilitates the continuing efforts to develop more rational treatment approaches.

Despite our expectations, the size of this volume remains similar to that of its predecessor. We have endeavored to reduce redundancy and to present information in an understandable yet disciplined and crisp style. We trust that we have succeeded in this endeavor well without reducing the richness of detail, language, and graphics.

We are deeply grateful to the many distinguished contributors who made this volume possible. Our charge to them was quite rigorous, and we believe that they have more than satisfied our expectations. We hope that we have met the expectations of readers as well.

Joyce H. Lowinson, M.D.
Pedro Ruiz, M.D.
Robert B. Millman, M.D.
John G. Langrod, Ph.D.

ACKNOWLEDGMENTS

We want to express a special note of gratitude to our managing editor, Katey Millet. Gentle, but firm and determined, she contributed to the conceptualization and implementation of this vastly expanded edition. Bonnie Montgomery, project editor, did an outstanding job during the critical phase of the production process. Above all, we wish to express our deep appreciation of the efforts made by our contributors to meet our deadline during an era when the pressures on everyone of them exceeded expectations.

CONTRIBUTORS

Robert M. Anthenelli, M.D.
Associate Professor of Psychiatry and Neuroscience
University of Cincinnati College of Medicine (UCCOM)
Director, Substance Dependence Programs
UCCOM and Cincinnati Veterans Administration Medical Center
Cincinnati, Ohio

Gerard M. Armstrong
Deputy Director, Managed Care, Health and Revenue Services
N.Y.S. Office of Alcoholism and Substance Abuse Services
New York, New York

James B. Bakalar, J.D.
Lecturer in Law
Department of Psychiatry
Harvard Medical School
Boston, Massachusetts

Steven L. Batki, M.D.
Clinical Professor of Psychiatry
University of California, San Francisco School of Medicine
Director, Division of Substance Abuse and Addiction Medicine
Department of Psychiatry
San Francisco General Hospital
San Francisco, California

Ann Bordwine Beeder, M.D.
Departments of Public Health and Psychiatry
Cornell University Medical College
New York, New York

Sheila B. Blume, M.D., FASAM
Medical Director, Alcoholism, Chemical Dependency and Compulsive Gambling Programs
South Oaks Hospital
Director, South Oaks Institute of Alcoholism and Addictive Behavior Studies
Amityville, New York
Clinical Professor of Psychiatry
State University of New York at Stony Brook
Stony Brook, New York

Elizabeth M. Botvin, M.D.
Research Associate, Department of Public Health
Cornell University Medical College
New York, New York

Gilbert J. Botvin, Ph.D.
Professor and Director
Institute for Prevention Research
Cornell University Medical College
New York, New York

Nancy M. Brehm, Ph.D.
Licensed Psychologist
Boston, Massachusetts

Vincent Brewington, M.A.
Deputy Director
Substance Abuse Division
Lincoln Hospital
Bronx, New York

Margaret K. Brooks, J.D.
Consultant, New Perspectives
Montclair, New Jersey

Lawrence S. Brown, Jr., M.D., M.P.H., FASAM
Senior Vice President, Division of Medical Services, Evaluation, and Research
Addiction Research and Treatment Corporation
Department of Medicine
Harlem Hospital
Columbia University College of Physicians and Surgeons
New York, New York

Betty J. Buchan, M.S., DFTCB
Department of Epidemiology and Biostatistics
University of South Florida College of Public Health
Tampa, Florida

Milton Earl Burglass, M.D., M.P.H., M.Div., M.S., CAS, FAAFP, FASAM
Clinical and Research Faculty
Zinberg Center for Addiction Studies
Harvard Medical School
Cambridge, Massachusetts

Robert P. Cabaj, M.D.
Medical Director, Mental Health Services
San Mateo County, California
Associate Professor in Clinical Psychiatry
University of California, San Francisco School of Medicine
San Francisco, California

John S. Cacciola, Ph.D.
Research Psychologist
Veterans Administration Medical Center
Philadelphia, Pennsylvania

Joseph A. Califano, Jr.
President
National Center on Addiction and Substance Abuse
New York, New York

Susie A. Carleton, Ph.N.
El Cerito, California

Kathleen M. Carroll, Ph.D.
Associate Professor of Psychiatry
Division of Substance Abuse
Yale University School of Medicine
New Haven, Connecticut

Grace Chang, M.D., M.P.H.
Assistant Professor of Psychiatry
Harvard Medical School
Brigham and Women's Hospital
Boston, Massachusetts

John N. Chappel, M.D.
Professor of Psychiatry
University of Nevada School of Medicine
Medical Director, Alcohol and Drug Programs
West Hills Hospital
Reno, Nevada

James R. Christopher, CAS
Founder and Executive Director
SOS/Save Our Selves/Secular Organizations for Sobriety
Los Angeles, California

Domenic A. Ciraulo, M.D.
Professor of Psychiatry and Chairman, Division of Psychiatry
Boston University School of Medicine
Chief, Psychiatry Service
Veterans Administration Medical Center, Outpatient Clinics
Boston, Massachusetts

Patricia D. Culliton, M.A., LAc
Director, Alternative Medicine
Department of Medicine
Hennepin County Medical Center
Minneapolis, Minnesota

Dennis C. Daley, M.S.W.
Assistant Professor of Psychiatry
Director, Center for Psychiatric and Chemical Dependency Services
University of Pittsburgh School of Medicine
Pittsburgh, Pennsylvania

David A. Deitch, Ph.D.
Clinical Professor of Psychiatry
University of California, San Diego
Director of the California Addiction Technology Transfer Center
San Diego, California

John C. Demers
National Center on Addiction and Substance Abuse
New York, New York

Don C. Des Jarlais, Ph.D.
Professor of Epidemiology and Community Medicine
Albert Einstein College of Medicine of Yeshiva University
Director of Research, Chemical Dependency Institute
Beth Israel Medical Center
New York, New York

Charles J. Devlin
Vice President
Daytop Village, Inc.
New York, New York

Vincent P. Dole, M.D.
Professor and Senior Physician, Emeritus
Rockefeller University
New York, New York

Ernest Drucker, Ph.D.
Professor of Epidemiology and Social Medicine
Albert Einstein College of Medicine of Yeshiva University
Director, Division of Community Health
Montefiore Medical Center
Bronx, New York
Senior Fellow, The Lindesmith Center
New York, New York

Linda Dusenbury, Ph.D.
Clinical Associate Professor of Public Health
Cornell University Medical College
New York, New York

Everett H. Ellinwood, Jr., M.D.
Professor of Psychiatry and Pharmacology
Duke University Medical Center
Durham, North Carolina

Paul F. Engelhart, M.A., M.S.
Director of Public Affairs and Development
Catholic Charities
Diocese of Rockville Centre
Hicksville, New York

Mathea Falco, J.D.
President
Drug Strategies
Washington, D.C.

Francisco Fernandez, M.D.
Associate Professor
Department of Psychiatry and Behavioral Sciences
Baylor College of Medicine
Houston, Texas

Loretta P. Finnegan, M.D.
Director, Women's Health Initiative
National Institutes of Health
Bethesda, Maryland

Samuel R. Friedman, Ph.D.
National Development and Research Institute, Inc.
New York, New York

Paul J. Fudala, Ph.D.
Assistant Professor of Pharmacology in Psychiatry
University of Pennsylvania School of Medicine
Clinical Toxicologist
Department of Psychiatry/Medical Research
Department of Veterans Administration Medical Center
Philadelphia, Pennsylvania

William F. Gabrielli, Jr., M.D., Ph.D.
Professor and Acting Chairman
Department of Psychiatry
University of Kansas School of Medicine
Kansas City, Kansas

Marc Galanter, M.D., FASAM
Professor of Psychiatry
New York University School of Medicine
New York, New York

Karl V. Gallegos, M.D.
Private Practice, Addiction Medicine
Atlanta, Georgia

Gantt P. Galloway, Pharm.D.
Assistant Professor of Clinical Pharmacy
University of California
Chief of Pharmacologic Research
Haight Ashbury Free Clinics, Inc.
San Francisco, California
Director of Research, New Leaf Treatment Center
Concord, California
Research Pharmacist, MPI Treatment Services
Summit Medical Center
Oakland, California

Steven R. Gambert, M.D.
Professor of Medicine
Associate Dean for Academic Programs
New York Medical College
Valhalla, New York

Eliot L. Gardner, Ph.D.
Professor of Psychiatry and Neuroscience
Director, Laboratory of Behavioral Neuropharmacology
Director, Division of Basic Research
Department of Psychiatry
Albert Einstein College of Medicine of Yeshiva University
Bronx, New York

Anne Geller, M.D.
Associate Professor of Clinical Medicine
Columbia University College Physicians and Surgeons
Chief, Smithers Center
St. Luke's/Roosevelt Hospital
New York, New York

Jane Glick, M.S.S.W., C.S.W.
The Presbyterian Hospital in the City of New York
New York, New York

Mark S. Gold, M.D.
Professor of Neuroscience, Psychiatry, and Community Health and
Family Medicine
University of Florida Brain Institute
University of Florida College of Medicine
Gainesville, Florida

Aviel Goodman, M.D.
Director
Minnesota Institute of Psychiatry
St. Paul, Minnesota

Carolyn Goodman, Ed.D.
Assistant Clinical Professor Emeritus
Albert Einstein College of Medicine of Yeshiva University
Founder and Director
PACE (Patient and Child Education)
Bronx Psychiatric Center
Bronx, New York

Donald W. Goodwin, M.D.
Distinguished University Professor
Department of Psychiatry
University of Kansas School of Medicine
Kansas City, Kansas

John F. Greden, M.D.
Professor and Chair of Psychiatry
Research Scientist, Mental Health Research Institute
University of Michigan
Ann Arbor, Michigan

Robert A. Greenstein, M.D.
Associate Professor of Psychiatry
University of Pennsylvania School of Medicine
Associate Chief, Behavioral Health
Philadelphia Veterans Administration Medical Center
Philadelphia, Pennsylvania

Lester Grinspoon, M.D.
Associate Professor of Psychiatry
Harvard Medical School
Boston, Massachusetts

Charles S. Grob, M.D.
Associate Professor of Psychiatry and Pediatrics
UCLA School of Medicine
Los Angeles, California
Director, Division of Child and Adolescent Psychiatry
Harbor-UCLA Medical Center
Torrance, California

Holly Hagan, M.P.H.
Epidemiologist
Seattle/King County Health Department
Seattle, Washington

James A. Halikas, M.D.
Professor of Psychiatry
Director of Addiction Medicine Postgraduate Training Program
Department of Psychiatry
University of Minnesota Medical School
Minneapolis, Minnesota

David A. Halperin, M.D., FAPA
Associate Clinical Professor of Psychiatry
Mt. Sinai School of Medicine
Adjunct Associate Professor of Psychology
John Jay College/CUNY
City University of New York
New York, New York

R. Adron Harris, Ph.D.
Department of Pharmacology
University of Colorado Health Sciences Center
Denver, Colorado

Harry W. Haverkos, M.D.
Intramural Research Program
National Institute on Drug Abuse
National Institutes of Health
Baltimore, Maryland

Anthony W. Heath, Ph.D.
Director, Division of Behavioral Sciences
McNeal Family Practice Residency Program
Berwyn, Illinois

Allen W. Heineman, Ph.D.
Professor of Physical Medicine and Rehabilitation
Northwestern University Medical School
Director, Rehabilitation Services Evaluation Unit
Rehabilitation Institute of Chicago
Chicago, Illinois

Sharon Hird, M.D.
Fellow
Departments of Public Health and Psychiatry
Division of Substance Abuse
The New York Hospital
Cornell University Medical College
New York, New York

Arthur T. Horvath, Ph.D.
Center for Cognitive Therapy
La Jolla, California
President, S.M.A.R.T. Recovery
Beachwood, Ohio

Robert L. Hubbard, Ph.D.
National Development and Research Institutes
Raleigh, North Carolina

Jerome H. Jaffe, M.D.
Adjunct Clinical Professor of Psychiatry
University of Maryland School of Medicine
Baltimore, Maryland

Murray E. Jarvik, M.D., Ph.D.
Chief, Psychopharmacology Unit
Veterans Administration Medical Center (Brentwood)
Los Angeles, California

Daniel C. Javitt, M.D., Ph.D.
Associate Professor of Psychiatry
New York University School of Medicine
Nathan Kline Institute for Psychiatric Research
Orangeburg, New York

Stanley John, M.D.
Acting Associate Director of Evaluation and Research
Addiction Research and Treatment Corp.
Brooklyn, New York

Bruce D. Johnson, Ph.D.
Director, Institute for Special Populations Research
National Development and Research Institutes, Inc.
New York, New York

Christopher R. Johnson, M.D.
Department of Psychiatry
Baylor College of Medicine
Houston, Texas

Steven Jonas, M.D., M.P.H.
Professor of Preventive Medicine
State University of New York at Stony Brook
School of Medicine
Stony Brook, New York

Herman Joseph, Ph.D.
Research Scientist
New York State Office of Alcohol and Drug Abuse
Adjunct Faculty
The Rockefeller University
New York, New York

Patti Juliana, M.S.W.
Director, Clinical Services
Division of Substance Abuse
Albert Einstein College of Medicine of Yeshiva University
Bronx, New York

Stephen R. Kandall, M.D.
Professor of Pediatrics
Albert Einstein College of Medicine of Yeshiva University
Bronx, New York
Chief, Division of Neonatology
Beth Israel Medical Center
New York, New York

Hannah Kates, M.A., CRC
Director, Vocational Education Services
National Association on Drug Abuse Problems
New York, New York

Edward J. Khantzian, M.D.
Clinical Professor of Psychiatry
Harvard Medical School at The Cambridge Hospital
Cambridge, Massachusetts
Associate Chief of Psychiatry
Hathorne Units
Tewksbury Hospital
Tewksbury, Massachusetts

Elizabeth T. Khuri, M.D.
Associate Professor of Clinical Public Health and Pediatrics
Cornell University Medical College
Clinical Director, Adolescent Development Program
New York Hospital
New York, New York

George R. King, Ph.D.
Assistant Research Professor
Duke University Medical Center
Durham, North Carolina

Herbert D. Kleber, M.D.
Professor of Psychiatry
College of Physicians and Surgeons, Columbia University
Director, Division on Substance Abuse
New York State Psychiatric Institute
Executive Vice President
National Center on Addiction and Substance Abuse
New York, New York

Clifford M. Knapp, Ph.D.
Assistant Professor of Psychiatry
Boston University School of Medicine

Clinical Director of Psychopharmacology
Medication Development Research Unit
Veterans Administration Medical Center Outpatient Clinic
Boston, Massachusetts

Thomas R. Kosten, M.D.
Professor of Psychiatry
Yale University School of Medicine
New Haven, Connecticut

Mary Jeanne Kreek, M.D.
Professor and Head
Laboratory on the Biology of Addictive Diseases
Senior Physician
The Rockefeller University Hospital
New York, New York

John G. Langrod, Ph.D., A.C.S.W.
Director of Admissions and Evaluation
Division of Substance Abuse
Albert Einstein College of Medicine of Yeshiva University
Bronx, New York

Mary Jo Larson, Ph.D., M.P.A.
Senior Research Associate
Institute for Health Policy
Heller School, Brandeis University
Waltham, Massachusetts

David C. Lewis, M.D.
Professor of Medicine and Community Health
Donald G. Millar Professor of Alcohol and Addiction Studies
Director, Center for Alcohol and Addiction Studies
Brown University
Providence, Rhode Island

Bruce S. Liese, Ph.D.
Associate Professor of Family Medicine and Psychiatry
University of Kansas Medical Center
Kansas City, Kansas
Director, Kansas City Center for Cognitive Therapy
Prairie Village, Kansas

Walter Ling, M.D.
Professor and Chief, Substance Abuse Program
University of California, Los Angeles, School of Medicine
Director, Los Angeles Addiction Treatment Research Center
Associate Chief of Psychiatry for Substance Abuse
West Los Angeles Veterans Administration Medical Center
Los Angeles, California

Joyce H. Lowinson, M.D.
Professor Emeritus of Psychiatry
Albert Einstein College of Medicine of Yeshiva University
Adjunct Faculty
The Rockefeller University
New York, New York

Nancy Mahon, Esq.
Director
Center on Crime, Communities and Culture
The Open Society Institute
New York, New York

Jorge Maldonado, M.D.
Clinical Fellow
Psychosomatic Medicine and Consultation Liaison Psychiatry
Baylor College of Medicine
Houston, Texas

Ira J. Marion, M.A.
Executive Director
Division of Substance Abuse
Albert Einstein College of Medicine of Yeshiva University
Bronx, New York

G. Alan Marlatt, Ph.D.
Professor of Psychology
Director, Addictive Behaviors Research Center
Department of Psychology
University of Washington
Seattle, Washington

Jennifer McNeely, B.A.
Senior Research Associate
The Lindesmith Center
Open Society Institute
New York, New York

Fernando L. Merino, M.D.
Fellow in Infectious Diseases
Department of Internal Medicine
Yale University School of Medicine
AIDS Program
Yale-New Haven Hospital
New Haven, Connecticut

Norman S. Miller, M.D.
Associate Professor of Psychiatry
Chief, Department of Addictions
University of Illinois at Chicago
College of Medicine
Chicago, Illinois

Robert B. Millman, M.D.
Saul P. Steinberg Distinguished Professor of Psychiatry and Public Health
Cornell University Medical College
Director, Division of Substance Abuse Services
New York Hospital-Payne Whitney Psychiatry Clinic
New York, New York

John P. Morgan, M.D.
Professor of Pharmacology
The City University of New York Medical School
The City College of New York
New York, New York

John Muffler, Ed.D.
Project Director, Center for Program Evaluation
National Development and Research Institutes, Inc.
New York, New York

David F. Musto, M.D.
Professor of Child Psychiatry and History of Medicine
Yale University School of Medicine
New Haven, Connecticut

Edgar P. Nace, M.D.
Clinical Professor of Psychiatry
University of Texas Southwestern Medical School
Medical Director
Charter Dallas Behavioral Health Systems
Dallas, Texas

Ethan Nadelmann, J.D., Ph.D.
Director, The Lindesmith Center
A Project of the Open Society Institute
New York, New York

Lisa M. Najavits, Ph.D.
Assistant Professor of Psychology
Harvard Medical School
Boston, Massachusetts
Associate Psychologist
Alcohol and Drug Treatment Center
McClean Hospital
Belmont, Massachusetts

Lorenz K. Y. Ng, M.D.
Washington, D.C.

David M. Novick, M.D., FACP
Associate Clinical Professor of Medicine
Wright State University School of Medicine
Dayton, Ohio
Active Staff, Department of Medicine
Kettering Medical Center
Kettering, Ohio
Adjunct Faculty
The Rockefeller University
New York, New York

Charles P. O'Brien, M.D., Ph.D.
Professor and Vice Chairman of Psychiatry
University of Pennsylvania
Veterans Administration Medical Center
Philadelphia, Pennsylvania

Monsignor William B. O'Brien
President and Founder
Daytop Village, Inc.
President and Founder
World Federation of Therapeutic Communities, Inc.
New York, New York

Denise Paone, Ph.D.
Assistant Professor of Epidemiology and Social Medicine
Albert Einstein College of Medicine of Yeshiva University
Bronx, New York
Assistant Director of Research
Chemical Dependency Institute
Beth Israel Medical Center
New York, New York

Richard Payne, M.D.
Professor of Medicine (Neurology)
Pain and Symptom Control Section
Department of Neuro-Oncology
M. D. Anderson Cancer Center
Houston, Texas

J. Thomas Payte, M.D.
Medical Director, Drug Dependence Associates
San Antonio, Texas

Robert N. Pechnick, Ph.D.
Associate Professor of Pharmacology
Department of Pharmacology and Experimental Therapeutics
Louisiana Sate University Medical Center
New Orleans, Louisiana

Russell E. Poland, Ph.D.
Professor of Psychiatry
Harbor-UCLA Medical Center
Torrance, California

Russell K. Portenoy, M.D.
Co-Chief, Pain and Palliative Care Service
Department of Neurology
Memorial Sloan-Kettering Cancer Center
New York, New York

Beny J. Primm, M.D.
Executive Director, Addiction Research and Treatment Corporation
Brooklyn, New York

Jonathan W. Reader, Ph.D.
Professor of Sociology
Drew University
Madison, New Jersey

Marc Reisinger, M.D.
Practicing Psychiatrist
Vice President, European Opiate Addiction
Treatment Association
Brussels, Belgium

James T. Richardson, Ph.D., J.D.
Professor of Sociology and Judicial Studies
Director, Master of Judicial Studies
University of Nevada, Reno
Reno, Nevada

Holly Robinson, M.A., CRC
Vocational Education Services
National Association on Drug Abuse Problems
New York, New York

Neil L. Rosenberg, M.D.
Associate Clinical Professor of Medicine
Division of Clinical Pharmacology and Toxicology
University of Colorado School of Medicine
Denver, Colorado

Marsha Rosenbaum, Ph.D.
Director
The Lindesmith Center
San Francisco, California

Bruce J. Rounsaville, M.D.
Professor of Psychiatry
Yale University School of Medicine
New Haven, Connecticut

Pedro Ruiz, M.D.
Professor and Vice Chair for Clinical Affairs
Department of Psychiatry and Behavioral Sciences
The University of Texas, Houston Health Science Center
Houston, Texas

Joy M. Schmitz, Ph.D.
Associate Professor of Psychiatry and Behavioral Sciences
University of Texas Health Science Center
Houston, Texas

Nina G. Schneider, Ph.D.
Department of Psychiatry and Biobehavioral Sciences
UCLA School of Medicine
Chief, Nicotine Research Unit
West Los Angeles Veterans Administration Medical Center
Los Angeles, California

Marc A. Schuckit, M.D.
Professor of Psychiatry
University of California at San Diego School of Medicine
Director, Alcohol Research Center
San Diego Veterans Administration Medical Center
San Diego, California

Peter A. Selwyn, M.D., M.P.H.
Associate Director
AIDS Program
Associate Professor of Medicine, Epidemiology, and Public Health
Yale University School of Medicine
Yale-New Haven Hospital
New Haven, Connecticut

Edward C. Senay, M.D.
Professor of Psychiatry Emeritus
Director of Research, Interventions
University of Chicago
Chicago, Illinois

Richard B. Seymour, M.A.
Managing Editor
Journal of Psychoactive Drugs
San Francisco, California

Howard J. Shaffer, Ph.D., CAS
Associate Professor and Director
Division on Addictions
Harvard Medical School
Boston, Massachusetts

Charles W. Sharp, Ph.D.
Associate Director for Special Programs
Division of Basic Research
National Institute on Drug Abuse
Rockville, Maryland

Eric J. Simon, Ph.D.
Professor of Psychiatry and Pharmacology
New York University Medical Center
New York, New York

Zili Sloboda, Sc.D.
Director
Division of Epidemiology and Preventive Research
National Institute on Drug Abuse
Rockville, Maryland

David E. Smith, M.D., FASAM
Founder and Medical Director, Haight Ashbury Free Clinics, Inc.
San Francisco, California
President, American Society of Addiction Medicine
Chevy Chase, Maryland

Michael O. Smith, M.D., DAc
Director, Substance Abuse Division
Lincoln Hospital
Bronx, New York

James L. Sorensen, Ph.D.
Adjunct Professor of Psychiatry
University of California, San Francisco
San Francisco, California

M. Duncan Stanton, Ph.D.
Professor of Psychiatry (Psychology)
University of Rochester School of Medicine and Dentistry
Division of Family Programs
Strong Memorial Hospital
Rochester, New York

Karen Stennie, M.D.
Department of Psychiatry
University of Florida College of Medicine
Gainesville, Florida

Kathleen A. Sullivan, RN, M.A., CEAP
Vice President, Ancillary Network Development
MultiPlan
New York, New York

C. Douglas Talbott, M.D., FASAM
Medical Director and President
Talbott Recovery Campus
President-Elect, American Society of Addiction Medicine
Clinical Professor of Family Practice
Morehouse Medical School
Atlanta, Georgia

Douglas W. Teller, M.D.
Associate Program Director
Internal Medicine Residency
Kettering Medical Center
Kettering, Ohio

J. Thomas Ungerleider, M.D.
Professor Emeritus of Psychiatry
UCLA School of Medicine
Los Angeles, California

C. Fernando Valenzuela, M.D., Ph.D.
Instructor
Department of Pharmacology
University of Colorado Health Sciences Center
Denver, Colorado

Karl G. Verebey, Ph.D., DABFT
Associate Professor of Psychiatry
SUNY Health Science Center
Brooklyn, New York
Resident and Director, Leadtech Corporation
North Bergen, New Jersey

Adale Walters, M.D., M.P.H.
The University of Michigan
Ann Arbor, Michigan

Arnold M. Washton, Ph.D., CSAC
Founder and Executive Director
The Washton Institute
New York, New York

Hsiang-lai Wen, M.D.
Hong Kong

Donald R. Wesson, M.D.
Medical Director and Scientific Director, MPI
Treatment Service
Summit Medical Center
Oakland, California

Joseph Westermeyer, M.D., M.P.H., Ph.D.
Professor of Psychiatry
University of Minnesota Medical School
Chief of Psychiatry
Minneapolis VA Medical Center
Minneapolis, Minnesota

Charles L. Whitfield, M.D., FASAM
Faculty, Rutgers Advanced Summer School on Alcohol and Drug Studies
Rutgers University
New Brunswick, New Jersey
Private Practice
Atlanta, Georgia

Charles Winick, Ph.D.
Professor of Sociology
The Graduate School and University Center
The City University of New York
New York, New York

Joycelyn Sue Woods, M.A.
Executive Vice President, National Alliance of Methadone Advocates
Research Associate, Chemical Dependency Research Working Group
New York, New York

George E. Woody, M.D.
Clinical Professor of Psychiatry
University of Pennsylvania School of Medicine
Chief
Substance Abuse Treatment Unit
Philadelphia VA Medical Center
Philadelphia, Pennsylvania

Stephen R. Zukin, M.D.
Director, Division of Clinical and Services Research
National Institute on Drug Abuse
Rockville, Maryland
Professor of Psychiatry and Neuroscience
Albert Einstein College of Medicine of Yeshiva University
Bronx, New York

CONTENTS

SECTION I. BACKGROUND

SECTION II. DETERMINANTS AND PERPETUATORS OF SUBSTANCE ABUSE

SECTION III. SUBSTANCES OF ABUSE

SECTION IV. RELATED COMPULSIVE AND ADDICTIVE BEHAVIORS

SECTION V. EVALUATION AND EARLY TREATMENT

SECTION VI. TREATMENT APPROACHES

SECTION VII. MANAGEMENT OF MEDICAL CONDITIONS ASSOCIATED WITH SUBSTANCE ABUSE

SECTION VIII. HIV INFECTION AND AIDS

SECTION IX. SPECIAL POPULATIONS

SECTION X. PREVENTION
AND EDUCATION

SECTION XI. MEDICAL EDUCATION
AND STAFF TRAINING

SECTION XII. POLICY ISSUES

SECTION I. BACKGROUND

1 HISTORICAL PERSPECTIVES

David F. Musto

The last three decades of the nineteenth century saw far-reaching transformations in American life. With immigration from all parts of Europe and from Asia, the population expanded greatly and became heterogeneous in speech, religion, and way of life. Many of the immigrants, unprepared to join the agricultural sector of the economy, crowded into the growing cities, which soon began to exhibit today's familiar urban problems. With the industrial revolution, large enterprises grew up and attained a new level of economic power; with the construction of the railroads, vast areas of the West were opened for settlement and exploitation of the timber and mineral resources. In social terms, the geographic dispersal of the population that occurred as many moved west spelled the end of the once close-knit family. In political terms, these changes terminated the hegemony of the Protestant, North European group that had controlled the affairs of the nation through the Civil War.

The variety of social ills that inevitably attended these rapid changes in all aspects of life gave rise to a spirit of reform that ran through American culture from the mid-nineteenth century to 1920. This reformist or "progressive" impulse stemmed largely from the fear of social disorder among the same middle- and upper-class citizens whose political and economic power was increasingly insecure. Rapid transformation seemed to threaten the heart of American life. While most reforms of the Progressive era (1890–1917) were aimed at curing the disorder itself, some movements naturally responded to specific evils that seemed to result from the upheaval (1). Increasingly, crime and immorality were blamed on easily obtained narcotics and alcohol. This goal of moral uplift of the underprivileged was shared by Progressive era temperance activists, political reformers, and crusaders against the indiscriminate use of psychoactive substances such as opium and cocaine.

THE BACKGROUND OF PROGRESSIVE ERA REFORMS

Alcohol and the Prohibition Movement

Alcohol had been the object of recurrent prohibition crusades in the nineteenth century, and as the Progressive era developed, some sociologists began to speculate that alcohol abuse was actually the result rather than the cause of poverty. However, alcohol seemed to exacerbate almost all the evils of a disorderly society. Even if it could not be wholly blamed for economic failure, it certainly did not help. Alcohol lowered efficiency and productivity and, in the eyes of the reformers, increased all the evils of the urban scene: Prostitutes worked in and around saloons; alcohol apparently made men more susceptible to the influence of corrupt city bosses; and it broke up families and invited violence. It reduced the chances for freedom, prosperity, and happiness and did not contribute to the virtue and enlightened character of an electorate needed by a democracy.

Furthermore, alcohol worsened the situation of Protestant Christianity. Not only was the saloon associated with Catholic immigrants, but also it seemed to make people incapable of responding to Evangelical Protestantism. If it made a person unconcerned about something as urgent as salvation, then surely it would make him or her oblivious to public concerns. Democratization, therefore, made it even more important that the saloon be abolished. Extending the powers of the landless class, in itself, posed quite a threat to stability; drunken masses would constitute an intolerable danger (2).

With the final temperance movement that led to the adoption in 1919 of the Eighteenth Amendment, the nation moved toward implementation of a prohibition justified on moral, religious, and scientific grounds (3). It is quite likely that by 1919 a majority of Americans believed that liquor prohibition would be a great benefit in reducing poverty, crime, broken families, lost work time, and immorality. Eventually, every state except two, Rhode Island and Connecticut, ratified the amendment.

Narcotics, Cocaine, and Cannabis

By the end of the nineteenth century, the narcotics problem was also worrying reform-minded legislators, health professionals, and the laity. Opium in its crude form had been imported into North America from the time of the earliest European settlements. Various medicines were made from it. Alcohol extracts of crude opium included laudanum and paregoric, and opium was mixed with other drugs in patent medicines, among the most popular of which was Dover's Powder, originating in England in the eighteenth century. American statistics on opium imports were not kept until the 1840s, but from that time on domestic consumption rose rapidly until the mid-1890s, when the annual importation of crude opium leveled off at about a half million pounds (4). After passage of federal laws in 1914 strictly limiting importation of opium, the import statistics became less helpful in estimating national consumption, and smuggling became a greater problem. Yet, statistics for the pre-World War I period provide good evidence that a steady increase of opium use in the United States occurred in the nineteenth century and that when the twentieth century began, there was already a substantial consumption of the drug for medicinal and nonmedicinal purposes. State laws regulating the availability of narcotics began to be enacted around the time of the Civil War, and many states attempted to control the drugs by the 1890s.

Several major technologic and chemical advances made the most powerful ingredients in opium available in pure, cheap form. In the first decade of the nineteenth century, morphine was isolated from opium, and by 1832, American pharmaceutical manufacturers were preparing morphine from imported crude opium. Codeine was isolated in 1832, and this less addicting substance became a common form of manufactured derivative, particularly after morphine and heroin were severely restricted in the United States after World War I (5, 6). Heroin, a trade name of the Bayer Company for diacetylmorphine, was introduced commercially in 1898 with the hope that acetylation of the morphine molecule would reduce its side effects while maintaining its effectiveness in suppressing the cough reflex. A similar hope was entertained the next year for acetylation of salicylic acid, a mild analgesic with undesirable side effects, which was then marketed as Aspirin, the Bayer trademark for sodium acetylsalicylic acid. Heroin, of course, proved to be at least as addictive as morphine and eventually ousted morphine as the drug of choice among American drug habitués (7). The increasing use of heroin in this period is an example of the effectiveness of three innovations adopted by nineteenth-century industrial enterprises—manufacturing, rapid distribution, and effective marketing techniques.

Coca leaves, in their indigenous growth areas in South America, were known to have stimulant properties and had been used for centuries by natives. Coca's unusual properties were popularized in Europe and America in the mid-nineteenth century, and an alcohol extract of the leaves, which contained some of the active stimulant cocaine, often appeared under the name *wine of coca*. In the 1880s, pure cocaine became more easily available because of advances in manufacturing technology, and it was immediately praised, especially in the United States. Its stimulating and euphoric properties were touted for athletes, workers, and students, and bottlers of popular soda drinks and easily obtained "tonics" added cocaine to obtain a stimulant effect. Medical uses were soon discovered, and worldwide experimentation established cocaine as an anesthetic for the surface of the eye and as a block to pain stimuli when injected near a nerve. The stimulant properties were bothersome side effects of cocaine when used as an anesthetic, but within a few decades satisfactory substitutes were developed that were considered less habituating, such as procaine in 1905. Cocaine was also convenient for shrinking nasal and sinus membranes, and it became one of the early effective remedies for "hay fever," allergies, and sinusitis. As an over-the-counter remedy for hay fever or "nasal catarrh," in powder form to be sniffed or as a spray, cocaine began to be criticized as misused or carelessly dispensed for mere pleasure or dissipation.

In the period from about 1895 to 1915, cocaine became associated in the popular and medical press with southern blacks' hostility to whites. Vicious crimes said to have been perpetrated by blacks were commonly attributed to the effects of cocaine. In efforts to pass antinarcotic legislation, this association was repeated by federal officials and spokesmen for the health professions, although direct evidence for such a close and specifically racial association was wanting or even contradictory (8). Eighty years ago, cocaine was considered a typically "Negro" drug, whereas opiates, and specifically heroin, were described as characteristically "white," illustrating the influence of social tensions and racial stereotypes on interpretation of the narcotics problem.

Cannabis, or marihuana, in the form of "reefers" or "joints," seems to have been unfamiliar in the United States until this century, yet there has been a long-standing fear of hashish, a concentrated and powerful form of cannabis. Hashish was known from its use as an esoteric and perilous drug popular in the Middle East and from description of its bizarre effects by literary figures who experimented with it in the mid-nineteenth century (9).

PROGRESSIVE ERA FOOD AND DRUG REFORMS
(1898–1906)

Faced with what they perceived as social breakdown associated with the pernicious effects of drugs and alcohol, reformers turned to the federal government. In the period leading to the Progressive era, state and local laws were losing credibility as effective measures to control distribution and consumption of both alcohol and psychoactive drugs. The failure was usually ascribed to the patchwork-quilt character of laws below the federal level of government (10). But federal action was limited by the few constitutional bases for laws that would affect abuses. Other than the tariff, the federal government was restricted mostly to regulating interstate commerce and levying taxes. Police and health powers, obviously the most appropriate for combating addiction and illicit drugs, were the province of the states. For example, the United States Public Health Service and its antecedent agencies were limited to dealing with communicable diseases and gathering and disseminating such medical information as vital statistics and public health advice; they could not provide direct delivery of health services except to their legal wards, chiefly the Merchant Marine and American Indians (11). The armed services excepted, federal police agencies included alcohol tax agents, members of the Coast Guard, and customs and immigration officers. Therefore, there was little precedent for federal regulation of dangerous drugs, and no federal policing agency could easily add this burden to its current duties. As a result, the range of activities that were left to an individual's or company's sense of fair play was remarkably large. In the nineteenth century, federal law did not require the labeling of drugs on over-the-counter proprietaries. Thus, these patent medicines could contain any amount of, say, morphine without acknowledgment and could even aver that the potion contained no morphine. The percentage of alcohol in some popular remedies was higher than that in many cocktails today. Claims that a proprietary could cure cancer, tuberculosis, or any other ailment were legally unchallengeable; no tests of efficacy, purity, or standardization were required. In addition, newspapers, the primary source of information for most Americans, were chary of offending their advertisers, and many papers had contracts with proprietary manufacturers that would become invalid with the enactment of any state law requiring disclosure of contents or any modification of advertising claims (12).

Hence, it is not surprising that no federal law requiring content information and some accuracy of claims was enacted until 1906, when public concern reached a pitch sufficient to propel the government to resort to its power over interstate commerce to enact such a measure. The law, the Pure Food and Drug Act, contained some of the earliest federal provisions affecting narcotics; if any over-the-counter remedy in interstate commerce contained an opiate, cannabis, cocaine, or chloral hydrate, the label was required to state its contents and percentage. The effect of this simple measure apparently was to reduce the amount of such drugs in popular remedies and also to hurt their sales, although other proprietaries flourished. The Proprietary Association of America, dismayed at the accusation of being "dopers," favored strict limitation of dangerous drugs in their products and ostracized manufacturers who continued to put such drugs as cocaine in "asthma cures."

Although a step had been taken to warn proprietary users of the amount of dangerous drugs in the remedies, still nothing had been done to bring under control another target of reform: "dope doctors" and pharmacists who purveyed opiates and cocaine to anyone who asked for them. The percentage of such deviants in each profession was not large, but they took advantage of the broad authority given to all licensed pharmacists and physicians to use their professional judgment in the delivery of medicines and services, and the dominance of the state in the licensing of the health professions seemed unassailable by the federal government. In addition to purchasing drugs from professional miscreants, one could order them from mail-order houses. How to rectify this promiscuous distribution of narcotics presented another difficult constitutional problem for federal action.

TOWARD PROHIBITION OF NARCOTIC DRUGS
(1909–1919)

The Shanghai Commission and the Smoking Opium Act (1909)

Several bills directed at the traffic in narcotics had been introduced into Congress before 1908, but federal legislation was accomplished only after President Theodore Roosevelt convened the Shanghai Opium Commission in 1909 to aid the Chinese Empire in its desire to stamp out opium addiction, particularly opium smoking (13). The measure, intended more as evidence of America's good faith in convening the commission than as an adequate weapon against American narcotic abuse, was modest and limited. Called The Smoking Opium Exclusion Act, it outlawed importation of opium prepared for smoking (14). Its passage while the Shanghai Commission was in session under the chairmanship of an American, the Right Reverend Charles H. Brent, Episcopal bishop of the Philippine Islands, was designed to show the delegates of other nations that the United States was willing to take steps to aid control of world opium traffic. American delegates reported back to the State Department that the announcement of the act's passage was met with an impressive response from the other 12 nations represented.

The American delegates, however, and indeed the departments most closely associated with narcotic policy planning—State, Treasury, and Agriculture—were aware that the legislation against smoking opium was but the first step in controlling a national problem described as serious and threatening to progress. The nation needed a law that more closely controlled sales of over-the-counter remedies, excessive or careless prescribing of narcotics, and other avenues of easy access to narcotics. The question, of course, was how the federal government could accomplish this by constitutional means. Both the power to regulate interstate commerce and to levy taxes provided some basis for federal narcotics control. The State Department, which coordinated domestic legislation and planning until 1914, eventually opted for the latter, reasoning that by using tax administration, all narcotics could be traced, not just drugs shipped from one state to another.

The first of the administration's proposed bills, drafted in 1909, provided for extremely harsh penalties and was intricately detailed but without exemption for proprietaries that contained very small amounts of the narcotics (15). The effect of such bills would have been to make the handling of narcotic preparations so risky and complicated for retail outlets that the whole narcotic traffic would fall into the hands of physicians. The physicians would be limited only by their good judgment and by restrictions that state legislatures might enact (e.g., record keeping, prohibiting the refilling of narcotic prescriptions, or maintaining addicts) (16).

Such tough proposals met with opposition from the rank and file of the drug trades, proprietary manufacturers, and some members of Congress who feared, among other things, that such a precedent might be extended to alcohol. Before the Webb-Kenyon Act was passed over President Taft's veto in 1913 and upheld by the Supreme Court, it was legal to live in a dry state, purchase liquor from a wet state, and have it delivered via interstate commerce.

The Hague Treaty (1912)

While domestic debate continued among the specific interests affected by the proposed narcotic legislation, the United States continued its campaign to regulate the international traffic in narcotics. Since the Shanghai Commission was not empowered to draft a treaty (the delegates could only make recommendations), American diplomats sought a second meeting for the preparation of an international treaty. After much persuasion and repeated setbacks, the Netherlands, at America's request, convened the International Opium Conference at The Hague in December 1911. Again Bishop Brent, head of the American delegation, was chosen to preside, and after weeks of debate and compromise, the delegates signed The Hague Opium Convention in January 1912 (4). The title is somewhat misleading; the treaty also sought to control cocaine. An American and Italian suggestion that cannabis be included was not accepted.

The Hague Treaty emphasized enactment of legislation in each nation to control the production of crude substances, their manufacture into pharmaceutical products, and their distribution within the nation and abroad (17). The United States government believed that its people were extravagant consumers of opiates; federal publications reported that the country was, by far, the largest consumer of opium per capita among Western nations. In the words of the State Department's opium commissioner, Dr. Hamilton Wright, "Uncle Sam is the worst drug fiend in the world," consuming, he claimed, more opium per capita than the fabled opium-using Chinese (18). The thought within the State Department was that if the nations that grew opium and coca enacted strict legislation in the spirit of the treaty, the American problem would be greatly reduced, perhaps vanish. The challenge was to persuade other nations to have a "correct" view of narcotic use and to enforce legislation in accord with this view.

Yet the stern international measures envisaged by such reformers as Dr. Wright were not adopted before the Great War. The Hague Treaty was not airtight; its vague phrases did not compel the ratifying nations to enact strict laws to reduce narcotic distribution to solely medical purposes. Moreover, American domestic legislation, now promoted as the American implementation of The Hague Treaty, was still hampered by doctrines of states' rights and constitutional interpretation, to say nothing of the competing interests of physicians, pharmacists, and manufacturers of proprietary medicines.

The Harrison Act (1914)

In 1913, the administration of President Woodrow Wilson drafted legislation grounded in its constitutional taxation power. Hopefully, the new measure would, at the very least, bring into the open the vast narcotic traffic so that the states could take appropriate health and police measures or step up enforcement of existing laws. At the most, Wright hoped the Harrison Act, as the legislation was called, would be recognized as the fulfillment of an international obligation in accord with Article VI of the Constitution and thus take precedence over the rights of states. If this were the case, the general phraseology of the Harrison Bill, such as requiring the prescription of narcotics "in good faith," could be interpreted broadly and would allow prosecution of "dope doctors," other malpracticing professionals, and peddlers.

The measure passed the House of Representatives relatively easily but slowed down in the Senate and did not finally pass into law until December 1914. It was to come into effect on March 1, 1915 (19). In its final form, the act allowed proprietary medicines to include small amounts of narcotics, and physicians were not required to keep records of medicines dispensed while they personally attended a patient. Legitimate purveyors of opiate and cocaine preparations were required to register with the Bureau of Internal Revenue and obtain a tax stamp, for which they paid one dollar per year. Detailed record keeping was required for most transactions, and legal possession by a consumer was made dependent on a physician's or dentist's prescription. Individual consumers were forbidden to register (20). But when federal personnel sought to arrest the dope doctors for prescribing, they discovered that many judges of federal district courts thought the action was an infringement of state police powers. In 1916, a crucial Supreme Court interpretation, known as the first Jin Fuey Moy decision, held that it was beyond federal powers to prohibit narcotics possession by anyone to whom the Treasury Department had refused registration, such as a peddler or addict (21).

Not until the height of the war effort—and in the midst of a zealous drive to rid the nation of perceived threats to its integrity and security—was a successful campaign mounted to strengthen the Harrison Act to prevent health professionals from dispensing narcotics to persons whose only problem was addiction itself.

DRUG CONTROL IN A PERIOD OF DIMINISHING USE (1919–1962)

Size and Symbolism of the Addiction Problem

The true size of the drug abuse problem in the early decades of the twentieth century (Dr. Wright's hyperbole not withstanding) was a matter of public debate, much as it is today. Whereas the Public Health Service in rather sober studies published in 1915 and 1924 argued that there were probably never more than a quarter million habitual users of opiates and cocaine in the nation, the Treasury Department assessed the number at slightly more than 1 million, who were described as moral wretches for the most part (22, 23). New York City officials claimed that heroin addicts were responsible for huge numbers of crimes and estimated that in 1924 the remarkable figure of 75% of all crimes were committed by addicts (24). The mayor of New York City in 1919 linked heroin with anarchism and political bombings (25)—and his was not an isolated opinion. There was fear in the nation concerning several groups considered extreme domestic threats: socialists, members of the Industrial Workers of the World, Bolsheviks, and addicts (26). The image of the addict as immoral and criminal, a belief dating back among respectable writers and observers well into the nineteenth century, made them an obvious target for serious social reformers as well as ambitious politicians and bureaucrats. If one accepted that they numbered more than 1 million in a nation of 100 million, stern action and uncompromising control seemed entirely justified. Nevertheless, this sentiment coexisted with experiments in public-health-based addiction management and medical theories of addiction as a treatable disease. When the results of attempts at treatment proved disappointing, faith in treatment waned, and the punitive model of drug abuse control won, as it were, by default.

Maintenance Clinics (1912–1925)

Beginning in 1912 in Jacksonville, Florida, 40-odd clinics had been established in various parts of the country to supply addicts with maintenance doses of narcotics in what were designed to be controlled conditions. The clients were usually those too poor or socially marginal to have access to private physicians. A relatively small percentage of the nation's addicts were enrolled in these clinics, particularly if one accepted the extravagant estimate of more than a million addicts for the whole nation. It is likely that the number of addicts registered at any one time in maintenance clinics did not exceed 5000 (27). The average age of patrons was about 30, and they had usually been addicts for at least several years before joining the clinic. Some clinics were operated by police departments (e.g., New Haven) and others by health departments (e.g., Atlanta), and attitudes toward the clinics varied from one city to another. Some were clearly operated under political patronage and for a profit. In a few instances, as in Albany, cocaine was dispensed as well as morphine.

An exception to the policy of almost all these clinics, which was to maintain addicts indefinitely on morphine, was the clinic operated in 1919 and 1920 by the New York City Department of Health. Here heroin was used to entice addicts into a detoxification and rehabilitation program. After almost a year of operation, the city ended its experiment. It found that almost all addicts, even if detoxified, returned to heroin after release from 6 weeks of hospital treatment. The Health Department concluded that restriction of availability by the police and federal agents was necessary if addiction was to be effectively diminished. About 7500 persons registered at the clinic, and almost all received gradually decreasing doses of heroin; 10% were under the age of 19 (28).

Adoption of a Federal Antimaintenance Policy

Given the inadequacy and variety of state laws, there seemed no way to control physicians and pharmacists—even though the unethical percentage was small—other than by imposition of federal authority. If a physician could exercise judgment as to when and whom to maintain in an opiate habit, it was certain that some physicians would be unscrupulous, thus spreading the habit and reaping a profit. Therefore, in addition to reforms in the medical and pharmaceutical professions, the goal of the federal government was to restrict that breadth of medical judgment by law. The undertaking was hazardous, for such federal encroachment on medicine was unprecedented; the physician would be allowed to maintain an opiate addict only if approved by a local narcotics agent. These exceptions would be chiefly iatrogenically addicted and middle-class patients. (One should keep in mind that some observers believed that physicians created about half of American opiate addiction.)

In 1918, partly to counteract the Jin Fuey Moy decision, the Treasury Department established a Special Committee on Narcotics Traffic. The committee helped persuade Congress to pass strengthening legislation in February 1919 (29). Then, aiding the government effort, the Supreme Court, in two fundamental interpretations of the act, rejected by a vote of 5 to 4 the argument that it was legal to maintain an addict by prescription if the addict had no problem except addiction (30). To carry out the strict Supreme Court ruling that addiction maintenance be severely limited in the United States, a Narcotics Division was established in the Treasury Department in December 1919. It was part of the newly formed Prohibition Unit of the Internal Revenue Bureau, which had been created to enforce liquor prohibition. Its first head was Levi G. Nutt, a pharmacist from Ohio who had risen in the ranks of the tax unit. He now oversaw about 150 narcotic agents scattered across the nation.

Addiction Disease and Law Enforcement

One result of antimaintenance law enforcement, which was backed by leading physicians and such reformers as Dr. Alexander Lambert, president of the American Medical Association (AMA) in 1919, was a curious decline in the respectability of a certain medical theory that would have admitted maintenance as a rational therapy response: the immunochemical theory of opiate addiction. This happened because both reformers and government agents feared maintenance and were disgusted by the subterfuges some health professionals used to justify a profitable trade. Their fear and disgust extended to suspicion of any justification for maintenance. Supplying drugs to an addict came to be considered a form of medical malpractice that endangered society by perpetuating criminal and immoral persons in their esoteric pleasures.

In the immunological reasoning that was popular among some addiction experts prior to 1919, the argument ran that ingestion of, say, morphine stimulated the formation of antibodies like those produced against smallpox virus or of antitoxins like those produced against the toxins of the diphtheria bacterium. Such theories were popular explanations for illnesses in the late nineteenth and early twentieth centuries and in many cases saved lives. With regard to addiction, and according to several competent and respected clinicians, the theory held that maintenance doses of an opiate would be required to bring an addict's physiology into balance with the level of antibodies or antitoxins present. If too little opiate were administered, the body would begin to experience withdrawal symptoms as a result of the action of unneutralized antibodies or antitoxins; if too much opiate were administered, the body would experience the physiologic effects of opiates. According to Dr. Ernest Bishop of New York, the amount of opiate required to balance an individual's physiology could be determined with great precision, and the addict would remain a fully normal person only so long as this exact dose was maintained. However, Dr. Bishop did not rule out cure in some instances by various popular medical regimens (31).

The intimate link between this scientific theory and its implications for public policy made its adherents suspect. Those who practiced medicine in accordance with the theory could be indicted and convicted of violating the 1919 Supreme Court interpretations of what was legitimate medical practice. When Dr. A. G. DuMez of the Hygienic Laboratory (now the National Institutes of Health), one of the leading addiction experts of the United States Public Health Service, published his endorsement of some of the immunological experiments in 1919, he was asked by the AMA's Committee on Addiction to retract his statement, which he did in part by qualifying his previous endorsement (32, 33). Within a year or two the question of the cause of addiction was so controversial that the Surgeon General of the Public Health Service wrote the president of the Louisiana State Board of Health to advise that the phrase "physiological balance" was too controversial to be included in a description of narcotic treatment and the enforcement problem (13).

It was soon demonstrated that immunological substances could not be found in the blood; the adherents of "addiction disease" caused by a simple and easily detectable immunological process were evidently in error. Yet the intense political nature of the addiction question and the fear of addicts, whose numbers were very likely overestimated, had an impact on the exchange of scientific information and medical practice. At the level of social planning, maintenance was judged poor public policy, and it was to be eliminated if at all possible. This decision might, indeed, have been the correct one, but the suddenness of implementation and the emotionally charged attitude toward addicts and their maintainers caused policy to collide dramatically with research and medical opinion.

The events of 1919 spelled the eventual end of the clinic experiment and of the concept of addiction as a health problem. Maintenance of nonmedical addicts had become illegal even if records were carefully kept and a physician examined every patient and tried to keep the drug down to a minimum. By 1925, all the clinics known to the Narcotics Division had been closed.

The rapidity with which opinion on controversial questions like addiction and narcotics can be crystallized is one of the most interesting features of narcotic control in the United States. To resist the closure of maintenance was difficult; the new policy ensued from the anger, scapegoating, fatigue, and frustration of the lawmakers because a simple answer to addiction was still not available. The burden for the next several decades would rest on law enforcement to prevent illegal access to narcotic supplies. The hope for a simple medical cure had been dashed.

Fear of Federal Control on the Part of Health Professions

Court decisions continued to restrict what remained of a physician's right to maintain an addict. Procedures used by agents to get information led to hostility and suspicion, but the reason that enforcement personnel used such methods as informers was that they had repeatedly encountered determined profit-making physicians whose concern for the welfare of their patients and the community was nil. A further disagreement between the federal government and the medical profession arose from a question even more fundamental than maintenance: Did the federal government have the right to interfere with medical practice and exempt certain classes of patients from a doctor's judgment? The medical profession came out of the social agitation associated with World War I with a fear that the federal government would enter into "state medicine" or compulsory health insurance. After 1920, the AMA greatly resisted the various federal measures concerning health, such as the Sheppard-Towner Act for Maternal and Child Care, which was to be financed by matching grants to the states. The medical profession fought such federal intervention with great vigor and generally with success (34).

Yet the Harrison Act remained a thorn in the side of professional medicine. If it was constitutional for government to say who could be maintained or not, a precedent was set for further incursions into medical practice. A similar problem for the AMA was the Willis-Campbell Act of 1921, which limited a physician's prescriptions for alcohol to a fairly modest number and placed other restrictions on the kind and amount of alcohol that could be prescribed. Hence, physicians were disturbed at the Harrison and Willis-Campbell Acts in part not because they wanted to maintain addicts or become saloonkeepers (although at times a few seemed quite willing to do just that) but because they were fearful of where this unprecedented use of federal power in the health fields might lead.

Narcotic Drugs Import and Export Act (1922)

After the outlawing of addiction maintenance, a series of federal statutes in the 1920s sought to fill gaps in the federal control of narcotics. The first, the Narcotic Drugs Import and Export Act of 1922, permitted only crude narcotics to enter the United States; American drug companies would manufacture them into pure substances (35). Any subsequently manufactured foreign narcotic product in the United States, like Swiss morphine or German cocaine, was illegal. Intricate restrictions were placed on American export and transshipment of narcotics because it was feared that a great deal of morphine was arriving in China, via Japan, in this manner or that it was being smuggled back into the United States after export to Canada or Mexico. Finally, the Federal Narcotic Control Board, composed of the Secretaries of Treasury, Commerce, and State, was established to authorize legitimate imports and exports.

Restrictions on Heroin (1924)

In the mid-1920s, the United States attempted to obtain international sanctions against the manufacture of heroin, which by then was considered the most dangerous narcotic, particularly for adolescents. Most of the crime in New York City was blamed on heroin, including daring bank robberies, senseless violence, and murders. The danger of heroin was exaggerated by respectable antinarcotic reformers in order to inform the American people of its peril. One excellent example is the educational campaign of Captain Richmond Pearson Hobson, a hero of the Spanish-American War, former congressman, and ardent Prohibitionist, who directed his speaking and organizational talents against narcotics shortly after the Eighteenth Amendment's ratification. Captain Hobson was wont to warn women who habitually used any particular face powder to have it checked for heroin, lest they become addicted. He claimed that one dose of heroin was addictive, and that an ounce of heroin could addict 2000 persons. He blamed a national crime wave on heroin, claiming that it was a stimulant to senseless violence. He desired that a compilation of such warnings be sent into every American home and requested Congress to print 50 million copies of his eight-page brochure, "The Peril of Narcotics" (36). The pamphlet was not printed, but a revised version of his message was printed in the Congressional Record and distributed by sympathetic congressmen (37). Hobson represents a popularizer of heroin dangers who disseminated grossly erroneous information on addiction that tended to alarm the public while providing a convenient explanation for unrelated, serious social problems.

In 1924, partly to encourage other nations to regulate narcotics and partly to assist in the American fight against addiction, Congress prohibited importation of crude opium into the United States for the manufacture of heroin (38). The author of this legislation, Representative Stephen Porter of Pittsburgh, chairman of the House Foreign Affairs Committee, took the leading congressional role in the international negotiations and planning for domestic control of narcotics in the 1920s.

Federal Narcotic Farms (1929)

Porter's second major effort was to provide for two "narcotic farms" where addicts could be treated as sick individuals and detoxified and where they could perhaps assist investigators in the search for a cure (39). A factor in this legislation was that federal prisons were becoming jammed with Harrison Act violators, most of whom were also addicts. Congress had to build either two new prisons or two treatment centers. Thus came into being the Lexington, Kentucky, and Fort Worth, Texas, narcotic hospitals operated by the United States Public Health Service. This legislation also provided for the Public Health Service Narcotics Division, which evolved into the present National Institute of Mental Health (NIMH) and National Institute on Drug Abuse (NIDA).

The Federal Bureau of Narcotics (1930)

Finally, Representative Porter sought the establishment in the Treasury Department of an independent narcotics agency. The Narcotics Division had accompanied the Prohibition Unit when the latter was raised to the rank of bureau in 1927, and although still subordinate and headed by an assistant commissioner, it was gradually expanding. In 1930, shortly before his death, Porter shepherded through Congress the act creating the Federal Bureau of Narcotics (FBN) (40). When the Prohibition Bureau moved from the Treasury Department to the Justice Department in the mid-1920s, the Narcotics Division remained behind, but its head, Levi G. Nutt, was not to become the first commissioner of narcotics. Nutt's son and son-in-law were implicated by a federal grand jury in "indiscreet" dealings with the recently slain New York narcotics underworld figure, Arnold Rothstein (41). Nutt was transferred from his post a week after the filing of the grand jury's report, which also touched on his own activities and those of the New York District Office. Assistant Prohibition Commissioner Harry J. Anslinger was picked from the international control section of the Prohibition Bureau to take temporary charge of the Narcotics Division.

Anslinger had not been deeply involved with narcotics; his training was in the foreign service and in international negotiations to cut off rum running. To Representative Porter, however, he seemed the ideal candidate. Accustomed to what Porter likely regarded as foreign wiles and ulterior motives in areas of American moral concern, he could ably represent the United States in its struggle, dating back to 1906, to achieve international control of narcotics traffic. The medical aspect of the question seemed secondary, for if smuggling could be ended, the narcotics problem would take care of itself.

Thus began the 32-year tenure of Commissioner Anslinger. Most of the enforcement questions had been settled: Maintenance was illegal; the image of the heroin addict was well-publicized by such spokesmen as Captain Hobson; a national system of agents was established with fairly well-defined styles of enforcement, although there was the eternal integrity problem in the agents' dealings with smugglers. The most profound effect on narcotics enforcement in the immediate future was not new policies but rather the Depression, which drastically reduced the FBN's budget, led to detailed scrutiny of even its telephone bills by Congress, and probably helped explain the parsimony characteristic of the Anslinger tenure. Even in the 1960s, the Bureau made a fetish of a low budget.

The Marihuana Problem (1930–1937)

Commissioner Anslinger's first major issue appeared even as he took office—a quickly burgeoning fear centered in the Southwest about a plant grown and used by Mexicans who had poured into the region as farm laborers in the prosperous 1920s. This drug or plant was known as locoweed, marihuana, or, more scientifically, cannabis. As the fear of marihuana grew, so did the belief that it stimulated violence and was being slyly sold to American school children. In the early 1930s, the FBN tried to minimize these fears and suggested that state laws were the appropriate response. The Uniform State Narcotic Drug Act proposed in 1932 included marihuana regulations as an option for state legislation; the Bureau thought it had found the solution. The plant grew in the United States, so the best response would be from local government, not from an agency that had its eyes on the smuggling of drugs from Turkey, France, Bolivia, China, and Siam.

Yet, recalled Anslinger, the Treasury Department decided to make marihuana use a federal offense, more as a gesture to the fearful Southwest than as a comprehensive and probably effective plan for marihuana control. The Department's bill was modeled on the National Firearms Act, which was declared constitutional by the Supreme Court in March 1937. In April, the Treasury representatives went before Congress to ask for a similar "transfer tax" and licensing system for marihuana. Congress passed the Marihuana Tax Act of 1937 without dissent, and by October it was in effect (42). Opposition to the act in committee came from an AMA representative, Dr. William C. Woodward, who stated that this was an area of state concern, and that it should not become one more example of federal encroachment on the medical profession.

In the enforcement of the act the Bureau described marihuana as a fearsome substance but played down any suggestion that it was a problem out of control. The apparent goal was to make the drug unattractive but not to create a panic over claims that it was widely disseminated to school children (9).

Adoption of Mandatory Minimum Sentences (1951–1956)

World War II brought narcotic use, particularly opiates, to a low point. Control over the growth of opium poppies had been sought in 1942 by the Opium Poppy Control Act (43). There was other legislation at this time to resolve technical problems, strengthen penalties, and include synthetic narcotics, such as meperidine, under federal regulations (44). At the close of hostilities, though, the FBN anticipated a resumption of illicit world narcotic trade. The Bureau looked back to World War I when, it was claimed, there had been a postwar upsurge. And so when there was a rise in addiction among ghetto youth in Chicago and New York in the late 1940s and authorities noted a lower age among those sent to prisons or narcotic hospitals, the Bureau asked Congress for stronger penalties. The variability in judges' sentences and disposition of cases—a short sentence or probation for a trafficker the Bureau might have spent years trying to convict—led to the proposal to take sentencing of certain offenders out of the hands of judges. Also, a mandatory sentence might deter the potential trafficker or even the drug user.

Such legislation was introduced by Representative Hale Boggs and enacted in 1951 (45). In 1956, after Senate hearings chaired by Senator Price Daniel, the death penalty was allowed at the jury's discretion in some instances of heroin sales (46). This was the peak of punitive legislation against drug addiction in the United States. In a half century the federal response to dangerous drugs had advanced from requiring accurate labeling of narcotics in over-the-counter remedies (but with no limit on how much could be present) to the possibility of the death penalty or, at least, a mandatory sentence for conveying heroin to a minor (regardless of the quantity of heroin).

Voices were raised against such harsh measures, but they were not very effective in modifying the course of events up to 1956. The American Bar Association (ABA) questioned the wisdom of mandatory minimum sentences, and a joint ABA-AMA committee began to examine the narcotics question with a philosophy far different from that embodied in the Boggs-Daniel Acts. Staff of the committee looked at the British experience, in which legal heroin maintenance was available to the several hundred known addicts, and wondered whether some similar system would be suitable for the United States (47). Presidential and congressional confidence in various forms of psychological and chemical treatment flourished and was expressed in such national projects as the Community Mental Health Center program of 1963. Narcotic maintenance programs reappeared, using the synthetic narcotic methadone. The police effort to make narcotic supplies scarce—which seemed so reasonable to progressive medical leadership in 1919—began to seem crude, ineffective, and conducive to gross malfeasance. A turning point in the national approach to narcotics was again at hand.

DRUG CONTROL IN A PERIOD OF RISING USE (1962–1980)

Medical and Psychological Response to Addiction (1962–1970)

After Anslinger announced his retirement in 1962—a sign of hope to those wanting to see some form of maintenance or at least less reliance on mandatory prison sentences—President John F. Kennedy called the White House Conference on Narcotics and Drug Abuse (48). Its participants represented the various conflicting points of view; after the conference was over, the President's Advisory Commission on Narcotics and Drug Abuse considered how to carry out the spirit of reexamination and make specific recommendations. The Commission's Final Report, published in 1963, marks a definite, if small, shift from the trend to see all "narcotics" as equal in the sight of the law. There was a suggestion that psychological treatment might be useful and that some variations in prison sentencing, such as civil commitment, might prove effective against addiction (49).

In the 1960s, the appearance of psychedelic substances, such as lysergic acid diethylamide (LSD), and the quick rise in marihuana use drew attention to the varieties of drugs available and abusable. Further studies of marihuana suggested that it was less dangerous than had been assumed in the early 1930s, and the fact that millions of individuals were estimated to have used it in the 1960s also suggested that marihuana was not so very dangerous in moderate use. Other drugs, like amphetamines and barbiturates, became as popular in the streets as they had previously been common in middle-class homes. The number of heroin addicts began to rise, and the nation perceived itself under attack by a "drug culture" linked by many observers to a youth "counterculture."

Both the legislative and executive branches of the government began to respond to the drug problem in ways that reflected, at the same time, concern about increasing drug use and changing opinions on the nature of drugs and the best ways to prevent abuse. The Drug Abuse Amendments of 1965 created the Bureau of Drug Abuse Control in the Department of Health, Education, and Welfare to address diversion and misuse of barbiturates and amphetamines; and the Narcotic Addict Rehabilitation Act of 1966 approved civil commitment as an alternative to prison for addicted drug offenders (50, 51).

The high hopes held for civil commitment of drug addicts were not to be realized. At first such commitment seemed in keeping with advanced notions of psychological and milieu treatment, but it was modified to guarantee that the addict would remain for treatment. Yet the cost and length of treatment as well as the dismal success rate brought this apparently more sophisticated form of confinement into question. Civil commitment may also have conflicted with the legal rights of the individual: An addict could be confined for several years, not for a crime but because he or she had a disease. These many difficulties with civil commitment caused a shift from optimism in the Advisory Commission's report of 1963 to a close questioning of the concept in the report of the President's Commission on Law Enforcement and the Administration of Justice in 1967 (52).

Reorganization of the Federal Drug Control Bureaucracy

In response to political and social pressures similar to those that had prompted the transfer of the Prohibition Unit from the Treasury Department to the Justice Department in the late 1920s, the Federal Bureau of Narcotics was joined with the Bureau of Drug Abuse and Control in 1968 and moved to Justice under the name, Bureau of Narcotics and Dangerous Drugs (BNDD).

When Richard Nixon took office in 1969, his advisors saw almost immediately that narcotics control offered an opportunity to make good on Nixon's campaign promise to reduce crime. The first major legislative initiative of the Nixon Administration was the Comprehensive Drug Abuse and Control Act of 1970, which brought together and rationalized all previous drug legislation under the interstate commerce powers of the federal government. The new law also established schedules that differentiated among the various drugs of abuse and formed the basis for a new penalty structure that abandoned mandatory minimum sentences (53).

In the spring of 1971, President Nixon issued an executive order that established the Special Action Office for Drug Abuse Prevention (SAODAP), a White House office that was meant to oversee the prevention and treatment programs of a host of cabinet departments and agencies. SAODAP was given statutory existence through the Drug Abuse Office and Treatment Act of 1972 (54). That same year a special unit in aid of local law enforcement called the Office of Drug Abuse Law Enforcement (ODALE) was also established through executive order as was the Office of National Narcotics Intelligence (ONNI). The expenditure of the Bureau of Narcotics and Dangerous Drugs in fiscal year 1972 was more than $60 million, a remarkable amount when compared with the FBN expenditures in 1962 of about $4 million.

In 1973, ODALE and ONNI were combined with BNDD to form the Drug Enforcement Administration. Also in 1973, the National Institute on Drug Abuse (NIDA) evolved from SAODAP and the Division of Narcotics and Drug Abuse of the National Institute of Mental Health (NIMH). To date, the Drug Enforcement Agency (DEA) and the NIDA have pursued the law enforcement and drug research components of national drug policy (15).

Methadone Maintenance

Perhaps the most fundamental change in narcotics control of this period was the widespread use of methadone maintenance in control and treatment of narcotic addiction. The technique, begun in the 1960s, was given enthusiastic support by the Nixon Administration, in no small measure because of its apparent effectiveness in reducing addict crime. Methadone is a long-acting synthetic narcotic developed in Germany during World War II. It is given orally to lessen or even eliminate the desire for heroin. Some of the similarities between the use of and theoretical justification for methadone maintenance now and morphine maintenance in the World War I period are obvious, and both have encountered some of the same practical problems.

Some experts say that methadone may be required by a hard-core addict indefinitely; i.e., it does not end narcotic addiction but makes it more socially acceptable or feasible. This policy runs counter to an old theme in American attitudes, namely, that addiction should be stopped, not catered to. As realized a half century ago, however, a maintenance system, if deployed across the nation, is difficult to regulate, and diversion of supplies to nonaddicts can be a problem. One objection to the old maintenance clinics was the enormous profits garnered by some individuals who operated them; the implication was that profits stimulated the distribution of narcotics and the temptation to recruit new customers. Another problem was the failure of neat scientific explanations, such as Dr. Bishop's theory that a patient in precise opiate maintenance balance is quite normal. This did not work out so conveniently in practice. Maintenance, which was legal, for example, in New York State in 1918 and 1919, eventually led to abuses among health professionals and, in times of national fear, made the thousands of addicts scapegoats for social problems. Legal maintenance systems can thus become unpalatable or abhorred. They are sensitive to public pressure and political influences, and their existence is precarious, especially when the public believes that addiction itself is the cause of immorality, criminal behavior, and loss of productivity.

CHANGING MORES, CHANGING LAWS

Gerald R. Ford brought a markedly different political style to the White House in August of 1974. The new president wanted to distance himself from Nixon's heated antidrug rhetoric and from his management style that had concentrated power in the White House at the expense of the cabinet departments. To these ends, Ford adamantly resisted congressional attempts to institute an Office of Drug Control Policy in the White House to continue SAODAP-style oversight functions. He did sign amendments to the Drug Abuse Office and Treatment Act of 1972 that mandated establishment of such a body in the Executive Office of the President but did not seek appropriations to fund it.

In March of 1975, in the face of what appeared to be a worsening drug situation, the administration ordered a comprehensive study of the nature and extent of drug use and directions for future remedial policy. The study, known at the *White Paper on Drug Abuse,* was published in September of 1975 and set a new tone for drug abuse policy in the years to come. It recognized that the "total elimination of drug abuse is unlikely, but government actions can contain the problem and limit its adverse effects," a view that presaged the "harm reduction" argument of today. It also established antidrug priorities: "All drugs are not equally dangerous, and all drug use is not equally destructive.... Priority in both supply and demand reduction should be directed toward those drugs which inherently pose a greater risk—heroin, amphetamines (particularly when used intravenously), and mixed barbiturates" (55).

In the end, Ford turned away from the spirit of the *White Paper* and, in an attempt to bolster his chances in the 1976 presidential elections, resorted to the law-and-order approach to narcotics control that still paralleled the sentiments of an ever-narrowing majority of voters. In April of that year he introduced the Narcotic Sentencing and Seizure Act of 1976, which tried to revive the concept of mandatory minimum sentences for drug-trafficking offenses, and established cabinet committees for drug policy oversight and coordination. Whatever the merits of the bill, Ford was defeated, and the trend toward greater toleration of drug use and less emphasis on control of abuse through law enforcement accelerated.

The election of Jimmy Carter was most welcome to those who supported profound revision of the laws governing possession and use of recreational drugs, particularly marihuana. Carter appointed Dr. Peter Bourne as his special assistant for health issues and decided after some delay to implement the legislation establishing the Office of Drug Abuse Policy with Dr. Bourne as its head. Dr. Bourne set a tone of accommodation to the view that possession of marihuana in small amounts for personal use ought to be decriminalized as a step toward wiser and more just use of law-enforcement resources. Dr. Bourne was also of the opinion, as he wrote in August 1974, that "Cocaine . . . is probably the most benign of illicit drugs currently in widespread use. At least as strong a case could be made for legalizing it as for legalizing marihuana. Short acting—about 15 minutes—not physically addicting, and acutely pleasurable, cocaine has found increasing favor at all socioeconomic levels in the last year" (56). But the career of Dr. Bourne dramatically illustrates that toleration of recreational drug use would not become characteristic of more than a significant and vocal minority of Americans.

Bourne served the Carter Administration from January 1977 until July of 1978. During this time, drug policy continued to focus on the international aspects of the heroin problem and on domestic control of barbiturates and amphetamines. The Drug Strategy Council was revitalized and published national strategies for the duration of the administration. Bourne was able to report an apparent reversal of the 1974 and 1975 trends that had indicated a worsening heroin situation: Overdose death rates were declining, as were heroin prices and purity. In early 1977, President Carter decided to advocate decriminalization of marihuana in accordance with a trend that was being acted on by state legislatures throughout the nation. This was startling evidence of the profound change in attitudes toward drug consumption that had taken place since the 60s. But in July of 1978, Dr. Bourne resigned because of allegations that he had written a fraudulent prescription for methaqualone for a member of his staff and that he himself had used cocaine—an accusation that Bourne denied; the Carter Administration was suddenly in no position to appear soft on the drug issue. Though not obvious to most observers at the time, the wave of toleration that had been rising since the 1960s had crested, and both public opinion and public policy were about to change course.

THE NEW WAR ON DRUGS (1980 TO THE PRESENT)

Cocaine and Drug Intolerance

As the 1980s opened, cocaine use became more common but seemed to be characteristic of an economic elite who preferred to sniff or inject it. But by the middle of the decade, the method of consuming cocaine was shifting to smoking. Cocaine hydrochloride had to be converted to a base form for successful volatilizing. At first, smokers would use a "free-base kit," a dangerous method involving open flames and ether, often purchased at a drug paraphernalia store or "head-shop." Then, about 1985, drug dealers began distributing "crack" to the streets of America's large urban centers. "Crack" was a rock-like base form of cocaine that could be volatilized easily without requiring any preliminary ether treatment. The extraordinary blood levels of cocaine one could achieve by inhaling cocaine fumes from "crack" and its availability in units costing only a few dollars greatly expanded the cocaine market among poor and minority populations. Accompanying the "crack epidemic" were turf wars in urban areas as sellers competed for territory. Through the latter part of the decade the street price drifted lower until eventually, in terms of equivalent value, crack sold for less than had cocaine on New York streets prior to the Harrison Act of 1914 (57).

The arrival of crack, coupled with the overdose deaths of well-known youthful sports stars, combined with growing political pressure from anxious and angry parents, contributed to a new sense of national crisis over the cocaine problem. From the historian's perspective, the shift in attitude was rapid, widespread, and profound. The perception of cocaine for many moved from that of a safe, nonaddictive tonic to that of a feared substance linked to ruined careers and families. The stereotypic "coke head"—anxious, fearful, paranoid, hyperactive, and out of touch with others—may be the most fear-producing drug image to the American public. Perhaps the change in attitude is so striking because the initial image of cocaine was so optimistic (58). The fear of cocaine as well as popular and, at times, expert opinion that cocaine use would continue unabated unless legislators took drastic action spurred Congress and President Reagan into dramatic attacks on the drug problem.

In the fall of 1986, shortly before congressional elections, the executive and legislative branches of the federal government competed to enact the most severe laws against drug use. Billions were authorized by the Anti-Drug Abuse Act of 1986, although much less was later appropriated by Congress (59). Many observers, especially those within the treatment community, believed that the actual impact and funding of the law was a discouraging anticlimax to the promises and expectations that had accompanied its passage.

In 1988, as the presidential election approached, the fear of cocaine was reflected in enormous media coverage. Democrats and Republicans were each expressing outrage over drugs and drug use, neither side wanting to appear less determined than its opponent. An emphasis on law enforcement, so characteristic of the decline phase of the earlier wave of drug use, was most clearly demonstrated by the competition between the two major presidential contenders in which the Democratic candidate proposed greatly expanding the number of DEA agents, a stance in favor of law enforcement that eloquently illustrated the great change that had taken place in American attitudes since the Carter-Ford campaign. In 1976, the candidates had vied with one another as to which would be more understanding of casual or recreational use of what were considered to be "soft" drugs.

The 1988 Anti-Drug Abuse Act, like the one passed 2 years earlier, authorized substantial sums for treatment, but about two-thirds of funding went to law enforcement (60). Also, the 1988 act targeted the casual user much more prominently, with provisions such as fines for possession of personal amounts of drugs. An indication that the concern over drugs was expanding to include alcohol was the 1988 act's provision that a year after enactment, every bottle of beverage alcohol manufactured in the United States would have to carry a warning label.

One of the most significant provisions of the 1988 law was its Title I known as the National Narcotics Leadership Act. Reaching back to the 1972 Drug Abuse Office and Treatment Act and the 1974 amendments to it, this title again established an Office of National Drug Control Policy (ONDCP) in the Executive Office of the President and with it the position of Director of National Drug Control Policy—the so-called "drug czar." The legislation also included a requirement that the executive branch provide a comprehensive national strategy with guidelines to measure its success. A series of federal strategies have been published since September 1989 including the latest one put out by the Clinton White House in February 1995.

Conclusion—the 1990s

We can now look back on a quarter century of continuous and widespread exposure to illicit drugs. Those who have lived through this most recent "drug epidemic" can testify to the remarkable change in attitude toward drugs from the 1970s to the current popular attitudes. When we recall Jerry Rubin's claim in 1970 that "marijuana makes each person God," Timothy Leary's recommendation to "turn on, tune in, and drop out," and a *Time* magazine cover in 1981 exhibiting cocaine in a martini glass, we know that a shift in social norms has taken place. This change in attitude is captured by a second *Time* cover, in 1986: solid black except for a distorted skull-like face announcing a story on "Drugs: The Enemy Within." We have moved from softening of antidrug laws in the mid-1970s to renewing their severity since the late 1980s.

The longitudinal studies of the University of Michigan are helpful in illustrating this change in attitude toward drug use. The surveys indicate that acceptance of marihuana use among high-school seniors peaked about 1979, the middle of the Carter administration. Thereafter, positive attitudes toward marihuana declined slowly until they reached a low point of less than half the 1979 level in 1991; regular use of marihuana declined by about 50% during the same period (61). The Michigan surveys have also produced very recent evidence of newly increased use of some drugs among young people and somewhat less inclination to regard drug use as very risky. It is too early to speculate on the long-term significance of these findings, but they may presage a new period of experimentation with psychoactive substances.

During the past few years, declines have been reported in casual cocaine use and related emergency room admissions, but as the National Household Survey indicates, frequent cocaine use seems to have stabilized over the past 8–10 years among a "hard core" group of about half a million people (62). Drug Use Forecasting (DUF) surveys of the National Institute of Justice suggest that cocaine use among arrestees (a group underrepresented in the NIDA survey) rose rapidly in the late 1980s (63). Both surveys suggest that use of cocaine is becoming concentrated at lower socioeconomic levels of society.

So we see that our society has been through two "experiments in nature" regarding cocaine in the United States: twice (once beginning in the 1880s and again around 1970), a young population with no deeply held antagonism to the drug or even information about it has been exposed to the euphoric effects of cocaine. In each instance, 15–20 years passed before the nation changed its mind on the value and risks of cocaine.

An important difference between the earlier cocaine problem and the present one is that the first anticocaine laws followed the change in public attitude toward the drug, while in the current episode severe anticocaine laws were on the statute books at the very beginning of the new infatuation when Dr. Bourne pronounced the drug "benign." The result has been a much longer controversy over control of cocaine and the efficacy of legal restrictions than was the case early in this century.

Debate over legalization of drugs received public prominence during the current wave of drug use, both as drug toleration was quickly rising—in the mid-1970s—and as drug toleration was rapidly falling—in the late 1980s. The dominant argument for legalizing or "decriminalizing" cocaine, marihuana, and opiates in each case reflects the shift in the public's assumptions about drugs. In the 1970s, the argument was commonly made that the drugs were relatively safe, especially when compared with alcohol or tobacco; in the recent controversy, the argument has seldom been made that a drug like cocaine is safe, but rather that availability of a cheaper product would end turf wars and allow the dollars spent on interdiction to be spent improving conditions in the inner city. Comparison with alcohol and tobacco seems to have diminished as the public has become increasingly alarmed at these two legal substances. If Americans continue moving toward intolerance of drugs and drug users, it is unlikely that legal restrictions will be relaxed or eliminated. One contrary pressure would be economic depression, which could make illegal drugs—as alcohol came to be seen in 1933—an attractive source of government revenue and reactivation of trade.

The rise of acquired immune deficiency syndrome (AIDS) adds another dimension to drug abuse control; the epidemic is now spreading most rapidly among intravenous drug users, many of whom engage in both needle sharing and unprotected sex. Here the debate about relaxing legal restrictions has centered on the wisdom of distributing sterile syringes and needles, condoms, and methadone without many of the elaborate regulations now controlling this opioid. The full social and medical impact of AIDS lies in the future, but we can assume that the stress of these concerns—if the history of chronic, often fatal diseases such as tuberculosis is a guide—will tend to restrict rather than relax public policies (64).

Changes in the perception of alcohol over the past 10 years are another marker of evolving attitudes toward psychoactive substances of all kinds. More people now regard alcohol as a dangerous substance rather than as a beverage to be used in moderation with meals and on festive occasions. In 1984, the federal government required states to raise the drinking age to 21 or lose a part of highway taxes; in 1989, as noted, all beverage alcohol had to carry warning labels; and now we hear discussions about prohibiting advertising of alcoholic beverages. The coming decade will probably see this trend toward intolerance of recreational substance use continue. In the past, antagonism to alcohol has first led to extreme restrictions, which, in turn,

have been followed by a backlash against alcohol's tarnished image. For almost 50 years following repeal of national prohibition in 1933, it was difficult to discuss the problems associated with alcohol consumption without being accused of sympathy with discredited prohibitionists. Now the mood has changed, and the task will be to see whether this time the nation can establish a sustainable alcohol and drug policy that will not be swept aside in frustration and resentment.

The most recent legislation bearing on drug abuse control attempts once again to make the consequences of violating drug laws more dire. The Violent Crime Control and Law Enforcement Act of 1994 enhanced penalties for drug trafficking in prisons and drug-free zones, allowed the president to declare a violent crime or drug emergency in a specific area on request of the state or local executive, and amended the National Narcotics Leadership Act of 1988 to strengthen ONDCP (65).

The question for public policy is the degree to which a growing reliance on law enforcement will be balanced by availability of treatment and sustained support for research.

References

1. Clark N. Deliver us from evil: an interpretation of American prohibition. New York: WW Norton, 1976:29.
2. Timberlake JH. Prohibition and the Progressive Movement. Cambridge, MA: Harvard University Press, 1963.
3. Sinclair A. Era of excess: a social history of the Prohibition Movement. New York: Harper & Row, 1962:36–49.
4. Terry CE, Pellens M. The opium problem. New York: Bureau of Social Hygiene, 1928:50–51, 929–937.
5. Sonnedecker G. Emergence of the concept of opiate addiction. 1. J Mon Pharm 1962;6:275.
6. Sonnedecker G. Emergence of the concept of opiate addiction. 2. J Mon Pharm 1963;7:27.
7. Musto DF. Early history of heroin in the United States. In: Bourne PG, ed. Addiction. New York: Academic Press, 1974:175–185.
8. Wright H. Report on the international opium commission and on the opium problem as seen within the United States and its possession. In: 61st Congress, 2nd Session. Opium problem: message from the President of the United States, February 21, 1910. Senate document no. 377. Washington, DC: Government Printing Office, 1910:49.
9. Musto DF. The marihuana tax act of 1937. Arch Gen Psychiatry 1972; 26:101.
10. Wilbert MI, Motter MG. Digest of laws and regulations in force in the United States relating to the possession, use, sale, and manufacture of poisons and habit-forming drugs. Public Health Bulletin no. 56. Washington, DC: Government Printing Office, 1912.
11. Dupree AH. Science in the federal government: a history of policies and activities to 1940. Cambridge, MA: Harvard University Press, 1957: 267–270.
12. Young JH. The toadstool millionaires: a social history of patent medicines in America before federal regulation. Princeton, NJ: Princeton University Press, 1961.
13. Taylor AH. American diplomacy and the narcotics traffic, 1900–1939: a study in international humanitarian reform. Durham, NC: Duke University Press, 1969:48–81.
14. United States 60th Congress. Public law no. 221. An act to prohibit the importation and use of opium for other than medicinal purposes. Approved February 9, 1909.
15. Musto DF. The American disease: origins of narcotic control. New Haven, CT: Yale University Press, 1973:41–42, 257–263.

16. State of Massachusetts, Acts of 1914, Chapter 694. An act to regulate the sale of opium, morphine and other narcotic drugs. Approved June 22, 1914.
17. Renborg BA. International drug control: a study of international administration by and through the League of Nations. Washington, DC: Carnegie Endowment for International Peace, 1947:15–17.
18. Wright H. Uncle Sam is the worst drug fiend in the world. New York Times 1911;March 12(sect 5):12.
19. United States 63rd Congress. Public law no. 233. To provide for the registration of, with collectors of internal revenue, and to impose a special tax upon all persons who produce, import, manufacture, compound, deal in, dispense, sell, distribute, or give away opium or coca leaves, their salts, derivatives or preparations. Approved December 17, 1914.
20. United States Treasury Department. Treasury decision no. 2172. March 9, 1915.
21. United States Supreme Court. U.S. versus Jin Fuey Moy, 241 U.S. 394, 1916.
22. Kolb L, DuMez AG. The prevalence and trend of drug addiction in the United States and factors influencing it. Public Health Rep 1924;39:1179.
23. United States Treasury Department. Traffic in narcotic drugs. Washington, DC: Government Printing Office, 1919.
24. Kuhne G. Statement of Gerhard Kuhne, head of Identification Bureau, New York City Department of Correction. In: Conference on narcotic education: hearings before the Committee on Education of the House of Representatives, December 16, 1925. Washington, DC: Government Printing Office, 1926:175.
25. Mayor appoints drug committee. New York Times 1919;May 27:9.
26. Murray RK. Red scare: a study of national hysteria, 1919–1920. Minneapolis: University of Minnesota, 1955.
27. Federal Bureau of Narcotics. Narcotic clinics in the United States. Washington, DC: Government Printing Office, 1955.
28. Hubbard SD. New York City narcotic clinic and differing points of view on narcotic addiction. New York City Department of Health Monthly Bulletin 1920;Jan:45–47.
29. United States 65th Congress. Public law no. 254, sections 1006 to 1009. An act to provide revenue, by paying special taxes for every person who imports, manufactures, produces, compounds, sells, deals in, dispenses or gives away opium. Approved February 24, 1919.
30. United States Supreme Court. Webb et al. versus

U.S. 249 U.S. 96, 1919; U.S. versus Doremus 249 U.S. 86, 1919.
31. Bishop ES. The narcotic drug problem. New York: Macmillan, 1920.
32. American Medical Association, House of Delegates. Report of the committee on the narcotic drug situation in the United States. JAMA 1920; 74:1326.
33. DuMez AG. Increased tolerance and withdrawal phenomena in chronic morphinism. JAMA 1919;72:1069.
34. Burrow JG. AMA, voice of American medicine. Baltimore: Johns Hopkins University Press, 1963.
35. United States 67th Congress. Public law no. 227. To amend the act of February 9, 1909, as amended, to prohibit the importation and use of opium for other than medicinal purposes. Approved May 26, 1922.
36. United States Senate, Committee on Printing. Use of narcotics in the United States, June 3, 1924. Washington, DC: Government Printing Office, 1924.
37. Hobson RP. The peril of narcotic drugs. Congressional Record 1925;Feb 18:4088–4091.
38. United States 68th Congress. Public law no. 274. Prohibiting the importation of crude opium for the purpose of manufacturing heroin. Approved June 7, 1924.
39. United States 70th Congress. Public law no. 672. To establish two United States narcotic farms for the confinement and treatment of persons addicted to the use of habit-forming narcotic drugs who have been convicted of offenses against the United States. Approved January 19, 1929.
40. United States 71st Congress. Public law no. 357. To create in the Treasury Department a Bureau of Narcotics. Approved June 14, 1930.
41. United States House of Representatives, Committee on Ways and Means. Bureau of Narcotics: presentment and report by the Grand Jury on the subject of the narcotic traffic. Filed February 19, 1930. Washington, DC: Government Printing Office, 1930;Feb 19:73–77.
42. United States 75th Congress. Public law no. 238. To impose an occupational excise tax upon certain dealers in marihuana, to impose a transfer tax upon certain dealings in marihuana. Approved August 2, 1937.
43. United States 77th Congress. Public law no. 797. Opium poppy control act of 1942. Approved December 12, 1942.
44. Udell GG, compiler. Opium and narcotic laws. Washington, DC: Government Printing Office, 1968.

45. United States 82nd Congress. Public law no. 255. To amend the penalty provision applicable to persons convicted of violating certain narcotic laws. Approved November 2, 1951.

46. United States 84th Congress. Public law no. 728. Narcotic control act of 1956. Approved July 18, 1956.

47. Joint Committee of the American Bar Association and the American Medical Association on Narcotic Drugs. Interim and final reports. Drug addiction: crime or disease? Bloomington, IN: Indiana University Press, 1961.

48. Proceedings of the White House Conference on Narcotic and Drug Abuse. Washington, DC: Government Printing Office, 1962.

49. President's Advisory Commission on Narcotics and Drug Abuse. Final report. Washington, DC: Government Printing Office, 1963.

50. United States 89th Congress. Public law no. 89–74. Drug abuse control amendment act of 1965. Approved February 1965.

51. United States 89th Congress. Public law no. 793. Narcotic addict rehabilitation act of 1966. Approved November 8, 1966.

52. President's Commission on Law Enforcement and the Administration of Justice. The challenge of crime in a free society. Washington, DC: Government Printing Office, 1967:228–229.

53. United States 91st Congress. Public law no. 513. Comprehensive drug abuse prevention and control act of 1970. Approved October 27, 1970.

54. United States 92nd Congress. Public law no. 92–255. Drug abuse office and treatment act of 1972. Approved March 21, 1972.

55. Domestic Council on Drug Abuse Task Force. White paper on drug abuse. Washington, DC: Government Printing Office, 1975:97–98.

56. Bourne PG. The great cocaine myth. Drugs and Drug Abuse Education Newsletter 1974;5:5.

57. Musto DF. Illicit price of cocaine in two eras: 1908–1914 and 1982–1989. Conn Med 1990; 54:321–326.

58. Musto DF. America's first cocaine epidemic. Wilson Q 1989;13:59–64.

59. United States 99th Congress. Public law no. 570. Anti-drug abuse act of 1986. Approved October 27, 1986. For summary, see: Congressional Quarterly Weekly Report 1986;44(Oct 25):2699–2707.

60. United States 100th Congress. Public law no. 690. Anti-drug abuse act of 1988. Approved November 18, 1988. For summary, see: Congressional Quarterly Weekly Report 1988;46(Nov 19):3145–3151.

61. Johnston LD, O'Malley PM, Bachman JG. Drug use, drinking and smoking: national survey results from high school, college and young adult populations, 1975–1988. Washington, DC: Government Printing Office, 1989:57.

62. United States Health and Human Services Department, Substance Abuse and Mental Health Services Administration. Preliminary estimates from the 1993 National Household Survey on Drug Abuse. Advance report no. 7, 1994; July:2.

63. United States Justice Department, National Institute of Justice. 1989 drug use forecasting annual report. Washington, DC: Government Printing Office, 1990.

64. Musto DF. Quarantine and the problem of AIDS. Milbank Q 1986;64(suppl 1):97–117.

65. United States 103rd Congress. Public law no. 103–322. Violent crime control and law enforcement act of 1994. Approved September 13, 1994.

2 EPIDEMIOLOGY

Charles Winick

Epidemiology is concerned with the distribution and determinants of disease occurrence involving alcohol, tobacco, and other drugs (ATOD). To understand the proportion of abusers or dependents, we need to know the number of users of each substance. Abuse is a lesser degree of impairment than dependence (1).

Classical, psychiatric, and social epidemiology can be distinguished (2). The classical approach tracks the movement of a disease through a population (3). Psychiatric epidemiology adds confirming criteria, and social epidemiology focuses on subgroups and trends.

DATA COLLECTION TECHNIQUES

Triangulation is the combination of different research methodologies with different perspectives. Cross-checks are provided by a range of methods, such as survey, ethnography, and arrest information.

The Community Epidemiology Work Group (CEWG) integrates various indicators of drug abuse. Data on morbidity, mortality, treatment, public health, ethnography, law enforcement, and surveys are detailed in the reports from the group's specialist epidemiologists in 20 cities. The introduction to each community report summarizes unique features of a location, such as its economy; access to major highways, ports, or airports; tourist popularity; recreational life-style and local colleges; availability of space for the cultivation of illegal drugs; ethnicity and distance from U.S. borders (4).

Twenty indicators of substance abuse in a community have been grouped in one analysis into five topic areas: availability/environment (two), use (five), prevention/treatment (three), enforcement/regulation (three), and harm (seven) (5).

Surveys

The probability sample survey has become the most important method of determining the number of substance users. A national study of drinking, which operationally defined various drinking levels, was followed by a study of illicit psychotherapeutic drugs (6, 7). The first large-scale household probability sample study that involved the full range of substance use was conducted by the Commission on Marihuana and Drug Abuse in 1972 (8). In 1974, the National Institute on Drug Abuse (NIDA) assumed sponsorship of what became known as the National Household Survey on Drug Abuse (NHSDA).

This study collects data on Americans' use of a wide variety of substances, including marihuana, inhalants, hallucinogens, cocaine, opiates, stimulants, sedatives, tranquilizers, alcohol, and cigarettes. The survey is conducted annually, with a sample of around 30,000 and sponsorship by the Substance Abuse and Mental Health Services Administration (SAMHSA).

The most influential single source of data on youth substance use is the Monitoring the Future (MTF) program. MTF, with a national sample of approximately 16,000 high-school seniors, 18,000 eighth graders, and 16,000 tenth graders in 1994, has collected self-report questionnaire data annually since 1975 (9). The survey tracks the prevalence of ATOD use among junior-high and high-school students, some of whom are followed into their adult years. Another widely used school-based survey instrument is the Centers for Disease Control and Prevention's Behavior Risk Factor Surveillance (BRFS).

The major national survey on drinking practices and problems is conducted by Berkeley's Alcohol Research Group, at approximately 5-year intervals (10).

For the National Comorbidity Survey (NCS), a structured psychiatric diagnostic personal interview is administered to a sample of 8098 persons aged 15–54 (11). Its questions were incorporated in the 1994 NHSDA, the federal government's 1996 Health Interview Survey, and telephone interviews in the evaluation of the Fighting Back community action program (12).

Samples from treatment agencies, mental health agencies, criminal justice welfare agencies, and hard-to-reach subgroups such as dropouts yield considerably higher prevalence estimates than a household survey (13, 14). Substantial attention has been paid to the quality of interview data (15–17). Survey reach has been extended by such approaches as network "small world" questions (18).

Collateral Rates of Other Diseases

The death rate from cirrhosis of the liver has been used to estimate the number of alcoholics (19). Heroin addicts' overdose-related deaths and death rates from alcoholism are used to estimate prevalence (20, 21). Hepatitis B is an indicator of intravenous drug abuse, although its rate is declining because of educational programs and the spread of vaccination.

One major epidemiological contribution to the study of acquired immune deficiency syndrome (AIDS) was the discovery of its link to drug use, by users sharing needles or engaging in sexual intercourse with intravenous (IV) drug users. The AIDS-needle injector relationship varies considerably among American cities, from 6.3% in Los Angeles to 54% in New York City (22).

Drug Abuse Warning Network (DAWN)

The Drug Abuse Warning Network (DAWN), via cooperating hospital emergency rooms (ERs) and medical examiners (MEs), crisis centers and coroners, provides an indirect approach to epidemiology in key metropolitan areas (23). ER episodes per 100,000 ranged from 174 in Minneapolis-St. Paul to 700 in San Francisco in 1992 (24).

In DAWN, a mention or occurrence of drug use reported during an ER visit may result from an inappropriate use of prescription drugs, inappropriate use of over-the-counter drugs, adverse reactions, or use of an illicit drug (25).

In recent years, heroin, cocaine, and alcohol-in-combination have been the substances most frequently mentioned in ER reports. Some communities have established their own adaptations of DAWN, like the Hawaii Emergency Room Episode Data (HEED).

Information on fatalities directly or indirectly related to drug misuse or abuse derive from the DAWN sample of MEs in 27 metropolitan areas. Some MEs report cases based on circumstantial evidence and others conduct toxicologic analysis.

Capture-Recapture

In estimating the number of narcotic addicts, the capture-recapture procedure was first used by Greenwood (26). An addict listed by the Drug Enforcement Administration (DEA) was said to be captured. If reappearing on the roster, the person was recaptured. Another application of the approach is the use of multivariate contingency table analysis in order to estimate the size of the population of unknown drug users in the community from any number of sources, whether or not they are statistically independent of each other (27).

Local Studies

Various techniques are employed in order to trace incidence and spread of local drug use. In the copping area approach, an intensive count is conducted of a small geographic area in which an addict operates by stationing a field team at these sites (28).

Ethnography originally became significant in studying use of illegal drugs in Chicago and New York City (29–31). It has figured in many studies of substance use, users at risk for HIV, and identified phenomena that would otherwise not be noticed (32–40).

Treatment Programs

Treatment programs can provide systematic data on alcohol and drug users in treatment (41). The three major national surveys to determine characteristics of people in treatment and its effectiveness are the Drug Abuse Reporting Program (DARP, 1969–1974), Treatment Outcome Prospective Study (TOPS, 1979–1981), and Drug Abuse Treatment Outcome Study (DATOS, 1991–1993) (42–44). In the course of a year, each treatment slot turns over an average of perhaps 3 times, so that the unduplicated number of persons in treatment in a year can be estimated (45). With the coming of managed care, there is likely to be an increase in the frequency with which the slots turn over, as treatment becomes shorter.

With hardcore heroin users, the probability of entering into treatment during 1989–1990 was about 0.33. If 1,550,000 persons entered treatment

for all drug problems in these 2 years and 12.4% of these were primary heroin users, some 192,000 heroin users received treatment in both 1989 and 1990. Applying the 0.33 probability would lead to an approximate total of 582,000 hardcore heroin users (46).

Rates of treatment as reported for 1992 by the National Drug and Alcoholism Treatment Unit Survey (NDATUS) range from 1.2 per 1000 (New York City) to 8.1 per 1000 (Baltimore). On a typical day, some 800,000 persons receive services in a special drug or alcohol program, for a prevalence rate of approximately 300 per 100,000 (46). Untreated users of heroin and cocaine differ in a number of ways from users in treatment (47). Other users are in treatment with nonspecialty providers that may not be included in NDATUS (48, 49).

Urine Testing

Urine testing to detect the presence of drugs in persons applying for a job or already employed involves over 10 million persons annually. Most large companies and a number of federal agencies test urine, and figures from such testing can be used to estimate the number of applicants or employees who are taking specific substances. From 7% to 10% of potential employees could test positive for the use of illegal substances (50).

Critics of urine testing have questioned the relationship between the presence of a drug in the body and the worker's ability to function effectively, the validity of the tests used, issues of invasion of privacy, and undue zealotry (51). However, it has generally been upheld in the courts.

Special Indices

Indices have been developed on the basis of composite measures that lead to an estimate of the number of users of a specific drug. The Heroin Problem Index (HPI), for example, was developed to determine the number of heroin addicts by using five indicators: treatment program admissions per 100,000 population, heroin emergency room episodes per 100,000 population, heroin-related deaths per 100,000 population, retail price of heroin, and purity of retail heroin (52).

Subgroups

The following discussion highlights some of the subgroups involved in various degrees of drug use.

GENDER DIFFERENCES

Prevalence rates of drug use are higher among males than females, and the differences increase with age and involvement. Cigarettes, alcohol, marihuana, and cocaine are used more frequently by males than females. Men are more likely, and women are less likely, to obtain psychotherapeutic drugs via illicit channels.

Although with cigarettes and alcohol the median age of onset is higher for women than for men, there is an overall convergence between men and women in age of initiation of drug use (53). There are few gender differences in the proportion of respondents starting to use marihuana or cocaine after age 20.

Sixty-nine percent of all psychotherapeutic drugs are prescribed for women. Because women have lower body-fluid ratios and less body weight than men, the central nervous system effects of drugs are observable sooner on women than on men (54, 55).

The average woman, who weighs perhaps 40 pounds less than the average man, could drink less than the 15 centiliters of absolute alcohol per day, which is the usual criterion for excessive drinking, and still be impaired (56). Women's drinking is relatively likely to be hidden (57). There is an underdiagnosis of alcoholism in women, and women who drink heavily are viewed more negatively than men who do so. Alcoholism begins at a later age in women than in men, although women have physical manifestations of alcoholism and enter treatment at approximately the same age as men (58).

Since the end of World War II, use of illegal drugs has been consistently highest among males in their late teens and through their 20s. Society has been especially concerned about drug misuse in this age group, because of its impact on social functioning and its prominence as perpetrators of street crime.

PREGNANT WOMEN

A national survey found that 6.7% of women in childbearing years of 15–44 had used an illicit drug in the preceding month, compared with 1.8% of pregnant women (59). The first (1993) National Pregnancy and Health Survey of 2613 mothers delivering liveborns interviewed at hospitals found that 5.5% had used illicit drugs at some time during their pregnancy.

The fetal alcohol syndrome in children born to alcoholic women may include midfacial anomalies, low birth weight and length, brain maldevelopment, and other substantial deficits (60). Large urban areas have reported many babies born to crack-using mothers. The babies may have attention arousal deficit, excitability, seizures, and other problems. Other infants have AIDS transmitted from their mothers (61).

COLLEGE STUDENTS

In a survey of 56 4-year and 22 2-year colleges, the proportion of students using various substances in the previous year was 85.2% for alcohol, 39.8% for tobacco, 26.4% for marihuana, 5.2% for cocaine, 4.9% for hallucinogens, and 4.9% for amphetamines (62). The students consumed an average of 5 drinks per week. Some 41.8% had binged (5+ drinks in one sitting in the previous 2 weeks). In another national study, 86% of fraternity men and 80% of sorority women had binged, compared with 45% of men and 36% of women who were not affiliated (63). There is no evidence that binge drinking in college leads to a lifelong habit (64).

THE ELDERLY

The aging of heavy-drug-using cohorts from earlier decades has resulted in a shift in the age distribution of drug users. NHSDA reported that 29% of illicit drug users in 1994 were over 35, compared with 10% in 1979 (65). In 1979, 12% of cocaine-related DAWN episodes involved persons over 35, who accounted for 38% of such episodes in 1993. In one Houston study, more than one-sixth (17.6%) of persons over 55 were using a psychoactive substance (66).

The incidence of heavy drinking and alcohol problems in men decreases with age, and the chronicity of the problems is highest in the middle years (67). However, several factors promote alcohol dependence in older men (68). The true incidence of alcoholism among the elderly could be 20–30% (69). Users of illegal drugs tend to mature out of their habit before becoming elderly (70).

ETHNIC GROUPS

Reports on ethnic substance abuse seldom control for socioeconomic status and must be read cautiously. At least in the case of opiates, blacks and Hispanics dominate statistics of arrest, treatment, and ER mentions (71).

Black teenagers have lower rates of alcohol use and abuse than do whites (72). Frequent heavy drinking, which levels off beyond age 20 for whites, increases in blacks. Binge drinking appears to be more prevalent among blacks, especially in their mid-20s. There is a significant increase in cirrhosis mortality in blacks compared with whites (73). One study found lifetime prevalence rates for alcoholism to be 19% for nonwhites and 5% for whites (74).

There is a greater prevalence of alcohol problems among Hispanics than in the general adult population. Mexican-Americans are less likely than whites or blacks to use stimulants or psychedelics. They are late in getting treatment and experience more arrests and longer prison terms than other minorities (75).

Native Americans are at relatively high risk for substance dependence (76). Native American youths probably use more alcohol, marihuana, and inhalants than other young people.

OCCUPATIONAL SUBSTANCE ABUSE

Occupational alcoholism emerged as an area of investigation with the support of the National Institute on Alcoholism and Alcohol Abuse (NIAAA) in the 1970s. Originally management oriented, the occupational substance abuse approach has been extended to labor unions (77). Employee assistance programs (EAPs) can provide data on workers' substance use that may be unavailable through other sources.

About one-third of full-time workers smoked, two-thirds consumed alcohol in the previous month, and 15% reported heavy use of illicit drugs in the past year (78). Of persons using illicit drugs in 1991, 55% worked full time, and 13% worked part time. Fifteen percent of illicit drug users and 6% of heavy alcohol users said that they had gone to work high or a little drunk during the past year.

Many young people in military service are away from home for the first time and subject to peer pressure. In a worldwide 1985 survey, 47% smoked cigarettes, about one-third had used marihuana in the preceding year, and one-fourth were moderate to heavy drinkers (79). In a 1992 survey, military personnel had lower rates of illicit drug use but higher rates of cigarette smoking and heavy alcohol use than civilians (80).

THE HOMELESS

There is a substantial population of homeless people among whom substance abuse is the major health problem and many of whom are also at risk for tuberculosis and AIDS (81). Perhaps 20–30% of the homeless have alcohol problems, and 30–40% may have drug problems. Since 650,000 Americans may be homeless at any one time and some 3 million will experience it at some time, alcohol and other drug dependence in this population is important.

MENTALLY ILL CHEMICAL ABUSERS (MICA)

Of persons with mental disorders, 29% also have a substance abuse disorder (82). Substance abuse problems are found in 47% of schizophrenics and 24% of those with anxiety disorders. Forty-seven percent of alcohol abusers and 53% of drug abusers also have mental disorders. A mental disorder or an alcohol problem is found in 72% of drug abusers. In New York State psychiatric hospitals, almost one-third of admissions had comorbid chemical abuse disorders (83).

In the NCS general population survey of psychiatric comorbidity, some 8% were drug dependent at some time in their lives, and 1.8% were dependent in the previous year (84). Substance abuse could be second to anxiety disorders as the most prevalent psychiatric condition (85).

ARRESTEES AND PRISONERS

The increase in the total prison population to 1,053,738 at the end of 1994 reflects drug sentences, which represented 22% of state and 60% of federal prisoners, respectively, at the end of 1993 (86).

In 1989, 27% of jail inmates were under the influence of a drug when committing an offense, and 44% had used an illegal drug in the month before the offense. In 1991, comparable figures for prison inmates were one-third and one-half, respectively. In 1991, 14% of prison inmates had been under the influence of cocaine when engaged in their offense, up from 1% in 1974 and 4.6% in 1979 (87–90). One-third to one-half of arrests for drug offenses result from police investigation of other crimes.

The number of black, Hispanic, and women drug offenders has been increasing. As more drug offenders are arrested, more are convicted, and sentences are longer. The average federal drug sentence increased from 47.1 months in 1980 to 84.7 months for 1991.

Drug Use Forecasting (DUF)

The Drug Use Forecasting (DUF) system, currently in 23 cities, involves urine specimens at each site from about 225 male and 100 female arrestees each quarter. The proportion of male arrestees testing positive for any drug during 1993 ranged from 54% (San Jose) to 81% (Chicago) (91). Cocaine was the most prevalent drug at all DUF sites in 1994.

Arrestee drug use has been consistently stable and high. The urine testing is complemented by information obtained through interviews, although a substantial proportion of arrestees lie about their drug use (92).

Fatal Accident Reporting System (FARS)

A number of larger communities have used FARS data on single-vehicle nighttime (6 pm to 6 am) fatal motor vehicle accidents that are alcohol related (93). FARS is a division of the National Highway Traffic Safety Administration (NHTSA). Some two-thirds of fatal crashes occur at night and approximately three-fifths involve single vehicles. In 1992, 45% of fatal crashes were alcohol related. FARS information is a proxy for the incidence of alcohol use while driving. However, the community must have enough motor vehicle traffic to provide a consistent base.

PATTERNS OF SUBSTANCE ABUSE

Simultaneous polydrug use (SPU) is the use of more than one drug at the same time or in close temporal proximity (94). Concurrent polydrug use (CPU) is the use of more than one drug in the same time period but not necessarily at the same time. Eighty percent of men and women in treatment had taken two or more substances, either simultaneously and/or concurrently, during their substance abuse careers (95). Almost all of the single substance abusers had been alcohol drinkers.

In an average month in a recent year, 13 million Americans used illicit drugs (96). Of these, 10 million used marihuana and 1.4 million used cocaine. Thirteen million Americans exhibited heavy alcohol use (5+ drinks per occasion on 5+ days during the month). Sixty million people, including 4 million aged 12–17, smoked cigarettes.

Using marihuana is a good predictor of the use of more serious drugs only if it begins early. Similarly, only drinking that begins early is a good predictor of marihuana use. Age of first use of entry drugs appears to be crucial for later drug involvement (97).

DEPRESSANTS

Alcohol

In a typical recent year, the approximately 140 million persons using alcohol made it the most popular psychoactive substance (98). However, the decline in the amount of alcohol consumed since 1981 probably reflects health considerations, raising the drinking age and antialcohol education. Other significant changes in the social climate of drinking includes a federal excise tax increase, bans on "Happy Hours," laws that hold the server legally responsible for alcohol-related accidents, and self-censorship of drinking portrayals in the media (99). Including wine, spirits, and beer, the 1991 apparent average per capita consumption of alcohol was 2.31 gallons (100). There is a range from 1.36 (Utah) to 4.36 gallons (Nevada).

Getting drunk is a more prevalent goal in lower socioeconomic and younger age groups. A subgroup with a high proportion of heavier drinkers does not necessarily have a high proportion of frequent drunks (101). Drinking problems are greatest among the young, male, single residents of wet regions and urban, less educated, and persons of lower socioeconomic characteristics. Heavy drinkers also smoke more heavily than smokers in the general population (102).

There appear to be no statistically significant differences in heavy alcohol use by ethnicity (6.4% of whites, 7.3% of Hispanics, and 4.8% of blacks) (103). Heavy use was more likely to be found among men (10.3%) than women (2.5%).

Analysis of BRFS data from 49 states reported the median prevalence for binge drinking (5+ drinks at least once in the previous month) to be 14.2%. The rate of chronic drinking (60+ drinks in the previous month) was 2.98%, and the rate of drinking and driving (1+ times) was 2.42% (104). Nationally, the top 2.5% drank from 31% to 36% of the nation's total alcohol consumption (105). The top 5% consumed 45–50% of the total.

Marihuana

Marihuana use has declined since 1979. Some 66 million persons have used it at least once, but 10 million had done so during 1994. Among persons over 35, lifetime prevalence is higher among blacks than whites or Hispanics.

The rate of marihuana use in the NHSDA surveys was 4.3% in 1993 and 4.7% in 1994. Use on a weekly basis during the past year has remained constant from 1990 through 1994 at about 2.7%. However, use among youths 12–17 years old increased sharply from 4% in 1992 to 4.9% in 1993 and 7.3% in 1994.

Similar results were reported by the MTF study. Lifetime prevalence among high-school seniors, which was 60.3% in 1980, dropped to 50.9% in 1986 and 32.6% in 1992 but rose to 38.2% in 1994 (106). Marihuana's annual prevalence among eighth graders rose from 6% in 1991 to 16% in 1995.

The marketing of marihuana is responsive to social changes. Recently popular, blunts (deriving from the Philly Blunt inexpensive cigar brand) are gutted cigars refilled with marihuana and sometimes with additional substances. They enhance the communal ritual experience of smoking marihuana, in that they are generally shared by users. Blunts are mentioned in rap music, and their shape contributes to the hip-hop concept of "phatness," or excellence, also expressed in 40-ounce bottles of beer, oversized baggy clothes, and similar subcultural manifestations (107).

Heroin

In recent years, there have been around 550,000 regular heroin users. About 2.1 million Americans have tried heroin. Many different sources supply the American market, and in some cities, there are established brand names. The jump in heroin-related ER admissions tracked by DAWN, from 38,063 in 1988 to 64,221 in 1994, is an indicator of how heroin use is becoming popular again. Males, blacks, and residents of large metropolitan areas and of the Northeast are most likely to be heroin users. Its new popularity reflects low prices and high potency. The potency attracts users who can get high by snorting, without intravenous injection and the associated possibility of contracting AIDS.

Since 1990, numbers of young people are increasingly initiated into heroin use by inhalation or smoking, as heroin has been losing some of its stigma from the 1960s, becoming a form of rejection of crack's harshness.

Barbiturates

Barbiturates are used as sedatives and together with substances such as heroin and alcohol. About 4% of the population have taken barbiturates for nonmedical purposes, with males ages 26–34 and those living in large metropolitan areas the most likely users. Pentobarbital (Nembutal) and secobarbital (Seconal) are among the widely used short-acting barbiturates.

Benzodiazepines

The benzodiazepines, such as chlordiazepoxide (Librium), diazepam (Valium), flurazepam (Dalmane), and oxazepam (Serax), figure prominently among licit drugs in the top 20 controlled substances. In benzodiazepine episodes involving multiple drugs, alcohol figured in more than two-fifths, and cocaine use was reflected in approximately 1 of 10 cases (108).

The most widely prescribed sleep aid is triazolam (Halcion) (109). Its relatively short half-life and minimal hangover effect helped it to achieve major popularity.

Flunitrazepam (Rohypnol, "rophies"), which has been widely abused in England and is several times more potent than diazepam, is growing in popularity among young people in the United States, together with or often after heroin or cocaine use.

STIMULANTS

Cocaine

Cocaine may be sniffed, taken intravenously, smoked in the form of crack crystals, or mixed with other drugs. Cocaine that is snorted is often placed in lines on a mirror, in powder form, and a straw or paper cone is used for the inhalation. Crack is cheap and was popular in urban ghetto areas through the late 1980s.

Cocaine use has been declining since 1987, even though the trend among poorer people is more modest. Between 1985 and 1994, the proportion of current cocaine users in the National Household Survey declined from 2.7% to 0.6%. In 1994, three-fifths of current cocaine users were aged 18–34. There were higher rates of cocaine use among blacks (1.3%) and Hispanics (1.1%) than whites (0.5%). Current cocaine use was higher among men, noncompleters of high school, and the unemployed.

Lifetime prevalence among high-school seniors declined from 16.9% (1986) to 12.1% (1988), 9.4% (1990), and 5.9% (1994). Cocaine users were significantly more likely than nonusers to have dropped out of high school, cohabited, collected unemployment or welfare, been fired from a job, been divorced, not desired a college degree, and not had a full-time job (110).

Amphetamines

Methamphetamine was widely distributed for some time in cities with Asian populations on the West Coast. In the last few years, its use has become a significant national phenomenon. Relatively pure methamphetamine can be synthesized without external heat from ephedrine, the widely available over the counter bronchodilator. Ephedrine is the most popular truck driver's stimulant, sometimes sold with names like "Go Power."

Tobacco

In a recent year, some 60 million persons smoked cigarettes in the previous month (111). Blacks, residents of nonmetropolitan areas, persons with less than a high-school education, and the unemployed were especially likely to be current smokers. Cigarette smoking is rising among young Americans. Eighth graders' rate of smoking in the past 30 days rose from 14.3% (1991) to 18.6% (1994) (112). There is a wide range by state in high-school students' smoking, from 17% in the District of Columbia to 39% in West Virginia, in the month surveyed (113).

Forty-four million Americans, or almost half of all American adults who ever smoked, have stopped (114). Of persons age 20 or more who have ever smoked, 19% never tried to quit, 20% had tried to quit but not in the last year, and 15% of current smokers had quit for some time in the past year. Five per-

cent were former smokers who had been abstinent for 3–12 months, and 41% had been abstinent for over 1 year.

Fourteen percent of smokers were heavy drinkers, and 13% were currently using illicit drugs, versus 3% for nonsmokers (115). Because of decreasing nicotine content, smokers use more cigarettes than in the past.

Other Substances

Pseudopharmaceuticals or "look-alikes" that physically resemble amphetamines are available on a limited basis (116). In recent years, there has been great interest in the designer drug methylenedioxymethamphetamine (X, Ecstasy, MDMA, ADAM) (117). Ecstasy is often the focus of raves, which are extended night dance parties with loud music, taking place in a large space with a disc jockey or music or tapes. Ecstasy use contributes to sensory overload in the rave experience (118).

THE ROLE OF EPIDEMIOLOGICAL INDICATORS

Multiple epidemiological indicators can indicate current information and trends locally, on a state or regional basis, or nationally and internationally. Such indicators also permit quantitative assessment of the achievement of specific goals of national policy. Thus, of the ten objectives in the 1989 and 1990 strategies of the Office of National Drug Control Policy (ONDCP), six employed NHSDA, one used DAWN, and one used MTF data as measures (119).

The power of valid epidemiology can be seen in the transformation of the alcoholism problem. Data from surveys established that alcohol problems are not concentrated among the disaffiliated. Acceptance of this new epidemiology, in turn, helped to create NIAAA, broaden health insurance coverage, and validate employee assistance programs (120).

Epidemiological data have not always had a major role in policy assessment. In the 1970s and 1980s, critics could scoff at "mythical numbers" that were not based on serious empirical data (121). The lack of justification for the numbers did not matter because they had few policy consequences (122).

Today, epidemiology numbers and indices represent formal measures of achievement of major objectives. There is spirited discussion about the relative merit of some indicators, but there is general agreement that American epidemiological measures of substance use and abuse represent the world standard.

References

1. American Psychiatric Association. Diagnostic criteria from DSM-IV. Washington, DC: American Psychiatric Association, 1994:108–112.
2. Clayton RR, Voss HL, Robbins C, Skinner WF. Gender differences in drug use: an epidemiological perspective. In: Ray BA, Braude MC, eds. Women and drugs: a new era for research. Rockville, MD: National Institute on Drug Abuse, 1986:80–99.
3. de Alarcon R. The spread of heroin abuse in a community. Bull Narc 1969;21:17–22.
4. Community Epidemiology Work Group. Epidemiological trends in drug abuse: proceedings June 1994. Rockville, MD: National Institute on Drug Abuse, 1994.
5. Larson MJ, Buckley J. A community substance abuse indicators handbook. Waltham, MA: Brandeis University Institute for Health Policy, 1995.
6. Cahalan D. American drinking practices. New Brunswick, NJ: Rutgers Center of Alcohol Studies, 1969.
7. Manheimer D. Use of mood-changing drugs among American adults. In: Winick C, ed. Sociological aspects of drug dependence. Cleveland: CRC Press, 1974:103–110.
8. Abelson H, Cohen R, Schrayer D. Drug experience, attitudes and related behavior among adolescents and adults. Princeton: Response Analysis Corporation, 1972.
9. Johnston LD, O'Malley PM, Bachman JG. National survey results on drug use from the Monitoring the Future study, 1975–1994. Rockville, MD: National Institute on Drug Abuse, 1995.
10. Clark WB. Some comments on methods. In: Clark WB, Hilton ME, eds. Alcohol in America. Albany, NY: State University of New York Press, 1991:19–25.
11. Kessler RC, McGonagle KA, Zhao S, et al. Lifetime and 12-month prevalence of DSM-III-R psychiatric disorders in the United States. Arch Gen Psychiatry 1994;51:8–19.
12. Saxe L, Kadushin C, Beveridge A, et al. Evaluation of Fighting Back. New York: City University of New York Graduate School, 1995.
13. Weisner C, Schmidt L, Tam T. Assessing bias in community based prevalence estimates: towards an unduplicated count of problem drinkers and drug users. Addiction 1995;90:391–405.
14. National Institute on Drug Abuse. Prevalence of drug use in the DC metropolitan area household and nonhousehold populations: 1991. Rockville, MD: National Institute on Drug Abuse, 1994.
15. Aquilino WS. Interview mode effects in surveys of drug and alcohol use. Public Opinion Q 1994;58:210–240.
16. Bonito AJ, Nurco D. Validity of addict self-report in social research. Int J Addict 1976;11:719–724.
17. Turner CF, Lessler JT, Gfroerer JC. Survey measurement of drug use: methodological studies. Rockville, MD: Department of Health and Human Services, 1992.
18. Killworth P, Robinson S. Estimating the size of an average personal network and of an event subpopulation. In: Cochen MK, Russell BH, Johnsen EC. eds. Small world. Norwood, NJ: Ablex, 1989:159–175.
19. Lieber CS. Alcohol and the liver: 1984 update. Hepatology 1984;4:1243–1260.
20. Baden M. Methadone-related deaths in New York City. Int J Addict 1970;5:489–498.
21. Van Natta P, Malin H, Bertolucci D, et al. The hidden influence of alcohol on mortality. Alcohol Health Res World 1984–1985;9:42–45.
22. Community Epidemiology Work Group. Epidemiologic trends in drug abuse: proceedings June 1994. Rockville MD: National Institute on Drug Abuse, 1994.
23. Person PH Jr. Indicators of drug abuse—DAWN. In: Richards LR, Blevens LB, eds. The epidemiology of drug abuse: current issues. Rockville, MD: National Institute on Drug Abuse, 1977:135–137.
24. Substance Abuse and Mental Health Services Administration. Annual emergency room data 1992: data from the Drug Abuse Warning Network. Rockville, MD: Department of Health and Human Services, 1994.
25. Wesson DR, Camber S. Phenylpropanolamine mentions in the Drug Abuse Warning Network: numbers plus interactions. In: Morgan JP, Kagan DV, Brody JS, eds. Phenylpropanolamine: risks, benefits, controversies. New York: Praeger, 1985:362–370.

26. Greenwood JA. Estimating the number of narcotic addicts. Document SCID-TR-3. Washington, DC: U.S. Department of Justice, 1971.

27. Bishop Y, Fienberg S, Holland P. Discrete multivariate analysis. Cambridge, MA: MIT Press, 1975.

28. Hughes PH, Jaffe JH. The heroin copping area: a location for epidemiologic study and intervention activity. Arch Gen Psychiatry 1971;24:394–400.

29. Dai B. Opium addiction in Chicago. Shanghai: Commercial Press, 1937. Reprinted, Montclair, NJ: Patterson Smith, 1970.

30. Lindesmith AR. Opiate addiction. Bloomington: Principia Press, 1947.

31. Preble E, Casey JJ. Taking care of business: the heroin user's life on the street. Int J Addict 1969; 4:1–24.

32. Agar M. Speaking of ethnography. Beverly Hills: Sage, 1976.

33. Adler PA. Wheeling and dealing. New York: Columbia University Press, 1985.

34. Johnson BD, Goldstein PJ, Preble E, et al. Taking care of business: the economics of crime by heroin abusers. Lexington, MA: Lexington Books, 1985.

35. Ramos R. Chicano intravenous drug users. In: Lambert EY, ed. The collection and interpretation of data from hidden populations. Rockville, MD: National Institute on Drug Abuse, 1990:128–145.

36. Weppner RS. Street ethnography: selected studies of crime and drug use in natural settings. Beverly Hills: Sage, 1977.

37. Hanson B, Beschner GM, Walters JM, Bovelle E. Life with heroin: voices from the inner city. Lexington, MA: Lexington Books, 1985.

38. Williams T. Crackhouse: notes from the end of the line. New York: Viking Penguin, 1993.

39. Feldman HW, Aldrich MR. The role of ethnography in substance abuse research and public policy: historical precedent and future prospects. In: Lambert EY, ed. The collection and interpretation of data from hidden populations. Rockville, MD: National Institute on Drug Abuse, 1990:12–30.

40. Feldman HW, Agar MH, Beschner G. Angel dust: an ethnographic study of PCP users. Lexington, MA: Lexington Books, 1979.

41. Waldorf D. Careers in dope. Englewood Cliffs, NJ: Prentice Hall, 1973.

42. Simpson DD, Sells S. Effectiveness of treatment for drug abuse: an overview of the DARP research program. Adv Alcohol Subst Abuse Treat 1982;2:7–29.

43. Hubbard FL, Marsden ME, Rachal JV. Drug abuse treatment: national study of effectiveness. Chapel Hill, NC: University of North Carolina Press, 1989.

44. Etheridge RM, Craddock SG, Dunteman GH, Hubbard RL. Treatment services in two national studies of community-based drug abuse treatment programs. J Subst Abuse Treat 1995;7:9–26.

45. ABT Associates. What America's users spend on illegal drugs. Washington, DC: Office of National Drug Control Policy, 1995.

46. Larson MJ, Buckley J. A community substance abuse indicators handbook. Waltham, MA: Brandeis University Institute for Health Policy, 1995:40–41.

47. Rounsaville BJ, Kleber HD. Untreated opiate addicts: how do they differ from those seeking treatment? Arch Gen Psychiatry 1985;42:1072–1075.

48. Baldwin WA, Rosenfeld BA, Breslow MJ, et al. Substance abuse-related admissions to adult intensive care. Chest 1993;103:21–25.

49. Eisenhandler J, Drucker E. Opiate dependency among the subscribers of a New York area private insurance plan. JAMA 1993;269:2890–2891.

50. Drug testing: what's at stake? Industrial Chem News 1986;April:61.

51. Morgan JP. The "scientific" justification for urine drug testing. Kans Law Rev 1988;36:683–697.

52. Person PH, Retka RL, Woodward AJ. Toward a heroin problem index: an analytic method for drug abuse indicators. Document no. 017–024–00522–3. Washington, DC: Department of Health, Education, and Welfare, 1977.

53. Ray BA, Braude MC, eds. Women and drugs: a new era for research. Rockville, MD: National Institute on Drug Abuse, 1986.

54. Cooperstock R. Sex differences in the use of mood-modifying drugs: an explanatory model. J Health Soc Behav 1971;12:238–244.

55. Naegle MA. Substance abuse among women: prevalence, patterns and treatment issues. Issues Ment Health Nurs 1988;9:127–137.

56. Homiller JD. Alcoholism among women. Chemical Depend Behav Biomed Issues 1980;4:1–31.

57. Wanberg KW, Knapp J. Differences in drinking symptoms and behavior of men and women alcoholics. Br J Addict 1970;64:347–355.

58. Blume SB. Women and alcohol: a review. JAMA 1986;256:1467–1470.

59. Office of Applied Studies. Preliminary estimates from the 1994 National Household Survey on Drug Abuse. Rockville, MD: Substance Abuse and Mental Health Services Administration, 1995.

60. Secretary of Health and Human Services. Fetal alcohol syndrome and other effects of alcohol in pregnancy outcome. Alcohol and health, seventh special report. Rockville, MD: National Institute on Alcohol Abuse and Alcoholism, 1990:139–162.

61. U.S. General Accounting Office. Drug-exposed infants: a generation at risk. Washington, DC: U.S. General Accounting Office, 1990.

62. Pressley SH, Mailman PWS, Lyerla R. Alcohol and drugs on American college campuses. Carbondale, IL: Southern Illinois University, 1993.

63. Honan WH. Study ties binge drinking to fraternity house life. New York Times 1995;Dec 6:B16.

64. Hanson DJ. Preventing alcohol abuse. New York: Praeger, 1995.

65. Office of Applied Studies. Preliminary estimates from the 1994 National Household Survey on Drug Abuse. Rockville, MD: Substance Abuse and Mental Health Services Administration, 1995.

66. Stephens RC, Haney CA, Underwood S. Psychoactive drug use and potential misuse among persons aged 55 years and older. J Psychoactive Drugs 1981;13:185–193.

67. Fillmore KM. Prevalence, incidence and chronicity of drinking patterns and problems among men as a function of age: a longitudinal and cohort analysis. Br J Addict 1987;82:77–83.

68. Brody JA. Aging and alcohol abuse. J Am Geriatr Soc 1982;30:123–126.

69. Hartford JT, Samoajski T. Alcoholism in the geriatric population. J Am Geriatr Soc 1982;30:18–24.

70. Prins EH. Maturing out: an empirical study of personal histories and processes in hard-drug addiction. Rotterdam: Van Gorcum, 1995.

71. Mandel J, Bordatto O. DAWN: a second look—its impact on minorities and public policy. Am J Drug Alcohol Abuse 1980;7:361–377.

72. Franklin JE. Alcoholism among Blacks. Hosp Community Psychiatry 1989;40:1120–1127.

73. Nace EP. Epidemiology of alcoholism and prospects for treatment. Ann Rev Med 1984;35:293–309.

74. Weissman MM, Myers SK, Harding PS. Prevalence and psychiatric heterogeneity of alcoholism in a United States urban community. J Stud Alcohol 1980;41:672–681.

75. Desmond DP, Maddux JF. Mexican-American heroin addicts. Am J Drug Alcohol Abuse 1985;103:317–346.

76. May PA. Substance abuse and American Indians: prevalence and susceptibility. Int J Addict 1982;17:1185–1209.

77. Winick C. A labor approach to alcohol and other substance abuse. In: Brill L, Winick C. eds. Yearbook of substance use and abuse. New York: Human Sciences Press, 1985:115–137.

78. Institute for Health Policy. Substance abuse: the nation's number one health problem. Waltham, MA: Institute for Health Policy, 1993.

79. Bray RM, Guess LL, Mason RE, et al. Highlights of the 1985 worldwide survey of alcohol and non-medical drug use among military personnel. Research Triangle, NC: Research Triangle Institute, 1986.

80. Research Triangle Institute. 1992 worldwide survey of substance abuse and health behaviors among military personnel. Chapel Hill, NC: Research Triangle Institute, 1992.

81. McCarty D, Argeriou M, Huebner RB, Lubran B. Alcoholism, drug abuse and the homeless. Am Psychol 1991;46:1139–1148.

82. Office of Policy and External Affairs. National conference on drug abuse research and practice: an alliance for the 21st century. Rockville, MD: National Institute on Drug Abuse, 1991:4.

83. Haugland G, Siegel C. Alexander MJ, Galanter M. A survey of hospitals in New York State treating psychiatric patients with chemical abuse disorders. Hosp Community Psychiatry 1991;42:1215–1220.

84. Kessler RC, McGonagle KA, Zhao S, et al. Lifetime and 12-month prevalence of DSM-III-R psychiatric disorders in the United States. Arch Gen Psychiatry 1994;51:8–19.

85. Regier D, Meyers JK, Kramer M, et al. The NIMH epidemiologic catchment area program. Arch Gen Psychiatry 1984;41:934–958.

86. Bureau of Justice Statistics. Prisoners in 1994. Washington, DC: U.S. Department of Justice, 1995;August.

87. Bureau of Justice Statistics. Drug law violators, 1980–86. Washington, DC: U.S. Department of Justice, 1988.

88. Bureau of Justice Statistics. Drugs and jail inmates. Washington, DC: U.S. Department of Justice, 1991.

89. Bureau of Justice Statistics. Federal criminal case processing, 1982–91. Washington, DC: U.S. Department of Justice, 1992.

90. Bureau of Justice Statistics. Survey of state prison inmates, 1991. Washington, DC: U.S. Department of Justice, 1993.

91. National Institute of Justice. Drug use forecasting 1993. Washington, DC: U.S. Department of Justice, 1994.

92. Stephens RC, Reucht TE. Reliability of self-reported drug use and urinalysis in the Drug Use Forecasting System. Prison J 1993;73:279–289.

93. National Highway Traffic Safety Administration. Traffic safety facts 1992: a compilation of motor vehicle crash data from the Fatal Accident Reporting System and the General Estimates System. Washington, DC: U.S. Department of Transportation, 1994.

94. Martin CS, Clifford PR, Clapper RL. Patterns and predictors of simultaneous and concurrent use of alcohol, tobacco, marihuana, and hallucinogens in first-year college students. J Subst Abuse 1992;4:319–326.

95. Carroll JE. Uncovering drug abuse by alcoholics and alcohol abuse by addicts. Int J Addict 1980;15:591–595.

96. Office of Applied Studies. Preliminary estimates from the 1993 National Household Survey on Drug Abuse. Rockville, MD: Substance Abuse and Mental Health Services Administration, 1995.

97. Robins LN. The natural history of adolescent drug use. Am J Public Health 1984;74: 656–657.

98. Office of Applied Studies. National Household Survey on Drug Abuse: population estimates 1994. Rockville, MD: Substance Abuse and Mental Health Services Administration, 1995:85.

99. Gerbner G. Stories that hurt: tobacco, alcohol and other drugs in the mass media. In: Resnik H, ed. Youth and drugs. Washington, DC: U.S. Department of Health and Human Services, 1990:53–127.

100. William GD, Clem DA, Dufour, MC. Apparent per capita alcohol consumption: national, state, and regional trends 1977–1991. Rockville, MD: National Institute on Alcoholism and Alcohol Abuse, 1993.

101. Clark W, Midanik L. Alcohol use and alcohol problems among U.S. adults. In: National Institute on Alcohol Abuse and Alcoholism: alcohol consumption and related problems. Washington, DC: Government Printing Office, 1982:3–52.

102. Kowlowski LT, Jelinek LC, Pope MA. Cigarette smoking among alcohol abusers: a continuing and neglected problem. Can J Public Health 1986;77:205–207.

103. Office of Applied Studies. Preliminary estimates from the 1994 National Household Survey on Drug Abuse. Rockville, MD: Substance Abuse and Mental Health Services Administration, 1995.

104. Larson MJ, Marsden ME. State-level substance abuse indicators for youth. Waltham, MA: Brandeis University Institute for Health Policy, 1995;June 15:25.

105. Greenfield TK. Who drinks most of the alcohol in the U.S.? The policy implications. Presented at 39th International Institute on the Prevention and Treatment of Alcoholism. Trieste, Italy, June 11–16, 1995.

106. Johnston LD, O'Malley PM, Bachman JG. National survey results on drug use from the Monitoring the Future study, 1975–1994. Rockville, MD: National Institute on Drug Abuse, 1995:78.

107. Sifaneck S. Regulating cannabis: an ethnographic analysis of the sale and use of cannabis in New York City and Rotterdam, Holland [PhD thesis]. New York: City University of New York, 1996.

108. Coach WF. Benzodiazepines: an overview. In: Community Epidemiology Work Group, Epidemiologic trends in drug abuse: proceedings December 1989. Rockville, MD: National Institute on Drug Abuse, 1990:88–99.

109. Moch JW. Halcion: the hot bed of controversy continues. Western St U Law Rev 1992;19: 453–462.

110. Newcomb MD, Bentler PM. Cocaine use among young adults. Adv Alcohol Subst Use 1986;6:73–96.

111. Office of Applied Studies. National Household Survey on Drug Abuse: population estimates 1994. Rockville, MD: Substance Abuse and Mental Health Services Administration, 1995.

112. News and Information Service. Smoking rates climb among American teenagers. Ann Arbor: University of Michigan, 1995;July 17.

113. Feder BJ. U.S. report on nation's tobacco use shows wide state by state disparities. New York Times 1996;Jan 26:A10.

114. U.S. Centers for Disease Control. The health benefits of smoking cessation. Rockville, MD: U.S. Department of Health and Human Services, 1990.

115. Office of Applied Studies. Preliminary estimates from the 1994 National Household Survey on Drug Abuse. Rockville, MD: Substance Abuse and Mental Health Services Administration, 1995.

116. Winick C. Phenylpropanolamine: toward resolution of a controversy. J Clin Psychopharmacol 1991;11:79–81.

117. National Institute on Drug Abuse. Drug abuse and drug abuse research: the second triennial report to Congress. Rockville, MD: National Institute on Drug Abuse, 1987:121–142.

118. Harrison L. "Raving" in Colorado—an amateur's field notes. In: Community Epidemiology Work Group. Epidemiologic trends in drug abuse: June 1994 proceedings. Rockville MD. National Institute on Drug Abuse, 1994:68–70.

119. Harrison LD. Trends and patterns of illicit drug use in the USA: implications for policy. Int J Drug Policy 1995;6:113–127.

120. Roman PM, Blum TC. Notes on the new epidemiology of alcoholism in the USA. J Drug Issues 1987;17:321–332.

121. Singer M. The vitality of mythical numbers. Public Interest 1971;23:3–9.

122. Reuter P. The (continued) vitality of mythical numbers. Public Interest 1984;75:135–147.

3 DRUG POLICY

Mathea Falco

INTRODUCTION

Americans view drugs and crime as two of the most important issues facing the nation, according to a December 1995 Wall Street Journal/NBC poll. Two-thirds of the public think that drug abuse is worse today than 5 years ago (1). Four out of five police chiefs rank drug and alcohol abuse as the top problem in their communities, ahead of gun availability and gang activity (2, 3). The health costs of leaving drug addiction untreated exceed $3 billion a year, according to a 1993 study by the Institute for Health Policy at Brandeis University (4).

Illegal drug use cuts across all economic and ethnic groups. Of the 12 million Americans who admit using drugs at least once a month, three-quarters are white and employed. Among young adults age 18 to 21, one in seven now reports using illicit drugs at least once a month (5). Direct experience with drug addiction is also widespread, although rarely discussed publicly. One in two Americans say they personally know someone who has been addicted to an illegal drug, according to a nationwide survey by Peter Hart Research Associates in 1995 (1).

This deep concern about drugs has made drug policy a top priority for several decades. Since 1980, we have spent about $290 billion on federal, state, and local antidrug efforts. This amount—some $20 billion a year—is twice as much as the federal government spends annually for all biomedical research, including research on heart disease, cancer, and AIDS (6, 7).

FEDERAL REGULATION OF PSYCHOACTIVE DRUGS

Since the early years of this century, the federal government has imposed regulatory controls over psychoactive drugs that officials believe threaten the public health because of their abuse potential. The most notable of these drugs have traditionally been heroin, cocaine, and marihuana, although amphetamines, barbiturates, and methaqualone also periodically dominate federal drug control concerns. Amphetamine abuse, for example, reached epidemic proportions in the 1960s, when the axiom "speed kills" ultimately turned a generation away from the drug, only to reappear as a major problem in the mid 1990s (8).

The Federal Controlled Substances Act is the legal framework that differentiates permissible medical drug use from prohibited drug abuse.[a] For example, drugs regulated in Schedule II of the Act (such as cocaine and amphetamines) are deemed to have limited prescribed uses but severe abuse potential; those drugs regulated in Schedule I (heroin and marihuana, for example) have no permitted medical use as well as a great abuse potential. Although the Act gives the Food and Drug Administration (FDA) an advi-

---

[a] The Controlled Substances Act, 21 U.S.C. Section 801 ff., was originally passed as Title II of the Comprehensive Drug Abuse Prevention and Control Act of 1970.

sory role, the Drug Enforcement Administration (DEA) ultimately determines how restrictively to schedule a particular drug.

This regulatory intersection of psychopharmacology and enforcement is sometimes caught up in larger political concerns. A striking example is the persistent policy debate over the medical use of marihuana. The FDA has recommended that marihuana be transferred to Schedule II so that the drug could be prescribed for certain conditions, such as glaucoma, severe chronic pain, and appetite loss associated with chemotherapy and AIDS. The DEA administrative judge upheld the FDA recommendation, but DEA has refused to modify marihuana's legal status. Arguing that other drugs can effectively be prescribed for these conditions, DEA believes that even limited medical use of marihuana will encourage increased nonmedical use by implicitly endorsing the drug's safety.

Whatever the pharmacological merits of these arguments concerning medical marihuana, it is clear that politics predominate. Despite the federal prohibition, 36 states have adopted laws that permit patients with certain conditions to use marihuana with a physician's approval. While the vast majority of Americans oppose the legalization or decriminalization of marihuana (9), most believe that the drug should be medically available (10).

In California, where Governor Pete Wilson has twice vetoed legislation permitting medical marihuana use, the issue is facing a voter referendum in November 1996. The initiative would permit seriously ill patients to use marihuana in their medical treatment, exempting them from the state's criminal marihuana laws. Although public opinion in the state strongly favors the proposal, both sides are waging vigorous political campaigns for and against the referendum. The intensity surrounding this issue suggests the larger landscape of federal drug policy, which seeks to protect Americans from drug abuse through a combination of supply control and demand reduction initiatives.

FEDERAL ANTIDRUG SPENDING TARGETS ILLEGAL DRUGS

In 1997, the federal antidrug budget will exceed $15 billion. These funds are targeted against illegal drugs, primarily heroin, marihuana, cocaine, and amphetamines. Every cabinet department has a substantial antidrug program, ranging from $7.14 billion in the Justice Department to $1.11 billion in the Treasury Department to $29 million in the Department of Agriculture. The Office of National Drug Control Policy (ONDCP) was created by Congress in 1988 to coordinate the multibillion dollar, multi-agency federal effort. The ONDCP director, known as the "Drug Czar," is also responsible for developing the national drug strategy.

Alcohol and tobacco, which are legal except for minors, are generally not considered part of federal drug control policy. Although these two drugs account for more than 500,000 deaths a year in the United States, they have traditionally been addressed as public health issues, quite separate from the government's "war on drugs." This distinction has begun to erode in recent years, as the FDA has attempted to extend its regulatory authority over nicotine as an addictive drug. Powerful industry interests have thus far prevailed in keeping tobacco relatively free of government control (11–14).

In the context of adolescent drug prevention efforts, however, underage smoking and drinking are addressed, and a substantial portion of the federal government's limited antidrug prevention budget goes towards school and community programs to curtail youthful substance abuse. Despite these efforts, alcohol use is increasing sharply among young teenagers. Drinking among 14-year-olds climbed 50% from 1992 to 1994, and all teens reported substantial increases in heavy drinking in the past 30 days. Two-thirds of high school seniors say they know a peer with a drinking problem (7).

More than one million teens become regular smokers each year, even though they cannot legally purchase tobacco. By twelfth grade, one in three students smokes. In 1995, one in five 14-year-olds reported smoking regularly, a 33% jump since 1991. Advertising plays a critical role in encouraging teens to smoke. In 1993, the tobacco industry spent $6 billion for advertising and promotions, much of it directed towards young people. Nicotine addiction is acquired early: 95% of all adult smokers began smoking before the age of 19 (15).

FEDERAL DRUG STRATEGY CONCENTRATES ON REDUCING SUPPLIES

The federal drug budget has grown ten-fold since 1981, when President Ronald Reagan radically changed the focus of drug policy. Under previous Republican and Democratic Administrations, prevention and treatment—efforts to reduce the demand for drugs—received at least as much funding as supply control initiatives. President Richard Nixon, faced with a heroin epidemic among U.S. personnel serving in the Vietnam War, actually devoted three-quarters of his drug budget to treatment during the early 1970s (16).

President Reagan, promising to end the "evil scourge" of drugs, more than doubled drug enforcement funding from 1981 to 1986. Reagan believed that the nation's borders could effectively be sealed against foreign drugs in much the same way Americans could be protected from the missiles of the "evil Empire" (the former Soviet Union) by the Strategic Defense Initiative. At the same time, federal funding for prevention, education, and treatment was substantially cut. From 1981 to 1985, prevention and education programs received an average of $23 million a year, less than 1% of the total federal drug budget (17). These cuts in demand reduction programs undermined the basic premise of earlier U.S. drug policy: that a reduction in illicit supplies would force addicts into treatment and prevent potential new users from trying drugs.

The primary concentration on supply control strategies has continued under both Presidents Bush and Clinton, whose antidrug budgets have generally allocated two-thirds of all funding to enforcement, interdiction, and source country programs. In part, these spending decisions reflect political pressures to appear "tough" on drugs, particularly in election years when voter concerns are more loudly expressed. The supply-side emphasis also reflects the strength of the popular view that other countries are largely responsible for America's drug problems. This view has deep historic roots dating back a hundred years. When the first drug laws were adopted early in this century, immigrant groups and minorities were linked in the public mind with drug abuse: opium was associated with Chinese laborers in the West, cocaine with blacks in the South, and marihuana with Mexican immigrants in the Southwest. These drugs were seen as foreign threats to America's social fabric, undermining traditional moral values and political stability (8, pp. 5–6).

Blaming foreigners for America's recurring drug epidemics continues to have powerful political appeal. Getting Mexican and Bolivian farmers to stop growing opium and coca seems easier than curbing America's demand for heroin and cocaine. The argument also seems logically compelling: if there were no drugs coming in, then there would be no drug problem. Even if some drugs got through, reduced supplies should drive up drug prices, cutting drug abuse within the United States. Unfortunately, the experience of the past two decades has demonstrated that supply control efforts themselves cannot reduce America's drug problems.

The Supply-Side Scorecard

Since 1981, American taxpayers have spent nearly $75 billion on federal efforts to reduce illicit drug supplies (through enforcement, interdiction, and international programs). Yet heroin and cocaine in the United States are more available at cheaper prices than ever before (6, 18). Over the last decade, worldwide opium production has more than doubled (exceeding 4100 tons per year, the equivalent of 410 tons of heroin), while coca production has also doubled (19). Heroin now sells for less than half its 1981 street price, and heroin purity exceeds 65% in many cities, compared with only 7% purity in 1981. Cocaine prices have dropped by two-thirds (20).

The "new" heroin epidemic widely described by the popular press that particularly afflicts affluent professionals, high fashion figures, and rock stars is driven in large part by the ready availability of high-quality, cheap heroin. Heroin can now be snorted or smoked, avoiding the dangers of HIV infection and unsightly track marks involved with intravenous heroin use. Like cocaine a decade ago, heroin offers the seductive illusion of a relatively safe, intensely pleasurable high. Unfortunately, the "new" heroin causes overdose deaths from snorting or smoking just as the old heroin did from mainlining. In New York City, heroin overdoses more than doubled from 1988 to 1994, while heroin emergency room episodes nationwide jumped 70% during the same period (21).

Some critics blame the apparent failure of interdiction on a lack of resources, arguing that the current $1.8 billion annual allocation should be many times as large. Others blame the Clinton Administration's moderated shift away from trying to intercept drugs in the "transit zones" through the Caribbean toward trying to curtail production of drugs in Bolivia, Colombia, and Peru. The underlying problem, however, is not operational but strategic: the supply-side approach is fatally flawed for fundamental structural reasons.

Structural Flaws in Supply-Side Strategy

In the past two decades, drug production has expanded rapidly into every region of the world. Poor farmers who do not have solid alternative sources of income have strong economic incentives to grow drug crops even under difficult circumstances. If one production area is wiped out, crops can easily be replaced. In the early 1990s, for example, a coca fungus in one region of Peru pushed cultivation into more remote, previously uncultivated areas. In the Central Asian republics of the former Soviet Union, opium has become an important source of revenue. In Kyrgyzstan, for example, a pound of opium brought $400 in 1994—two-thirds of the per capita GNP. The economics of drug cultivation make sustained worldwide reductions in supply very unlikely. Moreover, the American market does not need to depend on foreign drug supplies. Many psychoactive drugs like amphetamines, LSD, and MDMA are produced illicitly within the United States. Marihuana has also become a major crop in this country, despite its illegality: ONDCP estimates that 25% of all marihuana consumed here is domestically cultivated (6, p. 50).

America's drug requirements can be supplied from a relatively small growing area and transported in a few airplanes. Although the United States has large numbers of illicit drug users, Americans actually consume a relatively small portion of total worldwide drug production—about 5% of all heroin and less than one-third of all cocaine production. A 25-square mile poppy field (roughly the area of northwest Washington, DC) can supply the American heroin market for a year, while annual cocaine demand can be met from coca fields covering about 300 square miles (less than one-quarter of the size of Rhode Island). Three Boeing 747 cargo planes could transport the nation's annual cocaine supply of 250 metric tons; three much smaller DC-3A planes could carry the annual 8-metric-ton heroin supply. Given the country's long, porous borders and the high volume of cross-border air, sea, and land traffic, interdiction has not proved successful in markedly reducing drug availability within the United States.

Most important, however, is that the price structure of the drug market severely limits any impact interdiction efforts might have. The largest drug profits are made at the street level, not in foreign poppy or coca fields or on the high seas. The RAND Corporation estimates that the total cost of growing, refining, and smuggling cocaine to the United States accounts for less than 12% of retail prices. The total cost of producing and importing heroin accounts for an even smaller fraction of the retail price (22). Even if the United States were able to intercept half the cocaine coming from South America—or eradicate half the coca crop—the price of cocaine in cities would increase by only 5%. With cocaine prices at record lows, such a minor increase would be unlikely to affect consumption.

DEMAND REDUCTION SHOWS GREATER PROMISE

Recent history offers an important lesson: the steepest declines in illicit drug use occurred during a period when drug availability was rapidly increasing. For example, in 1985, 5.75 million Americans reported using cocaine during the past month. By 1991, when cocaine prices hit new lows, only 2.37 million Americans reported cocaine or crack use within the past month (23). This sharp drop reflected growing public awareness that drugs were harmful as well as a change in social attitudes towards drugs, particularly among Americans most responsive to health concerns.

Since 1992, however, public tolerance for drug use has increased; a majority of both teenagers and adults view drugs as less harmful than they did four years ago (24). During the same period, marihuana use among eighth graders has more than doubled. The link between social attitudes and drug use is clear: as public acceptance of drugs increases, so does use, particularly among young people.

PREVENTION REMAINS LOW PRIORITY IN FEDERAL POLICY

Despite the encouraging results of a wide range of prevention initiatives, including anti-tobacco and antidrug advertising, prevention remains the lowest policy priority. The federal government as well as most states and cities spend less than 15% of their total antidrug budgets on prevention. In the fiscal year 1996 federal drug budget, prevention programs received $1.43 billion, compared to $9.21 billion for domestic law enforcement, interdiction, and international efforts to curtail the supply of drugs. Despite the rapid increase in teenage drug use, Congress substantially cut prevention funding in the 1996 budget and threatens to do so again in 1997.

For officials whose horizons are often defined by election cycles, prevention may seem too long-term an investment to provide immediate political returns. The impact of prevention is difficult to capture visually, particularly in 30-second segments on the evening news. The results of good programs may require years to develop, and are often measured in negative terms, when something—like smoking or using drugs—*doesn't* happen. Drug seizures or arrests of drug dealers provide far more graphic demonstrations that officials are responding to voter concerns about drug abuse.

Although many Americans strongly support prevention, they often do not have a clear understanding of what actually works. Prevention research, which has received even lower funding priority than prevention itself, is often difficult for nonspecialists to interpret. Findings are generally published in academic journals, which lag behind the research by several years and which are intended for scholarly rather than lay audiences. As a result, the case for prevention in the public arena often lacks a sound research basis, leaving prevention funding vulnerable to rapid shifts in political direction.

As will be discussed in a later chapter, extensive studies over the past two decades have documented the cost-effectiveness of early prevention and education efforts. For example, two thoroughly evaluated school curricula, Life Skills Training (LST) and Students Taught Awareness and Resistance (STAR), have been found to reduce new smoking and marihuana use by half and drinking by one-third, and these results are sustained for at least three years (25). The cost of these programs range between $15 and $25 per pupil, including classroom materials and teacher training. By contrast, the cost for one year of outpatient drug treatment is about $5000; for residential treatment, about $18,000; and for incarceration, about $25,000.

Unfortunately, many of the programs currently being used in classrooms across the country do not cover the essential elements of prevention. Moreover, many have not been evaluated using large scale pretest, posttest control group designs that measure actual reductions in tobacco, drug, and alcohol use. Some programs that have been adequately evaluated, like LST, STAR, and Project Alert, have produced significant behavioral results. However, without booster sessions in subsequent years, these results tend to diminish over time. Yet any delay in starting to smoke, drink, and use drugs is beneficial, since children gain time to develop social competence and strength to resist peer and media influences to use.

While some school programs have produced impressive results, families, communities, and the media shape the larger social context in which children make decisions about alcohol, tobacco, and drug use. Prevention is most effective when school lessons are reinforced by a clear consistent message that teen alcohol, tobacco, and drug use is harmful, unacceptable, and illegal.

TREATMENT WORKS BUT IS OFTEN UNAVAILABLE

Although the public is skeptical about the efficacy of drug treatment, numerous long-term, large-scale studies report that treatment works—particularly for addicts who remain in treatment a year or longer (26, p. 135). Yet since the early 1980s, treatment has also been a far lower priority of federal drug policy than drug enforcement. As a result, less than one third of the nation's addicts can obtain treatment unless they can pay for private care. In many states, managed care is further eroding treatment availability as insurers reduce coverage for drug treatment (27, 28).

Treatment is effective in reducing the social, health, and lost productivity costs related to drug addiction. A major study in 1994, the California Drug and Alcohol Treatment Assessment, found that $1 invested in alcohol and drug treatment saved taxpayers $7.14 in future costs (29). Providing treatment to all addicts in the United States would save more than $150 billion in social costs over the next 15 years, while requiring $21 billion in treatment costs (30). In 1996, the federal drug budget allocated $2.68 billion to treatment, less than one-third the amount devoted to supply control efforts.

DRUG ABUSE PERVASIVE AMONG CRIMINAL OFFENDERS

In 1995, approximately 1.5 million people were incarcerated in the United States with an additional 3.5 million under the jurisdiction of the criminal justice system. At the time of arrest, on average two-thirds of arrestees nationwide (regardless of crime) tested positive for an illegal drug (31). Without treatment, nine out of ten incarcerated criminals return to crime and drugs after prison and the majority are re-arrested within three years (26, p. 184).

Treatment is cost-effective even for seriously addicted criminal offenders. A 1994 RAND Corporation study found that $34 million invested in treatment would reduce cocaine use as much as an expenditure of $246 million for domestic law enforcement (30). Extensive studies have shown that treatment of drug offenders does work. Therapeutic communities inside prisons reduce recidivism by a third to a half after inmates return to society. The most effective programs are extremely rigorous, demanding far more from offenders than passive incarceration, and they cost only $5000–8000 a year for each inmate (26, pp. 177–180).

Yet treatment for criminals is still very scarce. The General Accounting Office (GAO) reported in 1991 that only 364 of the 41,000 federal prisoners with drug abuse problems participated in intensive treatment programs (32). In addition, more than three quarters of all state prison and county jail inmates are drug abusers, but only 10% receive any help. Furthermore, the GAO concluded that even these numbers are inflated, since most prison treatment—which consists of drug education and occasional counseling—is ineffective (33, 34).

Within prisons, priority should be given to treating offenders with serious heroin and cocaine problems, since they are responsible for the largest proportion of predatory crimes. Intensive residential drug treatment, which has proven effective in reducing recidivism among this group, is the most cost-effective approach according to the Institute of Medicine. The Institute of Medicine estimates that there are at least 250,000 prison inmates and 750,000 offenders on probation and parole who need this kind of intensive treatment (26, p. 235).

Treatment should also be provided for parolees. Community supervision programs for offenders on parole or probation—regardless of their offense—usually fail unless drug treatment is provided (35). The more intensive and structured the treatment, the more likely it is to be effective. But because the number of treatment programs of any sort are woefully inadequate, offenders must compete with noncriminal addicts for limited treatment space. Some cities, such as Miami, have created special drug courts to provide immediate treatment for drug offenders. These programs have shown good results, with a treatment cost per offender of less than $1000. But in most cities, drug offenders do not get treatment, although most would participate if treatment were available.

POLARIZED DEBATE OVER FEDERAL POLICY

The public debate over drug policy, unlike many other areas of government action, is often polarized by deeply felt moral and philosophical differences. Some advocate even tougher drug enforcement and more prisons while others urge legalization of drugs. This debate, described more fully elsewhere, affects a wide range of issues involving the treatment of addicts and drug offenders (36).[b] A recent example of the "get tougher" view is legislation adopted by Congress in August 1996 making anyone convicted of a drug-related felony (possession, use, or distribution) ineligible for welfare (Aid for Families with Dependent Children) and food stamps.

The history of methadone maintenance treatment in this country has been seriously affected by the debate over policy. Developed 30 years ago as a legal synthetic narcotic, methadone has proved effective in reducing heroin use, increasing productivity, and curtailing criminal activity from the first day of treatment. Comprehensive methadone treatment combined with intensive counseling reduced illicit drug use by 79% according to a 1993 University of Pennsylvania study (37). Methadone clients were five times less likely to become infected with HIV than addicts not in treatment (38).

Despite the extensive evidence of methadone's efficacy as a treatment of last resort for heroin addicts, methadone maintenance remains quite limited as a treatment modality. In 1994, methadone programs served 115,000 clients—less than one-fifth of all heroin addicts in the United States. In 1995, the National Academy of Science's Institute of Medicine recommended that the federal government expand the availability of methadone treatment. The Institute also urged the government to simplify regulations governing dosage levels and take-home medication that currently discourage participation in treatment (38a). To date, however, government policy on methadone remains unchanged.

The government's reluctance to expand methadone availability reflects larger political questions concerning treatment. Some officials (particularly in Congress) argue that methadone simply substitutes one narcotic for another and does not produce abstinence, which should be the goal of treatment. In this view, making methadone more readily available would discourage addicts from becoming abstinent as well as deflect federal funds from drug-free treatment programs. On the other hand, some clinicians and researchers argue that methadone, the most extensively studied treatment modality in our history, should be allowed to play a larger role in reducing drug abuse and drug-related HIV infection—even if methadone-maintained addicts never achieve abstinence.

A similar philosophical conflict surrounds needle-exchange programs, designed to provide clean injection equipment to intravenous drug users. The percentage of AIDS cases attributed to injecting drug use has tripled since 1981, and now accounts for one-third of all AIDS cases nationwide. Drug use accounts for two-thirds of AIDS cases among women and more than half of all pediatric AIDS cases (39). In an effort to reduce HIV transmission by drug users, needle-exchange (or clean needle distribution) programs now operate in more than 60 cities across the country, although they are illegal in most states. The mayors of San Francisco and Los Angeles have declared states of emergency, which permit these programs to continue despite California law.

Since 1988, Congress has prohibited the use of federal funds to directly support needle exchange programs, largely because officials feared that these programs might encourage addiction by making needles easier to obtain and by tacitly communicating social approval of drug use. According to language adopted by Congress in 1992, the ban on federal funds for needle exchange programs is to remain in effect "unless the Surgeon General of the United States determines that such programs are effective in preventing the spread of HIV and do not encourage the use of illegal drugs" (40). Despite the ban on direct support, Congress *has permitted* the use of federal funds to conduct demonstration and research projects that involve the provision of needles (41). Studies in a number of cities—including a comprehensive evaluation commissioned by the U.S. Centers for Disease Control and Prevention—have found that needle exchange programs reduce the spread of HIV and hepatitis B without increasing drug use (42). In 1995, after a two-year review mandated by Congress (43), the National Academy of Sciences explicitly recommended that the Surgeon General rescind the prohibition

---

[b] The author strongly opposes drug legalization or decriminalization.

against applying any federal funds to support needle exchange programs (44). The American Medical Association, the American Academy of Pediatrics, and many other scientific organizations support this recommendation. However, the Administration has not acted, citing the need for more evidence that these programs do not increase drug use.

FEDERAL POLICY RESISTANT TO NEW DIRECTIONS

There are a number of reasons why federal drug policy continues to concentrate primarily on supply control rather than demand reduction. Bureaucratic inertia plays a considerable role: despite quite different political rhetoric under Republican and Democratic administrations, the policy remains essentially unchanged. In part, this reflects the interests of the many agencies involved in maintaining their share of the ever-larger federal drug budget, including personnel, equipment, and operating funds. More significant, however, is the historical legacy of the early drug laws and the traditional view of the nation's drug problem as predominantly criminal and foreign in origin.

As discussed earlier, Americans have traditionally blamed other countries for "supplying" domestic drug abusers. Recent history provides a number of dramatic examples of how this view affects policy. In the late 1960s, President Richard Nixon sealed a major border crossing point with Mexico in an effort to force the Mexican government to take action against marihuana and heroin production. At the same time, a U.S. Senator publicly threatened to bomb Istanbul, Turkey, if the Turkish government did not curtail illegal opium production used in the infamous "French Connection" heroin traffic. Since then, U.S. officials have issued similar threats against other drug producing countries, most recently in Latin America. In 1989, President George Bush invaded Panama and transported then-dictator General Manuel Noriega to the United States for trial because of his role in drug trafficking. (Notwithstanding Noriega's departure, Panama remains a major cocaine transshipment site. According to the U.S. Department of State [19], Panama is "ideal for narcotics smuggling and illicit financial transactions" and "has not yet developed the resources or expertise to interdict narcotics on a consistent basis.") In 1996, President Bill Clinton "decertified" Colombia for inadequate antidrug cooperation, which effectively means the cutoff of U.S. aid (except for drug control aid) and U.S. opposition to World Bank and other multilateral development loans (45).[c] Because of Colombian President Ernesto Samper's alleged connections to the Cali cartel, the U.S. Congress is currently threatening to impose trade sanctions on Colombia.

Although U.S.-supported foreign campaigns against drugs can produce temporary declines in supplies, they do not last. In the past two decades, the opium eradication programs in Mexico and Turkey were the only successes, and these were very short-lived. In both cases, other suppliers quickly filled the production gap. Within five years, Mexico resumed its major illegal production role while Turkey became prominent in drug trafficking (confining its opium production to the legal pharmaceutical market). In Colombia, when the Medellin cartel was broken up and its leaders killed by government forces in 1989 and 1990, cocaine prices in the United States temporarily increased (because of interrupted supplies). However, within six months, prices declined to their original levels as other trafficking groups (particularly the Cali cartel) took over the Medellin business (46).[d]

In addition to viewing other countries as the source for domestic drug abuse problems, Americans have traditionally looked to drug enforcement as the primary means to curb addiction and to protect citizens from drug offenders. The underlying assumption has been that the threat of jail is sufficient deterrence to keep people from using, buying, and selling illegal drugs. While the prospect of a criminal record is undoubtedly an effective deterrent for many Americans, it does not prevent everyone from trying drugs, as the rising rates of marihuana use among young teenagers demonstrate. And people who are already addicted are often not responsive to threats of punishment, since much of their lives focus on finding the next fix. Nor does time behind bars change addictive behavior for most drug offenders, judging from the high recidivism rates.

Yet arrest, prosecution, and incarceration provide tangible proof that the government is "doing something" about drugs. Sizeable drug seizures also provide concrete evidence of official vigilance, more easily understood than lengthy treatment and prevention programs that measure progress over years rather than months.

Only recently have Americans begun questioning whether this approach actually produces positive results, including lower rates of addiction, less drug crime, and safer schools and neighborhoods. A small mountain of cocaine seized by Customs officials projects a powerful image of enforcement effectiveness on the nightly news; however—as many community antidrug coalitions have discovered—these seizures don't necessarily translate into less cocaine or fewer addicts on their streets. Indeed, the experience of the past five years suggests that drug enforcement has its greatest impact at the street level when police are involved with communities in driving out drug dealers (36, 47). A recent nationwide survey reported that police chiefs by a margin of two to one believe that reducing drug and alcohol abuse is a more effective strategy for combating violent crime than longer prison sentences for criminals (2). There is a remarkable consensus among those who are directly involved in dealing with drug addiction and drug crime: new approaches are needed if lasting solutions are to be found.

Despite the urgent need for more effective strategies, research receives less than 4% of the drug budget—about $500 million a year—used primarily for treatment studies. Only one-tenth of the research budget is used to evaluate drug enforcement and interdiction, which in 1996 constitutes two-thirds of total antidrug spending (6). While enforcement must be an important part of any comprehensive national drug strategy, it cannot by itself solve the nation's drug abuse problems, as the experience of the past two decades has demonstrated. In the rapid buildup of drug enforcement since 1981, funding decisions have been driven largely by political pressures rather than research or empirical evidence.

The campaign rhetoric of the 1996 elections again focuses on whether candidates are "soft" or "tough" on drugs and drug crime. One measure of Presidential "toughness" appears to be the amount of the federal drug budget dedicated to interdiction and overseas source country programs. Reflecting Republican attacks on his drug-fighting record, President Clinton's requested funding for interdiction increased by nearly 20% from fiscal 1995 to fiscal 1997, while Clinton's requested funding for prevention fell by 22% over the same period. The recent budget increases for interdiction ignore the findings of a major National Security Council policy review in 1993 that concluded that interdiction had not succeeded in slowing the flow of cocaine into this country.[e] But the political stakes of changing policy direction are high: Republicans in Congress tried to eliminate the ONDCP, contending that budget would be better spent on interdiction than on coordinating the multi-agency federal antidrug effort (20, pp. 123). Although Clinton succeeded in having ONDCP's budget restored (under threat of a Presidential veto), he also moved to increase supply-side spending, particularly interdiction. As a result, the Clinton drug budget looks very much like the drug budgets of the past decade, with more than two-thirds of the funds supporting enforcement, interdiction, and source country programs.

---

[c] For a discussion of the annual process by which the President must certify whether or not other countries are cooperating with U.S. antidrug efforts, see reference 45. Subject to domestic political concerns as well as competing foreign policy interests, the certification process is a dubious gauge of antidrug cooperation, even as it provokes resentment toward the United States, especially in Latin America. Moreover, certification's exclusive focus on international drug control perpetuates the notion that supply rather than demand is at the heart of America's drug problem.

[d] For a discussion of fluctuations in illicit drug prices over time, see reference 47, Table 4. Apparently as a consequence of the 1989 crackdown in Colombia, the U.S. retail price per pure gram of cocaine rose by about $50 in 1990. However, in 1991 the average price had receded to the low levels of the late-1980s, and dropped still lower in 1992 and 1993. The continued low U.S. prices in the early 1990s occurred despite the fungal infestation of Peruvian coca, which resulted in an estimated 30% reduction in cocaine production from 1992 to 1993. Prices did not rise, in part, because cocaine suppliers stockpile supplies in anticipation of shortages.

---

[e] Presidential Decision Directive (PDD) 14, issued November 1993, called for a controlled shift in focus of cocaine interdiction operations from the transit zones to source countries, on the theory that it is more effective to attack drugs at the source of production rather than once they are in transit to the United States.

TOWARDS A MORE EFFECTIVE FEDERAL DRUG POLICY

The political obstacles facing any real change in policy direction are formidable. Nationwide surveys, however, indicate that the American people are more pragmatic and less ideological about drug policy than the polarized political debate suggests. Hart polls in 1995 and 1996 found that the public and the nation's police chiefs strongly favor a balanced approach, with an equal emphasis on reducing demand through education, prevention, and treatment (1, 2). The surveys convey above all that Americans want programs that work.

Yet most people do not have a clear sense of what does work to reduce drug abuse and drug crime. Nor do most officials know the results of recent research on prevention, treatment, and law enforcement. The information is often difficult to obtain and ambiguous, without sharply defined findings or apparent practical relevance. Indeed, our present knowledge could best be described as possible indicators for a map, pointing in promising directions, rather than a blueprint for a perfect strategy.

But we do know a great deal more about what works than we did in the 1960s when the current "war on drugs" began. Some of this knowledge has come from research; much has come from experience. From 1977 to 1981, the author was Assistant Secretary of State for International Narcotics Matters, responsible for designing and implementing many of the source-country programs still operating today. At the time, crop eradication and income substitution (to assist opium and coca farmers develop alternative livelihoods) seemed a promising approach to reducing illicit drug cultivation in underdeveloped countries. In the 1970s these programs were largely experimental, but later administrations expanded them significantly. From 1984 to 1994, for example, the United States provided nearly $2 billion in economic, police, and military aid to Bolivia, Peru, and Colombia (48). Despite this considerable effort, annual coca production nearly doubled over the course of the decade; after apparently leveling off in the early 1990s, more land was under coca and opium poppy cultivation in 1995 than ever before, setting new records for potential yields of cocaine and heroin.[f]

Despite continuing U.S. pressure, governments have been unwilling or unable to sustain drug-eradication campaigns. According to State Department figures, from 1989 through 1996, less than 3.5% of the Andean coca cultivation was eradicated. Any reductions in cultivation have been temporary and symbolic, since new plantings continue to expand. For example, from 1987 to 1993, the Bolivian government used $49 million in U.S. for-

eign aid to pay farmers to pull up 25,000 hectares of coca. During the same period, however, farmers planted more than 37,000 hectares of new coca (51). Ironically, this well-intended U.S. aid program became little more than a coca support program for Bolivian farmers. It has had no impact on America's cocaine problem.

At the same time that the inherent limitations of U.S. international supply control efforts have become apparent, research on prevention, treatment, and community-based law enforcement has pointed out new directions for effective action. The current laws provide sufficient flexibility for a major shift away from supply-control strategies toward demand-reduction initiatives. Law enforcement still has an important role to play, particularly in helping citizens restore the fabric and the safety of their communities. But the effectiveness of drug enforcement spending will have to be subject to the same scrutiny as prevention and treatment, so that our tax dollars support programs that measurably reduce addiction and crime.

The experience of many Western European countries is instructive, despite considerable cultural differences between those countries and ours. Like the United States, most European governments have laws prohibiting drug sales and possession. Some, notably the Netherlands, Spain, and Italy, impose administrative sanctions for possession for personal use and give wide enforcement discretion to the police. However, regardless of the legal framework, all countries give priority to demand reduction. Arrest and imprisonment are a last resort, reserved for dealers and addicts who repeatedly reject treatment. Social and health services as well as drug treatment are readily available and prevention is the primary strategy for reducing drug abuse (52).

In the United States, we have made considerable progress against occasional marihuana and cocaine use in the past decade. (The recent upsurge in drug use among young teens is cause for alarm, a warning that prevention and education are critical in sustaining progress over time.) Health concerns and social attitudes play a powerful role in shaping drug-taking behavior, as changes in adult cocaine, tobacco, and marihuana use have demonstrated. Studies have shown that prevention programs, reinforced by community efforts, can substantially reduce new drug and alcohol use among schoolchildren. Treatment also can be effective. Extensive research has found that three out of four addicts can learn to live without drugs if treatment is structured, sustained for a year or longer, and if meaningful alternatives are available (26, pp. 14–15). Within the criminal justice system, treatment can reduce recidivism among drug offenders by a third to a half (26, p. 184).

How do we translate this knowledge into federal drug policy so that federal spending priorities reflect the lessons learned from earlier approaches? Unless we are to remain prisoners of our past failures, drug policy should not be left to elected officials as it traditionally has been. Citizen coalitions, teachers, police, civic leaders, parents—all must play an active role in making sure the reality they experience in their homes, schools, and communities shapes the future direction of drug policy. The medical and scientific communities, too, must increase their involvement: their work lies at the heart of finding lasting solutions to America's drug problems.

---

[f] The International Narcotics Control Strategy Report (49), published annually since 1987 by the U.S. State Department, is regarded as more authoritative than any other report on illicit drug production, but its estimates are generally considered conservative and have displayed inexplicable inconsistencies over time. (Because the information sources and technology used to make the estimates are classified, the government's methodology cannot be evaluated independently.) According to Peter Reuter (50), the unnecessarily low credibility of the INCSR figures ultimately stems from the fact that such numbers have been and remain irrelevant to drug policy decision making.

References

1. Peter D. Hart Research Associates. Americans look at the drug problem. Washington, DC: Drug Strategies, 1995:2, 14.
2. Peter D. Hart Research Associates. Drugs and crime across America: Police chiefs speak out. Washington, DC: Drug Strategies and Police Foundation, 1996:2, 11–12.
3. Dieter RC. On the front line: Law enforcement views on the death penalty. Washington, DC: Death Penalty Information Center, 1995:3–6.
4. Institute for Health Policy, Brandeis University. Substance abuse: The nation's number one health problem. Princeton, NJ: Robert Wood Johnson Foundation, 1993.
5. U.S. Department of Health and Human Services. Preliminary estimates from the National Household Survey on Drug Abuse, 1990–1994. Wash-

ington, DC: U.S. Government Printing Office, 1995.
6. Office of National Drug Control Policy. The national drug control strategy: 1996, budget summary. Washington, DC: U.S. Government Printing Office, 1996.
7. Drug Strategies. Keeping score 1996. Washington, DC: Drug Strategies, 1996.
8. Musto DF. The American disease. 2nd ed. New York: Oxford University Press, 1987.
9. Maguire K, Pastore AL, eds. Sourcebook of criminal justice statistics 1994. Washington, DC: U.S. Department of Justice, 1995:196–197.
10. Grinspoon L, Bakalar J. Commentary: Marijuana as medicine. JAMA 1995;23:1875.
11. Bartecchi CE, MacKenzie TD, Schrier RW. The global tobacco epidemic. Sci Am 1995;272 (5):44–51.
12. Ferraro T. The tobacco lobby. Multinational Monitor 1992(Jan/Feb):19–22.

13. Kluger R. Ashes to ashes: America's hundred year cigarette war, the public health, and the unabashed triumph of Philip Morris. New York: Knopf, 1996.
14. Massing M. How to win the tobacco war. New York Review of Books 1996(11 July):32–36.
15. Lynch BS, Bonnie RJ, eds. Growing up tobacco free: Preventing nicotine addiction in children and youths. Washington, DC: National Academy Press, 1994.
16. Baum D. Smoke and mirrors: The war on drugs and the politics of failure. Boston: Little, Brown, 1996:56–57.
17. Falco M. Toward a more effective drug policy. In: University of Chicago Legal Forum, ed. Toward a rational drug policy. Chicago: University of Chicago Press, 1994:11.
18. Testimony of Thomas Constantine, DEA Administrator, before the House International Relations Committee, March 1995.

19. Bureau for International Narcotics and Law Enforcement Affairs. International narcotics control strategy report (INCSR), March 1996. Washington, DC: U.S. Department of State, 1996.

20. Falco M. U.S. drug policy: Addicted to failure. Foreign Policy 1996;102:124.

21. U.S. Department of Health and Human Services. Drug abuse warning network, 1993, 1994. Washington, DC: U.S. Government Printing Office, 1994, 1995.

22. Reuter P, Crawford G, Cave J. Sealing the borders: The effects of increased military participation in drug interdiction. Santa Monica, CA: RAND Corporation, 1988.

23. National Institute on Drug Abuse. National Household Survey on Drug Abuse: Main Findings 1985 and 1991. Washington, DC: Department of Health and Human Services, 1988, 1992.

24. U.S. Department of Health and Human Services. National survey results on drug abuse from the Monitoring the Future study, 1990–1994. Washington, DC: U.S. Government Printing Office, 1991–1995.

25. Botvin GJ, Baker E, Dusenbury L, Tortu S, Botvin EM. Preventing adolescent drug abuse through a multimodal cognitive-behavioral approach: Results of a 3-year study. J Consult Clin Psych 1992;58:437–446.

26. Gerstein DR, Harwood HJ, eds. Treating drug problems. Washington, DC: National Academy Press, 1992.

27. U.S. Bureau of Labor Statistics. Employee benefits in medium and large private establishments, 1993. Washington, DC: U.S. Government Printing Office, 1994.

28. Drug Strategies. Investing in the workplace: How business and labor address substance abuse. Washington, DC: Drug Strategies, 1996: 11–19.

29. Evaluating recovery services: The California drug and alcohol treatment assessment (CALDATA), executive summary. Sacramento, CA: Department of Alcohol and Drug Programs, 1994.

30. Rydell CP, Everingham SS. Controlling cocaine: Supply versus demand programs. Santa Monica, CA: RAND Corporation, 1994.

31. National Institute of Justice, U.S. Department of Justice. Drug use forecasting: Drugs and crime in America's cities, 1990–1994. Washington, DC: U.S. Government Printing Office, 1991–1995.

32. National Institute of Corrections. Intervening with substance-abusing offenders: A framework for action: The report of the National Task Force on Correctional Substance Abuse Strategies. Washington, DC: U.S. Government Printing Office, 1991.

33. U.S. General Accounting Office. Drug treatment: Despite new strategy, few federal inmates receive treatment. Washington, DC: U.S. Government Printing Office, 1991.

34. U.S. General Accounting Office. Drug treatment: State prisons face challenges in providing services. Washington, DC: U.S. Government Printing Office, 1991.

35. Petersilia J, Turner S. Evaluating intensive supervision probation/parole programs: Results of a nationwide experiment. Washington, DC: National Institute of Justice, 1991.

36. Falco M. The making of a drug-free America: Programs that work. New York: Times Books, 1994:175–188.

37. McLellan AT, Arndt IO, Woody GE, Metzger DS. The effects of psychosocial services in substance abuse treatment. JAMA 1993;269:1953–1959.

38. Metzger DS, Woody GE, McLellan AT, O'Brien CP, Druley P, Navaline H, et al. Human immunodeficiency virus seroconversion among in- and out-treatment intravenous drug users: an 18-month prospective follow-up. J AIDS 1993; 6:1049, 1056.

38a.Rettig RA, Yarmolinsky A, eds. Federal regulation of methadone treatment. Washington, DC: National Academy Press, 1995.

39. U.S. Department of Health and Human Services. HIV/AIDS surveillance report. Atlanta, GA: Centers for Disease Control and Prevention, 1995.

40. Departments of Labor, Health and Human Services, and Education, and Related Agencies Appropriation Act, P.L. 102–394, Section 514.

41. U.S. General Accounting Office. Needle exchange programs: Research suggests promise as an AIDS prevention strategy. Washington, DC: U.S. Government Printing Office, 1993.

42. Lurie P, Reingold AL. The public health impact of needle exchange programs in the United States and abroad. San Francisco, CA: University of California, 1993.

43. Alcohol, Drug Abuse and Mental Health Administration (ADAMHA) Reorganization Act of 1992, P.L. 102–321, Section 706.

44. Normand J, Vlahov D, Moses LE, eds. Preventing HIV transmission: The role of sterile needles and bleach. Washington, DC: National Academy Press, 1995:1–8.

45. Falco M. Passing grades: Branding nations won't resolve the U.S. drug problem. Foreign Affairs 1995;74(5):15–20.

46. Abt Associates. What America's users spend on illegal drugs, 1988–1993. Washington, DC: Office of National Drug Control Policy, 1995:18.

47. Kleiman MAR, Smith KD. State and local drug enforcement. In search of a strategy. In: Tonry M, Wilson JQ, eds. Drugs and crime. Chicago: University of Chicago Press, 1990:69–108.

48. U.S. Agency for International Development. Congressional presentations, fiscal years 1984–1994. Washington, DC: U.S. Government Printing Office, 1985–1995.

49. Bureau for International Narcotics and Law Enforcement Affairs. International Narcotics Control Strategy Reports (INCSRs), 1987–1996.

50. Reuter P. The mismeasurement of illegal drug markets: The implications of its irrelevance. In: Pozo S, ed. Exploring the underground economy. Kalamazoo, MI: W.E. Upjohn Institute, 1996.

51. Lee R. The economics of cocaine capitalism. Cosmos 1996(June):58–64.

52. Leuw E. Drugs and drug policy in the Netherlands. In: Tonry M, ed. Crime and justice: A review of research. Chicago: University of Chicago Press, 1991.

4 INTERNATIONAL PERSPECTIVES

Ethan Nadelmann, Jennifer McNeely, and Ernest Drucker

INTRODUCTION: REFRAMING THE ISSUE

The unparalleled global production and distribution of psychoactive substances confront us with a new and potent version of an old problem: While we have never satisfactorily resolved the basic issues of addiction for the individual, the role of drug use in the social, biological, and economic lives of nations has never been greater. A global drug economy currently estimated at hundreds of billions of dollars (290) and increasing illicit drug use in this century, along with the AIDS pandemic, force us to confront old ways of thinking about drugs and reconsider the set of policies we now employ for their control. Given the likelihood of continued drug availability and widespread use, this chapter seeks to reexamine drug use and addiction from a public health perspective and to offer strategies to reduce their harmful consequences.

During the past decade, municipal, state and national governments in many nations have responded to drug problems with a variety of initiatives based on the evolving notion of "harm reduction." These measures share an underlying assumption that it is better for both society and the individual to concentrate on reducing the risks and harms of (continued) drug use and drug control policies than to focus solely on the goal of making people drug-free (205, 246). Below, we describe and analyze these initiatives and discuss possible ways of reducing the scope and severity of drug problems in any society, but with particular reference to the United States.

Harm Reduction

In the harm reduction scheme, drug policy is regarded as part of broad social welfare and health policies that emphasize pragmatism and inclusiveness. Better social integration of all drug users, termed "normalization" in the Netherlands (194, 195, 317, 318), is, itself, a goal. Abstinence (total cessation of use) is viewed as one of several means of avoiding problems with drug use, and destructive use is distinguished from recreational or controlled use (344). Priority is placed on maximizing the amount of contact problematic drug users have with social, treatment, health, and other community services (159, 247).

Harm reduction is really a new name for an old concept. During the nineteenth and early twentieth centuries, when many potent new forms of several drugs (including heroin and cocaine) became available, drug control efforts focused more on ensuring quality, purity, and safe dose levels than on prohibiting their use. The new drugs (including heroin and cocaine) were regulated rather than banned (32, 222). Drug addiction (once it became known) was addressed by medical means, which often included the provision by physicians of safer forms of the problematic drugs to their addict patients. In the United Kingdom, the influential Rolleston Report of 1926 formalized the policy of allowing opiate users to obtain drugs from physicians (31, 306). The justification for this practice was that most addicts will use drugs regardless of their illegality, and that it is better—in terms of health, lifestyle, and criminal activity associated with illegal drug use—for addicts to get their drugs from a legal, unadulterated source than to get them illegally. Morphine maintenance programs in the United States, early in this century, similarly reflected harm reduction precepts (68, 222), as did efforts to persuade drug misusers to switch to safer drugs (67, 325). During the late nineteenth and early twentieth centuries, some physicians in the United States advised those alcoholic patients for whom abstinence did not seem a realistic option to switch from alcohol to opiates (285, 325).

Contemporary harm reduction notions first emerged in the formulation of Dutch drug policy during the late 1970s and early 1980s (195, 318). The singular modern event that made harm reduction official drug policy in the United Kingdom, Australia, Switzerland, and elsewhere was the recognition, during the mid-1980s, that injecting drugs with shared needles spreads HIV. In each of these countries, government health officials declared that, as the British Advisory Council on the Misuse of Drugs stated, "HIV is a greater threat to public and individual health than drug misuse" and that henceforth AIDS prevention efforts should be integrated with antidrug efforts, with emphasis on the former (1, 168, 289).

Harm reduction approaches start by asking: How can we reduce the likelihood of drug users suffering overdoses, contracting infectious diseases such as HIV, hepatitis, and tuberculosis, and developing abscesses and other drug use-related medical problems? How can we reduce the likelihood of drug users engaging in criminal and other undesirable behaviors? How can we increase the chances that drug users will act responsibly toward others, take care of their families, complete their education or training, and become legally employed? How can we make treatment and rehabilitation services more available to those drug users who have indicated a desire to change their patterns of drug use or stop altogether? And, more generally, how can we ensure that drug control policies do not cause more harm than drug use itself?

In the United States, although many government officials and informed citizens express interest in less punitive and more public health-oriented approaches to drug control, most American politicians and public officials have systematically refused to examine the underlying assumptions of our current drug policies: prohibition, criminalization, and a rigid drug-free ideology (33, 128, 162, 230). These policies have remained dominant in the United States, despite recommendations over the years to the contrary by several high-level scientific and governmental advisory bodies (204, 232, 240, 307,

312). The debate over "drug legalization" has increased awareness of the extent to which many drug problems are the result of prohibition rather than drug use per se (223, 229). But it has also been distorted by those who claim that any harm reduction initiatives are stepping-stones to or examples of drug legalization (28, 97, 225).

Drug Use and Public Health

In this chapter we examine treatment, prevention, and drug policy within the framework of public health concepts and practices. The model we have chosen conforms to the standard public health and preventive medicine framework outlined in most texts (310) and includes measures for primary, secondary, and tertiary prevention: Primary prevention is defined as prevention of addiction (not cessation of drug use per se), secondary prevention aims to limit the length and severity of individual disorders associated with continued drug use, and tertiary prevention involves limiting collateral medical and social consequences of addiction once it has become a prevalent and chronic condition (28, 96, 225) (Table 4.1).

The harm reduction practices discussed here are public health responses to two fundamental observations: (1) the well-documented difficulty in "curing" addiction, i.e., the limited efficacy of existing addiction treatment approaches in achieving a totally "drug-free" or abstinent condition (163), and (2) the complementary and equally well-documented observation that for most users of most drugs, controlled use (without treatment) is the norm (330, 344). The likelihood of controlled use is deemed a function more of policies that affect drug markets, public perception, and education about psychoactive drugs than of any pharmacological qualities of the drugs themselves.

Understanding drug use and addiction as a public health matter reflects a shift in perspective from viewing them as phenomena *caused by* individual psychological (or moral) factors (222) to potential *causes of* extensive social problems and threats to public health. Harm reduction thinking reflects this shift and goes a step further, holding that many of the most destructive consequences and refractory problems of illicit drug use are not attributable to drugs per se. Rather, they are closely linked to our drug control policies, especially to the prohibition of certain drugs and the criminalization of the drug user. Drug control policies shape the ways in which people use drugs. If well conceived, they can be powerful tools for minimizing the adverse consequences associated with the worldwide availability of psychoactive drugs, even under prohibition regimes (227). The wide range of individual, social, and cultural factors that determine patterns of drug use in general (e.g., personal interest, peer pressure, and style) and destructive drug use in particular (social and economic deprivation, psychopathology and, possibly, genetic factors) are all acknowledged. But in a world in which continued drug availability and use is a certainty, and new drugs appear each year, harm reduction takes a pragmatic approach, seeking only to change drug control policies, not to change the drugs themselves nor to alter human nature.

Three Caveats

Analysis of harm reduction efforts must be qualified by three important caveats. First, the scope and progress of harm reduction efforts in most countries has been somewhat overshadowed by the globalization of the "war on drugs." The international drug prohibition regime promoted by the United

Table 4.1. Level of Intervention in a Reduction Approach

Level of Intervention	Definition	Response	Example
Primary prevention	The absolute prevention of addiction, but not of drug use per se	Policy and law reform to reduce the harms of prohibitionist drug policy itself	Cannabis decriminalization
Secondary prevention	Limiting the length and severity of drug-related disorders	Interventions and education enabling safer drug use	Needle exchange
Tertiary prevention	Limiting the medical and social consequences of chronic addiction	Addiction treatment	Methadone maintenance

States since the early 1900s is now firmly established throughout the world: the Single Convention on Narcotic Drugs (1961) (310) and the 1988 United Nations Convention Against Illicit Traffic in Narcotic Drugs and Psychoactive Substances have both been ratified by over 100 governments (224, 290). Drug enforcement tactics and sanctions developed and refined in the United States (these tactics include undercover operations, extensive employment of paid informants and electronic surveillance, asset forfeiture laws, far-reaching conspiracy statutes, drug testing programs, and mandatory minimum and long-term prison sentences) have been adopted in many countries, and the amount and proportion of police resources and prison space devoted to drug law enforcement have increased dramatically (226). Even in Britain, Australia, Switzerland, and the Netherlands, advances in harm reduction have proceeded in tandem with tougher and more extensive efforts against drug traffickers (94, 290). It is within this largely hostile environment that harm reduction programs currently operate.

The second caveat concerns the methodological limitations encountered in evaluating different drug control policies and problems (155, 205, 266, 267). Data collection and analysis regarding illicit behavior, particularly drug dealing and other consensual crimes, are inherently difficult given the generally hidden nature of the activities and the strong disincentives for participants to disclose their involvement (266). Even in the United States, where data collection on illicit drug consumption and related behavior has advanced much further than elsewhere, informed analysts often differ widely in their estimations and analyses (266). Comparative analysis among countries presents further complications. Governments vary in how they collect and categorize data on illicit drug use and related public health and criminal justice information. Substantial variations within countries—such as among the 26 cantons in Switzerland, the six states and two territories in Australia, or the many cities and counties of the United Kingdom—render cross-national comparisons exceedingly difficult and problematic. Transnational movements of illicit drugs and drug users complicate efforts to assess the impact of national and local drug control policies. The same is true of intranational movements of illicit drug users, such as from rural, suburban, and small urban areas to large metropolitan centers. Most importantly, illicit drug use and drug-related behavior are shaped by so many societal influences—ranging from cultural norms to broader social welfare policies—that it is extremely difficult and sometimes impossible to determine the precise impact of specific drug control policies on drug-related behavior.

The third caveat concerns the adaptability and potential efficacy of foreign innovations in the United States. Most of the countries in which harm reduction policies are being implemented have much in common with the United States. They are advanced industrialized democracies shaped by Judeo-Christian ideals and traditions, populated principally by Caucasians of European origin but with growing ethnic and racial minorities, troubled by rising levels of crime and social deprivation, and increasingly hard pressed to sustain government support for social welfare services. They differ from the United States, however, in several respects. None has witnessed an explosion in "crack" cocaine use comparable to that which has occurred in the United States (although some must contend with extensive use of injectable amphetamine). None exhibits the magnitude and intensity of urban poverty, violence, and social dislocation found in many U.S. cities (261). None possesses ethnic and racial minorities in numbers comparable to those of African-Americans and Hispanics in the United States in terms of their share of both the overall population and the population of those most negatively affected by illicit drug use and drug control policies. Many European countries have demonstrated a commitment to universal access to health care and the provision of basic social services (e.g., housing) far beyond that found in the United States. Most European countries have proven more effective than the United States in balancing popular sentiments regarding the immorality of drug use and other deviant behavior with public health and broader social welfare concerns (86, 195). These differences do not undermine the relevance of harm reduction precepts and policies to the United States, but they do suggest that both the prospects and the efficacy of harm reduction initiatives in the United States will be influenced by the American context.

ADDICTION TREATMENT: A HARM REDUCTION VIEW

Addiction treatment addresses the needs of those who have been unable to manage their drug use or maintain a functional or productive life. In our framework, treatment of addiction represents "tertiary prevention." As the last step in "prevention," it seeks to help with problems coincidental to unmanaged drug use and to limit the harms associated with the chronic, recurrent condition of addiction without necessarily "curing" the condition itself. Drug users presenting for treatment typically have a host of social and medical problems stemming from their drug misuse and often even greater problems associated with the illegality of their drugs of choice. In some cases, the best course of treatment may be to attempt drug abstinence (a "drug-free" approach). But in other situations, the best way to manage an addict's social and medical problems may not be to insist on total abstinence as the first step. Rather, these situations call for accepting some form of drug dependence and arranging for legal drug maintenance, in the interest of promoting stability and health.

A harm reduction approach to drug treatment provides a spectrum of services that collectively meet the different needs of individual drug users. The services are offered in response to the needs and wishes of drug users, instead of demanding that users conform to rigid treatment program requirements. "Low-threshold" treatment, which offers help to drug users but places only minimal demands on them, is a crucial component of harm reduction drug treatment services. Controlled drug use, where some level of continued use is accepted but the goal is to reduce the amount of drugs used and to shift to safer forms of use, can, itself, be a treatment objective.

Drug Substitution and Maintenance Approaches

THE BRITISH SYSTEM

Drug maintenance approaches have a long history (216, 222). In the United Kingdom, physicians have always retained the freedom to prescribe heroin, cocaine, and most other drugs for their addict patients. The influential Rolleston Report of 1926 clearly identified addiction as a medical condition and placed addiction treatment in the hands of doctors, who were given the freedom to prescribe otherwise illegal drugs for medical purposes (296). Doctors were given the authority to maintain addicts or to gradually detoxify them by prescribing their drugs of choice. The report explicitly named heroin and morphine, though prescription of drugs such as pethidine, dipipanone, cyclimorph, dicanol, cocaine, and amphetamine was also permitted (172, 296). This flexibility and authority given doctors to treat addiction with pharmacological agents represents the core of what has long been known as the "British system."

That system ran smoothly in Great Britain from the 1920s to the 1960s, with the number of addicts never reaching much beyond a thousand at any one time and their characteristics being significantly different from those of today's stereotypical "junkies." Most addicts were middle class, and most could obtain their drugs of choice from physicians who perceived legal maintenance as preferable to the continued use of drugs obtained illegally. But the climate began to change—particularly in London—during the explosive rise of drug use in the mid-1960s, when the number of addicts began to increase and their age, profile, and the social nature of drug use shifted dramatically (253, 296). The irresponsible prescribing practices of a handful of physicians were blamed for the changes, though broader social, economic, and cultural trends were primarily responsible (a similar growth in drug use occurred throughout the United States and Europe in this period) (35, 254, 306).

Beginning in 1968, British physicians were required to obtain a special license to prescribe heroin and cocaine (although not methadone) to addicts. Oral methadone gradually began to replace heroin, morphine, and injectable methadone as the principal drug prescribed to addicts, and a more confrontational, abstinence-driven approach that sought to confine addicts to specialized drug clinics replaced the older tradition of normalizing addicts' lives with physician-prescribed maintenance doses. The proportion of opiate addicts seeking treatment dropped from at least 50% in the early 1970s to 10–25% in the mid-1980s, according to one estimate (154, 156). The British treatment system was thus poorly prepared to compete with the black market and attract illicit drug users when heroin use exploded in Britain during the 1980s, growing in the course of the decade to about 20 times the size of the mid-1960s "epidemic" (254).

But the key element of the British system, namely, the freedom of physicians to prescribe for addicts, survived these changes. During the late 1980s, largely in response to the spread of HIV, a few physicians began advocating a return to more flexible prescribing practices, a policy that was endorsed by the ministerial Advisory Council on the Misuse of Drugs (1). British physicians and clinics still rely primarily on oral methadone, but more than 10% of all methadone prescriptions are for injectable methadone (45, 302a), and a few physicians and clinics prescribe pharmaceutical versions of many of the drugs sold on the streets, including heroin, cocaine, amphetamines, and benzodiazepines (99, 250, 302a).

METHADONE MAINTENANCE TREATMENT: THE U.S. EXPERIENCE

The British system had parallels in the first period of addiction medicine (1900–1925) in the United States (225). Maintenance (or substitute) drugs were prescribed to chronic dependent users deemed incapable of stopping on their own. Drugs were dispensed by private physicians and by dozens of narcotics maintenance clinics, which provided maintenance doses of morphine and other narcotics—including, in some cases, heroin—to thousands of addicts between 1912 and 1923 (225). Some of these clinics—particularly one in Shreveport, Louisiana—proved successful both in normalizing the lives of opiate addicts and in virtually eliminating local illicit drug markets (222, 303). But the maintenance approach was soon overwhelmed in America by the militant temperance movement of the time and by federal and state drug enforcement agents (222). By 1925, organized medicine and the U.S. courts had rejected drug maintenance (197), largely silenced its proponents, and led American medicine to all but abandon not only maintenance treatment, but the entire field of addiction medicine, to law enforcement (67, 222).

It was not until the early 1960s, with the pioneering work of Drs. Vincent Dole and Marie Nyswander, that the concept of addiction treatment utilizing the prescription of maintenance drugs was reintroduced in the U.S (68, 89, 185). Methadone was presented and prescribed as a "medication" that treated a long-lasting neurometabolic imbalance associated with sustained opiate use. While speculative at the time, this idea has been borne out and elaborated by contemporary brain research on drug effects associated with long-term use, i.e., addiction, tolerance, withdrawal, and drug craving (85, 127, 232, 272). When properly prescribed, methadone provides relief from acute withdrawal symptoms and markedly reduces chronic narcotic craving by stabilizing blood levels of the drug and its metabolites, thereby permitting "normal" functioning (18, 90, 167, 326). The goal of methadone maintenance treatment (MMT) is not total drug abstinence but, rather, to allow the individual to live with a specific chemical dependency (to opiates) by minimizing the disruptive effects of poorly regulated opiate dependence (i.e., recurrent cycles of intoxication and withdrawal) on psychological and social well-being and the risk this poses to individual and public health.

Today, MMT is the preeminent harm reduction approach to addiction treatment. No method of treatment for addiction to opiates is so universally associated with success as is long-term, high-dose MMT (163, 167a, 326). Positive outcomes include decreases in heroin use (18, 163, 167, 236) and injecting (18, 73, 281, 326), reduction in criminal behavior and arrests (18, 163, 174, 239), reductions in death rates among addicts (58, 120, 143, 144), and increased employment (34, 167). While the safe and effective use of methadone maintenance antedates the AIDS epidemic (89, 186), it was the appearance of this new disease in 1981 (82, 114, 232) that renewed interest in drug maintenance treatment (262, 264, 265, 298, 326). MMT is powerfully associated with reduced risks of HIV/AIDS: The rate of HIV infection among those in MMT is generally inversely proportional to the time in treatment (23, 243, 287, 335). Thus, while today almost 50% of New York City's injectors are HIV positive, for those who have been in treatment since 1978, it is virtually zero (151). Retention in MMT is also associated with improved access to and utilization of other health and social services (309). Even for HIV-infected opiate addicts, the risk of infecting others is substantially

lower for methadone patients, because injecting and needle sharing are reduced with time in MMT (17, 18, 74, 281, 326). Additionally, many of the collateral health problems of addicts infected with HIV can be addressed through medical care services offered in conjunction with many MMT programs. Infectious diseases such as multi-drug-resistant tuberculosis (MDR/TB), for example, can be effectively controlled within the context of primary care offered in MMT programs (282). Prenatal care provided through MMT programs can help reduce adverse outcomes of pregnancy, including transmission of HIV from mother to the fetus.

Despite these overwhelmingly positive findings for MMT's impact on clinical, public health, and social outcomes (many of them from American studies), the United States has fallen far behind other western nations when it comes to its effective implementation (222a). Methadone is the most tightly regulated drug in the U.S. pharmacopoeia (167). With few exceptions, it may only be dispensed in licensed "programs" that are subject to strict federal and state regulations regarding dosage levels, pick-up times and locations, and other matters typically left to the discretion of physicians (87, 89). The United States established over 100,000 MMT slots from 1965 to 1980, but since then there has been little change in treatment methods (167), and the MMT system has failed to expand to anywhere near the levels required to effectively respond to the AIDS epidemic (167). In New York City, only one MMT clinic has opened in the past 20 years, while several have closed (personal communication, M. Livenstein, Committee of Methadone Program Administrators, June 15, 1995).

Most methadone maintenance programs in the United States are "high-threshold" and "user-unfriendly" (65), often expelling clients who use drugs illegally or otherwise violate program requirements (37, 222a, 309). The regulations dictate not only security and staffing requirements but also dosage levels, pick-up times and locations, and other matters typically left to the discretion of physicians when it comes to other medications (87, 89, 167). U.S. methadone clinics are also relatively expensive: Only 5–10% of the cost of methadone treatment is spent on the medication itself (167). In many states, methadone regulations are clearly in conflict with sound medical treatment practices (309). Patients have been consolidated into already overcrowded facilities, predictably increasing community hostility and the likelihood of loitering and drug transactions occurring around clinic sites. In California, privatization and limitations on the duration of publicly funded treatment have raised barriers to MMT (221, 273, 274). Similar threats to treatment quality and accessibility in other states include ceilings on methadone dose levels (309), prohibition of take-home medication (309), and arbitrary restrictions on the number of methadone clinics allowed within a certain area (e.g., Tennessee allows no more than one clinic within a 100-mile radius) (personal communication, S. Novick and J. Woods, National Alliance of Methadone Advocates, October 1994). Perhaps most remarkably, as of 1996, eight states had no methadone maintenance programs whatsoever. (Idaho, Mississippi, Montana, North Dakota, New Hampshire, South Dakota, Vermont, and West Virginia have no methadone programs (personal communication, M. Parrino, President, American Methadone Treatment Association, September 1996).)

Furthermore, the therapeutic efficacy of many MMT programs in the United States has been eroded, and the standards of clinical practice have deteriorated (222a). There is widespread ignorance of the proper use of this treatment and often hostility toward methadone among many of those working in MMT programs. Problems include administration of inadequate doses (57, 65, 71, 149) and a misguided orientation toward abstinence not just from illegal drugs but also from methadone itself, as a treatment goal (56, 71, 309). A 1992 study of data from a national survey of 172 methadone programs found that one-half of the programs encouraged patients to detoxify after only 6 months in treatment (71), notwithstanding abundant evidence that premature detoxification results in a return to heroin use in 80–90% of cases (309). This study also found that a full 68% of clinics kept patients at an average dose of 50 mg or less (71) (well below the minimum recommended dose) (167, 309), thus reiterating the critical findings of the U.S. General Accounting Office's 1990 report on methadone treatment programs.

The continued failure to relax counterproductive regulatory constraints on methadone treatment by U.S. government agencies ill-equipped to oversee clinical care and the continued punitive posture of drug enforcement authorities regarding MMT have taken a once successful modality of addiction treatment and driven it to the margins of medical practice and public health (87, 88). Despite its proven clinical effectiveness and over 3 million patient-years of positive experience with methadone, punitive prohibitionist attitudes and policies have had a huge adverse impact on public health by restricting access to this treatment, in the United States and around the world. Until 1994, France had only 52 patients in MMT (284); even in the mid-1980s, Belgium imprisoned doctors for dispensing methadone (256); and in Germany as of 1996, methadone maintenance is still only paid by the health care financing system if comorbidity (e.g., AIDS, pregnancy) is present (personal communication to J. McNeely from U. Weber, Integrative Drogenhilfe, Frankfurt, 1996) (320).

INTERNATIONAL DEVELOPMENTS IN METHADONE MAINTENANCE TREATMENT

With the growing international awareness of AIDS risks and the potential role of MMT in limiting its spread by reducing addicts' risky injecting behavior and needle sharing, most countries in the developed world are now initiating, expanding, and liberalizing methadone availability (60, 264, 265, 333). Australia increased its MMT slots by 10-fold between 1985 and 1994 (117). Germany did the same between 1990 and 1994, increasing total methadone slots from 200 in 1987 to 4500 in 1994 (9, 75, 238). Even France has begun to open MMTs and plans to reach 5000 patients by 1997 (personal communication, P. Aeberhard, Medecins du Monde, June 1996).

In a harm reduction framework, priority is placed on maintaining contact between illicit drug users and health care providers. Steps are taken to attract and retain a higher proportion of illicit opiate users in treatment, in part by better adapting methadone programs to the particular needs of clients. There is widespread support for the view that methadone maintenance need not be directed toward a goal of abstinence and that a "drug-free" therapeutic objective is neither universally desirable nor appropriate. Abstinence from illicit drug use is regarded as a desirable but clearly secondary objective, although it is worth observing that there is no evidence that entry to methadone maintenance reduces the likelihood of eventual stable abstinence from methadone and other drugs (206). Harm reduction-oriented methadone programs counsel patients who continue to use illicit drugs about safer drug use and HIV prevention and work with clients to set methadone dose levels that suit their individual needs (Fig. 4.1).

Outside the United States, methadone has been expanded largely by integrating it into "mainstream" medical practice (1, 29, 50, 54, 131, 254, 256, 262, 264, 294, 316). Thousands of general practitioners in community-based practices throughout Europe (personal communication, M. Reisinger, European Methadone Association, February 5, 1996) (257, 262, 264, 294, 316), Australia (54, 326), New Zealand, and Canada (98) are now involved in

methadone maintenance. In Belgium and Germany, this is the principal means of methadone distribution (personal communication, M. Reisinger, European Methadone Association, September 12, 1995) (256, 263). This approach makes methadone more readily available to heroin addicts who live far from methadone clinics, allocates counseling and other services more efficiently, and is less intrusive, less stigmatizing, and more flexible than U.S.-style methadone clinics (54, 244, 245). Enlisting physicians in regular medical practice to prescribe methadone has also played an important role in involving the mainstream medical community in addiction treatment.

Another foreign innovation is "low-threshold" MMT programs, which make treatment more readily accessible to the less highly motivated addicts in the community. These programs provide methadone but few other services, though referrals to more intensive care are usually available. They do not demand regular attendance, urine tests, or regular counseling contacts, all of which are standard in traditional methadone clinics.

Low-threshold programs are generally opposed in the United States and elsewhere on three grounds: that they are less effective than more "comprehensive" methadone programs in reducing illicit drug use and other undesirable drug-related behavior; that their availability offers a less demanding option for heroin addicts who would be better served by more comprehensive programs; and that their dramatically lower cost will undermine political support for traditional full-service programs. Support for low-threshold programs, on the other hand, is based on their relatively low cost, which greatly increases the number of people who can be provided with care; their proven success in establishing contact with illicit drug users put off by the rigorous requirements of programs that prioritize drug abstinence; and the fact that their clients typically fare better than do illicit drug users not enrolled in any programs (52, 114, 124, 211, 237, 341).

Low-threshold programs now operate in several cities in Europe (53, 129, 182, 257, 258), Australia (129, 326), and Hong Kong (237, 287). The Dutch were pioneers in deploying low-threshold "methadone buses"—mobile facilities that carry previously prescribed doses, free of charge, for a list of 100 or more patients who may meet the bus at any one of several predesignated locations daily (53, 257, 324)—an innovation that has also been adopted in Barcelona (258). In the Netherlands and, to a lesser extent, Switzerland, methadone is available in public and private health clinics and other government facilities (100). Some programs, including a few in the United States, deliver methadone to the homes of clients with AIDS and other immobilizing diseases. In Copenhagen (39) and in Amsterdam (257), methadone is available at police stations for addicts who have been arrested.

REINVENTING METHADONE IN THE UNITED STATES

These developments, as well as other initiatives to diversify and normalize methadone availability, offer numerous advantages over the U.S. model of confining MMT to specialized clinics. By distributing methadone treatment

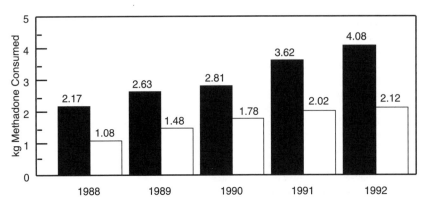

Figure 4.1.   Methadone consumption (*solid bar*) versus AIDS cases in intravenous drug users (*shaded bar*) (1993). All figures are per 100,000 population. (Source: INCB, 1993, and European Centre for the Epidemiological Monitoring of AIDS, 1993.) (Reproduced with permission from Farrell M, et al. Methadone provision in the European Union. Int J Drug Policy 1995;6(3):168–172.)

more evenly, they make it available to patients who live far from methadone clinics, reduce the amount of time and energy that methadone patients must devote to obtaining their prescribed drug, and alleviate some of the stigma associated with participation in methadone programs. They also play an important role in involving the medical community in the treatment of drug addiction and help to defuse and circumvent the "NIMBY" protests and zoning problems that often defeat efforts to establish new methadone clinics.

Though foreign developments in methadone maintenance have not been ignored in the United States, there has been considerable resistance to adopting or even experimenting with them. Except for a couple of "medical maintenance" experiments that have permitted some long-term methadone recipients to transfer from traditional methadone clinics to office-based physicians (242, 244, 245, 283), pharmacists and American doctors in general medical practice are virtually barred by federal regulations from playing any role in methadone maintenance. Methadone buses are used in Baltimore, Maryland, and Springfield, Massachusetts, but they operate much like traditional full-service programs (personal communication, J. Brady, The Johns Hopkins School of Medicine, December 15, 1995). Low-threshold "interim clinics," which provide methadone without extensive ancillary services, have been approved by federal regulators as a short-term option for addicts on waiting lists for traditional methadone programs (167). But Beth Israel Medical Center in New York City, the only provider of interim services, was forced by local political pressures to close its interim clinic in 1993, and there has yet to be another interim clinic opened anywhere in the United States.

One area in which the United States has made strides is in the provision of methadone to incarcerated addicts. The use of methadone in jails and prisons—in the United States and around the world—has generally been restricted to brief heroin detoxification programs. The largest in-jail methadone maintenance program in the world, with 3000 admissions per year, is the Key Extended Entry Program (KEEP) in New York City. Created in 1987 to provide maintenance doses of methadone to heroin users and methadone patients who had been arrested on misdemeanor charges and jailed at the Rikers Island jail facilities, it has proven effective in increasing the proportion of inmates who apply for and remain in drug treatment after release (207). Despite this success, it remains the only such program in the United States. Methadone maintenance programs can now be found in jails and even in prisons throughout Europe (91)—in Switzerland (2), Denmark, and the Netherlands—and in Australia (91, 148, 235). An evaluation of the methadone maintenance program initiated in January 1991 in two jails in Basel reported that it had drastically reduced illicit drug use among inmates receiving methadone (160).

In the Netherlands, the United Kingdom, Canada, and some parts of Australia, clients at many methadone programs need not submit to testing for drug use (129, 338). Further, syringe exchange programs (SEPs) (see below) are integrated or run in conjunction with many methadone programs. But in the United States, though some methadone programs have formal agreements to work with SEPs, they rarely translate into active cooperation (personal communication, A. Clear, Harm Reduction Coalition, June 18, 1996). Because U.S. methadone programs require abstinence from all illicit drugs, education on safer drug use is rare, despite the fact that many methadone patients do continue to use these drugs (personal communication, J. Woods, National Alliance of Methadone Advocates, 1996) (150). Most relationships between SEPs and methadone programs in the United States depend on individual methadone program counselors, who may tell their drug-using patients about SEPs, and on SEPs that take it upon themselves to operate near methadone programs.

OTHER DRUG SUBSTITUTION INITIATIVES

Methadone emerged as the most common maintenance drug because it is effective orally, is relatively long acting, produces less euphoria than injected heroin, presents relatively few undesirable side effects, and provokes cross-tolerance to heroin. The expansion of methadone maintenance through a diversity of providers—from low-threshold clinics to private doctors—can substantially increase the number of addicts in contact with drug treatment and other social services. But the capacity of MMT to reach many addicts is limited. Methadone is not a treatment for primary addiction to cocaine, amphetamine, alcohol, and other nonopiate drugs, though use of these drugs will often decline with time in MMT (18, 34, 102, 150, 187, 208). The minimal "high" makes it unattractive to many people who inject or smoke heroin. And oral consumption does not fill the needs of many users accustomed to the rituals of smoking or injecting drugs.

The result is that many who enter oral methadone maintenance programs either drop out or continue to use illicit drugs in addition to oral methadone (18, 121, 150, 163, 326). Some even inject the methadone—a potentially dangerous practice because most methadone prepared for oral consumption is not suitable for intravenous use (200). While those who persist in using illegal drugs still get significant benefits from oral methadone maintenance, their illegal drug use continues to pose significant personal and public health and safety risks.

Accordingly, in several countries there have been proposals to expand drug maintenance programs and practices beyond oral methadone to include injectable methadone, heroin, and other drugs in oral, injectable, and smokable forms. But in the United States, drug maintenance programs have been restricted to methadone, with the exception of some recent experiments with buprenorphine and the Food and Drug Administration's approval of l-α-acetylmethadol (LAAM)—essentially a longer acting form of methadone—for use in maintenance treatment, under similar conditions as methadone (69, 101, 109a, 184a, 212a, 259). During the 1970s, numerous proposals to prescribe heroin to addicts were advanced in the United States. One proposed the prescription of heroin as a lure and stepping-stone to oral methadone maintenance (126); another, as a supplement to oral methadone (345); and yet another, as a distinct program to attract heroin addicts unwilling to enter oral methadone or drug-free treatment programs (26, 27, 321). But these proposals were rejected on political grounds, and none was implemented (26, 27, 196, 215, 270).

Elsewhere, however, stimulated by increased concern about controlling the spread of AIDS, the medically supervised prescribing of other substitution drugs is entering a new phase of increased clinical experimentation. A "British system" approach, which allows physicians the freedom to prescribe a wide range of drugs for addiction treatment, can be evidenced throughout Europe and Australia and, to more limited extent, in parts of Asia and Latin America. Most of the experimentation has focused on maintaining addicts on different types of opiate drugs, both oral and injectable, though there have been some pilot programs of prescribing low-dose amphetamine and coca products to addicts. What all of these initiatives hold in common is the treatment of addiction as a medical problem, which physicians should have the freedom to address with pragmatism and flexibility.

In the Netherlands, a small morphine maintenance program was initiated in 1983 on an experimental basis in Amsterdam. Designed to manage a special group of 37 "extremely problematic addicts," the program provided a baseline dose of oral methadone, a dose of injectable morphine, and, in some cases, benzodiazepines and antipsychotics. Evaluated in a 2- to 3-year follow-up, the program was deemed modestly successful in improving the health and functioning of most of the addicts and in reducing their involvement in criminal activities (77, 78). Another program, operated by the Municipal Health Department in Amsterdam, prescribed injectable methadone and dextromoramide tartrate (Palfium)—an opiate that can be taken orally—to a group of long-term heavy opiate users (6).

In Italy during the late 1970s, a number of physicians dissatisfied with the quality of care for heroin addicts began providing addicts with injectable morphine on an outpatient basis. The Italian government legalized the prescribing experiment in 1980, but approval was abruptly withdrawn a few years later. No comprehensive evaluation of the program was ever conducted, although an estimated 1–4000 addicts were participating in 1982 (59, 78, 275). In Austria, private physicians have always been free to prescribe any legally available drug to addicts. In 1993, approximately a dozen addicts were receiving prescriptions for injectable morphine or methadone, and many others had prescriptions for codeine and other synthetic opiates (personal communication, A. David, Drug Policy Coordinator, Vienna, December 1993). A recent experiment substituting oral morphine sulfate for methadone found the morphine preferable for some patients who experienced negative methadone side effects (108). In Australia until the 1960s, physicians prescribed maintenance doses of opiates, principally morphine, to small numbers of white, middle-class addicts and to aging Chinese opium smokers (209). In Queensland, a small injectable methadone program has operated for decades (24). In these and other countries, moreover, addicts suffering from AIDS are entitled to opiates for pain relief.

More flexible prescribing practices also emerged in Edinburgh in 1988—a few years after local authorities realized that the prevalence of HIV infection among resident heroin users was, at over 50%, the highest in the United Kingdom (255, 271). Local physicians responded with more liberal prescription of methadone as well as oral versions of other drugs desired by addicts, such as dihydrocodeine, diazepam, and temazepam (though drug users were warned to steer clear of the last) (30, 132, 277). This policy—combined with the rapid expansion of needle distribution and exchange—is believed to have played an important role in reducing needle use and sharing, the rate of new HIV infections, and drug-related criminality (157).

Elsewhere, experimentation with oral opiates other than methadone has been prompted not so much by methadone's lack of acceptability to some addicts as by restricted methadone availability. This includes the use of codeine in Germany (185, 328), ethylmorphine in the Czech Republic (339), and buprenorphine in India (339). But as a wider range of substitution drugs—including methadone—becomes available, it has become clear that many patients prefer other orally consumed opiates over methadone. There is increasing interest among medical and treatment practitioners in having the freedom to prescribe different oral opiates for different patients, depending on circumstances and preference. In Germany, for example, a group of physicians has organized to resist pressures from the government and insurance companies to switch their codeine-maintained patients to methadone.

Heroin Prescription in Switzerland

The most significant extension of the "British system" approach has occurred in Switzerland, where a multicity study involving the prescription of injectable or smokable heroin, injectable morphine, and injectable methadone to hundreds of addicts began in January 1994 (25, 182, 228, 315). Participation is limited to drug users who are, at minimum, 20 years of age, demonstrate at least 2 years of opiate dependence, and have failed to benefit from at least two prior treatment attempts (313).

Though there is substantial variation between the clinics (based in 15 different cities), the basic program structure requires that all patients inject the heroin on site, under supervision. Some programs offer a maximum dose of 1 g of pharmaceutically pure heroin per day, in two or three injections, though some clinics allow greater variation and higher doses (199, 280). The programs also offer doses of oral methadone, which patients can take home, for those unable or unwilling to attend the clinic so frequently. These new Swiss programs offer substantial social and health services on site and are quite costly (at $10,000–$15,000 (U.S.) per year) but are far less costly than untreated addiction with its criminal liabilities and negative social impact.

Initial findings (January 1995) (301) and a follow-up evaluation (January 1996) (313) were positive regarding both the conduct of the programs and their outcomes. Through a variety of research designs, heroin prescription was deemed feasible, producing no black market in diverted heroin, and appears beneficial to the health of the clients in the program. There were no overdoses or serious complications with the prescribed heroin. Most impressively, 67% of the initial clients—all of whom had rejected methadone and done poorly in prior treatment attempts—were retained in the program after 15 months (314). Of those who did leave, almost 54% moved on to oral methadone and other treatment services, bringing the treatment retention rate above 80% (314). After 6 months in treatment, a 366-member study group showed substantial improvements in health, housing, and employment (199, 269). Nonopiate drug use—particularly cocaine use—remained a problem, but the percentage of clients testing positive for cocaine did decrease slightly (from 67% to 54%) following entry to the program (199). Self-reported *daily* cocaine use declined impressively, from 39% to 9% of patients after 6 months in the program (199).

Among the most interesting results of the Swiss program was the realization that heroin addicts, even when offered practically unlimited amounts of heroin each day, tended to stabilize and cut back on their daily dose. Research on one of the Zurich programs found that the average daily dose of injected heroin declined from 437 mg to 331 mg after 1 year of treatment (199). The programs consistently found that almost all addicts preferred heroin over morphine or injectable methadone. The rush was not as good as with heroin, the methadone caused constrictions in the veins, and the morphine produced uncomfortable side effects, typically a histamine reaction, which were particularly severe in women. In a double-blind experiment in the city of Thun, in which neither the doctor nor the patient knew whether the patient was receiving heroin or morphine, most patients were quickly able to identify the drug they were receiving (313).

Since the program's inception, the number of prescription slots has increased in stages, from the initial 700, with 250 for heroin, to 1000 by late 1995, with 800 for heroin (269). But even with this expansion, the experiment will probably still be too small to address the larger question of whether the controlled prescription of heroin to addicts can reduce profitability and deflate illegal heroin drug markets. Ability to test the impact of large-scale heroin prescription depends on government decisions about how to proceed with the program. The heroin prescription experiment is scheduled to conclude in December 1996, and the final evaluation will be completed by summer 1997, at which point the Swiss government must consider the evidence, confront the political issues, and decide whether the Swiss law on narcotics will be adapted to allow heroin maintenance as a regular treatment option for addicts.

The Swiss experiment has been watched carefully around the world and has prepared the way for the Netherlands, Australia, and Germany to consider similar approaches to prescribing injectable heroin. The Netherlands now plans a pilot program to prescribe injectable and noninjectable heroin to an initial 50 "hard-core" addicts, beginning in 1997 (158, 234). In Germany, the Deutsche Städtetag (German Associations of Cities) will ask the federal government to allow the legal prescription and dispensing of opiates, including heroin, as a scientific experiment (40). Though an initial request from the City of Frankfurt has been rejected by the federal government, experts believe that Germany will be engaging in these experiments by the end of the decade (41).

In Australia in 1991, the Australian National University sponsored, at the request of the Legislative Assembly of the Australian Capital Territory, the most thorough feasibility study of heroin maintenance ever undertaken (19, 153, 231) and concluded that the benefits of a heroin prescription trial outweighed the potential harms (20, 22). Researchers also found that the trial was widely supported by Canberra community residents, service providers, drug users, and ex-users, though 63% of police surveyed opposed it (21). A carefully constructed proposal for a pilot program in the Australian Capital Territory (ACT) was developed by the research team and submitted to the ACT Chief Minister in early 1996. The trial has been recommended based on thorough and expert scientific research, but political approval is needed before it can proceed (22, 337).

Prescription of Nonopiate Drugs

Opiate maintenance programs do not directly address the consumption of nonopiate drugs, such as amphetamines and cocaine. This is an increasingly important limitation given the dramatic growth since the late 1970s in cocaine and multidrug consumption—notably the use of "crack" cocaine and "cocktail" combinations of cocaine and heroin known as "speedballs." In the United States and most other countries, the notion of legally maintaining addicts with cocaine, amphetamine, and other stimulants, either alone or in combination with opiates, is rejected, and with a few exceptions (119, 179, 180), almost no effort has been made to investigate the feasibility of such a regimen. But in the United Kingdom, where some physicians reason that legal maintenance with this combination is preferable to illegal "maintenance" with illicit drugs, the practice of prescribing stimulants, typically in combination with heroin and/or methadone, has persisted for decades.

An initiative in Britain to prescribe injectable amphetamine during the amphetamine epidemic of 1968 was deemed a failure (217), but recent attempts to prescribe oral amphetamine appear more successful (109, 334). A 3-year study of a small oral amphetamine-prescribing program in Portsmouth found that over half of the 26 study participants (all daily amphetamine injectors upon entry) stopped injecting and that all decreased their sharing of injecting equipment and used less illicit amphetamine (109). The program was popular among users: It retained 67% of those who entered for at least 15 months, and of those who dropped out, two had stopped amphetamine use. The program also precipitated an increase in the number of primary amphetamine users presenting to treatment services in the area. Treatment services in Exeter (334) and a larger program in Cornwall (66, 332a) also achieved substantial drops in illicit amphetamine use and injecting with similar programs of oral amphetamine prescription. Utilizing oral and injectable methadone, oral amphetamine, codeine, and benzodiazepine prescription and a drug team that integrates needle exchange, prenatal and primary care health services, and mental health care, the Cornwall service exemplifies the flexible harm reduction-oriented approach that is the legacy of the British system (66, 332a).

In Switzerland, one of the heroin prescription clinics briefly experimented with prescribing smokable cocaine "reefers" to 12 patients. This part of the experiment was short-lived and not particularly successful—mostly due to the dissatisfaction of clients with the "reefers"—but it should open the possibility of prescribing cocaine in other forms, such as a nasal inhalant (199). Reports from Peru and the United States suggest that coca tea and other low-potency, cocaine-based beverages may also be useful in drug treatment programs (198, 286, 329). As with other experiments in addiction treatment, the principal obstacles to developing new substitution and maintenance programs are political, not scientific.

HARM REDUCTION WITH ACTIVE DRUG USERS: SECONDARY PREVENTION

Syringe (Needle) Exchange

Early in the AIDS epidemic, the role of injecting equipment—specifically the sharing of syringes contaminated with HIV—was clearly linked to HIV/AIDS transmission (82, 113, 232). The spread of HIV among injecting drug users (IDUs) was also associated with transmission to sexual partners and to the fetus during pregnancy and delivery. By 1995, most new cases of HIV in the United States were attributed directly or indirectly to drug use (161). According to the Centers for Disease Control and Prevention, drug injecting is the second most frequently reported risk behavior for HIV infection and over one-third of the 506,538 reported AIDS cases were among IDUs or heterosexual partners of IDUs by the end of 1995 (12, 61).

The institution of syringe exchange programs (SEPs) in the early years of the AIDS epidemic represented the first explicit harm reduction intervention to reduce HIV/AIDS risk without necessarily reducing illicit drug use. By addressing the linkage of injecting drug use and HIV, SEPs offered a way to hold the line on new transmission. However, SEPs have always met with strong opposition from proponents of punitive prohibitionist policies and from those committed to abstinence-only approaches (293, 299).

The positive effects of SEPs on syringe sharing and a wide range of other behaviors linked to HIV/AIDS risk have been well-documented in the United States, Great Britain, the Netherlands, and Australia (83, 204). In a review of 14 SEP studies, 10 illustrated reductions in the frequency of syringe sharing associated with SEPs, 4 showed no reductions, and none showed an increase (204). In Connecticut, the sharing of needles among IDUs dropped 40% after that state changed its paraphernalia laws in 1992 to allow for purchase and possession and sale of up to 10 syringes without a prescription (137, 323).

Another impact of SEPs on public health may be decreased marginalization of high-risk drug users (48, 83, 93, 115, 190, 232, 291, 307, 333). Active users of SEPs are often referred to medical care (e.g., for TB and HIV), and many use these programs to help users gain access to social and legal services and drug treatment (36, 51, 52, 81, 152, 190, 204). Since 1991, a Tacoma SEP has been the largest single source of recruitment to methadone maintenance programs in the region (personal communication to Marianne Apostolides, The Lindesmith Center, from D. Purchase, North American Syringe Exchange Network, 1995) (147). Of the first 569 clients in New Haven, Connecticut's SEP, 188 (33%) requested drug treatment, and 107 (57%) of those clients were placed in treatment programs (204). In the United Kingdom, where almost 60% of new SEP clients have no contact with other treatment or HIV prevention services, many clients are subsequently referred to such services (295).

Abundant evidence also points to the effectiveness of SEPs in disseminating information on HIV/AIDS risks, disposing of used syringes, and ultimately reducing the transmission of HIV and other infections by and among drug injectors (83, 137, 204). The claim that drug injectors will not alter their behavior to reduce the risks of contracting HIV and other infections has consistently been refuted (44, 115, 281, 292, 333). Surveys indicate that increasing numbers of drug injectors participate in SEPs and use only sterile syringes and that many now eschew syringe use in favor of oral and nasal means of consumption (though the latter may also be due to increased potency of noninjectable forms of heroin) (83, 111, 133, 279, 343). In cities that implemented SEPs in the mid-1980s, there is evidence of lower HIV prevalence among IDUs than in cities that did not offer SEPs until later in the AIDS epidemic (79). In Australia and the United Kingdom, where SEPs were instituted in the mid-1980s, HIV seroprevalence in drug injectors has remained lower than in most other countries (294, 335).

Yet, despite very favorable reports on the public health impact of SEPs in the United States and abroad by the National Commission on Acquired Immune Deficiency Syndrome (232), the Centers for Disease Control and Prevention (204), the General Accounting Office (312), the National Academy of Sciences' Institute of Medicine (240), and the Office of Technology Assessment (202, 247), these programs are still facing funding shortages, continued police harassment, and, in some cities, criminal prosecution for activists caught distributing syringes (13). Forty-five percent of SEPs operate without the legal sanction of local authorities (251), and all legal SEPs operate under strict rules. These rules—which may include limits on the number of syringes that can be dispensed to individual clients, restrictions on where SEPs can be located and what hours they are open, and eligibility and compliance requirements—can hinder the ability of SEPs to fulfill their public health mandate, in the same way that regulations on methadone maintenance treatment have often interfered with treatment goals (84). Many HIV/AIDS prevention programs are forced to rely on less effective bleach decontamination techniques because of local laws prohibiting needle exchange (11). The United States was also delinquent in allotting funds for research on needle exchange: The use of federal research funds for the evaluation of SEPs did not occur until 1992—the eleventh year of the AIDS epidemic. As of 1996, U.S. law still prohibits the use of federal funds to pay for SEPs. It is the private sector, charitable foundations, and community volunteers and activists, along with state and local officials, that have provided the funds and personnel for SEPs in the United States.

The availability of sterile syringes to IDUs in the United States varies substantially depending on local laws, policies, and attitudes. Only an approximate 10% of U.S. IDUs have access to U.S. SEPs, of which there were 101 (including Puerto Rico) as of 1996 (personal communication, D. Purchase, North American Syringe Exchange Network, August, 1996) (252). Local laws may prohibit the sale or possession of syringes without a prescription, as is the case in Washington, DC, and nine states—including those (New York, California, and Illinois) in which the vast majority of illicit drug injectors reside (204). Indeed, all but five states have drug paraphernalia laws that criminalize the possession or distribution of syringes except for "legitimate medical purposes" (137, 323). Even where over-the-counter sale is permitted, pharmacists may be prohibited or discouraged from selling syringes to anyone they suspect of illicit drug use (137). Even where no laws prohibit the sale and possession of syringes, they may not be readily available to those drug users who lead impoverished, disorganized, and itinerant lives on the streets. Paraphernalia laws also dissuade users from returning syringes to the exchanges, since they could be arrested if police find them in possession of syringes (137, 138, 141).

Syringe Exchange: Fine-Tuning the Model Outside the United States

The contrast between the United States and Europe, Canada, and Oceania is striking. Few of these countries ever enacted prescription or paraphernalia laws, and two that did—France (164, 165) and Austria—revoked them during the mid-1980s (204). By the late 1980s, virtually all developed countries allowed legal access to sterile injection equipment through syringe exchanges, over-the-counter sales, or both. Most public health authorities agree on the importance of reaching as many drug injectors as possible and minimizing the circulation of used syringes through aggressive syringe exchange and distribution efforts. Syringes are available around the clock, from pharmacies (178, 201, 204, 213), vending machines (8, 204), and even police stations (342). Circulation time of used syringes is minimized by encouraging or requiring drug injectors to return used syringes for clean ones and by providing multiple disposal sites for used syringes (176). Most SEPs abroad are strongly supported by government officials at the national and local level, most law enforcement officials, and a substantial majority of public opinion.

Syringe exchange programs are commonplace throughout the Netherlands (36, 48, 51, 152), Britain (93, 190), Switzerland (346), and Australia (16), and are present in dozens of other cities elsewhere in Europe (39). The first exchanges were established in 1981, in the Netherlands, and were a response to a hepatitis B epidemic among drug injectors (personal communication, J. P. Grund, June 26, 1996). These programs were rapidly expanded in the Netherlands in response to the threat of HIV later in the decade (36, 48, 51, 52, 152). In the United Kingdom, political support for syringe exchange arose in 1986 in response to evidence from Scotland that a shortage of syringes in Edinburgh had facilitated the spread of HIV. Over 200 SEPs now operate in England and two-thirds of all drug agencies maintain some syringe distribution or exchange scheme (93, 190). In Australia, SEPs began in the mid-1980s (16). As of 1996, all eight jurisdictions provide SEPs, and seven provide methadone as well (64). In Switzerland, syringe exchange is commonplace in most cities, though regions differ with regard to the means of distribution. Syringe exchanges also operate in most large cities in Germany as well as Vienna, Madrid, Bologna, Dublin, Oslo, and many smaller cities (39). In those major cities where no exchanges have been established, syringes are readily available in pharmacies (39).

Programs both in and out of the United States provide not only syringes but also alcohol swabs, sharps containers, medicinal ointments, bleach, cookers, cotton, sterile water, and usually condoms. Although injectors are strongly encouraged to return used syringes, the 1:1 requirement is not strictly enforced. Clients may be shown how to inject less hazardously so as to avoid complications (such as abscesses, septicemia, and endocarditis), and programs often provide primary health services and more generic advice on maintaining good health. The ethos is sympathetic to users, and drug injectors are not harassed about their drug use, although they are informed of and on request referred to drug treatment programs and other alternatives.

Some SEPs also provide detached or outreach services—such as mobile vans and pedestrian distributors—to deliver syringes more directly to homes or street corners. In Zurich, sterile syringes can be obtained around the clock via a network of distribution points that include contact centers for drug users, a "syringe van," mobile medical teams, pharmacies, and vending machines (346). In Vienna, syringes are exchanged in a mobile Ganslwirt bus, which reaches about 10–25% of all injectors (39). In Amsterdam, police stations will provide clean syringes in return for dirty ones (342). Many pharmacists now participate in such efforts also. In Liverpool, for instance, all pharmacies are entitled to sell injecting equipment while 20 operate free syringe exchanges (personal communication, M. A. Bellis, Centre for Environmental Epidemiology and Communicable Disease Control, Department of Public Health, Liverpool, England, 1996) (213). In New Zealand, 16% of all retail pharmacies were involved in syringe distribution and exchange by 1990 (201, 204).

Debates over syringe exchange in these countries focus not on whether they are desirable or necessary but on particular tactics and methods of distribution. Automated syringe exchange machines—which deliver a clean syringe when a used one is deposited—can now be found in more than a dozen European and Australian cities (8, 38, 204). These vending machines are relatively inexpensive, available 24 hours a day, and generally recognized as a useful complement to SEPs (204). Some public health officials worry that such machines and pharmacy sales decrease personal contact between drug injectors and health workers, but hard-pressed public health budgets and the benefits of enhanced availability may ultimately favor vending machines over staffed programs.

While Europeans and Australians established and expanded such programs in the 1980s (often in response to the all-too-apparent American catastrophe of HIV among IDUs), the United States resisted SEPs, arguing that syringe distribution encourages illicit drug use and "sends the wrong message" (14). Bitter confrontations blocked public and governmental action during the crucial early phase of our AIDS epidemic. It is now estimated that over 4300 HIV infections (and perhaps as many as 9,000–10,000 infections, depending on estimates of SEP effectiveness) could have been prevented between 1987 and 1995, had an effective program of needle exchange been implemented (203). Another 19,000 IDUs are still being infected with HIV in the United States each year (161). Fears that increased syringe availability would encourage illicit drug use and encourage injection drug use have proved unfounded (240, 327), making continued restrictions on the availability of sterile syringes unjustifiable on scientific or ethical grounds.

Peer Outreach and Education

Most needle and syringe exchange programs rely upon current drug users as outreach workers and volunteers. Their HIV prevention efforts engage active drug users outside of formal treatment settings—in local drug scenes, drop-in centers, and homes (49). Rather than aiming solely to lure drug users into treatment, they focus most of their energies on minimizing drug-related harms outside formal treatment settings (140). Some use vans or buses, while others have drop-in centers. These organizations typically offer information about safer drug use and safer sex, provide a link between drug users and social and/or medical services, distribute needles and condoms, and prove indispensable in collecting information about recent developments in the drug scene (49). A growing number are initiated and run by current drug users or ex-drug users and/or employ users as street outreach workers, program staff, leaders of peer counseling groups, etc. (personal communication, A. Clear, Harm Reduction Coalition, October, 1996).

Drug education targeted at current drug users dates back to the underground literature of the 1960s and early 1970s, when nongovernmental organizations published guidelines on how to minimize the risks associated with drug use. When drug prevention campaigns failed to stem rising solvent abuse in Britain during the late 1970s, the Institute for the Study of Drug Dependence published a guide for minimizing the dangers associated with solvent sniffing (166). During the late 1980s, the Lifeline Project in Manchester, England, began publishing *Smack in the Eye*, a comic book targeted at current opiate users that provided harm minimization information in a user-friendly style and language (122, 123). In 1990, it initiated a second comic book series, *Peanut Pete,* directed at young people engaged in recreational use of stimulants, hallucinogens, and other "party drugs." Similar publications are produced in the Netherlands (219), Australia, Germany, and, increasingly, the United States. They are straightforward about the possible pleasures of drug use but also contain information on drug-induced paranoia, dangers of particular types of drug use, and services of particular interest to drug users.

Harm reduction efforts also seek to reduce the damage resulting from drugs of unknown purity or potency. Users can be informed as to certain dangers, but most lack the resources to analyze the drugs they purchase. Some syringe exchanges have taken the initiative and distributed information gained from users about which drugs are particularly potent or have dangerous adulterants (169). This information, however, tends to be erratic, comes only after a hazardous batch of drugs hits the street, and reaches only a small fraction of users.

In the Netherlands, public health authorities recognized that one of the greatest dangers associated with the sudden expansion of the "rave scene" (gatherings, often at dance clubs, where young people consume MDMA and other stimulants and hallucinogens while dancing to high-energy music) was the sale of adulterated and unexpectedly high potency drugs. Private organizations, which later gained government support, responded by employing drug analysis units at raves where illicit drugs could be tested prior to consumption (116). Some cities in Germany (e.g., Berlin and Hannover) maintain silent or unspoken agreements between harm reduction groups and officials, allowing for inconspicuous drug analysis of MDMA and MDE, as well as heroin in the context of "fixer rooms" (see below) (41). Such initiatives resemble the Analysis Anonymous drug testing service in the United States, created by PharmChem Laboratories, Inc., in 1972 to provide a similar service to illicit drug users who mailed in samples (214).

Organized and subsidized self-help groups of illicit drug users play a modest but important role in the formulation and implementation of drug control policies in the Netherlands, Germany, and Australia and have begun to exercise some influence in Switzerland and the United States (112, 268). The Rotterdam "junkie union" began the first Dutch syringe exchange in response to the hepatitis B epidemic (personal communication, J. P. Grund, June 26, 1996). And Amsterdam's junkie union was decisive in initiating free SEPs in 1983–1984, after a major pharmacist in the central inner city "copping" area refused to sell needles to drug users. Similar groups in Canberra, Rotterdam, Groningen, Basel, Bern, and Bremen have worked with local public health officials on SEPs and other harm reduction initiatives (297, 336). Most of these groups also produce publications targeted at illicit drug users with information on reducing drug-related harms, kicking the habit, and identifying treatment alternatives. Although these groups tend to be short-lived and dependent on one or two highly motivated individuals, they play an important role in articulating the sentiments and perceptions of precisely those citizens who are most affected by local policies (46). They also offer valuable conduits between local policymakers and underground populations.

Municipal Zoning Policies

OPEN DRUG SCENES

In large part, public opposition to certain forms of drug use relates to their visible presence in the community, i.e., to public appearance of intoxicated individuals and to open drug dealing scenes with their associated loitering, violence, and disorderly conduct. Such open drug scenes are deeply embarrassing to city officials, especially in European cities that pride themselves on maintenance of public order. Like prostitution, homelessness, and public consumption of alcohol, they challenge community morals, appear disorderly or threatening, and effectively resist all attempts to be suppressed.

Alcohol use is generally accepted in private spaces (i.e., bars, restaurants, and homes), and public intoxication is tolerated under a broad (though declining) range of circumstances, from the office Christmas party to public sporting events. The use of illicit drugs is viewed quite differently. Though public cannabis use is viewed benignly in many cities, the use and sale of hard drugs is often seen as a sharp challenge to authority. Open drug dealing broadcasts to community residents that law enforcement has been displaced from power. Public consumption—particularly injection—of illicit drugs communicates a clear breakdown of public order and social control. Both attract political attention and create pressure for change that frequently—in the context of prohibition and its enforcement—takes the form of short-term solutions that do little more than conceal drug scenes or shift them to a different locale. This spawned the "shooting gallery"—a place where drug users could buy drugs and rent injecting equipment in a locale somewhat insulated from the view of the law (142). But this particular accommodation to prohibition occurred at a huge cost in public health: Shooting galleries fostered the sharing of injecting equipment and became the chief vector for HIV transmission among drug users in the U.S. cities of the East Coast (80, 142).

European and Australian police and public health officials, aware of this relationship early in the AIDS epidemic, officially tolerated certain spaces where drug use could be contained and health risk reduced while meeting the social requirements of drug law enforcement. "Open drug scenes" were allowed to develop in a few restricted areas. Early experiences with open scenes were sometimes adverse, as in Zurich's Platzspitz (220), but they became instructive for later attempts at steering the use of drugs to less publicly offensive locations and for the need to establish many small scenes rather than one central supermarket. An essential part of this process is that drug users and their advocates be integrated into the process of finding feasible solutions to local drug problems.

The city of Zurich attracted international notoriety during the late 1980s and early 1990s for its official toleration of an open drug scene in a public park, the Platzspitz, which became known as "Needle Park." The initial congregation of illicit drug injectors in the park during the mid-1980s was regarded by most city officials and residents, including the police, as an improvement after years of chasing drug users around the city. The concentration of drug users facilitated the provision of syringe exchange, emergency first aid, and other medical and social services.

During the early 1990s, public and official sentiment changed. City residents became upset by the growing numbers of drug injectors flocking to Zurich from elsewhere in Switzerland—about 70% of the approximately 2000 people entering the park each day were not city residents (220, 248)—and by increases in the number of robberies and car break-ins in the vicinity of the park. Within the park, competition among drug dealers—many of whom were of foreign origin—generated rising levels of violence, and general social and sanitary conditions deteriorated (220). The Platzspitz was closed in February 1992, and its successor, at the site of an old train station, was shut down as well when the city opted to focus on decentralized treatment, maintenance, and harm reduction services (145).

The lessons of Needle Park are disputed. Critics say that Zurich should adopt more punitive approaches and be less hospitable to illicit drug users. Antiprohibitionists argue that Needle Park proved the limits of liberalization within the broader context of drug prohibition. Its problems, they point out, were all a result of prohibition: the violent behavior and destructive impact of illicit drug dealers; overdoses and other adverse health effects from illicitly produced drugs of unknown potency and purity; robberies and other criminal activities committed by drug users requiring substantial sums of money to buy drugs at prices inflated by prohibition; and the unnatural congregation of many of the country's illicit opiate users in one place as a result of more severe drug policies elsewhere in Switzerland. Still others, including many of the city's public health and social welfare workers, reject the conclusion that Needle Park was a failure. They regard it instead as an experience that made the needs and the misery of drug users visible to everyone, thereby generating support for rapid implementation of SEPs and other harm reduction measures.

Zurich was not the only city to tolerate and attempt to regulate an open drug scene. Smaller scenes, in Bern's Kocherpark and along the river in Basel, evolved along much the same lines. As in Zurich, these scenes attracted significant numbers of young drug users from neighboring towns and generated strong opposition among local communities, which led to their dispersal (60, 170). In Rotterdam, police supervised an open drug scene next to the central railway station, known as "Platform Zero," with syringe exchange services and a mobile methadone unit readily available (personal communication, J. P. Grund, July 18, 1994). Because of a turn in public opinion, lack of political support, and an increase in the number of visitors, "Platform Zero" was closed and dismantled in 1994 (322).

In Frankfurt also, open heroin scenes emerged during the 1970s. They settled during the mid-1980s in two adjacent parks, the Gallusanlage and Taunusanlage, when top police officials decided that their decade-long efforts to suppress the local drug scenes had failed to halt their growth and merely shifted them from one neighborhood to another (278). Local authorities in Frankfurt established three crisis centers in the vicinity of the drug scenes, stationed a mobile ambulance to provide syringe exchange services and emergency medical assistance, offered first aid courses to junkies, and established a separate bus to provide services for drug-using prostitutes. Other services were provided in the vicinity of the main train station, where a "pill scene" had formed. The police continued their efforts to apprehend drug dealers but initiated a policy of tolerating an open scene within strictly defined borders in Taunusanlage Park. These initiatives were combined with efforts to lure users away from the drug scene by providing night lodgings, daytime residences, and methadone treatment centers in neighborhoods removed from the city center (238, 278). In conjunction with these measures, the open drug scene in the park was shut down in late 1992. The entire policy was coordinated and overseen by the "Monday Group"—a group of top city officials, including police, medical, public health, drug policy, and political officials, that met each Monday to assess local drug-related developments. By 1993, the new policy was believed responsible for significantly reducing the number of homeless drug users, drug-related robberies, and drug-related deaths in the city (107, 110, 260).

"SAFE SPACES" FOR DRUG USERS

Low-threshold facilities known as "contact centers," "street rooms," "health rooms, "harm reduction centers," etc. are officially tolerated and sometimes even government sponsored in many cities. These are places where drug users can meet, pick up injection equipment and condoms, and obtain simple medical care, advice, help with domestic problems, and sometimes a place to sleep. Most facilities allow drug users to remain anonymous. Many have qualified medical staff present (60), and some provide a "fixer room" where drug injectors can consume illicit drugs in a relatively hygienic environment (347). These facilities are regarded as preferable to the two most likely alternatives: open injection of illicit drugs in public places, which is widely regarded as distasteful and unsettling to most urban residents; or consumption of drugs in unsanctioned "shooting galleries," which are often dirty, sometimes violent, and frequently controlled by drug dealers and where needle sharing is often the norm. A few "street rooms" were quietly tolerated within drug agencies in England during the 1960s. During the late 1970s, a number of "drug cafes" for heroin users were established in Amsterdam, but they were later shut down when drug dealers effectively displaced social workers from control of the daily course of events (192). In Switzerland, the first *Gassenzimmer* ("fixer rooms") were established by private organizations in Bern and Basel during the late 1980s (146). By late 1993, eight were in operation, with most under the direct supervision of city officials: two in Bern, two in Basel, one in Luzern (in City Hall), and three in Zurich (60). An evaluation of the three *Gassenzimmer* in Zurich after their first year of operation concluded that they had proven effective in reducing the transmission of HIV and the risk of overdose (347). Three "injection rooms" have been in place in Frankfurt since 1995 (260).

Another innovation worth noting is the "apartment dealer" arrangement, adopted informally in Rotterdam, whereby police and prosecutors refrain from arresting and prosecuting apartment dealers—including sellers of heroin and cocaine—so long as they do not cause problems for their neighbors (139, 319, 342). This arrangement is viewed as part and parcel of broader "safe neighborhood" plans in which police and residents collaborate to keep neighborhoods safe, clean, and free of nuisances (38).

Toleration and regulation of open drug scenes and safe spaces for drug users both represent forms of informal zoning controls similar to those employed to regulate illegal prostitution (302). They also are consistent with the underlying philosophy of community policing in the United States. Law enforcement authorities recognize that they are unable to effectively suppress most illicit drug use and dealing and that chasing users and dealers from one neighborhood to another is costly and often counterproductive. Local residents express concern primarily with the safety and orderliness of their neighborhoods. And public health and social welfare officials find it easier to provide essential services when drug scenes are relatively stable and easily accessible. However, the challenges of maintaining control of such scenes are considerable, given both the illegality of the market and the social maladjustment of many hard-core drug users. No consensus has yet emerged on whether these scenes should be dispersed or tolerated and regulated.

DRUG POLICY REFORM AS PRIMARY PREVENTION

While addiction treatment innovations and preventive interventions such as SEPs play a crucial role in reducing the harms associated with drug use under prohibition (28, 225), it is changes in drug control policy that offer the best chance for primary prevention of drug-related harm. By reducing the association of drug use with criminal prosecution, a system that drives drug use and drug users to dangerous margins of society, the reform of punitive legal policies can produce clear benefits in the realm of public health and social order. In the United States in the 1970s, the movement to decriminalize marihuana was driven by the realization that criminal sanctions created greater harm than marihuana use itself (7, 177). In the same spirit, significant drug law reform has been undertaken in several European countries and Australia, in direct response to perceived public health needs and humanitarian concerns, starting with de facto decriminalization of marihuana. The case of Dutch regulation of cannabis is the most impressive example of this approach, both for its longevity (over 20 years) and its apparent success (171, 184, 193, 318).

Dutch Cannabis Policy

Decades ago, the Netherlands decriminalized cannabis at the national level. A 1976 report by the Baan Commission, a national drug policy working group, expressed the harm reduction sentiment that drug laws should not be more damaging to an individual than the use of the drug itself, and argued that the tendency of some cannabis users to move on to illicit opiate use could be reduced by separating the "soft-drug" and "hard-drug" markets (74). The Opium Law was revised to increase penalties for heroin and cocaine trafficking and cut penalties for the sale and consumption of small amounts of cannabis to misdemeanor offenses. Prosecutorial and police guidelines were also revised to de-emphasize enforcement of cannabis laws. The result was the creation of a relatively normalized, essentially noncriminal, and easily accessible cannabis distribution system in most Dutch cities (184). A clear-cut distinction was made between drug users and traffickers and between "hard" illegal drugs, with so-called unacceptable health risks (e.g., heroin, cocaine), and cannabis products.

The Netherlands permits the retail trade of cannabis products in local "coffee shops" under very specific conditions, i.e., no advertising, no hard drugs, no disturbance of public order, no sale to minors (under 18), and strict limits on the amount that can be sold to each customer. Enforcement of these guidelines falls to local "Triangle Committees" composed of the mayor, chief of police, and district attorney of each city. Today, the domestic Dutch market is a well-established commercial structure operating in a "gray economy" with legal tolerance and even some taxation. An estimated half-million regular customers are supplied by many small to midsize local producers plus a number of larger importers. So far there has been little evidence of organized crime in the coffee shop operations and virtually no violence associated with the domestic trade of cannabis in the Netherlands.

This tolerant policy toward the retail trade and use of cannabis for recreational purposes has had a positive effect in the Netherlands. Though cannabis consumption among Dutch teenagers has increased, the number of regular cannabis users in the Netherlands has remained significantly below U.S. levels (249, 276, 308). Rates of cocaine and heroin consumption among Dutch citizens are similarly modest, although the relatively high quality and low price of the drugs have attracted "drug tourists" from elsewhere in Europe (183). Dutch authorities express some concern about organized criminal involvement in wholesale production and sales of cannabis, and they contend with complaints from authorities in neighboring Germany, Belgium, and, lately, France; but by and large, the policy is supported by most of the public, politicians, and law enforcement officials. Cases of problematic cannabis use are rare, but cannabis users (like all Dutch drug users) who do develop problems have ready access to diverse and comprehensive treatment facilities based in the public health sector. Because of international pressures and some local discontent with the rapid growth in coffee shops, however, in 1995 the Dutch government resolved to substantially cut back the number of coffee shops (in some cities by as much as 50%) and to reduce the amount of cannabis allowed each customer from 30 to 5 g (234).

Other governments have also moved toward decriminalization of cannabis. During the 1970s, national drug commissions in many countries recommended cannabis decriminalization (63, 233, 331). In 1987, the South Australian government introduced a Cannabis Expiation Notice system that allows individuals apprehended with small quantities of cannabis (up to 100 g) to have their offense discharged—with no record of a criminal conviction—upon payment of a fine (300). A similar scheme was introduced in the Australian Capital Territory in 1992 (70). Although there has been a small consistent increase in cannabis use since 1985 (prior to the expiation system) (92), an analysis of the first 2 years of the expiation system by the South Australian Office of Crime Statistics found little evidence of any impact on the number or type of people detected using cannabis (76, 212). Its principal recommendation was that steps be taken to ensure that notice recipients pay their fines promptly to avoid court appearances.

In Switzerland, the Federal High Court decided in 1991 that penalties for dealing cannabis were unduly harsh and needed to be revised, given increasing evidence that the health hazards of cannabis consumption were relatively modest (105). A number of lower courts in Germany have ruled similarly, finding cannabis prohibition laws in conflict with the German constitution (188, 189). A German Supreme Court decision in May 1994 removed criminal penalties for possession of small amounts of cannabis (47), furthering an earlier decision that had given states the *option* not to prosecute for possession of small amounts of any drug. Although some states (i.e., Bavaria) responded by decreasing the amount necessary to trigger a "large amount" charge, many other state officials announced that they would no longer arrest people for possessing small amounts of any drug (181). The state of Hessen initiated federal legislation (Bundesratsdrucksache 582/92) in the Second Chamber (equivalent to the German senate), requesting the legalization of cannabis and its regulation by way of state monopoly. The state of Schleswig-Holstein received consent from the majority of state health ministers to dispense marihuana in pharmacies but will face opposition from the Federal Agency in Berlin (43, 175). Spain decriminalized private use of cannabis in 1983 but has since tightened its laws (55). Italy decriminalized possession of "moderate amounts for personal use" of any drug in 1975, toughened penalties in 1990, and then abolished criminal sanctions for illicit drug use altogether in April 1993 (15, 332). Although no government has advocated outright repeal of cannabis prohibition, an increasing number now favor decriminalization.

During the 1970s, 11 states in the United States decriminalized marihuana, effectively reducing the punishment for possession of small amounts to sanctions other than imprisonment. The impact on marihuana consumption and related problems was negligible (173, 218, 288, 304), but decriminalization did reduce the number of marihuana arrests and prosecutions. California saved an estimated $1 billion in the decade following the 1976 Moscone Act decriminalizing marihuana (3). While total drug arrests increased almost every year throughout the 1980s, arrests for marihuana consistently declined (103), leading many to suggest the drug had been effectively decriminalized. However, marihuana arrests have risen in recent years (over 400,000 in 1994), as drug arrests have continued to soar (in 1994, there were 1.35 million arrests nationally for drug law violations, 1 million of which were for drug possession) (104).

Medical Marihuana—A Special Case

One of the more interesting developments in U.S. drug policy is the debate over legalizing the medical use of marihuana. Increasing numbers of doctors and patients view marihuana as a legitimate medicine that can be highly effective in reducing the nausea associated with cancer chemotherapy, stimulating appetite for AIDS patients suffering from wasting syndrome, and reducing the intraocular pressure of glaucoma (134, 135). It is also commonly used as an anticonvulsant, muscle relaxant, and mild pain reliever for menstrual cramps and certain types of chronic pain (134). Polls indicate that a majority of Americans believe marihuana should be medically available (4, 118, 134), and numerous organizations, including the American Public Health Association and the American Federation of Scientists, have issued resolutions in support (5, 106). In 1988, a Drug Enforcement Administration administrative law judge ruled that marihuana should be moved to Schedule II, making it available for medical purposes (311), but the agency refused to comply. Thus marihuana remains a Schedule I drug, meaning that in the eyes of the government it has no legitimate use, and further research on its medical properties has been stifled (136).

Hundreds of individuals received marihuana for medical purposes in the 1980s, but this federal program was discontinued, and all but eight of the original recipients have either died or been cut from the program (135). In the meantime, there have been moves to provide marihuana to medical patients through "cannabis buyers' clubs," which are illegal but often tolerated by local police. Buyers' clubs, which supply marihuana to patients who have a doctor's prescription for marihuana, have sprung up across the country in recent years (62, 125, 305). Many of the clubs are private, underground operations, but others have achieved national attention (62, 125).

CONCLUSION

Harm reduction is not an alien philosophy unsuited to the United States. Its basic precepts can be discerned in the early history of U.S. drug control, in the institutionalization of methadone maintenance programs since the 1960s, in the decriminalization of marihuana during the 1970s, and in recent efforts to reduce the harms associated with alcohol and tobacco consumption. Both the philosophy and the language of harm reduction can be seen and heard in the recent proliferation of SEPs in the United States, in recent experiments with "interim" methadone maintenance and physician prescribing, in the creation of a methadone maintenance program in New York City's jail system, and in outreach efforts and other local initiatives to reduce the spread of HIV among illicit drug users. Interest in harm reduction is growing in some areas of the United States, where local politicians, health officials, and law enforcement leaders have expressed interest in many of the initiatives described in this article. Connecticut recently changed its needle laws. Baltimore's mayor, Kurt Schmoke, convened a Working Group on Drug Policy Reform in 1993 to consider harm reduction approaches to the city's drug problems (210). Local drug policy reform and harm reduction groups have sprung up across the country.

Harm reduction, it must be stressed, neither celebrates nor legitimates psychoactive drug use but acknowledges that it cannot be totally eliminated. Harm reduction does not disavow abstinence but recognizes that there are additional ways to reduce the harms of drug use. It does not repudiate the government's responsibility to "send the right message" but insists that government rhetoric and policy demonstrate concern for the health and welfare even of those who continue to use drugs illicitly. And it demands not that police abstain from drug enforcement but that they collaborate with public health officials and even drug users to reduce drug-related harms. Harm reduction represents a pragmatic and humane approach to reducing the damage associated with drug use and ineffective drug control policies. Indeed, it rests on a cornerstone of medicine's Hippocratic oath, "first do no harm."

Acknowledgments. *The authors would like to extend their thanks to Philip Coffin, Allison Orris and Leigh Hallingby of The Lindesmith Center for their valuable assistance.*

References

1. Advisory Council on the Misuse of Drugs. AIDS and drug misuse, part I: report of the Advisory Council on the Misuse of Drugs. London: Her Majesty's Stationery Office, 1988.
2. Albrecht HJ, van Kalmthout A. Drug policies in Western Europe. Freiburg, Germany: Max-Planck-Institut fur Auslandisches und Internationales Strafrecht, 1989.
3. Aldrich MR, Mikuriya T. Savings in California marijuana law enforcement costs attributable to the Moscone Act of 1976: a summary. J Psychoactive Drugs 1988;20(1):75–81.
4. American Civil Liberties Union. American voter's opinion on the use and legalization of marijuana for medical purposes. New York: American Civil Liberties Union, 1995.
5. American Public Health Association. Resolution for access to therapeutic marijuana/cannabis. Washington, DC: American Public Health Association, 1995.
6. Amsterdam Municipal Health Service. Jaarverslag 1991 Drugsafdeling. Amsterdam: Municipal Health Service, 1992.
7. Anderson P. High in America: the true story behind NORML and the politics of marijuana. New York: Viking Press, 1981.
8. Anonymous. Syringe exchange by Automat. Int J Drug Policy 1989;1(3):6.
9. Anonymous. Neue Zuercher Zeitung 1990;Sept 4:17.
10. Deleted in proof.

11. Anonymous. Special feature. J Acquir Immune Def Syndr 1994;7:741.
12. Anonymous. Injecting drug use second most frequently reported risk behavior for HIV infection. CESAR Fax 1996:5.
13. Anonymous. Arrest of needle-exchange workers draws national attention: New Brunswick, New Jersey Chai project. Alcohol Drug Abuse Wkly 1996;8(19):3.
14. Anonymous. New Jersey panel's support of needle exchange stirs debate. Alcohol Drug Abuse Wkly 1996;8(14):1.
15. Arnao G. Italian referendum deletes criminal sanctions for drug users. J Drug Issues 1994; 24(3):483–487.
16. Australian Government. Inter-Governmental report on AIDS: a report on HIV/AIDS activities in Australia, 1990–1991. Canberra: Australian Government Publishing, 1992.
17. Ball JC, Lange WR, Myers CP, Friedman SR. Reducing the risk of AIDS through methadone maintenance treatment. J Health Soc Behav 1988;29(3):214–226.
18. Ball JC, Ross A. The effectiveness of methadone maintenance treatment. New York: Springer-Verlag, 1991.
19. Bammer G. Should the controlled provision of heroin be a treatment option? Australian feasibility considerations. Addiction 1993;88(4): 467–475.
20. Bammer G. Report and recommendations of stage 2 feasibility research into the controlled availability of opioids. Canberra: Australian Institute of Criminology, National Centre for Epidemiology and Population Health, 1995.
21. Bammer G, Dance P, Stevens A, Mugford S, Ostini R, Crawford D. Attitudes to a proposal for controlled availability of heroin in Australia: is it time for a trial? Addict Res 1996;4(1):45–55.
22. Bammer G, Douglas RM. The ACT heroin trial proposal: an overview. Med J Aust 1996;164 (11):690–692.
23. Barthwell A, Senay EC, Marks R, White R. Patients successfully maintained with methadone escaped human immunodeficiency virus infection. Arch Gen Psychiatry 1989;46(10):957–958.
24. Battersby M, Farrell M, Gossop M, Robson P. Horse trading: prescribing injectable opiates to opiate addicts: a descriptive study. Drug Alcohol Rev 1992;11(1):35–42.
25. Baumann T, Battegay R, Rauchfleisch U. Drogen und Alkohol 1992:7.
26. Bayer R. Heroin maintenance, the Vera proposal and narcotics reform: an analysis of the debate. Contemp Drug Probl 1975;4:297–322.
27. Bayer R. Heroin maintenance: an historical perspective on the exhaustion of liberal narcotics reform. J Psychedelic Drugs 1976;8:157–165.
28. Bayer R, Oppenheimer GM. Confronting drug policy. New York: Cambridge University Press, 1993.
29. Bell J. Alternatives to non-clinical regulation: training doctors to deliver methadone maintenance treatment. Addict Res 1986;3:297–315.
30. Bennett W. Addicts forsake needles for drugs to addicts. Independent 1993;Aug 24.
31. Berridge V. Harm minimization and public health: an historical perspective. In: Heather N, Wodak A, Nadelmann EA, O'Hare P, eds. Psychoactive drugs and harm reduction: from faith to science. London: Whurr Publishers, 1993: 55–64.
32. Berridge V, Edwards G. Opium and the people. New Haven: Yale University Press, 1987.
33. Bertram E, Blachman M, Sharpe K, Andreas P. Drug war politics: the price of denial. Berkeley: University of California, 1996.

34. Bertschy G. Methadone maintenance treatment: an update. Eur Arch Psychiatry Clin Neurosci 1995;245(2):114–124.
35. Blackwell J. The saboteurs of Britain's opiate policy: overprescribing physicians or American style 'junkies'. Int J Addict 1988;23(5):517–526.
36. Blanken P. Spuiten Ruilen bij Hadon een Evaluatie van de Individuele en Collectieve Omruil. Rotterdam, Netherlands, 1990.
37. Blansfield HN. Medical mismanagement in public methadone programs. Conn Med 1994;58(3): 161–174.
38. Bless R, Freeman M, Korf D, Nabben T. Urban strategies to open drug scenes. Amsterdam: Amsterdam Bureau of Social Research and Statistics, 1993.
39. Bless R, Korf D, Freeman M. Urban drug policies in Europe. Amsterdam: Bureau of Social Research and Statistics, 1993.
40. Bollinger L. German drug law in action. In: Bollinger L, ed. Cannabis: from crime to human right. Frankfurt, NY: Peter Lang, 1996.
41. Bollinger L. German drug laws in the context of international pressure and internal conflicts—a theoretical approach to the evolution of drug policy. Unpublished manuscript, 1996.
42. Deleted in proof.
43. Bremen Institut fur Drogenforschung. Zur Cannabis—Situation in der Bundersrepublik Deutschland. Bremen: Bremen Institut fur Drogenforschung, 1995.
44. Brettle RP. HIV and harm reduction for injecting drug users. AIDS 1991;5:125.
45. Brewer C. Intravenous methadone maintenance: a British response to persistent opiate injectors. In: Loimer N, Schmid R, Springer A, eds. Drug addiction and AIDS. New York: Springer-Verlag, 1991:187–199.
46. Broadhead RS, Heckathorn DD, Grund JP, Stern LS, Anthony DL. Drug users versus outreach workers in combating AIDS: preliminary results of a peer driven intervention. J Drug Issues 1995;25(3):531–564.
47. Bundesverfassungsgericht. Beschluss, vom 9. Marz 1994–Az.: 2 BvL 43/92. Strafverteidiger 1994:295–303.
48. Buning EC. The effects of Amsterdam needle and syringe exchange. Int J Addict 1991;26 (12):1303–1311.
49. Buning EC. Outreach work with drug users: an overview. Int J Drug Policy 1993;4:78–82.
50. Buning EC. Involving G.P.'s in Paris. Euromethwork 1996;8:3–4.
51. Buning EC, Cohen P. AIDS und Drogenpolitik in den Niederlanden. Kriminalsoziol Bibliogr 1989;63/64.
52. Buning EC, Coutinho RA, Van Brussel GHA, Van Santen GW, Van Zadelhoff AW. Preventing AIDS in drug addicts in Amsterdam [letter]. Lancet 1986;1(8945):1435.
53. Buning EC, Van Brussel GHA, Van Santen GW. The 'Methadone by Bus' project in Amsterdam. Br J Addict 1990;85(10):1247–1250.
54. Byrne A, Wodak A. Census of patients receiving methadone in a general practice. Addict Res 1986;3:323–341.
55. Campbell D. Foreign focus: drugs and the law: possession may be the lesser evil. Guardian 1994;21:12.
56. Caplehorn JRM. A comparison of abstinence-oriented and indefinite methadone maintenance treatment. Int J Addict 1994;19:1361–1375.
57. Caplehorn JRM, Bell J. Methadone dosage and retention of patients in maintenance treatment. Med J Aust 1991;154:195–199.
58. Caplehorn JRM, Dalton MSYN, Haldar F, Petrenas AM, Nisbet JG. Methadone maintenance

and addicts' risk of fatal heroin overdose. Int J Addict 1996;31:177–196.
59. Catri F. Cooperativa Bravetta '80. Medicina Democratico 1981;23(4).
60. Cattaneo M, Dubois-Arber F, Leuthold A, Paccaud F. Evaluation of the federal measures to reduce the problems related to drug use: phase I: initial report 1990–1992. Zurich: Institut Universitaire de Medecine Sociale et Preventive, 1993.
61. Centers for Disease Control and Prevention. AIDS associated with injecting-drug use—United States 1995. MMWR Morb Mortal Wkly Rep 1996;86:392–398.
62. Christie J. Club medicine. Reason 1996;April: 54–57.
63. Commission of Inquiry into the Non-Medical Use of Drugs. Cannabis. Ottawa: Information, Canada, 1972.
64. Commonwealth Department of Human Services and Health. Review of methadone treatment in Australia: final report. Australia: Commonwealth Department of Human Services and Health, 1995.
65. Cooper JR. Ineffective use of psychoactive drugs: methadone treatment is no exception. JAMA 1992;267(2):281–282.
66. Cornwall Community Drugs Team. Annual report—1995. Cornwall, England.
67. Courtwright D. Dark paradise: opiate addiction in America before 1940. Cambridge: Harvard University Press, 1982.
68. Courtwright DT, Joseph H, Des Jarlais DC. Addicts who survived: an oral history of narcotic use in America, 1923–1965. Knoxville: University of Tennessee Press, 1989.
69. Cowan A, Lewis JW. Buprenorphine: combatting drug abuse with a unique opioid. New York: Wiley-Liss, 1995.
70. Criminal Justice Commission. Report on cannabis and the law in Queensland. Brisbane, Australia: Goprint, 1994.
71. D'Aunno T, Vaughn T. Variations in methadone treatment practices: results from a national study. JAMA 1992;267(2):253–258.
72. Deleted in proof.
73. Darke S, Hall W, Heather N, Ward J, Wodak A. The reliability and validity of a scale to measure HIV risk taking behavior among intravenous drug users. AIDS 1991;5(2):181–185.
74. de Kort M. The Dutch cannabis debate, 1968–1976. J Drug Issues 1994;24(3):417–427.
75. Degkwitz P, Chorzelski G, Krausz M. Five years of methadone prescription in Germany. In: Reisinger M, ed. AIDS and drug addiction in the European Community. Brussels: Commission of the European Communities, European Monitoring Centre on Drugs and Drug Addiction, 1993: 79–89.
76. Department of the Attorney General Office of Crime Statistics. Cannabis: the expiation notice approach. Adelaide, Australia: Department of the Attorney General, 1989.
77. Derks JTM. The efficacy of the Amsterdam morphine-dispensing programme. In: Ghodse HA, Kaplan CD, Mann RD, eds. Drug misuse and dependence. Park Ridge, NJ: Parthenon, 1990:85–108.
78. Derks JTM. Het Amsterdamse morfine-verstrekkingsprogramma: een longitudinaal onderzoek onder extreem problematische druggebruikers. Utrecht: Nederlands Centrum Geestelijke Volksgezondheid, 1990.
79. Des Jarlais DC. Characteristics of prevented HIV epidemics. Paper presented at the meeting of the 9th International Conference on AIDS, Berlin, Germany, June 7–11, 1993.
80. Des Jarlais DC, Friedman SR. Shooting galleries and AIDS: infection probabilities and

'tough' policies [Editorial]. Am J Public Health 1990;80(2):142–144.

81. Des Jarlais DC, Friedman SR. The AIDS epidemic and legal access to sterile equipment for injecting illicit drugs. Ann Am Acad Polit Soc Sci 1992;521:42–65.

82. Des Jarlais DC, Friedman SR, Choopanya K, Vanichseni S, Ward TP. International epidemiology of HIV and AIDS among injecting drug users. AIDS 1992;6(10):1023–1068.

83. Des Jarlais DC, Friedman SR, Sotheran JL, Wenston J, Marmor M, Yancovitz SR, Frank B, Beatrice S, Mildvan D. Continuity and change within an HIV epidemic: injecting drug users in New York City: 1984–1992. JAMA 1994;271(2):121–127.

84. Des Jarlais DC, Paone D, Friedman SR, Peyser N, Newman RG. Regulating controversial programs for unpopular people: methadone maintenance and syringe exchange programs. Am J Public Health 1995;85(11):1577–1584.

85. Diamond E. Paper presented at the meeting of the Albert Einstein Symposium on Opiates, New York Academy of Medicine, New York, NY, November 4, 1994.

86. Dixon D. From prohibition to regulation: bookmaking, anti-gambling and the law. Oxford: Clarendon Press, 1991.

87. Dole VP. Hazards of process regulations: the example of methadone maintenance. JAMA 1992;267(16):2234–2235.

88. Dole VP. Paper presented at the meeting of the Einstein Symposium on Opiates, New York Academy of Medicine, November 4, 1994.

89. Dole VP, Nyswander ME. Methadone maintenance treatment: a ten year perspective. JAMA 1976;235(19):2117–2119.

90. Dole VP, Nyswander ME, Kreek MJ. Narcotic blockade. Arch Intern Med 1966;118:304–309.

91. Dolan KA, Wodak A. An international review of methadone provision in prisons. Addict Res 1996;4(1):85–97.

92. Donnelly N, Hall W. Patterns of cannabis use in Australia. National Drug Strategy Monograph Series no. 27. Canberra: Australian Government Publishing Service, 1994.

93. Donoghoe MC, Stimson GV, Dolan K. Syringe exchange in England: an overview. London: Tufnell Press, 1992.

94. Dorn N, Murji K, South N. Traffickers: drug markets and law enforcement. New York: Routledge, 1992.

95. Deleted in proof.

96. Drucker E. Harm reduction: a public health strategy. Curr Issues Public Health 1995;1:64–70.

97. Drucker E. The failure of prohibition as a drug control strategy: the case of AIDS. AIDS (in press).

98. Drugs Directorate, H. P. Dispensing methadone for the treatment of opioid dependence. Ottawa: Drugs Directorate, 1994.

99. Duncan A. The quiet revolution. Int J Drug Policy 1990;2(3):23.

100. Eidgenoessige Betaubungsmittelkommission Arbeitsgruppe Methadon der Subkommission Drogenfragen. Methadonbericht:Suchtmittelersatz: Behandlung Heroinabhangiger in der Schweiz. 3rd ed. Bern: Bundesamt fur Gesundheitswesen, 1995.

101. Eissenberg T, Stitzer ML, Strain EC, Liebson IA, Bigelow GE. A placebo controlled clinical trial of buprenorphine as a treatment for opioid dependence. Drug Alcohol Depend 1995;40:17–25.

102. Fairbank A, Dunteman GH, Condelli WS. Do methadone patients substitute other drugs for heroin? Predicting substance use at 1-year fol-low-up. Am J Drug Alcohol Abuse 1993;19:465–474.

103. Federal Bureau of Investigation. Uniform crime reports, 1980–1994. Washington, DC: Federal Bureau of Investigation, 1994.

104. Federal Bureau of Investigation. Uniform crime reports. Washington, DC: Federal Bureau of Investigation, 1995.

105 Federal High Court of Switzerland. Auszug aus dem Aortal des Kassationshofes des Bundesgerichtes vom 29, August 1991. In: Sachen L, ed. Gegen Staatsanwaltschaft des Kantons Zurich (Nichtigkeitsbeschwerde). Luzern: Federal High Court of Switzerland, 1991.

106. Federation of American Scientists. Medical use of whole cannabis. Washington, DC: Federation of American Scientists, 1994.

107. Fischer B. Drugs, communities, and 'harm reduction' in Germany: the new relevance of 'public health' principles in local responses. J Public Health Policy 1995;16:389–411.

108. Fischer G, Presslich O, Kiamant K, Schneider C, Pezawas L, Kasper S. Oral morphine sulphate in the treatment of opiate dependent patients. Alcoholism 1996;32:35–43.

109. Fleming PM, Roberts D. Is the prescription of amphetamine justified as a harm reduction measure. J R Soc Health 1994;114(3):127–131.

109a. Fodero L. An alternative to methadone is approved in NY state. The New York Times 1996(Sept. 6).

110. City of Frankfurt. Drogenreferat der Stadt Frankfurt am Main: Tatigkeitsbericht: 1–10-92 bis 31–12-93. Frankfurt: City of Frankfurt, 1994.

111. French JF, Safford J. AIDS and intranasal heroin. Lancet 1989;1(8646):1082.

112. Friedman SR. Going beyond education to mobilising subculture subcultural change. Int J Drug Policy 1993;4(2):91–95.

113. Friedman SR, Des Jarlais DC. HIV among drug injectors: the epidemic and response. AIDS Care 1991;3:239–250.

114. Friedmann P, Des Jarlais DC, Peyser NP, Nichols SE. Retention of patients who entered methadone maintenance clinics via an interim methadone clinic. J Psychoactive Drugs 1994;26(2):217–221.

115. Frischer M, Bloor M, Green S. Reduction in needle sharing among community wide samples of injecting drug users. Int J STD AIDS 1992;3:288.

116. Fromberg E, Jansen F. Het drugs en monitoring system: Verslag 1–7-1992–1–7-1993. Utrecht: Netherlands Institute on Alcohol and Drugs, 1993.

117. Gaughwin M, Kliewer E, Ali R, Faulkner C, Wodak A, Anderson G. The prescription of methadone for opiate dependence in Australia. Med J Aust 1993;159(2):107–108.

118. Gauzer B. Should marijuana be legal? Parade Mag 1994;June 12.

119. Gawin F, Riordan C, Kleber H. Methylphenidate treatment of cocaine abusers without attention deficit disorder: a negative report. Am J Drug Alcohol Abuse 1985;11(3–4):193–197.

120. Gearing FR, Schweitzer MD. An epidemiologic evaluation of long term methadone maintenance treatment for heroin addiction. Am J Epidemiol 1974;100:101–112.

121. Gerstein DR, Harwood HJ. Treating drug problems: a study of the evolution, effectiveness, and financing of public and private drug treatment systems. Washington, DC: National Academy Press, 1990.

122. Gilman M. Smack in the eye! In: O'Hare P, Newcombe R, Matthews A, Buning EC, Drucker E, eds. The reduction of drug related harm. London: Routledge, 1992:137–145.

123. Gilman M. 'Smack in the eye', 'Peanut Pete' and the New Puritans. Int J Drug Policy 1993;4(1):28–31.

124. Glass RM. Methadone maintenance: new research on a controversial treatment. JAMA 1993;269(15):1995–1996.

125. Goldberg C. Marijuana club helps those in pain. N Y Times 1996;Feb 25:A16.

126. Goldstein A. New approaches to the treatment of heroin addiction: STEPS (Sequential Treatment Employing Pharmacological Supports). Arch Gen Psychiatry 1976;33(3):353–358.

127. Goleman D. Brain images of addiction in action show its neural basis. N Y Times 1996; Aug 13:C1–C3.

128. Gordon DR. The return of the dangerous classes: drug prohibition and policy politics. New York: WW Norton, 1994.

129. Gossop M, Grant M. The content and structure of methadone treatment programs: a study in six countries. Geneva: WHO, Programme on Substance Abuse, 1990.

130. Deleted in proof.

131. Greenwood J. Creating a new drug service in Edinburgh. Br Med J 1990;300:587–589.

132. Greenwood J. Persuading general practitioners to prescribe: good husbandry or a recipe for chaos? Br J Addict 1992;87(4):567–575.

133. Griffiths P, Gossap M, Powis B, Strang J. Extent and nature of transitions of route among heroin addicts in treatment. Br J Addict 1992; 87:485.

134. Grinspoon L, Bakalar J. Marijuana: the forbidden medicine. New Haven: Yale University Press, 1993.

135. Grinspoon L, Bakalar J. Marihuana as a medicine: a plea for reconsideration. JAMA 1995; 273(23):1875–1876.

136. Grinspoon L, Bakalar J. Marijuana, the AIDS wasting syndrome, and the US government. N Engl J Med 1995;333:670–671.

137. Groseclose SL, Weinstein B, Jones TS, Valleroy LA, Fehrs LJ, Kassler WJ. Impact of increased legal access to needles and syringes on practices of injecting-drug users and police officers—Connecticut, 1992–1993. J Acquir Immune Def Syndr Hum Retrovirol 1995;10:73–89.

138. Grove D. Negotiation: basing syringe distribution on actual need. Paper presented at the meeting of the North American Syringe Conference, Milwaukee, WI, April 1996.

139. Grund JP. Drug use as a social ritual: functionality, symbolism and determinants of self regulation. IVO series 4. Rotterdam: IVO, 1996.

140. Grund JP, Blanken P, Adriaans FP, Kaplan CD, Barendregt C, Meeuwsen M. Reaching the unreached: targeting hidden IDU populations with clean needles via known user groups. J Psychoactive Drugs 1992;24(1):41–47.

141. Grund JP, Heckathorn DD, Broadhead RS, Anthony DL. In Eastern Connecticut IDUs purchase syringes from pharmacies but don't carry syringes. J Acquir Immune Def Syndr Hum Retrovirol 1995;10:104–105.

142. Grund JP, Stern LS, Kaplan EH, Nico, Adriaans FP. Drucker E. Drug use contexts and HIV consequences: the effect of drug policy on patterns of everyday drug use in Rotterdam. Br J Addict 1992;87:381–392.

143. Gunne L-M, Gronbladh L. The Swedish methadone maintenance program: a controlled study. Drug Alcohol Depend 1981;7:249–256.

144. Gunne L-M, Gronbladh L. The Swedish meth-

adone maintenance program. In: Serban G, ed. The social and medical aspects of drug abuse. Jamaica, NY: Spectrum Publications, 1984: 205–213.

145. Guskind R. Needle Park's gone, addicts aren't. Natl J 1992;Oct 10:2315.

146. Haemmig RB. The streetcorner agency with shooting room ('Fixerstuebli'). In: O'Hare P, Newcombe R, Matthews A, Buning EC, Drucker E, eds. The reduction of drug related harm. London: Routledge, 1992:181–185.

147. Hagen H, Des Jarlais DC, Purchase D, Friedman SR, Reid T, Bell TA. An interview study of participants in the Tacoma, Washington, syringe exchange. Addiction 1993;88(12):1691–1697.

148. Hall W, Ward J, Mattick RP. Should methadone maintenance be provided in Australian prisons? Paper presented at the Second National Corrections Health Conference, Sydney, Australia, 1992.

149. Hargreaves WA. Methadone dose and duration for maintenance treatment. In: Cooper JR, ed. Research on the treatment of narcotic addiction: state of the art. Rockville, MD: National Institute on Drug Abuse, 1983.

150. Hartel D. Temporal patterns of cocaine use and AIDS in intravenous drug users in methadone maintenance [Abstract]. Paper presented at the 5th International Conference on AIDS, Montreal, Canada, June 1989.

151. Hartel D, Selwyn PA, Schoenbaum EE. Methadone maintenance treatment and reduced risk of AIDS and AIDS-specific mortality in intravenous drug users. Paper presented at the meeting of the 4th International Conference on AIDS, Stockholm, Sweden, 1988.

152. Hartgers C, Buning EC, Van Santen GW, Verster AD, Coutinho RA. The impact of the needle and syringe exchange programme in Amsterdam on injecting risk behavior. AIDS 1989; 3(9):571–576.

153. Hartland N, McDonald D, Dance P, Bammer G. Australian reports into drug use and the possibility of heroin maintenance. Drug Alcohol Rev 1992;11(2):175–182.

154. Hartnoll R. Going the whole way? Heroin maintenance and AIDS prevention. Int J Drug Policy 1993;4(1):36–41.

155. Hartnoll R. Improving the comparability of epidemiological data: why and how? In: Commission of the European Communities, ed. Health-related data and epidemiology in the European Community. Luxembourg: Office for Official Publications of the European Community, 1993:65–69.

156. Hartnoll RL, Lewis R, Mitcheson MC, Bryer S. Estimating the prevalence of opioid dependence. Lancet 1985;1(8422):203–205.

157. Haw S. Pharmaceutical drugs and illicit drug use in Lothian region. Scotland: Centre for HIV/AIDS and Drugs Studies, 1993.

158. Health Council of the Netherlands Committee on Pharmacological Interventions in Heroin Addicts. The prescription of heroin to heroin addicts. The Hague: Health Council of the Netherlands, 1995.

159. Heather N, Wodak A, Nadelmann EA, O'Hare P, eds. Psychoactive drugs and harm reduction: from faith to science. London: Whurr Publishers, 1993.

160. Herzog C. Basel prisons. Euro-methwork 1993;2:3.

161. Holmberg SD. The estimated prevalence and incidence of HIV in 96 large U.S. metropolitan areas. Am J Public Health 1996;86:642–654.

162. Horowitz C. War by other means. New York 1996;Feb 5:22–33.

163. Hubbard RL. Drug abuse treatment: a national study of effectiveness. Chapel Hill: University of North Carolina Press, 1989.

164. Ingold FR, Ingold S. The effects of liberalization of syringe sales on the behavior of intravenous drug users in France. Bull Narc 1989; 41(1–2):67–87.

165. Ingold FR, Toussirt M. Transmission of HIV among drug addicts in three French cities: implications for prevention. Bull Narc 1993; 45(1):117–134.

166. Institute for the Study of Drug Dependence. Teaching about a volatile situation: suggested health education strategies for minimizing casualties associated with solvent sniffing. London: Institute for the Study of Drug Dependence, 1979.

167. Institute of Medicine. Federal regulation of methadone treatment. Washington, DC: National Academy Press, 1995.

167a. Institute of Medicine. Treating drug problems. Washington, DC: National Academy Press, 1990;1:187.

168. Interdepartmental Stuurgroep Alcohol en Drugbeleid. Drugbeleid in beweging: naar een normalisering van de drugproblematiek. The Hague: Ministerie van Welzijn, Volksgezondheid en Culture, 1985.

169. Jacobs A. Neighborhood report: Lower Eastside: needle center sounds alarm on bad heroin. N Y Times 1996;13(April 7):7.

170. Jann M, Hemann R, Ramming P. Das Berner Anlaufstellenmodell: Evaluation des Betriebs der Anlaufstellen mit Drogenkonsumraum Munstergasse, Kleine Schanze und Nageligasse (1989–1991). Bern: Stiftung Contact, 1992.

171. Jansen ACM. Cannabis in Amsterdam. Muiderberg, Netherlands: Dick Coutinho, 1990.

172. Johnson BD. How much heroin maintenance (containment) in Britain? Int J Addict 1977;12 (2–3):361–398.

173. Johnston LD, O'Mally PM, Bachman JG. Monitoring the future. Occasional Paper Series no. 13. Ann Arbor: University of Michigan, 1981.

174. Joseph H. The criminal justice system and opiate addiction: an historical perspective. In: Leukefeld CG, Tims FM, eds. Compulsory treatment of drug abuse: research and clinical practice. Rockville, MD: National Institute on Drug Abuse, 1988:106–125.

175. Juso-Bundesverband. Materialien zur Drogenpolitik. Bonn: Juso-Bundesverband, 1995.

176. Kaplan EH. Probability models of needle exchange. Operations Res 1995;43:558–569.

177. Kaplan S. Marijuana: the new prohibition. New York: Pocket Books, 1970.

178. Keene J, Stimson GV. HIV prevention: the role of the community pharmacist. Pharm J 1991; 22:764.

179. Khantzian EJ. An extreme case of cocaine dependence and marked improvement with methylphenidate treatment. Am J Psychiatry 1983;140(6):784–785.

180. Khantzian EJ, Gawin F, Riordan CE, Kleber H. Methylphenidate (Ritalin) treatment in cocaine abuse: a preliminary report. J Subst Abuse Treat 1984;1(2):107–112.

181. Kinzer S. German state eases its policy on drug arrests. N Y Times 1994;May 18:A5.

182. Klingemann HKH. Drug treatment in Switzerland: harm reduction, decentralization and community response. Addiction 1996;91: 723–736.

183. Korf D. Heroinetoerisme II: resultaten van een veldonderzoek onder 382 buitenlandse dagelijkse opiaatgebruikers in Amsterdam. Amsterdam: Universiteit van Amsterdam, Instituut voor Sociale Geografie, 1987.

184. Korf D. Cannabis retail markets in Amsterdam. Int J Drug Policy 1990;2(1):23–27.

184a. Kosten TR, Schottenfeld R, Ziedonis D, Falcioni J. Buprenorphine versus methadone maintenance for opioid dependence. J Nerv Ment Dis 1993;181(6):358–363.

185. Krausz M. Vocational integration and additional drug consumption among addicts maintained on codeine/dihydrocodeine and methadone. Addiction (in press).

186. Kreek MJ. Health consequences associated with the use of methadone. In: Cooper JR, ed. Research on the treatment of narcotic addiction: state of the art. Rockville, MD: National Institute of Drug Abuse, 1983.

187. Lamb RJ, Kirby KC, Platt JJ. Treatment retention, occupational role, and cocaine use among those who remain in MMT. Am J Addict 1995; 4:1–6.

188. Landgericht (LG) Lubeck. Vorlagebeschluss zum Bundesverfassungsgericht vom 19. Dez. 1991 Az: 2 Ns Kl.167/90. Neue Juristische Wochenschr 1992:1571–1577.

189. Landgericht (LG) Frankfurt. Vorlagebeschluss zum Bundesverfassungsgericht. Strafverteidiger 1993:77–84.

190. Lart RA, Stimson GV. National survey of syringe exchange schemes in England. Br J Addict 1990;85(11):1433–1443.

191. Last JM, Wallace RB. Maxcy-Rosenau-Last public health and preventive medicine. 13th ed. Norwalk, CT: Appleton & Lange, 1992.

192. Leuw E. Door schade en schande: de geschiedenis van drugs-hulpverlening als sociaal beleid in Amsterdam. Tijdschrift voor Criminologie 1984;26:149.

193. Deleted in proof.

194. Leuw E. Drugs and drug policy in the Netherlands. Crime Justice Rev Res 1991;14: 229–276.

195. Leuw E, Marshall IH. Between prohibition and legalization: the Dutch experiment in drug policy. New York: Kugler, 1994.

196. Lewis DC, Gear CA, Rihs ME. Medical prescription of narcotics. Fribourg, Germany: Huber Verlag, 1996.

197. Lindesmith AR. The addict and the law. Bloomington, IN: Indiana University Press, 1965.

198. Llosa T. The standard low dose of oral cocaine used for treatment of cocaine dependence. Subst Abuse 1994;15(4):215–220.

199. Locher U. Switzerland's heroin prescription experiment: an update. Paper presented at The Lindesmith Center Seminar Series, New York, NY, January 4, 1996.

200. Loxley W, Carruthers S, Bevan J. In the same vein: first report of the Australian Study of HIV and Injecting Drug Use (ASHIDU). Perth: Curtin University of Technology, National Centre for Research into the Prevention of Drug Abuse, 1995.

201. Lungley S, Baker M. The needle and syringe exchange scheme in operation. Wellington: New Zealand Department of Health, 1990.

202. Lurie P. Policy experts unanimous: needle-exchange programs effective [Letter]. AIDS Wkly 1996:29.

203. Lurie P, Drucker E. An opportunity lost: esti-

mating the number of HIV infections associated with the U.S. government opposition to needle exchange programs. Paper presented at the 6th International Conference on AIDS, Vancouver, Canada, July 1996.

204. Lurie P, Reingold AL. The public health impact of needle exchange programs in the United States and abroad. Berkeley: University of California, Institute for Health Policy Studies, 1993.

205. MacCoun RJ, Saiger AJ, Kahan JP, Reuter P. Drug policies and problems: the promise and pitfalls of cross-national comparison. In: Heather N, Wodak A, Nadelmann EA, O'Hare P, eds. Psychoactive drugs and harm reduction: from faith to science. London: Whurr Publishers, 1993:103–117.

206. Maddux JF, Desmond DP. Methadone maintenance and recovery from opioid dependence. Am J Drug Alcohol Abuse 1992;18(1):63–74.

207. Magura S, Rosenblum A, Lewis C, Joseph H. The effectiveness of in-jail methadone-maintenance. J Drug Issues 1993;23(1):75–99.

208. Magura S, Siddiqi Q, Freeman RC, Lipton DS. Changes in cocaine use after entry to methadone treatment. In: Cocaine, AIDS, and intravenous drug use. New York: Haworth Press, 1991.

209. Manderson D. Rules and practices: the 'British System' in Australia. J Drug Issues 1992;22: 527.

210. Mayor's Working Group on Drug Policy Reform. Final report. Baltimore: City of Baltimore, 1993.

211. McClellan AT, Arndt IO, Metzger D, Woody G, O'Brien CP. The effects of psychosocial services in substance abuse treatment. JAMA 1993;269(15):1953–1959.

212. McDonald D, Moore R, Norberry J, Wardlaw G, Ballenden N. Legislative options for cannabis in Australia. National Drug Strategy Monograph Series no. 26. Canberra: Australian Government Publishing Service, 1996.

212a.Mello NK, Mendelson JH, Lukas SE, Gastfriend DR, Koon Teoh S, Holman LB. Buprenorphine treatment of opiate and cocaine abuse: clinical and preclinical studies. Harvard Rev Psychiatry 1993;1(3):168–183.

213. Mersey Drug Training and Information Centre. Reducing drug related harm in the Mersey Region. Liverpool: Mersey Drug Training and Information Centre, 1993.

214. Messinger TA. A decade of drug analysis results: 1973–1983. PharmChem Newsl 1984;13 (2/3).

215. Meyers EJ. American heroin policy: some alternatives. In: Drug Abuse Council, ed. The facts about "drug abuse". New York: Free Press, 1980:190–247.

216. Mino A. Analyse scientifique de la litterature pour la remise controlee d'heroine ou de morphine. Geneva: Office Federal de la Sante Publique, 1990.

217. Mitcheson M, Edwards G, Hawks D, Ogborne A. Treatment of methylamphetamine users during the 1968 epidemic. In: Edwards G, ed. Drugs and drug dependency. London: Saxon House, 1976:155–162.

218. Model KE. The effect of marijuana decriminalization on hospital emergency room drug episodes: 1975–1978. J Am Statist Assoc 1993;88(423):737–747.

219. Mol R, Otter E, van der Meer A. Drugs and AIDS in the Netherlands: the interests of drug users. Amsterdam: Interest Group for Drug Users MDHG, 1992.

220. Muller T, Grob P. Medizinische und soziale Aspekte der offenen Drogenszene Platzspitz in Zurich, 1991. Zurich, 1992.

221. Murphy S, Rosenbaum M. Money for methadone II: unintended consequences of limited-duration methadone maintenance. J Psychoactive Drugs 1988;20:397–402.

222. Musto DF. The American disease: origins of narcotic control. New York: Oxford University Press, 1987.

222a.Nadelmann E, McNeely J. Doing methadone right. Public Interest 1996;123:83–93.

223. Nadelmann EA. Drug prohibition in the United States: costs, consequences, and alternatives. Science 1989;245(Sept 1):939–946.

224. Nadelmann EA. Global prohibition regimes: the evolution of norms in international society. Int Organization 1990;44(4):479–526.

225. Nadelmann EA. Thinking seriously about alternatives to drug prohibition. Daedalus 1992; 121(3):85–132.

226. Nadelmann EA. Cops across borders: the internationalization of US criminal law enforcement. University Park, PA: Pennsylvania State University College Press, 1993.

227. Nadelmann EA. Europe's drug prescription. Rolling Stone 1995;Jan 26:38–39.

228. Nadelmann EA. Switzerland's heroin experiment. Natl Rev 1995;10:46–47.

229. Nadelmann EA. The war on drugs is lost. Natl Rev 1996;48(Feb 12):38–40.

230. Nadelmann EA, Wenner JS. Toward a sane national drug policy. Rolling Stone 1994;May 5:24–27.

231. National Center for Epidemiology and Population Health. Feasibility research into the controlled availability of opioids. Canberra: Australian National University, 1991.

232. National Commission on Acquired Immune Deficiency Syndrome. The twin epidemics of substance use and HIV. Washington, DC: National Commission on Acquired Immune Deficiency Syndrome, 1991.

233. National Commission on Marijuana and Drug Abuse. Marijuana: a signal of misunderstanding. Washington, DC: U.S. Government Printing Office, 1972.

234. Netherlands Ministry of Health Welfare and Sports, Netherlands Ministry of Justice. Drug policy in the Netherlands: continuity and change. The Hague, Netherlands: Ministry of Health, Welfare and Sports, 1995.

235. New South Wales Department of Corrective Services. Monitoring the NSW prison methadone program: a review of research 1986–1991. Australia: New South Wales Department of Corrective Services, 1992.

236. Newman RG. Methadone treatment in narcotic addiction. New York: Academic Press, 1977.

237. Newman RG. Narcotic addiction and methadone treatment in Hong Kong. J Public Health Policy (South Asian ed) 1985;6:526–538.

238. Newman RG. Another wall that crumbled— methadone maintenance treatment in Germany. Am J Drug Alcohol Abuse 1995;21(1): 27–35.

239. Newman RG, Peyser NP. Methadone treatment: experiment and experience. J Psychoactive Drugs 1991;23:115–121.

240. Normand J, Vlahov D, Moses LE. Preventing HIV transmission: the role of sterile needles and bleach. Washington, DC: National Academy Press, 1995.

241. North West Thames Regional Pharmaceutical Service. Supply of methadone within North West Thames. Unpublished manuscript, 1993.

242. Novick DM, Joseph H. Medical maintenance: the treatment of chronic opiate dependence in general medical practice. J Subst Abuse Treat 1991;8(4):233–239.

243. Novick DM, Joseph H, Croxson TS, Salsitz EA, Wang G, Richman BL, Poretsky L, Keefe JB, Whimbey E. Absence of antibody to human immunodeficiency virus in long–term socially rehabilitated methadone maintenance patients. Arch Intern Med 1990;150(1):97–99.

244. Novick DM, Joseph H, Salsitz EA, Kalin MF, Keefe JB, Miller EL, Richman BL. Outcomes of socially rehabilitated methadone maintenance patients in physicians' offices (medical maintenance): follow-up at three and a half to nine and a fourth years. J Gen Intern Med 1994;9(3):127–130.

245. Novick DM, Pascarelli EF, Joseph H, Salsitz EA, Richman BL, Des Jarlais DC, Anderson M, Dole VP, Nyswander ME. Methadone maintenance patients in general medical practice: a preliminary report. JAMA 1988;259 (22):3299–3302.

246. Office of Technology Assessment. The effectiveness of AIDS prevention efforts. Washington, DC: U.S. Government Printing Office, 1995.

247. O'Hare P, Newcombe R, Matthews A, Buning EC, Drucker E. The reduction of drug related harm. New York: Routledge, 1992.

248. Opernhaus Zurich AG. Geschaftbericht 1991/ 92. Zurich: Opernhaus Zurich AG, 1996.

249. Ossebaard HC. Netherlands cannabis policy [Letter]. Lancet 1996;347(9003):767–768.

250. Palombella A. Prescribing of smokable drugs. Int J Drug Policy 1990;1(6):31.

251. Paone D. Syringe exchange programs—United States, 1994–1995. MMWR Morb Mortal Wkly Rep 1995;44(37):684–691.

252. Paone D, Des Jarlais DC, Caloir S, Clark J, Jose B. Operational issues in syringe exchanges: the New York City Tagging Alternative Study. J Community Health 1995;20(2): 111–123.

253. Pearson G. The new heroin users. New York: Basil Blackwell, 1987.

254. Pearson G. Drug-control policies in Britain. Crime Justice Rev 1991;14:167.

255. Peutherer J, Simmonds EE, Dickson JD, Bath GE. HTVL III antibody in drug addicts. Lancet 1985;8464:1129–1130.

256. Picard E. Legal action against the Belgian Medical Association's restrictions of methadone treatment. In: Reisinger M, ed. AIDS and drugs addiction in the European Community. Brussels: Commission of the European Communities, European Monitoring Centre on Drugs and Drug Addiction, 1993:41–49.

257. Plomp HN, van der Hek H, Ader HJ. The Amsterdam dispensing circuit: genesis and effectiveness of a public health model for local drug policy. Addiction 1996;91(5):711–721.

258. Pompidou Group Co-operation Group to Combat Drug Abuse and Illicit Trafficking in Drugs. Multi-city study: drug misuse trends in thirteen European cities. Strasbourg: Council of Europe Press, 1994.

259. Prendergast ML, Grella C, Perry SM, Anglin MD. Levo-alpha-acetylmethadol (LAAM): clinical, research, and policy issues of a new pharmacotherapy for opioid addiction. J Psychoactive Drugs 1995;27(3):239–248.

260. Projekt Arbeit Technik und Kultur. Druckraum Moselstrasse 44 mobiler Spritzentausch (SAP). Integrative Drogenhilfe e v 1996:15–25.

261. Rainwater L. US doing poorly—compared to

others. News Issues Natl Ctr Child Poverty 1995:4–6.

262. Reisinger M. AIDS and drug addiction in the European Community. Brussels: Commission of the European Communities, European Monitoring Centre on Drugs and Drug Addiction, 1993.

263. Reisinger M. Methadone treatment and AIDS in Western Europe. Paper presented at National Conference on Methadone, Geneva, Switzerland, June 23, 1995.

264. Reisinger M. Methadone as a normal medicine. Euro-methwork 1996;8:9–10.

265. Reisinger M. Substitution treatment and the outbreak of AIDS epidemic in Western Europe. Pub of Seisida 1996;7(4):195.

266. Reuter P. Prevalence estimation and policy formulation. J Drug Issues 1993;23(2):167–184.

267. Reuter P, Falco M, MacCoun RJ. Comparing Western European and North American drug policies. Santa Monica, CA: Rand, 1993.

268. Rhodes TA, Hartnoll R, Johnson A, Holland J, Jones SS. Out of the agency into the streets: a review of outreach education in Europe and the United States. London: Institute for the Study of Drug Dependence, 1991.

269. Rihs M, Affentranger P. Status report on the Project Medical Prescription of Narcotics in Switzerland. Papers on Youth Policy. Bonn, Switzerland: SPD Party Committee, 1995;9.

270. Riordan CE, Gould LC. Proposal for the use of diacetyl morphine (heroin) in the treatment of heroin dependent individuals. New York: Vera Institute of Justice, 1972.

271. Robertson JR, Bucknall ABV, Welsby PD, Roberts JJ, Inglis JM, Peutherer J, Brettle RP. Epidemic of AIDS related virus (HTVL III/LAV) infection among intravenous drug abusers. Br Med J 1986;292(6519):527–529.

272. Robinson TE, Berridge KC. The renewal basis of drug craving: an incentive-sensitization theory of addiction. Brain Sci Res Rev 1993; 18:247–291.

273. Rosenbaum M, Irwin J, Murphy S. De facto destabilization as policy: the impact of short term methadone maintenance. Contemp Drug Probl 1988;15(4):491–517.

274. Rosenbaum M, Murphy S, Beck J. Money for methadone: preliminary findings from a study of Alameda County's new maintenance policy. J Psychoactive Drugs 1987;19:13–19.

275. Sagliocca L, Rezza G, Vlahov C, Baldassarre M, Siconolfi M, Nespoli P, Carrieri P. Did morphine prescription decrease the spread of HIV in Naples? A retrospective evaluation of a program implemented in early 1980's. Addict Res (in press).

276. Sandwijk JP, Cohen P, Musterd S, Langemeijer MPS. Licit and illicit drug use in Amsterdam II: report of a household survey in 1994 on the prevalence of drug use among the population of 12 and over. Amsterdam: University of Amsterdam, Department of Human Geography, 1995.

277. Schmidt WE. To battle AIDS, Scots offer oral drugs to addicts. N Y Times 1993;Feb 8:A3.

278. Schneider W. Report on the drug policy in the city of Frankfurt. Unpublished manuscript, 1993.

279. Schottenfeld RS, O'Mally S, Abdul-Salaam K, O'Connor PG. Decline in intravenous drug use among treatment seeking opiates users. J Subst Abuse Treat 1993;10(1):5–10.

280. Seidenberg A. Oral methadone and beyond: diversified drug prescription in Switzerland. Paper presented at a seminar at The Lindesmith Center, New York, NY, July 22, 1996.

281. Selwyn PA, Feiner C, Cox CP, Lipschutz C, Cohen RL. Knowledge about AIDS and high risk behavior among intravenous drug users in New York City. AIDS 1987;1(4):247–254.

282. Selwyn PA, Hartel D, Wasserman W, Drucker E. Impact of the AIDS epidemic on the morbidity and mortality among intravenous drug users in a New York City methadone maintenance program. Am J Public Health 1989;79:1358–1363.

283. Senay EC. Medical maintenance: an interim report. J Addict Dis 1994;13:65–69.

284. Serfaty A. HIV infection drug use in France: trends of the epidemic and governmental responses. In: Reisinger M, ed. AIDS and drug addiction in the European Community. Brussels: Commission of the European Communities, European Monitoring Centre on Drugs and Drug Addiction, 1993:61–70.

285. Siegal S. Alcohol and opiate dependence: reevaluation of the Victorian perspective. Res Adv Alcohol Drug Probl 1986;9:279.

286. Siegel RK. Intoxication: life in pursuit of artificial paradise. New York: EP Dutton, 1989.

287. Sinclair A. Hong Kong: low HIV rates in injection drug users. JAMA (Southeast Asia ed) 1994;10(5):11.

288. Single EW. The impact of marijuana decriminalization: an update. J Public Health Policy 1989;10:456–466.

289. Staples P. Reduction of alcohol- and drug-related harm in Australia: a government minister's perspective. In: Heather N, Wodak A, Nadelmann EA, O'Hare P, eds. Psychoactive drugs and harm reduction: from faith to science. London: Whurr Publishers, 1993:49–54.

290. Stares PB. Global habit: the drug problem in a borderless world. Washington, DC: Brookings Institution. 1996.

291. Stimson GV. Syringe exchange programs for injecting drug users. AIDS 1989;3:253.

292. Stimson GV. Risk reduction by drug users with regard to HIV infection. Int Rev Psychiatry 1991;3(3–4):401–405.

293. Stimson GV. The global diffusion of injecting drug use: implications for HIV infection. Bull Narc 1993;45:3–17.

294. Stimson GV. AIDS and injecting drug use in the United Kingdom, 1988–1993: the policy response and the prevention of the epidemic. Unpublished manuscript, 1994.

295. Stimson GV, Donoghoe MC, Donlon KA. In defense of legal syringe distribution: evidence from England. London: National Association of Attorneys General, 1992.

296. Stimson GV, Oppenheimer E. Heroin addiction: treatment and control in Britain. London: Tavistock, 1982.

297. Stover H, Schuller K. AIDS prevention with injecting drug users in the former West Germany. In: O'Hare P, Newcombe R, Matthews A, Buning EC, Drucker E, eds. The reduction of drug related harm. London: Routledge, 199:186–194.

298. Strang J, Stimson GV. AIDS and drug misuse: the challenge for policy and practice in the 1990s. New York: Routledge, 1990.

299. Stryker J, Smith MD. Dimensions of HIV prevention: needle exchange. Menlo Park, CA: Kaiser Family Foundation, 1993.

300. Sutton A, Sarre R. Monitoring the South Australian cannabis expiation notice system. J Drug Issues 1992;22(3):579–590.

301. Swiss Federal Office of Public Health. Status report on the medical prescription of narcotics. Liebefeld, Switzerland: Swiss Federal Office of Public Health, 1995.

302. Symanski R. The immoral landscape: female prostitution in Western societies. Toronto: Buttersworth, 1981.

302a. Task Force to Review Services for Drug Misusers. Reprt of an independent survey of drug treatment services in England. London: Department of Health, 1996.

303. Terry CE, Pellens M. The opium problem. New York: Bureau of Social Hygiene, 1928.

304. Thies CT, Register CA. Decriminalization of marijuana and the demand for alcohol, marijuana and cocaine. J Soc Sci 1993;30:385.

305. Treaster J. Healing herb or narcotic? Underground networks supplying the sick. N Y Times 1994;Nov 14:B1.

306. Trebach AS. The heroin solution. New Haven: Yale University Press, 1982.

307. Turner CF, Miller HG, Moses LE. AIDS, sexual behavior, and intravenous drug use. Washington, DC: National Academy Press, 1989.

308. U.S. Department of Health and Human Services Substance Abuse and Mental Health Services Administration. National Household Survey on Drug Abuse: main findings 1993. Washington, DC: U.S. Department of Health and Human Services, 1993.

309. U.S. Department of Health and Human Services Center for Substance Abuse Treatment. State methadone treatment guidelines. Rockville, MD: U.S. Department of Health and Human Services, Center for Substance Abuse Treatment, 1993.

310. U.S. Department of State Office of the Legal Adviser Treaty Affairs Staff. Treaties in force: a list of treaties and other international agreements of the United States in force as of January 1, 1995. Washington, DC: U.S. Department of State, 1995.

311. U.S. Drug Enforcement Administration. In the matter of marijuana rescheduling petition, Docket 86–22, opinion, recommended ruling, finding of fact, conclusions of law, and the decisions of administrative law judge. Washington, DC: U.S. Drug Enforcement Administration, 1988.

312. U.S. General Accounting Office. Needle exchange programs: research suggests promise as an AIDS prevention strategy: report to the Chairman, Select Committee on Narcotics Abuse and Control. (GAO/HRD-93–60). Washington, DC: U.S. General Accounting Office, 1993.

313. Uchtenhagen A. Current Swiss experience and future plans. Paper presented at a seminar at Beth Israel Medical Center, New York, NY, May 7, 1996.

314. Uchtenhagen A. Versuche fur eine aerztlichen Verschreibung von Betaeubungsmitteln, second intermediate report. Zurich, September, 1996.

315. Uchtenhagen A, Gutzwiller F, Dobler-Mikola A. General study design and implementation rules. In: Foundation for Social Therapy, eds. The connection between research and practice in drug therapy. Drogalkol 1994;3:187–198.

316. Van Brussel GHA. Methadone treatment in Amsterdam: the critical role of the general practitioners. Addict Res 1986;3:363–369.

317. van de Wijngaart GF. The Dutch approach: normalization of drug problems. J Drug Issues 1990;20(4):667–678.

318. van de Wijngaart GF. Competing perspectives on drug use: the Dutch experience. Berwyn, PA: Swets & Zeitlinger, 1991.

319. van der Hoeven R. Nota verdovende middelen. Unpublished manuscript, 1992.

320. Van Santen GW. Exchange of expertise in Europe: the Frankfurt experience. In: Reisinger M, ed. AIDS and drug addiction in the European Community. Brussels: Commission of the European Communities, European Monitoring Centre on Drugs and Drug Addiction, 1993:169–173.

321. Vera Institute of Justice. Heroin research and rehabilitation programme. New York: Vera Institute of Justice, 1971.

322. Visser H. Perron Nul: Opgang en ondergang (The rise and fall of Platform Zero). Netherlands: Meinema, 1996.

323. Vlahov D. Deregulation of the sale and possession of syringes for HIV prevention among injection drug users [Editorial]. J Acquir Immune Def Syndr Hum Retrovirol 1995;10(1): 71–72.

324. Vromen G. Amsterdam's controversial methadone buses help fight AIDS. Reuter Library Rep 1989;2.

325. Waldorf D, Orlick M, Reinarman C. Morphine maintenance: the Shreveport Clinic, 1919–1923. Washington, DC: Drug Abuse Council, 1974.

326. Ward J, Mattick RP, Hall W. Key issues in methadone maintenance treatment. Kensington, Australia: New South Wales University Press, 1992.

327. Watters JK, Estilo MJ, Clark GL, Lorvick J. Syringe and needle exchange as HIV/AIDS prevention for injection drug users. JAMA 1994;271(2):115.

328. Weber U. Maintenance with codeine in Germany: the supportive position. Unpublished manuscript, 1996.

329. Weil AT. The therapeutic value of coca in contemporary medicine. J Ethnopharmacol 1981; 3:367.

330. Weil AT. The natural mind: an investigation of drugs and the higher consciousness. Boston: Houghton Mifflin, 1986.

331. Werkgroep Verdovende Middelen. Rapport van de Werkgroep Verdovende Middelen. The Hague, Netherlands: Staatsuitgeverij, 1972.

332. Wever L. Drug policy changes in Europe and the USA: alternatives to international warfare. Int J Drug Policy 1992;3(4):176–181.

332a. White R. Amphetamine prescribing—interim report. Unpublished report. Cornwall, England: Cornwall Community Drugs Team, July, 1996.

333. WHO Collaborative Study Group. An international comparative study of HIV prevalence and risk behavior among drug injectors in 13 cities. Bull Narc 1993;45(1):19–47.

334. Willoughby S, Hager K, Miller J, Turner S. Harm minimization and amphetamine prescribing. In: Standing Committee on Drug Abuse, ed. SCODA conference volume. London: Standing Committee on Drug Abuse, 1992.

335. Wodak A. HIV infection and injecting drug use in Australia: responding to a crisis. J Drug Issues 1992;22(3):549–562.

336. Wodak A. Organizations of injecting drug users in Australia. Int J Drug Policy 1993; 4(2):96–97.

337. Wodak A. When medical research is beholden to politics. Med J Aust 1996;164(11):649–650.

338. Wolk J, Wodak A, Guinan JJ, Macaskill P, Simpson JM. The effect of needle and syringe exchange on a methadone maintenance unit. Br J Addict 1990;85(11):1445–1450.

339. World Health Organization Programme on Substance Abuse Drug Substitution Project. Report of WHO consultation, Geneva, 15–19 May 1995. Geneva: World Health Organization, 1996.

340. World Health Organization. WHO collaborative study on AIDS and drug addiction. Geneva: World Health Organization, 1996.

341. Yancovitz SR, Des Jarlais DC, Peyser NP, Drew E. A randomized trial of an interim methadone maintenance clinic. Am J Public Health 1991;81(9):1185–1191.

342. Zaal L. Police policy needed in Amsterdam. In: O'Hare P, Newcombe R, Matthews A, Buning EC, Drucker E, eds. The reduction of drug-related harm. New York: Routledge, 1996: 90–94.

343. Zeller R. Praventionskampagne gegen das Folienrauchen. Neue Zurcher Zeitung 1993:31.

344. Zinberg NE. Drug, set, and setting: the basics for controlled intoxicant use. New Haven: Yale University Press, 1984.

345. Zinberg NE, Harding WM. Control and intoxicant use: a theoretical and practical overview. J Drug Issues 1979;9:121–143.

346. Zurich Health Department Office of the Chief Medical Officer. AIDS prevention statistics on needle exchange 1992/1993. Zurich: Zurich Health Department, 1994.

347. Zurich Social Welfare Department. Erfahrungsbericht der Kontakt- und Anlaufstellen uber den Betrieb der Gassenzimmer. Zurich: Zurich Social Welfare Department, 1993.

SECTION II. DETERMINANTS AND PERPETUATORS OF SUBSTANCE ABUSE

5 GENETICS

Robert M. Anthenelli and Marc A. Schuckit

Several years ago, the *New York Times* (April 18, 1990) reported that "scientists [had] link[ed] alcoholism to a specific gene[,] . . . opening the 'window of hope' for prevention of a deadly disease." Although the accuracy of the finding on which this headline was based is controversial (1, 2), the story remains historically significant.

Fifty years ago there were those who doubted they would ever read such a headline (3). As our understanding of alcoholism (i.e., alcohol dependence) and other substance use disorders has advanced, so, too, have our ideas about their patterns of transmission. For instance, the moralistic idea of alcoholism as a characterological weakness has given way to the more contemporary view of the condition as a debilitating, heterogeneous group of disorders with multifactorial origins. The importance of environmental, developmental, and social factors championed by Jellinek and others in the 1940s has had to share the stage with a growing body of evidence supporting a genetic vulnerability to the disorder. All are important. No one headline tells the whole story.

This chapter reviews the role of genetic factors in the risk for substance abuse and dependence and outlines a methodological approach for study. Because the preponderance of data are from studies on alcohol, this drug is emphasized. Reflecting the clinical nature of this text and the authors' area of expertise, this chapter focuses primarily on human genetic aspects of substance disorders. Interested readers may wish to pursue a more comprehensive review of the animal and preclinical literature (4).

ALCOHOLISM AS A MODEL FOR STUDYING GENETIC VULNERABILITY TO SUBSTANCE ABUSE AND DEPENDENCE

Traditionally, the search for genetic influences in any complex disorder begins with studies of families, twins, and adoptees affected with the condition (5). These investigations can provide preliminary evidence on the probable importance of genetic factors and serve as the foundation for subsequent research. The following sections briefly review the results of more than three decades of family, twin, and adoption studies in alcoholism. Although these investigations are not unanimous in their results, when taken together, they provide compelling evidence for the importance of genetic factors in this disorder.

Family, Twin, and Adoption Studies of Alcoholism

FAMILY STUDIES

For centuries, philosophers, writers, and clergy have commented on the familial nature of alcoholism. Plutarch's assertion that "drunks beget drunkards" was based on anecdotal observation alone, and it was not until the past few decades that this contention came under careful scientific scrutiny (6). The basic design for family studies of any complex illness is to compare the risk for developing the disorder in relatives of probands (individuals manifesting the phenotype or trait) with the rate for relatives of control groups or for the general population (5).

Numerous studies have shown that rates of alcoholism are substantially higher in relatives of alcoholics than in relatives of nonalcoholics, with children of alcoholics demonstrating a 3- to 4-fold increased risk for developing the disorder (7, 8). This increased risk appears to be relatively specific for alcoholism, with most family studies showing an increased rate for the disorder among relatives of alcoholic probands, while the same group does not show higher rates of schizophrenia or bipolar disorder (7, 9).

Although family studies provide preliminary evidence that alcoholism might be inherited, they are, in themselves, inconclusive. Familial aggregation might also reflect the shared social and developmental influences of being raised in the same environment by biological parents. To disentangle these factors, other approaches are required.

TWIN STUDIES

Research with twins evaluates the relative contributions of genetic and environmental factors by comparing the similarity or concordance rates for illness in pairs of monozygotic twins with those of dizygotic twins. The twin study design allows researchers to estimate the contribution of genetic and environmental effects to the individual's liability for alcoholism and other substance use disorders. The liability identified in twin research generally has three components: *(1)* additive genetic effects; *(2)* common environmental effects shared by twins (e.g., intrauterine environment, parental upbringing); and *(3)* specific, nonshared environmental experiences (10). Identical twin pairs who share all of their genes should show higher concordance rates for gene-transmitted disorders than should fraternal twin pairs who, like ordinary siblings, generally share only half of their genes (10). On the other extreme, environmentally influenced disorders would show no difference between monozygotic and dizygotic twin pairs so long as both types of twins were exposed to the same childhood environment.

Several major twin studies have directly addressed the concordance rates for alcoholism in identical versus fraternal twins. In Sweden, Kaij found that the concordance rate for alcoholism in male monozygotic pairs was greater than that for dizygotic twins (approximately 60% versus 39%) (11). Interestingly, the discrepancy between concordance rates increased in proportion to the severity of alcoholism in these male twin pairs, favoring a genetic diathesis. A Veterans Administration twin register study in the United States revealed a similar higher concordance rate for identical male same-sex twin pairs (12) as did two other smaller studies (13, 14); however, not all studies agree (15).

While results among male same-sex twin pairs had consistently demonstrated that genetic factors were important in the etiology of alcoholism in men, results in women were less consistent. Thus, several smaller twin studies found no (14, 15) or relatively little (13) genetic influence in females compared to males. However, recently, in a large sample of female same-sex twin pairs in the United States, Kendler et al. reported that the concordance for alcoholism was greater in monozygotic than in dizygotic twin pairs (16).

Other investigations of twins have focused on how genetic factors might influence patterns of drinking and rates of absorption or elimination of ethanol in twins. Two Scandinavian studies of nonalcoholics have found that identical twins are more concordant for quantity and frequency of drinking but not for adverse consequences of drinking (17, 18). This latter point might reflect the twin sample under study, which was from the general population and not selected for drinking problems per se. Results from twin studies on concordance rates for alcohol absorption or elimination are conflicting, with some studies showing high levels of heritability for these parameters (19, 20) and others finding no such concordance (21). The disparity in results from these studies probably reflects the multiple factors that affect alcohol absorption and metabolism (e.g., use of other drugs, diet, etc.).

Thus, the majority of twin studies support the notion that alcoholism is genetically influenced and that heritable factors might play a role in the quantity and frequency of drinking *in both men and women.* The lack of unanimity of these studies points to the complexity of these issues and the interaction between genetic and environmental factors.

ADOPTION STUDIES

Perhaps the most convincing way to separate genetic from environmental effects is to study individuals separated soon after birth from their biological relatives and raised by nonrelative adoptive parents (22). This can be done through classical adoption studies or through a half-sibling approach (23).

There have been several half-sibling and adoption studies evaluating the possibility that alcoholism, at least in part, has genetic determinants. Schuckit and colleagues evaluated a group of individuals who had been raised apart from their biological parents but who had either a biological or surrogate parent with alcoholism (24). Subjects who had a biological parent with severe alcohol problems were significantly more likely to have alcoholism themselves than if their surrogate parent were alcoholic.

Over the past two decades, several adoption studies in Denmark, Sweden, and the United States have yielded similar results. In Denmark, Goodwin and coworkers found that the sons of alcoholics were about 4 times more likely to be alcoholic than sons of nonalcoholics and that being raised by either nonalcoholic adoptive parents or by biological parents did not affect this increased risk (25). Furthermore, although the sons of alcoholics were found to be at highest risk for developing alcoholism, they were no more likely to have other psychiatric disorders (22, 25). As with some of the twin studies cited above, results for women in the Copenhagen Adoption Study were not significant. Similar results were found in another large study done in Stockholm, Sweden, where Cloninger and colleagues showed significantly higher rates of alcohol abuse in adopted-out sons of biological fathers registered with alcohol problems (26). The Stockholm Adoption Study also suggested that, although significant, genes were less important as risk factors for alcoholism in women than men. Data from two smaller scale adoption studies in Iowa confirmed the results of the larger European studies (27, 28); however, Cadoret et al. did find important genetic influences in female adoptees (29). In fact, only one study, by Roe, has found contrary results (30), and most authors agree that the disparity probably reflects methodological problems in its design (e.g., small sample size and lack of rigorous diagnostic criteria for alcohol problems in the parents) or differences in the subpopulations of twins studied (6, 22, 31).

SUMMARY

The combination of family, twin, and adoption studies strongly suggests that genetic determinants play an important part in the etiology of alcoholism for both men and women. Unfortunately, with the possible exception of cigarette smoking, the case for other types of drug abuse is more complicated and less convincing. We will return to this issue in a later section, but will continue for now with alcoholism as our "model" for consideration.

THE SEARCH FOR GENETICALLY MEDIATED MARKERS OF ALCOHOLISM

The results of family, twin, and adoption studies offer enough support for genetic factors to justify a search for what might be inherited to increase the risk for this disorder. As a result, a number of laboratories have begun to look for trait or phenotypic markers of a vulnerability toward alcoholism (7, 32).

Such markers should be stable, easily measured properties that are themselves under genetic control and either directly influence the alcoholism risk or are linked to genes that affect the development of alcoholism.

The search for biological markers of alcoholism has been guided largely by three related premises. First, it is likely that there are measurable attributes associated with the risk for developing the disorder that differ in the frequency in which they are found in groups of high-and low-risk individuals; second, such properties are present before the illness develops and can be observed during remission from active drug use (7); and third, some trait markers may depend on the presence of active drug use for their expression to become overt.

The following sections outline an approach for looking for phenotypic markers of alcoholism. They begin by describing some of the options available for selecting populations at risk for developing the disorder and then address ways in which the homogeneity of these samples can be maximized.

Selecting High-Risk Populations

There are several possible approaches to the study of populations at high risk for the development of substance abuse and dependence, some of which are already paying dividends in the search for biological markers of alcoholism. Each of these methods has its own assets and liabilities, and no one approach is ideal. Choosing a sample for study depends on a number of practical and theoretic considerations; cost factors, the availability of subjects, and the suitability of the sample to the hypothesis being tested are all just some of the factors contributing to this decision (33).

ADOPTEE SAMPLES

Perhaps most informative, but also difficult to perform, are studies of children of alcoholics who have been adopted out and raised by nonalcoholic adoptive parents (34). These offspring are then followed longitudinally to determine differences from control subjects as possible leads to markers that might associate with the risk for developing alcoholism. Although such adoption studies offer the benefit of potentially separating genetic from environmental risk factors, they require years of study and are very expensive. To date, few appropriate groups have been available for study and relatively limited data have been reported (27, 35, 36); however, continued follow-up of these adoptees may yield useful results.

FAMILY PEDIGREES

Another approach is to study a limited number of pedigrees of alcoholics, looking for markers that are present in affected relatives but are absent in nonalcoholic family members (34). Variations of this method are currently in use at a number of centers, usually relying on "multiplex" or "high-density" families in which several members are affected with the disorder. This method is also time-consuming and expensive and, given the disorder's likely multifactorial polygenic origins, runs the risk of missing potential trait markers that may operate in disparate ways in different families (34). As is discussed later, pedigree studies can also provide the framework for more elaborate genetic analyses.

OTHER "HIGH-RISK" POPULATIONS

To avoid some of the problems inherent in the two approaches outlined above, most studies of populations at increased risk for alcoholism have examined nonalcoholic relatives of alcoholics from a wide range of families (7, 33). This method usually offers the advantages of a readily accessible control group and can identify potential markers to be intensively studied in more focused (i.e., selected pedigrees) ways (33). Most investigators using this method have focused on sons of alcoholic fathers, reflecting the expectation that sons will show higher rates of expression of alcoholism than daughters and the possibility that results from ethanol challenges could vary with the phase of the menstrual cycle (37).

There are important variations in the designs of studies using these high-risk populations. For example, some researchers have evaluated prepubertal boys in order to observe them before actual exposure to ethanol (38, 39). However, this approach risks missing potential markers that may appear only after puberty or that are triggered following modest alcohol consumption, and it requires a long follow-up period to see if future alcoholism develops (34). Other groups have selected older subjects, usually in their late teens to mid-20s. This decision avoids the problems mentioned above but adds the risk of leaving out early-onset alcoholics while creating the need to match subjects and controls on drinking histories. Such differences in sample selection probably explain some of the variance in the results obtained from these investigations.

Importance of Sample Homogeneity

Regardless of the specific approach selected, it is important to consider several major factors that can influence the results in studies evaluating potential trait markers.

ETIOLOGICAL HETEROGENEITY

First, when studying complex disorders like alcoholism or other kinds of drug dependence, it is essential to realize that, at best, one's diagnosis rests at the "clinical syndrome" level and that it is likely that many different pathways or etiologies can lead to this combination of symptoms and signs (34, 40). As a result of this etiological heterogeneity and the relatively early stage of this line of research, most investigators have chosen to focus on relatives of severely affected alcoholic individuals in the hope that genetic factors may be most obvious and identifiable in this group (7). Hence, we run the risk of identifying genetic factors that may be relevant to only the most severe forms of alcohol abuse.

COMORBIDITY WITH TWO SEPARATE DISORDERS

A second, related consideration is that life problems from excessive use of alcohol or other drugs may coexist with other disorders in the same patient. In fact, at least 30% of alcoholics have evidence of preexisting disorders (41). For instance, 70% of men with antisocial personality disorder (ASPD) have secondary alcohol problems during the course of their disorder; about 20% of patients during the manic phase of bipolar illness develop severe ethanol-related difficulties; and heroin addicts in methadone rehabilitation show high rates of secondary alcohol problems compared with their rate before treatment (41). The phenotypic variations between these groups of "alcoholics" having two disorders is obvious. If these men and women carry genetic factors related to their ASPD, mania, or heroin problems, it could be difficult to identify any inherited influences related to the alcohol dependence.

One approach that begins to address the vexing issue of comorbidity is that of *primary versus secondary alcoholism* (41, 42). Although various meanings have been linked with these terms in the past, one clinically relevant application uses the chronology of development of symptoms to classify alcoholics into two major groups. In primary alcoholism, the major life problems resulting from repeated excessive drinking are observed in men and women with no major preexisting psychiatric illness (41, 42). In contrast, individuals who develop ethanol-related life problems only after manifesting evidence of bipolar disorder or ASPD (e.g., secondary alcoholics) generally are not included in studies assessing the genetic susceptibility of alcoholism for fear that inherited factors contributing to the primary illness (e.g., ASPD) may obscure genetic determinants predisposing the subject to alcoholism. This distinction has clinical implications, with data from our laboratory and others showing that primary and secondary alcoholics demonstrate significantly different courses (23, 43) and outcomes at 1 year (23).

SUBTYPES OF ALCOHOLISM

Once the diagnosis of primary versus secondary alcoholism has been made, further classification into distinctive alcoholic subtypes may also increase the homogeneity of the sample population under study. Currently, several overlapping approaches are in use to categorize alcoholics into various subgroups based on family history, age of onset, clinical symptoms, and personality traits (22, 23, 44–46). Although each of these methods has its strengths and limitations, the validity of any one method over the others has not yet been established (45, 47). Although a review of all of the potential subtypes would require a separate chapter in its own right and is beyond the scope of this discussion, the underlying philosophy behind their use is an attempt to better define subsets of alcoholics who are at increased risk for developing the disorder.

Among the many different subtype classifications currently under study, one theory proposed by Cloninger, Bohman, Sigvardsson, and their colleagues has gained some popularity (26, 31, 44, 48, 49). Using a discriminant function analysis of their large sample of Swedish adoptees, this group initially proposed two forms of alcoholism (types 1 and 2) that could be distinguished on the basis of the biological parents' pattern of alcohol abuse and the degree to which postnatal environmental factors affected the inheritance of susceptibility to alcoholism (26, 48). Combining results from a variety of personality, clinical, and neuropsychopharmacological studies with the genetic epidemiological findings, these authors elaborated on this theory, expanding its original focus on the importance of gene-environment interactions in alcoholism.

Type 1 or "milieu-limited" alcoholism, thought to predominate among female alcoholics and their male relatives, is characterized by loss of control of drinking after the age of 25, pronounced environmental reactivity to drinking, minimal associated criminality, and "passive-dependent personality traits" marked by high degrees of harm avoidance, reward dependence, and low levels of novelty seeking as measured by Cloninger's Tridimensional Personality Questionnaire (TPQ) (44). In contrast, the type 2 or "male-limited" subgroup appears to have an inheritance pattern less dependent on environmental factors for phenotypic expression and has an earlier age of onset, more associated criminal behavior, and a triad of personality traits that run opposite those of the prototypic "milieu-limited" alcoholic (31, 44, 50). This group later refined their theory to include a *third* class of alcoholism, which they call "antisocial behavior disorder with alcohol abuse" (31, 50, 51).

Although parts of this theory have been tested (44, 49, 51), the results of these investigations must be considered preliminary (7). Results from our laboratory and others have tested features of the type 1/type 2 scheme in different populations of subjects in an effort to assess their generality. One major concern surrounds the possible overlap between the male-limited subtype and frank ASPD for which alcohol problems are only part of the syndrome. For example, when we examined the clinical course of primary alcoholic men (alcoholics without any major preexisting psychiatric disorder), we found that neither classification of these alcoholics into discrete type 1 and type 2 categories nor placing them along a continuum of type 2 characteristics was associated with the severity of their clinical course once age at onset was considered (52). In a different sample of male inpatient alcoholics, we further demonstrated that there was significant overlap between type 2 alcoholism and ASPD (47). Using another sample of young, nonalcoholic men at high risk for alcoholism and comparing them with matched controls, we found no difference in personality traits between groups as measured by the TPQ, nor was there any relationship between the severity of the fathers' alcoholism on a type 1/type 2 continuum and the sons' TPQ scores or their alcohol and drug pattern at an average of 21 years (53, 54). Different laboratories using other samples of alcoholics have found similar results (45, 55). Nonetheless, efforts to develop and empirically validate different methods of subtyping alcoholics should remain a priority, and the hypotheses put forward by Cloninger et al. have stirred active interest in this pursuit.

Babor and colleagues (46) used an empirical clustering technique and described a subgrouping scheme for alcoholics that included type A and type B alcoholics, named after the Roman gods Apollo and Bacchus. Type A alcoholics are characterized by later age-at-onset, fewer childhood risk factors, less severe dependence, fewer alcohol-related problems, and less psychopathological dysfunction. Type B alcoholics typically exhibit an early onset of alcohol-related problems, higher levels of childhood risk factors and familial alcoholism, greater severity of dependence, multiple substance use, a long-term treatment history, greater psychopathological dysfunction, and greater life stress (46, 56). The type A/B dichotomy was replicated in another large sample of alcohol-dependent subjects even after the exclusion of individuals with ASPD and those with an onset of alcohol dependence before age 25, further supporting this subtyping method's potential usefulness (57).

SUMMARY

An array of study approaches has been used to identify populations at elevated risk for developing alcoholism, usually evaluating children and young adults whose fathers have exhibited relatively severe manifestations of the disorder. Confounding factors such as etiological heterogeneity and the coexistence of two or more disorders in the same individual must be considered in the selection of populations for study and in the subsequent comparison of results. The next section reviews the results of studies of high-risk populations.

Results of Studies of Populations at High Risk for Alcoholism

The studies of alcoholic vulnerability are trying to learn more about the mechanisms by which the increased risk for the disorder is likely to be expressed (33). The following sections review evaluations of populations at elevated risk for developing alcoholism, briefly presenting some preliminary results. The characteristics of the sample populations differ for the studies presented here; most results, however, are based on comparisons of high- and low-risk groups.

To organize the vast array of findings, we find it convenient to somewhat arbitrarily divide the results regarding possible phenotypic markers into two broad categories: *studies evaluating baseline differences* in the usual attributes among high-risk and control groups; and *alcohol challenge protocols* that test for variations in response to ethanol between the two groups. Regarding the latter, an emphasis is placed on the finding of a decreased intensity of reaction to alcohol in sons and daughters of alcoholics (7, 34).

STUDIES OF BASELINE FUNCTIONING

Biochemical Markers

In keeping with our earlier comments about "prototypic" trait markers, a variety of biochemical gene-products have been evaluated for an association with the alcoholism risk. An array of proteins, antigens, and hormones have been studied in human beings, all of which share the attraction of being under some level of genetic control while at the same time being relatively accessible for measurement in a variety of tissues. Most of these potential markers were first identified in evaluations comparing alcoholics with nonalcoholic controls and thus run some risk of being "state" markers of heavy drinking (32). However, most studies take into consideration the need to assess the stability of the marker over time during periods of abstinence in order to test, at least indirectly, the marker's potential as a "trait" indicator associated with the predisposition toward alcoholism. Fewer studies have used nonalcoholic high-risk populations (e.g., sons of alcoholics), and these are usually limited by smaller sample sizes.

Among the proteins evaluated, one enzyme system important in the metabolism of ethanol in the liver has been shown to be under genetic control and may provide one of the best examples, to date, of how gene-environment interactions influence the risk for alcoholism (7, 58). Specifically, about 50% of Asians lack one of the isoenzyme forms of aldehyde dehydrogenase (ALDH), the major enzyme that degrades the first metabolite of ethanol, acetaldehyde, in the liver (59, 60). After imbibing alcohol, affected individuals develop higher blood acetaldehyde levels with associated facial flushing, tachycardia, and a burning sensation in the stomach. Not surprisingly, Asians missing this isoenzyme are less likely than others to drink heavily and appear to have a lower rate of alcoholism (58). Hence, the interaction between a genetically controlled enzyme system and environmental factors such as attitudes about drinking and drunkenness appears to contribute significantly to the lower alcoholism risk among a subgroup of Asians (58).

Monoamine oxidase (MAO), a major degradative enzyme system for many neurotransmitters, may also have potential importance for the risk of developing some subtypes of alcoholism and other substance use disorders (56). Monoamine neurotransmitters including dopamine, norepinephrine, and serotonin have all been implicated in various phenomena related to the risk of developing alcoholism. These phenomena include a preference for consuming alcohol, the development of tolerance to alcohol's rewarding effects, and personality characteristics (e.g., impulsivity) that predispose a person to repeated alcohol-related problems (56). Humans have two types of MAOs—MAO-A and MAO-B—that are the products of separate genes (56). Because certain blood cells (i.e., the platelets) also contain MAO-B and since platelet MAO-B activity is correlated with brain MAO-B activity (61), scientists have studied platelet MAO extensively as a surrogate for brain MAO-B. Several studies have indicated that low platelet MAO activity might be a marker for type 2 alcoholism (62, 63); however, the differences between type 1 and type 2 alcoholics have not been consistent across all studies (64). A recent analysis of data from an ongoing multisite study on the genetics of alcohol demonstrated, however, that regardless of the subgrouping scheme being employed (i.e., type 1 versus type 2, type A versus type B, or primary versus secondary alcoholism), men with an earlier age-at-onset and more severe course of alcohol-related problems had significantly lower platelet MAO levels than nonalcoholic men (56, 65). Alternatively, low platelet MAO activity may not be a specific marker for alcoholism per se but may be a more general indicator of a spectrum of disorders marked by disinhibition, impulsive aggression, and a predisposition for alcohol and other drug abuse (56).

Another platelet enzyme system is also being evaluated for a possible association with the risk of alcoholism. Tabakoff, Hoffman, and colleagues have demonstrated that following in vitro stimulation with several activating agents, platelet adenylate cyclase (AC) activity was significantly lower in abstinent alcoholics (66, 67). AC is an enzyme used by cells, including neurons, to relay signals from a cell's exterior to its interior (56, 66). AC activity levels are genetically determined and are frequently reduced in alcoholics compared with nonalcoholics even after alcoholics experience long periods of abstinence (56, 68). Thus, AC activity levels also may be a marker for alcoholism, although research findings indicate that low AC activity may be characteristic of a different alcoholism subtype than that associated with low MAO activity (56).

Genetic Polymorphisms

Whereas the biochemical markers discussed above represent gene products (i.e., proteins) associated with some alcoholic phenotypes, researchers have also reported gene variants (i.e., alleles) of specific genes in populations called polymorphisms that might be associated with alcoholism. Although the details of the molecular genetic techniques used to identify such genetic markers are beyond the scope of this chapter, briefly, they involve the meticulous dissection of deoxyribonucleic acid (DNA) into specific nucleotide (e.g., the building blocks of DNA) patterns called markers or microsatellites (for details see Refs. 69–71). Such markers are then analyzed to determine whether there is *linkage* between the marker and the phenotype (i.e., the marker is transmitted along with the disease in families) or whether there is an *association* between the polymorphism and the phenotype (72, 73) (i.e., a given marker allele is more common among those individuals with the disease in a population).

Indeed, as alluded to in the opening paragraphs of this chapter, the first report of an "alcoholism gene" occurred in 1990 when Blum et al. announced that he and his colleagues had identified a gene—an allele of dopamine receptor D2 (DRD2)—that appeared to be implicated in severe cases of alcoholism (74). The subject of much debate (1, 2, 72, 73, 75–77), the DRD2 controversy remains relevant because it heralded the advent of modern molecular genetic approaches to the complex genetic disease, alcoholism. Interestingly, there is also some evidence to implicate the DRD2 gene in other substance use disorders, leading some investigators to label it a potential "reward gene" (1).

Other molecular measures such as proteins (e.g., MNS) found on red blood cells and the red cells' esterase D enzyme system have been reported to be associated with alcoholism and were previously considered as potential trait markers of alcoholism (71, 78). However, recent data from the ongoing Collaborative Study on the Genetics of Alcoholism (COGA—see below) indicates that neither the esterase D enzyme polymorphism or MNS genotypes could distinguish between alcoholic and nonalcoholic people in more than 2000 subjects from alcoholic and control families (71). Furthermore, linkage analyses for hundreds of sibling pairs in the COGA families revealed no evidence that alcohol dependence was linked to regions on chromosome 13 containing the esterase D gene and the region on chromosome 4 containing the MNS genes (71). Thus, these results highlight that reports of associations between biochemical markers and alcoholism need to be viewed with caution until further confirmatory genetic analyses can be performed in larger samples.

Electrophysiological Markers

Electrophysiological measurements of brain activity have also been demonstrated as potentially promising neurobehavioral markers that might be associated with the predisposition toward alcoholism, at least among some subgroups of individuals (7, 38, 71). Like the biochemical markers, these parameters are appealing because they can be measured relatively easily and seem to be less influenced by subjective factors such as fatigue or inattention. These indicators are covered elsewhere in this text and are only briefly mentioned here.

Event-related potentials (ERPs) have been used extensively to study information processing in high- and low-risk populations (34). The amplitude of one important component of the ERP, the positive wave observed at approximately 300 msec after a rare but expected stimulus (P300), has been demonstrated to be significantly decreased in about one-third of the sons of alcoholic fathers compared with controls (38, 79). Although some studies do not agree with these results (80, 81), differences probably reflect variations in the studies' designs, including the sample population chosen. In addition to this elicited brain wave marker, a second approach has relied on measurements of the power of wave forms on the background cortical electroencephalogram (EEG) (34). Male alcoholics and their sons might demonstrate a decreased amount of slow wave (e.g., alpha wave) activity at baseline when compared with controls (82, 83). Similarly, our own laboratory has observed that sons of alcoholics differ from lower risk, matched controls at baseline on the amount of activity in one part of the frequency range of alpha waves (i.e., men with a positive family history of alcoholism had more energy in the fast alpha range compared with controls) (84). These preliminary results require replication, and as is discussed later, some of these electrophysiological markers also show group differences in response to an ethanol challenge.

Potential Differences in Cognitive Performance

There is disagreement about the relative importance of baseline neurocognitive test results and their relationship to the alcoholism risk (34). Much of this controversy can be attributed to the different sample populations under study. For example, comparisons of family history-positive (FHP) and family history-negative (FHN) subjects identified through their associations with juvenile authorities or from a Danish birth cohort have demonstrated lower verbal intelligence quotients (IQs) for the sons of alcoholics along with decreased auditory word span performance, impaired reading comprehension, a greater number of errors on the Category Test of the Halstead-Reitan Neuropsychological Test Battery, and problems with constructional praxis and abstract problem solving (85–88). In contrast, investigations from our laboratory, using a sample of college students and university employees (89), and from other groups selecting children of alcoholics from general population samples (90), have found few significant differences in cognitive performance between groups at higher and lower alcoholism risk (34). Differences in the results might reflect either higher rates of conduct and attention deficit disorders in the group selected because of their behavioral difficulties or environmental factors such as the disparity in the quality of education received. Hence, the association between cognitive variables and future alcoholism remains to be determined.

Personality Profiles

Baseline assessments of personality traits in high- and low-risk populations also provide conflicting results, with several factors likely to have contributed to the confusion (7, 34). First, during the course of heavy drinking and the period of early recovery, alcoholics are likely to show abnormalities on personality tests that might reflect the sequelae of ethanol's effects on brain functioning or the life stresses and mood swings inherent in an alcoholic life-style (91). As a result, studies assessing personality differences in alcoholics may be determining variables that were not observable before the alcoholism developed (92–94)or that may become normal with continued abstinence. Second, some personality traits that remain following abstinence may reflect other primary psychiatric diagnoses (e.g., ASPD) and not alcoholism per se (95). Finally, the diversity of personality measures used, questions about the cross-validity of the various test devices used, the variety of populations studied, and the multiple approaches to data analyses employed make it unlikely to expect unanimity of results (7).

With these caveats in mind, it is not surprising that various investigators have obtained different results on personality measures. For example, using a sample of Swedish adoptees, Cloninger et al. adapted information from a behavioral assessment and teacher interviews carried out when the children were 11 years of age and concluded that variations in childhood personality traits encompassed by the "tridimensional" personality theory described earlier (e.g., high novelty seeking and low harm avoidance) predicted the risk of later alcohol abuse (96). However, other prospective studies have demonstrated few differences between high- and low-risk populations (33, 97). In our own laboratory, studies of high-functioning nonalcoholic young men who differ in their family history for alcoholism revealed few baseline differences in most personality measures including items of the Minnesota Multiphasic Personality Inventory (MMPI), Spielberger Trait/State Anxiety Questionnaire, Eysenck Personality Inventory, or Rotter's Locus of Control (34, 98–100). More recently, preliminary work from our laboratory has demonstrated no significant relationships between any of the 18 TPQ scores and the subject's quantity and frequency of drinking or his family history of alcoholism (53). Although it is too early to draw conclusions from this or any other cross-sectional personality evaluation, it must be remembered that the relationship between personality profiles and the predisposition toward alcoholism remains speculative at this time. Clearly, further research, including long-term follow-up studies using valid, comparable, psychometric instruments that consider the clinical heterogeneity among alcoholics, is needed to test these hypotheses (7, 96).

Recently, Ebstein et al. (101) reported an association between a polymorphism of dopamine receptor D4 (DRD4) and the novelty-seeking subscale as measured by Cloninger's TPQ (44). That report, along with other confirmatory results (102) published in the same journal issue, provide the first replicated association between a specific genetic polymorphism and a personality trait (101). Although the subjects in this study were nonalcoholic normal controls, it is intriguing that a personality trait believed to predict an increased risk for alcoholism might have heritable components.

ALCOHOL CHALLENGE STUDIES

Along with the evaluation of baseline functioning, our laboratory and others have documented differences in the response to alcohol between high-risk and control populations. Although the details of our approach have been outlined extensively elsewhere (7, 34), we selected otherwise healthy groups of 18- to 25-year-old men who differed mainly in their respective family histories of alcoholism. Sons of primary alcoholic men were selected as higher risk or FHP subjects who were then compared with controls comprised of lower risk FHN individuals. The FHP and FHN subjects were matched on demographic characteristics (e.g., age, sex, race, educational level), along with variables that could influence their response to alcohol, such as quantity and frequency of drinking, substance intake history, height-to-weight ratio, and smoking history (7). Each FHP-FHN matched pair was carefully evaluated at baseline and then observed for 3–4 hours after consuming placebo, 0.75 mL/kg of ethanol, or 1.1 mL/kg of ethanol (i.e., the equivalent

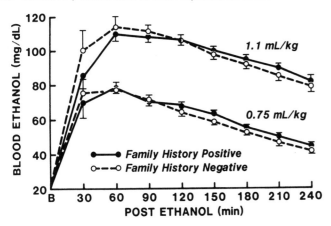

Figure 5.1. Mean blood alcohol concentrations for 22 matched pairs with positive and negative family histories after drinking 0.75 mL/kg of ethanol and 1.1 mL/kg of ethanol. *Bars* indicate SEs, and *B* indicates baseline. (Reproduced with permission from Schuckit MA. Subjective responses to alcohol in sons of alcoholics and control subjects. Arch Gen Psychiatry 1984;41:879–884. Copyright 1984, American Medical Association.)

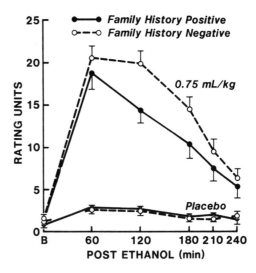

Figure 5.2. Mean self-ratings on 0–36 scale for intoxication after placebo and after 0.75 mL/kg of ethanol for 23 matched pairs with positive and negative family histories. *Bars* indicate SEs, and *B* indicates baseline. (Reproduced with permission from Schuckit MA. Subjective responses to alcohol in sons of alcoholics and control subjects. Arch Gen Psychiatry 1984;41:879–884. Copyright 1984, American Medical Association.)

of 3–5 drinks). The hypothesis behind this alcohol challenge paradigm was that one genetic vulnerability toward alcoholism could be mediated through an individual's response to ethanol, the very agent required for the development of the disorder (34).

Before the challenge sessions, the FHP and FHN subjects expressed similar expectations of the effects of ethanol. During the placebo session, there was no evidence of any differences between the two groups for the degree of body sway, the subjective feelings of intoxication, hormone levels, and most electrophysiological evaluations (34, 103). As shown in Figure 5.1, after drinking the alcohol, the two family history groups developed similar patterns of blood alcohol concentrations over time, making it unlikely that group differences depended on the rate of absorption or metabolism of ethanol (34, 104).

Differences in Subjective and Motor Responses

A major consistent difference between FHP and FHN subjects has been in the intensity of their subjective feelings of intoxication after imbibing alcohol (7, 34, 103–105). Using an analog scale and asking subjects to rate the intensity of different aspects of intoxication, including overall drug effect, level of "high," dizziness, etc., FHP men rated themselves as significantly less intoxicated than did their FHN matched controls after drinking ethanol (Fig. 5.2), with the maximum group difference observed 60–120 minutes after the drink had been consumed (7, 34, 103–105).

This decreased intensity of reaction to alcohol was also observed for at least one measure of motor performance. Here, to quantify the level of sway in the upper body, we asked subjects to stand still, with hands at the sides and feet together. FHN subjects showed a significantly greater increase in body sway after the alcohol challenge as shown in Figure 5.3 (106), a result corroborated elsewhere in daughters of alcoholics (107).

Less Intense Neurohormonal Changes

Because changes in subjective feelings and motor performance might be influenced by the differential expectations of the subjects, we next focused on alcohol-related changes in biological systems less likely to be sensitive to volitional control. After an ethanol challenge, FHPs also exhibited less intense change in the levels of cortisol and prolactin, two hormones shown to be altered after ethanol (108, 109). Similar results have been observed for the pattern of postdrinking changes in adrenocorticotropic hormone (ACTH), another important hormone in the hypothalamic-pituitary-adrenal axis (34, 110).

Diminished EEG Response

Along with baseline differences in potential electrophysiological markers observed in the two family history groups, sons of alcoholics demonstrated a less intense EEG response to the alcohol challenge (e.g., FHPs had less instability of alpha-range activity of the background cortical EEG) (84, 111). Although there are technical differences between this finding and the reports of Pollock et al., which are beyond the scope of this discussion (82), it is noteworthy that both groups have shown electrophysiological differences between FHPs and FHNs following an ethanol challenge; however, not all studies agree (80).

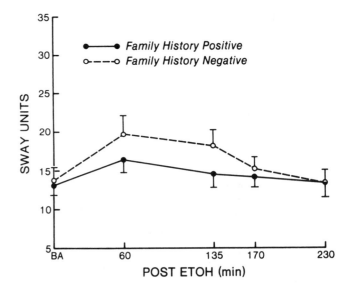

Figure 5.3. Mean total-body sway counts over time following ingestion of 0.75 mL/kg of ethanol for 34 matched pairs of young men with family histories negative (FHN) and positive (FHP) for alcoholism. (Reproduced with permission from Schuckit MA. Ethanol-induced changes in body sway in men at high alcoholism risk. Arch Gen Psychiatry 1985;42:375–379. Copyright 1985, American Medical Association.)

SUMMARY

The results of challenge studies of high-risk populations have provided several potential markers that might be associated with a genetic predisposition toward alcoholism (34). The decreased intensity of reaction to ethanol observed in a number of subjective, motor, hormonal, and electrophysiological measures has been reproduced in various forms by other laboratories in the United States and in Denmark (112, 113). Although the results of alcohol challenge studies are not unanimous (i.e., studies evaluating smaller sample sizes or not controlling for subjects' quantity and frequency of drinking provide unpredictable results) (114), it is hypothesized that a decreased intensity of reaction to lower doses of alcohol might make it more difficult for susceptible individuals to discern when they are becoming drunk at low enough blood levels to be able to stop drinking during an evening. Without this feedback, especially in the setting of a heavy drinking society, predisposed individuals may be inclined to drink more and, thus, run an increased risk for subsequent alcohol-related life problems (7). As with the other potential trait markers and hypotheses presented in this chapter, the relationship of these findings to actual alcoholism can be established only with appropriate follow-up evaluations of the high- and low-risk groups. These studies are described next.

Follow-up Studies in Sons of Alcoholics

The study of sons of alcoholics and controls was structured to facilitate a follow-up phase. Thus, interviewers blind to the initial family history and the determination of the level of response to alcohol located all 453 subjects an average of 8.2 years after the time of their initial evaluation (115, 116). Diagnoses were established using American Psychiatric Association criteria in the *Diagnostic and Statistical Manual of Mental Disorders,* third revised edition (DSM-III-R), as described in detail elsewhere (116). The data revealed that the family history groups had been correctly identified and that the sons of alcoholics had a 3-fold increased risk for alcohol dependence. The results also demonstrated a strong and significant relationship between a low level of response to alcohol and the future development of alcoholism. Thus, for example, sons of alcoholics who clearly demonstrated a low level of response to alcohol evidenced almost a 60% risk for alcohol abuse or dependence at follow-up, while the rate of alcoholism was less than 15% in the sons of alcoholics who clearly showed a higher level of sensitivity to alcohol. The relatively small number of FHN controls who showed low levels of response to alcohol at approximately age 20 were also at high risk for future alcoholism. The analyses demonstrated that for this white-collar and relatively highly functional group of men, the low level of response to alcohol was a mediator (or potential direct cause) of the high risk for alcoholism, explaining a great deal of the ability of family history to predict alcohol abuse or dependence (115–117).

These studies demonstrate some important attributes regarding genetic influences in the alcoholism risk. First, a family history of alcoholism is associated with increased risk for this disorder among people of diverse socioeconomic classes. Second, it is likely that there are multiple roads into the heightened alcohol risk, with, for example, some individuals developing their alcoholism in part through very high levels of impulsivity associated with the ASPD, but with others increasing their risk for alcoholism through a low level of response to alcohol in the context of a heavy drinking society, and so on. Third, it is not likely that a single gene explains the alcoholism risk, but rather it is multiple genes interacting with environment.

GENETIC ASPECTS OF DRUG ABUSE AND DEPENDENCE

There are a number of reasons why *most* of the information in this chapter on the genetics of substance abuse relates to alcohol and not to other drugs. Compared with other drug abuse disorders, alcoholism has consistently occurred at high rates in most societies for many decades. Despite some secular variations, overall, the disorder has remained highly prevalent in the population, allowing for its careful study over time. Similarly, enough time has elapsed for multiple generations of families affected with the dis-

order to be evaluated. These factors have contributed to the relative ease with which family, twin, and adoption study data have been gathered on alcohol dependence and help explain the comparable absence of similar studies of other drugs.

Studies of genetic influences in other types of drug abuse pose additional problems. First, there are many different substances of abuse, and dependency to any one drug might be uniquely related to a heterogeneous group of factors. As we expand the number of drugs and phenotypes under study, the level of complexity increases dramatically, and the relative contributions of genetic, sociocultural, and psychological determinants become even more difficult to discern. Second, the use of most drugs generally comes in waves or "fads," with secular effects taking on added significance compared with the *relative* stability seen for alcohol over time. For example, after reaching a peak prevalence in the mid-1970s, methaqualone (Quaalude) abuse in teenagers steadily declined in a linear trend as the availability of this drug was limited (118, 119). Partly as a result of these period effects, different generations of families have been exposed to different types of drugs, making it more difficult to perform the multigenerational studies described for alcoholism. Finally, ASPD, another syndrome that might have its own separate genetic underpinnings, is frequently associated with secondary drug problems. As was the case for alcoholism, studies of genetic factors in drug abuse will need to control carefully for this confounding diagnosis.

For all of these reasons, with the possible exception of cigarette smoking, it is difficult to marshal consistent evidence regarding genetic determinants as they relate to drugs other than alcohol. Nevertheless, in a manner similar to the approach outlined for alcoholism, the systematic study of genetic influences in drug abuse is beginning to produce some testable hypotheses. This section briefly reviews the information available from family, twin, and adoption studies of drug abuse. In addition, we highlight some preclinical work that offers examples of the ways that genetic influences affecting one category of drug might overlap with those impacting on other substances of abuse.

Some Preclinical Examples

Animal studies have demonstrated some preliminary evidence for the possible role of genetic factors in drug abuse (4, 120). Differences in the response to an assortment of drugs, including opiates (121), amphetamines (122), and barbiturates (123), in various inbred strains of rodents have been reported (120). However, some investigators believe that the use of more sophisticated selective breeding techniques to develop animal lines with a specific trait for drug taking (e.g., ones approximating "drug abuse" per se) has lagged behind the models developed for alcoholism (e.g., P line of alcohol-preferring rats) (120, 124). Also at the preclinical level, there is evidence that there may be an overlap in the initial reinforcing effects of ethanol, opioids, and psychostimulants that might be mediated via neurons that are part of the ventral tegmental area (VTA)-nucleus accumbens-pallidal-forebrain reward circuit (125). Hence, it might be difficult to target genetic factors associated with any one drug, and as described in other chapters of this text, it is possible that genetic factors may play a role in these complex brain systems related to drug sensitivity, neuroadaptation, and reward (4).

Human Studies

After the approach outlined above for alcoholism, the majority of studies have focused on the clustering of drug abuse in families. Several studies have documented correlations between drug use by teenagers and substance abuse by older family members (126–129). For example, a study of opioid-dependent probands revealed a prevalence of opiate abuse in family members that far exceeded the lifetime prevalence rate expected in the general population (130). However, these data are more complicated than they first appear. When these authors considered secular trends and the increase in availability of heroin and in the number of heroin-using peers, they found an intergenerational reversal: The siblings of probands had higher rates of opiate abuse than of alcoholism, but the parents of the subjects had higher rates of alcoholism than of opioid dependence. As is the case for alcoholism, family studies do little to sort out potential hereditary effects from environmental effects (5, 6).

Twin studies of genetic determinants of abuse of drugs other than alcohol are increasing in number but are still relatively rare (131). In general, the studies are limited by small sample sizes, and these investigations frequently focus on several drugs at once (132–134). With these caveats in mind, only tentative conclusions regarding genetic influences on specific drugs of abuse can be reached. However, there is some evidence that identical twins show higher concordance rates for use patterns of nicotine and caffeine (133) and for nonalcohol substance abuse (134, 135) and that genetic determinants might influence twins' responses to pain and its alleviation by morphine (136).

Similarly, adoption studies have provided limited data. In the Danish investigation of Goodwin et al., children of alcoholics raised by nonalcoholic adoptive parents were susceptible to alcohol abuse but not to other types of drug dependence (6). Perhaps the most informative statement on the genetic vulnerability of drug abuse has come from the Iowa sample of adoptees, which points to the importance of gene-environment interactions in drug abuse (137). Because the adoption agency records from which the investigators obtained their information did not include data on the biological parents' drug abuse history, their conclusions are quite speculative. These authors described two possible genetic routes to drug abuse in this sample. First, drug abuse was correlated with the ASPD, which was itself predicted by the biological parents' own antisocial behaviors. Second, in adoptees with no biological background for ASPD, parental alcohol abuse predicted drug abuse in the subjects. But along with these potential genetic relationships, the authors also showed the importance of environmental factors, in that divorce and psychiatric problems in the adoptive family were associated with the risk for drug abuse. More recently, Cadoret et al. (138) expanded on their earlier work in a study of male adoptees and again confirmed their earlier model.

GENETICS OF CIGARETTE SMOKING: A SPECIAL CASE?

In contrast to the relatively scant data available regarding heritable factors involved in illicit substance abuse and dependence, results from family, twin, and adoption studies indicate that genetic factors appear to influence cigarette smoking (139). For instance, in a genetic analysis of aspects of cigarette smoking behavior among male subjects in a large twin registry in the United States, Carmelli et al. reported moderate genetic influences on lifetime smoking practices (140). Because cigarette smoking is highly correlated with alcohol consumption and other consummatory behaviors, Swan et al. (141) adjusted for covariates in a sample of 360 adult male twin pairs and still demonstrated a genetic role for cigarette smoking. Thus, as was the case for alcoholism, smoking researchers are interested in identifying genetic factors that might help tailor prevention and treatment programs for nicotine dependence (139).

Summary

The systematic study of genetic factors in a predisposition to drug abuse is in its infancy compared with the past three decades of research addressing the biological susceptibility to alcoholism. This gap reflects the relatively stable prevalence of alcoholism in most populations, secular changes in substance abuse including the faddish nature of drug use, and the increased complexity of studying several different categories of drugs that appear to interact at multiple levels. Although, with the possible exception of cigarette smoking, too few studies are available to draw definite conclusions, our experience with alcoholism can provide some tools applicable to the task.

CONCLUSIONS AND IMPLICATIONS

In the opening paragraphs of this chapter, we alluded to the work being done in molecular genetics and the search for "the gene for alcoholism" (3, 74). One of the purposes of this chapter has been to provide the reader with much of the "small print" apt to be left out in headlines. As described, much work has preceded the preliminary molecular genetic studies now capturing the news. Our goal has been to organize more than two decades of diverse findings into a format that is understandable and illustrative of the promise of this line of research, while not minimizing the complexity of the issues at hand.

In many ways, the "window of hope" offered by better understanding of the probable genetic influences of alcoholism has already been opened and does not depend solely on identifying gene(s) at a molecular level. The clinical, societal, and research implications of this body of work are already emerging, with results from family, twin, and adoption studies helping to shape programs aimed at preventing the illness by educating children at high risk for alcoholism early on, allowing them to modify their drinking patterns. Individuals already suffering from the disorder are being matched to more appropriate therapies with information obtained in studies of alcoholic subtypes. The stigma once associated with the view of alcoholism as a "moral weakness" is fading with the accumulation of evidence supporting the importance of biological factors. The studies pointing to the importance of gene-environment interactions have demonstrated the need for cooperation among researchers in different disciplines, and they highlight the fact that unitary hypotheses arguing exclusively for any one approach are inadequate in explaining these heterogeneous disorders.

Advances in molecular genetics are adding important information to our understanding of the biological factors associated with the susceptibility to alcoholism. Many potential "candidate" genes have been identified that might be associated with the risk for the disorder (51, 70). Briefly, the rationale behind this approach is similar to that already described as part of our discussion of phenotypic markers. However, here the marker or phenotype (potentially, any of the phenotypic markers mentioned) is explicitly postulated to arise from either an "abnormal" gene product or from the product of a gene "linked" with or close by a gene associated with the disorder (5). Although the details of the molecular genetic techniques used in this approach are beyond the scope of this discussion and can be found elsewhere (5, 51, 142), recent advances in these areas have sparked a large multicenter effort (the Collaborative Study on the Genetics of Alcoholism or COGA) aimed at "identifying the gene(s) that influence susceptibility to alcoholism" (3, 71, 75). It is hoped that such a coordinated effort might provide insights into how the disorder is transmitted and might expand our knowledge about the biological basis of the inherited factors.

References

1. Noble EP. The D2 dopamine receptor gene: a review of association studies in alcoholism. Behav Genet 1993;23(2):119–229.
2. Goldman D, Brown GL, Albaugh B, Robin R, Goodson S, Trunzo M, Akhtar L, Wynne DK, Lucas-Derse S, Bolos AM, Tokola R, Virkkunen M, Linnoila M, Dean M. D2 receptor genotype and linkage disequilibrium and function in Finnish, American Indian and U.S. Caucasian patients. In: Gershon ES, Cloninger CR, eds. Genetic approaches to mental disorders. Washington, DC: American Psychiatric Press, 1994:327–344.
3. Goodwin DW. The gene for alcoholism. J Stud Alcohol 1989;50:397–398.
4. Crabbe JC, Belknap JK, Buck KJ. Genetic animal models of alcohol and drug abuse. Science 1994;264:1715–1723.
5. Pardes H, Kaufmann CA, Pincus HA, West A. Genetics and psychiatry: past discoveries, current dilemmas, and future directions. Am J Psychiatry 1989;164(4):435–443.
6. Goodwin DW. Alcoholism and genetics: the sins of the fathers. Arch Gen Psychiatry 1985;42:171–174.
7. Schuckit MA. Biological vulnerability to alcoholism. J Consult Clin Psychol 1987;55:1–9.
8. Cotton NS. The familial incidence of alcoholism. J Stud Alcohol 1979;40:1:89–116.
9. Schuckit MA. Genetic and clinical implications of alcoholism and affective disorder. Am J Psychiatry 1986;143:140–147.
10. Prescott CA, Kendler KS. Twin study design. Alcohol Health Res World 1995;19:200–205.
11. Kaij L. Studies on the etiology and sequels of abuse of alcohol. Lund: University of Lund Press, 1960.
12. Hrubec Z, Omenn GS. Evidence of genetic predisposition to alcohol cirrhosis and psychosis: twin concordances for alcoholism and its biological end points by zygosity among male veterans. Alcohol Clin Exp Res 1981;5:207–212.
13. Pickens RW, Svikis DS, McGue M, Lykken DT, Heston LL, Clayton PJ. Heterogeneity in the inheritance of alcoholism. Arch Gen Psychiatry 1991;48:19–28.
14. McGue M, Pickens RW, Svikis DS. Sex and age effects on the inheritance of alcohol problems: a twin study. J Abnorm Psychol 1992;101:3–17.
15. Gurling HM, Oppenheim BE, Murray RM. Depression, criminality and psychopathology associated with alcoholism: evidence from a twin

study. Acta Genet Med Gemellol (Roma) 1984; 33:333–339.

16. Kendler KS, Heath AC, Neale MC, Kessler RC, Eaves LJ. A population-based twin study of alcoholism in women. JAMA 1992;268:1877–1882.

17. Partanen J, Bruun K, Markkanen T. Inheritance of drinking behavior: a study on intelligence, personality, and use of alcohol of adult twins. Helsinki: Finnish Foundation for Alcohol Studies, 1966.

18. Jonsson E, Nilsson T. Alcoholism in monozygotic and dizygotic twins. Nor Psykiatr Tidsskr 1968;49:21.

19. Vesell ES, Page JG, Passananti GT. Genetic and environmental factors affecting ethanol metabolism in man. Clin Pharmacol Ther 1970;12: 192–201.

20. Radlow R, Conway TL. Consistency of alcohol absorption in human subjects. Paper presented at the American Psychological Association, Toronto, Canada, August 1978 [Abstract].

21. Kopun M, Propping P. The kinetics of ethanol absorption and elimination in twins and supplementary repetitive experiments in singleton subjects [Abstract]. Eur J Clin Pharmacol 1977; 11:337–344.

22. Goodwin DW. Familial alcoholism: a separate entity? Subst Alcohol Actions-Misuse 1983;4: 129–136.

23. Schuckit MA. The clinical implications of primary diagnostic groups among alcoholics. Arch Gen Psychiatry 1985;42:1043–1049.

24. Schuckit MA, Goodwin DW, Winokur GA. A study of alcoholism in half-siblings. Am J Psychiatry 1972;128:1132–1136.

25. Goodwin DW. Alcoholism and heredity. Arch Gen Psychiatry 1979;36:57–61.

26. Cloninger CR, Bohman M, Sigvardsson S. Inheritance of alcohol abuse: cross-fostering analysis of adopted men. Arch Gen Psychiatry 1981;38:861–868.

27. Cadoret RJ, Cain CA, Grove WM. Development of alcoholism in adoptees raised apart from alcoholic biologic relatives. Arch Gen Psychiatry 1980;37:561–563.

28. Cadoret RJ, Troughton E, O'Gorman TW. Genetic and environmental factors in alcohol abuse and antisocial personality. J Stud Alcohol 1987; 48:1–8.

29. Cadoret RJ, O'Gorman TW, Troughton E, Heywood E. Alcoholism and antisocial personality: interrelationships, genetic and environmental factors. Arch Gen Psychiatry 1985;42:161–167.

30. Roe A. The adult adjustment of children of alcoholic parents raised in foster homes. J Stud Alcohol 1994;5:378–393.

31. Cloninger CR, Sigvardsson S, Reich T, Bohman M. Inheritance of risk to develop alcoholism. In: Braude MC, Chao HM, eds. Genetic and biological markers in drug abuse and alcoholism. NIDA Res Monogr Ser 1986;66:86–96.

32. Schuckit MA. Trait (and state) markers of a predisposition to psychopathology. In: Judd LL, Groves P, eds. Physiological foundations of clinical psychiatry. Philadelphia: JB Lippincott, 1985.

33. Schuckit MA. Studies of populations at high risk for alcoholism. Psychiatr Dev 1985;3:31–63.

34. Anthenelli RM, Schuckit MA. Genetic studies on alcoholism. Int J Addict 1990;25:81–94.

35. Jacobsen B, Schulsinger F. Prospective longitudinal research: an empirical basis for the primary prevention of psychosocial disorders. In: Mednick SA, Baert AE, eds. The Danish adoption register. Oxford: Oxford University Press, 1981.

36. Utne HE, Hensen FV, Winkler K, Schulsinger F. Alcohol elimination rates in adoptees with and without alcoholic parents. J Stud Alcohol 1977; 38:1219–1223.

37. Jones BM, Jones MK. Women and alcohol: intoxication, metabolism, and the menstrual cycle. In: Greenblatt N, Schuckit MA, eds. Alcoholism problems in women and children. New York: Grune & Stratton, 1976.

38. Begleiter H, Porjesz B, Bihari B, Kissin B. Event-related brain potentials in boys at risk for alcoholism. Science 1984;227:1493–1496.

39. Behar D, Berg CJ, Rapoport JL, et al. Behavior and physiological effects of ethanol in high-risk and control children: a pilot study. Alcohol Clin Exp Res 1983;7:404–410.

40. McHugh PR, Slavney PR. The perspectives of psychiatry. Baltimore: Johns Hopkins University Press, 1983.

41. Schuckit MA. Drug and alcohol abuse. A clinical guide to diagnosis and treatment. 4th ed. New York: Plenum Medical Book Company, 1996.

42. Goodwin DW, Guze SB. Psychiatric diagnosis. 4th ed. New York: Oxford University Press, 1989.

43. Hesselbrock VM, Hesselbrock MN, Stabenau JR. Alcoholism in men patients subtyped by family history and antisocial personality. J Stud Alcohol 1985;46:59–64.

44. Cloninger CR. Neurogenetic adaptive mechanisms in alcoholism. Science 1987;236:410–416.

45. Penick EC, Powell BJ, Nickel EJ, Read MR, Gabrielli WF, Liskow BI. Examination of Cloninger's type I and type II alcoholism with a sample of men alcoholics in treatment. Alcohol Clin Exp Res 1990;14:623–629.

46. Babor TF, Hofmann M, DelBoca FK, Hesselbrock VM, Meyer RE, Dolinsky ZS, Rounsaville B. Types of alcoholics I: evidence for an empirically derived typology based on indicators of vulnerability and severity. Arch Gen Psychiatry 1992;49:599–608.

47. Anthenelli RM, Smith TL, Irwin MR, Schuckit MA. A comparative study of criteria for subgrouping alcoholics: the primary/secondary diagnostic scheme versus variations of the type 1/type 2 criteria. Am J Psychiatry 1994;151: 10:1468–1474.

48. Bohman M, Sigvardsson S, Cloninger CR. Maternal inheritance of alcohol abuse: cross-fostering analysis of adopted women. Arch Gen Psychiatry 1991;38:965–969.

49. von Knorring L, von Knorring AL, Smigan L, Lindberg U, Edholm M. Personality traits in subtypes of alcoholics. J Stud Alcohol 1987; 48:523–527.

50. Bohman M, Cloninger R, Sigvardsson S, von Knorring AL. The genetics of alcoholisms and related disorders. J Psychiatr Res 1987;21:4: 447–452.

51. Devor EJ, Cloninger CR. Genetics of alcoholism. Annu Rev Genet 1989;23:19–36.

52. Irwin M, Schuckit MA, Smith TL. Clinical importance of age at onset in type 1 and type 2 primary alcoholics. Arch Gen Psychiatry 1990; 47:320–324.

53. Schuckit MA, Irwin M, Mahler HIM. The tridimensional personality questionnaire scores for sons of alcoholics and controls. Am J Psychiatry 1990;147:481–487.

54. Schuckit MA, Irwin M. An analysis of the clinical relevance of type 1 and type 2 alcoholics. Br J Addict 1989;84:869–876.

55. Nixon SJ, Parsons OA. Application of the tridimensional personality questionnaire to a population of alcoholics and other substance abusers. Alcohol Clin Exp Res 1990;14:513–517.

56. Anthenelli RM, Tabakoff B. The search for biochemical markers. Alcohol Health Res World 1995;19:176–181.

57. Schuckit MA, Tipp J, Smith TL, Shapiro E, Hesselbrock V, Bucholz K, Reich T, Nurnberger JI. An evaluation of type A and B alcoholics. Addiction 1995;90:1189–1203.

58. Wall TL, Ehlers CL. Genetic influences affecting alcohol use among Asians. Alcohol Health Res World 1995;19:184–189.

59. Harada S, Agarwal DP, Goedde HW, Ishikawa B. Aldehyde dehydrogenase isozyme variation and alcoholism in Japan. Pharmacol Biochem Behav 1983;18:151–153.

60. Suwaki J, Ohara H. Alcohol-induced facial flushing and drinking behavior in Japanese men. J Stud Alcohol 1985;46:196–198.

61. Bench CJ, Price GW, Lammertsma AA, Cremer JC, Luthra SK, Turton D, Dolan D, Kettler R, Dingemanse J, Da Prada M, Biziere K, McClelland GR, Jamieson VL, Wood ND, Frackowiak SJ. Measurement of human cerebral monoamine oxidase type B (MAO-B) activity with positron emission tomography (PET): a dose ranging study with the reversible inhibitor Ro 19–6327. Eur J Clin Pharmacol 1991;40:169–173.

62. von Knorring AL, Bohman M, von Knorring L, Oreland L. Platelet MAO activity as a biological marker in subgroups of alcoholism. Acta Psychiatr Scand 1985;72:51–58.

63. Pandey GN, Fawcett J, Gibbons R, Clark DC, Davis JM. Platelet monoamine oxidase in alcoholism. Biol Psychiatry 1988;24:15–24.

64. Anthenelli RM, Smith TL, Craig CE, Tabakoff B, Schuckit MA. Platelet monoamine oxidase activity levels in subgroups of alcoholics: diagnostic, temporal, and clinical correlates. Biol Psychiatry 1995;38:361–368.

65. Anthenelli RM, Tipp J, Li TK, Magnes L, Schuckit MA, Rice J, Warwick D, Nurnberger JI. Platelet monoamine oxidase (MAO) activity in subgroups of alcoholics and controls: results from the COGA study. Alcohol Clin Exp Res 1996 (submitted for publication).

66. Tabakoff B, Hoffman PL. Genetics and biological markers of risk for alcoholism. In: Kiianmaa K, Tabakoff B, Saito T, eds. Genetic aspects of alcoholism. Helsinki: Finnish Foundation for Alcohol Studies, 1989:127–142.

67. Tabakoff B, Hoffman PL, Lee JM, Saito T, Willard B, Leon-Jones FD. Differences in platelet enzyme activity between alcoholics and nonalcoholics. N Engl J Med 1988;318:134–139.

68. Hoffman PL, Lee JM, Saito T. Platelet enzyme activities in alcoholics. In: Kiianmaa K, Tabakoff B, Saito T, eds. Genetic aspects of alcoholism. Helsinki: Finnish Foundation for Alcohol Studies, 1989.

69. Mullan M. Alcoholism and the 'new genetics'. Br J Addict 1989;84:1433–1440.

70. Goldman D. Identifying alcoholism vulnerability alleles. Alcohol Clin Exp Res 1995;19:824–831.

71. Begleiter H. The collaborative study on the genetics of alcoholism. Alcohol Health Res World 1995;19:228–236.

72. Cloninger CR. D2 dopamine receptor gene is associated but not linked with alcoholism. JAMA 1991;266:1833–1834.

73. Parsian A, Todd RD, Devor EJ, O'Malley KL, Suarez BK, Reich T, Cloninger CR. Alcoholism and alleles of the human D2 dopamine receptor locus. Arch Gen Psychiatry 1991;48:655–666.

74. Blum K, Noble EP, Sheridan PJ, Montgomery A, Ritchie T, Jagadeeswaran P, Nogami H, Briggs AH, Cohn JB. Allelic association of human dopamine D2 receptor gene in alcoholism. JAMA 1990;263:2055–2060.

75. Holden C. Probing the complex genetics of alcoholism. Science 1991;251:163–164.
76. Noble EP, Blum K, Ritchie T, Montgomery A, Sheridan PJ. Allelic association of the D2 dopamine receptor gene with receptor-binding characteristics in alcoholism. Arch Gen Psychiatry 1991;48:648–654.
77. Bolos AM, Dean M, Lucas-Derse S, Ramsberg M, Brown GL, Goldman D. Population and pedigree studies reveal a lack of association between the dopamine D2 receptor gene and alcoholism. JAMA 1990;264:3156–3160.
78. Hill SY, Goodwin DW, Cadoret R, Osterland CK, Doner SM. Association and linkage between alcoholism and eleven serological markers. J Stud Alcohol 1980;36:981–989.
79. Hesselbrock V, O'Connor S, Tasman A, Weidenman M. Cognitive and evoked potential indications of risk for alcoholism in young men. In: Kuriyamam K, Takada A, Ishii H, eds. Biomedical and social aspects of alcohol and alcoholism. Amsterdam: Elsevier Science Publishers, 1988.
80. Polich J, Bloom FE. Event-related brain potentials in individuals at high and low risk for developing alcoholism: failure to replicate. Alcohol Clin Exp Res 1988;12:368–373.
81. Hill SY, Steinhauer SR, Zubin J, Baughman T. Event-related potentials as markers for alcoholism risk in high density families. Alcohol Clin Exp Res 1988;12:368–373.
82. Pollock VE, Volavka J, Goodwin DW. The EEG after alcohol administration in men at risk for alcoholism. Arch Gen Psychiatry 1983;40:857–861.
83. Volavka J, Pollock VE, Gabrielli WF, Mednick SA. The EEG in persons at risk for alcoholism. In: Recent Developments in Alcoholism. 1985; 3:21–36.
84. Ehlers CL, Schuckit MA. Evaluation of EEG alpha activity in sons of alcoholics. Neuropsychopharmacology 1991;4:199–205.
85. Gabrielli WF, Mednick SA. Intellectual performance in children of alcoholics. J Nerv Ment Dis 1983;171:444–447.
86. Knop J, Goodwin DW, Teasdale TW, Mikkelsen U, Schulsinger F. A Danish prospective study of young males at high risk for alcoholism. In: Goodwin DW, Van Dusen K, Mednick SA, eds. Longitudinal research in alcoholism. Boston: Kluwer-Nijhoff, 1984.
87. Schaeffer KW, Parsons OA, Yohman JR. Neuropsychological differences between familial and nonfamilial alcoholics and nonalcoholics. Alcohol Clin Exp Res 1984;8:347–358.
88. Tarter RE, Hegedus AM, Goldstein G, Shelly C, Alterman A. Adolescent sons of alcoholics: neuropsychological and personality characteristics. Alcohol Clin Exp Res 1984;8:216–222.
89. Schuckit MA, Butters N, Lyn L, Irwin M. Neuropsychologic deficits and the risk for alcoholism. Neuropsychopharmacology 1987;1:45–53.
90. Drake RE, Vaillant GE. Predicting alcoholism and personality disorder in 33-year longitudinal study of children of alcoholics. Br J Addict 1988;83:799–807.
91. Schuckit MA, Haglund RM. An overview of the etiologic theories on alcoholism. In: Estes N, Heinemann E, eds. Alcoholism: development, consequences, and interventions. St. Louis: CV Mosby, 1982.
92. Kammeier ML Sr, Hoffmann H, Loper RG. Personality characteristics of alcoholics as college freshman and at the time of treatment. Q J Stud Alcohol 1973;34:390–397.
93. Vaillant GE. The natural history of alcoholism. Cambridge, MA: Harvard University Press, 1983.

94. Schuckit MA. Biomedical and genetic markers of alcoholism. In: Goedde HW, Agarwal PD, eds. Alcoholism: biomedical and genetic aspects. New York: Pergamon Press, 1989:290–302.
95. Schuckit MA. Alcoholism and sociopathy—diagnostic confusion. Q J Stud Alcohol 1973; 34:157–164.
96. Cloninger CR, Sigvardsson S, Bohman M. Childhood personality predicts alcohol abuse in young adults. Alcohol Clin Exp Res 1988;12:494–505.
97. Vaillant GE. Natural history of male psychological health. VIII. Antecedents of alcoholism and orality. Am J Psychiatry 1983;137:181–186.
98. Schuckit MA. Extroversion and neuroticism in young men at higher or lower risk for alcoholism. Am J Psychiatry 1983;140:1223–1224.
99. Morrison C, Schuckit MA. Locus of control in young men with alcoholic relatives and controls. J Clin Psychiatry 1983;44:306–307.
100. Saunders GR, Schuckit MA. Brief communication: MMPI scores in young men with alcoholic relatives and controls. J Nerv Ment Dis 1981;168:456–481.
101. Ebstein RP, Novick O, Umansky R, Priel B, Osher Y, Blaine D, Bennett ER, Nemanov L, Katz M, Belmaker RH. Dopamine D4 receptor (D4DR) rcon III polymorphism associated with the human personality trait of novelty seeking. Nat Genet 1996;12:78–80.
102. Benjamin J, Greenberg B, Murphy DL, Lin L, Patterson C, Hamer DH. Population and familial association between the D4 dopamine receptor gene and measures of novelty seeking. Nat Genet 1996;12:81–84.
103. Schuckit MA. Reactions to alcohol in sons of alcoholics and controls. Alcohol Clin Exp Res 1988;12:465–470.
104. Schuckit MA. Subjective responses to alcohol in sons of alcoholics and control subjects. Arch Gen Psychiatry 1984;41:879–884.
105. Schuckit MA, Gold EO. A simultaneous evaluation of multiple markers of ethanol/placebo challenges in sons of alcoholics. Arch Gen Psychiatry 1988;45:211–216.
106. Schuckit MA. Ethanol-induced changes in body sway in men at high alcoholism risk. Arch Gen Psychiatry 1985;42:375–379.
107. Lex BW, Lukas SE, Greenwald NE, Mendelson JH. Alcohol-induced changes in body sway in women at risk for alcoholism: a pilot study. J Stud Alcohol 1988;49:346–350.
108. Schuckit MA, Gold E, Risch C. Serum prolactin levels in sons of alcoholics and control subjects. Am J Psychiatry 1987;144:854–859.
109. Schuckit MA. Differences in plasma cortisol after ethanol in relatives of alcoholics and controls. J Clin Psychiatry 1984;45:374–379.
110. Schuckit MA, Risch SC, Gold ER. Alcohol consumption, ACTH level, and family history of alcoholism. Am J Psychiatry 1988;145: 1391–1395.
111. Ehlers CL, Schuckit MA. EEG responses to ethanol in sons of alcoholics. Psychopharmacol Bull 1988;24:434–437.
112. O'Malley SS, Maisto SA. Effects of family drinking and expectancies on response to alcohol in men. J Stud Alcohol 1985;46:289–297.
113. Pollock VE, Teasdale TW, Gabrielli WF, Knop J. Subjective and objective measures of response to alcohol among young men at risk for alcoholism. J Stud Alcohol 1986;47:297–304.
114. Schuckit MA. Advances in understanding the vulnerability to alcoholism. In: Advances in understanding the addictive states. New York: Raven Press, 1992:93–108.

115. Schuckit MA. A long-term study of sons of alcoholics. Alcohol Health Res World 1995;19: 172–175.
116. Schuckit MA, Smith TL. An 8-year follow-up of 450 sons of alcoholic and control subjects. Arch Gen Psychiatry 1996;53:202–210.
117. Schuckit MA. Low level of response to alcohol as a predictor of future alcoholism. Am J Psychiatry 1994;151:184–189.
118. O'Malley PM, Bachman JG, Johnston LD. Period, age, and cohort effects on substance use among young Americans: a decade of change, 1976–86. Am J Public Health 1988;78:1315–1321.
119. Anthenelli RM, Schuckit MA. Alcohol and cerebral depressants. In: Glass IB, ed. The international handbook of addiction behavior. London: Routledge, 1991:57–63.
120. Collins AC. Genetics as a tool for identifying biological markers of drug abuse. In: Braude MC, Chao HM, eds. Genetic and biological markers in drug abuse and alcoholism. NIDA research monograph no. 66. Rockville, MD: Department of Health and Human Services, 1986.
121. Collins RL, Horowitz GP, Passe DH. Genotype and test experience as determinants of sensitivity and tolerance to morphine. Behav Genet 1977;7:50.
122. Anisman H. Differential effects of scopolamine and d-amphetamine on avoidance: strain interactions. Pharmacol Biochem Behav 1975; 3:809–817.
123. Belknap JK, Ondrusek G, Waddingham S. Barbiturate dependence in mice induced by a single short-term oral procedure. Physiol Psychol 1973;1:394–396.
124. Li TK, McBride WJ, Waller MB, Murphy JM. Studies on an animal model of alcoholism. In: Braude MC, Chao HM, eds. Genetic and biological markers in drug abuse and alcoholism. NIDA research monograph no. 66. Rockville, MD: Department of Health and Human Services, 1986.
125. Koob GF, Bloom FE. Cellular and molecular mechanisms of drug dependence. Science 1988;242:715–723.
126. Gfroerer J. Correlation between drug use by teenagers and drug use by older family members. Am J Drug Alcohol Abuse 1987;13: 95–108.
127. Annis HM. Patterns of intrafamilial drug use. Br J Addict 1974;69:361–369.
128. Pickens RW, Svikis DS. Genetic vulnerability to drug abuse: biological vulnerability to drug abuse. NIDA research monograph 89. Rockville, MD: U.S. Department of Health & Human Services, 1988:1–7.
129. Ripple CH, Luthar SS. Familial factors in illicit drug abuse: an interdisciplinary perspective. Am J Drug Alcohol Abuse 1996;22:147–172.
130. Maddux JF, Desmond DP. Family and environment in the choice of opioid dependence or alcoholism. Am J Drug Alcohol Abuse 1989; 15:117–134.
131. Schuckit MA. Genetic and biological markers in alcoholism and drug abuse. In: Braude MC, Chao HM, eds. Genetic and biological markers in drug abuse and alcoholism. NIDA research monograph no. 66. Rockville, MD: Department of Health and Human Services, 1986.
132. Gershon ES. Behavorial and biological pharmacogenetics of d-amphetamine. Paper presented at the 3rd International Society for Twin Studies, Jerusalem, Israel, June 1980 [Abstract].

133. Pedersen N. Twin similarity for usage of common drugs. In: Gedda L, Parisi P, Nance W, eds. Twin research 3: epidemiological and clinical studies. New York: Alan R Liss, 1981.

134. Gynther LM, Carey G, Gottesman II, Vogler GP. A twin study of non-alcohol substance abuse. Psychiatry Res 1995;213:220.

135. Pickens RW, Svikis DS, McGue M. Genetic factors in human drug abuse. Paper presented at the CPDD 1991 Annual Scientific Meeting, June 1991 [Abstract].

136. Liston EH, Simpson JH, Jarvik LF, Guthrie D. Morphine and experimental pain in identical twins. In: Gedda L, Parisi P, Nance W, eds. Twin research 3: epidemiological and clinical studies. New York: Alan R Liss, 1981.

137. Cadoret RJ, Troughton E, O'Gorman TW, Heywood E. An adoption study of genetic and environmental factors in drug abuse. Arch Gen Psychiatry 1986;43:1131–1136.

138. Cadoret RJ, Yates WR, Troughton E, Woodworth G, Stewart MA. Adoption study demonstrating two genetic pathways to drug abuse. Arch Gen Psychiatry 1995;52:42–52.

139. Hughes JR. Genetics of smoking: a brief review. Behav Ther 1986;17:335–345.

140. Carmelli D, Swan GE, Robinette D, Fabsitz R. Genetic influence on smoking—a study of male twins. N Engl J Med 1992;327:829–833.

141. Swan GE, Carmelli D, Rosenman RH, Fabsiz RR, Christian JC. Smoking and alcohol consumption in adult male twins: genetic heritability and shared environmental influences. J Subst Abuse 1990;2:39–50.

142. Gershon ES, Merril CR, Goldin LR, DeLisi LE, Berrettini WH, Nurnberger JI Jr. The role of molecular genetics in psychiatry. Biol Psychiatry 1987;22:1388–1405.

6 Brain Reward Mechanisms

Eliot L. Gardner

Among the social and medical ills of the twentieth century, substance abuse ranks as one of the most devastating and costly. Although totally accurate data on the cost to society are difficult to arrive at, well-informed estimates of the yearly cost to just the United States alone are in the range of $250–300 billion (1, 2). Of course, substance abuse is not new. Descriptions of it are as old as the written word, with a particularly ancient one to be found in Genesis 9:20–23, in which Noah is described as becoming drunk with wine and found lying in a drunken stupor in his tent. At present, though, this age-old human scourge has taken on a new and frightening dimension with the realization that intravenous cocaine and heroin use now constitute the principal vector for the spread of acquired immunodeficiency syndrome (AIDS) in North America and Europe (3–5).

A question obviously arises—why do human beings initiate and persist in such an obviously self-destructive and aberrant behavior as substance abuse? As with all aberrant behavior patterns, compulsive drug-seeking and drug-taking pose two fundamental questions, one for the scientist and one for the clinician. For the scientist, the question is "What causes and perpetuates such patently self-destructive behavior?" For the clinician, the question is "How can such behavior be modified or curbed to the ultimate benefit of the patient?" In the absence of purely accidental or fortuitous discoveries of effective treatment methods for pathological drug-seeking and drug-taking, the scientific question becomes paramount, because from an understanding of the causes of drug self-administration can come rational hypothesis-driven treatment modalities.

Obviously, the causes of substance abuse are complex and multifactorial, including profoundly important social, economic, and educational factors. On the other hand, why is it that laboratory animals, on whom social, economic, and educational variables are inoperative, voluntarily (indeed, avidly) self-administer the same drugs that human beings use and abuse (6–9), and will *not* self-administer other drugs? This argues compellingly for a profoundly important biological basis for substance abuse. Also, the fact that laboratory animals will voluntarily self-administer these same drugs into highly selective and specific brain loci, and *not* others, argues that this core of basic biological causation for substance abuse is *neurobiological* in nature.

Historically, explanatory postulates of the neurobiological motivating forces behind the specific behavioral pattern of substance abuse have tended to parallel the more general explanatory postulates put forth by neurobehavioral theorists for the motivating forces behind *all* behavior. Early general theories of motivation, especially those of the nineteenth century, posited that behavior results primarily from subconscious "instincts" coded in the brain that impel certain behaviors to occur (10). Other early general theories of motivation, especially those popular during the first four decades of the twentieth century, posited that it is the activation of internal homeostatic brain mechanisms (e.g., hunger) that "drive" behavior (e.g., eating) to occur

(10). Thus, both concepts hold that behavior is primarily the result of activation of internal neuropsychobiological states within the organism, and the resulting behavior serves to relieve or reduce such internal activation. In quite parallel fashion, early explanations for substance abuse posited that compulsive drug users have a preexisting "psychic" disturbance (the so-called "addict" personality) that impels drug-taking behavior (11). Such "instinct-satisfaction" or "drive-reduction" theories do not explain why certain behaviors are preferred over others with presumably equivalent "instinct-satisfaction" or "drive-reduction" value (e.g., why some foods are preferred over others), and the postulation of a pre-coded "heroin drive" or "cocaine drive" in the central nervous system has seemed far-fetched to even the most dyed-in-the-wool instinct or drive-reduction theorists. There is also an unpleasing element of circularity to such concepts, i.e., a drug addict uses drugs because he or she has a predisposition to do so. True in some cases, no doubt, but hardly a richly satisfying explanation of the underlying neurobiological or psychobiological *mechanisms*. During the middle decades of the twentieth century, an alternative explanation came to dominate motivational theory in both psychology and psychiatry. This view, termed "reinforcement theory" (10, 12), explains behavior in terms of contingent associations between initially random behavioral elements and environmental stimuli. That is, if certain environmental stimuli ("reinforcers") are contingently paired with behavior, the future probability of that same behavior increases. Thus, reinforcement theory holds that behavior is primarily the result of the presence of salient environmental stimuli, which act on the central nervous system in such a way as to alter the future probability of behavior occurring in their presence (10, 12). The "reinforcement theory" explanation for substance abuse posits that compulsive substance abusers use drugs because these same drugs have been positive reinforcers on previous occasions. Once again, as with "instinct" and "drive-reduction" theories, there is an unpleasing circularity to such an explanation, i.e., a drug addict uses drugs because drugs have previously been "reinforcing." All very true in most cases, no doubt, but since reinforcement theory makes no attempt to describe the neurophysiological processes that occur in the presence of reinforcers, the "reinforcement" explanation for substance abuse is as unsatisfying with respect to underlying neurobiological or psychobiological substrates and mechanisms as are "instinct" and "drive-reduction" explanations. Seemingly more germane to these issues is the notion of "incentive stimulation" or "incentive motivation," a more modern concept in motivational theory (10). This view attempts to describe reinforcers as having the ability to activate internal sensory or affective processes within the organism that are inherently pleasurable or rewarding (i.e., subjectively pleasant), and which then organize and influence behavior to occur (10, 13–15). For example, if an organism ingests heroin or cocaine and finds that pleasure or reward ensues, the likelihood of future ingestion of heroin or cocaine increases. This position is, of course, strikingly close to the "common sense" hedonistic explanation for motivation which, as Young (13) notes, "implies that subjective feelings of pleasantness and unpleasantness influence behavior."

That drugs of abuse are positive reinforcers is clear. As early as 1940, it was demonstrated by Spragg's pioneering work (16) that laboratory animals will voluntarily engage in behaviors that lead to the injection of habit-forming drugs. Indeed, in Spragg's studies chimpanzees would drag the researcher to the cupboard where the morphine, syringes, and needles were stored, and voluntarily assume the proper position to receive the injections. In 1962, Weeks (6) demonstrated that animals will voluntarily self-administer habit-forming drugs if placed into a laboratory setting in which the animal's response on a manipulandum activates an automatic infusion system, which delivers a pre-set amount of drug through a surgically implanted venous catheter. Thus, the human researcher is totally out of the loop; drug delivery or non-delivery is totally under the voluntary control of the animal. This work set the stage for the now widely used paradigm of drug self-administration in laboratory animals as a tool for studying drug-induced reinforcement processes. One important ancillary result of the discovery of voluntary drug self-administration in animals is that it turned scientific attention away from hypothetical internal states within substance abusers (i.e., the "addict" personality) that supposedly "drove" them to abuse drugs, and focused attention instead on the drugs themselves and on the common neuropharmacological properties they might possess which make them positive reinforcers for man and animal alike.

As already noted, "incentive motivation" theory holds that positive reinforcers activate internal neural processes that are inherently pleasurable or rewarding (10, 13–15). The study of the nature of these inherently pleasurable or rewarding neural processes activated by positive reinforcers was advanced dramatically in 1954 with the seminal discovery by Olds and Milner that laboratory animals will voluntarily (indeed, avidly) self-administer electrical stimulation delivered through electrodes deep in the brain (17). This finding was of great importance for many reasons. First, such brain stimulation appears to act precisely as other positive reinforcers, and selectively strengthens any behavior linked contingently to it (17). Second, the finding that only a limited number of brain sites support such brain stimulation reward (18) strongly implies that there are anatomically specific circuits in the brain dedicated to the neural mediation of reward or pleasure (19–21). Third, the fact that electrical stimulation of brain reward sites can also evoke natural consummatory behaviors such as eating and drinking (22–26) implies that such electrical stimulation activates neural systems involved in natural reward and motivation.

Evidence that habit-forming drugs might derive their rewarding properties by activating such brain reward circuits was presented less than three years after the discovery of the brain-stimulation reward phenomenon (27), and has been amply confirmed in the more than three decades since. This acute enhancement of brain reward mechanisms now appears to be the single essential pharmacological commonality of abusable substances, and the hypothesis that abusable substances act on these brain mechanisms to produce the subjective reward that constitutes the reinforcing "high" or "rush" or "hit" sought by substance abusers is, at present, the most compelling hypothesis available on the neurobiology of substance abuse (28–31).

The remainder of this chapter addresses various aspects of this unifying conception of the neural nature of the positive reinforcement engendered by self-administration of abusable substances.

DRUG REWARD MODELS: SELF-ADMINISTRATION OF ABUSABLE SUBSTANCES BY LABORATORY ANIMALS

As stated previously, until approximately 20 years ago, the standard explanation for compulsive substance abuse emphasized predisposing internal drives (e.g., the "addict" personality) within the substance abuser that drove him or her to abuse drugs. Additionally, there was a second aspect to the standard 1950s and 1960s explanation for substance abuse—that substance abusers, driven to drug use by predisposing internal states, soon become caught up in a vicious cycle of drug administration, tolerance, physical dependence, withdrawal, and readministration. Driven by this vicious cycle, the sub-

stance abuser was believed to self-administer abusable substances primarily to ward off the unpleasant consequences of withdrawal. The emphasis of this explanatory rubric was thus negative—to ward off the negative physical consequences of drug withdrawal. No emphasis was placed on the possibility that abusable substance might have powerful *positively* reinforcing properties.

It was the demonstration that laboratory animals will voluntarily (often avidly) self-administer abusable substances (6–9) that decisively reoriented scientific attention onto the positively rewarding properties of the drugs themselves.

Self-Administration Paradigm

Abusable substances can be self-administered by laboratory animals using a variety of administration routes. The intravenous, intramuscular, intraperitoneal, and intracerebral injection routes have all been used, as have the oral ingestion, intragastric, and inhalation routes. The typical drug self-administration paradigm uses the intravenous route in laboratory animals surgically implanted with chronic indwelling intravenous catheters (6–9, 32, 33). Most typically rats (34, 35) or rhesus monkeys (36–40) are used, although other mammalian species have also been successfully used (41–43). Strikingly, animals will self-administer abusable substances in the absence of tolerance, physical dependence, withdrawal, or indeed any prior history of drug taking. The importance of this fact can hardly be overstated because it clearly shows that drug-taking behavior cannot be explained simply in terms of the ability of abusable drugs to ameliorate the withdrawal discomfort associated with abstinence from prior administration of such drugs. In addition, the use of operant conditioning procedures has shown that animal behavior can be controlled by abusable substances in much the same manner that food or water can control the behavior of a hungry or thirsty animal (39), with the obvious caveats that drugs can produce nonspecific increases or decreases in motoric behavior and that under certain operant schedules of drug self-administration (e.g., low fixed-ratio schedules) successive doses may cumulate rapidly within the body, resulting in limitations on rate of response (32). With ratio schedules of operant reinforcement, responding by laboratory animals for drug self-administration has been demonstrated for cocaine (39, 44–47), amphetamines (39, 43, 48–54), other stimulants (55, 56), caffeine (36), opiates (6, 36, 41, 45, 57–64), ethanol (65–66), sedative-hypnotics (36, 44, 67–70), dissociative anesthetics (71, 72), and other abusable substances (9, 33). With interval schedules of operant reinforcement, responding by laboratory animals for drug self-administration has been demonstrated for cocaine (47, 73–77), opiates (78–81), ethanol (80, 82, 83), sedative-hypnotics (70), and other abusable substances (9, 33). As with human substance abuse, drug self-administration in laboratory animals is profoundly influenced by the subject's previous experience with drugs and by the environmental context in which the drug administration takes place (32).

Typically, operant responding for drug self-administration in laboratory animals is compared against operant responding on a control manipulandum which does not deliver drug administration, or against operant responding for saline or vehicle administration. For some abusable substances, acquisition of operant responding for self-administration is rapid and facile—the catheterized laboratory animal is simply placed into the operant chamber and allowed to explore. Normal curiosity and exploratory behavior soon result in an initially random response on the manipulandum that delivers a drug injection. With the appropriate drug, dose, and reinforcement contingency, the animal experiences a subjective reward, with resulting "self-shaping" of behavior to the motor response that delivers the drug. Self-administration of the abusable substance ensues, with a characteristic learning curve and characteristic asymptotic self-administration behavior. For other abusable substances (presumably substances with a lower initial reward potency), such "self-learning" does not result in reliable self-administration behavior. In such cases, other experimental procedures are followed to obtain reliable self-administration behavior. These procedures include: (*a*) training the animal first to respond for a traditional reinforcer such as food and then substituting the drug reinforcer for the food (60), (*b*) training the animal first to respond for another drug with presumably higher initial reward potency and then substituting the drug under investigation for the original drug (52, 65,

84), (c) deliberately shaping the animal's operant behavior toward the manipulandum that delivers drug administration (55), (d) using noncontingent drug administration during the initial stages of the animal's exposure to the drug self-administration situation (85), (e) using an aversive stimulus such as foot-shock to initiate the operant responding for drug administration (38), (f) using food or water deprivation to encourage responding on the drug-administering manipulandum (86), and (g) first making the animal physically dependent upon the drug by programmed drug delivery and then allowing the animal to respond for drug injections after the termination of programmed delivery (6). Some authorities have argued that the use of such procedures constitute less rigorous demonstrations that a drug can serve as a reinforcer (33). Such arguments are debatable. So long as the final drug self-administration behavior is reliably higher than operant responding on a control manipulandum that does not deliver drug administration, or higher than operant responding for saline or vehicle administration, the laboratory "tricks" used to initiate or facilitate initial operant responding for drug reinforcement would seem more related to initial reward potency, which can have significant pharmacokinetic as well as pharmacodynamic components, than to basic reinforcement value. No matter how the drug self-administration is initiated, it can easily be determined whether the contingent drug administration is truly reinforcing the operant behavior by simply disabling the drug delivery system or substituting saline or vehicle for the active drug and seeing whether behavioral extinction (cessation of responding) occurs. If the drug is serving as a reinforcer, extinction ensues. If the drug is not serving as a reinforcer, the behavior continues unabated. Extinction of drug-reinforced responding follows a highly characteristic pattern essentially identical to extinction of food- or water-reinforced behavior—an initial increase in response rate (frustrative non-reward behavioral augmentation) followed by decreased responding and ultimate total cessation of responding. Recent demonstrations that extinction of responding for direct intracranial electrical brain-stimulation reward follows the same highly characteristic behavioral pattern as extinction of drug-reinforced responding (87; see also later discussion of this point) are an important element of the argument that drug self-administration activates the same brain-reward mechanisms activated by electrical brain-stimulation reward.

Characteristic Patterns of Drug Intake in the Self-Administration Paradigm

Patterns of drug intake in the self-administration paradigm in laboratory animals vary with drug class (33), and are provocatively similar to intake patterns seen in humans. With unlimited access to opiates, self-administration is quite uniform and constant, characterized by moderate and measured self-administration of modest doses without voluntary abstinence periods (36, 88). In contrast, unlimited self-administration of stimulants (cocaine, amphetamines, methylphenidate, caffeine) is characterized by alternating periods of drug-intake and drug-abstinence (36, 50, 52, 89–91). During drug-intake periods the self-administration behavior often reaches frenzied levels, accompanied by characteristic dopaminergic behavioral stereotypies, markedly reduced food and water intake, and total lack of sleep. During drug-abstinence periods, a semblance of normal eating, drinking, and sleeping returns. The alternating drug-intake and drug-abstinence periods can continue for months, and markedly resemble the alternating binge and abstinence pattern of human stimulant abuse (92). Unlimited ethanol self-administration in animals is also characterized by alternating binge and abstinence periods (65). Unlimited barbiturate and dissociative anesthetic (e.g., phencyclidine) self-administration in animals is characterized by maximum self-administration of available drug, without abstinence periods (36, 68, 93). Unlimited benzodiazepine self-administration is characterized by very modest intake patterns (68). Given the right reinforcement schedule and dose, nearly all intravenously self-administered drugs can be consumed by laboratory animals to the point of toxicity and/or death (36, 52, 65, 88). The death rate from unlimited stimulant self-administration is very high; that from opiates, ethanol, and barbiturates is very considerably lower although still significant. When drug availability is limited to a pre-set daily session, drug intake tends to be stable from session to session. Within each session, drug intake pattern varies with drug class. Opi-

ate self-administration is measured and steady, while stimulant self-administration is characterized by "mini-binges" at the start of test sessions followed by more measured self-administration for the remainder of the session. With different doses available during different test sessions, drug intake appears to be regulated by the animal to produce fairly uniform actual drug intake over a broad range of doses, a phenomenon that has been interpreted as supporting the concept that laboratory animals self-administer drugs to maintain a constant blood and brain level (94).

Modelling Drug Appetitiveness in Laboratory Animals: Drug Self-Administration under Progressive-Ratio Reinforcement Schedules

The self-administration paradigm in animals can be modified to assess the *relative* appetitive value of different addicting drugs. One such modification is the "progressive ratios" self-administration paradigm (95, 96), in which the amount of work an animal has to expend to receive a single intravenous injection is progressively increased in ratio fashion (e.g., 1 lever-press for the first injection, 2 lever-presses for the second injection, 4 lever-presses for the third injection, 8 lever-presses for the fourth injection, etc.) In any such progressive-ratio run, there comes a point where the animal simply gives up and abruptly stops lever-pressing (the "Oh hell, this ain't worth it anymore" point), the so-called "break-point." By comparing break-points between different classes of addicting drugs, one can establish hierarchies of appetitiveness. Such hierarchies closely resemble those observed in humans (e.g., cocaine extremely appetitive, morphine moderately appetitive, benzodiazepines marginally appetitive). Of course, there are individual differences amongst animals just as there are amongst humans. But cocaine is so appetitive to most laboratory animals that, if given continuous access, they will spend most of their waking hours self-administering the drug and will self-administer it to the point of starvation and death, even if hundreds or thousands of lever-presses are needed to obtain one dose of the drug (50, 89, 97). The parallels to the extreme appetitiveness of crack cocaine in vulnerable humans is striking.

Essential Commonalities of Substances Self-Administered by Laboratory Animals

Although *Chemical Abstracts* lists millions of different known chemicals, the number of chemicals voluntarily self-administered by laboratory animals is only a startlingly tiny fraction of that number—in fact, no more than a few score compounds (8, 9, 33). Also, the chemicals voluntarily self-administered by laboratory animals differ quite strikingly from each other in chemical structure and pharmacological class. The following questions obviously arise: (a) what do these self-administered compounds have in common, and (b) what distinguishes these compounds from the millions of other known compounds? The answers appear to be three-fold. First, although there are inexplicable exceptions (33), by and large the substances that are voluntarily self-administered by laboratory animals are the same ones that human beings also voluntarily self-administer (8, 9, 33, 98–102), and by and large the same drugs that are eschewed by animals are also eschewed by humans. Second, virtually all adequately studied abusable substances (including opiates, cocaine, amphetamines, dissociative anesthetics, barbiturates, benzodiazepines, alcohol, and marihuana) enhance brain-stimulation reward or lower brain reward thresholds in the mesotelencephalic dopamine (DA) system (28–31, 103–113). Third, virtually all adequately studied abusable substances enhance basal neuronal firing and/or basal neurotransmitter release in reward-relevant brain circuits (105, 114–124). These essential commonalities of substances self-administered by laboratory animals are important elements in the theory that drug self-administration activates the same brain-reward mechanisms activated by electrical brain-stimulation reward and that these brain-reward mechanisms include a mesotelencephalic DA component that runs through the medial forebrain bundle. In this last regard, it is compelling that animals voluntarily self-administer the DA reuptake blockers bupropion, mazindol, and nomifensine (55, 125–130), as well as 1-{2-[bis(4-fluorophenyl)methoxy]ethyl}-4-(3-phenylpropyl) piperazine (GBR 12909), a highly selective DA reuptake blocker (131, 132). It is similarly compelling in this regard that animals also voluntarily self-administer direct DA receptor agonists such as apomorphine and piribedil (84, 133–136).

An interesting variant of the drug self-administration paradigm in laboratory animals is one in which the drug infusion is automatically delivered and the animal can voluntarily respond to *terminate* the infusion (137). Just as the voluntarily self-administration paradigm assesses the positive reward of drugs, this voluntary termination-of-infusion paradigm assesses the negative reward value or aversive property of drugs. Interestingly, some drugs do act as negative reinforcers in this paradigm (137, 138). Provocatively, most drugs that act as negative reinforcers in this paradigm and may thus be inferred to have negative reward value are DA antagonists such as chlorpromazine and perphenazine (137, 138). Most humans find such drugs dysphorigenic (139, 140). These findings are additional important elements in the theory that the brain-reward mechanisms activated by drug self-administration include a crucial DA component.

Alteration of Drug Self-Administration by Pharmacological or Neurobiological Manipulations

One of the many approaches used to unravel the neuroanatomical, neurophysiological, and neurochemical substrates of drug-induced reward has been to attempt to alter systemic drug self-administration in laboratory animals by pharmacological manipulations or specific brain lesions. Obviously, when attempting to alter drug self-administration by administering another pharmacological agent, one has to be alert to the possibility of nonspecific drug effects on behavior. Thus, a compound could theoretically inhibit an animal's lever-pressing or bar-pressing for drug injections simply by being so powerful a sedative as to inhibit *all* motor behavior in a nonspecific fashion. The key, then, to inferring a specific effect on drug-induced reward is to look for specific effects on behavior maintained by drug reward (33). Thus, pharmacological manipulations that augment the reinforcing properties of a self-administered drug will selectively suppress drug responding (similar to increasing the unit dose of the self-administered drug) without altering other behaviors, while pharmacological manipulations that diminish the reinforcing properties of a self-administered drug will selectively increase drug responding (to compensate for the reduced effectiveness of the self-administered drug) without altering other behaviors. A manipulation that completely abolishes the reinforcing value of a self-administered drug should produce characteristic extinction of drug-reinforced responding—an initial increase in response rate (frustrative non-reward behavioral augmentation) followed by decreased responding and, finally, cessation of responding. Not unexpectedly, administration of opiate antagonists (e.g., naloxone, naltrexone) to animals self-administering morphine or heroin produces characteristic extinction of the drug responding (57, 81, 141–143). Provocatively, antibodies to morphine also produce a partial-extinction-like increase in heroin intake (144).

Pharmacological challenges that specifically disrupt individual neurotransmitter systems can obviously yield important information on the neurochemical substrates of drug-induced reward. In the many reports in which such neurotransmitter-specific pharmacological manipulations have been paired with drug self-administration in laboratory animals, a striking common thread stands out: Pharmacological challenges that disrupt brain DA systems interfere with the reward value of self-administered drugs. Thus, α-methyl-para-tyrosine (αMPT), a DA synthesis inhibitor, initially produces a partial-extinction-like increase in cocaine or amphetamine self-administration, followed by full extinction of the self-administration behavior as the αMPT dose increases (145–147). Similarly, gradually increasing doses of the DA antagonist pimozide produce an initial dose-dependent increase in self-administered amphetamine intake, followed at higher doses by cessation of self-administration (148). The stereoisomers (+)butaclamol (possessing potent DA antagonism) and (−)butaclamol (devoid of DA antagonism) have also been used to assess DA substrates of drug-induced reward (149). In these studies, (+)butaclamol produced partial and then complete extinction of amphetamine self-administration while (−)butaclamol had no effect on amphetamine self-administration (149). Similar patterns of increased drug self-administration after low-dose DA blockers followed by decreased drug self-administration after higher doses have also been reported from a large number of laboratories for animals

self-administering a wide range of abusable substances, including cocaine, amphetamine, and morphine (133, 142, 150–163). In contrast, noradrenergic blockers have no effect on drug self-administration in laboratory animals (147, 149, 150, 153, 155). In humans, DA antagonists and DA synthesis inhibitors blunt the euphorigenic effects of at least some abusable substances (164–167).

Another approach to pharmacological manipulation of drug self-administration in laboratory animals is the administration of neurotransmitter-specific agonists. The rationale for this approach is that of substitution—just as noncontingent administration of amphetamine temporarily decreases amphetamine self-administration, so too a neurotransmitter-specific agonist that activates the same brain-reward substrates should temporarily decrease drug self-administration. Such, in fact, is the case. Noncontingent administrations of the DA agonists apomorphine or piribedil dose-dependently decrease amphetamine self-administration (84).

A further approach to elucidating the neurochemical substrates of drug-induced reward is to study the effect on drug self-administration of selective lesions, induced either surgically or pharmacologically, of specific neurotransmitter systems in the brain. Obviously, such studies also help to elucidate the neuroanatomical substrates of drug-induced reward. Such studies typically are of two types: (*a*) studies of the effects of brain lesions on stable, previously-acquired drug self-administration, and (*b*) studies of the effects of brain lesions on acquisition of drug self-administration (168). In such studies, the use of neurotransmitter-specific neurotoxins to produce the desired lesion is generally preferable to non-neurotransmitter-specific knife-cuts, electrolytic lesions, or thermocoagulative lesions (168). When the catecholamine-specific neurotoxin 6-hydroxydopamine (6-OHDA) is used to selectively lesion the DA-rich nucleus accumbens, cocaine self-administration is disrupted but self-administration of the direct DA receptor agonist apomorphine in the same animals is unaffected (169). Similarly, when 6-OHDA is used to lesion the DA-rich ventral tegmental area, cocaine self-administration is disrupted but apomorphine self-administration is unaffected (170). 6-OHDA lesions of other brain sites do not affect cocaine self-administration (168–170). These data argue that cocaine self-administration is critically dependent upon a highly specific subset of the DA wiring of the mammalian brain—the mesolimbic DA system, which originates in the ventral tegmental area and projects importantly to the nucleus accumbens (171). In animals with 6-OHDA lesions of either of these two DA loci, the extent of 6-OHDA-induced DA depletion in the nucleus accumbens is highly predictive of duration of curtailment of cocaine self-administration. The greater the DA depletion, the longer the animal takes to recover drug self-administration behavior; animals with the greatest DA loss (more than 90%) often fail to recover at all (168). 6-OHDA lesions of the nucleus accumbens also block acquisition of amphetamine self-administration (172). Heroin and morphine self-administration in laboratory animals have been similarly demonstrated to be critically dependent upon the functional integrity of the mesolimbic DA system (173–175). It is compelling that the mesolimbic DA system constitutes a critical component of the reward system of the mammalian brain (29, 31, 104, 105; see also later discussion). In this regard, the previously reviewed data suggest that functional blockade, either pharmacologically-induced or lesion-induced, of brain reward substrates is the important commonality of manipulations blocking systemic drug self-administration. Thus, studies in which alteration of drug self-administration has been achieved by pharmacological or neurobiological manipulations are important elements in the theory that drug self-administration activates the same brain-reward mechanisms activated by electrical brain-stimulation reward and that these brain-reward mechanisms include the mesolimbic DA subsystem that runs through the medial forebrain bundle.

UNDERLYING NEUROBIOLOGY OF DRUG REWARD: ELECTRICAL SELF-STIMULATION OF BRAIN-REWARD CIRCUITS

Electrical Brain-Stimulation Reward Paradigm

To study electrical brain-stimulation reward, animals are first surgically implanted with chronic indwelling intracranial stimulating electrodes in specific brain loci, allowed to recover from the surgery, and then trained to self-administer the rewarding electrical stimulation by bar-pressing or lever-pressing in a standard operant chamber. The training techniques typically used are essentially identical to those employed to train animals for drug self-administration (see earlier discussion). Acquisition of lever-pressing for brain-stimulation reward is very rapid, with high asymptotic operant levels. Volitional self-administration of the rewarding electrical stimulation, often termed intracranial self-stimulation, is easily maintained by simple operant schedules of reinforcement. The reward engendered by such stimulation, and the brain substrates that support it, have been much studied and well characterized over the last 40 years (176–178). With electrodes in the proper brain loci, such direct brain-stimulation reward is intensely powerful. Hungry animals ignore food to get it and thirsty animals ignore water to get it, in strikingly similar fashion to the way in which cocaine self-administering animals ignore food and water during a drug binge. Animals even endure pain to reach the lever that delivers brain-stimulation reward. Response rates of animals self-stimulating for electrical brain reward are extremely high, often in excess of 100 lever-presses per minute. In short, electrical brain-stimulation reward is one of the most powerful rewards known to biology, rivaled only by the reward engendered by the most powerful self-administered drugs (e.g., cocaine). The few human studies of electrical stimulation of brain reward areas confirm this, the human experience being one of intense subjective pleasure or euphoria (179).

With simple operant schedules of reinforcement, lever-pressing for electrical brain-stimulation reward extinguishes essentially immediately upon termination of the reward, without the normal frustrative non-reward increase in responding that characterizes the early stages of extinction to lever-pressing for food, water, or drug reward. For many years, this was a major conundrum, with some workers arguing that this distinction between electrical brain-stimulation reward and drug self-administration reward implied that different brain substrates are activated by the two types of reward. Recently, however, Lepore and Franklin, in an extremely important piece of work, have shown that the rapid extinction of brain-stimulation reward behavior on low-ratio reinforcement schedules is essentially an artifact of the immediacy of the electrical brain-stimulation reward and of the operant behavioral schedules typically used in brain-stimulation reward studies (87). The paradigm developed by Lepore and Franklin, called "self-administration of brain-stimulation," delivers rewarding electrical brain stimulation in a manner deliberately designed to mimic the pharmacokinetics of drug self-administration as closely as possible. The animal's first response on the brain-stimulation reward lever turns on the brain stimulator, which then stays permanently on for the duration of the test session to deliver a continuous train of biphasic pulse-pairs of rewarding stimulation. However, the frequency of the pulse-pairs decreases with time, in much the same way that brain and blood levels of a self-administered drug decrease with time. Successive lever-presses increase the stimulation frequency by a pre-set amount. Since for any given set of electrical stimulation parameters (pulse-width, current, etc.) there is a range of stimulation frequencies that is optimally rewarding, animals in this paradigm typically lever-press enough times to bring the frequency into the optimal range, and then wait while it slowly decays (in much the same fashion that animals on drug self-administration wait for drug reward to decay after taking a few "hits"). When the stimulation frequency has decayed enough to bring it out of the rewarding range, the animals typically take a few more "hits" on the lever to once again bring the stimulation back up to the optimal range. In this paradigm, which so deliberately models the pharmacokinetics of drug self-administration, extinction is essentially identical to extinction of drug-reinforced behavior, complete with an initial frustrative non-reward increase in responding followed by a slow decrease and ultimate cessation of responding. The importance of this "self-administration of brain-stimulation" paradigm can hardly be overstated, for it shows that once the "pharmacokinetics" of electrical brain-stimulation reward are made to emulate those of drug reward, the difference between the two reward paradigms disappears. In view of these recent developments, the hypothesis that drug-reward and brain-stimulation reward activate the same brain-reward substrates appears more compelling than ever.

Neuroanatomy and Neurochemistry of Brain-Stimulation Reward

The neuroanatomical substrates of direct electrical brain-stimulation reward were initially unclear. Early anatomical mapping studies of the brain for positive brain-stimulation reward sites, carried out in the 1950s and 1960s, demonstrated that electrical brain-reward could be elicited in laboratory rats, cats, and monkeys from a wide variety of brain stem, midbrain, and forebrain loci, including the ventral tegmental area, substantia nigra, hypothalamus, medial forebrain bundle, septum, amygdala, neostriatum, nucleus accumbens, ventral forebrain olfactory nuclei, and portions of the cingulate cortex and frontal cortex (17, 180–185). Such a hodgepodge of sensory, motor, limbic, midbrain, diencephalic, and cortical domains made little sense at the time, although even the early workers noted that the vast majority of brain sites positive for electrical brain-stimulation reward correspond to the aggregate of ascending and descending tracts that comprise the medial forebrain bundle, the nuclei and projections of which extend from brain stem to cortex. Then, in the mid 1960s, pioneering Scandinavian neuroanatomists began to illuminate the monoaminergic anatomy of the brain using the newly developed neurotransmitter mapping technique of histofluorescence microscopy (186–189). A striking correspondence was noted between sites positive for brain-stimulation reward and the mesotelencephalic DA system, the major portions of which are carried through the medial forebrain bundle from the ventral mesencephalon to the limbic and cortical forebrain (171).

Guided by this anatomical correspondence, workers in many laboratories began to study the effects of pharmacological manipulation of DA neurotransmission on brain-stimulation reward. In 1969, the author and his colleagues found that selective inhibition of tyrosine hydroxylase profoundly inhibited brain-reward in monkeys, but that selective inhibition of DA-β-hydroxylase did not, prompting the postulation that brain-reward was critically dependent upon the functional integrity of DA neurotransmission. In 1972, Crow suggested that direct activation of the cell bodies or axons of the mesolimbic and mesostriatal DA systems was rewarding, and that DA was the crucial neurotransmitter of at least one major reward system in the brain (190). In 1980, Corbett and Wise, using movable electrodes to map brain-reward substrates in the ventral mesencephalon, showed that brain-stimulation reward thresholds were a function of the density of DA elements surrounding the electrode tip (191). Also compelling is that DA blockade disrupts brain-stimulation reward at all brain sites adequately tested (192–194), and that, following DA denervation that abolishes neostriatal brain-stimulation reward, direct electrical brain-reward can be restored in the denervated neostriatum by DA reinnervation from embryonic substantia nigra transplants (195). From these studies, and literally hundreds of other experiments (summarized in 31, 105, 194, 196–198), it has become abundantly clear that brain-reward is, in fact, critically dependent upon the functional integrity of DA neurotransmission within the mesotelencephalic DA systems, with the mesolimbic DA system constituting a particularly important focal point within these brain-reward systems. Compellingly, DA blockade mimics the effect of decreasing the electrical intensity of the rewarding brain stimulation (193).

However, the original supposition of many researchers that electrical brain-stimulation reward *directly* activates the DA fibers of the medial forebrain bundle appears contrary to the preponderance of recent evidence. This evidence derives in large part from the studies of Gallistel, Yeomans, Shizgal, and their colleagues (199–203), which argue persuasively on electrophysiological grounds that the primary medial forebrain bundle substrate directly activated by electrical brain-stimulation reward is a myelinated, caudally-running fiber system whose neurons have absolute refractory periods of 0.5–1.2 msec and local potential decay time-constants of approximately 0.1 msec. Since none of these neurophysiological properties agrees with those of the ascending mesotelencephalic DA neurons of the medial forebrain bundle, Wise and his colleagues have argued that the DA neurons cannot be the "first-stage" reward neurons preferentially activated by electrical brain-stimulation reward, but must instead constitute a crucial "second-stage" anatomical convergence within the reward circuitry of the brain, upon which the "first-stage" neurons (those preferentially activated by rewarding electrical stimulation) synapse to form an "in series" reward-relevant neural circuit (29, 104, 105). It is on this "second-stage" DA convergence—with its DA cell bodies in the ventral tegmental area and DA axon terminals in the nucleus accumbens (29, 104, 105)—that abusable substances appear to act to enhance brain reward and produce the euphorigenic effects that constitute the "high" or "rush" sought by substance abusers (29–31, 104, 105, 194; see also later discussion). Furthermore, it seems likely that only a small subset of these DA neurons are specialized for carrying reward-relevant information (105). Although apparently preferentially activated by abusable substances, these DA substrates also appear capable of direct activation by electrical brain-stimulation reward under proper conditions of electrical stimulation (204).

Recently, efforts have been directed toward determining: (a) the neuroanatomical site(s) of origin of the non-DA rostro-caudally conducting "first-stage" reward neurons within the medial forebrain bundle, and (b) whether a single, anatomically defined set of "third-stage" reward neurons carries the pleasure/reward neural signal even further (i.e., beyond the mesolimbic DA terminal loci that the "second-stage" DA caudo-rostrally conducting medial forebrain bundle reward neurons project to), and, if so, to what neuroanatomical site(s).

With respect to the first question, it has been clear for more than a decade (on the basis of electrophysiological studies employing anodal block [205]) that the majority of "first-stage" non-DA medial forebrain bundle reward neurons conduct their pleasure/reward neural signals caudally along axons projecting from the area of the lateral hypothalamus to the ventral tegmental area. This has led to the hypothesis that a majority of "first-stage" reward neurons arise rostral to the lateral hypothalamus and send their descending neuronal projections to the ventral tegmental area (205). To test this hypothesis, several research groups have studied the role of descending medial forebrain bundle neurons in electrical brain stimulation reward by damaging their various nuclei of origin. Lesions of a number of the descending inputs to the medial forebrain bundle have been found to *not* degrade the reward efficacy of medial forebrain bundle electrical brain stimulation reward. Thus, lesions of the amygdala (206), dorsomedial hypothalamus (207), frontal cortex (208, 209), medial preoptic area (210), medial septal area (210), or vertical limb of the diagonal band of Broca (210) produce no permanent or substantial effect on frequency or current thresholds for electrical brain stimulation reward in the medial forebrain bundle at the level of the lateral hypothalamus. Such lesion data can be reconciled with the hypothesis that "first-stage" non-DA reward neurons descend in the medial forebrain bundle if it is assumed that such "first-stage" neurons arise in one or several anterior medial forebrain bundle nuclei spared by such lesions—in particular, the rostral bed nuclei of the medial forebrain bundle, including the anterior lateral hypothalamus, horizontal limb of the diagonal band of Broca, interstitial nucleus of the stria medullaris, lateral preoptic area, magnocellular preoptic nucleus, olfactory tubercle, substantia innominata, and ventral pallidum (211–214). Recently, Shizgal and his colleagues, using electrophysiological and behavioral methods for inferring anatomical linkage between rewarding brain stimulation sites (201) and using lesion studies, have reported that psychophysical collision effects are obtained for electrical brain stimulation reward sites in the anterior lateral hypothalamus and the ventral tegmental area (213) and that sufficiently large lesions of the anterolateral medial forebrain bundle produce substantial and/or permanent elevations in brain reward thresholds at posterior medial forebrain bundle sites (212). This strongly suggests that descending "first-stage" reward neurons directly link the anterolateral medial forebrain bundle and the ventral tegmental area and that these axons may constitute a fairly heterogeneous population arising in a number of separate anterior bed nuclei of the medial forebrain bundle. Further, descending medial forebrain bundle axons arising from several of these anterior bed nuclei possess neural excitability properties closely matching behaviorally-derived estimates for the "first-stage" reward neurons of the medial forebrain bundle (214). Thus, the best current judgment is that the non-DA rostro-caudally conducting "first-stage" medial forebrain bundle reward neurons originate diffusely within the anterior bed nuclei of the medial forebrain bundle (anterior lateral hypothalamus, horizontal limb of the diagonal band of Broca, interstitial nucleus of the stria

medullaris, lateral preoptic area, magnocellular preoptic nucleus, olfactory tubercle, substantia innominata, and ventral pallidum), presumably constituting an anatomical convergence of disparate neurally-encoded information critical to the set point of hedonic tone. On the other hand, and stressing what they believe to be the *extremely* disparate neuroanatomical nature of this reward system, Gallistel and colleagues (215) have argued that the "first-stage" reward neurons are extensively collateralized bipolar neurons with both their cell bodies and the majority if not all of their terminals located in the midbrain. They base this argument on the facts that: (a) as noted earlier, forebrain lesions and knife cuts that transect most major medial forebrain bundle projection systems are remarkably ineffective in reducing the rewarding efficacy of medial forebrain bundle electrical brain stimulation reward (210); (b) nearly complete destruction of the medial forebrain bundle *rostral* to the brain stimulation site by as little as less than 1.0 mm often fails to alter both the efficacy of electrical brain stimulation reward *and* the number of neurons in the population of reward relevant fibers at the site of stimulation (the latter ascertained by quantitative psychophysical methods), while destruction *caudal* to the site of stimulation often significantly attenuates reward efficacy *and* substantially reduces the population of fibers carrying the reward signal (215); and (c) anodal electrical brain stimulation reward to the ventral tegmental area blocks cathodal electrical brain stimulation reward to the lateral hypothalamus, but not vice versa (205). This rather extreme view of the location, morphology, and distribution of the "first-stage" reward neurons implies that these neurons are distributed over so broad a midbrain region as to extend well beyond the conventionally defined borders of the medial forebrain bundle.

With respect to the second question, it is now clear that a "third-stage" reward pathway does exist, carrying the pleasure/reward neural signal beyond the nucleus accumbens, i.e., beyond the mesolimbic DA terminal loci to which the "second-stage" DA caudo-rostrally conducting medial forebrain bundle reward neurons project. Further, it is clear that this "third-stage" pathway uses the endogenous opioid peptide enkephalin as its primary neurotransmitter and projects anatomically to the ventral pallidum. Anatomical mapping and tracing studies show clearly that a major efferent pathway for nucleus accumbens output signals projects to the ventral pallidum, and that this pathway is enkephalinergic (216–219). Electrophysiological studies (220) show that a large majority of nucleus accumbens output neurons are opiate-sensitive and naloxone-blockable, tending to confirm that this is the major efferent pathway of the accumbens and tending to confirm its opioid peptidergic nature. This nucleus accumbens output pathway is known to be critical for expression of reward-related and incentive-related behaviors (as is the next-following transsynaptic pathway from the ventral pallidum to the pedunculopontine tegmental nucleus [221]). Manipulations of this nucleus accumbens–ventral pallidum pathway have clear effects on brain-stimulation reward and reward-driven behaviors. For example, lesions of this pathway significantly reduce both cocaine and opiate intravenous self-administration (222, 223). Such lesions also significantly attenuate acquisition of a drug-conditioned cue (place) preference (219). Very importantly, endogenous opioid release is selectively seen in the ventral pallidum as a consequence of rewarding electrical brain stimulation in other parts of the reward axis (e.g., ventral tegmental area [224]). Equally importantly, opioid microinjections into the ventral pallidum alter electrical brain-stimulation reward in an anatomically site-specific manner (225, 226). Provocatively, there are mutually reciprocal anatomical interconnections between the ventral pallidum, nucleus accumbens, and ventral tegmental area (227), which appear functionally relevant to the set-point of DA reward functions within the reward circuitry (228). Another nucleus accumbens output pathway—the medium spiny output neurons which use γ-aminobutyric acid (GABA) as a neurotransmitter—has been postulated on seemingly good neuroanatomical, neurochemical, and neuropharmacological grounds to constitute another brain reward final common output path (229–231). In fact, Carlezon and Wise (231) have very recently posited a model of drug-induced reward in which the critical event is inhibition of the GABAergic medium spiny output neurons in nucleus accumbens. However, since GABA appears to be co-localized with the opioid neuropeptide enkephalin in at least a portion of the medium spiny projection pathway from nucleus accumbens to

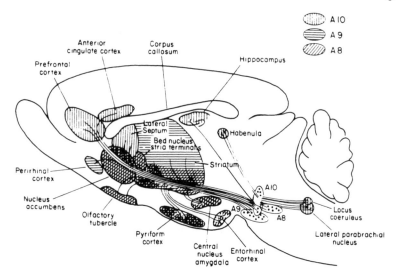

Figure 6.1. The mesotelencephalic dopamine (DA) circuitry of the mammalian (laboratory rat) brain. The primary brain-reward-relevant portion appears to be a subset of the mesolimbic projections originating in the ventral tegmental area (DA nucleus "A10") and terminating in the nucleus accumbens. Reproduced with permission from Cooper JR, Bloom FE, Roth RH. The biochemical basis of neuropharmacology. 5th ed. New York: Oxford University Press, 1986.

pallidum and from nucleus accumbens to ventral tegmental area (218, 232–238) (as well as apparently being co-localized with the opioid neuropeptide dynorphin and the non-opioid neuropeptide Substance P in at least a portion of the medium spiny projection pathway from nucleus accumbens to ventral tegmental area [232, 233, 235, 236]), this suggestion may well be fully congruent with the earlier-noted hypothesis that the "third-stage" reward neurons are co-extensive with at least a portion of the enkephalinergic pathway from nucleus accumbens to ventral pallidum.

A number of additional circuits synapse onto the "first-stage," "second-stage," or "third-stage" elements of this brain reward system, to apparently regulate and modulate the overall set-point of hedonic tone. The neurotransmitters of some of these additional circuits are known—including opioid peptides, serotonin, glutamate, and GABA (see later discussion of such modulatory systems).

Figure 6.1 illustrates some of the DA circuitry of the forebrain involved in these reward mechanisms.

Effects of Abusable Substances on Brain-Stimulation Reward

For studying the effects of abusable substances on these brain-reward mechanisms in the laboratory, a number of paradigms of electrical brain-stimulation reward have been used (see 105, 239 for reviews and discussions). Unfortunately, most early studies (1950s, 1960s, and early 1970s) used simple response-rate measures for brain-stimulation of fixed voltage or current and fixed stimulation frequency. Such response-rate studies were inadequate on many grounds, not the least being that some abusable substances are strong sedative-hypnotics and others are strong psychomotor stimulants. Such compounds may spuriously produce depressed or enhanced responding for brain-reward in a simple response-rate paradigm due simply to nonspecific motor effects. As a result, much of the early literature dealing with the effects of abusable substances on brain-reward is either difficult to interpret or, worse, leads to incorrect conclusions. For these reasons, attention in recent years has shifted to threshold measures, response-pattern analyses, choice measures, "curve-shift" rate-frequency function measures analogous to the dose-response paradigm of traditional pharmacology, and a host of other conceptually similar but operationally very distinct brain-stimulation reward paradigms (see 105, 239 for excellent discussions and comparisons amongst these paradigms). The author's laboratory has used a number of variants of the decremental titrating-threshold brain-reward paradigm, commonly known in the brain-reward literature as the "autotitration" para-

digm, which was developed by Stein and Ray (240). In one of the autotitration variants used (110, 111, 113, 241–244), the animal presses a "reward" lever to self-administer a brief (300 msec) train of rewarding brain stimulation, which automatically decreases in intensity with each successive lever-press. When this decremental stimulation passes through the threshold for activating the underlying neural substrate of reward, the animal presses a "reset" lever, which does not deliver any brain-reward, but resets the brain-reward intensity back to its initial level. By analyzing "reset" values, measure of the activation threshold (in microamperes of delivered current) of the neural system subserving brain-reward is obtained, which is independent of response rate and thus independent of the incidental sedation or psychomotor stimulation produced by many abusable drugs. In another autotitration variant (245–246), the "reset" of brain-reward intensity back to initial level is not controlled by a second lever, but rather by a time-delay circuit, which triggers only when the animal stops responding on the "reward" lever for a preset length of time (e.g., 5 seconds). Since animals will respond for even marginally rewarding brain-stimulation rather than none at all, this paradigm tends to give a more accurate measure of true threshold rather than threshold of a preferred range. Using these paradigms, the author has studied the effects on brain-stimulation reward of a wide range of abusable substances, including cocaine, amphetamines, opiates, barbiturates, ketamine, phencyclidine, benzodiazepines, alcohol, and marihuana (110, 111, 113, 242–244). In every case, robust enhancement of brain-stimulation reward is seen. Similar robust enhancement of brain-stimulation reward by representative compounds from virtually every class of abusable substance has also been reported from other laboratories (for reviews, see 29–31, 103, 194, 239; see also 110, 193, 247–263).

Arguing persuasively for the view that all abusable substances act by facilitating a common brain-reward substrate is the finding that abusable substances of *different* pharmacological classes (e.g., opiates and stimulants) have a synergistic effect on brain-stimulation reward thresholds when co-administered (249, 260).

Arguing persuasively for the view that facilitation of brain-reward mechanisms is closely related to abuse potential are findings with the class of compounds known variously as opiate partial agonists or mixed agonist-antagonists. This class, synthesized in large measure as part of a deliberate effort to develop effective narcotic analgesics with little or no abuse potential, contains some compounds that in fact appear to possess no abuse potential and others that do possess abuse potential (264). Amongst this class, the brain-stimulation reward paradigm discriminates nicely between those compounds having abuse potential and those devoid of it. Specifically, the abusable substance pentazocine lowers brain-reward thresholds while other mixed agonist-antagonists lacking abuse potential (e.g., cyclazocine, nalorphine) do not (257).

An intriguing finding is that brain-stimulation reward undergoes an age-related decline (253, 254), which is reversed by a single dose of d-amphetamine (253). It is tempting to conclude that this age-related decline in central reinforcement mechanisms may correlate with age-related decline in central DA function (265), which is temporarily restored by acute amphetamine.

A striking finding of many different laboratories is that DA antagonists, such as neuroleptics, *inhibit* electrical brain-stimulation reward of the medial forebrain bundle and associated DA loci (i.e., *raise* brain-reward thresholds) in a manner that appears diametrically opposite to the enhancement of brain-stimulation reward (*lowering* of brain-reward thresholds) produced by substances of abuse. This is a very robust and replicable finding, first reported 30 years ago by Stein and his colleagues (240, 248) and replicated many times since in a number of different laboratories (266–268; see also 198 for a review of related studies and a theoretical formulation of the role of DA antagonism in anhedonia). Such findings, coupled with the findings that animals volitionally terminate infusions of DA antagonists, and taken in the overall context of the findings already described that DA agonists are volitionally self-administered and enhance electrical brain-stimulation reward, are important elements in the theory that electrical brain-stimulation reward activates the same DA brain-reward substrates activated by drug self-administration, and that these substrates include the mesolimbic DA reward systems of the medial forebrain bundle.

For some abusable substances, the dose-range within which electrical brain-stimulation reward enhancement is seen is relatively narrow. Phencyclidine and ketamine, for example, produce brain-reward enhancement within a comparatively narrow range of low doses, but *inhibit* brain-reward, in neuroleptic-like fashion, at higher doses (243). The author has suggested that this low-dose brain-reward-enhancement, high-dose brain-reward-inhibition phenomenon in laboratory animals is homologous with the "low-dose good-trip," "high-dose bad-trip" phenomenon reported by street users of these drugs.

Provocatively, the author (110, 111, 242, 243, 250, 269) and others (259, 270, 271; see also 29, 104) have found that the brain-reward enhancement produced by abusable substances (including compounds in such different classes as opiates, amphetamines, cocaine, ethanol, barbiturates, benzodiazepines, phencyclidine, and ketamine) is in every case significantly attenuated by the opiate antagonists naloxone or naltrexone. Interestingly, naloxone not only attenuates the low-dose enhancement of brain stimulation reward produced by ketamine and phencyclidine, but also attenuates the high-dose inhibition of brain reward produced by these same drugs. Equally provocatively, naloxone has been reported to *augment* neuroleptic-induced inhibition of brain-stimulation reward (268). In view of the naloxone-induced attenuation of the brain-stimulation reward enhancement produced by all known classes of abusable substances, it would appear that there exists an important anatomical and functional interrelationship between the crucial drug-sensitive "second-stage" DA fibers of the reward system (29–31, 105, 194) and endogenous opioid peptide circuitry, and furthermore that this interrelationship is important for the brain-reward enhancement produced by *all* substances of abuse, not just opiates, and hence for their abuse liability. Anatomically, there are many brain loci where such a functional interaction between reward-relevant DA neurons and endogenous opioid peptide neurons could take place. Cell bodies, axons, and synaptic terminals of endogenous opioid peptidergic neurons are found in veritable profusion throughout the extent of the reward-relevant mesotelencephalic DA circuitry (272–273). The author (274) and others (275, 276) have shown that endogenous opioid peptide neurons synapse directly onto mesotelencephalic DA axon terminals, forming precisely the type of axo-axonic synapses one would expect of a system designed to modulate the flow of reward-relevant neural signals through the DA circuitry. In addition to the DA axon terminal regions (e.g., nucleus accumbens), other possible sites of DA-opioid peptide functional interaction include the DA cell body region of the ventral tegmental area (197) and transsynaptic modulation via afferents to the ventral mesencephalon from the region of the locus coeruleus (29), although there does not appear

to be direct synaptic interaction between coerulear noradrenergic efferent projections and either the "first-stage" or "second-stage" reward neurons in the ventral tegmental area. As noted above, there are excellent reasons for believing that opioid peptidergic (enkephalinergic) "third-stage" reward neurons project from the nucleus accumbens to the ventral pallidum (216–226), thus carrying the neural reward signal one synapse further. Additional evidence for believing that this is so includes the facts that: (a) the author has shown (242) that naloxone significantly attenuates the enhanced brain-stimulation reward induced by chronic pharmacological up-regulation of DA receptors in the mesolimbic DA system, suggesting that a crucial naloxone-blockable endogenous opioid peptide link lies *efferent* to the up-regulated DA receptors; and (b) the author has also shown (277) that naloxone significantly modulates behavioral responses induced by direct postsynaptic DA-receptor agonists in animals in whom the presynaptic DA fiber system has been destroyed by selective lesions of the DA mesotelencephalic system, again implicating a crucial naloxone-sensitive endogenous opioid peptide link *efferent* to the ascending DA mesotelencephalic DA system. Although some workers believe that the synaptic interaction in the nucleus accumbens between the "second-stage" DA reward neurons and the "third-stage" enkephalinergic neurons is an indirect one (i.e., mediated through interneurons), there is reason to believe that at least a portion of the "second-stage" DA reward neurons may synapse directly onto the "third-stage" endogenous opioid peptide neurons. Pickel et al. have presented evidence, from double-label electron microscopy studies, that a portion of the ascending mesotelencephalic DA fibers synapse directly onto endogenous opioid peptide neurons (278). A similar suggestion, again on the basis of ultrastructural evidence, had previously been made by Kubota et al. (279).

It seems, therefore, on the basis of the best presently available data, that likely sites for the interaction of abusable substances with endogenous brain opioid mechanisms that functionally modulate the intensity of reward signals carried through the DA reward system are (a) the ventral tegmental area, (b) the nucleus accumbens, and (c) the ventral pallidum.

CRITICAL NEUROANATOMY OF DRUG REWARD: INTRACRANIAL MICROINJECTION OF ABUSABLE SUBSTANCES

Although it is possible to infer anatomical sites of drug reward from studies such as these just described, there are other more direct ways of studying the neuroanatomy of drug-induced reward. Two such ways involve direct intracranial microinjections of abusable substances, in the first case coupled with the electrical brain-stimulation reward paradigm and in the second case coupled with self-administration methodologies.

Effects of Intracranial Microinjections of Abusable Substances on Electrical Brain-Stimulation Reward

When making intracranial microinjections of chemical substances to infer localized sites of action within the brain, a number of potentially serious methodological considerations arise, including the dangers of misinterpretation of data due to diffusion of the injected substance, local anesthesia within the injection site, and nonspecific irritation within the injection site. Also, local pressure effects and high local concentrations of the injected substance can be problematic. For a review of these and other important methodological considerations that apply to paradigms utilizing direct intracranial microinjections, the interested reader is directed to reviews by Routtenberg (280), Bozarth (281), and Broekkamp (282). With due regard for these methodological considerations, direct intracranial microinjections of abusable substances can be combined with electrical intracranial self-stimulation methods to infer the local site(s) of rewarding effects. Using these techniques, Broekkamp and colleagues found that the focal area for morphine's enhancing effects on electrical brain-stimulation reward lies within the ventral tegmental area and caudal hypothalamus (283, 284), with microinjections into the ventral tegmental area producing more immediate enhancement than microinjections into the caudal hypothalamus (285). In these studies, the latency time for enhancement of brain-stimulation reward was highly correlated with distance from the DA cells of the ventral mesencephalic DA nuclei that give rise to the mesotelencephalic DA fibers of the medial forebrain bundle (r = 0.83, p < 0.0001) (282, 285). These data are compelling, given the evidence already reviewed from other experimental paradigms and approaches for a focal role of the "second-stage" DA neurons of the mesotelencephalic DA system in mediating drug-induced reward. Using similar methods, Broekkamp and colleagues found that the focal area for amphetamine's enhancing effects on electrical brain-stimulation reward lies within the nucleus accumbens and neostriatal forebrain DA terminal projection loci of the "second-stage" mesotelencephalic DA reward-relevant systems (286). Microinjections of DA antagonists into these same DA terminal projection loci inhibit brain-stimulation reward (284, 287), with the DA axon terminals in the nucleus accumbens playing the most crucial role in hedonic set-point as measured by electrical brain stimulation reward (287). More recently, Wise and colleagues (288, 289) and Fibiger and colleagues (290) have confirmed that the ventral tegmental area is the crucial anatomical site for augmentation of electrical brain stimulation reward by opiates (288, 290), while the nucleus accumbens is the crucial anatomical site for augmentation of electrical brain stimulation reward by amphetamine (289). Opiate-induced augmentation of electrical brain stimulation in the ventral tegmental area appears to be mediated by μ and δ opioid receptors, but not by κ receptors (288).

Intracranial Self-Administration of Abusable Substances

A direct way to study the neuroanatomy of drug-induced reward is to meld intracranial microinjection technology with the self-administration paradigm, so that animals are allowed to work for direct intracranial self-administration of abusable substances into discrete brain loci. Although conceptually simple, this is actually a very difficult laboratory paradigm (for reviews, see 280, 281, 291–293). As noted by Olds (20), early work with intracranial self-administration was almost universally methodologically flawed. Even with sophisticated microinjection technologies (294), many conceptual and interpretational problems remain. For example, it is difficult with microinjection procedures (which must perforce be kept to sufficiently small volumes and forces as to preclude nonspecific neuronal effects) to duplicate the close time-link between behavioral response and reinforcement that occurs with natural rewards, and virtually impossible to duplicate the immediacy of electrical brain-stimulation reward. Since a reinforcement delay of only a few seconds is often enough to disrupt operant behavior (295, 296), this is a serious concern. Similarly, issues of drug diffusion, anatomical specificity, pharmacological specificity, and the multiple and distinct physiological systems activated by most drugs pose major methodological and conceptual problems. Also, as noted by Bozarth in his many insightful reviews of intracranial self-administration (281, 291), the fact that a given brain site does not support self-administration does not eliminate that site as a reward locus, since competing behaviors (e.g., sedation) produced by the drug injection may mask the reward behavior. Additionally, and again as noted by Bozarth (281), successful intracranial self-administration only identifies a site as being involved in the *initiation* of drug reward, not necessarily in the complex and multistepped neurophysiological components of the *overall* subjective experience of drug-induced reward or pleasure. In spite of the many methodological and interpretational problems that accrue to it, the paradigm's seeming face validity has made it appealing to researchers studying the neurobiology and neuroanatomy of drug-induced reward, and a number of laboratories have succeeded in overcoming most of the paradigm's problems and generating provocative and compelling data.

Thus, animals will voluntarily self-administer microinjections of amphetamine into the nucleus accumbens and prefrontal cortex (297–299), both of which are mesolimbic DA terminal projection loci, but not into other brain sites. Similarly, cocaine is voluntarily self-administered into the prefrontal cortex (300). Morphine is self-administered into the ventral tegmental area (301, 302), lateral hypothalamus (303, 304), and nucleus accumbens (305), all of which are either nuclei or terminal projection loci of the mesolimbic DA system (171), but not into other brain sites. Other opioids, both synthetic and endogenous, are also self-administered intracranially. Fentanyl is self-admin-

istered into the ventral tegmental area (306), met-enkephalin is self-administered into the nucleus accumbens (307), and the met-enkephalin analogue d-ala²-met-enkephalinamide is self-administered into the lateral hypothalamus (308). A related and conceptual derivative of these kinds of studies is the finding by Britt and Wise that microinjections of a hydrophilic opioid antagonist with limited diffusion characteristics (diallyl-normorphinium bromide) into the ventral tegmental area blocks intravenous opiate self-administration (309). Ethanol is self-administered into the ventral tegmental area, but—provocatively—only by animals with a genetic predisposition to high oral ethanol self-administration and *not* by animals with a genetic predisposition to ethanol abstinence (310). Phencyclidine is self-administered into the nucleus accumbens, and within that structure, preferentially self-administered into the "shell" subportion of nucleus accumbens as compared to the "core" subportion (231) (see later discussion of the apparent specialization of the "shell" subportion of nucleus accumbens for brain reward functions). Interestingly, the phencyclidine-related drugs MK-801 (dizoclipine) and CPP [3-((+/−)2-carboxypiperazinyl)propyl-1-phosphate], which share PCP's actions on excitatory amino acid receptor (NMDA) functions but not its direct DA reuptake blocking actions, are also self-administered preferentially into the accumbens "shell," suggesting that at least some of the rewarding effects of PCP-like dissociative anesthetics may be mediated through NMDA receptors on reward neurons or reward-modulating neurons (231).

An important theme in such intracranial microinjection studies, already alluded to, is the ability of such approaches to yield data showing which brain loci are responsible for the initiation of each separate and individual pharmacological action of any given abusable substance. So, for example, the analgesic effect of opiates is mediated by local action on opioid peptidergic circuits within the periaqueductal and periventricular gray matter of the brain stem (311, 312), the thermoregulatory effect by action in the preoptic area (313), while the rewarding effects appear mediated by action on the nuclei, tracts, and terminal projection loci of the mesolimbic DA system. Very importantly, physical dependence upon opiates has been shown by microinjection studies to be mediated by action on brain stem loci anatomically distinct and far removed from the mesolimbic DA loci mediating opiate-induced reward (314), and repeated morphine injections into the mesolimbic DA loci critical for drug-reward utterly fail to produce physiological dependence (314).

Despite the difficulties that the intracranial self-administration paradigm poses, completed studies add persuasively to the hypothesis that the "second-stage" DA neurons of the mesotelencephalic DA system play a focal and essential role in mediating drug-induced reward.

CRITICAL NEUROCHEMISTRY OF DRUG REWARD: *IN VIVO* BRAIN CHEMISTRY MEASUREMENTS DURING ADMINISTRATION OF ABUSABLE SUBSTANCES

If the ascending mesotelencephalic DA systems play the crucial role in drug-induced brain-reward that researchers in the field currently ascribe to them, one would expect abusable substances to act, at least indirectly or transsynaptically, in a DA-agonist-like fashion in these systems. For many years, this crucial derivative of the theory was untestable. However, two techniques have been developed which allow for *in vivo* real-time measurements of neurotransmitter release in discrete brain loci of living (indeed, in many cases, conscious, freely-moving) animals. These techniques are *in vivo* brain microdialysis and *in vivo* brain voltammetric electrochemistry (315, 316). Both of these paradigms have proven themselves to be valid and sensitive ways of measuring real-time neurotransmitter release in extremely discrete loci of the living brain, and both of these paradigms have now been applied to the question of which neurotransmitter substrates are activated by administration of abusable substances. Additionally, classical *in vivo* single-neuron electrophysiological recording techniques have also been applied to the same question. There is also an extensive literature on the use of push-pull cannula perfusion (317) for studying the effects of abusable substances on *in vivo* neurotransmitter release in forebrain reward-relevant loci (318, 319), but this literature will not be separately reviewed here, as the push-pull cannula perfusion technique is conceptually and even methodologically analogous to *in vivo* brain microdialysis and the effects of abusable substances on DA in forebrain reward loci as determined by *in vivo* push-pull perfusion have been found to be essentially identical to those determined by *in vivo* brain microdialysis.

Paradigms of *in vivo* Brain Microdialysis and *in vivo* Brain Voltammetric Electrochemistry

Although *in vivo* brain microdialysis (320–323) is conceptually similar to the much older push-pull cannula paradigm (317), it is technologically superior. For *in vivo* microdialysis studies, a microdialysis probe (324) is fabricated from miniature stainless steel and dialysis tubing and surgically implanted, by standard stereotaxic technique, into the desired brain locus. A pump is used to drive buffered Ringers solution (similar in ionic constituents and concentrations to the extracellular fluid of the brain) through the probe at a slow rate. At the tip of the probe, located in the brain site to be measured, extracellular neurotransmitters and metabolite molecules dialyze across the membrane and are carried out of the probe in the buffered Ringers solution to an analytical biochemistry apparatus. Typically, the analytic biochemistry apparatus is a high performance liquid chromatograph with electrochemical detection, although other analytic devices can also be used. If high performance liquid chromatography with electrochemical detection is used, the neurotransmitters and metabolites in the dialysate are first separated by reverse-phase column chromatography and the eluting species are then measured with an electrochemical detector. The *in vivo* sensitivity of this paradigm is excellent, allowing detection of basal DA release in even diffusely innervated DA terminal projection loci (e.g., prefrontal cortex). The selectivity of the paradigm is also excellent, because of the excellent separation of chemical species afforded by the chromatography columns. Time resolution is typically on the order of one measurement every 5 or 10 minutes, although much shorter sampling times (1 minute or less) are possible with microbore chromatography techniques (322).

In vivo brain voltammetric electrochemistry (316, 317, 322, 325–327) is based upon the fortuitous chemical coincidence that many neurotransmitters of interest (in the present instance, DA) and their metabolites are capable of electro-oxidation. Such oxidation yields an oxidation current, which can be measured using electrodes and apparatus essentially identical to that used in axon-conduction voltage-clamp measurements of traditional neurophysiology. The neurotransmitter molecules are identified by their characteristic oxidation potential, their characteristic electrochemical signatures (e.g., the shape of the voltammogram when performing fast cyclic voltammetry [322] or the characteristic oxidation-reduction ratios when performing high-speed chronoamperometry [322]), and by altering the physical-chemical nature of the electrode working surface, at which the electrochemical reactions take place, to produce electrodes with high selectivity for specific molecules (322, 328). For *in vivo* voltammetric electrochemistry studies, a "working" electrode (so called because the electrochemical reactions "work" at its surface) is fabricated, typically from carbon fibers and miniature glass tubing, and then calibrated for selectivity and sensitivity and characterized for response time. This working electrode is then surgically implanted, by standard stereotaxic technique, into the desired brain locus. At the same time, reference and auxiliary electrodes are implanted, typically at the brain surface. Electrochemical measurements are then begun, and continued for the duration of the experiment. The *in vivo* sensitivity of this paradigm is good, and the time resolution of high-speed versions (fast cyclic voltammetry, high-speed chronoamperometry) is excellent, allowing 10–20 independent measurements of neurotransmitter efflux per second (322).

Both *in vivo* brain microdialysis and *in vivo* brain voltammetric electrochemistry are markedly superior to older *in vitro* and *ex vivo* neurochemical paradigms, because they are real-time paradigms allowing correlations between neurochemistry and ongoing behavior, and because they eliminate the artifactual elevations in extracellular neurotransmitter concentrations seen at death with *in vitro* and *ex vivo* paradigms (329). In their most sophisticated usages, both *in vivo* brain microdialysis and *in vivo* brain voltammetric electrochemistry are carried out in awake animals to obviate artifacts introduced by anesthesia.

In vivo Brain Microdialysis Studies

Using *in vivo* brain microdialysis, a number of laboratories have shown that cocaine produces a robust enhancement of extracellular DA in the neostriatal and nucleus accumbens terminal projection areas of the reward-relevant mesotelencephalic DA system (117, 330–339). This enhancement of extracellular DA is more pronounced in the nucleus accumbens than in other forebrain DA loci (330), and is dose-dependent (339). The extracellular DA levels measured in forebrain DA loci after cocaine administration closely mirror the extracellular levels of cocaine itself in the same loci (331, 335, 340). The DA enhancing effect is seen whether the cocaine is exogenously administered by the experimenter or self-administered by the animal (332, 333). Relative re-elevation of extracellular DA evoked by cocaine, rather than absolute amount of extracellular DA evoked by cocaine, may be the critical factor correlating with cocaine self-administration, since animals self-administering cocaine who had lengthy previous repeated exposure to the drug show lower cocaine-induced enhancement of extracellular DA than animals self-administering cocaine who had no previous exposure to the drug (332, 333). Thus, repeated use of cocaine over extended time periods may reduce the reward threshold, i.e., the required amount of extracellular DA necessary for reward (332), perhaps due to the development of DA receptor supersensitivity (341, 342), which amplifies the reward signal. Alternatively, repeated cocaine use over extended time periods may result in decreased reward from the same amount of cocaine self-administered in the future, which would agree with some human reports, in which some cocaine users state that they continually "chase the first high" and never successfully re-achieve it. In animals repeatedly given cocaine so as to evoke cocaine sensitization (343, 344), enhanced DA efflux is observed in both the nucleus accumbens and neostriatum (335, 338), with cross-sensitization to methamphetamine (334). The enhanced DA efflux seen with cocaine sensitization may be in part accounted for by increased local concentrations of cocaine in relevant brain sites (335), a finding which gains special significance in view of reports that DA synthesis rate appears to decrease in cocaine sensitization (345–347). Cocaine's enhancing effects on extracellular DA in reward-relevant forebrain DA loci are blocked by tetrodotoxin, which prevents action potentials by blocking voltage-dependent Na^+ channels, indicating that cocaine's effects on forebrain DA reward neurons require the functional integrity of those neurons, which is congruent with cocaine's actions as a specific inhibitor of the reuptake of neuronally-released DA from the synaptic cleft (348, 349).

Combining *in vivo* microdialysis and drug self-administration, Pettit and Justice (339) showed that animals intravenously self-administering cocaine adopt a paced and measured pattern of self-infusion which, after an initial burst of responding to produce a loading dose of cocaine and quickly elevated extracellular DA levels in the nucleus accumbens, maintains extracellular DA levels in the nucleus accumbens at significantly elevated, stable levels that oscillate within a relatively constrained range. Thus, animals volitionally self-administering cocaine appear to regulate their self-infusion behavior so as to deliberately titrate a specific, set, stable level of extracellular DA in the reward-critical DA terminal projection fields of the nucleus accumbens (see later discussions for additional experiments using *combined* drug *self*-administration and *in vivo* neurochemistry or *in vivo* electrophysiology techniques).

Amphetamine also produces a robust enhancement of extracellular DA in reward-relevant neostriatal and nucleus accumbens DA terminal projection areas as measured by *in vivo* microdialysis (117, 123, 323, 330, 349–357), with stronger effect in the nucleus accumbens than in other forebrain DA loci (330, 350). When the amphetamine is microinjected directly into the DA reward loci, instead of administered systemically, the enhancing effect on extracellular DA is extremely potent (352, 357). Neither abolition of action potentials by tetrodotoxin nor depletion of vesicular DA pools by reserpine has any significant effect on amphetamine's extracellular DA-enhancing effects in reward loci. On the other hand, inhibition of DA synthesis by αMPT or inhibition of the membrane-bound DA uptake carrier by nomifensine effectively inhibits amphetamine's effect on extracellular DA in forebrain reward loci. Thus, amphetamine acts as a presynaptic DA releaser, in contrast to cocaine's reuptake blockade mechanism, but does not release DA by action-potential-dependent exocytosis (123, 353, 355). Rather, amphetamine appears to preferentially release DA from the newly-synthesized DA pool, possibly via a DA-carrier mediated mechanism (123, 353, 356). In animals given chronic amphetamine so as to produce amphetamine sensitization, a significantly increased DA efflux to amphetamine challenge is seen, but with no effect on basal DA efflux (355). 3,4-Methyl-enedioxymethamphetamine (MDMA), the amphetamine analogue known by the street name "Ecstasy," also robustly enhances extracellular DA levels in forebrain terminal loci of the reward-relevant mesotelencephalic DA system in freely-moving animals (358). This report also underscores the importance of doing these types of experiments in awake rather than anesthetized animals, since the same authors report that MDMA *decreases* extracellular DA levels in anesthetized animals (359).

Morphine also produces robust dose-dependent enhancement of extracellular DA in reward-relevant neostriatal and nucleus accumbens DA terminal loci as measured by *in vivo* microdialysis (123, 330, 360–362). This effect is duplicated by other μ opiate receptor agonists, including methadone, levorphanol, and fentanyl (115, 360), and by the μ-selective opioid peptide agonist [D-Ala^2,methyl-Phe^4,Gly^5-ol]-enkephalin (DAMGO) (362, 363). This effect is antagonized by low-dose naloxone and by the irreversible μ receptor antagonist β-funaltrexamine (360). DAMGO-enhanced extracellular DA in the nucleus accumbens is antagonized by the highly specific μ opioid antagonist D-Pen-Cys-Tyr-D-Trp-Orn-Thr-Pen-Thr-NH$_2$ (363), which does not itself affect basal DA levels. The δ-selective opioid peptide agonist [D-Pen^2,D-Pen^5]-enkephalin (DPDPE) also enhances extracellular DA in the nucleus accumbens when microinjected intracerebroventricularly (363), and the highly specific δ opioid antagonist N-allyl$_2$-Tyr-Aib-Aib-Phe-Leu-OH (ICI 174,864), which by itself has no effect on extracellular DA, blocks DPDPE's DA-enhancing effects (363). Provocatively, κ opiate receptor agonists (bremazocine, tifluadom, U-50,488, and the dynorphin derivative N-CH$_3$-Tyr-Gly-Gly-Phe-Leu-Arg-N-CH$_3$-Arg-D-Leu-NHC$_2$H$_5$ [E-2078]), which are *aversive* rather than appetitive to animals (364, 365), have been shown to *inhibit* rather than stimulate DA efflux in forebrain reward loci (330, 360). That this inhibition of DA efflux is mediated by endogenous κ opioid receptor mechanisms is buttressed by the finding that the selective κ opioid receptor antagonist norbinaltorphimine attenuates E-2078's inhibition of DA efflux in nucleus accumbens (363). The enhancing effect on DA efflux of morphine and other μ opiate receptor agonists is significantly stronger in the nucleus accumbens than in the neostriatum (330, 360). The enhanced DA efflux in nucleus accumbens is also seen with direct microinjection of μ opioid agonist into the ventral tegmental area, nucleus of origin of the mesolimbic DA reward neurons projecting to nucleus accumbens (362). Studies with tetrodotoxin show that opiate-agonist-induced enhancement of DA efflux in nucleus accumbens is action-potential-dependent (123, 363). Selective 5-HT$_3$ antagonism, either systemically administered or microinjected directly into the ventral tegmental area, antagonizes morphine's enhancement of DA release in nucleus accumbens (361, 362). Microinjections of baclofen, an agonist of the GABA$_B$ receptor, directly into the ventral tegmental area, blocks μ opiate-agonist-induced enhancement of DA release in nucleus accumbens (366), suggesting that activation of GABA$_B$ receptors on DA perikarya inhibits DA reward functions.

It should be noted that these *in vivo* microdialysis findings of opiate-induced enhancement of extracellular DA are in line with findings of opiate-induced enhancement of DA release *in vivo* as inferred from measurements of 3-methoxytyramine in discrete brain loci (see 367 for review).

It should also be noted that there is a remarkable correlation between the specific doses of μ, δ, and κ opioid agonists found to cause DA enhancement or inhibition in the nucleus accumbens (363) and the specific doses of μ, δ, and κ opioid agonists found to cause appetitive or aversive effects (364, 365) in the conditioned place preference paradigm of reward (see also later).

Nicotine enhances extracellular DA levels in both nucleus accumbens and neostriatum (120, 330, 368), with more pronounced effects in nucleus accumbens (120, 330). Muscarinic cholinergic agonists and antagonists are without effect on DA efflux in forebrain reward loci (368). Nicotine's enhancing effect on DA efflux is blocked by 5-HT$_3$ antagonists (362). Alcohol also enhances extracellular DA levels in both nucleus accumbens and neo-

striatum with more pronounced effects in nucleus accumbens (115, 119, 310, 330). This effect of alcohol is dose-dependent; low and moderate doses enhance DA efflux while the highest dose produces a biphasic effect—initial inhibition of DA release followed (as the high dose begins to wear off, as assessed by independent measures) by facilitation of DA efflux (119). The mechanism of action by which alcohol enhances DA efflux is not known, but some clues to its action may be that alcohol appears to potentiate L-dopa's augmentation of brain DA (369), and that low-dose γ-butyrolactone and low-dose apomorphine each block alcohol's enhancing effects on DA efflux (119). The abusable dissociative anesthetic phencyclidine also enhances extracellular DA levels in both nucleus accumbens (370) and neostriatum (114) after either systemic administration (114) or local intracranial microinjection (369), with preferential effects in the nucleus accumbens (371). Barbiturates, including pentobarbital, phenobarbital, and barbital, enhance extracellular DA levels in both nucleus accumbens and neostriatum, with more pronounced effects in nucleus accumbens (115). This effect of barbiturates is dose-dependent; low doses enhance DA efflux while high doses inhibit it (115). Δ^9-Tetrahydrocannabinol, the psychoactive constituent of marihuana and hashish, also enhances extracellular DA levels in nucleus accumbens (372), neostriatum (373, 374), and medial prefrontal cortex (375), all DA terminal fields of the reward-relevant mesotelencephalic DA system. At least in the nucleus accumbens, this effect is calcium-dependent and tetrodotoxin-sensitive (372).

As noted by Di Chiara, Imperato, and coworkers (330, 376), a common theme runs through all of these studies: drugs that are abused by humans and self-administered by laboratory animals act to produce enhanced extracellular DA levels in the terminal projection loci of the reward-relevant mesotelencephalic DA system, with the nucleus accumbens as a focal and extremely sensitive site of this action. Within the nucleus accumbens, drugs of abuse (cocaine, amphetamine, morphine) preferentially increase extracellular DA in the "shell" subportion of nucleus accumbens as compared to the "core" subportion [376], congruent with the suggestion that the "shell" subportion of nucleus accumbens is specialized for mediating brain reward functions (see [231] and later discussions of this point). Interactions have been noted between the enhanced DA produced in nucleus accumbens by abusable substances and normal biological reward functions apparently mediated by the nucleus accumbens (377).

Given naloxone's ability to block the brain-reward enhancing effects of a wide range of abusable substances as assessed in the already discussed electrical brain-stimulation reward paradigm, it would be interesting to know if naloxone similarly blocks the DA enhancing effects of abusable substances as assessed with the *in vivo* brain microdialysis paradigm. This has been tested only for opiates (115) and for Δ^9-tetrahydrocannabinol (372), and in both cases low doses of naloxone effectively block the enhancing effects on extracellular DA levels.

In Vivo Brain Voltammetric Electrochemistry Studies

Unfortunately, early *in vivo* brain voltammetric electrochemical techniques were flawed by an inability to distinguish between catecholamines and ascorbic acid (378–381), and between indoles and uric acid (382–384). Since ascorbate levels far exceed DA levels in forebrain DA terminal loci, and since at least some abusable substances (e.g., amphetamines) produce a profound elevation of brain ascorbate levels (380, 381, 385), this was a source of confounding in many early studies. Another major source of difficulty also attended early *in vivo* brain voltammetric electrochemical studies: with the combination of some early electrodes and the slow voltammetric scanning techniques used in many early studies, DA measurements were confounded by the electrocatalytic regeneration of DA in the presence of ascorbic acid (386, 387). Also, many early *in vivo* brain voltammetric electrochemical techniques were unable to distinguish DA from 3,4-dihydroxyphenylacetic acid (DOPAC) (for discussion, see 388). For these and other reasons, many early reports of enhanced DA release by abusable substances, assessed voltammetrically, are either erroneous or very difficult to interpret. Recently, however, *in vivo* voltammetric laboratory techniques have been improved by the development of neurotransmitter-selective recording procedures (322) involving, among other things, (a) alterations of electrode working surfaces to impart high selectivity for specific molecules and (b) use of molecule-specific electrochemical signatures. With these newer techniques, studies of the effects of abusable substances on extracellular DA in forebrain reward loci are less questionable.

Using these newer voltammetric techniques, cocaine has been shown to robustly augment extracellular DA in both the nucleus accumbens and neostriatum (389–391). The effect is seen both with systemic cocaine administration (389, 390) and with local cocaine microinjections directly into DA terminal regions (391). The effect is seen on both electrical- and K$^+$-stimulated DA release (389–391), but not on basal extracellular DA levels (391). Cocaine's augmentation of the extracellular DA electrochemical signal differs qualitatively from the augmentation produced by other monoamine uptake inhibitors (390, 391), suggesting that cocaine's mechanism of action may differ from that of other reuptake blockers (e.g., nomifensine). Cocaine's augmentation of extracellular DA in these studies is similar to its action in brain slice preparations using voltammetric electrochemical recordings (392). When cocaine is given chronically, both DA reuptake and electrically-stimulated (by stimulation of the medial forebrain bundle) DA release in the nucleus accumbens are robustly augmented (393). This augmentation is temporary, disappearing after 10 days of abstinence from cocaine, and may represent neuronal compensatory responses to prolonged uptake blockade of synaptic DA by cocaine (393).

Amphetamine also augments extracellular DA in forebrain reward loci as measured by in vivo brain voltammetric electrochemistry (394–407). This amphetamine-induced DA augmentation is seen in both mesolimbic (400, 403, 407) and neostriatal (394–402, 405, 406) reward-relevant DA terminal projection fields. A significant rostrocaudal gradient in amphetamine-induced extracellular DA augmentation is seen in the neostriatum (406), the DA increase being highest in rostral neostriatum (over 800% of pre-drug levels) and lowest in the most caudal neostriatum (425% of pre-drug levels). A similar rostrocaudal gradient in amphetamine-evoked extracellular DA in the neostriatum is seen with in vivo brain microdialysis measurements (406). The amphetamine analogue MDMA ("Ecstasy") also robustly enhances extracellular DA levels in forebrain terminal loci of the reward-relevant mesotelencephalic DA system in awake, freely-moving animals as measured by in vivo brain voltammetric electrochemistry (408). This effect of MDMA is dose-dependent and is seen in both nucleus accumbens and neostriatum (408). Methylphenidate similarly enhances extracellular DA in reward-relevant mesolimbic forebrain DA loci as assessed by in vivo brain electrochemistry (407).

In vivo brain voltammetric electrochemistry has been used less than other approaches to study opiate effects on DA release in forebrain reward loci. The extant studies do, however, appear to reveal a pattern of enhanced DA release. Thus, acute morphine administration produces robustly enhanced extracellular DA in the nucleus accumbens (409, 410) and a biphasic effect—early enhancement of extracellular DA followed by later inhibition—in the neostriatum (409–411). The biphasic pattern of enhancement and inhibition seen with voltammetric electrochemistry in the neostriatum after acute morphine is strikingly similar to the biphasic effect of morphine on reward-relevant mesostriatal DA neurons as assessed by single neuron electrophysiological recording studies (412) and by electrical brain-stimulation reward approaches (110). Acute morphine also produces a robust enhancement (≈100% increase) of the DA metabolite homovanillic acid (HVA) in nucleus accumbens (411). When administered systemically for two days in a row, morphine produces increased DA release in nucleus accumbens after a single repeated administration (413), suggesting that DA turnover mechanisms may be altered early in the course of chronic opiate administration. Fentanyl produces a robust (≈150%) increase in neostriatal DOPAC (414). The δ-selective opioid neuropeptide agonist [D-Ala^2,D-Pro^5]-enkephalin appears to be without effect on DA in nucleus accumbens, but inhibits DA release in the neostriatum (415). Provocatively, the κ opiate receptor agonist dynorphin-(1–13), which has the aversive properties common to κ agonists in animals rather than the appetitive properties seen with μ or δ agonists (364, 365), produces a profound and long-lasting inhibition rather than stimulation of DA efflux in the neostriatum as determined with in vivo voltammetric electrochemistry (416).

In awake, freely moving animals, caffeine and theophylline enhance extracellular DA levels in neostriatum as assessed by in vivo voltammetric electrochemistry (417). These effects are dose-dependent; low doses enhance DA efflux while high doses inhibit it (417). Noteworthily, the DA-enhancing effects of caffeine and theophylline are seen only in awake, unanesthetized animals—in anesthetized animals all doses inhibit DA efflux (417), stressing once again the importance of doing these types of in vivo experiments in awake, unanesthetized animals, since the high doses of anesthetics needed to produce immobilizing anesthesia are known to inhibit forebrain DA release signals as measured by in vivo voltammetric electrochemistry (418) (see also the earlier mention of this point with respect to in vivo brain microdialysis). Alcohol produces a robust enhancement of extracellular DA in reward-relevant forebrain DA loci as measured by in vivo voltammetric electrochemistry (419, 420). The effect is seen in both the nucleus accumbens and neostriatum (419, 420), and is seen in both anesthetized (419) and freely moving, unanesthetized (420) animals. Both DA release and DA metabolism are enhanced (419), and these effects are significantly antagonized by pretreatment with the calcium channel blocker nifedipine (419). Provocatively, the same dose of nifedipine which blocks alcohol-induced enhancement of DA metabolism and release in forebrain reward loci also blocks animal preference for alcohol, as determined by relative intake of alcohol versus water in a free-choice situation (419), suggesting that alcohol's rewarding properties may involve calcium-channel mechanisms modulating DA release in forebrain reward loci. The abusable dissociative anesthetic phencyclidine also enhances extracellular DA levels in neostriatum after local intracranial microinjection, as measured by in vivo voltammetric electrochemistry (421). The phencyclidine analog MK-801 markedly enhances DA metabolism in the nucleus accumbens at intraperitoneal doses as low as 0.1 mg/kg, as measured by in vivo voltammetric electrochemistry (422). Studies of benzodiazepine action on DA function in reward-relevant brain loci using in vivo voltammetric electrochemistry have been interpreted as indicating that benzodiazepines inhibit DA function. Thus, 10 mg/kg diazepam significantly reduces DOPAC levels in striatum (423) and 10 mg/kg flurazepam significantly reduces the normal nocturnal rise in both HVA levels and the DOPAC/DA ratio in nucleus accumbens (424, 425). However, several points regarding these studies must be made. First, the doses of benzodiazepines administered were massive, and since it is well established that, for some drugs of abuse, low doses enhance DA efflux in reward relevant DA brain loci while high doses inhibit it (see earlier discussion of this point), the benzodiazepine doses may simply have been out of the DA-enhancing range. Second, each of these studies (423–425) measures DA efflux inferentially (on the basis of DOPAC and HVA levels) rather than directly, and it is well established on the basis of in vivo brain microdialysis studies that some drugs of abuse increase extracellular DA while simultaneously decreasing DOPAC and HVA. Third, the pattern of benzodiazepine-induced changes in DOPAC and HVA reported in these studies is strikingly amphetamine-like. Fourth, low-dose benzodiazepines augment food consumption and induce spontaneous eating in many species (426–436), behaviors known to correlate with DA efflux in reward-relevant forebrain DA loci (117) and to even be mediated by the same neural fibers mediating electrical brain-stimulation reward (437, 438). In addition, this low-dose benzodiazepine-induced feeding is blocked by naloxone (431, 434) and appears identical to the augmented feeding induced by low-dose barbiturates (427, 433). For all these reasons, it does not appear to this reviewer that claims based on in vivo voltammetric electrochemistry that benzodiazepines inhibit DA function in brain reward loci can at this point be considered definitive. Δ^9-Tetrahydrocannabinol, the psychoactive constituent of marihuana and hashish, enhances extracellular DA levels in reward-relevant forebrain DA loci as measured by in vivo voltammetric electrochemistry (374).

Thus, the same common theme can be seen in these in vivo voltammetric electrochemistry studies as previously noted in the in vivo brain microdialysis studies—substances that are abused by humans and self-administered by laboratory animals act to produce enhanced extracellular DA levels in the terminal projection loci of the reward-relevant mesotelencephalic DA system, with the nucleus accumbens as a focal and extremely sensitive site of this action.

In Vivo Electrophysiological Studies

Clearly, one of the ways in which abusable substances can enhance extracellular DA release in reward-relevant brain loci is to increase the firing rate of reward-relevant DA neural fibers of the mesotelencephalic DA system. Thus, classical *in vivo* single-neuron electrophysiological recording techniques can also be applied to the question of activation of reward-relevant DA neural systems in the brain by abusable substances. There is in fact a large literature on this topic, and the present review must therefore perforce be selective.

Equally clearly, enhancement of presynaptic DA neuronal firing in reward relevant DA circuits would not be an appropriate mechanism of action for abusable substances acting directly on presynaptic DA release and/or reuptake (e.g., cocaine, amphetamines). In fact, due to compensatory neural feedback, autoreceptor-mediated, and/or enzymatic regulatory mechanisms, many such substances would be expected to inhibit presynaptic DA neural firing while enhancing overall synaptic function in reward-relevant DA synapses. Thus, single neuron microelectrode recording studies show that cocaine inhibits presynaptic DA neural firing (439) while enhancing extracellular DA in reward-relevant DA forebrain synapses (117, 330–339, 389–393) and enhancing the normal postsynaptic electrical effects of DA synaptic functioning in reward loci (440). Similarly, the acute inhibitory effect of amphetamine on the firing rate of mesotelencephalic DA neurons is well documented (441–444), but the overall net effect of amphetamine is one of enhanced DA synaptic action in reward-relevant DA synapses (117, 123, 323, 330, 349–357, 394–407). Interestingly, dose-response analyses of the electrophysiological effects of amphetamine on the activity of dopaminoceptive cells (i.e., neurons efferent to the ascending DA reward neurons) in forebrain reward loci reveal qualitative as well as quantitative changes in response to amphetamine (445–446). At low doses (less than 2.5 mg/kg), amphetamine dose-dependently increases synaptic DA levels and dose-dependently enhances the normal postsynaptic electrical effects of the dopaminoceptive cells, while dose-dependently inhibiting the firing rate of the presynaptic DA neurons. At high doses (greater than 2.5 mg/kg), however, a quantitative change occurs such that the dopaminoceptive cells become profoundly activated in the absence of further changes in synaptic DA levels (319, 445, 446).

Opiate-induced enhancement of the firing of reward-relevant mesotelencephalic DA neurons is well established (116, 118, 121, 122, 412, 447–452). Mesolimbic DA neurons originating in the ventral tegmental area and projecting to nucleus accumbens are preferentially sensitive to this opiate-induced activation (448). Opiate action on the firing rate of reward-relevant mesotelencephalic DA neurons is heterogeneous; some DA neurons are activated by opiates while others are inhibited (412, 450, 451). This dual action, with some DA reward neurons activated and some inhibited by opiates, may well constitute the neural substrate for the observation that electrical brain-stimulation reward is enhanced by opiates in some brain reward loci but inhibited in others (110) and also for the observation that extracellular DA is enhanced by opiates in some reward-relevant forebrain DA terminal loci but inhibited in others (409–411). While the action of μ opiate receptor agonists on the firing rate of mesotelencephalic DA neurons in reward-relevant brain loci is primarily an activating one, κ opiate receptor agonists (which have aversive rather than appetitive properties in animals [364, 365]) *inhibit* the firing rates of these same neurons (452). Although the neural mechanisms by which opiates activate the firing rates of DA neurons in reward-relevant loci are not known, some hypotheses are possible. A direct excitatory action mediated via either axo-axonic receptors or axo-somatodendritic receptors cannot be ruled out, in view of the presence of endogenous opioid peptide receptors on the axon terminals of mesotelencephalic DA neurons (274–276) and in view of recent demonstrations of direct excitatory effects of opiates on nerve membranes, as assessed by increased durations of calcium components of action potentials of dorsal root ganglion neurons in culture (453, 454). On the other hand, the widespread inhibitory effects of μ opiates on nerve membranes (455–457) makes a disinhibitory mechanism (458) more likely. Thus, abusable opiates may stimulate the firing of DA reward neurons by directly inhibiting other neurons, possibly in the ventral

tegmental area (459), which are tonically inhibitory to the mesolimbic DA reward neurons.

Nicotine also acutely activates mesotelencephalic DA neurons, as measured by single neuron electrophysiological recording techniques (460). The activating effect is dose-dependent within the range of 50–500 μg/kg administered intravenously. The same range of doses was more than three times as effective on mesolimbic DA neurons as on mesostriatal DA neurons, and all nicotine-induced activation of DA neurons was prevented or reversed by intravenous mecamylamine, implicating the involvement of nicotinic cholinergic receptors in mediating this neural activation (460). These results suggest that nicotine shares with other abusable substances the characteristic of being selectively effective in activating mesolimbic DA neurons that originate in the ventral tegmental area and project to the nucleus accumbens (460). Alcohol also enhances the firing rates of mesotelencephalic DA neurons in reward-relevant brain loci (461). The effects of phencyclidine and phencyclidine analogs on DA neuronal firing rates are interesting. When administered directly onto mesotelencephalic DA neurons, phencyclidine inhibits spontaneous DA neuronal firing in a manner similar to local applications of DA itself (462–466). When administered systemically, both phencyclidine itself and the phencyclidine analog N-[1-(2-thiophenyl)cyclohexyl]piperidine (TCP) elicit dose-dependent biphasic effects on the firing rate of identified mesotelencephalic DA neurons (464, 467). At low doses, an activation of DA neuron firing rate is seen, followed by inhibition at higher doses (464, 467). When administered systemically, the phencyclidine analogue MK-801 activates DA neurons in a manner equipotent to that of phencyclidine itself (468). Diazepam, the prototypical benzodiazepine, markedly excites mesolimbic DA neurons in the ventral tegmental area when administered intravenously (469). This excitation is reversed by the benzodiazepine antagonist Ro 15–1788. The same doses of diazepam potently inhibit non-DA substantia-nigra-pars-reticulata-like neurons in the ventral tegmental area, suggesting that benzodiazepines act directly on these latter non-DA cells to produce inhibition of neuronal activity and a disinhibition of the ventral tegmental area mesolimbic DA neurons (469). Curiously, at the doses tested, chlordiazepoxide and flurazepam did not mimic diazepam's potent activating effect on DA neurons (469).

In Vivo Brain Chemistry Measurements in Brain Reward Circuits during Self-Administration of Abusable Substances, as Assessed by Microdialysis, Voltammetric Electrochemistry, and Electrophysiology

As already noted, in the last few years a number of research groups have begun to combine *self*-administration techniques with *in vivo* microdialysis, *in vivo* voltammetric electrochemistry, and *in vivo* electrophysiology techniques for direct measurements of the functioning of the "second-stage" DA reward neurons (which, as noted earlier, appear to be the principal substrates for the reward-enhancing properties of abusable substances) during behaviorally separate subcomponents of volitional *self*-administration of abusable substances.

Using *in vivo* microdialysis techniques, four different laboratories (Hurd et al., Justice et al., Koob et al., and Wise et al.) have reported that nucleus accumbens extracellular DA levels are elevated during cocaine self-administration (333, 335, 339, 470–473). A relatively consistent picture emerges from these experiments. First, nucleus accumbens DA is *contingently* elevated by individual cocaine reinforcements during cocaine self-administration. Second, regardless of dosing regimen, nucleus accumbens DA levels are tonically elevated by a very large amount (200–800%) at the beginning of cocaine self-administration, and then for the duration of the drug-taking session fluctuate phasically—in a reinforcement-contingent fashion—within a relatively constrained range at the upper end of the large tonic elevation. Third, these phasic DA fluctuations are time-locked to the drug reinforcements. Fourth, when the drug amount received by the animal per reinforcement is varied, greater DA elevations and longer inter-response times follow injections of higher doses. Fifth, animals appear to regulate their drug-taking behavior so as to deliberately titrate a given level of extracellular DA within the reward-critical nucleus accumbens DA synapses. Sixth, the *absolute* amount of DA within the nucleus accumbens extracellular space does not appear to be the critical factor correlated with the self-administration behavior; rather, *relative* DA increases against the baseline of tonic elevation appear to be the critical factor. Seventh, the phasic DA fluctuations appear consistent with the multiple infusion pharmacokinetics of cocaine. Eighth, animals also appear to titrate drug-taking behavior so as to avoid aversive effects. Taken as a whole, these data strongly suggest that—during *volitional* drug-taking behavior—the rewarding properties of cocaine are primarily mediated by extracellular DA levels in the reward synapses of the nucleus accumbens. This conclusion is strongly congruent with the finding that microinjections of DA antagonists into the nucleus accumbens, but not into other brain areas, block voluntary intravenous cocaine self-administration in laboratory animals (290).

Using *in vivo* microdialysis techniques, Wise and colleagues have reported that nucleus accumbens extracellular DA levels are elevated during opiate (heroin) self-administration (470, 474). Dworkin, Smith, et al. have reported that while noncontingent intravenous heroin administration produced dose-dependent increases in nucleus accumbens extracellular DA, response-contingent heroin *self*-administration did not (475). The reason for this difference from the findings of Wise and colleagues (470, 474) is not apparent to this reviewer.

Also using *in vivo* microdialysis, Koob et al. have reported that nucleus accumbens extracellular DA levels are elevated during voluntary ethanol self-administration (476). Provocatively, dose-effect functions revealed significantly steeper slopes for the DA-enhancing effects of ethanol in rats of the alcohol-preferring P strain than in genetically heterogeneous non-preferring Wistar rats.

Studies using *in vivo* voltammetric electrochemistry techniques for measuring extracellular nucleus accumbens DA during drug self-administration are strangely at variance with those studies, just cited, using *in vivo* brain microdialysis techniques (470). Thus, Wise, Kiyatkin, Gratton, and Stein have reported that electrochemical signals presumably reflecting extracellular DA in nucleus accumbens *rise* phasically to a peak immediately prior to each cocaine or heroin self-administration, and then *fall* immediately after each self-administered intravenous drug injection (470, 477–482). This pattern of electrochemical changes is 180° out of phase with the findings from the *in vivo* microdialysis studies. The reasons for this variance are not apparent. Suggestions range from overstimulation of the DA neurons resulting in temporary depolarization inactivation to the temporary DA neuronal inhibition seen electrophysiologically in a subpopulation of nucleus accumbens neurons in animals working for food or drug reward (discussed later) to fundamental methodological flaws in the electrochemical technique that might permit other electro-oxidizable molecules to be mistaken for DA. In truth, the electrochemistry findings are a conundrum. As Wise has noted (470), ". . . since the voltammetric data that have been collected thus far show changes that are out of phase with the predictions of . . . current theories regarding the role of dopamine in addiction [and, as noted above, with *in vivo* microdialysis data], further studies with, and further refinements of, *in vivo* neurochemical methods are of major importance" (470, p.341).

Using *in vivo* single-neuron electrophysiological recording techniques, three research groups have studied the responses of DA neurons in the ventral tegmental area and nucleus accumbens (as well as other reward-related forebrain loci) to rewarding and reward-associated stimuli. Schultz and his colleagues (483–490) have found that individual DA neurons in both the ventral tegmental area and the nucleus accumbens are selectively activated during different components of a rewarded go–no go task in monkeys. Some DA neurons appear to signal the expectancy activated by the first instruction in each trial, others appear to signal the expectancy activated by specific visual trigger stimuli during each trial, others appear to signal preparation for movement or movement inhibition, others appear to signal the expectancy activated by conditioned stimuli associated with reward, and still others appear to signal the actual receipt of reward. The responses of some of the DA neurons that appear to signal reward expectancy were particularly interesting (484). These DA neuronal activations preceded the delivery of reward, were time-locked to the subsequent reward, and disappeared within a few trials when reward was omitted. Also, changes in the appetitive value of the reward modified the magnitude of these DA neuronal activations, suggesting a relationship between the DA neuronal signaling and the hedonic value of the expected reward (484). In the ventral mesencephalon, DA neurons signaling some aspect of reward or reward-associated stimuli were significantly more numerous in the ventral tegmental area than in adjacent DA loci (487). Since many of the reward-associated DA neurons identified in these experiments responded to reward during learning but not after the task was learned (at which time the same neurons responded to the conditioned, reward-predicting, stimulus), it would seem that DA neurons play an especially important role in reward-driven *learning* (488). Schultz and colleagues also hypothesize that many DA neurons may serve to signal the presence of *high-priority* reward-related stimuli (489), while others may serve to signal errors in reward-prediction (490).

Coupling single-neuron electrophysiological recording from the nucleus accumbens with voluntary intravenous cocaine self-administration in rats, Woodward and colleagues (491) have reported that approximately 20% of nucleus accumbens neurons exhibit altered firing rates in the few seconds *prior* to the rat's emission of the learned behavioral act (lever-pressing) that activated the cocaine infusion apparatus (anticipatory neural responses) while approximately 50% of nucleus accumbens neurons exhibit altered firing rates in the few minutes *after* the rat's emission of the learned behavioral act that activated the cocaine infusion apparatus (post-cocaine neural responses). Approximately two-thirds of the neurons showing anticipatory responses also showed post-cocaine responses. Neurophysiologically, the anticipatory responses were of two types: anticipatory excitatory responses (increased neuronal firing) and anticipatory inhibitory responses (decreased neuronal firing). The post-cocaine responses were similarly of two types: postcocaine excitatory responses and post-cocaine inhibitory responses. Behaviorally, the anticipatory responses were of two types: (*a*) "orienting-related" anticipatory responses (sustained alterations in neuronal firing with an onset centered around self-generated interruption of cocaine-induced behavioral stereotypy and orientation toward the lever), and (*b*) "lever-pressing-related" anticipatory responses (alterations in neuronal firing with a tight temporal relation to the sequences of movements directly related to lever-pressing for the next cocaine infusion). Very importantly, anticipatory-like neuronal activity was not observed during similar movements unrelated to lever-pressing for cocaine. Woodward and colleagues hypothesize that the "orienting-related" anticipatory responses reflect neural ". . . trigger systems activated by a *motivation to obtain reward*," while the "lever-pressing-related" anticipatory responses reflect the ". . . transformation of internal motivational states into components of a *sustained motor plan to acquire reward* (in this case, presumably a euphoric state elicited by cocaine)" (491, p.1239). Behaviorally, the post-cocaine neuronal responses (especially post-cocaine inhibition) were predictive of cocaine readministration: "The ramp-like return to baseline firing rates of some neurons . . . during post-cocaine inhibition proved to be a good predictor of the next lever-press" (491, p.1240). Furthermore, higher cocaine doses produced longer periods of post-cocaine inhibition that coincided with a longer self-administration interval, with the return to baseline firing rates of such neurons providing an accurate predictor of subsequent drug self-administration. Systemic administration of D1 or D2 DA receptor antagonists typically produced extinction of cocaine-taking behavior, and blocked the post-cocaine inhibitory response *of neurons that had anticipatory responses*. Neither DA antagonist modified anticipatory neural responses, nor did they affect post-cocaine inhibitory responses in neurons that did not show anticipatory responses. All together, these findings suggest that the role of nucleus accumbens neural circuitry in drug-taking behavior may be two-fold: (*a*) an initiation or trigger mechanism (represented by the anticipatory neuronal responses), which—considering that the anticipatory responses were not affected by DA receptor antagonists—may derive from neural signals carried by non-DA afferents to the nucleus accumbens; and (*b*) a reward mechanism *per se*, directly activated by drug reinforcement (represented by the post-cocaine responses) which—considering that the post-cocaine inhibitory response of neurons with anticipatory responses was blocked by DA receptor antagonists—presumably involves a DA substrate.

Koob and colleagues (492) coupled single-neuron electrophysiological recording from the nucleus accumbens with voluntary intravenous heroin self-administration in rats, and observed post-heroin neuronal inhibitory responses similar to the post-cocaine inhibitory responses observed by Woodward et al. (491). These neuronal inhibitory responses seemed clearly related to the drug-induced reward event, since non-rewarded behavioral responses (similar in behavioral topology to the heroin-reward behavioral responses) did not produce event-related neuronal inhibitory responses in the nucleus accumbens.

Taken altogether, these studies of concurrent *in vivo* microdialysis or *in vivo* single-neuron electrophysiology during volitional *self*-administration of abusable substances (or during volitional *self*-administration of other hedonically salient rewards) present a compelling argument for the intimate involvement of ventral tegmental area and nucleus accumbens DA neural circuits in the regulation of hedonic tone and in drug-induced reward (as well as in other reward-associated neural processes, such as reward expectancy and anticipation, that may well be involved in such clinically crucial phenomena as drug craving). As noted, the *in vivo* voltammetric electrochemistry studies are inexplicably at variance with the *in vivo* microdialysis studies.

PERTURBATIONS OF THE DOPAMINERGIC BRAIN REWARD SYSTEM LEADING TO INCREASED VULNERABILITY TO DRUG-TAKING BEHAVIOR

DA Reward Synapse and Modulatory Mechanisms Acting on the DA Reward System

From many of the separate strands of evidence reviewed here, inferences may be made regarding the neuroanatomy, neurophysiology, neurochemistry, and neuropharmacology of the pleasure/reward circuitry of the brain and of the crucial "second-stage" DA link within this pleasure/reward circuitry, which apparently constitutes the primary neuropharmacological site of action wherein abusable substances act to produce their intensely rewarding effects, and perhaps also wherein are encoded some neural aspects of substance abuse vulnerability and craving. First, the "first-stage" neurons of the reward system appear to originate within the anterior bed nuclei of the medial forebrain bundle, and project caudally along the medial forebrain bundle in a moderately fast-conducting, myelinated, heavily collaterized and diffuse neural system, of unknown neurotransmitter type(s), to synapse within the somato-dendritic zone of DA cell bodies in the ventral tegmental area. Second, these DA neurons of the ventral tegmental area constitute the "second-stage" neurons of the reward system. Third, the ventral tegmental area that gives rise to these "second-stage" DA reward neurons is heavily innervated, and neurophysiologically modulated (in some cases transsynaptically), by numerous synaptic inputs including GABAergic, glutamatergic, serotonergic, noradrenergic, opioid peptidergic (including enkephalinergic, endorphinergic, and dynorphinergic systems [see also 493–516]), cholecystokinergic (517–524), and neurotensinergic (525–533) neural systems. Fourth, the "second-stage" DA reward neurons project rostrally within the medial forebrain bundle to synapse in the nucleus accumbens. Fifth, these "second-stage" DA reward neurons constitute a critical locus for the addictive pharmacological actions of abusable substances. Sixth, within the region of their axonal terminal projections in the nucleus accumbens, these "second-stage" reward neurons are heavily innervated, and neurophysiologically modulated (in some cases transsynaptically), by numerous synaptic inputs including GABAergic, glutamatergic, serotonergic, opioid peptidergic, cholecystokinergic (518, 522, 534–540), and neurotensinergic (527, 530, 541–545) neural systems. Seventh, the most crucial reward synapses within the nucleus accumbens may be defined by their intra-accumbens locations and their synaptic connectivities—i.e., within the accumbens shell, in reward-relevant synaptic plexuses containing an opioid-DA axo-axonic link, a DA-opioid presynaptic-postsynaptic link, and neural inputs from limbic cortex and amygdala (409, 546–562). Eighth, from the nucleus accumbens, additional "third-stage" reward-relevant neurons, some of them opioid peptidergic and/or GABAergic, appear to carry the reward signal further, to or via the ventral pallidum (216–238). Ninth, the profuse, complex, and reciprocal neural interconnec-

tions between the ventral tegmental area, nucleus accumbens, ventral pallidum, amygdala, and bed nuclei of the medial forebrain bundle appear to be critically involved in regulating the functional set-point for hedonic tone (216–238, 546–567). In all of this complex neuronal computational machinery, the DA link between ventral tegmental area and nucleus accumbens seems central and crucial for drug-induced alterations in hedonic tone.

Although previously alluded to, it warrants reemphasis that the drug-sensitive DA "second-stage" component of the reward circuitry appears to be under the modulatory control of a wide variety of other neural systems, including GABAergic, glutamatergic, serotonergic, noradrenergic, and neuropeptide neurotransmitter and neuromodulatory mechanisms (see also 29, 241, 568–586), and theoretically an even wider variety of transsynaptic modulatory influences on the brain-reward systems are possible. Further, it appears that the functioning of the reward system, *and its sensitivity to abusable substances,* can be altered by directly manipulating these other neurotransmitter systems that synaptically interconnect with the DA substrates (241, 587–595), as well as manipulating the DA substrates directly.

Genetically-Imparted DA Reward Perturbations Leading to Increased Vulnerability to Drug-Taking Behavior

For many drugs of abuse, genetic differences influence both drug preferences and propensity for drug self-administration (596–600). Mouse strains that show high ethanol preference and high ethanol self-administration appear to generalize this increased vulnerability to other drugs of abuse such as nicotine and opiates (597, 601, 602). This suggests that some inbred animal strains may have a generalized vulnerability to the rewarding effects of abusable drugs. The Lewis rat strain is particularly interesting in this regard. Lewis strain rats have a high vulnerability for both ethanol and cocaine oral self-administration (601, 603). Furthermore, Lewis rats also: (*a*) learn cocaine or opiate self-administration more readily, (*b*) work harder for cocaine or opiate self-administration, and (*c*) cue-condition for cocaine or opiates more readily, all in comparison to other rat strains (603–605). The author and his coworkers have found that the brain-reward-enhancing property of Δ^9-tetrahydrocannabinol, the addictive substance in marihuana and hashish, is much more pronounced in Lewis rats than in other strains, as measured both by direct electrical brain-stimulation reward and by *in vivo* brain microdialysis of synaptic DA overflow in nucleus accumbens DA reward loci (606–609). This suggests that a *basal* dysfunction in DA regulation within the DA forebrain reward system may constitute a genetic vulnerability to the phenotypic polydrug preferences shown by Lewis rats (609). Congruent with this hypothesis, Nestler et al. have reported *basal* differences in DA neurotransmitter synthesis, transport, and release, as well as DA-dependent receptor, second messenger, and immediate early gene function in DA reward neurons in Lewis as compared to other rat strains (605, 610). Compellingly, the *same* dysfunctional differences in DA neurotransmitter synthesis, transport, and release, as well as DA-dependent receptor, second messenger, and immediate early gene function in DA reward neurons, can be induced by chronic drug administration in genetically *non-vulnerable* rats, and this results in the *same* behavioral phenotype of polydrug preference as seen in the genetically vulnerable Lewis rats (605).

Genetic contributions also appear to play a role in drug abuse vulnerability at the human level (603). Family, twin, and adoption studies all support a substantial genetic component in drug abuse vulnerability and ongoing drug dependence (reviewed in 611). Identifying genetic factors in drug abuse vulnerability is crucial to understanding addiction and, possibly, to identifying clinical subpopulations who may respond differently to potential pharmacotherapies. Linkage analysis in well-defined pedigrees is a powerful approach for studying single gene disorders (612). However, for complex inherited traits, association studies, which are statistical correlations between an inherited condition and polymorphisms occurring in strong candidate genes, may be a superior approach (613, 614). As drug abuse vulnerability does not follow clear Mendelian patterns of inheritance, most genetic studies on drug abuse have been association studies. Considering the wealth of data demonstrating the importance of DA in brain reward mechanisms, polymorphisms in genes that regulate DA neurotransmission are candidates as genetic vulnerability factors for drug abuse (615). The DA D2 and D4 receptors and the DA transporter are some of the candidate genes that have previously been analyzed. An allelic association to Taq I restriction fragment length polymorphisms (RFLPs) located in the D2 receptor gene has been found in alcoholics and drug abusers in some studies (616–619). These results are controversial, as negative association and linkage studies have also been reported (620, 621). However, a meta-analysis conducted on published studies supports a positive association to the D2 Taq A1 and B1 alleles (619). One problem with these polymorphisms is that they are generated by non-functional intronic mutations. Consequently, if the DA D2 gene is involved in drug abuse vulnerability, the Taq polymorphisms must be in linkage disequilibrium with functional alterations located elsewhere in the gene. So far, none have been found. A VNTR polymorphism in the 3′ untranslated region of the DA transporter gene, which has been linked to attention-deficit hyperactivity disorder, has shown a weak association in alcoholics who have specific aldehyde dehydrogenase-2 genotypes and in cocaine-induced paranoia (622–625). However, another association study in polysubstance abusers was negative (626). An association with attention-deficit hyperactivity disorder would be interesting, since a high percentage of children and adolescents with this condition become substance abusers. However, the VNTR polymorphism is nonfunctional and, so far, no significant alterations in the gene have been found that could explain the positive linkage and association findings. A VNTR in the third cytoplasmic loop of the DA D4 gene has been reported to be associated with both alcoholism and novelty seeking behavior (627, 628). The DA D4 gene differs from other DA candidate genes analyzed so far in that the polymorphism has been shown to be functionally significant, as differences in clozapine binding have been found in the 4 and 7 repeat polymorphisms (629). Additional evidence that the DA D4 polymorphism is functionally significant is the fact that it has been found to be associated with the behavioral trait of thrill-seeking (627, 628). No association to the DA D4 gene was detected in a study conducted on alcoholics (630). The DA D3 receptor gene has been found to have a common missense mutation that leads to a serine → glycine substitution (631), but thus far no significant association has been reported in drug or alcohol abusers (632).

Yet another DA-related candidate gene polymorphism for drug abuse vulnerability has recently emerged as a strong possibility—a codon 108/158 catechol-O-methyltransferase gene polymorphism. Catechol-O-methyltransferase plays an important role in regulating DA neurotransmission by inactivating synaptic DA (633). A single gene encodes membrane-bound and soluble forms of the enzyme, which differ by a 50 amino acid hydrophobic N-terminal anchoring sequence present in the membrane-bound form (634). A common enzyme activity polymorphism exists in humans that results in a 3- to 4-fold variation in enzymatic activity (635–639). Approximately 25% of Caucasians express a low activity form of the enzyme, another 25% have a high activity variant, and 50% display an intermediate level of activity (638, 639). In order to identify the genetic basis of this enzymatic variability, Lachman and his colleagues at the Albert Einstein College of Medicine have recently screened the catechol-O-methyltransferase gene by DNA sequence analysis of PCR-amplified genomic fragments, to identify allelic forms of the gene. They found a G → A transition at codon 158 of membrane-bound catechol-O-methyltransferase (corresponding to codon 108 of soluble catechol-O-methyltransferase) that results in a valine to methionine substitution. In retrospect, the two alleles were evident from a comparison of the two catechol-O-methyltransferase cDNA sequences published several years ago (640, 641). In collaboration with Uhl, Vandenbergh, and colleagues of the Addiction Research Center at the National Institute on Drug Abuse, Lachman and colleagues have recently found a significant increase in the frequency of catechol-O-methyltransferase 158[val], the high activity allele, in substance abusers (both opiate preferring and cocaine preferring). This finding is consistent with the hypothesis that blunted DA reward system function enhances vulnerability to drug abuse—as Schuckitt (642) has found for ethanol-responsiveness in alcoholics and sons of alcoholics—since expression of the high activity catechol-O-methyltransferase variant would magnify the decrease in DA. These data suggest that the DA-related codon 108/158 polymorphism could be a factor in genetic vulnerability to drug abuse.

Taking some of these concepts even further, Blum and colleagues (643) have postulated the existence of a generalized "reward deficiency syndrome," subsuming a large class of addictive, impulsive, and compulsive disorders (including drug abuse/dependence and nonchemical [behavioral] addictions) under a common rubric and positing that they have a common genetic basis. They postulate that all these disorders are connected by a common biological substrate—an alteration in the brain system that provides positive reinforcement (positive hedonic tone) for specific behaviors. They further postulate that "reward deficiency syndrome" results from a basal dysfunction of DA brain reward mechanisms. Evidence cited in support of this hypothesis includes the following facts: (a) as noted earlier in this chapter, drugs of abuse (which produce augmented hedonic tone) have one major commonality—they augment DA function as a final common neuropharmacological action, particularly in the DA mesocorticolimbic system so vital for the regulation of reward functions; (b) as also already noted, molecular biological, electrophysiological, and neurochemical studies show considerable differences in the DA reward systems of drug-preferring versus non-preferring genetic strains of rats (see also 644, 645); and (c) alcoholics, cocaine addicts, compulsive gamblers, and patients with obesity (a majority being compulsive eaters) or attention-deficit hyperactivity disorder are reported to possess the A1 D2 receptor allele (646–650). The number of D2 receptors in A1 carriers may be 20–30% lower than those lacking the A1 genotype (648). Also, the likelihood that an individual possesses the A1 genotype increases dramatically when two or more of the clinical conditions noted under (c) above are found to co-exist. Further, animal studies have shown that DA agonists can decrease the consumption/self-administration of various drugs of abuse or reduce drug craving, and that animals deliberately bred for high ethanol preference have *decreased* brain DA function (651–653). In addition, alcoholics possessing the A1/A1 genotype are more responsive to DA agonist therapy (e.g., bromocriptine) for treatment of alcohol craving (654). Provocatively, a predictive model based on Bayes' Theorem of Probability suggests that an individual with the A1 allele for the D2 receptor has a 74% chance of developing one of the disorders that comprises the "reward deficiency syndrome" (643). In sum, the "reward deficiency syndrome" theory holds that addictive, impulsive, and compulsive disorders may have a common genetic basis—DA hypoactivity in reward pathways.

DA Reward Mechanisms and Vulnerability to Drug-Taking Behavior

Whether increased vulnerability to drug-taking behavior is imparted genetically or by other factors, the bulk of the currently available evidence suggests a central role for aberrations of brain DA reward function in imparting such vulnerability. Thus, animals bred for high ethanol self-administration have been shown to have lower densities of DA receptors, lower extracellular DA levels, and lower DA innervation density in DA forebrain reward areas than animals bred for ethanol avoidance (652, 653). Notably, the lower DA innervation densities were found only in DA limbic cortex and the *shell of the nucleus accumbens* (653). There were no difference in DA innervation densities between ethanol preferring and non-preferring rats in other major DA mesolimbic brain loci (653). Moreover, the subpopulation of DA neurons in the ventral tegmental area that project to the nucleus accumbens was found to be smaller (as shown by horseradish peroxidase tracing and immunocytochemical double staining) in the ethanol-preferring as compared to the non-preferring rats (653). In outbred heterogeneous rat strains, propensity to drug self-administration is also correlated with aberrant DA reward system function (655–657). Glick and colleagues have found that low to moderate DA levels are positively correlated with cocaine self-administration rates whereas moderate to high DA levels are negatively correlated with self-administration rates (656). They also found that DA release in the medial prefrontal cortex appears to be an important predictor of initiation of drug-taking (657). They suggest that ". . . normal variability in drug seeking behavior is at least in part attributable to individual differences in the activity of brain DA systems." Differentiating between initiation and maintenance of drug-taking behavior, they conclude that the nucleus accumbens is a "critical component" in both mechanisms (656). Piazza, Le Moal, Simon and colleagues have reported that individual differences in locomotor responses to novelty are predictive of differences in rats' tendencies to begin amphetamine self-administration, and that endogenous variations in brain DA systems mediating both stress and drug reward are responsible for individual differences in propensity to engage in drug-taking behavior (655, 658, 659). Interestingly, they report that animals showing high DA responses to cocaine challenge have an increased vulnerability for cocaine self-administration (655).

DA Reward Mechanisms and Relapse to Drug-Taking Behavior

The phenomenon of drug "priming"—the ability of a "priming" drug dose to reinstate previously extinguished drug-taking (660)—has been studied in animals as a model of relapse to drug-taking, primarily by Stewart and her colleagues (661–666). In this paradigm, the ability of drugs (or other stimuli, including stressors and drug-associated sensory stimuli) to re-establish extinguished drug-taking habits in laboratory animals is measured. As noted by Stewart and Wise (664), "the most potent stimulus for renewed responding that has been demonstrated in this model is a free 'priming' injection of the training drug; a priming injection of the training drug can re-establish extinguished habits much as a single drink, cigarette, or injection are thought to re-establish such habits in detoxified ex-addicts." Provocatively, such priming injections can be successfully given intravenously *or directly into component parts of the brain reward circuitry— most crucially the ventral tegmental area or nucleus accumbens* (665, 666), *but not into other brain loci.* Equally provocatively, cross-priming (from one class of abusable substances to another) has been demonstrated. Thus, priming doses of morphine reinstate cocaine self-administration (665) and priming doses of amphetamine or the DA agonist bromocriptine reinstate heroin-trained responding (666, 667). In this reviewer's opinion, such cross-priming between drugs of different classes speaks powerfully to the existence of *common* neurobiological and *common* neuropharmacological substrates for the actions of abusable substances within the DA reward circuitry of the brain, as detailed in previous sections of this chapter. Importantly, the drugs and doses known to re-initiate drug self-administration in both humans and animals are drugs and doses known to *increase* DA function within the brain's reward circuitry, as detailed earlier in this chapter. Thus, acute administration of DA-mimetic compounds precipitates relapse to drug-taking, just as acute heroin precipitates clinical relapse in human opiate abusers, and just as a single cigarette precipitates relapse to smoking in former nicotine addicts.

Stress is also a precipitant of relapse to drug-taking at the human level, and consequently has been studied in several animal models of drug self-administration—including fixed ratio reinforcement, progressive ratio reinforcement, and the drug reinstatement model noted in the previous paragraph. Working in this area, Shaham and colleagues have shown that environmental stress (*a*) increases opiate self-administration and opiate preferences in animals (668); (*b*) increases opiate *appetitiveness* as assessed by self-administration performance and break-points on progressive ratio reinforcement schedules (669, 670); (*c*) enhances the *reinforcing efficacy* of drug self-administration (670); (*d*) promotes relapse to drug-taking behavior (671, 672); and (*e*) acutely precipitates reinstatement of drug self-administration (672). Provocatively, Shaham and Stewart report (672) that *the same parameters of stress that acutely reinstate drug-taking in the self-administration animals increase DA overflow in the nucleus accumbens in drug naive animals,* implicating a common DA-mediated neurobiological mechanism in drug-induced and stress-induced relapse to drug-taking behavior. Similarly, DA overflow in the nucleus accumbens was increased by systemic injections of morphine, an effect that was reversed by an injection of naltrexone given 40 minutes later to induce opiate withdrawal. As noted, an interpretation of these results is that stressors can reinstate drug-taking behavior by activating neural systems in common with those activated by drugs of abuse. Again, the crucial role of the DA reward system of the brain appears evident.

DA Reward Mechanisms and Drug Craving

DA REWARD MECHANISMS AND THE CONDITIONED PLACE PREFERENCE (CUE PREFERENCE) ANIMAL MODEL OF DRUG-SEEKING

Drug craving is widely accepted to be a major component of drug addiction and dependence (673–679). Drug and/or alcohol addicts frequently report intense and/or prolonged yearning for additional drug or alcohol while in either voluntary or enforced abstinence periods, and a causal relation between such yearnings and drug or alcohol readministration has been suggested by many observers (674, 676–679). Thus, craving is typically experienced by chronic substance abusers when they have been deprived of drug for a period of time. By definition, then, animal models of craving must differ from the acute-administration and self-administration paradigms detailed earlier. Since craving at the human level is often elicited by sensory stimuli previously associated with drug-taking, various conditioning paradigms have been used to model craving in laboratory animals. One of the most widely used is conditioned place preference (680–682) (also referred to as conditioned cue preference). In this paradigm, animals are tested (when free of drug) to determine whether they prefer an environment in which they previously received drug as compared to an environment in which they previously received saline or vehicle. If the animal, in the drug-free state, consistently chooses the environment previously associated with drug delivery, the inference is drawn not only that the drug was appetitive but also that the appetitive hedonic value was coded in the brain and is accessible during the drug-free state, which, if not craving *per se,* would appear to be closely related to craving. The questions obviously arise: (*a*) is craving coded in the same neural circuitry as drug-induced reward? and (*b*) do pharmacological manipulations and/or lesions of the reward-relevant DA circuitry alter conditioned place preferences induced by abusable substances? With respect to the first question, many workers have, out of simple regard for parsimony, posited that craving *is* coded in the reward circuitry of the forebrain, and some have even posited that craving results directly from a functional deficiency of DA in the reward-relevant DA circuitry (676). With respect to the second and closely related question, it is now quite clear, on the basis of much work (reviewed in 682), that pharmacological manipulations or lesions of the mesotelencephalic DA system profoundly alter place conditioning of abusable substances, and that the mesotelencephalic DA system almost certainly serves as an important substrate for the central encoding in the brain of the hedonic value imparted by abusable substances. Furthermore, and very provocatively, White and Hiroi have shown (546, 547, 683, 684) that different aspects of conditioned hedonic value appear to depend upon different neurochemically specific DA substrates. Specifically, in amphetamine place conditioning, the newly synthesized DA pool appears to subserve the neural *en*coding of hedonic value, while the vesicular DA pool appears crucial for the behavioral expression or readout of that previously encoded hedonic value (546, 547, 683). Furthermore, while systemically administered D1 and D2 DA antagonists blocked both acquisition and expression of conditioned place preference for amphetamine, selective D1 antagonism was significantly more effective at blocking behavioral expression or readout of previously encoded hedonic value than D2 antagonists. Also, pre-conditioning and post-conditioning lesions of the lateral amygdaloid nucleus impaired the conditioned place preference for amphetamine. It is concluded on the basis of these place experiments that the behavioral expression or readout of conditioned incentive stimuli for amphetamine (i.e., the animal homolog of amphetamine craving) is mediated by a DA neural system that involves the vesicular DA pool and the D1 DA receptor in the nucleus accumbens and the lateral amygdaloid nucleus (546, 547, 683). These workers have also demonstrated that the ventral pallidum is involved in the acquisition of amphetamine conditioned place preference but *not* its behavioral expression or readout (685). If the conditioned place preference paradigm validly models drug-conditioned incentive stimuli, as many believe, researchers may be on the road to understanding the neurochemical substrates for the craving that substance abusers feel when confronted visually with syringes, needles, crack vials, smoking pipes, or even the street corner where they normally buy their illicit drugs.

DA REWARD MECHANISMS DURING CHRONIC DRUG ADMINISTRATION AND WITHDRAWAL

In contrast to the clear-cut and agreed-upon effects of acute administration of addicting drugs on brain reward mechanisms cited previously, the effects of *chronic* administration of abuse-prone drugs on reward mechanisms are less clear-cut. With respect to neurochemical indices (*in vivo* brain microdialysis measures of DA overflow in forebrain reward loci), a clear difference appears to exist between the effects of *chronic or continuous* administration (or intermittent *high dose* treatment, which presumably produces *continuous* intoxication) and the effects of *intermittent low dose* treatment, which presumably produces *intermittent phasic* stimulation. With *intermittent low doses* of psychostimulants (cocaine, amphetamines), "reverse tolerance" or "sensitization" of DA overflow in forebrain reward loci is seen upon subsequent psychostimulant re-challenge (335, 338, 355, 686–692). Similar psychostimulant neurochemical sensitization has been reported with self-administered, rather than exogenous, dosing (693). This sensitization may extend to basal DA overflow as well as drug-challenge-evoked DA overflow (687, 694). Similar sensitization of DA overflow in forebrain reward loci has been reported for opiates (695, 696). With *chronic continuous administration or intermittent treatment involving high doses* of psychostimulants, decreased DA synthesis is seen (347), and, in withdrawal from such dose regimens, depletion of basal extracellular DA in such brain-reward loci as nucleus accumbens (697–699). When cocaine is administered to emulate human "binges," *decreased basal and cocaine-stimulated DA levels* are reported (700). Reward-related *functional and behavioral* sequelae have also been reported. With *continuous treatment or intermittent treatment with high doses,* acute tolerance to cocaine's rewarding effects develops (701, 702), and withdrawal from the continuous intoxication produced by frequent low-dose cocaine or amphetamine produces *elevations* in brain-stimulation reward thresholds (703–710). In *opiate withdrawal* from chronic dosing regimens (either abstinence withdrawal or precipitated withdrawal), a pattern of *decreased DA levels* in forebrain reward loci (particularly nucleus accumbens) similar to that seen in withdrawal from continuous or high-dose intermittent psychostimulant administration is seen (711–715). Clear reward-related *functional and behavioral* sequelae are also seen in opiate withdrawal (i.e., *elevated* electrical brain-reward thresholds [716, 717]). Also, opiate withdrawal produces conditioned cue *aversion* (715, 716, 718–726). Further, opiate self-administration increases significantly in withdrawal, and the increase correlates with severity of withdrawal (671, 727, 728). Significantly, the neural mechanisms underlying this withdrawal-produced presumptive negative hedonic tone or dysphoria may involve the nucleus accumbens (718, 719), just as the acute-drug-induced positive hedonic tone may. Congruent with these findings from a variety of paradigms, DA depletion in the nucleus accumbens and elevation in brain-reward thresholds have been proposed as neural substrates for post-drug-use anhedonia and drug craving (676, 718, 729). Very importantly, since DA depletion, *unlike other withdrawal symptoms* (730), offers a withdrawal symptom common to psychostimulants, opiates, and ethanol, it may offer a long-sought common denominator for addiction (731). Adding credence to this possibility are findings from studies in which animals are allowed to self-administer intravenous cocaine or heroin and *in vivo* DA neurochemistry is concomitantly monitored in nucleus accumbens by brief-sampling-time microdialysis (470, 471, 474). In these studies, noted earlier in this chapter, both tonic and phasic alterations in nucleus accumbens DA levels were observed as a function of drug self-administration. At the beginning of each self-administration session, an enormous tonic elevation in nucleus accumbens DA occurs after the first "loading" doses of self-administered drug. This tonic DA elevation plateaus quickly, and is then followed by small but significant phasic fluctuations that correlate very tightly with voluntary self-administration. Nucleus accumbens DA *decreases* prior to, and appears to predict, each drug self-administration, whereas nucleus accumbens DA *increases* immediately after each drug self-administration, and appears to correlate with behavioral indices of satiation.

DA REWARD MECHANISMS AND "OPPONENT PROCESS" THEORY OF DRUG CRAVING

From the previously cited evidence, and from "Opponent Process" theory (732, 733), Koob and his colleagues have proposed an opponent process theory of the motivation for drug-taking (718, 729, 734). This theory is based upon the negative reinforcement (i.e., relief from aversive stimuli) that drug-taking in the face of the dysphoria and anhedonia imputed from this evidence entails. The theory holds that drug reinforcers arouse *both* positive (appetitive, pleasurable) and negative (aversive, dysphoric) hedonic processes in the brain, and that these processes oppose one another in a simple dynamic system. The time-dynamics and tolerance patterns of the two processes are hypothesized to differ. The positive hedonic processes are hypothesized to be simple, stable, of short latency and duration, to follow the reinforcer closely, and to develop tolerance rapidly. The negative hedonic processes are hypothesized to be of longer latency and duration (thus, they build up strength and decay more slowly), and to be resistant to the development of tolerance. Thus, if self-administration of an abusable drug is frequently repeated, two correlated changes in hedonic tone are postulated to occur. First, tolerance to the euphoric effects of the drug develops, while at the same time the withdrawal or abstinence syndrome becomes more intense and of longer duration (615, 718, 729, 734). Thus, the positive reinforcing properties of the drug diminish while the negative reinforcing properties (relief of withdrawal-induced anhedonia) strengthen. Koob and colleagues propose that not only are the positive reinforcing properties of abusable drugs mediated by drug effects in the nucleus accumbens, but that opponent processes *within these same brain reward circuits become sensitized* during the development of dependence and thus become responsible for the aversive stimulus properties of drug withdrawal, and therefore ultimately for the negative reinforcement processes that come, in this view, to dominate the motivation for chronic drug abuse. Thus, brain DA reward mechanisms, and the regulatory neural mechanisms controlling them, are conceptualized to dominate not only the positively reinforcing acute "hit," "rush," or "high" resulting from early administration but *also the negatively reinforcing properties that develop with chronic drug use and that are important in the maintenance of drug habits.* Koob and colleagues have postulated that endogenous opioid peptide mechanisms intrinsic to, and synaptically interacting with, the DA reward circuitry of the forebrain are critically involved in this opponent process motivation for drug dependence and addiction. (Such negative hedonic processes within the reward-encoding circuitry of the brain *must differ* from the aversive *physical* abstinence symptoms produced by drug withdrawal, which are mediated by *non-reward-related* neural circuitry involving the periaqueductal gray, locus coeruleus, medial thalamus, and the diencephalic-mesencephalic juncture [314, 735, 736].) Congruent with this concept, the author has gathered evidence—using both *in vivo* electrical brain-stimulation reward and *in vivo* brain voltammetric electrochemistry— suggesting that drug administration *does* evoke both positive and negative affective/hedonic processes within the pleasure/reward DA circuitry of the forebrain (110, 410, 411, 737). Medial brain-reward DA circuitry, originating in the ventral tegmental area and projecting through the medial portions of the medial forebrain bundle to the nucleus accumbens, appears uniquely sensitive to the brain-reward *enhancing* properties of addicting drugs (110, 737). With electrodes in the *medial* portions of the reward circuitry, opiates *enhance* brain-stimulation reward, this enhancement dissipates as time passes following each daily injection, and tolerance to this brain reward enhancement develops with repeated daily morphine injections (110). With electrodes in the *lateral* portions of the reward circuitry, opiates *inhibit* brain-stimulation reward (are *dysphorigenic*), this inhibition dissipates as time passes following each daily injection, and a progressive *augmentation* of this brain reward *inhibition* develops with repeated daily injections (110, 737). Both the medial and lateral loci are DA-mediated (246, 738–740). Thus, these two anatomical domains (medial and lateral) within the DA reward circuitry of the ventral forebrain respond to drug administration in a manner consistent with the predicted behavior of the "positive hedonic processes" and "negative hedonic processes" of Koob et al. Using *in vivo* voltammetric electrochemistry, we have seen that some DA reward neurons respond to drug administration by *inhibition* of DA overflow while other DA neurons within the same circuitry (but anatomically distinct) respond to drug administration by *enhancement* of DA overflow (410, 411, 737). Congruent with these observations are electrophysiological data showing that some DA reward neurons respond to opiate administration by inhibiting their firing (741) rather than by the enhanced firing (116, 742) normally seen. This, in turn, is congruent with recent reports from Woodward et al. and from Schultz et al., reviewed earlier in this chapter, concerning the heterogeneity of response patterns of reward-related DA neurons in nucleus accumbens.

Also congruent with some of these concepts are (*a*) the findings of Aston-Jones (743) that nucleus accumbens DA neural mechanisms are not only important in the acute rewarding effects of abusable substances, but also important in drug withdrawal, with the latter effects mediated by DA D2 receptors; and (*b*) the findings of van der Kooy and colleagues that DA neural mechanisms are involved in the motivational effects produced by opiate withdrawal (744–746).

However, as the author has argued (737), *simple* "opponent-process" conceptions seem unlikely, on the preponderance of presently-available evidence, to constitute fully satisfactory explanations of the undoubtedly complex neurobiological phenomena subsumed under the term "craving." Also, given that the presently available data generated with the "reinstatement" paradigm of relapse to drug self-administration indicate that only a drug "priming" injection or environmental stress—*but not withdrawal-induced anhedonia*—provoke relapse to drug-taking in drug-taking-extinguished animals, one is left with the following conundrum: (*a*) opponent-process neural mechanisms seem to exist, either directly within the DA reward circuitry or intimately connected to it synaptically (or both); (*b*) such opponent-process mechanisms may well mediate some aspects of anhedonia or dysphoria; (*c*) such opponent-process mechanisms appear to be triggered by withdrawal from addictive drug use; *but* (*d*) there is no present evidence that such withdrawal-triggered dysphoric opponent neural processes provoke relapse to drug-taking in animal models such as the reinstatement paradigm of drug self-administration.

CONCLUSION

A summary description of the role of brain reward mechanisms in substance abuse may be derived from all the evidence cited in this chapter.

First, it appears that abusable substances have two fundamental commonalities: (*a*) that they are voluntarily self-administered by non-human mammals, and (*b*) that they acutely enhance brain reward mechanisms. From this latter property presumably derives their euphorigenic potency, their appeal to non-human mammals, and the "hit," "rush," or "high" sought by the human substance abuser. Second, the reward circuits of the brain, upon which abusable substances act to enhance brain reward, include "first-stage," "second-stage," and "third-stage" components. The "first-stage" component comprises descending, myelinated, moderately-fast-conducting neurons that run caudally within the medial forebrain bundle and are preferentially activated by direct electrical brain-stimulation reward. These "first-stage" fibers synapse into the ventral mesencephalic nuclei containing the cell bodies of the ascending mesotelencephalic DA system, the axons of which run rostrally through the medial forebrain bundle to limbic and cortical projection areas. These mesotelencephalic DA neurons constitute the "second-stage" fibers of the reward system, and form a crucial drug-sensitive component of the reward circuitry, which appears preferentially activated neurochemically and/or electrophysiologically by abusable substances to enhance brain-reward. The mesolimbic DA fibers terminating in the nucleus accumbens, and most especially in the nucleus accumbens "shell," appear to be the most crucial reward-relevant component of the ascending mesotelencephalic DA system. From the nucleus accumbens, "third-stage" reward-relevant neurons, some of them enkephalinergic and/or GABAergic, appear to carry the reward signal further, to or via the ventral pallidum. Third, abusable substances appear to act on or synaptically close to these DA fibers to produce their reward-enhancing actions, possibly via an opioid peptidergic mecha-

nism. This DA component appears crucial for drug self-administration, and self-administration can be attenuated (at least in laboratory animals) by manipulating these DA substrates. Fourth, different classes of abusable substances appear to act on these DA reward substrates at different anatomical levels and via different sites of action on or near the DA neurons. Fifth, this crucial drug-sensitive DA component of the reward system is functionally modulated by a wide variety of other neurotransmitter-specific neural systems (including GABAergic, glutamatergic, serotonergic, noradrenergic, enkephalinergic, endorphinergic, dynorphinergic, cholecystokinergic, and neurotensinergic neural systems), which appear importantly involved in setting the level of hedonic tone carried through the DA reward system. Drug self-administration can be attenuated (at least in laboratory animals) by manipulating these other neurotransmitter systems that modulate the DA reward system. Sixth, complex reciprocal neural interconnections between the "first-stage," "second-stage," and "third-stage" reward neurons also appear to be importantly involved in regulating the functional set-point for hedonic tone, and (at least in laboratory animals) manipulating these neural interconnections can alter drug taking-behavior. Seventh, perturbations in the neural substrates of the DA reward system (genetically-imparted or otherwise) may be capable of altering vulnerability to drug-taking behavior. Eighth, relapse to drug-taking behavior triggered either by re-exposure to drug or by stress appears to involve reactivation of DA reward-linked substrates. Ninth, the subjective experience of drug craving itself may also involve activation of DA reward-linked substrates. A clinically relevant derivative of such considerations is that pharmacotherapeutic interventions to alter drug-reward, drug-craving, or even preexisting drug-vulnerabilities could conceivably target an exceedingly wide range of neurotransmitter systems that synaptically modulate the reward circuitry.

The admittedly incomplete picture of the reward systems of the mammalian brain painted in the present chapter, and drug interaction therewith, is illustrated in Figure 6.2. It will be instructive for the reader to compare Figures 6.1 and 6.2 and to note therefrom how little we yet know about the *functional* anatomy of the brain, as compared to the static anatomy. It will also be obvious to the reader that Figure 6.2 represents a *reductio ad minima* approach to the anatomy, chemistry, pharmacology, and function of the reward systems of the mammalian brain. It will be remarkable indeed if the anatomy of brain-reward, and the actions of abusable substances thereon, turn out to be as simple as that sketched in this chapter and as simple as shown in Figure 6.2. At the same time, knowledge does accumulate from year to year, and it will be equally instructive for the reader to compare Figure 6.2 in the present chapter with Figure 6.2 from the same chapter in the previous edition of this textbook (747). It will be obvious from such a comparison that we have learned a great deal more about the underlying neuroanatomy, neurochemistry, and neuropharmacology of brain reward mechanisms than was known or even conjectured 5 short years ago. Of course, more complex and comprehensive conjectural pictures of the reward apparatus of the mammalian brain, and of abusable drug action on these systems, have been presented. Although some such schemes are arguably less defensible, at our present limited state of knowledge, than the deliberately simplified picture painted in the present chapter, the interested reader is referred to them (748–756).

What, then, is the actual role of the ascending DA reward-relevant neuron and the seemingly crucial DA synapse to which it feeds? Even after more than a decade and a half, no suggestion appears to have bettered Wise's hypothesis that "the dopamine junction represents a synaptic way station for messages signaling the rewarding impact of a variety of normally powerful rewarding events. It seems likely that this synapse lies at a critical junction between branches of the sensory pathways which carry signals of the intensity, duration, and quality of the stimulus, and the motivational pathways where these sensory inputs are translated into the hedonic messages we experience as pleasure, euphoria or 'yumminess' " (194, p.94). However, as noted repeatedly in this chapter, it has become clear in the years since Wise's suggestion that the encoding of hedonic tone by the DA reward system of the brain is far more complex and subtle than was realized 15 years ago, incorporating nuances of anticipatory and conditioned reinforcement as well as anhedonia/dysphoria, craving, and (some) neural mechanisms underlying

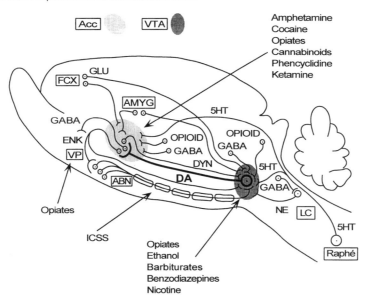

Figure 6.2.   Schematic diagram of the brain-reward circuitry of the mammalian (laboratory rat) brain, with sites at which various abusable substances appear to act to enhance brain-reward and thus to induce drug-taking behavior and possibly drug-craving. *ICSS*, descending, myelinated, moderately-fast-conducting component of the brain-reward circuitry that is preferentially activated by electrical intracranial self-stimulation; *DA*, subcomponent of the ascending mesolimbic dopaminergic system that appears preferentially activated by abusable substances; *Raphé*, brain stem serotonergic raphé nuclei; *LC*, locus coeruleus; *VTA*, ventral tegmental area; *Acc*, nucleus accumbens; *VP*, ventral pallidum; *ABN*, anterior bed nuclei of the medial forebrain bundle; *AMYG*, amygdala; *FCX*, frontal cortex; *5HT*, serotonergic (5-Hydroxytryptamine) fibers, which originate in the anterior raphé nuclei and project to both the cell body region (ventral tegmental area) and terminal projection field (nucleus accumbens) of the DA reward neurons; *NE*, noradrenergic fibers, which originate in the locus coeruleus and synapse into the general vicinity of the ventral mesencephalic DA cell fields of the ventral tegmental area; *GABA*, GABAergic inhibitory fiber systems synapsing upon the locus coeruleus noradrenergic fibers, the ventral tegmental area, and the nucleus accumbens, as well as the GABAergic outflow from the nucleus accumbens; *Opioid*, endogenous opioid peptide neural systems synapsing into both the ventral tegmental DA cell fields and the nucleus accumbens DA terminal projection loci; *ENK*, enkephalinergic outflow from the nucleus accumbens; *DYN*, dynorphinergic outflow from the nucleus accumbens; *GLU*, glutamatergic neural systems originating in frontal cortex and synapsing in both the ventral tegmental area and the nucleus accumbens.

both preexisting vulnerability to drug-taking and relapse to previously extinguished drug-taking.

Finally, the question arises as to the biological purposes these brain-reward systems evolved to serve. No one, after all, seriously believes that they emerged during the eons of evolution simply so that twentieth century man could inject himself with chemicals. What purposes, then, did these brain-reward systems evolve to serve? As Wise noted (194, p. 94), most workers believe that addictive drugs act on brain circuits that evolved to subserve the normal reinforcement functions of the central nervous system, for example, in reinforcing such biologically essential behaviors as feeding, as postulated more than 40 years ago in the pioneering ideas of Hebb (757), and as more recently stated in the eloquent writings of Goldstein (758). In fact, one of the oldest observations in the research literature on electrical stimulation of the brain is that stimulation in brain-reward areas can also evoke natural consummatory behaviors such as feeding and other species-typical biologically essential behaviors (22–25). Furthermore, the directly activated neural substrates of stimulation-induced feeding and brain-stimulation reward in the lateral hypothalamus and ventral tegmental area appear identical in terms of refractory periods, conduction velocities, and medial-lateral and dorsal-ventral alignment of the nerve fibers subserving the two stimulation-induced effects (feeding and reward), suggesting strongly that the same fibers mediate both effects (437, 438). It is intriguing in this regard to note that the same mesotelencephalic DA circuits that appear to subserve the reward induced by abusable drugs are also biochemically activated, in a manner seemingly identical to the DA activation produced by abusable drugs, by natural rewards (117, 759–762). Other more complex interactions between the DA reward system and natural rewards have also been reported (377). Is it possible, then, that some substance abusers have a defect in their ability to capture reward and pleasure from everyday experience, as postulated by some clinicians (763–765) and as postulated by Blum

and colleagues (643) in the context of their formulation of "reward deficiency syndrome"? Interestingly, this very concept—of a basal hypofunctionality in brain mechanisms subserving normal reward and pleasure functions—was originally postulated (albeit in rather elementary form) by Dole and his colleagues more than 30 years ago during the development of methadone maintenance therapy for heroin addiction (766, 767). If these conceptions have merit, they have profound implications: (a) our goals are not only to acutely rescue addicts from the clutches of their addictions, but also more importantly to restore their reward systems to a level of functionality that will enable them to "get off" on the real world; and (b) pharmacotherapeutic interventions for clinical treatment of substance abuse that are predicated on blockade of brain reward functions are doomed to failure.

Acknowledgments.   *Preparation of this manuscript was supported by grants from the Aaron Diamond Foundation and the National Institute on Drug Abuse, and by funds from the New York State Office of Alcohol and Substance Abuse Services. The author is indebted to William Paredes for his tireless assistance, and to Dr. T. Byram Karasu, Silverman Professor and Chairman, Department of Psychiatry, Albert Einstein College of Medicine, and Dr. Dominick P. Purpura, Dean, Albert Einstein College of Medicine, for their support. Work from the author's laboratory cited in this manuscript was supported by the U.S. Public Health Service under research grants DA-01560, DA-02089, and DA-03622 from the National Institute on Drug Abuse, research grant NS-09649 from the National Institute of Neurological Disorders and Stroke, research grant AA-09547 from the National Institute on Alcohol Abuse and Alcoholism, and research grant RR-05397 (Biomedical Research Support Grant) from the National Institutes of Health; by U.S. National Science Foundation research grant BNS-86–09351; by the U.S. Air Force Aeromedical Division, under research projects 6893–02-005 and 6893–02-039; by a research grant from the Natural Sciences and Engineering Research Council of Canada; and by very generous research grant and fellowship support from the Aaron Diamond Foundation of New York City.*

References

1. Lierman TL, ed. Building a healthy America. New York: Mary Ann Liebert, Inc., 1987.
2. Rice DP, Kelman S, Miller LS. Estimates of economic costs of alcohol and drug abuse and mental illness, 1985 and 1988. Public Health Rep 1991;106:280–292.
3. D'Aquila RT, Williams AB. Epidemic human immunodeficiency virus (HIV) infection among intravenous drug users (IVDU). Yale J Biol Med 1987;60:545–567.
4. Guinan ME, Hardy A. Epidemiology of AIDS in women in the United States: 1981 through 1986. JAMA 1987;257:2039–2042.
5. Des Jarlais DC, Friedman SR, Stoneburner RL. HIV infection and intravenous drug use: critical issues in transmission dynamics, infection outcomes, and prevention. Rev Infect Dis 1988;10:151–158.
6. Weeks JR. Experimental morphine addiction: method for automatic intravenous injections in unrestrained rats. Science 1962;138:143–144.
7. Schuster CR, Thompson T. Self administration of and behavioral dependence on drugs. Annu Rev Pharmacol 1969;9:483–502.
8. Griffiths RR, Bigelow CE, Liebson I. Experimental drug self-administration: generality across species and type of drug. NIDA Res Monogr 1978;20:24–43.
9. Brady JV, Lucas SE. Testing drugs for physical dependence potential and abuse liability NIDA Res Monogr 1984;52.
10. Bindra D, Stewart J, eds. Motivation. 2nd ed. Baltimore: Penguin, 1971.
11. Jaffe JH. Drug addiction and drug abuse. In: Goodman LS, Gilman A, eds. The pharmacological basis of therapeutics. 3rd ed. New York: Macmillan, 1965:285–311.
12. Skinner BF. The behavior of organisms: an experimental analysis. New York: Appleton-Century-Crofts, 1938.
13. Young PT. The role of affective processes in learning and motivation. Psychol Rev 1959;66:104–125.
14. Pfaffmann C. The pleasures of sensation. Psychol Rev 1960;67:253–268.
15. Young PT. Motivation and emotion: a survey of the determinants of human and animal activity. New York: Wiley, 1961.
16. Spragg SDS. Morphine addiction in chimpanzees. Comp Psychol Monogr 1940;15(7):1–132.
17. Olds J, Milner P. Positive reinforcement produced by electrical stimulation of septal area and other regions of rat brain. J Comp Physiol Psychol 1954;47:419–427.
18. Olds ME, Olds J. Approach-avoidance analysis of rat diencephalon. J Comp Neurol 1963;120:259–295.
19. Olds J. Pleasure centers in the brain. Sci Am 1956;194(4):105–116.
20. Olds J. Hypothalamic substrates of reward. Physiol Rev 1962;42:554–604.
21. Olds ME, Olds J. Drives, rewards and the brain. In: Newcomb TM, ed. New directions in psychology. New York: Holt, Rinehart & Winston, 1965:329–410.
22. Miller NE. Motivational effects of brain stimulation and drugs. Fed Proc 1960;19:846–853.
23. Margules DL, Olds J. Identical "feeding" and "rewarding" systems in the lateral hypothalamus of rats. Science 1962;135:374–375.
24. Hoebel BG, Teitelbaum P. Hypothalamic control of feeding and self-stimulation. Science 1962;135:375–377.
25. Coons EE, Levak M, Miller NE. Lateral hypothalamus: learning of food-seeking response motivated by electrical stimulation. Science 1965;150:1320–1321.
26. Hoebel BG. Feeding and self-stimulation. Ann N Y Acad Sci 1969;157:758–778.
27. Killam KF, Olds J, Sinclair J. Further studies on the effects of centrally acting drugs on self-stimulation. J Pharmacol Exp Ther 1957;119:157.
28. Kornetsky C. Brain-stimulation reward: a model for the neuronal bases for drug-induced euphoria. NIDA Res Monogr Ser 1985;62:30–50.
29. Wise RA. Action of drugs of abuse on brain reward systems. Pharmacol Biochem Behav 1980;13(suppl 1):213–223.
30. Wise RA. Neural mechanisms of the reinforcing action of cocaine. NIDA Res Monogr Ser 1984;50:15–33.
31. Wise RA, Bozarth MA. Brain substrates for reinforcement and drug self-administration. Prog Neuro-Psychopharmacol 1981;5:467–474.
32. Spealman RD, Goldberg SR. Drug self-administration by laboratory animals: control by schedules of reinforcement. Annu Rev Pharmacol Toxicol 1978;18:313–339.
33. Yokel RA. Intravenous self-administration: response rates, the effects of pharmacological challenges, and drug preferences. In: Bozarth MA, ed. Methods of assessing the reinforcing properties of abused drugs. New York: Springer-Verlag, 1987:1–33.
34. Weeks JR. Long-term intravenous infusion. In: Meyers RD, ed. Methods in Psychobiology. New York: Academic Press, 1972:2;155–168.
35. Smith SG, Davis WM. A method for chronic intravenous drug administration in the rat. In: Ehrenpreis S, Neidle A, eds. Methods in narcotics research. New York: Marcel Dekker, 1975:3–32.
36. Deneau G, Yanagita T, Seevers MH. Self-administration of psychoactive substances by the monkey: a measure of psychological dependence. Psychopharmacologia 1969;16:30–48.
37. Yanagita T, Deneau GA, Seevers MH. Evaluation of pharmacologic agents in the monkey by long-term intravenous self or programmed administration. Excerpta Med Int Congr Ser 1965;87:453–457.
38. Findley JD, Robinson WW, Peregrino L. Addiction to secobarbital and chlordiazepoxide in the rhesus monkey by means of a self-infusion preference procedure. Psychopharmacologia 1972;26:93–114.
39. Goldberg SR. Comparable behavior maintained under fixed-ratio and second-order schedules of food presentation, cocaine injection or d-amphetamine injection in the squirrel monkey. J Pharmacol Exp Ther 1973;18:30.
40. Stretch R, Gerber GJ. A method for chronic intravenous drug administration in squirrel monkeys. Can J Physiol Pharmacol 1970;48:575–581.
41. Jones BE, Prada JA. Relapse to morphine use in dog. Psychopharmacologia 1973;30:1–12.
42. Smith JM, Renault PF, Schuster CR. A mild restraint and chronic venous catherization system for cats. Pharmacol Biochem Behav 1975;3:713–715.
43. Balster RL, Kilbey MM, Ellinwood EH Jr. Methamphetamine self-administration in the cat. Psychopharmacologia 1976;46:229–233.
44. Goldberg SR, Hoffmeister F, Schlichting UU, Wuttke W. A comparison of pentobarbital and cocaine self-administration in rhesus monkeys: effects of dose and fixed-ratio parameter. J Pharmacol Exp Ther 1971;179:277–283.
45. Downs DA, Woods JH. Codeine- and cocaine-reinforced responding in rhesus monkeys: effects of dose on response rates under a fixed-ratio schedule. J Pharmacol Exp Ther 1974;191:179–188.
46. Pickens R, Thompson T. Cocaine-reinforced behavior in rats: effects of reinforcement magnitude and fixed ratio size. J Pharmacol Exp Ther 1968;161:122–129.
47. Goldberg SR, Kelleher RT. Behavior controlled by scheduled injections of cocaine in squirrel and rhesus monkeys. J Exp Anal Behav 1976;25:93–104.
48. Schlichting UU, Goldberg SR, Wuttke W, Hoffmeister F. d-Amphetamine self-administration by rhesus monkeys with different self-administration histories. Excerpta Med Int Congr Ser 1971;220:62–69.
49. Pickens R, Meisch R, McGuire LE. Methamphetamine reinforcement in rats. Psychonomic Science 1967;8:371–372.
50. Pickens R, Harris WC. Self-administration of d-amphetamine by rats. Psychopharmacologia 1968;12:158–163.
51. Balster RL, Schuster CR. A comparison of d-amphetamine, l-amphetamine and methamphetamine self-administration in rhesus monkeys. Pharmacol Biochem Behav 1973;1:167–172.
52. Yokel RA, Pickens R. Self-administration of optical isomers of amphetamine and methylamphetamine by rats. J Pharmacol Exp Ther 1973;187:27–33.
53. Risner ME. Intravenous self-administration of d- and l-amphetamine by dog. Eur J Pharmacol 1975;32:344–348.
54. Götestam KG, Andersson BE. Self-administration of amphetamine analogues in rats. Pharmacol Biochem Behav 1975;3:229–233.
55. Johanson CE, Schuster CR. A choice procedure for drug reinforcers: cocaine and methylphenidate in the rhesus monkey. J Pharmacol Exp Ther 1975;193:676–688.
56. Griffiths RR, Winger G, Brady JV, Snell JD. Comparison on behavior maintained by infusions of eight phenylethylamines in baboons. Psychopharmacology 1976;50:251–258.
57. Weeks JR, Collins RJ. Factors affecting voluntary morphine intake in self-maintained addicted rats. Psychopharmacologia 1964;6:267–279.
58. Hoffmeister F, Schlichting UU. Reinforcing properties of some opiates and opioids in rhesus monkeys with histories of cocaine and codeine self-administration. Psychopharmacologia 1972;23:55–74.
59. Collins RJ, Weeks JR. Relative potency of codeine, methadone and dihydromorphinone to morphine in self-maintained addict rats. Naunyn Schmiedebergs Arch Pharmacol 1965;249:509–514.
60. Talley WH, Rosenblum I. Self-administration of dextropropoxyphene by rhesus monkeys to the point of toxicity. Psychopharmacologia 1972;27:179–182.
61. Smith SG, Werner TE, Davis WM. Effect of unit dose and route of administration on self-administration of morphine. Psychopharmacology 1976;50:103–105.
62. Werner TE, Smith SG, Davis WM. A dose-response comparison between methadone and morphine self-administration. Psychopharmacology 1976;47:209–211.
63. Schuster CR, Balster RL. Self-administration of agonists. In: Kosterlitz HW, Collier HOJ, Villarreal JE, eds. Agonist and antagonist actions of narcotic analgesic drugs. Baltimore: University Park Press, 1973:243–254.
64. Moreton JE, Roehrs T, Khazan N. Drug self-administration and sleep-wake activity in rats dependent on morphine, methadone, or l-alpha-

acetylmethadol. Psychopharmacology 1976;47: 237–241.

65. Winger GD, Woods JH. The reinforcing property of ethanol in the rhesus monkey. I. Initiation, maintenance and termination of intravenous ethanol-reinforced responding. Ann N Y Acad Sci 1973;215:162–175.

66. Woods JH, Ikomi F, Winger G. The reinforcing property of ethanol. In: Roach MK, McIsaac WM, Creaven PJ, eds. Biological aspects of alcohol. Austin: University of Texas Press, 1971:371–388.

67. Winger G, Stitzer ML, Woods JH. Barbiturate-reinforced responding in rhesus monkeys: comparisons of drugs with different durations of action. J Pharmacol Exp Ther 1975;195:505–514.

68. Yanagita T, Takahashi S. Dependence liability of several sedative-hypnotic agents evaluated in monkeys. J Pharmacol Exp Ther 1973; 185:307–316.

69. Davis JD, Lulenski GC, Miller NE. Comparative studies of barbiturate self-administration. Int J Addict 1968;3:207–214.

70. Kelleher RT. Characteristics of behavior controlled by scheduled injections of drugs. Pharmacol Rev 1975;27:307–323.

71. Balster RL, Johanson CE, Harris RT. Phencyclidine self-administration in the rhesus monkey. Pharmacol Biochem Behav 1973;1:167–172.

72. Moreton JE, Meisch RA, Stark L, Thompson T. Ketamine self-administration by the rhesus monkey. J Pharmacol Exp Ther 1977;203:303–309.

73. Pickens R, Thompson T. Characteristics of stimulant drug reinforcement. In: Thompson T, Pickens R, eds. Stimulus properties of drugs. New York: Appleton, 1971:177–192.

74. Pickens R, Thompson T. Simple schedules of drug self-administration in animals. In: Singh JM, Miller L, Lal H, eds. Drug addiction. Experimental pharmacology. Mount Kisko, NY: Futura, 1972;1:107–120.

75. Goldberg SR, Kelleher RT. Reinforcement of behavior by cocaine injections. In: Ellinwood EH Jr, Kilbey MM, eds. Cocaine and other stimulants. New York: Plenum, 1977:523–544.

76. Balster RL, Schuster CR. Fixed-interval schedule of cocaine reinforcement: effect of dose and infusion duration. J Exp Anal Behav 1973; 20:119–129.

77. Dougherty J, Pickens R. Fixed-interval schedules of intravenous cocaine presentation in rats. J Exp Anal Behav 1973;20:111–118.

78. Woods JH, Schuster CR. Reinforcement properties of morphine, cocaine and SPA as a function of unit dose. Int J Addict 1968;3:231–237.

79. Schuster CR, Woods JH. The conditioned reinforcing effects of stimuli associated with morphine reinforcement. Int J Addict 1968;3: 223–230.

80. Carney JM, Llewellyn ME, Woods JH. Variable interval responding maintained by intravenous codeine and ethanol injections in the rhesus monkey. Pharmacol Biochem Behav 1977;5: 577–582.

81. Thompson T, Schuster CR. Morphine self-administration, food-reinforced and avoidance behaviors in rhesus monkeys. Psychopharmacologia 1964;5:87–94.

82. Anderson WW, Thompson T. Ethanol self-administration in water-satiated rats. Pharmacol Biochem Behav 1974;2:447–454.

83. Meisch RA, Thompson T. Ethanol as a reinforcer: an operant analysis of ethanol dependence. In: Singh JM, Lal H, eds. Drug addiction. Vol. 3. Neurobiology and influences on behavior. Miami: Symposia Specialists, 1974;3: 117–133.

84. Yokel RA, Wise RA. Amphetamine-type reinforcement by dopaminergic agonists in the rat. Psychopharmacology 1978;58:289–296.

85. Lyness WH, Friedle NM, Moore KE. Increased self-administration of d-amphetamine after destruction of 5-hydroxytryptaminergic neurons. Pharmacol Biochem Behav 1980;12: 937–941.

86. Lang WJ, Latiff AA, McQueen A, Singer G. Self-administration of nicotine with and without a food delivery schedule. Pharmacol Biochem Behav 1977;7:65–70.

87. Lepore M, Franklin KBJ. Modelling drug kinetics with brain stimulation: dopamine antagonists increase self-stimulation. Pharmacol Biochem Behav 1992;41:489–496.

88. Harrigan SE, Downs DA. Self-administration of heroin, acetylmethadol, morphine, and methadone in rhesus monkeys. Life Sci 1978;22:619–624.

89. Johanson CE, Balster RL, Bonese K. Self-administration of psychomotor stimulant drugs: the effects of unlimited access. Pharmacol Biochem Behav 1976;4:45–51.

90. Risner ME, Jones BE. Self-administration of CNS stimulants by dog. Psychopharmacologia 1975;43:207–213.

91. Risner ME, Jones BE. Characteristics of unlimited access to self-administered stimulant infusions in dogs. Biol Psychiatry 1976; 11:625–634.

92. Kramer JC, Fischman VS, Littlefield DC. Amphetamine abuse: pattern and effects of high doses taken intravenously. JAMA 1967;201: 305–309.

93. Yanagita T, Takahashi S. Development of tolerance to and physical dependence on barbiturates in rhesus monkeys. J Pharmacol Exp Ther 1970;172:163–169.

94. Yokel RA, Pickens R. Drug level of d- and l-amphetamine during intravenous self-administration. Psychopharmacologia 1974;34: 255–264.

95. Roberts DC, Bennett SA. Heroin self-administration in rats under a progressive ratio schedule of reinforcement. Psychopharmacology 1993;111:215–218.

96. Roberts DC. Self-administration of GBR 12909 on a fixed ratio and progressive ratio schedule in rats. Psychopharmacology 1993; 111:202–206.

97. Bozarth MA, Wise RA. Toxicity associated with long-term intravenous heroin and cocaine self-administration in the rat. JAMA 1985; 254:81–83.

98. Weeks JR, Collins RJ. Screening for drug reinforcement using intravenous self-administration in the rat. In: Bozarth MA, ed. Methods of assessing the reinforcing properties of abused drugs. New York: Springer-Verlag, 1987: 35–43.

99. Brady JV, Griffiths RR, Hienz RD, Ator NA, Lukas SE, Lamb RJ. Assessing drugs for abuse liability and dependence potential in laboratory primates. In: Bozarth MA, ed. Methods of assessing the reinforcing properties of abused drugs. New York: Springer-Verlag, 1987: 45–85.

100. Meisch RA, Carroll ME. Oral drug self-administration: drugs as reinforcers. In: Bozarth MA, ed. Methods of assessing the reinforcing properties of abused drugs. New York: Springer-Verlag, 1987:143–160.

101. Amit Z, Smith BR, Sutherland EA. Oral self-administration of alcohol: a valid approach to the study of drug self-administration and human alcoholism. In: Bozarth MA, ed. Methods

of assessing the reinforcing properties of abused drugs. New York: Springer-Verlag, 1987:161–171.

102. Yanagita T. Prediction of drug abuse liability from animal studies. In: Bozarth MA, ed. Methods of assessing the reinforcing properties of abused drugs. New York: Springer-Verlag, 1987:189–198.

103. Esposito RU, Kornetsky C. Opioids and rewarding brain stimulation. Neurosci Biobehav Rev 1978;2:115–122.

104. Wise RA, Bozarth MA. Brain reward circuitry: four circuit elements "wired" in apparent series. Brain Res Bull 1984;12:203–208.

105. Wise RA, Rompre P-P. Brain dopamine and reward. Annu Rev Psychol 1989;40:191–225.

106. Reid LD. Tests involving pressing for intracranial stimulation as an early procedure for screening likelihood of addiction of opioids and other drugs. In: Bozarth MA, ed. Methods of assessing the reinforcing properties of abused drugs. New York: Springer-Verlag, 1987:391–420.

107. Olds J, Travis RP. Effects of chlorpromazine, meprobamate, pentobarbital and morphine on self-stimulation. J Pharmacol Exp Ther 1960; 128:397–404.

108. Olds ME. Facilitatory action of diazepam and chlordiazepoxide on hypothalamic reward behavior. J Comp Physiol Psychol 1966;62: 136–140.

109. Olds ME. Comparative effects of amphetamine, scopolamine, chlordiazepoxide and diphenylhydantoin on operant and extinction behaviour with brain stimulation and food reward. Neuropharmacology 1970;9:519–532.

110. Nazzaro JM, Seeger TF, Gardner EL. Morphine differentially affects ventral tegmental and substantia nigra brain reward thresholds. Pharmacol Biochem Behav 1981;14:325–331.

111. Nazzaro JM, Gardner EL, Bridger WH, Carlson KR, Seeger TF. Pentobarbital induces a naloxone-reversible decrease in mesolimbic self-stimulation thresholds. Soc Neurosci Abstr 1981;7:262.

112. Herberg LJ, Rose IC. The effect of MK-801 and other antagonists of NMDA-type glutamate receptors on brain-stimulation reward. Psychopharmacology 1989;99:87–90.

113. Gardner EL, Paredes W, Smith D, Donner A, Milling C, Cohen D, Morrison D. Facilitation of brain stimulation reward by Δ9-tetrahydrocannabinol. Psychopharmacology 1988;96: 142–144.

114. Chen J, Gardner EL. In vivo brain microdialysis study of phencyclidine on presynaptic dopamine efflux in rat caudate nucleus. Soc Neurosci Abstr 1988;14:525.

115. Di Chiara G, Imperato A. Preferential stimulation of dopamine release in the nucleus accumbens by opiates, alcohol, and barbiturates: studies with transcerebral dialysis in freely moving rats. Ann N Y Acad Sci 1986;473:367–381.

116. Gysling K, Wang RY. Morphine-induced activation of A10 dopamine neurons in rats brains. Brain Res 1983;277:119–127.

117. Hernandez L, Hoebel BG. Food reward and cocaine increase extracellular dopamine in the nucleus accumbens as measured by microdialysis. Life Sci 1988;42:1705–1712.

118. Hommer DW, Pert A. The action of opiates in the rat substantia nigra: an electrophysiological analysis. Peptides 1983;4:603–608.

119. Imperato A, Di Chiara G. Preferential stimulation of dopamine release in the nucleus accumbens of freely moving rats by ethanol. J Pharmacol Exp Ther 1986;239:219–228.

120. Imperato A, Mulas A, Di Chiara G. Nicotine preferentially stimulates dopamine release in the limbic system of freely moving rats. Eur J Pharmacol 1986;132:337–338.

121. Kalivas PW, Widerlov E, Stanley D, Breese G, Prange AJ Jr. Enkephalin action on the mesolimbic system: a dopamine-dependent and a dopamine-independent increase in locomotor activity. J Pharmacol Exp Ther 1983;227:229–237.

122. Kalivas PW, Duffy P, Dilts R, Abhold R. Enkephalin modulation of A10 dopamine neurons: a role in dopamine sensitization. Ann N Y Acad Sci 1988;537:405–414.

123. Westerink BHC, Tuntler J, Damsma G, Rollema H, de Vries JB. The use of tetrodotoxin for the characterization of drug-enhanced dopamine release in conscious rats studied by brain dialysis. Naunyn Schmiedebergs Arch Pharmacol 1987;336:502–507.

124. Wise RA, Bozarth MA. A psychomotor stimulant theory of addiction. Psychol Rev 1987;94:469–492.

125. Wilson MC, Schuster CR. Mazindol self-administration in the rhesus monkey. Pharmacol Biochem Behav 1976;4:207–210.

126. Bergman J, Madras BK, Johnson SE, Spealman RD. Effects of cocaine and related drugs in nonhuman primates. III. Self-administration by squirrel monkeys. J Pharmacol Exp Ther 1989;251:150–155.

127. Woods JH, Katz JL, Medzihradsky F, Smith CB, Winger GD. Evaluation of new compounds for opioid activity: 1982 annual report. NIDA Res Monogr Ser 1983;43:457–511.

128. Winger G, Woods JH. Comparison of fixed-ratio and progressive-ratio schedules of maintenance of stimulant drug-reinforced responding. Drug Alcohol Depend 1985;15:123–130.

129. Risner ME, Silcox DL. Psychostimulant self-administration by beagle dogs in a progressive-ratio paradigm. Psychopharmacology 1981;75:25–30.

130. Corwin RL, Woolverton WL, Schuster CR, Johanson CE. Anorectics: effects on food intake and self-administration in rhesus monkeys. Alcohol Drug Res 1987;7:351–361.

131. van der Zee P, Koger HS, Gootjes J, Hespe W. Aryl 1,4-dialk(en)yl-piperazines as selective and very potent inhibitors of dopamine uptake. Eur J Med Chem 1980;15:363–370.

132. Heikkila RE, Manzino L. Behavioral properties of GBR 12909, GBR 13069 and GBR 13098: specific inhibitors of dopamine uptake. Eur J Pharmacol 1984;103:241–248.

133. Gill CA, Holz WC, Zirkle CL, Hill H. Pharmacological modification of cocaine and apomorphine self-administration in the squirrel monkey. In: Denker P, Radouco-Thomas C, Villeneuve A, eds. Proceedings of the tenth congress of the Collegium Internationale Neuro-Psychopharmacologicum. New York: Pergamon Press, 1978:1477–1484.

134. Woolverton WL, Goldberg LI, Ginos JZ. Intravenous self-administration of dopamine receptor agonists by rhesus monkeys. J Pharmacol Exp Ther 1984;230:678–683.

135. Baxter BL, Gluckman MI, Stein L, Scerni RA. Self-injection of apomorphine in the rat: positive reinforcement by a dopamine receptor stimulant. Pharmacol Biochem Behav 1974;2:387–391.

136. Davis WM, Smith SG. Catecholaminergic mechanisms of reinforcement: direct assessment by drug self-administration. Life Sci 1977;20:483–492.

137. Hoffmeister F, Wuttke W. Psychotropic drugs as negative reinforcers. Pharmacol Rev 1975;27:419–428.

138. Kandel DA, Schuster CR. An investigation of nalorphine and perphenazine as negative reinforcers in an escape paradigm. Pharmacol Biochem Behav 1977;6:61–71.

139. Baldessarini RJ. Drugs and the treatment of psychiatric disorders. In: Gilman AG, Goodman LS, Rall TW, Murad F, eds. Goodman and Gilman's the pharmacological basis of therapeutics. 7th ed. New York: Macmillan, 1985:387–445.

140. Rech R. Neurolepsis: anhedonia or blunting of emotional reactivity? Behav Brain Sci 1982;5:72–73.

141. Downs DA, Woods JH. Fixed-ratio escape and avoidance-escape from naloxone in morphine-dependent monkeys: effects of naloxone dose and morphine pretreatment. J Exp Anal Behav 1975;23:415–427.

142. Ettenberg A, Pettit HO, Bloom FE, Koob GF. Heroin and cocaine intravenous self-administration in rats: mediation by separate neural systems. Psychopharmacology 1982;78:204–209.

143. Goldberg SR, Hoffmeister F, Schlichting U, Wuttke W. Aversive properties of nalorphine and naloxone in morphine-dependent rhesus monkeys. J Pharmacol Exp Ther 1971;179:268–276.

144. Killian A, Bonese K, Rothberg RM, Wainer BH, Schuster CR. Effects of passive immunization against morphine on heroin self-administration. Pharmacol Biochem Behav 1978;9:347–352.

145. Baxter BL, Gluckman MI, Scerni RA. Apomorphine self-injection is not affected by alpha-methylparatyrosine treatment: support for dopaminergic reward. Pharmacol Biochem Behav 1976;4:611–612.

146. Pickens R, Meisch RA, Dougherty JA Jr. Chemical interactions in methamphetamine reinforcement. Psychol Rep 1968;23:1267–1270.

147. Wilson MC, Schuster CR. Aminergic influences on intravenous cocaine self-administration by rhesus monkeys. Pharmacol Biochem Behav 1974;2:563–571.

148. Yokel RA, Wise RA. Increased lever pressing for amphetamine after pimozide in rats: implications for a dopamine theory of reward. Science 1975;187:547–549.

149. Yokel RA, Wise RA. Attenuation of intravenous amphetamine reinforcement by central dopamine blockade in rats. Psychopharmacology 1976;48:311–318.

150. de Wit H, Wise RA. Blockade of cocaine reinforcement in rats with the dopamine receptor blocker pimozide, but not with the noradrenergic blockers phentolamine or phenoxybenzamine. Can J Psychol 1977;31:195–203.

151. Herling S, Woods JH. Chlorpromazine effects on cocaine-reinforced responding in rhesus monkeys: reciprocal modification of rate-altering effects of the drugs. J Pharmacol Exp Ther 1980;214:354–361.

152. Johanson CE, Kandel DA, Bonese K. The effects of perphenazine on self-administration behavior. Pharmacol Biochem Behav 1976;4:427–433.

153. Risner ME, Jones BE. Role of noradrenergic and dopaminergic processes in amphetamine self-administration. Pharmacol Biochem Behav 1976;5:477–482.

154. Risner ME, Jones BE. Characteristics of β-phenethylamine self-administration by dog. Pharmacol Biochem Behav 1977;6:689–696.

155. Risner ME, Jones BE. Intravenous self-admin-istration of cocaine and norcocaine by dogs. Psychopharmacology 1980;71:83–89.

156. Stretch R. Discrete-trial control of cocaine self-injection behaviour in squirrel monkeys: effects of morphine, naloxone, and chlorpromazine. Can J Physiol Pharmacol 1977;55:778–790.

157. Wilson MC, Schuster CR. The effects of chlorpromazine on psychomotor stimulant self-administration in the rhesus monkey. Psychopharmacologia 1972;26:115–126.

158. Wilson MC, Schuster CR. The effects of stimulants and depressants on cocaine self-administration behavior in the rhesus monkey. Psychopharmacologia 1973;31:291–304.

159. Davis WM, Smith SG. Noradrenergic basis for reinforcement associated with morphine action in nondependent rats. In: Singh JM, Lal H, eds. Drug addiction. Vol. 3. Neurobiology and influences on behavior. Miami: Symposia Specialists, 1974:155–168.

160. Hanson HM, Cimini-Venema CA. Effects of haloperidol on self-administration of morphine in rats. Fed Proc 1972;31:503.

161. Roberts DCS, Vickers G. Atypical neuroleptics increase self-administration of cocaine: an evaluation of a behavioral screen for antipsychotic activity. Psychopharmacology 1984;82:135–139.

162. de la Garza R, Johanson CE. Effects of haloperidol and physostigmine on self-administration of local anesthetics. Pharmacol Biochem Behav 1982;17:1295–1299.

163. Woolverton WL. Effects of a D_1 and D_2 dopamine antagonist on the self-administration of cocaine and piribedil by rhesus monkeys. Pharmacol Biochem Behav 1986;24:531–535.

164. Jönsson LE, Gunne LM, Änggard E. Effects of alpha-methyltyrosine in amphetamine-dependent subjects. Pharmacol Clin 1969;2:27–29.

165. Jönsson L, Änggard E, Gunne L. Blockade of intravenous amphetamine euphoria in man. Clin Pharmacol Ther 1971;12:889–896.

166. Jönsson LE. Pharmacological blockade of amphetamine effects in amphetamine dependent subjects. Eur J Clin Pharmacol 1972;4:206–211.

167. Gunne LM, Änggard E, Jönsson LE. Clinical trails with amphetamine-blocking drugs. Psychiat Neurol Neurochir 1972;75:225–226.

168. Roberts DCS, Zito KA. Interpretation of lesion effects on stimulant self-administration. In: Bozarth MA, ed. Methods of assessing the reinforcing properties of abused drugs. New York: Springer-Verlag, 1987:87–103.

169. Roberts DCS, Corcoran ME, Fibiger HC. On the role of ascending catecholamine systems in self-administration of cocaine. Pharmacol Biochem Behav 1977;6:615–620.

170. Roberts DCS, Koob GF. Disruption of cocaine self-administration following 6-hydroxydopamine lesions of the ventral tegmental area in rats. Pharmacol Biochem Behav 1982;17:901–904.

171. Moore RY, Bloom FE. Central catecholamine neuron systems: anatomy and physiology of the dopamine systems. Annu Rev Neurosci 1978;1:129–169.

172. Lyness WH, Friedle NM, Moore KE. Destruction of dopaminergic nerve terminals in nucleus accumbens: effect on d-amphetamine self-administration. Pharmacol Biochem Behav 1979;11:553–556.

173. Glick SD, Cox RS, Crane AM. Changes in morphine self-administration and morphine dependence after lesions of the caudate nucleus in rats. Psychopharmacologia 1975;41:219–224.

174. Bozarth MA, Wise RA. Heroin reward is dependent on a dopaminergic substrate. Life Sci 1981;29:1881–1886.

175. Spyraki C, Fibiger HC, Phillips AG. Attenuation of heroin reward in rats by disruption of the mesolimbic dopamine system. Psychopharmacology 1983;79:278–283.

176. Rolls ET. The brain and reward. Oxford: Pergamon Press, 1975.

177. Routtenberg A. The reward system of the brain. Sci Am 1978;239(5):154–164.

178. Olds ME, Fobes JL. The central basis of motivation: intracranial self-stimulation studies. Annu Rev Psychol 1981;32:523–574.

179. Heath RG. Pleasure response of human beings to direct stimulation of the brain: physiologic and psychodynamic considerations. In: Heath RG, ed. The role of pleasure in behavior. New York: Hoeber, 1964:219–243.

180. Bursten B, Delgado JMR. Positive reinforcement induced by intracerebral stimulation in the monkey. J Comp Physiol Psychol 1958; 51:6–10.

181. Wilkinson HA, Peele TL. Intracranial self-stimulation in cats. J Comp Neurol 1963; 121:425–440.

182. Briese E, Olds J. Reinforcing brain stimulation and memory in monkeys. Exp Neurol 1964; 10:493–508.

183. Valenstein ES. The anatomical locus of reinforcement. Prog Physiol Psychol 1966;1: 149–190.

184. Wetzel MC. Self-stimulation's anatomy: data needs. Brain Res 1968;10:287–296.

185. Routtenberg A, Malsbury C. Brainstem pathways of reward. J Comp Physiol Psychol 1969; 68:22–30.

186. Dahlström A, Fuxe K. Evidence for the existence of monoamine-containing neurons in the central nervous system: I. Demonstration of monoamines in the cell bodies of brainstem neurons. Acta Physiol Scand 1964;62(suppl 232):1–48.

187. Fuxe K. Evidence for the existence of monoamine neurons in the central nervous system: IV. Distribution of monoamine nerve terminals in the central nervous system. Acta Physiol Scand 1965;64(suppl 247):37–85.

188. Andén N-E, Dahlström A, Fuxe K, Larsson K, Olson L, Ungerstedt U. Ascending monoamine neurons to the telencephalon and diencephalon. Acta Physiol Scand 1966;67:313–326.

189. Ungerstedt U. Stereotaxic mapping of the monoamine pathways in the rat brain. Acta Physiol Scand 1971;82(suppl 367):1–48.

190. Crow TJ. A map of the rat mesencephalon for electrical self-stimulation. Brain Res 1972; 36:265–273.

191. Corbett D, Wise RA. Intracranial self-stimulation in relation to the ascending dopaminergic systems of the midbrain: a moveable electrode mapping study. Brain Res 1980;185:1–15.

192. Mogenson GJ, Takigawa M, Robertson A, Wu M. Self-stimulation of the nucleus accumbens and ventral tegmental area of Tsai attenuated by microinjections of spiroperidol into the nucleus accumbens. Brain Res 1979;171: 247–259.

193. Zarevics P, Setler PE. Simultaneous rate-independent and rate-dependent assessment of intracranial self-stimulation: evidence for the direct involvement of dopamine in brain reinforcement mechanisms. Brain Res 1979; 169:499–512.

194. Wise RA. The dopamine synapse and the notion of "pleasure centers" in the brain. Trends Neurosci 1980;3:91–95.

195. Fray PJ, Dunnett SB, Iversen SD, Björklund A, Stenevi U. Nigral transplants reinnervating the dopamine-depleted neostriatum can sustain intracranial self-stimulation. Science 1983;219: 416–420.

196. Wise RA. Brain dopamine and reward. In: Cooper SJ, ed. Theory in psychopharmacology. New York: Academic Press, 1981;1: 103–122.

197. Fibiger HC, Phillips AG. Mesocorticolimbic dopamine systems and reward. Ann N Y Acad Sci 1988;537:206–215.

198. Wise RA. Neuroleptics and operant behavior: the anhedonia hypothesis. Behav Brain Sci 1982;5:39–53.

199. Gallistel CR. Self-stimulation in the rat: quantitative characteristics of the reward pathway. J Comp Physiol Psychol 1978;92:977–998.

200. Gallistel CR, Shizgal P, Yeomans J. A portrait of the brain for self-stimulation. Psychol Rev 1981;88:228–273.

201. Shizgal P, Bielajew C, Corbett D, Skelton R, Yeomans J. Behavioral methods for inferring anatomical linkage between rewarding brain stimulation sites. J Comp Physiol Psychol 1980;94:227–237.

202. Yeomans JS. The absolute refractory periods of self-stimulation neurons. Physiol Behav 1979;22:911–919.

203. Yeomans JS, Matthews GG, Hawkins RD, Bellman K, Doppelt H. Characterization of self-stimulation neurons by their local potential summation properties. Physiol Behav 1979; 22:921–929.

204. Yeomans JS. Two substrates for medial forebrain bundle self-stimulation: myelinated axons and dopamine axons. Neurosci Biobehav Rev 1989;13:91–98.

205. Bielajew C, Shizgal P. Evidence implicating descending fibers in self-stimulation of the medial forebrain bundle. J Neurosci 1986;6:919–929.

206. Waraczynski MA, Ng Cheong Ton JM, Shizgal P. Failure of amygdaloid lesions to increase the threshold for self-stimulation of the lateral hypothalamus and ventral tegmental area. Behav Brain Res 1990;40:159–168.

207. Waraczynski MA, Conover K, Shizgal P. Rewarding effectiveness of caudal MFB stimulation is unaltered following DMH lesions. Physiol Behav 1992; 52:211–218.

208. Colle LM, Wise RA. Opposite effects of unilateral forebrain ablations on ipsilateral and contralateral hypothalamic self-stimulation. Brain Res 1987;407:285–293.

209. Ikemoto S, Panksepp J. The relationship between self-stimulation and sniffing in rats: does a common brain system mediate these behaviors? Behav Brain Res 1994;61:143–162.

210. Waraczynski MA. Basal forebrain knife cuts and medial forebrain bundle self-stimulation. Brain Res 1988;438:8–22.

211. Geeraedts LMG, Nieuwenhuys R, Veening JG. Medial forebrain bundle of the rat: III. Cytoarchitecture of the rostral (telencephalic) part of the medial forebrain bundle bed nucleus. J Comp Neurol 1990;294:507–536.

212. Murray B, Shizgal P. Attenuation of medial forebrain bundle reward by anterior lateral hypothalamic lesions. Behav Brain Res 1996; 75:33–47.

213. Murray B, Shizgal P. Behavioral measures of conduction velocity and refractory period for reward-relevant axons in the anterior LH and VTA. Physiol Behav 1996;59:643–652.

214. Murray B, Shizgal P. Physiological measures of conduction velocity and refractory period for putative reward-relevant MFB axons arising in the rostral MFB. Physiol Behav 1996; 59:427–437.

215. Gallistel CR, Leon M, Lim BT, Sim JC, Waraczynski M. Destruction of the medial forebrain bundle caudal to the site of stimulation reduces rewarding efficacy but destruction rostrally does not. Behav Neurosci 1996;110: 766–790.

216. Heimer L, Zahm DS, Churchill L, Kalivas PW, Wohltmann C. Specificity in the projections patterns of accumbal shell and core in the rat. Neuroscience 1991;41:89–125.

217. Mogenson GJ, Swanson LW, Wu M. Neural projections from nucleus accumbens to globus pallidus, substantia innominata, and lateral preoptic–lateral hypothalamic area: an anatomical and electrophysiological investigation in the rat. J Neurosci 1983;3:189–202.

218. Kalivas PW, Churchill L, Klitenick MA. GABA and enkephalin projection from the nucleus accumbens and ventral pallidum to the ventral tegmental area. Neuroscience 1993;57: 1047–1060.

219. McAlonan GM, Robbins TW, Everitt BJ. Effects of medial dorsal thalamic and ventral pallidal lesions on the acquisition of a conditioned place preference: further evidence for the involvement of the ventral striatopallidal system in reward-related processes. Neuroscience 1993;52:605–620.

220. Chrobak JJ, Napier TC. Opioid and GABA modulation of accumbens-evoked ventral pallidal activity. J Neural Transm Gen Sect 1993; 93:123–143.

221. Inglis WL, Dunbar JS, Winn P. Outflow from the nucleus accumbens to the pedunculopontine tegmental nucleus: a dissociation between locomotor activity and the acquisition of responding for conditioned reinforcement stimulated by d-amphetamine. Neuroscience 1994; 62:51–64.

222. Hubner CB, Koob GF. The ventral pallidum plays a role in mediating cocaine and heroin self-administration in the rat. Brain Res 1990; 508:20–29.

223. Robledo P, Koob GF. Two discrete nucleus accumbens projection areas differentially mediate cocaine self-administration in the rat. Behav Brain Res 1993;55:159–166.

224. Stein EA. Ventral tegmental self-stimulation selectively induces opioid peptide release in rat CNS. Synapse 1993;13:63–73.

225. Johnson PI, Stellar JR, Paul AD. Regional reward differences within the ventral pallidum are revealed by microinjections of a mu opiate receptor agonist. Neuropharmacology 1993; 32:1305–1314.

226. Johnson PI, Stellar JR. Comparison of delta opiate receptor agonist induced reward and motor effects between the ventral pallidum and dorsal striatum. Neuropharmacology 1994;33: 1171–1182.

227. Klitenick MA, Deutch AY, Churchill L, Kalivas PW. Topography and functional role of dopaminergic projections from the ventral mesencephalic tegmentum to the ventral pallidum. Neuroscience 1992;50:371–386.

228. Anagnostakis Y, Spyraki C. Effect of morphine applied by intrapallidal microdialysis on the release of dopamine in the nucleus accumbens. Brain Res Bull 1994;34:275–282.

229. Sesack SR, Pickel VM. Prefrontal cortical efferents in the rat synapse on unlabelled neuronal targets of catecholamine terminals in the nucleus accumbens septi and on dopamine neurons in the ventral tegmental area. J Comp Neurol 1992;320:145–160.

230. Self DW, Nestler EJ. Molecular mechanisms of drug reinforcement and addiction. Annu Rev Neurosci 1995;18:463–495.
231. Carlezon WA Jr, Wise RA. Rewarding actions of phencyclidine and related drugs in nucleus accumbens shell and frontal cortex. J Neurosci 1996;16:3112–3122.
232. Graybiel AM. Neurotransmitters and neuro-modulators in the basal ganglia. Trends Neurosci 1990;13:244–254.
233. Gerfen CR. The neostriatal mosaic: multiple levels of compartmental organization. Trends Neurosci 1992;15:133–139.
234. Kawaguchi Y, Wilson CJ, Augood SJ, Emson PC. Striatal interneurones: chemical physiological and morphological characterization. Trends Neurosci 1995;18:527–535.
235. Smith AD, Bolam JP. The neural network of the basal ganglia as revealed by the study of synaptic connections of identified neurons. Trends Neurosci 1990;13:259–265.
236. Bolam JP, Bennett BD. Microcircuitry of the neostriatum. In: Ariano MA, Surmeier DJ, eds. Molecular and cellular mechanisms of neostriatal function. New York: R.G. Landes, 1995:1–19.
237. Sesack SR, Pickel VM. Ultrastructural relationships between terminals immunoreactive for enkephalin, GABA, or both transmitters in the rat ventral tegmental area. Brain Res 1995;672:261–275.
238. Maneuf YP, Mitchell IJ, Crossman AR, Brotchie JM. On the role of enkephalin cotransmission in the GABAergic striatal efferents to the globus pallidus. Exp Neurol 1994;125:65–71.
239. Esposito RU, Porrino LJ, Seeger TF. Brain stimulation reward: measurement and mapping by psychophysical techniques and quantitative 2-[^{14}C]deoxyglucose autoradiography. In: Bozarth MA, ed. Methods of assessing the reinforcing properties of abused drugs. New York: Springer-Verlag, 1987:421–445.
240. Stein L, Ray OS. Brain stimulation reward "thresholds" self-determined in rat. Psycho-pharmacologia 1960;1:251–256.
241. Nazzaro JM, Gardner EL. GABA antagonism lowers self-stimulation thresholds in the ventral tegmental area. Brain Res 1980;189:279–283.
242. Seeger TF, Nazzaro JM, Gardner EL. Selective inhibition of mesolimbic behavioral supersensitivity by naloxone. Eur J Pharmacol 1980;65:435–438.
243. Nazzaro JM, Seeger TF, Gardner EL. Naloxone blocks phencyclidine's dose-dependent effects on direct brain reward thresholds. In: Proceedings of world conference on clinical pharmacology and therapeutics. London: British Pharmacological Society, 1980:949.
244. Gardner EL, Paredes W, Seeger TF, Smith D, van Praag HM. Mesolimbic DA antagonism by 5HT$_3$ receptor blockade. In: Book of abstracts, World Psychiatric Association regional symposium, The research and clinical interface for psychiatric disorders, October 13–16, 1988, Washington, DC. Washington, DC: American Psychiatric Association, 1988:222.
245. Gardner EL. An improved technique for determining brain reward thresholds in primates. Behav Res Meth Instrumentation 1971;3:273–274.
246. Seeger TF, Gardner EL. Enhancement of self-stimulation behavior in rats and monkeys after chronic neuroleptic treatment: evidence for mesolimbic supersensitivity. Brain Res 1979;175:49–57.

247. Esposito RU, Kornetsky C. Morphine lowering of self-stimulation thresholds: lack of tolerance with long-term administration. Science 1977;195:189–191.
248. Stein L. Effects and interactions of imipramine, chlorpromazine, reserpine, and amphetamine on self-stimulation: possible neurophysical basis of depression. In: Wortis J, ed. Recent advances in biological psychiatry. New York: Plenum Press, 1962;4:297–311.
249. Seeger TF, Carlson KR. Amphetamine and morphine: additive effects on ICSS threshold. Soc Neurosci Abstr 1981;7:974.
250. Seeger TF, Carlson KR, Nazzaro JM. Pentobarbital induces a naloxone-reversible decrease in mesolimbic self-stimulation threshold. Pharmacol Biochem Behav 1981;15:583–586.
251. Cassens GP, Mills AW. Lithium and amphetamine: opposite effects on threshold of intracranial reinforcement. Psychopharmacologia 1973;30:283–290.
252. Kelly K, Reid LD. Addictive agents and intracranial stimulation: morphine and thresholds for positive intracranial reinforcement. Bull Psychonomic Soc 1977;10:298–300.
253. Lewis MJ. Age related decline in brain stimulation reward: rejuvenation by amphetamine. Exp Aging Res 1983;7:225–234.
254. Lewis MJ, Phelps RW. A multifunctional on-line brain stimulation system: investigation of alcohol and aging effects. In: Bozarth MA, ed. Methods of assessing the reinforcing properties of abused drugs. New York: Springer-Verlag, 1987:463–478.
255. Marcus R, Kornetsky C. Negative and positive intracranial reinforcement thresholds: effects of morphine. Psychopharmacologia 1974;38:1–13.
256. Esposito RU, McLean S, Kornetsky C. Effects of morphine on intracranial self-stimulation to various brain stem loci. Brain Res 1979;168:425–429.
257. Kornetsky C, Esposito RU. Euphorigenic drugs: effects on the reward pathways of the brain. Fed Proc 1979;38:2473–2476.
258. Esposito RU, Motola AHD, Kornetsky C. Cocaine: acute effects on reinforcement thresholds for self-stimulation behavior to the medial forebrain bundle. Pharmacol Biochem Behav 1978;8:437–439.
259. Esposito RU, Perry W, Kornetsky C. Effects of d-amphetamine and naloxone on brain stimulation reward. Psychopharmacology 1980;69:187–191.
260. Hubner CB, Bain GT, Kornetsky C. Morphine and amphetamine: effect on brain stimulation reward. Soc Neurosci Abstr 1983;9:893.
261. Atrens DM, Von Vietinghoff-Reisch F, Der-Karabetian A, Masliyah E. Modulation of reward and aversion processes in the rat diencephalon by amphetamine. Am J Physiol 1974;226:874–880.
262. Liebman JM, Butcher LL. Comparative involvement of dopamine and noradrenaline in rate-free self-stimulation in substantia nigra, lateral hypothalamus and mesencephalic central gray. Naunyn Schmiedebergs Arch Pharmacol 1974;284:167–194.
263. Phillips AG, Fibiger HC. Dopaminergic and noradrenergic substrates of positive reinforcement: differential effects of d- and l-amphetamine. Science 1973;179:575–577.
264. Jaffe JH, Martin WR. Opioid analgesics and antagonists. In: Gilman AG, Goodman LS, Rall TW, Murad F, eds. Goodman and Gilman's the pharmacological basis of therapeu-

tics. 7th ed. New York: Macmillan, 1985:491–531.
265. Marshall JF, Rosenstein AJ. Age-related decline in rat striatal dopamine metabolism is regionally homogeneous. Neurobiol Aging 1990;11:131–137.
266. Franklin KBJ. Catecholamines and self-stimulation: reward and performance effects dissociated. Pharmacol Biochem Behav 1978;9:813–820.
267. Esposito RU, Faulkner W, Kornetsky C. Specific modulation of brain stimulation reward by haloperidol. Pharmacol Biochem Behav 1979;10:937–940.
268. Esposito RU, Perry W, Kornetsky C. Chlorpromazine and brain-stimulation reward: potentiation of effects by naloxone. Pharmacol Biochem Behav 1981;15:903–905.
269. Gardner EL, Paredes W, Smith D, Zukin RS. Facilitation of brain stimulation reward by Δ^9-tetrahydrocannabinol is mediated by an endogenous opioid mechanism. Adv Biosci 1989;75:671–674.
270. Lorens SA, Sainati SM. Naloxone blocks the excitatory effect of ethanol and chlordiazepoxide on lateral hypothalamic self-stimulation behavior. Life Sci 1978;23:1359–1364.
271. Kornetsky C, Bain G, Reidl EM. Effects of cocaine and naloxone on brain stimulation reward. Pharmacologist 1981;23:192.
272. Khachaturian H, Lewis ME, Schäfer MK-H, Watson SJ. Anatomy of the CNS opioid systems. Trends Neurosci 1985;8:111–119.
273. Mansour A, Khachaturian H, Lewis M, Akil H, Watson S. Anatomy of CNS opioid receptors. Trends Neurosci 1988;11:308–314.
274. Gardner EL, Zukin RS, Makman MH. Modulation of opiate receptor binding in striatum and amygdala by selective mesencephalic lesions. Brain Res 1980;194:232–239.
275. Pollard H, Llorens C, Bonnet JJ, Costentin J, Schwartz JC. Opiate receptors on mesolimbic dopaminergic neurons. Neurosci Lett 1977;7:295–299.
276. Pollard H, Llorens C, Schwartz JC, Gros C, Dray F. Localization of opiate receptors and enkephalins in the rat striatum in relationship with the nigrostriatal dopaminergic system: lesion studies. Brain Res 1978;151:392–398.
277. Hirschhorn ID, Hittner D, Gardner EL, Cubells J, Makman MH. Evidence for a role of endogenous opioids in the nigrostriatal system: influence of naloxone and morphine on nigrostriatal dopaminergic supersensitivity. Brain Res 1983;270:109–117.
278. Pickel VM, Chan J. Ultrastructural basis for interactions between opioid peptides and dopamine in rat striatum. Soc Neurosci Abstr 1989;15:810.
279. Kubota Y, Inagaki S, Kito S, Takagi H, Smith AD. Ultrastructural evidence of dopaminergic input to enkephalinergic neurons in rat neostriatum. Brain Res 1986;367:374–378.
280. Routtenberg A. Intracranial chemical injection and behavior: a critical review. Behav Biol 1972;7:601–641.
281. Bozarth MA. Intracranial self-administration procedures for the assessment of drug reinforcement. In: Bozarth MA, ed. Methods of assessing the reinforcing properties of abused drugs. New York: Springer-Verlag, 1987:173–187.
282. Broekkamp CLE. Combined microinjection and brain stimulation reward methodology for the localization of reinforcing drug effects. In: Bozarth MA, ed. Methods of assessing the reinforcing properties of abused drugs. New York: Springer-Verlag, 1987:479–488.

283. Broekkamp CLE, van den Bogaard JH, Cools AR, Heynen HJ, Rops RH, van Rossum JM. Separation of inhibiting and stimulating effects of morphine on self-stimulation behavior by intracerebral microinjections. Eur J Pharmacol 1976;36:443–446.

284. Broekkamp CLE, van Rossum JM. The effect of microinjections of morphine and haloperidol into the neostriatum and the nucleus accumbens on self-stimulation behavior. Arch Int Pharmacodyn Ther 1975;217:110–117.

285. Broekkamp CLE, Phillips AG, Cools AR. Facilitation of self-stimulation behavior following intracerebral microinjections of opioids into the ventral tegmental area. Pharmacol Biochem Behav 1979;11:289–295.

286. Broekkamp CLE, Pijnenburg AJJ, Cools AR, van Rossum JM. The effect of microinjections of amphetamine into the neostriatum and nucleus accumbens on self-stimulation behavior. Psychopharmacology 1975;42:179–183.

287. Stellar JR, Corbett D. Regional neuroleptic nicroinjections indicate a role for nucleus accumbens in lateral hypothalamic self-stimulation reward. Brain Res 1989;477:126–143.

288. Jenck F, Gratton A, Wise RA. Opioid receptor subtypes associated with ventral tegmental facilitation of lateral hypothalamic brain stimulation reward. Brain Res 1987;423:34–38.

289. Colle LM, Wise RA. Effects of nucleus accumbens amphetamine on lateral hypothalamic brain stimulation reward. Brain Res 1988;459:361–368.

290. Phillips AG, Broekkamp CL, Fibiger HC. Strategies for studying the neurochemical substrates of drug reinforcement in rodents. Prog Neuro-Psychopharmacol Biol Psychiatry 1983;7:585–590.

291. Bozarth MA. Opiate reward mechanisms mapped by intracranial self-administration. In: Smith JE, Lane JD, eds. Neurobiology of opiate reward processes. Amsterdam: Elsevier North Holland Biomedical Press, 1983:331–359.

292. Myers RD. Methods for chemical stimulation of the brain. In: Myers RD, ed. Methods in psychobiology. New York: Academic Press, 1972; 1:247–280.

293. Myers RD. Handbook of drug and chemical stimulation of the brain. New York: Van Nostrand Reinhold, 1974.

294. Bozarth MA, Wise RA. Electrolytic microinfusion transducer system: an alternative method of intracranial drug application. J Neurosci Meth 1980;2:273–275.

295. Renner KE. Delay of reinforcement: a historical review. Psychol Bull 1964;61:341–361.

296. Tarpy RM, Sawabini FL. Reinforcement delay: a selective review of the last decade. Psychol Bull 1974;81:984–997.

297. Phillips AG, Mora F, Rolls ET. Intracerebral self-administration of amphetamine by rhesus monkeys. Neurosci Lett 1981;24:81–86.

298. Monaco AP, Hernandez L, Hoebel BG. Nucleus accumbens: site of amphetamine self-administration. Comparison with the lateral ventricle. In: Chronister RB, DeFrance JF, eds. Neurobiology of the nucleus accumbens. Brunswick, ME: Haer Institute, 1981: 338–343.

299. Hoebel BG, Monaco AP, Hernandez L, Aulisi EF, Stanley BG, Lenard L. Self-injection of amphetamine directly into the brain. Psychopharmacology 1983;81:158–163.

300. Goeders NE, Smith JE. Cortical dopaminergic involvement in cocaine reinforcement. Science 1983;221:773–775.

301. Bozarth MA, Wise RA. Intracranial self-administration of morphine into the ventral tegmental area in rats. Life Sci 1981;28:551–555.

302. Bozarth MA, Wise RA. Localization of reward-relevant opiate receptors. NIDA Res Monogr Ser 1982;41:158–164.

303. Stein EA, Olds J. Direct intracerebral self-administration of opiates in the rat. Soc Neurosci Abstr 1977;3:302.

304. Olds ME. Hypothalamic substrate for the positive reinforcing properties of morphine in the rat. Brain Res 1979;168:351–360.

305. Olds ME. Reinforcing effects of morphine in the nucleus accumbens. Brain Res 1982;237: 429–440.

306. van Ree JM, De Wied D. Involvement of neurohypophyseal peptides in drug-mediated adaptive responses. Pharmacol Biochem Behav 1980;13(suppl 1):257–263.

307. Goeders NE, Lane JD, Smith JE. Self-administration of methionine enkephalin into the nucleus accumbens. Pharmacol Biochem Behav 1984;20:451–455.

308. Olds ME, Williams KN. Self-administration of d-ala²-met-enkephalinamide at hypothalamic self-stimulation sites. Brain Res 1980;194: 155–170.

309. Britt MD, Wise RA. Ventral tegmental site of opiate reward: antagonism by a hydrophilic opiate receptor blocker. Brain Res 1983;258: 105–108.

310. McBride WJ, Murphy JM, Gatto GJ, Levy AD, Yoshimoto K, Lumeng L, Li TK. CNS mechanisms of alcohol self-administration. Alcohol Alcohol Suppl 1993;2:463–467.

311. Pert A, Yaksh T. Sites of morphine induced analgesia in the primate brain: relation to pain pathways. Brain Res 1974;80:135–140.

312. Part A, Yaksh T. Localization of the antinociceptive action of morphine in primate brain. Pharmacol Biochem Behav 1975;3:135–138.

313. Teasdale JAP, Bozarth MA, Stewart J. Body temperature responses to microinjections of morphine in brain sites containing opiate receptors. Soc Neurosci Abstr 1981;7:799.

314. Bozarth MA, Wise RA. Anatomically distinct opiate receptor fields mediate reward and physical dependence. Science 1984;244:516–517.

315. Justice JB Jr, ed. Voltammetry in the neurosciences: principles, methods, and applications. Clifton, NJ: Humana Press, 1987.

316. Marsden CA, ed. Measurement of neurotransmitter release in vivo. IBRO handbook series: Methods in the neurosciences. Vol. 6. New York: Wiley, 1984.

317. Myers RD, Knott PJ, eds. Neurochemical analysis of the conscious brain: voltammetry and push-pull perfusion. Ann N Y Acad Sci 1986;473.

318. Leviel V, Guibert B. Involvement of intraterminal dopamine compartments in the amine release in the cat striatum. Neurosci Lett 1987; 76:197–202.

319. Kuczenski R. Dose response for amphetamine-induced changes in dopamine levels in push-pull perfusates of rat striatum. J Neurochem 1986;46:1605–1611.

320. Imperato A, Di Chiara G. Trans-striatal dialysis coupled to reverse phase high performance liquid chromatography with electrochemical detection: a new method for the study of the in vivo release of endogenous dopamine and metabolites. J Neurosci 1984;4:966–977.

321. Johnson RD, Justice JB Jr. Model studies for brain dialysis. Brain Res Bull 1983;10:567–571.

322. Gardner EL, Chen J, Paredes W. Overview of chemical sampling techniques. J Neurosci Meth 1993;48:173–197.

323. Zetterström T, Sharp T, Marsden CA, Ungerstedt U. In vivo measurement of dopamine and its metabolites by intracerebral dialysis: changes after d-amphetamine. J Neurochem 1983;41:1769–1773.

324. Paredes W, Chen J, Gardner E. A miniature microdialysis probe: a new simple construction method for making a chronic, removable and recyclable probe. Curr Separations 1989;9:94.

325. Adams RN, Marsden CA. Electrochemical detection methods for monoamine measurements in vitro and in vivo. In: Iversen LL, Iversen SS, Snyder SH, eds. Handbook of psychopharmacology. New York: Plenum, 1982;15:1–74.

326. Stamford JA. In vivo voltammetry: promise and perspective. Brain Res Rev 1985;10: 119–135.

327. Schenk JO, Adams RN. Chronoamperometric measurements in the central nervous system. In: Marsden CA, ed. Measurement of neurotransmitter release in vivo. IBRO handbook series: Methods in the neurosciences. Vol. 6. New York: Wiley, 1984:193–208.

328. Gerhardt GA, Oke AF, Nagy G, Moghaddam B, Adams RN. Nafion-coated electrodes with high selectivity for CNS electrochemistry. Brain Res 1984;290:390–395.

329. Vulto AG, Sharp T, Ungerstedt U. Rapid postmortal increase in extracellular concentration of dopamine in the rat brain as assessed by intra-cranial dialysis. Soc Neurosci Abstr 1985; 11:1207.

330. Di Chiara G, Imperato A. Drugs abused by humans preferentially increase synaptic dopamine concentrations in the mesolimbic system of freely moving rats. Proc Natl Acad Sci USA 1988;85:5274–5278.

331. Hurd YL, Kehr J, Ungerstedt U. In vivo microdialysis as a technique to monitor drug transport: correlation of extracellular cocaine levels and dopamine overflow in the rat brain. J Neurochem 1988;51:1314–1316.

332. Hurd YL, Weiss F, Koob G, And N-E, Ungerstedt U. Cocaine reinforcement and extracellular dopamine overflow in rat nucleus accumbens: an in vivo microdialysis study. Brain Res 1989;498:199–203.

333. Hurd YL, Weiss F, Koob G, Ungerstedt U. The influence of cocaine self-administration on in vivo dopamine and acetylcholine neurotransmission in rat caudate-putamen. Neurosci Lett 1990;109:227–233.

334. Akimoto K, Hamamura T, Kazahaya Y, Akiyama K, Otsuki S. Enhanced extracellular dopamine level may be the fundamental neuropharmacological basis of cross-behavioral sensitization between methamphetamine and cocaine—an in vivo dialysis study in freely moving rats. Brain Res 1990;507:344–346.

335. Pettit HO, Pan H-T, Parsons LH, Justice JB Jr. Extracellular concentrations of cocaine and dopamine are enhanced during chronic cocaine administration. J Neurochem 1990;55:798–804.

336. Nomikos GG, Damsma G, Wenkstern D, Fibiger HC. In vivo characterization of locally applied dopamine uptake inhibitors by striatal microdialysis. Synapse 1990;6:106–112.

337. Church WH, Justice JB Jr, Byrd LD. Extracellular dopamine in rat striatum following uptake inhibition by cocaine, nomifensine and benztropine. Eur J Pharmacol 1987;139:345–348.

338. Akimoto K, Hamamura T, Otsuki S. Subchronic cocaine treatment enhances cocaine-induced dopamine efflux, studied by in vivo intracerebral dialysis. Brain Res 1989;490: 339–344.

339. Pettit HO, Justice JB Jr. Dopamine in the nucleus accumbens during cocaine self-administration as studied by in vivo microdialysis. Pharmacol Biochem Behav 1989;34:899–904.

340. Nicolaysen LC, Pan H, Justice JB Jr. Extracellular cocaine and dopamine concentrations are linearly related in rat striatum. Brain Res 1988;456:317–323.

341. Goeders NE, Kuhar MJ. Chronic cocaine administration induces opposite changes in dopamine receptors in the striatum and nucleus accumbens. Alcohol Drug Res 1987;7:207–216.

342. Memo M, Pradhan A, Hanbauer I. Cocaine-induced supersensitivity of striatal dopamine receptors: role of endogenous calmodulin. Neuropharmacology 1981;20:1145–1150.

343. Post RM, Rose H. Increasing effects of repetitive cocaine administration in the rat. Nature 1976;260:731–732.

344. Shuster L, Yu G, Bates A. Sensitization to cocaine stimulation in mice. Psychopharmacology 1977;52:185–190.

345. Trulson ME, Ulissey MJ. Chronic cocaine administration decreases dopamine synthesis rate and increases [³H]spiroperidol binding in rat brain. Brain Res Bull 1987;19:35–38.

346. Kalivas PW, Duffy P, DuMars LA, Skinner C. Behavioral and neurochemical effects of acute and daily cocaine administration in rats. J Pharmacol Exp Ther 1988;245:485–492.

347. Brock JW, Ng JP, Justice JB Jr. Effect of chronic cocaine on dopamine synthesis in the nucleus accumbens as determined by microdialysis perfusion with NSD-1015. Neurosci Lett 1990;117:234–239.

348. Van Rossum J, Van Schoot J, Hurkman J. Mechanism of action of cocaine and amphetamine in the brain. Experientia 1982;18:229–230.

349. Reith MEA, Meisler BE, Sershen H, Lajtha A. Structural requirements for cocaine congeners to interact with dopamine and serotonin uptake sites in mouse brain and to induce stereotyped behavior. Biochem Pharmacol 1986;35:1123–1129.

350. Sharp T, Zetterström T, Ljungberg T, Ungerstedt U. A direct comparison of amphetamine-induced behaviours and regional brain dopamine release in the rat using intracerebral dialysis. Brain Res 1987;401:322–330.

351. Wood PL, Kim HS, Marien MR. Intracerebral dialysis: direct evidence for the utility of 3-MT measurements as an index of dopamine release. Life Sci 1987;41:1–5.

352. Hernandez L, Lee F, Hoebel BG. Simultaneous microdialysis and amphetamine infusion in the nucleus accumbens and striatum of freely moving rats: increase in extracellular dopamine and serotonin. Brain Res Bull 1987;19:623–628.

353. Butcher SP, Fairbrother IS, Kelly JS, Arbuthnott GW. Amphetamine-induced dopamine release in the rat striatum: an in vivo microdialysis study. J Neurochem 1988;50:346–355.

354. Zetterström T, Sharp T, Collin AK, Ungerstedt U. In vivo measurement of extracellular dopamine and DOPAC in rat striatum after various dopamine-releasing drugs: implications for the origin of extracellular DOPAC. Eur J Pharmacol 1988;148:327–334.

355. Robinson TE, Jurson PA, Bennett JA, Bentgen KM. Persistent sensitization of dopamine neurotransmission in ventral striatum (nucleus accumbens) produced by prior experience with (+)-amphetamine: a microdialysis study in freely moving rats. Brain Res 1988;462:211–222.

356. Westerink BH, Hofsteede RM, Tuntler J, de Vries JB. Use of calcium antagonism for the characterization of drug-evoked dopamine release from the brain of conscious rats determined by microdialysis. J Neurochem 1989;52:722–729.

357. Hoebel BG, Hernandez L, Schwartz DH, Mark GP, Hunter GA. Microdialysis studies of brain norepinephrine, serotonin, and dopamine release during ingestive behavior: theoretical and clinical implications. Ann N Y Acad Sci 1989;575:171–191.

358. Hiramatsu M, Cho AK. Enantiomeric differences in the effects of 3,4-methylenedioxymethamphetamine on extracellular monoamines and metabolites in the striatum of freely-moving rats: an in vivo microdialysis study. Neuropharmacology 1990;29:269–275.

359. Gazzara RA, Takeda H, Cho AK, Howard SG. Inhibition of dopamine release by methylenedioxymethamphetamine is mediated by serotonin. Eur J Pharmacol 1989;168:209–217.

360. Di Chiara G, Imperato A. Opposite effects of mu and kappa opiate agonists on dopamine release in the nucleus accumbens and in the dorsal caudate of freely moving rats. J Pharmacol Exp Ther 1988;244:1067–1080.

361. Imperato A, Angelucci L. 5-HT₃ receptors control dopamine release in the nucleus accumbens of freely moving rats. Neurosci Lett 1989;101:214–217.

362. Carboni E, Acquas E, Frau R, Di Chiara G. Differential inhibitory effects of a 5-HT₃ antagonist on drug-induced stimulation of dopamine release. Eur J Pharmacol 1989;164:515–519.

363. Spanagel R, Herz A, Shippenberg TS. The effects of opioid peptides on dopamine release in the nucleus accumbens: an in vivo microdialysis study. J Neurochem 1990;55:1734–1740.

364. Mucha RF, Herz A. Motivational properties of kappa and mu opioid receptor agonists studied with place and taste preference conditioning. Psychopharmacology 1985;86:274–280.

365. Shippenberg TS, Bals-Kubik R, Herz A. Endogenous opioids and reinforcement: role of multiple opioid receptor types and dopamine. NIDA Res Monogr Ser 1988;90:40.

366. Kalivas PW, Duffy P, Eberhardt H. Modulation of A10 dopamine neurons by gamma-aminobutyric acid agonists. J Pharmacol Exp Ther 1990;253:858–866.

367. Wood PL, Altar CA. Dopamine release in vivo from nigrostriatal, mesolimbic, and mesocortical neurons: utility of 3-methoxytyramine measurements. Pharmacol Rev 1988;40:163–187.

368. Damsma G, Westerink BH, de Vries JB, Horn AS. The effect of systemically applied cholinergic drugs on the striatal release of dopamine and its metabolites, as determined by automated brain dialysis in conscious rats. Neurosci Lett 1988;89:349–354.

369. Cashaw JL, Geraghty CA, McLaughlin BR, Davis VE. Effect of acute ethanol administration on brain levels of tetrahydropapaveroline in L-dopa-treated rats. J Neurosci Res 1987;18:497–503.

370. Hernandez L, Auerbach S, Hoebel BG. Phencyclidine (PCP) injected in the nucleus accumbens increases extracellular dopamine and serotonin as measured by microdialysis. Life Sci 1988;42:1713–1723.

371. Carboni E, Imperato A, Perezzani I, Di Chiara G. Amphetamine, cocaine, phencyclidine and nomifensine increase extracellular dopamine concentrations preferentially in the nucleus accumbens of freely moving rats. Neuroscience 1989;28:653–661.

372. Chen J, Paredes W, Li J, Smith D, Lowinson J, Gardner EL. Δ⁹-Tetrahydrocannabinol produces naloxone-blockable enhancement of presynaptic basal dopamine efflux in nucleus accumbens of conscious, freely-moving rats as measured by intracerebral microdialysis. Psychopharmacology 1990;102:156–162.

373. Ng Cheong Ton JM, Gardner EL. Effects of delta-9-tetrahydrocannabinol on dopamine release in the brain: intracerebral dialysis experiments. Soc Neurosci Abstr 1986;12:135.

374. Ng Cheong Ton JM, Gerhardt GA, Friedemann M, Etgen AM, Rose GM, Sharpless NS, Gardner EL. Effects of Δ⁹-tetrahydrocannabinol on potassium-evoked release of dopamine in the rat caudate nucleus: an in vivo electrochemical and in vivo microdialysis study. Brain Res 1988;451:59–68.

375. Chen J, Paredes W, Lowinson JH, Gardner EL. Δ⁹-Tetrahydrocannabinol enhances presynaptic dopamine efflux in medial prefrontal cortex. Eur J Pharmacol 1990;190:259–262.

376. Pontieri FE, Tanda G, Di Chiara G. Intravenous cocaine, morphine, and amphetamine preferentially increase extracellular dopamine in the "shell" as compared with the "core" of the rat nucleus accumbens. Proc Natl Acad Sci USA 1995;92:12304–12308.

377. Pothos EN, Creese I, Hoebel BG. Restricted eating with weight loss selectively decreases extracellular dopamine in the nucleus accumbens and alters dopamine response to amphetamine, morphine, and food intake. J Neurosci 1995;15:6640–6650.

378. Brazell MP, Marsden CA. Intracerebral injection of ascorbate oxidase—effect on in vivo electrochemical recordings. Brain Res 1982;249:167–172.

379. Mueller K. In vivo voltammetric recording with Nafion-coated carbon paste electrodes: additional evidence that ascorbic acid release is monitored. Pharmacol Biochem Behav 1986;25:325–328.

380. Ewing AG, Alloway KD, Curtis SD, Dayton MA, Wightman RM, Rebec GV. Simultaneous electrochemical and unit recording measurements: characterization of d-amphetamine and ascorbic acid on neostriatal neurons. Brain Res 1983;261:101–108.

381. Salamone JD, Hambry LS, Neill DB, Justice JB Jr. Extracellular ascorbic acid increases in striatum following systemic amphetamine. Pharmacol Biochem Behav 1984;20:609–612.

382. Crespi F, Sharp T, Maidment N, Marsden C. Differential pulse voltammetry: in vivo evidence that uric acid contributes to the indole oxidation peak. Neurosci Lett 1083;43:203–207.

383. Mueller K, Palmour R, Andrews CD, Knott PJ. In vivo voltammetric evidence of production of uric acid by rat caudate. Brain Res 1985;335:231–235.

384. Haskett C, Mueller K. The effects of serotonin depletion on the voltammetric response to amphetamine. Pharmacol Biochem Behav 1987;28:381–384.

385. Mueller K, Haskett C. Effects of haloperidol on amphetamine-induced increases in ascorbic acid and uric acid as determined by voltammetry in vivo. Pharmacol Biochem Behav 1987;27:231–234.

386. Dayton MA, Ewing AG, Wightman RM. Response of microvoltammetric electrodes to homogeneous catalytic and slow heterogeneous charge-transfer reactions. Anal Chem 1980;52:2392–2396.

387. Echizen M, Freed CR. Factors affecting in vivo

electrochemistry: electrode-tissue interactions and the ascorbate amplification effect. Life Sci 1986;39:77–89.

388. Gonon F, Buda M, Cespuglio R, Jouvet M, Pujol J-F. In vivo electrochemical detection of catechols in the neostriatum of anesthetized rats: dopamine or DOPAC? Nature 1980;286: 902–904.

389. Stamford JA, Kruk ZL, Millar J. Stimulated limbic and striatal dopamine release measured by fast cyclic voltammetry: anatomical, electrochemical and pharmacological characterisation. Brain Res 1988;454:282–288.

390. Stamford JA, Kruk ZL, Millar J. Dissociation of the actions of uptake blockers upon dopamine overflow and uptake in the rat nucleus accumbens: in vivo voltammetric data. Neuropharmacology 1989;28:1383–1388.

391. Gerhardt GA, Gratton A, Rose GM. In vivo electrochemical studies of the effects of cocaine on dopamine nerve terminals in the rat neostriatum. Physiol Bohemoslov 1988;37: 249–257.

392. Kelly RS, Wightman RM. Detection of dopamine overflow and diffusion with voltammetry in slices of rat brain. Brain Res 1987;423: 79–87.

393. Ng JP, Hubert GW, Justice JB Jr. Increased stimulated release and uptake of dopamine in nucleus accumbens after repeated cocaine administration as measured by in vivo voltammetry. J Neurochem 1991;56:1485–1492.

394. Forni C, Nieoullon A. Electrochemical detection of dopamine release in the striatum of freely moving hamsters. Brain Res 1984;297: 11–20.

395. Nieoullon A, Forni C, El Ganouni S. Contribution to the study of nigrostriatal dopaminergic neuron activity using electrochemical detection of dopamine release in the striatum of freely moving animals. Ann N Y Acad Sci 1986;473:126–134.

396. Gazzara RA, Fisher RS, Howard-Butcher S. The ontogeny of amphetamine-induced dopamine release in the caudate-putamen of the rat. Devel Brain Res 1986;28:213–220.

397. Stamford JA, Kruk ZL, Millar J. Measurement of stimulated dopamine release in the rat by in vivo voltammetry: the influence of stimulus duration on drug responses. Neurosci Lett 1986;69:70–73.

398. Knott PJ, Brannan TS, Andrews CD, Togasaki D, Young JG, Maker H, Yahr M. Drug, stress, and circadian influences on dopaminergic neuronal function in the rat studied by voltammetry and chronoamperometry. Ann N Y Acad Sci 1986;473:493–495.

399. Gazzara RA, Howard-Butcher S. A developmental study of amphetamine-induced dopamine release in rats using in vivo voltammetry. Ann N Y Acad Sci 1986;473:527–529.

400. Hughes CW, Pottinger HJ. Chronic CNS recording with in vivo electrochemistry in rats: monitoring biogenic amine release in behavioral and pharmacological models of depression. Ann N Y Acad Sci 1986;473:530–534.

401. Lane RF, Blaha CD, Hari SP. Electrochemistry in vivo: monitoring dopamine release in the brain of the conscious, freely moving rat. Brain Res Bull 1987;19:19–27.

402. Gonzalez-Mora JL, Sanchez-Bruno JA, Mas M. Concurrent on-line analysis of striatal ascorbate, dopamine and dihydroxyphenylacetic acid concentrations by in vivo voltammetry. Neurosci Lett 1988;86:61–66.

403. Gonon FG. Nonlinear relationship between impulse flow and dopamine released by rat mid-brain dopaminergic neurons as studied by in vivo electrochemistry. Neuroscience 1988;24: 19–28.

404. May LJ, Kuhr WG, Wightman RM. Differentiation of dopamine overflow and uptake processes in the extracellular fluid of the rat caudate nucleus with fast-scan in vivo voltammetry. J Neurochem 1988;51:1060–1069.

405. Forni C, Brundin P, Strecker RE, El Ganouni S, Björklund A, Nieoullon A. Time-course of recovery of dopamine neuron activity during reinnervation of the denervated striatum by fetal mesencephalic grafts as assessed by in vivo voltammetry. Exp Brain Res 1989;76:75–87.

406. Yamamoto BK, Pehek EA. A neurochemical heterogeneity of the rat striatum as measured by in vivo electrochemistry and microdialysis. Brain Res 1990;506:236–242.

407. Suaud-Chagny M-F, Buda M, Gonon FG. Pharmacology of electrically evoked dopamine release studied in the rat olfactory tubercle by in vivo electrochemistry. Eur J Pharmacol 1989;164:273–283.

408. Yamamoto BK, Spanos LJ. The acute effects of methylenedioxymethamphetamine on dopamine release in the awake-behaving rat. Eur J Pharmacol 1988;148:195–203.

409. Gardner EL. Cannabinoid interaction with brain reward systems—The neurobiological basis of cannabinoid abuse. In: Murphy LL, Bartke A, eds. Marijuana/cannabinoids: Neurobiology and neurophysiology. Boca Raton, FL: CRC Press, 1992:275–335.

410. Broderick PA, Gardner EL, van Praag HM. In vivo electrochemical evidence for an opiate-induced modulation of dopaminergic and serotonergic systems in rat striatum. Paper presented at meetings of American College of Neuro-Psychopharmacology, San Juan, Puerto Rico, 1983.

411. Broderick PA. In vivo electrochemical studies of rat striatal dopamine and serotonin release after morphine. Life Sci 1985;36:2269–2275.

412. Ostrowski NL, Paul I, Drnach M, Caggiula AR. Changes in locomotor activity and in the discharge rates of midbrain dopamine neurons with repeated administrations of low doses of morphine. Soc Neurosci Abstr 1983; 9:280.

413. Broderick PA, Phelan FT. Neurochemical aspects of morphine tolerance in the freely moving and behaving animal: voltammetric studies. Prog Clin Biol Res 1990;328:501–506.

414. Milne B, Quintin L, Pujol JF. Fentanyl increases catecholamine oxidation current measured by in vivo voltammetry in the rat striatum. Can J Anaesth 1989;36:155–159.

415. Broderick PA, Gardner EL, van Praag HM. In vivo electrochemical and behavioral evidence for specific neural substrates modulated differentially by enkephalin in rat stimulant stereotypy and locomotion. Biol Psychiatry 1984; 19:45–54.

416. Broderick PA. Striatal neurochemistry of dynorphin-(1–13): in vivo electrochemical semidifferential analyses. Neuropeptides 1987; 10:369–386.

417. Morgan ME, Vestal RE. Methylxanthine effects on caudate dopamine release as measured by in vivo electrochemistry. Life Sci 1989;45: 2025–2039.

418. Ford AP, Marsden CA. Influence of anaesthetics on rat striatal dopamine metabolism in vivo. Brain Res 1986;379:162–166.

419. Engel JA, Fahlke C, Hulthe P, Hard E, Johannessen K, Snape B, Svensson L. Biochemical and behavioral evidence for an interaction between ethanol and calcium channel antagonists. J Neural Transm 1988;74:181–193.

420. Signs SA, Yamamoto BK, Schechter MD. In vivo electrochemical determination of extracellular dopamine in the caudate of freely-moving rats after a low dose of ethanol. Neuropharmacology 1987;26:1653–1656.

421. Gerhardt GA, Pang K, Rose GM. In vivo electrochemical demonstration of the presynaptic actions of phencyclidine in rat caudate nucleus. J Pharmacol Exp Ther 1987;241:714–721.

422. Serrano A, D'Angio M, Scatton B. NMDA antagonists block restraint-induced increases in extracellular DOPAC in rat nucleus accumbens. Eur J Pharmacol 1989;162:157–166.

423. Crespi F, Keane PE. The effect of diazepam and Ro 15–1788 on extracellular ascorbic acid, DOPAC and 5-HIAA in the striatum of anesthetized and conscious freely moving rats, as measured by differential pulse voltammetry. Neurosci Res 1987;4:323–329.

424. Brose N, O'Neill RD, Boutelle MG, Fillenz M. Dopamine in the basal ganglia and benzodiazepine-induced sedation. Neuropharmacology 1988;27:589–595.

425. Brose N, O'Neill RD, Boutelle MG, Fillenz M. The effects of anxiolytic and anxiogenic benzodiazepine receptor ligands on motor activity and levels of ascorbic acid in the nucleus accumbens and striatum of the rat. Neuropharmacology 1989;28:509–514.

426. Randall LO, Schallek W, Heise GA, Keith EF, Bagdon RE. The psychosedative properties of methaminodiazepoxide. J Pharmacol Exp Ther 1960;129:163–197.

427. Soubrié P, Kulkarni S, Simon P, Boissier JR. Effets des anxiolytiques sur la prise de nourriture de rats et de souris placés en situation nouvelle ou familière. [The effects of anxiolytics on feeding behavior in rats and mice in novel or familiar environments.] Psychopharmacologia 1975;45:203–210.

428. Cooper SJ. Benzodiazepines as appetite-enhancing compounds. Appetite 1980;1:7–19.

429. Cooper SJ. A microgram dose of diazepam produces specific inhibition of ambulation in the rat. Pharmacol Biochem Behav 1985;22: 25–30.

430. Poschel BPH. A simple and specific screen for diazepam-like drugs. Psychopharmacologia 1971;19:193–198.

431. Stapleton JM, Lind MD, Merriman VJ, Reid LD. Naloxone inhibits diazepam induced feeding in rats. Life Sci 1979;24:2421–2426.

432. Wise RA, Dawson V. Diazepam-induced eating and lever pressing for food in sated rats. J Comp Physiol Psychol 1974;86:930–941.

433. Anderson-Baker WC, McLaughlin CL, Baile CA. Oral and hypothalamic injections of barbiturates, benzodiazepines and cannabinoids and food intake in rats. Pharmacol Biochem Behav 1979;11:487–491.

434. Britton DR, Britton KT, Dalton D, Vale W. Effects of naloxone on anti-conflict and hyperphagic actions of diazepam. Life Sci 1981; 29:1297–1302.

435. Cole, SO. Combined effects of chlordiazepoxide treatment and food deprivation on concurrent measures of feeding and activity. Pharmacol Biochem Behav 1983;18:369–372.

436. Della-Fera MA, Baile CA, McLaughlin CL. Feeding elicited by benzodiazepine-like chemicals in puppies and cats: structure-activity relationships. Pharmacol Biochem Behav 1980; 12:195–200.

437. Gratton A, Wise RA. Comparisons of refractory periods for medial forebrain bundle fibers

subserving stimulation-induced feeding and brain stimulation reward: a psychophysical study. Brain Res 1988;438:256–263.

438. Gratton A, Wise RA. Comparisons of connectivity and conduction velocities for medial forebrain bundle fibers subserving stimulation-induced feeding and brain stimulation reward. Brain Res 1988;438:264–270.

439. Pitts DK, Marwah J. Cocaine modulation of central monoaminergic neurotransmission. Pharmacol Biochem Behav 1987;26:453–461.

440. Peterson SL, Olsta SA, Matthews RT. Cocaine enhances medial prefrontal cortex neuron response to ventral tegmental area activation. Brain Res Bull 1990;24:267–273.

441. Bunney BS, Walters JR, Roth RH, Aghajanian GK. Dopaminergic neurons: effect of antipsychotic drugs and amphetamine on single cell activity. J Pharmacol Exp Ther 1973;185:560–571.

442. Bunney BS. The electrophysiological pharmacology of midbrain dopaminergic systems. In: Horn AS, Korf J, Westerink BHC, eds. The neurobiology of dopamine. New York: Academic Press, 1979:417–452.

443. Rebec GV. Electrophysiological pharmacology of amphetamine. Monogr Neural Sci 1987;13:1–33.

444. Chiodo LA. Dopamine-containing neurons in the mammalian central nervous system: electrophysiology and pharmacology. Neurosci Biobehav Rev 1988;12:49–91.

445. Rebec GV, Segal DS. Dose-dependent biphasic alterations in the spontaneous activity of neurons in the rat neostriatum produced by d-amphetamine and methylphenidate. Brain Res 1978;150:353–366.

446. Rebec GV, Alloway KD, Curtis SD. Apparent serotonergic modulation of the dose-dependent biphasic response of neostriatal neurons produced by d-amphetamine. Brain Res 1981;210:277–289.

447. Iwatsubo K, Clouet DH. Effects of morphine and haloperidol on the electrical activity of rat nigrostriatal neurons. J Pharmacol Exp Ther 1977;202:429–436.

448. Matthews RT, German DC. Electrophysiological evidence for excitation of rat ventral tegmental dopamine neurons by morphine. Neuroscience 1984;11:617–625.

449. Nowycky MC, Walters JR, Roth RH. Dopaminergic neurons: effect of acute and chronic morphine administration on single cell activity and transmitter metabolism. J Neural Transm 1978;42:99–116.

450. Hakan RL, Henriksen SJ. Systemic opiate administration has heterogeneous effects on activity recorded from nucleus accumbens neurons in vivo. Neurosci Lett 1987;83:307–312.

451. Henriksen SJ, Hakan RL. Responses of nucleus accumbens neurons to systemically and locally administered opiates provide evidence for dopamine (DA)-dependent and DA-independent circuitry underlying opiate self-administration. Adv Biosci 1989;75:675–678.

452. Walker JM, Thompson LA, Frascella J, Friederich MW. Opposite effects of mu and kappa opiates on the firing-rate of dopamine cells in the substantia nigra of the rat. Eur J Pharmacol 1987;134:53–59.

453. Crain SM, Shen K-F, Chalazonitis A. Opioids excite rather than inhibit sensory neurons after chronic opioid exposure of spinal cord–ganglion cultures. Brain Res 1988;455:99–109.

454. Crain SM, Shen K-F. Dual excitatory and inhibitory opioid modulation of the action potential duration of mouse dorsal root ganglion neurons in cultures. Adv Biosci 1988;75:189–192.

455. North RA. Opioid receptor types and membrane ion channels. Trends Neurosci 1986;9:114–117.

456. Nicoll RA, Siggins GR, Ling N, Bloom FE, Guillemin R. Neuronal actions of endorphins and enkephalin among brain regions: a comparative microiontophoretic study. Proc Natl Acad Sci USA 1977;74:2584–2588.

457. Duggan AW, North RA. Electrophysiology of opioids. Pharmacol Rev 1984;35:219–281.

458. Finnerty EP, Chan SHH. Morphine suppression of substantia nigra zona reticulata neurons in the rat: implicated role for a novel striato-nigral feedback mechanism. Eur J Pharmacol 1979;18:37–56.

459. Kelley AE, Stinus L, Iversen SD. Interaction between d-ala-met-enkephalin, A_{10} dopaminergic neurons and spontaneous behavior in the rat. Behav Brain Res 1980;1:3–24.

460. Mereu G, Yoon KW, Boi V, Gessa GL, Naes L, Westfall TC. Preferential stimulation of ventral tegmental area dopaminergic neurons by nicotine. Eur J Pharmacol 1987;141:395–399.

461. Mereu GP, Fadda F, Gessa GL. Ethanol stimulates the firing-rate of nigral-dopaminergic neurones in anaesthetized rats. Brain Res 1984;292:63–69.

462. Johnson SW, Haroldsen PE, Hoffer BJ, Freedman R. Presynaptic dopaminergic activity of phencyclidine in rat caudate. J Pharmacol Exp Ther 1984;229:322–332.

463. Johnson SW, Palmer MR, Freedman R. Effects of dopamine on spontaneous and evoked activity of caudate neurons. Neuropharmacology 1983;22:843–851.

464. Freeman AS, Bunney BS. The effects of phencyclidine and N-allylnormetazocine on midbrain dopamine neuronal activity. Eur J Pharmacol 1984;104:287–293.

465. Marwah J. Candidate mechanisms underlying phencyclidine-induced psychosis: an electrophysiological, behavioral, and biochemical study. Biol Psychiatry 1982;17:155–198.

466. Kirch DG, Palmer MR, Egan M, Freedman R. Electrophysiological interactions between haloperidol and reduced haloperidol, and dopamine, norepinephrine and phencyclidine in rat brain. Neuropharmacology 1985;24:375–379.

467. Rouillard C, Chiodo LA, Freeman AS. The effects of the phencyclidine analogs BTCP and TCP on nigrostriatal dopamine neuronal activity. Eur J Pharmacol 1990;182:227–235.

468. Steinfels GF, Tam SW, Cook L. Electrophysiological effects of selective sigma-receptor agonists, antagonists, and the selective phencyclidine receptor agonist MK-801 on midbrain dopamine neurons. Neuropsychopharmacology 1989;2:201–208.

469. O'Brien DP, White FJ. Inhibition of non-dopamine cells in the ventral tegmental area by benzodiazepines: relationship to A10 dopamine cell activity. Eur J Pharmacol 1987;142:343–354.

470. Wise RA. In vivo estimates of extracellular dopamine and dopamine metabolite levels during intravenous cocaine or heroin self-administration. Sem Neurosci 1993;5:337–342.

471. Wise RA, Newton P, Leeb K, Burnette B, Pocock DJB, Justice JB Jr. Fluctuations in nucleus accumbens dopamine concentration during intravenous cocaine self-administration in rats. Psychopharmacology 1995;120:10–20.

472. Pettit HO, Justice JB Jr. Effect of dose on cocaine self-administration behavior and dopamine levels in the nucleus accumbens. Brain Res 1991;539:94–102.

473. Parsons LH, Koob GF, Weiss F. Serotonin dysfunction in the nucleus accumbens of rats during withdrawal after unlimited access to intravenous cocaine. J Pharmacol Exp Ther 1995;274:1182–1191.

474. Wise RA, Leone P, Rivest R, Leeb K. Elevations of nucleus accumbens dopamine and DOPAC levels during intravenous heroin self-administration. Synapse 1995;21:140–148.

475. Hemby SE, Martin TJ, Co C, Dworkin SI, Smith JE. The effects of intravenous heroin administration on extracellular nucleus accumbens dopamine concentrations as determined by in vivo microdialysis. J Pharmacol Exp Ther 1995;273:591–598.

476. Weiss F, Lorang MT, Bloom FE, Koob GF. Oral alcohol self-administration stimulates dopamine release in the rat nucleus accumbens: genetic and motivational determinants. J Pharmacol Exp Ther 1993;267:250–258.

477. Gratton A, Wise RA, Kiyatkin EA. Chronoamperometric measurements of dopamine levels in rat nucleus accumbens during cocaine self-administration. Soc Neurosci Abstr 1992;18:1076.

478. Gratton A, Wise RA. Drug- and behavior-associated changes in dopamine-related electrochemical signals during intravenous cocaine self-administration in rats. J Neurosci 1994;14:4130–4146.

479. Kiyatkin EA, Stein EA. Biphasic changes in mesolimbic dopamine signal during cocaine self-administration. Neuroreport 1994;5:1005–1008.

480. Kiyatkin EA, Stein EA. Fluctuations in nucleus accumbens dopamine during cocaine self-administration behavior: an in vivo electrochemical study. Neuroscience 1995;64:599–617.

481. Kiyatkin EA, Wise RA, Gratton A. Drug- and behavior-associated changes in dopamine-related electrochemical signals during intravenous heroin self-administration in rats. Synapse 1993;14:60–72.

482. Kiyatkin EA. Behavioral significance of phasic changes in mesolimbic dopamine-dependent electrochemical signal associated with heroin self-administration. J Neural Transm Gen Sect 1994;96:197–214.

483. Apicella P, Ljungberg T, Scarnati E, Schultz W. Responses to reward in monkey dorsal and ventral striatum. Exp Brain Res 1991;85:491–500.

484. Schultz W, Apicella P, Scarnati E, Ljungberg T. Neuronal activity in monkey ventral striatum related to the expectation of reward. J Neurosci 1992;12:4595–4610.

485. Ljungberg T, Apicella P, Schultz W. Responses of monkey dopamine neurons during learning of behavioral reactions. J Neurophysiol 1992;67:145–163.

486. Apicella P, Scarnati E, Ljungberg T, Schultz W. Neuronal activity in monkey striatum related to the expectation of predictable environmental events. J Neurophysiol 1992;68:945–960.

487. Schultz W, Apicella P, Ljungberg T. Responses of monkey dopamine neurons to reward and conditioned stimuli during successive steps of learning a delayed response task. J Neurosci 1993;13:900–913.

488. Mirenowicz J, Schultz W. Importance of unpredictability for reward responses in primate dopamine neurons. J Neurophysiol 1994;72:1024–1027.

489. Schultz W. Behavior-related activity of pri-

mate dopamine neurons. Rev Neurologique 1994;150:634–639.

490. Mirenowicz J, Schultz W. Preferential activation of midbrain dopamine neurons by appetitive rather than aversive stimuli. Nature 1996; 379:449–451.

491. Chang JY, Sawyer SF, Lee RS, Woodward DJ. Electrophysiological and pharmacological evidence for the role of the nucleus accumbens in cocaine self-administration in freely moving rats. J Neurosci 1994;14:1224–1244.

492. Henriksen SJ, Callaway CW, Negus SS, Koob GF, Miller DE, Berg GI, Friedman LR, Engberg CC. Properties of neurons recorded in the rodent nucleus accumbens, in vivo: relationship to behavioral state and heroin self-administration. Soc Neurosci Abstr 1992;18:373.

493. Herz A, Shippenberg TS, Bals-Kubik R, Spanagel R. Opiatsucht. Pharmakologische und biochemische Aspekte. [Opiate addiction. Pharmacologic and biochemical aspects]. Arzneimittel-Forschung 1992;42:256–259.

494. Dauge V, Kalivas PW, Duffy T, Roques BP. Effect of inhibiting enkephalin catabolism in the VTA on motor activity and extracellular dopamine. Brain Res 1992;599:209–214.

495. Johnson SW, North RA. Opioids excite dopamine neurons by hyperpolarization of local interneurons. J Neurosci 1992;12:483–488.

496. Klitenick MA, DeWitte P, Kalivas PW. Regulation of somatodendritic dopamine release in the ventral tegmental area by opioids and GABA: an in vivo microdialysis study. J Neurosci 1992;12:2623–2632.

497. Heidbreder C, Gewiss M, Lallemand S, Roques BP, De Witte P. Inhibition of enkephalin metabolism and activation of mu- or delta-opioid receptors elicit opposite effects on reward and motility in the ventral mesencephalon. Neuropharmacology 1992;31:293–298.

498. Spanagel R, Herz A, Shippenberg TS. Opposing tonically active endogenous opioid systems modulate the mesolimbic dopaminergic pathway. Proc Natl Acad Sci USA 1992;89: 2046–2050.

499. Yoshida M, Yokoo H, Tanaka T, Mizoguchi K, Emoto H, Ishii H, Tanaka M. Facilitatory modulation of mesolimbic dopamine neuronal activity by a μ-opioid agonist and nicotine as examined with in vivo microdialysis. Brain Res 1993;624:277–280.

500. Noel MB, Wise RA. Ventral tegmental injections of morphine but not U-50,488H enhance feeding in food-deprived rats. Brain Res 1993; 632: 68–73.

501. Devine DP, Leone P, Wise RA. Mesolimbic dopamine neurotransmission is increased by administration of μ-opioid receptor antagonists. Eur J Pharmacol 1993;243:55–64.

502. German DC, Speciale SG, Manaye KF, Sadeq M. Opioid receptors in midbrain dopaminergic regions of the rat. I. Mu receptor autoradiography. J Neural Transm Gen Sect 1993;91: 39–52.

503. Speciale SG, Manaye KF, Sadeq M, German DC. Opioid receptors in midbrain dopaminergic regions of the rat. II. Kappa and delta receptor autoradiography. J Neural Transm Gen Sect 1993;91:53–66.

504. Bals-Kubik R, Ableitner A, Herz A, Shippenberg TS. Neuroanatomical sites mediating the motivational effects of opioids as mapped by the conditioned place preference paradigm in rats. J Pharmacol Exp Ther 1993;264:489–495.

505. Devine DP, Leone P, Pocock D, Wise RA. Differential involvement of ventral tegmental *mu*, *delta* and *kappa* opioid receptors in modulation of basal mesolimbic dopamine release: *in vivo* microdialysis studies. J Pharmacol Exp Ther 1993;266:1236–1246.

506. Mansour A, Fox CA, Burke S, Meng F, Thompson RC, Akil H, Watson SJ. Mu, delta, and kappa opioid receptor mRNA expression in the rat CNS: an in situ hybridization study. J Comp Neurol 1994;350:412–438.

507. Devine DP, Wise RA. Self-administration of morphine, DAMGO, and DPDPE into the ventral tegmental area of rats. J Neurosci 1994; 14:1978–1984.

508. Unterwald EM, Rubenfeld JM, Kreek MJ. Repeated cocaine administration upregulates kappa and mu, but not delta, opioid receptors. Neuroreport 1994;5:1613–1616.

509. Singh J, Desiraju T, Nagaraja TN, Raju TR. Facilitation of self-stimulation of ventral tegmentum by microinjection of opioid receptor subtype agonists. Physiol Behav 1994;55: 627–631.

510. Phillips GD, Robbins TW, Everitt BJ. Mesoaccumbens dopamine-opiate interactions in the control over behaviour by a conditioned reinforcer. Psychopharmacology 1994;114: 345–359.

511. Badiani A, Leone P, Noel MB, Stewart J. Ventral tegmental area opioid mechanisms and modulation of ingestive behavior. Brain Res 1995;670:264–276.

512. Noel MB, Wise RA. Ventral tegmental injections of a selective μ or δ opioid enhance feeding in food-deprived rats. Brain Res 1995; 673:304–312.

513. Badiani A, Leone P, Stewart J. Intra-VTA injections of the mu-opioid antagonist CTOP enhance locomotor activity. Brain Res 1995; 690:112–116.

514. Mansour A, Fox CA, Burke S, Akil H, Watson SJ. Immunohistochemical localization of the cloned mu opioid receptor in the rat CNS. J Chem Neuroanat 1995;8:283–305.

515. Klitenick MA, Wirtshafter D. Behavioral and neurochemical effects of opioids in the paramedian midbrain tegmentum including the median raphe nucleus and ventral tegmental area. J Pharmacol Exp Ther 1995;273:327–336.

516. Noel MB, Gratton A. Electrochemical evidence of increased dopamine transmission in prefrontal cortex and nucleus accumbens elicited by ventral tegmental μ-opioid receptor activation in freely behaving rats. Synapse 1995;21:110–122.

517. Derrien M, Durieux C, Dauge V, Roques BP. Involvement of D_2 dopaminergic receptors in the emotional and motivational responses induced by injection of CCK-8 in the posterior part of the rat nucleus accumbens. Brain Res 1993;617:181–188.

518. Hamilton ME, Freeman AS. Effects of administration of cholecystokinin into the VTA on DA overflow in nucleus accumbens and amygdala of freely moving rats. Brain Res 1995; 688:134–142.

519. Markowski VP, Hull EM. Cholecystokinin modulates mesolimbic dopaminergic influences on male rat copulatory behavior. Brain Res 1995;699:266–274.

520. Rompré PP, Boye SM. Opposite effects of mesencephalic microinjections of cholecystokinin octapeptide and neurotensin-(1–13) on brain stimulation reward. Eur J Pharmacol 1993;232:299–303.

521. Rasmussen K, Czachura JF, Stockton ME, Howbert JJ. Electrophysiological effects of diphenylpyrazolidinone cholecystokinin-B and cholecystokinin-A antagonists on midbrain

522. Tanaka J, Kariya K, Ushigome A, Matsuda M, Nomura M. CCK activates excitatory ventral tegmental pathways to the posterior nucleus accumbens. Neuroreport 1994;5:2558–2560.

523. Ladurelle N, Durieux C, Roques BP, Daugé V. Different modifications of the dopamine metabolism in the core and shell parts of the nucleus accumbens following CCK-A receptor stimulation in the shell region. Neurosci Lett 1994;178:5–10.

524. Rasmussen K, Howbert JJ, Stockton ME. Inhibition of A9 and A10 dopamine cells by the cholecystokinin-B antagonist LY262691: mediation through feedback pathways from forebrain sites. Synapse 1993;15:95–103.

525. Angulo JA, McEwen BS. Molecular aspects of neuropeptide regulation and function in the corpus striatum and nucleus accumbens. Brain Res Brain Res Rev 1994;19:1–28.

526. Nicot A, Rostene W, Berod A. Neurotensin receptor expression in the rat forebrain and midbrain: a combined analysis by in situ hybridization and receptor autoradiography. J Comp Neurol 1994;341:407–419.

527. Atoji Y, Watanabe H, Yamamoto Y, Suzuki Y. Distribution of neurotensin-containing neurons in the central nervous system of the dog. J Comp Neurol 1995;353:67–88.

528. Nicot A, Rostene W, Berod A. Differential expression of neurotensin receptor mRNA in the dopaminergic cell groups of the rat diencephalon and mesencephalon. J Neurosci Res 1995;40:667–674.

529. Jiang ZG, Pessia M, North RA. Neurotensin excitation of rat ventral tegmental neurones. J Physiol 1994;474:119–129.

530. Steinberg R, Brun P, Souilhac J, Bougault I, Leyris R, Le Fur G, Soubrié P. Neurochemical and behavioural effects of neurotensin vs [D-Tyr[11]]neurotensin on mesolimbic dopaminergic function. Neuropeptides 1995;28:43–50.

531. Steinberg R, Brun P, Fournier M, Souilhac J, Rodier D, Mons G, et al. SR 48692, a non-peptide neurotensin receptor antagonist differentially affects neurotensin-induced behaviour and changes in dopaminergic transmission. Neuroscience 1994;59:921–929.

532. Faure MP, Nouel D, Beaudet A. Axonal and dendritic transport of internalized neurotensin in rat mesostriatal dopaminergic neurons. Neuroscience 1995;68:519–529.

533. Mercuri NB, Stratta F, Calabresi P, Bernardi G. Neurotensin induces an inward current in rat mesencephalic dopaminergic neurons. Neurosci Lett 1993;153:192–196.

534. Kariya K, Tanaka J, Nomura M. Systemic administration of CCK-8S, but not CCK-4, enhances dopamine turnover in the posterior nucleus accumbens: a microdialysis study in freely moving rats. Brain Res 1994;657:1–6.

535. Li XM, Hedlund PB, Fuxe K. Cholecystokinin octapeptide in vitro and ex vivo strongly modulates striatal dopamine D_2 receptors in rat forebrain sections. Eur J Neurosci 1995;7: 962–971.

536. Corwin RL, Jorn A, Hardy M, Crawley JN. The CCK-B antagonist CI-988 increases dopamine levels in microdialysate from the rat nucleus accumbens via a tetrodotoxin- and calcium-independent mechanism. J Neurochem 1995; 65:208–217.

537. Ladurelle N, Roques BP, Dauge V. The transfer of rats from a familiar to a novel environment prolongs the increase of extracellular dopamine efflux induced by CCK8 in the pos-

terior nucleus accumbens. J Neurosci 1995;15: 3118–3127.

538. Morino P, Mascagni F, McDonald A, Hokfelt T. Cholecystokinin corticostriatal pathway in the rat: evidence for bilateral origin from medial prefrontal cortical areas. Neuroscience 1994;59:939–952.

539. Morency MA, Quirion R, Mishra RK. Distribution of cholecystokinin receptors in the bovine brain: a quantitative autoradiographic study. Neuroscience 1994;62:307–316.

540. Josselyn SA, Vaccarino FJ. Interaction of CCK_B receptors with amphetamine in responding for conditioned rewards. Peptides 1995; 16:959–964.

541. Wagstaff JD, Bush LG, Gibb JW, Hanson GR. Endogenous neurotensin antagonizes methamphetamine-enhanced dopaminergic activity. Brain Res 1994;665:237–244.

542. Diaz J, Levesque D, Griffon N, Lammers CH, Martres MP, Sokoloff P, Schwartz JC. Opposing roles for dopamine D_2 and D_3 receptors on neurotensin mRNA expression in nucleus accumbens. Eur J Neurosci 1994;6:1384–1387.

543. Ikemoto K, Satoh K, Maeda T, Fibiger HC. Neurochemical heterogeneity of the primate nucleus accumbens. Exp Brain Res 1995; 104:177–190.

544. Brun P, Steinberg R, Le Fur G, Soubrie P. Blockade of neurotensin receptor by SR 48692 potentiates the facilitatory effect of haloperidol on the evoked in vivo dopamine release in the rat nucleus accumbens. J Neurochem 1995;64: 2073–2079.

545. Diaz J, Levesque D, Lammers CH, Griffon N, Martres MP, Schwartz JC, Sokoloff P. Phenotypical characterization of neurons expressing the dopamine D_3 receptor in the rat brain. Neuroscience 1995;65:731–745.

546. Hiroi N, McDonald RJ, White NM. Involvement of the lateral nucleus of the amygdala in amphetamine and food conditioned place preferences (CPP). Soc Neurosci Abstr 1990; 16:605.

547. Hiroi N. A pharmacological and neuroanatomical investigation of the conditioned place preference produced by amphetamine. Montreal, Quebec: McGill University; 1990. Dissertation.

548. Hiroi N, White NM. The lateral nucleus of the amygdala mediates expression of the amphetamine-produced conditioned place preference. J Neurosci 1991;11:2107–2116.

549. White NM, Hiroi N. Amphetamine conditioned cue preference and the neurobiology of drug-seeking. Sem Neurosci 1993;5:329–336.

550. White NM, Hiroi N. Preferential localization of self-stimulation sites in striosomes/patches of rat caudate-putamen. Soc Neurosci Abstr 1995;21: 2079.

551. Ragsdale CW Jr, Graybiel AM. Fibers from the basolateral nucleus of the amygdala selectively innervate striosomes in the caudate nucleus of the cat. J Comp Neurol 1988;269:506–522.

552. Ragsdale CW Jr, Graybiel AM. Compartmental organization of the thalamostriatal connection in the cat. J Comp Neurol 1991;311: 134–167.

553. Ragsdale CW Jr, Graybiel AM. A simple ordering of neocortical areas established by the compartmental organization of their striatal projections. Proc Natl Acad Sci USA 1990; 87:6196–6199.

554. Gerfen CR. The neostriatal mosaic: striatal patch-matrix organization is related to cortical lamination. Science 1989;246:385–388.

555. Berendse HW, Galis-de Graaf Y, Groenewegen HJ. Topographical organization and rela-

tionship with ventral striatal compartments of prefrontal corticostriatal projections in the rat. J Comp Neurol 1992;316:314–347.

556. Groenewegen HJ, Room P, Witter MP, Lohman AHM. Cortical afferents of the nucleus accumbens in the cat, studied with anterograde and retrograde transport techniques. Neuroscience 1982;7:977–995.

557. Phillipson OT, Griffiths AC. The topographic order of inputs to nucleus accumbens in the rat. Neuroscience 1985;16:275–296.

558. Christie MJ, Summers RJ, Stephenson JA, Cook CJ, Beart PM. Excitatory amino acid projections to the nucleus accumbens septi in the rat: a retrograde transport study utilizing D[^{3}H]aspartate and [^{3}H]GABA. Neuroscience 1987;22:425–439.

559. Borg JS, Deutsch AY, Zahm DS. Afferent projection to the nucleus accumbens core and shell in the rat. Soc Neurosci Abstr 1991;17:454.

560. Kelley AE, Domesick VB, Nauta WJH. The amygdalostriatal projection in the rat—an anatomical study by anterograde and retrograde tracing methods. Neuroscience 1982;7: 615–630.

561. McDonald AJ. Topographical organization of amygdaloid projections to the caudatoputamen, nucleus accumbens, and related striatal-like areas of the rat brain. Neuroscience 1991; 44:15–33.

562. Robinson TG, Beart PM. Excitant amino acid projections from rat amygdala and thalamus to nucleus accumbens. Brain Res Bull 1988;20: 467–471.

563. Price JL, Amaral DG. An autoradiographic study of the projections of the central nucleus of the amygdala. J Neurosci 1981;1:1242–1259.

564. Haber SN, Groenewegen HJ, Grove EA, Nauta WJ. Efferent connections of the ventral pallidum: evidence of a dual striato pallidofugal pathway. J Comp Neurol 1985;235:322–335.

565. Oades RD, Halliday GM. Ventral tegmental (A10) system: neurobiology. 1. Anatomy and connectivity. Brain Res 1987;434:117–165.

566. Gonzales C, Chesselet MF. Amygdalonigral pathway: an anterograde study in the rat with Phaseolus vulgaris leucoagglutinin (PHA-L). J Comp Neurol 1990;297:182–200.

567. Canteras NS, Simerly RB, Swanson LW. Connections of the posterior nucleus of the amygdala. J Comp Neurol 1992;324:143–179.

568. de Belleroche JS, Bradford HF. Presynaptic control of the synthesis and release of dopamine from striatal synaptosomes: a comparison between the effects of 5-hydroxytryptamine, acetylcholine, and glutamate. J Neurochem 1980;35:1227–1234.

569. Chesselet MF. Presynaptic regulation of neurotransmitter release in the brain: facts and hypothesis. Neuroscience 1984;12:347–375.

570. Hetey L, Drescher K. Influence of antipsychotics on presynaptic receptors modulating the release of dopamine in synaptosomes of the nucleus accumbens of rats. Neuropharmacology 1986;25:1103–1109.

571. Tricklebank MD. Interactions between dopamine and 5HT_3 receptors suggest new treatment for psychosis and drug addiction. Trends Pharmacol Sci 1989;10:127–129.

572. Westfall TC, Titternary V. Inhibition of the electrically induced release of [^{3}H]dopamine by serotonin from superfused rat striatal slices. Neurosci Lett 1982;28:205–209.

573. Bissette G, Nemeroff CB. Neurotensin and the mesocorticolimbic dopamine system. Ann N Y Acad Sci 1988;537:397–404.

574. Hervé D, Tassin JP, Studler JM, Dana C, Kitagbi P, Vincent JP, Glowinski J. Dopaminergic control of ^{125}I-labelled neurotensin binding site density in corticolimbic structures of the rat brain. Proc Natl Acad Sci USA 1986;83:6203–6207.

575. Hökfelt T, Everitt BS, Theodorsson-Norheim E, Goldstein M. Occurrence of neurotensin-like immunoreactivity in subpopulations of hypothalamic, mesencephalic, and medullary catecholamine neurons. J Comp Neurol 1984; 222:543–559.

576. Kelley AE, Cador M. Behavioral evidence for differential neuropeptide modulation of the mesolimbic dopamine system. Ann N Y Acad Sci 1988;537:415–434.

577. Kelley AE, Stinus L, Iversen SD. Behavioural activation induced in the rat by substance P infusion into ventral tegmental area: implication of dopaminergic A10 neurones. Neurosci Lett 1979;11:335–339.

578. Kalivas PW, Jennes L, Miller JS. A catecholaminergic projection from the ventral tegmental area to the diagonal band of Broca: modulation by neurotensin. Brain Res 1985;326: 229–238.

579. Nemeroff CB, Cain ST. Neurotensin-dopamine interactions in the CNS. Trends Pharmacol Sci 1985;6:201–205.

580. Palacios JM, Kuhar MJ. Neurotensin receptors are located on dopamine-containing neurones in rat midbrain. Nature 1981;294:587–589.

581. Pernow B. Substance P. Pharmacol Rev 1983; 35:85–141.

582. Phillips AG, Blaha CD, Fibiger HC, Lane RF. Interactions between mesolimbic dopamine neurons, cholecystokinin, and neurotensin: evidence using in vivo voltammetry. Ann N Y Acad Sci 1988;537:347–361.

583. Pickel VM, Joh TH, Chan J. Substance P in the rat nucleus accumbens: ultrastructural localization in axon terminals and their relation to dopaminergic afferents. Brain Res 1988;444: 247–264.

584. Quirion R, Chiueh CC, Everist HD, Pert A. Comparative localization of neurotensin receptors on nigrostriatal and mesolimbic dopaminergic terminals. Brain Res 1985;327:835–839.

585. Studler J-M, Kitagbi P, Tramu G, Hervé D, Glowinski J, Tassin J-P. Extensive co-localization of neurotensin with dopamine in rat meso-cortico-frontal dopaminergic neurons. Neuropeptides 1988;11:95–100.

586. Voigt MM, Wang RY, Westfall TC. The effects of cholecystokinin on the in vivo release of newly synthesized [^{3}H]dopamine from the nucleus accumbens of the rat. J Neurosci 1985; 5:2744–2749.

587. Amit Z, Sutherland EA, Gill K, Ögren SO. Zimeldine: a review of its effects on ethanol consumption. Neurosci Biobehav Rev 1984; 8:35–54.

588. Gill K, Amit Z, Ögren SO. The effects of zimelidine on voluntary ethanol consumption: studies on the mechanism of action. Alcohol 1985; 2:343–347.

589. Le Bourhis B, Uzan A, Aufrere G, Lefur G. Effets de l'indalpine, inhibiteur spécifique de la récapture de la sérotonine sur la dépendance comportementale à l'éthanol et sur la prise volontaire d'alcool chez le rat. [Effects of indalpine, a specific serotonin reuptake inhibitor, on ethanol behavioral dependence and voluntary alcohol consumption in the rat]. Ann Pharm Fr 1981;39:11–20.

590. Leccese AP, Lyness WH. The effects of putative 5-hydroxytryptamine receptor active

agents on d-amphetamine self-administration in controls and rats with 5,7-dihydroxytryptamine medial forebrain bundle lesions. Brain Res 1984;303:153–162.

591. Murphy JM, Waller MB, Gatto GJ, McBride WJ, Lumeng L, Li T-K. Monoamine uptake inhibitors attenuate ethanol intake in alcohol-preferring (P) rats. Alcohol 1985;2:349–352.

592. Naranjo CA, Sellers EM, Lawrin MO. Modulation of ethanol intake by serotonin uptake inhibitors. J Clin Psychiatry 1986;47(4)[suppl]: 16–22.

593. Rockman GE, Amit Z, Carr G, Brown ZW, Ögren SO. Attenuation of ethanol intake by 5-hydroxytryptamine uptake blockade in laboratory rats: I. involvement of brain 5-hydroxytryptamine in the mediation of the positive reinforcing properties of ethanol. Arch Int Pharmacodyn Ther 1979;241:245–259.

594. Yu DSL, Smith FL, Smith DG, Lyness WH. Fluoxetine-induced attenuation of amphetamine self-administration in rats. Life Sci 1986; 39:1383–1388.

595. Zabik JE, Roache JD, Sidor R, Nash JF Jr. The effects of fluoxetine on ethanol preference in the rat. Pharmacologist 1982;24:204.

596. Cannon DS, Carrell LE. Rat strain differences in ethanol self-administration and taste aversion. Pharmacol Biochem Behav 1987;28: 57–63.

597. George FR. Genetic and environmental factors in ethanol self-administration. Pharmacol Biochem Behav 1987;27:379–384.

598. Li TK, Lumeng L. Alcohol preference and voluntary alcohol intakes of inbred rat strains and the National Institutes of Health heterogeneous stock of rats. Alcoholism 1984;8:485–486.

599. Ritz MC, George FR, DeFiebre CM, Meisch RA. Genetic differences in the establishment of ethanol as a reinforcer. Pharmacol Biochem Behav 1986;24:1089–1094.

600. Suzuki T, George FR, Meisch RA. Differential establishment and maintenance of oral ethanol reinforced behavior in Lewis and Fischer 344 inbred rat strains. J Pharmacol Exp Ther 1988; 245:164–170.

601. George FR, Meisch RA. Oral narcotic intake as a reinforcer: genotype x environment interaction. Behav Genet 1984;14:603.

602. Khodzhagel'diev T. Formirovanie vlecheniia k nikotinu u myshei linii C57BL/6 i CBA. [Development of nicotine preference in C57BL/6 and CBA mice.] Biull Eksp Biol Med 1986; 101:48–50.

603. George FR, Goldberg SR. Genetic approaches to the analysis of addiction processes. Trends Pharmacol Sci 1989;10:78–83.

604. Kosten TA, Miserendino MJ, Chi S, Nestler EJ. Fischer and Lewis rat strains show differential cocaine effects in conditioned place preference and behavioral sensitization but not in locomotor activity or conditioned taste aversion. J Pharmacol Exp Ther 1994;269: 137–144.

605. Nestler EJ. Molecular mechanisms of drug addiction in the mesolimbic dopamine pathway. Sem Neurosci 1993;5:369–376.

606. Gardner EL, Lowinson JH. Marijuana's interaction with brain reward systems: update 1991. Pharmacol Biochem Behav 1991;40:571–580.

607. Chen J, Paredes W, Lowinson JH, Gardner EL. Strain-specific facilitation of dopamine efflux by Δ⁹-tetrahydrocannabinol in the nucleus accumbens of rat: an in vivo microdialysis study. Neurosci Lett 1991;129:136–140.

608. Gardner EL, Paredes W, Smith D, Seeger T, Donner A, Milling C, Cohen D, Morrison D.

Strain-specific facilitation of brain stimulation reward by Δ⁹-tetrahydrocannabinol in laboratory rats. Psychopharmacology 1988;96[suppl]:365.

609. Lepore M, Liu X, Savage V, Matalon D, Gardner EL. Genetic differences in Δ⁹-tetrahydrocannabinol-induced facilitation of brain stimulation reward as measured by a rate-frequency curve-shift electrical brain stimulation paradigm in three different rat strains. Life Sci [Pharmacol Lett] 1996;25:PL365–372.

610. Guitart X, Beitner-Johnson D, Marby DW, Kosten TA, Nestler EJ. Fischer and Lewis rat strains differ in basal levels of neurofilament proteins and their regulation by chronic morphine in the mesolimbic dopamine system. Synapse 1992;12:242–253.

611. Uhl GR, Elmer GI, Labuda MC, Pickens RW. Genetic influences in drug abuse. In: Bloom FE, Kupfer DJ, eds. Psychopharmacology: the fourth generation of progress. New York: Raven Press, 1995:1793–1806.

612. Krugylak L, Lander ES. High resolution genetic mapping of complex traits. Am J Hum Genet 1995;56:1212–1223.

613. Lander ES, Schork NJ. Genetic dissection of complex traits. Science 1994;265:2037–2048.

614. Elston RC. Linkage and association to genetic markers. Exp Clin Immunogenet 1995;12: 129–140.

615. Koob GF, Bloom F. Cellular and molecular mechanisms of drug dependence. Science 1988;242:715–723.

616. Blum K, Noble E, Sheridan PJ, Montgomery A, Ritchie T, Jagadeeswaran P, Nogami H, Briggs AH, Cohn JB. Allelic association of human dopamine D₂ receptor gene in alcoholism. JAMA 1990;263:2055–2060.

617. Smith SS, O'Hara BF, Persico AM, Gorelick DA, Newlin DB, Vlahov D, Solomon L, Pickens R, Uhl GR. Genetic vulnerability to drug abuse: the D₂ dopamine receptor Taq I B1 restriction fragment length polymorphism appears more frequently in polysubstance abusers. Arch Gen Psychiat 1992;49: 723–727.

618. Noble EP. The D₂ dopamine receptor gene: a review of association studies in alcoholism. Behav Genet 1993;23:119–129.

619. Uhl G, Blum K, Noble E, Smith S. Substance abuse vulnerability and D₂ receptor genes. Trends Neurosci 1993;16:83–88.

620. Bolos AM, Dean M, Lucas-Derse S, Ramsburg M, Brown GL, Goldman D. Population and pedigree studies reveal a lack of association between the dopamine D₂ receptor gene and alcoholism. JAMA 1990;264:3156–3160.

621. Suarez BK, Parsian A, Hampe CL, Todd RD, Reich T, Cloninger CR. Linkage disequilibria at the D₂ dopamine receptor locus (DRD2) in alcoholics and controls. Genomics 1994;19: 12–20.

622. Vandenbergh DJ, Persico AM, Hawkins AL, Griffin CA, Li X, Jabs EW, Uhl GR. Human dopamine transporter gene (DAT1) maps to chromosome 5p15.3 and displays a VNTR. Genomics 1992;14:1104–1106.

623. Cook EH, Stein MA, Krasowski MD, Cox NJ, Olken DM, Kieffer JE, Leventhal BL. Association of attention deficit disorder and the dopamine transporter gene. Am J Human Genet 1995;56:993–998.

624. Muramatsu T, Higuchi S. Dopamine transporter gene polymorphism and alcoholism. Biochem Biophys Res Commun 1995;211: 28–32.

625. Gelernter J, Kranzler HR, Satel SL, Rao PA. Genetic association between dopamine transporter

protein alleles and cocaine-induced paranoia. Neuropsychopharmacology 1994;11:195–200.

626. Persico AM, Vandenbergh DJ, Smith SS, Uhl GR. Dopamine transporter gene polymorphisms are not associated with polysubstance abuse. Biol Psychiatry 1993;34:265–267.

627. Ebstein EP, Novick O, Umansky R, Priel B, Osher Y, Blaine D, Bennett ER, Nemanov L, Katz M, Belmaker RH. Dopamine D4 receptor (D4DR) exon III polymorphism associated with the human personality trait of novelty seeking. Nature Genet 1996;12:78–80.

628. Benjamin J, Li L, Patterson C, Greenberg BD, Murphy DL, Hamer DH. Population and familial association between the D4 dopamine receptor gene and measures of novelty seeking. Nature Genet 1996;12:81–84.

629. Van Tol HHM, Wu CM, Guan HC, Ohara K, Bunzow JR, Civelli O, Kennedy J, Seeman P, Niznik HB, Jovanovic V. Multiple dopamine D4 receptor variants in the human population. Nature 1992;358:149–152.

630. Adamson MD, Kennedy J, Petronis A, Dean M, Virkkunen M, Linnoila M, Goldman D. DRD4 dopamine receptor genotype and CSF monoamine metabolites in Finnish alcoholics and controls. Am J Med Genet 1995;60: 199–205.

631. Lannfelt L, Sokoloff P, Martes MP, Pilon C, Giros B, Jonsson E, et al. Amino acid substitution in the dopamine D-3 receptor as a useful marker to investigating psychiatric disorders. Psychiatr Genet 1992;2:249–256.

632. Rietschel M, Nöthen MM, Lannfelt L, Sokoloff P, Schwartz JC, Lanczik M, et al. A serine to glycine substitution at position 9 in the extracellular N-terminal part of the dopamine D₃ receptor protein: no role in the genetic predisposition to bipolar affective disorder. Psychiat Res 1993;46:253–259.

633. Axelrod J, Tomchick R. Enzymatic O-methylation of epinephrine and other catechols. J Biol Chem 1958;233:702–705.

634. Tenhunen J, Salminen M, Lundstrom K, Kiviluoto T, Savolainen R, Ulmanen I. Genomic organization of the human catechol-O-methyltransferase gene and its expression from two distinct promoters. Eur J Biochem 1994; 223:1049–1054.

635. Weinshilboum RM, Raymond FA. Inheritance of low erythrocyte catechol-O-methyl transferase activity in man. Am J Human Genet 1977;29:125–135.

636. Scanlon PD, Raymond FA, Weinshilboum RA. Catechol-O-methyl transferase: thermolabile enzyme in erythrocytes of subjects homozygous for the allele for low activity. Science 1979;203:63–65.

637. Spielman RS, Weinshilboum RM. Genetics of red cell COMT activity: analysis of thermal stability and family data. Am J Med Genet 1981;10:279–290.

638. Aksoy S, Klener J, Weinshilboum RM. Catechol-O-methyltransferase pharmacogenetics: photoaffinity labelling and Western blot analysis of human liver samples. Pharmacogenetics 1993;3:116–122.

639. Boudikova B, Szumlanski C, Maidak B, Weinshilboum RM. Human liver catecholamine-O-methyltransferase pharmacogenetics. Clin Pharmacol Ther 1990;48:381–389.

640. Bertocci B, Miggiano V, Da Prada M, Dembric Z, Lahm H-W, Malherbe P. Human catechol-O-methyltransferase: cloning and expression of the membrane associated form. Proc Natl Acad Sci USA 1991;88:1416–1420.

641. Lundstrom K, Salminen M, Jalanko A,

Savolainen R, Ulmanen I. Cloning and characterization of human placental catechol-O-methyltransferase cDNA. DNA Cell Biol 1991;10:181–189.

642. Schuckitt MA. Low level of response to alcohol as a predictor of future alcoholism. Am J Psychiatry 1994;151:184–189.

643. Blum K, Cull JG, Braverman ER, Comings DE. Reward deficiency syndrome. Am Sci 1996;84:132–145.

644. Minabe Y, Emori K, Ashby CR Jr. Significant differences in the activity of midbrain dopamine neurons between male Fischer 344 and Lewis rats: an in vivo electrophysiological study. Life Sci [Pharmacol Lett] 1995;56: PL135–141.

645. Beitner-Johnson D, Guitart X, Nestler EJ. Dopaminergic brain reward regions of Lewis and Fischer rats display different levels of tyrosine hydroxylase and other morphine- and cocaine-regulated phosphoproteins. Brain Res 1991;561:146–149.

646. Comings DE, Comings BG, Muhleman G, Deitz G, Shahbahrami B, Tast D, et al. The dopamine D_2 receptor locus as a modifying gene in neuropsychiatric disorders. JAMA 1991;266:1793–1800.

647. Blum K, Sheridan PJ, Wood RC, Braverman ER, Chen TJ, Comings DE. Dopamine D2 receptor gene variants: association and linkage studies in impulsive-addictive-compulsive behaviour. Pharmacogenetics 1995;5:121–141.

648. Noble EP, Blum K, Ritchie T, Montgomery A, Sheridan PJ. Allelic association of the D_2 receptor gene with receptor-binding characteristics in alcoholism. Arch Gen Psychiatry 1991; 48:648–654.

649. Noble EP, St Jeor ST, Ritchie T, Syndulko K, St Jeor SC, Fitch RJ, Brunner RL, Sparkes RL. D2 dopamine receptor gene and cigarette smoking: a reward gene? Med Hypotheses 1994;42:257–260.

650. Noble EP, Blum K, Khalsa ME, Ritchie T, Montgomery A, Wood RC, Fitch RJ, Ozkaragoz T, Sheridan PJ, Anglin MD, Paredes A, Treiman LJ, Sparks RS. Allelic association of the D2 dopamine receptor gene with cocaine dependence. Drug Alcohol Depend 1993;33:271–285.

651. Dyr W, McBride WJ, Lumeng TK, Murphy JM. Effects of D1 and D2 dopamine receptor agents on ethanol consumption in the high-alcohol-drinking (HAD) line of rats. Alcohol 1993;10:207–212.

652. McBride WJ, Chernet JE, Dyr W, Lumeng L, Li TK. Densities of dopamine D2 receptors are reduced in CNS regions of alcohol preferring P rats. Alcohol 1993;10:387–390.

653. Zhou FC, Zhang JK, Lumeng L, Li TK. Mesolimbic dopamine system in alcohol-preferring rats. Alcohol 1995;12:403–412.

654. Lawford BR, Young RM, Rowell JA, Qualichefski B, Fletcher BH, Syndulko K, Ritchie T, Noble EP. Bromocriptine in the treatment of alcoholics with the D_2 dopamine receptor A1 allele. Nature Med 1995;1:337–341.

655. Rouge-Pont R, Piazza PV, Kharouby M, Le Moal M, Simon H. Higher and longer stress-induced increase in dopamine concentrations in the nucleus accumbens of animals predisposed to amphetamine self-administration. A microdialysis study. Brain Res 1993;602:169–174.

656. Glick SD, Raucci J, Wang S, Keller RW Jr, Carlson JN. Neurochemical predisposition to self-administer cocaine in rats: individual differences in dopamine and its metabolites. Brain Res 1994;653:148–154.

657. Glick SD, Merski C, Steindorf S, Wang S, Keller RW Jr, Carlson JN. Neurochemical predisposition to self-administer morphine in rats. Brain Res 1992;578:215–220.

658. Piazza PV, Deminiere JM, Le Moal M, Simon H. Factors that predict individual vulnerability to amphetamine self-administration. Science 1989;245:1511–1513.

659. Piazza PV, Rouge-Pont R, Deminiere JM, Kharouby M, Le Moal M, Simon H. Individual vulnerability to amphetamine self-administration is correlated with dopaminergic activity in frontal cortex and nucleus accumbens. Soc Neurosci Abstr 1990;16:585.

660. Gerber GJ, Stretch R. Drug-induced reinstatement of extinguished self-administration behavior in monkeys. Pharmacol Biochem Behav 1975;3:1055–1061.

661. de Wit H, Stewart J. Drug reinstatement of heroin-reinforced responding in the rat. Psychopharmacology 1983;79:29–31.

662. Stewart J. Conditioned and unconditioned drug effects in relapse to opiate and stimulant drug self-administration. Prog Neuro-Psychopharmacol Biol Psychiatry 1983;7:591–597.

663. Stewart J, de Wit H. Reinstatement of drug-taking behavior as a method of assessing incentive motivational properties of drugs. In: Bozarth MA, ed. Methods of assessing the reinforcing properties of abused drugs. New York: Springer-Verlag, 1987:211–227.

664. Stewart J, Wise RA. Reinstatement of heroin self-administration habits: morphine prompts and naltrexone discourages renewed responding after extinction. Psychopharmacology 1992;108:79–84.

665. Stewart J. Reinstatement of heroin and cocaine self-administration behavior in the rat by intracerebral application of morphine in the ventral tegmental area. Pharmacol Biochem Behav 1984;20:917–923.

666. Stewart J, Vezina P. A comparison of the effects of intra-accumbens injections of amphetamine and morphine on reinstatement of heroin intravenous self-administration behavior. Brain Res 1988;457:287–294.

667. Wise RA, Murray A, Bozarth MA. Bromocriptine self-administration and bromocriptine-reinstatement of cocaine-trained and heroin-trained lever pressing in rats. Psychopharmacology 1990;100:355–360.

668. Shaham Y, Alvares K, Nespor SM, Grunberg NE. Effect of stress on oral morphine and fentanyl self-administration in rats. Pharmacol Biochem Behav 1992;41:615–619.

669. Shaham Y, Klein LC, Alvares K, Grunberg NE. Effect of stress on oral fentanyl consumption in rats in an operant self-administration paradigm. Pharmacol Biochem Behav 1993; 46:315–322.

670. Shaham Y, Stewart J. Exposure to mild stress enhances the reinforcing efficacy of intravenous heroin self-administration in rats. Psychopharmacology 1994;114:523–527.

671. Shaham Y. Immobilization stress-induced oral opioid self-administration and withdrawal in rats: role of conditioning factors and the effect of stress on "relapse" to opioid drugs. Psychopharmacology 1993;111:477–485.

672. Shaham Y, Stewart J. Stress reinstates heroin-seeking in drug-free animals: an effect mimicking heroin, not withdrawal. Psychopharmacology 1995;119:334–341.

673. Jaffe JH. Current concepts of addiction. Res Publ Assoc Res Nerv Ment Dis 1992;70:1–21.

674. O'Brien CP, Childress AR, McLellan AT, Ehrman R. A learning model of addiction. Res

Publ Assoc Res Nerv Ment Dis 1992;70: 157–177.

675. Kreek MJ. Rationale for maintenance pharmacotherapy of opiate dependence. Res Publ Assoc Res Nerv Ment Dis 1992;70:205–230.

676. Dackis CA, Gold MS. New concepts in cocaine addiction: the dopamine depletion hypothesis. Neurosci Biobehav Rev 1985;9:469–477.

677. Gawin FH, Kleber HD. Abstinence symptomatology and psychiatric diagnosis in cocaine abusers. Arch Gen Psychiat 1986;43:107–113.

678. Vaillant GE. What can long-term follow-up teach us about relapse and prevention of relapse in addiction? Br J Addict 1988;83: 1147–1157.

679. Hoffmann NG, Miller NS. Perspectives of effective treatment for alcohol and drug disorders. Psychiatr Clin North Am 1993;16: 127–140.

680. van der Kooy D. Place conditioning: a simple and effective method for assessing the motivational properties of drugs. In: Bozarth MA, ed. Methods of assessing the reinforcing properties of abused drugs. New York: Springer-Verlag, 1987:229–240.

681. Bozarth MA. Conditioned place preference: a parametric analysis using systemic heroin injections. In: Bozarth MA, ed. Methods of assessing the reinforcing properties of abused drugs. New York: Springer-Verlag, 1987: 241–273.

682. Phillips AG, Fibiger HC. Anatomical and neurochemical substrates of drug reward determined by the conditioned place preference technique. In: Bozarth MA. Methods of assessing the reinforcing properties of abused drugs. New York: Springer-Verlag, 1987: 275–290.

683. Hiroi N, White NM. The reserpine-sensitive dopamine pool mediates (+)-amphetamine-conditioned reward in the place preference paradigm. Brain Res 1990;510:33–42.

684. Hiroi N, White NM. The amphetamine conditioned place preference: differential involvement of dopamine receptor subtypes and two dopaminergic terminal areas. Brain Res 1991; 552:141–152.

685. Hiroi N, White NM. The ventral pallidum area is involved in the acquisition but not expression of the amphetamine conditioned place preference. Neurosci Lett 1993;156:9–12.

686. Pettit HO, Pettit AJ. Disposition of cocaine in blood and brain after a single pretreatment. Brain Res 1994;651:261–268.

687. Parsons LH, Justice JB Jr. Serotonin and dopamine sensitization in the nucleus accumbens, ventral tegmental area, and dorsal raphe nucleus following repeated cocaine administration. J Neurochem 1993;61:1611–1619.

688. Kalivas PW, Duffy P. Time course of extracellular dopamine and behavioral sensitization to cocaine. I. Dopamine axon terminals. J Neurosci 1993;13:266–275.

689. Wolf ME, White FJ, Hu XT. MK-801 prevents alterations in the mesoaccumbens dopamine system associated with behavioral sensitization to amphetamine. J Neurosci 1994;14:1735–1745.

690. Wolf ME, White FJ, Nassar R, Brooderson RJ, Khansa MR. Differential development of autoreceptor subsensitivity and enhanced dopamine release during amphetamine sensitization. J Pharmacol Exp Ther 1993;264: 249–255.

691. Horger BA, Valadez A, Wellman PJ, Schenk S. Augmentation of the neurochemical effects of cocaine in the ventral striatum and medial pre-

frontal cortex following preexposure to amphetamine, but not nicotine: an in vivo microdialysis study. Life Sci 1994;55:1245–1251.

692. Paulson PE, Robinson TE. Amphetamine-induced time-dependent sensitization of dopamine neurotransmission in the dorsal and ventral striatum: a microdialysis study in behaving rats. Synapse 1995;19:56–65.

693. Hooks MS, Duffy P, Striplin C, Kalivas PW. Behavioral and neurochemical sensitization following cocaine self-administration. Psychopharmacology 1994;115:265–272.

694. Weiss F, Paulus MP, Lorang MT, Koob GF. Increases in extracellular dopamine in the nucleus accumbens by cocaine are inversely related to basal levels: effects of acute and repeated administration. J Neurosci 1992;12:4372–4380.

695. Schrater PA, Russo AC, Stanton TL, Newman JR, Rodriguez LM, Beckman AL. Changes in striatal dopamine metabolism during the development of morphine physical dependence in rats: observations using in vivo microdialysis. Life Sci 1993;52:1535–1545.

696. Spanagel R, Shippenberg TS. Modulation of morphine-induced sensitization by endogenous kappa opioid systems in the rat. Neurosci Lett 1993;153:232–236.

697. Imperato A, Mele A, Scrocco MG, Puglisi-Allegra S. Chronic cocaine alters limbic extracellular dopamine: neurochemical basis for addiction. Eur J Pharmacol 1992;212:299–300.

698. Parsons LH, Smith AD, Justice JB Jr. Basal extracellular dopamine is decreased in the rat nucleus accumbens during abstinence from chronic cocaine. Synapse 1991;9:60–65.

699. Robertson MW, Leslie CA, Bennett JP Jr. Apparent synaptic dopamine deficiency induced by withdrawal from chronic cocaine treatment. Brain Res 1991;538:337–339.

700. Maisonneuve IM, Kreek JM. Acute tolerance to the dopamine response induced by a binge pattern of cocaine administration in male rats: an in vivo microdialysis study. J Pharmacol Exp Ther 1994;268:916–921.

701. Emmett-Oglesby MW, Lane JD. Tolerance to the reinforcing effects of cocaine. Behav Pharmacol 1992;3:193–200.

702. Fischman MW, Schuster CR, Javaid J, Hatano Y, Davis J. Acute tolerance development to the cardiovascular and subjective effects of cocaine. J Pharmacol Exp Ther 1985;235:677–682.

703. Kokkinidis L, Zacharko RM, Predy PA. Post-amphetamine depression of self-stimulation responding from the substantia nigra: reversal by tricyclic antidepressants. Pharmacol Biochem Behav 1980;13:379–383.

704. Kokkinidis L, McCarter BD. Postcocaine depression and sensitization of brain-stimulation reward: analysis of reinforcement and performance effects. Pharmacol Biochem Behav 1990;36:463–471.

705. Barrett RJ, White DK. Reward system depression following chronic amphetamine: antagonism by haloperidol. Pharmacol Biochem Behav 1980;13:555–559.

706. Cassens G, Actor C, Kling M, Schildkraut JJ. Amphetamine withdrawal: effects on threshold of intracranial reinforcement. Psychopharmacology 1981;73:318–322.

707. Leith NJ, Barrett RJ. Amphetamine and the reward system: evidence for tolerance and postdrug depression. Psychopharmacology 1976;46:19–25.

708. Simpson DM, Annau Z. Behavioral withdrawal following several psychoactive drugs. Pharmacol Biochem Behav 1977;7:59–64.

709. Wise RA, Munn E. Withdrawal from chronic amphetamine elevates baseline intracranial self-stimulation thresholds. Psychopharmacology 1995;117:130–136.

710. Frank RA, Martz S, Pommering T. The effect of chronic cocaine on self-stimulation train-duration thresholds. Pharmacol Biochem Behav 1988;29:755–758.

711. Pothos E, Rada P, Mark GP, Hoebel BG. Dopamine microdialysis in the nucleus accumbens during acute and chronic morphine, naloxone-precipitated withdrawal and clonidine treatment. Brain Res 1991;566:348–350.

712. Crippens D, Robinson TE. Withdrawal from morphine or amphetamine: different effects on dopamine in the ventral-medial striatum studied with microdialysis. Brain Res 1994;650:56–62.

713. Rossetti ZL, Hmaidan Y, Gessa GL. Marked inhibition of mesolimbic dopamine release: a common feature of ethanol, morphine, cocaine and amphetamine abstinence in rats. Eur J Pharmacol 1992;221:227–234.

714. Acquas E, Di Chiara G. Depression of mesolimbic dopamine transmission and sensitization to morphine during opiate abstinence. J Neurochem 1992;58:1620–1625.

715. Spanagel R, Almeida OF, Bartl C, Shippenberg TS. Endogenous κ-opioid systems in opiate withdrawal: role in aversion and accompanying changes in mesolimbic dopamine release. Psychopharmacology 1994;115:121–127.

716. Schulteis G, Markou A, Gold LH, Stinus L, Koob GF. Relative sensitivity of multiple indices of opiate withdrawal: a quantitative dose-response analysis. J Pharmacol Exp Ther 1994;271:1391–1398.

717. Schaefer GJ, Michael RP. Changes in response rates and reinforcement thresholds for intracranial self-stimulation during morphine withdrawal. Pharmacol Biochem Behav 1986;25:1263–1269.

718. Koob GF, Stinus L, Le Moal M, Bloom FE. Opponent process theory of motivation: neurobiological evidence from studies of opiate dependence. Neurosci Biobehav Rev 1989;13:135–140.

719. Stinus L, Le Moal M, Koob GF. Nucleus accumbens and amygdala are possible substrates for the aversive stimulus effects of opiate withdrawal. Neuroscience 1990;37:767–773.

720. Kelsey JE, Arnold SR. Lesions of the dorsomedial amygdala, but not the nucleus accumbens, reduce the aversiveness of morphine withdrawal in rats. Behav Neurosci 1994;108:1119–1127.

721. Nader K, Bechara A, Roberts DC, van der Kooy D. Neuroleptics block high- but not low-dose heroin place preferences: further evidence for a two-system model of motivation. Behav Neurosci 1994;108:1128–1138.

722. Kosten TA. Clonidine attenuates conditioned aversion produced by naloxone-precipitated opiate withdrawal. Eur J Pharmacol 1994;254:59–63.

723. Higgins GA, Nguyen P, Sellers EM. The NMDA antagonist dizocilpine (MK801) attenuates motivational as well as somatic aspects of naloxone precipitated opioid withdrawal. Life Sci 1992;50:PL167–72.

724. Harris GC, Aston-Jones G. Beta-adrenergic antagonists attenuate somatic and aversive signs of opiate withdrawal. Neuropsychopharmacology 1993;9:303–311.

725. Higgins GA, Nguyen P, Joharchi N, Sellers EM. Effects of 5-HT₃ receptor antagonists on behavioural measures of naloxone-precipitated

726. opioid withdrawal. Psychopharmacology 1991;105:322–328.

726. Mucha RF. Is the motivational effect of opiate withdrawal reflected by common somatic indices of precipitated withdrawal? A place conditioning study in the rat. Brain Res 1987;418:214–220.

727. Dai S, Corrigall WA, Coen KM, Kalant H. Heroin self-administration by rats: influence of dose and physical dependence. Pharmacol Biochem Behav 1989;32:1009–1015.

728. Young GA, Moreton JE, Meltzer LT, Khazan N. 1-alpha-acetylmethadol (LAAM), methadone and morphine abstinence in dependent rats: EEG and behavioral correlates. Drug Alcohol Depend 1977;2:141–148.

729. Markou A, Koob GF. Postcocaine anhedonia: an animal model of cocaine withdrawal. Neuropsychopharmacology 1991;4:17–26.

730. Kalant H. Comparative aspects of tolerance to, and dependence on, alcohol, barbiturates, and opiates. In: Gross MM, ed, Alcohol intoxication and withdrawal. New York: Plenum Press, 1977;169–186.

731. Wise RA. The role of reward pathways in the development of drug dependence. Pharmacol Ther 1987;35:227–263.

732. Solomon RL. The opponent process theory of acquired motivation. Am Psychol 1980;35:691–712.

733. Solomon RL, Corbit JD. An opponent-process theory of motivation: I. Temporal dynamics of affect. Psychol Rev 1974;81:119–145.

734. Koob GF, Markou A, Weiss F, Schulteis G. Opponent process and drug dependence: neurobiological mechanisms. Sem Neurosci 1993;5:351–358.

735. De Vry J, Donselaar I, Van Ree JM. Intraventricular self-administration of heroin in the rat: reward seems dissociated from analgesia and physical dependence. Eur J Pharmacol 1989;161:19–25.

736. Wei E, Loh HH, Way EL. Brain sites of precipitated abstinence in morphine dependent rats. J Pharmacol Exp Ther 1973;185:108–115.

737. Gardner EL, Lowinson JH. Drug craving and positive/negative hedonic brain substrates activated by addicting drugs. Sem Neurosci 1993;5:359–368.

738. Gardner EL, Walker LS, Paredes W. Clozapine's functional mesolimbic selectivity is not duplicated by the addition of anticholinergic action to haloperidol: a brain stimulation study in the rat. Psychopharmacology 1993;110:119–124.

739. Eichler AJ, Antelman SM, Fisher AE. Self-stimulation: site-specific tolerance to chronic dopamine receptor blockade. Soc Neurosci Abstr 1976;2:440.

740. Ettenberg A, Wise RA. Non-selective enhancement of locus coeruleus and substantia nigra self-stimulation after termination of chronic dopaminergic receptor blockade with pimozide in rats. Psychopharmacol Commun 1976;2:117–124.

741. Ostrowski NL, Hatfield CB, Caggiula AR. The effects of low doses of morphine on the activity of dopamine-containing cells and on behavior. Life Sci 1982;31:2347–2350.

742. Matthews RT, German DC. Electrophysiological evidence for excitation of rat ventral tegmental area dopaminergic neurons by morphine. Neuroscience 1984;11:617–626.

743. Harris GC, Aston-Jones G. Involvement of D2 dopamine receptors in the nucleus accumbens in the opiate withdrawal syndrome. Nature 1994;371:155–157.

744. Bechara A, Harrington F, Nader K, van der Kooy D. Neurobiology of motivation: double dissociation of two motivational mechanisms mediating opiate reward in drug-naive versus drug-dependent animals. Behav Neurosci 1992;106:798–807.

745. Nader K, Bechara A, Roberts DCS, van der Kooy D. Neuroleptics block high- but not low-dose heroin place preferences: further evidence for a two-system model of motivation. Behav Neurosci 1994;108:1128–1138.

746. Bechara A, Nader K, van der Kooy D. Neurobiology of withdrawal motivation: evidence for two separate aversive effects produced in morphine-naive versus morphine-dependent rats by both naloxone and spontaneous withdrawal. Behav Neurosci 1995;109:91–105.

747. Gardner EL. Brain reward mechanisms. In: Lowinson JH, Ruiz P, Millman RB, Langrod JG, eds. Substance abuse: A comprehensive textbook. 2nd ed. Baltimore: Williams & Wilkins, 1992:70–99.

748. Smith JE, Dworkin SI. Neurobiological substrates of drug self-administration. NIDA Res Monogr Ser 1986;71:127–145.

749. Goeders NE, Smith JE. Intracranial self-administration methodologies. Neurosci Biobehav Rev 1987;11:319–329.

750. Alheid GF, Heimer L. New perspectives in basal forebrain organization of special relevance for neuropsychiatric disorders: the striatopallidal, amygdaloid, and corticopetal components of substantia innominata. Neuroscience 1988;27:1–39.

751. Heimer L, de Olmos J, Alheid GF, Zaborszky L. "Perestroika" in the basal forebrain: opening the border between neurology and psychiatry. Prog Brain Res 1991;87:109–165.

752. Fibiger HC, Phillips AG, Brown EE. The neurobiology of cocaine-induced reinforcement. Ciba Found Symp 1992;166:96–111.

753. Koob GF. Neural mechanisms of drug reinforcement. Ann N Y Acad Sci 1992;654:171–191.

754. Amalric M, Koob GF. Functionally selective neurochemical afferents and efferents of the mesocorticolimbic and nigrostriatal dopamine system. Prog Brain Res 1993;99:209–226.

755. Koob GF. Neurobiological mechanisms in cocaine and opiate dependence. Res Publ Assoc Res Nerv Ment Dis 1992;70:79–92.

756. Koob GF. Drugs of abuse: anatomy, pharmacology and function of reward pathways. Trends Pharmacol Sci 1992;13:177–184.

757. Hebb DO. The organization of behavior: a neuropsychological theory. New York: Wiley, 1949.

758. Goldstein A. Addiction: from biology to drug policy. New York: WH Freeman, 1995.

759. Damsma G, Pfaus JG, Wenkstern D, Phillips AG, Fibiger HC. Sexual behavior increases dopamine transmission in the nucleus accumbens and striatum of male rats: comparison with novelty and locomotion. Behav Neurosci 1992;106:181–191.

760. Wilson C, Nomikos GG, Collu M, Fibiger HC. Dopaminergic correlates of motivated behavior: importance of drive. J Neurosci 1995;15:5169–5178.

761. Wenkstern D, Pfaus JG, Fibiger HC. Dopamine transmission increases in the nucleus accumbens of male rats during their first exposure to sexually receptive female rats. Brain Res 1993;618:41–46.

762. Maldonado-Irizarry CS, Swanson CJ, Kelley AE. Glutamate receptors in the nucleus accumbens shell control feeding behavior via the lateral hypothalamus. J Neurosci 1995;15:6779–6788.

763. Gawin FH, Kleber HD. Abstinence symptomatology and psychiatric diagnosis in cocaine abusers. Arch Gen Psychiatry 1986;43:107–113.

764. Siegel RK. Cocaine smoking. J Psychoactive Drugs 1982;14:321–337.

765. Weiss RD, Mirin SM, Michael JL, Sollogub AC. Psychopathology in chronic cocaine abusers. Am J Drug Alcohol Abuse 1986;12:17–29.

766. Dole VP, Nyswander ME, Kreek MJ. Narcotic blockade. Arch Intern Med 1966;118:304–309.

767. Dole VP. Implications of methadone maintenance for theories of narcotic addiction. JAMA 1989;261:1879–1880.

7 CRAVING

James A. Halikas

DEFINING "CRAVING"

Craving is defined as a "compelling urge" that intrudes upon the drug user's thoughts, affects the user's mood, and compels alteration in his or her behavior. This compelling urge has also been described as an "urgent and overpowering desire" or an "irresistible impulse" to use the substance. Craving, in the substance abuser, has been considered to be analogous to fear in the phobic, or panic in the anxious individual. This societal definition is applied casually to both pharmacological cravings and other pleasurable activities, particular foods, sexual activity, gambling, and even, paradoxically, self-injurious behaviors.

The World Health Organization has defined craving as, "a desire to experience the effect(s) of a previously experienced psychoactive substance" (1). This definition blurs the distinction between wish or desire, on the one hand, and compulsion, on the other. In 1991, Halikas et al. described the craving sensation for cocaine as being "so intense and intrusive that it disrupts concentration, interferes with performance, makes the individual acutely and extremely uncomfortable, and controls subsequent actions. In short, craving is an irresistible urge to use a substance that compels drug seeking behavior" (2). This definition recognizes the compulsive, or drive, aspect of craving, but fails to address the contribution to craving made by the hedonic value of the substance.

The heart of the problem of definition is in understanding the subjective nature of the phenomenon of craving. Behavioral science has repeatedly wrestled with how to assess a subjective experience so as to study it systematically. Some individual experiences have now yielded to scientific method, largely because of the development of an objective yardstick against which individual subjective experience can be measured. Perception of color can be measured using the precise spectrum in visible light compared across individuals; sound can be assessed by known frequency and objective volume; white light can be measured by intensity in lumens; taste can be assessed in terms of concentration of test chemical. The individual subjective experience of an external stimulus can be systematically compared among individuals when there is an external objective yardstick. To date such yardsticks have not been developed for any of the human emotions experienced by all, e.g., love, hate, fear, anxiety, or, in this case, craving.

Over the last 60 years, the clinical method used in the behavioral sciences to assess such subjective experiences has been the accumulation of the descriptions of individuals. In this way, perhaps, characteristics can be identified and isolated that are at the heart of the common experience. Some of the original work on craving was done by Arnold Ludwig at the University of Kentucky. Focusing on alcoholics, he identified how drug-dependent individuals themselves define craving, how craving may be molded by psychological factors and expectations in the individual's current setting, and how patterns of alcohol use in individuals can be conditioned. Ludwig's analysis suggested that craving was a label affixed by patients to some combination of internal and external dysphoric or discontented *feelings,* which the alcoholic then used as a reason or excuse to resume drinking (3, 4). In essence, "craving" meant different things to different people. Ludwig's work had direct therapeutic implications in suggesting that the treater must understand the individual addict's unique set of environmental triggers and psychological stresses to develop a specific treatment program. In addition, Ludwig and his colleagues were predicting the utility of coping strategies and relapse prevention.

By first suggesting that craving was a label placed on a discontented state, Ludwig helped initiate the debate regarding the existence and the nature of the phenomenon of "craving." When it becomes associated with other subjective feelings such as this vague discontentedness, or when it becomes associated with psychological concepts such as conditioning, reinforcement, social learning, or expectancy, the definition becomes both widened and subject to intense debate. Indeed, there are many in the scientific community who challenge the very existence of craving as a discrete phenomenon because it has been so elusive. Most of the scientific community, however, and all clinical experience point to the existence of craving as an actual phenomenon for which we have, still, only a limited understanding. In that, it is like other human experiences—love, fear, sadness—that are elusive but real.

Controversy regarding the utility of the term craving, and further, the basic validity of the term, has gone on for decades. Kozlowski and Wilkinson of the Addiction Research Foundation contributed a seminal article in 1987 (5) in which they argued that while craving existed, the problems related to defining it came from mixing the traditional layman's definition of craving with technical or scientific definitions predicated on specific hypotheses. It was noted that scientists have taken craving variously to be representative of physical dependence, or be the result of physical symptoms, or be one of several withdrawal symptoms, or to indicate a subset of cognitive processes about drug use, but have always connected the observed phenomenon of craving to an interpreted explanation. Instead, Kozlowski and Wilkinson suggested that "craving" be used only in a descriptive way, indicating a strong desire or urge to use the substance.

Stockwell supported the concept of craving by demonstrating a correlation of craving intensity with withdrawal symptoms among alcoholics (6). West concurred, and suggested that instruments could be constructed that get at those aspects of craving commonly agreed upon (7). Shiffman, however, suggested that there was an absence of empirical evidence documenting its existence as a distinct state (8).

Kozlowski et al. subsequently concluded that the term craving was not useful because alcoholics and smokers studied could not distinguish between craving as a compelling urge and craving as a wish or a desire (9).

MEASUREMENT OF CRAVING

Other attempts have been made to develop clinical verification of craving as a phenomenon. The most generic attempt has been the use of a subjective analog scale, that is, a 10 cm horizontal line that attempts to measure "craving" from a zero point on the left, meaning "no craving," to a 10 cm point on the right side of the scale, meaning the most intense craving "ever in one's life." Patients are asked to determine how bad their craving is or was on this 10 cm line by placing a mark along the severity continuum. These individual points are then plotted or averaged, across individuals, or across time for any one individual to assess craving fluctuations.

Hughes believed it was possible to use self-report as a way of rating craving, but urged that craving parameters be identified, such as time or intensity, rather than mere presence or absence (10). Using the model of the cocaine user's subjective craving, Halikas et al. sought to identify three separate characteristics of craving that seemed to exist clinically: frequency, duration, and intensity (2). It appeared to these investigators that craving was an episodic phenomenon, like other subjective events, that comes and goes over the course of a few minutes or a few hours. Thus, the duration of craving could be assessed in real time; the repetitiveness or frequency of craving during the course of a 24-hour or 7-day period could be recorded; and the intensity of individual episodes could be assessed. With that in mind, the Minnesota Cocaine Craving Scale was developed, which continued to use the analog scale for measuring the *intensity* of the craving, but aggregated the *frequency* and *duration* of the phenomenon separately into discrete intervals (2). Figure 7.1 presents this simple descriptive scale.

Ludwig administered a craving questionnaire to 60 male alcoholic inpa-

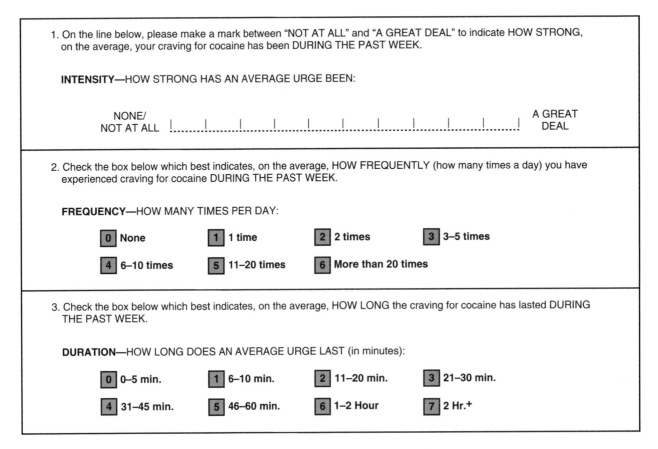

Figure 7.1. Simple descriptive scale. (Copyright 1989, James Halikas, M.D., Department of Psychiatry, Substance Abuse Disorder Program, University of Minnesota.)

tients showing that craving was defined in terms of the need for alcohol or the desired effects of alcohol (3). Here, craving was also associated with dysphoric mood and environmental frustration, and was noted to vary in intensity. Mathew et al. used a structured instrument with abstinent alcoholics, which found that craving was on a continuum that was modified by environmental factors and changes in mood, not an all-or-none phenomenon (11). Bradley et al. studied 78 opiate abusers after inpatient detoxification, looking for relapse precipitants (12). They categorized relapse precipitants into a variety of emotional, intellectual, interpersonal, and social areas.

Elaborate questionnaires have been designed for use with smokers, drinkers, and drug users to collect descriptions of craving by identifying the presence or absence of numerous characteristics thought to be associated with craving. In addition to elaborate questionnaires, systematic narrative data collection interviews have been performed with various populations of substance abusers in similar attempts to accurately define craving. Depending on the instrument and the investigator, craving has been found to be either a distinct phenomenon or a continuum that blends into normalcy.

The basic descriptive issues regarding craving continue to be:

1. In whom does this phenomenon occur?
2. With what substances does this phenomenon occur?
3. When does this phenomenon occur?
4. In what settings and under what circumstances does this phenomenon occur?
5. How do the characteristics of this phenomenon differ depending on the substance and user?
6. Why does this phenomenon occur in some, but not in all, individuals with similar characteristics?

We can conclude from the work to date that craving is hard to measure, hard to describe, and hard to delineate.

THE SUBJECTIVE EXPERIENCE OF CRAVING

The subjective phenomenon of craving has been extended and made to overlap with other equally elusive concepts in substance abuse such as tolerance, free choice, dependence, dysphoria, boredom, desire for an altered or heightened sensory state, etc.

Ludwig and Wikler suggested that craving for alcohol really represented a cognitive correlate for an alcohol withdrawal syndrome that was subclinical in nature (13). This term, "craving," summated the internal and external cues, and presented the addict with a potential source of relief, i.e., the substance.

Maisto and Schefft reviewed two theoretical constructs regarding alcoholism as a disease—one involving loss of control of alcohol, and the other involving overwhelming craving for alcohol (14). Both constructs had some utility but were still too nebulous for empirical analysis.

Childress et al. documented the association between negative mood states and craving and withdrawal symptoms (15). Here, they first presented their hypothesis that treatment should address both internal and external conditioned stimuli as part of the treatment approach. Marlatt suggested that craving was a component of expectation and anticipation—psychological qualities—rather than a physiological phenomenon (16). In 1990 he addressed the importance of cue exposure in developing relapse prevention methodologies, and suggested that the success of cue exposure was mediated by extinction of the pleasurable expectations associated with the substance (17).

Weddington et al. showed that, in cocaine addicts, craving was worse prior to admission for detoxification, thus relating it to internal psychological cues and expectations of withdrawal (18). Long found that craving for alcohol among problem drinkers increased after drinking low alcohol beers, indicating that the craving was not just associated with the alcohol, but with the rest of the drinking experience as well, thus adding another psychological dimension to the discussion of craving (19). Laberg took this concept further by suggesting that craving was entirely a conditioned response among alcoholics associated with environmental and intrapsychic cues relevant to drinking in the same way that fear was a conditioned response in phobias (20).

Sherman et al. studied drug-free heroin addicts for craving (21). They found that direct heroin cues were most effective in eliciting craving, and

also in eliciting withdrawal symptoms. Heroin cues were also associated with an increase in anxiety and tension in these addicts. The linkage between negative affects, craving, and withdrawal symptoms suggested that craving involved, at least in part, conditioned expectancies.

Clinical studies of craving have focused on the development of craving *triggers,* usually based on interview information from substance users with concurrent assessment of physiological correlates. For example, Russian scientists have measured cortical evoked potentials in association with charged word stimuli, such as "vodka." Russian work has also focused on galvanic skin response and skin conductance changes. Nemtsov and his colleagues from the Scientific Research Institute of Psychiatry in Moscow have demonstrated physiological changes in skin conductance response along with other psychophysiological indices, using the simple technique of charged words, such as "vodka" or "beer" (22). Genkina, in Moscow, showed that cortical evoked potentials varied with charged words such as "vodka," again pointing to direct physiological correlates to craving (23). Shostakovich, from the Serbskii Institute, also demonstrated this increase in the P300 wave in response to the word "vodka" in all cortical regions (24).

Ludwig described a semi-structured interview with 150 alcoholic patients that showed that craving was associated with cues or stimuli in virtually all individuals (25). This work suggested the use of desensitization to specific cues as a possible treatment tool.

Multiple other triggers in relapse related to both craving and loss of control have been noted by Maisto (14). Judith Wurtman showed that carbohydrate craving varied with menstrual cycle and serotonin stimulating medications (26). Satel and Gawin noted case reports where craving was triggered by depressive affect in male cocaine users (27). Rankin et al. showed that speed of drinking a prescribed amount of alcohol directly correlated with the intensity of craving previously reported by the alcoholic (28).

O'Brien and Childress have contributed enormously to the literature with studies of opiate and cocaine addicts in craving research paradigms and treatment protocols. They have determined that it is possible to use an extinction conditioning model to eliminate the subjective experience of craving, while the individual at the same time continues to manifest the physiological correlates of the no-longer-perceived subjective experience. In 1990 they demonstrated that an extinction protocol to drug-related cues that decreased craving helped significantly with retention of patients in outpatient cocaine treatment (29). Their work also demonstrated that there were strong signs of physiological arousal associated with these drug-related cues in addition to the subjective feelings of craving.

Several investigators have noted that some drugs of abuse seem to provide a feed-forward, which then causes a substantial increase in the drive to use the substance. This has been called "priming." While some authors have considered this to be synonymous with "craving," it may not be. Engle had indicated early on that priming was possibly not always a factor in craving by showing that one ounce of vodka, given to alcoholics double-blind, did not increase their desire for alcohol (30). Ludwig et al., however, suggested that low doses of alcohol could have a priming effect, which they labeled the "first drink" phenomenon (31). Bradley and Moorey also noted craving and priming as separate but related factors, thus distinguishing between craving for the substance and the priming effect of a small amount of the substance (32). Jaffe et al. demonstrated the priming effect of double-blind IV cocaine in increasing the subjective phenomenon of craving among cocaine users as ascertained by questionnaire (33).

Siegel suggested that drug tolerance and dependence were entirely the result of Pavlovian conditioning in humans (34). Childress et al. suggested that there was an association between conditioned drug-related responses and craving in all addicted populations (35). They suggested, therefore, that extinction procedures would be useful as a treatment technique. Powell et al. reviewed behavioral correlates for opiate craving and concluded that drug related cues could elicit craving as could both withdrawal symptoms and pleasurable symptoms (36). They felt that these all acted as conditioned responses. Monti et al. suggested that social learning, expectations, learned reactions, coping skills, etc. were the basis of development of craving (37).

Halikas and Kuhn suggested that cocaine craving in humans was a behavioral manifestation of "kindling," the neuronal supersensitivity induced by cocaine in animal studies (38). They further suggested that the symptoms seen in chronic cocaine users—irritability, restlessness, hypervigilance, and paranoia—may be the result of the same kindling phenomenon in some individuals.

All pharmacological strategies for reduction of drug consumption related to reduction in craving have also suggested a theoretical basis for craving based upon learning theory. Craving has been considered synonymous with the reinforcing effects of the substance. Drugs that reduce the pleasurable, or reinforcing, qualities of a substance are thought to be useful in reducing craving. But, animal studies in this regard have been disappointing; most drugs tested reduce reinforcement in animals, but when translated to humans, do not appear to reduce craving or the final common pathway of human drug use.

Craving can also be seen as an aspect of a prolonged subclinical abstinence or withdrawal syndrome, which suggests that an ultra-long-term withdrawal schedule of the substance, where the organism adapts to slowly decreasing levels of the substance, might reduce craving. Craving may be seen as being idiosyncratic in vulnerable individuals, whether based on concurrent psychiatric illness, some other pre-existing psychic or physiological damage, or some genetic vulnerability (39). Elsewhere in this text are detailed reviews of the pharmacology and complications of each abused substance, which will address all of these possible elements of craving.

ANIMAL MODELS OF CRAVING

There has been extensive work in the last 20 years to develop animal models of craving as part of finding an objective physiological yardstick for craving. This brief review of this work will rely heavily on Athina Markou et al.'s remarkably thorough review of animal models in craving published in *Psychopharmacology* in 1993 (40).

In preclinical research, craving is conceptualized within the *incentive-motivation theory of behavior,* an interaction between the incentive provided by the rewarding or pleasurable properties of the drug and the subsequent drive, or motivation, of the organism to use the drug, or to avoid withdrawal symptoms in the absence of the drug. Within this conceptualization, the drug has similar direct reinforcing properties for all similar animals. It is, in Pavlovian terms, the unconditioned stimulus, i.e., the food that makes the dog salivate. Like food, the drug has another aspect independent of the direct reinforcement effects of the substance; it is transferred to other previously neutral stimuli to give them conditioned reinforcement properties, i.e., the bell associated with the food that causes the Pavlovian dog to salivate. In humans, these would be the social or mechanical triggers to craving, such as the needle and syringe to the heroin addict, the sight of white powder to the cocaine addict, the smell of liquor to an alcoholic, etc.

These two aspects of the substance, its direct reinforcing or pleasurable effect, and its ability to "rub off" on previously neutral stimuli, both need to be studied and calibrated to develop an animal model of craving. The success of any animal model so created will be based on its ability to be replicated, its "reliability," and its ability to mimic the human condition, its "predictive validity."

Within the framework of incentive-motivational theory of behavior, it is also hypothesized that reinforcing drugs have, in addition to direct pleasurable properties, an ability to cause the organism *to seek out* the substance repetitively. This is the "feed-forward" element of this hypothesis. Whether this internalized motivation, or new drive, for subsequent drug use is mediated by the same neuronal systems as other more traditional organismic reinforcers (sex and food) need not be known to utilize the experimental knowledge base gained from studies of these traditional reinforcers. As with all learning theory, there is a continuous feedback postulated between the organism and its environment, and a constant attempt at maintaining homeostasis. Further, there is an implication that stimuli with a hedonic value, i.e., reinforcers, are reinforcing because they somehow help push the organism toward this self same homeostasis: This may be a debatable premise.

It is important to recognize that the incentive-motivation theory of craving is also predicated on the transference of these motivational feed-forward properties by what were originally neutral environmental stimuli, and have

now become conditioned stimuli on their own. Craving is thus seen as being on a spectrum from first use, *not* predicated upon any craving, and subsequent uses where each use increases the incentive-motivational value, as can be observed by the differential exertion the organism will put forth to obtain the substance.

While drug-taking supposedly moves the organism towards homeostasis, simultaneously, the organism seems to develop neuronal adaptive mechanisms to counteract the effects of the substance. When the substance is abruptly discontinued, these now unopposed counteractive effects present the syndrome of physiological and psychological withdrawal. With most substances, psychological withdrawal symptoms seem to last well beyond physiological symptoms and may be the stimulus of renewed drug craving. Using this conceptualization of craving, animal models based on craving for food, water, sex, etc., can be extended to become models of drug craving.

Five models of drug craving have been developed: progressive ratio, choice, extinction, conditioned reinforcement, and second order schedule paradigms. Progressive ratio and choice paradigms reflect both the reinforcing and the conditioned incentive properties of substances. Extinction, conditioned reinforcement, and second order schedules all assess drug-seeking behavior independent of the reinforcement property of substances by studying the incentive-motivational properties in the absence of the drug. The utility of all models is assessed by the reproducibility of the experimental observations across species and drug classes, and in different laboratories, and the consistency and correlation between the behavior in the model and in the human condition.

For example, in the progressive ratio paradigm, the "cost" of a drug to an animal is increased incrementally to determine how much "work" the creature will do to self-administer the substance. This model has been documented in a variety of species, both primate and non-primate, with a reproducibility and consistency across time and under a variety of research designs for most drugs of abuse including opiates, stimulants, and nicotine. Drug dose, interval between drug administration, and increments of work ratio all show relevance in this model. There is a "breaking point," which is the maximal effort that the animal will exert for any dose of the medication; this "breaking point" has also been shown to have a high predictive reliability in human studies, and is considered a useful index in modeling human drug craving.

This breaking point measure varies in drug-dependent animals compared with non–drug-dependent animals and seems to reflect the enhanced incentive-motivational properties of addictive drugs. This would be analogous to the observation that human addicts spend far more time and effort to obtain substances than nondependent individuals do.

NEUROLOGICAL CORRELATES OF CRAVING

This paradigm can also be used to study the effects of various pharmacological and anatomical central nervous system lesions in animals. Neurotransmitter antagonists, agonists, and inhibitors have all been demonstrated to affect the breaking point measure for different addictive substances.

Recent scientific definitions of craving have linked craving with acute changes in neurotransmitter concentrations, such as dopamine, with specific reference to cocaine, or changes in endorphin levels with respect to alcohol. Halikas and Kuhn suggested a neuroelectrical basis for cocaine craving in the form of "kindling" (38). Pharmacologically induced kindling in the animal model by stimulants has been well known for decades. It has been postulated that repeated intermittent exposure to cocaine in humans had a similar effect, which was manifested as craving. Other authors have also suggested that stimulant drugs have an auto-priming mechanism that generates a conditioned response of craving (within our hypothesis, kindling), which is concordant with the subjective experiences reported by cocaine-dependent individuals. Craving has been associated with the nucleus accumbens and also with the hippocampus. Since the hippocampus is associated with learning, memory, and long-term potentiation (the mechanism of kindling), its anatomical association with craving appears to have validity. An analogous theoretical view of craving related to kindling or sensitization has been propounded by Robinson and Barridge (41). Whether this is receptor sensitization or electrical sensitization through changes in long-term potentiation remains speculative.

Wise hypothesized at least a two-factor model for addiction involving both positive reinforcement properties and suppression of pain and dysphoric internal signals (42). This model suggests that the positive and negative reinforcement effects are anatomically and functionally distinct, and may involve different neurotransmitter systems.

Kleber and Gawin discussed the cocaine crash as being caused by decrease in dopamine after long-term stimulant use (43). They associated craving with this relative depletion of dopamine.

Jaffe suggested that craving can be evoked by internal and external stimuli long after physiological withdrawal has been completed (44). This may involve memory traces of the reinforcing effects of these substances. Jaffe also suggested that a small dose of a drug among these formerly dependent individuals could have a priming effect resulting in increased craving, whether on a physiological or a psychological basis.

Weiss recognized the association of sweets with craving among incarcerated drug addicts (45). They hypothesized that this craving for sweets reflected an infantile component in their personality makeup. Whatever the merits of that interpretation, the observation and association were clear.

TREATMENT OF CRAVING

The basic question of what is craving continues to exist. Until the phenomenon of craving is carved away from other human experiences precisely, and understood in a testable way, we will all continue to be forced to consider it as a present, but poorly understood, clinical phenomenon. This does not, nor should not, stop us from seeking to ameliorate it or treat it, either with psychological or physiological modalities.

Childress et al. have been remarkably consistent in their studies of modification of craving through the use of psychological modalities. In 1986 they showed that extinction procedures were effective in reducing both craving and conditioned withdrawal symptoms in opiate users as part of an inpatient treatment program (46). They also engage the cocaine patient in an extinction paradigm, during which he or she becomes desensitized to the cocaine cues. These patients are retained more effectively in treatment because of this extinction paradigm. On the other hand, Powell et al. concluded that success with the desensitization technique of exposure therapy used in eliminating such cravings was quite limited (36).

Several medications have been identified that may have some usefulness in the treatment of craving. The narcotic antagonist, naltrexone, reduces craving in some alcoholics as assessed in double-blind studies. Both O'Malley (47) and Volpicelli (48) found reductions in the subjective phenomenon of craving of alcohol with double-blind naltrexone using the analog scale. Unfortunately, naltrexone is not equally useful in reducing heroin craving, even though it was originally developed as a heroin blocker. To date, no medication has been found that reduces craving in the opiate-dependent individual.

Smoking of nicotine cigarettes and use of nicotine-based tobacco products have long been a source of study because of the enormous health consequences of smoking. Nicotine substitution products are available that appear to reduce use of tobacco products by providing direct substitution, either in gum or by patch delivery system, of nicotine, while extinguishing the associated conditioned cues, and then eventually withdrawing the nicotine.

A variety of medications has been tried in an effort to reduce cocaine craving and cocaine relapse (49). Everything from chocolate to buprenorphine (a narcotic) have been tried, usually with beginning optimism and with subsequent negative findings after systematic replication. Medications that fit this description include amantadine (50), bromocriptine (51), carbamazepine (52, 53), desipramine (54), virtually all of the antidepressant medications, many of the neuroleptic medications, many of the antianxiety medications, and most of the anticonvulsant medications (55). All seem to work in some people, some of the time. But whether this is related to treatment of the craving per se, or to general mood stabilization or modification, remains unknown. All of these are powerful medications with complex neurochemical effects, which may have, as a common end product, decreased use of cocaine.

CONCLUSION

The concept of craving appears to be valid. It seems to strike a knowledgeable chord in all individuals. The fact that the term is so apparently communicative among drug users certainly suggests its importance as a significant aspect of drug use and addiction, whether or not it is scientifically manageable, as yet. Craving is a clinically useful descriptive term that does not yet lend itself to quantitative reliable assessment. In that regard, it is not alone. Clinicians must also seek to deal with other phenomena, such as loss of control and denial, in working with these patients.

From this brief review, it can be seen that the "final common pathway" is drug use and return to drug use. Whether this behavior is a desire for an altered state of consciousness, desire for pleasurable state, or some other volitional reason, or whether this is truly a "compelling urge," that intrudes itself into the person's life, may not always be clear. It may be more useful for the clinician not to accept the word "craving" at face value when given by a patient, but to ask, "How does this craving show itself in you?", and pursue it with questions regarding set and setting, internal responses when this sensation is felt, and ability to reject or succumb to this sensation. Further, it is necessary for the clinician to appreciate the behavioral conditioning elements and also the possible physiological elements related to this person's return to substance use, and seek to individualize the treatment plan.

References

1. Informal Expert Committee on the Craving Mechanism. Report. United Nations International Drug Control Programme and World Health Organization technical report series (No. V. 92–54439T), 1992.
2. Halikas JA, Kuhn KL, Crosby RD, Carlson GA, Crea F. The measurement of craving in cocaine patients using the Minnesota Cocaine Craving Scale. Compr Psychiatry 1991;32(1):22–27.
3. Ludwig AM, Stark LH. Alcohol craving: Subjective and situational aspects. Q J Stud Alcohol 1974;35(3-A):899–905.
4. Ludwig AM. The mystery of craving. Alcohol Health & Research World 1986;11(1):12–17, 69–70.
5. Kozlowski LT, Wilkinson DA. Use and misuse of the concept of craving by alcohol, tobacco, and drug researchers. Br J Addiction 1987;82(1):31–36.
6. Stockwell T. Is there a better word than "craving"? Br J Addiction 1987;82(1):44–45.
7. West R. Use and misuse of craving. Br J Addiction 1987;82(1):39–41.
8. Shiffman S. Craving: Don't let us throw the baby out with the bath water. Br J Addiction 1987;82(1):37–38.
9. Kozlowski LT, Mann RE, Wilkinson DA, Poulos CX. "Cravings" are ambiguous: Ask about urges or desires. Addict Behav 1989;14(4):443–445.
10. Hughes JR. Craving as a psychological construct. Br J Addiction 1987;82(1):38–39.
11. Mathew RJ, Claghorn JL, Largen J. Craving for alcohol in sober alcoholics. Am J Psychiatry 1979;136(4-B):603–606.
12. Bradley BP, Phillips G, Green L, Gossop M. Circumstances surrounding the initial lapse to opiate use following detoxification. Br J Psychiatry 1989;154:354–359.
13. Ludwig AM, Wikler A. "Craving" and relapse to drink. Q J Stud Alcohol 1974;35(1-A):108–130.
14. Maisto SA, Schefft BK. The constructs of craving for alcohol and loss of control drinking: Help or hindrance to research. Addict Behav 1977;2(4):207–217.
15. Childress AR, McLellan AT, Natale M, O'Brien CP. Mood states can elicit conditioned withdrawal and craving in opiate abuse patients. National Institute on Drug Abuse Research Monograph Series 1987;76:137–144.
16. Marlatt GA. Craving notes. Br J Addiction 1987;82(1):42–44.
17. Marlatt GA. Cue exposure and relapse prevention in the treatment of addictive behaviors. Addict Behav 1990;15(4):395–399.
18. Weddington WW, Brown BS, Haertzen CA, Cone EJ, et al. Changes in mood, craving, and sleep during short-term abstinence reported by male cocaine addicts: A controlled, residential study. Arch Gen Psychiatry 1990;47(9):861–868.
19. Long CG, Cohen EM. Low alcohol beers and wines: Attitudes of problem drinkers to their use and their effect on craving. Br J Addiction 1989;84(7):777–783.
20. Laberg JC. What is presented, and what prevented, in cue exposure and response prevention with alcohol dependent subjects? Addict Behav 1990;15(4):367–386.

21. Sherman JE, Zinser MC, Sideroff SI, Baker TB. Subjective dimensions of heroin urges: Influence of heroin-related and affectively negative stimuli. Addict Behav 1989;14(6):611–623.

22. Nemtsov AV. The responses of skin resistance to alcohol-related verbal stimuli in alcoholic adolescents. Zh Nevropatol Psikhiatr Im S S Korsakova 1989;89(8):112–116.

23. Genkina OA, Shostakovich GS. Cortical evoked activity during conditioning with an unperceived word. Hum Physiol 1987;13(3):159–167.

24. Shostakovich GS. The neural mechanism of subconscious attraction to alcohol in chronic alcoholics. Soviet Neurol Psychiatry 1989–1990; 22(4):3–12.

25. Ludwig AM. Pavlov's "bells" and alcohol craving. Addict Behav 1986;11(2):87–91.

26. Wurtman JJ. Carbohydrate craving, mood changes, and obesity. J Clin Psychiatry 1988;49 (Suppl):37–39.

27. Satel SL, Gawin FH. Seasonal cocaine abuse. Am J Psychiatry 1989;146(4):534–535.

28. Rankin H, Hodgson RJ, Stockwell T. The concept of craving and its measurement. Behav Res Ther 1979;17(4):389–396.

29. O'Brien CP, Childress AR, McLellan T, Ehrman R. Integrating systematic cue exposure with standard treatment in recovering drug dependent patients. Addict Behav 1990;15(4):355–365.

30. Engle KB, Williams TK. Effect of an ounce of vodka on alcoholics' desire for alcohol. Q J Stud Alcohol 1972;33(4-A):1099–1105.

31. Ludwig AM, Wikler A, Stark LH. The first drink: Psychobiological aspects of craving. Arch Gen Psychiatry 1974;30(4):539–547.

32. Bradley BP, Moorey S. Extinction of craving during exposure to drug-related cues: Three single case reports. Behav Psychother 1988;16(1):45–56.

33. Jaffe JH, Cascella NG, Kumor KM. Cocaine-induced cocaine craving. Psychopharmacology 1989;97(1):59–64.

34. Siegel S. Drug anticipation and the treatment of dependence. National Institute on Drug Abuse Research Monograph Series 1988;84:1–24.

35. Childress AR, McLellan AT, Ehrman R, O'Brien CP. Classically conditioned responses in opioid and cocaine dependence: A role in relapse? National Institute on Drug Abuse Research Monograph Series 1988;84:25–43.

36. Powell J, Gray JA, Bradley BP, Kasvikis Y, et al. Effects of exposure to drug-related cues in detoxified opiate addicts: A theoretical review and some new data. Addict Behav 1990;15(4):339–354.

37. Monti PM, Rohsenow DJ, Abrams DB, Binkoff JA. Social learning approaches to alcohol relapse: Selected illustrations and implications. National Institute on Drug Abuse Research Monograph Series 1988;84:141–160.

38. Halikas JA, Kuhn KL. Possible neurophysiological basis of cocaine craving. Ann Clin Psychiatry 1990;2(2):79–83.

39. Halikas JA, Crosby RD, Pearson VL, Nugent SM, Carlson GA. Psychiatric comorbidity in treatment-seeking cocaine abusers. Am J Addictions 1993;3(1):1–11.

40. Markou A, Weiss F, Gold LH, Caine SB, Schulteis G, Koob GF. Animal models of drug craving. Psychopharmacology 1993;112:163–182.

41. Robinson TE, Barridge KC. The neural basis of drug craving: An incentive-sensitization theory of addiction. Brain Res Brain Res Rev 1993; 18:247–291.

42. Wise RA. The neurobiology of craving: Implications for the understanding and treatment of addiction. J Abnorm Psychol 1988;97(2):118–132.

43. Kleber HD, Gawin FH. "The physiology of cocaine craving and "crashing": In reply. Arch Gen Psychiatry 1987;44(3):299–300.

44. Jaffe JH. Addictions: What does biology have to tell? Special issue: Psychiatry and the addictions. Int Rev Psychiatry 1989;1(1–2):51–61.

45. Weiss G. Food fantasies of incarcerated drug users. Int J Addictions 1982;17(5):905–912.

46. Childress AR, McLellan AT, O'Brien CP. Abstinent opiate abusers exhibit conditioned craving, conditioned withdrawal and reductions in both through extinction. Br J Addiction 1986; 81(5):655–660.

47. O'Malley S, Jaffe AJ, Chang G, et al. Naltrexone and alcohol dependence: a controlled study. Arch Gen Psychiatry 1992;49:881–887.

48. Volpicelli JR, Alterman AI, Hayashida M, et al. Naltrexone and the treatment of alcohol dependence. Arch Gen Psychiatry 1992;49:876–880.

49. Crosby RD, Halikas JA, Carlson GA. Pharmacotherapeutic interventions for cocaine abuse: present practices and future directions. J Addict Dis 1991;11(2):13–30.

50. Gawin FH, Morgan C, Kosten TR, Kleber HD. Double-blind evaluation of the effect of acute amantadine on cocaine craving. Psychopharmacology 1989;97(3):402–403.

51. Dackis CA, Gold MS. Bromocriptine as a treatment for cocaine abuse. Lancet 1985;2:1151–1152.

52. Halikas JA, Crosby RD, Carlson GA, Crea F, Graves NM, Bowers LD. Cocaine reduction in unmotivated crack users using carbamazepine versus placebo in a short-term, double-blind crossover design. Clin Pharmacol Ther 1991; 50(1):81–95.

53. Halikas JA, Kuhn KL, Maddux TL. Reduction of cocaine among methadone maintenance patients using concurrent carbamazepine maintenance. Ann Clin Psychiatry 1990;2 (1):3–6.

54. Gawin FH, Kleber HD, Byck R, Rounsaville BJ, et al. Desipramine facilitation of initial cocaine abstinence. Arch Gen Psychiatry 1989;46(2):117–121.

55. Halikas JA, Crosby RD, Carlson GA. Valproate in the treatment of cocaine addiction. Ann Clin Psychiatry 1992;4:65–66.

8 PSYCHODYNAMICS

Nancy M. Brehm and Edward J. Khantzian

Unraveling the etiology of substance abuse continues to be a challenge. There have been many technological advances in understanding the chemistry of human behavior, including the highly significant discovery of opiate receptor sites and endorphins, as well as other neurotransmitter systems. However, the substance abuse field continues to be in a preparadigm stage of development (1), suggesting a lack of agreement between theory and treatment. Sederer (2, p. 71) notes:

To set foot into the field of psychiatry (or the addictions) is to encounter an overwhelming mass of clinical data, hypothetical notions, and theoretical constructs. Dopamine mingles with denial, and serotonin with symbiosis. Defenses and divorce appear as meaningful, and influential, as gamma aminobutyric acid and the endorphins. Urban drift, ego-deficits, and ventricular enlargement may be found rubbing conceptual shoulders.

However, during the past couple of decades, important shifts have occurred in psychodynamic thinking about substance abuse (3–10). This chapter first summarizes early psychoanalytic theories about addiction, which primarily emphasized the use of drugs as a regressive, pleasurable adaptation. Following recent developments in psychodynamic thinking, it then explores the gradual shift in emphasis to a view of substance abuse as progressive responses to psychological suffering and related self-regulatory deficiencies. These deficiencies include impaired self-care, vulnerabilities in self-development and self-esteem, troubled self-object relations, and affect deficits. Early theories had viewed addictive behavior as reminiscent of wishes for early infantile pleasure. By contrast, a progressive perspective views addiction as an adaptive effort for survival. The chapter then considers the treatment implications, based on current theory and experience.

EARLY PSYCHOANALYTIC THEORIES OF ADDICTION

Early psychodynamic writings about addiction reflected the predominant way of understanding the psyche at that time, namely, a topographic model of the mind (11–13). Hence, they stressed regressive behavior caused by unconscious conflicts about libidinal pleasures, homosexuality, and aggression. In a letter to Wilhelm Fliess, in late 1897, Freud wrote: "The insight has dawned on me that masturbation is the one major habit, the 'primary addiction,' and it is only as a substitute and replacement for it that the other addictions—to alcohol, morphine, tobacco and the like—come into existence"

(14, p. 287). From this statement we can deduce that Freud saw addictions as substitutions for a regressive infantile autoeroticism, which was first experienced as pleasurable, then unpleasurable, the vicious circle of most addictions. In this cycle, the wish for pleasure becomes gratified, but only with accompanying guilt and loss of self-esteem. These feelings produce unbearable anxiety, which, in turn, leads to repetition of the act in order to find relief. Hence, the cycle begins again. Thus, from this perspective, addictions not only are substitutions for the primary addiction but also are examples of the repetition compulsion. Attempts are made to master the painful feelings and to regain self-esteem (15).

Abraham (12) stressed the role of alcohol in reducing sexual inhibitions in men. He based his theory on the analyses of male alcoholics and emphasized the openly affectionate behavior between men when drinking in beer halls. He theorized that male alcoholics have intense conflicts about homosexuality and that alcohol allows them to express these unconscious feelings in a way that society deems acceptable.

Also, from the regressive perspective, Rado (13) emphasized the "elatant" effect of drugs to alter depressed moods. He suggested that an understanding of addiction came from the recognition that the strength of the impulse to use a substance was more important than the substance in determining whether or not an individual became an addict. Addicts take drugs in order to find relief from a specific type of depression. This "initial depression" is an emotional state in which intense, persistent suffering occurs when some individuals experience frustration. What makes the drug initially become so crucial to the user is the ability of the drug to raise self-esteem and to alter the depressed mood to "elation." This elation is reminiscent of the narcissism that a baby feels, "radiant with self-esteem, and full of belief in the omnipotence of its wishes, of its thoughts, gestures and words" (13).

In contrast to the emphasis on libidinal and erotic aspects of addiction, Glover (16) focused primarily on aggression and sadism as the factors most pivotal in addiction. The addict projects his or her conflicts onto drugs, as a defense against a regression to a more psychotic state. Glover viewed the addictions as fixations in a developmental system between the more primitive paranoid-schizoid state and the more advanced obsessional-neurotic state. Consistent with the view that addiction is a coping mechanism and primarily defensive in nature, Glover viewed the addict's obsessional involvement with drugs and the related unconscious homosexual fantasy systems as a progressive and successful defense against paranoid-sadistic tendencies and psychosis. Clearly, Glover's view of addiction as a progressive rather than a regressive adaptation marked the onset of a new perspective in the psychodynamic formulation of addiction.

Expanding on Glover's ideas, Knight (17) described alcoholism as "regressive acting out of unconscious libidinal and sadistic drives" (p. 234) and as progressive attempts at the solution of the conflict. By drinking, the alcoholic not only obtains forbidden gratifications and expresses unconscious hostilities (ego-alien impulses) but also dissolves his or her inhibitions and anxieties (ego-protective impulses).

Additionally, Knight was one of the first psychoanalysts to look at the effect of the interaction between parent and child on the etiology of alcoholism. He described the mothers of his male patients as overindulgent and overprotective. By overresponding to the infant, the mother eventually sets herself up for failure as the child becomes more demanding. His consequential rage at frustration eventually changes into hostility and disappointment in the mother. "Weaning such a child becomes extremely difficult and when accomplished, traumatic" (17, p. 237). Knight described his male patients' fathers as aggressive and dominating, particularly in the business world. The child sees his father as a person with whom he cannot compete. (Knight did qualify that his patients were perhaps more indulged growing up. Most of them came from families with means.) Influenced by similar ideas, recent research on the effect of the relationship of the mother-infant dyad and drug abuse (see Wilson, 18) supports the critical importance of the "good enough" mother (19).

Fenichel (20) saw alcoholism as a maladaptive defense mechanism employed in order to resolve neurotic conflict, particularly between dependence and the expression of anger. Balint (21) characterized the alcoholic as having a basic character flaw, which he called the "basic fault." "The patient says that he feels there is a fault within him, a fault that must be put right" (21, p. 21). According to Balint, alcoholics seek to alleviate these feelings by using alcohol. They achieve "inner harmony" from the effect of intoxication.

In summary, although much emphasis was placed on regressive aspects of addiction in early psychodynamic theories, we can see formulations suggesting that addiction is a progressive behavior. As is seen in the next decades, many of these seeds blossomed and shaped current psychodynamic thinking. The attempt to master (22), the use of a substance to relieve or "medicate" depression (13), the defense against drives and affects (16), and the resolution of intrapsychic conflict (17, 20) are themes that emerge in current psychodynamic hypotheses about etiology, course, and treatment of substance abuse.

DEVELOPMENT OF CONTEMPORARY THEORIES OF PSYCHOANALYSIS

The development of contemporary theories of substance abuse has closely paralleled the clinical and developmental theories of psychoanalysis in general, which have focused on different perspectives other than the early psychoanalytic theory of drive psychology. More recent formulations have placed greater emphasis on structural (ego and self) development, interpersonal (object relations) theories, and centrality of affects. As will be demonstrated, these viewpoints have influenced attempts to better understand the suffering of addicts. Expansion of psychoanalysis from solely a drive-conflict model is due in part to the broader range of emotional problems treated, to the expansion of child analysis, and to current research in infant and child behavior (23). (We believe infant research is particularly important in the understanding of addictive behavior.)

Drive psychology had been expanded from its initial emphasis on the instinctual drives of sexuality and aggression to early formulations about character development (24, 12), defense mechanisms (25), and compromise formations, which occur because of intrapsychic conflicts (i.e., between the ego and the id, and/or the superego) (26). Freud's ideas about dreams and repression suggested that there must be some thought processes or perceptual mechanisms in control (23). Hence, emphasis on the ego and its autonomy began.

Formulations about the ego and its conflict-free functions developed into the second of the psychologies, ego psychology. Clinicians noticed the remarkable abilities of the individual to adapt to suffering in creative ways, and these abilities were assigned to the ego. Hartmann (27) was one of the first psychoanalysts to write about the functions of the ego and its development through learning and maturation. The ego's function of regulating the tension between the inner world and the outer world and its organizational abilities to find solutions to problems in both the inner world and the outer world are of "primary importance for the self-preservation of man" (27, p. 84).

Rapaport (28) also reframed ideas about the importance of the ego's autonomy. He suggested that the external environmental influences and the inner drives must be balanced to achieve inner harmony and harmonious self-functioning. The autonomy of the ego keeps drives from being rampantly indulged, on the one hand, or the individual from becoming the slave of the environment, on the other. At the same time, the environment encourages autonomous ego functions, such as "motor capacity, thinking, memory, perceptual and discharge thresholds, and the capacity for logical communication" (cited in Zinberg, 29, p. 577).

Another area of importance in ego psychology is the concept of ego defect. Anna Freud (30) emphasized that ego defects had not received adequate attention. She differentiated between two types of pathology: (1) abnormalities caused by trauma and internal conflict, and (2) "defects in personality structure . . . , which were caused by . . . developmental irregularities and failures" (p. 70).

In further commenting on the development of the ego, Pine (23) suggested that internal self-regulation is paramount for the healthy development of the ego. For the child who comes to expect "satisfaction and/or relief, that very expectation is already a regulator of inner state" (p. 203). The baby who cries and sucks a thumb in anticipation that his or her needs will eventually be met is very different from the infant who has no internal sense of safety. As traumatized adults, these individuals will seek self-regulation outside of themselves "via alcohol or other drugs or via addictive relationships or magical expectations of others, or to a degree to which they give up in despair in the face of distress, or spill it out into action or diffuse affect outbursts" (23, p. 204). Deficiencies in internal self-regulation is a central theme in the understanding of substance abuse.

A shift in emphasis to the intrapsychic world of the child led to a better integration of drive psychology or need satisfaction with the importance of object ties of the developing infant through the writings of Klein (31) and Fairbairn (32) and, consequently, to the British school of object relations. Klein and Fairbairn spoke of early drives (aggressive and libidinal) in terms of internalized objects—both bad and good. Fairbairn coined the term *object relations theory* and spoke of the object-seeking nature of drives rather than the early psychoanalytic focus on pleasure seeking. From the direct experience of observing children and mothers, Winnicott (19, 33) attempted to experience the world of the early infant-mother dyad and described the importance of the perfectly attuned, "good-enough mother." These early experiences of the child with the mother have become increasingly important in understanding the etiology of the addictive core of the self (18).

The most recent psychology in psychoanalysis, that of the self (34–36), places great emphasis on the total experience of the self and the "confirming/mirroring/rewarding inputs of the other" (23, p. 31). Spitz (37) had emphasized the differentiation of the "me" from the "not me." Mahler (38) and Mahler et al. (39) had elaborated on the psychic birth of the infant and the affective consequences of inadequate mothering. Kohut (34–36) placed emphasis on the wholeness or fragmentation of the self, its continuity or discontinuity, and the esteem of the self. As we shall see, contemporary thinking about substance abuse has centered on stages of structural development, including appropriate functions of the ego and a secure sense of self (6, 18, 40).

In concurrence with formulations about self-development, clinicians and researchers have attempted to understand affective development prior to and after the development of the capacity for verbal and mental representation (9). Emde (41) stressed the importance of the affective life as giving continuity to our experience of ourselves, even before we have words or images. It is the way to know the uniqueness of ourselves and to understand the sameness of others. The ability to modulate affect (affect tolerance) is of particular importance to the understanding of substance abuse.

The genetic view of the development of affects theorized that affect precursors in the newborn consist basically of a state of contentment and a state of distress. From these two basic reaction patterns evolve all adult-type affects (9). Affect differentiation is continuous. For example, shame, rage, hate, and depression are further differentiations out of primitive, painful affects. Further differentiation of shame can be seen in dishonor, ridicule, humiliation, etc.

The development of affect is implemented by verbalization and desomatization. An infant can experience affect only as physical change and pain. As the child matures, and self and object representations become part of everyday life, an awareness emerges about the self-experience of "feeling." The child develops the ability to understand feelings and to undertake actions from the signals of the feelings. By adulthood, emotions are expressed mostly on the cognitive level, and the expressive component is seen much less frequently.

Affect tolerance is an equally important aspect of affect in relationship to the addictions. Sashin (42) defined "affect tolerance as the ability to respond to a stimulus, which would ordinarily be expected to evoke affects by the subjective experiencing of feelings, rather than by an apparent non-reaction response or a discharge pattern of response, such as impulsive behavior, somatic dysfunction, or personality disorganization" (42, p. 175). After reviewing the psychoanalytic literature on the development of affect tolerance, Sashin (42) concluded that "affect tolerance is particularly influenced by three variables—the capacity to fantasize, the state of the inner container, and the capacity to verbalize affect" (p. 179). (The *inner container* is defined as the relationship with a "good-enough" mother who can tolerate affect herself and provide the infant with a soothing and nurturing atmosphere.)

As we now focus on the contemporary psychodynamic theories of substance abuse, we will see that each psychological viewpoint—drive, ego, object, self, and affect—gives clues to understanding the puzzle of why destructive drugs and alcohol become an indispensable way of life for certain individuals. We will explore substance abuse seen as a response to psychological suffering and as self-regulatory deficiencies.

SUBSTANCE ABUSE—A RESPONSE TO PSYCHOLOGICAL SUFFERING

Although the literature does not specifically define addiction as an attempt to return to homeostasis, addicts frequently describe the use of a substance as an attempt to feel "okay," "better," "normal," "not panicked," "not anxious," "not overwhelmed," "not out of control," etc. What is crucial to each individual is

a sense of self-recognition built around familiar and ongoing subjective states and that certain forms of interruptions or threatened interruptions of those states trigger attempts to maintain the (psychological) steady state—to maintain homeostasis. The forms and tolerance levels of the particular subjective state will naturally vary over time, but the homeostatic tendencies nonetheless remain present [23, p. 84].

It is the premise of contemporary investigators that theories of substance abuse as drive defense and affect defense can be viewed as an attempt of the individual to return to homeostasis or as an adaptation to relieve emotional suffering.

Psychoanalytic ideas pertaining to this hypothesis first appeared in the writings of Gerard and Kornetsky (43, 44) and Chein et al. (45). They emphasized that adolescents "use drugs adaptively to cope with overwhelming (adolescent) anxiety in anticipation of adult roles in the absence of adequate preparation, models and prospects" (cited in Khantzian, 5, p. 1261). Chein et al. (45) stated that addiction was "adaptive and functional"; i.e., narcotics are used to help one cope and interact with one's emotions and the outside world.

Wieder and Kaplan (46) developed this perspective further by emphasizing that "the dominant conscious motive for drug use is not the seeking of 'kicks', but the wish to produce pharmacologically a reduction in distress that the individual cannot achieve by his own psychic efforts" (p. 403). The child cannot maintain psychic homeostasis alone. He or she must have an object until the ego has matured enough to function by itself. To a certain extent, the adult borderline and psychotic personalities remain attached to their objects for psychic homeostasis. For many drug users, the substance functions in the same way as an external object. The choice of a specific drug depends on the interaction between the idiosyncratic meaning and the physical effect of the drug "with the particular conflicts and defects in a person's psychic structure throughout his development" (46, p. 428). Therefore, drugs are not selected indiscriminately; they are chosen to act as "structural prostheses."

Based on the work of Wieder and Kaplan and the problems associated with adaptation and the ego function of addicts, Milkman and Frosch (47) tested the hypothesis that the self-selections of specific drugs are related to a preferred defensive style. Using the Bellack and Hurvich Interview and Rating Scale for Ego Functioning, they compared heroin and amphetamine addicts in drugged and nondrugged conditions. Their preliminary findings supported the hypothesis that heroin addicts prefer the calming and dampening effects of opiates; opiates also seem to strengthen the addicts' tenuous defenses while simultaneously reinforcing their tendencies toward withdrawal and isolation. Conversely, amphetamine addicts use the stimulating action of these drugs to induce an inflated sense of self-worth and a defensive style involving active confrontation of their environment.

The work of Wurmser (10, 48) and Khantzian (49–51) suggested that the excessive emphasis on the regressive effects of narcotics in the early psychoanalytic and some of the contemporary studies was unwarranted. Wurmser and Khantzian considered the specific pharmacological action of opiates as a progressive effect whereby regressive states may actually be reversed. Wurmser's work suggested that narcotics are used adaptively by narcotic addicts to compensate for defects in affect defense, particularly against feelings of rage, shame, and abandonment. Khantzian stressed the use of narcotics in the service of drive defense. Narcotics act to reverse regressive states by the direct antiaggression action of opiates; opiates serve to counteract the disorganizing influences of rage and aggression on the ego. The failures and deficits in defense are due to the failure of the child to internalize the "good-enough" caring environment. Internalization of the caring environment is the result of adequate nurturing (4).

Further expansion of these views led to a "self-medication" hypothesis, which focused on the use of heroin and cocaine dependence as an attempt to alleviate emotional suffering. Addicts do not choose drugs randomly to alleviate the painful affect states and underlying psychiatric disorders. Rather, drugs are chosen because of their specific psychopharmacological action, which helps alleviate the suffering (5). The evidence of underlying psychiatric disorders that supports a self-medication hypothesis of addictive disorders is found in reports by Weissman et al. (52), McLellan et al. (53), Rounsaville et al. (54, 55), Khantzian and Treece (56), and Blatt et al. (57). These researchers produced diagnostic findings documenting the co-occurrence of depression, personality disorder, and alcoholism.

Recently, more emphasis has been placed on understanding addiction as "self-medication" to alleviate suffering, with less emphasis on severe psychopathology (6). For example, pain-relieving properties of the opiates help the user modulate disturbing, rageful feelings that are the source of much suffering in their lives, often originating in past experiences in which they were victims, perpetrators, or both. The sedative-hypnotics can help tense, emotionally restricted individuals to experience walled-off affect and to overcome related fears concerning human closeness, dependency, and intimacy. Cocaine, because of its energizing and activating properties, appeals to both high-energy and low-energy type individuals. It can help overcome feelings of fatigue and depletion states associated with depression or boredom (10, 58), and persons with high-energy may be attracted to cocaine because it increases feelings of self-esteem and frustration tolerance (46) or augments a preferred hyperactive style and amplifies feelings of self-sufficiency (59). Paradoxically, stimulants also calm the restlessness and hyperactivity in individuals who suffer with attention deficit disorder (5).

In an update of the self-medication hypothesis, Khantzian has focused on subjective states of distress that are often as confusing and elusive as they are painful and unbearable. These states of subjective distress are involved in three areas not previously considered, namely *(1)* nicotine dependence, *(2)* self-medication of negative symptoms in schizophrenia, and *(3)* self-medication of psychic numbing and flooding involved in posttraumatic stress disorder (PTSD) (60).

Dodes (61) suggested that addiction is a response to feelings of helplessness that are experienced by addicts as a narcissistic injury. The addiction, in his view, is an active behavior that reverses the feeling of helplessness and restores a sense of internal power by controlling and regulating one's affective state (something that drugs are particularly suited to do). At the same time, the addictive behavior is an expression of the narcissistic rage that inevitably accompanies such states of helplessness. Indeed, Dodes suggested that the defining "addictive" qualities of addiction, its intensity and its limitless disregard of ordinary considerations, are due to the expression of this underlying narcissistic rage as a central factor in addiction.

Dodes (62) has expanded this theory of viewing addictions as a subset of compulsions. The action of using the drug is seen as a displacement or substitution for acting in a way that would correct the addict's helplessness and express his or her rage directly in the real world. "Thus the addiction contains within it a superego prohibition expressed in the (unconscious) requirement to displace the narcissistic imperative for mastery to the addictive behavior" (62, p. 821). Dodes notes that compulsions may be defined following Fenichel, as "intense ideas that have to be thought about (or acted upon); their persistence represents the energy of some other associatively connected impulsive idea that has been warded off" (20, p. 268). When addictive behavior is seen as the expression of an idea that must be acted on (the enraged impulse to reassert mastery against helplessness) and as an action that must be taken in displacement because of the need to ward off the direct expression of this feeling, then addiction can be understood to be a subset of compulsions. This hypothesis is significant because it suggests the treatability of addictions with a psychodynamic approach that has been accepted for many years for compulsions. This view also allows many compulsions to be better understood as true addictions. In considering the impli-

cations of this hypothesis for treatment, the therapist can reframe the impulse for the patient as a healthy drive for mastery of helplessness, but displaced. The drive can be seen as "a drive for life" that can help alleviate the feelings of shame and helplessness that are so painful for the abuser.

Contrasting the view of substance abuse as a compulsion, Wurmser (63) suggests that it is a defense of affect, which can be viewed as the mirror image of the "compulsive avoidance." He also conceptualizes substance abuse as an artificial affective defense against fending off overwhelming feelings of helplessness, suggestive of a "primary phobia." This phobia concerns fears about or wishes "for being closed in, captured, or trapped by structures and limitations, and any type of closeness" (p. 93). He suggests that the compulsive search of the addict for the addictive object (alcohol, drugs, etc.) is a mirror image of the usual avoidant behavior of the phobic. This external addictive object serves as a narcissistic protector against the primary phobia, becoming highly overvalued. Internally, a defense of narcissism is developed that produces "grandiosity, haughtiness, and withdrawal from the external world." This defense is experienced by others as ruthlessness and coldness, who punish the addict's perceived haughtiness with humiliation and shame.

The self of the substance abuser is highly unstable. Any narcissistic crisis may stimulate affective regressions and the need for the protection of the addictive object. Wurmser emphasizes the use of denial and reversal, suggesting that addicts employ acting out behavior as a way of turning passivity into activity—giving a paradoxical sense of mastery of feelings of helplessness (also see Dodes, 62). In an attempt at conflict resolution, the ego of the substance abuser joins the libidinal and aggressive drives of the id and wages war against the functions of the superego and the laws of rationality of the external world. Unfortunately, the superego is a formidable foe, and following the grandiose feelings of intoxication where the ego ideal becomes the person "I am good, grand and strong," the defense crumbles. Self-observation produces overwhelming feelings of shame, which become unbearable. Splitting, fragmentation, and massive depersonalization can occur. The limiting functioning of the superego is experienced as restricting and suffocating, reenacting the primary phobia. The protecting self-care functions of the superego fall victim to the defensive regression of affect.

In summary, whether the focus is on affect defense or drive defense, certainly the literature emphasizes the addict's tragic suffering and this person's attempts to alleviate or control his or her emotional state. Greenspan (64) suggested that "establishment of homeostasis was the most crucial achievement in the first 3 months of life." It is a most crucial task in the life of the substance abuser, and one he or she struggles constantly to master. In our opinion, much of the addicts' struggles derive from these earliest phases of development and are apparent in their self-regulatory deficits.

SELF-REGULATORY DEFICIENCIES

A main framework for understanding substance abuse emphasizes self-regulatory deficiencies, encompassing deficits in self-care, self-development and self-esteem, self-object relationships, and affects. The ego must serve as a signal and guide in protecting the self against realistic, external dangers and against instability and chaos in internal emotional life (40). Impairments can also be observed in the development of the self, where the sense of self and self-esteem wanes and waxes. It follows that many substance abusers describe stormy relationships or isolated existences because of their vulnerabilities in self-cohesiveness (40).

Zinberg (29) offered a slightly different perspective regarding self-regulation in the addict. Building on the ideas of Rapaport (28), which were discussed earlier, Zinberg emphasized the imbalance of the addict's ego, and the inability of the addict to maintain ego autonomy. Stressing the importance of the environment, Zinberg stated that "junkies have lost varied sources of [environmental] stimulus nutriment" (29, p. 578). Relationships from families and others have been so severed that the only input junkies have or obtain from the external world is negative. Junkies keep drives at high tension because of their desire for external gratification and the biological imperative of the withdrawal symptoms if they do not "cop" (i.e., obtain their drug). The ego regresses because it cannot maintain its relative autonomy from the id and the environment. Primary process thinking consisting of fantasies and delusional images precludes the addict's having a sense that he or she is in control. Addicts "are at the mercy of primitive impulses and an overwhelming sense of neediness that invades, or more nearly blocks out a capacity to perceive and integrate 'objective reality'" (29, p. 579).

Impairments in Self-Care

Corresponding to the shift in focus on ego (or structural) functions in psychoanalysis, contemporary formulations of addictive vulnerability have placed growing emphasis on the developmental and structural deficits in substance abusers that make it difficult to regulate their behavior (4, 40). Many patients who are drug dependent show a disregard of possible dangers to their "well-being," including the use of abusive substances. The inability to provide self-care is associated with a set of ego functions related to "signal-anxiety, reality-testing, judgment, and synthesis" (40, p. 165). The addict's disregard of self is not primarily the result of unconscious motivations of destructiveness but the "result of failures to adopt and internalize these functions from the caring parents in early and subsequent phases of development" (4, p. 193). Many problems in self-care are apparent in the histories of substance abusers prior to the use of a drug or subsequently even after long periods of abstinence.

Although adequate self-care functions are usually present in cocaine abusers, cocaine users also can seem oblivious in this respect, thus keeping themselves from adequately worrying about or considering the potential danger in a situation (6). Given that such individuals are often inordinately driven by achievement and performance concerns, they often override whatever self-care functions they might possess.

Another deficit related to problems in self-care is the inability of the addict and alcoholic to soothe and calm themselves, especially when stressed, and conversely, the inability to be active in situations that call for activity when their "well-being" depends on it (40, 65, 66). This vulnerability is also the result of difficulties the child has in internalizing the caring functions of the mother (6).

Empiric research by Shedler and Block (67) recently provided support for the hypotheses of inadequate internalization of caring functions as a cause of substance abuse. They found that psychological differences between frequent drug users, experimenters, and abstainers in an adolescent population are the result of the type of parenting each group has received. Mothers of frequent drug users are described as "relatively cold, unresponsive, and underprotective. They appear to give their children little encouragement, while[,] conjointly, they are pressuring and overly interested in their children's 'performance'" (67, p. 641).

Vulnerabilities in Self-Development and Self-Esteem

The boundary between defects in the ego and the self is somewhat arbitrarily drawn. The nature of self-disturbances to be discussed here certainly has impact on ego disturbances, and the nature of ego disturbances has impact on self-disturbances. However, subjective attitudes about the self, rather than functions in personality organization, and how they are integrated into character traits need to be further explored.

Although a thorough description of the pathological formations of the self in relationship to addictions is beyond the scope of this chapter, a short summary follows. (Readers are referred to Levin (15) for a more detailed discussion.)

Jacobson (68) first described the "primal psychophysiological self," which she saw as the initial stage of human development. This stage is composed of an "undifferentiated, psychosomatic matrix" in which there are neither self-representations nor object representations. Gradually, the child develops a sense of self as distinct from object, but these boundaries can become blurred at times of crisis or not "good-enough mothering." The blurring of the self and object boundaries creates vulnerabilities in reality testing that are characteristic of substance abusers.

Basing his work on Jacobson's concept of self and object, Kernberg (69) described four stages of human development. As in Jacobson's concept, Kernberg proposes an undifferentiated matrix of self (child) and object

(mother) as the first stage. In the second stage, self and object are not differentiated but are represented by internal structures, self-objects, that have affective memories, either positive or negative. In the third stage, self and object are differentiated, but there is no integration of bad and good self or bad and good mother. The mother who frustrates becomes totally bad, and likewise, the mother who pleases is all good. In the final stage, the child integrates the positive and negative self and object. When this stage is achieved, the child has a stable, cohesive sense of self and a constant representation of mother. Frustrations are tolerable because of the internalized, less-than-perfect, loving caretaker. Needs do not change the internal representations.

Because of the deficit of "good-enough mothering," most addicts and alcoholics do not progress to stage four. Rather, Kernberg believed that the alcoholic developed a pathological "grandiose self," which is refueled by alcohol. This entitled "grandiose self" perceives that the self is perfect and the object is loving, and any other perceptions are denied. The alcoholic then uses rigid and primitive defenses of splitting, denial, and projection to keep from his or her awareness the bad self or inadequate self at all costs.

Kohut (34, 36) defined the self "as a unit cohesive in space and enduring in time, which is a center of initiative and recipient of impressions" (cited in Levin (15, p. 230)). Human development consists of three stages: The first is a "fragmented self" in which boundaries or parts of self and objects are blurred. There is a sense of self in each body part, each sensation, or each mental content, but there is no integration of these experiences. At the next stage, an "archaic, nuclear self" develops as caretakers relate to the infant as a cohesive whole. The nuclear self is bipolar and consists of two parts: a grandiose self that is omnipotent and the idealized self-object. At this stage there is a self that is cohesive and enduring, but there are no differentiated objects. In order for the self to develop to stage three, the functions of the self-objects must be internalized. These self-object functions include "internalization of tension regulation; self-soothing and self-esteem regulation; and . . . a stimulus barrier for the fragile nuclear self" (15, p. 231). In stage three there is a clearly differentiated real self and a clearly differentiated object. Kohut (36) emphasized that the substance abuser does not internalize the functions of the self-object, which results in defects in the self. "It is the lack of self-esteem for the unmirrored self, the uncertainty about the very existence of the self, the dreadful feelings of the fragmentation of the self that the addict tries to counteract by his addictive behavior" (p. 197).

From his observations of patients, Khantzian (4) reported shifting bipolar affects experienced in the therapeutic relationships. Most of the time, patients show difficulties in having their needs met and are compliant, cooperative, and passive. Occasionally, however, they lapse into opposite attitudes of intrusiveness and demandingness, which reveal an enormous sense of entitlement.

Wurmser (10) further explored the narcissistic disturbances of self. He speculated that compulsive drug users try "to reestablish an omnipotent position where either their self is grandiose and without limitations" or where the other person, "the archaic self-object," is treated as all-giving and is required to live up to the highest ideals. When limitations are imposed, the painful affects of rage, shame, and abandonment are experienced. Rage ensues when the ideal self or the ideal world collapses. Shame is experienced because of discrepancies between the limited, disappointing self and the grandiose, ideal self. The feelings of abandonment become devastating when the self-objects are not as all-giving as expected. "The importance of narcotics . . . lies in their effect of reducing or even eliminating these three basic affects" (10, p. 833).

This overt grandiose self can be isolated both affectively and cognitively from an existing, enfeebled self who has chronic feelings of poor self-esteem, such as is frequently found in the addict and the alcoholic (15). Substance abusers do not develop a sufficient capacity for self-love and self-esteem. They do not enjoy confidence in themselves or their abilities and have difficulty feeling valued in the world (66). The effects of drugs and alcohol interact with the painful feelings of inadequacies and momentarily alleviate their pain or improve how they feel about themselves.

In addition, addicts cannot retain narcissistic supplies from external sources to maintain their fragile self-esteem (9). The only continuously available source is drugs. Hence, the addict craves drugs for their effect of maintaining a sense of self-worth and of dissipating feelings of depletion. This is a never-ending process. Krystal likened it to a "baby [who] constantly regurgitates and swallows the contents of the stomach" (9, p. 186), demonstrating possibly the precursor "of an inability to retain the yearned for supplies [of affection] that we see in drug dependent patients and in bulimia" (p. 186).

Troubled Self-Object Relations

Deficits in self-development and self-esteem of the substance abuser cause major problems in relationships (66). "As much as they need others to know how they feel, they often fear and distrust their dependency, disavow their needs, and act in counterdependent ways" (p. 264). They are experts in disguising their needs for nurturance, although these needs can be excessive. They are at the mercy of their "significant other" or external world to supply their self-esteem, but they are paralyzed in asking for validation. They tend to go to either extreme, of totally depending on and being subservient to the other, or they isolate themselves in a stand-offish position (4). Wherever they stand, their self-value is hopelessly intertwined with the other.

The autonomy of the self develops from the internalization of two separate functions of mother: mother as environment, where the nurturing and protective self-care functions are internalized, and mother as object, where a mother as relationship is internalized (19). If the latter happens prematurely before the former, then the child lacks the ability "to be" his or her own internalized environmental mother and is needful of (or addicted to) mother as object (70). McDougall (71) suggested also that some mothers were "addictive." "They encourage the babies to become dependent on them as an addict needs drugs, with total dependence on an external object—to deal with situations which should be handled by self-regulatory psychological means" (p. 448).

Wallant (72) emphasizes an oppositional point of view. She suggests that today's society has emphasized the goal of autonomy and independence, sacrificing the ability of the individual to form meaningful attachments. Because of this emphasis, the child (and the adult) is left alone at times with unbearable feelings of helplessness and powerlessness (normative abuse). Suggesting that an infant is born with a sense of separateness from the other, he wishes to remain close to the mother because of his smallness and helplessness, not because he thinks his mother is part of himself. Drawing on the concept of Winnicott's transitional space (73), Wallant describes the metaphorical space as "immersive moments"—moments of closeness with mother and child, lover and lover, adult and God (space suggests distance). "The affective experience of igniting an empathic connection between two separate beings is the magic of love, the holiness of spirituality, and the miracle of humanity" (p. 103). Wallant renames the transitional object (Winnicott, 73) as an immersive object because "such an object also serves to keep the child close to mother, to keep him intimately connected to her while she is gone" (72, p. 99).

Two patterns of defective attachments encourage the process of addiction. In both instances, the child has had too few immersive moments and too many moments of feeling helpless and alone. In the first pattern, "the mother is unempathically distant and controlling, the child is expected to attune to her needs" (72, p. 129). He learns to depend only on himself because he cannot trust he will receive the help he needs. In isolation, as a adult, he feels powerful and in control. He can control any substance he takes into his body. When, however, the drug controls him, he is again the weak, small helpless child.

In the second pattern, the mother is paradoxically the opposite—"overly attentive, overly gratifying, overly involved." The child retreats to an internal objectless space and does not develop a sense of his own power. The drug provides him with moments of merger, where he does not have to be alone. Tragically, as the drug begins to control him, he returns to the original experience of being controlled by "an overpowering, demanding other".

Deficits in Affect Tolerance

Deficits in affect tolerance have an important relationship to the craving for drugs or alcohol. Using Sashin's (42) definition of affect tolerance, problems in affect concerning the alcoholic and the drug abuser are defined within three areas: one, the state of the inner container; two, the capacity to verbalize feelings; and three, the capacity to fantasize.

The state of the inner container of the substance abuser has been described as being too porous, allowing the contents (e.g., rage and anger) to pour out uncontrollably (the narcotic addict); as overly restrictive and sealed, thus constricting experiences and communication (the alcoholic); or as depleted, resulting in emptiness (the cocaine abuser) (66). The condition of the container determines vulnerabilities in affect tolerance.

As previously discussed, the complex world of adult affects stems from two basic conditions: one of contentment and one of displeasure (9). A second developmental line involves the desomatization of affects. Affects that are experienced only as physiological experiences are overwhelming and considered very dangerous. The most critical job of the mother is to protect the infant from becoming overwhelmed by affects but at the same time to be able to help the child bear "increasingly affective tension" (8). Her only guide to this very delicate duet is her empathy. If the mother does not succeed in keeping the child from experiencing overwhelming affect, then psychic trauma occurs. For a child "to be overwhelmed with an adult type of affect, be it anxiety, rage, or guilt, may be most painful and terrifying" (8, p. 96–97). These traumatic feelings have been described as fragmentation of the self (34), an inconsolable state (8), or "Todesangst," mortal terror (Freud, cited in Stern, 74). Krystal and Raskin (7) believed that the drug abuser lives in constant dread of reexperiencing the traumatic feelings that occurred preverbally. "These persons function as though they have an unconscious memory of the danger of trauma" (p. 33). The use of drugs is seen as an attempt to shore up the defense against reexperiencing the chaos.

In a recent article summarizing his ideas about substance abuse, Krystal (75) again emphasizes the developmental process of affects. Affects consists of four components: a cognitive aspect, an expressive aspect, a hedonic aspect, and an activating aspect. The cognitive part consists of a recognizable emotion and the story behind it. The expressive part of affect is a physiological component. If the cognitive and expressive aspects simultaneously are recognized, in an undissociated way, a feeling can be experienced. In treating the addict the analytic therapist must first ask the question of how the patient experiences his emotions and how he reacts to them. These questions can lead to the discovery of preverbal trauma, where the infant has experienced overwhelming affects. "The patient may be caught in a involuntary, compulsive need to repeat the pattern of selectively retained excessive reaction to a specific affect or to the alexithymic undifferentiated affect pattern" (75, p. 74). The continued pattern of working himself into an unbearable state drives the addictive person to search for a substance that will give relief.

The hedonic aspect of an emotion suggests that emotions are either pleasurable or distressful. However, in the experience of the drug addict, pleasure is usually not experienced as the same phenomenon as gratification, and pain can be different and separate from suffering. Differentiating pleasure, gratification, pain, and suffering allows more understanding into one of the "addictive mechanisms." For example, in addiction, an abuser can anesthetize himself (reducing the pain) but become unmindful of the unsolved personal problems, which in the long run increases the suffering.

The activating aspect of emotion is defined as the state of "animation" of the organism. "The activating aspect of emotions is the link of mental function with all of psychobiology, and it regulates the whole—organism activation or deactivation" (75, p.77). Many addicts complain of feeling "dead" or "empty" and defend against feeling this emotion by the use of a substance of choice. Krystal emphasizes the importance of understanding which aspect of the emotions are affected in doing analytic therapy. For example, in isolation of affect the cognitive and expressive aspects of affect are emotionally separated and need to be integrated. In a regression of affect, where deverbalization and resomatization occurs, the activating aspect of emotion may become dominant, such as chronic hyperactivity.

In attempting to understand why a user continues, beyond physiological addictive factors, despite chronic suffering from their abuse (physical deterioration, psychological regression, and an internal world of chaos), Khantzian (76) speculated that the abuser feels some means of control in the active behavior of using. Thus, the suffering experienced from the drug or alcohol is more bearable because it is something the user understands. The feeling has a story. Thus, a hangover is much more tolerable than experiencing the preverbal affects of inconsolable feelings or fragmentation of the self.

The ability to verbalize one's feeling also has particular importance in understanding the etiology of substance abuse. Krystal (9) adopted the term *alexithymia*, originally used by Sifneos (77) and Nemiah (78), to describe the condition of patients who could not verbalize what they were feeling. Such patients, including psychosomatics and substance abusers, reacted basically in somatic ways, with affects expressed physiologically rather than verbally (9). These reactions can be very distressing because there is no conscious bridge between cognition and feelings. To experience and identify a feeling involves connecting the feeling to the story behind it. These patients cannot tell whether they are "sad, tired, hungry, or ill." Paradoxically, these patients can display intense affects in brief moments (9).

McDougall (79) has also described a similar inability to display affect in some of her patients. She used the term *disaffected* to describe the lifeless emotional experience that these patients bring into analysis. She noted that most of them were "pragmatic, unimaginative, factual and unemotional," even in describing events of intense emotional happenings in their lives. She hypothesized that their "narcissistic economy and the incapacity to contain and elaborate affective experience" was caused not only by mothers' being out of touch with their babies' needs but also squelching any outburst of spontaneous affective display. "The child would rather give up his own internal vitality than lose [mother]. He would rather freeze himself forever into the 'baby-sitting-in-the-snow' " (79, p. 405). In order to maintain the frozen quality of their affects, these patients drown their feelings in alcohol, bulimic bouts, or drug abuse. If the affects are allowed to be felt, there is danger of overwhelming affect and psychosomatic regression. Thus, an attempt to avoid intense feelings can greatly stimulate the use of substance abuse.

Lastly, the incapacity to fantasize has been associated with alexithymics, including psychosomatics and drug abusers. There is a cognitive inability to fantasize and symbolize. These patients tend to verbalize concrete facts and are devoid of wish-fulfilling fantasies. They are hindered in therapy by their inability to associate to events or dreams or their incapacity for fantasy-making. Because they cannot symbolize their conflict, they experience only the physiological aspects of their affect, which are painful. Thus, they turn to drugs to alleviate or block the affective responses (9).

de M'Uzan (80) commented on the sudden changes in the quality of verbalization of alexithymics, which accompany abrupt changes in affect. While such people usually present as "dull, mundane, and unimaginative," they occasionally are capable of rich verbal expression. "The symbolization, almost always poor, becomes dazzling at times but remains isolated and incapable of entering into a syntax" (81, p. 464).

In summary, the vulnerabilities of affect tolerance exhibited by alcoholics or addicts do not begin to describe the suffering they endure in their frantic attempts to block feelings either by shoring up the inner container so that it does not leak, by not connecting their affect with cognitions and therefore not feeling at all, or by being frozen without fantasy or metaphor.

Developmental Models

As we have seen, there are many hypotheses about substance abuse in this preparadigm state. We have explored the hypothesis that drugs and alcohol are adaptations to emotional suffering and/or deficiencies in self-regulation, involving underdeveloped functions of the ego, developmental deficits of the self, addictive object relations, and vulnerabilities in affect tolerance. How, then, can all these hypotheses about the substance abuser be integrated in a meaningful way, such that the disparate findings yield a synthesized approach in treatment planning?

Wilson et al. (18) proposed a hierarchic model of opiate addiction based on failures in self-regulation, a model that shows promise of understanding these deficits as impairments in developmental stages. They used the hierarchic (multimodal) epigenetic theory of self-organization, originally proposed by Gedo and Goldberg (82) and subsequently expanded on by Gedo (83–85) and Wilson et al. (86, 87). Gedo and Goldberg defined epigenesis as "the formation of structure as the result of successive transactions between the organism and its environment; the outcome of each phase is understood to depend upon the outcomes of all previous phases" (82, p. 12).

Each new phase (mode) has a higher level of organization in which there are specific developmental tasks and specific developmental dangers. For example, when the patient is functioning in the first phase (mode I), over-stimulation is a constant danger. The task of the therapist is one of pacification in order to control the threat of overwhelming excitation. In the second stage, mode II, the existing danger is a fragmentation of the newly formed and fragile self. The task is the reintegration of clusters of the nuclei of self. The child begins to internalize the caring functions of the caretaker; thus, the internalization of the ability to care for the self occurs.

With the shift from parts of the self to a cohesive self and the experience of the mother as separate, the task of the third phase, mode III, is gradual integration of reality or "optimal disillusion." However, in this stage there may not be an integration of the good and bad self and the good and bad mother (66). There is danger of a grandiose self, "usually disavowed and split off," which can distort perceptions of reality. A total disregard for danger in situations may exist, disavowed by feelings of omnipotence. At the same time, there is a paradoxic propensity for shame.

In the fourth phase, mode IV, the child and the mother are separate. Infantile grandiosity has been mastered. The vulnerabilities are those of infantile neuroses in which intrapsychic conflict occurs between the id, the ego, and the superego. The task in this phase is the resolution of conflicts. In the last phase, mode V, the residues of infantile behavior are slight and do not interfere with the goals of one's life. One can deal with the problems of everyday life through introspection.

Wilson et al. (18) hypothesized that the opiate addict's behavior can be understood to fluctuate among the first three stages (modes) of development. When the addict is functioning in the first stage, in which there is a failure to regulate stimulation and attachment processes, the danger to the addict is overstimulation, and hence the need for a drug as defense (4–6, 10). In the second stage, emotional experiences may result in interruptions of preverbal communications between child and mother, thus producing the disruption of self-cohesion. If this occurs, drugs become the replacement for the lost object (4, 9, 66, 71). Self and objects have obtained wholeness in the third stage. Omnipotent illusions remain only in the sphere of sexuality. The danger in this mode is the threat of castration. If the threat becomes overwhelming, regressive behavior occurs. Grandiosity and idealization return. Drugs then allow omnipotent control over the self and objects (7, 47).

Wilson et al. (18) hypothesized that the drug addict may be functioning in different modes at different times, depending on perceived dangers of his or her external reality. They used the Scale for Failures in Self-Regulation to measure verbal and nonverbal manifestation in self-regulation failures in addicts. Their study showed that addicts do have significantly greater difficulties in self-regulation than do normal subjects. Wilson et al. also found evidence of all three modes of functioning in the sample of addicts they tested.

Using a similar model, Berger (88) has analyzed the importance of psychological development in understanding the societal issues of substance abuse. Most of the psychoanalytic social analyses done in the past have emphasized "instinct, conflict, and defense—between drives and the desires of the person and the opposing . . . repressive requirements of culture" (88, p. 54). Berger suggests that in today's society the commonly found symptoms of painful inner experiences, such as boredom, helplessness, etc., are blotted out either by escaping to passivity (e.g., watching television) or to "compulsive, impulsive, immediate, short-term gratification." He describes a personality profile, which is ubiquitous in our culture, with deficits in ego functions (difficulties planning and working, magical solutions, impoverished languages relying on cliches, etc.) that all emphasize living in the immediate moment without contemplation of the future consequences. He emphasizes the inability of the person to create solutions to problems internally. Individual creativity has not been encouraged in a society that supplies the motivation and solutions.

Berger's model of development describes three phases: The first is a rudimentary existence (classically called primary narcissism); the second, the preverbal or pregenital stage; and third, the classic oedipal stage, where the child can now "talk, locomote, reason, symbolize, etc.," a very different existence from the first stage. Berger believes that many adults today get stuck in "the middle phase" (second stage) where "dipoles of existence—self and other, inside and outside, male and female, good and bad—have not yet jelled into a stable, flexible internal situation" (88, p. 76). In the middle phase, there are rapid shifts in polarization and self-cohesion leading to disintegration anxiety. When an adult is developmentally stuck in this stage, the unbearable feelings create an immediate need for an external self-soothing object. Substances of abuse are always available without a delay.

TREATMENT IMPLICATIONS

The goal of treatment is to attend to the patient and to administer to his or her needs in the most therapeutic manner at the moment (82). "The moment" encompasses constant shifts in developmental stages.

Initial Treatment Stage—Stabilization

Where overstimulation or dangerous loss of control is the danger and homeostasis or stabilization is the therapeutic task, the therapist must fulfill a special role initially as a caretaker. The patient must be provided with hope that relief from being overwhelmed will occur and with the expectation that homeostasis can be achieved. Thus, hope and expectation gradually become the "regulator of (the) inner state" (23).

In the initial stage of treatment, the therapist's role is expanded to the role of a "primary care therapist." The primary care therapist is concerned "about patients' needs for control, containment, contact, and comfort" (89, p. 169). In this role, the initial concern of the therapist is to help the patient gain control over the use of alcohol or drugs (40, 90). The first task of the therapist is to take an extensive drug and developmental history. Through the telling of his or her own life story, the alcoholic or drug abuser begins to be gently confronted with the "deleterious consequences" of the abused substance. At the same time, the therapist builds a therapeutic alliance through concern for the addict's suffering. He or she initiates treatment by an empathic investigation with the abuser to discover when the abuse first began, where the substance was used, the pattern and progression of use that developed, and how internal feeling states were changed (91).

The therapist and the patient carefully evaluate the severity of the substance abuse and the immediate and long-term steps whereby control can be achieved (89). Some patients may need immediate hospitalization or internment in order not to place themselves or others in a dangerous situation. However, many do not need this level of intervention. The therapist and patient can begin immediately in a therapeutic mode to determine what the best treatment plan is for the particular patient. The need for control rather than abstinence should be emphasized. "Keeping the focus on control allows a strategy to develop that avoids premature insistence on permanent abstinence, or an equally untenable permissive acceptance of uncontrolled drinking" (40, p. 173).

The "therapist's caring concern" may either immediately or gradually be internalized by the patient, thus allowing the "nucleus" of internal self-regulation to develop and control or abstinence to occur (92). This internalization is possible through the therapeutic alliance, i.e., the immediate identification with the therapist as the "idealized object" or the "aggressive object." However, drinking may continue to occur. Therapy may proceed if the drinking is intermittent. Therapy should focus on the reasons why abstinence or control cannot be reached. If the drinking continues and is destructive, there may be a need for hospitalization or interruption of therapy (92).

During the initial stage of therapy, where control is of paramount importance, the use of self-help groups such as Alcoholics Anonymous (AA) and Narcotics Anonymous (NA) can provide the patient with a social family in which life is bearable and manageable without alcohol and drugs (89). AA helps the individual to recognize the "powerlessness" that he or she feels and/or denies in relation to alcohol (93). It provides alcoholics with the steps whereby their "powerlessness" can be changed into power to manage their impulsivity. The function of AA is to provide the individual with a framework of "self-governance" in a social context (93). In the event that the patient resists the use of AA or NA, the therapist can offer other approaches, such as group or individual psychotherapy to help the patient achieve abstinence. AA and NA may not be appropriate for some patients who suffer from intense shame and anxiety or whose personality structure is too rigid to accept the AA/NA message of "surrender—belief in a higher power," etc. (94).

During the initial phases of therapy, the therapist must also make a careful evaluation of whether to use "adjunctive pharmacological agents" and other treatment strategies in order to help the patient achieve and maintain control" (89). For example, methadone maintenance can be effective not only in the achievement of biological homeostasis for narcotic addicts but also in the management of their painful feelings of aggression and rage. The use of Antabuse and naltrexone and other monitoring procedures, such as the screening of urine, can be powerful deterrents against the impulsivity of the patient. Acupuncture has also proved to be extremely useful as an adjunctive treatment modality (95) (see also Chapter 51 in this volume) and, from a developmental perspective, probably compensates for addicts' inability to comfort or soothe themselves. Another important treatment strategy is the education of the patient about the use of alcohol or drugs as "self-medication" and the underlying drive or affective vulnerabilities that make the use of alcohol or drugs necessary.

Some patients will decide not to continue in therapy once they have stabilized. The therapist helps patients to decide what is more helpful for them. Some patients, particularly patients who had previously abused alcohol, begin to function in a healthy, adaptive way so that therapy is not needed. Others are more vulnerable because of the absence of alcohol or drugs. Therapy at this stage proceeds more traditionally. However, the therapist cannot rely on interpretations alone. Using empathy as a guide, the therapist weaves an interaction with the client that allows for appropriate active helpfulness on the part of the therapist (96).

Building Internal Self-Regulation

When stabilization has occurred, the task of the therapist becomes focused on building internal self-regulation and cohesiveness of the self. This is provided through the reliability of the therapist's always being there—an uninterrupted relationship (82). The child begins to internalize the caring functions of mother because of a continuous relationship with her; thus, he or she internalizes the capacity for self-care (19). Mother also creates a safe place to play and a safe place to begin to differentiate feelings, particularly negative feelings.

To promote structural growth, the therapist must similarly provide a safe and secure environment in which the patient can begin to correct the "basic fault" (21) and begin to integrate ego functions of self-regulation in order to achieve "gradual mastery over narcissistic injuries" (82, p. 163). The therapist gradually becomes taken in as "environmental mother" and "relationship-mother."

A phased treatment approach appreciates and addresses initial needs for abstinence, safety and comfort, and, subsequently, the psychotherapeutic understanding and modification of self-regulation vulnerabilities. The role of the primary care therapist in early phases of treatment helps the patient to appreciate shared and real concerns for stabilization and control. The patient is encouraged to utilize 12-step groups in order to benefit from the containing and transforming influences that they supply. Subsequently, individual and group psychotherapy provide therapeutic contexts for the naturalistic unfolding of patients' characterological defenses and underlying self-regulation vulnerabilities. Interactive and focused individual and group treatment, supportive and expressive in mode, become important as crucial experiences in helping substance abusers to internalize self-regulating capacities for better affect management, self-other relations, and self-care that otherwise have been absent or underdeveloped (90, 96, 97). Kaufman (98) has recently focused on the benefits of psychotherapy for "the addicted person" and has emphasized the importance of integrating 12-step and psychotherapy approaches.

In addressing the narcissistic characteristics of the substance abuser, Derby (99) describes the difficulties the therapist encounters in surviving the interpersonal exploitation, grandiosity, and lack of empathy the substance abuser can exhibit. Derby believes that this behavior can quickly be interpreted by the therapist as sociopathic. The use of contracts (so many AA meetings, urine tests, etc.), which are useful with the sociopathic population, are doomed to failure with the substance abuser because he or she hides his or her reactions to intrusion. These hidden self states are "responses of rage, inadequacy, shame[,] and emptiness." The substance abuser has difficulty in finding words for expressing these feelings because of hyposymbolization and isolation of affect. Derby emphasizes the importance of the therapist's countertransference in the treatment of addicts. Preset ideas about addicts must be abandoned, and the therapist must be open to each individual story without countertransferential feelings of moral judgment.

Internalizing Self-Care Functions

Self-care functions are internalized as the result of the care and concern of the primary therapist (94). It is very important for the therapist to talk about the inability of substance abusers to take care of themselves, rather than to emphasize the destructiveness of their behavior. The therapist needs to explore with the addict the developmental deficiencies and defects that do not allow danger to be anticipated and to help him or her understand that this disability is correctable (94). Modified dynamic group therapy is especially helpful in the internalization of the self-care functions (96).

Related to self-care functions, the therapist instructs the patient in alternatives for self-soothing functions, rather than the use of alcohol or drugs. The auxiliary use of acupuncture, meditation, exercise, pharmacotherapy, hypnosis, etc. can help relieve the patient's emotional suffering or irritability. Sometimes, the suggestion of a warm bath or hot shower, however simplistic, can work wonders (96).

Repairing Self-Deficits and Enhancing Self-Esteem

The control of inner tension, establishing and prioritizing personal goals, and giving up illusions about oneself and others are therapeutic goals that help to repair self-deficits and enhance self-esteem (100). The establishment of a caring relationship in the therapy creates a "holding environment" in which lack of frustration allows for the new acquisition of psychological skills. It is important to emphasize the "opening up of the patient's inner (world), which at the start of therapy either was severely inhibited or chaotically eruptive" (88, p. 173). An environment of excessive frustration or disappointment previously created an atmosphere in which learning these skills could not take place and thus became the root of many self-deficits. However, a self-deficit cannot be repaired simply through didactic instruction. The circumstances surrounding its etiology must be first reconstructed and understood before acquisition of new ego functions can take place (100). "In a therapy that is going well, the manifestations of immature, archaic parts of the self . . . exhibit a trajectory of change, sometimes explicitly mirroring changes of various childhood phases" (88, p. 174). One of the most critical obstacles in learning new psychological skills is uncovering identifications with one of the primary caretakers. For example, before less destructive self-soothing activities can be internalized, the client and therapist must reconstruct that the safest, happiest time of the day in a woman's childhood, when there was minimal chaos, was the cocktail hour. Five o'clock and a drink meant reduction in tension.

A crucial task in this phase of therapy is the acquisition of a "shared language" (100). The therapist translates into mutual experiences the early messages that hinder the patient from acquiring phase-appropriate skills of adaptation. These skills relate to the "crucial areas of perception, cognition, . . . communication, . . . and the control and expression of affects" (100, p. 215). Affective childhood history acquires a mutually understood language.

As the story unfolds and solutions to problems are mutually resolved, patients gradually acquire the "know-how" that permits more autonomous functioning. Repeated successful maneuverings in a more adaptive mode allow the patient gradually to give up the propensity to rely on "a symbiotic partner"—alcohol, drugs, or therapist—and acquire self-mastery, so crucial in self-value and realistic self-esteem (100).

Maintaining Mature Self-Object Relationships

Because substance abusers usually disavow their needs for attachment by grandiose illusions about themselves, they typically keep themselves in functional and actual psychological isolation (66). The process of healing involves reversing this isolation. These dependency problems, which are usually so camouflaged, should not be exposed insensitively. They must be explored with respect and delicacy. However, the grandiose illusions, which are destructive in intimate relationships, gradually can be identified. The therapist treads a delicate balance to avoid colluding in the disavowal or in confronting the illusion too aggressively, thus rupturing the treatment. When the addict begins to view the therapist as a "transformational other" who is powerful enough to separate the addict from his or her drug or alcohol, feelings of idealization and love may be expressed toward the therapist (72). Self-help groups or group psychotherapy can often be used to give human support and contact or appropriate reality testing (96).

Modulating Affect

Krystal (101) suggested specific technical modifications to help patients understand their difficulties in the regulation of affect tolerance. The first task, that of managing one's feelings (the inner container), is critical in the therapeutic process. The therapist takes an active role in teaching the patient "what affect responses are and how one uses them to one's advantage" (101, p. 371). Because many of the feelings are experienced somatically, the therapist must understand the intense discomfort that feelings create and help the patient begin to contain them appropriately.

The therapist encourages the addict to nurture his or her ability to verbalize feelings. "Affect-naming and verbalization must be encouraged; supplying (to the patient) the words and names of emotions is a slow task, because verbalization represents just one half of the task. The other half consists in desomatization" (101, p. 371). A bridge must be built between the affective and cognitive components. The feeling must become attached to the story.

Finally, the therapist helps the addict to develop his or her capacity to fantasize. Wolff (102) suggested the use of play as a technique in helping the patient who is deprived of feelings. Using Winnicott's (73) hypothesis that the patient must learn to play before he or she can use psychotherapy, Wolff stressed the use of creative play, in which fantasies are encouraged and feelings, desires, and bodily sensations are explored. One of the current authors uses the metaphor of floating balloons to represent positive potential happenings in her work with alcoholic patients. The right to fantasize about positive potential happenings, or to float different balloons, does not initially exist for these patients. Play is especially helpful with patients who experience anhedonia.

Evaluations of Psychotherapy and Psychotherapists Treating Substance Abusers

An excellent summary of the views conceptualizing contemporary psychoanalytically oriented treatment practices has been described by Yaliscove (103). He emphasizes the effect of toxic substances on brain functioning, which can last for over a year after abstinence. He suggests that some of the regressed narcissistic behavior seen both during use and abstinence may be more neurologically based. He also emphasizes problems with growth of the autonomous ego functions that he names " failures of neutralizations." Suggesting that these deficits are the result of overstimulation in early childhood, the child never reaches the more peaceful stage of latency.

In a description of therapy for addicts he stresses the stages of therapy that are different from the traditional psychotherapeutic treatments. Emphasizing the role of protector in the stage before abstinence and the role of educator during the initial stages of treatment, he believes that interpretations about transference and countertransference must wait until an abstinent stable adjustment to reality has been reached. Prior to this stage, exploratory interpretations tend to reenact the overstimulating, overwhelming anxieties of early childhood.

Another summary of the treatment of the substance abuser is described by Rothschild (104). She also emphasizes the impairment of ego functions, which typically are defended against by denial. She also stresses the importance of grief work, as the substance abuser begins to separate from the drug of choice. An important ego function, the adaptive regression in the service of the ego, according to Rothschild, is woefully lacking in many addicts. They do not know how to play without alcohol or drugs; hence, when they become sober, they are vulnerable to a sense of boredom and narcissistic emptiness in their lives. Rothschild also emphasizes the initial role of the therapist is as teacher or expert.

She thinks it is important to see through the narcissistic defenses of the addict to help the addict learn to observe and empathize with his or her vulnerabilities of self.

CONCLUSIONS

The psychology of substance abuse, as formulated from a psychodynamic perspective, focuses on understanding addictions as adaptive attempts to alleviate emotional suffering and repair self-regulatory deficiencies. Treatment emphasizes mutual understanding of this suffering, gradual toleration and modulation of painful feelings, learning of psychological skills to care for and nurture the self, and the adoption of a reality not based on childhood illusions. The complexity of addictions still leaves much to be explored. The psychodynamic perspective is only one of many attempts to understand. Whatever the perspective, our greatest source of knowledge is our patients. We learn by listening attentively to the uniqueness of each story.

References

1. Shaffer HJ, Gambino B. Epilogue: integrating treatment choices. In: Milkman HB, Sederer LI, eds. Treatment choices for alcoholism and substance abuse. Lexington, MA: Lexington Press, 1990:351–375.
2. Sederer L. An organization model for those entering the field of psychiatry. J Psychiatr Educ 1988;12:71.
3. Khantzian EJ. Opiate addiction: a critique of theory and some implications for treatment. Am J Psychother 1974;28:59–74.
4. Khantzian EJ. The ego, the self and opiate addiction: theoretical and treatment considerations. Int Rev Psychoanal 1978;5:189–198.
5. Khantzian EJ. The self-medication hypothesis of addictive disorders [special article]. Am J Psychiatry 1985;142:1259–1264.
6. Khantzian EJ. Self-regulation factors in cocaine dependence: a clinical perspective. In: The epidemiology of cocaine use and abuse. NIDA Monograph no. 110. DHHS publication no. (ADM) 91–1787. Rockville, MD: National Institute of Drug Abuse, 1991:211–227.
7. Krystal H, Raskin HA. Drug dependence aspects of ego function. Detroit: Wayne State University Press, 1970.
8. Krystal H. Trauma and affects. Psychoanal Study Child 1978;33:81–116.
9. Krystal H. Integration and self-healing affect—trauma-Alexithymia. Hillsdale, NJ: Analytic Press, 1988.
10. Wurmser L. Psychoanalytic considerations of the etiology of compulsive drug use. J Am Psychoanal Assoc 1974;22:820–843.
11. Freud S. Three essays on the theory of sexuality. In: Standard edition. London: Hogarth Press, 1955;7:125–245 (original work published in 1905).
12. Abraham K. The psychological relation between sexuality and alcoholism. In: Selected papers of Karl Abraham. New York: Basic Books, 1964 (original work published in 1908).
13. Rado S. The psychoanalysis of pharmacothymia. Psychoanal Q 1933;2:1–23.
14. Freud S. The complete letters of Sigmund Freud to Wilhelm Fliess. Masson JM, trans/ed. Cambridge, MA: Harvard University Press, 1985:287.
15. Levin JD. Treatment of alcoholism and other addictions. Northvale, NJ: Jason Aronson, 1987.
16. Glover E. On the etiology of drug addiction. In: On the early development of mind. New York: International Universities Press, 1956.
17. Knight RP. The dynamics and treatment of chronic alcohol addiction. Bull Menninger Clin 1937;1:233–250.
18. Wilson A, Passik SD, Faude J, Abrams J, Gordon E. A hierarchical model of opiate addiction. Failures of self-regulation as a central aspect of substance abuse. J Nerv Ment Dis 1989;177:390–399.
19. Winnicott DW. The theory of the parent-infant relationship. In: The maturational processes and the facilitating environment. Madison, CT: International Universities Press, 1965:37–55 (original work published in 1964).
20. Fenichel O. The psychoanalytic theory of neurosis. New York: WW Norton, 1945:375–386.
21. Balint M. The basic fault: therapeutic aspects of regression. New York: Brunner/Mazel, 1968.
22. Freud S. Remembering, repeating, and working-through. In: Standard edition. London: Hogarth Press, 1955;12:145–156 (original work published in 1914).
23. Pine F. Drive ego, object, and self: a synthesis for clinical work. New York: Basic Books, 1990.
24. Freud S. Character and anal erotism. In: Standard edition. London: Hogarth Press, 1955; 9:169–175 (original work published in 1908).
25. Freud A. The ego and the mechanisms of defense. Vol II. New York: International Universities Press, 1966.
26. Brenner C. Mind in conflict. Madison, CT: International Universities Press, 1982.
27. Hartmann H. Ego psychology and the problem of adaptation. New York: International Universities Press, 1958 (original work published in 1939).
28. Rapaport D. The theory of ego autonomy: a generalization. In: Gill M, ed. The collected papers of David Rapaport. New York: Basic Books, 1967:722–744 (original work published in 1957).
29. Zinberg NE. Addiction and ego function. Psychoanal Stud Child 1975;30:567–588.
30. Freud A. A psychoanalytic view of developmental psychopathology. In: The writings of Anna Freud. New York: International Universities Press, 1981;8:57–74 (original work published in 1974).
31. Klein M. Contributions to psychoanalysis. London: Hogarth Press, 1948 (original work published in 1921–1945).
32. Fairbairn WRD. A revised psychopathology of the psychoses and psychoneuroses. Int J Psychoanal 1941;22:250–279.
33. Winnicott DW. The capacity to be alone. In: The maturational processes and the facilitating environment. Madison, CT: International Universities Press, 1965:29–36 (original work published in 1958).
34. Kohut H. The analysis of the self. New York: International Universities Press, 1971.
35. Kohut H. Thoughts on narcissism and narcissistic rage. Psychoanal Stud Child 1972;27:364–400.
36. Kohut H. The restoration of the self. New York: International Universities Press, 1977.
37. Spitz RA. No and yes. New York: International Universities Press, 1957.
38. Mahler MS. Notes on the development of basic moods: the depressive affect. In: Loewenstein RM, Newman LM, Schur M, Solnit AJ, eds. Psychoanalysis: a general psychology. New York: International Universities Press, 1966: 152–168.
39. Mahler MS, Pine F, Bergman A. The psychological birth of the human infant. New York: Basic Books, 1975.
40. Khantzian EJ. Some treatment implications of the ego and self disturbances in alcoholism. In: Bean MH, Zinberg NE, eds. Dynamic approaches to the understanding and treatment of alcoholism. New York: Macmillan, 1981: 163–193.
41. Emde RN. The prerepresentational self and its affective core. Psychoanal Stud Child 1983; 38:165–192.
42. Sashin JI. Affect tolerance: a model of affect-response using catastrophe theory. J Soc Biol Struct 1985;8:175–202.
43. Gerard DL, Kornetsky C. Adolescent opiate addiction: a case study. Psychiatr Q 1954;28: 367–380.
44. Gerard DL, Kornetsky C. Adolescent opiate addiction: a study of control and addict subjects. Psychiatr Q 1955;29:457–486.
45. Chein I, Gerard DL, Lee RS, Rosenfeld E. The road to H. New York: Basic Books, 1964.
46. Wieder H, Kaplan EH. Drug use in adolescents: psychodynamic meaning and pharmacogenic effect. Psychoanal Stud Child 1969;24:399–431.
47. Milkman H, Frosch WA. On the preferential abuse of heroin and amphetamine. J Nerv Ment Disord 1973;156:242–248.
48. Wurmser L. Methadone and the craving for narcotics; observations of patients on methadone maintenance in psychotherapy. In: Proceedings of the Fourth National Methadone Conference, San Francisco, 1972. New York: National Association for the Prevention of Addiction to Narcotics, 1972.
49. Khantzian EJ. A preliminary dynamic formulation of the psychopharmacologic action of methadone. In: Proceedings of the Fourth National Methadone Conference, San Francisco, 1971. New York: National Association for the Prevention of Addiction to Narcotics, 1972.
50. Khantzian EJ. An ego-self theory of substance dependence: a contemporary psychoanalytic perspective. In: Lettieri DJ, Sayers M, Pearson HW. Theories on drug abuse. NIDA research monograph 30. Rockville, MD: National Institute on Drug Abuse, 1980.
51. Khantzian EJ. Psychological (structural) vulnerabilities and the specific appeal of narcotics. Ann N Y Acad Sci 1982;398:24–32.
52. Weissman MM, Slobetz F, Prusoff B, Mezritz M, Howard P. Clinical depression among narcotic addicts maintained on methadone in the community. Am J Psychiatry 1976;133:1434–1438.
53. McLellan AT, Woody GE, O'Brien CP. Development of psychiatric illness in drug abusers. N Engl J Med 1979;201:1310–1314.
54. Rounsaville BJ, Weissman MM, Crits-Cristoph K, Wilbur C, Kleber H. Diagnosis and symptoms of depression in opiate addicts: course and relationship to treatment outcome. Arch Gen Psychiatry 1982;39:151–156.
55. Rounsaville BJ, Weissman MM, Kleber H, Wilber C. Heterogeneity of psychiatric diagnosis in treated opiate addicts. Arch Gen Psychiatry 1982;39:164–166.
56. Khantzian EJ, Treece C. Psychodynamics of drug dependence: an overview. In: Blaine JD,

Julius DA, eds. Psychodynamics of drug dependence. NIDA research monograph no. 12. DHEW publication no. (ADM) 77–470. Washington, DC: Government Printing Office, 1977: 11–25.

57. Blatt SJ, Berman W, Bloom-Feshback S, Sugarman A, Wilber C, Kleber H. Psychological assessment of psychopathology in opiate addiction. J Nerv Ment Dis 1984;172:156–165.

58. Khantzian EJ. Self-selection and progression in drug dependence. Psychiatry Dig 1975;10: 19–22.

59. Khantzian EJ. Impulse problems in addiction: cause and effect relationships. In: Wishnie H, ed. Working with the impulsive person. New York: Plenum, 1979.

60. Khantzian EJ. Unpublished manuscript.

61. Dodes LM. Addiction, helplessness, and narcissistic rage. Psychoanal Q 1990;59:398–419.

62. Dodes LM. Compulsion and addiction. J Am Psychoanal Assoc 1996;44:815–836.

63. Wurmser L. Psychology of compulsive drug use. In: Wallace B, ed. The chemically dependent—phases of treatment and recovery. New York: Brunner/Mazel, 1992.

64. Greenspan SI. Psychopathology and adaptation in infancy and early childhood. New York: International Universities Press, 1981.

65. Khantzian EJ, Mack JE. Self-preservation and the care of the self: ego instincts reconsidered. Psychoanal Stud Child 1983;28:209–232.

66. Khantzian EJ. Self-regulation and self-medication factors in alcoholism and the addictions: similarities and differences. In: Galanter M, ed. Recent developments in alcoholism. New York: Plenum, 1990;8:255–270.

67. Shedler J, Block J. Adolescent drug use and psychological health. Am Psychol 1990;45: 612–630.

68. Jacobson E. The self and the object world. New York: International Universities Press, 1964.

69. Kernberg O. Borderline conditions and pathological narcissism. New York: Jason Aronson, 1975.

70. Ogden TH. The matrix of the mind. Northvale, NJ: Jason Aronson, 1989.

71. McDougall J. Primitive communication and the use of the countertransference: reflections on early psychic trauma and its transference effects. In: Plea for a measure of abnormality. New York: International Universities Press, 1974: 247–298.

72. Wallant KB. Creating, the capacity for attachment—treating addictions and the alienated self. Northvale, NJ: Jason Aronson, 1995.

73. Winnicott DW. Playing and reality. London: Tavistock, 1971.

74. Freud S. Cited in Stern MM. Fear of death and neurosis. J Am Psychoanal Assoc 1968;16:3–31.

75. Krystal H. Disorders of emotional development in addictive behavior. In: Dowling S, ed. The Psychology and treatment of addictive behavior. Madison, CT: International Universities Press, 1995.

76. Khantzian EJ, Wilson A. Substance dependence, repetition and the nature of addictive suffering. Presented at 76th annual meeting, American Psychoanalytic Association, Chicago, IL, 1987. In: Wilson A, Gedo JE, eds. Hierarchical concepts in psychoanalysis. New York: Guilford Press, 1993:263–283.

77. Sifneos P. Clinical observations on some patients suffering from a variety of psychosomatic diseases. Proceedings of the 7th European Conference on Psychosomatic Research, Rome, September 11–16, 1967. Acta Med Psychosom 1967;452–458.

78. Nemiah JC. The psychological management and treatment of patients with peptic ulcer. Adv Psychosom Med 1970;6:169–173.

79. McDougall J. The. "dis-affected" patient; reflections on affect pathology. Psychoanal Q 1984; 53:386–409.

80. de M'Uzan M. Analytical process and the notion of the past. Int Rev Psychoanal 1974;1:464–480.

81. Marty P, de M'Uzan M. Le pensee operatorie. Rev Fr Psychoanal 1963;27(suppl):345–456.

82. Gedo JE, Goldberg A. Models of the mind: a psychoanalytic theory. Chicago: University of Chicago Press, 1973.

83. Gedo JE. Beyond interpretation: toward a unified theory of psychoanalysis. New York: International Universities Press, 1979.

84. Gedo JE. Psychoanalysis and its discontents. New York: International Universities Press, 1984.

85. Gedo JE. Conflict in psychoanalysis: essays in history and method. New York: Guilford Press, 1986.

86. Wilson A, Passil S, Faude J. Self regulation and its failures. In: Masling J, ed. Empirical studies in psychoanalytic theory. Hillsdale, NJ: Erlbaum, 1996;3:149–214.

87. Wilson A, Malatesta C. Affects and the compulsion to repeat: Freud's repetition compulsion revisited. Psychoanal Contemp Thought 1989; 12:265–312.

88. Berger LS. Substance abuse as symptom—a psychoanalytic critique of treatment approaches and the cultural beliefs that sustain them. Hillsdale, NJ: Analytic Press, 1991.

89. Khantzian EJ. The primary care therapist and patient needs in substance abuse treatment. Am J Drug Alcohol Abuse 1988;14:159–167.

90. Dodes LM, Khantzian EJ. Individual psychodynamic psychotherapy with addicts. In: Clinical textbook of addiction disorders. London: Guilford Press, 1991:391–405.

91. Khantzian EJ. Psychotherapeutic interventions with substance abusers—the clinical context. J Subst Abuse Treat 1985;2:83–88.

92. Dodes LM. Abstinence from alcohol in long-term individual psychotherapy with alcoholics. Am J Psychother 1984;36:248–256.

93. Mack JE. Alcoholism AA, the governance of the self. In: Bean MH, Zinberg NE, eds. Dynamic approaches to the understanding and treatment of alcoholism. New York: Free Press, 1981:163–188.

94. Khantzian EJ. A contemporary psychodynamic approach to drug abuse treatment. Am J Drug Alcohol Abuse 1986;12:213–222.

95. Ng LKY, Wen HL. Acupuncture in substance abuse. In: Lowinson JH, Ruiz P, eds. Substance abuse: clinical problems and perspectives. Baltimore: Williams & Wilkins, 1981:509–516.

96. Khantzian EJ, Halliday KS, McAuliffe WK. Addiction and the vulnerable self. New York: Guilford Press, 1990.

97. Khantzian EJ. Self-regulation vulnerabilities in substance abusers: treatment implications. In: Dowling S, ed. The psychology and treatment of addictive behaviors. Madison, CT: International University Press, 1995.

98. Kaufman E. The psychotherapy of addicted persons. New York: Guilford Press, 1994.

99. Derby K. Some difficulties in the treatment of character-disordered addicts. In: Wallace BC, ed. The chemically dependent—phases of treatment and recovery. New York: Brunner/Mazel, 1992.

100. Gedo JE. The mind in disorder: psychoanalytic models of pathology. Hillsdale, NJ: Analytic Press, 1988.

101. Krystal H. Alexithymia and the effectiveness of psychoanalytic treatment. Int J Psychoanal Psychother 1983;9:353–378.

102. Wolff HH. The contribution of the interview situation to the restriction in fantasy and emotional experience in psychosomatic patients. Psychother Psychosom 1977;28:58–67.

103. Yaliscove DL. Survey of contemporary psychoanalytically oriented clinicians on the treatment of the addictions: a synthesis. In: Wallace BC, ed. The chemically dependent—phases of treatment and recovery. New York: Brunner/Mazel, 1992.

104. Rothschild, DE. Treating the substance abuser: psychotherapy throughout the recovery process. In: Wallace BC, ed. The chemically dependent—phases of treatment and recovery. New York: Brunner/Mazel, 1992.

9 PSYCHOLOGY OF STAGE CHANGE

Howard J. Shaffer

Until recently, there has been no meaningful integration of theory, research, and practice in the addictions field (1, 2). Marlatt and other observers (3, 4) describe the emergence of a significant theoretical movement: the evolution of the concept of "stages of change" to understand and explain the entire addiction process. Vaillant's natural history approach to addictive disorders (5) provided the supportive conditions for this perspective to emerge. Prochaska and Di-Clemente (6) stimulated and nourished the movement by giving theoretical substance and empirical sustenance to the idea of discrete developmental stages of addiction. The stages of change concept has had a powerful heuristic effect in the development of models of addiction (7, 8), evaluating and understanding treatment (3), understanding natural recovery (4), and guiding the course of psychotherapy (9–11). Some theorists (12, 13) have gone so far as to conclude that "A zeitgeist has emerged in which therapists from different systems are searching for common processes of change" (13, p. 520).

By the beginning of the 1990s, discussions of contemporary approaches to the emergence and treatment of addiction were enhanced by illustrations of developmental stage change models; now, however, these considerations have become central to addiction theory, treatment, and policy. This chapter will examine three major areas. First, the chapter explores the development of addiction and the transition to recovery with emphasis on the psychodynamics of ambivalence. The emergence of ambivalence provides the infrastructure of resistance to abstinence, lifestyle change, and recovery. Next, the stage change model is examined to see how it can help clinicians manage countertransference hate (10). Finally, the chapter provides a report on how stage change strategies can be used to increase the efficacy of social programs and policies designed to prevent addiction or reduce the potential harm(s) associated with addiction.

This analysis will begin by presenting a model that extends the theory of stage change to an account of the "natural recovery" process reported by "cocaine quitters" (4) and intoxicant abuse in general (14). The following section will outline this model briefly by describing a common set of processes that may explain recovery from any addiction whether or not it occurs within the framework of formal treatment. While this model has much in common with earlier models (for example, it describes several stages similar to those of precontemplation, contemplation, and action [6]), it provides more detail about the role of psychodynamic events that occur during the emergence of addiction and the transition from addiction to recovery. (Readers interested in this transition should see Shaffer and Jones [4] and Shaffer and Robbins [11] for a more thorough discussion of this approach to stage change.)

A MODEL OF CHANGE AND RECOVERY

Shaffer and Jones (4) were the first to report that natural cocaine quitters recover their independence through a sequence of stages comprised of identifiable activities. By listening to addict's stories, their way of making sense of their addiction and recovery experience, Shaffer has elaborated a new addiction narrative that suggests fresh ways of utilizing different treatment frames over time. This approach suggests six stages of change that can describe both the emergence of addiction and the evolution of recovery. The major events associated with quitting are observable and thus provide the arena for a psychodynamic analysis of recovery. It appears that successful quitters pass through each of these stages, though at different rates. It does not follow, however, that if a person with addiction goes through these stages, they will be assured of breaking the habit. (Prochaska, Norcross and DiClemente [15] provide a very useful stage change guide to breaking habits.) Systematic research will be necessary to confirm this conclusion or the circumstances under which the sequence of quitting phases proves to be insufficient for recovery. At present, the identification of these stages, and recognition that various steps are an integral part of the quitting process, holds great promise for those who desire more effective behavior change skills. To recover from addiction, however, a sequence of well-defined events must occur. The intensity and duration of each milestone in the sequence will vary from person to person, but the sequence will be common to all.

Stage One: Initiation and Emergence of Addiction

To become addicted to any activity or substance and then to successfully quit, one must first engage in the activity. Everyone who uses a drug, however, does not become a drug abuser or addict. In fact, the vast majority of those who have tried a psychoactive drug (or engaged in gambling or other potentially addicting activities) do not become addicted (4, 16). However, for a wide array of interactive biological, psychological, and social reasons, some initial episodes of drug use provide a portal into the addictive process.

Stage Two: Substance Use Produces Positive Experiences

If an activity (e.g., drug use, gambling, overeating) is not associated with some positive consequences, it will be discontinued. Positive effects can be a direct result of the pharmacological properties of the drug or the psychological reinforcement it provides (e.g., relief of depression or reduced sexual inhibition). The consequences also can be positive in a more indirect manner. For example, some drug users experience more social rewards, are held in higher esteem, and have more to do when they are using the substance. Without some positive consequences, any activity or drug use would not be continued to the point that addiction could emerge. The experience of positive consequences is fundamental to understanding the development of ambivalence that emerges during the often repetitive cycle of addictive behaviors characterized by the next stage. In addition, an understanding of these positive consequences is essential if clinicians expect to manage effectively the feelings of countertransference hate that often emerge during the treatment of addiction.

Stage Three: Adverse Consequences Emerge

For drug use or any other activity to be considered an addiction, it must, by definition, be associated with adverse consequences. When adverse consequences emerge, most people restrict, regulate, or modify their behavior. They moderate their activities or abstain entirely. People with addiction, however, are unable to modify their behavior. For biological, psychological, or social reasons, they remain unable to temper their actions. At the beginning of this process, they do not even contemplate readjusting their behavior (6). The essence of this addiction predicament (17) is that the object of addiction continues to provide some of the previous positive consequences while simultaneously producing adversities that begin to weigh more heavily (9, 10). Addictive behaviors serve while they destroy. The reason that these repetitive behaviors can be so very destructive rests on the notion that people with addiction are not fully aware that the negative effects produced by their excessive substance abuse (or other addictive behaviors) are, in fact, the result of that behavior pattern. This period represents the "throes of addiction." Shaffer and Robbins (11) suggest that during this stage, people with addiction believe their behavior has little to do with their suffering. Instead, they perceive others as the source of their problems. The urging of friends and family to reduce or stop the addictive behavior is of little consequence; in fact, their pleading can become the fuel that energizes the addictive behavior so that the pattern intensifies further. At this level, people with addiction are capable of making sense of their world, with one exception: they cannot make any causal association between their addictive behavior and the life problems that they have had to endure. To minimize the discomfort associated with these problems, persons with addiction persist in engaging in those behaviors that previously had produced positive consequences. The result is the maintenance of repetitive, excessive behavior patterns—addictive behaviors—that repeat without the *apparent* presence of a regulatory mechanism capable of restoring control by breaking this cycle.

Stage Four: Turning Points and the Evolution of Quitting

For people who have experienced addiction and then successfully recover, adverse consequences of substance abuse enter into their awareness and life takes a turn. This *turning point* into awareness, or insight, has often been considered the end of denial. More accurately it is a reclaiming of the projections that characterize stage three. No longer are one's problems the result of external events; no longer can one continue to claim victimization. The adverse consequences associated with addictive behavior now are experienced as one's own. This is the beginning of an epistemological shift. The person with addiction is confronted by their own recognition of the causal connection between their drug using behaviors and such problems as poor health, financial difficulty, or family disintegration. They now realize that their behaviors are not anomalous and not without adverse effect. Often experienced as a life crisis, addicts recognize that their lifestyle must now change if they are to regain control. They begin to recognize that they must give up the positive consequences of their behavior that continue while they gain access to the negative outcomes that are connected with the addictive behavior pattern. The events associated with the turning point experience mark the beginning of the evolution of quitting.

A turning point represents the shift between unencumbered substance abuse and the realization that this abuse is directly responsible for the presence of profoundly negative life circumstances. The thought of quitting or controlling drug abuse first appears prior to the actual turning point. This thought represents ambivalence, which is at the core of addiction.

AMBIVALENCE

Addiction is a well-known destructive behavior. Like all patterns of human behavior, addictive behavior patterns perform some service. Usually, people have difficulty understanding the adaptive or useful value of these patterns. The result is that efforts to change these behaviors often fail. Whether recovery is initiated by self or other, it is very important to understand that addictive behaviors serve while they destroy.

This double-edged sword called addiction produces ambivalence for the person with addiction who is thinking about change. Ambivalence is a feeling of conflict. It is a simultaneous sense of both wanting and not wanting to change, of liking and disliking the experience. In spite of the obvious destructive power of addiction, people in the midst of addiction cling to the part of this experience that they like, the part that was adaptive originally and produced positive consequences during stage two. As drug abusers become aware of their ambivalence, they begin to express a wish that they want to quit. However, they do not yet want to stop. Increasing levels of self observation develop and the substance abuser now begins to realize that the costs of addictive behavior exceed the benefits. Substance abuse is explicitly identified as the major (and perhaps not the only) destructive agent in their life. It is at this point that a quitter often asks friends and significant others for help to stop. Before a turning point, the burden of self-control had been delegated more to others than oneself; *the acceptance of personal responsibility* represents the actual turning point.

A turning point is not simply a transition. It is actually the end of a complex dynamic process about drugs (or other addictive behavior). We consider it an end point even though abstinence and recovery might be months or years away. Needless to say, the experience of a turning point does not produce instantaneous results. Commonly experienced turning points have been described as periods of dissonance associated with feelings of self-loathing or a deterioration of personal values (4). Other turning point perceptions include the recognition that substance abuse is beginning to exacerbate rather than diminish intrapersonal and interpersonal conflict. An extremely important yet commonly reported turning point centers around the recognition that one's deteriorating physical condition is related to drug abuse. This is experienced as a do-or-die situation: if drugs are used, users believe that they may die as a result. Other turning points, less extreme but no less important, involve the recognition that drug involvement may cause users to lose what is important to them (e.g., a job or a special relationship).

Stage Five: Active Quitting

Once a turning point is reached, the process and task associated with active quitting can begin. Two basic approaches to quitting have been identified: "tapered" and "cold turkey" quitting. It is possible that a successful quitter will mix these approaches to find a method that works. The majority of quitters, however, fall predominately or entirely into one style or the other. Few successful quitters mix their stopping strategies.

The notion of *active* quitting is important. Successful quitters make observable changes during this stage of addiction. The methods for quitting drugs include energetic attempts to avoid the drug, gaining social support for personal change, and engaging in some form of self-development that also can help to manage stress (18). Thus, this stage is characterized neither by thoughtfulness nor ambivalence. It is identified by important and marked behavioral change and lifestyle reorganization. New activities are elevated to a position of prominence; they gain intrapersonal and interpersonal value. Old behaviors become devalued and less meaningful.

Stage Six: Relapse Prevention

Very few individuals who stop their drug use remain totally abstinent from that moment. Marlatt and Gordon (19) examined how slips, that is, single episodes of drug use, can lead to full blown relapse. Biological, psychological, and sociological factors interact to influence the risk of relapse for any individual. The final phase of quitting involves the maintenance of new skills and lifestyle patterns that promote positive, independent patterns of behavior. The integration of these behaviors into regular day-to-day activities is the essence of relapse prevention (20).

The experience of natural quitters suggests that having a number of strategies and tactics to draw upon is essential to maintaining abstinence. Successful quitters substitute a variety of behavior patterns for their old drug-using lifestyle. For example, they become regularly involved in physical exercise. At times these substitute patterns also can become excessive. This risk is most probable when (*a*) excessive behavior patterns serve as anodynes to uncomfortable affective states, and/or (*b*) self-observation skills are weak and poorly developed. Flights into spiritual or religious conversions also help many individuals sustain their abstinence. For some, relapse prevention is sustained by entry into formal treatment. Others occasionally substitute different drugs that they consider less troublesome than their drug of abuse. The use of pharmacological substitution is extremely risky and often backfires. The results of drug substitution can be as devastating and destructive as the original drug abuse.

In sum, there are six major stages that describe the cycle of addiction. The first three stages comprise the natural history stage of addiction, while the last three are associated with quitting, or the treatment history of the addictive disorder. The first phase serves as groundwork for the second phase and thus must not be lost sight of during the therapeutic process.

TOWARD CLINICAL INTEGRATION: FACILITATING STAGE CHANGE PSYCHOTHERAPEUTIC LANGUAGE[a]

Prochaska, DiClemente, and Norcross (21) persuasively demonstrate that the most robust and reliable predictor of treatment outcome, regardless of treatment strategy, is an index of patient readiness to change. Consequently, psychotherapists should attend to (*a*) the overall readiness of a patient to change and (*b*) a patient's specific stage of change. By identifying a patient's specific level of development within the natural history of addiction, treatment can be directed to facilitate movement to the next stage of development and not impede this natural process.

To help patients progress through the stages of quitting, clinicians must begin to speak a language that promotes and encourages this natural progression instead of inadvertently complicating the tasks of recovery with irrelevant or restricting ideas. To accomplish this goal, therapists must first learn to match the tasks of clinical work to the stage of change that clients are experiencing (7, 10). For example, it is not useful to explore ambivalence in detail when a patient has resolved their ambivalence and is ready to actively quit. Similarly, it is equally useless to help patients develop quitting strategies when they have not become resolute about their readiness to change because painful ambivalence is fueling denial. Helping individuals move from one stage of experience to the next requires clinicians to recognize and interact with their clients' particular frame of reference. In other words, clinicians must become fluent in the language of each stage of addiction and recovery for each patient. Clinicians must be adept listeners and observers as they inhabit the role of students learning to navigate their clients' subjective realities. Put simply, if clinicians fail to become "fluent" in their clients' particular "language," there is little hope that a genuine, empathic, meaningful dialogue, capable of facilitating change, will develop.

---

[a] This section derives from the work of Shaffer and Robbins (11).

Clinical Applications of a Stage Change Model[b]

According to a stage change model, clinicians should base treatment choices on which method of care is appropriate to the individual patient at any specific time during the process of recovery. Prescriptive treatment requires the integration and modification of clinical approaches. Wachtel (22) was one of the first to describe the integration of clinical approaches when he considered the movement toward an integration of psychoanalysis and behavior therapy. Khantzian, Halliday, and McAuliffe (23) modified traditional psychodynamic group psychotherapy techniques for substance abusers.

Integrating clinical methods is not as complicated as it first appears. Consider the third stage of the stage change model described earlier. When adverse consequences develop but remain out of awareness, most people do not seek treatment for addiction. Others (e.g., family, friends, doctor, lawyer) often entreat or coerce stage three addicts into a clinical setting. When treatment is available, confrontation and clarification are the most useful clinical interventions. These tactics help patients gain access to the ambivalence, fantasy, and wish that they would want to stop their addictive behavior.

To resolve impasses, clinicians must examine their motives for patient change. Patients resist change in response to the therapeutic context. What clinicians present to patients determines in large measure how patients respond (24). This view represents a significant shift from the common "patient must be motivated to change" view of psychotherapy. The task of therapists is simply to help patients (gradually) shift their experience so they can move to the next stage of a natural process. For example, when patients present for treatment experiencing adverse effects from their behavior and unaware that they are indeed causing these painful events (i.e., stage three of the stage change model presented earlier), the goal of treatment is not active quitting (i.e., stage five). The task of psychotherapy is for patients to experience and begin to tolerate their ambivalence so that denial is no longer necessary; consequently, patients naturally experience a turning point (stage four, when they begin to accept responsibility for their behavior). Similarly, when patients who have reached the relapse prevention stage of treatment do relapse, in addition to identifying the specific relapse "triggers" so that patients can learn the most from their experience, clinicians also must attend to any ambivalence that has resurfaced.

Miller and Rollnick (24) offer a variety of useful clinical suggestions that minimize countertransference and, as a consequence, therapeutic impasses. To begin, therapists must express empathy; this notion is similar to becoming fluent in a patient's representation and experience of the world. Instead of being argumentative, clinicians should develop discrepancies—between patients' behavior and their stated goals—to help them see the self-deception in either their goals or their behavior. This discrepancy is an expression of ambivalent conflict and must be exercised if it is to dissipate denial. Therapists need to roll with patient resistance; clinicians must remember that they stimulate defensiveness by their probing, confronting, and clarifying comments. Psychotherapists need to actively support patient self-efficacy. Thus, clinicians should implement strategies that will increase a patient's sense of hope, the range of alternatives, and ultimately the possibility of change. This can be accomplished through a variety of tactics. For example, during the course of therapy, a care giver can ask patients how uncomfortable they are at that moment along any emotional dimension (e.g., anxiety). Later in the very same session, usually as they leave the treatment office, the therapist can ask how the patient feels now along the same dimension. Inevitably, patients will respond with a somewhat different value to their feelings. Even if they are more uncomfortable, the therapist can note that "things are already beginning to change." (Sometime things do indeed get worse before getting better.)

TREATMENT OF PAINFUL AMBIVALENCE: THE ESSENCE OF PSYCHOTHERAPY FOR ADDICTION

Similar tactics can be used to explore and exercise the painful feelings associated with ambivalent conflicts. As I described earlier, it is essential to the psychotherapy of substance abuse that clinicians explore with patients *what addiction does for them* and not simply how it may hurt them. Denial is the result of painful ambivalence: the feeling that one both wants and does not want an object, feeling, or behavior. Denial is a defense mechanism that removes one side of the painful conflict by erasing it from consciousness. Overcoming denial within the context of psychotherapy requires clinicians to stimulate and exercise ambivalent feelings. Not only will this approach to treatment increase a patient's ability to tolerate painful ambivalence and, therefore, diminish the underlying need for denial, but this tactic adds considerable credibility to any therapist's position. Patients who abuse intoxicants know full well that these drugs reliably do something for them—even though they also may experience significant adverse effects. Once patients know that the therapist is aware of this fact and can tolerate a candid discussion of this matter, there is much less to be defensive about.

During psychotherapy sessions, ask open-ended questions, listen reflectively, and be affirmative—support clients' efforts to participate in change (24). This can be done by occasionally summarizing what has transpired during treatment, for example, "so far you have said that . . . and we have come to think . . . " Finally, elicit self-motivational statements by asking evocative questions. Help patients to recognize their responsibility by challenging their motivation to change (24). This requires patients to defend change; don't impose change so patients defend the status quo (e.g., patients struggling with addiction often say they are in treatment because their parent or spouse wanted them to come: "do you always do what they ask you to?") Guide patients to look both backward (before problem) and forward (after problem) so they can develop a mental image of their life before and after substance abuse. Finally, contact patients by telephone or mail after their first office visit. This tactic will minimize the dropout rate after evaluation and encourage the development of a treatment adherence (typically 30–60% of patients do not follow treatment prescriptions) (24).

Psychodynamics of Ambivalence: A Brief Treatment Guide

The psychodynamic rationale[c] for focusing on ambivalence rests on the assumption that a substance user's id-wishes stimulate ego-wants to stop. However, an addict's superego suppresses this and other wishes, including the wish to want to change. Instead, apprehension about wishing for anything develops. Drug users know that their prior wishes frequently resulted in episodes of substance abuse. Consequently, these wishes produced dysphoria and discomfort about how a drug wish was going to be fulfilled, usually through socially unacceptable and/or illicit behavior patterns (at least phenomenologically unacceptable). The subjective experience of intemperate guilt and shame is sufficiently painful to stimulate suppression of the experience of all wishes, regardless of drug involvement. An addict's ego responds to this emotional conflict by enacting social withdrawal, retreat, and the subjective experience of humiliation, remorse, and regret. Reduced self-efficacy and an increasing sense of being emotionally, cognitively, and behaviorally stuck soon follows.

---

[b] Much clinical evidence and experience support the clinical application of a stage change model as described in this section. However, systematic research is necessary to clarify the complex causal influences that affect treatment outcome.

[c] This rationale is a structural-conflict explanation of some essential psychological events that must be resolved during the transition from addiction to a turning point. Most patients, regardless of previous education and cultural background, are familiar with the notion of an unconscious aspect of mind. Many are also familiar with the structural elements of psychodynamic theory. Because this psychodynamic language is the most recognizable formulation for patients in treatment to grasp, this depiction of ambivalence is selected from several others (e.g., behavioral approach-avoidance or competing reference groups) for the present discussion. However, other models should not be neglected since these representations can stimulate an understanding essential to the future conduct of research that will explore the development, maintenance, and resolution of ambivalence.

Psychodynamic treatment for ambivalence begins with an exploration of this conflict followed by an explanation of the treatment rationale (a simple version of what's been already described). Superego pressure will begin to diminish simply by examining forbidden wishes in a safe and secure atmosphere (25). During this uncovering work, clinicians consider the role of wishes and fantasies. Psychodynamic psychotherapists permit an examination of how these desires translate to the awareness of wanting substances as a means to resolve inner conflict or deficiency.

As underlying belief systems are uncovered, clinicians must also be willing to explore behaviors that reflect the patient's ambivalence about both wanting to stop and continue drug use. By only confronting attitudes that encouraged drug use, therapists unwittingly stimulate and affirm these beliefs. In addition, failing to explore a patient's drug wishes, interests, and fantasies diminishes the credibility of treatment. Similarly, therapists must permit an exploration of the shortcomings and personal losses that come with a drug-free lifestyle. Clinicians also must permit open discussion of what happens to the patient when he or she acts out wants. During this dialogue, patients are encouraged to articulate their wishes for wants: what do they wish they would want? This is a difficult and complex process because countertransference often limits clinicians from permitting an open exploration of patient wishes and their positive experiences with drug use. However, clinicians must learn to recognize and use these experiences so that they can explore fully what drug use does for each patient; only by gaining access to such an understanding can ambivalent feelings be explored and tolerated. Substitutes for the object of addiction can be identified once patients discover how the original objects of their desire produced satisfaction and pleasure.

As these associative exercises strengthen the patient's capacity to recognize desires, ambivalence is piqued and denial diminished. This aroused emotional state provides the emotional environment within which drug abusers first recognize and then gradually accept responsibility for their addiction. Interest in stopping addiction becomes stronger as a drug abuser recognizes his or her capacity for producing as well as stifling substance abuse. With this realization, patients naturally enter the turning point crisis.

Throughout the course of treatment, substance abusers need to be held responsible for the adverse consequences of their drug abuse. During this period, some people unwittingly help the person with addiction keep these negative effects out of awareness. Consequently, family and systems treatments offer great utility. Group therapy also is very helpful if the patient is willing to participate. One patient's denial is another group member's irritation. Both of these treatments also are useful to explore ambivalence: the patient's ambivalence about change, the family's ambivalence about simultaneously loving and hating the patient for the current family crises. Behavioral treatments are of little assistance during this stage of addiction.

During a turning point, when an addict begins to realize that he or she wants to stop, psychodynamic treatments can be very useful. These techniques assist patients to understand their life and make sense out of chaotic emotions. In addition, dynamic therapies help manage the growing awareness of adverse consequences and mobilize the executive functions of the personality to regain control. During this stage of change, behavioral treatment remains premature because it is still too difficult for anyone to give up or change behaviors that some part of them actively desires. Research on natural recovery shows that people usually know exactly how to change their behavior (4). What keeps drug abusers from doing what they already know is their sense of ambivalence. Addiction treatment—whether self imposed or provided professionally—must help people work through their ambivalence. Psychodynamically oriented psychotherapy is arguably the best strategy for helping patients determine what substance abuse *does for* them and what it *means to* them.

However, once the patient resolves the ambivalence that is so very paralyzing and responsible for energizing their denial, they usually become sufficiently organized to consider actively changing and more directive behavior therapy becomes the most appropriate treatment of choice. During the fifth or active change stage, patients need to learn new behavior patterns and get support for testing their ability to carry these out; in particular they need to have the option of failing and resolving the associated negative affect. Consequently, behavior, psychodynamic, family or systems, and group ther-

apies can all be applied judiciously and effectively. Passive, nondirective therapies have little value at this point unless this strategy serves to help the patient integrate the emotional experience of actively changing.

During the relapse prevention stage, both behavioral and psychodynamic treatments are essential. Behavioral approaches help patients learn how to avoid or cope with risky situations, determine the cues that begin a sequence of events that threaten their sobriety, and successfully manage negative thoughts. The majority of relapse incidents involve negative emotional states, however, and can benefit from psychodynamic techniques. New research also emphasizes the importance of behavior change (26). This work reveals that for nonpsychiatric patients who are substance abusers those who sustain a regimen of physical exercise are less likely to relapse. Psychodynamic and pharmacological treatments will be most helpful for psychiatric patients during this stage of addiction treatment. These methods assist patients to manage the emotional turmoil that often predicts substance abuse relapse (19, 26).

Shaffer and Gambino (14) consider the question as to whether (a) therapists must cultivate a sufficiently broad base of clinical skills to provide continuous care or (b) the therapist should direct the patient to other clinicians during the course of treatment. Both possibilities are acceptable. Throughout the field of medical practice the idea of a primary care provider as case manager is common. For the therapist whose range of clinical skills is narrow, the clinical task is to coordinate treatment interventions prescriptively. This therapist need not deliver every treatment personally. They should, however, remain sensitive to the shifting needs of the patient throughout the course of recovery and then try to provide or access specialty treatments when appropriate.

It is crucial for addiction treatment specialists to determine how patients envision their place in the sequence of addiction stages. This process helps patients engage and remain in the therapeutic process. In addition, it aids both therapist and patient in accessing a useful rationale for the treatment program that will follow. If the treatment rationale is in conflict with the patient's perception of their problem, they often drop out of treatment. When therapy follows a formulation that is consistent with the patient's view, treatment compliance is common. In short, the patient's perception of their change process is essential to determining which clinical method should be applied.

Assessing the Patient's Perception

As stated earlier, psychodynamically oriented psychotherapy is arguably the best strategy for helping patients determine what substance abuse *does for* them and what it *means to* them. This task is essentially a problem in self and social perception. The most important view of addictive behavior for the drug treatment specialist is the patient's. The patient's perception of the disorder will determine when and how patients seek treatment. Understanding a patient's perception of his or her substance abuse permits the clinician to negotiate and navigate treatment interventions.

To develop an integrated model of substance abuse treatment, clinicians need to begin to learn how to *access* and then to *assess* their patient's view of addiction. While it may be possible to impose a clinical model on some patients, most patients bring their own view of addiction with them when they enter treatment. When the provider and patient see things similarly, treatment can go well. However, most clinicians recognize that the majority of substance abusers find it difficult to engage in treatment. Historically, this has been a patient problem: many treatment specialists blame the patient and their "disease of denial." More likely, however, this situation results when the patient's view does not match the therapist's.

Kleinman (27) and Pfifferling (28) discussed the importance of examining a patient's perspectives for the treatment of psychiatric disorders in general. Their work particularly influenced the research of Shaffer (10), who demonstrated that patients understand addictive behavior from at least 13 different perspectives. For example, in addition to the conventional view that addiction represents a disease process, patients often consider their intemperate behavior as the result of an excessive habit, a psychodynamic deficiency, or a biological dilemma. Some patients view their excessive behavior patterns as average and expectable for their social reference group.

There are more complex views. For example, there are patients who see their problems as a punishment. Some consider it a well-deserved penalty while others view it as unreasonable and unfortunate. Clinicians often view addiction as a challenge, something to overcome. Patients may see it as an enemy and deny their capacity to resist; alternatively, these patients may resist with pronounced hostility. Other patients view their addiction as direct evidence of personal weakness, a moral loss of control. For some, addiction is a strategy by which they manage their environment and their identity. Addiction also can provide relief from obligations and responsibilities. Quite often addiction is understood as a irrevocable personal loss; this view often leads to depression. Finally, patients can view addiction as an opportunity, a time for personal growth and reflection. This perspective can lead to personal development and significant changes in lifestyle.

STAGE CHANGE AND SOCIAL POLICY

Stage change models can be used effectively to guide the strategic implementation of prevention and treatment programs; in addition, stage change can help planners develop better social policy strategies and programs. For example, currently there is considerable concern about the capacity of primary prevention programs to yield effective results (29–31). However, it is very difficult to separate the problems of prevention programs from the improper application of this technology. Like drug policy, we must recognize that efforts to prevent the onset of drug use, the harms associated with drug use, or the progression of adversity once drug-using patterns have been established, can have both advantages and disadvantages. Stage change models guide us to recognize that better prevention programs can achieve a variety of positive objectives: (*a*) inhibit the development of drug-using behaviors (i.e., traditional primary prevention), (*b*) delay the onset of harm in drug users (i.e., contemporary harm reduction or secondary prevention); (*c*) arrest or delay harm in progression and scope (i.e., tertiary prevention). Any of these prevention strategies should be careful not to develop programs that inadvertently stimulate drug use or abuse or the potential harms associated with such use. However, while not widely prevalent, unfortunately, this prevention outcome is not extinct (31).

Stage change models can help program planners to better match interventions to the target population's natural place in the stages of change. For example, most traditional primary prevention programs, designed to limit the onset of any psychoactive substance use, are systematically applied long after such use started. In America most young people begin using alcohol with their family during religious rituals before they ever are exposed to alcohol and other drug prevention programs in the school system. Similarly, parents traditionally advise very young children to take vitamins or medicine because these substances "are good for you." When parents heap social approval upon their children during this family drug-taking ritual, young people learn rapidly that ingesting substances can indeed make them, and sometimes even others, "feel good." The well-learned lessons of ingesting substances to promote shifts in feeling states are very difficult to undo, particularly when the programs designed to change this already established behavior pattern are of the primary prevention variety. The stage change model teaches that once young people have experienced any positive consequences of substance use, secondary prevention programs are now in order and the time has passed for primary prevention strategies. These programs attempt to reduce drug use and any harm that may accrue to people who already use drugs. Secondary prevention programs are better matched to the experiences of most young people who are in stage two (i.e., positive consequences). These prevention efforts must account for any positive experiences people have had during their early stages of involvement with potentially addictive substances and activities.

Stage change models also encourage policy makers and program planners to recognize that the impact of any treatment program is not simply the consequence of its clinical efficacy (32). Treatment impact is a function of both efficacy and participation. Clinicians can maximize clinical impact by better matching treatments to prospective patients' stage of change within the natural history of addiction. To have impact, treatment programs must attract and engage sufficient numbers of people. Once in treatment, the effi-

cacy effects of the clinical intervention begin to exert influence. Prochaska (32) reminds us that even very effective treatments that attract or sustain few people in care have limited impact. To illustrate, a treatment program with 25% efficacy and 75% participation has dramatically more impact than another program with 30% efficacy and 1% participation. Program planners need to develop treatment programs that have more impact. This process will require a shift in how policy makers conceptualize treatment programs. Countering the push to establish new policies are the countertransferential forces that sustain the status quo. Rather than experience the discomforts usually associated with changing treatment strategies and programs, policy makers find it less irritating to blame patients for failing to thrive and attribute poor outcome efficacy to patient traits (e.g., intractability).

Research guided by stage change models reveals that the vast majority of people who need substance treatment are not ready to change or take direct action to counter their problems (21). That is, these people have not yet started to think about drug abuse as the cause of their suffering; they have not started to think that changing their behavior will change the quality of their lives. Consequently, this group of prospective patients may never enter the array of currently available treatments—whether effective or ineffective. New clinical technologies can engage this reluctant group more effectively. Instead of addressing denial as the major problem, clinical programs must appeal to the substance abuser's ambivalence about change. By "demanding" less change at the outset of treatment and featuring ambivalence oriented interventions (10, 11, 24), new clinical programs will engage more people in treatment. Consequently, these new treatment programs will have the opportunity to maximally affect public health in general and substance abuse in particular.

Stage change models encourage policy makers to recognize the need to establish programs that either inhibit the progression from initiation to adverse consequences during stages one through three (i.e., secondary prevention) or implement programs designed to reduce or restrict the development of harms that emerge from the activities associated with any one of the stages. Similarly, legal sanctions against psychoactive drug use minimizes the positive consequences that users experience during the positive consequences stage. Table 9.1 provides a brief summary of the stages of addiction and the prospects for matching social programs to a stage. While other pos-

Table 9.1 Matching Treatment with Stages of Change

Stages of Addictive Behavior	Range of Possible Modality Matches
1. Initiation	*Primary prevention* (e.g., public education and information programs, social resistance training)
2. Positive Consequences	*Secondary prevention* (e.g., public education, counseling, social resistance training)
3. Adverse Consequences	*Tertiary prevention* (e.g., counseling), *outpatient psychotherapy services*, or *self-help fellowships* (to stimulate ambivalence, dissonance, and a readiness for change), *DWI programs* or *acute inpatient services* (when there is a need for medical and psychiatric crisis management)
4. Turning Point(s)	*Acute inpatient and outpatient services* (e.g., detoxification, partial care, 12-step, and self-help programs)
5. Active Quitting	*Residential programs* (only for chronic substance abusers who have little or no social support systems available), *partial care* or *outpatient services* (chemical substitutions, counseling, 12-step, and self-help programs)
6. Relapse Prevention or Change Maintenance	*Outpatient, 12-step, self-help,* and *residential* (only for chronic substance abusers who have little or no social support systems available)

sible treatment and program matches exist, Table 9.1 illustrates the matching strategy as guided by a stage change model.

SUMMARY

This chapter considered the natural history of addictive disorders and the common processes of change that can characterize this process. A model was examined as a template to describe the emergence of addiction and the stages of recovery. Further, this discussion focused on the psychological events associated with stage change and the transitions between them. Of special interest, we considered the role that ambivalence plays in energizing the denial that sustains the status quo. A psychodynamic structural-conflict rationale was offered to explain the emergence and maintenance of addictive ambivalence. Just as this model is only one of many possible perspectives that can explain ambivalence, the chapter noted a variety of patient views that exist to explain addiction in general. This approach to understanding the social perception of addiction yields a functional approach to this disorder: emphasis on patient perceptions encourages clinicians to thoroughly assess the shifting meaning of addiction throughout the patient's life, reveals how addiction can work adaptively for a patient, and, therefore, stimulates more economical treatment tactics to help work through the ambivalence that often sustains addictive behaviors. In closing, this chapter considered some of the implications of a stage change model for developing social policies and programs.

Acknowledgments. *Prochaska and DiClemente (6), Marlatt and Gordon (19), Marlatt, Baer, Donovan, and Kivlahan (8), and Vaillant (5) provide the intellectual framework that stimulated much of the developmental stage change thinking that led to a modern reformation of addiction explanations. These workers are pioneers and I am indebted to them for providing the conceptual and intellectual platform upon which many of the ideas in this chapter rest.*

The author extends special thanks to Blase Gambino, Stephanie Jones, Janet Mann, and Melissa Robbins for their helpful comments on earlier versions of this chapter.

References

1. Tims FM, Leukefeld CG. Relapse and recovery in drug abuse: an introduction. In: Tims FM, Leukefeld CG, eds. Relapse and recovery in drug abuse. National Institute of Drug Abuse Research Monograph 72:1–4. Washington, DC: U.S. Government Printing Office, 1986.
2. Niaura RS, Rohsenow DJ, Binkoff JA, Monti PM, Pedraza M, Abrams DB. Relevance of cue reactivity to understanding alcohol and smoking relapse. J Abnorm Psychol 1988;97:133–152.
3. Maisto SA, Connors GJ. Assessment of treatment outcome. In: Donovan DM, Marlatt GA, eds. Assessment of addictive behaviors. New York: Guilford Press, 1988:421–453.
4. Shaffer HJ, Jones SB. Quitting cocaine: the struggle against impulse. Lexington, MA: Lexington Books, 1989.
5. Vaillant G. The natural history of alcoholism. Cambridge: Harvard University Press, 1983.
6. Prochaska JO, DiClemente CC. Common processes of self change in smoking, weight control, and psychological distress. In: Shiffman S, Wills TA, eds. Coping and substance abuse. New York: Academic Press, 1985.
7. Marlatt GA. Matching clients to treatment: treatment models and stages of change. In: Donovan DM, Marlatt GA, eds. Assessment of addictive behaviors. New York: Guilford Press, 1988: 474–484.
8. Marlatt GA, Baer JS, Donovan DM, Kivlahan DR. Addictive behaviors: Etiology and treatment. Annu Rev Psychol 1988;39:223–252.
9. Shaffer HJ. The psychology of stage change: the transition from addiction to recovery. In: Lowinson JH, Ruiz P, Millman RB, Langrod JG, eds. Substance abuse: a comprehensive textbook. Baltimore: Williams & Wilkins, 1992:100–105.
10. Shaffer HJ. Denial, ambivalence and countertransference hate. In: Levin JD, Weiss R, eds. Alcoholism: dynamics and treatment. Northdale, NJ: Jason Aronson, 1994:421–437.
11. Shaffer HJ, Robbins M. Psychotherapy for addictive behavior: a stage-change approach to meaning making. In: Washton AM, ed. Psychotherapy and substance abuse: a practitioner's handbook. New York: Guilford Press, 1995: 103–123.
12. Goldfried MR. Toward the delineation of therapeutic change principles. Am Psychol 1980;35: 991–999.
13. Prochaska JO, Velicer WF, DiClemente CC, Fava J. Measuring processes of change: applications to the cessation of smoking. J Consult Clin Psychol 1988;56:520–528.
14. Shaffer HJ, Gambino B. Epilogue: integrating treatment choices. In Milkman HB, Sederer LI, eds. Treatment choices for alcoholism and substance abuse. Lexington, MA: Lexington Books, 1990;351–375.
15. Prochaska JO, Norcross JC, DiClemente CC. Changing for good: a revolutionary six-stage program for overcoming bad habits and moving your life positively forward. New York: Avon, 1994.
16. Shaffer HJ. The epistemology of "addictive disease": the Lincoln-Douglas debate. J Subst Abuse Treat 1987;4:103–113.
17. Shaffer HJ, Gambino B. The epistemology of addictive disease: gambling as predicament. J Gambling Behavior 1989;5:211–229.
18. Carey MP, Kalra DL, Carey KB, Halperin S, Richards CS. Stress and unaided smoking cessation: a prospective investigation. J Consult Clin Psychol 1993;61:831–838.
19. Marlatt GA, Gordon JR, eds. Relapse prevention: maintenance strategies in the treatment of addictive behaviors. New York: Guilford Press, 1985.
20. Brownell KD, Marlatt GA, Lichtenstein E, Wilson GT. Understanding and preventing relapse. Am Psychol 1986;41:765–782.
21. Prochaska JO, DiClemente CC, Norcross JC. In search of how people change: applications to addictive behaviors. Am Psychol 1992;47: 1102–1114.
22. Wachtel PL. Psychoanalysis and behavior therapy: toward an integration. New York: Basic Books, 1977.
23. Khantzian EJ, Halliday KS, McAuliffe WE. Addiction and the vulnerable self: modified dynamic group therapy for substance abusers. New York: Guilford Press, 1990.
24. Miller WR, Rollnick S, eds. Motivational interviewing: preparing people to change addictive behavior. New York: Guilford Press, 1991.
25. Havens L. A safe place. Cambridge: Harvard University Press, 1989.
26. Svanum S, McAdoo WG. Predicting rapid relapse following treatment for chemical dependency: a matched-subjects design. J Consult Clin Psychol 1989;57:222–226.
27. Kleinman A. The illness narratives: suffering, healing and the human condition. New York: Basic Books, 1988.
28. Pfifferling JH. A cultural prescription for medicocentrism. In: Eisenberg L, Kleinman A, eds. The relevance of social science for medicine. Boston: D. Reidel, 1980;197–222.
29. Botvin GJ, Baker E, Dusenbury L, Botvin EM, Diaz T. Long-term follow-up results of a randomized drug abuse prevention trial in a white middle-class population. JAMA 1995;273: 1106–1112.
30. Bukstein OG. Adolescent substance abuse. New York: John Wiley, 1995.
31. Ellickson PL. Schools. In: Coombs RH, Ziedonis D, eds. Handbook on drug abuse prevention. Boston: Allyn and Bacon, 1995:93–120.
32. Prochaska JO. A transtheoretical approach to addiction treatment: considering stages of change to optimize treatment outcomes. Paper presented at the Drugs and Addictions Treatment Briefing, Harvard University, Cambridge, MA, May 6, 1996.

10 SOCIOCULTURAL

Bruce D. Johnson and John Muffler

The legacy of segregation and poverty helped create a black ghetto whose environment was destructive to many of its inhabitants—a ghetto "largely maintained by white institutions and condoned by white society" (1). These trends toward separate and unequal societies continued through the decades of the 1970s and 1980s, accelerating into the first half of the 1990s. Although research evidence is starting to demonstrate a national decline in the prevalence of abuse for almost all drugs, significant numbers of Americans continue to use alcohol and illicit drugs regardless of ethnic, racial, or socioeconomic group. Data from a variety of sources, however, suggest that minority peoples suffer adverse consequences in disproportionate numbers to their representation in the population. The 1991 National Household Survey on Drug Abuse, for example, indicated that of the more than 75 million people aged 12 and above who have used an illicit drug in their lifetime, approximately 5 million were Latino and 9 million African-American. Substance use and abuse also maintains its devastating impact upon the criminal justice, health care, and other human services systems, while contributing to the unraveling of productivity and the sense of personal well-being and community cohesion (2).

This chapter reviews sociocultural forces in American society that have propelled patterns of drug use and abuse during the 1980s and have continued unabated into the 1990s. Several socioeconomic forces in American society during the past 15 years have exacerbated multiple social crises. Principal among them are massive budget reductions at all levels of government, rampant downsizing in corporate and industrial America, and the decline in availability of needed social services shredding the historic "safety net." These have significantly worsened living standards for poor persons, especially in American inner cities. These multiple crises among low-income Americans, particularly minorities, have created a major reservoir of persons with numerous social problems and severe social deficits. During the last half of the 1980s and beginning of the 1990s, crack abuse has expanded dramatically and has greatly affected American society, inner-city communities, as well as the drug treatment and criminal justice systems. Virtually all social control and treatment systems are seriously impaired from habilitating and rehabilitating their clients because of constrictions imposed by legislation, funding, and professional staff practices, as well as by client perceptions of their needs and expectations of services. As a result, staff provide targeted services for a limited proportion of the multiple problems that individual clients present; such services alleviate only some symptoms and solve but a few problems. This review also includes a brief social history and epidemiology of drug use and abuse.

MULTIPLE SOCIAL CRISES

A major phenomenon of the modern city is the reality of the visibly poor living near rich or middle-income people. The stark contrast between the "haves" and "have nots" that emerged in the 1980s is the result of important structural shifts in American society. In particular, "ghettoization" has increased during the 1970s and 1980s. Inner-city neighborhoods comprised mainly of low-income, welfare, and poor people from minority (Hispanic and African-American) backgrounds have expanded in geographical area and population size (3, 4). The more successful and stable working people tend to move out of these ghettos, leaving behind the poorest and least successful (5). Such neighborhoods have a conspicuous absence of small businesses that create entry-level jobs and economic opportunities for youths and young adults (2, 6, 7). Even outside of inner-city ghettos similar trends have had a great impact upon the lives of low-income people and families (8).

Multiple social crises continue to persist in employment, housing, family composition, and education—setting a framework for the patterns of drug abuse and use to be chronicled later in this chapter. During the 1970s, but especially in the 1980s and early 1990s, American cities experienced a continued catastrophic decline in manufacturing and other labor-intensive industries that provide unskilled "working-class" jobs with steady employment and low but adequate incomes. When and if new jobs were created, they tended to require advanced education or skills. Other new jobs tended to be in fast food or other service industries paying a near-minimum wage, which was far less than needed to live. The result was that many minority males, especially, were unlikely to have any legal employment and to become "discouraged workers" who were "out of the labor force" (2, 9). The end result has been the marginalization of working-class and middle-class people, white and minority, who have limited access to legal jobs, diminished income and purchasing power, little access to affordable housing, and little financial support.

By 1960, many structurally sound housing units provided low-cost housing to working families living in the inner city. While the costs of maintaining and renovating such buildings climbed, rental income or income for maintenance did not increase substantially. Therefore, large segments of the low-cost housing stock deteriorated or were abandoned during the 1960s and 1970s, particularly in inner-city neighborhoods (10, 11). In the 1980s, real estate values in most major metropolitan areas soared. Affordable housing was beyond the economic reach of much of the population (12), and funds for subsidized housing for poor and middle-income families were reduced by more than 90% in the 1980s (13, 14).

Important shifts also occurred in family structure, particularly among minorities. The proportion of African-American children living in mother-only families increased from 30 to 51% between 1970 and 1985. Almost 90% of African-American children will experience poverty if the family is headed by a single woman under 30 (6). Poor families headed by single women will likely be without adequate financial support for housing, so they must live with other relatives, in public shelters, or in very deteriorated buildings (15). Even when a household is maintained, several different family members, relatives, and unaffiliated persons may reside in or be "couch persons" who contribute little to and consume much of the minimal fiscal resources provided by public transfers for the household head and children (16, 17).

Many other crises also affect inner-city residents and low-income persons. High school dropouts rarely find employment, and even high school graduates are fortunate to find jobs paying much above the minimum wage (18, 19). Inner-city hospitals have closed or reduced services. Health care and preventive health clinic services have been cut back (20). Youth recreation and service programs have been reduced. State mental health institutions have released large numbers of clients into communities with marginal support services (21, 22). Child abuse and neglect have increased (especially since parental drug abuse has been defined as neglect). Transfer payments such as home relief, Aid to Families with Dependent Children (AFDC), and Supplemental Security Income (SSI) have declined in purchasing power. The nearly complete absence of public transfer payments to young adults (especially males ages 18 to 25) without child-care responsibilities systematically impoverishes those who cannot obtain employment or training stipends. Homicide has become a leading killer of young African-American men (2, 6, 23, 24).

These multiple crises at the policy and social level have clear negative impacts upon families, households, and individuals. Particularly in inner-city neighborhoods, virtually every household and family is affected by several of these crises. A sizable proportion appear to be severely distressed household family units (25, 26). In such households, income from legal employment is usually unstable and insufficient to pay for family members' rent, food, and clothing. Transfer payments are always inadequate. Only a few people in the family or kin network can support marginally adequate housing. Family or kin without housing or shelter descend continuously upon such households, sleeping and eating "free" to themselves but at high cost to the householder's marginal budget (27, 28). Youths growing up in such households have no place to study and little time or support to do so. Facing many distractions, they do poorly in marginal inner-city schools. The household head is frequently a maternal figure. She is likely to be a grandmother or older aunt to the children who either replaces or accompanies the birth mother. Economic contributions to the family by the children's father are rare. At various times, family members or kin experience serious illness, mental health problems, drug or alcohol abuse, jail or prison, child abuse or neglect, or death by injury or disease (17, 25, 26). A situation has arisen that socializes many people into a cycle of deviant behaviors, helps perpetuate learned helplessness, and maintains the disenfranchisement of poor people and their communities within the larger society.

While households with multiple problems are most numerous and persistent in the inner cities and ghettos of major American cities, households in all segments of American society experience similar problems. Usually such households have slightly more resources (income, family members, access to help) to resolve issues privately (7) or they need limited assistance from publicly-funded programs. The end result is that the majority of clients of most publicly funded social service programs have been socialized in households and family/kin networks that experience chronic exposure to the multiple crises described earlier. Such individuals themselves have many episodes with their multiple social deficiencies. As adults, they need "habilitation" rather than "rehabilitation" to establish conventional practices and behaviors and to acquire the ability to contribute to the legitimate economic system.

People living in or moving into inner-city neighborhoods of American cities in the 1950s and 1960s that have deteriorated into ghettos in the 1970s and 1980s have been at very high risk for, and at the forefront of, most of the drug-related issues discussed below and constitute the core of the drug abuse problem in America in the 1990s.

EPIDEMIOLOGY OF DRUG USE AND ABUSE

Illicit drug use is widespread. It shifted substantially in the 1970s and 1980s, continues in the 1990s, and can be easily projected to remain a major problem for the first 20 years of the new millennium. The following analysis provides a framework for analyzing the shifts in patterns of drug use. A *drug era* (29–31) may be conceptualized as a time-bound sociohistorical period in which a new drug or "innovative" mode of use (e.g., heroin use, or crack use as an innovative mode of cocaine administration) is introduced and adopted by large numbers of people; its use becoming institutionalized within segments of the population. A drug era has four major phases (31). First is the *incubation* phase in which some "pioneers" begin use, refine innovations, and develop relatively standard patterns of use and/or selling practices. The *expansion* phase occurs when the pioneers "initiate" or "turn on" larger numbers of users, usually those with other illicit drug use experience, to the new drug or mode of consumption; sizable proportions become very regular users. The *plateau* phase occurs when most of those at highest risk for becoming regular users will have the opportunity to do so, but have not become regular users, although a steady flow of new initiates (usually persons under age 20) continues. The *decline* phase begins when smaller proportions (than in previous years) of "high risk" neophytes initiate the use of the given drug or regular users reduce their consumption, thus reducing overall demand and limiting economic returns. Nevertheless, many persons who initiated during the first and second phases become such persistent regular users of that substance or mode of consumption that their use will recur over many years of their lifetime, even when younger cohorts do not become users of that substance. The behavior of persons coming of age, mainly between ages 16 to 21, are particularly crucial for understanding at which phase a drug era finds itself. The drugs which persons initiate and regularly use (as well as the drugs they avoid using) during their transition to adulthood may form a cohort of the most committed users of that substance, so

that the drug using and selling behaviors of that cohort can be traced for many years during their adulthood.

The following sections describe complex patterns and central findings from three decades of epidemiology to document four drug eras: marihuana, heroin, cocaine powder, and crack cocaine. Two relatively distinct literatures exist: (*a*) distribution of drug use and regular use in the general population or significant subsamples of the population and (*b*) patterns of drug abuse among small subpopulations which are at very high-risk for multiple social problems. While the two groups of studies are not easily joined, the most serious drug abusers are often not included in general surveys, and the trends are generally similar for both sets of indicators.

Drug Use among High School Seniors and the General Population

Since 1970, two major sets of information have been systematically collected and published about drug use in the United States. National household surveys have collected data from a representative sample of all households during intermittent years from 1972 to 1995. Since 1975, a nationally representative sampling of high school seniors has been conducted. While these sources systematically undersample people at highest risk for drug abuse, they include very large samples and provide the important trend information summarized in this chapter. Many publications and excellent graphics from these studies are published as government documents (32, 33) and are available via the Internet at http://www.nida.nih.gov/.

MARIHUANA ERA (1965–1979)

The evidence from both households and high school seniors shows marihuana use growing from less than 5% during the mid 1960s, expanding during the 1970s, peaking around 1979, declining substantially during the 1980s with a slight upturn in the mid 1990s. Reported lifetime use of marihuana in the household population increased from 19% in 1972 to a peak of 37% in 1979, and it declined somewhat to 33% in 1983 and 31 percent in 1994 (32). Current (within the past 30 days) marihuana use increased from less than 10% in 1972 to a peak of 17% in 1979; it has declined to 5% in 1994 (the lowest this figure has been since the 1960s) (32). Marihuana use among high school seniors has been approximately twice as high. Lifetime marihuana use increased from less than 5% in 1965 (33) to 47% in 1975, peaked at more than 60% in 1979, and declined steadily through the 1980s to 33% in 1992, but had increased somewhat to 38% in 1994 (33). Similar shifts in current marihuana use occurred: a quarter of high school seniors were current users in 1975; this rose to 36% in 1979 and has declined to about 12% in 1992, but increased to 19 percent in 1994 (33). Clearly, a declining proportion of high school seniors (many turn age 18) become and might remain current users of marihuana. Nevertheless, more than a third of American youths continue to initiate marihuana use before reaching adulthood, and a third to half of the lifetime initiates are current (and half of these are weekly) marihuana users. Thus, projections of trends from the 1980s and early 1990s suggest that marihuana use may continue to decline, but with perhaps modest increases, among both high school seniors and the household population, in the last half of the 1990s. During the 1990s, most of the marihuana users are likely to be those whose marihuana use began in the 1960s and 1970s and who persist in its use on an irregular basis.

A variety of other research shows that marihuana use became institutionalized and widespread among American youths and young adults in the 1970–1990 period. Longitudinal research (34–39) shows that sizable proportions of people who initiated marihuana use and became regular users in the 1970s have remained persistent users during the 1980s, especially those who have not settled into usual adult roles (e.g., those who remain unmarried, have no children, are cohabiting, have irregular or marginal employment, etc.). While probably half of current marihuana users do not use other drugs, the more regular the use of marihuana, the higher the probability of being a user of cocaine, heroin, and other drugs, and of selling marihuana or other drugs. Virtually all users of other illegal drugs also use marihuana, and daily marihuana use is common among abusers of other drugs (36). In short, marihuana is a common secondary drug (along with alcohol and cigarettes) used by most drug abusers. It is the most frequently used illicit drug among the nation's numerous intermittent and recreational drug users. Eras of use of LSD and other psychedelics, amphetamines, and barbiturates occurred parallel to the marihuana era, with important increases during the 1970s, peaking around 1979, and declining in the 1980s with negligible increases in 1993 and 1994 (33).

COCAINE HYDROCHLORIDE ERA (1974–1985)

As with marihuana, the use of cocaine (powder) hydrochloride was uncommon in 1965. Local, national surveys in the 1960s did not include questions about cocaine. In spring 1970, college students in the New York area were asked to report lifetime use of several drugs as high school seniors; this suggests that less than 1% in 1966 and 3.4% by 1969 had used cocaine or heroin; 7% reported cocaine use as college students in 1970 (38). Lifetime cocaine use in the general population grew from 3.3% in 1972 to about 12% in first half of the 1980s but declined to 11% in 1990 and to 10% in 1994 (32). The proportion of those who used cocaine in the past 30 days increased from 0.2% in 1972 to about 3% in the first half of the 1980s, but this declined to 0.7% in 1994 (32). Probably less than 4% of high school seniors or of the general population had any cocaine use prior to 1970 (36). Among high school seniors, the proportion of those using cocaine increased from 9% in 1975 to 17% in 1985, then declined steadily to 6% in 1994. Current cocaine use increased from 2% in 1972 to a peak of 6.7% in 1985, and declined substantially to about 1.5% in 1994 (33). Nevertheless, high proportions of high school seniors report that cocaine is easily available in their community. In short, while cocaine use remains widespread, the decline phase appears to be well underway among high school seniors and other young adults.

Most cocaine use among students and the general population (including middle-income and upper-income groups) involves snorting (nasal inhalation) of cocaine powder (39). Virtually all cocaine users are (or have been) regular marihuana users and regular consumers of alcohol. Longitudinal research has indicated that substantial proportions of marihuana users from the 1970s initiated cocaine use and became regular users in the 1980s (36). Relatively smaller proportions inject or smoke cocaine or crack (39–42). Particularly among white cocaine users, a variety of informal norms were followed to "limit" cocaine use by defining it as a "recreational" drug whose use was limited to weekends, parties, and social occasions (40–42).

Analysis of the heroin and crack eras, however, necessitate shifting from measures of use in school and general populations to analysis of patterns of substance use and abuse, primarily among low-income groups where such use patterns are most clearly established.[a] An especially important source of information about heroin and crack abuse among the very highest risk subpopulations is the Drug Use Forecasting (DUF) program (1987–present). This program interviews 350 recent arrestees each quarter in 24 cities across the nation; urine specimens are obtained from almost all arrestees and tested for 10 different drugs (43). DUF documents that Manhattan arrestees always have the highest proportion detected as opiate (heroin) positive and the proportion cocaine positive is usually among the highest in the country (44). That is, the magnitude of problems with heroin, cocaine, and crack abuse are the nation's most severe in New York City (as are the closely related HIV and AIDS epidemics). Several analyses of data from crack users and from DUF-Manhattan arrestees document (45–47) that shifts in drug use patterns (1987–1995) among arrestees in Manhattan have *not* been substantially due to changes in arrest charges, gender, ethnic composition, or ages; rather, shifts in drug use patterns have occurred primarily among specific birth co-

horts, which are interpreted in this chapter as representing differential exposure during ages 16–21 to different drug eras.

HEROIN INJECTION ERA (1965–1973)

Heroin has never become a commonly used drug among students or the general population; generally less than 2% report any lifetime heroin use, and less than 0.5% report heroin use in the past 30 days in most surveys (32, 33). Rather, the heroin era (and the crack era as described later in this section) has occurred primarily among inner-city youths in some large cities, and typically involves what may be termed "abuse" (very regular use on a near daily, daily, and multiple-times-daily basis). Moreover, the nature of heroin and crack eras is relatively specific to a given geographic locale. In the following discussion, trends are provided for New York City; similar heroin epidemics have been documented for other cities as well (48–51), although the precise years and indicators may not be as well-documented as for New York City.

Heroin was known among white ethnics and a relatively small number of jazz musicians prior to the 1950s. Heroin use began to spread among males in Harlem during the 1950s (52, 53). Among young men in Manhattan, heroin use increased from 3% in 1963 to a peak of 20% in 1972, and the decline phase began as only 13% used heroin in 1974 (54, 55). Among those who initiated heroin injection during this heroin era (born 1945–1959 and reached adulthood in the 1960s or 1970s), sizable proportions became addicted within two years. While less than half of these persisted for several years in their addiction (56), this heroin era cohort constitutes the vast majority of heroin addicts who are in their 30s and 40s in the mid 1990s. Persons addicted during this heroin era primarily consume heroin (often mixed with cocaine powder as a speedball) via intravenous injection. Figure 10.1 shows that among DUF-Manhattan arrestees born in 1945–1959 (these birth cohorts reached age 18 in 1963–1976 during the expansion and plateau phases of the heroin era), up to one third of these cohorts are detected as opiate abusers and over three-quarters of the self-reported heroin users claim any drug injection at their current arrest (in a DUF-Manhattan interview) conducted nearly 20–28 years later (during 1987–1995). In short, members of the 1945–1959 birth cohorts who have remained active as criminals (and are rearrested in 1987–1995), have among the highest proportions of opiate positives—their heroin use and injection patterns have persisted among this birth cohort for nearly a quarter century as they have become middle-age adults (57).

During the expansion phase of the heroin era, approximately 120,000 heroin abusers were estimated for 1970 and 160,000 for 1972 (58); statistical extrapolations to 1978 suggested a range of 140,000 to 240,000 (depending upon assumptions of inactivation rates). A conservative estimate would be 125,000 to 150,000 heroin abusers in New York City during the 1975 to 1995 period.

In response to this heroin era, the foundations of the current drug treatment system were established during the late 1960s and early 1970s. Methadone maintenance expanded from less than 100 clients to about 20,000 clients between 1965 and 1974; by 1975, the number of readmissions to methadone exceeded new (not previously known) heroin abusers (see Chapter 42). Most therapeutic communities were established by the early 1970s, as were most outpatient drug-free programs (59). Federal- and state-sponsored "civil" and "criminal" commitment programs begun in the 1960s placed heroin abusers in prison-like facilities with mandated aftercare programs. They were found to be very expensive, rehabilitated few, and were closed in the midst of fiscal crises during the 1970s (60). The criminal commitment program in California was modestly successful in interrupting runs of heroin addiction, but methadone treatment was more successful at reducing criminality (61, 62). The drug treatment system that evolved between 1965 and 1980 was focused primarily upon rehabilitation of heroin abusers. In the early 1980s, about three-quarters of those admitted to public drug treatment programs had heroin as their primary drug of abuse, but this was to change in the mid 1980s.

One piece of "good news" in inner-city New York's hard drug scene is that declining proportions of youths reaching adulthood after 1975 initiated

---

[a] The hard drug abuse problem has always been most severe in New York. Such abusers frequently were trendsetters and suppliers to the nation's Northeast. A variety of drug abuse indicators have been systematically monitored for three decades (58, 94) which are unavailable elsewhere. A wide variety of major studies of drug use and abuse in New York City and State have been conducted by several investigators (Denise Kandel, Ann Brunswick, Division of Substance Abuse Services, Bruce Johnson, Paul Goldstein, John Ball, and many others).

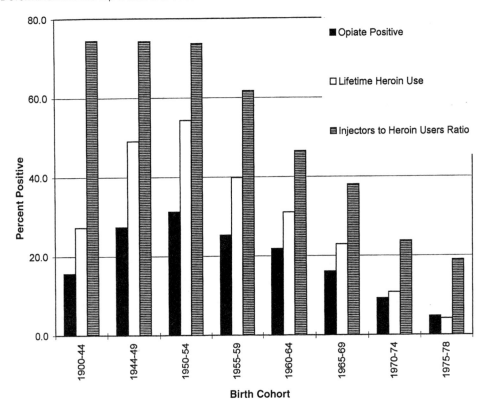

Figure 10.1.   Percent opiate positive, self-reported heroin use, and ratio of injectors to heroin users by birth cohort (Adapted using special computations from Golub A, Johnson BD. A recent decline in cocaine use among youthful arrestees in Manhattan (1987–1993). Am J Public Health 1994; 84:1250–1254.)

or became regular users of heroin; a definite norm against any heroin use—and especially against heroin injection—has become widespread among arrested persons born after 1970 (see Fig. 10.1). The proportion using heroin among younger birth cohorts has declined further and has remained low in the 1980s and 1990s. Thus, only about 9% of DUF-Manhattan arrestees born 1970–1974 (age 21–25 in 1995) are detected as opiate positive, and only a quarter of these heroin users report drug injection (e.g., they mainly snort heroin) at arrests occurring 1987–1995 (57). Compared to their counterparts 20 years earlier (e.g., those born 1950–1959 and who were often their parents), the birth cohort born 1970–1975 has "turned off" to heroin (or more precisely not "turned on" to heroin) and has developed strong norms against heroin use, and especially against injection drug use. The 1975–1979 cohort by 1995 is too young to have established clear heroin use patterns, but early indications suggest that they will be somewhat less likely than the 1970–1974 birth cohort to become heroin users and to inject heroin.

COCAINE AND THE FREEBASE ERA (1975–1984)

Cocaine snorting (nasal inhalation) became popular among increasingly larger proportions of nonheroin drug users in the inner city. From 1975 to 1983, cocaine gained a reputation of "status drug" that was relatively innocuous; large numbers of inner-city drug users were snorting cocaine when they could afford its high price in the 1970s. In New York, "after hours clubs" became a gathering place for cocaine users and dealers (42). By 1980, the number of cocaine powder sellers outnumbered that of heroin sellers by two to one. By 1984, 43% of all Manhattan arrestees tested positive for cocaine, while only 22% were positive for heroin; more than half of the latter were also positive for cocaine (63) and were probably "speedballers" (64).

"Freebasing" emerged on the West Coast (65) but began to spread in New York in the early 1980s. This process converts adulterated cocaine hydrochloride powder into alkaloidal cocaine or "free base." Cocaine freebase is not water soluble and cannot be snorted or injected. When the freebase is

heated at low temperatures and the fumes inhaled, the user becomes euphoric within seconds. The high from freebase lasts less than 20 minutes and is followed by rapid dysphoria in which the user feels worse than usual (28, 66). Rapid episodes of use recur. Freebasing became increasingly popular in New York from 1980 to 1984; many after hours clubs became "base houses" where cocaine could be purchased and someone would "cook it up" or "base it" (16, 67). Although some base houses were in transitional areas, most were located in minority low-income neighborhoods and run by minority owners (67, 68).

CRACK ERA (1985–1989)

In 1984 and 1985, New York officials saw dealers selling vials containing what users called "crack" (69–72)—also frequently called "rock" and sold in baggies on the West Coast. Crack is cocaine freebase packaged in retail form, typically a small plastic vial (about the size of a perfume sample) with a watertight cap. The asking price in 1985 was $20 for a standard vial containing several chunks of freebase. Prices, vial shapes, and the amounts in vials have dropped dramatically in the past decade with most vials selling for $3–5 in 1995 and containing only one or two small chunks of freebase (73). While the cost of a retail dosage unit is low, users typically buy several vials at a time or repeatedly return to purchase more within an hour or two. Multiple purchases and use episodes occur during a typical use day. The major limitation facing users is money to purchase crack (28, 67).

Crack use exploded during 1984–1986 in New York, Miami, Detroit, Washington, DC, and elsewhere, quickly dominating illicit drug markets in many inner-city neighborhoods (69–72). While the numbers of cocaine users apparently did not increase substantially, the evidence suggests that the relatively few regular cocaine users increased the frequencies of their consumption (73). While crack selling was based predominantly in inner-city neighborhoods and among minorities, crack use and crack sellers had spread to virtually all neighborhoods of the New York City region by the late 1980s (74). The history of the crack era in New York has been documented with some precision (31, 44, 73): the expansion phase lasted from 1984–1986, the plateau phase lasted from 1986–1989, the decline phase began in 1990 and continues through 1995. In particular, among DUF-Manhattan arrestees, the 1965–1970 birth cohort had the highest rates of detected cocaine use (over 60 percent) (45–47) and may be considered the "crack generation" in New York City. They were joined, however, by very sizable proportions of older birth cohorts that had equally high levels of detected cocaine use. This cohort of persons who initiated and participated in the crack era have had, and are likely to continue having, a substantial impact upon New York and American society.

The crack era contributed a major expansion of the existing drug abuse and sales patterns in inner-city communities (16, 75). Recent research (73–80) suggested several major findings about the crack era. Almost no drug neophytes "turned on" to crack as their first drug. The vast majority of crack abusers had prior histories of regular illicit use of marihuana or cocaine powder, and a sizable proportion were heroin injectors (77). Such drug abusers tended to "add" crack to their already existing patterns of drug consumption. Apparent remission to their "old drugs" probably occurred because they expended most of their funds for crack. Two-thirds of crack abusers consumed crack on a daily basis and more than half used crack four or more times daily; more than half of the crack abusers used more than $1000 per month of crack (75). By contrast, about a third of heroin injectors used heroin daily, but few used heroin four or more times daily. In short, crack was used more intensively (higher frequencies and expenditures, especially among daily users) than were heroin and cocaine powder.

Crack abusers were significantly different from other drug user subgroups on many dimensions. They generally had the highest proportions of people involved in and receiving high incomes from drug sales and other criminality. Among crack abusers, crack use greatly exceeded the cost and frequency of use of the other drugs that they also consumed. Crack abusers had higher frequencies of and cash incomes from other crimes (robbery, burglary, thefts, etc.) than did cocaine powder users. By 1988, crack had become the most frequently sold and lucrative drug in the street drug market (75). Crack selling became the most common crime and generated the largest cash income for all illicit drug user subgroups studied. Crack sales generated higher cash incomes than did the sales of heroin, cocaine powder,

or marihuana, or the commission of other crimes (robbery, burglary, thefts, etc.). Crack use did not greatly increase violence among drug abusers; rather, persons who were already violent (robbers, assaulters, etc.) tended to become crack abusers and spent large amounts on crack (85). Many people who became crack abusers between 1985 and 1989 were children of alcoholics or heroin abusers, or were otherwise abused or neglected in childhood (81, 82), and came from severely distressed households or families (16, 17, 25, 26, 83).

Overall, during the crack era, a substantial expansion in the number of daily drug abusers occurred. In New York City, a substantial majority of an estimated 150,000 persistent heroin injectors appear to have added crack abuse and sale to their daily activities. A relatively smaller proportion (probably less than 20%) of recreational cocaine snorters (who avoided heroin) have become crack abusers (39, 84). But since recreational cocaine snorters were so numerous, substantial numbers became crack abusers. While precise estimates are not available, the Committee on the Judiciary (84) estimates that New York State had 434,000 cocaine/crack addicts. This report estimated that 2.2 million people are cocaine addicts nationally; a Rand report (85) estimates approximately 2.5 million monthly or more frequent users of cocaine. Among reported daily users, most are crack users who consume the majority of the total volume of cocaine.

While thousands of people are seeking treatment for crack addiction, thousands more are being convicted of crack sales and sent to jail or prison (86–87), and many thousands more are on the streets at any given time. No treatment regime for cocaine or crack has been demonstrated to be effective in preventing relapse to cocaine for large proportions of dependent users (88). No long-acting cocaine derivative (like methadone for heroin) has been developed to prevent the rapid swings between euphoria and depression, although some new drugs and acupuncture may help alleviate symptoms (88) (Smith M. Personal communication. Acupuncture Clinic, Lincoln Hospital, Bronx, 1988).

Beginning in early 1990, a variety of indicators suggested that the crack era entered the decline phase and this has continued through the first half of the 1990s (45–47, 89, 90). The cocaine use patterns in Figure 10.2 somewhat conceal the incubation, expansion, and plateau phase of the crack era, because almost all of the heroin era and the cocaine powder era cohorts (e.g.,

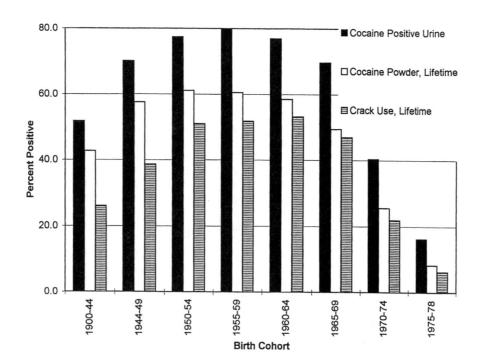

Figure 10.2. Percent cocaine positive and reporting lifetime use of cocaine and crack (Adapted using special computations from Golub A, Johnson BD. A recent decline in cocaine use among youthful arrestees in Manhattan (1987-1993). Am J Public Health 1994; 84:1250-1254.)

those born between 1944 and 1965) were very regular consumers of cocaine powder (either by snorting or injection as speedballs); almost all of these users also initiated to crack cocaine in 1983–1987; hence, their levels of cocaine use are nearly identical (or slightly higher) than that of the key birth cohort (those born 1965–1969); the decline phase was primarily ushered in by cohorts born after 1969.

Among DUF-Manhattan arrestees, birth cohorts born 1971 and later had decreased proportions who were detected as cocaine users. Specifically, while 78 percent of those born in 1968 (and turned 18 in the crack era) were detected as cocaine positive, only 45% of those born in 1971 tested cocaine positive (45–47). The vast majority of high-risk (e.g., arrested) inner-city adults under age 21 in 1986, but less than 10 percent of those born after 1974, were cocaine positive in the 1990s (45–47). Reversing a trend, the vast majority of high-risk inner-city adults under age 21 in the 1990s were apparently avoiding cocaine and crack; yet their counterparts only 4–5 years earlier were the core group who became persistent crack abusers and sellers. "Crack head" has become one of the most disparaging and stigmatized names on the streets (91). Some who were actively abusing crack between 1986 and 1988 appear to be desisting for longer periods of time (92, 93). Nevertheless, through the first half of the 1990s, it is clear that the cohorts (especially those born 1965–1970) who became key participants in the crack era will likely persist as crack users for a decade or two in the future. The major hope is that the cohorts born in the 1970s continue to avoid heroin, cocaine, and crack as DUF data from the 1990s suggest. At this point, available data suggest that no "new" drug such as methamphetamine, or consumption technique such a heroin smoking has "replaced" heroin or crack. No "new" drug era, therefore, is evident in New York City, although inner-city marihuana consumers now commonly place their marihuana into a tobacco cigar and smoke it as a "blunt." The period 1990–1995 might best be characterized as a "post-crack era" in which the three major drugs (heroin, cocaine, and crack) appear to be in a slow decline phase.

In addition to affecting patterns of drug abuse, drug sales, and nondrug criminality by users, the crack era had a substantial impact upon the drug treatment system, the criminal justice system, and the health care system. The major social response to crack has been primarily punitive—with substantial increases in arrests and jail or prison sentences (some with mandatory minimums), but with virtually no increases in drug treatment.

Impact of the Crack Era on Drug Treatment

Crack has had a far more substantial impact upon the drug treatment system than documented in the statistical data on drug treatment admissions (Fig. 10.3). During the late 1970s in New York City (94) approximately 25,000 admissions for drug abuse treatment occurred annually. Heroin was the primary drug of abuse for more than 90% of these admissions. In the early 1980s, the number of heroin admissions declined to about 21,000 in 1981 and 17,000 in 1983 to 1984. Between 1985 and 1994, however, the number of heroin admissions declined and stabilized at 11,000 to 14,000 annually. Heroin as a proportion of admissions declined from 81% in 1984 to 45%.[b]

Beginning in 1984, cocaine as the primary drug of abuse at admission began to increase substantially; it rose from about 2,000 in 1983, to more than 8,000 in 1986, to 11,000 in 1989 (surpassing heroin for the first time), to

13,000 in 1992, and to 12,000 in 1994–1995. Most of these cocaine admissions were for crack abuse. Cocaine snorters rarely applied for admission (92–94). These figures do not include the numerous cocaine and crack abusers with concurrent alcohol abuse problems who seek treatment at alcohol treatment programs or attend meetings of Alcoholics Anonymous and Narcotics Anonymous. Virtually all drug treatment programs indicate that they routinely cannot admit the many crack abusers who seek help. The need for crack treatment by crack abusers without heroin addiction greatly exceeds the available slots. At drug-free residential and outpatient programs, approximately 80% of admissions listed cocaine or crack as the primary drug of abuse (94).

Unfortunately, a decade of research has not developed effective treatments for cocaine. Scientific efforts to develop a cocaine antagonist (like naltrexone for opiates or antabuse for alcohol) or a long-acting substitute (like methadone for heroin) have had little success (see Chapters 16 and 17). Only a few crack detoxification programs have been established (81, 82), and these appear to have little or no measurable effect in preventing relapse to cocaine and crack abuse.

Hence, a crying need is for a new treatment approach that is even modestly effective in helping crack abusers "come off" crack and—most importantly—in preventing relapse to regular crack abuse. In the absence of such a new approach, a significant expansion of the treatment system is essential, but unlikely in the current political climate. Such an investment in crack treatment must rival the investment made by society in the criminal justice system to control crack abusers.

Impact of the Crack Era on the Criminal Justice System

Urine testing in several major cities documents the widespread nature of recent (within the past 48 hours) cocaine use among arrestees. The Drug Use Forecasting (DUF) project (44) shows that more than two-thirds of arrestees tested positive for cocaine at arrest in Manhattan in 1994 (the highest of 24 DUF cities). More than 50 percent of arrestees were detected as cocaine positive in several DUF cities including Atlanta, Birmingham, Chicago, Cleveland, Miami, St. Louis, and Philadelphia (44). In most major cities, a sizable majority of persons arrested for a variety of criminal offenses were positive for cocaine (the exact proportion due to crack cannot be determined). Cocaine and crack abuse and sales have been common among most criminal offenders in the 1990s (73, 74).

The public and politicians have demanded a harsh approach for crack sellers. In New York (as elsewhere), police have received funding to "crack down" on crack dealers. In New York City, Operation Pressure Point (1983–1986) was instituted to "take back" the streets from heroin and cocaine dealers (95). Tactical Narcotic Teams (1987–1990) consisted of roving squads designed to make numerous buy-bust arrests of dealers, especially crack sellers. Community policing (1991–1995) now focuses on drug sellers and "quality of life" crimes (like prostitution, shoplifting, and fare beating). The number of heroin arrests has increased from about 17,000 in 1987, to 24,000 in 1990, to 33,000 in 1994 (94). Cocaine and crack arrests nearly doubled from 28,600 in 1986 to 54,000 in 1989, then declined to 31,300 in 1993 with an increase to 38,200 in 1994. The total number of drug-related arrests went from 58,000 in 1986 to almost 90,000 in 1989. Such mass arrest strategies as a means of controlling drug selling remain politically popular, but the effectiveness of this strategy remains unresolved (95–97).

The arrests of thousands of crack sellers, however, has had a great impact upon the rest of the criminal justice system (98). At every stage in the New York criminal courts, persons arrested on crack sale charges from 1986 to 1988 were treated more harshly than were cocaine powder arrestees in 1983 and 1984. They were more likely to receive jail and prison sentences (99), although this discrepancy changed towards more equality in the late 1980s and early 1990s (100). Likewise, when compared with cocaine arrestees from 1983 to 1984, matched crack arrestees in 1986 were more likely to have higher rearrest rates for drug sales and some nondrug crimes in the subsequent three years (69–72, 100).

The most substantial impact has occurred within the correctional system.

---

[b] The proportion of heroin admissions is likely to remain high in New York, primarily because 23,000 treatment slots exist in methadone maintenance programs; this is half of all treatment slots in the city. Evidence of heroin abuse is required for entry, and heroin is routinely listed as the "primary drug of abuse." Since 1985, all methadone programs have had to contend with extensive crack abuse among their patients, especially persons seeking readmission (Magura S, Siddiqui Q, Freeman RC, Lipton DS. Cocaine use and help-seeking among methadone patients. J Drug Issues 1991;21:617–633). For many heroin-plus-crack abusers seeking methadone treatment, crack abuse may actually be their most intense problem, but methadone programs will list heroin as the "primary drug of abuse" at admission to satisfy the various regulatory agencies. If staff could truthfully record the client's "true" primary drug of abuse, methadone programs might admit more than half with crack as the primary drug of abuse.

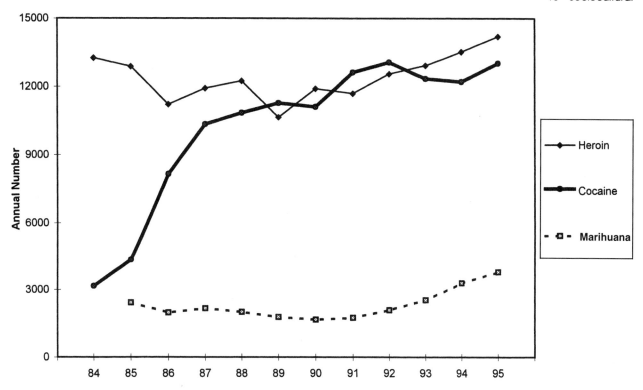

Figure 10.3. Trends in primary drug of abuse to drug treatment programs in New York City, 1984-1995. (Reproduced with permission from Frank B, Galea J. Current drug abuse trends in New York City. Community epidemiological trends in drug abuse: community epidemiological work group. Vol. II proceedings. Rockville, MD: National Institute on Drug Abuse, 1996.)

Most of the dramatic rise in correctional populations in the mid 1980s was due to convictions for drug sales (101–102), primarily crack. At year end, prison populations grew from 196,007 in 1969 to 301,470 in 1979 (103)—a 6% annual average increase—which grew to 462,002 by 1984—a 10% annual average increase—to 710,054 by year end 1989 and surpassed a million (1,053,738) by year end 1994 (104), an average increase of 8.7 percent annually since 1980. In short, the prison population more than tripled since 1980 and the imprisonment rate increased from 139 in 1980 to 387 per 100,000 U.S. residents (104).

The jail population increased at an annual average of 8% as well, from 163,994 in 1980, to 234,500 in 1984, to 395,553 in 1989, and to 490,442 in 1994. Over 1.5 million people were in jails and prisons at the end of 1994 (105). Probationers have increased from 1,086,535 in 1979, to 1,740,948 in 1984, to 2,356,990 in 1988 (106), to 2,900,000 in 1994, an annual average increase of nearly 7% during the 15 years. Parolees have also increased from 218,690 in 1979, to 266,992 in 1984, to 407,977 in 1988 to 510,000 in 1994 (106), an average annual increase of 9.6%. Moreover, the annual percentage increases accelerated sharply between 1987 and 1989, when more than 100,000 additional persons were added to each system: prison, jail, probation, and parole. More than 5 million persons were under criminal supervision or incarcerated in 1994, compared with less than 2 million in 1980.

Using the average annual increase during the 1980s to make projections throughout the 1990s for each system, the nation's prison population exceeded 1 million by year end 1994 (104) and will likely exceed 1.5 million by year end 1999. Assuming that the same growth rate in jail and prison populations occurring in the 1980s continues throughout the 1990s, more than 2.2 million people will be in prison and jail at the end of the millennium. In addition, projecting over 8% annual growth rate to the end of the 1990s, more than 5 million people are likely to be on parole or probation. Perhaps a significant downturn in crack abuse during the 1990s might slightly reduce the annual percentage increases in the criminal justice populations; however, social, economic, and political forces suggest that such "slowing" appears more unlikely in the 1990s than an "accelerated" increase in criminal justice populations.[c]

Much of the growth in criminal justice populations is due to convictions for drug crimes. The proportion of drug offenders rose from 8 to 26% between 1980 and 1994, forcing down the proportion imprisoned for violent and property crimes. Especially in federal prisons, the proportion serving sentences for drug crimes increased from 25 to 60% (101–102, 104). A careful analysis of this increase indicated that much of the increase was due to mandatory sentences imposed upon crack sellers possessing more than 5 grams of crack, almost all of whom were African-American. Indeed, the U.S. Sentencing Commission (107) recommended that penalties for crack sales be set equal to those for cocaine powder (where 500 grams must be sold to invoke five-year mandatory minimum penalties). In order to maintain the political appearance of being "tough" on crack sellers, however, both President Clinton and Congress voted to maintain the current harsh mandatory penalties for sales involving only 5 grams of crack.

In 1989, one quarter of all young African-American males were under criminal justice supervision (in jail or prison or on parole or probation); this figure reached one third in 1994 (108–109) and is likely to exceed 50% early in the twenty-first century. Most data show that minorities are disproportionately arrested and incarcerated for drug offenses. Popular support for the "in-

---

[c] The National Council on Crime and Delinquency (NCCD) (101–102) has been making prison projections since 1982 for eight (now 12) states; most of their projections have been underestimates, due mainly to the unrelenting passage of "tougher" laws that mean more time in prison for larger numbers of offenders. NCCD shows an annual growth rate of 13% for 12 states through 1994, a rate of growth more than twice the NCCD 1988 forecast. A less rigorous estimate based upon the 1978 to 1985 period with a 6.8% annual growth in the correctional population led to projections for year end 1994 with 157,000 less than the 1,056,738 figure (Johnson BD, Lipton DS, Wish E. Facts about the criminality of heroin and cocaine abusers and some new alternatives to incarceration. New York: Narcotic and Drug Research, 1986). More conservative projections have consistently been underestimated.

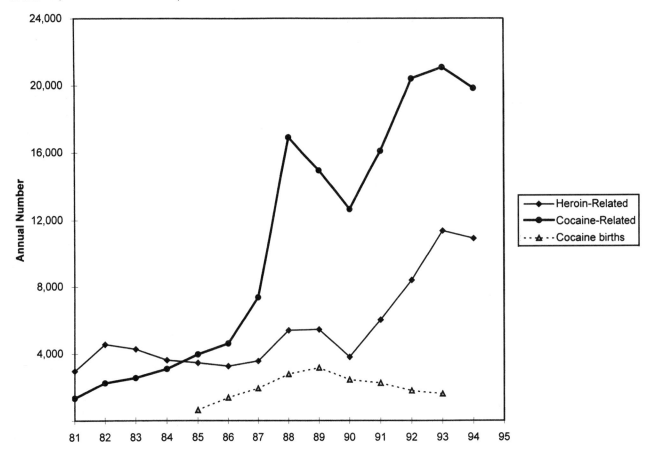

Figure 10.4. Changes in the number of heroin- and cocaine-related emergency room mentions and births to women using cocaine in New York City, 1981–1994. (Reproduced with permission from Frank B, Galea J. Current drug abuse trends in New York City. Community epidemiological trends in drug abuse: community epidemiological work group. Vol. II proceedings. Rockville, MD: National Institute on Drug Abuse, 1996.)

carceration" solution to the crack problem proved very expensive during the 1980s. In 1979, the nation's corrections (jail and prison) costs were about $5 billion; this rose to $19 billion by 1988 (110), a nearly four-fold increase during the 1980s. Given inflation and the rapid growth in correctional populations, the projected cost for corrections is likely to increase by four to five times during the 1990s and to approach $80–100 billion annually by the year 2000.

Impact of Crack on the Public Health System

Crack has also had a substantial impact on the public health and social service delivery system in New York City and elsewhere. Figure 10.4 shows that the number of emergency room mentions in New York for heroin declined slightly in the early 1980s and rose to about 5,000 per year in the last years of the 1980s, but has nearly doubled to over 10,000 in 1993 and 1994 (94). The number of cocaine-related emergency room mentions, however, increased much more drastically from 1324 in 1981, to 3,102 in 1984, and to 14,925 in 1989, with further increases to about 20,000 in 1992–1994 (94).

The number of births in which cocaine use by the mother was detected rose from 628 in 1985 to 3,168 in 1989 but has declined to about 1,700 in 1993–1994 (94). The number of children placed in foster care in New York City more than quadrupled in the last half of the 1980s. In many other areas of the public health system, crack abusers and their chronic problems have placed major strains upon all public systems.

The AIDS epidemic is directly linked to the heroin epidemic of the early 1970s. The numerous heroin addicts who shared needles and routinely went to shooting galleries in the 1970s and 1980s have become the major carriers and transmitters of HIV and AIDS (111). Thousands have died from AIDS-related illnesses, and possibly half of the heroin era cohort will not live to see their 50th birthday. Along the way, they will transmit HIV to their sexual partners and, among needle-using women, transmit HIV to their children (111) (see Chapters 59–62). In a similar fashion, increasing evidence suggests that cocaine and crack may decrease immune system function and increase the speed of dying from AIDS-related illnesses. Moreover, some new (and yet unanticipated) disaster like AIDS could possibly emerge among crack abusers within the next several years. In short, the public health consequences of the crack era are likely to continue in the future.

Local Drug Subcultures

The research data reviewed above for New York City and much other material indicate substantial variation in "local subcultures" of drug abuse. That is, every locality with significant numbers of drug abusers is affected by both macro level trends (e.g., the spread of crack cocaine) and by the prior histories and activities of local drug abusers and dealers. Local subcultures create their own unique patterns of drug consumption and argot, which may be rare or unknown in other localities.

For example, the New York City "local subculture" is unique in several ways. Many of the heroin abusers inject speedballs (heroin and cocaine in the same shot). Persons who only inject cocaine (but avoid heroin) are very rare. In the 1990s, heroin snorting (but avoidance of injection) has become common among persons seeking admission for heroin addiction (94). Likewise, in the 1950s–1990s, heroin addicts frequented "shooting galleries" where they "rented works," bought heroin, and shared syringes and drugs with total strangers. Addicts frequently shared their drugs and needles with other users in many other settings as well (16, 28). New York cocaine abusers were rarely good at "freebasing" cocaine themselves (67, 68); therefore, a few "chemists" freebased cocaine for others. Most now buy crack without ever having cocaine. Almost all crack is sold in small plastic vials

(73), rarely in plastic "baggies" (which are the common sales units for heroin and cocaine powder).

By contrast, the local subculture in Miami has relatively little heroin and few heroin abusers. Many heroin users do not inject it; speedballs are uncommon and shooting galleries are very rare. Drug abusers commonly engage in cocaine injections (but without heroin). Crack is known as "rock" and sold in baggies, not vials (112). Washington, DC, has a vigorous market in PCP ("angel dust") and a substantial proportion of PCP users, a drug rarely found in other major cities. San Diego has a strong market (and other Western cities a weak market) in methamphetamine—a drug that was unavailable in East coast cities as recently as 1994 (44). In each city, the local drug argot and terminology may be unknown to drug abusers and treatment staff in other cities. Even within major metropolitan areas, drug argot may vary substantially by community and ethnic group. Likewise, the extent and timing of various drug eras may vary dramatically in different cities.

CONCLUSION

This chapter has reviewed some of the broader sociocultural factors that influence drug use, abuse, and treatment within American society. Both clientele and drug/alcohol treatment programs have been harmed by "ghettoization." Since the 1960s, the continued growth and economic decline of inner cities in America as "separate and unequal" communities (1) has been due mainly to shifts in the economy and the persistence of multiple social crises: declining employment opportunities for low-income people; the shortage of, and rapidly rising costs of, housing and shelter; shifts toward less stable families; high rates of school dropout and difficulty in gaining advanced education; and a variety of other crises (declines in health care, youth services, transfer payments).

The persistence of these crises during three decades has had cumulative negative effects. Many families growing up in inner cities have been consistently battered by these larger social crises, and as individuals they have developed multiple social problems (unemployment, lack of permanent housing or homelessness, poor health, mental illness, incomplete high school education, lack of or few skills, little legal income, criminal activity, etc.). These many problems have been chronically present during their lives and crisis episodes occur regularly. These problems have seriously undermined the likelihood that such people will make positive contributions to American society.

Such multiple-problem people, having grown up in severely distressed households, were at high risk for drug use, abuse, and sales activity during the period from 1960 to 1995. This trend is expected to continue into the twenty-first century. While patterns of monthly marihuana and cocaine use occurred in many segments of American society, the abuse (near-daily and daily) of heroin, cocaine, and crack was particularly prominent among inner-city residents with multiple social problems. Initiation to addiction during the heroin era (1965–1973) in New York further exacerbated the multiple social problems present in their lives. When the crack era (1985–1989) exploded, numerous heroin abusers and cocaine snorters quickly added crack to their daily drug patterns and became even more regular (multiple-times-daily) users of crack. Many financed their crack (and other drug) abuse by engaging in crack sales or distribution. While the crack era may have plateaued from 1987 to 1989 and began to decline in the 1990s, many indi-

viduals and families have been badly damaged. Members of this crack era cohort now constitute a major segment of the inner-city community that has been seriously harmed by unemployment, homelessness, drug abuse, criminality, etc. These crack abusers and their descendants will prove to be one of the major problem populations confronting drug/alcohol treatment programs, the criminal justice system, and many other agencies in the 1990s. The 1990 census data show that half of the population of the United States live in large metropolitan areas (1,000,000 or more people). These data also indicate that minority persons are overrepresented in central city and metropolitan areas. For example, African-Americans account for 12% of the United States population and 57% reside in these areas; while only 26% of whites, who constitute 84% of the nation's population, reside in central cities and large metropolitan areas. Minority health issues and adequate access to care are growing in importance as they become an increasingly larger segment of the American population.

The disproportionate number of African-Americans and Latinos with HIV/AIDS is explained, in part, by their overrepresentation among injecting drug users and crack users. The data are not clear concerning the significance of other issues such as differences in drug use practice or general health status. It is clear that AIDS associated with drug injectors has a significant and disproportionate presence among African-Americans and Latinos.

Most of the "gains" (e.g., declines in drug use) documented by the national household surveys and high school senior surveys have occurred outside the inner city where the most severe drug abuse problems have been concentrated. As America moves into the next millennium, the prognosis for improving the prospects of inner-city hard drug and alcohol abusers is not good: almost all the social crises and factors in the American economy suggest that "ghettoization" is continuing. The number of multiple-problem people has apparently expanded due to heroin and crack abuse. Criminal justice approaches to crack have tripled correctional populations during a 15-year period from 1980 to 1995, but have had marginal impacts upon crime levels. Almost no efforts at substantial reform are underway as politicians battle to be "tougher" on crack sellers than other politicians (73, 113–114). Breakthroughs in treatment of heroin or crack abuse have yet to materialize. The past (1) has provided good insights about the general direction of the future since the 1960s. The already disastrous situation in the inner city could significantly worsen by century's end and in the first decade of the twenty-first century.

Acknowledgments. *This research was supported primarily by the National Institute on Drug Abuse grant for "Behavioral Sciences Training in Drug Abuse Research" (5 T32 DA07233–12), and in part by the "Natural History of Crack Distribution" (1 R01 DA05126–08) and the National Institute of Justice for "Changing Patterns of Drug Use and Criminality among Crack Cocaine Users" (87-IJ-CX-0064) and the Drug Use Forecasting Program (94-IJ-R-013). Additional support was provided by National Development and Research Institutes (formerly Narcotic and Drug Research, Inc.)*

Points of view and the opinions in this paper do not necessarily represent the official positions of the United States Government or National Development and Research Institutes.

The authors wish to thank Dr. Blanche Frank of the New York State Office of Alcohol and Substance Abuse Services for collecting, maintaining, and providing the epidemiological data on drug abuse for three decades; these data are included in Figures 10.3 and 10.4.

References

1. National Advisory Commission on Civil Disorder. U.S. Riot Commission report. New York: Bantam Books, 1968.
2. Jaynes GD, Robin WM Jr. A common destiny: blacks and American society. Washington, DC: National Academy Press, 1989.
3. Hughes MA. Concentrated deviance or isolated deprivation? The 'underclass' idea reconsidered. Report prepared for the Rockefeller Foundation. Princeton, NJ: Princeton University, Princeton Urban and Regional Research Center, 1988.
4. Ricketts E, Sawhill I. Defining and measuring the underclass. J Policy Analysis Management 1988;7(2):316–325.
5. Wilson WJ. The truly disadvantaged. Chicago: University of Chicago Press, 1988.
6. Gibbs TJ, ed. Young, black, and male in America: an endangered species. Dover, MA: Auburn House, 1988.
7. Sullivan M. Getting paid. New Brunswick, NJ: Rutgers University Press, 1989.
8. Sandefur GD, Tienda M. Divided opportunities: minorities, poverty, and social policy. New York: Plenum Press, 1988.
9. Larson, TE. Employment and unemployment of young black males. In: Gibbs JT, ed. Young, black, and male in America: an endangered species. Dover, MA: Auburn House, 1988.
10. Dolbeare C. The low income housing crisis. In: Hartman C, ed. Housing crisis: what is to be done? Boston: Routledge and Kegan Paul, 1983.
11. Hartman C, Keating D, Le Gates R. Displacement: how to fight it. Berkeley, CA: National Housing Law Project, 1986.
12. Tucker W. The excluded Americans. Homelessness and housing politics. San Francisco: Laissez Faire Books, 1989.
13. Downs A. Rental housing in the 1980s. Washington, DC: Brookings, 1983.
14. Sanjek R. Federal housing programs and their impact on homelessness. New York: National Coalition for the Homeless, 1986.
15. Smith JP. Poverty and the family. In: Sandefur GD, Tienda M, eds. Divided opportunities. Mi-

norities, poverty, and social policy. New York: Plenum Press, 1988:141–192.

16. Johnson BD, Williams T, Dei K, Sanabria H. Drug abuse in the inner city: impact on hard drug users and the community. In: Tonry M, Wilson JQ, eds. Drugs and crime. Chicago: University of Chicago Press, 1990;13:9–67.

17. Dunlap E. Inner city crisis and drug dealing: portrait of a drug dealer and his household. In: Suzanne MacGregor, ed. Crisis and resistance: social relations and economic restructuring in the city. London: University of Minnesota and Edinburgh Press, 1995.

18. Glasgow D. The black underclass. New York: Vintage Books, 1981.

19. Reed RJ. Education and achievement of young black males. In: Gibbs JT, ed. Young, black, and male in America: an endangered species. Dover, MA: Auburn House, 1988:37–96.

20. Health problems of inner-city poor reach crisis point. New York Times 1990(December 24):1, 24.

21. Bachrach L. The homeless mentally ill: an analytic review of the literature. Washington, DC: Alcohol and Drug Abuse and Mental Health Administration, 1984.

22. Hope M, Young J. The faces of homelessness. Lexington, MA: Lexington Books, 1986.

23. Brunswick AF. Young black males and substance use. In: Gibbs JT, ed. Young, black, and male in America: an endangered species. Dover, MA: Auburn House, 1988:166–187.

24. Dembo R. Young black males and delinquency. In: Gibbs JT, ed. Young, black, and male in America: an endangered species. Dover, MA: Auburn House, 1988.

25. Dunlap, E, Johnson BD. The setting for the crack era: Macro forces, micro consequences (1960–92). J Psychoactive Drugs 1992;24(3): 307–321.

26. Dunlap E, Johnson BD. Family/resources in the development of a female crack seller career: Case study of a hidden population. J Drug Issues 1996;26(1):175–198.

27. Johnson BD, Goldstein P, Preble E, et al. Taking care of business: the economics of crime by heroin abusers. Lexington, MA: Lexington Books, 1985.

28. Johnson BD, Hamid A, Sanabria H. Emerging models of crack distribution. In: Mieczkowksi T, ed. Drugs and crime: a reader. Boston: Allyn and Bacon, 1991.

29. Becker HS. History, culture, and subjective experience: an exploration of the social bases of drug-induced experiences. J Health Soc Behav 1967;8:163–176.

30. Musto D. Historical perspectives on alcohol and drug abuse. In: Lowinson J, Ruiz P, Millman R, Langrod J, eds. Substance abuse: a comprehensive textbook. Baltimore: Williams & Wilkins, 1992:2–14.

31. Golub A, Johnson BD. The crack epidemic: empirical findings support a hypothesized diffusion of innovation process. Socio-Economic Planning Sciences (in press).

32. Substance Abuse, Mental Health Services Administration. Office of Applied Studies. National household survey on drug abuse: population estimates 1994. Washington, DC: U.S. Department of Health and Human Services, 1995.

33. Johnston LD, O'Malley PM, Backman JG. National survey results on drug use from the Monitoring the Future Study, 1975–1994. Vol. II. Secondary school students. Rockville, MD: National Institute on Drug Abuse, 1995.

34. Elliott DB, Huizinga D, Menard S. Multiple problem youth: delinquency, substance use, and

35. Kandel DB. Yamaguchi K. Job mobility and drug use: an event history analysis. Am J Sociol 1987;92:836–878.

36. Kandel DB, Murphy D, Karus D. Cocaine use in young adulthood: patterns of use and psychosocial correlates. In: Kozel NJ, Adam EH, eds. Cocaine use in America: epidemiologic and clinical perspectives. NIDA Research Monograph no. 61. Rockville, MD: National Institute on Drug Abuse, 1985:76–110.

37. Yamaguchi K, Kandel DB. Patterns of drug use from adolescence to young adulthood. Sequences and predictors of progression. Am J Public Health 1984;74:668–681.

38. Johnson BD. Marijuana users and drug subcultures. New York: Wiley-Interscience, 1973.

39. Frank B, Morel R, Schmeidler J, Maranda M. Cocaine and crack use in New York State. New York: Division of Substance Abuse Services, 1988.

40. Zinberg N. Drugs, set, and setting. New Haven: Yale University Press, 1984.

41. Spotts JV, Shontz FC. Cocaine users: a representative case approach. New York: Free Press, 1980.

42. Williams T. The cocaine culture in after hours clubs. New York: City University of New York; 1978. Thesis.

43. Wish ED, Gropper B. Drug testing in the criminal justice system: methods, research, and applications. In: Tonry M, Wilson JQ, eds. Drugs and crime. Chicago: University of Chicago Press, 1990;13:321–392.

44. National Institute of Justice. Drug use forecasting 1995.. Annual report on adult and juvenile arrestees. Washington, DC: Government Printing Office, 1996.

45. Golub A, Johnson BD. A recent decline in cocaine use among youthful arrestees in Manhattan (1987–1993). Am J Public Health 1994; 84:1250–1254.

46. Golub A, Johnson BD. The shifting importance of alcohol and marijuana as gateway substances among serious drug abusers. J Alcohol Stud 1994;55:607–614.

47. Golub A, Johnson BD. Cohort differences in drug use pathways to crack among current crack abuser in New York City. Criminal Justice and Behavior 1994;21:403–422.

48. Hunt LG, Chambers CD. The heroin epidemics: a study of heroin use in the U.S., 1965–75 (part II). Holliswood, NY: Spectrum, 1976.

49. Rittenhouse JD, ed. The epidemiology of heroin and other narcotics. NIDA Research Monograph no. 16. Rockville, MD: National Institute on Drug Abuse, 1977.

50. Hunt L. Heroin epidemics: a quantitative study of current empirical data. Washington, DC: Drug Abuse Council, 1978.

51. Hughes PH. Behind the walls of respect: community experiments in heroin addiction control. Chicago: University of Chicago Press, 1977.

52. Brown C. Manchild in the promised land. New York: Macmillan (Signet Books), 1965.

53. Haley A. Autobiography of Malcolm X. New York: Signet, 1965.

54. Clayton RR, Voss HL. Young men and drugs in Manhattan: a causal analysis. Rockville, MD: National Institute on Drug Abuse, 1981.

55. Boyle J, Brunswick AF. What happened in Harlem? Analysis of a decline in heroin use among a generation unit of urban black youth. J Drug Issues 1980;10:109–130.

56. Johnson BD. Once an addict, seldom an addict. Contemp Drug Probl 1978;Spring:35–53.

57. Johnson BD, Thomas G, Golub A. Trends in heroin use among Manhattan arrestees from the heroin and crack eras. In: Inciardi JA, ed. Heroin in the crack era (in press).

58. Frank B, Schmeidler J, Johnson BD, Lipton DS. Seeking the truth in heroin indicators: the case of New York City. Drug Alcohol Depend 1978; 3:345–358.

59. Brecher EM. Licit and illicit drugs. Boston: Little, Brown, 1972.

60. Anglin MD, ed. Special issue: a social policy analysis of compulsory treatment for opiate dependence. J Drug Issues 1988;18(4).

61. McGlothlin WH, Anglin MD, Wilson BD. Narcotic addiction and crime. Criminology 1978; 16:293–315.

62. Anglin MD, Hser Y. Treatment of drug abuse. In: Tonry M, Wilson JQ, eds. Drugs and crime. Chicago: University of Chicago Press, 1990.

63. Wish ED, Brady E. Cuadrado M. Drug use and crime of arrestees in Manhattan. Paper presented at the 47th meeting of the Committee on Problems of Drug Dependence. New York: Narcotic and Drug Research, 1984.

64. Sanchez JE, Johnson BD. Woman and the drug-crime connection: crime rates among drug-abusing women at Rikers Island. J Psychedelic Drugs 1987;19:200–216.

65. Seigel RK. Cocaine smoking. J Psychoactive Drugs 1982;14:277–359.

66. Van Dyke C, Byck R. Cocaine. Sci Am 1983; 246:128–141.

67. Williams T. The cocaine kids. New York: Addison-Wesley, 1989.

68. Williams T. The crack house. Reading MA: Addison-Wesley, 1991.

69. Johnson BD, Golub A, Fagan J. Careers in crack, drug use, drug distribution, and nondrug criminality. Crime and Delinquency 1995;41: 275–295.

70. Brody J. Crack: a new form of cocaine. New York Times 1985 (November 29):1.

71. Kids and cocaine: an epidemic strikes middle America. Newsweek 1986(March 17):58–65.

72. Crack and crime. Newsweek 1986(June 16): 15–22.

73. Johnson BD, Dunlap E, Associates. Crack selling: The economy, "get tough" policies, and selling crack cocaine. New York: Cambridge University Press (in preparation).

74. Belenko S, Fagan J. Crack and the criminal justice system. New York: New York City Criminal Justice Agency, 1987.

75. Johnson BD, Natarajan M, Dunlap E, Elmoghazy E. Crack abusers and noncrack abusers: Profiles of drug use, drug sales, and nondrug criminality. J Drug Issues 1994;24:117–141.

76. Fagan J, Chin K. Social processes of initiation into crack. J Drug Issues 1991;21:313–344.

77. Fagan J, Chin K. Initiation into crack and cocaine: a tale of two epidemics. Contemp Drug Probl 1989;16:579–618.

78. Fagan J, Chin K. Violence as regulation and social control in the distribution of crack. In: De La Rosa M, Lambert E, Gropper B, eds. Drugs and violence. NIDA Research monograph no. 103. Rockville, MD: National Institute on Drug Abuse, 1991:8–43.

79. Fagan J, ed. Special issues on crack cocaine. Contemp Drug Probl 1989;16(4) and 1990;17(1).

80. Frank B, Morel R, Schmeidler J, Maranda M. Illicit substance use among Hispanics in New York State. New York: Division of Substance Abuse Services, 1988.

81. Wallace B. Crack addiction: treatment and recovery issues. Contemp Drug Probl 1990; 17:79–120.

82. Wallace B. Crack cocaine: a practical treatment approach for the chemically dependent. New York: Bruner/Mazel, 1991.
83. Dunlap E. Impact of drugs on family life and kin networks in the inner-city African-American single parent household. In: Harrell A, Peterson G, eds. Drugs, crime, and social isolation: barriers to urban opportunity. Washington, DC: Urban Institute Press. 1992:181–207.
84. U.S. Senate Committee on the Judiciary. Hardcore cocaine addicts: measuring—and fighting—the epidemic. A staff report. Washington, DC: Government Printing Office, 1990.
85. Rydell CP, Everingham SS. Controlling cocaine: Supply vs demand programs. Santa Monica, CA: Rand Drug Policy Research Center, 1994.
86. Division of Substance Abuse Services. Five year plan: 1984–1985 through 1988–1989. Fourth annual update, December. Albany, NY: 1988.
87. Ross RA, Cohen M. New York: State trends in felony drug processing 1983–87. Albany: New York: State Division of Criminal Justice Services, 1988.
88. Breaking the cycle of addiction. Science 1988; 241:1029–1030.
89. New York reports a drop in crack traffic. New York Times 1990(December 27):B1, B4.
90. Johnson BD, Dunlap E, Hamid A. Changes in New York's crack distribution scene. In: Vamos P, Corriveau P, eds. Drugs and society to the year 2000. Montreal: Portage Program for Drug Dependencies, 1992:360–364.
91. Furst T. The stigmatized image of the "crack head." Paper presented at American Society of Criminology, Washington, DC, November, 1995.
92. Rainone G, Frank B, Kott A, Maranda M. Crack users in treatment. New York: Division of Substance Abuse Services, 1987.

93. Simeone R. The problem of crack in New York: City. New York: Division of Substance Abuse Services, 1989.
94. Frank B, Galea J. Current drug abuse trends in New York City. Community epidemiological trends in drug abuse: community epidemiological work group. Vol. II proceedings. Rockville, MD: National Institute on Drug Abuse, 1996.
95. Zimmer L. Operation pressure point: the disruption of street-level trade on New York's lower east side. Occasional paper from the Center for Research in Crime and Justice. New York: University School of Law, 1987.
96. Kleiman MAR, Smith KD. State and local drug enforcement: in search of a strategy. In: Tonry M, Wilson JQ, eds. Drugs and crime. Chicago: University of Chicago Press, 1990;13:68–108.
97. Moore M. Supply reduction and law enforcement. In: Tonry M, Wilson JQ, eds. Drugs and crime. Chicago: University of Chicago Press, 1990;13:109–159.
98. Belenko S. The impact of drug offenders on the criminal justice system. In: Weisheit RA, ed. Drugs, crime, and the criminal justice system. Cincinnati, Ohio: Anderson, 1990:27–78.
99. Belenko S, Fagan J, Chin K. Criminal justice responses to crack. J Res Crime Delinquency 1991;28:55–74.
100. Belenko S. Crack and the evolution of anti-drug policy. Westport, CT: Greenwood, 1993.
101. Austin J, McVey A. The impact of the war on drugs. Focus [newsletter]. San Francisco: National Council on Crime and Delinquency, December 1989.
102. Join Together Policy Panel. Fixing a failing system. National policy recommendations. How the criminal justice system should work with communities to reduce substance abuse. Boston: MA: Join Together (Boston University School of Public Health), 1996.

103. Number of prisoners, jail inmates and probation and parole. In: Source book of criminal justice statistics. Washington, DC: National Institute of Justice, 1994.
104. Bureau of Justice Statistics. Prisoners in 1994. Washington, DC: Government Printing Office, 1995.
105. Bureau of Justice Statistics. Jail inmates 1994. Washington, DC: Government Printing Office, 1995.
106. Bureau of Justice Statistics. Update. Probation and parole 1994. Washington, DC: Government Printing Office, 1995.
107. Meierhoefer, BS. The general effect of mandatory minimum prison terms: A longitudinal study of federal sentences imposed. Washington, DC: Federal Judicial Center, 1992.
108. Mauer M. Young black men and the criminal justice system: a growing national problem. Washington, DC: The Sentencing Project, 1990.
109. Mauer M. Young black Americans and the criminal justice system: Five years later. Washington, DC: The Sentencing Project, 1995.
110. Bureau of Justice Statistics. Justice expenditure and employment 1990. Washington, DC: Government Printing Office, 1991.
111. Turner CF, Miller HG, Moses LE. AIDS, sexual behavior, and intravenous drug use. Washington, DC: National Research Council, 1989.
112. Inciardi JA, Lockwood D, Pottieger A. Women and crack cocaine. New York: Macmillian, 1993.
113. Reuter P. Hawks ascendant: the punitive trend in American drug policy. Daedalus 1992; 121(3): 15–52.
114. Reuter P. On the consequences of toughness. In: Lazear E, Krauss M, eds. Searching for alternatives. Stanford, CA: Hoover Institution Press, 1991:138–164.

11 ALCOHOL: NEUROBIOLOGY

C. Fernando Valenzuela and R. Adron Harris

Discussion of the effects of alcohol (ethanol) on brain function should begin with the chemistry of ethanol itself. Ethanol is a small organic molecule consisting of a two-carbon backbone surrounded by hydrogen atoms, with a hydroxyl group attached to one of the carbons. The hydroxyl group provides ethanol with its water-soluble (hydrophilic) properties, while the hydrocarbon backbone gives ethanol some of its lipid-soluble (hydrophobic) properties. Thus, ethanol has the capacity to interact with and dissolve into both water and lipid. Consequently, ethanol has been thought to produce its effects in the nervous system by acting on hydrophobic sites, hydrophilic sites, or both. However, several questions remain about the site and mechanism of action of ethanol in the central nervous system (CNS). Traditionally, many investigators believed that ethanol acts nonspecifically by perturbing neuronal membrane lipids. More recently, data suggest that ethanol acts by interacting specifically with membrane proteins, such as neurotransmitter receptors. In the past decade, attention has gradually shifted from the effects of ethanol on membrane lipids to its effects on membrane receptors and intracellular signaling systems. We begin this chapter by reviewing the effects of ethanol on membrane lipids.

EFFECTS OF ETHANOL ON MEMBRANE LIPIDS

The hypothesis that ethanol produces intoxication through perturbation of neuronal membrane lipids originated with Meyer and his students at the beginning of this century (1). These early studies compared the anesthetic effects of ethanol with other anesthetics in goldfish and tadpoles (2) and demonstrated that the effects of ethanol and other alcohols, as well as of other anesthetics, could be correlated with the ratio of distribution of the compound of interest between oil and water. The more lipid soluble the alcohol or anesthetic, the greater its potency in producing anesthesia. The correlation between lipid solubility and potency of the alcohol's *anesthetic* actions was interpreted to signify that cellular lipids were the site of alcohol actions (2). The later electrophysiological demonstrations of the importance of the neuronal plasma membrane in conduction and transduction of information in the nervous system (3) and the neurochemical modeling of the neuronal plasma membranes as lipid bilayers by Singer and Nicholson (4) promoted an extrapolation of the earlier correlative studies and focused attention on the neuronal plasma membrane as a major site of ethanol's actions in the CNS. The actual demonstrations that ethanol, in concentrations relevant to human intoxication (25–100 mM; i.e., 115–460 mg/100 mL), can produce measurable changes in membrane fluidity occurred only during the past 15 years (5). Studies using the sensitive physicochemical techniques of electron paramagnetic resonance (EPR) and fluorescence polarization provided evidence that ethanol at concentrations as low as 25 mM could increase membrane fluidity (6, 7) and that changes in membrane fluidity could be correlated with ethanol-induced anesthesia (8). However, the transition between correlation and/or extrapolation and causality in relating the phospholipid fluidization and/or disordering effects of ethanol to intoxication has not occurred. Although the abilities of alcohols and other anesthetics to fluidize phospholipid bilayers correlate well with their lipid partition (solubility) characteristics and, in turn, with their anesthetic potencies, Pang et al. (9) and other investigators (10) point out that such correlations can lead to erroneous conclusions. For instance, Franks and Lieb (11) have shown that inhibition of the water-soluble, lipid-free enzyme luciferase by anesthetics, including alcohols, correlates well with the solubility of these anesthetics in a lipid bilayer. Since luciferase is a lipid-free protein, it can be concluded that correlations between potency of action on a particular system and lipid solubility do not demonstrate a priori that lipids are necessary for alcohol's actions.

When further considering the membrane lipid perturbation hypothesis as an explanation of the intoxicating effects of ethanol, one also has to realize that the ethanol-induced fluidity changes in neuronal plasma membranes are relatively small. Anesthetic concentrations of ethanol (~100 mM) cause a 0.6% decrease in the order parameter measured with EPR. Subanesthetic concentrations of ethanol produce even smaller changes. Changes in order parameter induced by 100 mM ethanol can be mimicked by increases of temperature of 0.5°C (5, 12). Since such fluctuations in temperature occur daily in the course of normal human physiology function, a number of investigators have commented that ethanol-induced increases in membrane fluidity are simply too small to be pharmacologically relevant. For example, Pringle et al. (13) have stated that "until it can be shown either that some bilayer of different lipid composition, or that proteins very sensitive to small changes in (lipid) order, exist, the disordered lipid hypothesis must be regarded with reservation." It should be emphasized, however, that the possibility that a hydrophobic environment forms part of the site of action of ethanol cannot be ruled out. The reader is referred to earlier editions of this textbook (14) and to a review by Miller (10) for more details on the lipid theories of ethanol's actions.

EFFECTS OF ETHANOL ON LIGAND-GATED ION CHANNELS

Members of the superfamily of ligand-gated ion channels mediate fast synaptic chemical neurotransmission in the CNS (reviewed in Ref. 15). These channels open in response to a specific neurotransmitter and selectively conduct cations or anions to the intracellular or extracellular neuronal compartments. The anion-conducting ligand-gated ion channels are the type-A γ-aminobutyric acid receptor (GABA$_A$-R) and the glycine receptor. The cation-conducting ligand-gated ion channels are the nicotinic acetylcholine (nAChR), the glutamate, and the 5-hydroxytryptamine type-3 (5-HT$_3$) receptors. In the next sections, we discuss the acute and chronic effects of ethanol on the function of these ligand-gated ion channels and the involvement of these channels in some of the consequences of chronic ethanol administration, such as reinforcement, tolerance, and withdrawal. The reader is referred to earlier editions of this chapter for a discussion of the effects of ethanol on neurotransmitter turnover (14).

GABA$_A$ Receptors

GABA mediates the majority of inhibitory neurotransmission in the vertebrate CNS. GABA interacts with three types of membrane receptors. GABA$_A$ receptors are ligand-gated ion channels that selectively conduct Cl$^-$ and other anions to the intracellular space causing hyperpolarization. Five different GABA$_A$ receptor subunit families, each with multiple subunit subtypes, have been cloned. These families (and their subtypes) are $\alpha_{(1-6)}$, $\beta_{(1-4)}$, $\delta_{(1-3)}$, and δ. GABA$_B$ receptors are G protein-coupled receptors. GABA$_C$ receptors are also ligand-gated ion channels that are insensitive to classical $GABA_A$ antagonists, such as bicuculline, and are mainly present in the retina. Two classes of $GABA_C$ receptor subunits have been identified, p(1–2). By analogy to other members of the ligand-gated ion channel family of receptors, $GABA_A$ receptors are believed to be formed by five subunits arranged pseudosymmetrically around a central ion pore (reviewed in Ref. 16). Each subunit is believed to transverse the membrane 4 times, forming the M1–M4 transmembrane domains. These transmembrane domains are thought to form the walls of the pore. $GABA_A$ receptors can be modulated by a number of compounds including benzodiazepines, barbiturates, anesthetics, zinc, and alcohols (reviewed in Ref. 17). In this section, we discuss the acute and chronic effects of ethanol on $GABA_A$ receptors and the involvement of this neurotransmitter-gated ion channel in reinforcement, tolerance, and ethanol withdrawal.

Acute Effects

A number of studies suggest that $GABA_A$ receptors are targets for the acute actions of ethanol. The duration of ethanol-induced loss of righting reflex in mice is increased or decreased by $GABA_A$ agonists or antagonists, respectively (18, 19). The benzodiazepine partial inverse agonist Ro 15–4513 abolishes some but not all behavioral actions of ethanol; ethanol-induced low-dose anticonflict effects such as intoxication, consumption, and hypoactivity are abolished, whereas locomotor stimulation, hypothermia, and conditioned taste aversion are not (reviewed in Ref. 20). Pharmacogenetic studies with selected lines have also implicated $GABA_A$ receptors as mediators of the acute actions of ethanol. Mice have been selected for the duration of loss of righting reflex in response to acute ethanol administration. These selected mouse lines are the long-sleep (LS) (ethanol-sensitive) and short-sleep (SS) (ethanol-resistant) mice. These mouse lines not only differ in their sensitivity to ethanol but also display different sensitivity to drugs that modulate $GABA_A$ receptor function, such as benzodiazepines and anesthetics. Ethanol potentiates the $GABA_A$ receptor-mediated $^{36}Cl^-$ uptake in brain membrane vesicles from LS mice and $GABA_A$ receptor function in *Xenopus* oocytes expressing LS mice brain mRNA (21, 22) whereas it does not potentiate $^{36}Cl^-$ uptake in vesicles from SS mice and it inhibits $GABA_A$ receptors in oocytes expressing SS brain mRNA. Pharmacogenetic experiments with the alcohol-nontolerant (ANT) (alcohol-sensitive) and alcohol-tolerant (AT) (alcohol-insensitive) rats also suggest that ethanol interacts with $GABA_A$ receptors. These rat lines display different sensitivities to ethanol- and benzodiazepine-induced motor impairment (reviewed in Ref. 23). In the ANT rats, the cerebellar granule cell layer becomes sensitive to benzodiazepine agonists as a result of a mutation in the one-hundredth codon of the α_6 $GABA_A$ receptor subunit sequence (23, 24). This mutation could explain the abnormal benzodiazepine and the increased ethanol sensitivity of these rats. Other behavioral experiments with inbred strains and selected rodent lines suggest that $GABA_A$ receptors are involved in ethanol's mechanism of action in the CNS, and these are discussed elsewhere (25).

Functional studies with neuronal preparations also showed that ethanol acutely modulates $GABA_A$ receptor function. Ethanol was shown to stimulate GABA-mediated $^{36}Cl^-$ uptake into membrane vesicles purified from cerebral cortex and in cultured spinal chord neurons (26, 27). Ethanol also potentiates $GABA_A$ receptor function in cultured neurons from rat dorsal root ganglion (28) and spinal cord neurons (27). The potentiating effects of ethanol on neuronal $GABA_A$ receptor function appear to depend on the brain region and the species studied. Ethanol potentiated $GABA_A$ receptor function in some but not all cells from each region examined (hippocampus, cerebral cortex, cerebellum, and spinal cord), with mouse hippocampal neurons being more sensitive that neurons derived from chick or rat (29). Moreover, other factors appear to influence $GABA_A$ receptor sensitivity to the potentiating effects of ethanol; it appears to depend on many experimental variables such as temperature, length of incubation, incubation with $GABA_B$ agonists, and method of membrane vesicles preparation (reviewed in Ref. 20).

Electrophysiological studies using in vivo preparations also showed that systemic ethanol enhances GABA-mediated neuronal firing rates

(30). Other in vivo studies suggested that the effects of ethanol also appear to be dependent of the brain region examined. It was shown that ethanol enhances the effects of iontophoretically applied GABA in medial septal areas, inferior colliculus, substantia nigra reticulata, ventral palidum, and the band of Broca but not in the lateral septum, ventral tegmental area (VTA), and CA1 region of the hippocampus (31). However, other studies have failed to confirm these differential brain regional sensitivity of $GABA_A$ receptors to ethanol's effects. For example, Soldo et al. (32) found that $GABA_A$ receptors in slice preparations from both the rat medial and the rat lateral septum were sensitive to ethanol. Moreover, Weiner et al. (33) found that under conditions that increase protein kinase C (PKC)-dependent phosphorylation, hippocampal $GABA_A$ receptors in slice preparations are indeed potentiated by ethanol. More recently, Harris et al. (34) reported that null mutant mice lacking the γ isoform of PKC display reduced sensitivity to the effects of ethanol on loss of righting reflex and hypothermia and that ethanol did not potentiate $GABA_A$ receptor function in brain membrane vesicles prepared from these mutant mice. Consequently, the sensitivity of different $GABA_A$ receptor populations to ethanol depends on other modulatory systems such as protein phosphorylation. These factors appear to play a role in the ethanol-induced enhancement of GABAergic function in cerebellar Purkinje cells (35). Systemic administration of ethanol enhanced $GABA_A$-mediated inhibition of Purkinje cell firing only if the β-adrenergic receptor agonists norepinephrine or isoproterenol were concomitantly applied with GABA. One possibility is that ethanol potentiates $GABA_A$ receptor function only in receptors that have been previously sensitized via activation of β-adrenergic receptors, which activate cyclic adenosine 3',5,-monophosphate (cAMP)-dependent protein kinase A (PKA). It should be emphasized that phosphorylation may not be the only factor that determines $GABA_A$ receptor sensitivity to ethanol. In a recent paper, it was shown that microtubule depolymerization blocked the ethanol-induced enhancement of muscimol-stimulated $^{36}Cl^-$ uptake in stably-transfected cells expressing $\alpha_1\beta_1\gamma_{2L}$ $GABA_A$ receptor subunits (36).

The effects of ethanol on $GABA_A$ receptor function have also been studied by varying the subunit composition of the receptor. These studies have suggested that γ_2 $GABA_A$ receptor subunits might play an important role in ethanol's actions. The γ_2 subunit exists in two forms produced by alternative splicing, the short (γ_{2S}) and the long (γ_{2L}) forms. These two forms differ in that the γ_{2L} form contains an additional stretch of eight amino acids that included a PKC consensus phosphorylation site. Wafford et al. (37) reported that $GABA_A$ receptors expressed in *Xenopus* oocytes containing the γ_{2L} form, but not receptors containing the γ_{2S} form, were potentiated by low concentrations of ethanol. In addition, site-directed mutagenesis of the PKC phosphorylation site present in the eight amino acid stretch of the γ_{2L} subunit (serine 343) blocked the potentiating effects of ethanol (38). Consequently, it was postulated that PKC-dependent phosphorylation of $GABA_A$ receptor γ_2 subunits was required for ethanol's mechanism of action. The findings of Wafford et al. (37) were partially corroborated by a recent study with transiently transfected cells where it was demonstrated that the receptors composed of $\alpha_1\beta_1$ subunits are not potentiated by low concentrations of ethanol and that receptors composed of $\alpha_1\beta_1\gamma_{2L}$ subunits are potentiated by ethanol (39). This study did not compare the effects of ethanol on receptors containing γ_{2S} versus γ_{2L} subunits, and consequently, it was not confirmed that the γ_{2L} version is required for ethanol's actions. It should be kept in mind that other studies did not find a requirement of the γ_{2L} subunit for the effects of high ethanol concentrations. Sigel et al. (40) found that higher concentrations of ethanol than those used by Wafford et al. (37) produced a small but significant potentiation of GABAergic responses in *Xenopus* oocytes and that this potentiation did not require the γ_{2L} subunit. Anesthetic concentrations of ethanol (50–400 mM) have been shown to potentiate equally well $GABA_A$ receptors containing $\alpha_1\beta_1$ or $\alpha_1\beta_1\gamma_{2S}$ subunits (41). Moreover, Kurata et al. (42) reported that anesthetic concentrations of octanol produced a shift to the left in the GABA dose/response curve and that this shift was similar in cells expressing $\alpha_1\beta_2$ or $\alpha_1\beta_2\gamma_{2S}$ subunits. Consequently, the γ_2 subunit appears to be required for the actions of low, but not high, concentrations of ethanol on $GABA_A$ receptors.

Chronic Effects and Withdrawal

Several studies have looked at the effects of chronic ethanol exposure on $GABA_A$ receptor function (20, 43). Morrow et al. (44) found that chronic ethanol treatment caused a 26% decrease in maximal $^{36}Cl^-$-dependent chloride flux but only when animals attained blood alcohol levels $\geq$ 150 mg/100 mL. Sanna et al. (45) also observed a reduction in GABA-stimulated $^{36}Cl^-$ uptake in cortical microsacs prepared from rats chronically treated with ethanol. A reduction in $GABA_A$ receptor function after chronic ethanol treatment was reported with the use of electrophysiological techniques in neurons of the medial septal nucleus (31) and in *Xenopus* oocytes expressing brain mRNA (46). Moreover, behavioral responses to muscimol injections in the substantia nigra are also found to be reduced in ethanol-treated animals (47). However, chronic treatment of mice with ethanol did not affect basal and/or muscimol-stimulated $^{36}Cl^-$ into brain membrane vesicles (48–51).

The modulation of $GABA_A$ receptor function by drugs other than muscimol was reported to be affected by chronic treatment with ethanol. Both the direct effects of pentobarbital on $^{36}Cl^-$ uptake and its effects on GABA-mediated $^{36}Cl^-$ uptake appear to be reduced in microsacs prepared from animals chronically treated with ethanol (44). However, others found no change in the direct effects of pentobarbital (50, 51). In addition, other studies reported no changes in $GABA_A$ receptor function after chronic treatment with ethanol. Several studies have also failed to demonstrate an effect of chronic ethanol on [^3H]muscimol or [^3H]flunitrazepam binding to brain $GABA_A$ receptors (reviewed in Ref. 43), whereas other studies have found increases in binding of the type-I benzodiazepine ligand [^3H]zolpidem and of the partial inverse agonist [^3H]Ro 15–4513 in some regions of the CNS (43, 52). A more consistent finding has been that ethanol affects the coupling between the benzodiazepine and the GABA sites in the $GABA_A$ receptor complex. Chronic ethanol treatment has been shown to decrease *(a)* the benzodiazepine-induced enhancement of muscimol-stimulated $^{36}Cl^-$ uptake in mouse brain microsacs or stably-transfected cells (50, 51, 53) and *(b)* the benzodiazepine-induced increase of GABA-gated currents in *Xenopus* oocytes expressing brain mRNA (46). Conversely, benzodiazepine inverse agonist modulation of $GABA_A$ receptors appears to be increased by chronic exposure to ethanol (51, 54). Interestingly, $GABA_A$ receptor-mediated $^{36}Cl^-$ uptake was decreased in brain membrane vesicles prepared from benzodiazepine-tolerant mice, which also displayed cross-tolerance to both ethanol and barbiturates (55).

The effects of chronic ethanol on $GABA_A$ receptor subunit expression have also been the focus of intense research. It has been reasoned that cells chronically exposed to ethanol might attempt to restore homeostasis by altering the level of expression of membrane receptors. The chronic effects of ethanol on $GABA_A$-R subunit expression have been studied by measuring subunit mRNAs and/or subunit protein levels (20, 43). Some studies have found decreases in cerebral cortical α_1, α_2, α_3, α_6, and γ_{2S} and in cerebellar α_1 mRNA after chronic ethanol exposure. Others have found no change in the mRNA levels of cortical α_3 and both cortical and cerebellar β_2 subunits. Moreover, it was recently reported that chronic ethanol also affects the levels of α_4-subunit mRNA (56). Interestingly, mRNA levels for both cerebellar α_6 and β_2 subunits and for cortical γ_{2L} subunits have been reported to increase upon chronic ethanol treatment (20, 43). It should be noted that ethanol can also affect the function of $GABA_A$ receptors not only at the mRNA transcription level but also at the posttranscriptional and/or posttranslational levels. Klein et al. (53) demonstrated that chronic ethanol exposure affects the benzodiazepine/GABA site coupling in a fibroblast cell line stably expressing $GABA_A$ receptors composed of $\alpha_1\beta_1\gamma_{2L}$ subunits. In these stably transfected cells, $GABA_A$ receptor subunit expression cannot occur at the transcriptional level because subunit expression is controlled by an exogenous dexamethasone-sensitive promoter. Consequently, the effects of chronic ethanol on GABA/benzodiazepine coupling are likely to occur at the posttranslational level in these stably transfected cells.

Chronic ethanol administration results in changes in the function of the $GABA_A$ receptor-Cl^- channel complex and the N-methyl-D-aspartate (NMDA) receptor-channel complex that would be expected to promote ethanol withdrawal seizures by acting in concert. Here, we review the role of $GABA_A$ receptors on ethanol withdrawal, whereas we review the role of NMDA receptors below (see Glutamate Receptors below). Breese and his colleagues have reported that administration of the $GABA_A$ antagonist bicuculline into the inferior colliculus, but not the medial geniculate nucleus or the substantia nigra, produced seizures similar to audiogenic seizures in ethanol-withdrawn rats (49). These authors also reported a similar regional specificity in the ability of muscimol, injected into the inferior colliculus, to suppress audiogenic ethanol withdrawal seizures (49). More recent work examined the mechanism by which multiple withdrawals from chronic ethanol treatment facilitate the rate of kindling from the inferior collicular cortex (57). The authors found that multiple ethanol withdrawals increase seizure sensitivity in the inferior colliculus via a local decrease in GABA inhibitory function. A similar conclusion was reached by other investigators (58). Recent work by Peris et al. (59) examined GABAergic transmission in substantia nigra and superior colliculus in ethanol-withdrawn animals. An increase in GABAergic transmission in pathways connecting the striatum and substantia nigra and a decrease in GABAergic transmission in pathways connecting the substantia nigra and the superior colliculus have been postulated to play a role in ethanol withdrawal seizures. The authors found that ethanol withdrawal caused an increase in the number of $GABA_A$ receptors in the striatum, a decrease in [^3H]GABA release in the substantia nigra, and an increase in GABA release in the superior colliculus. Thus, for the acute effects of ethanol on $GABA_A$ receptor function, ethanol withdrawal appears to produce changes in GABAergic neurotransmission that are brain region-dependent. These studies, as well as earlier work indicating that $GABA_A$ agonists, can suppress ethanol withdrawal seizures (60–62), support the hypothesis that subsensitivity of the $GABA_A$ receptor-Cl^- channel complex in certain brain areas, which may occur as an adaptive response of the system to chronic stimulation by ethanol, contributes to ethanol withdrawal seizures.

Tolerance

The function of the $GABA_A$ receptor-Cl^- channel complex in the brains of animals treated chronically with ethanol appears to become resistant to the acute effect of $GABA_A$ agonists, benzodiazepines, and ethanol. Buck and Harris (46) reported that chronic in vitro exposure to ethanol (50 mM, 2–4 days) of *Xenopus* oocytes expressing mouse brain mRNA resulted in a selective decrease in response to muscimol (see previous section for details). A number of behavioral studies also indicate a decreased response to $GABA_A$ agonists in animals that have been chronically treated with ethanol (e.g., motor incoordination, locomotor activity) (19, 47, 63). Moreover, Volkow et al. (64, 65) demonstrated that recently detoxified alcoholic subjects display abnormal lorazepam-induced responses in brain glucose metabolism as measured by positron emission tomography and [^{18}F]fluorodeoxyglucose. Consequently, chronic ethanol treatment affects the sensitivity of $GABA_A$ receptors not only to agonists for the GABA-binding site but also to agonists for the benzodiazepine-binding site.

In addition to changes in sensitivity to GABA agonists and benzodiazepines (cross-tolerance or heterologous desensitization) produced by chronic alcohol exposure, there is also evidence for a rapid tolerance to the actions of ethanol. For example, consumption of ethanol for 1 week resulted in complete tolerance to the enhancing action of ethanol on $GABA_A$ receptor function measured in vitro (48). Furthermore, this tolerance developed rapidly, as it was detected following a single injection of ethanol (48). Thus, a decreased modulation of the $GABA_A$ receptor by ethanol may be one mechanism underlying the "acute" or "rapid" tolerance that develops to ethanol actions in vivo.

A most interesting observation regarding the role of changes in the characteristics of the $GABA_A$ receptor in ethanol tolerance is the recent finding that a single injection of the benzodiazepine antagonist Ro 15-1788 (flumazenil) reversed tolerance, measured at 24 hours after a single ethanol injection, to ethanol-induced motor incoordination (but not hypothermia) (66). This effect was observed whether flumazenil was given 26 or 2 hours before the second injection of ethanol. Similarly, flumazenil was reported to reverse tolerance to the anticonflict (anxiolytic) action of ethanol (67). It was suggested that the maintenance of tolerance to certain effects of ethanol (those thought to be mediated by the GABA$_A$ receptor-channel complex) might depend on the occupation of benzodiazepine receptors by an endogenous agonist and that brief exposure to the benzodiazepine antagonist might "reset" the mechanisms that maintain tolerance (66). Similar results and conclusions were recently put forward by June et al. (68).

Reinforcement

The possible links between ethanol's effects on this neurotransmitter system and ethanol-induced reinforcement and/or alcohol abuse is derived from two types of behavioral pharmacology studies. The first type of study examined the effects of GABA receptor-related ligands in ethanol discrimination paradigms, and the second type of study examined the effects of GABA receptor agonists and antagonists on voluntary ethanol ingestion. Experiments with drug discrimination use animals that are trained by operant methods to respond in a particular manner (press a specific lever) in the presence of a drug stimulus and to respond on an alternative lever in the absence of the specific drug stimulus. It is assumed that drugs can change the subjective state of the animal and generate interoceptive cues that act as the discriminative stimulus. As Johanson (69) has stated, "drugs of abuse . . . produce changes in subjective state[,] and to the extent that these changes are related to their abuse, drug discrimination procedures may be useful for predicting the dependence potential of drugs."

Rees and Balster (70) trained mice to discriminate an injection of ethanol, pentobarbital, or the benzodiazepine oxazepam from an injection of saline (vehicle). They then tested whether the benzodiazepine partial inverse agonist Ro 15-4513 could alter the subjective effects of these three drugs in the animals. Ro 15-4513 was shown to block the ability of an animal to discriminate ethanol; i.e., ethanol-trained animals given a combination of ethanol and Ro 15-4513 responded primarily on the lever associated with saline administration. The discriminative stimulus properties of oxazepam were also antagonized by Ro 15-4513, but Ro 15-4513 failed to antagonize the discriminative properties of pentobarbital. These results indicate that the subjective, interoceptive cues produced by ethanol administration might mimic more closely the cues produced by benzodiazepines as compared with pentobarbital. It is also of interest that Ro 15-4513 was less effective in reversing the biochemical effects of pentobarbital at the GABA receptor-Cl$^-$ channel complex (71), compared with its ability to reverse ethanol's actions at this receptor-ionophore complex. Both the biochemical and behavioral studies indicate that a significant component of the interoceptive cues associated with ethanol ingestion may depend on ethanol's actions at the GABA receptor-Cl$^-$ channel complex. A number of other pharmacological agents such as naloxone and propranolol (72) have not been able to antagonize the discriminative stimulus properties of ethanol, thus indicating the select importance of the GABA receptor-Cl$^-$ channel system. However, as is discussed in a later section, antagonists acting at the 5-HT$_3$ receptor also effectively block the discriminative stimulus properties of ethanol.

Studies of GABA receptor-active agents on voluntary ethanol ingestion have focused on the effects of benzodiazepine receptor antagonists and partial inverse agonists. Samson et al. (73) used a procedure in which rats were allowed to lever press for access to oral doses of ethanol or sucrose. After a stable response level was obtained during a limited daily period of access to ethanol or sucrose, the animals were injected with GABA receptor modulators prior to being given access to the ethanol or sucrose. The benzodiazepine receptor antagonist Ro 15–1788 produced no visible effect on the animals' lever pressing for the ethanol reward. The benzodiazepine partial inverse agonists Ro 15-4513 and FG-7142 both produced a dose-dependent decrease in lever pressing for ethanol. When the antagonist (Ro 15-1788) and the partial inverse agonist (Ro 15-4513) were administered together, the antagonist blocked the actions of Ro 15-4513 (i.e., the Ro 15-4513-induced decrease in lever pressing for ethanol was blocked by Ro 15-1788). This type of antagonism of the effects of Ro 15-4513 bespeaks benzodiazepine receptor-specific effects of Ro 15-4513 on ethanol self-administration. Care must be exercised in interpreting the neurochemical specificity of such studies, since the proconvulsant effects of the benzodiazepine receptor inverse ago-

nists may produce a general malaise that would be reflected in diminished responding for any reinforcer. The benzodiazepine receptor antagonist would, of course, reverse the malaise and restore responding. Interestingly, however, in the studies of Samson et al. (73), the responding for sucrose reinforcement was undiminished by Ro 15-4513.

Ro 15-4513 has also been shown to decrease the consumption of ethanol in a two-bottle choice situation in which the rats can select either ethanol solution or water (74, 75). Low doses of Ro 15-4513 (0.375–3.0 mg/kg intraperitoneally) reduced responses for ethanol, whereas high doses (6.0 mg/kg intraperitoneally) reduced both ethanol and water responses. Self-administration to saccharin in a similar free-choice paradigm was unaffected by Ro 15-4513, suggesting that the effects of the GABA$_A$/benzodiazepine receptor inverse agonist do not generalize to other reinforcers. Moreover, low doses of a GABA$_A$ receptor antagonist (isopropylbicyclophosphate, a picrotoxin-type ligand) selectively blocked responses to ethanol. In some of these experiments, both randomly bred rats and rats selected for ethanol preference showed qualitatively similar responses. The pattern of effects of Ro 15-4513 and Ro 15-1788 on the quantities of ethanol ingested by the experimental animals was quite similar to what was witnessed in the studies of Samson et al. (73). In addition, another benzodiazepine receptor inverse agonist (Ro 19–4603) reduced voluntary ethanol consumption by the Sardinian ethanol-preferring rats (76) and in the alcohol-preferring (P) rats (77). Thus, the importance of the GABA receptor-Cl$^-$ channel system in the reinforcing effects of ethanol is beginning to emerge from the results of the current studies and should be given further serious consideration. However, it should be kept in mind that interactions between GABAergic and dopaminergic systems might be important for the reinforcing effects of ethanol (78). These effects of ethanol are discussed below in the section on dopamine receptors.

Glycine Receptors

Glycine is the major inhibitory neurotransmitter in the spinal cord and brainstem and is also found in most brain regions. Like GABA$_A$ receptors, glycine receptors are Cl$^-$-conducting channels that belong to the superfamily of ligand-gated ion channels. These glycine receptors are also termed "strychnine-sensitive" receptors because they are inhibited by strychnine and to distinguish them from glycine-binding sites on NMDA receptors that are not affected by strychnine. Two types of glycine receptor subunits, α and β, have been cloned, and four subtypes of α subunits (α_{1-4}) have been identified (reviewed in Ref. 79).

Like GABA$_A$ receptors, glycine receptors also appear to be modulated by ethanol. It was reported that injection of glycine enhanced the ethanol-induced loss of righting reflex in mice (80). Celentano et al. (81) demonstrated that ethanol (50 mM) caused a persistent increase in the sensitivity to glycine of cultured chick spinal cord neurons, and Engblom and Åkerman (82) found that ethanol directly stimulated chloride fluxes through glycine receptors in synaptoneurosomes in the absence of glycine. Recently, it has been reported than ethanol (40 mM) potentiates glycine-activated Cl$^-$ currents in cultured mouse hippocampal and spinal cord neurons (83) and in *Xenopus* oocytes expressing homomeric receptors composed of α_1 or α_2 glycinergic subunits (84). Interestingly, receptors composed of α_1 subunits were more sensitive to ethanol than receptors composed of α_2 subunits, and a single amino acid mutation in the amino terminal segment of the α_1 subunit (alanine 52 to serine) decreased the sensitivity of α_1-containing receptors to the same level as α_2-containing receptors (84). More recent work showed that the "cut off" for the effect of long-chain alcohols on glycine receptors is between decanol and dodecanol (85). Although more work is required to understand the role of glycine receptors in ethanol's mechanism of action, these studies suggest that the function of glycine-gated ion channels is enhanced by alcohol.

Glutamate Receptors

Glutamate and aspartate are the neurotransmitters that mediate the majority of excitatory synaptic neurotransmission in the mammalian CNS. These neurotransmitters bind to a family of receptors that can be divided into two main categories. The first category of glutamate receptors comprises the

NMDA- and non-NMDA-gated ion channels. Non-NMDA receptors can be subdivided into amino-3-hydroxy-5-methyl-4-isoxazolepropionic acid (AMPA) and kainate receptors. Glutamate-gated ion channels conduct Ca^{2+} and Na^+ into the cell and K^+ from the cell. In addition to glutamate (or NMDA), glycine is required as a "co-agonist." In contrast to the glycine-binding sites on glycine receptors, the NMDA receptor glycine-binding sites are strychnine-insensitive. NMDA channels are blocked by Mg^{2+} in a voltage-sensitive manner. Two main classes of NMDA receptor subunits have been cloned (NR1 and NR2); each has several splice variants. Nine non-NMDA receptor subunit subtypes have been cloned (GluR 1–7 and KA 1–2). GluR 1–4 subunits are considered to belong to the AMPA subtype of non-NMDA receptors, whereas the GluR 5–7 and KA 1–2 subunit subtypes are considered to belong to the kainate subtypes. The second main category of glutamate receptors consists of the metabotropic glutamate receptors, which are coupled to G protein signal transduction systems. The following discussion focuses on the effects of ethanol on the glutamate-gated ion channels.

NMDA RECEPTORS

Acute Effects

Behavioral studies suggested that ethanol inhibits NMDA receptor function. Ethanol was shown to reduce NMDA-induced convulsions (86, 87) and NMDA-induced hyperalgesia in rodents (88). Moreover, duration of loss of righting reflex in mice injected intraperitoneally with ethanol was greatly increased by NMDA antagonists (89, 90), and noncompetitive antagonists of NMDA receptors produced ethanol-like effects in rats trained to discriminate ethanol from vehicle (91). NMDA receptor agonists decreased sensitivity to ethanol, whereas antagonists increased sensitivity to the hypnotic effects of ethanol in both LS and SS mice. SS mice were more sensitive to the effects of the antagonist dizocilpine than were LS mice (92).

Biochemical and electrophysiological studies also showed that ethanol acutely inhibits NMDA receptor function. Ethanol produced a dose-dependent inhibition of NMDA-stimulated $^{45}Ca^{2+}$ uptake in rat cerebellar granule cells and in dissociated brain cells from newborn rats (93–95) and of glutamate-stimulated cyclic guanosine monophosphate (cGMP) production (93). Ethanol inhibited NMDA-stimulated release of endogenous dopamine and norepinephrine in rat brain slices (96, 97), and inhibited NMDA-stimulated nitric oxide production in rat cortical cultures in the presence of Mg^{2+} or Zn^{2+} (98). Moreover, ethanol inhibited NMDA-induced currents in rat hippocampal neurons and acutely dissociated adult rat dorsal root ganglia (99–100) and increased the frequency of channel openings (at 1.7–8.6 mM ethanol) or decreased open channel probability and mean open time (at >86 mM ethanol) in cultured rat hippocampal neurons (101). Ethanol also inhibited NMDA-dependent excitatory postsynaptic potentials in adult rat hippocampal slices (102, 103). Ethanol inhibited NMDA-gated currents in Xenopus oocytes expressing hippocampal or cerebellar rat brain mRNA (104). Experiments with recombinant receptors expressed in Xenopus oocytes demonstrated that ethanol inhibits NMDA receptors in a manner that is dependent of subunit composition and phosphorylation factors. Differentially spliced variants of NMDA receptor NR1 subunits vary in their sensitivity to ethanol (105), and heteromeric NMDA receptors containing NR1/2A or NR1/2B subunits are more sensitive to the inhibitory actions of ethanol than receptors containing NR1/2C or NR1/2D subunits (106–108). In addition to subunit composition, recent evidence suggests that other factors such as protein kinase C-dependent phosphorylation might modulate the sensitivity of NMDA receptors to ethanol (109).

The NMDA (and non-NMDA (see below)) receptors are intimately involved in the acquisition of long-term synaptic potentiation (LTP), an electrophysiologically measured phenomenon that is a model for learning and memory in the nervous system (110, 111). LTP has mainly been studied in the hippocampus where it can be induced by several experimental paradigms including stimulation with brief, high-frequency trains of stimuli delivered to certain neuronal pathways; these stimuli induce a sustained enhancement of synaptic responses (112). The mechanisms underlying the induction, expression, and maintenance of LTP are poorly understood. As pointed out by Gozlan et al. (111), "This is probably due to the fact that LTP is not a unique process and indeed recent studies have shown that several forms of LTP could be generated depending on the experimental conditions." The effects of ethanol on LTP have been studied by several laboratories. Morrisett and Swartzwelder (113) found that LTP induced by θ-like stimulation in the perforant path-dentate gyrus was completely antagonized by ethanol. The authors concluded that the effects of ethanol were primarily due to an action at NMDA receptors. Ripley and Little (114) found that the Ca^{2+} channel blocker nitrendipine prevents the decrease caused by chronic ethanol intake in the maintenance of tetanic long-term potentiation in mice. Wayner et al. (115) demonstrated that acute administration of ethanol and/or diazepam inhibited hippocampal LTP and that this effect can be blocked by the angiotensin II receptor antagonists saralasin and losartan. Therefore, it appears that the effects of ethanol on LTP may be mediated in part by angiotensin II and/or angiotensin II type-1 receptors and Ca^{2+} channels. Taken together, these studies suggest that ethanol affects LTP; consequently, they offer an attractive explanation for some of the cognitive effects of ethanol.

Chronic Effects and Withdrawal

NMDA receptors appear to adapt to the initial ethanol-induced inhibition of their function with an upregulation that ultimately leads to increased function. In mice that were fed ethanol chronically (7 days), the number of hippocampal-binding sites for the noncompetitive NMDA antagonist, dizocilpine (MK-801) was significantly increased (116). This ligand binds to a site within the NMDA receptor-coupled ion channel, and its binding is thought to reflect the number of NMDA receptor-channel complexes. Autoradiographic analysis indicated that dizocilpine binding was also increased in several other brain regions of ethanol-fed mice (117). Membrane-binding investigations have demonstrated an increase in NMDA-specific glutamate binding in the hippocampus of ethanol-fed mice (118), similar to the previously reported increase in glutamate binding in brain membranes of rats treated chronically with ethanol (119). However, there was no change in the binding of glycine to the strychnine-insensitive site in hippocampal membranes of ethanol-fed mice (118). Recent work by Hu and Ticku has confirmed that chronic ethanol increases the specific binding of dizocilpine in a cortical membrane preparation (120). The same group also demonstrated that chronic ethanol caused an increase in NMDA receptor NR2A and NR2B subunits in hippocampus and cerebral cortex but did not affect the levels of NR1 subunits. Consequently, it is possible that chronic ethanol treatment differentially affects the upregulation of NMDA receptor subunits in some regions of the CNS and that this change is reflected in the alterations in ligand binding to the receptor. Alternatively, the NMDA receptor-binding results could indicate a change in the sensitivity of the system to glycine, which is known to increase glutamate and dizocilpine binding (121). It is not clear at present whether the upregulation of the NMDA receptor-channel complex represents an adaptive response to inhibition of the system by ethanol. Support for this postulate comes from a study in which chronic phencyclidine (PCP) (another inhibitor of NMDA receptor function) treatment was also reported to result in an increase in binding in the brain of a ligand that binds to the PCP site (122). However, in another study, in which animals were given repeated injections of dizocilpine, there was no change in PCP binding, although there was a decrease in binding of a competitive inhibitor at the NMDA receptor (123).

The question of whether the increased glutamate and dizocilpine binding observed after chronic ethanol ingestion is reflected in increased function of the NMDA receptor-channel complex has been addressed with several experimental approaches. Studies using primary cultures of cerebellar granule cells, where NMDA-stimulated increases in intracellular Ca^{2+} were measured with the fluorescent dye Fura-2, indicate that chronic ethanol increases NMDA receptor function (120, 124). Hoffman and collaborators found that when cells were exposed for 1–5 days to 100 mM ethanol or for 3 or more days to 20 mM ethanol, there was an increased response to all concentrations of NMDA tested (in the presence of glycine), with no change in the EC_{50} for NMDA. Similarly, the maximal response to glycine (in the presence of NMDA) was increased in the ethanol-treated cells, while the glycine EC_{50} was unaltered (124). The data suggested an increased number of NMDA receptor-channel complexes, with no change in the properties of the receptor, since there was no alteration in (percent) inhibition of the NMDA response by Mg^{2+} or dizocilpine in the chronically ethanol-treated cells (124). There was also no change in the acute (percentage) inhibition of the NMDA response by ethanol in the chronically ethanol-exposed cells (124). This finding is comparable to previous electrophysiological data (125) and suggests that "tolerance" to the acute effect of ethanol does not occur in this system.

The increase in NMDA receptor function in ethanol withdrawal has also been studied with electrophysiological techniques. Morrisett (126) recently reported that in vitro ethanol withdrawal in rat dentate gyrus slices significantly enhanced the duration of high-frequency stimuli-induced afterdischarges. Moreover, ethanol withdrawal was associated to an increase in NMDA-dependent excitatory postsynaptic potentials in mouse hippocampal pyramidal neurons (127). Interestingly, the authors observed an increase in the synaptic activation of calcium spikes, which suggests that NMDA and Ca^{2+} channels might have a synergistic effect to contribute to the hyperexcitability that takes place during ethanol withdrawal. Consequently, work using a wide variety of experimental approaches indicates that NMDA receptor function is increased during ethanol withdrawal.

It should be emphasized that this increase in NMDA receptor function might be responsible for the neurotoxic effects seen during ethanol withdrawal (reviewed in Ref. 128). Chronic exposure of rat cerebellar granule cells to ethanol is associated with an increase in glutamate-induced neurotoxicity as measured by a fluorescence assay. The neurotoxic effects of glutamate can be blocked by antagonists of NMDA receptors; consequently, pharmacological manipulations at this level could be useful in the treatment of alcohol-related excitotoxicity. In this regard, Hoffman et al. (129) found that treatment with ganglioside GM_1 attenuated glutamate-induced excitotoxicity in chronically ethanol-exposed cerebellar granule cells.

There is evidence, in intact animals, that upregulation of the NMDA receptor-coupled channel and the accompanying increase in function play a role in ethanol withdrawal seizures. The time course of the upregulation paralleled the time course for the appearance and disappearance of handling-induced ethanol withdrawal seizures in ethanol-withdrawn mice (117). Furthermore, treatment of mice with competitive and noncompetitive antagonists of the NMDA receptor attenuated these ethanol withdrawal seizures, and administration of NMDA, at a dose that had no effect in control animals, exacerbated the seizures (116). Similarly, treatment of rats with dizocilpine and other noncompetitive NMDA receptor antagonists attenuated audiogenic ethanol withdrawal seizures (130), and focal microinjection of NMDA receptor antagonists into the inferior colliculus and pontine reticular formation blocked seizures during ethanol withdrawal (131). The genetic evidence for a role of NMDA receptors in ethanol withdrawal seizures is inconclusive. Dizocilpine binding was measured in the brains of mice that were selectively bred to be prone (WSP) or resistant (WSR) to ethanol withdrawal seizures and genetic differences were found in one study (132) but not in another (133).

The overall results are compatible with the hypothesis that both $GABA_A$ receptor subsensitivity and an upregulation of NMDA receptors contribute to ethanol withdrawal seizures. Since there appears to be no change in the *properties* of the NMDA receptor-channel complex after chronic ethanol ingestion, it may be speculated that decreased sensitivity to GABA would simply allow activation of a greater number of NMDA receptors in the ethanol-fed animals, thus generating the withdrawal seizures (once ethanol is eliminated from the brain). However, it should be noted that many of these experiments have been carried out in different brain areas or in cells in culture. Given the regional differences in response of brain GABA and NMDA receptors to ethanol treatment and the demonstration that $GABA_A$ receptors in circumscribed brain regions appear to influence ethanol withdrawal seizures (although this seizure activity occurs throughout the brain (134)), one must exercise caution in extrapolating the results from one model system or brain area to another. For example, the increased *function* of the NMDA receptor after chronic ethanol treatment has been demonstrated in primary cultures of cerebellar granule cells, whereas the adult cerebellum has few NMDA receptors (117). Thus, the ethanol-induced changes in the GABA and glutamate systems suggest a testable hypothesis for the biochemical changes that underlie at least one important ethanol withdrawal symptom.

The synaptic plasticity associated with NMDA receptor activation is also important in neuronal development and, in particular, for activity-dependent synaptic modification (135). For example, it has been shown that administration of a specific antagonist of the NMDA receptor blocks the ability of the visual cortex in the newborn cat to respond to a period of monocular deprivation, which normally alters the sensitivity of neurons to visual stimulation (135). The authors suggested that "activation of visual cortical NMDA receptors is required both for the modification and maintenance of the neuronal response properties that depend on visual experience." This type of data suggests that inhibition of NMDA receptor function by ethanol during neuronal development could interfere with the establishment of normal neuronal connections. This possibility is relevant to the fetal alcohol syndrome (FAS), which is a pattern of congenital malformations that can occur in the children of alcoholic mothers (136) and for which a number of animal models have been developed (137). In humans, one of the characteristics of FAS is mental retardation, and in animals born to mothers treated chronically with ethanol, various deficits in learning and memory, as well as hippocampal abnormalities, have been reported (137). To date, there have been only a few examinations of NMDA receptor function in the offspring of animals treated with ethanol during gestation. Electrophysiological investigations in rats were performed with use of hippocampal slices from adult offspring of alcohol-treated animals (ethanol in a liquid diet was administered throughout gestation) (138). The response to NMDA of extracellular population field potentials was measured. In the offspring of the ethanol-treated animals, the response to NMDA was significantly reduced, and this reduction seemed to result from an enhanced sensitivity to Mg^{2+} (138). Somewhat similar results were obtained in biochemical studies of adult offspring of rats fed an ethanol-containing liquid diet beginning on day 12 of pregnancy and continuing until parturition. It was found that the stimulation of hippocampal polyphosphoinositide metabolism by the agonists quisqualate and ibotenate (acting at the metabotropic glutamate receptor) and the inhibition of carbachol-stimulated polyphosphoinositide metabolism by kainate (acting at the kainate receptor) and NMDA were all reduced in the offspring of the ethanol-fed animals, as compared with controls (139). Thus, in both studies, there was a reduced response to NMDA in the hippocampus of the offspring of ethanol-treated animals. However, in the biochemical study, a generalized depression in response to several glutamate agonists was found, while in the electrophysiological experiments, it was reported that there was little or no change in response to agonists acting at non-NMDA glutamate receptors (i.e., ethanol exposure of the mother had a selective effect on the response to NMDA in the offspring). It is not absolutely clear from these studies whether the inhibition of the NMDA response by ethanol in the fetus during gestation resulted in the observed deficits in the NMDA response in the animals that were exposed to ethanol prenatally when they grew to adulthood. However, the deficits seen in studies with animals could well contribute to the behavioral and/or intellectual impairment demonstrated in human offspring of ethanol-ingesting mothers.

Tolerance

Glutamate receptors (in particular the NMDA subtype) appear to play a role in the development of tolerance to ethanol (reviewed in Refs. 140 and 141). The NMDA receptor blockers dizocilpine and ketamine block the development of rapid and chronic tolerance to ethanol-induced motor impairment and hypothermia (142–145). Moreover, the agonist of the glycine site on NMDA receptors, d-cycloserine, enhances the development of rapid tolerance to ethanol (146). The ability of NMDA antagonists to block tolerance has been attributed to the effects of this blocker on learning, a process that is believed to be mediated, in part, by NMDA receptors. In this regard, it was found that the noncompetitive NMDA antagonist dizocilpine blocked the development of environment-dependent tolerance, which is believed to be governed by learning, but not the development of environment-independent tolerance, which is believed to be independent of learning processes (147). This finding has recently been confirmed by Rafi-Tari et al. (148) who report that dizocilpine prevents the development of chronic tolerance in rats on a circular maze test that is claimed to assess the effects of ethanol on learning and memory independently of its influence on motor capability. The results of the experiments described above, taken together with the evidence that chronic ethanol produces upregulation of NMDA receptors, suggest that NMDA receptors play a role in the development of tolerance to ethanol.

NON-NMDA RECEPTORS

Several lines of evidence suggest that non-NMDA glutamate receptors are also modulated by ethanol. Some studies have shown that ethanol inhibits non-NMDA receptor function less than that of NMDA receptors (93, 99, 102). However, other studies have demonstrated that ethanol inhibits, to a similar degree, non-NMDA and NMDA responses in *Xenopus* oocytes expressing rat hippocampal mRNA (104, 149). The high sensitivity of non-NMDA receptors to ethanol has also been observed in striatal (150, 151) and hippocampal (152) neurons. The inhibition of non-NMDA receptors depends on the agonist concentration and the subunit(s) expressed (149, 153). Recent work has demonstrated that the ethanol-induced inhibition of non-NMDA responses might involve both a PKC-dependent and PKC-independent mechanism (153). Interestingly, recent evidence suggests that the non-NMDA glutamatergic system also plays a role in alcohol withdrawal hyperexcitability. In hippocampal CA1 neurons, withdrawal from chronic alcohol treatment resulted in increased activity of this glutamatergic system (154). Consequently, non-NMDA receptors, like NMDA receptors, appear to be targets for the acute and chronic actions of ethanol in the CNS.

Cholinergic Systems

A significant amount of work has indicated that, at the biochemical level, cholinergic systems are sensitive to perturbation by ethanol. This work has been reviewed previously (14, 155). In general, ethanol inhibits the release of acetylcholine in the brain, with some brain areas being more affected than others. Pharmacological studies of the behavioral interactions between ethanol and cholinergic systems have often focused on the sedative and/or hypnotic or depressant effects of ethanol, and the results have been conflicting. For example, the cholinesterase inhibitor physostigmine reportedly decreased the duration of loss of righting reflex in mice, but neither acetylcholine nor cholinergic receptor blockers affected ethanol-induced depression of activity in an active avoidance paradigm (156, 157). More recently, cholinergic agonists, as well as a cholinesterase inhibitor, were found to *increase* the sensitivity of SS mice (but not LS mice) to ethanol (158). One problem with these studies may be that the drugs used have multiple actions. For example, the anticholinesterase agent physostigmine (eserine) was shown to display unexpected agonist actions on both muscle- and neuronal-type nicotinic acetylcholine receptors (nAChRs) (159).

nAChRs are the prototypes of the ligand-gated ion channel family of receptors. nAChRs can be divided into two categories: the muscle type and the neuronal type. Muscle-type nAChRs are formed by 2 α_1, β_1, γ_1, δ_1 (or ϵ_1 in the adult) subunits, whereas the neuronal-type nAChRs are formed by two types of subunits, α_{2-9} and or β_{2-4}. Although the muscle-type nAChR is likely not to be involved in the mechanism of action of ethanol, it has been used as a model system to study the molecular mechanism of the interaction between relatively high concentrations of short- and long-chain alcohols and ligand-gated ion channels (160, 161). On the other hand, little is known about the effects of alcohols on neuronal-type nAChR, which could mediate some actions of ethanol in the nervous system. Behavioral experiments suggest that common genes regulate sensitivity to an acute dose of ethanol and nicotine (162). For example, LS and SS mice, which were selected for differential sensitivity to ethanol-induced sleep time, display cross-tolerance between ethanol and nicotine (162, 163). Another study showed that nicotine altered the stimulatory effect of ethanol on locomotor activity and that the blood-brain barrier permeable blocker of neuronal nAChRs, mecamylamine, partially counteracted this stimulatory effect of ethanol and the ethanol-induced increase in dopamine overflow in the rat nucleus accumbens (164, 165). More recent investigations have reported that ethanol inhibits native neuronal nAChR in isolated neurons from the pond snail *Lymnaea stagnalis* (166) and recombinant nAChRs expressed in *Xenopus* oocytes (167). Because the principal role of neuronal-type nAChRs in the CNS appears to be the control of neurotransmitter release at the presynaptic level (168), it should be keep in mind that nAChRs might be important targets for ethanol's actions in the CNS.

5-Hydroxytryptamine Type 3 Receptors

Relatively little is known about the effects of ethanol on 5-HT$_3$ receptors, another member of the superfamily of ligand-gated ion channels. It was shown that ethanol potentiates 5-HT$_3$ receptor-mediated currents in neuroblastoma cells (169) and in nodose ganglion neurons (170) at concentrations ranging between 25 and 100 mM. The potentiation by ethanol decreased with increasing concentrations of 5-HT, and ethanol treatment affected the decay rate of 5-HT$_3$ receptor responses (170). Recent experiments with recombinant 5-HT$_3$ receptors expressed in *Xenopus* oocytes yielded similar results (171).

EFFECTS OF ETHANOL ON VOLTAGE-GATED ION CHANNELS

Ca^{2+} Channels

Acute Effects

Three main types of voltage-gated Ca^{2+} channels can be found in sensory neurons: the T type (small conductance and transient fast current), the N type (neuronal type, intermediate conductance and transient fast current), and the L type (large conductance and long-lasting slow current) (15). Ca^{2+} channels are composed of a principal subunit (α_1) and several auxiliary subunits (α_2, β, γ, and δ; N-type channels do not appear to have γ subunits) (172).

Evidence for a role for Ca^{2+} in the sedative and/or hypnotic effect of ethanol was the finding that intracerebroventricular administration of Ca^{2+} increased sensitivity to the hypnotic action of ethanol in SS, but not in LS, mice and that there was a correlation in these lines between calcium-induced enhancement of behavioral and electrophysiological responses to ethanol (173). More recent work showed that administration of nitrendipine and Ω-conotoxin, blockers of voltage-sensitive calcium channels (VGCC), enhance the motor-incoordinating and sleep-inducing effects of ethanol (174, 175). The effects of nitrendipine and Ω-conotoxin are in line with biochemical studies of the effect of ethanol on Ca^{2+} flux through VGCC in various brain membrane preparations (reviewed in Ref. 176). In general, it appears that ethanol (>50 mM) inhibits Ca^{2+} entry into synaptosomal preparations over very short depolarization times (176). It is not clear which subtype of VGCC is inhibited by ethanol, since nitrendipine, an L-channel blocker, was reported to enhance the behavioral effect of ethanol and ethanol had little effect on ligand binding to L-channels in brain membranes (177). Electrophysiological evidence for an effect of ethanol on VGCC has been sparse. It has been suggested that most of the data obtained in electrophysiological studies could be explained by an ethanol-induced increase in intracellular Ca^{2+}, which then blocks inward Ca^{2+} flux (178). In a synaptosomal preparation, high concentrations of ethanol (350–700 mM) did increase resting intracellular Ca^{2+} (179, 180), and it was postulated that this primary effect of ethanol could account for the ability of ethanol both to stimulate neurotransmitter release and to inhibit Ca^{2+} influx (179). It was also found that ethanol inhibited VGCC in a cultured abdominal ganglion neuron from *Aplysia*, although high ethanol concentrations (>100 mM) were necessary to produce inhibition (181). These data are also compatible with other recent work in cultured neuroblastoma and neuroblastoma × glioma cells, indicating that ethanol (>30 mM) inhibited Ca^{2+} flux through VGCC (182). Interestingly, it has been reported that G$_i$ subtypes of the family of the guanine nucleotide-binding protein family might be involved in the ethanol inhibition of L-type Ca^{2+} channels in undifferentiated pheochromocytoma cells (183). While some of the data described above suggest that inhibition of Ca^{2+} flux may play a role in the sedative and/or hypnotic effect of ethanol, there is in fact no clear behavioral correlate for this acute neurochemical effect. On the other hand, the role of dihydropyridine-sensitive (L-type), voltage-sensitive calcium channels in neuroadaptation to ethanol has received a significant amount of attention and is discussed below.

Chronic Effects and Withdrawal

It is believed that Ca^{2+} flux into neuronal cells is involved in the electrophysiological events associated with seizures, and many calcium channel antagonists are effective anticonvulsants (184). Since ethanol inhibited Ca^{2+} flux through these channels (although at higher concentrations than are necessary to inhibit responses at NMDA receptor-gated channels), it seemed possible that chronic ethanol administration might also produce an upregulation of VGCC as an adaptive response to the initial inhibitory effect of ethanol. When dihydropyridine binding to L-type VGCC in the brain was investigated, an increased number of binding sites for the L-channel antagonist nimodipine was found in the whole brains of rats exposed chronically (7 or more days) to ethanol by inhalation (185). This change appeared to be reflected in channel function as an increased effect of the VGCC agonist Bay-K 8644 on polyphosphoinositide metabolism, and dopamine release in certain brain areas was also found (185). In another study, rats were fed ethanol in a liquid diet for 8 weeks, and only a slight, nonsignificant increase in striatal nitrendipine binding, accompanied by a *decrease* in Bay-K 8644-induced Ca^{2+} influx and dopamine release, was reported (186); similarly, no increase in baseline calcium currents was observed in cultured *Aplysia* neurons after exposure to 200 mM ethanol for 21 days (181). However, rats that were given ethanol in their drinking water for 25 days demonstrated an increased number of striatal nitrendipine-binding sites (187), and in PC12 cells exposed to ethanol in vitro (200 mM, 2–6 days), there was also an increase in nitrendipine-binding sites as well as in voltage-sensitive, dihydropyridine-sensitive Ca^{2+} influx (188). More recently, it has been reported that a 6- to 10-day exposure to ethanol vapor caused an increase in the number of binding sites (B_{max}) for [^{3}H]nitrendipine without changing the affinity of this ligand for VGCC (189). Although there was no increase in the binding of an L-channel antagonist in brain tissue obtained from alcoholics at the time of autopsy (190), it is difficult to compare these data with the more controlled data in animals. In particular, the patients whose brains were studied had been abstinent from alcohol for weeks to months, and there was a rather long delay between death and freezing of the samples, both of which factors could affect the ligand-binding data. Overall, much of the evidence from the various studies in cells and animals suggests that chronic ethanol treatment produces an increase in dihydropyridine-sensitive calcium channels that is evident at the time of ethanol withdrawal and is reversible with time after withdrawal. Future studies with humans will need to take these findings into consideration.

Several dihydropyridine L-channel antagonists were found to attenuate handling-induced ethanol withdrawal seizures in rats when the antagonists were administered during withdrawal (191). Furthermore, concurrent chronic treatment of rats with ethanol and nitrendipine prevented the ethanol-induced increase in dihydropyridine-binding sites in the brain (192), and administration of nitrendipine to mice during their chronic exposure to ethanol vapor blocked ethanol withdrawal seizures (193), suggesting a correlation between an increase in VGCC after chronic ethanol treatment and the occurrence of ethanol withdrawal seizures. More recently, it was found that pharmacological manipulations with isomers of Bay K-8644 that increase or decrease the function of the VGCC produce enhancement or reduction, respectively, of hippocampal slice hyperexcitability in ethanol-withdrawn mice (194). Moreover, the VGCC blockers nifedipine and flunarizine attenuated the ethanol withdrawal-induced potentiation of 2-deoxyglucose uptake impairment in hippocampal slices (195).

The molecular mechanism of the chronic ethanol-induced increase in VGCC has been examined in several studies. The upregulation may not represent a direct adaptation to the inhibitory effect of ethanol, since chronic treatment of animals with nifedipine did not result in L-channel upregulation (174). Similarly, chronic (6 days) exposure of PC12 cells to several types of L-channel antagonists, including nifedipine, did not alter the binding of an L-channel antagonist, PN 200-110, although 6 days of ethanol exposure induced an increase in binding (196). Interestingly, in these studies, exposure of the PC12 cells to the calcium channel *agonist* Bay-K 8644 increased PN 200-110 binding, similar to ethanol (196). The authors suggested that the upregulation of dihydropyridine-sensitive calcium channels after chronic

ethanol treatment could represent a response to ethanol-induced increases in intracellular calcium levels rather than the inhibition of calcium flux, which in part may also be a result of the increased intracellular Ca^{2+} levels (196). The ability of chronic ethanol exposure to upregulate VGCC in PC12 cells was eliminated by inhibitors of protein kinase C, suggesting a role for this enzyme in the molecular mechanism of the upregulation. Whether direct phosphorylation of the calcium channel is involved (an effect of ethanol on posttranslational modification of protein structure) or there is a more indirect effect on gene expression (an effect of ethanol on transcription or translation), as suggested by Messing et al. (192), needs further investigation.

Although there is evidence for the dissociation of ethanol tolerance and physical dependence, it is of interest to note that experiments with VGCCs suggest that their upregulation is involved in both phenomena. When rats were given injections of nitrendipine during chronic ethanol administration (also by repeated injection), tolerance to the motor-incoordinating effect of ethanol did not develop (197). Similarly, in mice given the L-channel antagonist PN 200–110 during chronic ethanol treatment, tolerance to the hypnotic effect of ethanol did not develop (174). The chronic treatment with channel antagonists also prevented the ethanol-induced upregulation of VGCC, as discussed. The data are all correlational but are compatible with the suggestion that the upregulation of VGCC is associated with both tolerance to and physical dependence on ethanol.

Na$^+$ and K$^+$ Channels

Much less in known about the effects of ethanol on the function of other voltage-gated ion channels, such as potassium and sodium channels. In rodent brain synaptosomes, high concentrations of ethanol (>350 mM) inhibited batrachotoxin- and veratridine-stimulated ^{22}Na$^+$ uptake (reviewed in Ref. 198). Recent work by Kukita and Mitaku (199) showed that high concentrations of various aliphatic alcohols produced an irreversible suppression of sodium currents in squid giant axons. The irreversible effects of the alcohols appeared to be due to denaturation of the sodium channels.

Potassium channels also appear to be affected by alcohol. Low concentrations of ethanol inhibited a voltage-dependent potassium channel in CA1 hippocampal pyramidal neurons (200). Anantharam et al. (201) examined the effects of ethanol on 10 different classes of voltage-gated potassium channels expressed in *Xenopus* oocytes. Although there are some differences in the sensitivity of the channels to high concentrations of ethanol (>200 mM), none of the potassium channels examined was particularly sensitive to low concentrations of ethanol. An exception appears to be the large-conductance, Ca^{2+}-activated K^+ channels in neurohypophysial terminals (202). These channels are involved in the control of hypophyseal hormone release. Ethanol increases the activity of these Ca^{2+}-activated K^+ channels by a mechanism that involves a change in the channel gating properties (202). Thus, inhibitory effects of ethanol on release of hormones such a vasopressin and oxytocin could, at least in part, be due to neuronal hyperpolarization produced by the stimulation of these K^+ channels.

Recent work (203) presents interesting details of the interaction between potassium channels and alcohols. Concentrations of ethanol between 17 and 170 mM selectively inhibited a noninactivating cloned K^+ channel from *Drosophila*. Competition experiments among alcohols and site-directed mutagenesis experiments indicate that the alcohols act on a discrete site, possibly a putative hydrophobic pocket, in the potassium channel. Consequently, it appears as if some voltage-gated potassium channels are targets for the acute actions of ethanol. A challenging task for future research is to determine whether the effects of ethanol on potassium or sodium channels are involved in any of the behavioral effects of ethanol.

EFFECTS OF ETHANOL ON G PROTEIN-COUPLED RECEPTORS

The family of G protein-coupled receptors, which currently includes more than 300 members, is one of the most important systems for transmembrane signal transduction in living cells (reviewed in Refs. 204 and 205). G protein-coupled receptors can be activated by a myriad of ligands, including amines (dopamine, noradrenaline, 5-hydroxytryptamine (5-HT), acetylcholine), amino acids (glutamate and GABA), peptides and proteins (vasopressin, oxytocin), nucleosides (adenosine), and fatty acid and phospholipid derivatives. In general, G protein-coupled receptors consist of seven transmembrane domains, an extracellular N-terminal domain, and an intracellular C-terminal domain. These receptors couple to one or more classes of heterotrimeric G proteins formed by α, β, and γ subunits. G proteins have been classified into four major subfamilies on the basis of α subunit homology; these families are: G_s, G_i, G_q, and G_{12} (205). Members of the G_s subfamily, which includes G_s (S and L) and G_{olf}, stimulate adenylyl cyclase activity. Members of the G_i family produce a variety of effects, such as inhibition of adenylyl cyclase (G_{i1-3}) and inhibition of Ca^{2+} channels in neuronal and endocrine cells (G_{o1-2}). The G_q subfamily (G_q, $G_{11,14,15,16}$) stimulates phospholipase C-β in many cells. The functions of G_{12} proteins are still under investigation. In the following sections, we discuss the role of G protein-coupled systems in the actions of ethanol in the nervous system. First, we discuss the effects of ethanol on adenylyl cyclase-coupled systems. Next, we examine the importance of specific G protein-coupled systems (dopamine, 5-HT, opiates, arginine-vasopressin) in processes associated with alcohol intake. The reader is referred to an earlier version of this chapter (14) for a discussion of ethanol's effects on the turnover of neurotransmitters coupled to G protein receptors.

Adenylyl Cyclase-Coupled Systems

Eight forms of adenylyl cyclase have been cloned; they have been classified into five families, based on their sequence homology (206). Adenylyl cyclases are integral membrane glycoproteins that are formed by two sets of six transmembrane domains (connected by a large intracellular loop) and intracellular amino- and carboxy-terminal domains. The activity of the majority of adenylyl cyclases is stimulated by G_s-α and the diterpene, forskolin, and is inhibited by G_i-α. We review the acute and chronic effects of ethanol on adenylyl cyclase systems next (for a more detailed review see Refs. 207 and 208).

Acute Effects

The effects of ethanol on adenylyl cyclase activity have been studied by several laboratories. Rabin and Molinoff (209) found that ethanol (>68 mM) caused an increase in basal and dopamine-stimulated adenylyl cyclase activity in mouse striatum, cerebellum, and cerebral cortex. Similarly, Saito et al. (210) found that ethanol (20–500 mM) acutely increased β-adrenergic receptor-coupled adenylyl cyclase activity in mouse cerebral cortex, without having a significant effect on basal adenylyl cyclase activity. Ethanol also potentiated the stimulatory effects on adenylyl cyclase activity of the nonhydrolyzable guanosine 5'-triphosphate (GTP) analog, Gpp(NH)p, and decreased the EC_{50} for magnesium required for maximal stimulation of this enzyme. These investigators proposed that ethanol was acting at multiple sites, i.e., the β-adrenergic receptor, the G proteins, and the adenylyl cyclase catalytic subunit itself. In another study, it was found that ethanol reversibly altered isoproterenol binding to mouse cerebral cortical β-adrenergic receptors in vitro (211). Ethanol selectively increased the EC_{50} of isoproterenol binding to the high-affinity form of the β-adrenergic receptor, which is believed to reflect the assembly of a ternary complex containing the receptor, the G_s protein, and adenylyl cyclase.

The findings with mouse cerebral tissue have been confirmed by some studies with cultured neuronal and nonneuronal cells. Ethanol significantly enhanced the adenosine receptor-induced increase in cAMP levels in neuroblastoma × glioma NG 108–15 cells (212). A similar enhancing effect of ethanol on receptor-stimulated adenylyl cyclase activity was also found in another murine neuroblastoma clonal cell line (213). In wild-type and mutant (with altered coupling between β-adrenergic receptor, G_s, and adenylyl cyclase) S49 lymphoma cells, ethanol increased basal and guanine nucleotide- and fluoride-stimulated adenylyl cyclase activity (214). In mutant S49 cells, lacking the α_s subunit of G_s, ethanol had little effect on guanine nucleotide- and fluoride-stimulated adenylyl cyclase activity. This study sug-

gested that G_s played an important role in the actions of ethanol on S49 cells. It should be noted that not all studies with cultured cell lines show that ethanol enhances agonist-stimulated adenylyl cyclase activity. Chik and Ho (215) showed that ethanol does not enhance the norepinephrine-induced stimulation of cAMP levels but inhibits the norepinephrine-induced stimulation of N-acetyltransferase and melatonin. Consequently, ethanol might exert different effects on cells expressing particular classes of adenylyl cyclases. Indeed, a recent study suggests that this might be the case. Yoshimura and Tabakoff (216) measured the effects of acute ethanol treatment on the activity of various isoforms of adenylyl cyclases that were transiently expressed in human embryonic kidney cells. Ethanol alone did not have an effect on adenylyl cyclase activity. However, in the presence of prostaglandin E_1, cAMP generation by adenylyl cyclase types II, IV, V, VI, and the recently cloned VII (217) was significantly increased. Adenylyl cyclase type VII was the most ethanol-sensitive isoform. These results indicate that ethanol preferentially interacts with some but not all isoforms of adenylate cyclase and that this could be important for determining the mechanism of action of ethanol in the CNS. Interestingly, adenylate cyclase type VII is mainly expressed in the cerebellar granule cell layer, and as mentioned before, cAMP-dependent signaling is important for the modulation of ethanol sensitivity of $GABA_A$ receptors (35).

The effects of ethanol on agonist-induced inhibition of adenylyl cyclase have also been studied, but to a lesser extent than those effects of ethanol on agonist-induced stimulation of adenylyl cyclase. Some investigators found that ethanol does not affect the opiate-induced inhibition of striatal adenylyl cyclase in an in vitro assay (218). Others reported that ethanol blocks the adenosine receptor-induced inhibition of adenylyl cyclase in preparations from brain cortical membranes (219). Therefore, more work is required to determine the effects of ethanol on agonist-induced inhibition of adenylyl cyclase activity.

Chronic Effects

The effects of chronic ethanol treatment on agonist-stimulated adenylyl cyclase activity have also been the focus of intense research. The guanine nucleotide analog-induced stimulation of adenylyl cyclase activity was found to be reduced in the brains of mice that were chronically fed with ethanol (220). A similar finding was reported by Saffey et al. (221) with adult female rats. Treatment of these rats with ethanol for 6 days resulted in a decrease in basal and in guanosine analog- or norepinephrine-stimulated adenylyl cyclase activity. Chronic ethanol ingestion was also reported to affect the binding of β-adrenergic agonists to high-affinity sites in the hippocampus and frontal cortex and to decrease stimulated adenylyl cyclase activity (222, 223). Ethanol did not have these effects in the cerebellum, which indicates that ethanol might exert specific effects depending on the brain region examined (222, 223). Interestingly, loss of high-affinity binding to β-adrenergic receptors was also found in the cerebral cortex but not in the cerebellum of alcoholics (224). However, the finding that cerebellar adenylyl cyclase is not affected by ethanol has not been corroborated in all cases. Chronic ethanol treatment of cultured cerebellar granule cells produced a decrease in the isoproterenol- and adenosine-induced increase in cAMP levels. Moreover, 7-day ethanol treatment produced a reduction in stimulated adenylyl cyclase activity in cerebellar and pons membranes of long-sleep (LS) and short-sleep (SS) mice. Pretreatment of membranes with pertussis toxin, which inhibits G_i, blocked the ethanol induced-inhibition of adenylyl cyclase activity (225). Consequently, cerebellar adenylyl cyclase activity appears to be sensitive to chronic ethanol treatment in some cases. Regarding the sensitivity of adenylyl cyclase to ethanol in murine lines selected for ethanol sensitivity, Wand and Levine (226) reported that chronic ethanol exposure reduced GTP-γS-, AlF_3-, and $MnCl_2$-stimulated adenylyl cyclase activity in homogenates from the anterior pituitary of LS mice. Adenylyl cyclase activity in SS mice was not affected by ethanol. The authors also found a decrease in G_s protein in LS mice that paralleled the changes in adenylyl cyclase activity. Taken together, these results indicate that ethanol exerts differential effects in some, but not all, brain regions of these lines of mice.

Studies with cultured cells also indicate that ethanol chronically decreases adenylyl cyclase activity. Gordon et al. (212) found that chronic ethanol treatment of neuroblastoma $\times$ glioma NG 108-15 hybrid cells reduced adenosine-stimulated cAMP levels. The same effect of chronic ethanol treatment was observed in stimulated adenylyl cyclase activity in murine neuroblastoma N1E-115 cells (227), in S49 lymphoma cells (228), and pheochromocytoma-derived PC12 cells (229). In some cases, the mechanism of action of chronic ethanol may be due to accumulation of extracellular adenosine and adenosine receptor desensitization. Nagy et al. (230) demonstrated that chronic incubation of neuroblastoma $\times$ glioma NG 108-15 hybrid and S49 lymphoma cells with ethanol, in the presence of adenosine deaminase to eliminate the extracellular adenosine, blocked the ability of ethanol to produce heterologous desensitization of adenosine receptor- and prostaglandin E_1 receptor-induced cAMP accumulation. However, not all investigators have found that the effects of chronic ethanol depend on extracellular adenosine. Williams et al. (231) recently reported that ethanol (200 mM for 2 days) increased agonist-stimulated cAMP accumulation in NG 108-15 cells. This effect of ethanol was not reversed by removal of extracellular adenosine and was not mimicked by prolonged treatment with an adenosine agonist. Interestingly, chronic ethanol treatment also increased basal cAMP levels in NG 108–15 cells, and this effect was blocked by adenosine deaminase treatment. Consequently, chronic treatment with ethanol can affect adenylyl cyclase function differentially, depending on the cell type studied.

Several studies have also examined at the effects of chronic ethanol on the levels of G proteins. It was reasoned that one of the possible mechanisms by which chronic ethanol treatment could inhibit adenylyl cyclase activity may be via a decrease in the stimulatory G_s protein levels. Mochly-Rosen et al. (232) and Charness et al. (233) found that chronic treatment with ethanol of NG 108-15 neuroblastoma cells resulted in a decrease in both the mRNA and protein levels of the α_s subunit of G_s. Similarly, Rabin (234) reported that chronic ethanol treatment caused a reduction in α_s in pheochromocytoma-derived PC12 cells. This author also reported that this effect of ethanol was not seen in a cell line that is functionally deficient in protein kinase A, indicating that changes in protein phosphorylation may mediate the effects of chronic ethanol on α_s levels. The finding that ethanol decreased levels of α_s in cultured cells was corroborated by a study with LS and SS mice. Wand and Levine (226) showed that chronic ethanol treatment decreased protein levels of α_s in anterior pituitary. However, other studies with brain tissue have not found decreased α_s levels in chronically treated animals. Wand et al. (225) found that exposure of LS and SS mice for a 7-day period did not alter levels of α_s. Tabakoff et al. (235) reported that levels of α_s were not changed in the cerebral cortex, hippocampus, or cerebellum of C57BL/6 mice chronically treated with ethanol. A similar result was obtained by Pellegrino et al. (236) in the substantia nigra, striatum, globus pallidus, frontal cortex, nucleus accumbens, ventral tegmental area (VTA), and ventral pallidum of male Fisher 344 rats treated with ethanol for 4 weeks. Consequently, chronic ethanol may alter the levels of brain α_s only in selected regions of the CNS, such as the pituitary.

Another possible mechanism by which chronic ethanol treatment causes a decrease in adenylyl cyclase activity is via an increase in levels of the inhibitory G_i protein. In favor of this mechanism are the findings of Wand et al. (225) who showed that levels of the α_1 and α_2 subunits of G_i were significantly increased in cerebellar and pons membranes from ethanol-exposed LS and SS mice. Moreover, Pellegrino et al. (236) also found increase in levels of the α_3 subunit of G_i in Fisher 344 rats in some of the brain regions associated with the nigrostriatal and mesolimbic dopaminergic systems. However, other studies have detected no changes in the levels of G_i and its subunits. Charness et al. (233) and Rabin (234) did not find significant changes in the levels of G_i in a NG 108–15 neuroblastoma-derived cell line and in pheochromocytoma-derived PC12 cells, respectively. The same observation was made by Tabakoff et al. (235) in mouse cerebral cortex, hippocampus, or cerebellum of male C57BL/6 mice chronically treated with ethanol, except for a small increase in the levels of $G_i\alpha_1$ detected in the striatum. Taken together, these findings suggest, as for the case of G_s, that ethanol may affect adenylyl cyclase activity via brain region-specific changes in the levels of G proteins.

Phospholipase C-Phosphoinositide Metabolism

Initial studies suggested that acute treatment with ethanol does not affect phosphoinositide (PI) turnover in murine brain (237, 238). However, more recent evidence suggests that acute ethanol treatment might affect PI turnover in some cases. Ethanol (50–200 mM) inhibited neurotensin- and bradykinin-stimulated PI turnover (239). In vivo administration of high ethanol levels to C57B1/6J mice (injected intracerebroventricularly with [^{3}H]inositol) resulted in a decrease in the formation of inositol monophosphates in brain and cerebellum. More recently, it was shown that ethanol acutely affects the function of G_q-protein-coupled receptors such as the 5-HT type-2c and muscarinic type-1 receptors (240). Ethanol (25–200 mM) produced a dose-dependent inhibition of currents evoked by 5-HT and acetylcholine in Xenopus oocytes expressing brain mRNA. In contrast, metabotropic glutamate receptor responses were much less sensitive to ethanol. Ethanol did not inhibit the currents produced by a nonhydrolyzable analog of GTP or by myo-inositol-1,4,5-triphosphate. The ethanol-induced inhibition of serotonin responses was blocked by a specific inhibitor of protein kinase C (240). These results suggest that some classes of G-protein-coupled receptors are more sensitive to ethanol and that the mechanism of this inhibition involves protein kinase C.

Chronic ethanol treatment also appears to have effects on PI turnover, especially when its effects are studied in cultured cells. In N1E-115 (241) and NG 108-15 (242) cells, chronic ethanol treatment resulted in a decrease in bradykinin-stimulated PI turnover. Interestingly, in the N1E-115 cells, there was no change in the stimulation of PI turnover by neurotensin and a guanine nucleotide analog. This finding suggests that ethanol selectively affected the coupling between the bradykinin receptor and G_q protein. Conversely, chronic ethanol affected the guanine-nucleotide-stimulated PI turnover in the NG 108-15 cells, suggesting that it affected the function of the G_q protein itself in these cells. In contrast to the effects of ethanol on cultured cells, it was reported that chronic ethanol treatment of young mice produced an increased PI turnover in cerebral cortex and hippocampus (243) and that it had no acute effect on norepinephrine-stimulated PI turnover in the cortex of mice chronically treated with ethanol (237). Clearly, more work is required to understand fully the effects of ethanol on G-protein-and/or phospholipase-C-dependent PI turnover.

Adenosine Systems

In the brain, adenosine is believed to serve as a neuromodulator rather than a neurotransmitter. Specific neurons that contain adenosine have not been identified; however, the levels of this compound in the brain appear to be sufficient to activate adenosine receptors on neuronal membranes (244). Four subtypes of adenosine receptors have been identified; activation of A_1 receptors produces inhibition of adenylate cyclase activity, activation of A_{2a} and A_{2b} receptors stimulates this activity, and activation of A_3 receptors activates phospholipase C (244, 245). Although a group of studies was performed to investigate ethanol's actions on adenosine-stimulated adenylate cyclase activity (see above), most of the evidence for an interaction of ethanol with adenosine systems comes from behavioral studies. Treatment of mice with adenosine antagonists (e.g., caffeine, theophylline) reduced the sedative and/or hypnotic and motor-incoordinating effects of ethanol, while treatment with agonists or adenosine uptake inhibitors enhanced the responses to ethanol (246). The actions of the agonists and antagonists were not due simply to peripheral effects, since similar results were obtained with compounds administered either systemically or intracerebroventricularly (247). Studies have also been carried out in which adenosine agonists and antagonists were administered chronically to mice, and the motor-incoordinating effect of ethanol was measured. In animals receiving chronic treatment with caffeine or isobutylmethylxanthine (but not theophylline), adenosine receptors were increased in the brain, and the response to ethanol was also increased (248). While these data might suggest that adenosine receptors are directly involved in the motor incoordination produced by ethanol, studies with LS and SS mice do not completely support such a conclusion. It was found that LS mice were more sensitive to the depressant actions of an adenosine agonist and to the excitatory actions of an adenosine antagonist than were SS mice. However, no difference has been detected between LS and SS mice in the number of adenosine receptors or in the electrophysiological response to adenosine in the hippocampus (12). It is possible that adenosine receptors are more important in mediating the motor-incoordinating than the sedative and/or hypnotic effects of ethanol (although the measure used to assay the sedative and/or hypnotic effect, duration of loss of righting reflex, contains a component of motor coordination). However, it should also be pointed out that some of the methylxanthine adenosine receptor antagonists that have been used to link the adenosine systems to the motor-incoordinating effects of ethanol could have other effects in the brain. For example, these compounds have stimulatory effects in animals that could result in antagonism of the depressant effects of ethanol by a simple additive mechanism.

Assuming that adenosine does play a role in the motor-incoordinating and/or hypnotic effect of ethanol, biochemical studies have attempted to determine the mechanism by which ethanol influences this system. Ethanol could act directly at the adenosine receptor(s), and it has been found that ethanol enhances cAMP responses to adenosine in human lymphocytes and in neuroblastoma $\times$ glioma (NG 108-15) cells in culture (212, 249). In the cells in culture, effects were detectable at 50 mM ethanol, a concentration that could be obtained in vivo. However, this effect of ethanol may not be specific for adenosine, since ethanol has been reported to enhance the cAMP response to a number of stimulatory agonists in brain and other tissue and seems to act primarily at G_s, the stimulatory guanine nucleotide-binding protein that couples receptors to adenylate cyclase rather than at the receptors per se (207). Recent experiments have shown that a selective adenosine receptor antagonist or agonists can block the ethanol-induced inhibition of potassium-stimulated glutamate release in near-term fetal guinea pig hippocampus (250). Consequently, ethanol could have direct or indirect effects on the function of the adenosine A_1 receptor. As mentioned in the Adenylyl Cyclase section, a more specific action of ethanol on adenosine systems has also been proposed. In NG 108-15 cells and in S49 lymphoma cells, ethanol (100–200 mM) increased the accumulation of extracellular adenosine. It was

suggested that ethanol inhibited the bidirectional adenosine transporter, since cellular mutants that do not contain the transporter did not respond to ethanol with an increase in extracellular adenosine (230, 251, 252). The authors proposed that in the NG 108-15 and S49 cells the enhancement of adenylate cyclase activity by ethanol was due to the presence of increased extracellular adenosine, which secondarily activated A_2 receptors and increases cAMP and/or protein kinase A activity. This mechanism could account for the ability of adenosine agonists to increase behavioral responses to ethanol, although direct tests of the ability of ethanol to increase brain adenosine have been negative (253).

Several lines of evidence suggest that acetate, the primary product of ethanol catabolism, mediate some effects of ethanol in the CNS (254). Ethanol and acetate produced similar effects on motor coordination and anesthetic potency tests, and the effects of acetate and ethanol were blocked and partially blocked, respectively, by the adenosine receptor antagonist 8-phenyltheophylline. However, acetate inhibited locomotor activity in mice, whereas ethanol enhanced it. The effects of acetate on locomotor activity were blocked by 8-phenyltheophylline, while those of ethanol were enhanced. The authors conclude that the effects of ethanol on locomotor activity result from a combination of the effects of ethanol and acetate. In another study, Cullen and Carlen (255) demonstrated that acetate, ethanol, and adenosine produced similar hyperpolarizing effects in rat hippocampal dentate granule cells and that these effects were blocked by 8-phenyltheophylline. It should be noted, however, that other effects of adenosine cannot be induced by acetate in CA1 pyramidal hippocampal neurons (256) (Fig. 11.1).

Dopamine

Five different subtypes of dopamine receptors have been cloned (257). These subtypes are the D_{1A}, D_{1B}, $D_{2S/2L}$, D_3, and D_4 receptors. D_{1A} and D_{1B} receptors activate adenylyl cyclase and increase cAMP levels. D_2, and D_4 receptors inhibit adenylyl cyclase, and D_2 receptors stimulate K^+ channels and inhibit Ca^{2+} channels. At present, effector pathways for D_3 receptors are not

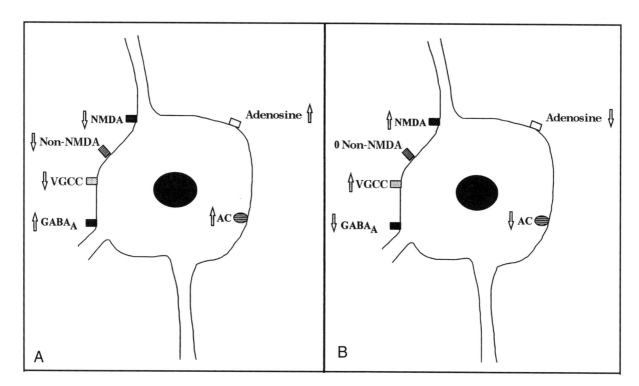

Figure 11.1. Summary of the effects of acute **(A)** and chronic **(B)** ethanol on neuronal receptors and signal transduction. Acute ethanol exposure increases GABA$_A$ receptor function and the activity of adenylate cyclase. The function of the NMDA and non-NMDA subtypes of glutamate receptors is inhibited. Voltage-gated Ca^{2+} channels (VGCC) are also inhibited. Adenosine receptor function may be increased. Chronic ethanol exposure increases NMDA and VGCC function, whereas GABA$_A$ and adenylate cyclase activity are reduced. Adenosine receptor function may be reduced. Non-NMDA glutamate receptors appear not to be affected by chronic ethanol.

completely understood. A number of addictive substances, including opiates and cocaine, have been postulated to be positive reinforcers because of their ability to activate the mesolimbic dopaminergic pathway (from the VTA to the nucleus accumbens). Drugs that block dopamine receptors and lesions of the VTA dopaminergic pathways reduce the rewarding effects of opiates and cocaine (258). Agonists acting at dopamine D_2 receptors (e.g., bromocriptine) decrease cocaine self-administration in animals, reportedly by substituting for the increase in synaptic dopamine usually produced by cocaine administration (259). Given the postulated involvement of specific dopaminergic pathways in the rewarding (reinforcing) effects of other addictive substances, the effects of ethanol on dopamine systems of the brain have been examined. Also, a number of studies have examined the effects of dopamine receptor agonists and antagonists on ethanol self-administration.

Earlier biochemical studies on the effects of ethanol on the dynamic state of dopamine systems of the brain relied on the measurements of the rates of accumulation of the precursor of dopamine (i.e., dihydroxyphenylalanine or DOPA) after inhibition of DOPA decarboxylase or on measurement of the metabolites of dopamine such as dihydroxyphenylacetic acid (DOPAC) as an indication of dopamine release rates. It was assumed that dopamine synthesis and release were positively coupled to the electrophysiological activity of the dopamine neurons (260). These studies showed that ethanol, in general, produces an increase in the synthesis and release (turnover) of dopamine (reviewed in Ref. 155). Advances in technology have allowed more direct measurements of dopamine release in particular brain areas. The technique of brain dialysis (261), with which released dopamine can be sampled directly in brain areas of an unanesthetized animal, was used in a number of earlier studies to measure dopamine metabolites. Using brain dialysis techniques, Imperato and Di Chiara (262) demonstrated that systemically administered ethanol produced a significant increase in dopamine release in the nucleus accumbens and that the nucleus accumbens area was more sensitive to ethanol's action than the striatum. Conversely, a dramatic and ethanol-reversible decrease in dopamine release after ethanol withdrawal was found in the nucleus accumbens (263) and striatum (264). Electrophysiological measurements of the activity of dopamine neurons in the VTA and the substantia nigra after systemic or in vitro acute administration of ethanol also demonstrated an increased firing rate of these neurons (260, 265). On the other hand, others have found that the number of spontaneously active dopaminergic neurons and their firing rates are reduced in the VTA during ethanol withdrawal (263, 266) and that these effects are reversed on ethanol administration. Administration of ethanol *directly* into the nucleus accumbens and corpus striatum and measurement of dopamine release by dialysis techniques substantiated the dopamine-releasing properties of ethanol but did not generate evidence for a greater sensitivity of the nucleus accumbens to ethanol (267). A particularly compelling study showed that alcohol self-administration increased the release of dopamine in the rat nucleus accumbens. This effect was greater in P rats than in Wistar rats and was not observed during self-administration of saccharin (268). It is entirely probable (see below) that systemic administration of ethanol may have effects on other neuronal systems that modulate the sensitivity of dopamine neurons to the direct effects of ethanol.

Other studies have led to the postulate that a connection probably exists between the number of D_2 receptors in the limbic system and ethanol preference and/or reinforcement (reviewed in Ref. 269). Korpi et al. (270) and Stefanini et al. (271) found small reductions in the number of D_2 receptors in the caudate nucleus, nucleus accumbens, and olfactory tubercle in alcohol-preferring and Sardinian ethanol-preferring rats, respectively. These findings with D_2 receptors were confirmed by autoradiography experiments (272). In addition, others found that D_1 receptors are also reduced in limbic areas of Sardinian ethanol-preferring rats (273). It should be emphasized that one study found decreases in the number of D_2 receptors on ethanol withdrawal (274), whereas another did not (275).

Several studies examined the effects of manipulations of dopaminergic neurotransmission on the reinforcing actions of ethanol. Studies with rats that were trained to press a lever to receive an oral dose of ethanol demonstrated that pretreatment of the animal with dopamine receptor agonists apomorphine (73), bromocriptine or Sandoz 205–152 (74), or quinpirole

(276) significantly decreased ethanol intake. Similar results were found in rats bred for preference for ethanol (P line rats) and in unselected Wistar rats (74). Moreover, intraperitoneal injection of alcohol-preferring rats with the dopamine receptor agonists bromocriptine and quinpirole caused a decrease in ethanol drinking (276, 277). On the other hand, others have found that microinjections of the nonspecific dopamine agonist *d*-amphetamine and the D_2 and/or D_3 agonist quinpirole into the nucleus accumbens increase reinforcement responses to ethanol (278). Thus, mesolimbic dopaminergic systems appear to interact with ethanol by various mechanisms. The decrease in ethanol ingestion after administration of dopamine receptor agonists has been interpreted (73, 74) to indicate that, as for cocaine, these agonists are in some way substituting for the ethanol-induced stimulation of the dopamine system. Some human studies with dopamine agonists also support the role of dopamine systems in ethanol reinforcement. Apomorphine, given to human male "moderate drinkers," has been shown to enhance ethanol's actions on several behavioral measures of ethanol intoxication (279), while drugs such as α-methyl-*p*-tyrosine, which block the synthesis of catecholamines and deplete brain dopamine, antagonize ethanol-induced euphoria and stimulant effects in humans (280). In addition, a double-blind clinical trial showed that bromocriptine reduced alcohol craving in chronic alcoholics (281).

The use of dopamine receptor antagonists in studies of dopamine involvement in ethanol self-administration or preference has produced somewhat equivocal results. Earlier studies by Davis et al. (282), in which animals were trained to press on a lever for intragastric administration of ethanol, demonstrated that the dopamine receptor antagonist haloperidol *did not* alter the pattern of pressing for ethanol. More recent studies by Pfeffer and Samson (283), in which rats lever pressed for oral doses of ethanol, demonstrated that haloperidol, in a dose-dependent manner, reduced ethanol intake during a restricted period of access to ethanol. The effect of haloperidol was primarily restricted to a reduction of ethanol intake later in the test session, and little effect was seen on the initial high rate of ethanol intake (283). Depending on dose and time of administration, haloperidol may produce a variety of effects on dopamine neurotransmission, since it acts not only at neurons postsynaptic to the dopamine neuron but also on the dopamine neurons themselves to interfere with the normal feedback control of dopamine neuronal firing (284). Therefore, significantly more work may be necessary to clarify the interactions of drugs such as haloperidol with ethanol during periods of ethanol ingestion or other forms of self-administration. In this regard, Dyr et al. (276) found that the D_2 receptor antagonist spiperone increased ethanol intake at low doses (10 µg/kg) and decreased ethanol intake at higher doses (30 µg/kg). Moreover, D_1 receptor antagonists decreased ethanol intake. Consequently, the effects of dopamine receptor antagonists appear to be complex as a result of the contribution of more than one subtype of dopamine receptors in ethanol-induced consumption.

Samson et al. (285) have recently reviewed the effects of dopaminergic agonists and antagonists on the reinforcing actions of ethanol. The authors conclude, from microinjection of these dopaminergic drugs, that only part of the control of ethanol drinking is mediated by the mesolimbic dopaminergic system. The authors mention that both dopamine agonists and antagonists decrease ethanol-reinforced responding and total ethanol self-administration. The dopamine antagonist raclopride produced a rapid termination of drinking, whereas the dopaminergic activator *d*-amphetamine both slows down the initial drinking response rate and prolongs drinking by interfering with normal drinking termination processes (285, 286). An interaction between mesolimbic GABAergic and dopaminergic systems appears to be involved in ethanol reinforcement. Hodge et al. (287) recently reported that muscimol administration into the nucleus accumbens decreases ethanol self-administration by terminating responding to a lever in Long-Evans rats and that this effect is blocked by doses of bicuculline that were ineffective by themselves.

Experiments with the neurotoxin 6-hydroxydopamine also suggest that mesolimbic dopaminergic systems are involved in the control of ethanol drinking. This neurotoxin causes degeneration of dopaminergic and noradrenergic neurons and decreases preference to ethanol in rats (288). Others have found that 6-hydroxydopamine-induced lesions enhance ethanol intake

(289–291). More recently, Rassnick et al. (292) found that 6-hydroxy-dopamine-induced lesions of the nucleus accumbens and olfactory tubercle did not affect ethanol self-administration in rats. It should be emphasized that different rat strains and experimental paradigms were used in the different studies mentioned above and that this could account for the variety of results obtained by different laboratories. In a very interesting recent study, Lança (293) shows that intrastriatal transplantation of fetal dopaminergic grafts reduced voluntary ethanol intake in rats. Taken together, these experiments suggest that the dopaminergic mesolimbic system plays a role in the mechanism of ethanol-induced reinforcement.

It should be mentioned in this section that the D_2 receptor gene has been implicated in alcoholism. Blum et al. (294, 295) found a correlation between alcoholism and a restriction fragment length polymorphism in the $3'$ and $5'$ regions of the D_2 receptor gene. Others, however, have not found such a correlation (296, 297). The reader is referred to recent articles for more details on the controversy surrounding the possible involvement of this gene in alcoholism (269, 298).

The serotonin (5-HT$_3$) receptor *antagonist* ICS-205-930, administered prior to the administration of ethanol to rats, has been shown to block the stimulation of dopamine release in the nucleus accumbens produced by ethanol (299), but significantly higher doses of ICS-205-930 were necessary to block the effects of ethanol when the ethanol was administered directly into the nucleus accumbens (267). These data suggest that the effects of ethanol on dopamine release may be modulated by brain serotoninergic systems. Ethanol's actions on serotonergic neurotransmission are discussed below, but it should be noted that selective 5-HT$_3$ receptor *agonists* have been shown to increase dopamine release from slices of rat striatum (300). In addition, as discussed in the next section, ICS-205-930 acts as a benzodiazepine inverse agonist as well as a 5-HT$_3$ antagonist, and some of its anti-ethanol effects could be due to actions on GABA$_A$ receptors (301).

5-Hydroxytryptamine

5-Hydroxytryptamine (5-HT) receptors were recently classified into seven categories (5-HT$_{1-7}$) (reviewed in Ref. 302). Five subtypes of 5-HT$_1$ receptors (A–F) and three subtypes of 5-HT$_2$ receptors have been identified. 5-HT receptors exert a wide variety of actions, including inhibition of neurotransmitter release (5-HT$_{1B}$ and 5-HT$_{1D}$), increase in phosphoinositide turnover (5-HT$_{2A-C}$), and decrease (5-HT$_{1E-F}$) or increase (5-HT$_{4,6,7}$) in cAMP levels (302). 5-HT$_3$ receptors are ligand-gated ion channels, and their involvement in ethanol's actions was described above, in the section entitled, Effects of Ethanol on Ligand-Gated Ion Channels. The role of 5-HT systems on alcohol intake has been reviewed recently (303, 304). LeMarquand et al. (303) summarized studies examining ethanol intake after several manipulations that increase or decrease serotoninergic function. The majority of the studies support the hypothesis that an increase in serotoninergic function leads to a decrease in ethanol consumption. In these studies, serotonin function was increased by means of brain or peripheral injections of serotonin or its precursors, serotonin uptake inhibitors, serotonin releasers, or serotonin agonists. Conversely, the majority of the studies do not support the hypothesis that a decrease in serotoninergic function leads to an increase in ethanol consumption. Serotonin function was decreased by means of serotoninergic neurotoxins, electrolytic lesions of serotoninergic pathways, serotonin receptor antagonists, and serotonin uptake enhancers. The reasons for these apparent inconsistencies can be related to experimental factors such as doses, times of exposure, and animal species used (reviewed in Ref. 155). Nevertheless, some studies with serotonergic drugs on ethanol discrimination suggest that serotonin may play a role in ethanol reinforcement.

Working with the hypothesis that drugs that potentiate serotonergic neurotransmission could substitute for ethanol, 5-HT uptake inhibitors have been administered to humans and other animals. Earlier work with zimelidine (305) and more recent studies with citalopram and fluoxetine indicate that these 5-HT uptake inhibitors can reduce ethanol intake in human heavy drinkers (306), in animals trained to self-administer ethanol (73), or in animals selectively bred to voluntarily consume large quantities of ethanol

(307). The reduction in alcohol intake in humans treated with 5-HT uptake inhibitors is modest but provides evidence that ethanol intake may be controlled by mechanisms that control other ingestive behaviors. In this regard, one should also consider that reductions in ethanol intake by agents that increase 5-HT neurotransmission may not result from an ethanol substitution phenomenon but may reflect serotonin's actions on systems that more directly control ethanol and other fluid intake. Brain serotonin exerts an important control on the renin-angiotensin system (308); Grupp and his colleagues have demonstrated that angiotensin II can decrease ethanol intake in rats and have proposed that angiotensin serves as a signal of satiety for ethanol intake (309). Another interesting finding with regards to the interaction between ethanol and serotonin receptors was that the 5-HT$_3$ receptor antagonist MDL-72222 exacerbated ethanol withdrawal seizures in mice (310). However, this antagonist also interacts with GABA$_A$ receptors (301). Serotoninergic drugs, acting more specifically, were shown to modify the actions of ethanol. Buspirone, a 5-HT$_{1A}$ receptor agonist, has been shown to reduce alcohol consumption in several species, including humans (311), without reducing food and/or fluid intake (269).

Experiments with rats selectively bred for ethanol preference (preferring (P) and nonpreferring (NP) rats) also implicate serotoninergic systems in alcohol abuse. Wong et al. (312) found that 5-HT$_{1A}$ receptors were more abundant in membranes isolated from the cortical brain areas of P rats than in membranes from NP rats. Conversely, levels of 5-HT$_2$ receptors labeled with [^{3}H]ketanserin were found to be reduced in several brain regions of P rats in comparison with NP rats (313). Furthermore, the serotonin content and density of serotonin immunoreactive fibers appear to be reduced in P rats compared with NP rats in the forebrain and dorsal and medial raphe (314, 315).

As noted above, a number of electrophysiological and neurochemical studies have demonstrated that serotonin modulates the activity of dopamine neurons (300, 316). Microdialysis experiments demonstrated that ethanol not only stimulates the release of dopamine in the nucleus accumbens but also that of serotonin (262, 317). It was shown that serotoninergic neurons from the anterior raphe nuclei project and make synaptic contacts with dopaminergic neurons in the VTA (318). Moreover, microinjections of serotonin into the VTA enhance dopamine release in the nucleus accumbens (319). This process might occur via 5-HT$_3$ receptors because their stimulation with agonists increases release of dopamine in the nucleus accumbens (320). Conversely, antagonists of this receptor decrease the stimulatory effects of ethanol on dopamine release in this brain region (317). Consequently, serotoninergic systems might be important mediators of the actions of ethanol on dopaminergic neurotransmission. For recent reviews containing more details about the role of 5-HT$_3$ receptors on ethanol's reinforcement, see Grant (304) and LeMarquand et al. (303).

Serotonergic systems, in addition to being implicated in ethanol reinforcement and other responses to ethanol, are also candidates for systems that modify the characteristics of functional tolerance to ethanol. Combined destruction of noradrenergic and serotonergic systems in the brain completely eliminated ethanol tolerance development in the rat (321). Depletion of A$_1$ alone, particularly the serotonergic pathway connecting the median raphe nucleus to the hippocampus, *delayed* the development of tolerance to the motor-impairing and hypothermic effects of ethanol in rats (290). Similarly, in mice, the development of "environment-dependent" or conditional tolerance was slowed by the depletion of brain A$_1$ (322). The results of these studies suggested that there may be species differences with respect to the primary neurotransmitter systems that influence the development of tolerance to different effects of ethanol, but that interactions between noradrenergic and serotonergic systems are important in determining the rate and extent of tolerance development in both species studied. It is of interest that differences in the characteristics of serotonin- and norepinephrine-containing pathways have been described in selected lines and inbred strains of animals (323), emphasizing the genetic variability that exists in these systems and that would also be expected to influence development of tolerance to ethanol. Another important conclusion from the described studies is that the presence of ethanol in the brain is a necessary, but not sufficient, condition for the development of ethanol tolerance; in addition, the concomitant activity of certain neuronal (e.g., noradrenergic, serotonergic) pathways is required.

Brain Opiate Systems

The involvement of endogenous opiate systems in the reinforcing or other actions of ethanol is inherently attractive as a hypothesis because of numerous studies demonstrating the reinforcing or addictive properties of opiates. A demonstration of a significant effect of ethanol on the endogenous opiate systems could indicate common mechanisms in the addictive actions of ethanol and opiates. A number of approaches have provided evidence that ethanol's effects on brain opiate systems might play a role in reinforcement.

Three major subtypes of opiate receptors (μ, κ, and δ) have been identified to date (reviewed in Ref. 324), and the effects of ethanol on the binding of ligands to the various subtypes of opiate receptors have been extensively investigated and reviewed elsewhere (207). Ethanol has selective effects on ligand binding to opiate receptor subtypes. In mouse striatal tissue, ethanol had a biphasic effect on dihydromorphine (DHM) binding to μ opiate receptors: Lower concentrations of ethanol (50 mM) increased binding, whereas higher concentrations (200 mM) inhibited binding (325). Ethanol inhibited the binding of (2-D-Ala, 5-D-Leu)enkephalin (ENK) to striatal δ opiate receptors (325). The striatal δ receptors were more sensitive than the μ receptors to the inhibitory effect of ethanol, as was also found in whole rat brain (326). In mouse frontal cortex, however, ethanol had an approximately equal inhibitory effect on ligand binding to μ and δ opiate receptors, whereas binding to M receptors was unaffected by ethanol (327).

Investigations of the effects of ethanol on opiate peptide dynamics in the brain have been difficult to perform. Because of the relatively complex mechanisms for synthesis and release of endogenous opiates, the results obtained so far are equivocal. Studies by Herz and his colleagues (328) indicated that acute ethanol treatment of rats resulted in increased striatal levels of methionine enkephalin. On the other hand, Ryder et al. (329) found that administration of a higher dose of ethanol to rats did not alter levels of leucine enkephalin. The radioimmunoassays for measuring peptide levels and the methods for isolating the peptides vary significantly among laboratories, and these variations can influence the results and interpretations. Measurement of mRNA levels for the β-endorphin precursor pro-opiomelanocortin (POMC) can overcome some of these difficulties for this particular opioid peptide. In cultured rat pituitary cells and transformed pituitary cells, ethanol reduces mRNA for POMC (i.e., reduce synthesis) and reduces β-endorphin release (330). It is interesting that alcoholics have been reported to have *reduced* CSF levels of β-endorphin when sober (331) and possibly to exhibit a trend toward lower CSF levels of enkephalin (332). In an interesting series of recent pharmacogenetic studies, it was found that there are differences between the brain and pituitary β-endorphin systems of the high-alcohol-drinking Alko-alcohol (AA) and low-alcohol-drinking Alko-nonalcohol (ANA) rats (333–335). POMC mRNA or β-endorphin-like peptide levels were significantly higher in some brain regions of the AA rats compared with ANA rats (333). Moreover, voluntary ethanol consumption in the AA rats was reduced by intracerebroventricular injections of a selective μ-receptor antagonist (334). Furthermore, spontaneous in vivo release of β-endorphin from the hypothalamus was higher in AA than in ANA rats, but the ethanol-induced increase in β-endorphin release was similar in both rat lines (335). Consequently, ethanol appears to have effects on opiate peptide dynamics in some brain regions. Assessments of brain enkephalin levels in alcohol-preferring and alcohol-avoiding mice and other aspects of the literature regarding endogenous opiate system characteristics in humans and animals have led Blum and his colleagues (336, 337) to enunciate an "opioid deficiency hypothesis." Simply stated, the hypothesis indicates that alcoholics are inherently deficient in the "activity" of their opiate systems and that intake of ethanol compensates for such a deficiency. The compensation by ethanol could occur by way of ethanol-induced increases in brain enkephalin levels (328) or by ethanol-generated opiate-like alkaloids (tetrahydropapaveroline (THP), salsolinol) that arise through actions of the acetaldehyde generated by metabolism of ethanol (338). Acetaldehyde may directly condense with dopamine to form salsolinol or compete with the metabolism of biogenic aldehydes to promote the condensation of the biogenic amine transmitters with their own aldehyde metabolites to form compounds such as THP (339). It should be noted that the "opiate deficiency hypothesis" is inconsistent with the decreased alcohol consumption produced by opiate antagonists in animals and humans (see below).

Reid et al. (340), on the other hand, have proposed an "opiate surfeit hypothesis" to explain "loss of control" type of ethanol intake by alcoholics. This hypothesis indicates that "loss of control is a product of an excess or surfeit in opioidergic activity." A corollary to this hypothesis would be that initial intake of ethanol would exacerbate the surfeit in opioidergic activity and result in loss of control drinking. Opioids acting at the level of the μ and δ opioid receptors are reinforcing in experimental animals (reviewed in Ref. 341). Consequently, if this hypothesis is correct, blockade of the actions of this endogenous opioids should decrease alcohol intake. Indeed, this finding has been reported in several studies. Opioid receptor antagonists decrease alcohol drinking or alcohol self-administration in monkeys and rodents. Moreover, low doses of morphine appear to stimulate alcohol intake in rats, while high doses of morphine, methadone, or several opioid peptides decrease alcohol drinking in rodents (341). The mechanism by which ethanol increases opioidergic activity remains unknown, but it could involve an increase in transcriptional and/or translational or posttranslational mechanisms (341, 342).

The importance of the opioid system in alcohol reinforcement and dependence has been underscored by the recent approval of naltrexone for the treatment of alcoholism. A double-blind, placebo-controlled clinical trial with 70 male alcohol-dependent patients demonstrated that naltrexone significantly reduced craving and days in which alcohol was consumed, which was reflected by a reduction in the number of relapses in the treated group (343). A similar conclusion was reached by O'Malley et al. (344) in a double-blind, placebo-controlled, randomized study with 97 alcohol-dependent patients. A more recent study (345) reports that naltrexone treatment reduced the "high" produced by ethanol and the amount of ethanol consumed during the first drinking episode. The authors conclude that "the lower alcohol consumption by the naltrexone-treated subjects may have resulted from naltrexone's blockage of the pleasure produced by alcohol." Consequently, blockade of the opioid system appears to reduce the reinforcing or euphoriant effects of ethanol. Naltrexone is the first clinically approved pharmacological agent capable of blocking the reinforcing properties of ethanol.

Arginine Vasopressin

Arginine vasopressin (AVP) is a mammalian antidiuretic hormone that is synthesized primarily in the hypothalamus and in some extrahypothalamic brain areas. AVP exerts a number of actions on neuroadaptive processes (i.e., learning, memory) in addition to its peripheral effects on the circulatory system (346). It was shown that in both mice and rats the administration of AVP or an analog will maintain (reduce the rate of loss of) functional ethanol tolerance, once that tolerance has been acquired, even in the absence of further ethanol intake by the animals (347, 348). In mice, AVP has been found to maintain tolerance to the hypnotic, hypothermic, and motor-impairing effects of ethanol; in rats, AVP has been found to maintain tolerance to the motor-impairing effect (347–349). The action of AVP on tolerance is mediated by CNS receptors, since the effect is observed after intracerebroventricular administration of doses that have no detectable peripheral effects (350).

There are two subtypes of vasopressin receptors: V_2 receptors are found in the kidney and are coupled with adenylate cyclase, while V_1 receptors were first identified in the liver and vascular smooth muscle and are coupled with polyphosphoinositide metabolism and increases in intracellular Ca^{2+} (351, 352). Studies with selective agonists and antagonists for these two receptor subtypes indicated that the effect of vasopressin on tolerance is mediated by V_1 receptors in the brain (353), consistent with binding studies and the demonstration that vasopressin can stimulate polyphosphoinositide metabolism in the hippocampus and lateral septum (areas with a high concentration of V_1 receptors) (346, 354, 355).

The mechanism by which vasopressin modulates the rate of loss of tolerance may involve effects on neurotransmitter release. In mice, depletion of norepinephrine after tolerance had been developed (this depletion did not affect *expression* of tolerance (356)) blocked the ability of vasopressin to maintain tolerance (357). More recent autoradiographic studies demonstrated that the 6-hydroxydopamine treatment that blocked the effect of vasopressin on tolerance also reduced the number of vasopressin V_1 receptors in the lateral septum (354). Since 6-hydroxydopamine acts by destroying catecholaminergic neuronal terminals, these data suggested that a portion of septal vasopressin receptors are localized on the terminals of catecholaminergic neurons. Vasopressin may act at these presynaptic terminals to directly modulate the release of norepinephrine (and/or dopamine). Although direct effects of vasopressin on the release of norepinephrine in hippocampal slices could not be demonstrated (358), these experiments have not yet been done with tissue from the lateral septum.

In rats, serotonergic systems appear to play an important role in the maintenance of ethanol tolerance by a vasopressin analog. Specifically, the analog could no longer maintain tolerance in animals in which the dorsal serotonergic afferent pathways to the hippocampus had been chemically denervated (359). The effect of serotonin depletion on the action of vasopressin in the mouse has been recently studied in more detail (360, 361). The authors found that intracerebroventricular injection of 5,7-dihydroxytryptamine into mice, which destroys serotonergic terminals from the raphe to the forebrain, impaired the ability of AVP to maintain tolerance. Continuous intracerebroventricular infusion of serotonin or a selective agonist for 5-HT$_2$ receptors was able to restore the effect of AVP (360). Serotoninergic pathways appear to be important not only for the effects of vasopressin on tolerance maintenance but also for the effects of this hormone in the development of tolerance. Wu et al. (361) recently reported that AVP facilitates the development of tolerance to a single intraperitoneal injection (1.8 g/kg) of ethanol. The destruction of serotonin neuronal terminals by intracerebroventricular injection of 5,7-dihydrotryptamine prevented the facilitatory effect of vasopressin to the development of tolerance. Destruction of catecholaminergic terminals did not prevent development of tolerance. Together, these results suggest that serotoninergic systems mediate, at least in part, the vasopressin-dependent maintenance and development of tolerance to ethanol.

In addition to the postulated presynaptic action of vasopressin in maintaining ethanol tolerance, recent data suggest an intriguing postsynaptic action of the peptide that may affect the rate of loss of tolerance. Vasopressin, administered intracerebroventricularly, was found to increase the levels of mRNA for the immediate early gene (IEG) c-fos in the lateral septum and hippocampus via an action at V_1 receptors (362, 363). This IEG, which is a cellular homolog of viral oncogenes, is normally involved in growth and development (364). However, its expression can also be stimulated by neurotransmitters, leading to the suggestion that it is involved in synaptic plasticity that may underlie various forms of neuroadaptation (365). The c-fos gene encodes a protein, Fos, that, in combination with the products of another IEG, c-jun, binds to specific sequences of DNA and increases the expression of other genes (366). Thus, the expression of c-fos provides a mechanism whereby the short-lived peptide vasopressin (which has a half-life of minutes) can induce long-term changes in CNS function that may be involved in the actions of the peptide on neuroadaptive processes such as memory and tolerance (346). Comparison of the effects of several peptides on the maintenance of ethanol tolerance and on c-fos expression revealed a correlation between the ability of the peptides to prolong tolerance and to increase c-fos expression in the lateral septum (as opposed to the hippocampus). Hence, if the effect of vasopressin on c-fos expression is important for the maintenance of tolerance; the data suggest that the site of action of vasopressin is the lateral septum (362). Interestingly, peripheral injection of AVP increases c-fos in specific brain areas, such as the suprachiasmatic, supraoptic, and paraventricular nuclei of the hypothalamus. Thus, this specificity on the actions of AVP may be important for the ability of this hormone to maintain tolerance to ethanol.

Most of the studies of the ability of AVP to maintain tolerance have examined the effect of administered peptide. However, there is also some evidence that endogenous AVP plays a role in the normal maintenance of ethanol tolerance. For example, intracerebroventricular administration of a V_1 receptor antagonist increased the rate of loss of tolerance in mice, presumably by blocking the action of endogenous peptide (353). Another piece of evidence supporting a role for endogenous AVP in modulation of ethanol tolerance comes from studies by Pittman et al. (367) who reported that ethanol tolerance did not develop in Brattleboro rats exposed chronically to ethanol. These rats are genetically deficient in vasopressin (368). In this study of Brattleboro rats, tolerance was measured 48 hours after the animals were removed from the ethanol inhalation chambers, and it is possible that they had also developed tolerance but lost it more rapidly than controls; i.e., that endogenous vasopressin actually plays a role in modulating the rate of loss of tolerance.

EFFECTS OF ETHANOL ON NEUROTROPHIC FACTORS

Growth factors and their receptors are another important component of cellular signal transduction in the nervous system. The broad term neurotrophic factor refers to a growth factor that is important for the development and/or maintenance of the nervous system (reviewed in Ref. 369). The list of neurotrophic factors includes fibroblast growth factor (FGF), epidermal growth factor (EGF), insulin and insulin-related growth factor (IGF), platelet-derived growth factor (PDGF), vascular endothelial growth factor (VEGF), and the neurotrophins. The term neurotrophin is used to collectively designate the following neurotrophic factors: nerve-derived growth factor (NGF), brain-derived neurotrophic factor (BDNF), and neurotrophins 3 and 4/5. These neurotrophic factors bind to one of six classes of tyrosine kinase-coupled receptors designated as the EGF (class I), IGF (class II), PDGF (class III), FGF (class IV), eph (class V; orphan receptor), and Trk (class VI) family of receptors (369). In most cases, binding of the growth factors to their receptors produces dimerization or conformational changes that lead to the activation of the receptor's intrinsic tyrosine kinase activity and autophosphorylation on tyrosine residues (370). These autophosphorylated tyrosine residues act as docking sites for the binding and activation of proteins containing src homology-2 (SH$_2$) domains (369, 370). The list of SH$_2$-domain-containing proteins that are activated by neurotrophic factor receptors include the src family of tyrosine kinases, phosphatidylinositol 3-kinase, ras-GTPase-activating protein (GAP), protein tyrosine phosphatase 1D, phospholipase C-γ (PLC-γ), and several adaptor proteins (Shc, Grb2, Nck) involved in the ras signal transduction cascade (369, 370).

A growing body of experimental evidence indicates that ethanol interacts with the NGF-coupled signaling systems. Ethanol administration in ovo to chick embryos induces a decrease in choline acetyltransferase activity of both brain and spinal cord that can be reversed by concomitant administration of NGF (or EGF) (371). Moreover, ethanol induced an increase in cholinergic and a decrease in GABAergic neuronal expression in cultures from chick embryo cerebral hemispheres (372). The ethanol-induced decrease in GABAergic neuronal expression was blocked by NGF, whereas the NGF-induced increase in cholinergic neuronal expression was affected by ethanol (372). NGF was also shown to ameliorate ethanol-induced toxicity in cultured dorsal root ganglion neurons (373) and in dissociated septal neuronal cultures from fetal rats (374). Consequently, NGF appears to exert protective actions against the neurotoxic actions of ethanol in different neuronal populations.

Other investigators found that NGF (and FGF) can enhance potentially neurotoxic effects induced by ethanol. Messing et al. (375) found that ethanol potentiated NGF- and FGF-induced neurite outgrowth in cultured neurons derived from pheochromocytomas (PC12 cells). These authors postulate that ethanol could affect the normal functioning or development of the nervous system by increasing the growth of neural processes and disturbing synaptic organization. Recent work by the same group determined more details of the mechanism of action of ethanol on neurite outgrowth in growth factor-treated PC12 cells. Ethanol increased NGF- and FGF-induced activation of mitogen-activated protein (MAP) kinases, which relays trophic signals from membrane growth factor receptors to the nucleus (376). This increase in growth factor-activated MAP kinase activity was blocked by downregulation of the isoforms β, δ, and ε of PKC. Consequently, ethanol appears to enhance growth factor-dependent signal transduction downstream of growth factor receptors, and its effects seem to involve other signaling molecules such as PKC.

Ethanol was also shown to affect levels of NGF and/or NGF receptors under some experimental conditions. Valles et al. (377) found that prenatal ethanol treatment of rats resulted in an increase in the number of NGF receptors and in the intracellular pool of NGF and NGF receptors in cultured cortical astrocytes. It was also found that these astrocytes secreted less NGF, which could have harmful effects for cortical neuronal migration during development. The NGF signaling system in the adult brain also appears to be sensitive to ethanol. Aloe and Tirassa (378, 379) reported that chronic exposure of rats to ethanol causes a reduction of NGF in the hippocampus and in the hypothalamus and a reduction of NGF receptors in the septum and nucleus of Meynert. Intracerebral injection of NGF returned NGF receptor expression to normal levels. However, other investigators have failed to reproduce these findings. Chronic treatment with ethanol of rats did not affect the mRNA or protein NGF levels or the neurotropic activity of this growth factor in the hippocampus (380). Therefore, more research is required to determine the details of ethanol's effects on NGF signaling systems in the developing and adult brain.

The effects of ethanol on insulin and IGF-coupled signaling systems in the brain have also been studied. Prenatal exposure to ethanol of rats affected the normal developmental regulation, but not the localization, of IGF-1 mRNA expression in the brains of the offspring (381). Quantitative autoradiography and in situ hybridization showed no alteration in the numbers of IGF-1 and IGF-2 receptors, indicating that ethanol's effects are not at the level of the IGF receptor but at the level of the growth factor itself. However, it should be noted that ethanol was shown to affect the function of IGF receptors, although different laboratories reported different results. Resnicoff et al. (382, 383) showed that ethanol inhibited IGF-1-induced proliferation of cultured fibroblasts and blocked IGF-1 receptor tyrosine autophosphorylation, tyrosine phosphorylation of insulin receptor substrate 1, and the association of phosphatidylinositol 3-kinase. A similar inhibitory effect of ethanol on insulin-induced tyrosine phosphorylation of insulin receptor substrate 1 was found by Xu et al. (384), along with an ethanol-induced inhibition of insulin-stimulated neuronal thread protein gene expression in a primitive neuroectodermal tumor cell line. Conversely, others have shown that ethanol enhances the stimulatory effects of insulin and IGF-1 on DNA synthesis in fibroblasts (385). Obviously, more work will be required to determine the reasons for the discrepancies between the findings of these studies. It should be noted here that some of these studies also measured the effects of ethanol on the PDGF receptor system (382, 383, 385) and found no effects. A lack of effects of ethanol was found in *Xenopus* oocytes expressing recombinant human PDGF receptors (386). Thus, not all growth factor receptors appear to have the same sensitivity to the actions of ethanol.

In summary, several lines of experimental evidence suggest that some neurotrophic factor-dependent signaling systems are affected by ethanol. In addition, these factors might protect neuronal cells against ethanol's neurotoxic effects. Since these factors are important during the development of the CNS, the interaction between ethanol and neurotrophic factors might be of special importance in the pathogenesis of the fetal alcohol syndrome. In addition, the effects of ethanol on these neurotrophic signaling systems might also be important in the adult brain because these factors produce short- and long-term modulatory effects on neuronal signaling and synaptic plasticity (387–389). An interesting challenge for future research will be to determine the precise role of the neurotrophic factors in the acute and chronic actions of ethanol in the developing and mature nervous system.

CONCLUSIONS

During the past decade, tremendous advances have occurred in understanding the neurobiology of alcohol actions. However, key questions regarding the precise sites of action of ethanol remain unanswered. Here we briefly discuss what we have learned and what questions remain.

With regard to the acute actions of ethanol, major advances include the demonstration that ethanol, like other drugs of abuse, increases the firing (and release of dopamine) in mesolimbic pathways, particularly the VTA and nucleus accumbens. This action is likely critical to the rewarding actions of ethanol, but the neurochemical and biophysical mechanisms responsible for this effect remain to be elucidated. The reductionist approach of searching for synaptic receptors sensitive to ethanol has been successful, and the ligand-gated ion channels (e.g., GABA$_A$, glycine, NMDA, AMPA, kainate receptors, and neuronal nAChRs) have emerged as likely sites of alcohol action. However, there is not definitive evidence linking any of these receptors to specific behavioral actions of alcohol. Likewise, the mechanisms by which ethanol affects the function of these receptors is not clear. Specifically, is there a direct interaction between ethanol and specific amino acids of these receptors, or is it a less direct mechanism? In this respect, there is considerable evidence that protein phosphorylation either determines or modifies the actions of ethanol on some of these receptors. An unanswered question is whether ethanol directly affects the activity of protein kinases or phosphatases. Although much attention has been given to the ligand-gated ion channels, it is important to remember that several voltage-gated channels, most notably calcium channels, are also quite sensitive to ethanol. There are also rather selective effects of ethanol on several G-protein-coupled receptors and effectors (e.g., adenylyl cyclase). Now that these actions of ethanol have been identified in isolated systems, the challenge is to determine which sites are important for specific electrophysiological and behavioral actions of alcohol.

Studies of chronic exposure to alcohol have delineated a number of neurochemical responses, but their relationship to tolerance and dependence has yet to be rigorously defined. There appear to be changes in the expression of numerous genes (e.g., G proteins, c-*fos*, GABA$_A$, and NMDA receptor subunits, chaperonin proteins) during chronic ethanol exposure, changes in protein kinase activity, and changes in the function of ligand-gated ion channels. Thus, chronic alcohol treatment produces a fascinating example of "molecular rewiring" of the brain. The critical question is, which of these many neurochemical changes are really important for tolerance or dependence? Answering this question may be critical to the evolution of new therapeutic interventions for alcohol dependence.

Both acute and chronic alcohol treatments clearly have widespread and complex neurobiological actions. How can a causal relationship be established between a neurochemical or electrophysiological change and a behavior for a drug with such diverse actions? Perhaps the most powerful approach is a combination of molecular and behavioral genetics. Actions of ethanol such as severe intoxication, acute tolerance, and withdrawal seizure severity have been studied genetically in mice and rats. Recent advances in molecular genetics make it feasible to define the genes that regulate these actions of ethanol in these animal models. This may provide a strategy for linking specific proteins to behavioral actions of alcohol. In addition, the relationship of the corresponding human genes to alcoholism can then be determined, again leading to the possibility of new therapeutic interventions. It appears that alcohol research is entering a synergistic phase in which rapid advances in molecular and biophysical analysis of brain function will be combined with molecular genetic analysis of animal models to answer some of the long-standing questions regarding the neurobiology of alcohol action.

Acknowledgment. *Portions of this chapter have been modified from a previous edition of this textbook (14). We thank Drs. Boris Tabakoff, Paula Hoffman, and Kathy Grant for advice and assistance with this chapter.*

References

1. Meyer HH. Zur Theorie der Alcolnarkose: der Einfluss wechselnder Temperatur auf Wirkungs-Starke und Teilungs Coefficient der Narkotica. Naunyn Schmiedebergs Arch Exp Pathol Pharmacol 1901;46:338–346.
2. Lipnick RL. Hans Horst Meyer and the lipid theory of narcosis. Trends Pharmacol Sci 1989;10: 265–269.
3. Brinley FJ Jr. Excitation and conduction in nerve fibers. In: Mountcastle VB, ed. Medical physiology. St. Louis: CV Mosby, 1980:46–81.
4. Singer SJ, Nicholson GL. The fluid mosaic model of the structure of cell membranes. Science 1972;175:720–731.
5. Tabakoff B, Hoffman PL, McLaughlin A. Is ethanol a discriminating substance? Semin Liver Dis 1988;8:26–35.
6. Chin JH, Goldstein DB. Drug tolerance in biomembranes: a spin label study of the effects of ethanol. Science 1977;196:684–685.
7. Harris RA, Schroeder F. Ethanol and the physical properties of brain membranes: fluorescence studies. Mol Pharmacol 1981;20:128–137.
8. Goldstein DB, Chin JH, Lyon RC. Ethanol disordering of spin-labeled mouse brain membranes—correlation with genetically-determined ethanol sensitivity of mice. Proc Natl Acad Sci U S A 1982;79:4231–4233.

9. Pang KY, Braswell LM, Chang L, Sommer TJ, Miller KW. The perturbation of lipid bilayers by general anesthetics: a quantitative test of the disordered lipid hypothesis. Mol Pharmacol 1980; 18:84–90.

10. Miller KW. The nature of the site of general anesthesia. Int Rev Neurobiol 1985;27:1–61.

11. Franks NP, Lieb WR. Do general anesthetics act by competitive binding to specific receptors? Nature 1984;310:599–601.

12. Deitrich RA, Dunwiddie TV, Harris RA, Erwin VG. Mechanism of action of ethanol: initial central nervous system actions. Pharmacol Rev 1989;41:489–537.

13. Pringle MU, Brown KB, Miller KW. Can the lipid theories of anesthesia account for the cutoff in anesthetic potency in homologous series of alcohols? Mol Pharmacol 1981;19:49–55.

14. Tabakoff B, Hoffman PL. Alcohol: neurobiology. In: Lowinson JH, Ruiz P, Millman RB, Langrod JG, eds. Substance abuse: a comprehensive textbook. 2nd ed. Baltimore: Williams & Wilkins, 1992:152–185.

15. Hille B. Ionic channels of excitable membranes. 2nd ed. Sunderland, MA: Sinauer, 1992:1–170.

16. McDonald RL, Olsen RW. GABA_A receptor channels. Annu Rev Neurosci 1994;17:569–602.

17. Sieghart W. Structure and pharmacology of γ-aminobutyric acid_A receptor subtypes. Pharmacol Rev 1995;47:181–234.

18. Liljequist S, Engel JA. Effects of GABAergic agonists and antagonists on various ethanol-induced behavioral changes. Psychopharmacology 1982;78:71–75.

19. Martz A, Deitrich RA, Harris RA. Behavioral evidence for involvement of γ-aminobutyric acid in the actions of ethanol. Eur J Pharmacol 1983;89:53–62.

20. Mihic SJ, Harris RA. Alcohol actions at the GABA_A receptor/chloride channel complex. In: Deitrich RA, Erwin G, eds. Pharmacological effects of ethanol on the nervous system. Boca Raton, FL: CRC Press, 1995.

21. Allan AM, Harris RA. Gamma-aminobutyric acid and alcohol actions: neurochemical studies of long sleep and short sleep mice. Life Sci 1986;39:2005–2015.

22. Wafford KA, Burnett DM, Dunwiddie TV, Harris RA. Genetic differences in the ethanol sensitivity of GABA_A receptors expressed in Xenopus oocytes. Science 1990;249:291–293.

23. Korpi ER. Role of GABA_A receptors in the actions of alcohol and in alcoholism: recent advances. Alcohol Alcohol 1994;29:115–129.

24. Uusi-Oukari M, Korpi AT. Specific alterations in the cerebellar GABA_A receptors of an alcohol-sensitive ANT rat line. Alcohol Clin Exp Res 1991;15:241–248.

25. Allan AM, Harris RA. Neurochemical studies of genetic differences in alcohol action. In: Crabbe JC, Harris RA, eds. The genetic basis of alcohol and drug action. New York: Plenum Press, 1991.

26. Allan AM, Harris RA. Ethanol and barbiturates enhance GABA-stimulated influx of ^{36}Cl in isolated brain membranes. Pharmacologist 1985; 27:125.

27. Ticku MK, Lowrimore P, Lehoullier P. Ethanol enhances GABA-induced ^{36}Cl influx in primary spinal cord cultured neurons. Brain Res Bull 1986;17:123–126.

28. Nishio M, Narahashi T. Ethanol enhancement of GABA-activated chloride current in rat dorsal root ganglion neurons. Brain Res 1990;518: 283–286.

29. Reynolds JN, Prasad A, MacDonald JF. Ethanol modulation of GABA receptor-activated Cl$^-$ currents in neurons of the chick, rat and mouse central nervous system. Eur J Pharmacol 1992; 224:173–181.

30. Givens BS, Breese GR. Site-specific enhancement of γ-aminobutyric acid-mediated inhibition of neural activity by ethanol in the rat medial septal area. J Pharmacol Exp Ther 1990; 254:528–538.

31. Criswell HE, Simson PE, Duncan GE, et al. Molecular basis for regionally specific action of ethanol on γ-aminobutyric acid_A receptors: generalization to other ligand-gated ion channels. J Pharmacol Exp Ther 1993;267:522–537.

32. Soldo BL, Proctor WR, Dunwiddie TV. Ethanol differentially modulates GABA_A receptor-mediated chloride currents in hippocampal, cortical and septal neurons in rat brain slices. Synapse 1994;18:94–103.

33. Weiner JL, Zhang L, Carlen PL. Potentiation of GABA_A-mediated synaptic current by ethanol in hippocampal CA1 neurons: possible role of protein kinase C. J Pharmacol Exp Ther 1994;268: 1388–1395.

34. Harris RA, McQuilkin SJ, Paylor R, Abeliovich A, Tonegawa S, Wehner JM. Mutant mice lacking the γ isoform of protein kinase C show decreased behavioral actions of ethanol and altered function of γ-aminobutyrate type A receptors. Proc Natl Acad Sci U S A 1995;92:3658–3662.

35. Lin AM-Y, Bickford PC, Palmer MR. The effects of ethanol on δ-aminobutyric acid-induced depressions of cerebellar Purkinje neurons: influence of β adrenergic receptor action in young and aged Fisher 344 rats. J Pharmacol Exp Ther 1993;264:951–957.

36. Whatley VJ, Brozowski SJ, Hadingham KL, Whiting PJ, Harris RA. Microtubule depolymerization inhibits ethanol-induced enhancement of GABA_A responses in stably transfected cells. J Neurochem 1996;66:1318–1321.

37. Wafford KA, Burnett DM, Leidenheimer NJ, et al. Ethanol sensitivity of the GABA_A receptor expressed in Xenopus oocytes requires eight amino acids contained in the γ_{2L} subunit of the receptor complex. Neuron 1991;7:27–33.

38. Wafford KA, Whiting PJ. Ethanol potentiation of GABA_A receptors requires phosphorylation of the alternatively spliced variant of the gamma 2 subunit. FEBS Lett 1992;313:113–117.

39. Harris RA, Proctor WR, McQuilkin SJ, Klein RL, Mascia MP, Whatley V, Whiting PJ, Dunwiddie TV. Ethanol increases GABA_A responses in cells stably transfected with receptor subunits. Alcohol Clin Exp Res 1995;19: 226–232.

40. Sigel E, Baur R, Malherbe P. Recombinant GABA_A receptor function and ethanol. FEBS Lett 1993;324:140–142.

41. Mihic SJ, Whiting PJ, Harris RA. Anaesthetic concentrations of alcohols potentiate GABA_A receptor-mediated currents: lack of subunit specificity. Eur J Phamacol 1994;268:209–214.

42. Kurata Y, Marszalec W, Hamilton BJ, Carter DB, Narahashi T. Alcohol modulation of cloned GABA_A receptor-channel complex expressed in human kidney cell lines. Brain Res 1993; 631:143–146.

43. Morrow AL. Regulation of GABA_A receptor function and gene expression in the central nervous system. Int Rev Neurobiol 1995;38:1–41.

44. Morrow AL, Suzdak PD, Karanian JW, Paul SM. Chronic ethanol administration alter γ-aminobutyric acid, pentobarbital, and ethanol-mediated ^{36}Cl$^-$ uptake in cerebral cortical synaptoneurosomes. J Pharmacol Exp Ther 1988;246:158–164.

45. Sanna, E, Serra M, Cossu A, Colombo G, Follesa P, Cuccheddu T, Concas A, Biggio G. Chronic ethanol intoxication induces differential effects on GABA_A and NMDA receptor function on the rat brain. Alcohol Clin Exp Res 1993;17:115–123.

46. Buck KJ, Harris RA. Chronic ethanol exposure of Xenopus oocytes expressing mouse brain mRNA reduced GABA_A receptor-activated current and benzodiazepine modulation. Mol Neuropharmacol 1991;1:59–64.

47. Gonzalez LP, Czachura JF. Reduced behavioral responses to intranigral muscimol following chronic ethanol. Physiol Behav 1988;46: 473–477.

48. Allan AM, Harris RA. Acute and chronic ethanol treatments alter GABA receptor-operated chloride channels. Pharmacol Biochem Behav 1987;27:665–670.

49. Frye GD, McCown TJ, Breese GR. Characterization of susceptibility to audiogenic seizures in ethanol-dependent rats after microinjection of γ-aminobutyric acid (GABA) agonists into the inferior colliculus, substantia nigra or medial septum. J Pharmacol Exp Ther 1983;227:663–670.

50. Mihic SJ, Kalant H, Liu JF, Wu PH. Tole of the GABA-receptor/chloride-channel complex in tolerance to ethanol and cross tolerance to diazepam and pentobarbital. J Pharmacol Exp Ther 1992;261:108–113.

51. Buck KJ, Harris RA. Benzodiazepine agonist and inverse agonist actions on GABA_A receptor-operated chloride channels. II. Chronic effects of ethanol. J Pharmacol Exp Ther 1990;253: 713–719.

52. Mahtre MC, Mehta AK, Ticku MK. Chronic ethanol administration increases the binding of the benzodiazepine inverse agonist and alcohol antagonist [^{3}H]Rl 15–4513 in rat brain. Eur J Pharmacol 1988;153:141–145.

53. Klein RL, Mascia MP, Whiting PJ, Harris RA. GABA_A receptor function and binding in stably transfected cells: chronic ethanol treatment. Alcohol Clin Exp Res 1995;19:1338–1344.

54. Mehta AK, Ticku MK. Chronic ethanol treatment alters the behavioral effects of Ro 15-4513, a partially negative ligand for benzodiazepine binding sites. Brain Res 1989;489: 93–100.

55. Allan AM, Baier LD, Zhang X. Effects of lorazepam tolerance and withdrawal on GABA_A receptor-operated chloride channels. J Pharmacol Exp Ther 1992;261:395–402.

56. Devaud LL, Smith FD, Grayson DR, Morrow AL. Chronic ethanol consumption differentially alters the expression of γ-aminobutyric acid_A receptor subunit mRNAs in rat cerebral cortex: competitive, quantitative reverse transcriptase-polymerase chain reaction analysis. Mol Pharmacol 1995;48:861–868.

57. McCown TJ, Breese GR. A potential contribution to ethanol withdrawal kindling: reduced GABA function in the inferior collicular cortex. Alcohol Clin Exp Res 1993;17:1290–1294.

58. Faingold CL, Riaz A. Ethanol withdrawal increases firing in inferior colliculus neurons associated with audiogenic seizure susceptibility. Exp Neurol 1995;132:91–98.

59. Peris J, Coleman-Hardee M, Burry J, Pecins-Thompson M. Selective changes in GABAergic transmission in substantia nigra and superior colliculus caused by ethanol and ethanol withdrawal. Alcohol Clin Exp Res 1992;16: 311–319.

60. Cooper Br, Viik K, Ferris RM, White HL. Antagonism of the enhanced susceptibility to audiogenic seizures during alcohol withdrawal in the rat by γ-aminobutyric acid (GABA) and

"GABA-mimetic" agents. J Pharmacol Exp Ther 1979;209:396–403.

61. Goldstein DB. Alcohol withdrawal reactions in mice: effect of drugs that modify neurotransmission. J Pharmacol Exp Ther 1973;186:1–9.

62. Gonzalez LP, Hettinger MK. Intranigral muscimol suppresses ethanol withdrawal seizures. Brain Res 1984;298:163–166.

63. Taberner PV, Unwin JW. Behavioral effects of muscimol, amphetamine, and chlorpromazine on ethanol tolerant mice. Br J Pharmacol 1981; 74:2761–2762.

64. Volkow ND, Wang G-J, Hitzemann R, Fowler JS, Wolf AP, Pappas N, Biegon A, Dewey S. Decreased cerebral response to inhibitory neurotransmission in alcoholics. Am J Psychiatry 1993;150:417–422.

65. Volkow ND, Wang G-J, Begleiter H, et al. Regional brain metabolic response to lorazepam in subjects at risk for alcoholism. Alcohol Clin Exp Res 1995;19:510–516.

66. Buck KJ, Heim H, Harris RA. Reversal of alcohol dependence and tolerance by a single administration of flumazenil. J Pharmacol Exp Ther 1991;257:984–989.

67. Criswell HE, Breese GR. Evidence for involvement of an endogenous benzodiazepine inverse agonist in tolerance to the anticonflict action of ethanol. Alcohol Clin Exp Res 1990;14:279.

68. June HL, Duemler SE, Greene TL, et al. Effects of the benzodiazepine inverse agonist Ro 19-4603 on the maintenance of tolerance to a single dose of ethanol. J Pharmacol Exp Ther 1995; 274:1105–1112.

69. Johanson CE. Discriminative stimulus effects of diazepam in humans. J Pharmacol Exp Ther 1991;257:634–643.

70. Rees DC, Balster RL. Attenuation of the discriminative stimulus properties of ethanol and oxazepam, but not of pentobarbital, by Ro 15-4513 in mice. J Pharmacol Exp Ther 1988;244: 592–598.

71. Allan AM, Huidobro-Toro JP, Bleck V, Harris RA. Alcohol and the GABA receptor-chloride channel complex of brain. Alcohol Alcohol 1987;1(suppl):643–646.

72. Winter JC. The stimulus properties of morphine and ethanol. Psychopharmacology 1975;44: 209–214.

73. Samson HH, Tolliver GA, Schwarz-Stevens K. Oral ethanol self-administration: a behavioral pharmacological approach to CNS control mechanisms. Alcohol 1990;7:187–191.

74. Koob GF, Weiss F. Pharmacology of drug self-administration. Alcohol 1990;7:193–197.

75. Rassnick S, D'amico E, Riley E, Koob G. GABA antagonist and benzodiazepine partial inverse agonist reduce motivated responding for ethanol. Alcohol Clin Exp Res 1993;17:124–130.

76. Balakleevsky A, Colombo G, Fadda F, Gessa GL. Ro 19-4603, a benzodiazepine receptor inverse agonist, attenuates voluntary ethanol consumption in rats selectively bred for high ethanol preference. Alcohol Alcohol 1990;25: 449–452.

77. June HL, Murphy JM, Mellor-Burke JJ, Lumeng L, Li TK. The benzodiazepine inverse agonist Ro 19-4603 exerts prolonged and selective suppression of ethanol intake in alcohol-preferring (P) rats. Psychopharmacology 1994;115:325–331.

78. Harris RA, Brodie MS, Dunwiddie TV. Possible substrates of ethanol reinforcement: GABA and dopamine. Ann N Y Acad Sci 1992;654:61–69.

79. Bechade C, Sur C, Triller A. The inhibitory neuronal glycine receptor. Bioessays 1994;16: 735–744.

80. Williams KL, Ferko AP, Barbieri EJ, DiGrego-

rio GJ. Glycine enhances the central depressant properties of ethanol in mice. Pharmacol Biochem Behav 1995;2:199–205.

81. Celentano JJ, Gibbs TT, Farb DH. Ethanol potentiates GABA- and glycine-induced chloride currents in chick spinal cord neurons. Brain Res 1988;455:377–380.

82. Engblom AC, Åkerman KEO. Effect of ethanol on δ-aminobutyric acid and glycine receptor-coupled Cl⁻ fluxes in rat brain synaptoneurosomes. J Neurochem 1991;57:384–390.

83. Aguayo LG, Pancetii FC. Ethanol modulation of the γ-aminobutyric acid$_A$- and glycine-activated Cl⁻ current in cultured mouse neurons. J Pharmacol Exp Ther 1994;270:61–69.

84. Mascia MP, Mihic SJ, Valenzuela CF, Schofield PR, Harris RA. A single amino acid determines differences in ethanol actions on strychnine-sensitive glycine receptors. Mol Pharmacol 1996;50:402–406.

85. Mascia MP, Machu TK, Harris RA. Enhancement of homomeric glycine receptor function by long-chain alcohols and anaesthetics. Br J Pharmacol (in press).

86. Kulkarni SK, Mehta AK, Ticku MK. Comparison of anticonvulsant effects of ethanol against NMDA-, kainic acid-, and picrotoxin-induced convulsions in rats. Life Sci 1990;46:481–487.

87. Sharma AC, Thorat SN, Nayar U, Kulkarni SK. Dizocilpine, ketamine and ethanol reverse NMDA-induced EEG changes and convulsions in rats and mice. Indian J Physiol Pharmacol 1991;35:111–116.

88. Meller ST, Dykstra C, Pechman PS, Maver TJ, Gebhart GF. Ethanol dose-dependently attenuates NMDA-mediated thermal hyperalgesia in the rat. Neurosci Lett 1993;154:137–140.

89. Daniell LC. The noncompetitive N-methyl-D-partate antagonists, MK-801, phencyclidine and ketamine, increase the potency of general anesthetics. Pharmacol Biochem Behav 1990;36: 111–115.

90. Daniell LC. Effect of CGS 19755, a competitive N-methyl-D-aspartate antagonist, on general anesthetic potency. Pharmacol Biochem Behav 1991;40:767–769.

91. Grant KA, Colombo G. Discriminative stimulus effects of ethanol: effect of training dose on the substitution of N-methyl-D-aspartate antagonists. J Pharmacol Exp Ther 1993;264:1241–1247.

92. Wilson WR, Bosy TZ, Ruth JA. NMDA agonists and antagonists alter the hypnotic response to ethanol in LS and SS mice. Alcohol 1990; 7:389–395.

93. Hoffman PL, Moses F, Tabakoff B. Selective inhibition by ethanol of glutamate-stimulated cyclic GMP production in primary cultures of cerebellar granule cells. Neuropharmacology 1989;28:1239–1243.

94. Dildy JE, Leslie SW. Ethanol inhibits NMDA-induced increases in intracellular Ca²⁺ in dissociated brain cells. Brain Res 1989;499:383–387.

95. Rabe CS, Tabakoff B. Glycine site-directed agonists reverse the actions of ethanol at the N-methyl d-aspartate receptor. Mol Pharmacol 1990;38:753–757.

96. Woodward JJ, Gonzales RA. Ethanol inhibition of N-methyl-D-aspartate-stimulated endogenous dopamine release from rat striata slices: reversal by glycine. J Neurochem 1990;45:712–715.

97. Fink K, Gothert M. Inhibition of N-methyl-D-aspartate-induced noradrenaline release by alcohols is related to their hydrophobicity. Eur J Pharmacol 1990;191:225–229.

98. Chandler LJ, Guzman NJ, Sumners C, Crews FT. Magnesium and zinc potentiate ethanol inhibition of N-methyl-D-aspartate-stimulated ni-

tric oxide synthase in cortical neurons. J Pharmacol Exp Ther 1994;271:67–75.

99. Lovinger DM, White G, Weight FF. Ethanol inhibits NMDA-activated ion current in hippocampal neurons. Science 1989;243:1721–1724.

100. White G, Lovinger DM, Weight FF. Ethanol inhibits NMDA-activated current but does not alter GABA-activated current in an isolated adult mammalian neuron. Brain Res 1990;507: 332–336.

101. Lima-Ladman MTR, Albuquerque EX. Ethanol potentiates and blocks NMDA-activated single-channel currents in rat hippocampal pyramidal cells. FEBS Lett 1989;247: 61–67.

102. Lovinger DM, White G, Weight FF. NMDA receptor-mediated synaptic excitation selectively inhibited by ethanol in hippocampal slice from adult rat. J Neurosci 1990;10: 1372–1379.

103. Morrisett RA, Martin D, Oetting TA, Lewis DV, Wilson WA, Swartzwelder HS. Ethanol and magnesium ions inhibit N-methyl-D-aspartate-mediated synaptic potentials in an interactive manner. Neuropharmacology 1991; 30:1173–1178.

104. Dildy-Mayfield JE, Harris RA. Comparison of ethanol sensitivity of rat brain kainate, dl-α-amino-3-hydroxy-5-methyl-4-isoxolone propionic acid and N-methyl-D-aspartate receptors expressed in Xenopus oocytes. J Pharmacol Exp Ther 1992;262:487–494.

105. Koltchine V, Anantharam V, Wilson A, Bayley H, Treistman SN. Homomeric assemblies of NMDAR1 splice variants are sensitive to ethanol. Neurosci Lett 1993;152:13–16.

106. Kuner T, Schoepfer R, Korpi ER. Ethanol inhibits glutamate-induced currents in heteromeric NMDA receptor subtypes. Neuroreport 1993;5:297–300.

107. Chu B, Anantharam V, Treistman SN. Ethanol inhibition of recombinant heteromeric NMDA channels in the presence and absence of modulators. J Neurochem 1995;65:140–148.

108. Mirshahi T, Woodward JJ. Ethanol sensitivity of heteromeric NMDA receptors: effects of subunit assembly, glycine and NMDAR1 Mg²⁺-insensitive mutants. Neuropharmacology 1995;34:347–355.

109. Snell LD, Tabakoff B, Hoffman PL. Involvement of protein kinase C in ethanol-induced inhibition of NMDA receptor function in cerebellar granule cells. Alcohol Clin Exp Res 1994;18:81–85.

110. Izquierdo I, Medina JH, Bianchin M, Walz R, Zanatta MS, Da Silva RC, Bueno e Silva M, Ruschel AC, Paczko N. Memory processing by the limbic system: role of specific neurotransmitter systems. Behav Brain Res 1993;58: 91–98.

111. Gozlan H, Khazipov R, Ben-Ari Y. Multiple forms of long-term potentiation and multiple regulatory sites of N-methyl-D-aspartate receptors: role of the redox site. J Neurobiol 1995; 26:360–369.

112. Bliss TVP, Lomo T. Long-lasting potentiation of synaptic transmission in the dentate area of the anesthetized rabbit following stimulation of the perforant path. J Physiol (Lond) 1973; 232:357–374.

113. Morrisett RA, Swartzwelder HS. Attenuation of hippocampal long-term potentiation by ethanol: a patch-clamp analysis of glutamatergic and GABAergic mechanism. J Neurosci 1993;13:2264–2272.

114. Ripley TL, Little HJ. Nitrendipine prevents the

decrease caused by chronic ethanol intake in maintenance of tetanic long-term potentiation. Exp Brain Res 1995;103:1–8.

115. Wayner MJ, Armstrong DL, Polan-Curtain JL, Denny JB. Ethanol and diazepam inhibition of hippocampal LTP is mediated by angiotensin II and AT1 receptors. Peptides 1993; 14:441–444.

116. Grant KA, Valverius P, Hudspith M, Tabakoff B. Ethanol withdrawal seizures and the NMDA receptor complex. Eur J Pharmacol 1990;176: 289–296.

117. Gulya K, Grant KA, Valverius P, Hoffman PL, Tabakoff B. Brain regional specificity and time course of changes in the NMDA receptor-ionophore complex during ethanol withdrawal. Brain Res 1991;547:129–134.

118. Snell LD, Tabakoff B, Hoffman PL. The density of NMDA but not glycine binding sites is increased in ethanol-dependent mice. Alcohol Clin Exp Res 1991;15:333.

119. Michaelis EK, Mulvaney MJ, Freed WJ. Effects of acute and chronic ethanol intake on synaptosomal glutamate binding activity. Biochem Pharmacol 1978;27:1685–1691.

120. Hu XJ, Ticku MK. Chronic ethanol treatment upregulates the NMDA receptor function and binding in mammalian cortical neurons. Brain Res 1995;30:347–356.

121. Monaghan DT, Olverman HJ, Nguyen L, Watkins JC, Cotman CW. Two classes of N-methyl-D-aspartate recognition sites: differential distribution and differential regulation by glycine. Proc Natl Acad Sci U S A 1988;85: 9836–9840.

122. Massey BW, Wessinger WD. Changes in phencyclidine (PCP) receptor binding following cessation of chronic PCP administration. Pharmacologist 1990;32:192.

123. Beart PM, Lodge D. Chronic administration of MK-801 and the NMDA receptor: further evidence for reduced sensitivity of the primary acceptor site from studies with the cortical wedge preparation. J Pharm Pharmacol 1990; 42:354–355.

124. Iorio KR, Reinlib L, Tabakoff B, Hoffman PL. NMDA-induced [Ca^{2+}]i enhanced by chronic ethanol treatment in cultured cerebellar granule cells. Alcohol Clin Exp Res 1991;15:333.

125. White G, Lovinger DM, Grant KA. Ethanol (EtOH) inhibition of NMDA-activated ion current is not altered after chronic exposure of rats or neurons in culture. Alcohol Clin Exp Res 1990;14:352.

126. Morrisett RA. Potentiation of N-methyl-D-aspartate receptor-dependent afterdischarges in rat dentate gyrus following in vitro ethanol withdrawal. Neurosci Lett 1994;167:175–178.

127. Whittington MA, Lambert JD, Little HJ. Increased NMDA receptor and calcium channel activity underlying ethanol withdrawal hyperexcitability. Alcohol Alcohol 1995;30:105–114.

128. Hoffman PL. Glutamate receptors in alcohol withdrawal-induced neurotoxicity. Metabol Brain Dis 1995;10:73–79.

129. Hoffman PL, Iorio KR, Snell LD, Tabakoff B. Attenuation of glutamate-induced neurotoxicity in chronically ethanol-exposed cerebellar granule cells by NMDA receptor antagonists and ganglioside GM₁. Alcohol Clin Exp Res 1995;19:721–726.

130. Morrisett RA, Rezvani AH, Overstreet D, Janowsky DS, Wilson WA, Swartzwelder HS. MK-801 potently inhibits alcohol withdrawal seizures in rats. Eur J Pharmacol 1990;176: 103–105.

131. Riaz A, Faingold CL. Seizures during ethanol withdrawal are blocked by focal microinjection of excitant amino acid antagonists into the inferior colliculus and pontine reticular formation. Alcohol Clin Exp Res 1994;18:1456–1462.

132. Valverius P, Crabbe JC, Hoffman PL, Tabakoff B. NMDA receptors in mice bred to be prone or resistant to ethanol withdrawal seizures. Eur J Pharmacol 1990;184:185–189.

133. Carter LA, Belknap JK, Crabbe JC, Janowsky A. Allosteric regulation of the N-methyl-D-aspartate receptor-linked ion channel complex and effects of ethanol in ethanol-withdrawal seizure-prone and -resistant mice. J Neurochem 1995;64:213–219.

134. Walker DW, Zornetzer SF. Alcohol withdrawal in mice: electroencephalographic and behavioral correlates. Electroencephalog Clin Neurophysiol 1974;36:233–244.

135. Kleinschmidt A, Bear MF, Singer W. Blockade of "NMDA" receptors disrupts experience-dependent plasticity of kitten striate cortex. Science 1987;238:355–358.

136. Clarren SK, Smith DW. The fetal alcohol syndrome. N Engl J Med 1978;298:1063–1067.

137. Abel EL. The fetal alcohol syndrome: behavioral teratology. Psychol Bull 1980;87:29–50.

138. Morrisett RA, Martin D, Wilson WA, Savage DD, Swartzwelder HS. Prenatal exposure to ethanol decreases the sensitivity of the adult rat hippocampus to N-methyl-D-aspartate. Alcohol 1989;6:415–420.

139. Noble EP, Ritchie T. Prenatal ethanol exposure reduces the effects of excitatory amino acids in the rat hippocampus. Life Sci 1989;45: 803–810.

140. Kalant H. Problems in the search for mechanisms of tolerance. Alcohol Alcohol 1993; suppl 2:1–8.

141. Trujillo KA, Akil H. Excitatory amino acids and drugs of abuse: a role for N-methyl-D-aspartate receptors in drug tolerance, sensitization and physical dependence. Drug Alcohol Dependence 1995;38:139–154.

142. Khanna JM, Wu PH, Weiner JL, Kalant H. NMDA antagonist inhibits rapid tolerance to ethanol. Brain Res Bull 1991;26:643–645.

143. Khanna JM, Kalant H, Shah G, Chau A. Effects of (+)MK-801 and ketamine on rapid tolerance to ethanol. Brain Res Bull 1992;28:311–314.

144. Khanna JM, Mihic SJ, Weiner J, Shah G, Wu PH, Kalant H. Differential inhibition by NMDA antagonists of rapid tolerance to, and cross-tolerance between, ethanol and chlordiazepoxide. Brain Res 1992;574:251–256.

145. Khanna KM, Shah G, Weiner J, Wu PH, Kalant H. Effect of NMDA receptor antagonists on rapid tolerance to ethanol. Eur J Pharmacol 1993;230:23–31.

146. Khanna KM, Kalant H, Shah G, Chau A. Effect of D-cycloserine on rapid tolerance to ethanol. Pharmacol Biochem Behav 1993;45:983–986.

147. Szabò G, Tabakoff B, Hoffman PL. The NMDA receptor antagonists dizocilpine differentially affects environment-dependent and environment-independent ethanol tolerance. Psychopharmacology 1994;113:511–517.

148. Rafi-Tari S, Kalant H, Liu JF, Silver I, Wu PH. Dizocilpine prevents the development of tolerance to ethanol-induced error on a circular maze test. Psychopharmacology 1996;125: 23–32.

149. Dildy-Mayfield JE, Harris RA. Acute and chronic ethanol exposure alters the function of hippocampal kainate receptors expressed in Xenopus oocytes. J Neurochem 1992;58:1569–1572.

150. Teichberg VI, Tal N, Goldberg O, Liuni A. Barbiturates, alcohols, and the CNS excitatory neurotransmission: specific effects of the kainate and quisqualate receptors. Brain Res 1984;292:285–292.

151. Lovinger DM. High ethanol sensitivity of recombinant AMPA-type glutamate receptors expressed in mammalian cells. Neurosci Lett 1993;159:83–87.

152. Martin D, Tayyeb MI, Swartzwelder HS. Ethanol inhibition of AMPA and kainate receptor-mediated depolarization of hippocampal area CA1. Alcohol Clin Exp Res 1995; 19:1312–1316.

153. Dildy-Mayfield JE, Harris RA. Ethanol inhibits kainate responses of glutamate receptors expressed in Xenopus oocytes: role of calcium and protein kinase C. J Neurosci 1995;15: 3162–3171.

154. Molleman A, Little HJ. Increases in non-N-methyl-D-aspartate glutamatergic transmission, but no change in γ-aminobutyric acidB transmission, in CA1 neurons during withdrawal from in vivo chronic ethanol treatment. J Pharmacol Exp Ther 1995;272:1035–1041.

155. Hoffman PL, Tabakoff B. Ethanol's action on brain biochemistry. In: Tarter RE, van Thiel DH, eds. Alcohol and the brain: chronic effects. New York: Plenum Press, 1985:19–68.

156. Erickson CK, Burnam WL. Cholinergic alteration of ethanol-induced sleep and death in mice. Agents Actions 1971;21:8–13.

157. Graham DT, Erickson CK. Alteration of ethanol-induced CNS depression: ineffectiveness of drugs that modify cholinergic transmission. Psychopharmacology 1974;34:173–180.

158. Erwin VG, Korte A, Jones BC. Central muscarinic cholinergic influences on ethanol sensitivity in long-sleep and short-sleep mice. J Pharmacol Exp Ther 1988;247:857–862.

159. Pereira EF, Alkondon M, Reinhardt S, et al. Physostigmine and galanthamine: probes for a novel binding site on the α₄β₂ subtype of neuronal nicotinic acetylcholine receptors stably expressed in fibroblast cells. J Pharmacol Exp Ther 1994;270:768–778.

160. Valenzuela CF, Kerr J, Duvvuri P, Johnson DA. Modulation of PCP-sensitive ethidium binding to the Torpedo acetylcholine receptor: interaction of noncompetitive inhibitors with carbamylcholine and cobra α-toxin. Mol Pharmacol 1992;41:331–336.

161. Tonner PH, Miller KW. Molecular sites of general anaesthetic action on acetylcholine receptors. Eur J Anesth 1995;12:21–30.

162. Collins AC, Romm E, Selvaag S, Turner S, Marks MJ. A comparison of the effects of chronic nicotine infusion on tolerance to nicotine and cross-tolerance to ethanol in long- and short-sleep mice. J Pharmacol Exp Ther 1993; 266:1390–1397.

163. Luo T, Marks MJ, Collins AC. Genotype regulates the development of tolerance to ethanol and cross-tolerance to nicotine. Alcohol 1994; 11:167–176.

164. Blomquist O, Soderpalm B, Engel JA. Ethanol-induced locomotor activity: involvement of central nicotinic acetylcholine receptors? Brain Res Bull 1992;29:173–178.

165. Blomquist O, Engel JA, Nissbrandt H, Soderpalm B. The mesolimbic dopamine-activating properties of ethanol are antagonized by mecamylamine. Eur J Pharmacol 1993;249: 207–213.

166. McKenzie D, Franks NP, Lieb WR. Actions of general anesthetics on a neuronal nicotinic acetylcholine receptor in isolated identified

neurons of *Lymnaea stagnalis*. Br J Pharmacol 1995;115:275–282.

167. Convernton PJO, Duvoisin RM, Connolly JG. Modulation of the activity of the nicotinic $\alpha_3\beta_4$ receptor subtype by alcohol. Soc Neurosci Abst 1995;21:528.13.

168. McGehee DS, Heath MJS, Gelber S, Devay P, Role LW. Nicotinic enhancement of fast excitatory synaptic transmission in CNS by presynaptic mechanisms. Science 1995;269:1692–1696.

169. Lovinger DM. Ethanol potentiation of 5-HT$_3$ receptor-mediated ion current in NCB-20 neuroblastoma cells. Neurosci Lett 1991;122:57–60.

170. Lovinger DM, White G. 5-Hydroxytryptamine$_3$ receptor-mediated ion current in neuroblastoma cells and isolated adult mammalian neurons. Mol Pharmacol 1991;40:263–270.

171. Machu TK, Harris RA. Alcohols and anesthetics enhance the function of 5-hydroxytryptamine$_3$ receptors expressed in *Xenopus* laevis. J Pharmacol Exp Ther 1994;271:898–905.

172. Isom LL, Ragsdale DS, De Jongh DS, et al. Structure and function of the β_2 subunit of brain sodium channels, a transmembrane glycoprotein with a CAM motif. Cell 1995;83:433–442.

173. Palmer MR, Morrow EL, Erwin VG. Calcium differentially alters behavioral and electrophysiological responses to ethanol in selectively bred mouse lines. Alcohol Clin Exp Res 1987;11:457–463.

174. Dolin SJ, Little HJ. Are changes in neuronal calcium channels involved in ethanol tolerance? J Pharmacol Exp Ther 1989;250:985–991.

175. Brown LM, Sims JS, Randall P, Wilcox R, Leslie SW. Ω-Conotoxin increases sleep time following ethanol injection. Alcohol 1993;10:159–162.

176. Leslie SW. Sedative-hypnotic drugs: interaction with calcium channels. Alcohol Drug Res 1986;6:371–377.

177. Harris RA, Jones SB, Bruno P, Bylund DB. Effects of dihydropyridine derivatives and anticonvulsant drugs on [^{3}H]nitrendipine binding and calcium and sodium fluxes in brain. Biochem Pharmacol 1985;34:2187–2191.

178. Carlen PL, Wu PH. Calcium and sedative-hypnotic drug actions. Int Rev Neurobiol 1988;29:161–189.

179. Daniell LC, Brass EP, Harris RA. Effect of ethanol on intracellular ionized calcium concentrations in synaptosomes and hepatocytes. Mol Pharmacol 1987;32:831–837.

180. Shah J, Pant HC. Spontaneous calcium release induced by ethanol in the isolated rat brain microsomes. Brain Res 1988;474:94–99.

181. Treistman SN, Wilson A. Effects of chronic ethanol on currents carried through calcium channels in *Aplysia*. Alcohol Clin Exp Res 1991;15:489–493.

182. Twombly DA, Herman MD, Kye CH, Narahashi T. Ethanol effects on two types of voltage-activated calcium channels. J Pharmacol Exp Ther 1990;254:1029–1037.

183. Mullikin-Kilpatrick D, Mehta ND, Hildebrandt JD, Treistman SN. Gi is involved in ethanol inhibition of L-type calcium channels in undifferentiated but not differentiated PC-12 cells. Mol Pharmacol 1995;47:997–1005.

184. Rogawski MA, Porter RJ. Antiepileptic drugs: pharmacological mechanisms and clinical efficacy with consideration of promising developmental stage compounds. Pharmacol Rev 1990;42:223–286.

185. Dolin S, Hudspith M, Pagonis C, Little H, Littleton J. Increased dihydropyridine-sensitive Ca^{2+} channels in rat brain may underlie ethanol physical dependence. Neuropharmacology 1987;26:275–279.

186. Woodward JJ, Machu T, Leslie SW. Chronic ethanol treatment alters GV-conotoxin and Bay K 8644 sensitive calcium channels in rat striatal synaptosomes. Alcohol 1990;7:279–284.

187. Lucchi L, Govoni S, Battaini F, Pasinetti G, Trabucchi M. Ethanol administration in vivo alters calcium ions control in rat striatum. Brain Res 1985;332:376–379.

188. Greenberg DA, Carpenter CL, Messing RO. Ethanol-induced component of ^{45}Ca^{2+} uptake in PC12 cells is sensitive to Ca^{2+} channel modulating drugs. Brain Res 1987;410:143–146.

189. Guppy LJ, Littleton JM. Binding characteristics of the calcium channel antagonist [^{3}H]nitrendipine in tissues from ethanol-dependent rats. Alcohol Alcohol 1994;29:283–293.

190. Marks SS, Watson DL, Carpenter CL, Messing RO, Greenberg DA. Calcium channel antagonist receptors in cerebral cortex from alcoholic patients. Brain Res 1989;478:196–198.

191. Little HJ, Dolin SJ, Halsey MJ. Calcium channel antagonists decrease the ethanol withdrawal syndrome. Life Sci 1986;39:2059–2065.

192. Messing RO, Sneade AB, Savidge B. Protein kinase C participates in up-regulation of dihydropyridine-sensitive calcium channels by ethanol. J Neurochem 1990;55:1383–1389.

193. Little HJ, Dolin SJ, Whittington MA. Possible role of calcium channels in ethanol tolerance and dependence. Ann N Y Acad Sci 1988;560:465–466.

194. Whittington MA, Little HJ. Changes in voltage-operated calcium channels modify ethanol withdrawal hyperexcitability in mouse hippocampal slices. Exp Physiol 1993;78:347–370.

195. Shibata S, Shindou T, Tominaga K, Watanabe S. Calcium channel blockers improve hypoxia/hypoglycemia-induced impairment of rat hippocampal 2-deoxyglucose uptake in vitro after ethanol withdrawal. Brain Res 1995;673:320–324.

196. Marks SS, Watson DL, Carpenter CL, Messing RO, Greenberg DA. Comparative effects of chronic exposure to ethanol and calcium channel antagonists on calcium channel antagonist receptors in cultured neural (PC12) cells. J Neurochem 1989;53:168–172.

197. Wu PH, Pham T, Naranjo CA. Nifedipine delays the acquisition of ethanol tolerance. Eur J Pharmacol 1987;139:233–236.

198. Sanna E, Harris RA. Neuronal ion channels. Recent Dev Alcohol 1994;11:169–186.

199. Kukita F, Mitaku S. Kinetic analysis of the denaturation process by alcohols of sodium channels in squid giant axon. J Physiol 1993;463:523–543.

200. Moore SD, Madamba SG, Siggins GR. Ethanol diminishes a voltage-dependent K$^+$ current, the M-current, in CA1 hippocampal pyramidal neurons in vitro. Brain Res 1990;516:222–228.

201. Anantharam V, Bayley H, Wilson A, Treistman SN. Differential effects of ethanol on electrical properties of various potassium channels expressed in oocytes. Mol Pharmacol 1992;42:499–505.

202. Dopico AM, Lemos JR, Treistman SN. Ethanol increases the activity of large conductance, Ca^{2+}-activated K$^+$ channels in isolated neurohypophysial terminals. Mol Pharmacol 1996;49:40–48.

203. Covarrubias M, Vyas TB, Escobar L, Wei A. Alcohols inhibit a cloned potassium channel at a discrete saturable site. J Biol Chem 1995;270:19408–19416.

204. Gudermann T, Nürnberg B, Schultz G. Receptors, G proteins as primary components of transmembrane signal transduction. Part 1. G-protein-coupled receptors: structure and function. J Mol Med 1995;73:51–63.

205. Gudermann T, Nürnberg B, Schultz G. Receptors, G proteins as primary components of transmembrane signal transduction. Part 2. G-proteins: structure and function. J Mol Med 1995;73:123–132.

206. Iyengar R. Molecular and functional diversity of mammalian G$_s$-stimulated adenylyl cyclases. FASEB J 1993;7:768–775.

207. Hoffman PL, Tabakoff B. Ethanol and guanine nucleotide binding proteins: a selective interaction. FASEB J 1990;4:2612–2622.

208. Tabakoff B, Hoffman PL. Effect of alcohol on neurotransmitters and their receptors. In: Begleiter H, Kissin B, eds. The pharmacology of alcohol and alcohol dependence. 2nd ed. New York: Oxford University Press, 1996;356–430.

209. Rabin RA, Molinoff PB. Activation of adenylate cyclase by ethanol in mouse striatal tissue. J Pharmacol Exp Ther 1981;216:129–134.

210. Saito T, Lee JM, Tabakoff B. Ethanol's effects on cortical adenylate cyclase activity. J Neurochem 1985;44:1037–1044.

211. Valverius P, Hoffman PL, Tabakoff B. Effect of ethanol on mouse cerebral cortical β-adrenergic receptors. Mol Pharmacol 1987;32:217–222.

212. Gordon AS, Collier K, Diamond I. Ethanol regulation of adenosine receptor-stimulated cAMP levels in a clonal neural cell line: an in vitro model of cellular tolerance to ethanol. Proc Natl Acad Sci U S A 1986;83:2105–2108.

213. Stenstrom S, Richelson E. Acute effect of ethanol on prostaglandin E$_1$-mediated cyclic AMP formation by a murine neuroblastoma clone. J Pharmacol Exp Ther 1982;221:334–341.

214. Rabin RA, Molinoff PB. Multiple sites of action of ethanol on adenylate cyclase. J Pharmacol Exp Ther 1983;227:551–556.

215. Chik CL, Ho AK. Ethanol reduces norepinephrine-stimulated melatonin synthesis in rat pinealocytes. J Neurochem 1992;59:1280–1286.

216. Yoshimura M, Tabakoff B. Selective effects of ethanol on the generation of cAMP by particular members of the adenylyl cyclase. Alcohol Clin Exp Res 1995;19:1435–1440.

217. Hellevuo K, Yoshimura M, Mons N, Hoffman PL, Cooper DMF, Tabakoff B. The characterization of a novel human adenylyl cyclase which is present in brain and other tissues. J Biol Chem 1995;270:11581–11589.

218. Hoffman PL, Tabakoff B. Ethanol does not modify opiate-mediated inhibition of striatal adenylate cyclase. J Neurochem 1986;46:812–816.

219. Bauché F, Bourdeaux-Jaubert AM, Giudicelli Y, Nordmann R. Ethanol alters the adenosine receptor-Ni-mediated adenylate cyclase inhibitory response in rat brain cortex in vitro. FEBS Lett 1987;219:296–300.

220. Saito T, Lee JM, Hoffman PL, Tabakoff B. Effects of chronic ethanol treatment on the β-adrenergic receptor-coupled adenylate cyclase system of mouse cerebral cortex. J Neurochem 1987;48:1817–1822.

221. Saffey K, Gillman MA, Cantrill RC. Chronic in vivo ethanol administration alters the sensitivity of adenylate cyclase coupling in homo-

genates of rat brain. Neurosci Lett 1988; 84:317–322.

222. Valverius P, Hoffman PL, Tabakoff B. Brain forskolin binding in mice dependent on and tolerant to ethanol. Brain Res 1989;503:38–43.

223. Valverius P, Hoffman PL, Tabakoff B. Hippocampal and cerebellar β-adrenergic receptors and adenylate cyclase are differentially altered by chronic ethanol ingestion. J Neurochem 1989;52:492–497.

224. Valverius P, Borg S, Valverius MR, Hoffman PL, Tabakoff B. Beta-adrenergic receptor binding in brain of alcoholics. Exp Neurol 1989;105:280–286.

225. Wand GS, Diehl AM, Levine MA, Wolfgang D, Samy S. Chronic ethanol treatment increases expression of inhibitory G-proteins and reduces adenylyl cyclase activity in the central nervous system of two lines of ethanol-sensitive mice. J Biol Chem 1993;268:2595–2601.

226. Wand GS, Levine MA. Hormonal tolerance to ethanol is associated with decreased expression of the GTP-binding protein, G_s alpha, and adenylyl cyclase activity in ethanol-treated LS mice. Alcohol Clin Exp Res 1991;15:705–710.

227. Richelson E, Stenstrom S, Forray C, Enloe L, Pfenning M. Effects of chronic exposure to ethanol on the prostaglandin E_1 receptor-mediated response and binding in a murine neuroblastoma clone (N1E-115). J Pharmacol Exp Ther 1986;239:687–692.

228. Bode DC, Molinoff PB. Effects of chronic exposure to ethanol on the physical and functional properties the plasma membrane of S49 lymphoma cells. Biochemistry 1988;27: 5700–5707.

229. Rabin RA. Chronic ethanol exposure of PC 12 cells alters adenylate cyclase activity and intracellular cyclic AMP content. J Pharmacol Exp Ther 1990;252:1021–1027.

230. Nagy LE, Diamond I, Collier K, Lopez L, Ullman B, Gordon AS. Adenosine is required for ethanol-induced heterologous desensitization. Mol Pharmacol 1989;36:744–748.

231. Williams RJ, Veale MA, Horne P, Kelly E. Ethanol differentially regulates guanine nucleotide-binding protein α subunit expression in NG108-15 cells independently of extracellular adenosine. Mol Pharmacol 1993;43: 158–166.

232. Mochly-Rosen D, Chang F-H, Cheever L, Kim M, Diamond I, Gordon AS. Chronic ethanol causes heterologous desensitization of receptors by reducing α_s messenger RNA. Nature 1988;333:848–850.

233. Charness ME, Querimit LA, Henteleff M. Ethanol differentially regulates G proteins in neural cells. Biochem Biophys Res Commun 1988;155:138–143.

234. Rabin RA. Ethanol-induced desensitization of adenylate cyclase: role of the adenosine receptor and GTP-binding proteins. J Pharmacol Exp Ther 1993;264:977–983.

235. Tabakoff B, Whelan JP, Ovchinnikova L, Nhamburo P, Yoshimura M, Hoffman M. Quantitative changes in G proteins do not mediate ethanol-induced down regulation of adenylyl cyclase in mouse cerebral cortex. Alcohol Clin Exp Res 1995;19:187–194.

236. Pellegrino SM, Woods JM, Druse MJ. Effects of chronic ethanol consumption on G proteins in brain areas associated with the nigrostriatal and mesolimbic dopamine systems. Alcohol Clin Exp Res 1993;17:1247–1253.

237. Hoffman PL, Moses F, Luthin GR, Tabakoff B. Acute and chronic effects of ethanol on receptor-mediated phosphatidylinositol 4,5-bisphos-phate breakdown in mouse brain. Mol Pharmacol 1986;30:13–18.

238. Gonzales RA, Theiss C, Crews FT. Effects of ethanol on stimulated inositol phospholipid hydrolysis in rat brain. J Pharmacol Exp Ther 1986;237:92–98.

239. Smith TL. The effects of acute exposure to ethanol on neurotensin and guanine-nucleotide-stimulation of phospholipase C activity in intact N1E-115 neuroblastoma cells. Life Sci 1990;47:115–119.

240. Sanna E, Dildy-Mayfield JE, Harris RA. Ethanol inhibits the function of 5-hydroxytryptamine type 1c and muscarinic M1 G protein-linked receptors in Xenopus oocytes expressing brain mRNA: role of protein kinase C. Mol Pharmacol 1994;45:1004–1012.

241. Smith TL. Selective effects of acute and chronic ethanol exposure on neuropeptide and guanine nucleotide stimulated phospholipase C activity in intact N1E-115 neuroblastoma cells. J Pharmacol Exp Ther 1991;258:410–415.

242. Simonsson P, Rodriguez FC, Loman N, Alling C. G proteins coupled to phospholipase C: molecular targets of long-term ethanol exposure. J. Neurochem 1991;56:2018–2026.

243. Sun GY, Navidi M, Yoa F-G, Wood WG, Sun AY. Effects of chronic ethanol administration on poly-phosphoinositide metabolism in the mouse brain: variance with age. Neurochem Int 1993;22:11–17.

244. Dunwiddie TV. The physiological role of adenosine in the central nervous system. Int Rev Neurobiol 1985;27:63–139.

245. Olah ME, Stilles GL. Adenosine receptor subtypes: characterization and therapeutic regulation. Annu Rev Pharmacol Toxicol 1995;35: 581–606.

246. Dar MS, Mustafa SJ, Wooles WR. Possible role of adenosine in the CNS effects of ethanol. Life Sci 1983;33:1363–1374.

247. Dar MS. Central adenosinergic system involvement in ethanol-induced motor incoordination in mice. J Pharmacol Exp Ther 1990; 255:1202–1209.

248. Dar MS, Wooles WR. Effect of chronically administered methylxanthines on ethanol-induced motor incoordination in mice. Life Sci 1986;39:1429–1437.

249. Nagy LE, Diamond I, Gordon A. Cultured lymphocytes from alcoholic subjects have altered cAMP signal transduction. Proc Natl Acad Sci U S A 1988;85:6973–6976.

250. Reynolds JD, Brien JF. The role of adenosine A1 receptor activation in ethanol-induced inhibition of stimulated glutamate release in the hippocampus of the fetal and adult guinea pig. Alcohol 1995;12:151–157.

251. Krauss SW, Ghirnikar RB, Diamond I, Gordon AS. Inhibition of adenosine uptake by ethanol is specific for one class of nucleoside transporters. Mol Pharmacol 1993;44:1021–1026.

252. Sapru MK, Diamond I, Gordon AS. Adenosine receptors mediate cellular adaptation to ethanol in NC108–15 cells. J Pharmacol Exp Ther 1994;271:542–548.

253. Clark M, Dar MS. The effects of various methods of sacrifice and of ethanol on adenosine levels in selected areas of rat brain. J Neurosci Meth 1988;25:243–249.

254. Israel Y, Orrego H, Carmichael FJ. Acetate-mediated effects of ethanol. Alcohol Clin Exp Res 1994;18:144–148.

255. Cullen N, Carlen PL. Electrophysiological actions of acetate, a metabolite of ethanol, on hippocampal dentate granule neurons: interactions with adenosine. Brain Res 1992;588:49–57.

256. Brundege JM, Dunwiddie TV. The role of acetate as a potential mediator of the effects of ethanol in the brain. Neurosci Lett 1995; 186:214–218.

257. Sibley DR, Monsma FJ, Shen Y. Molecular neurobiology of dopaminergic receptors. Int Rev Neurobiol 1993;35:391–415.

258. Koob GF, Vaccarino F, Amalric M, Bloom FE. Positive reinforcement properties of drugs: search for neural substrates. In: Engel J, Oreland L, eds. Brain reward systems and abuse. New York: Raven Press, 1987:35–50.

259. Heikkila RE, Orlansky H, Cohen G. Studies on the distinction between uptake inhibition and release of [³H]dopamine in rat brain tissue slices. Biochem Pharmacol 1975;241: 847–852.

260. Gessa GL, Muntoni F, Collu M, Vargiu L, Mereu G. Low doses of ethanol activate dopaminergic neurones in the ventral tegmental area. Brain Res 1985;348:201–203.

261. Di Chiara G, Imperato A. Drugs abused by humans preferentially increase synaptic dopamine concentrations in the mesolimbic system of freely moving rats. Proc Natl Acad Sci U S A 1988;85:5274–5278.

262. Imperato A, Di Chiara G. Preferential stimulation of dopamine release in the nucleus accumbens of freely moving rats by ethanol. J Pharmacol Exp Ther 1986;239:219–228.

263. Diana M, Pistis M, Carboni S, Gessa GL, Rosseti ZL. Profound decrement of mesolimbic dopaminergic neuronal activity during ethanol withdrawal syndrome in rats: electrophysiological and biochemical evidence. Proc Natl Acad Sci U S A 1993;90:7966–7969.

264. Rossetti ZL, Hmaidan Y, Gessa GL. Marked inhibition of mesolimbic dopamine release: a common feature of ethanol, morphine, cocaine and amphetamine abstinence in rats. Eur J Pharmacol 1992;221:227–234.

265. Mereu G, Fadda F, Gessa GL. Ethanol stimulates the firing rate of nigral dopaminergic neurons in unanesthetized rats. Brain Res 1984; 292:63–69.

266. Shen RY, Chiodo LA. Acute withdrawal after repeated ethanol treatment reduces the number of spontaneously active dopaminergic neurons in the ventral tegmental area. Brain Res 1993; 622:289–293.

267. Wozniak KM, Pert A, Linnoila M. Antagonism of 5-HT₃ receptors attenuates the effects of ethanol on extracellular dopamine. Eur J Pharmacol 1990;187:287–289.

268. Weiss F, Lorang MT, Bloom FE, Koob GF. Oral alcohol self-administration stimulates dopamine release in the rat nucleus accumbens: genetic and motivational determinants. J Pharmacol Exp Ther 1993;267:250–258.

269. Nevo I, Hamon M. Neurotransmitter and neuromodulatory mechanisms involved in alcohol abuse and alcoholism. Neurochem Int 1995;26: 305–336.

270. Korpi ER, Sinclair JD, Malminen O. Dopamine D₂ receptor binding in striatal membranes of rat lines selected for differences in alcohol-related behaviors. Pharmacol Toxicol 1987;61: 94–97.

271. Stefanini E, Frau M, Garau MG, Garau B, Fadda F, Gessa GL. Alcohol-preferring rats have fewer dopamine D₂ receptors in the limbic system. Alcohol Alcohol 1992;27: 127–130.

272. McBride WJ, Chernet E, Dyr W, Lumeng L, Li TK. Densities of dopamine D₂ receptors are reduced in CNS regions of alcohol-preferring P rats. Alcohol 1993;10:387–390.

273. De Montis MG, Gambarana C, Gessa GL, Meloni D, Tagliamonte A, Stefanini E. Reduced [^{3}H]SCH 23390 binding and DA-sensitive adenylyl cyclase in the limbic system of ethanol-preferring rats. Alcohol Alcohol 1993; 28:397–400.

274. Rommelspacher H, Raeder C, Kaulen P, Bruning G. Adaptive changes of dopamine-D$_2$ receptors in rat brain following ethanol withdrawal: a quantitative autoradiographic investigation. Alcohol 1992;9:355–362.

275. May T. Striatal dopamine D$_1$-like receptors have higher affinity for dopamine in ethanol-treated rats. Eur J Pharmacol 1992;215: 313–316.

276. Dyr W, McBride WJ, Lumeng L, Li TJ, Murphy JM. Effects of D$_1$ and D$_2$ dopamine receptor agents on ethanol consumption in the high-alcohol-drinking (HAD) line of rats. Alcohol 1993;10:207–212.

277. Weiss F, Mitchiner M, Bloom FE, Koob GF. Free-choice responding for ethanol versus water in alcohol preferring (P) and unselected Wistar rats is differentially modified by naloxone, bromocriptine, and methysergide. Psychopharmacology 1990;101:178–186.

278. Hodge CW, Samson HH, Haraguchi M. Microinjections of dopamine agonists in n. accumbens increase ethanol reinforced responding. Pharmacol Biochem Behav 1992;43: 249–254.

279. Alkana RL, Parker ES, Malcolm RD, Cohen HB, Birch H, Noble EP. Interaction of apomorphine and amantadine with ethanol in men. Alcohol Clin Exp Res 1982;6:403–411.

280. Ahlenius SD, Carlsson A, Engel J, Svensson T, Sodersten P. Antagonism by α-methyltyrosine of the ethanol-induced stimulation and euphoria in man. Clin Pharmacol Ther 1973;14:586–593.

281. Borg V. Bromocriptine in the prevention of alcohol abuse. Acta Psych Scand 1983;68: 100–110.

282. Davis WM, Smith SG, Werner TE. Noradrenergic role in the self-administration of ethanol. Pharmacol Biochem Behav 1978;9:369–374.

283. Pfeffer AO, Samson HH. Haloperidol and apomorphine effects on ethanol reinforcement in free feeding rats. Pharmacol Biochem Behav 1988;29:343–350.

284. Morgenroth VH, Walters JR, Roth RH. Dopaminergic neurons—alteration in the kinetic properties of tyrosine hydroxylase after cessation of impulse flow. Biochem Pharmacol 1976;25:655–661.

285. Samson HH, Tolliver GA, Haraguchi M, Hodger CW. Alcohol self-administration: role of mesolimbic dopamine. Ann N Y Acad Sci 1992;654:242–253.

286. Hodge CW, Samson HH, Tolliver GA, Haraguchi M. Effects of intraaccumbens injections of dopamine agonists and antagonists on sucrose and sucrose-reinforced responding. Pharmacol Biochem Behav 1994;48:141–150.

287. Hodge CW, Chappelle, AM, Samson HH. GABAergic transmission in the nucleus accumbens is involved in the termination of ethanol self-administration in rats. Alcohol Clin Exp Res 1995;19:1486–1493.

288. Brown ZW, Amit Z. The effects of selective catecholamine depletions by 6-hydroxydopamine on ethanol preference in rats. Neurosci Lett 1977;5:333–336.

289. Lê AD, Khanna JM, Kalant H, LeBlanc AE. Effect of modification of brain serotonin (5-HT), norepinephrine (NE) and dopamine (DA) on ethanol tolerance. Psychopharmacology 1981;75:231–235.

290. Lê AD, Khanna JM, Kalant H, LeBlanc AE. The effect of lesions in the dorsal, median and magnus raphe nuclei on the development of tolerance to ethanol. J Pharmacol Exp Ther 1981;218:525–529.

291. Quarfordt SD, Kalmus GW, Myers RD. Ethanol drinking following 6-OHDA lesions of nucleus accumbens and tuberculum olfactorium of the rat. Alcohol 1991;8:211–217.

292. Rassnick S, Stinus L, Koob GF. The effects of 6-hydroxydopamine lesions of the nucleus accumbens and the mesolimbic dopamine system on oral self-administration of ethanol in the rat. Brain Res 1993;623:16–24.

293. Lança AJ. Reduction of voluntary alcohol intake in the rat by modulation of the dopaminergic mesolimbic system: transplantation of ventral mesencephalic cell suspensions. Neuroscience 1994;58:359–369.

294. Blum K, Noble EP, Sheridan PJ, Montgomery A, Ritchie T, Jagadeeswaran P, Nogami H, Briggs AH, Cohn JB. Allelic association of human dopamine D$_2$ receptor gene in alcoholism. JAMA 1990;263:2055–2060.

295. Blum K, Noble EP, Sheridan PJ, et al. Genetic predisposition in alcoholism: association of the D$_2$ dopamine receptor TAz I B1 RFLP with severe alcoholics. Alcohol 1993;10:59–67.

296. Bolos AM, Dean M, Lucas-Derse S, Ramsburg M, Brown GL, Goldman D. Population and pedigree studies reveal a lack of association between the dopamine D$_2$ receptor gene and alcoholism. JAMA 1990;264:3156–3160.

297. Gelernter J, Goldman D, Risch N. The A1 allele at the D$_2$ dopamine receptor gene and alcoholism. JAMA 1993;269:1673–1677.

298. Gejman PV, Ram A, Gelerneter J, et al. No structural mutation in the dopamine D$_2$ receptor gene in alcoholism or schizophrenia: analysis using denaturing gradient gel electrophoresis. JAMA 1994;271:201–208.

299. Carboni E, Acquas E, Frau R, Di Chiara G. Differential inhibitory effects of a 5-HT$_3$ antagonist on drug-induced stimulation of dopamine release. Eur J Pharmacol 1989; 164:515–519.

300. Blandina P, Goldfarb J, Craddock-Royal B, Green JP. Release of endogenous dopamine by stimulation of 5-hydroxytryptamine$_3$ receptors in rat striatum. J Pharmacol Exp Ther 1989; 251:803.

301. Klein RL, Sanna E, McQuilkin SJ, Whiting PJ, Harris RA. Effects of 5-HT$_3$ receptor antagonists on binding and function of mouse and human GABA$_A$ receptors. Eur J Pharmacol 1994; 268:237–246.

302. Hoyer D, Clarke DE, Fozard JR, et al. VII. International union of pharmacology classification of receptors for 5-hydroxytryptamine (serotonin). Pharmacol Rev 1994;46:157–203.

303. LeMarquand D, Pihl RO, Benkelfat C. Serotonin and alcohol intake, abuse, and dependence: findings from animal studies. Biol Psychiatry 1994;36:395–421.

304. Grant KA. The role of 5-HT$_3$ receptors in drug dependence. Drug Alcohol Depend 1995;38: 155–171.

305. Naranjo CA, Sellers EM, Roach CA, et al. Zimelidine-induced variations in alcohol intake by nondepressed heavy drinkers. Clin Pharmacol Ther 1984;35:374–381.

306. Naranjo CA, Sellers EM, Sullivan JT, Woodley DV, Kadlec K, Sykora K. The serotonin uptake inhibitor citalopram attenuates ethanol intake. Clin Pharmacol Ther 1987;41:266–274.

307. Murphy JM, Waller MB, Gatto GJ, McBride WJ, Lumeng L, Li TK. Effects of fluoxetine on the intragastric self-administration of ethanol in the alcohol preferring P line of rats. Alcohol 1988;5:283–286.

308. Van de Kar LD, Wilkinson CW, Ganong WF. Pharmacological evidence for a role of brain serotonin in the maintenance of plasma renin activity in unanesthetized rats. J Pharmacol Exp Ther 1981;219:85–90.

309. Grupp LA, Perlanski E, Stewart RB. Angiotensin II-induced suppression of alcohol intake and its reversal by the angiotensin antagonist Sar-1, Thr-8 angiotensin II. Pharmacol Biochem Behav 1989;31:813–816.

310. Grant KA, Hellevuo K, Tabakoff B. The 5-HT3 antagonist MDL-72222 exacerbates ethanol withdrawal seizures in mice. Alcohol Clin Exp Res 1994;18:410–414.

311. Bruno F. Buspirone in the treatment of alcoholic patients. Psychopathology 1989;22(suppl 1):49–59.

312. Wong DT, Reid LR, Li TK, Lumeng L. Greater abundance of serotonin$_{1A}$ receptor in some brain areas of alcohol-preferring (P) rats compared to nonpreferring (NP) rats. Pharmacol Biochem Behav 1993;46:173–177.

313. McBride WJ, Chernet E, Rabold JA, Lumeng L, Li TK. Serotonin-2 receptors in the CNS of alcohol-preferring and -nonpreferring rats. Pharmacol Biochem Behav 1993;46:631–636.

314. Zhou FC, Bledsoe S, Lumeng L, Li TK. Reduced serotoninergic immunoreactivity fibers in the forebrain of alcohol-preferring rats. Alcohol Clin Exp Res 1994;18:571–579.

315. Zhou FC, Pu CF, Murphy J, Lumeng L, Li TK. Serotoninergic neurons in the alcohol preferring rats. Alcohol 1994b;11:397–403.

316. Richardson BP, Engel G, Donatsch P, Stadler PA. Identification of serotonin M-receptor subtypes and their specific blockade by a new class of drugs. Nature 1985;316:126–131.

317. Yoshimoto K, McBride WJ, Lumeng L, Li TK. Alcohol stimulates the release of dopamine and serotonin in the nucleus accumbens. Alcohol 1991;9:17–22.

318. Herve D, Pickel VM, Joh TH, Beaudet A. Serotonin axon terminals in the ventral tegmental area of the rat: fine structure and synaptic input to dopaminergic neurons. Brain Res 1987; 435:71–83.

319. Guan XM, McBride WJ. Serotonin microinfusion into the ventral tegmental area increases accumbens dopamine release. Brain Res Bull 1989;23:541–547.

320. Jiang LH, Ashby CR, Dasser RJ, Wang RY. The effect of intraventricular administration of the 5-HT$_3$ receptor agonist 2-methylserotonin on the release of dopamine in the nucleus accumbens: an in vivo chroniculometric study. Brain Res 1990;513:156–160.

321. Lê AD, Khanna JM, Kalant H, LeBlanc AE. Effect of modification of brain serotonin (5 HT), norepinephrine (NE) and dopamine (DA) on ethanol tolerance. Psychopharmacology 1981;75:231–235.

322. Melchior CL, Tabakoff B. Modification of environmentally cued tolerance to ethanol in mice. J Pharmacol Exp Ther 1981;219:175–180.

323. Murphy JM, McBride WJ, Lumeng L, Li T-K. Contents of monoamines in forebrain regions of alcohol-preferring (P) and -nonpreferring (NP) lines of rats. Pharmacol Biochem Behav 1987;26:389–392.

324. Knapp RJ, Malatynska E, Collins N, Fang L, Wang JY, Hruby VJ, Roeske WR, Yamamura H. Molecular biology and pharmacology of cloned opioid receptors. FASEB J 1995;9: 516–525.

325. Tabakoff B, Hoffman PL. Alcohol interactions with brain opiate receptors. Life Sci 1983;32:197–204.

326. Hiller JM, Angel JM, Simon EJ. Characterization of the selective inhibition of the delta subclass of opioid binding sites by alcohols. Science 1981;214:468–469.

327. Khatami S, Hoffman PL, Shibuya T, Salafsky B. Selective effects of ethanol on opiate receptor subtypes in brain. Neuropharmacology 1987;26:1503–1507.

328. Seizinger BR, Bovermann K, Maysinger D, Hollt V, Herz A. Differential effects of acute and chronic ethanol treatment on particular opioid peptide systems in discrete regions of brain and pituitary. Pharmacol Biochem Behav 1983;18(suppl 1):361–369.

329. Ryder S, Straus E, Lieber CS, et al. Cholecystokinin and enkephalin levels following ethanol administration in rats. Peptides 1981;2:223–226.

330. Dave JR, Tabakoff B, Hoffman PL. Ethanol withdrawal seizures produce increased c-fos mRNA in mouse brain. Mol Pharmacol 1990;37:367–371.

331. Genazzani AR, Nappi G, Facchinetti F, et al. Central deficiency of β-endorphin in alcohol addicts. J Clin Endocrinol Metab 1982;55:583–586.

332. Borg S, Kvande H, Rydberg U, et al. Endorphin levels in human cerebrospinal fluid during alcohol intoxication and withdrawal. Psychopharmacology 1982;78:101–103.

333. Gianoulakis C, De Waele JP, Kiianmaa K. Differences in the brain and pituitary β-endorphin system between the alcohol-preferring AA and alcohol avoiding ANA rats. Alcohol Clin Exp Res 1992;16:453–459.

334. Hyytia P. Involvement of μ-opioid systems in alcohol drinking by alcohol preferring rats. Pharmacol Biochem Behav 1993;45:697–701.

335. De Waele JP, Kiianmaa K, Gianoulakis C. Spontaneous and ethanol-stimulated in vitro release of β-endorphin by the hypothalamus of AA and ANA rats. Alcohol Clin Exp Res 1994;1468–1473.

336. Blum K, Briggs AH, Elston SFA, Hirst M, Hamilton MG, Verebey K. A common denominator theory of alcohol and opiate dependence: review of similarities and differences. In: Rigter H, Crabbe JC, eds. Alcohol tolerance and dependence. New York: Elsevier Biomedical Press, 1980:371–391.

337. Blum K, Briggs AH, Trachtenberg MC, Delallo L, Wallace JE. Enkephalinase inhibition: regulation of ethanol intake in genetically predisposed mice. Alcohol 1987;4:449–456.

338. Davis VE, Walsh MJ. Alcohol, amines, and alkaloids: a possible biochemical basis for alcohol addiction. Science 1970;167:1005–1007.

339. Cohen C, Collins M. Alkaloids from catecholamines in adrenal tissue: possible role in alcoholism. Science 1970;167:1749–1751.

340. Reid LD, Delconte JD, Nichols ML, Bilsky EJ, Hubbell CL. Tests of opioid deficiency hypotheses of alcoholism. Alcohol 1991;8:247–257.

341. Froehlich JC, Li TK. Opioid involvement in alcohol drinking. Ann N Y Acad Sci. 1994;739:156–167.

342. Froehlich JC. Interactions between alcohol and the endogenous opioid system. In: Zakhari S, ed. Alcohol and the endocrine system. NIAAA research monograph series. NIH publication. Washington, DC: National Institutes of Health, 1993:21–35.

343. Volpicelli JR, Alterman AI, Hayashida M, O'Brien CP. Naltrexone in the treatment of alcohol dependence. Arch Gen Psychiatry 1992;49:876–880.

344. O'Malley SS, Jaffe AJ, Chang G, Schottenfeld RS, Meyer RE, Rounsaville B. Naltrexone and coping skills therapy for alcohol dependence. A controlled study. Arch Gen Psychiatry 1992;49:881–887.

345. Volpicelli JR, Watson NT, King AC, Sherman CE, O'Brien CP. Effect of naltrexone on alcohol "high" in alcoholics. Am J Psychiatry 1995;152:613–615.

346. Hoffman PL. Central nervous system effects of neurohypophyseal peptides. In: Smith CW, ed. The peptides. New York: Academic Press, 1987:239–295.

347. Hoffman PL, Ritzmann RF, Walter R, Tabakoff B. Arginine vasopressin maintains ethanol tolerance. Nature 1978;276:614–616.

348. Lê AD, Kalant H, Khanna JM. Interaction between des-9-glycinamide-[8-Arg]vasopressin and serotonin on ethanol tolerance. Eur J Pharmacol 1982;80:337–345.

349. Hoffman PL, Tabakoff B. Neurohypophyseal peptides maintain tolerance to the incoordinating effects of ethanol. Pharmacol Biochem Behav 1984;21:539–543.

350. Hung C-R, Tabakoff B, Melchior CL, Hoffman PL. Intraventricular arginine vasopressin maintains ethanol tolerance. Eur J Pharmacol 1984;106:645–648.

351. Jard S. Vasopressin isoreceptors in mammals: relation to cyclic AMP-dependent and cyclic AMP-independent transduction mechanisms. Curr Top Membr Transp 1983;18:255–285.

352. Mohr E, Meyerhof W, Richter D. Vasopressin and oxytocin: molecular biology and evolution of the peptide hormones and their receptors. Vitam Horm 1995;51:235–266.

353. Szabò G, Tabakoff B, Hoffman PL. Receptors with V_1 characteristics mediate the maintenance of ethanol tolerance by vasopressin. J Pharmacol Exp Ther 1988;247:536–541.

354. Ishizawa H, Tabakoff B, Mefford IN, Hoffman PL. Reduction of arginine vasopressin binding sites in mouse lateral septum by treatment with 6-hydroxydopamine. Brain Res 1990;507:189–194.

355. Shewey LM, Dorsa DM. V_1-type vasopressin receptors in rat brain septum: binding characteristics and effects on inositol phospholipid metabolism. J Neurosci 1988;8:1671–1677.

356. Tabakoff B, Ritzmann RF. The effects of 6-hydroxydopamine on tolerance to and dependence on ethanol. J Pharmacol Exp Ther 1977;203:319–332.

357. Hoffman PL, Melchior CL, Tabakoff B. Vasopressin maintenance of ethanol tolerance requires intact brain noradrenergic systems. Life Sci 1983;32:1065–1071.

358. Hagan JJ, Balfour DJK. Lysine vasopressin fails to alter (^{3}H)noradrenaline uptake or release from hippocampal tissue in vitro. Life Sci 1983;32:2517–2522.

359. Speisky MB, Kalant H. Site of interaction of serotonin and desglycinamide-arginine vasopressin in maintenance of ethanol tolerance. Brain Res 1985;326:281–290.

360. Wu PH, Liu JF, Lança AJ, Kalant H. Selective involvement of central 5-HT$_2$ receptors in the maintenance of tolerance to ethanol by arginine (8)-vasopressin. J Pharmacol Exp Ther 1994;270:802–808.

361. Wu PH, Liu JF, Wu WL, Lança AJ, Kalant H. Development of alcohol tolerance in the rat after a single exposure to combined treatment with arginine (8)-vasopressin and ethanol. J Pharmacol Exp Ther 1996;276:1283–1291.

362. Rathna Giri P, Dave JR, Tabakoff B, Hoffman PL. Arginine vasopressin induces the expression of c-fos in the mouse septum and hippocampus. Mol Brain Res 1990;7:131–137.

363. Hoffman PL. Neuroadaptive functions of the neuropeptide arginine vasopressin. Ann N Y Acad Sci 1994;739:168–175.

364. Curran T. The fos oncogene. In: Reddy EP, Skalka AM, Curran T, eds. The oncogene handbook. Amsterdam: Elsevier Science Publishers, 1988:307–325.

365. Greenberg ME, Ziff EB, Greene LA. Stimulation of neuronal acetylcholine receptors induces rapid gene transcription. Science 1986;234:80–83.

366. Halazonetis TD, Georgopoulos K, Greenberg ME, Leder P. c-Jun dimerizes with itself and c-fos, forming complexes of different DNA binding affinities. Cell 1988;55:917–924.

367. Pittman QJ, Rogers J, Bloom FE. Arginine vasopressin deficient Brattleboro rats fail to develop tolerance to the hypothermic effects of ethanol. Regul Pept 1982;4:33–41.

368. Schmale H, Ivell R, Breindl M, Darmer D, Richter D. The mutant vasopressin gene from diabetes insipidus (Brattleboro) rats is transcribed but the message is not efficiently translated. EMBO J 1984;3:3289–3293.

369. Weiner HL. The role of growth factor receptors in central nervous system development and neoplasia. Neurosurgery 1995;37:179–194.

370. Heldin C-H. Dimerization of cell surface receptors in signal transduction. Cell 1995;80:213–223.

371. Brodie C, Kentroti S, Vernadakis A. Growth factors attenuate the cholinotoxic effects of ethanol during early neuroembryogenesis in the chick embryo. Int J Dev Neurosci 1991;9:203–213.

372. Brodie C, Vernadakis A. Ethanol increases cholinergic and decreases GABAergic neuronal expression in cultures derived from 8-day-old chick embryo cerebral hemispheres: interaction of ethanol and growth factors. Dev Brain Res 1992;65:253–257.

373. Heaton MB, Paiva M, Swanson DJ, Walker DW. Modulation of ethanol neurotoxicity by nerve growth factor. Brain Res 1993;620:78–85.

374. Heaton MB, Paiva M, Swanson DJ, Walker DW. Responsiveness of cultured septal and hippocampal neurons to ethanol and neurotrophic substances. J Neurosci Res 1994;39:305–318.

375. Messing RO, Henteleff M, Park JJ. Ethanol enhances growth factor-induced neurite formation in PC12 cells. Brain Res 1991;565:301–311.

376. Roivainen R, Hundle B, Messing RO. Ethanol enhances growth factor activation of mitogen-activated protein kinases by a protein kinase C-dependent mechanism. Proc Natl Acad Sci U S A 1995;92:1891–1895.

377. Valles S, Lindo L, Montoliu C, Renau-Piqueras J, Guerri C. Prenatal exposure to ethanol induces changes in the nerve growth factor and its receptor in proliferating astrocytes in primary culture. Brain Res 1994;656:281–286.

378. Aloe L, Tirassa P. The effect of long-term ethanol intake on brain NGF-target cells of aged rats. Alcohol 1992;9:299–304.

379. Aloe L, Bracci-Laudiero L, Tirassa P. The effect of chronic ethanol intake on brain NGF level and on NGF-target tissues of adult mice. Drug Alcohol Depend 1993;31:159–167.

380. Baek JK, Heaton MB, Walker DW. Chronic al-

cohol ingestion: nerve growth factor gene expression and neurotrophic activity in rat hippocampus. Alcohol Clin Exp Res 1994;18:1368–1376.

381. Breese CR, D'Costa A, Sonntag WE. Effect of in utero ethanol exposure on the postnatal ontogeny of insulin-like growth factor-1, and type-1 and type-2 insulin-like growth factor receptors in the rat brain. Neuroscience 1994;63:579–589.

382. Resnicoff M, Sell C, Ambrose D, Barsega R, Rubin R. Ethanol inhibits the autophosphorylation of the insulin-like growth factor 1 receptor and the IGF-1-mediated proliferation of 3T3 cells. J Biol Chem 1993;268:21777–21782.

383. Resnicoff M, Rubini M, Barsega R, Rubin R. Ethanol inhibits insulin-like growth factor-1-mediated signalling and proliferation of C6 glioblastoma cells. J Clin Invest 1994;71:657–662.

384. Xu YY, Bhavani K, Wands JR, de la Monte SM. Ethanol inhibits insulin receptor substrate-1 tyrosine phosphorylation and insulin-stimulated neuronal thread protein gene expression. Biochem J 1995;310:125–132.

385. Tomono M, Kiss Z. Ethanol enhances the stimulatory effects of insulin and insulin-like growth factor-1 on DNA synthesis in NIH 3T3 fibroblasts. Biochem Biophys Res Com 1995;208:63–67.

386. Valenzuela CF, Harris RA. Effects of ethanol on PDGF receptor-dependent signal transduction. Alcohol Clin Exp Res 1995;19 (suppl):32A.

387. Valenzuela CF, Kazlauskas A, Brozowski SJ, Weiner JL, DeMali KA, McDonald BJ, Moss SJ, Dunwiddie TV, Harris RA. Platelet-derived growth factor is a novel modulator of type A γ-aminobutyric acid-gated ion channels. Mol Pharmacol 1995;48:1099–1107.

388. Valenzuela CF, Xiong Z, MacDonald JF, et al. Platelet-derived growth factor (PDGF) induces a long-term inhibition of NMDA receptor function. J Biol Chem 1996;271:16151–16159.

389. Lo DC. Neurotrophic factors and synaptic plasticity. Neuron 1995;15:979–981.

12 ALCOHOL: CLINICAL ASPECTS

Donald W. Goodwin and William F. Gabrielli, Jr.

DEFINITION

There are many definitions of alcoholism. Keller and his associates (1) defined alcoholism as the "repetitive intake of alcoholic beverages to a degree that harms the drinker in health or socially or economically, with indication of inability consistently to control the occasion or amount of drinking." Charles Jackson, author of the *Lost Weekend,* said the alcoholic was a person who could take it or leave it, so he took it. This concept embodies two important features of alcoholism: denial and rationalization. The American Psychiatric Association in the *Diagnostic and Statistical Manual of Mental Disorders: DSM-IV,* fourth edition, defines *alcohol dependence* (2). The criteria for diagnosis are the same as for dependence of any substances of abuse. These are listed in Table 12.1. For the purpose of this chapter, alcoholism and alcohol dependence are synonymous. The term "alcoholism" is still widely used. The term "alcoholism" is retained in this chapter.

HISTORY

Six millennia ago at the Sumerian trading post of Godin Tepe in what is now western Iran, people were drinking beer and wine. In 1992, chemists analyzed a residue in pottery jars found in the ruins of Godin Tepe and identified it as wine or beer. The Sumerians were among the first people to develop a complex, literate society of prospering city-states based on irrigation, agriculture, and widespread trade (3). Apparently, the societal development at least paralleled the use of beer or wine.

Beer making began almost as soon as Mesopotamians domesticated barley to make bread in the early transition to agriculture around 8000 BC. Alcohol goes back at least to Paleolithic times. Paleolithic humans had fermented fruit juice (wine), fermented grain (beer), and fermented honey (mead). The word "methanol" (alcohol) derives from the Greek word *methy* and the Sanskrit word *madhu,* which mean both "honey" and "intoxicating drink" (4).

Descriptions of drunkenness fill the writings of antiquity, but so do pleas for moderation. Moderation was recommended in the East by Genghis Khan. Ancient Egypt invented the first temperance tract. The Old Testament condemns drunkenness but not alcohol.

The process of distillation was discovered about 800 AD in Arabia. The word "alcohol" comes from the Arabic *alkuhl,* meaning essence. Alcoholism in the modern era usually embodies the easier route to drunkenness, the distilled spirit.

The disease concept of alcoholism originated in the writings of Benjamin Rush, M.D. (widely recognized as the father of American Psychiatry) and by the British physician, Thomas Trotter (5). The first hospital for alcoholics was opened in Boston in 1841. In 1904, the Medical Temperance Society changed its name to the American Medical Association for the Study of Inebriety and Narcotics. Although waxing and waning in popularity with the introduction and repeal of prohibition, the disease concept of alcoholism has continued through the twentieth century, remaining one of the more difficult medical management problems. During the 1960s and 1970s, strong evidence suggested a biological, familial, and even hereditary role in the etiology of some alcoholism. Even today, despite numerous treatment programs and methods, no universally effective treatment option exists for this very old disease.

PREVALENCE AND EPIDEMIOLOGY

Today, in the United States, the reported consumption of alcohol is less than 3 gallons per year per person over the age of 14 (6). This figure is based on tax data. Untaxed sales, such as those on military installations, are not included, so per capita estimates may be low. Most adults in the United States are light drinkers or rarely drink. Thirty-five percent claim they do not drink at all, and 55% drink less than 3 drinks per week. Only 11% of the adult population drink an average of at least 1 ounce of alcohol per day (6). Most alcohol is consumed by a small percentage of people. Ten percent of drinkers consume more than half of all alcohol consumed.

Although the drinking behavior of Americans is known, the prevalence of alcoholism is not known. This should not be surprising, given the diversity of definitions. The alcoholism rate is not the same as the rate of heavy drinkers, however defined. Estimates of the extent of alcoholism range from 5 million to 14 million Americans, although the higher figures almost always include "problem drinkers." Older studies in European countries (7) have reported a lifelong expectancy rate for alcoholism among men of about 3–5%; the rate for women ranges from 0.1% to 1%. Weissman and Myers found similar rates in a late-1970s household survey in Connecticut (8). It has been speculated that the cultural trend toward more women working outside the home might unmask or stimulate more alcoholism among women, but there is no evidence of this yet.

More is known about patterns of "normal" drinking than about the prevalence of alcoholism. In 1985, the federal government studied the drinking habits of more than 30,000 households, dividing drinkers into abstainers, moderate drinkers, and heavy drinkers (9). A moderate drinker was defined as one who drank 4–13 drinks per week. A heavy drinker averaged 2 or more drinks per day, or more than 14 drinks per week. A drink was defined as a 1½-ounce highball, a bottle of beer, or 4 ounces of wine.

Table 12.1. Diagnostic Criteria for Substance Dependence

A maladaptive pattern of substance use, leading to clinically significant impairment of distress, as manifested by three (or more) of the following, occurring in the same 12-month period:

(1) Tolerance, as defined by either of the following:
    (a) A need for markedly increased amounts of the substance to achieve intoxication or desired effect
    (b) Markedly diminished effect with continued use of the same amount of the substance
(2) Withdrawal, as manifested by either of the following:
    (a) The characteristic withdrawal syndrome for the substance (refer to Criteria A and B of the criteria sets for Withdrawal from the specific substances)
    (b) The same (or closely related) substance is taken to relieve or avoid withdrawal symptoms
(3) The substance is often taken in larger amounts or over a longer period than was intended
(4) There is a persistent desire or unsuccessful efforts to cut down or control substance use
(5) A great deal of time is spent in activities necessary to obtain the substance (e.g., visiting multiple doctors or driving long distances), use the substance (e.g., chain smoking), or recover from its effects
(6) Important social, occupational, or recreational activities are given up or reduced because of substance use
(7) The substance use is continued despite knowledge of having a persistent or recurrent physical or psychological problem that is likely to have been caused or exacerbated by the substance (e.g., recurrent cocaine use despite recognition of cocaine-induced depression, or continued drinking despite recognition that an ulcer was made worse by alcohol consumption)

Specify if:

With Physiological Dependence: evidence of tolerance or withdrawal (i.e., either Item 1 or 2 is present)
Without Physiological Dependence: no evidence of tolerance or withdrawal (i.e., neither Item 1 nor 2 is present)

From American Psychiatric Association. Diagnostic and statistical manual of mental disorders: DSM-IV. 4th ed. Washington, DC: American Psychiatric Association, 1994:181.

Using these definitions, the researchers found that 13% of men and 3% of women were heavy drinkers. Heavy drinkers were concentrated in the highest income groups and among whites. There is some inconsistency about the social class correlation, since higher rates among blue-collar workers and urban blacks have been found in other studies, including an earlier nationwide survey of drinking practices by Cahalan and associates (10). Regarding drinkers in general, this survey also demonstrated that more drinkers live in cities and suburbs than in rural regions and small towns. To some extent, religion determined whether a person was a drinker or a teetotaler: Almost all urban Jews and Episcopalians drank on occasion; fewer than half of rural Baptists drank. The drinking patterns revealed by this study were highly changeable. It was common for individuals to be heavy drinkers for long periods and then become moderate drinkers or teetotalers.

Blacks in city ghettos have a particularly high rate of alcohol-related problems; whether rural blacks have comparably high rates of alcohol problems is unknown (11). Native Americans are also said to have high rates of alcoholism (12), but this does not apply to all tribes, and books have been written debunking the "firewater myth" (13). Orientals, on the other hand, generally have low rates of alcoholism.

Alcoholism is a serious problem in France and Russia (14). Although Italy, like France, is a "vinocultural" country (where wine is a popular beverage), Italians are alleged to have a lower rate of alcoholism than do the French (15). Estimates of alcoholism rates are usually based on cirrhosis rates and admissions to psychiatric hospitals for alcoholism. France has the highest cirrhosis rate in the world. Ireland has a relatively low cirrhosis rate, despite its reputation for a high rate of alcoholism. There is a correlation between consumption of alcohol and cirrhosis rates. Both cirrhosis rates and alcoholism are correlated with the total amount of alcohol consumed by the population of that country (16). Cirrhosis rates themselves are probably somewhat unreliable, especially with the complicating risk associated with possible simultaneous infection by hepatitis C, a factor that significantly in-

creases the risk of cirrhosis development (17). Further, estimates of the prevalence of alcoholism in different countries tend to change from time to time as new information is obtained (18).

Cirrhosis data suggest that individuals in certain occupations are more vulnerable to alcoholism than those doing other types of work. Waiters, bartenders, longshoremen, authors, and reporters have relatively high cirrhosis rates; accountants, mail carriers, and carpenters have relatively low rates (16).

Alcohol problems are associated with a history of school difficulty (19). High-school dropouts and frequent truancy and delinquency have a particularly high association with alcoholism.

Age is also correlated with alcoholism. Urban blacks begin drinking at an earlier age than do whites of comparable socioeconomic status (11). Women generally begin heavy drinking at a later age than men (20).

CLINICAL PICTURE

Alcoholism is at least partly a behavioral disorder. The specific behavior that causes problems is the consumption of large quantities of alcohol on repeated occasions. The motivation underlying this behavior is often obscure. When asked why they drink excessively, alcoholics occasionally attribute their drinking to a particular mood, such as depression or anxiety, or to stressful circumstances. They sometimes describe an overpowering "need" to drink, variously described as a craving or compulsion. Just as often, however, the alcoholic is unable to give a plausible explanation of his or her excessive drinking (21).

Like other drug dependencies, alcoholism is marked by a preoccupation with ensuring the availability of the drug in quantities sufficient to produce intoxication. Early on, the patient may deny this preoccupation or rationalize the need by assertions that he or she drinks no more than his or her friends. Accordingly, alcoholics tend to spend their time with other heavy drinkers. They may not drink more than their "alcoholic" friends.

An insurance salesman writes (3):

My need was easy to hide from myself and others (maybe I'm kidding myself about the others). I only associated with people who drank. I married a woman who drank. There were always reasons to drink. I was low, tense, tired, mad, happy. I probably drank as often because I was happy as for any other reason. And occasions for drinking—when drinking was appropriate, expected—were endless. Football games, fishing trips, parties, holidays, birthdays, Christmas, or merely Saturday night. Drinking became interwoven with everything pleasurable—food, sex, social life. When I stopped drinking, these things, for a time, lost all interest for me, they were so tied to drinking.

As alcoholism progresses and problems from drinking become more serious, alcoholics may drink alone, sneak drinks, hide the bottle, and otherwise conceal the seriousness of their condition. This is accompanied by guilt and remorse, which produce more drinking, relieving the feelings. Remorse may be intense enough to provoke more drinking as the alcohol seems to temporarily blunt the feeling. This may influence morning drinking when remorse may be most intense. An alcoholic writes (3):

For years, I drank and had very little hangover, but now the hangovers were gruesome. I felt physically bad—headachy, nauseous, weak, but the mental part was the hardest. I loathed myself. I was waking early and thinking what a mess I was, how I had hurt so many others and myself. The words "guilty" and "depression" sound superficial in trying to describe how I felt. The loathing was almost physical—a dead weight that could be lifted in only one way, and that was by having a drink, so I drank, morning after morning. After two or three, my hands were steady, I could hold some breakfast down, and the guilt was gone, or almost.

Drinking relieves guilt and anxiety, then produces anxiety and depression (22). Symptoms associated with depression and anxiety disorders—terminal insomnia, low mood, irritability, and anxiety attacks with chest pain, palpitations, and dyspnea—often occur. Alcohol relieves these symptoms, resulting in a vicious circle of drinking, then depression, and then more drinking. When the circle is ultimately stopped, a withdrawal syndrome may follow. Often, the patient succeeds in stopping drinking for several days or weeks, only to "fall off the wagon" again (3):

At some point I was without wife, home or job. I had nothing to do but drink. The drinking was now steady, days on end. I lost appetite and missed meals (besides money was short). I awoke at night, sweating and shaking, and had a drink. I awoke in the morning vomiting and had a drink. It couldn't last. My ex-wife found me in my apartment shaking and seeing things and got me in the hospital. I dried out, left, and went back to drinking. I was hospitalized again, and this time stayed dry for 6 months. I was nervous and couldn't sleep, but got some of my confidence back and found a part-time job. Then my ex-boss offered me my job back and I celebrated by having a drink. The next night I had two drinks. In a month I was drinking as much as ever and again unemployed.

Despair and hopelessness seem to be inevitable. By the time patients consult a physician, they have often reached rock bottom. Their situation seems hopeless. Their problems have become so numerous that they feel nothing can be done about them. At this point, they may be ready to acknowledge their alcoholism but feel powerless to stop drinking. But many do stop—some permanently—as is discussed later.

Alcohol occasionally produces amnesia. Nonalcoholics, when drinking, also experience this amnesia (blackouts), but they experience them less often than do alcoholics (23). Amnesia is particularly distressful to alcoholics because they fear that they have harmed someone or behaved imprudently while intoxicated (24).

> A 39 year old salesman awoke in a strange hotel room. He had a mild hangover but otherwise felt normal. His clothes were hanging in the closet; he was clean-shaven. He dressed and went down to the lobby. He learned from the clerk that he was in Las Vegas and that he had checked in 2 days previously. It had been obvious that he had been drinking, the clerk said, but he hadn't seemed very drunk. The date was Saturday the fourteenth. His last recollection was of sitting in a St. Louis bar on Monday the ninth. He had been drinking all day and was drunk, but could remember everything perfectly until about 3 P.M., when "like a curtain dropping," his memory went blank. It remained blank for approximately 5 days. Three years later, those 5 days were still a blank. He was so frightened by the experience that he abstained from alcohol for 2 years (3).

The amnesia is anterograde (25). During a blackout, individuals have relatively intact remote and immediate memory but experience a specific short-term memory deficit in which they are unable to recall events that happened 5 or 10 minutes before. Because other intellectual faculties are well preserved, they can perform complicated acts and appear normal to the casual observer. Blackouts probably represent impaired consolidation of new information rather than repression motivated by a desire to forget events that happened while drinking (24).

Sometimes, a curious thing happens: The drinker recalls things that happened during a previous drinking period that, when sober, he or she had forgotten. This is a phenomenon called state-dependent memory. For instance, alcoholics often report hiding money or alcohol when drinking, forgetting it when sober, and having their memory return when drinking again (24):

> A 47-year-old housewife often wrote letters when she was drinking. Sometimes she would jot down notes for a letter and start writing it but not finish it. The next day, sober, she would be unable to decipher the notes. Then she would start drinking again, and after a few drinks the meaning of the notes would become clear and she would resume writing the letter. "It was like picking up the pencil where I had left off."

Benzodiazepines combined with alcohol apparently increase the likelihood of blackouts with smaller amounts of alcohol than are usually required (26). Orally, benzodiazepines produce a mild impairment of short-term memory (27) but are not associated with blackouts of the type produced by alcohol (unless given intravenously).

IDENTIFICATION

Before alcoholism can be treated it must be diagnosed. Physicians are in a good position to identify a drinking problem. A physical examination and laboratory tests may reveal the following:

1. Arcus senilis—a ringlike opacity of the cornea—occurs commonly with age and is considered an innocent condition. The ring forms from fatty material in the blood. Alcohol increases fat in the blood and more alcoholics have the ring than do others their age (28).
2. A red nose (acne rosacea) occurs more commonly in those who drink. Occasionally, however, people with red noses are teetotalers and may resent the insinuation.
3. Red palms (palmar erythema) are suggestive but not diagnostic of alcoholism.
4. Asterixis, otherwise known as liver flap, points to the alcoholic with concurrent liver disease.
5. Cigarette burns between the index and middle fingers or on the chest and contusions and bruises suggest periods of alcoholic stupor.
6. Painless enlargement of the liver suggests a larger alcohol intake than the liver can cope with. Severe, constant upper abdominal pain and tenderness radiating to the back indicates pancreatic inflammation, and alcohol sometimes is the cause.
7. Spider angiomas, spider-like groupings of blood vessels in the skin, are common in long-standing alcoholism.
8. Reduced sensation and weakness in the feet and legs may occur from excessive drinking. This is also seen in diabetes and other long-standing metabolic disorders.
9. Laboratory tests provide other clues. More than half of alcoholics have increased amounts of γ-glutamyl transpeptidase (GGTP) in their blood, which is unusual in nonalcoholics. After GGTP, elevations in the following tests are most often associated with heavy drinking: mean corpuscular volume (MCV), uric acid, triglycerides, aspartate aminotransferase, and urea (29).

Another approach is to "score" several common blood chemistry values according to a formula derived from a discriminant function analysis of values obtained from alcoholics and controls. A distinctive "fingerprint" may suggest recent heavy drinking but not necessarily alcoholism (30).

In searching for signs of alcohol abuse, physicians sometimes slip into a moralistic attitude that offends the patient. For personal reasons, physicians may believe any drinking is wrong. They still should be aware of findings suggesting that moderate drinking may actually contribute to longevity (31). Turner and associates (32) in their review of the "beneficial" effects of alcohol surveyed a number of well-designed studies indicating that the risk of coronary heart disease is lower in persons who use alcohol moderately than in abstainers. Increased levels of high-density lipoproteins (HDL)—a negative risk factor for myocardial infarction—are associated with moderate and even (in some studies) heavy alcohol use. Moderate drinking is defined by Turner et al. as an intake that exceeds neither 0.8 g/kg of ethanol per day (up to a limit of 80 g) nor an average of 0.7 g/kg for 3 successive days.

None of this should be interpreted as encouragement of immoderate use of alcohol. For alcoholics, no level of intake is considered beneficial. Moreover, uncertainties exist concerning the effects of moderate drinking on the unborn child and the relationship of moderate drinking to automobile accidents.

NATURAL HISTORY AND GENDER DIFFERENCES

The natural history of alcoholism seems to be different for men and women (33). Onset is usually at a younger age for men, often in the late teens or early 20s. The course is insidious, with the individual not fully realizing that there is a problem until the 30s. The first hospitalization may not occur until the late 30s or the 40s (34). Rarely does alcoholism occur de novo after the age of 45 (3). The onset of alcoholism often occurs later in women and is more variable (33). Women alcoholics may also be more likely to suffer from affective disorder (depression or manic-depressive illness) (35).

Patterns of drinking are variable. Jellinek (36) divided alcoholics into various types according to their drinking pattern. One type, which he called the "gamma alcoholic" is common in America. The key feature is problems with "control": Once they begin drinking they are unable to stop at a reasonable point. Once the episode is terminated, however, these individuals can maintain sobriety and function rather well until the next episode. Another type of alcoholic (found more often in France according to Jellinek) has "control" but is unable to "abstain": He must drink a given quantity of alcohol every day. This person may not realize he has a problem until he is unable to drink on a given day. He may alter his life-style in order to accomplish the drinking. He may go into withdrawal if unable to drink on a given day. Others have postulated other types of alcoholics. Although these "pure" types of alcoholics may exist, many individuals do not conform to any specific type. A person may drink moderately for a long time before his or her drinking begins to interfere with health or social functioning (37).

COMPLICATIONS

Complications from alcohol use can be divided into social and medical. Alcoholics have a high rate of marital separation and divorce. They often have job troubles, including frequent absenteeism and job loss. They have frequent accidents in the home, on the job, and while driving automobiles. About 40% of highway fatalities in the United States involve a driver who has been drinking (38). Nearly half of convicted felons are alcoholic (39), and about half of police activities in large cities are associated with alcohol-related offenses.

Medical complications fall into three categories: (a) acute effects, (b) chronic effects, and (c) withdrawal effects.

Consumption of very large amounts of alcohol can lead directly to death by depressing the respiratory center in the medulla. Acute hemorrhagic pancreatitis occasionally occurs from a single heavy drinking episode.

Nearly every organ system can be affected by heavy use of alcohol. Gastritis and diarrhea are common. Gastric ulcer may also occur, although the evidence that alcohol directly produces ulceration is equivocal.

Liver damage is the most serious effect of alcohol on the gastrointestinal tract (40). Cirrhosis results from the combined effects of alcohol, possibly diet, and other factors, possibly including heredity. Human and animal studies indicate that a single large dose of alcohol combined with a diet rich in fat produces a fatty liver (41). The connection between fatty liver and cirrhosis is unclear. The fatty changes in the liver after acute alcohol intoxication are reversible. Most patients with portal (Laënnec's) cirrhosis are excessive drinkers. However, most severe alcoholics do not develop cirrhosis (probably less that 15%).

Alcoholism is associated with pathology of the nervous system, principally owing to vitamin deficiencies. Peripheral neuropathy, the most common neurologic complication, results from multiple vitamin B deficiencies (42). It is usually reversible with adequate nutrition. Retrobulbar neuropathy may lead to amblyopia (sometimes called tobacco-alcohol amblyopia), also usually reversible with vitamin therapy.

Other neurologic complications include anterior lobe cerebellar degenerative disease (43) and the Wernicke-Korsakoff syndrome (44). The latter results from thiamine deficiency. The acute Wernicke stage consists of ocular disturbances (nystagmus or sixth nerve palsy), ataxia, and confusion. It usually clears in a few days but may progress to a chronic brain syndrome (Korsakoff psychosis). Short-term memory loss (anterograde amnesia) is the most characteristic feature of Korsakoff's psychosis. "Confabulation" (narration of fanciful tales) may occur. The Wernicke-Korsakoff syndrome is associated with necrotic lesions of the mammillary bodies, thalamus, and other brainstem areas. Thiamine corrects early Wernicke signs rapidly and *may* prevent development of an irreversible Korsakoff dementia. Once the dementia is established, thiamine usually does not help.

A 48-year-old divorced housepainter has been admitted to the hospital with a history of 30 years of heavy drinking. He has had two previous admissions for detoxification but the family states that he has not had a drink in several weeks and shows no sign of alcohol withdrawal. He looks malnourished, however, and on examination is found to be ataxic and have a bilateral sixth cranial nerve palsy. He appears confused and mistakes one of his physicians for a dead uncle.

Within a week the patient walks normally, and there is no sign of a sixth nerve palsy. He seems less confused and can now find his way to the bathroom without direction. He remembers the names and birthdays of his siblings but has difficulty naming the past five presidents.

More strikingly, he has great difficulty in retaining information for longer than a few minutes. He can repeat back a list of numbers immediately after he

has heard them, but a few minutes later does not recall being asked to perform the task. Shown three objects (keys, comb, ring), he cannot recall them 3 minutes later. He does not seem worried about this. Asked if he can recall the name of his doctor, he replies, "Certainly," and proceeds to call the doctor "Dr. Masters" (not his name) whom he claims he first met in the Korean War. He tells a long untrue story about how he and "Dr. Masters" served as fellow soldiers in the Korean War.

The patient is calm, alert, friendly. One could be with him for a short period and not realize he has a severe memory impairment, in view of his intact immediate memory and spotty but sometimes impressive remote memory. His amnesia, in short, is largely anterograde. Although treated with high doses of thiamine, the short-term memory deficit persists and appears to be irreversible.

Whether excessive use of alcohol produces cortical atrophy has been debated for many years (45). Computed tomography (CT) scans of alcoholics have been contradictory, with some showing cerebral atrophy (46), some showing none (47), and one showing *reversible* atrophy (48). In a 1987 study, computer technology was used to count brain cells in alcoholics who came to autopsy; alcoholics had fewer neurons in the frontal cortex than did nonalcoholics (49). If confirmed by further studies, this would support the long-held but poorly documented view that excessive use of alcohol produces cortical atrophy of the frontal lobes. The extensive psychometric literature on intellectual impairment in alcoholics is also contradictory (50). Most studies performed soon after drinking bouts show intellectual deficits, but the deficits vary from study to study. The most consistent results have involved use of the categories test of the Halstead Battery, indicating that alcoholics have difficulty in "conceptual shifting." Many of the deficits found in alcoholics undergoing detoxification are reversible. No studies have reported a decline in alcoholics' IQs.

Other medical complications of alcoholism include cardiomyopathy, thrombocytopenia and anemia, and myopathy. Two studies (51, 52) showed an increase in breast cancer in women who were light or moderate drinkers. Not having previously been reported, the association awaits further study for confirmation. It has also been reported that alcoholics have an increased risk of stroke (53). This could be related to alcohol-induced hypertension, although the relationship between alcohol and sustained hypertension remains controversial (54, 55). The effect of alcohol on stroke was lost when adjusted for smoking in another study (56).

A possible teratogenic effect of alcohol has been suspected for centuries, but it was not until the work of Lemoine in 1968 (57) and the independent observations of Jones et al. in 1973 (58) that a distinct dysmorphic condition associated with maternal alcoholism during pregnancy was described in the medical literature. The abnormalities most typically associated with alcohol teratogenicity can be grouped into four categories: central nervous system dysfunction, birth deficiencies, a characteristic cluster of facial abnormalities, and variable major and minor malformations. Animal studies have now demonstrated specific teratogenic properties of ethyl alcohol in a variety of species, with many of the abnormalities being similar to those described in humans (59).

Despite this growing body of evidence, the so-called fetal alcohol syndrome remains a subject of controversy. Large-scale longitudinal studies are needed to definitely establish the teratogenicity of alcohol in humans. This is because alcoholic women are often malnourished, take other drugs, smoke heavily, and in general have life-styles that differ from those of nonalcoholic women. Most clinicians considering present evidence believe women should be cautioned against drinking excessively during pregnancy and perhaps should avoid alcohol altogether, since "safe" levels of alcohol have not been ascertained (20).

WITHDRAWAL

The term *alcohol withdrawal syndrome* is preferable to *delirium tremens* (DTs). The latter refers to a specific manifestation of the syndrome. The most common withdrawal symptom is tremulousness, which occurs a few hours after cessation of drinking. Transitory hallucinations may occur. If so, they usually begin 12–24 hours after drinking stops (42).

After a week of heavy drinking and little food, a 30-year-old newspaper reporter tried to drink a morning cup of coffee and found that his hands were shaking so violently he could not get the cup to his mouth. He managed to pour some whisky into a glass and drank as much as he could. His hands became less shaky but now he was nauseated and began having "dry heaves." He tried repeatedly to drink but could not keep the alcohol down. He felt ill and intensely anxious and decided to call a doctor friend. The doctor recommended hospitalization.

On admission, the patient had a marked resting and exertional tremor of the hands, and his tongue and eyelids were tremulous. He also had feelings of "internal" tremulousness. Lying in the hospital bed, he found the noises outside his window unbearably loud and began seeing "visions" of animals and, on one occasion, a dead relative. He was terrified and called a nurse, who gave him a tranquilizer. He became quieter, and his tremor was less pronounced. At all times he realized that the visual phenomena were "imaginary." He always knew where he was and was oriented otherwise. After a few days the tremor disappeared and he no longer hallucinated. He still had trouble sleeping but otherwise felt back to normal and vowed never to drink again.

Grand mal convulsions (rum fits) occur occasionally, sometimes as long as 2 or 3 days after drinking stops. As a rule, alcoholics experiencing convulsions do not have epilepsy; they have normal electroencephalograms (EEGs) when not drinking and experience convulsions only during withdrawal (60).

Delirium tremens is infrequent and, when it occurs, is often associated with medical illness. For diagnosis of delirium tremens, gross memory disturbance should be present, plus other withdrawal symptoms, such as agitation and hallucinations. Typically, delirium tremens begins 2 or 3 days after drinking stops and subsides within 1–5 days (61). One should always suspect intercurrent medical illness when delirium occurs during withdrawal. The physician should be particularly alert to hepatic decompensation, pneumonia, subdural hematoma, pancreatitis, and fractures.

DUAL DIAGNOSIS

The *DSM-IV* definition of alcohol dependence quoted above (2) allows alcoholism to coexist with other diagnoses. This is a relatively new concept. In the past, alcoholism was only diagnosed if it was "primary," meaning that it was not associated with other pathophysiologic states. Diagnoses of other disorders, including depression and anxiety disorders, could not be made when active or recent drinking had occurred. A good deal of evidence now indicates that many, and perhaps most, alcoholics do *not* have primary alcoholism. Their alcoholism *is* associated with other psychopathology, including addiction to other drugs, depression, manic-depressive illness, anxiety disorder, or antisocial personality.

Studies indicate that between 30% and 50% of alcoholics meet diagnostic criteria for major depression. About one-third of alcoholics fulfill criteria for one of the anxiety disorders, particularly social phobia in men and agoraphobia in women. Many alcoholics have an antisocial personality (the figures vary too much to warrant quoting). Finally, many alcoholics are addicted to other drugs (62).

The coexistence of alcoholism and drug addiction, in fact, seems to be increasing. A 1989 survey of Alcoholics Anonymous (AA) members (63) found that 36% of respondents reported addiction to drugs as well as alcohol—an increase over the 38% recorded in the 1986 survey, reflecting a trend first tracked in 1977, when the proportion of such respondents was 18%. Age and sex were major factors: About 75% of young people reported previous drug addiction, and there was a greater percentage of women than men.

The survey has been conducted every 3 years since 1968. A tendency for more and more young people to join AA had declined sharply in the latest survey. In a previous survey, there had been an increase of 22% in the number of members under age 31 in a 3-year period, compared with an increase of 1% in the latest survey. Those under 21 made up 3% of the 1989 respondents.

AA, which usually discourages research, came up with other interesting figures. The marked increase in women members (34% in 1986) rose only 1% in the 1989 survey. Among members, 50 months was the average sobriety length. The survey underscored a continuing problem—half of those who

come to AA do not remain for more than 3 months. Former surveys had indicated that only about 15% continued attending meetings. The fate of alcoholics who reject AA is not clear, but treatment evaluation studies indicate that many of them reduce their drinking or stop altogether without the help of AA. Most of these improvements can be described as "spontaneous," inasmuch as professional help did not seem responsible.

One final word should be said about alcohol use in the United States. According to the Centers for Disease Control and Prevention (CDC), per capita consumption of ethanol—the actual alcohol in alcoholic beverages—was 2.58 gallons from all beverages in 1986, the lowest since 2.64 gallons in 1977. The CDC report noted that two of three American adults drink but that a relatively small number consume most of the alcoholic beverages: 10% of drinkers, or 6.5% of the U.S. adult population, drink half of all the alcohol consumed in the nation (64).

TREATMENT

The treatment of alcoholism and the management of alcohol withdrawal symptoms present separate problems.

In the absence of serious medical complications, alcohol withdrawal syndrome is usually transient and self-limited; the patient recovers within several days regardless of treatment (33). Insomnia and irritability may persist for longer periods.

Treatment for withdrawal is symptomatic and prophylactic. Relief of agitation and tremulousness can be achieved with a variety of drugs, including barbiturates, paraldehyde, chloral hydrate, the phenothiazines, and the benzodiazepines. Currently, the benzodiazepines (e.g., chlordiazepoxide) are widely considered the drugs of choice for withdrawal. They have little, if any, synergistic action with alcohol and, compared with barbiturates and paraldehyde, relatively little abuse potential. They can be administered parenterally to intoxicated patients without apparent risk and continued orally during the withdrawal period. There is some evidence that mortality is increased when the phenothiazines are used, reportedly from hypotension or hepatic encephalopathy.

Administration of large doses of vitamins—particularly the B vitamins—is obligatory, given the role of these vitamins in preventing peripheral neuropathy and the Wernicke-Korsakoff syndrome (42). The B vitamins are water soluble, and there is no apparent danger in administering them in large doses.

Unless the patient is dehydrated because of vomiting or diarrhea, there is no reason to administer fluids parenterally. Contrary to common belief, alcoholics are usually not dehydrated; they may be overhydrated from consumption of large volumes of fluid (65). During withdrawal, hyperventilation may cause respiratory alkalosis, and this, together with hypomagnesemia, has been reported to produce withdrawal seizures (66). If the individual has a history of withdrawal seizures, diphenylhydantoin (Dilantin) may be prescribed, although there is no evidence that it prevents withdrawal seizures.

If patients develop delirium, they should be considered dangerous to themselves and others, and protective measures should be taken. Ordinarily, tranquilizers will calm the patient sufficiently to control agitation, and restraints will not be necessary. Administration of intravenous barbiturates may be necessary for severe agitation. Most importantly, if delirium occurs, further exploration should be conducted to rule out serious medical illness missed in the original examination. When a patient is delirious, an attendant should always be present. It is sometimes helpful to have a friend or relative present (67).

The treatment of alcoholism should not begin until withdrawal symptoms subside. Treatment has two goals: (*a*) sobriety and (*b*) amelioration of psychiatric conditions associated with alcoholism (68). A small minority of alcoholics are eventually able to drink in moderation, but for several months after a heavy drinking bout, total abstinence is desirable, for two reasons. First, the physician must follow the patient, sober, for a considerable period to diagnose a coexistent psychiatric problem. Second, it is important for the patient to learn that he or she can cope with ordinary life problems without alcohol. Most relapses occur within 6 months of discharge from the hospital; they become less and less frequent after that (69).

For many patients, disulfiram (Antabuse) is helpful in maintaining abstinence (70). By inhibiting aldehyde dehydrogenase, the drug leads to an accumulation of acetaldehyde if alcohol is consumed. Acetaldehyde is highly toxic and produces nausea and hypotension. The latter condition, in turn, produces shock and may be fatal. In recent years, however, Antabuse has been prescribed in a lower dosage (250 mg) than was employed previously, and no deaths from its use have been reported for a number of years. One study indicates that the dose is irrelevant; the deterrent effect is psychological and not dose dependent (71).

Discontinuation of Antabuse after administration for several days or weeks still deters drinking for a 3- to 5-day period because the drug requires that long to be excreted. Hence, it may be useful to give patients Antabuse during office visits at 3- to 4-day intervals early in the treatment program.

Until recent years, it was recommended that patients be given Antabuse for several days and challenged with alcohol to demonstrate the unpleasant effects that follow. This procedure was not always satisfactory because some patients showed no adverse effects after considerable amounts of alcohol were consumed and other patients became very ill after drinking small amounts of alcohol. At present, the alcohol challenge test is considered optional. The principal disadvantage of Antabuse is not that patients drink while taking the drug but that they stop taking the drug after a brief period. This, again, is a good reason to give the drug on frequent office visits during the early crucial period of treatment.

In recent years, a wide variety of procedures, both psychological and somatic, have been tried in the treatment of alcoholism. None has proved definitely superior to others (72). There is no evidence that intensive psychotherapy helps most alcoholics. Nor are tranquilizers usually effective in maintaining abstinence or controlled drinking. Aversive conditioning techniques have been tried, with such agents as apomorphine and emetine to produce vomiting, succinylcholine to produce apnea, and electrical stimulation to produce pain. The controlled trials required to show that these procedures are effective have not been conducted, but a high rate of success has been reported for the apomorphine treatment in well-motivated patients (73). Although it is not known how many alcoholics benefit from participation in AA, most clinicians agree that alcoholics should be encouraged to attend the meetings on a trial basis.

Serotonin reuptake blockers have been reported to reduce drinking in animals and heavy drinking humans (74). Clinical trials are being conducted at this time to determine whether available serotonin reuptake blockers have a similar effect. The available serotonin reuptake blockers are marketed for treatment of depression, obsessive compulsive disorder, obesity, and panic disorder.

In three double-blind studies (75–77), lithium carbonate was found superior to placebo in reducing drinking in depressed alcoholics. The dropout rate was high in all three studies. A fourth study failed to confirm the efficacy of lithium for alcoholism (78).

In conclusion, it should be emphasized that relapses are characteristic of alcoholism and that physicians treating alcoholics should avoid anger or excessive pessimism when such relapses occur. Alcoholics see nonpsychiatric physicians as often as they see psychiatrists (probably more often), and there is evidence that general practitioners and internists are sometimes more helpful (79). This may be particularly true when the therapeutic approach is warm but authoritarian, with little stress on "insight" or "understanding." Since the cause of alcoholism is unknown, "understanding," in fact, means acceptance of a particular theory. That may provide temporary comfort but probably rarely provides lasting benefit.

References

1. Keller M, McCormick M, Efron V. A dictionary of words about alcohol. 2nd ed. New Brunswick, NJ: Rutgers University Center of Alcohol Studies, 1982.
2. American Psychiatric Association. Diagnostic and statistical manual of mental disorders: DSM-IV. 4th ed. Washington, DC: American Psychiatric Association, 1994.
3. Goodwin DW. Alcoholism: the facts. New York: Oxford University Press, 1995.
4. Roueché B. Alcohol. New York: Grove Press, 1960.
5. Rush B. An inquiry into the effects of ardent spirits upon the human body and mind. 6th ed. New York: 1811.
6. National Institute on Alcohol Abuse and Alcoholism. Epidemiol Rep 1992;Aug–Dec.
7. Slater E. The incidence of mental disorder. Ann Eugenics 1935;6:172.
8. Weissman MM, Myers JK. Clinical depression in alcoholism. Am J Psychiatry 1980;137:3.
9. U.S. Government. Public Health Rep 1985;101:593–598.
10. Cahalan D, Cisin IH, Crossley HM, eds. American drinking practices: a national survey of behavior and attitudes. Monograph no. 6. New Brunswick, NJ: Rutgers University Center of Alcohol Studies, 1969.
11. Robins LN, Murphy GE, Breckenridge MB. Drinking behavior of young Negro men. Q J Stud Alcohol 1968;29:657–684.
12. Dozier EP. Problem drinking among American Indians: the role of socio-cultural deprivation. Q J Stud Alcohol 1966;27:71–87.
13. Leland J. Firewater myths. New Brunswick, NJ: Rutgers University Center of Alcohol Studies, 1976.
14. Sadoun R, Lolli G, Silverman M. Drinking in French culture. Monograph no. 5. New Brunswick, NJ: Rutgers University Center of Alcohol Studies, 1965.
15. Bales RF. Cultural differences in rates of alcoholism. Q J Stud Alcohol 1946;5:480.
16. DeLint J, Schmidt W. The epidemiology of alcoholism. Biological basis of alcoholism. Toronto: Wiley-Interscience, 1971.
17. Pares A, Barrera JM, Caballeria J, Guadalupe E, Bruguera M, Gaballeria L, Castillo R, Rodes J. Hepatitis C virus antibodies in chronic alcoholic patients: association with severity of liver injury. Hepatology 1990;12:1295–1299.
18. Popham RE. Indirect methods of alcoholism prevalence estimation: a critical evaluation. In: Alcohol and alcoholism. Toronto: University of Toronto Press, 1970.
19. McCord W, McCord J. A longitudinal study of the personality of alcoholics. Society, culture and drinking patterns. New York: Wiley, 1962.
20. Wilsnack SC, Beckman LJ, eds. Alcohol problems in women. New York: Guilford Press, 1984.
21. Ludwig AM. On and off the wagon. Q J Stud Alcohol 1972;33:91–96.
22. Davis D. Mood changes in alcoholic subjects with programmed and free-choice experimental drinking. In: Recent advances in studies of alcoholism. Washington, DC: U.S. Department of Health, Education, and Welfare, 1971.
23. Goodwin DW, Crane JB, Guze SB. Alcoholic "blackouts": a review and clinical study of 100 alcoholics. Am J Psychiatry 1969;126:191–198.
24. Goodwin DW. Blackouts and alcohol-induced memory dysfunction. In: Recent advances in studies of alcoholism. Washington, DC: U.S. Department of Health, Education, and Welfare, 1971.
25. Tamerin JS, Weiner S, Poppen R, Steinglass P, Mendelson JH. Alcohol and memory: amnesia and short-term memory function during experimentally induced intoxication. Am J Psychiatry 1971;127:1659–1664.
26. Morris HH, Estes ML. Traveler's amnesia. JAMA 1987;258:945–946.
27. Kumar R, Mac DS, Gabrielli WF, Goodwin DW. Anxiolytics and memory: a comparison of lorazepam and alprazolam. J Clin Psychiatry 1987;48:158–160.
28. Ewing JA, Rouse BA. Corneal arcus as a sign of possible alcoholism. Clin Exp Res 1980;4:104.
29. Whitefield JB. Alcohol-related biochemical changes in heavy drinkers. Aust N Z J Med 1981;11:132.
30. Ryback RS, Eckardt MJ, Felsher B. Biochemical and hematological correlates of alcoholism and liver disease. JAMA 1982;248:2261–2265.
31. Anderson KM, Casteeli WP, Levy D. Cholesterol and mortality: 30 years of follow-up from the Framingham study. JAMA 1987;257:2176–2180.
32. Turner TB, Bennett VL, Hernandez H. The beneficial side of moderate alcohol use. Johns Hopkins Med J 1981;148:53.
33. Pemberton DA. A comparison of the outcome of treatment in female and male alcoholics. Br J Psychiatry 1967;113:367–373.
34. Drew LRH. Alcoholism as a self-limiting disease. Q J Stud Alcohol 1968;29:956–967.
35. Schuckit M, Pitts FN Jr, Reich T, King LJ, Winokur G. Alcoholism. Arch Environ Health 1969;18:301–306.
36. Jellinek EM. The disease concept of alcoholism. New Brunswick, NJ: Rutgers University Center of Alcohol Studies, 1960.
37. Vaillant GE. The natural history of alcoholism. Cambridge, MA: Harvard University Press, 1983.
38. Sixth special report to the United States Congress on alcohol and health. Rockville, MD: National Institute on Alcohol Abuse and Alcoholism, 1987.
39. Goodwin DW, Crane JB, Guze SB. Felons who drink. Q J Stud Alcohol 1971;32:136–147.
40. Lieber CS, DeCarli LM. An experimental model of alcohol feeding and liver injury in the baboon. J Med Primatol 1974;3:153–163.
41. Lieber CS. Metabolic effects produced by alcohol in the liver and other tissues. Adv Intern Med 1968;14:151–199.

42. Victor M, Adams RD. The effect of alcohol on the nervous system. In: Proceedings of the Association for Research in Nervous and Mental Disease. Baltimore: Williams & Wilkins, 1953.
43. Romano J, Michael M Jr, Merritt HH. Alcoholic cerebellar degeneration. Arch Neurol Psychiatry 1940;44:1230–1236.
44. Victor M, Adams RD, Collins GH. The Wernicke-Korsakoff syndrome. Philadelphia: FA Davis, 1971.
45. Courville C. The effects of alcohol on the nervous system of man. Los Angeles: San Lucas, 1955 (privately printed).
46. Epstein PS, Pisani VD, Fawcett JA. Alcoholism and cerebral atrophy. Alcohol Clin Exp Res 1977;1:61–65.
47. Hill SY, Reyes RB, Mikhael M, Ayre F. A comparison of alcoholics and heroin abusers: computerized transaxial tomography and neuropsychological functioning. In: Sexias F, ed. Currents in alcoholism. New York: Grune & Stratton, 1977.
48. Carlen PL, Wortzman G, Holgate RC, Wilkinson DA, Rankin JG. Reversible cerebral atrophy in recently abstinent chronic alcoholics measured by computed tomography scans. Science 1978;200:1076–1078.
49. Harper C, Kril J, Daly J. Are we drinking our neurones away? Br Med J 1987;294:534–536.
50. Goodwin DW, Hill SY. Chronic effects of alcohol and other psychoactive drugs on intellect, learning and memory. In: Chronic effects of alcohol and other psychoactive drugs on cerebral function. Toronto: Addiction Research Foundation Press, 1975.
51. Harvey EB, Schairer C, Brinton LA, Hoover RN, Fraumeni JF. Alcohol consumption and breast cancer. J Natl Cancer Inst 1987;78:657–661.
52. Willett WC, Stampfer MJ, Colditz GA, Rosner BA, Hennekens CH, Speizer FE. Moderate alcohol consumption and the risk of breast cancer. N Engl J Med 1987;316:1174–1180.
53. Gill JS, Zezulka AV, Shipley MJ, Gill SK, Bevers DJ. Stroke and alcohol consumption. N Engl J Med 1986;315:1041–1046.
54. MacMahon S. Alcohol consumption and hypertension. Hypertension 1987;9:111–121.
55. Regan TJ. Alcohol and the cardiovascular system. JAMA 1990;264:377–381.
56. Gorelick PB, Rodin MB, Langenberg P, et al. Is acute alcohol ingestion a risk factor for ischemic stroke? Results of a controlled study in middle-aged and elderly stroke patients at three urban medical centers. Stroke 1987;18:359–364.
57. Lemoine P, Harousseau H, Borteyru JP, et al. Les enfants de parents alcooliques: anomalies observees. Quest Med 1968;25:476–482.
58. Jones KL, Smith DW, Ulleland CM, et al. Pattern of malformation in offspring of chronic alcoholic mothers. Lancet 1973;1:1267–1271.
59. Randall C, Taylor W, Walker D. Ethanol-induced malformations in mice. Alcohol Clin Exp Res 1977;1:219–223.
60. Marinacci AA. Electroencephalography in alcoholism. In: Alcoholism. Springfield, IL: Charles C Thomas, 1956:484–536.
61. Tabakoff B, Sutker PB, Randall CL, eds. Medical and social aspects of alcohol abuse. New York: Plenum Press, 1983.
62. Penick EC, Nickel EJ, Powell BJ, et al. A comparison of familial and nonfamilial men alcoholic patients without a co-existing psychiatric disorder. J Stud Alcohol (in press).
63. Alcoholism Rep [Newsletter] 1990;June:5.
64. Centers for Disease Control. MMWR Morb Mortal Wkly Rep 1989;Dec 15.
65. Jellinek EM. Phases of alcohol addiction. Q J Stud Alcohol 1952;13:673–684.
66. Mendelson JH. Biologic concomitants of alcoholism. N Engl J Med 1970;283:24–32.
67. Goodwin DW. Alcoholism. In: Psychiatric diagnosis. New York: Oxford University Press, 1988.
68. Castaneda R, Cushman P. Alcohol withdrawal: a review of clinical management. J Clin Psychiatry 1989;50:278–284.
69. Glatt MM. An alcoholic unit in a mental hospital. Lancet 1959;2:397–398.
70. Fuller RK, Branchey L, Brightwell DR, et al. Disulfiram treatment of alcoholism. JAMA 1986;256:1449–1455.
71. Fuller RK, Williford WO. Life-table analysis of abstinence in a study evaluating the efficacy of disulfiram. Alcohol Clin Exp Res 1980;4:298.
72. Institute of Medicine. Prevention and treatment of alcohol problems. Washington, DC: National Academy Press, 1989.
73. Smith JW, Frawley PJ. Long-term abstinence from alcohol in patients receiving aversion therapy as part of a multimodal inpatient program. J Subst Abuse Treat 1990;7:77–82.
74. Liskow BI, Goodwin DW. Pharmacological treatment of alcohol intoxication withdrawal and dependence: a critical review. J Stud Alcohol 1987;48:356–370.
75. Fawcett J, Clark DC, Aagesen CA, et al. A double-blind placebo-controlled trial of lithium carbonate therapy for alcoholism. Arch Gen Psychiatry 1987;44:248–256.
76. Kline NS, Wren JC, Cooper TB, Varga E, Canal O. Evaluation of lithium therapy in chronic and periodic alcoholism. Am J Med Sci 1974;268:15–22.
77. Merry J, Reynolds CM, Bailey J, Coppen A. Prophylactic treatment of alcoholism by lithium carbonate. Lancet 1976;2:481–482.
78. Goodwin DW. Alcoholism and affective disorders. In: Alcoholism and clinical psychiatry. New York Academy of Medicine. New York: Plenum Press, 1982.
79. Gerard DL, Saenger G. Outpatient treatment of alcoholism. Toronto: University of Toronto Press, 1966.

13 OPIATES: NEUROBIOLOGY

Eric J. Simon

Since the previous edition of this book there have been a number of major developments in the area of the biology of the opiate drugs, in particular in our understanding of the endogenous opioid system. The most important advance was the cloning of the three major types of opioid receptors. The meaning and the importance of this are explained and other recent developments are summarized in this chapter.

The demonstration of receptors for the opiate narcotic analgesics in animal and human central nervous systems (CNSs), followed by the discovery that the body produces its own opiate-like substances, was hailed as a major breakthrough in neuroscience. It was widely felt that these discoveries would lead to an understanding of the biochemical basis of analgesia and pain regulation as well as narcotic addiction. The molecular basis of narcotic addiction is still unknown in spite of the strides made in information concerning the endogenous opioid system and other neurotransmitter systems likely to be of importance. However, progress is being made and is summarized.

This chapter is a review of the current status of our knowledge of the biology of the endogenous opioid system and provides a summary of some of its postulated functions with emphasis on the question of its possible relevance to narcotic addiction. Finally, it provides some speculations as to where the field may be going in the next few years and how it may ultimately benefit clinical medicine, in particular our ability to prevent and treat narcotic addiction.

DISCOVERY OF OPIOID RECEPTORS AND ENDOGENOUS OPIOID PEPTIDES

Opium, an extract derived from the poppy, *Papaver somniferum,* is one of the oldest medications known. Its psychological effects and usefulness in relieving pain and diarrhea were already known to the ancient Sumerians (4000 BC) and Egyptians (2000 BC). The main active ingredient of opium is the alkaloid morphine, which is still the most effective and widely used pain-relieving drug. The wide variety of pharmacological activities of morphine have long fascinated scientists, who have attempted to understand the mechanisms that underlie these activities. The most interesting actions of morphine and related drugs are those affecting the CNS, such as the control of pain, mood changes, and the phenomena of tolerance and physical and psychological dependence, which together make up the major undesirable side effects of the opiate drugs, namely, narcotic addiction.

In the 1940s and 1950s, a very active synthetic program was mounted by the pharmaceutical industry in an attempt to produce a nonaddictive analgesic, a goal that has, unfortunately, not been achieved to this day. This effort did, however, result in a large number of clinically useful medications, many of which are still in use. The work also yielded a number of scientific findings that gave rise to the hypothesis that opiate drugs must bind to highly specific sites or receptors on nerve cells in order to exert most of their effects. This hypothesis was based on the observation that many of the pharmacological effects of these drugs, including analgesia, are highly stereospecific; i.e., the levorotatory enantiomer is usually active, and the dextrorotatory form is essentially inactive. In 1973, our laboratory (1) and two others (2, 3) simultaneously published biochemical evidence for the existence of stereospecific binding sites for opiates in animal brain. This was quickly followed by our finding that such sites also exist in human brain (4). There is now strong evidence that these binding sites are receptors that mediate various pharmacological effects of the opiate drugs.

The important finding that specific receptors for opiate drugs exist in every vertebrate and even in some invertebrate species studied led to yet another very exciting discovery. Scientists posed the question why such receptors are so widespread and why they have survived eons of evolution. This led to the postulate that they must have endogenous functions and, as a corollary, that endogenous opiate-like ligands are likely to exist. An exhaustive study of the known neurotransmitters and neurohormones did not reveal any that had high affinity for the newly found binding sites. This stimulated a number of laboratories to begin the tedious work of trying to isolate from animal brain a novel substance with the appropriate characteristics. In 1975, Hughes in Kosterlitz's laboratory (5) and Terenius and Wahlstrom (6) reported the detection in brain extracts of substances that exhibited opiate-like (opioid) activity. Success in purifying and characterizing the structure of endogenous molecules with opioid activity was first achieved by Hughes and Kosterlitz and their coworkers (5). These substances proved to be two closely similar pentapeptides, Tyr-Gly-Gly-Phe-Met and Tyr-Gly-Gly-Phe-Leu, which they named methionine and leucine enkephalin (Greek for *in the brain*), respectively. Since then, at least 12 peptides with opioid activity have been found, including the endorphins, derived from the previously known pituitary hormone β-lipotropin, of which the most important is β-endorphin (7, 8). Dynorphin (9) is a very potent opioid peptide with Leu-enkephalin at its N-terminal. It is a very basic peptide; i.e., it contains many basic amino acids, such as lysine and arginine, and is clearly not derived from β-lipotropin.

Since these opioid peptides are thought to be the natural ligands of the opiate receptors, the latter have been renamed "opioid" receptors, a term used throughout the rest of this review. The name "endorphin" was suggested by the author of this chapter in 1975 as a useful generic term for all peptides with endogenous opiate-like activity. It is a contraction of "endogenous" and "morphine" (the terminal "e" was dropped at the suggestion of Avram Goldstein to conform to nomenclature for peptides). This term is used interchangeably with the more cumbersome term "endogenous opioid peptides" throughout this review.

It should be mentioned that two laboratories have found that authentic morphine and codeine exist in animal CNS (10, 11). The significance of the presence of these alkaloids, formerly thought to be the products of plants only, is intriguing and remains to be determined. It has not yet been proven that these molecules are indeed synthesized by animal cells.

OPIOID PEPTIDES

A considerable body of knowledge has been accumulated regarding the pharmacology and molecular biology of the opioid peptides, which is summarized in this section.

The complexity of the endogenous opioid system is considerably greater than originally suspected. Approximately a dozen endogenous peptides with opioid activity are known, and as is discussed later, there are also multiple types of receptors.

The techniques of molecular biology have permitted some order to be established among the many opioid peptides known. As shown in Figure 13.1,

it is now clear that all of the known opioid peptides are derived from three large precursor proteins, proopiomelanocortin, proenkephalin, and prodynorphin, with each encoded by a separate gene. As discussed below and depicted in Figure 13.2, the structures of the genes are also known.

The discovery of proopiomelanocortin (POMC) (12, 13) was of considerable importance, not only for opioid research but for the entire field of biology. It was the first protein precursor found to give rise to several different and seemingly unrelated biologically active peptides. In addition to being the precursor of the endorphins, this protein gives rise to adrenocorticotropin (ACTH) and a family of melanocyte-stimulating hormones (α-, β-, and γ-MSH), as indicated by its name coined by Sidney Udenfriend. The intermediate lobe of the pituitary is the major source of POMC, and β-endorphin is the major opioid peptide derived from this precursor. It exists mainly in the pituitary gland and the CNS.

POMC was the first of the opioid peptide precursors to be sequenced (14). Its gene structure has also been determined, and it contains three expressed sequences (these are the translated regions of the DNA called *exons* for short) and two intervening sequences (these are sequences called *introns* for short, which are often quite long and which are "spliced out" and therefore no longer present in mature messenger RNA (mRNA)). POMC is the primary gene product, which is subsequently processed into the various biologically active peptides. Pairs of basic amino acids (in rare cases a single basic amino acid) border each peptide present in the precursor proteins and are the targets for proteolytic cleavage by "processing" enzymes. The extent and the nature of the processing vary from tissue to tissue. A number of the processing enzymes are known and have been cloned and thoroughly characterized.

Proenkephalin was first discovered in bovine adrenal cortex, where enkephalin biosynthesis was elucidated by Udenfriend and collaborators (15). It has been cloned and sequenced from bovine and human (16) tissues. It contains one copy of Leu-enkephalin, four copies of Met-enkephalin, and two copies of C-terminal-extended Met-enkephalin peptides, a heptapeptide and an octapeptide. The gene coding for proenkephalin contains four exons and five introns.

Prodynorphin, the last of the opioid peptide precursors to be characterized (17, 18), has been isolated from various mammalian tissues, including brain and spinal cord, pituitary, adrenal, and reproductive organs. All of the opioid peptides derived from this protein, dynorphin A and B and α- and β-neo-endorphin, are C-terminal extensions of Leu-enkephalin. The prodynorphin gene has four exons and three introns (19).

There is considerable similarity between the three precursors and between their genes. They contain almost the same total number of amino acids. All have several opioid peptides contained in the C-terminal half of the molecule and, as stated, framed by pairs of basic amino acids. They all possess a cysteine-rich N-terminal sequence preceded by similarly sized signal peptides. There is considerable amino acid sequence homology, which in the case of proenkephalin and prodynorphin exceeds 50%. The genes also exhibit similarity in the placement and size of their respective introns and exons. All this evidence has given rise to the hypothesis that the three genes have developed from a common ancestor gene by gene duplication.

All of the opioid peptides produce a variety of pharmacological effects when injected intraventricularly. These effects include analgesia, respiratory depression, and a wide variety of behavioral changes, including the production of a rigid catatonia. It is evident that they are remarkably similar to the opiate drugs in the types of changes they produce. The peptides do not pass very efficiently through the blood-brain barrier, but a number of effects, particularly on memory and learning, have been reported for systemically administered opioid peptides (20). Presumably only very tiny amounts of the peptides are required. The actions of the enkephalins tend to be short-lived, presumably as a result of their rapid destruction by peptidases. In fact, several peptidases capable of hydrolyzing enkephalins have been studied in detail by a number of laboratories. Inhibitors of these enzymes have been found to cause analgesia (21), presumably by conserving the brain's enkephalins, and some may be useful (nonaddictive?) analgesic agents. The longer chain peptides tend to be more stable and produce effects of long duration. Thus, β-endorphin can produce analgesia that can last 3–4 hours. All of the re-

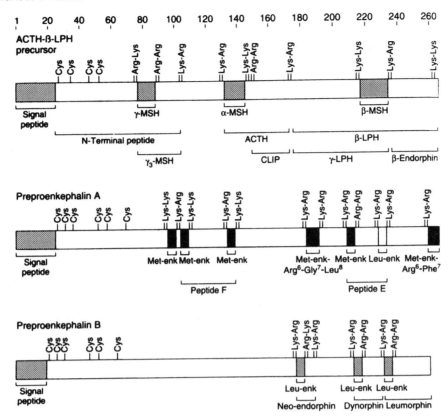

Figure 13.1. Diagrammatic representation of structures of opioid peptide precursors, Met-enkephalin *(Met-enk)*, Leu-enkephalin *(Leu-enk)*, signal peptides, and MSH units are shown. Cysteine and dibasic acid residues are shown *above,* and major peptides derived from each precursor are shown *below* each diagram. *LPH,* lipotropin; and *CLIP,* corticotropin-like intermediate lobe peptide. (Reproduced with permission from Imura H. J Endocrinol 1985;107:147–157, reproduced by permission of the Journal of Endocrinology Ltd.)

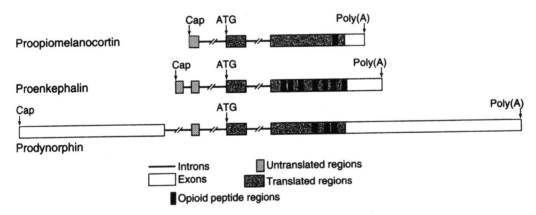

Figure 13.2. Opioid peptide gene family. *Cap,* start of transcription; *ATG,* start of translation; *Poly(A),* start of polyadenylation; and *solid bars,* opioid peptide regions, i.e., Met-enkephalin and/or Leu-enkephalin. (Reproduced with permission from Höllt V. In: Almeida OFX, Shippenberg TS, eds. Neurobiology of opioids. Heidelberg: Springer-Verlag, fig 1, 1991:12, ©Springer-Verlag.)

sponses to endogenous opioids are readily reversed by opiate antagonists, such as naloxone and naltrexone.

The distribution of the major opioid peptides, enkephalins, β-endorphin, and dynorphin A, has been mapped in rat brain by the powerful technique of immunocytochemistry (for review, see Ref. 22). It was found that many groups of cell bodies throughout the brain and spinal cord contain and probably produce enkephalins. Dynorphins also seem to be produced in a considerable number of cell groups. This is in contrast to β-endorphin, which is found in cell bodies of only two brain areas, the arcuate nucleus of the hypothalamus and the nucleus tractus solitarius of the brainstem. All of the

peptides seem to be moved to nerve terminals in many regions by means of axonal transport.

MULTIPLE OPIOID RECEPTORS, PROPERTIES, AND DISTRIBUTION

When opioid receptors were first demonstrated, it was thought that only a single type existed. However, this idea quickly changed, based on the fact that there are multiple opioid peptides and that some of these may be neurotransmitters. It is a well-known fact that the classical neurotransmitters tend to have more than one receptor each. The first definitive evidence for multiple opioid receptors was obtained by Martin and coworkers (23, 24) who studied the pharmacology of morphine and its congeners in chronic spinal dogs. Their findings appeared to be consistent with the existence of at least three types of opioid receptors, which they named μ (for morphine), κ (for ketocyclazocine), and σ (for SKF-10047, N-allyl-normetazocine). These drugs exhibited quite different pharmacological profiles and were unable to replace each other in the suppression of withdrawal symptoms in dogs treated chronically with one of them. Separate receptors appeared to be the simplest explanation. Experiments in whole animals, in vitro bioassay systems, and binding studies in cell membrane preparations have continued to confirm the existence of the receptor types postulated by Martin and coworkers.

The discovery of the enkephalins by Hughes and Kosterlitz led to the postulate of another receptor type with preference for these opioid pentapeptides. The first evidence for this came from work in Kosterlitz's laboratory with isolated organ systems (25). Enkephalins were much less effective than morphine in inhibiting electrically evoked contractions of the isolated guinea pig ileum, whereas the reverse was true in the isolated mouse vas deferens. The enkephalin-preferring receptor that seemed to predominate in the latter tissue was named δ (for deferens). Further support for this hypothesis came from competition binding studies and from the finding that the receptors in the mouse vas deferens were significantly more resistant to naloxone than those in the guinea pig ileum; i.e., 10 times as much naloxone was required for the same degree of reversal of opioid inhibition of contraction. The receptors that predominate in the guinea pig ileum were similar to Martin's μ receptor and were therefore assumed to be the same receptor type.

Since then, several additional types of receptors has been postulated, most notably a specific receptor for β-endorphin called ε (26) and another receptor for the enkephalins, different from δ receptors, called ι (27), because it seemed to predominate in intestines. Subtypes of receptors, such as μ_1 and μ_2, δ_1 and δ_2, and κ_1 and κ_2, have also been suggested. Space does not permit discussion of these additional, less well established opioid receptors, but this should not be interpreted to mean that they may not be real and of considerable importance. The σ receptor is very interesting but is perhaps not truly an opioid receptor, since actions mediated via this receptor are not reversed by the opiate antagonist naloxone, an operational definition of opioid receptors that is widely accepted. There is considerable evidence suggesting that the σ receptors are binding sites for another abused drug, phencyclidine, also known as "angel dust" or PCP (28). The rest of this review concentrates on the three major and best studied types of opioid receptors, μ, δ and κ.

The fine mapping of the three major types of opioid receptors in rat brain has been accomplished primarily by the technique of autoradiography (29, 30), using radiolabeled highly selective ligands (see below). All three major types of opioid receptors are widely distributed throughout the gray areas of the brain and spinal cord, with limbic and limbic-associated areas tending to have the highest levels. While there is some overlap, the μ, δ, and κ receptors show quite distinct localizations, suggesting that they are likely to be different molecular species rather than different forms of a single receptor.

Distribution of opioid receptors in other species, including human brain (4), has also been studied. The distribution tends to be quite similar from species to species. There are, however, some interesting and poorly understood species differences. An example is the cerebellum, which is high in M receptors in the guinea pig, high in κ receptors in the rabbit, and virtually devoid of any opioid receptors in the rat. All of these receptors have been shown to bind their ligands stereospecifically and with affinities in the nanomolar range. The naturally occurring peptides have a preference for a particular receptor type but are not highly selective. It has been postulated that enkephalins are endogenous ligands for δ receptors and dynorphins are endogenous ligands for κ receptors, whereas there are several candidates for the μ receptor, including β-endorphin and morphine. Even the enkephalins have significant affinity at this receptor which could serve as a second or "iso" receptor for them. More work is needed to establish definitively which peptides (or natural alkaloids) go with which receptors.

The lack of selectivity of the natural opioid peptides presented serious problems for the characterization of the different types of opioid receptors

and led to a major effort by organic chemists to synthesize analogs that are highly selective ligands for the three major types. This quest has met with considerable success. Highly specific agonists are now available. For the μ site, there is a gly-ol derivative of D-Ala²-enkephalin, called DAMGO (31); for δ, there are the dipenicillamine analogs of enkephalin, DPDPE and DPLPE (32) and a hexapeptide called DSBuLET (33); for κ receptors, there are stable derivatives of dynorphin (34, 35) and nonpeptide derivatives synthesized by scientists at the Upjohn Company, called U 50,488H (36) and U 69,593 (37). All the compounds discussed so far are agonists, but specific antagonists have also become available for all three receptor types. For μ receptors, cyclic derivatives of somatostatin have been shown to be highly selective antagonists (38). For δ receptors, a peptide synthesized at ICI (39) and a derivative of naltrexone called naltrindole (40) serve as selective antagonists, while a "double-headed" molecule called nor-binaltorphimine (41) proved to antagonize effects mediated via κ receptors.

A most surprising and intriguing finding was the natural existence in unexpected places of highly selective ligands. Thus, selective ligands for μ opioid receptors were found in casein hydrolysates (42) called casomorphin and in frog skin (43) named dermorphin. Several δ-receptor-selective agonists, called deltorphins, were also isolated from frog skin (44).

CLONING OF OPIOID RECEPTORS

Though cloning was briefly alluded to in the discussion of the sequencing of the genes that encode the opioid peptide precursor proteins, a brief explanation of precisely what cloning is and what it can do is deemed to be appropriate for the diverse readership of this book. As explained in the next paragraph, it is merely a more rapid and convenient way to obtain the amino acid sequence of a protein by sequencing the DNA that encodes it.

The opioid receptors, like the peptide precursors, are protein molecules; i.e., they are long chains of amino acids. There are 20 amino acids of which all proteins are composed, and it is the amino acid sequence or primary structure that confers uniqueness on each protein. The amino acid sequence dictates the three-dimensional structure, i.e., the way the protein is folded and displayed in the cell, which in large measure is responsible for the unique function of a protein, such as that of an enzyme, receptor, or ion channel. To understand the structure and function of a protein, therefore, it is essential to know its amino acid sequence. After the classical work of Fred Sanger in Cambridge, England, who sequenced the short protein, insulin, it became evident that direct sequencing of very large proteins is very tedious and labor-intensive. It proved much easier to sequence the DNA of the gene encoding the protein and to use the genetic code to translate the nucleotide triplets or codons into amino acids. This has the additional advantage of providing the sequence for the coding region of the gene as well as of the protein. The reverse, obtaining the DNA sequence from the amino acid sequence, would be much more difficult because the genetic code is "degenerate"; i.e., in many cases there are as many as 4–6 codons for the same amino acid.

The technique, which has become known as cloning, consists of isolating the mRNA from an appropriate source. The mRNA is converted to its complementary DNA (cDNA) by the enzyme, reverse transcriptase. Cloning can also be done with genomic DNA, but using cDNA is easier because the mRNA from which it is made has been processed to remove the large, confusing introns usually present in the gene. Pieces of the cDNA are placed into a vector (DNA that can replicate, such as phage or plasmid DNA). The vector is introduced into a bacterium (a strain of *Escherichia coli* is most commonly used), which are grown into colonies. This step is the cloning, since it results in bacterial colonies or clones that contain the gene in question, and these can be greatly amplified by simply growing up large amounts of the bacteria from the appropriate clone. A suitable analytical method to determine the colonies that contain the DNA to be sequenced is required. If a portion of the sequence is known, hybridization of the clones with a labeled oligonucleotide probe, prepared from the known sequence, can be used for identification. If not, expression cloning can be used, in which the DNA is transferred to an appropriate mammalian cell (*Xenopus* oocytes have also been used) capable of expressing the gene product. The presence of the gene product, the protein encoded by the gene, is detected by measuring a function, such as receptor binding, enzymatic activity, or ion channel function or by selection with a specific antibody against the protein. If the gene is found to be expressed, the DNA is amplified, purified, and sequenced.

For several years, many laboratories, including ours, tried hard but in vain to clone and sequence DNA encoding opioid receptors. It was usually done by purifying the receptor (in our case the μ receptor) and obtaining a short amino acid sequence from the purified protein to be translated into nucleotide sequence, labeled with a radioisotope. This labeled probe was then used to recognize the clones containing the gene by hybridization with the appropriate DNA. For various reasons, too complex to discuss here, this did not succeed. Expression cloning proved successful in two laboratories. In this technique, pieces of DNA are transfected into mammalian cells and assayed for expression of the receptor, i.e., for opioid ligand binding. Such cells have received the cDNA encoding the receptor, which can be isolated and sequenced.

Kieffer et al. (45) and Evans et al. (46), using this approach, simultaneously and independently succeeded in cloning the δ opioid receptor from a neuroblastoma × glioma hybrid cell line, NG 108–15. Since that time, based on the expected similarity between opioid receptor types, all three major opioid receptors have been sequenced for several species, including humans (for a review of this field, read Ref. 47). It is noteworthy that, as this is being written, no subtypes of μ, δ or κ receptors have been cloned. This may simply mean that they are sufficiently different to have so far escaped detection. It could also signify that the subtypes, postulated on the basis of pharmacology, are not encoded by separate genes but are modifications of the cloned proteins, which occurred after protein synthesis, i.e., so-called posttranslational modifications. Such posttranslational changes include the addition of sugars (glycosylation), of phosphate groups (phosphorylation), or of lipids (lipidation).

WHAT CAN WE LEARN FROM CLONING?

The availability of the complete amino acid sequences of all three major types of opioid receptors and knowledge of the structure of the genes encoding these receptors have already led to considerable progress in our understanding of how these receptors function. Though it had been hypothesized, based on pharmacological data, it was the sequencing that proved that the opioid receptors belong to the large family of receptors that can couple to guanine nucleotide-regulatory proteins (G proteins). This means that the signal generated when an opioid agonist binds to its receptor is transduced and propagated via G proteins and second messenger systems. This is discussed in somewhat more detail later in this chapter. Structurally, opioid receptors appear to traverse the cell membrane 7 times, a characteristic of all G protein-coupled receptors. This has been most thoroughly studied with rhodopsin, the vision protein, a prototypical member of this group, whose "ligand" happens to be light.

A great deal has been learned about the nature of the opioid binding site on the receptor by mutating the cDNA so as to change or delete one or more amino acids in the protein and transfecting the mutated DNA into suitable cells for expression. These techniques are known as deletion and site-directed mutation analyses. Another clever technique, widely used now, is the creation of cDNA that gives rise to molecules that are hybrids between two receptors, e.g., molecules that are part μ and part δ receptor. These new receptors are called chimeras, after the Greek mythological monster with the head of a lion, the body of a she-goat and the tail of a dragon. Studies of these chimeras permit analysis, for example, of what region confers ligand specificity for one or the other type of receptor and which region is responsible for signal transduction by a particular activated receptor. A detailed discussion of these studies is not possible in this chapter. Suffice it to say that the ligand binding site, even for relatively hydrophilic ligands, is not on the outer surface of the cell membrane, as was expected, but deep inside the rather hydrophobic (fatty) membrane itself. When this was first discovered for the β-adrenergic receptor, a member of the same family, it was a great surprise to scientists in this field. For readers who wish to know more about this fascinating area of research, excellent reviews have appeared (47, 48).

PURIFICATION OF OPIOID RECEPTORS

Isolation and purification of opioid receptors is an important endeavor. Only by studying isolated, highly purified receptor proteins and their structures will we obtain answers to many important questions about their functions. For example, much can be learned about the structure of a protein and its posttranslational modifications (phosphorylation, glycosylation, lipidation, etc.) by the use of modern physical chemical techniques, such as mass spectrometry. It has also been possible, though difficult, to crystallize pure proteins and establish their precise three-dimensional structure and location of each atom by the powerful technique of x-ray diffraction. I briefly summarize progress in the area of receptor purification, especially since it is one in which my own laboratory has pioneered.

The first purification to apparent homogeneity of a μ opioid binding site was reported from our laboratory (49). The starting tissue was a membrane fraction prepared from bovine striatum. The major purification step was affinity (also called biospecific) chromatography on a column in which a derivative of naltrexone was coupled to agarose beads. Since only opioid receptors bind to this matrix with high affinity, this step resulted in 3000- to 5000-fold purification. A second step made use of our knowledge that the receptors are glycoproteins containing the sugar N-acetylglucosamine (50) and involved (a) absorption on a wheat germ lectin column specific for this sugar and (b) elution by competition with high concentrations of N-acetylglucosamine. The purified protein showed a single band with a molecular weight of 65 kDa on SDS-polyacrylamide gel electrophoresis (SDS-PAGE). Its specific binding activity (15,000 pmol/mg protein) is close to the theoretical value for a pure protein of this size. Purification to homogeneity of μ receptors has since been reported by Cho et al. (51) and Ueda et al. (52).

The δ receptor has been purified by Klee and coworkers (53) from NG 108–15 neuroblastoma × glioma hybrid cell cultures known to contain high levels of only this receptor type. This purification was done by affinity-labeling the receptor with an irreversible, δ-selective ligand, [³H]-3-methylfentanylisothiocyanate, called "superFIT." The purified protein showed a single band on SDS-PAGE with a molecular weight of 58 kDa. The amount of superFIT bound per mg protein was in agreement with the expected theoretical value. This purified δ receptor is covalently bound to superFIT and is therefore inactive. The purification of active δ binding sites has recently been reported (54).

The purification of κ sites has been reported from frog brain (55) and from human placenta (56). The purification of this receptor from mammalian nervous system has not yet been reported.

One molecule that has been purified and cloned is called opioid binding cell adhesion molecule, OBCAM (57). It belongs to the immunoglobulin superfamily and is clearly not one of the opioid receptors. Since it binds opioids, it is of interest, and studies on this molecule are continuing.

Our laboratory has been able to purify enough μ opioid binding protein to generate some amino acid sequences, two peptides of 21 and 13 amino acids in length, respectively. We have produced antibodies to these sequences, which immunoprecipitate efficiently our purified receptor. These antibodies also give immunoblots of the correct molecular weight with the purified protein as well as with brain regions high in μ opioid receptors (58). Immunohistochemical studies in our laboratory (59) have shown that the distribution of the immune reactivity of these peptides strongly parallels that of μ receptors, as established by autoradiography.

RECONSTITUTION OF M OPIOID RECEPTORS IN ARTIFICIAL MEMBRANES

The μ opioid receptor protein we have purified is capable of binding opioid antagonists with high affinity but has very low affinity for agonists. This is not surprising, since it is well known that receptors of this family must be coupled to a G protein in order to bind agonists with high affinity. In recent papers (60, 61) we reported that we have succeeded in reconstituting our purified opioid receptor in lipoprotein particles or liposomes (sometimes referred to as artificial membranes) and to recouple it with various highly purified isoforms of G proteins. The coupled receptor, in this system containing only pure proteins and a defined phospholipid, is now able to bind agonists with high affinity, comparable to that of the native, membrane-bound receptor. Moreover, the binding is highly selective for μ agonists compared to δ or κ agonists.

G proteins all contain an enzymatic activity, namely an enzyme that hydrolyzes guanosine 5′-triphosphate (GTP) to guanosine 5′-diphosphate (GDP), called GTPase. This enzyme is known to be stimulated when a receptor coupled to the G protein is activated by an agonist ligand. We showed in the same study that when μ agonists bind to the purified, reconstituted μ receptor, GTPase is stimulated up to 100%. This stimulation is again highly specific for μ agonists, and no stimulation is seen with either δ or κ agonists. These experiments constitute the final proof that we have indeed purified a μ opioid receptor. All G protein isotypes seem to work in the system. Thus, other approaches are needed to determine which are the physiologically important ones.

FUNCTIONS OF ENDOGENOUS OPIOIDS AND THEIR RECEPTORS

Table 13.1 represents the major functions in which the endogenous opioid system has been implicated in the literature. It is evident that they may play a role in a wide variety of physiological and pharmacological phenomena, though the evidence in some cases is still quite preliminary. Our interest is, of course, primarily in the behavioral effects of the opiates, but actions on the autonomic nervous system and the endocrine system are of considerable importance, especially since these systems are known to interact with the CNS. A relatively recent discovery is the cross-talk between the immune system and the CNS in which the endorphins appear to play a role. This is an exciting research area, since it has the potential to explain many aspects of diseases that are now poorly understood, such as the effect of stress in exacerbating many diseases as well as on the susceptibility to diseases.

One caveat that should be kept in mind is that changes seen in or produced by endogenous opioids may be important but such changes need not signify primary involvement of this system. The observed changes could be a secondary or tertiary consequence of some other perturbation of the nervous system.

Table 13.1. Functions in Which Endorphins Have Been Implicated

Behavioral and mood changes
  Supraspinal and spinal analgesia
  Stress-induced analgesia
  Euphoria and dysphoria
  Sedation
  Locomotor activity
  Tolerance
  Withdrawal signs
  Appetite suppression
  Anticonvulsant activity
  Mental disorders

Endocrine system
  ACTH-cortisol release
  Prolactin release
  GH release
  ADH inhibition
  LH and testosterone inhibition

Autonomic effects
  Mydriasis
  Miosis
  Smooth muscle motility
  Body temperature
  Respiratory depression
  Heart rate
  Blood pressure
  Endotoxic and hemorrhagic shock
  Spinal cord injury

Immune system
  Monocyte and leukocyte chemotaxis
  Mitogen-induced proliferation
  Antibody production
  Natural killer activity

GH, growth hormone; ADH, antidiuretic hormone; and LH, luteinizing hormone.

vous system. Because of limitations of space and in deference to the central theme of this book, I discuss only two possible functions, namely the control of pain and the development of addictive behavior, i.e., tolerance and physical and psychic dependence. Before beginning a discussion of these functions, it is appropriate to summarize the current ideas about how the endorphins and their receptors act in order to exert their physiological effects.

Mechanism of Action

From a biochemical viewpoint, the opioid peptides are thought to exert their actions at neuronal synapses as either neurotransmitters or neuromodulators. It is likely that the peptides act as neurotransmitters, i.e., by altering (generally decreasing) the transsynaptic potential, when their receptors are localized presynaptically. On the other hand, evidence suggests that many opioid receptors are localized postsynaptically. In this case, the peptides modulate the release of a neurotransmitter, which can be one of the classical amines, such as acetylcholine, norepinephrine, or serotonin, or another peptide, such as substance P or neurotensin.

An interesting series of experiments performed by Schoffelmeer and coworkers (62) points to a possible functional difference between opioid receptor types with respect to modulation of transmitter release. These workers found that activation of μ receptors in cortical slices from rat brain led to inhibition of norepinephrine release, activation of δ receptors in striatal slices inhibited acetylcholine release, and the activation of κ receptors inhibited the release of striatal dopamine. Each of these effects seemed to be quite specifically manifested by a particular type of receptor, suggesting a different function for each type.

As stated earlier, it is now definitely established that all three major types of opioid receptors are coupled to G proteins. The early results were obtained in cell cultures, but more recent results show this to be true in the brain. This area of investigation has been reviewed (63).

The G proteins, in turn, can couple the receptors either to second messenger systems or directly to ion channels. It is thought that the slower effects of opioids may be exerted via an inhibition of the enzyme adenylate cyclase, which synthesizes the second messenger, cyclic adenosine 3′,5′-monophosphate (cAMP). The level of cAMP affects the activity of an enzyme that is able to phosphorylate proteins (cAMP-activated protein kinase A).The phosphorylation of synaptic proteins would have relatively immediate effects. It is also possible that other proteins that act on gene expression can be phosphorylated, resulting in a downregulation or upregulation of gene transcription. This could be responsible for some of the very long lasting changes produced by opiates.

The rapid effects are most likely due to direct action on ion channels. It was established that the μ and δ opioid receptors open potassium channels (64), which results in reduction of calcium conductance. The activation of κ receptors was found to reduce calcium conductance by closing calcium channels (65). It has recently been found that all three types of opioid receptors can act by both mechanisms; i.e., they can open potassium channels or close calcium channels (personal communication, R. A. North).

Pain and Its Modulation

Inasmuch as it was work on the opiate analgesics that led to the discovery of the endorphins and their receptors, it was natural to postulate that the endogenous opioid system may be involved in endogenous pain modulation as well as in analgesia. This notion was supported by the finding that all CNS regions known to be implicated in the conduction and dampening of pain impulses have high levels of opioid receptors. The application of opiates was found to inhibit selectively the firing of nociceptive neurons in the substantia gelatinosa of the spinal cord (66). Moreover, as mentioned earlier, the intraventricular injection of all opioid peptides produces analgesia. These findings were sufficiently suggestive to encourage further work in this area.

Many early experiments involved attempts to demonstrate that non-drug-induced types of analgesia could be reversed by naloxone. If successful, this would suggest the involvement of endorphin release onto their receptors. Akil and coworkers (67) showed partial reversal by naloxone of analgesia induced by electrical brain stimulation in rats. Such reversal has also been observed in human patients with chronic pain in whom stimulation of the periaqueductal gray area provided effective pain relief for prolonged periods (68).

Acupuncture and electroacupuncture have also been shown to be reversed by opiate antagonists (69, 70), and some provocative studies in humans (71) suggest that the endogenous opioids may also play a role in placebo-induced analgesia, which is effective in about 30% of subjects tested.

It was postulated that pain thresholds could be related to receptor occupancy by endorphins. If so, the administration of opiate antagonists should lower pain thresholds. Such an effect has been surprisingly difficult to demonstrate in animals or humans. Jacob et al. (72) have been able to demonstrate a lowering of the pain threshold in rats in carefully controlled experiments, with a hotplate used as a source of thermal pain.

More direct evidence for the release of opioid peptides during analgesia has been obtained. Using indwelling intraventricular cannulae, Akil et al. (73) observed a large increase in the amount of β-endorphin released into the cerebrospinal fluid of terminal cancer patients after analgesia due to stimulation of electrodes implanted in the central gray region of the brain. These workers (74) also found an increased release of enkephalins during pain stimulation, though this increase was much less robust (about 2-fold), which is not surprising in view of the instability of these peptides.

A study by Han and coworkers (75) in Beijing, China, indicates release of endorphin during electroacupuncture in rats. Using radioimmunoassays, these workers found that low-frequency electroacupuncture resulted in the release of enkephalins into spinal perfusate while high-frequency stimulation led to release of dynorphin A. The injection of antibodies to either enkephalins or dynorphin blocked analgesia produced at the appropriate frequencies. These studies suggest that δ (or μ) receptors may be involved at low frequency while κ receptors play a predominant role at high frequencies. This raises the interesting question as to which types of opioid receptors play a role in pain modulation.

It is now widely accepted that all three of the major receptor types are involved in analgesia, but some evidence that they may be implicated in different kinds of pain is also becoming available. Thus, most reports suggest that supraspinal analgesia may be mediated via μ rather than δ or κ receptors (76, 77). However, lest this finding be taken too seriously, I hasten to add that there are also reports of supraspinal analgesia mediated via δ (78) and κ (79) receptors. At the spinal level, analgesia against thermal pain stimuli seems to be mediated by both μ and δ mechanisms, while κ receptors seem to preferentially mediate analgesia against chemically induced visceral pain (80).

It is evident that much is yet to be learned regarding the mechanisms underlying analgesia and endogenous pain modulation. However, the evidence that suggests that the endogenous opioid system is involved in at least some of these mechanisms is quite impressive.

Narcotic Addiction

There were and continue to be great expectations that the discovery of the endogenous opioid system would lead to major advances in our understanding of the molecular mechanism of drug addiction. Virtually all of the work leading to the discoveries of opioid receptors and endogenous opioid peptides was supported by grants from the National Institute on Drug Abuse (NIDA) and was therefore directed toward learning about the biochemical basis of drug addiction. NIDA is still the largest supporter of research in this area. Though we cannot state at this time that the molecular basis of drug addiction has been elucidated, there has been much progress toward this goal since the earlier edition of this book. Moreover, we are able to suggest some possible reasons why progress has not been more rapid. Early work on possible changes in the number or properties of opioid receptors after chronic morphine administration was negative (81, 82). However, this work was carried out before it became known that there are a number of different types and subtypes of receptors. It is evident that these experiments had to be redone on individual receptor types.

One report details such experiments for μ receptors (83). Some subtle changes in binding of the highly selective μ ligand, DAMGO, were observed, namely a decrease in the number of high-affinity binding sites, which

resulted in a small change in total receptor number. A more striking and perhaps more important finding was the loss of the normal sensitivity of these receptors toward inhibition by GTP and its analogs. This could be construed as confirmation of earlier reports suggesting that uncoupling of receptors from G proteins may be a mechanism of tolerance development rather than changes that occur at the binding sites.

Considerable evidence suggests that tolerance can develop selectively to a given receptor type with little cross-tolerance toward the others. Such studies were first carried out on the isolated mouse vas deferens (84), but similar results in whole animals have also been obtained (85).

When animals are treated chronically with opiate antagonists such as naloxone or naltrexone, there is an upregulation, i.e., an increase in the number of opioid receptors in many brain areas (86–89). This has been observed for all three types of opioid receptors, though the extent tends to vary from one brain region to another (90). Downregulation of receptors due to chronic treatment with agonists has been more difficult to demonstrate, but some reports have appeared (for a review of opioid receptor regulation, see Ref. 91).

Another theory suggested that the chronic administration of opiate drugs would lead to a decrease in the synthesis and/or release of endorphins. Efforts to show changes in the levels of these peptides were negative. Clearly, these experiments should be repeated for all of the endogenous opioids now known. However, recent studies suggest that such changes in endorphin metabolism do occur but require more sophisticated experiments than were available when the earlier experiments were done.

When the processing of the precursor of β-endorphin, POMC, was examined, it was found to give rise to two major species, β-endorphin, which contains 31 amino acids, and β-endorphin$_{1-27}$, which has had its 4 C-terminal amino acids removed. These peptides exist in brain regions of naive rats in a ratio of 1:1 to 1.5:1. When this ratio was examined in rats made tolerant to and dependent on morphine (treated for 3 days with subcutaneous morphine pellets) (92), it was found to be almost 2:1 in favor of β-endorphin$_{1-27}$. This subtle change could not be observed with the usual rapid procedures, such as radioimmunoassays, but required sophisticated separation techniques, such as high-performance liquid chromatography (HPLC). It is made more intriguing by the finding (93) that the shorter form of β-endorphin seems to be an antagonist capable of reversing many of the effects of β-endorphin. It is evident that this result can give rise to interesting hypotheses regarding the mechanism of tolerance and/or dependence.

An additional important result was obtained in the same laboratory, showing that the biosynthesis of β-endorphin is, in fact, reduced in chronically morphinized rats. This was determined by demonstrating a reduction in the amount of mRNA for POMC present in the cells of the hypothalamus of morphine-treated rats. The reason why this is not reflected in the peptide level is that peptide release is closely coupled to synthesis and that a decrease in release compensates for the reduced production. This pseudo-feedback inhibition by the exogenous drugs could also play a role in the effects produced by chronic opiates.

It was observed very early (94) that tolerance and physical dependence develops to pharmacological doses of the opioid peptides. Cross-tolerance with synthetic and natural opiates has also been shown. This should not, however, be interpreted to mean that we develop tolerance and dependence to our endogenous opioid peptides. They are sequestered and released as needed in very small quantities, which may be the body's way to prevent the formation of tolerance to and dependence on its own substances.

There is an abundant literature that suggests that many of the symptoms of opiate withdrawal are the result of interactions between the opioid and other neurotransmitter systems. This has been studied in detail for the noradrenergic system. Gold et al. (95) have treated human heroin addicts with clonidine, an α_2-noradrenergic agonist, in a double-blind, placebo-controlled study. They found that clonidine eliminated or reduced many objective signs and subjective symptoms of withdrawal for 4–6 hours in all addicts. In an open pilot study the patients did well on clonidine for periods of 1 week. All of the patients had been addicted to opiates for 6–10 years and had been on methadone for 6–60 months at the time of the study. This clinical study is an interesting and successful follow-up of the basic research on interactions between the opioid and the noradrenergic system in the locus ceruleus, which is summarized next.

The failure to demonstrate good correlation between effects of chronic opiates and changes in opioid receptor binding prompted scientists to look for changes in the postreceptor cascade of events. The pioneering paper was that of Collier and Roy (96), who showed that morphine and other opiates inhibit cAMP formation in rat brain homogenates. This was followed quickly by another important paper by Sharma et al. (97), who demonstrated a similar inhibition in NG 108–15 cells in culture. They went on to show that chronic opiate treatment of NG 108–15 cells leads to a compensatory increase in adenylyl cyclase, which blunts the inhibition of the enzyme by opiates (tolerance?) and leads to an overshoot in cAMP production on antagonist-precipitated withdrawal (dependence?). These findings stimulated considerable work in a number of laboratories. In particular, a detailed study of acute and chronic effects of opiates on signal transduction has been carried out in the locus ceruleus. This brain region was chosen based on evidence for interaction between the opioid and noradrenergic systems, summarized above. The most important impetus was the seminal electrophysiological research of Aghajanian and coworkers (98–100), indicating an important role for this region in opiate tolerance and withdrawal. In a series of important papers, it was shown by Nestler and colleagues that chronic morphine causes a compensatory increase in all of the components of the cAMP signal transduction pathway, including G proteins, adenylyl cyclase, cAMP-dependent protein kinase, and several protein substrates for this kinase. Some such protein substrates have been identified in the locus ceruleus and other brain regions of chronically morphinized rats (101). Increased phosphorylation was found for tyrosine hydroxylase (102), an important enzyme in the synthesis of catecholamines, and for myelin basic proteins (103), components of myelin. It is evident that alteration in this important signaling pathway could account for tolerance and many features of opiate dependence. Changes in the phosphorylation of proteins that can regulate gene transcription (transcription factors) could lead to even longer term effects by changing the level of gene expression for certain proteins. This would explain very early findings that tolerance development was attenuated by inhibitors of protein and nucleic acid synthesis (104) and could explain effects in chronic opiate users that appear to last months or even years, including the high rate of recidivism. An excellent review of these studies by Nestler et al. (105) is available.

A very important observation was made by Trujillo and Akil (106, 107), who found that tolerance as well as physical dependence was dramatically reduced when MK-801, a noncompetitive antagonist at the *N*-methyl-D-aspartate (NMDA) glutamate receptor, was administered to rats along with chronic morphine. Excitatory amino acid receptors and, in particular, this glutamate receptor have been shown to have a crucial function in brain development, long-term potentiation, and learning. The Pasternak and Inturrisi laboratories (108, 109) have shown that competitive antagonists of the NMDA receptor also attenuate tolerance. They also found that this effect appears to be mediated via the gaseous neurotransmitter, nitric oxide (NO), since inhibitors of the enzyme NO synthase also profoundly reduce tolerance to opiates. These investigators found (108) that the NMDA receptor seems to be involved in the development as well as the maintenance of tolerance; i.e., antagonists also reverse established tolerance, whereas the Akil group did not find reversal of established tolerance. The reason for this discrepancy is not known, but there are a number of important differences in the way the experiments were performed. Moreover, the NMDA antagonists exert behavioral effects of their own, which, according to Akil, could compete with and thus mask the withdrawal symptoms.

Two mechanisms of tolerance development have been defined. Pharmacological (nonassociative) tolerance is a direct physiological response to chronic drug treatment. Associative or behavioral tolerance is the result of conditioning, i.e., learning of associations between drug effects and environmental cues. It is interesting that several laboratories (see, for example, Refs. 110 and 111) found that NMDA antagonists inhibit pharmacological tolerance but do not seem able to inhibit associative tolerance (107). This is surprising in view of the well-known role of excitatory amino acid receptors in memory, including previous evidence that MK-801 interferes with some types of learning.

An investigation of the anatomical site at which NMDA receptor antagonists exert their effect on tolerance and dependence led to a surprising finding. Tolerance was found to be inhibited at the spinal level by Kest et al. (112), who used intrathecal administration. Moreover, studies in spinalized rats (113, 114) provided evidence that inhibition at the spinal level was sufficient to inhibit tolerance to morphine analgesia. This suggests that the NMDA receptors, which are crucial for tolerance development, are located in the spinal cord. An excellent review of these studies on the role of excitatory amino acid receptors in the development of tolerance and physical dependence has been published (115).

CONCLUDING COMMENTS

It is a considerable task to review the developments in a field that moves as rapidly as the neurobiology of the opiate drugs and of the endogenous opioid system. It is an even more daunting task to try to make this chapter relevant to the readers of a book on substance abuse. I have tried to do my best to meet both goals.

It is evident that there have been many major developments in this field since the appearance of the earlier edition. Because of limitations in both space and the author's expertise, many developments had to be given short shrift or left out altogether. This overview gives the interested reader an idea of the state of the art in many aspects of this exciting area of research and provides comprehensive reviews and original papers for those who wish more in-depth information. This research domain continues to be an extremely active one and findings in this area impinge on many other areas of neuroscience.

One important area I did not cover is the research using self-administration and investigator-initiated administration of opiates in animals ranging from rats to monkeys. A great deal has been learned from these studies about the brain areas responsible for the hedonistic aspects of drug use. The mesolimbic dopamine system, which consists of dopaminergic neurons in the ventral tegmentum and the regions to which they project, particularly the nucleus accumbens, has emerged as an important system for the reinforcing effects of opiates and other drugs of abuse. A review of this research can be found in Reference 116 and is covered in Chapter 6, Brain Reward Mechanisms, by Dr. Eliot Gardner.

It is difficult and probably foolish to try to predict the future. However, I cannot resist making a few comments. There is considerable optimism that an understanding of the biochemistry and physiology of the endogenous opioid system will permit a more rational approach to the synthesis of medication for the treatment and prevention of drug addiction. It is also quite likely that the design of nonaddictive analgesic agents will be facilitated by a knowledge of the structures and functions of the different types of opioid receptors. If one of the receptors is found to mediate analgesia but to have little or no role in addiction, ligands could be tailor-made for it. The κ receptor is currently the favorite candidate for this approach. As stated earlier, analgesia can be produced by raising the level of endogenous enkephalins, which is deemed unlikely to be highly addictive. Powerful inhibitors of the enkephalin-splitting enzymes, synthesized in Dr. Bernard Roques' laboratory in Paris, are currently in clinical trial.

There are more and more indications for the involvement of the endogenous opioid system in the chronic effects of opiate drugs. The hopes of scientists that the discoveries of opioid receptors and their endogenous ligands will give us important answers about the molecular mechanisms involved in narcotic addiction are higher than ever.

The reasons for the relatively slow progress in our understanding of the molecular mechanism of drug abuse are becoming clear. It is a very complex process involving not only the endogenous opioid system but many other neurotransmitter and neuropeptide systems and their signal transduction cascades. Our understanding of these processes is nevertheless improving rapidly, and there is light at the end of the tunnel.

The multitude of functions attributed to the endorphins makes it probable that they are brain chemicals, rivaling in importance the "classical" neurotransmitters. In fact, this seems to be true of a large number of neuropeptides, the study of which was greatly revitalized by the discovery of the endorphins.

No disease involving genetic alterations of the opioid peptides or their receptors has yet been discovered. However, I am willing to predict that such diseases will eventually be found. Hereditary insensitivity to pain is a candidate for such a genetic defect, though the evidence is still sparse. Addictive disorders could prove to involve genetic and/or environmentally induced changes in the endogenous opioid machinery or elsewhere, and there are signs pointing to this.

The question of whether there is a common mechanism for all addictive disorders is intriguing and much debated. While the evidence to sustain this idea is still not very strong, it is a working hypothesis that certainly deserves to be submitted to experimental testing, whenever possible. There have been many papers that have provided evidence for the involvement of the endogenous opioid system in the effects of chronic cocaine, alcohol, and other abused drugs. The alterations in the signaling systems also seem to be quite similar for various drugs of abuse. Much of the evidence for such common mechanisms underlying drug abuse are summarized in the two reviews (117, 118).

The methadone maintenance program, conceived and started by Vincent Dole and Marie Nyswander and now used worldwide for the treatment of heroin addiction, came out of the sound application of receptor theory and pharmacokinetics to the problem of drug abuse. The day when all types of drug abuse and compulsive behaviors can be prevented and successfully treated may not yet be around the corner, but the very active research effort in this area and the progress made during the past two decades provide reasons for optimism.

Acknowledgments. *The research performed in the author's laboratory was supported by grant DA-00017 from the National Institute on Drug Abuse. The long-standing support by NIDA is gratefully acknowledged.*

References

1. Simon EJ, Hiller JM, Edelman I. Stereospecific binding of the potent narcotic analgesic ^{3}H-etorphine to rat brain homogenate. Proc Natl Acad Sci U S A 1973;70:1947–1949.
2. Pert CB, Snyder SH. Opiate receptor: demonstration in nervous tissue. Science 1973;179:1011–1014.
3. Terenius L. Stereospecific interaction between narcotic analgesics and a synaptic plasma membrane fraction of rat cerebral cortex. Acta Pharmacol Toxicol 1973;32:317–320.
4. Hiller JM, Pearson J, Simon EJ. Distribution of stereospecific binding of the potent narcotic analgesic etorphine in the human brain: predominance in the limbic system. Res Commun Chem Pathol Pharmacol 1973;6:1052–1062.
5. Hughes J, Smith TW, Kosterlitz HW, Fothergill LA, Morgan BA, Morris HR. Identification of two related pentapeptides from the brain with potent opiate agonist activity. Nature 1975;258:577–579.
6. Terenius L, Wahlstrom A. Inhibitor(s) of narcotic receptor binding in brain extracts and cerebrospinal fluid. Acta Pharmacol Toxicol 1974;35(suppl 1):55.
7. Bradbury AF, Smyth DG, Snell CR, Birdsall NJM, Hulme CC. C-fragment of lipotropin has a high affinity for brain opiate receptors. Nature 1976;260:793–795.
8. Cox BM, Goldstein A, Li CH. Opioid activity of a peptide, β-lipotropin-(61–91) derived from β-lipotropin. Proc Natl Acad Sci U S A 1976;73:1821–1823.
9. Goldstein A, Tachibana S, Lowney LI, Hunkapiller M, Hood L. Dynorphin-(1–13), an extraordinarily potent opioid peptide. Proc Natl Acad Sci U S A 1979;76:6666–6670.
10. Donnerer J, Oka K, Brossi A, Rice KC, Spector S. Presence and formation of codeine and morphine in the rat. Proc Natl Acad Sci U S A 1986;83:4566–4567.
11. Goldstein A, Barrett RW, James IF, et al. Morphine and other opiates from beef brain and adrenal. Proc Natl Acad Sci U S A 1985;82:5203–5207.
12. Mains RE, Eipper BA, Ling N. Common precursor to corticotropins and endorphins. Proc Natl Acad Sci U S A 1977;74:3014–3018.
13. Roberts JL, Herbert E. Characterization of a common precursor to corticotropin and β-lipotropin: cell-free synthesis of the precursor and identification of corticotropin peptides in the molecule. Proc Natl Acad Sci U S A 1977;74:4826–4830.
14. Nakanishi S, Inoue A, Kita T, et al. Nucleotide sequence of cloned cDNA for bovine corticotropin β-lipotropin precursor. Nature 1979;278:423–428.

15. Udenfriend S, Kilpatrick DL. Proenkephalin and the products of its processing: chemistry and biology. In: Udenfriend S, Meienhofer J, eds. The peptides. New York: Academic Press, 1984;VI:25–68.
16. Comb M, Seeburg PH, Adelman J, Eiden L, Herbert E. Primary structure of the human Met- and Leu-enkephalin precursor and its mRNA. Nature 1982;295:663.
17. Kakidani H, Furutani Y, Takahashi H, et al. Cloning and sequence analysis of cDNA for porcine β-neoendorphin/dynorphin precursor. Nature 1982;298:245–248.
18. Civelli O, Douglass J, Goldstein A, Herbert E. Sequence and expression of the rat prodynorphin gene. Proc Natl Acad Sci U S A 1985;82:4291–4294.
19. Horikawa S, Takai T, Toyosato M, et al. Isolation and structural organization of the human preproenkephalin B gene. Nature 1983;306:611–614.
20. Martinez JL, Weinberger SB, Schulteis G. Enkephalins and learning and memory: a review of evidence for a site of action outside the blood-brain barrier. Behav Neural Biol 1988;49:192–221.
21. Fournie Zaluski MC, Chaillet P, Bouboutou R, et al. Analgesic effects of kelatorphan, a new, highly potent inhibitor of multiple enkephalin degrading enzymes. Eur J Pharmacol 1984;102:525–528.
22. Watson SJ, Akil H, Khachaturian H, Young EA, Lewis ME. Opioid systems: anatomical, physiological and clinical perspectives. In: Hughes J, Collier HOJ, Rance MJ, Tyers MB, eds. Opioids past, present and future. London: Taylor & Francis, 1984:145–178.
23. Martin WR, Eades CG, Thompson JA, Huppler RE, Gilbert PE. The effects of morphine- and nalorphine-like drugs in the nondependent and morphine-dependent chronic spinal dog. J Pharmacol Exp Ther 1976;197:517–532.
24. Gilbert PE, Martin WR. The effects of morphine- and nalorphine-like drugs in the nondependent morphine-dependent and cyclazocine-dependent chronic spinal dog. J Pharmacol Exp Ther 1976;198:66–82.
25. Lord JAH, Waterfield AA, Hughes J, Kosterlitz HW. Endogenous opioid peptides: multiple agonists and receptors. Nature 1977;267:495–499.
26. Schulz R, Faase E, Wuster M, Herz A. Selective receptors for β-endorphin on the rat vas deferens. Life Sci 1979;24:843–850.
27. Oka T. Enkephalin receptor in the rabbit ileum. Br J Pharmacol 1980;68:193–195.
28. Zukin SR, Zukin RS. Specific ^{3}H-phencyclidine binding in rat central nervous system. Proc Natl Acad Sci U S A 1979;76:5372–5376.
29. Mansour A, Khachaturian H, Lewis ME, Akil H,

Watson SJ. Autoradiographic differentiation of μ, δ and κ opioid receptors in the rat forebrain and midbrain. J Neurosci 1987;7:2445–2464.
30. Tempel A, Zukin RS. Neuroanatomical patterns of the μ, δ and κ opioid receptors of rat brain as determined by quantitative in vitro autoradiography. Proc Natl Acad Sci U S A 1987;84:4308–4312.
31. Handa BK, Lane AC, Lord JAH, Morgan BA, Rance MJ, Smith CFC. Analogues of β-LPH 61–64 possessing selective agonist activity at μ opiate receptors. Eur J Pharmacol 1981;70:531–540.
32. Mosberg HI, Hurst R, Hruby VJ, et al. Bis-penicillamine enkephalins possess highly improved specificity toward δ opioid receptors. Proc Natl Acad Sci U S A 1983;80:5871–5874.
33. Delay-Goyet P, Seguin C, Gacel G, Roques BP. ^{3}H-[D-Ser^2(O-tert-butyl),Leu^5]enkephalyl-Thr^6 and [D-Ser^2(O-tert-butyl),Leu^5]enkephalyl-Thr^6 (O-tert-butyl), two new enkephalin analogs with both a good selectivity and a high affinity toward δ-opioid binding sites. J Biol Chem 1988;263:4124–4130.
34. Gairin JE, Mazarguil H, Alvinerie P, Saint Pierre S. Synthesis and biological activities of dynorphin A analogues with opioid antagonist properties. J Med Chem 1986;29:1913–1917.
35. Goldstein A, Nestor JJ Jr, Naidu A, Newman SR. "DAKLI": a multipurpose ligand with a high affinity and selectivity for dynorphin (κ) binding sites. Proc Natl Acad Sci U S A 1988;85:7375–7379.
36. Von Voigtlander PF, Lahti RA, Ludens JH. U 50,488H: a selective and structurally novel non-μ (M) opioid agonist. J Pharmacol Exp Ther 1983;224:7–12.
37. Lahti RA, Mickelson MM, McCall JM, Von Voigtlander PF. ^{3}H-U-69,593, a highly selective ligand for the opioid κ receptor. Eur J Pharmacol 1985;109:281–284.
38. Gulya K, Gehlert DR, Wamsley JK, Mosberg H, Hruby VJ. Light microscopic autoradiographic localization of δ opioid receptors using a highly selective bis-penicillamine cyclic enkephalin analog. J Pharmacol Exp Ther 1986;238:720–726.
39. Cotton R, Giles MG, Miller L, Shaw JS, Timms D. ICI 174864: a highly selective antagonist for the opioid δ receptor. Eur J Pharmacol 1984;97:331–332.
40. Portoghese PS, Sultana M, Takemori AE. Naltrindole, a highly selective and potent non-peptide δ opioid receptor agonist. Eur J Pharmacol 1988;146:185–186.
41. Portoghese PS, Lipowski AW, Takemori AE. Binaltorphimine and nor-binaltorphimine, potent and selective κ-opioid receptor antagonists. Life Sci 1987;40:1287–1292.

42. Chang K, Killian S, Hazum E, Cuatrecasas P, Chang J. Morphiceptin: a potent and specific agonist for morphine (μ) receptors. Science 1981; 212:75–77.

43. Broccardo M, Erspamer V, Falconieri Erspamer G, et al. Pharmacological data on dermorphins, a new class of potent opioid peptides from amphibian skin. Br J Pharmacol 1981;73:625–631.

44. Erspamer V, Melchiorri P, Falconieri-Erspamer G, et al. Deltorphins: a family of naturally occurring peptides with high affinity and selectivity for δ opioid binding sites. Proc Natl Acad Sci U S A 1989;86:5188–5192.

45. Kieffer BL, Befort K, Gaveriaux-Ruff C, Hirth CG. The δ-opioid receptor: isolation of a cDNA by expression cloning and pharmacological characterization. Proc Natl Acad Sci U S A 1992;89:12048–12052.

46. Evans CJ, Keith DEJ, Morrison H, Magendzo K, Edwards RH. Cloning of a δ opioid receptor by functional expression. Science 1992;258:1952–1955.

47. Minami M, Satoh M. Molecular biology of the opioid receptors: structures, functions and distributions. Neurosci Res 1995;23:121–145.

48. Knapp RJ, Malatynska E, Collins N, et al. Molecular biology and pharmacology of cloned opioid receptors. FASEB J 1995;9:516–525.

49. Gioannini TL, Howard AD, Hiller JM, Simon EJ. Purification of an active opioid binding protein from bovine striatum. J Biol Chem 1985; 260:15117–15121.

50. Gioannini TL, Foucaud B, Hiller JM, Hatten ME, Simon EJ. Lectin binding of solubilized opiate receptors: evidence for their glycoprotein nature. Biochem Biophys Res Commun 1982; 105:1128–1134.

51. Cho TM, Hasegawa J, Ge BL, Loh HH. Purification to apparent homogeneity of a μ-type opioid receptor from rat brain. Proc Natl Acad Sci U S A 1986;83:4138–4142.

52. Ueda H, Harada H, Misawa H, Nozaki M, Takagi H. Purified opioid μ receptor is of a different molecular size than δ and κ receptors. Neurosci Lett 1987;75:339–344.

53. Simonds WF, Burke TR, Jr, Rice KC, Jacobson AE, Klee WA. Purification of the opiate receptor of NG 108–15 neuroblastoma glioma hybrid cells. Proc Natl Acad Sci U S A 1985;82: 4974–4978.

54. Loukas S, Merkouris M, Panetsos F, Zioudrou C. Purification to homogeneity of an active opioid receptor from rat brain by affinity chromatography. Proc Natl Acad Sci U S A 1994;91 (10):4574–4578.

55. Simon J, Benye S, Hepp J, et al. Purification of a κ-opioid receptor subtype from frog brain. Neuropeptides 1987;101:19–28.

56. Ahmed MS, Zhon D, Cavinato AG, Maulik D. Opioid binding properties of the purified κ receptor from human placenta. Life Sci 1989;44: 861–871.

57. Schofield PR, McFarland KC, Haflick JS, et al. Molecular characterization of a new immunoglobulin superfamily protein with potential roles in opioid binding and cell contact. EMBO J 1989;8:489–495.

58. Gioannini TL, Yao Y, Hiller JM, Taylor LP, Simon EJ. Antisera against peptides derived from a purified μ-opioid binding protein recognize the protein as well as μ-opioid receptors in brain regions and a cell line. Mol Pharmacol 1993; 44:796–801.

59. Hiller JM, Zhang Y, Bing G, Gioannini TL, Stone EA, Simon EJ. Immunohistochemical localization of μ opioid receptors in rat brain using antibodies generated against a peptide sequence present in a purified μ opioid binding protein. Neuroscience 1994;62:829–841.

60. Gioannini TL, Fan LQ, Hyde L, et al. Reconstitution of a purified μ-opioid binding protein in liposomes: selective, high affinity, GTP-γS-sensitive μ-opioid agonist binding is restored. Biochem Biophys Res Commun 1993;194: 901–908.

61. Fan LQ, Gioannini TL, Wolinsky TD, Hiller JM, Simon EJ. Functional reconstitution of a highly purified μ-opioid receptor protein with purified G-proteins in liposomes. J Neurochem 1995;65:2537–2542.

62. Schoffelmeer ANM, Rice KC, Jacobson AE, et al. μ, δ and κ receptor-mediated inhibition of neurotransmitter release and adenylate-cyclase activity in rat brain slices: studies with fentanyl isothiocyanate. Eur J Pharmacol 1988;154: 169–178.

63. Childers SR. Minireview. Opioid receptor-coupled second messenger systems. Life Sci 1991; 48:1991–2003.

64. North RA, Williams JT, Surprenant A, Christi MJ. μ and δ receptors belong to a family of receptors that are coupled to potassium channels. Proc Natl Acad Sci U S A 1987;84:5487–5491.

65. Gross RA, Macdonald RL. Dynorphin A selectively reduces a large transient (N-type) calcium current of mouse dorsal root ganglion neurons in cell culture. Proc Natl Acad Sci U S A 1987; 84:5469–5473.

66. Duggan AW, Hall JG, Headley PM. Suppression of transmission of nociceptive impulses by morphine: selective effects of morphine administered in the region of the substantia gelatinosa. Br J Pharmacol 1977;61:65–67.

67. Akil H, Mayer DJ, Liebeskind JC. Antagonism of stimulation-produced analgesia by naloxone, a narcotic antagonist. Science 1976;191:961–962.

68. Richardson DE, Akil H. Pain reduction by electrical brain stimulation in man. Part II: chronic self administration in the periaqueductal gray matter. J Neurosurg 1984;47:184–194.

69. Pomeranz B, Chiu D. Naloxone blockade of acupuncture analgesia: endorphin implicated. Life Sci 1976;19:1757–1762.

70. Mayer DJ, Price DD, Rafii A. Antagonism of acupuncture analgesia in man by the narcotic antagonist naloxone. Brain Res 1977;121: 368–372.

71. Levine JD, Gordon NC, Fields HL. The mechanism of placebo analgesia. Lancet 1978;2: 654–657.

72. Jacob JJ, Tremblay EC, Colombel MC. Facilitation de reactions nociceptives par la naloxone chez la souris et chez le rat. Psychopharmacology 1974;37:217–219.

73. Akil H, Richardson ED, Barchas JD, Li CH. Appearance of β-endorphin-like immunoreactivity in human ventricular cerebrospinal fluid upon analgesic electrical stimulation. Proc Natl Acad Sci U S A 1978;75:5170–5172.

74. Akil H, Richardson DE, Hughes J, Barchas JD. Enkephalin-like material elevated in ventricular cerebrospinal fluid of pain patients after analgesic focal stimulation. Science 1978;201: 463–464.

75. Han JS, Xie GX, Zhou ZF. Acupuncture mechanisms in rabbits studied with micro-injection of antibodies against β-endorphin, enkephalin and substance P. Neuropharmacology 1984;23:1–5.

76. Chaillet P, Coulaud A, Zajac JM, Fournie Zaluski MC, Constantin J, Roques BP. The μ rather than the δ subtype of opioid receptors appears to be involved in enkephalin induced analgesia. Eur J Pharmacol 1984;101:83–90.

77. Wood PL, Rackham A, Richard J. Spinal analgesia: comparison of the μ agonist morphine and the κ agonist ethylketocyclazocine. Life Sci 1981;28:2119–2125.

78. Porreca F, Heyman JS, Mosberg HI, Omnzas JR, Vaught JL. Role of μ and δ receptors in the supraspinal and spinal analgesic effects of (D-Pen^2, D-Pen^5)enkephalin in the mouse. J Pharmacol Exp Ther 1987;241:389–393.

79. Carr KD, Bonnet KA, Simon EJ. μ and κ opioid-agonists elevate brain stimulation threshold for escape by inhibiting aversion. Brain Res 1982; 245:389–393.

80. Yaksh TL. Multiple spinal opiate receptor systems in analgesia. In: Kruger L, Liebeskind J, eds. Advances in pain research and therapy. New York: Raven Press, 1984:197–215.

81. Bonnet KA, Hiller JM, Simon EJ. The effects of chronic opiate treatment and social isolation on opiate receptors in the rodent brain. In: Kosterlitz HW, ed. Opiates and endogenous opioid peptides. Amsterdam: Elsevier Press, 1976: 335–343.

82. Klee WA, Streaty RA. Narcotic receptor sites in morphine dependent rats. Nature 1974;248: 61–63.

83. Werling LL, McMahon PN, Cox BM. Selective changes in μ opioid receptor properties induced by chronic morphine exposure. Proc Natl Acad Sci U S A 1989;86:6393–6397.

84. Schulz R, Wuster M, Krenss H, Herz A. Lack of cross-tolerance on multiple opiate receptors in the mouse vas deferens. Mol Pharmacol 1980; 18:395–401.

85. Schulz R, Wuster M, Herz A. Differentiation of opiate receptors in the brain by the selective development of tolerance. Pharmacol Biochem Behav 1981;14:75–79.

86. Lahti RA, Collins RJ. Chronic naloxone results in prolonged increases in opiate binding sites in brain. Eur J Pharmacol 1978;51:185–186.

87. Zukin RS, Sugarman JR, Fitz-Syage ML, Gardner EL, Zukin SR, Gintzler AR. Naltrexone-induced opiate receptor supersensitivity. Brain Res 1982;245:285–292.

88. Tempel A, Zukin RS, Gardner EL. Supersensitivity of brain opiate receptor subtypes after chronic naltrexone treatment. Life Sci 1982;31: 1401–1404.

89. Yoburn BC, Shah S, Chan K, Duttaroy A, Davis T. Supersensitivity to opioid analgesics following chronic opioid antagonist treatment: relationship to receptor selectivity. Pharmacol Biochem Behav 1995;51:535–539.

90. Morris BJ, Millan MJ, Herz A. Antagonist-induced opioid receptor upregulation. II. Regionally specific modulation of μ, δ and κ binding sites in rat brain revealed by quantitative autoradiography. J Pharmacol Exp Ther 1988;247: 729–736.

91. Zukin RS, Pellegrini-Giampietro DE, Knapp CM, Tempel A. Opioid receptor regulation. In: Herz A, Akil H, Simon EJ, eds. Opioids. Berlin: Springer-Verlag, 1993;I:107–123.

92. Bronstein DM, Przewlocki R, Akil H. Effect of morphine treatment on pro-opiomelanocortin systems in rat brain. Brain Res 1990;519: 102–111.

93. Hammonds RGH Jr, Nicolas P, Li CH. β-Endorphin (1–27) is an antagonist of β-endorphin analgesia. Proc Natl Acad Sci U S A 1984;81: 1389–1390.

94. Wei E, Loh HH. Physical dependence on opiate-like peptides. Science 1976;193:1262–1263.

95. Gold M, Redmond DEJ, Kleber HD. Clonidine blocks acute opiate withdrawal symptoms. Lancet 1978;2:599–600.

96. Collier HOJ, Roy AC. Morphine-like drugs inhibit the stimulation by E prostaglandins of cyclic AMP formation by rat brain homogenate. Nature 1974;248:24–27.

97. Sharma SK, Klee WA, Nirenberg M. Dual regulation of adenylate cyclase accounts for narcotic dependence and tolerance. Proc Natl Acad Sci U S A 1975;72:3092–3096.

98. Rasmussen K, Beitner-Johnson D, Krystal DB, Aghajanian GK, Nestler EJ. Opiate withdrawal and the rat locus coeruleus: behavioral, electrophysiological and biochemical correlates. J Neurosci 1990;10:2308–2317.

99. Aghajanian GK. Tolerance of locus coeruleus neurones to morphine and suppression of withdrawal response by clonidine. Nature 1978;276:186–188.

100. Aghajanian GK, Wang YY. Common α_2 and opiate effector mechanisms in the locus coeruleus: intracellular studies in brain slices. Neuropharmacology 1987;26:789–800.

101. Guitart X, Nestler EJ. Identification of morphine- and cyclic AMP-regulated phosphoproteins (MARPP's) in the locus coeruleus and other regions of rat brain: regulation by acute and chronic morphine. J Neurosci 1989;9:4371–4387.

102. Guitart X, Hayward M, Nisenbaum LK, Beitner-Johnson DB, Haycock JW, Nestler EJ. Identification of MARPP-58, a morphine- and cyclic AMP-regulated phosphoprotein of 58 kDa, as tyrosine hydroxylase: evidence for regulation of its expression by chronic morphine in the rat locus coeruleus. J Neurosci 1990;10:2649–2659.

103. Guitart X, Nestler EJ. Identification of MARPP-14–20, morphine- and cyclic AMP-regulated phosphoproteins of 14–20 kD, as myelin basic proteins. Evidence for their acute and chronic regulation by morphine in rat brain. Brain Res 1990;516:57–65.

104. Cox BM, Osman OH. Inhibition of the development of tolerance to morphine in rats by drugs which inhibit ribonucleic acid or protein synthesis. Br J Pharmacol 1970;38:157–170.

105. Nestler EJ, Hope BT, Widnell KL. Drug addiction: a model for the molecular basis of neural plasticity. Neuron 1993;11:995–1006.

106. Trujillo KA, Akil H. Inhibition of morphine tolerance and dependence by the NMDA receptor antagonist MK-801. Science 1991;251:85–87.

107. Trujillo KA, Akil H. Inhibition of opiate tolerance by non-competitive N-methyl-D-aspartate receptor antagonists. Brain Res 1994;633:178–188.

108. Elliott K, Minami N, Kolesnikov YA, Pasternak GW, Inturrisi CE. The NMDA receptor antagonists, LY274614 and MK-801, and the nitric oxide synthase inhibitor, NG-nitro-l-arginine, attenuate analgesic tolerance to the μ-opioid morphine but not to M opioids. Pain 1994;56:69–75.

109. Tiseo PJ, Cheng J, Pasternak GW, Inturrisi CE. Modulation of morphine tolerance by the competitive N-methyl-D-aspartate receptor antagonist LY274614: assessment of opioid receptor changes. J Pharmacol Exp Ther 1994;268:195–201.

110. Marek P, Ben-Eliyahu S, Vaccarino AL, Liebeskind JC. Delayed application of MK-801 attenuates development of morphine tolerance in rats. Brain Res 1991;558:163–165.

111. Ben-Eliyahu S, Marek P, Vaccarino AL, Mogil JS, Sternberg WF, Liebeskind JC. The NMDA receptor antagonist MK-801 prevents long-lasting non-associative morphine tolerance in the rat. Brain Res 1992;575:304–308.

112. Kest B, Mogil JS, Shamgar B-E, Kao B, Liebeskind JC, Marek P. The NMDA receptor antagonist MK-801 protects against development of morphine tolerance after intrathecal administration. Proc West Pharmacol Soc 1993;36:307–310.

113. Gutstein HB, Trujillo KA. MK-801 inhibits the development of morphine tolerance at spinal sites. Brain Res 1993;626:332–334.

114. Gutstein HB, Trujillo KA, Akil H. Does MK-801 inhibit the development of morphine tolerance in the rat at spinal sites? Anesthesiol 1992;77:A737.

115. Trujillo KA, Akil H. Excitatory amino acids and drugs of abuse: a role for N-methyl-D-aspartate receptors in drug tolerance, sensitization and physical dependence. Drug Alcohol Depend 1995;38:139–154.

116. Koob GF, Bloom FE. Cellular and molecular mechanisms of drug dependence. Science 1988;242:715–723.

117. Nestler EJ. Molecular neurobiology of drug addiction. Neuropsychopharmacology 1994;11:77–87.

118. Self DW, Nestler EJ. Molecular mechanisms of drug reinforcement and addiction. Ann Rev Neurosci 1995;18:463–495.

14 OPIATES: CLINICAL ASPECTS

Jerome H. Jaffe, Clifford M. Knapp, and Domenic A. Ciraulo

This chapter summarizes the pharmacology of opioid drugs and relates this knowledge to the phenomenon of repetitive opioid use and its complications.

OPIOID ACTIONS

Opioid drugs exert their actions by binding to receptors on the cell membranes of neurons and certain other cells, such as white blood cells (1). Three major types of opioid receptors have been identified (mu, delta, and kappa), which appear to subserve different physiological functions. While the physiological role of each of the three receptor types is not yet fully known, it does appear that mu and delta receptors are involved in systems that influence mood, reinforcing effects, respiration, pain, blood pressure, and endocrine and gastrointestinal function (2). Kappa receptors, when activated, can produce endocrine changes and analgesia; however, while animals self-administer mu and delta agonists under experimental conditions, they do not self-administer pure kappa receptor agonists. Instead, kappa agonists appear to produce aversive effects in animals (3) and dysphoria, rather than euphoria, in human subjects (4).

The three major classes of opioid receptors may be further subdivided into different receptor subtypes, for example, the mu_1 and mu_2 receptors and $kappa_1$ and $kappa_3$ receptors (5, 6). Different opioid receptor subtypes may be associated with distinct effects. Knowledge about the actions of these different receptor subtypes is limited at present to information obtained from animal experiments. The mu_1 receptors may mediate the supraspinal analgesic effects of opioids while the mu_2 receptors have been implicated in spinal analgesia and the regulation of gastrointestinal motility and respiration (6). The $delta_2$ and $kappa_1$ receptors may play a role in spinal analgesia while the $delta_1$ and $kappa_3$ receptors may mediate the analgesic actions of opioids at the supraspinal level. The $delta_2$ receptor may also mediate opioid analgesic actions in brain neurons. The role of the $kappa_2$ receptor has yet to be established.

Opioid drugs now are defined and categorized in terms of their capacity to bind and activate these various receptor types (Table 14.1). Those drugs that bind and activate a receptor are *agonists* at that receptor. Those that bind but do not activate a receptor function as *antagonists* at that receptor. Opioids can differ greatly in their relative affinity for the various receptor types. They can also differ in intrinsic activity, in that they may bind very well to a receptor but may produce less than full receptor activation. A weak or partial agonist at a receptor can, under some circumstances, act as an antagonist at that same receptor (2). For example, after surgical procedures involving the potent mu agonists fentanyl and sufentanil, respiratory depression can be reversed by naloxone, an antagonist that binds preferentially at the mu receptor. However, naloxone-induced reversal of respiratory depression can be accompanied by a reversal of analgesic actions or sometimes by acute opioid withdrawal. It is also possible to use a partial mu agonist such as buprenorphine to alleviate fentanyl respiratory depression (2). By displacing fentanyl, buprenorphine alleviates severe respiratory depression but continues to exert some mu agonist activity, including analgesia.

Table 14.1 Selectivities of Opioid Analgesics for Opioid Receptor Classes

Drugs	mu	delta	kappa1	kappa3
Morphine	+++		+	+
Methadone	+++			
Levorphanol	+++			+++
Fentanyl	+++			
Sufentanil	+++	+	+	
Butorphanol	P		+++	
Buprenorphine	P		—	
Nalbuphine	—		++	++
Pentazocine	P		++	+

Table modified from Reisine T, Pasternak G. Opioid analgesics and antagonists. In: Hardman JG, Limbird LE, Molinoff RW, Ruddon RW, Gilman AG, eds. Goodman and Gilman's the pharmacologic basis of therapeutics. 9th ed. New York: McGraw-Hill, 1995:521–556.
Legend: +, agonist; P, partial agonist; —, antagonist.

Until the latter part of the twentieth century, the opioids commonly abused were prototypical mu agonists exerting preferential binding at the mu receptor and acting as full agonists. Most of the opioids that are readily available, either legally or illegally, are either prototypical mu agonists, partial mu agonists, or mixed agonist-antagonists. The latter are agents exerting some agonist actions at kappa receptors and either antagonist or weak agonist actions at mu and delta receptors. Opioid agonists and antagonists have been developed that act much more specifically at delta and kappa receptors, but these are not currently in clinical use (2). Some of the available agents also bind to a sigma receptor. Because binding to a sigma receptor is not antagonized by naloxone, it is no longer thought of as an opioid receptor. It was once believed that the dysphoric and hallucinatory effects seen with some mixed agonists/antagonists were a result of actions at the sigma receptor, but with the recognition that kappa activation can produce dysphoric effects, the significance of sigma binding is now uncertain (2, 4).

Opioid receptors are found throughout the brain and spinal cord, in neural plexuses in the gastrointestinal tract and other parts of the autonomic nervous system, and on white cells. Not surprisingly, therefore, opioid drugs have diverse actions on many organ systems. The most prominent effects, and the effects for which the opioids are most commonly prescribed, are exerted on the central nervous system (CNS) and the gastrointestinal tract.

Acting in the CNS, the opioids produce analgesia, a sense of tranquillity and decreased sense of apprehension, and a suppression of the cough reflex. These are the CNS actions for which they are prescribed. However, opioids also can produce nausea, vomiting, depression of respiration, constriction of the pupils, alterations in temperature regulation, and a variety of changes in the neuroendocrine system. These are the generally unwanted side effects that clinicians as well as illicit users of the drugs try to avoid (2).

Effects of opioids on pain and anticipation of pain and distress can be profound. At high enough doses, indifference to pain is sufficient to permit major surgery, but the profound respiratory depression that accompanies this level of opioid effect requires mechanical support of respiration (7). More commonly, however, opioids are used as analgesics in much lower doses, such as 10 mg of morphine or 1.5 mg of hydromorphone (Dilaudid). At such doses the analgesia is marked but there is no loss of consciousness, and other senses and cognition are generally unaffected. The use of opioids in treatment of acute and chronic pain is discussed at length in Chapter 57. This chapter focuses on those other effects of opioids that are, in all likelihood, the reason that they are self-administered by individuals who are not in pain.

Even at analgesic doses, opioids produce changes in mood and feeling. Typically, among medical patients, these are described as decreased anxiety, drowsiness, and a sense of tranquility (2). There appear to be significant differences among individuals in the way they feel when they take opioids. Postaddict volunteers usually experience an elevation of mood and increased sense of self-esteem (i.e., euphoria). Others given the same dose may complain of a sense of confusion and drowsiness, which they experience as unpleasant (8, 9). Such dysphoric responses are aggravated by opioid-induced

nausea, but it is not the nausea that causes the dysphoria. Heroin addicts who do not have a high tolerance sometimes experience nausea and vomiting along with a sense of euphoria. As is discussed in more detail later, it is likely that repeated opioid use is motivated by a desire to reexperience this sense of euphoria. The complex of euphoria and decreased concern with anticipated problems is often referred to as a "high." When mu agonist opioids are self-administered intravenously (or, sometimes, when heroin or opium is smoked) there is a sharp and rapid increase in brain opioid levels that produces a distinct, intense, and generally pleasurable sensation often referred to by heroin addicts as a "flash" or "rush." Some users liken the feeling to sexual orgasm. Since "rush" is not experienced with a slower onset of opioid action (oral or subcutaneous routes), addicts may persist in intravenous use despite its risks (10). Descriptions of "rush" can be surprisingly varied (11).

For some individuals, opioids appear to have the capacity to ameliorate certain varieties of depression, to control anxiety, to reduce anger, and to blunt paranoid feelings and ideation (12, 13). Chapter 8 discusses at greater length the notion that some individuals take opioids as a form of self-medication for emotions that are otherwise abnormally painful. The neural mechanisms by which opioids produce reinforcing effects in animals and, presumably, their mood elevating effects in humans are discussed here briefly and also more extensively in Chapter 6. Mu opioids inhibit the activity of the locus coeruleus, the principal clustering of noradrenergic neurons in the brain. Activity in these neurons is associated with subjective symptoms and autonomic signs of anxiety (14). The antianxiety actions of opioids are probably due in part to their capacity to inhibit locus coeruleus activity. The significance of this action is that alpha$_2$ adrenergic agonists, which can also inhibit the locus coeruleus, can be used to control some of the signs of opioid withdrawal (discussed later in this chapter).

Included among the many other effects opioids produce through their CNS action are suppression of the cough reflex (which makes them useful antitussives) and effects on the neuroendocrine system. Most of these neuroendocrine effects, such as the inhibition of gonadotropin-releasing hormone, which results in decreased luteinizing hormone (LH) and follicle stimulating hormone (FSH) and, ultimately, in decreased testosterone levels in males and disturbed menstrual function in females, are unwanted side effects (2); they are discussed further in Chapter 41. The opioid inhibition of corticotrophin releasing factor (CRF) results in decreased adrenocorticotropic hormone (ACTH) and decreased levels of cortisol. It is conceivable that for some individuals the inhibition of CRF is useful in dealing with anxiety or stress.

Mu agonist opioids have many effects on the gastrointestinal system, slowing passage of food in the stomach and in the small and large intestine. Because of this action, opioid drugs are still key therapeutic agents in the treatment of diarrhea. Drugs such as diphenoxylate (the main active ingredient in Lomotil) and loperamide (Imodium) are actually specialized opioids. The latter can be sold without special controls because very little of it gets into the CNS and therefore it acts primarily on the gut. Because little tolerance develops to this gut-slowing effect, patients with chronic pain given large doses of opioids are often constipated, as are heroin addicts if their supply is uninterrupted over long periods. (Opioid withdrawal generally produces cramps and diarrhea.) As described in Chapter 41, former addicts maintained on methadone also typically have problems with constipation. Mixed agonist/antagonists (such as pentazocine, butorphanol, and nalbuphine) and kappa agonists have less prominent constipating effects.

Some opioids, such as morphine, produce histamine release, which is associated with vasodilatation of skin vessels and itching. The nose scratching that is seen when addicts are quite intoxicated is probably related, in part, to this effect. However, pruritus is also seen with opioids that do not release histamine and may, therefore, be related to opioid effects on neurons (2). The effects of opioids on the cardiovascular system are not prominent except under special circumstances; one of these is hypovolemia, in which opioids can aggravate shock. Opioids also have effects on the bladder. They tend to increase sphincter tone and decrease the voiding reflexes, and in this way they can increase the likelihood of urinary retention (1).

SOME CLINICAL IMPLICATIONS OF DIFFERENCES IN DRUG DISPOSITION

In the United States there are at least 20 drugs available that have opioid actions; additional opioids are available in other countries (2). As has already been mentioned, many of these drugs may be thought of as prototypical mu agonists; some have actions on other receptors as well or act preferentially at other receptors. However, differences in receptor activity profiles are not the only clinically important ways in which specific drugs differ. They may also differ in the way in which they are absorbed, metabolized, and eliminated by the body. For example, some opioids, such as sufentanil, may be metabolized so rapidly as to be of limited use as oral analgesics but are quite useful when given intravenously in managing anesthesia for major surgery (6). In contrast, levo-alpha-acetylmethadol (LAAM) with a half-life of 2.5 days is very slowly cleared from the body, as are its active metabolites, noracetylmethadol and di-noracetylmethadol, whose half-lives are two and four days, respectively. These slow rates of elimination allow LAAM to be administered as infrequently as three times a week as a maintenance agent for opioid dependence (1).

Major pathways for morphine metabolism include its conversion to morphine-3-glucuronide, and to lesser extent morphine-6-glucuronide (15). Morphine-6-glucuronide is a more potent analgesic agent than is morphine and may contribute significantly to the analgesic effects of morphine treatment (16). Renal insufficiency can lead to reduction in the clearance rate of morphine-6-glucuronide and the resultant high concentrations of this compound may have toxic effects (17). The meperidine metabolite normeperidine may also accumulate to produce toxicity in patients with renal dysfunction (18). Normeperidine has no analgesic activity but can induce seizures (2, 19) and cause other serious problems, such as twitching, tremors, and mental confusion (19). Problems can also arise when excessive amounts of meperidine are used, as in meperidine addiction, a problem occasionally seen among physicians, nurses, and other medical personnel with access to meperidine. In these cases it is not unusual for the problem to come to attention because the user has a grand mal seizure as a result of the build-up of normeperidine (10).

In some instances, the drug administered is actually quite inactive as an opioid, and only when it is metabolized by the body does it become able to attach to and activate opioid receptors (a prodrug). At least three examples are relevant to problems of drug dependence. The most obvious is the case of heroin (diacetylmorphine). Heroin is not a potent mu agonist. Because heroin is more lipid soluble than morphine, it can more rapidly enter the brain, where it is converted to 6-mono-acetyl-morphine. In the brain, heroin and morphine produce virtually identical effects because heroin acts primarily as morphine and as 6-acetyl-morphine (2). Very little heroin is detected in the urine of heroin addicts because heroin is excreted as morphine. Heroin may be preferred by addicts because they value the rapid onset of effects, which may be linked to the sensation of "rush," and because they dislike the histamine release produced by morphine.

Codeine, perhaps the most commonly used opioid in medicine, is also primarily a prodrug. Codeine (3-methoxy-morphine or morphine-3-methyl ether) does not bind significantly to opioid receptors. However, in the body, a small percentage of codeine is converted to morphine, which then produces its characteristic effects (2). Codeine is valuable clinically because it is well absorbed when given by mouth and not much of it is deactivated by the liver as it is absorbed into the bloodstream. Individuals taking codeine for medical purposes usually will have traces of morphine in their urine.

The metabolism of codeine is catalyzed by cytochrome P450 (CYP) enzymes as is biotransformation of several of other opioids. The cytochrome P450 enzymes are produced by twelve different gene families, three of which, CYP 1, 2, and 3, may play a major role in drug metabolism in humans. These families are further divisible into several subfamilies, each of which are to some extent selective for the drug reactions that they will catalyze. The conversion of codeine to morphine is catalyzed to a large extent by the isoform CYP2D6, as is the transformation of hydrocodone into hydromorphone (20) and oxycodone into oxymorphone. A small subpopulation of individuals are poor metabolizers of these drugs as compared to most of the population who extensively metabolize these agents. These individu-

als will obtain less analgesia from a given dose of codeine or hydrocodone than will extensive metabolizers of these agents. Differences in individual drug metabolism rates may be attributable to genetic polymorphism. A deficiency in the ability of individuals to metabolize codeine may result from one or more mutations of the CYP2D6 genes, which results in altered enzyme activity. Genotypes can be determined by challenging subjects with a pharmacological probe such as dextromethorphan, which is mostly metabolized by CYP2D6. Between 4 to 10% of the Caucasian population are poor metabolizers of dextromethorphan (21).

DRUG INTERACTIONS

Many compounds may selectively inhibit the activity of different isoforms of the cytochrome P450 enzymes. Some of these enzyme inhibitors may be substrates of specific enzymes (i.e., their transformation is catalyzed by that enzyme, and inhibit metabolism through competitive inhibition). Other compounds inhibit enzymes but are not substrates of these enzymes. These inhibitors may reduce enzyme activity by mechanisms such as noncompetitive inhibition.

Quinidine can inhibit the activity of CYP2D6, and the administration of this drug has the potential to reduce the analgesic potency of codeine and related compounds. Quinidine may inhibit the metabolism of tramadol (Ultram), which is also dependent on CYP2D6 for its biotransformation into an active metabolite. The rate of biotransformation of tramadol, codeine, and related compounds by CYP2D6 may also be decreased by fluoxetine and paroxetine (22). Methadone also has inhibitory actions on CYP2D6 and as a result may interfere with the metabolism of substrates of this enzyme, which include desipramine, amitriptyline, and many other agents (23). The metabolism of the potent analgesic opioid alfentanil is dependent on the enzyme CYP3A4 (22). Agents such as erythromycin, troleandomycin, midazolam, ketoconazole, and nefazodone may inhibit CYP3A4 from catalyzing the biotransformation of alfentanil (24, 25).

Although the enzymes that are involved in the interaction between opioids and many other compounds have yet to be identified, these interactions may be of clinical importance. Propoxyphene (Darvon), which is structurally related to methadone, can inhibit the metabolism of carbamazepine (Tegretol) (26). Chronic administration of rifampin (27), phenytoin (28), or carbamazepine can increase methadone metabolism and, as a result, precipitate withdrawal. The metabolism of meperidine is increased by either phenytoin (Dilantin) (29) or phenobarbital (30) treatment and normeperidine levels may increase as a result (31). Chronic carbamazepine treatment induces tramadol metabolism.

Certain opioid-related drug interactions do not involve drug metabolizing enzymes. Many CNS depressants including barbiturates and neuroleptics may potentiate the sedative actions of opioids. The administration of either meperidine or of tramadol to patients being treated with a monoamine oxidase inhibitors such as phenelzine (Nardil) or tranylcypromine (Parnate) can cause toxic reactions to occur. These reactions may result from alterations in cerebral serotonin levels and in the case of tramadol also norepinephrine levels. The administration of meperidine to a patient being treated with a monoamine oxidase inhibitor may lead to hypertension, excitement, hyperreflexia, hyperthermia, and tachycardia (32). This reaction may progress to coma and sometimes death. The administration of tramadol may increase the risk of seizures occurring in patients also being treated with tricyclic antidepressants, cyclobenzaprine, promethazine, selective serotonin reuptake inhibitors (e.g., fluoxetine, sertraline, paroxetine), and neuroleptic agents. There have been isolated clinical reports of a serotonergic syndrome with the combination of tramadol and selective serotonergic reuptake inhibitors.

HOW CAN THE ACTIONS OF OPIOIDS EXPLAIN CONTINUED OPIOID USE?

For more than a century, three major hypotheses have been put forth to account for continued opioid use (33). The first is that after a period of opioid use for whatever reason, people become physically dependent and then continue use to avoid the distress of withdrawal. The characteristics of opioid physical dependence and withdrawal are described here and in Chapter 36. A second hypothesis is that people continue to use opioids because they like the effects (e.g., euphoria) produced. Although many behavioral psychologists reject words such as "liking" or "euphoria," preferring terms such as "positive reinforcing effects" to explain repeated drug taking in the absence of physical dependence, in practice, volunteers in laboratories studying opioid effects are asked to answer to questions such as: "How much do you 'like' the drug's effects?" and "How 'high' do you feel?" The third major hypothesis is that, for some people, even on initial use, opioids alleviate some preexisting dysphoric or painful affective state. Hence, for these individuals, opioid use is repeated not because of a desire for euphoria but to relieve some psychological distress that is not being caused by withdrawal (i.e., it is used for self-medication). This latter notion is discussed at length in Chapter 8.

Over the years there have been a number of elaborations, variations, and combinations of these three basic hypotheses, each with different implications for understanding and management of opioid dependence. For example, it has been postulated that euphoria is an atypical response to opioids that occurs primarily in individuals with psychopathology (34). Continued opioid seeking and opioid use despite societal prohibitions against such use was viewed, in part, as a manifestation of the antecedent psychopathology that caused the individual to experience euphoria initially. Another variation is that psychopathology is the basis for both the initial experimentation and the initial experience of euphoria, but that after repeated use the avoidance of withdrawal becomes the major motivation for continued use (34). Other recent variations on these themes are that individuals who respond positively to opioids have some neurophysiological deficit, e.g., deficient endorphins, that is corrected by exogenous opioids (13), or that repeated use of opioids (for whatever reason) produces a relatively permanent dysfunction in some biologic system (e.g., an endogenous opioid system), such that normal mood and function require the continuous use of exogenous opioids (35).

While there is some comfort in the hypothesis that only a limited percentage of the population will experience opioid euphoria and, therefore, be vulnerable to opioid dependence, the proportion of the population that is vulnerable must be quite large. When heroin was widely available to U.S. Army personnel in Vietnam, 42% of enlisted men experimented with opioids and, of these, about half became physically dependent. Of those who tried it at least five times, 73% became physically dependent. Interestingly, the characteristics that predicted who would become dependent in Vietnam were not the same as the characteristics that predicted who would relapse to opioids after return to the United States (36).

One of the most significant advances in understanding how opioids can lead to sustained drug-using behavior and relapse to opioid use after a period of withdrawal has been the recognition that both drug effects and drug withdrawal phenomena can become linked through learning to environmental cues and internal mood states (37–39). Since the concept of learned or conditioned craving tends to amplify and extend both the motivating effects of opioid withdrawal and their positive reinforcing actions, it is presented here not as a distinct hypothesis about continued opioid use but as a process that should be considered whatever the initial or primary motives for use may have been.

There is little question that opioid withdrawal produces dysphoria and significant distress (described later) and that avoidance of opioid withdrawal can be a major motive for continuing opioid use if there is a significant degree of physical dependence (10, 35). However, avoidance of withdrawal does not readily explain relapse once acute and protracted withdrawal phenomena have abated. Consequently, much current work focuses on how the acute effects of drugs come to have so much value for the individual that other values are subordinated to the goal of obtaining and using opioids, and on how emotions and environmental cues re-evoke the distress of withdrawal or the memory of opioid euphoria or opioid reduction of dysphoria. Chapters 7 and 8 consider the issues at greater length.

OPIOID REINFORCEMENT AND OTHER DRUGS

As described in Chapter 6, there has been a remarkable increase in knowledge about the neurophysiological substrates of the positive reinforcing actions of opioid drugs. Multiple lines of evidence point to a critical role for

dopaminergic neurons originating in the ventral tegmental area and ascending to the nucleus accumbens and frontal cortex. Mu agonist opioids appear to increase activity in this system with a resultant increase in dopamine release in the nucleus accumbens. In contrast, kappa agonists tend to have no effect or to decrease dopamine release (2). Cocaine and amphetamines, although acting on different receptors, also produce increases in dopamine release at the nucleus accumbens. On the basis of such findings, it is postulated that cocaine and opioids (as well as certain other commonly abused drugs) share a common pathway that is critical for their reinforcing actions (40, 41). These common actions on dopaminergic pathways may account for the well-known synergistic effects of opioids and agents such as cocaine and amphetamines that induce euphoric effects by releasing or inhibiting reuptake of dopamine. Addicts frequently inject heroin and cocaine simultaneously (a "speedball") and claim that the euphoria is in some ways more intense or satisfying than with either agent alone. Opioids and amphetamines are also synergistic in producing both analgesia and euphoria. It is interesting that the combinations do not produce additive side effects or toxicity; instead the combination of morphine and amphetamine produces more analgesia and more euphoria, but fewer unwanted side effects, than morphine alone (42, 43). Addicts have long recognized that opioids can ameliorate some of the anxiogenic effects of cocaine. In mice, mu agonist opioids can significantly attenuate the lethality of cocaine, an effect that is antagonized by naloxone (44).

PHYSICAL DEPENDENCE (NEUROADAPTATION) AND TOLERANCE

Physical dependence is usually defined as an altered state of biology induced by a drug, such that when the drug is withdrawn (or displaced from its receptors by an antagonist), a complex set of biologic events (withdrawal or abstinence phenomena) ensue that are typical for that drug (or class of drugs) and that are distinct from a simple return to normal function (2, 10). So defined, physical dependence may develop within a single cell (e.g., a neuron in a culture), a complex of cells (e.g., the spinal cord), or the whole organism. Physical dependence can be observed with a number of classes of pharmacological agents that have psychoactive effects, including opioids, CNS depressants, caffeine, and nicotine, to name but a few, as well as with drugs that are not ordinarily thought of as psychoactive agents (10).

The type of physical dependence induced by opioids is one of the most thoroughly studied, in part because the clinical manifestations of the opioid withdrawal syndrome are easily measured, and because the availability of specific antagonists, such as naloxone, has facilitated research in human and infrahuman species.

Recent research has shed new light on the mechanisms involved in the development of tolerance and dependence. Stimulation of opioid receptors located on critical cells such as those located in the locus coeruleus produces a decrease in cell firing. This effect reflects cellular hyperpolarization that results from both the activation of potassium channels and the inhibition of slowly depolarizing sodium channels (45). These actions occur in conjunction with a decrease in intracellular cyclic AMP levels. Following chronic exposure to opioids, potassium channel currents become reduced while cyclic AMP pathways become up-regulated, which leads to an increase in the phosphorylation of slowly depolarizing sodium channels. These events cause cells to become hyperexcitable (45). Experiments with transgenic mice have implicated the transcription factor Cyclic AMP-Responsive Element Binding protein (CREB) as being critical in the changes produced by chronic opioid treatment (46). Symptoms of opioid withdrawal are markedly less in mice missing two CREB proteins. The actions of CREB may result from its effects on key signaling proteins. The basic cellular mechanisms underlying opioid dependence are considered in greater detail in Chapter 13.

The biological changes responsible for opioid physical dependence begin as soon as opioid receptors are activated by opioid agonists. With prototypical mu opioid agonists such as morphine, some degree of physical dependence can be induced in nontolerant human volunteers by single doses of opioids in the same dose range used for analgesia (15–30 mg). The low degree of physical dependence induced in this way is of little clinical significance, and withdrawal symptoms are not typically seen when opioids are given briefly for acute pain. However, even this degree of physical dependence can easily be demonstrated by administering a specific antagonist such as naloxone. Subjects given up to 10 mg of naloxone 6–24 hours after a dose of morphine (18–30 mg/70 kg) report nausea and other feelings of dysphoria and exhibit yawning, sweating, tearing, and rhinorrhea (47). Animals previously made physically dependent on opioids and then withdrawn appear to become physically dependent more rapidly upon a second exposure to opioids, and it is likely that this is also the case with humans who were previously dependent. Certainly, *tolerance* to opioids can develop quite rapidly in opioid users, and in experiments with formerly dependent volunteers the dose of morphine can be increased from ordinary clinical doses (e.g., 60 mg/day) to 500 mg/day over as short a period as 10 days (10).

Although the characteristics of the opioid withdrawal syndrome produced by a variety of available mu-opioid agonists are all qualitatively similar, they can differ considerably with respect to the time of onset of symptoms, peak intensity, time to peak intensity, and duration of signs and symptoms (10). The signs and symptoms selected by the fourth edition of the *Diagnostic and Statistical Manual of Mental Disorders* (DSM-IV) as criteria for diagnosing the opioid withdrawal syndrome are shown in Table 14.2. In general, the time course and intensity of the opioid withdrawal syndrome are related to how quickly the specific agonist is removed from its receptors. Drugs such as heroin, morphine, and hydromorphone (Dilaudid) have relatively short biologic half-lives (2–3 hours). When these drugs are stopped after a period of chronic use, the receptors are cleared relatively quickly. The onset of observable withdrawal is typically within 8–12 hours, and the acute syndrome reaches peak intensity within 48 hours and then begins to subside over a period of about 5–7 days. With drugs such as methadone or l-acetylmethadol, which have half-lives after chronic administration ranging from 16 to more than 60 hours (see Chapter 41) and are sequestered in body tissues, observable withdrawal may not develop until 36–48 hours or more after the last dose. Peak intensity may not develop until the fourth to sixth day, and some signs may persist for more than 14 days. When naloxone is used to displace methadone from its receptors, the onset of withdrawal is within minutes and a brief (30–60 minutes) but severe syndrome develops (10). As the naloxone is excreted, the methadone that is still in the body again binds to the receptors and withdrawal subsides.

In considering the older literature on the characteristics of the syndromes produced by drugs such as heroin, morphine, methadone, and buprenorphine, it is important to recognize that most of this classic work was carried out at the Addiction Research Center at Lexington, Kentucky, where the primary instrument used for measuring withdrawal intensity was the Himmelsbach Scale. This scale focused exclusively on observable physiological or behavioral signs such as blood pressure, pulse, temperature, lacrimation, pupillary size, sweating, piloerection, vomiting, diarrhea, and insomnia. No

weight was given to more subjective manifestations of opioid withdrawal such as anxiety, drug craving, depression, irritability, muscle cramps, backache, bone pains, and general dysphoria (48). Hence, with certain mu agonists, the onset of peak severity and duration of withdrawal when described by the Himmelsbach Scale may not always truly reflect the time course of dysphoria, craving, or sense of need for withdrawal relief experienced by a drug user. Two examples of this discrepancy are seen with methadone and buprenorphine. While it is generally reported that the withdrawal from methadone is milder yet more protracted than that of heroin and morphine, this generality does not necessarily reflect the subjective sense of distress (muscle aches, bone pains, dysphoria, depression) that drug addicts may experience during withdrawal. These symptoms are measurable using symptom checklists. When account is taken of these symptoms, withdrawal after cessation of methadone is found to develop in some drug-dependent individuals less than 24 hours after the last dose, and in some individuals it persists for weeks. Buprenorphine is a partial mu agonist, but it binds quite firmly to the receptors. Buprenorphine is associated with little or no withdrawal phenomena when these are measured by the Himmelsbach Scale (49, 50); however, using a symptom checklist, withdrawal (although generally not severe) is easily measurable starting about 30–48 hours after the last dose, and the onset and time course of the syndrome generally correlate with subjects' sense of wanting something (a drug) to alleviate the discomfort. The experienced subjects in the studies rated the intensity of buprenorphine withdrawal as less than that which they had experienced with other opioid drugs such as heroin and methadone (50).

Protracted Abstinence

It has been long recognized that, after the more obvious and measurable manifestations of opioid withdrawal have subsided, many previously physically dependent individuals continue to experience unwanted feelings ranging from a vague sense of not feeling normal to more easily described symptoms of depression and abnormal responses to stressful situations. In two prospective studies in which former heroin users were stabilized on opioids (in one study the drug was morphine, in the second, methadone), there continued to be deviations from baseline on several physiological measures (respiration, temperature, etc.) for up to 24 weeks after withdrawal. These were associated with feelings of decreased self-esteem, anxiety, and other indices of psychological disturbances (51, 52). These physiological and psychological deviations from baseline have been referred to frequently as the *protracted abstinence syndrome,* and it is postulated that this state contributes to relapse following withdrawal (35). As described in Chapter 41, patients who have successfully participated in methadone maintenance programs often complain of protracted abstinence symptoms even when withdrawal has been carried out quite slowly. In many cases there is also a return of thoughts about opioid use (drug hunger). The biologic basis for protracted opioid abstinence is largely unexplored. Among the factors complicating the study of this phenomenon is the high prevalence of other psychiatric disorders (e.g., affective disorders, antisocial personality) among those who become heroin dependent (see Chapter 8). Hence, the appearance of depression, anxiety, or irritability during the weeks following withdrawal cannot usually be attributed exclusively to opioid withdrawal.

Receptor Specificity of Tolerance and Physical Dependence

It is also of clinical significance that the phenomena of tolerance and physical dependence appear to be relatively receptor specific. Hence, induction of tolerance to a mu agonist such as morphine will induce some degree of tolerance to other mu agonists such as hydromorphone (Dilaudid), levorphanol, and methadone but little cross-tolerance to drugs acting primarily at kappa receptors (2). However, tolerance to mu agonists is generally accompanied by mu agonist physical dependence, and, therefore, any effort to abruptly substitute a kappa agonist with either no action or antagonistic actions at the mu receptor will generally be associated with varying degrees of withdrawal. However, if such an agent were available, it might be possible

---

Table 14.2   Diagnostic Criteria for Opioid Withdrawal

A. Either of the following
   (1) cessation of (or reduction in) opioid use that has been heavy and prolonged (several weeks or longer)
   (2) administration of an opioid antagonist after a period of opioid use
B. Three (or more) of the following, developing within minutes to several days after Criterion A:
   (1) Dysphoric mood
   (2) Nausea or vomiting
   (3) Muscle aches
   (4) Lacrimation or rhinorrhea
   (5) Pupillary dilation, piloerection, or sweating
   (6) Diarrhea
   (7) Yawning
   (8) Fever
   (9) Insomnia
C. The symptoms in Criterion B cause clinically significant distress or impairment in social, occupational, or other important areas of functioning.
D. The symptoms are not due to a general medical condition and are not better accounted for by another mental disorder.

Table from Diagnostic and Statistical Manual of Mental Disorders. 4th edition, revised. Washington, DC: American Psychiatric Press, 1994. Copyright 1994, American Psychiatric Association.

to use a drug that has mu as well as delta and kappa actions, thereby exerting analgesic effects through the non-mu receptors. Conversely, if tolerance develops to a relatively selective kappa agonist, substitution of an opioid with actions at other receptors might still yield analgesia. Because clinically available opioids have somewhat different profiles of relative receptor affinity, some patients may respond better to one than to another and cross-tolerance is often incomplete. Yet, as described in Chapter 41, the cross-tolerance between methadone and other mu agonists is such that patients maintained on doses of 60–100 mg of methadone orally report little or no euphoria from a dose of heroin up to 25 mg.

While the currently available opioids may exhibit preferential binding to one or another of the receptor types (e.g., morphine and methadone bind preferentially to mu receptors), at very high doses even these drugs may begin to exert some of their effects through other receptors to which they bind with lesser affinity.

Some available agents categorized as agonist/antagonists (such as butorphanol, nalbuphine, and pentazocine) appear to exert either weak agonist or antagonist actions at the mu receptor, but their actions at other receptors such as kappa are such as to render them useful analgesics. However, if such agents are administered to individuals dependent on a mu agonist such as morphine or heroin, by displacing the more potent agonists they may precipitate mu agonist withdrawal. In general, these agonist/antagonists have lower abuse potential than prototypical mu agonists, probably because their actions at kappa receptors are such that, when the dose is increased, most individuals begin to experience dysphoria rather than greater euphoria (2). However, when pentazocine is combined with the antihistamine tripelennamine (T's and Blues—Talwin and blue-colored pyribenzamine tablets), the combination appears to be more euphorigenic than is either agent alone. Interestingly, in rats, combining tripelennamine with pentazocine or nalbuphine results in a significantly greater lowering of the threshold for electrical self-stimulation than do the opioids alone (53, 54).

Kappa agonist physical dependence has been studied in animals and appears to be distinct from mu agonist physical dependence, although there are some common elements (55). Physical dependence on relatively pure kappa agonists has not been thoroughly studied in humans, in part because volunteers are reluctant to take high dosages because of the dysphoric effects. Physical dependence on nalorphine, an opioid with mu antagonist and kappa agonist actions, has been studied in humans, and while there is a measurable syndrome when nalorphine is discontinued, and while the syndrome shares some features with morphine withdrawal, it is not characterized by drug-seeking behavior (56).

Buprenorphine is best characterized as a partial mu agonist. Given to nontolerant and nondependent volunteers, it is generally identified as an opioid drug and produces elevation of mood and other effects typical of morphine-like agents (49). Therefore, it is considered to have abuse potential and is subject to regulation under the Controlled Substances Act. However, it appears to exhibit a different slope for its dose-effect curve so that increasing doses do not produce comparable increases in euphoria or mu agonist toxicity (i.e., respiratory depression). At low levels of mu agonist physical dependence, buprenorphine can substitute for morphine or heroin in suppressing mu agonist withdrawal. However, at very high levels of mu agonist physical dependence it may not substitute completely or may precipitate withdrawal. Another interesting characteristic of buprenorphine is the tenacity with which it binds to the mu receptor. One consequence of this characteristic is that unusually high doses of naloxone are required to reverse effects of overdoses or to precipitate withdrawal (49). Buprenorphine is now being studied as an alternative to methadone for detoxification from heroin for opioid maintenance treatment, and as a transitional agent that facilitates transfer from methadone to treatment with an antagonist such as naltrexone (described later).

Managing Opioid Physical Dependence

There are many ways to deal with the development of opioid neuroadaptation (physical dependence). As is emphasized in Chapter 33, *physical dependence* and *addiction* are not (or should not be) interchangeable terms.

When a patient with intractable pain becomes physically dependent, the situation should not evoke any sense of urgency about "getting the patient off narcotics." Ideally, in such a situation the issue is proper pain management and withdrawal from opioids is undertaken only when there is some confidence that pain can be managed without opioid drugs. However, circumstances are not always ideal and doctors are often pressured to withdraw patients from opioids even when there is no medical indication for doing so or clear plan for alternative pain relief.

Treatment of individuals who are dependent on illicit opioids may involve either the use of maintenance therapies or of medically managed withdrawal. Maintenance therapy until recently relied solely on the use of methadone. In 1993, L-alpha-acetylmethadol (Orlaam) received approval for use as an opioid maintenance agent. This drug and its metabolites act as mu receptor agonists. The metabolites of LAAM have a much greater affinity for the mu receptor and have more agonist activity than does the parent compound (57). This may account for the LAAM's slow onset of action. These compounds have long half-lives that allow LAAM to be administered as infrequently as three times a week. Withdrawal from LAAM is characterized by the slow onset of mild abstinence symptoms and a protracted course.

As an alternative to either methadone or LAAM maintenance regimens researchers have focused on the use of buprenorphine as a maintenance agent. Buprenorphine offers the advantage of a good safety profile, a lower potential for abuse than full mu receptor agonists, and an ability to block the reinforcing effects of other opioids. The lower abuse liability holds promise for less drug diversion and the possibility of opioid replacement therapy in settings other than the typical methadone clinic. It must noted, however, that injectable buprenorphine has been abused by heroin addicts in other countries (58, 59). Buprenorphine has poor oral bioavailability but is well absorbed when administered sublingually. Sublingual tablets are not yet commercially available, but such tablets, formulated to include naloxone to discourage parenteral use, are currently in the development stage. Buprenorphine has been compared to methadone as an agent for maintenance treatment of opioid dependence by several groups of investigators. In one double-blind, placebo-controlled study, an 8 mg per day dose of buprenorphine did not differ significantly from a 60 mg per day dose of methadone in its ability to reduce illicit opioid use as determined by urinalysis while both buprenorphine and 60 mg methadone were superior to 20 mg of methadone (60). In another equally well-controlled study, an 80 mg per day dose of methadone was significantly more effective than 8 mg per day of sublingual buprenorphine at keeping patients opioid free and in reducing symptoms of opioid craving (61). In this study 8 mg of buprenorphine was comparable to 30 mg of methadone. These findings suggest that further research is required to determine the optimal maintenance dose for buprenorphine.

The use of methadone and LAAM for purposes of maintenance therapy is restricted to approved treatment programs. Many opioid-dependent persons in the United States do not have access to these programs. Thus, it is often necessary to consider how best to accomplish opioid withdrawal even when the clinician believes that maintenance would be a better option. Also, many individuals who have been maintained on methadone at some point elect (or are pressured) to seek to withdraw from methadone. In each situation the approach to withdrawal must take into account the current clinical situation of the patient (what specific opioid, for how long, at what dose, and for what reason), any associated medical or psychiatric problems, past experiences with withdrawal, the motives of the patient in seeking withdrawal, the available clinical resources, and the patient's social support network (see also Chapter 36).

The objective of medically managed withdrawal is to make the syndrome more tolerable for the individual so that complete withdrawal can be accomplished. Hence, the technique selected often depends in part on how much discomfort the individual is willing to tolerate and the support system that is available. In a hospital situation, the standard method has been to substitute oral methadone for shorter-acting opioids such as morphine or heroin, then after a day or two of stabilization to reduce the methadone by about 20% per day. With few exceptions (e.g., medical personnel on very high doses of pure opioids), initial stabilization rarely requires more than 40 mg/day, usually given in divided doses. Because of the kinetics of methadone, with this approach some modest withdrawal discomfort begins about the third or fourth day and often persists for a number of days after the dose has been reduced to zero. Sedatives help to deal with the restless sleep and insomnia that often persist for many days or weeks. Temptations to use opioids are typically fewer in a hospital than in an outpatient setting and patients are generally better able to tolerate some discomfort and craving in a hospital setting. Unfortunately, because of the costs of in-hospital treatment, patients who are withdrawn by using methadone typically are discharged still experiencing low-level withdrawal and still having a relatively high craving for opioids. Relapse to opioids after brief in-hospital detoxification is quite high.

Hospital stays can be further shortened by managing withdrawal with clonidine or other alpha$_2$-adrenergic agonists (62–64). Lofexidine, a structural analog of clonidine, may cause less sedation and hypotension than clonidine, but is not yet available in the United States. These agents act on autoreceptors, which inhibit locus coeruleus neurons that become hyperactive during mu agonist opioid withdrawal (10, 14). Clonidine suppresses many of the autonomic signs and symptoms of withdrawal (e.g., nausea, vomiting, sweating, intestinal cramps, and diarrhea) (62–65), although it does little to alleviate the muscle aches, back pain, insomnia, and craving for opioids (65). By omitting the substitution of methadone, the duration of the acute heroin withdrawal syndrome is shortened. Clonidine can also be used to facilitate withdrawal from methadone. Clonidine is usually given orally, 0.1–0.3 mg every 6 hours up to a total of 2 mg in hospitalized patients, and 1.2 mg per day in outpatients. Even at these doses hypotension is a limiting side effect. More experienced clinicians have given higher doses, but the sedation and marked hypotension associated with higher doses can make nursing care a problem.

Clonidine has also been used to facilitate precipitated withdrawal and the initiation of treatment with the opioid antagonist naltrexone. With this technique the entire course of the *acute* opioid withdrawal syndrome can be compressed to 2–4 days (63, 64). Further, if patients can be persuaded to continue taking naltrexone for a week after withdrawal, the probability of early relapse can be reduced. Clonidine-managed rapid opioid withdrawal and clonidine-managed antagonist-precipitated opioid withdrawal have also been carried out in outpatients (64), but the facilities required are better described as day hospital, rather than outpatient clinics.

Buprenorphine appears to be a very useful agent for managing opioid withdrawal. In contrast to clonidine, buprenorphine does not tend to produce marked decreases in blood pressure. Patients transferred to buprenorphine experience little or no withdrawal and craving is generally suppressed (66). Buprenorphine can then be discontinued or naltrexone treatment can be initiated. During acute detoxification of opioid dependent patients including methadone-dependent individuals, buprenorphine reduces subjective and physiological withdrawal symptoms with an efficacy comparable or greater than that of clonidine (67, 68). There is, however, a mild withdrawal syndrome when buprenorphine is discontinued or reduced.

Still another variation on managed antagonist-precipitated opioid withdrawal involves heavy sedation with short-acting benzodiazepines, (e.g., intravenous midazolam [Versed]), followed by naloxone and naltrexone. It has been reported that with such an approach few or no withdrawal symptoms are observed when the effects of the benzodiazepine wear off. In short, the patient is able to tolerate naltrexone only hours after being dependent on opioids (69). A "24-hour detoxification" procedure is being advertised in several countries including the United States. The procedure involves tracheal intubation, induction of anesthesia with the intravenous anesthetic propofol, supplemented with benzodiazepines and clonidine. Opioid withdrawal is precipitated with intravenous naloxone or naltrexone via an intragastric tube. Anesthesia is maintained 6–8 hours. Patients are discharged (usually in 24–48 hours) on oral naltrexone. Relapse rates are influenced by including follow-up visits and supervised naltrexone in the initial fee. Agents that raise endogenous opioid levels by inhibiting opioid peptide degradation (e.g., acetorphan) also have been used to treat symptoms of opioid withdrawal (70). NMDA antagonists and nitric oxide synthase inhibitors have reduced opioid withdrawal symptoms in animal models, but studies in humans are preliminary (71).

Researchers have tried for some years without much success to find evidence that opioid tolerance is related to a "down-regulation" of opioid receptors (decrease in receptor number or receptor sensitivity) (see Chapter 13). However, there is some evidence that chronic administration of an opioid antagonist such as naltrexone produces an up-regulation of opioid receptors. Following discontinuation of naltrexone there is increased sensitivity to opioid actions (72, 73). In recently detoxified heroin addicts this could result in an increased risk of overdosage if they experiment with opioids soon after naltrexone discontinuation.

The most common approach to opioid withdrawal for those who were heroin addicts is to stabilize the patient on relatively low doses of oral methadone (20–40 mg) and then, while the patient remains ambulatory in the community, to gradually reduce this dose to zero over a period of several weeks. For a number of years, treatment programs in the United States were obliged to withdraw heroin addicts who were not eligible for methadone maintenance within 21 days. The rate of relapse to heroin was exceedingly high. Clinical studies of the relative effects of different rates of withdrawal suggested that some patients were more likely to avoid relapse if methadone was reduced by very small increments of 1–3 mg per week over a period of up to 6 months (74). Federal regulations governing methadone programs now allow for more flexible and extended periods of dose reduction and withdrawal (up to 180 days).

In summary, there are a number of pharmacological options and techniques available for withdrawing opioids from individuals who have become physically dependent. More recently, clinical research has focused on psychological and social support techniques for reducing the high rate of relapse following withdrawal (see Chapter 48). What remains to be learned is which pharmacological approach, if any, combines best with which relapse prevention approach to yield the best long-term outcome.

OPIOID TOXICITY

When opioids are given orally under medical supervision, even prolonged periods of use appear to produce no major toxic effects on physiologic systems. However, it is likely that prolonged exposure to opioids induces, in some individuals, long-lasting adaptive changes that require continued administration of an opioid to maintain normal mood states and normal responses to stress (see Chapter 14). In contrast to the modest effects of medically supervised oral opioids, the toxic effects associated with unsupervised use of illicit, often contaminated opioids by parenteral routes are severe and quite common. These toxic effects range from acute and sometimes fatal overdoses to a wide range of infections associated with shared or contaminated injection implements, to neurological, muscular, pulmonary, and renal damage, the etiology of which is sometimes obscure. These toxic effects and medical complications are described in detail in Chapter 55. Opioid users are more likely than age-matched controls to die as a result of suicide or violence. Prior to the beginning of the human immunodeficiency virus (HIV) epidemic, mortality among illicit opioid users was two to three times higher than that of age- and gender-matched controls for older addicts, and 20-fold higher for younger addicts. However, since in some cities 50% of intravenous drug users are HIV seropositive, these older estimates of excess mortality among opioid users of 1.5–2% per year grossly understate the situation now emerging (10).

Acute opioid overdose is not uncommon among opioid addicts despite the remarkable tolerance that can develop to mu agonists such as morphine. For example, patients with terminal cancer may sometimes require doses in excess of 500 mg of morphine per hour intravenously. However, as noted in Chapter 57, a high degree of tolerance to opioids is not inevitable and many cancer patients can be managed for long periods without sharp escalation of dosage. This variability in the development of opioid tolerance, as well as the fluctuating levels of purity of illicit opioids, may help to explain why even opioid users with some degree of tolerance may experience severe opioid overdoses. Other factors that may contribute to overdosage is the tendency to combine other drugs such as alcohol or sedatives with opioids, or the return to opioid use shortly after a period of detoxification that is associated with significant loss of acquired tolerance.

The characteristic signs of acute opioid toxicity include varying degrees of clouded consciousness (up to complete and unresponsive coma), severe respiratory depression, and markedly constricted (pinpoint) pupils. Not infrequently, there is pulmonary edema associated with the severe respiratory depression. While blood pressure is reduced by such doses of opioids, severe hypotension and cardiovascular collapse do not generally occur unless hypoxia is severe and prolonged. In such situations, the pupils may be dilated (10).

The first response should be to reestablish adequate ventilation and to administer an opioid antagonist such as naloxone. This should be given intravenously, if possible, with cautious increments to avoid precipitation of opioid withdrawal. Doses of less than 0.5 mg of naloxone (Narcan) are sometimes adequate to reverse respiratory depression, and the response is typically seen within 1 or 2 minutes of initial intravenous administration. Generally, if there is no substantial response to 5–10 mg of naloxone, there is little likelihood that the coma and respiratory depression are due solely to opioid overdose. One possible exception is in the case of buprenorphine. As noted earlier, buprenorphine appears to bind firmly to receptors so that if an overdose does occur it is likely to require in excess of 10 milligrams of naloxone to antagonize its effects. Notably, this amount requires 25 ampules of Narcan. Mild degrees of pulmonary edema may clear when the respiratory rate is normalized. More severe pulmonary edema may require positive pressure ventilation.

Naloxone is a short-acting drug. If the opioid overdose is caused by an agent with a much longer half-life such as methadone, the patient may lapse back into coma when the naloxone is metabolized and the methadone still present reattaches to the receptors (10). In such instances, continued observation of the patient is called for. Alternatively, it may be possible to follow naloxone with a longer-acting antagonist such as naltrexone orally, recognizing that, unless used judiciously, naltrexone could precipitate severe withdrawal.

References

1. Jaffe JH. Opioid-related disorders. In: Kaplan HI, Sadock BJ, eds. Comprehensive textbook of psychiatry. 6th ed. Baltimore: Williams & Wilkins, 1995.
2. Jaffe JH, Martin WR. Opioid analgesics and antagonists. In: Gilman AG, Rall TW, Nies AS, Taylor P, eds. Goodman and Gilman's the pharmacological basis of therapeutics. 8th ed. New York: Pergamon Press, 1990:485–521.
3. Woods JH, Winger G. Behavioral characterization of opioid mixed agonist-antagonists. Drug Alcohol Depend 1987;20:303–315.
4. Musacchio JM. The psychotomimetic effects of opiates and the sigma receptor. Neuropsychopharmacology 1990;3:191–200.
5. Pasternak GW. Pharmacological mechanisms of opioid analgesics. Clin Neuropharmacol 1993; 16:1–18.
6. Reisine T, Pasternak G. Opioid analgesics and antagonists. In: Hardman JG, Limbird LE, Molinoff RW, Ruddon RW, Gilman AG, eds. Goodman and Gilman's the pharmacologic basis of therapeutics. 9th ed. New York: McGraw-Hill, 1995:521–556.
7. Marshall BE, Longnecker DE. General anesthetics. In: Gilman AG, Rall TW, Nies AS, Taylor P, eds. Goodman and Gilman's the pharmacological basis of therapeutics. 8th ed. New York: Pergamon Press, 1990:311–331.
8. Lasagna L, Von Felsinger JM, Beecher HK. Drug-induced changes in man. 1. Observations on healthy subjects, chronically ill patients, and 'postaddicts'. JAMA 1955;157:1106–1120.
9. Von Felsinger JM, Lasagna L, Beecher HK. Drug-induced changes in man. 2. Personality and reactions to drugs. JAMA 1955;157: 1113–1119.
10. Jaffe JH. Drug addiction and drug abuse. In: Gilman AG, Rall TW, Nies AS, Taylor P, eds. Goodman and Gilman's the pharmacological basis of therapeutics. 8th ed. New York: Pergamon Press, 1990:522–573.
11. Seecof R, Tennant FS. Subjective perceptions of the intravenous "rush" of heroin and cocaine in opioid addicts. Am J Drug Alcohol Abuse 1986;12:79.
12. McKenna GJ. Methadone and opiate drugs: psychotropic effect and self-medication. In: Verebey K, ed. Opioids in mental illness: theories, clinical observations, and treatment possibilities. New York: New York Academy of Sciences, 1982:44–55.
13. Gold MS, Pottash AC, Sweeney D, Martin D, Extein I. Antimanic, antidepressant, and antipanic effects of opiates: clinical, neuroanatomical, and biochemical evidence. In: Verebey K, ed. Opioids in mental illness: theories, clinical observations, and treatment possibilities. New York: New York Academy of Sciences, 1982: 141–150.
14. Redmond DE, Krystal JH. Multiple mechanisms of withdrawal from opioid drugs. Annu Rev Neurosci 1984;7:443–478.
15. Hasselström J, Säwe J. Morphine pharmacokinetics and metabolism in humans: enterohepatic cycling and relative contribution of metabolites to active opioid concentrations. Clin Pharmacokinet 1993;24:344–354.
16. Portenoy RK, Thaler HT, Inturrisi CE, Friedlander-Klar H, Foley KM. The metabolite morphine-6-glucuronide contributes to analgesia produced by morphine infusion in patients with pain and normal renal function. Clin Pharmacol Ther 1992;51:422–431.
17. Osborne RJ, Joel SP, Slevin ML. Morphine intoxication in renal failure: the role of morphine-6-glucuronide. Br Med J 1986;292:1548–1549.
18. Szeto HH, Inturrisi CE, Houde R, Saal S, Cheigh J, Reidenberg MM. Accumulation of normeperidine, an active metabolite of meperidine, in patients with renal failure of cancer. Ann Intern Med 1977;86:738–741.
19. Houde RW. Misinformation: side effects and drug interactions. In: Hill CS Jr, Fields WS, eds. Advances in pain research and therapy. Vol. 11. Drug treatment of cancer pain in a drug-oriented society. New York: Raven Press, 1989: 145–161.
20. Otton SV, Schadel M, Cheung SW, Kaplan HL, Busto UE, Sellers EM. CYP2D6 phenotype determines the metabolic conversion of hydrocodone to hydromorphone. Clin Pharmacol Ther 1993;54:463–472.
21. Schmid B, Bircher J, Preisig R, Kupfer A. Polymorphic dextromethorphan metabolism: co-segregation of oxidative O-demethylation with debrisoquin hydroxylation. Clin Pharmacol Ther 1985;38:618–624.
22. Ciraulo DA, Shader RI, Greenblatt DJ, Barnhill JG. Basic concepts. In: Ciraulo DA, Shader RI, Greenblatt DJ, Creelman W, eds. Drug interactions in psychiatry. 2nd ed. Baltimore: Williams & Wilkins, 1995:1–28.
23. Wu D, Otton SV, Sproule BA, Busto U, Inaba T, Kalow W, Sellers EM. Inhibition of human cytochrome P450 2D6 (CYP2D6) by methadone. Br J Pharmacol 1993;35:30–34.
24. Bartowski RR, Goldberg ME, Larijani GE, Boerner T. Inhibition of alfentanil metabolism by erythromycin. Clin Pharmacol 1989;46: 99–102.
25. Labroo RB, Thummel KE, Kunze KL Podoll T, Trager WF, Kharasch ED. Catalytic role of cytochrome P4503A4 in multiple pathways of alfentanil metabolism. Drug Metab Dispos 1995;23:490–496.
26. Ciraulo DA, Slattery M. Anticonvulsants. In: Ciraulo DA, Shader RI, Greenblatt DJ, Creelman W, eds. Drug interactions in psychiatry. 2nd ed. Baltimore: Williams & Wilkins, 1995: 249–310.
27. Kreek MJ, Garfield JW, Gutjahr CL, Giusti LM. Rifampin-induced methadone withdrawal. N Engl J Med 1976;294:1104–1106.
28. Tong TG, Pond SM, Kreek MJ, Jaffery NF, Benowitz NL. Phenytoin-induced methadone withdrawal. Ann Intern Med 1981;94:349–351.
29. Pond SM, Kretschzmar KM. Effect of phenytoin on meperidine clearance and normeperidine formation. Clin Pharmacol Ther 1981;30:680–686.
30. Strambaugh JE, Wainer IW, Hemphill DM, Schwartz I. A potentially toxic drug interaction between pethidine (meperidine) and phenobarbitone. Lancet 1977;1:398–399.
31. Edwards DJ, Svensson CK, Visco JP, Lalka D. Clinical pharmacokinetics of pethidine. Clin Pharmacokinet 1982;7:421–433.
32. Creelman WL, Ciraulo DA. Monoamine oxidase inhibitors. In: Ciraulo DA, Shader RI, Greenblatt DJ, Creelman W, eds. Drug interactions in psychiatry. 2nd ed. Baltimore: Williams & Wilkins, 1995:249–310.
33. Jaffe JH, Jaffe FK. Historical perspectives on the use of subjective effects measures in assessing the abuse potential of drugs. NIDA Monogr Res Ser 1989;92:43–72.
34. Kolb L. Pleasure and deterioration from narcotic addiction. Mental Hygiene 1925;9:699–724.
35. Dole V, Nyswander M. Heroin addiction—a metabolic disease. Arch Intern Med 1967;120: 19–24.
36. Robins LN. Addict careers. In: DuPont RL, Goldstein A, O'Donnell J, eds. Handbook on drug abuse. Washington, DC: U.S. Government Printing Office, 1979:325–336.
37. Childress AR, McLellan AT, O'Brien CP. Conditioned responses in a methadone population. J Subst Abuse Treat 1986;3:173–179.
38. Wikler A. Opioid dependence: mechanisms and treatment. New York: Plenum Press, 1980.
39. Meyer RE, Mirin SM. The heroin stimulus: implication for a theory of addiction. New York: Plenum Press, 1979.
40. Wise RA. The neurobiology of craving: implications for the understanding and treatment of addiction. J Abnorm Psychol 1988;2:118–132.
41. Koob GF, Bloom FE. Cellular and molecular mechanisms of drug dependence. Science 1988; 242:715–723.
42. Forrest WH Jr, Brown BW Jr, Brown CR, et al. Dextroamphetamine with morphine for the treatment of postoperative pain. N Engl J Med 1977;296:712–715.
43. Jasinski DR, Preston K. Evaluation of mixtures of morphine and D-amphetamine for subjective

and physiological effects. Drug Alcohol Depend 1986;17:1–13.

44. Witkin JM, Johnson RE, Jaffe JH, et al. The partial opioid agonist, buprenorphine, protects against lethal effects of cocaine. Drug Alcohol Depend 1991;27:177–184.

45. Hyman SE. Shaking out the cause of addiction. Science 1996;273:611–612.

46. Maldonado R, Blendy JA, Tzavara E, Gass P, Roques BP, Hanoune J, et al. Reduction of morphine abstinence in mice with a mutation in the gene encoding CREB. Science 1996;273: 657–659.

47. Heishman SJ, Stitzer ML, Bigelow GE, Liebson IA. Acute opioid physical dependence in postaddict humans: naloxone dose effects after brief morphine exposure. J Pharmacol Exp Ther 1989;248:127–134.

48. Kolb L, Himmelsbach CK. Clinical studies of drug addiction. III. A critical review of withdrawal treatments with method of evaluating abstinence syndromes. Am J Psychiatry 1938; 94:759–799.

49. Jasinski DR, Pevnick JS, Griffith JD. Human pharmacology and abuse potential of the analgesic buprenorphine. Arch Gen Psychiatry 1978;35:501–516.

50. Fudala PJ, Jaffe JH, Dax EM, Johnson RE. Use of buprenorphine in the treatment of opioid addiction. II. Physiologic and behavioral effects of daily and alternate-day administration and abrupt withdrawal. Clin Pharmacol Ther 1990; 47:525–534.

51. Martin WR, Jasinski DR. Physiological parameters of morphine dependence in man—tolerance, early abstinence, protracted abstinence. J Psychiatr Res 1969;7:9–17.

52. Martin WR, Jasinski DR, Haertzen CA, et al. Methadone—a reevaluation. Arch Gen Psychiatry 1973;28:286–295.

53. Unterwald EM, Kornetsky C. Effects of concomitant pentazocine and tripelennamine on brain-stimulation reward. Pharmacol Biochem Behavior 1984;21:961–964.

54. Unterwald EM, Kornetsky C. Effects of nal-

buphine alone and in combination with tripelennamine on rewarding brain stimulation thresholds in the rat. Pharmacol Biochem Behavior 1986;25:629–632.

55. Gmerek DE, Dykstra LA, Woods JH. Kappa opioids in rhesus monkeys. III. Dependence associated with chronic administration. J Pharmacol Exp Ther 1987;242:428–436.

56. Martin WR, Fraser HF, Gorodetzky CW. Demonstration of tolerance and physical dependence on N-allyl-normorphine (nalorphine). J Pharmacol Exp Ther 1965;150:437–442.

57. Bertalmio AJ, Medzihradsky, Winger G, Woods JH. Differential influence of N-Dealkylation on the stimulus properties of some opioid agonists. J Pharmacol Exp Ther 1992;261:278–284.

58. Forsyth AJ, Farquhar D, Gemmell M, Shewan D, Davies JB. The dual use of opioids and temazepam by drug injectors in Glasgow (Scotland). Drug Alcohol Depend 1993;32: 277–280.

59. San L, Torrens M, Castilio C, Porta M, de la Torre R. Consumption of buprenorphine and other drugs among heroin addicts under ambulatory treatment, results from cross-sectional studies 1988 and 1990. Addiction 1993;88:1341–1349.

60. Johnson RE, Jaffe JH, Fudala PJ. A controlled trial of buprenorphine treatment for opioid dependence. JAMA 1992;267:2750–2755.

61. Ling W, Wesson DR, Charuvastra C, Klett JC. A controlled trial comparing buprenorphine and methadone maintenance in opioid dependence. Arch Gen Psychiatry 1996;53:401–407.

62. Washton AM, Resnick RG. Clonidine in opiate withdrawal: review and appraisal of clinical findings. Pharmacotherapy 1981;1:140–146.

63. Kleber HD, Topazian M, Gaspari J, Kosten TR. Clonidine and naltrexone in outpatient treatment of opioid withdrawal. Am J Drug Alcohol Abuse 1987;13:1–18.

64. Vining E, Kosten TR, Kleber HG. Clinical utility of rapid clonidine-naltrexone detoxification for opioid abusers. Br J Addict 1988;83: 567–575.

65. Jasinski DR, Johnson RE, Kocher TR. Clonidine in morphine withdrawal. Differential effects on signs and symptoms. Arch Gen Psychiatry 1985; 42:1063–1065.

66. Johnson RE, Cone EJ, Henningfield JE, Fudala PJ. Use of buprenorphine in the treatment of opiate addiction. I. Physiologic and behavioral effects during a rapid dose induction. Clin Pharmacol Ther 1989;46:335–343.

67. Cheskin LJ, Fudala PJ, Johnson RE. A controlled comparison of buprenorphine and clonidine for acute detoxification from opioids. Drug Alcohol Depend 1994;36:115–121.

68. Janiri L, Mannelli P, Persico AM, Serretti A, Tempesta E. Opiate detoxification of methadone maintenance patients using lefetamine, clonidine, and buprenorphine. Drug Alcohol Depend 1994;36:139–145.

69. Loimer N, Lenz K, Schmid R, Presslich O. Technique for greatly shortening the transition from methadone to naltrexone maintenance of patients addicted to opiates. Am J Psychiatry 1991;148:933–935.

70. Hartmann F, Poirier M-F, Bourdel M-C, Loo H, Lecomte J-C, Schwartz J-C. Comparisons of acetorphan with clonidine for opiate withdrawal symptoms. Am J Psychiatry 1991; 148:5.

71. Herman BH, Vocci F, Bridge P. The effects of NMDA receptor antagonists and nitric oxide synthase inhibitors on opioid tolerance and withdrawal. Neuropsychopharmacology 1995; 13:269–293.

72. Zukin RS, Sugarman JR, Fitz-Syage ML, Gardner EL, Zukin SR, Gintzler AR. Naltrexone-induced opiate receptor supersensitivity. Brain Res 1982;245:285–292.

73. Sicuteri F, Nicolodi M, Del Bene E, Poggioni M. Chronic naloxone improves migraine and modifies iris reactivity to morphine [abstract]. Biol Psychiatry 1991;29:5035.

74. Senay EC, Dorus DW, Goldberg F, Thornton W. Withdrawal from methadone maintenance: rate of withdrawal and expectation. Arch Gen Psychiatry 1977;34:361–367.

15 COCAINE (AND CRACK): NEUROBIOLOGY

Mark S. Gold and Norman S. Miller

The study of cocaine addiction is both exciting and instructive to the experienced professional and the layperson, despite the tragic and far-reaching consequences experienced by the victims (1–3). The course of addiction to cocaine is intense and can be measured in weeks and months, in contrast to years with alcohol and other drugs of addiction. As a result, clinicians and researchers can more easily study many of the principles that are generalizable to other forms of drug and alcohol addiction. The behavioral components identifiable in cocaine addiction are observable in virtually all forms of addiction: the intense preoccupation with acquiring the substance, the compulsive use despite adverse consequences, and the pattern of relapse.

Perhaps the greatest legacy in the study of cocaine addiction has been the elucidation of several important neurochemical factors that appear to link the original drive for the drug in all addictive behaviors. The discovery that a number of neurotransmitters, residing in discrete brain sites, play a role in the initiation and propagation of cocaine addiction has changed the attitudes and perspectives of researchers and clinicians regarding the etiology and course of cocaine and other addictive diseases. The discovery of underlying neurological mechanisms contributing to cocaine addiction has led to the acceptance that addiction is a true disease state with its own unique pathology (4–6), with or without a dramatic abstinence syndrome.

EPIDEMIOLOGY

Prevalence

Annual Monitoring the Future surveys and other less formally structured sources of information have shown decreases in the lifetime, annual, monthly, and daily use of cocaine. The lifetime use of an illicit drug in 1994 was 45.6%, down from its peak of 66% in 1982, and less than the 58% observed when the survey was initiated in 1975. The peak lifetime use of cocaine by seniors was 17.3% in 1985, down to 9.4% in 1990, and 5.9% in 1994. By contrast, the peak annual rate of cocaine use was 12.7% in 1986, compared with 5.3% in 1990, and 3.6% in 1994. More frequent use, binge or daily use that can be considered addictive use of cocaine, has shown a decrease from a peak for use within 30 days of 6.7% in 1985 to 1.9% in 1990,

Lifetime Use of Cocaine

Figure 15.1. 1995 school survey results for lifetime use of cocaine among 8th, 10th, and 12th grade students. (Data from Johnston L. NIDA Monitoring the Future Study. Ann Arbor: University of Michigan, 1995.)

and for daily use from a peak of 0.4% in 1986, to 0.1% in 1990, to 0.1% in 1994. Data from 1995 has been recently reported by the University of Michigan (Fig. 15.1) suggesting continued decreases in use have ended and may begin a reversal as perception of cocaine danger falls.

Crack use also has decreased significantly among high school seniors between 1989 and 1990, but additional decreases have been difficult to demonstrate. Annual cocaine use dropped from 3.5% in 1991 to 3.1% in 1992, but increased to 3.6% in 1994. Current use decreased by half, but returned to 1.5% of seniors in 1994. Similarly, daily use also diminished by half, from 0.2% in 1989 to 0.1% in 1990, but has remained at this level since 1994. Data acquisition regarding use of crack began in 1987, 2 years after this pretreated freebase form of cocaine became available on the illicit market. In the 1995 survey annual crack use was 1.3% in 8th graders, 1.4% in 10th graders, and 1.9% in 12th graders; 0.8% of twelfth graders use crack at least once a month (Fig. 15.2).

The 1993 National Household Survey on Drug Abuse estimated that 4.5 million Americans used cocaine in 1992, 1.3 million of whom used at least monthly. Clinical experience and some governmental data suggest that most surveys underestimate the number of cocaine addicts in the United States. Surveying only 10 cities, the Department of Justice urine tests identified about 650,000 cocaine addicts through urine testing (7). In a study of 1116 patients admitted for alcohol and drug treatment, 150 patients qualified for cocaine dependence, or 12% of the inpatient population (8, 9). Cocaine abuse and dependence is a common problem that is part of the increasing population of poly-drug abusers, dependent on alcohol, nicotine, opiates, and/or cocaine. Cocaine and heroin users account for a major new group of persons with human immunodeficiency virus infection. The Drug Abuse Warning Network reported over 30,000 cocaine-related emergency room visits during the third quarter of 1992 (9a).

Drug use by 12th Graders

Figure 15.2. 1995 high school survey results for drug use by high school seniors in the past year and past month for crack, alcohol, and marihuana. (Data from Johnston L. NIDA Monitoring the Future Study. Ann Arbor: University of Michigan, 1995.)

Patterns of Addictive Use

The patterns of cocaine use in particular vary, and no one stereotype prevails. Cocaine may be used continuously for days in "runs" or "binges" or at regular intervals when a paycheck is received (that is, only for a day or so every 2 weeks). Others use once or twice a month, while still others use daily for prolonged periods of weeks, months, and years if not interrupted.

Cocaine users come from all social strata, all races, and both sexes. Demographically, the cocaine addicts are young (12–39 years of age), are dependent on at least three drugs (including alcohol), and are predominantly male (75%). Many, if not most, have important comorbid psychiatric and addictive illnesses. Alcohol dependence is exceedingly common among cocaine users. In the Epidemiological Catchment Area Study, 84% of those with cocaine dependence were also alcohol dependent (9b).

While the glamour of cocaine use of the late 1970s and early 1980s has subsided, it appears that so-called "recreational use" has also lost some of its appeal. It is not known beyond the surveys already mentioned just how many individuals can and do use cocaine for "sport" or "pleasure" without significant abuse and addiction liability. However, there is clearly a substantial number of users who have tried cocaine once or more without serious consequence and who have now stopped as a result of education, prevention, or changes in attitudes. If one of every two Americans between the ages of 25 and 30 has used cocaine, then the overwhelming majority have stopped on their own. What is certain is that the risk for developing cocaine addiction is substantial and the morbidity and mortality high (10, 11).

Cocaine and Alcohol (Cocaethylene)

Researchers have clearly demonstrated that in the presence of two drugs of abuse, cocaine and alcohol, the body creates a third. Additive myocardial depressant effects, not related to ischemia, but rather a direct toxic effect of cocaine plus ethanol have similarly been reported (12). Small, "recreational" doses of cocaine produce coronary vasoconstriction and impair myocardial function. Ethanol has coronary vasoconstrictive and myocardial depressant effects as well. Additive effects on the nucleus locus coeruleus may also contribute to the panic and anxiety produced by cocaine and alcohol. Since cocaine is most often taken with other drugs like alcohol, many of the findings that clinicians attribute to cocaine may in fact be due to the combination of drugs. Ethanol plus cocaine appears to increase the period of time associated with cocaine-related increases in blood pressure. Such an interaction between cocaine and alcohol might increase the likelihood of small vessel, intracerebral ischemic infarcts. Ethanol use increases cocaine use and liking for cocaine possibly by the association of combined used with cocaethylene production. In a recent study, nondependent cocaine users were chosen on the basis of ability to choose cocaine versus placebo. Thereafter they were pretreated with small social doses of alcohol and given choices of cocaine and money. Alcohol pretreatment significantly increased choice of cocaine (13) over the alternative reinforcer, money. Alcohol can make it particularly difficult to reduce or abstain from cocaine use.

Chronic cocaine abusers often experience persistent panic attacks or bouts of anxiety, which are reported to persist months after discontinuation of cocaine (14, 15). These consequences may be linked to cocaine and alcohol use. Heuristically consistent with reports of cocaine kindling and cocaine modification of benzodiazepine receptor binding (16) and withdrawal "anxiety" in animals (17) combined use of cocaine and alcohol is quite common among cocaine users (18) with approximately 12 million combination users (19). While initially used by the addict to modify the anxiogenic effects of cocaine and reduce the likelihood of insomnia (20) upon withdrawal, anxiety is increased and possibly prolonged well into abstinence (21).

The longer half-life of cocaethylene (2 hours compared with 38 minutes for cocaine) and additive effect of cocaethylene on the dopamine (DA) transporter (22) and the 40-fold greater affinity for the serotonin transporter may explain the occurrence of lethal heart attacks and stroke (18-fold increase in the risk of sudden death compared to cocaine alone [23]) and the greater irritability, prolonged toxicity (24), and withdrawal complaints.

In a study of 103 inpatient alcoholics and 51 outpatient alcoholics, 49% and 51%, respectively, were also cocaine dependent. Cocaine addiction is also common along heroin addicts; studies show ranges between 20 and 50% for concomitant cocaine addiction (25). Moreover, the studies clearly show that alcohol is so commonly used that it is the first drug of addiction for cocaine addicts, followed closely by cannabis. Studies further show that people who have never used marihuana do not generally use cocaine. Early National Institute of Drug Abuse data suggested that if a person has used marihuana fewer than 10 times he or she is not as likely to use cocaine as if marihuana was used 100 times. Viewed conversely, 98% of cocaine addicts have used marihuana (26–28).

Preparations and Routes of Administration

Cocaine is known by names that reflect both appearance and effects. Coca paste is known as "base," "pasta," "pitillo," and "buscuso." The powdered crystalline form is known as "snow" and "coke" and the rock base form as "crack." Cocaine is an alkaloid that is found in the leaves of Erythroxylon coca, a tree or shrub indigenous to western South America. That nearly all of the world's coca-producing countries are concentrated in one geographical area has led some to conclude cocaine eradication possible if the "Drug War" was viewed as an actual war. Abundant numbers of the plant are found in the wild state in Peru, Colombia, Ecuador, and Bolivia. Coca paste is prepared by dissolving dried coca leaves in a solution of kerosene or gasoline, alkaline bases, potassium permanganate, and sulfuric acid. The resultant coca paste contains not only cocaine but also adulterants, diluents, sulfates, and other coca alkaloids. The other forms of cocaine are prepared from coca paste: cocaine hydrochloride, by the mixture of hydrochloric acid and paste, and crack, by the mixture of bases and paste.

While clinical wisdom and some systematic studies have suggested that certain preparations of cocaine are more addictive, some notable exceptions make a generalization impossible at this time (29). The principal routes of administration are oral, intranasal, intravenous, and inhalation. The slang terms for these routes are, respectively, "chewing," "snorting," "mainlining," and "smoking." Oral absorption is the slowest, within 45–60 minutes. While there is evidence that the quicker and higher peak absorption of cocaine leads to greater intoxication and addiction rates, any of the routes of administration can lead to absorption of large and toxic amounts of cocaine, especially once the onset of regular and addictive use is established. The absorption patterns parallel the behavioral and subjective effects of cocaine. Most controlled studies report close correlation between the plasma levels of cocaine and the physiological and behavioral effects. Also, the toxicities are believed to reflect the route of administration. There is sufficient evidence that acute administration follows differential effects on routes of cocaine administration, with greater toxicity for inhalation than for intravenous than for intranasal than for oral.

The purity of the preparations influences the rate and completeness of absorption of cocaine. In coca leaf chewing, the purity is 0.5%, and it is higher for the cocaine hydrochloride form taken via the oral or intranasal route, with a wide range of 20–80%. The purity for intravenous preparations and the smoked form also varies, from 7–100% for the former and 40–100% for the latter.

Orally consumed cocaine has an area under the curve, or total amount absorbed, equal to that of the intranasal route, with similar bioavailability of 20–30%. The loss of cocaine after oral absorption is due to the first pass hepatic biotransformation, which metabolizes 70–80% of the dose. For oral absorption, the cocaine concentrations in the blood rise slowly such that at 10–15 minutes, levels are 30–50 ng/ml, with a peak of 160 ng/ml at about 60 minutes. The slow and more sloped peak blood level is thought to be responsible for the oral route's apparent low rate of addiction.

After intranasal absorption, the loss of cocaine is due to the ionized form of cocaine's (cocaine HCl) poor penetration of biologic membranes, particularly the nasal mucosa; the vasoconstricting properties of cocaine limit its own passage into blood vessels. The onset of activity is within 3–5 minutes and the blood level peaks at 10–20 minutes, fading in 45–60 minutes. Because cocaine has a biologic half-life of 1 hour, repeated self-administrations are necessary to maintain an effect.

After intravenous (IV) injection, the entire bolus of cocaine is delivered to the vessel chamber and has a bioavailability of 100%. The limiting factor for IV cocaine concentration is the original purity of the injected sample. The onset of activity is within 30 seconds, with a duration of action of 10–20 minutes. The venous system must still be traveled, with the sequence being from the peripheral veins back to the heart and subsequently through the pulmonary system for ejection by the left ventricle to the brain.

Cocaine inhalation became popular because it produces the quickest and highest peak blood levels to the brain without the risks attendant to IV use. Freebase cocaine, whether in coca paste, freebase, or crack form, is much more volatile and lipid soluble than the leaf and powder forms. Because the freebase can be inhaled and thus delivered to the pulmonary bed, it is pumped by the heart directly into the brain. The bioavailability is low, at 6–32%, due to the pyrolysis that occurs on heating the cocaine for vaporization.

With all the routes of administration, chronic and repetitive use of cocaine produces high blood levels. In this regard, the various routes of administration tend to merge and clinical distinctions may be more difficult to make. One study found no significant differences among the routes of administration on several measures of behavioral effects, including paranoia and violence (30).

While cocaine has reliable effects, the state of the organism at the time of the cocaine challenge is an important, often neglected factor. Cocaine appears to produce its greatest effects when the user is not full from overeating or sexually exhausted from recent activity. Chronic food deprivation decreases extracellular DA in the nucleus accumbens providing more motivation and reward for the animal who has learned how to inject cocaine for DA release (31). Cocaine reward may also be influenced by genetic factors and in utero exposure.

Prenatal cocaine exposure led to a marked and stable enhancement of the rates of self-administration for all periods examined suggesting that prenatal exposure to cocaine alters cocaine reinforcement properties for adults (32). Increases in DA in nucleus accumbens and other systems and serotonin systems in brain have been demonstrated for prenatally exposed animals.

What the host brings to the drug challenge may help us ultimately explain pathological attachment to drugs and relative aversion and resistance of others to the same drugs at the same time.

PHARMACOLOGY

Chemistry

Cocaine was the first local anesthetic to be discovered. The pure alkaloid was first isolated in 1860 by Niemann, who noted that it had a bitter taste and produced a peculiar effect on the tongue by making it devoid of sensation. Cocaine is benzoylmethylecgonine and is an ester of benzoic acid and a nitrogen-containing base. Ecgonine is an amino alcohol base closely related to tropine, the amino alcohol in atropine. Cocaine has the base structure of the synthetic local anesthetics. The structure contains hydrophilic tertiary amine and hydrophobic aromatic residue that are separated by an intermediate alkyl chain.

Neurophysiology

Cocaine's most important clinical action is its ability to block the initiation or conduction of the nerve impulse following local application. Its most striking systemic effect is its stimulation of the central nervous system (CNS). Cocaine is a stimulant by means of its potentiation of the responses of sympathetically innervated organs to norepinephrine and, to a lesser extent, epinephrine. Cocaine has its most important actions on neurotransmitters centrally by inhibiting the reuptake of norepinephrine and serotonin as well as DA. Cocaine causes an extremely rapid and powerful inhibition, which can be quite long-lasting. Cocaine also facilitates the release of norepinephrine and DA, activates tyrosine hydroxylase, increases acutely the levels of neurotransmitters in synapses, and increases adrenergic beta-cell populations and the inhibition of neurotransmitter release via action of autoreceptors on presynaptic sites. It binds to the DA transporter labeled by mazindol and to imipramine binding sites on serotonergic neurons. The net effect of the blockage is an increase in the amount of neurotransmitter available at the postsynaptic site for a putative enhanced effect at the postsynaptic sites. Cocaine does not directly activate opioid receptors but may indirectly influence these systems. Cocaine also affects neurotransmission in histamine, acetylcholine, and phenethylamine pathways (33, 34). Cocaine blocks DA uptake into presynaptic terminals and the acute systematic administration of cocaine transiently and dose-dependently increases the extracellular concentration of DA in the nucleus accumbens of rats (35–38) associated in humans with mood elevation and arousal.

There are specific neuroanatomical sites that underlie these fundamental functions, as the mesolimbic system is related to expression of mood and the reticular activation system to arousal. The neurotransmitters interact in excitatory and inhibitory synapses to produce a yet only minimally understood myriad of behavioral effects (Table 15.1).

While DA appears essential to cocaine reward, other evidence suggests that no single neurotransmitter is responsible for the clinical or experimental effects of cocaine in that other pharmacological agents have effects similar to cocaine on these neurotransmitters without the prominent clinical characteristics of cocaine such as euphoria, addiction, and cardiovascular acceleration. Serotonergic activation modulates the reward potency of both cocaine and amphetamines, and pharmacological agents that activate dopaminergic systems without affecting the serotonergic systems do not produce typical self-administration as in addictive use by animals or humans. Correspondingly, pure serotonin agonists and antagonists that lack DA-stimulating properties do not produce reward behavior, further indicating that both systems are required for the expression of compulsive use of cocaine. Problems exist with these hypotheses. Antidepressants characteristically affect the same neurotransmitter systems as do cocaine and amphetamines by inducing a presynaptic blockade of the reuptake of these neurotransmitters, but are not drugs of abuse. Neuroleptics block DA transmission at the postsynaptic site but clinically do not stop cocaine use. While it is relatively clear that these neurotransmitters are required for these functions, and interactions between them or other systems appear important, there are limitations in our present knowledge and ability to link together all the phenomena in cocaine addiction.

Considerable animal and human data suggest that high-dose cocaine use over prolonged periods of time leads to sustained neurophysiological changes in the brain that are responsible for mood and reward behavior. Studies of electrical and pharmacological self-stimulation of brain sites for drive states provide a model for some of the behaviors witnessed in cocaine addiction. Chronic cocaine administration increases the threshold voltage required to elicit self-stimulation behavior in dopaminergic areas such as the nucleus accumbens. The increased voltage requirement indicates subsensitive or down-regulated brain sites as responsible for compulsive use of cocaine. The dysregulation appears to represent a depletion of dopaminergic neurons that may also contribute to the anhedonia and depression during acute and subacute withdrawal in animals and humans following chronic cocaine stimulation (39, 40). Interesting data from humans suggests that tolerance may develop to cocaine's effects but that the rewarding aspects of the cocaine experience are not decreased. In animals, evidence for a reverse tolerance, learning-related increases in cocaine's rewarding properties have been reported.

Behavioral sensitization produced by repeated cocaine is associated with enhanced response in caudate and nucleus accumbens. Such an important effect, which may explain cocaine binges, suggests that the DA transporter is induced by DA blockade during cocaine self-administration to produce compensatory increases in the DA uptake carrier (41).

DOPAMINE

Central dopaminergic, alpha-adrenergic, and beta-adrenergic receptor supersensitivity induced by chronic cocaine administration has been demonstrated in animals and inferred in humans. Naturally, with significant advances in receptor isolation and cloning, researchers have tried to determine which of the many DA receptor subtypes is most responsible for cocaine reward. Researchers have identified seven different proteins that can act as DA receptors (D1a, D1b, D2short, D2long, D3, D4, D5), all of which are distinct from the DA transporter(s). The assumption that cocaine affinity for the DA transporter is directly related to self-administration underlies the DA hypothesis of cocaine reward. According to this theory, the DA transporter serves as the primary means of removing DA from the synaptic cleft after its release; inhibition of this uptake results in an acute excess of DA in the synaptic cleft (1). It has been hypothesized the DA transporter *is* the cocaine receptor, i.e., the initial site of action that ultimately leads to the reinforcement associated with the drug (42). The recent cloning of the DA transporter and study of D3 agonists and antagonists may someday lead to a greater understanding of the mechanisms mediating cocaine and other drug and natural reward and treatments for addiction (43, 44).

Furthermore, the rewarding effects of cocaine self-administration are reduced by D1, D2, and D3 receptor antagonists but not by noradrenergic receptor antagonists (45). Self-administration of cocaine is reduced or eliminated following lesions of the dopaminergic innervation of the nucleus accumbens or lesions of nucleus accumbens cell bodies. In contrast, lesions of noradrenergic or dopaminergic terminals in the striatum or prefrontal cortex are without effect. Finally, evidence suggests that the DA receptors of the nucleus accumbens may function as part of a neuronal mechanism responsible for endogenous reward, which reinforces behaviors leading to natural stimuli such as food and water. Thus, operant conditioning experiments with animals indicate that the rewarding properties of food, water, or intracranial brain stimulation may depend on the nucleus accumbens DA receptor activation. Therefore, the rewarding properties of drugs that lead to excessive self-administration may result from the ability of one or a combination of compounds to activate this neural substrate for endogenous reward (43, 44).

Recent data suggest that cocaine has many but not all of the same effects on DA systems as primary reinforcers. In a recent study, monkeys were trained to work to obtain intravenous cocaine and juice rewards. During these rewards the investigators recorded 62 neurons with both cocaine and juice rewards producing characteristic changes. However, the neuronal release produced by rewards were independent: a response to one did not predict the other. The neural basis for rewards for cocaine do not appear to be the same as for juice. Signals generated for juice and cocaine reward are at least partially separable at the neuronal levels within the ventral striatum and cocaine does not act on the reward system in the same ways as a natural reward or reinforcer (46).

The DA depletion hypothesis suggests that repetitive stimulation by cocaine and the subsequent chronic blockade of reuptake lead to a depletion of presynaptic DA stores. Because reuptake of DA is the principal source of DA for future release, a chronic blockade understandably would result in a relative decrease in DA transmission. A neuroadaptive mechanism of a nerve ending to the severing of its stimulation is an up-regulation or enhanced sensitivity of the postsynaptic sites, hence, receptor supersensitivity (47).

The D2 receptor is an autoreceptor whose agonist action is to decrease the release of DA, and supersensitivity of this receptor would lead to decreased DA release, as suggested by animal studies. Other possible mecha-

Table 15.1 Diagnostic Criteria for Cocaine Intoxication (DSM-IV)

Cocaine intoxication usually begins with a "high" feeling and includes one or more of the following:
- euphoria with enhanced vigor
- gregariousness
- hyperactivity
- interpersonal sensitivity
- affective blunting with fatigue or sadness and social withdrawal
- talkativeness
- anxiety
- tension
- alertness
- grandiosity
- sterotyped and repetitive behavior
- anger
- impaired judgment

Reproduced with permission from Diagnostic and statistical manual of mental disorders. 4th edition. Washington, DC: American Psychiatric Association, 1994:223–224.

nisms for decreased DA function are neurotoxic degeneration of dopaminergic neurons, D1-receptor-mediated feedback innervation to the cell bodies of mesolimbic DA neurons, and multiple feedback loops involving serotonergic, noradrenergic, enkephalinergic, and GABAergic synapses. Relapse appears to be related to the DA system as well. The priming effects of cues in cocaine-seeking behavior can be mimicked by activation of the mesolimbic DA system. DA acts at two general classes of DA receptors termed D1 like and D2 like distinguished by structure, opposite modulation of adenylate cyclase, and differential localization. Priming ability of the D1 like and D2 like selective agonists was assessed by their ability to reinstate nonreinforced lever-pressing (48). Priming effect was selectively induced by D2 like and not D1 like DA receptor agonists. Moreover the D1 like agonists prevented cocaine-seeking behavior induced by cocaine itself whereas D2 like agonists enhanced this behavior. These recent data suggest that D1 like agonists may be useful pharmacotherapies for cocaine addiction.

These neurophysiological changes have been understandably difficult to measure, and those studies in animals have not always closely followed the long-term patterns of use that are frequently observed in cocaine addicts. However, in some studies of humans, decreased DA transmission has been documented. Both homovanillic acid, the principal metabolite of DA in humans, and prolactin, the hormone whose release is inhibited by DA, have been found in decreased amounts in humans who consumed cocaine addictively. Moreover, other studies have shown that transiently increased dopaminergic transmission is associated with recurrent desire to use cocaine.

The cocaine-DA hypothesis is supported by the following studies:

- Selective 6-hydroxydopamine lesions of DA terminals in the nucleus accumbens but not caudate nucleus abolish cocaine self-administration (49).
- Intra-accumbens administration of selective D1 and D2 antagonist drugs attenuate cocaine reinforcement in a dose-dependent manner (50).
- Using in vivo microdialysis, it has been demonstrated that a single injection of cocaine increases the concentration of extracellular DA in the nucleus accumbens with a maximal effect reached at peak reported cocaine euphoria in humans, approximately 30–40 minutes postexposure (51). Other changes in dopaminergic neurotransmission may appear only after cocaine administration has been terminated, including persistently reduced DA metabolism and decreased DA synthesis. Postmortem binding to DA transporters in striatum is also reduced in humans with a history of cocaine abuse (52–54).
- Repeated IV administration of cocaine followed by its withdrawal persistently reduces the number of DA transporters in the nucleus accumbens, but not in the striatum (55, 56).
- Adaptive regulation of DA transporter function appears to be more pronounced in the nucleus accumbens than striatum in chronic administration studies (57).
- Both decreased synthesis and concentrations of DA have been reported for cocaine in the nucleus accumbens and frontal cortex following chronic administration with long-lasting decreases in extracellular DA in the nucleus accumbens after just 10 days of cocaine administration. The decreased density of D1 receptor binding sites in various areas of the brain have been reported to persist for at least 2 weeks after cocaine use (58).
- Weiss et al. (59) findings of a significant decrease in basal DA release as early as 2–4 hours after discontinuation of a self-administration demonstrated in 1992 that the onset of the synaptic DA deficiency is greatly accelerated by sustained cocaine self-administration. These data support the Dackis and Gold 1985 hypothesis that cocaine craving and withdrawing are due to deficiency of mesolimbic DA which could involve a depletion of intraneuronal DA pools or autoregulation of DA neurons as suggested by intermittent cocaine modifications administration studies (60, 61).
- Bromocriptine is somewhat efficacious in acute cocaine withdrawal. Bromocriptine is a DA agonist that is widely used without abuse in the treatment of infertility, amenorrhea-galactorrhea, and Parkinson's disease. It has also shown promise in reducing acute cocaine craving and withdrawal dysphoria (61–68).
- Prolactin is increased in chronic users (69–73).

- Some corresponding neurochemical data have been obtained from humans by brain imaging. Humans withdrawn from cocaine 10 days show decreased cerebral blood flow and changes in brain glucose metabolism in the frontal cortex and were accompanied by significant decreases in DA D2 receptors in basal ganglia. The combined findings led these researchers to propose that a long-lasting deficit in dopaminergic neuronal function may occur in this group of patients (74–76).
- PET studies in humans and non-human primates demonstrate cocaine binding to DA transporters in vivo at pharmacological and subpharmacological levels (73–75).
- Mice lacking the DA transporter (77) lends evidence to the critical role of DA, specifically the DA's reuptake transporter in the reinforcing and biochemical actions of cocaine. The transporter controls the levels of DA in the synapse by feedback after cocaine binding blocks reuptake. DA remains at very high concentrations in the synapse during cocaine intoxication. Giros and coworkers (77) studied a mouse strain in which the gene encoding the DA transporter was disabled by a knockout. Without functioning DA transporters these mice do not respond to cocaine. Cocaine produced no changes in DA or behavior demonstrating that the DA transporter is absolutely necessary for cocaine to produce its psychostimulant effects.

Toxicity

While there are general ranges for doses and blood levels that produce toxicity, considerable individual variation in response exists so that caution is urged in interpreting predicted conditions of use for the development of toxicity. The majority of the organ-specific toxicities are referable to the CNS and cardiovascular system; however, other organ systems may be involved.

Cocaine also lowers the seizure threshold, and seizures are the most common serious neurological complication, followed by stroke from cerebral hemorrhage or infarction, ischemia of the spinal cord, hyperpyrexia, and coma from respiratory depression. Other less common and severe symptoms are dizziness, headache, paresthesias, tremor, and syncope. Cardiovascular toxicity includes cocaine-induced cardiac cell death, reduced oxygenation, myocarditis, high-output cardiac failure, dilated cardiomyopathy, aortic dissection, rhabdomyolysis with acute renal and hepatic failure, and disseminated intravascular coagulopathy. Cocaine has been shown to increase plasminogen activator inhibitor activity resulting in antifibrinolytic activity and increased likelihood of producing ischemia (78). Other less severe acute cocaine-related symptoms are chest pain, shortness of breath, palpitations, and diaphoresis. Gastrointestinal complaints include nausea, abdominal pain, and vomiting. Relatively common head and throat complaints, especially from smoking, are throat tightness and cough with production of black sputum. Nasal congestion and frank necrosis of the nasal septum commonly occur following intranasal use of cocaine. More general constitutional symptoms and signs are weakness, chills, myalgias, fever, back pain, fatigue, and insomnia. Cocaine has been implicated in ischemia and infarction of many organs, especially the heart and brain, although ischemic small bowel, kidneys, spleen, and legs have been reported. Vasospasm, platelet activation, and accelerated atherosclerosis have been suggested as causing the increased incidence of cocaine-induced ischemia (79).

Cocaine use is associated with poor concentration and judgment, making accidents and injuries more common. Recent data indicate that cocaine-related injuries are an important cause of death among young adults (80).

ACUTE INTOXICATION

Psychological Effects

As a CNS stimulant, cocaine has many psychological effects that are predictable and similar to those of other stimulants such as amphetamines and caffeine. As with toxicity, psychological variations exist and are dependent on the user, environment, dose, and route of administration. Nonetheless, the intensity and duration of the acute manifestations correlate with the rate of rise and height of the peak blood level and are subsequently reflected in brain

Table 15.2 Signs and Symptoms of Cocaine Use

Cocaine behavioral and psychological changes are accompanied by two or more of these signs and symptoms that develop during or shortly after cocaine use:

- tachycardia or bradycardia
- pupillary dilation
- elevated or lowered blood pressure
- perspiration or chills
- nausea or vomiting
- evidence of weight loss
- psychomotor agitation or retardation
- muscular weakness
- respiratory depression
- chest pain
- cardiac arrhythmia
- confusion
- seizures
- dyskinesias
- dystonias
- coma

Reproduced with permission from Diagnostic and statistical manual of mental disorders. 4th edition. Washington, DC: American Psychiatric Association, 1994:223–224.

concentrations. Crack smoking produces a faster rise and higher blood levels result in the earlier-onset and most prominent clinical psychological signs and symptoms. As discussed, the dose and route of administration determine these pharmacokinetic parameters for cocaine absorption and distribution in the body.

The acute psychological effects begin when cocaine reaches the brain, which occurs within seconds by any route of administration. The major psychological functions affected by cocaine are mood, cognition, drive states such as hunger, sex, and thirst, and consciousness (Table 15.2). An immediate and intense euphoria, analogous to a sexual orgasm, occurs and may last seconds or minutes, depending on the dose, route of administration, and tolerance of the user. Other alterations arising from elevation in mood include giddiness, enhanced self-confidence, and a forceful boisterousness. The subsequent level of mood is milder euphoria mixed with anxiety, which can last for minutes, followed by a more protracted anxious state that persists for hours. During intoxication, a state virtually indistinguishable from hypomania or frank mania is typical. Thoughts race and the user speaks in a rapid, often pressured manner. The user is garrulous and grandiose with tangential and incoherent speech. Appetite is suppressed during the period of intoxication usually followed by a rebound increased appetite as the cocaine is eliminated. In low doses, the libido is stimulated and sexual performance in men is reported to be enhanced by a prolonged erection and a heightened orgasm. In high doses, spontaneous ejaculation and orgasm can occur. The level of sensory awareness is altered and hypervigilance is typical. The user may develop ideas of reference and other mental alterations. Insomnia is common. With increasing doses, acts and decisions of poor judgment and indiscretions are more common. Motor activity is increased, as are driven atypical behaviors. Cocaine restlessness and fidgety behavior are accompanied by a driven state of perpetual motion.

Physiological Effects

The acute physiological effects result from sympathetic nervous discharge after cocaine releases norepinephrine, epinephrine, and DA. Activation of the cardiovascular system results in tachycardia, hypertension, and diaphoresis. CNS stimulation lowers seizure threshold and causes other changes such as tremor, arousal electrographic changes, emesis, and hyperpyrexia. Peripheral nervous system stimulation results in urinary and bowel delay and retention, muscular contractions, and cutaneous flushing.

Again, the magnitude and direction of the cocaine-induced behavioral and physiological changes depend on many variables such as the dose used and individual characteristics of the person using the cocaine. Cocaine intoxication effects such as euphoria, increased pulse and blood pressure, and psychomotor activity are expected. Depressant effects such as sadness, bradycardia, decreased blood pressure, and decreased psychomotor activity are less common in naive users, but can be seen in chronic high-dose users.

Acute intoxication is accompanied by tachycardia, bradycardia, pupil-

lary dilation, elevated or lowered blood pressure, perspiration or chills, nausea or vomiting, confusion, seizures, dyskinesias, dystonias, or coma, evidence of weight loss, psychomotor agitation or retardation, muscular weakness, respiratory depression, chest pain, or cardiac arrhythmia (81).

CHRONIC INTOXICATION

Psychological Effects

Chronic, persistent, and regular use of cocaine by any route of administration has characteristic consequences that are commonly identified by the clinician who is informed about and alert to them. Chronic administration of cocaine produces and can easily be confused with virtually all of the psychiatric syndromes and disorders (i.e., mania, depression, eating disorders, schizophrenic syndromes, and personality disturbances). When cocaine is included in the differential diagnosis, urine testing is necessary. Tolerance and dependence do develop immediately to cocaine use and have been demonstrated at wide ranges of doses, particularly at higher doses, and withdrawal from chronic cocaine use also has a predictable and stereotypical, protracted psychological and physiologic course in some addicts.

The development of tolerance is reflected by the waning of some of the acute effects of intoxication, which become less intense and shorter in duration with continued and chronic use and are only partly overcome by escalation of the dose. The euphoria lessens with the onset of tolerance, and an extremely interesting phenomenon is that most cocaine addicts recall that their very early trials of cocaine yielded the greatest and most satisfying euphoria, even more than that experienced during a cocaine "run" or "binge" or following reinstitution of use after a period of prolonged abstinence. Most cocaine addicts will reliably choose cocaine over other drugs even if they say that they are not getting the quality of the high and work to acquire and use it suggesting that sensitization has occurred and also that some aspects of cocaine reward are not consciously appreciated. While not as dramatic as reported for MDMA or Ecstasy, subsequent use of cocaine may produce less and less euphoria. Episodes of cocaine-induced euphoria typically are not as long, despite larger doses taken more frequently in shorter intervals. The euphoria diminishes increasingly with further cocaine use over months and years, despite increasingly higher doses—up to several grams of cocaine a day. The cocaine addict in a sense continues to chase the original "high" with lesser results.

Adverse psychological effects commonly follow chronic cocaine use including anxiety and a depression with panic and hopelessness. Many of these effects may be as a result of cocaine-induced changes in the brain, which are quite persistent. Cocaine increases the coagulability of platelets, increases the intracerebral blood pressure and produces ischemic cerebrovascular insults, which have become evident on scanning and in the course of detailed neuropsychological testing of addicts. Chronic cocaine abuse is associated with a number of very important long-lasting changes in the CNS. Neuropathological changes include cerebrovascular events, lacunar events, DA transporter deficits, EEG abnormalities, vasculitis, seizures, and decrements in neurobehavioral performance (87). In some cases, cocaine addiction induces a neuropsychiatric disease more like Parkinson's disease with cell loss and functional decrements related to the drug self-administration.

The sensation of being out of control accompanied by intense apprehension of impending doom is a regular occurrence with addictive cocaine use and is indistinguishable from panic disorder. The subjective feelings of helplessness and hopelessness lead to eventual suicidal thinking and behavior in many cocaine addicts. The paranoid delusions are common and quite distressing to the addict, who mistakenly believes that others are "spying on him" or "out to get her" and who already may be suspicious because of the illicit nature of cocaine use and the sometimes devious means required to obtain it (88).

Adverse Physiological Effects

Insomnia, anorexia, and increased motor activity conflicts with simultaneous feelings of hunger and fatigue. The chronic user is physically and mentally exhausted from the effects of the cocaine but "needs" cocaine to function at all.

Cocaine use has been found to cause a number of serious cardiac conditions, including arrhythmia, coronary atherosclerosis, cardiomyopathy, and congestive heart failure. Cocaine users frequently report an elevated or irregular heart rate, conditions that can result in fibrillation. Cocaine has also been reported to cause cardiac spasms that can lead to myocardial infarction in otherwise healthy individuals.

In addition, cocaine use may also cause silent myocardial ischemia. Death of heart muscle fibers can result when cocaine simultaneously increases cardiac oxygen demand while the vasoconstricting effects of cocaine decrease blood flow to the heart.

Patients with premature coronary artery disease may find that cocaine use hastens coronary atherosclerosis. The risk of myocardial infarction may be further increased, as cocaine use has been associated with blood clot formation.

Cocaine use also elevates blood pressure, sometimes to the point at which spontaneous bleeding and stroke occur. The elevated blood pressure also places an additional strain upon the heart and further increases the risk of myocardial infarction.

The libido is depressed and sexual performance is impaired, with consequent impotency in males and anorgasmy in females during chronic cocaine use. Men may have difficulty in achieving and maintaining erections and initiating ejaculation, whereas females may be sexually unresponsive and anorgasmic following prolonged bouts of cocaine intake. Muscular twitches, tremors, and generalized weakness are common, especially with high-dose inhalation as in freebasing. Weight loss (sometimes extreme), malnutrition, and poor hygiene and self-care can result from heavy, prolonged cocaine use.

Cocaine was at one time thought to be a short-acting drug, but the effects on the brain appear persistent and difficult to reverse. Volkow (89) reported on her work with positron emission tomography (PET).

The main finding was the first documentation of disruption in cerebral blood flow in the cocaine abusers. Since then several investigators have replicated these findings clearly corroborating her earlier studies showing areas of very low blood flow in the brains of cocaine abusers. As a result of these studies it has become clear that the use of cocaine places the individual at risk for cerebrovascular accident both from strokes as well as hemorrhages. Cocaine is a vasoconstrictor and if the vasoconstriction is severe and prolonged, it can lead to ischemia and necrosis with a consequent disruption in brain function. Its consequences will necessarily depend on the location and extent of the vascular insult. Thus pathology can range from mild facial paralysis to hemiplegia.

Another important finding from Volkow's PET studies in cocaine abusers is the documentation of a significant decrease in DA D2 receptors that persist even after protracted withdrawal. The reduction in D2 receptors is associated with functional changes in the brain that involve among others the orbitofrontal cortex and the cingulate gyrus. Because the orbitofrontal cortex is important in the regulation of repetitive behavior and its function is also disrupted in patients with compulsive behaviors Volkow has postulated that it could also underlie the compulsive patterns for drug self-administration in cocaine abusers.

NEUROBIOLOGY

Neurotransmitter Systems

The brain mechanisms of addiction evolved long before the clinical phenomenon of addiction was first recorded, in Biblical scripture. The neurological substrate for addiction is located in the limbic system, the phylogenetically old portion of the brain that contains prehistoric and primitive instincts for survival. This system apparently was unprepared for the intensity and duration of stimulation produced by cocaine leading to the misinterpretation that something of major organismic significance has occurred after cocaine use. Within the limbic system is housed the biologically primitive circuitry for the drive states such as hunger, sex, and thirst as well as mood and memory. The limbic system is composed of various centrally located structures loosely organized but richly interconnected by neuronal pathways that use certain neurotransmitters at the synapses.

DOPAMINE AND THE MESOLIMBIC SYSTEM

The DA-containing neurons have cell bodies that are part of the ventral tegmentum and whose fibers project to "reward cells" located in the hippocampus as well as send fibers to the nucleus accumbens to form the mesolimbic pathway. It has been clear for some time that the reinforcing effects of amphetamines and cocaine result from their ability to elevate synaptic concentrations of DA. The reduction in gene expression appears to be related to the reduction in transporter sites because both occur in the same anatomical pathway. This suggests that the regulation of uptake in the mesolimbic neuron is separate or different from that in nigrostriatal neurons. The reduction in transporters is specific to the mesolimbic DA neurons, which are intimately involved with the reinforcing properties of psychostimulants. This association strongly supports a role for these neurons in the acquisition and/or maintenance of cocaine-seeking behavior (82, 83). The abrupt withdrawal of cocaine from rats that have self-administered it for long periods increases the threshold for intracranial self-stimulation 5 days after their last exposure to cocaine. These investigators suggest that the elevation of this threshold may represent a measure of the animal's hedonic state, as the magnitude and duration of the increase in threshold was proportional to the amount of cocaine previously self-administered by the rat. These changes suggest that withdrawal of cocaine alters many functional constituents of the mesolimbic DA neuron. The reduction in DA transporters in rats withdrawn from cocaine depends on the history of use, the dose of cocaine, and the pattern of drug administration. Although the significance of a loss of DA transporters in the nucleus accumbens is unknown, such a reduction may affect CNS function, which may be manifested as a behavioral change. Pharmacological blockade and neurotoxin lesions of noradrenergic and serotonergic systems spare the compulsive self-stimulation of the stimulants, but pharmacological blockade or lesions of the mesolimbic DA system attenuate or eliminate these effects. In fact, rewarding actions of amphetamine can be produced by microinjections directly into the nucleus accumbens, the terminus for the presynaptic DA neurons.

SEROTONIN AND THE DORSAL RAPHE NUCLEI

The raphe nuclei of the dorsal pons contain serotonin cell bodies that project fibers to the various aspects of the forebrain, importantly, to areas responsible for mood and arousal. Serotonin input to the met-enkephalin system that synapses on DA neurons in the ventral tegmentum modulates the "reward" center. As previously mentioned, an interaction via opiate transmission may be important in addictive behavior. Opiate interactions appear important for "classical opiates" widely used in medicine for analgesia (84).

Typically the effects of the opiate analgesics are morphine-like and attributed to the stimulation of mu opioid receptors. Meperidine intoxication itself shares certain features with cocaine intoxication. Differences between the pharmacology of meperidine and other mu opioid agonists have been suspected and documented. Chronic exposure to meperidine produces stimulant effects, including tremor and convulsions, hyperreflexia and increased startle. These effects do not occur with morphine. Haloperidol is a meperidine with some analgesic activity of its own in addition to DA antagonism. Many of the effects of meperidine are not reversible by opiate antagonists. High doses of meperidine and morphine produces seizures antagonized by naloxone but meperidine reversal is minimal. Some studies had suggested that the non-opioid effects of meperidine might be due to inhibition of serotonin uptake but now research has demonstrated that it is due to cocaine-like effects of meperidine at the DA transporter (85).

NOREPINEPHRINE AND THE LOCUS COERULEUS

Noradrenergic cell bodies are located in the pons near the fourth ventricle and project to various aspects of the limbic system and cerebral cortex. While these neurons have been implicated in withdrawal from various drugs, including opiates and alcohol, and are stimulated during cocaine intoxication, they have been shown to play only a permissive role in addictive behaviors (86).

TOLERANCE AND DEPENDENCE

Tolerance and dependence are best viewed as neuroadaptations to the presence of a foreign drug and are related on a continuum of neurochemical changes and clinical expression. Tolerance and dependence are not specific for addiction, occur in the absence of addiction, and develop in response to a wide variety of addictive and nonaddictive drugs. The overemphasis on the inclusion of tolerance and dependence for diagnosis has led to confusion, misdiagnosis, and underdiagnosis (90).

In brief, tolerance is the adaptation of the brain to the effects of the drug and dependence is the de-adaptation to the absence of the drug. In the case of cocaine, tolerance develops to some of its central effects. As described, tolerance to the euphoria develops quickly and has been measured within an hour after a single intravenous dose so that the dose must be escalated or the route *and* dose changed in order to experience desired effects of equal intensity. Some small degree of tolerance to effects on heart rate and blood pressure develops during the infusion of cocaine over the course of 4 hours; however, it is unlikely that significant tolerance to its cardiovascular actions is usually achieved. Also, in controlled studies performed in the laboratory, cocaine addicts did not achieve tolerance to the paranoia induced by cocaine. In large surveys of 452 cocaine addicts, it was reported that the paranoia and suspiciousness actually worsened with increasing use of cocaine over time and in larger doses (91). What is clear although not well documented in studies is that cocaine addicts typically increase the dose of cocaine both throughout the natural history of their addiction over months and years and during a cocaine binge over days. It is not unusual to find in clinical practice cocaine addicts who have reached intranasal doses of 1–3 grams per day or more, and many state that they would use more if their supply did not become exhausted. Tolerance does not seem to drive the use of cocaine. The adverse effects of anxiety, depression, financial expense, suicidal thinking, disrupted lives, and others increase as the euphoria decreases, so that tolerance would seem to be a rate-limiting factor at best.

WITHDRAWAL

Until the mid 1980s organized psychiatry discounted the possibility that cocaine use was associated with an abstinence syndrome of any consequence (92–95). Such mythology only added to the widespread notion that cocaine was safe and non-addicting. Organized psychiatry was not immune to the cocaine misinformation as current practice considered drugs most addicting on the basis of the withdrawal syndrome produced upon discontinuation. Observations in humans (96) and, more recently, animal studies (97, 98) support the concept of a sometimes subtle but important cocaine abstinence state (99, 100). Even the current DSM-IV recognizes the existence and importance of cocaine withdrawal:

> The essential feature of cocaine withdrawal is the presence of a characteristic withdrawal syndrome that develops within a few hours to several days after the cessation of (or reduction in) cocaine use that has been heavy and prolonged. The withdrawal syndrome is characterized by the development of dysphoric mood accompanied by two or more of the following physiological changes: fatigue, vivid and unpleasant dreams, insomnia or hypersomnia, increased appetite, and psychomotor retardation or agitation. Anhedonia and drug craving can often be present but are not part of the diagnostic criteria. These symptoms cause clinically significant distress or impairment in social, occupational, or other important areas of functioning (100a, p. 225).

A definite, stereotypical withdrawal syndrome is observed in some users following either long-term use or even a binge of a few days. On abrupt cessation, withdrawal can be accompanied by depression, anxiety, and craving for the drug that is soon followed by general fatigue and a need for sleep ("crash"). Upon initial awakening, hyperphagia, continued sleepiness, depression, and anhedonia ensue. Mood returns to normal over a period of days, although in some cases dysphoria and anhedonia may persist for weeks. Craving for the drug may wax and wane over weeks in response to emotions and cocaine-related stimuli. Although these signs and symptoms meet the requirement for withdrawal and are similar to those of the withdrawal from other drugs, there are no consistent measurable or observable

physiological disruptions that require gradual withdrawal of the drug or pharmacological intervention.

The occurrence of a withdrawal dysphoria with neurovegetative symptoms that occurs within hours after a binge is now generally accepted by cocaine users and psychiatrists as "the crash" (101, 102). In human beings, the acute abstinence state is of variable intensity and symptomatology (103) but includes irritability, anxiety, and depression, which can, and often is, self-medicated with cocaine. Acute withdrawal symptoms ("a crash") are often seen after periods of repetitive high-dose use ("runs" or "binges"). These periods are characterized by intense and unpleasant feelings of lassitude and depression, generally requiring several days of rest and recuperation. Depressive symptoms with suicidal ideation or behavior can occur and are generally the most serious problems seen during "crashing" or other forms of cocaine withdrawal. A substantial number of individuals with cocaine dependence have few or no clinically evident withdrawal symptoms on cessation of use.

However, a more complicated three-phase abstinence symptomatology has been proposed to characterize cocaine withdrawal (101). The phases represent progression of signs and symptoms of withdrawal subsequent to cocaine cessation. The three phases are crash, withdrawal, and extinction. According to this model, the crash is exhaustion lasting from hours to 4 days, associated with intense depression, agitation, anxiety, hypersomnolence, hyperphagia, and craving for cocaine. The withdrawal phase ranges from 1 to 10 weeks, with an absence of craving in the early weeks and a reemergence of craving in the middle weeks. Toward the end of withdrawal the symptoms of anhedonia, anergia, anxiety, and high cocaine craving appear gradually. Extinction lasts indefinitely and consists of normal mood and recurrent craving for cocaine, either spontaneously or in response to cues.

Other studies have not supported the three-phase abstinence syndrome for cocaine. Two major studies (103, 104) have differed in that craving was greatest in the 24 hours before admission (day 1) and was associated with intense depression. No definite crash was observed, and mood states, craving, and sleep disturbances gradually yet perceptibly improved during the initial 4 weeks. In these studies the withdrawal was most severe in the initial days and gradually subsided over the ensuing weeks before discharge without pharmacological intervention. In general, cocaine withdrawal is neither acutely life threatening nor problematic in a secure, locked environment but is easily provoked by a host of conditioned cues (104).

COCAINE AND CONDITIONING

Cocaine users describe intense craving for cocaine when cocaine is made available to them or merely when the word cocaine is uttered in conversation. Handling paper money or seeing a bill rolled may produce intense craving. Seeing places or people where cocaine was used, smelling cocaine, seeing a cocaine pipe, seeing a friend who they used cocaine with, hearing a song that they used cocaine to, and numerous other casual smells, sights, and sounds can trigger an intense reaction in the user or the person who has used in the past but is now abstinent (105). Users report tasting cocaine, craving cocaine, sweating and experiencing shortness of breath, feeling faint, smelling cocaine, and feeling a little of the cocaine euphoria. All of these experiences contribute to cocaine taking and the persistence of cocaine dependence. In humans even the presentation of cocaine paraphernalia after weeks or months of abstinence produces intense cravings and withdrawal-like symptoms (106, 107). In experimental studies in humans, individuals with a history of cocaine use show greater physiological reactivity in response to cocaine cues than do cocaine-naive individuals. The greater responses were also demonstrated to cocaine stimuli rather than powerful opiate cues. Cocaine-related stimuli elicit conditioned physiological and subjective states in cocaine users (108).

COMPARISON BETWEEN AMPHETAMINE AND COCAINE

Amphetamine, cocaine, and methylphenidate have quite similar pharmacological and clinical characteristics and are almost identical in their sympathetic properties. They differ mainly in onset of action and half-life. Amphetamine and cocaine are potent CNS stimulants that have almost equal reinforcing properties in self-administration studies in animals and humans. In rankings of toxicity from self-administration, both cocaine and amphetamines are more reinforcing than opiates, barbiturates, benzodiazepines, and alcohol. The patterns of addictive use for amphetamines and cocaine in humans are similar, and both drugs typically are taken in binges until either the supply of the drug or the user is exhausted. However, daily or weekly repetitive use of the drug consistently over months and weeks is also common. Amphetamines are often taken orally, but intravenous use is also not uncommon among established addicts. With either route, the addiction is identifiable and not fixed in outward appearances. What is clear about the addictive pattern is that no one route of administration, sequence, or interval is the rule for either drug, and a variety of patterns that depend on the user, supply, and purity of the drug is possible (109).

The effects of the drugs are so similar that cocaine users describe the euphoric effects of cocaine in terms that are almost indistinguishable from those used by amphetamine users. In laboratory studies, subjects familiar with cocaine cannot distinguish between the subjective effects of 16 mg of cocaine and a dose of 10 mg of dextroamphetamine when both are given intravenously. However, the duration of cocaine's effects are shorter than that of amphetamines, with a half-life of 1 hour for cocaine and 10 hours for amphetamines. As a result, addictive or repeated use may be more common with cocaine and the withdrawal syndrome may be more protracted with amphetamines. Otherwise, the toxicities from cocaine are clinically indistinguishable from those produced by amphetamines.

Clinically, while amphetamine use and addiction remain, their prevalence has not returned to that of the 1960s, when both "street addicts" and "housewives" typified the greatest consumer of the drug. The largest sources of amphetamines remain physicians' illicit methamphetamine laboratories and pharmaceutical manufacturers who illegally produce and distribute them, whereas cocaine is imported chiefly from South America, albeit illegally. It also is not clear whether a diminished supply of cocaine would correspondingly increase the rate of amphetamine addiction (110). In the case of psychostimulants, rats will self-administer amphetamine and DA directly into the nucleus accumbens. Although cocaine is not self-administered into the nucleus accumbens, bilateral injections of DA receptor antagonists into the nucleus accumbens or lesions of the mesoaccumbens DA system attenuate the reinforcing effects of intravenously self-administered cocaine. These studies provide strong evidence that DA receptors in the nucleus accumbens mediate the reinforcing effects of psychostimulants. A large body of evidence suggests that the reinforcing effects of drugs as diverse as psychostimulants and opiates are mediated by a common neurobiological substrate. In particular, psychostimulants and opiates are thought to produce reinforcement by direct or indirect actions on the dopaminergic neurons in the ventral tegmental area or on their target neurons in the nucleus accumbens.

NEUROTOXICITY

One new area of investigations is the role of persistent deficits produced by drug-related effects. The optimistic assertions that illicit drug use could be discontinued and the user would be able to return to normal is at odds with developmental theories that would assert that drug intoxication and addiction might interfere with normal development and further that drugs taken for their specific effects and target in the brain appear equally proficient at inducing changes in heart, brain, and other vital organs. Cocaine use is associated with increases in blood pressure that are much greater in small vessels in brain and increase the oxygen demands on the heart but decrease the available blood. Ischemic cerebrovascular accidents occur commonly in cocaine users and their significance extends beyond the PET scan deficits reported for addicts to persistent neuropsychological deficits. Abstinence may simply allow certain addicts to recognize that they cannot function at their premorbid level or that they cannot hit a curve ball as they did before cocaine. Volkow has reported that cocaine causes a decrease in the number of D2 receptors with corresponding decreases in brain metabolism especially in the frontal cortex (111). These drug-induced changes apparently persist for many months or even years after abstinence. Such changes could underlie craving or the perception

that the addict would be better, would feel and think better, if they only had their drug to use. The more cocaine use the more DA is released and available to act at DA receptors but the greater the need for animals to electrically self-stimulate pleasure systems when cocaine is no longer available. Similar findings suggesting acute and persisting anhedonia on withdrawal have been reported by Weiss for cocaine, alcohol, nicotine, and opiates (112). Once changes occur in neurotrophin, neurofilaments, glutamate receptors, and glial filaments use become addiction as brains are changed and trained. Exposure to conditioned cues, stress, D2 agonists, and so on all make use more likely and driven. Cocaine-related ischemic strokes and gross anatomical changes and also more subtle ventral tegmental, nucleus accumbens cell, and nuclear program changes produce neurotoxic consequences, which may suggest that any short-term treatment approach is questionable with long-term abstinence assumed to be necessary for full return to premorbid functioning. While there are multiple DA receptors on the postsynaptic membrane that respond differently to different compounds and certainly serve different biological functions, Self and coworkers (113) have suggested that new pharmacotherapies target the D1 receptor system. D1 receptor agonists may diminish episodes of intense cocaine craving and reduce relapse in addicts who have stopped using the drug. D2 agonists, stress, and conditioned cues might increase cocaine seeking and drive to use.

Adaptive changes are referred to as tolerance or a reduction in the drug's effects after repeat administration or the need to increase the dose to maintain the same effect. Addiction is a drug-induced brain change, which presumably can be studied in animals to generate neural change models and once these changes are understood, new treatments can be tried in these animal models. Investigators look for the changes cocaine produces in the brain that cause addiction and possibly specific interactions between genetic and environmental factors that make certain animals or people more likely to become addicts.

COCAINE ADDICTION AS A DRIVE STATE

It has been suggested that humans and lower animals have an aberrant or "fourth" drive for drugs. It appears that the brain mechanisms for feeding account for self-intoxication, at least in lower animals. Studies of the neurobiology of the DA system confirm that the brain circuits that play a role in food-rewarded behavior are the brain circuits that play a role in drug-rewarded behavior. DA antagonists block the rewarding effects of food and water just as they block the self-administration of stimulants such as cocaine.

Recent studies using in vivo voltametry and microdialysis make it possible to monitor the synaptic levels of brain DA in the nucleus accumbens of freely moving animals. The studies suggest that drugs of addiction have much more powerful effects on the mesolimbic DA system than do most natural rewards. Only very palatable foods and highly potent sex-related stimuli seem capable of activating the mesolimbic system with anywhere near the potency of ventral tegmentum–injected morphine or nucleus accumbens–injected amphetamine (114).

Dissociations of Addiction and Pharmacological Dependence

Opiates have two clearly established sites of reinforcing self-administration of drugs, namely, the ventral tegmental area of the dopaminergic cells and the nucleus accumbens, to which these cell project to form the mesolimbic pathway. The ventral tegmental cells contain opiate receptors, and the main output of the nucleus accumbens uses gamma-aminobutyric acid (GABA) as a neurotransmitter. These GABA neurons project to the pedunculopontine nucleus, which may be a final common pathway for addictive behavior, since lesions of this nucleus block the self-administration of both amphetamine and morphine (115).

Important neurochemical evidence for the dissociation of addiction from pharmacological tolerance is obtained by the finding that classic opiate withdrawal signs do not occur in animals whose stimulation of the ventral tegmentum is terminated, whereas if the same morphine injections are given a few millimeters distant in the periaqueductal gray matter, the animals do

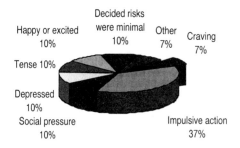

Figure 15.3. Cocaine addicts' reasons for relapse. Automatic or impulsive action is the principal reason given by addicts for their relapse. (Reproduced with permission from Miller NS, Gold MS. Dissociation of "conscious desire" (craving) from and relapse in alcohol and cocaine dependence. Ann Clin Psychiatry 1994;6(2):99–106.)

develop physical dependence and hence do express withdrawal signs when the opiate injections are terminated or blocked. Other animal experiments support the finding that addictive behavior can be demonstrated with the very first injection of morphine (116, 117).

This dissociation of addiction sites from pharmacological to dependence sites can also be inferred from the relapse of an addict to a drug long after pharmacological withdrawal has been completed. Relapse (118) to cocaine despite well-known and previously experienced adverse side effects cannot be explained by withdrawal (Fig. 15.3). Moreover, the term *reward behavior* for addictive use of a drug is ill conceived, since the addict relapses and continues to use drugs after suffering a sometimes excruciating withdrawal. The negative, unpleasant, and unrewarding effects of the drug begin to far outweigh the pleasure derived, yet the addict continues to pursue the drug.

Common Biological Mechanisms with Other Drugs and Alcohol

Alcohol, through a cascade of reactions, activates the norepinephrine fibers of the mesolimbic circuitry. More directly, alcohol, through the formation of condensation products such as tetrahydroisoquinolines (TIQs), interacts at opiate receptors. In noncovalent reactions, acetaldehyde reacts with DA to form salsolinol and DA reacts with its aldehyde product to form tetrahydropapaveroline (THP), both of which have been shown to act at opiate receptors (119, 120).

Support for the final common pathway for these drugs is provided by the finding that kainic acid lesions of the nucleus accumbens and 6-hydroxydopamine lesions of the mesolimbic DA system disrupt heroin, cocaine, and alcohol self-administration. Moreover, blockade of DA receptors prevents the reinforcing properties of opiates and cocaine, whereas blockade of norepinephrine sites similarly blocks the threshold-lowering effect of cocaine, reduces heroin reward, and attenuates self-administration of ethanol in animals. Additionally, opiate antagonists prevent postshock increase of ethanol consumption in rodents. In humans, naltrexone significantly reduced the relapse rate over a 95-day post-detoxification period in recovering alcoholics.

Naloxone and/or naltrexone attenuation of many drugs of abuse in self-administration and human paradigms is consistent with the modulatory role of opioids. Recently, naltrexone has been directly demonstrated to reverse ethanol-induced increases in extracellular DA but not serotonin (121). DA neurons appear to discharge under conditions consistent with an attribution of incentive salience suggesting that DA functions to give survival meaning to a particular occurrence (122). Mu and kappa opioid receptor antagonists have been shown to modify basal DA release within the nucleus accumbens (123) suggesting that tonically active endogenous opioid systems may actually regulate mesolimbic DA neurons. Naltrexone could reduce alcohol and other drug relapse by altering the organismic significance attributed to the drug event and ultimately altering the endogenous reward produced by ethanol

and other drugs. If endogenous opioid systems play such an important role in ongoing survival behavior reward and attribution of salience, then chronic treatment with naltrexone may have anti-drug reward but subjectively unrewarding effects, which may limit medication compliance or the duration of antagonist treatment. Serotonergic medications may also be found to be useful on the basis of specific effects on DA systems (124). A number of compounds under current investigation look quite promising at modifying the 5-HT-endorphin-DA circuits of drug reward. Of these, amperozide inhibits the voluntary consumption of ethyl alcohol by rats (125, 126) and more recently amperozide has been demonstrated to have a potent inhibitory effect on cocaine consumption with a minimal effect on food consumption or body weight (127). Both ritanserin and amperozide are active at the 5-HT2 sites and have promise in reducing the consumption of drugs as apparently different as alcohol and cocaine. The early studies suggest that common effects on reward pathways may be responsible for the common effects reported rather than direct effects on DA systems. Neither ritanserin the prototypical 5-HT2 receptor antagonist or amperozide have been well-studied to date in humans and further basic studies of their effects at the nucleus accumbens and mesocorticolimbic DA pathways are necessary to help understand the neuroanatomical and receptor basis of their apparent activity in reducing rewarding drug self-administration. Again, anti-craving and other human reports of compounds from carbamazepine to methylphenidate to mazindol suggest that cocaine abuse can be modified by a wide range of compounds without therapeutic efficacy. A specific compound that alters cocaine reward and cocaine taking is needed to improve clinical treatment outcomes.

FAMILY HISTORY AND GENETIC STUDIES

In one prospective study of 56 cocaine addicts, the rate for familial alcoholism was 52% in male and 60% in female cocaine dependents (128, 129). In a later study of 31 cocaine addicts, 68% had a family history positive for alcoholism without a significant gender difference (130).

The prevalence of familial alcoholism among male alcoholics has been well documented in numerous studies. The rate of familial alcoholism is 50% according to most studies, while the rate for familial alcoholism among females is generally more variable, with prevalence rates above and below 50%. The prevalence of familial alcoholism was 50% among males and 80% among females in a retrospective study of 150 cocaine dependents.

Opiate dependents with a parental history of alcoholism were more frequently diagnosed with concurrent alcoholism. In one study, 21.3% of the opiate dependents with a diagnosis of alcohol dependence had at least one parent with alcohol dependence. Opiate dependents without the diagnosis of alcohol dependence (4, 22) had a 12.5% rate of alcohol dependence in their families. The familial transmission of non-alcohol drug use and dependence in combination and for specific drug types has been only incompletely studied. In family members of drug addicts, rates for drug abuse or addiction range between 15 and 20%, and in family members of drug addicts with alcohol addiction, rates are approximately 25%. The rate for familial drug addiction in alcoholics only (without drugs) is lower, at 3%. The drugs in these studies were stimulants, opiates, cannabis, and barbiturates or benzodiazepines. Some familial studies have shown that the drug type in probands follows that of parents (131, 132).

While several twin studies show that monozygotic twins are concordant for alcoholism significantly more than are dizygotic twins, only one study shows a similar twin difference for monozygotic twins for illicit drugs. Also, only one adoption study is available that examines the transmission of drugs from biological parents to adopted-out offspring. This study shows that drug abuse in the adoptees was significantly more likely to be associated with drug abuse in the biological parent than in the adopted, nonbiological parents (133–136).

The implications of these familial and genetic studies and of the high rate of comorbidity of drugs with other drugs and alcohol are that alcohol and drug dependents have a generalized vulnerability to both alcohol and drugs. Whereas an alcoholic has an increased risk of developing a drug dependence, often to cocaine, a drug dependent or cocaine addict has an increased risk of developing alcohol dependence. The substitution of one drug for another and between alcohol and drugs, and the simultaneous and concurrent use of drugs and alcohol, compels investigators to search for common denominators on all levels, including biological and environmental.

PSYCHIATRIC COMORBIDITY

Comorbid psychiatric syndromes occur commonly in patients with cocaine dependence because (*a*) intoxication and withdrawal from cocaine and other drugs produce psychiatric syndromes; (*b*) both categories of disorders are common, and the chance of co-occurrence is high; and (*c*) the psychopathology of the disorders is greater when they are found together in the same individual.

There is confirmatory evidence that cocaine and other drugs can produce psychiatric syndromes through several pharmacological and psychological mechanisms. Acute and chronic intoxication with stimulants as well as withdrawal from depressants can cause many symptoms of anxiety syndromes that are indistinguishable from phobias, obsessive-compulsiveness, panic, and generalized anxiety. Conversely, acute and chronic intoxication with depressants or withdrawal from stimulants can cause a severe and incapacitating depression indistinguishable from major depression from other causes (137–139).

Psychotic symptoms, particularly of the paranoid type, are produced during intoxication with stimulants and during withdrawal from depressants. For example, cocaine or amphetamine administration can result in hallucinations and delusions during intoxication. In contrast, alcohol and sedative-hypnotic administration can result in these same symptoms during withdrawal. Personality disturbances are less clear, but it has been documented that chronic drug and alcohol use in an addictive fashion often leads to severe alterations in attitudes and behaviors in the addict. These frequently resemble antisocial, borderline, dependent, immature, and narcissistic personality disorders and ameliorate or disappear with abstinence from drugs and alcohol and especially with specific treatment of the addictive disorder (140, 141). There is no familial and genetic evidence to support a high rate of primary anxiety or affective or psychotic disorders among drug addicts, including cocaine addicts and alcoholics. Familial, adoption, and twin studies have found these psychiatric disorders to be independent of drug and alcohol dependence. Moreover, the sociodemography, early life course, and prognosis of the drug addicts and alcoholics more closely resemble those observed for drug addiction and alcoholism than for those with the psychiatric disorders.

There are several Axis I diagnoses in the DSM-IV that require the exclusion of drug and alcohol use diagnoses before the psychiatric diagnoses can be made (142).

Treatment of Comorbid Psychiatric and Substance Abuse Disorders

Treatment intervention for psychiatric disorders in cocaine addicts usually can be applied only after abstinence has been achieved and treatment for the addictive disorder has been initiated. For those patients with psychiatric disorders and concurrent cocaine, drug, and/or alcohol dependence, specific pharmacological therapies can be instituted when indicated for the psychiatric disorders. In general, the comorbid psychiatric disorder improves and the response to treatment is more efficacious with abstinence and specific treatment of the addictive disorder.

In general, the same pharmacological approaches already mentioned can be used in the addicted patient with a psychiatric disorder, with notable exceptions. Specifically, antidepressants and antipsychotic medications with low anticholinergic and low sedative properties are preferred because of established abuse and addiction potential of medications with stronger anticholinergic and sedative effects. Importantly, the use of sedative-hypnotics and tranquilizers, including benzodiazepines, is to be avoided because of their clearly documented addictive potential, particularly in the high-risk population of alcoholics and drug addicts. Moreover, a poorly accepted clinical caveat is that alcoholics and drug addicts do not respond well to drug effects in their attempts to achieve and maintain abstinence, so that a conservative approach for all medications is strongly suggested (143, 144).

Interactions between Addiction and Psychiatric Disorder

There is little direct evidence for the self-medication hypothesis that purports that addicts use because of underlying psychiatric disorders. The bulk of the evidence is to the contrary. Alcoholics and drug addicts use despite the adverse, toxic, and countertherapeutic effects of addictive use of drugs and alcohol. In animal studies, cocaine is self-administered in spite of serious and often fatal adverse consequences. Rhesus monkeys and rats have been reported to continue to press a bar in order to receive injections of cocaine to the point of convulsions, inanition, exhaustion, and death. In these animals, the pursuit of cocaine itself and not some underlying psychological factors motivated this extraordinary addictive cocaine use. The animals pursue cocaine for its pharmacological effects, as no personality factors or underlying psychopathology has been identified in these experiments (145–147).

Clinical experience and controlled studies of human cocaine addicts bear out the findings in the animal studies. Stimulants and other drugs, including alcohol, have powerfully controlling effects on mind and behavior. The morbidity and mortality arising from cocaine addiction and the pursuit and self-administration of cocaine by humans are staggering.

Some authors have speculated that it is the poverty of inner city conditions and the poverty of addicts' social interactions that are the primary factors in drug use and addiction. However, laboratory animals find these drugs powerfully reinforcing whether they are raised in isolation or in groups and regardless of whether they are experimentally stressed or coddled. Conditions of housing and stress can influence how rapidly animals learn to self-administer these drugs and whether they will learn to self-administer marginally effective doses. However, in most experiments with these animals and drugs, all healthy animals were reasonably quick to self-administer moderate intravenous doses of cocaine, heroin, and alcohol. The combination of a powerful reinforcing drug and motivated goal-directed behavior aimed toward euphoria production morbidly accelerated the addiction process. Just receiving the same amount of drug previously would not pose a great threat.

COCAINE ADDICTION TREATMENTS
Neurobiological Treatments

Throughout the 1980s as more cocaine addicts came to medical attention looking for treatment, addiction specialists and researchers responded with a series of frantic efforts to find therapeutic modalities specific enough to "treat" cocaine abuse. Yet, at the same time, exactly what was to be treated has remained an issue of considerable debate. Pharmacological treatments were necessary for cocaine overdose; cocaine toxicity; to replace cocaine, blunt, or block the effects of cocaine; to support cocaine abstinence; to reduce cocaine dysphoria; or to produce nausea or vomiting when cocaine was taken. None were discovered (148).

No potential new treatment was more important than the development of medicine that could separate the cocaine urge from drug-taking or alter the attachment of the addict for the drug. Naturally, progress came at a slow pace and without regard for the needs of the physicians and clinics. More effective management of acute cocaine intoxication, early diagnosis, urine and blood testing for cocaine and benzoylecgonine, the discovery of the uniquely toxic properties of cocaine when taken with alcohol, and the treatment of medical and psychiatric complications of cocaine have been important advances. All have combined to reduce cocaine-related morbidity and mortality. These and other efforts helped dispel the notion so prevalent in the late 1970s and early 1980s that cocaine was a "safe" drug of abuse—an oxymoron if there ever was one. Significant progress has been made in the laboratory allowing for a clearer understanding of cocaine's effects on the brain and relationship to the endogenous reinforcement systems. Significant progress has been made in understanding and targeting with psychopharmacological agents what patients describe as cocaine craving. Yet continued use of cocaine in the absence of craving has been reported.

Theories of cocaine abstinence and reward have led to large numbers of human clinical trials with a variety of disparate substances: amantadine, bromocriptine, buprenorphine, bupropion, carbamazepine, desipramine, fluoxetine, flupentixol, gepirone, imipramine, lithium, levodopa-carbidopa, maprotiline, mazindol, methadone, methylphenidate, naltrexone, pergolide, phenelzine, ritanserin, sertraline, trazodone, tryptophan, and tyrosine have all been reported or proposed as treatments. In general, all medications tried have been demonstrated to have some subjective effect on the cocaine experience or craving but do not alter or interfere with the natural history of cocaine dependence and use as assessed by testing, or euphoria (149–154).

Serotonergic agents such as fluoxetine, ritanserin, and sertraline have effects on human reports of cocaine craving and cocaine responding in animals, but generally only at doses that suppress behaviors maintained by food and other reinforcers (155). As one of the new avenues for pharmacotherapy of cocaine dependence, 5-HT agents have not been well studied. They may find a niche in the treatment of the patient with obsessive ruminations about cocaine, or they may simply go the way of desipramine. At this point it is safe to say that none of the currently available psychopharmacological treatment approaches has shown the relative strength of cocaine reward and attachment. Available data suggest that cocaine abuse can be modified by a wide range of compounds. Developing safe and effective medications to treat cocaine abuse and dependence is an ongoing challenge (156).

At present, no drug or drugs exist that are effective in treating cocaine abuse, overdose, or dependence. A number of medications have been tried without enduring success. However, a specific compound that alters cocaine taking is needed to improve treatment.

New behavioral models in animals (157, 158) and the characterization of the cocaine receptor site on the DA transporter molecule appear to offer promise for identifying new treatments that might prevent relapse or cocaine euphoria. The fact that not all DA uptake inhibitors exert reinforcing properties similar to cocaine (159) suggests that once the neuronal DA transporter is purified and cloned, new nonaddicting pharmacological treatments for human cocaine addicts might be developed. To date, the bulk of work has focused on the ability of pharmacological agents to attenuate craving. Further work is needed to see what effect on recovery and relapse these agents have. Finally, the progress in understanding the role of the DA system, the DA transporter, and the pharmacokinetics of cocaine reward has led to development of a vaccine for cocaine. One vaccine or immunotherapy appears to prevent the uptake of cocaine into critical brain reward sites in rats (160). Other immunological techniques may target the degradation of cocaine and speed the breakdown into inactive benzoylecgonine. These approaches are critical and emphasize the severity of cocaine use and the importance of prevention with the evidence of persistence of behavioral and neuropathology now commonly observed by clinicians.

Behavioral Interventions

Physicians are frequently in a position to identify, treat, and refer cocaine addicts for further treatment. It has been reported that more than 50% of patients in psychiatric settings, including inpatients and outpatients, suffer from a drug or alcohol dependence. Moreover, it has been found that 25–50% of a general medical practice is made up of drug and alcohol dependents (161).

The physician can initiate an intervention through prompt and proper diagnosis and treatment in clinical practice. It is imperative to develop diagnostic skills that are focused on the behaviors and consequences of addiction and to become knowledgeable in the laboratory confirmation of use and addiction. The physician often may not be the primary caregiver but frequently is involved through a particular specialty with the recovered drug addict. Because addiction often requires continuous treatment for an indefinite time, the physician will have many opportunities to continue to intervene in positive ways in the long-term treatment of addictive disorders (162). The clinical findings and natural history of cocaine dependence, the attachment of the user for the drug, and the power of the cocaine reward in shaping, conditioning, and modifying behavior have contributed to the current therapeutic approach, which combines a number of modalities. Current treatment strate-

gies are not one or another but always combine rehabilitative, psychodynamic, and behavioral approaches with pharmacological treatment during the acute withdrawal period and during early abstinence. Pharmacological agents have been successfully used to decrease abstinence complaints and decrease early treatment dropout rates.

Recent behavioral techniques of relapse prevention based on principles of behavioral therapies have been employed. In this type of treatment, patients are encouraged to identify internal and external precipitants of drug urges, to restructure their lifestyles in order to engage in healthy activities and avoid drug-oriented situations, to understand in detail the process of relapse in order to avoid it, and to stop relapses early (in the "lapse" stage) before they cause severe problems. Also, patients are exposed to increasingly vivid reminders of their cocaine use, while concomitantly being taught various cognitive behavioral techniques and relaxation exercises in order to reduce conditioned craving and learn alternative methods of dealing with their drug urges (163). Higgins and coworkers (13) at Vermont have reported on the use of a novel behavioral model of cocaine addiction treatment commonly called the incentive method. They give patients an increasing incentive payment for each clean urine specimen with the possibility of earning $1,000 over a 3-month period. At the end of a 12-week study period more than 60% of patients achieved stable abstinence that was two times greater than those patients treated without incentive payments. At the 1-year follow-up these differences persisted. The contingency payments may not be a treatment per se but a mechanism to keep the patient in treatment while behavioral treatment including relapse prevention was prescribed.

We have successfully used contingency approaches concurrently with other approaches in the treatment of physicians, health providers, and athletes.

The mainstay of treatment for cocaine dependence remains psychological (164). Treatment for cocaine dependence and prevention of relapse has been tried for the past decade and has now evolved to include elements of relapse prevention, 12-step programs, and other therapies to stop drug use and reduce recidivism (165–168). Recovery is a process that begins with a break in denial, a learning process of breaking old habits, friendships, and "triggers" to the first desire to use cocaine, and leading to eventual new healthy patterns of living shifting the locus of control from external to internal. Patients are encouraged to identify internal and external precipitants of drug urges and to restructure their lifestyles to avoid drug situations and relapse in relapse prevention protocols, as compared with behavioral treatment that focuses on extinguishing conditioned craving responses. Community reinforcement, payment for abstinence, and relapse prevention are the three major types of cocaine treatment programs in widespread use in the United States.

All of the therapies, including behavioral techniques, psychotherapy, and abstinence-based approaches, use the goal of abstinence and promote participation in self-help groups such as Alcoholics Anonymous (AA), Narcotics Anonymous (NA), and Cocaine Anonymous (CA) in their treatment programs (169). Initially, some cocaine-dependent patients might need alcohol detoxification, others might need alcohol detoxification plus the nicotine patch. Others might be candidates for immediate antidepressant treatment. All might be candidates for 12-step fellowship and some might need some kind of psychotherapy. Cocaine addicts are also comorbid for medical disorders like hepatitis or bronchitis, personality disorders like antisocial personality disorder, other drug use, and a number of psychiatric disorders ranging from major depression and bipolar illness to eating disorders and anxiety disorders. As demonstrated in a recent study of alcoholics, vigorous treatment for nicotine dependence (170) is absolutely essential in preventing relapse morbidity and mortality.

Pharmacological agents have been used to reverse the acute abstinence-related anergia, dysphoria, and depression. Pharmacological agents have also been used to reduce craving for cocaine with a hope that relapse might be prevented or made less likely.

Long-term treatment in self-help groups has arisen for specific drug types, such as CA and NA. These are similar to AA and suggest abstinence and adherence to a 12-step program of recovery from both alcohol and other drugs. Importantly, the principles of an abstinence-based treatment program that includes AA, CA, and NA will work for the alcoholic who has an additional drug dependence or the multiple drug dependent with an alcohol dependence diagnosis. The similarities in the treatment of the addictive disorders are greater than the differences, so that recovery by most cocaine addicts is possible in any of these groups (171–173).

Cocaine addiction differs from opiate and other addictions in many important ways. Cocaine does not produce an opiate calming effect or brief euphoria but is used in binges, frantically, until the supply or the user is exhausted. Satiety for the drug does not exist or develop and use can take place every 15–30 minutes for hours or days. The euphoric effect is a function of host factors, blood concentration, rapidity, and rise of cocaine concentrations in brain DA systems. Prolonged blockade of the DA transporter by cocaine results in long-term adaptive changes that can markedly impair mesolimbic DA function and also induce a state of supersensitivity. Adaptive changes in G proteins and the cAMP pathway have been implicated by

Nestler (174). Neurobiological research may help us understand the complex relationship between cocaine addiction and major psychological, psychosocial, cognitive, and neurological impairments, which persist long after detoxification. Those patients in need of the most intense medical and psychiatric evaluation are those who use by inhalation and intravenously (175). Scientific understanding of the mechanistic basis of the effects of cocaine is rudimentary and developing relevant and effective treatments slower than expected. Cocaine induces a complex state with alternating euphoria and dysphoria supporting binge use. Cocaine is taken whether the user defines the effect as positive or negative or both. Use of cocaine reinforces compulsive thinking about and use of cocaine regardless of consequences. Cocaine addiction is a heterogenous disorder where specialized treatments targeted to clinically distinct subgroups are desperately needed.

References

1. Dackis CA, Gold MS. New concepts in cocaine addiction: the dopamine depletion hypothesis. Neurosci Biobehav Rev 1985;9:469–477.
2. Kleber HD. Cocaine abuse: historical, epidemiological and psychological perspectives. J Clin Psychiatry 1988;49(2 suppl):3–6.
3. Gold MS, Verebey K. The psychopharmacology of cocaine. Psychiatr Ann 1984;14:714–723.
4. Wise RA. The brain and reward. In: Liebman JM, Cooper SJ, eds. The neuropharmacological basis of reward. Oxford, England: Oxford University Press, 1989:377–424.
5. Gawin FH. Cocaine addiction, psychology, and neurophysiology. Science 1991;251:1580–1586.
6. Gawin FH, Ellinwood EH. Cocaine and other stimulants. N Engl J Med 1988;318:1173–1182.
7. Senate Judiciary Committee. Joseph Biden Committee Report.
8. Miller NS, Gold MS, Belkin BM, Klahr AI. Family history and diagnosis of alcohol dependence in cocaine dependence. Psychiatry Res 1989;29:113–121.
9. Miller NS, Gold MS. Alcohol and other drug dependence and withdrawal characteristics. In: Gold MS, ed. Alcohol. New York: Plenum Books, 1991.
9a. U.S. Department of Health and Human Services. Drug abuse warning network, 1992. Washington, DC: U.S. Government Printing Office, 1993.
9b. Klerman GL, Weissman MM. The course, morbidity, and cost of depression. Arch Gen Psychiatry 1992;49(10):831–834.
10. Gold MS. The cocaine epidemic: what are the problems, insights, and treatments? Pharmacy Times 1987;3:36–42.
11. Miller NS, Gold MS, Millman RB. Cocaine: general characteristics, abuse and addiction. N Y State J Med 1989;89:390–395.
12. Uszenski RT, Gills RA, Schaer GL, Analouei AR, Kuhn FE. Additive myocardial depressant effects of cocaine and ethanol. Am Heart J 1992;124:1276–1283.
13. Higgins ST, Roll JM, Bickel WK. Alcohol pretreatment increases preference for cocaine over monetary reinforcement. Psychopharmacology 1996;123:1–8.
14. Washton AM, Gold MS, chronic cocaine abuse: evidence for adverse effects on health and functioning. Psychiatr Ann 1984;14:733–739.
15. Louie AK, Lannon RA, Keiter TA. Treatment of cocaine-induced panic disorder. Am J Psychiatry 1989;146:40–44.
16. McAllister K, Goeders N, Dworkin S. Chronic cocaine modifies brain benzodiazepine receptor densities. NIDA Res Monogr 1988;81:101–108.
17. Wood DM, Lal H. Anxiogenic properties of cocaine withdrawal. Life Sci 1987;41:1431–1436.
18. Grant BF, Harford TC. Concurrent and simultaneous use of alcohol with cocaine: results of a national survey. Drug Alcohol Depend 1990;25:97–104.
19. Randall T. Cocaine, alcohol mix in body to form even longer lasting, more lethal drugs. JAMA 1992;267:1043–1044.
20. Sands BF, Ciraulo DA. Cocaine drug-interactions. J Clin Psychopharmacol 1992;12:49–55.
21. Prather PL, Lal H. Protracted withdrawal: sensitization of the anxiogenic response to cocaine in rats concurrently treated with ethanol. Neuropsychopharmacology 1992;6:23–29.
22. Hearn WL, Flynn DD, Hime GW, Rose S, Cofino JC, Mantero-Atienza E, et al. Cocaethylene: a unique cocaine metabolite displays high affinity for the dopamine transporter. J Neurochem 1991;56:698–701.
23. Rose S, Hearn WL, Hime GW, Wetli CV, Ruttenberg AI, Mash DC. Cocaine and cocaethylene concentrations in human post mortem cerebral cortex. Soc Neurosci Abst 1990;11.6:14.
24. Fowler JS, Volkow ND, MacGregor RR, Logan J, Dewey SL, Gatley SJ, Wolf AP. Comparative PET studies of the kinetics and distribution of cocaine and cocaethylene in baboon brain. Synapse 1992;12:220–227.
25. Kosten TR, Rounsaville BJ, Kleber HD. Parental alcoholism in opioid addicts. J Nerv Ment Dis 1987;173:461–468.
26. Kandel DB, Raveis VH. Cessation of illicit drug use in young adulthood. Arch Gen Psychiatry 1989;46:109–116.
27. Verebey K, Gold MS. From coca leaves to crack: the effects of dose and routes of administration in abuse liability. Psychiatr Ann 1988;18:513–520.
28. Strang J, Edwards G. Cocaine and crack: the drug and the hype are both dangerous. Br Med J 1989;299:337–338.
29. Smart RG. Crack cocaine use: a review of prevalence and adverse effects. Am J Drug Alcohol Abuse 1991;17:13–26.
30. VanDyke C, Ungerer J, Jatlow P, et al. Intranasal cocaine: dose relationship of psychological effects and plasma levels. Int J Psychiatry Med 1982;12:1–13.
31. Pothos EN, Hernandez L, Hoebel BG. Chronic food deprivation decreases extracellular dopamine in the nucleus accumbens: Implications for a possible neurochemical link between weight loss and drug abuse. Obesity Research 1995;3:525s–529s.
32. Keller RW, LeFevre R, Raucci J, Carlson JN, Glick SD. Enhanced cocaine self-administration in adult rats prenatally exposed to cocaine. Neurosci Lett 1996;205:153–156.
33. Jaffe JH. Drug addiction and drug abuse. In: Gilman AG, Rall TW, Nies AS, Taylor P, eds. Goodman and Gilman's the pharmacological basis of therapeutics. 8th edition. New York: Pergamon Press, 1990:522–573.
34. Hoffman BB, Lefkowitz RJ. Catecholamines and sympathomimetic drugs. In: Gilman AG, Rall TW, Nies AS, Taylor P, eds. Goodman and Gilman's the pharmacological basis of therapeutics. 8th edition. New York: Pergamon Press, 1990:187–220.
35. Harris JE, Baldessarini RJ. Uptake of (3H)-catecholamines by homogenates of rat corpus striatum and cerebral cortex: Effects of amphetamine and analogues. Neuropharmacology 1973;12:659–679.
36. Heikkila RE, Orlansky H, Cohen G. Studies on the distinction between uptake inhibition and release of [³H]-dopamine in rat brain and tissue slices. Biochem Pharmacol 1975;103:241–248.
37. Hurd YL, Kehr J, Ungerstedt U. In vivo microdialysis as a technique to monitor drug transport: correlation of extracellular cocaine levels and dopamine overflow in the rat brain. J Neurochem 1988;51:1314–1316.
38. Pettit JP, Justice JB. Dopamine in the nucleus accumbens during cocaine self-administration as studies by in vivo microdialysis. Pharmacol Biochem Behav 1989;34:899–904.
39. deWit H, Stewart J. Reinstatement of cocaine-reinforced responding in the rat. Psychopharmacology 1981;75:134–143.
40. Fischman MW, Schuster CR, Resnekov L, et al. Cardiovascular and subjective effects of intravenous cocaine administration in humans. Arch Gen Psychiatry 1976;33:983–989.
41. Segal DS, Kuczenski R. Repeated cocaine administration induces behavioral sensitization and corresponding decreased extracellular dopamine response in caudate and accumbens. Brain Res 1996;577:351–355.
42. Wise RA, Rompre P-P. Brain dopamine and reward. Annu Rev Psychol 1989;40:191–225.
43. Gold MS. Drugs of abuse: a comprehensive series for clinicians. Vol III. Cocaine. New York: Plenum, 1993.
44. Gold MS. Clinical implications of the neurobiology of addiction. In: Miller, NS, ed. Principles of addiction medicine. Chevy Chase, MD: American Society of Addiction Medicine, 1995.
45. Koob GF, Vaccarino FJ, Amalric M, Swerdlow NR. Neural substrates for cocaine and opiate reinforcement. In: Fischer S, Raskin A, Uhlenhuth EH, eds. Cocaine: clinical and behavioral aspects. New York: Oxford University Press, 1987:80–108.
46. Bowman EM, Aigner TG, Richmond BJ. Neural signals in the monkey ventral striatum related to motivation for juice and cocaine rewards. J Neurophysiol 1996;75:1061–1073.
47. Callahan PM, Appel JB, Cunningham KA. Dopamine D1 and D2 mediation of the discriminative stimulus properties of d-amphetamine

and cocaine. Psychopharmacology 1991;103: 50–55.

48. Self DW, Barnhart WJ, Lehman DA, Nestler EJ. Opposite modulation of cocaine-seeking behavior by D1- and D2-like dopamine receptor agonists. Science 1996;271:1586–1589.

49. Roberts DC, Koob GF, Klonoff P, Fibiger HC. Extinction and recovery of cocaine self-administration following 6-hydroxydopamine lesions of the nucleus accumbens. Pharmacol Biochem Behav 1980;12:781–787.

50. Robledo P, Maldonado LR, Koob GF. Role of dopamine receptors in the nucleus accumbens in the rewarding properties of cocaine. Ann N Y Acad Sci 1992;654:509–512.

51. Hernandez L, Hoebel BG. Food reward and cocaine increase extracellular dopamine in the nucleus accumbens as measured by microdialysis. Life Sci 1988;42:1705–1712.

52. Karoum F, Suddath RL, Wyatt RJ. Chronic cocaine and rat brain catecholamine. Long-term reduction in hypothalamic and frontal cortex dopamine metabolism. Eur J Pharmacol 1990; 186:1–8.

53. Brock JW, et al. Effect of chronic cocaine on dopamine synthesis in the nucleus accumbens as determined by microdialysis perfusion with NSD-1015. Neurosci Lett 1990;117:234–239.

54. Hurd YL, Herkenham M. Molecular alteration in the neostriatum of human cocaine addicts. Synapse 1993;13:357–369.

55. Deleted in proof.

56. Pilotte NS, Sharpe LG, Kuhar MJ. Withdrawal of repeated intravenous infusions of cocaine persistently reduces binding to dopamine transporters in the nucleus accumbens of Lewis rats. J Pharmacol Exp Ther 1994;269:963–969.

57. Izenwasser S, Cox BM. Inhibition of dopamine uptake by chronic cocaine and nicotine: tolerance to chronic treatments. Brain Res 1992; 573:119–125.

58. Zahniser NR, Peris J, Dworkin LP, Curella P, Yasuda RP, O'Keefe L, et al. Sensitization to cocaine in the nigrostriatal dopamine system. NIDA Res Monogr 1988;88:55–77.

59. Weiss F, Markou A, Lorang MT, Koob GF. Basal extracellular dopamine levels in the nucleus accumbens are decreased during cocaine withdrawal after unlimited-access self-administration. Brain Res 1992;593:314–318.

60. Weiss F, Hurd YL, Ungerstedt U, Koob GF. Repeated cocaine administration potentiates the hypomotility effects of apomorphine. Soc Neurosci Abstr 1989;15:250.

61. Dackis CA, Gold MS. Bromocriptine as treatment of cocaine abuse. Lancet 1985;1(8438): 1151–1152.

62. Nunes EV, McGrath PJ, Stewart JW, Quitkin FM. Bromocriptine treatment for cocaine addiction. Am J Addictions 1992;2:169–172.

63. Moskovitz H, Brookoff D, Nelson L. A randomized trial of bromocriptine for cocaine users presenting to the emergency department. J Gen Intern Med 1993;8:1–4.

64. Giannini AJ, Bilet W. Bromocriptine therapy in cocaine withdrawal. J Clin Pharmacol 1987;27: 267–270.

65. Dackis CA, Gold MS, Sweeney DR, Byron JP, Climko R. Single-dose bromocriptine reverses cocaine craving. Psychiatry Res 1987;20:261–264.

66. Giannini AJ, Folts DJ, Feather JN, Sullivan BS. Bromocriptine and amantadine in cocaine detoxification. Psychiatry Res 1989;29:11–16.

67. Tennant FS, Sagherian A. A double-blind comparison of amantadine and bromocriptine for ambulatory withdrawal from cocaine dependence. Arch Intern Med 1987;147:109–112.

68. Kosten TR, Schumann B, Wright D. Bromocriptine treatment of cocaine abuse in patients maintained on methadone. Am J Psychiatry 1988; 145:381–382.

69. Bradberry CW, Roth RH. Cocaine increases extracellular dopamine in rat nucleus accumbens and ventral tegmental area as shown by in vivo microdialysis. Neurosci Lett 1989;103: 97–102.

70. Kalivas PW, Duffy P. Effect of acute and daily cocaine treatment on extracellular dopamine in the nucleus accumbens. Synapse 1990;5:48–58.

71. Mendelson JH, Mello NK, Teoh SK, Ellingboe J, Cochin J. Cocaine effects on pulsatile secretion of anterior pituitary, gonadal, and adrenal hormones. J Clin Endocrinol Metab 1989; 69:1256–1260.

72. Krantzler HR, Wallington DJ. Serum prolactin level, craving, and early discharge from treatment in cocaine-dependent patients. Am J Drug Alcohol Abuse 1992;18:187–195.

73. Mello NK, Sarnyai Z, Mendelson JH, Drieze JM, Kelly M. Acute effects of cocaine on anterior pituitary hormones in male and female rhesus monkeys. J Pharmacol Exp Ther 1993; 266:804–811.

74. Volkow ND, Mullani N, Gould KL, Adler S, Krajewski K. Cerebral blood flow in chronic cocaine users: A study with positron emission tomography. Br J Psychiatry 1988;152:641–648.

75. Volkow ND, Hitzemann R, Wang GJ, Fowler JS, Wolf AP, Dewey SL. Long-term frontal brain metabolic changes in cocaine abusers. Synapse 1992;11:184–190.

76. Volkow ND, Fowler JS, Wang GJ, Hitzemann R, Logan J, Schlyer DJ, et al. Decreased dopamine D_2 receptor availability is associated with reduced frontal metabolism in cocaine abusers. Synapse 1993;14:169–177.

77. Giros B, Jaber M, Jones SR, Wightman RM, Caron MG. Hyperlocomotion and indifference to cocaine and amphetamine in mice lacking the dopamine transporter. Nature 1996;379: 606–612.

78. Moliterno DJ, Lange RA, Gerard RD, Willard JE, Lackner C, Hillis LD. Influence of intranasal cocaine on plasma constituents associated with endogenous thrombosis and thrombolysis. Am J Med 1994;96:492–496.

79. Chen JC, Hsiang N, Morris C, Benny WB. Cocaine-induced multiple vascular occlusions. J Vasc Surg 1996;23:719–723.

80. Marzuk PM, Tardiff K, Leon AC. Fatal injuries after cocaine use as a leading cause of death among young adults in New York City. N Engl J Med 1995;332:1753–1757.

81. Hollander JE. The management of cocaine-associated myocardial ischemia. N Engl J Med 1995; 333:1267–1272.

82. Koob GF, Bloom FE. Cellular and molecular mechanisms of drug dependence. Science 1988; 242:715–723.

83. Koob GF. Dopamine addiction and reward. Semin Neurosci 1992;4:139–148.

84. Izenwasser S, Newman AH, Cox BM, Katz, L. The cocaine-like behavioral effects of meperidine are mediated by activity at the dopamine transporter. Eur J Pharmacol 1996;297:9–17.

85. Izenwasser S, Newman AH, Cox BM, Katz JL. The cocaine-like behavioral effects of meperidine are mediated by activity at the dopamine transporter. Eur J Pharmacol 1996;297:9–17.

86. Gold MS, Pottash ALC. Endorphins, locus coeruleus, clonidine, and lofexidine: a mechanism for opiate withdrawal and new nonopiate treatments. Adv Alcohol Subst Abuse 1981; 3:33–51.

87. Cadet JL, Bolla KI. Chronic cocaine use as a neuropsychiatric syndrome: a model for debate. Synapse 1996;22:28–34.

88. Siegal RK. Cocaine smoking disorders: diagnosis and treatment. Psychiatr Ann 1984;14: 728–732.

89. University of Florida. Facts About Tobacco, Alcohol, Other Drugs 1996;5(2).

90. Miller NS, Dackis CA, Gold MS. The relationship of addiction, tolerance and dependence: a neurochemical approach. J Subst Abuse Treat 1987;4:197–207.

91. Satel SL, Southwick SM, Gawin FH. Clinical features of cocaine-induced paranoia. Am J Psychiatry 1991;148:495–498.

92. Grinspoon L, Bakalar JB. Drug dependence: non-narcotic agents. In: Kaplan HI, Freedman AM, Sadock BJ, eds. Comprehensive textbook of psychiatry. 3rd edition. Baltimore: Williams & Wilkins, 1980.

93. Washton AM, Gold MS. Successful use of naltrexone in addicted physicians and business executives. Adv Alcohol Subst Abuse 1984; 4(2):89–96.

94. Washton AM, Gold MS. Intranasal cocaine addiction. Lancet 1983;2(8363):1374.

95. Gold MS. Science sizes up cocaine. In: Medical and health annual of the encyclopedia Britannica, 1987:184–203.

96. Dackis CA, Gold MS, Sweeney DR. The physiology of cocaine craving and "crashing". Arch Gen Psychiatry 1987;44(3):298–299.

97. Markou A, Koob GF. Post cocaine anhedonia: an animal model of cocaine withdrawal. Neuropsychopharmacology 1991;4:17–26.

98. Kokkindis L, McCarter BD. Post cocaine depression and sensitization of brain-stimulation reward: analysis of reinforcement and performance effects. Pharmacol Biochem Behav 1990;36:463–471.

99. Gold MS. Dopamine depletion hypothesis for acute cocaine abstinence: clinical observations, prolactin elevations, and persistent anhedonia/dysphoria. Neuroendocrinol Lett 1993;15(4): 271.

100. Gold MS, Miller NS, Jonas JM. Cocaine (and crack): neurobiology. In: Lowinson JH, Ruiz P, Millman RB, eds. Substance abuse: a comprehensive textbook. 2nd edition. Baltimore: Williams & Wilkins, 1992:222–235.

100a. Diagnostic and statistical manual of mental disorders. 4th edition. Washington, DC: American Psychiatric Association, 1994.

101. Gawin FH, Kleber HD. Abstinence symptomatology and psychiatric diagnosis in cocaine abusers: clinical observations. Arch Gen Psychiatry 1986;43:107–113.

102. Gold MS, Vereby K. The psychopharmacology of cocaine. Psychiatr Ann 1984;14:714–723.

103. Satel SL, Price LH, Palumbo JM, McDougle CJ, Krystal JH, Gawin F, et al. Clinical phenomenology and neurobiology of cocaine abstinence: a prospective inpatient study. Am J Psychiatry 1991;148:1712–1716.

104. Weddington WW, Brown BS, Haertzen CA, et al. Changes in mood, craving, and sleep during short-term abstinence reported by male cocaine addicts. Arch Gen Psychiatry 1990;47:861–868.

105. Gold MS. 800-COCAINE. New York: Bantam, 1984.

106. Dackis CA, Gold MS. Addictiveness of central stimulants. Adv Alcohol Subst Abuse 1990; 9:9–26.

107. Childress AR, McLellan AT, Ehrman RN, O'Brien CP. Extinction of conditioned responses in abstinent cocaine or opioid users. NIDA Res Monogr 1987;76:189–195.

108. Ehrman RN, Robbins SJ, Childress AR, O'Brien CP. Conditioned responses to cocaine-related stimuli in cocaine abuse patients. Psychopharmacology 1992;107:523–529.

109. Roache JD, Meisch RA. Drug self-administration in drug and alcohol addiction. In: Miller NS, ed. Comprehensive handbook of drug and alcohol addiction. New York: Marcel Dekker, 1991:625–640.

110. Miller NS. Amphetamines. In: Miller NS, ed. Comprehensive handbook of drug and alcohol addiction. New York: Marcel Dekker, 1991: 427–435.

111. Volkow ND. Imaging pharmacological actions of psychostimulants during drug addiction. Paper presented at the Institute of Medicine Symposium on Neuroscience Research: Advancing our Understanding of Drug Addiction. Washington, DC, July 29, 1996.

112. Weiss F. Neuroscience of addiction. The state of the science. Paper presented at the Institute of Medicine Symposium on Neuroscience Research: Advancing our Understanding of Drug Addiction. Washington, DC, July 29, 1996.

113. Self DW, Barnhart WJ, Lehman DA, Nestler EJ. Opposite modulation of cocaine-seeking behavior by D1 and D2 like dopamine receptor antagonists. Science 1996;271:1586–1589.

114. DiChiara G, Imperato A. Drugs of abuse preferentially stimulate dopamine release in the mesolimbic system of freely moving rats. Proc Natl Acad Sci U S A 1988;85:5274–5278.

115. Bechara A, Vander Kooy D. The tegmental pedunculo-pontine nucleus: a brain stem output of the limbic system critical for the conditioned place preferences produced by morphine and amphetamine. J Neurosci 1989;9:3400–3409.

116. Bozarth MA, Wise RA. Anatomically distinct opiate receptor fields mediate reward and physical dependence. Science 1984;224:516–517.

117. Bozarth MA, Wise RA. Dissociation of the rewarding and physical dependence-producing properties of morphine. In: Harris LS, ed. Problems of drug dependence. NIDA Res Monogr 1983;43:171–177.

118. Miller NS, Gold MS. Dissociation of "conscious desire" (craving) from and relapse in alcohol and cocaine dependence. J Clin Psychiatry 1994;6:99–106.

119. Trachtenberg MC, Blum K. Alcohol and opioid peptides: neuropharmacological rationale for physical craving of alcohol. Am J Drug Alcohol Abuse 1987;13:365–372.

120. Blum K. A commentary on neurotransmitter restoration as a common mode of treatment for alcohol, cocaine and opiate abuse. Integr Psychiatry 1989;6:199–204.

121. Benjamin D, Grant ER, Poherecky LA. Naltrexone reverses ethanol-induced dopamine release in the nucleus accumbens in awake, freely moving rats. Brain Res 1993;621: 137–140.

122. Robinson TE, Berridge KC. The neural basis of drug craving: an incentive-sensitization theory of addiction. Brain Res Brain Res Rev 1993; 18:247–291.

123. Spanagel Herz A, Shippenbert TS. Opposing tonically active endogenous opioid systems modulate the mesolimbic dopaminergic pathway. Proc Natl Acad Sci U S A 1993;89: 2046–2050.

124. Wozniak KM, Pert A, Mele A, Linnoila M. Focal application of alcohol elevates extracellular dopamine in rat brain: a microdialysis study. Brain Res 1991;540:31–40.

125. Myers RD. Psychopharmacology of alcohol. Annu Rev Pharmacol Toxicol 1978;18:125–144.

126. Myers RD, Lankford M, Bjork A. 5-HT2 receptor blockade by amperozide suppresses ethanol drinking in genetically preferring rats. Pharmacol Biochem Behav 1993;45:741–747.

127. McMillen BA, Jones EA, Hill LJ, Williams HL, Bjork A, Myers RD. Amperozide, a 5-HT2 antagonist, attenuates craving for cocaine by rats. Pharmacol Biochem Behav 1993;46:125–129.

128. Miller NS, Belkin BM, Gold MS. Multiple addictions: cosynchronous use of alcohol and drugs. N Y State J Med 1990;90:596–600.

129. Helzer JE, Przybeck TR. The co-occurrence of alcoholism with other psychiatric disorders in the general population and its impact on treatment. J Stud Alcohol 1988;49:219–224.

130. Miller NS. Comorbidity of psychiatric alcohol/drug disorders: interactions and independent status. J Addict Dis 1993;12(3):5–16.

131. Hill SY, Cloninger CR, Ayre FR. Independent familial transmission of alcoholism and opiate abuse. Alcohol Clin Exp Res 1977;1:335–342.

132. Meller WH, Rinehart R, Cadoret RJ, Troughton E. Specific familial transmission in substance abuse. Int J Addict 1988;23:1029–1039.

133. Miller NS, Gold MS. Research approaches to inheritance to alcoholism. Subst Abuse 1988; 9:157–163.

134. Pickens RW. Genetic vulnerability to drug abuse. NIDA Res Monogr 1988;89:41–51.

135. Pickens RW, Svikis DS, McGue M, Lykken DT, Heston LL, Clayton PJ. Heterogeneity in the inheritance of alcoholism: a study of male and female twins. Arch Gen Psychiatry 1991; 48:19–28.

136. Cadoret RJ, Troughton E, O'Gorman TW, Heywood E. An adoption study of genetic and environmental factors in drug abuse. Arch Gen Psychiatry 1986;43:1131–1136.

137. Miller NS, Mahler JC, Belkin BM, Gold MS. Psychiatric diagnosis in alcohol and drug dependence. Ann Clin Psychiatry 1991;3:79–89.

138. Gold MS. The good news about panic, anxiety and phobias. New York: Villard Books, 1989.

139. Gold MS. The good news about depression. New York: Villard Books, 1987.

140. Gold MS, Slaby AE. Dual diagnosis in substance abuse. New York: Marcel Dekker, 1991.

141. Schuckit MA. Alcoholism and other psychiatric disorders. Hosp Community Psychiatry 1983;34:1022–1027.

142. Schuckit MA. Genetic and clinical implications of alcoholism and genetic disorders. Am J Psychiatry 1986;143:140–147.

143. Dilsaver SC, Alessi NE. Antipsychotic withdrawal symptoms: phenomenology and pathophysiology. Acta Psychiatr Scand 1988;77: 241–246.

144. Dilsaver SC, Greden JF, Snider RM. Antidepressant withdrawal syndromes: phenomenology and pathophysiology. Int Clin Psychopharmacol 1987;2(1):1–19.

145. Miller NS, Gold MS. Dependence syndrome: a critical analysis of essential features. Psychiatr Ann 1991;21:282–290.

146. Mayfield D. Psychopharmacology of alcohol. II. Affective tolerance in alcohol intoxication. J Nerv Ment Dis 1968;146:322–327.

147. Mayfield DG. Alcohol and effect: experimental studies. In: Goodwin DW, Erickson CK, eds. Alcoholism and affective disorders. New York: SP Medical and Scientific Books, 1979: 99–107.

148. Leshner AI, Molecular mechanisms of cocaine addiction. N Engl J Med 1996;335:128–129.

149. Weiss SRB, Post RM, Aigner TG. Carbamazepine in the treatment of cocaine-induced disorders. In: Watson RR, ed. Drug and alcohol abuse reviews: treatment of drug and alcohol abuse. Totowa, NJ: Humana Press, 1992:149.

150. Berger P, Gawin F, Kosten TR. Treatment of cocaine abuse with mazindol. Lancet 1989;1: 283.

151. Gawin FH, Riordan C, Kleber HD. Methylphenidate treatment of cocaine abusers without attention deficit disorder: A negative report. Am J Drug Alcohol Abuse 1985;11: 193–197.

152. Jaffe JH, Witkin JM, Goldberg SR, Katz JL. Potential toxic interactions of cocaine and mazindol. Lancet 1989;8654:111.

153. Kosten TR, Steinberg M, Diakogiannis IA. Crossover trial of mazindol for cocaine dependence. Am J Addictions 1993;2:161–164.

154. Shottenfeld RS, Pakes J, Ziedonis D, Kosten TR. Buprenorphine: dose-related effects on cocaine and opioid use in cocaine-abusing opioid-dependent humans. Biol Psychiatry 1993; 34:66–74.

155. Kleven MS, Woolverton WL. Effects of three monoamine uptake inhibitors on behavior maintained by cocaine or food presentation in rhesus monkeys. Drug Alcohol Depend 1993; 31:149–158.

156. Mendelson JH, Mello NK. Management of cocaine abuse and dependence. N Engl J Med 1996;334:965–972.

157. Markou A, Koob GF, Bromocriptine reverses the elevation in intracranial self-stimulation thresholds observed in a rat model of cocaine withdrawal. Neuropharmacology 1992; 7:213–224.

158. Markou A, Weiss F, Gold LH, Caine SB, Schulteis G, Koob GF. Animal models of drug craving. Psychopharmacology 1992;112: 163–182.

159. Rothman RB. High affinity dopamine reuptake inhibitors as potential cocaine antagonists: a strategy for drug development. Life Sci 1990; 46:17–21.

160. Carerra MR, Ashley JA, Parsons LH, Wisching P, Koob GE, Janda KD. Suppression of psychoactive effects of cocaine by active immunization. Nature 1995;378:727–730.

161. Vaillant GE. The course of alcoholism and lessons of treatment. In: Grinspoon L, ed. Psychiatry update. Washington, DC: American Psychiatric Press, 1984.

162. Mersy DJ. Interventions for recovery in drug and alcohol addiction. In: Miller NS, ed. Comprehensive handbook of drug and alcohol addiction. New York: Marcel Dekker, 1991: 1063–1078.

163. Marlatt GA. Relapse prevention: a self-controlled program for the treatment of addictive behaviors. In: Stuart RB, ed. Adherence compliance and generalization in behavioral medicine. New York: Brunner-Mazel, 1982.

164. Dackis CA, Gold MS, Estroff TW. Inpatient treatment of addiction. In: Karasu TB, ed. Treatments of psychiatric disorders. A task force report of the American Psychiatric Association. Washington, DC: American Psychiatric Press, 1989;2:1359–1379.

165. Weiss RD, Mirin SM. Cocaine. Washington DC: American Psychiatric Press, 1987.

166. Washton AM. Nonpharmacologic treatment of cocaine abuse. Psychiatr Clin North Am 1986: 563–571.

167. Marlatt GA. Relapse prevention: A self-control program for the treatment of addictive behaviors. In: Stuart RB, ed. Adherence, compliance, and generalization in behavioral medicine. New York: Brunner/Mazel, 1982.

168. Miller NS, Gold MS. The psychiatrist's role in integrating pharmacological and nonpharmacological treatments for addictive disorders. Psychiatr Ann 1992;22(8):436–440.

169. Chappel JN. The use of Alcoholics Anonymous and Narcotics Anonymous by the physician in treatment of drug and alcohol addiction. In: Miller NS, ed. Comprehensive handbook of drug and alcohol addiction. New York: Marcel Dekker, 1991:1079–1090.

170. Hurt RD, Offord KP, Croghan IT, Gomez-Dahl L, Kottke TE, Morse RM, Melton J. Mortality following inpatient addictions treatment. JAMA 1996;275:1097–1103.

171. Schulz JE. 12 step programs in recovery for drug and alcohol addiction. In: Miller NS, ed. Comprehensive handbook of drug and alcohol addiction. New York: Marcel Dekker, 1991: 1255–1274.

172. Gold MS. The facts about drugs and alcohol.

3rd edition. New York: Bantam Books, 1991.

173. Washton A, Gold MS. Cocaine: a clinician's manual. New York: Guilford Press, 1985.

174. Nestler, EJ. The molecular neurobiology of drug addiction. Neuropsychopharmacology 1994;11:77–87.

175. Mendelson JH, Mello NK. Management of cocaine abuse and dependence. N Engl J Med 1996;334:965–972.

16 Cocaine (and Crack): Clinical Aspects

Mark S. Gold

To the Incas of Peru, cocaine was a gift from the gods. In our own age, cocaine is seen by many to be a curse from the Devil. Dr. Howard P. Rome, editorial director of *Psychiatric Annals,* commented that the ravages of cocaine "have added the fifth pale horseman as civilization hurtles toward its Apocalypse" (1).

Although cocaine abuse in this country had reached epidemic proportions, as early as 1990, the National Household Survey on Drug Abuse found cause for hope. Data from that survey showed that the number of current cocaine users—people who had used the drug within the past 30 days—had decreased from 5.8 million in 1985 to 1.6 million in 1990. The number of people who had used cocaine within the year fell from 12 million to 8 million between 1985 and 1988. Cocaine-related emergency room visits declined 26% between 1988 and 1990. To a significant degree, the decline can be attributed to widespread public education about the dangers of cocaine.

The bad news is that the number of people using cocaine every day or every week rose during the same period. In addition, among the nearly 3 million current users are a half million people who use crack, the highly addictive smokable form of cocaine and the most dangerous development in the long history of this deadly drug. With an estimated 80 tons of cocaine having entered the United States in 1990, it is not surprising that 10% of children ages 9–12 report that it is easy to obtain cocaine. More bad news is on the horizon. 1995 PRIDE data and 1995 UM/NIDA data concur that illicit drug use in general is resurgent after declines in use after 1988. Crack, cocaine, and other drug use appears to be slowly increasing again (2, 3).

This chapter summarizes the clinical and epidemiological features of cocaine abuse. Following a discussion of the psychopharmacology of cocaine use and the wide-ranging medical complications experienced by cocaine users, there is a discussion of approaches to treatment for cocaine addiction, including some promising clinical treatment strategies.

EPIDEMIOLOGY

The history of cocaine has been thoroughly discussed elsewhere (4–6). The relevant clinical issues related to cocaine's history have to do largely with the changes over time in dosage, route of administration, patterns of use, and the technology of cocaine production.

The amount of cocaine ingested by the Incas was probably low. It is estimated that the average user chewed 60 grams of coca leaves a day. Given that the alkaloid content of a coca leaf is about 0.5–0.7% and that only a portion of the alkaloid is absorbed in digestion, the total dosage would have been 200–300 mg over a 24-hour period (7).

Word about cocaine first spread to Europe through reports by explorers and later by naturalists and botanists (8). By 1860 essays about the virtues of cocaine inspired makers of wines and tonics to add the drug to their formulations. Within 15 years people could also buy snuff that contained pure cocaine and that was touted as a remedy for asthma and hay fever. These new cocaine preparations, doses, and routes of administration marked the first change in the pattern of cocaine use in more than 4000 years (9). The established daily doses of cocaine ingested via these products would have ranged from about 225 to 1620 mg—more than five to eight times the cocaine intake of the coca chewer in Peru.

In 1884 Sigmund Freud published his essay "Uber Coca" (10) in which he advocated the therapeutic use of cocaine as a stimulant, an aphrodisiac, a local anesthetic, and a medicine for treating asthma, wasting diseases, digestive disorders, nervous exhaustion, hysteria, syphilis, and even altitude sickness (11). Freud, who himself used cocaine in dosages of about 200 mg a day, recommended cocaine in oral doses of 50–100 mg as a stimulant and as a euphoriant in depressive states (12, 13). For 90 years his essay was the only report that used controlled studies to document the effects of cocaine on humans (14).

Freud also prescribed cocaine to alleviate the symptoms of withdrawal from alcohol and morphine addiction. Because the addictive power of cocaine was not then recognized, some patients who used cocaine as a substitute for alcohol or morphine became addicted to cocaine instead. As these and other adverse consequences of cocaine use soon became apparent, Albrecht Ehrlenmeyer accused Freud of having unleashed "the third scourge of humanity," the other two being alcohol and opiates (14).

In America, during the mid 1880s, Atlanta druggist John Pemberton devised a patent medicine that contained two naturally occurring stimulants: cocaine and caffeine (15). Because it contained no alcohol, he advertised his product—eventually known as Coca-Cola—as an "intellectual beverage," a "temperance drink," and a "brain tonic" (16–18). Until 1903, Coca-Cola contained approximately 60 mg of cocaine per 8-ounce serving. The maker voluntarily removed cocaine from the formulation in response to public pressure and news reports about the dangers of cocaine.

The turn of the century thus also marked a turn in public attitudes about cocaine. The American Medical Association, seeking to raise the standards of medical practice, lobbied to curb the sales of patent medicines, including those containing cocaine. The Harrison Narcotic Act of 1914, which mistakenly listed cocaine as a narcotic, banned the use of cocaine in proprietary medications and tightened the restrictions on the manufacture and distribution of coca products (4).

Due to these restrictions, and for other reasons as well, drug users turned to amphetamines and other centrally stimulating drugs that were developed starting in the 1930s. These drugs easily substituted for cocaine because they cost less, were more widely available, and induced a sense of euphoria that lasted longer (18). They were also deadly. By the late 1960s the drug-using subculture recognized the danger in amphetamines, as reflected in the contemporary slogan "speed kills." Eventually amphetamines were listed as Schedule II drugs (drugs with a high abuse potential and prescription limitations), making them much more difficult to obtain.

Stimulant abusers searching for a "safe" recreational euphoria soon rediscovered cocaine (19). In the early 1970s, cocaine abuse skyrocketed, especially among middle and upper middle class populations, where it became known as "the champagne of pharmaceuticals." The warnings of cocaine's dangers from the previous cocaine epidemic during the late nineteenth century had long since been forgotten.

During the 1970s cocaine was usually administered intranasally. A typical user bought a gram of cocaine for approximately $150 and snorted the drug from a tiny "coke spoon" or perhaps even a fingernail cultivated for the purpose. Such methods delivered between 5 and 10 mg of the drug. A "line" of cocaine inhaled through a straw delivered approximately 25 mg. Typical users would repeat the dose in both nostrils, thus taking between 10 and 50 mg of cocaine at a time (20).

The perception among users was that cocaine was safe and nonaddictive. Perception of safety appears necessary for widespread use of illicit drugs. Drugs of abuse tend to be viewed as safe until proven dangerous—the opposite burden of proof applied to new pharmaceuticals. The medical literature of the time did little to contradict this false perception. An article appearing in 1977 claimed that "aside from financial depletion, the main undesirable effects of 'social snorting' are nervousness, irritability, and restlessness from overstimulation" (21). The authors went on to state that cocaine may improve physical performance, cure stage fright, and fortify the body and mind without the risk of causing withdrawal syndrome marked by prolonged cravings for the drugs. The same authors, writing in the 1980 edition of the *Comprehensive Textbook of Psychiatry* (22), stated: "Used no more than two or three times a week, cocaine creates no serious problems. In daily and fairly large amounts, it can produce minor psychological disturbances. Chronic cocaine abuse usually does not appear as a medical problem."

People willing or prone to misuse drugs interpreted these and other similar statements from medical "experts" as a license to try and then to use cocaine freely. As the supply of cocaine rose, the price dropped and the amount of a typical dose increased. A new method called "freebasing" made cocaine smokable, allowing rapid self-administration of high blood and brain levels without intravenous injection. Freebase allowed users to ingest much higher doses than ever before (6). Some users combined cocaine and heroin in a drug cocktail known as a "speedball"—the combination that killed comedian John Belushi.

Another smokable form of cocaine in the mid 1980s opened another tragic chapter in the history of the drug. Essentially mass-produced freebase cocaine, crack is low priced (as little as $2 a dose), making it available to younger users and sending the average age of the user spiraling downward. Crack users feel more confident, more intelligent, more in control, and sexier; smoked cocaine is rapidly addicting and produces medical effects previously seen only in long-term intranasal users (23). Recently Kandel and Yamaguchi reported that crack smoking was the last drug in a long chain of substances used by youth, often after cocaine hydrochloride (24).

Crack differs from cocaine hydrochloride, the powdered form of cocaine, in several ways (23). Because it is smoked, the user feels a "high" in less than 10 seconds. Conditioning can cause euphoria to be reported when the warm pipe touches the lips of the experienced user. In contrast, sniffing cocaine produces a high after a delay of 1–2-minutes. The feeling of euphoria from crack wears off after 5–15 minutes; the effects of snorted cocaine may last slightly longer. Another difference is that the user reports that the crack-induced euphoria is far more powerful than that created by powder. Pharmacokinetic studies of intranasal and intravenous cocaine administration have been reviewed elsewhere (25). Following intranasal administration of 96 mg of cocaine, peak venous plasma levels of between 150 and 200 ng/ml are reached in 30 minutes. Intravenous administration of 32 mg produce peak venous plasma levels of 250–300 ng/ml after only 4 minutes. A similar rise in plasma levels occur following the smoking of 50 mg of cocaine base (26). The levels of cocaine reaching the heart and brain after either smoking or intravenous administration are much greater and faster peaking in seconds when arterial rather than venous sampling is done. Concurrent use of alcohol can increase blood levels of cocaine. The smoked drug is absorbed rapidly from the lungs to the heart and then to the brain, rather than passing incompletely and slowly through the nasal membrane on the long route to the brain. Cocaine smoking and intravenous use tend to be particularly associated with a rapid progression from use to abuse or dependence, often occurring over weeks to months. Intranasal use is associated with a more gradual progression, usually occurring over months to years. Cocaine is metabolized by cholinesterase present in plasma and liver into two metabolites, benzoylecgonine and ecgonine methyl ester, which are excreted and can be measured in urine for 36 hours or longer after last use. Dependence is commonly associated with a progressive tolerance to the desirable effects of cocaine, leading to increasing doses and/or changes in route of administration. With continuing use, there is a diminution of pleasurable effects due to tolerance and an increase in dysphoric effects. While reporting decreased pleasure, use continues unabated. It may even accelerate.

COCAINE USE TODAY

Surveys of callers to the National Helpline conducted from 1983 to 1989 have identified some persistent shifts in the current cocaine epidemic (27). For example, in 1983 the typical caller was a 31-year-old intranasal cocaine user, college educated, and employed with an income of more than $25,000. By 1989, the typical caller was less educated, unemployed, a non-intranasal user, and had an income of less than $25,000. Since 1989 these early findings have been replicated and it has become routine to consider crack use an urban drug and a poor drug and consider cocaine hydrochloride as a suburban and middle class drug of abuse. Patients report that it is easy to find crack cocaine in any city at any time by simply finding the poorest neighborhoods or looking for a ghetto. While crack has been the focus of media reports, cocaine is linked to violence, irritable aggression, and even traffic accidents and dangerous driving. It is now clear that driving under the influence of intoxicating drugs other than alcohol may be an important cause of traffic injuries. Using a rapid urine test to identify reckless drivers who were under the influence of cocaine or marihuana (28), of 150 subjects stopped for reckless driving and providing a urine, 59% tested positive. A community survey conducted in the United States in 1991 reported that 12% of the population had used cocaine one or more times in their lifetime; 3% had used it in the last year; and less than 1% had used it in the last month. As with amphetamines, cocaine dependence is associated with either of two patterns of self-administration: episodic or daily (or almost daily) use. Serious medical, social, and other consequences have been reported with experimental, episodic, and also daily use. Cocaine use separated by 2 or more days of nonuse is episodic. "Binges" are characterized by use that typically involve continuous high-dose use over a period of hours or days. Binges usually terminate only when cocaine supplies are depleted or the user is so exhausted that they "pass out" or so experienced that they realize that a rest is necessary for neurotransmitter repletion and renewed feeling of cocaine's euphoric effects. In chronic daily use, there are generally no wide fluctuations in dose on successive days, but an increase in dose over time. In summary, epidemiological data indicate that crack has spread throughout America but taken particular hold in urban areas of the country. Cocaine and crack use have been reported to occur in all groups and among all demographic groups, at all levels of society.

Crack use has been associated with binge use, addiction, urban decay, crime, and violence. Cocaine hydrochloride causes these consequences as well. Just being shot appears to be associated with the presence of cocaine in the blood. Commission of a felony is similarly highly associated with the presence of cocaine or another illicit drug in the body of the perpetrator. Still, the association between crack, violence, and medical emergencies has been compelling. A way of measuring the impact of cocaine and then crack use is by looking at changes in emergency room (ER) visits. Between 1976 and 1986 there was a 15-fold increase in the number of emergency room visits due to cocaine and in the number of admissions to public treatment programs for cocaine (29). These were cocaine hydrochloride effects. Cocaine-related ER visits jumped again by 86% in 1987, largely because of the invention and use of crack (30). Nearly one in four drug-related ER visits involved some combination of drugs and alcohol (31). A 1988 survey by the Drug Abuse Warning Network (DAWN) found that 1 of 4 cocaine-related emergency room visits was related to crack smoking, compared with 1 of 20 in the previous survey (32). By 1989, cocaine was the number one cause of emergency room visits in Washington, DC, and New York as well as Atlanta, Baltimore, Chicago, Indianapolis, Detroit, Los Angeles, New Orleans, and many other cities (33). Similarly, more than 70% of arrestees in such major cities as New York, Philadelphia, and Washington, DC, tested positive for one or more drugs, usually including cocaine (34). Recent cocaine use is associated with a range of violent premature deaths, including homicides, suicides, accidents (35), and reckless driving (28). In 1994 emergency room visits were rising again.

Autopsies revealed the presence of cocaine in more than 18% of motor vehicle fatalities in New York City between 1984 and 1987 (36). These data are consistent with the recent driving impaired report of Brookhoff (28). It is likely that the well-known direct effects of cocaine—feelings of alertness, euphoria, aggressiveness, and irritability, psychotic distortions and increased risk-taking behavior—diminish a driver's ability to control the vehicle (29, 37). It is evident that cocaine is a major cause of traumatic accidents (38).

Cocaine has changed society in other ways as well. It has changed professional and nonprofessional sports. It has altered the process by which businesses screen job candidates and has led to the development of employee assistance programs in the workplace. It has thwarted decades of progress in international diplomacy and threatened the relationships between our nation and other parts of the world.

In summary, the abuse of cocaine reached epidemic proportions in the last two decades with disastrous consequences for individuals and communities. Although a general downward trend in total drug consumption since the mid-1980s has been reported, that trend has been reversing since 1992.

The proportion of individuals abusing psychoactive substances, legal and illegal, remains at alarming levels in the United States. According to a recent comprehensive report by the Robert Wood Johnson Foundation (39), substance abuse is the number one health problem in the United States with more deaths and disabilities from substance abuse than from any other preventable cause. The Robert Wood Johnson Foundation also reports a direct link between illicit drugs (including cocaine) and violent crime. Our own recent reports correlate illicit drug use with carrying weapons and violence among sixth through twelfth grade students (40).

As a result of widespread education and prevention and the harsh reality that most Americans knew or could readily identify with a victim of the cocaine epidemic, self-reported perception of danger ("using cocaine once or twice") has increased throughout the 1980s and with it cocaine use fell. However, continued decreases in addictive use did not follow and recent use has rebounded since 1993. Figure 16.1 presents trends from 1975 to 1994 on perceived risk and availability, as well as past year use, for high school seniors.

Recent data from the annual PRIDE survey and also the Monitoring the Future UM/NIDA data released in December, 1995, point to a resurgence in cocaine and crack use (2, 3). After steady decreases in use from 1984 until 1994, cocaine, especially crack, appears in the early stages of a resurgence (Fig. 16.2)

In summary, dramatic changes in the patterns of cocaine use, the typical dosage, and the route of administration have combined to produce a deadly epidemic of addiction to a drug once touted by medical experts as "safe." Experimental use has decreased in response to massive re-education of the American people. However, addiction continues to be a major public health problem and rates of adolescent use may have begun a new upward trend.

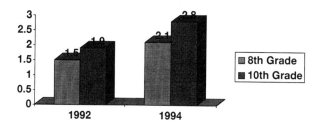

Annual Use of Cocaine

Figure 16.2. Cocaine, especially crack, appears in the early stages of a resurgence.

COCAINE INTOXICATION AND ADDICTION

By claiming that cocaine was relatively harmless and dismissing the notion that the drug could be addictive, medical experts ignored Freud's own observation, published in an 1887 paper, that cocaine was "a far more dangerous enemy to health than morphine" (41). The result was that cocaine was essentially field-tested on the public, with deadly results.

Many people whose use of cocaine could be described as "moderate" or "recreational" claimed that cocaine was not addictive. A June 1990 survey of callers to the National Helpline found that even callers using cocaine once or twice a week (the "recreational" users) report severe problems stemming from their drug use. Cocaine is taken for the positive or expected cocaine intoxication state DSM-IV criteria as described in Table 16.1.

Addiction Liability

Clearly, the addictive power of cocaine is deceptive. In fact, most users who deny that they are addicted cannot say no to cocaine if it is made available. Typically, addicts continue to seek the drug even though their lives are being destroyed. Cocaine must produce a state similar to a delusion in users. Loved ones see a fragile, sickly, imperiled addict and at the same time the users say that they see nothing of the kind and are simply fine. Our past failure to recognize the delusionary and addictive power of cocaine is in part responsible for the current cocaine epidemic (42).

A person's susceptibility to cocaine addiction depends to a large degree on the dose, duration, and route of administration. Anecdotal data suggest that cocaine smokers are twice as likely to fail to complete their treatment program as are intranasal abusers. Other elements that determine addiction susceptibility are (*a*) the psychological and physical changes brought about

Table 16.1 Diagnostic Criteria for Cocaine Intoxication

A. Recent use of cocaine
B. Clinically significant maladaptive behavioral or psychological changes: euphoria or affective blunting; changes in sociability; hypervigilance; interpersonal sensitivity; anxiety, tension, or anger; stereotyped behaviors; impaired judgment; impaired social or occupational functioning that developed during or shortly after use of cocaine.
C. Two or more of the following, developing during, or shortly after, cocaine use:
    Tachycardia *or* bradycardia
    Pupillary dilation
    Elevated or lowered blood pressure
    Perspiration or chills
    Nausea or vomiting
    Evidence of weight loss
    Psychomotor agitation or retardation
    Muscular weakness, respiratory depression, chest pain, or cardiac arrhythmias
    Confusion, seizures, dyskinesias, dystonias, or coma
D. The symptoms are not due to a general medical condition and are not better accounted for by another mental disorder.

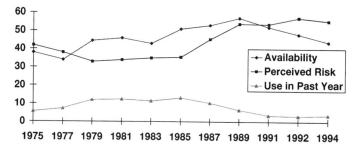

Figure 16.1. Trends in cocaine availability, perceived risk, and use in past year for high school seniors.

by drug use, (b) the degree of that change, (c) the speed of onset of the change, (d) the duration of change, and (e) the post-drug effects (43).

Cocaine tends to be less addictive if the dose is small, the peak plasma levels low, the onset of activity slow, the duration of action long, and the unpleasant withdrawal effects absent or very mild. If cocaine is taken by means of chewed coca leaves, through oral ingestion, or, to some extent, through intranasal use, consequences are generally slow to develop. Swallowing or snorting cocaine is an inefficient way of using the drug, since cocaine penetrates biological membranes poorly. Hepatic biotransformation prevents 70–80% of the oral or intranasal dose from reaching the circulatory system (44).

Acute intoxication with high doses of cocaine may be associated with rambling speech, headache, transient ideas of reference, and tinnitus. There may also be paranoid ideation, auditory hallucinations in a clear sensorium, and tactile hallucinations ("coke bugs"), which the user usually recognizes as effects of cocaine. Extreme anger with threats or acting out of aggressive behavior may occur. Mood changes such as depression, suicidal ideation, irritability, anhedonia, emotional lability, or disturbances in attention and concentration are common. After oral administration, cocaine concentrations in the blood rise slowly, peaking approximately 1 hour after ingestion. Behavioral effects of the drug tend to follow the same curve. In contrast, intranasal use produces a quicker onset of drug effects, shorter duration of action, and higher peak blood levels. Hence the addiction potential of intranasal cocaine abuse is higher than that of oral use, largely because of the more rapid onset of pharmacological effects.

Intravenous (IV) cocaine use ranks higher on the addiction potential scale than intranasal use. Given unlimited access to the drug, IV cocaine abusers will escalate the dose until they deteriorate physically and mentally. The onset of the IV cocaine "rush" is within 30–45 seconds, and the drug's effects last for 10–20 minutes. Peak blood levels can be more than twice those that occur following intranasal ingestion. What is more, 100% of an IV dose is delivered to the circulatory system, compared with 20–30% of an intranasal dose (43). For many reasons—pain of injection, difficulty of finding and using needles and syringes, risk of infectious disease—IV administration is less appealing to cocaine abusers than other methods.

Given the parameters that define addiction susceptibility, choosing to take cocaine in any smokable form has the highest addictive potential. Cocaine can be smoked as coca paste, as freebase, or as crack, which is simply freebase prepared by a different method. The popularity of crack compared with freebase is largely a product of marketing techniques that make small amounts of high-quality cocaine available at low prices and without having to undertake a dangerous chemical process to convert cocaine to a smokable form.

In actuality, smoking is not the most efficient system for delivering cocaine to the body. A significant portion of the drug dose is lost to pyrolysis. Nonetheless, the remaining dose produces potent effects. The resulting high is intense—some users describe it as "full body orgasm." The onset is extremely rapid; only 8–10 seconds elapse before the user experiences the high. The concentration of the drug in the brain also occurs more rapidly than following IV use, resulting in greater behavioral effects.

Addiction implies goal-directed behavior aimed at finding and using cocaine to produce maximal euphoria. The user is not primarily focused on neural adaptation or withdrawal. Recent studies have tried to separate addiction from neural adaptation by comparing volitional self-administration from passive drug injections, which are involuntary. Not only does addiction develop in the former but neurochemical changes appear maximized during the self-administration model. It is as if wanting to be high and finding and self-administering cocaine combines to produce maximal brain rewarding and dependency producing effects. Chronic self-administration of cocaine, but not passive receipt of the same doses at the same frequency, in yoked animals is associated with addiction and markedly elevated dopamine (DA) and serotonin levels. These brain neurochemical effects can be followed in the amygdala, suggesting altered neuronal activity in this brain area underlies drug-seeking behavior. The amygdala receives dopaminergic innervation from the ventral tegmental area and serotonergic innervation from the midbrain and pontine raphe as well as extensive communication from the nucleus accumbens. Although the nucleus accumbens plays a critical role in the

Table 16.2 Diagnostic Criteria for Cocaine Withdrawal

A. Cessation of (or reduction in) cocaine use that has been heavy and prolonged.
B. Dysphoric mood and two (or more) of the following physiological changes, developing within a few hours to several days after Criterion A:
   1. fatigue
   2. unpleasant dreams
   3. insomnia or hypersomnia
   4. increased appetite
   5. psychomotor retardation or agitation
C. The symptoms in Criterion B cause clinically significant distress or impairment in social, occupational, or other important areas of functioning.
D. The symptoms are not due to a general medical condition and are not better accounted for by another mental disorder.

Table based on Diagnostic and statistical manual of mental disorders. 4th edition (DSM-IV). Copyright American Psychiatric Association, Washington, DC, 1994. Used with permission.

reinforcing properties of cocaine and other stimulants the amygdala might be involved in the acquisition of stimulus-reward associations or the motivational aspects of drug-seeking (45). The danger and allure of the streets may actually increase the reinforcing potency of crack cocaine.

Also contributing to the addiction potential of crack is the fact that the effects of the drug last only 5–10 minutes. After the high is over, the crack user feels anxious, depressed, and paranoid. Such a rapid shift between positive and negative effects of the drug makes users crave another "hit" of the drug to restore the euphoria they felt just moments before. These cravings form a distinct part of the withdrawal syndrome associated with cocaine.

Withdrawal symptoms are the inverse of cocaine's effects. Most troubling to the clinician and addict is the dysphoria and drive for a cocaine remedy so typically reported by crack addicts. Removal of the withdrawal anhedonia by taking crack, is another positive reinforcer, adding to addiction liability of cocaine and crack. Cocaine withdrawal symptoms (Table 16.2) include decreased energy, dysphoric and anhedonic psychomotoric retarded state with concurrent limited interest in the environment, and limited ability to experience pleasure. These symptoms are mildest immediately following cessation of cocaine use but increase in intensity and remind the addict that this state is cocaine-reversible during the next 96 hours (44).

For years experts assumed cocaine was not addictive ; however, DSM IV has now not only said that cocaine causes addiction but has established criteria for dependence and for cocaine withdrawal (Table 16.2).

NEUROBIOLOGIC AND PSYCHOPHARMACOLOGIC EFFECTS OF COCAINE USE

Cocaine's addictive potential is the result of the interaction of goal-directed volitional self-administration and profound drug-related effects on many of the most critical neurochemical systems of the brain. While amphetamine has a number of direct DA releasing and DA storage vesicle effects, both amphetamine and cocaine produce positive reinforcement blocking the reuptake of DA into the presynaptic neuron and causing an acute increase in synaptic DA availability. By preventing DA reuptake, greater concentrations of DA remain in the synaptic cleft with more DA available at the postsynaptic site for stimulation of receptors. The abnormally high levels of DA in the synapse inhibit the firing-rate of dopaminergic cells. Numerous studies have supported the positive reinforcement effects associated with increased synaptic levels of DA. Recent laboratory research has established that cocaine acts directly on the so-called reward pathways. These pathways are indirectly activated by pleasurable stimuli from other activities, including eating, drinking, and sex. So powerful is the direct stimulation provided by cocaine that sleep, safety, money, morality, loved ones, responsibility, even survival become largely irrelevant to the cocaine user. In a sense, cocaine "short circuits" the process by which people normally achieve gratification and security (46). Cocaine access to primitive brain reward mechanisms appears to be the target of cocaine self-administration.

One of cocaine's primary effects in the brain is to block the presynaptic reuptake of neurotransmitters including serotonin, norepinephrine, and DA. Cocaine binds to the presynaptic transporter complexes inhibiting reuptake of DA, noradrenaline, and serotonin prolonging monoamine neurotransmission. The reinforcing properties of cocaine are believed to be associated with enhanced dopaminergic neurotransmission in mesocorticolimbic pathways. Hence there is a surplus of these neurotransmitters at the postsynaptic receptor sites (47). This surplus in turn activates responses along the sympathetic nervous system, producing such effects as vasoconstriction and acute increases in heart rate and blood pressure (48, 49). Within the past few years a receptor for cocaine has been identified in the brain. This receptor appears to be the cocaine binding site on the DA transporter on dopaminergic nerve terminals (50). By interfering with neurochemical activity, cocaine acts in many ways like a neuromodulatory neurotransmitter.

Starting with the hypothesis that activation of DA systems in the mesocorticolimbic areas of the brain are responsible for the motor and reinforcing effects of cocaine, DA activation has been described as essential in most, if not all, drug reinforcement (51). Petit (52) showed that the elevation of synaptic levels of DA in response to cocaine is augmented in the nucleus accumbens after repeated administration, explaining users' reports of continued and sometimes increasing euphoria early in a binge. Kalivas and Duffy (53) placed dialysis probes in the ventral tegmental area DA cell bodies that terminate in the nucleus accumbens; this gave evidence for a specific role for this neural structure in sensitization. Petit and Justice (54) using microdialysis in the nucleus accumbens have demonstrated that extracellular DA levels are increased during cocaine self-administration with the behavior directed towards attaining specific, almost optimal DA levels. DA levels attained were dose dependent and correlated with increased cocaine intake (55). DA neurons and DA release appear to demonstrate tolerance and diminished responses to chronic self-administration consistent with the notion of a functional DA deficit over time. By preventing DA reuptake, greater concentrations of DA remain in the synaptic cleft with more DA available at the postsynaptic site for brain reinforcement, reward, or stimulation of specific salience supporting receptors. Cocaine reward or a particular drug experience is commonly explained by addicts in terms such as "hunger," "taste," and "sex." This may not be at all a coincidence. Users, by their choice of words and descriptions, may be confirming the similarities in critical brain sites for natural and drug reward. The nucleus accumbens and DA are critical in food, drinking, and sex reward (56, 57) as well as drug reward.

Most recently, investigators using a binge administration paradigm found that cocaine significantly lowers basal DA levels and alters the pattern but not the magnitude of the response to cocaine itself (58). Binge use is supported by the cocaine-DA connection. It is, therefore, well accepted that the mesolimbic and mesocortical dopaminergic systems are critical in the acute and binge reinforcing effects of cocaine and also cocaine-induced euphoria. Volkow and colleagues have characterized cocaine binding in the brain to a high-affinity on the DA transporter using positron emission tomography (PET) and tracer doses of [11C]cocaine in the baboon in vivo (59). At subpharmacological doses, [11C]cocaine binds predominantly to a high-affinity site on the DA transporter. Using PET and [11C]cocaine Volkow demonstrated cocaine binding to DA transporters in vivo. Because the studies with [11C]cocaine were done at subpharmacological levels of cocaine, [11C]co-

caine's binding to the DA transporter probably represented high-affinity sites. This may, however, not be the only pharmacologically relevant binding site when cocaine is administered in behaviorally active, pharmacological doses.

There is a wealth of evidence implicating DA in incentive motivational effects of drugs as well as of food, sex, and other natural incentives (60–63). The treatment conundrum is how to have a treatment dose, power of therapy, or incentives that can match the access and reinforcement produced by cocaine.

Table 16.3 lists the basic effects of cocaine; Table 16.4 compares the drug's effects following different routes of administration. The precise psychological and behavioral effects depend on many factors: the purity of the drug, route of administration, chronicity of use, the personality and mental health of the user, past and present use of drugs and alcohol, the environment in which the drug is used, and other drugs taken at the same time.

CLINICAL PHARMACOLOGY

The purer the drug, the greater its effects. As a rule, pure cocaine is unavailable on the street. Instead, cocaine is usually adulterated with other substances such as mannitol, lactose, or glucose to add weight, and caffeine, lidocaine, amphetamines, quinine, or even heroin to add taste and to provide additional central nervous system (CNS) stimulant effects (64). The typical concentration of cocaine in street preparations ranges from 10 to 50%; rarely, samples can contain as much as 70% cocaine. Both the cocaine concentration and the adulterants affect the user's response to the drug.

Whether a user enjoys or dislikes cocaine may depend on the individual's normal level of excitation, which is controlled by the adrenergic system, the thyroid hormone thyroxin, and other regulators (43). Certain people in their normal state are more subdued, while others are more excitable. Because cocaine stimulates the CNS, a person with a low level of arousal or excitement may be more likely to enjoy the changes in alertness and energy cocaine provides. On the other hand, people who are normally hyperexcited may feel uncomfortable and dysphoric, and may even develop paranoid psychosis due to the major sympathetic discharge triggered by cocaine.

Once consumed, cocaine triggers the series of physiological responses

Table 16.3 Effects of Cocaine[a]

Generally enjoyable effects with great increase in self-image. A rapid onset of "high" with the following components:
1. Euphoria, seldom dysphoria
2. Increased sense of energy
3. Enhanced mental acuity
4. Increased sensory awareness (sexual, auditory, tactile, visual)
5. Decreased appetite (anorexia)
6. Increased anxiety and suspiciousness
7. Decreased need of sleep
8. Postponement of fatigue
9. Increased self-confidence, egocentricity
10. Delusions—dependence
11. Physical symptoms of a generalized sympathetic discharge

[a]Low to average doses (25 to 150 mg) (approximately 20 to 30 mg/line).

Table 16.4 Differential Effects Dependent on Routes of Cocaine Administration

Route	Mode	Initial Onset of Action (sec)	Duration of "High" (min)	Average Acute Dose (mg)	Peak Plasma Levels (ng mL)	Purity (%)	Bioavailability (percent absorbed)
Oral	Coca leaf chewing	300–600	45–90	20–50	150	0.5–1	—
Oral	Cocaine HCl	600–1800		100–200	150–200	20–80	20–30
Intranasal	"Snorting" cocaine HCl	120–180	30–45	5 × 30	150	20–80	20–30
Intravenous	Cocaine HCl	30–45	10–20	25–50	300–400	7–100 × 58	100
				> 200	1000–1500		
Smoking	Coca paste	8–10	5–10	60–250	300–800	40–85	6–32
Intra-pulmonary	Freebase			250–1000	800–900	90–100	
	Crack				?	50–95	

Reprinted with permission from Verebey K, Gold MS. From coca leaves to crack: the effects of dose and routes of administration in abuse liability. Psychiatr Ann 1988;18:514.

that make up the natural "fight or flight" response to an impending threat. By affecting the release and reuptake of epinephrine, cocaine causes a shift in the blood supply from the skin and the viscera into the skeletal musculature. Oxygen levels rise, as do concentrations of sugar in the blood. After the acute dose of cocaine wears off, the user's body usually returns to its more normal state. Following chronic use, however, the body's reservoirs of neurotransmitters and hormones may be depleted. In addition, the drug may compromise the body's ability to regenerate these biochemicals. As a result, the chronic user may experience symptoms of withdrawal (42).

The cocaine-induced feeling of increased alertness is reported subjectively and can be confirmed by electroencephalogram and electrocardiogram recordings, which show a general desynchronization of brain waves after cocaine administration (65). Such desynchronization, which indicates arousal, occurs in the part of the brain that is thought to be involved in the regulation of conscious awareness, attention, and sleep. Despite the feeling of arousal, individuals using cocaine do not gain any particular superior ability or greater knowledge. Their sense of omnipotence is only an illusion; they tend to misinterpret their enhanced confidence and lowered inhibitions as signs of enhanced physical or mental acuity. The motivational symptoms of drug withdrawal are presumably mediated by molecular and cellular adaptations to chronic cocaine exposure but appear to occur in brain regions also associated with reinforcement. Cocaine is self-administered directly into the prefrontal cortex although dopaminergic innervation of this structure is not essential for maintaining intravenous self-administration.

The nucleus accumbens is a central hub in a functional circuit that allows drug reinforcement to occur through simultaneous activation of multiple reward sites and is considered a logical final common anatomical target for drugs acting on receptors in other reinforcing nuclei. The G-protein-cAMP system in the nucleus accumbens is involved in acute drug reinforcement and is an important component of the adaptations that occur during chronic drug self-administration (66).

Through its impact on neurotransmitters, particularly DA, cocaine can affect sexual excitation. Cocaine used intravenously or in smokable form can produce spontaneous ejaculation without direct genital stimulation (67). In extreme cases cocaine even replaces the sex partner. Tolerance to the sexual stimulation of cocaine develops rapidly, sometimes resulting in impotence or sexual frigidity. Cocaine use can therefore replace the natural sex drive, which in turn threatens long-term relationships and can disrupt family stability. In some cases women cocaine users trade sexual favors for crack. During a short period of time these women may have sex with many partners, putting themselves and others at risk of infection (68).

By inactivating the feeding center located in the lateral hypothalamus, cocaine also supersedes the primary eating drive, thus leading to severe loss of appetite and loss of body weight. Cocaine is commonly used by women with and without primary eating disorders to curb appetite or lose weight. The cocaine user's decreased need for sleep may also result from the drug's effects on neurotransmitters, including serotonin, which at times functions as the "sleep transmitter."

Many clinical manifestations of cocaine intoxication are also found in cases of hyperthyroidism. Some of these manifestations include hypertension, hyperkinesis, sweating, rapid heartbeat, tremor, anxiety, and hyperthermia. Conversely, the cocaine "crash" following use shares many of the signs and symptoms with the hypothyroid state: low energy, depression, bradykinesia, weight gain, and hypersomnia. From such evidence it can be assumed that cocaine activates the thyroid axis (69).

DA inhibits secretion of prolactin. Hyperprolactinemia is the endocrine abnormality most often reported in clinical studies of cocaine abusers (70) with clear elevations in prolactin observed during abuse and withdrawal (71–78) and in animals. Loss of interest in sex and poor sexual performance noted by cocaine addicts may be related to this DA-prolactin release from inhibition.

Another neuroendocrine abnormality related to the DA deficiency hypothesis is the study by Hollander (79), where recently abstinent cocaine users were found to have a 580% peak growth hormone response to apomorphine. Symptoms include gynecomastia, galactorrhea, and sexual dysfunctions such as infertility, impotence, and amenorrhea.

Laboratory evidence suggests that cocaine can cause adrenocortical hypertrophy, stimulating the release of high doses of cortisol in animals. It is possible that similar effects occur in humans. Hence another aspect of cocaine use may be its impact on the hypothalamic-pituitary-adrenal axis (69). Because it affects the supply of acetylcholine, cocaine can lead to mental confusion and loss of coordination (80).

Cocaine users report feeling more alert and more energetic. This reaction in turn produces a tremendous increase in self-confidence, self-image, and egocentricity; in some individuals this manifests as megalomania and feelings of omnipotence. Some groups, including athletes, salespeople, entertainers, musicians, and physicians, sometimes use cocaine to provide them with these effects, to enhance their energy, confidence, and "star image."

But there are limits to the degree to which CNS activity can be artificially stimulated. After chronic use, or following a prolonged binge, symptoms of depression, lack of motivation, sleeplessness, paranoia, irritability, and outright acute toxic psychosis may develop (42). States of severe transient panic accompanied by a terror of impending death can occur in persons with no preexisting psychopathologic conditions, as can paranoid psychoses (29, 81, 82).

All of these effects return investigators to DA but there are at least five DA-receptor subtypes. Their respective roles in cocaine reinforcement remains to be demonstrated. Studies in rats suggest that the D3 DA receptors play an important role (83) but numerous questions remain unanswered. Clinicians focus on the rapidity of deterioration, addiction, and change. The tremendous attachment for cocaine and desire to repeat the pleasurable aspects of the cocaine experience and to counteract the depressive effects of the postcocaine crash can lead to compulsive chronic use of the drug. Such activity leads to a decrease or depletion in the neurotransmitter supply. The long-term results of such depletion include overt depression, dysphoria, hallucinatory experiences, and destructive antisocial behavior. More subtle changes in behavior include irritability, hypervigilance, psychomotor agitation, and impaired interpersonal relations (29).

Cocaine is known to worsen the symptomatology of depression. People with major depression are likely to experience dysphoria after cocaine use, although in other individuals cocaine acts in some ways like an antidepressant. Paranoia is another commonly seen product of cocaine abuse. In its ability to induce a state resembling functional paranoid psychosis, cocaine is similar to other central stimulants, including amphetamines (84).

Use of cocaine can also produce a psychotic syndrome characterized by paranoia, impaired reality testing, anxiety, a stereotyped compulsive repetitive pattern of behavior, and vivid visual, auditory, and tactile hallucinations such as the delusion that insects are crawling under the skin (84). Subjective and clinical data also show that cocaine can induce panic attacks (85).

A further complication of cocaine abuse is that many users ameliorate some of the unpleasant stimulating effects of the drug by concomitantly or subsequently ingesting sedating agents such as alcohol or marihuana (29, 44). The combined use of cocaine and alcohol is common, with reports of 62–90% of cocaine abusers also concurrent ethanol abusers (86). Cocaine users report that concurrent ethanol use prolongs the "high" and attenuates a number of the unpleasant physical and psychological effects of cocaine. Cocaethylene, the ethyl ester of benzoylecgonine, is similar to cocaine in neurochemical and pharmacological properties and behavioral effects. Cocaethylene binds to the DA transporter blocking DA uptake and increasing extracelluar concentrations of DA in the nucleus accumbens but unlike cocaine it has little effect on the serotonin transporter. While similar to cocaine and having at least addictive effects on heart rate and reward, there have been reports of increased lethality. Autopsies revealed that between 1984 and 1987, 56% of all drivers killed in traffic accidents in New York City were found to have used either cocaine, alcohol, or both (36).

Cocaine memory of euphoria appears to peak immediately preceding cocaine self-administration and be important in supporting a cocaine binge. Vivid, long-term memories of being high tend to persecute the drug abuser by invoking powerful cravings for the next high (29). Cocaine users describe intense craving for cocaine when cocaine is made available to them or merely when the word cocaine is uttered in conversation. Seeing places or people where cocaine was used, smelling cocaine, seeing a cocaine pipe, seeing a friend who they used cocaine with, hearing a song that they used cocaine to, and numerous other casual smells, sights, and sounds can trigger an intense reaction in the user or the person who has used in the past but is now abstinent (87). Users report tasting cocaine, craving cocaine, sweating, feeling faint and short of breath, smelling cocaine, and feeling a little of the cocaine euphoria. All of these experiences contribute to cocaine taking and the persistence of cocaine dependence. In man even the presentation of cocaine paraphernalia after weeks or months of abstinence produces intense cravings and withdrawal-like symptoms (88, 89). In experimental studies in humans, individuals with a history of cocaine use show greater physiological reactivity in response to cocaine cues than do cocaine-naive individuals. The greater responses were also demonstrated to cocaine stimuli rather than powerful opiate cues. Cocaine-related stimuli elicit conditioned physiological and subjective states in cocaine users (90).

Many cocaine-dependent individuals respond to drug cues in the human laboratory as well. They report increased craving for cocaine and have clear physiological evidence of intense arousal. Such changes are being tested as treatment predictors and strategies for treatment itself. In a cue-reactivity protocol that concluded with relaxation exercises, patients who achieved abstinence were predicted by craving reported after relaxation training. Patients who subsequently initiated abstinence reported a reduction in cue-elicited craving to below baseline levels while those who did not succeed in treatment remained elevated (91). As is discussed later in the section "Treatment of Cocaine Addiction," these cravings are one of the most difficult aspects in weaning addicts from cocaine.

MEDICAL COMPLICATIONS OF COCAINE ABUSE

The medical and psychiatric complications associated with cocaine use are so numerous (92) and severe that it would take an entire book to describe them completely. Benowitz (93) has recently reviewed the organ toxicity of cocaine including toxic paranoid psychosis, panic disorder, suicide, convulsions, cerebrovascular accidents, cardiotoxicity, and hepatotoxicity. Among the complications are cardiovascular effects, including arrhythmias and myocardial infarctions; respiratory effects such as chest pain and respiratory failure; neurological effects such as seizure and headache; gastrointestinal complications, including abdominal pain and nausea; and many others. For the purposes of this chapter, a brief description of cocaine's far-ranging and troubling medical consequences must suffice.

Cardiovascular System

The first clinical report of cocaine abuse–associated cardiac toxicity appeared in 1978 (94). A review of the recent medical literature reveals that cocaine use has been linked to virtually every type of heart disease (95).

Cocaine produces a number of cardiovascular effects that may lead to the development of different forms of arrhythmia. Tachycardia often occurs within minutes of cocaine ingestion. Other forms of arrhythmia associated with cocaine use include sinus bradycardia, ventricular premature depolarization, ventricular tachycardia degenerating to defibrillation, and asystole. Crumb and Clarkson (96) suggest that cocaine may induce arrhythmias because it slows impulse conduction by blocking cardiac sodium channels. Tachycardia is also partly due to cocaine's local anesthetic activity and to indirect stimulation of alpha-receptors (97). One study found a greater acceleration in heart rate and blood pressure associated with cocaine smoking than with IV cocaine use (98).

Cocaine is known to elevate blood pressure through adrenergic stimulation. The pressor effects of cocaine continue to rise as dosage increases (99). The sudden increase in blood pressure may cause spontaneous bleeding in people with normal blood pressure and may underlie many incidents of cerebrovascular accidents associated with cocaine use (100).

Evidence suggests that cocaine can induce spasms in a number of vascular systems, including the coronary arteries (101). These spasms can produce myocardial infarction even in a person whose endothelium is otherwise intact (102). The pathological changes in the vasculature, regardless of route of cocaine self-administration, that place individuals at high risk for a cardiovascular or cerebrovascular accident appear to include arteriolar thickening, increased perivascular deposits of collagen and glycoprotein, and inflammation (103).

Most of the case reports of cocaine-related cardiovascular toxicity involve myocardial infarctions, which may occur regardless of dosage level or route of administration (104). Cocaine increases myocardial oxygen consumption, but at the same time it interferes with the coronary circulation's ability to adjust to this increased demand by decreasing its resistance to blood flow (105). Cocaine users also frequently develop silent myocardial ischemia (106). This problem may also arise during the first weeks of withdrawal. So common is the incidence of myocardial infarction due to cocaine that its occurrence in young patients who lack the usual coronary risk factors suggests a diagnosis of cocaine abuse (107).

In a recent study (108) wholebody timed distribution of pharmacological doses of C-cocaine was studied in rats using quantitative autoradiographic microimaging. Rapid, intense uptake was seen in the brain, spinal cord, adrenals, and nuchal brown fat pad. Cocaine appears to bind in the brain to the DA transporter and to a lesser extent to transporters for norepinephrine and serotonin. Microvascular spasm may also be a major factor in producing thallium-201 defects in the presence of normal coronaries. In patients with nominal narrowing coronaries, cocaine-induced microvascular spasm may cause coronary thrombosis and infarction. The demonstration of cocaine binding in the heart and its time sequence is of relevance in understanding the cardiotoxicity of cocaine. Further support on the relevance of direct effect of cocaine on the heart is given by our studies showing decreased myocardial perfusion in naive anesthetized animals. These studies indicate that central effects are not essential in causing cardiovascular perturbations.

Cocaine addiction can accelerate coronary atherosclerosis. Cocaine use by patients with premature artery disease can exacerbate the problem and may result in death (109). Either directly or indirectly, cocaine may affect platelets, possibly causing them to form thrombi that can plug small vessels (110). Finally, long-term abuse of cocaine may lead to interstitial fibrosis and eventually to congestive heart failure (111). The cardiac effects of cocaine have previously been treated with propranolol and may respond to the calcium channel blocker nitrendipine (69).

Respiratory System

Smoking crack can induce severe chest pain or dyspnea (112). One explanation for this effect may be that cocaine significantly reduces the ability of the lungs to diffuse carbon monoxide (113). Often it is this symptom of chest pain that drives patients to seek medical attention.

Other respiratory effects of cocaine smoking include lung damage, pneumonia, pulmonary edema, cough, sputum production, fever, hemoptysis, pulmonary barotrauma, pneumomediastinum, pneumothorax, pneumopericardium, and diffuse alveolar hemorrhage (114–116). Cocaine inhalation can cause or contribute to asthma (117). Respiratory failure, resulting from cocaine-induced inhibition of medullary centers in the brain, may lead to sudden death (118).

Recently a new syndrome entered the medical terminology: "crack lung" (119). People with this condition present with the symptoms of pneumonia—severe chest pains, breathing problems, high temperatures. Yet x-rays reveal no evidence of pneumonia and the condition does not respond to standard treatments. Anti-inflammatory drugs may relieve symptoms of crack lung. People with this syndrome may suffer oxygen starvation or loss of blood with potentially fatal results.

Neurotoxicity

As even Freud was aware, cocaine is an epileptogenic agent that can provoke generalized seizures, even after a single dose (14, 120). With repeated administration, the ability of cocaine to produce clonic convulsions increases (121). This phenomenon, known as "kindling," may result from sensitization of receptors in the brain. Since seizure disorders can be unmasked or induced by cocaine's kindling effect on the brain, proper medical evaluation of patients must rule out epilepsy (69).

Volkow et al. (122) has studied postsynaptic DA receptor density in PET studies using (^{18}F)N-methylspiroperidol. Subjects abstinent for less than 1 week showed significantly lower values for uptake of the ligand in the striatum when compared to non–drug-using control subjects. The subjects abstinent for 4–5 weeks showed values comparable to normal. These findings suggest decreased density of postsynaptic DA receptors rather than a change in receptor affinity. Volkow has also reported on the Swiss-cheese, multiple, often silent, infarcts and neural change associated with cocaine and crack use.

Other researchers' work supports Volkow and indicates that cocaine significantly constricts the cerebral vasculature and can lead to ischemic brain infarction. Long-term effects of intermittent or casual cocaine use in patients without symptoms of stroke or transient ischemic attack were investigated by Strickland et al. (123). Single-photon emission computed tomography with xenon-133 and (⁹⁹ᵐTc)hexamethylpropyleneamine oxime, magnetic resonance imaging, and selected neuropsychological measures were used to study cerebral perfusion, brain morphology, and cognitive functioning. Patients were drug free for at least 6 months before evaluation. All showed regions of significant cerebral hypoperfusion in the frontal, periventricular, and/or temporal-parietal areas. Deficits in attention, concentration, new learning, visual and verbal memory, word production, and visuomotor integration were observed. This study by Strickland and coworkers indicates that long-term cocaine use may produce sustained brain perfusion deficits and persistent neuropsychological compromise. As noted, cocaine abuse is associated with intracranial hemorrhage. CNS stimulants such as cocaine may also cause tics, persistent mechanical repetition of speech or movement, ataxia, and disturbed gait, which may disappear after drug use is stopped (124). When high-dose users (2.2 g/day) are drug free for 6 months, they still show decreased brain function and decreased blood flow, suggesting that brain changes may persist long after cessation of use. Marihuana and cocaine are commonly used at the same time. While not entirely clear from anecdotal reports, marihuana may potentiate cocaine's effects. Smoking placebo, 1.24%, or 2.64% THC-containing marihuana cigarettes followed by 0.9 mg/kg intranasal cocaine in a random design, marihuana pretreatment significantly reduced the latency to peak cocaine euphoria from 1.87 to 0.53 minutes, decreased the duration of dysphoric or bad effects and increased peak cocaine levels and apparent bioavailability by area under the curve analysis when highest dose marihuana preceded cocaine (173). Marihuana-induced vasodilatation of the nasal mucosa attenuates the vasoconstrictive effects of cocaine and thus increases absorption (125).

Impact on Sexuality

Many users claim that cocaine is an aphrodisiac. Indeed, as mentioned earlier, the feeling of sexual excitement that sometimes accompanies cocaine use may be the result of its impact on the DA system and may produce spontaneous orgasm. Nonetheless, chronic cocaine abuse causes derangements in reproductive function including impotence and gynecomastia (126). These symptoms may persist for long periods, even after use of cocaine has stopped. Men who abuse cocaine chronically and in high doses may have difficulty maintaining an erection and ejaculating. Many men report experiencing periods when they completely lose interest in sex (7)—not surprising, perhaps, given the direct effects of cocaine on the primary reward systems of the brain.

In women, cocaine abuse has adverse effects on reproductive function, including derangements in the menstrual cycle function, galactorrhea, amenorrhea, and infertility (7). Some women who use cocaine report having greater difficulty achieving orgasm (127). To be detailed later, children born to women who use cocaine during pregnancy are at high risk of congenital malformations and perinatal mortality (128).

Other Adverse Effects

Chronic cocaine abuse may induce persistent hyperprolactinemia (129), apparently because it disrupts DA's ability to inhibit prolactin secretion (130). This effect may continue for long periods even after a person has stopped using cocaine (69).

As a result of the drug's effects on the primary eating drive, many individuals who use cocaine compulsively lose their appetites and can experience significant weight loss (131).

Cocaine has also been shown to produce hyperpyrexia, or extremely elevated body temperatures (47), which can contribute to the development of seizures, life-threatening cardiac arrhythmias, and death (132, 133). This effect results from hypermetabolism combined with severe peripheral vasoconstriction and the impact of cocaine on the ability of the thalamus to regulate body heat (134). Experimental evidence suggests that treatment for hyperpyrexia may involve vigorous cooling of the body by immersing the trunk and the extremities in cold water (135).

Several investigators (136, 137) implicate cocaine in the development of the muscle wasting condition known as rhabdomyolysis. Why the drug should produce this effect is unclear. Roth and colleagues (138) suggest that it may arise due to arterial vasoconstriction, which can lead to tissue ischemia, or that it may be due to a direct toxic effect of cocaine on muscle metabolism. A study of 39 patients with acute rhabdomyolysis found that onset was rapid and occurred in previously healthy individuals who used cocaine hydrochloride. A third of this group had acute renal failure, often together with severe hepatic dysfunction and disseminated intravascular coagulation. Seven patients became oliguric and eight required hemodialysis. Six of the 13 patients with acute renal failure died, adding yet another fatal side effect to cocaine's already long list.

Sudden death from respiratory or cardiac arrest, myocardial infarction, and stroke have been associated with cocaine use among young and otherwise healthy persons. These incidents are probably caused by the ability of cocaine to increase blood pressure, cause vasoconstriction, or alter the electrical activity of the heart. Seizures have been observed in association with cocaine use as have palpitations and arrhythmias. Traumatic injuries due to disputes resulting in violent behavior are common, especially among persons who sell cocaine.

Different routes of cocaine administration can produce different adverse effects. Intranasal use can lead to sinusitis, loss of the sense of smell, atrophy of the nasal mucosa, nosebleeds, perforation of the nasal septum, problems with swallowing, and hoarseness (139, 140). Ingested cocaine can cause severe bowel ischemia or gangrene due to vasoconstriction and reduced blood flow (141). Persons who inject cocaine have puncture marks and "tracks," most commonly on their forearms, as seen in those with opioid dependence. HIV infection is associated with cocaine dependence due to the frequent intravenous injections and the increase in promiscuous sexual behavior. HIV seropositivity is associated with crack smoking without intravenous use. Recently (142), the clear association between the smoking of crack and high-risk sexual practices have been reported and linked to acceleration in the spread of the HIV virus. A study of 2323 young adults of 18–29 in cities from New York to Miami to San Francisco found a 15.7% HIV positive rate among crack smokers and 5.2% among non–crack smokers. The prevalence of HIV was highest among crack smoking women in New York (29.6%) and Miami (23.0%). Further analysis of 283 women who had sex in exchange for money or crack showed 30.4% were HIV infected. Women who had had unprotected sex in exchange for money or drugs were as likely to be infected with the HIV virus as men who had had recent anal sex with men. Other sexually transmitted diseases, hepatitis, and tuberculosis and other lung infections are also seen. Intravenous use is associated with diseases introduced by dirty needles contaminated with the blood of previous users as well as with extra substances in the drug. The most common severe complications from IV cocaine use are bacterial or viral endocarditis, hepatitis, and AIDS (143). Other conditions arising from parenteral cocaine use include cellulitis, cerebritis, wound abscess, sepsis, arterial thrombosis, renal infarction, and thrombophlebitis. As mentioned earlier, crack smoking can lead to the pneumonia-like symptoms of crack lung. Those who smoke cocaine are at increased risk for respiratory problems such as coughing, bronchitis, and pneumonitis due to irritation and inflammation of the tissues lining the respiratory tract. Deaths have occurred from all forms of cocaine administration (144, 145).

Other medical complications include headache, thallium poisoning, retinal artery occlusion, dermatological problems, and muscle and skin infarction. Persons who lack the enzyme pseudocholinesterase are at risk for sudden death from cocaine use because the enzyme is essential for metabolizing the drug. Derlet and Albertson (92) found that 9.5% of patients attempted suicide with cocaine or as a result of cocaine intoxication.

COCAINE AND PREGNANCY

One of the most troubling aspects of the current cocaine epidemic, especially crack smoking, is its use by pregnant women. The available data have been at times conflicting and difficult to understand. Pregnancy increases a woman's susceptibility to the toxic cardiovascular effects of cocaine (146). Placental abruption, or premature separation of a normally implanted placenta, occurs in approximately 1% of pregnancies in women who use cocaine, making the drug a significant cause of maternal morbidity as well as fetal mortality (147). Women who use cocaine during pregnancy have a rate of spontaneous abortion even higher than that of heroin users (128).

Cocaine may produce toxic effects on the fetus at concentrations that are apparently nontoxic to the mother. The drug decreases blood flow to the uterus, increases uterine vascular resistance, and reduces fetal oxygen levels. The vasoconstriction, tachycardia, and increased blood pressure associated with cocaine use increase the risk of intermittent intrauterine hypoxia, preterm or precipitous labor, and placental abruption (148). Cocaine has a significant effect on the ability of fetal hearts to produce action potentials of normal rising velocity, amplitude, and duration (149). Cocaine can cause fetal cerebral infarction (128), growth retardation (150), and fetal death (151). In an interesting pilot study with implications for long-term development, cardiovascular effects of prenatal cocaine exposure in a small group of newborns were compared with a group of normal controls. Results from complete echocardiographic study indicated that the left ventricular (LV) posterior wall and septum were significantly thicker in the exposed group. In addition, the exposed group had significantly larger LV mass, suggestive of the LV hypertrophy found in adult cocaine users (152). The most noncontroversial finding regarding in utero cocaine exposure involves impaired somatic growth and decreased head circumference. Infant gestational age, birth weight, head circumference, and length were decreased, and the rate of low birth weight increased in the majority of studies of the offspring of cocaine-using women (153, 154). Maternal cocaine use was also independently associated with reduced head circumference in a large, prospective survey in Boston. This finding was particularly compelling because all mothers received prenatal care. It seems clear that maternal cocaine use is related to lower infant birth weight and decreased head circumference (155).

Experts have also argued over the prevalence of in utero cocaine exposure. The National Association for Perinatal Addiction Research and Education has estimated that 11% of women studied in 36 hospitals had used illicit drugs during pregnancy. Several prospective surveys demonstrate a prevalence of drugs of abuse of 0.4–44% among pregnant patients. Study of the prevalence of intrauterine cocaine exposure revealed that meconium analysis was able to detect 2.68 times more instances of drug abuse in patients than corresponding urine analysis. Lewis and co-authors' 25.8% prevalence rate compares with a 31% positive cocaine rate in other studies on urban patients and an 11.8% rate in the suburbs (156). While precise data are unavailable in many parts of the country, between 15 and 25% of babies are born with cocaine already in their system (157).

The syndrome associated with cocaine-addicted infants has been given the name "jittery baby" (149). In one series, 34 or 39 infants exposed to cocaine before birth displayed CNS irritability (158). Such children frequently present with such abnormalities as decreased birth weight, length, and head circumference, genitourinary malformations, and neurologic and behavioral impairments (128, 159–161). Much of the early clinical research giving rise to crack baby reports was flawed by failing to consider the relative importance and frequency of poly-drug use among pregnant women. In fact a recent meta-analysis failed to confirm a number of cocaine-related effects in utero with the exception of low birth weight (162). Infants of substance-abusing mothers often have a decreased ventilatory response to carbon dioxide and a 5–10 times increased risk of sudden infant death syndrome (SIDS) (163). Chasnoff (164) reports that the incidence of SIDS in infants exposed to cocaine is 15% more than three times that of infants exposed to heroin or methadone. Cocaine can be passed to infants through breast milk and can be found in milk up to 60 hours after the mother used the drug. Infants intoxicated by cocaine ingested via breast milk may present with hypertension, tachycardia, sweating, dilation of the pupils, and apnea (165).

Early studies of infants who were exposed prenatally to cocaine suggested that neurological and developmental sequelae were common. One explanation of these findings is based on cocaine's action as a potent vasoconstrictor that causes decreased uterine and placental blood flow and that had been related to fetal hypoxia in animal models. Cocaine readily crosses the placenta and can cause fetal cerebral vasoconstriction and ischemia directly. Cocaine-induced CNS malformations theoretically may result if the alteration in fetal cerebral blood flow occurs at a critical time in brain development. Cocaine also inhibits neurotransmitter reuptake, which theoretically may result if the alteration in fetal cerebral blood flow occurs at a critical time in brain development. Cocaine also inhibits neurotransmitter reuptake, which theoretically could result in long-lasting effects on CNS function. Several recent reviews of the effects of prenatal cocaine exposure suggest that caution is warranted in the interpretation of these early reports because of numerous methodological weaknesses inherent in the study designs (166).

It is clear that a significant number of fetuses are exposed to cocaine in utero. Developmental consequences are likely. It is important to remember that historical accounts tend to minimize exposure. This "denial" has been demonstrated by a recent study of 3010 neonates. Although 11% of the women reported using illicit drugs during pregnancy, 31% of infants meconium tested positive for cocaine alone (167).

Cocaine's effects on the unborn and newborn may also be related to poor nutrition, poor hygiene, and neglect. Cocaine compromises the mother or any caregiver's ability to respond to their new baby through talking, eye contact, and tactile stimulation. Such disconnection and indifference to the infant's behavioral cues, which is necessary for optimal intellectual and emotional infant development, creates additional problems. It has been suggested that drug-dependent mothers are impaired in the ability to respond to their infants; the specific interactional behavior of cocaine-using mothers is still under investigation (152).

COCAINE AND OTHER PSYCHIATRIC DISORDERS

A patient who suffers from a psychiatric illness often appears more susceptible to stimulant toxicity and abuse. Some people with depression will experiment with cocaine, amphetamines, or even excessive caffeine and tobacco to lift themselves out of their fatigue, low energy, and disinterest in activities. They generally find that cocaine makes them no better and sometimes more depressed and hopeless. Recent use often appears temporarily related to depressive exacerbations and medication resistance. Surveys of people undergoing treatment for cocaine abuse reveal that at least half of a given patient population meet the diagnostic criteria for mood disorders (44, 168). A similar incidence of depression can be seen among opiate addicts. However, 20% of cocaine abusers experience cyclic mood disorders such as bipolar disorders (manic-depressive illness) and cyclothymic disorder; the incidence of these conditions in opiate addicts is only 1%. Such findings suggest that people who experience mood swings prefer stimulants over other illicit drugs. Another commonly seen condition among cocaine patients is residual attention deficit disorder (hyperactivity).

People with borderline personality disorder are likely to turn to mood-altering drugs for relief. They may use stimulants to induce feelings of pleasure or depressants to reduce internal distress. Since these people are already on edge, use of stimulants and depressants may trigger a flare-up of anger or violence.

Perhaps more than those with any other personality disorder, people diagnosed as having antisocial personality disorder are prone to use mood-altering drugs. Alcohol is often the drug of choice in such individuals, but many also use cocaine or amphetamines or a combination of several drugs. People with this disorder are distressed, tense, unable to tolerate boredom, and agitated to the point of discomfort. Their use of drugs often removes any remaining inhibitions, increasing the risk of anger, violence, and actions that violate the rights or property of others. Since cocaine is by definition an illicit substance, use of the drug in itself constitutes a form of antisocial behavior.

Like a person with schizophrenia, a person in the throes of cocaine delirium may lose contact with reality and become confused and disoriented. Paranoia is a trait commonly seen in both schizophrenia and cocaine abuse.

In both conditions the patient may experience auditory hallucinations. The delirium of cocaine usually dissipates within a few days, although some symptoms of delirium may persist for up to a year (169).

Many people with eating disorders—anorexia and bulimia—take diet pills containing amphetamines to suppress the appetite. Some of these people progress to using cocaine or illicitly acquired amphetamines, such as "crank" or "ice," the smokable version of methamphetamine. Over time they may become tolerant to these drugs and eventually dependent on them. In severe cases, use of amphetamines may lead to chronic intoxication and psychosis that resembles schizophrenia. Withdrawal produces symptoms including fatigue and depression.

In a survey conducted by the National Helpline, 50% of callers reported experiencing cocaine-induced panic attacks. Treatment facilities specializing in panic and anxiety disorders also report that onset of panic attacks often begins with cocaine use (170). It appears that through the process of kindling—lowering the stimulation threshold of the brain—cocaine may increase the risk of panic. Over time, and following ingestion of large amounts of the drug, such reactions may occur spontaneously, without drug-induced stimulation. Panic reactions may persist even after use of cocaine has stopped.

As in other medical conditions, the results of treatment depend on a variety of factors. Persistent, untreated depression may compromise recovery. Moreover, abrupt cessation from cocaine use has been suggested with depressive symptoms (44). This is corroborated by the finding of high rates of depressive disorders among treatment-seeking cocaine abusers (171). Because serotonin uptake inhibitors are antidepressants (172), this type of agent is further suggested for treatment of depressive cocaine abusers.

Overall rates for active psychiatric disorders appear to be approximately 50% currently in cocaine abusers and 75–85%, lifetime. Some published literature and studies in progress report extremely high comorbidity for cocaine dependence. Such high rates of comorbidity may be related to poor outcome reported for cocaine treatment and numerous positive treatment reports which are tantalizing but difficult to replicate. The authors and other investigators have reported important associations between cocaine use and dependence and bipolar disorders, depression, marihuana abuse and dependence, and alcohol abuse and dependence (44, 172). Some investigators have reported comorbidity of up to 25% for bipolar-spectrum illnesses (mania, hypomania, cyclothymia) in cocaine-dependent patients. Lifetime major depression is diagnosed in approximately 50% of subjects, whereas dysthymia is diagnosed in another 25–50% (170, 172). Rates for alcoholism are quite high, with as many as 60% having clear lifetime diagnoses. Marihuana use is common and may be related to cocaine pharmacokinetics. Marihuana and cocaine are commonly used at the same time. As described earlier in the chapter, marihuana may potentiate cocaine's effects (125, 173).

Some clinicians suggest that a history of attention-deficit hyperactivity disorder (ADHD) is common. Individuals with a cocaine dependence diagnosis often have temporary depressive symptoms that meet symptomatic and duration criteria for major depressive disorder that are difficult to characterize. Cocaine-using patients give compelling histories consistent with repeated panic attacks, social phobic-like behavior, and generalized anxiety-like syndromes. Eating disorders are also commonly reported on the basis of pathological starvation, satiety or more traditional bulimia. Cocaine-induced psychotic disorder with delusions and hallucinations that resembles mania or schizophrenia, paranoid type can occur and persist. More commonly, mental disturbances that occur in association with cocaine use resolve within hours to days after cessation of use.

Superstition and unusual behavior and thoughts are common. Individuals with cocaine dependence develop these "superstitions" as conditioned responses to cocaine-related stimuli and, unfortunately for them, they cannot successfully recognize the total number of such stimuli. They may say they feel better in Florida or give a history of seasonal affective changes, but really have so many associations that they are asking for a geographic cure. They may have extreme agitation, provoked nausea, provoked drive for the drug in the absence of a clear association with a sight or sound associated with the drug. Most common is their reaction to seeing, holding, or rolling paper money. These responses probably contribute to relapse, are difficult to extinguish, and typically persist long after detoxification is completed. Co-

caine use disorders are often associated with other substance dependence or abuse, especially involving alcohol, marihuana, and benzodiazepines, which are often taken to reduce the anxiety and other unpleasant stimulant side effects of cocaine. Cocaine dependence may be associated with post-traumatic stress disorder, antisocial personality disorder, ADHD, and pathological gambling. Cocaine addicts take alcohol and benzodiazepines in an effort to reduce the negative consequences of cocaine intoxication but intravenous users commonly use cocaine in combination with heroin to produce a speedball effect which is described as better than either alone.

Mello and coworkers have developed an animal model to evaluate the speedball phenomenon (174) in rhesus monkeys who simultaneously self-administer cocaine and heroin. Pretreatment with an opiate antagonist, quadazocine (0.1 mg/kg IM), had no effect on the discriminative stimulus effects of cocaine but antagonized the cocaine-like discriminative stimulus effects of heroin. Pretreatment with a DA antagonist, flupentixol (0.018 mg/kg), antagonized the discriminative stimulus effects of cocaine but did not affect the cocaine-like effects of heroin. The pharmacological systems mediating the stimulus properties of cocaine and heroin in rhesus monkeys are not only distinct but also functionally independent. The pharmacological classification of cocaine as a stimulant and heroin as an opiate tends to divert attention from exploration of the ways in which these drugs may have similar effects. This complex poly-drug use is extremely compelling and further study may yield important information on the DA-endorphin-serotonin systems interplay in maximizing drug-induced brain reward. The addiction psychiatrist must always weigh the risk of withholding psychiatric treatment as one tries to establish a clear diagnosis and the propensity for relapse when comorbid psychopathology goes untreated.

TREATMENT OF COCAINE ADDICTION

The evaluation and initial treatment of cocaine-using patients is a complex, demanding, and sometimes confusing process (175). Thorough treatment requires the physician to integrate a range of medical, psychiatric, social, and drug counseling services. Adding to the complexity is the need to address family issues and to anticipate the risk of relapse. Although currently the success rate of treatment for drug addiction is less than would be desired, new treatment strategies, including some pharmacological interventions, offer hope for improving the outcome.

In recent years many treatment facilities have adopted the chemical dependency model, which regards drug dependence as a primary condition—a disease unto itself—not a secondary problem arising from some other underlying psychopathology (176). Such programs take a multidisciplinary approach to drug treatment and provide a range of behavioral, cognitive, educational, and self-control techniques aimed at reducing drug cravings and the potential for relapse. Significantly, these programs also require patients to abstain from all drugs and to participate actively in 12-step programs such as Alcoholics Anonymous (AA) or Cocaine Anonymous (CA). The advantage in doing so is that patients learn to consider themselves as being continually at risk and in a recovering—rather than a recovered—state. They also learn to see themselves as chemically dependent, not crazy. Such a fundamental shift in perspective improves the chances that the patient will live a happy, healthy, and drug-free life.

Diagnosis

The first step in treatment, of course, is to diagnose the patient's condition accurately. A list of the clinical criteria for cocaine dependency appears in Table 16.5 (177). Of course, the clinical use of supervised urine testing for drugs, including cocaine, in diagnosis has been underutilized.

A diagnosis of cocaine withdrawal (see Table 16.2) can be made if the patient has stopped or reduced heavy use of the drug after a prolonged period (several days or longer) and experiences dysphoric mood (depression, irritability, anxiety) and fatigue, sleep disturbance, or psychomotor agitation persisting for at least 24 hours. Many patients report having "coke dreams" with themes involving the repeated pursuit or use of cocaine.

Other related diagnoses include cocaine delirium and cocaine delusional disorder. In the former, the patient develops delirium, marked by disorga-

Table 16.5   Diagnostic Criteria for Cocaine Dependency

Loss of control
  Inability to stop using or refuse cocaine
  Failure to self-limit use
  Predictable or regular use
  Binges for 24 hours or longer
  Urges and cravings for cocaine
Exaggerated involvement
  Self-proclaimed need for cocaine
  Fear of distress without cocaine
  Feelings of dependency on cocaine
  Feelings of guilt about using cocaine and fear of being discovered
  Preference for cocaine over family, friends, and recreational activities
Continued use despite adverse effects
  Medical problems (e.g., fatigue, insomnia, headaches, nasal problems, bronchitis)
  Psychological problems (e.g., irritability, depression, loss of sex drive, lack of motivation, memory impairment)
  Social/interpersonal problems (e.g., loss of friends or spouse, job difficulties, social withdrawal, involvement in traffic accidents, excuse-making behavior)

Washton AM, Gold MS, Pottash AC. Opiate and cocaine dependencies: techniques to help counter the rising tide. Postgrad Med 1985;77:293–300.

nized thinking, sensory misperceptions, and disorientation within 24 hours after drug use. Typically patients experience tactile or olfactory hallucinations. Affect is often labile. Because violent or aggressive behavior is common, especially after use of crack cocaine, restraint may be required. When the pharmacological effects of cocaine have worn off, the delirium usually disappears.

The essential feature of cocaine delusional disorder involves the presence of persecutory delusions developing shortly after the use of cocaine. At first, the patient may experience the feelings of suspiciousness and curiosity as a source of pleasure or entertainment. In the later phases the suspiciousness, anxiety, and paranoia may provoke violent or aggressive behavior, often accompanied by hallucinations that further distort reality. Delusions may persist up to a year following use of cocaine.

In all cases, regardless of the exact diagnosis, toxicological analysis of body fluids should be made to confirm the findings.

Inpatient versus Outpatient Care

If circumstances permit, outpatient treatment is the preferred modality for delivery of care, for several reasons. Many cocaine abusers can be treated as outpatients, since use of the drug usually can be stopped abruptly without medical risk or significant discomfort. The goal of treatment is to return the patient to a normal life; by definition there can be no "normal" life inside the hospital. The cost of outpatient treatment is lower (although some insurance companies may refuse to pay for care delivered in the outpatient setting). Many patients are more willing to accept help on an outpatient basis since it carries less of a social stigma and is less disruptive to daily life. Entering a hospital or a rehabilitation center as an inpatient with their fewer privileges and liberties conveys an acceptance that the disease is an imminent danger to themselves. Perhaps the most important consideration, however, is that in all cases of substance abuse, outpatient care will eventually be needed, given the lifelong risk of relapse and the need for ongoing support (178). However, inpatient or residential treatment provides an ideal transition from drug use and dependency to abstinence and daily meetings.

When drug use is severe, or if outpatient care is not possible or has failed in the past, hospitalization is called for. While not a complete listing, indications for inpatient care include:

1. Chronic crack, freebase, or intravenous use
2. Concurrent dependency on other addictive drugs or alcohol
3. Serious concurrent medical or psychiatric problems
4. Severe impairment of psychological or neurological functioning
5. Insufficient motivation for outpatient treatment
6. Lack of family and social supports
7. Failure in outpatient treatment (177)

One important advantage of a treatment facility is removing patients from the environment—the home, the streets—that may be contributing to their drug use. Patients under round-the-clock supervision are unable (in most cases) to obtain illicit drugs. They can take daily advantage of the many types of therapy the hospital offers. Another advantage is that patients are available for full medical and psychiatric evaluations, which will reveal whether any coexisting problems such as HIV infection, hepatitis, or clinical depression exist (179). Many of these problems emerge, and can be properly evaluated, only after detoxification and during observation over a period of several drug-free days. Successful initial treatment in a residential setting may facilitate the integration and retention by the patient of outpatient and self-help meetings.

Treatment Strategies

Planning treatment requires a comprehensive assessment of the psychobiological, social, and pharmacological aspects of the patient's substance abuse. For many patients, cocaine use is the focus of their entire life. They become totally preoccupied with drug-seeking and drug-taking behaviors. They may have become accustomed to the mood changes invoked by cocaine and have forgotten what life without drugs is like. Thus they come to regard the drugged state as "normal" and may not believe any treatment is necessary. For this reason they may refuse to acknowledge the need for help. Many patients hence enter treatment only under pressure from family, friends, employers, or the judicial system (169). In severe cases, the patient perceives such pressure to be a threat from "enemies," which only serves to reinforce drug-induced feelings of suspicion, persecution, and paranoia. For this and other reasons, families often need guidance in staging an intervention on a cocaine-abusing relative.

The initial contact with a patient may occur after the crash and during the withdrawal phase. The physician should take a complete family, medical, and forensic history, as well as a history of all drug use. However, information obtained from chemically dependent people can be incomplete or highly unreliable. For this reason the patient should undergo a thorough physical and dental examination. Chest x-rays and electrocardiograms may supply useful information and may help to reassure patients about their state of health. Any severe conditions or impending medical emergencies may necessitate transfer to the medical floor or hospital. One concern is that patients about to enter the hospital may ingest huge and potentially lethal doses of one or more drugs (175).

Immediately following the physical examination, blood and/or supervised urine samples should be collected and sent for analysis. If possible, a sample of the cocaine used by the patient should also be submitted to the laboratory. All subsequent urine collections should be supervised and taken first thing in the morning. Temperature and/or specific gravity should be measured to confirm that the sample has not been adulterated. Although expensive, antibody tests and gas chromatography-mass spectrography testing are many times more sensitive and specific than thin layer chromatography or urine drug screens. Blood is the preferred sample for forensic purposes or to evaluate whether the person is under the influence at the time of the psychiatric exam (175). Frequent urine laboratory testing is valuable because it eliminates the need to continually question the patient about current drug use, uncovers any drug use by the patient, and provides a strong motivation for the patient to remain drug free.

Medical Treatment of Withdrawal and Cocaine-Related Emergencies

As a rule, symptoms of cocaine withdrawal are not medically dangerous (180). Detoxification from cocaine requires no treatment other than abstinence (175). However, many patients find the symptoms of withdrawal intensely dysphoric, so much so that they feel driven to continue acquiring and using cocaine in order to fend off the symptoms. Any medical treatment that helps relieve withdrawal symptoms therefore improves the initial prognosis. A DA theory may explain drug reward, survival drive reward, symptoms or complaints common to acute drug withdrawal states (including cocaine withdrawal), and be a useful or predictor or model to identify potential new treatments. However, early in clinical trials it became quite clear that successful amelioration of withdrawal appears to be of limited clinical significance. Painless and symptomless cocaine withdrawal was often followed by relapse and re-addiction just as clonidine detoxification was followed by opiate re-addiction and success with the nicotine patch was followed by a return to smoking. New treatments directed at reversal of post-abstinence craving—like bromocriptine or desipramine (181–185) on cocaine abstinence—were based on the assumption that successful craving reduction would in some way reduce drug use or relapse. These and other recent treatments have been surprisingly ineffective in stopping relapse or cocaine-taking. They offered clinical support for the DA theory of abstinence and craving but also convinced researchers that drug use and recidivism was clearly separable from drug withdrawal. More recently, researchers have focused the development of treatments on the direct prevention of further drug use as measured by urinalysis or tried to reduce the likelihood of relapse.

The choice of treatment for cocaine toxicity depends on the clinical signs and symptoms. Supportive therapy is the rule. Treating hyperthermia with vigorous body cooling may be a positive first step. Cardiac and neurological status should be monitored closely, with medical strategies directed at providing symptom relief. Use of phenothiazines, especially chlorpromazine (Promapar, Thorazine) or of haloperidol (Haldol) is contraindicated for acute reactions because these drugs may lower the seizure threshold. Spontaneous cocaine-induced seizures can be treated with intravenous administration of 25–50 mg of a short-acting barbiturate such as pentobarbital sodium (Nembutal) (177).

Hospitalization with respiratory assistance and a life support system may be necessary in cases of severe cocaine overdose reaction. Treatment of overdose is often complicated by the presence of sedative-hypnotics, opiates, or alcohol, drugs that are frequently taken to mitigate the unpleasant effects of excessive cocaine use.

Typically, cocaine psychosis lasts for 3–5 days following cessation of use; if it persists for a longer period or if the patient becomes increasingly difficult to manage, a reevaluation of the diagnosis is indicated and an antipsychotic medication such as haloperidol may be tried.

Long-term Treatment of Cocaine Dependency

Patients with dependency problems usually experience the best outcome if treated by physicians, psychologists, and other caregivers who specialize in managing addictive disorders (177). In recent years increasing demand for treatment has led to the burgeoning availability of specialized treatment centers in many parts of the country. Addiction specialists understand that animals and humans, whether bred for drug preference or not, whether dependent or drug-naive, whether reared in Milan or Miami, self-administer drugs of abuse. The reinforcing properties of drugs are powerful motivational forces, which are preferred by the subject to natural reinforcers. Addicts or subjects in self-administration studies perform many difficult and time-consuming tasks to gain access to drugs. Drug users make active choices between the drug over work, spouse, friends, and other reinforcers. The drugs that stimulate their own taking and are positively reinforcing in animals do the same in humans. This relationship is so strong that drug self-administration in animals is now viewed as predictive of human drug abuse potential. The data derived from animal and human self-administration of abused drugs support the notion that drug reinforcement is the unifying feature of drug abuse and dependence. It is also true that drug abstinence is the behavioral and physical state "released" by the absence of the drug of abuse to which the chronic user has adapted. So, it is also positive reinforcement to reverse the negative hedonic state released by drug abstinence. Addiction specialists focus on the motivational rather than the physical aspects of the withdrawal syndrome. Malaise, boredom, depression, anhedonia, decreased appetite, brain stimulation changes, increased behavioral responsiveness to stressors, and increases in reward thresholds are all part of the withdrawal syndrome. Human addicts report that they need cocaine to return to normal or simply to think straight after prolonged use. Musicians report a loss of creativity, authors report "writer's block," and others report a loss of color or brightness in their lives after abstinence. Reward and withdrawal mechanisms are associated with both positive and negative reinforcement in ways that are not easily separated clinically. The "good feeling" that is the goal of cocaine use usually involves both euphoria (positive reinforcement) and reversal of cocaine-absence dysphoria. The failure of cocaine addiction treatment was attributed to incomplete medical science and poor medical treatment options rather than to the positive drive of motivated behavior directed at the use of cocaine. While a desirable outcome over a period of many years was virtually unheard of following repeated detoxifications, it was remarkable how slow the medical profession was to recognize the implications of this observation. Rather than question the underlying assumption, which placed medical skills essential in the diagnosis and treatment of withdrawal at the center of the problem of addiction treatment, physicians seemed resigned to recycle addicted people through one emergency room or detoxification experience after another for what often proved to be an addiction-shortened lifetime.

Clinical Treatment Model

Whether it serves as the primary mode of care or as a sequel to hospitalization, a comprehensive outpatient program should include a range of treatment strategies. These include supportive counseling, drug education, peer support groups, and family meetings. Exercise therapy may also prove to be a helpful adjunct (169). For a period of time, caregivers should follow the patient on a daily basis. Severe depression may require psychotherapy and perhaps the use of medications. Regular telephone support should continue for several months. Many treatment centers offer ongoing group therapy sessions for patients and their families for a period of years following discharge.

In all cases, patients should be given frequent urine tests to screen for all drugs of abuse. Even in prisons and other criminal justice settings, urine testing is the most useful barometer of treatment outcome. The goal must be to achieve abstinence from mood-altering chemicals, including alcohol. Attaining this goal cannot be determined simply by asking the patient, family, or loved ones if he or she "is still using drugs." We should ask this question *and* look for drugs in the urine. There is no hope for effective treatment so long as the patient continues to use drugs. Personality problems, emotional difficulties, and psychiatric disorders should be addressed as they arise, but the chances of success are virtually nil unless the patient is drug free.

Another crucial element of long-term treatment is participation in a 12-step recovery program. In recent years the medical and psychiatric professions have come to recognize the significant contributions that AA and similar programs can make to the lives of substance abusers. Members draw strength and security from meeting with others who understand and share their concerns and can offer practical strategies for surviving "one day at a time." Any treatment program that does not embrace the 12-step approach and encourage patients to participate stands little chance of long-term success.

When considering the treatment of addictive disease, it is useful to recall that the use of medicines remains limited when compared to the role of medicines in many other mental disorders, including the affective and the anxiety disorders, the two diagnostic groupings that share with addiction the distinction of being the most prevalent classes of mental disorders. While cognitive-behavioral approaches have been effective in the treatment of both affective and anxiety disorders, pharmacotherapy dominates the clinical management of these diseases. In contrast to the treatment of affective and anxiety disorders, when it comes to substance use disorders, pharmacotherapy plays a relatively minor role and the 12-step programs, the most potent cognitive-behavioral approach, are ascendant. Chapter 37 describes in detail the Twelve Steps and how they are put into practice.

The dream of modern pharmacological research is to find more specific and effective treatments that block ready access to the drug-induced effects of both the reward and the withdrawal pathways, without producing agonist effects or other effects. Naturally, antagonists that reverse the effects of cocaine and marihuana, like naloxone reverses the effects of opiates, are essential for emergency rooms and pharmacotherapies for relapse prevention. Relapse-preventing psychopharmacology is an important new addition to this phase. Medications that deny brain reward access to rewarding drugs of abuse rather than punish the addict for using are in the early phases of a dramatic change in the field of addiction medicine and addiction psychiatry (186).

Comorbid cocaine patients may represent up to 80% of patients with cocaine dependency according to recent studies reported at the 1995 meeting of the American Psychiatric Association. They need simultaneous and aggressive cocaine and psychiatric treatments. Patients need to find thorough treatment of their mental disorder, which will improve quality of life and reduce the risk for depression-related and anxiety-related relapses and suicides.

The 12-step programs use a unitary approach to addictive disease by largely disregarding the specific substances being used. AA takes a unitary view on addiction by making clear that staying sober means not only not drinking alcohol but also not using other brain-rewarding chemicals. Beyond not using alcohol or other drugs, AA works to change the addict's lifestyle to a better, less self-centered life (18).

Preventing Relapse

Despite progress in treatment for cocaine use, the risk of relapse is extremely high. As noted, the memory of cocaine euphoria is so powerful that it can produce overwhelming urges to revert to drug use. Patients whose lifestyles revolved around cocaine are susceptible to being reminded of the drug in surprising ways. For example, a patient who sees talcum powder, bread crumbs, or snow may be reminded of cocaine. Seeing cocaine-using friends or locations, smelling cocaine, or even hearing a song associated with cocaine use can trigger drug urges. The click of a cigarette lighter or the light from a match is enough to remind some patients of their cocaine-smoking habit. Apparently, almost any stimulus that has been repeatedly associated with obtaining and using cocaine can become a cocaine "reminder" (187).

Gawin and Ellinwood (188) describe a four-step treatment approach to the extinction of cocaine cravings. In the first phase, patients are isolated from the events, objects, people, and locations that may provoke urges. Next, some of these stimuli are gradually reintroduced as mental images during psychotherapy sessions. Patients then discuss and rehearse strategies for managing the temptations arising from such provocation. In the third stage patients reenter their former environments gradually and under the guidance of their caregivers. In the final phase of consolidation, patients continue to participate in self-help and aftercare groups or resume treatment as necessary to counteract any recurring drug cravings.

Persistence of cocaine abstinence may be manifested in persistent dysphoria and cocaine self-administration. Recent data support persistent neural dysregulation in cocaine dependence. It is not uncommon for such persistent dysphoria or anxiety or panic symptoms to persist after discontinuation of cocaine and thus constitute a feature of the prolonged abstinence phase. We have seen patients who complain of panic attacks that continue for years.

Neurobiological changes that persist after prolonged abstinence have been reported by a number of different groups who have studied prolactin as a marker of abnormal dopaminergic function (189–195). One investigator (76) found persistent hyperprolactinemia in 14 male and 2 female cocaine abusers at admission and at inpatient day 28. Teoh et al. (196) also found that the relative duration and severity of hyperprolactinemia in abstinent cocaine addicts predicted enhanced risk of relapse.

Like our pioneering work (71) these studies suggest that cocaine-induced derangement of the dopaminergic system is consistent with decreased dopaminergic tone and consequent disinhibition of the DA-regulated prolactin system. Persistent abstinence manifested by continuing neural dysregulation and resultant dysphoria may be an unrecognized consequence of cocaine dependence.

Persistent neural compromise suggests that limitations may exist for the cocaine-dependent person even after abstinence. The mechanisms underlying cocaine-induced ischemic stroke are not well understood. Strategies for treatment do not exist. Generally these patients demonstrated multifocal areas of cortical hypoperfusion and scalloping of periventricular regions indicating that SPECT is sensitive to perfusion abnormalities associated with cocaine use (197–200). Cerebral blood flow abnormalities and cognitive abnormalities may persist following extended periods of drug abstinence, particularly in chronic, long-term users. Moreover, there is evidence that there may be minimal recovery of some cognitive abilities following abstinence, especially recovery of short-term verbal memory deficits (201).

These studies and clinical experience suggest that prolonged crack cocaine self-administration and even cocaine hydrochloride use (202–204) are often accompanied by structural neuronal change and compromise that are not readily reversed.

Relapse prevention strategies developed according to a social learning theory model have been adapted to chemical dependency treatment that follows the disease model. Some of these techniques are: helping the patient recognize the warning signs of relapse; combating the powerful memories of euphoria; reinforcing the negative aspects of drugs; overcoming the desire to attempt to regain control over drug use; avoiding the people, places, and things that may trigger drug urges; preventing occasional "slips" from developing into full-blown binges; learning other ways to cope with dysphoric feelings that in the past may have led to drug use; developing an array of pleasurable and rewarding alternatives to drugs (205). As the early preoccupation with withdrawal as the central focus of addictive disease was excessive, so perhaps today's dismissal of withdrawal as a major factor in addiction is an overreaction. If generally effective ways were found to treat the withdrawal symptoms resulting from the physiological dependence on any substance, whether taken medically or nonmedically, such treatments might have broad application both in addiction treatment and in medical practice.

The most promising approach to treatment of cocaine abuse is one that recognizes the high risk of relapse and applies a range of cognitive and behavioral strategies, including a 12-step program, to minimize the risk. New treatment approaches include financial incentive motivation and cue-related relaxation have been reported and appear to offer some promise in prediction of high relapse potential patients and possibly in adding to what is the current approach to treatment. A recent study (206) confirmed that many cocaine-dependent individuals respond to drug cues in the laboratory with increased craving for cocaine and demonstrable physiological arousal. They studied 19 patients in a cue-reactivity protocol that concluded with relaxation exercises. Self-reported craving and skin conductance levels were measured. Patients who achieved abstinence were predicted by craving reported after relaxation training. Patients who subsequently initiated abstinence reported a reduction in cue-elicited craving to below baseline levels, while those who did not succeed in treatment remained elevated.

The Future of Treatment for Cocaine Abuse

New treatments must be assessed over long periods with regular independent urine and other testing to confirm efficacy. Recidivism is a major area for future research. Recidivism among cocaine patients is high; most treatment specialists acknowledge that they offer treatment, not a cure, for addiction. However, there is reason for hope. Perhaps a decade ago, only 10–20% of drug addicts recovered following treatment. More recently a study found that, on average, up to 80% of substance abusers treated for 3 months or longer had reduced their drug use significantly, and that fully 50% were still completely drug free a year after treatment ended (207). Some programs today report a success rate of 60–70%. However, most programs have a high initial dropout rate and even patients who succeed in treatment with one program frequently may have benefited from previous attempts at treatment with different programs. Furthermore, a treatment program may have a different success rate with various types of drug users. For example, a program that helps a 40-year-old college-educated executive to recover may not succeed in treating a 19-year-old unemployed high school dropout. Five-year follow-up data on truly similar patients, with random assignment of treatment and confirmation by urine testing, are necessary to evaluate treatment success claims.

Most agents used to treat cocaine abuse target the DA system because of its role in reinforcement (208). However, serotonin (5-HT) has also been implicated in reinforcement (209) and is affected by cocaine. Acutely, cocaine increases DA and norepinephrine and also serotonergic activity by inhibiting uptake of neurotransmitter release in the synaptic cleft (210). When cocaine is used chronically, the increased neurotransmitter levels induced by cocaine cause an inhibition of transmitter synthesis (211). When chronic cocaine self-administration is stopped, DA in the DA system and also the 5-HT system may decrease synaptic transmitter levels (71).These changes may be related to cocaine craving and possibly relapse. In addition to DA treatments, pharmacological treatment agents for cocaine craving might inhibit 5-HT uptake, like cocaine, but would be nonaddicting (212).

The 5-HT3 antagonist ondansetron reduced the "rush" produced by cocaine and the 5-HT2 antagonist ritanserin has been reported to reduce cocaine self-administration in rats. In a study 25 cocaine-dependent males were exposed to cocaine craving cues while their 5-HT levels were reduced by tryptophan depletion. Serotonin appeared to be related to cue-induced craving since they found a decreased desire for cocaine stimulated by cue exposure (212).

Serotonergic agents have been used to treat other addictive disorders, such as alcoholism (213) and obesity (214). Fluoxetine, a 5-HT uptake inhibitor, is associated with reduced cocaine use among methadone-maintained patients (215) and may be tried (214, 215).

Some reports have suggested that methylphenidate (Ritalin) reduces cocaine cravings in patients with attention deficit disorder, possibility because of its ability to stimulate the CNS. However, the abuse potential of methylphenidate and similar drugs severely limits their usefulness (216). The antidepressants bupropion (Wellbutrin) or trazodone (Desyrel), or the anticonvulsant carbamazepine (Tegretol), may be effective in relieving acute withdrawal symptoms and in maintaining abstinence from cocaine. Lack of patient compliance and the risk of extrapyramidal side effects may preclude the use of DA receptor neuroleptics, even though such drugs are known to block the euphoria caused by amphetamines. In general, all medications tried have been demonstrated to have some subjective effect on the cocaine experience or craving but do not alter or interfere with the natural history of cocaine dependence or euphoria (217). For example, lithium carbonate has been reported by some, but not others, to reduce the intensity of euphoria (218). While lithium is not currently used to treat cocaine dependence, the clinical utility of lithium in cocaine-abusing manic depressive or bipolar patients appears clear. Desipramine has been reported to reduce cocaine craving in a number of studies and was thought to promote abstinence (219–222). Tricyclics like desipramine appeared well suited to correct the catecholamine receptor supersensitivity that could accompany DA and norepinephrine depletion in chronic cocaine users. Yet, as a treatment for cocaine dependence it has been quite disappointing. Desipramine, imipramine, doxepin, and other tricyclics have been tried and while effects may be demonstrated for short periods, cocaine use and relapse are not prevented by such treatment. This was not as surprising to the basic researchers in the field who reported that desipramine has little or no effect on cocaine self-administration in animals (223) or humans (217, 224). Desipramine was prescribed to large numbers of cocaine dependent patients and has clearly been a disappointment as a promising pharmacotherapy. Still, this clinical experience may provide important clues regarding cocaine cues, craving, and euphoria. Carbamazepine was believed to be an important treatment on the basis of animal models and reversal of cocaine-related kindling (225). Again, clinicians reported clinical success but double-blind and long-term studies with carbamazepine have been as disappointing as for those with desipramine. This has been the pattern for cocaine dependence treatment development, where many seemingly promising compounds from methylphenidate to mazindol were reported "to work" and ultimately failed as new treatments (217, 226–232).

While recent studies found that disulfiram reduced cocaine use in concomitant cocaine and alcohol abusers (233) Hameedi et al. recently (234) studied the effect of disulfiram pretreatment on the behavioral, physiological, and pharmacological effects of an acute dose of cocaine using a double-blind, placebo-controlled, within-subject design. This study did not support the hypothesis that disulfiram affects cocaine-induced euphoria. They also showed that cocaine and disulfiram together increased nervousness and paranoia in three subjects, while not increasing heart rate and blood pressure more than cocaine alone. Unexpectedly, disulfiram also increased plasma cocaine levels suggesting that disulfiram use in cocaine addicts may be problematic.

Cocaine has humbled many researchers and research groups with its early and late recidivism, persistent attachment of the user to the drug easily triggered by known and unrecognized environmental cues, and willingness to "respond" to one or another experimental measures but do not stop continued use in clinical trials (29, 235–245).

With continued understanding of the cellular basis for drug reward and the possibility that drug and other rewards are separable, new pharmacological treatments that focus on the positive aspects of the drug-taking experience and reduce drug reward and drug taking may be possible. While the brain produces neurotransmitters to maintain homeostasis, a drug like cocaine alters normal brain function to induce a sense of well-being. Repeated administration of cocaine causes the brain to function as if this new, drug-dependent, state was "normal." Our task in developing new and effective treatments is first to truly understand the effects of illicit drugs, then to establish a model for the abstinent state, and finally to provide a treatment that allows the person to feel safe and comfortable while permitting the brain the opportunity to return to its predrug normal state. Without an antidote to cocaine toxicity, it is doubtful that we will know enough about cocaine's effects to successfully undo them. It is hoped that cocaine treatment will soon evolve to match our treatment options for heroin.

The clinical findings and natural history of cocaine dependence, the attachment of the user to the drug, and the power of the cocaine reward in shaping, conditioning, and modifying behavior have contributed to the current therapeutic approach, which combines a number of modalities. Current treatment strategies are not one or another but are always a combined rehabilitation, psychodynamic, and behavioral with pharmacological treatment during the acute withdrawal period and during early abstinence. Pharmacological agents have been successfully used to decrease abstinence complaints and decrease early treatment drop-out rates. Pharmacological agents have been used to reverse the acute abstinence-related inertia, dysphoria, and depression. Pharmacological agents have also been used to reduce craving for cocaine with a hope that relapse might be prevented or made less likely. Finally, pharmacological treatments have been given which have been believed to modify cocaine's positive, rewarding effects to reduce relapse or the impact of a slip.

The mainstay of treatment for cocaine dependence remains behavioral. In treating physicians and celebrities addicted to cocaine persistent abstinence can be achieved by contingent urine-related contracting with swift losses related to abstinence violation. For others opposite reinforcement paradigms with monetary reward for abstinence have been quite successful. Community payment for abstinence or the "Reinforcement Approach" has shown more efficacy than traditional counseling or pharmacotherapies. Payment for abstinence by focusing on drug and cocaine-free urines rather than a more amorphous outcome can succeed where standard drug abuse counseling fails in retaining cocaine-dependent individuals in outpatient treatment. In one early study a surprising 85% of patients completed 12 weeks of incentive treatment and 65–70% achieved 6 or more weeks of continuous cocaine abstinence across the two trials. By contrast, less than 45% of patients assigned to standard counseling completed 12 weeks of treatment. Higgins and colleagues (246) at Vermont documented 6 or more weeks of continuous cocaine abstinence in only 5–10% of the non-incentive patients similar to results by other clinicians trying to treat cocaine dependence. Their early work was followed by a random assignment test of incentives wherein patients earn vouchers exchangeable for retail items contingent on documentation of cocaine abstinence via urinalysis. Considering the widespread use of incentives in our capitalistic society the systematic use of incentives to foster cocaine abstinence may be warranted. Community reinforcement, payment for abstinence, and relapse prevention are the three major types of cocaine treatment programs in widespread use in the United States. A recent study by Higgins et al. (247) assessed whether incentives improved treatment outcome in ambulatory cocaine-dependent patients. They studied 40 cocaine-dependent adults randomly assigned to behavioral treatment with or without an added incentive program. The behavioral treatment was based on the "Community Reinforcement Approach" and was provided to both groups. Subjects in the group with incentives received vouchers exchangeable for retail items contingent on submitting cocaine-free urine specimens during weeks 1 through 12 of treatment; the group without incentives received no vouchers during that period. The two groups were treated the same during weeks 13–24. In this important study 75% of patients in the group with vouchers completed 24 weeks of treatment versus 40% in the group without vouchers. Average duration of continuous cocaine abstinence documented via urinalysis during weeks 1–24 of treatment were 11.7 ± 2.0 weeks in the group with vouchers versus 6.0 ± 1.5 weeks in the group without vouchers. At 24 weeks after treatment entry, the voucher group evidenced significantly greater improvement than the no-voucher group on the Drug scale of the Addiction Severity Index (ASI), and only the voucher group showed significant improvement on the ASI Psychiatric scale. Their data support a greater role for incentives in cocaine relapse prevention. Incentives delivered contingent on submitting cocaine-free urine specimens significantly improve treatment outcome in ambulatory cocaine-dependent patients. Standard treatment for cocaine dependence and prevention of relapse has been tried for the past decade and has now evolved to include elements of relapse prevention, 12-step programs, treatment of comorbid disorders and other therapies to stop drug use and reduce recidivism. Recovery is a process which begins with a break in denial, a learning process of breaking old habits, friendships, and "triggers" to the first desire to use cocaine, and leading to eventual new healthy patterns of living centering the locus of control from an external one to an internal one. Patients are encouraged to identify internal and external precipitants of drug urges and to restructure their lives to avoid drug situations and relapse as compared with behavioral treatment, which focuses on extinguishing conditioned craving responses.

While much is to be learned about the most effective approach for a particular patient, it does appear that cocaine addiction is a virulent disease where intensity of intervention and frequency of treatment contacts are quite important variables. All psychosocial treatments attempt to help the patient understand their ambivalence to give up cocaine and clarify the importance of cocaine in the present problems. At the same time the clinician and treatment program tries to reduce cocaine availability through encouraging avoidance of people, places, and things associated with their addiction. Active participation in a viable recovery group or program can reduce cocaine availability by supporting abstinence. The addict is encouraged to identify high risk environments, feelings and attitudes and to prescribe a sponsor or group meeting rather than a relapse. Conditioned cues and cravings are identified in the context of the group meetings and the patient learns that an impulse does not mean an automatic action. In every drug challenge or potential use event the user is asked to weigh the risks and benefits of a slip. Just coming to a daily treatment program is a lifestyle modification that can have a very positive impact on recovery. Meetings provide an opportunity to learn and share with others and also develop new associates and coping skills. Finally, a slip does not automatically become a relapse and many intensive treatment programs manage such events by using them to prevent others. Recovery in such a model is very much like the recovery programs and attitudes commonly found in 12-step and other alcohol treatment programs—recovery is a marathon, not a sprint.

THE BEST TREATMENT IS PREVENTION

Cocaine dependence remains an intractable public health problem in the United States that contributes to many of our most disturbing social crises, including violent crime, unsafe streets, urban decay, accidents, unnecessary

Table 16.6 Recent Trends in Alcohol and Drug Use

Substance	1985	1992	% Change
Alcohol	113,000,000	98,200,000	−13%
Cigarettes	60,000,000	54,000,000	−10%
Marihuana	18,000,000	9,000,000	−50%
Cocaine	6,000,000	1,300,000	−79%

Current Use (within previous 30 days) of Drugs in USA, 1985–1992.

medical costs, the spread of infectious disease (e.g., AIDS, hepatitis, and tuberculosis), failures in school and work performance, and neonatal drug exposure. Every physician should realize that the experience of recent years has proved that effective education prevents drug abuse and results in abstinence. Beginning in the mid 1980s, America under the influence of President and Mrs. Reagan began to emphasize demand reduction through education. A wide range of efforts based in schools, the community, the workplace, religious groups, and the family aimed at reducing drug use has resulted in a dramatic reduction of drug use. In addition, the Partnership for a Drug-Free America, an organization that uses many of this country's best advertising and marketing minds, has created a remarkable series of advertisements aimed at "unselling" drugs. These ads, in a direct and powerful manner, demystify and deglamorize drug use. These ads have helped to reduce drug use in general, but they have had an especially significant effect upon adolescents and children.

Three national studies, the National Household Survey, the National High School Senior Survey, and the PRIDE Survey substantiate the recent reversal of the previous decline in recent drug use (Table 16.6). Furthermore, the National High School Senior Survey reveals that drug use declines when adolescents understand the risks associated with drug use—even though the *availability* of the drug increased (Fig. 16.1).

Education for prevention actually should begin before a child is conceived. Prospective parents should know the severe physical and mental side effects that may afflict their offspring if they use drugs prior to conception. After birth, drug education should begin at home and be reinforced by pediatricians and family physicians. A broad-based school program should start with kindergarten and end with college. Employers and governmental agencies must also share in this drug education program. Physicians should play a significant role in reducing the cocaine epidemic by never failing to consider the possibility of substance abuse in their patients and by inoculating their patients, especially their younger ones, with accurate information about this dangerous and deadly drug.

Prevention and education are supported by a social climate where danger of cocaine is clear and social policies prohibit use on the basis of the hypothesis that safe use is an oxymoron. Dupont and Voth (248) have recently reviewed current and historical trends in United States drug policy. A restrictive cocaine and other drug policy is a deterrent to drug use and helps reduce drug-related costs and societal problems. Although legalization or decriminalization of cocaine and other drugs might reduce some of the legal consequences of drug use, increased drug use would result and harmful consequences would far outweigh these initial benefits.

References

1. Rome HP. Personal reflections—cocaine. Psychiatr Ann 1988;18(9):505.
2. Johnston LD, O'Malley PM, Bachman JG. National survey results on drug use from the Monitoring the Future study, 1975–1994. Rockville, MD: National Institute on Drug Abuse, 1995.
3. Pride Survey, 1994–1995. National Summary, United States, Grades 6–12. Bowling Green, KY: PRIDE, 1995.
4. Petersen RC. Cocaine: an overview. NIDA Res Monogr 1977;13:5–15.
5. Carroll E. Coca: the plant and its use. NIDA Res Monogr 1977:13:35–45.

6. Siegel RK. Cocaine smoking. J Psychoactive Drugs 1982;14:277–359.
7. Phillips J, Wynne RD. Cocaine: the mystique and the reality. New York: Avon Books, 1980.
8. Morimer WG. Peru: history of coca, the "devine plant" of the Incas. With an introductory account of the Incas and of the Andean Indians of today. New York: Vail, 1901; New York: AMS Press, 1978 (reprint).
9. Siegel RK. New patterns of cocaine use: changing dose and routes. NIDA Res Monogr 1985; 61:204–220.
10. Freud S. Uber Coca [On cocaine]. In: Byck R, ed. Cocaine papers. New York: Stonehill Publishing, 1974:49–73.
11. Kleber HD. Introduction. Cocaine abuse: histori-

cal, epidemiological and psychological perspectives. J Clin Psychiatry 1988;49(suppl 2):3–6.
12. Freud S. On the general effects of cocaine (1885). Drug Depend 1970;5:15–17.
13. Jones E. The cocaine episode. In: Trilling L, Marcus S, eds. The life and work of Sigmund Freud. New York: Basic Books, 1953:52–67.
14. Byck R. Cocaine papers: Sigmund Freud. New York: Stonehill Publishing, 1974.
15. Louis JC, Yazijian HZ. The cola wars. New York: Everest House Publishers, 1980:13–38.
16. Graff H. The Coca-Cola conspiracy. High Times 1977;24:47–50, 76, 78.
17. Beattie GF. Soft drink flavours: their history and characteristics. Perfumery and Essential Oil Record 1956;47:437–442.

18. Estroff TW, Gold MS. Medical and psychiatric complications of cocaine abuse with possible points of pharmacological treatment. Adv Alcohol Subst Abuse 1986;5(1–2):61–76.

19. Van Dyke C, Byck R. Cocaine use in man. Adv Alcohol Subst Abuse 1983;3:1–24.

20. Siegel RK. Cocaine: recreational use and intoxication. NIDA Res Monogr 1977;13:119–136.

21. Grinspoon L, Bakalar JB. A kick from cocaine. Psychology Today 1977:41–42, 78.

22. Grinspoon L, Bakalar JB. Drug dependence: nonnarcotic agents. In: Kaplan HI, Freedman AM, Sadock BJ, eds. Comprehensive textbook of psychiatry. 3rd edition. Baltimore: Williams & Wilkins, 1980:1621.

23. Gold MS. Crack abuse: its implications and outcomes. Resident & Staff Physician 1987; 33(8):45–53.

24. Kandel DB, Yamaguchi K. From beer to crack: developmental patterns of involvement in drugs. Am J Public Health 1993;83:851–855.

25. Johanson CE, Fischman MF. The pharmacology of cocaine related to its abuse. Pharmacol Rev 1989;41:3–52.

26. Foltin RW, Fischman MW. Smoked and intravenous cocaine in humans: acute tolerance, cardiovascular and subjective effects. J Pharmacol Exp Ther 1991;257:247–261.

27. Roehrich H, Gold MS. 800 COCAINE: origin, significance and findings. Yale J Biol Med 1988; 61:149–155.

28. Brookoff D, Cook CS, Williams C, Mann CS. Testing reckless drivers for cocaine and marijuana. N Engl J Med 1994;331:518–522.

29. Gawin FH, Ellinwood EH Jr. Cocaine and other stimulants. N Engl J Med 1988;318:1173–1182.

30. Adler J. Hour by hour crack. Newsweek 1988 (November 28):64–79.

31. Miller NS, Mirin SM. Multiple drug use in alcoholics: practical and theoretical implications. Psychiatr Ann 1989;19:248–255.

32. National Institute on Drug Abuse. Cocaine tops list of drugs sending users to emergency rooms. NIDA Notes 1988:22–23. (DHHS Publication no. (ADM)88–1488)

33. National Institute on Drug Abuse. Statistical series: semiannual report: trend data through July–December 1988. Data from the Drug Abuse Warning Network, series G, number 23, p. 8 ff.

34. Wish ED, O'Neil JA. Drug use forecasting (DUF) research update. U.S. Department of Justice Newsletter, September 1989.

35. Tardiff DP, Gross EM, Wu J, Stajic M, Millman R. Analysis of cocaine positive fatalities. J Forensic Sci 1989;34:53–63.

36. Marzuk PM, Tardiff K, Leon AC, Stajic M, Morgan EB, Mann JJ. Prevalence of recent cocaine use among motor vehicle fatalities in New York City. JAMA 1990;263:250–256.

37. Lowenstein DH, Massa DM, Rowbotham MC, Collis SD, McKinney HE, Simon RP. Acute neurologic and psychiatric complications associated with cocaine abuse. Am J Med 1987;83: 841–846.

38. Lindenbaum GA, Carroll SF, Daskal I, Kapusnick R. Patterns of alcohol and drug abuse in an urban trauma center: the increasing role of cocaine abuse. J Trauma 1989;29:1654–1658.

39. Substance abuse. The nation's number one health problem. The Robert Wood Johnson Foundation, 1993.

40. Gold MS, Gleaton TJ. Cocaine, marijuana, alcohol, violence. Results of annual high school survey. Biol Psychiatry 1995;37:627.

41. Brain PF, Coward GA. A review of the history, actions, and legitimate uses of cocaine. J Subst Abuse 1989;1:431–451.

42. Gold MS, Verebey K. The psychopharmacology of cocaine. Psychiatr Ann 1984;140:714–723.

43. Verebey K, Gold MS. From coca leaves to crack: the effects of dose and routes of administration in abuse liability. Psychiatr Ann 1988; 18:513–521.

44. Gawin FH, Kleber HD. Abstinence symptomatology and psychiatric diagnosis in cocaine abusers: clinical observations. Arch Gen Psychiatry 1986;43:107–113.

45. Wilson JM, Nobrega JN, Corrigall WA, Coen KM, Shannak K, Kish SJ. Amygdala dopamine levels are markedly elevated after self—but not passive—administration of cocaine. Brain Res 1994;668:39–45.

46. Dunwiddie TV. Mechanisms of cocaine abuse and toxicity: an overview. NIDA Res Monogr 1988;88:185–198.

47. Ritchie JM, Greene NM. Local anesthetics. In: Gilman AG, Goodman LS, Rall TW, et al., eds. Goodman and Gilman's the pharmacological basis of therapeutics. 7th edition. New York: Macmillan, 1985:309–310.

48. Javaid J, Fischman MW, Schuster CR, Dekirmenjian H, Davis JM. Cocaine plasma concentrations: relationship to physiological and subjective effects in humans. Science 1978;202: 227–228.

49. Resnick R, Schuyten-Resnick E. Clinical aspects of cocaine: assessment of cocaine abuse behavior in man. In: Mulé SJ, ed. Cocaine. Boca Raton, FL: CRC Press, 1977.

50. Kuhar MJ, Ritz MC, Sharkey J. Cocaine receptors on dopamine transporters mediate cocaine-reinforced behavior. NIDA Res Monogr 1988; 88:14–22.

51. Wise RA, Bozarth MA. A psychomotor stimulant theory of addiction. Psychol Rev 1987; 94(4):469–492.

52. Petit Ho, Pan HT, Parsons LH, Justice JB. Extracellular concentrations of cocaine and dopamine are enhanced during chronic cocaine administration. J Neurochem 1990;55: 798–804.

53. Kalivas PW, Duffy P. Time course of extracellular dopamine and behavioral sensitization to cocaine. II. Dopamine perikarya. J Neurosci 1993;13:276–284.

54. Petit H, Justice J. Dopamine in the nucleus accumbens during cocaine self-administration as studied by in vivo microdialysis. Pharmacol Biochem Behav 1989;34:899–904.

55. Petit H, Justice JB. Effect of dose on cocaine self-administration behavior and dopamine levels in the nucleus accumbens. Brain Res 1991; 539:94–102.

56. Yoshida M, Yokoo H, Mizoguchi Y, Kawahara H, Tsuda A, Nishikawa T, Tanaka M. Eating and drinking cause increased dopamine release in the nucleus accumbens and ventral tegmental area in the rat: measurement by in vivo microdialysis. Neurosci Lett 1992;139:73–76.

57. Hernandez L, Hoebel BG. Food reward and cocaine increase extracellular dopamine in the nucleus accumbens as measured by microdialysis. Life Sci 1988;42:1705–1712.

58. Maisonneuve IM, Ho A, Kreek MJ. Chronic administration of a cocaine "binge" alters basal extracellular levels in male rats: an in vivo microdialysis study. J Pharmacol Exp Ther 1995; 272:652–657.

59. Volkow ND, Fowler JS, Logan J, Gatley SJ, Dewey SL, MacGregor RR, et al. Carbon-11-cocaine binding compared at subpharmacological and pharmacological doses: a PET study. J Nucl Med 1995;36:1289–1297.

60. Robbins TW, Everitt BJ. Functions of dopamine in the dorsal and ventral striatum. Semin Neurosci 1992;4:119–127.

61. White NM, Milner PM. The psychobiology of reinforcers. Annu Rev Psychol 1992;43:443–471.

62. Wise RA, Rompre PP. Brain dopamine and reward. Annu Rev Psychol 1989;40:191–225.

63. Robinson TE, Berridge KC. The neural basis of drug craving: an incentive-sensitization theory of addiction. Brain Res Brain Res Rev 1993; 18:247–291.

64. Bastos ML, Hoffman DB. Detection and identification of cocaine, its metabolites and its derivatives. In: Mulé SJ, ed. Cocaine: chemical, biological, clinical, social and treatment aspects. Boca Raton, FL: CRC Press, 1976:45.

65. Wallach MB, Gerson S. A neuropsychopharmacological comparison of d-amphetamine, l-DOPA and cocaine. Neuropharmacology 1971;10:743.

66. Self DW, Nestler EJ. Molecular mechanisms of drug reinforcement and addiction. Annu Rev Neurosci 1995;18:463–495.

67. Dimijian GG. Contemporary drug abuse. In: Goth A, ed. Medical pharmacology, principles and concepts. 7th edition. St. Louis: CV Mosby, 1974:313.

68. Sterk C. Cocaine, HIV seropositivity. Lancet 1988;1:1052–1053.

69. Dackis CA, Gold MS. Biological aspects of cocaine addiction. In: Volkow ND, Swann AC, eds. Cocaine in the brain. New Brunswick, NJ: Rutgers University Press, 1988.

70. Mello NK, Sarnyai Z, Mendelson JH, Drieze JM, Kelly M. Acute effects of cocaine on anterior pituitary hormones in male and female rhesus monkeys. J Pharmacol Exp Ther 1993; 266:804–811.

71. Dackis CA, Gold, MS. New concepts in cocaine addiction: the dopamine depletion hypothesis. Neurosci Biobehav Rev 1985;9:469–477.

72. Kranzler HR, Wallington DJ. Serum prolactin level, craving and early discharge from treatment in cocaine-dependent patients. Am J Drug Alcohol Abuse 1992;18:187–195.

73. Krystal JH, Gawin F, Charney DS, Heninger GR, Kleber HD. Clinical phenomenology and neurobiology of cocaine abstinence: A prospective inpatient study. Am J Psychiatry 1991; 148:1712–1716.

74. Mello NK, Teoh SK, Ellingboe J, Cochin J, Mendelson JH. Cocaine effects on pulsatile secretion of anterior pituitary, gonadal, and adrenal hormones. J Clin Endocrinol Metab 1989;69:1256–1260.

75. Mello NK, Sarnyai Z, Mendelson JH, Drieze JM, Kelly M. Acute effects of cocaine on anterior pituitary hormones in male and female rheusus monkeys. J Pharmacol Exp Ther 1993; 266:804–811.

76. Teoh SK, Mendelson JH, Mello NK, Weiss R, McElroy S, McAfee B. Hyperprolactinemia and risk for relapse of cocaine abuse. Biol Psychiatry 1990;28:824–828.

77. Krantzler HR, Wallington DJ. Serum prolactin level, craving, and early discharge from treatment in cocaine-dependent patients. Am J Drug Alcohol Abuse 1992;18:187–195.

78. Gold MS. Cocaine. New York: Plenum Medical Books, 1993.

79. Hollander E, Nunes E, DeCaria CM, Quitkin FM, Cooper T, Wager S, Klein DF. Dopaminergic sensitivity and cocaine abuse: response to apomorphine. Psychiatry Res 1990;33:161–169.

80. Mulé SJ. The pharmacodynamics of cocaine abuse. Psychiatr Ann 1984;14:724–727.

81. Weinstein SP, Gottheil E, Smith RH, Migrala KA. Cocaine users seen in medical practice. Am J Drug Alcohol Abuse 1986;12:341–354.

82. Jeri FR, Sanchez CC, Del Pozo T, Fernandez M, Carbajal C. Further experience with the syndromes produced by coca paste smoking. In: Jeri FR, ed. Cocaine 1980. Lima, Peru: Pacific Press, 1980.

83. Caine S, Koob GF. Modulation of cocaine self-administration in the rat through D-3 dopamine receptors. Science 1993;260:1814–1816.

84. Jaffee JH. Drug addiction and drug abuse. In: Gilman AG, Goodman LS, Rall TW, et al., eds. Goodman and Gilman's the pharmacological basis of therapeutics. 7th edition. New York: Macmillan, 1985:532–581.

85. Anthony JC, Tien AY, Petronis KR. Epidemiologic evidence on cocaine use and panic attacks. Am J Epidemiol 1989;129:543–549.

86. Jatlow P. Cocaethylene. Pharmacologic activity and clinical significance. Ther Drug Monit 1993;15:533–536.

87. Gold MS. 800-COCAINE. New York: Bantam, 1984.

88. Dackis CA, Gold MS. Addictiveness of central stimulants. Adv Alcohol Subst Abuse 1990; 9:9–26.

89. Childress AR, McLellan AT, Ehrman RN, O'Brien CP. Extinction of conditioned responses in abstinent cocaine or opioid users. NIDA Res Monogr 1987;76:189–195.

90. Ehrman RN, Robbins SJ, Childress AR, O'Brien CP. Conditioned responses to cocaine-related stimuli in cocaine abuse patients. Psychopharmacology 1992;107:523–529.

91. Margolin A, Avants K, Kosten TR. Cue-elicited cocaine craving and autogenic relaxation: association with treatment outcome. J Subst Abuse Treat 1994;11:549–552.

92. Derlet RW, Albertson TE. Emergency department presentation of cocaine intoxication. Ann Emerg Med 1989;18:115–119.

93. Benowitz NL. How toxic is cocaine? In: Cocaine: scientific and social dimensions. Ciba Found Symp 1992;166:125–148.

94. Benchimol A, Bartall H, Desser KB. Accelerated ventricular rhythm and cocaine abuse. Ann Intern Med 1978;88:519–520.

95. Karch SB, Billingham ME. The pathology and etiology of cocaine-induced heart disease. Arch Pathol Lab Med 1988;112:225–230.

96. Crumb WJ Jr, Clarkson CW. Characterization of cocaine-induced block of cardiac sodium channels. Biophys J 1990;57:589–599.

97. Jones LF, Tackett RL. Central mechanisms of action involved in cocaine-induced tachycardia. Life Sci 1990;46:723–728.

98. Perez-Meyes M, DiGiuseppi S, Ondrusek G, Jeffcoat AR, Cook CE. Free-base cocaine smoking. Clin Pharmacol Ther 1982;32:459–465.

99. Foltin RW, Fischman MW, Pedroso JJ, Pearlson GD. Repeated intranasal cocaine administration: lack of tolerance to pressor effects. Drug Alcohol Depend 1988;22:169–177.

100. Lichtenfeld PJ, Rubin DB, Feldman RS. Subarachnoid hemorrhage precipitated by cocaine snorting. Arch Neurol 1984;41:223–224.

101. Smith HWB, Lieberman HA, Brody SL, Battey LL, Donohue BC, Morris DC. Acute myocardial infarction temporally related to cocaine use. Ann Intern Med 1987;107:13–18.

102. Vitullo JC, Karam R, Mekhail N, Wicker P, Engelmann A, Khairallah PA. Cocaine-induced small vessel spasm in isolated rat hearts. Am J Pathol 1989;135:85–91.

103. Chow JM, Menchen SKL, Paul BD, Stein RJ. Vascular changes in the nasal submucosa of chronic cocaine addicts. Am J Forensic Med Pathol 1990;11:136–143.

104. Isner HM, Estes North AM III, Thompson PD, et al. Acute cardiac events temporally related to cocaine abuse. N Engl J Med 1986;315:1438–1443.

105. Wilkerson RD. Cardiovascular toxicity of cocaine. NIDA Res Monogr 1988;88:304–324.

106. Nadamanee K, Gorelick DA, Josephson MA, et al. Myocardial ischemia during cocaine withdrawal. Ann Intern Med 1989;111:876–880.

107. Schachne JS, Roberts BH, Thompson PD. Coronary-artery spasm and myocardial infarction associated with cocaine use. N Engl J Med 1984;310:1665–1666.

108. Som P, Oster ZH, Wans GJ, Volkow ND, Sacker DF. Spatial and temporal distribution of cocaine and effects of pharmacological interventions: wholebody autoradiographic microimaging studies. Life Sci 1994;55:1375–1382.

109. Dressler FA, Malekzadeh S, Roberts WC. Quantitative analysis of amounts of coronary arterial narrowing in cocaine addicts. Am J Cardiol 1990;65(5):303–308.

110. Togna G, Tempesta E, Togna AR, Doci N, Cebo B, Caprino I. Platelet responsiveness and biosynthesis of thromboxane and prostacyclin in response in in vitro cocaine treatment. Haemostasis 1985;15:100–107.

111. Peng SK, French WJ, Pelikan PCD. Direct cocaine cardiotoxicity demonstrated by endomyocardial biopsy. Arch Pathol Lab Med 1989; 113:842–845.

112. Wiener MD, Putnam CE. Pain in the chest in a user of cocaine. JAMA 1987;258:2087–2088.

113. Itkonen J, Schnoll A, Glassroth J. Pulmonary dysfunction in "freebase" cocaine users. Arch Intern Med 1984;144:2195–2197.

114. Hoffman CK, Goodman PC. Pulmonary edema in cocaine smokers. Radiology 1989;172:462–465.

115. Cregler LL, Mark H. Medical complications of cocaine abuse. N Engl J Med 1986;315:1495–1500.

116. Murray RJ, Albin RJ, Mergner W, et al. Diffuse alveolar hemorrhage temporally related to cocaine smoking. Chest 1988;93:427–429.

117. Rebhum J. Association of asthma and freebase smoking. Ann Allergy 1988;60:339–342.

118. Jonsson S, O'Meara M, Young JB. Acute cocaine poisoning: importance of treating seizures and acidosis. Am J Med 1983;75:1061–1064.

119. Barden JC. Crack smoking seen as a peril to the lungs. New York Times 1989 (December 24):19.

120. Merriam AE, Medalia A, Levine B. Partial complex status epilepticus associated with cocaine abuse. Biol Psychiatry 1988;23:515–518.

121. Post RM, Kopanda RT, Black KE. Progressive effects of cocaine on behavior and central amine metabolism in the rhesus monkey: relationship to kindling and psychosis. Biol Psychiatry 1976;11:403–419.

122. Volkow ND, Fowler JS, Wolf AP, Schlyer D, Shiue C-Y, Alpert R, et al. Effects of chronic cocaine abuse on postsynaptic dopamine receptors. Am J Psychiatry 1990;147:719–724.

123. Strickland TL, Mena I, Villanueva-Meyer J, Miller BL, Cummings J, Mehringer M, et al. Cerebral perfusion and neuropsychological consequences of chronic cocaine use. J Neuropsychiatry Clin Neurosci 1993;5:419–427.

124. Estroff TW, Gold MS. Chronic medical complications of drug abuse. Psychiatr Med 1987;3:267–286.

125. Lukas SE, Sholar M, Kouri E, Fukuzako H, Mendelson JH. Marijuana smoking increases plasma cocaine levels and subjective reports of euphoria in male volunteers. Pharmacol Biochem Behav 1994;48:715–721.

126. Ashley R. Cocaine: its history, uses and effects. New York: St. Martin's Press, 1975:240.

127. Smith DE, Wesson DR, Apter-Marsh M. Cocaine- and alcohol-induced sexual dysfunction in patients with addictive diseases. J Psychoactive Drugs 1984;16:359–361.

128. Chasnoff IJ, Burns WJ, Schnoll SH, Burns KA. Cocaine use in pregnancy. N Engl J Med 1985;313:666–669.

129. Mendelson J, Teoh S, Lange U, Mello N, Weiss R, Skupny A. Hyperprolactinemia during cocaine withdrawal. NIDA Res Monogr 1988;81:67–73.

130. Mendelson JH, Mello NK, Teoh SK, Ellingboe J, Cochin J. Cocaine effects on pulsatile secretion of anterior pituitary, gonadal, and adrenal hormones. J Clin Endocrinol Metab 1989;69:1256–1260.

131. Jonas JM, Gold MS. Cocaine abuse and eating disorders. Lancet 1986;1:390–391.

132. Roberts DCS, Quattrocchi E, Howland MA. Severe hyperthermia secondary to intravenous drug abuse. Am J Emerg Med 1984;2:373.

133. Loghmanee F, Tobak M. Fatal malignant hyperthermia associated with recreational cocaine and ethanol abuse. Am J Forensic Med Pathol 1986;7:246–248.

134. Goldfrank LR, et al., eds. Toxicologic emergencies. 3rd edition. Norwalk, CT: Appleton-Century-Crofts, 1986:477–486.

135. Gold MS. Medical implications of cocaine intoxication. Alcoholism Addiction 1989 (October):16.

136. Merigian KS, Roberts JR. Cocaine intoxication: hyperpyrexia, rhabdomyolysis, and acute renal failure. J Toxicol Clin Toxicol 1987; 25:135–148.

137. Krohn KD, Slowman-Kovacs S, Leapman SB. Cocaine and rhabdomyolysis. Ann Intern Med 1988;208:639–640.

138. Roth D, Alarcon FJ, Fernandez JA, Preston RA, Bourgoignie JJ. Acute rhabdomyolysis associated with cocaine intoxication. N Engl J Med 1988;319:673–677.

139. Schweitzer VG. Osteolytic sinusitis and pneumomediastinum: deceptive otolaryngologic complications of cocaine abuse. Laryngoscope 1986;96:206–210.

140. Vilensky W. Illicit and licit drugs causing perforation of the nasal septum. J Forensic Sci 1982;27:958–962.

141. Van Dyke C, Jatlow P, Ungerer J, et al. Oral cocaine: plasma concentrations and central effects. Science 1978;200:211–213.

142. Edlin BR, Irwin KL, Faruque S, McCoy CB, Word C, Serrano Y, et al. Intersecting epidemics—crack cocaine use and HIV infection among inner-city young adults. N Engl J Med 1994;331:1422–1427.

143. Kreek MJ. Multiple drug abuse patterns and medical consequences. In: Meltzer HY, ed. Psychopharmacology: the third generation of progress. New York: Raven Press, 1987:1600–1603.

144. Cregler LL, Mark H. Cardiovascular dangers of cocaine abuse. Am J Cardiol 1986;57:1185–1186.

145. Kosten TR, Kleber HD. Sudden death in cocaine abusers: relation to neuroleptic malignant syndrome. Lancet 1987;1(8543):1198–1199.

146. Woods JR Jr, Plessinger MA. Pregnancy increases cardiovascular toxicity to cocaine. Am J Obstet Gynecol 1990;162:529–533.

147. Pritchard JA, MacDonald PC, Gant NF.

Williams obstetrics. Norwalk, CT: Appleton-Century-Crofts, 1985:395–407.

148. Finnegan L. The dilemma of cocaine exposure in the perinatal period. NIDA Res Monogr 1988;81:379.

149. Richards IS, Kulkarni AP, Remner WF. Cocaine-induced arrhythmia in human foetal myocardium in vitro: possible mechanism for foetal death in utero. Pharmacol Toxicol 1990; 66:150–154.

150. Hadeed AJ, Siegel SR. Maternal cocaine use during pregnancy: effect on the newborn infant. Pediatrics 1989;84:205–210.

151. Critchley HOD, Woods SM, Barson AJ, et al. Fetal death in utero and cocaine abuse. Case report. Br J Obstet Gynecol 1988;95:195–196.

152. Singer L, Arendt R, Minnes S. Neurodevelopmental effects of cocaine. Clin Perinatol 1993; 20:245–261.

153. Bingol N, Fuchs M, Diaz V, Stone RK, Gromisch DS. Teratogenicity of cocaine in humans. J Pediatr 1987;110:93–96.

154. Cherukuri R, Minkoff H, Feldman J, Parekh A, Glass L. A cohort study of alkaloidal cocaine (crack) in pregnancy. Obstet Gynecol 1989;72: 145–151.

155. Zuckerman B, Amaro H, Bauchner H, Cabral H. Depressive symptoms during pregnancy: relationship to poor health behaviors. Am J Obstet Gynecol 1989;160:1107–1111.

156. Lewis DE, Moore CM, Leikin JB, Koller A. Meconium analysis for cocaine: a validation study and comparison with paired urine analysis. J Anal Toxicol 1995;19:148–150.

157. Bateman DA, Heagarty MC. Passive freebase cocaine ('crack') inhalation by infants and toddlers. Am J Dis Child 1989;134:25–27.

158. Dobersczak TM, Shanzer S, Senie RT, Kandall SR. Neonatal neurologic and electroencephalographic effects of intrauterine cocaine exposure. J Pediatr 1988;113:354–358.

159. Zuckerman B, Frank DA, Hingson R, et al. Effects of maternal marijuana and cocaine use on fetal growth. N Engl J Med 1989;320:762–768.

160. Chasnoff IJ, Lewis DE, Squires L. Cocaine intoxication in a breast-fed infant. Pediatrics 1987;80:836–838.

161. Newald J. Cocaine infants: a new arrival at hospitals' step? Hospitals 1986;60(7):96.

162. Lutiger B, Graham K, Einarson TR, Koren G. Relationship between gestational cocaine use and pregnancy outcome: a metanalysis. Teratology 1991;44:405–414.

163. Ward SLD, Schuetz S, Krishna V, et al. Abnormal sleeping ventilatory pattern in infants of substance-abusing mothers. Am J Dis Child 1986;140:1015–1020.

164. Chasnoff IJ. Perinatal effects of cocaine. Contemp OB/GYN 1987(May):163–179.

165. Chasnoff IJ. Cocaine intoxication in an infant via maternal milk. Pediatrics (in press).

166. Hofkosh D, Pringle JL, Wald HP, Switala J, Hinderliter SA, Hamel SC. Early interactions between drug-involved mothers and infants. Within-group differences. Arch Pediatr Adolesc Med 1995;149(6):665–672.

167. Ostrea EM, Brady M, Gause S, Raymundo AL, Stevens D. Drug screening of newborns by meconium analysis: a large-scale, prospective, epidemiologic study. Pediatrics 1992;89: 107–113.

168. Gold MS. Cocaine. In: Medical and health annual. Chicago: Encyclopedia Britannica 1988: 277–284.

169. Siegel RK. Cocaine smoking disorders: diagnosis and treatment. Psychiatr Ann 1984;14: 728–732.

170. Gold MS. The good news about panic, anxiety, and phobias. New York: Villard Books, 1989.

171. Rounsaville BJ, Anton SF, Carroll K, et al. Psychiatric diagnosis of treatment seeking cocaine abusers. Arch Gen Psychiatry 1991;48: 43–51.

172. Asberg M, Errikson B. The effects of serotonin re-uptake blockers on depression. J Clin Psychiatry 1986;41:23–35.

173. Lukas SE, Sholar M, Kouri E, Fukuzako H, Mendelson JH. Marijuana smoking increases plasma cocaine levels and subjective reports of euphoria in male volunteers. Pharmacol Biochem Behav 1994;48:715–721.

174. Mello NK, Negus SS, Scott E, Lukas SE, Mendelson JH, Sholar JW, Drieze J. A primate model of polydrug abuse: cocaine and heroin combinations. J Pharmacol Exp Ther 1995; 274:1325–1337.

175. Gold MS, Estroff TW. The comprehensive evaluation of cocaine and opiate abusers. In: Hall RCW, Beresford TP, eds. Handbook of psychiatric diagnostic procedures. Vol. 2. Spectrum Publications, 1985.

176. Millman RB. Evaluation and clinical management of cocaine abusers. J Clin Psychiatry 1988;49(suppl 2):27–33.

177. Washton A, Gold MS, Pottash AC. Opiate and cocaine dependencies. Postgrad Med 1985; 77:297.

178. Roehrich H, Gold MS. Emergency presentations of crack abuse. Emerg Med Serv 1988; 17(8):41–44.

179. Dackis CA, Gold MS, Estroff TW. Inpatient treatment of addiction. In: Treatments of psychiatric disorders: a task force report of the American Psychiatric Association. Washington, DC: American Psychiatric Association, 1989:1359–1379.

180. Gold MS. Diagnosis and treatment of cocaine abuse — II. In: Symposium of cocaine proceedings. New York: American Psychiatric Association, 1982:3–4.

181. Roehrich H, Gold MS. Cocaine. In: Ciraulo DA, Shader RI, eds. Clinical manual of chemical dependence. Washington, DC: American Psychiatric Press, 1991:195–231.

182. Jonas JM, Gold MS. The pharmacologic treatment of alcohol and cocaine abuse. Psychiatr Clin North Am 1992;15:179–190.

183. Gold MS. Cocaine (and crack):clinical aspects. In: Lowinson JH, Ruiz P, Millman RB, Langrod JG, eds. Substance abuse: a comprehensive textbook. 2nd edition. Baltimore: Williams & Wilkins, 1992:205–221.

184. Roehrich H, Dackis CA, Gold MS. Bromocriptine. Med Res Rev 1987;7(2):243–269.

185. Extein IL, Gold MS. The treatment of cocaine addicts: Bromocriptine or desipramine. Psychiatr Ann 1988;18(9):535–537.

186. Gold MS, Miller NS. The biology of addictive and psychiatric disorders. In: Miller NS, ed. Treating coexisting psychiatric and addictive disorders. Center City, MN: Hazelden, 1994: 35–52.

187. Childress A, Ehrman R, McLellan AT, O'Brien C. Conditioned craving and arousal in cocaine addiction: a preliminary report. NIDA Res Monogr 1988;81:74–80.

188. Gawin F, Ellinwood E. Stimulants. In: Kleber HD, ed. Treatment of psychiatric disorders: a task force report of the American Psychiatric Association. Washington, DC: American Psychiatric Association, 1989:1218–1241.

189. Mendelson JH, Teoh SK, Lange U, Mello NK, Weiss R, Skupny A, Ellingboe J. Anterior pituitary, adrenal, and gonadal hormones during cocaine withdrawal. Am J Psychiatry 1988; 145:1094–1098.

190. Teoh SK, Mendelson JH, Mello NK, Weiss R, McElroy S, McAfee B. Hyperprolactinemia and risk for relapse of cocaine abuse. Biol Psychiatry 1990;28:824–828.

191. Swartz CM, Breen K, Leone F. Serum prolactin levels during extended cocaine abstinence. Am J Psychiatry 1990;147:777–779.

192. Lee MA, Bowers MM, Nash JF, Meltzer HY. Neuroendocrine measures of dopaminergic function in chronic cocaine users. Psychiatry Res 1990;33:151–159.

193. Kranzler H, Wallington D. Serum prolactin, craving and early discharge from treatment in cocaine-dependent patients. Am J Drug Alcohol Abuse 1992;18:187–196.

194. Hollander E, Nunes E, DeCaria C, Quitkin FM, Cooper T, Wager S, Klein DF. Dopaminergic sensitivity in cocaine abuse: response to apomorphine. Psychiatry Res 1990;33:161–169.

195. Mendelson JH, Teoh SK, Lange U, Mello NK, Weiss R, Skupny A, Ellingboe J. Anterior pituitary, adrenal, and gonadal hormones during cocaine withdrawal. Am J Psychiatry 1988; 145:1094–1098.

196. Teoh SK, Mendelson JH, Mello NK, Weiss R, McElroy S, McAfee B. Hyperprolactinemia and risk for relapse of cocaine abuse. Biol Psychiatry 1990;28:824–828.

197. Miller BL, Cummings JL, Villanueva-Meyer J, et al. Frontal lobe degeneration: clinical, neuropsychological, and SPECT characteristics. Neurology 1991;41:1374–1382.

198. Tumeh S, Nagel JS, English RJ, et al. Cerebral abnormalities in cocaine abusers: demonstration by SPECT perfusion brain scintigraphy. Radiology 1990;176:821–824.

199. Volkow ND, Mullani N, Gould KL, et al. Cerebral blood flow in chronic cocaine users: a study with positron emission tomography. Br J Psychiatry 1988;152:641–648.

200. Holman BL, Moretti J-L, Hill TC. SPECT perfusion imaging in cerebrovascular disease. In: Noninvasive imaging of cerebrovascular disease. New York: Allan R Liss, 1989:147–162.

201. Manschreck TC, Margert L, Schneyer C, et al. Freebase cocaine and memory. Compr Psychiatry 1990;31:369–375.

202. Lichtenfeld PJ, Rubin DB, Feldman RS. Subarachnoid hemorrhage precipitated by cocaine snorting. Arch Neurol 1984;41:223–224.

203. Wojak JC, Flamm ES. Intracranial hemorrhage and cocaine abuse. Stroke 1987;18:712–715.

204. Kaye BR, Fainstat M. Cerebral vasculitis associated with cocaine abuse. JAMA 1987;258: 2104–2106.

205. Washton AM. Nonpharmacologic treatment of cocaine abuse. Psychiatr Clin North Am 1986; 9:563–571.

206. Margolin A, Avants K, Kosten TR. Cue-elicited cocaine craving and autogenic relaxation: association with treatment outcome. J Subst Abuse Treat 1994;11:549–552.

207. The White House. National drug control strategy. Office of National Drug Control Policy, September 1989.

208. Wise RA. Catecholamine theories of reward: a critical review. Brain Res 1978;152:215–247.

209. Montgomery AM, Rose IC, Herberg LJ. 5-HT1A agonists and dopamine: the effects of 8-OH-SPAT and buspirone on brain stimulation reward. J Neural Transm 1991;83:139–158.

210. Cunningham KA, Lakokski JM. Electrophysiological effects of cocaine and procaine on dorsal raphe serotonin neurons. Eur J Pharmacol 1988;148:457–462.

211. Galloway MP. Regulation of dopamine and serotonin synthesis by acute administration of cocaine. Synapse 1990;6:63–72.

212. Satel SL, Krystal JH, Delgado PL, Kosten TR, Charney DS. Tryptophan depletion and attenuation of cue-induced craving for cocaine. Am J Psychiatry 1995;152:778–783.

213. Naranjo CA, Kadlec KE, Sanhueza P, et al. Fluoxetine differentially alters alcohol intake and other consummatory behaviors in problem drinkers. Clin Pharmacol Ther 1990;47:490–498.

214. Shopsin B. Second generation antidepressants: a clinical pharmacotherapeutic research strategy. Psychopharmacol Bull 1981;17:33–35.

215. Batki SL, Manfredi LB, Sorensen JL, et al. Fluoxetine for cocaine abuse in methadone patients: preliminary findings. NIDA Res Monogr 1990;105:516–517.

216. Herridge P, Gold MS. Pharmacological adjuncts in the treatment of opioid and cocaine addicts. J Psychoactive Drugs 1988;20:233–242.

217. Meyer RE. New pharmacotherapies for cocaine dependence revisited. Arch Gen Psychiatry 1992;49:900–904.

218. Gawin FH, Kleber HD, Byck R, Rousanville BJ, Kosten TR, Jatlow PI, et al. Desipramine facilitation of initial cocaine abstinence. Arch Gen Psychiatry 1989;46:117–121.

219. Gawin FH, Byck R, Kleber HD. Desipramine augmentation of cocaine abstinence: initial results. Clin Neuropharmacol 1986;9(supp 4):202–204.

220. Gawin FH, Kleber HD, Byck R, Rousanville BJ, Kosten TR, Jatlow PI, et al. Desipramine facilitation of initial cocaine abstinence. Arch Gen Psychiatry 1989;46:117–121.

221. Kosten TR. Pharmacotherapeutic interventions for cocaine abuse matching patients to treatments. J Nerv Ment Dis 1989;177:379–389.

222. Kosten TR. Pharmacotherapies for cocaine abuse: neurobiological abnormalities reversed with drug intervention. The Psychiatric Times 1993(February):25–27.

223. Mello NK, Lukas SE, Bree MP, Mendelson JH. Desipramine effects on cocaine self-administration by rhesus monkeys. Drug Alcohol Depend 1990;26:103–116.

224. Fischman MW, Foltin RW, Nestadt G, Pearlson GD. Effects of desipramine maintenance on cocaine self-administration by humans. J Pharmacol Exp Ther 1990;253:760–770.

225. Baptista T, Weiss SRB, Post RM. Carbamazepine attenuates cocaine-induced increases in dopamine in the nucleus accumbens: an in vivo dialysis study. Eur J Pharmacol 1993;236:39–42.

226. Weiss SRB, Post RM, Aigner TG. Carbamazepine in the treatment of cocaine-induced disorders: In: Watson RR, ed. Drug and alcohol abuse reviews: treatment of drug and alcohol abuse. Totowa, NJ: Humana Press, 1992:149.

227. Gawin FH. Cocaine addiction: psychology and neurophysiology. Science 1991;251:1580–1586.

228. Berger P, Gawin F, Kosten TR. Treatment of cocaine abuse with mazindol. Lancet 1989;1:283.

229. Gawin FH, Riordan C, Kleber HD. Methylphenidate treatment of cocaine abusers without attention deficit disorder: a negative report. Am J Drug Alcohol Abuse 1985;11:193–197.

230. Jaffe JH, Witkin JM, Goldberg SR, Katz JL. Potential toxic interactions of cocaine and mazindol. Lancet 1989;8654:111.

231. Kosten TR, Steinberg M, Diakogiannis IA. Crossover trial of mazindol for cocaine dependence. Am J Addictions 1993;2:161–164.

232. Shottenfeld RS, Pakes J, Ziedonis D, Kosten TR. Buprenorphine: dose-related effects on cocaine and opioid use in cocaine-abusing opioid-dependent humans. Biol Psychiatry 1993;34:66–74.

233. Carroll K, Ziedonis M, O'Malley L, McCance-Katz E, Gordon L, Rounsaville B. Pharmacologic interventions for alcohol and cocaine abusing individuals: a pilot study of disulfiram vs. naltrexone. Am J Addictions 1993;2(1):77–79.

234. Hameedi FA, Rosen MI, McCance-Katz EF, McMahon TJ, Price LH, Jatlow PI, et al. Behavioral, physiological, pharmacological interaction of cocaine, disulfiram in humans. Biol Psychiatry 1995;37:560–563.

235. Weiss RD. Relapse to cocaine abuse after initiating desipramine treatment. JAMA 1988;260:2545–2546.

236. Weiss RD, Mirin SM. Psychological and pharmacological treatment strategies in cocaine dependence. Ann Clin Psychiatry 1990;2:239–243.

237. Avants SK, Margolin A, Chang P, Kosten TR, Birch S. Acupuncture for the treatment of cocaine addiction. Investigation of a needle puncture control. J Subst Abuse Treat 1995;12(3):195–205.

238. Kosten TA, Kosten TR, Gawin FH, Gordon LT, Hogan I, Kleber HD. An open trial of sertraline for cocaine abuse. Am J Addictions 1992;1:349–353.

239. Kosten TA, Kosten TR. Pharmacological blocking agents for treating substance abuse. J Nerv Ment Dis 1991;179:583–592.

240. Kosten T, Silverman DG, Fleming J, Kosten TA, Gawin FH, Compton M, et al. Intravenous cocaine challenges during naltrexone maintenance: a preliminary study. Biol Psychiatry 1992;32:543–548.

241. Mello NK, Mendelson JH, Bree MP, Lukas SE. Buprenorphine and naltrexone effects on cocaine self-administration by rhesus monkeys. J Pharmacol Exp Ther 1990;254:926–939.

242. Meert TF, Janssen PAJ. Ritanserin, a new therapeutic approach for drug abuse. Part 2. Effects on cocaine. Drug Dev Res 1992;25:39–53.

243. Ichikawa J, Meltzer HY. Amperozide, a novel antipsychotic drug, inhibits the ability of d-amphetamine to increase dopamine release in vivo in rat striatum and nucleus accumbens. J Neurochem 1992;58:2285–2291.

244. Markou A, Koob GF. Post cocaine anhedonia: An animal model of cocaine withdrawal. Neuropsychopharmacology 1991;4:17–26.

245. Gawin FH. Cocaine addiction: psychology and neurophysiology. Science 1991;251:1580–1586.

246. Higgins ST, Budney AJ, Bickel WK, Hughes JR, Foerg F, Badger G. Achieving cocaine abstinence with a behavioral approach. Am J Psychiatry 1993;150:763–769.

247. Higgins ST, Budney AJ, Bickel WK, Foerg FE, Donham R, Badger GJ. Incentives improve outcome in outpatient behavioral treatment of cocaine dependence. Arch Gen Psychiatry 1994;51:568–576.

248. DuPont RL, Voth EA. Drug legalization, harm reduction and drug policy. Ann Intern Med 1995;123:461–465.

17 MARIHUANA

Lester Grinspoon and James B. Bakalar

The present generation of young people cannot remember when marihuana was an exotic weed with an aura of mythical power and mysterious danger. Although still illegal, it has become a commonplace part of the American social scene, used regularly by millions and occasionally used by millions more. A realistic view of this drug is now both more important and easier to achieve.

The use of marihuana reached a high point in the late 1970s and early 1980s, declined until the early 1990s, than began to rise slightly. In a 1978 NIDA survey, 37% of high school seniors said that they had smoked marihuana in the past 30 days. In 1989 that number fell to 17%, but by 1994 it had risen again to 19%. Trends at ages 18 to 25 have been similar. In 1969, 20% of high school seniors had used marihuana at least once; in 1979, 60% had; in 1989, 44%; and in 1994, 38%. Use in the past year reached a low of 22% in 1992 and rose to 30% in 1994. The perceived risk of regular marihuana use has also been falling slightly. In 1978, 35% of high school seniors said it was very risky; in 1986, 71%; in 1992, nearly 80%; and in 1994, closer to 60%.

HISTORY

The earliest record of human cannabis use is a description of the drug in a Chinese compendium of medicines, the Herbal of Emperor Shen Nung, dated 2737 BC according to some sources and 400 to 500 BC according to others. Marihuana was a subject of controversy even in ancient times. Some warned that the hemp plant lined the road to Hades while others thought it led to paradise. Its intoxicating properties were known in Europe during the nineteenth century and for a much longer time in South and Central America; thousands of tons of Indian hemp (the common name of the Cannabis sativa plant from which the drug is obtained) were produced for its commercially useful long bast fiber beginning in Jamestown, Virginia, in 1611. Nevertheless, during the early American history of cannabis, nothing was known of its intoxicating properties.

In 1857 Fitz Hugh Ludlow (1), largely influenced by those members of the French romantic literary movement who belonged to "Le Club des Haschischins," published *The Hasheesh Eater: Being Passages from the Life of a Pythagorean* and made a number of American literati aware of cannabis' euphoriant properties. Unlike his European counterparts, Ludlow did not use hashish but, rather, Tilden's Solution, one of a number of proprietary preparations of Cannabis indica (an alcoholic extract of cannabis), which he could obtain from his local apothecary. Ludlow established a link in the public mind, albeit a very narrow segment of it, between cannabis the medicine and cannabis the intoxicating drug. However, in the half-century from the publication of his book to the appearance, across the southern border, of what we now commonly call marihuana, grass, pot, or dope (all names for the dried and chopped flowering pistillate and staminate tops and leaves of the hemp plant), even this limited awareness all but completely vanished.

In any case, throughout history the principal interest in the hemp plant has been in its properties as an agent for achieving euphoria. In this country, it is almost invariably smoked, usually as a cigarette called a "joint" or "doobie"—but elsewhere the drug is often taken in the form of a drink or in foods such as candy.

Drug preparations from the hemp plant vary widely in quality and potency, depending on the type (there are possibly three species or, alternatively, various ecotypes), climate, soil, cultivation, and method of preparation. When the cultivated plant is fully ripe, a sticky, golden yellow resin with a minty fragrance covers its flower clusters and top leaves. The plant's resin contains the active substances. Preparations of the drug come in three grades, identified by Indian names. The cheapest and least potent, called bhang, is derived from the cut tops of uncultivated plants and has a low resin content. Much of the marihuana smoked in the United States, particularly a few years ago, is of this grade. Ganja is obtained from the flowering tops and leaves of carefully selected, cultivated plants, and it has a higher quality and quantity of resin. The third and highest grade of the drug, called charas in India, is largely made from the resin itself, obtained from the tops of mature plants; only this version of the drug is properly called hashish. Hashish can also be smoked, eaten, or drunk. Recently, more potent and more expensive marihuana from Thailand, Hawaii, and California has become available in this country. Some California growers have been successful in cultivating an unpollinated plant by the early weeding out of male plants; the product is the much sought-after sinsemilla. Such new breeding and cultivation techniques have raised the tetrahydrocannabinol content of marihuana smoked in the United States over the last 20 years; while there have been some extravagant claims about the size of this increment, most authorities believe it has been modest. On average, street cannabis is not much more potent than it was in the 1960s.

The chemistry of the cannabis drugs is extremely complex and not completely understood. In the 1940s it was determined that the active constituents are various isomers of tetrahydrocannabinol. The delta-9 form (hereafter called THC) has been synthesized and is believed to be the primary active component of marihuana. However, the drug's effects probably also involve other components and the form in which it is taken. There are more than 60 cannabinoids in marihuana and a number of them are thought to be biologically active. This activity is apparently mediated by the recently discovered receptors in the brain and elsewhere in the body which are stimulated by THC (2). This exciting discovery implied that the body produces its own version of cannabinoids for one or more useful purposes. The first of these cannabinoid-like neurotransmitters was identified in 1992 and named anandamide (*ananda* is the Sanskrit word for bliss) (3). Cannabinoid receptor sites occur not only in the lower brain but also in the cerebral cortex and the hippocampus.

The psychic effects of the drug have been described in a very extensive literature. Hashish long ago acquired a lurid reputation through the writings of literary figures, notably the group of French writers—Baudelaire, Gautier,

Dumas père, and others—who formed "Le Club des Haschischins" in Paris in the 1850s. Their reports, written under the influence of large amounts of hashish, must be largely discounted as exaggerations that do not apply to moderate use of the drug. There is a story that hashish was responsible for Baudelaire's psychosis and death; the story overlooks the fact that he had relatively little experience with hashish, was in all probability actually writing about his experience with laudanum, and, moreover, had been an alcoholic and suffered from tertiary syphilis.

Bayard Taylor—the American writer, lecturer, and traveler best known for his translation of Goethe's *Faust*—wrote one of the first accounts of a cannabis experience in terms that began to approach a clinical description. He tried the drug in a spirit of inquiry during a visit to Egypt in 1854. His narrative of the effects follows (4):

> The sensations it then produced were . . . physically of exquisite lightness and airiness—mentally of a wonderfully keen perception of the ludicrous in the most simple and familiar objects. During the half hour in which it lasted, I was at no time so far under its control that I could not, with the clearest perception, study the changes through which I passed. I noted with careful attention the fine sensations which spread throughout the whole tissue of my nervous fibers, each thrill helping to divest my frame of its earthly and material nature, till my substance appeared to me no grosser than the vapors of the atmosphere, and while sitting in the calm of the Egyptian twilight I expected to be lifted up and carried away by the first breeze that should ruffle the Nile. While this process was going on, the objects by which I was surrounded assumed a strange and whimsical expression. . . . I was provoked into a long fit of laughter. . . . [The effect] died away as gradually as it came, leaving me overcome with a soft and pleasant drowsiness, from which I sank into a deep, refreshing sleep.

Perhaps a better clinical account is that of Walter Bromberg, a psychiatrist, who described the psychic effects on the basis of his own experience and many observations and talks with people while they were under the influence of marihuana (5):

> The intoxication is initiated by a period of anxiety within 10 to 30 minutes after smoking, in which the user sometimes . . . develops fears of death and anxieties of vague nature associated with restlessness and hyperactivity. Within a few minutes he begins to feel more calm and soon develops definite euphoria; he becomes talkative . . . is elated, exhilarated . . . begins to have . . . an astounding feeling of lightness of the limbs and body . . . laughs uncontrollably and explosively . . . without at times the slightest provocation . . . has the impression that his conversation is witty, brilliant. . . . The rapid flow of ideas gives the impression of brilliance of thought and observation . . . [but] confusion appears on trying to remember what was thought . . . he may begin to see visual hallucinations . . . flashes of light or amorphous forms of vivid color which evolve and develop into geometric figures, shapes, human faces, and pictures of great complexity. . . . After a longer or shorter time, lasting up to two hours, the smoker becomes drowsy, falls into a dreamless sleep and awakens with no physiologic after-effects and with a clear memory of what happened during the intoxication.

Most observers confirm Bromberg's account as a composite, somewhat exaggerated and overinclusive description of marihuana highs. They find that the effects from smoking last from 2 to 4 hours, the effects from ingestion 5 to 12 hours. For a new user, the initial anxiety that sometimes occurs is alleviated if supportive friends are present. The intoxication heightens sensitivity to external stimuli, reveals details that would ordinarily be overlooked, makes colors seem brighter and richer, and brings out values in works of art that previously had little or no meaning to the viewer. It is as though the cannabis-intoxicated adult perceives the world with some of the newness, wonder, curiosity, and excitement of a child; the person's world becomes more interesting and details that had been taken for granted now attract more attention. The high also enhances the appreciation of music; many jazz and rock musicians have said that they perform better under the influence of marihuana, but this effect has not been objectively confirmed.

The sense of time is distorted: 10 minutes may seem like an hour. Curiously, there is often a splitting of consciousness, so that the smoker, while experiencing the high, is at the same time an objective observer of his or her own intoxication. The person may, for example, be afflicted with paranoid thoughts yet at the same time be reasonably objective about them: laughing or scoffing at them and, in a sense, enjoying them. The ability to retain a degree of objectivity may explain the fact that many experienced users of marihuana manage to behave in a perfectly sober fashion in public even when they are highly intoxicated.

Although the intoxication varies with psychological set and social setting, the most common response is a calm, mildly euphoric state in which time slows and sensitivity to sights, sounds, and touch is enhanced. The smoker may feel exhilaration or hilarity and notice a rapid flow of ideas with a reduction in short-term memory. Images sometimes appear before closed eyes; visual perception and body image may undergo subtle changes. It is dangerous to operate complex machinery, including automobiles, under the influence of marihuana, because it slows reaction time and impairs attention and coordination. There is uncertainty as to whether some impairment persists for several hours after the feeling of intoxication has passed (6, 7).

Marihuana is sometimes referred to as a hallucinogen. Many of the phenomena associated with lysergic acid diethylamide (LSD) and LSD-type substances can be produced by cannabis. As with LSD, the experience often has a wave-like aspect. Other phenomena commonly associated with both types of drugs are distorted perception of various parts of the body, spatial and temporal distortion, depersonalization, increased sensitivity to sound, synesthesia, heightened suggestibility, and a sense of thinking more clearly and having deeper awareness of the meaning of things. Anxiety and paranoid reactions are also sometimes seen as consequences of either drug. However, the agonizingly nightmarish reactions that even the experienced LSD user may endure are quite rare among experienced marihuana smokers, not simply because they are using a far less potent drug but also because they have much closer and continuing control over the extent and type of reaction they wish to induce. Furthermore, cannabis has a tendency to produce sedation, whereas LSD and LSD-type drugs may induce long periods of wakefulness and even restlessness. Unlike LSD, marihuana does not dilate the pupils or materially heighten blood pressure, reflexes, and body temperature. (On the other hand, it does increase the pulse rate.) Tolerance develops rapidly with LSD-type drugs but little with cannabis. Finally, marihuana lacks the potent consciousness-altering qualities of LSD, peyote, mescaline, psilocybin, and other hallucinogens; it is questionable whether in doses ordinarily used in this country it can produce true hallucinations. These differences, particularly the last, cast considerable doubt on marihuana's credentials for inclusion among the hallucinogens.

HEALTH EFFECTS OF MARIHUANA USE

In recent years the psychological and physical effects of long-term use have caused most concern. Studies are often conflicting and permit various views of marihuana's possible harmfulness. This complicates the task of presenting an objective statement about the issue.

One of the first questions asked about any drug is whether it is addictive or produces dependence. This question is hard to answer because the terms addiction and dependence have no agreed-upon definitions. Two recognized signs of addiction are tolerance and withdrawal symptoms; these are rarely a serious problem for marihuana users. In the early stages, they actually become more sensitive to the desired effects. After continued heavy use, some tolerance to both physiological and psychological effects develops, although it seems to vary considerably among individuals. Almost no one reports an urgent need to increase the dose to recapture the original sensation. What is called behavioral tolerance may be partly a matter of learning to compensate for the effects of high doses, and may explain why farm workers in some Third World countries are able to do heavy physical labor while smoking a great deal of marihuana.

A mild withdrawal reaction also occurs in animal experiments and possibly in some human beings who take high doses for a long time. The rarely reported mild symptoms are anxiety, insomnia, tremors, and chills, lasting for a day or two. It is unclear how common this reaction is; in a Jamaican study, heavy ganja users did not report abstinence symptoms when withdrawn from the drug. In any case, there is little evidence that the withdrawal reaction ordinarily presents serious problems to marihuana users or causes them to go on taking the drug.

In a more important sense, dependence means an unhealthy and often unwanted preoccupation with a drug to the exclusion of most other things. People suffering from drug dependence find that they are constantly thinking about the drug, or intoxicated, or recovering from its effects. The habit impairs their mental and physical health and hurts their work, family life, and friendships. They often know that they are using too much and repeatedly make unsuccessful attempts to cut down or stop. These problems seem to afflict proportionately fewer marihuana smokers than users of alcohol, tobacco, heroin, or cocaine. Even heavy users in places like Jamaica and Costa Rica do not seem to be dependent in this damaging sense. Marihuana's capacity to lead to psychological dependence is not as strong as that of either tobacco or alcohol.

It is often difficult to distinguish between drug use as a cause of problems and drug use as an effect; this is especially true in the case of marihuana. Most people who develop a dependency on marihuana would also be likely to develop other dependencies because of anxiety, depression, or feelings of inadequacy. The original condition is likely to matter more than the attempt to relieve it by means of the drug. The troubled teenager who smokes cannabis throughout the school day certainly has a problem, and excessive use of marihuana may be one of its symptoms.

The idea has persisted that in the long run smoking marihuana causes some sort of mental or emotional deterioration. In three major studies conducted in Jamaica, Costa Rica, and Greece, researchers have compared heavy long-term cannabis users with nonusers and found no evidence of intellectual or neurological damage, no changes in personality, and no loss of the will to work or participate in society. The Costa Rican study showed no difference between heavy users (seven or more marihuana cigarettes a day) and lighter users (six or fewer cigarettes a day). Experiments in the United States show no effects of fairly heavy marihuana use on learning, perception, or motivation over periods as long as a year (8–11).

On the other side are clinical reports of a personality change called the amotivational syndrome. Its symptoms are said to be passivity, aimlessness, apathy, uncommunicativeness, and lack of ambition. Some proposed explanations are hormone changes, brain damage, sedation, and depression. Since the amotivational syndrome does not seem to occur in Greek or Caribbean farm laborers, some writers suggest that it affects only skilled and educated people who need to do more complex thinking (12–14). However, there is no credible evidence that what is meant by this syndrome is related to any inherent properties of the drug rather than to different sociocultural adaptations on the part of the users.

The problem of distinguishing causes from symptoms is particularly acute here. Heavy drug users in our society are often bored, depressed, and listless, or alienated, cynical, and rebellious. Sometimes the drugs cause these states of mind and sometimes they result from personality characteristics that lead to drug abuse. Drug abuse can be an excuse for failure or a form of self-medication. Because of these complications and the absence of confirmation from controlled studies, the existence of an amotivational syndrome caused by cannabis use has to be regarded as unproved.

Much attention has also been devoted to the idea that marihuana smoking leads to the use of opiates and other illicit drugs: the stepping stone hypothesis, now commonly referred to as the gateway hypothesis. In this country, almost everyone who uses any other illicit drug has smoked marihuana first, just as almost everyone who smokes marihuana has drunk alcohol first. Anyone who uses any given drug is more likely to be interested in others, for some of the same reasons. People who use illicit drugs, in particular, are somewhat more likely to find themselves in company where other illicit drugs are available. None of this proves that using one drug leads to or causes the use of another. Most marihuana smokers do not use heroin or cocaine, just as most alcohol drinkers do not use marihuana. The metaphor of stepping stones suggests that if no one smoked marihuana it would be more difficult for anyone to develop an interest in opiates or cocaine. There is no convincing evidence for or against this. What is clear is that at many times and places marihuana has been used without these drugs, and that these drugs have been used without marihuana.

Only the unsophisticated continue to believe that cannabis leads to violence and crime. Indeed, instead of inciting criminal behavior, cannabis may tend to suppress it. The intoxication induces a mild lethargy that is not conducive to any physical activity, let alone the commission of crimes. The release of inhibitions results in fantasy and verbal (rather than behavioral) expression. During the high, marihuana users may say and think things they would not ordinarily say and think, but they generally do not do things that are foreign to their nature. If they are not already criminals, they will not commit crimes under the influence of the drug.

Does marihuana induce sexual debauchery? This popular impression may owe its origin partly to writers' fantasies and partly to the fact that users in the Middle East once laced the drug with what they thought were aphrodisiacs. In actuality, there is little evidence that cannabis stimulates sexual desire or power. On the other hand, there are those who contend, with equally little substantiation, that marihuana weakens sexual desire. Many marihuana users report that the high enhances the enjoyment of sexual intercourse. This appears to be true in the same sense that the enjoyment of art and music is apparently enhanced. It is questionable, however, that the intoxication breaks down barriers to sexual activity that are not already broken.

Does marihuana lead to physical and mental degeneracy? Reports from many investigators, particularly in Egypt and parts of the Orient, indicate that long-term users of the potent versions of cannabis are, indeed, typically passive, nonproductive, slothful, and totally lacking in ambition. This suggests that chronic use of the drug in its stronger forms may have debilitating effects, as prolonged heavy drinking does. There is a far more likely explanation, however. Many of those who take up cannabis in these countries are poverty stricken, hungry, sick, hopeless, or defeated, seeking through this inexpensive drug to soften the impact of an otherwise unbearable reality. This also applies to many of the "potheads" in the United States. In most situations one cannot be certain which came first: the drug, on the one hand, or the depression, anxiety, feelings of inadequacy, or the seemingly intolerable life situation on the other.

There is a substantial body of evidence that moderate use of marihuana does not produce physical or mental deterioration. One of the earliest and most extensive studies of this question was an investigation conducted by the British Government in India in the 1890s. The investigating agency, called the Indian Hemp Drugs Commission, interviewed some 800 people—including cannabis users and dealers, physicians, superintendents of mental asylums, religious leaders, and a variety of other authorities—and in 1894 published a report of more than 3000 pages. It concluded that there was no evidence that moderate use of the cannabis drugs produced any disease or mental or moral damage or that it tended to lead to excess any more than did the moderate use of whiskey (15, 16).

In the La Guardia study in New York City, an examination of chronic users who had averaged about seven marihuana cigarettes a day (a comparatively high dosage) over a long period (the mean was eight years) showed that they had suffered no demonstrable mental or physical decline as a result of their use of the drug (17). The 1972 report of the National Commission on Marihuana and Drug Abuse (18), although it did much to demythologize cannabis, cautioned that, of people in the United States who used marihuana, 2% became heavy users and that these abusers were at risk, but it did not make clear exactly what risk was involved. Furthermore, since the publication of this report, several controlled studies of chronic heavy use have been completed that have failed to establish any pharmacologically induced harmfulness, including personality deterioration or the development of the so-called amotivational syndrome (8, 11, 14, 19–22). The most recent government sponsored review of cannabis, *Marijuana and Health,* conducted by the Institute of Medicine, while cautious in its summary statement, found little documentation for most of the alleged harmfulness of this substance (23).

A common assertion made about cannabis is that it may lead to psychosis. The literature on this subject is vast, and it divides into all shades of opinion. Many psychiatrists in India, Egypt, Morocco, and Nigeria have declared emphatically that the drug can produce insanity; others insist that it does not. One of the authorities most often quoted in support of the indictment is Benabud of Morocco. He believes that the drug produces a specific syndrome called "cannabis psychosis." His description of the identifying symptoms is far from clear, however, and other investigators dispute the existence of such a psychosis. The symptoms said to characterize this syndrome are also common to other acute toxic states, including, particularly in Morocco, those associated with malnutrition and endemic infections. Benabud estimates that the number of kif (marihuana) smokers suffering from all types of psychosis is not more than 5 in 1000 (24); this rate, however, is lower than the estimated total prevalence of all psychoses in populations of other countries. One would have to assume either (*a*) that there is a much lower prevalence of psychoses other than cannabis psychosis among kif smokers in Morocco or (*b*) that there is no such thing as a cannabis psychosis and the drug is contributing little or nothing to the prevalence rate for psychoses.

Bromberg, in a report of one of his studies, listed 31 patients whose psychoses he attributed to the toxic effects of marihuana. Of these 31, however, 7 patients were already predisposed to functional psychoses that were only precipitated by the drug, 7 others were later found to be schizophrenics, and 1 was later diagnosed as a manic-depressive (25). The Chopras in India, in examinations of 1238 cannabis users, found only 13 to be psychotic, which is about the usual prevalence of psychosis in the total population in Western countries (26). In the La Guardia study, 9 of 77 people who were studied intensively had a history of psychosis; however, this high rate could be attributed to the fact that all those studied were patients in hospitals or institutions. Allentuck and Bowman, the psychiatrists who examined this group, concluded that "marihuana will not produce psychosis de novo in a well-integrated, stable person" (27).

An article by Thacore and Shukla in 1976 revived the concept of the cannabis psychosis (28). The authors compared 25 people with what they call a paranoid psychosis precipitated by cannabis with an equal number of paranoid schizophrenics. The cannabis psychotics were described as patients in whom there had been a clear temporal relation between prolonged abuse of cannabis and the development of a psychosis on more than two occasions. All had used cannabis heavily for at least 3 years, mainly in the form of bhang, the weakest of the three preparations common in India (it is usually drunk as a tea or eaten in doughy pellets). In comparison with the schizophrenics, the cannabis psychotics were described as more panicky, elated, boisterous, and communicative; their behavior was said to be more often violent and bizarre and their mental processes characterized by rapidity of thought and flight of ideas without schizophrenic thought disorder. The prognosis was said to be good; the symptoms could be easily relieved by phenothiazines and recurrence prevented by a decision not to use cannabis again. The syndrome was distinguished from an acute toxic reaction by the absence of clouded sensorium, confusion, and disorientation. Thacore and Shukla did not provide enough information to justify either the identification of their 25 patients' conditions as a single clinical syndrome or the asserted relation to cannabis use. They had little to say about the amount of cannabis used, except that relatives of the patients regarded it as abnormally large; they did not discuss the question of why the psychosis is associated with bhang rather than the stronger cannabis preparations ganja and charas. The meaning of "prolonged abuse on more than two occasions" in the case of men who were constant heavy cannabis users was not clarified, and the temporal relation between this situation and psychosis was not specified. Moreover, the cannabis-taking habits of the control group of schizophrenics were not discussed—a serious omission where use of bhang is so common. The patients described as cannabis psychotics were probably a heterogeneous mixture, with acute schizophrenic breaks, acute manic episodes, severe borderline conditions, and a few symptoms actually related to acute cannabis intoxication: mainly anxiety-panic reactions and a few psychoses of the kind that can be precipitated in unstable people by many different experiences of stress or consciousness change (28).

The explanation for such psychoses is that a person maintaining a delicate balance of ego functioning—so that, for instance, the ego is threatened by a severe loss or a surgical assault or even an alcoholic debauch—may also be overwhelmed or precipitated into a psychotic reaction by a drug that alters, however mildly, his or her state of consciousness. This concatenation of factors—a person whose ego is already overburdened in its attempts to manage a great deal of anxiety and to prevent distortion of perception and body image, plus the taking of a drug that, in some persons, promotes just these effects—may, indeed, be the last straw in precipitating a schizophrenic break. Of 41 first-break acute schizophrenic patients studied by Dr. Grinspoon at the Massachusetts Mental Health Center, it was possible to elicit a history of marihuana use in 6 (29). In 4 of the 6 it seemed quite improbable that the drug could have had any relation to the development of the acute psychosis, because the psychosis was so remote in time from the drug experience. Careful history taking and attention to details of the drug experiences and changing mental status in the remaining 2 patients failed either to implicate or exonerate marihuana as a precipitant in their psychoses.

Our own clinical experience and that of others (30) suggests that cannabis may precipitate exacerbations in the psychotic processes of some schizophrenic patients at a time when their illnesses are otherwise reasonably well-controlled with antipsychotic drugs. In these patients it is often difficult to determine whether the use of cannabis is simply a precipitant of the psychosis or whether it is an attempt to treat symptomatically the earliest perceptions of decompensation; needless to say, the two possibilities are not mutually exclusive. There is little support for the idea that cannabis contributes to the etiology of schizophrenia (31). And in one recently reported case, a 19-year-old schizophrenic woman was more successfully treated with cannabidiol (one of the cannabinoids in marihuana) than she had been with haloperidol (32).

Although there is little evidence for the existence of a cannabis psychosis, it seems clear that the drug may precipitate in susceptible people one of several types of mental dysfunction. The most serious and disturbing of these is the toxic psychosis. This is an acute state that resembles the delirium of a high fever. It is caused by the presence in the brain of toxic substances that interfere with a variety of cerebral functions. Generally speaking, as the toxins disappear, so do the symptoms of toxic psychosis. This type of reaction may be caused by any number of substances taken either as intended or inadvertent overdoses. The syndrome often includes clouding of consciousness, restlessness, confusion, bewilderment, disorientation, dreamlike thinking, apprehension, fear, illusions, and hallucinations. It generally requires a rather large ingested dose of cannabis to induce a toxic psychosis. Such a reaction is apparently much less likely to occur when cannabis is smoked, perhaps because not enough of the active substances can be absorbed sufficiently rapidly, or possibly because the process of smoking modifies in some yet unknown way those cannabinoids that are most likely to precipitate this syndrome.

Some marihuana users suffer what are usually short-lived, acute, anxiety states, sometimes with and sometimes without accompanying paranoid thoughts. The anxiety may reach such proportions as properly to be called panic. Such panic reactions, although uncommon, probably constitute the most frequent adverse reaction to the moderate use of smoked marihuana. During this reaction, the sufferer may believe that the various distortions of bodily perceptions mean that he or she is dying or is undergoing some great physical catastrophe, and similarly the individual may interpret the psychological distortions induced by the drug as an indication of his or her loss of sanity. Panic states may, albeit rarely, be so severe as to incapacitate, usually for a relatively short period of time. The anxiety that characterizes the acute panic reaction resembles an attenuated version of the frightening parts of an LSD or other psychedelic experience—the so-called "bad trip." Some proponents of the use of LSD in psychotherapy have asserted that the induced altered state of consciousness involves a lifting of repression. Although the occurrence of a global undermining of repression is questionable, many effects of LSD do suggest important alterations in ego defenses. These alterations presumably make new percepts and insights available to the ego; some, particularly those most directly derived from primary process, may be quite threatening, especially if there is no comfortable and supportive setting to facilitate the integration of the new awareness into the ego organization. Thus, psychedelic experiences may be accompanied by a great deal of anxiety, particularly when the drugs are taken under poor conditions of set and setting; to a much lesser extent, the same can be said of cannabis.

These reactions are self-limiting, and simple reassurance is the best method of treatment. Perhaps the main danger to the user is that she will be diagnosed as having a toxic psychosis. Users with this kind of reaction may be quite distressed, but they are not psychotic. The sine qua non of sanity, the ability to test reality, remains intact, and the panicked user is invariably able to relate the discomfort to the drug. There is no disorientation, nor are there true hallucinations. Sometimes this panic reaction is accompanied by paranoid ideation. The user may, for example, believe that the others in the room, especially if they are not well known, have some hostile intentions or that someone is going to inform on the user, often to the police, for smoking marihuana. Generally speaking, these paranoid ideas are not strongly held, and simple reassurance dispels them. Anxiety reactions and paranoid thoughts are much more likely in someone who is taking the drug for the first time or in an unpleasant or unfamiliar setting than in an experienced user who is comfortable with the surroundings and companions; the reaction is very rare where marihuana is a casually accepted part of the social scene. The likelihood varies directly with the dose and inversely with the user's experience; thus, the most vulnerable person is the inexperienced user who inadvertently (often precisely because he or she lacks familiarity with the drug) takes a large dose that produces perceptual and somatic changes for which the user is unprepared.

One rather rare reaction to cannabis is the flashback, or spontaneous recurrence of drug symptoms while not intoxicated. Although several reports suggest that this may occur in marihuana users even without prior use of any other drug (32), in general it seems to arise only in those who have used more powerful hallucinogenic or psychedelic drugs. There are also some people who have flashback experiences of psychedelic drug trips while smoking marihuana; this is sometimes regarded as an extreme version of a more general heightening of the marihuana high that occurs after the use of hallucinogens. Many people find flashbacks enjoyable, but to others they are distressing. They usually fade with the passage of time. It is possible that flashbacks are attempts to deal with primary process derivatives and other unconscious material that has breached the ego defenses during the psychedelic or cannabis experience.

Rarely, but especially among new users of marihuana, there occurs an acute depressive reaction. It is generally rather mild and transient but may sometimes require psychiatric intervention. This type of reaction is most likely to occur in a user who has some degree of underlying depression; it is as though the drug allows the depression to be felt and experienced as such. Again, set and setting play an important part.

Most recent research on the health hazards of marihuana concerns its long-term effects on the body. The main physiological effects of cannabis are increased appetite, a faster heartbeat, and slight reddening of the conjunctiva. Although the increased heart rate could be a problem for people with cardiovascular disease, dangerous physical reactions to marihuana are almost unknown. No human being is known to have died of an overdose. By extrapolation from animal experiments, the ratio of lethal to effective (intoxicating) dose is estimated to be on the order of thousands to one.

Studies have examined the brain, the immune system, the reproductive system, and the lungs. Suggestions of long-term damage come almost exclusively from animal experiments and other laboratory work. Observations of marihuana users and the Caribbean, Greek, and other studies reveal little disease or organic pathology associated with the drug (12–14).

For example, there are several reports of damaged brain cells and changes in brain-wave readings in monkeys smoking marihuana, but neurological and neuropsychological tests in Greece, Jamaica, and Costa Rica found no evidence of functional brain damage. Damage to white blood cells has also been observed in the laboratory, but again, its practical importance is unclear. Whatever temporary changes marihuana may produce in the immune system, they have not been found to increase the danger of infectious disease or cancer. If there were significant damage, we might expect to find a higher rate of these diseases among young people beginning in the 1960s, when marihuana first became popular. There is no evidence of that.

The effects of marihuana on the reproductive system are a more complicated issue. In men, a single dose of THC lowers sperm count and the level of testosterone and other hormones. Tolerance to this effect apparently develops; in the Costa Rican study, marihuana smokers and controls had the same testosterone levels. Although the smokers in that study began using marihuana at an average age of 15, it had not affected their masculine development. There is no evidence that the changes in sperm count and testosterone produced by marihuana affect sexual performance or fertility.

In animal experiments THC has also been reported to lower levels of female hormones and disturb the menstrual cycle. When monkeys, rats, and mice are exposed during pregnancy to amounts of THC equivalent to a heavy human smoker's dose, stillbirths and decreased birth weight are sometimes reported in their offspring. There are also reports of low birth weight, prematurity, and even a condition resembling the fetal alcohol syndrome in some children of women who smoke marihuana heavily during pregnancy. The significance of these reports is unclear because controls are lacking and other circumstances make it hard to attribute causes. To be safe, pregnant and nursing women should follow the standard conservative recommendation to avoid all drugs, including cannabis, that are not absolutely necessary.

A well-confirmed danger of long-term, heavy marihuana use is its effect on the lungs. Smoking narrows and inflames air passages and reduces breathing capacity; damage to bronchial cells has been observed in hashish smokers. The possible side effects include bronchitis, emphysema, and lung cancer. Marihuana smoke contains the same carcinogens as tobacco smoke, usually in somewhat higher concentrations. Marihuana is also inhaled more deeply and held in the lungs longer, which increases the danger (45, 46). On the other hand, almost no one smokes 20 marihuana cigarettes a day. Marihuana of higher potency may reduce the danger of respiratory damage, because less smoking is required for the desired effect. There is now some experimental evidence demonstrating that high-potency THC cigarettes are smoked less vigorously than those of low potency; the user takes smaller and shorter puffs, inhaling less with each puff (34).

It is hard to generalize about abuse or define specific treatments, because the problems associated with marihuana are so vague, and cause and effect so hard to determine. Marihuana smokers may be using the drug as a facet of adolescent exploration, to demonstrate rebelliousness, cope with anxiety, medicate themselves for early symptoms of mental illness, or most commonly, simply for pleasure.

The complexity of the problem is illustrated by a most important long-term study by two Berkeley psychologists (35). Shedler and Block followed the progress of 101 San Francisco children of both sexes from ages 5 to 18, and gave them personality tests at 7, 11, and 18 years of age. By the end of the study, 68% had used marihuana and 39% had used it once a week or more; large minorities had also used cocaine, hallucinogens, and prescription stimulants and sedatives. Three main groups could be distinguished: 29 "abstainers" who had used no illicit drugs; 36 "experimenters" who had used marihuana no more than once a month and had tried at most one other drug; and 20 "frequent users" who had smoked marihuana at least once a week and had used at least one other drug. The other 16 fit into none of these categories and were not included in the study.

Striking personality differences among the three groups appeared in childhood, long before any drug use. The frequent users, as early as age 7, got along poorly with other children and had few friends. They found it difficult to think ahead and lacked confidence in themselves. They were untrustworthy and seemingly indifferent to moral questions. At age 11 they were described as inattentive, uncooperative, and vulnerable to stress. At 18, they were insecure, alienated, impulsive, undependable, self-indulgent, inconsiderate, and unpredictable in their moods and behavior; they overreacted to frustration; they felt personally inadequate and also victimized and cheated. They had lower high school grades than adolescents in the other two groups.

Abstainers, at age 7, were described as inhibited, conventional, obedient, and lacking in creativity. At age 11 they were shy, neat and orderly, eager to please, but lacking in humor, liveliness, and expressiveness. The terms that best described them at 18 were tense, overcontrolled, moralistic, anxious, and lacking in social ease or personal charm. Their high school grades were average.

The happy mean, statistically, was found in the "experimenters." They were more likely to be warm, responsive, curious, open, active, and cheerful from the age of 7 on. In the three broad categories of personal happiness, relations with others, and rational self-control, frequent users were doing worst and experimental users best. The authors pointed out that studies comparing moderate drinkers with alcoholics and abstainers have found similar personality differences.

To find some sources of these differences, the authors examined experiments conducted when the children were only 5 years old. Their parents' behavior was observed as they worked with the child on a laboratory task involving blocks and mazes. Mothers of both frequent users and abstainers tended to be cold and unresponsive. They gave their children little encouragement but insisted that they perform well; and the experience seemed unpleasant for both mother and child. Fathers of frequent users did not differ from fathers of experimenters, but abstainers' fathers were impatient, hypercritical, and domineering.

According to the authors, frequent drug users believe that they have nothing to look forward to and are therefore drawn to the immediate gratification provided by drugs. Their alienation and impulsiveness might have roots in their relationship with their mothers. The problems of abstainers are also serious, but they attract less attention, because they are less troublesome for society. Abstainers suppress their impulses to avoid feeling vulnerable, perhaps because they have internalized the attitudes of harsh, authoritarian fathers. Experimental users are the largest and most typical group. At least in the San Francisco area in the 1980s, reasonably inquisitive, open, and independent adolescents experimented with marihuana as part of growing up.

The inverted U-shaped relationship between the degree of drug use and psychological health suggests that the need for therapy would also describe such a curve. The fact that among the abstainers are to be found many individuals who could profit from psychotherapy is not relevant to this discussion of marihuana. The important question concerns the indications for therapy for those who comprise the other two arms of the curve. Given the current prevalence of drug use in our society, the developmentally appropriate propensity of adolescents to explore and experiment, and the relatively benign sequelae of such experimentation with cannabis, it is obvious that therapy is not properly indicated for young people who fit the description of the "experimenter."

It is appropriate to consider psychotherapy for the frequent adolescent users of marihuana. The picture that emerges is "one of a troubled adolescent who is interpersonally alienated, emotionally withdrawn, and manifestly unhappy, and who expresses his or her maladjustment through undercontrolled, overtly antisocial behavior" (35). They are described as being "overreactive to minor frustrations, likely to think and associate to ideas in unusual ways, having brittle ego-defense systems, self-defeating, concerned about the adequacy of their bodily functioning, concerned about their adequacy as persons, prone to project their feelings and motives onto others, feeling cheated and victimized by life, and having fluctuating moods."

Obviously, psychotherapy is not inappropriate for individuals who exemplify this description. But it should be emphasized that this is not psychotherapy for marihuana abuse; it is therapy for the underlying psychopathology, one of whose symptoms is the abuse of cannabis. It is no more appropriate to see marihuana as the cause of the problem here than it is to see repetitive handwashing as the cause of obsessive-compulsive disorder. The individual may be brought to psychiatric attention because of the hand-washing, but the therapy will address the underlying disorder. Becoming attached to cannabis is not so much a function of any inherent psychopharmacological property of the drug as it is emotionally driven by the underlying psychopathology. Success in curtailing cannabis use requires dealing with that pathology.

MEDICINAL USES OF MARIHUANA

The history of cannabis as a Western medicine begins in 1839 with a publication by W. B. O'Shaughnessy, a British physician working in Calcutta (36). He reported on the analgesic, anticonvulsant, and muscle relaxant properties of the drug. His paper generated a good deal of interest, and there are about 100 other papers in the Western medical literature from 1840 to the turn of the century. In the nineteenth century the drug was widely prescribed in the Western world for various ailments and discomforts, such as coughing, fatigue, rheumatism, asthma, delirium tremens, migraine headache, and painful menstruation. Although its use was already declining somewhat because of the introduction of synthetic hypnotics and analgesics, it remained in the United States Pharmacopoeia until 1941. The difficulties imposed on its use by the Marihuana Tax Act of 1937 completed its medical demise, and, from that time on, physicians allowed themselves to become ignorant about the drug.

The greatest advantage of cannabis as a medicine is its unusual safety. The ratio of lethal dose to effective dose is estimated on the basis of extrapolation from animal data to be about 20,000:1. Huge doses have been given to dogs without causing death, and there is no reliable evidence of death caused by cannabis in a human being. Cannabis also has the advantage of not disturbing any physiological functions or damaging any body organs when it is used in therapeutic doses. It produces little physical dependence or tolerance; there has never been any evidence that medical use of cannabis has led to habitual use as an intoxicant.

Whole cannabis preparations have the disadvantages of instability, varying strength, and insolubility in water, which makes it difficult for the drug to enter the bloodstream from the digestive tract. Another problem is that marihuana contains so many ingredients with possible disadvantageous effects, including too high a degree of intoxication. This multitude of ingredients is also an opportunity, since it suggests the manufacture of different cannabinoids, synthetic or natural, with properties useful for particular purposes; some of these have now become available (37). One which is presently legally available for the treatment of nausea and vomiting of cancer chemotherapy and the AIDS weight loss syndrome is dronabinol (Marinol), a synthetic THC. While it is not as useful medicinally as whole smoked marihuana, it is legally available as a Schedule II drug. Smoking generates quicker and more predictable results because it raises THC concentration in the blood more easily and predictably to the needed level. Also, it may be hard for a nauseated patient in chemotherapy to take oral medicine. But many patients dislike smoking or cannot inhale (38).

There are many anecdotal reports of marihuana smokers using the drug to reduce postsurgery pain, headache, migraine, menstrual cramps, phantom limbs, and other kinds of pain. It is possible that cannabis acts by mechanisms different from those of other analgesics, but the literature does not indicate a specific effect of cannabis on pain pathways or suggest that it is likely to be more effective than other analgesics. Again, some new synthetic derivative might prove useful as an analgesic, but this is not an immediate prospect.

Because of reports that some people use less alcohol when they smoke marihuana, cannabis has been proposed as an adjunct to alcoholism treatment, but so far it has not been found useful (39–41). Most alcoholics neither want to substitute marihuana nor find it particularly helpful. But there might be some hope for use of marihuana in combination with disulfiram (Antabuse) (42). Certainly a cannabis habit would be preferable to an alcohol habit for anyone who could not avoid dependence on a drug but was able to substitute one drug for another.

About 20% of epileptic patients do not get much relief from conventional anticonvulsant medications. Cannabis has been explored as an alternative, at least since a case was reported in which marihuana smoking, together with the standard anticonvulsants phenobarbital and diphenylhydantoin (Dilantin), was apparently necessary to control seizures in a young epileptic man (43). Marihuana also reduces muscle spasm and tremors in some people who suffer from cerebral palsy or multiple sclerosis (44). The cannabis derivative that is most promising as an anticonvulsant is cannabidiol. In one controlled study, cannabidiol in addition to prescribed anticonvulsants produced improvement in seven patients with grand mal seizures; three showed great improvement. Of eight patients who received a placebo instead, only one improved (45).

Anecdotal reports of the use of cannabis for the relief of asthma abound. The antiasthmatic drugs that are available all have drawbacks—limited effectiveness or side effects. Because marihuana dilates the bronchi and reverses bronchial spasm, cannabis derivatives have been tested as antiasthmatic drugs. Smoking marihuana would probably not be a good way to treat asthma because of chronic irritation of the bronchial tract by tars and other substances in marihuana smoke, so recent research has sought a better means of administration. THC in the form of an aerosol spray has been investigated extensively (46, 47). Other cannabinoids such as cannabinol and cannabidiol may be preferable to THC for this purpose. An interesting finding for future research is that cannabinoids may affect the bronchi by means of a different mechanism from that of the familiar antiasthmatic drugs.

A promising new medical use for cannabis is treatment of glaucoma, the second leading cause of blindness in the United States. About a million Americans suffer from the form of glaucoma (wide angle) treatable with cannabis. Marihuana causes a dose-related, clinically significant drop in intraocular pressure that lasts several hours in both normal subjects and those with the abnormally high ocular tension produced by glaucoma. Oral or intravenous THC has the same effect, which seems to be specific to cannabis derivatives rather than simply a result of sedation. Cannabis does not cure the disease, but it can retard the progressive loss of sight when conventional medication fails and surgery is too dangerous (48).

It remains to be seen whether topical use of THC or a synthetic cannabinoid in the form of eyedrops will be preferable to smoking marihuana for this purpose. So far THC eyedrops have not proved effective, and in 1981 the National Eye Institute announced that it would no longer approve human research using these eyedrops (42). Studies continue on certain synthetic cannabis derivatives and other natural cannabinoids. Smoking marihuana is a better way of titrating the dose than is the taking of an oral cannabinoid, and most patients seem to prefer it. Unfortunately, many patients, especially elderly ones, dislike the psychoactive effects of marihuana.

Cannabis derivatives have several minor or speculative uses in the treatment of cancer, and one major use. As appetite stimulants, marihuana and THC may help to slow weight loss in cancer patients (49). THC has also retarded the growth of tumor cells in some animal studies, but results are inconclusive, and another cannabis derivative, cannabidiol, seems to increase tumor growth (50). Possibly cannabinoids in combination with other drugs will turn out to have some use in preventing tumor growth.

But the most promising use of cannabis in cancer treatment is the prevention of nausea and vomiting in patients undergoing chemotherapy. About half of patients treated with anticancer drugs suffer from severe nausea and vomiting. In 25 to 30% of these cases, the commonly used antiemetics do not work (38). The nausea and vomiting are not only unpleasant but a threat to the effectiveness of the therapy. Retching can cause tears of the esophagus and rib fractures, prevent adequate nutrition, and lead to fluid loss.

The antiemetics most commonly used in chemotherapy are prochlorperazine (Compazine) and the newer ondansetron (Zofran) and granisetron (Kytril). The suggestion that cannabis might be useful arose in the early 1970s when some young patients receiving cancer chemotherapy found that marihuana smoking, which was, of course, illegal, reduced their nausea and vomiting. In one study of 56 patients who got no relief from standard antiemetic agents, 78% became symptom-free when they smoked marihuana (51).

Several of the most urgent medical uses of cannabis are the treatment of the nausea and weight loss suffered by many AIDS patients. The nausea is often a symptom of the disease itself and a side effect of some of the medicines (particularly AZT). For many AIDS patients the most distressing and threatening symptom is cachexia. Marihuana will retard weight loss in most patients and even helps some regain weight (38).

A committee of the Institute of Medicine of the National Academy of Sciences remarked in a report in 1982 (23, p. 139):

> Cannabis shows promise in some of these areas, although the dose necessary to produce the desired effect is often close to one that produces an unacceptable frequency of toxic [undesirable] side effects. What is perhaps more encouraging . . . is that cannabis seems to exert its beneficial effects through mechanisms that differ from those of other available drugs. This raises the possibility that some patients who would not be helped by conventional therapies could be treated with cannabis. . . . It may be possible to reduce side effects by synthesizing related molecules that could have a more favorable ratio of desired to undesired actions; this line of investigation should have a high priority.

The committee recommended further research, especially in the treatment of nausea and vomiting in chemotherapy, asthma, glaucoma, and seizures and spasticity.

Under federal and most state statutes, marihuana is listed as a Schedule I drug: high potential for abuse, no currently accepted medical use, and lacking in accepted safety for use under medical supervision. It cannot ordinarily be prescribed and may be used only under research conditions.

The potential of cannabis as a medicine is yet to be realized, partly because of its reputation as an intoxicant, ignorance on the part of the medical establishment, and legal difficulties involved in doing the research. Recreational use of cannabis has affected the opinions of physicians about its medical potential in various ways. When marihuana was regarded as the drug of blacks, Mexican-Americans, and bohemians, doctors were ready to go along with the Bureau of Narcotics, ignore its medical uses, and urge prohibition. For years the National Organization for the Reform of Marijuana Laws and other groups have been petitioning the government to change this classification. Now that marihuana has become so popular among a broad section of the population, we have been more willing to investigate its therapeutic value. Recreational use now spurs medical interest instead of medical hostility.

The potential dangers of marihuana when taken for pleasure and its possible usefulness as a medicine are historically and practically interrelated issues: historically, because the arguments used to justify public and official disapproval of recreational use have had a strong influence on opinions about its medical potential; practically, because the more evidence accumulates that marihuana is relatively safe even when used as an intoxicant, the clearer it becomes that the medical requirement of safety is satisfied. Most recent research is tentative, and initial enthusiasm for drugs is often disappointed after further investigation. But it is not as though cannabis were an entirely new agent with unknown properties. Studies done during the past 10 years have confirmed a centuries-old promise. With the relaxation of restrictions on research and the further chemical manipulation of cannabis derivatives, this promise will eventually be realized. The weight of past and contemporary evidence will probably prove cannabis to be valuable in several ways as a medicine.

References.

1. Ludlow FH. The hasheesh eater: being passages from the life of a Pythagorean. New York: Harper and Bros., 1857.
2. Matsuda LA, Lolait SJ, Brownstein MJ, Young AC, Bonner TI. Structure of a cannabinoid receptor and functional expression of the cloned cDNA. Nature 1990;346:561–564.
3. Devane WA, et al. Isolation and structure of a brain constituent that binds to the cannabinoid receptor. Science 1992;258:1946–1949.
4. Ebin D, ed. The drug experience. New York: Grove Press, 1961.
5. Bromberg W. Marihuana intoxication: a clinical study of Cannabis sativa intoxication. Am J Psychiatry 1934;91:303.
6. Chait LD. Subjective and behavioral effects of marijuana the morning after smoking. Psychopharmacology 1990;100:328–333.
7. Yesavage JA, Leirer VO, Denari M, Hollister LE. Carry-over effects of marijuana intoxication on aircraft pilot performance: a preliminary report. Am J Psychiatry 1985;142:1325–1329.
8. Braude MC, Szara S, eds. Pharmacology of marihuana. 2 vols. New York: Raven Press, 1976.
9. Culver CM, King FW. Neurophysiological assessment of undergraduate marihuana and LSD users. Arch Gen Psychiatry 1974;31: 707–711.
10. Lessin PJ, Thomas S. Assessment of the chronic effects of marihuana on motivation and achievement: a preliminary report. In: Braude MC, Szara S, eds. Pharmacology of marihuana. New York: Raven Press, 1976.
11. Stefanis C, Boulougouris J, Liakos A. Clinical and psychophysiological effects of cannabis in longterm users. In: Braude MC, Szara S, eds. Pharmacology of marihuana. New York: Raven Press, 1976.
12. Canter W, Doughty P. Social and cultural aspects of cannabis use in Costa Rica. Ann N Y Acad Sci 1976;282:1–16.
13. Rubin V, Comitas L. Ganja in Jamaica. Garden City, NY: Doubleday, 1976.
14. Stefanis C, Dornbush R, Fiuk M. Hashish: studies of long-term use. New York: Raven Press, 1977.
15. Report of the Indian Hemp Drugs Commission, 1893–94. 7 vols. Simla, India: Government Central Printing Office, 1894.
16. Solomon D, ed. The marihuana papers. Indianapolis: Bobbs-Merrill, 1966.
17. Mayor's Committee on Marihuana. The marihuana problem in the city of New York: Lancaster, PA: Jacques Cattell Press, 1944.
18. National Commission on Marihuana, Drug Abuse. Marihuana: a signal of misunderstanding: first report of the National Commission on Marihuana and Drug Abuse. Washington, DC: Government Printing Office, 1972.
19. Beaubrun MH, Knight F. Psychiatric assessment of 30 chronic users of cannabis and 30 matched controls. Am J Psychiatry 1973;130:309.
20. Dornbush RL, Freedman AM, Fink M, eds. Chronic cannabis use. Ann N Y Acad Sci 1976;282.
21. Hochman JS, Brill NQ. Chronic marijuana use and psychosocial adaptation. Am J Psychiatry 1973;130:132.
22. Rubin V, Comitas L. Ganja in Jamaica. The Hague: Mouton, 1975.
23. Institute of Medicine. Marijuana and health. Washington, DC: National Academy Press, 1982.
24. Benabud A. Psychopathological aspects of the cannabis situation in Morocco: statistical data for 1956. Bull Narc 1957;9:2.
25. Bromberg W. Marihuana: a psychiatric study. JAMA 1939;113:4.
26. Murphy HBM. The cannabis habit: a review of the recent psychiatric literature. Addictions 1966;13:3. [Citing Chopra RN, Chopra GS. The present position of hemp drug addiction in India. Indian Med Res Mem 1939;31].
27. Allentuck S, Bowman KM. The psychiatric aspects of marihuana intoxication. Am J Psychiatry 1942;99:248.
28. Thacore VR, Shukla SRP. Cannabis psychosis and paranoid schizophrenia. Arch Gen Psychiatry 1976;33:383.
29. Grinspoon L. Marihuana reconsidered. 2nd ed. Cambridge, MA: Harvard University Press, 1977.
30. Treffert DA. Marihuana use in schizophrenia: a clear hazard. Am J Psychiatry 1978;135:10.
31. Andreasson S, Allebeck P, Rydberg U. Schizophrenia in users and nonusers of cannabis: a longitudinal study in Stockholm County. Acta Psychiatr Scand 1989;79:505–510.
32. Zuardi AW, Morais SL, Guimarãs FS, Mechoulam R. Antipsychotic effect of cannabidiol [letter]. J Clin Psychiatry 1995;56:485–486.
33. Ganz VP, Volkman F. Adverse reactions to marijuana use among college students. J Am Coll Health Assoc 1976;25:93.
34. Heishman SJ, Stitzer ML, Yingling JE. Effects of tetrahydrocannabinol content on marijuana smoking behavior, subjective reports, and performance. Pharmacol Biochem Behav 1989; 34(1):173–179.
35. Shedler J, Block J. Adolescent drug use and psychological health: a longitudinal inquiry. Am Psychologist 1990;45:612–630.
36. O'Shaughnessy WB. On, the preparation of the Indian hemp, or gunjah (*Cannabis indica*): the effect on the animal system in health, and their utility in the treatment of tetanus and other convulsive diseases. Trans Med Phys Soc Bombay 1842;8:421.
37. Mechoulam R, Carlini EA. Toward drugs derived from cannabis. Naturwissenschaften 1978; 65:174–179.
38. Grinspoon L, Bakalar J. Marihuana, the forbidden medicine. New Haven, CT: Yale University Press, 1993.
39. Roffman RA. Marihuana as medicine. Seattle: Madrona, 1982:99.
40. Rosenberg CM. The use of marihuana in the treatment of alcoholism. In: Cohen S, Stillman RC, eds. The therapeutic potential of marihuana. New York: Plenum, 1976.
41. Rosenberg CM, Gerrein JR, Schnell C. Cannabis in the treatment of alcoholism. J Stud Alcohol 1978;39:155–158.
42. Roffman RA. Marihuana as medicine. Seattle: Madrona, 1982:82–83.
43. Consroe PF, Wood GC, Buchsbaum H. Anticonvulsant nature of marihuana smoking. JAMA 1975;234:306–307.
44. Petro DJ. Marihuana as a therapeutic agent for muscle spasm or spasticity. Psychosomatics 1980;21:81–85.
45. Cunha JM, Carlini EA, Pereira AE, et al. Chronic administration of cannabidiol to healthy volunteers and epileptic patients. Pharmacology 1980;21:175–185.
46. Tashkin DP, Shapiro BJ, Lee YE, Harper CE. Effects of smoked marijuana in experimentally induced asthma. Am Rev Respir Dis 1975; 112:377–386.
47. Tashkin DP, Reiss S, Shapiro BJ, Calvarese B, Olson JL, Lodge JW. Bronchial effects of aerosolized delta-9-tetrahydrocannabinol in healthy and asthmatic subjects. Am Rev Respir Dis 1977;115:57–65.
48. Hepler RS, Rank IM, Petrus R. Ocular effects of marihuana smoking. In: Braude MC, Szara S, eds. Pharmacology of marihuana. New York: Raven Press, 1976.
49. Regelson W, Butler JR, Schulz J, et al. Delta-9-tetrahydrocannabinol as an effective antidepressant and appetite-stimulating agent in advanced cancer patients. In: Braude MC, Szara S, eds. Pharmacology of marihuana. New York: Raven Press, 1976.
50. White AC, Munson JA, Munson AE, Carchman RA. Effects of delta-9-tetrahydrocannabinol in Lewis lung adenocarcinoma cells in tissue culture. J Natl Cancer Inst 1976;56: 655–658.
51. Vinciguerra V, Moore T, Brennan E. Inhalation marijuana as an antiemetic for cancer chemotherapy. N Y State J Med 1988;88:525–527.

18 AMPHETAMINES AND OTHER STIMULANTS

George R. King and Everett H. Ellinwood, Jr.

The use of stimulant compounds has a long history. Chinese native physicians have been using the drug Ma-huang for more than 5000 years. In 1887 Nagai found the active agent in Ma-huang to be ephedrine (31). Amphetamine proper was first synthesized in 1887 by Edeleau as part of a systematic program to manufacture aliphatic amines. Early investigations of the properties of amphetamine focused on the peripheral effects and found that amphetamine was a sympathomimetic agent with bronchodilator properties (31). Oddly, the central nervous system actions were not reported until approximately 1933, and this was closely followed by the first reports of amphetamine abuse. Amphetamines produce feelings of euphoria and relief from fatigue, may improve performance on some simple tasks, increase activity levels, and produce anorexia (31). The abuse liability of the amphetamines is thought to be primarily related to their euphorigenic effects.

This chapter reviews the literature regarding the use and abuse of the amphetamines. First, the basic behavioral neuropharmacology of the amphetamines is reviewed, followed by a brief discussion of the metabolism and toxic consequences of the amphetamines. Next, the epidemiology and economics of amphetamine use and abuse is discussed to put in context the social development and extent of abuse. The medical uses of amphetamine are then presented with a focus on the use of stimulants to treat attention-deficit hyperactivity disorder. Following the review of medical uses, the literature regarding amphetamine abuse is also reviewed, and where appropriate, the physiological and potential neurobiological bases for such effects are discussed. Finally, the chapter presents a brief overview of some treatments of stimulant abuse.

PHARMACOLOGY

The present section describes the basic neurochemical, physiological, and behavioral actions of acute and subchronic administration of amphetamines. The effects of chronic amphetamine administration are discussed under later sections entitled "Toxicity" and "Abuse." This section extensively examines the literature regarding high-dose effects in nonhumans, rather than extensively reviewing the low- to moderate-dose effects in humans. Unlike the causes and effects of many "natural" diseases, those of drug abuse are known (e.g., pharmacological and toxic), and the results of animal experimentation allow for detailed research into these neurobiological processes underlying the development of drug abuse.

Central Effects

NEUROCHEMICAL

The amphetamines are indirect catecholamine agonists and administration results in the release of newly synthesized norepinephrine and dopamine (36–38, 52, 68, 75, 110, 136, 144, 166, 201, 204, 205, 221, 235, 239, 259, 286, 303, 309). Several lines of evidence indicate that amphetamine acts on newly synthesized, versus stored, pools of catecholamines. First, reserpine pretreatment, which depletes stored catecholamines in synaptic vesicles, does not affect the central stimulating properties of amphetamine. Second, treatment with alpha-methyltyrosine inhibits the rate-limiting step of catecholamine biosynthesis and blocks the central stimulating properties of amphetamine (170, 309). High doses of amphetamines will also decrease tyrosine hydroxylase (TH) activity in the neostriatum (190, 191) and the substantia nigra (192).

In addition, high doses of amphetamines release 5-hydroxytryptamine and may affect serotonergic receptors (52, 110, 241, 306). In much the same way that amphetamine affects TH activity, amphetamine also results in a decrease of tryptophan hydroxylase activity following acute administration (152, 189, 226). These synthesis-sensitive mechanisms are in contrast to other types of stimulants such as methylphenidate and cocaine, which act through storage pools (but not on newly synthesized pools) of catecholamines.

Amphetamine administration also influences various neuropeptide systems (136). Peptidergic systems are associated with mesostriatal dopamine circuitry and are thought to play a modulatory role in dopaminergic activity. For example, substance P-containing neurons, whose cell bodies originate in the striatum, have terminal fields in the substantia nigra; Reid et al. (240) found that intranigral substance P injections result in striatal dopamine release. Furthermore, intranigral injections also result in increased locomotor activity (145); these locomotor-stimulating properties of substance P are blocked by mesostriatal 6-hydroxydopamine (6-OHDA) (145).

Neurotensin (NT) pathways also serve to modulate dopaminergic activity. First, in the rat brain, NT receptors are extensively co-localized with dopamine (234). It has been argued that NT preferentially activates somatodendritic receptors, which inhibits terminal activity and neurotransmitter release (217). Given the modulatory effects of neuropeptides on dopaminergic functioning, one would expect that amphetamine would influence these systems. Hanson et al. (136) reported that 18 hours after five injections of amphetamine (15 mg/kg/injection; each injection separated by 6 hours), the levels of NT and substance P were elevated in the striatum. These changes in neuropeptide levels may mediate some of the behavioral effects to be described later (e.g., loss of baseline activity levels and anergia) of repeated doses of amphetamine.

ELECTROPHYSIOLOGICAL

The systemic administration of amphetamines generally results in a dose-dependent depression of the firing rate of catecholaminergic neurons (27, 237), and noradrenergic neurons in the locus ceruleus (124). This suppression of firing rate is caused by somatodendritic autoregulation. For example, Groves and colleagues have infused low doses of amphetamine into the substantia nigra pars compacta while simultaneously recording electrical activity (126, 130–132). These authors found a dose-dependent inhibition of firing rate that lasted approximately 90 minutes. This result was not due to a generalized neuronal suppression, as nondopaminergic neurons were not inhibited. Furthermore, lesions anterior to the substantia nigra attenuate this inhibitory effect (25, 26, 131); second, pretreatment with the synthesis blocker α-MT also abolishes this effect (25, 131), whereas these treatments do not abolish the inhibitory effects of the direct dopamine agonist apomorphine (26, 27).

In contrast to the inhibitory effects of amphetamine on dopaminergic neurons in the substantia nigra, the effects of amphetamine in the neostriatum are biphasic (127, 236, 237). Low doses of amphetamine inhibit the firing rate of spontaneously active neostriatal neurons, while at higher doses there is an excitation of the firing rate. In the caudate putamen, administration of d-amphetamine results in a transient increase in the firing rate of dopaminergic neurons within the first 10 minutes and then a profound inhibition of the firing rate of these neurons (126). This dissociation of the effects of amphetamine on neostriatum and substantia nigra firing rates may underlie some of the behavioral effects of amphetamine to be described later.

Stimulants also have potent effects on electroencephalogram (EEG) recordings. Amphetamine accelerates and desynchronizes the EEG while also shifting the resting EEG toward higher frequencies. During sleep, the amplitude and duration of large delta waves are truncated (307). Furthermore, high-dose intravenous amphetamines and especially cocaine induce sinusoidal high-voltage waves of 20–50 Hz (i.e., spindling) in the olfactory and amygdaloid structures of rats (283), and cats (91, 94).

STRUCTURE-ACTIVITY RELATIONS

Amphetamine is a β-phenylisopropylamine. The critical structural components of amphetamine are an unsubstituted phenyl ring, the alpha-methyl group, the two-carbon side chain between the phenyl ring and the nitrogen, and the primary amino group (16). Research indicates that all the components are necessary for the typical biochemical and pharmacological effects of amphetamine. Different structural modifications accentuate or attenuate various actions of the amphetamines and related compounds. These structure-activity relationships become ever more important in a culture in which tailor-made "designer" drugs increasingly include recreational drugs flowing from clandestine laboratories. The following section provides a brief description of the structure-activity relationships for the amphetamines and related compounds.

Dopamine

Amphetamine blocks the reuptake of and directly releases dopamine from newly synthesized pools. Unlike the reported differential affinity of the d- and l-isomers of amphetamine for norepinephrine release and uptake, such stereospecificity does not seem to exist for the dopaminergic system (68, 75, 279, 289); these researchers found that the dextro and levo isomers were equipotent in inhibiting dopaminergic uptake from rat hypothalamic and corpus striatum synaptosomes.

Norepinephrine

Amphetamine blocks the reuptake of norepinephrine and also causes its release. The beta-phenethylamine structure is critical for the actions of amphetamine; for example, increasing and/or decreasing the number of carbons between the phenyl ring and the nitrogen attenuates the effects of amphetamine on norepinephrine release and reuptake (16).

The alpha-methyl group also seems to be of importance in determining the activity of amphetamine on norepinephrine efflux. For example, the configuration of this group is responsible for the difference in the inhibitory dose 50 (ID_{50}) of d- and l-amphetamine (16); continued methylation in the alpha position to form phentermine and mephentermine extensively decreases the actions on norepinephrine uptake and release (16).

Serotonin

In general, the amphetamines do not have a strong effect on the serotonergic system. However, there are some exceptions to this general rule. For example, an early report by Pletscher et al. (231) indicated that p-chloro-N-methylamphetamine resulted in depleted 5-HT and 5-hydroxyindoleacetic acid (5-HIAA) levels, while norepinephrine and dopamine levels were unchanged; similar results have been reported by Fuller et al. (108), Fuller and Molloy (107), and Moller-Nielsen and Dubnick (212). These results indicate that amphetamine derivatives with strong electron-withdrawing substituents on the phenyl ring affect the serotonergic system.

The 4-chlorinated derivatives of both amphetamine and methamphetamine have strong serotonergic depleting properties, and it appears that there must be at least a two-carbon chain between the phenyl ring and the nitrogen for such effects to occur (107, 212). Both p-chloro-N-methylphenethylamine and p-chloromethamphetamine are potent depleters of serotonin, but p-chloro-a-methylbenzylamine is not (16).

CNS STIMULATORY EFFECTS

One of the primary effects of the amphetamines and related compounds is central nervous system stimulation, which results in the characteristic activation of behavior. Early reports indicated that a two-carbon chain between the nitrogen and the phenyl ring was necessary for these stimulatory effects; Van der Shoot et al. (300) reported that two-carbon chain amphetamine derivatives increased the spontaneous locomotor activity of mice, while derivatives containing 1–3 or more carbon chains did not result in increased activity. These authors also reported that increasing the alkyl chain length on the amino group progressively decreased psychomotor stimulation. [cf9]N-Di-

methylation resulted in similar effects. These results would seem to indicate that the binding of an amino group to a secondary carbon seems to be necessary for the psychomotor stimulation produced by the amphetamines (16).

The alpha-methyl group also appears to be a critical determinant of stimulatory action: beta-phenethylamine is minimally active, and phentermine is approximately half as active as amphetamine (16). Further evidence indicating the importance of the alpha-methyl group are results indicating that the dextro isomers of both amphetamine and methamphetamine are significantly more potent in stimulating behavior than are the levo isomers (213, 250, 279, 286, 289, 301).

Behavioral Effects

The following section briefly reviews the immense literature regarding the major behavioral effects of acute and subchronic administration of amphetamines, and the possible neural substrates for these effects. These effects are: (a) locomotor stimulation, (b) stereotypy induction, (c) aggression, and (d) anorexia.

LOCOMOTION

Role of Dopamine: Acute Effects

Low doses of amphetamine result in increased locomotor activity, running, and forward motion associated with exploratory behaviors (89, 159). Several lines of evidence indicate that this increase in locomotor activity is mediated by the mesolimbic dopaminergic system. First, Pijnenburg and van Rossum (228) found that dopamine injected into the nucleus accumbens increased locomotor activity, while intrastriatal injections did not increase activity. Second, this increase in locomotor activity is blocked by the administration of dopaminergic antagonists (229). Third, Thornburg and Moore (297) found that, while blockage of dopamine synthesis by alpha-methyltyrosine inhibited the locomotor-stimulating effects of amphetamine, subsequent blockage of norepinephrine synthesis by the potent dopamine-beta-hydroxylase inhibitor U-14,624 had no effect on this property of amphetamine. These results indicate that the locomotor-stimulating properties of amphetamine are selectively mediated by dopaminergic transmission.

Localization of the locomotor-stimulating properties of amphetamine to the mesolimbic system come from a variety of lesion studies. First, electrolytic (215) and 6-hydroxydopamine (10, 69, 182) lesions of the neostriatum fail to effect locomotion induced by amphetamine. Second, electrolytic lesions of the rostral hypothalamus, resulting in an interruption of mesolimbic dopaminergic input, reduce amphetamine-induced locomotion (65). Third, 6-OHDA lesions of the nucleus accumbens abolish the effects of amphetamine (160, 173, 181, 182, 287, 299). Last, the locomotor stimulation produced by amphetamine injection into the nucleus accumbens is far more intense than the activity induced by amphetamine injection into the neostriatum (228, 229).

Role of Dopamine: Chronic Effects

The effects of chronic stimulant (amphetamine and cocaine) administration on behavior and dopaminergic neurotransmission depend on the route and temporal pattern of administration. Daily intermittent injections induce enhanced locomotion and stereotypies (183–185), while the continuous infusion of an equivalent daily dose of cocaine induces tolerance to the behavioral effects of cocaine (183–185, 242). These behavioral effects are associated with alterations in dopaminergic neurotransmission in several brain areas. Daily intermittent administration of stimulants induce augmented dopamine release in several brain areas (3, 175–179, 185). In contrast, the continuous administration of an equivalent daily dose of cocaine induces attenuated dopamine release in several brain areas (46, 161, 185).

Role of Serotonin

Although this research indicates that the locomotor properties are mediated by the mesolimbic dopamine system, several lines of evidence indicate that the serotonergic system plays an inhibitory modulating role on the effects of amphetamine. First, midbrain serotonergic raphe (65, 163, 216) or medial forebrain bundle lesions (125) enhance the locomotor-stimulating effects of amphetamine. Furthermore, administration of parachlorophenylalanine or 5,6- or 5,7-dihydroxytryptamine also enhances the locomotor-stimulating properties of the amphetamines (22, 206, 218, 288). Therefore, the overall pattern of results indicates that increased serotonergic neurotransmission inhibits the locomotor-stimulating properties of amphetamines.

Role of Endogenous Opiates

Several reports indicate that endogenous opiate systems are important in the regulation of amphetamine induced locomotion and dopamine release. For example, Schad et al. (270) recently reported that administration of naloxone, followed by amphetamine significantly reduced amphetamine-induced increase in extracellular dopamine in the nucleus accumbens and striatum and also attenuated the increase in locomotor activity elicited by amphetamine, suggesting that endogenous opiate systems are critical in modulating the behavioral and neurochemical effects of amphetamine. Similar behavioral results have been reported by Motles et al. (214).

STEREOTYPIES

Acute Effects

High doses of amphetamines result in stereotyped behaviors that are representative for the respective species. These behaviors are continually repetitive acts that serve no apparent purpose (see, e.g., references 235 and 305). The stereotyped behavior elicited in the rat generally consists of sniffing, licking, biting, or gnawing (102). Although amphetamine will elicit all of these behaviors, several lines of research indicate that they do not form a unitary package, to the extent that different behaviors seem to be under different neural control. First, at lower, stereotypy-inducing doses, the behavioral pattern consists mainly of sniffing and head and limb movements (65). At progressively higher doses, these behaviors are supplanted by biting, gnawing, and licking behaviors (65). Second, amantadine, phenylethylamine, and piribedil will induce only limb movements and sniffing but will not elicit the gnawing and biting behaviors (21, 64, 66). Third, biting and gnawing, but not limb movements and sniffing, are elicited by (ƒ)(N-n-propylnorapomorphine (66). Fourth, amantadine inhibits biting while alpha-methylparatyrosine inhibits sniffing (66, 67, 133). Fifth, lesioning of different brain areas results in differential inhibition of various behaviors; Creese and Iversen (69) found that 6-OHDA lesions of the substantia nigra induced supersensitivity to sniffing caused by direct dopamine agonist treatment (i.e., apomorphine) but that the gnawing and biting components of the stereotypy were unaffected. On the other hand, 6-OHDA lesions of the caudate abolish the intense gnawing and biting components of the stereotypy (10, 182). 6-OHDA lesions of the nucleus accumbens attenuate the sniffing component of the stereotypy while the biting/gnawing component is unaffected (10, 182). The overall pattern of these results would seem to indicate that an intact caudate putamen is necessary for the development of the intense gnawing/biting portion of the stereotypy (66).

Chronic Effects

The effects of chronic amphetamine and cocaine administration depend, in part, on the dosing regime used. Use of a daily, intermittent dosing regime results in sensitization (i.e., an augmentation of the effects of amphetamine). Daily injections of amphetamine result in the preempting of locomotor stimulation by periods of intense, focused stereotypies (24, 200, 238, 265, 266, 267). As the duration of amphetamine administration lengthens, tolerance to the dopamine effects of amphetamine develops and various "end-stage" behaviors appear; these behaviors are characterized by limb flicks, abortive grooming, increased startle responses to existent and nonexistent stimuli, and abnormal dystonic postures (43, 83, 86, 91, 146, 233, 283). In other words, animals progress from an initial stage in which they exhibit "exploratory, investigative," and repetitive movements, to a stage characterized by intense stereotypies interspersed with bizarre behavior. This behavior is unrelated to environmental cues and may consist of "bits and pieces" of earlier patterns and sequences of behavior that at one time served a purpose.

SOCIAL BEHAVIOR

Chronic amphetamine administration also has a profound effect on social behavior. For example, Schiorring (262) found that both acute and chronic amphetamine dosing resulted in extreme withdrawal from social activity in monkeys; social activity was replaced by stereotyped self-grooming or staring into space. Similar results on social behavior have been reported by Angrist and Gershon (6, 7), Cole et al. (59), Ellinwood (84), Ellinwood et al. (95), and Ellinwood and Kilbey (90).

These results suggest increasing behavioral disintegration and social isolation during chronic amphetamine administration. The behavioral repertoire becomes increasingly restricted, and the animal becomes increasingly responsive to existent and nonexistent stimuli. In other words, the animal is increasingly losing contact with reality. Even months after withdrawal, a single moderate dose of amphetamine can reintroduce the original repertoire of intense bizarre behaviors that originally may have taken months to develop; thus, the behavior remains long-term in a residual latent state. At the abuse level, these latent behavioral residuals may include drug acquisition behaviors that become incorporated into the stereotyped patterns. In part, these acquisition residuals may provide the basis for the "greased slide" fall into intense drug-seeking behavior after reinitiation of human abusers to a single dose of amphetamines (91, 200).

The neurobiological basis for such effects is currently under investigation. The effects apparently are not the result of changes in the number or affinity of postsynaptic dopamine receptors, since studies using chronic low, moderate, or high doses of amphetamine have not demonstrated consistently or sufficiently large enough changes in these parameters of dopamine neurons to account for the effects (28, 62, 219, 220). The effects also apparently do not result from changes in the pharmacokinetics of amphetamine (79, 80, 172, 197, 224).

Chronic amphetamine administration has, however, been associated with decreased dopamine stores and TH activity (96–98, 260, 266, 282). Although these studies have consistently described monoamine depletions in the striatum, no consistent depletions in the nucleus accumbens have been reported; however, any mesoaccumbens depletions are of considerably smaller magnitude than those found in the caudate (199). In addition to the effects on dopaminergic functioning, a profound depletion of serotonin and tryptophan hydroxylase activity has also been reported, although it seems that this effect is more specific to methylamphetamine than to d- or l-amphetamine (152).

AGGRESSION

The effects of amphetamine on aggressive behavior are complex and as yet poorly understood. However, as a general statement, the effects seem to depend on the dose, the environment, and the individual. Amphetamine use has been associated with the potential for sudden violent outbursts for quite a while; indeed, a common street warning of the 1960s and 1970s was "speed kills." Since this is such an important but controversial topic, the present section reviews the experimental and clinical literature regarding the effects of amphetamine on aggressive behavior.

Several descriptions of murders and other violent offenses have been attributed to amphetamine intoxication (8, 85, 275). For example, Ansis and Smith (8) describe a case of a male who murdered two individuals and shot several others. This individual had been consuming amphetamines in increasing doses for three weeks. The individual developed paranoid delusions and killed these people in a blind rage. (A more complete discussion of amphetamine psychosis is presented below in the section entitled "Abuse.") Several surveys of prison inmates have also found that a large percentage of inmates and juvenile delinquents have committed their crimes while intoxicated by amphetamines (142, 274). Such findings led Ellinwood (86) to conclude that stimulants (including the amphetamines) have a specific association with violent behavior. Furthermore, Ellinwood (86) found that many homicides were committed due to misinterpretation or, more often, hallucinatory delusional reasons; they were not simply due to the violence of the drug marketplace. In other words, the homicides were a consequence of drug consumption.

Some experimental research in humans indicates that acute doses of amphetamine can increase aggressiveness in humans. For example, Cherek et al. (48) exposed humans to a competitive task involving money. As part of the task, subjects could deliver blasts of white noise or take money from a competitor. The results indicated that 5 and 10 mg doses increased the frequency of noise deliveries and the taking away of money, suggesting an increase in aggressive behavior. In contrast to these results, caffeine reduced the frequency of such aggressive behavior, indicating that the effects are specific to amphetamine (47).

In spite of this evidence indicating that amphetamine increases aggressive behavior, other evidence indicates that amphetamine can decrease aggressive behavior. Amphetamine treatment has been used to treat aggression in children diagnosed with hyperkinesis and/or attention-deficit hyperactivity disorder (20). This effect has been repeatedly confirmed in controlled, double-blind studies (5, 61). Not all surveys of prison populations and juvenile delinquents have reported finding a relation between aggression or hostility and amphetamine abuse (122, 295, 296).

ANOREXIA

The amphetamines are potent anorectics and have been used clinically for such purposes for a long time (89, 93). The evidence indicates that this effect of the amphetamines is mediated by dopaminergic neurotransmission. First, pretreatment with alpha-methyl-p-tyrosine reduces the anorectic effects of amphetamine in rats (1, 2, 12, 56, 106, 141, 150, 309). Second, administration of α- and β-blockers (e.g., phentolamine, phenoxybenzamine piperoxan, yohimbine, tolazine, propranolol, pindolol, and dichloroisoproterenol) has no effect on amphetamine-induced anorexia (2, 195, 208, 261). Third, administration of dopamine antagonists such as haloperidol, pimozide, penfluridol, and spiroperidol reduces the anorectic effects of amphetamine (2, 56–58, 106, 141, 194, 195, 257). Fourth, lesions of the dopaminergic system with 6-OHDA attenuate amphetamine-induced anorexia (100, 141, 147, 256).

More specifically, this anorectic effect of amphetamine is probably mediated by the lateral hypothalamus. For example, Glick (120) reported that lateral hypothalamic lesions result in an attenuation of the anorectic effects of amphetamine (17, 35, 100, 252). Furthermore, bilateral lesions of the nigrostriatal dopaminergic system induce the same aphagic-adipsic syndrome as do lateral hypothalamic lesions (33, 100). Nigrostriatal dopamine neurons pass through the internal capsule, which is adjacent to the lateral hypothalamus, and the results of studies involving lateral hypothalamic lesions could also be attributed to destruction of these dopaminergic neurons (89).

Although the preceding research indicates that the amphetamines probably work through a dopaminergic mechanism, several lines of evidence indicate that structurally related compounds such as fenfluramine (N-ethyl-alpha-methyl-3-trifluoromethyl-beta-phenylethylamine, a ring-substituted phenylisopropylamine) seem to act via a serotonergic mechanism. First, the administration of serotonin (5-HT) antagonists attenuates fenfluramine-induced anorexia (2, 14, 18, 56, 106, 109, 111, 112, 169, 195, 261). Second, administration of the 5-HT uptake inhibitor chlorimipramine reduces fenfluramine-induced anorexia (56, 58, 78, 112, 116, 169). Third, serotonergic lesions (18) and lesions produced by 5-dihydroxytryptamine (55) attenuate the effects of fenfluramine-induced anorexia.

Elimination and Pharmacokinetics

There are two primary modes of eliminating the amphetamines from a biological system: (a) renal excretion and (b) metabolism. Both may be important in understanding pathophysiology and treatment, especially the treatment of overdoses in which facilitation of excretion is important.

RENAL EXCRETION

Amphetamine is a basic (pK$_a$ 9.90), highly lipid-soluble drug. Because amphetamine is a basic drug, one of the primary modes of elimination is excretion of the unchanged drug in the urine; indeed, in some instances, most of a dose of amphetamine may be excreted in this way (307). Renal excretion is strongly determined by the pH of the urine; with acidic urine (e.g., pH 5) approximately 99% of a dose of amphetamine is ionized by glomular filtration, and only the remaining nonionized portion of the drug is reabsorbed into the circulatory system (304). Hence a treatment of amphetamine overdose is to acidify the urine (31).

METABOLISM

There are several metabolic pathways for the biotransformation of the amphetamines. One pathway is aromatic hydroxylation (31). Aromatic hydroxylation is apparently restricted to the 4′ position, as no evidence for 2′- or 3′-hydroxylation has been obtained (29, 76); this hydroxylation results in phenolic amines, which are subsequently excreted in the urine or conjugated with sulfate, and then excreted (29, 269). Ring substitution (e.g., fenfluramine) of amphetamine blocks this metabolic pathway (29, 31).

p-Hydroxyamphetamine, a major metabolite of this metabolic pathway, is also extremely biologically active. For example, p-hydroxyamphetamine is three times more potent in inhibiting noradrenaline uptake than is amphetamine (158). The hydroxylated metabolite is also a potent pressor agent (119). When p-hydroxyamphetamine is administered intracerebrally, it is also a locomotor stimulant (290).

A second metabolic pathway is beta-hydroxylation. This process is carried out by the enzyme dopamine beta-hydroxylase, which converts dopamine to norepinephrine, and it is apparently restricted to the primary amines (29, 31). The metabolites resulting from beta-hydroxylation have the hydroxyl group in the 1r-(−)configuration (29, 31, 168). This metabolic route is blocked by the second alpha-methyl group in the phentermine derivatives (29, 31). When the ring hydroxylated metabolites (e.g., p-hydroxyamphetamine) undergo beta-hydroxylation, p-hydroxynorephedrine is produced. p-Hydroxynorephedrine can be taken up into norepinephrine terminals and probably can act as a "false transmitter," thereby enhancing the effects of amphetamine (76, 121, 202).

By far, the most important metabolic pathways for the amphetamines are those involving oxidation of the nitrogen and its alpha-carbons (i.e., N-dealkylation and deamination). Both reactions result in a primary amine and a carbonyl function (31). During N-dealkylation, the alkyl or arylalkyl groups on the nitrogen atom are removed by the microsomal mixed function oxidase system. The process requires metabolic oxygen and NADPH$_2$ and results in equal portions of the primary amine and the aldehyde (29, 31).

Deamination results in the excretion of the corresponding ketone, secondary alcohol, or benzoic acid, although the major metabolite excreted is benzoic acid (31). Ketone is formed via oxidation of the alpha-carbon and N-oxidation (29, 30, 315); hydroxylation of the alpha-carbon results in the formation of an unstable alpha-carinolamine, which decays to the ketone and ammonia (15). N-oxidation may contribute to the metabolism of amphetamine by an N-hydroxylation, which results in N-hydroxyamphetamine (15, 31, 42). N-hydroxyamphetamine forms strong complexes with cytochrome P450 (103–105, 164). This complex is then further oxidized to the nitro (54) or nitroso (207) compound. This nitrocompound is then converted to a ketone via an oxidative process involving a hydrolytic step (29, 171).

After chronic administration of amphetamines, the tissue and brain contents of p-hydroxyamphetamine and p-hydroxynorephedrine are not significantly different from those of saline-treated control subjects, indicating that the rate of removal of amphetamine is not affected by chronic administration (196). These results are consistent with other findings that indicate that the urinary ratio of unchanged amphetamine to hydroxylated metabolites is unaltered following chronic amphetamine administration (201). However, following chronic amphetamine administration, the uptake of (3)H-amphetamine into the pons medulla is accelerated (196); furthermore, chronic amphetamine treatment also accelerates the uptake of (3)H-norepinephrine in the pons medulla (63, 294).

These results indicate that the metabolism of amphetamine is different from that of most other drugs. Chronic amphetamine administration does not seem to result in enzyme induction as indicated by the lack of an increase in the rate of removal, or the production of hydroxylated metabolites. However, during chronic administration, amphetamine and p-hydroxyephedrine may accumulate in a pool that could eventually disrupt cellular functioning (196). Finally, the brain and heart levels of amphetamine in chronically treated animals are significantly higher than those in control animals, and this difference may in part account for the sensitization often produced by chronic amphetamine administration (196).

Toxicity

The chronic high-dose abuse of amphetamines results in toxic pathophysiological changes. The present section describes these toxic effects. Table 18.1 presents some of the toxic effects of high-dose and chronic amphetamine use.

CENTRAL TOXICITIES

Norepinephrine

Chronic and high-dose amphetamine use induces substantive toxic alterations in central monoaminergic systems. In one set of experiments examining the toxicity of amphetamines, Seiden et al. (268) injected rhesus monkeys eight times daily (final dose 3–6.5 mg/kg/injection) for 3–6 months and then assessed acute and residual withdrawal effects. Subjects sacrificed 24 hours after the final injection exhibited a depletion of norepinephrine in all brain regions examined (pons medulla, midbrain, hypothalamus, and frontal cortex). In the subjects sacrificed 3–6 months after the final injection, the brain norepinephrine levels were still depressed in the midbrain and the frontal cortex but had returned to control levels in the hypothalamus and the pons medulla.

Dopamine

In contrast to the generalized effects on norepinephrine levels, only dopamine levels in the caudate putamen were depressed, with other brain regions showing no effect in the subjects sacrificed 24 hours after the last injection. Furthermore, this depletion appeared to be permanent since the degree of dopaminergic depletion was the same in the subjects sacrificed 24 hours or 3–6 months after the last injection (see also 245). These results are consistent with the results of Tonge (298), who found depressed norepinephrine levels for up to 36 hours after chronic oral amphetamine intake in rats, and the results of Harris and Baldessarini (137), who found that chronic amphetamine intake depresses TH activity in the corpus striatum. These results indicate that chronic amphetamine administration is toxic to the dopamine system.

More recent work has also demonstrated extensive toxicities induced by chronic amphetamine administration. First, dopamine and tyrosine-beta-hydroxylase levels are reduced for extended periods following chronic amphetamine administration (153, 244, 246). Second, the number of dopaminergic uptake sites has been found to be reduced (244, 246). Third, there is evidence of neuronal degeneration, chromatolysis, and decreased catecholamine histofluorescence (77, 246, 246). Fourth, the number of dopamine transporters has been found to be reduced. All apparent evidence indicates that these effects are more severe following continuous or high-dose administration regimes (199).

Serotonin

These changes are not restricted to catecholamine neurons. The amphetamines also produce toxic effects in the serotonergic system. Chronic methamphetamine administration has been shown to induce long-term changes in tryptophan hydroxylase activity (153), as well as 5-HT content and uptake sites (244). The clinical significance of these changes is unclear, since a nonstimulant, FDA-approved anorectic agent that has been extensively used clinically induces analogous changes. Fenfluramine produces long-lasting changes in 5-HT and 5-HIAA content in the rat brain (57, 139, 140, 188, 263, 281). Chronic fenfluramine administration also results in decreased numbers of 5-HT uptake sites (263) and depresses tryptophan hydroxylase activity (281). Finally, fenfluramine also produces morphological damage to the terminal fields of serotonergic neurons (9).

CEREBRAL VASCULATURE

Changes in cerebral vasculature have also been reported following chronic amphetamine administration. For example, Rumbaugh (251) reported that monkeys treated with methamphetamine for 1 year demonstrated extensive changes in the small arterioles and capillary beds; the changes were characterized by patchy areas of beading, vascular filling or nonfilling, and fragmentation of the vessels. Further changes included loss of neurons with increased numbers of glial cells, satellitosis, and microhemorrhage in the cerebellum and hypothalamus. Similar results were obtained with animals who were treated only with methamphetamine for 3 months. This pattern of results indicates that chronic amphetamine users are at a high risk for cerebrovascular damage. In addition, high-dose amphetamines, both experimentally and clinically, induce hypertensive episodes associated with cerebral hemorrhage. Indeed, several cases of death have been attributed to hemorrhages induced by chronic amphetamine use (see reference 174 for a review). These results indicate that the amphetamines are potentially highly toxic and can result in severe brain damage even after a short period of use.

Peripheral Toxicities

CARDIOVASCULAR EFFECTS

The cardiovascular effects of amphetamine are prominent. Amphetamine raises both systolic and diastolic blood pressure, and heart rate is reflexively slowed (307). Tachycardia and cardiac arrhythmias are not uncommon following high doses of amphetamines (93). Catecholamines have the effect of sensitizing the myocardium to ectopic stimuli, thereby increasing the risk of fatal cardiac arrhythmias. There are recorded cases of myocardial lesions in chronic amphetamine users. These lesions may have served as ectopic arrhythmogenic sites during amphetamine intoxication, resulting in cardiac arrest and death (247).

THERMAL REGULATION

The amphetamines result in peripheral hyperthermia via activation of the sympathoadrenal system (115, 134, 167). However, the amphetamines produce hypothermia centrally, and this seems to be mediated by the activity of the anterior hypothalamus (162, 167, 211). Another major cause of death related to amphetamine abuse is hyperpyrexia (174). This effect is directly related to the catecholamine effects of amphetamine (93) and, if not fatal in and of itself, leads to a cascade of convulsions, coma, and cerebral hemorrhage.

Table 18.1. Toxic Consequences of High-Dose and Chronic Use of Psychomotor Stimulants

Pattern of Use	Toxic Consequence
High-dose	Slowing of cardiac conduction
	Ventricular irritability
	Hypertensive episode
	Hyperpyrexic episode
	CNS seizures and anoxia
Dose escalation	Hyperpyrexia
	Cardiovascular hypertension
	Slowing of cardiac conduction
Binge	Physical exhaustion resulting in impaired judgment and insight
	Development of psychotic ideation
	Potential for sudden violence
	Neurotransmitter depletion
	Neuronal destruction
	High-risk behaviors (e.g., needle sharing, automobile accidents, sexual promiscuity, etc.)
Chronic	Long-term neurotransmitter depletion
	Neuronal destruction
	Cerebrovascular damage
	Psychosis

Adapted from Gawin FH, Ellinwood EH. Cocaine and other stimulants. N Engl J Med 1988;318:1173; and Ellinwood EH, Lee TH. Dose- and time-dependent effects of stimulants. NIDA Res Monogr Ser 1989;94:323–340.

EPIDEMIOLOGY, SOCIOLOGY, AND ECONOMICS

The amphetamines have been abused almost since their introduction (8, 19, 113). For example, benzedrine inhalers were abused by a wide segment of the population (e.g., athletes, professionals, and students) during the 1930s to overcome fatigue and increase alertness (8). Amphetamines were routinely available to soldiers during World War II and the Vietnam War to keep soldiers alert during combat conditions (8). Indeed, Grinspoon and Hedblom (129) reported that from 1966 to 1969, soldiers consumed more amphetamines than did the combined totals of British and American soldiers during World War II.

Amphetamine Epidemics

Amphetamine epidemics have been reported in Japan (180), Sweden (128), and the United States (53). These epidemics are generally associated with increasing levels of violence and the development of a "speed culture" (129). For example, Smith (277) extensively interviewed amphetamine addicts who had been part of the "speed scene" in the 1950s and 1960s. These individuals were primarily heroin addicts who received amphetamine prescriptions to wean them away from the heroin addiction. Many of these heroin addicts found that the use of amphetamines was advantageous: it was legal and inexpensive, and the increase in energy allowed them to better engage in "street hustles" (8). However, this attempt at the treatment of heroin addiction did not work: the individuals reported becoming paranoid and unable to engage in street hustles. (See the section entitled "Abuse" for a more complete discussion of amphetamine psychosis.)

An examination of these epidemics indicates that several factors are involved in their development: (a) the introduction of large segments of the population to the use of amphetamines for medical, recreational, and antifatigue purposes; (b) the widespread dissemination of knowledge regarding the amphetamine experience; (c) the development of a core of chronic amphetamine users who establish a stable illegal market; (d) increasing use of rapid routes of administration (intravenous and smoking); (e) an initial oversupply of amphetamine that is directed to both the legal and illegal markets; and finally, (f) the development of clandestine laboratories for the production and distribution of amphetamines (87).

The Drug Subculture

During the 1960s and early 1970s, there were several ways to be introduced to the use of amphetamines. For example, one of the most common modes of introduction was the medical use of amphetamines for their anorectic properties. In 1967, at the peak of the amphetamine epidemic, Balter (1972, as cited in reference 87) estimated that there were 31 million prescriptions for anorectic agents, of which 14.5 million were new prescriptions. Of these 31 million prescriptions, 23 million were for amphetamines. Thus, approximately 6–8% of the American population were legally exposed to the amphetamines. Other, not necessarily illegal modes of introduction include professionals' (e.g., doctors, lawyers, musicians, etc.) use of amphetamines for their antifatigue properties.

The illegal introduction of individuals to the use of amphetamines is exemplified by the Haight-Ashbury speed scene. An ethnographic analysis of this drug "subculture" provides a valuable glimpse into the dynamics of drug addiction and the interactions that occur among the abused drug, the individual, and the environment. This drug scene was primarily composed of young, white, middle-class, well-educated males who came to the Haight-Ashbury district as part of the "hippie" movement. These individuals generally had experience with marihuana and psychedelics and could therefore be considered receptive to drug experimentation. Introduction to the use of amphetamines was generally determined by the community in which the individual resided, as opposed to any predisposition for amphetamines or other personality factors (276). The individual was inducted into the amphetamine community and generally progressed from casual, experimental use to continuous high-dose use. As more and more people became involved in the use of amphetamines, a specific amphetamine subculture developed, with its own patterns of behavior, mores, and "laws."

In this community, amphetamines were consumed in large groups at places called "flash houses" (8). In these houses individuals would inject large amounts of amphetamine for an extended period of time; individual users would drift into a flash house until the physical limits of the house were reached. Carey and Mandel (34) provide a graphic description of the frenetic pace and extreme crowding typical of a flash house; the abuse of amphetamines would continue for weeks or months until the individuals were so paranoid and physically exhausted that the slightest provocation could result in violent retaliation. Indeed, massive violent retaliation was the expected norm in the community (129). It is tempting to speculate that much of the violence associated with methamphetamine use was the result of the high-dose use coupled with the crowded living conditions; Chance (44, 45) reported high rates of violence and increased lethality in mice that were given near-toxic doses of amphetamines and housed in groups (i.e., amphetamine rage). Many of these individuals progressed to barbiturate and heroin addiction because they disliked the anxiety and paranoia associated with chronic amphetamine abuse (277).

Economics of Illicit Amphetamines

The methamphetamine industry is an extremely lucrative business. Before the laws were changed and amphetamine was restricted to medical use only by the Controlled Substances Act of 1970, a major source of supply was the diversion of commercially produced amphetamine to a well-developed "black market." This diversion had two sources. One source was what were called "script doctors," who may have begun their illegal careers prescribing amphetamines for weight loss purposes. For example, O'Conner (223) describes a case of a physician in the San Francisco Bay area who dispensed approximately 1 million units of amphetamine in a 1-year period. The procedure for script doctors was reasonably simple: an individual would enter the doctor's office and pay a fee for a prescription of amphetamines; it was not uncommon for busloads of people to be shipped to a doctor's office to receive a prescription for a dealer (223). O'Conner (223) has estimated that such script doctors accounted for roughly 7% of the illegal distribution of illegal amphetamines. Since the late 1970s such practices have been severely curtailed by medical licensing boards and the Drug Enforcement Administration.

A second source of diversion during the 1960s was phony companies acting as distributors for commercially produced amphetamines. Sadusk (253) estimated that approximately 50% of all commercially made amphetamines were routed to the black market. This was reasonably simple because of lax investigation and supervisory practices by the state and federal governments. Indeed, Grinspoon and Hedblom (129) describe a company that received 13.5 million units of amphetamine after its license had been revoked for illegal sales of amphetamines.

Today, the underground production of amphetamine in the United States is controlled by small clandestine laboratories, concentrated largely in Texas and southern California but that periodically can flourish in any area of the country. Amphetamine production is estimated to be a $3 billion a year industry, with every indication of expansion (53). Cho (53) estimated that production of amphetamine from phenylacetic acid would cost approximately $700 per pound (assuming a 10% yield); the street value would be approximately $225,000. As Cho (53) concludes, with such a profit margin, the prices of amphetamine could be reduced to increase the competition with the cocaine market. In addition, methamphetamine, including "ice" coming out of the Pacific Basin, has periodically made inroads into the United States. The marketplace is often driven by adequate distribution networks; current lore is that motorcycle gangs provide the basic synthesis ingredients to "franchise" labs and then distribute the product (personal communication, David Smith). Hence, one might predict an increase in the use of amphetamines; this is especially true considering that the duration of amphetamine's effects is approximately 10–12 hours, versus 45 minutes for cocaine. Therefore, the drug user may see amphetamine as a cost-effective replacement for cocaine. These factors predict an increase in the use of amphetamines; yet so far the pattern has been mini-epidemics in specific locales such as San Diego and Philadelphia.

MEDICAL USES OF AMPHETAMINES

As stated earlier, in the late 1960s, at the height of amphetamine abuse epidemic in the United States, there were approximately 31 million prescriptions for anoretic stimulant drugs, yet enough was legally manufactured for 8 billion pills. This lax legal and social attitude of prescription and supply regulation was followed in most of the industrial nations by very strict control. From 1969 to 1971, the U.S. government: (a) markedly reduced the production of amphetamines by 80%; (b) physicians were alerted to the dependence-producing effects; and (c) amphetamines were rescheduled to Schedule II by the Food and Drug Administration (FDA). The pendulum has swung back to the point that potentially important clinical uses are being avoided by physicians. Pitts (230) lamented that the usefulness of amphetamines in treating medically ill (see 89, 149) and treatment failure depressed patients had been discounted to the point that physicians were afraid to even consider their use. To provide balance for the clinician, potential usefulness of amphetamines other than the well-known, FDA approved indications for narcolepsy and attention deficit disorder will be discussed here. In the United States, there are only two FDA approved indications for dextroamphetamine and methylphenidate: (a) narcolepsy and (b) attention-deficit hyperactivity disorder, although it has been used to treat other disorders in the past.

Treatment of Attention-Deficit Hyperactivity Disorder (ADHD)

The diagnosis of ADHD is fairly common: ADHD is thought to affect 2–5% of elementary school children, with the diagnosis 3–6 times more common in boys than in girls (32, 143). For a diagnosis, the symptoms should develop before the age of seven, and be present for at least 6 months. The disorder is characterized by frequent fidgeting, difficulties in focussing on classroom assignments, impulsivity, excessive talking and interruption of others, and repeated shifting from one activity to another (143, 210). The treatment of first choice for ADHD involves the use of psychostimulants, primarily methylphenidate, dextroamphetamine, or pemoline. An excellent review of stimulant treatment of ADHD can be found in Shenker (271).

STIMULANT TREATMENT OF ADHD

The most common pharmacotherapies for ADHD are methylphenidate, dextroamphetamine, and pemoline. Methylphenidate, the most common treatment, is a piperidine derivative structurally related to amphetamine, and is a milder central nervous system stimulant than amphetamine. Numerous studies have indicated that methylphenidate is highly effective in increasing attentiveness, reducing hyperactivity and destructive behavior, and improving classroom behavior and academic performance (see references 138, 254, 273 and 302 for reviews). The improvements in behavior and academic performance seem to persist as long as the drug is taken, with the behavior problems returning upon cessation of methylphenidate (23, 151, 157, 302). Second-line stimulants used in the treatment of ADHD, for those individuals who may not respond to methylphenidate, are dextroamphetamine and pemoline. These drugs have been reported to be as effective as methylphenidate in the treatment of ADHD (81, 227). For example, Pelham et al. (227) reported that, while dextroamphetamine and pemoline produced more consistent effects on behavioral improvement, methylphenidate induced better improvement in academic improvement.

The literature indicates that approximately 30% of children diagnosed with ADHD will still have ADHD at 18 years of age, and approximately 8% of children with ADHD will have ADHD at 26 years of age (see reference 187 for a review). Several recent reports suggest that stimulants are also efficacious treatments for adult attention deficit disorder. For example, Matochik et al. (209) reported that both chronic (minimum of 6 weeks' treatment) methylphenidate and d-amphetamine decreased restlessness and improved attention, although neither drug had any effect on whole brain metabolism (as measured by positron emission tomography). These authors reported similar effects following an acute dose of d-amphetamine and methylphenidate. Similar results following chronic methylphenidate were

reported by Spencer et al. (280) using a randomized, 7-week, placebo-controlled, crossover study of methylphenidate in 23 adult patients.

SIDE EFFECTS IN THE USE OF STIMULANTS TO TREAT ADHD

Considerable concern surrounds the use of methylphenidate and, to a lesser extent, amphetamine and pemoline in hyperactivity or ADHD in children and possible detrimental effects on general physical and emotional growth and central nervous system development. The United States FDA Psychopharmacology Pediatric Subcommittee reviewed the literature relevant to growth suppression by stimulants in the treatment of hyperkinetic syndrome. There is clear evidence of temporary retardation in growth in weight and suggestion of temporary slowing of stature growth related to drug dose and absence of drug holidays during the prepubertal period (74, 249, 255). To allow for growth rebound, the importance of drug holidays is evident in children requiring higher doses and manifesting drug plateaus.

NONSTIMULANT-BASED TREATMENTS OF ADHD

Several studies have suggested that clonidine may be useful in the treatment of ADHD (138, 154–156, 312). Tricyclic antidepressants have been shown to be effective in treating ADHD (see references 255 and 271 for a discussion), although their use is not generally recommended in treating ADHD: Tolerance develops to their effects (232) and several deaths have been reported following tricyclic antidepressants treatment of ADHD (248). Lastly, the MAO-A inhibitors clorgyline and tranylcypromine (318), but not the MAO-B inhibitor deprenyl (316, 317), have been reported to be therapeutically beneficial in the treatment of ADHD.

Use of Stimulants as Anorectics

The effectiveness of stimulants as anorectics is well documented. In 1972, a study (264) using 206 anorectic drug trials, found in a meta analysis of the data that these anorectic drugs were effective for weight loss at least out to 16 weeks of treatment. The problem with the use of anorectics, besides their abuse potential, is that only a small percentage maintain weight loss after cessation of anorectics for one year (284). Where possible, stimulants with lower abuse potential should be used. For example, fenfluramine and chlorpheniramine are amphetamine congeners that appear to work primarily on the serotonergic system without major psychostimulant effects (123).

More recently, Weintraub et al. (308) have clearly demonstrated that, combined with behavioral therapy, sustained dosing of fenfluramine plus phentermine is effective in initiating and maintaining long-term weight loss. In a study extending out beyond 3 years, fenfluramine (60 mg) and phentermine (15 mg/day) were remarkably effective compared to placebo in reducing weight and maintaining weight control, with a very small incidence of side effects. In summary, this type of study indicates that, when a serotonergic releasing-type anorectic and a lower abuse potential catecholamine-type anorectic are combined, there is a sustained improvement in weight control.

Finally, with any clinical use of psychostimulants, careful history taking of previous drug misuse is warranted. We think that previous abusers of other stimulants obviously should be excluded from treatment even when medically warranted.

Stimulant Treatment of Depression

In Europe, some countries have prohibited any use of stimulants. In 1968 an English report concluded that, with regard to the previous clinical use for depression, "amphetamines . . . have no place in the treatment of depression" (314). Several prominent psychopharmacologists in the late 1960s and 1970s concluded that the addictive properties and the cardiovascular and CNS side effects of amphetamines outweighed the meager therapeutic effects in most psychiatric conditions (148, 310). The reinterpretation of these older studies of depression by Satel and Nelson (258) and Chiarello and Cole (49) is still not resolved, but on balance, there is no evidence to justify the use of stimulants as a first-line or routine treatment with usual depression patients (99). In their careful review, Fawcett and Busch (99) concluded that in endogenous depressed patients stimulants may be useful to potentiate other antidepressant medications when used judiciously by experienced clinicians. They warn, clearly, of side effects but review a number of studies that conclude that augmentation with stimulants may be effective in treatment failure depressions.

Potential Therapeutic Niche in Medically Ill and Geriatric Depression

Satel and Nelson (258) reviewed the placebo-controlled studies of methylphenidate in senile and chronic brain syndrome patients and found that four out of five of these studies found methylphenidate superior to placebo in improving the energy, mental alertness, and competence in self-care; all of which are not necessarily depressive symptoms. Another group of patients that reported to respond rapidly and effectively to stimulants are medically ill or post-stroke depressed patients (11, 99, 198). More recently, case reports have appeared indicating that 65–85% of patients with human immunodeficiency virus (HIV)-related neuropsychiatric symptoms, including depression, show some to marked improvement (5, 149, 174).

ABUSE

The amphetamines are widely abused drugs, and this abuse has been present almost since the introduction of amphetamine for medical use. The abuse of amphetamine undoubtedly results from its euphoric and psychomotor-stimulating properties. In 1994, emergency room visits involving cocaine reached a record high 142,000 with an additional 17,400 visits related to methamphetamine and other stimulants.

The development of stimulant abuse follows a developmental pattern that has been qualitatively described (92, 113). This profile describes the behavioral pathologies that emerge during the active abuse and withdrawal phases. A description of the underlying structural and functional phases has only recently begun to be elucidated (described earlier). A description of the relationship between the neurobiological changes and the behavioral pathologies that develop is one of the major tasks that remains in the analysis of drug abuse.

Table 18.2 illustrates the different phases of stimulant abuse, the symptoms and behaviors of abuse, and the toxic side effects associated with each phase. Drug effects relating to abuse should be considered in relation to three phases of the establishment of an abusive pattern: initiation, consolidation, maintenance, and withdrawal. Each phase has its own unique profile of mechanisms that are involved in the drug effect reinforcement profile.

Initiation Phase

During the initial, single-dose phase, the acute reinforcing actions of amphetamine are determined by the pharmacological effects (i.e., release of dopamine) and the resulting euphoria, increase in energy, and enhancement of vocational and social interactions that occur following consumption. The individual may initially increase the number of settings and occasions on which the drug is used (i.e., for studying, at parties, etc.). During this phase, conditioning occurs: settings in which the drug is consumed become associated with the euphoriant and energizing effects of the drug, and this is especially true for individuals using rapid routes of administration (such as intravenous or smoking). This conditioning process is critical for the development of drug urges and cravings that manifest themselves during withdrawal (92).

The initiation phase is primarily concerned with classical conditioning of drug cue or reinforcement properties (225). During the initiation phase, both anticipatory acts and the stimulus properties of the drug are gradually linked in appropriate classically and operantly conditioned sequences. Anticipatory acts may include drug-seeking behaviors. Drug stimulus properties include not only the reinforcing efficacy of the drug but also the cascade of other discriminative or internally appreciated drug cues (e.g., subjective effects) associated with the consumption of the drug. In the drug culture vernacular, drug cues are described by such terms as a "taste." An anticipatory taste in human drug users or abusers often leads to associated autonomic responses

Table 18.2. Phases of Development of Amphetamine Abuse: Factors Mediating Abuse Dependence, Proposed Mechanisms[a]

Phase	Abuse dependence	Mechanism
Single dose	Conditioned cues High-dose rush	Mesolimbic dopamine release Classical conditioning Operant conditioning Enhancement of social/ sexual activity Antifatigue properties
Dose escalation	Acute tolerance results in increasing dose and frequency of use	Rapid routes of administration, resulting in fast delivery to CNS with resulting dopamine release and euphoria Onset of neurotransmitter depletion
Binge	Compulsive frequent use that may be related to stereo- typical patterns of use	Neurotransmitter depletion Neuronal destruction Impulsivity due to serotonin depletion Conditioned urges and memories of drug effects Acute tolerance coupled Drug acquisition behaviors become stereotyped
Crash Early	Depression Agitation Anxiety High drug craving	Neurotransmitter depletion Dopaminergic autoreceptor supersensitivity Memories of drug effects and conditioned urges
Middle	Fatigue No drug craving Insomnia with a high desire for sleep	
Late	Hyperphagia Hypersomnolence	
Withdrawal Intermediate	Reemergence of conditioned drug urges and cravings	Conditioned drug urges and cravings Impulsivity due to serotonin depletion
Late	Gradual extinction of conditioned drug urges and cravings	Extinction of urges Possible restoration of neurotransmitter functioning

Adapted from Gawin FH, Ellinwood EH. Cocaine and other stimulants. N Engl J Med 1988;318:1173; and Ellinwood EH, Lee TH. Dose- and time-dependent effects of stimulants. NIDA monograph no. 94. Pharmacology and toxicology of amphetamine and related designer drugs. 1989:323–340.

and urges. Current theoretical formulations of these responses also include anticipatory conditioned effects that are opposite to the drug effect, not unlike a mini-withdrawal episode.

Consolidation Phase

With prolonged, intermittent consumption, the user discovers that higher doses produce greater effects; the individual starts to consume higher doses regularly, if the resources are available. Indeed, before the development of tolerance, the euphoriant effects of stimulants are proportional to amphetamine plasma levels (101, 165). However, as stimulant use continues, tolerance to the euphoriant effects develops, and the individual starts to escalate the frequency and dose in an attempt to chase the "flash" or "rush" of amphetamine administration. During the high-dose transition phase, the individual resorts to rapid routes of administration such as smoking or intravenous administration. In spite of any tolerance that may have developed, these routes of administration result in a rapid rise in plasma amphetamine levels, which produces an intense euphoria (i.e., "flash").

The individual may start binging during this period. A binge is characterized by the repeated readministration of the drug, resulting in frequent mood swings. Binges typically last 12–18 hours but may last as long as 2, 3 or even 7 days (113). Such binges are facilitated by acute tolerance; the effects of the drug diminish rapidly. Acute tolerance, coupled with the memory of the preceding "flash," produces the desire to reinstate the drug effect;

this is accomplished by the repeated consumption of the drug. These euphoric states result in strong memories of the drug effects and in the conditioning of previously neutral stimuli to the drug effects.

During this high-dose period of binges the individual comes to focus on the internally generated sensations produced by stimulant consumption (e.g., energy and euphoria). As a result, the chronic user withdraws from social activities and pursues the direct pharmacological effects, including sensations as well as stereotyped noninteractive behaviors, of amphetamine. Over time, in high-dose regimes, these stereotyped behaviors disintegrate into remnants of the original behaviors. During this period, the pattern of acquisition and intake becomes stereotyped and restricted; the individual's behavior focuses on the purchase and consumption of amphetamine, and the number of settings in which amphetamine is consumed becomes progressively restricted. This is functionally similar to the development of intense stereotypies and the withdrawal from the earlier described social interactions in nonhumans.

Withdrawal Phase

EARLY WITHDRAWAL PHASE

At the end of a binge, the individual enters the "crash" phase, which is characterized by initial depression, agitation, anxiety, anergia, and high drug craving (113). The memories of the drug effects and the stimuli associated with these effects can result in the conditioned drug craving experienced during the early crash phase.

In the middle period of the crash phase drug craving is replaced by fatigue, depression, loss of desire for the drug, and insomnia accompanied by an intense desire for sleep. During this time, the individual may use alcohol, benzodiazepines, or opiates to induce the desired sleep.

During the late period of the crash phase, hypersomnolence is followed by awakening in a hyperphagic state (113).

INTERMEDIATE WITHDRAWAL PHASE

Following the crash period, if individuals remain abstinent, they enter an intermediate withdrawal phase with effects that are generally opposite those of the drug: loss of physical and mental energy necessary to most naturally occurring incentive behaviors. During withdrawal, individuals experience fatigue, decreased mental energy, limited interest in the environment, and anhedonia. These symptoms gradually increase in intensity during the 12–96 hours following the crash phase (113). At this time memories of euphoria induced by amphetamine consumption stand in marked relief to the anhedonia being experienced at the moment. This results in intense drug craving, and the individual is highly prone to relapse by starting another binge cycle. If the individual can remain abstinent for 6–18 weeks, the anhedonia and dysphoria attenuate but may wax and wane over the next 6–9 months (113).

LATE WITHDRAWAL PHASE

During the extinction phase, brief periods of drug craving can occur. The individual may experience conditioned combinations of stimulus properties of both the drug and withdrawal "hunger" effects in the form of "urges" or "cravings." These episodes of craving are triggered by conditioned stimuli (circumstances and objects) that were previously associated with the drug effects. If the individual experiences these cues without the associated drug effects, then the ability of these cues to elicit drug craving will diminish over time; over time the individual will experience less intense drug cravings, which should lessen the probability of relapse (113).

Amphetamine Psychosis

During the phase of chronic, high-dose consumption of amphetamines, the individual may develop "amphetamine psychosis." The stimulant psychosis is more prevalent with amphetamine than with cocaine, probably due to the difficulty in sustaining high chronic levels of cocaine. This psychosis has several profiles. First, and most commonly, the individual develops paranoid ideation (60, 82, 278). This paranoia usually is accompanied by ideas of reference and an extremely well-formed delusional structure. The para-

noid structure is facilitated by a heightened awareness of the environment, coupled with the increasing social isolation induced by amphetamine use (72, 87). In the beginning there is an exploratory, pleasurable, vague suspiciousness in which the individual continually wants to look beneath the surface of things (i.e., from the original term *subspicio*), and the individual watches others intensely (82, 87). Later there is a phase reversal in which the person feels that others are watching and following him or her (95). As consumption continues, the individual may overreact to stimuli in the peripheral field of vision and may start to hallucinate (95). This pattern of hyperreactivity to environmental stimuli may be functionally similar to the hyperstartle reaction described previously in animals. During the later stages of psychosis development, the individual may lose all insight and develop extremely well-structured delusions of persecution (72). These delusions, when coupled with the loss of insight, the exhaustion produced by a binge, or the co-administration of sedatives, and the hyperreactivity to stimuli can produce a confused, panicky, fugue-like state that can result in sudden acts of violence (95).

Another prominent aspect of amphetamine psychosis is the development of stereotyped behavior patterns that are more complex than those found in animals and that typically consist of activities that the individual normally engaged in and enjoyed doing. Many psychotic and prepsychotic individuals engage in the repetitive disassembling and reassembling of radios, engines, and various gadgets (82). Although individuals engaged in such activities are aware that the behavior is meaningless and serves no purpose, they report being unable to stop and become irritable and anxious if forced to stop. Furthermore, during engagement in the activity, the individuals report feeling an exploratory pleasure; they do not feel anxious (72).

The clinical description of human stimulant abuse presents all indications of a progressive behavioral and personality disintegration of the individual. Initially, the individual consumes the drug for the euphoric feelings. However, as consumption progresses, the individual switches to rapid routes of administration and starts binging. With prolonged consumption, the individual starts withdrawing from social interactions, and bizarre, even paranoid, ideations start developing. With further consumption, the individual becomes increasingly exhausted, loses insight into his or her actions, and may become violent or increasingly psychotic.

TREATMENT OF AMPHETAMINE ABUSE

An enormous research effort is based on the assumption that an understanding of the rate-limiting mechanisms underlying stimulant (a) reinforcement, (b) residual withdrawal states, and (c) toxic consequences would lead to effective treatment regimes. Although a great deal has been learned about the neurobiological mechanisms underlying these aspects of high-dose stimulant use, the development of rational treatment strategies has lagged behind. There is virtually no controlled treatment literature specifically regarding amphetamine abuse. However, the rise in cocaine abuse has resulted in a controlled treatment literature that can be applied to amphetamines. Table 18.3 presents the different types of pharmacological and behavioral therapies applied to amphetamine and cocaine abuse, along with possible mechanisms underlying their efficacy.

No specific medication has gained widespread acceptance as having broad clinical effectiveness in the treatment of stimulant dependence (272). Nevertheless, medications are useful in managing particular manifestations of dependence in selected patients. Potential indications for pharmacotherapy include treatment of co-morbid psychiatric disorders, management of stimulant withdrawal and other drug-induced mental disorders, treatment of concurrent substance use disorders (e.g., alcohol dependence), and facilitation of initial abstinence.

Pharmacotherapy

Clinical evidence indicates that pharmacotherapy can be effective in the treatment of stimulant abuse, putatively by reversing or compensating for the long-term residual neuroadaptations produced by chronic abuse. Pharmacological treatments of stimulant abuse generally rest on one of the two following approaches: (a) blockade of the reinforcing actions of amphetamines,

Table 18.3. Proposed Treatments for Stimulant Abuse: Symptoms Treated, Possible Mechanisms of Treatment Efficacy

Treatment	Symptoms	Mechanism
PHARMACOTHERAPY		
Dopamine agonist	Dysphoria-anergia	Increased dopaminergic activity
Classical antidepressants	Depression, craving, dysphoria	Provision of low-grade enhancement of "energy activating" or affective tone Reduction of fantasy urges
Fluoxetine	Reinforcing efficacy Residual impulsivity	Increased serotonergic activity
BEHAVIORAL		
Extinction	Conditioned urges and craving	Extinction of conditioned responses
Self-mastery	Relapse prevention	Self-mastery and control over urges and situations that can trigger use
Contingency contracting	Relapse prevention (drug-free urine tests)	Aversive consequences for failure to adhere to the conditions of the contract Positive consequences for adhering to the conditions of the contract
Increasing natural reinforcement density	Relapse prevention	Reduction of the reinforcing value of the drug

or (b) the provision of low-grade enhancement of "energy-activating" or affective tone with direct dopamine agonists, or with classical antidepressants. The latter approach is thought to reduce the "fantasy urges" that trigger use.

DOPAMINE AGONISTS

Dopamine agonists have been used to attenuate the anergia-dysphoria experienced during withdrawal from stimulants (e.g., cocaine). For example, several controlled, double-blind studies have indicated that the dopamine agonists bromocriptine and amantadine alleviate the craving and dysphoria during cocaine withdrawal (70, 71, 117, 292). Indeed, in the Tennant and Sagherian (292) report three subjects indicated that bromocriptine almost completely eliminated the euphoric effects of cocaine during treatment.

TRICYCLIC ANTIDEPRESSANTS

Tricyclic antidepressants were first used to treat the amphetamine withdrawal anergic state in the 1970s. For example, imipramine and desipramine were used during this period, based largely on clinical case studies, and were especially effective during the early weeks of withdrawal for the waxing and waning period of psychasthenia and anergia (88). However, during this era there were no controlled studies. Subsequently, amphetamine abuse mini-epidemics have been scattered and sporadic, and most recent controlled studies have focused on cocaine abuse treatment (113). Of the numerous medications that have been evaluated in the treatment of cocaine dependence, the tricyclic antidepressant desipramine has been the most extensively studied. In a double-blind, placebo-controlled, outpatient trial, desipramine was found to be superior to placebo or lithium in facilitating initial abstinence from cocaine (311); however, there is a delay of 2–3 weeks in onset of medication effect, and outpatient drop-out rates are very high during this period (311, 313). Controlled studies examining the use of desipramine in the treatment of cocaine dependence in methadone-maintained opioid addicts failed to demonstrate superiority over placebo (272, 285). In a 12-week trial of psychotherapy and pharmacotherapy (desipramine versus placebo) in outpatients, with follow-up extending to one year, Carroll et al. (39, 40) found that desipramine-treated subjects had less cocaine use at 6 weeks, but not at 12 weeks or at the 6- and 12-month follow-ups. Desipramine appeared to be most effective in subjects with lower severity of dependence (39, 40). The precise role of desipramine and other antidepressants in the treatment of co-

caine dependence has yet to be established; they may help relieve severe withdrawal symptoms when these are present, and is probably useful in treating stimulant addicts with persistent depressive symptoms (see 193 for animal model of this approach). Several other studies have indicated that desipramine can be effective in attenuating the depressive symptoms and craving associated with cocaine withdrawal (114, 118, 291, 293). Other potential new treatments proposed for cocaine addiction (see Chapters 15 and 16) would apply equally to amphetamine abuse; these include the administration of D1-receptor antagonists and low-dose flupentixol. However, the sporadic, area-specific rise and fall of amphetamine mini-epidemics make this type of research extremely difficult.

Behavioral Therapy

As stated earlier, drug abuse is a behavioral problem that is initially maintained and partly sustained by the euphoric and behavioral activating effects of the stimulants. In other words, drugs act as reinforcers to partly maintain drug-seeking and drug-taking behaviors. Thus, nonpharmacological treatments of stimulant abuse can be derived from an understanding of the conditioning process.

EXTINCTION

As described earlier, during the active abuse phase the pharmacological effects of amphetamine consumption (e.g., euphoria and behavioral activation) become associated with various environmental stimuli via the process of classical conditioning. During the withdrawal phase exposure to these same stimuli can elicit drug craving and urges. These cravings and urges are conditioned responses that extinguish slowly and that are not systematically affected by detoxification or the simple passage of time (i.e., forgetting). Hence, one behavioral treatment would be to accelerate the extinction of these conditioned responses by exposing the individual, in a laboratory or clinical setting, to drug-related stimuli in the absence of any drug effects. Over repeated exposures the cravings and urges would diminish. The therapist would start by having the individual create a hierarchy of stimuli that elicit craving and urges, and then successively expose him or her to these stimuli; this is similar to systematic desensitization for anxiety and phobic disorders (13).

This type of treatment has been used with some success in the treatment of cocaine and opiate abusers (50, 51, 222). The efficacy of this treatment depends on several factors. First, the stimuli used for extinction training must be stimuli that are very similar to those the individual actually experienced. For example, if the individual were an intravenous user of amphetamine, then the therapist could expose the abuser to a needle and syringe, or other related paraphernalia. However, the use of a pipe, as in the case of the ice or crack user, would be inappropriate because such items would not represent conditioned stimuli for that particular individual. Second, the efficacy depends on the degree of generalization of the extinction training from the laboratory or clinical setting to the individual's natural environment. This generalization can be maximized by appropriately selecting conditioned stimuli and by making the therapeutic setting as similar to the natural environment of the abuser as possible, or by conducting the training in as many different settings as possible.

Much of the current literature on desensitization focuses on the automatic processes involved in the stimulus properties of abuse (e.g., contiguous pairings, generalization, etc.) without considering the sense of self-mastery. There is a very meager literature on facilitating the stimulant abuser's development of strategies to cope with, adapt to, and master the autonomic-automatic conditioned responses that develop during the course of abuse. The authors' own work with abusers includes several steps in strategy development for the abuser. These steps include: (a) extensively identifying conditioned cues and the internal responses generated by these cues; (b) prioritizing the potency of these stimuli (i.e., creating a stimulus hierarchy); (c) bringing these conditioned stimuli to the forefront of one's thinking so that one tries not to forget about them; (d) identifying mood-setting events that may set the stage for conditioned stimuli to become prepotent (e.g., domestic quarrels, job stress, etc.); (e) developing strategies for anticipating and confronting these events ahead of time; (f) setting sequential "stops" in the steps needed for drug acquisition; (*g*) systematic reviewing and diary charting of "near misses" every day; (*h*) developing self-mastery from these near misses; and (*i*) developing emergency procedures for seeking immediate help in stopping if the abuser succumbs to the urge to use the drug. Obviously, the strategy development requires an assessment of the individual's personality and ego assets, along with a tailoring of the strategies to the capabilities and circumstances of the individual abuser.

CONTINGENCY CONTRACTING

In contingency contracting the abuser signs a "contract" stating that he or she will perform certain behaviors; in some contracts failure to perform these behaviors results in aversive consequences (e.g., the abuser's money being sent to his or her most disliked charity, the loss of a license to practice profession); conversely, the fulfillment of the conditions of the contract may result in positive consequences (e.g., receiving money). Some behavioral contracts incorporate both positive and negative consequences.

Contingency contracts are commonly used in urine-monitoring programs (135). In this treatment procedure the individual agrees to participate in a urine-monitoring program, and failure to provide either a drug-free urine or a scheduled urine sample results in an aversive consequence; this aversive consequence is obtained from the abuser's own statements (186, 243). It is important that any positive or negative consequences be derived from the abuser's own statements; otherwise, they will not be optimally effective. This form of treatment will probably be effective only in the mild abuser, because individuals with more severe abuse problems will be aware of their degree of craving and will probably be unable to abstain from the drug; hence, the severe abuser would never agree to the conditions of the contract (135).

INCREASING NATURAL REINFORCEMENT DENSITY

Basic behavioral research indicates that the reinforcing value (efficacy) of an event is inversely related to the overall density of reinforcement in the environment. In other words, a given event will be a more potent reinforcer in a relatively impoverished environment, as compared with the same event in a relatively enriched environment (see, e.g., reference 73 for a review of this literature). Drug abuse is more likely to be found in lower socioeconomic conditions (87), where the number of available reinforcers are likely to be limited. Thus, drugs are more efficacious reinforcers under these conditions, as compared with higher socioeconomic strata. Furthermore, this analysis would predict that, as the abuse continues and the behavioral repertoire becomes increasingly focused on drug-seeking and drug-taking, the reinforcing efficacy of the drug increases independent of any concomitant neurochemical changes.

This analysis implies that one potential method of treating stimulant abusers would be to reinstate former natural behaviors such as sports, nondrug social activities, etc. This would increase the overall reinforcement density that the individual experiences, thereby decreasing the reinforcing efficacy of the drug. Indeed, Carroll, Lac, and Nygaard (41) have found that both the acquisition and rate of cocaine self-administration in rats decreases simply by introducing a second response alternative that delivers a glucose-saccharin solution.

Much research must still be conducted on the treatment of amphetamine and stimulant abuse; our limited knowledge regarding the residual behavioral and neurochemical changes produced by chronic, high-dose stimulant abuse precludes any definitive statement regarding the most efficacious treatments for the abuser. However, effective treatments are likely to contain a behavioral component to reduce conditioned craving and teach the necessary strategic coping skills for dealing with the original environment that contributed to the development of the abuse. Pharmacotherapy is also likely to be an important component, especially in dealing with the craving and depressive symptoms that occur during withdrawal. Ultimately, any treatment package must be tailored to the specific needs and situations of the individual.

CONCLUSION

The consumption of amphetamines for nonmedical reasons probably occurs because of their euphoriant and psychomotor-stimulating properties. Chronic consumption of amphetamine results in the development of stereotyped behavior, paranoia, and possibly aggression. During the protracted withdrawal phase from amphetamine, individuals experience anhedonia and anergia. This may be the result of long-lasting, and possibly permanent, changes in the neurobiological substrates that mediate reward (178). In addition to these effects, acute and chronic consumption of amphetamine can be highly toxic. Deaths from amphetamine overdose are not uncommon and are caused by hyperpyrexia, cardiac failure, convulsions, and cerebral hemorrhage.

The neurobiological substrates that mediate the effects of amphetamine and normally occurring behaviors are beginning to be elucidated. The effects of amphetamine are probably mediated by the mesolimbic dopaminergic system. Chronic amphetamine use results in permanent depletions of dopamine from a variety of brain regions. This depletion may mediate some of the tolerance, anhedonia, and anergia experienced by amphetamine users. Furthermore, chronic amphetamine use results in changes in somatodendritic and terminal autoreceptor sensitivity, which may negatively affect natural reinforcers.

In addition to the effects on the dopaminergic system, methamphetamine has also been reported to deplete the serotonergic system, which may have several functional effects. Examination of the clinical psychiatric literature indicates that depletion of the serotonin system is associated with impulsive behavior (i.e., disinhibition of behavior); for example, Linnoila et al. (203) found that violent offenders with a diagnosis of personality disorder associated with impulsivity had lower 5-HIAA levels than did other offenders. Relating the amphetamine abuse syndrome and the literature on serotonergic activity and impulsivity provides for an operating hypothesis that the lower serotonergic activity during chronic amphetamine consumption, and the resulting impulsivity (disinhibition of behavior) that may result from this depletion, may result in amphetamine abusers being more likely to relapse. Furthermore, if the individual relapses, consumption of amphetamines will have a greater reinforcing effect because of the absence of the normal inhibitory effects of the serotonergic system on dopamine release.

The likelihood of relapse and disinhibition is further enhanced by the presence of stimuli that were previously associated with drug consumption and drug effects, similar to effects found with the conditioned place preference paradigm. During withdrawal, these stimuli can elicit conditioned craving that would further tend to result in relapse and resumption of the binge cycle.

The current federal effort to curb cocaine importation and use, coupled with the large profit margins associated with amphetamine production, may result in an increase in the number of individuals abusing amphetamines. The individual who is prone to drug abuse may see the use of amphetamines as an economical alternative to cocaine abuse. This may be especially true given that the effects of amphetamine last longer than the effects of cocaine. If this increase does occur, then one would expect to see an increase in the number of individuals admitted to hospital emergency rooms for the treatment of the physical and behavioral effects of acute and chronic amphetamine use.

Acknowledgments. *Preparation of this chapter was supported by NIDA grant 1-R29-DA08899, G. R. King, Ph.D., principal investigator, and grant SRCD-5P5D-DA05303, E. H. Ellinwood principal investigator.*

References

1. Abdallah AH. On the role of norepinephrine in the anorectic effect of D-amphetamine in mice. Arch Int Pharmacodyn Ther 1971;192:72–77.
2. Abdallah AH, Roby DM, Boeckler WH, Riley CC. Role of dopamine in the anorexigenic effect of DITA, comparison with d-amphetamine. Eur J Pharmacol 1976;40:39–44.
3. Akimoto K, Hammamura T, Otsuki S. Subchronic cocaine treatment enhances cocaine-induced dopamine efflux studied by in vivo intracerebral dialysis. Brain Res 1989;490:339–344.
4. Angrist B, D'Hollosy M, Sanfilipo M, et al. Central nervous system stimulants as symptomatic treatments for AIDS-related neuropsychiatric impairment. J Clin Psychopharmacol 1992;12:268–272.
5. Arnold LE, Kirilcuk V, Corson SA, Corson EO. Levoamphetamine and dextroamphetamine: differential effect on aggression and hyperkinesis in children and dog. Am J Psychiatry 1973;130:165–170.

6. Angrist BM, Gershon S. The phenomenology of experimentally induced amphetamine psychosis: preliminary observations. Biol Psychiatry 1970;2:95–107.

7. Angrist BM, Gershon S. Some recent studies on amphetamine psychosis—unresolved issues. In: Ellinwood EH, Cohen S, eds. Current concepts on amphetamine abuse. Rockville, MD: National Institute on Mental Health 1972:193–204.

8. Ansis SF, Smith RC. Amphetamine abuse and violence. In: Smith DE, ed. Amphetamine use, misuse, and abuse. Boston: G.K. Hall & Co., 1979:205–217.

9. Appel NM, De Souza EB. Fenfluramine selectively destroys serotonin terminals in brain. Immunocytological evidence. Soc Neurosci 1988;14:556.

10. Asher IM, Aghajanian GK. 6-Hydroxydopamine lesions of olfactory tubercules and caudate nuclei: effect on amphetamine-induced stereotyped behaviour in rats. Brain Res 1974; 82:1–12.

11. Ayd FJ, Zohar J. Psychostimulant (amphetamine of methylphenidate) therapy for chronic and treatment-resistant depression. In: Zohar J, Belmaker RH, eds. New York: PMA Publishing, 1987:343–355.

12. Baez LA. Role of catecholamines in the anorectic effects of amphetamine in rats. Psychopharmacologia (Berlin) 1974;35:91–98.

13. Bandura A. Principles of behavior modification. New York: Holt, Rinehart, and Winston, 1969.

14. Barrett AM, McSharry L. Inhibition of drug-induced anorexia in rats by methysergide. J Pharm Pharmcol 1975;27:889–895.

15. Beckett AH, Al-Saraj S. The mechanism of oxidation of amphetamine enantiomorphs by liver microsomal preparations from different species. J Pharm Pharmacol 1972;24:174.

16. Biel JH, Bopp BA. Amphetamine: structure-activity relationships. In: Iversen LL, Iversen SD, Snyderman SH, eds. Handbook of psychopharmacology. Vol. 11. Stimulants. New York: Plenum Press, 1978:1–39.

17. Blundell JE, Leshem MB. Central action of anorexic agents: effects of amphetamine and fenfluramine in rats with lateral hypothalamic lesions. Eur J Pharmacol 1974;28:81–88.

18. Blundell JE, Latham CJ, Leshem MB. Biphasic action of a 5-hydroxytryptamine inhibitor on fenfluramine-induced anorexia. J Pharm Pharmacol 1973;25:492–494.

19. Blum K. Handbook of abusable drugs. New York: Gardner, 1984:306–312.

20. Bradley C. The behavior of children receiving benzedrine. Am J Psychiatry 1937;94:577–585.

21. Braestrup C, Anderson H, Randrup A. The monoamine oxidase B inhibitor deprenyl potentiates phenylethylamine behaviour in rats without inhibition of catecholamine metabolite formation. Eur J Pharmacol 1975;34:181–189.

22. Breese GR, Cooper Br, Mueller RA. Evidence for involvement of 5-hydroxytryptamine in the actions of amphetamine. Br J Pharmacol 1974; 52:307–314.

23. Brown RT, Wynne ME, Borden KA, Clingerman SR, Genisses R, Sunt AL. Methylphenidate and cognitive therapy in children with attention deficit disorder: a double-blind trial. J Dev Behav Pediatr 1986;7:163–174.

24. Browne RG, Segal DS. Metabolic and experiential factors in the behavioral response to repeated amphetamine. Pharmacol Biochem Behav 1977;6:545–552.

25. Bunney BS, Aghajanian GK. Electrophysiological effects of amphetamine on dopaminergic neurons. In: Usdin E, Snyder SH, eds. Frontiers in catecholamine research. Oxford: Pergamon Press, 1973:957–962.

26. Bunney BS, Aghajanian GK. d-amphetamine-induced inhibition of central dopaminergic neurons: mediation by a striato-nigral feedback pathway. Science 1976;192:391–393.

27. Bunney BS, Aghajanian GK, Roth RH. Comparison of the effects of L-dopa, amphetamine, and apomorphine on firing rate of rat dopaminergic neurons. Nature New Biol 1973;245: 123–125.

28. Burt DR, Creese I, Snyder SH. Anti-schizophrenic drugs: chronic treatment elevates dopamine receptor binding in brain. Science 1977; 196:326–328.

29. Caldwell J. Metabolism of amphetamines in mammals. Drug Metab Rev 1976;5:219.

30. Caldwell J. Round table discussion on mechanisms of amphetamine deamination. In: Gorrod JW, ed. Biological oxidation of nitrogen. Amsterdam: Elsevier/North Holland, 1978:495.

31. Caldwell J. The metabolism of amphetamines and related stimulants in animals and man. In: Caldwell J, ed. Amphetamines and related stimulants: chemical, biological, clinical, and social aspects. Boca Raton, FL: CRC Press, 1980.

32. Calia KA, Grothe DR, Elia J. Attention-deficit hyperactivity disorder. Clin Pharm 1990;9: 632–642.

33. Carey RJ, Goodall EB. Attenuation of amphetamine anorexia by unilateral nigral striatal lesions. Neuropharmacology 1975;14:827.

34. Carey JT, Mandel J. A San Francisco Bay Area "speed" scene. J Health Soc Behav 1968;9: 164–174.

35. Carlisle HJ. Differential effects of amphetamine on food and water intake in rats with lateral hypothalamic lesions. J Comp Physiol Psychol 1964;58:47–54.

36. Carlsson A. Amphetamine and brain catecholamines. In: Costa E, Garattini S, eds. Amphetamines and related compounds. New York: Raven Press, 1970:289–299.

37. Carlsson A, Waldeck B. Effects of amphetamine, tyramine, and protriptyline on reserpine resistant amine-concentrating mechanisms of adrenergic nerves. J Pharm Pharmacol 1966;18: 252–253.

38. Carlsson A, Lindqvist M, Dahlstroem A, Fuxe K, Masuoka D. Effects of the amphetamine group on intraneuronal brain amines in vivo and in vitro. J Pharm Pharmacol 1965;17:521–524.

39. Carroll KM, Rounsaville BJ, Gordon LT, et al. One-year follow-up of psychotherapy and pharmacotherapy for cocaine dependence. Arch Gen Psychiatry 1994;51:989–997.

40. Carroll KM, Rounsaville BJ, Gordon LT, et al. Psychotherapy and pharmacotherapy for ambulatory cocaine abusers. Arch Gen Psychiatry 1994;51:177–187.

41. Carrol ME, Lac ST, Nygaard ST. A concurrently available nondrug reinforcer prevents the acquisition or decreases the maintenance of cocaine-reinforced behavior. Psychopharmacology 1989;97:23–29.

42. Castagnoli N Jr. Drug metabolism: review of principles and the fate of one-ring psychotomimetics. In: Iversen LL, Iversen SD, Snyderman SH, eds. Handbook of psychopharmacology. Vol. 11. Stimulants. New York: Plenum Press, 1978:335–387.

43. Castellani S, Ellinwood EH, Kilbey MM. Behavioral analysis of chronic cocaine intoxication in the cat. Biol Psychiatry 1978;13:203–205.

44. Chance MRA. A peculiar form of social behavior induced in mice by amphetamine. Behaviour 1946;1:60–70.

45. Chance MRA. Aggregation as a factor influencing the toxicity of sympathomimetic amines in mice. J Pharmacol Exp Ther 1946;87:214–219.

46. Chen N-H, Reith MEA. Dopamine and serotonin release-regulation autoreceptor sensitivity in A_9/A_{10} cell body and terminal areas after withdrawal of rats from continuous infusion of cocaine. J Pharmacol Exp Ther 1993;267:1445–1453.

47. Cherek DR, Steinberg JL, Baruchi JT. Effects of caffeine on human aggressive behavior. Psychiatry Res 1983;8:137–145.

48. Cherek DR, Steinberg JL, Kelly TH. Effects of d-amphetamine on human aggressive behavior. Psychopharmacology 1986;88:381–386.

49. Chiarello RJ, Cole JO. The use of psychostimulants in general psychiatry. Arch Gen Psychiatry 1987;44:286–295.

50. Childress AR, McLellan AT, O'Brien CP. Abstinent opiate abusers exhibit conditioned craving. Br J Addict 1986;81:701–706.

51. Childress AR, McLellan AT, Ehrman R, et al. Extinction of conditioned responses in abstinent cocaine or opioid users. NIDA Res Monogr Ser 1987;76:189–195.

52. Chiueh CC, Moore KE. In vivo evoked release of endogenously synthesized catecholamines from the cat brain evoked by electrical stimulation and d-amphetamine. J Neurochem 1974;23: 159–168.

53. Cho AK. Ice: a new dosage form of an old drug. Science 1990;249:631–634.

54. Cho AK, Wright J. Pathways of metabolism of amphetamine and related compounds. Life Sci 1978;22:363.

55. Clineschmidt BV. 5,6-Dihydroxytryptamine: suppression of the anorexigenic action of fenfluramine. Eur J Pharmacol 1973;24:405.

56. Clineschmidt BV, McGuffin JC, Werner AB. Role of monoamines in the anorexigenic actions of fenfluramine, amphetamine, and p-chloromethamphetamine. Eur J Pharmacol 1974;27: 313–323.

57. Clineschmidt BV, McGuffin JC, Pflueger AB, Totaro JA. A 5-hydroxytryptamine-like mode of anorectic action for 6-chloro-2- (1-piperazinyl]-pyrazine (MK-212). Br J Pharmacol 1978;62: 579–589.

58. Clineschmidt BV, Zacchei AG, Totaro JA, Pflueger AB, McGuffin JC, Wishousky TI. Fenfluramine and brain serotonin. Ann N Y Acad Sci 1978;305:222–241.

59. Cole JO, Freedman AM, Friedhoff AJ. Psychopathology and psychopharmacology. Baltimore: Johns Hopkins University Press, 1973.

60. Connell PH. Amphetamine psychosis. Maudsley monograph number 5. London: Oxford University Press, 1958.

61. Conners CK. A teacher rating scale for use in drug studies with children. Am J Psychiatry 1969;126:152–156.

62. Conway PG, Uretsky NJ. Role of striatal dopaminergic receptors in amphetamine-induced behavioral facilitation. J Pharmacol Exp Ther 1982;221:650–655.

63. Cook J, Schanberg SM. Effect of methamphetamine on norepinephrine metabolism in various regions of the brain. J Pharmacol Exp Ther 1975;194:87–93.

64. Costall B, Naylor RJ. The site and mode of action of ET-495 for the mediation of stereotyped behaviour in the rat. Naunyn Schmiedebergs Arch Pharmacol 1973;278:117–133.

65. Costall B, Naylor RJ. Extrapyramidal and mesolimbic involvement with the stereotypic activity of d- and l-amphetamine. Eur J Pharmacol 1974; 25:121–129.

66. Costall B, Naylor RJ. Mesolimbic and extrapyramidal sites for the mediation of stereotyped behaviour patterns and hyperactivity by amphetamine and apomorphine in the rat. In: Ellinwood E, Kilbey M, eds. Cocaine and other stimulants. New York: Plenum Press, 1975: 47–76.

67. Cox B, Tha SJ. Effects of amantadine and l-dopa on apomorphine and d-amphetamine induced stereotyped behaviour in rats. Eur J Pharmacol 1973;24:96–101.

68. Coyle JT, Snyder SH. Catecholamine uptake by synaptosomes in homogenates of rat brain: stereospecificity in different areas. J Pharmacol Exp Ther 1969;170:221–231.

69. Creese I, Iversen SD. The role of forebrain dopamine systems in amphetamine induced stereotyped behaviour in the rat. Psychopharmacologia 1975;39:345–357.

70. Dackis CA, Gold MS. Pharmacological approaches to cocaine addiction. J Subst Abuse Treat 1985;2:139–145.

71. Dackis CA, Gold MS, Sweeney DR, Byron JP Jr, Climko R. Single-dose bromocriptine reverses cocaine craving. Psychiatry Res 1987;20: 261–264.

72. Davis JM, Schlemmer RF Jr. The amphetamine psychosis. In: Caldwell J, ed. Amphetamines and related stimulants: chemical, biological, clinical, and sociological aspects. Boca Raton, FL: CRC Press, 1980:161–173.

73. Davison M, McCarthy D. The matching law: a research review. Hillsdale, NJ: Erlbaum, 1988.

74. Dickinson LD, Lee J, Ringdah IC, et al. Impaired growth in hyperkinetic children receiving pemoline. J Pediatr 1979;94:538.

75. Dingell JV, Owens ML, Norvich MR, Sulser F. On the role of norepinephrine biosynthesis in the central action of amphetamine. Life Sci 1967; 6:1155–1162.

76. Dring LG, Smith RL, Williams RT. The metabolic fate of amphetamine in man and other species. Biochem J 1970;116:425.

77. Duarte-Escalante O, Ellinwood EH Jr. Central nervous system cytopathological changes in cat with chronic methedrine intoxication. Brain Res 1970;21:151–155.

78. Duhalt J, Boulanger M, Voisin C, Malen CL, Schmitt H. Fenfluramine and 5-hydroxytryptamine. Part 2: involvement of brain 5-hydroxytryptamine in the anorectic activity of fenfluramine. Arzneimittelforschung 1975;25: 1758–1762.

79. Eison MS, Eison AS, Ellison G. The regional distribution of d-amphetamine and local glucose utilization in rat brain during continuous amphetamine administration. Exp Brain Res 1981; 43:281–288.

80. Eison MS, Ellison G, Eison AS. The regional distribution of amphetamine in rat brain is altered by dosage and by prior exposure to drug. J Pharmacol Exp Ther 1981;218:237–241.

81. Elia J, Borcherding BG, Rapoport JL, Keysor CS. Methylphenidate and dextroamphetamine treatments of hyperactivity: are there true nonresponders? Psych Res 1991;36:141–155.

82. Ellinwood EH Jr. Amphetamine psychosis. I. Description of the individuals and process. J Nerv Ment Disord 1967;144:273.

83. Ellinwood EH Jr. Effect of chronic methamphetamine intoxication in rhesus monkeys. Biol Psychiatry 1971;3:25–32.

84. Ellinwood EH Jr. Comparative methamphetamine intoxication in experimental animals. Pharmakopsychiatr Neuro-Psychopharmakol 1971; 4:351–361.

85. Ellinwood EH Jr. Assault and homicide associated with amphetamine abuse. Am J Psychiatry 1971;127:90–95.

86. Ellinwood EH Jr. Amphetamine psychosis: individuals, settings, and sequences. In: Ellinwood EH, Cohen S, eds. Current concepts in amphetamine abuse. Rockville, MD: National Institute on Mental Health, 1972: 143–157.

87. Ellinwood EH Jr. Amphetamine and stimulant drugs. In: Drug use in America: problem in perspective. Second report, Marihuana and Drug Abuse Commission, 1973:140–157.

88. Ellinwood EH Jr. Amphetamine and cocaine. In: Jarvik ME, ed. Psychopharmacology in the practice of medicine. New York: Appleton-Century-Crofts, 1977:467–479.

89. Ellinwood EH. Neuropharmacology of amphetamines and related stimulants. In: Caldwell J, ed. Amphetamines and related stimulants: chemical, biological, clinical, and sociological aspects. Boca Raton, FL: CRC Press, 1980:69–84.

90. Ellinwood EH Jr, Kilbey MM. Species differences in responses to amphetamine. In: Eleftheriou BE, ed. Psychopharmacogenetics. New York: Plenum Press, 1975:323–375.

91. Ellinwood EH, Kilbey MM. Chronic stimulant models of psychosis. In: Hanin I, Usdin E, eds. Animal models of psychiatry. New York: Pergamon Press, 1977.

92. Ellinwood EH, Lee TH. Dose- and time-dependent effects of stimulants. In: Asghar K, De Souza E, eds. Pharmacology and toxicology of amphetamine and related designer drugs. NIDA Res Monogr Ser 1989;94:323–340.

93. Ellinwood EH, Rockwell WJK. Central nervous system stimulants and anorectic agents. In: Blackwell B, ed. Meyler's side effects of drugs. Amsterdam: Elsevier, 1988:1–26.

94. Ellinwood EH, Sudilovsky A, Nelson LM. Behavior, EEG analysis of chronic amphetamine effect. Biol Psychiatry 1974;8:169–176.

95. Ellinwood EH, Sudilovsky A, Nelson LM. Evolving behavior in the clinical and experimental amphetamine (model) psychosis. Am J Psychiatry 1973;130:1088–1093.

96. Ellison G, Eison MS, Huberman HS, Daniel F. Long-term changes in dopaminergic innervation of caudate nucleus after continuous amphetamine. Science 1978;201:276–278.

97. Ellison G, Morris W. Opposed stages of continuous amphetamine administration: parallel alterations in motor stereotypies and in vivo spiroperidol accumulation. Eur J Pharmacol 1981;74:207–214.

98. Ellison G, Rattan R. The late stage following continuous amphetamine administration to rats is correlated with altered dopamine but not serotonin. Life Sci 1982;31:771–777.

99. Fawcett JF, Busch KA. Stimulants in psychiatry. In: Schatzberg AF, Nemeroff CB, eds. The American Psychiatric Press textbook of psychopharmacology. Washington, DC: American Psychiatric Press, 1995:417–435.

100. Fibiger HC, Zis AP, McGeer EG. Feeding and drinking deficits after 6-hydroxydopamine administration in the rat: similarities to the lateral hypothalamic syndrome. Brain Res 1973; 55:135.

101. Fischman MW, Schuster CR, Resnekov L, Shick JFE, Krasnegor NA, Fennell W, Freedman DX. Cardiovascular and subjective effects of intravenous cocaine administration in humans. Arch Gen Psychiatry 1976;33: 983–989.

102. Fog R. On stereotypy and catalepsy: studies on

the effect of amphetamine and neuroleptics in the rat. Acta Neurol Scand 1972;48(suppl):50.

103. Franklin MR. The formation of a 455 nm complex during cytochrome P-450-dependent N-hydroxyamphetamine metabolism. Mol Pharmacol 1974;10:975–985.

104. Franklin MR. Complexes of metabolites of amphetamines with hepatic cytochrome P-450. Xenobiotica 1974;5:133–142.

105. Franklin MR. Inhibition of the metabolism of N-substituted amphetamines by SKF 525-A and related compounds. Xenobiotica 1974;4: 143–150.

106. Frey H-H, Schulz R. On the central mediation of anorexigenic drug effects. Biochem Pharmacol 1973;22:3041–3049.

107. Fuller RW, Molloy BB. Recent studies with 4-chloroamphetamine and some analogues. In: Costa E, Gessa GL, Sandler M, eds. Advances in biochemical psychopharmacology. New York: Raven Press, 1974;10:195–205.

108. Fuller RW, Snoddy HD, Roush BW, Molloy BB. Further structure-activity studies on the lowering of brain 5-hydroxyindoles by 4-chloroamphetamine. Neuropharmacology 1973; 12:33–42.

109. Funderburk WH, Hazelwood JC, Ruckart RT, Ward JW. Is 5-hydroxytryptamine involved in the mechanism of action of fenfluramine? J Pharm Pharmacol 1971;23:468–470.

110. Fuxe K, Ungerstedt U. Histochemical, biochemical and functional studies on central monoamine neurons after acute and chronic amphetamine administration. In: Costa E, Garattini S, eds. Amphetamines and related compounds. New York: Raven Press, 1970: 257–288.

111. Garattini S, Buczko W, Jori A, Samanin R. The mechanism of fenfluramine. Postgrad Med J 1975;51(suppl 1):27–35.

112. Garattini S, Bizzi A, De Gaetano G, Jori A, Samanin R. Recent advances in the pharmacology of anorectic agents. In: Howard I, ed. Recent advances in obesity research. London: Newman Publishing, 1975:354–367.

113. Gawin FH, Ellinwood EH. Cocaine and other stimulants. N Engl J Med 1988;318:1173.

114. Gawin FH, Kleber HD. Cocaine abuse treatment: open pilot trial with desipramine and lithium carbonate. Arch Gen Psychiatry 1984; 41:321–327.

115. Gessa GL, Clay GA, Brodie BB. Evidence that hyperthermia produced by d-amphetamine is caused by peripheral action of the drug. Life Sci 1969;8:135–141.

116. Ghezzi D, Samanin R, Bernasconi S, Tognoni G, Gerna M, Garattini S. Effect of thymoleptics of fenfluramine-induced depletion of brain serotonin in rats. Eur J Pharmacol 1973;24: 205–210.

117. Giannini AJ, Baumgartel P, DiMarzio LR. Bromocriptine therapy in cocaine withdrawal. J Clin Pharmacol 1987;27:267–270.

118. Giannini AJ, Malone DA, Giannini MC, Price WA, Loiselle RH. Treatment of depression in chronic cocaine and phencyclidine abuse with desipramine. J Clin Pharamcol 1986;26: 211–214.

119. Gill JR, Mason DT, Bartter FC. Effects of hydroxyamphetamine (paredrine) on the function of the sympathetic nervous system in normotensive subjects. J Pharmacol Exp Ther 1967;155:288.

120. Glick SD. Brain damage and changes in drug sensitivity. In: Glick SD, Goldfarb J, eds. Behavioral pharmacology. St. Louis, MO: CV Mosby, 1976:97.

121. Goldstein M, Anagoste B. The conversion in vivo of d-amphetamine to p-hydroxynorephedrine. Biochim Biophys Acta 1965;107:166–168.

122. Gossop MR, Roy A. Hostility and drug dependence: its relation to specific drugs, and oral or intravenous use. Br J Psychiatry 1976;128:188–193.

123. Gotestam KG, Gunne L. Subjective effects of two anorexigenic agents, fenfluramine and AN488, in amphetamine-dependent subjects. Br J Addictions 1972;67:39–44.

124. Graham AW, Aghajanian GK. Effects of amphetamine on single cell activity in a catecholamine nucleus, the locus coeruleus. Nature 1971;234:100–102.

125. Green TR, Harvey JA. Enhancement of amphetamine action after interruption of ascending serotonergic pathways. J Pharmacol Exp Ther 1974;190:109.

126. Groves PM, Rebec GV. Changes in neuronal activity in the neostriatum and the reticular formation following acute or long-term amphetamine administration. In: Ellinwood E, Kilbey M, eds. Cocaine and other stimulants. New York: Plenum Press, 1977:269–301.

127. Groves PM, Rebec GV, Segal DS. The action of d-amphetamine on spontaneous activity in the caudate nucleus and reticular formation of the rat. Behav Biol 1974;11:33–47.

128. Goldberg L. Epidemiology of drug abuse in Sweden. In: Zarafonetis CJD, ed. Drug abuse: proceedings of an international conference. Philadelphia: Lea & Febiger, 1972:27–66.

129. Grinspoon L, Hedblom P. The speed culture. Cambridge, MA: Harvard University Press, 1975.

130. Groves PM, Wilson CJ, Young SJ, Rebec GV. Self-inhibition by dopaminergic neurons. Science 1975;190:522–529.

131. Groves PM, Young SJ, Wilson CJ. Self-inhibition by dopaminergic neurons: disruption by (+−)-alpha-methyl-para-tyrosine pretreatment or anterior diencephalic lesions. Neuropsychopharmacology 1976;15:755–762.

132. Groves PM, Young SJ, Wilson CJ. Nigro-striatal relations and mechanisms of action of amphetamine. In: Butcher LL, ed. Cholinergic-monoaminergic interactions in the brain. New York: Academic Press, 1978:177–218.

133. Hackman, Pentikaeinen P, Neuroven RJ, Vapaatalo H. Inhibition of apomorphine gnawing compulsion by amantadine. Experentia 1973;29:1524–1525.

134. Haefely W, Bartholini G, Pletscher A. Monoaminergic drugs: general pharmacology. Pharmacol Ther 1976;2:185–218.

135. Hall WC, Talbert RL, Ereshefsky L. Cocaine abuse and its treatment. Pharmacotherapy 1990;10:47–65.

136. Hanson GR, Sonsalla P, Letter A, et al. Effects of amphetamine analogs on central nervous system neuropeptide systems. In: Asghar K, De Souza E, eds. Pharmacology and toxicology of amphetamine and related designer drugs. NIDA Res Monogr Ser 1989;94:259–269.

137. Harris E, Baldessarini R. Amphetamine-induced inhibition of tyrosine hydroxylation in homogenates of rat corpus striatum. J Pharm Pharmacol 1973;25:755–757.

138. Hart-Santora D, Hart L. Clonidine in attention-deficit hyperactivity disorder. Ann Pharmacol 1992;26:37–39.

139. Harvey JA, McMaster SE. Fenfluramine: evidence for a neurotoxic action on a long-term depletion of serotonin. Comm Psychopharmacol 1975;1:217–228.

140. Harvey JA, McMaster SE. Cumulative neurotoxicity after chronic treatment with low dosages in the rat. Comm Psychopharmacol 1977;1:3–17.

141. Heffner TG, Zigmond MJ, Stricker EM. Effects of dopaminergic agonists and antagonists on feeding in intact and 6-hydroxydopamine-treated rats. J Pharmacol Exp Ther 1977;201:386–399.

142. Hemmi T. How we handled the problem of drug abuse in Japan. In: Sjoqvist F, Tottie M, eds. Abuse of central stimulants. Stockholm: Almquist and Wiksell, 1969:147–153.

143. Henker B, Whalen CK. Hyperactivity and attention deficits. Am Psychol 1989;44:216–223.

144. Herman ZS. Influence of some psychotropic and adrenergic blocking agents upon amphetamine stereotyped behavior in white rats. Psychopharmacologia 1967;11:136–142.

145. Herrera-Marschitz M, Christensson-Nylander I, Sharp T, et al. Striatonigral dynorphin and substance P pathways in the rat. II. Functional analysis. Exp Brain Res 1986;64:193.

146. Ho BT, Taylor DL, Estevez VS, Englert LF, McKenna ML. Behavioral effects of cocaine: metabolic and neurochemical approach. In: Ellinwood E, Kilbey M, eds. Cocaine and other stimulants. New York: Plenum Press, 1977.

147. Hollister AS, Ervin GN, Cooper Br, Breese GR. The roles of monoamine neural systems in the anorexia induced by (+)-amphetamine and related compounds. Neuropharmacology 1975;14:715–723.

148. Hollister LE. Drugs for mental disorders of old age. JAMA 1975;6:195–198.

149. Holmes VF, Fernandez F, Levy JK. Psychostimulant response in AIDS-related complex patients. J Clin Psychiatry 1989;50(1):5–8.

150. Holtzman SG, Jewett RE. The role of brain norepinephrine in the anorexic effects of dextroamphetamine and monoamine oxidase inhibitors in the rat. Psychopharmacologia (Berlin) 1971;22:151–161.

151. Horn WF, Ialongo NS, Pascoe JM, et al. Additive effects of psychostimulants, parent training, and self-control therapy with ADHD children. J Am Acad Child Adolesc Psychiatry 1991;30:233–240.

152. Hotchkiss AJ, Gibb JW. Long-term effects of multiple doses of methamphetamine on tryptophan hydroxylase and tyrosine hydroxylase activity in rat brain. J Pharmacol Exp Ther 1980;214:257–262.

153. Hotchkiss AJ, Morgan ME, Gibb JW. The long-term effects of multiple doses of methamphetamine on neostriatal tryptophan hydroxylase, tyrosine hydroxylase, choline acetyltransferase and glutamate decarboxylase activities. Life Sci 1979;25:1373–1378.

154. Hunt RD. Treatment effects of oral and transdermal clonidine in relation to methylphenidate: an open pilot study in ADD-H. Psychopharmacol Bull 1987;23:111–114.

155. Hunt RD, Capper L, O'Connell P. Clonidine in child and adolescent psychiatry. J Child Adolesc Psychopharmacol 1990;1:87–102.

156. Hunt RD, Minderra RB, Cohen DJ. Clonidine benefits children with attention deficit disorder and hyperactivity: report of a double-blind placebo-crossover therapeutic trial. J Am Acad Child Psychiatry 1985;24:617–629.

157. Ialongo NS, Horn WF, Pascoe JM, et al. The effects of a multimodal intervention with attention-deficit hyperactivity disorder children: a 9-month follow-up. J Am Acad Child Adolesc Psychiatry 1993;32:182–189.

158. Iversen LL. The uptake and storage of noradrenaline in sympathetic nerves. Cambridge: Cambridge University Press, 1967.

159. Iversen SD. Neural substrates mediating amphetamine responses. In: Ellinwood E, Kilbey M, eds. Cocaine and other stimulants. New York: Plenum Press, 1975:31–45.

160. Iversen SD, Kelly PH, Miller RJ, Seviour P. Amphetamine and apomorphine responses in the rat after lesion of the mesolimbic or striatal dopamine neurones. Br J Pharmacol 1975;54:244P.

161. Izenwasser S, Cox BM. Inhibition of dopamine uptake by cocaine and nicotine: tolerance to chronic treatments. Brain Res 1992;573:119–125.

162. Jacob J, Snaudeau C, Michaud G. Actions de la noradrenaline, de la dopamine, de l'isopropyladrenaline et de la 5-hydroxytryptamine administre par voie intracisternale et souscutanee sur la temperature du rat eveille. J Pharmacol Paris 1971;2:401–422.

163. Jacobs BL, Wise WD, Taylor KM. Is there a catecholamine-serotonin interaction in the control of locomotor activity? Neuropharmacology 1975;14:501–506.

164. James RC, Franklin MR. Comparisons of the formation of cytochrome P-450 complexes absorbing at 455 nm in rabbit and rat microsomes. Biochem Pharmacol 1975;24:835–838.

165. Javaid JI, Fischman MW, Schuster CR, Dekirmenjian H, Davis JM. Cocaine plasma concentration: effects in humans. Science 1978;202:227–228.

166. Javoy F, Hamon H, Glowinski J. Disposition of newly synthesized amines in cell bodies and terminals of central catecholaminergic neurons. I. Effect of amphetamine and thioproperazine on the metabolism of CA in the caudate nucleus, the substantia nigra and the ventromedial nucleus of the hypothalamus. Eur J Pharmacol 1970;10:178–188.

167. Jellinek P. Dual effect of dexamphetamine on body temperature in the rat. Eur J Pharmacol 1971;15:389–392.

168. Jenner P, Testa B. The influence of stereochemical factors on drug disposition. Drug Metab Rev 1973;2:117.

169. Jespersen S, Scheel-Kruger J. Evidence for a difference in mechanism of action between fenfluramine- and amphetamine-induced anorexia. J Pharm Pharmacol 1973;25:49–54.

170. Joensson L-E, Gunne L-M, Aenggaerd E. Effects of alpha-methyltyrosine in amphetamine dependent subjects. Pharmacol Clin 1969;2:27.

171. Jonsson J. Hydroxylation of amphetamine to parahydroxyamphetamine by rat liver microsomes. Biochem Pharmacol 1974;23:3191.

172. Jori A, Caccia S, Dolfini E. Tolerance to anorectic drugs. In: Garattini S, Samanin R, eds. Central mechanism of anorectic drugs. New York: Raven Press, 1978:179–189.

173. Joyce EM, Koob GF. Amphetamine-, scopolamine-, and caffeine-induced locomotor activity following 6-hydroxydopamine lesions of the mesolimbic dopamine system. Psychopharmacology 1981;73:311–313.

174. Kalant H, Kalant O. Death in amphetamine users: causes and rates. In: Smith DE, ed. Amphetamine use, misuse, and abuse. Boston: G. K. Hall & Co., 1979:169–188.

175. Kalivas PW, Duffy P. Effects of daily cocaine and morphine treatment on somatodendritic and terminal field DA release. J Neurochem 1988;50:1498–1504.

176. Kalivas PW, Duffy P, Dumars LA, Skinner C. Behavioral and neurochemical effects of acute and daily cocaine administration in rats. J Pharmacol Exp Ther 1988;245:485–492.

177. Kalivas PW, Duffy P, Barrow J. Regulation of the mesocorticolimbic dopamine system by glutamic acid receptor subtypes. J Pharmacol Exp Ther 1989;251:378–387.

178. Kalivas PW, Duffy P. Effect of acute and daily cocaine treatment on extracellular dopamine in the nucleus accumbens. Synapse 1990;5: 48–58.

179. Kalivas PW, Stewart J. Dopamine transmission in the initiation and expression of drug and stress induced sensitization of motor activity. Brain Res Rev 1991;16:223–244.

180. Kato M. Epidemiology of drug dependency in Japan. In: Zarafonetis CJD, ed. Drug abuse: proceedings of an international conference. Philadelphia: Lea & Febiger, 1972:67–72.

181. Kelly PH, Iversen SD. Selective 6-OHDA-induced destruction of mesolimbic dopamine neurons: abolition of psychostimulant induced locomotor activity in rats. Eur J Pharmacol 1976;40:45–56.

182. Kelly PH, Seviour PW, Iversen SD. Amphetamine and apomorphine responses in the rat following 6-OHDA lesions of the nucleus accumbens septi and corpus striatum. Brain Res 1975;94:507–522.

183. King GR, Joyner C, Lee T, Kuhn C, Ellinwood EH Jr. Intermittent and continuous cocaine administration: residual behavioral states during withdrawal. Pharmacol Biochem Behav 1992; 43:243–248.

184. King GR, Joyner C, Lee TH, Ellinwood EH Jr. Withdrawal from continuous or intermittent cocaine: effects of NAN-190 on cocaine-induced locomotion. Pharmacol Biochem Behav 1993;44:253–262.

185. King GR, Kuhn C, Ellinwood EH Jr. Dopamine efflux during withdrawal from continuous or intermittent cocaine. Psychopharmacology 1993;111:179–184.

186. Kleber HD, Gawin FH. The spectrum of cocaine abuse and its treatment. J Clin Psychiatry 1984;45(12, sec 2):18–23.

187. Klein RG, Mannozza S. Long-term outcome of hyperactive children: a review. J Am Acad Child Adolesc Psychiatry 1991;30:383–387.

188. Kleven MS, Schuster CR, Seiden LS. The effect of depletion of brain serotonin by repeated fenfluramine on neurochemical and anorectic effects of acute serotonin. J Pharmacol Exp Ther 1988;246:1–7.

189. Knapp S, Mandell AJ, Geyer MA. Effects of amphetamine on regional tryptophan hydroxylase activity and synaptosomal conversion of tryptophan to 5-hydroxytryptamine in rat brain. J Pharmacol Exp Ther 1974;189: 676–689.

190. Koda LY, Gibb JW. The effect of repeated doses of methamphetamine on adrenal and brain tyrosine hydroxylase. Pharmacologist 1971;13:253.

191. Koda LY, Gibb JW. Adrenal and striatal tyrosine hydroxylase activity after methamphetamine. J Pharmacol Exp Ther 1973;185: 42–48.

192. Kogan FJ, Nichols WK, Gibb JW. Influence of methamphetamine on nigral and striatal tyrosine hydroxylase activity and on striatal dopamine levels. Eur J Pharmacol 1976;36: 363–371.

193. Kokkinidis L, Zacharko RM, Predy PA. Post-amphetamine depression of self-stimulation responding from the substantia nigra: reversal by tricyclic antidepressants. Pharmacol Biochem Behav 1980;13:379–383.

194. Kruk ZL. Dopamine and 5-hydroxytryptamine inhibit feeding in rats. Nature 1973;246:52–53.

195. Kruk ZL, Smith LA, Zarrindast MR. Antagonism of responses to anorectics by selective receptor blockers. Br J Pharmacol 1976;58: 468–469.

196. Kuhn CM, Schanberg SM. Distribution and metabolism of amphetamine in tolerant animals. In: Ellinwood E, Kilbey M, eds. Cocaine and other stimulants. New York: Plenum Press, 1975:161–177.

197. Kuhn CM, Schanberg SM. Metabolism of amphetamine after acute and chronic administration to the rat. J Pharmacol Exp Ther 1978; 207:544–554.

198. Lazarus LW, Winemiller DR, Lingam VR, et al. Efficacy and side effects of methylphenidate for post-stroke depression. J Clin Psychiatry 1992;53:447–449.

199. Lee T, Ellinwood EH. Time-dependent changes in the sensitivity of dopamine neurons to low doses of apomorphine following amphetamine infusion: electrophysiological and biochemical studies. Brain Res 1989;483: 17–29.

200. Lee TH, Ellinwood EH, Nishita JK. Dopamine receptor sensitivity changes with chronic stimulants. In: Kalivas W, Nemeroff CB, eds. The mesocorticolimbic system. New York: Academy of Sciences, 1988:324–329.

201. Lewander T. A mechanism for the development of tolerance to amphetamine in rats. Psychopharmacologia 1971;21:18.

202. Lewander T. Displacement of brain and heart noradrenaline by p-hydroxyephedrine after administration of p-hydroxyamphetamine. Acta Pharmacol Toxicol 1971;29:20–32.

203. Linnoila M, Virkkunen M, Scheinin M, et al. Low cerebrospinal fluid 5-hydroxyindoleacetic acid concentrations differentiates impulsive from nonimpulsive violent behavior. Life Sci 1983;33:2609–2614.

204. Littleton JM. The interaction of dexamphetamine with inhibitors of noradrenaline synthesis in rat brain in vivo. J Pharm Pharmacol 1967; 19:414–415.

205. Lundborg P. Amphetamine-induced release of 3H-metaraminol from subcellular fractions of the mouse heart. J Pharm Pharmacol 1969; 21:266–268.

206. Mabry PD, Campbell BA. Serotonergic inhibition of catecholamine-induced behavioral arousal. Brain Res 1973;49:381–391.

207. Mansuy D, Beaune P, Chottard JC, Bartoli JF, Gans P. The nature of the "455 absorbing complex" formed during cytochrome P-450 dependent oxidative metabolism of amphetamine. Biochem Pharmacol 1976;25:609–612.

208. Mantegazza P, Naimzada KM, Riva M. Effects of propranolol on some activities of amphetamine. Eur J Pharmacol 1968;4:25–30.

209. Matochik JA, Liebenauer LL, King AC, Szymanski HV, Cohen RM, Zametkin AJ. Cerebral glucose metabolism in adults with attention deficit hyperactivity disorder after chronic stimulant treatment. Am J Psychiatry 1994; 151:658–664.

210. Meller W, Lyle K. Attention deficit disorder in childhood. Prim Care 1987;14:745–759.

211. McCullough D, Milberg J, Robinson SM. A central site for the hypothermic effects of (+)-amphetamine sulfate and p-hydroxyamphetamine hydrobromide in mice. Br J Pharmacol 1970;40:219–226.

212. Moller-Nielsen I, Dubnick B. Pharmacology of chlorphentermine. In: Costa E, Garattini S, eds. Amphetamines and related compounds. New York: Raven Press, 1970:63–73.

213. Moore KE. Toxicity and catecholamine releasing activities of d- and l-amphetamine in isolated and aggregated mice. J Pharmacol Exp Ther 1963;142:6–12.

214. Motles E, Tetas M, Gonzalez M. Effects of naloxone on the behaviors evoked by amphetamine and apomorphine in adult cats. Prog Neuropsychopharmacol Biol Psychiatry 1995; 19(3):475–490.

215. Naylor RJ, Ollay JE. Modification of the behavioural changes induced by amphetamine in rats by lesions in the caudate nucleus, the caudate-putamen and the globus pallidus. Neuropharmacology 1974;11:91–99.

216. Neill DB, Grant LD, Grossman SP. Selective potentiation of locomotor effects of amphetamine by midbrain raphe lesions. Physiol Behav 1972;9:655.

217. Nemeroff C. The interaction of neurotensin with dopaminergic pathways in the central nervous system: basic neurobiology and implications for the pathogenesis and treatment of schizophrenia. Psychoneuroendocrinology 1986;11:15–37.

218. Neuberg J, Thut PD. Comparison of the locomotor stimulant mechanisms of the action of d-amphetamine and d-amphetamine plus l-dopa: possible involvement of serotonin. Biol Psychiatry 1974;8:139–150.

219. Nielsen EB, Nielsen M, Ellison G, Braestrup C. Decreased spiroperidol and LSD binding in rat brain after continuous amphetamine. Eur J Pharmacol 1981;66:149–154.

220. Nielsen EB, Nielsen M, Braestrup C. Reduction of (3)H-spiroperidol binding in rat striatum and frontal cortex by chronic amphetamine: dose response, time course, and role of sustained dopamine release. Psychopharmacology 1983;81:81–85.

221. Obianwu HO. Possible functional differentiation between the stores from which adrenergic nerve stimulation, tyramine and amphetamine release noradrenaline. Acta Physiol Scand 1969;75:92–101.

222. O'Brien CP, Childress AR, Arndt IO, McLellan AT, Woody GE, Maany I. Pharmacological and behavioral treatments of cocaine dependence: controlled studies. J Clin Psychiatry 1988;49(suppl):17–22.

223. O'Conner MM. The arrest of doctors, pharmacists, and other medical licentiates. In: Smith DE, ed. Amphetamine use, misuse, and abuse. Boston: G. K. Hall & Co., 1979:297–302.

224. Orzi F, Dow-Edwards D, Jehle J, Kennedy C, Sokoloff L. Comparative effects of acute and chronic administration of amphetamine on local cerebral glucose utilization in the conscious rat. J Cereb Blood Flow Metab 1983;3: 154–160.

225. Pavlov IP. Conditioned reflexes. New York: Dover Publications, 1970.

226. Peat MA, Warren PF, Gibb JW. Effects of a single dose of methamphetamine and iprindole on the serotonergic and dopaminergic system of the rat brain. J Pharmacol Exp Ther 1983; 255:126–131.

227. Pelham WE, Greenslade KE, Vodde-Hamilton M, et al. Relative efficacy of long-acting stimulants on children with attention deficit-hyperactivity disorder: a comparison of standard methylphenidate, sustained-release methylphenidate, sustained-release dextroamphetamine, and pemoline. Pediatrics 1990;86: 226–237.

228. Pijnenburg AJJ, van Rossum JM. Stimulation of locomotor activity following injection of dopamine into the nucleus accumbens. J Pharm Pharmacol 1973;25:1003.

229. Pijnenburg AJJ, Honig WMM, van Rossum JM. Inhibition of d-amphetamine induced locomotor activity by injection of haloperidol into the nucleus accumbens of the rat. Psychopharmacologia (Berlin) 1975;41:87–95.

230. Pitts FN Jr. The use of dextroamphetamine in mentally ill depressed patients. J Clin Psychiatry 1982;43:438.

231. Pletscher A, Bartholini G, Bruderer H, Burkard WP, Gey KF. Chlorinated arylalkylamines affecting the cerebral metabolism of 5-hydroxytryptamine. J Pharmacol Exp Ther 1964; 145:334–350.

232. Pliszka SR. Tricyclic antidepressants in the treatment of children with attention deficit disorder. J Am Acad Child Psychiatry 1987;26: 127–132.

233. Post RM. Progressive changes in behavior and seizures following chronic cocaine administration: relationship to kindling and psychosis. In: Ellinwood E, Kilbey M, eds. Cocaine and other stimulants. New York: Plenum Press, 1977.

234. Quirion R, Chiueh C, Everist H, Pert A. Comparative localization of neurotensin receptors on nigrostriatal and mesolimbic dopaminergic terminal. Brain Res 1985;327:385–389.

235. Randrup DB, Munkvad I. Pharmacology and physiology of stereotyped behavior. J Psychiatric Res 1974;11:1.

236. Rebec GV, Groves PM. Differential effects of the optical isomers of amphetamine on neuronal activity in the reticular formation and caudate nucleus of the rat. Brain Res 1975; 83:301–318.

237. Rebec GV, Segal DS. Dose-dependent biphasic alterations in the spontaneous activity of neurons in the rat neostriatum produced by d-amphetamine and methylphenidate. Brain Res 1978;150:353–366.

238. Rebec GV, Segal DS. Enhanced responsiveness to intraventricular infusion of amphetamine following repeated system administration. Psychopharmacology 1979;62:101–102.

239. Rech RH. Antagonism of reserpine behavioral depression by d-amphetamine. J Pharmacol Exp Ther 1964;146:369–376.

240. Reid M, Herrera-Marschitz M, Hokfelt T, Terenius L, Ungerstedt U. Differential modulation of striatal dopamine release by intranigral injection of gamma-aminobutyric acid (GABA), dynorphin A and substance P. Eur J Pharmacol 1988;147:411–420.

241. Reid WD. Turnover rate of brain 5-hydroxytryptamine increased by d-amphetamine. Br J Pharmacol 1970;40:483.

242. Reith MEA, Benuck M, Lajtha A. Cocaine disposition in the brain after continuous or intermittent treatment and locomotor stimulation in mice. J Pharmacol Exp Ther 1987;243: 281–287.

243. Resnick RB, Resnick EB. Cocaine abuse and its treatment. Psychiatr Clin North Am 1984; 7:713–728.

244. Ricaurte GA, Schuster CR, Seiden LS. Long-term effects of repeated methylamphetamine administration on dopamine and serotonin neurons in the rat brain: a regional study. Brain Res 1980;193:153–163.

245. Ricaurte GA, Seiden LS, Schuster CR. Further evidence that amphetamines produce long-lasting dopamine neurochemical deficits by destroying dopamine nerve fibers. Brain Res 1984;303:359–364.

246. Ricaurte GA, Guillery RW, Seiden LS, Schuster CR, Moore RY. Dopamine nerve terminal degeneration produced by high doses of methylamphetamine in the rat brain. Brain Res 1982;235:93–103.

247. Richards HGH, Stephens A. Sudden death associated with the taking of amphetamines. Med Sci Law 1973;13:35–38.

248. Riddle MA, Geller B, Ryan N. Another sudden death in a child treated with desipramine. J Am Acad Child Psychiatry 1993;32:792–795.

249. Roche AF, Lipman RS, Overall JE, et al. The effects of stimulant medication of growth of hyperkinetic children. Pediatrics 1979;63:847.

250. Roth LW, Richards RK, Shemano I, Morphis BB. A comparison of the analeptic, circulatory and other properties of d-and l-desoxyephedrine. Arch Int Pharmacodyn Ther 1954; 98:362–368.

251. Rumbaugh CL. Small vessel cerebral vascular changes following chronic amphetamine intoxication. In: Ellinwood E, Kilbey M, eds. Cocaine and other stimulants. New York: Plenum Press, 1977:241–251.

252. Russek M, Rodriguez-Zendejas AM, Teitelbaum P. The action of adrenergic anorexigenic substances on rats recovered from lateral hypothalamic lesions. Physiol Behav 1973;10: 329–333.

253. Sadusk JR. Non-narcotic addiction: size and extent of the problem. JAMA 1966;196: 707–709.

254. Saffer DJ. Major treatment considerations for attention-deficit hyperactivity disorder. Curr Prob Pediatr 1995;25:137–143.

255. Safer JJ, Allen RP, Barr E. Growth rebound after termination of stimulant drugs. J Pediatr 1975;86:709.

256. Samanin R, Bernassconi S, Garattini S. The effect of selective lesioning of brain catecholamine-containing neurons on the activity of various anorectics in the rat. Eur J Pharmacol 1975;34:373–375.

257. Samanin R, Bendotti C, Bernasconi S, Pataccini R. Differential role of brain monoamines in the activity of anorectic drugs. In: Garattini S, Samanin R, eds. Central mechanisms of anorectic drugs. New York: Raven Press, 1977:233–242.

258. Satel SL, Nelson JC. Stimulants in the treatment of depression: a critical overview. J Clin Psychiatry 1989;50(7):241–249.

259. Scheel-Krueger J. Comparative studies of various amphetamine analogues demonstrating different interactions with the metabolism of the catecholamines in the brain. Eur J Pharmacol 1971;14:47–59.

260. Schmidt CJ, Ritter JK, Sonsalla PK, Hanson GR, Gibb JW. Role of dopamine in the neurotoxic effects of methamphetamine. J Pharmacol Exp Ther 1985;233:539–544.

261. Schmitt H. Influence d'agents interferant avec les catecholamines et la 5-hydroxytryptamine sur les effets anorexigenes de l'amphetamine et de la fenfluramine. J Pharmacol (Paris) 1973; 4:285–294.

262. Schiorring E. Changes in individual and social behavior induced by amphetamine and related compounds. In: Ellinwood E, Kilbey M, eds. Cocaine and other stimulants. New York: Plenum Press, 1977:481.

263. Schuster CR, Lewis M, Seiden LS. Fenfluramine. neurotoxicity. Psychopharmacol Bull 1986;22:148–151.

264. Scoville BA. Review of amphetamine-like drugs by the Food and Drug Administration. In: Bray GA, ed. Obesity in perspective. Washington, DC: DHEW Publication No. NIH (75–707), 1975:441–443.

265. Segal DS. Behavioral and neurochemical correlates of repeated d-amphetamine administration. In: Mandell AJ, ed. Advances in biochemical psychopharmacology. Vol. 13. New York: Raven Press, 1975.

266. Segal DS, Weinberger SB, Cahill J, McCunney SJ. Multiple daily amphetamine administration: behavioral and neurochemical alterations. Science 1980;207:904–906.

267. Segal DS, Mandell AJ. Long-term administration of d-amphetamine: progressive augmentation of motor activity and stereotypy. Pharmacol Biochem Behav 1974;2:249–255.

268. Seiden LS, Fischman MW, Schuster CR. Changes in brain catecholamines induced by long-term methamphetamine administration in rhesus monkeys. In: Ellinwood E, Kilbey M, eds. Cocaine and other stimulants. New York: Plenum Press, 1977:179–185.

269. Sever PW, Dring LG, Williams RT. Urinary metabolites of p-hydroxyamphetamine in man, rat and guinea pig. Xenobiotica 1976;6:345.

270. Schad CA, Justice JB Jr, and Holtzman SG. Naloxone reduces the neurochemical and behavioral effects of amphetamine but not those of cocaine. Eur J Pharmacol 1995;275(1):9–16.

271. Shenker A. The mechanism of action of drugs used to treat attention-deficit disorder hyperactivity disorder: focus on catecholamine receptor pharmacology. In: Barness LA, ed. Advances in pediatrics. St. Louis: Mosby Year Book, 1992;39:337–382.

272. Shuckit MA. Drug and alcohol abuse: a clinical guide to diagnosis and treatment. 4th ed. New York: Plenum, 1995:118–144.

273. Simeon JG, Wiggins DM. Pharmacotherapy for attention-deficit hyperactivity disorder. Can J Psychiatry 1993;38:443–448.

274. Simonds JF, Kashani J. Drug abuse and criminal behavior in delinquent boys committed to training school. Am J Psychiatry 1979;136: 1444–1448.

275. Siomopoulos V. Violence: the ugly facet of amphetamine abuse. Illinois Med J 1981; 159:375–377.

276. Smith R. The world of the Haight-Ashbury speed freak. J Psychedelic Drugs 1969: 172–188.

277. Smith R. The marketplace of speed: violence and compulsive methamphetamine abuse. Final report of the Amphetamine Research Project to the National Institute on Mental Health. Washington, DC: NIMH, 1972.

278. Snyder SH. Catecholamines in the brain as mediators of amphetamine psychosis. Arch Gen Psychiatry 1972;27:169.

279. Snyder SH, Taylor KM, Coyle JT, Meyerhoff JL. The role of brain dopamine in behavioral regulation of the actions of psychotropic drugs. Am J Psychiatry 1970;127:199–207.

280. Spencer T, Wilens T, Biederman J, Faraone SV, Ablon JS, Lapey K. A double-blind, crossover comparison of methylphenidate and placebo in adults with childhood-onset attention-deficit hyperactivity disorder. Arch Gen Psychiatry 1995;52:434–443.

281. Steranka LR. Long-term decreases in striatal dopamine 3,4-dihydroxyphenylacetic acid after a single injection of amphetamine: time-course and time-dependent interactions with amfonelic acid. Brain Res 1982;234:123–126.

282. Steranka LR, Sanders-Bush E. Long-term effects of fenfluramine on central serotonergic mechanisms. Neuropharmacology 1979;18: 895–903.

283. Stripling JS, Ellinwood EH. Augmentation of the behavioral and electrophysiological response to cocaine by chronic administration in the rat. Exp Neurol 1977;54:546–564.

284. Stunkard A, McLaren-Hume M. The results of treatment for obesity. Arch Intern Med 1959; 103:79–85.

285. Substance Abuse, Mental Health Services Administration. Reported by Associated Press, November 7, 1995.

286. Svensson TH. The effect of inhibition of catecholamine synthesis on dexamphetamine induced central stimulation. Eur J Pharmacol 1970;12:161–166.

287. Swerdlow NR, Koob GF. Separate neural substrates of the locomotor-activating properties of amphetamine, heroin, caffeine and corticotropin releasing factor (CRF) in the rat. Pharmacol Biochem Behav 1985;23:303–307.

288. Swonger AK, Rech RH. Serotonergic and cholinergic involvement in habituation of activity and spontaneous alterations of rats in a Y maze. J Comp Physiol Psychol 1972;81: 509–522.

289. Taylor KM, Snyder SH. Amphetamine: differentiation by d-and l-isomers of behavior involving brain norepinephrine or dopamine. Science 1970;168:1487–1489.

290. Taylor WA, Sulser F. Effects of amphetamine and its hydroxylated metabolites on central noradrenergic mechanisms. J Pharmacol Exp Ther 1973;185:620.

291. Tennant FS Jr, Rawson RA. Cocaine and amphetamine dependence treated with desipramine. In: Harris LS, ed. Problems in drug dependence. NIDA Res Monogr Ser 1983; 43:351–355.

292. Tennant FS Jr, Sagherian AA. Double-blind comparison of amantadine and bromocriptine for ambulatory withdrawal from cocaine dependence. Arch Intern Med 1987;147: 109–112.

293. Tennant FS Jr, Tarver AL. Double-blind comparison of desipramine and placebo in withdrawal from cocaine dependence. In: Harris LS, ed. Problems in drug dependence. NIDA Res Monogr Ser 1984;55:159–163.

294. Thierry A, Javoy F, Glowinski S, Kety S. Effects of stress on the metabolism of norepinephrine, dopamine and serotonin in the central nervous system of the rat. I. Modification of norepinephrine turnover. J Pharmacol Exp Ther 1968;163:163–171.

295. Tinklenberg JR, Roth WT, Kopell BS, Murphy P. Cannabis and alcohol effects on assaultiveness in adolescent delinquents. Ann N Y Acad Sci 1977;282:85–94.

296. Tinklenberg JR, Woodrow KM. Drug use among youthful assaultive and sexual offenders. In: Frazier SH, ed. Aggression. Research Publication Association for Research in Nervous and Mental Disease. Baltimore: Williams & Wilkins, 1974;52:209–224.

297. Thornburg JE, Moore KE. The relative importance of dopaminergic and noradrenergic neuronal systems for the stimulation of locomotor activity induced by amphetamine and other drugs. Neuropharmacology 1973;12:853.

298. Tonge SR. Noradrenaline and 5-hydroxytryptamine metabolism in six areas of rat brain during post-amphetamine depression. Psychopharmacologia (Berlin) 1974;38:181–186.

299. Vaccarino FJ, Amalric M, Swerdlow NR, Koob GF. Blockade of amphetamine but not opiate induced locomotion following antagonism of dopamine function in the rat. Pharmacol Biochem Behav 1986;24:61–65.

300. Van der Shoot JB, Ariens EJ, Van Rossum JM, Hurkmans JA. Phenylisopropylamine derivatives, structure, and action. Arzneimittelforschung 1961;9:902–907.

301. Van Rossum JM. Mode of action of psychomotor stimulant drugs. Int Rev Neurobiol 1970;12:309–383.

302. Vinson, DC. Therapy for attention-deficit hyperactivity disorder. Arch Fam Med 1994;3: 445–451.

303. Von Voigtlander PF, Moore KE. Involvement of nigro-striatal neurons in the in vivo release of dopamine by amphetamine, amantadine and tyramine. J Pharmacol Exp Ther 1973; 184:542–552.

304. Vree TB, Henderson PTH. Pharmacokinetics of amphetamines: in vivo and in vitro studies of the factors governing their elimination. In: Cadwell J, ed. Amphetamines and related stimulants: chemical, biological, clinical, and social aspects. Boca Raton, FL: CRC Press, 1980.

305. Wallach MB. Drug-induced stereotyped behavior: similarities and differences. In: Ungerstedt E, ed. Neuropsychopharmacology of monoamines and their regulatory enzymes. New York: Raven Press, 1974:241–260.

306. Weiner N. Pharmacology of central nervous system stimulants. In: Zarafonetis CJD, ed. Drug abuse: proceedings of the international conference. Philadelphia: Lea & Febiger, 1972:243–251.

307. Weiner N. Norepinephrine, epinephrine, and the sympathomimetic amines. In: Gilman AG, Goodman LS, Rall TW, Murad F, eds. The pharmacological basis of therapeutics. New York: Macmillan, 1985:145–180.

308. Weintraub M, Sundaresan PR, Schuster B, et al. Long-term weight control study III (weeks 104 to 156). Clin Pharmacol Ther 1992;51: 602–607.

309. Weissman A, Koe BK, Tenen SS. Antiamphetamine effects following inhibition of tyrosine hydroxylase. J Pharmacol Exp Ther 1966;151: 339–352.

310. Wheatley D. Amphetamines in general practice: their use in depression and anxiety. Seminars in Psychiatry 1969;1:163–173.

311. Wilkins JN, Gorelick DA. Management of stimulant dependence and withdrawal. In: Miller NS, ed. Principles of addiction medicine. Chevy Chase, MD: American Society of Addiction Medicine, 1994:1–8.

312. Willens TE, Biederman J, Spencer T. Clonidine for sleep disturbances associated with attention-deficit hyperactivity disorder. J Am Acad Child Adolesc Psychiatry 1994;33: 424–426.

313. Withers NW, Pulvirenti L, Koob GF, Gillin JC. Cocaine abuse and dependence. J Clin Psychopharmacology 1995;15:63–78.

314. Working Party of the British Medical Association. Control of amphetamine preparations. Br J Psychiatry 1968;114:572–573.

315. Wright J, Cho AK, Gal J. The role of N-hydroxyamphetamine in the metabolic deamination of amphetamine. Life Sci 1977; 20:467.

316. Zametkin AJ, Rapoport JL. Neurobiology of attention deficit disorder with hyperactivity: where have we come in 50 years? J Am Acad Child Psychiatry 1987;26:676–686.

317. Zametkin AJ, Rapoport JL. Noradrenergic hypothesis of attention deficit disorder with hyperactivity: a critical review. In: Meltzer HY, ed. Psychopharmacology: the third generation of progress. New York: Raven Press, 1987: 837–842.

318. Zametkin AJ, Rapoport JL, Murphy DL, et al. Treatment of hyperactive children with monoamine oxidase inhibitors I. Clinical efficacy. Arch Gen Psychiatry 1985;42:962–966.

19 SEDATIVE-HYPNOTICS AND TRICYCLICS

Donald R. Wesson, David E. Smith, Walter Ling, and Richard B. Seymour

Sedative-hypnotics are drugs and medications that have, as prominent pharmacological effects, the ability to reduce anxiety or induce sleep. Medications that reduce anxiety without producing unwanted sedation are also called tranquilizers. Alcohol and marihuana would be classified pharmacologically as sedative-hypnotics; however, because alcohol and marihuana are also important drugs of abuse, alcohol and marihuana are the subjects of their own chapters. The sedative-hypnotics included in this chapter are prescription medications that are manufactured by pharmaceutical companies for treatment of medical disorders.

This chapter focuses on the benzodiazepines and newer sedative-hypnotics because they have largely replaced the short-acting barbiturates and other nonbarbiturate hypnotics in medical therapeutics. Abuse of nonbenzodiazepine sedative-hypnotics has been greatly curtailed by controls on their availability, by the availability of new medications for the indications that they were previously prescribed for, and by changes in physician prescribing practices.

Some tricyclic antidepressants, such as amitriptyline, have sedation as a prominent side effect. Their propensity to produce sedation is sometimes used therapeutically as an alternative to sedative-hypnotics for treatment of insomnia, although they are not sedative-hypnotics. They are included in this chapter because they are prescription medications that are sometimes misused by drug addicts for their sedative effects.

Although the use of sedative-hypnotics is ubiquitous in American society, mainstream society is ambivalent about the appropriate role of sedative-hypnotics. As a consequence, laws relating to sedative-hypnotics are complex, bewildering, and inconsistent. Alcohol is socially sanctioned as an intoxicant, marihuana is grudgingly tolerated, and medical prescription of sedative-hypnotics is increasingly subjected to controls (e.g., benzodiazepines have been put on triplicate prescription in New York, and because of its abuse, methaqualone has been removed from the American market).

Sedative-hypnotic abuse is often attributed to physicians' overprescribing. What constitutes overprescribing, however, is a complex judgment that is molded by beliefs about the cause and appropriate treatment of anxiety and insomnia. Because everyone has experienced anxiety or transient difficulty sleeping, almost everyone presumes expertise about the most appropriate treatment of these conditions. Most people formulate their ideas about appropriate use of sedative-hypnotics from their personal experience with them and the experiences of family or friends. The unrecognized pitfall in their thinking is that people who have not experienced a pathological anxiety disorder believe that everyone's anxiety is the same as theirs and that anxiety is just a normal reaction to adversity. For this reason, they may oppose treating anxiety or insomnia with medications.

Opposition to treating anxiety with tranquilizers also comes from psychotherapists. Psychotherapists with a psychodynamic orientation view anxiety as a secondary symptom of underlying psychopathology. Psychotherapeutic treatment is directed toward understanding and resolving the underlying *reasons* for anxiety. Because anxiety is the symptom that causes people to seek psychotherapy, many psychodynamically oriented therapists are concerned that tranquilizers will undermine their patients' motivation for psychotherapeutic work.

Drug abuse counselors also may oppose medication, particularly treatment with sedative-hypnotics. All mood-altering prescription medications are viewed as risky for a drug addict because the medication may trigger a return to drug-seeking behavior, particularly among recovering addicts who previously abused prescription medications. Even therapeutically prescribed medications that have little abuse potential in non-drug addicts, such as antidepressants, are viewed as risky because they may produce desirable sedative or stimulant effects in drug addicts and because it is easier to define a line of "complete abstinence" than to figure out which medications are or are not risky for a particular addict.

Within the context of recovery-oriented drug abuse treatment, most counselors and nurses and some physicians are, themselves, recovering addicts and alcoholics. Patients usually feel that the recovering addict or alcoholic is better able to understand their experience of addiction because "they have been there, and their knowledge does not just come from books." Further, recovering treatment personnel provide a valuable role model and an affirmation that "recovery is possible." Recovering treatment personnel may, however, have difficulty with regard to use of medications. They may feel, for example, that their own recovery is jeopardized by patients who take medications that they may desire. If they did not use medications during their own early recovery, they may believe that medications are not necessary or that the anxiety, mood, and sleep disturbances, common in early recovery, are events that the recovering addict needs to learn to cope with. Finally, many recovering addicts and alcoholics believe that physicians enabled their drug use or contributed to their relapse to drug use because they inappropriately prescribed psychotropic medications.

Although physicians may view disabling anxiety as a disease process, many people believe that physicians have been overly influenced by pharmaceutical companies' advertising that promotes all human misery and suffering as an illness amenable to pharmacological treatment. Although few people would find moral value in withholding penicillin for pneumococcal pneumonia, many would view the pharmacotherapy of other people's anxiety objectionable from a moral perspective.

Pharmacological Calvinism causes needless human suffering. Some people who could benefit from sedative-hypnotics do not seek medical treatment even when anxiety is disabling and treatment alternatives to medication are not accessible.

Physicians are often faulted for "giving in" to their patients' request (or demand) for sedative-hypnotics. Clinically experienced physicians know, however, that trying to talk some patients out of taking sedative-hypnotics is futile, even when the distress is due to family discord, grief, an intolerable life situation, or an acute loss. When a physician refuses a patient's request for sedative-hypnotic medication, the patient generally concludes that the physician does not understand the severity of his or her distress and consults another physician. The physician-patient transaction is often further distorted by patients who are drug dependent (1).

Prescribing guidelines for therapeutic use of benzodiazepines other than for treatment of addiction is beyond the scope of this chapter. Guidelines have been compiled in a publication of the American Psychiatric Association (2).

BENZODIAZEPINES

Benzodiazepine use and abuse continues to generate professional controversy, legislative hearings, and articles in the lay press. Because of psychiatrists' concerns about benzodiazepine dependence, the American Psychiatric Association formed a task force that reviewed the issue and published a report in book form (3). Legislative concern about benzodiazepines generally involve benzodiazepines' contribution to the cost of medical care or to benzodiazepine abuse and dependence.

"Abuse" is a difficult concept when applied to prescription medications. In common use, concepts of drug abuse, misuse, and addiction are deeply rooted in social values and attitudes and have been inconsistently encoded into laws. For example, moderate use of alcohol is widely sanctioned for adults; but public intoxication or driving with an alcohol blood level above 0.8–1 mg/100 mL is generally considered alcohol abuse. Any use of prescription medications to produce intoxication is generally considered abuse, although it would not necessarily qualify as "abuse" according to criteria of the *Diagnostic and Statistical Manual of Mental Disorders: DSM-IV* (4).

The term "misuse" is commonly applied to prescription sedative-hypnotics, but unlike abuse and dependence, *DSM-IV* does not provide specific criteria for "misuse." When medications are taken in higher doses or more frequently than prescribed, or taken by someone other than the person for whom the medication was prescribed, or taken for reasons other than what would normally be considered "medical use," the behavior is generally considered misuse of the medication.

DSM-IV defines abuse and dependence in terms of behavioral and physiological consequences to the person taking the medication. The criteria for abuse and dependence apply as uniformly as possible across classes of drugs, and the criteria do not distinguish the source of the medication or the intended purpose for which it was taken. Further, when most people, including physicians, speak of drug "dependence," they are referring to "physical dependence." *DSM-IV* uses the term "dependence" to denote a more severe form of substance use disorder than "abuse," and uses the specifier "with or without physiological dependence," to indicate whether or not the patient has significant physical dependence. Physiological dependence is not required for a *DSM-IV* diagnosis of "drug dependence." A diagnosis of substance dependence is only made when a patient has dysfunctional behaviors *that are a result of the drug use.*

The qualification that the dysfunctional behavior be the *result* of drug use is extremely important but in a practical sense is often difficult to establish with certainty. In considering the diagnosis of sedative-hypnotic dependence among patients who are being treated for an anxiety disorder, it is not always possible to ascertain with certainty whether the behavioral dysfunction is produced by the underlying psychiatric disorder or by the drug use. Different attribution is often the basis of disagreement among psychiatrists, patients, and patient families. A patient whose "panic attacks" are ameliorated by a medication may exhibit what may be interpreted as "drug-seeking behavior" if their access to the medication is threatened.

In a regulatory context, "benzodiazepine abuse" can mean many things: self-administration of a benzodiazepine to produce intoxication, or long-term prescription of benzodiazepines at therapeutic doses to patients who subsequently develop physical dependence on the benzodiazepines, or patients' escalating their dose of benzodiazepines beyond that prescribed by their physicians, or use of a benzodiazepine by heroin or cocaine addicts to self-medicate symptoms of heroin withdrawal or cocaine toxicity, or intentional benzodiazepine overdose in a suicide or suicide attempt.

Often, legislative hearings use data from the National Institute on Drug Abuse's Drug Abuse Warning Network (DAWN). DAWN is a national reporting system that tabulates "mentions" of psychotropic medications and drugs from patients treated in participating emergency rooms. In DAWN, drug abuse is defined as "the nonmedical use of a substance to obtain its psychic effect, or the use of a drug because of drug dependence, or the use of a drug to commit suicide, or the use of a medication inconsistent with accepted medical practice."

Effective legislative strategies for reducing or preventing benzodiazepine abuse must focus on the different behaviors that are often lumped together in a general category of "benzodiazepine abuse." The various forms of benzodiazepine abuse delineated above differ in their risk to public health and social cost, and they need different prevention and treatment approaches.

Epidemiology of Benzodiazepine Abuse

The incidence and prevalence of benzodiazepine abuse depend on how abuse is defined. If any nonmedical use of a benzodiazepine is defined as abuse, then benzodiazepine abuse is common. If, however, *DSM-IV* criteria are used, the prevalence of abuse is much lower.

Given the frequency that the benzodiazepines are prescribed, the rates of their abuse, even those such as alprazolam that are widely prescribed, is remarkably low (5). The abuse of benzodiazepines and other sedative-hypnotics is, however, a significant problem among some subgroups of patients, such as those on methadone maintenance (6–9).

Benzodiazepines are generally not primary drugs of abuse; i.e., they are rarely taken by themselves to produce intoxication. Most people who take benzodiazepines do so for anxiolysis or sleep induction. After chronic use, they may also be taking them to ameliorate benzodiazepine withdrawal symptoms. Some alcoholic and sedative-hypnotic abusers find the subjective effects of benzodiazepines desirable, but even among this population, benzodiazepines are rarely used alone to produce intoxication.

The subjective effects of benzodiazepines on non-drug addicts have similarities to alcohol. In a double-blind, crossover study (10), intravenous diazepam 0.12 mg/kg (or 72 mg in a 60-kg person) or 0.20 mg/kg (or 120 mg in a 60-kg person) or alcohol 0.75 mg/kg (about three shots of 86 proof liquor) were compared on various subjective and performance measures. On the Subjective High Assessment Scale, a visual analog scale, peak subjective "drug effects," "drunk" and "high," were not statistically different between the low-dose diazepam and the alcohol dose. The higher dose of diazepam produced statistically greater effects on most scales except "drunk" and "nauseated," and the higher dose of diazepam produced greater impairment on all measures of performance. In normal-subject challenge studies, benzodiazepines generally produce dose-dependent increases in self-report levels of sedation and fatigue (11).

Benzodiazepines are commonly self-administered by drug addicts, sometimes to ameliorate withdrawal from heroin, alcohol, or other drugs or to attenuate the side effects of cocaine or methamphetamine intoxication. Addicts may also combine benzodiazepines with heroin, marihuana, or alcohol to enhance their effects.

During the first half of the 1990s, flunitrazepam (Rohypnol) gained popularity among some adolescents, particularly in Florida and Texas, as a drug that could be taken at school without the telltale odor of alcohol or marihuana.

Flunitrazepam is an effective hypnotic marketed in many countries for treatment of insomnia. Although not marketed in the United States or Canada, 1- and 2-mg tablets of flunitrazepam are available by prescription in Mexico, Central and South America, and many countries in Europe, Asia, and Africa. Until 1996, small quantities of flunitrazepam could be brought legally into the United States, but flunitrazepam is now subject to confiscation by U.S. Customs. Flunitrazepam abuse is most visible in Florida and Texas, although sporadic reports from drug abuse treatment clinics and po-

lice seizures of flunitrazepam in other areas suggest a broader distribution. Street names of flunitrazepam vary by region. In Florida, flunitrazepam is most often referred to as "roSHAY" or "roofies"; in Texas, it is often called "Roche." In the street-drug marketplace, deception is common, and many different kinds of tablets are being sold under these street names.

The popular media has given flunitrazepam abuse considerable attention in the United States. Newspapers and television coverage have focused on its use for "date rape." While the publicity is framed to warn women that men may slip flunitrazepam into their drinks, another potential result of the publicity is to instruct unscrupulous men in its use.

A study of "Roche" abuse along the Texas-Mexico border from Brownsville to Laredo found that flunitrazepam abuse was only one of many benzodiazepines being abused (12). Although users in the area prefer white tablets imprinted with Roche and the number 2, many were not specifically seeking Rohypnol. From users' descriptions of the tablets and from police seizures of tablets at schools, it appears that many users are taking Rivotril (the trade name for clonazepam marketed in Mexico), Lexotán (the trade name for bromazepam, another benzodiazepine-hypnotic marketed in Mexico), and Valium, which is different in appearance from the Valium marketed in the United States. There is a great deal of misinformation among users, school nurses, police, and drug treatment personnel about what "Roche" tablets are. Many users believe that "Roche" is the name of the drug. Some thought that the tablets were animal tranquilizers. Many users who had heard about Rohypnol thought all white tablets imprinted with "Roche" and the number 2 were Rohypnol.

Medical Uses of Benzodiazepines

Benzodiazepines have many important medical uses. Treatment of anxiety disorders, short-term treatment of insomnia, treatment of seizure disorders, and preoperative sedation and anesthesia are the most common uses. From an addiction medicine perspective, it is easy to lose site of their medical utility because addiction medicine specialists treat patients who often misuse or abuse benzodiazepines or patients who have developed dependence on them.

Benzodiazepines are still among the most widely prescribed medications, although there has been a steady decline in their prescription worldwide because new medications have been introduced for the same purposes and because there is concern about their overuse, misuse, and abuse. Benzodiazepines have been subject to increasing control and, in New York, have been placed on triplicate status. Benzodiazepines have a significant advantage over the previously available sedative-hypnotics. The short- and intermediate-acting barbiturates, meprobamate and ethchlorvynol, are lethal if taken in excess of 10 times a single therapeutic dose. Benzodiazepines, on the other hand, are virtually nonlethal unless combined with alcohol or other drugs. Because children may accidentally overdose on prescription medications and adults who overdose in suicide attempts often take everything in the family medicine cabinet, it is of significant public health benefit to have nonlethal medications in the family medicine cabinet.

Some patients with debilitating anxiety symptoms derive great benefit from benzodiazepine treatment, even from long-term treatment, and tolerance to the therapeutic effects and physical dependence do not inevitably occur.

Adverse Effects of Benzodiazepines

Separate from issues of addiction and dependence, the prescription of benzodiazepines can be associated with adverse effects that may bring patients to the attention of addiction specialists. Alprazolam (Xanax) is noteworthy because it is prescribed for treatment of panic attacks (13) and depression (14, 15) in relatively high doses (4–10 mg/day) for extended periods of time. Initial clinical trials suggested few side effects or adverse events (16). With accumulated clinical experience, there have been case reports of alprazolam-released hostility (17–19), rebound insomnia (20), major depression (21), amnesia (22), and aggressive and violent behavior (23). As is subsequently discussed in more detail, physical dependence can result when higher-than-usual therapeutic doses are used daily for about a month and when usual therapeutic doses are used for several months.

The prescription of psychotropic medications is malevolent only when medication robs a patient of the opportunity to develop a more satisfactory nonpharmacological solution or when the patient develops drug dependence or other adverse effects that compound the patient's difficulties.

Benzodiazepine Abuse Potential

The abuse potential of a drug or medication is often used to refer to the likelihood that addicts will self-administer the drug or medication to produce intoxication. In laboratory self-administration models, abuse potential is often inferred from addicts' comparison of their liking of the drug compared to other established drugs of abuse or to placebo.

LIKING OF DRUG BY ADDICTS

Current and ex-drug abusers may have different subjective responses to psychoactive drugs than non-drug abusers. The different response may have a biological component, as altered response to benzodiazepines has been observed in children of alcoholics (24). The extent to which altered drug effects are learned, the result of some genetically determined biochemical or receptor site differences, or are caused by perturbations of metabolism or receptor site function induced by long-term exposure to drugs is not well delineated. Whatever the cause, some drugs have desirable or reinforcing effects in people with current or past histories of alcohol and other drug abuse that are not present in non-drug abusers (25). Most non-drug abuser or nonanxious people do not like the effects of benzodiazepines and prefer placebo. Studies in ex-drug abusers generally show that benzodiazepines are reinforcing but less so than short-acting barbiturates. Of the benzodiazepines, addicts generally prefer diazepam or alprazolam (26) to other benzodiazepines. Outside the laboratory setting, the benzodiazepine actually used by addicts is determined both by preference and accessibility.

VALUE ON THE "STREET-DRUG" BLACK MARKET

Availability of a drug or medication on the street-drug black market establishes that it has value to the drug abuser, although its availability does not necessary mean that the drug or medication is a drug of abuse. For example, the antihypertensive medication, clonidine, is effective in reducing opiate withdrawal symptoms and is sold on the street-drug black market. Clonidine is not used, however, to produce intoxication but is used by opiate addicts to self-medicate opiate withdrawal symptoms when heroin is not available.

The uses of benzodiazepines by addicts are varied. Benzodiazepines are used by cocaine addicts to ameliorate anxiety and agitation induced by cocaine or methamphetamine abuse or by heroin addicts to "self-medicate" opiate withdrawal symptoms. Benzodiazepines are also used by methadone-maintained patients to "boost" the subjective effects of methadone or to produce intoxication.

Diazepam is commonly sold or traded on the street-drug black market. Current price on the West Coast is $1 or $2 for a 10-mg Valium tablet. More commonly available and used by methadone-maintained patients is clonazepam (Klonopin). Klonopin is popular, in part, because it is not readily detectable in the drug screens commonly used by methadone-maintained programs and because it is the only benzodiazepine still on the California State formulary. Street price ranges from $1 to $3 for a 2-mg clonazepam tablet.

OTHER SEDATIVE-HYPNOTICS

When the short-acting sedative-hypnotics such as secobarbital and pentobarbital were commonly prescribed, they were often taken orally or by injection to produce intoxication. Intoxication with sedative-hypnotics is qualitatively similar to intoxication with alcohol. The desired effect is a state of "disinhibition" in which mood is elevated, self-criticism, anxiety, and guilt are reduced, and energy and self-confidence are increased. During intoxication, the mood is often labile and may shift rapidly from euphoria to sadness. The user does not always obtain the desired effects and, while intoxicated, may be irritable, hypochondriacal, anxious, and angry to the point of rage.

Preexisting personality, expectations, and circumstances under which the drug is used all interact. Users' perception that a drug effect is pleasurable is partly learned and partly the pharmacology of the drug.

A person intoxicated on sedative-hypnotics commonly has an unsteady gait, slurred speech, sustained horizontal nystagmus, and poor judgment. Intoxication with sedative-hypnotics may produce an amnesia for events that occur while intoxicated that is similar to alcoholic blackouts. Amnesia appears particularly likely to occur with benzodiazepine intoxication.

SEDATIVE-HYPNOTIC WITHDRAWAL

The sedative-hypnotic withdrawal syndrome is a spectrum of signs and symptoms that occur after stopping or markedly reducing the daily intake of a sedative-hypnotic. Signs and symptoms do not always follow a specific sequence. Common signs and symptoms include anxiety, tremors, nightmares, insomnia, anorexia, nausea, vomiting, postural hypotension, seizures, delirium, and hyperpyrexia. The withdrawal syndrome is similar for all sedative-hypnotics, but the severity and time course depend on the particular sedative-hypnotic. With short-active medications such as pentobarbital, secobarbital, meprobamate, and methaqualone, withdrawal symptoms typically begin 12–24 hours after the last dose and peak in intensity between 24 and 72 hours. If the patient has liver disease or is elderly, symptoms may develop more slowly. With long-active medications such as phenobarbital, diazepam, and chlordiazepoxide, the withdrawal syndrome usually begins 24–48 hours after the last dose and peaks on the fifth to eighth day.

During untreated sedative-hypnotic withdrawal, the electroencephalogram may show bursts of high-voltage, slow-frequency activity that precede clinical seizure activity. The withdrawal delirium may include disorientation to time, place, and situation and auditory and visual hallucinations. The delirium generally follows a period of insomnia. Some patients may have only delirium, others only seizures, and some may have both delirium and seizures.

The classical studies of barbiturate withdrawal were conduced in the 1950s (27). In the early 1960s, Hollister et al. reported on experimental studies of the physical dependence producing effects of high-dose chlordiazepoxide (28) and diazepam (29). Clinical case reports of withdrawal leave little doubt that a similar withdrawal syndrome is produced by methaqualone (30), ethchlorvynol (31) and meprobamate (32).

With the exception of buspirone, which apparently does not have a withdrawal syndrome, the other sedative-hypnotics listed in Table 19.1 can produce clinically significant withdrawal signs and symptoms when taken at two or more times the maximum therapeutic range for more than a month.

Low-Dose Benzodiazepine Withdrawal Syndromes

Many patients who have taken benzodiazepines in therapeutic doses for months to years can abruptly discontinue the drug without developing withdrawal symptoms. The symptoms for which the benzodiazepine was being taken often return or intensify. The return of symptoms is called "symptom reemergence" (or recrudescence). Patients' symptoms of anxiety, insomnia, or muscle tension abate during benzodiazepine treatment. When the benzodiazepine is stopped, symptoms return to the same level as before benzodiazepine therapy. The reason for making a distinction between symptom rebound and symptom recurrence is that symptom recurrence suggests persistence of the original symptoms, whereas symptom rebound suggests a transient withdrawal syndrome.

Other patients chronically taking similar amounts of a benzodiazepines in therapeutic doses develop symptoms ranging from mild to severe when the benzodiazepine is stopped or when the dosage is substantially reduced. Characteristically, patients tolerate a gradual tapering of the benzodiazepine until they are at 10–20% of their peak dose. Further reduction in benzodiazepine dose causes patients to become increasingly symptomatic. In addiction medicine literature, the low-dose benzodiazepine withdrawal syndrome may be called *therapeutic-dose withdrawal, normal-dose withdrawal,* or *benzodiazepine discontinuation syndrome.*

Many patients experience a transient increase in symptoms for 1–2 weeks after benzodiazepine withdrawal. The symptoms are an intensified return of the symptoms for which the benzodiazepine was prescribed. The

Table 19.1 Common Sedative-Hypnotics and their Phenobarbital Withdrawal Equivalency

Generic Name	Trade Name(s)	Common Therapeutic Indication	Usual Therapeutic Dose Range (mg/day)	Dose Equal to 30 mg of Phenobarbital for Withdrawal (mg)
Barbiturates				
Butabarbital	Butisol	Sedative	45–120	100
Butalbital[a]	Fiorinal, Sedapap	Sedative/ analgesic	100–300	100
Pentobarbital	Nembutal	Hypnotic	50–100	100
Secobarbital	Seconal	Hypnotic	50–100	100
Benzodiazepines				
Alprazolam	Xanax	Antianxiety	0.75–4	1
Chlordiazepoxide	Librium	Antianxiety	15–100	25
Clonazepam	Klonopin	Anticonvulsant	0.5–4	1
Clorazepate	Tranxene	Antianxiety	15–60	30
Diazepam	Valium	Antianxiety	4–40	10
estazolam	ProSom	Hypnotic	1–2	1
Flumazenil	Romazicon	Antagonist		
Flunitrazapam[b]	Rohypnol	Hypnotic	1–2	1
Flurazepam	Dalmane	Hypnotic	15–30	30
Lorazepam	Ativan	Antianxiety	1–16	16
Midazolam	Versed	Anesthesia		
Oxazepam	Serax	Antianxiety	10–120	30
Quazepam	Doral	Hypnotic	15	15
Temazepam	Restoril	Hypnotic	7.5–30	15
Trizolam	Halcion	Hypnotic	0.125–0.5	0.125
Others				
Chloral hydrate	Noctec, Somnos	Hypnotic	250–1000	500
Ethchlorvynol	Placidyl	Hypnotic	500–1000	500
Meprobamate	Miltown	Antianxiety	1200–2400	1200
Zolpidem	Ambien	Hypnotic	5–10	5

[a]Butalbital is an ingredient in many combination analgesics.
[b]Not marketed is the United States.

transient form of symptom intensification is called "symptom rebound." The term comes from sleep research in which "rebound insomnia" is commonly observed following sedative-hypnotic use. Symptom rebound lasts a few days to weeks following discontinuation of the benzodiazepine. Symptom rebound is the most common withdrawal consequence of prolonged benzodiazepine use.

A few patients experience a severe, protracted withdrawal syndrome that includes symptoms (e.g., paresthesias and psychosis) that were not present before. It is this latter withdrawal syndrome that has generated much of the concern about the long-term "safety" of the benzodiazepines when taken daily for months to years.

Protracted Benzodiazepine Withdrawal Syndrome

In some patients, protracted benzodiazepine withdrawal consists of relatively mild withdrawal symptoms such as mild to moderate anxiety, mood instability, and sleep disturbance. In others, however, the protracted withdrawal syndrome consists of increased sensitivity to light and sound, psychosis, and severe insomnia. The symptoms can be severe and disabling and last many months.

There is considerable controversy surrounding even the existence of this syndrome. The notion of a protracted withdrawal syndrome evolves primarily from the addiction medicine literature (33). Many symptoms are nonspecific and often mimic an obsessive-compulsive disorder with psychotic features. As a practical matter, it is often difficult in the clinical setting to separate symptom reemergence from protracted withdrawal. New symptoms such as paresthesias and increased sensitivity to sound, light, and touch are particularly suggestive of low-dose withdrawal.

The protracted benzodiazepine withdrawal has no pathognomonic signs or symptoms, and the broad range of nonspecific symptoms produced by the protracted benzodiazepine withdrawal syndrome also could be the result of agitated depression, generalized anxiety disorder, panic disorder, partial complex seizures, or schizophrenia. The time course of symptom resolution

is the primary differentiating feature between symptoms generated by withdrawal and symptom reemergence. Symptoms from withdrawal gradually subside with continued benzodiazepine abstinence, whereas symptom reemergence does not.

The waxing and waning of symptom intensity from day to day is characteristic of the low-dose protracted benzodiazepine withdrawal syndrome. Patients are sometimes asymptomatic for several days; then, without apparent reason, they become acutely anxious. Often there are concomitant physiological signs, e.g., dilated pupils, increased resting heart rate, and increased blood pressure. The intense waxing and waning of symptoms is important in distinguishing low-dose withdrawal symptoms from symptom reemergence.

Risk Factors for Low-Dose Withdrawal

Some drugs or medications may facilitate neuroadaptation by increasing the affinity of benzodiazepines for their receptors. Phenobarbital, for example, increases the affinity of diazepam to benzodiazepine receptors, and prior treatment with phenobarbital has been found to increase the intensity of chlordiazepoxide (45 mg/day) withdrawal symptoms (34). Patients at increased risk for development of the low-dose withdrawal syndrome are those with a family or personal history of alcoholism, those who use alcohol daily, or those who concomitantly use other sedatives. Case control studies suggest that patients with a history of addiction, particularly to other sedative-hypnotics, are at high risk for low-dose benzodiazepine dependence. The short-acting, high-milligram-potency benzodiazepines appear to produce a more intense low-dose withdrawal syndrome.

Pharmacological Treatment of Withdrawal

The strategies for treating physical dependence on sedative-hypnotics involve gradual reduction of a sedative-hypnotic or substitution of an anticonvulsant medication that allows the physiological readjustment to occur gradually. There are three basic strategies. The first is to use gradually decreasing doses of the sedative-hypnotic (27). The second is to substitute another long-active barbiturate for the sedative-hypnotic of abuse and to gradually withdraw the substitute medication (35–37). The third is to substitute an anticonvulsant such as carbamazepine (38–42) or valproate (43, 44).

Abrupt discontinuation of a sedative-hypnotic in a patient who is physically dependent on it is not acceptable medical practice. Unlike opiate withdrawal, whose withdrawal symptoms are unpleasant but not life-threatening in an otherwise healthy patient, abrupt withdrawal of sedative-hypnotics can be fatal (32, 45).

WITHDRAWAL WITH THE DRUG OF DEPENDENCE

The classical treatment of a sedative-hypnotic patient is a gradual withdrawal of the drug of dependence (27). While the method is sound from a pharmacological point of view, it has some disadvantages. When the drug of dependence is a short-acting hypnotic, such as a short-acting barbiturate, patients may become intoxicated and disinhibited, resulting in behavior problems. Giving an addict their drug of abuse, even in a therapeutic context, is problematic.

A gradual taper of the drug of dependence is more often used in the context of therapeutic discontinuation of patients from long-acting sedative-hypnotics. With long-term benzodiazepine therapy, for instance, physical dependence can develop in patients who do not have a substance abuse disorder. In this situation, gradual taper of the drug of dependence can be an appropriate therapeutic strategy.

SUBSTITUTION OF PHENOBARBITAL

Phenobarbital substitution has a number of advantages over withdrawal from the drug of dependence. First, phenobarbital is long-acting, and small changes in blood levels of phenobarbital occur between doses, allowing the safe use of smaller daily doses. Second, phenobarbital is safer than the shorter-acting barbiturates, as the lethal dose of phenobarbital is many times higher than the toxic dose and the signs of toxicity (e.g., sustained nystagmus, slurred speech, and ataxia) are easy to observe. Third, phenobarbital intoxication does not usually produce disinhibition, so most patients view it as a medication, not as a drug of abuse. Finally, the phenobarbital technique can be applied to a broad range of sedative-hypnotics and with patients who abuse a mixture of alcohol and/or sedative-hypnotics.

The disadvantages to phenobarbital substitution is that the calculations for making the conversion between the drug or drugs of abuse are tedious, and 1–5% of patients treated with phenobarbital develop a rash.

Stabilization Phase

The substitution dose of phenobarbital is calculated by substituting 30 mg of phenobarbital for each hypnotic dose of the drug of abuse. The hypnotic dose of sedative-hypnotics is not obvious for medications that are not used as hypnotics. For sedative-hypnotics that are not marketed as sleeping pills, the upper recommended therapeutic single dose is considered equivalent to the hypnotic dose. Except under unusual circumstances, the maximum daily dose of phenobarbital is 500 mg/day. Table 19.1 shows the phenobarbital conversion for common sedative-hypnotics.

The phenobarbital withdrawal conversion equivalence is not the same as therapeutic dose equivalency. The phenobarbital withdrawal equivalence is the amount of phenobarbital that can be substituted to prevent serious sedative-hypnotic withdrawal signs and symptoms.

Although sedative-hypnotics abusers may exaggerate the number of pills that they are taking, the patient's history is the best guide to initial therapy. If the patient has overstated the amount of drug used, they will become intoxicated during the first few days of treatment. Intoxication is easily managed by omitting one or more doses of phenobarbital and adjusting the daily phenobarbital dose downward as described later under withdrawal.

If, on initial evaluation, the patient is in acute sedative-hypnotic withdrawal and has had a withdrawal seizure, the initial dose of phenobarbital is administered by injection. If nystagmus, slurred speech, or ataxia develop 1–2 hours after the intramuscular dose, the patient is in no immediate danger from sedative-hypnotic withdrawal. Patients are maintained on the initial calculated schedule of phenobarbital for 2 days. If the patient has neither signs of sedative-hypnotic withdrawal nor signs of phenobarbital intoxication, he or she is ready to begin withdrawal.

Withdrawal Phase

For inpatients the daily phenobarbital dose is decreased 30 mg/day unless the patient develops signs or symptoms of phenobarbital toxicity or sedative-hypnotic withdrawal. (Outpatient withdrawal generally proceeds more slowly.) If signs of phenobarbital toxicity appear, the daily phenobarbital dose is decreased by 50%, and the 30-mg-per-day withdrawal is continued from the reduced phenobarbital dose. If the patient has objective signs of sedative-hypnotic withdrawal, the daily phenobarbital dose in increased 50%, and the patient is restabilized before continuing the withdrawal.

SUBSTITUTION OF AN ANTICONVULSANT

Protocols using carbamazepine (Tegretol) or valproic acid (Depakote, Depakene) have been used clinically for treatment of sedative-hypnotic withdrawal. Both medications enhance γ-aminobutyric acid (GABA) function. Both are effective in suppressing benzodiazepine withdrawal symptoms. Neither carbamazepine nor valproic acid produce effects that sedative-hypnotic abusers find desirable.

The use of valproate as a withdrawal protocol was suggested in 1989 (43), and clinical case reports of its use in benzodiazepine withdrawal have appeared (44, 46). Valproic acid in a dosage up to about 1200 mg/day is useful both in acute withdrawal and in treatment of persistent symptoms following withdrawal.

Carbamazepine has been reported useful in benzodiazepine withdrawal (38, 41, 42, 47–49) and in alcohol withdrawal (50, 51). It has also been useful in treating benzodiazepine withdrawal in benzodiazepine-dependent, methadone-maintained patients. Both carbamazine and phenobarbital may increase the metabolism of methadone and require that the dose of methadone be adjusted.

In patients with seizure disorders (52), valproic acid appears to be better tolerated than carbamazepine.

ZOLPIDEM

Zolpidem (Ambien) is an imidazopyridine hypnotic, chemically unrelated to the benzodiazepines. Although zolpidem is not chemically a benzodiazepine, its pharmacological profile is similar to a benzodiazepine, and it binds to a subunit of the same GABA/benzodiazepine receptor as the benzodiazepines (53, 54). Its sedative effects are reversed by the benzodiazepine antagonist, flumazenil. Zolpidem is rapidly absorbed and has a short half-life ($T_{1/2}$ = 2.2 hours). Its sedative effects are additive with alcohol. Like triazolam, zolpidem decreases brain metabolism of glucose (55).

Zolpidem has been extensively used in Europe, and only a few cases of abuse have been reported. In Italy (56), a case report suggests that some patients increase dosage many times that prescribed and that zolpidem produces a withdrawal syndrome similar to that of other sedative-hypnotics. The case histories illustrated significant tolerance to zolpidem and the rapid production of withdrawal symptoms that might be expected from a potent, short-acting sedative-hypnotic.

Some investigators suggest that zolpidem does not produce tolerance or physical dependence (57). Mice were administered zolpidem or midazolam (both 30 mg/kg) by gastric intubation for 10 days. Animals treated with midazolam, but not zolpidem, showed tolerance to the drug's sedative effects and lowered seizure threshold after the drug was stopped. Further, the benzodiazepine antagonist, flumazenil, precipitated withdrawal in the midazolam-treated animals, but not those treated with zolpidem.

Studies with baboons suggest that zolpidem is reinforcing and that it produces tolerance and physical dependence (58). In a free-choice paradigm, baboons consistently self-administered zolpidem intravenously at higher rates than either the vehicle solution alone or triazolam. After 2 weeks of zolpidem self-administration, substitution of the vehicle solution alone resulted in suppression of food pellet intake, which the investigators interpreted as zolpidem withdrawal. Baboons trained to discriminate oral doses of either phenobarbital (10 mg/kg) or lorazepam (1.8 mg/kg) from placebo responded to zolpidem as though it were the active drug more than 80% of the time. In another experiment, animals developed tolerance to zolpidem-induced ataxia and sedation over 7 days of drug administration. The investigators concluded that the rates of self-administration of zolpidem were similar to pentobarbital and higher than those maintained by 11 benzodiazepines that they had studied.

BUSPIRONE

Buspirone (BuSpar) is a anxiolytic that is not chemically or pharmacologically related to the benzodiazepines, barbiturates, or other sedative-hypnotics. Buspirone is not cross-tolerant with classical sedative-hypnotics and will not prevent acute benzodiazepine withdrawal signs and symptoms (59, 60) even when the buspirone is begun 4 weeks before benzodiazepine withdrawal is initiated (61).

From the neuropharmacology of benzodiazepine withdrawal, buspirone has been proposed as a potential adjunct in managing symptoms of withdrawal following acute withdrawal (62) and appears to have clinical utility in benzodiazepine discontinuation (47).

Buspirone's anxiolytic effects take days to weeks to develop. Buspirone has been proposed as an alternative to benzodiazepines in postdetoxification treatment of anxiety in patients who are alcohol or sedative-hypnotic dependent (63–68).

TRICYCLIC ANTIDEPRESSANTS

Tricyclic antidepressants are not drugs of abuse, although they are misused in several ways. They are commonly involved in suicide attempts. Amitriptyline (Elavil) and other tricyclics have sedative and other mood-altering effects that some patients find desirable, and they may escalate their dose and develop toxicity (69). Methadone-maintained patients use amitriptyline or other antidepressants to "boost" the sedative effects of methadone. Studies in the 1970s found that the frequency of urine samples positive for amitriptyline in methadone-maintained patients ranged from 2.5% (70) to 34% (71).

Tricyclic antidepressants sometimes become snared in the lexicon of drug abuse. For example, a case report of a woman who covertly took amitriptyline to induce seizures was reported as amitriptyline abuse (72).

Blood levels of desipramine may be increased in methadone-maintained patients, and smaller doses of tricyclics may be indicated when treating depression in methadone-maintained patients (73). Tricyclic antidepressants are commonly used in the treatment of cocaine abuse among methadone-maintained patients. Clinical trial of antidepressants in the treatment of cocaine abuse has shown mixed results, although improvement in cocaine abuse among depressed, methadone-maintained patients has been reported (74).

References

1. Wesson DR, Smith DE. Prescription drug abuse. Patient, physician, and cultural responsibilities. West J Med 1990;152(5):613–616.
2. Roy-Byrne P, Crowley D, eds. Benzodiazepines in clinical practice: risk and benefits. Washington, DC: American Psychiatric Press, 1991.
3. American Psychiatric Association Task Force on Benzodiazepine Dependency. Benzodiazepine dependency, toxicity, and abuse. Washington, DC: American Psychiatric Press, 1990.
4. American Psychiatric Association. Diagnostic and statistical manual of mental disorders: DSM-IV. Washington, DC: American Psychiatric Association, 1994.
5. Sellers EM, Ciraulo DA, DuPont RL, et al. Alprazolam and benzodiazepine dependence. J Clin Psychiatry 1993;54(10 [suppl]):64–75.
6. Iguchi MY, Handelsman L, Bickel WK, Griffiths RR. Benzodiazepine and sedative use/abuse by methadone maintenance clients. Drug Alcohol Depend 1993;32(3):257–266.
7. Barnas C, Rossman M, Roessler H, Riemer Y, Fleischhacker WW. Benzodiazepines and other psychotropic drugs abused by patients in a methadone maintenance program: familiarity and preference. Clin Neuropharmacol 1992;15 (suppl 1, pt A):110A–111A.
8. DuPont RL, Saylor KE. Marijuana and benzodiazepines in patients receiving methadone treatment [Letter]. JAMA 1989;261(23):3409.
9. Iguchi MY, Griffiths RR, Bickel WK, Handelsman L, Childress AR, McLellan AT. Relative abuse liability of benzodiazepines in methadone maintained populations in three cities. NIDA Res Monogr 1989;95:364–365.
10. Schuckit MA, Greenblatt D, Gold E, Irwin M. Reactions to ethanol and diazepam in healthy young men. J Stud Alcohol 1991;52(2): 180–187.
11. Shader RI, Pary RJ, Harmatz JS, Allison S, Locniskar A, Greenblatt DJ. Plasma concentrations and clinical effects after single oral doses of prazepam, clorazepate, and diazepam. J Clin Psychiatry 1984;45(10):411–413.
12. Calhoun SR, Wesson DR, Galloway GP, Smith D. Abuse of flunitrazepam (Rohypnol) and other benzodiazepines in Austin and South Texas. J Psychoactive Drugs 1996;28(2):183–189.
13. Nightingale S. New indication for alprazolam. JAMA 1990;264(22):2863.
14. Rickels K, Feighner JP, Smith WT. Alprazolam, amitriptyline, doxepin, and placebo in the treatment of depression. Arch Gen Psychiatry 1985; 42(2):134–141.
15. Kravitz HM, Fawcett J, Newman AJ. Alprazolam and depression: a review of risks and benefits. J Clin Psychiatry 1993;54(20 [suppl]): 78–84.
16. Noyes RJ, DuPont RLJ, Pecknold J, et al. Alprazolam in panic disorder and agoraphobia: results from a multicenter trial II. Patient acceptance, side effects, and safety. Arch Gen Psychiatry 1988;45:422–428.
17. Rosenbaum JF, Woods SW, Groves JE, Klerman GL. Emergence of hostility during alprazolam treatment. Am J Psychiatry 1984;141 (6):792–793.
18. Rapaport M, Braff DL. Alprazolam and hostility [Letter]. Am J Psychiatry 1985;142(1):146.
19. Gardner DL, Cowdry RW. Alprazolam-induced dyscontrol in borderline personality disorder. Am J Psychiatry 1985;142(1):98–100.
20. Kales A, Bixler EO, Vala-Bueno A, et al. Alprazolam: effects on sleep and withdrawal phenomena. J Clin Pharmacol 1987;27:508–515.
21. Lydiard RB, Laraia MT, Ballenger JC, Howell EF. Emergence of depressive symptoms in patients receiving alprazolam for panic disorder. Am J Psychiatry 1987;144(5):664–665.
22. Curran HV. Tranquilizing memories: a review of the effects of benzodiazepines on human memory. Biol Psychol 1986;23(2):179–213.
23. Brown CR. The use of benzodiazepines in prison populations. J Clin Psychiatry 1978;39 (3):219–222.
24. Ciraulo DA, Barnhill JG, Ciraulo AM, et al. Parental alcoholism as a risk factor in benzodiazepine abuse: a pilot study. Am J Psychiatry 1989;146:1333–1335.
25. Griffiths R, Roache J. Abuse liability of benzodiazepines. A review of human studies evaluating subjective and/or reinforcing effects. In: Smith D, Wesson D, eds. The benzodiazepines: current standards for medical practice. Hingham, MA: MTP Press; 1985:209–225.
26. Schmauss C, Apelt S, Emrich HM. The seeking and liking potentials of alprazolam [Letter]. Am J Psychiatry 1988;145(1):128.
27. Isbell H. Addiction to barbiturates and the barbiturate abstinence syndrome. Ann Intern Med 1950;33:108–120.
28. Hollister L, Motzenbecker E, Degan R. Withdrawal reactions from chlordiazepoxide (Librium). Psychopharmacologia 1961;2:63–68.
29. Hollister LE, Bennett LL, Kimbell I, Savage C, Overall JE. Diazepam in newly admitted schizophrenics. Dis Nerv Syst 1963;24(12):746–750.
30. Swartzburg M, Lieb J, Schwartz AH. Methaqualone withdrawal. Arch Gen Psychiatry 1973; 29:46–47.
31. Flemenbaum A, Gunby B. Ethchlorvynol (Placidyl) abuse and withdrawal. Dis Nerv Syst 1971;32(3):188–192.
32. Swanson LA, Okada T. Death after withdrawal of meprobamate. JAMA 1963;184(10): 780–781.
33. Lader M. History of benzodiazepine dependence. J Subst Abuse Treat 1991;8(1–2):53–59.
34. Covi L, Lipman RS, Pattison JH, Derogatis LR, Uhlenhuth EH. Length of treatment with anxiolytic sedatives and response to their sudden withdrawal. Acta Psychiatr Scand 1973;49: 51–64.
35. Smith D, Wesson D. A new method for treatment of barbiturate dependence. JAMA 1970; 213:294–295.
36. Smith D, Wesson D. A phenobarbital technique for withdrawal of barbiturate abuse. Arch Gen Psychiatry 1971;24:56–60.
37. Vestal RE, Rumack BH. Glutethimide dependence: phenobarbital treatment. Ann Intern Med 1974;80(5):670.
38. Garcia-Borreguero D, Bronisch T, Apelt S, Yassouridis A, Emrich HM. Treatment of benzodiazepine withdrawal symptoms with carbamazepine. Eur Arch Psychiatry Clin Neurosci 1991;241(3):145–150.
39. Neppe VM, Sindorf J. Carbamazepine for high-dose diazepam withdrawal in opiate users. J Nerv Ment Dis 1991;179(4):234–235.
40. Roy-Byrne PP, Sullivan MD, Cowley DS, Ries RK. Adjunctive treatment of benzodiazepine discontinuation syndromes: a review. J Psychiatr Res 1993;27(suppl 1):143–153.
41. Ries R, Cullison S, Horn R, Ward N. Benzodiazepine withdrawal: clinicians' ratings of carbamazepine treatment versus traditional taper methods. J Psychoactive Drugs 1991;23(1): 73–76.
42. Schweizer E, Rickels K, Case WG, Greenblatt DJ. Carbamazepine treatment in patients discontinuing long-term benzodiazepine therapy. Effects on withdrawal severity and outcome. Arch Gen Psychiatry 1991;48(5):448–452.
43. Roy-Byrne PP, Ward NG, Donnelly P. Valproate in anxiety and withdrawal syndromes. J Clin Psychiatry 1989;50:44–48.
44. Apelt S, Emrich HM. Sodium valproate in benzodiazepine withdrawal [Letter]. Am J Psychiatry 1990;147(7):950–951.
45. Fraser HF, Shaver MR, Maxwell ES, Isbell H, Wilker A. A fatal termination of barbiturate abstinence syndrome in man. J Pharmacol Exp Ther 1952;106:387.
46. McElroy SL, Keck PE, Jr, Lawrence JM. Treatment of panic disorder and benzodiazepine withdrawal with valproate [Letter]. J Neuropsychiatry Clin Neurosci 1991;3(2):232–233.
47. Rickels K, Case WG, Schweizer E, Garcia-Espana F, Fridman R. Benzodiazepine dependence: management of discontinuation. Psychopharmacol Bull 1990;26(1):63–68.
48. Ries RK, Roy-Byrne PP, Ward NG, Neppe V, Cullison S. Carbamazepine treatment for benzodiazepine withdrawal. Am J Psychiatry 1989; 146(4):536–537.
49. Klein E, Uhde TW, Post RM. Preliminary evidence for the utility of carbamazepine in alprazolam withdrawal. Am J Psychiatry 1986;143: 235–236.
50. Malcolm R, Ballenger JC, Sturgis ET, Anton R. Double-blind controlled trial comparing carbamazepine to oxazepam treatment of alcohol withdrawal. Am J Psychiatry 1989;146(5): 617–621.
51. Stuppaeck CH, Pycha R, Miller C, Whitworth AB, Oberbauer H, Fleischhacker WW. Carbamazepine versus oxazepam in the treatment of alcohol withdrawal: a double-blind study. Alcohol Alcohol 1992;27(2):153–158.
52. Richens A, Davidson DL, Cartlidge NE, Easter DJ. A multicentre comparative trial of sodium valproate and carbamazepine in adult onset epilepsy. J Neurol Neurosurg Psychiatry 1994; 57(6):682–687.
53. Byrnes JJ, Greenblatt DJ, Miller LG. Benzodi-

azepine receptor binding of nonbenzodiazepines in vivo: alpidem, zolpidem and zopiclone. Brain Res Bull 1992;29(6):905–908.

54. Langer SZ, Arbilla S, Benavides J, Scatton B. Zolpidem and alpidem: two imidazopyridines with selectivity for omega 1- and omega 3-receptor subtypes. Adv Biochem Psychopharmacol 1990;46:61–72.

55. Piercey MF, Hoffman WE, Cooper M. The hypnotics triazolam and zolpidem have identical metabolic effects throughout the brain: implications for benzodiazepine receptor subtypes. Brain Res 1991;554(1–2):244–252.

56. Cavallaro R, Regazzetti MG, Covelli G, Smeraldi E. Tolerance and withdrawal with zolpidem [Letter]. Lancet 1993;342(8867): 374–375.

57. Perrault G, Morel E, Sanger DJ, Zivkovic B. Lack of tolerance and physical dependence upon repeated treatment with the novel hypnotic zolpidem. J Pharmacol Exp Ther 1992;263 (1):298–303.

58. Griffiths RR, Sannerud CA, Ator NA, Brady JV. Zolpidem behavioral pharmacology in baboons: self-injection, discrimination, tolerance and withdrawal. J Pharmacol Exp Ther 1992;260 (3):1119–1208.

59. Lader M, Olajide D. A comparison of buspirone

and placebo in relieving benzodiazepine withdrawal symptoms. J Clin Psychopharmacol 1987;7(1):11–15.

60. Schweizer E, Rickels K. Failure of buspirone to manage benzodiazepine withdrawal. Am J Psychiatry 1986;143(12):1590–1592.

61. Ashton CH, Rawlins MD, Tyrer SP. A double-blind, placebo-controlled study of buspirone in diazepam withdrawal in chronic benzodiazepine users. Br J Psychiatry 1990;157(7):232–238.

62. File SE, Andrews N. Benzodiazepine withdrawal: behavioral pharmacology and neurochemical changes. Biochem Soc Symp 1993;59: 97–106.

63. Bruno F. Buspirone in the treatment of alcoholic patients. Psychopathology 1989;22(suppl 1): 49–59.

64. Kranzler HR, Meyer RE. An open trial of buspirone in alcoholics. J Clin Psychopharmacol 1989;9:379–380.

65. Malcolm R, Anton RF, Randall CL, Johnston A, Brady K, Thevos A. A placebo-controlled trial of buspirone in anxious inpatient alcoholics. Alcohol Clin Exp Res 1992;16:1007–1013.

66. Olivera AO, Servis S, Heard C. Anxiety disorders coexisting with substance dependence: treatment with buspirone. Curr Ther Res 1990; 47:52–61.

67. Taylor DP, Moon SL. Buspirone and related compounds as alternative anxiolytics. Neuropeptides 1991;19[suppl]:15–19.

68. Tollefson GC, Montague-Clouse J, Tollefson SL. Treatment of comorbid generalized anxiety in a recently detoxified alcoholic population with a selective serotonergic drug (buspirone). J Clin Psychopharmacol 1992;12: 19–26.

69. Delisle JD. A case of amitriptyline abuse [Letter]. Am J Psychiatry 1990;147(10):1377–1378.

70. Cantor R. Methadone maintenance and amitriptyline [Letter]. JAMA 1979;241(22): 1278.

71. Cohen MJ, Hanbury R, Stimmel B. Abuse of amitriptyline. JAMA 1978;240(13):1372–1373.

72. O'Rahilly S, Turner T, Wass J. Factitious epilepsy due to amitriptyline abuse. Irish Med J 1985;78(6):166–167.

73. Maany I, Dhopesh V, Arndt IO, Burke W, Woody G, O'Brien CP. Increase in desipramine serum levels associated with methadone treatment. Am J Psychiatry 1989;146(12):1611–1613.

74. Ziedonis DM, Kosten TR. Pharmacotherapy improves treatment outcome in depressed cocaine addicts. J Psychoactive Drugs 1991;23(4): 417–425.

20 HALLUCINOGENS

Robert N. Pechnick and J. Thomas Ungerleider

This chapter focuses on the major current and past hallucinogens of abuse: the prototype ergot hallucinogen lysergic acid diethylamide (LSD); other indolealkylamines such as psilocybin, psilocin, and dimethyltryptamine (DMT); and the phenethylamines, including mescaline, methylenedioxymethamphetamine (MDMA or "ecstasy"), methylenedioxyamphetamine (MDA or "Eve"), and dimethoxymethylamphetamine (DOM). Marihuana and phencyclidine (PCP), which are sometimes classified as hallucinogens, are covered in other chapters in this volume. Comprehensive reviews of hallucinogenic substances not covered in this chapter, such as the piperidyl benzilate esters, as well as the historical use of hallucinogens by other cultures, are available elsewhere (1–3).

In the 1990s, the "war on drugs" continues; however, the focus has begun to change with respect to the hallucinogens. First, there are now data indicating that the use of hallucinogens is on the rise, especially among adolescents. Thus, the trend of decreased use of the hallucinogens from the mid 1970s through the 1980s has begun to reverse. Second, although during the 1980s little research was conducted wherein humans were administered hallucinogens, over the last few years there has been a resurgence of clinical studies carried out under highly controlled conditions (4–10). The results obtained from controlled clinical studies should provide important and unbiased information, in contrast to some of the clinical data that previously have come from anecdotal information obtained from limited first-person accounts (11), "street pharmacologists," or from hospital emergency room records. Third, this resurgence in clinical research has taken place at the same time that there have been major advances regarding the possible mechanisms of action of the hallucinogens. For example, much more is now known about the effects of hallucinogens on the synthesis, release, and metabolism of indoleamines and catecholamines, and their interactions with specific pre- and postsynaptic receptor subtypes. Although in the past decade there had been an ever-widening discrepancy between our limited knowledge of the clinical pharmacology of the hallucinogens and information on their mechanisms of action obtained from preclinical studies, we now may be reaching a point where we can begin to develop a unified conceptual framework regarding the fundamental mechanisms underlying their pharmacological effects in humans. This chapter reviews the current information on the clinical effects of the hallucinogens, potential mechanisms of action, and the pathophysiological sequelae of their use. The reader also is directed to some other recent reviews (9, 12–14).

HISTORICAL PERSPECTIVE

To a large degree, the revolution in the drug abuse field that began in the United States in the mid-1960s and continues today came from concern over the use of hallucinogens, particularly LSD. A detailed consideration of these events provides a window to view how the widespread concern about drug abuse in the United States first began. Until the mid-1960s, the use of illicit drugs in the United States largely had been limited to specific populations or subcultures: heroin, used by those in the inner-city ghettos; marihuana, used by jazz musicians and Hispanic immigrants; and amphetamine and amphetamine analogues, originally used by women who had them prescribed for weight loss. Prescription antianxiety agents, including meprobamate and benzodiazepines such as chlordiazepoxide (Librium), also were commonly used at that time. Moreover, most Americans drank alcohol.

In the early 1960s, Timothy Leary, then a young psychology instructor at Harvard, began experimenting with hallucinogens, particularly LSD. He claimed that it provided instant happiness, enhanced creativity in art and music, facilitated problem-solving ability in school and at work, increased self-awareness, and might be useful as an adjunct to psychotherapy. Leary popularized this on college campuses, coining the phrase "turn on, tune in, drop out." When he was not reappointed to the faculty at Harvard he became a highly publicized self-proclaimed martyr to his cause, and his followers began to proselytize for LSD. Leary's advocates organized their lifestyle around LSD and developed a subculture of fellow LSD users who shared this common interest. They would never give it to anyone without their knowledge, and they would not use other classes of drugs. For example, they would not smoke tobacco, use amphetamine or amphetamine-like psychostimulants, barbiturates, or even drink alcohol. Thus, very little polydrug abuse occurred among these LSD users. In contrast to later patterns of hallucinogen use, the early users of LSD were older; a study published in 1968 revealed that the average age of persons using and in difficulty from LSD was 21 years (15). At that time the quality of street LSD ("Owsley's acid" or "Stanley's stuff") was equivalent to that made by legitimate chemists at Sandoz Laboratories, the original manufacturer of the drug.

The lay press repeatedly kept "discovering" LSD and, in effect, advertising it. As publicity increased, subcultures experimenting with LSD began to emerge in many East and West Coast cities. Other hallucinogenic compounds, such as mescaline and psilocybin, began to be taken as well, although LSD remained the most widely-used hallucinogen because it was the most readily available on the street. Musicians, rock music, the hippie lifestyle, and "flower children" were loosely joined with Leary's philosophy. There were highly publicized festivals celebrating LSD such as "The Summer of Love" in the Haight-Ashbury district of San Francisco. Later, younger individuals began to experiment with LSD, and its use began to increase in all socioeconomic groups, particularly middle-class and affluent youth. Moreover, many of these individuals also became active in various "protest" movements, speaking out against such governmental policies as the war in Vietnam and about other national issues such as civil rights and "free speech." About this time various adverse reactions began to be recorded from medical centers around the country. The whole phenomenon continued to be widely publicized, and in many cases sensationalized (16), by the press. The populace reacted with anxiety and fear, worrying that many of the young would soon become "acid-heads."

Eventually, many of the LSD users became involved in polydrug abuse, using other drugs besides hallucinogens. This included the extensive use of marihuana, hashish, and in some cases methamphetamine or even heroin. Various "street" substances, whose identity was frequently unknown, as well as combinations of drugs, were consumed. In addition, in the search for new drugs with different and improved characteristics, such as more or less euphoria, hallucinogenic activity or stimulant properties, longer or shorter duration of action, literally hundreds of so-called "designer drugs" were synthesized (DOM, MDMA, DMT, etc.).

Concern about drug abuse rose until it finally was perceived as one of the nation's most pressing problems, along with the economy and the war in Vietnam (17). The nation geared up to declare war on drug abuse, and the national drug abuse effort expanded from a relatively small research-oriented program under the National Institutes of Mental Health (NIMH) to the then newly created National Institute on Drug Abuse (NIDA) and the National Institute on Alcohol Abuse and Alcoholism (NIAAA). Eventually a new "super-agency," ADAMHA (Alcohol, Drug Abuse, and Mental Health Administration), was established to oversee NIDA, NIAAA, and NIMH. In 1995 the combined NIDA and NIAAA annual budgets have risen to more than $654 million dollars, and this does not include the Drug Enforcement Agency (DEA) or the Bureau of Alcohol, Tobacco and Firearms, who also have considerable budgets that are directed towards drug abuse enforcement. More recently, ADAMHA has merged into the National Institutes of Health (NIH).

By the mid-1960s more than a thousand articles on LSD had appeared in the medical literature. Sandoz Laboratories stopped distributing the drug in late 1966 due to the reported adverse reactions and the resulting public outcry. At that time all of the existing supplies of LSD were turned over to the government, which was to make the drug available for legitimate and highly controlled research; however, research on humans essentially was discontinued. Although some of the hallucinogens originally were developed and studied for use in chemical warfare, the results of these experiments have remained classified. Today, LSD, along with heroin and marihuana, remains classified as a Schedule I drug according to the Comprehensive Drug Abuse Prevention and Control Act of 1970. Legally, LSD is regarded as having no currently accepted medical use in the United States, a high potential for abuse, and to be unsafe even when administered by a physician. The thera-

peutic potential of LSD as an adjunct to psychotherapy, in the management of the dying patient, and in the treatment of alcoholism remains unresolved. Nevertheless, "black market" LSD has always been and remains widely available on the street.

DEFINITIONS AND TERMINOLOGY

The term *hallucinogen* means "producer of hallucinations." Many drugs, when taken in sufficient quantity, are psychoactive and can cause auditory and/or visual hallucinations. Such hallucinations may be present as part of a delirium, accompanied by disturbances in judgment, orientation, intellect, memory, emotion, and level of consciousness (e.g., organic brain syndrome). Delirium also may result from drug withdrawal (e.g., sedative-hypnotic withdrawal or delirium tremens in alcohol). The term *hallucinogen,* however, generally refers to compounds that alter consciousness without producing delirium, sedation, excessive stimulation, or intellectual or memory impairment as prominent effects. This label actually is inaccurate because true LSD-induced "hallucinations" are rare; what are commonly seen are illusory phenomena. An illusion is a perceptual distortion of an actual stimulus in the environment; to see someone's face seeming to be melting is an illusion; whereas to see a melting face when no face is present is a hallucination.

There are a variety of widely accepted synonyms for the hallucinogens, including the terms *psychedelic,* which was coined in 1957 by Osmond in the hope of finding a nonjudgmental term (18). Unfortunately, those who use the term *psychedelic* have been criticized as being "prodrug" much as those who use the term *hallucinogen* have been accused of being "antidrug." Other suggested names have included *phantastica, psychotaraxic, psycholeptic,* and *psychotomystic* (19–21). The term *psychotomimetic,* meaning "a producer of psychosis," also has been widely used. For a review of Lewin's (22) original terminology and a classification system for the hallucinogenic drugs, see Shulgin (1).

EPIDEMIOLOGY

The epidemiological data on the use of hallucinogens centers on the use of LSD and, more recently, MDMA. Both the use of LSD and its availability decreased from the mid-1970s through the 1980s (23). These downward trends appear to be reversing in the 1990s (14, 24). In 1992 there was an increase in prevalence in the use of LSD by school-age children and young adults, but there are indications that since that time increases have continued only in high school students (24). In 1994, the annual prevalence rates for LSD use were 7% in high school students and 5% in college students, and the lifetime prevalence rates for LSD and hallucinogens were 3.7% and 2.2% for students in the eighth grade, and 13.8% and 7.4%, respectively, in young adults (24). There are ethnic differences in the use of hallucinogens; in the twelfth grade whites have the highest usage of LSD and hallucinogens compared to blacks and Hispanics (24). Other studies have shown higher rates of hallucinogen usage. For example, a random survey of Tulane University undergraduates in 1990 indicated that the number of students reporting having tried LSD was more than 17% (25).

Hallucinogens appear to be readily available on the street. In 1994 more than 24% of 18-year-olds said that they were "exposed" (friends using drug or around people using drug) to LSD, whereas 14% said that they were "exposed" to other hallucinogens (24). Aside from increases in prevalence and use of hallucinogens, there also have been changes in attitudes towards their use. In high school students there has been a decrease in the proportions disapproving of LSD use and associating risk with its use; in contrast, older groups are more likely to perceive LSD as dangerous (24). These changes in attitude are likely linked to the increase in use in those age groups.

The lifetime prevalence of MDMA use in young adults in 1994 was estimated to be 3.8% (24); however, a random survey of Tulane University undergraduates in 1990 indicated that 23% of the respondents reporting trying either MDMA or mescaline/psilocybin (25). Moreover, it was found that the number of students trying MDMA increased from 1986 to 1990. A study published in 1987 found that 39% of randomly polled undergraduates at Stanford University had used MDMA at least once (26). Therefore, the use of some hallucinogens among certain populations could be far greater than currently appreciated. However, it is important to note that it has been reported that college students show annual usage of LSD and hallucinogens that is not greater than non–college-enrolled peers; in fact, college students show a lower annual usage of MDMA compared to non–college-enrolled peers (24).

PATTERNS OF ABUSE

In the 1960s, LSD was used primarily by those interested in its ability to alter perceptual experiences (sight, sound, taste, and even feeling states). Much attention was paid to *set,* the expectation of what the drug experience would be like, and *setting,* the environment in which the drug was used. The early drug missionaries promulgated the erroneous notion that only good LSD "trips" would result if the prospective user ensured a number of pre-conditions before their drug experience. Those relating to set included:

- being relaxed and largely stress/anxiety free;
- having no major resentment or anger and no recent arguments at home, school or work;
- freeing up several days, often an entire weekend, for the drug experience and its aftermath.

Those relating to setting included:

- having a close friend present as a sitter or guide for the experience;
- being in quiet, comfortable surroundings, particularly outdoors, or sitting on soft, thick carpeting;
- listening to pleasant sounds (originally, the music of Ravi Shankar);
- reading reassuring passages (originally, from the *Tibetan Book of the Dead.*)

In more recent times users often attended concerts, dances ("raves") or films (particularly psychedelic or brightly colored ones) during the drug experience. Use is rarely more than once weekly because tolerance to LSD and other hallucinogens occurs so rapidly (see later section "Effects of Chronic Use").

CHEMICAL CLASSIFICATION

The commonly abused hallucinogenic substances can be classified according to their chemical structure. Figure 20.1 shows the structures of these hallucinogens. Note that all of these drugs are organic compounds and some occur naturally.

Indolealkylamines

All of the indole-type hallucinogens have structural similarities to the neurotransmitter serotonin (5-hydroxytryptamine [5-HT]), suggesting that their mechanism of action could involve the alteration of serotonergic neurotransmission.

LYSERGIC ACID DERIVATIVES

Lysergic acid is one of the constituents of the ergot fungus that grows on rye. It has inadvertently been baked into bread, with profound mental changes occurring in those who consumed it (27). Because the presence of the diethylamide group is a prerequisite for hallucinogenic activity, it is not clear whether these reported epidemics actually were due to ergot in the bread, or to some other related substances or (psychological) phenomena. LSD was first synthesized by Hofmann in 1938, and it was called LSD-25 because it was the 25th compound made in this series of experiments on ergot derivatives. In 1943, Hofmann accidentally ingested some of the compound, and soon had the first LSD "trip," a famous bicycle ride home from his laboratory. The seeds of the morning glory (*Ipomoea*) contain lysergic acid derivatives, particularly lysergic acid amide. Although they are packaged commercially, many varieties, such as Heavenly Blue and Pearly Gates, have been treated with insecticides, fungicides, and other toxic chemicals.

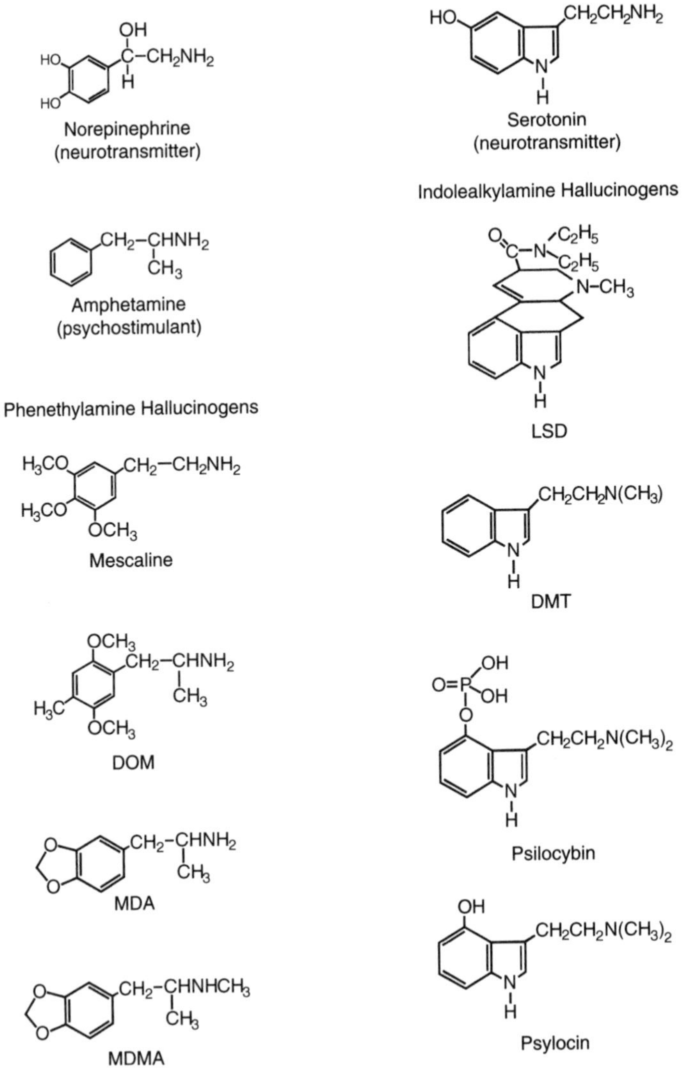

Figure 20.1. Structures of phenethylamine- and indolealkylamine-type hallucinogens.

SUBSTITUTED TRYPTAMINES

Psilocybin and *psilocin* occur naturally in a variety of mushrooms that have hallucinogenic properties. The most publicized is the Mexican or "magic" mushroom, *Psilocybe mexicana,* which contains both psilocybin and psilocin, as do some of the other *Psilocybe* and *Conocybe* species. *Dimethyltryptamine* (DMT), although found in small concentrations in certain plants, is usually produced synthetically.

Substituted Phenethylamines

The substituted phenethylamine-type hallucinogens are structurally related to the catecholamine neurotransmitters dopamine, norepinephrine and epinephrine.

MESCALINE

Mescaline is a naturally occurring hallucinogen present in the peyote cactus (*Lophophora williamsii* or *Anhalonium lewinii*), which is found in the Southwestern United States and Northern Mexico. Peyote was used by the Indians in these areas in highly structured tribal religious rituals.

PHENYLISOPROPYLAMINES

The phenylisopropylamine hallucinogens *2,5-dimethoxy-4-methylamphetamine* (DOM or STP, from "serenity, tranquility and peace"), *3,4-methylenedioxyamphetamine* (MDA or "Eve"), and *3,4-methylenedioxymethamphetamine* (MDMA or "ecstasy") are synthetic compounds and are structurally similar to mescaline as well as the psychostimulant amphetamine. They have inaccurately been called "psychotomimetic amphetamines," and sometimes are referred to as "stimulant-hallucinogens." It should be pointed out that literally hundreds of analogues of the aforementioned compounds have been synthesized (11) and sometimes are found on the street, the so-called "designer drugs."

ACUTE PSYCHOLOGICAL EFFECTS

The overall psychological effects of many of the hallucinogens are quite similar; however, the rate of onset, duration of action, and absolute intensity of the effects differ among the drugs. Moreover, the various hallucinogens vary widely in potency and the slope of the dose-response curve. Thus, some of the apparent qualitative differences among hallucinogens may be due, in part, to the amount of drug ingested relative to its specific dose-response characteristics.

LSD is one of the most potent hallucinogens known, with behavioral effects occurring in some individuals after doses as low as 20 micrograms. Typical street doses range from 50 to 300 micrograms. Because of its high potency, LSD can be applied to paper blotters or the backs of postage stamps. The absorption of LSD from the gastrointestinal tract occurs rapidly, with drug diffusion to all tissues, including the brain. The onset of psychological and behavioral effects occurs approximately 60 minutes after oral administration, peaks 2 to 4 hours after administration, with a gradual return to the predrug state in 10 to 12 hours. Both Hofmann (28) and Hollister (2) have described the effects of LSD in great detail.

The first 4 hours are sometimes called a "trip." The subjective effects of LSD are dramatic (2), and can be divided into somatic (dizziness, paresthesias, weakness, and tremor), perceptual (altered visual sense and changes in hearing), and psychic (changes in mood, dreamlike feelings, altered time sense, and depersonalization). The somatic symptoms usually occur first. Later, visual alterations are marked and sounds are intensified. Visual distortions and illusory phenomena occur, but true hallucinations are rare. Dreamlike imagery may develop when the eyes are closed, and afterimages are prolonged. Sensory input becomes mixed together, and synesthesia ("seeing" smells, "hearing" colors) is commonly reported. Touch is magnified and time is markedly distorted. Feelings of attainment of true insight are common, as is the experience of delusional ideation. Separating one object from another and self from environment becomes difficult, and depersonalization can develop. Emotions become intensified, and extreme lability may be observed, with rapid and extreme changes in affect. Several emotional feelings may occur at the same time. Performance on tests involving attention, concentration, and motivation is impaired. Several hours later, subjects sometimes feel that the drug is no longer active, but later they recognize that at that time they had paranoid thoughts and ideas of reference. This is a regular but little publicized aftereffect which finally dissipates 10 to 12 hours after the dose. From 12 to 24 hours after the trip there may be some slight letdown or a feeling of fatigue. There is no immediate craving to take more drug to relieve this boredom; one trip usually produces "satiation" for some time. Memory for the events that occurred during the trip is quite clear.

DMT produces effects that are similar to those produced by LSD, but DMT is inactive after oral administration and must be injected, sniffed, or smoked. It has a rapid onset, almost immediately after intravenous administration, and a short duration of action, about 30 minutes (8). Because of its short duration of action, DMT was once known as the "businessman's LSD" (i.e., one could have a psychedelic experience during the lunch hour and be back at work in the afternoon). However, the sudden and rapid onset of a period of altered perceptions that soon terminates is disconcerting to some. DMT has never been a widely, steadily available or popular drug on the streets.

In contrast to DMT, the effects of DOM have a very slow onset, but it has been reported to last more than 24 hours.

Mescaline is approximately two to three orders of magnitude less potent than LSD, and its effects last about 6 to 10 hours.

It is not clear whether the stimulant hallucinogens, MDMA and MDA, should be classified with the other hallucinogens. Acute effects of MDMA include euphoria, increased physical and emotional energy, and heightened sensual awareness (29). Both MDA and MDMA produce fewer perceptual phenomena, less emotional lability, less depersonalization, and fewer disturbances of thought than do other hallucinogens (4, 29–30). Martin and Sloan (31), using three criteria for characterizing LSD-like drugs, have categorized MDA as "probably LSD-like, but with other properties." MDMA and MDA do have some properties in common with other hallucinogens. For example, in rats trained to discriminate mescaline from saline, both MDMA and MDA produced mescaline-like discrimination responses (32). As would be expected from their structural resemblance to amphetamine, MDMA and MDA have psychostimulant properties, and they do reduce appetite. However, unlike the other hallucinogens, MDMA is self-administered by monkeys, possibly due to its psychostimulant properties (33).

AUTONOMIC AND OTHER EFFECTS

The hallucinogens also possess significant autonomic activity. LSD produces marked pupillary dilation, hyperreflexia, increases in blood pressure and body temperature, tremor, piloerection, and tachycardia. Some of these autonomic effects of the hallucinogens are variable and might be due, in part, to the anxiety state of the user. DMT also increases heart rate, pupil diameter, and body temperature (7), and MDA and MDMA increase heart rate and blood pressure (6, 10, 29), possibly due to their amphetamine-like effects. LSD also can cause nausea, and nausea and vomiting are especially noteworthy after the ingestion of mescaline or peyote. The hallucinogens also alter neuroendocrine function. For example, in humans DMT and MDMA have been found to elevate plasma levels of ACTH, cortisol, and prolactin (7, 10), and MDE has been found to elevate serum cortisol levels (6). Similarly, LSD (34), the hallucinogen DOI [1-(2,5-dimethoxy-4-iodophenyl)-2-aminopropane] (35), and MDMA (36) increase plasma glucocorticoids in the rat.

EFFECTS OF CHRONIC USE

A high degree of tolerance develops to the behavioral effects of LSD after repeated administration. Such behavioral tolerance develops very rapidly, after only several days of daily administration, and tolerance is also lost rapidly after the individual stops taking the drug for several days. Because of this rapid development of tolerance, LSD users usually limit themselves to taking the drug once or twice weekly (37). Cross-tolerance develops between LSD and other hallucinogens such as mescaline and psilocybin, suggesting a similar mechanism of action. However, cross-tolerance does not develop to other classes of psychotropic agents that are thought to have different underlying mechanisms of action, such as amphetamine, phencyclidine, and marihuana. It should be pointed out that little tolerance develops to the various autonomic effects produced by the hallucinogens. There is no withdrawal syndrome after the cessation of the chronic administration of the hallucinogens.

MECHANISMS OF ACTION

The exact mechanisms of action of LSD and other hallucinogens still remain unclear. LSD affects the electrical activity of neurons in the locus ceruleus and certain cortical regions, and at a systems level, these effects could change how the brain handles sensory information as well as alter cognitive and perceptual processing (13). Although hallucinogenic drugs interact with several neurotransmitter systems (38), their ability to alter neurotransmission mediated by the neurotransmitter serotonin appears to be of critical importance (39, 40). It is important to note that an ever increasing number of serotonin receptors have been identified, and the terminology for these serotonin receptor families and subtypes is in a state of flux (41–43). Some of the receptors have been renamed and/or reclassified, and caution must be used in comparing results and conclusions drawn from older studies with the nomenclature currently used.

Early on it was noted that many hallucinogens, including LSD, were structurally similar to serotonin (see Fig. 20.1). Later, studies demonstrated that LSD could block the contractile effects of serotonin in isolated smooth muscle preparations, suggesting that LSD might produce its psychic effects by having similar antagonist activity at central serotonergic synapses. However, it was found that brom-LSD, an LSD analogue that does not produce hallucinations, also has serotonergic antagonist activity. Thus, the mechanism of the hallucinogenic activity of LSD could not be explained solely by its direct serotonergic antagonist activity.

In 1961, Freedman (44) was the first to provide direct evidence that LSD acted upon serotonergic systems within the central nervous system. He found that LSD increases the levels of serotonin in rat brain, but decreases the levels of serotonin metabolites, whereas the non-hallucinogenic analogue brom-LSD failed to have the same effects. As brom-LSD does not produce hallucinatory phenomena, these results suggested that the hallucinogenic effects of LSD might be due to LSD-induced decreases in serotonin turnover (synthesis and release) in the brain. Other evidence supporting the interaction of hallucinogens with serotonergic systems: (a) the chronic administration of monoamine oxidase inhibitors decreases the density of serotonin receptors and reduces the behavioral effects of LSD (45, 46), and (b) treatments that decrease brain levels of serotonin (e.g., lesions, reserpine, parachloroamphetamine or other neurotoxins), up-regulate postsynaptic serotonin receptors and increase the behavioral effects of LSD (39).

Aghajanian and coworkers (47) found that LSD inhibits the firing of serotonergic neurons in the dorsal raphe nucleus, most likely by interacting with presynaptic autoreceptors (48), now termed 5-HT_{1A} receptors. Other indole-type hallucinogens, such as psilocin and DMT, also produce this effect (48). A decrease in firing rate of serotonergic neurons would account for Freedman's (44) observation that LSD increases the levels of serotonin, but decreases the levels of serotonin metabolites. However, strong evidence refutes a direct linkage between the presynaptic effects of LSD and its hallucinogenic activity: (a) phenethylamine hallucinogens, such as mescaline, do not have the same inhibitory effects on the firing of serotonergic neurons (49); (b) there is no correlation between the activity of drugs at presynaptic 5-HT_{1A} receptors and their hallucinogenic activity (13); and (c) tolerance does not develop to the effects of the hallucinogens on neuronal firing, but behavioral tolerance rapidly develops after the repeated administration of hallucinogens (50). These findings suggest that interactions with presynaptic 5-HT_{1A} receptors cannot be the sole mechanism of action of the hallucinogens, and other factors must be involved.

Both indole- and phenethylamine-type hallucinogens have been found to bind to the serotonin 5-HT_{2A} receptor subtype (formerly called the 5-HT_2 receptor) (51–56), where they act as agonists or partial agonists (54, 56). This receptor subtype is found in high concentrations in cortical and limbic regions (57), and interactions with these receptors appear to underlie the mechanism of action of the hallucinogens. For example: (a) there are very high correlations between the binding affinities of both indolealkylamine- and phenethylamine-type hallucinogens for the 5-HT_{2A} receptor and their hallucinogenic activity in humans and their potency in behavioral studies in laboratory animals (51, 56); (b) the chronic administration of LSD, but not the nonhallucinogenic analogue brom-LSD, has been found to decrease the density of 5-HT_{2A} receptors, an effect that would be associated with the development of tolerance to the behavioral effects of LSD (58); and (c) in preclinical studies it has been found that many of the effects of hallucinogens are blocked by 5-HT_{2A} receptor antagonists (56, 59).

Even though the interaction of hallucinogens with 5-HT_{2A} receptors appears to be critical, other serotonergic receptor subtypes also might be involved. For example, interactions with the closely related 5-HT_{2C} receptors (formerly called 5-HT_{1C} receptors) might contribute to the psychoactive effects (53, 60). Although apparently not critical for hallucinogenic activity, interactions with presynaptic 5-HT_{1A} receptors might contribute to the effects of some hallucinogens. The differential interactions of the various hallucinogens with numerous sites and systems might underlie the qualitative differences between the drugs. However, the commonality of interactions with 5-HT_{2A} receptors suggests that selective 5-HT_{2A} receptor antagonists might be useful in blocking the behavioral effects of the hallucinogens in humans.

Like amphetamine and amphetamine-like analogues, MDMA and MDA cause the release of both dopamine and serotonin (61, 62). Both drugs bind to serotonin 5-HT_{2A} receptors, but they do so with relatively low affinity (52–54), suggesting that their psychoactive effects are not mediated by direct interactions with this receptor subtype. These characteristics, along with the differences in the subjective effects that they produce compared to the "classical" hallucinogens, support the conjecture that MDMA and MDA should not be classified with the other hallucinogens.

ADVERSE REACTIONS

Strassman (63) has characterized adverse reactions according to the temporal relationship between drug exposure and symptomatology, with acute and chronic reactions at the end of the continuum, and delayed (subsequent panic attacks) and intermittent (flashback phenomena) between the ends of the continuum. Although the existence of some of the acute adverse reactions is clear-cut and not subject to debate, some of the purported long-term adverse effects remain controversial. One of the problems is that many of the studies reporting long-term adverse reactions lack adequate predrug data.

Acute Adverse Reactions

Social factors, media presentations, and public fear all have shaped perceptions of the effects of LSD and other hallucinogens. A person's reaction to the effects of a drug may be felt to be either a pleasant or an unpleasant experience; a perceptual distortion or illusion may cause intense anxiety in one person and be a pleasant and amusing interlude in another. Individuals who place a premium on self-control, advance planning, and impulse restriction may do particularly poorly on LSD. Traumatic and stressful external events can precipitate an adverse reaction (e.g., being arrested and read one's rights in the middle of a pleasant experience may precipitate an anxiety reaction). Prediction of who will have an acute (or other) adverse reaction is unreliable (15), and the occurrence of multiple previous pleasurable LSD experiences renders no immunity from an adverse reaction. Adverse reactions have occurred after doses of LSD as low as 40 micrograms, and no adverse effects have been observed in some individuals after ingesting 2000 micrograms, although in general the hallucinogenic effects are proportional to dosage levels. Thus, acute adverse behavioral reactions generally are not dose-related, but a function of personal predisposition, setting, and circumstance. Because of the perceptual distortions (and subsequent deficits in judgment), there is always the risk that self-destructive behavior will occur. Some of the adverse reactions that occur after ingesting hallucinogens can be due to other contaminants in the product, such as strychnine, phencyclidine, or amphetamine. Once commonly reported by medical facilities (64), acute adverse LSD reactions are rarely seen today, yet the drug remains in use. Moreover, the paucity of users seeking emergency medical treatment may reflect increased knowledge of how to deal with such situations on the part of the "drug-using community."

Acute anxiety or panic reactions, the so-called "bad trip," are the most commonly reported acute adverse reactions. They usually wear off before medical intervention is sought; most LSD is metabolized and excreted within 24 hours, and acute panic reactions usually subside within this time frame. Depression with suicidal ideation can occur several days after LSD use (65).

Paranoid ideation, "hallucinations," and a confusional state (organic brain syndrome) are other commonly reported acute adverse reactions (66, 67). Initially it was thought that LSD could replicate the signs and symptoms of schizophrenia in some subjects, and the induction of such a model psychosis could be used to study and potentially find a cure for this major psychiatric illness. These hopes did not materialize, as major differences have been found between hallucinogen-induced psychosis and the schizophrenic state (68). More recently, using single photon emission computed tomography (SPECT), it was found that the administration of mescaline to controls produced a "hyperfrontal" pattern, whereas "hypofrontality" has been observed in schizophrenics (4).

Diagnostically, it is important to make a differential diagnosis between

LSD psychosis and paranoid schizophrenia, particularly since patients, who in fact are paranoid, now often complain of being poisoned with LSD. A history of prior mental illness, a psychiatric examination that reveals the absence of an intact or observing ego, and auditory (rather than visual) hallucinations all suggest schizophrenia. Other drug-induced psychoses, including those from psychostimulants or PCP, must be ruled out. An organic brain syndrome in general speaks against LSD, especially when obtunded consciousness is present. Toxicologic analysis of body fluids can be helpful in making the ultimate diagnosis, but supportive treatment must not be withheld. Atropine poisoning can be differentiated by the presence of prominent anticholinergic effects such as dry mouth and blurred vision. Patients with amphetamine psychosis often fail to differentiate their perceptual distortions from reality, whereas LSD users are aware of the difference.

In terms of adverse physiological effects, LSD has a very high therapeutic index. An elephant was killed after the experimental administration of a massive dose relative to brain weight, 0.15 mg/kg, or approximately 300,000 micrograms of LSD (19). The lethal dose in humans has not been determined, and fatalities that have been reported usually are secondary to perceptual distortions with resultant accidental death (e.g., "flying" off a roof, merging with an oncoming automobile on the freeway) (69). Hemiplegia has been reported after taking LSD, possibly due to the production of vasospasm (70).

Users of MDMA have reported nausea, jaw clenching and teeth grinding, increased muscle tension, and blurred vision. Less common adverse effects include anxiety, panic attacks, and psychosis. A type of "hangover" the day after taking the drug has been described, manifested by insomnia, fatigue, drowsiness, sore jaw muscles, loss of balance, and headache (29). Hyperthermia, rhabdomyolysis, and hepatotoxicity can occur, and there have been a few reports of death after ingestion of the drug (71, 72). In a controlled setting, the administration of MDA produced episodes of anxiety, a toxic psychosis, and dysphoria (5).

Treatment of Acute Adverse Reactions

Treatment of the acute adverse reactions to hallucinogens first must be directed toward preventing the patient from physically harming self or others. Anxiety can be handled by means of interpersonal support and reassurance. Psychotherapeutic intervention consists of reassurance, placing the patient in a quiet room, and avoidance of physical intrusion until the patient begins to calm down. The use of a benzodiazepine, such as lorazepam, also can be effective. The oral route can be used for administering such medication in mildly agitated patients; however, it can be difficult to convince severely agitated and/or paranoid patients to swallow a pill, in which case parenteral administration might be necessary. Severely agitated patients who fail to respond to a benzodiazepine may be given a neuroleptic agent. Caution must be used in administering neuroleptics as they can lower the seizure threshold and elicit seizures, especially if the hallucinogen has been cut with an agent that has convulsant activity, such as strychnine. Phenothiazines, such as chlorpromazine, given orally or intramuscularly can end an LSD trip and have been found effective in treating LSD-induced psychosis (20, 73–75). Because anticholinergic crises can develop with chlorpromazine in combination with other drugs with anticholinergic activity (PCP and DOM), haloperidol is a safer drug to use when the true nature of the drug ingested is unknown. It has been suggested that a combination of intramuscular haloperidol and lorazepam is particularly effective in treating acute adverse reactions (76). Theoretically, selective $5\text{-}HT_{2A}$ antagonists should block the effects of hallucinogens; however, other drugs with significant $5\text{-}HT_{2A}$ antagonist activity (clozapine and risperidone) also might be effective (13).

Drug Interactions

Drugs interactions involving the hallucinogens do not appear to be an important source of adverse reactions. There are reports that the effects of LSD are reduced after the chronic administration of monoamine oxidase inhibitors or specific serotonin reuptake inhibitor antidepressants such as fluoxetine (77–80), whereas the effects of LSD are increased after the chronic administration of lithium or tricyclic antidepressants (79, 80).

Long-Term Adverse Effects

Chronic adverse reactions include psychoses, depressive reactions, acting out, paranoid states, and flashbacks (21, 81). Flashbacks have been a well-publicized adverse reaction. They now have been renamed "hallucinogen persisting perception disorder," and have specific diagnostic criteria (82). In the past, the use of variable definitions of what constitutes a flashback was a major problem (83), and hopefully the establishment of specific diagnostic criteria will facilitate studying and understanding this problem. Only a small proportion of LSD and other hallucinogenic users experience flashbacks (84). They can occur spontaneously a number of weeks or months after the original drug experience, appear not to be dose-related, and can develop after a single exposure to the drug (85). During a flashback, the original drug experience is recreated complete with perceptual and reality distortion. Even a previously pleasant drug experience may be accompanied by anxiety when the person realizes that they have no control over its recurrence. In time flashbacks decrease in intensity, frequency, and duration (although initially they usually last only a few seconds), whether treated or not. Flashbacks may or may not be precipitated by stressors or the subsequent use of other psychoactive drugs, such as psilocybin or marihuana. The administration of specific serotonin reuptake inhibitor antidepressants has been reported to initiate or exacerbate flashbacks in individuals with a history of LSD use (86). Flashbacks usually can be handled with psychotherapy. An anxiolytic or neuroleptic may be indicated, but probably is as much for the reassurance of the therapist as for the patient. The exact mechanism underlying this phenomenon remains obscure. Individuals with flashbacks have a high lifetime incidence of affective disorder compared to non–LSD-abusing substance abusers (67). LSD users have been shown to have long-term changes in visual function (12, 87, 88). For example, a visual disturbance consisting of prolonged afterimages (palinopsia) has been found in individuals several years after the last reported use of LSD (89). Such changes in visual function might underlie flashbacks.

Psychosis can develop and persist after hallucinogen use, but it remains unclear whether hallucinogen use can "cause" long-term psychosis, or if it has a role in precipitating the onset of illness. For example, hallucinogens may have a variety of effects in a person who is genetically predisposed to schizophrenia: (a) they may cause the psychosis to manifest at an earlier age; (b) they may produce a psychosis that would have remained dormant if drugs had not been used; or (c) they may cause relapse in a person who has previously suffered a psychotic disorder (68). Although there is some evidence that prolonged psychotic reactions tend to occur in individuals with poor premorbid adjustment, a history of psychiatric illness and/or repeated use of hallucinogens, severe and prolonged illness has been reported in individuals without such a history (63).

Chronic personality changes with a shift in attitudes and evidence of magical thinking can occur after the use of hallucinogens. There is always the risk that such thinking can lead to destructive behavior, in acute as well as chronic reactions. The effects of the chronic use of LSD must be differentiated from the effects of personality disorders, particularly in those who use a variety of drugs in polydrug abuse patterns. In some individuals with well-integrated personalities and with no previous psychiatric history, chronic personality changes have resulted from repeated LSD use. Personality changes that result from LSD use can occur after a single experience, unlike other classes of drugs (PCP, perhaps, excepted) (81). In addition, the hallucinogenic drugs interact in a variety of nonspecific ways with the personality, which may particularly impair the developing adolescent (73). The suggestibility that may come from many experiences with LSD may be reinforced by the social values of a particular subculture in which the drug is used. For example, if some of these subcultures embrace withdrawal from society, that is to say, a noncompetitive approach toward life, the person who "withdraws" after the LSD experience may be suffering from a side effect that represents more of a change in social values than a true drug effect. Treatment of chronic hallucinogen abuse can include psychotherapy on a long-term basis in order to determine what needs are being fulfilled by the use of the drug for this particular person. Twelve-step meetings also might be crucial for reinforcement of the decision to remain abstinent.

There is no generally accepted evidence of brain cell damage, chromosomal abnormalities, or teratogenic effects after the use of the indole-type hallucinogens and mescaline (63). However, great controversy currently surrounds the possible neurotoxic effects of MDMA and MDA in humans (29). The controversy centers on the suitability of extrapolating results from studies using laboratory animals to human MDMA users, the way in which neurotoxicity is defined, and the degree and manner in which neurochemical changes caused by exposure to MDMA diminish over time. The issue of potential neurotoxic effects of MDMA is made more meaningful because of the high use of this drug in some populations (25, 26).

In 1985, Ricaurte et al. (90) reported that MDA produced long-lasting changes in brain serotonergic systems, and similar effects later were found after the administration of MDMA (91). The neurotoxic effects of both MDA and MDMA appear to be limited to serotonergic neurons, causing degeneration of serotonergic cell bodies and axons, decreases in the levels of enzymes involved in the biosynthesis of serotonin, and long-term depletions of serotonin, serotonin metabolites, and serotonin reuptake sites (91–95). Even though LSD affects serotonergic neurotransmission, the administration of massive doses of LSD does not damage serotonergic neurons. In contrast, a single dose of MDMA approximately three times higher than the typical "street" dose has been shown to affect central serotonergic systems for several weeks in rodents, and in some studies neurochemical markers did not return to normal until one year after drug administration. Moreover, it is not apparent whether there is actual regeneration of neurons or only compensatory changes in the remaining undamaged neurons. The neurotoxic effects of MDMA appear to be a function of total exposure, that is, both the dose administered and the number of times the drug was given.

The exact mechanism of MDMA-induced neurotoxicity is unknown, and might be due to MDMA itself or involve the formation of a neurotoxic metabolite.

MDMA-induced neurotoxicity has been found in nonhuman primates (29), but it is not known whether similar effects occur in humans. Moreover, it is not clear whether these changes in serotonergic neurons have functional consequences, either in laboratory animals or humans. Studies have found decreased levels of the serotonin metabolite 5-hydroxyindoleacetic acid (5-HIAA) (96, 97), differences in personality traits (97), and alterations in sleep patterns (98) in MDMA users. Although the subjective effects of DMT are not different (8), the pupillary response to DMT are reduced (7) in subjects who had a history of MDMA use. Thus, to date the physiological and psychological changes found in MDMA users have been subtle.

Although the functional consequences of alterations in serotonergic neurotransmission in young users are unknown, it is possible that some effects of MDMA-induced toxicity will manifest themselves as the users age. Cells die as part of the aging process, and if exposure to MDMA kills or, for that matter, damages or weakens a certain proportion of cells, cell loss due to aging could be compounded, producing substantial impairment in the functioning of specific cell groups and/or neurochemical systems. As serotonergic systems have been implicated in the control of sleep, food intake, sexual behavior, anxiety, and mood, disruption due to cell loss could have major consequences. The actual functional consequences of MDMA exposure remain to be determined.

Acknowledgments. *The authors would like to thank Mr. Michael P. Bova for preparing the figure. R. N. P. (Robert N. Pechnick) is supported by the National Institute on Drug Abuse.*

References

1. Shulgin AT. Psychotomimetic drugs: structure-activity relationships. In: Iversen LL, Iversen SD, Snyder SH, eds. Handbook of psychopharmacology. New York: Plenum Press, 1978; 11:243–333.
2. Hollister LE. Psychotomimetic drugs in man. In: Iversen LL, Iversen SD, Snyder SH, eds. Handbook of psychopharmacology. New York: Plenum Press, 1978;11:389–424.
3. Siegel RK. The natural history of hallucinogens. In: Jacobs BL, ed. Hallucinogens: neurochemical, behavioral, and clinical perspectives. New York: Raven Press, 1984:1–18.
4. Hermle L, Fünfgeld M, Oepen G, et al. Mescaline-induced psychopathological, neuropsychological, and neurometabolic effects in normal subjects: experimental psychosis as a tool for psychiatric research. Biol Psychiatry 1992;32: 976–991.
5. Hermle L, Spitzer M, Borchardt D, Kovar K-A, Gouzoulis E. Psychological effects of MDE in normal subjects. Neuropsychopharmacology 1993;8:171–176.
6. Gouzoulis E, von Bardeleben U, Rupp A, Kovar K.-A., Hermle L. Neuroendocrine and cardiovascular effects of MDE in healthy volunteers. Neuropsychopharmacology 1993;8:187–193.
7. Strassman RJ, Qualls CR. Dose-response study of N,N-dimethyltryptamine in humans. I. Neuroendocrine, autonomic and cardiovascular effects. Arch Gen Psychiatry 1994;51:85–97.
8. Strassman RJ, Qualls CR, Uhlenhuth EH, Kellner R. Dose-response study of N,N-dimethyltryptamine in humans. II. Subjective effects and preliminary results of a new rating scale. Arch Gen Psychiatry 1994;51:98–108.
9. Strassman RJ. Hallucinogenic drugs in psychiatric research and treatment; perspectives and prospects. J Nerv Ment Dis 1995;183:127–138.
10. Grob CS, Poland RE, Chang C, Ernst T. Psychobiologic effects of 3,4-methylenedioxymethamphetamine in humans: methodological considerations and preliminary observations. Behav Brain Res 1996;73:103–107.
11. Shulgin A, Shulgin, A. PIHKAL: A chemical love story. Berkeley: Transform Press, 1991.
12. Abraham HD, Aldridge AM. Adverse consequences of lysergic acid diethylamide. Addiction 1993;88:1327–1334.
13. Aghajanian GK. Serotonin and the action of LSD in the brain. Psychiatric Annals 1994;24: 137–141.
14. Schwartz RH. LSD: its rise, fall, and renewed popularity among high school students. Pediatr Clin North Am 1995;42:403–413.
15. Ungerleider JT, Fisher DD, Fuller MC, Caldwell A. The bad trip: the etiology of the adverse LSD reaction. Am J Psychiatry 1968;125:1483–1490.
16. Weil A. Natural mind. Boston: Houghton Mifflin, 1972:10.
17. National Commission on Marijuana and Drug Abuse. Appendices to marijuana: signal of misunderstanding, and drug abuse: problem in perspective. Washington, DC: Government Printing Office, 1972, 1973.
18. Osmond H. A review of the clinical effects of psychotomimetic agents. Ann N Y Acad Sci 1957;66:418.
19. Cohen S. A quarter century of research with LSD. In: Ungerleider JT, ed. The problems and prospects of LSD. Springfield, IL: Charles C Thomas, 1972:20–45.
20. Cohen S. Psychotomimetics (hallucinogens) and cannabis. In: Clark WG, del Gudice J, eds. Principles of psychopharmacology. New York: Academic Press, 1978:357–371.
21. Shick JFE, Freedman DX. Research in non-narcotic drug abuse. In: Arieti S, ed. American handbook of psychiatry. New York: Basic Books, 1975;6:552–622.
22. Lewin L. Phantasica: narcotic and stimulating drugs. Tras. Wirth, PHA, London: Kegan Paul; Trench, Trubner and Co, 1924 (1931).
23. Johnston L. "Monitoring the future"—the National High School Senior Survey. Washington, DC: National Institute of Drug Abuse, 1990.
24. Johnston LD, O'Malley PM, Bachman JG. National survey results on drug use from the Monitoring the Future Study, Vol. II, 1975–1994. NIH Publication 96–4027, 1996.
25. Cuomo MJ, Dyment PG, Gammino VM. Increasing use of "ecstasy" (MDMA) and other hallucinogens on a college campus. J Am Coll Health 1994;42:271–274.
26. Peroutka SJ. Incidence of the recreational use of 3,4-methylenedioxymethamphetamine (Ecstasy) on an undergraduate campus. N Engl J Med 1987;317:1542–1543.
27. Fuller JG. The day of St. Anthony's fire. New York: Macmillan, 1968.
28. Hofmann A. Chemical, pharmacological and medical aspects of psychotomimetics. J Exp Ment Dis 1961;5:31–51.
29. Steele TD, McCann UD, Ricaurte GA. 3,4-methylenedioxymethamphetamine (MDMA, "ecstasy"): pharmacology and toxicology in animals and humans. Addiction 1994;89:539–551.
30. Peroutka SJ, Newman H, Harris H. Subjective effects of 3,4-methylenedioxymethamphetamine in recreational users. Neuropsychopharmacology 1988;1:273–277.
31. Martin WR, Sloan JW. Pharmacology and classification of LSD-like hallucinogens. In: Martin WR, ed. Drug addiction II: amphetamine, psychotogen, and marijuana dependence. Handbuch der experimentellen pharmakologie. Berlin: Springer-Verlag, 1977; 45(2):305–368.
32. Callahan PM, Appel JB. Differences in the stimulus properties of 3,4-methylenedioxyamphetamine and 3,4-methylenedioxymethamphetamine in animals trained to discriminate hallucinogens from saline. J Pharmacol Exp Ther 1988;246:866–870.
33. Lamb RJ, Griffiths RR. Self-injection of d, 1–3,4-methylenedioxymethamphetamine (MDMA) in the baboon. Psychopharmacology 1987;91:268–272.
34. Halaris AE, Freedman DX, Fang VS. Plasma corticoids and brain tryptophan after acute and

chronic dosage of LSD. Life Sci 1975; 17:1467–1472.

35. Nash FJ, Meltzer HY, Gudelsky GA. Selective cross-tolerance to 5-HT$_{1A}$ and 5-HT$_2$ receptor-mediated temperature and corticosterone responses. Pharmacol Biochem Behav 1989; 33:781–785.

36. Nash FJ, Meltzer HY, Gudelsky GA. Elevation of serum prolactin and corticosterone concentration in the rat after the administration of 3,4-methylenedioxymethamphetamine. J Pharmacol Exp Ther 1988;245;873–879.

37. Ungerleider JT, Fisher DD. The problems of LSD and emotional disorders. Calif Med 1967; 106:49–55.

38. Hamon M. Common neurochemical correlates to the action of hallucinogens. In: Jacobs BL, ed. Hallucinogens: neurochemical, behavioral and clinical perspectives. New York: Raven Press, 1984:143–169.

39. Freedman DX. Hallucinogenic drug research—if so, so what? Symposium summary and commentary. Pharmacol Biochem Behav 1986;24: 407–415.

40. Jacobs BL. How hallucinogenic drugs work. Am Sci 1987;75:386–392.

41. Saxena PR. Serotonin receptors: subtypes, functional responses and therapeutic relevance. Pharmacol Ther 1995;66:339–368.

42. Humphrey PPA, Hartig PD. A proposed new nomenclature for 5-HT receptors. Trends Pharmacol Sci 1993;14:233–236.

43. Teitler M, Herrick-Davis K. Multiple serotonin receptor subtypes: molecular cloning and functional expression. Crit Rev Neurobiol 1994;8: 175–188.

44. Freedman DX. Effects of LSD-25 on brain serotonin. J Pharmacol Exp Ther 1961;134: 160–166.

45. Grof S, Dytrych Z. Blocking of LSD reaction by premedication with Niamid. Activitas Nervosa Superior 1965;7:306.

46. Lucki I, Frazer A. Prevention of the serotonin syndrome in rats by repeated administration of monoamine oxidase inhibitors but not tricyclic antidepressants. Psychopharmacology 1981;77: 205–211.

47. Aghajanian GK, Foote WE, Sheard MH. Lysergic acid diethylamide: sensitive neuronal units in the midbrain raphe. Science 1968;161:706–708.

48. Aghajanian GK, Sprouse JS, Rasmussen K. Physiology of the midbrain serotonin system. In: Meltzer HY, ed. Psychopharmacology: the third generation of progress. New York: Raven Press, 1987:141–149.

49. Trulson ME, Heym J, Jacobs BL. Dissociations between the effects of hallucinogenic drugs on behavior and raphe unit activity in freely moving cats. Brain Res 1981;215:275–293.

50. Trulson ME, Jacobs BL. Dissociations between the effects of LSD on behavior and raphe unit activity in freely moving cats. Science 1979; 205:515–518.

51. Glennon RA, Titeler M, McKenney JD. Evidence for 5-HT$_2$ involvement in the mechanism of action of hallucinogenic agents. Life Sci 1984;35:2505–2511.

52. Lyon RA, Glennon RA, Titeler M. 3,4-Methylenedioxymethamphetamine (MDMA): stereoselective interactions at brain 5-HT$_1$ and 5-HT$_2$ receptors. Psychopharmacology 1986;88: 525–526.

53. Titeler M, Lyon RA, Glennon RA. Radioligand binding evidence implicates the brain 5-HT$_2$ receptor as a site of action for LSD and phenylisopropylamine hallucinogens. Psychopharmacology 1988;94:213–216.

54. Sadzot B, Baraban JM, Glennon RA, et al. Hallucinogenic drug interactions at human 5-HT$_2$ receptors: implications for treating LSD-induced hallucinogens. Psychopharmacology 1989;98:495–499.

55. Pierce PA, Peroutka SJ. Hallucinogenic drug interactions with neurotransmitter receptor binding sites in human cortex. Psychopharmacology 1989;97:118–122.

56. Glennon RA. Do classical hallucinogens act as 5-HT2 agonists or antagonists? Neuropsychopharmacology 1990;3:509–517.

57. Pazos A, Cortes R, Palacios JM. Quantitative autoradiographic mapping of serotonin receptors in the rat brain. II. Serotonin-2 receptors. Brain Res 1985;346:231–249.

58. Buckholtz NS, Zhou D, Freedman DX, Potter WZ. Lysergic acid diethylamide (LSD) administration selectively downregulates serotonin receptors in rat brain. Neuropsychopharmacology 1990;3:137–148.

59. Glennon RA, Young R, Rosecrans JA. Antagonism of the effects of the hallucinogen DOM and the purported 5-HT agonist quipazine by 5-HT$_2$ antagonists. Eur J Pharmacol 1983;91:189–196.

60. Burris KD, Breeding M, Sanders-Bush E. (+)Lysergic acid diethylamide, but not its nonhallucinogenic congeners, is a potent serotonin 5-HT$_{1C}$ receptor agonist. J Pharmacol Exp Ther 1991;258:891–896.

61. Johnson MP, Hoffman AJ, Nichols DE. Effects of enantiomers of MDA, MDMA and related analogues on [^{3}H]serotonin and [^{3}H]dopamine release from superfused rat brain slices. Eur J Pharmacol 1986;132:269–276.

62. Hiramatsu M, Cho AK. Enantiomeric differences in the effects of 3,4-methylenedioxymethamphetamine on extracellular monoamines and metabolites in the striatum of freely-moving rats: an in vivo microdialysis study. Neuropharmacology 1990;29: 269–275.

63. Strassman RJ. Adverse reactions to psychedelic drugs: a review of the literature. J Nerv Ment Dis 1984;172:577–595.

64. Ungerleider JT, Fisher DD, Goldsmith SR, Fuller MC, Forgy E. A statistical survey of adverse reactions to LSD in Los Angeles County. Am J Psychiatry 1968;125:352–357.

65. Madden JS. LSD and post-hallucinogen perceptual disorder. Addiction 1994;86:762–763.

66. Ungerleider JT. The acute side effects from LSD. In: Ungerleider JT, ed. The problems and prospects of LSD. Springfield, IL: Charles C Thomas, 1972:61–68.

67. Abraham HD, Aldridge AM. LSD: a point well taken. Addiction 1994;89:763.

68. Bowers MB Jr. The role of drugs in the production of schizophreniform psychoses and related disorders. In: Meltzer HY, ed. Psychopharmacology: the third generation of progress. New York: Raven Press, 1987:819–823.

69. Ungerleider JT, Fisher DD, Fuller MC. The dangers of LSD: analysis of seven months' experience in a university hospital's psychiatric service. JAMA 1966;197:389–392.

70. Sobel J, Espinas O, Friedman S. Carotid artery obstruction following LSD capsule ingestion. Arch Intern Med 1971;127:290–291.

71. Dowling GP, McDonough ET, Bost RO. "Eve and ecstasy": a report of five deaths associated with the use of MDEA and MDMA. JAMA 1987;257:1615–1617.

72. Henry JA, Jeffreys KJ, Dawling S. Toxicity and deaths from 3,4-methylenedioxymethamphetamine ("ecstasy"). Lancet 1992;340:384–387.

73. Miller D. The drug dependent adolescent. In:

Feinstein SC, Giovachini P, eds. Adolescent psychiatry. New York: Basic Books, 1973.

74. Neff L. Chemicals and their effects on the adolescent ego. In: Feinstein S, Giovacchini P, Miller A, eds. Adolescent psychiatry. New York: Basic Books, 1971.

75. Dewhurst K, Hatrick JA. Differential diagnosis and treatment of lysergic acid diethylamide-induced psychosis. Practitioner 1972;209: 327–332.

76. Miller PL, Gay GR, Ferris KC, Anderson S. Treatment of acute, adverse reactions: "I've tripped and I can't get down." J Psychoactive Drugs 1992;24:277–279.

77. Resnick O, Krus DM, Raskin M. LSD-25 action in normal subjects treated with a monoamine oxidase inhibitor. Life Sci 1964;3:1207–1214.

78. Strassman RJ. Human hallucinogen interactions with drugs affecting serotonergic neurotransmission. Neuropsychopharmacology 1992;7: 241–243.

79. Bonson KR, Murphy DL. Alterations in responses to LSD in humans associated with chronic administration of tricyclic antidepressants, monoamine oxidase inhibitors or lithium. Behav Brain Res 1996;73:229–233.

80. Bonson KR, Buckholtz JW, Murphy DL. Chronic administration of serotonergic antidepressants attenuates the subjective effects of LSD in humans. Neuropsychopharmacology 1996;14:425–437.

81. Fisher DD. The chronic side effects from LSD. In: Ungerleider JT, ed. The problems and prospects of LSD. Springfield, IL: Charles C Thomas, 1972:69–80.

82. Diagnostic and statistical manual of mental disorders: DSM-IV. Washington, DC: American Psychiatric Association, 1994.

83. Frankel FH. The concept of flashbacks in historical perspective. Int J Clin Exp Hypn 1994; 42:321–335.

84. Shick JFE, Smith DE. An analysis of the LSD flashback. J Psychedelic Drugs 1970;3:13–19.

85. Levi L, Miller NR. Visual illusions associated with previous drug abuse. J Clin Neuro-ophthalmol 1990;10:103–110.

86. Markel H, Lee A, Holmes RD, Domino EF. LSD flashback syndrome exacerbated by selective serotonin reuptake inhibitor antidepressants in adolescents. J Pediatr 1994;125:817–819.

87. Abraham HD. A chronic impairment of colour vision in users of LSD. Br J Psychiatry 1982; 140:518–520.

88. Abraham HD, Wolf E. Visual function in past users of LSD: psychophysical findings. J Abnorm Psychol 1988;97:443–447.

89. Kawasaki A, Purvin V. Persistent palinopsia following ingestion of lysergic acid diethylamide (LSD). Arch Ophthalmol 1996;114:47–50.

90. Ricaurte GA, Bryan G, Strauss L, Seiden L, Schuster C. Hallucinogenic amphetamine selectively destroys brain serotonin nerve terminals. Science 1985;229:986–998.

91. Gibb JW, Johnson M, Stone D, Hanson GR. MDMA: historical perspectives. Ann N Y Acad Sci 1990;600:601–611.

92. Molliver ME, Berger UV, Mamounas LA, Molliver DC, O'Hearn E, Wilson MA. Neurotoxicity of MDMA and related compounds: anatomic studies. Ann N Y Acad Sci 1990; 600:640–661.

93. Schmidt CJ, Kehne JH. Neurotoxicity of MDMA: neurochemical effects. Ann N Y Acad Sci 1990;600:665–680.

94. De Souza EB, Battaglia G, Insel TR. Neurotoxic effects of MDMA on brain serotonin neurons: evidence from neurochemical and radioligand

binding studies. Ann N Y Acad Sci 1990; 600:682–697.

95. Ricaurte GA, Forno LS, Wilson MA, et al. (±)3,4-Methylenedioxymethamphetamine (MDMA) selectively damages central serotonergic neurons in non-human primates. JAMA 1988;260:51–55.

96. Ricaurte GA, Finnegan KT, Irwin I, Langston JW. Aminergic metabolites in cerebrospinal fluid of humans previously exposed to MDMA: preliminary observations. Ann N Y Acad Sci 1990;600:699–708.

97. McCann UD, Ridenour A., Shaham Y, Ricaurte GA. Serotonin neurotoxicity after (±)3,4-meth-

ylenedioxymethamphetamine (MDMA; "ecstasy"): a controlled study in humans. Neuropsychopharmacology 1994;10:129–138.

98. Allen RP, McCann UD, Ricaurte GA. Persistent effects of (±)3,4-methylenedioxymethamphetamine (MDMA, "ecstasy") on human sleep. Sleep 1993;16:560–564.

21   PHENCYCLIDINE (PCP)

Stephen R. Zukin, Zili Sloboda, and Daniel C. Javitt

HISTORY

Phencyclidine (1–1(phenylcyclohexyl)piperidine; PCP; "angel dust") was developed by Parke-Davis under the trade name Sernyl during the 1950s in a research program targeting general anesthetics. In certain respects clinical trials in anesthesia were promising. Patients anesthetized with PCP did not manifest the depression of vital cardiovascular and respiratory functions typical of classical general anesthetic agents. In fact, the PCP-induced anesthetic state differed sharply from the state of relaxed sleep induced by barbiturates or opiates in nearly every respect (1–3). Patients appeared catatonic, displaying flat faces, open mouth, and fixed, sightless staring, with rigid posturing, and sometimes waxy flexibility. It was inferred that without overt loss of consciousness, patients were sharply dissociated from the environment. For this reason PCP and the related compounds cyclohexamine (1) and ketamine (4) were classified as "dissociative anesthetics."

Despite its physiological advantages over traditional anesthetics, PCP was removed from the market in 1965 and officially limited thereafter to veterinary applications. Up to half of patients subjected to PCP anesthesia developed severe intraoperative reactions including agitation and hallucinations (1–3). Many of these patients went on to develop psychotic reactions, which persisted beyond emergence from anesthesia and in some cases persisted for an additional 12–240 hours (2, 5). Qualitatively similar effects were observed when much lower doses of PCP were tried for chronic pain (5). As a result of these findings, PCP and cyclohexamine were abandoned for clinical use, although the shorter acting and less potent PCP derivative ketamine did find a place in the anesthetic pharmacopoeia. The fact that drugs with such well-documented negative and aversive behavioral effects became widely abused during the 1970s is one of the most remarkable developments in psychopharmacology.

EPIDEMIOLOGY

The nature of phencyclidine and the characteristics of its abuse affect its epidemiological features. Because it is water soluble, PCP is often adulterated and misrepresented on the street as THC (tetrahydrocannabinol, the principal psychoactive substance in marihuana), LSD, mescaline, psilocybin, amphetamine, or cocaine. Because of this variability and the high frequency with which it is used in combination with other drugs, the user may not be aware that he or she has ingested PCP. To add to the confusion, the street names for PCP vary considerably within and between regions of the country: angel dust, dust, crystal, cyclones, embalming fluid, wet, killer weed, mintweed, PeaCe Pill, goon, surfer, and as recently as 1994, Illy, crazy Eddie, Purple Rain, and Milk. Its abuse was first noted on the West Coast in 1965 (6). Its negative effects quickly made it an undesirable drug and it had limited popularity on the streets. Analyses of street samples collected on the West Coast between 1971 and 1974 found that, in about half of the PCP samples, PCP was mixed with other drugs. However, during the last half of the 1970s, almost three-quarters of the street samples were found to be pure PCP. It was originally ingested orally but as the risk of overdose is greater with the oral form of the drug, it is now more commonly smoked or snorted,

allowing the user more control of dosage. It has also been injected. Ethnographic studies of users of PCP in four metropolitan areas (7) found regional differences in first time use: snorting in Chicago and Philadelphia, smoking in Seattle, and both smoking and snorting in Miami.

Initial use is usually in a smoking form (about 1–100mg of PCP per joint) in conjunction with marihuana, tobacco, or parsley. Chronic users may take from 100 mg to 1 gram within a single 24-hour period. The effects last between 4 and 6 hours with a longer "coming down" period. It is most often used as a social drug, with other users. PCP is used by people from all socioeconomic backgrounds with and without formal premorbid psychopathology. For those who become chronic users, PCP is generally a primary drug of choice. Studies of chronic users show persistent cognitive and memory problems, speech difficulties, mood disorders, loss of purposive activities, and weight loss, lasting a year or more after last use. Late-stage chronic use has been associated with paranoia and violent behavior with auditory hallucinations (6).

Certain specific characteristics of PCP abuse render its study particularly difficult: episodic peaks of abuse, wide regional variations, media attention, public misconceptions, and sharp decline in use. However, a good epidemiological picture of PCP use can be obtained by examining all the data sources together. The following sections will present the extent of PCP use in the United States over time and describe the characteristics of those persons who use PCP.

PCP "Epidemics"

The previously cited data sources suggest that there was an epidemic of phencyclidine use in the period between 1973 and 1979 and again perhaps, between 1981 and 1984 (8–10). These increases in PCP use stimulated a number of scientific articles in professional journals, which examined the question of whether the epidemic was real or was a pseudoepidemic brought into being by exploitation of the most dramatic cases by the media. (11). However, the national data systems as well as many regional systems (12) support the increases in use in the late 1970s, but only the indicator data support the increases noted in the 1980s. By their very nature, indicator data represent legal or health problems associated with drug use; therefore, they are not good indicators of new users. Except, perhaps for acute overdoses seen in the emergency room, those who represent the "statistics" in hospitals, the medical examiners' offices, drug abuse treatment, and jails are more likely to be intermediate or chronic users of drugs and as such represent the lag-end of an "epidemic."

Review of Household Survey data for these periods indicate that in 1976 it was estimated that 9.5% of those aged 18–25 had ever used PCP; however, the estimates for 1977 and 1979 show increases to 13.9% and 14.5%, respectively. Estimates of PCP use for those aged 12–17 were 3.0% in 1976, 5.8% in 1977, and 3.9% in 1979. By 1982 these percentages began to decline significantly for both age groups (for those 12–17, 2.2% and for those 18–25, 10.5%). For the 1985 and 1988 Surveys, these figures were 1.1% and 1.2% for those 12–17 and 5.6% and 4.4% for those 18–25. Prior to 1985 survey data were reported for three age groups: 12–17, 18–25, and over 25. In 1985, the oldest group was divided into two groups, those 26–34 and those over 34. In that same year the higher PCP use rates (10.6%) were noted for those 26–34. Subsequently, although rates have always been highest within the 26–34 age group, they have been decreasing.

As a source of information on young people, the Monitoring the Future study provides a better database for estimating the extent of "new" use of drugs specifically because of the age groups involved. PCP was added to the questionnaire in 1979. The percentage of high school seniors reporting use of PCP was 12.8% in 1979 and decreased over time to its lowest level of about 3% in 1987 where it has remained stable through 1995 (2.7%) (13). Data are not available for the 8th and 10th graders.

During the same periods, increases were noted in the numbers of persons reported to DAWN for drug-related problems associated with PCP and in drug abuse treatment admissions. The numbers of PCP-related emergency room mentions increased from 1,934 in 1974 to 4,993 in 1977, 9,877 in 1978 to a high of 10,288 in 1979 (14). After a decline to 5,840 in 1981, increases were again noted in 1982 and 1983 (8,067 and 9,782, respectively). Crider (15) points out that between 1973 and 1975, among treatment admissions, the rate of first-time users of PCP increased more rapidly than was observed in the emergency room data system (3,420 in 1973; 4,240 in 1974; 7,180 in 1977; peaking at 9,130 in 1979; and declining to 1,270 by 1981). She attributes the observed increases to a change in route of administration from oral (tablet or capsule) to smoking (along with tobacco or marihuana). The subsequent decline in PCP use has been thought to be the result of a number of activities aimed to make the population more aware of the abuse potential and dangers associated with PCP. At the same time the drug was rescheduled on the Controlled Substances Act from Schedule III to Schedule II, restricting its availability. In addition, reporting on the production of the precursor drug, piperidine, was made a requirement in 1979. Finally, penalties for the possession of PCP with the intent to sell were increased. All of the activities were thought to be associated with the declines in use in the early 1980s. The increases that are noted in the DAWN system, for example, during the mid 1980s may actually represent a continuation of the "epidemic" from the late 1970s. This hypothesis is supported by the characteristics of the populations constituting those being seen in these agencies. First of all, they seem to come principally from Los Angeles, Washington, DC, and New York City. They are older and more likely to be African-American. Finally, they seem to be using PCP in combination with alcohol and/or heroin (15).

Current Trends in PCP Use

Preliminary analyses of the 1994 Household Survey estimates that approximately nine million people had used phencyclidine at least once in their lives, representing 4.3% of household residents aged 12 years and older (16). The percent of persons reporting "lifetime" use of PCP has been increasing since 1985 when the estimate was 2.9%. Information available in detail from the 1993 Household Survey (17) show higher rates of use estimated for those between the ages of 26 and 34 years (8.2%) with the lowest rates reported for those 12–17 years of age (1.0%). About twice as many males (5.5%) report use as females (2.7%). Whites are more likely to use PCP (4.5%) as the other groups, with Hispanics reporting higher rates of use (3.2%) than African-Americans (1.9%). Use tends to be greater in the western part of the country (5.9%). When lifetime use is compared across the six cities that were oversampled in the survey, these regional differences are underscored. In 1993, the city with the highest estimate of use was Denver with 6.5%. The next highest cities were Los Angeles (4.3%) and then Washington, DC (4.2%). The city with the lowest percentage of use was Miami, 0.8%. These relationships have remained the same since 1991, with Denver having the highest percentage of users and Miami the lowest (18). Examination of these percentages by socioeconomic status shows that there are no differences in almost all the cities except perhaps Chicago where the percentage of users was somewhat higher for the middle and upper socioeconomic status populations (16–18).

These "lifetime" estimates provide a proxy assessment of cohort differences over time. For many illicit drugs, including PCP, changes in lifetime use patterns have been associated with changes in perceptions of the "harm-fulness" of their use and in reports as to the ease with which the drugs can be obtained. For PCP, the relationship between these perceptions and use have held steady. In 1994, 73% of those interviewed indicated that there were "great risks" associated with the use of PCP even if tried once or twice. The percentage reporting that PCP was easy to obtain in 1994 was 29%. Lifetime estimates of use and for these measures of perception have not changed significantly over the last six years for the total population, within age groups, between sexes, among racial or ethnic groups, or by region of the country. However, when the data on perceptions of risk associated with PCP use are compared to reported use across age groups, it is difficult to assess the relationship of these measures. The group that has the lowest rates of use (those 12–17) also has the fewest people who believe there is great risk associated with using PCP. Those who report the second lowest rate of use, those 35 and older, were the most likely to believe that PCP use poses great risk. About two thirds of those in the age group with the highest rates of use, those 26–34, report that use is risky (16).

Annual prevalence, use within the year prior to survey, is a better estimate to use for public health programming as it represents the current picture of use. With this in mind, in 1994, 0.02%, or 478,000, people were estimated to have used PCP at least once in the prior year. Although involving a large number of cases, PCP use is dwarfed by annual rates of marihuana, cocaine, crack, and inhalant use (8.5%, 1.7%, 0.6%, and, 1.1%, respectively) (16).

Earlier it was mentioned that since 1987 about 3% of high school seniors reported PCP use sometime in their lifetimes. The characteristics of the 1994 high school seniors who reported using PCP are similar to those mentioned above for the Household Survey: mostly male and from the northeast and western regions. When the senior class of 1994 who reported use of PCP were asked about when they began its use, the mode was within the two to three years prior to interview (while in grades 10 and 11) (19). This survey also examines noncontinuation of drugs, defined as the proportion of people who ever tried a drug but do not continue to use it in the 12 months prior to the survey. In 1994, PCP ranked among the top seven most often discontinued drugs after inhalants (56%), heroin (50%), methamphetamine (47%), steroids (46%), tranquilizers (44%), and methaqualone (43%).

Although information on use is not available for the 8th and 10th graders, questions were included on their questionnaires as to perceptions regarding the difficulty in obtaining PCP. In 1994, about 18% of the 8th graders and 24% of the 10th graders thought that PCP was "fairly easy" or "very easy" to obtain compared to 31% of the 12th graders. Similar questions regarding marihuana elicited higher percentages for the 8th and 10th graders (49% and 75%, respectively) compared to 85% for 12th graders. However, the proportion of 8th and 10th graders who thought PCP was easy to get was similar to those who thought heroin and crystal methamphetamine were easy to get (13).

Indicator Data

National data systems of indicators vary with regard to the specificity of the drug implication. As the Drug Abuse Warning Network (DAWN) was designed to ascertain emerging patterns of drug use it is a much better drug abuse surveillance indicator system. Reports from DAWN prior to 1989 were limited to sentinel cities and were not truly representative of the nation although projected national estimates were made. Detailed national estimates are available for 1989 through 1993 when the system was based on a representative sample of hospitals. The ranking of PCP, relative to other drugs mentioned in the DAWN emergency room system, has changed from 19th in 1990 to 27th in 1991 and 22nd in 1992 and 1993 (20, 21). Throughout these years the cases were about 72% male, over 40% in their mid-twenties and about 40–43% African-American. In 1990, 1991, and 1992, the percentages who were white were 26, 29.6, and 20.8% and the percentages who were Hispanic were 16.4, 35.5, and 22.0%, respectively. The overall DAWN cases for these years are about half male, mostly white (about 60%), and between the ages of 26 and 34.

Over 38% of the PCP users reported that PCP was the only drug they had used prior to their admission to the emergency room compared to 28% for all admissions. About one third of the DAWN PCP cases reported that they used the drug for recreational reasons and about another 30% mentioned they were dependent compared to total DAWN cases where about one third mentioned dependence and over 43% mentioned suicidal intent. For all three years, the same cities reported the highest numbers of emergency room admissions associated with PCP (in rank order): Los Angeles, Chicago, Washington, DC, New York City, San Francisco, Baltimore, and Philadelphia. These cities varied as to the race or ethnic groups involved, with African-Americans and Hispanics more often mentioned for Los Angeles, New York City, and San Francisco; African-Americans in Chicago, whites in Baltimore, and whites and African-Americans in Philadelphia and Washington, DC.

The National Institute on Drug Abuse (NIDA) supports the Community Epidemiology Work Group (CEWG), which twice a year brings together drug abuse researchers and program managers from 21 cities across the country to exchange data on drug use in their areas, including indicator data from the emergency rooms, medical examiners' offices, arrest records, and drug abuse treatment facilities; information on price and purity of drugs seized; and other data for their communities. Through this mechanism it has been possible to identify emerging drug patterns as targets for study. In the most recent meetings, in June and December 1995, reports were made indicating a rebound of PCP use in Washington, DC, Philadelphia, and New York City in emergency rooms; in Washington, DC, and Chicago among juvenile arrestees; and in Miami among treatment admissions particularly in conjunction with marihuana (22, 23). Future Household and Monitoring the Future surveys will show whether these increases represent a significant trend.

NEUROBIOLOGY

Identification and Characterization of the PCP Receptor

The central nervous effects of PCP are initiated by binding of the drug to high-affinity PCP receptors whose existence in rat brain membranes was demonstrated in 1979 (24, 25). PCP receptors are highly selective for drugs that elicit PCP-like effects on behavior, including PCP and related arylcyclohexylamines, the F-opioids, the dioxolanes (a class of dissociative anesthetics), and dizocilpine (MK-801) (24–31). Several classes of drugs not chemically derived from PCP, including the F-opiates (27, 32–34), the dioxolane derivatives dexoxadrol and etoxadrol (29), and the anticonvulsant MK-801 (31), are active in the [^{3}H]PCP binding assay and exhibit PCP-like behavioral activity. All of these drugs mimic PCP in conditioned and unconditioned behavioral assays and generalize to PCP in the highly selective rat two-lever drug discriminative stimulus test. The relative potencies of these drugs in eliciting PCP-like behaviors are proportional to their potencies in competing for radioligand binding to the PCP receptor. More than 100 such derivatives have been so characterized. Drugs that exhibit PCP-like behavioral effects also block NMDA-activated channels in electrophysiologic assays. The rank order of potency of such drugs as channel blockers parallels their behavioral potencies and their potencies in binding to the PCP receptor. By contrast, a wide range of neurotransmitters, known agonists, and antagonists of other receptors (including the classical opiates and the psychotomimetic drugs LSD, THC, cocaine, and mescaline) are inactive in the PCP-binding assay and fail to elicit PCP-like behaviors or channel-blocking activity.

PCP–N-methyl-D-aspartate (NMDA) Receptor Interactions

Following the demonstration of PCP receptors, the next major advance in determining the molecular mechanism of PCP occurred in the early 1980s with the demonstration that PCP receptor ligands potently inhibit neurotransmission mediated at NMDA-type glutamate receptors. NMDA receptors are one of several receptor types for the excitatory amino acid neurotransmitter glutamate. As opposed to other glutamate receptors, NMDA channels are permeable to Ca^{2+} along with Na^+. Following NMDA receptor activation, therefore, NMDA-mediated Ca^{2+}-flux may lead to stimulation of calmodulin-dependent kinases, and activation of postsynaptic second messenger pathways (35). A unique functional property of the NMDA channel is that it is blocked in a voltage-dependent manner by the endogenous Mg^{2+} ion. The dual voltage- and ligand-dependence of NMDA receptors permits

them to function in a Hebbian manner to integrate information from multiple input streams (36–38). One stream is represented as a modulation of presynaptic glutamate release; additional streams are reflected in modulation of resting membrane potential on the postsynaptic NMDA-bearing dendrites. Ca^{2+} flowing through open, unblocked NMDA channels may serve as the trigger for long-term potentiation, which, in turn, may represent the neurophysiological substrate underlying learning and memory formation. In rodents, PCP and other NMDA antagonists lead to profound memory disturbances that are linked to inhibition of hippocampal long-term potentiation (39). Profound amnesia is also characteristic of both PCP psychosis and ketamine anesthesia.

Glycine Sensitivity of NMDA Receptor Activation

As opposed to most receptors, which require the presence of only a single neurotransmitter, NMDA receptors possess two distinct agonist binding sites, one for glutamate and other excitatory amino acids, and a second for glycine. Binding of both glycine and glutamate are required for NMDA receptor activation to occur, and, in vitro, total removal of glycine from the incubation medium prevents NMDA receptor activation by glutamate. From a technical viewpoint, therefore, glutamate and glycine should be considered co-agonists at the NMDA receptor complex (40). However, the functional roles played by glutamate and glycine in vivo appear quite different. Thus, glutamate is released from presynaptic nerve endings in a pulsatile fashion and rapidly deactivated following release, as is the case for most classical neurotransmitters. In contrast, glycine in forebrain does not appear to be concentrated in presynaptic nerve endings nor released in response to electrical stimulation. Moreover, endogenous glycine levels are typically at or above the K_d of the NMDA-associated glycine site for these agents, indicating that activity-stimulated release of glycine is not required for neurotransmission. It has even been suggested that the glycine site may be saturated under normal brain conditions, and thus physiologically irrelevant, although this appears not to be the case (40). Instead, glycine appears to set the tonic level of NMDA excitability, determining the degree to which presynaptic glutamate release leads to postsynaptic excitation. Postsynaptic excitation, however, is triggered by presynaptic glutamate release. Functionally, therefore, glycine functions more similarly to a neuromodulator than a classical neurotransmitter. In addition to glycine, the NMDA-associated glycine site shows high affinity for D-serine, which therefore may also serve as an endogenous NMDA agonist (41). The high affinity of the NMDA-associated glycine site for D-serine stands in contrast to the classical, strychnine-sensitive inhibitory glycine receptor found primarily in hindbrain, which binds D-serine with low affinity.

Use-Dependent Blockade

Because PCP mediates its effects at a binding site located within the NMDA channel, access of PCP to its site of action is affected by the degree of NMDA receptor activation. Opening of the NMDA channel facilitates access of PCP to its receptor, accelerating the rate at which PCP-induced blockade of NMDA receptor-mediated neurotransmission is observed. Thus, in vitro, NMDA currents show marked use-dependence, with greater use being associated with more rapid blockade over the course of seconds to minutes (42). However, the phenomenon of use-dependence appears to be true only over the course of minutes. When incubations are continued for several hours, significant PCP receptor occupancy is observed even in the absence of NMDA activation. The slow onset of closed channel blockade is most likely due to the ability of PCP receptor ligands, all of which are highly lipophilic, to reach the NMDA channel by diffusion through the lipid bilayer (43).

Neurotoxicity

In the range of concentrations most associated with behavioral hyperactivity, PCP does not appear to cause significant long-lasting brain toxicity. At doses significantly above those used for behavioral studies (e.g., 5–50 mg/kg), however, PCP induces neuronal vacuolization, particularly in neurons in posterior cingulate/retrosplenial cortex (44). Similar vacuolization is observed following of administration of MK-801 (dizocilpine) and ketamine, indicating that the effect is probably NMDA receptor-mediated. The effect is initially observed in layers III and IV of cortex. At lower doses (e.g., 5 mg/kg), the effect is transient, reaching peak levels approximately 12 hours after PCP or MK-801 administration and then resolving over 12–18 hours. Extremely large doses of drug, however, may lead to neuronal necrosis which is apparent even 48 hours after drug administration. Although posterior cingulate/retrosplenial cortex appears most susceptible to the effects of PCP, other hippocampus and other limbic brain regions may be affected at higher doses. Along with vacuolization, administration of high-dose PCP leads to elevation of glucose uptake (45), expression of heat shock (46), and glial fibrillary acidic protein (47) in the affected regions. Vacuolization can be inhibited by prior administration of antipsychotic, anticholinergic, or GABAergic agents, and is potentiated by administration of pilocarpine.

Behavioral Pharmacology

The behavioral effects of PCP in animals depend upon species (48). In rodents, PCP induces a characteristic syndrome of hyperactivity and stereotypies (48). These behavioral effects respond partially to treatment with neuroleptics (49), and may also be reversed by agents such as glycine that augment NMDA receptor-mediated neurotransmission (50). Because the serum half-life of PCP is shorter and the volume of distribution is larger, rodents typically require doses of PCP higher than those used clinically than in humans (51). Sensitization to the behavioral effects of PCP may occur following daily administration (52). In rodents, PCP may also inhibit social behavior. The effects of PCP on social behaviors are poorly reversed by typical or atypical antipsychotic agents (53).

PCP-induced hyperactivity in rodents is mediated at least in part by disruption of NMDA-mediated interaction with ascending midbrain dopamine systems (54). PCP-induced hyperactivity appears to be reflective of increased dopaminergic neurotransmission within nucleus accumbens, since this effect can be selectively inhibited by accumbens lesions (55–57). Other components of the PCP-induced behavioral syndrome (e.g., alterations in social behavior, stereotypies) persist even following accumbens lesion (57), however, suggesting that those behaviors may be mediated by other brain regions. In addition to being present in dopaminergic terminal fields, NMDA receptors are also present in substantia nigra (A9) and ventral tegmental area (A10). Glutamatergic innervation of substantia nigra from prefrontal cortex is a major determinant of dopaminergic activity levels and NMDA receptors appear to be the primary mediators of glutamate-induced stimulation of midbrain dopaminergic neurons (58). To the extent that NMDA receptors stimulate A9 and A10 neurons, PCP would, paradoxically, be expected to decrease dopaminergic outflow in striatum and accumbens. However, it has been found that direct application of PCP to A10 does not inhibit dopamine cell firing or alter dopamine release in accumbens, although it does prevent NMDA-induced neuronal activation (59). Thus, the predominant behavioral effects of PCP in rodents appear to be due to its interactions within dopamine terminal fields rather than within dopaminergic midbrain nuclei.

In monkeys, doses of approximately 0.5 mg/kg PCP produce a tranquilization in which animals appear awake but unresponsive to the environment (60). At doses of 1.0 mg/kg, PCP induces a cataleptoid state in which animals show waxy flexibility and rigidity closely resembling catatonic schizophrenia. Doses of 2.5 mg/kg lead to stupor; 5.0 mg/kg, to surgical anesthesia; and 15 mg/kg to convulsive seizures.

In both rats and monkeys, PCP administration also leads to profound disruption in learning and memory. In rodents, noncompetitive NMDA antagonists lead to disruptions in spatial delayed alteration performance, which can be reversed by dopamine (D2) receptor antagonists (61). Thus, in cortex, as in striatum, the effects of NMDA antagonists may, in part, reflect secondary dysregulation of dopaminergic neurotransmission. In monkeys, NMDA antagonists lead to impairments in learning and working memory performance that are not reproduced by amphetamine (62), indicating that the effect cannot be wholly attributed to increased dopaminergic neurotransmission. However, NMDA antagonists do lead to potentiation of the disruptive effects of amphetamine on learning in monkeys, indicating that interactions between the NMDA and dopamine systems may nevertheless be important.

Table 21.1 Densities of Receptors Labeled by (^{3}H)TCP and (^{3}H) (+)SKF-10,047

Region	Receptor Densities (fmol/mg tissue)	
	(^{3}H)TCP site[a]	(^{3}H)(+)SKF-10,047 sites[b]
Hippocampus		
CA1	104	200
CA2	105	217
CA3	66	173
Dentate	111	200
Subiculum	84	—
Frontal cortex	83	134
Superior colliculus	65	134
Nucleus accumbens	52	100
Cerebellum	47	145
Locus ceruleus	46	140
Amygdala	42	—
Dorsomedial hypothalamus	40	162
Central gray	26	167
Substantia nigra	14	145
Pontine reticular nucleus	8	84
Globus pallidus	0	—
Corpus callosum	0	6

[a]See reference 25.
[b]See reference 127.

Anatomic Localization

The anatomic localization of the PCP receptor in the rat brain has been determined by receptor autoradiography using [^{3}H]PCP (63) and [^{3}H]TCP (64) as radioligands (Table 21.1). High densities of PCP receptors are found in anterior forebrain areas, including neocortex and olfactory structures. The highest selective localization is observed in the dentate gyrus and the CA1 and CA2 subfields of the hippocampus. [^{3}H]TCP binding displays low density in midbrain/pontine areas. White matter areas (including corpus callosum and anterior commissure) as well as certain gray matter areas (including globus pallidus, the ventral tegmental area, and some pontine and thalamic nuclei) show near background levels of [^{3}H]TCP binding. Within the spinal cord [^{3}H]TCP-labeled sites are localized primarily to laminae I and II in cervical and thoracic spinal segments. In lamina I the density of sites decreases along a rostral to caudal gradient (65). Autoradiographic evidence indicates that PCP receptors are located postsynaptically rather than presynaptically in the perforant path-dentate granule cell system of the adult rat (66). A phylogenetic study indicates that PCP receptors are old from an evolutionary standpoint, occurring in the neural tissue of a large number of animal species, including monkey, guinea pig, chicken, turtle, frog, goldfish, shark, planarian, and sea anemone, although their pharmacology in invertebrates is not congruent with that found in vertebrates (67).

Molecular Characterization of the PCP Receptor

On a molecular level, the NMDA receptor complex is heteroligemeric in structure, consisting of combinations of NMDAR1 and NMDAR2 subunits. NMDAR1 is the key subunit in the formation of the receptor complex (35). All functional NMDA receptor complexes contain a Type 1 (NR1) subunit; complexes may also contain variable numbers of modulatory subunits (NR2A-D). The sensitivity of NMDA receptors to modulatory effects of glycine are conferred by residues within the NR1 subunit itself (68–69). Thus, in general, all functional NMDA receptor complexes should be sensitive to glycine. Eight variants of NMDAR1 (NMDAR1a–h) have been identified which reflect alternative mRNA splicing. These clones have distinct sensitivities to agonists, antagonists, Zn^{2+}, and polyamines. Polyamines are also conferred by regulatory (NR2) subunits which are differentially expressed across brain regions (70). NMDA receptors are primarily postsynaptic in localization and occur on both projection- and interneurons (71–72). In some brain regions, however, and especially in target areas of the mesolimbic/mesocortical system, NMDA receptors may also be localized presynaptically and thus may regulate release of dopamine from presynaptic terminals (56, 73–75). It has been suggested that such receptors consist solely of NR1 subunits and thus may have a different pharmacological profile from postsynaptic receptors (76).

Effects of PCP at Non-NMDA Receptor Molecular Targets

At doses at least 10-fold higher than those at which it exerts its unique behavioral effects by blocking NMDA receptor-mediated neurotransmission, PCP also blocks presynaptic monoamine reuptake, thus directly increasing synaptic levels of dopamine and noradrenaline. Levels sufficient to block monoamine reuptake may be achieved during high-dose intoxication and may contribute to the stimulatory effects of PCP seen at those doses. Ketamine, even at high dose, fails to block monoamine transporters. This observation may contribute towards explaining the apparently lower incidence of episodes of extreme agitation and violence following ketamine, rather than PCP, intoxication. At doses associated with extremely high-dose intoxication, PCP blocks neuronal Na^+ and K^+ channels. Such effects may be relevant to the seizures observed following PCP overdose. PCP also interacts with a variety of other central nervous system (CNS) receptors including cholinergic, opiate, and GABA/benzodiazepine receptors. However, the majority of such effects take place at concentrations that are not likely to be encountered in clinical situations.

PSYCHOPHARMACOLOGY

Pharmacokinetics

In practical terms PCP must be considered an extremely potent compound among drugs of abuse. It is extremely lipid-soluble and can reach significant brain levels upon administration via routes including oral, inhalation, smoking, and topical (77). A typical street dose is about 5 mg (one pill, joint, or line) (see reference 103). Based upon the pharmacokinetics of PCP, such a dose would result in a serum PCP concentration between 0.01 and 0.1 μM. Marked psychotic reactions have been observed associated with undetectably low serum concentrations (< 0.02 μM), while concentrations of > 0.4 μM induce gross impairment of consciousness. Abusers characteristically titrate their dose in an effort to maximize the "high" while avoiding unconsciousness. Failures of judgment or variations in purity of supplies often result in inadvertent overdose, which may lead to severe medical complications. Serum concentrations above 1.0 μM are strongly associated with coma, seizures, respiratory arrest, and death (78–79). The highest recorded serum and cerebrospinal fluid concentrations are in the range of 1.0 to 2.0 μM.

PCP manifests a volume of distribution of 6.2 l/kg (80). Its lipophilicity facilitates accumulation in fatty body tissues, including the brain (81–82). Mobilization of adipose stores, as with exercise, may release sequestered PCP, leading to "flashbacks" (81–82).

Metabolism is primarily hepatic, with renal secretion of hydroxylase metabolites (83). The pK_a of 8.5 implies that PCP is largely ionized while in the stomach or the urinary tract. In passing through the pyloric valve PCP enters a nonacidic environment in the small intestine in which it becomes largely nonionized and readily absorbed across the mucosal membrane, whereupon enterohepatic recalculation can account for the fluctuating clinical course so often observed in intoxication.

Chemistry

A phenylcyclohexylamine, PCP is easily synthesized from the starting materials piperazine, cyclohexanone, and potassium cyanide. The synthesis proceeds through the intermediate 1-piperidinocyclohexanecarbonitrile (PC), which is reacted with phenylmagnesium bromide to form PCP (84). The simplicity of this reaction, which enables PCP to be synthesized with almost no training or equipment, suggests that a resurgence of PCP abuse may follow successful efforts to eliminate from the marketplace drugs of abuse derived from natural products. During the 1970s analytic surveys of street samples revealed that a large portion of drugs marketed as THC, mescaline, and LSD were actually PCP (85). Another consequence of the ease of synthesis is the contamination of significant percentages of analyzed street samples of PCP by dangerously high amounts of residual PC (86). In physiologic saline, PC decomposes to hydrocyanic acid (87). When PC-contaminated PCP is smoked, about 58% of the PC breaks down to cyanide and organic by-products (88). Although devoid of PCP-like pharmacological activity, PC is thus more acutely toxic and may be implicated in some PCP-related fatalities.

Psychotomimetic Effects

In normal volunteers, single small intravenous subanesthetic doses (0.05–0.1 mg/kg) of PCP acutely induced a psychotic state in which subjects became withdrawn, autistic, negativistic, and unable to maintain a cognitive set, and manifested concrete, impoverished, idiosyncratic, and bizarre responses to proverbs and projective testing. Some subjects showed catatonic posturing (89–95). These schizophrenia-like alterations in brain functioning went beyond the symptom level; thus, in formal studies of neuropsychological function, PCP induced a spectrum of specific disturbances in attention (96), perception (93–96), and symbolic thinking (92, 96) strikingly similar to those seen in schizophrenia. The most severe impairment caused by PCP was observed in tests requiring selective attention and paired-association learning (89). An important clinical correlate of this data is that any person under the influence of even a small dose of PCP or a similar drug will have profound alterations of higher emotional functions affecting judgment and cognition, even in the absence of gross neurological findings.

In recompensated schizophrenic subjects, single low doses of PCP caused rekindling of presenting symptomatology lasting as long as 6 weeks, without evocation of any symptoms or signs not typical of the schizophrenic illness (90, 91, 93, 97). An important clinical correlate of this data is that schizophrenics or preschizophrenics abusing a PCP-type drug run an extremely high risk of severe psychiatric morbidity.

The epidemic of PCP abuse during the 1970s yielded considerable data on psychotomimetic effects in other than experimental subjects. This literature cannot be used directly to ascertain risks because no firm evidence is available of what percentage of recreational PCP users sought or were brought to medical attention. However, it is striking that in retrospective studies of patients hospitalized for complications of PCP use, the PCP-intoxicated patients could not be distinguished from schizophrenics based upon presenting symptomatology (98, 99).

Reinforcing Effects

SELF-ADMINISTRATION

A series of studies established that experimental monkeys avidly self-administer large doses of PCP intravenously (100–102) and orally (103). In such studies the finding that the monkeys, given unlimited access to PCP, maintained nearly continuous intoxication distinguished abuse patterns of PCP from those of classical stimulants. In this respect the reinforcing properties of PCP resemble those of opiates and CNS depressants more than those of stimulants (104). Furthermore, as distinct from findings on opiate self-administration, monkeys self-administered doses of PCP high enough to cause marked behavioral effects (104). Given the similarities between behavioral effects of PCP in monkeys and humans, this research validates the clinical impression of avid human self-administration of PCP. PCP-like drugs have been shown to stimulate brain reward areas, lowering the threshold for intracranial self-stimulation (105, 106). Such effects define a classical profile for drugs abused by humans and are shared by other abused compounds, including opiates and benzodiazepines, despite their differing mechanisms of action.

TOLERANCE

In rats and monkeys, repeated administration of PCP on a daily or more frequent schedule leads to two- to fourfold rightward shifts in dose-response curves. The major determinant of this moderate tolerance appears to be biodispositional (107–109). As opposed to the modest degree of tolerance observed upon intermittent dosing, it appears that much greater degrees of tolerance are induced by continuous self-administration (104). In human subjects, there is a paucity of scientific data on PCP tolerance, but tolerance has been observed in burn patients given repeated ketamine for analgesia (110).

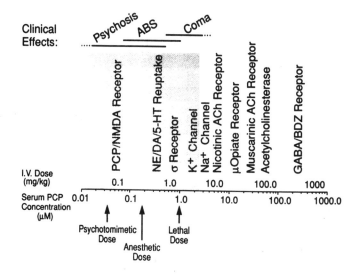

Figure 21.1. Dose range of PCP effects. The relationship is shown among dose, serum concentration, molecular target sites, and clinical effects. The shaded area represents clinically relevant interactions. (Reprinted with permission from Javitt DC, Zukin SR. Recent advances in the phencyclidine model of schizophrenia. Am J Psychiatry 1991;148:1301–1308. Copyright 1991, the American Psychiatric Association.)

DEPENDENCE

After unlimited-access self-administration of PCP for a month or longer, severe signs of withdrawal reaction were observed in monkeys when the drug was discontinued. These included vocalizations, bruxism, oculomotor hyperactivity, diarrhea, piloerection, somnolence, tremor, and seizures (111). Similarly severe reactions might be expected following binging upon PCP by human abusers.

In summary, primate research has established a compelling case that PCP is a strongly addictive drug. Despite a paucity of controlled studies of tolerance and dependence in humans, PCP must be considered comparable to classical drugs of abuse in this respect.

CLINICAL TOXICOLOGY

The range of clinical effects of PCP can be correlated with dose and serum PCP concentration (Fig. 21.1). The variety of effects of PCP are due to its interaction with a variety of molecular target sites.

The highest-affinity target site is the CNS PCP/NMDA receptor, which would be the only system affected significantly at very low PCP doses. Serum PCP levels up to about 0.1 μM would correspond with a clinical state manifesting psychotomimetic symptoms without overt physiological disturbances of vital functions. Serum levels just higher than 0.1 μM correspond to dissociative anesthesia. At still higher doses, as additional receptor sites are occupied, acute brain syndrome accompanied by prominent neurological and cardiovascular complications ensues. Serum levels of 1.0 μM and above are associated with coma and lethal complications. The PCP-induced organic mental syndrome and coma result from the summation of PCP's actions noncompetitively inhibiting the PCP/NMDA receptor, blocking the reuptake sites for catecholamines and indolamines, and blocking sodium and potassium channels and nicotinic and muscarinic cholinergic receptors. It is not currently feasible to design and administer treatments specifically targeting each of the molecular sites at which PCP exerts its toxic effects. Therefore, treatment must address each symptom cluster and organ system.

MEASURES TO REDUCE SYSTEMIC PCP LEVELS

Trapping of ionized PCP in the stomach has led to the suggestion of continuous nasogastric suction for PCP intoxication (112, 113). However, such a strategy can be needlessly intrusive and can lead to complications such as electrolyte imbalances. The same principle can be more safely implemented by administration of activated charcoal, which has been shown to bind PCP and to diminish toxic effects of PCP in animals (114).

Trapping of ionized PCP in urine has led to the suggestion of urinary acidification as an aid to drug elimination. Current thinking (115) is that this strategy is ineffective and potentially dangerous, since only a small portion of PCP is excreted in urine; that metabolic acidosis itself carries significant risks; and that acidic urine would increase the risk of renal failure secondary to rhabdomyolysis (116, 117).

Finally, the extremely large volume of distribution of PCP implies that neither hemodialysis nor hemoperfusion significantly promote drug clearance (115).

At present no drug has been shown to function as a "PCP antagonist." No drug will work for PCP as naloxone works for heroin because any compound binding to the PCP receptor, which is located within the ion channel of the NMDA receptor, would block NMDA receptor-mediated ion fluxes as does PCP itself. Recent progress in elucidation of NMDA receptor mechanisms suggests concepts that could lead to pharmacological strategies promoting NMDA receptor activation, such as administration of glycine or polyamines (or derivatives or precursors of such substances). Increasing channel open time would promote dissociation of PCP from its binding sites. There is evidence that oral glycine in massive doses can antagonize PCP-induced behaviors in the mouse (118). However, no clinical trials of such strategies for PCP intoxication in humans have been carried out to date. Therefore, treatment must be supportive and directed at specific symptoms and signs of toxicity. It is important to remember that especially after oral administration, PCP levels may continue to rise unevenly over many hours or even days. Therefore, a prolonged period of clinical observation is mandatory before concluding that no serious or life-threatening complications will ensue.

NEUROLOGICAL TOXICITY

The majority of PCP-intoxicated patients manifest nystagmus, which may be horizontal, vertical, or rotatory (119). Nystagmus is one of the crucial signs that can help distinguish PCP intoxication from a naturally occurring psychotic state. Coma can occur at any point during intoxication (120). There is a dose-dependent neuronal hyperexcitability ranging from increased deep tendon reflexes through opisthotonos to seizure states, generalized or focal, up to status epilepticus (119, 121–123). Focal neurological findings may arise on the basis of cerebral vasoconstriction (121, 124). Seizures are managed with intravenous benzodiazepines (120).

BEHAVIORAL TOXICITY

As noted earlier, a schizophrenia-like psychotic state can be observed after extremely low doses of PCP. In fact, such cognitive and emotional alterations are the threshold effects of this drug. The question of whether specific PCP-induced psychotic symptoms respond to treatment with neuroleptics has not been addressed. Clinically urgent behavioral complications of PCP abuse stem not from the "core" psychotic symptoms themselves but rather from behavioral disinhibition, which can be coupled with severe anxiety, panic, rage, and aggression. Such reactions are more common with somewhat higher doses, at which some degree of delirium as well as neurological symptoms and other medical derangements can be observed. The behavioral manifestations can severely compromise the clinician's ability to treat the medical complications.

The disruption of sensory input by PCP causes unpredictable, exaggerated, distorted, or violent reactions to environmental stimuli. A cornerstone of treatment is therefore minimization of sensory inputs to PCP-intoxicated patients. Patients should be evaluated and treated in as quiet and isolated an environment as possible. Precautionary physical restraint is recommended by some authorities (115) with the risk of rhabdomyolysis balanced by the avoidance of violent or disruptive behavior.

DRUG TREATMENT

Since no specific PCP antagonist is available, the goal of drug therapy for PCP-induced behavioral toxicity is sedation. This can be accomplished by using benzodiazepines or neuroleptics. There is no convincing evidence that either class of compounds is clinically superior.

Benzodiazepines are effective via either oral or parenteral (intramuscular) routes. Diazepam is effective via the oral route but may be poorly or erratically absorbed intramuscularly. Lorazepam may be given via either route of administration.

Haloperidol is the neuroleptic most commonly used for this indication. Because of the anticholinergic actions of PCP, neuroleptics with potent intrinsic anticholinergic properties should be avoided.

AUTONOMIC TOXICITY

Severe hyperthermia has been observed, which can arise in a delayed fashion and can be of fatal proportions (125, 126). The anticholinergic properties of PCP can dose-dependently evoke a full spectrum atropine-like toxicity and can be managed accordingly when life-threatening.

CARDIOVASCULAR TOXICITY

Mild hypertension may be seen even in minimal PCP intoxication. At higher doses hypertension may be severe and hypertensive crisis with CNS complications has been reported.

RHABDOMYOLYSIS

This potentially devastating complication arises from multiple sources. First, PCP in high doses has a direct excitatory action upon the muscle endplate. Second, the behavioral toxicity of high doses of PCP frequently leads to muscle trauma. This combination of factors can lead to severe rhabdomyolysis, myoglobinuria, and renal failure.

CONCLUSION

Phencyclidine stands as the prototype of a unique category of drugs—NMDA channel blockers—that have high abuse potential and severe adverse medical effects in the abuse situation. The epidemic of phencyclidine abuse in the late 1970s and early 1980s, in focusing scientific attention upon the basic mechanisms by which these drugs exert their singular combination of psychotomimetic, cognitive, and abuse-promoting effects, played a key role in advancing research in a major new area of neuroscience. Future scientific progress in elucidating mechanisms of NMDA receptor function may lead to specific pharmacotherapeutic approaches to treatment of PCP abuse and toxicity.

References

1. Collins VJ, Gorospe CA, Rovenstine EA. Intravenous nonbarbiturate, nonnarcotic analgesics: preliminary studies. I. Cyclohexylamines. Anesth Analg 1960;39:303–306.
2. Greifenstein FE, Yoskitake, J, DeVault M, Gajewski JE. A study of 1-aryl cyclohexylamine for anesthesia. Anesth Analg 1958;37:283–294.
3. Johnstone M, Evans V, Baigel S. Sernyl (Cl-395) in clinical anesthesia. Br J Anaesth 1958; 31:433–439.
4. Corssen G, Domino EF. Dissociative anesthesia: further pharmacologic studies and first clinical experience with the phencyclidine derivative CI-581. Anesth Analg 1966;45:29–40.
5. Meyer JS, Greifenstein F, DeVault M. A new drug causing symptoms of sensory deprivation. J Nerv Ment Dis 1959;129:54–61.
6. Petersen RC, Stillman RC. Phencyclidine: a review. National Institute on Drug Abuse publication no. 1980-0-341-166/614. Washington, DC: U.S. Government Printing Office, 1980.
7. Waldorf D, Beschner G. PCP use. Services research notes. Washington, DC: National Institute on Drug Abuse, 1979.
8. Fishburne PM, Cisin I. National survey on drug abuse: main findings 1979. National Institute on Drug Abuse publication no. (ADM) 80–976. Washington, DC: U.S. Government Printing Office, 1980.
9. Miller JD, Cisin I, et al. National survey on drug abuse: main findings 1982. National Institute on Drug Abuse publication no. (ADM) 83–1263. Washington, DC: U.S. Government Printing Office, 1983.
10. National Institute on Drug Abuse. National survey on drug abuse: main findings 1985. National Institute on Drug Abuse publication no. (ADM) 88–1586. Washington, DC: U.S. Government Printing Office, 1988.
11. Davis BL. The PCP epidemic: a critical review. Int J Addictions 1982;17(7):1137–1155.
12. Newmeyer JA. The epidemiology of PCP use in the late 1970s. J Psychedelic Drugs 1980;12: 211–215.
13. Johnston LD, Bachman JG, O'Malley PM. National survey results on drug use from the Monitoring the Future study, 1975–1994: Volume I: secondary school students. National Institute on Drug Abuse publication no. 95–4026. Washington, DC: U.S. Government Printing Office, 1995.
14. Hinkley S, Greenwood J. Emergency room visits in DAWN projected to the nation. A report from the Drug Enforcement Administration. Washington, DC: U.S. Government Printing Office, 1981.
15. Crider R. Phencyclidine: changing abuse patterns. In: Clouet DH, ed. Phencyclidine: an update. NIDA Res Monogr Ser 1986;64.
16. Substance Abuse and Mental Health Services Administration, Office of Applied Studies. National survey on drug abuse: population estimates 1994. DHHS Publication No. (SMA) 95–33063. Washington, DC: U.S. Government Printing Office, 1995.
17. Substance Abuse and Mental Health Services Administration, Office of Applied Studies. National survey on drug abuse: main findings 1993. DHHS Publication No. (SMA) 95–3020.Washington, DC: U.S. Government Printing Office, 1995.
18. Substance Abuse and Mental Health Services Administration, Office of Applied Studies. National survey on drug abuse: main findings 1992. DHHS Publication No. (SMA) 94–3012. Washington, DC: U.S. Government Printing Office, 1994.
19. National Institute on Drug Abuse. Release of national survey results on drug use from the Monitoring the Future study, 1995. Press Release, December 15, 1995.
20. Substance Abuse and Mental Health Services Administration, Office of Applied Studies. Annual emergency room data 1992. DHHS Publication No. (SMA) 94–2080. Washington, DC: U.S. Government Printing Office, 1994.
21. Substance Abuse and Mental Health Services Administration, Office of Applied Studies. Annual emergency room data 1993. DHHS Publication No. (SMA) 95–3019. Washington, DC: U.S. Government Printing Office, 1995.
22. National Institute on Drug Abuse. Epidemiologic trends in drug abuse, community epidemiology work group, June 1995; Volume 1: highlights and executive summary. National Institutes of Health publication no. 95–3990. Washington, DC: U.S. Government Printing Office, 1995.
23. National Institute on Drug Abuse. Epidemiologic trends in drug abuse, community epidemiology work group, December 1995; Volume 1: highlights and executive summary. National Institutes of Health publication no. 96–4128. Washington, DC: U.S. Government Printing Office, 1996.
24. Vincent JP, Kartalouski B, Geneste P, Kamenka JM, Lazdunski M. Interaction of phencyclidine ("angel dust") with a specific receptor in rat brain membranes. Proc Natl Acad Sci USA 1979;76:4678–4682.
25. Zukin SR, Zukin RS. Specific ^{3}H-phencyclidine binding in rat central nervous system. Proc Natl Acad Sci USA 1979;76:5372–5376.
26. Holtzman SG. Phencyclidine-like discriminative effects of opioids in the rat. J Pharmacol Exp Ther 1980;214:614–619.
27. Holtzman SG. Phencyclidine-like discriminative stimulus properties of opioids in the squirrel monkey. Psychopharmacology (Berl) 1982;77: 295–300.
28. Quirion R, Hammer RP Jr, Herkenham M, Pert CB. Phencyclidine (angel dust) F "opiate" receptor: visualization by tritium-sensitive film. Proc Natl Acad Sci USA 1981;78:5881–5885.
29. Hampton RY, Medzihradsky F, Woods JH, Dahlstrom PJ. Stereospecific binding of ^{3}H-phencyclidine in brain membranes. Life Sci 1982;30:3147–3154.
30. Mendelsohn LG, Kalra V, Johnson BG, Kerchner GA. F opioid receptor: characterization and co-identity with the phencyclidine receptor. J Pharmacol Exp Ther 1985;233:597–602.
31. Sircar R, Rappaport M, Nichtenhauser R, Zukin SR. The novel anticonvulsant MK-801; a potent and specific ligand of the brain phencyclidine/F receptor. Brain Res 1987;435:235–240.
32. Zukin SR, Temple A, Gardner EL, Zukin RS. Interaction of [^{3}H](!)SKF 10,047 with brain F receptors: characterization and autoradiograph visualization. J Neurochem 1986;46:1032–1041.
33. Zukin SR. Differing stereospecificities distinguish opiate receptor subtypes. Life Sci 1982; 31:1307–1310.
34. Holtzman SG. Phencyclidine-like discriminative stimulus properties of opioids in the squirrel monkey. Psychopharmacology 1982;77:295–300.
35. Michaelis EK (1996) Glutamate neurotransmis-

sion: characteristics of the NMDA receptors in mammalian brain. Neural Notes 2:3–7.

36. Cotman CW, Monaghan DT, Ganong AH. Excitatory amino acid neurotransmission: NMDA receptors and Hebb-type synaptic plasticity. Annu Rev Neurosci 1988;11:61–80.

37. MacDermott AB, Mayer ML, Westbrook GL, Smith SJ, Barker JL. NMDA-receptor activation increases cytoplasmic calcium concentration in cultured spinal cord neurones. Nature 1985; 321:519–522.

38. Mayer ML, MacDermott AB, Westbrook GL, Smith SJ, Barker JL. Agonist- and voltage-gated calcium entry in cultured mouse spinal cord neurons under voltage clamp measured using arsenazo III. J Neurosci 1987;7:3230–3244.

39. Morris RGM. Synaptic plasticity and learning: selective impairment of learning in rats and blockade of long-term potentiation in vivo by the N-methyl-D-aspartate receptor antagonist AP5. J Neurosci 1989;9:3040–3057.

40. Wood PL. The co-agonist concept: is the NMDA-associated glycine receptor saturated in vivo? Life Sci 1995;57:301–310.

41. Schell MJ, Molliver ME, Snyder SH. D-serine, an endogenous synaptic modulator: localization to astrocytes and glutamate-stimulated release. Proc Natl Acad Sci USA 1995;92:3948–3952.

42. Lerma J, Zukin RS, Bennett MV. Interaction of Mg2+ and phencyclidine in use-dependent block of NMDA channels. Neurosci Lett 1991; 123:187–191.

43. Javitt DC, Zukin SR. Biexponential kinetics of [3H]MK-801 binding: evidence for access to closed and open N-methyl-D-aspartate receptor channels. Mol Pharmacol 1989;35:387–393.

44. Olney JW, Labruyere J, Price MT. Pathological changes induced in cerebrocortical neurons by phencyclidine and related drugs. Science 1989; 244:1360–1362.

45. Ellison G. The N-methyl-d-aspartate antagonists phencyclidine, ketamine, and dizocilpine as both behavioral and anatomical models of the dementias. Brain Res Rev 1995;20:250–267.

46. Sharp FR, Butman M, Aardalen K, Nickolenko J, Nakki R, Massa SM, et al. Neuronal injury produced by NMDA antagonists can be detected using heat shock proteins and can be blocked with antipsychotics. Psychopharmacol Bull 1994;30:555–560.

47. Fix AS. Pathological effects of MK-801 in the rat posterior cingulate/retrosplenial cortex. Psychopharmacol Bull 1994;30:577–582.

48. Chen G, Ensor CR, Russell D, Bohner B. The pharmacology of 1-(1-phenylcychohexyl) piperidine-HCl. J Pharmacol Exp Ther 1959;127: 240–250.

49. Jackson DM, Johansson C, Lindgren L-M, Bengtsson A. Dopamine receptor antagonists block amphetamine and phencyclidine-induced motor stimulation in rats. Pharmacol Biochem Behav 1994;48:465–471.

50. Toth E, Lajtha E. Antagonism of phencyclidine-induced hyperactivity by glycine in mice. Neurochem Res 1986;11:393–400.

51. Owens SM, Hardwick WC, Blackall D. Phencyclidine pharmacokinetic variability among species. J Pharmacol Exp Ther 1987;242:96–101.

52. Xu X, Domino EF. Phencyclidine-induced behavioral sensitization. Pharmacol Biochem Behav 1994;47:603–608.

53. Steinpreis RE, Sokolowski JD, Papnikolaou A, Salamone JD. The effects of haloperidol and clozapine on PCP- and amphetamine-induced suppression of social behavior in the rat. Pharmacol Biochem Behav 1994;47:579–585.

54. Irifune M, Shimizu T, Nomoto M, Fukuda T. Involvement of N-methyl-D-aspartate (NMDA) receptors in noncompetitive NMDA receptor antagonist-induced hyperlocomotion in mice. Pharmacol Biochem Behav 1995;51: 291–296.

55. French ED, Vantini G. Phencyclidine-induced locomotor activity in the rat is blocked by 6-hydroxydopamine lesion of the nucleus accumbens: comparisons to other psychomotor stimulants. Psychopharmacol 1984;82:83–88.

56. French ED, Pilapil C, Quirion R. Phencyclidine binding sites in the nucleus accumbens and phencyclidine-induced hyperactivity are decreased following lesions of the mesolimbic dopamine system. Eur J Pharmacol 1985; 116:1–9.

57. Steinpreis RE, Salamone JD. The role of nucleus accumbens dopamine in the neurochemical and behavioral effects of phencyclidine: a microdialysis and behavioral study. Brain Res 1993; 612:263–270.

58. Wang T, French ED. L-Glutamate excitation of A10 dopamine neurons is preferentially mediated by activation of NMDA receptors: extra-intracellular electrophysiological studies in brain slices. Brain Res 1993;627:299–306.

59. Wang T, O'Connor WT, Ungerstedt U, French ED. N-methyl-D-aspartic acid biphasically regulates the biochemical and electrophysiological response of A10 dopamine neurons in the ventral tegmental area: in vivo microdialysis and in vitro electrophysiological studies. Brain Res 1994;666:255–262.

60. Chen GM, Weston JK. The analgesic and anesthetic effect of 1-(1-phenylcyclohexyl) piperidine-HCl on the monkey. Anesth Analg 1960; 39:132–138.

61. Verma A, Moghaddam B. NMDA receptor antagonists impair prefrontal cortex function as assessed via spatial delayed alternation performance in rats: modulation by dopamine. J Neurosci 1996;16:373–379.

62. Moersbaecher JM, Thompson DM. Effects of phencyclidine, pentobarbital, and d-amphetamine on the acquisition and performance of conditional discriminations in monkeys. Pharmacol Biochem Behav 1980;13:887–894.

63. Quirion R, Hammer RP Jr, Herkenham M, Pert CB. Phencyclidine (angel dust)/sigma "opiate" receptor: visualization by tritium-sensitive film. Proc Natl Acad Sci USA 1981;78:5881–5885.

64. Sircar R, Zukin SR. Quantitative localization of [3H]TCP binding in rat brain by light microscopy autoradiography. Brain Res 1985;344: 142–145.

65. Annonsen LM, Seybold VS. Phencyclidine and F receptors in rat spinal cord: binding characterization and quantitative auto radiography. Synapse 1989;4:1–10.

66. Bekenstein JW, Bennett JP Jr, Wooten GF, Lothman EW. Autoradiographic evidence that NMDA receptor-coupled channels are located postsynaptically and not presynaptically in the perforant path-dentate granule cell system of the rat hippocampal formation. Brain Res 1990; 514:334–342.

67. Vu TH, Weissman D, London ED. Pharmacological characteristics and distributions of F- and phencyclidine receptors in the animal kingdom. J Neurochem 1990;54:598–604.

68. Hirai H, Kirsch J, Laube B, Betz H, Kuhse J. The glycine binding site of the N-methyl-D-aspartate receptor subunit NR1: Identification of novel determinants of co-agonist potentiation in the extracellular M3-M4 loop region. Proc Natl Acad Sci USA 1996;93:6031–6036.

69. Wafford KA, Kathoria M, Bain CJ, et al. Identification of amino acids in the N-methyl-D-aspartate receptor NR1 subunit that contribute to the glycine binding site. Mol Pharmacol 1995; 47:374–380.

70. Rock DM, MacDonald RL. Polyamine regulation of N-methyl-D-aspartate receptor channels. [review]. Annu Rev Pharmacol Toxicol 1995; 35:463–482.

71. Huntley GW, Vickers JC, Morrison JH. Cellular and synaptic localization of NMDA and non-NMDA receptor subunits in neocortex: organizational features related to cortical circuitry, function and disease. Trends Neurosci 1994;17: 536–542.

72. Landwehrmeyer GB, Standaert DG, Testa CM, Penney JB Jr, Young AB. NMDA receptor subunit mRNA expression by projection neurons and interneurons in rat striatum. J Neurosci 1995;15:5297–5307.

73. Javitt DC. Negative schizophrenic symptomatology and the phencyclidine (PCP) model of schizophrenia. Hillside J Clin Psychiatry 1987; 9:12–35.

74. Krebs MO, Desce JM, Kemel ML, Gauchy C, Godeheu G, Cheramy A, Glowinski J. Glutamatergic control of dopamine release in the rat striatum: evidence for presynaptic N-methyl-D-aspartate receptors. J Neurochem 1991;56: 81–85.

75. Koek W, Colpaert FC, Woods JH, Krebs MO, Desce JM, Kemel ML, et al. Glutamatergic control of dopamine release in the rat striatum: evidence for presynaptic N-methyl-D-aspartate receptors on dopaminergic nerve terminals. J Neurochem 1991;56:81–85.

76. Wang JK, Thukral V. Presynaptic NMDA receptors display physiological characteristics of homomeric complexes of NR1 subunits that contain the exon 5 insert in the N-terminal domain. J Neurochem 1996;66:865–868.

77. Burns RS, Lerner SE. Perspectives: acute phencyclidine intoxication. Clin Toxicol 1976;9: 477–501.

78. Walberg CB, McCarron MM, Schulze BW. Quantitation of phencyclidine in serum by enzyme immunoassay: results in 405 patients. J Anal Toxicol 1983;7:106–110.

79. Pearce DS. Detection and quantitation of phencyclidine in blood by use of [2H5]phencyclidine and select ion monitoring applied to non-fatal cases of phencyclidine intoxication. Clin Chem 1976;22:1623–1626.

80. Cook CE, Brine DR, Jeffcoat AR. Phencyclidine disposition after intravenous and oral doses. Clin Pharmacol Ther 1982;31:625–634.

81. James SH, Schnoll SH. Phencyclidine: tissue distribution in the rat. Clin Toxicol 1976; 9:573–582.

82. Misra AL, Pontani RB, Bartolomeo J. Persistence of phencyclidine (PCP) and metabolites in brain and adipose tissue and implications for long-lasting behavioural effects. Res Commun Chem Pathol Pharmacol 1979;24:431–445.

83. Wong LK, Biemann K. Metabolites of phencyclidine. Clin Toxicol 1976;9:583–591.

84. Soine WH. Clandestine drug synthesis. Med Res Rev 1986;6(1):41–74.

85. Lerner SE, Burns RS. Phencyclidine use among youth: History, epidemiology, and chronic intoxication. In: Petersen RC, Stillman RC, eds. Phencyclidine (PCP) abuse: an appraisal. NIDA Res Monogr Ser 1978;21:66–118.

86. Soine WH, Vincek WC, Agee DT, et al. Contamination of illicit phencyclidine with 1-piperidinocyclohexanecarbonitrile. J Anal Toxicol 1980;4:217–221.

87. Soine WH, Brady KT, Balster RL, Underwood JQ III. Chemical and behavioral studies of 1-piperidinocyclohexanecarbonitrile (PCC): evidence for cyanide as the toxic component. Res Commun Chem Pathol Pharmacol 1980; 30(1):59–70.
88. Lue LP, Scimeca JA, Thomas BF, Martin BR. Pyrolyte fate of piperidinocyclohexanecarbonitrile, a contaminant of phencyclidine during smoking. J Anal Toxicol 1988;12:57–61.
89. Bakker CB, Amini FB. Observations on the psychotomimetic effects of Sernyl. Compr Psychiatry 1961;2:269–280.
90. Luby ED, Cohen BD, Rosenbaum F, Gottlieb J, Kelley R. Study of a new schizophrenomimetic drug Sernyl. Arch Neurol Psychiatry 1959;81:363–369.
91. Ban TA, Lohrenz JJ, Lehmann HE. Observations on the action of Sernyl—a new psychotropic drug. Can Psychiatr Assoc J 1961;6: 150–156.
92. Davies BM, Beech HR. The effect of 1-arylcyclohexylamine (Sernyl) on twelve normal volunteers. J Ment Sci 1960;106:912–924.
93. Domino EF, Luby E. Abnormal mental states induced by phencyclidine as a model of schizophrenia. In: Domino EF, ed. PCP (phencyclidine): historical and current perspectives. Ann Arbor, MI: NPP Books, 1981:37–50.
94. Rodin EA, Luby ED, Meyer JS. Electroencephalographic findings associated with Sernyl infusion. EEG Clin Neurophysiol 1959;11: 796–798.
95. Rosenbaum G, Cohen BD, Luby ED, Gottlieb JS, Yelen D. Comparisons of Sernyl with other drugs. Arch Gen Psychiatry 1959;1:651–656.
96. Cohen BD, Rosenbaum G, Luby ED, Gottlieb JS. Comparison of phencyclidine hydrochloride (Sernyl) with other drugs. Arch Gen Psychiatry 1961;6:79–85.
97. Itil T, Keskiner A, Kiremitci N, Holden JMC. Effect of phencyclidine in chronic schizophrenics. Can Psychiatr Assoc J 1967;12: 209–212.
98. Erard R, Luisada PV, Peele R. The PCP psychosis: prolonged intoxication or drug-precipitated functional illness? J Psychedelic Drugs 1980;12:235–245.
99. Yesavage JA, Freeman AM III. Acute phencyclidine (PCP) intoxication: psychopathology and prognosis. J Clin Psychiatry 1978;44: 664–665.
100. Balster RL, Johanson CE, Harris RT, Schuster CR. Phencyclidine self-administration in the rhesus monkey. Pharmacol Biochem Behav 1973;1:167–172.
101. Lukas SE, Griffiths RR, Brady JV, Wurster RM. Phencyclidine-analogue self-injection by the baboon. Psychopharmacology (Berl) 1984; 83:316–320.
102. Risner ME. Intravenous self-administration of phencyclidine and related compounds in the dog. J Pharmacol Exp Ther 1982;221:627–644.
103. Carroll ME, Meisch RA. Oral phencyclidine (PCP) self-administration in rhesus monkeys: effects of feeding conditions. J Pharmacol Exp Ther 1980;214:339–346.
104. Balster RL. Clinical implications of behavioral pharmacology research on phencyclidine. In: Clouet DH, ed. Phencyclidine: an update. NIDA Res Monogr Ser 1986;64:148–161.
105. Nazzaro JM, Seeger TF, Gardner EL. Naloxone blocks phencyclidine's dose-dependent effects on direct brain reward thresholds. In: Proceedings of World Conference on Clinical Pharmacology and Therapeutics. London: British Pharmacological Society, 1980:949.
106. Herberg LJ, Rose IC. The effect of MK-801 and other antagonists of NMDA-type glutamate receptors on brain-stimulation reward. Psychopharmacology (Berl) 1989;99:87–90.
107. Woolverton WL, Balster RL. Tolerance to the behavioral effects of phencyclidine: importance of behavioral and pharmacological variables. Psychopharmacology (Berl) 1979;64: 19–24.
108. Johnson KM, Balster RL. Acute and chronic phencyclidine administration: relationship between biodispositional factors and behavioral effects. Subst Alcohol Actions Misuse 1981; 2:131–142.
109. Freeman AS, Martin BR, Balster RL. Relationship between the development of behavioral tolerance and the biodisposition of phencyclidine in mice. Pharmacol Biochem Behav 1984; 20:373–377.
110. Carroll ME. PCP, the dangerous angel. In: Snyder SH, ed. The encyclopedia of psychoactive drugs. New York: Chelsea House, 1985.
111. Balster RL, Woolverton WL. Continuous access phencyclidine self-administration by rhesus monkeys leading to physical dependence. Psychopharmacology (Berl) 1980;70:5–10.
112. Aronow R, Done AK. Phencyclidine overdose: an emerging concept of management. JACEP 1978;7:56–59.
113. Done AK, Aronow R, Miceli JN. The pharmacokinetics of phencyclidine in overdosage and its treatment. In: Petersen RC, Stillman RC, eds. Phencyclidine (PCP) abuse: an appraisal. NIDA Res Monogr Ser 1978;21:210–217.
114. Picchioni AL, Consroe PF. Activated charcoal—a phencyclidine antidote, or hog in dogs [letter]. N Engl J Med 1979;300:202.
115. Baldridge EB, Bessen HA. Phencyclidine. Emerg Med Clin North Am 1990;8(3): 541–550.
116. Bywaters EGL, Stead JK. The production of renal failure following injection of solutions containing myohaemoglobin. Q J Exp Physiol 1944;33:53–70.
117. Perri GC, Gorini P. Uraemia in the rabbit after injection of crystalline myoglobin. Br J Exp Pathol 1952;33:440–444.
118. Toth E, Lajtha A. Antagonism of phencyclidine-induced hyperactivity by glycine in mice. Neurochem Res 1986;11:393–400.
119. McCarron MM, Schulze BW, Thompson GA, et al. Acute phencyclidine intoxication: incidence of clinical findings in 1,000 cases. Ann Emerg Med 1981;10:237–242.
120. McCarron MM, Schulze BW, Thompson GA, et al. Acute phencyclidine intoxication: clinical patterns, complications, and treatment. Ann Emerg Med 1981;10:290–297.
121. Crosley CJ, Binet EF. Cerebrovascular complications in phencyclidine intoxication. J Pediatr 1979;94:316–318.
122. Kessler GF, Demers LM, Berlin C, et al. Phencyclidine and fatal status epilepticus [letter]. N Engl J Med 1974;291:979.
123. Patel R, Connor G. A review of thirty cases of rhabdomyolysis-associated acute renal failure among phencyclidine users. Clin Toxicol 1986;23:547–556.
124. Altura BT, Altura BM. Phencyclidine, lysergic acid diethylamide, and mescaline: cerebral artery spasms and hallucinogenic activity. Science 1981;212:1051–1052.
125. Stine RJ. Heat illness. JACEP 1979;8: 154–160.
126. Thompson TN. Malignant hyperthermia from PCP [letter]. J Clin Psychiatry 1979;40:327.
127. Sircar R, Nichtenhauser R, Ieni JR, Zukin SR. Characterization and autoradiographic visualization of $(+)-[3H]SKF10,047$ binding in rat and mouse brain: further evidence for phencyclidine/"sigma opiate" receptor commonality. J Pharmacol Exp Ther 1986; 237:681–688.

22 INHALANTS

Charles W. Sharp and Neil L. Rosenberg

Volatile substances are ubiquitous and varied. Numerous substances are currently abused, yet inhalation to produce euphoria can be traced to the ancient Greeks (1). With the advent of the use of anesthetics in the mid-1800s, chloroform and ether parties occurred, and these substances are still used today (2, 3). Another anesthetic, euphemistically called "laughing gas," accurately describes one of the recreational uses of another anesthetic, nitrous oxide, which also originated in the late 1800s. It is stated that the use of ether and nitrous oxide at parties initiated the use of these compounds as anesthetics (4). With the increased use of gasoline at the turn of the century, many more substances became available through the process of petroleum "cracking" and distillation and were included in many types of solvents, cleaners, degreasers, and glues. These products can be found everywhere, in industry, in the workplace, and in the home. Thus it is not surprising that anyone could find a favorite sweet smelling substance to "get high on." These substances are a bargain when one compares the going price of a "toke" or a "hit" of marihuana or cocaine. With that in mind, this chapter reviews many of those substances most commonly now known to be abused through inhalation of "unheated" vapors.

The practice of "sniffing," "snorting," "huffing," "bagging," or inhaling to get high describes various forms of inhalation. If the substance is glue or some other dissolved solid, the user will empty the can's contents (or a gas) into a plastic bag and then hold the bag to the nose and inhale ("bagging"). Another method is to soak a rag with the mixture and then stick the rag in the mouth and inhale the fumes ("huffing"). A simple but more toxic approach is to spray the substance directly into the oral cavities. This allows these abusers to be identified by various telltale clues, e.g., organic odors on the breath or clothes, stains on the clothes or around the mouth, empty spray paint or solvent containers, and other unusual paraphernalia. These telltale clues may enable one to identify a serious problem of solvent abuse before it causes serious health problems or death.

EPIDEMIOLOGY

Prevalence

The extent of this drug problem is greater than most realize. Inhalant use exists not only in developed countries but also in underdeveloped countries. Other countries, e.g., England (5, 6) and countries in the American hemisphere (7), are systematically evaluating the abuse of solvents (8–18). Several recent reports have identified inhalant (solvent) abuse as a problem of serious proportion (7, 19). In the United States, the pattern of inhalant abuse is exemplified by national studies, the annual "high-school" (20), "young adults" (21), and "national household" surveys (22) and by state surveys such as the New York (23) and Texas surveys (24, 25).

Although we primarily rely on broad state or national surveys, these surveys do not clearly delineate many regions where high populations of inhalant use occurs, such as in some inner cities that include impoverished or ethnic minorities or other isolated communities, especially those of Native Americans. In most surveys, there appears to be an underrepresentation of blacks in the solvent-abusing populations (26). Although Hispanic groups are considered to be overrepresented in the solvent-abusing population, surveys generally do not show a much greater percentage of this group who abuse solvents than of the more general "Anglo-American" population or of the population as a whole. The extent of use in these groups is difficult to evaluate properly, as many of the inhalant abuse individuals are not accessed by survey systems. To look at the regional problems of solvent abuse, Beauvais and Oetting have comprehensively studied many Native American groups (7); others have studied Hispanic communities (27).

Not readily observed in the nationwide surveys, a higher use of inhalants was observed for Hispanic groups residing outside New York City (28). Of greater interest is their recent study of "transients" (23). Although the lifetime prevalence of inhalants by the household adult population was 2–4%, the lifetime use of "transients" was 15–18%. Cocaine use and heroin use (in New York City) were higher in this group also (45% and 27%, respectively).

Individual states as well as the national government began to evaluate the extent of the problem of inhalant abuse in the late 1960s and early 1970s. Updates are available nationally from the National Institute on Drug Abuse, the Substance Abuse and Mental Health Services Administration, and various state drug agencies. The extent of use of inhalants has been compared (29, 30) to that of cocaine and/or other stimulants (amphetamines or "uppers"). It is still interesting to make that comparison (see Table 22.1). In most surveys, more subjects under 18 have used inhalants (and stimulants) on either an experimental (ever used) or a more frequent (current use) level of exposure. In this age group, inhalant use compares to that observed for stimulants only on an "ever used" basis in the high-school survey. Use of any drug by this age group is higher only for marihuana, alcohol, and cigarettes. In the next age group (18–25 years), the use of cocaine is increased and now exceeds that for use of either inhalants or stimulants. The experimental and/or current use of most drugs had been declining until 1995, when an upward trend in drug use was observed. However, for many years, the level of every category of use of inhalants by those under 18 has been steadily increasing except for the use of organic nitrites, which has decreased. What is most startling is the use of inhalants by younger aged groups (e.g., eighth graders). Use of inhalants by this group is highest (31) and seems to be growing, as noted by the Johnston et al. 1995 national high-school report (20). Some decline in inhalant use has been noted in the Liu and Maxwell 1995 Texas surveys (25).

By analyzing patterns of use over a time period (representative of an individual's maturation through comparison of different age groups) and utilizing data from various surveys, use of inhalants appears to decline during or after the "teen years." With most other drugs, the use increases during one's maturation. This would indicate that there are few new initiates into inhalants (as compared to other drugs) during the 20s (age) and that there are fewer inhalant "heavy" users during these years of maturity. With cocaine, the opposite trend occurs. In summary, the annual prevalence rates of inhalants in young adults appears to be lower than in younger populations. Several hypotheses exist for this: (a) a loss of this population to the survey, (b) a forgetfulness about this type of behavior, or (c) a downgrading of this event in their conscious thinking.

Often a topic of discussion, what drug use occurs first? In the high-school survey (20), the percentage of first use of inhalants occurred at about the same rate in all the grades measured. However, the rate of initiation was slightly higher in the eighth grade. The rate of first use of inhalants was the same as for marihuana in the sixth grade and much lower than that for alcohol or cigarettes. The ninth grade (followed by the tenth) is the grade where most initiate any form of drug abuse. Thus, inhalants or marihuana was cho-

Table 22.1   Drug Prevalence

	% Ever Used						Current Use (Within Past 30 Days)					
	Inhalants		Stimulants		Cocaine		Inhalants		Stimulants		Cocaine	
	1988	1994	1988	1994	1988	1994	1988	1994	1988	1994	1988	1994
High school (20)												
Eighth graders[a]		19.9		12.3		3.6		5.6		3.6		1.0
Seniors	17.5	17.7	19.8	15.7	12.1	5.9	3.0	2.7	4.6	4.0	3.4	1.5
Young adults (21)												
Young adults (19–28)	15	13.2	28.8	17.1	28.2	15.2	0.6	0.5	2.7	1.7	5.7	1.3
College students	12.6	12	17.7	9.2	15.8	5.0	1.3	0.6	1.8	1.5	4.2	0.6
Others	12.5		27.4		24.1		1.2		4.5		6.4	
Household (29a, 46)												
12–17 yr olds	8.8	7.0	4.2	1.9	3.4	1.7	2.0	1.6	1.2	0.5	1.1	0.3
18–25 yr olds	12.5	10	11.3	3.3	19.7	12.1	1.7	0.8	2.4	0.5	4.5	1.2
26–34 yr olds	9.8	11.1	15.4	7.8	26.5	23	0.6	0.4	0.9	0.4	2.6	1.3
35+ yr olds	1.8	3.1	3.6	4.5	4.0	7.9	0.5	0.1	0.4	0.2	0.4	0.4
Texas secondary (24)												
Grade 7	33.1	20.2	10.5	2.5	4.0	2.8	11.8	7.1	4.5	1.1	1.1	1.0
Grade 8	32	23.8	12.3	5.5	5.2	4.7	9.4	7.5	5.4	2.3	2.7	1.4
Grade 12	25.5	14.5	25	9.9	11.6	8.3	3.3	2.0	6.8	2.6	4.2	2.4
Texas Inmates (25, 29b)												
Youth (10–17 yr olds)	39	33.4	29	16.5	47	38.5	13	11	10	4.1	23	15.7
Adult (18 and older)	27.2	15.7	50.5	28.4	60.4	55.4	2.1	0.6	10.3	3.5	25.2	17.9

aData not adjusted for nitrite use.

sen equally in these very early years, but at a lower rate than was alcohol or tobacco.

One of the more grim statistics gathered regarding drug abuse relates to death. There is no current U.S. government group gathering data on the number of deaths associated with inhalant use. In 1970, and more recently, Bass attempted to obtain these statistics (32–34). Deaths are reported to Poison Control Centers but are related to products and include accidental deaths as well as those caused by the subject using the product to get high. Even though this data cannot be used to determine prevalence of deaths resulting from inhalation to get high, the Annual Report of the American Association of Poison Control Centers (35) lists many deaths caused by hydrocarbons; and many of these are related to butane deaths. This report includes only a fraction of the deaths relating to solvent abuse. Anderson noted their concern about an increasing number of deaths caused by these gases (36). This group in England has been accumulating data on deaths related to inhalant abuse for over two decades. They reported 63 in 1982, 117 in 1985, 116 in 1987, 113 in 1989, 151 in 1990 (the highest number), 122 in 1991, and 73 in 1993. Gas fuels are accounting for increasing proportions of the deaths (33% in 1989 to over 50% in 1992–1993). Other products classified as aerosols (mainly fluorocarbons), solvents in adhesives, and other solvents (mainly trichloroethane) contributed almost equally to account for about 70% of the deaths in 1989. Most deaths are attributed to direct toxic effects (19, 37). These include direct toxic effects (e.g., cardiotoxic actions of butane, fluorocarbons, and other gases), inhalation of gastric contents, trauma, and suffocation (19, 37). There are also other causes of death related to inhalation of these substances (e.g., running in front of a car during or after intoxication). Garriott et al. have documented such occurrences in their compilation of similar data for the Dallas and San Antonio areas (38, 39).

Sociocultural Factors

The bases for inhaling solvents are similar to those described over a decade ago by Cohen (40). These substances are widely available, are readily accessible, cheap, and legally obtained. The substances make the solvent abuser forget and relieve the solvent abuser's boredom. These substances provide a quick high, with a rapid dissipation of the high and with a minimal hangover. However, subjects who use heavily over short periods often complain of headaches. Many solvent abusers, more than other drug users, are poor, come from broken homes, and do poorly in school (41, 42). However, reports generally indicate a lower-than-expected use of inhalants by blacks than socioeconomic indicators would indicate. Some Hispanic groups, especially recent immigrants from Latin-American countries, and Native Americans on reservations have a higher percentage of inhalant users than the population as a whole. Difficulty with acculturation and strong peer influence enhance the entrance into inhalant use as well as other drug use (29). The family atmosphere is often disruptive for the abuser and has been identified as less adjusted or more conflictual than for controls (43).

Oetting et al. (42) have categorized those who use inhalants into three groups: (a) inhalant-dependent adults, (b) polydrug users, and (c) young inhalant users. The first group will have the most serious health problems because they have used heavily for a long time; the latter will be those for whom treatment is most desirable to keep them from progressing to the other groups and for whom there may be hope for successful intervention. Although all inhalant abusers use other drugs or alcohol, the first group predominately use inhalants, even though other drugs are available. The second group infrequently uses inhalants primarily because they cannot get their drug of choice; their problems will arise more from the use of other drugs and not be related to those outlined in this chapter. Those in this last group, the young inhalant users, are in the experimentation period of solvents, having started with either tobacco, alcohol, and possibly even marihuana as well as inhalants. Before any of this group matures into the first group, intervening behavioral modifications are very important.

One trait that is often associated with sniffers is disruptive behavior. Some report them to be more violent. However, in a carefully controlled study, the only aggressive feature that stood out is the self-directed aggression (41). Cognitive measures of these groups support the antisocial and self-

destructive nature of inhalant abusers. At least two major studies found these groups to have lower Wechsler verbal scores; it remains unanswered today as to whether these groups self-selected inhalant abuse because of these predilections or whether the deficiencies came about as the result of inhalant abuse (41). In some instances, examination of school records indicates that cognitive deficits probably occurred before inhalant use began. Although it is uncertain how they became dysfunctional, it is very likely that inhalants prevent their continued growth and development (42). For further reading on the nature of the problem, especially the social-cultural conditions, we refer the reader to other reviews (29, 40, 44).

Substances Inhaled

Despite the widespread availability and inhalation of these substances, it was not until the 1950s that nationwide attention focused on what was euphemistically called "glue sniffing" by reporters (45) and by judicial action. The term is still widely used today to describe a myriad of substances that now include special shoe polishes, glue, gasoline, thinners, solvents, aerosols (paint, cooking lubricant spray, deodorant, hair spray, electronic cleaners and others), correction fluids, cleaning fluids, refrigerant gases (e.g., fluorocarbons and the newer incompletely halogenated replacements (46), anesthetics, whippets (whipped cream propellants), organic nitrites, and even cooking or lighter gas. In this context, it is not unheard of to find kids selling toluene obtained from large commercial drums or to see vendors distributing nitrous oxide from commercial cylinders of the gas, which are easily transported in cars. It is important to keep in mind that there are many different chemicals in these different products, all of which have different physiological effects and different toxicities as well as different chemical properties. Sometimes, the substances are listed on the container with or without the proportion of each. Some of the possible substances found in different products are listed in Table 22.2.

One aspect of the inhalant abuse problem is often brought up but not an-

Table 22.2. Chemicals Commonly Found in Inhalants

Adhesives	
Airplane glue	Toluene, ethyl acetate
Rubber cement	Hexane; toluene; methyl chloride; acetone; methyl ethyl ketone; methyl butyl ketone
PVC cement	Trichloroethylene
Aerosols	
Paint sprays	Butane; propane (U.S.); fluorocarbons; toluene; hydrocarbons ("Texas Shoe Shine," a spray paint containing toluene)
Hair sprays	Butane; propane (U.S.); fluorocarbons
Deodorants; air fresheners	Butane; propane (U.S.); fluorocarbons
Analgesic spray	Fluorocarbons
Asthma spray	Fluorocarbons
Anesthetics	
Gaseous	Nitrous oxide
Liquid	Halothane; enflurane
Local	Ethyl chloride
Cleaning agents	
Dry cleaning	Tetrachloroethylene; trichloroethane
Spot removers	Tetrachloroethylene; trichloroethane; trichloroethylene
Degreasers	Tetrachloroethylene; trichloroethane; trichloroethylene
Solvents	
Polish remover	Acetone, ethyl acetate, toluene
Paint remover	Toluene; methylene chloride; methanol
Paint thinners	Toluene; methylene chloride; methanol
Correction fluid thinners	Trichloroethylene; trichloroethane
Fuel gas	Butane
Lighter	Butane; isopropane
Fire extinguisher	Bromochlorodifluoromethane
Food products	
Whipped cream	Nitrous oxide
Whippets	Nitrous oxide
"Room odorizers" (Locker room; Rush; Poppers)	(Iso)amyl nitrite; (iso)butyl nitrite; isopropyl nitrite; butyl nitrite, cyclohexylnitrite

swered to anyone's satisfaction. That is, why are certain specific substances inhaled. Some consider the odor to be important; others believe that the feeling one gets is most important. It is difficult to say what substances are preferred. Rankings of ever used substances may put glue and gasoline at the top (22). However, a more detailed questionnaire (24) ranked correction fluids at the top with glue, gasoline, and spray paint being the next most frequent. A survey of delinquent children ranked paint sprays as the most frequently used substance (24) with nitrites also high on the list. Thinners and other solvents (including toluene per se) were noted to be used more frequently than "Texas shoe shine," a favorite of solvent abusers in the Texas region. The now less-accessible fluorocarbons seem to be used very little (according to this Texas survey), possibly because they are readily available only in the more expensive pressurized refrigerant replacement cans. However, there are still numerous deaths attributed to the inhalational abuse of these fluorocarbons (35).

The very limited abuse of some spray products (e.g., frying pan coaters) today could indicate a low desire for the butane and isopropane used to replace the fluorocarbons. However, the use of butane lighter and other "cooking" gases here and in England (19, 47–49) refute that hypothesis. The availability of the pure gas in pressurized containers nullifies the need for separating these gases from other substances in aerosols. It is indeed unusual that these very dangerous substances are inhaled, and it is hard to tell whether this is a passing fancy or whether some really like to get "dizzy" on the butane and propane gases.

A recent report of this problem in the Cincinnati region would indicate that this use of butane gas causes enough deaths in this country to be concerned about the abuse of fuel gases, whether or not it is a passing form of inhalant abuse (50). Other cases continue to be reported. The bottom line is that there are a variety of substances used, probably based more on availability than individual preference. Yet, sniffers seem to go out of their way to get their favorite, e.g., Texas "shoe shine," or clear lacquer or gold spray paints, or other local or current favorites. In other regions, the fad may almost exclusively be limited to other inhalants, e.g., nitrous oxide, butane gases, or gasoline.

Evans and Raistrick (51) summarized the "sniffer's" conception of phenomenology when they sniffed butane gas or toluene. Moods, thoughts, hallucinations (except tactile), and colors appeared similar under either compound. However, time passed slowly under butane and more rapidly under toluene. This one study would indicate that butane may be an acceptable substitute for one of the most widely used substances, toluene (and related products), and be used for some time to come. In an effort to reduce the undesired exposure to cooking gases, it is now mandatory to add thiols to some portable gas containers such as propane tanks and has been suggested to be added to all forms of gas containers similar to that added to our natural gas supply.

One study is notable because it evaluated the inhalation event and did not rely on retrospective evaluation (52). This was only possible because nitrous oxide is an approved anesthetic. The investigators measured moods over time at different doses resembling those of the "recreational user." They noted that the effects lasted only a couple of minutes, and word tests demonstrated that memory retention within 5 minutes of the event was reduced. Some liked the effect, while others did not. Other studies have measured the neuropsychological effects of nitrous oxide on humans after lower 1-hour doses (53) or after anesthesia (54). The abuse of this substance may also be related to prior exposure in a medical situation. Reports discuss the use of nitrous oxide for anxiety reduction, especially for children in dental treatment (55, 56); another even suggests use of nitrous oxide for treatment of alcoholism (57), an untested and unapproved treatment. Most tragically, deaths are still noted following abuse of this substance (58–61).

The addictive nature of fluorocarbons is exemplified by cases of asthma inhalers who inhale beyond the point of medication (62). This is one of the few marketable forms of fluorocarbons in substances used by the public, except for the pressurized refrigerant refillers for air conditioner systems, as the United States banned the use of fluorocarbons, as the propellant for most commercial aerosols, at the onset of the 1980s because of atmospheric pollution.

Not only are various commercial household products used for "pleasure," many anesthetics are often utilized (63–65). That these substances are abused by middle-class professionals not only demonstrates the diversity of the groups that abuse inhalants but also focuses on the basic nature of the physical properties of most of these volatile agents. Almost all solvents produce anesthesia if sufficient amounts are inhaled; some of them are described in a detailed study (66). Although this is an important property of the agent, the ability to produce anesthesia does not seem to correlate with the extent of abuse of any given substance.

Because of the diversity and complex composition of the products, there are often incorrect referrals to what particular solvents are being abused. Toluene is often quoted as the substance involved when other substances are also present and may contribute to the problem or be the primary substance at issue. This can best be visualized by the following example. Transmission fluid has been reported to be abused and identified to contain toluene. However, there is no toluene in transmission fluid. However, there is toluene in "Trans-go," a wax stripper, which is a substance of abuse in the same Florida area where transmission fluid is reportedly abused. When inquiries are made of users as to the substances they are abusing, it is easy to see how the above transliteration (misnomer) could easily occur, and a reporting error, result. Also some reports associating toluene with a particular syndrome may have missed the correct substance that is the cause of that syndrome. To correctly identify the substance, it is critical that clinical measures of body fluids be conducted to correlate a clinical syndrome with a particular substance. Clues may be derived from containers, but that is often not helpful, as many products do not identify all the substances and may often only refer to some of the ingredients as nontoxic hydrocarbons.

TOXICOLOGY OF INHALANT ABUSE

Acute Intoxication

Most commercial products that are inhaled contain several distinctly different solvents, each with its own potential distinct toxicity. In addition, most "inhalant abusers" have inhaled a variety of products to excess before they appear in a treatment facility. An exception would be a novice experiencing an overdose—usually resulting in anoxia and possibly death. The majority of inhalant abusers never reach a hospital or an outpatient facility.

To understand the solvent abuser, one can conceive of the intoxicated state as a quick "drunk," as many of the symptoms resemble alcohol intoxication. Evaluation of these individuals provide several of the following symptoms: initial excitation turning to drowsiness, disinhibition, lightheadedness, and agitation. With increasing intoxication, individuals may develop ataxia, dizziness, and disorientation. In extreme intoxications, they may show signs of sleeplessness, general muscle weakness, dysarthria, nystagmus, and occasionally hallucinations or disruptive behavior. Several hours after, especially if they have slept, they are likely to be lethargic, hungover with mild to severe headaches. Chronic abuse is associated with more serious complications including weight loss, muscle weakness, general disorientation, inattentiveness, and lack of coordination.

Most reports have described the acute intoxication in heavy users of toluene vapors. Acute intoxication with toluene produces headache, euphoria, giddiness, and cerebellar ataxia. At lower levels (just over 200 ppm), fatigue, headache, paresthesia, and slowed reflexes appear (67). Exposure at levels approaching 1000 ppm causes confusion or delirium, and euphoric effects appear at or above that level. Although solvent abusers have favorites, as described above, they often use an unpredictable array of solvents. Multiple components in the mixtures may enhance the net toxicity in a synergistic or additive manner. More specific syndromes and details of the clinical features of the chronic inhalant abuser are described below and are related as closely as possible to specific substances.

Death is rare in the course of acute intoxication, but when it does occur, it is usually the result of asphyxia or ventricular fibrillation or induced cardiac arrhythmia following high exposures to identified mixtures of solvents. "Cerebral anoxia associated with VSA [volatile substance abuse] fatalities may be related to multiple factors including asphyxia, cerebral and pulmonary oedema, cardiac arrhythmias and arrest, terminal unconsciousness, hyperpyrexia[,] and others" (Ref. 68, p. 194). Bass showed a high association of deaths with the abuse of substances containing fluorocarbon propellants and other solvents as well. Although these types of incidences may have declined in the United States because of the restriction of the use of fluorocarbons in aerosols in 1980, fluorocarbon-related deaths still appear to be of major concern (19, 68–70) in work-related accidents (71) and elsewhere. It is not as evident, but the results of several cases link fibrillation or other cardiac insufficiencies to the use of other halocarbons (3, 36, 72–77). These types of products range from anesthetics (halothane) used by hospital and other medical personnel to the more common solvents (dichloroethanes, trichloroethanes, tetrachloroethanes, trichloroethylene) contained in cleaning fluids and typing correction fluid solvents. The chlorohydrocarbons derived from correction fluids have been judged the cause of recent deaths (78–80). Some cardiac arrhythmias have also been reported following abuse of substances containing toluene, as well as a nonfatal respiratory arrest (81). Today, sudden deaths are more often associated with some inhalants containing butane and propane (49).

Although not common, anesthetics have also been indicated as the cause of deaths (2, 64, 82). Severe problems, even deaths, have resulted from the abuse of these compounds by medical professionals, especially nitrous oxide (60, 61, 83). It is well known that oxygen should be mixed with nitrous oxide when inhaled for several minutes to an hour. Apparatuses are available for this when it is being used as an anesthetic. However, in some instances (homes, food services, or the ophthalmologist's office where it may be used as a cryogen), there are no masks for mixing these gases, and death has occurred (60). Also, freezing of the lips to the cylinder may occur (84).

In evaluating any patient suspected of inhaling solvents either accidentally or to get "high," it is important to determine as precisely as possible not only the solvent(s) but also other contributing factors (including other drugs such as alcohol, cigarettes, or marihuana, malnutrition, or respiratory irritants such as fumes or viruses) before beginning treatment. These interrelating factors are often more important for some groups of inhalant abusers, in that they use more drugs, are less well nourished, and live in more "polluted" areas than other types of drug abusers.

General Considerations

Although treatments are usually not specific or designed for different solvents, it is important to identify the major contributing factors in order to understand the prognosis and recovery of the individual and in the design of treatment. This is not easy, as it is difficult to identify the causative agents even if one obtains the container or product most often used.

Labels are often insufficient to identify even the major element, let alone any minor elements, that could be contributory to the disease state. It is common for toluene to be listed, but as yet other toxic substances are not identified. For example, one of the more toxic agents, hexane, affects the peripheral nervous system and has been identified in products that did not list it on the product's label. Only through an analysis of the products used (e.g., by quantitative gas chromatography) will it be possible to determine most of the volatile solvents therein. This, of course, may not be sufficient, as identification of one product sniffed by the user does not reveal all the toxicants that should be considered in his or her diagnosis. A "sniffer's" repertoire is quite varied in the type of solvents as well as other drugs used.

In anticipation that the physician, forensic toxicologist, or others will be able to identify the major substances contributing to the disease state, we will attempt herein to delineate the symptoms most often encountered in inhalant abusers and, hopefully on a rational basis, correlate them where possible with the substances that are most likely to be the cause. We will include, where possible, any specific treatments that will be used in addition to the provision of the usual basic supportive care.

To correlate those specific clinical symptoms that result from exposure to various volatile chemicals is not easy, as suitable animal studies have not corroborated many clinical evaluations. Also, months to years of exposure are often necessary for the expression of some disease states. As many inhalant abuse subjects are not admitted to hospitals or outpatient clinics or placed in any drug treatment program for problems associated with inhalant

abuse overdose or dependency, little information has surfaced detailing many of their problems. Therefore, this review utilizes retrospective clinical case studies of inhalant abusers and other solvent-related accidents, whether from abuse or occupational exposures, along with the information derived from animal studies, to identify particular hazards that may result from inhalation exposure.

Recognition of and Criteria for Defining Neurotoxicity

The nervous system may be affected at many levels by organic solvents as well as other neurotoxic substances. As a general rule, resultant syndromes are diffuse in their manifestations (85). Because of their nonfocal presentation, neurotoxic disorders may be confused with metabolic, degenerative, nutritional, or demyelinating disease (85). This principle is illustrated in the setting of chronic toluene abuse, which may resemble the multifocal demyelinating disease, multiple sclerosis, in the findings on neurological examination (86–88). In addition, neurotoxic syndromes rarely have specific identifying features on diagnostic tests such as computed tomography (CT), magnetic resonance imaging (MRI), or nerve conduction studies (85). As a result, mild cases of intoxication may be very difficult to diagnose. The most reliable information, in fact, comes from documented cases of massive exposure, and details of low-level exposure and presymptomatic diagnosis are vague at best.

Acute, high-level exposure to most, if not all, solvents will induce short-lasting effects on brain function, most of which are reversible. Acute incidents that are irreversible probably act by producing secondary systemic effects such as cerebral hypoxia or a metabolic acidosis (89), and none of these incidents has been proven to act by inducing an irreversible functional abnormality. In general, both acute high-level and low-level exposure to organic solvents are associated with full reversibility, and the acute toxicity with high-level exposure in no way predicts whether chronic low-level exposure will lead to an irreversible neurological disease.

Chronic high-level exposure to organic solvents occurs only in the inhalant abuse setting, where levels several thousand fold higher than the occupational setting frequently occur. Chronic neurotoxic disease related to solvent abuse is slowly and incompletely reversible, and usually does not progress after cessation of exposure (87, 88). Both acute and chronic neurotoxicity from organic solvents are functions predominantly related to the dose and duration of exposure.

There may be no relationship between the mechanism of acute neurotoxicity and the clinical manifestations of chronic neurotoxicity. For example, an acute effect of a particular organic solvent may be attributable to the parent compound, while a chronic effect may be associated with a metabolite of this compound. In addition, in several known cases, a solvent has been reported to either diminish or potentiate the neurotoxic potency of a second solvent (90–92).

There is little or no apparent individual variability or altered susceptibility to the neurotoxic effects of either acute or chronic exposure to organic solvents. Except for other toxic exposures or illnesses that also cause neurological sequelae, individuals will likely develop a similar clinical picture when exposed to solvents at equivalent doses for equivalent durations of time.

Chemical structure can predict the neurotoxic effects. An example of this is seen with two closely related compounds: 2,5-hexanedione (the toxic metabolite of *n*-hexane) and 2,4-hexanedione. A fixed dose of 2,5-hexanedione produces axonal degeneration in a particular species very similarly to that produced by hexane, whereas 2,4-hexanedione never produces these changes. Thus, a small but important change in the compound's structure elicits a change from a positive to a negative pharmacological action.

TREATMENT OF THE INHALANT ABUSER

There is no accepted treatment approach for inhalant abusers. Many drug treatment facilities refuse treatment of the inhalant abuser, because many feel that inhalant abusers are resistant to treatment. One program that focusses solely on the comprehensive treatment of inhalant abusers, the International Institute for Inhalant Abuse (IIIA), based in Colorado, uses a 3-phase model that allows for longer periods of treatment. Longer periods of

Table 22.3. Clinical Classification of Inhalant Abusers

Transient social	Transient isolate
Short history of use	Short history of use
Use with friends	Use alone
Petty offenses while intoxicated	No legal involvement
Average intelligence	Average/above intelligence
Possible learning disabilities	No learning disabilities
10–16 years of age	10–16 years of age
Chronic social	Chronic isolate
Long history of use (>5 years)	Long history of use (>5 years)
Daily use with friends	Daily use alone
Legal involvement—misdemeanors	Legal involvement—assaults common
Poor social skills	Poor social skills
Ninth grade education	Ninth grade education
Brain damage	Brain damage
Mid-20s to early 30s	Mid-20s
Mental retardation prevalent	Preuse psychopathology prevalent

Table 22.4. Major Neurologic Syndromes Produced by Organic Solvents

Encephalopathy
  Acute encephalopathy—nonspecific; high-level exposure
  Chronic encephalopathy—seen with repeated high-level exposure over years
Cerebellar ataxia
Peripheral neuropathy—distal axonopathy
Cranial neuropathy—primarily cranial nerves V and VII
Parkinsonism
Visual loss—optic neuropathy
Multifocal
  Central nervous system (e.g., toluene)
  Central and peripheral

treatment are needed to be able to address the complex psychosocial, economic, and biophysical issues of the inhalant abuser. When brain injury, primarily in the form of cognitive dysfunction, is present, the rate of progression in the treatment process is even slower.

The inhalant abuser typically does not respond to usual drug rehabilitation treatment modalities. Several factors may be involved, particularly in situations of the chronic abuser, where significant psychosocial problems may be present. Treatment becomes slower and progressively more difficult when the severity of brain injury worsens as abuse progresses through transient social use (experimenting in groups) to chronic use in isolation (Table 22.3).

Drug screening may be useful in monitoring inhalant abusers (93, 94). Routine urine screens for hippuric acid, the major metabolite of toluene (95), performed 2–3 times weekly will detect the high level of exposure to toluene usually seen in inhalant abusers. It should be noted that the metabolism of any one compound may be modified by the presence of another, either increased (following inducement by drugs, e.g., barbiturates) or decreased (benzene metabolism reduced in the presence of toluene (96)).

Neuroleptics and other forms of pharmacotherapy are usually not useful in the treatment of inhalant abusers. However, as alcohol is a common secondary drug of abuse among inhalant abusers, a monitored program for alcohol abuse may be necessary.

NEUROLOGICAL SEQUELAE OF CHRONIC INHALANT ABUSE

Organic solvents are widely prevalent compounds and inadvertent exposure, primarily industrial, as well as volitional abuse occurs primarily by inhalation, with significantly less absorption occurring via skin or gastrointestinal routes. These compounds are highly lipophilic, which explains their distribution to organs rich in lipids (e.g., brain, liver, adrenal). Unexpired solvents absorbed by the tissues are then eliminated through the kidneys following metabolism of the solvents to more water soluble compounds. In addition, metabolism of some solvents may create additional compounds that are sometimes more toxic than the parent chemical (97–99).

Although most organic solvents produce nonspecific effects following absorption of extremely high concentrations (i.e., encephalopathy), a few produce relatively specific neurological syndromes with low-level, chronic exposure. Table 22.4 lists those syndromes associated with organic solvent exposure. Most of the early animal studies, which served as the basis for the setting of tolerance levels in industry, utilized acute studies to measure the effects, often including high-level exposures that produced lethality. More recent experimental studies have focused on chronic low-level and/or high-level exposures to solvents that result in peripheral and central nervous system syndromes. Major neurotoxic syndromes occurring in individuals chronically exposed to select organic solvents include a peripheral neuropathy, ototoxicity, and an encephalopathy. Less commonly, a cerebellar ataxic syndrome, parkinsonism, or a myopathy may occur alone or in combination with any of these clinical syndromes. In some instances, solvents interact and cause synergistic effects, resulting in multifocal central and peripheral nervous system damage.

Compounds of Interest

The organic solvents described in detail below are not intended to be a complete listing of compounds with associated neurotoxicity. They represent those organic solvents that have been more commonly associated with abuse or where clear neurotoxicity is associated with exposure.

N-HEXANE AND METHYL BUTYL KETONE

These two organic solvents are classified together because both n-hexane and methyl butyl ketone (MBK) are metabolized to the same neurotoxin, 2,5-hexanedione (2,5-HD) and produce a similar peripheral neuropathy. 2,5-HD is responsible for most, if not all, of the neurotoxic effects that follow exposure to n-hexane or MBK (100–102). Methyl ethyl ketone (MEK) alone produces neither clinical nor pathological evidence of a peripheral neuropathy in experimental animals (100). The importance of MEK is related to a synergistic effect between MEK and MBK and between MEK and n-hexane detected in experimental animals and probably in humans (90–92). This potentiation of toxicity of one compound (MBK or n-hexane) by an otherwise nontoxic compound (MEK) underscores the difficulty with sorting out toxic effects of individual solvents contained within a mixture and suggests that occupational exposure to solvent mixtures should be minimized or avoided altogether.

Methyl Butyl Ketone

MBK had limited industrial use until the 1970s when it became more widely used as a paint thinner, clearing agent, and a solvent for dye printing. Soon afterward, numerous outbreaks of polyneuropathy associated with chronic exposure to MBK were being reported (103–107). Originally, MEK had been used as a solvent, followed by a mixture of MEK (90%)/methyl isobutyl ketone (10%). When the methyl isobutyl ketone was replaced by MBK (10%), reports of polyneuropathy began to appear in the literature. The route of exposure is usually inhalation, but exposure has also occurred by the oral route through ingesting contaminated food in work areas and by cutaneous contact.

The clinical syndrome is characterized by the insidious onset of an initially painless sensorimotor polyneuropathy, which begins several months after continued chronic exposure. Even following cessation of exposure, the neuropathy may develop or may continue to progress for up to 3 months. In severe cases, an unexplained weight loss may be an early symptom. Sensory and motor disturbance begins initially in the hands and feet, and sensory loss is primarily small fiber (i.e., light touch, pinprick, temperature) with relative sparing of large-fiber sensation (i.e., position and vibration). Electrophysiological studies reveal an axonal polyneuropathy and pathologically multifocal axonal degeneration and multiple axonal swellings, and neurofilamentous accumulation at paranodal areas is seen (108). Overlying the axonal swellings, thinning of the myelin sheath occurs. These findings are typical of a distal axonopathy or "dying-back" neuropathy described in other toxic and metabolic causes of peripheral neuropathy.

Prognosis for recovery correlates directly with the intensity of the neurological deficit before removal from toxic exposure, with mild to moderate residual neuropathy seen in the most severely affected individuals up to 3 years after exposure.

n-Hexane

Until the 1970s, n-hexane was considered an innocuous solvent. n-Hexane is used in the printing of laminated products, in the extraction of vegetable oils, as a diluent in the manufacture of plastics and rubber, in cabinet finishing, as a solvent in biochemical laboratories, and as a solvent for glues and adhesives.

Cases of n-hexane polyneuropathy have been reported both after occupational exposure (109) and after deliberate inhalation of vapors from products containing n-hexane, such as glues (110–118). Clinically and pathologically, the neuropathy occurring with n-hexane is that of a distal axonopathy (119), indistinguishable from that associated with MBK.

When glues have been analyzed in past reports of polyneuropathy occurring after glue sniffing, n-hexane has been a major component of the products' composition (up to 50% by weight). Another major component of these glues has been toluene. However, polyneuropathy does not occur from inhalation of toluene alone, and in previous reports of n-hexane neuropathy, the neuropathy did not appear until the subject switched to a product containing n-hexane. In contrast to toluene, n-hexane does not usually induce significant signs of central nervous system (CNS) dysfunction, except with high-level exposures where an acute encephalopathy may occur.

Both clinical and experimental studies have shown evidence of CNS effects from n-hexane. Experimental animal studies have shown n-hexane to cause axonal degeneration in the CNS (119, 120). Clinically, cranial neuropathy, spasticity, and autonomic dysfunction occasionally occur (90). Abnormalities on electrophysiological tests of CNS function, including electroencephalography, visual evoked responses, and somatosensory evoked responses, have also been seen (121, 122). In spite of these finds, clinical effects of chronic low-level exposure to n-hexane is restricted to the peripheral nervous system.

TOLUENE (METHYL BENZENE)

Toluene is one of the most widely used solvents and is employed as a paint and lacquer thinner, as a cleaning and drying agent in the rubber and lumber industries, and in the motor and aviation fuels and chemical industries. It is a major component in many paints, lacquers, glues and adhesives, inks, and cleaning liquids. As with other solvents, inhalation is the major route of entry, though some absorption occurs percutaneously. Of all the solvents, toluene-containing substances seem to have the highest potential for abuse (24, 122a).

In 1961, Grabski (123) reported the first patient with persistent neurological consequences of chronic toluene inhalation. Since then, many reports of neurotoxicity, often of a severe nature, have appeared in the literature (86–88, 124–147).

Experience is still not sufficient to determine the incidence of chronic effects of toluene and other volatile hydrocarbons. The neurological pattern, however, has been very clearly delineated, with effects only on the CNS. Syndromes of persistent and often severe neurotoxicity include cognitive dysfunction (86–88, 131, 133, 141, 142, 144, 148–150), cerebellar ataxia (86, 88, 123, 126, 130, 137, 144, 145), optic neuropathy (128, 134), sensorineural hearing loss (128), and an equilibrium disorder (143). Most commonly, toluene neurotoxicity includes several of the above syndromes and has been described as multifocal CNS involvement (86–88, 138, 141, 142, 144). Despite the many instances of "persistent" neurological deficits, in only one study was abstinence documented prior to clinical evaluation (87). This point is of great importance, since it has already been noted that some individuals will go into complete remission with prolonged abstinence (126, 151).

In a study of 20 chronic abusers of spray paint, which almost entirely consisted of toluene, abstinence was documented for at least 1 month prior to evaluation (87). In those chronic solvent abusers, 65% showed neurological impairment. This was a small and unselected sample, so the findings

probably do not reflect the true prevalence of neurological damage. However, there was a fairly consistent pattern of neurological abnormality. As has been suggested, the CNS is selectively vulnerable. In fact, no peripheral neuropathy was found, and there is no convincing evidence that pure toluene or other aromatic hydrocarbons cause peripheral neuropathy. Aliphatic hydrocarbons such as n-hexane, as noted earlier, cause predominantly peripheral nerve damage.

Neurological abnormalities varied from mild cognitive impairment to severe dementia, associated with elemental neurological signs such as cerebellar ataxia, corticospinal tract dysfunction, oculomotor abnormalities, tremor, deafness and hyposmia. Cognitive dysfunction was the most disabling and frequent feature of chronic toluene toxicity and may be the earliest sign of permanent damage. Dementia, when present, was typically associated with cerebellar ataxia and other signs (87). One patient had pyramidal and cerebellar signs without cognitive impairment. Oculomotor dysfunction, deafness, and tremor were seen only in severely affected individuals. Cranial nerve abnormalities were confirmed to olfactory and auditory dysfunction. Toluene-induced optic neuropathy, previously reported (134), was not reported in the larger studies (87, 142) but was not specifically addressed. In a more recent study, visual evoked potential abnormalities were found in a large percentage of chronic toluene abusers and other drug-abusing controls (152).

Other investigators have found a similar syndrome after chronic exposure to toluene (86, 88, 126, 137). Although some investigators emphasized the cerebellar disorder, they noted that most cases also showed impairment in a variety of cerebral functions. In one study, there was a similar pattern of cognitive impairment with neurological abnormality, but the individuals were studied as soon as 3 days after the last exposure, and there have been no data on long-term cognitive outcome long after cessation of prolonged toluene abuse. It should be noted, however, that many chronic toluene abusers have had no persistent cognitive impairment despite approximately calculated cumulative doses equivalent to those in individuals with cognitive impairment (87, 142). This suggests either that the abuse histories obtained were not accurate or that other factors possibly play a role in those individuals.

The clinical data suggest that the cognitive, cerebellar, corticospinal, and brainstem signs are due to diffuse effects of toluene on the CNS. In one prior report of an autopsy of a chronic solvent abuser, there was prominent degeneration and gliosis of ascending and descending long tracts with cerebral and cerebellar atrophy (153). Unfortunately, as in most reports of toluene neurotoxicity, this patient was abusing many solvents contained in several different mixtures, so the effects of individual solvents could not be determined.

A recent report has demonstrated that chronic abuse of toluene-containing substances causes diffuse CNS white matter changes (141). This was based on the findings on MRI of the brain in six individuals and the neuropathological changes in one abuser not studied by MRI. All individuals abused the same toluene-containing mixture, which contained primarily toluene (61%) and methylene chloride (10%). MRI of the six individuals revealed the following abnormalities: (a) diffuse cerebral, cerebellar, and brainstem atrophy; (b) loss of differentiation in the gray and white matter throughout the CNS; and (c) increased periventricular white matter signal intensity on T2-weighted images. More recent MRI studies have supported these original observations (125, 127, 139, 146, 147).

Another recent study attempted to find correlation between the severity of the clinical involvement in 11 chronic toluene abusers and the findings on brainstem auditory evoked responses (BAERs) and MRI (142). Neurological abnormalities were seen in 4 of 11 individuals and included cognitive, pyramidal, cerebellar, and brainstem findings. MRI of the brain was abnormal in 3 of 11 individuals, and all 3 also had abnormalities on neurological examination. Abnormalities on MRI were the same as those reported previously (141). BAERs were found to be abnormal in 5 of 11 individuals and were similar to those previously reported in toluene abusers (86, 138). In this study (142), all three individuals with abnormal MRI scans and neurological examinations also had abnormal BAERs. Two of five individuals with abnormal BAERs, however, had normal neurological examinations and MRI scans. This study suggests that BAERs may detect early CNS injury from toluene inhalation even at a time when neurological examination and MRI scans are normal. These results suggested that BAERs may be a screening test to monitor individuals at risk from toluene exposure for early evidence of CNS injury. However, a more recent study (152) determined that while certain abnormalities on BAERs are very specific for effects of toluene abuse, they are too insensitive to observe in the usual clinical setting.

Neuropathology Section

The neuropathology of chronic inhalant abuse is poorly described, but recent studies have begun to shed some light on possible pathogenetic mechanisms. The first report of neuropathological changes was in an individual who was primarily an abuser of paint thinner containing toluene (153). Closer examination of the case revealed that this individual abused many different volatile substances over more than a decade and the neuropathological changes cannot be considered the result of just toluene. However, there were changes seen diffusely in the white matter that would correlate well with the MRI data. Rosenberg et al. (141) reported the neuropathological findings in one individual who had only changes in the white matter, diffusely, again correlating with the MRI changes. The changes revealed diffuse, ill-defined myelin pallor, which was maximal in the cerebellar, periventricular, and deep cerebral white matter. Neurons were preserved throughout, axonal swelling or beading was not seen, gliosis was minimal, and occasional, scant perivascular macrophage collections were seen. These findings were supported in a more recent neuropathological study (154). In this latter report, the neuropathological and biochemical changes seen in the brains of chronic toluene abusers were identical with those seen in those with adrenoleukodystrophy (ALD). ALD is a rare X-linked disorder associated with accumulation of very long chain fatty acids in certain tissues, including brain (155). These findings suggest that toluene is a white matter toxin; the mechanism of action, however, needs to be explained.

A possible explanation for the effect of toluene on white matter was raised by Unger et al. (146). In this study, the MRI spectroscopic characteristics of liposomes both with and without toluene embedded in the membrane of the liposome were described. The characteristics of the toluene liposomes suggest that there was increased water content, which was the same as the MRI characteristics in the brains of chronic toluene abusers. Their hypothesis is that toluene somehow changes the configuration of certain membrane lipoproteins, making them hydrophilic. Perhaps the gradual accumulation of water is only a marker for the molecular injury that occurs. This may also explain reports of some chronic toluene abusers who, following prolonged abstinence, will have gradual, though incomplete, improvement in their neurological deficit. In other words, since neurons are not being destroyed and membrane components may be replaced over time, clinical improvement may be seen, even in the most severely affected individuals.

Although an exact dose-effect relationship cannot be drawn yet for chronic toluene exposure, it is clear that all severely affected individuals have had heavy and prolonged exposure. The lack of correlation between the type or duration of exposure and neurological impairment may be due to unreliable histories or other factors, such as genetic predisposition (unlikely) or hypoxemia resulting from "huffing" or "bagging." Nutritional factors and other concomitantly used substances may also be involved. Gradual resolution of acute toxicity and absence of withdrawal symptoms were probably due to slow elimination of toluene from the CNS.

Basic Studies

Animals have proved valuable in resolving the basis of the *n*-hexane peripheral neuropathy and have clarified some of the apparent "toluene-induced" neurotoxicities (156–160). Most noteworthy are the studies of Pryor et al. (158, 161) that demonstrate persistent irreversible midfrequency hearing loss by cued behavioral responses, BAERs, and pathology. Other studies (162–164) have extended these findings. Hearing deficits are produced after as little as 2 weeks of exposure to 1200 ppm or 1400 ppm of toluene. This was attributed to cochlear dysfunction rather than the central conduction pathology found in the human studies noted above. Other studies from this group have measured a toluene-induced motor syndrome that is characterized by a widened landing foot splay and a short and widened gait

that may relate to the cerebellar syndrome in humans (165). Mergler and Beauvais (166) have studied olfactory responses to toluene.

TRICHLOROETHYLENE

Trichloroethylene (TCE) is an important organic solvent used extensively in industry in metal degreasing, in extracting oils and fats from vegetable products, in cleaning optical lenses and photographic plates, in paints and enamels, in dry cleaning, and as an adhesive in the leather industry. Although its use in recent years has diminished somewhat as a result of concern that it could be a human carcinogen (167), NIOSH estimates the total number of individuals exposed to TCE to be in excess of 3.5 million (NIOSH 1978).

TCE has been recognized for over 50 years as an industrial hazard with neurotoxic properties (168). It was once commonly used as an anesthetic agent despite early reports of toxicity (169–172). TCE was abandoned as an anesthetic agent, however, apparently not because of its toxicity but because its anesthetic action was weak and eventually better agents became available (173). Clinical experience suggested that it was safe in minimal concentrations and useful, since at the time it was one of the few nonexplosive agents that could supplement nitrous oxide and did not produce significant respiratory depression (173, 174).

Its major neurological manifestation is related to a slowly reversible trigeminal neuropathy (168–170, 175–178), although involvement of other cranial nerves and peripheral nerves has also been described (168, 179, 180). The trigeminal neuropathy associated with TCE intoxication was recognized as characteristic and for a time intentional exposure was considered a useful treatment of trigeminal neuralgia (176). Cranial neuropathies after general anesthesia with TCE were noted over 40 years ago (169, 170, 172). Of 13 cases of multiple cranial nerve palsies following general anesthesia, 2 were related to TCE anesthesia. Twenty-four to forty-eight hours after general anesthesia, individuals developed paresthesia around the lips that then spread to involve the entire trigeminal distribution bilaterally over the ensuing 2–3 days. Motor weakness also occasionally occurred in the trigeminal distribution, and other cranial nerves including facial (VII), optic (II) and other lower cranial nerves also became affected (168, 169). Resolution of the trigeminal neuropathy occurs slowly in an "onion-peel" distribution, felt to be indicative of segmental or nuclear trigeminal involvement (168, 180).

Most importantly, much of the earlier literature on the neurotoxicity of TCE includes observations that were most likely due to decomposition products (e.g., dichloroacetylene) rather than TCE itself (170, 172, 181, 182). Dichloroacetylene, produced most prominently under alkali conditions, reacts violently with air to produce two noxious gases, phosgene and carbon monoxide (182). Dichloroacetylene disrupts the region of the brainstem where the trigeminal nucleus is located in experimental animals and is therefore probably responsible for the neurotoxic properties of TCE (183). Short-term exposure to narcotizing levels of TCE in the industrial setting has also been reported to induce a transverse myelopathy (184). This report is of interest because it has also been shown that a transverse myelopathy can be experimentally induced in the rat with dichloroacetate, which is a possible metabolite of TCE/dichloroacetylene (185). Attempts to experimentally reproduce the neurotoxicity associated with the industrial use of TCE have not been successful with pure grades of TCE (186–189). Pryor's group were the first to identify in rats a midfrequency hearing loss similar to that observed for toluene exposure (190). Others have since corroborated these studies (162, 191, 192). This neurotoxicity may also be peripheral, i.e., cochlear in origin.

Little data are available on the neuropathological changes after TCE exposure. A single autopsied case of an individual who died 51 days after industrial exposure to TCE and TCE decomposition products (probably dichloroacetylene) revealed bilaterally symmetric brainstem lesions (175). These changes were most prominent in the fifth nerve nuclei, spinal tracts, and nerve roots. The fifth nerves both within and outside the brainstem showed extensive myelin and axonal degeneration. Other neuropathological changes were seen but were less prominent.

Although the higher level exposures to TCE and its decomposition products are well-described, reports of long-term, low-level exposure occurring in the industrial setting are relatively few. These reports have focused on neuropsychiatric and behavioral effects including a neurasthenic syndrome with subjective complaints of dizziness, headache, nausea, fatigue, anxiety, and insomnia (193–198). Although these disorders reportedly become more severe with length of employment and degree of exposure, the neurobehavioral and neuropsychological literature on the toxic effects of TCE is so fragmented and poorly documented that it is impossible to make any firm conclusions regarding the low-level, chronic exposure to TCE and its neurotoxic potential (199). Neurobehavioral disturbances to acute, high-level exposure have included severe psychiatric presentations (200, 201).

Several studies have been performed in order to study the behavioral effects of single short-term exposure to TCE (197, 202–205). These studies have indicated that while fatigue and sleepiness occur in humans following exposure to TCE concentrations above 100 ppm for 2 hours, no deterioration in performance or manual dexterity occurs following exposure to levels up to 300 ppm. In one study, adverse effects on performance were seen at levels of 1000 ppm, but no significant effects were seen at lower concentrations (206). In a frequently cited study, detrimental effects of 8 hours of exposure to TCE concentrations of 110 ppm were found on performing tests of perception, complex reaction time, memory, and manual dexterity (197). Others have been unable to replicate this study (202, 205). In a study where subjects were exposed to TCE concentrations of 1000 ppm and optokinetic nystagmus was measured, minimal effects were seen and found to persist for only up to 2 hours (206). Somewhat increased effects are seen when ethanol ingestion is added to the TCE exposure (203, 204), and it has been demonstrated that ethanol will inhibit metabolism of TCE to its breakdown products, trichloroethanol and trichloroacetic acid, thereby increasing TCE concentration in blood (207). In general, however, these studies have shown that the behavioral effects of ethanol are more pronounced than those of TCE.

METHYLENE CHLORIDE (DICHLOROMETHANE)

Methylene chloride is widely used in industry for paint stripping, as a blowing agent for foam, as solvent for degreasing, in the manufacture of photographic film, as the carrier in rapid-dry paints, and in aerosol propellants. It is also used in the diphasic treatment of metal surfaces, in the textile and plastics industry, and for extracting heat-sensitive edible fats and essential oils. It is estimated that almost 100,000 individuals are exposed to methylene chloride in the workplace alone.

As with other solvents, methylene chloride has CNS depressant properties at high levels of exposure and may lead rapidly to unconsciousness and death (208–212). This has been reported both in industrial settings (208, 210) and as a result of solvent inhalation abuse (211, 212).

Methylene chloride has generally been considered safer than other chlorinated hydrocarbons and has not attracted the attention it deserves as a possible cause of chronic CNS dysfunction. Methylene chloride is metabolized to carbon monoxide (213–216), and therefore, both its hypoxia effect as well as its narcotic actions must be considered with regard to its CNS-depressant effects. Carbon monoxide, at high levels, and other forms of cerebral hypoxia are known to cause permanent neurological sequelae.

The acute effects of exposure to methylene chloride have been studied in controlled experiments in humans (217–219). In one study, 11 healthy nonsmokers were exposed to levels of methylene chloride up to 1000 ppm for 1–2 hours (217). Inhalation of methylene chloride at levels of 500–1000 ppm for this length of time was followed promptly by a sustained (at 24 hours postexposure) elevation of carboxyhemoglobin. These levels never reached above 10% saturation, however. Visual evoked responses in the three subjects tested showed an increase in peak-to-peak amplitudes after 2 hours of exposure and returned to baseline 1 hour after termination of exposure. No untoward subjective symptoms occurred at levels of exposure below 1000 ppm. At exposure to concentrations of 1000 ppm, two of three subjects reported "mild lightheadedness," which promptly resolved after cessation of exposure.

The effects of methylene chloride exposure on three tests of cognitive function (reaction time, short-term memory, calculation ability) were tested in 14 normal subjects (218). Repeated tests at different exposures up to 3.5 g/m^3 methylene chloride showed no statistically significant impairment in

performance, although at the highest exposure levels, a greater variation in the responses was obtained for reaction time than under control conditions.

Controlled exposure of normal volunteers for up to 24 hours to various concentrations (up to 800 ppm) of methylene chloride in five separate studies showed the following abnormalities: After 2.5 hours of exposure to 500 ppm, complaints of "general uneasiness" were noted. After 4 hours of exposure to 300 and 800 ppm in only one experiment were mood rating scales noted to be significant for depression. There was no impairment of cognitive performance as measured by tests of short-term memory and calculation ability in any of these studies after 2.5 hours of exposure to methylene chloride at levels up to 1000 ppm. Some impairment was noted in psychomotor performance and vigilance after 3–4 hours of exposure to 800 ppm.

Overall, studies of controlled human exposure to methylene chloride do not show effects of CNS toxicity, except at higher levels of exposure, and even then, the effects are minimal and rapidly reversible. The one exception may be in those inhalant abusers described where methylene chloride is a major component of the compound that they are abusing (87, 141, 142).

There have been few attempts to address the issue of chronic exposure and permanent neurological sequelae to methylene chloride. A group of 46 men working in a factory making acetate film reported an excess of neurological symptoms, compared to a nonexposed referent group (220). These individuals were exposed to a methylene chloride:methanol (9:1) mixture, and methylene chloride concentrations were below 100 ppm. Although neurological symptoms were increased in the exposed group, no abnormalities were detected on neuropsychological tests. No evidence was found of long-term damage that could be attributed to exposure to methylene chloride. In a larger study to assess the potential chronic health effects of methylene chloride, no increase in the number of expected deaths resulting from diseases of the nervous system were seen among 1013 workers chronically exposed to methylene chloride (221).

In summary, the evidence suggests that methylene chloride does not produce permanent neurological sequelae except with massive acute exposures that are associated with hypoxic encephalopathy. No evidence exists that chronic low-level exposure causes any long-term CNS injury.

1,1,1-TRICHLOROETHANE

1,1,1-Trichloroethane is widely used as an industrial degreasing solvent and, compared with other solvents, is relatively less toxic, although several reports of severe toxicity and deaths exist in the literature (75, 76, 222, 223). Its acute toxicity has made it unsuitable as a volatile anesthetic, and its use as a carrier in aerosols was abandoned in the United States in 1973.

In those cases where postmortem examination of the brain was undertaken, the pathological changes suggested cerebral hypoxia either primary to CNS depressant effect (76) or secondary to cardiac or respiratory arrest (75, 76). The possible mechanisms of the effects of 1,1,1-trichloroethane have been postulated to be related to its effect on either the autonomic nervous system (224) or central sleep apnea (225). Chronic cardiac toxicity along with possible sensitization to other inhalation anesthetics has also been suggested as a possible mechanism of 1,1,1-trichloroethane toxicity (77).

There are several reports of the acute behavioral and neuropsychological changes occurring after voluntary exposure of humans to 1,1,1-trichloroethane (226–229). No impairment on a series of psychomotor tests following several days of exposure to 500 ppm of 1,1,1-trichloroethane (226). In another study, no behavioral effects were seen after two 4.5-hour exposures to 450 ppm of 1,1,1-trichloroethane (227). Two studies demonstrated some performance deficits (228, 229). In one study, after 3.5 hours of exposure to 0, 175, and 350 ppm of 1,1,1-trichloroethane, abnormalities were seen on some behavioral tests, most notably those tests concerned with attention and concentration and those concerned with analysis of grammatical statements (229). Overall, these studies suggest mild, if any, acute effects of exposure of individuals to levels of trichloroethane up to 500 ppm.

With regard to low-level, chronic exposure to 1,1,1-trichloroethane, a clinical, neurophysiological and behavioral study of female workers chronically exposed to this agent at levels up to 1000 ppm found no differences, compared to a reference solvent-unexposed group (230).

It appears that 1,1,1-trichloroethane is not associated with either acute or chronic neurotoxicity at levels below 1000 ppm and that the only permanent neurological sequelae are related to cerebral hypoxia after massive exposure. In contrast to trichloroethylene, equivalent doses of trichloroethane do not produce hearing loss when administered to rats (231).

GASOLINE

Gasoline is a complex mixture of organic solvents and other chemicals and metals. The sniffing of gasoline is common among various solvent abusers, especially on some remote Native American reservations. Although some CNS or peripheral neuropathies may occur as a result of the solvents in gasoline, other toxicities may result from tetraethyllead (or its metabolite triethyllead) (232–242). In cases where high lead levels were observed, various disorders have been observed, including hallucinations and disorientation, dysarthria, chorea, and convulsions. The symptoms include moderate to severe ataxia, insomnia, anorexia, slowed peripheral nerve conduction, limb tremors, dysmetria, and sometimes limb paralysis. In most cases, the electroencephalogram (EEG) is normal, but in severe states, an abnormal to severely depressed cortical EEG is observed. Only in one lethal case was there any kidney damage noted; electrolytes are usually in the normal range. Because many of these symptoms in the early stages of the disease can be reversed by parenteral chelation therapy with ethylenediaminetetraacetic acid (EDTA), British anti-Lewisite (BAL) (dimercaprol), and/or penicillamine, it is important to check the serum lead levels in any chronic inhalant abuser to see if this treatment should be prescribed. This type of therapy has recently been reviewed for gasoline alkyllead additives. They did find it to be generally effective and discussed the complications surrounding the treatment of these individuals (243).

ALCOHOLS AND SOLVENTS

One interesting phenomenon has been observed following the exposure to two or more solvents. Degreaser's flush was ascribed to a flushing of the face when occupational workers left their degreasing vats and drank alcohol after leaving work (244, 245). Also, heavy drinking has been associated with toluene exposure (246). More recently, both humans and rats have been noted to be thirsty when exposed to toluene and alcohol (247, 248). Also, animal studies have shown that solvents alter the metabolism of alcohol and prolong its action (93, 249). This might explain the "flushing phenomenon" but may or may not relate to the psychological dependence of solvents or to the development of thirst. An attempt to study the acute effects of alcohol and toluene, at low exposures in human volunteers, failed to produce any interaction by their behavioral measures. This may be indicative that the interaction takes some time and/or high levels of exposure to develop.

Methanol intoxication was identified in an individual intoxicated on a spray can of carburetor cleaner containing toluene (42%), methanol (23%), and methylene chloride (20%) (250). Although mild acidosis did occur, the main concern was the high blood level of methanol. Ethanol therapy was utilized to prevent formation of high levels of formic acid. The above mixture is commonly abused and is very similar in composition to paint thinner; yet the repercussions of prolonged use are unclear.

NITROUS OXIDE

Although nitrous oxide is not an organic solvent, it is discussed here because of its potential for abuse. Nitrous oxide is a commonly used anesthetic and has been noted for some unusual toxicities. This substance is usually not thought of when one discusses inhalants, as it is unique both chemically and in its physiological action. Although it is often abused by youthful experimenters; it is also abused by medical personnel. This substance, nitrous oxide, is used as an anesthetic, as a propellant for whipped cream, and as a octane booster. Laughing gas (N_2O), as it is euphemistically called, was abused soon after it was discovered in the nineteenth century. More recently, it was shown that central and peripheral nerve damage resulted following high levels of N_2O exposure, even in the presence of adequate oxygen (251) and even in short-term use when nitrous oxide was used as an anesthetic (252).

Patients with vitamin B_{12} deficiencies are especially sensitive (253). The symptoms include numbness and weakness in the limbs, loss of dexterity, sensory loss, and loss of balance. The neurological examination indicates sensorimotor polyneuropathy. There is also a combined degeneration of the posterior and lateral columns of the cord that resembles B_{12} deficiencies (251). Studies focusing on the mechanism of action indicate that cobalamins (vitamin B_{12}) are inactivated by N_2O; more recent studies have focused on the methionine synthase enzyme that needs vitamin B_{12} to function (254). Vitamin B_{12} (or folinic acid) did not aid recovery from this disease in some patients (254, 255) but did in others (256). Dietary methionine might be helpful as indicated by studies in rats (257). Rehabilitation proceeds with abstinence and is relative to the extent of neurological damage. Recent reviews cover many of the medical aspects of the adverse effects of and the pros and cons of using nitrous oxide (254, 258–260). Despite the widespread distribution of this information to the medical community and the reduced availability of pressurized cylinders, cases are still being observed (61, 83, 261). The authors also get many calls regarding serious problems related to abuse of nitrous oxide.

In regard to the dependency of nitrous oxide, animal studies on selectively bred mice for alcohol dependence showed a cross-dependency on nitrous oxide (262). They also observed handling-induced convulsions shortly after cessation of nitrous oxide, which could be prevented by either alcohol or nitrous oxide. This might indicate a physical dependence on nitrous oxide that needs to be dealt with in the treatment of patients in this drug abuse state.

PSYCHIATRIC DISTURBANCES IN ORGANIC SOLVENT ABUSE

Psychiatric disorders related to solvent abuse are rare if existent. Ron (263) reviewed the subject and concluded that psychiatric morbidity is "highest in those referred to psychiatric hospitals and lowest in clinics dealing exclusively with volatile substance (VS) (solvent) abuse. The psychiatric diagnoses of these patients do not appear to differ in type or frequency from those given to well-matched populations of nonabusers, and there is little evidence to suggest that specific or persistent psychiatric disability results from this practice." On the other hand, there is little doubt that personality disorders of an antisocial type are common in VS abusers. In an earlier edition (29), Korman summarized an earlier study (264) of psychiatric emergency room admittants as follows: "inhalant users differed significantly from matched other drug users in that they displayed significantly more self-directed destructive behavior, as well as some degree of recent suicidal and homicidal behavior."

A more recent study of older adult subjects (265) observed that most of the patients had antisocial personality disorders. Although they were admitted for their drug dependency, especially on solvents (most for 5–13 years), they also used marihuana, alcohol, stimulants, and other drugs. They interpret this as indicative of the progression of the dependent state with age for a select group of solvent abusers. This chronically disturbed group was also refractory to treatment at this setting. Another study of psychiatric subjects did not identify any group of patients as being inhalant abusers, although 9% used inhalants and other drugs (266). Thus, they could not associate any disorder with the use of inhalants either because it does not exist or because they did not have the appropriate group of patients.

Only one report (267) has identified a personality disorder with inhalant abuse. In a group of 22 randomly selected subjects from a number of patients over a 5-year period, several were considered to have a personality deviation on admission. These were subsequently diagnosed as substance abusers. These patients had inhaled a "toluene-based" glue daily for 2 years or more. Paranoid psychosis was diagnosed for 19 of the subjects; 3 patients had temporal lobe epilepsy. Family alcoholism, crime, and other negative life-styles were present, but no family history of hospitalization for severe mental illnesses was found. Another group studied whether drug abuse (including "glue") at age 11 predicted the development of attention deficit/hyperactivity disorder or depression 4 years later (268).

Some reports of single cases have identified a psychiatric illness associated with solvent overexposure from paints, glues and pure solvents, xylene, or trichlorohydrocarbons (137, 269–272). Subjects showed mild tremors and ataxia as well as disorientation, impaired attention and memory, and hallucinations. Subjects improved with time with supportive care and, in one case, with neuroleptics. However, only the latter case was identified as having irreversible schizophreniform psychosis (269).

Hallucinations are often associated with inhalant abuse (149, 271, 273). This seldom is seen or identified in studies of groups of inhalant abusers. Thus, this may be the expression of susceptible individuals or of a high degree of intoxication. One such case has been described as neurological discharges that mimic a "crawling insect feeling" (234). One group was able to relate these hallucinations to abnormal EEG recordings (149). It is evident that a more comprehensive study of these conditions and/or individuals is needed. This issue is far from being resolved. A recent letter points to the need for further studies.

NON-NERVOUS SYSTEM TOXICITY OF INHALANT ABUSE

Most of the adverse clinical effects of inhalant abuse are on the nervous system. There are however, other significant adverse effects on other organ systems, including kidney, liver, lung, heart, and blood.

Renal Toxicity

Currently, spray paints are widely abused substances, at least in the United States. The abuse of these substances occurs not only among polydrug users but also by painters. The exposure to these and similar substances has resulted in the hospitalization of inhalant abusers for various kidney disorders (144, 147, 274–291). A 32-year-old woman, identified as having renal distal acidosis after sniffing spray paint (287), presented to the hospital with severe quadriparesis. These subjects often have associated gastrointestinal involvement, including nausea, vomiting, and severe abdominal cramps. Lauwerys et al. (292) have reviewed the reports on nephrotoxicity in humans.

In one of the early reports, Streicher et al. (144) examined several cases and described them in detail, eliciting the nature of distal renal acidosis in groups of paint and/or glue sniffers from the Southwest and Hawaii. These and others have noted the recurrence of renal dysfunction associated with solvent abuse; the disease state reappears in many individuals who return to their habit after release from the hospital. Their symptoms include hyperchloremic metabolic acidosis, hypokalemia, hypocalcemia, and other electrolyte imbalances. Solvents usually cause a unique distal-type tubular acidosis, but proximal tubules are also affected. Although the distal tubule is responsible for the known electrolyte and metabolic imbalance, the proximal type is responsible for the wasting of amino acids and other proteins. In spite of this tubular damage being reversible; other organs, particularly brain, are the target of repetitive acidosis, plus a depletion of important amino acids. A slightly different kidney dysfunction, glomerulonephritis, has also been identified in workers using solvents (293), especially painters (288), and reviewed by Daniell et al. (278). In addition, an interstitial nephritis leading to renal failure has been recently reported by Taverner et al. (289). Rhabdomyolysis is sometimes observed after exposure to solvents (294). All of these reports indicate that kidney dysfunction is one of the most common toxicities noted for solvent abusers. Even of greater concern might be the diabetic who presents after an overdose of solvents. Solvent odors might cover up the "acetone breath" of the diabetic and prevent the identification of the condition and/or the basis of the acidosis if the patient is unconscious (295).

There are also reports that halohydrocarbons—chloroform and others (296), methylene chloride (297, 298), trichloroethylene (299), methoxyflurane (300), and dichloropropane (301)—may contribute to, if not cause, renal damage. The nephrotic pathological changes reported include tubular necrosis and calcification. The reversibility of these changes is unknown and is likely dependent on the extent of the damage. Others (302, 303) observed signs of Goodpasture's syndrome.

Although toluene is often proposed as the toxic agent and is present in most of the substances abused by these subjects, there has been no animal data to verify that toluene is the primary agent or even one of a group of substances that can cause renal dysfunction. Recently, Batlle et al. (276) have exposed the turtle bladder to high concentrations of toluene and observed a diminished hydrogen ion transport that had no affect on the sodium transport. Also, toluene did not reduce the pH gradient across the bladder. Efforts to reproduce these nephrotic changes in rodents have met with limited success. These studies indicate that hypocalcemia occurs only in a near-lethal situation (303a).

Other animal studies have identified the nature of some of these nephrotic changes (296, 299). Animal studies have also shown mild nephrotic changes following exposure to hydrocarbons (304). In most cases, more than one substance is present; this may indicate that the most severe nephrotic changes occur in the presence of two or more of these solvent compounds.

Thus several kinds of solvent mixtures are associated with either glomerulonephritis, distal renal tubular acidosis, or other nephrotic changes. Usually, these different kidney disorders do not occur in the same individual and may be related to individual and/or other environmental factors. Although metallic spray paints are frequently used by these subjects, they also use paint thinners and glues and other solvents. It would appear reasonable to conclude that toluene may account for some but not all of these renal abnormalities, which are likely due to a combination of toxicants in these toluene products—possibly including the metals contained in the spray paint, such as cadmium and lead, which are known to be nephrotoxic (305), or concurrent alcohol use (280, 306) and/or infections (288, 307, 308). As more cases of renal toxicity are being reported, it is important that individuals exposed to high doses of solvents be checked for renal changes and metabolic imbalance.

For most of these subjects, electrolyte repletion usually restores the kidney function and eliminates the muscle spasms, even in the more severely affected patients, in a few days. Caution about the use of bicarbonate early in the treatment of these subjects has been discussed by Lavoie et al. (283). Correction of salt and electrolyte imbalance, including potassium, calcium, magnesium, and chloride, should be considered in the treatment of solvent abusers for muscle fatigue, even in the absence of more severe kidney disorders.

RENAL TOXICITY IN PREGNANCY

One must be alert for nephrotoxicity in pregnant women who abuse solvents (290, 309–311). Numerous pregnant women have presented with renal tubular acidosis. In one report (309), three of the five infants showed growth retardation. These women often, but not always, respond to treatment for their metabolic imbalance after 72 hours and abstinence of solvent abuse.

Hepatotoxicity

Chlorohydrocarbons (e.g., trichloroethylene, chloroform, halothane) have been known for years to produce hepatotoxicities (312). Several reports describe solvent-related toxicities (2, 274, 300, 308, 313–320). Any individual who is chronically exposed to these compounds would expect to develop hepatorenal toxicities, depending on the dose and length of exposure (313). Buring et al. (321) evaluated the effects of low levels of exposure measured retrospectively by several investigators. They concluded there is increased risk for operating room personnel where these chlorohydrocarbon anesthetics are used. However, Brown and Gandolfi (300) have questioned that liver toxicity occurs very often after use of halothane as an anesthetic. Shaw et al. (322) review these rare occurrences and their etiological factors. In addition, the situations where halothane hepatitis occurs has been reviewed by Neuberger and Davis (323) who have proposed a hypoxic model to explain those occurrences of hepatitis.

The recent increase in the inhalation of correction fluids for "pleasure," which contain trichloroethylene and trichloroethanes or tetrachloroethanes (324), increases the likelihood of observing more of these toxicities in inhalant abusers (325). This disease state is exemplified in two recent reports of apparent occupational (poorly ventilated areas) overexposure. Nephronecrosis and/or hepatotoxicity was observed after exposure to mixtures containing methylene chloride and other solvents (297, 315, 326) and trichloroethane (302, 327). Methylene chloride has been considered not to be hepatotoxic (298). However, a recent report may have identified an upper limit that may occur in inhalant abuse (315) where hepatotoxicity does occur. Ketones including acetone potentiate halocarbon hepatotoxicity (328). So far, there have been few inhalant abusers noted to have irreversible liver damage. This low incidence of liver damage so far noted for this group may be due to a low rate of use of chlorinated solvents. However, the frequent heavy use of alcohol concurrently with inhalants should be of concern for this group, especially as they become older and have used these substances for many years. When these patterns of "drug" exposure are known, it would be advisable to conduct liver function tests.

Hepatocellular and other carcinomas are observed at high doses of trichloroethylene (299) and halothane (329). Anesthetic chlorinated hydrocarbons (halothane, trichloroethylene, chloroform) are also considered to be carcinogenic (330).

Pulmonary Toxicity

Despite the likelihood that solvents irritate the lungs, there have been few cases noted where the pulmonary system is severely compromised. Solvents have, nevertheless, been noted to cause pulmonary hypertension, acute respiratory distress, increased airway resistance, and residual volume and restricted ventilation. Increased airway resistance or residual volume may be more clearly noted following an exercise challenge (331). Additionally, response to an aerosolized bronchodilator is suggestive of an airway involvement perhaps induced by habitual inhalation of hydrocarbons. Smoking may have been a contributory factor in one study (332) and was not ruled out in the others. In studies of workers using waterproofing aerosols containing trichloroethane (333) or using a paint stripper (334), acute respiratory distress has been correlated with the chlorinated hydrocarbon exposure. Although solvents irritate the pulmonary system, it is not at all clear from the limited case studies reported, to date, how extensive or what types of pulmonary damage occur that can be primarily due to solvent exposure and not to other inspired substances that are dissolved in the solvents. For example, a recent report of a homicidal case (a spray paint "sniffer") noted metallic deposition along with hemorrhagic alveolitis (335). It is uncertain how to generalize the impact of dual exposure of solvent and infection, but an animal study showed decreased pulmonary bacteriocidal activity after exposure to dichloroethylene (336).

Any change may be very slow in onset but most likely will be enhanced by the other substances volatilized along with the solvent (e.g., polystyrenes, tars) or utilized by the subject (tobacco and marihuana). Because of the potential for cause and augmentation by other substances, the amount of smoking should always be considered in any treatment of these individuals.

Cardiotoxicity

Many solvent abusers may die from direct or indirect cardiotoxic actions of solvents without note of any public or private record. More specifically, several recent reports have identified ventricular fibrillation and cardiac arrest in hospitalized patients (77, 337–342). Some of the subjects had inhaled trichloroethylene- (343) or trichloroethane-containing solvents (77, 342) and were additionally compromised by anesthesia (e.g., halothane) (77). Fluorocarbons have been shown to cause arrhythmias in animals (344). Chenoweth and colleagues have shown that butane, hexane, heptanes, gasoline, some anesthetics, and toluene also produce these arrhythmias (345). More recently, two reports (338, 339) have linked glue sniffing to arrhythmias and dilated cardiomyopathy. However, the linkage of arrhythmia to glue sniffing is not well supported by animal studies. Glues usually do not contain halocarbons but do contain toluene and other hydrocarbons. The somewhat different cardiotoxicities noted above are not all easily explained, but congenital or other environmental causes were not ruled out. When they are observed, antiarrhythmic therapy should be used (77). Exercise and adrenaline exacerbate these cardiotoxicities, and efforts to minimize these situations should therefore be instituted. Also, anesthesia should not be induced in patients shortly after intoxication, and one should probably avoid the use of halogenated hydrocarbons in other circumstances where heavy solvent exposure is suspected.

Hematological Toxicity

There are three areas of concern in regards to solvent inhalation and the hematopoietic system. Two of these relate to blood dyscrasias as the result of the abuse of solvents. First, methylene chloride exposure can increase the carboxyhemoglobin levels (212), a change that also occurs with cigarette smoking. The levels of carboxyhemoglobin may become sufficiently high to cause brain damage (346) or death (347). A second group of substances, the organic nitrites, produce methemoglobinemia and hemolytic anemia (348–351). A third substance, benzene, has been identified as causing aplastic anemia and acute myelocytic leukemia (292, 352). Benzene is present in thinners, varnish removers and other solvents and in varying proportions in gasoline.

One group of substances, the volatile liquid "amyl" and "butyl" nitrites, deserve special discussion. During the late nineteenth and early twentieth centuries, amyl nitrite was used in clinical practice as a vasodilator to treat angina pectoris. Although this use of the drug is uncommon today, it is used for diagnostic purposes in echocardiogram examinations (353, 354) and for cyanide poisoning (355). These drugs are not the typical solvents previously described; however, they are often included in the "inhalant abuse" category. As with nitrous oxide, different individuals (predominately homosexuals) are the primary abusers of isoamyl ("amyl"), isobutyl or butyl nitrites, propyl nitrites, cyclohexyl nitrites, and maybe others. They may use them for sphincter dilation and penile engorgement. Use by others for nonsexual purposes is unclear. A recent study could not correlate changes in regional blood flow with any psychological measures or somatic changes (356); also, isoamyl nitrite did not substitute for barbiturates, as do toluene and other solvents (357). These studies do not offer any explanation for why individuals become dependent on nitrites. However, the finding by Mathew et al. (356) that nitrites reduce anger, fatigue, and depression may offer a clue.

The nitrites are usually not considered toxic during inhalation because of syncope (fainting). However, Guss et al. (358) noted a dangerously high 37% methemoglobin level in a normal subject who had used isobutyl nitrite. This methemoglobinemia is the major identified toxicity and is the cause of several deaths (159). There is a specific treatment for nitrite overdose. The high and slowly reversible reduction of methemoglobin can be aided by the use of methylene blue (359).

Organic nitrites have also been reported to produce bradycardia (354), reduce killer cell activity (360), produce allergic reactions (361), and be potentially carcinogenic (362). These latter effects are of special concern in the development of AIDS, in that there is an association between the development of Kaposi's sarcoma and high amyl-butyl nitrite use (363–365). The ability to produce nitrosamines has fueled the speculation that nitrites are carcinogenic (362, 366, 367). Yet, in contrast to sodium nitrite, organic nitrites produce methemoglobin instantly in vitro (368) and may therefore not be around long enough to produce nitrosamines. Thus, the rapid oxidation of organic nitrites by hemoglobin and the fact that detectable levels of organic nitrites in blood are noted only briefly after administration (369) question this hypothesis. While mutagenicity appears possible under special conditions, carcinogenicity is far from proven.

Organic nitrites also modulate the immune capacity of animals (370–372). Soderberg reviews the potential for nitrites to impair the immune system (373). In his studies, after inhalation exposure of mice for 14 days to isobutyl nitrite, there is a reduced capacity for the concanavalin A (but not lipopolysaccharide) stimulation of T-cell functions. He states (373) that nitrites may reduce immune capacity while augmenting viral growth and tumor growth.

Also, hematopoietic effects were identified in a subject using glue (trichloroethylene) in his hobby; cessation of the symptoms occurred when he ceased his hobby (374).

NEONATAL SYNDROME

There is increasing evidence that solvent inhalation during pregnancy produces a "fetal solvent syndrome." There are numerous cases of infants of mothers who chronically abuse solvents (124, 290, 309–311, 318, 375–378) diagnosed with this syndrome. These mothers inhaled paint reducer (thinner?) and paint sprays and drank various quantities of alcohol. Whether toluene alone (often noted as the major solvent), other solvent components, and/or these components in combination with alcohol or other environmental factors are responsible is still unsubstantiated by laboratory studies; yet toluene appears to be a major contributor. Toluene embryopathy is compared to the more well recognized fetal alcohol syndrome (377). The infants present with problems ranging from hyperchloremic acidosis to microencephaly (124, 310).

It is difficult to produce these abnormalities in rodents. Growth retardation occurred in rats with doses of toluene that produce high fetal mortality without producing skeletal anomalies (379), and an ataxic syndrome has been identified in young rats exposed to high levels of toluene throughout pregnancy (380).

Nitrous oxide (50–75% for 24 hours on day 8) has been shown to produce some "major visceral and minor skeletal (fetal) abnormalities" (381). Surprisingly, these abnormalities are protected against by 0.27% halothane, but not by folinic acid. Also, animal fetal liver toxicities occur after administration of carbon tetrachloride (382) or malformations following chloroform (383). With so little knowledge and yet with all the potential dangers, it is very important that pregnant women not be exposed to very high concentrations of solvents. It is encouraging to know that a critical prospective study of workers exposed to low levels of solvent showed no more abnormalities than the carefully matched controls (384). This does not, however, diminish the need for the avoidance of exposure of pregnant women to moderate to high levels of solvent.

References

1. Carroll E. Notes on the epidemiology of inhalants. In: Sharp CW, Brehm M. eds. Review of inhalants: euphoria to dysfunction. NIDA research monograph series no. 15, DHEW publication ADM 77–553. Washington, DC: Department of Health, Education, and Welfare, 1977: 14–24.
2. Hutchens KS, Kung M. "Experimentation" with chloroform. Am J Med 1985;78:715–718.
3. Kringsholm B. Sniffing-associated deaths in Denmark. Forensic Sci Int 1980;l5:2l5–225.
4. Smith TC, Cooperman LH, Wollman H. History and principles of anesthesiology. In: Goodman GA, Goodman LS, Gilman A, eds. Goodman and Gilman's the pharmacological basis of therapeutics. 6th ed. New York: Macmillan, 1980:258.
5. Flanagan RJ, Ives RJ. Volatile substance abuse. Bull Narc 1994;46(2):49–78.
6. Gilvary E, McCarthy S, McArdle P. Substance use among school children in the north of England. Drug Alcohol Depend 1995;37:255–259.
7. Kozel N, Sloboda Z, De La Rosa M. Epidemiology of inhalant abuse: an international perspective. NIDA research monograph series no. 148, NIH publication 95–3831. Washington, DC: National Institutes of Health, 1995.
8. Adelekan ML. Self-reported drug use among secondary school students in the Nigerian state of Ogun. Bull Narc 1989;41(1–2):109–116.
9. Alvarez FJ, Queipo D, Del Rio MC, Garcia MC. Patterns of drug use by young people in the rural community of Spain. Br J Addict 1989;84: 647–652.
10. Beauvais F, Oetting ER. Inhalant abuse by young children. In: Crider RA, Rouse BA, eds. Epidemiology of inhalant abuse: an update. NIDA research monograph series no. 85, DHHS publication ADM 88–1577. Washington, DC: Department of Health and Human Services, 1988:30–49.
11. Carlini-Cotrim B, Carlini EA. The use of solvents and other drugs among children and adolescents from a low socioeconomic background: a study in São Paulo, Brazil. Int J Addict 1988; 23:1145–1156.
12. Cooke BR, Evans DA, Farrow SC. Solvent misuse in secondary school children—a prevalence study. Community Med 1988;10:8–13.
13. Diamond ID, Pritchard C, Choudry N, Fielding M, Cox M, Bushnell D. The incidence of drug and solvent misuse among southern English normal comprehensive school children. Public Health 1988;102:107–114.
14. Levy SJ, Pierce JP. Drug use among Sydney teenagers in 1985 and 1986. Community Health Stud 1989;13:161–169.
15. Medina-Mora E, Ortiz A. Epidemiology of solvent/inhalant abuse in Mexico. In: Crider RA,

Rouse BA, eds. Epidemiology of inhalant abuse: an update. NIDA research monograph series no. 85, DHHS publication ADM 88–1577. Washington, DC: Department of Health and Human Services, 1988:140–171.
16. Pedersen W, Clausen SE, Lavik NJ. Patterns of drug use and sensation-seeking among adolescents in Norway. Acta Psychiatry Scand 1989; 79:386–390.
17. Smart RG. Inhalant use and abuse in Canada. In: Crider RA, Rouse BA, eds. Epidemiology of inhalant abuse: an update. NIDA research monograph series no. 85, DHHS publication ADM 88–1577. Washington, DC: Department of Health and Human Services, 1988:121–139.
18. Tapia-Conyer R, Cravioto P, De La Rosa B, Velez C. Risk factors for inhalant abuse in juvenile offenders: the case of Mexico. Addiction 1995;90:43–49.
19. Taylor JC, Norman CL, Bland JM, Anderson HR, Ramsey JD. Trends in deaths associated with abuse of volatile substances, 1971–1993. Report 8. London: St. George's Hospital Medical School, 1995;June.
20. Johnston LD, O'Malley PM, Bachman JG. National survey results on drug use from the Monitoring the Future Study, Vol I, 1975–1994. NIH publication 95–4026. Washington, DC: National Institutes of Health, 1995.
21. Johnston LD, O'Malley PM, Bachman JG. National survey results on drug use from the Monitoring the Future Study, Vol II, 1975–1994. NIH publication 96–4027 95–4026. Washington, DC: National Institutes of Health, 1996.
22. Substance Abuse and Mental Health Services Administration. National Household Survey on Drug Abuse: population estimates 1994. DHHS publication (SMA) 95–3063.Washington, DC: Department of Health and Human Services, 1995.
23. Johnson BD, Frank B, Marel R, Schmeidler J, Maranda M, Gillman C. Statewide household survey of substance abuse, 1986: illicit substance use among adults in New York State's transient population. New York: New York State Division of Substance Abuse Services, 1988.
24. Fredlund EV, Spence RT, Maxwell JC. Substance use among students in Texas secondary schools, 1988. Austin: Texas Commission on Alcohol and Drug Abuse, 1989;March.
25. Liu LY, Maxwell JC. Texas school survey of substance use among students: grades 7–12, 1994. Austin: Texas Commission on Alcohol and Drug Abuse, 1995;March.
26. Fredlund EV, Spence RT, Maxwell JC, Kavinsky JA. Substance use among Texas Department of Corrections inmates, 1988. Austin: Texas Commission on Alcohol and Drug Abuse, 1990; Feb.
27. Padilla ER, Padilla AM, Morales A, Olmedo

EL, Ramirez R. Inhalant, marijuana, and alcohol abuse among barrio children and adolescents. Int J Addict 1979;14:945–964.
28. Frank B, Marel R, Schmeidler J. The continuing problem of youthful solvent abuse in New York State. In: Crider RA, Rouse BA, eds. Epidemiology of inhalant abuse: an update. NIDA research monograph series no. 85, DHHS publication ADM 88–1577. Washington, DC: Department of Health and Human Services, 1988: 77–105.
29. Sharp CW, Korman M. Volatile substances. In: Lowinson JH, Ruiz P, eds. Substance abuse: clinical problems and perspectives. Baltimore: Williams & Wilkins, 1981:233–255.
30. Sharp CW, Rosenberg NL. Volatile substances. In: Lowinson JH, Ruiz P, Millman RB, Langrod JG, eds. Substance abuse: A comprehensive textbook. 2nd ed. Baltimore: Williams & Wilkins, 1990:303–327.
30a. National Household Survey on Drug Abuse: Population estimates 1988. Department of Health and Human Services publication 89–1636. Washington, DC: Department of Health and Human Services, 1988.
30b. Fredlund WV, Farabee D, Blair LA, Wallisch LS. Substance use and delinquency among youths entering Texas Youth Commission facilities, 1994. Austin, TX: Texas Commission on Alcohol and Drug Abuse, 1995.
31. Edwards RW. Drug use among 8th grade students is increasing. Int J Addict 1993;28: 1621–1623.
32. Bass M. Sudden sniffing death. JAMA 1970; 212:2075–2079.
33. Bass M. Death from sniffing gasoline. N Engl J Med 1978;299:203.
34. Bass M. Abuse of inhalation anesthetics. JAMA 1984;251:604.
35. Litovitz TL, Felberg L, Soloway RA, Ford M, Geller R. 1994 annual report of the American Association of Poison Control Centers Toxic Exposure Surveillance System. Am J Emerg Med 1995;13:551–597.
36. Anderson HR. Increase in deaths from deliberate inhalation of fuel gases and pressurised aerosols [Letter]. BMJ 1990;301:41.
37. Shepherd RT. Mechanism of sudden death associated with volatile substance abuse. Hum Toxicol 1989;8:287–291.
38. Garriott J, Petty CS. Death from inhalant abuse: toxicological and pathological evaluation of 34 cases. Clin Toxicol l980;l6:305–315.
39. Garriott J. Death among inhalant abusers. In: Sharp CW, Beauvais F, Spence R, eds. Inhalant abuse: a volatile research agenda. NIDA research monograph series no. 129, NIH publication 93–3480. Washington, DC: National Institutes of Health, 1992:181–192.
40. Cohen S. Inhalant abuse: an overview of the problem. In: Sharp CW, Brehm M. eds. Review

of inhalants: euphoria to dysfunction. NIDA research monograph series no. 15, DHEW publication ADM 77–553. Washington, DC: Department of Health, Education, and Welfare, 1977:2–10.

41. Korman M, Matthews RW, Lovitt R. Neuropsychological effects of abuse of inhalants. Percept Mot Skills 1981;53:547–553.

42. Oetting ER, Edwards RW, Beauvais F. Social and psychological factors underlying inhalant abuse. In: Crider RA, Rouse BA, eds. Epidemiology of inhalant abuse: an update. NIDA research monograph series no. 85, DHHS publication ADM 88–1577. Washington, DC: Department of Health and Human Services, 1988:172–203.

43. Matthews RW, Korman M. Abuse of inhalants: motivation and consequences. Psychol Rep 1981;49:519–526.

44. Oetting ER, Webb J. Psychosocial characteristics and their links with inhalants, a research agenda. In: Sharp CW, Beauvais F, Spence R, eds. Inhalant abuse: a volatile research agenda. NIDA research monograph series no. 129, NIH publication 93–3480. Washington, DC: National Institutes of Health, 1992:59–98.

45. Kerner K. Current topics in inhalant abuse. In: Crider RA, Rouse BA, eds. Epidemiology of inhalant abuse: an update. NIDA research monograph series no. 85, DHHS publication ADM 88–1577. Washington, DC: Department of Health and Human Services, 1988:8–29.

46. Trochimowicz HJ. Development of alternative fluorocarbons. In: Sharp CW, Beauvais F, Spence R, eds. Inhalant abuse: a volatile research agenda. NIDA research monograph series no. 129, NIH publication 93–3480. Washington, DC: National Institutes of Health, 1992:287–300.

47. Mathew B, Kapp E, Jones TR. Commercial butane abuse, a disturbing case. Br J Addict 1989;84:563–564.

48. Evans AC, Raistrick D. Patterns of use and related harm with toluene-based adhesives and butane gas. Br J Psychiatry 1987;150:773–776.

49. Siegel E, Wason S. Sudden death caused by inhalation of butane and propane. N Engl J Med 1990;323:1638.

50. Siegel E, Wason S. Sudden sniffing death following inhalation of butane and propane: changing trends. In: Sharp CW, Beauvais F, Spence R, eds. Inhalant abuse: a volatile research agenda. NIDA research monograph series no. 129, NIH publication 93–3480. Washington, DC: National Institutes of Health, 1992:193–202.

51. Evans AC, Raistrick D. Phenomenology of intoxication with toluene-based adhesives and butane gas. Br J Psychiatry 1987;150:769–773.

52. Zacny JP, Coalson DW, Lichtor JL, Yajnik S, Thapar P. Effects of naloxone on the subjective and psychomotor effects of nitrous oxide in humans. Pharmacol Biochem Behav 1994;49:573–578.

53. Fagan D, Paul DL, Tiplady B, Scott DB. A dose-response study of the effects of inhaled nitrous oxide on psychological performance and mood. Psychopharmacology (Berl) 1994;116:333–338.

54. Cheam EW, Dob DP, Skelly AM, Lockwood GG. The effect of nitrous oxide on the performance of psychomotor tests. A dose-response study. Anaesthesia 1995;50:764–768.

55. Veerkamp JS, Gruythuysen RJ, Hoogstraten J, van Amerongen WE. Anxiety reduction with nitrous oxide: a permanent solution? ASDC J Dent Child 1995;62:44–48.

56. Stach DJ. Nitrous oxide sedation: understanding the benefits and risks. Am J Dent 1995;8:47–50.

57. Daynes G. Nitrous oxide for alcohol withdrawal [Letter]. S Afr Med J 1994;84:708.

58. Winek CL, Wahba WW, Rozin L. Accidental death by nitrous oxide inhalation. Forensic Sci Int 1995;73:139–141.

59. DiMaio VJM, Garriott JC. Four deaths resulting from abuse of nitrous oxide. J Forensic Sci 1978;23:169–172.

60. Fraunfelder FT. Nitrous oxide warning. Am J Ophthalmol 1988;105:688.

61. Wagner SA, Clark MA, Wesche DL, Doedens DJ, Lloyd AW. Asphyxial deaths from the recreational use of nitrous oxide. J Forensic Sci 1992;37:1008–1015.

62. Thompson PJ, Dhillon P, Cole P. Addiction to aerosol treatment: the asthmatic alternative to glue sniffing. BMJ 1983;287:1515.

63. Nordin C, Rosenqvist M, Hollstedt C. Sniffing of ethyl chloride—an uncommon form of abuse with serious mental and neurological symptoms. Int J Addict 1988;23:623–627.

64. Krause JG, McCarthy WB. Sudden death by inhalation of cyclopropane. J Forensic Sci 1989;34:1011–1012.

65. Jacob B, Heller C, Daldrup T, Burrig KF, Barz J, Bonte W. Fatal accidental enflurane intoxication. J Forensic Sci 1989;34:1408–1412.

66. Eger EI II, Liu J, Koblin DD, Laster MJ, Taheri S, Halsey MJ, et al. Molecular properties of the ideal inhaled anesthetic: studies of fluorinated methanes, ethanes, propanes, and butanes. Anesth Analg 1994;79:245–251.

67. Benignus VA. Health effects of toluene: a review. Neurotoxicology 1981;2:567–588.

68. al-Alousi LM. Pathology of volatile substance abuse: a case report and a literature review. Med Sci Law 1989;29:189–208.

69. Fitzgerald RL, Fishel CE, Bush LL. Fatality due to recreational use of chlorodifluoromethane and chloropenta-fluoroethane. J Forensic Sci 1993;38:477–483.

70. Groppi A, Polettini A, Lunetta P, Achille G, Montagna M. A fatal case of trichlorofluoromethane (Freon 11) poisoning. Tissue distribution study by gas chromatography-mass spectrometry. J Forensic Sci 1994;39:871–876.

71. Clark MA, Jones JW, Robinson JJ, Lord JT. Multiple deaths resulting from shipboard exposure to trichlorotrifluoroethane. J Forensic Sci 1985;30:1256–1259.

72. Spencer JD, Raasch FO, Trefny FA. Halothane abuse in hospital personnel. JAMA 1976;235:1034–1035.

73. Yamashita M, Matsuki A, Oyama T. Illicit use of modern volatile anaesthetics. Can Anaesth Soc J 1984;31:76–79.

74. Nouchi T, Miura H, Kanayama M, Mizuguchi O, Takano T. Fatal intoxication by 1,2-dichloroethane—a case report. Int Arch Occup Environ Health 1984;54:111–113.

75. Gresham GA, Treip CS. Fatal poisoning by 1,1,1-trichloroethane after prolonged survival. Forensic Sci Int 1983;23:249–253.

76. Jones RD, Winter DP. Two case reports of deaths on industrial premises attributed to 1,1,1-trichloroethane. Arch Environ Health 1983;38:59–61.

77. McLeod AA, Marjot R, Monaghan MJ, Hugh-Jones P, Jackson G. Chronic cardiac toxicity after inhalation of 1,1,1-trichloroethane. BMJ 1987;294:727–729.

78. King GS, Smialek JE, Troutman WG. Sudden death in adolescents resulting from the inhalation of typewriter correction fluid. JAMA 1985;253:1604–1606.

79. Macdougall IC, Isles C, Oliver JS, Clark JC, Spilg WG. Fatal outcome following inhalation of Tipp-Ex. Scott Med J 1987;32:55.

80. Troutman WG. Additional deaths associated with the intentional inhalation of typewriter correction fluid. Vet Hum Toxicol 1988;30:130–132.

81. Cronk SL, Barkley DEH, Farrell MF. Respiratory arrest after solvent abuse. BMJ 1985;290:897–898.

82. Allan AR, Blackmore RC, Toseland PA. A chloroform inhalation fatality—an unusual asphyxiation. Med Sci Law 1988;28:120–122.

83. Suruda AJ, McGlothlin JD. Fatal abuse of nitrous oxide in the workplace. J Occup Med 1990;32:682–684.

84. Rowbottom SJ. Nitrous oxide abuse [Letter]. Anaesth Intensive Care 1988;16:241–242.

85. Schaumburg HH, Spencer PS. Recognizing neurotoxic disease. Neurology 1987;37:276–278.

86. Lazar RB, Ho SU, Melen O, Daghestani AN. Multifocal central nervous system damage caused by toluene abuse. Neurology 1983;33:1337–1340.

87. Hormes JT, Filley CM, Rosenberg NL. Neurologic sequelae of chronic solvent vapor abuse. Neurology 1986;36:698–702.

88. Fornazzari L, Wilkinson DA, Kapur BM, Carlen PL. Cerebellar, cortical and functional impairment in toluene abusers. Acta Neurol Scand 1983;67:319–329.

89. Rosenberg NL. Neurotoxicology. In: Sullivan JB, Krieger GR, eds. Medical toxicology of hazardous materials. Baltimore: Williams & Wilkins, 1992:145–153.

90. Altenkirch H, Wagner HM, Stoltenburg-Didinger G, Steppat R. Potentiation of hexacarbon-neurotoxicity by methyl-ethyl-ketone (MEK) and other substances: clinical and experimental aspects. Neurobehav Toxicol Teratol 1982;4:623–627.

91. Altenkirch H, Mager J, Stoltenburg G, et al. Toxic polyneuropathies after sniffing a glue thinner. J Neurol 1977;214:137–152.

92. Saida K, Mendell JR, Weiss HS. Peripheral nerve changes induced by methyl n-butyl ketone and potentiated by methyl ethyl ketone. J Neuropathol Exp Neurol 1976;35:207–225.

93. Takahashi S, Kagawa M, Inagaki O, Akane A, Fukui Y. Metabolic interaction between toluene and ethanol in rabbits. Arch Toxicol 1987;59:307–310.

94. Selden A, Hultberg B, Ulander A, Ahlborg G Jr. Trichloroethylene exposure in vapour degreasing and the urinary excretion of N-acetyl-β-D-glucosaminidase. Arch Toxicol 1993;67:224–226.

95. Meulenbelt J, de Groot G, Savelkoul TJ. Two cases of acute toluene intoxication. Br J Ind Med 1990;47:417–420.

96. Plappert U, Barthel E, Seidel HJ. Reduction of benzene toxicity by toluene. Environ Mol Mutagen 1994;24:283–292.

97. Allen N. Solvents and other industrial organic compounds. In: Vinken PJ, Bruyn GW, eds. Handbook of clinical neurology. New York: Elsevier, 1979;36:361–389.

98. Goetz CG. Organic solvents. In: Goetz CG, ed. Neurotoxins in clinical practice. Jamaica, NY: Spectrum, 1985:65–90.

99. Spencer PS, Schaumburg HH. n-Hexane and methyl n-butyl ketone. In: Spencer PS, Schaumburg HH, eds. Experimental and clinical neurotoxicology. Baltimore: Williams & Wilkins, 1980:456–475.

100. Spencer PS, Schaumburg HH, Sabri MI, Veronesi B. The enlarging view of hexacarbon neurotoxicity. Crit Rev Toxicol 1980;7:279–356.

101. Graham DG, Carter AD, Boekelheide K. In vitro and in vivo studies of the molecular pathogenesis of *n*-hexane neuropathy. Neurobehav Toxicol Teratol 1982;4:629–634.

102. Perbellini L, Brugnone F, Gaffuri E. Neurotoxic metabolites of "commercial hexane" in the urine of shoe factory workers. Clin Toxicol 1981;18:1377–1385.

103. Menkes JH. Toxic polyneuropathy due to methyl *n*-butyl ketone. Arch Neurol 1976; 33:309.

104. Billmaier D, Yee HT, Allen N, Craft B, Williams N, Epstein S, et al. Peripheral neuropathy in a coated fabrics plant. J Occup Med 1974;16:665–671.

105. McDonough JR. Possible neuropathy from methyl *n*-butyl ketone. N Engl J Med 1974; 290:695.

106. Allen N, Mendell JR, Billmaier DJ, Fontaine RE, O'Neill J. Toxic polyneuropathy due to methyl *n*-butyl ketone: an industrial outbreak. Arch Neurol 1975;32:209–218.

107. Mallov JS. MBK neuropathy among spray painters. JAMA 1976;235:1455–1457.

108. Spencer PS, Schaumburg HH, Raleigh RL, Terhaar CJ. Nervous system degeneration produced by the industrial solvent methyl *n*-butyl ketone. Arch Neurol 1975;32:219–222.

109. Herskowitz A, Ishii N, Schaumburg H. *n*-Hexane neuropathy: a syndrome occurring as a result of industrial exposure. N Engl J Med 1971;285:82–85.

110. Gonzalez EG, Downey JA. Polyneuropathy in a glue sniffer. Arch Phys Med Rehab 1972; 53:333–337.

111. Shirabe T, Tsuda T, Terao A, Araki S. Toxic polyneuropathy due to glue-sniffing: report of two cases with a light and electron-microscopic study of the peripheral nerves and muscles. J Neurol Sci 1974;21:101–113.

112. Goto I, Matsumura M, Inove N, et al. Toxic polyneuropathy due to glue sniffing. J Neurol Neurosurg Psychiatry 1974;37:848–853.

113. Prockop LD, Alt M, Tison J. "Huffer's" neuropathy. JAMA 1974;229:1083–1084.

114. Korobkin R, Asbury AK, Sumner AJ, Nielsen SL. Glue-sniffing neuropathy. Arch Neurol 1975;32:158–162.

115. Oh SJ, Kim JM. Giant axonal swelling in "huffer's" neuropathy. Arch Neurol 1976;33: 583–586.

116. Towfighi J, Gonatas NK, Pleasure D, Cooper HS, McCree L. Glue sniffer's neuropathy. Neurology 1976;26:238–243.

117. Dittmer DK, Jhamandas JH, Johnson ES. Glue-sniffing neuropathies. Can Fam Physician 1993;39:1965–1971.

118. Takeuchi Y. *n*-Hexane polyneuropathy in Japan: a review of *n*-hexane poisoning and its preventive measures. Environ Res 1993;62: 76–80.

119. Schaumburg HH, Spencer PS. Degeneration in central and peripheral nervous systems produced by pure *n*-hexane: an experimental study. Brain 1976;99:183–192.

120. Frontali N, Amantini MC, Spagnolo A, Guarcini AM, Saltari MC. Experimental neurotoxicity and urinary metabolites of the C5-C7 aliphatic hydrocarbons used as glue solvents in shoe manufacture. Clin Toxicol 1981; 18:1357–1367.

121. Seppalainen AM, Raitta C, Huuskonen MS. *n*-Hexane induced changes in visual evoked potentials and electroretinograms of industrial workers. Electroencephalogr Clin Neurophysiol 1979;47:492–498.

122. Mutti A, Ferri F, Lommi G, Lotta S, Lucertini S, Franchini I. *n*-Hexane-induced changes in nerve conduction velocities and somatosensory evoked potentials. Int Arch Occup Environ Health 1982;51:45–54.

122a. Sharp CW, Beauvais F, Spence R. Inhalant abuse: a volatile research agenda. NIDA research monograph series no. 129, NIH publication 93–3480. Washington, DC: National Institutes of Health, 1992.

123. Grabski DA. Toluene sniffing producing cerebellar degeneration. Am J Psychiatry 1961; 118:461–462.

124. Arnold GL, Kirby RS, Langendoerfer S, Wilkins-Haug L. Toluene embryopathy: clinical delineation and developmental follow-up. Pediatrics 1994;93:216–220.

125. Ashikaga R, Araki Y, Miura K, Ishida O. Cranial MRI in chronic thinner intoxication. Neuroradiology 1995;37:443–444.

126. Boor JW, Hurtig HI. Persistent cerebellar ataxia after exposure to toluene. Ann Neurol 1977;2:440–442.

127. Caldemeyer KS, Pascuzzi RM, Moran CC, Smith RR. Toluene abuse causing reduced MR signal intensity in the brain. AJR Am J Roentgenol 1993;161:1259–1261.

128. Ehyai A, Freemon FR. Progressive optic neuropathy and sensorineural hearing loss due to chronic glue sniffing. J Neurol Neurosurg Psychiatry 1983;46:349–351.

129. Ikeda M, Tsukagoshi H. Encephalopathy due to toluene sniffing. Report of a case with magnetic resonance imaging. Eur Neurol 1990;30: 347–349.

130. Kelly TW. Prolonged cerebellar dysfunction associated with paint-sniffing. Pediatrics 1975; 56:605–606.

131. King MD. Neurological sequelae of toluene abuse. Human Toxicol 1982;1:281–287.

132. King PJL, Morris JGL, Pollard JD. Glue sniffing neuropathy. Aust N Z J Med 1985;15: 293–299.

133. Knox JW, Nelson JR. Permanent encephalopathy from toluene inhalation. N Engl J Med 1966;275:1494–1496.

134. Keane JR. Toluene optic neuropathy. Ann Neurol 1978;4:390.

135. Lolin Y. Chronic neurological toxicity associated with exposure to volatile substances. Hum Toxicol 1989;8:293–300.

136. Maas EF, Ashe J, Spiegel P, Zee DS, Leigh RJ. Acquired pendular nystagmus in toluene addiction. Neurology 1991;41:282–285.

137. Malm G, Lying-Tunell U. Cerebellar dysfunction related to toluene sniffing. Acta Neurol Scan 1980;62:188–190.

138. Metrick SA, Brenner RP. Abnormal brainstem auditory evoked potentials in chronic paint sniffers. Ann Neurol 1982;12:553–556.

139. Ohnuma A, Kimura I, Saso S. MRI in chronic paint-thinner intoxication. Neuroradiology 1995;37:445–446.

140. Poungvarin N. Multifocal brain damage due to lacquer sniffing: the first case report of Thailand. J Med Assoc Thai 1991;74:296–300.

141. Rosenberg NL, Kleinschmidt-DeMasters BK, Davis KA, Dreisbach JN, Hormes JT, Filley CM. Toluene abuse causes diffuse central nervous system white matter changes. Ann Neurol 1988;23:611–614.

142. Rosenberg NL, Spitz MC, Filley CM, Davis KA, Schaumburg HH. Central nervous system effects of chronic toluene abuse—clinical, brainstem evoked response and magnetic resonance imaging studies. Neurotoxicol Teratol 1988;10:489–495.

143. Sasa M, Igarashi S, Miyazaki T, Miyazaki K, Nakano S, Matsuoka I. Equilibrium disorders with diffuse brain atrophy in long-term toluene sniffing. Arch Oto-Rhino-Laryngol 1978;221: 163–169.

144. Streicher HZ, Gabow PA, Moss AH, Kono D, Kaehny WD. Syndromes of toluene sniffing in adults. Ann Intern Med 1981;94:758–762.

145. Takeuchi Y, Hisanaga N, Ono Y, Ogawa T, Hamaguchi Y, Okamoto S. Cerebellar dysfunction caused by sniffing of toluene-containing thinner. Ind Health 1981;19:163–169.

146. Unger E, Alexander A, Fritz T, Rosenberg N, Dreisbach J. Toluene abuse: physical basis for hypointensity of the basal ganglia on T2-weighted MR images. Radiology 1994;193: 473–476.

147. Xiong L, Matthes JD, Li J, Jinkins JR. MR imaging of spray heads: toluene abuse via aerosol paint inhalation. AJNR Am J Neuroradiol 1993;14:1195–1199.

148. Berry JG, Heaton RK, Kirby MW. Neuropsychological deficits of chronic inhalant abusers. In: Rumack B, Temple A, eds. Management of the poisoned patient. Princeton: Science Press, 1977:9–31.

149. Channer KS, Stanley S. Persistent visual hallucination secondary to chronic solvent encephalopathy: case report and review of the literature. J Neurol Neurosurg Psychiatry 1983; 46:83–86.

150. Tsushima WT, Towne WS. Effects of paint sniffing on neuropsychological test performance. J Abnorm Psychol 1977;86:402–407.

151. Wiedmann KD, Power KG, Wilson JTL, Hadley DM. Recovery from chronic solvent abuse. J Neurol Neurosurg Psychiatry 1987;50: 1712–1713.

152. Levisohn PM, Kramer RE, Rosenberg NL. Neurophysiology of chronic cocaine and toluene abuse [Abstract]. Neurology 1992; 42(suppl 3):434.

153. Escobar A, Aruffo C. Chronic thinner intoxication: clinico-pathologic report of a human case. J Neurol Neurosurg Psychiatry 1980;43: 986–994.

154. Kornfeld M, Moser AB, Moser HW, Kleinschmidt-DeMasters B, Nolte K, Phelps A. Solvent vapor abuse leukoencephalopathy comparison to adrenoleukodystrophy. J Neuropath Exp Neurol 1994;53:389–398.

155. Poser C. The dysmyelinating diseases. In: Joynt RJ, ed. Clinical neurology. Philadelphia: Lippincott-Raven Publishers, 1983:31–36.

156. Miyake H, Ikeda T, Maehara N, Harabuchi I, Kishi R, Yokota H. Slow learning in rats due to long-term inhalation of toluene. Neurobehav Toxicol Teratol 1983;5:541–548.

157. Lorenzana-Jimenez M, Salas M. Neonatal effects of toluene on the locomotor behavioral development of the rat. Neurobehav Toxicol Teratol 1983;5:295–299.

158. Pryor GT, Dickinson J, Howd RA, Rebert CS. Transient cognitive deficits and high-frequency hearing loss in weanling rats exposed to toluene. Neurobehav Toxicol Teratol 1983; 5:53–57.

159. Wood RW, Cox C. Acute oral toxicity of butyl nitrite. J Appl Toxicol 1981;1:30–31.

160. Rees DC, Knisely JS, Jordan S, Balster RL. Discriminitive stimulus properties of toluene in the mouse. Toxicol Appl Pharmacol 1987;88: 97–104.

161. Rebert CS, Sorenson SS, Howd RA, Pryor GT. Toluene-induced hearing loss in rats evidenced by the brainstem auditory-evoked response. Neurobehav Toxicol Teratol 1983;5:59–62.

162. Niklasson M, Tham R, Larsby B, Eriksson B.

Effects of toluene, styrene, trichloroethylene, and trichloroethane on the vestibulo- and opto-oculo motor system in rats. Neurotoxicol Teratol 1993;15:327–334.

163. Nylen P, Hagman M, Johnson AC. Function of the auditory and visual systems, and of peripheral nerve, in rats after long-term combined exposure to *n*-hexane and methylated benzene derivatives. I. Toluene. Pharmacol Toxicol 1994;74:116–123.

164. Li HS, Johnson AC, Borg E, Hoglund G. Auditory degeneration after exposure to toluene in two genotypes of mice. Arch Toxicol 1992; 66:382–386.

165. Pryor GT. A toluene-induced motor syndrome in rats resembling that seen in some solvent abusers. Neurotoxicol Teratol 1991;13:387–400.

166. Mergler D, Beauvais B. Olfactory threshold shift following controlled 7-hour exposure to toluene and/or xylene. Neurotoxicology 1992; 13:211–215.

167. Lloyd JW, Moore RM, Breslin P. Background information on trichloroethylene. J Occup Med 1975;17:603–605.

167a. National Institute for Occupational Safety and Health. Special occupational hazard review with control recommendations: trichloroethylene. DHEW publication no. 78–130. Washington, DC: Department of Health, Education, and Welfare 1978.

168. Feldman RG. Trichloroethylene. In: Vinken PJ, Bruyn GW, eds. Handbook of clinical neurology. Intoxications of the nervous system, part I. Amsterdam: North-Holland, 1979;36: 457–464.

169. Humphrey JH, McClelland M. Cranial-nerve palsies with herpes following general anesthesia. BMJ 1944;1:315–318.

170. McClelland M. Some toxic effects following trilene decomposition products. Proc R Soc Med 1944;37:526–528.

171. Enderby GEH. The use and abuse of tri-chlorethylene. BMJ 1944;2:300–302.

172. Firth JB, Stuckey RE. Decomposition of trilene in closed circuit anaesthesia. Lancet 1945;1: 814–816.

173. Atkinson RS. Trichlorethylene anesthesia. Anesthesiology 1960;21:67–77.

174. Hewer CL. Further observations on trichlorethylene. Proc R Soc Med 1943;36:463–465.

175. Buxton PH, Hayward M. Polyneuritis cranialis associated with trichloroethylene poisoning. J Neurol Neurosurg Psychiatry 1967;30: 511–518.

176. Glaser MA. Treatment of trigeminal neuralgia with trichlorethylene. JAMA 1931;96:916–920.

177. Defalque RJ. Pharmacology and toxicology of trichlorethylene: a critical review of the world literature. Clin Pharmacol Ther 1961;2: 665–688a.

178. Mitchell ABS, Parsons-Smith BG. Trichloroethylene neuropathy. BMJ 1969;1:422–423.

179. Gwynne EI. Trichloroethylene neuropathy. BMJ 1969;2:315.

180. Feldman RG, Mayer RM, Taub A. Evidence for peripheral neurotoxic effect of trichloroethylene. Neurology 1970;20:599–606.

181. Defalque RJ. The "specific" analgesic effect of trichlorethylene upon the trigeminal nerve. Anesthesiology 1961;22:379–384.

182. Waters EM, Gerstner HB, Huff JE. Trichloroethylene. I. An overview. J Toxicol Environ Health 1977;2:671–707.

183. Schaumburg HH, Spencer PS, Thomas PK. Disorders of peripheral nerves. Philadelphia: FA Davis, 1983.

184. Sagawa K. Transverse lesion of the spinal cord after accidental exposure to trichloroethylene. Int Arch Arbeitsmed 1973;31:257–264.

185. Spencer PS, Bischoff MC. Spontaneous remyelination of spinal cord plaques in rats orally treated with sodium dichloroacetate. J Neuropathol Exp Neurol 1982;41:373.

186. Adams EM, Spencer HC, Rowe VK, McCollister DD, Irish DD. Vapor toxicity of trichloroethylene determined by experiments on laboratory animals. Arch Ind Hyg Occup Med 1951;3:469.

187. Utesch RC, Weir FW, Bruckner JV. Development of an animal model of solvent abuse for use in the evaluation of extreme trichloroethylene inhalation. Toxicology 1981;19:169.

188. Tucker AW, Sanders VM, Barnes DW, Bradshaw TJ, White KL Jr, Sain LE, et al. Toxicology of trichloroethylene in the mouse. Toxicol Appl Pharmacol 1982;62:351.

189. Dorfmueller MA, Henne SP, York RG, Bornschein RL, Manson JM. Evaluation of teratogenicity and behavioral toxicity with inhalation exposure of maternal rats to trichloroethylene. Toxicology 1979;14:153.

190. Rebert CS, Day VL, Matteucci MJ, Pryor GT. Sensory-evoked potentials in rats chronically exposed to trichloroethylene: predominant auditory dysfunction. Neurotoxicol Teratol 1991;13:83–90.

191. Crofton KM, Zhao X. Mid-frequency hearing loss in rats following inhalation exposure to trichloroethylene: evidence from reflex modification audiometry. Neurotoxicol Teratol 1993; 15:413–423.

192. Jaspers RM, Muijser H, Lammers JH, Kulig BM. Mid-frequency hearing loss and reduction of acoustic startle responding in rats following trichloroethylene exposure. Neurotoxicol Teratol 1993;15:407–412.

193. Andersson A. Health dangers in industry from exposure to trichloroethylene. Acta Med Scand 1957;157(suppl 323):7–220.

194. Bardodej Z, Vyskocil J. Trichloroethylene metabolism and its effects on the nervous system as a means of hygienic control. Arch Ind Health 1956;13:581–592.

195. Grandjean E, Murchinger R, Turrian V, Haas PA, Knoepfel H-K, Rosenmund H. Investigations into the effects of exposure to trichloroethylene in mechanical engineering. Br J Ind Med 1955;12:131–142.

196. Lilis R, Stanescu D, Muica N, Roventa A. Chronic effects of trichloroethylene exposure. Med Lav 1969;60:595–601.

197. Salvini M, Binaschi S, Riva M. Evaluation of the psychophysiological functions in humans exposed to trichloroethylene. Br J Ind Med 1971;28:293–295.

198. Smith GF. Investigations of the mental effects of trichloroethylene. Ergonomics 1970;13:580.

199. Annau Z. The neurobehavioral toxicity of trichloroethylene. Neurobehav Toxicol Teratol 1981;3:417–424.

200. Todd J. Trichlorethylene poisoning with paranoid psychosis and Lilliputian hallucination. BMJ 1954;7:439–440.

201. Harenko A. Two peculiar instances of psychotic disturbance in trichloroethylene poisoning. Acta Neurol Scand 1967;31(suppl): 139–140.

202. Stewart RD, Dodd HC, Gay HH, Erley DS. Experimental human exposure to trichloroethylene. Arch Environ Health 1970;20:64–71.

203. Ferguson RK, Vernon RJ. Trichloroethylene in combination with CNS drugs: effects on visual-motor tests. Arch Environ Health 1970;20: 462–467.

204. Winneke G. Acute behavioral effects of exposure to some organic solvents—psychophysiological aspects. Acta Neurol Scand 1982;66 (suppl 92):117–129.

205. Vernon RJ, Ferguson RK. Effects of trichloroethylene on visual-motor performance. Arch Environ Health 1969;18:894–900.

206. Kylin B, Axell K, Samuel HE, Lindborg A. Effect of inhaled trichloroethylene on the CNS: as measured by optokinetic nystagmus. Arch Environ Health 1967;15:49–52.

207. Muller G, Spassowski M, Henschler D. Metabolism of trichloroethylene in man. III. Interaction of trichloroethylene and ethanol. Arch Toxicol 1975;33:173–189.

208. Moskowitz S, Shapiro H. Fatal exposure to methylene chloride vapor. Arch Ind Hyg Occup Med 1952;6:116–123.

209. Winek CL, Collum WD, Esposito F. Accidental methylene chloride fatality. Forensic Sci Int 1981;18:165–168.

210. Tariot PN. Delirium resulting from methylene chloride exposure: case report. J Clin Psychiatry 1983;44:340–342.

211. Sturmann K, Mofenson H, Caraccio T. Methylene chloride inhalation: an unusual form of drug abuse. Ann Emerg Med 1985;14:903–905.

212. Horowitz BZ. Carboxyhemoglobinemia caused by inhalation of methylene chloride. Am J Emerg Med 1986;4:48–51.

213. Stewart RD, Fisher TN, Hosko MJ, Peterson JE, Baretta ED, Dodd HC. Experimental human exposure to methylene chloride. Arch Environ Health 1972;25:342–348.

214. Kubic VL, Andres MW, Engel RR, Barlow CH, Caughey WS. Metabolism of dihalomethanes to carbon monoxide. I. In vivo studies. Drug Metab Dispos 1974;2:53–57.

215. Ratney RS, Wegman DH, Elkins HB. In vivo conversion of methylene chloride to carbon monoxide. Arch Environ Health 1974;28: 223–226.

216. Astrand I, Ovrum P, Carlsson A. Exposure to methylene chloride. I. Its concentration in alveolar air and blood during rest and exercise and its metabolism. Scand J Work Environ Health 1975;1:78–94.

217. Stewart RD, Fisher TN. Carboxyhemoglobin elevation after exposure to dichloromethane. Science 1972;176:295–296.

218. Gamberale F, Annwall G, Hultengren M. Exposure to methylene chloride. II. Psychological Functions. Scand J Work Environ Health 1975; 1:95–103.

219. Winneke G. The neurotoxicity of dichloromethane. Neurobehav Toxicol Teratol 1981;3: 391–395.

220. Cherry N, Venables H, Waldron HA, Wells GG. Some observations on workers exposed to methylene chloride. Br J Ind Med 1981;38: 351–355.

221. Hearne FT, Grose F, Pifer JW, Friedlander BR, Raleigh RL. Methylene chloride mortality study: dose-response characterization and animal model comparison. J Occup Med 1987;29: 217–228.

222. Silverstein MA. Letter to the editor. Arch Environ Health 1983;38:252.

223. McCarthy TB, Jones RD. Industrial gassing poisonings due to trichlorethylene, perchlorethylene, and 1,1,1-trichloroethane, 1961–80. Br J Ind Med 1983;40:450–455.

224. Kobayashi H, Hobara T, Kawamoto T, Sakai T. Effect of 1,1,1-trichloroethane inhalation on heart rate and its mechanism: a role of autonomic nervous system. Arch Environ Health 1987;42:140–143.

225. Wise MG. Trichloroethane (TCE) and central sleep apnea: a case study. J Toxicol Environ Health 1983;11:101–104.

226. Stewart RD, Gay HH, Schaffer AW, Erley DS, Rose VK. Experimental human exposure to methyl chloroform vapor. Arch Environ Health 1969;19:467–472.

227. Salvini M, Binaschi S, Riva M. Evaluation of the psychophysiological functions in humans exposed to the 'threshold limit value' of 1,1,1-trichloroethane. Br J Ind Med 1971;28:286–292.

228. Gamberale F, Hultengren M. Methylchloroform exposure. II. Psychophysiological functions. Work Environ Health 1973;10:82–92.

229. Mackay CJ, Campbell L, Samuel AM, Alderman KJ, Idzikowski C, Wilson HK, Gompertz D. Behavioral changes during exposure to 1,1,1-trichloroethane: time-course and relationship to blood solvent levels. Am J Ind Med 1987;11:223–239.

230. Maroni M, Bulgheroni C, Cassitto G, Merluzzi F, Gilioli R, Foa V. A clinical, neurophysiological and behavioral study of female workers exposed to 1,1,1-trichloroethane. Scand J Work Environ Health 1977;3:16–22.

231. Pryor GT. Solvent-induced neurotoxicity: effects and mechanisms. In: Chang LW, Dyer RS, eds. Handbook of toxicology. New York: Marcel Dekker, 1995.

232. Coodin FJ, Dawes C, Dean GW, Desjardins PR, Sutherland JB. Riposte to "Environmental lead and young children." Can Med Asoc J 1980;123:469–471.

233. Eastwell HD. Elevated lead levels in petrol "sniffers." Med J Aust 1985;143:563–564.

234. Goldings AS, Stewart RM. Organic lead encephalopathy: behavioral change and movement disorder following gasoline inhalation. J Clin Psychiatry 1982;43:70–72.

235. Goodheart RS, Dunne JW. Petrol sniffer's encephalopathy. A study of 25 patients. Med J Aust 1994;160:178–181.

236. Hansen KS, Sharp FR. Gasoline sniffing, lead poisoning, and myoclonus. JAMA 1978;240:1375–1376.

237. Prockop LD, Karampelas D. Encephalopathy secondary to abusive gasoline inhalation. J Fla Med Assoc 1981;68:823–824.

238. Reese E, Kimbrough RD. Acute toxicity of gasoline and some additives. Environ Health Perspect 1993;101(suppl 6):115–131.

239. Remington G, Hoffman BF. Gas sniffing as a form of substance abuse. Can J Psychiatry 1984;29:31–35.

240. Robinson RO. Tetraethyl lead poisoning from gasoline sniffing. JAMA 1978;241:1373–1374.

241. Tenenbein M, deGroot W, Rajani KR. Peripheral neuropathy following intentional inhalation of naphtha fumes. Can Med Assoc J 1984;131:1077–1079.

242. Valpey R, Sumi SM, Copass MK, Goble GJ. Acute and chronic progressive encephalopathy due to gasoline sniffing. Neurology 1978;28:507–510.

243. Burns CB, Currie B. The efficacy of chelation therapy and factors influencing mortality in lead intoxicated petrol sniffers. Aust N Z J Med 1995;25:197–203.

244. Pardys S, Brotman M. Trichloroethylene and alcohol: a straight flush. JAMA 1974;229:521–522.

245. Stewart RD, Hake CL, Peterson JE. "Degreasers' Flush," dermal response to trichloroethylene and ethanol. Arch Environ Health 1974;29:1–5.

246. Antti-Poika M, Juntunen J, Matikainen E, Suoranta H, Hanninen H, Seppalainen AM, Liira J. Occupational exposure to toluene: neurotoxic effects with special emphasis on drinking habits. Int Arch Occup Environ Health 1985;56:31–40.

247. Kira S, Ogata M, Ebara Y, Horii S, Otsuki S. A case of thinner sniffing: relationship between neuropsychological symptoms and urinary findings after inhalation of toluene and methanol. Ind Health 1988;26:81–85.

248. Pryor GT, Howd RA, Uyeno ET, Thurber AB. Interactions between toluene and alcohol. Pharmacol Biochem Behav 1985;23:401–410.

249. Cunningham J, Sharkawi M, Plaa GL. Pharmacological and metabolic interactions between ethanol and methyl n-butyl ketone, methyl isobutyl ketone, methyl ethyl ketone, or acetone in mice. Fundam Appl Toxicol 1989;13:102–109.

250. McCormick MJ. Methanol poisoning as a result of inhalational solvent abuse. Ann Emerg Med 1990;19:639–642.

251. Layzer RB. Myeloneuropathy after prolonged exposure to nitrous oxide. Lancet 1978;2:1227–1230.

252. Kinsella LJ, Green R. 'Anesthesia paresthetica': nitrous oxide-induced cobalamin deficiency. Neurology 1995;45:1608–1610.

253. Flippo TS, Holder WD Jr. Neurologic degeneration associated with nitrous oxide anesthesia in patients with vitamin B_{12} deficiency. Arch Surg 1993;128:1391–1395.

254. Nunn JF. Clinical aspects of the interaction between nitrous oxide and vitamin B_{12}. Br J Anaesth 1987;59:3–13.

255. Chanarin I. Nitrous oxide and the cobalamins. Clin Sci 1980;59:151–154.

256. Vishnubhakat SM, Beresford HR. Reversible myeloneuropathy of nitrous oxide abuse: serial electrophysiological studies. Muscle Nerve 1991;14:22–26.

257. Fujinaga M, Baden JM. Methionine prevents nitrous oxide-induced teratogenicity in rat embryos grown in culture. Anesthesiology 1994;81:184–189.

258. Brodsky JB, Cohen EN. Adverse effects of nitrous oxide. Med Toxicol 1986;1:362–374.

259. Gillman MA. Nitrous oxide has a very low abuse potential [Letter]. Comment on: Addiction 1994;89(7):831–839 [Comment]. Addiction 1995;90(3):439.

260. Jastak JT. Nitrous oxide and its abuse. J Am Dent Assoc 1991;122:48–52.

261. Schwartz RH, Calihan M. Nitrous oxide: a potentially lethal euphoriant inhalant. Am Family Pract 1984;30:171–172.

262. Belknap JK, Laursen SE, Crabbe JC. Ethanol and nitrous oxide produce withdrawal-induced convulsions by similar mechanisms in mice. Life Sci 1987;41:2033–2040.

263. Ron MA. Volatile substance abuse: a review of possible long-term neurological, intellectual and psychiatric sequalae. Br J Psychiatry 1986;148:235–246.

264. Korman M, Semler I, Trimboli F. A psychiatric emergency room study of 162 inhalant users. Addict Behav 1980;5:143.

265. Dinwiddie SH, Zorumski CF, Rubin EH. Psychiatric correlates of chronic solvent abuse. J Clin Psychiatry 1987;48:334–337.

266. Fernandez-Pol B, Bluestone H, Mizruchi MS. Inner-city substance abuse patterns: a study of psychiatric inpatients. Am J Drug Alcohol Abuse 1988;14:41–50.

267. Byrne A, Kirby B, Zibin T, Ensminger S. Psychiatric and neurological effects of chronic solvent abuse. Can J Psychiatry 1991;36:735–738.

268. Henry B, Feehan M, McGee R, Stanton W, Moffitt TE, Silva P. The importance of conduct problems and depressive symptoms in predicting adolescent substance use. J Abnorm Child Psychol 1993;21:469–480.

269. Goldbloom D, Chouinard G. Schizophreniform psychosis associated with chronic industrial toluene exposure: case report. J Clin Psychiatry 1985;46:350–351.

270. Katzelnick DJ, Davar G, Scanlon JP. Reversibility of psychiatric symptoms in a chronic solvent abuser: a case report. J Neuropsychiatry Clin Neurosci 1991;3:319–321.

271. Levy AB. Delirium induced by inhalation of typewriter correction fluid. Psychosomatics 1986;27:665–666.

272. Roberts FP, Lucas EG, Marsden CD, Trauer T. Near-pure xylene causing reversible neuropsychiatric disturbance [Letter]. Lancet 1988;8605:273.

273. Chadwick OF, Anderson HR. Neuropsychological consequences of volatile substance abuse: a review. Hum Toxicol 1989;8:307–312.

274. Baerg RD, Kimberg DV. Centrilobular hepatic necrosis and acute renal failure in "solvent sniffers." Ann Intern Med 1970;73:713–720.

275. Bennett RH, Forman HR. Hypokalemic periodic paralysis in chronic toluene exposure. Arch Neurol 1980;37:673.

276. Batlle DC, Sabatini S, Kurtzman NA. On the mechanism of toluene-induced renal tubular acidosis. Nephron 1988;49:210–218.

277. Carlisle EJ, Donnelly SM, Vasuvattakul S, Kamel KS, Tobe S, Halperin ML. Glue-sniffing and distal renal tubular acidosis: sticking to the facts. J Am Soc Nephrol 1991;1:1019–1027.

278. Daniell WE, Couser WG, Rosenstock L. Occupational solvent exposure and glomerulonephritis. JAMA 1988;259:2280–2283.

279. Gupta RK, van der Meulen J, Johny KV. Oliguric acute renal failure due to glue-sniffing. Case report. Scand J Urol Nephrol 1991;25:247–250.

280. Jone CM, Wu AH. An unusual case of toluene-induced metabolic acidosis. Clin Chem 1988;34:2596–2599.

281. Kamijima M, Nakazawa Y, Yamakawa M, Shibata E, Hisanaga N, Ono Y, et al. Metabolic acidosis and renal tubular injury due to pure toluene inhalation. Arch Environ Health 1994;49:410–413.

282. Kaneko T, Koizumi T, Takezaki T, Sato A. Urinary calculi associated with solvent abuse. J Urol 1992;147:1365–1366.

283. Lavoie FW, Dolan MC, Danzl DF, Barber RL. Recurrent resuscitation and 'no code' orders in a 27-year-old spray paint abuser [Clinical conference]. Ann Emerg Med 1987;16:1266–1273.

284. Marjot R, McLeod AA. Chronic nonneurological toxicity from volatile substance abuse. Hum Toxicol 1989;8:301–306.

285. Mizutani T, Oohashi N, Naito H. Myoglobinemia and renal failure in toluene poisoning: a case report. Vet Hum Toxicol 1989;31:448–450.

286. Nelson NA, Robins TG, Port FK. Solvent nephrotoxicity in humans and experimental animals. Am J Nephrol 1990;10:10–20.

287. Patel R, Benjamin J Jr. Renal disease associated with toluene inhalation. Clin Toxicol 1986;24:213–223.

288. Ravnskov U. Exposure to organic solvents—a missing link in poststreptococcal glomerulonephritis? Acta Med Scand 1978;203:351–356.

289. Taverner D, Harrison DJ, Bell GM. Acute renal failure due to interstitial nephritis induced by 'glue-sniffing' with subsequent recovery. Scott Med J 1988;33:246–247.

290. Wilkins-Haug L, Gabow PA. Toluene abuse during pregnancy: obstetric complications and perinatal outcomes. Obstet Gynecol 1991;77:504–509.

291. Will AM, McLaren EH. Reversible renal damage due to glue sniffing. BMJ 1981;283:525–526.

292. Lauwerys R, Bernard A, Viau C, Buchet JP. Kidney disorders and hematotoxicity from organic solvent exposure. Scand J Work Environ Health 1985;11(suppl 1): 83–90.

293. Harrison DJ, Thomson D, MacDonald MK. Membranous glomerulonephritis. J Clin Pathol 1986;39:167.

294. Anetseder M, Hartung E, Klepper S, Reichmann H. Gasoline vapors induce severe rhabdomyolysis. Neurology 1994;44:2393–2395.

295. Brown JH, Hadden DR, Hadden DS. Solvent abuse, toluene acidosis and diabetic ketoacidosis. Arch Emerg Med 1991;8:65–67.

296. Lock EA. Mechanism of nephrotoxic action due to organohalogenated compounds. Toxicol Lett 1989;46:93–106.

297. Miller L, Pateras V, Friederici H, Engel G. Acute tubular necrosis after inhalation exposure to methylene chloride. Report of a case. Arch Intern Med 1985;145:145–146.

298. Rioux JP, Myers RA. Methylene chloride poisoning: a paradigmatic review. J Emerg Med 1988;6:227–238.

299. Kimbrough RD, Mitchell FL, Houk VN. Trichloroethylene: an update. J Toxicol Environ Health 1985;15:369–383.

300. Brown BR, Gandolfi AJ. Adverse effects of volatile anaesthetics. Br J Anaesth 1987;59:14–23.

301. Pozzi C, Marai P, Ponti R, Dell'oro C, Sala C, Zedda S, Locatelli F. Toxicity in man due to stain removers containing 1,2-dichloropropane. Br J Ind Med 1985;42:770–772.

302. Keogh AM, Ibels LS, Allen DH, Isbister JP, Kennedy MC. Exacerbation of Goodpasture's syndrome after inadvertent exposure to hydrocarbon fumes. BMJ 1984;288:188.

303. Nathan AW, Toseland PA. Goodpasture's syndrome and trichloroethane intoxication. Br J Clin Pharmacol 1979;8:28406.

303a. Pryor GT, Rebert CS. Neurotoxicology of Inhaled Substances, National Institutes on Drug Abuse Contract 271-90-7202 report, November 1992.

304. Short BG, Burnett VL, Cox MG, Bus JS, Swenberg JA. Site-specific renal cytotoxicity and cell proliferation in male rats exposed to petroleum hydrocarbons. Lab Invest 1987;57:564–577.

305. Wedeen RP. Occupational renal disease. Am J Kidney Dis 1984;111:241–257.

306. Sarmiento Martinez J, Guardiola Sala JJ, Martinez Vea A, Campãna Casals E. Renal tubular acidosis with an elevated anion gap in a 'glue sniffer' [Letter]. Hum Toxicol 1989;8:139–140.

307. Yamaguchi K, Shirai T, Shimakura K, Akamatsu T, Nakama H, Kono K, et al. Pneumatosis cystoides intestinalis and trichloroethylene exposure. Am J Gastroenterol 1985;80:753–757.

308. Farrell G, Prendergast D, Murray M. Halothane hepatitis. Detection of a constitutional susceptibility factor. N Engl J Med 1985;313:1310–1314.

309. Goodwin TM. Toluene abuse and renal tubular acidosis in pregnancy. Obstet Gynecol 1988;71:715–718.

310. Lindemann R. Congenital renal tubular dysfunction associated with maternal sniffing of organic solvents. Acta Paediatr Scand 1991;80:882–884.

311. Paraf F, Lewis J, Jothy S. Acute fatty liver of pregnancy after exposure to toluene. A case report. J Clin Gastroenterol 1993;17:163–165.

312. Stewart A, Witts LJ. Chronic carbon tetrachloride intoxication. 1944 [Classical article]. Br J Ind Med 1993;50:8–18.

313. Benjamin SB, Goodman ZD, Ishak KG, Zimmerman HJ, Irey NS. The morphologic spectrum of halothane-induced hepatic injury: analysis of 77 cases. Hepatology 1985;5:1163–1171.

314. Clearfield HR. Hepatrenal toxicity from sniffing spot-remover (tichloroethylene). Dig Dis 1970;15:851–856.

315. Cordes DH, Brown WD, Quinn KM. Chemically induced hepatitis after inhaling organic solvents. West J Med 1988;148:458–460.

316. Dossing M. Occupational toxic liver damage. J Hepatol 1986;3:131–135.

317. Hakim A, Jain AK, Jain R. Chloroform ingestion causing toxic hepatitis. J Assoc Physicians India 1992;40:477.

318. Hodgson MJ, Furman J, Ryan C, Durrant J, Kern E. Encephalopathy and vestibulopathy following short-term hydrocarbon exposure. J Occup Med 1989;31:51–54.

319. McCunney RJ. Diverse manifestations of trichloroethylene. Br J Ind Med 1988;45:122–126.

320. McIntyre AS, Long RG. Fatal fulminant hepatic failure in a 'solvent abuser'. Postgrad Med J 1992;68:29–30.

321. Buring JE, Hennekens CH, Mayrent SL, Rosner B, Greenberg ER, Colton T. Health experiences of operating room personnel. Anaesthesiology 1985;62:325–330.

322. Shaw J, Brooks PM, McNeil JJ, Moulds RFW, Ravenscroft PJ, Smith AJ. Modern inhalational anesthetic agents. Med J Aust 1989;150:95–102.

323. Neuberger J, Davis M. Advances in understanding of halothane hepatitis. Trends Pharmacol Sci 1983;Jan:19–20.

324. Ong CN, Koh D, Foo SC, Kok PW, Ong HY, Aw TC. Volatile organic solvents in correction fluids: identification and potential hazards. Bull Environ Contam Toxicol 1993;50:787–793.

325. Greer JE. Adolescent abuse of typewriter correction fluid. South Med J 1984;77:297–298.

326. Mizutani K, Shinomiya K, Shinomiya T. Hepatotoxicity of dichloromethane. Forensic Sci Int 1988;38:113–128.

327. Hodgson MJ, Heyl AT, Van Thiel DH. Liver disease associated with exposure to 1,1,1-trichloroethane. Arch Intern Med 1989;149:1793–1798.

328. Plaa GL. Experimental evaluation of haloalkanes and liver injury. Fundam Appl Toxicol 1988;10:563–570.

329. Redfern N. Morbidity among anaesthetists. Br J Hosp Med 1990;43:377–381.

330. Cohen EN. Inhalation anesthetics may cause genetic defects, abortions and miscarriages in operating room personnel. In: Eckenhoff JE, ed. Controversy in anesthesiology. Philadelphia: WB Saunders, 1979:47–57.

331. Reyes de la Rocha S, Brown MA, Fortenberry JD. Pulmonary function abnormalities in intentional spray paint inhalation. Chest 1987;92:100–104.

332. Schikler KN, Lane EE, Seitz K, Collins WM. Solvent abuse associated pulmonary abnormalities. Adv Alcohol Subst Abuse 1984;3:75–81.

333. Woo OF, Healey KM, Sheppard D, Tong TG. Chest pain and hypoxemia from inhalation of a trichloroethane aerosol product. J Toxicol Clin Toxicol 1983;20:333–341.

334. Buie SE, Pratt DS, May JJ. Diffuse pulmonary injury following paint remover exposure. Am J Med 1986;81:702–704.

335. Engstrand DA, England DM, Huntington RW 3d. Pathology of paint sniffers' lung. Am J Forensic Med Pathol 1986;7:232–236.

336. Sherwood RL, O'Shea W, Thomas PT, Ratajczak HV, Aranyi C, Graham JA. Effects of inhalation of ethylene dichloride on pulmonary defenses of mice and rats. Toxicol Appl Pharmacol 1987;91:491–496.

337. Boon NA. Solvent abuse and the heart [Editorial]. BMJ 1987;294:722.

338. Cunningham SR, Dalzell GWN, McGirr P, Khan MM. Myocardial infarction and primary ventricular fibrillation after glue sniffing. BMJ 1987;294:739–740.

339. Wiseman MN, Banim S. "Glue sniffer's" heart? BMJ 1987;294:739.

340. Wright MF, Strobl DJ. 1,1,1-Trichloroethane cardiac toxicity: report of a case. J Am Osteopath Assoc 1984;84:285–288.

341. Ong TK, Rustage KJ, Harrison KM, Brook IM. Solvent abuse. An anaesthetic management problem. Br Dent J 1988;164:150–151.

342. Wodka RM, Jeong EW. Cardiac effects of inhaled typewriter correction fluid [Letter]. Ann Intern Med 1989;110:91–92.

343. Mee AS, Wright PL. Congestive (dilated) cardiomyopathy in association with solvent abuse. J R Soc Med 1980;73:671–672.

344. Taylor GJ, Harris WS. Cardiac toxicity of aerosol propellants. JAMA 1970;214:81–85.

345. Chenoweth MB. Abuse of inhalation anesthetic drugs. In: Sharp CW, Brehm M. eds. Review of inhalants: euphoria to dysfunction. NIDA research monograph series no. 15, DHEW publication ADM 77–553. Washington, DC: Department of Health, Education, and Welfare, 1977:102–111.

346. Barrowcliff DF, Knell AJ. Cerebral damage due to endogenous chronic carbon monoxide poisoning caused by exposure to methylene chloride. J Soc Occup Med 1979;29:12–14.

347. Manno M, Chirillo R, Daniotti G, Cocheo V, Albrizio F. Carboxyhaemoglobin and fatal methylene chloride poisoning [Letter]. Lancet 1989;2(8657):274.

348. Wason S, Detsky AS, Platt OS, Lovejoy FH Jr. Isobutyl nitrite toxicity by ingestion. Ann Intern Med 1980;92:637–638.

349. Brandes JC, Bufill JA, Pisciotta AV. Amyl nitrite-induced hemolytic anemia. Am J Med 1989;86:252–254.

350. Machabert R, Testud F, Descotes J. Methaemoglobinaemia due to amyl nitrite inhalation: a case report. Hum Exp Toxicol 1994;13:313–314.

351. Edwards RJ, Ujma J. Extreme methaemoglobinaemia secondary to recreational use of amyl nitrite. J Accident Emerg Med 1995;12:138–142.

352. Austin H, Delzell E, Cole, P. Benzene and leukemia. A review of the literature and a risk assessment. Am J Epidemiol 1988;127:419–439.

353. Marwick TH, Nakatani S, Haluska B, Thomas JD, Lever HM. Provocation of latent left ventricular outflow tract gradients with amyl nitrite and exercise in hypertrophic cardiomyopathy. Am J Cardiol 1995;75:805–819.

354. Rosoff MH, Cohen MV. Profound bradycardia after amyl nitrite in patients with a tendency to

vasovagal episodes. Br Heart J 1986;55: 97–100.

355. Klimmek R, Krettek C. Effects of amyl nitrite on circulation, respiration and blood homeostasis in cyanide poisoning. Arch Toxicol 1988;62:161–166.

356. Mathew RJ, Wilson WH, Tant SR. Regional cerebral blood flow changes associated with amyl nitrite inhalation. Br J Addict 1989;84: 293–299.

357. Rees DC, Knisely JS, Balster RL, Jordan S, Breen TJ. Pentobarbital-like discriminative stimulus properties of halothane, 1,1,1-trichloroethane, isoamyl nitrite, flurothyl and oxazepam in mice. J Pharmacol Exp Ther 1987;241:507–515.

358. Guss DA, Normann SA, Manoguerra AS. Clinically significant methemoglobinemia from inhalation of isobutyl nitrite. Am J Emerg Med 1985;3:46–47.

359. Smith M, Stair T, Rolnick MA. Butyl nitrite and a suicide attempt. Ann Intern Med 1980; 92:719–720.

360. Lotzova E, Savary CA, Hersh EM, Khan AA, Rosenblum M. Depression of murine natural killer cell cytotoxicity by isobutyl nitrite. Cancer Immunol Immunother 1984;17:130–134.

361. Dax EM, Lange WR, Jaffe JH. Allergic reactions to amyl nitrite inhalation. Am J Med 1989;86:732.

362. Osterloh J, Goldfield D. Butyl nitrite transformation in vitro, chemical nitrosation reactions, and mutagenesis. J Anal Toxicol 1984;8:164–169.

363. Newell GR, Adams SC, Mansell PWA, Hersh EM. Toxicity, immunosuppressive effects and carcinogenic potential of volatile nitrites: possible relationship to Kaposi's sarcoma. Pharmacotherapy 1984;4:284–291.

364. Haverkos HW, Kopstein AN, Wilson H, Drotman P. Nitrite inhalants: history, epidemiology and possible links to AIDS. Environ Health Perspect 1994;102:858–861.

365. Moss AR, Osmond D, Bacchetti P, Chermann J, Barre-Sinoussi F, Carlson J. Risk factors for AIDS and HIV seropositivity in homosexual men. Am J Epidemiol 1987;125: 1035–1047.

366. Mirvish SS, Haverkos HW. Butyl nitrite in the induction of Kaposi's sarcoma in AIDS [Letter]. N Engl J Med 1987;317:1603.

367. Yamamoto M, Ishiwata H, Yamada T, Yoshihira K, Tanimura A, Tomita I. Studies in the guinea-pig stomach on the formation of N-nitrosomethylurea, from methylurea and sodium nitrite, and its disappearance. Food Chem Toxicol 1987;25:663–668.

368. Klimmek R, Krettek C, Werner HW. Ferrihaemoglobin formation by amyl nitrite and sodium nitrite in different species in vivo and in vitro. Arch Toxicol 1988;62:152–160.

369. Osterloh JD, Goldfield D. Uptake of inhaled n-butyl nitrite and in vivo transformation in rats. J Pharm Sci 1985;74:780–782.

370. Dunkel VC, Rogers-Back AM, Lawlor TE, Harbell JW, Cameron TP. Mutagenicity of some alkyl nitrites used as recreational drugs. Environ Mol Mutagen 1989;14:115–122.

371. Lewis DM, Lynch DW. Toxicity of inhaled isobutyl nitrite in BALB/c mice: systemic and immunotoxic studies. In: Haverkos HW, Dougherty JA, eds. Health hazards of nitrite inhalants. NIDA research monograph series no. 83, DHHS publication ADM 88–1573. Washington, DC: Department of Health and Human Services, 1988:50–58.

372. Jacobs RF, Marmer DJ, Steele RW, Hogue TR. Cellular immunotoxicity of amyl nitrite. J Toxicol Clin Toxicol 1983;20:421–449.

373. Soderberg LSF. Immunomodulation by nitrite inhalants may predispose abusers to AIDS and Kaposi's sarcoma. In: Sharp CW, ed. Pharmaconeuroimmunology, a review. Advances in Neuroimmunology. Elmsford, NY: Pergamon Press, 1996.

374. Pinkhas J, Cohen I, Kruglak J, de Vries A. Hobby induced factor VII deficiency. Haemeostasis 1972;1:52–54.

375. Hersh JH, Podruch PE, Rogers G, Weisskopf B. Toluene embryopathy. J Pediatr 1985;106: 922–927.

376. Hersh JH. Toluene embryopathy: two new cases. J Med Genet 1989;26:333–337.

377. Pearson MA, Hoyme HE, Seaver LH, Rimsza ME. Toluene embryopathy: delineation of the phenotype and comparison with fetal alcohol syndrome. Pediatrics 1994;93:211–215.

378. Donald JM, Hooper K, Hopenhayn-Rich C. Reproductive and developmental toxicity of toluene: a review. Environ Health Perspect 1991;94:237–244.

379. Ono A, Sekita K, Ohno K, Hirose A, Ogawa Y, Saito M, et al. Reproductive and developmental toxicity studies of toluene. I. Teratogenicity study of inhalation exposure in pregnant rats. J Toxicol Sci 1995;20:109–134.

380. Pryor GT. Animal research on solvent abuse. In: Sharp CW, Beauvais F, Spence R, eds. Inhalant abuse: a volatile research agenda. NIDA research monograph series no. 129, NIH publication 93–3480. Washington, DC: National Institutes of Health, 1992:233–258.

381. Mazze RI, Fujinaga M, Baden JM. Halothane prevents nitrous oxide teratogenicity in Sprague-Dawley rats; folinic acid does not. Teratology 1988;38:121–127.

382. Cagen SZ, Klaassen CD. Hepatoxicity of carbon tetrachloride in developing rats. Toxicol Appl Pharmacol 1979;50:347–354.

383. Murray FJ, Schwetz BA, McBride JG, Staples RE. Toxicity of inhaled chloroform in pregnant mice and their offspring. Toxicol Appl Pharmacol 1979;50:515–522.

384. Eskenazi B, Gaylord L, Bracken MB, Brown D. In utero exposure to organic solvents and human neurodevelopment. Dev Med Child Neurol 1988;30:492–501.

23 DESIGNER DRUGS

John P. Morgan

INTRODUCTION

"Designer" jeans all resemble Levi's®. Similarly, "designer drugs" are imitative but not innovative. As a slogan, the phrase has notable media persistence because it provokes the image of a clever unaffiliated chemist in a hidden laboratory manipulating psychoactive chemicals toward new highs and dangers. However, most of the illegally designed drugs have been made by underground chemists simply following published syntheses. A search of the biomedical literature in 1996 using the subject heading *designer drug* locates papers almost always about methylenedioxymethamphetamine (MDMA). This chemical was first synthesized in 1910 and was patented by a pharmaceutical company in 1914 (1).

Until one hundred years ago, only plants yielded psychoactive drug products. However, in the late nineteenth and early twentieth centuries, medicinal chemists began producing synthetic chemicals which could alter mood, change consciousness, induce pleasure, and modify unwanted feelings. Essentially all of the synthetic chemicals that have been used illicitly for psychoactivity (amphetamine, barbiturates, amyl nitrite, methaqualone) were initially made by pharmaceutical chemists seeking better treatments for disease. Sometime during their approved history, they were diverted for unsanctioned use. Additionally, some psychoactive chemicals never became commercial products. Illicit synthesis using methods published by pharmaceutical chemists always supplied the market for unsanctioned use. Among these are phencyclidine, LSD, 4-methyl aminorex, and MDMA.

When Henderson (2) coined the term *designer drug*, he was characterizing successful attempts to produce fentanyl analogues that were *legal* as well as potent and lucrative. The volume of use (and manufacture) of synthetic illegal drugs remains low in comparison to the ingestion of the botanical psychoactives cocaine, heroin, and cannabis; although it has been said that as much MDMA is now consumed in Great Britain as is marihuana (3). The products of illegal chemists are much feared. However, their output is modest. Since the 1992 edition of this book (4) only one new illicitly synthesized chemical, methcathinone, has become of any clinical importance. There is no evidence that difficult syntheses are undertaken underground and there is no evidence of increasing precision promoting bioavailability, distribution to the brain, or receptor-tuning. The toxic opioid analogue MPTP is produced by careless management of temperature and pH during the attempted manufacture of MPPP, as discussed later in this chapter. For a synthesized product to enter the illicit psychoactive market, it must produce a desired effect but should also be economical for clandestine manufacture. It must be easily made, and the precursors easily obtained.

The phrase *controlled substance analogues* could replace the confusing term *designer drug,* if any classification other than *synthetic* is needed. The Controlled Substances Act was amended to include the Controlled Substances Analogues Enforcement Act in 1986. According to this law, a controlled substance analogue to be classified as illegal is "substantially similar" to the chemical structure of an already controlled substance in Schedule I or II. Shulgin (5) believes that the phrase is essentially imprecise. Is a chemical substantially similar if it is an analogue; a homologue; or an isomer? Early decisions classified MDMA as "substantially similar" to methamphetamine. Some decisions evoke the pornography allusion of Supreme Court Justice Potter Stewart. No one can exactly define the standard but jurists and jurors know a "controlled substance analogue" when they see it.

The analysis that follows discusses only five important synthetic products (and a few analogues):

1. congeners of the potent synthetic opioid, fentanyl
2. the meperidine congener MPPP and its highly toxic contaminant, MPTP
3. MDMA and some analogous phenethylamines
4. 4-methylaminorex ("U4Euh") and its precedent analogue, aminorex
5. methcathinone (ephedrone) sometimes called "cat" or "jeff"

The section on MDMA is longer than all other discussions combined because its use is common, its market may be expanding, and toxicity is frequently reported.

OPIOID ANALOGUES

Opioid products are at the heart of the concern over controlled substance analogues. A number of congeners of the potent opioid fentanyl have appeared in illicit trade and have been responsible for death in heroin injectors who were insufficiently tolerant. A meperidine analogue, (1-methyl-4-propionoxy-4-phenylpyridine) (MPPP) was synthesized illicitly but because of preparation problems became contaminated with 1-methy-4-phenyl-1,2,3,6-tetrahydropyridine (MPTP). This drug causes a parkinsonian syndrome in humans and has become an important research tool in understanding pathology in the basal ganglion.

Fentanyl Analogues

In 1979, a series of unusual deaths occurred in Orange County, California. The fatalities occurred in heroin injectors and resembled heroin overdose but toxicological analysis was negative. By the end of 1980, 15 such fatalities had been recorded. The toxin was later identified as an analogue of the legal opioid fentanyl, alpha-methyl-fentanyl. It had been promoted in street sales as "China White" (sometimes a name for purported high-quality heroin). Between 1981 and 1984, at least three other analogues were identified in street drug samples and in the bodily fluids of overdose victims: alpha-methyl-acetyl-fentanyl, 3-methyl-fentanyl, and para-fluoro-fentanyl (Fig. 23.1). 3-methyl-fentanyl (TMF) is approximately 6000 times as potent as morphine. By the end of 1984, an apparent decline in use of these products had occurred as had the number of deaths, although perhaps 10 even more unusual analogues were identified. Writing in 1988, Henderson estimated that more than 100 deaths had occurred (only three outside California) (6).

However, TMF moved to the East Coast during 1988 and at least 16 overdose deaths occurred in and around Pittsburgh (7). TMF was not always identifiable as the sole cause of death but was detected in bodily fluids. The article describing the Pittsburgh deaths appeared in the *Journal of the American Medical Association* shortly after more deaths secondary to TMF were reported in *The New York Times*. The *Times* article described at least 17 deaths and a number of hospitalizations in New York City, Hartford, Connecticut, and Patterson, New Jersey (8).

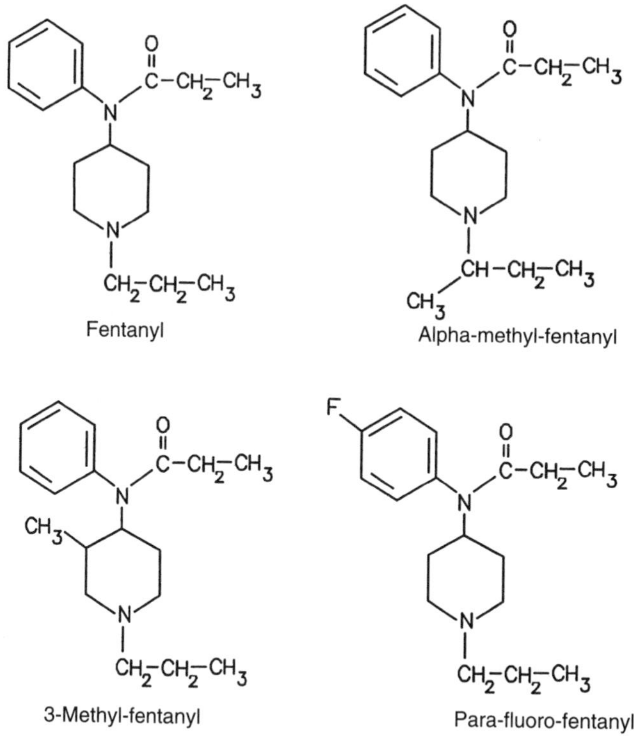

Figure 23.1. Chemical structure of fentanyl, alpha-methyl-fentanyl, 3-methyl-fentanyl, and para-fluoro-fentanyl.

Potency

Although it is likely that any marketed controlled substance analogue will be relatively potent, a potent opioid has particular dangerous significance. Many users of street heroin do not attain significant levels of tolerance even though previously low-quality, adulterated street heroin has improved. Additionally, "regular" injectors of heroin spend much time not using (9) and may often be susceptible to overdose with any potent material. It is not that fentanyl or its profoundly potent analogues cause a better high or more respiratory depression than heroin, it is that they do it in such a small volume of white powder.

MPTP

The illicit synthesis of the meperidine congener MPPP (Fig. 23.2) was effected as early as 1977 by a young man in Bethesda, Maryland. He developed Parkinson's disease and the sequence was understood and described by Davis and his coworkers in 1979 (10).

MPPP, a close relative of meperidine, had previously been tested as an analgesic but possessed insufficient activity. The synthesis is particularly likely to be contaminated with the MPTP congener under conditions of inadequate control of temperature and pH. In 1982 in California, a number of injectors who had purchased "street heroin" developed parkinsonian symptoms and subsequent analysis of the product identified both MPTP and MPPP. The scientists who described this phenomenon reported that the description of the synthesis of MPPP had been carefully excised from journal pages in the Stanford Medical School library (11). Primates given MPTP develop a parkinsonian syndrome secondary to destruction of dopaminergic neurons in the substantia nigra (12). MPTP may cause occupational Parkinson's disease. One reported case involved a chemist who had conducted repeated synthetic reactions involving MPTP. Exposure may have occurred through accidental inhalation or skin contamination (13). Follow-up studies indicate that susceptibility to the toxicity is variable. All exposed to MPTP do not necessarily become ill. A review article in 1985 (14) estimated that of 300 exposed individuals, only 20 developed Parkinson's disease.

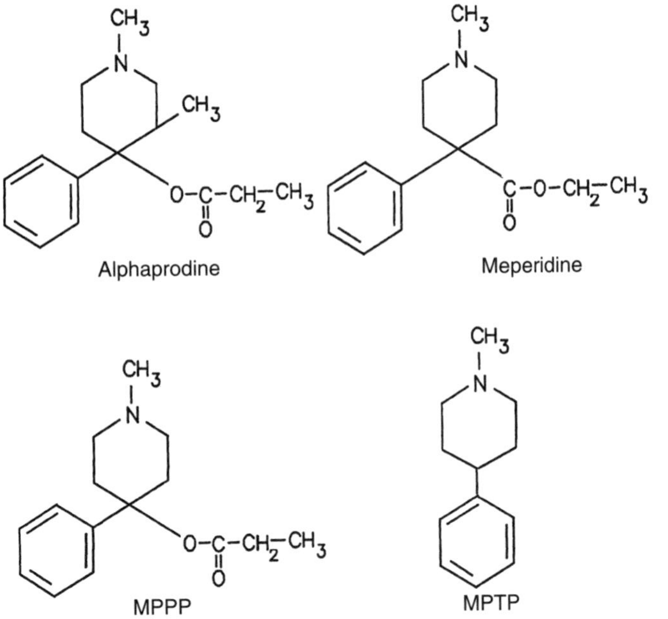

Figure 23.2. *Chemical structure of alphaprodine, meperidine, MPPP, and MPTP.*

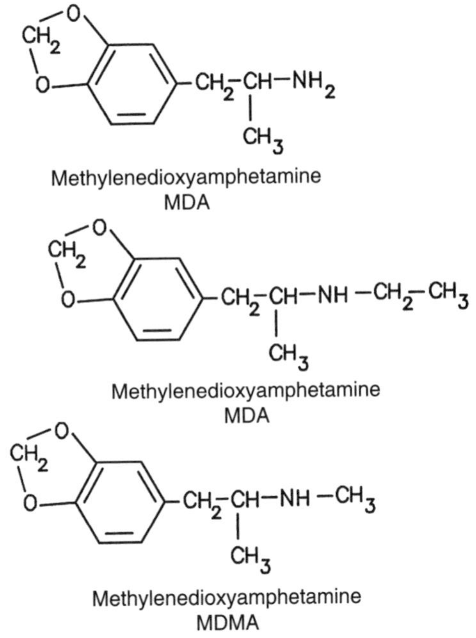

Figure 23.3. Chemical structure of methylenedioxyamphetamine (MDA), methylenedioxyethylamphetamine (MDEA), and methylenedioxymethamphetamine (MDMA).

Mechanism of Action

The neurotoxicity is not caused by MPTP itself but by a toxic metabolite. MPTP binds with high affinity to neural monoamine oxidase B and is converted to methylphenyldihydropyridine (MPP+). Interference with conversion by prior treatment with a monoamine oxidase inhibitor will prevent experimental toxicity. MPP+ is taken up by sensitive cells in the substantia nigra, reaches high intramitochondrial concentration, interferes with oxidative phosphorylation, and causes cellular death (15).

MDMA

MDMA and MDA (frequently referred to as designer amphetamines) were synthesized in 1910 (1) and patented by 1914 (Fig. 23.3). MDA was studied in humans as an appetite suppressant in the 1950s and 1960s but never marketed. It appeared as an illicit psychedelic in the late 1960s in the Haight-Ashbury district in San Francisco (16). Some early Canadian reports of serious toxicity may actually have involved paramethoxyamphetamine (PMA), an analogue believed to provoke severe hypertension (17). MDA was included in Schedule I of the (new) 1970 Controlled Substances Act. MDMA was ignored.

The author had an unusual personal experience in 1979 or 1980 involving the then largely unknown MDMA.

Two of my students approached me in 1979 or 1980 with two large, opaque white capsules. They had been purchased for $12 each at a party. The seller provided the students with an informational sheet I still possess. Copied from Wet—The Magazine of Gourmet Bathing, the article describes a drug called "XTC," identifying it as a close relative of MDA. The writer stated that some psychotherapists had found the drug useful, particularly in couples being counseled together, as a promoter of intimacy and communication. The article described the drug as legal under the Controlled Substance Act because of its chemical difference from MDA.

I told my student about reports of the hazards of MDA and also informed them that the claims in Wet were almost certain to be untrue, because claims regarding psychedelic exotica were frequently exaggerated. I was completely wrong. I sent a portion of the powder from one capsule for analysis. The first laboratory reported that the drug behaved as methamphetamine on thin layer chromatography, but that this was not definitive. Later, a skilled analyst using gas chromatography and mass spectrometry identified the drug as "N-methylmethylene-dioxyamphetamine." Unfortunately, I had given my stu-

dents the news of the first analysis and one consumed the "methamphetamine" to stay awake for an all-night study session. He felt that it worked but not particularly well. A letter from Dr. A. T. Shulgin confirmed what Wet had published.

Shulgin and Nichols had referred to MDMA in 1978, describing the drug as producing an "easily managed" euphoria with emotional and sensual overtones (18). In correspondence, Shulgin described a group of psychotherapists who had begun to use the drug to facilitate therapeutic sessions and to promote communication and intimacy. This use of a phenethylamine psychedelic compound to assist psychotherapy had actually begun with MDA (19). Between 1978 and 1985, a network of such therapists and clients had grown in the United States. Most reports of the therapeutic outcome (admittedly uncontrolled) were positive. No serious toxicity occurred in these settings.

Two other recreational settings of use emerged by 1984. Groups of friends and invitees took the drug in small group social settings for fun and to enhance communication and intimacy. To some degree, this use related to the psychotherapeutic ideology. Later, a college-based urban party and dancing scene emerged (20). Large volumes of the drug were being manufactured in Boston, Arlington (Texas), and other cities. This casual and frequent use by young people attracted attention and, in 1984, the DEA applied under the Controlled Substances Act to place MDMA in Schedule I on an emergency basis. Although there was evidence of widespread synthesis, marketing, and consumption, there was little evidence of harm. The only claim of toxicity presented by the DEA was a report of neurotoxic damage to rodent serotonergic brain cells not by MDMA but by MDA (21). There was significant legal opposition to the rescheduling by a group of psychotherapists and MDMA advocates who believed the drug to have legitimate value (22).

Effects

George Greer, a Santa Fe psychiatrist, had devised a protocol for MDMA use in therapy by 1983. He described administering the drug to 29 patients, usually beginning with 100–150 mg by mouth followed by an optional dose of 50–75 mg in 2 hours. His subjects reported positive feelings of closeness and an expanded perspective and insight into problematic conflicts or feelings (23). Other positive studies and reports were generated, including that of Liester et al. who questioned 20 psychiatrists who had previously taken

MDMA (24). This report was also positive but listed some adverse effects, including a decreased desire to perform mental or physical work, decreased appetite, and trismus.

After 1986, when the drug was placed in Schedule I, use continued by young people in clubs. This early dance phenomenon (referred to as Acid House) evolved particularly in Britain, Ireland, Western Europe, and later North America into "raves." These are organized, large social events initially held in large warehouses—later in dance halls and clubs. Young people would often dance all night to recorded and programmed "house" music accompanied by light shows and computer-generated video images. The preferred drug was MDMA and dancers consumed uncertain amounts of the illicit material. This phenomenon continues in Europe and North America and accounts for what is apparently an enormous volume of consumption. The phenomenon of social contemplative small group use also continues—probably supplied by the same illicit market—although at a smaller volume (20).

Neuropharmacology

MDMA possesses a variety of psychoactive properties and interacts with a variety of neurotransmitters. It is a stimulant with amphetamine-like actions and users may, soon after ingestion, experience tachycardia, increased blood pressure, dry mouth, anorexia, diminished fatigue, mood elevation, and jaw clenching. Frank hallucinations are rarely, if ever, experienced. The desired effects, which may occur in any of the situations of use, include euphoria, heightened sensuality, enhanced feeling of closeness, affection, and comfort in communication. Many subjects report a remarkable diminution of self-consciousness and embarrassment. Adverse consequences (seldom causing major distress) include gait instability, jaw clenching, a distaste for mental or physical tasks, fatigue, and nausea. Some MDMA effects are mediated by displacement of dopamine and norepinephrine. In discrimination studies, MDMA will substitute for D-amphetamine in animals trained to distinguish that stimulant from saline. Most studies also point to serotonergic activity. MDMA displaces serotonin from nerve terminals but shows little affinity for postsynaptic 5-HT receptors. It seems very likely that the positive feelings reported by users have much to do with enhanced availability of serotonin at the synapse (25).

Neurotoxicity

MDMA produces, in many animal species, dose-related reductions in brain serotonin (5-HT) and 5-hydroxyindoleacetic acid (5-HIAA). There is diminution of 5-HT uptake sites and diminished activity of tryptophan hydroxylase—a necessary enzyme for serotonin synthesis. This neurotoxicity has been seen with other serotonin displacers including MDA, methamphetamine, and the widely prescribed appetite suppressant fenfluramine (26). The toxic dose in many animal species is quite high compared to the "usual" human dose of 1.0–2.0 mg/kg. However, in some non-human primates, the toxic dose is closer to the recreational dose in humans. The dosage issues have been closely examined in a 1995 review by Granquist (27). In non-human primates, the toxicity is usually produced by a course of intramuscular or subcutaneous injection. Typically, primates are given, by injection, 5–20 mg/kg twice per day for four days. Not only does this exceed the usual human dose (often taken as a single dose), but injection increases the likelihood of toxicity (28). One study in non-human primates administered 2.5 mg/kg by mouth once every two weeks for a total of 8 doses over 4 months. In this study, there was no evidence of neurotoxic response in assays of 5-HT and 5-HIAA in a number of regions of the brain (27). Another study in primates (2.5 mg/kg × 8 doses) produced decreases in 5-HT and 5-HIAA but [³H]paroxetine binding was not altered. Such a finding suggests (but does not prove) that 5-HT synaptic terminals were intact despite the decreases in neurotransmitter and metabolite concentrations (29). There have been few published studies assessing serotonergic functions in humans. One 1994 study comparing frequent users to controls identified a decrease of 32% in cerebrospinal fluid concentration of 5-HIAA. There were no other indications of neurotoxicity and these subjects also had significantly greater non-MDMA amphetamine experience than the controls. Extensive psychological testing in these users documented the "abnormalities" of decreased impulsivity and hostility (30).

Another human study examined serum prolactin following injection of L-tryptophan. This assessment of serotonergic function identified some diminution of prolactin blood levels but the study was preliminary and uncontrolled (31). A similar study measuring serum prolactin and cortisol after D-fenfluramine injection in a group of extremely frequent British users is planned (32). A dose-ranging NIDA-funded study in humans is largely completed (33). It has assessed many important outcome variables including pharmacokinetic and cardiovascular data, sleep encephalopathy, fenfluramine challenge, and a variety of neuroimaging studies (positron emission tomography [PET] and single photon emission computed tomography [SPECT]).

General Toxicity

In England, there have been many reports of systemic toxic effects. These include reports of cardiac arrhythmia (34), aplastic anemia (35), and hepatotoxicity (36). There have been more frequent reports of a syndrome at raves probably related to extreme hyperthermia and dehydration. Some of these dancers underwent rhabdomyolysis, disseminated intravascular coagulation, renal failure, and death (34). It is generally believed that these disastrous clinical events are preventable by adequate hydration and adequate room cooling. Such advice is frequently provided to ravers. These serious consequences have been confined to England with no such reports in Holland or the United States.

Assays of MDMA

Some of the toxicities may relate to contamination and impurities in the illicit MDMA marketplace. A number of assays of MDMA preparations have been conducted and regular postings of assays and appearance of European products occur on the World Wide Web (http://www.ecstasy.org). A recent survey of 22 American samples revealed that 8 had no MDMA at all but 2 of these contained the MDMA analogue methylenedioxyethylamphetamine (MDE). This congener (also illegal) appears in European samples as well. Some American samples contained over-the-counter pharmaceuticals including phenylpropanolamine, dextromethorphan, ephedrine guaifenesin, and caffeine. Unidentified fillers, binders, and "cuts" were included. Despite frequent claims (particularly in New York City), there were no American products containing heroin, ketamine, rat poison, or ground glass (37).

Nexus

The DEA has placed one other analogue, 4-bromo,3–4,dimethoxy-phenethylamine in Schedule I. This drug, often called "nexus" or 2-CB, has MDMA-like properties in much lower doses (0.1–0.2 mg/kg) but is not widely distributed (38). 2-CB is also discussed in a remarkable and well-written novel, linking drug experience narratives to 179 distinct phenethylamines. This *roman à clef* also contains information on the synthesis of the drugs. The book has focused much attention (wanted and unwanted) on its authors—a medicinal chemist and his spouse. The title *PIHKAL* stands for "Phenethylamines I Have Known and Loved" (39).

4-Methylaminorex (4MAM OR "U4Euh")

This compound was the first example of a controlled substance analogue stimulant. Currently, there is little evidence of widespread use, and clinical importance is unassessed. The widespread availability of cocaine and synthetic methamphetamine may deter attempts to manufacture stimulant controlled substance analogues. 4-methylaminorex has generally been sold in illicit markets as "U4Euh." This product was first synthesized by McNeil Laboratories in the 1960s and, like MDA, evaluated as an anorectic. It is illicitly synthesized from the widely available over-the-counter drug phenylpropanolamine. It has been associated with one fatality and has been moved to Schedule I by the DEA (40). This drug was never marketed, but a non-methylated version (aminorex) was marketed in Europe as an appetite depressant in 1965. It was frequently associated with severe pulmonary hypertension and was withdrawn in 1968 (41). Reportedly, aminorex itself has recently appeared in illicit trade in America (42). Structurally, it most resembles the relatively mild prescription stimulant pemoline (Fig. 23.4). 4-

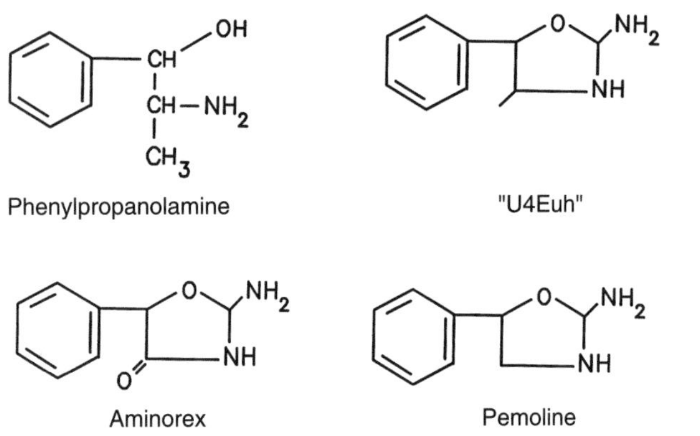

Figure 23.4. Chemical structure of phenylpropanolamine, "U4Euh," aminorex, and pemoline.

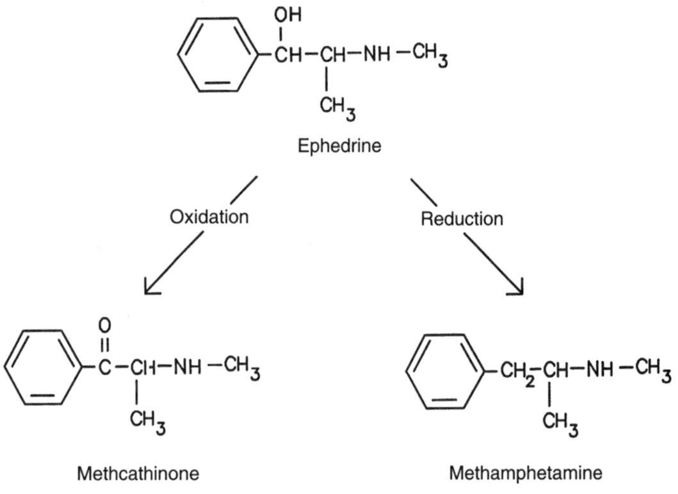

Figure 23.5. Chemical structure of ephedrine, an oxidative precursor to methcathinone and a reductive precursor to methamphetamine.

MAM provokes at oral doses of 10–20 mg a reportedly smooth episode of enhanced intellectual energy lasting 10–12 hours. Its advocates claim that work is facilitated not only without agitation but with a diminution of anxiety. There is one published opinion that it should be carefully assessed in humans for potential benefits (43).

METHCATHINONE

A number of possible stimulant compounds appear in the Khat plant (catha edulis). It is now believed that cathinone is the chief active ingredient producing amphetamine-like effects when the leaves are chewed in the Khat ceremony (44). In the 1950s, Parke-Davis conducted studies on an analogue of cathinone, methcathinone. There are no available human data but animal studies revealed a series of effects closely parallel to those of D-amphetamine. In 1987, Glennon et al. performed a number of behavioral studies confirming the stimulant actions of this product. Animals trained to discriminate d-amphetamine from saline would substitute methcathinone. Methcathinone, like amphetamine, displaces [^{3}H] dopamine from rat cells in the caudate nucleus (45).

Methcathinone (called ephedrone) emerged as a marketed illicit drug in Russia. It was prominently used by heroin injectors in a "speedball" combination (46). Reportedly, Russian users would also use the drug alone in IV binges resembling a methamphetamine pattern first reported in the United States in the late 1960s.

The drug appeared in commerce in rural Michigan in 1991, reportedly having been manufactured in clandestine laboratories in the upper peninsula of that state. It was quickly placed into Schedule I of the Controlled Substances Act in 1992. Emerson and Cisek described four patients admitted to Michigan emergency rooms after episodes of IV use. These physicians also collected questionnaire data from 17 users in Michigan who sought the drug for its stimulant properties. Many were intranasal users. Snorting was followed by euphoria and excitement with enhancement of visual perception. Such use produced 5–8 hours of enhanced energy, feelings of toughness and invincibility, and increased sexual desire. Subsequent doses were said to push users from "speeding" to "tripping" with more visual effects and even hallucinations. Use was frequently accompanied by headaches, abdominal cramps, sweating, and tachycardia (47).

The drug is said to have spread from Michigan to other Midwestern states. Its appearance may lead to further restrictions on the availability of ephedrine—an oxidative precursor to "cat" and a reductive precursor to "ice" (Fig. 23.5).

CONCLUSION

It is unclear how often and with what impact synthetic chemicals will emerge onto the illicit psychoactive market. It is also unclear how toxic such products are likely to be. The assessment of toxicity is always difficult because of the overheated character of media and police reports when such products appear (48). Ten years after the emergence of "designer drugs," their continuing impact remains poorly defined.

References

1. Mannich C, Jacobson W. Uber oxyphenylalkylamine und Dioxyphenylalkylamine. Berl Dtsch Chem Ges 1910;43:189.
2. Henderson GL. Designer drugs: past history and future prospects. J Forensic Sci 1988;33:569–575.
3. Karch S. Ecstasy in Europe. Forensic Drug Abuse Advisor (FDAA) 1995;7:78.
4. Lowinson J, Ruiz P, Millman RB. Substance abuse: a comprehensive textbook. 2nd ed. Baltimore: Williams & Wilkins, 1992.
5. Shulgin AT. How similar is substantially similar? J Forensic Sci 1990;35:10–12.
6. Henderson GL. Blood concentration of fentanyl and its analogs in overdose victims. Proc West Pharmacol Soc 1983;26:287–290.
7. Hibbs J, Perper J, Winek C. An outbreak of designer-drug related deaths in Pennsylvania. JAMA 1991;265:1011–1013.
8. Nieves E. Toxic heroin has killed 12, officials say. The New York Times 1991(4 February):B1–B2.
9. Johnson BD, Goldstein PJ, Preble E, et al. Taking care of business: the economics of crime by heroin users. Lexington, MA: Lexington Books, 1985.
10. Davis GC, Williams AS, Markey SP, et al. Chronic parkinsonism secondary to intravenous injection of meperidine analogues. Psychiatry Res 1979;1:249–254.
11. Langston JW, Ballard PA, Tetrud JW, Irwin I. Chronic parkinsonism in human due to a product of meperidine-analogue synthesis. Science 1983;219:979–980.
12. Burns RS, Chiueh CC, Markey SP, Ebert MH, Jacobowitz DM, Kopin IJ. A primate model of parkinsonism: selective destruction of dopaminergic neurons in the pars compacta of the substantia nigra by 1-methyl-4-phenyl-1,2,3,6-tetrahydropyridine. Proc Natl Acad Sci 1983;80:4546–4550.
13. Langston JW, Ballard PA. Parkinson's disease in a chemist working with 1-methyl-4-phenyl-1,2,3,6-tetrahydropyridine. N Engl J Med 1983;309:310.
14. Bianchine JR, McGhee B. MPTP and parkinsonism. Rational Drug Ther 1985;19:5–7.
15. D'Amato RJ, Lipman LP, Synder SH. Selectivity of the parkinsonian neurotoxin MPTP: toxic metabolite MPP+ binds to neuromelanin. Science 1986;231:987–989.
16. Meyers F, Rose A, Smith D. Incidents involving the Haight-Ashbury population and some uncommonly used drugs. J Psychedelic Drugs 1967–1968;1:140–146.
17. Beck J. MDMA: The popularization and resultant implications of a recently controlled psychoactive substance. Contemp Drug Probl 1986;13:23–63.
18. Shulgin AT, Nichols D. Characterization of three new psychotomimetics. In: Stillman RC, Willette RE, eds. The psychopharmacology of hallucinogens. New York: Pergamon Press, 1978.
19. Naranjo C, Shulgin AT, Sargent T. Evaluation

of 3,4-methylenedioxyamphetamine (MDA) as an adjunct to psychotherapy. Medicine et Pharmacologia Experimentalis 1967;17:359–364.

20. Beck J, Rosenbaum M. Pursuit of Ecstasy: the MDMA experience. Worlds of Ecstasy: who uses Ecstasy? Albany: SUNY Press, 1994: 27–55.

21. Ricaurte G, Bryan G, Strauss L, Seiden L, Schuster C. Hallucinogenic amphetamine selectively destroys brain serotonin nerve terminals. Science 1985;229:986–988.

22. Beck J, Rosenbaum M. Scheduling of MDMA ("Ecstasy"). In: Inciardi J, ed. The handbook of drug control in the United States. Westport, CT: Greenwood Press, 1990.

23. Greer G. MDMA: a new psychotropic compound and its effect in humans. Sante Fe, NM: self-published manuscript, 1983.

24. Liester MB, Grob CS, Bravo GL, Walsh RN. Phenomenology and sequelae of 3,4-methylenedioxymethamphetamine use. J Nerv Ment Dis 1992;180:345–352.

25. Steele TD, McCann UD, Ricaurte GA. 3,4-Methylenedioxymethamphetamine (MDMA, "Ecstasy"): pharmacology and toxicology in animals and human. Addiction 1994;89:539–551.

26. Schuster C, Lewis M, Seiden L. Fenfluramine: neurotoxicity. Psychopharmacol Bull 1988;22: 148–151.

27. Granquist L. Neurochemical markers and MDMA neurotoxicity. Multidisciplinary Association for Psychedelic Studies (MAPS) Newsletter 1995;5:10–13.

28. Ricaurte GA, DeLanney LE, Irwin I, Langston JW. Toxic effects of MDMA on central serotonergic neurons in the primate: importance of route and frequency of administration. Brain Res 1988;446:165–168.

29. Insel TR, Battaglia G, Johannessen JN, Marra S, DeSouza EB. 3–4 methylenedioxymethamphetamine ('Ecstasy') selectively destroys brain serotonin terminals in Rhesus monkeys. J Pharmacol Exp Ther 1989;249:713–720.

30. McCann UD, Ridenour A, Shaham Y, Ricaurte GA. Serotonin neurotoxicity after (±) 3,4-methylenedioxymethamphetamine (MDMA, "Ecstasy"): a controlled study in humans. Neuropsychopharmacology 1994;10:129–138.

31. Price LH, Ricaurte GA, Krystal JH, Heninger GR. Neuroendocrine and mood responses to intravenous L-tryptophan in (±)3,4-methylenedioxymethamphetamine (MDMA) users. Arch Gen Psychiatry 1989;46:20–22.

32. Jansen KLR. MDMA (ecstasy) studies at the Maudsley Hospital. Multidisciplinary Association for Psychedelic Studies (MAPS) Newsletter 1996;6:7.

33. Grob C. Harbor-UCLA MDMA project update Feb. Multidisciplinary Association for Psychedelic Studies (MAPS) Newsletter 1995;5:2.

34. Henry J, Jeffreys K, Dawling S. Toxicity and deaths from 3,4-Methylenedioxymethamphetamine ("Ecstasy"). Lancet 1992;340:384–387.

35. Marsh JC, Abboudi ZH, Gibson FM, Scopes J, Daly S, O'Shaunnessy DF, Baugham AS. Aplastic anaemia following exposure to 3,4-methylenedioxymethamphetamine ('Ecstasy'). Br J Haematol 1994;88:281–285.

36. O'Connor B. Hazards associated with the recreational drug 'ecstasy'. Br J Hosp Med 1994; 52:507, 510–514.

37. Doblin R. MDMA analysis project. Multidisciplinary Association for Psychedelic Studies (MAPS) Newsletter 1996;6:11–13.

38. Karch S. Nexus banned by DEA. Forensic Drug Abuse Advisor (FDAA) 1994;6:12.

39. Shulgin AT, Shulgin A. PIHKAL: a chemical love story. Berkeley, CA: Transform Press, 1991.

40. Davis FT, Brewster ME. A fatality involving "U4Euh," a cyclic derivative of phenylpropanolamine. J Forensic Sci 1988;33:549–553.

41. Follath F. Drug induced pulmonary hypertension? Br Med J 1971;1:265–266.

42. Karch S. Aminorex banned. Forensic Drug Abuse Advisor (FDAA) 1994;6:38.

43. Doblin R. 4-methylaminorex. Multidisciplinary Association for Psychedelic Studies (MAPS) Newsletter 1996;6:121.

44. Kalix P. Pharmacological properties of the stimulant khat. Pharmacol Ther 1990;48:397–416.

45. Glennon RA, Yousif M, Naiman N, Kalif P. Methcathinone: a new and potent amphetamine-like agent. Pharmacol Biochem Behav 1987; 26:547–551.

46. Zhinge YK, Dovensky BS, Crossman A, et al. Ephedrone: 2-methylamine-1-phenylpropan-1-one (Jeff). J Forens Sci 1991;36:915–920.

47. Emerson TS, Cisek JE. Methcathinone: A Russian designer amphetamine infiltrates the rural Midwest. Ann Emerg Med 1993;22:1897–1903.

48. Hettena S. Year of the cat. Spin 1995;10:67–69, 90.

24 MDMA

Charles S. Grob and Russell E. Poland

MDMA (3,4-Methylenedioxymethamphetamine) is a novel psychoactive compound with structural similarities to both amphetamine and the psychedelic phenethylamine, mescaline. As was the case with the psychedelics three decades ago, MDMA has since the early 1980s been at the center of a virulent controversy pitting proponents of its use as an adjunctive psychiatric treatment against those who have argued that it poses a grave threat to public health and safety. By recapitulating the generational and cultural divides catalyzed by widespread use of lysergic acid diethylamide (LSD) and related compounds in the 1960s, the growing use of MDMA by young people has confounded and shifted debate from one examining the relative risks and benefits of a putative psychiatric treatment to questions addressing social control and protection of youth. Encompassing challenges to conventional cultural norms, defenses of social stability, and the inevitable media distortion and sensationalism, MDMA, as did psychedelics 30 years earlier, has become an issue of "more than medical significance" (81).

HISTORICAL BACKGROUND

MDMA was first synthesized in 1912 by chemists working for Merck Pharmaceuticals in Germany searching for a new class of appetite suppressant drugs, and patented in 1914. With the outbreak of World War I, however, industrial scientists were forced to turn their attention elsewhere, and further explorations of the properties and potential applications of MDMA were halted (108, 110). In the early 1950s, as part of systematic U.S. Army Intelligence research on potential psychotropic drug applications to espionage and counter-espionage endeavors, MDMA once again came to the attention of research pharmacologists. Allocated to the Edgewood Arsenal's Chemical Warfare Service, and provided the code name EA-1475, MDMA was administered to a variety of animals for standard LD_{50} screening. Plans to initiate human trials with MDMA were abandoned, however, following the tragic and untimely death in 1953 of a subject enrolled in a U.S. Army contract study at the New York State Psychiatric Institute who had received "forced injections" of EA-1298, or MDA (3,4-methylenedioxyamphetamine), an analogue and an active metabolite of MDMA (62). As a testimony to the capricious and often unethical "research" conducted under the auspices of U.S. Intelligence services during this period, one of the lead investigators of the fatal MDA study would later state, "We didn't know whether it was dog piss or what it was we were giving him" (67).

As with many of the powerful consciousness-altering compounds examined by the CIA and U.S. Army Intelligence, the 1960s witnessed a proliferation of information and interest in the phenethylamine psychedelics within the growing counter-culture movement. MDA in particular enjoyed a brief period of popularity in the late 1960s and early 1970s, when it was euphemistically attributed the exotic name of the "love drug." MDMA, though, remained largely unknown to psychedelic enthusiasts and would not be examined until the mid 1970s when University of California Berkeley biochemist and toxicologist, Alexander Shulgin, acting on the suggestion of a student who claimed to have successfully alleviated a severe stutter with the drug, synthesized and self-administered 120 mg of the compound (110). He would later describe MDMA as evoking "an easily controlled altered state of consciousness with emotional and sensual overtones, and with little hallucinatory effect" (109).

Highly impressed with the drug's apparent capacity to induce heightened states of empathic rapport, a critical component of successful psychotherapy, Shulgin introduced several psychiatrist and psychologist acquaintances to MDMA's unusual profile of action. Their responses, both to their own subjective experience, as well as to those of patients to whom they had administered the drug, were an unequivocal endorsement of MDMA's apparent capacity to facilitate the process of psychotherapy. For the remainder of the 1970s, a quiet underground of psychotherapists, particularly on the West coast of the United States, conducted thousands of MDMA-augmented treatments with what at that time was still a legal and uncontrolled substance. Although unfortunately no methodological research was conducted to substantiate MDMA's alleged efficacy in alleviating psychological distress and modifying maladaptive personality structures, testimonials to its therapeutic range of action abounded. Unbridled enthusiasm for this novel and as yet unsubstantiated treatment was best summed up by a psychiatrist colleague of Shulgin's who told him, "MDMA is penicillin for the soul, and you don't give up penicillin, once you've seen what it can do" (110).

Sensitive to the fate suffered in the 1960s by proponents of psychiatric research and treatment with psychedelics once word of their highly unusual effects had been disseminated to the culture at large (49), knowledge of MDMA remained a tightly guarded secret among practitioners of its use and their patients for several years. By the early 1980s, however, word of MDMA had filtered out, abetted by media accounts of a new psychotherapeutic "miracle medicine" and the spread of an alternative recreational drug on some college campuses (particularly in California and Texas), where for a period of time MDMA replaced cocaine as a new drug of choice. First popularly called Adam during its early phase of use among psychotherapists, to signify "the condition of primal innocence and unity with all life" (1), it soon acquired the alternative appellation of "Ecstasy," the name by which it is popularly known to this day. Indeed, the transformation of MDMA as "Adam" into MDMA as "Ecstasy" appears to have been a marketing decision reached by an enterprising distributor searching for an alternative code name, who concluded that it would not be profitable to take advantage of the drug's most salient features. "Ecstasy was chosen for obvious reasons," this individual later reported, "because it would sell better than calling it 'Empathy.' 'Empathy' would be more appropriate, but how many people know what it means?" (34).

By 1984, with growing use on college campuses and increased media attention and embellishment, political pressure was placed on federal regulators to establish tight controls on what was still a legal drug. Consequently, in 1985 the U.S. Drug Enforcement Agency (DEA) convened hearings to determine the fate of MDMA. These highly publicized hearings achieved the unintended effect of further raising public awareness of MDMA as well as interest in experimentation. Media accounts further polarized opinion, pitting enthusiastic claims of MDMA by proponents on the one hand, versus dire warnings of unknown dangers to the nation's youth on the other. Coverage of the MDMA scheduling controversy included a national daytime television talk show (the Phil Donahue program) highlighting the surprising disclosure by a prominent University of Chicago neuroscientist that recent (but as yet unpublished) research had detected "brain damage" in rats injected with large quantities of MDA, an analogue and metabolite of MDMA. Public debate was further confounded by the frequent confusion of MDMA with MPTP, a dopaminergic neurotoxin that had recently been revealed to have induced severe Parkinson's-like disorders in users seeking synthetic heroin substitute highs. With growing concern over the dangers of new "designer drugs," public discussion took an increasingly discordant tone (11). In the spring of 1986, following a series of scheduling hearings on MDMA conducted by the DEA in several U.S. cities, the DEA administrative law judge presiding over the case determined on the weight of the evidence presented that there was sufficient indication for safe utilization under medical supervision and recommended Schedule III status (124). Not obliged to follow the recommendation of his administrative law judge, however, and expressing grave concerns that MDMA's growing abuse liability posed a serious threat to public health and safety, the DEA director overruled the advisement and ruled that MDMA be placed in the most restrictive category, Schedule I (61). Since then, with the exception of a three-month period in early 1988 when it

was briefly unscheduled due to a court challenge, MDMA has remained classified as a Schedule I substance.

In the decade following the MDMA scheduling controversy, patterns of use have undergone a marked shift. With the failure to establish official sanction for MDMA treatment, most psychotherapists who had used the drug adjunctively in their work ceased to do so, unwilling to violate the law and jeopardize their livelihoods through the use of a now illegal drug. In the wake of the highly publicized scheduling hearings, however, use among young people escalated. By the late 1980s, interest in MDMA had spread from the United States across the Atlantic to Europe, where it became the drug of choice at marathon dance parties called "raves." Beginning on the Spanish island of Ibizia, spreading across the Continent, and then back to the United States, MDMA-catalyzed "raves" have drawn large numbers of young people, often attracting greater than 10,000 individuals at a single event (100). Although use in the United States has tended to be cyclical, waxing and waning depending upon an often erratic supply, popularity in Europe has remained high (20, 99). With multiple illicit laboratories, including pharmaceutical manufacturers in former "Iron Curtain" countries, the European youth market appears to have become saturated with the drug in recent years (117).

EPIDEMIOLOGY

Although various estimates have been given on the extent of current illicit MDMA use in the United States and western Europe, the exact prevalence remains unknown. Saunders (98) has stated that "millions" of young people in the United Kingdom have taken MDMA. A Harris Opinion Poll (55) for the BBC in Great Britain presented data that 31% of people between the ages of 16 and 25 admitted to taking MDMA, most often at "dance clubs," and that 67% reported that their friends had tried the drug. In a survey of school children across the whole of England, 4.25% of 14-year-olds and, in another survey, 6.0% of those ages 14 and 15, were reported to have taken MDMA (100). The popular British press have recently reported that an estimated 500,000–1,000,000 young people in Great Britain take MDMA every weekend (107, 117). The "rave scene" in particular appears to be responsible for the explosive growth of MDMA in the United Kingdom (74), and has been described as developing into what many believe to be the "largest youth movement in British history" (10).

In the United States, according to a 1993 National Institute on Drug Abuse survey, 2.0% of all United States college students had admitted to taking MDMA in the previous 12 months (83a). An interview study of Stanford University undergraduate students reported that 39% had taken MDMA at least once in their lives (85), while a Tulane University survey revealed that 24.3% of over 1,200 students questioned had experimented with the drug (26). MDMA has been described as having the "greatest growth potential among all illicit drugs" in the United States, with tens of thousands of new users being introduced to the drug every month, particularly within the context of the "rave scene" (82).

POTENTIAL TREATMENT APPLICATIONS

Psychopharmacological modification of psychotherapy is a treatment modality with prehistoric roots in the shamanic healing application of psychedelic plants within a societally sanctioned and ritualized context (17). Evidence has accumulated that the controlled utilization of psychedelics for therapeutic and initiatory purposes has played a vital role in aboriginal and preindustrial societies from before recorded history to the present (28, 29, 52). Indeed, over the last four decades the advent of psychopharmacological treatments has transformed the theory and practice of psychiatry; nevertheless, their impact upon psychotherapeutic technique and efficacy has been marginal (48). From 1950 to the mid 1960s, over 1,000 professional papers were published in the clinical psychiatric literature in Europe and the United States describing the treatment of an estimated 40,000 patients with psychedelic substances (47), yet this era in the history of psychiatry has been virtually forgotten.

Beginning in the late 1970s, proponents of this form of drug-enhanced psychotherapy began to investigate the therapeutic potential of the still-legal

MDMA. Compared to LSD, the prototype psychedelic of the twentieth century, MDMA was judged to possess distinct advantages as a therapeutic adjunct. MDMA was described as being a relatively mild, short-acting drug capable of facilitating heightened states of introspection and intimacy along with temporary freedom from anxiety and depression, yet without distracting alterations in perception, body image, and sense of self. Patients were reported as losing defensive anxiety, feeling more emotionally open and accessing feelings and thoughts not ordinarily available to them. Lasting improvement was often reported in patients' self esteem, ability to communicate with significant others, capacity for achieving empathic rapport, interest in and capacity for insight, strengthened capacity for trust and intimacy, and enhanced therapeutic alliance (48).

A variety of treatment applications were explored prior to MDMA's scheduling in the mid 1980s, including the physical pain and emotional distress associated with severe medical illness, posttraumatic stress disorders, depression, phobias, addictions, psychosomatic disorders, and relationship (marital) problems (2, 32, 45, 62). In reviewing their work with 80 patients treated with MDMA-augmented psychotherapy, Greer and Tolbert (46) have noted long lasting benefits in symptom reduction, particularly in diminishing the pathological effects of prior traumatic experience, as well as sustained improvement in effective and empathic communication skills with family members. More recently, Riedlinger and Riedlinger (91) have examined the putative rationale for treating suicidal depression with MDMA.

Unfortunately, before MDMA's value as a treatment modality could be subjected to rigorous, methodological research evaluation in the United States, the drug was placed in the most restrictive Schedule I status. All applications since the mid 1980s to conduct clinical trials with MDMA have consequently been rejected, although an approved Phase I investigation of physiological and psychological effects in normal volunteers with prior MDMA experience was recently concluded by the authors at Harbor-UCLA Medical Center (53). Because clinical patient populations have never been subjected to formal examination with MDMA, only anecdotal case reports have been available for examination. In addition to accounts of treatment outcome, the experiences of long-term users of MDMA have also been systematically examined. One study (65), which subjected 20 psychiatrists with past personal histories of MDMA use to extensive semi-structured interviews, reported that 85% had increased ability to interact with or be open with others, 80% had decreased defensiveness, 65% had decreased fear, 60% had decreased sense of separation or alienation from others, 50% had increased awareness of emotions, and 50% had decreased aggression. One-half of these psychiatrists with MDMA use experience also reported long-term improvement in social and interpersonal functioning.

In Europe, opportunities for more systematic study of MDMA treatment have been possible. Between 1988 and 1993, permission was granted by public health officials in Switzerland to several psychiatric clinicians, under the auspices of the Swiss Medical Society for Psycholytic Therapy, to treat patients with MDMA. Although authorities neglected to insist upon the implementation of prospective research designs, a retrospective analysis of treatment outcomes was recently conducted (41, 42). One hundred and twenty-one former patients consented to examination, on average two years following termination of treatment. Patients (predominantly diagnosed with affective disorders, adjustment disorders, and personality disorders) had been engaged in long-term psychotherapy augmented with an average of 6.8 MDMA sessions over three years. Overall, 90.9% of patients reported to have experienced improved clinical status as a result of their prior treatment with MDMA, while 2.5% claimed to have clinically "deteriorated." Significant decreases were noted in self-administration of nicotine, alcohol, and cannabis in the years following MDMA treatment, and significant improvements were noted in self-acceptance, autonomy, and overall quality of life.

ADVERSE CLINICAL EFFECTS

When examining adverse effects of MDMA, it is important to distinguish between relatively benign, transient effects experienced by healthy, occasional users ingesting relatively moderate dosages versus more dangerous sequelae reported to occur in a small minority of individuals taking MDMA, often in the context of significant premorbid pathology, adverse settings, polysubstance use, and excessive dosing. Liester et al. (65) have reported in their evaluation of psychiatrists with past, personal use that common short-term side effects of MDMA were similar to effects induced by amphetamines, including trismus, bruxism, restlessness, anxiety, and decreased appetite. Other investigators have reported tachycardia, palpitations, dry mouth, and insomnia (45, 87).

With substantial alterations in patterns of use over the past decade, from occasional use for therapeutic and spiritual purposes (119) to frequent, repeated ingestion at large rave dances, the reported risks have increased significantly (90). Although earlier investigations had concluded that MDMA was a drug with a relatively low potential for abuse (9, 59, 111, 114) and where persistent use patterns were described as "extremely rare" (88), the likelihood of individuals frequently ingesting higher dosages of MDMA, often in association with other drugs or alcohol, appears to be increasing (99). Most reports of severe adverse effects over the past several years have in fact occurred in Europe, particularly Great Britain, where the phenomenon of widespread, frequent use among youth is far more prevalent than in the United States. It is also critical to note that given the clandestine (and often amateur) context within which MDMA is manufactured for the escalating mass market, the available black market drug is often not necessarily what it is advertised as being (15, 122), nor is it necessarily free of contaminants and adulterants (19, 125). As was the case with psychedelics in the 1960s, following the transition over time from limited and legal use by relatively well-educated aficionados to mass market consumption for illicit and "recreational" purposes by youth, the purity and quality of MDMA has progressively declined while the associated risks to the user have climbed.

Given the extent to which MDMA has been subject to widespread use and abuse in the past decade, it is somewhat surprising that more reports of serious adverse effects have not been reported. Particularly within a context of grave concerns raised over potential risks, fueled by media publicity and hyperbole, only a relatively small number of fatal reactions to the drug have made their way into the medical literature. Nevertheless, serious attention needs to be accorded the potential for catastrophic medical reactions, as they have occurred and are likely to continue, particularly to individuals with pre-existing vulnerabilities (both medical and psychological) who take the drug under circumstances that accentuate the risks.

The first reports of fatalities associated with MDMA ingestion occurred in the United States in 1987. Dowling et al. (31) described five cases of individuals who had precipitously died; they had detected at postmortem positive toxicological screens for MDMA or MDEA, an MDMA analogue. One of these cases was an individual who was electrocuted while under the influence of MDMA, whereas the other four were all associated with individuals who sustained fatal cardiovascular events. Three of these individuals apparently had pre-existing severe cardiac or respiratory disease (atherosclerotic coronary artery disease, idiopathic hypertrophic cardiomyopathy, and bronchial asthma), which were felt to have played a primary role in their sudden death. Alcohol and drugs in addition to MDMA were also found to have been associated with the four cases of death induced by cardiovascular collapse. In two of these cases alcohol use occurred shortly before death; in one case alcohol along with a narcotic analgesic were found to be positive on post-mortem toxicological screen; and in one case presence of a barbiturate was detected. Individuals who may be at heightened risk of life-threatening cardiac arrhythmias and associated cardiovascular collapse are those having underlying illnesses with heightened sensitivity to exogenous-induced adrenergic stimulation, such as ischemic heart disease, cardiac conduction defects, cardiomyopathy and mitral valve prolapse (19, 83). When MDMA is taken by such individuals with pre-existing medical vulnerabilities, and particularly in the presence of alcohol or other drugs, licit or illicit, the risks for life-threatening events are compounded.

Several cases have also been reported over the last few years in the medical literature of severe cerebrovascular accidents apparently induced by MDMA. Manchanda and Connolly (66) described a young man who experienced a cerebral infarction after having consumed "several" MDMA tablets. Similarly, Rothwell and Grant (98) reported a young woman who had taken MDMA who subsequently sustained a cerebral venous sinus thrombosis after engaging in an extended period of prolonged dancing and associated dehydration. Pre-existing neurological vulnerabilities appear to accentuate the risks for devastating cerebrovascular events, as was the case of a young woman who had an intracerebral bleed from an aneurysm of the left posterior communicating artery shortly after ingesting two and a half MDMA tablets (43). Associated polysubstance and alcohol use also appear to potentiate the dangers of MDMA use, inducing injury to central nervous system structures (116). Damage to subcortical structures through a mechanism of vasoconstriction brought on by enhanced serotonin neurotransmission has also been suggested as the pathogenesis of some strokes associated with MDMA (54).

With increasing use of MDMA, often of indeterminate quality and excessive quantity, cases of apparent hepatotoxicity have begun to emerge, particularly in Great Britain. Henry et al. (56) have reported six young men and one young woman who had used MDMA within the previous few weeks who presented with jaundice, elevated bilirubin, and abnormal liver chemistries. Each was without a known history of heavy alcohol use, intravenous drug use, or evidence of infectious hepatitis. Dykhuizen et al. (33) have also reported on three cases of idiosyncratic toxic hepatitis, presumably secondary to MDMA. Whether the liver damage in these cases was caused by an idiosyncratic reaction to MDMA or to some contaminant ingested along with it is not known (58). Although such case reports provoke the need to inquire about MDMA use histories in young people presenting with unexplained jaundice and hepatomegaly, they do appear to be extremely rare, even in the context of increasing usage of an often impure, illicit compound. Basic 28-day toxicological studies in dogs and rats have reported no evidence of liver damage (40). Thus, the mechanism underlying the reported liver damage remains to be determined.

Additional case reports have surfaced over the past several years of isolated instances of catastrophic hyperthermic reactions leading to disseminated intravascular coagulation (DIC), rhabdomyolysis, acute renal failure, and, on occasion, death (56). Virtually all of such reported cases have occurred in the setting of prolonged vigorous dancing in poorly ventilated environments and were associated with inadequate fluid replacement. To date, all known fatalities caused by malignant hyperthermia have occurred in Great Britain and have been in rave dance club settings. These environments are described as being very crowded with exceedingly high ambient temperatures (90). Indeed, in some British rave dance halls, including settings where deaths from hyperthermia had occurred, supplies of water were often restricted by club management in order to increase the sales of soft drinks. In one particularly unscrupulous establishment the water taps were reportedly turned off in the bathrooms while tap water was sold over the counter at the bar for the same price as beer (68).

Given that the degree of MDMA use has climbed well into the millions, particularly in Europe, it is not surprising that cases of psychiatric disturbance have been reported. Such adverse psychiatric events reported have included panic disorder (70, 84, 121), paranoid psychoses (24, 75, 76) and depression (69). What is remarkable about many of these reports, apart from the surprisingly small numbers of presenting cases contrasted to the exceedingly large potential pool of (mostly young) individuals who have used MDMA, is the extremely high and frequent dosages of the drug that had been consumed by many of those individuals who had experienced adverse psychiatric sequelae (69, 75, 76, 101, 120). In the face of significant premorbid psychopathology, and often in combination with other drugs or alcohol, frequent use of high-dose MDMA does appear to heighten risks for deterioration of psychiatric status. The evidence, however, for occasional, low-dose MDMA use, taken in controlled settings without additional drugs or alcohol by individuals with negative histories for psychiatric disorders, appears to be considerably lower.

NEUROTOXICITY

Since the mid 1980s, evidence has existed that MDMA and its analogues are capable of inflicting profound changes on brain serotonin systems in laboratory animals (92). Preclinical studies have consistently demonstrated that MDMA causes an acute, but reversible, depletion of serotonin (77). Unlike other amphetamine-like compounds, which exert comparable effects on both serotonergic and dopaminergic neurons (106), MDMA's predominant target is the serotonin system (although dopamine systems also can be affected) (123).

Effects of serotonin systems in laboratory animals subjected to administration of large dosages of MDMA has been divided into short-term and long-term effects. Some of the acute effects of MDMA, including the rapid release of intracellular serotonin, are presumed to mediate the behavioral and psychological profile observed in humans (53), whereas in animals the neurotoxic effects are not manifested until days later (7). It would appear that neurotoxicity is not inextricably linked to the acute effects of the drug. Administration of fluoxetine prior to, or up to six hours after, MDMA administration blocks or attenuates the development of neurotoxicity (44), whereas some acute effects of MDMA (e.g., behavioral, neuroendocrine, and temperature) occur within minutes and peak within a few hours (18, 53, 80) (Poland and Grob, unpublished data). The majority of work on MDMA has revolved around its neurotoxic effects and the mechanisms by which these effects are produced. Rats administered multiple doses of MDMA undergo serotonergic neurotoxic changes that can last for many months before neurochemical recovery occurs (7), although there can be considerable interanimal variability in the degree of neurotoxicity, as well as in the extent of recovery, from the same dosage regimen. In rats, neurotoxicity appears to be limited to axon terminals, with relative sparing of cell bodies (8). Regeneration and resprouting of brain serotonin axonal projections do occur, yet may take up to a year to develop in rodents, and perhaps longer in non-human primates (95). The question of whether these axonal connections observed during recovery are "normal" or not, however, remains to be elucidated. In squirrel monkeys administered MDMA (5.0 mg/kg, subcutaneous) twice daily for four consecutive days, profound reductions of brain serotonin, 5-hydroxyindole acetic acid (5-HIAA), the primary metabolite of serotonin, and serotonin uptake sites, persist even at 18 months. Interestingly, the thalamus shows some recovery, while the hypothalamus shows an (apparent) overshoot in regeneration (3), suggesting that under some circumstances MDMA administration can lead to a lasting reorganization of ascending 5-HT axon projections (36). A single oral dose of 5.0 mg/kg in primates, only 2–3 times higher than that usually taken by humans, produces thalamic and hypothalamic effects observed only at two weeks after administration (93). A no-effect level in monkeys, however, has been reported between 2.5–5.0 mg/kg (Ricaurte GA, unpublished data). Despite the widespread damage to 5-HT neurons produced by high doses of the drug, few functional changes have been found (39, 63, 97). However, the authors (53) (Poland and Grob, unpublished data) have found that the neuroendocrine response to acute fenfluramine challenge is altered for up to one year in rats treated with high doses of MDMA (20 mg/kg, bid × 4 days). In contrast, we have not found such changes in humans with a history of MDMA use.

The mechanisms underlying MDMA-induced serotonin neurotoxicity are thought to occur by the uptake of MDMA into serotonin nerve terminals, causing an initial reduction of serotonin levels. A second phase of serotonin reduction follows, possibly due to the formation of neurotoxic metabolites (5) or by generation of free radicals (8), which causes degeneration of serotonin terminals (and in some cases axons) for weeks to months, depending upon the species and dosage regimen employed. Additional data indicate that dopamine also plays a role in the mechanism underlying the neurotoxic effects of MDMA on serotonin neurons (105), as does glutamate, since various N-methyl-D-aspartate antagonists can inhibit or attenuate MDMA induced neurotoxicity (44). Other compounds that have been shown to modulate or prevent long-term serotonergic neurotoxic changes in laboratory animals administered MDMA include the serotonin re-uptake inhibitors fluoxetine and citalopram (102, 103), the serotonin antagonist ritanserin (104), the dopamine antagonist haloperidol (57), and the monoamine oxidase-B inhibitor L-Deprenyl (115), as well as the N-methyl-D-aspartate antagonists dizocilpine (22, 57) and dextromethorphan (35). Furthermore, in addition to pure neurochemical modulators, temperature appears to be another variable in the mediation of MDMA neurotoxicity (18).

Whereas multiple studies have established and reconfirmed that MDMA provokes profound changes in brain serotonin systems of laboratory animals, there has been virtually no demonstration that functional or behavioral abnormalities have been induced. Similarly, no data are available addressing the issue of whether normal function is restored following biochemical recovery. It has long been demonstrated that at least in some species serotonin and other monoaminergic neurons can undergo extensive regeneration following neurotoxin-induced degenerative change (13). As determined by immunocytochemical and autoradiographic techniques, regeneration of serotonin fibers have been observed in the hypothalamus following serotonin lesions induced by the experimental neurotoxin 5,7-dihydroxytryptamine (5, 7-DHT). This reinnervation appears to be *structurally* normal (38). Although it is not known to what extent regenerated (or sprouted) fibers are able to re-establish original synaptic contacts (36), some recently published data suggest that the observed patterns of re-innervation are abnormal (36). The degree to which such biochemical alterations affect functional normality is a question still awaiting elucidation. Indeed, it appears that it is the specific "damage" to serotonin fibers, (primarily serotonergic axonal terminals originating from the dorsal raphe), induced by neurotoxins causing significant declines in serotonin levels, which ultimately reactivate latent developmental signals in the brain. Most likely, this occurs at the genomic level, thus encouraging resprouting and regeneration along with the stimulation of an astrocytic growth factor (6). Whether the degenerative axonal changes associated with the phenomenon of serotonergic neurotoxicity is simply a prelude to what may eventually be recognized as a healthy and adaptive neuroplasticity response, or whether it is the substrate for what will eventuate in neuropsychiatric pathology, is not yet known.

MDMA is not the only drug known to induce long standing effects on indices of serotonergic neurotransmission (12, 16). However, the drug with the greatest relevance to MDMA in its effects on serotonergic function is fenfluramine. Marketed as an anorectic drug for the treatment of obesity, fenfluramine has been administered to over 50 million patients during the past 25 years (27). Fenfluramine has also been explored in controlled trials as a putative treatment for a variety of psychopathological conditions, including infantile autism (96), attention deficit hyperactivity disorder (30), eating disorders (14), depression (118), and suicidal behavior (79). In spite of such a long history of clinical application without reports of adverse outcome, fenfluramine has come under increasing attack in recent years because preclinical investigations have identified that its effects on the brains of laboratory animals induce what has been described as serotonergic neurotoxicity (72). In rats as well as non-human primates, fenfluramine has been shown to cause long-standing depletions of regional brain 5-HT and 5-HIAA, changes very similar to those induced by MDMA. Indeed, some fenfluramine-induced neurotoxicity has been described as being the same as for MDMA-induced neurotoxicity (71). Recently, a vigorous debate occurred at the FDA over approval of the more 5-HT–active optical isomer of fenfluramine, D-fenfluramine. Many of the same concerns over the long-term effects of serotonergic neurotoxicity as during the MDMA debates were raised; nevertheless, the decision of the FDA advisory panel was to recommend approval without restriction for the prescription drug D-fenfluramine. Although without the high public profile and notoriety of MDMA, fenfluramine is not itself lacking in potential for abuse (64). Nevertheless, the government approval for the use of D-fenfluramine was no doubt influenced by the aggressive lobbying efforts of the pharmaceutical industry, a fact which underscores the intrusion of political and economic agendas into the realm of scientific policy.

Efforts to extend the neurotoxicity hypothesis to human populations have met with mixed results. Measurements of neurotransmitter metabolites in the cerebrospinal fluid of MDMA users were assessed in one early study as be-

ing within normal limits (86). A subsequent study (94), which reported lower levels of CSF 5-HIAA in MDMA users, is difficult to interpret because the control population employed was a group of patients with chronic back pain. Such a choice for the control group is suspect because of evidence that serotonergic mechanisms are involved in pain control (25, 78) as well as the known association of increased levels of CSF 5-HIAA in patients suffering from chronic non-malignant and malignant pain (21, 23). Additional studies which reported serotonergic abnormalities in MDMA subjects (60, 89), as reflected by abnormal neuroendocrine response to l-tryptophan and by mild to moderate cognitive impairment, need to be interpreted cautiously due to methodological concerns surrounding subject recruitment and assessment (50, 51, Doblin, personal communication). The most methodologically sound retrospective evaluation of human MDMA users, although finding no differences between prolactin secretion induced by the l-tryptophan challenge test, did find significantly lower levels of cerebral spinal fluid 5-HIAA in MDMA users compared to controls (73). Surprisingly, however, and confounding expectations inferred by the neurotoxicity hypothesis, these same MDMA subjects with relatively low levels of cerebral spinal fluid 5-HIAA were also assessed as having significantly lower scores on personality measures of impulsivity and hostility; opposite results would have been expected (37, 112, 113). Finally, a decrease in stage II sleep and sleep time has been reported in subjects with a history of MDMA (4). This is both an interesting and perplexing observation. Given the prominent role that serotonin plays in the regulation of both slow wave and REM sleep, one would have expected that these sleep EEG measures might have been most affected by MDMA. In summary, most, if not all, of the observed changes reported thus far are compatible with a general effect of MDMA on serotonin neurotransmission independent of neurotoxicity, although the latter effect cannot be ruled out.

Unfortunately, the question of MDMA's potential neurotoxicity in humans has been marked by unwelcome and excessive attention by the media. This has led not only to often sensationalized and distorted media reportage, but also to implicit and explicit pressures on scientific researchers to align their findings with conventional expectations. Needless to say, MDMA's role as a recreational drug for millions of young people worldwide is worrisome, particularly within the context of ill-prepared and vulnerable individuals consuming an illicitly manufactured and marketed drug of dubious quality in unpredictable and often dangerous settings. Nevertheless, for a true appreciation of MDMA's range of effects, it is imperative that objective investigation be conducted in an impartial and fair scientific environment. As previously mentioned, the authors have recently been granted permission for the first FDA-sanctioned administration of MDMA to human normal volunteers with prior experience with the drug, in order to accurately determine its range of physiological effects, safety parameters, and central nervous system mechanisms (53). In addition to standard Phase I investigational measures, brain imaging studies and neuropsychological testing will be administered in a prospective manner, to more clearly delineate MDMA's psychobiological effects and potential to cause injury to brain function. Hopefully, the future will provide additional controlled and methodologically sound investigations probing the full range of MDMA's effects, and begin to answer the questions surrounding the drug's capacity to cause harm versus its innate potential under optimal conditions to facilitate beneficial outcomes.

Acknowledgments. *This work was supported in part by National Institutes of Health grants MH00534, DA06863 and by General Clinical Research Center grant RR 00425. We thank Mrs. Debbie Hanaya for expert administrative assistance.*

References

1. Adamson S, Metzner R. Through the gateway of the heart: accounts of experiences with MDMA and other empathogenic substances. San Francisco: Four Trees Publications, 1985.
2. Adamson S, Metzner R. The nature of the MDMA experience and its role in healing, psychotherapy, and spiritual practice. ReVision 1988;10:59–72.
3. Ali SF, Newport GD, Scallet AC, Binienda Z,

Ferguson SA, Bailey JR, et al. Oral administration or MDMA produces selective 5-HT depletion in the non-human primate. Neurotoxicol Teratol 1993;15:91–96.
4. Allen R, McCann U, Ricaurte G. Persistent effects of MDMA (Ecstasy) in human sleep. Sleep 1993;16:560–564.
5. Axt KJ, Commins D, Seiden LS. Alphamethyl-paratyrosine prevents methylamphetamine induced formation of endogenous 5,6-DHT in rat hippocampus. Soc Neurosci Ab 1985;11:1193.

6. Azmitia EC, Whitaker-Azmitia, PM. Awakening, the sleeping giant: anatomy and plasticity of the brain serotonergic system. J Clin Psychiatry 1991;52(suppl):4–16.
7. Battaglia G, Yeh SY, DeSouza EB. MDMA-induced neurotoxicity: parameters of degeneration and recovery of brain serotonin neurons. Pharmacol Biochem Behav 1988;29:269:274.
8. Baumgarten HG, Zimmermann B. Neurotoxic phenylalkylamines and indolealkylamines. In:

Herken H, Hucho F, eds. Selective neurotoxicity. Berlin: Springer-Verlag, 1992:225–291.

9. Beck J. The public health implications of MDMA use. In: Peroutka SJ, ed. The clinical, pharmacological, and neurotoxicological effects of the drug MDMA. Holland: Kluwer, 1990.

10. Beck J. Ecstasy and the rave scene: historical and cross-cultural perspectives. CEWG 1993; Dec:424–431.

11. Beck J, Morgan PA. Designer drug confusion: a focus on MDMA. J Drug Education 1986; 16:287–302.

12. Benwell MEM, Balfour DJK, Anderson JM. Smoking-associated changes in the serotonergic systems of discrete regions of human brain. Psychopharmacology 1990;102:68–72.

13. Bjorklund A, Stenevi U. Regeneration of monoaminergic and cholinergic neurons in the mammalian central nervous system. Physiol Rev 1979;59:62–100.

14. Blouin AG, Blouin J, Perez EL, Bushnik, Zuro C, Mulder E. Treatment of bulimia with fenfluramine and desipramine. J Clin Psychopharmacol 1988;8:261–269.

15. Bost RO. 3,4-Methylenedioxymethamphetamine (MDMA) and other amphetamine derivatives. J Forensic Sci 1988;22:576–587.

16. Bowers MB. Amitriptyline in man: decreased formation of central 5-hydroxyindoleacetic acid. Clin Pharmacol Ther 1974;15:167–170.

17. Bravo GL, Grob CS. Shamans, sacraments and psychiatrists. J Psychoactive Drugs 1989;21: 123–128.

18. Broening HW, Bowyer JF, Slikker W. Age-dependent sensitivity of rats to the long-term effects of the serotonergic neurotoxicant (±) 3,4-methylenedioxymethamphetamine (MDMA) correlates with the magnitude of the MDMA-induced thermal response. J Pharmacol Exp Ther 1995;275:325–333.

19. Buchanan JF, Brown CR. Designer drugs: a problem in clinical toxicology. Med Toxicol 1988;3:1–17.

20. Capdevila M. MDMA o el extasis quimico. Barcelona: Los Libros De La Liebre De Marzo, 1995.

21. Ceccherelli F, Costa C, Ischia S, Ischia A, Giron G, Allegri G. Cerebral tryptophan metabolism in humans in relation to malignant pain. Funct Neurol 1989;4:341–353.

22. Colado MI, Murray TK, Green AR. 5-HT loss in rat brain following 3,4-methylenedioxymethamphetamine (MDMA), p-chloroamphetamine and fenfluramine administration and effects of chlormethiazole and dizocilpine. Br J Pharmacol 1993;108:583–589.

23. Costa C, Ceccherelli F, Bettero A, Marin G, Mancusi L, Allegri G. Tryptophan, serotonin and 5-hydroxyindoleacetic acid levels in human CSF in relation to pain. In: Schlossberger HG, Kochen W, Linzen B, Steinhart H, eds. Progress in tryptophan and serotonin research. New York: DeGruyter, 1984:413–416.

24. Creighton FJ, Black DL, Hyde CE. "Ecstasy" psychosis and flashbacks. Br J Psychiatry 1991; 159:713–716.

25. Crisp T, Stafinsky JL, Boja JW, Schecter MD. The antinociceptive effects of 3,4-methylenedioxymethamphetamine (MDMA) in the rat. Pharmacol Biochem Behav 1989;34:497–501.

26. Cuomo MJ, Dyment PG, Gammino VM. Increasing use of "ecstasy" (MDMA) and other hallucinogens on a college campus. J Amer College Health Assoc 1994;42:271–274.

27. Derome-Tremblay M, Nathan C. Fenfluramine studies. Science 1989;243:991.

28. Dobkin de Rios, M. Hallucinogens: cross-cultural perspectives. Albuquerque: University of New Mexico Press, 1984.

29. Dobkin de Rios M, Grob CS. Hallucinogens, suggestibility and adolescence in cross-cultural perspective. Yearbook Ethnomedicine 1994;3: 113–132.

30. Donnelly M, Rapoport JL, Potter WZ, Oliver J, Keysor CS, Murphy DL. Fenfluramine and dextroamphetamine treatment of childhood hyperactivity: clinical and biochemical findings. Arch Gen Psychiatry 1989;46:205–212.

31. Dowling GP, McDonough ET, Bost RO. "Eve" and "ecstasy": a report of five deaths associated with the use of MDEA and MDMA. JAMA 1987;257:1615–1617.

32. Downing J. The psychological and physiological effects of MDMA on normal volunteers. J Psychoactive Drugs 1986;18:335–339.

33. Dykhuizen RS, Brunt PW, Atkinson P, Simpson JG, Smith CC. Ecstasy induced hepatitis mimicking viral hepatitis. Gut 1995;36:939–941.

34. Eisner B. Ecstasy: the MDMA story. Berkeley: Ronin Publishing, 1989.

35. Finnegan KT, Skratt JJ, Irwin I, Langston JW. The N-methyl-D-aspartate (NMDA) receptor antagonist, dextromethorphan, prevents the neurotoxic effects of 3,4-methylenedioxymethamphetamine (MDMA) in rats. Neurosci Let 1990; 105:300–306.

36. Fischer C, Hatzidimitriou G, Wlos J, Katz J, Ricaurte G. Re-organization of ascending 5HT axon projections in animals previously exposed to the recreational drug MDMA ("Ecstasy"). J Neurosci 1995;15:5476–5485.

37. Fishbein DH, Lozovsky D, Jaffe J. Impulsivity, aggression, and neuroendocrine responses to 5-HT stimulation in substance abusers. Biol Psychol 1989;25:1049–1066.

38. Frankfurt M, Azmitia E. Regeneration of 5-HT fibers in the rat hypothalamus following unilateral 5,7 DHT injection. Brain Res 1984;298: 272–282.

39. Frederick DL, Ali SF, Alikker W, Gillam MP, Allen RR, Paule MG. Behavioral and neurochemical effects of chronic methylenedioxymethamphetamine (MDMA) treatment in rhesus monkeys. Neurotoxicol Teratol 1995;17: 531–543.

40. Frith C, Chang L. Toxicity of methylenedioxymethamphetamine (MDMA) in the dog and rat. Fundam Appl Toxicol 1987;9:110–119.

41. Gasser P. Die psycholytische psychotherapie in der Schweiz (1988–1993). Jahrbuch fur Transkulturelle Medizin und Psychotherapie 1995; 6:143–162.

42. Gasser P. The psycholytic therapy in Switzerland from 1988–1993: a follow-up study. MAPS 1995;5:3–7.

43. Gledhill JA, Moore DF, Bell D, Henry JA. Subarachnoid hemorrhage associated with MDMA abuse. J Neurol Neurosurg Psychiatry 1993; 56:1036–1037.

44. Green AR, Cross AJ, Goodwin GM. Review of the pharmacology and clinical pharmacology of MDMA ("Ecstasy"). Psychopharmacology 1995;119:247–260.

45. Greer G, Tolbert R. Subjective reports of the effects of MDMA in a clinical setting. J Psychoactive Drugs 1986;18:319–327.

46. Greer G, Tolbert R. The therapeutic use of MDMA. In: Peroutka SJ, ed. Ecstasy: the clinical pharmacological and neurotoxicological effects of the drug MDMA. Holland: Kluwer, 1990.

47. Grinspoon L, Bakalar JB. Psychedelic drugs reconsidered. New York: Basic Books, 1979.

48. Grinspoon L, Bakalar JB. Can drugs be used to enhance the psychotherapeutic process? Am J Psychotherapy 1986;40:393–404.

49. Grob CS. Psychiatric research with hallucinogens: what have we learned? Yearbook Ethnomedicine 1994;3:91–112.

50. Grob CS, Bravo GL, Walsh RN. Second thoughts on 3,4-methylenedioxymethamphetamine (MDMA) neurotoxicity. Arch Gen Psychiatry 1990;47:288.

51. Grob CS, Bravo GL, Walsh RN, Liester MB. The MDMA-neurotoxicity controversy: implications for clinical research with novel psychoactive drugs. J Nerv Ment Dis 1992;180: 355–356.

52. Grob CS, Dobkin de Rios M. Adolescent drug use in cross-cultural perspective. J Drug Issues 1992;22:121–138.

53. Grob CS, Poland RE, Chang L, Ernst T. Psychobiologic effects of 3,4-methylenedioxymethamphetamine in humans: methodological considerations and preliminary observations. Behav Brain Res 1996;73:103–107.

54. Hanyu S, Ikeguchi K, Imai H, Imai N, Yoshida M. Cerebral infarction associated with 3,4-methylenedioxymethamphetamine ("ecstasy") abuse. Eur Neurol 1995;35:173.

55. Harris Research Center. Young peoples poll. January 1992.

56. Henry JA, Jeffreys KJ, Dawling S. Toxicity and deaths from 3,4-methylenedioxymethamphetamine ("ecstasy"). Lancet 1992;340:384–387.

57. Hewitt KE, Green AR. Chlormethiazole, dizocilpine and haloperidol prevent the degeneration of serotonergic nerve terminals induced by administration of MDMA ("Ecstasy"). Neuropharmacology 1994;33:1589–1595.

58. Karch SB. The pathology of drug abuse. Boca Raton, FL: CRC Press, 1993:210–218.

59. Korf D, Blanken P, Nabben T. Een nieuwe wonderpil? Amsterdam: Korf, 1991.

60. Krystal JH, Price LH, Opsahl C, Ricaurte GA, Heninger GR. Chronic 3,4-methylenedioxymethamphetamine (MDMA) use: effects on mood and neuropsychological function? Am J Drug Alcohol Abuse 1992;18:331–341.

61. Lawn JC. Schedules of controlled substances: scheduling of 3,4-methylenedioxymethamphetamine (MDMA) into schedule I. Federal Register 1986;51:36552–36560.

62. Lee MA, Shlain B. Acid dreams: the CIA, LSD and the sixties rebellion. New York: Grove Weidenfeld, 1985.

63. LeSage M, Clark R, Poling A. MDMA and memory: the acute and chronic effects of MDMA in pigeons performing under a delayed-matching-to-sample procedure. Psychopharmacology 1993;110:327–332.

64. Levin A. Abuse of fenfluramine. Br Med J 1973;2:49.

65. Liester MB, Grob CS, Bravo GL, Walsh RN. Phenomenology and sequelae of 3,4-methylenedioxymethamphetamine use. J Nervous Mental Disease 1992;180:343–352.

66. Manchanda S, Connolly MJ. Cerebral infarction in association with ecstasy abuse. Postgrad Med J 1993;69:874–879.

67. Marks J. The search for the "Manchurian candidate." New York: Dell, 1979.

68. Matthews A, Jones C. Spate of British ecstasy deaths puzzles experts. Int J Drug Policy 1992;3:4.

69. McCann UD, Ricaurte GA. Lasting neuropsychiatric sequelae of (±)methylenedioxymethamphetamine ("ecstasy") in recreational users. J Clin Psychopharmacol 1991;11: 302–305.

70. McCann UD, Ricaurte GA. MDMA ("ecstasy"),

71. McCann UD, Ricaurte GA. On the neurotoxicity of MDMA and related amphetamine derivatives. J Clin Psychopharmacol 1995;15:295–296.

72. McCann U, Hatzidimitriou G, Ridenour A, Fischer C, Yuan J, Katz J, Ricaurte G. Dexfenfluramine and serotonin neurotoxicity: further preclinical evidence that clinical caution is indicated. J Pharmacol Exp Ther 1994;269:792–798.

73. McCann UD, Ridenour BS, Shaham Y, Ricaurte GA. Serotonin neurotoxicity after (±)3,4-methylenedioxymethamphetamine (MDMA; "ecstasy"): a controlled study in humans. Neuropsychopharmacology 1994;10:129–138.

74. McDermott P, Matthews A, O'Hare P, Bennett A. Ecstasy in the United Kingdom: recreational drug use and subcultural change. In: Heather N, Wodak A, Nadelman E, O'Hare P, eds. Psychoactive drugs and harm reduction: from faith to science. London: Whurr Publishers, 1993.

75. McGuire PK, Cope H, Fahy TA. Diversity of psychopathology associated with use 3,4-methylenedioxymethamphetamine ('ecstasy'). Br J Psychiatry 1994;165:391–395.

76. McGuire P, Fahy T. Chronic paranoid psychosis after misuse of MDMA ("ecstasy"). Br Med J 1991;302:697.

77. McKenna DJ, Peroutka SJ. Neurochemistry and neurotoxicity of 3,4-methylenedioxymethamphetamine. J Neurochem 1990;54:14–22.

78. Messing RB, Fisher L, Phebus L, Lytle LD. Interaction of diet and drugs in the regulation of brain 5-hydroxyindoles and the response to painful electric shock. Life Sci 1976;18:707–714.

79. Meyendorff E, Jain A, Traskman-Bendz L, Stanley B, Stanley M. The effects of fenfluramine on suicidal behavior. Psychopharmacol Bull 1986;22:155–159.

80. Nash FJ, Meltzer HY, Gudelsky GA. Elevation of serum prolactin and corticosterone concentrations in rat after administration of MDMA. J Pharmacol Exp Ther 1988;245:873–879.

81. Neill JR. "More than medical significance": LSD and American psychiatry 1953–1966. J Psychoactive Drugs 1987;19:39–45.

82. Newmeyer JA. X at the crossroads. J Psychoactive Drugs 1993;25:341–342.

83. Nichols GR, Davis GJ, Corrigan CA, Ransdell JS. Death associated with abuse of a "designer drug." Kentucky Med Assoc J 1990;88:601–603.

83a. NIDA Capsules, CAP 16. U.S. Department of Health and Human Services, National Institute on Drug Abuse, July, 1993.

84. Pallanti S, Mazzi D. MDMA (ecstasy) precipitation of panic disorder. Biol Psychiatry 1992;32:91–95.

85. Peroutka SJ. Incidence of recreational use of 3,4-methylenedioxymethamphetamine (MDMA, "ecstasy") on an undergraduate campus. N Engl J Med 1987;317:1542–1543.

86. Peroutka SJ, Pascoe N, Faull KF. Monoamine metabolites in the cerebrospinal fluid of recreational users of 3,4-methylenedimethoxymethamphetamine (MDMA; "Ecstasy"). Res Commun Subst Abuse 1987;8:125–138.

87. Peroutka SJ, Newman H, Harris H. Subjective effects of 3,4-methylenedioxymethamphetamine in recreational users. Neuropsychopharmacology 1988;1:273–277.

88. Peroutka SJ. Ecstasy: a human neurotoxin? Arch Gen Psychiatry 1989;46:191.

89. Price LH, Ricaurte GA, Krystal JH, Heninger GR. Neuroendocrine and mood responses to intravenous L-tryptophan in 3,4-methylenedioxymethamphetamine (MDMA) users. Arch Gen Psychiatry 1989;46:20–22.

90. Randall T. Ecstasy-fueled "rave" parties become dances of death for English youths. JAMA 1992;268:1505–1506.

91. Riedlinger TJ, Riedlinger JE. Psychedelic and entactogenic drugs in the treatment of depression. J Psychoactive Drugs 1994;26:41–55.

92. Ricaurte G, Bryan G, Strauss L, Seiden L, Schuster C. Hallucinogenic amphetamine selectively destroys brain serotonin nerve terminals. Science 1985;229:986–988.

93. Ricaurte GA, DeLanney LE, Irwin I, Langston JW. Toxic effects of MDMA on 5-HT neurons in the primate: importance of route and frequency of administration. Brain Res 1988;446:165–168.

94. Ricaurte GA, Finnegan KT, Irwin I, Langston JW. Aminergic metabolites in cerebrospinal fluid of humans previously exposed to MDMA: preliminary observations. N Y Acad Sci 1990;600:699–708.

95. Ricaurte GA, Martello A, Katz JL, Martello MB. Lasting effects of (±)3,4-methylenedioxymethamphetamine on central serotonergic neurons in non-primates. J Pharmacol Exp Ther 1992;261:616–622.

96. Ritvo ER, Freeman BJ, Geller E, Yuwiler A. Effects of fenfluramine on fourteen autistic outpatients. J Am Acad Child Psychiatry 1983;222:549–558.

97. Robinson T, Castaneda E, Whishaw I. Effects of cortical serotonin depletion induced by 3,4-methylenedioxymethamphetamine (MDMA) on behavior, before and after additional cholinergic blockade. Neuropsychopharmacology 1993;8:77–85.

98. Rothwell PM, Grant R. Cerebral venous sinus thrombosis induced by "ecstasy." J Neurol Neurosurg Psychiatry 1993;56:1035.

99. Saunders N. E for ecstasy. London: Saunders, 1993.

100. Saunders N. Ecstasy and the dance culture. London: Saunders, 1995.

101. Schifano F, Magni G. MDMA ("ecstasy") abuse: psychopathological features and craving for chocolate: a case series. Biol Psychiatry 1994;36:763–767.

102. Schmidt CJ. Neurotoxicity of the psychedelic amphetamine, methylenedioxymethamphetamine. J Pharmacol Exp Ther 1987;240:1–7.

103. Schmidt CJ, Taylor VL. Depression of rat brain tryptophan hydroxylase following the acute administration of methylenedioxymethamphetamine. Biochem Pharmacol 1987;36:4095–4102.

104. Schmidt CJ, Abbate GM, Black CK, Taylor VL. Selective 5-HT2 receptor antagonists protect against the neurotoxicity of methylenedioxymethamphetamine in rats. J Pharmacol Exp Ther 1990;255:478–483.

105. Schmidt CJ, Sullivan CK, Fadayel GM. Blockade of striatal 5-HT2 receptors reduces the increase in extracellular concentrations of dopamine produced by MDMA. J Neurochem 1994;62:1382–1389.

106. Seiden LS, Ricaurte GA. Neurotoxicity of methamphetamine and related drugs. In: Meltzer HY, ed. Psychopharmacology: the third generation of progress. New York: Raven Press, 1987.

107. Sharkey A. Sorted or distorted. The Guardian 1996(26 Jan):2–4.

108. Shulgin AT. History of MDMA. In: Peroutka SJ, ed. Ecstasy: the clinical, pharmacological and neurotoxicological effects of the drug MDMA. Holland: Kluwer, 1990.

109. Shulgin AT, Nichols DE. Characterization of three new psychotomimetics. In: Stillman R, Willete R, eds. The psychopharmacology of hallucinogens. New York: Pergamon Press, 1978:74–83.

110. Shulgin A, Shulgin A. PIHKAL. Berkeley: Transform Press, 1991.

111. Siegel RK. MDMA: nonmedical use and intoxication. J Psychoactive Drugs 1986;18:349–354.

112. Siever LJ, Coccaro EF, Zemishalny Z, Silverman J, Klar H, Loscneczy MF, et al. Psychobiology of personality disorders: pharmacologic implications. Psychopharmacol Bull 1987;23:333–336.

113. Siever LJ, Davis KL. A psychological perspective on personality disorders. Am J Psychol 1991;148:1647–1658.

114. Solowij J, Lee N. Survey of ecstasy (MDMA) users in Sydney. Rozelle, New South Wales, Australia: New South Wales Health Department Research Grant Report Series DAD, 1991:91.

115. Sprague JE, Nichols DE. The monoamine oxidase-B inhibitor l-deprenyl protects against 3,4-methylenedioxymethamphetamine-induced lipid peroxidation and long-term serotonergic deficits. J Pharmacol Exp Ther 1995;273:667–673.

116. Squier MV, Jalloh S, Hilton-Jones D, Series H. Death after ecstasy ingestion: neuropathological findings. J Neurol Neurosurg Psychiatry 1995;58:756–764.

117. Sylvester R. Ecstasy: the truth. The Sunday Telegraph 1995(19 Nov):24.

118. Ward NG, Ang J, Pavinich G. A comparison of the acute effects of dextroamphetamine and fenfluramine in depression. Biol Psychiatry 1985;20:1090–1097.

119. Watson L, Beck J. New age seekers: MDMA use in spiritual pursuit. J Psychoactive Drugs 1991;23:261–270.

120. Winstock AR. Chronic paranoid psychosis after misuse of MDMA. Br Med J 1991;302:1150–1151.

121. Whitaker-Azmitia PM, Aronson TA. "Ecstasy" (MDMA)-induced panic. Am J Psychiatry 1989;146:119.

122. Wolff K, Hay AWM, Sherlock K, Conner M. Contents of "ecstasy." Lancet 1996;346:1100–1101.

123. Yamamoto BK, Nash JF, Gudelsky GA. Modulation of methylenedioxymethamphetamine-induced striatal dopamine release by the interaction between serotonin and gamma-aminobutyric acid in the substantia nigra. J Pharmacol Exp Ther 1995;273(3):1063–1070.

124. Young F. Opinion and recommended ruling, findings of fact, conclusions of law and decision of administrative law judge: submitted in the matter of MDMA scheduling. U.S. Drug Enforcement Administration Docket No. 84–88, 22 May 1986.

125. Ziporyn T. A growing industry and menace: makeshift laboratory's designer drugs. JAMA 1986;256:3061–3063.

panic disorder: induction by a single dose. Biol Psychiatry 1992;32:950–953.

25 NICOTINE

Joy M. Schmitz, Nina G. Schneider, and Murray E. Jarvik

About 30 years ago the Surgeon General of the United States identified cigarette smoking as a major *preventable* cause of death and disability. Over the ensuing years, the study of smoking and nicotine dependence experienced unprecedented growth. Today, the scientific literature clearly establishes nicotine as a powerful drug of addiction, with neurobiological effects similar to those of most drugs of abuse. Cigarette smoking is the most prevalent form of nicotine addiction in the United States, involving over 25% of the adult population. The interplay of biological, psychological, social, and other factors contribute to the development and maintenance of smoking behavior. This multiplicity of determinants also contributes to the difficulty of smoking cessation. Despite progress in the understanding and treatment of nicotine dependence, the National Health Objectives of attaining a smoke-free society by the year 2000 will not be achieved. This chapter reviews the current status of tobacco use, nicotine pharmacokinetics, pharmacodynamics, and actions, and currently available pharmacological and behavioral interventions for the treatment of nicotine dependence.

TOBACCO USE

Prevalence

Currently, an estimated 25% of adults in the United States smoke (1). This figure represents a gradual, but substantial decline from 42.4% in 1965. Recent estimates suggest a leveling off in smoking prevalence, with rates unchanged from 1990 to 1992. Extrapolation of current trends suggests that by the year 2000, about 22% of the U.S. adult population will be smokers. Of the 46 million adults who currently smoke, 24 million (27.7%) are men and 22 million (22.5%) are women (2). Since 1965, differences in smoking prevalence between the sexes have narrowed, in part due to the faster rate of decline in smoking prevalence among men, compared to women (3, 4). The percentage change in smoking prevalence from 1965 to 1991 was 46% among men and 31% among women (1). Smoking prevalence has been consistently higher among blacks than whites, although the rate of decline in prevalence per year has been approximately the same (5). Hispanics generally have lower smoking rates than non-Hispanics.

Over the years, differences in smoking rates across educational groups have widened. In 1965, 33.7% of adults with a college degree smoked compared to 36.5% of adults with less than a high school education, a nonsignificant difference. In 1990, the differences in smoking rates between college graduates (13.5%) and high school dropouts (31.8%) were highly significant (4). The divergent trends by level of education can be illustrated by comparing the rate of decline (in percentage points per year) from 1965 to 1990 for high school dropouts (0.20), high school graduates (0.48), persons with some college education (0.81), and college graduates (0.84). Consequently, educational status has become the best sociodemographic predictor of differential smoking prevalence rates (6).

Other Forms of Tobacco

Since the late 1970s, there has been a substantial increase in the sale and consumption of smokeless tobacco (SLT) products (7). In 1986, the Surgeon General's report estimated that 12 million Americans used smokeless tobacco (8). SLT use is predominantly an activity of young, white males. Its prevalence is most concentrated in rural, southern regions of the United States, and among blue-collar workers (9). The recent resurgence in the use of SLT was accompanied by accumulating documentation of the harmful consequences of SLT. Not only does SLT use increase the risk of health problems (e.g., oral cancer) (8), but it raises the probability of subsequent

cigarette smoking or use of other nicotine-containing substances (10). Furthermore, it has been confirmed that regular use of smokeless tobacco causes physical dependence (11, 12). Systemic levels of nicotine are generally similar in users of smokeless tobacco and cigarette smokers, although smoke inhalation produces more rapid uptake (13).

Smoking Cessation

The prevalence of cessation (also referred to as the quit ratio), or the percentage of former smokers among ever smokers, has been used to describe patterns of smoking cessation. This index shows an increasing trend in quitting from 29.6% in 1965 to 44.8% in 1987 (3). More recently, the 1993 quit ratio was 49.6%, representing almost half of an estimated 46 million former smokers (2). Cessation prevalence was higher among men (51.9%), whites (51.6%), and increased directly with age. Survey results indicate that most smokers (70%) want to stop smoking, with 34% attempting to quit each year. Of those who attempt to quit, only 2.5% are successful (2).

HEALTH IMPLICATIONS

Risks of Smoking

Cigarette smoking is a profound contributor to mortality. Each year more than 400,000 deaths, or 20% of the total deaths in the United States, are caused by smoking (14). Cigarette smoking substantially increases the risk of cardiovascular disease (e.g., stroke, sudden death, heart attack) (3), non-malignant respiratory diseases (e.g., emphysema, asthma, chronic bronchitis, chronic obstructive pulmonary disease) (15), lung cancer (3), and other cancers (e.g., mouth, pharynx, larynx, esophagus, stomach, pancreas, uterus, cervix, kidney, ureter, and bladder) (16, 17). The harmful effects of smoking on reproduction and pregnancy include reduced fertility and fetal growth, as well as increased risk of ectopic pregnancy and spontaneous abortion (18). Finally, nonsmokers who are exposed to environmental tobacco smoke, i.e., "passive smoking", appear to be at increased risk for many of the same health problems and complications as smokers (19), although the evidence for heart disease caused by ETS is mixed.

Risks of Nicotine

Some of the actions of nicotine (e.g., sympathetic activation, changes in lipid metabolism, platelet aggregation, hypercoagulability, circulating catecholamines) could contribute to the pathogenesis of cardiovascular disease (20); however, the evidence for a causal role of nicotine in heart disease is weak. The magnitude of increased risk associated with these and other effects of nicotine on the cardiovascular system depends on the rate of nicotine absorption (21). The more slowly absorbed nicotine from nicotine replacement products does not appear to increase cardiovascular risk to healthy individuals (20, 22, 23), or cause adverse cardiac effects in patients with coronary artery disease (e.g., 24). Nicotine does not appear to have carcinogenic activity (20). It has been suggested that endogenous formation of nicotine-derived nitrosoamines are found in substantial concentrations and could contribute to cancer in humans (20), but there is little evidence to support this theory. Studies of pulmonary toxicity suggest that nicotine may contribute to the development of emphysema by increasing levels of elastase, an enzyme that destroys alveolar structure (25). In smokers who already have lung disease, acute exposure to nicotine may worsen pulmonary function by inducing constriction of both central and peripheral airways (20, 26). Nicotine may cause adverse reproductive outcomes by reducing uteroplacental blood flow (27, 28), producing fetal hypoxia (29, 30), and impairing development of the fetal brain (31, 32). Some evidence suggests that the adverse obstetrical effects are less during steady-state nicotine gum use than during smoking (e.g., 29, 33–36).

In summary, although the independent contribution of nicotine to the development of tobacco-related health problems has not been fully elucidated, its potential toxicity appears to be substantially less than that associated with tobacco use.

Benefits of Smoking Cessation

The 1990 Report of the Surgeon General concluded that smoking cessation has major and immediate health benefits for men and women of all ages (18). In people with existing conditions or disease states, quitting smoking has been shown to reduce further impairment and disability (37–41). Overall, people who quit smoking live longer than those who continue smoking, because of the reduction in risk of dying from smoking-related diseases. The extent of risk reduction depends on several factors, however, such as number of years of smoking, number of cigarettes smoked per day, and the presence or absence of disease at the time of quitting. In general, the decline in risk of all-cause mortality begins shortly after quitting and continues for about 10–15 years, eventually approximating the mortality risk of never-smokers (18). In terms of pregnancy, smoking cessation prior to attempting to conceive returns fertility to a level comparable to never-smokers and prevents birth weight deficits (18). Indeed, stopping smoking at any time during pregnancy is beneficial because of increased availability of oxygen to the fetus (18).

In summary, there is overwhelming evidence that smoking cessation is beneficial, yet people continue to smoke. It is believed that the tenacity of smoking can be explained by recognizing tobacco use as an addiction to nicotine.

SMOKING AS NICOTINE ADDICTION

Evidence from both the human and animal literature clearly demonstrates that nicotine is a psychoactive drug of dependence and the primary controlling variable in cigarette smoking (18, 20, 42). Nicotine produces "dependence" and "withdrawal," as specified in the 1994 *Diagnostic and Statistical Manual of Mental Disorders,* fourth edition (DSM-IV) (43). Almost all people who smoke more than five cigarettes per day meet the DSM-IV diagnostic criteria for tobacco dependence, which include (*a*) tolerance, (*b*) withdrawal, (*c*) used in larger amounts or over a longer period than intended, (*d*) a persistent desire or unsuccessful efforts to cut down or quit, (*e*) a great deal of time spent using the substance, (*f*) giving up important social, occupational, or recreational activities because of substance use, and (*g*) continued use despite knowledge of medical problems related to use. Earlier views of nicotine as a drug of "habituation" (44) have been largely replaced by the current consensus, which regards nicotine as an addictive substance comparable to heroin, cocaine, and alcohol. Arguments against nicotine as an addictive drug (45, 46) have generally been refuted (e.g., 47).

PHARMACOLOGY OF NICOTINE

The pharmacological effects of nicotine are essential to sustaining cigarette smoking. This section reviews several important aspects of nicotine's pharmacological profile, including pharmacokinetic, pharmacodynamic, reinforcing actions, and conditioning factors. Understanding tobacco dependence requires knowledge of the interplay of these multiple, complex processes.

Nicotine Pharmacokinetics

DOSING AND ABSORPTION

Nicotine is readily absorbed from every site on or in the body, including the lungs, buccal and nasal mucosa, skin, and gastrointestinal tract. Cigarette smoke contains fine particles or droplets of tar averaging less than a micron in size. Absorption is influenced by the pH of the preparation. Most cigarette tobacco is acid flue-cured with a pH around 5.5. Nicotine is mostly ionized at this level and therefore little is absorbed through the oral mucosa (48). Tobacco in a single cigarette contains about 10 mg of nicotine, regardless of brand and Federal Trade Commission rated nicotine yield. The average nicotine intake from a single cigarette is about 1.0 mg, but may exceed 3 mg (49, 50). Constituents of tobacco smoke are shown in Figure 25.1.

Cigarette smoking delivers nicotine very rapidly, with an initial distribution half-life of approximately 10–20 minutes followed by an elimination half-

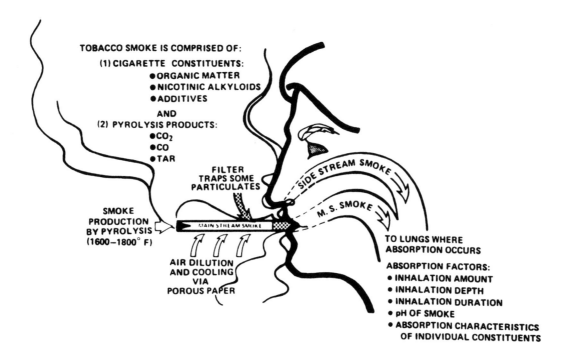

Figure 25.1. Production and rate of cigarette smoke constituents. (Reproduced with permission from Henningfield JE. Behavioral pharmacology of cigarette smoking. In: Thompson T, Dews PD, Barrett JE, eds. Advances in behavioral pharmacology. Vol. 4. Orlando: Academic Press, 1984:138.)

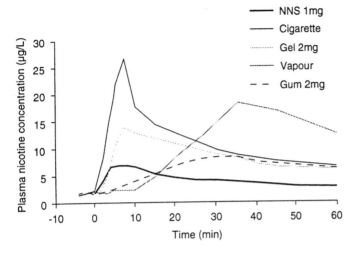

Figure 25.2. Venous plasma nicotine concentrations over time for a single cigarette and single dose of each of 4 nicotine delivery systems. (Reproduced with permission from Schneider NG, Lunell E, Olmstead RE, Fagerstrom KO. Clinical pharmacokinetics of nasal nicotine delivery: a review and comparison to other nicotine systems. Clinical Pharmacokinet 1996;31:65–80.)

life of 2–3 hours (51). As nicotine gets into the bloodstream it is immediately delivered to the brain by means of the heart. Delivery of nicotine to the brain is estimated to take less than 20 seconds (52, 53). Brain concentrations decline quickly as nicotine is redistributed to other body tissues. Approximately 90% of nicotine is metabolized to cotinine by C-oxidation. Cotinine has a long biological half-life (19–24 hours). Recently published research suggests that metabolism of nicotine is dose-independent and that nicotine and cotinine elimination pharmacokinetics are similar in smokers and nonsmokers (54).

The dose of nicotine delivered and the rate of delivery critically determine its potential for abuse. Nicotine delivery devices other than cigarettes (e.g., polacrilex gum, transdermal nicotine) do not produce the rapid and large increase in arterial nicotine concentration observed with cigarettes (55). Absorption of nicotine from the transdermal patch systems is gradual and slow. Absorption from gum is faster and strongly determined by the chewing patterns of the user (56). Absorption of nicotine from the transdermal systems allows for more steady delivery of measured nicotine doses. The commercially available transdermal patch systems vary in their rate of nicotine delivery and absorption. These variations do not appear to be related to overall differential clinical effect (57). However, further study may show that individuals will find patches differentially effective. Delivery of nicotine in the form of nasal spray shows a rise time of nicotine in venous blood faster than for the other replacement systems (58) (Figure 25.2). Whereas transdermal systems reach peak venous levels between 10 and 15 ng/ml after 4–6 hours (59), a single dose of 1 mg nicotine nasal spray has been shown to produce mean peak venous levels of 8.1 ng/ml within 11.5 minutes (60).

In summary, the kinetic profile of nicotine delivery by cigarette smoking supports its categorization as an addictive drug. The rapid transfer of inhaled nicotine into the arterial circulation and into the brain provides the maximum opportunity for behavioral reinforcement from smoking. The abuse liability of nontobacco nicotine delivery systems, while generally low, may depend on the extent to which these devices closely mimic the kinetics of cigarette smoking. Factors other than kinetic profile, however, can affect or predict the abuse liability of a drug delivery system (61). Dose of the drug, cost, availability, and social acceptability are some of the other aspects affecting degree of dependence (62).

TOLERANCE, SENSITIZATION, AND WITHDRAWAL

Repeated exposure to nicotine, as to many other psychoactive substances, can result in neural adaptations that are reflected in nicotine tolerance, sensitization, and withdrawal. Indeed, such adaptations may contribute

to, and define, the development of an addictive state (47). Studies have documented the development of tolerance to some, but not all, of nicotine's effects (20). In humans, substantial acute tolerance develops to the behavioral arousal and cardiovascular effects of nicotine within the course of a single day. In most smokers the first cigarette of the day produces stronger subjective and cardiovascular effects (i.e., increase in heart rate) compared with cigarettes later in the day, thereby demonstrating a loss of some tolerance to the effects of nicotine during overnight abstinence from smoking (63, 64).

An exposure model of tolerance posits that chronic tolerance develops in proportion to the extent of nicotine exposure (65). People who are initially less sensitive to nicotine's aversive effects may be more likely to have further exposure to nicotine self-administration, resulting in the development of a higher degree of tolerance. Others have put forth an alternative conceptualization of tolerance in which differences in constitutional factors (i.e., initial sensitivity to nicotine), in combination with environmental factors, determine the degree of tolerance (66). According to the "sensitivity" model of tolerance, people with high innate sensitivity experience more intense aversive and rewarding effects of nicotine, and thus are more likely to develop the consequent pattern of smoking. Findings from animal and human studies have generally supported the hypothesis that tolerance to nicotine is linked to initial sensitivity (e.g., 67, 68). The evidence to date, while provocative, is limited and awaits further examination of innate differences in sensitivity in people with different levels of nicotine exposure and smoking patterns.

Because of tolerance characteristics, most smokers smoke a similar number of cigarettes per day to achieve the desired effects of nicotine and to minimize withdrawal discomfort throughout the day. Daily plasma levels of nicotine usually seen in smokers reach a peak of 10–40 ng/ml in late afternoon, declining to 5–10 ng/ml after overnight abstinence (69). Manipulating the nicotine yield of the cigarette causes smokers to change their smoking behavior in an effort to regulate or titrate levels of nicotine within certain limits (21, 70). The smoker quickly learns that negative symptoms associated with short periods of abstinence can be rapidly reversed by nicotine use. Thus, nicotine withdrawal signs and symptoms, while not life threatening, can affect behavior and serve as a strong impetus for continued smoking.

Diagnostic criteria for nicotine withdrawal according to DSM-IV include at least four of the following signs occurring within 24 hours of abrupt cessation of nicotine use or reduction in the amount of nicotine use: (a) dysphoric or depressed mood, (b) insomnia, (c) irritability, frustration, or anger, (d) anxiety, (e) difficulty concentrating, (f) restlessness, (g) decreased heart rate, (h) increased appetite or weight gain (Table 25.1). Craving for nicotine, although no longer listed as a diagnostic criteria, is considered to be an important element in nicotine withdrawal. There are other reported clinical manifestations of nicotine withdrawal, as can be seen in Table 25.1, that do not appear among the limited list of DSM-IV items (71). Increases in aggressive responding (72), as well as decreases in social cooperative behavior (73), have been observed during periods of acute nicotine abstinence. Withdrawal symptoms are believed to be due primarily to nicotine deprivation. Nevertheless, other nonpharmacological factors such as conditioning (74) and expectancy (75) have been shown to influence aspects of behavior during nicotine withdrawal.

Nicotine-specific withdrawal effects are measurable in laboratory settings (e.g., 76–78), and in clinical trials of nicotine replacement therapy (e.g., 79, 80). In laboratory experiments (76–78), nicotine deprivation in heavy smokers produces increases in subjective desire to smoke, impaired performance on computerized cognitive tasks (i.e., logical reasoning, digit recall, arithmetic), and decreases in heart rate. Nicotine replacement in the form of gum largely attenuates these abstinence effects, although effects on desire to smoke are less well established (76). Withdrawal data from clinical trials of nicotine replacement therapy are generally concordant with laboratory study results. Cessation from tobacco leads to increases in withdrawal symptoms, with nicotine replacement decreasing the severity of most symptoms (79, 80). Taken together, these findings clearly demonstrate the occurrence of abstinence-related signs and symptoms, most of which are reversible by nicotine administration.

In summary, chronic self-administration of nicotine, like other psychoactive substances, leads to tolerance, sensitization, and withdrawal. The

Table 25.1 Signs and Symptoms of Withdrawal

Mood changes
    * Irritability/Frustration/Anger
    * Anxiety
    * Depression
      Hostility
      Impatience
Physiological symptoms:
      Drowsiness
      Fatigue
    * Restlessness
    * Difficulty concentrating
      Decreased alertness
      Lightheadedness
      Headaches
      Tightness in chest
      Bodily aches and pains
      Tingling sensation in limbs
      Stomach distress
    * Hunger
      Urges to smoke
      Craving
Physiological signs:
    * Weight gain
    * Decrease in heart rate
      Increased peripheral circulation
      Drop in urinary adrenalin, noradrenalin, cortisol
      Changes in electroencephalogram
      Changes in endocrine functions
      Neurotransmitter changes
      Performance deficits
    * Sleep disturbance
      Constipation
      Sweating
      Mouth ulcers
      Increased coughing

* These items are represented in DSM-IV criteria for nicotine withdrawal.

following section reviews some of the neuropharmacological mechanisms that may underlie these effects of nicotine dependence.

Nicotine Pharmacodynamics

The brain is an important site of nicotine's actions. As mentioned previously, the immediacy of inhaled nicotine absorption results in nicotine reaching the brain within 7–19 seconds of puffing (53, 81). Nicotine produces a wide range of effects in the peripheral and central nervous system (CNS), including changes in cardiovascular, neural, endocrine, and skeletal muscle functions. Recent studies indicate that these diverse behavioral effects are most likely mediated through multiple subtypes of nicotinic receptors in different parts of the brain (82, 83).

Peripheral effects occur with stimulation of nicotinic cholinergic receptors in the parasympathetic and sympathoadrenal systems. Nicotine increases blood pressure (by 5–10 mm Hg), heart rate (by 10–20 beats/min), cardiac output, coronary blood flow, and cutaneous vasoconstriction (84). Endocrine and metabolic effects are known to occur. These include the release of prolactin, growth hormone, vasopressin, β-endorphins, cortisol and adrenocorticotrophic hormone (ACTH) (85, 86). Some of these peripheral effects may be mediated by CNS stimulation.

Other pharmacodynamic effects of nicotine occur in the CNS. These nicotinic cholinergic receptors appear to be stimulated as well as desensitized by nicotine inhaled from tobacco smoke (87–89). Moreover, prolonged smoking leads to repetitive receptor desensitization, evoking up-regulation and increasing receptor density (90). The family of nicotinic cholinergic receptors is known to have different physiological and pharmacological properties (91, 92). An interesting proposition is that smokers may adjust their smoking habits to achieve the balance of receptor stimulation and desensitization which they find most reinforcing (88, 93). For instance, heavy smokers may smoke in a way to maintain their nicotinic receptors in a desensitized state. In contrast, other smokers who maintain relatively low plasma nicotine concentrations might smoke in a way that causes stimulation of central nicotinic receptors.

Autoradiographic studies in laboratory animals have been conducted in an effort to map the distribution of nicotine receptors to different brain areas (94). These studies find cholinergic nicotinic receptors located in the interpeduncular nucleus and medial habenula of the limbic system, as well as in the thalamic nuclei and cerebral cortex. Brain imaging using positron emission tomography, reveal densest binding in the anterior nuclei of the thalamus and in the cerebral cortex (95). Metabolic mapping with deoxyglucose suggests that nicotine stimulates glucose utilization, with these effects localized primarily to brain regions that show high densities of nicotinic receptors (96).

Heterogeneity in receptor function and site has been shown in recent attempts to correlate behavioral effects of novel nicotinic agonists with the high affinity binding site for [^{3}H]nicotine. For example, evaluation of the effects of various nicotinic agonists in rats suggest unique dose-response curves across behaviors of drug discrimination, locomotor decreases, and locomotor increases (97–99). Studies examining the cognitive effects of neuronal nicotinic acetylcholine receptor (nAChRs) agonists also reveal differences in effects (e.g., 100). This line of research raises the possibility that nicotinic agonists with selective actions on cognition might be developed for the therapeutic management of Alzheimer's disease (83).

Primary actions taking place at nicotinic-cholinergic receptors appear to be followed by those involving the dopaminergic system. Recent evidence supporting the involvement of dopamine comes from studies of lesions of forebrain dopamine systems on nicotine-induced locomotor activation and self-administration (e.g., 101–103). In a study by Corrigall and associates (102), rats with lesions of the mesolimbic dopamine system showed marked decreases in rate of nicotine self-administration compared to sham-lesioned rats who displayed a relatively stable pattern of behavior across the 3-week testing period. More recent data suggest that self-administered nicotine activates the mesolimbic dopamine system directly at the level of the ventral tegmental area (104). Finally, Pontieri and colleagues (105) demonstrated that intravenous nicotine in the rat produces neurochemical changes (i.e., cerebral glucose utilization and extracellular dopamine) in the shell of the nucleus accumbens that resemble those implicated in other classes of dependence-producing drugs, such as cocaine (106, 107).

The development of chronic tolerance to nicotine appears to be related to an increase in the number of binding sites (108, 109). More recently, studies have suggested a possible role for endogenous glutamate in the development of sensitization and tolerance to psychoactive compounds, including nicotine. Administering an antagonist at the N-methyl-D-aspartate (NMDA) glutamate receptor has been shown to weaken or prevent tolerance to nicotine (110). Further evidence suggests that tolerance to nicotine-induced dopamine release in the nucleus accumbens may be at least in part mediated by activation of NMDA receptors (110). Other factors interacting with the glutamaterigic systems, such as glucocorticoids, are likely to be involved in nicotine tolerance.

In summary, recent advances in neurobiological research have increased our understanding of the heterogeneity of nicotinic receptors and sites of activity in the brain. Recent evidence negates the earlier notion that all the diverse central effects of nicotine are mediated through one type of receptor that originates in one region of the brain. Further behavioral research is needed in order to better characterize the multiple brain nicotinic receptors.

Actions

REINFORCING EFFECT OF NICOTINE

A key characteristic of addiction is repetitive self-administration due to the reinforcing effect of the drug. Numerous animal and human experimental findings have shown that, in appropriate conditions, the reinforcing effect of nicotine can maintain rates of responding. Not all nicotine self-administration studies have yielded positive findings, however (111, 112). The mixed findings are most likely related to inexact laboratory models of drug self-administration for nicotine. That is, the conditions and techniques that support the reinforcing efficacy of one drug (e.g., cocaine) may be inappropriate for another drug to serve as a reinforcer (47). In summary, available research on nicotine self-administration suggests that intravenous nicotine can maintain rates of responding above control levels under a variety of conditions, although intravenous nicotine appears to be a less generalizable reinforcer than intravenous cocaine (113). The determinants of its reinforcing value are complex, and will require further investigation across different experimental conditions.

COGNITIVE EFFECTS OF NICOTINE

Smokers often report that smoking helps them to concentrate and sustain attention over long periods of time. As mentioned earlier, impairment of these cognitive abilities is a characteristic of nicotine withdrawal.

Nicotine's potential as a cognitive enhancer has been extensively studied in animals and humans. Animal studies suggest that nicotine and nicotine agonists can enhance acquisition and retention of spatial tasks in normal and aged animals (e.g., 114, 115). In humans, the performance-enhancing effects of nicotine are most prominently seen in abstinent smokers. In such studies, nicotine appears to reverse deprivation-induced deficits in sensory abilities, finger tapping, and selective and sustained attention (116). These performance tasks do not appear to be reliably enhanced in nonabstinent smokers and nonsmokers (116). In their critical review of experimental research findings from 1970 to 1993, Heishman, Taylor, and Henningfield (116) concluded that slower cognitive performance in smokers deprived of nicotine is attributable to nicotine withdrawal reducing normal levels of performance. Others (117–119), however, have reported data more consistent with a nicotine-facilitation or enhancement (rather than nicotine withdrawal) explanation of cognitive effects. Debate continues over the question of whether people smoke cigarettes primarily to enhance cognitive performance (e.g., mental alertness), as suggested by Warburton (120), or because they are dependent on the drug nicotine and its psychoactive effects (20).

Cognitive impairments of dementia, as seen in Alzheimer's disease for example, have been associated with losses of central nicotinic receptors. These observations further support the hypothesized role of nicotinic mechanisms in cognition and suggest that nicotine may have some therapeutic value for improving cognitive function in this special population. There have been only a few clinical trials with nicotine given to demented patients, but the promising results warrant further investigation (121–123).

Hunger and Body Weight

Nicotine's role as an anorectic agent, capable of suppressing hunger and eating, has been proposed on the basis of several observations. Cigarette smoking is associated with reduced body weight, i.e., smokers tend to weigh about 3–4 kg less than nonsmokers (124, 125). Weight gain is a commonly reported consequence of smoking cessation (18, 126). Nicotine replacement therapy has been shown to attenuate weight gain following smoking cessation in some studies (e.g., 127).

Weight changes associated with smoking or smoking cessation appear to be transient, however, and may be due to both eating and metabolic effects of nicotine (128). During the first few weeks postcessation, increases in eating and hunger rise sharply, but gradually decline toward baseline levels at lengthier follow-ups (126, 129, 130). Relapse to smoking following cessation appears to cause only a short-term decrease in eating (131, 132). Similarly, metabolic rate is acutely increased by nicotine, but removal of these acute effects (i.e., smoking cessation) does not appear to result in a chronic decrease in metabolism (133, 134).

Recently, a "set point" explanation of the effect of smoking on body weight and energy balance has been put forth (128). Accordingly, nicotine (or its removal) lowers (or raises) body weight set point, or the level around which body weight is regulated. This set-point hypothesis explains why, once body weight has stabilized during regular smoking or prolonged cessation, caloric intake is the same for smokers, ex-smokers, and never-smokers. The notion of nicotine lowering body weight set point has been supported in animal research (135, 136).

The set-point hypothesis, if confirmed by further research, has important treatment implications. It suggests that weight gain after smoking cessation, often viewed as a promoting relapse, might be difficult to prevent. Indeed, smoking cessation interventions that attempt to prevent cessation-related weight gain have been largely ineffective.

Mood

Smokers report smoking as a means of reducing negative affect and stress, and enhancing positive feeling states. As with hunger and weight, negative mood is listed as a symptom of nicotine withdrawal (43), and has been linked to smoking relapse following cessation (137).

The issue as to whether nicotine actually provides psychological improvements or simply reverses the mood impairing effects of deprivation has been debated in the literature. The "nicotine-resource" model views nicotine as a positive resource (138, 139), whereas the "deprivation-reversal" model suggests that smokers gain nothing from cigarettes except a delay in the onset of nicotine withdrawal effects (140). Recently, Parrott (141) addressed this issue in a series of studies involving the monitoring of mood states over a day of repetitive cigarette use in adult smokers. The resulting pattern of fluctuation in feeling states was suggestive of improved moods immediately after smoking, but mood deteriorations between cigarettes. Moreover, smokers showed no evidence of acute tolerance to these psychological effects of nicotine.

Although smokers anecdotally report using cigarettes to cope with environmental stressors, there is no evidence of any particular advantage associated with this coping method. In fact, nicotine's pharmacological effects are largely stimulatory (e.g., increased heart rate), despite smokers' subjective effects of "calmness" when smoking in a stressful situation (142, 143). It has been argued that smokers actually have higher levels of stress than nonsmokers, based on the hypothesis that nicotine depletion (between cigarettes) leads to feelings of stress (144). Quitting smoking eventually removes this source of stress associated with nicotine withdrawal. Some evidence suggests that smokers report higher levels of anxiety compared to nonsmokers (145, 146), and that former smokers experience reduced levels of daily stress relative to precessation levels (e.g., 147, 148).

In summary, recent findings are most consistent with the deprivation-reversal model of stress modulation. Smoking appears to provide relief of adverse moods such as anxiety and stress, rather than the attainment of beneficial moods (141, 144). Thus, the effects of nicotine on mood reinforce tobacco use and may increase the difficulty in quitting smoking (see discussion of treatment later in this chapter).

Conditioning

Frequent, repeated pairings of cigarette smoking and its reinforcing effects over time are subject to conditioning mechanisms that further maintain the complex behavior. From an operant learning model, the smoker associates smoking a cigarette in specific situations with the rewarding effects of nicotine. Eventually, specific environmental situations, such as after a meal, with coffee or an alcoholic beverage, or around other smokers, become powerful cues capable of eliciting conditioned responses. Thus, conditioning develops through the pairing of the pharmacological actions of nicotine with drug-seeking behaviors in various environments.

Experimental studies have shown that exposure to environmental cues associated with smoking can elicit physiological responses consistent with conditioning effects (149, 150) and that pattern of responsivity may be related to risk for smoking relapse (151, 152). Theoretically, conditioning loses its power through the disassociation of cues and drug effects. Most behavioral therapies for smoking cessation include strategies aimed at eliminating drug-seeking responses to conditioned cues.

TREATMENT

Nicotine dependence is persistent and not easily mutable; however, the past decade of research has generated a broad range of innovative pharmacological adjuncts. To date, nicotine is the only pharmacological agent approved by the Food and Drug Administration (FDA) for use in smoking-cessation therapy. Non-nicotine medications have shown some degree of efficacy; however, the results are equivocal. The potential efficacy of combining nicotine medications with each other or with non-nicotine medications is the focus of several ongoing trials. In contrast to pharmacotherapies, there have been relatively fewer new developments in behavioral technologies for smoking cessation. Approaches that combine pharmacological and behavioral therapy can substantially increase smoking cessation over either therapy alone (153); however, mechanisms for explaining the positive effects of combined therapy are not fully understood. The following sections review literature on currently available treatment approaches, practice recommendations, and special population considerations.

Nicotine Replacement Systems

Nicotine replacement systems in the form of gum (nicotine polacrilex), patch (transdermal nicotine), and nasal spray have been approved for use in the United States, based on current scientific data, with others in development, such as the oral nicotine inhaler, and the oral transmucosal nicotine stick. In contrast to smoking, the absorption of nicotine via these alternative delivery systems is slower, produces lower plasma nicotine concentrations (58, 154), and does not produce the high arterial blood levels associated with smoking (55) (see Figure 25.2). Herein lies the rationale for using nicotine as an agonist drug replacement: to enable the smoker to reduce nicotine previously obtained from cigarettes with a system that provides substantially reduced toxicity and elimination of the arterial "boli", or rapid entry of nicotine to the brain (81). All of the nicotine replacement systems eliminate the carcinogens and gases associated with tobacco smoke.

Several mechanisms of action explain the potential benefits of nicotine replacement or reduction therapy (NRT) in the enhancement of smoking cessation (154). First, NRT systems can reduce the severity of withdrawal symptoms usually reported after abrupt cessation of cigarette smoking (71, 79, 80). While receiving some relief from nicotine withdrawal, the individual can focus on other aspects of quitting, such as developing coping skills to resist smoking cues. Second, nicotine delivery systems may provide some degree of cross-tolerance with cigarettes, resulting in decreased smoking desire (155–158). Finally, replacement medications may produce some of the desirable nicotine-related mood and cognitive changes previously provided by cigarettes (159).

NICOTINE POLACRILEX

Transmucosally delivered nicotine in the form of polacrilex ("nicotine gum") was the first replacement therapy, receiving FDA-approved labeling for use in a 2-mg form and 4-mg form in 1984 and 1991, respectively. Nicotine, bound to an ion-exchange resin and incorporated into a gum base, is released and absorbed into the circulation solely across the mucosal surfaces in the oral cavity (160). The medication is buffered to alkaline pH to facilitate absorption of the nicotine. Nicotine gum releases nicotine only when used according to certain parameters of chewing; thus, persons without proper instructions may underdose and fail to achieve effective levels of nicotine absorption from the gum (56, 161). For instance, consumption of acidic beverages decreases the amount of nicotine absorbed (56). Even when used optimally, only 54% of the nicotine in the gum is extracted, whereas 46% remains bound to the ion-exchange resin (162). Venous plasma nicotine concentrations achieved with *ad libitum* use of nicotine gum in clinical trials fall in the range of 8–13.3 μg/L for 2 mg gum and 22.5 μg/L for 4 mg gum (58).

There is clear evidence of nicotine gum's effectiveness in relieving many of the acute tobacco-withdrawal symptoms. Schneider and colleagues (80) were among the first to provide support for the efficacy of nicotine gum in the relief of withdrawal. In their double-blind, placebo-controlled clinic trial, subjects receiving nicotine gum (2 mg) reported less severe total withdrawal discomfort over five days of smoking abstinence, compared to placebo subjects. Other nicotine gum studies have demonstrated relief of specific withdrawal symptoms, including psychological distress (163), cognitive impairment (164), and appetite and weight (163). The assumption that higher doses of nicotine replacement provide better relief of withdrawal has been empirically supported in some (164) but not all studies (165). Dose-related effects of nicotine gum on cigarette withdrawal appear to be more pronounced in women than in men (166, 167).

Nicotine gum has been shown to reliably improve smoking-cessation outcomes (168–173). In a meta-analytic review of 39 studies, Silagy and colleagues (172) reported that the odds of abstinence at long-term follow-up (at least 6 months) were 1.6 higher for nicotine gum users than for controls. This review also found evidence that nicotine gum (versus placebo) produces highest quit rates when given with behavioral therapy in a smoking clinic setting than with brief advice, as in a primary care or hospital setting (172). Two other determinants of the effectiveness of nicotine gum include level of nicotine dependence and dosage of nicotine gum. For high nicotine dependent smokers, defined as scoring seven or more points on the Fagerström Tolerance Questionnaire (FTQ) (174), the 4 mg gum appears to be more effective than the 2 mg dose or placebo (175–177). Finally, one study reported superior treatment effects associated with a fixed regimen for gum use compared to an ad lib treatment condition (178). However, the authors acknowledge that subjects in the fixed regimen condition chewed more gum than subjects given ad lib chewing instructions, which may have accounted for the observed treatment effects.

In summary, research supports the clinical efficacy of nicotine gum in suppressing withdrawal symptoms and improving abstinence outcomes. When administered in a setting that provides some degree of counseling or behavioral therapy, nicotine gum use results in significantly better success than that seen with placebo gum. The higher dose of nicotine polacrilex (4 mg) produces improved treatment results compared with lower doses, especially for high-dependent smokers; however, this effect becomes most evident when the patient is compliant with a fixed-dosing regimen (177).

TRANSDERMAL NICOTINE SYSTEMS

Transdermal nicotine delivery systems, or nicotine patches, were first approved by the FDA in late 1991 and 1992, and, for nonprescription use, in 1996. Advantages of transdermal systems include ease of application, steady-state dosing, and minimal side effects. Commercially available patches come in 16-hour and 24-hour delivery systems. Whereas 24-hour therapy provides a higher blood nicotine concentration on awakening and may control smoking better during the morning hours, sleep disturbance may be less likely with the 16-hour application (179). One study comparing the 16-hour versus 24-hour patch therapy did not show any difference in efficacy (180). The pharmacokinetic characteristics of transdermal nicotine suggest a slower rising time in plasma nicotine concentration, ranging from peak level occurring within 2 to 10 hours after application (depending on the patch) compared to other delivery systems (59, 154). Venous plasma nicotine concentrations achieved with fixed dose clinical use of the patch (7–22 mg/day) fall in the range of 6–23 μg/L (58). The elimination half-life of transdermally administered nicotine ranges from 3 to 6 hours (57). The recommended course of transdermal nicotine therapy ranges from 8 to 18 weeks, with gradual reduction of patch dosage prior to treatment termination. However, recent review of patch efficacy studies calls into question the need for long-term nicotine patch treatment (greater than 8 weeks) and weaning before termination (181). Transdermal nicotine therapy has a relatively benign side effect profile; however, a significant proportion of patients experience mild to moderate dermatological reactions (182).

Nicotine patch therapy has been shown to provide withdrawal symptom relief, with significant effects observed in both individual symptom ratings, such as irritation, anger, restlessness, difficulty in concentrating (183), as well as in overall withdrawal scores (180, 184). Transdermal nicotine patches have been shown to significantly decrease cigarette craving (184–186). Recent data suggest an inverse relationship between withdrawal symptoms and serum nicotine and cotinine levels in abstinent smokers receiving nicotine patch therapy (187). This raises the possibility that a higher dose of transdermal nicotine may be necessary for the relief of withdrawal symptoms, particularly in heavier smokers (188–190). In addition to its therapeutic effect on withdrawal symptomatology, new findings from Cinciripini and colleagues (191) suggest that transdermal nicotine, when combined with behavior therapy, produces favorable concomitant changes in negative affect, coping, and self-efficacy. Presumably, by easing withdrawal discomfort, nicotine patch therapy facilitates the learning of skills to cope with urges and negative mood.

Recent reviews (153, 172, 173, 181) conclude that the nicotine patch more than doubles quit rates over those produced by placebo treatment. As with nicotine polacrilex, the highest rates of abstinence occur in studies involving intensive adjuvant behavioral counseling therapy (181). Unlike nicotine gum, when combined with low-intensity nonpharmacological interventions, transdermal nicotine therapy is effective (192–195). In one study in a general-practice setting, long-term abstinence rates (at two years) were significantly higher in the nicotine (12%) compared to the placebo (3%) groups (196). Although absolute rates of quitting are lower when the nicotine patch is combined with low-intensity nonpharmacological support, this finding has important public health implications, since the majority of smokers do not undergo intensive smoking cessation counseling. The patch's clinical efficacy in the relative absence of intensive counseling may be attributable to good compliance, and thus, more stable nicotine serum levels.

In an effort to improve the relative efficacy of the patch, Jorenby and colleagues (190) tested the hypothesis that higher transdermal nicotine doses would produce more adequate replacement and better cessation rates than lower doses. Their results showed little evidence of superior treatment outcome in the 252 individuals receiving the 44-mg dose relative to the same size group of individuals receiving the 22-mg dose. The prediction that the 44-mg nicotine patch dose might be more effective with heavily dependent subjects was not substantiated. These findings stand in contrast to another recent study on high-dose nicotine patch therapy and smoking cessation. In this latter study, Dale and colleagues (188) found that achieving a greater percentage of nicotine replacement increases the efficacy of nicotine patch therapy. Although data from these studies allay concerns about potential nicotine toxicity, the clinical benefits of routinely using higher-dose nicotine patch therapy are debatable (197, 198). Smokers who fail with standard patch doses, however, may prove to be appropriate candidates for higher nicotine replacement doses (189).

A limitation of transdermal nicotine is its passive and slow system of administration. The fixed, as opposed to *ad libitum,* nature of patch treatment provides no means of responding to triggers or acute high-risk situations, or titration of dose for withdrawal relief. Consequently, the development of other systems has proceeded, along with combined treatments using the patch for steady administration of nicotine with a faster system for immediate relief.

NASAL SPRAY

The recent development of nasal administration systems for nicotine replacement is based on the rationale that a faster-acting preparation might speed relief of withdrawal and thus be of significant relevance in smoking cessation. As shown in Figure 25.2, the nasal spray has a faster rising time compared to other non-cigarette delivery systems. Blood concentrations achieved with ad libitum use of nicotine administered nasally appear to be moderate, and in the same range as 2 mg nicotine gum and low-to-moderate dose patches (58). The prescribed nicotine nasal spray (NNS) device consists of a small bottle fitted for insertion into the nostril. Pressing a pump mechanism releases a fine mist of nicotine 0.5 mg, prepared in a water-based, pH buffered solution. One metered dose consists of 2 squirts (one in each nostril) for a total of 1.0 mg. The average frequency of spray use ranges from 13 to 20 doses per day (58, 199). The NNS is easier to use than the gum, and, in contrast to the more passive administration system of the patch, provides the user with more flexible, self control dosing for withdrawal and craving relief.

Findings from early placebo-controlled clinical trials lend support to the safety and efficacy of NNS as an alternative replacement therapy for smoking cessation. In 1992, Sutherland et al. (199) published 1-year validated abstinence rates of 26% in the active spray group, compared with 10% in the placebo group. In this study, NNS was offered as an adjunct to group treatment. In a later study using a similar design, Hjalmarson et al. (200) also reported significant differences in active (34%) versus placebo (18%) success rates at one year. More recent findings reported by Schneider et al. (201) provide further support of the efficacy and acceptability of NNS. This third trial used a stricter "no-slips" outcome criteria, and found that NNS significantly enhanced success rates over follow-up time points, including at one year

(18% versus 8%). The most commonly reported adverse effects with NNS use include nasal irritation, throat irritation, sneezing, runny nose, watery eyes, and coughing. While these symptoms appear to be well-tolerated and transient in clinical trials, they may deter compliance in general practice settings.

NICOTINE INHALER

The nicotine inhaler originated from the earlier development of a "less harmful", noncombustible cigarette called Favor (202) (see "Harm Reduction" section later in this chapter). The inhaler, or mouthpiece, produces slower and lower plasma nicotine levels compared to cigarettes, and allows for flexible *ad libitum* dosing (58, 203) (see Figure 25.2). Unlike other NRT systems, the mouthpiece allows for some of the oral and handling reinforcement associated with cigarette smoking. Some have proposed that the sensory stimulation effects (e.g., throat irritation) may actually assist with cessation (204, 205). Each mouthpiece contains a 10 mg porous plug of nicotine, and delivers up to 400 puffs of vaporized nicotine. Absorption of nicotine from the inhaler is primarily buccal rather than pulmonary (206). The amount of nicotine obtained depends on number of puffs and environmental temperature. At room temperature, one puff delivers up to 13 micrograms of nicotine. It takes at least 80 puffs to obtain the nicotine delivery typically provided by one cigarette (154, 207). In clinical trials subjects are generally instructed to puff frequently, using at least 4 inhalers per day at a rate of about 100 puffs per use (e.g., 208).

Double-blind controlled trials of the safety and efficacy of the inhaler have been encouraging (208–210). Tønnesen et al. (210) found higher rates of abstinence in the first year for the active inhaler group (15%) compared with the placebo inhaler group (5%). In the other two trials, results were significant in early cessation but not at one year (208, 209). Thus far, the inhaler appears to be safe and effective for early cessation. The unique oral, handling, and other sensory characteristics of the inhaler may enhance its appeal to certain types of smokers (207). Comparative studies among all NRT systems (gum, patch, nasal spray, and inhaler) are needed in order to evaluate their potential differential effectiveness with specific subgroups of smokers.

SUMMARY

Currently available forms of NRT are effective in smoking cesssation. Comparisons between the relative effectiveness of the different forms of NRT can only be made indirectly at present. Figure 25.3 shows the median of the distributions of abstinence rates reported in 61 published studies of NRT (41 gum, 21 patch, 3 nasal spray, and 3 inhaler). Most of the studies were randomized, controlled comparisons of NRT versus placebo; however, there was considerable variation in methodological characteristics (e.g., duration of use, dose, follow-up period, allowances for slips). With these caveats in mind, the results generally suggest that across all four types of NRT, median abstinence levels decline over time, from about 40% at 3 months to 22% at 12 months. In addition, the level of nonpharmacological support appears to affect outcome (Fig. 25.3B), with higher abstinence rates found in gum and patch studies involving a high level of support (e.g., formal multisession smoking programs) compared to low support (e.g., brief advice, self-help). This finding is consistent with other reviews (153, 172).

Applications of Nicotine Replacement Therapies: Further Considerations

INDIVIDUALIZATION OF NRT

The previous sections clearly indicate that each of the different nicotine replacement delivery systems is safe and effective, especially when used with behavioral therapy. Consequently, clinicians and patients have more options than ever before when it comes to selecting the most appropriate replacement formulation. Efforts to individualize nicotine replacement therapies based on specific patient characteristics might lead to improved efficacy (154). For example, heavily dependent smokers seem to respond better to

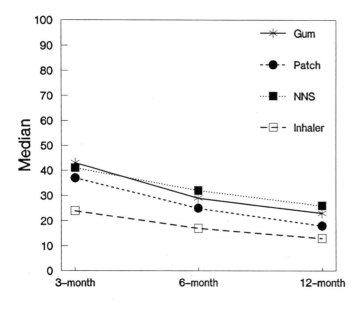

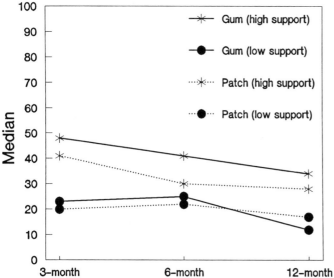

Figure 25.3. Median abstinence levels across nicotine replacement therapy studies. Data based on the following studies: gum (165, 175, 176, 178, 211–247); patch (179, 180, 182, 184, 185, 190–195, 248–257); nasal spray (199–201); inhaler (208–210).

higher doses of nicotine replacement therapy (175, 177, 239). According to Sachs (177), the 4-mg dose of nicotine polacrilex should be used as an initial treatment for high-dependent smokers, defined according to FTQ score ($\geq$ 7) and baseline carbon monoxide level ($>$ 15 ppm). Other individual differences to consider include past treatment success and failure experiences. Having a history of poor compliance with the more acute systems may be an indicator for use of once-a-day dosing nicotine patch. On the other hand, the faster acting systems may be critical for smokers who need to titrate dose or satisfy oral-handling needs previously associated with smoking. As discussed in the next section, combination nicotine therapy may offer an effective patient-to-treatment matching approach.

COMBINING NRT

The potential efficacy of combining nicotine replacement products has been the focus of recent study. For example, mutual advantages might result from combining two preparations with dissimilar pharmacokinetic profiles (e.g., rapid and slow delivery systems). Smokers might need both a self-dos-

ing, fast-acting system, such as NNS or nicotine gum, to respond to acute, high-risk craving situations, as well as a slow, steady system, such as the patch, to maintain plasma nicotine concentrations sufficient for relief of withdrawal (258, 259). Tentative conclusions drawn from two recent studies suggest that combining the transdermal system with nicotine gum is more effective in reducing withdrawal (260) and increasing abstinence rates (261, 262) than either treatment alone. Further trials are needed to determine whether the beneficial effects are attributable to the higher doses of nicotine produced by the two therapies, or to their combined, complementary mechanisms of action (58, 258). The therapeutic effects of nicotine medications in combination with other non-nicotine agents have been evaluated in a few recent studies. For example, the combined administration of nicotine replacement and nicotinic blockade (with the antagonist mecamylamine) may attenuate the rewarding effects of cigarettes smoking more than the same doses of nicotine or mecamylamine alone (263). The question of whether nicotine medications can interact effectively with other medications to maximize treatment outcome is the focus of other ongoing studies. In addition to concurrent use of different forms of NRT, Henningfield (154) has proposed "sequential" use whereby people who have achieved abstinence with the patch then use another NRT such as gum occasionally or as needed to avoid relapse.

OTHER THERAPEUTIC USES OF NICOTINE

Nicotine delivery systems discussed thus far are distinguishable from cigarette smoking or tobacco use in that they do not expose the individual to carbon monoxide, tars, or any of the other harmful carcinogenic elements found in tobacco. There is growing interest in the possibility that nicotine, delivered in this safer, noncontaminated form, has therapeutic applications per se (264–266). Small scale, preliminary studies have examined the potential value of nicotine as a pharmaceutical agent in the treatment of Alzheimer's disease (122–124, 267), Parkinson's disease (268–271), ulcerative colitis (272–275), Tourette's syndrome (276, 277), and sleep-disordered breathing (278). Much of this work has been prompted by clinical observations that certain diseases affect nonsmokers more than smokers (e.g., ulcerative colitis, Parkinson's), or by neurological discoveries of nicotinic receptor function (e.g., Alzheimer's disease). Importantly, there is little, if any, evidence of the development of dependence in the therapeutic use of nicotine in nonsmokers at dosing levels which appear to be adequate to provide therapeutic benefit (264). Data on the safety and long-term health effects of nicotine treatment would help determine the absolute benefit of replacement medications for nonsmoking indications.

OVER-THE-COUNTER USE OF NRT

The development of nicotine replacement therapy over-the-counter (OTC) represents a substantial paradigm shift in smoking cessation therapy in the United States. The increased availability of these smoking cessation products is likely to facilitate quitting behavior among more smokers (279), since the majority of smokers prefer to quit on their own, thus avoiding the cost and inconvenience of treatment by a physician. This expected increase in quitting attempts, however, may not translate into high success rates per quit attempt. One potential concern related to OTC nicotine is the lack of provision of supportive, behaviorally-based therapy. As already mentioned, the efficacy of replacement therapies is significantly enhanced (doubled) when prescribed within the context of nonpharmacological support (153). Another concern with OTC nicotine is its potential for abuse, including nontherapeutic use. Abuse liability tests in smokers clearly indicate that cigarettes are more reinforcing and have greater abuse potential than the gum (156), patch (280), spray, and inhaler (281).

TREATMENT DEPENDENCE ON NRT

All nicotine medications have the potential to sustain tolerance and physical dependence (154). NRT does not generally lead to continued, long-term use beyond recommendation (also referred to as *dependence or addiction*); however, some people who achieve tobacco abstinence using NRT are either unable or unwilling to discontinue NRT use. According to Hughes (62), the probability of treatment dependence increases to the extent that the treatment system produces rapid onset of action, high blood nicotine levels, few side effects, and high frequency of use. Transdermal nicotine, with its slower onset of action, has very little likelihood of treatment dependence, compared to more rapid delivery systems, such as the gum or NNS. Indeed, there have been no reports of transdermal nicotine use beyond recommended treatment duration. Continued nicotine dependence has been studied most in patients using 2-mg nicotine polacrilex. Findings from a randomized, double-blind study revealed a higher incidence of long-term (10-month) postcessation use among abstinent smokers receiving nicotine gum (17%), compared to abstinent smokers receiving placebo gum (6%) (282). Withdrawal symptoms have been observed in long-term users receiving abrupt placebo substitution (283, 284); however, gradual tapering approaches seem to effectively abate withdrawal (285, 286). For NNS, the rate of long-term (one year) use among successful subjects was 43% in one study (199) and 38% in the other (200). In both studies NNS use was permitted to one year. Schneider et al. (201) found that limiting use of NNS to six months was sufficient for most subjects, and may be as effective as longer treatment durations.

Questions concerning the therapeutic utility of prolonged NRT use cannot be answered on the basis of available data. Little is known about the adequate duration of NRT use, or whether maintained use of NRT might offset high relapse rates. An important observation is that most long-term gum users are abstinent from smoking (285, 287). In addition, findings from one study suggest that heavier smokers with higher nicotine dependence scores need to use more gum for a longer duration than lighter, less-dependent smokers (287). The risks of long-term NRT use have not been thoroughly studied, but are considered to be much less than those associated with continued use of cigarettes. In addition to exposure to lower amounts of nicotine (285), NRTs eliminate the carcinogens and gases of cigarette smoke.

In summary, it remains to be seen whether NRT produces higher rates of treatment dependence and whether OTC access increases that further. Factors such as instructions, cost, and social acceptability are likely to influence the duration of NRT use. Varying the duration of the NRT regimen may be important in efforts to individualize treatment. For most nonprescription NRT products, the inclusion of specific dose tapering instructions might reduce problems associated with dependence and discontinuation (288).

Other Pharmacological Agents for Smoking Cessation

A host of other non-nicotine medications have been tested in smokers with varying degrees of success. These include agents hypothesized to (a) abate withdrawal, (b) treat associated psychopathology, (c) block the reinforcing effects of nicotine, and (d) make nicotine intake aversive. Although some of these appear promising, none have received consistent positive results from long-term trials.

Clonidine, a nonreceptor antagonist, has been reported to reduce withdrawal symptoms (289–292); however, its benefit in promoting smoking cessation is questionable (292, 293). Clonidine does, however, appear to be advantageous for a select group of smokers, i.e., women with a history of recurrent depression, multiple previous quit attempts, or a high level of nicotine dependence (293–295). Transdermal clonidine, compared to pill form, appears to be associated with less frequent dosing, more stable clonidine blood levels, fewer side effects (296), and better smoking cessation outcomes (297). In general, the effects of clonidine on smoking cessation, when positive, appear to be short-lived, with most smokers relapsing by 6 months (e.g., 293, 298, 299).

Anxiolytic and antidepressant medications were originally proposed as symptomatic treatments for the effects of nicotine administration and deprivation in smokers who claim to have specific "reasons for smoking", (e.g., reduce anxiety, regulate mood) (300, 301). Of the antianxiety agents investigated, buspirone has received the most attention (e.g., 302–308) yet results are inconclusive. In a double-blind, placebo-controlled trial (302), high-anxiety smokers who received buspirone and cognitive-behavioral treatment had significantly higher one-month abstinence rates (88%) compared to the placebo-treated high-anxiety smokers (61%). The abstinence advantage for the buspirone high-anxiety group relative to placebo high-anxiety disappeared, however, by 3-month follow-up. Schneider and colleagues (307) failed to find significant treatment effects per se, or in high versus low anxiety smokers, using a stratification procedure similar to Cinciripini. In this second study the investigators used a strict, "no slips" criteria for defining abstinence, which may explain the conflicting findings.

As with anxiolytics, the original rationale for using antidepressants was based on evidence that affective symptomatology related to nicotine withdrawal, if left untreated, may lead to relapse for certain smokers. More recent support for this treatment strategy comes from evidence of an association between cigarette smoking and major depression. A bidirectional relationship has been described such that each disorder (nicotine dependence and major depression) increases the odds for onset of the other (309, 310). Moreover, smokers with histories of major depression experience more depressive symptoms of withdrawal and have lower rates of quitting success than smokers without a history of depression (311–314). Surprisingly, there have been relatively few studies of antidepressants in smokers with a history of depression. Preliminary studies of doxepin in *unselected* groups of smokers were largely unsuccessful (315, 316). More recent focus has been on other agents, such as bupropion (317) and fluoxetine (318). In a randomized, placebo-controlled, double-blind study, Ferry and colleagues (317) showed significantly higher cessation rates in bupropion-treated depressed male smokers compared to placebo-treated smokers. In another preliminary study of 39 smokers with a past but not present depression, double-blind treatment with fluoxetine for 3 weeks prior to quitting smoking resulted in decreases in subsyndromal depressive symptoms (318). Whether fluoxetine has significant efficacy as an adjunct to smoking cessation in this select population of smokers remains to be seen.

As a nicotinic blocker, the antagonist mecamylamine has been shown to decrease smoking satisfaction, as well as many other physiological, behavioral, and reinforcing effects of nicotine (319–321). When administered alone to smokers, mecamylamine increases ad lib smoking behavior, presumably in an attempt to overcome blockade (322). Theoretically, long-term use of this blocking agent should lead to extinction; however, poor compliance and prohibitive side effects have hindered efforts to empirically validate this therapeutic strategy. Rose and colleagues (323) recently proposed a solution based on an agonist-antagonist treatment model. Co-administration of nicotine and mecamylamine may act in a complementary fashion to reduce the number of receptors available for activation by additional nicotine. Indeed, this research team (323) has shown that, in humans, the combination of nicotine and mecamylamine produces attenuation of smoking satisfaction and reduction of adverse side effects. In a randomized, double-blind, placebo-controlled clinical trial (n ° 48) the concurrent administration of oral mecamylamine with transdermal nicotine produced higher rates of continuous abstinence compared to patch treatment alone (at 12 months, 37.5% versus 4.2%, respectively) (323). Other trials of this novel combination treatment are under way.

Agents such as silver nitrate work by making drug use cause unpleasant effects. When silver nitrate combines with smokers' saliva, it produces silver sulfide, which produces a bad taste in the mouth. This and other aversive medications suffer from compliance problems that interfere with effective use (300, 324). For these reasons, silver nitrate was recently removed from the market as an over-the-counter product for smoking cessation.

Harm Reduction and the Concept of the "Safer Cigarette"

Efforts to develop a less hazardous cigarette began with the evolution of filters and low tar/nicotine smokes as a means of preventing smoker's cough and other adverse effects related to the inhalation of toxins in tobacco smoke (325). Filters, if properly used, could reduce nicotine and tar delivery by diluting smoke with air. However, smokers, unlike smoking machines, compensate by adjusting their smoking behavior (e.g., increasing puff volume, depth of inhalation) or blocking the filter vents (326). In practice, use of filtered cigarettes and "so-called" low yield cigarettes have led to little, if any, reduction of toxicological effects (327, 328) or health risks (3, 329–331).

Moreover, a majority of smokers reject ultra-low-yield cigarettes (1 mg tar) as unsatisfying (327).

Subsequent efforts to develop a less harmful cigarette were based on the logic of lowering tar to nicotine ratios (332). In other words, because nicotine intake is essential to smokers' satisfaction and nicotine is less harmful than other components in the smoke, a reasonable approach is to lower tar but maintain, or enhance, nicotine yields. An alternative approach is to replace cigarettes with nicotine delivery devices that eliminate *all* burned constituents of tobacco, as represented by the Favor device (202), once marketed as a smoke-free alternative. Favor resembled a cigarette in shape and size, but contained none of the harmful products of combustion (202). Although the product was poorly accepted as an alternative to cigarettes, it provided the basis for development of the nicotine inhaler as a smoking cessation treatment (described earlier).

R. J. Reynolds introduced a virtually tar-free cigarette (Premier) that heated, rather than burned tobacco. Smoke particles were comprised mainly of glycerol and water, rather than tar (333). Tests of glycerol particle cigarettes found evidence of substantial (90%) tar reduction, but problematic acceptability, because of low nicotine yield and poor taste (333). The newest device, the Eclipse, developed by R. J. Reynolds, "primarily heats tobacco instead of burning it" (RJR Tobacco Company). Preliminary data, not yet available, was presented at a meeting at Duke University, cosponsored by Rose and Levin (334) and RJR. Eclipse is purported to reduce tar, and is believed to be more acceptable, but problems remain, e.g., high CO levels (Benowitz, personal communication). Nicotine levels produced with this product have yet to be determined.

The question of whether less harmful cigarettes will discourage cessation attempts among smokers who would otherwise quit, or permit a safer alternative for chronic smokers who absolutely cannot quit, must be addressed. It is also not known whether a safer cigarette will substantially reduce health risks. Longitudinal studies are needed in order to arrive at cost-benefit decisions concerning the long-term health value of these products.

Behavioral Treatments

Behavioral treatment for smoking has become commonplace (335). Over the past decade this approach has spread from primarily clinic-based, formal smoking cessation programs to applications in community and public health settings (336). Clinic-based behavioral technologies have also been incorporated into various self-help approaches. However, the past decade has witnessed a relative slowdown in the development of new behavioral methods, especially in comparison to pharmacological advances. As noted by Shiffman (336), this trend seems to parallel the lack of improvement in treatment outcomes over the years.

Although a review of the many behavioral techniques developed and tested over the years is beyond the scope of this chapter (see 335, 337, 338), some of the more common methods deserve comment. These include reduced smoking and nicotine fading, contingency management, relapse prevention, and cue exposure. In practice, these and other elements of treatment are typically combined in a multicomponent program (339). Most formal smoking cessation programs consist of multiple treatment sessions, delivered in a group setting by trained facilitators (340–342). Whereas the success of multicomponent treatment programs is generally well-established (335), much less is known about the relative effectiveness of each component. With few exceptions, most of the studies described in this section were published prior to 1990, again reflecting a decline in the development of new behavioral treatments (336), along with a marked shift toward integrating behavioral therapies with medications in the treatment of tobacco dependence (20, 153).

The procedure of *reduced smoking* involves the gradual tapering of cigarette consumption prior to cessation, so as to ameliorate withdrawal discomfort. After reducing to a target level (e.g., 50% of initial cigarette consumption) abrupt cessation is recommended (343). In *nicotine fading*, smokers are instructed to systematically switch to lower nicotine and tar brands of cigarettes (344). Nicotine fading procedures have been shown to reduce nicotine intake (345, 346); however, treatment findings have been mixed (344, 347–349). When offered in the context of a multicomponent intervention,

good outcomes have been reported (340). In sum, nicotine fading is a simple procedure, with high face-validity and acceptability. Behavioral fading and reduction approaches may be useful alternatives for reducing withdrawal and enhancing success in cases where pharmacological treatments are contraindicated (e.g., pregnant women, patients with active cardiovascular disease). In all applications, however, these interventions should be used to prepare the smoker for *cessation,* not as a recommendation to reduce to a "safe" level of smoking. Finally, the benefits of brand switching may be offset by smokers who compensate for reduced nicotine yields by altering their smoking topography (e.g., deeper inhalations, more frequent puffs).

Scheduled smoking is a variation of reduced smoking and involves progressively increasing the intercigarette interval and reducing smoking frequency. This reduction procedure was first demonstrated by Shapiro (350), who used a portable signaling device to cue subjects to smoke at random times of decreasing frequency. In a recent study by Cinciripini et al., (351), higher one-year abstinence rates were found in subjects treated according to a scheduled reduced smoking method, compared to subjects receiving the nonscheduled reduced smoking method (i.e., gradual reduction with no specific changes in the intercigarette interval). The authors suggest that imposing a fixed smoking schedule may facilitate cessation by breaking the smoker's well-established pattern of ad-lib nicotine self-administration and promoting the use of coping and urge management skills. Moreover, scheduled smoking gives the patient an opportunity to adapt to the progressively longer time intervals between cigarettes, thereby decreasing withdrawal symptoms following cessation (351).

In *contingency management,* contracted rewards or punishments are delivered upon performance of the targeted behavior (e.g., maintained abstinence). These methods are generally designed to enhance motivation to not smoke or remain in treatment. Several early studies showed that refunding monetary deposits contingent upon abstinence was effective (352–354), at least in the short term. Larger payment amounts appear to promote longer periods of abstinence (355). Another method of contingency management involves the delivery of reinforcement for reduced carbon monoxide (CO) levels. Breath CO levels provide an indication of smoke exposure and generally correlate with self-reported number of cigarettes smoked per day (356). In addition to assessing smoking status, CO readings can serve as motivational feedback to patients in treatment for smoking cessation. Beyond feedback, however, CO readings have been effectively used as a target for reinforcement interventions. Stitzer and colleagues (357–359) demonstrated that smokers were more likely to achieve CO reduction targets when contingent monetary payments were available (357), and that the amount of smoking behavior change was related in an orderly way to the amount of payment available (358, 359). As a simple, quick, and transportable device, CO-based reinforcement procedures have applicability across diversity of settings and populations, including employees at a worksite (360, 361) to methadone maintenance patients in a drug treatment program (362, 363).

The *relapse prevention* (RP) treatment model (364) emphasizes the role of situational variables and coping responses in relation to relapse versus abstinence. Theoretically, successful coping decreases the probability of relapse by increasing self-efficacy. Support for the theoretical interrelationship between coping, self-efficacy, and relapse exists (e.g., 342, 365–374). For example, it is generally accepted that coping in terms of either behavioral and/or cognitive responses are equally effective in preventing relapse, and that treatment approaches should teach ex-smokers a broad repertoire of coping responses and to overcome inhibitions in the use of such coping responses (373). In addition, the ex-smoker must be taught skills for handling lapses to avoid self-defeating beliefs, feelings, and expectations that may lead to a relapse (364). The notion that lapses associated with negative attributional and emotional reactions increase the probability of relapse, referred to as the Abstinence Violation Effect, has received some empirical support (375–377).

Given its theoretical support, it is surprising that the treatment effects of RP have been modest, at best (e.g., 378–381). A recent review of controlled clinical trials shows evidence for the effectiveness of RP compared to no-treatment controls, but weaker evidence of RP's superiority over discussion controls or other active treatments (382). A study by Stevens and Hollis

(342) is often cited as yielding the most positive findings for RP training. Importantly, these investigators evaluated an RP intervention that provided individually tailored coping skills training during postcessation maintenance. Their findings support the usefulness of the relapse prevention model in applications where sufficient time is spent having subjects successfully develop and rehearse appropriate coping strategies. Other studies have shown that the combination of RP and nicotine replacement therapy improves abstinence rates over either treatment used alone (233, 383). Finally, there is limited but intriguing evidence from at least one study to suggest that RP training may be most efficacious among certain subgroups of smokers. Curry et al. (379) found that women were more likely to benefit from the RP program than from a more traditional abstinence program, whereas men showed the opposite pattern of outcome.

Cue exposure techniques stem from principles of classical conditioning in relation to drug addiction. Environmental cues become associated with drug use (cigarette smoking) and become conditioned stimuli, capable of eliciting conditioned responses (e.g., craving) that lead to drug seeking behavior. The elicitation of conditioned responses to discriminant cues for smoking has been demonstrated in many human experimental studies (e.g., 149, 384–389), and has been shown to be predictive of treatment progress and relapse (152, 384, 390). In the clinic setting, however, application of extinction-based procedures in smoking cessation has been modest and mostly disappointing. In an early study, Corty and McFall (391) showed that relevant smoking cues could be used to elicit urges, and, by preventing smoking, the conditioned responses diminished, but did not improve cessation outcome. Future research should explore various parameters of cue exposure (e.g., saliency, duration, timing, and cognitive mediating factors), so that mechanisms underlying an extinction treatment approach are better understood.

In summary, the degree to which each of the behavioral techniques described in this section is essential to success in quitting smoking is difficult to determine. Most programs offered today contain one or more of these treatment components. Given that nicotine dependence is a multi-faceted disorder, involving biological, social, behavioral, and psychological factors, it is reasonable to assume that a successful treatment must target as many of these factors as possible. An advantage of multicomponent treatment programs is that it allows participants to select options from a menu of choices, or tailor treatment to their own needs (392).

Less Intensive Interventions

Intensive clinic-based treatment programs have been credited with providing the necessary setting for the development and testing of new smoking cessation techniques. Indeed, the success of formal clinic programs largely affects the direction of public health smoking-control programs (336). Most smokers, however, do not have the interest, need, or resources to seek formal smoking cessation treatment (153, 393). Moreover, such programs are not always readily available or accessible to smokers. It has been suggested that less intensive interventions be tried first, before offering more costly, clinic-based programs (339). Not only does this "stepped-care" model approach make sense from a large-scale, cost-effectiveness perspective, it provides an organizing framework for the delivery of smoking cessation interventions across a range of professionals and modalities (394).

The recently published *Smoking Cessation Clinical Guideline* (395) offers key recommendations for increasing the role of primary care clinicians (e.g., physicians, nurses, respiratory therapists) in assisting patients who smoke. Most health care professionals have the opportunity to interact with smokers and convey a powerful and motivational message about smoking cessation (396). At a minimum, primary care clinicians should systematically identify all smokers, strongly advise smokers to quit, and determine the patients' willingness to make a quit attempt. It is also recommended (395) that assistance be given to those patients who are willing to make a quit attempt, such as setting a quit date, explaining nicotine replacement therapy, providing self-help materials, problem-solving advice, and social support. Patients not willing to set a quit date should receive motivational intervention (e.g., reviewing the benefits of quitting) to promote subsequent quit at-

tempts. Finally, follow-up contacts to re-assess smoking status should be scheduled with all patients. Relapses should be carefully reviewed as a learning experience, rather than a sign of failure. Recommitment to abstinence, and/or referral to a more intensive program, should be considered.

Smoking and Other Addictions

Tobacco dependence is common among users of other drugs, with smoking prevalence ranging from 85% to 100% in abusers of alcohol, opioids, and cocaine (397–399). Not only do alcoholic patients tend to smoke more heavily than their smoking, nonalcoholic counterparts (397, 400, 401), they are also less likely to achieve abstinence from cigarettes, even though the number of attempts to stop is the same in both groups (398, 402). Several studies report a significant positive correlation between degree of alcohol dependence and tobacco dependence (398, 403–406).

The observed correlation between cigarette smoking and other drug use has been extended by laboratory studies demonstrating direct, dose-dependent relationships between these variables. Acute administration of ethanol (407, 408), heroin (409), psychomotor stimulants (410, 411), and sedatives (412) have produced increases in rates of cigarette smoking. In both laboratory and clinic setting, the administration of methadone results in substantial, dose-related changes in rates of cigarette smoking by methadone-maintained smokers (413, 414).

Despite the fact that nicotine has been and continues to be one of the most common drugs of dependence among patients with alcohol and drug problems, very little is known about optimal treatments for the reduction and cessation of tobacco use in these dually dependent patients. In the past, substance abuse programs have been reluctant to intervene on smoking due to presumed negative effects. Current evidence dispels these myths that have kept smoking interventions and other substance abuse programs separate. Several survey studies have reported an overwhelming favorable response to implementing concurrent intervention for nicotine and other substance dependence (415–417). Data indicate that smoking cessation programs can be delivered within the context of alcohol treatment without negative consequences (417–420). More recently, Hurt and colleagues (421) published findings from a prospective, nonrandomized, controlled trial on the effect of treating nicotine dependence in smokers undergoing inpatient treatment from other addictions. At the time of hospital discharge, 21.6% of the smoking intervention group and 10% of the control group were not smoking. At one year, confirmed smoking cessation rates differed significantly between the intervention group (11.8%) and the control group (0.0%). These initial studies point to the feasibility and promising benefits of treating cigarette smoking in the context of alcohol and drug treatment.

Tobacco-related diseases are the leading cause of death in patients previously treated for alcoholism and/or other non-nicotine drug dependence (422). The time has come to direct smoking treatment research to this high-risk group of smokers. Future studies must determine if existing behavioral and pharmacological interventions, tested extensively in the general smoking population, prove to be equally effective in patients with other chemical dependencies.

SUMMARY

Few drugs have been as thoroughly researched as nicotine. As noted by the former Surgeon General Antonia Novello, "smoking represents the most extensively documented cause of disease ever investigated in the history of biomedical research" (18). The psychopharmacological literature provides unequivocal evidence that nicotine is the critical abuse-producing agent in tobacco use, similar to the role of ethanol in alcoholic beverage consumption, or cocaine in coca leaf use (423). These and other discoveries about the nature of nicotine dependence have been used to advance treatment development, particularly pharmacological approaches. Nicotine itself, in the form of replacement therapy, has become the most widely used pharmacotherapy for tobacco dependence. The beneficial effects of nicotine medications are generally enhanced when used in combination with behavioral treatment. Newer nicotine formulations, as well as non-nicotine agents and medication combinations, have received considerable attention over the last several years. Relatively less attention has been paid to understanding and treating nicotine dependence in special high risk groups of smokers, i.e., patients with other addictive disorders, psychiatric comorbidity, medical disorders. Improved smoking cessation and prevention programs are needed to reverse trends that show an upward surge in smoking prevalence and tobacco-related disease among certain minority populations (424). Continued investigation of the potential therapeutic value of nicotine for specific diseases will be part of the research agenda for the next decade. Nicotine delivery systems can be used to better define the mechanisms of disease, drug actions, and prospects for clinically useful applications.

Acknowledgments. *This research was supported in part by a grant from the National Institute on Drug Abuse to Dr. Schmitz (R01 DA08888), and by the Research Service of the West Los Angeles Veterans Affairs Medical Center (VA Merit Review Awards of Drs. Schneider and Jarvik). We thank Jack Henningfield for his helpful comments on an earlier version of the manuscript.*

References

1. U.S. Centers for Disease Control and Prevention. Preventing tobacco use among young people: a report of the Surgeon General. MMWR 1994;43(RR-4):1–10.
2. U.S. Centers for Disease Control and Prevention. Cigarette smoking among adults—United States, 1993. MMWR 1994;43:925–929.
3. U.S. Department of Health and Human Services. Reducing the health consequences of smoking: 25 years of progress: A report of the surgeon general. (DHHS Publication no. (CDC) 89–8411). U.S. Department of Health and Human Services, Public Health Service, Centers for Disease Control, Center for Health Promotion and Education, Office on Smoking and Health, 1989.
4. U.S. Centers for Disease Control and Prevention. Cigarette smoking among adults—United States. MMWR 1992;41:354–355.
5. Fiore MC, Novotny TE, Pierce JP, Hatziandreu EJ, Patel KM, Davis RM. Trends in cigarette smoking in the United States. The changing influence of gender and race. JAMA 1989; 261:49–55.
6. Fiore MC, Newcomb P, McBride P. Natural history and epidemiology of tobacco use and addiction. In: Orleans CT, Slade J, eds. Nicotine addiction: principles and management. New York: Oxford University Press, 1993:245–261.
7. Gritz ER, Ksir C, McCarthy WJ. Smokeless tobacco use in the United States: past and future trends. Ann Behav Med 1985;7:24–27.
8. U.S. Department of Health and Human Services. The health consequences of using smokeless tobacco: a report of the Advisory Committee to the Surgeon General. (NIH Publication no. 86–2874), U.S. Department of Health and Human Services, Public Health Service, 1986.
9. Marcus AC, Crane LA, Shopland DR, Lynn WR. Use of smokeless tobacco in the United States: Recent estimates from the Current Population Survey. Natl Cancer Inst Monogr 1989; 8:17–23.
10. Severson HH, Lichtenstein E, Gallison C. A pinch or a pouch instead of a puff? Implications of chewing tobacco for addictive processes. Bull Soc Psychol Addict Behav 1985;4:85–92.
11. Hatsukami DK, Gust SW, Keenan RM. Physiologic and subjective changes from smokeless tobacco withdrawal. Clin Pharmacol Ther 1987; 41:103–107.
12. Hatsukami D, Anton D, Keenan R, Callies A. Smokeless tobacco abstinence effects and nicotine gum dose. Psychopharmacology 1992;106: 60–66.
13. Benowitz NL. Nicotine and smokeless tobacco. CA Cancer J Clin 1988;38:244–247.
14. U.S. Centers for Disease Control and Prevention. Cigarette smoking attributable mortality and years of potential life lost—United States, 1993. MMWR 1993;42:645–649.
15. U.S. Department of Health and Human Services. The health consequences of smoking: chronic obstructive lung disease. A report of the Surgeon General. (DHHS Publication no. 84–50205). U.S. Department of Health and Human Services, Public Health Service, 1984.
16. American Cancer Society. Cancer facts and figures—1993. New York: American Cancer Society 1993.
17. U.S. Department of Health and Human Services. The health consequences of smoking: cancer. A report of the Surgeon General. (DHHS Publication no. 82–50179). U.S. Department of Health and Human Services, Public Health Service, 1982.
18. U.S. Department of Health and Human Services. The health benefits of smoking cessation: a report of the Surgeon General (DHHS Publication no. CDC 90–8416). U.S. Department of Health and Human Services, Public Health Service, 1990.
19. U.S. Environmental Protection Agency. Respiratory health effects of passive smoking: lung cancer and other disorders. Washington, DC: Office of Health and Environmental Assessment, 1992.
20. U.S. Department of Health and Human Services. The health consequences of smoking: nicotine addiction: a report of the Surgeon General (DHHS Publication no. CDC 88–8406). U.S. Department of Health and Human Services, Public Health Service, 1988.
21. Benowitz NL. Pharmacologic aspects of cigarette smoking and nicotine addiction. N Engl J Med 1988;319:1318–1330.
22. Fagerström KO, Säwe U. The pathophysiology of nicotine dependence: treatment options and the cardiovascular safety of nicotine. Cardiovascular Risk Factors 1996;6:135–143.
23. Murray RP, Bailey WC, Daniels K, Bjornson WM, Kurnow K, Connett JE, et al. Safety of nicotine polacrilex gum used by participants in the Lung Health Study. Chest 1996;108: 438–445.
24. Transdermal Nicotine Study Group. Nicotine replacement therapy for patients with coronary artery disease. Arch Intern Med 1994;154: 989–995.
25. Morosco GJ, Nightingale TE, Frasinel C, Goeringer GC. Pancreatic elastase activation as a possible indicator of the relative hazard of different cigarettes. J Toxicol Environ Health 1981;8:89–94.
26. Yamatake Y, Sasagawa S, Yanaura S. Drug responses of canine trachea, bronchus and bronchiole. Chem Pharm Bull 1978;26:318–320.
27. Lehtovirta P, Forss M. The acute effect of smoking on intervillous blood flow of the placenta. Br J Obstet Gynaecol 1978;85:729–731.
28. Philipp K, Pateisky N, Endler M. Effects of smoking on uteroplacental blood flow. Gynecol Obstet Invest 1984;17:179–182.
29. Lehtovirta P, Forss M, Rauramo I, Kariniemi V. Acute effects of nicotine on fetal heart rate variability. Br J Obstet Gynaecol 1983;90:710–715.
30. Manning FA, Feyerabend C. Cigarette smoking and fetal breathing movements. Br J Obstet Gynaecol 1976;83:262–270.
31. Navarro HA, Seidler FJ, Whitmore WL, Slotkin TA. Prenatal exposure to nicotine via maternal infusions: effects on development of catecholamine systems. J Pharmacol Exp Ther 1988; 244:940–944.
32. Navarro HA, Seidler FJ, Eylers JP, et al. Effects of prenatal nicotine exposure on development of central and peripheral cholinergic neurotransmitter systems: evidence of cholinergic trophic influences in developing brain. J Pharmacol Exp Ther 1989;251:894–900.
33. Bruner JP, Forouzan I. Smoking and bucally administered nicotine: acute effects on uterine and umbilical artery Doppler velocity waveforms. J Reprod Med 1991;36:435–440.
34. Lindblad A, Marsal K, Andersson KE. Effect of nicotine on human fetal blood flow. Obstet Gynecol 1988;72:371–382.
35. Lindblad A, Marsal K. Influence of nicotine chewing gum on fetal blood flow. J Perinat Med 1987;15:13–19.
36. Oncken CA, Hatsukami DK, Lupo VR, Lando HA, Gibeau LM, Hansen RJ. Effects of short-term use of nicotine gum in pregnant smokers. Clin Pharmacol Ther 1996;59:654–661.
37. Aberg A, Bergstrand R, Johnansson S, Ulvenstan G, Vedin A, Wedd A, Wilhelmsen L. Cessation of smoking after myocardial infarction: effects of mortality after 10 years. Br Heart J 1983;49:416–422.
38. Daly LE, Mulcahy R, Graham LM, Hickey N. Long-term effect on mortality of stopping smoking after unstable angina and myocardial infarction. Br Med J 1983;287:324–326.
39. Mulcahy R. Influence of cigarette smoking on morbidity and mortality after myocardial infarction. Br Heart J 1983;49:410–415.
40. Salonen JT. Stopping smoking and long-term mortality after acute myocardial infarction. Br Heart J 1980;43:463–469.
41. Vliestra RE, Kronmal RA, Oberman A, Frye RL, Killip T III. Effect of cigarette smoking on survival of patients with angiographically documented coronary artery disease. Report from the CASS registry. JAMA 1986;255:1023–1027.
42. The ICD-10 classification of mental and behavioral disorders. Geneva, Switzerland: World Health Organization, 1992.
43. American Psychiatric Association. Diagnostic and statistical manual of mental disorders. 4th edition. Washington, DC: American Psychiatric Press, 1994.
44. Smoking and health: report of the Advisory Committee to the Surgeon General of the Public Health Service. Washington, DC: U.S. Department of Health, Education and Welfare, 1964.
45. Robinson JH, Pritchard WS. The role of nicotine in tobacco use. Psychopharmacology 1992;108: 397–407.
46. Warburton DM. Is nicotine use an addiction? Psychologist: Bull Br Psychol Soc 1989;4: 166–170.
47. Stolerman IP, Jarvis MJ. The scientific case that nicotine is addictive. Psychopharmacology 1995;117:2–10.
48. Jarvik ME, Schneider NG. Nicotine. In: Lowinson JH, Ruiz P, Millman RB, eds. Substance

abuse: a comprehensive textbook. 2nd edition. Baltimore: Williams & Wilkins, 1992.

49. Benowitz NL, Hall SM, Herning RI, Jacob P III, Jones RT, Osman AL. Smokers of low-yield cigarettes do not consume nicotine. N Engl J Med 1983;309:139–142.

50. Henningfield JE, Kozlowski LT, Benowitz NL. A proposal to develop meaningful labeling for cigarettes. JAMA 1994;272:312–314.

51. Benowitz NL, Jacob P, Denaro C, Jenkins R. Stable isotope studies of nicotine kinetics and bioavailability. Clin Pharmacol Ther 1991;49: 270–277.

52. Benowitz NL. Clinical pharmacology of inhaled drugs of abuse: implications in understanding nicotine dependence. NIDA Res Monogr 1990; 99:12.

53. Benowitz NL. Cigarette smoking and nicotine addiction. Med Clin North Am 1992;76: 415–437.

54. Benowitz NL, Jacob P. Nicotine and cotinine elimination pharmacokinetics in smokers and nonsmokers. Clin Pharmacol Ther 1993;53: 316–323.

55. Henningfield JE, Stapleton JM, Benowitz NL, Grayson RF, London ED. Higher levels of nicotine in arterial than in venous blood after cigarette smoking. Drug Alcohol Depend 1990;33: 23–29.

56. Henningfield JE, Radzius A, Cooper TM, Clayton RC. Drinking coffee and carbonated beverages blocks absorption of nicotine from nicotine polacrilex gum. JAMA 1990;264:1560–1564.

57. Palmer KJ, Bucklet MM, Faulds D. Transdermal nicotine: a review of its pharmacodynamic and pharmacokinetic properties, and therapeutic efficacy as an aid to smoking cessation. Drugs 1992;44:498–529.

58. Schneider NG, Lunell E, Olmstead RE, Fagerstrom KO. Clinical pharmacokinetics of nasal nicotine delivery: a review and comparison to other nicotine systems. Clin Pharmacokinet 1996;31:65–80.

59. Benowitz NL. Nicotine replacement therapy: what has been accomplished—Can we do better? Drugs 1993;45:157–170.

60. Johansson CJ, Olsson P, Bende M, Carlsson T, Gunnarsson PO. Absolute bioavailability of nicotine applied to different nasal regions. Eur J Clin Pharmacol 1991;41:585–588.

61. Henningfield JE, Keenan RM. Nicotine delivery kinetics and abuse liability. J Consult Clin Psychol 1993;61:743–750.

62. Hughes JR. Dependence potential and abuse liability of nicotine replacement therapies. Biomed Pharmacother 1989;43:11–17.

63. Henningfield JE. Behavioral pharmacology of cigarette smoking. In: Thompson T, Dews PB, eds. Advances in behavioral pharmacology. New York: Academic Press, 1984;4:131–210.

64. West RJ, Russell MAH. Cardiovascular and subjective effects of smoking before and after 24 h of abstinence from cigarettes. Psychopharmacology 1987;92:118–121.

65. Gurling HMD, Grant S, Dangl J. The genetic and cultural transmission of alcohol use, alcoholism, cigarette smoking and coffee drinking: a review and an example using a log-linear cultural transmission model. Br J Addiction 1985; 80:269–279.

66. Pomerleau OF, Collins AC, Shiffman S, Pomerleau CS. Why some people smoke and others do not: new perspectives. J Consult Clin Psychol 1993;61:723–731.

67. Collins AC, Marks MJ. Progress towards the development of animal models of smoking-related behaviors. J Addict Dis 1991;10:109–126.

68. Pomerleau OF, Hariharan M, Pomerleau CS, Cameron OG, Guthrie SK. Differences between smokers and never-smokers in sensitivity to nicotine: a preliminary report. Addiction 1993; 88:113–118.

69. Benowitz NL, Kuyt F, Jacob P. Circadian blood nicotine concentrations during cigarette smoking. Clin Pharmacol Ther 1982;32:758–764.

70. Russell MAH. Nicotine and its control over smoking. In: Wonnacott S, Russell MAH, Stolerman JP, eds. Nicotine psychopharmacology: molecular, cellular and behavioral aspects. Oxford, England: Oxford University Press, 1990:374.

71. Schneider NG. Clinical signs and symptoms of withdrawal during smoking cessation. In: Future directions in nicotine replacement therapy: proceedings. Paris: Adis International, 1994.

72. Cherek DR, Bennett RH, Grabowski J. Human aggressive responding during acute tobacco abstinence: effects of nicotine and placebo gum. Psychopharmacology 1991;104:317–322.

73. Spiga R, Bennett RH, Schmitz J, Cherek DR. Effects of nicotine on cooperative responding among abstinent male smokers. Behavioural Pharmacology 1994;5:337–343.

74. Siegel S. Classical conditioning, drug tolerance and drug dependence. In: Smart RG, Glaser FB, Israel Y, Kalent H, Popham RE, Schmidt W, eds. Research advances in alcohol and drug problems. New York: Plenum Press, 1983;7: 207–246.

75. Tate JC, Stanton AL, Green SB, Schmitz JM, Le T, Marshall B. An experimental analysis of the role of expectancy in nicotine withdrawal. Psychol Addict Behav 1994;8:169–178.

76. Henningfield JE, Nemeth-Coslett R. Nicotine dependence: interface between tobacco and tobacco-related disease. Chest 1988;93:37S–55S.

77. Pickworth WB, Herning RI, Henningfield JE. Spontaneous EEG changes during tobacco abstinence and nicotine substitution in human volunteers. J Pharmacol Exp Ther 1989;251:976–982.

78. Snyder FR, Davis FC, Henningfield JE. The tobacco withdrawal syndrome: performance decrements assessed on a computerized test battery. Drug Alcohol Depend 1989;23:259–266.

79. Hughes JR, Gust SW, Skoog K, Keenan RM, Fenwick JW. Symptoms of tobacco withdrawal: a replication and extension. Arch Gen Psychiatry 1991;48:52–59.

80. Schneider NG, Jarvik ME, Forsythe AB. Nicotine versus placebo gum in the alleviation of withdrawal during smoking cessation. Addict Behav 1984;9:149–156.

81. Russell MAH, Feyerabend C. Cigarette smoking: a dependence on high-nicotine boli. Drug Metabol Rev 1978;80:29–57.

82. Abood LG, Banerjee S, Kanne DB. Sites, mechanisms, and structural characteristics of the brain's nicotine receptor. J Subst Abuse 1989; 1:259–271.

83. Stolerman IP, Mirza NR, Shoaib M. Nicotine psychopharmacology: addiction, cognition, and neuroadaptation. Med Res Rev 1995;15:47–72.

84. Benowitz NL. Clinical pharmacology of nicotine. Annu Rev Med 1986;37:21–32.

85. Seyler LE, Pomerleau OF, Fertig JB, Hunt D, Parker K. Pituitary hormone response to cigarette smoking. Pharmacol Biochem Behav 1986; 24:159–162.

86. Wilkins JN, Carlson HE, van Vunakis H, Hill MA, Gritz E, et al. Nicotine from cigarette smoking increases circulating levels of cortisol, growth hormone, and prolactin in male chronic smokers. Psychopharmacology 1982; 78:305–308.

87. Balfour DJK. The neurochemical mechanisms underlying nicotine tolerance and dependence. In: Pratt JA, ed. The biological basis of drug tolerance and dependence. London: Academic Press, 1991:121–151.

88. Balfour DJK. Neural mechanisms underlying nicotine dependence. Addiction 1994;89: 1419–1423.

89. Wonnacott S. Characterization of brain nicotine receptor sites. In: Wonnacott S, Russell MAH, Stolerman IP, eds. Nicotine psychopharmacology: molecular, cellular, and behavioural aspects. New York: Oxford University Press, 1990:226–265.

90. Benwell MEM, Balfour DJK, Anderson JM. Evidence that smoking increases the density of nicotine binding sites in human brain. J Neurochem 1988;50:1243–1247.

91. Deneris ES, Connolly J, Rogers SW, Duvoisin R. Pharmacology and functional diversity of neuronal nicotinic acetylcholine receptors. Trends Pharmacol Sci 1991;12:34–40.

92. Lindstrom J, Schoepfer R, Conroy WG, Whiting P. Structural and functional heterogeneity of nicotinic receptors. Ciba Found Symp 1990; 152:23–42.

93. Benwell MEM, Balfour DJK, Birrell CE. Desensitization of the nicotine-induced mesolimbic dopamine responses during constant infusion with nicotine. Br J Pharmacol 1995;114: 454–460.

94. London ED, Waller SB, Wamsley JK. Autoradiographic localization of [^{3}H] binding sites in the rat brain. Neurosci Lett 1985;53:179–184.

95. Broussolle EP, Wong DF, Fanelli RJ, London ED. In vivo specific binding of [^{3}H]l-nicotine in the mouse brain. Life Sci 1989;44: 1123–1132.

96. London ED. Effects of nicotine on cerebral metabolism. Ciba Found Symp 1990;152: 131–146.

97. Reavill C, Walther B, Stolerman IP, Testa B. Behavioural and pharmacokinetic studies on nicotine, cytisine and lobeline. Neuropharmacology 1990;29:619–624.

98. Reavill C, Waters JA, Stolerman IP, Garcha HS. Behavioural effects of the nicotinic agonists N-(3-pyridylmethyl)pyrrolidine and isoarecolone in rats. Psychopharmacology 1990; 102:521–528.

99. Reavill C, Spivak CE, Stolerman IP, Waters JA. Isoarecolone can inhibit nicotine binding and produce nicotine-like discriminative stimulus effects in rats. Neuropharmacology 1987;26:789–792.

100. Decker MW, Brioni JD, Bannon AW, Arneric SP. Diversity of neuronal nicotinic acetylcholine receptors: lessons from behavior and implications for CNS therapeutics. Life Sci 1995;56:545–570.

101. Clarke PBS, Fu DS, Jakubovic A, Fibiger HC. Evidence that mesolimbic dopaminergic activation underlies the locomotor stimulant action of nicotine in rats. J Pharmacol Exp Ther 1988;246:701–708.

102. Corrigall WA, Franklin KBJ, Coen KM, Clarke PBS. The mesolimbic dopaminergic system is implicated in the reinforcing effects of nicotine. Psychopharmacology 1992;107: 285–289.

103. Balfour DJK, Graham CA, Vale AL. Studies on the possible role of brain 5-HT systems and adrenocortical activity in the behavioral responses to nicotine and diazepam. Psychopharmacology 1986;90:528–532.

104. Corrigall WA, Coen KM, Adamson KL. Self-administered nicotine activates the mesolimbic

dopamine system through the ventral tegmental area. Brain Res 1994;653:278–284.

105. Pontieri FE, Tanda G, Orzi F, Di Chiara G. Effects of nicotine on the nucleus accumbens and similarity to those of addictive drugs. Nature 1996;382:255–257.

106. Pettit HO, Justice JB. Effect of dose on cocaine self-administration and dopamine levels in the nucleus accumbens. Brain Res 1991;539: 94–102.

107. Wise RA, Rompre PP. Brain dopamine and reward. Annu Rev Psychol 1989;40:191–225.

108. Ksir C, Hakan R, Hall DP, Kellar KJ. Exposure to nicotine enhances the behavioral stimulant effect of nicotine and increases binding of [3H]acetylcholine to nicotinic receptors. Neuropharmacology 1985;24:527–531.

109. Schwartz RD, Kellar KJ. Nicotinic cholinergic receptor binding sites in the brain: regulation in vivo. Science 1983;220:214–216.

110. Shoaib M, Benwell MEM, Akbar MT, Stolerman IP, Balfour DJK. Behavioural and neurochemical adaptations to nicotine in rats: influence of NMDA antagonists. Br J Pharmacol 1994;111:1073–1080.

111. Henningfield JE, Goldberg SR. Stimulus properties of nicotine in animals and human volunteers: a review. In: Seiden LS, Balster RL, eds. Behavioral pharmacology: the current status. New York: Alan R Liss, 1984:433–449.

112. Swedberg MDB, Henningfield JE, Goldberg SR. Nicotine dependency: animal studies. In: Wonnacott S, Russell MAH, Stolerman IP, eds. Nicotine psychopharmacology: molecular, cellular, and behavioural aspects. Oxford, England: Oxford Science Publications, 1990: 38–76.

113. Henningfield JE, Cohen C, Slade JD. Is nicotine more addictive than cocaine? Br J Addict 1991;86:565–569.

114. Engstrom DA, Bickford P, de la Garza R, Young D, Rose GM. Increased responsiveness of hippocampal pyramidal neurons to nicotine in aged, learning-impaired rats. Neurobiol Aging 1993;14:259–266.

115. Stolerman IP. Behavioural pharmacology of nicotine in animals. In: Wonnacott S, Russell MAH, Stolerman IP, eds. Nicotine psychopharmacology: molecular, cellular and behavioural aspects. Oxford, England: Oxford University Press, 1990:279–294.

116. Heishman SJ, Taylor RC, Henningfield JE. Nicotine and smoking: a review of effects on human performance. Exp Clin Psychopharmacol 1994;2:345–395.

117. Hughes JR. Distinguishing withdrawal relief and direct effects of smoking. Psychopharmacology 1991;104:409–410.

118. Sherwood N. Effects of nicotine on human psychomotor performance. Hum Psychopharmacology 1993;8:155–184.

119. Shiffman S, Paty JA, Gnys M, Kassel JD, Elash C. Nicotine withdrawal in chippers and regular smokers: subjective and cognitive effects. Health Psychol 1995;14:301–309.

120. Warburton DM. The pleasures of nicotine. In: Adlkofer F, Thurau K, eds. Effects of nicotine on biological systems. Basel: Birkhauser Verlag, 1990:473–483.

121. Jones GMM, Sahakian BJ, Levy R, Warburton DM, Gray JA. Effects of acute subcutaneous nicotine on attention, information processing and short-term memory in Alzheimer's disease. Psychopharmacology 1992;108:485–494.

122. Newhouse PA, Sunderland T, Tariot PN, Blumhardt CL, Weingartner H, Mellow A, Murphy DL. Intravenous nicotine in Alzheimer's disease: a pilot study. Psychopharmacology 1988;95:171–175.

123. Sahakian BJ, Coull JT. Nicotine and tetrahydroaminoacradine: evidence for improved attention in patients with dementias of the Alzheimer type. Drug Devel Res 1994;31: 80–88.

124. Klesges RC, Meyers AW, Klesges LM, LaVasque ME. Smoking, body weight, and their effects on smoking behavior: a comprehensive review of the literature. Psychol Bull 1989;106:204–230.

125. Wack JT, Rodin J. Smoking and its effects on body weight and the systems of caloric regulation. Am J Clin Nutr 1982;35:366–380.

126. Gritz ER, Carr CR, Marcus AC. The tobacco withdrawal syndrome in unaided quitters. Br J Addiction 1991;86:57–69.

127. Gross J, Stitzer ML, Maldonaldo J. Nicotine replacement: effects on postcessation weight gain. J Consult Clin Psychol 1989;57:87–92.

128. Perkins KA. Weight gain following smoking cessation. J Consult Clin Psychol 1993;61: 768–777.

129. Hatsukami D, McBride C, Pirie P, Hellerstedt W, Lando H. Effects of nicotine gum on prevalence and severity of withdrawal in female cigarette smokers. J Subst Abuse 1991;3: 427–440.

130. Hughes JR. Tobacco withdrawal in self-quitters. J Consult Clin Psychol 1992;60:689–697.

131. Moffatt RJ, Owens SG. Cessation from cigarette smoking: changes in body weight, body composition, resting metabolism and energy consumption. Metabolism 1991;40:465–470.

132. Perkins KA, Epstein LH, Pastor S. Changes in energy balance following smoking cessation and resumption of smoking in women. J Consult Clin Psychol 1990;58:121–125.

133. Perkins KA, Epstein LH, Stiller RL, Marks BL, Jacob RG. Acute effects of nicotine on resting metabolic rate in cigarette smokers. Am J Clin Nutr 1989;50:545–550.

134. Perkins KA. Metabolic effects of cigarette smoking. J Appl Physiol 1992;72:401–409.

135. Levin ED, Morgan MM, Galvez C, Ellison GD. Chronic nicotine and withdrawal effects on body weight and food and water consumption in female rats. Physiol Behav 1987;39: 441–444.

136. Schwid SR, Hirvonen MD, Keesey RE. Nicotine effects on body weight: a regulatory perspective. Am J Clin Nutr 1992;55:878–884.

137. Hall SM, Muñoz RF, Reus VI, Sees KL. Nicotine, negative affect, and depression. J Consult Clin Psychol 1993;61:761–767.

138. Warburton DM. The puzzle of nicotine use. In: Lader M, ed. The Psychopharmacology of addiction. Oxford, England: Oxford University Press, 1988.

139. Warburton DM. Smoking within reason. Journal of Smoking-Related Disorders 1992;3:55–59.

140. Schachter S. Pharmacological and psychological determinants of smoking. In: Thornton RE, ed. Smoking behaviour, physiological, and psychological influences. Edinburgh: Churchill-Livingstone, 1978.

141. Parrott AC. Stress modulation over the day in cigarette smokers. Addiction 1995;90:233–244.

142. Gilbert DG. Paradoxical tranquilizing and emotion-reducing effects of nicotine. Psychol Bull 1979;86:643–661.

143. Perkins KA, Grobe JE, Fonte C, Breus M. "Paradoxical" effects of smoking on subjective stress versus cardiovascular arousal in males and females. Pharmacol Biochem Behav 1992; 42:301–311.

144. Parrott AC. Smoking cessation leads to reduced stress, but why? Int J Addictions 1995; 30:1509–1516.

145. Houston JP, Schneider NG. Further evidence on smoking and anxiety. Psychol Rep 1973; 32:322.

146. Schneider NG, Houston JP. Smoking and anxiety. Psychol Rep 1970;26:941–942.

147. Carey MP, Kalra DL, Carey KB, Halperin S, Richards CS. Stress and unaided smoking cessation: a prospective investigation. J Consult Clin Psychol 1993;61:831–838.

148. Cohen S, Lichtenstein E. Perceived stress, quitting smoking, and smoking relapse. Health Psychol 1990;9:466–478.

149. Rickard-Figueroa K, Zeichner A. Assessment of smoking urge and its concomitants under an environmental smoking cue manipulation. Addict Behav 1985;10:249–256.

150. Samuet JL, Dittmar A. Heat loss and anticipatory finger vasoconstriction induced by a smoking of a single cigarette. Physiol Behav 1985;35:229–232.

151. Niaura RS, Rohsenow DJ, Binkoff JA, Monti PM, Pedraza M, Abrams DB. Relevance of cue reactivity to understanding alcohol and smoking relapse. J Abnorm Psychol 1988;97:133–152.

152. Niaura R, Abrams D, Demuth B, Pinto R, Monti P. Responses to smoking-related stimuli and early relapse to smoking. Addict Behav 1989;144:419–428.

153. Hughes JR. Combining behavioral therapy and pharmacotherapy for smoking cessation: an update. NIDA Res Monogr 1995;150:92–109.

154. Henningfield JE. Nicotine medications for smoking cessation. N Engl J Med 1995;333: 1196–1203.

155. Buchkremer G, Bents H, Horstmann M, Opitz K, Tolle R. Combination of behavioral smoking cessation with transdermal nicotine substitution. Addict Behav 1989;14:229–238.

156. Nemeth-Coslett R, Henningfield JE. Effects of nicotine chewing gum on cigarette smoking and subjective and physiologic effects. Clin Pharmacol Ther 1986;39:625–630.

157. Perkins KA, Grobe JE, Stiller RL, et al. Nasal spray nicotine replacement suppresses cigarette smoking desire and behavior. Clin Pharmacol Ther 1992;52:627–634.

158. Rose JE, Herskovic JE, Trilling Y, et al. Transdermal nicotine reduces cigarette craving and nicotine preference. Clin Pharmacol Ther 1985;38:450–456.

159. Resnick MP. Treating nicotine addiction in patients with psychiatric co-morbidity. In: Orleans CT, Slade J, eds. Nicotine addiction: principles and management. New York: Oxford University Press, 1993:327–336.

160. Sachs DPL. Nicotine polacrilex: practical use requirements. Curr Pulmonol 1989;10:141–159.

161. Schneider NG. Nicotine gum in smoking cessation: rationale, efficacy, and proper use. Compr Ther 1987;13:32–37.

162. Benowitz NL, Jacob P III, Savanapridi C. Determinants of nicotine intake while chewing nicotine polacrilex gum. Clin Pharmacol Ther 1987;41:467–473.

163. Gross J, Stitzer ML. Nicotine replacement: ten-week effects on tobacco withdrawal symptoms. Psychopharmacology 1989;93:334–341.

164. Snyder FR, Henningfield JE. Effects of nicotine administration following 12 hours of tobacco deprivation: assessment on computerized performance tasks. Psychopharmacology 1989;97:17–21.

165. Hughes JR, Gust SW, Keenan RM, Fenwick JW. Effect of dose on nicotine's reinforcing, with-

drawal-suppression and self-reported effects. J Pharmacol Exp Ther 1990;252:1175–1183.

166. Hatsukami D, Skoog K, Allen S, Bliss R. Gender and the effects of different doses of nicotine gum on tobacco withdrawal symptoms. Exp Clin Psychopharmacol 1995;3:163–173.

167. Leischow SJ, Sachs DPL, Bostrom AG, Hansen MD. Effects of differing nicotine-replacement doses on weight gain after smoking cessation. Arch Fam Med 1992;1:233–237.

168. Cepeda-Benito A. Meta-analytic review of the efficacy of nicotine chewing gum in smoking treatment programs. J Consult Clin Psychol 1993;61:822–830.

169. Hughes JR. Combined psychological and nicotine gum treatment for smoking: a critical review. J Subst Abuse 1991;3:337–350.

170. Hughes JR. Pharmacotherapy for smoking cessation: unvalidated assumptions, anomalies, and suggestions for future research. J Consult Clin Psychol 1993;61:751–760.

171. Lam W, Sze PC, Sacks HS, Chalmers TC. Meta-analysis of randomised controlled trials of nicotine chewing-gum. Lancet 1987;2 (8549):27–30.

172. Silagy C, Mant D, Fowler G, Lodge M. Meta-analysis on efficacy of nicotine replacement therapies in smoking cessation. Lancet 1994; 343:139–142.

173. Tang JL, Law M, Wald N. How effective is nicotine replacement therapy in helping people to stop smoking? BMJ 1994;308:21–26.

174. Fagerström KO, Schneider NG. Measuring nicotine dependence: a review of the Fagerström Tolerance Questionnaire. J Behav Med 1989;12:159–182.

175. Herrera N, Franco R, Herrera L, Partidas A, Rolando R, Fagerstrom KO. Nicotine gum, 2 and 4 mg, for nicotine dependence. Chest 1995;108:447–451.

176. Kornitzer M, Kittel F, Dramaix M, Bourdoux P. A double-blind study of 2 mg versus 4 mg nicotine-gum in an industrial setting. J Psychosom Res 1987;31:171–176.

177. Sachs DPL. Effectiveness of the 4-mg dose of nicotine polacrilex for the initial treatment of high-dependent smokers. Arch Intern Med 1995;155:1973–1980.

178. Killen JD, Fortmann SP, Newman B, Varady A. Evaluation of a treatment approach combining nicotine gum with self-guided behavioral treatments for smoking relapse prevention. J Consult Clin Psychol 1990;58:85–92.

179. Fiore MC, Kenford SL, Jorenby DE, et al. Two studies of the clinical effectiveness of the nicotine patch with different counseling treatments. Chest 1994;105:524–533.

180. Daughton DM, Heatley SA, Prendergast JJ, et al. Effect of transdermal nicotine delivery as an adjunct to low-intervention smoking cessation therapy: a randomized, placebo-controlled, double-blind study. Arch Intern Med 1991; 151:749–752.

181. Fiore MC, Smith SS, Jorenby DE, Baker TB. The effectiveness of the nicotine patch for smoking cessation: a meta-analysis. JAMA 1993;271:1940–1947.

182. Sachs DPL, Sawe U, Leischow SJ. Effectiveness of a 16-hour transdermal nicotine patch in a medical practice setting, without intensive group counseling. Arch Intern Med 1993; 153:1881–1890.

183. Fagerström KO, Lunell E, Molander L. Continuous and intermittent transdermal delivery of nicotine: blockade of withdrawal symptoms and side effects. Journal of Smoking-Related Diseases 1991;2:173–180.

184. Transdermal Nicotine Study Group. Transdermal nicotine for smoking cessation: results of two multicenter controlled trials. JAMA 1991; 266:3133–3138.

185. Abelin T, Ehrsam R, Buhler-Reichert A, Imhof PR, Muller P, et al. Effectiveness of a transdermal nicotine system in smoking cessation studies. Meth Find Exp Clin Pharmacol 1989;11: 205–214.

186. Krumpe P, Malani N, Adler J, Ramoorthy S, Asadi S, et al. Efficacy of transdermal nicotine administration as an adjunct for smoking cessation in heavily nicotine addicted smokers [abstract]. Am Rev Resp Dis 1989;139:A337.

187. Hurt RD, Dale LC, Offord KP, et al. Serum nicotine and cotinine levels during nicotine-patch therapy. Clin Pharmacol Ther 1993;54: 98–106.

188. Dale LC, Hurt RD, Offord KP, Lawson GM, Croghan IT, Schroeder DR. High-dose nicotine patch therapy: percentage of replacement and smoking cessation. JAMA 1995;274:1353–1358.

189. Hughes JR. Treatment of nicotine dependence: is more better? JAMA 1995;274:1390–1391.

190. Jorenby DE, Smith SS, Fiore MC, Hurt RD, Offord KP, Croghan IT, et al. Varying nicotine patch dose and type of smoking cessation counseling. JAMA 1995;274:1347–1352.

191. Cinciripini PM, Cinciripini LG, Wallfisch A, Haque W, Van Vunakis H. Behavior therapy and the transdermal nicotine patch: effects on cessation outcome, affect, and coping. J Consult Clin Psychol 1996;64:314–323.

192. Hurt RD, Dale LC, Fredrickson PA, Caldwell CC, Lee GA, Offord KP, et al. Nicotine patch therapy for smoking cessation combined with physician advice and nurse follow-up. JAMA 1994;271:595–600.

193. Russell MAH, Stapleton JA, Feyerabend C, et al. Targeting heavy smokers in general practice: Randomised controlled trial of transdermal nicotine patches. BMJ 1993;306:1308–1312.

194. Tønnesen P, Nørregaard J, Simonsen K, et al. A double-blind trial of a 16-hour transdermal nicotine patch in smoking cessation. N Engl J Med 1993;325:311–315.

195. Westman EC, Levin ED, Rose JE. The nicotine patch in smoking cessation: a randomized trial with telephone counseling. Arch Intern Med 1993;153:1917–1923.

196. Tønnesen P, Nørregaard J, Säwe U. Two-year outcome in a smoking cessation trial with a nicotine patch. Journal of Smoking-Related Disease 1992;3:241–245.

197. Jorenby DE, Smith SS, Fiore MC, Baker TB, Hurt RD. Do heavy smokers need a higher replacement dose of nicotine to quit? A reply. JAMA 1996;275:1882–1883.

198. Westman EC, Rose JE. Do heavy smokers need a higher replacement dose of nicotine to quit? Letter. JAMA 1996;275:1882.

199. Sutherland G, Stapleton JA, Russell MAH, et al. Randomised controlled trial of nasal nicotine spray in smoking cessation. Lancet 1992; 340:324–329.

200. Hjalmarson A, Franzon M, Westin A, Wiklund O. Effect of nicotine nasal spray on smoking cessation: A randomized placebo-controlled, double-blind study. Arch Intern Med 1994; 154:2567–2572.

201. Schneider NG, Olmstead R, Mody FV, Doan K, Franzon M, Jarvik ME, Steinberg C. Efficacy of a nicotine nasal spray in smoking cessation: a placebo-controlled, double-blind trial. Addiction 1995;90:1671–1682.

202. Jacobson NL, Jacobson AA, Ray JP. Noncombustible cigarette: alternative method of nicotine delivery. Chest 1979;76:355–356.

203. Russell MAH, Jarvis MJ, Sutherland G, Feyerabend C. Nicotine replacement in smoking cessation: absorption of nicotine vapor from smoke-free cigarettes. JAMA 1987;257:3262–3265.

204. Glover ED. The nicotine vaporizer, nicotine nasal spray, combination therapy, and the future of NRT: a discussion. Health Values 1994; 18:22–28.

205. Rose JE, Behm FM, Levin ED. Role of nicotine dose and sensory cues in the regulation of smoke intake. Pharmacol Biochem Behav 1993;44:891–900.

206. Schneider NG. Nicotine nasal spray. Health Values 1994;18:10–14.

207. Leischow SJ. The nicotine vaporizer. Health Values 1994;18:4–9.

208. Schneider NG, Olmstead R, Nilsson F, Mody F, Franzon M, Doan K. Efficacy of a nicotine inhaler in smoking cessation: a double-blind, placebo-controlled trial. Addiction 1996;91: 1293–1306.

209. Leischow SJ, Nilsson F, Franzon M, Hill A, Otte P, Merikle EP. Efficacy of the nicotine inhaler as an adjunct to smoking cessation. Am J Health Behav 1996;20(5):364–371.

210. Tønnesen P, Nørregaard J, Mikkelsen K, Jørgensen S, Nilsson F. A double-blind trial of a nicotine inhaler for smoking cessation. JAMA 1993;269:1268–1271.

211. Areechon W, Punnotok J. Smoking cessation through the use of nicotine chewing gum: a double-blind trial in Thailand. Clin Ther 1988; 10:183–186.

212. Blondal T. Controlled trial of nicotine polacrilex gum with supportive measures. Arch Intern Med 1989;149:1818–1821.

213. Brantmark B, Ohlin P, Westling H. Nicotine-containing chewing gum as an anti-smoking aid. Psychopharmacologia 1973;31:191–200.

214. British Thoracic Society. Comparison of four methods of smoking withdrawal in patients with smoking related diseases. Br Med J 1983; 286:595–597.

215. Campbell IA, Lyons E, Prescott RJ. Stopping smoking: do nicotine chewing gum and postal encouragement add to doctors' advice? Practitioner 1987;231:114–117.

216. Christen AG, McDonald JL, Olson BL, Drook CA, Stookey GK. Efficacy of nicotine chewing gum in facilitating smoking cessation. J Am Dent Assoc 1984;108:594–597.

217. Clavel F, Benhamou S, Company-Huertas A, Flamant R. Helping people to quit smoking: randomized comparison of groups being treated with acupuncture and nicotine gum with control group. Br Med J 1985;291: 1538–1539.

218. Cohen SJ, Stookey GK, Katz BP, Drook CA, Christen AG. Helping smokers quit: a randomized controlled trial with private practice dentists. J Am Dent Assoc 1989;118:41–45.

219. Cohen SJ, Stookey GK, Katz BP, Drook CA, Smith DM. Encouraging primary care physicians to help smokers quit: a randomized, control trial. Ann Intern Med 1989;110:648–652.

220. Fagerstrom KO. Effects of nicotine chewing gum and follow-up appointments in physician-based smoking cessation. Prev Med 1984; 13:517–527.

221. Fee WM, Stewart MJ. A controlled trial of nicotine chewing gum in a smoking withdrawal clinic. Practicioner 1982;226:148–149.

222. Gilbert JR, Wilson DMC, Best JA, Taylor W,

Linsday EA, Singer J, Willms DG. Smoking cessation in primary care: a randomized controlled trial of nicotine-bearing chewing gum. J Fam Pract 1989;28:49–55.

223. Hall SM, Tunstall CD, Ginsberg D, Benowitz NL, Jones RT. Nicotine gum and behavioral treatment: a placebo controlled trial. J Consult Clin Psychol 1987;55:603–605.

224. Hall SM, Tunstall C, Rugg D, Jones R, Benowitz N. Nicotine gum and behavioral treatment in smoking cessation. J Consult Clin Psychol 1985;53:256–258.

225. Harackiewicz JM, Blair LW, Sansone C, Epstein JA, Stuchell RN. Nicotine gum and self-help manuals in smoking cessation: an evaluation in a medical context. Addict Behav 1988; 13:319–330.

226. Hjalmarson AIM. Effect of nicotine chewing gum in smoking cessation: a randomized, placebo controlled, double-blind study. JAMA 1984;252:2835–2838.

227. Huber D. Combined and separate treatment effects of nicotine chewing gum and self-control method. Pharmacopsychiatry 1988;21:461–462.

228. Hughes JR, Gulliver SB, Amori G, Mireault GC, Fenwick JF. Effect of instructions and nicotine of smoking cessation, withdrawal symptoms and self-administration of nicotine gum. Psychopharmacology 1989;99:486–491.

229. Hughes JR, Gust SW, Keenan RM, Fenwick JW, Healey ML. Nicotine vs. placebo gum in general medicine practice. JAMA 1989;261: 1300–1305.

230. Jamrozik K, Fowler G, Vessey M, Wald N. Placebo controlled trial of nicotine chewing gum in general practice. Br Med J 1983; 289:794–797.

231. Jarvik ME, Schneider NG. Degree of addiction and effectiveness of nicotine gum therapy for smoking. Am J Psychiatry 1984;141:790–791.

232. Jarvis MJ, Raw M, Russell MAH, Feyerabend C. Randomised controlled trial of nicotine chewing gum. Br Med J 1982;285:537–540.

233. Killen JD, Maccoby N, Taylor CB. Nicotine gum and self-regulation training in smoking relapse prevention. Behav Ther 1984;15: 234–248.

234. Malcolm RE, Sillett RW, Turner JA, Ball KP. The use of nicotine chewing gum as an aid to stop smoking. Psychopharmacology 1980;70: 295–296.

235. Ockene JK, Kristeller J, Goldberg R, Amick TL, Pekow PS, Hosmer D, et al.. Increasing the efficacy of physician-delivered smoking interventions: a randomized clinical trial. J Gen Intern Med 1991;6:1–8.

236. Page AR, Walters DJ, Schlegel RP, Best JA. Smoking cessation in family practice: the effects of advice and nicotine chewing gum prescription. Addict Behav 1986;11:443–446.

237. Puska P, Bjorkqvist S, Koskela K. Nicotine containing chewing gum in smoking cessation: a double-blind trial with half year follow up. Addict Behav 1979;4:141–146.

238. Schneider NG, Jarvik ME, Forsythe AB, Read LL, Elliot ML, Schweiger A. Nicotine gum in smoking cessation: a placebo-controlled, double-blind trial. Addict Behav 1983;8:253–261.

239. Tonnesen P, Fryd V, Hansen M, Helsted J, Gunnersen AB, Forchammer H, Stockner M. Two and four mg nicotine chewing gum and group counselling in smoking cessation: an open, randomized, controlled trial with a 22 month follow-up. Addict Behav 1988;13: 17–27.

240. Tonnesen P, Fryd V, Hansen M, Helsted J, Gunnersen AB, Forchammer H, et al. Effect of nicotine chewing gum in combination with group counselling on the cessation of smoking. N Engl J Med 1988;318:15–18.

241. Russell MAH, Merriman R, Stapleton J, Taylor W. Effect of nicotine chewing gum as an adjunct to general practitioners' advice against smoking. Br Med J 1983;287:1782–1785.

242. Fagerstrom KA. A comparison of psychological and pharmacological treatment in smoking cessation. J Behav Med 1982;5:343–351.

243. Fortmann SP, Killen JD. Nicotine gum and self-help behavioral treatment for smoking relapse prevention: results from a trial using population-based recruitment. J Consult Clin Psychol 1995;63:460–468.

244. Nebot M, Cabezas C. Does nurse counselling or offer of nicotine gum improve the effectiveness of physician smoking cessation advice. Fam Pract Res J 1992;12 (3):263–270.

245. Marshall A, Raw M. Nicotine chewing gum in general practice: effect of follow-up appointments. Br Med J 1985;290:1397–1398.

246. McGovern PG, Lando HA. An assessment of nicotine gum as an adjunct to freedom from smoking cessation clinics. Addict Behav 1992; 17(2):137–147.

247. Zelman DC, Brandon TH, Jorenby DE, Baker TB. Measures of affect and nicotine dependence predict differential response to smoking cessation treatments. J Consult Clin Psychol 1992;60(6):943–952.

248. Abelin T, Buehler A, Muller P, Vesanen K, Imhof PR. Controlled trial of transdermal nicotine patch in tobaco withdrawal. Lancet 1989; 1:7–10.

249. Buchkremer G, Bents H, Horstmann M, Opitz K, Tolle R. Combination of behavioral smoking cessation with transdermal nicotine substitution. Addict Behav 1989;14:229–238.

250. Hurt RD, Lauger GG, Offord KP, Kottke TE, Dale LC. Nicotine replacement therapy with use of a transdermal nicotine patch: a randomized, double-blind, placebo-controlled trial. Mayo Clin Proc 1990;65:1529–1537.

251. Imperial Cancer Research Fund General Practice Research Group. Effectiveness of a nicotine patch in helping people stop smoking: Results of a randomized trial in a general practice. Br Med J 1993;306:1304–1308.

252. Mulligan SC, Masterson JG, Devane JG, Kelly JG. Clinical and pharmacokinetic properties of a transdermal nicotine patch. Clin Pharmacol Ther 1990;47:331–337.

253. Mankani SK, Garabrant DH, Homa DM. Effectiveness of nicotine patches in a workplace smoking cessation program. An eleven-month follow-up study. J Occup Environ Med 1996; 38(2):184–189.

254. Stapleton JA, Russell MA, Feyerabend C, Wiseman SM, Gustavsson G, Sawe U, Wiseman D. Dose effects and predictors of outcome in a randomized trial of transdermal nicotine patches in general practice. Addiction 1995; 90(1):31–42.

255. Richmond RL, Harris K, de Almeida NA. The transdermal nicotine patch: Results of a randomised placebo-controlled trial. Med J Aust 1994;161(2):130–135.

256. Hilleman DE, Mohiuddin SM, Delcore MG. Comparison of fixed-dose transdermal nicotine, tapered-dose transdermal nicotine, and buspirone in smoking cessation. J Clin Pharmacol 1994;34(3):222–224.

257. Foulds J, Stapleton J, Hayward M, Russell MA, Feyerabend C, Fleming T, Costello J. Transdermal nicotine patches with low-intensity support to aid smoking cessation in outpa-tients in a general hospital. A placebo-controlled trial. Arch Fam Med 1993;2(4): 417–423.

258. Fagerström KO. Combined use of nicotine replacement products. Health Values 1994;18: 15–20.

259. Schneider NG. Nicotine therapy in smoking cessation: pharmacokinetic considerations. Clin Pharmacokinet 1992;23:169–172.

260. Fagerström KO, Schneider NG, Lunell E. Effectiveness of nicotine patch and nicotine gum as individual versus combined treatments for tobacco withdrawal symptoms. Psychopharmacology 1993;111:271–277.

261. Kornitzer M, Boutsen M, Dramaix M, Thijs J, Gustavsson G. Combined use of nicotine patch and gum in smoking cessation: a placebo-controlled clinical trial. Prev Med 1995;24:41–47.

262. Puska P, Korhonen HI, Vartiainer E, Urjanheimo E-L, Gustavsson G, Westin A. Combined use of nicotine patch and gum compared with gum alone in smoking cessation: a clinical trial in North Karelia. Tobacco Control 1995; 4:231–235.

263. Rose JE, Behm FM, Westman EC, Levin ED, Stein RM, Lane JD, Ripka GV. Combined effects of nicotine and mecamylamine in attenuating smoking satisfaction. Exp Clin Psychopharmacol 1994;2:328–344.

264. Balfour DJK, Fagerstrom KO. Pharmacology of nicotine and its therapeutic use in smoking cessation and neurodegenerative disorders. Pharmacol Ther (in press).

265. Jarvik ME. Beneficial effects of nicotine. Br J Addiction 1991;86:571–575.

266. Westman EC, Levin ED, Rose JE. Nicotine as a therapeutic drug. NCMJ 1995;56:48–51.

267. Wilson AL, Langley LK, Monley J, Bauer T, Rottunda S, McFalls E, et al. Nicotine patches in Alzheimer's disease: pilot study on learning, memory, and safety. Pharmacol Biochem Behav 1995;51:509–514.

268. Fagerström KO, Pomerleau O, Giordani B, Stelson F. Nicotine may relieve symptoms of Parkinson's disease. Psychopharmacology 1994;116:117–119.

269. Marshall J, Schnieden H. Effect of adrenaline, noradrenaline, atropine, and nicotine on some types of human tremor. J Neurol Neurosurg Psychiatry 1966;29:214–218.

270. Moll H. The treatment of post-encephalitic Parkinsonism by nicotine. Br Med J 1926: 1079–1081.

271. Reavill C. Action of nicotine on dopamine pathways and implications for Parkinson's disease. In: Wonnacott S, Russell MAH, Stolerman IP, eds. Nicotine psychopharmacology: molecular, cellular, and behavioural aspects. Oxford, England: Oxford University Press, 1990.

272. Lashner BA, Hanauer SB, Silverstein MD. Testing nicotine gum for ulcerative colitis patients. Experience with single-patient trials. Dig Dis Sci 1990;35:827–832.

273. Pullan RD, Rhodes J, Ganesh S, et al. Transdermal nicotine for active ulcerative colitis. N Engl J Med 1994;330:811–815.

274. Rhodes J, Thomas G. Nicotine treatment in ulcerative colitis. Current status. Drugs 1995; 49:157–160.

275. Srivastava UD, Russell MAH, Feyerabend C, et al. Transdermal nicotine in active ulcerative colitis. Eur J Gastroenterol Hepatol 1991;3: 815–818.

276. McConville BJ, Sanberg PR, Fogelson MH, King J, Cirino P, Parker KW et al. The effects of nicotine plus haloperidol compared to nico-

tine only and placebo nicotine only in reducing tic severity and frequency in Tourette's disorder. Biol Psychiatry 1992;31:832–840.

277. Silver AA, Sandberg PR. Transdermal nicotine patch and potentiation of haloperidol in Tourette's syndrome. Lancet 1993;342 (8864):182.

278. Davila DG, Hurt RD, Offord KP, Harris CD, Shepard JW. Acute effects of transdermal nicotine on sleep architecture, snoring, and sleep-disordered breathing in nonsmokers. Am J Respir Crit Care Med 1994;150:469–474.

279. Oster G, Delea TE, Huse DM, Regan MM, Colditz GA. The benefits and risks of over-the-counter availability of nicotine polacrilex. Med Care 1996;34:389–402.

280. Pickworth WB, Bunker EB, Henningfield JE. Transdermal nicotine: reduction of smoking with minimal abuse liability. Psychopharmacology 1994;115:9–14.

281. Schuh KJ, Schuh LM, Henningfield JE, Stitzer ML. Nicotine nasal spray and nicotine vapour inhaler: abuse liability determination. (unpublished manuscript).

282. Hughes JR, Gust SW, Keenan R, Fenwick JW, Skoog K, Higgins ST. Long-term use of nicotine vs. placebo gum. Arch Intern Med 1991; 151:1993–1998.

283. Hughes JR, Hatsukami DK, Skoog KP. Physical dependence on nicotine in gum: a placebo substitution trial. JAMA 1986;255:3277–3279.

284. West R, Russell MAH. Effects of withdrawal from long-term nicotine gum use. Psychol Med 1984;15:891–893.

285. Hurt RD, Offord KP, Lauger GG, Marusic Z, Fagerstrom KO, Enright PL, et al. Cessation of long-term nicotine gum use—a prospective, randomized trial. Addiction 1995;90:407–413.

286. Tate JC, Schmitz JM, Spiga R. Reducing long-term nicotine gum use: the role of nonpharmacological factors. In: Harris LS ed. Problems of drug dependence, 1992: proceedings of the 54rd annual scientific meeting, the College on Problems of Drug Dependence. Washington, DC: U.S. Government Printing Office, 1993:268.

287. Hajek P, Jackson P, Belcher M. Long-term use of nicotine chewing gum occurrence, determinants, and effect on weight gain. JAMA 1988; 260:1593–1596.

288. Schneider NG. How to use nicotine gum and other strategies to quit smoking. New York: Simon & Schuster, 1988.

289. Glassman AH, Jackson WK, Walsh BT, Roose SP, Rosenfeld B. Cigarette craving, smoking withdrawal, and clonidine. Science 1984;226: 864–866.

290. Gourlay S, Forbes A, Marriner T, et al. A placebo-controlled study of three clonidine doses for smoking cessation. Clin Pharmacol Ther 1994;55:64–69.

291. Ornish SA, Zisook S, McAdams LA. Effects of transdermal clonidine treatment on withdrawal symptoms associated with smoking cessation: a randomized, controlled trial. Arch Intern Med 1988;148:2027–2031.

292. Prochazka AV, Petty TL, Nett L, et al. Transdermal clonidine reduced some withdrawal symptoms but did not increase smoking cessation. Arch Intern Med 1992;152:2065–2069.

293. Hilleman DE, Mohiuddin SM, Delcore MG, et al. Randomized, controlled trial of transdermal clonidine for smoking cessation. Ann Pharmacother 1993;27:1025–1028.

294. Glassman AH, Stetner F, Walsh BT, et al. Heavy smokers, smoking cessation, and clonidine: results of a double-blind, randomized trial. JAMA 1988;259:2863–2866.

295. Glassman AH, Covey LS, Dalack GW. Smoking cessation, clonidine, and vulnerability to nicotine among dependent smokers. Clin Pharmacol Ther 1993;54:670–679.

296. Langley MS, Heel RC. Transdermal clonidine. Drugs 1988;25:123–142.

297. Covey LS, Glassman AH. A meta-analysis of double-blind placebo-controlled trials of clonidine for smoking cessation. Br J Addiction 1991;86:991–998.

298. Davison R, Kaplan K, Fintel D, Parker M, Anderson L, Haring O. The effect of clonidine on the cessation of cigarette smoking. Clin Pharmacol Ther 1988;44:265–267.

299. Niaura R, Brown RA, Goldstein MG, Murphy JK, Abrams DB. Transdermal clonidine for smoking cessation: a double-blind randomized dose-response study. Exp Clin Psychopharmacol 1996;4:285–291.

300. Jarvik ME, Henningfield JE. Pharmacological treatment of tobacco dependence. Pharmacol Biochem Behav 1988;30:279–294.

301. Jarvik ME, Henningfield JE. Pharmacological adjuncts for the treatment of nicotine dependence. In: Orleans CT, Slade J, eds. Nicotine addiction: principles and management. New York: Oxford University Press, 1993:245–261.

302. Cinciripini PM, Lapitsky L, Seay S, Wallfisch A, Meyer WJ, Vunakis H. A placebo-controlled evaluation of the effects of buspirone on smoking cessation: differences between high- and low-anxiety smokers. J Clin Psychopharmacol 1995;15:182–191.

303. Gawin F, Compton M, Byck R. Buspirone reduces smoking [letter]. Arch Gen Psychiatry 1989;46:288.

304. Hillemann DE, Mohiuddin SM, Del Core MG, Sketch MH. Effect of buspirone on withdrawal symptoms associated with smoking cessation. Arch Intern Med 1992;152:350–352.

305. Robinson MD, Smith WA, Cederstrom EA, Sutherland DE. Buspirone effect on tobacco withdrawal symptoms: a pilot study. J Am Board Fam Pract 1991;4:89–94.

306. Robinson MD, Pettice YL, Smith WA, Cederstrom EA, Sutherland DE, Davis H. Buspirone effect on tobacco withdrawal symptoms: a randomized placebo-controlled trial. J Am Board Fam Pract 1992;5:1–9.

307. Schneider NG, Olmstead RE, Sloan K, Steinberg C, Daims R, Brown HV. Buspirone in smoking cessation: A placebo-controlled trial. Clin Pharmacol Ther 1996;60(5):568–575.

308. West R, Hajek P, McNeill A. Effect of buspirone on cigarette withdrawal symptoms and short-term abstinence rates in a smokers clinic. Psychopharmacology 1991;104:91–96.

309. Breslau N, Fenn N, Peterson EL. Early smoking initiation and nicotine dependence in a cohort of young adults. Drug Alcohol Depend 1993;33:129–137.

310. Breslau N. Psychiatric comorbidity of smoking and nicotine dependence. Behav Genet 1995; 25:95–101.

311. Anda RF, Williamson DF, Escobedo LG, Mast EE, Giovino GA, Remington PL. Depression and the dynamics of smoking. JAMA 1990; 264:1541–1545.

312. Covey LS, Glassman AH, Stetner F. Depression and depressive symptoms in smoking cessation. Compr Psychiatry 1990;31:350–354.

313. Glassman AH, Helzer JE, Covey LS, Cottler LB, Stetner F, Tipp JE, et al. Smoking, smoking cessation and major depression. JAMA 1990;264:1546–1549.

314. Hughes JR, Hatsukami DK, Mitchell JE, Dahlgren LA. Prevalence of smoking among

psychiatric outpatients. Am J Psychiatry 1986; 143:993–997.

315. Edwards NB, Murphy JK, Downs AD, et al. Doxepin as an adjunct to smoking cessation: a double-blind pilot study. Am J Psychiatry 1989;146:373–376.

316. Murphy JK, Edwards NB, Downs AD, et al. Reduction of nicotine withdrawal symptoms with doxepin. Am J Psychiatry 1990;147: 1353–1357.

317. Ferry LH, Robbins AS, Scariati PD, et al. Enhancement of smoking cessation using the antidepressant bupropion hydrochloride [abstract]. Circulation 1992;86(suppl):I-671.

318. Dalack GW, Glassman AH, Rivelli S, Lirio C. Mood, major depression, and fluoxetine response in cigarette smokers. Am J Psychiatry 1995;152:398–403.

319. Clarke PBS. Nicotinic receptor blockade therapy and smoking cessation. Br J Addiction 1991;86:501–555.

320. Rose JE, Sampson A, Levin ED, Henningfield JE. Mecamylamine increases nicotine preference and attenuates nicotine discrimination. Pharmacol Biochem Behav 1989;32:933–938.

321. Stolerman IP. Could nicotine antagonists be used in smoking cessation? Br J Addiction 1986;81:47–53.

322. Nemeth-Coslett R, Henningfield JE, O'Keefe MD, Griffiths RR. Effects of mecamylamine on human cigarette smoking and subjective ratings. Psychopharmacology 1986;88:420–425.

323. Rose JE, Behm FM, Westman EC, Levin ED, Stein RM, Ripka GV. Mecamylamine combined with nicotine skin patch facilitates smoking cessation beyond nicotine patch treatment alone. Clin Pharmacol Ther 1994;56:86–99.

324. Jensen EJ, Schmidt E, Pedersen B, Dahl R. Effect on smoking cessation of silver acetate, nicotine and ordinary chewing gum. Psychopharmacology 1991;104:470–474.

325. Slade J. Nicotine delivery devices. In: Orleans CT, Slade J, eds. Nicotine addiction: principles and management. New York: Oxford University Press, 1993:3–23.

326. Kozlowski LT, Pope MA, Lux JE. Prevalence of the misuse of ultra-low-tar cigarettes by blocking filter vents. Am J Public Health 1988; 78:694–695.

327. Kozlowski LT. Less hazardous smoking and the pursuit of satisfaction. Am J Public Health 1989;77:539–541.

328. Maron DJ, Fortmann SP. Nicotine yield and measures of cigarette smoke exposure in a large population: are lower yield cigarettes safer? Am J Public Health 1987;77:546–549.

329. Kaufman DW, Palmer JR, Rosenberg L, Stolley P, Warshauer E, Shapiro S. Tar content of cigarettes in relation to lung cancer. Am J Epidemiol 1989;129:703–711.

330. Wilcox HB, Schoenberg JB, Mason TJ, Bill JS, Stemhagen A. Smoking and lung cancer: risk as a function of cigarette tar content. Prev Med 1988;17:263–272.

331. Palmer JR, Rosenberg L, Shapiro S. Low yield cigarettes and the risk of nonfatal myocardial infarction in women. N Engl J Med 1989;320: 1569–1573.

332. Russell MAH. Are cigarettes getting safer? Br J Addiction 1984;79:241–243.

333. Sutherland G, Russell MAH, Stapleton JA, Feyerabend C. Glycerol particle cigarettes: a less harmful option for chronic smokers. Thorax 1993;48:385–387.

334. Rose JE, Levin ED. Eclipse and the harm reduction strategy for smoking. Special conference at Duke University, August 23, 1996.

335. Schwartz JL. Methods of smoking cessation. Med Clin North Am 1992;76:451–476.

336. Shiffman S. Smoking cessation treatment: any progress? J Consult Clin Psychol 1993;61:718–722.

337. Schwartz JL. Review and evaluation of smoking cessation methods: the United States and Canada, 1978–1985 (Report No. 81–2940). Bethesda, MD: U.S. Public Health Service, 1987.

338. Law M, Tang JL. An analysis of the effectiveness of interventions intended to help people stop smoking. Arch Intern Med 1995;155:1933–1941.

339. Lichtenstein E, Glasgow RE. Smoking cessation: what have we learned over the past decade? J Consult Clin Psychol 1992;60:518–527.

340. Lando HA, McGovern P, Sipfle C. Public service application of an effective clinic approach to smoking cessation. Health Educ Res 1989;4:103–109.

341. Schmitz JM, Tate JC. Treatment session frequency and smoking cessation. J Subst Abuse 1994;6:77–85.

342. Stevens VJ, Hollis JF. Preventing smoking relapse using an individually tailored skills-training technique. J Consult Clin Psychol 1989;57:420–424.

343. Flaxman J. Quitting smoking now or later: gradual, abrupt, immediate, and delayed quitting. Behav Res Ther 1978;9:260–270.

344. Foxx RM, Brown RA. A nicotine fading and self-monitoring program to produce cigarette abstinence or controlled smoking. J Appl Behav Anal 1979;12:111–125.

345. McGovern PG, Lando HA. Reduced nicotine exposure and abstinence outcome in two nicotine fading methods. Addict Behav 1991;16:11–20.

346. West RJ, Russell MAH, Jarvis MJ, Feyerabend C. Does switching to an ultra-low nicotine cigarette induce nicotine withdrawal effects? Psychopharmacology 1984;84:120–123.

347. Beaver C, Brown RA, Lichtenstein E. Effects of monitored nicotine fading and anxiety management training on smoking reduction. Addict Behav 1981;6:301–305.

348. Lando HA. Lay facilitators as effective smoking cessation counselors. Addict Behav 1987;12:69–72.

349. Lando HA, McGovern P. Nicotine fading as a nonrisky alternative in a broad-spectrum treatment for eliminating smoking. Addict Behav 1985;10:153–161.

350. Shapiro D, Schwartz GE, Tursky B, Shnidman SR. Smoking on cue: a behavioral approach to smoking reduction. J Health Soc Behav 1971;12:108–113.

351. Cinciripini PM, Lapitsky L, Seay S, Wallfisch A, Kitchens K, Van Vunakis H. The effects of smoking schedules on cessation outcome: can we improve on common methods of gradual and abrupt nicotine withdrawal? J Consult Clin Psychol 1995;63:388–399.

352. Elliott R, Tighe T. Breaking the cigarette habit: effects of a technique involving threatened loss of money. Psychol Record 1968;18:503–513.

353. Lando HA. Aversive conditioning and contingency management in the treatment of smoking. J Consult Clin Psychol 1976;44:312.

354. Paxton R. The effects of a deposit contract as a component in a behavioral programme for stopping smoking. Behav Res Ther 1980;18:45–50.

355. Paxton R. Deposit contracts with smokers: varying frequency and amount of repayment. Behav Res Ther 1981;19:117–123.

356. Henningfield JE, Stitzer ML, Griffiths RR. Expired air carbon monoxide accumulation and elimination as a function of number of cigarettes smoked. Addict Behav 1980;5:265–272.

357. Stitzer ML, Bigelow GE. Contingent reinforcement for reduced carbon monoxide levels in cigarette smokers. Addict Behav 1982;7:403–412.

358. Stitzer ML, Bigelow GE. Contingent payment for carbon monoxide reduction: effects of pay amount. Behavior Therapy 1983;14:647–656.

359. Stitzer ML, Bigelow GE. Contingent reinforcement for carbon monoxide reduction: within-subject effects of pay amount. J Appl Behav Anal 1984;17:477–483.

360. Rand CS, Stitzer ML, Bigelow GE, Mead AM. The effects of contingent payment and frequent workplace monitoring on smoking abstinence. Addict Behav 1989;14:121–128.

361. Stitzer ML, Rand CS, Bigelow GE, Mead AM. Contingent payment procedures for smoking reduction and cessation. J Appl Behav Anal 1986;19:197–202.

362. Schmitz JM, Grabowski J, Rhoades H. Contingent reinforcement for reduced carbon monoxide levels in methadone maintenance patients. Addict Behav 1995;20:171–179.

363. Shoptaw S, Jarvik ME, Ling W, Rawson RA. Contingency management for tobacco smoking in methadone-maintained opiate addicts. Addict Behav 1996;21:409–412.

364. Marlatt GA, Gordon JR, eds. Relapse prevention. New York: Guilford Press, 1985.

365. Baer JS, Holt CS, Lichtenstein E. Self-efficacy and smoking reexamined: construct validity and clinical utility. J Consult Clin Psychol 1986;54:846–852.

366. Bliss RE, Garvey AJ, Heinold JW, Hitchcock JL. The influence of situation and coping on relapse crisis outcomes after smoking cessation. J Consult Clin Psychol 1989;57:443–449.

367. Brandon TH, Tiffany ST, Obremski KM, Baker TB. Postcessation cigarette use: the process of relapse. Addict Behav 1990;15:105–114.

368. Curry SG, Marlatt GA. Unaided quitters' strategies for coping with temptations to smoke. In: Shiffman S, Wills TA, eds. Coping and substance abuse. New York: Academic Press, 1985:243–265.

369. Colletti G, Supnick JA, Payne TJ. The smoking self-efficacy questionnaire (SSEQ): preliminary scale development and validation. Behavioral Assessment 1985;7:249–260.

370. Garcia ME, Schmitz JM, Doerfler LA. A fine-grained analysis of the role of self-efficacy in self-initiated attempts to quit smoking. J Consult Clin Psychol 1990;58:317–322.

371. Schmitz JM, Rosenfarb IS, Payne TJ. Cognitive and affective responses to successful coping during smoking cessation. J Subst Abuse 1993;5:61–72.

372. Shiffman S. Relapse following smoking cessation: a situational analysis. J Consult Clin Psychol 1982;50:71–86.

373. Shiffman S. Coping with temptations to smoke. J Consult Clin Psychol 1984;52:261–267.

374. Shiffman S. A cluster-analytic classification of smoking relapse episodes. Addict Behav 1986;11:295–307.

375. Baer JS, Kamarck T, Lichtenstein E, Ransom CC. Prediction of smoking relapse: analyses of temptations and transgressions after initial cessation. J Consult Clin Psychol 1989;57:623–627.

376. Grove JR. Attributional correlates of cessation self-efficacy among smokers. Addict Behav 1993;18:311–320.

377. Spanier CA, Shiffman S, Maurer A, Reynolds W, et al. Rebound following failure to quit smoking: the effects of attributions and self-efficacy. Exp Clin Psychopharmacol 1996;4:191–197.

378. Brown RA, Lichtenstein E, McIntyre KO, Harrington-Kostur J. Effects of nicotine fading and relapse prevention on smoking cessation. J Consult Clin Psychol 1984;52:307–308.

379. Curry SJ, Marlatt GA, Gordon J, Baer JS. A comparison of alternative theoretical approaches to smoking cessation and relapse. Health Psychol 1988;7:545–556.

380. Davis JR, Glaros AG. Relapse prevention and smoking cessation. Addict Behav 1986;11:105–114.

381. Glasgow RE, Klesges RC, Klesges LM, Vasey MW, Gunnarson DF. Long-term effects of a controlled smoking program. Behavior Therapy 1985;16:303–307.

382. Carroll KM. Relapse prevention as a psychosocial treatment: A review of controlled clinical trials. Exp Clin Psychopharmacol 1996;4:46–54.

383. Buchkremer G, Minneker E, Block M. Smoking-cessation treatment combining transdermal nicotine substitution with behavioral therapy. Pharmacopsychiatry 1991;24:96–102.

384. Killen JD, Maccoby N, Taylor CB. Nicotine gum and self-regulation training in smoking relapse prevention. Behavioral Therapy 1984;15:234–248.

385. Abrams DB, Monti PM, Carey KB, Pinto RP, Jacobus SI. Reactivity to smoking cues and relapse: two studies of discriminant validity. Behav Res Ther 1988;26:225–233.

386. Payne TJ, Etscheidt M, Corrigan SA. Conditioning arbitrary stimuli to cigarette smoke intake: a preliminary study. J Subst Abuse 1990;2:119–125.

387. Payne TJ, Schare ML, Levis DJ, Colletti G. Exposure to smoking-relevant cues: effects on desire to smoke and topographical components of smoking behavior. Addict Behav 1991;6:467–479.

388. Payne TJ, Smith PO, Sturges LV, Holleran SA. Reactivity to smoking cues: mediating roles of nicotine deprivation and duration of deprivation. Addict Behav 1996;21:139–154.

389. Tiffany ST, Drobes DJ. Imagery and smoking urges: the manipulation of affective content. Addict Behav 1990;15:531–539.

390. Zinser MC, Baker TB, Sherman JE, Cannon DS. Relation between self-reported affect and drug urges in continuing and withdrawing smokers. J Abnorm Psychol 1992;101:617–629.

391. Niaura R, Abrams DB, Monti PM, Pedraza M. Reactivity to high risk situations and smoking cessation outcome. J Subst Abuse 1989b;1:393–405.

392. Corty E, McFall RM. Response prevention in the treatment of cigarette smoking. Addict Behav 1984;9:405–408.

393. Lando HA. Formal quit smoking treatments. In: Orleans CT, Slade J, eds. Nicotine addiction: principles and management. New York: Oxford University Press, 1993:221–244.

394. Fiore MC, Novotny TE, Pierce JP, Giovino GA, Hatziandreu EJ, Newcomb PA, et al. Methods used to quit smoking in the United States: do cessation programs help? JAMA 1990;263:2760–2765.

395. Orleans CT. Treating nicotine dependence in medical settings: a stepped-care model. In: Orleans CT, Slade J, eds. Nicotine addiction: principles and management. New York: Oxford University Press, 1993:145–161.

395. The Agency for Health Care Policy and Research smoking cessation clinical practice guideline. JAMA 1996;275:1270–1280.

396. Russell MH, Wilson C, Taylor C, Baker CD. Effect of general practitioners' advice against smoking. Br Med J 1979;2:231–235.

397. Burling TA, Ziff DC. Tobacco smoking: a comparison between alcohol and drug abuse inpatients. Addict Behav 1988;13:185–190.

398. DiFranza JR, Guerrera MP. Alcoholism and smoking. J Stud Alcohol 1990;51:130–135.

399. Istvan J, Matarazzo JD. Tobacco, alcohol, and caffeine use: a review of their interrelationships. Psychol Bull 1984;95:301–326.

400. Kozlowski LT, Jelinek LC, Pope MA. Cigarette smoking among alcohol abusers: a continuing and neglected problem. Can J Public Health 1986;77:205–207.

401. Zeiner AR, Stanitis T, Spurgeon M, Nichols N. Treatment of alcoholism and concomitant drugs of abuse. Alcohol 1985;2:555–559.

402. Bobo JK, Gilchrist LD, Schilling RF II, Noach B, Schinke SP. Cigarette smoking cessation attempts by recovering alcoholics. Addict Behav 1987;8:209–215.

403. Abrams DB, Rohsenow DJ, Niaura RS, Pedraza M, Longabaugh R, Beattie MC, et al. Smoking and treatment outcome for alcoholics: effects on coping skills, urge to drink, and drinking rates. Behavior Therapy 1992;23:283–297.

404. Batel P, Pessione F, Maitre C, Rueff B. Relationship between alcohol and tobacco dependencies among alcoholics who smoke. Addiction 1995;90:977–980.

405. Carmody TP, Brischetter CS, Matarazzo JD. Co-occurrent use of cigarettes, alcohol, and coffee in healthy, community-living men and women. Health Psychol 1985;4:323–335.

406. Gulliver SB, Rohsenow DJ, Colby SM, Dey AN, Abrams DB, Niaura RS, et al. Interrelationship of smoking and alcohol dependence, use and urges to use. J Stud Alcohol 1995;56:202–206.

407. Griffiths RR, Bigelow GE, Liebson I. Facilitation of human tobacco self-administration by ethanol: a behavioral analysis. J Exp Anal Behav 1976;25:279–292.

408. Mello NK, Mendelson JH, Sellers ML, Kuehnle JC. Effect of alcohol and marijuana on tobacco smoking. Clin Pharmacol Ther 1980;27:202–209.

409. Mello NK, Mendelson JH, Sellers ML, Kuehnle JC. Effects of heroin self-administration on cigarette smoking psychopharmacology. Psychopharmacology 1980;67:45–52.

410. Henningfield JE, Griffiths RR. Cigarette smoking and subjective response: effects of d-amphetamine. Clin Pharmacol Ther 1981;30:497–505.

411. Schuster CE, Lucchesi BR, Emley GS. The effects of d-amphetamine, meprobamate, and lobeline on cigarette smoking behavior in normal human subjects. NIDA Res Monogr 1979;23:91–99.

412. Henningfield JE, Chait LD, Griffiths RR. Cigarette smoking and subjective response in alcoholics: effects of pentobarbital. Clin Pharmacol Ther 1983;33:806–812.

413. Chait LD, Griffiths RR. Effects of methadone on human cigarette smoking and subjective ratings. J Pharmacol Exp Ther 1984;229:636–640.

414. Schmitz JM, Grabowski J, Rhoades H. The effects of high and low doses of methadone on cigarette smoking. Drug Alcohol Depend 1994;34:237–242.

415. Joseph AM. Nicotine treatment at the drug dependency program of the Minneapolis VA Medical Center. J Subst Abuse Treat 1993;10:147–152.

416. Kozlowski LT, Skinner W, Kent C, Pope MA. Prospects for smoking treatment in individuals seeking treatment for alcohol and other drug problems. Addict Behav 1989;14:273–278.

417. Orleans CT, Hutchinson D. Tailoring nicotine addiction treatments for chemical dependency patients. J Subst Abuse 1993;10:197–208.

418. Burling TA, Marshall GD, Seidner AL. Smoking cessation for substance abuse inpatients. J Subst Abuse 1991;3:269–276.

419. Joseph AM, Nichol KL, Willenbring ML, Korn JE, Lysaght LS. Beneficial effects of treatment of nicotine dependence during an inpatient substance abuse program. JAMA 1990;263:3043–3046.

420. Story J, Stark MJ. Treating cigarette smoking in methadone maintenance clients. J Psychoactive Drugs 1991;23:203–215.

421. Hurt RD, Eberman KM, Croghan IT, Offord KP, Davis LJ, Morse RM, et al. Nicotine dependence treatment during inpatient treatment for other addictions: a prospective intervention trial. Alcoholism Clin Exp Res 1994;18:867–872.

422. Hurt RD, Offord KP, Croghan IT, Gomez-Dahl L, Kottke TE, Morse RM, Melton LJ. Mortality following inpatient addictions treatment: role of tobacco use in a community-based cohort. JAMA 1996;275:1097–1103.

423. Henningfield JE, Cohen C, Pickworth WB. Psychopharmacology of nicotine. In: Orleans CT, Slade J, eds. Nicotine addiction: principles and management. New York: Oxford University Press, 1993:24–45.

424. Ramirez AG, Gallion KJ. Nicotine dependence among blacks and Hispanics. In: Orleans CT, Slade J, eds. Nicotine addiction: principles and management. New York: Oxford University Press, 1993:350–364.

26 CAFFEINE

John F. Greden and Adale Walters

INTRODUCTION

The vast majority of adults in the world consume caffeine. In the United States, more than 80% report regular daily intake (1, 2). The majority have moderate consumption, and perhaps as many as one in five adults consume doses generally considered large enough to cause clinical symptoms. Caffeine is the most widely consumed psychoactive agent in the world, far ahead of alcohol (second place) and nicotine (third place) (1, 3–5).

Yet, for most of the twentieth century, few were concerned about caffeine's potential health consequences, including the Food and Drug Administration (FDA) which categorized caffeine as one of many substances that are "generally recognized as safe" (GRAS) (6–7), the American Psychiatric Association's Diagnostic and Statistical Manual Second Edition (DSM-II) (8), which had no official mention of caffeine, or the vast majority of physicians who infrequently asked patients about their caffeine intake.

Knowledge modifies viewpoints, however. Beginning in the 1970s, a growing number of clinical reports noted caffeine had significant clinical consequences when ingested in adequate amounts (9–13). Surveys of general populations and clinical settings began to confirm the widespread nature of consumption (4, 14). The name "caffeinism" was attached to the syndrome of clinical features which stemmed from acute or chronic overuse (9). Specific neurochemical studies of caffeine and other adenosines helped call attention to underlying neurobiological mechanisms (15–19).

By 1978, viewpoints had shifted enough so that the FDA (20) commissioned a committee to reinvestigate substances "generally recognized as safe" (GRAS) and subsequently published a report on caffeine. In 1980, just six years after the first modern report on "caffeinism" (indicating that it could induce a syndrome indistinguishable from anxiety), the diagnosis of *caffeine intoxication* was incorporated into the third edition of the American Psychiatric Association's DSM-III (21). As part of America's fitness craze, the media and the general public both became interested in caffeine's health consequences, resulting in a flourish of articles, health books, and discussions on talk shows.

Clinicians began to accept that caffeine does have reinforcing properties, produces tolerance in some situations, induces a characteristic constellation of clinical symptoms when acute or chronic overuse occurs (22–24), and frequently leads to withdrawal symptoms if use is suddenly discontinued. For these and other reasons, caffeinism and caffeine withdrawal were incorporated into both previous editions of this textbook (25, 26). This chapter seeks to provide an updated perspective.

Table 26.1 Sources of Caffeine in Beverages and Food

Source	approximate mg/unit	"Rule of 25s"
Fresh drip coffee	100–140	150
Brewed coffee	90–110	100
Decaffeinated coffee	2–4	0
Instant coffee	66–100	75
Tea (leaf)	30–75	50
Tea (bag)	42–100	50
Cocoa	5–50	25
Soft drinks[a]	25–50	50
Traditional cola drinks (Pepsi, Coke, Tab, Royal Crown, Dr. Pepper)	25–50	
Mountain Dew, selected orange soft drinks	25–50	
Water with caffeine (Water Joe)	50–75	
Chocolate bar or ounce of baking chocolate	25–35	

[a]All soft drink names are registered trademarks.

DEFINITIONS

Caffeine

Caffeine is a member of the chemical class of alkaloids (27–29), specifically a xanthine derivative (1-, 3-, 7-trimethylxanthine). The drug occurs naturally in a multitude of sources, notably coffee, tea, cocoa, soft drinks, chocolate, and maté (Table 26.1). It is added pharmaceutically to hundreds of prescription drugs and over-the-counter analgesics, stimulants, diet preparations, and cold products (Table 26.2). There are few soft drinks or over-the-counter analgesics that contain no caffeine (Table 26.3); caffeine is difficult to avoid.

Caffeinism

Caffeinism is the term coined to describe the clinical syndrome produced by acute or chronic overuse of caffeine (9). The syndrome is usually characterized by central nervous system and peripheral manifestations that are directly linked to expected pharmacological actions of caffeine and include anxiety, psychomotor alterations, sleep disturbances, mood changes, and psychophysiological complaints.

REINFORCING PROPERTIES

As recently reviewed by Griffiths and Mumford (30), human studies under double blind conditions demonstrate that caffeine has reinforcement properties in most people with a history of heavy prior use (31, 32). Such reinforcement is clearly a function of dose and prior exposure, characterized by a classic inverted U-shaped curve. Doses of 25 mg or higher are reinforcing; the rate of self-administration begins to decrease above 50 or 100 mg; doses in the high range (e.g., 400 mg and higher) actually induce avoidance. Those who select or "choose" caffeine also differ from "nonchoosers" (33). Choosers associate favorable effects with caffeine when it is compared with placebo. They state the drug makes them feel energetic, content, and alert, whereas nonchoosers describe anxiety, jitteriness, and mood changes. Prior physical dependence also appears to be a factor in caffeine's reinforcing properties. As an illustration, those who experience caffeine withdrawal (e.g., headache when switched to decaffeinated products) are far more likely to show caffeine reinforcement, i.e., choose caffeinated products when given a choice (34). Whereas prior exposure with physical dependence promotes reinforcement, pilot studies suggest that individuals with high levels of anxiety are least likely to choose caffeine (33, 35), which may partially explain the observation that patients with diagnosed panic disorder are especially vulnerable to future episodes of panic attacks if caffeine is consumed (36).

TOLERANCE

If an individual's responses to a drug begin to change following repeated exposure and an increased dose is required to produce the same responses that occurred earlier, tolerance has developed. After years of uncertainty, it

Table 26.2 Sources of Caffeine in Medications

Source	mg/unit
Prescription analgesics	
APC (aspirin, phenacetin, and caffeine)	32
Cafergot	100
Darvon compound	32
Fiorinal	40
Over-the-counter analgesics	
Aspirin compound	32
BC tablet	16
Bromo-Seltzer	32.5
Capron	32
Comeback	100
Cope	32
Dolor	30
Easy-Mens	32
Excedrin	60
Goody's Headache Powder	32.5
Medache	32
Moranox	15
Midol	32
Nilain	32
PAC	32
Pre-mens	66
Stanback tablets	16
Stanback Powder	32
Trigesic	30
Vanquish	32
Many cold preparations	30
Over-the-counter stimulants and appetite suppressants	
Amostat tablets	100
Anorexin capsules	100
Appedrine tablets	100
Caffedrine capsules	250
Dexatrim capsules	200
Double-E Alertness	180
Nodoz tablets	100
Odrinex tablets	50
Prolamine capsules	140
Quick-Pep tablets	150
Spantrol capsules	150
Tirend tablets	100
Verb TD capsules	200
Vivarin tablets	200
Wakoz	200

is apparent from both preclinical research and human studies that regular caffeine use does induce tolerance. This is reflected in a range of physiological effects including sleep (37, 38).

HISTORY

Caffeine's history is global in scope, centuries in duration, and as provocative as most other drugs of abuse. Caffeine is available in more than 60 plant species around the world. Caffeine is everywhere. The vehicle for ingestion may change, but the drug's effects are largely the same. In South America, caffeine-containing beverages, generally made from plants such as guarana, maté, and yoco (11, 39–40), have always been an integral part of the culture. In Arabia, China, Europe, and North America, caffeine's history is inseparable from coffee and tea. The word "caffeine" is believed to originate from the Arabic term "gawah," a word for wine (11, 41). Folklore and sketchy records suggest that people probably began ingesting caffeine in Arabia approximately 1,000 years ago (its actual use probably preceded that date). According to legend, a goatherder named Kaldi observed energetic behavior among his goats after they ate red berries from a shrub. Kaldi allegedly tried the berries himself, and sleepiness was counteracted, presumably a desired result for a goatherder. As with most products possessing reinforcing properties in the central nervous system, usage spread. Rather

Table 26.3   Beverages and Over-the-Counter Analgesics Without Caffeine

Beverages
Canada Dry Ginger Ale
Coke Caffeine-Free
Pepsi Free
7-Up
Sprite
Squirt
Tab Caffeine-Free
Over-the-counter analgesics
Anacin
Aspirin
Empirin
Pamprin
Tylenol

than directly eating berries, more palatable preparations were discovered, such as preparing the berries in a hot drink, the first "coffee." Just as predictably, increased use led to proliferation of both advocates and opponents. Some religious leaders reportedly defended consumption of Kaldi's hot drink, claiming that caffeine assisted in lengthy prayer. Others criticized users as not being "true followers" (42).

The word "tea" presumably originated from the Chinese "tay" in the dialect of Amoy. Tea was believed to have been present in China as early as 2737 BC, was first mentioned in writing approximately 350 AD, and was introduced into Europe in approximately 1600 AD (43). Society's response to the introduction of tea was similar to that of coffee (40). Advocates and opponents vociferously debated the drug; its use quickly spread. Caffeine was introduced to European countries during the sixteenth century and brought to America by European explorers. Debates again percolated to the surface, with some suggesting caffeine was a terrible drug of abuse comparable in scope to opioids and alcohol; others considered it a medical treatment.

Centuries may pass, but subjective descriptions of caffeine's effects have remained remarkably the same. In 1601, Parry wrote that "a certain liquor which they call caffeine . . . will soon intoxicate the brain" (41). Others concurred, emphasizing that caffeine produced "nervousness and palsies." The chronic consumer was described as someone who is (44):

> . . . tremulous and loses his self-command; he is subject to fits of agitation and depression; he loses his color and has a haggard appearance. The appetite falls off . . . the heart also suffers; it palpitates, or it intermits.

This description, almost four centuries old, appears to meet currently-existing DSM-IV criteria for substance intoxication: (a) development of a substance-specific syndrome due to recent ingestion of a psychoactive substance, and (b) maladaptive behavior during the waking state due to the effect of the substance on the central nervous system, e.g., belligerence, impaired judgment, impaired social or occupational functioning.

Historical commentaries also preceded current debates about whether caffeine can induce physical dependency. Colonial American women were described as "such slaves to it that they would rather go without their dinners than without a dish of tea" (46). English in the Victorian era claimed that "a renewed dose of the poison gives temporary relief, but at the cost of future misery" (44). Others suggested that tea and coffee promoted use of tobacco, alcohol, opium, and other stimulants; our forbears also were concerned about the problems of a "domino effect" and "comorbidity." Not surprisingly, systematic data were rarely collected.

Throughout history, societies have sought to counteract substance abuse by declaring drug use as illegal, immoral, unhealthful, or a combination of all three. Legal banishment of caffeine was often tried and often failed. Caffeine, generally in the form of coffee and tea, has been outlawed at one time or another in most parts of the world. Bans were usually defied and eventually rescinded, often with the concomitant adoption of taxation. The following sixteenth century text is typical:

> the (coffee) habit had become so strong, and the use of it so generally agreeable, that the people continued, notwithstanding all prohibitions, to drink it in their own houses. The officers of the police, seeing they could not suppress

the use of it allowed the selling of it, on paying a tax; and the drinking it provided it was not done openly; so that it was drunk in particular places, with the doors shut, or in the back room of some of the shopkeepers houses . . . (42)

One of the factors contributing to caffeine's widespread consumption among all ages was its introduction in cola-type soft drinks (43). In the late 1800s, the drug began appearing in Dr. Pepper, Coca-Cola, and Pepsi-Cola. In the early 1900s, legal statutes required that it be included in cola drinks, intended to replace cocaine, which would subsequently be banned from such beverages (another of the many examples where societies attempt to eliminate one psychoactive agent by substituting another deemed less harmful).

EPIDEMIOLOGY

Caffeine *consumption* in the world is huge. It exceeds several billion kilograms annually (1, 3–5). Approximately 80% of adults in North America report regular intake. Per capita intake for the entire world's population approximates 70 mg/day (3, 43). In the United States, this figure is considerably larger at 220 to 240 mg.

Data about caffeinism are sketchy. The *incidence and prevalence* are relatively unknown throughout most of the world, and it is unknown whether they are rising or declining. Reasons are summarized in Table 26.4. These issues are of special relevance for investigators.

As reflected in Tables 26.1–26.3 and Figure 26.1, caffeine is present in a *wide variety of products*. Caffeinated coffee is the major source for most of the American population, but many people consume the drug predominantly or exclusively via other vehicles (e.g., tea), and millions use a multitude of agents (e.g., a blend of coffee, tea, cola drinks, analgesics, cocoa). To inquire about "how many cups of coffee" one drinks each day is only a rough estimate. Intake from all sources should ideally be determined and summed.

Individual variation in response to caffeine is well known. While there is ample documentation of dose-response relationships in large sample studies and a greater likelihood that caffeinism will develop as daily dosage increases, caffeinism has been documented among some individuals who use only low or moderate amounts, and a few large consumers are seemingly immune to symptoms.

Tolerance is a third factor that must be considered in determining the incidence and prevalence of caffeinism. Acute caffeine use clearly produces different biological consequences than chronic use. Most scientific studies are conducted with acute-use paradigms; most cases of caffeinism result from chronic use.

Finally, *age, body mass,* concomitant use of *other psychoactive agents* such as nicotine or alcohol, and differing *ambient state* at the time of ingestion (e.g., fatigue, sleep deprivation, stress, etc.) may contribute to the well-recognized differential response to the same dosage and confuse the issue of whether an individual is caffeine dependent. While there is no clear-cut

Table 26.4   Confounding Variables in Epidemiology of Caffeine Intake and Caffeinism

- Surveys that emphasize "coffee" consumption vs. total "caffeine" consumption
- Changing patterns in consuming caffeinated coffee vs. decaffeinated coffee
- Increased use of soft drinks, most caffeinated
- Decreases in percolated brewing (less caffeine concentration) and increases in fresh drip brewing (greater caffeine concentration) (see Figure 26.1)
- Upsurge of coffee houses in many American cities
- Perception that consumers are becoming attracted to concentrated coffees (e.g., espresso)
- Introduction of new caffeinated products, e.g., caffeinated water
- Tea consumption has increased
- Tolerance develops among most users and disguises "symptoms" for many
- Acute use studied most often, but chronic use most often leads to caffeinism
- Age alters responses to caffeine
- Co-existing medical and psychiatric conditions, other comorbid drug use, and pharmaceutical treatments may predispose to or disguise the diagnosis

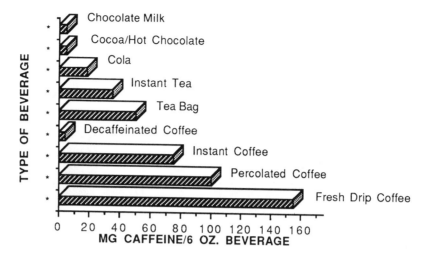

Figure 26.1. Average caffeine content of beverages. (Adapted from Barone JJ, Roberts H. Human consumption of caffeine. In: Dews PB, ed. Caffeine. New York: Springer-Verlag, 1984:59–76.)

dosage at which all people can be expected to develop the syndrome (as summarized in Table 26.5), there are dosage conventions that have become generalized to "low," "moderate," or "high" intake.

When considering epidemiology of caffeinism in America, an important question that begs for additional study is whether *total* average daily intake of caffeine from all sources is increasing or decreasing. Unfortunately, this question cannot be answered. While reasonable data are available for *coffee* consumption (collected from industrial surveys) (1, 5–7), other sources have usually not been assessed at the same time. The percentage of coffee drinkers began dropping progressively and significantly between 1962 (used as a point of reference since survey assessments began in the early 1960s) and the late 1980s, but stabilization of coffee use occurred during the 1990s. The vast majority of caffeine consumption in America occurs via ingestion of regular (caffeinated) coffee so it is tempting to conclude that total caffeine use diminished in the years prior to 1985, but such a conclusion may be erroneous for all the reasons listed in Table 26.4. In 1962, only one third of the population reported drinking soft drinks "the day before," compared with two thirds by 1989 (47), and most soft drinks are caffeinated. Similarly, increased tea drinking, the shift to fresh drip brewing, and other variables all lead to the conclusion that, while regular coffee drinking reportedly decreased meaningfully during the past several decades, it is safe to say that total intake of caffeine remains high and has, possibly, increased.

Most caffeine is ingested in the morning hours (47). There are only slight differences in use patterns across various regions of the country. The percentage of coffee drinkers tends to increase with age (Fig. 26.2), but there is a gradual decline in elderly populations in the actual intake per day, and there may be greater use of decaffeinated beverages. Infants and children, because of their small size, consume relatively large amounts of caffeine on a mg/kg basis (Fig. 26.3).

For all these reasons, the prevalence of caffeinism can only be estimated by coupling known pharmacokinetics and dose-effect relationships with reported intakes of total caffeine from survey data. Pharmacologically, the risk of developing some meaningful clinical manifestations becomes high—perhaps even predictable among most people—when intake exceeds 500 mg/day. This places 20–30% of North Americans at risk (4, 10). Recogniz-

ing that there are individual variations and accepting a conservative approach, these data suggest that perhaps 10–20% of the North American adult population probably have meaningful clinical symptoms consistent with a diagnosis of caffeinism. This prevalence exceeds that for most substances of abuse.

Truly large intake is not common, but some report ingestion of 2000–5000 mg/day (12, 48). Despite their frequent denials ("I have been drinking large amounts of coffee all my life, and it's never given me any trouble"), symptoms of caffeinism almost certainly exist among such individuals.

There is considerable variability in common sources of caffeine, but some generalizations are possible. Common sources are provided in Table 26.1. This table also summarizes the "Rule of 25s", which suggests that the easiest way to remember caffeine quantities in the various beverage sources is to "round off" to multiples of 25. Figure 26.1 schematically illustrates the different contents of the major groupings.

PHARMACOLOGY, NEUROPHARMACOLOGY, AND NEUROBIOLOGY

Chemically isolated more than 170 years ago (49) and structurally characterized in 1875 (50), caffeine has been well studied. Absorption from the gastrointestinal tract is rapid and complete (51). Peak plasma levels tend to occur 30–45 minutes following oral intake. Once absorbed, caffeine is poorly bound (10–30%) to plasma albumin (52), promptly crosses the blood-brain barrier, and enters into relative equilibrium between plasma and brain (53). Ingested dosages are closely correlated with brain concentrations.

Caffeine is measurable in most body fluids, such as plasma, saliva, breast milk (a factor that should be considered in those that breastfeed their infants), urine, cerebrospinal fluid, semen, and amniotic fluid (54). Liquid chromatography currently is the assay method of choice.

Approximately 15% of the circulating drug is metabolized per hour (51). The half-life in humans is approximately 3.5–5 hours. A comprehensive and detailed metabolic pathway, relying predominantly upon liver biotransformation, has been well characterized (49). Caffeine is quite safe, with relatively low toxicity (27, 37, 55). For a death to occur from overdose for an average adult male, 5–10 grams, the equivalent of 50–100 cups of regular brewed coffee, would probably be required, necessitating ingestion in non-beverage form.

For decades, investigators have been seeking to understand caffeine's mechanisms of action in the brain (25). It increases norepinephrine secretion, inhibits phosphodiesterase breakdown of cyclic 3',5'-adenosine monophosphate (cyclic AMP) in high concentrations, sensitizes central catecholamine postsynaptic receptors, enhances cyclic guanosine 3',5'-monophosphate (cyclic GMP), modulates acetylcholine and serotonin activ-

Table 26.5 Caffeine Dosage vs. Conventional Terminology

Dosage terminology	Dosage (mg/kg)	Average daily intake for a 70 kg person (mg)
"Low"	3.5 or less	245 or less
"Moderate"	3.5–10	245–700
"High"	10 or more	700 or more

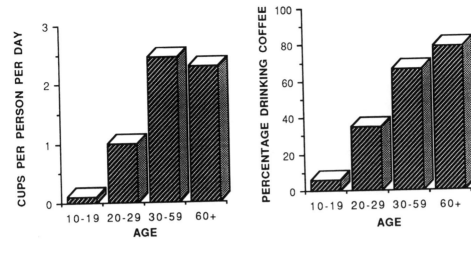

Figure 26.2.   Consumption of coffee in different age ranges (1989).

ity, modifies calcium metabolism, and antagonizes central nervous system (CNS) adenosine receptors. This latter appears to be most important (56–58).

Adenosine, a constituent of ATP and nucleic acids, is a neuromodulator that influences a number of metabolic functions in the CNS. There do not appear to be discrete adenosinergic pathways in the CNS (59). Rather, adenosinergic neurons in the brain form a diffuse and important system sometimes labeled as "depressant." More accurately, adenosine and its agonists have sedative, anxiolytic, and anticonvulsant actions. Once released, adenosine binds to cell surface receptor sites. These sites have been relatively well characterized using radioreceptor ligand binding techniques, and several subtypes have been distinguished. Caffeine competes with adenosine for binding at the high-affinity adenosine receptor sites. When adenosine binds to its receptor sites, "tranquilizing" or hypnogenic effects occur, and blood vessels are dilated in cerebral and coronary circulatory networks (57, 58). Considering the profile of actions stemming from adenosine, it is not

surprising that caffeine's antagonism produces actions that are often considered "stimulating" or "anxiogenic."

While adenosine continues to receive most of the attention as the probable mechanism of anxiety induction, a recent study suggests that many of the alerting effects of caffeine could be linked to caffeine's actions on serotonin neurons (60) or to kynurenine, a neuroactive tryptophan metabolite. Orlikov and Ryzov (61) induced anxiety in 15 healthy volunteers by administering an anxiogenic dose of caffeine and noted that kynurenine concentration was markedly increased at the peak of anxiety and returned to normal after anxiety had dissipated. Additional studies of these hypotheses are indicated.

Regional blood flow studies using positron emission tomography (PET) or single photon emission tomography (SPECT) imaging reveal, somewhat counter-intuitively, that 200 mg of caffeine produces a diffuse *decrease* in cerebral blood flow of approximately 30% (62, 63). These vasoconstrictive effects undoubtedly contribute to caffeine's efficacy in patients with migraine headaches. These potent results are illustrated in Figure 26.4.

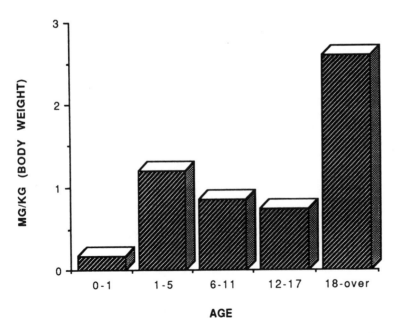

Figure 26.3.   Mean daily consumption of caffeine: age influence. (Reproduced with permission from Little AD. Comments on the health aspects of caffeine, especially the contribution of soft drinks, with particular reference to the report of the Select Committee on GRAS substances. Cambridge, MA: Little, 1977.)

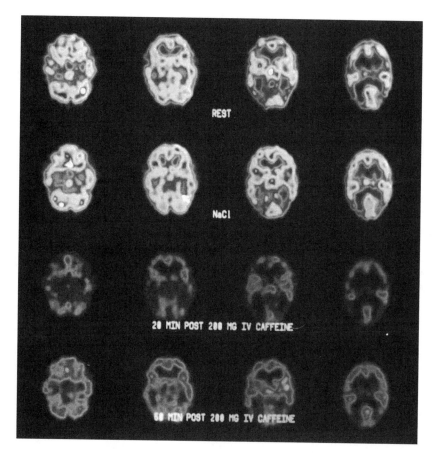

Figure 26.4. Positron-emission tomographic measurements of regional cerebral blood flow in a normal adult human subject, using the oxygen-15 water method. Horizontal slices at four brain levels (highest to lowest levels, right to left) were made under four different conditions: (**A**) resting; (**B**) after a saline–NaCl–placebo infusion; (**C**) 20 minutes after an intravenous infusion of 200 mg of caffeine; and (**D**) 50 minutes after caffeine infusion. These results represent a decrease in whole brain blood flow of approximately 30% (scan generously provided by Oliver G. Cameron, M.D., Ph.D. Results published in Cameron OG, Modell JG, Hariharan M. Caffeine and human cerebral blood flow: a positron emission tomography study. Life Sci 1990;47:1141–1146.)

Recent investigations confirm that most psychoactive agents influence gene expression, including alteration of the immediate early gene activation system. Expression of c-fos mRNA in rat brain has been shown to be induced by caffeine, possibly the result of antagonism of adenosine receptors (64).

Caffeine's actions in other physiological systems are well documented. In the cardiovascular system, the drug increases heart rate and force of contraction (65). Because its action in the CNS may be in the opposite direction, many individuals may notice no change in heart rate, most report mild tachycardia, and a few have significant increases in heart rate. Rarely, subjects will experience bradycardia following caffeine. Arrhythmias are relatively common and are sometimes the presenting complaint for patients (9).

Caffeine has prompt and powerful diuretic effects (66). Many individuals, especially males in their 50s and older, also describe "bladder irritation," manifested by urethral spasm, urinary frequency, and urgency 1–2 hours following caffeine ingestion. It is not known whether this phenomenon is related to prostatic hypertrophy or to other changes associated with aging. Such urinary discomfort may contribute to the observed diminished intake as people age.

Increased gastric secretion and enhanced gastric acidity commonly follow caffeine use (9, 67). Accordingly, patients with peptic ulcer have been advised for decades to avoid caffeine. Gastric physiological consequences ("coffee upsets my stomach") make consumption of caffeine-containing beverages unpleasant for some people.

Caffeine's neurobiological actions sometimes are reported to be conflicting because different actions may occur at different concentrations or at different time points following ingestion. This is not surprising. Alterations of one neurotransmitter system often produce sequential changes and receptor upregulation and downregulation in other systems at a later time point. These variations may explain why caffeine's effects are sometimes described as bimodal, (e.g., with psychomotor anxiety at lower doses and lethargy at higher doses) and why conventional dose-response relationships may appear to be absent at higher dosage or toxic levels (17, 18, 27).

Age (49) should receive greater attention when considering the clinical consequences of caffeinism. Animal studies of intravenous administration confirm an *age-dependent increase* in the rate of demethylation of caffeine. Thus, without considering differences in CNS function, newborns, infants, and young children probably have less tolerance for caffeine than do adults because of metabolic differences. Indeed, newborn humans have been shown to have a limited capacity for caffeine metabolism, with slow urinary excretion of unchanged caffeine and consequent prolonged half-lives (68). These developmental metabolic differences probably have even greater clinical importance *in utero,* especially when coupled with the observation that pregnant women have decreased ability to metabolize methylxanthines (67). Caffeine use should be discouraged during pregnancy.

ETIOLOGY OF CAFFEINISM

How and when does caffeine ingestion begin? Why should it ever begin, considering there are actual barriers to starting ingestion? Infants and children do not seem to have any *innate* craving for caffeine, the taste is actually perceived as bitter for a large percentage of individuals of all ages, and acute exposure to doses of 200–250 mg in the uninitiated may actually produce symptoms of anxiety and other types of distress (37, 51, 69). These observations

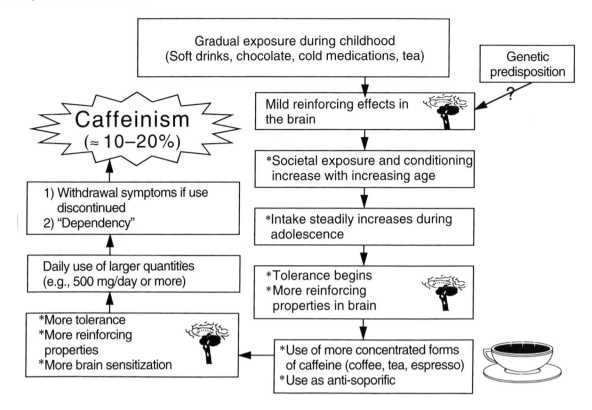

Figure 26.5.   Illustration of increasing exposure and progressively greater consumption, leading toward caffeinism.

indicate that gradual exposure, reinforcement, tolerance, and increasing dosages all play a role. A likely sequence is illustrated in Figure 26.5.

The progression is similar to that for most drugs of abuse. Most individuals in our society are gradually exposed to caffeine early in their lives, intake slowly increases, and the majority of users progress to a pattern of frequent or daily consumption. Approximately one quarter eventually begin consuming large quantities, exceeding 500 mg/day, and conservatively 10% of all adults then progress to develop the syndrome of caffeinism. To plan preventive interventions, we must understand this progression of use. To understand this progression of use, we must understand the drug's reinforcing properties. Caffeine use starts for most during childhood. Mean daily consumption of caffeine in American children is surprisingly high. For example, consumption in the age range of one to five is 1.20 mg/kg body weight from all sources (70). This compares with 2.60 mg/kg for people 18 and over. In America, initial use usually occurs via soft drinks or chocolate products, but exceptions do occur. In some settings, for example, serving tea to children is common.

Few or no data are available to indicate how children respond to these first exposures. Just as importantly, few or no data are available to indicate whether young children preferentially seek caffeine once they have been introduced to it. These voids in the knowledge base need to be filled.

It is known that when significant exposure occurs during adolescence or young adulthood, not all the initial consequences are considered positive; the feeling of being "wired" may be intense. Yet through "trial and error" many individuals develop a pattern of actively seeking the caffeine "high," while controlling adverse effects. Dosage increments are sometimes driven by apparently extraneous reasons. For example, many young people report beginning a pattern of high consumption during their college years, to aid them in studying during late hours. Clinical impressions indicate that it is CNS stimulation that is actively sought by most high consumers. The key reinforcing factor promoting caffeine usage and dosage increase may be the drug's reinforcing effects upon pleasure and reward centers of the brain (18, 19, 71–81). These pleasure centers, whether in the hypothalamus, median forebrain bundle, or elsewhere, seemingly are stimulated by adrenergic output of dopamine and norepinephrine, secondary effects of caffeine. (The role of the competitive antagonism of adenosine in this sequence is not well known.) Caffeine's actions appear comparable (although less potent) in some aspects to those of other stimulants, such as amphetamines and cocaine. Drug self-administration studies reveal that caffeine does maintain self-administration under some conditions, but not as reliably as classic drugs of abuse such as cocaine, d-amphetamine or pentobarbital. If tolerance is a factor in the development of caffeinism, then heavy users should find the drug reinforcing after abstinence. This is precisely what Goldstein (14, 82–85) reported—pleasant and desirable effects following ingestion after overnight abstinence.

It is not known whether there are genetic predispositions to the development of caffeinism (86, 87). Suggestions that heritability may influence the amount of coffee consumed and that genetically transmitted variations may be seen in sleep after caffeine use have been hypothesized, but mechanisms are not well substantiated. As stated previously, caffeine does alter gene expression.

In summary, the dual desires to seek repetitive consumption so as to stimulate the brain's diffuse "reward centers" and to avoid withdrawal symptoms may be the most important variables encouraging people to move from that relatively positive and innocuous stage of controlled input to the stage of caffeinism (see Fig. 26.5).

THE CULTURE OF CAFFEINE

Societal conditioning also affects caffeine use (88). Promoters include the intimacy of social conversations in coffee shops, the pleasure of "coffee breaks" in America or the 4:00 PM tea time in England, the desire to display fine dishware or other elaborate paraphernalia, the gathering for a hot cup of coffee or tea on a cold winter day, and other comparable factors. This conditioning undoubtedly contributed to the remarkable domestication of this drug. Stress is also part of societal conditioning—passing college examinations, meeting the boss's deadline, finishing a grant proposal—and it appears that for many stress actually enhances intake.

In recent years there has been an explosion in the growth of espresso shops, especially in metropolitan and college environments. It has become a part of the American vernacular to order a shot or double shot of espresso, latté, or cappuccino at the local espresso cafe. In this new culture of caffeine, the consumer is feted with a variety of beans from different countries. The manner in which the bean is processed, packaged, and delivered will affect how much caffeine the consumer will be exposed to. This may be an unpredictable determination, depending on the country's standards and regulation of export. The method of preparation may be varied depending on the sophistication of the espresso shop. Other factors, such as cleaning and maintenance of the apparatus, as well as the maceration process of the coffee bean itself, will affect the ultimate amount of caffeine delivered in the beverage at point of consumption.

The espresso shop is a vehicle for socialization, and this in turn affects the number of "cups" of espresso consumed. The consumer can order a single or double shot of espresso and vary the vehicle of presentation by ordering it as a latté or cappuccino. This urban beverage may be delivered in a demitasse or decorative glass concealing the real amount of caffeine to be ingested by the consumer. There is a glamour and cosmopolitan air to sipping espresso at an outdoor cafe. Likewise, it is part of the intelligentsia to order an international bean to be ground for espresso. These variables become important in disguising the amount of caffeine ingested by the urban espresso consumer. The end result of a couple hours of conversation at the local espresso shop may lead to a higher than usual exposure of caffeine to the unwary consumer.

Another part of the culture of caffeine is found on the Internet. One can find frequently asked questions about caffeine on the World Wide Web. The computer literate espresso consumer can have their questions answered about the different bean varieties as well as the amounts of caffeine in different preparations. Interactive networks respond to questions about types of preparations and health interactions. Article references are given as well as amounts of caffeine in non-coffee preparations. The Mountanos Brothers Coffee Company in San Francisco offers a list of the amount of caffeine in straight and blended bean products from across the world. Another Web network answers questions on the safe to lethal amounts of coffee. One can find humorous barbs and poems on the joy and ecstasy of caffeine as well. The culture of caffeine is significant and will inevitably affect the number of exposures and subsequent chances of health interactions in the population. It will be important for clinicians to be aware of this information database and its impact on the lives of their patients.

DIAGNOSTIC TERMINOLOGY

The term "caffeinism" has come to denote the generic syndrome of clinical features secondary to intake of caffeine, but official diagnostic nomenclatures have employed more specific terms. "Caffeine intoxication" is the only official diagnosis associated with caffeinism in the American Psychiatric Association's Diagnostic and Statistical Manual of Mental Disorders, 4th edition (DSM-IV) (45). The criteria for this diagnosis are listed in Table 26.6.

If symptoms should exceed those for caffeine intoxication and require independent clinical intervention, it is permissible to diagnose "caffeine-induced anxiety disorder" and/or "caffeine-induced sleep disorder." All DSM-IV caffeine-related disorders are listed in Table 26.7.

Drugs of abuse have two major characteristics: they are reinforcing and they produce adverse effects. While "intoxication" is recognized as a syndrome, caffeine withdrawal, dependence, and abuse are not. Should they be?

With regard to *withdrawal,* Hughes and colleagues (34, 89) and Griffiths and his collaborators (90) have demonstrated that abstinence from caffeine induces a distinct withdrawal syndrome (headache, fatigue, and drowsiness beginning approximately 18–24 hours after the last dose and tapering over the next week). Remarkably, withdrawal manifestations can occur even with doses as modest as 100 mg/day. Double-blind tests also confirm that a subset of coffee and soda drinkers reliably self-administer caffeinated beverages in preference to uncaffeinated beverages, sometimes to avoid withdrawal. These data arguably support the view that caffeine withdrawal should be included as a diagnosis in DSM-IV and ICD nosological systems. Meanwhile, only research criteria for caffeine withdrawal have been compiled (Table 26.8).

Table 26.6 Diagnostic Criteria for Caffeine Intoxication

A. Recent consumption of caffeine, usually in excess of 250 mg (e.g., more than 2–3 cups of brewed coffee).
B. Five (or more) of the following signs, developing during or shortly after caffeine use:
1. restlessness
2. nervousness
3. excitement
4. insomnia
5. flushed face
6. diuresis
7. gastrointestinal disturbance
8. muscle twitching
9. rambling flow of thought and speech
10. tachycardia or cardiac arrhythmia
11. periods of inexhaustibility
12. psychomotor agitation
C. The symptoms in criterion B cause clinically significant distress or impairment in social, occupational, or other important areas of functioning.
D. The symptoms are not due to a general medical condition and are not better accounted for by another mental disorder (e.g., an anxiety disorder).

Table based on Diagnostic and Statistical Manual of Mental Disorders, 4th edition (DSM-IV). Copyright American Psychiatric Association, Washington, DC, 1994. Used with permission.

The situation is less clear for *caffeine dependence.* Self-administration of coffee to obtain the effects of caffeine occurs under selected circumstances (24, 90–92) but with lesser elevations in ratings of "euphoria" and "well-being" than when amphetamines are taken (93–95). A telephone survey designed to determine what would be found if DSM-III-R criteria for drug dependence were applied to caffeine found that 44% of current users (or approximately one third of the total population) would have met three or more of the criteria and been diagnosed as having a dependency on caffeine (92). Most reported a "desire to reduce" or "prior lack of success in reducing." Hughes and colleagues (89) reviewed the issue of caffeine dependence and showed that the clinical patient database was almost nonexistent. Until controlled clinical studies convincingly demonstrate meaningful clinical dependence and "use despite harm," it will be difficult to convince a skeptical public that as many as one third of the general population should be potential candidates for a diagnosis of caffeine abuse or dependence in DSM or ICD classifications (21, 45, 96).

CLINICAL DESCRIPTION

Consistent with the gradual progression of intake to moderate or large doses, the clinical features of caffeinism tend to develop insidiously, after months or years of intake, unless there are preceding comorbid disorders such as panic disorder. Potential reasons for this insidious pattern are that there may have been a simple steady increase over years until "intoxication" is reached, symptom onset only because of CNS neurotransmitter or receptor changes associated with chronic use, or biological changes associated with aging. Most patients diagnosed as having caffeinism are older than 35 years. Because of the gradual development of symptoms, the majority of subjects with caffeinism still are reluctant to link anxiety, sleep disruption, or other troubling symptoms with their long-standing ingestion of caffeine.

Table 26.7 Caffeine-Related Disorders

Caffeine-induced disorders
Caffeine intoxication
Caffeine-induced anxiety disorder
  Specify if: with onset during intoxication
Caffeine-induced sleep disorder
  Specify if: with onset during intoxication
Caffeine-related disorder not otherwise specified

Table based on Diagnostic and Statistical Manual of Mental Disorders, 4th edition (DSM-IV). Copyright American Psychiatric Association, Washington, DC, 1994. Used with permission.

Table 26.8   Research Criteria for Caffeine Withdrawal

A. Prolonged daily use of caffeine.
B. Abrupt cessation of caffeine use or reduction in the amount of caffeine used, closely followed by headache and one (or more) of the following symptoms:
    1. marked fatigue or drowsiness
    2. marked anxiety or depression
    3. nausea or vomiting
C. The symptoms in criterion B cause clinically significant distress or impairment in social, occupational, or other important areas of functioning.
D. The symptoms are not due to the direct physiological effects of a general medical condition (e.g., migraine, viral illness) and are not better accounted for by another mental disorder.

Table based on Diagnostic and Statistical Manual of Mental Disorders, 4th edition (DSM-IV). Copyright American Psychiatric Association, Washington, DC, 1994. Used with permission.

Most sufferers of "caffeinism" present with other complaints (9). Rarely do people enter medical circles with the request that they need help to counteract their excessive caffeine intake. It is reasonable to hypothesize that those with caffeinism may seek medical attention more than nondependent individuals (although this hypothesis has not been tested systematically), if only because most high consumers describe their health as being fair or poor (10).

CAFFEINE-INDUCED ANXIETY DISORDER

Anxiety is the recognized *sine qua non* of caffeinism. The folklore of "coffee nerves" has a long history (40, 42, 46, 97, 98), but few systematic studies were conducted until the causal links between anxiety and caffeinism were re-emphasized in 1974 (9).

Features of caffeine-induced anxiety include restlessness, nervousness, excitement, insomnia, diuresis, flushing, gastrointestinal disturbance, muscle twitching, irritability, and jitteriness. Everyday terms are used for these features, of course, such as "tense," "wired," "high strung," "stressed out," and "juiced." More sophisticated consumers have been heard to describe being "high on caffeine." Cartoonists often use the coffee high as a theme. Those with caffeinism are noted by others to talk somewhat faster and louder, to appear energetic, but also to be less tolerant, to perhaps be more intrusive in conversation, to respond with greater irritation to work stressors, and to live with a "driven" quality. Perhaps because of these associated interpersonal manifestations, friends and family members often encourage high users to "get off caffeine."

Quantitative assessments generally confirm correlations between increasing caffeine and increasing anxiety. For example, individuals with the highest caffeine intakes report significantly greater levels of "state" anxiety (how one feels at the moment) on the State-Trait Anxiety Index (STAI) (99). Trait anxiety scores (how one generally feels) are also elevated to an abnormal level, consistent with the fact that most patients with caffeinism have chronic, daily patterns of use.

Clinicians have long speculated that patients with generalized anxiety disorder (GAD) are more sensitive to caffeine than those without the disorder. To study possible sensitivity, Bruce and colleagues (100) compared a number of measures in those with GAD versus normal controls after administering two doses of oral caffeine (250 and 500 mg) and placebo. Caffeine produced significantly greater decreases in auditory-evoked potential amplitudes, greater increases in skin conductance levels, greater systolic and diastolic blood pressure increases, higher critical fusion flicker frequency, and higher self-ratings of anxiety and sweating in patients with GAD than in normal patients. These data suggest that those with GAD manifest greater sensitivity to caffeine.

The same is true for those afflicted with panic disorder. Because generalized anxiety disorder is "related" to panic disorder, this is not surprising. The drug does not appear to cause panic attacks in normal individuals, but it did in 71% of subjects already diagnosed with the disorder (36). The drug seems to produce excessive adrenergic stimulation, with panic patients showing greater blood pressure increases than controls following a caffeine challenge. Caffeine intensifies the CNS symptoms of panic attacks in people with the disorder, which probably explains why people with panic disorder report consuming less caffeine than normal controls or patients with other types of psychiatric disorders but report more symptoms from the caffeine consumed than do depressed or normal controls (101). These observations suggest that the disorder underlying panic attacks has some common neurobiological underpinnings with the mechanisms of action for caffeine.

It is unknown whether caffeine may cause or accentuate other psychiatric diagnoses commonly considered to be in the "anxiety spectrum" (e.g., social phobia, post-traumatic stress disorder, obsessive compulsive disorder) or if individuals with these diagnoses might be more sensitive to the drug, but intriguingly, those with social phobia did not differ from a controlled population of "community subjects" in weekly consumption of caffeinated beverages (102).

Paradoxically, a small number of individuals report mild improvement in attention deficit and hyperactivity symptoms when they receive caffeine (103, 104). All these illustrations reveal that caffeine's effects must be interpreted within the context of underlying neurobiological function.

CAFFEINE-INDUCED SLEEP DISORDER

Caffeine's ability to overcome sleepiness (14, 83) is actively sought by many at times when vigilance or sustained performance seem desirable. Unfortunately, the drug's effects cannot always be titrated or "turned off" at will, and sought-after actions may quickly become undesired insomnia. At such times, if specific clinical treatment is required, caffeine-induced sleep disorder (DSM-IV) is an appropriate diagnosis.

If given acutely to nontolerant individuals, caffeine interferes with sleep in most people (5, 10, 14, 83, 105–107). In those with tolerance, the incidence of reported sleep abnormalities decreases considerably. For example, in one study (10), 53% of low consumers (<250 mg/day) agreed that caffeine before bedtime would prevent sleep compared to 43% of moderate consumers (250–749 mg/day) and only 22% of high consumers (750 mg/day or more). Despite these subjective denials among high consumers, almost all objective sleep laboratory testing studies indicate that caffeine consumers do have greater delays in sleep onset, more frequent awakenings, and altered sleep architecture and that these effects are dose related (5). It seems as if many of these individuals simply have adapted to this pattern of subtly impaired sleep and do not consider it abnormal.

Age and concomitant medication use may be confounding variables, with the elderly being more sensitive to caffeine's sleep impairment. Median caffeine concentration has been demonstrated to be higher in elderly hospitalized individuals reporting sleep problems than in those without (108), and caffeine was noted to counteract the sedative-hypnotic effect of barbiturates (109). Highest users also reported greater use of sedative-hypnotics to aid sleep induction. These factors should be considered before prescribing sedative-hypnotics. In community populations, median plasma caffeine concentrations also have been shown to significantly correlate with sleep quality.

Geriatric patients often consume medications that contain caffeine, sometimes without being aware that the drug is being ingested. In one cross-sectional analysis, the prevalence of caffeinated medication use was 5.4%, and predictably, those reporting the use of caffeine-containing medications were at increased risk of having trouble falling asleep. Clinicians should encourage their geriatric patients to read the label on medications and to select those that are caffeine-free whenever possible (110).

Caffeine's competitive antagonism of adenosine receptors is likely the underlying mechanism for sleep impairments since adenosine induces sedation (58).

CAFFEINE-RELATED MOOD DISORDERS

The relationship between caffeine and mood disorders has received too little attention among investigators. It is not recognized in DSM-IV. Considering caffeine's categorization as a "stimulant," a report by Greden et al. in 1976 (10) paradoxically suggested high caffeine consumption among psychiatric patients might be associated with greater depressive symptoms. These investigators showed that depression rating scores increased steadily among 83 hospitalized psychiatric patients as caffeine intake increased, and a large percentage of the highest users had clinically significant elevations. Overall, 17% of the low users (0–249 mg/day) compiled Beck scores greater than 23, compared to 34% of moderate users (250–749 mg/day) and 50% of high users (750 mg/day or more) (p<.05). The study design did not permit an answer to the question of whether caffeine use was causal, an attempt at "self-medication" to counteract the depressive symptoms, or an epiphenomenon. A more recent clinical assessment (111) compared caffeine intake among normal volunteers, patients with major depression, seasonal affective disorder, alcohol dependence, and comorbid primary depression with secondary alcohol dependence and determined that patients of *all* diagnostic groups were more likely than normal volunteers to report using caffeine, although the responses of the patient groups did not differ from each other. Another study concluded that, while depressed patients did not differ from control subjects in total caffeine intake, more depressed patients report that caffeine induces anxiety (101).

There was a recent suggestion from a large epidemiological study that nurses who consumed more coffee per day had a lower suicide risk than those who drank none, but there were enough methodological concerns that any conclusions seem premature (112).

Of indirect relevance to treatment of mood disorders, it has been found that caffeine lengthens seizures during electroconvulsive therapy (ECT) (113). This observation has led to occasional administration of caffeine prior to ECT in the hope of augmenting treatment response.

Yohimbine is an alpha-2 antagonist marketed as an agent for treating male impotence. Recently, it has been prescribed to some patients receiving selective serotonin receptor inhibitor antidepressants (SSRIs) in attempts to counteract sexual side effects of the medications. If the alpha-2 receptor is blocked, then appropriate negative feedback about adrenergic output cannot be obtained, and secretion of adrenergic transmitters tends to continue. Charney et al. (36) showed that yohimbine produced elevations in anxiety, blood pressure, and MHPG levels. Because of the prevalence of caffeine use, it is predictable that most users of yohimbine also will be caffeine users and that the effects of the two agents might be interactive, producing even greater likelihood of anxiety, panic, or sleep disturbances. This prospect warrants study and caution.

CAFFEINE-RELATED SOMATIC MANIFESTATIONS

While epidemiological data are not available, most individuals with caffeinism probably confront the health care system in primary care offices. Psychophysiological symptoms probably are the most common reasons for them to seek evaluation. The majority of high users experience one or more of the common cluster of caffeine-induced somatic symptoms, including urinary frequency and diuresis, headache, tachycardia, arrhythmias, tremulousness, diarrhea, gastrointestinal pain or discomfort, or lightheadedness (66). Less frequent symptoms include seeing "spots" in front of the eyes, "ringing" in the ears, a feeling of being unable to breathe (perhaps attributable to caffeine-induced panic attack), "tingling" in fingers and toes, and excessive perspiration.

These psychophysiological symptoms sometimes can be frightening to patients, especially since few individuals make any association with caffeine intake. The worst is imagined: "I have an ulcer." "I am having a stroke." "This must be a 'heart attack'." " I am going to die." In such circumstances, patients seek evaluation from physicians, often precipitating an extensive medical evaluation, many laboratory tests, but inconclusive results. If the evaluation does not include a consideration of caffeinism and this diagnosis is missed, other medical interventions usually are prescribed to counteract the troublesome symptoms.

CAFFEINE-RELATED COMORBID DISORDERS

Caffeine and Eating Disorders

Intriguingly, Keys et al. (114) reported increased caffeine ingestion during starvation. Because of this report, Krahn and colleagues (116) measured caffeine use of 171 patients with eating disorders and compared clinical profiles of high, moderate, and low caffeine consumers. Mean caffeine intake was not elevated compared to the general population. However, 14.6% of eating disorder patients were high consumers (more than 750 mg/day), and they consumed more than 15 mg/kg/day compared to the 7.0 mg/kg/day consumed by the top 10% of caffeine users in the general population (43). The highest consumers also reported higher anxiety, a trend toward worse depression on the Beck Depression Scale, more binge eating, greater use of diet pills, alcohol, and tobacco. In summary, some symptoms previously attributed to eating disorders might be linked to concomitant caffeine use.

Comorbid Substance-Related Disorders

Highest caffeine consumers report significantly greater use of sedative-hypnotics and antianxiety agents ("minor tranquilizers") than low or moderate users. A somewhat startling figure is that approximately two thirds of highest caffeine users reported using an antianxiety agent within the past month (116). Obviously, when evaluating and treating patients who might have developed anxiety because of caffeine use, it would be preferable to discontinue the offending agent rather than adding another psychoactive agent to counteract its effects. Caffeine, alcohol, and tobacco use cluster together in the same individuals probably because all common substances of abuse induce sensitization of brain reward pathways. Recently, some systematic data have been collected in an attempt to document these purported linkages. Studies have revealed that more smokers consume coffee than nonsmokers (117) and are more likely to drink caffeinated coffee; also, ex-smokers use more coffee than nonsmokers but less than smokers. While probably due to common CNS reinforcing mechanisms, smoking also alters caffeine metabolism, with smokers showing an approximate doubling of the exhalation curve (116). In abstinent smokers, blood caffeine levels increase and remain elevated for as long as 6 months. This observation may have clinical relevance, possibly being sufficient to produce caffeine toxicity. Investigators should consider the possibility that presumed nicotine withdrawal symptoms may actually represent a blend of nicotine withdrawal and caffeine toxicity (118).

Caffeine has been incorrectly touted as an antidote to alcohol intoxication (119). Indeed, animal studies suggest caffeine does not effectively ameliorate but may worsen ethanol intoxication (120). Reformed alcoholics often are noted to vociferously consume caffeine. The reasons for this claimed excessive use are unknown. Of relevance, many alcoholics develop hepatic abnormalities, and hepatic abnormalities have been shown to change caffeine demethylation, with resultant changes in exhalation curves of a specific-$^{14}CO_2$-methyl-labeled caffeine (121). Studies to determine whether caffeine metabolism is altered in alcoholic cirrhotics revealed that exhalation curves were clearly different, with alcoholics showing a slower rise than normal subjects.

Since smokeless tobacco has increased in popularity over the past two decades, it is of relevance to determine if interactions are also found between this form of administration and caffeine. Siegel and colleagues (122) found that smokeless tobacco users reported heavier consumption of alcohol and had higher mean caffeine levels (p<.001) than those who did not use smokeless tobacco.

Caffeine and Postsurgical Headaches

Many cases of headache that occur after general anesthesia may be related to caffeine withdrawal. Fennelly et al. (123) reported a highly significant difference between the caffeine consumption of patients with and without preoperative and postoperative headaches. With each 100 mg increase in reported caffeine consumption, they noted a 12% increase of headache developing in the immediate preoperative period (p<.007) and a 16% increase in the odds of postoperative headache (p<.0001).

Hampl and colleagues (124) sought to assess the therapeutic implications of perioperative caffeine by studying 40 patients undergoing minor surgical procedures with general anesthesia. They were randomly allocated to placebo or caffeine tablets at dosages equal to their average daily consumption. Fifty percent of the patients who received placebo reported headaches; no patient receiving caffeine substitution therapy reported headache. Anesthesiologists and surgeons should begin routinely documenting caffeine consumption and, whenever possible, suggest tapering prior to operative procedures. Prophylactic administration of caffeine tablets also might be considered for surgical patients who report high daily intake of caffeine (124).

Caffeine and Weekend Headaches

Headache specialists have long recognized that caffeine might be related to weekend headaches. Sometimes such headaches have been misdiagnosed as migraines or attributed to social or psychological stressors associated with being at home over the weekend. Recent reports again confirm that patients with high daily caffeine intake and excessively delayed wakening on weekends had a 69% risk of weekend headache, compared with only 4% of controls. Such data support clinical observations that weekend headaches often may be linked to caffeine withdrawal and, while confounded with chronobiological sleep rhythms, prolonged sleeping, per se, may not be the cause of such headaches (125).

Caffeine and Cardiovascular Disease

Cardiovascular specialists recognize caffeine use as a potential risk factor. A recent study confirms prior reports that caffeine may interact with stressful behavioral situations. Caffeine or placebo was given to two groups: (a) low-risk men who were negative for parental hypertension and had low-to-normal resting blood pressure and (b) high-risk men who were positive for family history and had high normal blood pressure. When confronted with a stressful psychomotor task, caffeine plus the task resulted in approximately half of the high-risk group having transient blood pressures of 140/90 mm Hg or greater. This would suggest that caffeine in combination with mental stress may be associated with a risk for unacceptably high levels of blood pressure in those with positive family histories of hypertension or those with borderline elevations of blood pressure themselves (126).

Caffeine and Chronobiology

Chronobiological regulation plays a major role in many psychiatric syndromes, especially mood, sleep, and eating disorders. Individuals with different diurnal rhythms (e.g., "morning-types" and "evening-types") also report different patterns of consumption of alcohol, caffeine, and nicotine. Evening-types are reported to consume more alcohol, nicotine, and caffeine from both coffee and cola, while morning types reported greater consumption of caffeine from tea.

OTHER PSYCHOACTIVE AGENTS ASSOCIATED WITH CAFFEINE

Coffee and tea contain a large number of additional psychoactive products besides caffeine and the other xanthines (theophylline and theobromine). Chocolate contains phenylethylamine. Some analgesics with caffeine also contain barbiturates, and many cold products contain antihistamines. These illustrations indicate that interactive drug effects are likely. These other substances may themselves induce pharmacological responses, interact with caffeine in altering CNS or peripheral transmitter activity, or change the metabolism of caffeine. The primary focus of this chapter is caffeine, but it should be noted that these other agents exist and may be clinically relevant. Unfortunately, interactive effects have received too little scientific attention.

CAFFEINE WITHDRAWAL

Caffeine withdrawal is a physiological syndrome resulting when individuals who have been previously consuming the drug on a regular basis suddenly discontinue their intake (12). The research criteria are provided in Table 26.8. The syndrome presumably stems from prior development of physiological dependence on caffeine. Principal manifestations of withdrawal include headache, drowsiness, and fatigue. Less frequent manifestations include impaired psychomotor performance, difficulty concentrating, psychophysiological complaints (e.g., nausea, excessive yawning), and craving. Onset usually is within 18–24 hours, a figure that is consistent with the known half-life of caffeine (12). Since caffeine consumption among many individuals is linked to employment, the withdrawal syndrome often occurs on weekends (especially among those inclined to sleep late) or at vacation times. If unrecognized, its origins may be attributed incorrectly to difficulties coping with the home setting or to marital or family conflicts.

The frequency of the caffeine withdrawal syndrome is not well known, but it may be common. Dreisbach and Pfeiffer (127), in an experimental setting where placebo was substituted for caffeine, induced headaches in 25–35% of laboratory volunteers by stopping caffeine suddenly. Greden et al. (12) noted that 20% of a hospitalized patient population reported *being aware* of previous caffeine withdrawal headache. The number who actually had the syndrome may have been higher, since some probably were unaware of any association.

Caffeine withdrawal headaches start with a sense of fullness in the head, and progress to throbbing, diffuse pain, accentuated by movement. If untreated, the pain peaks 3–6 hours after beginning, Approximately one quarter may report mild nausea. As Goldstein stated in 1969 (84, 85), there is no doubt that the caffeine withdrawal headache is a "real phenomenon." Many report concomitant features now known to be attributable to the withdrawal syndrome (lethargy, rhinorrhea, yawning, irritability).

Caffeine consumers with withdrawal headaches and drowsiness were approximately 2.5 times more likely to self-administer caffeinated coffee in double-blind tests (34).

Topographic quantitative EEG measures of alpha and theta power reveal significant increases during caffeine withdrawal, with return to the pre-abstinent EEG levels when caffeine usage is resumed (128).

Perhaps the most effective "treatment" for the withdrawal syndrome is renewed caffeine consumption. Relief tends to occur within 30–60 minutes. Perhaps this partially explains why so many analgesics sold in over-the-counter "pain" products contain caffeine. It also suggests that many individuals who develop caffeine withdrawal headaches may drift toward frequent and exclusive use of analgesics that contain caffeine, and that these products then become another significant source of caffeine intake.

In summary, the caffeine withdrawal syndrome is found commonly among individuals with caffeinism, occurs frequently on weekends, is often associated with headaches (with a diagnostic clue being that these headaches characteristically respond best to analgesics that contain caffeine), and probably helps promote the pattern on ongoing caffeine consumption among many heavy consumers.

DIFFERENTIAL DIAGNOSIS

Caffeinism may present with different displays of clinical features, mimic other clinical entities, exist comorbidly with other disorders, and be confounded by other drugs and medications. Any clinical differential must consider caffeinism when confronting those common entities that present with one or more of the major constellations associated with caffeinism, i.e., anxiety and panic, sleep disorders, somatic or psychophysiological disorders, affective or mood disorders, and other types of substance abuse. Syndromes that should be explored specifically include hyperthyroidism, hypomania or mania, electrolyte disturbances, pheochromocytoma (with its four p's—head *p*ain, *p*alpitations, *p*allor, and *p*erspiration), delayed sleep phase insomnia or other sleep disorders, and other types of substance abuse, especially cocaine, amphetamine, phenylpropanolamine (PPA), and ephedrine. In addition to careful clinical history, physical examination and appropriate laboratory testing are usually essential to rule out some of these conditions.

Considering the widespread pattern of caffeine intake, it is reasonable to suggest that self-rating survey forms (10) might be appropriately included in the routine assessment of all new patients in primary care medical settings. As suggested previously, if caffeine consumption exceeding 500 mg/day is found and the user has clinical symptoms and signs compatible with caffeinism, the clinician can assume that a direct correlation between drug intake and symptoms is probable and needs to be ruled out. This presumption is necessary to avoid the common pattern of overlooking caffeine in favor of other, often more esoteric, presumed causes.

A presumptive diagnosis of caffeinism then needs to be tested with a withdrawal paradigm. The key clinical symptoms are listed and quantified with simple rating scales at baseline, caffeine intake is withdrawn, and changes following the discontinuation are monitored. If clinical features are due to caffeinism, they characteristically will lessen in intensity or even disappear within 1–2 weeks after the withdrawal paradigm. Of course, new symptoms (e.g., sleepiness, yawning, headache) sometimes develop transiently because of caffeine withdrawal. Causal association is strongly suggested if the troublesome symptoms fade. If further documentation is desired, a caffeine challenge can be employed. The caffeine intake is reinstituted at prior levels, and symptoms again are monitored. If due to caffeine, the symptoms usually recur within 1–2 days, sometimes even within hours. This "A-B-A" design often seems necessary to convince skeptical patients that caffeine is truly the offending agent.

TREATMENT

The treatment of caffeinism can be stated simply: caffeine intake should be reduced or discontinued. Statement is easy; attainment is not. Subjects with caffeinism often minimize the importance of caffeine, sometimes despite the "A-B-A" challenge, or seem willing to tolerate the unpleasant, troubling components of caffeinism to retain the drug's reinforcing qualities. The widespread availability of the agent also makes it difficult to avoid future ingestion. Finally, the withdrawal manifestations that occur for some may discourage attempts to discontinue use.

To counteract these barriers, an imaginative educational program is necessary. The clinician should explain caffeine's pharmacological actions, listing the common consequences and their known mechanisms. Brochures may aid in this process. A list of products that contain caffeine, comparable to that printed in this chapter, should be given to the patient, since it is not uncommon for individuals to "give up coffee" and substitute an alternative source such as tea or cola drinks. Caffeine-containing products already available at home (e.g., in the medicine chest), at work, or in the automobile should be discarded (resistance to this "housecleaning" often is a clue to future difficulty with compliance). Family members or significant partners should be included in this educational effort. It is more difficult for one individual to be caffeine-free in a household where others are regular consumers.

If acute withdrawal produces troublesome symptoms and interferes with progress, a staged reduction may be tried. A gradual substitution of decaffeinated beverages may help. Clinical experience suggests, however, that total discontinuation may be more effective than gradual withdrawal programs in preventing "relapse," which usually develops by a gradual increase of daily dosage.

Patients, family, and friends may benefit from practical hints that help them modify their prior patterns of intake. They should be encouraged to drink water when thirsty (including having a pitcher of ice water instead of a pot of coffee in key locations, such as on their work desk), suck sugarless mints, routinely request decaffeinated coffee in restaurants, consume decaffeinated soft drinks (usually displayed prominently on the containers), limit caffeine consumption to one or at most two specified times of the day (e.g., morning breakfast and afternoon coffee break), and avoid use of analgesics that contain caffeine (these should be discarded to limit availability). Many individuals whose symptoms became troublesome only when dosage is in-creased past certain threshold levels may find that it is adequate to simply limit intake below that level; however, as indicated previously, chronicity, tolerance with increasing dosage, and increasing age may lead to development of symptoms in subsequent years even if dosage remains stable. The problem of caffeinism should not be counteracted by recommending a switch to other herbal preparations (these products have their own patterns of toxicity) (129) or by treating symptoms with additional prescription medications. Special attention should be given to assessing and counteracting concomitant drug use, as already described. Use of over-the-counter products by the patient also should be discouraged. In contrast to some types of substance abuse (e.g., nicotine or opioids), there are no available "substitutes" that seemingly diminish craving by counteracting withdrawal but are considered safer alternatives.

This condition often is remitting in nature. Clinicians should understand this and respond to patients with support and encouragement to continue in their efforts ("don't quit quitting"). The overall objective is the patient's well-being and prolongation of time periods without symptoms. Intermittent periods of relapse should not be perceived as failure.

As indicated earlier, for some individuals dosage reduction may be adequate. Some patients, however, are especially vulnerable to any caffeine intake, and total abstinence should be emphasized. Clearly, patients with panic disorder should refrain from caffeine use. Most already do. Anyone with well-documented histories of cardiovascular disease, especially arrhythmias, should totally refrain as should people with prior stroke or transient ischemic attacks. Those with gastrointestinal disorders and peptic ulcer disease should be totally abstinent. Patients with bipolar mood disorder (manic-depression) and schizophrenia should be encouraged to totally refrain, as should pregnant women.

PREVENTION

Our population is better educated about caffeine than in the past, although much remains to be done. Brewed decaffeinated coffee now is widely available as an alternative beverage in most restaurants, airlines, and other public service-related settings. The soft-drink industry seems to have responded to public concerns by offering more noncaffeinated selections. Some analgesic products have removed caffeine. These steps should be encouraged. Similarly, caffeine use during pregnancy and by young children should not be treated as harmless.

FUTURE OUTLOOK

Caffeine is a domesticated, popular, widely-consumed drug. It appears to be undergoing a surge in popularity. It will continue to be a component of our society. Safe use is certainly possible; it continues to be the norm in most people. However, caffeinism and caffeine withdrawal also continue to be common and clinically important but unrecognized, underdiagnosed even when recognized, and untreated in many treatment settings. Research on caffeine has flourished. More knowledge is needed and can be anticipated. Meanwhile, clinicians who actively consider the diagnosis of caffeinism in their patients will be surprised at how many afflicted subjects are identified, impressed at how many are helped by removal of the offending agent, and pleased to know that almost all are grateful.

References

1. Graham DM. Caffeine—Its identity, dietary sources, intake, and biological effects. Nutr Rev 1978;36:97–102.
2. Hughes JR, Oliveto AH, Helzer JE, Bickel WK, Higgins ST. Indications of caffeine dependence in a population-based sample. In: Harris LS, ed. Problems of drug dependence, 1992. NIDA Res Monogr Ser 1993;132:194.
3. Gilbert RM. Caffeine consumption. In: Spiller GA, ed. The methylxanthine beverages and foods: chemistry, consumption, and health effects. New York: Alan R. Liss, 1984:185–213.
4. Gilbert RM. Caffeine as a drug of abuse. In: Gibben RG, Hiklart YI, Pophom RE, Schmidt W, Smart RG, eds. Research addresses in alcohol and drug problems. New York: John Wiley & Sons, 1976.
5. Levy M, Zylber-Katz E. Caffeine metabolism and coffee-attributed sleep disturbances. Clin Pharmacol Ther 1983;33:770–775.
6. U.S. Food and Drug Administration. Caffeine: deletion of GRAS status, proposed declaration that no prior sanction exists, and use on an interim basis pending additional study. Federal Register 1980;45/205:69817–69838.
7. U.S. Food and Drug Administration. Caffeine content of various products. FDA Talk Paper, T80–45. Washington, DC: U.S. Food and Drug Administration, 1980.
8. Diagnostic and Statistical Manual of Mental Disorders, Second Edition (DSM-II). Washington, DC: American Psychiatric Association, 1968.
9. Greden JF. Anxiety or caffeinism: a diagnostic dilemma. Am J Psychiatry 1974;131:1089.
10. Greden JF. Anxiety and depression associated with caffeinism among psychiatric inpatients. Am J Psychiatry 1978;135:963.
11. Greden JF. Coffee, tea and you. Sciences 1979;19:6.

12. Greden JF, Victor V, Fontaine P, Lubetsky M. Caffeine-withdrawal headache: a neglected syndrome. In: Scientific proceedings of the 132nd annual meeting, American Psychiatric Association. Chicago: American Psychiatric Association, 1979:389.

13. Winstead DK. Coffee consumption among psychiatric inpatients. Am J Psychiatry 1976; 133:1447.

14. Goldstein A, Warren R, Kaizer S. Psychotropic effects of caffeine in man I. Individual differences and sensitivity to caffeine-induced wakefulness. J Pharmacol Exp Ther 1965;49:156.

15. Waldeck B. Sensitization by caffeine of central catecholamine receptors. J Neural Transm 1973; 34:61–72.

16. Waldeck B. Modification of a caffeine-induced locomotor stimulation by a cholinergic mechanism. J Neurol Transm 1974;35:195.

17. Waldeck B. Ethanol and caffeine: A complex interaction with respect to locomotor activity and central catecholamines. Psychopharmacologia 1974;36:209–220.

18. Waldeck B. Effect on locomotor activity and central catecholamine mechanisms: A study with special reference to drug interaction. Acta Pharmacol Toxicol (Suppl IV) 1975;36:1.

19. Fuxe K, Ungerstedt U. Action of caffeine and theophylline on supersensitive dopamine receptors: Considerable enhancement of receptor response to treatment with dopa and dopamine receptor agonists. Med Biol 1974;52:48–54.

20. SCOGS. Evaluation of health aspects of caffeine as a food ingredient, SCOGS-89. Bethesda, MD: Federation of American Societies for Experimental Biology, 1978.

21. Diagnostic and Statistical Manual of Mental Disorders, Third Edition (DSM-III). Washington, DC: American Psychiatric Association, 1980.

22. Griffiths RR, Woodson PP. Caffeine physical dependence: a review of human and laboratory animal studies. Psychopharmacology 1988;94: 437–451.

23. Griffiths RR, Woodson PP. Reinforcing properties of caffeine: studies in humans and laboratory animals. Pharmacol Biochem Behav 1988; 29:419–427.

24. Hughes JR, Higgins ST, Bickel WK, Hunt WK, Fenwick JW, Gulliver SB, et al. Caffeine self-administration, withdrawal and adverse effects among coffee drinkers. Arch Gen Psychiatry 1991;48:611–617.

25. Greden JF. Caffeinism and caffeine withdrawal. In: Lowinson JH, Ruiz P, eds. Substance abuse: clinical problems and perspectives. Baltimore: Williams & Wilkins, 1981:274.

26. Greden JF, Walters A. Caffeine. In: Lowinson JH, Ruiz P, Millman RB, eds. Substance abuse: a comprehensive textbook. 2nd ed. Baltimore: Williams & Wilkins, 1992:357–370.

27. Weiss B, Laties VG. Enhancement of human performance by caffeine and the amphetamines. Pharmacol Rev 1962;14:1.

28. Phillis JW, Kostopoulos GK, Limacher JJ. Depression of corticospinal cells by various purines and pyrimidines. Can J Physiol Pharmacol 1974;52:1226.

29. Phillis JW, Kostopoulos GK, Limacher JJ. A potent depressant action of adenosine derivatives on cerebral cortical neurons. Eur J Pharmacol 1975;30:125.

30. Griffiths RR, Mumford GK. Caffeine—a drug of abuse? In: Bloom FE, Kupfer DJ, eds. Psychopharmacology: the fourth generation of progress. New York: Raven Press, 1995:1699–1713.

31. Griffiths RR, Bigelow GE, Liebson IA. Human coffee drinking: reinforcing and physical dependence producing effects of caffeine. J Pharmacol Exp Ther 1986;239:416–425.

32. Griffiths RR, Bigelow GE, Liebson IA. Reinforcing effects of caffeine in coffee and capsules. J Exp Anal Behav 1989;52:127–140.

33. Evans SM, Griffiths RR. Caffeine tolerance and choice in humans. Psychopharmacology (Berlin) 1992;108:51–59.

34. Hughes JR, Oliveto AH, Bickel WK, Higgins ST, Badger GJ. Caffeine self-administration and withdrawal: incidence, individual differences and interrelationships. Drug Alcohol Depend 1993;32:239–246.

35. Griffiths RR, Woodson PP. Reinforcing effects of caffeine in humans. J Pharmacol Exp Ther 1988;246:21–29.

36. Charney DS, Heninger GR, Jatlow PI. Increased anxiogenic effects of caffeine in panic disorders. Arch Gen Psychiatry 1985;42:233–243.

37. Colton T, Gosselin RE, Smith RP. The tolerance of coffee drinkers to caffeine. Clin Pharmacol Ther 1968;9:31–39.

38. Eddy NB, Downs AW. Tolerance and cross-tolerance in the human subject to the diuretic effect of caffeine, theobromine and theophylline. J Pharmacol Exp Ther 1928;33:167–174.

39. Rall TW. The xanthines. In: Gilman AG, Goodman LS, Gilman A, eds. The pharmacological basis of therapeutics. 6th ed. New York: Macmillan, 1980:592–607.

40. Greden JF. The tea controversy in Colonial America. JAMA 1976;236:63.

41. Gilbert RM. Caffeine beverages and their effects. Addictions 1974;21:68.

42. Ellis J. An historical account of coffee. London: Edward and Charles Dilly, 1774.

43. Barone JJ, Roberts H. Human consumption of caffeine. In: Dews PB, ed. Caffeine. New York: Springer-Verlag, 1984:59–76.

44. Siegerist HE. Literary controversy over tea in 18th-century England. Bull Hist Med 1943; 13:185.

45. Diagnostic and Statistical Manual of Mental Disorders, Fourth Edition (DSM-IV). Washington, DC: American Psychiatric Association, 1994.

46. Kalm P. Travels into North America. Warrington, PA: William Eyres, 1770;1:372.

47. International Coffee Organization. United States of America, coffee drinking study—winter. London, 1989.

48. Molde DA. Diagnosing caffeinism. Am J Psychiatry 1975;132:202.

49. Arnaud MJ. Products of metabolism of caffeine. In: Dews PB, ed. Caffeine. New York: Springer-Verlag, 1984:3–38.

50. Medicus L. Zur Constitution der Harnsauregruppe. Liebigs Ann Chem 1875;175:230–251.

51. Axelrod R, Reichenthal J. The fate of caffeine in man and a method for its estimation in biological material. J Pharmacol Exp Ther 1953;107: 519–523.

52. Bonati M, Lantini R, Galetti F, Young JF, Tognoni G, Garattini S. Caffeine disposition after oral doses. Clin Pharmacol Ther 1982;32:98–106.

53. Kaplan GB, Greenblatt DJ, LeDuc BW, Thompson ML, Shader RI. Relationship of plasma and brain concentrations of caffeine and metabolites to benzodiazepine receptor binding and locomotor activity. J Pharmacol Exp Ther 1989;248: 1078–1083.

54. Christensen HD, Neims AH. Measurement of caffeine and its metabolites in biological fluids. In: Dews PB, ed. Caffeine. New York: Springer-Verlag, 1984:39–45.

55. Boyd EM, Dolman M, Knight LM. The chronic oral toxicity of caffeine. Can J Physiol Pharmacol 1965;43:995.

56. Holloway FA, Modrow HE, Michaelis RC. Methylxanthine discrimination in the rat: possible benzodiazepine and adenosine mechanisms. Pharmacol Biochem Behav 1985;22:815–824.

57. Snyder SH, Katims JJ, Annau Z, Bruns RF, Daly JW. Adenosine receptors and behavioral actions of methylxanthines. Proc Natl Acad Sci USA 1981;78:3260–3264.

58. Snyder SH. Adenosine as a mediator of the behavioral effects of xanthines. In: Dews PB, ed. Caffeine. New York: Springer-Verlag, 1984: 129–152.

59. Williams M. Adenosine—a selective neuromodulator in the mammalian CNS? TINS 1984 (May):164–168.

60. Klein E, Zohar J, Geraci MF, Murphy DL, Uhde TW. Anxiogenic effects of m-CPP in patients with panic disorder: comparison to caffeine's anxiogenic effects. Biol Psychiatry 1991;30: 973–984.

61. Orlikov A, Ryzov I. Caffeine-induced anxiety and increase of kynurenine concentration in plasma of healthy subjects: a pilot study. Biol Psychiatry 1991;29:391–396.

62. Cameron OG, Modell JG, Hariharan M. Caffeine and human cerebral blood flow: a positron emission study. Life Sci 1990;47:1141–1146.

63. Mathew RJ, Wilson WH, Tant S. Caffeine-induced cerebral blood flow changes in schizophrenia. Eur Arch Psychiatry Neurol Sci 1986; 235:206–209.

64. Wilce PA, Le F, Matsumoto I, Shanley BC. Ethanol inhibits NMDA-receptor mediated regulation of immediate early gene expression. Alcohol Alcohol Suppl 1993;2:359–363.

65. von Borstel RW, Wurtman RJ. Caffeine and the cardiovascular effects of physiological levels of adenosine. In: Dews PB, ed. Caffeine. New York: Springer-Verlag, 1984:142–152.

66. Victor BS, Lubetsky M, Greden JF. Somatic manifestations of caffeinism. J Clin Psychiatry 1981;42:185.

67. Levi L. Effect of coffee on the function of the sympatho-adrenomedullary system in man. Acta Med Scand 1967;181:431.

68. Leviton A. Epidemiologic studies of birth defects. In: Dews PB, ed. Caffeine. New York: Springer-Verlag, 1984:188–200.

69. Peters JM. Factors affecting caffeine toxicity: a review of the literature. J Clin Pharmacol 1967; 7:131.

70. Little AD. Comments on the health aspects of caffeine, especially the contribution of soft drinks with particular reference to the report of the Select Committee on GRAS substances. Cambridge, MA: Little, 1977.

71. Anden NE, Jackson DM. Locomotor activity stimulation in rats produced by dopamine in the nucleus accumbens: Potentiation by caffeine. J Pharm Pharmacol 1975;27:666–670.

72. Arnold MA, Carr DB, Togasaki DM, Pian MC, Martin JF. Caffeine stimulates B-endorphin release in blood but not in cerebrospinal fluid. Life Sci 1982;32:1017–1024.

73. Berkowitz BA, Tarver JH, Spector S. Release of norepinephrine in the central nervous system by theophylline and caffeine. Eur J Pharmacol 1970;10:64.

74. Clubley M, Bye CE, Henson TA, Peck AW, Riddington CJ. Effects of caffeine and cyclizine alone and in combination on human performance, subjective effects and EEG activity. Br J Clin Pharmacol 1979;7:157–163.

75. Corrodi H, Fuxe K, Jonsson G. Effects of caf-

feine on central monoamine neurons. J Pharm Pharmacol 1972;24:155–158.

76. Fernstrom JD, Fernstrom MH. Effects of caffeine on monoamine neurotransmitters in the central and peripheral nervous system. In: Dews PB, ed. Caffeine. New York: Springer-Verlag, 1984:107–115.

77. Geyer MA, Dawsey WJ, Mandell AJ. Differential effects of caffeine, d-amphetamine, and methylphenidate on individual raphe cell fluorescence: A microspectrofluorimetric demonstration. Brain Res 1975;85:135–139.

78. Grant SJ, Redmond DE. Methylxanthine activation of noradrenergic unit activity and reversal by clonidine. Eur J Pharmacol 1982;85:105–109.

79. Joyce EM, Koob GF. Amphetamine-, scopolamine-, and caffeine-induced locomotor activity following 6-hydroxydopamine lesions of the mesolimbic dopamine system. Psychopharmacology (Berlin) 1981;73:311–313.

80. Karasawa T, Furakawa K, Yoshida K, Shimizu M. Effect of theophylline on monoamine metabolism in the rat brain. Eur J Pharmacol 1976; 37:97–104.

81. Ravitz AJ, Moore KE. Effects of amphetamine, methylphenidate and cocaine on serum prolactin concentrations in the male rat. Life Sci 1977; 21:267–272.

82. Goldstein A. Wakefulness caused by caffeine. Exp Pathol Pharmacol 1964;248:269.

83. Goldstein A, Kaizer S. Psychotropic effects of caffeine in man. II. Alertness, psychomotor coordination and mood. J Pharmacol Exp Ther 1965;150:146.

84. Goldstein A, Kaizer S. Psychotropic effects of caffeine in man. III. A questionnaire survey of coffee drinkers and its effects in a group of housewives. Clin Pharmacol Ther 1969;10:477.

85. Goldstein A, Kaizer S, Whitby O. Psychotropic effects of caffeine in man. IV. Quantitative and qualitative differences associated with habituation to caffeine. Clin Pharmacol Ther 1969;10:489.

86. Abe K. Reactions to coffee and alcohol in monozygotic twins. J Psychosom Res 1968;12:199.

87. Perry A. The effect of heredity on attitudes toward alcohol, cigarettes and coffee. J Appl Psychol 1973;58:275.

88. Wikler A. Dynamics of drug dependence: Implications of a conditioning theory for research and treatment. Arch Gen Psychiatry 1973;28:611.

89. Hughes JR, Oliveto AH, Helzer JE, Higgins ST, Bickel WK. Should caffeine abuse, dependence, or withdrawal be added to DSM-IV and ICD-10? Am J Psychiatry 1992;149:33–40.

90. Strain EC, Mumford GK, Silverman K, Griffiths RR. Caffeine dependence syndrome. Evidence from case histories and experimental evaluations. JAMA 1994;272:1043–1048.

91. Evans SM, Griffiths RR. Low-dose caffeine physical dependence in normal subjects: dose-related effects. In: Harris LS, ed. Problems of drug dependence 1990. NIDA Res Monogr Ser 1991;105:446.

92. Griffiths RR, Evans SM, Heishman SJ, Preston KL, Sannerud CA, Wolf B, et al. Low-dose caffeine physical dependence in humans. J Pharmacol Exp Ther 1990;255:1123–1132.

93. Chait LD. Factors influencing the subjective response to caffeine. Behav Pharmacol 1992;3: 219–228.

94. Chait LD, Griffiths RR. Effects of caffeine on human cigarette smoking behavior and subjective response. Clin Pharmacol Ther 1983;34: 612–622.

95. Weiss B, Laties VG. Enhancement of human performance by caffeine and the amphetamines. Pharmacol Rev 1962;14:1–36.

96. World Health Organization. The ICD-10 classification of mental and behavioural disorders, clinical descriptions and diagnostic guidelines. Geneva: World Health Organization, 1992.

97. Erhardt E. Psychic disturbances in caffeine intoxication. Acta Med Scand 1929;71:94.

98. Powers H. The syndrome of coffee. Med J Record 1925;121:745.

99. Speilberger CO, Gorsuch RL, Lushene RE. State-trait anxiety inventory manual. Palo Alto, CA: Consulting Psychologists Press, 1970.

100. Bruce M, Scott N, Shine P, Lader M. Anxiogenic effects of caffeine in patients with anxiety disorders. Arch Gen Psychiatry 1992;49: 867–869.

101. Lee M, Cameron OG, Greden JF. Anxiety and caffeine consumption in people with anxiety disorders. Psychiatry Res 1985;15:211–217.

102. Holle C, Heimberg RG, Sweet RA, Holt CS. Alcohol and caffeine use by social phobics: an initial inquiry into drinking patterns and behavior. Behav Res Ther 1995;33:561–566.

103. Arnold LE, Christopher J, Huestis R. Methylphenidates vs. dextroamphetamine vs. caffeine in minimal brain dysfunction. Arch Gen Psychiatry 1978;35:463.

104. Schnackenberg RD. Caffeine as a substitute for schedule II stimulants in hyperkinetic children. Am J Psychiatry 1973;130:796.

105. Furlong FFW. Possible psychiatric significance of excessive coffee consumption. Can Psychiatr Assoc J 1975;20:577.

106. Neil JF, Himmelhoch JM, Mallinger AG, Mallinger J, Hanin I. Caffeinism complicating hypersomnic depressive episodes. Compr Psychiatry 1978;19:377.

107. Silver W. Insomnia, tachycardia and cola drinks. Pediatrics 1971;47:635.

108. Curless R, French JM, James OF, Wynne HA. Is caffeine a factor in subjective insomnia in elderly people? Age Ageing 1993;22:45–45.

109. Forrest WH, Bellville JW, Brown BW. The interaction of caffeine with pentobarbital as a nighttime hypnotic. Anesthesiology 1972; 36:37.

110. Brown SL, Salive ME, Pahor M, Foley DJ, Corti MC, Langlois JA, Wallace RB, Harris TB. Occult caffeine as a source of sleep problems in an older population. J Am Geriatr Soc 1995;43:860–864.

111. Leibenluft E, Fiero PL, Bartko JJ, Moul DE, Rosenthal NE. Depressive symptoms and the self-reported use of alcohol, caffeine, and carbohydrates in normal volunteers and four groups of psychiatric outpatients. Am J Psychiatry 1993;150:294–301.

112. Kawachi I, Willett WC, Colditz GA, Stampfer MJ, Speizer FE. A prospective study of coffee drinking and suicide in women. Arch Intern Med 1996;156:521–525.

113. McCall WV, Reid S, Rosenquist P, Foreman A, Kiesow-Webb N. A reappraisal of the role of caffeine in ECT. Am J Psychiatry 1993; 150:1543–1545.

114. Keys A, Brozek J, Henschel A. The biology of human starvation. Minneapolis: University of Minnesota Press, 1950.

115. Krahn DD, Hasse S, Ray A, Gosnell B, Drenowski A. Caffeine consumption in patients with eating disorders. Hosp Community Psychiatry 1991;42:313–315.

116. Greden JF, Procter A, Victor B. Caffeinism associated with greater use of other psychotropic agents. Compr Psychiatry 1981;22:565.

117. Klesges RC, Ray JW, Klesges LM. Caffeinated coffee and tea intake and its relationship to cigarette smoking: an analysis of the Second National Health and Nutrition Examination Survey (NHANES II). J Subst Abuse 1994;6: 407–418.

118. Swanson JA, Lee JW, Hopp JW. Caffeine and nicotine: a review of their joint use and possible interactive effects in tobacco withdrawal. Addict Behav 1994;19:229–256.

119. Newman HW, Newman EJ. Failure of Dexedrine and caffeine as practical antagonists of the depressant effect of ethyl alcohol in man. Q J Stud Alcohol 1956;17:406.

120. Kuribara H, Tadokoro S. Caffeine does not effectively ameliorate, but rather may worsen the ethanol intoxication when assessed by discrete avoidance in mice. Jpn J Pharmacol 1992;59: 393–398.

121. Wietholtz H, Boegelin M, Arnaud MJ, Bircher J, Preisig R. Assessment of the cytochrome P-448 dependent liver enzyme system by a caffeine breath test. Eur J Clin Pharmacol 1981; 21:53–59.

122. Siegel D, Benowitz N, Ernster VL, Grady DG, Hauck WW. Smokeless tobacco, cardiovascular risk factors, and nicotine and cotinine levels in professional baseball players. Am J Public Health 1992;82:417–421.

123. Fennelly M, Galletly DC, Purdie GI. Is caffeine withdrawal the mechanism of postoperative headache? Anesth Analg 1991;72: 449–453.

124. Hampl KF, Schneider MC, Ruttimann U, Ummenhofer W, Drewe J. Perioperative administration of caffeine tablets for prevention of postoperative headaches. Can J Anaesth 1995; 42:789–792.

125. Couturier EG, Hering R, Steiner TJ. Weekend attacks in migraine patients; caused by caffeine withdrawal? Cephalalgia 1992;12:99–100.

126. Lovallo WR, Pincomb GA, Sung BH, Everson SA, Passey RB, Wilson MF. Hypertension risk and caffeine's effect on cardiovascular activity during mental stress in young men. Health Psychol 1991;10:236–243.

127. Dreisbach RH, Pfeiffer C. Caffeine-withdrawal headache. J Lab Clin Med 1943;28: 1212.

128. Reeves RR, Struve FA, Patrick G, Bullen JA. Topographic quantitative EEG measures of alpha and theta power changes during caffeine withdrawal: preliminary findings from normal subjects. Clin Electroencephalogr 1995;26: 154–162.

129. Lightfoot CJ, Blair HJ, Cohen JR. Lead intoxication in an adult caused by Chinese herbal medication. JAMA 1977;238:1539.

27 ANABOLIC-ANDROGENIC STEROIDS

Gantt P. Galloway

Humans have observed for millennia that the testes play a role in producing and maintaining male sexual characteristics. The hormonal nature of this action was demonstrated in 1849, and the endogenous anabolic-androgenic steroid (AAS) testosterone was isolated in 1935 (1). The first use of AASs as performance enhancers purportedly dates to World War II, when they were administered to German soldiers prior to combat (2). Use in sports, which began in the 1940s, first brought AASs widespread public attention. Due to limitations of analytic technology, testing of athletes for AAS use did not begin until the 1976 Olympic Games, when eight samples that had screened positive by a newly developed radioimmunoassay technique were confirmed by gas chromatography-mass spectroscopy (3). Additional notoriety accrued to AASs in 1988; in that year Ben Johnson, a world record-holding runner, tested positive at the Olympic Games (4) and survey results showed that the lifetime prevalence of AAS was 6.6% in male high school seniors in the United States (5). Subsequent survey work (Table 27.1) has confirmed that AAS use is no longer confined to elite athletes.

The term anabolic-androgenic steroid is used in this chapter to denote that all steroids exhibiting myotrophic actions also promote the expression of male sexual characteristics (although the ratio of these effects varies). Common street names for AASs include 'roids' and 'juice,' although some users of illicit AASs are surprisingly knowledgeable about nomenclature and endocrine physiology. Different types of steroids may be confused with one another because the term steroid also encompasses glucocorticoids, mineralocorticoids, estrogens, and progestins (6). The actions of these other classes of steroids are distinct from and, in some cases, opposed to those of AASs.

PHYSIOLOGY AND PHARMACOLOGY

Testosterone is produced in males by Leydig cells in the testes in response to luteinizing hormone, a gonadotropin secreted by the pituitary. Testosterone acts directly on target cells, binding to an intracellular receptor. This androgen-receptor complex binds to chromosomes, leading to increases in the synthesis of specific RNAs and proteins (7). Expression of these protein products mediates the anabolic and androgenic effects of testosterone. 5-α-dihydrotestosterone, produced by the action of 5-α-reductase enzymes on testosterone, also produces these effects with a much greater potency. 5-α-reductase enzymes are limited to target tissues such as prostate, seminal vesicles, and pubic skin, serving to amplify the actions of testosterone in those tissues (8). Testosterone is also metabolized by aromatase enzymes to estradiol, an estrogen. The role of endogenous estrogen in males remains unclear. The mechanism of action of AASs, particularly at supraphysiologic doses, is further complicated by interactions with other steroid receptor systems, including those for estrogens, progestins, and glucocorticoids (9).

Although testosterone is the major androgenic hormone, its clinical utility is limited by extensive first-pass hepatic metabolism and brief (10-minute) elimination half life. Esterification of the 17-β-hydroxyl group, alkylation of the 17-α-position, and modification of the steroid nucleus have been undertaken to increase the oral bioavailability, absorption half life, elimination half life, and ratio of anabolic to androgenic effects (10). 17-β-esterification increases the lipophilicity of testosterone, increasing the absorption half life when administered intramuscularly in oil. 17-α-alkylation slows hepatic metabolism and enhances the bioavailability when administered orally.

The metabolism of testosterone to estradiol, 5-α-dihydrotestosterone, and the inactive metabolites androsterone and etiocholanolone is well defined. The metabolism of 17-β-esterified derivatives by rapid deesterification to testosterone is also well defined. The metabolism of testosterone de-

rivatives with modifications to the steroid nucleus or 17-α-alkyl substitutions is considerably more complex, with each of the dozens of compounds available having a separate pattern of biotransformation. 17-epimerization (11, 12) and 6-β-hydroxylation (13, 14) emerge as important pathways, although many others contribute (Table 27.2). Although important, the androgen and estrogen receptor binding profiles of AAS metabolites have, for the most part, not been defined. The reader is referred elsewhere for more thorough reviews of AAS pharmacology and physiology (7, 8, 15).

EPIDEMIOLOGY AND USE PATTERNS

Incidence and Prevalence

The spread of AAS use has been largely a silent phenomenon, yet the estimate from the Substance Abuse and Mental Health Services Administration published in 1995 is 1,084,000 Americans had ever used AASs and that 312,000 (29%) of those had used in the prior year (16). The comparable figures for heroin use are 2,083,000 and 281,000 (13%), respectively. AAS use is not confined to the United States; surveys have revealed use in the United Kingdom, Sweden, and South Africa (see Table 27.1). Prevalence is higher in males than females: lifetime estimates from population and school based surveys are 1.8–11% in males and 0.2–3.2% in females. Athletes, particularly weight lifters, have a greater prevalence of use than do non-athletes, but the difference is surprisingly small in some studies, pointing to the importance of other factors in the decision to use AASs.

Reasons for Use

Body builders generally start AAS use seeking psychological rewards from attention to and admiration of a muscular physique. Athletes use AASs seeking to improve their performance; this performance enhancement may be due to objective effects of increased muscle mass in weight lifters and linebackers or due to subjective effects such as increased levels of aggression or increased confidence. Coaches and parents of adolescent athletes may encourage use of AASs (17, 18). Law enforcement and corrections officers may use AASs seeking an intimidating physique and fighting proficiency. Material benefits from use of AASs may include college athletic scholarships and employment opportunities. Direct pharmacological actions of AASs result in euphoria and a subjective "high" in some individuals (19, 20). Withdrawal symptoms can also become important factors in continued use. Etiologic classifications of psychosocial factors, reality factors, and directly reinforcing effects have been presented elsewhere (21).

Personality Type

Clinical observations of preoccupation with self and self-image has led to investigations into personality characteristics of AAS abusers. In the first study examining personality traits in AAS abusers, Perry et al. compared rates of DSM-III personality disorders and traits in 20 AAS using weight lifters, 20 non-using weight lifter controls, and 20 non-using non-athletic controls (22). The AAS users had more personality disorders (85%) than either the non-using weight lifters (50%), or the community controls (35%). Although no individual personality disorder or trait was noted to occur with a significantly greater frequency in any of these groups, the authors did note that there was a 27-fold higher incidence of personality disorders in the histrionic, narcissistic, antisocial, and borderline grouping in AAS users than in community controls and a nine-fold higher incidence when compared to non-using weight lifters (22). In a subsequent study of personality characteristics in adolescents with the same three-group design with 24 subjects per

Table 27.1   Prevalence of AAS Use

Ref. no.	Year	Location	Respondents	Timeframe	N	Prevalence
19	1991	MI, US	weight lifters	lifetime	404 M, 45 F	12% M, 4% F
5	1988	US	12th grade students	lifetime	3403 M	6.6% M
96	1993	GA, US	high school students	lifetime	962 M, 919 F	6.5% M, 1.9% F
26	1984	IL, US	weight lifters	lifetime	250 M and F, total	44%
129	1990	OR, US	high school football players	current	191 M	1.1% M
130	1989	AR, US	11th grade students	lifetime	853 M, 914 F	11% M, 0.5% F
131	1995	US	8th grade students	prior year	c. 17,300	1.8% M, 0.6% F
			10th grade students		c. 15,800	1.9% M, 0.4% F
			12th grade students		c. 15,400	2.1% M, 0.5% F
				lifetime	M and F, total	2.4%
132	1992	AR, US	11th grade students	lifetime	672 M, 806 F	7.6% M, 1.5% F
133	1995	US	college students	past year	75,169 M and F, total	0.9%
134	1995	MA, US	high school students	lifetime	1,501 M, 1,549 F	5.7% M, 1.7% F
32	1995	Falkenberg, Sweden	high school students	lifetime	688 M, 695 F	5.8% M
135	1993	CA, US	7th grade students	lifetime	782 M and F, total	4.7% M, 3.2% F
27	1992	western Cape, South Africa	high school seniors	lifetime	1,361 M and F, total	0.6% overall 1.2% M, 1.3% M sports participants
16	1995	US	residents of households, age 12 and over	lifetime	7,950 M, 9,859 F	0.9% M, 0.2% F
136	1990	IL, US	high school students	lifetime	1,028 M, 1,085 F	6.5% M, 2.5% F, 5.5% athletes, 2.4% nonathletes
137	1992	WV, US	high school students	lifetime	3900 M	5.3% M
138	1993	Scotland, UK	college students	lifetime	341 M, 292 F	4.4% M, 1.0% F

Table 27.2   Metabolic Pathways of Selected AASs

Parent drug	Major metabolic pathways
Fluoxymesterone	6-β-hydroxylation, 4-ene-reduction, 3-keto-reduction, and 11-hydroxy-oxidation (13)
Methandrostenolone	17-epimerization (12)
Stanozolol	4-β-hydroxylation, 16-α-hydroxylation, 16-β-hydroxylation, and 3-hydroxylation on the pyrazole ring (128)

Disorders of Body Image

Dissatisfaction with body image, specifically the perception of being too small or insufficiently muscular, is common in AAS users and is associated with AAS dependence (19). One case report (25) and data from a comparison of 88 AAS-using male athletes and 68 non-using male athletes (24) indicate that this dissatisfaction with body image reaches pathological levels in some AAS users. This was observed in 10 (11%) of AAS users, as compared to none of the non-users. The following description was given of this condition:

> Individuals with this disorder believed that they looked small and weak, even though they were large and muscular. They declined to be seen in public, refused invitations to the beach, or wore baggy sweatclothes even in summer to avoid being seen as "small."

This disorder has been termed "reverse anorexia nervosa," although these individuals appear to meet diagnostic criteria for body dysmorphic disorder. Anorexia nervosa and bulimia nervosa were also diagnosed at high rates, 3 (3%) and 1 (1%), respectively, compared to 1 (1%) and none in the non-user group, although neither of these differences reached statistical significance.

Sources

AASs are typically not acquired by prescription (26, 27). The proportion of AASs prescribed by physicians in the United States has probably decreased since AASs were added to Schedule III of the Controlled Substances Act in 1990. Small-scale importation of pharmaceutical AASs from Mexico may be one source of supply for the illicit market (28). Most people who sell AASs are themselves users of AASs and they often recruit new users at gymnasiums. The illicit market for AASs raises concerns about purity and safety; these concerns are particularly acute for injectable AASs. Table 27.3 lists AASs available on the world market.

Patterns of Use

AASs are typically abused in a cyclic fashion, with "cycles" of 4–18 weeks on AASs and one month to one year off (19, 22, 26, 29). In some instances the quest for maximal results leads to continuous administration, although sometimes periods of modest doses of a single AAS are interspersed between high dose use of many AASs. Cycles that involve building up to a peak dose then tapering down are called "pyramids" (26). Multiple AASs—up to eight—are often used simultaneously, a practice referred to as "stacking," with both oral and injectable preparations combined (19, 22, 24–26, 29–31). Administration of multiple steroids in ascending and tapering doses is known as "stacking the pyramid" (26). Users often meticulously plan and record their use of AASs and may be able to give detailed histories. Injection is a common route of administration, even in adolescents (32). The patterns of cyclic use, variable doses, simultaneous use of multiple AASs, and use of grossly supratherapeutic doses makes extrapolations from therapeutic and experimental data problematic.

Other Drugs Used

AAS users frequently use a wide variety of other drugs. Concurrent abuse of or dependence on other psychoactive drugs may exist and other drugs may be used for purported anabolic effects, to evade detection of AAS use, to treat AAS adverse effects, or for other performance or appearance enhancing effects.

group, Burnett et al. were not able to find statistically significant differences between athletic users and non-using athletes, although trends toward greater forcefulness, greater impulsivity, and less cooperativeness as measured by the Millon Adolescent Personality Inventory were observed in the athletic users; similar trends were evident when comparing non-AAS using athletes to non-athlete, non-using controls (23). The prevalence of antisocial personality disorder (and no other personality disorders) was ascertained in 88 AAS-using athletes and 68 non-using control athletes. A trend toward a higher incidence of antisocial personality disorder as diagnosed with the Structured Clinical Interview for DSM-III-R was found: 9 (10%) of the AAS users and only 2 (3%) of the controls (24). Narcissism and empathy were examined in 16 weight lifters who had used AASs and 20 weight lifters who had not used AASs. The AAS users had lower ratings of empathy and higher ratings on the three (of seven) dimensions of narcissism most associated with psychopathology: exploitativeness, exhibitionism, and entitlement (21). Although none of these studies can rule out the possibility that AAS use causes symptoms that lead to assessment of personality disorders, clinicians should be aware that antisocial and narcissistic behavior are relatively common in AAS abusers.

Table 27.3 Commercially Available Anabolic-Androgenic Steroids

Generic names	Brand names	Route, recommended dosage	Abused doses and reference numbers
Boldenone undecenoate	Equipoise	veterinary only (horses: 0.5 mg/kg once/3 wks)	50–200 mg/wk (22, 24, 29, 31)
Calusterone Dimethyltestosterone	—	—	—
Clostebol[b]	Clostene Steranabol Megagrisevit (multi-ingredient) Trofoseptine (multi-ingredient) Alfa-Trofodermin	IM: 40 mg two times/wk topical	DNS (35)
Danazol[a,c] (a partial androgen agonist)	Cyclomen Danatrol Danazant Danocrine (U.S.) Danol Ladazol Mastodanatrol Winbanin	PO: 100–800 mg/d	—
Dromostanolone[b] Drostanolone Methyldihydrotestosterone Propionate	Masterid Masteril Permastril	IM: 100 mg 3×/wk	800 mg/wk (44)
Epitiostanol	—		
Ethylestrenol[b] Ethyloestrenol	Orabolin	PO: up to 4 mg/d	6–8 mg/d (68) 10–12 mg/d (31)
Fluoxymesterone[a,c]	Android-F Halotestin (U.S) Halodrin (multi-ingredient)	PO: 1–20 mg/d	—
Formebolone[b]	Esiclene	PO: 5–10 mg/d IM	
Furazabol[b]	Androfurazanol	PO: up to 3 mg/d IM: 25 mg 1–2×/wk	
Mepitiostane	Thioderon	PO	
Mesterolone[b]	Mestoranum Proviron	PO: 50–100 mg/d	25 mg/d (44) 350–700 mg/wk (34) DNS (24)
Methandrostenolone[b] Methandienone Metandienone	Metaboline (multi-ingredient)	PO: 4 mg/d for 6 wks alternating with 2–4 wks drug free periods	40 mg/d (48) 15 mg/d for 9 years (118) mean, 28 mg/d in a group of of 20 (22) 15 mg/d (119) 5–50 mg/d (36) 25–50 mg/d (44), 15–40 mg/d (29) DNS (25)
Methandriol Mestenediol Methylandrostenediol	Otormon F (multi-ingredient)	—	—
Methenolone[b] Methenolone Acetate Methenolone Enanthate	Primobolan Primobolan Depot Primobolan S AntiFocal N	PO (acetatate): up to 20 mg/d IM (enanthate): 100 mg/2–4 wks	100 mg/wk (34) 20 mg/wk (31) 200 mg/wk (44) 4 cc IM/wk (concentration unknown) (29)
Metenolone Enantate Metenolone Enanthate Methenolone Oenanthate	(multi-ingredient) NeyChondrin (multi-ingredient) NeyGeront (multi-ingredient) NeyPulpin (multi-ingredient) NeyTumorin (multi-ingredient)		
Methyltestosterone[a,c]	Android-10, 25 (U.S.) Metandren Testomet Testovis Testred (U.S.) Virilon (U.S.) multi-ingredient preparations: Eldec, Estratest, Estratest H.S., Mediatric, Mixogen, Pasuma, Premarin with Methyltestosterone, Prowess, and Tylosterone	PO: 10–50 mg /d	DNS (24)

Table 27.3 Commercially Available Anabolic-Androgenic Steroids—*Continued*

Generic names	Brand names	Route, recommended dosage	Abused doses and reference numbers
Methyltestosterone[a,c]	Oreton Methyl (U.S.)	buccal: 5 to 25 mg/d	—
Mibolerone	Mibolerone	veterinary only	—
Nandrolone[a,b] Nortestosterone in various salts and esters:	Activin Androlone-D Deca-Durabolin (U.S.)	IM: 25–200 mg/1–4 wks	mean dose 197 mg/wk (22) 100 mg/wk (31) 100–200 mg/wk (60) 100 mg/3 ds (48)
Cyclohexylpropionate Decanoate Hemisuccinate Laurate Phenylpropionate Sodium Sulfate Undecanoate	Deca-Durabol Durabolin (U.S.) Dynabolon Fherbolico Hybolin Decanoate Hybolin Improved (U.S.) Kabolin Kératyl Nandrobolic (U.S.) Nandrol Stenabolin multi-ingredient preparations: Dexatopic Dinatrofon Docabolin Docabolina Trophobolène		100 mg/wk to 200 mg/d (44) 600 mg/wk–200 mg/d (29) DNS (24, 25, 35, 43, 114)
Norclostebol Acetate	—	IM	—
Norethandrolone[b]	Nilevar	PO: up to 30 mg/d	—
Oxandrolone[a]	Lonavar Oxandrin (U.S.)	PO: 2.5 mg 2–4×/d	25 mg/d (25) mean, 14 mg/d (22) 70–175 mg/wk (34) 25 mg/d (48) 12.5–15 mg/d (31) 20–40 mg/d (29)
Oxymetholone[a]	Adroyd Anadrol-50 (U.S.) Anapolon Oxitosona Plenastril	PO: 1–5 mg/kg/d	mean, 46 mg/d (22) 250 mg/d (36) 100 mg/d (44)
Prasterone Sodium Sulfate	multi-ingredient preparations:	IM: 200 mg/4 to 6 wks	—
Prasterone Enanthate[b]	Gynodian Gynodian Depot		
Quinbolone[b]	Anabolicum Vister	PO: up to 30 mg/d	—
Stanolone Androstanolone Dihydrotestosterone	Andractim Gelovit Ophtovitol (multi-ingredient)	topical sublingual sublabial	—
Stanozolol[a,b] Androstanazole Methylstanazole	Stromba Strombaject Winstrol (U.S.)	[a]PO: initial dose of 2 mg three times/d, maintenance dose of 2 mg/d[b] PO: 2.5 mg 3 times/wk to 10 mg/d IM: 50 mg every 2 to 3 wks	30 mg/d–250 mg/wk (44) 10 mg/d (36) DNS (31, 35) (22)
Testosterone[a] transdermal patches	Testoderm (U.S.) Androderm (U.S.)	transdermal: 4–6 mg/d	—
Testosterone[a] in aqueous suspension	Testandro (U.S.) Histerone (U.S.) Tesamone (U.S.)	IM: 25–50 mg/2 to 3 wks	—
Testosterone[c] subcutaneous pellets	Testopel Pellets	subcutaneous implantation: 150–450 mg/ 3–4 months	—
Testosterone esters[a,c]: Acetate Cypionate Decanoate Enanthate Hexahydrobenzoate Hexahydrobenzylcarbonate Isocaproate Phenylpropionate Propionate Undecanoate	Andro L.A. 200 (U.S.) Andropository-200 (U.S.) Delatestryl (U.S.) Durathate-200 (U.S.) Everone 200 (U.S.) Andro-Cyp 100, −200 depAndro 100, −200 (U.S.) Depotest 100, −200 (U.S.) Depo-Testosterone (U.S.) Duratest 100, −200 (U.S.) T-cypionate many other brand names, including combination products	IM: cypionate: 50–400 mg/2–4 wks enanthate and propionate: 40–50 mg/2–4 wks to 100 mg 3 times/wk	100 mg/3 days (17, 22, 24, 101) 269–1400 mg/wk (17, 22, 24, 29, 36, 48, 101)
Trenbolone		veterinary	76 mg/wk (34) mean, 93 mg/3 days (22) 76 mg/wk (44)

[a] Dose information from Kastrup E, ed. Facts and comparisons. St. Louis: Facts and Comparisons, Inc., 1996.
[b] Dose information from Reynolds J, Parfitt K, Parsons A, Sweetman S, eds. Martindale: the extra pharmacopoeia. 30th ed. London: The Pharmaceutical Press, 1993.
[c] Dose information from McEvoy G, ed. AHFS 96 drug information. Bethesda, MD: American Society for Health-System Pharmacists, 1996.
Legend: DNS, abuse reported, dose not stated; *IM,* intramuscular; *PO,* oral.

PSYCHOACTIVE DRUGS

Abuse of and dependence on other psychoactive drugs is not unknown in AAS users, although concerns about health and appearance may moderate use of other drugs. In one group of 20 AAS-using weight lifters, 7 (35%) were alcohol abusers, 2 (10%) were alcohol dependent, and 1 (5%) was a drug abuser compared to 13 (65%) alcohol abusers and 1 (5%) drug abuser in a control group of non–AAS-using weight lifters (22). In a convenience sample of 41 AAS users recruited from gymnasiums, 4 (9.8%) smoked cigarettes, 6 (14.6%) had past diagnoses of alcohol abuse or dependence, and 13 (31.7%) had prior diagnoses of other drug abuse or dependence, mostly marihuana (7) and cocaine (5), but none had current substance abuse dependence, except for nicotine dependence (29). Other studies have reported higher levels of substance abuse and dependence between cycles. One series of 23 AAS users included several subjects who only used between cycles (33). In another group of 88 athletes who used AASs, 28 (32%) had diagnoses of current substance abuse or dependence while off-cycle, but only 1 (1%) had a diagnosis of current substance abuse or dependence while on-cycle; in a comparison group of non-users 15 out of 68 (22%) had current substance abuse or dependence diagnoses (24). It is not clear from these data that abuse and dependence diagnoses for drugs other than AASs are any more common in AAS users than in the general population; AASs users' preoccupation with health and performance may even confer some degree of protection against use of other drugs of abuse.

OTHER PERFORMANCE ENHANCING DRUGS

A wide variety of psychomotor stimulants—from ephedrine, caffeine, and phenylpropanolamine to cocaine and methamphetamine—are used by athletes who also use AASs (34, 35). Although some of these may be used for therapeutic indications and some may be abused for their psychoactive properties, this class of drugs is accepted by segments of the athletic community as enhancing performance.

Human growth hormone (HGH) is anabolic and has been used by AAS users (26, 34, 36). A lifetime HGH use prevalence of 5% was found in a survey of 224 male tenth grade students, suggesting that abuse of HGH may also be widespread (37). A variety of substances purported to increase release of endogenous HGH are also abused, notably gamma-hydroxybutyrate (38).

The β-2 adrenergic agonist clenbuterol has been observed to increase the deposition rate of lean mass and retard adipose gain in animal husbandry. Based on this information clenbuterol has entered into use by athletes as an anabolic agent (39). Other agents reportedly abused to enhance performance include deprenyl, β-adrenergic antagonists, levothyroxine, and erythropoietin (34, 35, 40). AAS users also often consume prodigious amounts of dietary supplements, which may be associated with their own hazards (41).

DRUGS TO EVADE DETECTION

The threat of disqualification for athletes found to have abused AASs has led to use of pharmacological aids to evade detection. Detecting testosterone abuse is complicated by the fact that it occurs endogenously. Detection of testosterone abuse therefore relies on the ratio of testosterone to epitestosterone. Normal ratios of testosterone to epitestosterone in urine are 1–2.5:1 and ratios of 6:1 or greater are considered positive, which has led to some athletes to self-administer epitestosterone in combination with testosterone (35). Probenecid and a wide variety of diuretics are used to decrease urinary concentrations of AASs (35). Diuretics are also used by body builders to counter the fluid retention caused by AASs and to increase muscle definition—to create a more 'ripped' or 'cut up' look with increased definition of superficial vasculature, muscular shape, and muscular striations (23, 31, 34). Supplemental potassium may also be taken, leading to a risk of hyperkalemia, particularly when potassium-sparing diuretics are used (42, 43).

DRUGS TO TREAT SIDE EFFECTS

Estrogenic effects of AASs and their metabolites can lead to gynecomastia. The partial estrogen antagonists tamoxifen (34, 44, 45) and clomiphene (46) are used to prevent and treat this complication of AAS abuse.

Human chorionic gonadotropin (HCG) stimulates androgen production by the interstitial cells of the testis. To counter the profound suppression of endogenous androgen suppression and testicular atrophy caused by exogenous AASs, HCG is administered intramuscularly in doses of 3000 U.S.P. units every week to 2000 U.S.P. units every 2 days either simultaneously with AASs or between cycles (22, 26, 29, 31, 35, 44, 46–48). Human chorionic gonadotropin is one of the most common adjunctive medications used by AAS abusers, with use reported by 17 out of 53 (32%) users in one study (34).

CONSEQUENCES OF USE

Therapeutic Uses

The therapeutic utility of AASs is limited, both with respect to the number of indications and the number of patients with those indications. AASs have therapeutic utility in primary and secondary hypogonadism in males and are frequently used in delayed puberty in males. They are effective in some cases of refractory anemia, especially aplastic anemia and Fanconi's anemia. AASs are sometimes effective in palliation of carcinoma of the breast in women. 17-α-alkylated AASs are useful in the treatment of hereditary angioedema. Difficulty in distinguishing between these legitimate therapeutic uses and abuse for athletic or appearance enhancement rarely arises. Uses of AASs that are currently experimental, including replacement therapy in older men in whom serum testosterone concentrations decline—"male menopause"—and as a component of male contraceptive regimens, may lead to great increases in legitimate use (49).

Effectiveness in Increasing Muscle Mass and Strength

The ability of AASs to promote weight gain and muscle growth in healthy adults was for many decades subject to divergent opinions from the athletic and medical communities. As late as 1977 the American College of Sports Medicine stated that AASs had no value in enhancing athletic performance (50). In 1984 the College acknowledged the potential effectiveness of AASs (51) and in 1987 stated that:

1. Anabolic-androgenic steroids in the presence of an adequate diet can contribute to increases in body weight, often in the lean mass compartment.
2. The gains in muscular strength achieved through high-intensity exercise and proper diet can be increased by the use of anabolic-androgenic steroids in some individuals. (52)

The initial reluctance to acknowledge the effectiveness of AASs in enhancing athletic performance stemmed in part from the limitations of the clinical trials that had been conducted. Those early trials were often poorly controlled with respect to diet, level of exercise, and blinding, and used doses of AASs much smaller than those used by competitive athletes. It is also important to remember that changes of a very few percent in a competition may make the difference between obscurity and a world record setting performance and that such small changes require large sample sizes to detect. A review of the best clinical trials indicates that strength gains on the order of 5% can be achieved with doses of AASs that are modest compared to those used illicitly (53). The ability of AASs to increase strength and muscle mass but not aerobic performance is supported by a study of ultrastructural changes in muscle, in which fiber cross-sectional area increased but capillary density was unchanged (54). The myotrophic action of AASs appears to stem not only from actions at androgen receptors but also from competitive antagonism at catabolism-mediating corticosteroid receptors (55, 56). AASs may also enhance athletic performance through erythropoiesis and psychological effects (10, 57).

Adverse Effects

VASCULAR AND CARDIAC

Many nonfatal (42, 58–61) and fatal (62–64) myocardial infarctions have been attributed to AAS use. Other fatal cardiac events associated with AAS use include myocarditis with dilated cardiomyopathy (65), cardiac arrest with cardiomegaly and myocardial fibrosis and necrosis (43), and cardiac arrest with cardiomegaly (66). Noncardiac vascular events that have occurred in AAS abusers include hemorrhagic cerebrovascular accident (62), ischemic cerebrovascular accident (67, 68), severe lower limb ischemia due to diffuse arterial thrombosis (67), and pulmonary embolism (69, 70).

The causal relationship between AASs and the adverse cardiac and vascular events is difficult to establish. Changes in coagulation, serum lipid profiles, hypertension, cardiomegaly (71), and direct cardiac toxicity leading to arrhythmogenic foci have all been implicated. Investigation into coagulation changes has led to contradictory data with some studies suggesting increased fibrinolytic activity (72) and others suggesting increased platelet activation (73) and activation of the hemostatic system (74). Hemoconcentration with hematocrits of up to 71% has been reported in AAS abusers, possibly due to coadministration of diuretics; the resulting increase in blood viscosity may increase the risk for thromboembolic phenomena (31). Supraphysiologic doses of AASs as a class are capable of producing marked adverse changes in serum lipids, with increases on the order of 35% of atherogenic low-density lipoprotein (LDL) and decreases on the order of 60% of cardioprotective high-density lipoproteins (HDL) (24, 44, 75). The aromatizable 17-β-esterified AASs such as nandrolone have much milder effects on serum lipid profiles (76, 77). Physiological levels of testosterone in males, whether from endogenous or exogenous sources, may not have adverse effects on serum lipids but rather may be associated with higher HDL levels (78). Hypertension has long been identified as an adverse effect of AASs, and, although a cause and effect relationship is supported by some recent work (79, 80), other studies have cast doubts on this relationship (34, 81, 82).

HEPATIC

AASs are associated with a number of deleterious effects on the liver. AASs can cause acute elevation of transaminases (44, 83) and fatal hepatitis (84). Chronic use of AASs may cause gross changes in the liver including hepatomegaly (43) and peliosis (85). Hepatocellular carcinoma also occurs in AAS users, although the tumors are often relatively benign compared to typical hepatocellular carcinoma (86–88). Although 17-α-alkylated AASs have been implicated in these adverse hepatic effects, the possibility that other AASs, particularly in the doses used illicitly, may be hepatotoxic cannot be excluded.

MUSCULOSKELETAL

There have been several case reports of tendon ruptures and avulsions in AAS users (71, 89, 90). Increased force generated by hypertrophied muscles and abnormal tendon morphology may each play a role in increasing this risk (91). Although being tall is typically a desired outcome for AAS users, users who are still growing may not attain their full stature because of premature closure of epiphyses (92).

COMPLICATIONS SECONDARY TO INJECTION DRUG USE

Injection of AASs is common (80% in one sample) (19) and puts users at risk for a variety of complications, including HIV infection. Three case reports are consistent with HIV infection from AAS injection (93–95). Although the risk of HIV transmission in adults appears to be low, based on the paucity of case reports and unanimous denial of sharing of injection equipment in two samples of 21 (44) and 39 (19) AAS injectors, the data from adolescents are alarming. Eighteen of 20 AAS-injecting high school students had shared needles in the preceding 30 days (96). Further studies are plainly needed to assess the risk of HIV transmission associated with injection of AASs and to assess the need for targeted HIV risk reduction interventions. Clinicians should encourage abstinence from AASs on the basis that the substantial medical and psychiatric risks outweigh the short-term benefits. For patients who continue to use AASs the risks should be explained and patients should be instructed in safe injection techniques. Safe injection techniques include use of alcohol swabs for cleaning injection sites and not sharing injection equipment or multi-dose vials. Other reported complications of AAS injection include hepatitis B infection (93), local infection with the atypical mycobacterium *M. smegmatis* (97), and pseudotumor (98).

GYNECOMASTIA AND MASTODYNIA

Testosterone and other aromatizable AASs are metabolized in part to estradiol and other estrogen agonists. These estrogen agonists can lead to breast pain in men (34) and gynecomastia (23, 24, 45, 47, 71, 99). Gynecomastia is a sufficiently common adverse effect that staging criteria and techniques for surgical management have been presented (100).

MALE GENITOURINARY

Case reports of testicular atrophy in AAS users are common (23, 30, 47, 101). Testicular atrophy has also been documented in controlled work (24) and is an expected effect given the negative feedback exerted by AASs on the testes. Azoospermia may also follow AAS use and may resolve spontaneously (102) or require gonadotropin treatment (103). Prostate volume is responsive to AASs and resultant increases may lead to bladder outflow obstruction (25, 104).

VIRILIZATION OF WOMEN

Supraphysiologic doses of AASs in women leads to masculinization. Specifically, women taking AASs have been reported to have voice instability and deepening, clitoral hypertrophy, shrinking of the breasts, menstrual irregularities, and hirsutism (29, 105, 106). In contrast to side effects that also occur in males, these side effects are largely irreversible.

DERMATOLOGICAL

Sebaceous gland hypertrophy and cysts, increased skin surface fatty acids and increased cutaneous populations of *Proprionobacteria acnes* put AAS abusers at increased risk for acne vulgaris (23, 107, 108). Indeed, acne is one of the most common side effects of AASs, self-reported by 21 out of 53 (40%) AAS abusers in one series and 12 out of 22 (55%) in another (30, 34). The high incidence of acne in AAS users makes this a useful finding when screening for use of AASs. Other dermatological sequelae of AAS abuse may include linear keloids, striae (43), oily hair, androgenic alopecia (in both men and women), hirsutism, seborrheic dermatitis, and secondary infections including furunculosis (43, 107, 109).

OTHER PHYSICAL EFFECTS

AASs have been associated with a wide variety of other adverse effects, including induction of an attack of coproporphyria (110), splenic peliosis and rupture (85), and aggravation of tics in Gilles de la Tourette's syndrome (111). Fluid retention is commonly reported by AAS users (23, 30, 34) and largely drives their use of diuretics, as previously described. Alterations in thyroid function occur, most notably a decrease in thyroid binding globulin, but the clinical significance is unclear (112). AASs exert negative feedback on the hypothalamic-pituitary-gonadal axis and cause predictable depression in follicle stimulating hormone, luteinizing hormone, and testosterone, unless testosterone is the exogenous AAS being administered (47).

AGGRESSION

Endogenous testosterone has long been postulated as mediating aggressive behavior in males through brain AAS receptors. Many case reports lend credence to the hypothesis that exogenous AASs may increase aggressive behavior and violence (17, 25, 36, 48, 63, 71, 101, 104, 111, 113). Explosive outbursts are well known among AAS abusers who refer to them as "roid rages." Violent behavior can occur in individuals with no prior history or other risk factors and may culminate in fatal and near-fatal outcomes (36). Aggression and hostility are reported at high rates in case series, e.g., 19 of 20 weight lifters (22).

Controlled studies are required to document aggression and other effects of AAS abuse but are complicated by difficulties in blinding and safety concerns that prevent administration of the extreme doses of multiple AASs commonly abused. Nonetheless, many controlled studies have been conducted that both demonstrate aggression as a consequence of AAS use and illustrate experimental techniques useful in defining other sequelae of AAS use.

Studies comparing AAS abusers to non-using controls permit evaluation of actual drugs and doses of abuse, but random assignment is impossible. Careful selection of controls such as non-abusing athletes or body builders is important as they may differ significantly from the general population. In a study of 46 male strength athletes (16 current users of anabolic steroids, 16 former users and 14 non-users) there was a trend toward higher self-ratings of impatience and belligerence in current users (114). The Profile of Mood States (POMS), Buss-Durkee Hostility Inventory, and subjective ratings of aggression and irritability were administered to 50 male weight lifters—12 current (within last 30 days) AAS users, 14 previous users, and 24 non-users. Using Likert scales, current and former users reported greater aggression and irritability during periods of AAS use than was reported by controls. No differences in composite or individual scale scores from either the POMS or Buss-Durkee Hostility Inventory (former AAS users were not asked to use these instruments to rate their past moods) calls into question the sensitivity of these standard measures in this context (30).

Comparing on-cycle behavior with off-cycle behavior is a sensitive technique that can be embedded in studies that compare users with non-users. POMS anger-hostility scores were higher in 5 on-cycle, adolescent, weight-lifting AAS users than in 19 AAS users who were between cycles (23). Twenty-three AAS-using male strength athletes reported significantly more fights, verbal aggression, and violence toward their significant others when using AAS than when not using AAS, although when not using they did not differ from 14 non-using control athletes (33).

Finally, aggression from AASs can be assessed in prospective controlled trials in which AASs are administered, although only a limited dose range has been used. Another point of caution in interpreting these trials concerns blinding: the effectiveness of blinding is not reported in most trials, but in one placebo-controlled crossover trial of physiologic doses of testosterone 12 of 13 subjects were able to break the blind (115). In an open-label trial, 30 subjects divided into four groups were administered testosterone enanthate 100 mg per week, testosterone enanthate 300 mg per week, nandrolone decanoate 100 mg per week, or nandrolone decanoate 300 mg per week for 6 weeks. Minnesota Multiphasic Personality Inventory hostility and aggression subscale scores increased compared to baseline with greater increases in the high-dose groups (116). One controlled, prospective trial of the psychiatric effects of supratherapeutic doses of AASs has been conducted (20). Twenty healthy males without histories of AAS use were given 40 and then 240 mg per day of methyltestosterone in a double-blind inpatient trial. Irritability, mood swings, violent feelings, and hostility were greater during the high-dose period than at baseline (20).

The clear ability of AASs to promote aggression and irritability raises several specific concerns. Although there have been no clear reports in the biomedical literature of sexual assault in connection with AAS use (just one report of an AAS user who was "irritable and 'rough' with his wife, both physically and sexually") (17), increases in both aggression and libido have lead to concerns that AAS users may be likely to commit sexual assault (46). Female sex partners of male AAS abusers may be at high risk for nonsexual assault (17, 33). Abuse of AASs by law enforcement and corrections (36) personnel is of particular concern as individuals in these professions have an ongoing need for carefully measured levels of violent and aggressive behavior.

LIBIDO AND SEXUAL FUNCTION

AASs can have marked effects on sexual function. There are many case reports of men experiencing increased libido (104), decreased libido (47), and impotence (47, 101). In a study of all 53 AAS using body builders who attended one gymnasium, 18 (34%) reported increased libido and 16 (30%) reported impotence (34). Both increases and decreases in libido were reported in a study comparing AASs using to non-using athletes (30). Increased sexual arousal compared to baseline was demonstrated in a controlled inpatient trial of methyltestosterone, but other aspects of male sexual function were not evaluated (20). A study of three groups of male body builders (15 current AAS users, 15 former AAS users, and 15 who had never used AAS) who all had available sexual partners revealed higher levels of both erectile difficulties and orgasmic and coital frequency in current AAS

users (46). Differences in dose, duration of use, and presence or absence of metabolites with estrogenic properties may account for the variable effects of AASs; evaluation of these factors will require further investigation.

MOOD CHANGES AND PSYCHOTIC SYMPTOMS

Beyond aggression and libido changes, many other psychiatric effects of AAS use have been reported. When considering psychiatric effects of AASs, diagnoses are considered for which organic causes, such as AAS use, are exclusion criteria. The reader is advised that, per DSM-IV criteria, those diagnoses are then substance induced disorders. Abundant case reports exist of hypomania (117) and mania (36), along with reports of irritability, elation, recklessness, racing thoughts, and feelings of power and invincibility that did not clearly meet diagnostic criteria for hypomania or mania (25, 36, 48, 111, 113). One of these cases of hypomania resolved 3–4 days after discontinuation of AAS use and recurred after resumption of AAS use, suggesting a causal relationship (117). Depressed mood (25, 118) and major depression with psychotic features (119) have also been reported during periods of AAS use, as have paranoia and auditory and tactile hallucinations (36).

In a series of 53 AAS-using body builders—the entire population of AAS-using regular attendees at a Swedish gymnasium—27 (51%) reported unspecified mood disturbances (34). Burnett et al. found on-cycle users (N = 5) to have higher depression, vigor, and total mood disturbance on the POMS than 19 off-cycle users (23). In a study of 20 AAS-using athletes and 20 non-using athletes, 14 (70%) of the AAS users reported increased frequency of depression while on-cycle, 14 (70%) reported an increase in paranoid thoughts while on-cycle, and 13 (65%) reported an increase in other psychotic symptoms, although the only psychiatric diagnoses per DSM-III was major depression, single episodes in one AAS user and two non-user controls (22). Pope and Katz reported on a series of 41 AAS users: five (12%) had psychotic symptoms while on AASs, four (10%) had subthreshold psychotic symptoms while on AASs, but none had symptoms when off AASs (29). Five of these 41 subjects met criteria for manic episodes while on AASs and an additional eight met two of the first three DSM-III-R criteria (120) for mania (29). In the largest study examining psychiatric diagnoses, mood disorders were more common in male AAS users (N = 88) while they were on-cycle (23%) than while they were off-cycle (10%) or among male non-users (N = 68, 6%) (24). These mood disorders experienced by AAS users while on-cycle were major depression (13%), hypomanic episode (10%), and manic episode (5%); a dose-response relationship was noted for each of these mood disorders. Psychotic symptoms were diagnosed in 3 (3%) of on-cycle users but not in any off-cycle users or non-users.

Two prospective, controlled trials involving blinded administration of AASs also indicate that AASs can cause mood changes. Increased confidence in performance on a pegboard task was noted in subjects receiving nandrolone decanoate 300 mg per week or testosterone enanthate 100 or 300 mg per week (116). In Su et al.'s trial of administration of 0 mg, 40 mg, and then 240 mg per day of methyltestosterone, increases in euphoria, energy, and mood swings were noted; one of 20 subjects (5%) had an acute manic episode and an additional subject had a hypomanic episode (20). There is a clear relationship, in at least some individuals, between mood changes and AASs; the ability of AASs to induce psychotic symptoms independent of mania has not been definitively established.

COGNITIVE CHANGES

Cognitive impairment, including distractibility, forgetfulness, and confusion has been demonstrated in two controlled trials (20, 114). Improvement in performance of a psychomotor task (a pegboard test) was noted in another controlled trial (116). While these changes are usually subtle, there may be significant impairment in a subset of AAS users (20).

DEPENDENCE

Although abuse of AASs dates back several decades, the first reports of dependence did not emerge until the late 1980s (48, 121). From these initial reports, a subsequent case report (25) and survey work by Brower et al. (19,

Table 27.4 Symptoms of Dependence Reported by AAS Using Male Weight Lifters

Symptom	Percentage
Withdrawal symptoms	84
More substance taken than intended	51
Large time expenditure on substance related activity	40
Continued AAS use despite problems caused or worsened by use	37
Social, work, or leisure activities replaced by AAS use	29
Tolerance	18
Desire yet unable to cut down or control use	16
Frequent intoxication or withdrawal symptoms when expected to function or when physically hazardous	9
Substance used to relieve or avoid withdrawal symptoms	4

Table from Brower KJ, Blow FC, Young JP, Hill EM. Symptoms and correlates of anabolic-androgenic steroid dependence. Br J Addict 1991;86(6):759–768.

Table 27.6 Signs of AAS Abuse

Musculoskeletal
  Hypertrophied muscles
Dermatologic
  Acne
  Striae
  Oily skin
  Needle punctures over large muscles
  Male pattern baldness in men and women
  Hirsutism in females
Genitourinary
  Testicular atrophy
  Prostatic hypertrophy
  Clitoral hypertrophy
Chest
  Gynecomastia
Abdomen
  Hepatomegaly
Head and neck
  Deep, unstable voice in women
  Enlarged larynx in women
Body as a whole
  Edema
  Jaundice

118), it has become apparent that dependence on AASs per DSM-III-R (120) criteria is a real phenomenon. The full range of symptoms of dependence can exist, including loss of control, interference with other activities, and withdrawal symptoms (19) (Table 27.4). Although the data are sparse, dependence appears to be common in AAS users, with 6 of 8 (75%) (118) and 28 of 49 (57%) (19) respondents in each of two studies of weight lifters having three or more symptoms, as required for DSM-III-R diagnosis of dependence (120). Commonly reported symptoms during withdrawal include fatigue, depressed mood, and desire to take more AASs (Table 27.5). The depressed mood following discontinuation of AAS use may resolve within days (48) or may persist for more than a year (122). It is unclear whether persistent depression following withdrawal of high dose AAS is a withdrawal phenomenon, an ongoing process triggered by withdrawal, or a recrudescence of depression obscured by AAS use. Prolonged depression following withdrawal of high-dose AAS has responded to fluoxetine in four cases (122); electroconvulsive therapy was used successfully in a fifth case that had not responded to fluoxetine or desipramine with lithium augmentation (101).

The neurochemical basis of AAS withdrawal symptoms has not been fully elucidated. The opiate system has been implicated based on a case report in which 0.2 mg of naloxone was administered to a patient in AAS withdrawal, eliciting a constellation of symptoms consistent with opiate withdrawal (121). These symptom diminished after four hours and continued to resolve with clonidine treatment over the next six days, although on the seventh day the patient complained of craving, depression, and fatigue and apparently relapsed. The role of clonidine in ameliorating these withdrawal symptoms is unclear as the time course of AAS withdrawal has not been defined. Rosse and Deutsch postulated a role for the benzodiazepine/gamma-aminobutyric acid$_A$ receptor complex, citing tolerance to the anticonvulsant effects of flurazepam in mice chronically exposed to exogenous testosterone (123). While these observations provide a basis for further investigation, neither can be construed as indicating efficacy of any specific pharmacotherapy for AAS withdrawal.

EVALUATION AND TREATMENT

Diagnosis

The prevalence of AAS use in athletes is high enough that it should always be entertained as a possibility. The combination of muscular hypertrophy with testicular atrophy, gynecomastia, needle punctures over large muscles, any signs of virilization in women, or severe acne also suggest the possibility of AAS use. Use of AASs may cause a wide range of signs on physical examination and many laboratory abnormalities. These are summarized in Tables 27.6 and 27.7.

As with other drugs of abuse, toxicological testing for AASs can be helpful in both diagnosis and treatment. Most testing for AASs occurs in the context of athletic competition, where the object is to "level the playing field" by prohibiting a wide variety of performance enhancing drugs. This rationale stands in contrast to testing in the workplace where the goal is to detect drug use associated with performance impairment. Several points of caution need to be raised when considering testing for AASs. Few clinical laboratories are equipped to conduct these tests and the tests for AASs are quite expensive (35). Even those laboratories that test for some AASs may not test for all of the dozens of different compounds that are abused, leading to possibility of false-negative results. The prolonged half-life of some AASs needs to be considered when evaluating repeatedly positive results. Finally, the possibility exists that dietary intake of AASs used in animal husbandry may lead to positive test results (124).

Table 27.5 Symptoms Reported by Male Weight Lifters During AAS Withdrawal

Symptom	Percentage
Desire to take more AASs	52
Fatigue	43
Dissatisfaction with body image	42
Depressed mood	41
Restlessness	29
Anorexia	24
Insomnia	20
Decreased libido	20
Headaches	20
Suicidal thoughts	4

Reprinted with permission from Brower KJ, Blow FC, Young JP, Hill EM. Symptoms and correlates of anabolic-androgenic steroid dependence. Br J Addict 1991;86(6):759–768.

Table 27.7 Common Laboratory Abnormalities in AAS Abusers

Elevated hemoglobin
Elevated hematocrit
Elevated low-density lipoprotein cholesterol
Depressed high-density lipoprotein cholesterol
Elevated[a] or depressed[b] serum testosterone
Decreased luteinizing hormone
Decreased follicle stimulating hormone
Urinary testosterone:epitestosterone ≥6[a]
Elevated serum estradiol[a]
Elevated alanine aminotransferase [c]
Elevated aspartate aminotransferase [c]
Elevated alkaline phosphatase
Elevated lactate dehydrogenase [c, d]

[a]in users of testosterone esters
[b]in non-users of testosterone esters or during withdrawal
[c]also elevated by muscle damage from intense exertion
[d]isozyme analysis can distinguish hepatic from muscular contributions

Treatment

Controlled trials of psychosocial treatment for AAS dependence have not been reported and AAS users infrequently present to substance abuse treatment programs (125). Nonetheless, tentative treatment recommendations can be made based on treatment of other dependencies, the pharmacology of AASs, and the characteristics of AAS users. Assessment of psychiatric status is essential; severe symptoms are an indication for inpatient treatment. AAS users may have a variety of relationship problems. Assault may occur in AAS users' relationships. Ongoing assessment of sexual function is indicated as decreased sexual function may occur upon discontinuation of AASs (118) and has been reported to lead to relapse (47). Persistent decrease in sexual function below that achieved prior to AAS use is an indication for consultation with an endocrinologist.

Psychosocial treatment must include an understanding and acknowledgment of the motivation for continued use. Treatment approaches will differ for individuals whose use persists due to euphoria, versus those who continue to use because they experience depressed mood upon discontinuation, versus those who use it to enhance body image (particularly those with distorted body image), versus those who use for performance enhancement. The nature and course of AAS withdrawal should be reviewed with the user. Conventional drug abuse treatment is appropriate for those who abuse AASs for their mood-altering effects or are dependent on additional substances. For people on a quest for body building or increased athletic performance, realistic goals with respect to performance and appearance must be set, and a diet and exercise plan should be agreed upon to achieve these goals. Peer counseling by former body builders and group support may be of particular value for these users. Nutritional counseling and consultation with a fitness expert may be helpful. Gymnasiums are a frequent locale for acquisition of AASs and need to be avoided until recovery is firmly established. While a wide variety of individuals can deliver psychosocial treatment to AAS users, those who are physically fit or former AAS users will have certain advantages. The reader is referred to a recent review for a more complete discussion of psychosocial treatment issues (126).

The role of pharmacotherapy in treatment of AAS dependence is also poorly defined. While depression, mania, and psychosis may be induced by AAS use or withdrawal and may resolve with prolonged abstinence, their etiology may be difficult to establish with certainty. Pharmacotherapy for psychiatric symptoms should based on a consideration of the risks and benefits, including the potential side effects of the medications and the consequences of inaction, which may include problems with retention in treatment. Maintenance and controlled taper have not been reported as therapeutic modalities, and no other pharmacotherapy can be routinely recommended.

PREVENTION

The development of interventions to reduce the initiation of AAS use is in its infancy. The benefits of AASs with respect to muscular development raises the possibility that comprehensive and accurate information about AASs might serve to increase use. Nonetheless, simply informing potential users of the risks of AASs may not be effective. In a randomized trial in high school football players of a balanced presentation discussing risks and benefits (N = 65), risks only (N = 70), and a control group (N = 57), only those in the balanced group increased their belief in adverse affects from AASs, although subjects in the risks only group decreased their belief in the benefits of AASs (127). No prevention trials with AAS use as an outcome measure have been conducted. There is a real possibility that interventions designed to prevent AAS use could have the opposite effect if applied to populations in which there is little familiarity with AASs. Controlled trials of interventions should be conducted in groups with different levels of familiarity with AASs (e.g., athletes vs. students who are not athletes) with AAS use as an outcome before those interventions are put into general practice.

Acknowledgments. *The author gratefully acknowledges the research assistance of Michael Lim and Judith Rosen, M.P.H. and the encouragement and editorial suggestions of Donald Wesson, M.D.*

References

 1. Kochakian CD. History of anabolic-androgenic steroids. In: Lin G, Erinoff L, eds. Anabolic steroid abuse. Rockville, MD: National Institute on Drug Abuse, 1990:29–59.
 2. Wade N. Anabolic steroids: Doctors denounce them, but athletes aren't listening. 1972;176:1399–1403.
 3. Hatton C, Catlin D. Detection of androgenic anabolic steroids in urine. Clin Lab Med 1987;7:655–668.
 4. Marshall E. The drug of champions. Science 1988;242:183–184.
 5. Buckley W, Yesalis C, Freidl K, et al. Estimated prevalence of anabolic steroid use among male high school seniors. JAMA 1988;260:3441–3445.
 6. Higgins G. Adonis meets Addison: another potential cause of occult adrenal insufficiency [letter]. J Emerg Med 1993;11(6):761–762.
 7. Wilson J. Androgen abuse by athletes. Endocrine Rev 1988;9(2):181–199.
 8. Winters S. Androgens: endocrine physiology and pharmacology. In: Lin G, Erinoff L, eds. Anabolic steroid abuse. Rockville, Maryland: National Institute on Drug Abuse, 1990:113–130.
 9. Jänne O. Androgen interaction through multiple steroid receptors. In: Lin G, Erinoff L, eds. Anabolic steroid abuse. Rockville, Maryland: National Institute on Drug Abuse, 1990:178–186.
10. Kleiner SM. Performance-enhancing aids in sport: health consequences and nutritional alternatives. J Am Coll Nutr 1991;10(2):163–176.
11. Schanzer W, Opfermann G, Donike M. 17-Epimerization of 17 alpha-methyl anabolic steroids in humans: metabolism and synthesis of 17 alpha-hydroxy-17 beta-methyl steroids. Steroids 1992;57(11):537–550.
12. Harrison LM, Fennessey PV. Methandrostenolone metabolism in humans: potential problems associated with isolation and identification of metabolites. J Steroid Biochem 1990;36(5):407–414.
13. Kammerer RC, Merdink JL, Jagels M, Catlin DH, Hui KK. Testing for fluoxymesterone (Halotestin) administration to man: identification of urinary metabolites by gas chromatography-mass spectrometry. J Steroid Biochem 1990;36(6):659–666.
14. Schanzer W, Horning S, Donike M. Metabolism of anabolic steroids in humans: synthesis of 6 beta-hydroxy metabolites of 4-chloro-1,2-dehydro-17 alpha-methyltestosterone, fluoxymesterone, and metandienone. Steroids 1995;60(4):353–366.
15. Wilson J. Androgens. In: Hardman J, Limbird L, Molinoff P, Ruddon R, Gilman A, eds. Goodman & Gilman's The pharmacological basis of therapeutics. 9th ed. New York: McGraw-Hill, Health Professions Division, 1996.
16. Substance Abuse and Mental Health Services Administration. National household survey on drug abuse: population estimates 1994. Washington, DC: U.S. Department of Health and Human Services, 1995.
17. Schulte HM, Hall MJ, Boyer M. Domestic violence associated with anabolic steroid abuse [letter]. Am J Psychiatry 1993;150(2):348.
18. Salva PS, Bacon GE. Anabolic steroids: interest among parents and nonathletes. South Med J 1991;84(5):552–556.
19. Brower KJ, Blow FC, Young JP, Hill EM. Symptoms and correlates of anabolic-androgenic steroid dependence. Br J Addict 1991;86(6):759–768.
20. Su TP, Pagliaro M, Schmidt PJ, Pickar D, Wolkowitz O, Rubinow DR. Neuropsychiatric effects of anabolic steroids in male normal volunteers. JAMA 1993;269(21):2760–2764.
21. Porcerelli JH, Sandler BA. Narcissism and empathy in steroid users. Am J Psychiatry 1995;152(11):1672–1674.
22. Perry PJ, Andersen KH, Yates WR. Illicit anabolic steroid use in athletes. A case series analysis. Am J Sports Med 1990;18(4):422–428.
23. Burnett KF, Kleiman ME. Psychological characteristics of adolescent steroid users. Adolescence 1994;29(113):81–89.
24. Pope HJ, Katz DL. Psychiatric and medical effects of anabolic-androgenic steroid use. A controlled study of 160 athletes. Arch Gen Psychiatry 1994;51(5):375–382.
25. Hays LR, Littleton S, Stillner V. Anabolic steroid dependence [letter]. Am J Psychiatry 1990;147(1):122.
26. Frankle M. Use of androgenic anabolic steroids by athletes [letter]. JAMA 1984;252(4):482.
27. Schwellnus MP, Lambert MI, Todd MP, Juritz JM. Androgenic anabolic steroid use in matric pupils. A survey of prevalence of use in the western Cape. S Afr Med J 1992;82(3):154–158.
28. Shepherd M, McKeithan K. Examination of the type and amount of pharmaceutical products being declared by U.S. residents upon returning to the U.S. from Mexico at the Laredo, Texas border crossing. Austin: The University of Texas, 1996.

29. Pope H, Katz D. Affective and psychotic symptoms associated with anabolic steroid use. Am J Psychiatry 1988;145(4):487–490.

30. Bahrke MS, Wright JE, Strauss RH, Catlin DH. Psychological moods and subjectively perceived behavioral and somatic changes accompanying anabolic-androgenic steroid use. Am J Sports Med 1992;20(6):717–724.

31. Hickson JJ, Johnson TE, Lee W, Sidor RJ. Nutrition and the precontest preparations of a male bodybuilder. J Am Diet Assoc 1990;90(2):264–267.

32. Nilsson S. Androgenic anabolic steroid use among male adolescents in Falkenberg. Eur J Clin Pharmacol 1995;48(1):9–11.

33. Choi PY, Pope HJ. Violence toward women and illicit androgenic-anabolic steroid use. Ann Clin Psychiatry 1994;6(1):21–25.

34. Lindstrom M, Nilsson AL, Katzman PL, Janzon L, Dymling JF. Use of anabolic-androgenic steroids among body builders—frequency and attitudes. J Intern Med 1990;227(6):407–411.

35. Benzi G. Pharmacoepidemiology of the drugs used in sports as doping agents. Pharmacol Res 1994;29(1):13–26.

36. Pope HJ, Katz DL. Homicide and near-homicide by anabolic steroid users. J Clin Psychiatry 1990;51(1):28–31.

37. Rickert VI, Pawlak MC, Sheppard V, Jay MS. Human growth hormone: a new substance of abuse among adolescents? Clin Pediatr (Phila) 1992;31(12):723–726.

38. Galloway G, Frederick S, Staggers F, Gonzales M, Stalcup S, Smith D. Gamma-hydroxybutyrate: an emerging drug of abuse that causes physical dependence. Addiction (in press).

39. Prather ID, Brown DE, North P, Wilson JR. Clenbuterol: a substitute for anabolic steroids? Med Sci Sports Exerc 1995;27(8):1118–1121.

40. Gareau R, Audran M, Baynes R, et al. Erythropoietin abuse in athletes. Nature 1996;380:113.

41. Pearl JM. Severe reaction to "natural testosterones": how safe are the ergogenic aids? [letter]. Am J Emerg Med 1993;11(2):188–189.

42. Appleby M, Fisher M, Martin M. Myocardial infarction, hyperkalaemia and ventricular tachycardia in a young male body-builder. Int J Cardiol 1994;44(2):171–174.

43. Luke JL, Farb A, Virmani R, Sample RH. Sudden cardiac death during exercise in a weight lifter using anabolic androgenic steroids: pathological and toxicological findings. J Forensic Sci 1990;35(6):1441–1447.

44. Morrison CL. Anabolic steroid users identified by needle and syringe exchange contact. Drug Alcohol Depend 1994;36(2):153–155.

45. Salaman J. Misuse of anabolic drugs [letter]. BMJ 1993;306(6869):62.

46. Moss HB, Panzak GL, Tarter RE. Sexual functioning of male anabolic steroid abusers. Arch Sex Behav 1993;22(1):1–12.

47. Bickelman C, Ferries L, Eaton RP. Impotence related to anabolic steroid use in a body builder. Response to clomiphene citrate. West J Med 1995;162(2):158–160.

48. Brower K, Blow F, Beresford T, Fuelling C. Anabolic-androgenic steroid dependence. J Clin Psychiatry 1989;50(1):31–33.

49. Bagatell C, Bremner W. Androgens in men—uses and abuses. N Engl J Med 1996;334(11):708–714.

50. American College of Sports Medicine. Position statement on the use and abuse of anabolic-androgenic steroids in sports. Med Sci Sports Exerc 1977;9:11–13.

51. American College of Sports Medicine. Position stand on the use and abuse of anabolic-androgenic steroids in sports. Am J Sports Med 1984;12:13–18.

52. American College of Sports Medicine. Position stand on the use of anabolic-androgenic steroids in sports. Med Sci Sports Exerc 1987;19(5):534–539.

53. Elashoff JD, Jacknow AD, Shain SG, Braunstein GD. Effects of anabolic-androgenic steroids on muscular strength. Ann Intern Med 1991;115(5):387–393.

54. Kuipers H, Peeze BF, Hartgens F, Wijnen JA, Keizer HA. Muscle ultrastructure after strength training with placebo or anabolic steroid. Can J Appl Physiol 1993;18(2):189–196.

55. Mayer M, Rosen F. Interaction of glucocorticoids and androgens with skeletal muscle. Metabolism 1977;27:937–962.

56. Raaka B, Finnerky M, Samuels H. The glucocorticoid antagonist 17 alpha-methyltestosterone binds to the 10S glucocorticoid receptor and blocks antagonist-mediated disassociation of the 10S oligomer to the 4S deoxyribonucleic acid-binding sub-unit. Mol Endocrinol 1989;3:322–341.

57. Smith DA, Perry PJ. The efficacy of ergogenic agents in athletic competition. Part I: Androgenic-anabolic steroids. Ann Pharmacother 1992;26(4):520–528.

58. Toyama M, Watanabe S, Kobayashi T, et al. Two cases of acute myocardial infarction associated with aplastic anemia during treatment with anabolic steroids. Jpn Heart J 1994;35(3):369–373.

59. Kennedy C. Myocardial infarction in association with misuse of anabolic steroids. Ulster Med J 1993;62(2):174–176.

60. Huie MJ. An acute myocardial infarction occurring in an anabolic steroid user. Med Sci Sports Exerc 1994;26(4):408–413.

61. Ferenchick GS, Adelman S. Myocardial infarction associated with anabolic steroid use in a previously healthy 37-year-old weight lifter. Am Heart J 1992;124(2):507–508.

62. Kennedy MC, Corrigan AB, Pilbeam ST. Myocardial infarction and cerebral haemorrhage in a young body builder taking anabolic steroids [letter]. Aust N Z J Med 1993;23(6):713.

63. Kennedy MC, Lawrence C. Anabolic steroid abuse and cardiac death. Med J Aust 1993;158(5):346–348.

64. Lyngberg KK. [Myocardial infarction and death of a body builder after using anabolic steroids]. Ugeskr Laeger 1991;153(8):587–588.

65. Schollert PV, Bendixen PM. [Dilated cardiomyopathy in a user of anabolic steroids]. Ugeskr Laeger 1993;155(16):1217–1218.

66. Dickerman RD, Schaller F, Prather I, McConathy WJ. Sudden cardiac death in a 20-year-old bodybuilder using anabolic steroids. Cardiology 1995;86(2):172–173.

67. Laroche GP. Steroid anabolic drugs and arterial complications in an athlete—a case history. Angiology 1990;41(11):964–969.

68. Akhter J, Hyder S, Ahmed M. Cerebrovascular accident associated with anabolic steroid use in a young man. Neurology 1994;44(12):2405–2406.

69. Robinson RJ, White S. Misuse of anabolic drugs [letter]. Br Med J 1993;306(6869):61.

70. Siekierzynska CA, Polowiec Z, Kulawinska M, Rowinska ZE. [Death caused by pulmonary embolism in a body builder taking anabolic steroids (metanabol)]. Wiad Lek 1990;43(19–20):972–975.

71. Visuri T, Lindholm H. Bilateral distal biceps tendon avulsions with use of anabolic steroids. Med Sci Sports Exerc 1994;26(8):941–944.

72. Ansell JE, Tiarks C, Fairchild VK. Coagulation abnormalities associated with the use of anabolic steroids. Am Heart J 1993 125(2 pt 1):367–371.

73. Ferenchick G, Schwartz D, Ball M, Schwartz K. Androgenic-anabolic steroid abuse and platelet aggregation: a pilot study in weight lifters. Am J Med Sci 1992;303(2):78–82.

74. Ferenchick GS, Hirokawa S, Mammen EF, Schwartz KA. Anabolic-androgenic steroid abuse in weight lifters: Evidence for activation of the hemostatic system. Am J Hematol 1995;49(4):282–288.

75. Glazer G. Atherogenic effects of anabolic steroids on serum lipid levels. A literature review. Arch Intern Med 1991;151(10):1925–1933.

76. Glazer G, Suchman AL. Lack of demonstrated effect of nandrolone on serum lipids. Metabolism 1994;43(2):204–210.

77. Bagatell CJ, Bremner WJ. Androgen and progestagen effects on plasma lipids. Prog Cardiovasc Dis 1995;38(3):255–271.

78. Barrett CE. Testosterone and risk factors for cardiovascular disease in men. Diabete Metab 1995;21(3):156–161.

79. Kuipers H, Wijnen JA, Hartgens F, Willems SM. Influence of anabolic steroids on body composition, blood pressure, lipid profile and liver functions in body builders. Int J Sports Med 1991;12(4):413–418.

80. Riebe D, Fernhall B, Thompson PD. The blood pressure response to exercise in anabolic steroid users. Med Sci Sports Exerc 1992;24(6):633–637.

81. Pascual J, Teruel JL, Marcen R, Liano F, Ortuno J. Blood pressure after three different forms of correction of anemia in hemodialysis. Int J Artif Organs 1992;15(7):393–396.

82. Thompson PD, Sadaniantz A, Cullinane EM, et al. Left ventricular function is not impaired in weight-lifters who use anabolic steroids. J Am Coll Cardiol 1992;19(2):278–282.

83. Wood P, Yin JA. Oxymetholone hepatotoxicity enhanced by concomitant use of cyclosporin A in a bone marrow transplant patient. Clin Lab Haematol 1994;16(2):201–204.

84. Tsukamoto N, Uchiyama T, Takeuchi T, Sato S, Naruse T, Nakazato Y. Fatal outcome of a patient with severe aplastic anemia after treatment with metenolone acetate. Ann Hematol 1993;67(1):41–43.

85. Hirose H, Ohishi A, Nakamura H, Sugiura H, Umezawa A, Hosoda Y. Fatal splenic rupture in anabolic steroid-induced peliosis in a patient with myelodysplastic syndrome. Br J Haematol 1991;78(1):128–129.

86. Friedl K. Reappraisal of the health risks associated with high doses of oral and injectable androgenic steroids. NIDA Res Monogr Ser 1990;102:142–177.

87. Goldman B. Liver carcinoma in an athlete taking anabolic steroids. J Am Osteopath Assoc 1985;85:56.

88. Creagh T, Rubin A, Evans D. Hepatic tumours induced by anabolic steroids in an athlete. J Clin Pathol 1988;41:441–443.

89. Stannard JP, Bucknell AL. Rupture of the triceps tendon associated with steroid injections. Am J Sports Med 1993;21(3):482–485.

90. Liow RY, Tavares S. Bilateral rupture of the quadriceps tendon associated with anabolic steroids. Br J Sports Med 1995;29(2):77–79.

91. Laseter JT, Russell JA. Anabolic steroid-induced tendon pathology: a review of the literature. Med Sci Sports Exerc 1991;23(1):1–3.

92. Moore W. Anabolic steroid use in adolescence. JAMA 1988;260:3484–3486.

93. Sklarek H, Mantovani R, Erens E, Heisler D, Niederman N, Fein A. AIDS in a bodybuilder using anabolic steroids [letter]. N Engl J Med 1984;311:1701.

94. Scott M, Scott M, Jr. HIV infection associated with injections of anabolic steroids [letter]. JAMA 1989;262:207–208.

95. Henrion R, Mandelbrot L, Delfieu D. Contamination par le VIH à la suite d'injections d'anabolisants [letter]. Presse Med 1992;21(5):218.

96. DuRant RH, Rickert VI, Ashworth CS, Newman C, Slavens G. Use of multiple drugs among adolescents who use anabolic steroids. N Engl J Med 1993;328(13):922–926.

97. Plaus WJ, Hermann G. The surgical management of superficial infections caused by atypical mycobacteria. Surgery 1991;110(1):99–103.

98. Khankhanian NK, Hammers YA, Kowalski P. Exuberant local tissue reaction to intramuscular injection of nandrolone decanoate (Deca-Durabolin)—a steroid compound in a sesame seed oil base—mimicking soft tissue malignant tumors: a case report and review of the literature. Mil Med 1992;157(12):670–674.

99. Spiga L, Gorrini G, Ferraris L, Odaglia G, Frassetto G. [Unilateral gynecomastia induced by the use of anabolic steroids. A clinical case report]. Minerva Med 1992;83(9):575–580.

100. Reyes RJ, Zicchi S, Hamed H, Chaudary MA, Fentiman IS. Surgical correction of gynaecomastia in bodybuilders [see comments]. Br J Clin Pract 1995;49(4):177–179.

101. Allnutt S, Chaimowitz G. Anabolic steroid withdrawal depression: a case report [letter]. Can J Psychiatry 1994;39(5):317–318.

102. Sorensen MB, Ingerslev HJ. [Azoospermia in 2 body-builders after taking anabolic steroids]. Ugeskr Laeger 1995;157(8):1044–1045.

103. Turek PJ, Williams RH, Gilbaugh Jr, Lipshultz LI. The reversibility of anabolic steroid-induced azoospermia. J Urol 1995;153(5):1628–1630.

104. Wemyss HS, Hamdy FC, Hastie KJ. Steroid abuse in athletes, prostatic enlargement and bladder outflow obstruction—is there a relationship? Br J Urol 1994;74(4):476–478.

105. Gerritsma EJ, Brocaar MP, Hakkesteegt MM, Birkenhager JC. Virilization of the voice in post-menopausal women due to the anabolic steroid nandrolone decanoate (Decadurabolin). The effects of medication for one year. Clin Otolaryngol 1994;19(1):79–84.

106. Strauss R, Liggett M, Lanese R. Anabolic steroid use and perceived effects in ten weight-trained woman athletes. JAMA 1985;253:2871–2873.

107. Scott M, Scott AM. Effects of anabolic-androgenic steroids on the pilosebaceous unit. Cutis 1992;50(2):113–116.

108. Merkle T, Landthaler M, Braun FO. [Acne conglobata-like exacerbation of acne vulgaris following administration of anabolic steroids and vitamin B complex-containing preparations]. Hautarzt 1990;41(5):280–282.

109. Scott M, Scott M, Scott AM. Linear keloids resulting from abuse of anabolic androgenic steroid drugs. Cutis 1994;53(1):41–43.

110. Lane PR, Massey KL, Worobetz LJ, Jutras MN, Hull PR. Acute hereditary coproporphyria induced by the androgenic/anabolic steroid methandrostenolone (Dianabol). J Am Acad Dermatol 1994;30(2 Pt 2):308–312.

111. Leckman JF, Scahill L. Possible exacerbation of tics by androgenic steroids [letter]. N Engl J Med 1990;322(23):1674.

112. Deyssig R, Weissel M. Ingestion of androgenic-anabolic steroids induces mild thyroidal impairment in male body builders. J Clin Endocrinol Metab 1993;76(4):1069–1071.

113. Dalby JT. Brief anabolic steroid use and sustained behavioral reaction [letter]. Am J Psychiatry 1992;149(2):271–272.

114. Bond AJ, Choi PY, Pope HJ. Assessment of attentional bias and mood in users and non-users of anabolic-androgenic steroids. Drug Alcohol Depend 1995;37(3):241–245.

115. Tenover JS. Effects of testosterone supplementation in the aging male. J Clin Endocrinol Metab 1992;75:1092–1098.

116. Hannan CJ, Friedl KE, Zold A, Kettler TM, Plymate SR. Psychological and serum homovanillic acid changes in men administered androgenic steroids. Psychoneuroendocrinology 1991;16(4):335–343.

117. Freinhar J, Alvarez W. Androgen-induced hypomania. J Clin Psychiatry 1985;46(8):354–355.

118. Brower KJ, Eliopulos GA, Blow FC, Catlin DH, Beresford TP. Evidence for physical and psychological dependence on anabolic androgenic steroids in eight weight lifters. Am J Psychiatry 1990;147(4):510–512.

119. Pope HG Jr, Katz DL. Bodybuilder's psychosis [letter]. Lancet 1987;1(8537):863.

120. American Psychiatric Association. Diagnostic and statistical manual of mental disorders. 3rd edition, revised. Washington, DC: American Psychiatric Press, 1987.

121. Tennant F, Black D, Voy R. Anabolic steroid dependence with opioid-type features [letter]. N Engl J Med 1988;319:578.

122. Malone DJ, Dimeff RJ. The use of fluoxetine in depression associated with anabolic steroid withdrawal: a case series. J Clin Psychiatry 1992;53(4):130–132.

123. Rosse R, Deutsch F. Hooked on hormones [letter]. JAMA 1990;263:2048–2049.

124. Kicman AT, Cowan DA, Myhre L, Nilsson S, Tomten S, Oftebro H. Effect on sports drug tests of ingesting meat from steroid (methenolone)-treated livestock. Clin Chem 1994;40(11 Pt 1):2084–2087.

125. Clancy GP, Yates WR. Anabolic steroid use among substance abusers in treatment. J Clin Psychiatry 1992;53(3):97–100.

126. Corcoran JP, Longo ED. Psychological treatment of anabolic-androgenic steroid-dependent individuals. J Subst Abuse Treat 1992;9(3):229–235.

127. Goldberg L, Bents R, Bosworth E, Trevisan L, Elliot DL. Anabolic steroid education and adolescents: do scare tactics work? Pediatrics 1991;87(3):283–286.

128. Schanzer W, Opfermann G, Donike M. Metabolism of stanozolol: identification and synthesis of urinary metabolites. J Steroid Biochem 1990;36(1–2):153–174.

129. Goldberg L, Bosworth EE, Bents RT, Trevisan L. Effect of an anabolic steroid education program on knowledge and attitudes of high school football players. J Adolesc Health Care 1990;11(3):210–214.

130. Johnson MD, Jay MS, Shoup B, Rickert VI. Anabolic steroid use by adolescents. 1989;83:921–924.

131. Johnston L, O'Malley P, Bachman J. National survey results from the Monitoring the Future Study, 1975–1994. Rockville, MD: National Institute on Drug Abuse, 1995.

132. Komoroski EM, Rickert VI. Adolescent body image and attitudes to anabolic steroid use. Am J Dis Child 1992;146(7):823–828.

133. Meilman PW, Crace RK, Presley CA, Lyerla R. Beyond performance enhancement: polypharmacy among collegiate users of steroids. J Am Coll Health 1995;44(3):98–104.

134. Middleman AB, Faulkner AH, Woods ER, Emans SJ, DuRant RH. High-risk behaviors among high school students in Massachusetts who use anabolic steroids. 1995;96(2 Pt 1):268–272.

135. Radakovich J, Broderick P, Pickell G. Rate of anabolic-androgenic steroid use among students in junior high school [published erratum appears in J Am Board Fam Pract 1993;6(6):616]. J Am Board Fam Pract 1993;6(4):341–345.

136. Terney R, McLain LG. The use of anabolic steroids in high school students. Am J Dis Child 1990;144(1):99–103.

137. Whitehead R, Chillag S, Elliott D. Anabolic steroid use among adolescents in a rural state. J Fam Pract 1992;35(4):401–405.

138. Williamson DJ. Misuse of anabolic drugs [letter]. BMJ 1993;306(6869):61.

28 EATING DISORDERS

Mark S. Gold, Christopher R. Johnson, and Karen Stennie

INTRODUCTION

Addiction is a chronic disease characterized by compulsive self-administration without apparent regard to the consequences of consuming the addictive substance. The process of addiction is mediated through brain mechanisms underlying reward or reinforcement. Reinforcement can be accomplished through both positive and negative mechanisms. Positive reinforcement promotes continued use to attain and maintain a state desirable to the organism (e.g., initially euphoria). Conversely, negative reinforcement promotes continued use to avoid an undesirable state associated with decreasing or stopping use (e.g., abstinence syndrome). Paradoxically, the use of drugs to terminate negative reinforcement is particularly compelling because it is also positively rewarding.

The ultimate expression of reinforcement is in the brain's hierarchical organization and promotion of behaviors through neurobiological mechanisms that reward and thereby make survival and other desirable behaviors more likely to occur. Basic research has been conducted to elucidate the fundamental processes of reward of primitive species survival drives and the usurpation of these existing systems by exogenous agents. This addiction research has enhanced our ability to treat this chronic problem and understand the common brain mechanisms involved in pain, appetite, drug reinforcement, and sexual behaviors.

The definition of addiction has gone through considerable evolution. The focus in the past was that addiction results as a means of avoiding the distress of withdrawal. Addiction was inadvertent or somehow passive or an unintended consequence of these pernicious agents. This model for addiction had a potent impact on both theory and treatment by putting a bizarre emphasis on neuroadaptation. Thus, by emphasizing abstinence symptomatology and treating withdrawal we thought we understood addiction and its treatment. Treatment of addiction was often considered the same as or equivalent to treating withdrawal. Unfortunately, astounding success in the development of anti-withdrawal agents did little to improve treatment outcomes. The high rates of relapse after this "treatment" have lead many to believe that positive reinforcement may be more active, purposeful, and important than anything else in the process of addiction and the persistence of relapse (1).

The brain's reinforcing pathways share common mesocorticolimbic projections, also known as the medial forebrain bundle. The brain does not seem to differentiate whether the reward is provoked by licit or illicit drugs, by extreme environmental manipulations, or by fasting. This much-studied area of the brain, which includes the ventral tegmental area (VTA) and the nucleus accumbens (nAC), is considered the neural center modulating positive reinforcement (2). Feeding, sex, and other survival behaviors are reinforced or made more likely by events occurring within the VTA and nAC. The central neurotransmitter involved in these events is dopamine (DA), although many other neurotransmitters modulate the effects of DA and the development of addiction. Intracerebral microdialysis allows scientists to study awake, freely moving animals given drugs like cocaine, before and after eating (2).

Intracerebral microdialysis enables the study of neurotransmitters in the nAC and other localized brain regions in awake, freely moving and behaving animals (3–6). An increase in the extracellular level of DA in the nAC, a major target of the mesolimbic dopaminergic system (MDS) (7), during ingestion of food has been reported by numerous authors (8–13). This is quite similar to the result produced by cocaine or after other drug self-administra-tion (14). This suggests that there is a relationship between food intake and the activity of the MDS just as it has been suggested that there is a relationship between reward (13), illicit drug reinforcement (14–16), self-stimulation and sexual behavior (17–19), and MDS dopaminergic activity. Eating behavior is complex but it appears that the MDS is activated by food reward. Food is reported to be addicting or extremely rewarding by some patients who complain of compulsive candy, potato chip, or other food consumption. In animals it appears that food reward depends in part on its palatability or the hedonic component related to the sensory properties of foods (15, 16). Like recent immigrants to the United States, when animals are offered a more palatable diet, most animal species eat more and become obese (17–19). Passive drug administration is not addicting while active goal-directed behavior seeking and using drugs for euphoria production is addicting. Being stuffed with cake is a markedly different experience than sneaking around and raiding the refrigerator after midnight. Host factors such as genetic vulnerability at conception or acquired in utero or early in life will play an important role in determining the pathological reward produced by drugs or food or some micronutrient, thus underlying the acquisition of a pathological attachment we call addiction or binge eating or obesity.

Consumption of food and water and copulative behavior increase the extracellular level of DA in conscious and freely moving animals. Many studies of addictive drugs including cocaine, ethanol, opiates, and nicotine also show such increases in DA within the nAC following their administration (20). We believe that this primitive reward system is central to the development of both eating disorders and addiction. The numerous associations between eating disorders and drug addictions, co-morbidity, genetic links, high recidivism, and common neurobiological pathways, modification of drug reward by eating or starvation lead us to consider the possibility that binge eating disorders represent a drug-free auto-addiction for a significant subset of the addiction-prone. In others it is a trigger leading to a drug or alcohol relapse. In others it is an apparent result of alcohol or drug abstinence. Mesolimbic DA activity is but one common thread attributing rewarding properties of both food and illicit drugs.

DRUG REWARD

Drug reward was reviewed in detail in Chapter 6. The mesocorticolimbic dopaminergic system is thought to act as an interface between the midbrain and forebrain (21). It seems to function as a modulator, integrating emotion into directed behavior (22). Drug reward also confers importance or significance upon certain behaviors and not others. Species-specific survival drives (feeding, drinking, and copulation) have been demonstrated by many studies to be reinforced or given salience through this system. Many studies of substance abuse disorders in animal models demonstrate that the addictive nature of these drugs is mediated by their direct effect upon this reward system (1, 23). All drugs of abuse are self-administered by animals and man. Cocaine is self-administered to death in paradigms where use and access are unlimited (24). However, the most convincing evidence that drugs access this primitive system is that they decrease the amount of brain stimulation required to motivate baseline responding (25). Drug use motivates repetition of the behavior and creates a feeling of satisfaction like that produced by completion of a biological imperative or normal survival behavior. Drug use produces the same sense of accomplishment and may be seen by the addict as tantamount to survival. The normal survival behaviors become less compelling as they are bypassed by the normal reinforcement system (26). In many instances cocaine addicts stop eating, drinking, washing, talking and interacting with others and look like patients with a primary eating disorder (27). The studies of divergent drugs of abuse from heroin to nicotine to cocaine all involve the VTA-nAC dopaminergic system; thus, it is thought to be the core neuroanatomy for addiction medicine and central to brain control of any goal-directed rewarding behavior (28).

Primary Reinforcers

Feeding, like drinking and copulation, is considered a specific species-survival behavior reinforced through the medial forebrain bundle. These survival behaviors are primary reinforcers; that is, they have a direct effect upon the medial forebrain bundle. Drugs of abuse are also primary reinforcers. Feeding within the arena of eating is also a primary reinforcer. But normal feeding behavior and eating disorders differ in the purpose they serve. Feeding behavior is typically a response to hunger. Hunger may have been a more important reason to eat in our past than it is in the United States today. Hunger is likely generated by depletion of nutrient and energy stores. The reward generated by feeding, paired with the state of hunger and its resolution into satiety, thus positively reinforces feeding behavior in a state of hunger. Studies show that a state of hunger via food deprivation in rats actually enhances the reward effect of feeding. A state of hunger also potentiates illicit drug reward. In this sense hunger and craving could be seen as secondary reinforcers paired with the primary reward generated by feeding. Eating or the use of cocaine produces satiation. In this sense illicit drugs acquire the organismic significance attributed to food. They become an acquired primary drive equated with survival. Feeding is a behavior that promotes survival of the health and survival of the organism, which ultimately translates into a greater chance of survival of the species.

Neurobiology of Feeding

The neurobiology of feeding involves a complex interplay of peripheral afferent signaling, central modulation, and nutrient composition. This is a dynamic process of hunger, feeding, satiation, and satiety. The effect of these processes in food reward and the effect of many addictive drugs on these regulatory systems may help to explain the relationship between substance abuse and eating disorders. It is becoming apparent that eating and drug disorders share a common neuroanatomical and neurochemical basis (29). The latter may access brain reward through exogenous, illicit drugs and the former through dietary and environmental manipulations. Understanding this relationship of substance abuse and eating disorders will allow us to create more effective and focused treatment strategies.

The concepts of hunger, satiation, and satiety have variable definitions. They may also be relative to a culture and the availability of food. In cultures without starvation and where few individuals eat in response to hunger, eating disorders appear much more common. Hunger can be thought of as both a physiological drive to eat and also as a perceived desire to eat. Satiation is generally recognized as the process that ends eating behavior. Satiety is then the state after the completion of eating behavior in which further eating is inhibited. Eating disorders and obesity may be divided into related groups just as neural messengers are being discovered that affect either aspect of the eating process.

While the precise physiological mechanisms regulating feeding behavior have not been fully described, research studying the role of various neurotransmitters and neuropeptides has contributed to a greater understanding of this complex process. The overall regulation of feeding includes central nervous system (CNS) integration of peripheral afferent signals, reward, endocrine responses, energy states, drive and mood states, micronutrient intake and supply, neurotransmitter responses, and efferent motor commands into a coordinated system of assuring the organism's metabolic needs in the face of more global environmental factors. Our interest is in how disruptions in this system give rise to self-perpetuating, maladaptive behaviors. Furthermore, once established, the primitive reward systems seems to function as to preserve these maladaptive behaviors. We will mainly consider the role of

neurotransmitter systems in the pathogenesis of eating disorders and their similarity with substance abuse disorders.

NEUROBIOLOGY OF EATING DISORDERS AND REWARD

The defined teleology of eating disorders has changed considerably during this century. Early studies on eating disorders including obesity were primarily defined in psychological terms as the consequence of emotional upheaval, displacement of other psychological drives, or as the means to satisfy some unfulfilled psychological need. In the latter half of this century the focus changed more toward physiological mechanisms arising from work studying the effects of hypothalamic lesions and their subsequent effect upon feeding behavior and weight change. More recently the physiological mechanisms regulating feeding, diet, and weight have been under increasing scrutiny particularly in light of the unfortunate trends of the increasing prevalence of eating disorders in industrialized nations. The definitive work in this area stems from the results of studies where microinjections of drugs are delivered to specific brain foci. Microdialysis studies of neurotransmitters in conjunction with the microinjection studies have allowed unprecedented access to brain mechanisms and a new understanding of the neurochemistry of addictive and eating disorders. Recently, many new neuropeptides have been discovered with crucial roles in regulating feeding. Furthermore, advances in neuroimaging and immunochemistry have also added to the evolving renaissance of neurobiological understanding (30).

NEUROPEPTIDES

Many studies of brain lesions, microinjection of drugs, neuropeptides, and microdialysis studies of neurotransmitter levels in freely moving and behaving animals indicate that the control of feeding behavior can be localized to the hypothalamus. The paraventricular nucleus (PVN) seems to be the part of the hypothalamus that is most critical to this process. Lesions of these areas have been demonstrated to cause obesity, increased parasympathetic tone, and hyperphagia (31).

A significant amount of data suggests that eating disorders represent dysregulations in the neurotransmitter pathways involving DA, serotonin (5HT), endogenous opioids, and other neuropeptides. The role of the dopaminergic system in eating disorders links them with the pathway of brain reward in which all the classical addictions appear to converge. This reality seems obvious considering the common desire for a cigarette or coffee after a good meal and the stereotypical use of alcohol before sex and a cigarette afterwards. Patients in early alcoholism recovery begin eating ice cream and potato chips, binging at night. They note that this behavior calms them down. It seems likely that one of the stimulatory peptides is involved in the release of driven eating. Still, eating is much more complex, involving numerous stimulatory and inhibitory peptides and messengers.

Some of the major neuropeptides involved in regulating appetite and feeding are listed in Table 28.1. Of the inhibitory neuropeptides, neurotensin (NT) has a known important relationship with DA. In the mesencephalon, NT-containing neurons originate in the VTA and terminate in the substantia nigra pars compacta (SNC), the nAC, the caudate putamen, prefrontal cortex, and the central median amygdala. In the diencephalon NT is found within the zona incerta and the median eminence.

NT and DA are both colocalized in neuronal projections from the VTA to the SNC, the prefrontal cortex and within the tuberoinfundibular DA system, particularly the median eminence (32). The importance of NT is evinced through the studies of the effects of cocaine administration and withdrawal on the NT system. Chronic cocaine administration and withdrawal seem to disrupt the normal NT-DA interactions at the nerve cell bodies and terminals. Cocaine induced increased NT binding in the prefrontal cortex and the SNC may be due to selective depletion of NT from NT-DA nerve terminals as a result of upregulation of postsynaptic NT receptors. This is analogous to the enhancement of DA binding. Since peptides are not conserved after uptake as are monoamines, NT would be lost more readily than DA in the prefrontal cortex. Thus chronic administration of cocaine may selec-

Table 28.1 Neuropeptides that Regulate Food Intake and Affect Eating and Energy Expenditure

Stimulate feeding Usually decrease energy expenditure	Inhibit feeding Usually increase energy expenditure
Neuropeptide Y	Serotonin
Galanin	Insulin
Dynorphin	Neurotensin
β-endorphin	CRF
GHRH	Dopamine
Norepinephrine	Cholecystokinin
Anandamide	Leptin
GABA	TRH, MSH, glucagon, enterostatin, calcitonin, amylin, bombesin, somatostatin, cytokines

Adapted from Sahu A, Kalra SP. Neuropeptide regulation of feeding behavior: neuropeptide Y. TEM 1993;4(7):217–224.

tively deplete NT from VTA projections to the prefrontal cortex and SNC without markedly affecting levels of DA or the reinforcing effects associated with enhanced DA levels (33). DA, norepinephrine, and 5HT appear involved in eating and satiety.

NEUROPEPTIDE Y

Neuropeptide Y (NPY) is a good place to start as a model for uncontrolled hyperphagia. NPY is one of the most abundant and widely distributed neuropeptides known. It is a member of the pancreatic polypeptide family but has a number of unique actions in the regulation of body weight by driving food intake. NPY is involved in the regulation of other hormones and neurotransmitters and appears involved in circadian rhythms. Studies indicate that 5HT may play an antagonistic role with NPY in the regulation of feeding (34). 5HT neurons innervate NPY-containing neurons in the arcuate nucleus. Central injections of 5HT inhibit food intake through NPY as we might expect serotonin-specific reuptake inhibitors (SSRIs) to act. NPY infusions in the hypothalamus decreases 5HT release. NPY is the most potent activator of feeding behavior yet discovered. Its levels seem to vary inversely with those of 5HT. Administration of NPY into the hypothalamic PVN induces feeding in satiated animals and may selectively induce extraordinary carbohydrate intake. Administration of anti-NPY decreases spontaneous carbohydrate intake in animals. Chronic administration of NPY produces an obesity syndrome indistinguishable from naturally-occurring obesity. NPY is clearly the single most potent orexigenic compound known and a viable model for driven overeating and obesity.

Neuroanatomical studies show that links exist between these systems, possibly indicating a feedback system (35). NPY and endorphin relationships have been studied in animals. NPY administered intracerebroventricularly and into the PVN of the hypothalamus stimulates feeding and decreases brown adipose tissue thermogenesis. Although specific NPY antagonists are not yet available (phase one trials are expected to begin in March), studies have shown that the opioid antagonist naloxone blocked NPY-induced feeding when both drugs were injected intracerebroventricularly. Peripheral naloxone blocked intracerebroventricular NPY-induced feeding and brown fat alterations. Fourth ventricular naloxone decreased PVN NPY-induced feeding and naltrexone given into the nucleus of the solitary tract blocked PVN NPY-induced alterations in feeding and brown fat. These data indicate that NPY–endorphin interactions in the PVN may act on feeding and the nucleus of the solitary tract (36). NPY has a number of known and probably some unknown receptors in brain and elsewhere. Which receptor is responsible for NPY effect on feeding and carbohydrate drive is unknown. It is also possible that neuropeptides reinforce existing macronutrient preference and simply increase the attachment for the preferred food, especially those with specific taste, smell, or texture. NPY and also galanin may induce eating in satiated animals and preferentially stimulate carbohydrate and fat intake, respectively, by this mechanism.

Elevated levels of NPY have been demonstrated in bulimic patients (37). d-fenfluramine, a potent 5HT agonist widely used in the treatment of human obesity, blocks or attenuates NPY-induced or driven feeding in animals. Acute d-fenfluramine administration actually has been shown to decrease NPY content in the hypothalamus, selectively in the paraventricular and arcuate nuclei. While the precise mechanism of fenfluramine's effects on eating is unknown, it does appear that it is an effect dependent on the presence of the medication and related to inducing a NPY store deficiency in the hypothalamus. These are very exciting and important studies because of the basic literature that supports a critical role for NPY and suggests it is the most potent orexigenic agent known. Studies of NPY microinjections into the hypothalamic PVN elicit a binge type behavior similar to the binges of bulimic patients, even overriding states of satiety. NPY may be the brain's physiological signal that means hunger and is the physiological signal that drives feeding.

Neuroscientific progress allows certain patients with eating disorders to be categorized according to neuropeptide and treated accordingly. For example, testing patients for NPY or galanin abnormalities may identify important obesity subgroups, which may also explain clinical characteristics like excessive fat eating. Leptin or other chemical abnormalities may also be defined. Neurotransmitter modulation of neuropeptides may also yield new treatments. 5HT is demonstrated in animal and human studies to inhibit feeding and produce satiety. Administration of 5HT agonists including dexfenfluramine (38–40), sertraline (41) and fluoxetine (42, 43) all result in weight loss and decreased food intake for as long as they are administered. New treatments for eating disorders may lead to novel approaches to cocaine and other addictions.

BEHAVIORAL SIMILARITIES

Addictions and eating disorders share many common clinical features. Some have suggested that classifying eating disorders as addictions based on phenomenological analogy is an example of overgeneralization and selective reduction (44). However, it is clear that the commonalties between these disorders are not limited to behavioral observations but involve an array of still to be elucidated neurotransmitter abnormalities that converge in the centers of brain reward. Addiction has been defined as a disease characterized by the repetitive and destructive use of one or more mood altering drugs that stems from a biological vulnerability exposed or induced by environmental factors (45). It is a maladaptive pattern of substance use leading to clinically significant impairment or distress with three or more of the following in the same 12 months period:

1. Tolerance
2. Withdrawal
3. The substance is often taken in larger amounts or over longer periods than was intended.
4. Persistent desire or unsuccessful efforts to cut down or control use
5. A great deal of time is spent in activities necessary to obtain the substance, use the substance, or recover from its effects.
6. Important social, occupational or recreational activities are given up or reduced because of substance abuse.
7. Continued substance use despite knowledge of having a persistent or recurrent physical or psychological problem that was likely to have been caused or exacerbated by the substance.

If current psychiatric diagnostic categories did not define addiction in terms of a psychoactive substance, would eating disorders qualify? Yes. The phenomenological similarities between eating disorders and traditionally recognized substance abuse disorders are (a) a higher than average family history of alcohol or drug abuse, (b) cravings for food or a psychoactive substance, (c) cognitive dysfunction, (d) the use of food or psychoactive substances to relieve negative affect (e.g., anxiety and depression), (e) secretiveness about the problem behavior, (f) social isolation and maintenance of the problem behavior despite adverse consequences, (g) denial of the presence and severity of the disorder, (h) depression, and (i) experience of a transition where food or the psychoactive substance no longer relieves negative affect but creates the feelings they were originally used to allay. With the change away from considering tolerance and withdrawal as essential pieces of dependence, eating disorders share many of the most salient features of addictions (46). In the eating disorders currently classified in the *Diagnostic and Statistical Manual of Mental Disorders,* 4th edition (DSM-IV), anorexia nervosa, bulimia nervosa, and binge eating disorder, food is a substance used both repetitively and destructively by either its prolonged restriction or episodic overconsumption (47).

EATING DISORDERS

Weight and food preoccupation are the primary symptoms in both anorexia nervosa and bulimia nervosa. Many patients demonstrate both anorexic and bulimic behaviors. Obese, especially morbid obese, patients describe similar preoccupations. The prevalence of eating disorders appears to be increasing and may range from 1–4% of adolescent and young adult women in predominantly white, upper-middle and middle-class student groups. Obesity is also increasing in these groups despite personal trainers, home exercise equipment, and other fitness developments. Bulimia nervosa is more common than anorexia nervosa. The majority of eating disorder cases are females, with males constituting only approximately 5% of the total cases (48). Anorexia nervosa appears in restricting and bulimic subtypes. Up to 50% of anorexia nervosa patients develop bulimic symptoms; significant numbers of patients who are initially bulimic develop anorexic symptoms and restricting and bulimic subtypes may occasionally alternate in the same patient. The diagnostic process is confusing or confused.

Eating disorders also share the primary reward of feeding but differ in the paired stimuli. Feeding in this context is typically not a response which promotes survival, but rather serves to satisfy other paired stimuli. Various classifications of eating disorders abound in the literature. These classifications have established objective diagnostic criteria that are not correlated with neurotransmitter or other medical abnormality. The recent basic neurobiological studies show a plethora of neurotransmitter systems are involved in the regulation of feeding, mood, and in the pathogenesis of psychiatric and addictive disorders. While we have reported similarities between certain patients with eating disorders and those with addictive illness, others have argued for the inclusion of bulimia nervosa and anorexia nervosa into depressive illness or as an obsessive-compulsive spectrum disorder following from the many similarities between obsessive-compulsive disorder and eating disorders (49). They even further suggest that these disorders appear to be related to mood disorder, thus the obsessive-compulsive spectrum disorder family may be a subset of an affective disorder spectrum family (50).

Anorexia nervosa and bulimia nervosa are the two eating disorder syndromes recognized in the current DSM-IV, which was published in 1994 (47). Binge-eating disorder, while officially classified as an eating disorder not otherwise specified (NOS), is being considered for acceptance as a distinct diagnostic entity.

Anorexia Nervosa

Anorexia nervosa is a disease that has been documented back to at least the seventeenth century. While some experts suggest that there are no cases of anorexia nervosa, only starvation, in cultures without food abundance, it appears across the globe in various cultures. Biological explanations for the occurrence of this disease date back to the early 1950s when scientists found that lesions of the lateral hypothalamus lead to an avoidance of food in malnourished rats. More recent research indicates that the lateral hypothalamic area may be involved in the discrimination between food and non-food through both visual and gustatory stimuli. This area also appears to mediate perception of reward and drive for food (51). A genetic association or common neurobiological risk is also evident from the high concordance of this disease between monozygotic twins (52). Pathogenesis is unknown, though numerous investigations have identified reproducible abnormalities.

The diagnostic criteria for anorexia nervosa in the DSM-IV are listed in Table 28.2. The name anorexia is a misnomer because loss of appetite is actually rare. Anorexics tend to be obsessed with food, and may even hoard food and exercise for hours daily. They become socially isolated and depressed. Despite steady diminution in social and occupational functioning and the appearance of life-threatening physical disturbances, they will typi-

Table 28.2 Diagnostic Criteria for Anorexia Nervosa

A. Refusal to maintain body weight at or above a minimally normal weight for age and height (e.g., weight loss leading to maintenance of body weight less than 85% of that expected; or failure to make expected weight gain during period of growth, leading to body weight less than 85% of that expected).

B. Intense fear of gaining weight or becoming fat, even though underweight.

C. Disturbance in the way in which one's body weight or shape is experienced, undue influence of body weight or shape on self-evaluation, or denial of the seriousness of the current low body weight.

D. In postmenarchal females, amenorrhea, i.e., the absence of at least three consecutive menstrual cycles. (A woman is considered to have amenorrhea if her periods occur only following hormone, e.g., estrogen administration.)

Table based on Diagnostic and Statistical Manual of Mental Disorders, 4th edition (DSM-IV). Copyright American Psychiatric Association, Washington, DC, 1994. Used with permission.

cally deny the severity of their symptoms and respond with disinterest and even resistance to treatment attempts (53). A cognitive distortion develops in which the anorexic's self-worth becomes inexplicably tied to her ability to achieve and maintain an emaciated state. Amenorrhea can appear before noticeable weight loss has occurred. Delayed sexual development in adolescents and poor sexual adjustment in adults is common (53).

Anorexics are classified into two subtypes. The restricting subtype limit their weight loss techniques to calorie restriction and excessive exercise. They tend to exhibit obsessive-compulsive behaviors (54) including but not limited to bizarre diet and exercise routines, and express diminished sexual interest. The binge eating/purging subtype regularly engages in binge eating and purging. Purging methods include self-induced vomiting and the abuse of laxatives, diuretics, or enemas. The presence of binging and purging in anorexics is associated with impulsive behaviors, such as substance abuse, promiscuity, suicide attempts, self-mutilation, and stealing (54). Bulimic symptoms occur in 30–80% of anorexics (55) and subtypes can alternate in the same patient (54).

Although anorexia has been reported as early as the Middle Ages in female Christian saints (56), its incidence has increased in the past 30 years (53) to approximately 4 cases per 100,000 (57). Males comprise only 5% of cases (58). Prevalence is 0.5–1% among late adolescents and adult females with subsyndromal cases even more common (47). Anorexia is more prevalent in industrialized societies where "one can never be too rich or too thin." It also occurs, however, in non-Western cultures where weight concern is not apparent (59) and the expressed motivation for food restriction may be epigastric discomfort or distaste for food (47). The mean age of onset is 17 years and occurrence is rare over 40 years of age (53). Anorexia has an impressive mortality rate of 0.5–1% per observational year. Death is due to suicide in 30–50% of the cases with the remaining morbidity secondary to medical complications (60). There is complete recovery in about 40% of anorexic patients. In another 20% there is resolution of the eating disorder, but subsequent emergence of other significant psychiatric pathology including schizophrenia, bipolar disorder, depression, personality disorders, and substance abuse.

5HT, DA, opioid peptides, and other food-relevant messengers may have a critical role in the pathogenesis of anorexia nervosa. Many studies show that 5HT activity parallels behavioral characteristics of anorexia nervosa. 5HT levels have been shown to diverge between the sexes. While men have been reported with anorexia nervosa, cases are extremely rare (61). Anorexia nervosa occurs before the onset of menses in approximately one third of patients but is commonly followed by correlating amenorrhea and active disease state. Rather than thinking of the disease of some sort of rejection of adult sexuality, brain mechanisms common to luteinizing hormone rhythmicity and food reward may be particularly vulnerable in early adolescence. In all women, changes in levels of sex hormones during the normal menstrual cycle appear to affect 5HT's influence on appetite. 5HT seems to be more potent as an appetite suppressant in women. Although the exact pathological significance is unknown, increased levels of 5HT have been found in the cerebrospinal fluid (CSF) of treated anorexics. It seems that increased release of 5HT may be involved in the development of anorexia nervosa. Cocaine, which increases 5HT and other essential brain messengers, produces anorexia in men and women who chronically self-administer cocaine; it can be associated with amenorrhea and a delusion of well-being.

Anorexia nervosa is also described by some as an "auto-addiction." The absence of food produces a state of strikingly bizarre well-being, which is supported by continued starvation. Increased levels of endogenous opioids activity have been discovered in the CSF of patients with anorexia nervosa (62). Marrazzi and Luby (63) proposed that, in an auto-addictive model, the disease may begin as a phobic fear arising from more general concerns about body image. Secondarily the patient develops a ritualistic behavior revolving around dieting, exercise, and burning calories. Finally, chronicity leads to the condition of anorexia nervosa. They suggest that this psychobiological process alters brain feeding mechanisms that gradually are recognized as a "normal" state, much like drug addicts of all types consume their drugs of choice in order to feel normal. In this sense, the disease state is a result of tolerance, dependence, and neuroadaptive mechanisms at a critical period in the developing organism's existence. Central to this model is the role of opioids (63). It is during the initial period of dieting that opioids are released, reflected in increased CSF activity. This release of opioids affects the primitive dopaminergic reward system so as to reinforce the dieting behavior. The result is that the anorexic behavior of suppressing the drive for food is reinforced by the very signal which causes the drive to eat, namely increased opioid activity: opioids not only downregulate metabolism as an adaptation to starvation but physical exercise is also known to increase opioid activity. The result is the potentially tragic consequences of anorexia nervosa (64).

The etiology of anorexia is unknown. Many psychosocial and psychodynamic theories have tried to explain its resurgence in modern times, but none define a mechanism for understanding the persistence of this unique symptom complex. The prelude to anorexia is exposure to severe food deprivation (53). This can occur both voluntarily to improve one's appearance or professional performance (e.g., ballet dancers, gymnasts, jockeys) (65) and involuntarily due to illness, severe stress, or involuntary starvation (53). But as Halmi asks "what is unique about the individual who goes on to develop anorexia nervosa?" (53) This same question has been contemplated by addiction specialists for decades; that is, why are millions exposed to drugs such as alcohol and tobacco, but only a smaller percentage become addicts? Exposure is the common risk factor, but a common neurobiological process must be operant in all those who use a substance (food in case of anorexics) in a manner that is dangerous to their survival with little insight or regard for negative consequences.

Bulimia Nervosa

Like adolescent alcohol and drug use, while many young men and women experiment with severe diets, starvation, fasting, and self-induced vomiting, few apparently lose control and become anorexic or bulimic. Despite the significant negative consequences, approximately 0.5% of the women between the ages of 15 and 40 years exhibit anorexia nervosa (66) and 1–1.5% of women exhibit symptoms of bulimia (67).

The diagnostic criteria for bulimia nervosa in the DSM-IV are listed in Table 28.3. As initially described by Russell in 1979 (55), the defining behaviors in bulimia nervosa are episodes of binge eating combined with compensatory techniques to avoid gaining weight. Whether it is planned or spontaneous, the impulse to binge is perceived as irresistible by the bulimic. There is a subjective loss of control during the binge, with rapid consumption until the bulimic is uncomfortably or even painfully full. Because of significant shame engendered by this behavior, binge eating is typically done only in private and stopped if inadvertently discovered (47). After the binge has run its course, the individual will be left with feelings of depression, guilt, or self-disgust.

As with classical addictions, eating disorders interfere with normal life patterns. Preoccupation with the substance in question, such as supermarket gazing and cooking for others, is common (52). Just as with other addictive substances, the overconsumption of food or binging is frequently conducted at night or in secret, both historically and in current practice (68). The

Table 28.3 Diagnostic Criteria for Bulimia Nervosa

A. Recurrent episodes of binge eating. An episode of binge eating is characterized by both of the following:
 1. eating, in a discrete period of time (e.g., within any 2-hour period), an amount of food that is definitely larger than most people would eat during a similar period of time and under similar circumstances
 2. a sense of lack of control over eating during the episode (e.g., a feeling that one cannot stop eating or control what or how much one is eating)
B. Recurrent inappropriate compensatory behavior in order to prevent weight gain, such as self-induced vomiting; misuse of laxatives, diuretics, enemas, or other medications; fasting; or excessive exercise
C. The binge eating and inappropriate compensatory behaviors both occur, on average, at least twice a week for 3 months.
D. Self-evaluation is unduly influenced by body shape and weight.
E. The disturbance does not occur exclusively during episodes of Anorexia Nervosa.

Table based on Diagnostic and Statistical Manual of Mental Disorders, 4th edition (DSM-IV). Copyright American Psychiatric Association, Washington, DC, 1994. Used with permission.

chronic compromised nutritional state induced by both of these disorders (69) produces the cognitive changes, mood lability, apathy, irritability, decreased libido, and sleep disturbances commonly seen in other addictions (47). Eating disorders, like classical addictions, can have quite tragic outcomes with a high degree of mortality. Anorexia nervosa mortality as estimated from (42) published studies in a recent meta-analysis is substantially greater than for female psychiatric outpatients, 200 times greater than the suicide rate in the general population at approximately 5.6% per decade (70).

Bulimics, like other addicts, appear to have a favorite "drug" of abuse, consuming proportionally more sweet, high-fat foods during larger meals (37). It is quite common to hear of a bulimic trigger in the same way an addict describes a drug cue that precipitates intense cravings and use. Bulimics describe external and internal cues such as seeing a pizza delivery truck or feeling depressed as triggering thoughts that they are fat or in need of a binge-purge episode. They describe rituals similar to drug-using rituals with similar foods and environments.

The compensatory methods in bulimia are categorized as purging and non-purging. Purging behaviors are self-induced vomiting and abuse of laxatives, diuretics, or enemas. Self-induced vomiting is practiced by 80–90% of patients. If fingers are used, scars and abrasions can often be found on the dorsum of the hand known as "Russell's sign." Other implements and, rarely, syrup of ipecac are used to induce vomiting, but most bulimics eventually learn how to vomit spontaneously. For some bulimics vomiting becomes a reinforcing goal in itself, occurring even after small meals. Laxatives, either alone or in combination with other purging methods, are employed by 38–75% of bulimic women (71). Bulimics practicing laxative abuse appear to exhibit greater psychiatric pathology, as reflected by an increased frequency of suicide attempts, self injurious behaviors, and hospitalized depression (72), than do bulimics who use self-induced vomiting only.

Non-purging compensatory methods include fasting, excessive exercise, surreptitious use of thyroid hormone, and reduction of insulin dosage by diabetics to avoid metabolism of consumed food. Bulimics try to restrict caloric intake between binges and avoid foods that are binge triggers for them.

Bulimia nervosa is more common than anorexia nervosa, with a prevalence among women of 1–3% (73, 74). Only 10–15% of bulimics are men. Bulimia nervosa has traditionally been regarded as a disease afflicting middle to upper class Caucasian women (75), but recent reports suggest that its prevalence among ethnically diverse groups, although not as great, is significant (76). The age of onset ranges from 12 to 35 years of age, with a mean of 18 years of age (77). It is thought that bulimia nervosa tends to occur in overweight individuals during or following a dieting attempt (47) and up to a third may be previous anorexics (53). The body weight of bulimics fluctuates but tends to remain in the normal range. There is an increased incidence of mood disorders, specifically dysthymia and major depression; the prevalence of borderline personality disorder in bulimics ranges from 25 to 48% (78). The reported incidence of drug abuse among bulimics is as high as 46%

(79). Bulimia has a significant relapse rate (31%) within two years following treatment, but relapse after 6 months of symptom control is unusual (80). Relapse occurs more often in patients who are vomiting than in those who are binging, but the significance of this fact is unknown.

Bulimia nervosa, like anorexia nervosa, has been postulated to be characterized by abnormalities in the regulation of feeding. It has long been known to have a high co-morbidity with substance abuse (81), particularly alcoholism (82). 5HT and opioids also seems to be important neurotransmitters involved in the pathogenesis of bulimia nervosa. Studies show low levels of 5HT metabolite (5-HIAA) and low DA metabolite (HVA) in the CSF of bulimic patients compared with normal controls. Low 5HT and low DA in nAC and elsewhere is the critical chemical link to pathological alcohol reward or preference (83). Decreased release of DA in the mesocorticolimbic system may affect taste preference of bulimic patients resulting in a decreased enjoyment of food. Bulimics' preference for high sucrose solutions may indicate that the impaired reward function could contribute to addictive cravings for food (84). Low 5HT levels are also known to be associated with increased appetite alcoholism and impassivity as previously discussed. 5HT is an inhibitor of feeding and would be increased by administration of an SSRI, like fluoxetine, which has been successfully used in some patients with bulimia.

Binge-Eating Disorder

Obesity has many possible causes and may be divided into groups including hypothyroidism, diabetes mellitus, or binge-eating disorders. Binge-eating disorder is perhaps the most common yet least studied of the eating disorders (85). Binge-eating disorders, like drug addiction, are characterized by a pathological attachment. Both include obsessive thoughts about food and compulsions to eat more food than most people would eat within similar periods of time and in similar circumstances. Like cocaine addiction or alcoholism, the binge eater cannot take or leave it. They "can't eat just one." The binge episodes generally cause the binge eater much distress leaving them with feelings of guilt, disgust, and depression. Some studies show that the amount of food consumed is directly proportional to the amount of DA released in the lateral hypothalamic area (86). Binging episodes may also reflect an effect of endogenous opiates. Studies show that food restriction increases the rewarding effect of food, addictive drugs, and intracranial self-stimulation. State dependent opioid modulation of reward has been identified as a possible mechanism facilitating this response (87). Naltrexone and naloxone have been shown to block the opioid dependent increase in palatability and also to selectively reduce episodes of binge eating without affecting normal food consumption (88–90). These opiate blockers have also been effective in reducing binge episodes associated with bulimia nervosa and anorexia nervosa (91). Naltrexone is widely used to treat alcoholics and also opiate addicts.

Research criteria for binge-eating disorder in DSM-IV are listed in Table 28.4. Binge-eating disorder as defined is essentially bulimia nervosa in the absence of regular inappropriate compensatory behaviors, that has a duration of at least 6 months (92). A large multisite DSM-IV field trial with 2727 subjects found a prevalence rate of 4.6% in a community sample and 28.7% among weight loss program patients (93). The prevalence was significantly greater among women in the weight loss patients (29.7% vs. 21.8%), yet the rate among men was substantial. As McElroy et al. note, "given that 34 million adults in the United States are overweight, even if only a small fraction of these individuals had binge-eating disorder, it would represent a large number of individuals" (50). By contrast, purging bulimia was found in only 0.5% of the community sample and 6.7% of the weight loss patients.

Also in contrast to bulimia nervosa, binge-eating disorder appears to occur at least as often among ethnic minorities as among Caucasians (94). Smith (76) suggests that such a finding should be anticipated because binge-eating disorder is more common in the obese (95) and obesity is more prevalent in minorities such as Native Americans, Hispanics, and African-Americans. In some individuals binge eating occurs prior to the development of obesity (96). Wurtman has previously described what she calls carbohydrate craving obesity (96a). In this disorder subjects preferentially consume car-

Table 28.4 Diagnostic Criteria for Binge-Eating Disorder

A. Recurrent episodes of binge eating. An episode of binge eating is characterized by both of the following:
  1. eating, in a discrete period of time (e.g., within any 2-hour period), an amount of food that is definitely larger than most people would eat in a similar period of time under similar circumstances
  2. a sense of lack of control over eating during the episode (e.g., a feeling that one cannot stop eating or control what or how much one is eating)
B. The binge-eating episodes are associated with three (or more) of the following:
  1. eating much more rapidly than normal
  2. eating until feeling uncomfortably full
  3. eating large amounts of food when not feeling physically hungry
  4. eating alone because of being embarrassed by how much one is eating
  5. feeling disgusted with oneself, depressed, or very guilty after overeating
C. Marked distress regarding binge eating is present.
D. The binge eating occurs, on average, at least 2 days a week for 6 months.
E. The binge eating is not associated with the regular use of inappropriate compensatory behaviors (e.g., purging, fasting, excessive exercise) and does not occur exclusively during the course of Anorexia Nervosa or Bulimia Nervosa.

Table based on Diagnostic and Statistical Manual of Mental Disorders, 4th edition (DSM-IV). Copyright American Psychiatric Association, Washington, DC, 1994. Used with permission.

bohydrates at particular times during the day, typically in the early evening. Commonly these patients meet DSM-IV criteria for binge-eating disorder. Many of these patients give a strong family history for alcoholism and multiple previous attempts and failures in dieting, exercising, and surgeries. Studies show that consumption of carbohydrates can selectively increase the levels of 5HT in the brain (97). This process involves consumption of carbohydrates, which increases levels of tryptophan in the blood. Tryptophan is subsequently transported across the blood-brain-barrier where it is converted to 5HT. The studies show that consumption of carbohydrates is likely a specific response to decreased brain 5HT. (Subjects with carbohydrate craving obesity are thought to have lower 5HT levels than control subjects.) Thus, carbohydrates are not necessarily consumed during times of food hunger, but instead are likely consumed to correct this deficit in 5HT. Lowered brain 5-HT function may be caused by a calorie restricted, carbohydrate-limited weight loss regimen and result in negative mood changes leading to termination of the diet (98). These studies also show that the consumption is specific to carbohydrates: consumption of protein and fat does not increase. Consumption of carbohydrate-rich, protein-poor foods has been shown to result in an increased uptake of tryptophan and increased serotonergic synthesis and activity. Foods rich in protein inhibit this effect. Consumption of proteins may increase blood levels of tryptophan as well as other similar amino acids but all compete for transport into the brain; thus, there is no appreciable rise in brain tryptophan. Studies of 5HT replacement also show decreases in the amounts of carbohydrate consumed, further indicating that increased carbohydrate consumption is in likely response to decreased brain 5HT (97). Extrapolating from this example one can see how feeding in eating disorders is a result of the reward of feeding becoming paired with stimuli other than hunger resulting in an excess of feeding which bypasses or disrupts the normal mechanisms of appetite, hunger, and satiety control. Medications that increase available 5HT decrease carbohydrate consumption (98a). Combination medical therapy as first described by Weintraub in 1984 may help these patients (99). This combination of pharmaceuticals, starting at fenfluramine 10 mg daily and phentermine 8–19 mg daily, is in widespread use to control obesity as part of an organized obesity treatment program (100). These medications in well-selected, truly obese patients can successfully reduce body weight and the complications normally associated with obesity. These medications should be used in appropriate patients as they are commonly associated with side effects from dry mouth, fatigue, and hair loss to memory loss, constipation, and insomnia. Co-morbid major psychiatric disease such as panic, addictive disease, and anorexia nervosa are contraindications to use.

BINGE CO-MORBIDITY

Higher rates of depression, psychological distress, and impulsivity have been reported among those who binge than among obese subjects who do not (101). Preliminary studies have not consistently demonstrated an increased incidence of substance abuse or dependence in individuals with binge-eating disorders (102–105). However, the rate of substance abuse among their first degree relatives was reported to be 49% (103), greater than the rate of 37% in the first-degree relatives of bulimics (106).

Eating disordered patients, especially bulimics, are commonly found to be using or dependent on drugs of abuse. A review of 51 co-morbidity studies conducted since 1977 found that greater co-morbidity with substance abuse was present among bulimics than anorexics and among bulimic anorexics than restrictor anorexics (107). In a recent co-morbidity study, 37% of 105 female patients with eating disorders met DSM III-R criteria for either alcohol or drug dependence (108). The most commonly abused drugs were cannabis, cocaine, stimulants, and diet pills. Substance dependence was more common in patients with personality disorders. Thirty-one percent of the bulimic subgroups had Cluster B personality disorders, with borderline personality disorder the most common, while none of the restrictor anorexics had a Cluster B disorder. Restrictor anorexics were significantly less likely to be alcohol or drug dependent than the group as a whole. Similarly, in retrospective review of female psychiatric inpatient records from 1978 to 1990, the high incidence of alcohol abuse in the patients with eating disorders was accounted for by the subset of patients with borderline personality disorders. The occurrence of borderline personality disorders was significantly higher (11.4% vs. 2.9%) in patients with eating disorders than in others (109). While some findings are controversial it is clear that there is a very high incidence of alcohol abuse, drug abuse, or both among bulimic women. Garfinkel and Garner (110) reported that 18.3% of their bulimics used alcohol at least weekly and 21.2% were frequent illicit drug users. Mitchell and co-workers (111) found that 34.4% of bulimics had a history of drug or alcohol problems and 23% had very serious alcohol abuse with 17.7% having treatment for a chemical dependency. These data are consistent with the Yager et al. survey of 628 women with eating disorders (112), where 38% reported weekly alcohol use and 22.7% reported daily alcohol use. These authors also reported on a very high level of illicit drug use with daily use in excess of 10% for marihuana alone. The authors have reported, as have others, that the converse is also true and that eating disorders are very common among cocaine addicts, alcoholics, and other addicts in primary addiction treatment.

Alcoholics commonly report eating disorders in their children and families. Alcoholism can be conceptualized as either a psychiatric or a substance use disorder. However, it appears genetic factors are more important in alcoholism than eating or other disorders. One of the most striking results of Kendler's recent analysis (113) was the pattern of genetic risk factors for broadly defined alcoholism and other "disorders" in women. Alcoholism was substantially more heritable than any other disorder. More importantly, 12% of the genetic variation for alcoholism resulted from each of the two major genetic factors that are unique to alcoholism. That is, most of the genetic variation that influences vulnerability to broadly defined alcoholism in a general population of women is unrelated to the genetic factors that alter liability to the common mood, anxiety, and eating disorders. In accord with previous findings, Kendler's data demonstrate that the family environment appeared to play little etiologic role in alcoholism in women. The question remains, what can be inherited and can what is inherited explain other addictions and eating?

A review of 12 studies found the prevalence of borderline personality disorder in bulimics to range from 25 to 48% (78). The realization that bulimia, substance abuse, and borderline personality disorder all involve the impulsive-compulsive, self-injurious behaviors that produce a transient reduction in tension and that they tend to be co-morbid is strongly suggestive of common neurotransmitter dysregulation most likely involving 5HT, DA, and endorphins. Sweet cravings occur with opiate addiction (114) and sweets can sometimes improve opiate withdrawal (115). Drugs affecting the same neurotransmitter systems have been found to be efficacious in treating both eating disorders and the classical drug addictions. The serotonergic agent fenfluramine in combination with the weak amphetamine phentermine that is currently being used in the treatment of obesity has been reported to decrease craving and self-reported use in cocaine addicts (116). Naltrexone, which reduces the frequency of binge eating, reduces craving and relapse in alcoholics (117). A careful look at the neural events involved in pathological drug attachment appears essential in links to pathological eating.

INHERITANCE OF PATHOLOGICAL ATTACHMENT

The motivation to drink alcohol and the risk of becoming addicted are in part genetically determined (118). Opioid peptides are considered central to motivated behaviors possibly with or through DA. Certain inbred animal strains show preference for alcohol or drugs and easily become dependent. Alcohol preference may be linked to opioid peptides since among a long list of supporting evidence interference with opioid system decreases drinking while potentiating endogenous enkephalins increase drinking. There are large differences between AA and ANA rats in baseline and after drinking. AA rats have lower dynorphin levels in nAC which may increase the sensitivity to the reinforcing effects of DA. AA rats who have lower met-enkephalin levels in the nAC respond by increasing alcohol intake, which may strengthen the motivation to continue drinking alcohol. Inheriting the vulnerability to develop alcoholism, conceptualized as more brain reward and less toxicity and impairment, alcoholism may predispose women to develop eating disorders.

Koob (119) reported at the 1995 ASAM meeting the work of his group headed by Weiss where, during self administration, a cannula placed in the nAC monitors the actual amount of DA released in a freely moving and behaving animal. Monitoring of DA release regularly as the animal is living, self-administering drug, and so on can lead to gratification of DA reward per dose of rewarding substance. When an animal is self administering ethanol there is a rise in the amount of DA released. But alcohol preferring strain of rats who have behavioral responses or lack of them to alcohol have more dramatic increases in DA after alcohol self-administration. So, more DA is released per ethanol for the genetically-biased animals than the animals not bred for alcohol-liking or preference. Similar findings might be demonstrated for fatty food preference. DA is important but other systems are also very much involved. Opioid peptides are also involved. We have known for years that antagonists for opioid peptides, like naloxone and naltrexone, reduce alcohol self-administration. Koob wondered whether reduction in the alcohol's ability to interact with the brain's reinforcement pathways could be localized to a region or cell body. Exactly where in the brain does the reproducible reduction of ethanol self-administration after opiate antagonists occur? By microinjection into brain sites, he found the nAC and the amygdala are prime sites, but the amygdala is the major area where a direct injection of opioid antagonist could reverse alcohol self-administration. The amygdala is the most sensitive site. The reinforcing effects of alcohol now appear to be localized to a brain area strikingly similar to the same brain area and brain circuits that we have described as operative in heroin. Alcohol self-administration may be quite similar to heroin self-administration in this respect. There is a clear neuropharmacology of alcohol reinforcement—DA, GABA, opioid peptides, 5HT, glutamate, and NMDA are all involved and important. Most recently we have shifted to study more than the acute drug effects.

Koob's newest data suggest that the same brain systems important in the acute self-administration of alcohol are important in supporting alcohol dependence. Spontaneous physical withdrawal does not drive ethanol self-administration but rather the reward system drives motivation and directed goal-oriented, drug seeking and taking. During ethanol withdrawal and dependence, we have just found that brain stimulation thresholds are elevated. Just like a pain threshold elevation this elevated hedonic threshold provides clear evidence that the hedonic or pleasure responses are off and dysfunctional. The chronic use animals need more brain current to produce the same effect as a result of the withdrawal-induced dysfunction in the medial forebrain bundle. During ethanol withdrawal there is a decrease in DA in the nAC but if self-administration is allowed during withdrawal, DA levels return to normal. It is as if alcohol intake is a way to return DA levels to normal. The animal can rapidly reinstate their DA levels. This alcohol reward and dependence model appears quite relevant to binge eating and obesity. Furthermore, hunger and its relationship to eating appears a useful construct related to drug craving and use (120).

SEROTONIN (5HT)

Data from both animal and human studies support a role for 5HT dysregulation in bulimia and in other eating disorders. Injection of 5HT into the hypothalamus PVN of the rat produces dose-related inhibition of food intake by reducing the size and duration of the first meal and by lengthening the interval between the first and second meal without affecting meal initiation or "hunger" (121). In humans, the serotonergic drug d-fenfluramine decreases appetite and increases satiety (122). Fenfluramine's effects appear to persist as long as the medication is taken and can be demonstrated in mild, moderate, and morbid obesity. Chronic use has begun supporting an important role for 5HT in normal and pathological eating. The phenomenology of anorexia nervosa has also been related to serotonergic hyperactivity (123). These authors relate the disparity in gender prevalence to the greater hypophagic effect of serotonergic agents in female versus male rats (124, 125). Furthermore, they compare the sexual repression frequently observed in anorexics to the inhibition of female sexual behavior in other species by 5HT (126).

In actuality, however, the level of the major brain metabolite of 5HT, 5-hydroxyindoleacetic acid (5-HIAA) appears to be reduced in the cerebral spinal fluid of anorexics rather than elevated (127), and the serotonergic antidepressant fluoxetine has shown some favorable results in uncontrolled clinical trials with anorexics (128, 129). To incorporate the observed efficacy of a serotonergic agent into the hyperserotonergic model it has been postulated that the chronic use of fluoxetine, through the downregulation of 5HT receptors (130) results in a decrease in serotonergic hypersensitivity (131). Alternatively, fluoxetine's beneficial effect may be on obsessive-compulsive symptomatology (131). Certainly the SSRIs are not a cure for anorexia nervosa and are of limited value in supporting a 5HT hypothesis. Another confounding finding is the modest response obtained with the antiserotonergic agent cyproheptadine (132).

In the case of bulimia nervosa, an inverse theory of 5HT hypoactivity has been posited (37). According to this model, bulimics binge to improve their mood (i.e., self-medicate) by elevating brain 5HT levels (37). Cocaine acutely elevates brain 5HT and, while producing euphoria, inhibits appetite. High carbohydrate, low protein meals favor the transport of tryptophan into the CNS, which is the rate-limiting step in the synthesis of 5HT (133). CSF 5-HIAA was found to be reduced in bulimic patients who binged at least twice a day (84) and in bulimic women acute tryptophan depletion caused significant increased food intake, mood lability, irritability, and retarded affect over controls (134). Further support for serotonergic involvement is the seasonal variation in mood and eating symptoms among 10–45% of bulimic patients (135–138). Light therapy improved mood and eating behavior in a preliminary study with 17 bulimic patients (139). Light therapy may influence serotonergic pathways (140), as well as correct circadian rhythm disturbances (141, 142). Serotoninergic theories appear to be the most relevant to bulimia, and a 5HT subgroup may be quite important. Still, there are major problems with this theory. Problems with the 5HT theory of bulimia nervosa are the observations that (*a*) binge meals do not generally contain a higher proportion of carbohydrates than do non-binge meals (143) and (*b*) selective serotonergic antidepressants are no more efficacious than other antidepressant classes in the treatment of bulimia (131).

Recently, there has been increased interest in the study of CNS 5HT function and its general relationship to behavior (144). This research had produced an array of findings which have been among the most replicated in modern biological psychiatry. Central to these studies is the finding that a low CSF concentration of 5-HIAA, a measure of CNS 5HT activity, is correlated with impaired impulse control and with violence towards others and self. In contrast, other evidence suggests that high concentrations of CSF 5-HIAA are often found in individuals exhibiting psychopathological problems characterized by overly inhibited or obsessive symptoms. Markuu Linnoila, at the 1995 ASAM (119) meeting, described his work "as on the verge of establishing linkages to antisocial alcoholism genes."

Impulsive low 5-HIAA non-human primates and alcoholics have been described in the literature (144). Markku Linnoila (145) found a number of interesting interactions between CSF 5-HIAA and behaviors. First, CSF 5-HIAA is a meaningful and highly heritable biological trait. For example, low 5-HIAA monkeys raised with parental neglect when given ethanol in adolescence, "drink like fish . . . the monkeys have to be protected from their drinking." In all rearing conditions the low 5-HIAA monkeys drink alcohol without the ability to control. Low 5-HIAA personality indices observed in human studies include chronic irritability, low grade chronic somatic anxiety, dysphoria, violence (acting or lashing out), alcohol-related problems, and suicide attempts. Finally, the increased frequency of anger attacks among patients with eating disorders (146) have been attributed to central serotonergic dysregulation that has been previously associated with impulsive aggressive behavior (147). Patients with eating disorders exhibit several clinical features and biological findings indicative of 5HT dysregulation including feeding abnormalities, depression, suicide, impulsivity, violence, anxiety, harm-avoidance, obsessive-compulsive features, seasonality, and simultaneous disturbances in neuroendocrine and neurochemical systems linked to 5HT (148).

Consistent with this hypothesis, many bulimic patients are successfully treated today with SSRIs; Prozac is actually approved for this use by the FDA. Patients treated with MAO inhibitors, which increase 5HT, especially in high doses, report binge eating as a side effect of their treatment; however, it is not certain that this is a drug-driven effect and not a rebound from depressive illness. Still, bipolar patients certainly have episodes of excessive food intake followed by periods of no appetite and weight loss. As such, bipolar patients may offer a clue to the pathophysiology of naturally occurring eating disorders. Clinical psychiatrists have often pointed to their hyperphagic depressions as suggestive of bipolar rather than unipolar diathesis. Researchers, on the other hand, focus on the effects of the newly discovered peptides regulating eating and suggest a possible role in eating disorders for these compounds.

OPIOIDS

Evidence for involvement of endogenous opioids in bulimic behavior is suggested by successful clinical treatment of some bulimic patients with the opioid antagonist naltrexone (149–153). Although using a low dose of naltrexone was shown to be ineffective (106) in a double-blind, placebo-controlled trial, naltrexone significantly decreased binge duration but not binge frequency (154). Naltrexone was also shown to be effective, in conjunction with psychotherapy, in reducing binging behavior in a case study of binge-eating disorders (90). It is interesting to note that the patient's scores for interpersonal distrust, maturity fears, and drive for thinness transiently improved during naltrexone therapy. Bulimic patients were found to exhibit higher pleasantness ratings for highly sweetened sucrose solution than controls or bulimics with a history of anorexia. These foods might produce a pathological reward and attachment in the same way that alcohol produces excessive mesolimbic DA release in response to alcohol availability or use in alcohol preferring animals. Perceived deprivation of the normal level of hedonistic response to food could induce an addiction-like craving for food, culminating in a binge episode. Again, like alcohol, there is evidence that the hedonistic response to sweet taste involves both endogenous opioids (77) and central DA in the mesolimbic reward pathways. Interestingly, in addition to decreased CSF b-endorphin levels, bulimic patients with frequent binge episodes have lower CSF concentrations of the DA metabolite homovanillic acid (84). Decreased central DA appears to be a common feature of early drug abstinence and is related to dysphoria and craving as well as depression. CSF b-endorphin levels in bulimic patients were found to be lower than in controls (155), which interestingly has been reported for alcoholic patients who have also responded to naltrexone.

IMPORTANCE OF DRUG STATE TO BEHAVIOR

Most current drugs of abuse have profound and important effects on eating and food preference. Alcoholics report appetite loss during intoxication and specific food cravings during abstinence. Nicotine dependence is associated with loss of weight and weight gain with abstinence. Marihuana induces eating and specific eating patterns descried as the "munchies." Co-

Table 28.5   Effects of Addictive Drugs on Eating

Drug	Administration	Withdrawal
Nicotine	decreases	increases
Stimulants	decreases	increases
Marihuana	increases	—
Opiates	increases fat intake	—
Ethanol	decreases by providing empty calories	increases sugar, carbohydrate intake

caine and amphetamines are potent anorexics. Opiates appear to induce and opiate antagonists decrease eating (Table 28.5). Drug abstinence states are referred to in terms of food. Hunger for drugs, the taste of drugs, and cravings are commonplace and can just as easily be heard on an eating disorder ward as an addiction service.

There have been numerous reports of co-morbidity between eating disorders and substance abuse (33, 156). Eating disorders run in addiction families and vice versa. Eating patterns change among alcoholics and other addicts depending on their drug status. Alcoholics in early abstinence report carbohydrate craving. NPY is a primary mediator of carbohydrate "drive" and norepinephrine is also a possible mediator but DA is not. While norepinephrine and NPY drive carbohydrate cravings and intake, 5HT is a primary inhibitor of carbohydrate intake. While humans have well-developed and highly regulated drives for micronutrients in food, we appear to have poorly developed satiety. If we are deprived of a food or drink which we are accustomed to the brain increases appetite for nutrients, appetites for specific foods and/or alcohol ingestion causing decreased perception of anxiety and stress. NPY appears to reduce anxiety, so carbohydrate or alcohol intake can actually increase self-perceptions of well-being. Another neuromodulator of eating, galanin, is also known to be a potent analgesic. This suggests that eating, especially eating fat, may reduce pain. Just putting a galanin antagonist in the hypothalamus of animals totally stops the eating of fat. Like opioids and other drugs, the more fat we eat the more we want. The more eating of fat the more galanin Liebowitz and her colleagues (145) find in the brain. In this way she explains the "drive" for fat and a mechanism for fat craving. The resultant obesity occurs as a consequence of our poor fat satiety control. We eat carbohydrates generally in the morning, we eat fat between lunch and dinner. Alcoholics in early abstinence report binging not only on fats but also on carbohydrates throughout the day.

Tobacco, alcohol, and other drug use starts and increases dramatically during adolescence. Fat intake rises dramatically at puberty. Just after puberty changes can be demonstrated, gender differences that are real and important. Appetite for ethanol also rises at puberty. Are the new appetites and drives that come along after puberty related? NPY stimulates intake of carbohydrate, galanin stimulates fat and some carbohydrate intake, opiates stimulate fat and some protein intake after direct injection into the brain. Fluoxetine suppresses carbohydrate with no change in fat or protein. Opiate antagonists work in a different system and more generally stop fat intake. 5HT works at special times in circadian and developmental stages, not at all times. Drug experimentation is a necessary precondition to abuse and addiction. Brain reward is essential in making the experimentation more likely to continue and in cementing the attachment necessary for dependence to occur. Dieting may be essential in the onset of anorexia nervosa, bulimia, and even obesity. In many cases overeating is a paradoxical consequence of attempts at caloric restriction including dieting. Losing weight is the motivation behind diets and diets are rarely successful in achieving the desired effects. What diets may be doing is priming the neurotransmitter and neuromodulator systems to eat more and may be triggers for disinhibited eating.

CONCLUSION

As the twentieth century concludes, the American media has expanded the country's interpretation of addictions and substance abuse. Pop culture has broadened its concept of addictions to encompass other self-destructive, yet seemingly compulsive behaviors. These include "workaholics," gamblers, compulsive spenders, and food addicts, the self-confessed "foodaholics." While this process may provoke a knee-jerk rejection of common-

alties, this chapter has addressed the issue of whether the eating disorders should legitimately be considered as forms of addiction. It appears that this tendency to consider every potentially harmful compulsive or repetitive behavior as an addiction is one of the major considerations for not considering some eating disorders as addictive, auto-addictive disorders. Some believe that the conception of eating disorder as another form of addiction disorder is a "therapeutic dead end" (157). One concern raised is that the addiction-as-disease model is primarily an abstinence model and dieting and food avoidance are risk factors for eating disorders. It must be recognized, however, that with the evolution of our understanding of brain reward systems, the future addiction-as-disease model will include appropriate medication management for relapse prevention. It has also been proposed that patients with eating disorders embrace the suggestion that they have an addiction because then no self-responsibility is involved (44). However, it is clear that eating disorders are not due to a lack of self-control. In addition to the neurotransmitter aberrations that have been described on single photon emission computed tomography (SPECT) imaging, bulimics exhibit low or negative changes in regional blood flow to the frontal lobe area (158). In answer to the initial question as to whether eating disorders should be classified as addictions, we would propose that both disorders involve similar brain systems and result in similar behaviors and feeling states. Both are important diseases where loss of control and compulsive use are preeminent. Both are diverse groups of people with illnesses of unknown etiology, characterized by a chronic relapsing course without specific pathophysiology or treatment. Both involve the acquired pathological attachment with the agent(s) of their ultimate compromise and possible destruction. Both may involve host or risk factors which predispose a person to extreme reward after consumption or use thereby making repetition more likely to occur. Both involve denial and reluctance to accept that they are in fact ill and in need of treatment. Both can result in early death. Both generally require early experimentation, one with drugs, the other with dieting. Both can be relapse triggers for each other. Drugs are used to decrease eating and eating is used to decrease drug-taking. Both are used to accentuate the other. The similarities are numerous and striking. But as long as the diagnostic scheme is descriptive and not neurobiological it will be difficult to identify which patients have one disorder and which have two. Food is a powerful mood-altering substance that is repetitively and destructively used (or restricted) in eating disorders, and there is considerable experimental evidence of biological vulnerability. Finally, categorizing eating disorders as addictions also has ramifications for prevention. Epidemiological studies among high school students show that eating disorders are associated with alcohol use (159) and that even dieting in adolescents is related to alcohol and tobacco abuse (160). With our current appreciation of eating disorders as yet another form of dangerous addiction, it is time that educational efforts be targeted to the adolescent population to halt its current burgeoning growth in our society (161). It is time that individuals with eating disorders are not held "responsible" for disease process any more than patients with diabetes or heart disease. Hopefully, this is true for other addicts. Experts worry whether such a discussion might lead to gambling or compulsive sexual behaviors being proposed for inclusion as addictions. However, as the well-known adage goes, if it looks like a duck, acts like a duck, and quacks like a duck, it must be a duck: patients with binge eating, obesity, anorexia, and bulimia have a chronic disorder characterized by loss of control, relapse, compulsivity, re-prioritization, and continuation despite severe and adverse consequences.

The DSM-IV eating disorder category naturally encompasses a diverse patient group. Some have a history of anorexia nervosa without obesity, while others are restrictors, some purge, and still others have amenorrhea. Arguments have been made to consider eating disorders as personality disorders, obsessive-compulsive disease, depression and as an addictive disorder. Addiction treatment programs have alerted us to the high co-morbidity of eating disorders in addiction patients, the high degree of eating disorders that appear to run in families, the common occurrence of eating binges or starvation as relapse triggers in newly abstinent patients and patient reports of enhancing drugs' euphorigenic properties through starvation or purging. These observations support the importance of continued questioning and consideration to the hypothesis that eating disorders are related to tobacco, alcohol, and other addictive disorders.

References

1. DuPont RL, Gold MS. Withdrawal and reward: implications for detoxification and relapse prevention. Psychiatric Ann 1995;25(11):663–668.
2. Gold MS. Clinical implications of the neurobiology of addiction. In: ASAM Official Manual, Basic Science, Section 1, Chapter 4. Bethesda, MD: American Society of Addiction Medicine, 1994.
3. Benveniste H, Huttmeir PC. Microdialysis—theory and application. Prog Neurobiol 1990;35:195–215.
4. Church WH, Justice JB, Neill DB. Detecting behaviorally relevant changes in extracellular dopamine with microdialysis. Brain Res 1987;412:397–399.
5. Imperato A, Di Chiara G. Trans-striatal dialysis coupled to reverse phase high performance liquid chromatography with electrochemical detection: A new method for the study of the in vivo release of endogenous dopamine and metabolites. J Neurosci 1984;4:966–977.
6. Ungerstedt V, Hallstrom A. In vivo microdialysis. A new approach to the analysis of neurotransmitters in the brain. Life Sci 1987;41:861–864.
7. Fuxe K, Hokfelt T, Johansson O, Jonsson G, Lidbrink P, Ljungdahl A. The origin of the dopamine nerve terminals in limbic and frontal cortex: Evidence for mesocortico dopamine neurons. Brain Res 1974;82:349–355.
8. Hernandez L, Hoebel B. Feeding and hypothalamic stimulation increase dopamine turnover in the accumbens. Physiol 1988;44:599–606.
9. Hernandez L, Hoebel BG. Feeding can enhance dopamine turnover in the prefrontal cortex. Brain Res Bull 1990;24:975–979.
10. Mogenson GJ. Studies of the nucleus accumbens and its mesolimbic dopaminergic affects in relation to ingestive behaviors and reward. In: Hoebel GB, Noving D, eds. Neural basis of feeding and reward. Brunswick: Haer Institute 1982:275–506.
11. Radhakishun FS, van Ree JM, Westerink BH, Cools AR. Scheduled eating increases dopamine release in the nucleus accumbens of food-deprived rata as assessed with on-line brain dialysis. Neurosci Lett 1988;82:351–356.
12. Yoshida M, Yokoo H, Mizoguchi K, Kawahara H, Tsuda A, Nishikawa T, et al. Eating and drinking cause increased dopamine release in the nucleus accumbens and ventral tegmental area in the rat: Measurement by in vivo microdialysis. Neurosci Lett 1992;139:73–76.
13. Young AM, Joseph MN, Gray JA. Increased dopamine release in vivo in nucleus accumbens and caudate nucleus of the rat during drinking: A microdialysis study. Neuroscience 1992;48:871–876.
14. Miller NS, Gold MS. A hypothesis for a common neurochemical basis for alcohol and drug disorders. Psychiatr Clin North Am 1993;16:105–117.
15. Fantino M. Properties sensorielles des aliments et controle de la prise alimentaire. Sci Alim 1987;7:5–16.
16. Grill HJ, Berridge KC. Taste reactivity as a measure of the neural control of palatability. Prog Psychobiol Physiol Psychol 1985;11:1–61.
17. Louis-Sylvestre J, Giachetti I, Le Magnen J. Sensory vs. dietary factors in cafeteria-induced overweight. Physiol Behav 1984;32:901–905.
18. Rolls BJ. Palatability and food preference. In: Diaffi AL, et al., eds. The body weight regulatory system: normal and disturbed mechanisms. New York: Raven Press, 1981:271–278.
19. Sclafani A, Berner CN. Influence of diet palatability on the meal taking behavior of hypothalamic hyperphagic and normal rats. Physiol Behav 1976;16:355–363.
20. Gold MS. Drugs of abuse: a comprehensive series for clinicians. Vol. IV. Nicotine. New York: Plenum, 1995.
21. Dackis CA, Gold MS. New concepts in cocaine addiction: the dopamine depletion hypothesis. Neurosci Biobehav Rev 1985;9(3):469–477.
22. Koob GF. Drugs of abuse: anatomy, pharmacology and function of reward pathways. Trends Pharmacol Sci 1992;13:177–184.
23. Gold MS. Neurobiology of addiction and recovery: the brain, the drive for the drug and the 12-step fellowship. J Subst Abuse Treat 1994;11(2):93–97.
24. Gold, MS. Drugs of abuse: a comprehensive series for clinicians. Vol. III. Cocaine. New York: Plenum, 1993.
25. Kornetsky CR, et al. Intracranial self-stimulation thresholds: a model for the hedonic effects of drugs of abuse. Arch Gen Psychiatry 1979;36:289–292.
26. Gold MS, Miller NS. Seeking drugs/alcohol and avoiding withdrawal: the neuroanatomy of drive states and withdrawal. Psych Ann 1992;22(8):430–435.
27. Jonas JM, Gold MS. Cocaine abuse and eating disorders. Lancet 1986;1(8477):390.
28. Wise RA. The role of reward pathways in the development of drug dependence. Pharmacol Ther 1987;35:227–263.
29. Gold MS, Miller NS. A hypothesis for a common neurochemical basis for alcohol and drug disorders. Psychiatric Clin North Am 1993;16(1):105–117.
30. Blundell JE. Appetite disturbances and the problems of overweight. Drugs 1990;39(suppl 3):1–19.
31. Weingarten HP, Parkinson W. Ventromedial hypothalamic lesions eliminate acid secretion elicited by anticipated eating. Appetite 1988;10:205–219.
32. Kaschow J, Nemeroff CB. The neurobiology of neurotensin: focus on neurotensin-dopamine interactions. Regulatory Peptides 1991;26:153–164.
33. Gold MS. Are eating disorders addictions? Adv Biosci 1993;90:455–463.
34. Sahu A, Kalra SP. Neuropeptide regulation of feeding behavior: neuropeptide Y. TEM 1993;4(7):217–224.
35. Guy J, et al. Serotonin innervation of neuropeptide-Y containing neurons in the rat arcuate nucleus. Neurosci Lett 1988;85:9–13.
36. Kotz, CM, Grace MK, Briggs J, Levine AS, Billington CJ. Effects of opioid antagonists naloxone and naltrexone on neuropeptide Y-induced feeding and brown fat thermogenesis in the rat. J Clin Invest 1995;96:163–170.
37. Kaye WH, Weltzin TE. Neurochemistry of bulimia nervosa. J Clin Psychiatry 1991;52(10 suppl):21–28.
38. Sugrue MF. Neuropharmacology of drugs affecting food intake. Pharmacol Ther 1987;32:145–182.
39. McTavish D, Heel RC. Dexfenfluramine. A review of its pharmacological properties and therapeutic potential in obesity. Drugs 1992;43(5):713–733.
40. O'Conner HT, Richman RM, Steinbeck KS, Caterson ID. Dexfenfluramine treatment of obesity: a double blind trial with post trial follow up. Int J Obesity 1995;19:181–189.
41. Nielson JA, Chapin DS, Johnson JL Jr, Torgerson LK. Sertraline, a serotonin-uptake inhibitor, reduces food intake and body weight in lean rats

and genetically obese mice. Am J Clin Nutr 1992;55:5s–8s.
42. Wise SD. Clinical studies with fluoxetine in obesity. Am J Clin Nutr 1992;55:181s–184s.
43. Spring S, Wurtman J, Wurtman R, El-Khoury A, Goldberg H, McDermott J, Pingitore R. Efficacies of dexfenfluramine and fluoxetine in preventing weight after smoking cessation. Am J Clin Nutr 1995;62:1181–1187.
44. Vandereycken W. The addiction model in eating disorders: Some critical remarks and selected bibliography. Int J Eat Disord 1990;9:95–101.
45. Gold MS. The good news about drugs, alcohol. New York: Villard Books, 1991.
46. Varner LM. Dual diagnosis. Patients with eating and substance-related disorders. J Am Diet Assoc 1995;95(2):224–225.
47. American Psychiatric Association. Diagnostic and Statistical Manual of Mental Disorders. 4th edition. Washington, DC: American Psychiatric Association, 1994.
48. Kaplan AS, Garfinkel PR. General principles of outpatient treatment—eating disorders. In: Gabbard GO, ed. Treatments of psychiatric disorders. Vol. 2 Washington, DC: American Psychiatric Press, 1995.
49. McElroy SL, Keck PE Jr, Phillips KA. Kleptomania, compulsive buying and binge-eating disorder. J Clin Psychiatry 1995;56(suppl 4):14–26.
50. McElroy SL, Phillips KA, Keck PE Jr. Obsessive compulsive spectrum disorder. J Clin Psychiatry 1994;55(suppl):33–51.
51. Fukuda M, Ono T, Nishino H, Nakamura K. Neuronal responses in monkey lateral hypothalamus during operant feeding behavior. Brain Res Bull 1986;17:879–884.
52. Treasure J, Campbell I. Editorial: a biological hypothesis for anorexia nervosa. Psychol Med 1994;24:3–8.
53. Halmi K. Eating disorders: anorexia nervosa, bulimia nervosa, and obesity. Washington, DC: American Psychiatric Press, 1994–1995.
54. American Psychiatric Association. Practice guidelines for eating disorders. Washington, DC: American Psychiatric Press, 1993.
55. Russell G. Bulimia nervosa: an ominous variant of anorexia nervosa. Psychol Med 1979;429–448.
56. Bell RM. Holy anorexia. Chicago: University of Chicago Press, 1985.
57. Szmukler GI. The epidemiology of anorexia nervosa and bulimia. J Psychiatr Res 1985;19:1243–1253.
58. Halmi KA. Anorexia nervosa: demographic and clinical features in 94 cases. Psychosom Med 1974;36:18–26.
59. Palmer RL. Weight concern should not be a necessary criterion for the eating disorders: a polemic. Int J Eat Disord 1993;14:459–466.
60. Herzog W, Rathner G, Vandereychken W. Long-term course of anorexia nervosa: a review of the literature. In: Herzig W, Deter HC, Vandereychken W, eds. The course of eating disorders. New York: Springer-Verlag, 1992:15–29.
61. Olivardia R, Pope HG Jr, Mangweth B, Hudson JI. Eating disorders in college men. Am J Psychiatry 1995;152(9):1279–1285.
62. Kaye WH, Pickar DM, Naber D, Ebert MH. Cerebrospinal fluid opioid activity in anorexia nervosa. Am J Psychiatry 1982;139:643–645.
63. Marrazzi MA, Luby ED. An auto-addiction opioid model of chronic anorexia nervosa. Int J Eat Disord 1986;5(2):191–208.
64. Marrazzi MA, Luby ED. Anorexia nervosa as an auto-addiction. Ann N Y Acad Sci 1989;575:545–547.

65. Halmi K. Princess Margaret of Hungary, 1242–1271. Am J Psychiatry 1994;151:1216.

66. Willi J, Giacometti G, Limacher B. Update on the epidemiology of anorexia nervosa in a defined region of Switzerland. Am J Psychiatry 1990;158:495–502.

67. Fairburn CG, Beglin SJ. Studies of the epidemiology of bulimia nervosa. Am J Psychiatry 1990;147:401–408.

68. Parry-Jones WL, Parry-Jones B. Implications of historical evidence for the classification of eating disorders. Br J Psychiatry 1994;165:287–292.

69. Pirke KM, Pahy S, Schweiger V, Warnoff M. Metabolic and endocrine indices of starvation in bulimia: a comparison with anorexia nervosa. Psychiatry Res 1985;15:33–39.

70. Sullivan PF. Mortality in anorexia nervosa. Am J Psychiatry 1995;152:1073–1074.

71. Bulik CM. Abuse of drugs associated with eating disorders. J Subst Abuse 1992;4:69–90.

72. Mitchell JE, Boutacoff LI, Hatsukami D, Pyle RL, Eckert ED. Laxative abuse a variant of bulimia. J Nerv Ment Dis 1986;174:174–176.

73. Garfinkel PE, Lin E, Goening P, Spegg C, Goldbloom DS, Kennedy S. Bulimia nervosa in a Canadian community sample: Prevalence and comparison of subgroups. Am J Psychiatry 1995;152:1052–1058.

74. Kendler KS, Maculae C, Neil M, Kestrel R, Health A, Eaves L. The genetic epidemiology of bulimia nervosa. Am J Psychiatry 1991;148:1627–1637.

75. Striegel-Moore RH, Silberstein LR, Roudin J. Toward an understanding of risk of factors for bulimia. Am Psychol 1986;41:246–263.

76. Smith D. Binge eating in ethnic minority groups. Addict Behav 1995;20:695–703.

77. Drewnowski A. Metabolic determinants of binge eating. Addict Behav 1995;20:733–745.

78. Rossiter EM, Agras WS, Telch CF, Schneider JA. Cluster B personality characteristics predict outcome in the treatment of bulimia nervosa. Int J Eat Disord 1993;13:349–357.

79. Powers PS, Coovert DL, Brightwell DR, Stevens BA. Other psychiatric disorders among bulimic patients. Compr Psychiatry 1988;29:503–508.

80. Olmstead MP, Kaplan AS, Rockert W. Rate and prediction of relapse in bulimia nervosa. Am J Psychiatry 1994;151:738–743.

81. Mitchell JE, Specker SM, de Zwaan M. Comorbidity and medical complications of bulimia nervosa. J Clin Psychiatry 1991;52(10 suppl):13–20.

82. Epik A, Arikan Z, Boratav C, Isik E. Bulimia in a male alcoholic: a symptom substitution in alcoholism. Int J Eat Disord 1995;17(2):201–204.

83. McBride WJ, Bodart B, Lumberg L, Li TK. Association between low contents of dopamine and serotonin in the nucleus accumbens and high alcohol preference. Alcohol Clin Exp Res 1995;19:1420–1422.

84. Jimerson DC, Lesem MD, Kaye WH, Brewerton TD. Low serotonin and dopamine metabolite concentrations in cerebrospinal fluid from bulimic patients with frequent binge episodes. Arch Gen Psychiatry 1992;49:132–137.

85. Bruce B, Wilfley D. Binge eating among the overweight population: a serious and prevalent problem. J Am Diet Assoc 1996;96(1):58–61.

86. Meguid MM, Yang ZJ, Koseki M. Eating induces rise in LHA-dopamine correlates with meal size in normal and bulbectomized rats. Brain Res Bull 1995;36(5):487–490.

87. Carr KD, Papadouka V. The role of multiple opioid receptors in the potentiation of reward by food restriction. Brain Res 1994;639(2):253–260.

88. Levine AS, Weldon DT, Grace M, Cleary JP, Billington CJ. Naloxone blocks that portion of feeding driven by sweet taste in food-restricted rats. Am J Physiol 1995;268(1, pt 2):R248–252.

89. Drewnowski A, Krahn DD, Demitrack MA, Nairn K, Gosnell BA. Naloxone, an opiate blocker, reduces the consumption of sweet high-fat foods in obese and lean female binge eaters. Am J Clin Nutr 1995;61(6):1206–1212.

90. Marrazzi MA, Markham KM, Kinzie J, Luby ED. Binge eating disorder: response to naltrexone. Int J Obes Relat Metab Disord 1995;19(2):143–145.

91. De Zwaan M, Mitchell JE. Opiate antagonists and eating behavior in humans: a review. J Clin Pharmacol 1992;32:1060–1072.

92. Marcus MD. Introduction—binge eating: clinical and research directions. Addict Behav 1995;20:691–693.

93. Spitzer RL, Yanovski S, Wadden T, Wing R, Marcus MD, Stunkard A, et al. Binge eating disorder: its further validation in a multisite study. Int J Eat Disord 1993;13:137–153.

94. Bruce B, Agras WS. Binge eating disorder in females: a population-based investigation. Int J Eat Disord 1992;12:365–373.

95. Telch CF, Agras WS, Rossiter EM. Binge eating increases with increasing adiposity. Int J Eat Disord 1988;7:115–119.

96. Mussell MP, Mitchell JE, Weller CL, Raymond NC, Crow SJ, Crosby RD. Onset of binge eating, dieting, obesity, and mood disorders among subjects seeking treatment for binge eating disorder. Int J Eat Disord 1995;14:395–401.

96a. Wurtman JJ. Depression and weight gain: the serotonin connection. J Affective Disorders 1993;29:183–192.

97. Fernstrom JD. Food-induced changes in brain serotonin synthesis: is there a relationship to appetite for specific macronutrients? Appetite 1987;8:163–182.

98. Walsh A, Oldman A, Franklin M, Fairburn C, Cowen P. Dieting decreases plasma tryptophan and increases the prolactin response to d-fenfluramine in women but not men. J Affective Dis 1995;33:89–97.

98a. Wurtman JJ, Wurtman RJ. Drugs that enhance central serotonergic transmission diminish elective carbohydrate consumption by rats. Life Sci 1979;24:895–904.

99. Weintraub M, Hasday JD, Mushlin AI, Lockwood DH. A double blind clinical trial in weight control: use of fenfluramine and phentermine alone and in combination. Arch Intern Med 1984;144:1143–1148.

100. Weintraub M. Long-term weight control: The National Heart, Lung, and Blood Institute funded multimodal intervention study. Clin Pharmacol Ther 1992;51:581–646.

101. Mitchell JE, Mussell MP. Comorbidity and binge eating disorder. Addict Behav 1995;20:725–732.

102. Marcus MD, Wing RR, Ewing L, Kern E, Gooding W, McDermott M. Psychiatric disorders among obese binge eaters. Int J Eat Disord 1990;9:69–77.

103. Yanovski SZ, Nelson JE, Dubbert BK, Spitzer R. Association of binge eating disorder and psychiatric comorbidity in obese subjects. Am J Psychiatry 1993;150:1472–1479.

104. Brody ML, Walsh T, Devlin MJ. Binge eating disorder: reliability and validity of a new diagnostic category. J Consult Clin Psychol 1994;62:381–386.

105. Specker S, deZwaan M, Raymond N, Mitchell J. Psychopathology in subgroups of obese women with and without binge eating disorder. Compr Psychiatry 1994;35:185–190.

106. Mitchell JE, Hatsukami D, Pyle R, Eckert E. Bulimia with and without a family history of drug abuse. Addict Behav 1988;13:245–251.

107. Holderness CC, Brooks P Gunn J, Warren MP. Co-morbidity of eating disorders and substance abuse. Review of the literature. Int J Eat Disord 1994;16:1–34.

108. Braun DL, Sunday SR, Halmi KA. Psychiatric co-morbidity in patients with eating disorders. Psychol Med 1994;24:859–867.

109. Koepp W, Schildbach S, Schmager C, Rohner R. Borderline diagnosis and substance abuse in female patients with eating disorders. Int J Eat Disord 1993;14:107–110.

110. Garfinkel PE, Garner DM. Anorexia nervosa: a multidimensional perspective. New York: Brunner Mazel, 1982.

111. Mitchell JE, Hatsukami DK, Eckert ED, Pyle RL. Characteristics of 275 patients with bulimia. Am J Psychiatry 1985;142:482–485.

112. Yager J, Landsverk J, Edelstein CK, Jarvik M. A 20 month follow-up study of 628 women with eating disorders: II. Course of associated symptoms and related features. Int J Eat Disord 1988;7:503–513.

113. Kendler KS, Walters EE, Neals MC, Kessler RC, Heath AC, Eaves LJ. The structure of the genetic and environmental risk factors for six major psychiatric disorders in women. Arch Gen Psychiatry 1995;52:374–383.

114. Willenbring ML, Morley JE, Krahn DD, Carlson G, Levine AS, Shafer RB. Psychoneuroendocrine effects of methadone maintenance. Psychoneuroendocrinology 1989;14:371.

115. Moraia A, Fabre J, Chee E, Zeger S, Orsat E, Robert A. Diet and opiate addiction, a quantitative assessment of the diet of non-institutionalized opiate addicts. Br J Addiction 1989;84:173–180.

116. Rothman RB, Gendron T, Hitzig P. Letter to the editor. J Subst Abuse Treat 1994;11:273–275.

117. Volpicelli JR, Alterman AI, Hayashida M, O'Brien CP. Naltrexone in the treatment of alcohol dependence. Arch Gen Psychiatry 1992;49:876–880.

118. Nylander I, Hyytia P, Forsander O, Terenius L. Differences between alcohol-preferring (AA) and alcohol-avoiding (ANA) rats in prodynorphin and proenkephalin systems. Alcohol Clin Exp Res 1994;18:1272–1279.

119. University of Florida. Facts about tobacco, alcohol, other drugs 1995;4:3.

120. Kassel JD, Shiffman S. What can hunger teach us about drug craving. Adv Behav Res Ther 1992;14:141–167.

121. Shor-Posner G, Grinker JA, Marinescu C, Brown O, Leibowitz SF. Hypothalamic serotonin in the control of meal patterns and macronutrient selection. Brain Res Bull 1986;17:663–671.

122. Hill AJ, Bundell JE. Food selection, body weight and the premenstrual syndrome (PMS). Effect of D-fenfluramine [abstract]. Int J Obesity 1991;15:215.

123. Treasure J, Campbell I. Editorial: the case for biology in the etiology of anorexia nervosa. Psychol Med 1994;24:3–8.

124. Rowland NE. Effect of continuous infusions of dexfenfluramine on food intake, body weight and brain amines in rats. Life Sci 1986;39:2581–2586.

125. Haleem DJ. Serotonergic functions in rat brain: sex-related differences and responses to stress. University of London, 1988. Ph.D. thesis.

126. Carter A, Davis ST. Biogenic amines, reproductive hormones and female sexual behavior. A review. Behav Res 1977;1:213–225.

127. Kaye WH, Ebert MH, Gwirtsman HE, et al. Differences in brain serotonergic metabolism between nonbulimic and bulimic patients with anorexia nervosa. Am J Psychiatry 1984; 141:1598–1601.

128. Gwirtsman HE, Guze BH, Yager J, Gainsley B. Fluoxetine treatment of anorexia nervosa: an open clinical trial. J Clin Psychiatry 1990;51: 378–382.

129. Kaye WH, Weltzin TE, Hsu LKG, Bulik CM. An open trial of fluoxetine in patients with anorexia nervosa. J Clin Psychiatry 1991; 52:464–471.

130. Beasley CM, Masica DN, Potvin JH. Fluoxetine. A review of receptor and functional effects and their clinical implications. Psychopharmacology (Berl) 1992;107:1–10.

131. Advokut C, Kutlesic V. Pharmacotherapy of the eating disorders: A commentary. Neurosci Biobehav Rev 1995;19:59–66.

132. Halmi KA, Eckert E, LaDu TJ, et al. Anorexia nervosa: treatment efficacy of cyproheptadine and amitriptyline. Arch Gen Psychiatry 1986; 43:177–181.

133. Wallin MS, Rissanen AM. Food and mood: relationship between food, serotonin and affective disorders. Acta Psychiatr Scand Suppl 1994;377:36–40.

134. Weltzin TE, Fernstrom MH, Fernstrom JD, Neuberger SK, Kaye WH. Acute tryptophan depletion and increased food intake and irritability in bulimia nervosa. Am J Psychiatry 1995;152:1668–1671.

135. Fornari VM, Braun DL, Sunday SR, Sandberg DE, Matthews M, Chen IL, et al. Seasonal patterns in eating disorder subgroups. Compr Psychiatry 1994;35:450–456.

136. Hardin TA, Wehr TA, Brewerton T, Kasper S, Berrettini W, Rabkin J, et al. Evaluation of seasonality in six clinical populations. J Psychiatr Res 1991;25:75–87.

137. Fornari WM, Sandberg DE, Lachenmeyer J, Cohen D, Matthews M, Montero G. Seasonal variations in bulimia nervosa. Ann N Y Acad Sci 1989;575:509–511.

138. Lam RW, Solyom L, Tompkins A. Seasonal mood symptoms in bulimia nervosa and seasonal affective disorder. Compr Psychiatry 1991;32:552–558.

139. Lam RW, Goldner EM, Solyom L, Remick RA. A controlled study of light therapy for bulimia nervosa. Am J Psychiatry 1994;151: 744–750.

140. Lewy AJ, Sack RL, Miller LS, Hoban TM. Antidepressant and circadian phase-shifting effects of light. Science 1987;235:352–354.

141. Lewy AJ, Sack RL, Singer CM, White DM, Hoban TM. Winter depression and the phase-shift hypothesis for bright light's therapeutic effects: history, theory, and experimental evidence. J Biol Rhythms 1988;3:121–134.

142. Jacobsen FM, Murphy DL, Rosenthal NE. The role of serotonin in seasonal affective disorder and the antidepressant response to phototherapy. In: Rosenthal NE, Blehar M, eds. Seasonal affective disorders and phototherapy. New York: Guilford Press, 1989.

143. Kales EF. Macronutrient analysis of binge eating in bulimia. Physiol Behav 1990;48:837–840.

144. Mehlman PT, Higley JD, Faucher I, Lilly AA, Taub DM, Vickers J, et al. Correlation of SCF 5-HIAA concentration with sociality and the timing of emigration in free-ranging primates. Am J Psychiatry 1995;152:907–913.

145. University of Florida. Facts about tobacco, alcohol, other drugs 1994;3:3.

146. Fava M, Rappe SM, West J, Herzog DB. Anger attacks in eating disorders. Psychiatry Res 1995;56:205–212.

147. Coccaro EF, Seiver LJ, Klar HM, Maruer G, Cochrane K, Cooper TB, Mohs RC, Davis KL. Serotonergic studies in patients with affective and personality disorders. Arch Gen Psychiatry 1989;46:587–599.

148. Brewerton TD. Toward a unified theory of serotonin dysregulation in eating and related disorders. Psychoneuroendocrinology 1995; 20:561–590.

149. Gold MS, Sternbach HA. Endorphins in obesity and in the regulation of appetite and weight. Integrative Psychiatry 1984;2(6):203–210.

150. Jonas JM, Gold MS. Naltrexone treatment of bulimia: clinical and theoretical findings linking eating disorders and substance abuse. Adv Alcohol Subst Abuse 1988;7(1):29–37.

151. Jonas JM, Gold MS. The use of opiate antagonists in treating bulimia: a study of low dose versus high dose naltrexone. Psychiatry Res 1988;24:195–199.

152. Jonas JM, Gold MS. Opiate antagonists as clinical probes in bulimia. In: Hudson JI, Pope HG Jr, eds. The psychobiology of bulimia. Washington, DC: American Psychiatric Association Press, 1987:115–127.

153. Jonas JM, Gold MS. Naltrexone reverses bulimic symptoms. Lancet 1986;1(8484):807.

154. Alger SA, Schwalberg MD, et al. Effect of a tricyclic antidepressant and opiate antagonist on binge-eating behavior in normoweight bulimic and obese, binge-eating subjects. Am J Clin Nutr 1991;53:865–871.

155. Brewerton TD, Lydiard RB, Laraia MT, Shook JE, Ballinger JC. CSF beta-endorphin and dynorphin in bulimia nervosa. Am J Psychiatry 1992;149:1086–1090.

156. Gold MS. Are eating disorders addictions? Adv Biosci 1993;990:55–63.

157. Wilson GT. The addiction model of eating disorders: a critical analysis. Adv Behav Res Ther 1991;13:27–72.

158. Nazoe S, Naruo T, Yonekura R, Nakabeppu Y, Soojima Y, Nagal N, et al. Comparison of regional cerebral blood flow in patients with eating disorders. Brain Res Bull 1995;36(3): 251–255.

159. Watts WD, Ellis AM. Drug abuse and eating disorders: prevention implications. J Drug Educ 1992;22(3):223–240.

160. French SA, Story M, Duwnes B, Resnick MD, Blum RW. Frequent dieting among adolescents: psychosocial and health behavior correlates. Am J Public Health 1995;85:695–701.

161. Ash JB, Piazza E. Changing symptomatology in eating disorders. Int J Eat Disord 1995;18: 27–38.

29 Pathological Gambling

Sheila B. Blume

INTRODUCTION

Gambling in one form or another has been part of human behavior since prehistory. Records of games of chance and related artifacts have been discovered among the ruins of the ancient city of Babylon, dating from 3000 BC (1). Gambling is mentioned in both the Old and New Testaments and in the classical literature of many cultures (e.g., the Sanskrit epic *The Mahabahrata*). Private lotteries were common in Europe throughout the Middle Ages, while Elizabeth I of England chartered the first government-sponsored lottery in 1566 (2).

European settlers who came to North America employed lotteries as a means of raising funds in all of the original 13 colonies. The first great universities established in the New World (e.g., Yale, Columbia, Harvard, Princeton) also relied on lotteries to raise money (2).

Along with the human tendency to gamble has come gambling-related problems, including the loss of control of gambling behavior, commonly referred to as compulsive gambling. *The Mahabahrata,* for example, tells the story of how a fair and wise king is brought low by his only fault, his addiction to gambling. He gambles away his wealth, his kingdom, his brothers and himself (into slavery) and, finally, his wife. Famous compulsive gamblers in modern history have included a seventeenth century Venetian rabbi (3) and the Russian novelist Feodor Dostoyevsky. Dostoyevsky wrote a novel called *The Gambler* in 1866, during a period of catastrophic gambling losses, in an effort to preserve his financial integrity (4).

In a 1928 essay entitled *Dostoyevsky and Parricide* (5) Sigmund Freud discussed the writer's compulsive gambling and hypothesized its relationship to traumatic events in his life, particularly his father's death. Interestingly, Freud conceptualized Dostoyevsky's behavior as gambling for its own sake (rather than as a means to acquire money) and considered it an addiction (6). Several psychoanalysts studied and treated compulsive gamblers from the 1920s through the 1960s (6). However, there was relatively little interest in scientific research in the field of compulsive gambling or in the treatment of this disorder until the 1970s and 1980s. These decades saw an increased focus on gambling problems, which had several roots. The first treatment unit for compulsive gamblers was established by Dr. Robert Custer at the Brecksville, Ohio, Veterans Administration Hospital in 1971 (7). This unit adapted the treatment methods used in alcoholism rehabilitation to the treatment of gambling disorders, relying on group, individual, and family therapies and employing self-help fellowships, such as Gamblers Anonymous (GA) and Gam-Anon, as adjuncts to professional treatment. The model was found effective and subsequently adopted by other addiction treatment facilities throughout the United States. Articles in the popular press alluded to these treatment programs and to GA as a means of helping troubled gamblers. In addition, the 1980s and 1990s saw a worldwide trend toward governmental legalization of many types of gambling. Legislatures looked increasingly to state lotteries and taxes from legal gambling as revenue sources in an atmosphere of rising government expenses and citizen unwillingness to accept tax increases. The result was an explosive growth in the availability of a wide variety of games of chance to the general public. The ready availability of gambling caused both an increase in the amount gambled by the population at large and an increase in the visibility of gambling problems. As of 1992, gambling had become a major industry in the United States, with a total of about $330 billion bet during that year and a profit of nearly $30 billion (8). Recent surveys indicate that 80–90% of American adults gamble to some extent (9), a significantly greater proportion than those who use alcohol or other drugs.

TERMS AND DEFINITIONS

For the purpose of understanding gambling problems, it is important to define gambling narrowly rather than using a broad definition (for example, considering sky-diving or other high-risk behavior as "gambling with one's life"). Gambling or wagering involves either playing a game for money (e.g., betting on a game of golf) or staking something of value (usually money) on an event influenced by chance (e.g., betting on whether a specific set of numbers will be picked in a lottery). To be important to the development of gambling problems, this wagering must be short term, so that a feeling of excitement can be produced while awaiting the outcome. Thus, a long-term financial investment would not be considered gambling for this purpose, although chance may play a role in its gain or loss of value.

The term "gambling problems" is used as an umbrella term for a wide range of problems related to gambling activities, such as underage gambling, illegal gambling, and dishonest games, in addition to personal and family problems related to excessive gambling by an individual. "Problem gambler" is sometimes used to refer to a person whose gambling creates problems, while "compulsive gambler" or "pathological gambler" applies specifically to an individual suffering from the disorder described in the Diagnostic and Statistical Manual of the American Psychiatric Association as Pathological Gambling (10).

Different varieties of currently popular gambling involve differing proportions of chance and skill. Playing chess for money involves significantly more skill than chance. Betting on horse races may involve considerable knowledge of the competitors and skill in handicapping, while playing the lottery or roulette relies entirely on chance. Forms of gambling also differ in the immediacy of their payoff. Casino games such as blackjack tend to be short interval gambling, and slot machines offer an almost immediate payoff. Slot machines are the predominant type of betting reported by pathological gamblers in Germany and Holland, and such gambling is associated with high rates of gambling problems among English school-aged children (11, 12). There is some evidence that pathological gamblers who prefer different types of wagering may differ in some characteristics (13). However, little research has been devoted to such distinctions and most ideas about these differences are based on clinical experience.

DIAGNOSIS OF PATHOLOGICAL GAMBLING

The Diagnostic and Statistical Manual (DSM) of the American Psychiatric Association first included pathological gambling among the mental disorders in its third edition (14). The diagnostic criteria were altered in 1987 and again in 1994. In the current edition, DSM-IV (10), the disorder is char-

acterized as persistent and recurrent maladaptive gambling behavior, not better accounted for as a component of a manic episode. At least five of the following 10 criteria must be present for the diagnosis to be made:

1. "*Is preoccupied with gambling (e.g., preoccupied with reliving past gambling experience, handicapping or planning the next venture, or thinking of ways to get money with which to gamble).*" Preoccupation is sometimes extreme. Pathological gamblers have been known to go to the racetrack on their wedding day. Pathological sports bettors may follow several games simultaneously on two or three radios or television sets.
2. "*Needs to gamble with increasing amounts of money in order to achieve the desired excitement.*" This phenomenon is comparable to the tolerance seen in substance dependence.
3. "*Has repeated unsuccessful efforts to control, cut back, or stop gambling.*" This criterion refers to impaired control.
4. "*Is restless or irritable when attempting to cut down or stop gambling.*" This describes the equivalent of a withdrawal state in substance dependence. About 65% of GA members reported such withdrawal symptoms, which also included insomnia, headaches, upset stomach or diarrhea, anorexia, palpitations, weakness, shaking, sweating and breathing problems (15).
5. "*Gambles as a way of escaping from problems or relieving a dysphoric mood (e.g., feelings of helplessness, guilt, anxiety, depression).*" Female pathological gamblers often describe such "escape" as a primary reason for gambling (16).
6. "*After losing money gambling, often returns another day to get even ("chasing" one's losses).*" Chasing is a common symptom of this disorder (17). It has no equivalent in alcohol or other drug addictions.
7. "*Lies to family members, therapist, or others to conceal the extent of involvement with gambling.*"
8. "*Has committed illegal acts such as forgery, fraud, theft, or embezzlement to finance gambling.*" Individuals who are normally honest and law-abiding often begin to appropriate other people's money when they develop pathological gambling. They characteristically rationalize this activity as temporary borrowing, but their need for money eventually overpowers their moral standards. Pathological gambling is closely associated with criminal activity, especially white-collar crime (18, 19).
9. "*Has jeopardized or lost a significant relationship, job, or educational or career opportunity because of gambling.*" Marital and other family relationships are usually the first to be affected as the gambler becomes preoccupied with gambling activity, although all relationships and activities are eventually damaged by the disease.
10. "*Relies on others to provide money to relieve a desperate financial situation caused by gambling.*" This is generally known as a "bailout" and is often elicited from family or friends without revealing that the indebtedness is due to gambling. If the donors of the funds are aware of the gambling, they often insist on a promise that the pathological gambler will give up or reduce this activity.

Pathological gambling is a progressive disease that often has its onset in adolescence, but may begin at any age. Its characteristics may differ with age and sex. Female pathological gamblers are less likely to commit crimes than males and report less indebtedness (16). The latter may be a reflection of the economic reality that women have less access to credit than men and less ability to borrow large sums. Women also more often report gambling to escape from the psychological distress produced by a painful situation, for example, an abusive relationship or a husband who is often absent (16).

Pathological gambling tends to run in families, so that children of pathological gamblers are at increased risk for developing the disorder. Males have higher rates than females, and, as discussed later in this chapter, those suffering from alcoholism or other addictions have particularly high prevalence rates.

EPIDEMIOLOGY OF GAMBLING PROBLEMS

Studies of the prevalence of pathological gambling in the United States over the past 20 years are difficult to compare because of differences in methodology (9, 20). A series of studies performed during the 1980s in the eastern United States and in California, using the South Oaks Gambling Screen (SOGS) in a general population sample, found that approximately 4% of adults reported some gambling-related problems in their lifetime, while 1.2–2.3% fell into the category of "probable pathological gambler." Using the same methodology, a study in Iowa at about the same time found much lower prevalence rates (1.6% reporting gambling problems and 0.1% probable pathological gamblers). This difference was thought to be related to the absence of a state lottery in Iowa and thus the relative unavailability of legal gambling. These results also echoed the findings of a 1974 survey, using a different method, in which residents of Nevada (the only state in which legal gambling had been available for a considerable time) had a pathological gambling rate of 2.5%, compared to 1% for the rest of the country (21).

Studies in six states were conducted during the early 1990s, using a modified version of the South Oaks Gambling Screen in a total of about 14,000 adults. The lifetime prevalence of problem gambling ranged from 2.8% to 3.6% in Midwestern states and was 4.8% in Texas, 5.1% in the state of Washington, and 6.3% in Connecticut. The differences in rates were again related to variations in gambling availability (9). In all studies, males showed higher rates than females.

Prevalence rates for pathological gambling are higher among patients in treatment for substance use disorders than in the general population. In a 1986 study of 458 alcoholic and drug dependent adult inpatients at South Oaks Hospital, Lesieur, Blume, and Zoppa (22) reported that 89% had gambled at some time and 72% during the previous year. These patients tended to use substances and gamble at the same time. Considering the patient group as a whole, 9% satisfied criteria for a lifetime diagnosis of pathological gambling and an additional 10% reported some gambling problems, but did not meet criteria for the diagnosis. Rates were highest among those addicted to drugs alone (18% pathological gamblers plus an additional 11% with gambling problems), next most common among those dependent on both alcohol and drugs (12% and 10%), and lowest among those dependent on alcohol alone (5% and 10%). Rates were higher among males, 25% of whom were problem gamblers compared to 6% of the females. Patients who reported heavy or compulsive gambling by a father, mother, or sibling had problem gambling rates of 62%, 30%, and 40%, respectively. Among those with an alcoholic father, 25% reported gambling problems.

A study of 100 adolescent inpatients in treatment for substance use disorders at the same hospital reported lifetime prevalence of pathological gambling of 14%, with an additional 14% reporting some gambling problems but not meeting diagnostic criteria (23).

A 1992 study examined 298 cocaine abusers in treatment (24). A concurrent diagnosis of pathological gambling was found in 19% of the male and 5.5% of female patients, with an overall rate of 15%. Those who were also pathological gamblers were more likely to be dependent on additional drugs and alcohol as well as cocaine, and to have a history suggestive of attention deficit disorder. Although an association between gambling problems and attention deficit disorder has been postulated (25) further research is needed to elucidate this relationship.

The prevalence of pathological gambling among psychiatric patients has also been studied. Lesieur and Blume (26) found a lifetime prevalence of 6.7% for probable pathological gambling in a survey of 105 patients admitted to an acute adult psychiatric service for primary psychiatric problems. Nine percent of the males and 4% of the female patients scored more than 5 on the South Oaks Gambling Screen. Gambling problems were most prevalent among patients with comorbid substance-use disorders, among whom 11% were probable pathological gamblers.

Although gambling problems occur throughout the world, there is a lack of comparative epidemiological data in the literature. One study of over 7,000 residents of a Hong Kong community found pathological gambling in 3% of the male and 0.16% of the female subjects (27).

PHENOMENOLOGY OF PATHOLOGICAL GAMBLING

Pathological gambling is currently understood as a disease characterized by an addiction to what gamblers call "being in action" (28). This term describes an aroused state compared by some gamblers to the "high" experi-

enced after using stimulants such as cocaine. A gambler is "in action" while awaiting the result of a significant wager (e.g., watching a football game, playing a slot machine). In some cases, a feeling of altered identity or dissociation is experienced (29). Both the "high" and the dissociated state afford a relief from dysphoric feelings such as boredom, anxiety, and depression. They allow a reduction in self-criticism, worry, and guilt, and permit the gambler to indulge in fantasies about the next "big win."

Pathophysiology

The physiological basis of these altered states is not understood. Little research has been devoted to the subject so far. The most extensive study has been that of Roy et al. (30). This group measured several neurotransmitters and their metabolites in the body fluids of 20 male pathological gamblers who had been gambling actively until the time of the study, in comparison to 20 normal controls. They found increased levels of centrally-produced metabolites of the neurotransmitter norepinephrine in the cerebrospinal fluid of the gamblers. In addition, they found an increased urinary output of norepinephrine. A second article reported that scores on the extraversion scale of the Eysenck Personality Questionnaire were correlated with these altered physiological findings (31). The authors postulated that abnormalities in the norepinephrine system might be related to the disease. Their theory is reminiscent of a remark made by a pathological gambler telling his story at an open GA meeting who stated, "I had the feeing that I had become addicted to my own adrenalin."

Other studies have found electroencephalogram abnormalities among pathological gamblers similar to those seen in attention deficit disorder (25, 32). In addition, a study of beta-endorphins among pathological gamblers found lower baseline levels in those who gambled on horse races as compared to slot machine gamblers and normal controls (13). Deficits in the endorphin system could link at least some types of pathological gambling to other addictive disorders. However, far more research will be required before these relationships are understood.

Psychodynamics

Considerable attention has been devoted to the study of psychodynamic factors involved in pathological gambling. Rosenthal (6) and Lesieur and Rosenthal (19) have reviewed the psychoanalytic literature dating back to 1917, including Freud's 1928 essay. The earlier studies stressed themes of gambling as an eroticized activity and a form of masochism. More recently, parental identification has been emphasized as well as narcissistic traits and several types of omnipotent fantasies (e.g., of "controlling the uncontrollable") (19).

Psychological research has focused on sensation-seeking and deficits in impulse control (19). A study of personality structure by McCormick and Taber (33) described five personality dimensions relevant to pathological gambling: a mood factor (from depression through hypomania), an obsessive-compulsive factor, a factor related to stressful life experiences, a socialization factor, and a substance-related factor.

Course of the Disease

The progressive course of pathological gambling is usually described in the three phases originally elucidated by Dr. Robert Custer, based on his experience at the Brecksville treatment unit. He described these as the winning, losing, and desperation phases (7). To this, Rosenthal has added the hopeless or "giving-up" phase (19). Since nearly all of Custer's patients were male, whereas about a third of probable pathological gamblers identified in general population studies are female, it is not surprising that this progression of phases may not be for characteristic of all gamblers. Women tend to start their gambling problems later than men and are less likely to experience a winning phase (16).

WINNING PHASE

In some cases, the career of the pathological gambler begins with a big win (equal to half the individual's annual earnings or more). Dostoyevsky describes such a progression in a character in *The Gambler*, with a rapid development of preoccupation, tolerance, and loss of control (4). For most gamblers, however, the winning phase reflects the time and effort they devote to gambling on skill-related forms of wagering such as horse race betting, playing the stock market, or playing cards. Winning induces a feeling of power, wealth, and omnipotence. As the gambler's involvement with gambling grows, he or she depends increasingly on the "high" derived from being in action and less on other mechanisms of defense to deal with problems and to counteract negative emotional states. He or she pulls away from intimate interpersonal relationships and derives a growing proportion of his or her self-esteem from both gambling skill and the feeling of being favored by God, Fate, or Lady Luck. While others must work for a living, the gambler feels empowered to obtain money through magical means. While pathological gamblers both win and lose during this phase, they tend to recall and talk about their wins and deny, rationalize, or minimize their losses. For this reason they are often unable to account for money claimed to be won. The winning phase is more characteristic of pathological gamblers whom Lesieur describes as "action-seekers" as opposed to initial "escape-seekers" who begin their gambling involvement as a way to relieve situation-related dysphoria. In a study of female members of GA, more than half started as "escape-seekers" (16). Gambling for escape is also associated with the kinds of "hypnotic," "blackout," or dissociated status described by Jacobs (29).

LOSING PHASE

This phase often begins with the kind of unpredictable losing streak experienced by anyone who gambles. Sometimes it begins with a "bad beat" (an unexplained bizarre circumstance that turns an expected win into a loss) (34). For example, a horse approaching the finish line well in front of the pack suddenly drops dead, or a winning horse is disqualified because of a technicality irrelevant to the race itself. The experience of losing would be distressing for the ordinary gambler, but for the pathological gambler it is experienced as a severe narcissistic blow, and may begin a pattern of "chasing" losses (17). This experience may be related to the phenomenon described by gamblers as "going on tilt" (an acute deterioration of play). In any case, the gambler now feels compelled to win back money he or she has lost and begins to gamble less cautiously, thereby compounding losses. As losses mount, gambling becomes more urgent and also more solitary. Lying to cover losses, appropriating assets from family members, taking out loans, and continually searching for money become prevalent activities. Interpersonal relationships are further strained. Family members find themselves isolated and confused by the gambler's behavior and the disappearance of family funds. Spouses sometimes suspect the gambler is having an affair. Even when they know about the gambling, spouses are usually unaware of the extent of the gambler's indebtedness.

Comorbidities, including affective disorders, may become more apparent during this phase (35), described by some patients and families as "like being on an emotional rollercoaster." The gambler both wins and loses during this phase but money won is only partially used to pay debts. Most of it is gambled.

During this phase the gambler may seek a bailout, promising to cut down or stop gambling in return. The bailout, however, is treated like a "big win," partly gambled and accepted as further evidence of the gambler's omnipotence (19).

DESPERATION PHASE

This phase may begin with the gambling away of funds from a bailout or some other grave disappointment. The gambler is now desperate. Immoral and/or illegal acts (e.g., fraud, embezzling, writing bad checks) become a necessity, as does the compensatory belief in a big win "just around the corner." Irritability, mood swings, isolation, escape fantasies, and suicidal ideation or attempts are common. Debts mount. Additional bailouts are sought. The gambler may be arrested and prosecuted.

Most members of GA who come for help reporting they have "hit bottom" do so in this phase. Surveys of GA members have reported severe depression in 72% and suicidal attempts in 17–24% (35).

GIVING UP PHASE

Pathological gamblers who reach this phase no longer cling to the fantasy of "winning it all back." They gamble sloppily. Their goal is just to stay in action.

Comorbid psychiatric conditions have already been mentioned. Depression, bipolar disorder, and suicidal attempts are particularly common, as are substance use disorders (19). Physical conditions generally thought of as stress-related (e.g., hypertension, gastrointestinal problems, respiratory symptoms) are also common at all stages of the disease. Spouses of pathological gamblers often suffer from a variety of physical and emotional disorders, and may experience several phases in their own reactions, as the disease develops. These have been described as denial (broken through in "cycles of discovery"), stress, and exhaustion (19). Studies of children of pathological gamblers have found increased rates of such health-threatening behaviors as drinking, drug use, smoking, overeating, and gambling. These problems are especially evident in children of parents with comorbid conditions such as combined pathological gambling and substance dependence (36, 37).

PATHOLOGICAL GAMBLING AND SUBSTANCE-USE DISORDERS: IDENTIFICATION IN CLINICAL POPULATIONS

Because of the high prevalence of pathological gambling among persons suffering from substance use disorders, all such patients should be evaluated for gambling problems (22, 23). The relationship between substance use and gambling is a complex one (21). The two activities are often combined. Alcoholic beverages are served in casinos and at sports events. Both licit and illicit gambling activities may be centered at bars, where illicit drugs are also sold. Substance dependence may develop simultaneously with pathological gambling or may develop before or afterward. It is, therefore, important to assess risk in substance dependent patients who do not report current gambling problems. Patients with a history of intense interest in gambling before the onset of substance dependence, patients with a family history of pathological gambling, and patients with a history of gambling problems in remission are at special risk. The altered psychological state experienced during gambling may lead to relapse in a newly-abstinent substance dependent patient. Alternatively, abstinence from alcohol and drugs may be sustained, but a "switch of addictions" experienced (38). The action of gambling is easily substituted for the substance-induced "high" in the patient's pattern of dependence, leading to a rapid development of pathological gambling.

Patients in treatment for substance-use disorders who have a history of gambling problems, either current or in remission, should be treated simultaneously for both disorders. All other patients should be educated about gambling problems and the risk of switching addictions. In addition, addiction treatment programs should structure their recreation programs to avoid encouraging gambling-related activities such as cards, bingo, or dice games. Even though "house rules" usually forbid gambling, betting is often carried on surreptitiously. Newly abstinent patients often have difficulty structuring the time they formerly spent in substance-related activities. Efforts should be made to encourage constructive non–gambling-related recreation as a preventive measure.

The South Oaks Gambling Screen (SOGS) (Fig. 29.1) is available to screen clinical populations (39). It can be administered as a pencil-and-paper test or a clinical interview. It should be scored with the score sheet (Fig. 29.2) since not all questions are counted in the total score. The first few questions, although not scored, give the evaluator a quick survey of the kinds and amounts of wagering done by the subject, and of family history. The amounts wagered must be evaluated relative to the subject's total disposable income. The family history is useful in judging risk. Question 12 is not scored, but acts as a lead-in to question 13. In addition, although questions 16 (j) and (k) are not scored, they provide valuable information to the rater. The maximum SOGS score is 20. Scores of 5 or more are indicative of probable pathological gambling, while a score of between 1 and 4 may indicate some gambling problem. Note that the questions are written in a lifetime mode. Patients who score 5 or more should be evaluated using DSM-IV diagnostic criteria for pathological gambling (10), either current or in remission.

Name_____ Date _____

1. Please indicate which of the following types of gambling you have done in your lifetime. For each type, mark one answer: "not at all," "less than once a week," or "once a week or more."

	not at all	less than once a week	once a week or more	
a.	_____	_____	_____	play cards for money
b.	_____	_____	_____	bet on horses, dogs or other animals (at OTB, the track or with a bookie)
c.	_____	_____	_____	bet on sports (parlay cards, with a bookie, or at Jai Alai)
d.	_____	_____	_____	played dice games (including craps, over and under or other dice games) for money
e.	_____	_____	_____	gambled in a casino (legal or otherwise)
f.	_____	_____	_____	played the numbers or bet on lotteries
g.	_____	_____	_____	played bingo for money
h.	_____	_____	_____	played the stock, options and/or commodities market
i.	_____	_____	_____	played slot machines, poker machines or other gambling machines
j.	_____	_____	_____	bowled, shot pool, played golf or some other game of skill for money
k.	_____	_____	_____	pull tabs or "paper" games other than lotteries
l.	_____	_____	_____	some form of gambling not listed above
				(please specify) _____

2. What is the largest amount of money you have ever gambled with on any one day?

_____ never have gambled　　　　_____ more than $100 up to $1,000
_____ $1 or less　　　　_____ more than $1,000 up to $10,000
_____ more than $1 up to $10　　　　_____ more than $10,000
_____ more than $10 up to $100

3. Check which of the following people in your life has (or had) a gambling problem.

_____ father　　　　_____ mother　　　　_____ a brother or sister　　　　_____ a grandparent
_____ my spouse or partner　　　　_____ my child(ren)　　　　_____ another relative
_____ a friend or someone else important in my life

4. When you gamble, how often do you go back another day to win back money you lost?

_____ never
_____ some of the time (less than half the time I lost)
_____ most of the time I lost
_____ every time I lost

5. Have you ever claimed to be winning money gambling but weren't really? In fact, you lost?

_____ never (or never gamble)
_____ yes, less than half the time I lost
_____ yes, most of the time

6. Do you feel you have ever had a problem with betting money or gambling?

_____ no
_____ yes, in the past but not now
_____ yes

7. Did you ever gamble more than you intend to? . . . . _____ yes　_____ no

8. Have people criticized your betting or told you that you had a gambling problem,
regardless of whether or not you thought it was true? . . . . _____ yes　_____ no

9. Have you ever felt guilty about the way you gamble or what happens when you gamble?. . . . . _____ yes　_____ no

10. Have you ever felt like you would like to stop betting money or gambling but didn't think you could? . . . . _____ yes　_____ no

11. Have you ever hidden betting slips, lottery tickets, gambling money, I.O.U.s or other signs of betting
or gambling from your spouse, children or other important people in your life? . . . . _____ yes　_____ no

12. Have you ever argued with people you live with over how you handle money?. . . . . _____ yes　_____ no

13. (If you answered yes to question 12): Have money arguments ever centered on your gambling? . . . . _____ yes　_____ no

14. Have you ever borrowed from someone and not paid them back as a result of your gambling?. _____ yes　_____ no

15. Have you ever lost time from work (or school) due to betting money or gambling? . . . . _____ yes　_____ no

16. If you borrowed money to gamble or to pay gambling debts, who or where did you borrow from? (check "yes" or "no" for each)

	no	yes
a. from household money_____	( )	( )
b. from your spouse _____	( )	( )
c. from other relatives or in-laws _____	( )	( )
d. from banks, loan companies or credit unions_____	( )	( )
e. from credit cards_____	( )	( )
f. from loan sharks _____	( )	( )
g. you cashed in stocks, bonds or other securities _____	( )	( )
h. you sold personal or family property _____	( )	( )
i. you borrowed on your checking account (passed bad checks)_____	( )	( )
j. you have (had) a credit line with a bookie _____	( )	( )
k. you have (had) a credit line with a casino _____	( )	( )

Figure 29.1. South Oaks Hospital gambling screen form. Copyright 1992, South Oaks Foundation.

Scores on the SOGS itself are determined by adding up the number of questions which show an "at risk" response:

Questions 1, 2 & 3 not counted:

_____ Question 4 — most of the time I lost
or
every time I lost

_____ Question 5 — yes, less than half the time I lost
or
yes, most of the time

_____ Question 6 — yes, in the past but not now
or
yes

_____ Question 7 — yes

_____ Question 8 — yes

_____ Question 9 — yes

_____ Question 10 — yes

_____ Question 11 — yes

Question 12 not counted

_____ Question 13 — yes

_____ Question 14 — yes

_____ Question 15 — yes

_____ Question 16a — yes

_____ Question   b — yes

_____ Question   c — yes

_____ Question   d — yes

_____ Question   e — yes

_____ Question   f — yes

_____ Question   g — yes

_____ Question   h — yes

_____ Question   i — yes

questions 16j & k not counted

Total = _____ (there are 20 questions that are counted)

0 = no problem
1–4 = some problem
5 or more = probable pathological gambler

Figure 29.2. South Oaks Hospital gambling screen score sheet. Copyright 1992, South Oaks Foundation.

The SOGS has been translated into many languages, including Spanish, Italian, German, Turkish, Japanese, and several Southeast Asian languages, and adapted to different cultures (40).

In addition to screening for pathological gambling in chemically dependent populations, the SOGS is recommended for patients in mental health and general medical settings and in employee assistance programs (EAPs) (41). In a poll of 86 programs and EAP professionals, 64% reported having had experience with pathological gamblers among their caseloads (42). Jail and prison populations should also be screened, as pathological gamblers who complete their sentences are highly likely to resume criminal activity if their disease is untreated.

Pathological gamblers do not usually seek treatment spontaneously until they reach the desperation phase of illness. The populations previously mentioned as candidates for screening can often be identified and treated in earlier stages of illness, before the most serious damage has been done.

TREATMENT OF PATHOLOGICAL GAMBLING

Current treatment for pathological gambling is in many ways similar to the treatment of substance use disorders. Most of the treatment is delivered on an outpatient basis, with inpatient care reserved for patients in a crisis of some kind, treatment failures, and patients with comorbid disorders. Treatment programs may be organized to treat pathological gambling primarily, dealing with comorbid disorders as needed, or as specialized tracks within addiction treatment programs (43, 44).

Modalities employed include psychoeducation, individual and group therapies, and family involvement, either in conjoint family sessions or in separate individual or group therapy for "significant others." Family members can and should be referred for help whether or not the problem gambler accepts treatment (45).

Referrals to GA and Gam-Anon (a 12-step fellowship for family members) are often made and attendance is encouraged as an adjunct to treatment. GA was established in 1957, based on the 12 steps of Alcoholics Anonymous (AA), as adapted to the recovery of pathological gamblers. GA differs in several respects from AA (46). Among these are a reduced emphasis on a belief in "God as we understand Him," replaced, for example, in the third step, by "this Power of our own understanding." GA has also developed several specific strategies in dealing with the extreme financial indebtedness of new members and their initial difficulties in handling money. GA has a "big book" explaining its philosophy and methods (47).

In addition to these methods of treatment, a variety of behavioral techniques have been employed to treat pathological gambling, including desensitization and aversive techniques (19, 48). Behavioral techniques may be employed in combination with any of those already listed and/or with GA.

Initial Treatment

Patients may begin treatment for a variety of reasons. There may be an external motivation, for example, an arrest or threatened arrest, pressure from the family as a condition of providing a bailout, or job jeopardy. There may be a crisis such as a suicide attempt, or the patient may have been diagnosed through screening while in treatment for a psychiatric or substance use disorder. Structured intervention techniques involving family members, friends, and/or an employer, similar to those used to motivate alcoholics and other addicts, are also effective in pathological gamblers.

The initial therapeutic challenges are to engage the trust of the gambler, to educate him or her about the nature of the disease and recovery, to assess and intervene in any immediate physical, psychiatric or social problems, and to establish initial abstinence.

Once this is accomplished, treatment aims at developing a more internalized and stable motivation for recovery.

Rehabilitation

Continued treatment includes exploring the role of gambling in the patient's life and helping him or her develop other, healthier means to satisfy these needs. Understanding relapse triggers, learning relapse prevention techniques and practicing stress management are helpful, as are measures to improve the interpersonal and social functioning of the patient. Family treatment is also critical to rehabilitation. In some patients long-term psychodynamic psychotherapy is required for stable recovery.

Abstinence is the ultimate goal in most treatment programs, although reduction or control of gambling is sought in some programs, presumably for earlier-stage problem gamblers. Addiction-model programs favor abstinence goals, and this is the most practical objective in combined substance-use disorder/pathological gambling treatment.

Long-Term Follow-Up

Pathological gambling is a lifelong disorder. As with substance dependence, patients may relapse after years of abstinence. Therefore, long-term follow-up in GA is helpful, with the availability of professional assistance as needed in times of increased stress or risk of relapse. Likewise, long-term

Gam-Anon involvement is helpful for family members. Unfortunately, Gamateen, a self-help, 12-step-based fellowship for adolescent children of pathological gamblers, is not yet widely available.

A limited number of outcome studies have been published to date demonstrating the efficacy of pathological gambling treatment (19, 49, 50). Lesieur and Blume (51) followed 72 patients, treated for pathological gambling in a special track of an inpatient addiction program, for a period of 6–14 months. Some were treated for pathological gambling alone, but most had alcohol and/or other drug problems as well, and some had their gambling problem discovered through use of the South Oaks Gambling Screen (SOGS). A modification of the Addiction Severity Index (ASI) was used (52). At the time of follow-up, 64% were abstinent from gambling, 65% from alcohol, and 80% from drugs. The ASI scores reflected marked improvement in all scales except those measuring health and employment (several patients had lost their jobs immediately before admission and, therefore, showed a worsening on this scale).

A 1985 study examined the cost-effectiveness of pathological gambling treatment (53). The authors concluded that an overall benefit to cost ratio of 20:1 was realized to society.

PREVENTION OF PATHOLOGICAL GAMBLING

In spite of the immense social and personal costs of pathological gambling there has been very little research or programmatic attention paid to the prevention of this disorder (54). Although 48 states have legalized gambling and gambling continues to spread rapidly in the country as a whole, only 13 states devote any funds to prevention and treatment. There is no federal contribution, and no national policy on gambling problems.

Some attempts at prevention have been made through public education (e.g., posting signs in casinos) and the establishment of toll-free referral numbers. However, the shortage of treatment resources and the long waiting lists at many clinics hamper efforts to connect individuals and families in need with professional help. As of 1993, there were only about 100 treatment programs for pathological gambling in the United States compared with more than 13,000 for alcoholism (54). Until the public and policymakers become aware of the seriousness of this illness and are willing to devote resources to research, prevention, and treatment, millions of Americans will continue to suffer from its effects without societal recognition or help.

References

1. Fleming AM. Something for nothing: a history of gambling. New York: Delacorte Press, 1978. Cited by McGurrin MC, ed. Pathological gambling: conceptual, diagnostic, and treatment issues. Sarasota: Professional Resource Press, 1992.
2. Clotfelter CT, Cook PJ. Selling hope: state lotteries in America. Cambridge, MA: Harvard University Press, 1989.
3. Hertzberg L. Leon Modena, Renaissance rabbi. 1571–1648. Harvard Magazine 1985(Sept–Oct):41–43.
4. Dostoyevsky F; Coulson J, trans. The gambler/bobok/a nasty story. New York: Penguin Books, 1966:7–16.
5. Freud S. Dostoyevsky and parricide. In: Collected Papers. Vol. III. London: Hogarth Press, 1928.
6. Rosenthal RJ. The psychodynamics of pathological gambling: a review of the literature. In: Galski T, ed. The handbook of pathological gambling. Springfield, IL: Charles C Thomas, 1987.
7. Custer R, Milt H. When luck runs out: help for compulsive gamblers and their families. New York: Facts On File Publications, 1985.
8. Christiansen EM. The 1992 gross annual wagering of the United States: Parts I and II. International Gaming and Wagering Business Part I 1993;14(7):12–33; Part II 1993;14(8):12–30.
9. Volberg RA. Prevalence studies of problem gambling in the United States. J Gambl Stud 1996;12(2):111–128.
10. American Psychiatric Association. Diagnostic and statistical manual of mental disorders. 4th ed. Washington, DC: American Psychiatric Association, 1994.
11. Fisher S, Griffiths M. Current trends in slot machine gambling: research and policy issues. J Gambl Stud 1995;11(3):239–247.
12. Fisher S. Measuring pathological gambling in children: the case of fruit machines in the U.K. J Gambl Stud 1992;8(3):263–285.
13. Blaszczynski A, Winter SW, McConaghy N. Plasma endorphin levels in pathological gambling. J Gambl Behav 1986;2:3–14.
14. American Psychiatric Association. Diagnostic and statistical manual of mental disorders. 3rd ed. Washington, DC: American Psychiatric Association, 1980.
15. Rosenthal RJ, Lesieur HR. Withdrawal symptoms and pathological gambling. Paper presented at the International Conference on Gambling and Risk Taking. London, 1990.
16. Lesieur HR, Blume SB. When lady luck loses: women and compulsive gambling. In: Van Den Bergh N, ed. Feminist perspectives on addictions. New York: Springer-Verlag, 1991: 181–197.
17. Lesieur HR. The chase: career of the compulsive gambler. Cambridge, MA: Schenkman, 1984.
18. Rosenthal RJ, Lorenz VC. The pathological gambler as criminal offender: comments on evaluation and treatment. Clinical Forensic Psychiatry 1992;15(3):647–660.
19. Lesieur HR, Rosenthal RJ. Pathological gambling: a review of the literature (prepared for the American Psychiatric Association Task Force on DSM-IV Committee on Disorders of Impulse Control Not Elsewhere Classified). J Gambl Stud 1991;7(1):5–39.
20. Volberg RA. The prevalence and demographics of pathological gamblers: implications for public health. Am J Public Health 1994;84(2): 237–241.
21. Lesieur HR, Blume SB. Pathological gambling, eating disorders, and the psychoactive substance use disorders. J Addict Dis 1993;12(3):89–92.
22. Lesieur RH, Blume SB, Zoppa RM. Alcoholism, drug abuse and gambling. Alcohol Clin Exp Res 1986;10(1):33–38.
23. Lesieur HR, Heineman M. Pathological gambling among youthful multiple substance abusers in a therapeutic community. Br J Addict 1988;83:765–771.
24. Steinberg MA, Kosten TA, Rounsaville BJ. Cocaine abuse and pathological gambling. Am J Addict 1992;1(2):121–132.
25. Carlton P, Goldstein L. Physiological determinants of pathological gambling. In: Galski T, ed. The handbook of pathological gambling. Springfield, IL: Charles C Thomas, 1987.
26. Lesieur HR, Blume SB. Characteristics of pathological gamblers identified among patients on a psychiatric admissions service. Hosp Community Psychiatry 1990;41(9):1009–1012.
27. Chen MB, Wong MA, Lee N, Chan-Ho MW, Lau J, Fung M. The Shatin community mental health survey in Hong Kong. Arch Gen Psychiatry 1993;50:125–133.
28. Blume SB. Compulsive gambling and the medical model. J Gambl Behav 1988;3:237–247.
29. Jacobs DF. Evidence for a common dissociative-like reaction among addicts. J Gambl Behav 1988;4(1):27–37.
30. Roy A, Adinoff B, Roehrick L, et al. Pathological gambling: a psychobiological study. Arch Gen Psychiatry 1988;45:369–373.
31. Roy A, DeJong J, Linnoila M. Extraversion in pathological gamblers, correlates with indices of noradrenergic function. Arch Gen Psychiatry 1989;46:679–681.
32. Goldstein L, Manowitz P, Nora R, Swartzburg M, Carlton PL. Differential EEG activation and pathological gambling. Biol Psychiatry 1985; 20:1232–1234.
33. McCormick RA, Taber JI. The pathological gambler: salient personality variables. In: Galski, T, ed. The handbook of pathological gambling. Springfield, IL: Charles C Thomas, 1987:9–40.
34. Rosecrance J. Attributions and the origins of problem gambling. Sociological Q 1986;27: 463–477.
35. Linden RD. Pathological gambling and major affective disorder: preliminary findings. J Clin Psychiatry 1985;47:201–203.
36. Jacobs DF, Marston AR, Singer RD, et al. Children of problem gamblers. J Gambl Behav 1989; 5(4):261–268.
37. Lesieur HR, Rothschild J. Children of Gamblers Anonymous members. J Gambl Behav 1989; 5(4):269–281.
38. Blume SB. Pathological gambling and switching addictions: report of a case. J Gambl Stud 1994;10(1):87–96.
39. Lesieur HR, Blume SB. The South Oaks gambling screen (SOGS): a new instrument for the identification of pathological gamblers. Am J Psychiatry 1987;144(9):1184–1188.
40. Lesieur HR, Blume SB. Revising the South Oaks gambling screen in different settings. J Gambl Behav 1992;9(3):213–219.
41. Lesieur HR. Pathological gambling, work, and employee assistance. J Empl Assistance Professionals Assoc 1992;1(1):32–62.
42. Lesieur HR. Experience of employee assistance programs with pathological gamblers. J Drug Issues 1989;19(4):425–436.
43. Blume SB. Treatment for the addictions: alcoholism, drug dependence and compulsive gambling in a psychiatric setting. J Subst Abuse Treat 1986;3:131–133.
44. Blume SB. Treatment for the addictions in a psychiatric setting. Br J Addict 1989;84: 727–729.
45. Heineman M. Losing your shirt. Minneapolis: CompCare Publishers, 1992.

46. Browne BR. The selective adaptation of the Alcoholics Anonymous program by Gamblers Anonymous. J Gambl Behav 1991;7(3):187–206.

47. Gamblers Anonymous. Sharing recovery through Gamblers Anonymous. Los Angeles, CA: Gamblers Anonymous Publications, 1984.

48. Taber JI, McCormick RA. The pathological gambler in treatment. In: Galski T, ed. The handbook of pathological gambling. Springfield, IL, Charles C Thomas, 1987:137–168.

49. Taber JI, McCormick RA, Russo AM, Adkins BJ, Ramirez LF. Follow-up of pathological gamblers after treatment. Am J Psychiatry 1987; 144:757–761.

50. Russo AM, Taber JI, McCormick RA, et al. An outcome study of an inpatient treatment program for pathological gamblers. Hosp Community Psychiatry 1984;35:823–827.

51. Lesieur HR, Blume SB. Evaluation of patients treated for pathological gambling in a combined alcohol, substance abuse and pathological gambling treatment unit using the addiction severity index. Br J Addict 1991;86:1017–1028.

52. Lesieur HR, Blume SB. Modifying, the addiction severity index for use with pathological gamblers. Am J Addict 1992;1(3):240–247.

53. Politzer RM, Morrow JS, Leavey SB. Report on the cost-benefit/effectiveness of treatment at the Johns Hopkins Center for Pathological Gambling. J Gambl Behav 1985;1:131–142.

54. The need for a national policy on problem and pathological gambling in America. New York: National Council on Problem Gambling, November 1, 1993.

30   SECTS AND CULTS

David A. Halperin

The interface between drugs and religious activity predates recorded history. Within this realm of interactions, one sees not only drugs used as an aspect of religious activity but also religion practiced as if it were a drug. This chapter deals with both facets of this interaction. Of particular interest within our modern society has been the transformation of mainstream individuals (primarily youth and young adults) into cult members who are described by their parents and associates as "drugged" or "spaced out." And, the reality that the extent of their commitment such as that shown at Jonestown, within the confines of the meeting houses of the Order of the Solar Temple, or as members of Aum Shinrkyu was so exaggerated that intelligent, superficially intact individuals were able to commit murder and suicide without apparent compunction or compassion, as if they were under the influence of a mind altering substance. An example of the powerful impact of cultism on the individual is illustrative of the manner in which cult affiliation parallels in its effect and intensity the mind-altering substance.

THE CULT AS DRUG

Alison was the oldest daughter of a middle class family of professionals. Her father was an academic. During his pursuit of tenure, the family was forced to move to a number of campuses, often in relatively remote and unsophisticated locations. Throughout her childhood, Alison seemed to have the sense of being the disfavored sibling. She always pointed to her parent's "preferential" treatment of her younger siblings, particularly her sister, Jacqueline. She pointed to her younger sister's having attended a boarding preparatory school as evidence of her parents obvious if unstated preference. Nonetheless, Alison did well in school and was admitted to a prestigious college in the New York area. During her freshman year, she appeared to become depressed. Her parents attributed her depression to separation from home and the normative anxiety attendant on being a college freshman subject to a more competitive educational environment. Her mother contacted the college's student mental health center, which provided a list of mental health professionals who were considered particularly attuned to the needs of adolescents. Alison was then referred for psychotherapy. Unknown to both college and parents, Alison's therapist, Dr. Q, was a member of a psychoanalytic group that had become a psychoanalytic cult, the Sullivanian Institute Fourth Wall Theater.

The history of the Sullivanian Institute Fourth Wall Theater is a fascinating reflection of both the history of the psychoanalytic movement and its interaction with the prevailing culture. Harry Stack Sullivan was a significant figure in the growth and development of the psychoanalytic movement in the United States. His work (unfortunately obscured by his own neologisms, which have not become part of the mainstream parlance of psychoanalysis) focussed on careful observation and the interpersonal aspect of the therapist-patient dyad. However, like many other facets of American professional culture during the 1960s, some significant change in terms of a fusion of traditional approaches and a heightened consciousness of the changing world was considered de rigeur. It was during this "Greening of America" that Saul Newton, the registrar of the William Alanson White Institute (the New York branch of Sullivan's Washington Institute of Psychoanalysis) and a psychoanalyst at the Institute, Janet Pearce, wrote the book *The Conditions of Human Growth*. This book fused the apocalyptic thinking common to that era with a "psychoanalytic" perspective (1). The Sullivanian Institute was formed to propagate their ideas and to train psychoanalysts at the dawn of this new departure in human history (2). The Sullivanian Institute differed from more conventional institutes in a number of significant ways. Psychoanalysts and patients would interact on a social basis. The leader, Saul Newton, reputedly interacted with both patients and supervisors on a very intimate basis. Therapists and patients would spend their vacations together initially at Amagansett and later at Accord in the Catskills. Moreover, patients would live together in a commune-like setting. An aspect of the Sullivanian Institute that garnered it particular publicity and notoriety was the practice of encouraging members to schedule periods of sexual activity among one another, to break down the "artificiality" of conventional sexual mores. Another destructive aspect of the Sullivanian Institute was its view of the nuclear family as being the fountainhead of all evil. Members were ordered to raise their children in a communal setting and severely criticized for taking an individual interest in their own children. Since the family of origin was viewed as the site of all pathology, members were encouraged by their psychoanalysts to terminate all contact with their family. Members would visit their family, however, to collect artifacts associated with their childhood and to solicit for funds. Family members, specifically parents, would receive a letter announcing that their child would no longer be in contact with them and would prosecute them if they attempted to contact them. The sense of loss among family members who were totally disowned by their children is difficult to exaggerate. Individuals within the Sullivanian Institute were encouraged to socialize only with fellow members, to devote all their income to paying for their "psychoanalysis" and to live their lives according to paths directed by their therapist and the overall Stalinesque figure of Saul Newton. In a very real sense, the Institute provided an anodyne in which individuals were discouraged from developing any sense of autonomy. Within the course of their "psychoanalysis" all initiates were encouraged to place their difficulties and the very course of their lives at the feet of their "omniscient" analysts. The Sullivanian Institute treated psychoanalysis as a soma—a drug—to wash out the sin of individual autonomy, relabelled narcissism (2, 3).

After her entry into treatment with Dr. Q, Alison's therapy conformed to the Sullivanian norm. Initially, she continued to stay in contact with her family; however, she gradually began to approach her family with an increasingly cynical perspective. Her interactions became increasingly routinized and infrequent, losing the spontaneity and informality which had previously characterized their interactions. Finally, the contact ceased entirely, and Alison's parents received the expected letter whose arrival they dreaded. In the years that followed, Alison's life became a mystery. Occasionally, Alison would contact them to solicit money for a group project. Or, the family would be contacted by a group defector, one of whom informed them that they were grandparents. Alison did not attend her father's funeral. Alison's mother entered therapy to deal with her daughter's status as "nearly dead," alive but unreachable. The mother's treatment focussed on supporting her in her efforts to contact a daughter who never answered her letters or returned her calls. Ex-members assured parents that these efforts at communication were important because despite their children's "drugged" states the very persistence of the parents' efforts reenforced their children's awareness that a world existed outside the cult. In addition, the mother's therapy focussed on her profound sense of guilt at her daughter's cult affiliation. Had her problems so afffected her daughter that she was forced into the cult? And had the mother not been the person who found Dr. Q? An additional factor that troubled her mother was the extent of her daughter's psychopathology and to what degree this had lead to Alison's continued cult affiliation. The experience of working with other cult members unfortunately emphasizes that cult affiliation is not necessarily the product of a specific diagnostic paradigm. Nonetheless, cult members such as Alison appear to be quite dysphoric individuals who are often profoundly affected by the experience of separation from their family. Alison conformed to this model: her dysphoria attendant on separation is suggestive of a borderline personality disorder. With supportive psychotherapy tempered with compassion for her profound concern for an unavailable child, Alison's mother's chronic depression lifted. Her sense of empowerment was increased by the formation of a support group, Parents Against Cult Therapy, of parents of children who were within the cult group. Over time, the parents' efforts increased publicity about the group's activities and heightened pressure against its leaders. In this regard, the experience of Alison's mother resembles that of other parents and professionals who have joined self-help groups and scholarly organizations such as the American Family Foundation.

The support Alison's mother received enabled her later to be of great assistance when Alison ultimately left the group. Alison had given birth to a daughter; when the child was six months old, the group decided that Alison was too "enmeshed" with her daughter, and that she should no longer have any contact with her baby. This deprivation helped Alison decided to leave. She "kidnapped" her child, went underground, and contacted her mother. Reconciliation followed. Unfortunately, not every individual is able to leave cult groups so easily. Many individuals require intense follow-up because of post-cult symptomatology, which includes severe depression, anxiety, fear of retaliation or pursuit by the cult group, and periods of dissociation including the "snapping" phenomenon, which have been regarded as symptomatic of Atypical Dissociative Disorder. For these individuals, residential treatment centers such as WellSpring (4, 5) or a period of therapy with therapists familiar with post-cult symptomatology may be very useful. The importance of follow-up for cult affiliation parallels the need for follow-up with former substance abusers. It is of interest that with the death of Saul Newton and increasing publicity about the group's increasingly bizarre isolation from the outside world, it imploded (6, 7).

Pharmacologically active substances are not the only mind altering agents. Alison's history illustrates the profoundly destructive potential of group pressures, group processes, control over sources of information, restriction on outside contacts, and continual resort to a few psychoanalytic phrases as mantras to control individual awareness as well as the use of medication itself (8). In a profound sense, the Sullivanian Institute acted as a drug by limiting Alison's ability to participate in the world and by altering in a most profound manner the character and content of her encounters with others. If her history illustrates the cult as drug, an examination of the use of drugs within cults is also pertinent.

DRUG USE WITHIN CULTS

The earliest cultures encountered by anthropologists used a variety of mind-altering substances as part of their religious activity. The use of peyote within the Native American Church described by Preston and Hammerschlag (9) is representative. Within the rites and rituals of the Native American Church, the ingestion of peyote is a fundamental sacrament accompanied by lengthy preparations of purification and introspection; it is used within a rigidly proscribed pattern with the anticipation of a significant and transcendent experience for the initiate. Such a preparation for the use of a drug precludes its use for promiscuous purposes. In this context, the initiate regards the use of peyote as an aspect of a spiritual odyssey without any sense of being involved in a secular hedonistic activity; it is a preparation for growth. Reports of shamanic activity within a wide variety of other cultures such as the Inuit emphasize that the substance in question is regarded with the sanctity accorded other sacraments within "civilized" society and as an aid in a spiritual quest. It is in recognition of this structure that recent United States judicial decisions have protected and reaffirmed the right to use peyote during religious ceremonies. Many pre-Columbian American cultures used a wide variety of substances (e.g., mescaline and yohimbine) for religious and shamanic rituals. Indeed, Aldous Huxley's provocative essay "The Doors of Perception" (1963) popularized the use of peyote and mescaline as a pharmacological aid in producing the transcendent experience within the broader society. But the use of substances within religious ritual has not been restricted to nonliterate cultures. The parallelism between these nonliterate societies and other cultures are striking and foreshadows the national experience during the "Decade of Love."

In classical Greece, the use of ergot derivatives appears to have been a significant aspect of the rituals performed within the Eleusinian mysteries; as poets noted "I have seen the truth within the kernel of wheat." It is likely that the actual agent involved was an ergot derivative. In this regard, the Eleusinian mysteries present a parallelism to the more modern use made in the 1960s of LSD, a purified ergot derivative celebrated by figures as diverse as the late Timothy Leary and the Beatles. Such phenomena were portrayed on a more enigmatic level by Stephen King in "The Children of the Corn," a story of regressive savagery fueled by adepts using ergot derivatives. However, drug use was and is not restricted to such relatively marginal cultures. The ceremony of Havdalah—Division—which marks the end of the Jewish Sabbath is marked by smelling nutmeg—Basamim/spices—which are said to be a foretaste of the holiness that has been exemplified by the peace of the Sabbath.

The 1960s were characterized by an extraordinary efflorescence of interest in the cultic and the occult and by the popularization of drug use within mainstream American society. As the "Greening of America" proceeded apace, the use of mind-altering substances other than alcohol, caffeine, or nicotine were no longer confined to the marginal, the disenfranchised, or the ethnic minorities. There was an increasing confluence of interest in the transcendent religious experience and substance abuse. This confluence was anticipated by a comparable period of rapid social and intellectual change in nineteenth century France. One has only to read Rimbaud in his manifesto written to his former mentor:

Right now, I'm depraving myself as much as I can. Why? I want to be a poet, and I am working at making myself a visionary: you won't understand all, and I'm not even sure I can explain it to you. The problem is to attain the unknown by disorganizing all the senses. The suffering is immense, but you have to be strong, and to have been born a poet. And I have realized that I am a poet. . . . (10, p. 71)

These ideas were developed at greater length when he refers to:

A poet makes himself a visionary through a long, boundless, and systematized disorganization of all senses. (10, p. 72)

However, while Rimbaud is both an avatar and precursor of the alienated and isolated adolescent that became such a stock figure in that tumultuous decade, he was by no means unique. Coleridge's Xanadu was apocryphally created during an opium reverie. Thomas de Quincey's *Memoirs of an Opium Eater* (11, 12) was both a warning and enticement to generations of British Romantics. Baudelaire, also, referred to his use of hashish and opium. In a very real sense, Rimbaud only plowed a prepared ground with his extraordinary adolescent intensity. Even less manic figures such as Flaubert referred to the use of substances. And within the English culture, so noteworthy a protector of the innocent, Sherlock Holmes, was reputed to use cocaine. Within the "religious" framework, a figure such as Alaister Crowley, the self-professed Beast of the Book of Revelation (he would sign his letters with the 666), linked an interest in occult religiosity and substance abuse. William Butler Yeats, who was briefly a follower of Crowley and a member of the Order of the Golden Dawn, dabbled in the use of opium during his early, less-focussed period. There was ample precedent for the Beatles' dual embrace of Transcendental Meditation and LSD, in which the group members both experimented with and promoted the use of hallucinogens as providing a readily accessible transcendental experience—an ostensibly pain free mysticism in which the consumer could readily unlock the secrets of the Absolute. Aldous Huxley spoke from an aristocratic English background. His espousal of Vedanta and mescaline came in the context of his general skepticism about the positive aspects (if any) of mass culture. In contrast, the Beatles, in their embrace of mass culture, disdained elitism and proclaimed the desirability of enlightening the masses as opposed to restricting the benefits of the transcendental to an educated elite. In a characteristic literary work of that era, Tom Wolfe's *Electric Kool-Aid Acid Test,* characters routinely use mind-altering substances without any apparent appreciation of their darker potential. Nor was there any appreciation that drug use, in and of itself, may encourage cult affiliation.

The relationship of cults and drug use is marked by paradox. As Deutsch (13) noted:

All but three of the subjects had made at least moderate use of LSD and other hallucinogens prior to meeting Baba. These drug users saw their psychedelic experiences as influential or even essential in their embrace of Hinduism and Baba. The notion of this influence is commonplace among American followers of Eastern religions; Baba himself referred to the psychedelic experience as a "preview of coming attractions." The trips that the devotees believed had influenced their conversion typically had a "mystical" content such as experiences of unity with others or the cosmos, and revelations of universal love along with sensations of utter certainty and intense elation. At least two subjects had sensations of being God associated with their elation. . . ."

The small cult group described by Deutsch reflects the pursuit of Freud's "oceanic feeling" that was so characteristic of the Decade of Love. The darker potential of this pursuit of the Total was presented in the Charles Manson family. Manson recruited his followers within the naive and idealistic culture of San Francisco during the "summer of love." His theology, a complex blend of apocalyptic fantasy and Satanism, appealed to a members of the alienated and isolated psychedelic subculture that effloresced in that era diligently nurtured by an abundance of mind altering drugs. The cults seemed to offer a "philosophical" parallel to drugs because both cults and drugs promised an immediacy and a certainty in their quest of the transcendent. In neither the cult nor the drug experience is there room for doubt or hesitation—in both consumption of theology and consumption of the mind-altering substance are seen alike as promising a guarantee of transcendence. Drugs inevitably yield a sense of disappointment. The promise of transcendence is never quite realized, or even if realized initially, is never repeated with quite the same impact. Moreover, the social and economic aspects of the drug culture inevitably take their toll, leaving many individuals searching for a means of reaching transcendence without engaging in obviously self-destructive behavior. It is in this context that many cult groups offer themselves to the vulnerable individuals as a quasi therapeutic environment in which transcendence and a sense of community will enable the individual to deal with their problems in the area of substance abuse.

CULTS AND DRUGS: THE THERAPEUTIC DIMENSION?

That intense religious or quasi religious group experiences may enable the individual to deal with substance abuse has been well recognized for many years. In groups as diverse as Alcoholics Anonymous or many fundamentalist Protestant denominations, there is the appropriate recognition that the substance abuser often requires a strong sense of support to deal successfully with substance abuse (6). The reliance on intense quasi religious feelings as part of a treatment program for substance abuse has not been limited to alcoholism, although Alcoholics Anonymous is the most prominent and is the prototype of the self-help, 12-step recovery movement. All 12-step programs emphasize the importance of a belief in "God as we understand him" as a major factor in enabling the substance abuser to achieve sobriety or to end substance abuse. The importance of this emphasis on the role of God's intervention to enable the abuser to end his or her abuse has been and remains controversial. However, its presence underlies the reality that the chronic substance abuser has often grown up within a chaotic and unstructured environment—that substance abuse occurs within a context marked by the absence of those essential continuities that everyone requires. The immanence of divine intervention provides this sense of continuity, which is such a significant aspect of all human interaction and often so woefully absent from the substance abuser's life.

A sense of continuity can also be provided by intense commitment to a community or group. This aspect of group commitment has been exploited by cult groups offering themselves to vulnerable individuals as a quasi therapeutic environment in which abstinence is reenforced by a reliance on the theological guidance of the cult leader. This aspect of cult appeal has been noted in many groups; it is exemplified by the Reverend Jim Jones, who emphasized that his organization, the People's Temple, could cure substance abuse. (Apocryphally, the physician who ultimately mixed the Kool-Aid at Jonestown was a former substance abuser whom Jones assisted to stop his drug abuse and become a physician.) The People's Temple was not unique; other drug treatment groups state that their treatment of narcotics addiction reflects the approaches and teachings of their founders.

Intense emotional commitment is a significant aspect of many drug treatment programs. There has been continuing concern over the potential for drug treatment and rehabilitation programs to transmute into a species of cult. Rebhun (14) commented on this potential for cultic evolution in referring to the

paraprofessional ex-addict staffed drug program models that have emerged since the 1950s with the founding of Synanon. Some of the main characteristics in these types of programs include the use of a "second-chance family" or "communitas" treatment structure, the presence of a charismatic leader (who is usually an ex-addict) and the use of encounter or confrontation types of treatment modalities. The roles contained within these programs rely heavily upon the use of "charismatic experience" and a shared but highly structured milieu experience of members as the basis for the helping process. (p. 187)

Synanon was founded by a charismatic ex-addict, Charles Diedrich. Originally, a residential treatment center focussed on substance abuse, it expanded in a "utopian" community with grandiose claims for healing all matter of illness. Ultimately, members were tried and convicted of attempting to murder "heretics" (15, 16). Synanon was not unique. The history of residential drug treatment centers includes other organizations initially formed on the basis of an intense commitment to a charismatic leader mutated into hierarchical, authoritarian organizations. The experience of Odyssey House, whose members reportedly burnt candles at the feet of the group's leader "as a sign of respect," provides another illustration of a "mainstream" program being transformed into a quasi cult-like organization (6). Eventually, Odyssey House was transformed by the members and associated professionals because they found it impossible to function in providing responsible and meaningful service. It is not surprising that these organizations undergo this destructive change. The difficulty in surmounting chronic substance abuse, in members and staff alike, may lead to a search for magical, transcendent solutions to what appear to be intractable problems. In their search, a false resolution to these problems may be fashioned on the basis of fusion with an authoritarian, charismatic leader who promises to provide the continuity, structure, and control that is otherwise lacking. Even when the organization does not undergo a cultic transformation, the difficulty that recovered substance abusers appear to experience upon leaving the therapeutic community and in becoming independent members of society who are able to function autonomously in non–drug-related areas is a testimonial to the intensity of the feelings mobilized within these groups.

SUMMARY

The relationship between mind-altering chemical substances and intense religious feeling predates civilization. Even in nonliterate societies there is a confluence of religious practice and the use of mind-altering substances. More recently, intense drug use has provided an entry path into cultic groups because such groups function like drugs that enable vulnerable individuals to transcend their alienation, isolation, and discontinuity. Conversely, groups formed to help substance abusers recover may transform themselves into quasi cultic organizations because of the members' object-hunger and need for structure, support, and charismatic leadership to provide sustenance.

References

1. Pearce J, Newton S. Conditions of human growth. New York: Citadel, 1963.
2. Halperin D. The dark underside: cultic misappropriation of psychiatry and psychoanalysis. Cultic Studies Journal 1993;10:1:33–45.
3. Siskind AB. The Sullivanian Institute/Fourth Wall community: radical psychotherapy as quasi religion. In: Robbins T, Grail A, eds. Between sacred and secular. Greenwich, CT: JAI Press, 1994.
4. Martin PR. Post cult recovery. Assessment and rehabilitation. In: Langone M, ed. Recovery from cults. New York: WW Norton, 1993: 203–231.
5. Martin PR. Description of WellSpring. In: Singer M, ed. Cults in our midst. San Francisco. Jossey-Bass, 1996:290.
6. Halperin D, Markowitz A. Residential treatment: the potential for cultic evolution. Cultic Studies Journal 1991;8:1:46–61.
7. Hoban P. Psycho drama. The chilling story of how the Sullivanian Cult turned a utopian dream into a nightmare. New Yorker, June 19, 1989.
8. Halperin D. Group processes in cult recruitment and affiliation. In: Halperin DA, ed. Psychodynamic perspectives on religion, sect and cult. Littleton, MA: James Wright-PSG, 1983.
9. Preston R, Hammerschlag C. The Native American Church. In: Halperin DA, ed. Psychodynamic perspectives on religion, sect and cult. Littleton, MA: James Wright-PSG, 1983:93–105.
10. Halperin D. Artur Rimbaud: the poet as adolescent. Adolesc Psychiatry 1985;15:70–85.
11. Baudelaire C; Steueble-Lipman Wulf, ed. Un mangeur d'opium/Charles Baudelaire avec le texte parallele de Confessions of an English Opium Eater et des Suspira de profundis de Thomas de Quincey. Neuchatel: Payot, 1976.
12. De Quincey T. Confessions of an English opium eater. New York: AL Burt, 1856.
13. Deutsch A. Psychiatric perspectives on an Eastern-style cult. In: Halperin DA, ed. Psychodynamic perspectives on religion, sect and cult. Littleton, MA: James Wright-PSG, 1983.
14. Rebhun J. The drug rehabilitation program: cults in formation? In: Halperin DA, ed. Psychodynamic perspectives on religion, sect and cult. Littleton, MA: James Wright-PSG, 1983.
15. Ofshe R. The social development of the Synanon cult: the managerial strategy of organizational transformation. Sociological Analysis 1980;441(2):109–127.
16. Mitchell D, Mitchell C, Ofshe R. The light on Synanon: how a country newspaper exposed a corporate cult. New York: Seaview, 1982.

31 SEXUAL ADDICTION
Aviel Goodman

TERMINOLOGY: COMPULSION, IMPULSIVITY, OR ADDICTION?

Over one hundred years ago, Krafft-Ebbing described a condition in which a person's sexual appetite is abnormally increased

> to such an extent that it permeates all his thoughts and feelings, allowing of no other aims in life, tumultuously, and in a rut-like fashion demanding gratification without granting the possibility of moral and righteous counter-presentations, and resolving itself into an impulsive, insatiable succession of sexual enjoyments. . . . This pathological sexuality is a dreadful scourge for its victim, for he is in constant danger of violating the laws of the state and of morality, of losing his honor, his freedom and even his life. (1, pp. 70–71).

Most clinicians agree that what Krafft-Ebbing described as pathological sexuality does exist in the form of paraphilias and syndromes of similarly driven nonparaphilic sexual behavior. Questions remain, however, about how this condition should be classified: as an obsessive-compulsive disorder (2–8), as an impulse-control disorder (9, 10), or as an addictive disorder (11–16).

Obsessive-Compulsive Disorder

Arguments in favor of classifying this syndrome of sexual behavior as a form of obsessive-compulsive disorder (OCD) emphasize the defensive function of the sexual activity, how it operates to reduce anxiety and other painful affects. Proponents of these arguments further note that when sexual activity is blocked, individuals who suffer from this condition experience discomfort (7, 8). Compulsions, however, are defined in DSM-IV as "repetitive behaviors (e.g., hand washing, ordering, checking) or mental acts (e.g., praying, counting, repeating words silently) the goal of which is to reduce anxiety or distress, not to provide pleasure or gratification" (17, p. 418). In most cases, compulsive behaviors are intended to prevent a dreaded event or to reduce distress, and patients do not experience them as pleasurable. The sexual behavior in this syndrome, meanwhile, is rarely intended consciously to prevent a dreaded event; and, while reduction of distress contributes to motivation to engage in the sexual behavior, pleasure or gratification also contributes significantly. Moreover, most of the symptomatic behaviors in the sexual syndrome are more complex and less stereotyped than are typical compulsive behaviors; and, during their enactment, they are more often ego-syntonic (that is, accepted by the subject as consistent with his or her sense of self). "Compulsion," as it is defined in DSM-IV, thus does not seem to be an appropriate designation for the sexual behavior that characterizes this syndrome.

Additional evidence against classifying this syndrome as a compulsive disorder emerged from studies that assessed response to treatment with antidepressant medications. A study by Kafka (18) found no significant difference between the response of paraphilic symptoms to imipramine and their response to fluoxetine, while another study by Kruesi and his colleagues (19) found no significant difference between the response of paraphilic symptoms to desipramine and their response to clomipramine. This pattern of similar response to serotonergic and noradrenergic antidepressants resembles the response pattern that is typically observed in depression, but differs from the response pattern that is typically observed in OCD. The symptoms of OCD typically respond significantly more strongly to fluoxetine or clomipramine than they do to tricyclic antidepressants; and they respond particularly poorly to desipramine, which has relatively little serotonergic activity. The study by Kruesi's group (19) also noted a placebo response rate of 17%, while placebo response in adults with OCD is rare. Meanwhile, Stein and his colleagues (20) observed that serotonin reuptake blockers were helpful in treating paraphilias and "sexual addictions," but in a less robust and specific way than they were helpful in treating sexual obsessions or compulsions that occurred in OCD. Stein's group, moreover, found that the sexual symptoms of patients with these conditions and comorbid depression improved when their mood improved, while those of patients with these conditions and comorbid OCD often did not improve when their OCD improved. These findings suggest that, while this sexual syndrome could be related to OCD, it is unlikely to be a form of OCD.

Impulse-Control Disorder

Barth and Kinder (9) argued that this sexual syndrome should be designated "sexual impulsivity," since it met the diagnostic criteria for atypical impulse control disorder in the then-current DSM-III. DSM-IV includes the following description of impulse-control disorders:

> The essential feature of Impulse-Control Disorders is the failure to resist an impulse, drive, or temptation to perform an act that is harmful to the person or to others. For most of the disorders in this section, the individual feels an increasing sense of tension or arousal before committing the act and then experiences pleasure, gratification, or relief at the time of committing the act. Following the act there may or may not be regret, self-reproach, or guilt. (17, p. 609)

The DSM description of impulse-control disorder does indeed seem to accurately characterize this sexual syndrome. At the same time, it seems to characterize substance dependence equally well. If substance dependence, which is readily acknowledged to be an addictive disorder, is also an impulse-control disorder, then a condition that meets the diagnostic criteria for impulse-control disorder is not thereby precluded from classification also as an addictive disorder.

Addictive Disorder

What, then, is the difference between impulse-control disorder and addictive disorder? This question can be answered only if a behaviorally nonspecific definition of addictive disorder is available. The definition of addiction is itself a matter of controversy, and DSM-IV does not employ the term at all. A provisional set of diagnostic criteria for addictive disorder can, however, be derived from the DSM-IV criteria for substance dependence, the prototypal addictive disorder, by replacing the specific terms *substance* and *substance use* with the nonspecific term *behavior,* and by replacing "characteristic withdrawal syndrome for the substance" with a general definition of withdrawal that applies to all categories of behavior. Table 31.1 lists Goodman's (21) proposed set of behaviorally nonspecific diagnostic criteria for addictive disorder. This set of diagnostic criteria for addictive disorder is provisional and, like the sets of diagnostic criteria in the DSM series, it may need to be revised in the light of further developments in scientific research or theory. The important point is that behaviorally nonspecific diagnostic criteria for addictive disorder can be formulated that are consistent with the form and content of DSM-IV, are expressed in the same descriptive language, and are no less reliable and valid than are the DSM-IV diagnostic criteria for substance dependence. Goodman (21, 22) also proposed a simple definition of addiction, which facilitates preliminary diagnosis of an addictive disorder. Addiction was defined as a condition in which a behavior that can function both to produce pleasure and to reduce painful affects is employed in a pattern that is characterized by two key features: (a) recurrent failure to control the behavior, and (b) continuation of the behavior despite significant harmful consequences. "Recurrent failure to control" was noted to mean not that addicted individuals invariably lose control when they engage in the behavior, but that their predictions that they would remain in control of the behavior have repeatedly proved to be unreliable.

The relationship between addictive disorder and impulse-control disorder can now be elucidated, along with the relationship between addictive disorder and OCD. All three types of disorder involve difficult-to-resist drives to engage in overt behaviors that entail consequences that are harmful or unpleasant for the individual. The primary function of impulsive behavior is to produce pleasure or gratification: in terms of learning theory, it is motivated primarily by positive reinforcement. Meanwhile, the primary function of compulsive behavior is to reduce anxiety or other painful affects: in terms of learning theory, it is motivated primarily by negative reinforcement. Finally, addictive behavior functions both to produce pleasure and to reduce painful affects: it is motivated by positive reinforcement and by negative reinforcement. Addictive behavior thus shares core characteristics with both impulsive behavior and compulsive behavior.

The foregoing discussion leads us to conclude that "sexual addiction" is the most appropriate designation for the syndrome of sexual behavior that we are considering. Grouping this syndrome with the substance addictions is further supported by their phenomenological similarities. Orford (23) observed that patients' descriptions of their subjective experience of the sexual behavior syndrome are qualitatively similar to patients' descriptions of their experience of drug addiction. Goodman (21) expanded on Orford's observation and noted a number of other characteristic features that are shared by sexual addiction and substance addiction. These characteristic features include: (a) characteristic course—the disorder typically begins in adolescence or early adulthood and follows a chronic course with remissions and exacerbations; (b) behavioral features—narrowing of behavioral repertoire, continuation of the behavior despite harmful consequences; (c) individuals' subjective experience of the condition—sense of craving, preoccupation, excitement during preparatory activity, mood-altering effects of the behavior, sense of loss of control; (d) progressive development of the condition—craving, loss of control, narrowing of behavioral repertoire, and harmfulness of consequences all tending to increase as the duration of the condition increases; (e) experience of tolerance—as the behavior is repeated, its potency to produce reinforcing effects tends to diminish; (f) experience of withdrawal phenomena—psychological and/or physical discomfort when the behavior is discontinued; (g) tendency to relapse—that is, to return to harmful patterns of behavior after a period of abstinence or control has been achieved; (h) relationship between the condition and other aspects of affected individuals' lives—for example, neglect of other areas of life as the behavior assumes priority; and (i) recurrent themes in the ways individuals with these conditions relate to others and to themselves—including low self-esteem, self-centeredness, denial, rationalization, and conflicts over dependency and control. Significantly, the recognized hallmarks of addiction—experiences of craving, loss of control, tolerance, and withdrawal—characterize sexual addiction as well as substance addiction.

A common objection to the concept of sexual addiction is based on the idea that addiction is properly a physiological condition that must be defined in terms of physiological dependence on a foreign substance and physical withdrawal syndromes that emerge when the substance is no longer administered (9, 24). However, current psychobiological theories of addiction to alcohol and other drugs tend to emphasize the emotional effects that addicts wish to achieve (25) and the activation of centrally coded affect systems (26), rather than unmediated chemical effects or physical withdrawal symptoms. Many investigators of the neurobiology of drug addiction, including Goldstein (27), Jaffe (28), and Miller, Dackis, and Gold (29), agree that tolerance and neuroadaptation can contribute to maintaining or increasing drug use, but are neither necessary nor sufficient for the development of addiction. In agreement with these investigators, the description of substance dependence in DSM-IV includes the sentence, "Neither tolerance nor withdrawal is necessary or sufficient for a diagnosis of Substance Dependence." (p. 178). Furthermore, psychological research has demonstrated that withdrawal in drug addiction is not simply an automatic physiological response to decreased levels of exogenous chemicals, but is a complex process that is shaped significantly by learning (30–40). The objection to the concept of sexual addiction on the grounds that addiction is a physiological condition can be answered also at a philosophical level. According to this objection, the sexual behavior syndrome cannot be an addictive disorder because it is a psychological condition, while addictions are physiological conditions. This argument presupposes a dichotomy between psychological states and physiological states. Meanwhile, contemporary psychiatric and philosophical

---

Table 31.1 Proposed Diagnostic Criteria for Addictive Disorder

A maladaptive pattern of behavior, leading to clinically significant impairment or distress, as manifested by three (or more) of the following, occurring at any time in the same 12-month period:
   (1) tolerance, as defined by either of the following:
      (a) a need for markedly increased amount or intensity of the behavior to achieve the desired effect
      (b) markedly diminished effect with continued involvement in the behavior at the same level of intensity
   (2) withdrawal, as manifested by either of the following:
      (a) characteristic psychophysiological withdrawal syndrome of physiologically described changes and/or psychologically described changes upon discontinuation of the behavior
      (b) the same (or a closely related) behavior is engaged in to relieve or avoid withdrawal symptoms
   (3) the behavior is often engaged in over a longer period, in greater quantity, or at a higher level of intensity than was intended
   (4) there is a persistent desire or unsuccessful efforts to cut down or control the behavior
   (5) a great deal of time is spent in activities necessary to prepare for the behavior, to engage in the behavior, or to recover from its effects
   (6) important social, occupational, or recreational activities are given up or reduced because of the behavior
   (7) the behavior continues despite knowledge of having a persistent or recurrent physical or psychological problem that is likely to have been caused or exacerbated by the behavior

Table from Goodman A. Addictive disorders: an integrated approach. Part one. An integrated understanding. J Min Addict Recovery 1995;2:33–76.

theory affirms an essential unity of psychological and physiological, in which every event that is described in psychological terms is identical with an event that is described in some set of physiological terms (41–44). Thus, to speak of dependence or distress that is psychological but not physiological is not meaningful.

DIAGNOSIS AND EPIDEMIOLOGY

Diagnosis of Sexual Addiction

Diagnostic criteria for sexual addiction can be derived from the behaviorally nonspecific criteria for addictive disorder that were outlined in Table 31.1, by replacing "behavior" with "sexual behavior." A definition of sexual addiction, which facilitates preliminary diagnosis of the disorder, can be similarly derived from the simple definition of addiction by replacing "behavior" with "sexual behavior." Accordingly, sexual addiction is defined as a condition in which some form of sexual behavior that can function both to produce pleasure and to reduce painful affects is employed in a pattern that is characterized by two key features: (a) recurrent failure to control the sexual behavior, and (b) continuation of the sexual behavior despite significant harmful consequences. In sum, sexual addiction is a syndrome in which some form of sexual behavior relates to and affects an individual's life in such a manner as to accord with the simple definition of addiction or to meet the diagnostic criteria for addictive disorder.

Significantly, no form of sexual behavior is in itself defined as sexual addiction. A pattern of sexual behavior is designated sexual addiction, not on the basis of what the behavior is, but on the basis of how the behavior relates to and affects a person's life. Any sexual behavior has the potential to be engaged in addictively, but constitutes an addictive disorder only to the extent that it occurs in a pattern that meets the diagnostic criteria or accords with the definition. Whether a pattern of sexual behavior qualifies as sexual addiction is determined not by the type of behavior, its object, its frequency, or its social acceptability, but by the relationship between this behavior pattern and an individual's life, as indicated in the definition and specified in the diagnostic criteria.

Differential Diagnosis

The paraphilic behavior and hypersexual behavior that characterize sexual addiction can occur also as manifestations of underlying organic pathology, and occasionally are its earliest or most prominent symptoms. Paraphilic or hypersexual behavior can be a symptom of a brain lesion, particularly a lesion in the medial basal-frontal, diencephalic, or septal region. Anomalous sexual behavior can occur also in the context of a seizure disorder, especially in association with temporal lobe epilepsy (45–50). More broadly, any disorder that is associated with an impairment of cerebral functioning can weaken normal inhibitory controls and thereby allow the expression of sexual behaviors that ordinarily are suppressed. Hypersexual behavior can occur also as a side effect of medication, particularly antiparkinsonian agents. Finally, sexually aggressive behavior has been associated with elevated levels of testosterone (51, 52). The differential diagnosis is usually facilitated by the presence of additional symptoms or circumstances that suggest the underlying etiology, although altered sexual behavior may be the earliest manifestation in some cases of brain pathology. Clues that invite an organic evaluation include onset in middle age or later, regression from previously normal sexuality, excessive aggression, report of auras or seizure-like symptoms prior to or during the sexual behavior, abnormal body habitus, and presence of soft neurological signs. Also of value in determining whether a case of paraphilia or hypersexuality represents sexual addiction are the diagnostic criteria for sexual addiction. Tolerance, psychophysiological withdrawal symptoms on discontinuation of the sexual behavior (usually affective discomfort, irritability, or restlessness), and persistent desire to cut down or control the behavior are generally not observed in a paraphilia or hypersexuality that is not part of the sexual addiction syndrome.

Obsessions and compulsions with sexual content can occur in OCD. In contrast with sexual addiction, sexual obsessions and compulsions typically are not accompanied by sexual arousal and do not provide or lead to sexual pleasure (53, 54). Most often, patients experience repugnance and fear of acting on sexual obsessions that occur in OCD (54, 55).

A syndrome that meets the diagnostic criteria for sexual addiction can occur in the context of other psychiatric disorders, including manic-depressive disorder and its variants, schizophrenia, borderline personality disorder, and substance dependence. When the diagnostic criteria for both sexual addiction and another psychiatric disorder are met, both diagnoses are warranted, regardless of whether sexual addiction might be secondary to the other psychiatric disorder. The diagnosis of sexual addiction is a descriptive designation of how a pattern of sexual behavior relates to and affects an individual's life. It does not presume a particular etiology, nor is it precluded by the presence of other conditions that may be etiologically relevant.

Prevalence

Carnes (12) reported that 3–6% of Americans suffer from sexual addiction, and Coleman (5) reported that approximately 5% of the population meet diagnostic criteria for "sexual compulsivity." Neither report indicated how the data were obtained. A literature review at the end of 1995 revealed no further data on the prevalence of sexual addiction.

Gender and Age Features

The majority of individuals who use sexual behavior addictively are men. Gender differences in prevalence are greater for paraphilias than for nonparaphilic sexual addictions. In the majority of cases, onset is prior to age 18 (56, 57). While sexual addiction tends to be a chronic, lifelong disorder, the frequency of addictive sexual behavior typically peaks between the ages of 20 and 30, and then gradually declines.

Comorbidity and Familial Patterns

Researchers have noted significant comorbidity among different forms of sexual addiction; that is, individuals who engage addictively in one form of sexual behavior are likely also to engage addictively in other forms of sexual behavior. High frequencies of comorbidity have been observed not only within the category of paraphilias (19, 58–60), but also between paraphilias and nonparaphilic sexual addictions (12, 61, 62). The disorders that have been most widely reported to be comorbid with sexual addiction are depressive disorders, anxiety disorders, personality disorders, substance addiction, and other addictive disorders (18, 19, 58, 62–66). The prevalence of these disorders in sex addicts was found to be significantly higher than it is in the general population. Meanwhile, a higher frequency of sexually addictive behavior patterns than is prevalent in the general population has been observed in chemically dependent individuals (4, 67) and in compulsive gamblers (68, 69). The only family history study that was available for review (67) indicated a significant history of sexual addiction and of other addictive disorders in parents of sex addicts. Clearly, more research needs to be conducted in the areas of sexual addiction comorbidity and family history, particularly in light of the usefulness of such findings in understanding etiology and in formulating treatment plans.

ETIOLOGY

Theories of the etiology of sexual addiction can be grouped into four general categories: biological, cognitive-behavioral, psychoanalytic, and integrated. As we consider these theories, let us keep in mind that sexual addiction is not a unitary disorder but a heterogeneous group of disorders. Thus, a variety of different theories could be useful in explaining and understanding sexual addiction, each within its own realm of applicability; and the usefulness of a particular theory could vary from one case of sexual addiction to another.

Biological Theories

Biological theories of the etiology of sexual addiction include those that attribute the disorder to an endocrine abnormality, those that attribute it to brain pathology, and those that consider it to be a "spectrum disorder," a member of a family of psychiatric disorders that share significant features.

ENDOCRINE ABNORMALITY

Recent reviews of endocrinologic studies indicated little support for theories that attribute paraphilias or sexually aggressive behavior to abnormalities of androgen metabolism (70–72). In a review of theories of sexual offending, Marshall and Barbaree (72) concluded that, while there may be a few sex aggressive offenders whose sexual behavior is driven by high androgen levels, the primary problem for the majority appears to be impaired inhibitory control over sex and aggression.

BRAIN PATHOLOGY

Most studies of the relationship between hypersexual or paraphilic behavior and brain pathology have focused on the temporal lobes. Several studies by groups of investigators that were led by Hendricks (73), Hucker (74, 75), and Langevin (71, 76, 77) were consistent in their findings of right temporal lobe abnormalities in sexual sadists and left temporal lobe abnormalities in pedophiles. Flor-Henry's group (78, 79) recorded EEGs on 50 exhibitionists, and reported that the recordings showed altered left hemisphere function and disruption of interhemispheric EEG relationships. These findings indicate that brain abnormalities may be correlated with some forms of paraphilia; however, they do not, in themselves, provide sufficient basis for an etiologic theory of sexual addiction. Formulation of an etiologic theory would require, in addition, an understanding of how such brain abnormalities develop, and an integration of this understanding with the brain-behavior correlations.

"SPECTRUM DISORDER" THEORIES

Hollander and his colleagues (2, 6, 20) identified sexual addiction as an obsessive-compulsive spectrum disorder, a member of a family of disorders that share with OCD some symptoms, comorbidity, possible causes, familial transmission, and response to specific pharmacological and behavioral treatments. These investigators conceptualized OCD spectrum disorders as being distributed along a phenomenological and neurobiological spectrum of harm avoidance, from a compulsive, risk-aversive pole to an impulsive, risk-seeking pole. In the terms of this theory, the sexual obsessions and compulsions of OCD are at the more compulsive end of the spectrum, whereas paraphilias and nonparaphilic sexual addictions are at the more impulsive end. Hollander and his colleagues hypothesized that the central component of the neurobiological abnormalities that are associated with OCD spectrum disorders is a disturbance in serotonergic function.

In 1992, both Kafka and Prentky (62) and McElroy and her colleagues (10) proposed that sexual addiction is an affective spectrum disorder, a member of a family of disorders that share with affective disorders a number of clinically significant features, including demographic and clinical characteristics, phenomenology, family history, biology, and response to treatment. Both groups of investigators speculated that impulse-control disorders, among which they included sexual addiction, share the same postulated underlying physiological abnormality that characterizes other forms of affective spectrum disorder. They both then reviewed studies that provided evidence that impulse-control disorders, like other forms of affective spectrum disorder, may be associated with an abnormality in central serotonergic physiology.

These two theories, obsessive-compulsive spectrum disorder theory and affective spectrum disorder theory, have much in common, from the manner in which the theories were presented to their emphasis on abnormalities in serotonergic function. In fact, obsessive-compulsive spectrum disorders could be understood to represent a subset of affective spectrum disorders, a relationship that was implied in the paper by McElroy's group (10). The spectrum disorder theories considerably enhance our understanding of sexual addiction and its relationship to other psychiatric disorders. At the present point in the development of biological psychiatry, though, these theories are more theories of classification and pathophysiology than theories of etiology. The spectrum disorder theories hypothesize that sexual addiction, along with a large number of other psychiatric disorders, is associated with abnormalities in serotonergic function. They also suggest that a genetically transmitted diathesis predisposes an individual to develop one or more of these disorders. We could speculate further that this diathesis involves a predisposition to develop an abnormality in serotonergic function. In order to proceed beyond this speculation, biological theories of the etiology of sexual addiction would need to address (a) how sexual addiction (or addiction in general) differs neurobiologically from other affective spectrum and obsessive-compulsive spectrum disorders, and (b) how the neurobiological abnormalities that are associated with sexual addiction (or addiction in general) develop.

Cognitive-Behavioral Theories

A number of investigators have proposed psychological theories of sexual addiction, which the investigators identified as cognitive-behavioral theories. These theories incorporate elements of social learning, family systems, and psychodynamic approaches, as well as cognitive and behavioral theories.

Schwartz and Brasted (16) attributed the origin of "sexual impulsivity" to an irrational belief system that consists of poor self-image, unrealistic expectations of what life has to offer, anticipation of personal failure, and a general feeling of helplessness. They added that religious beliefs and social expectations also play roles in the development of the disorder, by burdening the individual with shame, guilt, and subsequently low self-esteem. Finally, they proposed that marital difficulties can lead to or exacerbate addictive sexual behavior.

The theory that was presented by Coleman (3, 4) attributed the development of "compulsive sexual behavior" to two dynamics, one that predisposes an individual to compulsively use substances or behaviors as means of alleviating emotional pain, and a second that leads individuals who are thus predisposed to select certain sexual behaviors as their preferred mode of pain alleviation. According to Coleman's theory, the basis of the predisposition is some type of intimacy dysfunction in an individual's family of origin, such as child abuse or neglect. In response to this trauma, the child develops a sense of shame. He or she perceives himself or herself to have been the cause of the abuse or neglect, and experiences feelings of unworthiness and inadequacy. Shame and low self-esteem interfere with healthy interpersonal functioning, intimate relationships are dysfunctional or nonexistent, and loneliness compounds the individual's low self-esteem. Coleman identified these events and feelings as the origin of the compulsive predisposition:

> All of these events and feelings cause psychological pain for the client, and in order to alleviate this pain, the client begins to search for a "fix," or an agent which has analgesic qualities to it. For some, this agent is alcohol. For others, it could be drugs, certain sexual behaviors, particular foods, working patterns, gambling behaviors, etc. All seem to cause physical and psychological changes which alleviate the pain and provide a temporary relief. (3, p. 9; 4, pp. 196–197)

Coleman hypothesized that the specific dynamic that then leads predisposed individuals to use sexual behavior for their "fix" is a background of restrictive and conservative attitudes regarding sexuality.

Carnes (12) also distinguished between an individual's general addictive tendencies and the catalytic events and/or environments that interact with the addictive tendencies to precipitate a specific addictive problem. He represented the general addictive tendencies as a set of three core beliefs: (a) I am a bad, unworthy person; (b) no one would love me as I am; and (c) my needs will not be met if I have to depend on others. Carnes attributed the development of addictive core beliefs to addicts' families of origin. He characterized these families as unbalanced along the dimensions of structure and intimacy, with structure being either chaotic or rigid and intimacy being either enmeshed or disengaged. As a result of this family pathology, many of the child's basic human needs remain unmet. The child, consequently, not only fails to develop healthy self-esteem, but also learns that other people are unreliable, that one can count only on oneself, and that to survive one must remain in control. What has been discussed so far applies to all forms of addiction. Sex addicts then develop a fourth core belief that distinguishes them from other addicts: (d) sex is my most important need. Carnes ascribed the development of this core belief to childhood experiences of being sexually abused, either overtly or covertly. He noted that "covert incest," in which parents are flirtatious, suggestive, or sexually titillating with their children, may be even more pathogenic than is overt incest. In addition to the distress and shame that are experienced by victims of overt incest, covert incest children are likely also to feel crazy, doubting that their sense of reality is reliable.

The theories that were presented by Schwartz and Brasted, Coleman, and Carnes are quite compatible with each other. While they vary in breadth and depth, none of the theories seems to be saying anything with which any of the others would seriously disagree. The most purely cognitive-behavioral of the three, Schwartz and Brasted's theory focuses on a system of irrational beliefs that resemble those that Beck and others (80, 81) described in cognitive theories of depression. Schwartz and Brasted offered no etiologic hypothesis about how the irrational belief system develops. Moreover, they did not consider what distinguishes those individuals with low self-esteem and depressing thoughts who become sexually impulsive from those who become depressed (and not sexually impulsive). Coleman's most important theoretical contribution seems to have been his identification of two dynamics in the development of compulsive sexual behavior, one that predisposes an individual to compulsively use substances or behaviors as means of alleviating emotional pain, and a second that leads predisposed individuals to select certain sexual behaviors as their preferred "fix." Coleman's description of the development of the first dynamic was clear, intuitively sound, and consistent with the more detailed psychoanalytic theories. His account of the second dynamic as being the result of restrictive and conservative attitudes regarding sexuality, however, seems unable to withstand scrutiny. Sexually compulsive individuals come from a broad range of cultural backgrounds, and not every compulsively predisposed individual who grows up in a sexually restrictive or conservative subculture becomes sexually compulsive. Selection of sexual behavior by compulsively predisposed individuals, therefore, must be guided by factors that are more specific than are cultural attitudes about sexuality. Carnes's account of sexual addiction synthesized cognitive-behavioral and family systems approaches to yield a theory that was both far-reaching and experience-near. His thoughts on the development of general addictive tendencies probably deserved more attention in the substance addiction field than they received. Interestingly, Carnes focused on the use of sexual behavior as a substitute means of gratifying unmet needs. As we considered earlier, gratification represents the primary function of impulsive behavior. Coleman, meanwhile, focused on the use of sexual behavior as a means of alleviating emotional pain, which represents the primary function of compulsive behavior. Addiction, we recall, involves both gratification and alleviation of emotional pain. Carnes and Coleman thus seemed to be emphasizing complementary aspects of addiction.

Psychoanalytic Theories

More material on the etiology of sexual addiction is available in the psychoanalytic literature than in the literature of all other areas of psychiatry and psychology combined. While this body of literature spans 90 years and a variety of theoretical orientations, the themes around which it crystallizes have remained remarkably stable. Moreover, the underlying processes that psychoanalytic theories describe for perversions or paraphilias not only are fairly consistent with each other, but they also are fairly consistent with the underlying processes that other psychoanalytic theories describe for nonparaphilic sexual addictions. While the latter have not been addressed as extensively as have the former, the etiologic theories that have been proposed for perversions seem to be applicable, for the most part, to nonparaphilic sexual addictions as well. In deference to space constraints, this literature will be summarized, rather than reviewed (with a consequent sacrifice of specificity and of attention to differences among the theories). The psychoanalytic investigators whose work was incorporated into the summary include: Bak (82, 83), Chasseguet-Smirgel (84, 85), Coen (86), Eber (87), Fenichel (88), Freud (89, 90), Gillespie (91), Glasser (92, 93), Glover (94), Goldberg (95, 96), Greenacre (97, 98), Hammer (99), Hershey (100), Hoffman (101), Kernberg (102, 103), Khan (104–106), Kohut (107), McDougall (108, 109), Myers (110), Ovesey and Person (111, 112), Payne (113), Rosen (114, 115), Socarides (116), Stoller (117), Stolorow (118, 119), and Trop and Alexander (120).

If we consider the work of these psychoanalytic investigators as a whole, the psychodynamic and etiologic factors in perversion and pathological hypersexuality can be grouped in two categories: nonspecific factors that promote the development of addictive patterns in general, and specific factors that foster sexualization and thus promote the development of sexual addiction in particular.

The primary nonspecific factors are ego weakness, unusually intense castration anxiety (anxiety about the vulnerability of one's body self to mutilation), the fantasy of gender bipotentiality, splitting, and superego pathology. These factors are interrelated, and are understood to originate in some combination of constitutional factors and disturbances in the mother-child relationship. The central difficulty is seen to concern deficiencies and distortions in the mother's responsiveness to the child's needs, which result from the mother's narcissistic pathology and her use of the child as a means of meeting her own emotional and narcissistic needs. While different authors emphasized different aspects of the etiologic process, three consequences of deficient and distorted maternal responsiveness seem to promote the development of addictive behavior patterns in general: (a) impaired internalization of a variety of self-regulatory ego and superego functions; (b) a disrupted transition through the separation-individuation process; and (c) abnormally high levels of aggression, which derives primarily from the frustration of early needs. The sequelae of these factors can then be summarized as (a) deficits in psychic structuralization and development, with specific impairments in affect regulation, self-comforting, superego functions (including ego ideal), object relations, and self-system; and (b) reliance on some form of pleasure-producing behavior as an attempt to regulate feelings and self-esteem, to repair narcissistic balance, to manage aggression, and to compensate for missing pieces in the psychic structure and in the inner object world.

The specific factors that typically foster sexualization, and that thus promote the development of sexual addiction in particular, are seductiveness and sexualization on the mother's part, which induce precocious genitalization and identification with the mother's sexualization. Maternal seductiveness can be either overtly sexual or covert and more subtly narcissistic, and the sexual nature of the mother's interest is usually repressed or disavowed. Constitutional contributions to the etiology of sexual addiction were not excluded by any of the reviewed psychoanalytic theories, but were specifically mentioned only by Freud (89) and Bak (82), as possible factors in the ego's impaired ability to manage castration anxiety, and by Kernberg (102), as a possible source of an excessive intensity of aggression.

Before we proceed, let us consider the relationship between the cognitive-behavioral theories and the psychoanalytic theories. Overall, the two groups of theories are mutually compatible. For the most part, the cognitive-behavioral theories can be understood as simplified versions of the psychoanalytic theories, with four major differences. First of all, the cognitive-behavioral theories place greater emphasis on beliefs as etiologic factors, while the psychoanalytic theories place greater emphasis on affects and psychological functions. Second, the psychoanalytic theories discuss the mother-child relationship as the nucleus of the etiologic matrix, and they explore in detail its pathogenic dynamics. The cognitive-behavioral theories, meanwhile, expand the etiologic matrix to include the entire family of origin and the sociocultural milieu, but they say little about the mother-child relationship or about specific pathogenic interactional patterns other than sexual abuse. Third, the cognitive-behavioral theories hardly mention aggression or sadism at all, while aggression and sadism are prominent as both etiologic and dynamic factors in the psychoanalytic theories. Finally, the psychoanalytic theories emphasize overt sexual abuse less, and covert seduction and narcissistic exploitation more, than do the cognitive-behavioral theories. Also, the pathogenic interactions on which the psychoanalytic theories focus occur earlier in life than do those that the cognitive-behavioral theories typically discuss.

Integrated Theories

The human being is both biological and psychological, and the etiology of sexual addiction is likely to be most fully understood through a theory that integrates both biological and psychological understandings. Prior to the 1990s, the theory of fetishism that was proposed by Epstein (46) was the only coherent attempt to integrate biological theory and psychological theory (in this case, psychoanalytic theory) to account for a form of sexual addiction. Epstein identified the primary disturbance in fetishism as a state of increased organismic excitability or impaired organismic control, which he regarded as the product of cerebral pathophysiology. We can infer that the heightened excitability or dyscontrol that Epstein described would amplify the child's sensori-affective responsiveness, with the result that the child's affects and inner conflicts would be unusually intense. Epstein characterized the typical mother-child relationship of the fetishist in much the same way as did other psychoanalytic investigators of perversion. He added, though, that increased organismic excitability or dyscontrol intensifies the child's responses to disturbed maternal behavior, thereby exacerbating its pathogenic potential. Fetishistic behavior, according to Epstein's theory, represents a result of both the forces of excitability-dyscontrol and attempts to establish control by providing a focus toward which sexual and aggressive drives are directed.

More recently, Goodman (14, 121) proposed an integrated theory of sexual addiction that was based on a comprehensive theory of addictive disorders. In his presentation of the comprehensive theory, Goodman (21, 122) began by reviewing literature that addressed comorbidity, family history, neurobiological relationships, response to pharmacotherapy, psychometric assessment, and longitudinal and archival studies of premorbid personality measures in disorders that he grouped together as addictive disorders: alcoholism, drug addiction, bulimia, pathological gambling, and sexual addiction. On the basis of the similarities and interconnections that this review revealed, he proposed (a) that these addictive disorders have in common an underlying biopsychological process, and (b) that this biopsychological process precedes the onset of the disorders and is thus not simply a consequence of addictive behavior or an addictive lifestyle. Extrapolating from these findings, Goodman hypothesized that all addictive disorders, whatever the types of behavior that characterize them, share an underlying biopsychological process, which he designated the *addictive process*. He originally suggested that the addictive process could be understood as compulsive dependence on external action as a means of regulating one's internal (or subjective) states, one's feelings and sense of self. More recently, he defined the addictive process as *an enduring, inordinately strong tendency to engage in some form of pleasure-producing behavior as a means of relieving painful affects and/or regulating one's sense of self*. Goodman's theory of addictive disorders identified two sets of factors and predisposing conditions: those that concern the underlying addictive process, and those that relate to the selection of a particular substance or behavior as the one preferred for addictive use. According to this theory, the addictive process is both biological and psychological, and it can be described and understood in either biological or psychological terms. While Epstein (46) developed his integrated biopsychological theory within a framework of mental-physical interaction, Goodman developed his within a framework of mental-physical identity (41–44).

BIOLOGICAL FORMULATION OF THE ADDICTIVE PROCESS

Goodman (21, 122) reviewed neurobiological theories of alcoholism, drug addiction, bulimia, and pathological gambling, and developed a biological formulation of the addictive process on the foundation that was provided by the components of these theories that could fit together. (He proceeded from the premise that research findings sufficiently supported the hypothesis of the addictive process. Consequently, in developing this formulation, his intention was not to prove that the addictive process existed, but to demonstrate that a biological theory of the addictive process was possible.) According to Goodman's hypothesized biological formulation, the addictive process involves impaired affect regulation, impaired behavioral inhibition, and aberrant function of the motivational-reward system. Impaired affect regulation renders individuals chronically vulnerable to painful affect-states and affective instability. In the context of impaired affect regulation, behaviors that are associated with escape from or avoidance of painful affect-states are more strongly reinforced than they otherwise would have been. Aberrant function of the motivational-reward system subjects the individual to unsatisfied states of restless anhedonia or emptiness. In the context of aberrant motivational-reward function, behaviors that are associated

with activation of the reward system are more strongly reinforced than they otherwise would have been. Impaired behavioral inhibition increases the likelihood that an urge for some form of reinforcement (negative, positive, or both) in the short term will override consideration of longer term consequences, both negative and positive. When affect regulation is impaired and motivational-reward function is aberrant, impaired behavioral inhibition means that urges to engage in behaviors that are associated with both (a) escape from or avoidance of painful affect-states and (b) activation of the reward system are extraordinarily difficult to resist, despite the harmful consequences that they entail.

Goodman hypothesized that impaired affect regulation, impaired behavioral inhibition, and aberrant function of the motivational-reward system are primarily associated (but not in a simple one-to-one fashion) with dysfunctions in the norepinephrine, serotonin, and dopamine systems, and that dysfunction in the endogenous opioid system can contribute to all of these functional aberrations. Activity of the norepinephrine system is associated with affect regulation and ability to manage emotional stress (123–125). Serotonin system activity is associated with behavioral inhibition (126, 127), emotional stabilization (128), appetite modulation (129), sensory reactivity (130, 131), and pain sensitivity (131, 132). Dopamine is the principal neurotransmitter in the brain reward system, and activity of dopaminergic pathways is associated also with behavioral activation, novelty seeking, and incentive functions (133–135). Endogenous opioids are involved in reward, alleviation of pain (psychosocial as well as somatic) (136, 137), and hedonic tone (138). They also have an ancillary role in appetitive, emotional, and behavioral regulation (139–143). Goodman speculated that the addictive process may develop concurrently with a similar primary defect in each of these systems: low basal activity of the neuromodulator, which is associated with supersensitivity of postsynaptic receptors in the cases of norepinephrine and dopamine, and perhaps also in the case of endogenous opioids. Dysfunction of the serotonergic system may be the most critical neurochemical correlate of the addictive process. Serotonin is released from all of the axonal varicosities where it is concentrated, not only from those that make typical synaptic contacts (144, 145). Such widespread release suggests that serotonin diffuses as a neurohumoral agent to reach relatively distant targets. The serotonergic system is moreover characterized by tonic activity, with serotonergic neurons firing at rates of about one spike per second (146). These findings suggest that the serotonergic system serves a widespread pacemaker or homeostatic regulatory function (147).

The neuroanatomical correlates of the addictive process, Goodman hypothesized, may involve dysfunctions in two systems within the brain: one that is constituted by the orbitofrontal cortex, the septum, and the hippocampus; and one that includes the nucleus accumbens, the ventral tegmental area, and related structures. Dysfunction in the former system may be primarily associated with impaired affect regulation and impaired behavioral inhibition (148–152). Dysfunction in the latter system may be primarily associated with aberrant function of the motivational-reward system (153, 154) and with dysregulation of the orbitofrontal cortex (149), which is the cortical component of the former system.

Goodman proposed that these impairments in neurochemical and neuroanatomical functioning develop out of the interaction between genetic propensities and deficiencies in the early caregiving environment. He suggested that this interaction is particularly important in the developmental critical periods of the first years of life, during which the maturing brain is most sensitive to environmental influences and is dependent on particular qualities of environmental interchange for its healthy development (124, 152, 155–161).

While this formulation brought us a step closer to understanding the neurobiology of the addictive process, we can note that it was a heuristic oversimplification. Each neuromodulator involves a diverse system of connections and receptors, and interactions among the neuromodulator systems are complex. Functional neuroanatomy also is more complex than Goodman's formulation can accommodate. Brain regions are interconnected by tangled networks through which they influence each other, and serious questions have been raised by neuroscientists about the extent to which functions can be meaningfully localized within the brain (148, 162–164).

PSYCHOLOGICAL FORMULATION OF THE ADDICTIVE PROCESS

Goodman (21, 165) also reviewed psychoanalytic and learning theory-based theories of alcoholism, drug addiction, bulimia, pathological gambling, and sexual addiction, and developed a psychological formulation of the addictive process on the foundation that was provided by core features that these theories shared. According to this formulation, the addictive process originates in impairment of the self-regulation system, the internal psychobiological system that regulates one's subjective subjective (sensory, emotional, and cognitive) states and one's behavioral states. Impaired internal regulation of their subjective states leads individuals to depend on external actions to regulate their feelings and sense of self. Impaired internal regulation of their behavioral states limits individuals' capacity to modulate or inhibit such compensatory actions. Addictive behavior thus represents both an attempt to cope with the subjective consequences of impaired subjective consequences of impaired self-regulatory functioning, and an overt manifestation of impaired self-regulatory functioning.

Goodman identified the self-regulation system as a complex system of functions that are interrelated both functionally and developmentally. He focused on three primary components: (a) affect regulation functions (the most basic and significant)—self-soothing, self-enlivening, keeping feelings in balance, tolerating feelings without being overwhelmed; (b) self-care functions—self-protection, self-nurturing, taking care of one's needs; and (c) self-governance functions—values, standards, self-esteem, self-punishment, maintenance of a stable and cohesive sense of self.

The self-regulation system is believed to develop through the interaction of multiple systems that involve both genetic endowment and the child's relationship with his or her primary caregiver during the first years of life. The essential process in the development of self-regulatory functions is "internalization," a dialectical process whereby regulatory functions that had been provided for the child by the caregiver gradually become integrated into the child's autonomous functional system through interactions between the maturing child and the responsive caregiver.

Goodman noted that various combinations of genetic and environmental factors can interfere with the development of the self-regulation system, and that each of the three primary components may be impaired to varying degrees. To the extent that affect regulation is impaired, affect-states tend to be unstable, intense, and disorganizing. Affect-dysregulated individuals are vulnerable to being traumatically overwhelmed by affects that an intact individual does not experience as potentially traumatic. To the extent that self-care is impaired, individuals are deficient in their abilities to avoid danger, to protect themselves, and to take care of their needs, both physical and emotional. As a result, they are particularly susceptible to getting hurt and to being chronically dissatisfied. To the extent that self-governance is impaired, individuals lack a stable self-esteem, a consistent sense of self, and a clear sense of direction. They may have skewed or fragmented values, ideals, and sense of meaning. Their behavior tends to oscillate between extremes, and they may swing from actions that violate their values to actions that are self-injurious or that invite punishment from the environment.

Impaired self-regulation thus leaves individuals abnormally vulnerable to being overwhelmed by intense affect-states and loss of self-coherence, a danger that they experience as a threat to their very existence. They consequently turn to a variety of self-protective mental and behavioral processes in order to attenuate or to avoid this danger. Such individuals typically must evoke and employ object representations to perform for them the functions that individuals with an intact and well-structuralized self-regulation system are able to do automatically. They then externalize these self-regulation–endowed object representations, or self-object representations, onto persons, institutions, nonhuman objects, substances, activities, or bodily states, which thereby come to function for the individuals as self-objects: that is, nonself entities or processes that serve self-regulatory functions. These individuals are subsequently inclined to depend on their artificial self-objects for the provision of self-regulatory functions that they are not sufficiently able to provide for themselves. Insofar as these individuals experience (consciously or unconsciously) their deficient or missing self-regulatory functions to be necessary for their survival, they are highly motivated (a) to control their artificial self-objects, and (b) to externalize their self-regulatory potential onto, and thereby to create artificial self-objects of, objects over which they believe (consciously or unconsciously) that they have control. Furthermore, insofar as these individuals experience their deficient or missing self-regulatory functions to be necessary for their survival, their urges to engage in behavior that conjures (or attempts to conjure) self-regulatory functions from their artifical self-objects are typically so imperative that their patterns of engaging in such behavior are likely to be characterized by recurrent loss of control and by continuation of the behavior despite significant harmful consequences. This, then, is the essence of the addictive process: (a) due to some combination of genetic and environmental factors, individuals' self-regulatory functions are impaired; (b) impaired self-regulation leaves these individuals abnormally vulnerable to being overwhelmed by intense affect-states and by loss of self-coherence; and (c) in attempts to attenuate or to avoid the danger of being thus overwhelmed, these individuals externalize their self-regulatory potential onto nonself entities or processes over which they believe that they have control. Individuals whose externalizations of this type lead them to engage in some form of behavior in a pattern that is characterized by recurrent loss of control and by continuation of the behavior despite significant harmful consequences can then be characterized as "addicts," whatever the behavior(s) in which they addictively engage. Many such addicts learn to ward off traumatic affect-states and self-states by engaging in a rewarding activity: for example, eating, taking a mood-altering substance into their bodies, gambling, or engaging in some form of sexual behavior. With practice, this response can evolve into a self-protective way of being. External or internal cues that are associated with intense affect-states or loss of self-coherence can then trigger or be experienced as urges to engage in addictive behavior.

THE "DRUG OF CHOICE" QUESTION

As we noted earlier, Goodman's theory identified two sets of factors that influence the development of addictive disorders: those that concern the underlying addictive process, and those that relate to the selection of a particular form of behavior (and further, in the case of psychoactive substance use addiction, a particular substance) as the one that is preferred for addictive use. Goodman focused on the former set because he believed it to be the more important, both in terms of etiologic significance and as a guide in treatment. He did, however, also consider what he termed the "drug of choice" question: Given a sufficient degree of predisposition to develop addictive behavior patterns, as represented in the addictive process, what determines which substances or behaviors are selected for addictive use?

Goodman observed that the selection of a substance or a behavior for addictive use seems to depend both on factors of learning and on genetic factors. He identified three components of the learning process that may be particularly influential in the selection of an addictive means: affect, expectancy, and exposure. The affect(s) from which an individual is most motivated to seek relief are those that he or she experiences as most painful or dangerous. The substance or experience that brings relief from the affects that an individual experiences as most painful or dangerous is thereby most strongly reinforced (via negative reinforcement). Meanwhile, learned expectations about how a substance or a behavior will alter one's affective state or sense of self are an integral part of the substance's or behavior's effects, and controlled studies have found the subjective and behavioral effects of psychoactive substances to be determined as much by expectancies as by the pharmacological properties of the substances (166–168). The third component, exposure, can consist of either direct experience or modeling of (identification with) another person who engages in the behavior. Direct experience can occur through either experimentation or adventitious contact. Exposure gives the contingencies of reinforcement a chance to operate.

The selection process is influenced also by genetic factors, especially those that affect the hedonic quality of specific experiences. The sensitivity of the reward system to different substances is subject to genetically-based variation (169, 170). Greater sensitivity of the reward system to a particular substance (or behavior) enhances its positive reinforcement value, relative to other substances and behaviors. Genetically based biological variations can also render an individual more or less sensitive to the immediate aversive consequences of a substance or a behavior, such as standing ataxia or flushing after ingestion of alcohol (171). The immediate aversive consequences that the individual experiences then influence the frequency and extent to which he or she ingests the substance or engages in the behavior.

The addictive process is not separable from the addict's personality and character organization, except by theoretical abstraction, and neither is the addict's selection of a particular substance or behavior for addictive use. An addict's drug-of-choice or behavior-of-choice is typically an agent or action that is congruent with his or her characteristic modes of adaptation: one that facilitates the addict's pre-existing means of managing and integrating affective, behavioral, and cognitive responses. The selection of a particular substance or behavior is facilitated also by its capacity to enhance the individual's adaptation, by compensating for defects or weaknesses in his or her adaptational system. An individual's affective, behavioral, and cognitive response tendencies, and the ego processes that function to manage and to integrate them, also are the products of the interaction between genetic factors and factors of learning.

The development of a particular addictive disorder thus seems to have three components: (a) an individual is predisposed to depend on some form of pleasure-producing behavior to regulate his or her (dysregulated) internal states, by virtue of the addictive process; (b) the individual takes a mood-altering substance into his or her body, or engages in some other rewarding behavior; and (c) the effects of the substance or behavior (negatively reinforcing, positively reinforcing, and aversive), the individual's expectations about its effects in the future, and the fit between the substance or behavior and the individual's characteristic modes of adaptation, combine to determine the likelihood that the individual will select that substance or behavior as his or her addictive "drug of choice." These effects and expectations are determined by both genetic and environmental factors. Meanwhile, the adaptive human organism, once having developed the capacity to use an external action as a means of regulating internal states, can shift among different behaviors (and substances) or combine them, according to the opportunities and limitations of the situation.

SELECTION OF SEXUAL BEHAVIOR

Goodman's formulation of the "drug of choice" process suggests that sexual addiction develops in addictively predisposed individuals who experience some form of sexual stimulation, either directly or through identification with a parental figure (usually the mother) who sexualizes, and who learn to expect that sexual behavior not only will provide pleasure but also (a) will relieve the affects that they experience as most painful or dangerous, through (b) means that are congruent with their characteristic modes of adaptation. Children naturally explore their bodies with their hands and their physical surroundings with their bodies, so exposure to sexual sensations is virtually inevitable. Yet, not all addictively predisposed individuals become sex addicts. The selection of sexual behavior as an addictive preference thus seems to depend not only on exposure to sexual stimulation, but also on the interpersonal context of the exposure. The kind of exposure that leads to the development of sexual addiction in addictively predisposed individuals typically results from sexual seduction, which, as a number of investigators (12, 106, 107, 172) have noted, can be overt or covert. Exposure to sexual sensations can also occur fortuitously, since children naturally explore their bodies with their hands and their physical surroundings with their bodies. In addition to overt or covert seduction, other characteristics of the mother-child relationship that promote sexualization, including the mother's reliance on sexualization in her defensive activities and in her relationship with her child (86), are likely also to contribute to the predisposed individual's selection of some form of sexual behavior as his or her addictive "drug of choice."

TREATMENT

The modalities that have been employed in treating sexual addiction include medication, behavior modification, cognitive-behavioral therapy, therapeutic groups, couples or family therapy, and psychodynamic psychotherapy.

Medication

The category of medication comprises two different kinds of pharmacological treatment, antiandrogenic agents and affect-regulating agents (antidepressants and mood stabilizers).

ANTIANDROGENIC AGENTS

Antiandrogenic agents that are in use at this time include medroxyprogesterone acetate and cyproterone acetate, the latter of which is not currently available in the United States. A number of clinical studies have demonstrated that medroxyprogesterone acetate can reduce sex drive, sexual thoughts, sexual behavior, and aggressiveness (173–184). Cyproterone acetate has been reported to decrease sexually driven aggression, and to reduce arousal responses to pedophilic and coercive sexual stimuli but not to mutually consenting adult sex scenes (185–192). Administration of these agents is, however, frequently associated with unpleasant side effects, and serious side effects (including thrombophlebitis, pulmonary embolism, and hepatic dysfunction) occasionally occur. Noncompliance also is a significant problem, and one study (173) had a dropout rate of greater than 50%. Most reviewers agree that antiandrogenic agents do not by themselves constitute adequate treatment for paraphilias, but that they can be a valuable adjunct to behavior modification, group therapy, or individual psychotherapy with some patients, particularly during early stages of treatment (176, 193–195).

AFFECT-REGULATING AGENTS

A number of reports have provided evidence for the efficacy of affect-regulating agents in the treatment of paraphilias, even in patients who are not suffering from a major affective disorder. Agents that have been found to be effective include fluoxetine (18, 62, 187–200), sertraline (63), imipramine (18, 201), desipramine (19), clomipramine (202–205), lithium (18, 206–208), buspirone (209), and electroconvulsive therapy (210). Kafka (18, 63) and Kafka and Prentky (62) treated nonparaphilic sexual addictions as well as paraphilias with affect-regulating agents, and found that both conditions responded favorably. Sexual addiction symptoms have been reported to respond almost equally well to different kinds of affect-regulating agents (18, 19). While such a large number of positive findings is encouraging, the confidence with which conclusions can be drawn from these findings is limited by the paucity of controlled studies.

Behavior Modification

Behavioral methods have been employed in the treatment of paraphilias, but not in the treatment of nonparaphilic sexual addictions. They are oriented toward assisting individuals to reduce the erotic quality of their paraphilic interests, or to shift the balance of erotic arousal potential from paraphilic interests to nonparaphilic interests. The primary forms of behavioral treatment for paraphilias are aversion conditioning, covert sensitization, masturbatory training, and imaginal desensitization. Some behavioral methods also teach patients a self-administered treatment that they can perform on their own. Such methods can help not only to diminish paraphilic behavior but also to enhance feelings of self-control.

AVERSION CONDITIONING

In aversion conditioning, unwanted patterns of sexual behavior are linked repeatedly with unpleasant stimuli, most often electric shock or foul odors. This classical or Pavlovian conditioning procedure is intended to transform stimulus features of the sexual behavior into conditioned stimuli or triggers for the aversive responses to the unpleasant stimuli. A number of uncontrolled studies (211–219) found that aversion conditioning yielded positive results, while one study (220) found no significant effects and another (221) found that the success of aversion conditioning depended on the availability of appropriate sexual outlets and the absence of severe nonsexual pathology.

COVERT SENSITIZATION

Covert sensitization was developed as an imaginary version of aversion conditioning, in which fantasies of paraphilic arousal are paired with fantasies of aversive events to promote a learned association between paraphilic themes and unpleasant feelings. In covert sensitization, patients are first led through a relaxation exercise, and then are instructed to visualize themselves engaging in some aspect of their paraphilic behaviors. At that point, they are told to imagine either an unpleasant event, such as nausea and vomiting (which can be reinforced by a nauseating odor), or an aversive consequence that could follow the behavior in reality, such as public humiliation or shame at being discovered by a superego figure. Studies have found covert sensitization to be effective in the treatment of exhibitionism and pedophilia (222–229).

MASTURBATORY TRAINING

Masturbatory training attempts to shift paraphilic patients' arousal patterns in the conventional direction by controlling the fantasies or visual stimuli that they experience while masturbating. The two main forms of masturbatory training are satiation and fading. Satiation involves instructing male patients to masturbate to orgasm with conventional sexual stimuli or fantasies, and then to continue masturbating while visualizing their deviant objects. The idea is that masturbating after orgasm will extinguish erotic arousal to paraphilic fantasies. In the fading technique, paraphilic patients' fantasies are gradually shifted from deviant to conventional during periods of sexual arousal. Patients may be provided with visual stimuli on which to focus, such as photographic slides that automatically fade from one kind of scene to another; or they may be instructed to gradually alter the scenarios that they fantasize while masturbating. One study (230) of masturbatory satiation reported mild success, but other therapeutic modalities were provided at the same time and no post-treatment follow-up was mentioned.

IMAGINAL DESENSITIZATION

The technique of imaginal desensitization is based on the theory that, once an individual has developed a sequence of sexual activity, which begins with a sexual thought or fantasy and ends with overt behavior, interruption of the sequence results in anxiety that then motivates completion of the sequence. Imaginal desensitization uses the methods of systematic desensitization to diminish the anxiety that is aroused by interruption of the sequence that leads to paraphilic behavior. After relaxation is induced, the patient visualizes performing a sequence of behaviors that lead to noncompletion of the act. Relaxation is allowed to develop with each visualized behavior before the patient proceeds to the next behavior in the sequence. The patient is thus trained to visualize not completing the sexual act, while remaining relaxed. One study (231) reported imaginal desensitization to be more effective than covert sensitization.

Cognitive-Behavioral Therapies

Quadland (7), Schwartz and Brasted (16), and Carnes (11, 12) described programs for treating sexual addiction that were predominantly cognitive-behavioral (or social-cognitive-behavioral) in their approach. In addition to their cognitive-behavioral orientation, the three programs shared a reliance on group therapy as their primary form of treatment.

Quadland (7) described a group therapy program for treating "compulsive sexual behavior." The program was intended to help group members both (a) to change their sexual behavior and (b) to recognize and understand the factors that drove their sexual behavior. Quadland identified two cognitive-behavioral techniques that the program employed, self-monitoring and contracting. In the self-monitoring component, participants kept journals of their sexual thoughts, feelings, and experiences. They then talked in group sessions about what they had entered in their journals. In the contracting component, participants made contracts with the group about changes that they wanted to make each week. Group sessions then usually began with a review of contracts from the previous week. Quadland noted the benefits of

mutual support and of confrontation by peers with participants who seemed to be less than honest with themselves or with the group.

Schwartz and Brasted (16) presented a cognitive-behavioral treatment program that involved six stages. The first stage focused on stopping the undesired sexual behavior. Behavior modification techniques and/or pharmacotherapy were employed, as needed, to modify patients' sexual drives. The goal of the second stage was for the patient to accept the existence of a problem and to promise to keep no secrets from the therapist or from fellow group members. In the third stage, patients were taught anxiety reduction techniques, so they would no longer need to rely on sexual behavior to alleviate their anxiety. The fourth stage consisted of cognitive therapy that was directed toward modifying the irrational beliefs that Schwartz and Brasted hypothesized to underlie the sexual addiction. In the fifth stage, patients were trained in such skills as assertiveness and problem solving in order to facilitate adaptive social functioning. Finally, the sixth stage focused on resolving whatever residual problems the individual had in establishing a primary sexual relationship. This stage most often involved couples therapy with the pretreatment sexual partner.

The program for treating sexual addiction that was developed by Carnes (11, 12) shared with Schwartz and Brasted's program an initial focus on stopping the addictive sexual behavior and a subsequent emphasis on altering the maladaptive core beliefs that were thought to underlie the patient's addictive system. It differed from the programs that were described by Quadland and by Schwartz and Brasted in several ways that reflected the more complete adoption by Carnes of the addiction model. Carnes developed a structured, intensive program that resembled the traditional substance addiction treatment program. A series of lectures and workshops were interwoven with group therapies and homework assignments. The program incorporated principles and methods from the 12-step approach, and participants were encouraged to regularly attend meetings of a 12-step fellowship for recovering sex addicts after they had completed the program. Carnes's program also directly involved members of sex addicts' families, who were invited to participate in special lectures and groups. Finally, Carnes's program was distinguished from the others by its inclusion of relapse prevention techniques. Participants were guided in compiling an inventory of their relapse risk factors, and then in preparing for what could be done before a "slip" (an episode of symptomatic behavior), during a slip, and after a slip had occurred. They learned to anticipate slip-inducing possibilities and to devise a series of action steps that could serve to prevent a slip. Participants were then instructed to rehearse the slip prevention steps so thoroughly that, when a potentially seductive situation occurred, they would be able to perform the steps automatically.

Quadland (7) reported that participants in his program indicated a decrease in their frequency of compulsive sexual behavior at follow-up 6 months after treatment. No other studies have been published that specifically assessed the efficacy of cognitive-behavioral treatment for sexual addiction. In a review of treatment outcomes with sex offenders (a category that overlaps but is not identical with the category of sex addicts), Marshall and his colleagues (193) concluded that evaluations of comprehensive cognitive-behavioral programs were encouraging, at least for the treatment of child molesters and exhibitionists. However, they noted, the programs were not uniformly effective.

Therapeutic Groups

Many clinicians believe that group therapy and self-help groups are the most effective modalities for the treatment of individuals who use sexual behavior addictively. The types of therapeutic group that have been employed in treating sex addicts include cognitive-behavioral groups, psychodynamic psychotherapy groups, and support groups. While group therapy can range from highly structured to relatively unstructured, most investigators have concluded that individuals who use sexual behavior addictively seem to do best in groups that are at least moderately structured. Mathis and Collins (232) and Truax (233) emphasized the importance of treating paraphilic patients in groups that consist of individuals with similar problems, where shared experiences and needs can help to dissolve rationalization, isolation, and denial. Ganzarain and Buchele (234) noted that, for many paraphilic patients, groupmates and the group peer culture become a surrogate benign superego. Group members often can more readily receive guidance, confrontation, and support from groupmates than from therapists or other individuals in their lives. Three studies reported positive results from psychodynamic group psychotherapy treatment of patients who suffered from perversions (234–236).

The most common self-help groups for individuals who use sexual behavior addictively are the 12-step groups that are modeled on Alcoholics Anonymous. Since the 1970s, four 12-step fellowships of recovering sex addicts have developed, each based on the model of Alcoholics Anonymous and adapted for sexual addiction: Sex Addicts Anonymous (SAA), Sex and Love Addicts Anonymous (SLAA), Sexaholics Anonymous (SA), and Sexual Compulsives Anonymous (SCA). The primary differences between the four fellowships are encapsulated in their definitions of sobriety. Sobriety in SAA is defined as no "out-of-bounds" sex. In consultation with their sponsors and fellow group members, sex addicts in SAA identify the sexual behaviors that are likely to lead to harmful consequences, and then define "boundaries" that exclude these behaviors (237). In SLAA, sobriety is similarly defined as no "bottom-line" sex: "Define your bottom-line behavior . . . any sexual or emotional act which, once engaged in, leads to loss of control over rate, frequency or duration of its recurrence, resulting in worsening self-destructive consequences" (238, p.4). Sobriety in SA is more strictly defined as no sexual activity other than with a spouse: "Any form of sex with one's self or with partners other than the spouse is progressively addictive and destructive" (239, p.4). In SCA, members are encouraged to define sexual sobriety for themselves, to develop sexual recovery plans that are consistent with their own values (240). The differences between the 12-step fellowships may, however, be less important than the differences between individual groups. Since the fellowships lack formal leadership structures and internal controls, the characteristics of a particular group are determined primarily by the individuals who attend it.

Couples and Family Therapy

As we noted earlier, the sexual addiction treatment programs that were presented by Schwartz and Brasted (16) and by Carnes (11, 12) both involved couples or family therapy. The inclusion of couples or family therapy in the treatment of sexual addiction has been recommended also by psychiatric and psychoanalytic clinicians. Reid (195) and Gabbard (241) observed that marital therapy can elucidate pathogenic factors in the marital relationship, while Wise (242) emphasized that marital therapy can engage the spouse and the energy in the relationship as agents of therapeutic change. Both the cognitive-behaviorally oriented therapists and the psychodynamically oriented therapists, while noting that couples or family therapy can be important in the treatment of sexual addiction, accorded it a supplemental or adjunctive status.

Psychodynamic Psychotherapy

A number of psychoanalytically oriented clinicians have stated that intensive psychodynamic psychotherapy is the treatment of choice for paraphilias (241–244). Significantly, Stein and his colleagues (20) observed that the beneficial effect of antidepressant medications in sexual addiction may be seen only when they are combined with intensive psychotherapy. The primary focus of psychodynamic treatment is on patients' character pathology, rather than on their pathological behavior. Thus, as Rosen (244) noted, the more pronounced the accompanying personality disorder, the greater the need for psychodynamic therapy that emphasizes transference work. All of the investigators who recommended psychodynamic psychotherapy qualified their recommendations with statements to the effect that the general criteria of suitability for psychodynamic psychotherapy apply to sex addicts as well. One study (244) reported that five of six exhibitionists who were treated in individual psychodynamic psychotherapy for an average of 21 sessions lost all urges to expose themselves and had not relapsed at the 24-month follow-up.

Integrated Treatment

Many investigators have concluded that no single treatment is effective for all paraphilic patients, and that the best approach for most patients seems to be to provide individually tailored combinations of behavioral, psychosocial, psychodynamic, and pharmacological modalities (195, 241, 243, 245–247). A number of clinicians have presented programs for treating sexual addiction that combined two or more therapeutic modalities. Interestingly, those multimodality programs that had a cognitive-behavioral core were usually described by their authors as "cognitive-behavioral," while those multiple-modality programs that had a psychodynamic core were described as "integrated."

Travin and Protter (248, 249) were the first to introduce an integrated paradigm for the treatment of paraphilic disorders. They described their "bimodal approach" as a synthesis of cognitive-behavioral and focused psychodynamic treatment modalities, with which could be integrated other modalities, such as medication, family therapy, and longer term psychodynamic psychotherapy. The cognitive-behavioral protocol that Travin and Protter recommended consists of (a) measures that enhance behavioral control, which include covert sensitization and/or masturbatory satiation, and (b) measures that address social-interpersonal deficits, which include stress management, assertiveness training, and social-communicative skills training. While relapse prevention was included among the self-control techniques that were identified in the authors' book (249), it was not further discussed in the book, and it was not mentioned at all in the initial paper by Protter and Travin (248) or in a more recent paper by Travin (250). Travin and Protter described the psychodynamic component of their approach as more active, more directive, and more focused on symptoms than is psychoanalytic psychotherapy. They focused on sexual fantasy both as a bridge that links the cognitive-behavioral and psychodynamic components, and as an organizing schema for treatment intervention. In the psychotherapy component of their approach, the therapist treats the patient's conscious fantasy productions and ritualized sexual behavior as symbolic transformations of the unconscious perverse fantasy that organizes the patient's sexual life. Travin and Protter noted that the way in which the various components of their treatment approach are implemented depends on a variety of factors that concern the patient, the severity of the disorder, and the treatment context. With patients who have little behavioral control and are at risk for victimizing others, covert sensitization and masturbatory satiation are initiated immediately, in order to promote the development of self-control. Until symptomatic control stabilizes, psychodynamic intervention assumes a secondary role. Such patients are likely also to require fairly comprehensive social rehabilitation. Meanwhile, the treatment of patients whose disorder is less severe and whose behavior is less likely to be harmful to others consists primarily of psychodynamic psychotherapy that addresses characterological issues. Specific cognitive-behavioral interventions are then added, as they are needed. More recently, Travin (250) fine-tuned his bimodal approach in a few ways. He singled out Kohut's self psychology as a particularly useful framework for the psychodynamic psychotherapy of patients with "compulsive sexual behaviors"; and he observed that, among the medications that are available, serotonergic agents seemed to be the most effective. Travin also identified group therapy as the primary means of treatment in his approach, noting that patients were seen individually as well when such treatment was deemed to be appropriate.

Goodman (14, 121, 249) presented a system for treating sexual addiction that brought together psychodynamic psychotherapy, cognitive-behavioral treatment, therapeutic groups, and pharmacotherapy. Goodman's treatment system developed in the context of his theory that sexual addiction represents an expression through sexual behavior of the addictive process: an enduring, inordinately strong tendency to engage in some form of pleasure-producing behavior as a means of regulating affects and/or self-states that are painful and potentially overwhelming due to impaired self-regulation. Consequently, the treatment system was designed to address both the addictive sexual behavior and the underlying addictive process. Goodman's system addressed addictive sexual behavior through relapse prevention and other cognitive-behavioral techniques. Relapse prevention strategies help individuals who use sexual behavior addictively (*a*) to recognize factors and situations that are associated with an increased risk of acting out sexually, (*b*) to cope more effectively with sexual urges, (*c*) to recover rapidly from episodes of symptomatic behavior, and (*d*) to use such "slips" as opportunities to learn about how their recovery plans can be improved. Goodman's approach to relapse prevention conceptualizes urges to engage in addictive sexual behavior as signals of disruptive feeling-states that the addict needs to develop healthier, more adaptive means to manage. In thus shifting the focus from controlling the behavior to understanding the feelings, relapse prevention provides a natural bridge from behavior management to psychodynamic psychotherapy.

Goodman's system for treating sexual addiction addressed the addictive process primarily through psychodynamic psychotherapy and therapeutic groups, as means of promoting self-regulation and fostering the development of meaningful interpersonal connections. Goodman described psychodynamic psychotherapy as a process that helps individuals to become more aware of their feelings, needs, inner conflicts, core beliefs, and automatic ways of protecting themselves from emotional pain. With this awareness, individuals then have opportunities to amend their maladaptive core beliefs and to develop more healthy, adaptive means of managing their feelings, getting their needs met, resolving their inner conflicts, and taking care of themselves. Psychodynamic psychotherapy, moreover, affords opportunities for integration of the personality and for internalization of self-regulatory functions that were not adequately internalized during childhood. Goodman observed that therapeutic groups, including 12-step groups, could facilitate the development of abilities to make meaningful connections with others and to turn to people in times of need instead of turning to addictive sexual behavior. He noted that groups provide some therapeutic factors that are not available in individual therapy. The function of psychiatric pharmacotherapy in Goodman's system was to enhance affect regulation and to stabilize psychobiological functioning, as well as to treat the symptoms of comorbid psychiatric disorders. The rationale for using affect-regulating medication in the treatment of sexual addiction, even in the absence of major affective comorbidity, was that enhancement of affect regulation diminishes the frequency and intensity of addictive urges, while more stable psychobiological functioning is associated with better behavioral control and improved assessment of reality.

Goodman's treatment system represented a coherent integration of the various therapeutic modalities, but it devoted insufficient attention to group therapy and it neglected behavior modification, family therapy, and antiandrogen pharmacotherapy. These deficiencies of the system can be remedied with four modifications. The first and most important modification incorporates the recognition that recovery from sexual addiction proceeds in stages (more or less), and that treatment should be appropriate to the patient's current stage of recovery. Four stages of recovery can be distinguished: Stage One, Initial Behavior Modulation; Stage Two, Stabilization (of behavior and affect); Stage Three, Character Healing; and Stage Four, Self-Renewal. This modification of Goodman's system facilitates the formulation of treatment plans that are individually tailored and that are designed to evolve, in terms of both therapeutic focus and primary modalities employed, as individuals who have used sexual behavior addictively progress through the four stages of recovery.

During Stage One, most individuals who suffer from sexual addiction can begin to modulate their sexual behavior by means of a combination of inner motivation, psychological support, and affect-regulating medication. Many sex addicts do not require affect-regulating medication, but some who are able to modulate their behavior without medication may still benefit from the medication's attenuation of addictive urges and from its alleviation of the affective distress that often accompanies the initial modulation of addictive behavior. A number of sex addicts, meanwhile, may need more specific intervention, in the form of behavior modification or antiandrogen pharmacotherapy or both. The progressive modulation of addictive sexual behavior marks the transition from Stage One to Stage Two. At this point, the therapeutic focus can shift to relapse prevention as the primary modality for stabilizing abstinence from addictive behavior. Supportive psychotherapy may be helpful at this time, but exploratory-expressive psychotherapy is likely to

be more beneficial in most cases if it is deferred until the latter part of Stage Two, when behavior and affect are more stable. Meanwhile, psychodynamically oriented interventions may be needed during Stages One and Two to address psychodynamically based resistances to pharmacological, behavioral, and cognitive-behavioral interventions, lest the entire treatment be disrupted. Stage Three is the period during which the therapeutic focus can turn to psychodynamic psychotherapy as the therapeutic modality that is most effective in treating character pathology. Psychodynamic psychotherapy, however, is not equally effective in all cases. Both the need for and the capacity for psychodynamic therapy vary considerably among individuals who use sexual behavior addictively. Also worth noting is that the initiation of psychodynamic psychotherapy does not entail that relapse prevention is no longer needed. Couples therapy or family therapy, when indicated, is likely to be most helpful after the individual's major disorder has stabilized and, if significant character pathology was part of the presenting picture, after character healing is well under way. However, some form of couple or family intervention may be necessary earlier in treatment if the couple or family system is in crisis. Self-help groups, such as 12-step groups, are typically most helpful during Stages One and Two and early in Stage Three. A good self-help group—one that is composed of relatively healthy, growing individuals with whom the patient fits well—can be helpful also later in Stage Three and in Stage Four. The second modification of the treatment system alters the system's guidelines to recommend that relapse prevention be conducted in a group therapy setting, where it is likely to be not only more resource-efficient than in an individual therapy setting, but also more effective. The third modification, including behavior modification and antiandrogen pharmacotherapy in the treatment system, and the fourth, adding couples and family therapy to the list of therapeutic options, were addressed in the discussion of the first modification. (A more detailed and comprehensive discussion of this treatment system, and of the theoretical material that has been presented in this chapter, can be found in reference 252.)

To date, no studies have been conducted to evaluate the effectiveness of integrated treatment for sexual addiction.

Prognosis

The data that could provide an empirical basis for most statements about the prognosis of sexual addiction are not yet available. While the long-term response of sexual addiction to various types of treatment cannot at this time be reliably predicted, a number of factors have been identified that seem to influence the prognosis. These factors can be clustered in three groups: (*a*) illness factors (that complicate the prognosis), which include early age of onset, high frequency of symptomatic sexual behavior, concomitant use of alcohol or other drugs, and absence of anxiety or guilt about the behavior; (*b*) recovery support factors (that improve the prognosis), which include a stable job, a stable primary relationship, a supportive social network, availability of appropriate sexual outlets, and environmental monitoring; and (*c*) personality factors (that improve the prognosis), which include intelligence, creativity, self-observatory capacity, sense of humor, capacity to form interpersonal connections, and motivation for change—which is a function of one's ability to experience oneself as responsible, as well as one's degree of subjective distress. Prognosis is influenced also by comorbidity with other psychiatric disorders and by the degree of associated character pathology.

Many clinicians agree that sexual addiction, like other addictive disorders, is a chronic condition. However much they may have benefited from treatment, most addicts (of all behavioral types) will to some extent remain vulnerable to being overwhelmed by intense affect-states and loss of self-coherence in situations that would be neither traumatic nor disorganizing for individuals whose self-regulation systems are intact. And sex addicts, in particular, will remain vulnerable to experiencing threats of being overwhelmed by these internal states as urges to engage in sexual behavior. Even after stable recovery has been achieved, ongoing maintenance activity may be required indefinitely to prevent relapse. Like other addictive disorders, sexual addiction does not get cured. Nonetheless, as Camus (250) observed in "The Myth of Sisyphus" (in an apparently unrelated context), "The important thing . . . is not to be cured, but to live with one's ailments" (p. 38).

References

1. Krafft-Ebbing R; Rebman FJ, trans. Psychopathia sexualis (1886). New York: Paperback Library, 1965.
2. Anthony DT, Hollander E. Sexual compulsions. In Hollander E, ed. Obsessive-compulsive related disorders. Washington, DC: American Psychiatric Association, 1993:139–150.
3. Coleman E. Sexual compulsion vs. sexual addiction: the debate continues. SIECUS Report 1986:7–11.
4. Coleman E. Sexual compulsivity: definition, etiology and treatment considerations. In: Coleman E, ed. Chemical dependency and intimacy dysfunction. New York: Haworth Press, 1987.
5. Coleman E. Is your patient suffering from compulsive sexual behavior? Psychiatric Ann 1992; 22:320–325.
6. Hollander E. Introduction. In: Hollander E, ed. Obsessive-compulsive related disorders. Washington, DC: American Psychiatric Association, 1993:1–16.
7. Quadland MC. Compulsive sexual behavior: definition of a problem and an approach to treatment. J Sex Marital Ther 1985;11:121–132.
8. Weissberg JH, Levay AN. Compulsive sexual behavior. Med Aspects Human Sexuality 1986; 20:127–128.
9. Barth RJ, Kinder BN. The mislabeling of sexual impulsivity. J Sex Marital Ther 1987;13:15–23.
10. McElroy SL, Hudson JI, Pope HG, Keck PE, Aizley HG. The DSM-III-R impulse control disorders not elsewhere classified: clinical characteristics and relationship to other psychiatric disorders. Am J Psychiatry 1992;149:318–327.
11. Carnes P. Out of the shadows: understanding sexual addiction. Minneapolis: CompCare, 1983.
12. Carnes P. Contrary to love: helping the sexual addict. Minneapolis: CompCare, 1989.
13. Goodman A. Sexual addiction: designation and treatment. J Sex Marital Ther 1992;18:303–314.
14. Goodman A. Diagnosis and treatment of sexual addiction. J Sex Marital Ther 1993;19(3): 225–251.
15. Marks I. Behavioural (non-chemical) addictions. Br J Addict 1990;85:1389–1394.
16. Schwartz MF, Brasted WS. Sexual addiction. Med Aspects Human Sexuality 1985;19: 103–107.
17. American Psychiatric Association. Diagnostic and statistical manual of mental disorders. 4th edition. Washington, DC: American Psychiatric Press, 1994.
18. Kafka MP. Successful antidepressant treatment of nonparaphilic sexual addictions and paraphilias in men. J Clin Psychiatry 1991;52:60–65.
19. Kruesi MJP, Fine S, Valladares L, Phillips RA, Rapoport JL. Paraphilias: a double-blind crossover comparison of clomipramine versus desipramine. Arch Sex Behav 1992;21: 587–593.
20. Stein DJ, Hollander E, Anthony DT, et al. Serotonergic medications for sexual obsessions, sexual addictions, and paraphilias. J Clin Psychiatry 1992;53:267–271.
21. Goodman A. Addictive disorders: an integrated approach. Part one. An integrated understanding. J Min Addict Recovery 1995;2:33–76.
22. Goodman A. Addiction: definition and implications. Br J Addict 1990;85:1403–1408.
23. Orford J. Hypersexuality: implications for a theory of dependence. Br J Addict 1978;73: 299–310.
24. Levine MP, Troiden RR. The myth of sexual compulsivity. J Sex Res 1988;25:347–363.

25. Cox WM, Klinger E. A motivational model of alcohol use. J Abnorm Psychol 1988;97:168–180.
26. Baker TB, Morse E, Sherman JE. The motivation to use drugs: a psychobiological analysis of urges. In: Rivers PC, ed. Nebraska symposium on motivation: alcohol and addictive behavior. Lincoln, NE: University of Nebraska Press, 1987:34;257–323.
27. Goldstein A. Introduction. In: Goldstein A, ed. Molecular and cellular aspects of the drug addictions. New York: Springer-Verlag, 1989.
28. Jaffe JH. Current concepts of addiction. In: O'Brien CP, Jaffe JH, eds. Addictive states. New York: Raven Press, 1992:1–21.
29. Miller NS, Dackis CA, Gold MS. The relationship of addiction, tolerance, and dependence to alcohol and drugs: a neurochemical approach. J Subst Abuse Treat 1987;4:197–207.
30. Childress AR, Ehrman R, Rohsenow DJ, Robbins SJ, O'Brien CP. Classically conditioned factors in drug dependence. In: Lowinson JH, Ruiz P, Millman RB, Langrod JG. Substance abuse: a comprehensive textbook. Baltimore: Williams & Wilkins, 1992:56–69.
31. Childress AR, McLellan AT, O'Brien CP. Abstinent opiate abusers exhibit conditioned craving, conditioned withdrawal, and reductions in both through extinction. Br J Addict 1986;81: 701–706.
32. Leventhal H, Cleary PD. The smoking problem: a review of the research and theory in behavioral risk modification. Psychol Bull 1980;88: 370–405.
33. Ludwig AM, Wikler A. Craving and relapse to drink. Q J Stud Alcohol 1974;35:108–130.
34. O'Brien C. Experimental analysis of conditioning factors in human narcotic addiction. Pharmacol Rev 1975;27:533–543.
35. Sherman JE, Jorenby DE, Baker TB. Classical conditioning with alcohol: acquired preferences and aversions, tolerance, and urges/craving. In Chaudron CD, Wilkinson DA, eds. Theories on alcoholism. Toronto: Addiction Research Foundation, 1988:173–237.
36. Sideroff S, Jarvik ME. Conditioned responses to a videotape showing heroin-related stimuli. Int J Addict 1980;15:529–536.
37. Wikler A. Some implications of conditioning theory for problems of drug abuse. Behav Sci 1971;16:92–97.
38. Wikler A. Dynamics of drug dependence: implications of a conditioning theory for research and treatment. In: Fisher S, Freedman A, eds. Opiate addictions: origins and treatment. Washington, DC: L Winston & Sons, 1973:7–21.
39. Wikler A. A theory of opioid dependence. In: Lettieri D, Sayers M, Pearson H, eds. Theories on drug abuse: selected contemporary perspectives. NIDA Res Monogr Ser 1980;30:174–178.
40. Wikler A. Opioid dependence: mechanisms and treatment. New York: Plenum, 1980.
41. Goodman A. Organic unity theory: the mind-body problem revisited. Am J Psychiatry 1991; 148:553–563.
42. Goodman A. Organic unity theory: a foundation for integrative psychiatry. I. Philosophical theory. Integrative Psychiatry (in press).
43. Goodman A. Organic unity theory. a foundation for psychiatry as an integrative science. In: Bittar EE, ed. Principles of medical biology. Greenwich, CT: Jai Press (in press).
44. Goodman A. Organic unity theory: an integrative mind-body theory for psychiatry. Theoretical Medicine (in press).
45. Blumer D. Changes in sexual behavior related to temporal lobe disorders in man. J Sex Research 1974;42:155–162.

46. Epstein AW. Fetishism: a study of its psychopathology with particular to a proposed disorder in brain mechanism as an etiological factor. J Nerv Ment Dis 1960;130:107–119.
47. Epstein AW. Relationship of fetishism and transvestism to brain and particularly to temporal lobe dysfunction. J Nerv Ment Dis 1961; 133:247–253.
48. Hoenig J, Kenna J. EEG abnormalities and transsexualism. Br J Psychiatry 1979;134:293–300.
49. Kolarsky A, Freund K, Machek J, Polak O. Male sexual deviation: association with early temporal lobe damage. Arch Gen Psychiatry 1967;17: 735–743.
50. Mohan KJ, Salo MW, Nagaswami S. A case of limbic system dysfunction with hypersexuality and fugue state. Dis Nerv Syst 1975;36: 621–624.
51. Raboch J, Cerna H, Zemek P. Sexual aggressivity and androgens. Br J Psychiatry 1987;151: 398–400.
52. Seim HC. Evaluation of serum testosterone and luteinizing hormone levels in sex offenders. Fam Pract Res J 1988;7:175–180.
53. Abel G. Paraphilias. In: Kaplan HI, Sadock BJ, eds. Comprehensive textbook of psychiatry, 5th ed. Baltimore: Williams & Wilkins, 1989: 1069–1085.
54. Rasmussen SA, Tsuang MT. Clinical characteristics and family history in DSM-III obsessive-compulsive disorder. Am J Psychiatry 1986; 143:317–322.
55. Warwick HMC, Salkovskis PM. Unwanted erections in obsessive-compulsive disorder. Br J Psychiatry 1990;157:919–921.
56. Abel GC, Osborn C. The paraphilias: the extent and nature of sexually deviant and criminal behavior. Psychiatr Clin N Am 1992;15:675–687.
57. Abel GG, Rouleau J-L. The nature and extent of sexual assault. In: Marshall WL, Laws DR, Barbaree HE, eds. Handbook of sexual assault: issues, theories, and treatment of the offender. New York: Plenum, 1990:9–21.
58. Chalkley AJ, Powell GE. The clinical description of forty-eight cases of sexual fetishism. Br J Psychiatry 1983;142:292–295.
59. Rooth FG. Exhibitionism, sexual violence and paedophilia. Br J Psychiatry 1973;122:705–710.
60. Wilson GD, Gosselin C. Personality characteristics of fetishists, transvestites, and sadomasochists. Person Ind Diff 1980;1:289–295.
61. Breitner IE. Psychiatric problems of promiscuity. South Med J 1973;66:334–336.
62. Kafka MP, Prentky R. Fluoxetine treatment of nonparaphilic sexual addictions and paraphilias in men. J Clin Psychiatry 1992;53:351–358.
63. Kafka MP. Sertraline pharmacotherapy for paraphilias and paraphilia-related disorders: An open trial. Ann Clin Psychiatry 1994;6: 189–195.
64. Fagan PJ, Wise TN, Schmidt CW, Ponticas Y, Marshall RD. A comparison of five-factor personality dimensions in males with sexual dysfunction and males with paraphilia. J Pers Assess 1991;57:434–448.
65. Blair CD, Lanyon RI. Exhibitionism: etiology and treatment. Psychol Bull 1981;89:439–463.
66. Washton AM. Cocaine may trigger sexual compulsivity. US J Drug Alcohol Depend 1989; 13:8.
67. Schneider JP, Schneider B. Sex, lies, and forgiveness: couples speaking out on healing from sexual addiction. Center City, MN: Hazelden Educational Materials, 1991.
68. Lesieur HR. Report on pathological gambling in New Jersey. In: Report and recommendations of the governor's advisory commission on gam-

bling. Trenton, NJ: Governor's Advisory Commission on Gambling, 1988.

69. Steinberg MA. Sexual addiction and compulsive gambling. Am J Prevent Psychiatry Neurol 1990;2:39–41.

70. Hucker SJ, Bain J. Androgenic hormones and sexual assault. In: Marshall WL, Laws DR, Barbaree HE, eds. Handbook of sexual assault: issues, theories, and treatment of the offender. New York: Plenum, 1990:94–102.

71. Langevin R, Ben-Aron MH, Coulthard R, et al. Sexual aggression: constructing a predictive equation: A controlled pilot study. In: Langevin R, ed. Erotic preference, gender identity, and aggression in men: new research studies. Hillsdale, NJ: Erlbaum, 1985:39–76.

72. Marshall WL, Barbaree HE. An integrated theory of the etiology of sexual offending. In: Marshall WL, Laws DR, Barbaree HE, eds. Handbook of sexual assault: issues, theories, and treatment of the offender. New York: Plenum, 1990:209–229.

73. Hendricks SE, Fitzpatrick DF, Hartman K, Quaife MA, Stratbucker RA, Graber B. Brain structure and function in sexual molesters of children and adolescents. J Clin Psychiatry 1988;49:108–112.

74. Hucker S, Langevin R, Wortzman G, et al. Neuropsychological impairment in pedophiles. Can J Behav Sci 1986;18:440–448.

75. Hucker S, Langevin R, Wortzman G, et al. Cerebral damage and dysfunction in sexually aggressive men. Ann Sex Res 1988;1:33–47.

76. Langevin R. Sexual anomalies and the brain. In: Marshall WL, Laws DR, Barbaree HE, eds. Handbook of sexual assault: issues, theories, and treatment of the offender. New York: Plenum, 1990:103–113.

77. Langevin R, Bain J, Wortzman S, Hucker S, Dickey R, Wright P. Sexual sadism: brain, blood, and behavior. Ann N Y Acad Sci 1988; 528:163–171.

78. Flor-Henry P, Koles ZL, Reddon JR, Baker L. Neuropsychological studies (EEG) of exhibitionism. In: Shagrasi MC, Josiassen RC, Roemer RA, eds. Brain electrical potentials and psychopathology. Amsterdam: Elsevier, 1986: 279–306.

79. Flor Henry P, Lang R. Quantitative EEG analysis in genital exhibitionists. Ann Sex Res 1988; 1:49–62.

80. Beck AT. Depression: clinical, experimental and theoretical aspects. New York: Harper & Row, 1967.

81. Beck AT, Rush AJ, Shaw BF, Emery G. Cognitive therapy of depression. New York: Guilford Press, 1979.

82. Bak RC. Fetishism. J Am Psychoanal Assoc 1953;1:285–298.

83. Bak RC. Aggression and perversion. In: Lorand S, ed. Perversions: psychodynamics and therapy. London: Ortol, 1965:231–240.

84. Chasseguet-Smirgel J. Perversion, idealization and sublimation. Int J Psycho-Anal 1974;55: 349–357.

85. Chasseguet-Smirgel J. Loss of reality in perversions—with special reference to fetishism. J Am Psychoanal Assoc 1981;29:511–534.

86. Coen SJ. Sexualization as a predominant mode of defense. J Am Psychoanal Assoc 1981;29: 893–920.

87. Eber M. Don Juanism: a disorder of the self. Bull Menninger Clinic 1981;45:307–316.

88. Fenichel O. The psychoanalytic theory of neurosis. New York: WW Norton, 1945.

89. Freud S. Three essays on the theory of sexuality. In: Strachey J, ed and trans. The standard edition of the complete psychological works of Sigmund Freud. London: Hogarth Press, 1905 (1953);7:123–245.

90. Freud S. Fetishism. In: Strachey J, ed and trans. The standard edition of the complete psychological works of Sigmund Freud. London: Hogarth Press, 1927(1953);21:149–157.

91. Gillespie WH. Notes on the analysis of sexual perversions. Int J Psycho-Anal 1952;33: 397–402.

92. Glasser M. Some aspects of the role of aggression in the perversions. In: Rosen I, ed. Sexual deviation. 2nd edition. Oxford: Oxford University Press, 1979:278–305.

93. Glasser M. Identification and its vicissitudes as observed in the perversions. Int J Psycho-Anal 1986;67:9–17.

94. Glover E. Agression and sado-masochism. In: Rosen I, ed. Pathology and treatment of sexual deviation: a methodological approach. London: Oxford University Press, 1964: 146–162.

95. Goldberg A. A fresh look at perverse behavior. Int J Psycho-Anal 1975;56:335–342.

96. Goldberg A. The problem of perversion: the view from self psychology. New Haven, CT: Yale University Press, 1995.

97. Greenacre P. Further considerations regarding fetishism. Psycho-Anal Study Child 1955;10: 187–194.

98. Greenacre P. Fetishism. In: Rosen I, ed. Sexual deviation. 2nd edition. Oxford: Oxford University Press, 1979:79–108.

99. Hammer EF. Symptoms of sexual deviation: dynamics and etiology. Psychoanal Rev 1968;55:5–27.

100. Hershey DW. On a type of heterosexuality, and the fluidity of object relations. J Am Psychoanal Assoc 1989;37:147–171.

101. Hoffman M. Drug addiction and "hypersexuality": related modes of mastery. Compr Psychiatry 1964;5:262–270.

102 Kernberg OF. Borderline personality organization. J Am Psychoanal Assoc 1967;15: 641–685.

103. Kernberg OF. Aggression in personality disorders and perversions. New Haven, CT: Yale University Press, 1992.

104. Khan MMR.The role of polymorph-perverse body-experiences and object-relations in ego-integration. Brit J Med Psychol 1962;35: 245–261.

105. Khan MMR. Role of the 'collated internal object' in perversion-formations. Int J Psycho-Anal 1969;50:555–565.

106. Khan MMR. Alienation in perversions. London: Hogarth Press, 1979.

107. Kohut H. The analysis of the self: a systematic approach to the psychoanalytic treatment of narcissistic personality disorders. New York: International Universities Press, 1971.

108. McDougall J. Primal scene and sexual perversion. Int J Psycho-Anal 1972;53:371–384.

109. McDougall J. Identifications, neoneeds and neosexualities. Int J Psycho-Anal 1986;67: 19–31.

110. Myers W. Sexual addiction. In: Dowling S, ed. The psychology and treatment of addictive behavior. Madison, CT: International Universities Press, 1994.

111. Ovesey L, Person E. Gender identity and sexual psychopathology in men: a psychodynamic analysis of homosexuality, transsexualism, and transvestism. J Am Acad Psychoanal 1973;1: 53–72.

112. Person E, Ovesey L. Transvestism: new perspectives. J Am Acad Psychoanal 1978;6: 301–323.

113. Payne SM. Some observations on the ego development of the fetishist. Int J Psycho-Anal 1939;20:161–170.

114. Rosen I. The general psychoanalytic theory of perversion: a critical review. In: Rosen I, ed. Sexual deviation. 2nd edition. Oxford: Oxford University Press, 1979:29–64.

115. Rosen I. Perversion as a regulator of self-esteem. In: Rosen I, ed. Sexual deviation. 2nd edition. Oxford: Oxford University Press, 1979:65–78.

116. Socarides CW. The preoedipal origin and psychoanalytic therapy of sexual perversions. Madison, CT: International Universities Press, 1988.

117. Stoller RJ. Perversion: the erotic form of hatred. New York: Pantheon, 1975.

118. Stolorow RD. The narcissistic function of masochism (and sadism). Int J Psycho-Anal 1975;56:441–448.

119. Stolorow RD. Psychosexuality and the representational world. Int J Psycho-Anal 1979;60: 39–45.

120. Trop JL, Alexander R. The concept of promiscuity: a self psychological perspective. In: Stern EM, ed. Psychotherapy and the promiscuous patient. New York: Haworth Press, 1992:39–49.

121. Goodman A. Dépendence sexuelle (Sexual addiction). Médicine & Hygiène 1995;53:1575–1577.

122. Goodman A. The addictive process: a neurobiological understanding. (unpublished manuscript).

123. Gold PW, Goodwin FK, Chrousos GP. Clinical and biochemical manifestations of depression: relation to the neurobiology of stress (first of two parts). N Engl J Med 1988;319:348–353.

124. Kraemer GW. Causes of changes in brain noradrenaline systems and later effects on responses to social stressors in rhesus monkeys: the cascade hypothesis. Antidepressants and Receptor Function (CIBA Foundation Symposium 123). New York: Wiley, 1986.

125. Post RM. Transduction of psychosocial stress into the neurobiology of recurrent affective disorder. Am J Psychiatry 1992;149:999–1010.

126. Coccaro EF, Siever LJ, Klar HM, et al. Serotonergic studies in patients with affective and personality disorders. Arch Gen Psychiatry 1989;46:587–599.

127. Stein DJ, Hollander E, Liebowitz MR. Neurobiology of impulsivity and the impulse control disorders. J Neuropsychiatry Clin Neurosci 1993;5:9–17.

128. Mandell AJ, Knapp S. Asymmetry and mood, emergent properties of serotonin regulation. Arch Gen Psychiatry 1979;36:909–916.

129. Blundell JE. Serotonin and appetite. Neuropharmacology 1984;23:1537–1552.

130. Sheard MH, Aghajanian GK. Stimulation of midbrain raphe neurons: behavioral effects of serotonin release. Life Sci 1968;7:19–25.

131. Harvey JA, Yunger LM. Relationship between telencephalic content of serotonin and pain sensitivity. In: Barchas J, Usdin E, eds. Serotonin and behavior. New York: Academic Press, 1973:179–189.

132. Akil H, Liebeskind JC. Monoaminergic mechanisms of stimulation produced analgesia. Brain Res 1975;94:279–296.

133. Cloninger CR. Neurogenetic adaptive mechanisms in alcoholism. Science 1987;236: 410–416.

134. Ramsey NF, Van Ree JM. Reward and abuse of opiates. Pharmacol Toxicol 1992;71:81–94.

135. Wise RA. The role of reward pathways in the development of drug dependence. Pharmacol Ther 1987;35:227–262.

136. Amir S, Brown ZW, Amit Z. The role of endorphins in stress: evidence and speculations. Neurosci Behav Rev 1980;4:77–86.

137. Panksepp J, Herman B, Conner R, Bishop P, Scott JP. The biology of social attachments: opiates alleviate separation distress. Biol Psychiatry 1978;13:607–618.

138. Herz A, Shippenberg TS. Neurochemical aspects of addiction: 0pioids and other drugs of abuse. In: Goldstein A, ed. Molecular and cellular aspects of the drug addictions. New York: Springer-Verlag, 1989.

139. Baile CA, McLaughlin CL, Della-Fera MA. Role of cholecystokinin and opioid peptides in control of food intake. Physiol Rev 1986; 66:172–234.

140. Morley JE, Levine AS. Pharmacology of eating behavior. Annu Rev Pharmacol Toxicol 1985;25:127–146.

141. Morley JE, Levine AS, Rowland NE. Stress-induced eating. Life Sci 1983;32:2169–2182.

142. Pfaus JG, Gorzalka BB. Opioids and sexual behavior. Neurosci Biobehav Rev 1987;11: 1–34.

143. Graeff FG. Neuroanatomy and neurotransmitter regulation of defensive behaviors and related emotions in mammals. Brazil J Med Biol Res 1994;27:811–829.

144. Chan-Palay V. Cerebellar dentate nucleus: organization, cytology and transmitters. Berlin: Springer-Verlag, 1977.

145. Beaudet A, Descarries L. Quantitative data on serotonin nerve terminals in adult rat neocortex. Brain Res 1976;111:301–309

146. Aghajanian GK, Wang RY. Physiology and pharmacology of central serotonergic neurons. In: Lipton MA, DiMascio A, Killam KF, eds. Psychopharmacology: a generation of progress. New York, Raven Press, 1978: 171–183.

147. Smith BH, Sweet WH. Monoaminergic regulation of central nervous system function: I. Noradrenergic systems. Neurosurgery 1978;3: 109–119.

148. Gorenstein EE, Newman JP. Disinhibitory psychopathology: a new perspective and a model for research. Psychol Rev 1980;87:301–315.

149. Modell JG, Mountz JM, Beresford TP. Basal ganglia/limbic striatal and thalamocortical involvement in craving and loss of control in alcoholism. J Neuropsychiatry Clin Neurosci 1990;2:123–144.

150. Tarter RE, Alterman AI, Edwards KL. Vulnerability to alcoholism in males: a behavior-genetic perspective. J Stud Alcohol 1985;4: 329–356.

151. Eyzaguirre C, Fidone SJ. Physiology of the nervous system. 2nd edition. Chicago: Year Book Medical Publishers, 1975.

152. Schore AN. Affect regulation and the origin of the self: the neurobiology of emotional development. Hillsdale, NJ: Lawrence Erlbaum, 1994.

153. Watson SJ, Trujillo KA, Herman JP, Akil H. Neuroanatomical and neurochemical substrates of drug-seeking behavior: overview and future directions. In: Goldstein A, ed. Molecular and cellular aspects of the drug addictions. New York: Springer-Verlag, 1989:29–91.

154. Louilot A, Taghzouti K, Simon H, Le Moal M. Limbic system, basal ganglia, and dopaminergic neurons: executive and regulatory neurons and their role in the organization of behavior. Brain Behav Evol 1989;33:157–161.

155. Edelman GM. Neural darwinism: the theory of neuronal group selection. New York: Basic Books, 1987.

156. Greenough WT, Black JE. Induction of brain structure by experience: substrates for cognitive development. In: Gunnar MR, Nelson CA, eds. Minnesota symposium on child psychology. Developmental behavioral neuroscience. Hillsdale, NJ: Lawrence Erlbaum, 1992; 24:155–200.

157. Greenough WT, Black J, Wallace C. Experience and brain development. Child Dev 1987; 58:539–559.

158. Kraemer GW. Effects of differences in early social experience on primate neurobiological-behavioral development. In: Reite M, Field T, eds. The psychobiology of attachment and separation. New York: Academic Press, 1985: 135–161.

159. Kraemer GW, Ebert MH, Schmidt DE, McKinney WT. A longitudinal study of the effects of different rearing environments on cerebrospinal fluid norepinephrine and biogenic amine metabolites in rhesus monkeys. Neuropsychopharmacology 1989;2:175–189.

160. Kraemer GW, Ebert MH, Schmidt DE, McKinney WT. Strangers in a strange land: a psychobiological study of infant monkeys before and after separation from real or inanimate mothers. Child Dev 1991;62:548–566.

161. Tucker DM. Developing emotions and cortical networks In: Gunnar MR, Nelson CA, eds. Minnesota symposium on child psychology. Developmental behavioral neuroscience. Hillsdale, NJ: Lawrence Erlbaum, 1992;24:75–128.

162. Kiernan RJ. Localization of function: the mind-body problem revisited. J Clin Neuropsychol 1981;3:345–352.

163. Luria AR. The working brain. New York: Basic Books, 1973.

164. Miller L. 'Narrow localizationism' in psychiatric nosology. Psychol Med 1986;16:729–734.

165. Goodman A. The addictive process: a psychoanalytic understanding. J Am Acad Psychoanal 1993;21:89–105.

166. Wilson GT. Alcohol use and abuse: a social learning analysis. In: Chaudron CD, Wilkinson DA, eds. Theories on alcoholism. Toronto: Addiction Research Foundation, 1988:239–287.

167. Cooper ML, Russell M, George WH. Coping, expectancies, and alcohol abuse: a test of social learning formulations. J Abnorm Psychol 1988;97:218–230.

168. Hull JG, Bond CF. Social and behavioral consequences of alcohol consumption and expectancy: a meta-analysis. Psychol Bull 1986; 99:347–360.

169. Besnard F, Kempf E, Fuhrmann G, Kempf J, Ebel A. Influence of mouse genotype on responses of central biogenic amines to alcohol intoxication and aging. Alcohol 1986;3: 345–350.

170. Fadda F, Colombo G, Gessa GL. Genetic sensitivity to effect of ethanol on dopaminergic system in alcohol preferring rats. Alcohol Alcohol Suppl 1991;1:439–442.

171. Schuckit M. Genetics and the risk for alcoholism. JAMA 1985;18:2614–2617.

172. Johnson AM, Robinson DB. The sexual deviant (psychopath)—causes, treatment, and prevention. JAMA 1957;164:1559–1565.

173. Berlin FS. Sex offenders: a biomedical perspective and a status report on biomedical treatment. In: Greer JG, Sturat IR, eds. The sexual aggressor: current perspectives on treatment. New York: Van Nostrand Reinhold, 1983:83–123.

174. Berlin FS, Meinecke CF. Treatment of sex offenders with antiandrogenic medications: conceptualization, review of treatment modalities, and preliminary findings. Am J Psychiatry 1981;138:601–607.

175. Bradford JM. Organic treatment for the male sexual offender. Ann N Y Acad Sci 1988; 528:193–202.

176. Bradford JMW. The antiandrogen and hormonal treatment of sexual offenders. In: Marshall WL, Laws DR, Barbaree HE, eds. Handbook of sexual assault: issues, theories, and treatment of the offender. New York: Plenum, 1990:297–310.

177. Cordoba OA, Chapel JL. Medroxyprogesterone acetate antiandrogen treatment of hypersexuality in a paedophilic sex offender. Am J Psychiatry 1983;140:1036–1039.

178. Freund K. Therapeutic sex drive reduction. Acta Psychiatr Scand Suppl 1980;287:5–38.

179. Gagne P. Treatment of sex offenders with medroxyprogesterone acetate. Am J Psychiatry 1981;138:644–646.

180. Hermann WM, Beach RC. Pharmacotherapy for sexual offenders: review of the actions of antiandrogens with special s to their psychic effects. Mod Prob Pharmacopsychiatry 1908;15: 182–194.

181. Maletzky BM. Somatic therapies. In: Maletzky BM, ed. Treating the sexual offender. Newbury Park, CA: Sage, 1991.

182. Money J. Use of androgen depleting hormone in the treatment of male sex offenders. J Sex Res 1970;6:165–172.

183. Money J. The therapeutic use of androgen depleting hormone. Int Psychiatry Clin 1972; 8:165–174.

184. Wincze JT, Bansai S, Malamud M. Effects of medroxyprogesterone acetate on subjective arousal, arousal through erotic stimulation, and nocturnal penile tumescence in male sexual offenders. Arch Sex Behav 1986;15:293–305.

185. Bancroft J, Tennent G, Loucas K, Cass J. The control of deviant sexual behavior by drugs: behavioural changes following estrogens and anti-androgens. Br J Psychiatry 1974;125: 310–315.

186. Bradford JMW, Pawlak A. The effects of cyproterone acetate in the treatment of the paraphilias. Arch Sex Behav 1993;22: 383–402.

187. Bradford JMW, Pawlak A. The effects of cyproterone acetate on the sexual arousal patterns of pedophiles. Arch Sex Behav 1993; 22:629–641.

188. Cooper AJ. A placebo-controlled trial of antiandrogen cyproterone acetate in deviant hypersexuality. Compr Psychiatry 1981;22: 458–465.

189. Gilby R, Wolf L, Goldberg B. Mentally retarded adolescent sex offenders: a survey and pilot study. Can J Psychiatry 1989;34: 452–458.

190. Laschet U. Antiandrogen in the treatment of sex offenders: mode of action and therapeutic outcome. In: Zubin J, Money J, eds. Contemporary sexual behavior: critical issues in the 1970s. Baltimore: Johns Hopkins University Press, 1973:311–319.

191. Laschet U, Laschet L. Antiandrogens in the treatment of sexual deviations in men. J Steroid Biochem 1975;6:821–826.

192. Murray MAF, Bancroft JHH, Anderson DC, Tennent TG, Carr PJ. Endocrine changes in male sexual deviants after treatment with antiandrogens, oestrogens or tranquilizers. J Endocrinol 1975;67:179–188.

193. Marshall WL, Jones R, Ward T, Johnson P, Barbaree HE. Treatment outcome with sexual offenders. Clin Psychol Rev 1991;11:465–485.
194. Marshall WL, Barbaree HE. Outcome of comprehensive cognitive-behavioral treatment programs. In: Marshall WL, Laws DR, Barbaree HE, eds. Handbook of sexual assault: issues, theories, and treatment of the offender. New York: Plenum, 1990:363–385.
195. Reid WH. Sexual disorders. In: Reid WH, ed. The treatment of psychiatric disorders: revised for the DSM-III-R. New York: Brunner/Mazel, 1989:273–295.
196. Bianchi MD. Fluoxetine treatment of exhibitionism [letter]. Am J Psychiatry 1990;147:1089–1090.
197. Emmanuel NP, Lydiard RB, Ballenger JC. Fluoxetine treatment of voyeurism [letter]. Am J Psychiatry 1991;148:950.
198. Jorgensen VT. Cross-dressing successfully treated with fluoxetine [letter]. N Y State J Med 1990;90:566–567.
199. Lorefice LS. Fluoxetine treatment of a fetish. J Clin Psychiatry 1991;52:41.
200. Perilstein RD, Lipper S, Friedman LJ. Three cases of paraphilias responsive to fluoxetine treatment. J Clin Psychiatry 1991;52:169–170.
201. Snaith RP, Collins SA. Five exhibitionists and a method of treatment. Br J Psychiatry 1981;138:126–130.
202. Casals-Ariet C, Cullen K. Exhibitionism treated with clomipramine [letter]. Am J Psychiatry 1993;150:1273–1274.
203. Clayton AH. Fetishism and clomipramine [letter]. Am J Psychiatry 1993;150:673–674.
204. Torres AR, de Abreu Cerquiera AT. Exhibitionism treated with clomipramine [letter]. Am J Psychiatry 1993;150:1274.
205. Wawrose FE, Sisto TM. Clomipramine and a case of exhibitionism [letter]. Am J Psychiatry 1992;149:843.
206. Bartova D, Nahumek K, Svestke J. Pharmacological treatment of deviant sexual behavior. Activ Nerv Sup (Praha) 1978;20:72–74.
207. Cesnik JA, Coleman E. Use of lithium carbonate in the treatment of autoerotic asphyxia. Am J Psychother 1989;63:277–286.
208. Ward NG. Successful lithium treatment of transvestism associated with manic-depression. J Nerv Ment Dis 1975;161:204–206.
209. Federoff JP. Buspirone hydrochloride in the treatment of transvestic fetishism. J Clin Psychiatry 1988;49:408–409.
210. Eyres A. Transvestism: employment of somatic therapy with subsequent improvement. Dis Nerv Syst 1960;(Jan):52–53.
211. Abel GG, Lewis DJ, Clancy J. Aversion therapy applied to taped sequences of deviant sexual behavior in exhibitionism and other sexual deviations: a preliminary report. J Behav Ther Exp Psychiatry 1970;1:59–66.
212. Birk L, Huddleston W, Miller E, Cohler B. Avoidance conditioning in homosexuality. Arch Gen Psychiatry 1971;25:314–323.
213. Evans DR. Masturbatory fantasy and sexual deviation. Behav Res Ther 1968;6:17–19.
214. Evans DR. Subjective variables and treatment effects in aversion therapy. Behav Res Ther 1970;8:147–152.
215. Fookes BH. Some experience in the use of aversion therapy in male homosexuality, exhibitionism, and fetishism-transvestism. Br J Psychiatry 1969;115:339–341.
216. MacCulloch MJ, Williams C, Birtles CJ. The successful application of aversion therapy to an adolescent exhibitionist. J Behav Ther Exp Psychiatry 1971;2:61–66.
217. Marks IM, Gelder MG, Bancroft JHJ. Sexual deviants two years after electric aversion. Br J Psychiatry 1970;117:173–185.
218. Marks IM, Rachman S, Gelder MG. Methods for assessment of aversion treatment in fetishism with masochism. Behav Res Ther 1965;3:253–258.
219. Wijesinghe B. Masses aversion treatment of sexual deviance. J Behav Ther Exp Psychiatry 1977;8:135–137.
220. Quinsey VL, Bergersen SG, Steinman CM. Changes in physiological and verbal responses of child molesters during aversion therapy. Can J Behav Sci 1976;8:202–212.
221. Feldman MP, MacCulloch MJ. The aversion therapy treatment of a heterogeneous group of five cases of sexual deviation. Acta Psychiatrica Scand 1968;44:113–123.
222. Abel GG, Osborn C. Stopping sexual violence. Psychiatric Ann 1992;22:301–306.
223. Alford GS, Webster JS, Sanders SH. Covert aversion of two interrelated sexual practices: obscene phone calling and exhibitionism. A single case analysis. Behav Ther 1980;11:15–25.
224. Brownell KD, Hayes SC, Barlow DH. Patterns of appropriate and deviant sexual arousal: the behavioral treatment of multiple sexual deviations. J Consult Clin Psychol 1977;45:1144–1155.
225. Callahan EJ, Leitenberg H. Aversion therapy for sexual deviation: contingent shock and covert sensitization. J Abnorm Psychol 1973;81:60–73.
226. Hayes SC, Brownell KD, Barlow DH. The use of self-administered covert sensitization in the treatment of exhibitionism and sadism. Behav Ther 1978;9:283–289.
227. Lamontagne Y, Lesage A. Private exposure and covert sensitization in the treatment of exhibitionists. J Behav Ther Exp Psychiatry 1986;17:197–201.
228. Maletzky BM. "Assisted" covert sensitization in the treatment of exhibitionism. J Consult Clin Psychol 1974;42:34–40.
229. Maletzky BM. Self-referred versus court-referred sexually deviant patients: success with assisted covert sensitization. Behav Ther 1980;11:306–314.
230. Hunter JA, Goodwin DW. The clinical utility of satiation therapy with juvenile offenders: variations and efficacy. Ann Sex Res 1992;5:71–80.
231. McConaghy N, Armstrong MS, Blaszczynski A. Expectancy, covert sensitization and imaginal desensitization in compulsive sexuality. Acta Psychiatr Scand 1985;72:176–187.
232. Mathis JL, Collins M. Mandatory group therapy for exhibitionists. Am J Psychiatry 1970;126:1162.
233. Truax RA. Discussion of Mathis and Collins. Am J Psychiatry 1970;126:1166.
234. Ganzarain R, Buchele BJ. Incest perpetrators in group therapy: a psychodynamic perspective. Bull Menninger Clin 1990;54:295–310.
235. Rosen I. Exhibitionism, scopophilia and voyeurism. In: Rosen I, ed. Pathology and treatment of sexual deviation: a methodological approach. London: Oxford University Press, 1964:293–350.
236. Witzig JS. The group treatment of male exhibitionists. Am J Psychiatry 1968;125:179–185.
237. Abstinence and boundaries in S.A.A. (booklet). Minneapolis: Sex Addicts Anonymous, 1986.
238. Suggestions for newcomers (pamphlet). Boston: The Augustine Fellowship, Sex and Love Addicts Anonymous, 1986.
239. Sexaholics Anonymous. Simi Valley, CA. SA Lit, 1989.
240. SCA—a program of recovery (booklet). New York: SCA, 1989.
241. Gabbard G. Paraphilias and sexual dysfunctions. In: Gabbard G, ed. Psychodynamic psychiatry in clinical practice. Washington, DC: American Psychiatric Press, 1994:327–357.
242. Wise TN. Fetishism and transvestism. In: Karasu TB, ed. Treatment of psychiatric disorders: a task force of the American Psychiatric Association. Washington, DC: American Psychiatric Press, 1989;1:633–646.
243. Wakeling A. A general psychiatric approach to sexual deviation. In: Rosen I, ed. Sexual deviation. 2nd ed. Oxford: Oxford University Press, 1979:1–28.
244. Rosen I. Exhibitionism, scopophilia, and voyeurism. In: Rosen I, ed. Sexual deviation. 2nd ed. Oxford: Oxford University Press, 1979:139–194.
245. Adson PR. Treatment of paraphilias and related disorders. Psychiatric Ann 1992;22:299–300.
246. Kilmann PR, Sabalis RF, Gearing ML, Bukstel LH, Scovern AW. The treatment of sexual paraphilias: a review of outcome research. J Sex Res 1982;18:193–252.
247. Schwartz MF. Effective treatment for sex offenders. Psychiatric Ann 1992;22:315–319.
248. Protter B, Travin S. Sexual fantasies in the treatment of paraphilic disorders: a bimodal approach. Psychiatr Q 1987;58:279–297.
249. Travin S, Protter B. Sexual perversion: integrative treatment approaches for the clinician. New York: Plenum Press, 1993.
250. Travin S. Compulsive sexual behaviors. Psychiatr Clin North Am 1995;18:155–169.
251. Goodman A. Addictive disorders: an integrated approach. Part two. An integrated treatment. J Min Addict Recovery 1996 3:49–77.
252. Goodman A. Sexual addiction: an integrated approach. Madison, CT: International Universities Press (in press).
253. Camus A. The myth of sisyphus. In: Camus A. The myth of sisyphus and other essays (1955; O'Brien J, trans). New York: Vintage International, 1991:1–138.

32 COLLECTION AND ACCUMULATION

Jane Glick and David A. Halperin

"Some people are actor junkies, some people are music junkies, I'm an art junkie." —Lizzie Himmel, noted New York photographer

Few human activities are as subject to varying interpretations as the collection and accumulation of objects. On one level, the accumulation of objects—the formation of a collection and the acquisitive actions that accompany it—can be seen in diagnostic terms as comparable to pathological gambling because it becomes a preoccupation, requires the expenditure of increasing amounts of money, resists efforts to control it, becomes a way of escaping from problems or of relieving dysphoria, may require concealing from family members the extent of expenditure or shopping activity, may lead to jeopardizing or losing significant relationships, and may lead the individual to rely on others to relieve the desperate straits to which their expenditures have led. Or, acquisitive activities may be seen as comparable to binge-eating in which there are "recurrent episodes . . . associated with subjective and behavioral indicators of impaired control over, and significant distress about, the binge eating" (1). Indeed, one collector has noted an almost narcotic-like effect when in the throes of a collecting frenzy: until the preoccupation with acquisition subsided, the collector was unaware of a chronic and debilitating lumbosacral pain. Similarly, concerns about a current acquisition enabled this collector to temporarily suppress or dissociate other, more usual, obsessive concerns. In more dynamic terms, collecting and hoarding can be seen as overdetermined activities subject to a variety of interpretations. The possibility that collection or accumulation may be related to other forms of addiction is suggested by the intriguing conjunction of collection, accumulation, and creativity to the use of cocaine illustrated by Charcot and Freud in the medical literature and in the world of fiction by Huysman's Des Esseintes and Arthur Conan Doyle's Sherlock Holmes. Thus, Edmond de Goncourt stated that the mature Doctor Charcot relied on a powerful narcotic potion of bromide, morphine, and codeine to "produce" such "exhilarating dreams on a daily basis" (2, p. 106). This relationship of collection and accumulation to addiction and its potential association with addictions of other types—comorbidity—is an issue that will be highlighted in this chapter by an examination of clinical examples.

Collection and accumulation should not be examined under a lens totally focused on their pathological dimensions. As a notable example, John Gedo (3) attributes Freud's being a "passionate" collector of antiquities to a multiplicity of causes, including his ambivalence about his identification with the Jewish people, his attempts at identification with his Germanic surround with "a commitment to classical ideals" acted out in the "struggle between Aryan Rome and Semitic Carthage, a conflict in which he identified with both sides"; and, the role played by his antiquities as transitional objects allowing Freud to transcend his background and achieve a more cosmopolitan identification. As illustrated in his discussion of Freud's collection and accumulation of antiquities, Gedo's analysis demonstrates that the acquisition of objects is overdetermined, and it can be understood only if intrapsychic, historical, and a wide variety of other factors are considered. Thus, the individual must be examined within specific historical contexts that may make the acquisition of many objects normative, e.g., the hoards of antiquities and objects d'art accumulated by wealthy Englishmen or Americans during grand tours of Europe, or the Tulipmania which swept Holland during the seventeenth century. This chapter examines the accumulation of objects—the collecting and/or the hoarding of objects in which individuals act out across a broad spectrum of activity from the appropriate and creative to the pathological and addictive, illustrates the treatment issues that arise in working with the "passionate collector," suggests therapeutic approaches, and examines the question of the proper nosological classification of accumulating the hoard.

GENERAL CONSIDERATIONS ON COLLECTION AND ACCUMULATION

The values that enter into the accumulation of objects—hoarding and accumulation—form the subtexts of works of literature such as Ben Johnson's play, *Volpone,* or Gogol's masterful short story, "The Coat." In more modern times, accumulation and its implications forms the basis of T. Coraghessian Boyle's recent short story, "Filthy with Things" (4). Here, the protagonist requests the assistance of an individual for help in organizing his life, and watches helplessly as his helper arrives, immediately diagnoses the story's protagonist as a "pathological accumulator" and prescribes radical therapy—removal of all accumulated objects leaving the "victim" in a totally pure, white minimalist environment. The description of "pathological accumulator" begs the question of whether this does, indeed, constitute a diagnostic entity with its own symptoms and deserves its own treatment approaches. The premise of this chapter is that pathological accumulation does, indeed, warrant such classification and treatment—that the use of terms such as "shop-aholic" trivializes what often is a severe disability and discourages the mental health professional from examining and treating such dysfunctional behavior with the seriousness that it merits. Moreover, the resort to accumulative behavior may enable the individual to avoid either recognizing or dealing with other significant pathology, which should be the focus of treatment.

The minimalism—the esthetic that "less is more" (as contrasted with the accumulator's retort that "less is a bore")—advocated as "radical" therapy is in direct contrast to the more humanistic approach described by X, the distinguished Italian author, who wrote his memoirs in the form of a dialog conducted in his apartment in Rome between himself and the objects whose past he lovingly recalls. On a more philosophical level, Claude Levi-Strauss, in his fascinating and magisterial *Tristes Tropiques,* notes that the mere act of acquisition of an object may be perceived as an act of defilement of its mana (inherent power) when it is valued exclusively or even primarily in terms of the purely Western esthetic. To Levi-Strauss the act of accumulation or collection becomes an attempt to retrieve the magic inherent in objects—paradoxically undertaken within a culture so intent on denying the existence of magic (5).

Freud's collection of antiquities marched across his office desk. Except in unusual circumstances, the home or the office becomes the arena in which the collection or accumulation is displayed. Most individuals will experience the minimalism inherent in the label of "pathological accumulator" as a denial of a sense of continuity and a denigration of their sense of individuality. Our dwellings and offices function as esthetic expressions, although we may not completely share the attitudes of Des Esseintes, the fin-de-siècle esthete, portrayed in Huysman's novel, *A rebours:* " . . . through the unfolding of his experience in a succession of elaborate interiors he himself had crafted. The objects in those interiors were the vehicles for his synaesthesia and visual fantasies; his dependence on this continuous aesthetic stimulation consigned him to physical lassitude and nervous hypersensitivity" (2, p. 77).

The manner in which an interior space is transformed from a house into a home with all its potentially accumulative connotations is a matter of great individuality. The space is considered a tabula rasa onto which the resident imposes his esthetic sensibility. Within limits, form inevitably follows function. Hoarding and accumulation to the detriment of efficiency is suspect. Nonetheless, perhaps in homage to his *maître,* Charcot, Freud's office was dominated by his striking collection of antiquities, which functioned as a museum from whose valences Freud drew inspiration. In this multidetermined relationship between collection and art, Freud was not unique. He acknowledged that Charcot introduced into the clinical studies of psychopathology "the sensibility of the artist." A recent study has noted that Freud's master, Charcot, was fascinated by the fantastic in art. Freud, himself, characterized Charcot's home as the "magic castle in which he lives . . . in short, a museum" (2, p. 102). For Charcot, it is clear that there was a relationship between the act of collecting and the act of creation. "The tension between reason and fantasy, order and disorder that shaped Charcot's artistic-medical persona was expressed in his personal practice of interior design. Charcot collaborated with his family to create a unified personal environment where historical materials were animated by private memories and exteriorized dreams" (2, p. 102). For Freud, as well, there is a relationship between collection and creation. Intriguingly, his first attempt at applied psychoanalysis, *Delusions and Dreams in Jensen's Gradiva* (6), examines the tension between an artist and his possession. For the psychoanalyst whose passion for antiquities and fascination with the archeology of the individual—whose interest in "applied psychoanalysis" with its attempt at an uncovering of the sources of creativity as in his studies of Leonardo—his collection was regarded as the markers in his trip of exploration.

In his ingathering of antiquities, Freud remains a model more discussed than emulated. Even within the mental health field, the configuration of the therapist's office has long been a matter of dispute. There is a continuing conflict between minimalist-impersonal and accumulative-personal perspectives. Many psychoanalysts adopt Freud's metaphor of surgical sterility and preserve the neutrality of the psychoanalytic field—leaving it "uncontaminated" by personal artifacts, essentially decorating their offices in black and white. In their zeal to remove any sense of individuality, these minimalists approach Freud's attitude towards his office decor with a therapeutic skepticism suggestive that they regard his "passionate collecting" as being akin to an addiction. If addiction it was, then it was self-controlled addiction indeed. This skepticism about the intrusion of the individualistic into the decoration of the therapist's office was highlighted in a recent article in the *New York Times*, which discussed the dimensions of the analytic couch in comparable terms (7). One of the authors of this chapter was mindful of these divergences when he was opening his own office and he remembered a colleague whose office was filled with an accumulation of objects because "my patients come from backgrounds where there has been little warmth" and contrasted it with the shabby room of an office reputedly maintained in a species of genteel poverty ostensibly to focus the attention of patients, without the possible distraction, on issues presented within the conscious and unconscious. The possibility that creating a space with warmth and individuality might be a corrective emotional experience was adopted.

THE COLLECTOR IN CONTROL?

The varying attitudes towards collection and accumulation illustrated by the differing attitudes towards furnishing the therapist's office are paralleled as well in the residential space. This parallelism is recounted by Tracey, a "self-regulating" addict.

Tracey has assembled a tasteful collection of twentieth century art, which was recently exhibited in a prominent New York gallery. However, when questioned about her collection, she comments that "I never planned it; it just happened." She notes that she had always liked art and objects of beauty. A factor of particular importance was her pleasure in looking at art museums and galleries and her enjoyment of the camaraderie of dealer and fellow collectors on her "rounds." In college, however, she decided that while she could never become a great artist, she could become a great art collector. The subliminatory aspect of being a great collector in lieu of being an artist—that the great collector is often an *artiste manqué* or failed artist has been frequently noted. But pleasure in sublimation or sociability provides only a partial explanation for the activity which occupies a great deal of the collector's time and energy. A parallelism between the collector and the hunter has also been noted as another significant factor in the development of the "committed" collector. Olmstead (8) has noted that the hunting metaphor is often used in the title of books about collecting. Of particular interest is the addictive aspect of collecting or hunting. Tracey notes that "I've gone through phases. I kept seeing things I liked and enjoyed owning things I wanted and seeing them around all the time." She describes the satisfaction of being able to have things that

were denied to her in the past. However, following her parent's deaths, one closely after the other, she became depressed. There was a moratorium on many aspects of her life including her collecting (unlike Freud who began to collect after his father's death, perhaps because he felt liberated to pursue an expansion of his area of identification). After about two years, she felt a renewed interest in life and in collecting. She characterized her renewed impetus as expressing the realization that "You can't take it with you." However, acquisition in and of itself became an egodystonic activity. Pure possession did not seem to afford sufficient gratification. This changing attitude towards collection has enabled Tracey to impose some measure of self-regulation. This modification of her behavior is a product of her increased sense of satiation but also of a number of other limiting factors. They include Tracey's sense that she has reached the point beyond which it becomes increasingly difficult to find objects she would prefer to those she has already acquired. An important reality factor is that the rapidly appreciating cost of artwork has made further acquisitions more difficult. At this point, "It stopped as rapidly as it started." Tracey considers herself "a controlled (self-regulated) addict." She acknowledges that she had an addiction for a time, but adds that she now has the ability to "hold tight and stop." She has adopted a variety of measures to maintain her sense of control. She imposes limits on herself such as frequenting only "safe" shows, i.e., exhibitions in which objects are either prohibitively expensive or not for sale. She relates her current attempts to maintain control as comparable to her mother's attempts to limit a smoking addiction by not allowing herself (an observant Jew) to smoke on the Sabbath or in certain rooms of the house. And, the imposition of compulsive controls (i.e., two drinks per day, no more no less) is often of benefit to the addict in recovery. Nonetheless, such approaches do not deal with underlying aspects of an addiction and appear to become less effective over time. Thus, despite her attempts at control, Tracey comments that she would still like to find things that are "very special." She notes that while making her rounds, she does not feel as driven and is able to accept "just looking" in the same fashion that passing a bakery and merely inhaling the scent of pastries satisfies her. Yet, with her sense of accomplishment at self control, there is the caveat of acknowledging that were she to move to a larger apartment. . . .

THE COLLECTOR AS AN UNREGULATED ADDICT

Tracey has the potential to behave in an addictive manner. She has never sought treatment because she currently feels her "addiction" is under control. However, Ted M. presents a less benign scenario:

Ted M. is an architect. He entered treatment in his mid 30s ostensibly because of his inability to decide if he wanted to divorce his wife for his girlfriend. A talented architect, Ted had married soon after receiving his degree at a prestigious school of architecture. His work has been illustrated in a number of professional publications, and he has received commissions for many projects in the New York metropolitan area. A few years after his marriage, he began a series of long-term extramarital relationships. These relationships were characteristically intense and volatile. He would explosively enter into consuming relationships with his partners. During the course of the relationships, he would respond to any separation from his partners in an equally intense fashion. On one occasion when his girlfriend, Opal, suggested that they cool things off, Ted was so offended by his girlfriend's "daring" to suggest any degree of separation or suggesting that she be free to pursue any contact with another man, that he threw a computer monitor through a glass wall at her. Despite this display of involvement, he remained quite unable to resolve his own exceedingly ambivalent relationship with his wife. He rationalized his inactivity as a necessary sacrifice because his passive, helpless, and phobic wife would be unable to survive his departure. In diagnostic terms, Ted was characterized as a borderline personality disorder. He fit the DSM IV diagnostic criteria of borderline personality disorder because of his (*a*) pattern of unstable and intense interpersonal relationships characterized by alternating between extremes of over idealization and devaluation; (*b*) impulsiveness in at least two areas that are potentially self-damaging, e.g., spending, sex; (*c*) affective instability; (*d*) inappropriate, intense anger or lack of control of anger; (*e*) marked persistent identity disturbance manifested by uncertainty about self-image, sexual orientation, type of friends desired, and preferred values. Ted did not simply form relationships with friends—he collected friends. For example, even after terminating the sexual aspect of a relationship with his girlfriends, he would maintain them—often as employees—lending them large sums of money, etc. Ted was also an object collector. If he found a shirt style he liked, then he would buy the same shirt in every available color. His wardrobe was enormous, but Ted rarely wore many items of his accumulation of clothing. Rather, his acquisition of clothing reflected "A chronic restiveness . . . an unrelenting need, even hunger for acquisitions . . . which derives from a memory of deprivation . . . and a subsequent longing for substitution" (9, p. 3). Ted collected other objects as well. He developed a focus for elephants, and collected hundreds of objects d'art in the form of elephants. His collection of elephants was not fetishistic in nature. In a profound manner it reflected the sense that "the collector, not unlike the religious believer, assigns power and value to these objects . . . [in which] affection becomes attached to things, which . . . can become animated like the amulets and fetishes of preliterate humankind or the holy relics of the religionist. Such special objects may even be given a name . . . and help assure the child of companionship . . . [G]iving an object a 'soul' or name . . . is known as animism. In psychological terms, it has been described as 'attachment' " (9, p. 9–10). On a more creative level, Ted assembled sculptures of elephants from debris found around his house and discarded objects. Eventually, he moved to a larger apartment in part to have space to store his collections of elephants and clothing. Ted also collected other objects. Every room in his house had many telephones ostensibly because that would ensure that he would be available for important phone calls; however, this also reflected Ted's fear of missing a "important" message during a childhood filled with a profound sense of having been ignored or deprived of attention he felt was his due. Borderline personality disorder is often characterized by identity disturbance. And, the formation of collections and the accumulation is often related to the expression of ambivalence around identity issues. Thus, it is not surprising that Ted's pathology expressed itself in his collections, but also expressed itself in his identity disturbance. Not only did he collect an enormous amount of clothing, but the clothing, itself, was often bizarre and inappropriately androgynous in fashion. In addition, he changed his professional name to create an alternative identity. Thus, he saw himself as transformed from the identity inherent in his given Jewish name to that of his Anglophilic professional name—as if to collect another personality.

Ted M. illustrates the importance of the formation of collections and the accumulation of objects as an aspect in the formation of individual identity. However, the appropriation of objects and the formation of collections also plays a significant role in the creation of societal and cultural identity. As a prime example, transporting the Elgin Marbles from the Acropolis to the British Museum may have been an act of esthetic appreciation that preserved vulnerable marble sculptures, but it was also an act of appropriation both illustrating and establishing the "benign" nature of the British Empire—labeling the accumulation of territories as an advance in "civilization" and as an extension of the "benefits" of civilization to those "benighted savages" otherwise deprived of "progress." And, even when the appropriated object has been preserved, it is preserved in so sanitized a setting that little remains of its inherent authority of power to bear real witness to its culture of origin. In other cases, the appropriated objects are destroyed or placed in a deliberately transformed setting to erase the cultural memory of conquered people as Cortés accomplished in Mexico.

Therapeutic work with Ted focused around issues of identification in sexual and vocational terms, his inability to separate from individuals and objects, and his development of other means of dealing with anxiety than the accumulation of objects. The therapist undertook the therapeutic task of enabling Ted to deal with his profound anxiety over the loss of objects, animate and inanimate—to separate from old relationships and objects and to form new relationships or purchase new objects which met his standards. In esthetic terms, the goal of treatment was the transformation of Ted from being an accumulator to becoming a connoisseur. In this context, the accumulator is seen as an individual who acquires objects for the sake of accumulation whereas the connoisseur is seen as the individual who ostensibly acquires only those objects which meet carefully defined esthetic standards. Or, the accumulator merely increases the size of his accumulation, whereas the connoisseur "upgrades" his collection. For the accumulator, the sequestration of increasing numbers of objects is the primary or exclusive focus of activity, as contrasted with the connoisseur's activity which acquires a sublimatory cast or is characterized by an artistic sensibility. As a result of treatment, Ted was able to make distinctions and separate from many of his possessions. He was able to adopt others which

were much more meaningful in both personal and objective terms. A primary aspect of this change was enabling Ted to face his *temor vacuui*—his fear of emptiness. Despite his professional success, Ted had always regarded his work as the product of a species of esthetic subservience. By supporting his adoption of a more personalized and esthetically consistent attitude towards his clients, he was able to enhance his *sense* and a *sense* of empowerment. As a result, he felt a heightened *sense* of the correctness of his individual choice of an item of clothing and a lessened need for accumulation and storage of a "wardrobe." He was ultimately able to form a lasting relationship with one woman. These issues—the relationship between collection or accumulation and addiction are presented in more grandiose terms in the case of Charles.

THE ACCUMULATOR AS CITY FOUNDER

Charles was the only son of wealthy parents. His father had helped to create a Fortune 500 company and after his retirement had been active in philanthropic activity. Charles graduated from a prestigious national university (as his father had not). Soon after graduation, he began to work for an investment firm. His progress within the firm was steady but slow. In the meantime, he developed an interest in real estate development, and he began to acquire property. He began to envisage his accumulating a sufficiently large tract to enable him to develop and promote the creation of a "new city." His wife, Ruth, panicked at his ever-increasing commitment of his fortune to this vision. She feared that this insatiable need to buy property would lead Charles to invest all of his sizable fortune in this scheme for urban development. Ultimately, she succeeded in referring Charles for psychiatric consultation. On mental status examination, Charles was an appropriately dressed male oriented in all spheres. His speech was loosely goal directed and under considerable pressure. He constantly returned to the discussion of his grandiose plans for his "city." And, he was not amenable to any discussion of the practical issues which his plans involved. He was totally unable to appreciate the potential self-destructive nature of his ambitions. After consultation, he was hospitalized with his consent. Upon hospitalization, he was diagnosed as having a bipolar affective disorder and placed on a mood stabilizer, lithium. He was initially reluctant to use lithium because he felt it might interfere with his enjoyment of cannabis, but the medical staff prevailed upon him to cooperate. He rapidly recovered and soon was discharged to his home for follow-up.

Charles' illness manifested itself in the accumulation of acreage. While superficially the purchase of real estate may appear to be a less frivolous and more reality-oriented decision in contradistinction to the accumulation of shoes, blouses, or other objects of fashion, there is a deeper logic at work. For Charles as for other accumulators, his acreage was an object which existed primarily as an abstraction—it was an accumulation assembled without any realistic regard for its intrinsic utility. Charles had no clearly formulated plan to utilize his acreage. His land existed as a demarcation on a map no more to be used than the 4000 shoes of Imelda Marcos, who purchased them presumably more for their symbolic value or as a concrete representation of some inner state than as objects to be worn. For the hoarder the hoard is its own reward. Charles' accumulation of acreage ostensibly represented the nidus of the plan to create "a new city," but a cursory discussion of his projected plan immediately revealed its unrealistic and unsubstantial nature. Yet, in Charles' plan, there is the distorted reflection of the great urbanist and architect, Daniel Burnham "Make no small plans, they have not the spark to stir the blood of men." And, in his plan to create a city, Charles reflected one of the ultimate phases in the formation of a collection which the noted auctioneer, Jim Julia, has characterized as the "final phase. It's the point at which you present it to the public and people come, fight over it, and walk away with these treasures in their arms . . . [thus] passing antiques [or acreage] along is the consummation of the collector's passion" (10). Accumulation and collection may also form a significant aspect of the creative process as illustrated by the artist, Andy Warhol.

ANDY WARHOL: THE ACCUMULATOR/ COLLECTOR AS CREATOR OR AS ADDICT?

Andy Warhol was an extraordinarily influential artist. He helped define art and fashion for an entire generation. He was also a collector and accumulator on a truly remarkable scale. His creative energy is unquestionable. Was his accumulative activity just another facet of his creative process or was it simply an addiction? Hellinger noted in *The Archives of the Andy Warhol Museum* (11, p. 195) that

> Warhol filled his town house at 57 East 66th Street with a treasure trove of fine art, furnishings, objects d'art, and jewelry—all uncatalogued and much of it tucked into shopping bags and boxes stacked in rooms so full that the door could not be opened or closed . . . [only five rooms] out of the 27 room town house had [not] served as warehouse for the objects he acquired each day. . . . A team of appraisers labored for months, producing a six-volume auction catalog. News of Warhol's limitless collecting interests ranging from "Canova to cookie jars." . . . The auction resulted in the sale of a staggering amount of collectibles. . . . The auction established Andy Warhol as an insatiable collector who was interested in everything and could part with nothing.

The question remains—was Andy Warhol a Collier brother with taste? Hellinger considers his accumulations to have been Warhol's "source material": "letters from a Warhol Superstar are found in a cookie tin containing used batteries and a broken camera" (11, p. 196). Hellinger contends that Warhol intentionally produced these "time capsules," a dumping place for seemingly unrelated materials that were products of a certain period of creative activity. Hellinger comments that the Archives have chosen to preserve these "time capsules" in their original form because they reflect Warhol's perceptions of a particular period, and that Warhol filled these "time capsules" with "selected and manipulated mass produced images of American pop culture—to transform some of the most poignant and at times horrific representations of our culture into fine art." From another perspective, however, it is difficult to see in this anything other than Warhol's inability to decrease his expanding hoard.

Andy Warhol's collection of objects was both an addiction and an artistic statement. On one level, it constituted a breach of the border demarcating the boundaries between the antique and the "collectible" or in other terms, high art from kitsch-elitism versus popular preference. The objects themselves, mass-produced cookie jars etc., stand apart from the elite products of high art. In the emergence of the "collectible," there is the recognition and a heightened appreciation of the merits of popular creations—a recognition manifested by the growth of a new industry celebrated every weekend across the country at flea markets. Warhol's refusal to accept the strictures dividing high art and its esthetic from kitsch with its acceptance of sentimentality and nostalgia, provided an antidote to the anhedonic, almost puritanical strictures of modernism. His activities provided the theoretical backdrop to the development of the modern "collectible" industry. It should be noted that collectibles, unlike antiques, are objects considered worthy of attention without formally considering their esthetic merit because of the role that the object played in particular context or the feeling tone it elicits (hence the cookie jar with its redolence of nurturing and comfort). Warhol presided with the other "pop" artists over a transformation which eliminated culture as an object of derision and transformed it into the substance of exhibitions at temples of the elite such as the Museum of Modern Art or into objects of reverence by the presence of baseball cards within the august precincts of Sotheby's or Christie's. But, this transfiguration of popular culture into high realms begs the question: When does the accumulation of collectibles or objects become the pathological expression of an addiction as opposed to being the expression of an esthetic passion? This question arises because it represents a central conflict within the groves of academe—between elite and popular art. What standards are appropriate? What do standards represent? And, what, other than price, is the difference in significance between the objects on sale at Sotheby's or Christie's or at a tag sale?

Andy Warhol's need to acquire objects reflected his ideological convictions and his restless intellectual and esthetic curiosity. He (and his fellow archeologists of the "collectible") transformed "old junk into antiques." But there was a darker side to his transformation of standards. Warhol, himself, was not addicted to drugs but many of his collaborators were. Indeed, the 1996 film *Basquiat* highlights the relationship between Warhol and Basquiat and Warhol's particular ambivalence towards Basquiat's substance abuse. It may be that in a profound sense Warhol's addictive accumulation of objects provided an area of transcendence which allowed him to avoid prolonged substance abuse.

Warhol's accumulations demonstrate that the hoard may present an esthetic challenge to elitism. Charles' accumulation of acreage illustrates that accumulation may be symptomatic of manic behavior and the expression of a bipolar disorder. Ted, as an individual with borderline personality disorder, attempted to avoid severe depressive affects with a flight into manic behavior. The accumulation of these hoards was disruptive on a personal level. The expenditure of significant amounts of monies in each of these accumulations either led or could have been potentially led the accumulators to accumulate not only objects but debt. Indeed, the motive behind the entry of Charles and Ted into psychiatric treatment was dictated, in part, by their families' concern for their financial future. And, it behooves the therapist whose patient discusses accumulations as a form of "investment" and reassures both the therapist and himself that the accumulation of objects will provide secure and superior financial returns, to help that patient carefully examine the reality of his financial situation. On a broader scale, the need to hoard vast amounts of property without consideration of the human cost of its acquisition is a tragic aspect of human history. In the recent past, the human cost of the depredations and accumulations by Hermann Goering demonstrated the need to accumulate on an archetypal scale. His actions went beyond any usual boundaries and deserve examination as representing an example of accumulation by an individual with profoundly psychopathic traits and a significant history of narcotics addiction.

HERMANN GOERING: THE ADDICT AS ACCUMULATOR

Hermann Goering has been characterized as the "most complex and many-sided of all Nazi leaders, at once a figure of ridicule and of fear, a man of huge talents and of strange flaws. . . . He was also a drug addict, a glutton, a dandy, the greediest and most insatiable of art collectors" (12). Goering presents the remarkable picture of an individual seemingly addicted to whatever object appeared to arrest his attention. While the florid, epicene figure of him in later years is certainly an accurate portrayal, he also presents the complex union of a war hero and an apparently effective military leader in World War I joined to a history of narcotics addiction and art addiction—activities he pursued while acquiring numerous extraordinarily gaudy uniforms, palaces, hunting lodges, and economic control over much of Germany and Occupied Europe. Ostensibly, Goering's morphine addiction was the product of wounds sustained during the Beerhall Putsch in 1923. His addiction lasted for the next 2–3 years and was treated in a succession of Swedish sanatoria by enforced abstinence. His later desire to accumulate a vast art collection may have reflected some genuine appreciation and connoisseurship of the objects themselves. Yet, much of Goering's activity appears to have been the product of his ambivalent and competitive relationship with Hitler. Goering identified with the condottiere and seemingly needed to establish himself as a "type of Renaissance man." To establish himself as a twentieth century Maecenas, he planned to open his museum, Carin Hall, as the Hermann Goering Museum in 1953 to celebrate his 60th birthday, characteristically later than Hitler's planned 1951 opening of his museum in Linz (12, p. 319). The vast number of works of art acquired by Goering appears to reflect art's traditional role as an icon of possession and conquest. But, in addition, Goering would acquire and sell pieces of art as a demonstration of his control of the men who were his underlings within the Nazi hierarchy and as an expression of his grandiosity: "Goering sold pictures to Gauleiters, as he told me with a childlike smile, for many times what he had paid—adding, moreover, an extra something to the price for the glory of the painting having come from the famous Goering collection." His accumulative activity may be compared to Napoleon's if only to illustrate Marx's dictum that "when history repeats itself it does so the first time as tragedy and the second time as farce." Nonetheless, it is important to consider Goering as an exemplar of the manner in which addictions to drugs, clothing, possessions, and fine art can be joined in an individual who, when placed in a structured setting, was tragically able to function in a very efficient manner.

SUMMARY

Collection and accumulation are activities which are overdetermined and characterized all societies since Maecenas and his colleagues who transported Greek statues from Athens to Rome. The acquisition of objects may be viewed as an expression of some intrapsychic conflict in which the objects acquired allow the collector or accumulator to avoid a sense of loss or deprivation. It may reflect some retentive need to continually acquire and to accumulate objects without regard to their merit or the individual's needs— no matter how broadly defined. In a profound sense, the acquisition of objects is tied to a system in which "life is a game and he who dies with the most toys wins." However, during the course of the individual's lifetime, the very acquisition of objects is seen both as a display of the inherent power or mana of the objects and as an attempt to incorporate the power, which is seen as resident in the objects themselves. On a less pathological level, the accumulation of objects may be part of a creative process in which the artist acquires objects as part of the exploration and transformation accompanying the creative process. However, the process of accumulation and collection may share many characteristics of an addiction. Here, the process of accumulation of a hoard supersedes any other aspect of the process of collection. There is no simple means to differentiate between the addictive accumulation or the esthetic collection of objects. However, when the growing collection appears to be fueled by a need to acquire objects driven primarily by its own inner dynamic—the presence of severe pathology should become a matter of primary concern for the therapist. Timely intervention by the therapist with an exploration of the need to acquire objects in the presence of severe borderline pathology or of a bipolar disorder for which aggressive accumulation may be a significant marker—may enable the addict to avoid personal and financial ruin.

References

1. Frances A, Pincus HA, First MB, eds. Diagnostic and statistical manual of mental disorders. 4th edition. Washington, DC: American Psychiatric Press, 1994.
2. Silverman DL. Art nouveau in fin-de-siecle France: politics, psychology and style. Berkeley, CA: University of California Press, 1989.
3. Gedo JE. Art alone endures. J Am Psychoanal Assoc 1992;40(2)501–516.
4. Boyle TC. Filthy with things. New Yorker 1993;68:52.
5. Levi-Strauss C. Tristes Tropiques. New York: Viking-Penguin, 1992.
6. Freud S. (1907) Delusions and dreams in Jensen's Gradiva. In: Standard edition, vol. 7. London: Hogarth Press, 1955.
7. New York Times 1996(29 Feb):C1, C6.
8. Olmstead AD. Justifying collecting—metaphors and functions. Brimfield Antique Guide 1996(Fall):9–10.
9. Muensterberger W. Collecting: an unruly passion—psychological perspectives. Princeton, NJ: Harcourt Brace, 1994.
10. The biggest auction in the world. Down East 1996(August):90.
11. Hellinger R. Archives of the Andy Warhol Museum; 1994:195.
12. Mosley L. The reich marshal: a biography of Hermann Goering. New York: Dell, 1974.

SECTION V. EVALUATION AND EARLY TREATMENT

33 DIAGNOSIS AND CLASSIFICATION: DSM-IV AND ICD-10

George E. Woody and John Cacciola

The Diagnostic and Statistical Manual of Mental Disorders, 4th edition, (DSM-IV) (1) is the diagnostic classification system developed by the American Psychiatric Association. The Tenth Revision of the International Classification of Disease (ICD-10) (2) is the system used by the World Health Organization. The substance abuse sections of previous iterations of each classification system differed significantly from each other, though many of the concepts they contained were similar. As a result, considerable efforts were made to make the current versions of these two systems as similar as possible and these efforts were mostly successful. ICD-10 actually has two versions, the clinical and the research versions. The clinical version is the manual that is used in clinical practice and will be the main focus of attention in this chapter, although the research version of ICD-10 will be mentioned briefly in the discussion of course modifiers for dependence.

This chapter compares the sections of ICD-10 and DSM-IV that deal with substance-related disorders. Many details are only mentioned or described in very general terms so as to present an easily readable and memorable comparison of the two systems.

OVERVIEW

Psychiatric disorders attributable to abusable substances are of two general types: (*a*) disorders related to the pattern and/or consequences of substance use itself (i.e., dependence, abuse, and [in ICD-10] harmful use) and (*b*) disorders produced by the pharmacological effects of the substances themselves (i.e., intoxication, withdrawal, and substance-induced mental disorders).

The edition preceding DSM-IV, DSM-III-R, organized these two general types of disorders into two areas, whereas ICD-10 placed them in one section. In DSM-III-R, the substance-induced disorders were found in a section entitled "Psychoactive Substance-Induced Organic Mental Disorders," whereas dependence and abuse were found in the "Psychoactive Substance Use Disorder" section. A major accomplishment of DSM-IV was to place all of these disorders into one section "Substance Related Disorders" consisting of two parts: "Substance Use Disorders" includes dependence and abuse; "Substance-Induced Disorders" includes intoxication, withdrawal, and substance-induced mental disorders. This major change in the organization of DSM-IV has made its overall organization much more similar to that of ICD-10.

In each classification system, abusable substances or their general drug class are listed and criteria are provided so that any of the disorders attributable to that substance can be identified and numbered. For example, Alcohol Withdrawal in DSM-IV is described and diagnostic criteria are summarized and coded as 291.8; Amphetamine-Induced Mood Disorder is identified and coded as 292.84; Cocaine Dependence is described and coded as 304.20; etc. In general, the descriptive text for each of the diagnostic categories in DSM-IV is more detailed than that found in ICD-10.

Differences remain, however, the most prominent of which is found in the use of the terms "abuse" in DSM-IV and "harmful use" in ICD-10. Most importantly, each classification system is founded on the Edwards and Gross definition of the dependence syndrome (3, 4), a concept that was originally developed from work with individuals having problems with alcohol but later expanded to all abusable substances.

DEPENDENCE AND ITS COURSE MODIFIERS, ABUSE, AND HARMFUL USE

Dependence

DSM-IV has seven criteria items for dependence and ICD-10 has six. In each classification system, three items are necessary to make a diagnosis of dependence. Specific items are ordered differently in each system; however, their similarities are readily apparent when compared in Table 33.1.

In DSM-IV, dependence is specified as being either *with* or *without* physiological features. Dependence with physiological features is present if there is evidence of tolerance or withdrawal (i.e., criterion items (1) or (2) are present). Dependence without physiological features is present if three or more items are present but none of these are items (1) or (2). There is no comparable subtyping of dependence in ICD-10.

Both DSM-IV and ICD include course modifiers for dependence. DSM-IV expanded the limited number of course modifiers that were present in DSM-III-R, again resulting in greater consistency between DSM-IV and ICD-10. The course modifiers for both classification systems apply only to dependence and not to abuse or harmful use.

DSM-IV

DSM-IV organizes its course modifiers in terms of stage of remission, agonist therapy, or being in a controlled environment.

Remission

A person is not classified as being in remission until he or she has been free of all criteria items for dependence and all of the "A" items for abuse (to be described later) for at least one month. The first 12 months following cessation of problems with the substance is a period of particularly high risk for relapse; thus, it is given a special designation of Early Remission. There are two categories:

Early Full Remission: No criteria for dependence, and none of the "A" criteria for abuse, have been met for the last 1–12 months.
Early Partial Remission: Full criteria for dependence or abuse have not been met for the last 1–12 months; however, one or two dependence, or one or more of the "A" abuse criteria have been met, intermittently or continuously, during this period of Early Remission.

When 12 months of Early Remission have passed without relapse to dependence, the person is in Sustained Remission. There are two categories:

Sustained Full Remission: None of the criterion items for dependence and none of the criterion items for abuse have been present in the last 12 months.
Sustained Partial Remission: Full criteria for dependence have not been met for a period of 12 months or longer. However, one or two dependence, or one or more of the "A" criteria for abuse have been met, either continuously or intermittently, during this period of Sustained Remission.

Table 33.1 Comparison of DSM-IV and ICD-10 Criteria Items for Dependence

DSM-IV	ICD-10
Three or more of:	same
1) tolerance	iv) same
2) withdrawal	iii) same
3) the substance is often taken in larger amounts or over a longer period than was intended	ii) difficulties in controlling substance-taking behavior in terms of its onset, termination, or levels of use
4) any unsuccessful effort or a persistent desire to cut down or control substance use	no corresponding ICD category
5) a great deal of time is spent in activities necessary to obtain substance or recover from its effects	v) increased amounts of time necessary to obtain or take the substance or recover from its effects. Note: (v) item has two parts; this phrase represents one part
6) important social, occupational, or recreational activities given up or reduced because of substance use	v) progressive neglect of the alternative pleasures or interests. Note: (v) item has two parts; this phrase represents one part
7) continued substance use despite knowledge of having had a persistent or recurrent physical or psychological problems that are likely to be caused or exacerbated by the substance	vi) persisting with substance use despite evidence of overtly harmful problem consequences
no corresponding DSM category	i) a strong desire or sense of compulsion to take the substance

On Agonist Therapy

On prescribed, supervised agonist medication related to the substance and the criteria for dependence or abuse (other than tolerance or withdrawal) have not been met for the agonist medication in the last month.

This category also applies to persons being treated for dependence using an agonist/antagonist having prominent agonist properties.

In a Controlled Environment

No criteria for dependence or abuse are met but the person has been in an environment for one month or longer where controlled substances are highly restricted. Examples are closely-supervised and substance-free jails, therapeutic communities, or locked hospital units. Occasionally persons will be on agonist therapy while also in a controlled environment. In such cases, both course modifiers apply.

Just as the remission categories require a transitional month without any criteria for dependence or abuse, the one month period after cessation of agonist therapy or release from a controlled environment is a corresponding transition period. Thus, persons in this one month period are still considered dependent. They will move into an early remission category after being free of all criteria for dependence and of the "A" abuse criteria for one month.

ICD-10

The course modifiers for ICD are similar but not identical and are as follows:

- Currently abstinent
- Currently abstinent, but in a protected environment (e.g., in hospital, in a therapeutic community, in prison, etc.)
- Currently on a clinically supervised maintenance or replacement regime [controlled dependence] (e.g., with methadone; nicotine gum or nicotine patch)
- Currently abstinent, but receiving treatment with aversive or blocking drugs (e.g., naltrexone or disulfiram)
- Currently using the substance [active dependence]
- Continuous use
- Episodic use [dipsomania]

After publication of the ICD-10 clinical criteria, the ICD-10 research criteria were published. The section on course modifiers in the research criteria

were made even more similar to those of DSM-IV by adding three subcategories to "Currently abstinent": "Early remission," "Partial remission," and "Full remission." Two subcategories were added to "Currently using the substance": "Without physical features" and "With physical features." The phrase "The course of the dependence may be further specified, if desired, as follows:" was added before the terms "Continuous use" and "Episodic use [dipsomania]." These changes to the ICD-10 research criteria set the stage for even more integration between the next iterations of the ICD and DSM criteria.

Abuse and Harmful Use

Though the current ICD and the DSM definitions of dependence are very similar, they differ sharply on the concepts of abuse and harmful use. In DSM-IV, abuse is defined in social terms: i.e., problematic use in the absence of compulsive use, tolerance, and withdrawal. ICD has been reluctant to accept criteria items that are defined in terms of social impairment. However, ICD recognizes a nondependent type of substance use disorder. In ICD-10, this disorder is called Harmful Use and involves substance use that results in actual physical or mental damage.

This difference between DSM and ICD in the acceptability of social criteria for defining a disorder is primarily because ICD must be applicable to a wide range of cultures. Social mores differ so markedly between countries that it is difficult to develop socially-defined criteria that can be applied across cultures. For example, any use of alcohol in a Moslem country can lead to major adverse social consequences, whereas Western societies have integrated alcohol use into their social fabric. The ICD-10 category of harmful use is one that can be applied cross-culturally, and is the closest that ICD comes to the DSM concept of abuse. However, harmful use is really a different construct since it is limited to use which causes actual physical or mental damage. Harmful use is in many ways a more restrictive category than abuse, and some persons having a DSM-IV abuse diagnosis do not meet criteria for harmful use. A summary comparison of Abuse and Harmful Use is listed in Table 33.2.

In addition to pointing out the major differences between DSM-IV and ICD-10 in this area, the Table 33.2 summary also reflects a major change made to the definition of abuse. Unlike DSM-III-R and other earlier iterations of the DSM, DSM-IV clearly separated the criteria items for abuse from those for dependence. This change was done by attempting to identify only items that signify problematic or hazardous use as abuse and by leaving only items signifying compulsive use, tolerance, or withdrawal as dependence.

Four DSM-IV criteria items were developed for abuse. One (hazardous use) had been part of earlier definitions. Another (use resulting in failure to fulfill role obligations) was moved from a DSM-III-R dependence criterion item to abuse. The third and fourth items (recurrent substance-related legal

Table 33.2 A Comparison of Abuse and Harmful Use

DSM-IV	ICD-10
Abuse	**Harmful Use**
One or more of the following occurring over the same twelve month period:	Clear evidence that the substance use was responsible for (or substantially contributed to) physical or psychological harm, including impaired judgment or dysfunctional behavior.
1) recurrent substance use resulting in a failure to fulfill major role obligations at work, school, or home	
2) recurrent substance use in situations in which it is physically hazardous	
3) recurrent substance-related legal problems	
4) continued substance use despite having persistent or recurrent social or interpersonal problems caused or exacerbated by the effects of the substance	
Never met criteria for dependence	

Table 33.3   Diagnoses Associated with Class of Substances

	Dependence	Abuse	Intoxication	Withdrawal	Intoxication Delirium	Withdrawal Delirium	Dementia	Amnestic Disorder	Psychotic Disorder	Mood Disorders	Anxiety Disorders	Sexual Dysfunctions	Sleep Disorders
Alcohol	X	X	X	X	I	W	P	P	I/W	I/W	I/W	I	I/W
Amphetamines	X	X	X	X	I				I	I/W	I	I	I/W
Caffeine			X								I	I	I
Cannabis	X	X	X		I				I		I		
Cocaine	X	X	X	X	I				I	I/W	I/W	I	I/W
Hallucinogens	X	X	X		I				I*	I	I		
Inhalants	X	X	X		I		P		I	I	I		
Nicotine	X			X									
Opioids	X	X	X	X	I				I	I		I	I/W
Phencyclidine	X	X	X		I				I	I	I		
Sedatives, hypnotics, or anxiolytics	X	X	X	X	I	W	P	P	I/W	I/W	W	I	I/W
Polysubstance	X												
Other	X	X	X	X	I	W	P	P	I/W	I/W	I/W	I	I/W

*Also Hallucinogens Persisting Disorder (Flashbacks).

Note: X, I, W, I/W, or P indicates that the category is recognized in DSM-IV. In addition, *I* indicates that the specifier With Onset During Intoxication may be noted for the category (except for Intoxication Delirium); *W* indicates that the specifier With Onset During Withdrawl may be noted for the category (except for Withdrawal Delirium); and *I/W* indicates that either With Onset During Intoxication or With Onset During Withdrawal may be noted for the category. *P* indicates that the disorder is Persisting.
Reproduced with permission from Frances A. Pincus HA, First MB, eds. Diagnostic and statistical Manual of Mental Disorders. 4th edition. Washington, DC: American Psychiatric Association Press, 1994; 177.

problems; continued use despite having recurrent social or interpersonal problems) were split from one DSM-III-R dependence item and moved to abuse. Portions of that item (recurrent substance-related medical or psychiatric problems) remained in a DSM-IV dependence item.

SUBSTANCE-INDUCED DISORDERS

As described above, intoxication, withdrawal, and the wide range of substance-induced mental disorders are included in one single section in both DSM-IV and ICD-10. DSM-IV provides a brief description of the clinical manifestations of intoxication and withdrawal for each substance; exceptions are those few substances that do not have an identified withdrawal syndrome, such as LSD. ICD-10 provides less detail about each substance but provides general criteria that allow for classification of intoxication or withdrawal according to specific substances.

DSM-IV also provides considerable detail for the substance-induced mental disorders. The wide range of mental disorders that can be produced by substances are identified in the text and summarized in Table 33.3.

Each of the mental disorders that are listed in this table are referenced and coded in the text accompanying that specific substance. They are also cross-referenced with the section of DSM-IV that deals with that type of disorder. For example, psychotic disorders attributable to alcohol intoxication or withdrawal are mentioned and coded in the text dealing with alcohol, and the reader is directed to the psychotic disorders section of DSM-IV for a more complete description of these disorders. ICD-10 provides a more general format that allows for classification of substance-induced mental disorders, but provides much less substance-specific detail than DSM-IV.

COMPARISONS OF DIFFERENCES IN SPECIFIC DIAGNOSTIC CATEGORIES

There are a few other important categories that are found in one system but not the other. For instance, DSM-IV has three categories that are not specified in ICD-10. These are Polysubstance Dependence; Other (or Unknown) Substance-Related Disorders; and Phencyclidine (or Phencyclidine-Like)-Related Disorders. These categories would likely be classified under the ICD-10 heading of "Disorders Resulting from Multiple Drug Use and Use of Other Psychoactive Substances."

A number of substances have limited diagnostic possibilities in DSM-IV but have a wider range of ICD-10 diagnostic labels. For instance, caffeine is included in the stimulant section of ICD-10 and thus is open to a wide range of subcategories. In contrast, Caffeine Intoxication, Caffeine-Induced Anxiety Disorder, and Caffeine-Induced Sleep Disorder are the only categories available for this substance in DSM-IV. Similarly, DSM-IV has only two categories involving nicotine: dependence and withdrawal. ICD-10 has the same wide range of diagnostic categories for nicotine that is available for all other substances.

ICD-10 has a section (listed as a subsection of "Behavioural Syndromes Associated with Physiological Disturbances and Physical Factors") that is separate from the psychoactive substance use section and that is used for classifying abuse of non–dependence-producing substances. This includes problematic use of antidepressants, laxatives, steroids, and hormones. A comparable section in DSM-IV is found under Other (or Unknown) Substance-Related Disorders.

SUMMARY

As shown, many of the major differences between the DSM and ICD classification systems have been eliminated or considerably reduced by DSM-IV and ICD-10. The most prominent remaining difference is in the concepts underlying abuse and harmful use. Less prominent differences are found in the less detailed descriptions of the various clinical syndromes in ICD-10 as compared to DSM-IV, and in ICD-10's ability to attach the entire range of substance-related diagnoses to any drug class while DSM-IV provides more limits on the number of diagnostic possibilities. Generally, ICD-10 has more categories available for each substance than DSM-IV, but many of these categories are never used because they do not exist. An example is hallucinogen withdrawal—a possible category in ICD-10 that is not present in DSM-IV, but that is probably never used in ICD-10 because there is little evidence that it ever occurs.

Overall, there are many more similarities than differences, especially when one focuses on the specific categories described (with the exception of abuse and harmful use), and on the similarities in the ways dependence and its course modifiers are defined. It is hoped that future work will succeed in creating even more consistency between these two classification systems.

References

1. Frances A, Pincus HA, First MB, eds. Diagnostic and statistical manual of mental disorders. 4th edition. Washington, DC: American Psychiatric Press, 1994.

2. World Health Organization. Tenth revision of the international classification of disease (ICD-10). Geneva: World Health Organization, 1992.

3. Edwards G, Gross MM. Alcohol dependence: provisional description of a clinical syndrome. Br J Med 1976;1:1058–1061.

4. Edwards G. The alcohol dependence syndrome: a concept as stimulus to enquiry. Br J Addict 1986; 81:171–183.

34 Diagnostic Interview and Mental Status Examination

Edward C. Senay

A substance abuse history should be obtained in every medical or psychiatric diagnostic examination, no matter how remote substance abuse may appear to be. A comatose 4-month-old child may not appear to be a likely candidate for substance abuse but, considering that death has been reported in infants from passive inhalation of phencyclidine (PCP) or cocaine base vapors, the need for examination for substance abuse in every instance should be clear. Substance abuse is a frequent problem for medical and social agencies, with recent studies indicating, for the entire U.S. population, a 26.6% lifetime prevalence for substance abuse disorders (1). These figures underscore the need for every clinician to have a high index of suspicion. This chapter reviews what constitutes an adequate psychiatric and substance abuse history and discusses attitudes and techniques of interviewing to insure that these areas are well covered. If drug effects are at all in question, the history should be supplemented with a urine screen, with special requests if difficult-to-detect drugs are in question (e.g., fentanyl may not be picked up by current standard toxicological techniques). In addition, most experts in the field suggest that family members, friends, or significant others should be interviewed if the patient agrees to such interviews (2–5).

SETTING AND PSYCHOLOGY OF THE DIAGNOSTIC INTERVIEW

If at all possible, an interview should be conducted in privacy. Questions about drugs and symptoms of mental disorders may raise feelings of shame and guilt, cause fears of possible legal consequences or of incriminating peers or family members, or evoke other emotions that are best managed by both patient and diagnostician in a private setting. If privacy is not possible in a crowded hospital ward or emergency room, the clinician may try writing simple questions and soliciting "yes" or "no" answers from patients or perhaps delaying the substance abuse history until privacy is possible. Responding to and/or taking control of the environment may be a positive message to the patient that the clinician is sensitive to the complex emotions that may be generated by asking about drugs and symptoms of other mental disorders.

Another frequently important psychological consideration in interviewing substance abusers is that they may be in "crisis." In the alcohol treatment community's term, they have "bottomed out"—that is, their spouses have said "Do something or I'm going to divorce you," or they have experienced threatened or actual job loss, or some serious health problem has resulted from the drug habit (e.g., carcinoma of the lung from nicotine addiction). The point is that their psychology, because of being in crisis, is characterized by passivity, suggestibility, uncertainty about the full meaning of what has happened to them, and a considerable degree of demoralization.

Given these psychological characteristics, the clinician, if at all possible, should be able to give the patient undivided attention for at least 20–30 minutes in a private place. If the clinician cannot give this much time and/or a private place is not available, it is better to tell the patient that what he or she needs cannot be provided at the moment but may be possible at the close of the day or the next morning. If it is possible then to operate in privacy for 20–30 minutes without any kind of interruption, the effects will be far superior to those obtained while trying to operate in less-than-optimal conditions.

Classically, the defining characteristic of the substance abuser has been denial. It is true just often enough to confirm what is basically a stereotype. There are substance abusers who never overcome denial and whose drinking, smoking, or shooting drugs continues uninterrupted until they die. The majority of substance abusers, however, are not defined by denial alone, nor do they use drugs every day until they develop a problem or die. Large numbers of substance abusers have decades-long careers consisting of episodes of addiction interspersed with periods of abstinence. They are intensely ambivalent, which means that there is another psychological pole, separate from and opposite to denial, that is in delicate, frequently changing balance with denial and that is a pole of healthy striving. Most substance abusers are quite aware that what they are doing is destructive, that they have been deceived by the culture of drugs and alcohol, and that they want to change. If this were not true, there would be no Alcoholics Anonymous, Cocaine Anonymous, or Narcotics Anonymous, and no success in methadone maintenance or therapeutic communities. The job of a clinician is to appeal to this pole of healthy striving. Even for those in complete denial, one must assume that there is a positive pole, because one can be sure that it was not there only in retrospect.

The goal of the clinician in the diagnostic interview is to begin to reverse the passivity, suggestibility, and demoralization of the patient by identifying the problem and by offering a way out. At this point the reader should be reminded of the importance of being nonjudgmental and accepting of substance abusers. Chappel (6) deals with the issue in more detail. Suffice it to say here that substance abusers come from every ethnic group, social class, and educational group. It is not a question of "them" and "us" because, if one is willing to look, one finds that half of "them" are "us" and vice versa. Most substance abusers respond well to a nonjudgmental, accepting attitude that suggests that the clinician genuinely is interested in learning about the drug abuser and his or her problems.

Experience teaches that it is a good interviewing technique to give the patient a few minutes to give the history without intrusion. If the patient takes the initiative and starts talking, let the patient proceed. If the patient waits for directions one might ask, "What brings you to see me?" "Tell me why you're here" or some such opening to permit the patient to begin to talk. Once the patient is talking, one can simply pick up on the last thing said, e.g., "your boss said that if you want your job back you have to get into treatment." The goal of this strategy is to learn how the patient defines his or her problem. If this strategy is successful, it will determine how the rest of the interview should be conducted. (Most people like to be listened to, so it helps to build a therapeutic relationship.) At one extreme, for example, one may have a patient with long-term recognition that drug abuse is a problem, that the spouse would react by threatening divorce, and that it would take a threat of divorce to enable the patient to gain control over the drug problem. The technical details on what drugs, how much, how often, etc. of history taking should be straightforward in such a case. At the other extreme there may be a patient who states that he or she has no drug problem, that the spouse is "sick," not the patient, and that he or she is coming only to appease the spouse. In such an instance details may require more probing than would otherwise be the case. The value of the initial strategy of allowing the patient to define the problem rapidly becomes apparent to anyone who adopts it.

After giving the patient some "free" time, so to speak, one must move to a much more active, controlling, and detailed mode of history taking (the medical model). The points to be asked about are outlined in the next section. After this medical phase, the interviewer enters a diagnostic phase that summarizes the evidence and determines a diagnosis. The final phase of the interview is prescriptive. The physician discusses what is needed to treat the problem; this phase should include a discussion with the patient to determine how, when, and why the prescription will be implemented.

As noted above, an important aspect of the psychology of addiction involves an intense, chronic, alternating ambivalence. Another important aspect is that the drug—its taking, its seeking, and its effects—come to take on the characteristics of a relationship with another living being. This is reflected in language that depicts "a monkey on my back," "my friend the bottle," or, in the heroin subculture, "I've got a Jones," to signify that one is addicted. Relationships with people usually have been put aside and have become secondary to the relationship with the habit. The clinical implications of this in the initial interview are complex. The clinician is in the position of recommending, quite rightfully, a change in behavior. But the addict will experience this as a threat to a relationship that he or she values highly. The physician should not be surprised if anger and denial or displeasure with the prescription becomes apparent. However, the addict must be assisted in starting the process of mourning for a relationship that must be lost if he or she is to succeed in changing.

The clinician should also keep in mind that the patient may be suffering from cognitive deficits secondary to drug use. Such cognitive deficits may be significant and may not be diagnosable by ordinary inspection. Cocaine "basers" or users of crack may appear to be functioning normally, but when they are reinterviewed the next day, the clinician may be surprised at the level of forgetfulness and misunderstanding about the contents of the initial interview because of the acute toxic effects of the drug on memory and cognition.

One should not try to interview an intoxicated patient unless compelling medical reasons are present, e.g., acute pancreatitis or hepatic encephalopathy. If it is medically feasible, the interview should be deferred until the patient is sober.

It is good practice routinely to interview people close to the patient—if the patient will permit this—to corroborate the history. Patients should be told that a workup is not complete without such an interview. If the patient refuses, one must respect the patient's wishes but should continue to seek permission to interview significant others. The presence of a medical emergency such as delirium compels interviewing significant others with or without patient permission.

BASIC POINTS IN A SUBSTANCE ABUSE HISTORY

The previous chapter reviewed the *Diagnostic and Statistical Manual of Mental Disorders,* 4th edition (DSM-IV) criteria for diagnosis (7). This information usually will be developed fully by asking about or defining the points outlined in this section.

Confidentiality

Before asking specific questions in relation to the drug history, the interviewer should tell the patient how the interviewer defines confidentiality. With minors, for example, some states permit a physician to keep a minor's drug abuse history confidential from the patient's parents; other states do not. Confidentiality laws are different for different classes of drugs; e.g., if federal funds support the treatment of a narcotic addict, then confidentiality is guarded closely and a physician could be fined or jailed for any breach of confidentiality. In these instances the patient should be told that the physician is liable for a fine or imprisonment for any release of information without the patient's signed informed consent, a court order, a medical emergency, or a federal inspector's review of records. Because this is the most stringent view of confidentiality, it is the safest. As noted earlier, the law with respect to minors may vary from state to state. The physician should seek a legal opinion if unsure of any local rules concerning minors, drug abuse, or confidentiality.

The hospital or clinic chart is, of course, an extension of the clinician, and both the clinician and the chart are covered by the general laws on confidentiality. The validity of the history may hinge on the patient's perception of what may happen if his or her confidentiality is threatened.

Drugs to be Asked About

There is a core set of drug classes that should be asked about in all settings, and this core set may need to be supplemented by the inclusion of local fads, as there is considerable variation in drug usage from area to area.

For example, in New York City from 1978 to 1979, among methadone maintenance patients, tricyclic antidepressants were more abused than cocaine; in Chicago between 1974 and 1982 the combination of pentazocine and tripelennamine, so-called "T's and Blues," was more popular than heroin. The clinician should also be aware that a buyer may get a drug on the street different from the one he or she intends to purchase and that the dealer may sell a drug different from the one he or she thinks is being sold; however, in the main, drug reports usually are validated by urine screens. Questions about quantity and frequency should be asked about the following:

1. Alcohol—beer, wine, whiskey, gin, etc.
2. Nicotine—cigarettes, chewing tobacco, pipes, etc.
3. Cannabis—"pot," "hashish"
4. Central nervous system (CNS) depressants—barbiturates, benzodiazepines
5. Stimulants—amphetamine, cocaine, cocaine "base," crack, etc.
6. Opioids—heroin, codeine, methadone
7. Hallucinogens—lysergic acid diethylamide (LSD), methylenedioxyamphetamine (MDA), mescaline
8. PCP—arylcyclohexylamines
9. Inhalants—glue, paint, aromatic hydrocarbons
10. Caffeine
11. Other drugs—over-the-counter (OTC) drugs with sedative effects

Most experts in the field believe that the more specific the questions, the better the history obtained. Asking about these 11 general classes obtains more and better information than only asking, "Do you use any drugs or alcohol?"

Age of First Use

"How old were you when you first used drugs?" is a relevant question because length of addiction may give some rough prognostic information. A 39-year-old drug user who started daily intoxication at age 16 and continued to his or her present age is a different patient from another 39-year-old who started at age 35. This information explains only some of the variation, however, since patients from both ends of this spectrum can do well in treatment, just as those from both ends can do badly. The clinician may also learn what the patient defines as a drug; e.g., the patient may exclude alcohol or marihuana or nicotine from his or her answer, thus indicating a belief that these are not drugs.

Period of Heaviest Lifetime Use

Interviewers new to the field of substance abuse commonly assume that drug users, particularly heavy drug users, use drugs for the pleasurable effects. In the early stages of the development of drug dependence pleasure may be one of the strong motivations, but as dose and duration of use increase, pleasure becomes less and less a motivation and other variables begin to control drug behavior. For example, many chronic heroin addicts report having received no pleasure from heroin injections for many years. Injecting heroin "takes away the sick"; that is, it relieves withdrawal but it does not induce pleasure. When one interviews an alcoholic whose intake exceeds the "fifth a day" level, it is difficult to conclude, after the clinical interview, whether the alcoholic has pleasure in any sphere of life, since dysphoria and depression usually predominate; this level of alcohol use has a mechanical, compelled quality that is not pleasurable in any sense.

Pleasure seeking, then, is not a very powerful determinant of drug use, particularly in the middle or end stages of a career of drug dependence. The question is, then, what is motivating the drug use? Answers to the question "When did you use the highest doses of drugs in your life?" may give some clues; e.g., there are many female heroin addicts who are addicted only when in a relationship with a drug-using male. When not in such a relationship they may use much less heroin or none at all.

The Past Three Weeks

If there has been no drug use during the previous three weeks, then the possibility of drug withdrawal is remote and the clinician does not have to worry about a fatal arrhythmia or status epilepticus complicating a medical or surgical procedure or entrance to a therapeutic community. Withdrawal from alcohol and CNS depressants can be lethal, and heavy intake during the past three weeks may require hospitalization. Research has demonstrated, however, that most alcoholic withdrawal syndromes can be managed in nonmedical settings. Dependence on CNS depressants above a daily dose of 3–5 times the therapeutic dose range of the drug involved is best managed in a hospital setting. A history of convulsions from any cause indicates hospital management rather than a nonmedical setting for alcohol or CNS depressant dependence.

Withdrawal from opioids, stimulants, PCP, and hallucinogens may be marked by depression or psychoses but is not lethal. The fetal or neonatal period is the only time in which opioid withdrawal can be fatal.

Validity of Drug and Alcohol Histories

The validity of the drug and alcohol history depends upon the degree of trust that the interviewer is able to establish with the patient. It also depends on the patient's perception of the identity of the interviewer. A heroin addict coming into a drug treatment clinic that is culturally and racially sensitive to the addict's needs and that is located in the addict's neighborhood will give a history as reliable as medical histories obtained in any private care setting. There are, of course, addicts who respond positively to every question in the review of systems or, conversely, deny any problems even though the problems are quite apparent, just as is the case in general medical settings.

The medical history obtained in established drug and alcohol clinics is reasonably reliable and valid, and drug use reports usually are confirmed and validated by urine screens.

One may be less confident of the validity and reliability of the history when one is taking a history that is not necessarily focused on the direct care of the addict or alcoholic (e.g., in military or court-ordered histories, etc.). The existence of urine testing increases reliability, because recent use of most common intoxicants is detected and most addicts and alcoholics know this.

Presence of Tolerance and Dependence

Specific questions should be asked about the need to increase the dose of the drug to obtain desired effects and about what symptoms occurred when doses were decreased. In general, tremulousness is the hallmark of withdrawal. The drug-specific withdrawal syndromes are described elsewhere in this text. The reader is reminded that multiple drug use is the modal pattern currently, so a complete history is required. When very high doses of intoxicants have been used, memory capacity may have become so impaired that the addict or alcoholic may not be able to report accurately. The clinician then must try to fill in the blanks. In the case of a patient reporting high doses of cocaine with resulting "edginess" or feelings of "being wired" so that rest or sleep is impossible, this would lead, for example, to a suspicion of the use of high doses of alcohol, barbiturates, or benzodiazepines to treat the dysphoric state of "being wired" and a recognition that a high enough dose of alcohol or depressants may have been used to induce physical dependence on the depressants. One would then have a high index of suspicion for two withdrawal syndromes—cocaine and alcohol, or cocaine and benzodiazepines.

Mental Status Examination (Psychiatric Interview)

Substance abuse disorders and other DSM-IV conditions have high concurrence (see previous chapter). Understanding the temporal relationship between symptoms indicating schizophrenia or bipolar affective disorder and the onset of drug use may be important in understanding and managing patients. The order in which the interviewer asks about symptoms relating to drug abuse and symptoms relating to other DSM-IV disorders should be determined by the presenting complaints of the patient. If, for example, the patient (or others) expresses a belief that drugs are the problem, it is probably best to obtain the drug history before exploring the history of psychiatric symptoms; if the patient expresses a belief that psychiatric symptoms are the problem, the same holds true. What is of overriding importance is that both spheres are adequately explored. Mood disorders, anxiety disorders, and an-

tisocial personality disorders appear to be more common in substance abusers than in the general population, so it is probably best to begin with these in a person who defines himself or herself as having a substance abuse disorder. One would next ask about symptoms related to other DSM-IV disorders.

For the interviewer with clinical training in psychiatry, psychology, or social work, taking a psychiatric history should present no problem. The substance abuse history may be more difficult, at least at first, but when more experience is gained the two will flow together smoothly. The reverse situation is more difficult. Many workers in the substance abuse field have had no training in mental disorders other than substance abuse and need more training, supervision, and experience to make the transition to complete history taking. The subject of taking histories from seriously ill psychiatric patients is sufficiently complex to preclude an in-depth review in a chapter of this nature. What is germane is that the substance abuse counselor should recognize the need for training and supervision to learn how to relate to the seriously ill psychiatric patient who has a complicating substance abuse disorder. The fundamental skill in psychiatric interviewing is listening. Listening, in a clinical sense, implies a good deal of cognitive activity on the part of the psychiatrist, who, while listening, is making judgments about the presence or absence of diagnostic criteria and is scanning the data both for what is and what is not being stated by the patient. In addition to these diagnostic activities, the psychiatrist is monitoring how the patient is expressing emotion in relation to the content of the patient's speech and in relation to the evolving relationship with the psychiatrist (the transference). The psychiatrist is also monitoring the feelings evoked in himself or herself by the patient (the countertransference). It should be obvious that "listening" is a very active mode of relating and is in no sense passive.

Common clinical issues important in treating "dual diagnosis" patients have been reviewed in depth and in excellent fashion by Kaufman (8). What is relevant for this discussion is the frequent volatility of the relationship with some "dual diagnosis" patients who in initial interviews appear to relate in one way but then change dramatically when trying to cope both with withdrawal and a major mental illness. What the clinician sees in an initial workup may change as the relationship develops. We are just beginning to understand how disruptive even low levels of common intoxicants are on cognition, memory, and judgment. In patients with major mental illnesses disruptive effects of common intoxicants may be more pronounced than they would be otherwise.

The term *mental status examination* refers to the entire psychiatric history. It is distinguished from the *mental status section,* which is only a portion of the entire history and in which the interviewer describes the immediate behavior, appearance, and affect of the patient. The mental status examination, however, begins with the demographics of the patient—age, sex, race, occupation, marital status, and presence or absence of children. It then describes the chief complaint, e.g., "suicidal thoughts." Next, the *history of the present illness* is presented. The organizing principle in the mental status examination is time. When was the first time a suicidal thought was noticed? A history of the present illness will then tell the reader in chronological order what symptoms and behavior followed. A well-written history of present illness will also give negative information; e.g., "suicidal thoughts were accompanied by feelings of depression but no specific plans for suicide have ever been made by the patient." In addition, negative information relevant to differential diagnosis can be presented in the history of present illness; e.g., in the case sketched in this paragraph there would be complete information on all the symptoms of depression (e.g., anorexia, insomnia, etc.) but also information on the presence or absence of mania and other symptoms relevant to the differential diagnosis.

As noted by MacKinnon and Yudofsky, a large number of formats are possible for the write-up of a psychiatric history and no one format has emerged as a standard (9). Despite the lack of standardization of formats most authorities do agree on content, and the information that follows covers the generally agreed upon areas of importance (10–13). The history of present illness is followed by the *past history,* sometimes called "previous illness," sometimes "personal history." The past history describes the functioning of the individual prior to the onset of illness: e.g., "prior to the onset of depression the patient had never suffered from dysphoric moods or other psychiatric problems." The past history also may involve relevant dynamics that are not presented directly in the present illness: e.g., "the patient describes a life-long tendency to procrastinate and to be self-critical."

The next section of the mental status examination describes the *growth and development of the patient*. Usually in this section material is obtained that permits judgment about the presence or absence of mental retardation, chronic mental illness, and other conditions that may complicate the present illness. In this section the examiner asks about problems with early illnesses or accidents, the patient's progress in school, the patient's family and social development, and details of the school, sexual, and social history.

The *family history* gives information on genetic tendencies, such as the presence or absence of alcohol or other substance abuse, depression, antisocial tendencies, and the like in relatives. Such information may be important in understanding the present illness. The family history usually is followed by the *medical history* of the patient.

The *mental status section* usually is next. In this section of the mental status examination, the examiner reports on the appearance, behavior, and speech of the patient in addition to observations on stream of thought, affect, thought content, sensorium and mental capacity, and insight and judgment. This section also gives the examiner's estimate of the reliability of the history obtained. It focuses on observable behavior but also may comment on significant negative information: "there was no evidence of hallucinations or delusions and the patient denies any history of these symptoms." Affect (immediate, expressed emotion) and mood (sustained emotional state) are specifically noted in this section. The degree of clarity of consciousness (sensorium) is noted: "the patient appeared mildly sedated but was oriented to time, place, and person." Material about the orientation of the patient is obtained by asking questions such as, "What is today's date?" and "Where are we?" Memory is tested by asking about recent events that one would expect most people to be aware of. Concentration is tested by asking the patient to perform simple arithmetic: "Please subtract 7 from 100, then take away 7 from the remainder, then 7 from that remainder." The patient's thinking ability can be tested by asking the patient to interpret proverbs. What does it mean when someone says, "People who live in glass houses shouldn't throw stones?" It is good practice to preface these kinds of questions with statements to the effect that these are parts of standard examinations so that the patient does wonder at the motivation for asking such questions.

Obviously there is a good deal of cultural and racial variation with respect to exposure to proverbs. If one is not sure of the patient's background one can ask, "Have you ever heard this proverb?" until one is found that is familiar to the patient. If there is a considerable cultural difference between examiner and examinee, it should be noted in this section. The significance of the difference can be commented upon in the diagnosis: e.g., a person who feels dominated by an agent of external control and comes from a culture in which "voodoo spells" or "magic" are accepted as reality may have a different problem than does a patient from a Eurocentric heritage who fears that television is controlling his or her thoughts. Asking the patient about similarities and differences is another way of exploring thinking abilities: "In what way is an apple like an orange?" and "What are differences between them?"

In this section the examiner also presents a judgment of the patient's insight. Does the patient understand the fact of his or her illness? Does the patient appreciate what must be done? Obviously this is a judgment by the examiner that takes into account all the data obtained. Is the patient competent to participate voluntarily in treatment? In some instances, the examiner will conclude that the patient is not competent to make important life decisions. In these instances detailed reasons should be given for this judgment: "The patient has suffered a stroke with a severe paralysis of his right arm and left leg, yet he insists that he can walk normally."

The mental status section is followed by a *formulation*. The elements of a formulation are as follows: (*a*) genetics or biological predisposition; (*b*) major psychological relationships and their history—e.g., family dynamics throughout childhood and adolescence; (*c*) characteristic defense mechanisms and coping style; and (*d*) stressors. The foregoing then should be integrated with the onset of the present illness. In the event that a diagnosis of personality disorder or mental retardation is made, the present illness section will contain some or all of the points covered in the formulation.

The next element in a psychiatric examination is a *presentation on five axes*. On axis 1 the examiner presents all diagnoses except personality disorder and developmental disorders. These, if present, are described on axis 2. Axis 3 presents medical conditions; axis 4 describes psychosocial and environmental problems in the past year; axis 5 presents a global assessment of functioning, both current and in the past year.

The final component of the mental status examination is the *management plan*.

A sample history, illustrative of many of these points, follows.

This is a 28-year-old white, married, female bank clerk who has two children, a 6-year-old boy and a 4-year-old girl.

CHIEF COMPLAINT

"I can't stay away from crack cocaine."

PRESENT ILLNESS

The patient dates her first use of cocaine to 10 years ago when she "snorted" cocaine at a party. She liked the effects of the drug. She then used cocaine by snorting once or twice a month for many years. In the past 6 months she has been smoking crack cocaine and her use has escalated dramatically. In recent weeks she has been using one-half to 1 gram daily with a feeling of compulsion that has frightened her, since she has always believed that she could control her use of substances. She states, for example, that, during her pregnancies, she completely avoided alcohol and tried to stop smoking nicotine cigarettes but was unable to do so. In recent weeks, she describes use of cocaine throughout the day. In recent weeks she has also noted that her memory and her ability to communicate with and care for her children have been seriously impaired. Her ability to work has also suffered. Her decision to come for treatment was based on a number of factors. She has been spending money on drugs in amounts she cannot afford. She describes her marriage as "on the rocks," but she has been most motivated by reports from her mother that her children have been frightened of her; this report together with her observation that the children have been having nightmares has been a strong motivation. She reports frequently feeling threatened and vaguely suspicious after using crack.

She first used alcohol at age 12 and began to use nicotine cigarettes and marihuana at age 13. Her use of alcohol and marihuana has always been episodic, usually at parties on weekends. Within a few months of beginning with nicotine she became and has remained a daily user. She now smokes two packs a day. She used hallucinogens on two occasions in her teens. She has no history of use of opioids, PCP, or inhalants. In the past few weeks she has been consuming alcohol, marihuana, and benzodiazepines to control the dysphoric hyperstimulation of crack cocaine. Her memory of the doses consumed is not clear.

She has had frequent severe mood lability with her menstrual periods but denies depressed moods, periods of overactivity, or suicidal thoughts. She denies any hallucinations or delusions and has never been in treatment for a psychiatric disorder.

PAST MEDICAL HISTORY

Throughout her life she has had many workups for "feeling sick to her stomach." There are cramps, on occasion so painful that she must stop whatever she is doing. She states that she is much more likely to have these problems when she is under stress. She has refused prescriptions by her family physician to treat these symptoms. She cannot articulate any reason for the refusal but has noted that alcohol, marihuana, and benzodiazepines relieve the pain and cramping.

FAMILY HISTORY

She believes that both parents are alcoholics. She states that she doesn't understand how this happened, since both maternal and paternal grandparents were very strict and did not use any drugs or alcohol to her knowledge. She has a maternal aunt with repeated severe depressions.

GROWTH AND DEVELOPMENT

The patient was born and raised in the metropolitan New York area. As far as she knows, she was delivered from a full-term pregnancy and began walking and talking at expected ages. She maintained good grades in school but remembers feeling very nervous and fearful that the other children didn't like her. She did make two friends in grammar school and has maintained periodic contact with them to this day. Her family attended church sporadically. The patient states that she never was able to develop a real belief system, because she felt that going to church was superficial and not taken seriously by anyone she knew.

Her early family life was marked by considerable tension between her mother and father, both of whom drank alcohol heavily and often argued. The patient usually retreated to her room during these prolonged fights. She remembers fantasies that she had an older woman friend who was "caring." She had no siblings. She remembers occasional warm moments with her mother and with her father, but never when father and mother were together.

Menses began at age 11, and although she was very shy and nervous around boys, she found herself quite interested in them. She engaged in "petting" in high school but has had sexual relations only with her husband, whom she married 6 years ago. She graduated from college with a business degree. Her husband is a successful businessman who sometimes celebrates business successes with cocaine use. It was after a business success that he first brought home crack cocaine 6 months ago. The patient reports that her husband has become "like a stranger" to her. She cannot tolerate the idea of his touching her and they have been fighting constantly for the past 2 years. They have had no sexual relations for more than a year. She states that she has recognized that she or they should get help but has felt overwhelmed and has turned increasingly to cocaine to deal with her conflicts. Her husband would not agree to accompany her to this interview. He expressed the belief, to her, that neither he nor she had any real problem and that she was overreacting.

MENTAL STATUS

The patient is a well-dressed, attractive young woman who appears to be her stated age. She relates well to the examiner, although her anxiety level appears to be quite high based on her self-report and her observable restlessness. Eye contact is broken off when she mentions her husband, children, or cocaine. Her speech is not pressured. She has a normal range of affects. The history appears to be quite reliable. The patient's IQ is estimated to be high normal. There are no hallucinations, delusions, thought blocking, or inappropriate affect.

She is oriented to time, place, and person. She has a good fund of information. She named the past five presidents, performed serial 7's, and remembered three items 5 minutes later easily. She gave an abstract answer to the proverb "People who live in glass houses.": "Take care of your own problems first, not someone else's." Similarities and differences were not tested because of time limitations.

Her insight and judgment are intact. She has recognized that she has to take action. She believes that she needs inpatient treatment for a few weeks while her mother takes care of the children. Given her loss of control and high degree of stress, this judgment is reasonable.

FORMULATION

Both parents appear to have problems with alcohol, and there is a history of severe depression in a maternal aunt. The patient's early life was characterized by her withdrawal from constant parental fighting. The patient's adjustment in school was successful academically but only partly successful socially. She remembers always being "shy" and "nervous." She has had severe premenstrual distress both as an adolescent and as an adult. She made few friends in school but has maintained relationships with two girlfriends since her grammar school years. She noted that drugs helped her to overcome her shyness but believed until a few months ago that she could control her use. She has been severely anxious since discovering that she could not control her use of cocaine, alcohol, and marihuana. She has used denial in dealing with this problem.

Her marriage is severely stressful, and it has been in this setting of increasing responsibilities for her children and marital stress that she has lost control over her intake of drugs. Her reality testing is intact and she recognizes that she must do something to help herself.

DIAGNOSIS

Axis 1: 304.20 Cocaine dependence
      305.10 Nicotine dependence
      300.70 Undifferentiated somatoform disorder

Axis 2: No Dx

Axis 3: No Dx

Axis 4: Severe marital problems; children have developed severe behavior problems. Severity: 4.

Axis 5: Current global assessment of functioning (GAF): 55. Higher GAF of 65 (at the beginning of the year).

The foregoing illustrative workup would, of course, be followed up by a detailed treatment plan.

USE OF INSTRUMENTS

Some clinicians use instruments such as the Michigan Alcoholism Screening Test (MAST), CAGE, or the Addiction Severity Index (ASI), while many others do not. This author does not use instruments when functioning as a clinician outside of a research context. Many of the instruments developed tap only one drug or class of drugs (e.g., CAGE, MAST), thus leaving open the question of use of other drugs such as nicotine, heroin, cocaine, etc. Instruments also miss local fads. Various cities or regions tend to have stable use of alcohol, nicotine, cocaine, heroin, and the like but frequently also have drugs used only locally (e.g., "T's and Blues"). Another potential problem with instruments is that the interviewer may relate to the instrument rather than to the patient. In the author's opinion, it is better for the patient to experience the interviewer as someone who can and will remember what the patient is saying because the examiner is interested in and is responsive to the patient's needs. Instruments can detract from this process if not used with sensitivity. On the other hand, some patients believe that the doctor should write down what they are saying and feel more "attended to" if the interviewer is using an instrument and/or taking notes.

Instruments are thorough for the range of data for which they are designed, and they provide a useful record that may spare long writings. Hester and Miller provide the best review of the large number of instruments that have appeared in recent years (14). Of those reviewed, only the ASI is comprehensive and has a scale that measures psychopathology. However, this scale cannot substitute for a formal clinical psychiatric history. The use of instruments is a clinical choice with some experienced clinicians preferring to use instruments and other, equally experienced clinicians preferring not to use them at all.

INTERVIEWER TECHNIQUES

Empathy and Sympathy

Empathy is the ability of one person to understand the emotions and thoughts of another by putting himself or herself in the other person's position. Empathy is essential for effective work with patients and is to be distinguished from *sympathy,* which refers to identifying with the other person while suspending critical intellect. In empathy one feels as the other person does but recognizes that other feelings are possible, and there is no fusion or identification with the patient. Sympathy implies identifying with the patient uncritically.

Summarizing with the Patient

A useful technique in diagnostic interviewing is to take a few minutes after completing the interview to summarize findings with the patient. For the illustrative case given above, the summary might proceed as follows:

You're 28, married, working in a bank, and have two children. Cocaine has become a severe problem for you, interfering with your ability to mother your children and to work. You have used alcohol, nicotine, cocaine, and, on occasion, marihuana since your teens and always believed that you had control. You're scared now because your cocaine use is out of control and you want help.

Your general health has been good except for recurring severe stomach pain for which you have no diagnosis, but you note that the symptoms are probably stress related.

You want to get help, and we both agree that you will start an inpatient program. We've also discussed the chronic nature of the problem you have and your probable need for a self-help group and other assistance for the foreseeable future.

The technique of reviewing a brief summary of the history with the patient often has some surprising consequences. For example, the patient may remember some critical event such as the death of a parent in close temporal relationship with the onset of illness or other psychologically meaningful material. The review also demonstrates to the patient that the interviewer has been listening and is responsive to the patient's needs.

Maintaining Eye Contact

A good interviewer listens empathically and makes frequent eye contact with the patient. How much eye contact is a matter to be sensed during the interview. A paranoid, suspicious patient may feel that you can read his or her mind if you make eye contact too often and too directly. Other patients may feel quite comforted by the fact that you are listening to them and looking at them frequently in an attempt to understand and to help them.

Picking Up on the Patient's Last Statement

In the initial phase of the interview when the interviewer is trying to obtain the patient's history to see how the person defines his or her own problems, a good technique is to repeat the last sentence or sentence fragment spoken by the patient: "You said that you were fighting with your husband and you knew that it was bad for the kids, who could hear you fighting." If the patient does not pick up on this, the interviewer might ask, "What feelings did you have when you were fighting with your husband?"

Use of Open-Ended Questions

Most writers on the question of interviewing believe that open-ended questions elicit more useful information in initial interviews. With the model case described previously, for example, one would ask, "Tell me more about feeling nervous." What the interviewer needs to know is whether the person has anxiety that is appropriate—any child would probably feel nervous while listening to parents argue—or whether the patient has anxiety that is not connected with immediate stressors, such as panic attacks—in other words, an anxiety disorder.

The foregoing sketches of interview techniques are intended to stimulate interest in the clinician who has had no formal training in psychiatry. The interested reader is urged to read further in any of this chapter's references to pursue this fascinating topic (15–17).

References

1. Kessler RC, McGonagle KA, Zhao S, et al. Lifetime and 12-month prevalence of DSM-3-R psychiatric disorders in the United States. Arch Gen Psychiatry 1994;51:8–19.
2. Schottenfeld RS. Assessment of the patient. In: Galanter M, Kleber HD, eds. Textbook of substance abuse treatment. Washington, DC: American Psychiatric Press, 1994.
3. Schuckit M. Drug, alcohol abuse. 4th edition. New York: Plenum Press, 1995.
4. Zimberg S. The clinical management of alcoholism. New York: Bruner/Mazel, 1982.
5. Gallant D. Alcoholism: a guide to diagnosis, intervention and treatment. New York: WW Norton, 1987.
6. Chappel JN. Attitudes toward the treatment of substance abusers. In: Lowinson JH, Ruiz P, Millman RB, Langrod JG, eds. Substance abuse: a comprehensive textbook. 2nd edition. Baltimore: Williams & Wilkins, 1992:983–996.
7. Diagnostic and statistical manual of mental disorders. 4th edition. Washington, DC: American Psychiatric Association, 1995.
8. Kaufman E. The psychotherapy of dually diagnosed patients. J Subst Abuse Treat 1989;6:9–18.
9. MacKinnon RA, Yudofsky SC. The psychiatric evaluation in clinical practice. Philadelphia: JB Lippincott, 1986.
10. Nicholi AM. The new Harvard guide to psychiatry. Cambridge, MA: Harvard University Press, 1988.
11. Stevenson I. The psychiatric interview. In: Arieti S, ed. American handbook of psychiatry. 2nd edition. New York: Basic Books, 1974;1:1138.
12. Stevenson I, Sheppe WM Jr. The psychiatric examination. In: Arieti S, ed. American handbook of psychiatry. 2nd edition. New York: Basic Books, 1974;1:1157.
13. Lazare A, Eisenthal S, Alonso A. Clinical evaluation: a multi-dimensional hypothesis testing, negotiated approach in psychiatry. Revised edition. New York: Basic Books, 1987.
14. Hester RK, Miller WR. Handbook of alcoholism treatment approaches: effective alternatives. New York: Pergamon Press, 1989.
15. Strayhorn JM Jr. Foundations of clinical psychiatry. Chicago: Yearbook Medical Publishers, 1982.
16. Sullivan HS. The psychiatric interview. New York: Morton, 1956.
17. Kaplan HI, Sadock BS, Grebb JA. Synopsis of psychiatry. 5th edition. Baltimore: Williams & Wilkins, 1988.

35 Diagnostic Laboratory: Screening for Drug Abuse

Karl G. Verebey and Betty J. Buchan

Alcohol and drug abuse are two major health care problems in America. This has prompted advancement in laboratory methods diagnosing substance abuse in psychiatric patients and suspected drug abusers. Physicians are more knowledgeable today than in the past about the nature of drug abuse, yet uncertainty remains in the use of the "diagnostic laboratory." The confusion surrounding drug abuse testing is a result of many variables. Each individual drug is unique, and detectability depends on the type of drug, size of the dose, frequency of use, the type of biological specimen tested, differences in individual drug metabolism, sample collection time in relation to use, and sensitivity of the analytical method (1). All these variables make each test request an individual case, and there are no general rules for all drugs and all situations.

This chapter reviews testing of drugs of abuse from several perspectives. A brief history of drug testing is followed by a section on the reasons for testing. Described in detail are the available methodologies, testing strategies, and data interpretation methods.

HISTORY OF DRUG TESTING

The modern drug abuse testing laboratory is a very recent development. Initially, drug testing was exclusively part of the pathology services in which usually overdose or fatal toxicity cases were investigated for the causative agents. Very large sample volumes were processed with crude, nonspecific methodology. As drugs of abuse became a major social problem, overdose cases also became more common. Hospital laboratories were called upon to perform emergency toxicology procedures to identify drug classes or specific drugs.

Another branch of testing developed when identified drug abusers in treatment programs needed follow-up to objectively monitor abstinence from drugs. Such rehabilitation testing was performed in hospitals or private clinical laboratories that initially were not designed for drug testing.

Drug testing has increased rapidly over the last decade due to widespread employee testing by the federal government, the military, and private industry. This has influenced the rapid development of specific urine drug testing laboratories.

Forensic drug testing is the newest to appear on the scene, forced upon the clinical laboratories by the legal profession. Positive results were sometimes questioned or flatly denied, and lawyers started to scrutinize every step of the testing process from collection to reporting of results. Forensic accountability was then required to protect the "due process rights" of clients. After losing court cases, clinical laboratories that performed legally sensitive testing began to reorganize. "Chain of custody" procedures were designed, and quality control and quality assurance procedures were implemented to promote reliability and reproducibility of test results. Drug testing procedures and instrumentation became more sophisticated, more sensitive, and more specific. As a result, extremely small amounts of drugs can be determined reliably at the nanogram range, and gas chromatography-mass spectrometry (GC/MS) provides assurance of specific analyte identification (2).

RATIONALE FOR TESTING

Drug abuse is characterized by impulsive drug-seeking behavior with occasional breaks and almost certain relapses. A common feature of drug abusers is *denial*. Abusers lie to themselves and the forbidding outside world to protect their continued, obsessive addiction to drugs and/or alcohol. For this reason, physicians seldom are given voluntarily the diagnostically important information about addictive habits.

The drug choice and the abuse pattern are important parts of the medical history. The attending physician cannot properly design treatment when kept in the dark about the patient's addiction. Symptoms of physical and/or psychiatric illness may be simulated by the presence or absence of certain drugs. The dichotomy of symptoms associated with the presence or absence of a drug is best illustrated by the opioid class of drugs (3). While under the influence of an opioid, the addict experiences euphoric, anxiolytic sedation, mental clouding, sweating, and constipation. The common opioid withdrawal signs and symptoms appear characterized by pupillary mydriasis, agitation, anxiety, panic, muscle aches, gooseflesh, rhinorrhea, salivation, and diarrhea. Thus, the two different sets of symptoms belong to the abuse of the same drug, observed at times of opioid presence and opioid absence.

In predisposed individuals, drugs can trigger behavior similar or identical to psychosis. For example, phencyclidine (PCP), d-lysergic acid diethylamide (LSD), amphetamines, or cocaine can cause toxic psychosis that is indistinguishable from paranoid schizophrenia. These drugs can produce model psychosis in anyone given an adequate dose. Drug-induced psychosis has a different prognosis and must be treated differently from psychosis related to endogenous organic, anatomical, or neurochemical disorders (4).

Treatment of drug abusers in therapy would be extremely handicapped if testing were not used. Therefore, comprehensive drug testing is important for making precise follow-up evaluations and selecting appropriate treatment (5). Thus, the first good reason for laboratory drug testing is to provide objective identification of drug abusers and identify the substance abused.

Testing is also important after drug abusers are identified. Treatment strategies are intimately connected to frequent urinalyses to monitor recovering addicts. Negative results support the success of treatment, while positive results alert the physician to relapses. Objective testing, therefore, is a necessary component of modern treatment (5).

Drug abuse testing may also be forensic in nature. Parole officers monitor ex–drug abusers after release from incarceration. A positive drug test may signal to law enforcement the parolee's involvement with drugs and may invalidate the parole.

More often than is seen in the general population, health professionals such as doctors, dentists, and nurses are afflicted with drug abuse problems. Once involvement with drugs is exposed, professional medical licenses are in danger of suspension. Rehabilitation of addicted health professionals is linked to drug testing as a condition of probation.

Professional athletes often abuse drugs. Teams and national or international sport associations may prohibit the use of performance-enhancing drugs (6). Staying drug-free is often a prerequisite for athletes to be allowed to compete. Laboratory testing of body fluids for drugs of abuse is the objective technique used to enforce these rules.

Finally, the conduct of business and the public's safety may be endangered by impaired or intoxicated employees. Bankers and stockbrokers who handle investors' money should not be influenced by psychoactive drugs, especially drugs that cause delusions and impulsive risk-taking behavior. Similarly, other drug-abusing professionals may endanger the public. Drug abuse has been identified among airline pilots, bus drivers, railroad engineers, and police officers. In all these examples, drug abuse testing is advantageous to the drug abuser and the general public. The abuser gets early treatment and a chance for early rehabilitation, and the public is saved from drug-related wrongdoing.

A decrease in drug abuse as a result of testing has been demonstrated clearly in the military. Prior to the institution of testing in 1981, 48% of armed forces personnel used illegal drugs. Three years after testing began, fewer than 5% were using drugs (7). Although critics often attack testing as ineffective, drug use clearly decreases where effective drug testing exists.

ABUSED DRUGS TESTED

Epidemiological studies expose the types of drugs used, new trends, and frequency of drug abuse by different populations in specific geographical regions and countries. In effective drug abuse testing, such information is used to help identify drug abusers. The testing of five drugs, selected by the Department of Health and Human Services Substance Abuse and Mental Health Services Administration (DHHS/SAMHSA), is required for accreditation by their National Laboratory Certification Program (NLCP) (Table 35.1). Panel I testing includes amphetamines, cannabinoids, cocaine, opioids, and phencyclidine. Panel II represents other commonly abused drugs, such as barbiturates, benzodiazepines, methaqualone, propoxyphene, methadone, and ethanol. Interestingly, some powerful hallucinogens seldom are tested routinely. They are listed in Panel III: LSD, methylenedioxyamphetamine (MDA), methylenedioxymethamphetamine (MDMA), psilocybin, and other designer drugs. These drugs are psychoactive in very low doses. Therefore, when they are diluted in total body water, detection is difficult or impossible unless large doses are taken or samples are collected immediately after drug use.

Table 35.1   Panel Groups of Abused Drugs: Tests Performed by Laboratories

I:Required[a]	II:Commonly performed	III:Not commonly performed
Amphetamines	Barbiturates	LSD
Cannabinoids	Benzodiazepines	Fentanyl
Cocaine	Methadone	Psilocybin
Opioids	Propoxyphene	MDMA
Phencyclidine	Methaqualone	MDA
	Ethanol	Designer drugs

[a]Testing required for certification by the DHHS/SAMHSA National Laboratory Certification Program.

"Designer drugs" are structural congeners of common drugs of abuse. Often they are not yet regulated when sold and used. "Street chemists" are occasionally synthesizing new and often dangerous drugs. They will operate as long as abusers will try new drugs, and their trade remains profitable. The laboratory's role is to develop sensitive methods for the detection of designer drugs in the urine of users.

TESTS AVAILABLE

A number of different laboratory methods are available for comprehensive drug screening. When the drug abuse habit of the patient is unknown, physicians usually request a "comprehensive drug screen." Some laboratories may perform the inexpensive thin-layer chromatography (TLC) procedure. Many results are negative because of the low sensitivity of TLC, not because a drug or its metabolite is not present in the sample (8). Different laboratories have different definitions of the term *comprehensive drug testing*. The physician should be very familiar with laboratory procedures to ensure effective use of the drug testing laboratory.

Urine samples are most commonly sent for the "routine drug screen." Psychiatrists and other physicians assume that this test detects all abused drugs. Routine TLC is not sensitive enough to detect marihuana, PCP, LSD, MDA, MDMA, mescaline, and fentanyl, among others. Thus, a negative TLC drug screen may mean there is no evidence of high-dose and/or recent abuse of drugs commonly detected by TLC. Low-level abuse of drugs is not likely to be detected, therefore "false negatives" are very common for routine drug screens performed by TLC (9).

If, for example, a physician suspects marihuana abuse, he or she must specifically request that a marihuana screen be performed. Currently, screening for prescription drugs and drugs of abuse is performed by enzyme immunoassay (EIA), such as the enzyme multiplied immunoassay test (EMIT), radioimmunoassay (RIA), or fluorescent polarization immunoassay (FPIA), and a modern version of the TLC, the high performance TLC (HPTLC), which has improved sensitivity over that of conventional TLC systems. In a very few laboratories drug screening is performed by capillary gas-liquid chromatography (GLC). In a single GLC analysis more than 25 compounds can be identified. This system is advantageous when there is no clue to the identity of the abused substance; however, GLC and GC/MS are time consuming, labor intensive, and usually expensive. High-performance liquid chromatography (HPLC) is similar to GLC in principle. It is usually less sensitive than GLC but sample preparation is easier. The EIA and RIA tests are significantly less expensive and more practical than the more specific GC/MS methods. These procedures are easily adaptable for high-volume automated screening of drugs. In fact, most good laboratories offer a 5 or 10 drug panel, with or without alcohol, performed by EIA.

ANALYTIC METHODOLOGIES
Alcohol Methods of Analysis

Alcohol abuse is a legal version of drug abuse in the United States and most parts of the world. The addictive chemical substance in all alcoholic beverages is ethanol or ethyl alcohol. Ethanol is present in beer (3–6%), wine (11–13%) and distilled beverages (22–60%). A 160-pound subject must ingest four to five drinks (12 oz beer, 4 oz wine, or 1 oz whiskey) in one hour to reach an ethanol level of 0.10 g/100 ml blood, or 100 mg/100 ml blood, which is the per se illegal limit to operate an automobile in most states.

Ethanol is one of the few drugs for which blood levels can be correlated with levels of intoxication or impairment, although large individual variations do exist. Ethanol is analyzed by means of chemical assays, EIAs, and GLC methods (10). The most specific quantitative method for blood alcohol determination is GLC or "head space" analysis by GLC. Volatile substances such as ethanol are driven out of aqueous biofluids into the "head space" or air space of a sealed test tube. Air samples are taken from the test tube by an air-tight syringe and injected into a gas chromatograph for separation and quantitation. This method separates ethanol from other alcohols and other volatile substances.

If ethanol analysis is performed on breath by means of a breathalyzer or on blood or urine by one of the chemical or immunoassays, the results are reliable for general use. Some states allow breathalyzer results, as acceptable values, to determine legal impairment while driving. In most forensic cases, however, results should be confirmed with a blood specimen using the GLC "head space" method. Alcoholism, like drug addiction, is hidden by denial. Therefore, when drug screening is requested, ethanol analysis should also be ordered. Ethanol measurement must be requested in addition to a drug screen because alcohol testing is not performed routinely by most laboratories.

Thin-Layer Chromatography (TLC)

TLC is a qualitative method and it is the least sensitive analytic technique for most drugs. Visualization of the spots on TLC is achieved by illumination with ultraviolet or fluorescent lights or by color reactions of the spots after spraying with chemical dyes. Identical molecules are expected to migrate to the same area and to give specific color reactions. Thus migration and color give TLC specificity not recognized in recent years with the advancement of more sophisticated techniques.

Radioimmunoassay (RIA) and Enzyme Immunoassay (EIA)

Figure 35.1 depicts the principle of immunoassays in drug detection. Antibodies are used to seek out specific drugs in biofluids. In samples containing one or more drugs, competition exists for available antibody-binding sites. The presence or absence of specific drugs is determined by the percent binding.

The specificity and sensitivity of the antibodies to a given drug differ depending on the particular drug assay and the assay manufacturer. Immunoassay can be very specific; however, compounds structurally similar to the drug of interest (i.e., the metabolites) often cross-react. Interaction of the antibody with a drug plus its metabolites increases the sensitivity of the assay.

EIA and FPIA are commonly used for drug abuse screening because no complicated extraction is required and the system lends itself to easy automation. EIA is more sensitive for most drugs and detects lower drug concentrations than TLC.

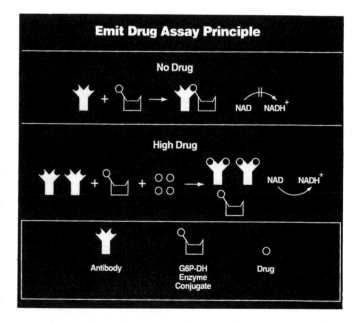

Figure 35.1. The basic principle of enzyme immunoassay (EIA) reactivity as it relates to drug detection. Molecules with similar functional groups cross-react, hence immunoassays have less specificity than do chromatographic assays. EIA is the most popular screening procedure. (Reproduced with the permission of Syva Company, Inc.)

On-site Screening Immunoassays

The increased prevalence of drug use has prompted the development of new drug screening technology that will produce results in as little as 10 minutes. Many situations require immediate testing and results for drugs of abuse. Hospital emergency departments have an immediate need for detecting drug overdoses. In addition, rapid results are useful for monitoring psychiatric patients, monitoring compliance within a drug rehabilitation program, and supervising parolees. Because these tests are designed to be performed *on-site* they may be performed directly in front of the person being tested or, certainly, at the site of collection. This is particularly useful for pre-employment screening, random or probable cause workplace testing, and for workplace accident-related injuries. It may also be important to conduct drug testing on-site in safety-oriented occupations, such as public transportation.

Visually interpreted competitive immunoassays that require no instrumentation have been developed in recent years. These kits are particularly effective because there is no calibration, maintenance, or down-time required and no special skills are needed to perform these tests. Most kits have built-in quality control zones in each panel, which ensures reagent integrity, and most have an extended shelf-life at room temperature.

There are currently a half dozen or more *on-site* kits on the market. Two kits use novel approaches. The Triage Panel for Drugs of Abuse plus Tricyclic Antidepressants (Biosite Diagnostics, Inc., San Diego, CA) is based on the use of Ascend Multiimmunoassay (AMIA) technology for simultaneous detection of multiple analytes in a sample. The Triage test device is shown in Figure 35.2. A urine sample is placed in the reaction cup in contact with lyophilized reagents and the reaction mixture is allowed to come to equilibrium for 10 minutes. The chemically labeled drugs (drug conjugate) compete with drugs that may be present in the urine for antibody binding sites. The reaction mixture is transferred to the solid phase membrane in the detection area that contains various immobilized antibodies in discrete drug class–specific zones. After a washing step, the operator visually examines each zone for the presence of a red bar. The method incorporates preset threshold concentrations that are independent for each drug. The assay response is proportional to the concentration of the unbound drug conjugate so that no signal is observed at drug concentrations less than the threshold concentrations (11). A positive specimen produces a distinct red bar in the drug detection zone adjacent to the drug name. A negative specimen does not pro-

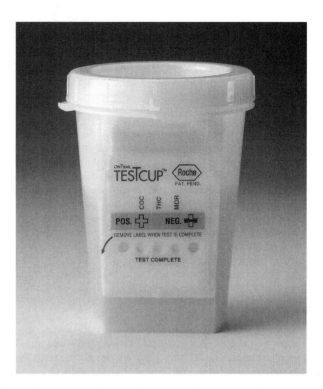

Figure 35.3. The OnTrak TesTcup Collection/Urinalysis Panel. (Reprinted with permission of Roche Diagnostic Systems, Inc., Somerville, NJ.)

duce a colored bar. The Triage Panel for Drugs of Abuse plus Tricyclic Antidepressants is available for the following drugs with their respective threshold or cut-off concentrations: phencyclidine (PCP) (25 ng/ml), benzodiazepines (BZO) (300 ng/ml), cocaine (COC) (300 ng/ml), amphetamines/methamphetamines (AMP) (1000 ng/ml), tetrahydrocannabinol (THC) (50 ng/ml), opiates (OPI) (300 ng/ml), barbiturates (BAR) (300 ng/ml), and tricyclic antidepressants (TCA) (1000 ng/ml).

Another new and unique screening device is the OnTrak TesTcup Collection/Urinalysis Panel (Roche Diagnostic Systems, Inc., Somerville, NJ). The OnTrak TesTcup, shown in Figure 35.3, simultaneously tests for the presence of three drugs (with respective threshold/cut-off concentrations): cocaine (COC) (300 ng/ml), tetrahydrocannabinol (THC) (50 ng/ml), and morphine (MOR) (300 ng/ml) and has the capability for a total of 5 different drugs. OnTrak TesTcup assays are based on the principle of microparticle capture inhibition. The test relies on the competition between drug, which may be present in the urine being tested, and drug conjugate immobilized on a membrane in the test chamber. Urine is collected directly in the OnTrak TesTcup and therefore provides the advantage of eliminating transfer or direct contact with the sample. After closing the cap and moving it to the test position, the sample reservoir is filled by tilting the cup for 5 seconds. Urine proceeds down immunochromatographic strips by capillary action and reacts with antibody-coated microparticles and drug conjugate present on the membrane. In approximately 3–5 minutes, the Test Valid bars appear, a decal is removed from the detection window and the results are interpreted as positive or negative. In the absence of drug, the antibody is free to interact with the drug conjugate, causing the formation of a blue band as a negative sign. When drug is present in the specimen, it binds to the antibody coated microparticles and no blue band is formed. A positive sample causes the membrane to remain white (OnTrak TesTcup package insert, April 1995).

These on-site screening kits have demonstrated greater than 97% agreement with confirmatory tests such as GC/MS (11). However, it must be stressed that these kits provide only preliminary analytical test results just like immunoassay tests run in a laboratory. A more specific alternate chemical method must be used to confirm positive screening results. GC/MS is the most specific confirmation method.

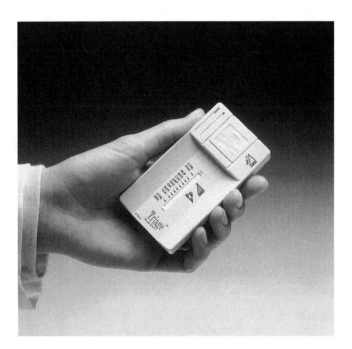

Figure 35.2. The Triage Panel for Drugs of Abuse plus Tricyclic Antidepressants. (Reprinted with permission of Biosite Diagnostics, Inc., San Diego, CA.)

Gas Liquid Chromatography (GLC) and Gas Chromatography-Mass Spectrometry (GC/MS)

GLC is an analytic technique that separates molecules by migration as described for TLC. The TLC plate is replaced by lengths of glass or metal tubing called columns, which are packed or coated with stationary materials of variable polarity. Figure 35.4 is an example of a GLC tracing showing separation of drugs in a mixture. The extracted analyte is carried through the column to the detector by a steady flow of heated gas. The detector responds to the drugs and other molecules. This response is graphically recorded and quantified, and is proportional to the amount of substance present in the sample. Identical compounds travel through the column at the same speed because they have identical interaction with the stationary column packing. The time between injection and an observed response at the recorder is the retention time. Identical retention times of substances on two different polarity columns constitute strong evidence that the substances are identical.

Stronger evidence can be obtained by the use of GC/MS, which identifies substances by gas chromatography separation and mass spectrometry fragmentation patterns. Figure 35.5 shows a GC/MS separation and fragmentation pattern of cocaine and its major metabolite benzoylecgonine. The separation is shown at the bottom of the figure, while the fragmentation is shown in the top two panels. Cocaine has the fragments 82, 182, and 303, while benzoylecgonine has 82, 240, and 361.

Not all bonds in molecules are of equal strength. The weak bonds are more likely to break under stress. In the mass spectrometer detector, electron beam bombardment of molecules breaks weak bonds. The exact mass and quantity of the molecular fragments or breakage products are measured by the mass detector. The breakage of molecules results in fragments unique for a drug. They occur in specific ratios to one another, thus the GC/MS method is often called "molecular fingerprinting." GC/MS is the most reliable, most definitive procedure in analytic chemistry for drug identification (12).

The fragmentation pattern of unknowns is checked against a computer library that lists the mass of drugs and related fragments. Matching a control's

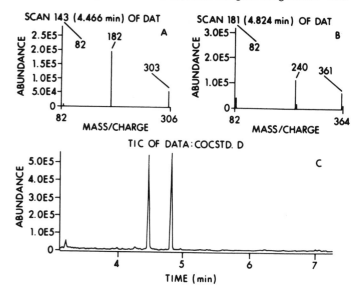

Figure 35.5. Gas chromatography-mass spectrometry showing and the fragmentation pattern of cocaine (**A**) and benzoylecgonine (**B**). **C,** the chromatographic separation of cocaine (4 min, 28 sec) and benzoylecgonine (4 min, 51 sec). (Reproduced with the permission of Drs. R. W. Taylor, N. C. Jain, and the *Journal of Analytical Toxicology.*)

fragments and fragment ratios is considered absolute confirmation of a particular compound. The sensitivity of GLC for most drugs is in the nanogram range, but with special detectors some compounds can be measured at picogram levels. GLC and GC/MS can also be used quantitatively, which provides additional information helping to interpret a clinical syndrome or explain corroborating evidence in forensic cases.

When a routine toxicology screen is ordered, the physician is often not aware that options are available for more specific screening and confirmation. Table 35.2 shows the performance characteristics of different types of assays for drugs of abuse.

CHOICE OF BODY FLUIDS AND TIME OF SAMPLE COLLECTION

Some drugs are metabolized extensively and are excreted very quickly, whereas others stay in the body for a long time (1). Thus, success of detection depends not only on the time of sample collection after last use but also on the drug used and whether the analysis is performed for the drug itself or

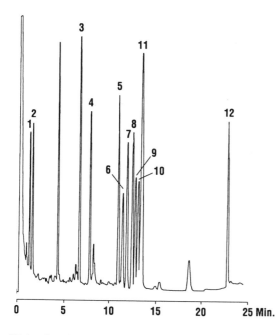

Figure 35.4. Gas liquid chromatographic (GLC) tracing showing separation of a drug mixture. The abscissa is time in minutes, the ordinate is detector response. The different drugs are number coded on the tracing. The drugs are: *1,* amphetamine; *2,* methamphetamine; *3,* meperidine; *4,* phencyclidine (PCP); *5,* methadone; *6,* amitriptyline; *7,* imipramine; *8,* cocaine; *9,* desipramine; *10,* pentazocine; *11,* codeine; and *12,* oxycodone. (Reprinted with permission of Alltech Associates, Inc., Deerfield, IL.)

Table 35.2 Performance Characteristics of Different Assays for Drugs of Abuse

Assay	Sensitivity	Specificity	Accuracy	Turn-Around time	Cost ($)
On-site EMIT; FPIA;	Moderate-high	Moderate	Qualitative[a]	Minutes	4–25
RIA; KIMS	Moderate-high	Moderate	Low-high	1–4 hours	1–5
TLC	Low-high	High	Qualitative[a]	1–4 hours	1–4
GC	High	High	High	Days	5–20
GC/MS	High	High	High	Days	10–100

Table from Cone EJ. New developments in biological measures of drug prevalence. In: Harrison LD, Hughes A, eds. The validity of self-reported drug use: Improving the accuracy of survey estimates. NIDA Res Monogr Ser 1986;167:104–126.
Legend: EMIT, enzyme multiplied immunoassay technique; *FPIA,* fluorescent polarization immunoassay; *RIA,* radioimmunoassay; *KIMS,* kinetic interaction of microparticles in solution; *TLC,* thin layer chromatography; *GC,* gas chromatography; *GC/MS,* gas chromatography/mass spectrometry.
[a] Results are generally expressed only in qualitative terms (i.e., positive/negative); consequently, accuracy may be difficult to assess.

Table 35.3 Typical Screening and Confirmation Cutoff Concentrations and Detection Times for Drugs of Abuse

Drug	Screening cutoff concentrations (ng/ml)	Analyte tested in confirmation	Confirmation cutoff concentrations (ng/ml)	Urine detection time
Amphetamine	1000	amphetamine	500	2–4 days
Barbiturates	200	amobarbital; secobarbital; other barbiturates	200	2–4 days for short acting; up to 30 days for long acting
Benzodiazepines	200	oxazepam; diazepam; other benzo-diazepines	200	Up to 30 days
Cocaine	300	benzoylecgonine	150	1–3 days
Codeine	300	codeine	300	
		morphine	300	1–3 days
Heroin	300	morphine	300	1–3 days
		6-acetylmorphine	10	
Marihuana	100; 50; 20	tetrahydro-cannabinol	15	1–3 days for casual use; up to 30 days for chronic use
Methadone	300	methadone	300	2–4 days
Methamphet-amine	1000	methamphetamine	500	2–4 days
		amphetamine	200	
Phencyclidine	25	phencyclidine	25	2–7 days for casual use; up to 30 days for chronic use

Table from Cone EJ. New developments in biological measures of drug prevalence. In: Harrison LD, Hughes A, eds. The validity of self-reported drug use: improving the accuracy of survey estimates. NIDA Res Monogr 1986;167:104–126.

for its metabolites. Table 35.3 illustrates the typical screening and confirmation cutoff concentrations, and the expected time scales of detectability for some commonly abused drugs.

When drug abuse detection is the goal, the following questions should be asked: (*a*) How long does the suspected drug stay in the body, or, what is its biologic half-life? (*b*) How fast and how extensively is the drug biotransformed? Should one look for the drug itself or its metabolites? (*c*) Which body fluid is best for analysis, or, what is the major route of excretion? Intravenous use or smoking drugs of abuse provides nearly instantaneous absorption into the bloodstream and excretion of the drug and/or metabolites in urine occurs almost immediately. Inhalation (smoking or snorting) or oral use of drugs will result in slower absorption and excretion in urine may not be detected immediately after use.

Cocaine is rapidly biotransformed into benzoylecgonine and ecgonine methyl ester. Less than 10% unchanged cocaine is excreted into the urine and is detectable only for 12–18 hours after use. What does this suggest to the clinician who wants to identify cocaine abusers? Because cocaine has a short half-life, unless use is suspected within hours or the patient is suspected to be under the influence of cocaine at the time of sample collection, the parent compound is not likely to be found in detectable concentrations in either blood or urine (13, 22). Plasma enzymes continue to metabolize cocaine even after blood is taken out of the body. Therefore, blood samples must be collected into tubes containing sodium fluoride to inactivate the enzymes. Benzoylecgonine is the major metabolite of cocaine; its half-life is about 6 hours and it is excreted in urine at levels totaling approximately 45% of the dose. Thus, cocaine abuse detection is best accomplished by collecting urine and analyzing it for benzoylecgonine.

Cocaine metabolism and disposition is contrasted with methaqualone, which is also very lipid-soluble but has a half-life of 20–60 hours due to slow biotransformation. Thus, either blood or urine tests are effective for many days to detect methaqualone itself. Methaqualone was detected for 21 days in urine after a single 300 mg oral dose and in blood for 7 days (14). Phar-

macokinetic and drug excretion information are important to determine target chemicals (drug or metabolite) for detection. Many physicians prefer blood to urine for drug screening because blood levels constitute stronger evidence of recent use and are related more closely to brain levels and drug-related behavioral changes than are urine levels.

The collection of urine specimens must be supervised to ensure donor identity and to guarantee the integrity of the specimen. It is not unusual to receive someone else's urine or a highly diluted sample when collection is not supervised or screened by the laboratory for pH, specific gravity, and creatinine levels. As a rule, first morning urine samples are more concentrated, therefore, drugs are easier to detect than in more diluted samples. The decision to use blood or urine must be based on the information needed and the specific drug's pharmacokinetic and excretion data. Drug levels in urine are higher than in blood, therefore, urine is usually the biofluid of choice for drug detection.

INTERPRETATION OF RESULTS

Psychoactivity of most drugs lasts only a few hours, while urinalysis can detect some drugs and/or metabolites for days or even weeks (15). Thus, the presence of a drug (or metabolite) in urine is only an indication of prior exposure, not proof of intoxication or impairment at the time of sample collection. In some cases, quantitative data in blood or urine can corroborate observed behavior or action of a subject, especially when the levels are so high that it is impossible for the subject to be free of drug effects. Nevertheless, laboratory data and corroborating drug-induced behavior must be interpreted by experts in pharmacology and toxicology with experience in drug biotransformation and pharmacokinetics.

Drug analysis reports, either positive or negative, may raise questions about the absolute truth of the results. The usual questions are: (*a*) What method was used? (*b*) Did the laboratory analyze for the drug only, the metabolite only, or both? (*c*) What is the "cut-off" value for the assay? and (*d*) Was the sample time close enough to the suspected drug exposure?

False-negative results occur more easily than false-positives, mainly because once a test is screened negative it is not tested further. Negative reports based on TLC alone are not conclusive due to lack of sensitivity. Additionally, if the screening method is RIA or EIA, the cut-off may have been set too high. Thus, drugs present below the cut-off concentration are reported as negative. It is imperative for the physician to know the cut-off for each drug tested and, for diagnostic purposes, ask for any drug presence above the blank. Another possibility for false negatives is that the sample was taken too long after the last drug exposure. Whatever the case may be, if the suspicion of drug use is strong, the clinician must repeat testing and inquire at the laboratory for more sensitive drug screening procedures.

In general, analytic methods have improved significantly in the past decades and the trend is toward further improvement (16). As technology advances, more drugs and chemicals will be analyzed in biofluids at the nanogram and picogram level. Advancement, however, does not mean that modern methodologies are infallible, nor that they replace clinical judgment. Theoretically and practically, technical or human error can influence testing results. A nationally certified laboratory, with a full spectrum of drug abuse tests, enables the well-trained clinician to make drug abuse diagnoses that were not possible in the past. With knowledge of the available analytic methods, one can scrutinize laboratory results with confidence as to their validity.

CLINICAL DRUG TESTING

Clinical drug testing has three components: emergency toxicology, rehabilitation toxicology, and diagnostic toxicology. Each has slightly different goals and requirements. *Emergency toxicology* requires quick analysis, responding to critical situations in overdose cases. Sometimes the clinical symptoms or the leftover drug is a sufficient clue to the laboratory for what drug to test, but most often the chemist must determine the toxic compound's identity. Thus, the emergency toxicology laboratory must be located near emergency services for speedy response and must use proved methods to provide quick answers. TLC is still widely used for screening; however, on-site, one step, nontechnical kit screening is becoming more common. Instrumental immunoassays are also quick and practical, but as in all screening techniques, they give only "yes" or "no" results for each drug or drug class tested. If the target drug is not tested, identification is not possible, and tracking down the unknown one by one is a slow process. However, if there is a clue to drug identity, immunoassays provide quick answers. Confirmation of positive results is performed by an alternate scientific method and is at the discretion of the physician.

In *rehabilitation programs,* drug testing is of foremost importance. Identified ex–drug abusers need to know that the therapist or the counselor knows objectively that they are in good standing or in danger of relapsing to drug use. In this situation drug abuse testing is a deterrent and an important component of the treatment process. However, from the laboratory's point of view, testing is significantly different from emergency toxicology. The test results may not be available for at least 24 hours, and large numbers of samples are analyzed in a batch for rehabilitation clinics. The laboratory usually performs a screening test recheck and/or confirms positives by means of an alternate scientific method. The choice of method depends on assay sensitivity, specificity, expense, and practicality. Instrumental immunoassay methods, such as EIA, are used most frequently for screening when large numbers of samples must be tested at a reasonable cost. An emerging FDA-approved sweat patch will aid rehabilitation drug testing. The patch placed on the skin is worn for several days and will detect any drug used during that period, thus timing and use of short-acting drugs will also be detected (17).

Testing for diagnostic drugs of abuse is another important and slightly different area. Denial is typical of drug abusers. Astute physicians are now frequently testing their patients for drug abuse. The critical role of diagnostic testing is to prevent false negatives when a drug is abused by the patient. The essence of diagnostic testing is *sensitivity.* From the laboratory's perspective, the most sensitive methods and a large drug panel screening technique are most appropriate. Immunoassays and GLC techniques must be used for ultimate sensitivity.

FORENSIC DRUG TESTING

Forensic drug testing has three components: workplace testing, medical examiner or postmortem testing, and correctional and parole testing.

Historically, *forensic drug testing* developed from clinical and pathologic testing. Laboratories had to implement numerous legally acceptable procedures and testing also needed improvement. Certified laboratories must be able to prove that positive test results are accurate and reliable and that the tests performed were from the individual listed on the report. Weak links in external or internal chain of custody procedures or poor standards and/or quality control in the testing process provide sufficient ammunition to defense attorneys and expert witnesses to contradict the validity of results. For this reason the forensic drug testing facility must be significantly more secure and better organized than that of a clinical drug testing laboratory.

Workplace testing is performed on subjects at their place of employment. Many industries and governmental agencies mandate testing of individuals performing critical duties. These places of employment have strict drug policies in place, informing employees that drug abuse is not tolerated and that tests are performed to protect the public interest. The different types of tests performed are pre-employment, for cause, and random drug testing. Positive findings can result in loss of job opportunity. The consequences of workplace testing are very serious and often disputed. People's livelihoods depend on laboratory results; therefore, sufficient safeguards must be built into the system to provide assurance that the results are reliable. In forensic testing the usual procedure is screening with a large-volume automated immunoassay analyzer (i.e., EIA and FPIA) and confirmation of positives by GC/MS.

Other forms of forensic drug testing requiring "litigation documentation" are *medicolegal cases* and *postmortem analysis* of body fluids for the presence of drugs and poisons. Before workplace testing became common, even the medicolegal or postmortem toxicology testing was less stringent. As a result of the very strict rules and regulations governing workplace testing,

more rigorous and complete evidence documentation and more accurate methods also are required in medicolegal and postmortem testing.

Another example of drug testing is in *correctional cases* and *testing in the prison system.* A very large percentage of the prisoners' criminal activity is connected either with drug use or drug trafficking. It is not unusual to find that drug abuse continues in the prisons. Therefore, correctional facilities have adopted a drug abuse testing policy in the prison system and also during parole. Although the consequences of testing are potentially punitive, testing of inmates in many states does not require confirmation of positive results.

TESTING DRUGS IN SALIVA, SWEAT, AND HAIR

Most drugs enter saliva by passive diffusion. The major advantages of saliva as a test specimen are that it is readily available, collection is non-invasive, the presence of parent drug is in higher abundance than metabolites, and a high correlation of saliva drug concentration that can be compared with the free fraction of drug in blood (17). The use of saliva to predict blood concentrations is limited because of the possibility of contamination of saliva from drug use by oral, smoked, and intranasal routes. Cone (18) reported that marihuana smoking produced contamination of the oral cavity by tetrahydrocannabinol (THC). Even though saliva concentrations of THC were derived from contamination, they were highly correlated with plasma concentrations (17). However, even with this precaution in mind and the short window of detectability of drugs in saliva, saliva measurements can be used to detect very recent drug use. This may be useful in testing automobile drivers involved in accidents.

Sweat is approximately 99% water and is produced by the body as a heat regulation mechanism. Since the amount of sweat produced is dependent on environmental temperatures, routine sweat collection is difficult due to a large variation in the rate of sweat production and the lack of adequate sweat collection devices. However, cocaine, morphine, nicotine, amphetamine, ethanol, and other drugs have been identified in sweat (17). A recently developed "sweat patch" resembles a Band-Aid and is applied to the skin for a period of several days to several weeks. Sweat is absorbed and concentrated on the cellulose pad, which is then removed from the skin and tested for drug content. Sweat testing for cocaine was recently evaluated by Cone et al. (19). Generally, there appeared to be a dose-concentration relationship; however, there was wide intersubject variability, which is a disadvantage of this technology. Research in this testing technology is still developing and is indicating apparent advantages of the sweat patch such as high subject acceptability of wearing the patch for drug monitoring and the ability to monitor drug intake for a period of several weeks with a single patch (17).

Testing for drugs in hair is also a recent addition to the drug abuse detection technology (20). Due to the very low concentrations of drugs incorporated in hair, very sensitive methodology must be used. Screening is performed by RIA with ultrasensitive antibodies and confirmation by GC/MS or mass spectrometry-mass spectrometry. Drug representatives from virtually all classes of abused drugs have now been detected in hair (17). It remains unclear how drugs enter the hair although the most likely entry routes involve: (*a*) diffusion from blood into the hair follicle and hair cells with subsequent binding to hair cell components (Fig. 35.6); (*b*) excretion in sweat, which bathes hair follicles and hair strands; (*c*) excretion in oily secretions into the hair follicle and onto the skin surface; and (*d*) entry from the environment (17). Two controversial issues in hair drug testing are the environmental contamination of hair that may result in a false positive test result and the interpretation of dose and time relationships. Although it has been generally assumed that the hair strand, when sectioned, provides a long-term time course of drug abuse history, studies with labeled cocaine have not supported this interpretation. Henderson et al. (21) concluded that ". . . there is not, at present, the necessary scientific foundation for hair analysis to be used to determine either the time or amount of cocaine use." In spite of some controversial aspects of hair testing, this technique is being used on an increasingly broad scale in a variety of circumstances (17). This

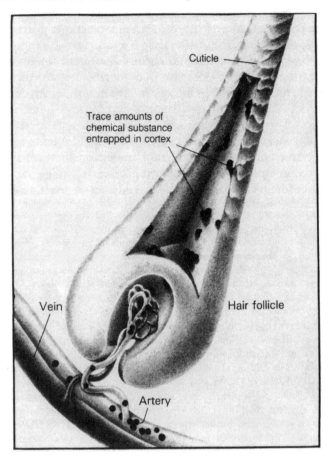

Figure 35.6. A conceptual drawing of drug transfer from the blood to hair follicle and its subsequent encapsulation in the hair shaft. (Reproduced with the permission of Psychemedics, Inc., Santa Monica, CA.)

It is important that this new, powerful tool, drug testing, be used judiciously as a means of early detection, rehabilitation, and prevention. Test results must be interpreted only by individuals who understand drugs of abuse medically and pharmacologically. The federal government requires that in its drug-testing program the results go directly to medical review officers, who are supposed to be trained to interpret such reports. Improper testing or improper interpretation of drug testing data must be prevented.

CONCLUSION

As long as illegal drug use is prevalent in our society, drug abuse testing will have an important clinical and forensic role. Testing in the clinical setting aids the physician who treats subjects with psychiatric signs and symptoms secondary to drug abuse, monitors treatment outcome, and handles serious overdose cases. Drug testing in the forensic setting will be used for workplace testing and monitoring of parolees convicted of drug-related charges.

Civil rights must be respected to protect the innocent. Names of subjects should be known only to the medical office where the sample is collected. Testing must follow strict security and chain of custody procedures to ensure anonymity and prevent sample mix-up during testing. Most progressive laboratories have instituted bar-code labeling of samples and related documents to ensure confidentiality. Bar-coding also improves accuracy of reporting and tracking of samples and records. This system ultimately prevents sample mix-up due to human error during accessioning and processing.

The reliability of testing procedures is also of foremost importance. Good laboratories institute internal open, blind and external quality control systems to assure high quality of testing (2). Reliability depends on three major factors: well-qualified and well-trained laboratory personnel, state-of-the-art instrumentation, and logical organization of the testing laboratory.

Before issuing certification, governmental agencies require laboratories to adhere to strict standards in personnel qualifications, experience, quality control, quality assurance programs, chain of custody procedures, and multiple data review prior to reporting results.

Two nationally recognized agencies protect the rights of individual citizens by assuring proper procedures in forensic drug testing. DHHS/SAMHSA administers its National Laboratory Certification Program and the

technology may be used to estimate the drug abuse habit of the patient who is in denial. Self-reported drug use over a period of several months can be compared to hair test results from a hair strand (about 3.9 cm long) representative of the same time period (17). It is expected that this type of comparison would be more effective than urine testing since urine provides a historical record of only 2–4 days under most circumstances (17). Since denial is a major problem with drug abusers, this technology is an invaluable tool in drug abuse diagnosis and therapy. Table 35.4 illustrates the comparison of usefulness of urine, saliva, sweat and hair as a biological matrix for drug detection.

ETHICAL CONSIDERATIONS

Legitimate need for drug abuse testing in the clinical setting is indisputable. Denial makes identification of drug abuse difficult; therefore, testing is necessary both for identification of drug abusers and monitoring of treatment outcome. Drug testing in the workplace and in sports is more controversial because positive test results may be used in termination of long-time employees or refusal to hire new ones.

Private companies believe that it is their right to establish drug and alcohol–free workplaces and sport arenas. The opposition believes that one is ill advised to terminate individuals for a single positive test result, even when it is confirmed by forensically acceptable procedures. A testing program is reasonable when a chance for rehabilitation is offered. Probationary periods provide an opportunity to stop using drugs through treatment or self-help programs. Employee assistance programs, which refer employees to drug counseling, are available in larger companies and governmental organizations.

Table 35.4   Comparative Usefulness of Urine, Saliva, Sweat, and Hair as a Biological Matrix for Drug Detection

Biological matrix	Drug detection time	Major advantages	Major disadvantages	Primary use
Urine	2–4 days	Mature technology; on-site methods available; established cutoffs	Only detects recent use	Detection of recent drug use
Saliva	12–24 hours	Easily obtainable; samples "free" drug fraction; parent drug presence	Short detection time; oral drug contamination; collection methods influence pH and s/p ratios; only detects recent use; new technology	Linking positive drug test to behavior and performance impairment
Sweat	1–4 weeks	Cumulative measure of drug use	High potential for environmental contamination; new technology	Detection of recent drug use (days–weeks)
Hair	months	Long-term measure of drug use; similar sample can be recollected	High possibility for environmental contamination; new technology	Detection of drug use in recent past (1–6 months)

Table from Cone EJ. New developments in biological measures of drug prevalence. In: Harrison LD, Hughes A, eds. The validity of self-reported drug use: improving the accuracy of survey estimates. NIDA Res Monogr 1986;167:104–126.

College of American Pathologists runs its Forensic Toxicology Proficiency Program. In addition, numerous state and city regulatory agencies inspect and certify drug-testing laboratories. Good laboratories are easily identified by having current certificates of qualification issued by national and local regulatory agencies.

In conclusion, drug abuse testing has come a long way in terms of accu-

racy and reliability (16). Testing started in traditional "wet chemistry" laboratories, using huge sample volumes and crude methodologies of low sensitivity. Now, autoanalyzers perform hundreds of tests on minute sample volumes, accurately measuring low-nanogram amounts of substances. Thus, the insecurity of the physician and counselor about drug abuse testing should not be a concern when using properly certified laboratories.

References

1. Chiang NC, Hawks RL. Implications of drug levels in body fluids: basic concepts. In: Hawks RL, Chiang NC, eds. Urine testing for drugs of abuse. NIDA Res Monogr 1986;73:62–83.
2. Blanke RV. Accuracy in urinalysis. In: Hawks RL, Chiang NC, eds. Urine testing for drugs of abuse. NIDA Res Monogr 1986;73:43–53.
3. Jaffee JH, Martin WR. Opioid analgesics and antagonists. In: Gilman AG, Goodman LS, et al., eds. The pharmacological basis of therapeutics. 7th ed. New York: Macmillan, 1985: 491–531.
4. Gold MS, Verebey K, Dackis CA. Diagnosis of drug abuse: drug intoxication and withdrawal states. Fair Oaks Hospital Psychiatry Letter 1980;3(5):23–34.
5. Pottash ALC, Gold MS, Extein I. The use of the clinical laboratory. In: Sederer LI, ed. Inpatient psychiatry: diagnosis and treatment. Baltimore: Williams & Wilkins, 1982:205–221.
6. Wadler GI, Heinline B. Drugs and athletes. Philadelphia: FA Davis, 1989: [chapter 18] Drug testing pg 195–210.
7. Willette E. Drug testing programs. NIDA Res Monogr 1986;73:5–12.
8. Verebey K, Martin D, Gold MS. Drug abuse: interpretation of laboratory tests. In: Hall W, ed. Psychiatric medicine. Washington, DC: U.S. Government Printing Office, 1982:155–167.
9. Manno JE. Interpretation of urinalysis results. In: Hawks RL, Chiang NC, eds. Urine testing for drugs of abuse. NIDA Res Monogr 1986;73: 54–61.
10. Baselt RC, Cravey RH, eds. Disposition of toxic drugs and chemicals in man. 4th edition. Foster City, CA: Chemical Toxicology Institute, 1995.
11. Buechler KF, Moi S, Noar B, et al. Simultaneous detection of seven drugs of abuse by the Triage Panel for Drugs of Abuse. Clin Chem 1992; 38:1678–1684.
12. Hawks RL. Analytical methodology. In: Hawks RL, Chiang NC, eds. Urine testing for drugs of abuse. NIDA Res Monogr 1986;73:30–42.
13. Verebey K. Cocaine abuse detection by laboratory methods. In: Washton AM, Gold MS, eds. Cocaine: a clinician's handbook. New York: Guilford Press, 1987:214–228.
14. Kogan MJ, Jukofsky D, Verebey K, et al. Detection of methaqualone in human urine by radio immunoassay and gas-liquid chromatography after a therapeutic dose. Clin Chem 1987;24: 1425–1427.
15. Dackis CA, Pottash ALC, Annitto W, et al. Persistence of urinary marijuana levels after supervised abstinence. Am J Psychiatry 1982;139: 1196–1198.
16. Frings CS, Battaglia DJ, White RM. Status of drugs of abuse testing in urine under blind conditions: an AACC study. Clin Chem 1989;35(5): 891–944.
17. Cone EJ. New developments in biological measures of drug prevalence. In: Harrison LD, Hughes A, eds. The validity of self-reported drug use: Improving the accuracy of survey estimates. NIDA Res Monogr 1986;167: 104–126.
18. Cone EJ. Saliva testing for drugs of abuse. Ann N Y Acad Sci 1993;694:91–127.
19. Cone EJ, Hillsgrove MJ, Jenkins AJ, Keenan RM, Darwin WD. Sweat testing for heroin, cocaine, and metabolites. J Anal Toxicol 1994; 18(6):298–305.
20. Baumgarten WA, Hill VA, Blahd WH. Hair analysis for drugs of abuse. J Forensic Sci 1989; 34(6):1433–1453.
21. Henderson GL, Harkey MR, Jones R. Hair analysis for drugs of abuse. Final report, grant no. NIJ 90-NIJ-CX-0012. National Institute on Justice, National Institute on Drug Abuse, September, 1993.
22. Cone EJ. Testing human hair for drugs of abuse. I. Individual dose and time profiles of morphine and codeine in plasma, saliva, urine, and beard compared to drug induced effects on pupils and behavior. J Anal Toxicol 1990;14:1–7.

36 DETOXIFICATION

Grace Chang and Thomas R. Kosten

Detoxification can be defined as a period of medical treatment, usually including counseling, during which time an individual is helped to overcome physical and psychological dependence on alcohol or drugs. Achievement of a substance-free state is preparatory to the even more challenging, but also more rewarding, period of sustained abstinence from alcohol and drugs.

DETOXIFICATION SITES

Detoxification can take place in either inpatient or outpatient settings. Selection of the setting will reflect the patient's clinical needs and circumstances, such as the availability of psychosocial supports, motivation for treatment, presence of comorbid conditions, and previous treatment and detoxification history. For example, outpatient detoxification may be appropriate for a highly motivated patient with mild-to-moderate dependence on alcohol, a supportive family, no concomitant significant medical or psychiatric illnesses, active participation in substance abuse treatment, and no previous withdrawals complicated by seizures or delirium tremens. While choice of the detoxification setting is ultimately a clinical decision to be made by a physician in collaboration with the patient, insurance case managers may exert some influence in the decision making process since they authorize payment for treatment and may rec-

ommend specific treatment facilities because of contractual arrangements.

The American Society of Addiction Medicine, with the National Association of Alcohol and Drug Programs, has formulated criteria for patient placement that include admission, continuation, and discharge criteria for each level of care. Four levels of substance abuse care have been identified: (*a*) outpatient, (*b*) intensive outpatient, (*c*) residential that is medically supervised, and (*d*) medically managed inpatient treatment. Patient placement is based on six factors: (*a*) patient's state of intoxication or potential for experiencing withdrawal symptoms, (*b*) biomedical comorbidity, (*c*) emotional symptoms or behavioral conditions, (*d*) patient's response to treatment recommendations, (*e*) relapse potential, and (*f*) environment for recovery (1, 2).

Thus, an accurate and competent clinical assessment of the patient is essential when referral to detoxification is made. Structured clinical interviews, such as the Addiction Severity Index, may assist in systematic assessment of the patient's substance abuse or dependence (3). The Clinical Institute Withdrawal Assessment for Alcohol (CIWA-A) is a widely used scale for the clinical quantification of the severity of the alcohol withdrawal syndrome and can be helpful in deciding between inpatient and outpatient detoxification (4). Scales for the assessment of opiate withdrawal (5, 6) and benzodiazepine withdrawal (7) are also available.

EMERGENCY DETOXIFICATION

Conducting an orderly and systematic history as well as physical and laboratory examination is frequently impractical in patients with acute alcohol and drug intoxications in emergency situations (8). The first priority is general supportive care and resuscitative measures, if needed. Airway obstruction, adequacy of ventilation, vital signs, cardiac rhythm, and level of consciousness should be evaluated; any findings of concern warrant immediate attention. The initial determination of the severity of a drug ingestion or poisoning includes the patient's general status and level of consciousness at arrival, alleged drug and dose involved, and complicating clinical situations particular to the patient or to the drug ingested (9).

IDENTIFYING SPECIFIC INTOXICANTS

Patients may be screened for use of specific substances by direct interview or laboratory analysis of body fluids. Each approach has advantages and disadvantages, but consistent evaluation of substance use will ensure due consideration of all diagnostic possibilities.

Patient History

Directly asking the patient about the quantity and frequency of alcohol and other drug consumption is an important means of detecting abuse and dependence (10). However, the patient must not only be able to communicate the necessary data, but also be willing to disclose accurate information on the amount and type of substance ingested. The patient's companions or family may be available to provide history as well. Although it has been demonstrated that patients do reveal the extent and type of substances used (11), such information may not be forthcoming in certain settings where patients may have concerns about self-incrimination. In addition, the adulteration of many illicit substances with other psychoactive substances may further obscure the clinical history, since patients are unaware of the exact nature of the additives. The same limitations may apply when interviewing collateral reporters.

Nonetheless, seeking information about an acute episode of intoxication may also allow the clinician to inquire about chronic patterns of dysfunctional substance use and select appropriate treatment protocols. Screening questionnaires for alcohol abuse and drug dependence continue to be refined by researchers so that the reliability of the information obtained can be increased.

Toxicology Screening

Emergency or admission screening can provide valuable information to physicians confronted with a confusing clinical presentation with atypical symptoms or signs and little or no history (12). Urine is the most common specimen for drug testing, because it can be collected noninvasively, is available in large volume, contains higher concentrations of drugs and their metabolites than do other tissues and fluids, is easier to analyze than blood or other tissues, and can be frozen, with drugs and their metabolites remaining stable during long-term storage (13). Although informed voluntary consent must be obtained when performing urine tests for individuals 18 years or older, urine testing may be completed even without this consent if a medical emergency exists (14).

DETOXIFICATION BY SUBSTANCE

Alcohol Intoxication

Mild to moderate alcohol intoxication may be characterized by impaired attention, poor motor coordination, dysmetria, ataxia, nystagmus, slurred speech, prolonged reaction time, flushed face, orthostatic hypotension, hematemesis, and stupor. Patient symptoms may include alcohol on the breath, loquacity, impaired judgment, inappropriate behavioral and emotional responses, euphoria, dizziness, and blurred vision. It is usually unnecessary to admit a conscious intoxicated patient to the hospital. The patient should be placed in a side-lying or face-down position to avoid aspiration of vomitus. Once other causes of intoxication have been ruled out, close observation is sufficient (15). The differential diagnosis of alcohol intoxication includes: sedative hypnotic intoxication, hypoglycemia, diabetic ketoacidosis, subdural hematoma or head injury, postictal status, hepatic encephalopathy, encephalitis, and other causes of ataxia, such as neurodegenerative diseases (16).

Pathologic intoxication is characterized by an excited, combative, psychotic state following minimal alcohol consumption in a susceptible individual. The patient must be prevented from harming self and others, either with parenteral sedatives or physical restraints (8).

The belligerent intoxicated patient warrants serious consideration of his or her potential for violence. According to Hackett, five principles guide the management of a "boisterous drunk." First, hospital police or security should be notified before the interview begins. Second, the interviewer should be tolerant and nonthreatening, making no attempt to change the patient's behavior. Third, an offer of food in a quiet, comfortable environment may calm the patient. Fourth, a low dose of a sedative such as lorazepam, 1–2 mg by mouth, or liquid haloperidol, 5 mg by mouth, for a patient near violence might be offered. Fifth, physical restraint and further sedation using haloperidol, 5 mg intramuscular, are necessary if the patient becomes violent (17).

Alcohol Withdrawal

Reduction or cessation of prolonged heavy alcohol consumption in tolerant individuals may be followed by alcohol withdrawal or life-threatening alcohol withdrawal delirium. The essential features of alcohol withdrawal include cessation of (or reduction in) alcohol use that has been heavy and prolonged, and two or more of the following developing within several hours to a few days after last use: (a) autonomic hyperactivity; (b) increased hand tremor; (c) insomnia; (d) nausea or vomiting; (e) transient hallucinations or illusions; (f) psychomotor agitation; (g) anxiety; (h) grand mal seizure (18). These symptoms cause clinically significant distress and are not due to other medical conditions. Differential diagnoses include sedative, hypnotic, or anxiolytic withdrawal, or generalized anxiety disorder. The early onset of withdrawal can begin within 6–8 hours of a substantial decline of blood alcohol levels and usually begins within the first 24 hours of abstinence (15). In rare cases, it may begin 10 days after the last drink. The duration of withdrawal may range from a few hours to 2 weeks. Mild-to-moderate alcohol withdrawal may be managed on an outpatient basis, using benzodiazepines on a tapered schedule, a parenteral dose of thiamine 100 mg and then a week's regimen of thiamine 50 mg, multivitamins, and folate 1 mg, all by mouth. Since hypomagnesemia has been closely associated with tremor in alcoholics and may play a role in the genesis of seizures, 100 mg thiamine and 4 g magnesium sulfate in 1 liter of 5% dextrose/normal saline can be administered intravenously over the course of one to 2 hours instead of the parenteral thiamine alone (19). Fever, serious underlying medical illness, seizures, signs of organic brain syndromes, or inability for self-care are contraindications to outpatient management.

Generalized tonic-clonic seizures may develop within 24 hours of abstinence. Among patients with seizures, two thirds will develop multiple seizures, while the remaining third will have only one. The rare patient who develops status epilepticus is likely to have epilepsy. Severe or repeated seizures can be treated with intravenous diazepam 5–10 mg or lorazepam 1–2 mg given slowly. Uncomplicated alcohol withdrawal seizures do not require the long-term use of antiepileptics such as phenytoin (Dilantin) (26).

Alcohol induced psychotic disorder may develop during intoxication or withdrawal. It is distinguished from a primary psychotic disorder because alcohol is determined to be etiologically related to the symptoms, which are assessed to be excessive and severe enough to merit independent clinical attention (18).

Alcohol withdrawal delirium usually develops within 1 week following recent cessation or reduction in alcohol consumption. The essential features of delirium are reduced ability to maintain attention or to shift attention appropriately to new external stimuli, and disorganized thinking, as manifested by rambling, irrelevant, or incoherent speech (18). Immediate hospitalization is indicated. Despite optimal therapy, delirium tremens results in 5–10% mortality, due to volume depletion, electrolyte imbalance, infection, cardiac arrhythmias, or suicide (15). The patient with alcohol withdrawal delirium requires hospitalization to achieve stabilization and to rule out delirium due to a general medical condition (such as head injury), dementia, primary psychotic disorders, malingering, and factitious disorder.

WERNICKE-KORSAKOFF SYNDROME

The acute presentation of Wernicke-Korsakoff syndrome, also known as Wernicke's psychosis, an organic mental syndrome secondary to alcoholism and thiamine depletion, is Wernicke's encephalopathy. Sixth-nerve palsy or oculomotor paralysis, ataxia, and dysarthria constitute the acute clinical presentation. Intravenous administration of 500–1000 mg thiamine is required (19). Exacerbation of the clinical picture may occur if carbohydrates, as in the form of dextrose solutions, are administered prior to thiamine therapy.

Psychological symptoms, anterograde amnesia, confabulation, and some degree of retrograde amnesia constitute Wernicke-Korsakoff syndrome. The emergence of Wernicke-Korsakoff syndrome is correlated with a poor prognosis, with only 20% of patients improving substantially (16). Fortunately, Wernicke-Korsakoff syndrome is seen in fewer than 5% of alcoholics (20).

Cocaine and Other Central Nervous System Stimulants

Central nervous system (CNS) stimulants are sympathomimetic substances that elicit states of heightened alertness, elevated mood, and enhanced psychomotor activity. Amphetamines and cocaine are the principal drugs of abuse in the group (8).

Amphetamines may be taken by mouth, absorbed through the nasal mucosa, or injected intravenously. Cocaine may be taken intranasally ("snorting"), injected intravenously, or smoked as cocaine "freebase" or "crack."

Stimulation by cocaine and amphetamines at high doses may result in peculiar stereotyped behavior, bruxism, formication, irritability, restlessness, confusion, emotional lability, and paranoia. Although patients may remain fully oriented, they may develop paranoid psychosis similar to mania or paranoid schizophrenia that may result in violent behavior. Hyperthermia and seizure activity may also accompany stimulant toxicity (21).

CNS depression follows stimulation, and can result in paralysis of motor activity, hyperreflexia with eventual areflexia, stupor progressing to coma, loss of vital functions, and death. Recent data support the causal relationship between increasing dosage of cocaine and a direct toxic effect on the myocardium. Some clinicians believe that the occurrence of acute myocardial infarction in any patient younger than 40 years of age without a history of other cardiac risk factors is presumptive of coronary spasm secondary to stimulant abuse until proven otherwise (22).

Supportive measures are the first priority in the treatment of stimulant toxicity (9). Agitation may respond to benzodiazepines. Management of psychosis can be achieved with chlorpromazine or haloperidol. Haloperidol may be the pharmacological agent of choice because of its dopaminergic activity and because chlorpromazine may slow the metabolism of amphetamine (22). Hyperthermia requires external cooling. If feasible, acidification of urine by oral administration with ammonium chloride will hasten urinary excretion of the stimulants. Seizure activity can be controlled by diazepam (21) or phenytoin (9). Severe hypertension or tachycardia have been treated by a variety of agents and their management would benefit from the expertise of a medical specialist.

Withdrawal from CNS stimulants may be characterized by hypersomnia, depression, fatigue, or apathy. Such symptoms are usually transient and do not require inpatient hospital care (23). For example, outpatient acupuncture has been used for over 40,000 cocaine or crack abusers at Lincoln Hospital in New York City, with 40% showing substantial evidence of improvement after several weeks (24). On the other hand, some clinical reports suggest that stimulant withdrawal can lead to depression of life-threatening intensity that may require brief hospitalization and step down to a less intensive form of treatment once the patient is stabilized (25).

Hallucinogens and Marihuana

The hallucinogens and marihuana can change level of consciousness and induce hallucinations, although marihuana is usually ingested at doses that produce euphoria and rarely leads to a psychiatric emergency (24). Cross-tolerance exists among most of the hallucinogens, but apparently not with marihuana (20).

The most potent hallucinogen is LSD, lysergic acid diethylamide. It is usually taken orally as a pill or dissolved on a piece of paper. Intoxication can result from doses as low as 50 micrograms (21). Sympathomimetic effects develop within an hour of ingestion. Peak effects, including visual hallucinations and novelty of perceptions, occur 2–3 hours after ingestion. Most effects subside within 8 hours, although some people complain of prolonged psychic numbness (8, 21).

Phencyclidine (PCP) is a drug of increasing abuse. Developed as a general anesthetic over three decades ago, PCP is usually smoked with tobacco or marihuana. It can also be taken orally, intranasally, or intravenously. Dose-related side effects can range from muscular incoordination, nystagmus, slurred speech, ataxia, and hyperreflexia at lower doses (5–10 mg) to seizures, hypertensive crisis, respiratory depression, coma, and death at higher doses (>20 mg). Effects persist for 4–6 hours (21).

The number of regular marihuana users is not known, but estimates for experimental marihuana use in the United States range from 26 to over 60 million Americans trying it at least once (8, 20, 21). Smoking produces effects that are manifest from seconds to minutes and disappear within a few hours. Marihuana that is eaten results in delayed onset and prolongation of effects.

Adverse reactions to hallucinogen and marihuana use include panic, delirium, psychosis, and flashbacks. With respect to marihuana, most of the adverse reactions do not require specific pharmacological intervention. Reassurance and observation appear to be sufficient (23). The treatment of PCP adverse reactions is controversial (9, 21, 22, 25). The consensus thus far is that supportive "talking down," suitable for reactions to other hallucinogens, may exacerbate PCP intoxication. Thus, close observation in a quiet environment may be the most appropriate approach, while ensuring both patient and staff safety. PCP-induced psychosis, which may last days to months, responds slowly to neuroleptics. Low-potency antipsychotics are not recommended, since they can cause hypotension, reduce the seizure threshold, and accentuate anticholinergic effects (8). Although use of gastric lavage followed by activated charcoal may enhance drug elimination, some degree of patient cooperation or endotracheal intubation is necessary for this to be a practical intervention.

The general approach to adverse reactions associated with ingestion of hallucinogens is reassurance for panic, delirium, or flashbacks. Because the patient may attempt to undertake impulsive behavior during a delirious state, the patient should not be left unobserved. Hallucinogen psychosis may persist for indefinite periods of time. Assessment of preexisting psychopathology and neurologic status, if possible, is recommended. No particular regimen of medications is indicated for this type of psychosis.

Opioids

Commonly abused opioids include heroin, hydromorphone hydrochloride, oxycodone, propoxyphene, meperidine, opium, and codeine. While patients rarely seek medical attention for opiate intoxication, they do seek treatment for overdose, withdrawal, or medical complications.

OVERDOSE

Opioid overdose is a medical emergency that can result in respiratory and CNS depression, gastric hypomotility with ileus, and noncardiogenic pulmonary edema. First measures for respiratory depression include airway support and naloxone hydrochloride, 0.4 mg or 0.01 mg/kg intravenously to reverse cardiorespiratory depression. Larger doses may be required if the opioid was codeine, pentazocine, or propoxyphene. Repeat antagonist dosing may be necessary, since the effects of naloxone last for 40 minutes, while opioid agonists can remain at potentially lethal blood levels for several hours. Failure to respond to several doses of the narcotic agonist suggests that other causes of respiratory depression and coma should be evaluated. Naloxone infusion at 0.4 mg/hour should then follow for those who respond to the initial naloxone challenge for a minimum of 12 hours, since most opioids have a longer half-life than naloxone (26). Ipecac-induced emesis or gastric lavage followed by the administration of activated charcoal is indicated when it is known that the route of opioid overdose was oral. Intubated comatose patients may have their stomachs emptied if they, too, overdosed by mouth. Patients identified to have pulmonary edema are at high risk, and require intubation, positive pressure ventilation, and intensive care (8, 9).

When the patient is stabilized, infectious complications may require the physician's attention. Acquired immunodeficiency syndrome (AIDS), hepatitis, and local and systemic bacterial infections may require treatment. Precautions in handling blood and secretions are necessary.

An assessment of the patient's suicidal intent at the time of overdose will provide the clinician with a better understanding of the circumstances of the overdose, as well as guide further treatment if necessary. Results from blood or urine toxicology screens may also provide important information by identifying other ingested substances.

WITHDRAWAL

Manifestation of the withdrawal symptoms depends on the duration of action and usual dose of opioid. Heroin has a brief duration of action and the first withdrawal symptoms appear 8 hours after last use (8). Symptoms include lacrimation, rhinorrhea, diaphoresis, yawning, and sneezing, followed by later symptoms of malaise, irritability, nausea, vomiting, diarrhea, myalgia, and arthralgia. Although not life threatening, these uncomfortable withdrawal symptoms may lead to narcotic seeking behavior by opiate addicts.

The signs and symptoms of opiate withdrawal may be minimized by a planned opiate detoxification. Due to the development of new medications and treatment philosophies, many more detoxification options are available, and include: (a) opiate substitution and detoxification using methadone, codeine, buprenorphine, or an opiate of the patient's choice; (b) clonidine — alone, with an opiate antagonist, following methadone, via a transdermal patch, or as an adjunct; (c) detoxification using other medications such as neuroleptics, diphenoxylate, beta-adrenoreceptor blocking drugs, sedative-hypnotics; or (d) auricular acupuncture (27). Management of opiate withdrawal may span a few days on an inpatient service to an outpatient 6-month methadone detoxification, depending on treatment availability and patient motivation (28).

Given the abundance of treatment choices available, the general principles of opiate detoxification will instead be described (27). The total amount of opiate consumed by a patient in a 24-hour period will be ascertained and then converted to the dosage equivalence of the opiate selected for detoxification. The dose can be titrated according to observed physical findings of withdrawal, staff and patient report. Opiate withdrawal scales, described earlier, can be used to quantify patient response to the process. Any opiate can be selected for detoxification, but an opiate with a long half-life, such as methadone, will be associated with milder withdrawal symptoms.

Once the correct daily dose of the detoxification opiate is established, the rate of tapering from the detoxification opiate can be rapid or slow, depending on the treatment plan formulated for the patient. Detoxification can be "blind," with the patient unaware of dose and rate of taper, or "open," with the patient aware of the dose and rate. The rate of daily dosing change can range from 5 to 75%, with greater reductions possible at initial high-dose levels.

Clinicians may consider using the naloxone challenge test prior to initiating detoxification to ensure that the patient is, in fact, physically dependent on opiates. Another potential advantage of the naloxone challenge is to precipitate withdrawal and accelerate detoxification.

At this point, no one detoxification approach has been demonstrated to be superior to others. For example, one double-blind, placebo controlled inpatient trial of clonidine in association with gradual methadone detoxification of 86 subjects concluded that clonidine is not a useful adjunct (29). However, outpatient trials comparing methadone tapering to clonidine alone found equivalent efficacy, and clonidine has been used with success by other investigators (30).

Innovative approaches to the management of opiate withdrawal include investigations of primary care–based ambulatory detoxification and 180-day methadone detoxifications. As a result of a prospective nonrandomized clinical trial comparing clonidine and clonidine plus naltrexone of 142 intravenous drug users, it appears that primary care providers might assume a larger role in the treatment of opiate dependent patients (31). An extended 180-day methadone detoxification offering psychosocial services that would not be possible for 21-day detoxification protocols, for patients who do not meet federal requirements for methadone maintenance or who do not desire maintenance, has been described to be effective (28). The generalizability of these new treatment approaches remains to be demonstrated under more rigorous investigation.

Sedative-Hypnotics

Sedative-hypnotics are widely prescribed and potentially abused. Acute intoxication, which resembles that occurring with alcohol, is rarely the cause for presentation to treatment. A paradoxical reaction, characterized by hyperexcitability secondary to disinhibition, may occur, but clears within hours and requires no more treatment than general support and reassurance (20).

Accidental and deliberate overdose with sedative-hypnotics, frequently in combination with alcohol, may be characterized by progressive depression of consciousness and respiratory and cardiovascular failure. Treatment is primarily supportive, with efforts aimed at preventing respiratory and cardiovascular collapse. Gastric lavage may be undertaken after endotracheal intubation (20). A naloxone challenge may be undertaken if opioid ingestion is a possibility and the history is unclear.

Withdrawal from sedative-hypnotics, in contrast to opiate withdrawal, is a potential medical emergency. Seizures, delirium, and death may follow, if untreated. Medically supervised detoxification is indicated. Onset of withdrawal symptoms depends on the amount regularly used and the substance's duration of action, ranging from 12–16 hours after a short-acting barbiturate to 7–10 days after diazepam. Symptoms include anxiety, restlessness, nausea, vomiting, weakness, and abdominal cramps progressing to tachycardia and hyperreflexia. In the case of acute withdrawal from short-acting or intermediate-acting barbiturates, the risk for grand mal seizures and delirium begins 24 hours after the last dose and peaks within the next 48 hours.

If the dose of the sedative-hypnotic is known and there are no additional complicating factors such as untreated psychosis, it may be possible to effect a medically supervised outpatient taper by decreasing the dose on a weekly basis. The exact reduction will reflect the drug used and the patient's clinical condition. If the withdrawal occurs on an inpatient setting, a more rapid schedule of tapering is feasible.

For example, Alexander and Perry divide the management of benzodiazepine tolerance into low-dose and high-dose withdrawal (32). Low-dose withdrawal is for patients who have exceeded manufacturer-recommended doses on a daily basis for longer than 1 month and who can have their benzodiazepines gradually tapered over the course of 4 weeks on an outpatient basis. High-dose withdrawal is considered for patients who have been taking more than the equivalent of 40 mg of diazepam daily for more than 8 months. Such patients might be tolerance tested with diazepam, and if demonstrated to be tolerant, tapered off medications at the rate of 10% a day in an inpatient setting.

If the dose of the sedative-hypnotic is unknown, and the patient may be using several simultaneously, a common strategy is to substitute the substances of abuse with phenobarbital, after a pentobarbital tolerance test is performed to establish the correct starting dose. It is also possible to estimate phenobarbital equivalences for drugs of abuse, with the proviso that no more than 500–600 mg of phenobarbital should be given in divided doses in any one 24-hour period (21, 33).

The details of the pentobarbital tolerance test are widely described, but can be summarized as follows. A sober patient is given 200 mg of pentobarbital by mouth and then carefully observed. If the patient falls asleep, then it is most likely that the patient is not dependent on sedative-hypnotics and the treatment plan should be revised. If the patient appears to be intoxicated, demonstrating nystagmus, ataxia, or dysarthria, then the patient's 6-hour pentobarbital requirement is between 100 and 200 mg. If the patient does not appear to be intoxicated, then a 100 mg pentobarbital challenge can be administered every 2 hours until intoxication is achieved or a maximum of 500–600 mg of pentobarbital is given. The total pentobarbital dose is calculated and then converted to phenobarbital, where 100 mg of pentobarbital is equivalent to 30 mg of phenobarbital. The patient is then administered standing doses of phenobarbital for 2 days, after which point the daily dose is decreased by 30 mg until detoxification is achieved.

It is not uncommon for individuals to abuse multiple substances, and a frequently observed behavior is for opiate-dependent individuals to abuse benzodiazepines. Methadone-maintained patients have been reported to "boost" their medication with benzodiazepines, in the past with diazepam and more recently with alprazolam. Once stabilized on methadone, an outpatient benzodiazepine detoxification procedure is possible (34).

SUMMARY

Detoxification can take place in either inpatient or outpatient settings, depending on the patient's clinical needs and other psychosocial factors. An accurate and competent clinical assessment is essential when detoxification and subsequent treatment plans are formulated. Uncomplicated alcohol withdrawal can be managed with a benzodiazepine taper and oral and parenteral vitamins. Withdrawal from stimulants usually does not require medications for its transient symptoms. Supportive care is usually sufficient for hallucinogen detoxification. Opiate withdrawal is not life threatening, but uncomfortable; so opiate substitution and detoxification or clonidine are two common management techniques. In contrast to opiate withdrawal, untreated sedative hypnotic withdrawal is a potential medical emergency that requires a medically supervised detoxification. Achievement of a substance-free state is preparatory for the more challenging but also more rewarding period of sustained abstinence.

References

1. Goldsmith RJ. Substance abuse and mental illness. In: Thienhas OJ, ed. Manual of clinical hospital psychiatry. Washington, DC: American Psychiatric Press, 1995:333–354.
2. American Society of Addiction Medicine. Patient placement criteria for treatment of psychoactive substance use disorders. Washington, DC: American Society of Addiction Medicine, 1991.
3. McLellan AT, Luborsky L, Woody GE, O'Brien CP. An improved diagnostic instrument for substance abuse patients: The addiction severity index. J Nerv Ment Dis 1980;168:26–33.
4. Sullivan JT, Sykora K, Schneiderman J, Naranjo CA, Sellers EM. Assessment of alcohol withdrawal: the revised clinical institute withdrawal assessment for alcohol scale (CIWA-Ar). Br J Addict 1989;84:1353–1357.
5. Bradley BP, Gossop M, Phillips GT, Legarda JJ. The development of an opiate withdrawal scale (OWS). Br J Addict 1987;82:1139–1142.
6. Kosten TR, Rounsaville BJ, Kleber HD. Comparison of clinician's ratings to self reports of withdrawal during clonidine detoxification of opiate addicts. Am J Drug Alcohol Abuse 1985;11:1–10.
7. Busto UE, Skyora K, Sellers EM. A clinical scale to assess benzodiazepine withdrawal. J Clin Psychopharmacol 1989;9:412–416.
8. Levine DG, Schwartz GR, Ungar JR. Drug abuse. In: Schwartz GR, Safar P, Stone JG, Storey PB, Wagner DK, eds. Principles of emergency medicine. Philadelphia: WB Saunders, 1986:1744–1757.
9. Gross PL. Toxicologic emergencies. In: Wilkins EW, ed. MGH textbook of emergency medicine. 2nd edition. Baltimore: Williams & Wilkins, 1989:395–422.
10. U.S. Preventive Services Task Force. Screening for alcohol and other drug abuse. AFP 1989;40:137–146.
11. Babor TF, Stephens RS, Marlatt GA. Verbal report methods in clinical research on alcoholism: response bias and its minimization. J Stud Alcohol 1987;48:410–424.
12. Kellermann AL, Fikn SD, LoGerto JP, Copass MK. Impact of drug screening in suspected overdose. Ann Emerg Med 1987;16:1206–1216.
13. Council on Scientific Affairs. Scientific issues in drug testing. JAMA 1987;257:3110–3115.
14. Schwartz RH. Urine testing in the detection of drugs of abuse. Arch Intern Med 1988;148:2407–2412.
15. Gallant DM. Acute alcohol intoxication and alcohol withdrawal. In: Gallant DM, ed. Alcoholism, a guide to diagnosis, intervention, and treatment. New York: WW Norton, 1987:105–118.
16. Hyman SE. Alcohol-related emergencies. In: Hyman SE, Tesar GE, eds. Manual of psychiatric emergencies. 3rd edition. Boston, MA: Little, Brown, 1994:294–303.
17. Hackett TP. Alcoholism: acute and chronic states. In: Hackett TP, Cassem NH, eds. Massachusetts General handbook of general hospital psychiatry. 2nd edition. Littleton, MA: PSG Publishing, 1987:419–437.
18. American Psychiatric Association. Diagnostic and statistical manual of mental disorders. 4th edition. Washington, DC: American Psychiatric Association, 1994.
19. Berk WA, Henderson WV. Alcohols. In: Tintinalli JE, Ruiz E, Krome RL, eds. Emergency medicine, a comprehensive study guide. 4th edition. New York: McGraw-Hill, 1995.
20. Schuckit MA. Drug and alcohol abuse, a clinical guide to diagnosis and treatment. 3rd edition. New York: Plenum, 1989.
21. Weiss RD, Greenfield SF, Mirin SM. Intoxication and withdrawal syndromes. In: Hyman SE, Tesar GE, eds. Manual of psychiatric emergencies. 3rd edition. Boston, MA: Little, Brown, 1994:279–293.
22. Ungar JR. Current drugs of abuse. In: Schwartz GR, Bucker N, Hanke BK, Mangeben MA, Mayer T, Ungar GR, eds. Emergency medicine: the essential update. Philadelphia: WB Saunders, 1989:210–224.
23. Penalaver AA, Burki VV. Psychiatric emergencies. In: Stine RJ, Chudnofsky CR, eds. A practical approach to emergency medicine. Boston, MA: Little, Brown, 1994:888–909.
24. Lipton DS, Brewington V, Smith M. Acupuncture for crack cocaine detoxification: experimental evaluation of efficacy. J Subst Treat 1994;7:205–215.
25. Ellison JM, Jacobs D. Emergency psychopharmacology: a review and update. Ann Emerg Med 1986;15:962–968.
26. Litovitz T. Sedatives and opiates. In: Callahan ML, ed. Current therapy in emergency medicine. Philadelphia: BC Decker, 1987:962–965.
27. Fishbain DA, Rosomoff HL, Cutler R, Rosomoff RS. Opiate detoxification protocols, a clinical manual. Ann Clin Psychiatry 1993;5:53–65.
28. Reilly PM, Banys P, Tusel DJ, et al. Methadone transition treatment: a treatment model for 180 day methadone detoxification. Int J Addictions 1995;30:387–402.
29. Ghodse H, Myles J, Smith SE. Clonidine is not a useful adjunct to methadone gradual detoxification in opioid addiction. Br J Psychiatry 1994;165:370–374.
30. Kleber HD, Riordan CE, Rounsaville BJ, et al. Clonidine in outpatient detoxification from methadone maintenance. Arch Gen Psychiatry 1985;42:391–394.
31. O'Connor PG, Waugh ME, Carroll KM, et al. Primary care-based ambulatory opioid detoxification, the results of a clinical trial. J Gen Internal Med 1995;10:255–260.
32. Alexander B, Perry PJ. Detoxification from benzodiazepines: schedules and strategies. J Subst Abuse Treat 1991;8:9–17.
33. Alling FA. Detoxification and treatment of acute sequelae. In: Lowinson J, Ruiz P, Millman R, Langrod J, eds. Substance abuse, a comprehensive textbook. Baltimore: Williams & Wilkins, 1992:402–415.
34. McDuff DR, Schwartz RP, Tommasello A, et al. Outpatient benzodiazepine detoxification procedure for methadone patients. J Subst Abuse Treat 1993;10:297–302.

37 ALCOHOLICS ANONYMOUS

Edgar P. Nace

For more than five decades Alcoholics Anonymous (AA) has influenced, guided, and shaped the treatment of alcoholism. It would be difficult today to find a substance abuse treatment program that does not espouse the principles of AA. The appeal of AA's Twelve Step program has been extended to other disorders including drug addiction (Narcotics Anonymous), eating disorders (Overeaters Anonymous), gambling (Gamblers Anonymous), and others.

From an inauspicious founding by two chronic alcoholics, AA has grown in numbers and scope to reach around the world. Men and women whose lives have been touched, even saved, by the program's deceptively simple Twelve Steps offer fervent testimony to AA's efficacy. This chapter highlights some of the history, growth, and dynamics of AA. A more indepth understanding can be acquired through reading the "Big Book," *Alcoholics Anonymous* (1), *Twelve Steps and Twelve Traditions* (2), Kurtz's *Not-God: A History of Alcoholics Anonymous* (3), and Bean's series of articles (4).

WHAT IS AA?

AA is a fellowship, that is, a "mutual association of persons on equal and friendly terms; a mutual sharing, as of experience, activity or interest" (5). AA is open to all men and women who want to do something about their drinking problems. Interestingly, members need not consider themselves alcoholics or seek abstinence. AA is nonprofessional, self-supporting, nondenominational, apolitical, and multiracial. There are no age or education requirements (6).

At the start of an AA meeting the "AA preamble" is usually read. The preamble is a concise description of AA (7):

Alcoholics Anonymous is a fellowship of men and women who share their experience, strength, and hope with each other that they may solve their common problem and help others to recover from alcoholism. The only requirement for membership is a desire to stop drinking. There are no dues or fees to AA membership; we are self-supporting through our own contributions. AA is not allied with any sect, denomination, politics, organization, or institution; does not wish to engage in any controversy, neither endorses nor proposes any causes. Our primary purpose is to stay sober and help other alcoholics to achieve sobriety.

The Program of AA

The program of AA consists of studying and following the "Twelve Steps" of AA (Table 37.1). In addition, AA groups are careful to adhere to the "Twelve Traditions" of AA (Table 37.2). The Twelve Steps offer the alcoholic a satisfying way of life without alcohol. This program is presented, described, and discussed in AA meetings. Meetings may be "open" or "closed." *Closed meetings* are for AA members only or prospective AA members, whereas *open meetings* are for nonalcoholics as well. AA meetings usually last 1 hour and are preceded and followed by informal socializing. There are different types of meetings: In *speaker meetings,* AA members tell their "stories." They describe their experiences with alcohol and their recovery—what it was like, what happened, and what it is like now. In *discussion meetings,* an AA member briefly describes some of his or her experiences and then leads a discussion on a topic related to recovery. *Step*

meetings usually are closed meetings and consist of a discussion of the meaning and ramifications of one of the Twelve Steps.

AA groups are autonomous. Some groups provide proof of attendance that may be required by a court or probation office, whereas other groups choose not to sign court slips.

Sponsorship is an essential function of AA. Each person who joins AA is encouraged to obtain a sponsor, that is, another AA member willing to offer person-to-person guidance in working the AA program. A sponsor typically is a person who has a substantial period of sobriety and who personally has studied and worked the Twelve Steps. The sponsorship relationship is informal, and the styles of sponsorship vary greatly. The neophyte to AA need not hesitate to ask another member to be a sponsor for fear of being a burden. Members who become sponsors do so, in part, because it helps them in recovery as well—"you keep it [sobriety] by giving it away."

That AA is a fellowship distinguishes it from professional treatment or programs. Alcoholism provides a bond between one AA member and another. In contrast, professional relationships establish a boundary between doctor and patient or therapist and client. The clinician, when confronted with an alcoholic patient, uses the diagnosis of alcoholism to erect a boundary from which role relationships are carefully defined. From the structure of the professional relationship the clinician applies his or her skills and technologies. There is no mutual sharing of experience or any pretense of equality in the relationship. According to Bean, the nonalcoholic professional often seems unattainably happy to the alcoholic, and the professional may "reinforce the picture of himself [or herself] as superior, powerful, and omniscient. The moral culpability of the alcoholic and the moral superiority of the helper, even though unstated, are always clearly understood" (4, p. 32).

What AA Promises

Working the Twelve Steps and adhering to the Twelve Principles leads to possibilities contained in the Twelve Promises:

1. We are going to know a new freedom and a new happiness.
2. We will not regret the past nor wish to shut the door on it.
3. We will comprehend the word serenity.
4. We will know peace.
5. No matter how far down the scale we have gone, we will see how our experience can benefit others.
6. That feeling of uselessness and self-pity will disappear.
7. We will lose interest in selfish things and gain interest in our fellows.
8. Self-seeking will slip away.
9. Our whole attitude and outlook on life will change.
10. Fear of people and economic insecurity will leave us.
11. We will intuitively know how to handle situations which used to baffle us.
12. We will suddenly realize that God is doing for us what we could not do for ourselves. (1, pp. 83–84)

The "Big Book" (*Alcoholics Anonymous*) goes on to say: "Are these extravagant promises? We think not. They are being fulfilled among us—sometimes quickly, sometimes slowly. They will always materialize if we work for them" (1, p. 84).

Table 37.1 The Twelve Steps of Alcoholics Anonymous

1. We admitted we were powerless over alcohol and that our lives had become unmanageable.
2. Came to believe that a Power greater than ourselves could restore us to sanity.
3. Made a decision to turn our will and our lives over to the care of God as we understood Him.
4. Made a searching and fearless moral inventory of ourselves.
5. Admitted to God, to ourselves, and to another human being the exact nature of our wrongs.
6. Were entirely ready to have God remove all these defects of character.
7. Humbly asked Him to remove our shortcomings.
8. Made a list of all persons we had harmed, and became willing to make amends to them all.
9. Made direct amends to such people wherever possible, except when to do so would injure them or others.
10. Continued to take personal inventory and when we were wrong promptly admitted it.
11. Sought through prayer and meditation to improve our conscious contact with God as we understood Him, praying only for knowledge of His will for us and the power to carry that out.
12. Having had a spiritual awakening as the result of these steps, we tried to carry this message to alcoholics, and to practice these principles in all our affairs.

The Twelve Steps and Twelve Traditions are reprinted with permission of Alcoholics Anonymous World Services, Inc. Permission to reprint this material does not mean that AA has reviewed or approved the contents of this publication, nor that AA agrees with the views expressed herein. AA is a program of recovery from alcoholism. Use of the Twelve Steps and Twelve Traditions in connection with programs and activities which are patterned after AA but which address other problems does not imply otherwise.

Table 37.2 The Twelve Traditions of Alcoholics Anonymous

1. Our common welfare should come first; personal recovery depends upon AA unity.
2. For our group purpose there is but one ultimate authority—a loving God as He may express himself in our group conscience. Our leaders are but trusted servants; they do not govern.
3. The only requirement for AA membership is a desire to stop drinking.
4. Each group should be autonomous except in matters affecting other groups or AA as a whole.
5. Each group has but one primary purpose—to carry its message to the alcoholic who still suffers.
6. An AA group ought never endorse, finance, or lend the AA name to any related facility or outside enterprise, lest problems of money, property, and prestige divert us from our primary purpose.
7. Every AA group ought to be fully self-supporting, declining outside contributions.
8. Alcoholics Anonymous should remain forever nonprofessional, but our service centers may employ special workers.
9. AA, as such, ought never be organized; but we may create service boards or committees directly responsible to those they serve.
10. Alcoholics Anonymous has no opinion on outside issues; hence the AA name ought never be drawn into public controversy.
11. Our public relations policy is based on attraction rather than promotion; we need always maintain personal anonymity at the level of press, radio, and films.
12. Anonymity is the spiritual foundation of all our Traditions, ever reminding us to place principles before personalities.

The Twelve Steps and Twelve Traditions are reprinted with permission of Alcoholics Anonymous World Services, Inc. Permission to reprint this material does not mean that AA has reviewed or approved the contents of this publication, nor that AA agrees with the views expressed herein. AA is a program of recovery from alcoholism. Use of the Twelve Steps and Twelve Traditions in connection with programs and activities which are patterned after AA but which address other problems does not imply otherwise.

What AA Does Not Do

Part of appreciating the role of AA in the recovery of alcoholics is understanding what AA does not do. From such an understanding, we will be better prepared to focus on what it does do. The list below was obtained from AA literature (6). AA does not

1. Furnish initial motivation for alcoholics to recover
2. Solicit members
3. Engage in or sponsor research
4. Keep attendance records or case histories
5. Join "councils" of social agencies
6. Follow up or try to control its members
7. Make medical or psychological diagnoses or prognoses
8. Provide drying-out or nursing services, hospitalization, drugs, or any medical or psychiatric treatment
9. Offer religious services
10. Engage in education about alcohol
11. Provide housing, food, clothing, jobs, money, or any other welfare or social services
12. Provide domestic or vocational counseling
13. Accept any money for its services, or any contributions from non-AA sources
14. Provide letters of reference to parole boards, lawyers, court officials

THE GROWTH OF AA

The birth date of AA is given as June 10, 1935. On this date Dr. Bob Smith, the Akron surgeon who co-founded AA with Bill Wilson, had his last drink. The official founding of AA was established with that event. Two and one-half years later "Dr. Bob" and "Bill W." estimated that as a result of their combined efforts in both Akron and New York City there were nearly 40 sober recovering alcoholics. The co-founders knew they were onto something (one alcoholic talking to another) and continued the struggle of carrying their hope, strength, and experience to other alcoholics. Most of those they contacted, however, were not maintaining sobriety nor had any interest in their ideas (3). But by the end of 4 years, membership was estimated to be about 100, and by the end of 1941, 8000 members could be counted. By 1968, 170,000 members were estimated (8). In spite of early

periods of discouragement, the growth of AA has been phenomenal and continues today.

Anonymous surveys of AA have been conducted every three years since 1968 by the AA General Services Office. The 1989 survey (available from AA World Services) determined that there are 47,973 AA groups in the United States and Canada. This is an increase of 5000 groups over the 1986 survey.

COMPOSITION OF AA

Approximately 12,000 members in AA were surveyed in 1989; 9394 completed and returned the questionnaires. Twenty-two percent of AA members were under 31 years of age, and 3% were under age 21. These percentages are essentially unchanged from the 1986 survey.

Similarly, the percentage of women in AA changed only from 34% in 1986 to 35% in 1989. However, this is a considerable increase from the 1968 figure of 22%.

An interesting trend is the percentage of AA members reporting addiction to drugs. In 1977, 18% reported drug addiction, but by 1989, 46% were reporting a history of drug addiction. Women and younger people in AA were more likely to report a history of drug addiction.

THE ORIGINS OF AA

The origins of AA must necessarily be seen to arise from the experience and insight of Bill Wilson ("Bill W.") The sequence of events and the major influences affecting him have been described by Ernest Kurtz (3).

Kurtz described four founding moments of AA. Carl Jung played a role in the first founding moment through his extended and frustrating treatment of an American businessman. Jung eventually advised this man (Roland H.) that medicine and psychiatry had no more to offer. Only a spiritual change or awakening, however unlikely, could be expected to release the continuing compulsion to drink. Roland H. proceeded to join the Oxford Group, a popular nondenominational religious group that sought to recapture the essence of first century Christianity and was interested in alcoholics. Roland H.'s successful conversion and abstinence constituted the first founding moment.

Roland H.'s experience was shared with an old friend and alcoholic, Edwin T. ("Ebby"). He, too, found the evangelical efforts of the Oxford Group sufficient to release him from further drinking (at least, temporarily). Ebby, a friend of Bill Wilson, called on Bill in November 1934. Wilson was at his home in New York City drinking. Ebby refused a drink, stating, "I don't need it anymore. I've got religion" (3, p. 7), and described his recent success in giving up alcohol. This conversation (between Bill and Ebby) was the second founding moment. In spite of Bill's disdain for his friend's newfound "religion," he couldn't shake the image of his friend—sober and confident. Bill was influenced through his conversation with Ebby to try again. Bill had himself admitted to the Charles B. Towns Hospital under the care of a psychiatrist, Dr. William Silkworth.

During this hospitalization Bill became increasingly depressed. Concomitant with his worsening condition there occurred one of those inexplicable events that one describes as a spiritual experience. Wilson experienced "ecstasy." He couldn't describe it, and he feared that it indicated brain damage. Dr. Silkworth reassured him concerning the latter, and Bill began to read James's *Varieties of Religious Experience* (9) in an effort to understand what had happened to him. The spiritual experience, the influence of James's writings, and the recognition of the utter hopelessness of his drinking were the third founding moment.

Bill then imagined that conversations between one alcoholic and another, such as his with Ebby, could lead to a "chain reaction" among alcoholics. Months later, in May 1935, an opportunity occurred in Akron, where Bill, a stockbroker, was on a business trip. A deal had fallen through, and Bill felt a mounting urge to drink. It was late Saturday afternoon, the day before Mother's Day. He consulted a church directory, reached an Oxford Group minister, and ultimately was referred to a woman who was receptive to his need to talk to another alcoholic. Mrs. Henrietta Sieberling arranged for Bill to come to her house and meet with Dr. Bob Smith, a deteriorating alcoholic surgeon. Dr. Smith was reluctant to accept this invitation but went with his wife to meet Bill W. Their historic meeting, the fourth founding moment, is described (3, p. 29):

> . . . here was someone who did understand, or perhaps at least could. This stranger from New York didn't ask questions and didn't preach; he offered no "you musts" or even "let's us's." He had simply told the dreary but fascinating facts about himself, about his own drinking. And now, as Wilson moved to stand up to end the conversation, he was actually thanking Dr. Smith for listening. "I called Henrietta because I needed another alcoholic. I needed you, Bob, probably just more than you'll ever need me. So, thanks a lot for hearing me out. I know now that I'm not going to take a drink, and I'm grateful to you." While he had been listening to Bill's story, Bob had occasionally nodded his head, muttering "Yes, that's like me, that's just like me." Now he could bear the strain no longer. He'd listened to Bill's story, and now, by God, this "rum hound from New York" was going to listen to him. For the first time in his life, Dr. Bob Smith began to open his heart.

Bill Wilson and Bob Smith became the co-founders of AA. Wilson went on to develop the fellowship of AA and to provide a remarkable chapter in the social history of twentieth century America. Bill W. learned to weave a careful course between religious dogma, on the one hand, and a humanistic liberal psychology on the other. The AA program was successful in incorporating the concepts of "surrender," "powerlessness," and appeal to a "Higher Power." These elements reflect its roots in the evangelical Christianity of the Oxford Group. Yet Bill W. avoided the Oxford Group's focus on attaining "Four Absolutes": absolute honesty, absolute purity, absolute unselfishness, and absolute love (3). He was aware of the psychological vulnerability of the alcoholic to strive for "absolutes," and, when the mark is missed, to indulge in self-castigation, self-hatred, and, finally, drunkenness.

The AA Fellowship evolved a system and a way of life reflected in the Twelve Steps and Twelve Traditions. The Traditions of AA are less familiar to most clinicians (see Table 37.2) than the Steps. Even a cursory reading of the Traditions conveys these three principles:

1. The singleness of purpose of AA
   - "The only requirement for AA membership is a desire to stop drinking" (Tradition 3)
   - " . . . primary purpose—to carry its message to the alcoholic who still suffers" (Tradition 5)

2. The avoidance of personal power and influence
   - " . . . there is but one ultimate authority—a loving God . . ." (Tradition 2)
   - " . . . each group should be autonomous . . ." (Tradition 4)
   - "An AA group ought never endorse, finance, or lend the AA name to any related facility or outside enterprise . . ." (Tradition 6)
   - "AA, as such ought never be organized . . ." (Tradition 9)

3. The need for humility
   - "Our common welfare should come first . . ." (Tradition 1)
   - "Alcoholic Anonymous should remain forever nonprofessional" (Tradition 7)
   - "Alcoholics Anonymous has no opinion on outside issues . . ." (Tradition 10)
   - "Our public relations policy is based on attraction rather than promotion . . ." (Tradition 11)
   - " . . . place principles before personalities" (Tradition 12)

The AA program counters pathological narcissism by assisting the alcoholic to be "not-God," to accept limitations, and to serve others. Further, the AA program provides a means for overcoming guilt, for example, by taking a personal inventory (Step 4) and making amends (Step 9) without triggering harsh superego responses. Although the origins of AA are rooted in the sacred and the religious, it has widened its appeal by cloaking the program in spiritual and secular garb.

AFFILIATION WITH AA

The 1989 AA General Services Office survey reports that 40% of newcomers were referred to AA by counselors and rehabilitation facilities, an increase of 4% from 1986. Thirty-four percent were attracted to AA by an AA member, 27% reported being self-motivated, 19% were influenced by a family member, and 7% were referred by a physician.

It would seem that AA could receive greater emphasis from physicians. Historically, things got off to a slow start with doctors. The first edition of *Alcoholics Anonymous* was published in 1939 (1). AA members were enthusiastic about reaching out to the medical community and sent 20,000 announcements of the "Big Book." Only two orders for *Alcoholics Anonymous* were received (10). Since then, of course, physicians have become much more aware of AA; one study from Great Britain reports that 65% of general practitioners believed that AA had something to offer beyond what could be obtained through medical efforts (11). However, as noted, only 7% of AA members in 1989 reported being referred by a physician, a decline from the 10% reported in the 1986 survey.

Once someone gets to AA, what are the chances he or she will stay? Figures from AA General Services Office surveys indicate that only 50% of those who come to AA remain more than 3 months. In a review of AA affiliation (12), about 20% of problem drinkers referred to AA were found to attend regularly. In a 4-year follow-up of alcoholism treatment (13), 27% of those who had ever gone to AA reported attendance at AA the month prior to follow-up, and of those who reported attending AA regularly, 39% had attended a meeting during the month prior to follow-up. In a more recent review of the literature (13), dropout rates from AA varied from 68% before 10 meetings were attended to 88% by 1 year after discharge.

The "dropout" problem raises the question of who is likely to make a stable affiliation with AA. Early research on this problem (4, 12, 14) suggests that those who join AA are middle-class, guilt-ridden, sociable, cognitively rigid, and socially stable. They also are more likely to be chronic alcoholics or loss-of-control drinkers and to have more alcohol-related problems. A comprehensive recent review (13) of the affiliation process fails to support earlier findings. Emrick (13) compared variables used to distinguish between stable and unstable affiliations and found that 64% bear no relationship, 29% show a positive relationship favoring AA affiliation, and only 7% bear a negative relationship to AA affiliation. This leads to the conclusion that most alcoholics have the possibility of making an affiliation with AA. Only those whose goal is not to abstain from alcohol would be seen as exceptions. Demographic variables such as education, employment, socioeconomic status of the alcoholic or of the parents, social stability, religion, and measures of social competence are unrelated to the affiliation process. Age favors, though not consistently, older alcoholics' making a positive affiliation. Marital status (married) and gender (male) also show some positive relationship to affiliation. Alcoholism variables bear little relationship to making a positive affiliation. For example, loss of control, quantity drunk daily, age at first drink, degree of physiological dependence, and drinking style bear no consistent relationship to affiliation.

Currently, research indicates an *unpredictability* as to who will affiliate with AA, which again emphasizes the importance of recommending AA to all possible members.

AA OUTCOME

Many efforts have been made to assess the effectiveness of AA attendance. Measurement of "outcome" typically is limited to abstinence or lack of abstinence from alcohol. In studies of AA from the 1940s to the early 1970s (15), sampling difficulties and other methodological problems were immense. Nevertheless, the findings indicated that thousands of AA members had achieved sobriety through AA. In a study of 393 AA members conducted by an AA member, it was determined that 70% who stayed sober for 1 year would be sober at 2 years, and that 90% of those sober at 2 years would be sober at 3 years (15). In two early studies of AA, sobriety of more than 2 years' duration was found in 46% of those sampled (16, 17).

A recent review of survey studies (13) found that 35–40% of respondents reported abstinence of less than 1 year, with 26–40% reporting abstinence of 1–5 years, and 20–30% having been sober 5 or more years. Overall, 47–62% of active AA members had at least 1 year of continuous sobriety.

The 1989 AA General Services Office survey consisting of 9,994 responses from a mailing of 12,000 reported an average sobriety length of 50 months. This figure was somewhat lower than the 52-month average in the 1986 survey, but higher than the 45-month average reported in 1983.

AA involvement has been found to correlate favorably with a variety of outcome measures. Those patients who attend AA before, during, or after a treatment experience have a more favorable outcome in regard to drinking (13). In the few studies available that assess the outcome on other variables, AA involvement is associated with a more stable social adjustment, more active religious life, internal locus of control, and better employment adjustment (13). Increased ethical concern for others, an increased sense of well-being, and increasing dependence on a Higher Power with less dependence on others also have been described (18). Finally, there is a positive relationship between outcome and extent of AA participation (13). Outcome is more favorable for those who attend more than one meeting per week and for those who have a sponsor, sponsor others, lead meetings, and work Steps Six through Twelve after completing a treatment program. Taking Step Four or Five is not consistently related to outcome, nor is telling one's story or doing Twelve Step work.

THE DYNAMICS OF AA

The reasons for AA's effectiveness may be as varied as the individuals involved. At the most basic level, the program works because one follows the Twelve Steps. It may be that these deceptively simple steps provide a concrete, tangible course of action; they may trigger cognitive processes previously unformed, unfocused, or abandoned; and they may encapsulate powerful dynamics capable of having an impact on craving, conditioning, and character. The AA program revolves around the Twelve Steps, and most members would offer the common-sense explanation that working the steps keeps them sober. This sentiment is reflected in the Big Book's chapter on how it works: "Rarely have we seen a person fail who has thoroughly followed our path" (1).

GROUP PROCESS

The utility of the slogan "keep it simple" is well-known to AA members but need not deter further inquiry into the process or dynamics of AA's effectiveness. Any effort to understand the efficacy of AA must take into ac-

count the ubiquitous group process that is operating. The elements of group therapy as enumerated by Yalom (19) are apparent:

1. *Hope* is provided by associating with other alcoholics who are not drinking and who apparently are happy, satisfied, or, indeed, grateful not to be drinking. In other words, change is possible.
2. *Universality* is formed through sharing stories and experiences involving alcohol. The newcomer is struck by the value of his or her experience as AA members identify with it and express thanks and gratitude to the newcomer for sharing the story. Instead of feeling condemned, the newcomer feels bonded to these other alcoholics by virtue of his or her experience.
3. *Information* is provided informally through conversations, through literature published by AA, and through the topics and content of the meetings themselves.
4. *Imitation* is a very prominent aspect of the group process. Phrases are repeated and rituals followed.
5. *Learning* occurs at multiple levels and includes how sober alcoholics view their disease, how they relate to others, and what they do to stay sober. The member also learns that the problem is alcohol (not a spouse, or job, or a lack of willpower). It is learned that one has a disease and that alcoholism is cunning, powerful, and baffling.
6. *Catharsis* can occur. The opportunity is provided (but not demanded) through discussion, speaker, and Step study meetings. Again, one's experiences are appreciated and not subjected to condemnation or judgment.
7. *Cohesiveness* follows from the ability to identify, usually quickly, with the viewpoints and experiences of fellow members. Cohesiveness is also facilitated by participating in the informal socializing characteristic of AA meetings. One feels at home by helping to make coffee, set up chairs, and eventually greet newcomers.

The beneficial aspects of group process may be found in many settings, for example, group therapy, religious groups, and organizational activities. The dynamics operative in coherent group settings as described by Yalom (19) cannot fully account for the impact of AA on alcoholics. If group process variables were the key to the transformation from inebriety to sobriety, substantial progress in arresting alcoholism could have been expected before the establishment of the AA program. Equal success might have been expected from a variety of group approaches. This has not been the case. It is necessary to look further. This chapter describes several formulations of AA effectiveness. These formulations, or explanations of the efficacy of AA, are superordinate to the group process variables described above, are not mutually exclusive, and are not necessarily contradictory.

EGO FUNCTIONS

The first formulation is the psychodynamic explanation forwarded by Mack (20) and Khantzian and Mack (21). Mack (20) introduces the concept of "self-governance," which refers to an aspect of the ego (or self) concerned with choosing, deciding, and directing the personality. Self-governance, according to Mack, encompasses a group of functions in the ego system and provides the individual with a sense of being and a sense of power to be in charge of oneself. Self-governance differs somewhat from the concept of autonomous and executive functions of the ego in that it acknowledges the interdependence among the ego and other individuals and groups. The concept of self-governance allows a sharing of control with others, and, indeed, indicates that survival and sense of personal value require interdependent participation in social structures.

The success of AA, according to Mack, is "due to its intuitive and subtle grasp of the complex psychosocial and biological nature of self-governance, not only for the control of problem drinking but in a far more general sense" (20, p. 134). The alcoholic has lost control over alcohol, and alcohol is making life unmanageable. AA recognizes the powerlessness of the individual in the face of the drive to drink and provides a counterforce to the drive to drink through caring, supportive interaction with others. The social aspects of group process operating in AA strengthen the individual's capacity for self-governance by "borrowing" such capacity from fellowship with AA members, the group process, and the acceptance of a Higher Power. In the most simple terms, the alcoholic learns to substitute people for alcohol.

Khantzian and Mack (21) further implicate ego functions in the etiology of and recovery from alcoholism. They view the alcoholic as not necessarily suffering from structural defects in the ego (as is more commonly noted in drug addicts) but rather see certain ego functions as being poorly developed. One such ego disability commonly observed in alcoholics and other addicts is a diminished capacity to recognize, regulate, and tolerate affect. Feelings may seem unmanageable and, therefore, threatening. The ability to describe how one feels may be lacking. The individual who feels overwhelmed, confused, or intolerably uncomfortable with affect is subject to develop counterdependent personality traits or other exaggerated character traits that serve as an affect defense (22). Such defenses constitute, in part, the defects of character that the AA Step program seeks to remove. Thus AA, through the working of the Steps (see Steps 6, 7, and 10), challenges the past faulty coping strategies of the alcoholic through its recognition that failure to do so will lead back to drinking.

Another ego function that may be deficient in substance-abusing individuals is that of "self-care." This capacity is part of the larger function of self-governance and involves reality testing, judgment, anticipation of consequences, and impulse control. AA may strengthen the self-care capacity of the individual by offering self-soothing slogans ("Easy does it"; "One day at a time"; "Live and let live") and by providing a caring milieu the alcoholic gradually identifies with, internalizes, and uses to modulate his or her behavior.

PATHOLOGICAL NARCISSISM

In addition to the specific ego dysfunctions mentioned earlier, Khantzian and Mack (21) emphasize the importance of pathological narcissism in substance abusers. Strands of pathological narcissism that may be observed in alcoholics and other addicts include the belief that they can take care of problems themselves, that they are self-sufficient, and that they are able to retain the necessary control over alcohol as well as other areas of their lives. Further, alcohol induces a feeling of personal power and adequacy (23). The person vulnerable to alcoholism or drug addiction may enter adult life wounded by empathic failures in being parented and therefore may retain archaic narcissistic tendencies such as grandiosity (including self-sufficiency), an overvaluation or devaluation of others, and a reliance on external supplies and sources to feel complete (24). An adult burdened by these narcissistic themes is doomed to continuous disappointment in self and others. Depression, anxiety, guilt, and shame can be expected. It is a short step to the discovery of relief from such emotional pain through alcohol. In addition, alcohol's pharmacological restoration of a feeling of personal power (23) reinforces the original pathological narcissism (25). As Mack (20) points out, AA tradition recognized the artificial inflation of the self in alcoholism and the chance of stimulating "power drives" by fostering an authoritarian system. Thus, the AA traditions (see Traditions 1, 2, 6, 9, 10, and 11) de-emphasize and discourage prestige, status, and power. A focus is kept on Tradition 5. At a very practical level, AA groups do not let money from their collections accumulate lest ambitious members covet a special project. The emphasis in Tradition 2 is to serve, not govern. The Traditions of AA, therefore, serve to curb and discourage expressions of unhealthy narcissism.

Even more cogent to the theme of narcissism are the Twelve Steps. The First Step, acknowledging powerlessness and loss of control, is the sine qua non of recovery. Without the recognition and acceptance of one's loss of control, recovery remains postponed. Brown (26) places particular emphasis on the alcoholic's need to accept loss of control (that is, accept Steps 1 and 2), for such acceptance is considered the nucleus of one's identity as an alcoholic from which the stages of recovery may unfold. A reading of the Steps makes clear how they offer a healthy alternative to pathological expressions of personality, whether the latter are premorbid or secondary to chronic intoxication. Humility, powerlessness, consideration of others, the need for self-examination, and service are clearly put forth, not as abstract ideals, but as tools to ward off a return to the insanity of alcoholism.

The narcissistic problems just described were recognized earlier by Tiebout (27). He points out that defiance and grandiosity stand in the way of the alcoholic's "surrender" and result in fleeting states of compliance but not a deep acceptance of defeat at the hands of alcohol.

The problem of retained pathological narcissistic traits is more central to the recovery process than are the ego functions described by Khantzian and Mack (21). This assertion is based on the unlikelihood of achieving a mature capacity for self-governance in the face of grandiosity, self-sufficiency, and a devaluing of others. Such narcissistic defenses shut out the social field from which mature self-governance may grow. Narcissistic pathology necessarily results in a diminished capacity for self-governance. Thus the modification of narcissistic traits, as facilitated by the caring confrontation of AA, opens the door to an improvement in other areas of ego development.

AN EMPATHIC UNDERSTANDING OF THE ALCOHOLIC

In a series of classic papers, Bean provides a second description of the mechanisms of AA's effectiveness, integrating its phenomenological and psychodynamic aspects: AA has "accomplished a shift from a society-centered view of alcoholism to an abuser-centered one" (4, p. 6). For the bereft or discouraged alcoholic, this shift is a startling, powerful encounter. AA provides the alcoholic with a protected environment. After years of feeling debased and worthless, the alcoholic is offered an environment free from the conventional view of drunken behavior. The alcoholic discovers that his or her experience is of value and even interesting to others. Further, the alcoholic's experiences may be useful to someone else, and others thank him or her for sharing it. As Bean explains, "This idea, that a person's experience is of value, is gratifying to anyone and is especially heady stuff to the chronically self-deprecating alcoholic" (4, p. 10).

Along with the shift in how alcoholism is viewed, AA provides a shift in what is expected of the alcoholic. First, the alcoholic is not asked to admit that he or she is an alcoholic. AA simply asks that one have a sincere desire to stop drinking. There is no effort to point out the error of one's ways or the evils of drink. In fact, the attraction of alcohol and the pleasure of alcohol are openly acknowledged but linked with the statement that "we couldn't handle it." The alcoholic who comes to AA is not asked to change, only to listen, identify, and keep coming back. The style of interpersonal contact is nonthreatening. Last names are not given, attendance is not taken, the setting is casual, and humor and friendliness abound. Nevertheless, the meeting is serious. Each member conveys that there is a lot to lose, regardless of how much has actually been lost, but also that there is much to gain—sobriety. Sobriety is the focus, and remains so, unvaryingly. Not drinking is the coin of the realm. Relapses or "slips" do not represent a failure on the part of the alcoholic or of AA. Rather, slips are further demonstration of the power of alcohol and, therefore, the necessity of AA as a counterforce.

Bean (4) emphasizes the regressive effect of alcohol on the alcoholic's personality functioning. The regression results from the toxic disinhibiting effect of alcohol on the brain, the stress of losing control, and the impact of opprobrium, failure, and stigma. AA is seen by Bean to facilitate surrendering immature defenses for mature defenses. Denial is relinquished partly as a result of the crisis that usually brings the alcoholic to AA in the first place, but also because the alcoholic is offered hope that there is a way out. The alcoholic is not expected to appreciate fully the consequences of his or her behavior. This would be overwhelming. The only expectation is to stop drinking one day at a time. Repression, therefore, replaces denial, according to Bean. Reaction formation and undoing are manifested in the change from love of drinking to love of sobriety.

The central point in Bean's explication of psychodynamic change through AA is that the drinking alcoholic is accepted as he or she presents (4). One is permitted to express oneself as he or she is rather than as others may wish him or her to be. The alcoholic in AA may continue unchanged in character and so is granted the opportunity to put his or her energy into abstinence. Not drinking allows the brain to heal and nurtures confidence, hope, and the gradual restoration of self-esteem. Not drinking and following the AA way promote maturity, that is, a shift from primitive defenses to higher-order defenses (25).

As the alcoholic advances in recovery, self-esteem is protected by abstinence but threatened by remorse over the past. According to Bean, AA techniques to handle this aspect of recovery are

1. The decision not to drink—repent and reform to build upon the wreckage of the past
2. Place blame on the illness, not the alcoholic
3. Avoid censure
4. Reward good behavior—this is done by dispensing 30-day, 60-day, 90-day, or 1 year "chips" as milestones in sobriety are achieved
5. Allow expression of low self-esteem in nondestructive ways rather than by drinking

AA does not ask the alcoholic to get a job, be a better family member, or become more responsible. Sobriety is the goal from which other desirable efforts may emerge. The "depressurization" techniques of AA ("one day at a time"; "keep it simple"; etc.) and the social dimension—sharing "experiences, strength, and hope"—are from Bean's perspective critical components of the AA experience.

ACCEPTING LIMITATIONS

The writings of Kurtz provide not only a definitive history of AA but also critical insights into AA's effectiveness (3, 28). The core dynamic of AA therapy, according to Kurtz, is "the shared honesty of mutual vulnerability openly acknowledged . . ." (28, p. 30).

An essential insight of AA for the alcoholic is its recognition and acceptance that one is "not-God" (3). With this term Kurtz is referring to the necessity for the alcoholic to accept personal limitation. The First Step of AA communicates to the alcoholic: "We admitted we were powerless over alcohol and that our lives had become unmanageable." The acceptance of personal limitation—a condition of existence for all—is a life or death matter for the alcoholic. AA, in teaching that the first drink gets the alcoholic drunk, implies that the alcoholic does not have a drinking limit, the alcoholic is limited (28). To experience limitation is tantamount to experiencing shame. As painful as the shame is, it is an affect pivotal to recovery. Acceptance of shame distinguishes the alcoholic who, in Tiebout's (27) terms, complies rather than surrenders. Compliance is motivated by guilt, is superficial, and ultimately is useless to extended recovery. Surrender involves recognition of powerlessness (and the affect associated with feeling limited or of having fallen short). Through surrender the alcoholic becomes open to the healing forces within AA. Kurtz (28) considers that Steps 2, 6, 7, and 10 influence the experience of shame in the alcoholic. The AA program treats shame by enabling the alcoholic to accept his or her need for others, by promoting the acceptance of others as they are ("live and let live"), and by valuing and reinforcing traits of honesty, sharing, and caring.

SPIRITUAL DIMENSION

Earlier it was noted that the effectiveness of AA could not be explained fully by the variables operating within group dynamics. Other mechanisms or explanations have been reviewed in the effort to understand better the dynamics of AA. Among these explanations are AA's impact on ego functions and pathological narcissism (20, 21), AA's understanding of the alcoholic and alcoholism from the viewpoint of the alcoholic (4), AA's confrontation of the powerlessness and loss of control of the alcoholic (26), and AA's ability to shift the alcoholic from self-centeredness to self-acceptance (28). These analyses of AA's effectiveness (like examination of group process variables) contribute to our understanding of the AA program but are incomplete in their capture of the AA process. The dimension of spirituality must be introduced and considered in the equation of our understanding.

At the beginning of this chapter it was suggested that working the Twelve Steps is what makes AA effective. This simple explanation may disguise the impact of spirituality on the recovery process. Spirituality rarely is part of the lexicon of the mental health professional but is a dimension of the AA program understood by those who work and live the Twelve Steps. The spirituality of the AA program is distinct from religious dogma and may be understood as a series of overlapping themes (29). The first theme is *release*. Release refers to the "chains being broken"—freedom from the compulsion to drink. The experience of release is a powerful and welcome event for the alcoholic and seems to occur naturally or to be given rather than achieved.

A second theme of spirituality is *gratitude*. Gratitude may flow from the feeling of release and includes an awareness of what we have—for example, the gift of life. According to Kurtz, the words "think" and "thank" share a common derivation (29). Thinking leads to remembrance (for example, as the AA speaker tells his or her story), and from remembrance an attitude of thankfulness (gratitude) may be experienced—gratitude, for example, that one is now sober.

The third theme is *humility*. Humility conveys the attitude that it is acceptable to be limited, to be simply human. The alcoholic's awareness of powerlessness over alcohol engenders humility.

Finally, a fourth theme or component to spirituality is *tolerance*. A tolerance of differences and limitations fosters the serenity often experienced by AA members.

These themes of spirituality are very similar to the healing process in mystical traditions as described by Deikman (30). According to Deikman, the process of attaining higher psychological development involves renunciation, humility, and sincerity. *Renunciation* refers to an attitude, that is, a giving up of the attachment to the things of the world. The alcoholic's giving up alcohol would demonstrate renunciation. *Humility,* according to Deikman, is "the possibility that someone else can teach you something you do not already know, especially about yourself" (30, p. 81), and *sincerity* simply refers to honesty of intention. It is apparent that the alcoholic working the Twelve Steps (see Table 37.1) is involving himself or herself in the processes of renunciation, humility, and sincerity.

In addition to the spiritual themes mentioned earlier, an additional healing dynamic may be significant: forgiveness. The seeking of forgiveness is implied, not directly expressed, in the Twelve Steps. For example, Steps 6 and 7 (see Table 37.1) ask God to remove defects of character and remove shortcomings. The behavior of AA members toward newcomers (welcoming, accepting, friendly, caring) communicates forgiveness. Forgiveness is neither asked for nor offered at AA. The word itself may or may not be heard at AA meetings, but its meaning pervades the transactions of the meetings. For example, Bean writes (4, p. 10):

> Alcoholics know how deeply and painfully ashamed and guilty other alcoholics are about their drinking, how they lie and minimize it, and how this reinforces their sense of worthlessness. The discovery that others have committed what they thought was their own uniquely unforgivable crime brings longed-for solace. Speakers repeatedly report their sense of relief when they first come to AA. They had no further need for dissembling and fear. Here they were among their own kind and were accepted.

Forgiveness may be a precondition for the dynamic forces described in this chapter to be operative. For example, forgiveness precedes hope. Hope is necessarily very tenuous for a newcomer to AA and requires a future orientation, an orientation minimized by AA's emphasis on "one day at a time." Forgiveness is experienced in a moment and may be the foundation for a growing sense of hope. Abandoning narcissistic defenses, strengthening the capacity for self-governance, and accepting "powerlessness" over alcohol all may be contingent on feeling forgiven or feeling capable of being forgiven. To be forgiven, to feel forgiven implies being accepted, a common description of the AA experience. The experience of shame (28) as a pivotal affect and the treatment of shame in AA may become possible only if preceded by a sense of being forgiven.

The concepts of spirituality, including forgiveness, are put forth only as one further effort to explain the impact and mechanisms of the AA program. Perhaps that which is effective in the AA program varies considerably from member to member. An AA member may have limited awareness of (and equally little interest in) the dynamic forces accounting for AA's effectiveness. But, possibly, for some, the program may be a secular expression of the Christian concept of grace—an unmerited gift from God.

LIMITATIONS OF AA

AA is predominantly a white, middle-class organization consisting of middle-aged married males (4). This broad demographic characterization of AA does not indicate a limitation of the AA program itself but may impose some barriers for those out of the mainstream. AA has been attracting a younger population. Three percent of members are under age 21, and 22% are 30 years of age or younger. The percentage of women has increased from 22% in 1968 to 35% in 1989 (31). Adoption of the AA program by minorities has been slower to occur. Yet, most urban areas have several meetings with a predominantly black or Hispanic population.

Psychiatric comorbidity may impede AA affiliation for some alcoholics. Personality disorders of the schizoid, avoidant, or paranoid type may not adapt well to the interaction and emotionality of AA meetings. At times, a patient on medications is thrown into conflict by AA members who may advise against the use of any drugs. AA as an organization does not hold opinions on psychotropic medications, but occasionally an AA member may inappropriately influence a fellow member who requires specific psychiatric treatment. An alcoholic persuaded to discontinue lithium or neuroleptics may relapse into psychosis, at great personal expense. As more alcoholics are reaching AA through rehabilitation programs, AA's familiarity with and understanding of individual needs may be increased, and the AA member under psychiatric treatment will be less likely to experience conflict and inappropriate advice.

Should AA be recommended only for certain alcoholics? There is no empirical base from which such a decision-making process could follow. AA generally seems to accommodate a wide variety of personalities and backgrounds. On a case-by-case basis, social or psychodynamic factors may deter the efficacy of AA utilization, but that can be ascertained on an individual basis only, not by currently available data. The question of whether some alcoholics are suited for AA and others not is seen by Brown less as an empirical question and more as reflecting a misunderstanding of or bias toward AA (26, p. 187):

> The position that AA is for some and not for others widens the gap between professionals and AA members. Patients and therapists alike tend to believe that being able to stay sober without the use of AA is superior to using it. Patients and therapists may both believe that AA is not for bright, capable people who can make use of a therapist.

Brown recommends that anyone concerned about drinking be referred to AA.

Apart from the issue of whether every alcoholic should be referred to AA, there are specific limitations to the AA method. These have been summarized by Bean (4) and include AA's being rigid, superficial, regressive, inspirational, fanatical, stigmatizing, and focusing only on alcohol. The rigidity is more likely to lie in individual members than the AA program itself. Questioning and intellectualizing are discouraged, but this seems more a means to hold back the ever-present threat of denial than a commitment to absolute dogma. The criticism of superficiality is appropriate if one's goals are to unravel the complex etiologies of alcoholism or to understand the dynamics of behavior change. AA chooses to put its energy into abstaining from drinking and simultaneously providing and tolerating a system that fosters dependency (hence the criticism of being regressive). AA certainly is inspirational rather than reflective, but again, the alcoholic early in recovery cannot be expected to obtain or use insight. Morale is of critical concern, and the emotional pitch of AA strikes a respondent chord in the demoralized. Unfortunately, fanaticism or zealotry may form part of the operation of AA loyalty. Such members are repellent to some newcomers, who may feel that their emotional needs are not understood or validated. Some charismatic AA members convert many alcoholics but alienate others, including the professionals to whom they relate in a condescending manner. Is there a stigma about attending AA? If there is, it is less than in past years, since acclaim for AA is easily found in popular literature and the media. At the least, any stigma attached to the AA program would be substantially less than that of chronic drunkenness.

To conclude, AA, like all other therapies for alcoholism, is limited. Considering our current state of knowledge, the clinician is obligated to become conversant with the purpose, principles, and utility of the AA program. By gaining an understanding of this Twelve Step program the clinician will be prepared to motivate and advocate AA to his or her alcoholic patients. This understanding is gained best by attending AA meetings, discussing AA with experienced members, and reading widely, including the AA literature as well as professional writings on AA. From this effort the physician can inform each patient appropriately of the advantages of AA as well as any potential drawbacks he or she may encounter.

THE MENTAL HEALTH PROFESSIONS AND AA

The clinician would be remiss to overlook, ignore, or disparage the value of AA for any patient with a substance use disorder. Familiarity with AA can be obtained by attending open AA meetings, developing friendly relation-

Table 37.3 Modulation of Differences between AA and Psychiatry

Subject	AA	Psychiatry	Modulation
Cause of drinking	One drinks because one is an alcoholic. Therapy can lead to intellectualization and denial.	One needs to understand the dynamics that influence behavior in order for change to be lasting.	Initially, the emphasis is put on cessation of drinking; later, an understanding of one's emotional pain or vulnerabilities.
Recovery	Simple—just follow the program.	Lengthy therapeutic quest.	Explore with the alcoholic resistances to AA, and/or why he or she can't avoid people, places, or things that facilitate drinking.
AA	A divine gift. It saved my life.	It's rigid.	It's both. Early in treatment the alcoholic needs a concise, rigid formula to contain drinking impulses and to counter despair.
Controlled drinking	A myth that kills.	Sometimes it seems possible.	Controlled drinking is a very unlikely outcome for the large majority of alcoholics. Mildly dependent, early-stage alcoholics sometimes reverse loss of control.
Medication	It's bad.	Good—corrects biochemical defects.	Medication may be essential during detoxification and in cases of psychiatric comorbidity.
Psychopathology	Alcoholics are normal once they stop drinking.	All alcoholics have specific conflicts that predate their alcoholism.	Psychopathology often predates the alcoholism but many times is the result of drinking. Sobriety leads to improvement in either case, but additional treatment is often useful.
Treatment	The Twelve Steps	Medical and psychological.	The two are not contradictory but can be used effectively by most alcoholics, with one receiving more emphasis at certain times.
Basis of treatment	Personal experience of others.	Scientifically based and empirically validated procedures.	Divergent sources of understanding enable the experience of many to make an impact on a complex disease.

ships with AA members, and insisting that one's patients meet with AA members for an initial, informed introduction to AA. Such efforts can facilitate an alliance with the AA community and foster the development of mutual respect.

Such grassroots efforts, however, do not dispel conceptual differences between AA and the treatments offered by the mental health field. Table 37.3 outlines potential differences, and, for the sake of comparison, presents these differences in extreme form. A modulation of the differences is suggested.

Chappel (32) effectively integrates working the Steps with the process of psychotherapeutic change. For example, Step One requires self-examination and honesty and is critical to overcoming the defense of denial; Step Three is, in part, a process of "letting go" and ridding oneself of obsessive tendencies; and Step Four promotes the development of an observing ego as one confronts issues of guilt and shame. If one conscientiously applies the Twelve Steps to one's life an openness to new experiences will be gained, the courage to attempt personal change will be acquired, and a greater acceptance of oneself and others can be expected (32).

CONCLUSION

This chapter outlines the origins of AA and describes its growth and basic situations. AA works. How well and for whom remain unsatisfactorily researched.

Particular emphasis is placed on reviewing the dynamics of AA. Just as group process variables seem to have only partial explanatory power, the same may be said of sophisticated psychodynamic formulations. The under-acknowledged, understudied area of spirituality bears serious consideration by the clinician. The theme of spirituality and the homilies expressed in AA slogans may someday catalyze an understanding of behavior change.

References

1. Alcoholics Anonymous. 2nd edition. New York: AA World Services, 1955.
2. Twelve steps, twelve traditions. New York: AA World Services, 1978.
3. Kurtz E. Not-God: a history of Alcoholics Anonymous. Center City, MN: Hazelden, 1979.
4. Bean MH. Alcoholics Anonymous: AA. Psychiatr Ann 1975;5(2):3–64.
5. Webster's new twentieth century dictionary of the English language. Unabridged 2nd edition. New York: William Collins Publishers, 1980.
6. Alcoholics Anonymous. Information on Alcoholics Anonymous. New York: AA World Services, 1988.
7. Alcoholics Anonymous. Grapevine. New York: The AA Grapevine, Inc., 1992.
8. About AA: a newsletter for professional men and women. Fall, 1984.
9. James W. The varieties of religious experience. New York: Mentor, 1958.
10. Thomsen R. Bill W. New York: Harper and Row, 1975.
11. Henry S, Robinson D. Understanding Alcoholics Anonymous. Lancet 1978;2:372–375.
12. Ogborne AC, Glaser FB. Characteristics of affiliates of Alcoholics Anonymous. J Stud Alcohol 1981;42(7):661–675.
13. Emrick C. Alcoholics Anonymous: affiliation processes and effectiveness as treatment. Alcoholism (NY) 1987;11:416–423.
14. Boscarino J. Factors related to "stable" and "unstable" affiliation with Alcoholics Anonymous. Int J Addict 1980;15(6):839–848.
15. Leach B, Norris JL. Factors in the development of Alcoholics Anonymous (AA). In: Kissin B, Begleiter H, eds. The biology of alcoholism: treatment and rehabilitation of the chronic alcoholic. New York: Plenum Press, 1977;5:441–543.
16. Bailey MB, Leach B. Alcoholics Anonymous: pathway to recovery: a study of 1058 members of the AA fellowship in New York City. New York: National Council on Alcoholism, 1965.
17. Edwards G, Hensman C, Haukes A, Williamson V. Alcoholics Anonymous: the anatomy of a self-help group. Soc Psychiatry 1967;1:195.
18. Eckhardt W. Alcoholic values and Alcoholics Anonymous. Q J Stud Alcohol 1967;28:277–288.
19. Yalom ID. The theory and practice of group psychotherapy. 2nd edition. New York: Basic Books, 1975.
20. Mack JE. Alcoholism, AA, the governance of the self. In: Bean MH, Zinberg NE, eds. Dynamic approaches to the understanding and treatment of alcoholism. New York: The Free Press, 1981.
21. Khantzian EJ, Mack JE. Alcoholics Anonymous and contemporary psychodynamic theory. In: Galanter M, ed. Recent developments in alcoholism. New York: Plenum Press, 1989.
22. Wurmser L. Psychoanalytic considerations of the etiology of compulsive drug use. J Am Psychoanal Assoc 1974;22:820–843.
23. McClelland DC, Davis WN, Kelin R, Wanner E. The drinking man. New York: The Free Press, 1972.
24. Kohut H. The restoration of the self. New York: International Universities Press, 1977.
25. Nace EP. The treatment of alcoholism. New York: Brunner/Mazel, 1987.
26. Brown S. Treating, the alcoholic: a developmental model of recovery. New York: John Wiley, 1985.
27. Tiebout HM. Surrender versus compliance in therapy. Q J Stud Alcohol 1953;14:58–68.
28. Kurtz E. Shame and guilt: characteristics of the dependency cycle. Center City, MN: Hazelden Foundation, 1981.
29. Kurtz E. Alcoholics Anonymous and spirituality. Workshop presented by Green Oaks Psychiatric Hospital, Dallas, TX, June 9, 1989.
30. Deikman AJ. The observing self—mysticism and psychotherapy. Boston: Beacon Press, 1982.
31. AA membership survey. New York: AA World Services, 1989.
32. Chappel JN. Teaching, learning recovery. Substance Abuse—AMERSA 1995;16(3):141–153.

38 ALTERNATIVE SUPPORT GROUPS

Arthur T. Horvath

This chapter presents an overview of five support groups for addictive behavior. These support groups are in many aspects fundamentally different from and hence alternatives to 12-step groups such as Alcoholics Anonymous (AA). These five groups, in order of longevity, are Women for Sobriety (WFS), Rational Recovery (RR), Moderation Management (MM), Men for Sobriety (MFS), and S.M.A.R.T. Recovery (SMART). A sixth alternative, Secular Organizations for Sobriety/Save Our Selves (SOS), is covered in Chapter 39. Chapter 37 covers 12-step groups. This chapter will be oriented toward providing information that would help professionals and their patients identify whether alternatives in general, and which alternative in particular, might be helpful for a particular patient.

These alternatives are relatively young and unknown. AA began in 1935. The oldest of the alternatives, WFS, began in 1976. Despite the continued predominance of 12-step groups in the United States, the alternatives appear to be gaining recognition. Where available, they have become options for professionals and their patients to consider in treatment planning.

Each alternative will be covered regarding its history, primary publications, intended membership, program, meeting format, and organizational aspects. A literature review of the limited empirical findings is also presented. Contact information for each group (and SOS) is included at the end of the chapter.

These alternatives (and SOS) have significant similarities with 12-step groups. All are without substantial empirical support of effectiveness. All offer 60–90 minute meetings at no charge, but request donations. All are essentially self-supporting, primarily through member donations and the sale of a variety of recovery materials (including books, workbooks, audio and videotapes, and software, some of which may be produced by lay individuals or professionals not directly affiliated with the organization). All publish, or intend to publish, newsletters or similar publications. All (except MM) are abstinence-oriented. All (except SMART) were founded by one or two individuals who had a vision about recovery from addictive behavior. All (except RR) are nonprofit corporations.

The programmatic and organizational differences between these alternatives (and SOS) and 12-step groups are substantial and numerous. Although WFS and MFS understand addictive behavior to involve a disease process, none emphasize reliance on a "higher power" for recovery. On the other hand, none are opposed to religious or spiritual beliefs in their members. None offer formal sponsorship of new members by experienced members. All (except RR) are supportive, both in principle and in practice, of appropriate professional treatment for addictive behavior. None expect members to attend for life, but rather to attend for as long as (or whenever) it is helpful. Typical attendance during the period of active involvement is 1–3 meetings per week, but there are few guidelines about frequency of attendance (versus AA's "90 meetings in 90 days"). All apparently appeal primarily to higher functioning individuals (although this may be an artifact of the effort often required to locate these alternatives). All are accepting, both in principle and in practice, of individuals with neurotic (but not necessarily psychotic) comorbidity, and all encourage professional treatment of these conditions. All are flexible in the application of their program principles to the individual case. All are supportive of 12-step groups for individuals who benefit from them. All suggest that some individuals may be impeded in their recovery by 12-step groups, or benefit more from alternative groups, or both. All are small (in comparison to AA's more than 90,000 meetings worldwide). All operate on very limited budgets.

The differences with respect to meetings and meeting leaders are also substantial and numerous. All groups typically devote major portions of their meetings to discussion ("crosstalk"). None have speaker meetings (although their leaders may give separate public presentations). All have, or prefer to have, small meetings (approximately 6–12 members), to allow ample opportunity for individual participation. All have meeting formats, but tolerate (or even encourage) significant variation based on local custom or preference. None have extensive meeting rituals. All are led by a facilitator who guides the discussion. The facilitator is typically a peer, and a member of the group's recovery program (but a significant minority of facilitators in some alternatives are behavioral health professionals). Because of the responsibility involved in being a facilitator, all appear to experience difficulty finding facilitators. Because of the lack of a lifetime membership requirement, all experience difficulty retaining facilitators. All aspire to international availability, as qualified facilitators can be identified.

These six organizations appear to be the only nationally available alternative addictive behavior support groups, as of 1996. Contact information is also provided for the American Self-Help Clearinghouse, which maintains a database of 750 nationally available support groups, many of them for addictive behavior. Specialized support groups with a 12-step or similar orientation are available for various faiths, occupations, and addictive behaviors (1).

Several issues pertinent to alternative support groups can be identified but are not explored here. Serious ethical and possibly legal issues may arise when an individual, for considered and responsible reasons, chooses to pursue an alternative approach to recovery, but a treatment provider or third party insists on 12-step-oriented treatment. The conditions which have allowed the alternatives to emerge may facilitate the emergence of others. The alternatives may increase the number of individuals involved in recovery, or they may draw their participants only from those who otherwise would have attended 12-step groups.

WOMEN FOR SOBRIETY (WFS)

History

WFS was founded in 1976 by Jean Kirkpatrick, Ph.D., to address the unique problems of women alcoholics. These problems are suggested to include the issues of self-value, self-worth, guilt, and humiliation. Kirk-

patrick's own experience was that AA was only partially helpful to her as a woman alcoholic.

Despite professional treatment and AA attendance, Kirkpatrick had a 30-year drinking history, including hospital and mental hospital admissions, hit-and-run accidents (during blackouts), and jail time. She had recurring episodes of depression and attempted suicide several times. She nevertheless managed to earn a doctorate in sociology from the University of Pennsylvania by age 50.

Kirkpatrick's AA experience was one that she believes is typical for women. The recounting of the harm caused by drinking seemed to be good for men in AA and reminded them of their reasons not to relapse. For her, however, recounting painful and often humiliating past drinking experiences seemed to make even more difficult the task of accepting herself and gaining mastery of her life. Additionally, AA did not address how societal views of women (versus men) alcoholics posed additional challenges for recovering women.

Kirkpatrick was ultimately able to stop drinking in her early 50s by relying on the philosophies of the Unity Church, Emerson, and Thoreau. Several years after achieving sobriety she formulated the principles of WFS, based in part on these philosophies. She also included in WFS cognitive-behavioral change techniques, and an emphasis on health promotion and peer support.

Primary Publications

WFS has two primary publications (2, 3). The WFS newsletter is *Sobering Thoughts*.

Intended Membership

WFS is intended for women alcoholics (including those who also have prescription medication problems). Kirkpatrick has suggested that for some women AA may be more effective at achieving initial sobriety, because initially a woman may be overwhelmed by the complexity of the WFS program. After several months of abstinence, however, most women are believed to be ready to appreciate the idea that women need a different approach to recovery.

Program

WFS views alcoholism as a physical disease that a woman can grow beyond by learning new self-enhancing behavior via

1. Positive reinforcement (approval and encouragement),
2. Cognitive strategies (positive thinking),
3. Letting the body help (relaxation techniques, meditation, diet, and physical exercise), and
4. Dynamic group involvement (4).

The WFS "New Life" Acceptance Program is presented in Table 38.1.

Meeting Format

WFS meetings are lead by a Certified Moderator. Certification is based on having at least one year of sobriety, reading *Turnabout* (2), subscribing to the WFS newsletter, and passing a written test about WFS principles and their application in meetings. WFS instituted certification to assure that moderators with a history of AA attendance understood the differences between WFS and AA principles and meeting formats.

Meetings are open to all women alcoholics. Newcomers are given a packet of introductory information. Meetings begin with a reading of the Statement of Purpose, followed by introductions ("Hello, my name is Jean, and I'm a competent woman"). Most of the meeting is devoted to discussion of member's concerns, and how the 13 Statements (Table 38.1) can be applied to them. Following discussion each member is asked to describe something positive she has accomplished in the past week.

The meeting closes with the members standing, holding hands, and saying: "We are capable and competent, caring and compassionate, always willing to help another, bonded together in overcoming our addictions."

Table 38.1   The WFS "New Life" Acceptance Program

Level I: Accepting alcoholism as a physical disease.
"I have a life-threatening (drinking) problem that once had me." (#1)

Level II: Discarding negative thoughts, putting guilt behind, and practicing
   new ways of viewing and solving problems.
"Negative thoughts destroy only myself." (#2)
"Problems bother me only to the degree I permit them to." (#4)
"The past is gone forever." (#9)

Level III: Creating and practicing a new self-image.
"I am what I think." (#5)
"I am a competent woman and have much to give life." (#12)

Level IV: Using new attitudes to enforce new behavior patterns.
"Happiness is a habit I will develop." (#3)
"Life can be ordinary or it can be great." (#6)
"Enthusiasm is my daily exercise." (#11)

Level V: Improving relationships as a result of our feelings about self.
"Love can change the course of my world." (#7)
"All love given returns." (#10)

Level VI: Recognizing life's priorities: emotional and spiritual growth, self-
   responsibility.
"The fundamental object of life is emotional and spiritual growth." (#8)
"I am responsible for myself and my actions." (#13)

From Kirkpatrick J. WFS "new life" acceptance program (brochure). Quakertown, PA:
Women for Sobriety, 1993. Copyright Jean Kirkpatrick, 1993.

Organizational Aspects

As of January, 1996, WFS reports approximately 300 meetings in 40 states, and 50 meetings in other countries (primarily Canada, Australia, New Zealand, Ireland, and Finland). Kirkpatrick is the full-time Executive Director of WFS. The 12-member Board of Directors is composed of professional women who have recovered through WFS and who lead groups. In Australia and New Zealand WFS receives some government funding.

Empirical Findings

Kaskutas (5, 6) collected responses from 579 women who attended WFS only, or both WFS and AA. These responses support the suggestion that women may need a different approach to recovery. Women who attended only WFS reported that they did not feel that they fit in at AA, that AA was too negative, that they disliked the "drunkalogues" and the focus on the past, and that AA is better suited to men's needs than women's. Women attended WFS for support and nurturance, for a safe environment, for discussion about women's issues, and for the emphasis on positives and self-esteem. For women who attended both WFS and AA, insurance against relapse and AA's availability were frequently cited reasons to attend AA. Talan (7) studied 115 women in AA or WFS, and found no differences between groups on reaction to the groups, length of time attending, or treatment outcome.

RATIONAL RECOVERY (RR)

History

Rational Recovery was founded by Jack Trimpey, LCSW, in 1985, to provide a rational (as opposed to spiritual) approach to recovery from alcohol and drug dependence. His own experience was that only by demanding of his own thinking a high level of rationality was he able to overcome his own drinking problems.

Trimpey credits Albert Ellis and Rational Emotive Behavior Therapy (REBT) (8, 9) with providing the initial guidance Trimpey needed to pursue a rational approach to recovery. However, he states that the foundation of his recovery was the development of a technique he later formalized as Addictive Voice Recognition Technique (AVRT). Rational Recovery was therefore initially formulated (10) as a combination of REBT techniques (for resolution of emotional problems that impede the accomplishment and maintenance of sobriety) and AVRT (for overcoming the addiction itself).

Trimpey's thinking about the role of support groups in recovery, and the relationship between REBT and AVRT in RR, has evolved since the publication of his first book (10). He has recently written that AVRT can "teach moderately to seriously addicted people how to quit an addiction without entering *addiction* 'treatment,' without attending recovery groups, and without otherwise improving oneself" (11, p. 4).

Beginning about 1993 RR groups transitioned to a primary focus on AVRT, with a minor focus on helping participants work on personal problems using REBT and related techniques. Because AVRT can also be taught through written material or at an educational workshop, Rational Recovery Systems, the parent organization of RR, has shifted its primary focus from providing support groups to providing education about AVRT.

Primary Publications

RR has three primary publications (10, 12, 13). The RR newsletter is the *Journal of Rational Recovery*.

Intended Membership

RR is primarily intended for individuals with substance abuse, but individuals with other addictive behaviors may also attend. As RR is currently practiced it is no longer (and no longer considers itself to be) a support group in the traditional sense, nor does it consider itself to have members. Meetings are viewed as primarily an opportunity to learn AVRT, and not especially useful (and possibly counterproductive) after this learning has occurred.

Program

RR views "thinking about drinking or drugging" as the unimpeded working of "the Beast" or Addictive Voice, a part of the brain which seeks intoxication purely for the pleasure of it. Responding forcefully to this Beast ("killing" it) by means of AVRT is considered the essential step.

The goal of AVRT is lifetime abstinence, and this goal is achieved by monitoring one's awareness for any thoughts or images that would lead back to drinking or using. AVRT suggests that "I want to drink/drug" is more accurately stated "It (the Beast) wants to drink/drug." Such thoughts or images are immediately responded to by pointing out the short-sighted nature of the pleasure to be obtained, and by re-asserting the absolute and non-negotiable decision to abstain for life (the the "Big Plan").

The REBT aspect of pre-1993 RR is illustrated by the rational counterpoints Trimpey makes to what he terms the "philosophy of alcoholism." He suggests that the irrationalities of this philosophy can perpetuate the relapse cycle. The first irrational idea (of 15 total) of this philosophy, and the rational idea to counteract it, is "*I am powerless over my alcoholic cravings, and therefore not responsible for what I put in my mouth*, **instead of the rational idea that** I have considerable control over my extremities and facial muscles." (10, p. 102).

Meeting Format

RR meetings are open only to individuals with addictive behavior. Meetings are conducted by a coordinator, who usually opens the meeting with the question: "Who has been thinking about drinking or using?" The discussion that follows attempts to help members use AVRT to recognize the Addictive Voice. Trimpey suggests that "RR meetings have little structure, but there is certainly a weighty agenda" (10, pg. 259).

Organizational Aspects

RR no longer maintains an exact meeting census, but estimates that as of January, 1996, there are several hundred meetings throughout the United States, and several dozen in other countries. RR groups are provided as a community service of Rational Recovery Systems, which is owned and operated by Jack Trimpey and his wife, Lois Trimpey. Rational Recovery Systems also conducts educational workshops and offers franchises for Rational Recovery Centers.

Empirical Findings

Taken together the literature supports the suggestion that RR may be an effective option for selected individuals. RR reports that three additional studies are in progress.

Galanter (14) studied 433 members of 63 RR groups. The sample was on average well-educated, employed, male, and relatively uninvolved in religious activities. The average length of substance problems was almost 25 years. Most subjects had previously attended 12-step groups. "Recruits" to RR (having less than one month of membership) were compared to "engaged members" (first meeting at least 3 months before). The average length of attendance for engaged members was 10 months. Comparisons suggested that RR helped maintain or initiate abstinence in a significant portion of engaged members. Reinert (15, 16) studied 45 subjects who attended AA, and 10 who attended RR, and found that RR attenders could be distinguished from AA attenders by lower levels of "surrender." Atkinson (17) surveyed 268 community college students and found some more willing to use an RR model of addiction treatment than an AA model.

MODERATION MANAGEMENT (MM)

History

MM was founded in 1993 by Audrey Kishline, to support individuals who desire to moderate their alcohol consumption. Her own experience had been that it was difficult to obtain support for this goal.

Kishline reports that during her twenties her drinking increased to the level of a moderate problem. She eventually sought treatment. Ultimately this treatment included two inpatient stays, an aftercare program, and consultation with at least 30 alcoholism treatment professionals, all of whom diagnosed her as "alcoholic." She also attended AA regularly for several years, attending hundreds of meetings. Her initial reaction to treatment was that her drinking became more severe. She suggests that at least in part this increase was a self-fulfilling prophecy based on what she had learned about alcoholism as a disease over which she was powerless. She also suggests that over several years she gradually matured out of her drinking problem, as she became more involved in the responsibilities and activities of life (e.g., marriage, children, homemaking, college courses, hobbies, and friends). As this maturing occurred, her beliefs about herself also evolved. Rather than believing herself to have a disease, she chose to abstain because of the kind of life she wanted to lead.

Several years prior to writing her 1994 book (18), Kishline chose to return to moderate drinking. She asserts that she was misdiagnosed initially, and that moderation of her alcohol consumption had been overlooked as an option for her. She founded MM in the hope that the moderation option would not be overlooked for others in similar situations.

Primary Publications

MM has one primary publication (18). A newsletter is planned.

Intended Membership

MM is intended for individuals who fit the description "problem drinker" rather than "alcoholic." There are two fundamental requirements for membership: A willingness to accept responsibility for one's own behavior and a desire to moderate drinking. MM is not aimed at individuals who have experienced significant withdrawal symptoms from alcohol, who have medical conditions exacerbated by alcohol (e.g., heart disease, diabetes, gastrointestinal problems, etc.), or who are experiencing other relevant conditions including pregnancy or desired pregnancy, a behavioral health disorder, being on medications that interact negatively with alcohol, or being in personal crisis. Lastly, MM is not designed for individuals who are already abstaining successfully after a history of severe dependence.

MM also recommends that prospective members complete the Short Alcohol Dependence Data Questionnaire (SADD) (19), which is reproduced in the MM book. On this test scores from 1 to 9 suggest low dependence on alcohol, 10 to 19 medium dependence, and 20 or higher (maximum score 45) high dependence. Those who score below 16 are considered good candidates for MM. Those who score between 16 and 19 are encouraged to obtain professional assessment before attending a moderation program. Those who score 20 and above are encouraged to pursue abstinence. Even individuals with low scores are not discouraged from pursuing abstinence, but are offered the alternative of MM.

MM hopes to reach problem drinkers early in their problem drinking career by offering an approach that appeals to common sense and does not require excessive effort (relative to the intensity of the problem). MM is therefore partly a prevention program. If an individual is not successful following MM's moderation guidelines, the individual is encouraged to pursue abstinence.

Program

MM views drinking problems as arising from bad habits, rather than being the manifestations of a disease. MM is based on empirically supported cognitive-behavioral moderation training programs, and they are referred to frequently in the MM book (20–22). The Nine Steps of MM are reprinted in Table 38.2. MM suggests that 6–18 months of once-weekly attendance is usually needed for successful completion of its program.

MM understands moderate drinking to be (for men) no more than 4 standard drinks per day, no more than 4 drinking days per week, and no more than 14 standard drinks per week. A standard drink is the amount of alcohol in a 12-ounce bottle of beer, a 5-ounce glass of wine, or a 1.5-ounce shot of liquor, all of which, because of differing concentrations, have approximately equal amounts of pure alcohol. For women, moderate drinking is understood to be no more than 3 standard drinks per day, no more than 4 drinking days per week, and no more than 9 standard drinks per week. Both sexes are encouraged not to drink and drive, or to drink in situations where the drinker or others might be endangered.

Meeting Format

Meetings are led by a moderator, and begin with the reading of an opening statement describing the purpose of MM, followed by a reading of the Nine Steps (see Table 38.2) and ground rules for members. Visitors (the meetings are open) and newcomers are invited to introduce themselves. Announcements and a treasurer's report are made. Anyone who has recently completed the recommended initial 30 days of abstinence is acknowledged.

The first working section of the meeting is devoted to giving every member the opportunity to update the group on their activities since the member's last meeting. Feedback by others may be offered. The next working section is general discussion. If no one has a topic to discuss, the moderator suggests one, which would typically be one of the ideas or techniques covered in the MM book. The meeting ends with the reading of a closing statement.

Table 38.2 The Nine Steps of Moderation Management

1. Attend meetings and learn about the program of Moderation Management.
2. Abstain from alcoholic beverages for 30 days and complete steps three through six at this time.
3. Examine how drinking has affected your life.
4. Write down your priorities.
5. Take a look at how much, how often, and under what circumstances you used to drink.
6. Learn the MM guidelines and limits for moderate drinking.
7. Set moderate drinking limits and start weekly "small steps" toward positive lifestyle changes.
8. Review your progress at meetings and update your goals.
9. After achieving your goal of moderation, attend MM meetings any time you feel the need for support, or would like to help newcomers.

From Kishline A: Moderate drinking: The Moderation Management Guide for people who want to reduce their drinking, New York: Crown, 1995. Copyright Audrey Kishline, 1994.

Organizational Aspects

As of January, 1996, MM reports 10 meetings in 8 states, and plans 42 additional meetings in 17 additional states. Kishline is the volunteer full-time Executive Director. The 10-member Board of Directors is composed primarily of addictive behavior professionals and writers. MM seeks inquiries from behavioral health professionals, who are welcome to function as meeting moderators.

Empirical Findings

No studies of MM have been published, but MM reports that two studies are in progress.

MEN FOR SOBRIETY (MFS)

MFS was founded in 1994 by Jean Kirkpatrick, Ph.D., after she had received requests to form a group for men based on the principles of WFS. MFS is still developing primary publications, and for these currently relies largely upon WFS, of which it is a distinct organizational component. With respect to its intended membership and meeting format, MFS is analogous to WFS. The MFS program attempts to identify and address issues unique to recovering men. As of January, 1996, MFS reports approximately 15 meetings in three states, and two meetings in Canada. No literature currently is published about MFS.

S.M.A.R.T. RECOVERY (SMART)

History

SMART (*Self Management and Recovery Training*) incorporated as a nonprofit organization in 1992 under the name Rational Recovery Self-Help Network. The organization entered into an agreement with Jack Trimpey, the founder and owner of Rational Recovery Systems, to use the name Rational Recovery and to operate Rational Recovery support groups. The Board of Directors, of which Trimpey was a member, had evolved from an informal group of advisors, mostly mental health professionals, which Trimpey had assembled for an initial meeting in 1991. Trimpey took the leading role in establishing and incorporating the organization.

Beginning about 1993 there was increasing disagreement between Trimpey and the organization about how the organization would be managed, and the nature of its program. These developments culminated in 1994 with the mutual agreement between Trimpey and the organization to separate. This separation was accomplished by changing the organization's name. The separation and related issues have been described in a series of articles (11, 23–26). Individual support groups made their own decisions about which affiliation to maintain.

Primary Publications

SMART's two primary publications (27, 28) are available only through SMART. The SMART newsletter is *S.M.A.R.T. Recovery: News and Views*.

Intended Membership

SMART is intended for individuals who desire to abstain from addictive behavior, or who are considering abstinence. Addictive behavior is understood as possibly arising from both substance use (e.g., psychoactive substances of all kinds, including alcohol, nicotine, caffeine, food, illicit drugs, and prescribed medications), and involvement in activities (e.g., gambling, sexual behavior, eating, spending, relationships, exercise, etc.). SMART assumes that there are degrees of addictive behavior, and that all individuals to some degree experience it. Individuals for whom the negative consequences of addictive behavior have become considerable are the ones likely to be considering or desiring abstinence.

Table 38.3   S.M.A.R.T. Recovery Purposes and Methods

1. We help individuals gain independence from addictive behavior.
2. We teach how to
   enhance and maintain motivation to abstain
   cope with urges
   manage thoughts, feelings and behavior
   balance momentary and enduring satisfactions
3. Our efforts are based on scientific knowledge, and evolve as scientific knowledge evolves.
4. Individuals who have gained independence from addictive behavior are invited to stay involved with us, to enhance their gains and help others.

Table from S.M.A.R.T. Recovery. S.M.A.R.T. Recovery purposes and methods (brochure). Beachwood, OH. Copyright S.M.A.R.T. Recovery, 1996.

Program

The SMART program is consistent with a cognitive-behavioral perspective, and views addictive behavior as a complex maladaptive behavior. The SMART Purposes and Methods statement is reprinted in Table 38.3.

There are four primary goals for an individual in the SMART program: motivational maintenance and enhancement, effective urge coping, rational thinking (leading to effective emotional and behavioral management), and lifestyle balance. In service of these goals many cognitive-behavioral and other psychological techniques are taught. With respect to changing addictive behavior itself, the program draws from established references of the cognitive-behavioral approach (e.g., 29–33). Self-help literature on addictive behavior (e.g., 10, 34–38), as well as cognitive-behavioral self-help literature on a broad range of topics, including mood management, assertiveness training, relationships, effective communication, and stress management is also recommended (39), and techniques derived from this literature are incorporated into the SMART program. Consistent with SMART's previous affiliation with RR, as well as its cognitive-behavioral orientation, REBT techniques and terms (8, 9) are a prominent aspect of the SMART program.

SMART does not employ "steps," or have a suggested sequence for change. It is assumed that each of the four primary goals will be important for most members, but the relative importance at different times, and the degree to which applicable ideas and techniques will need to be employed, is left to the individual. SMART suggests that there are as many routes to gaining independence from addictive behavior as there are individuals.

Although SMART limits its discussions to how to achieve abstinence, individuals unsure about adopting this goal are also encouraged to attend. SMART has a broad definition of abstinence, in part because individuals with any addictive behavior are invited to attend (e.g., abstinence from over involvement with food or sex, versus abstinence from all involvement, would be acceptable). SMART also encourages individuals unwilling to make a lifetime commitment to abstinence to consider a trial of abstinence.

Meeting Format

Meetings are open or closed to visitors according to local custom. Meetings begin with an opening statement by the Coordinator. The statement describes the four primary goals of the SMART program, and outlines the meeting to follow. Members begin by giving brief reports about recent successes they have experienced.

The major portion of the meeting follows, consisting of discussion guided by the Coordinator on the four primary goals of the SMART program. One of the principal discussion approaches is to consider "activating events" volunteered by the members. Activating events can include urges, life circumstance changes, thoughts, social interactions, or other experiences that lead or potentially lead to undesired emotions or behavior. Activating events are typically analyzed using Ellis' ABCDE method (8, 9). The Disputation step, in which irrational ideas are disputed, can draw upon the entire range of scientific knowledge about addictive behavior.

The formal meeting concludes with each member being asked to consider a personal homework project, which would put into action the ideas or techniques from the meeting that have been significant for the member. An informal discussion period follows, which includes socializing, the exchange of news, and the sale of publications.

Organizational Aspects

As of January, 1996, SMART reports approximately 200 meetings in 32 states. There are two part-time paid staff. The 15-member Board of Directors is composed primarily of addictive behavior professionals. An International Advisory Board is planned.

SMART meeting Coordinators have the opportunity to consult with a Professional Advisor, who typically is a behavioral health professional. Depending on local circumstances and traditions, either the Professional Advisor or the Coordinator handles administrative matters at the local level. Often a Professional Advisor consults with more than one Coordinator. SMART seeks inquiries from behavioral health professionals who may be interested in serving as Professional Advisors.

Empirical Findings

No studies of SMART have yet been published. One study is in progress.

CHOOSING AN ALTERNATIVE SUPPORT GROUP

If an individual has no experience with addictive behavior support groups, sampling all that are available would seem most sensible. If an individual has no strong preferences, 12-step groups would seem more desirable than the alternatives simply because of their availability and size (which increase the likelihood that suitable models of success would be identified). If alternatives are preferred, and more than one is reasonably proximate and not inappropriate for one's gender (WFS) or goal (MM), on what basis might one be selected over another? Although the information provided here may be helpful, probably the best test of compatibility is the individual's reaction to each available meeting. Because the quality of these meetings is quite dependent on the style and ability of the facilitator, it seems likely that the group environment the facilitator engenders may be a larger factor in the desirability of an individual meeting than the organization's official program or meeting format. Consequently, where more than one alternative is available, it should not be unexpected that an individual might attend selected meetings of each. Just as there is presumably a high degree of variability in the helpfulness of 12-step sponsors, there is presumably a high degree of variability in the helpfulness of the individual meetings of alternative support groups.

Excellent advice has been offered on how to integrate mental health treatment with 12-step attendance (40, 41). This advice is needed because of the apparent contradictions between these two perspectives. There appear to be far fewer of such contradictions for the individual attending an alternative. On the other hand, contradictions are likely to arise if the individual attending an alternative is also attending 12-step-oriented addictive behavior treatment.

If no suitable group is available, an option for the motivated individual, depending on the desired affiliation, would be to start one's own group. Given that teaching a subject is often the best way to learn it, this option has much to recommend it. The objection that those in early recovery should be guided by those in long-term recovery overlooks the fact that recoveries without this guidance occur routinely (42). If attending or starting a group is not an option, the literature of one or more of these alternatives may by itself be helpful. MM and SMART sponsor Internet discussion groups (called "listserves"), which may be of benefit to those who can access them. When there are not enough weekly meetings in a given locality to provide the level of support an individual desires, the literature and clinical experience suggest that some individuals may benefit from also attending 12-step groups (despite the programmatic contradictions).

Further research may provide guidance regarding matching individuals to addictive behavior support groups. However, the ultimate justification of a support group could not be established by an efficacy study. Millions have attended 12-step groups although there is little solid evidence of their efficacy. Support groups exist because recovering individuals choose to attend them. The primary question regarding these alternatives appears to be whether in the years ahead enough individuals will attend that the groups come to exist as equal members of the recovery community and not merely as "alternatives."

CONTACT INFORMATION

Women for Sobriety (WFS)
P.O. Box 618
Quakertown, PA 18951–0618
215-536-8026 (voice and fax)
WFSobriety@aol.com
http://www.mediapulse.com/wfs

Rational Recovery Systems (RR)
Box 800
Lotus, CA 95651
916-621-4374, 800–303-CURE (voice)
916-621-2667 (voice and fax)
rr@rational.org
http://www.rational.org/recovery

Moderation Management (MM)
P.O. Box 6005
Ann Arbor, MI 48106
313-677-6007 (voice)
To subscribe to MM (an Internet discussion group):
    Send message on next line to listserv@sjuvm.stjohns.edu
    subscribe MM yourfirstname yourlastname

Men for Sobriety (MFS)
(see Women for Sobriety)

S.M.A.R.T. Recovery (SMART)
24000 Mercantile Road, Suite 11
Beachwood, Ohio 44122
216-292-0220 (voice)
216-831-3776 (fax)
SRMail1@aol.com
To subscribe to SMARTREC (an Internet discussion group):
    Send message on next line to listserv@sjuvm.stjohns.edu
    subscribe SMARTREC yourfirstname yourlastname

Secular Organizations for Sobriety/Save Our Selves (SOS)
5521 Grosvenor Blvd.
Los Angeles, CA 90066
310-821-8430 (voice)
310-821-2610 (fax)
http://www.codesh.org/sos/

American Self-Help Clearinghouse
Northwest Covenant Medical Center
25 Pocono Road
Denville, NJ 07834
Group Information: 201–625-7101
Administration: 201–625-9565
201-625-9053 (TDD)
201-625-8848 (fax)

Acknowledgments. *The author gratefully acknowledges the review of relevant sections of this chapter by Jean Kirkpatrick and Beatrice (Cookie) Scott (WFS, MFS), Lois Trimpey (RR), Audrey Kishline (MM), Philip Tate, Michler Bishop, Rob Sarmiento, and Randy Cicen (SMART), and Jim Christopher (SOS). Vince Fox and Barbara McCrady provided conceptual guidance. Nevertheless, all opinions and any errors are attributable solely to the author. Kris Figueroa provided editorial assistance.*

References

1. American Self-Help Clearinghouse. The self-help source book. 5th edition. Denville, NJ: American Self-Help Clearinghouse, 1995.
2. Kirkpatrick J. Turnabout. New help for the woman alcoholic. New York: Bantam Books, 1990.
3. Kirkpatrick J. Goodbye hangovers, hello life: self-help for women. New York: Ballantine Books, 1986.
4. Women for Sobriety. Women and addictions: a way to recovery [brochure]. Quakertown, PA: Women for Sobriety, undated.
5. Kaskutas LA. What do women get out of self-help? Their reasons for attending Women for Sobriety and Alcoholics Anonymous. J Subst Abuse Treat 1994;11:185–195.
6. Kaskutas LA. An analysis of "Women For Sobriety." Berkeley, CA: University of California, 1993. Dissertation.
7. Talan BS. Power and control: predictors for the alcoholic woman's choice and effectiveness of treatment. Detroit, MI: University of Detroit, 1982. Dissertation.
8. Ellis A, Harper RA. A new guide to rational living. Englewood Cliffs, NJ: Prentice-Hall, 1975.
9. Ellis A, McInerney JF, DiGiuseppe R, Yeager RJ. Rational-emotive therapy with alcoholics and substance abusers. Elmsford, NY: Pergamon Press, 1989.
10. Trimpey J. The small book. New York: Delacorte Press, 1992.
11. Trimpey J. Rational Recovery update. The addictions newsletter [Newsletter of the American Psychological Association Division on Addictions] 1995;2:4, 14–15.
12. Trimpey J. The final fix for alcohol and drug addiction: addictive voice recognition technique. Lotus, CA: Lotus Press, 1994.
13. Trimpey J, Trimpey L. Taming, the feast beast. New York: Delacorte Press, 1994.
14. Galanter M, Egelko S, Edwards H. Rational Recovery: alternative to AA for addiction? Am J Drug Alcohol Abuse 1993;19:499–510.
15. Reinert DF, Estadt BK, Fenzel LM, Allen JP. Relationship of surrender and narcissism to involvement in alcohol. Alcohol Treat Q 1995;12:49–58.
16. Reinert DF. Effects of participation in alcohol self-help groups on surrender and narcissism among adult males. Baltimore, MD: Loyola College, 1993. Dissertation.
17. Atkinson DR, Abreu J, Ortiz-Bush Y, Brewer S. Mexican American and European American ratings of four alcoholism treatment programs. Hispanic J Behav Sci 1994;16:265–280.
18. Kishline A. Moderate drinking: The Moderation Management guide for people who want to reduce their drinking. New York: Crown, 1995.
19. Raistrick D, Dunbar G, Davidson R. Development of a questionnaire to measure alcohol dependence. Br J Addiction 1983;78:89–95.
20. Miller WR, Munoz RF. How to control your drinking: a practical guide to responsible drinking. Revised edition. Albuquerque: University of New Mexico, 1982.
21. Sanchez-Craig M. Saying when: how to quit drinking or cut down. Toronto: Addiction Research Foundation, 1993.
22. Sobell MB, Sobell LC. Problem drinkers: guided self-change treatment. New York: Guilford, 1993.
23. Bishop FM, Tate P, Horvath AT, Robb H. SMART Recovery/Rational Recovery update. The addictions newsletter [Newsletter of American Psychological Association Division on Addictions] 1995;2:4,12–13.
24. McCrady BS. Don Cahalan was right—the alcohol field does act like a "Ship of Fools": commentaries on "SMART Recovery/Rational Recovery update" and "Rational Recovery update." The addictions newsletter [Newsletter of the American Psychological Association Division on Addictions] 1995;2:5,16–17.
25. Trimpey J. Ship of fools or riverboat casino? Response to Barbara McCrady. The addictions newsletter [Newsletter of the American Psychological Association Division of Addictions] 1995;3:6,23–24.
26. Bishop M. SMART Recovery. Response to Barbara McCrady. The Addictions Newsletter [Newsletter of the American Psychological Association Division of Addictions] 1995;3:7–8.
27. SMART Recovery. Member's manual. Beachwood, OH: SMART Recovery, 1996.
28. SMART Recovery. Coordinator's manual. Beachwood, OH: SMART Recovery, 1996.
29. Marlatt GA, Gordon JR, eds. Relapse prevention: maintenance strategies in the treatment of addictive behaviors. New York: Guilford, 1985.
30. Miller WR, Rollnick S. Motivational interviewing: preparing people to change addictive behavior. New York: Guilford, 1991.
31. Monti PM, Abrams DB, Kadden RM, Cooney NL. Treating alcohol dependence: a coping skills training guide. New York: Guilford, 1989.
32. Beck AT, Wright FD, Newman CF, Liese BS. Cognitive therapy of substance abuse. New York: Guilford, 1993.
33. Prochaska JO, DiClemente CC, Norcross JC. In search of how people change: applications to addictive behavior. Am Psychol 1992;47:1102–1114.
34. Ellis A, Velten E. When AA doesn't work for you: rational steps to quitting alcohol. Fort Lee, NJ: Barricade, 1992.
35. Tate P. Alcohol. How to give it up and be glad you did. Altamonte Springs, FL: Rational Self-Help Press, 1993.
36. Fox V. Addiction, change and choice: the new view of alcoholism. Tucson, AZ: See Sharp, 1993.
37. Peele S, Brodsky A, Arnold M. The truth about addiction and recovery. New York: Simon & Schuster, 1989.
38. Prochaska JO, Norcross JC, DiClemente CC. Changing for good: the revolutionary program that explains the six stages of change and teaches you how to free yourself from bad habits. New York: William Morrow, 1994.
39. Santrock JW, Minnett AM, Campbell BD. The authoritative guide to self-help books. New York: Guilford Press, 1994.
40. McCrady B, Delaney, SI. Self-help groups. In: Hester RK, Miller WR, eds. Handbook of alcoholism treatment approaches: effective alternatives. Boston: Allyn & Bacon, 1995: 160–176.
41. Emrick CD. Alcoholics Anonymous and other 12-step groups. In: Galanter M, Kleber HD, eds. The American Psychiatric Press textbook of substance abuse treatment. Washington, DC: American Psychiatric Press, 1994:351–358.
42. Sobell LC, Cunningham JA, Sobell MB. Recovery from alcohol problems with and without treatment: prevalence in two population surveys. Am J Public Health 1996;86:966–972.

39   SECULAR ORGANIZATION FOR SOBRIETY

James R. Christopher

The Secular Organization for Sobriety (also known as SOS or Save Our Selves) is an abstinence–human support movement. Its effective self-empowerment method for achieving and maintaining a lasting sobriety, the Sobriety Priority Program, has helped thousands of alcoholics and addicts achieve and maintain sobriety, many of whom could not have done so in other programs.

WHAT IS SOS?

SOS is an alternative recovery method for those alcoholics or drug addicts who are uncomfortable with the spiritual content of widely available 12-step programs. SOS takes a reasonable, secular approach to recovery and maintains that sobriety is a separate issue from religion or spirituality. SOS credits the individual with achieving and maintaining his or her own sobriety. SOS respects recovery in any form, regardless of the path by which it is achieved. It is not opposed to or in competition with any other recovery programs. SOS supports healthy skepticism and encourages the use of the scientific method to understand alcoholism.

GENERAL PRINCIPLES

All those who sincerely seek sobriety are welcomed as members in any SOS group. SOS is not a spin-off of any religious group. There is no hidden agenda—SOS is concerned with sobriety, not spirituality. SOS seeks only to promote sobriety amongst those who suffer from alcoholism or other drug addictions. As a group, SOS has no opinion on outside matters and does not wish to become entangled in outside controversy.

Although sobriety is an individual responsibility, life does not have to be faced alone. The support of other alcoholics and addicts is a vital adjunct to recovery. In SOS, members share experiences, insights, information, strength, and encouragement in friendly, honest, anonymous, and supportive group meetings. To avoid unnecessary entanglements each SOS group is self-supporting through contributions from its members and refuses outside donations. Sobriety is the number one priority in an alcoholic's or addict's life. As such, he or she must abstain from all drugs or alcohol. Honest, clear, and direct communication of feelings, thoughts, and knowledge aids in recovery and in choosing nondestructive, nondelusional, and rational approaches to living sober and rewarding lives. As knowledge of drinking or addiction might cause a person harm or embarrassment in the outside world, SOS guards the anonymity of its membership and the contents of its discussions from those not within the group. SOS encourages the scientific study of alcoholism and addiction in all their aspects. SOS does not limit its outlook to one area of knowledge or theory of alcoholism and addiction.

HISTORY

In 1985, James Christopher, an alcoholic sober since 1978, published an account of the path he took to sobriety in *Free Inquiry* magazine, a secular humanist journal (1). This path had led Christopher from 17 years of a fearful and guilty alcoholism to a fearful and guilty sobriety with Alcoholics Anonymous (AA). Uncomfortable with the AA approach, Christopher broke from AA early in his recovery. He felt that there must be other alcoholics who wanted to achieve and maintain sobriety through personal responsibility and self-reliance rather than to turn one's life over to a "higher power." As a result of the tremendous response to the article from alcoholics and addicts who wanted to maintain sobriety as a separate issue from religion or spirituality, Christopher founded Secular Organizations for Sobriety. Its first self-help support group meeting was held in November, 1986, in North Hollywood, California. SOS has grown to over 2,000 meetings and over 20,000 members in the United States; with international affiliations, it numbers over 5,000 meetings and 100,000 members worldwide.

Christopher has since authored three books: *How to Stay Sober: Recovery without Religion* (2), *Unhooked: Staying Sober and Drug-Free* (3), and *SOS Sobriety: The Proven Alternative to 12-step Programs* (4). The SOS International Clearinghouse is a nonprofit organization based in Los Angeles; it publishes a quarterly newsletter.

PHILOSOPHY

Each SOS meeting is autonomous and held on an anonymous basis at no charge to participants, and stresses Christopher's "Sobriety Priority." The Sobriety Priority, accepted and maintained as a separate issue from anything else in the alcoholic's life, empowers one to choose his or her own plan or design for living. SOS deliberately offers no quality-of-life program and does not tell its members how to live. Consequently, SOS eschews "sponsorship" (the AA system of members with longer term sobriety acting as mentors to newcomers); instead, members approach each other as equals, respectful of diversity.

Research has shown that all people who drink, whether or not they are alcoholics, drink for the same reasons. Some will get hooked, others will not. One's original reasons for drinking may have dissipated over time or may remain in full force. But if one has acknowledged and accepted the fact that one cannot drink and get away with it, and if one maintains awareness of that fact as a required life-and-death necessity, one has no real choice. Therefore, drinking is not an option when one's survival is seriously threatened.

Sips of alcohol imprint on the limbic system as instantaneous pleasure, not pain. Sticking one's hand in a flame imprints as instantaneous pain. So one automatically avoids this behavior in the future. Alcohol avoidance can become immediate if a person accepts that alcohol threatens his or her survival. A person's recognition of his or her survival can compensate for that person's natural selective memory and negate denial. Rather than resolving issues that may have been one's original reasons to drink, rather than attempting to live in a certain way to avoid certain human emotions or circumstances any human being is likely to experience, one can choose to stay sober and to avoid alcohol "no matter what"—because no reason in the universe exists for a drink if one acknowledges and accepts that it threatens one's very survival. For alcoholics drink = pain, or drink = death. Survival is at stake. Therefore, the limbic system's false equation of alcohol with pleasure is challenged by passionate realizations of truth: "My name is Jim. I am a sober alcoholic. I cannot and do not drink no matter what, because I cannot drink and get away with it." This is not a statement about one's "character"; rather, it is an acknowledgment and acceptance of truth regarding the addict.

How do SOS members deal with their personal unresolved issues? Like most people, they (now being free to get on with their lives) can choose to work on certain aspects of themselves that they would like to change, perhaps with the aid of professional counseling, secular or spiritual; perhaps by way of returning to school or college, reading and exploring any of a number of fresh options. Recovering people—all people, really—are generally doing the best they can, moving at their own pace through life. As SOS members achieve and maintain sobriety, they tend to grow individually. Some issues in one's life may never come to a resolution. Knowing how to "do sobriety" as a protected separate issue does guarantee an end to problems with alcohol or other drugs; it does not guarantee that unrelated life circumstances will change without work.

As an abstinence movement, SOS offers a free-thought forum providing an informal support system for recovery. All persons grow at their own pace. SOS members share in confidence with each other their separate-issue life challenges. Some people initially attend some SOS meetings and then choose to attend no longer. Research has shown that many persons achieve a "clean and sober" lifestyle without support of any kind. Their recovery, as is the recovery of those in AA, Women for Sobriety, and other organizations, is as valid as anyone else's recovery.

SOS members tend to view SOS meetings as an awareness tool. Most do not "play out their lives" in daily meetings of any kind. Most members use the "citizens of the world" concept; i.e., members get on with their lives as clean and sober alcoholics or addicts, while continuing to take full advantage of SOS group support and to feel good from giving back support to those new to recovery.

The vast majority of members in any abstinence group interpret recovery as abstaining from all alcohol and drugs. However, some alcoholics and addicts also suffer from what treatment professionals call "dual diagnosis." They may be manic-depressive or schizophrenic, requiring medications responsibly prescribed by physicians to treat their physiological chemical imbalance. This is a medical matter, not an SOS "policy" matter.

SOS offers support from fellow alcoholics and addicts who can empathize from their own personal experiences and serve as models of successful long-term sobriety. SOS also offers a variety of recovery "tools": printed materials, audio and video tapes. SOS offers mutual respect, focusing on "doing sobriety," deliberately not offering a step program or "design for living." Although personal sobriety is not dependent on the continuing existence of SOS—and that is the general viewpoint of SOS members regarding dependency on any group—SOS fills a need, as evidenced by its rapid growth in the first decade of its existence.

THE SOBRIETY PRIORITY

The SOS program is offered as a suggested strategy. It can help people to achieve and maintain a lasting, continual abstinence from alcohol and drugs. Persons grappling with issues other than alcoholism (overeaters, gamblers, etc.) have successfully used the SOS approach as well. The Sobriety Priority approach for achieving and maintaining freedom from alcohol and other mind-altering drugs is a cognitive strategy. It can be applied on a daily basis to prevent relapse as long as one lives.

The Sobriety Priority approach respects the power of "nature" (genetic inheritance, progressive disease processes) and of "nurture" (learned habit, behaviors, and associations) by showing how to achieve the initial arrest of cellular addiction and stave off the chronic habits that result from this addiction.

The "cycle of addiction" contains three debilitating elements: chemical need (at the physiological cellular level), learned habit (chronic, drinking/using behaviors and associations), and denial of both need and habit. The cycle of alcohol addiction usually develops over a period of years. Cycles have been found to be much shorter with other drugs, especially cocaine. In all cases, however, the addiction becomes "Priority One," a separate issue from everything else. And as the addiction progresses, it begins to negate everything else. The cycle of addiction can be successfully replaced by another cycle: the cycle of sobriety. This cycle contains three essential elements: acknowledgment of one's addiction to alcohol or drugs, acceptance of one's disease or habit, and prioritization of sobriety as the primary issue in one's life.

The daily cognitive application of a new "Priority One," the Sobriety Priority, as a separate issue arrests the cycle of addiction. It frees the sober alcoholic or addict to experience "everything else" by teaching him or her to associate "everything else" with sobriety, not with drinking or using behaviors. The cycle of sobriety remains in place only so long as the sober alcoholic or addict cognitively chooses to continue to acknowledge the existence of his or her alcoholism or drug addiction.

The Sobriety Priority, applied daily, gradually weakens alcohol and drug associations, halting the cycle of addiction and allowing time for new associations to form as one experiences life without addictive chemicals. As one continues to make peace with the facts regarding his or her arrested addiction—that is, as one comes to prefer a sober lifestyle: one longs to preserve it, to respect the arrested chemical addiction, and to protect the new, sober life.

FAMILY AND FRIENDS

Many family members and friends of alcoholics and individuals addicted to other drugs come to a program of recovery reaching out for help. They come desperately looking for help in the way of answers to their questions about chemical dependency and the difficulties in their relationships that this dependency has caused. Although they are not the ones who are addicted, their lives have been greatly affected by the addiction of someone they love.

Until these family members and friends learn about chemical dependency, their well-meaning actions may further alienate relationships; they may escalate conflict and violence with the chemically dependent person.

By coming to SOS, family members and friends can learn about the Cycle of Addiction. When they can perceive the phases of chemical need and denial of learned habits within the chemically dependent person, the Cycle of Sobriety will be understood as an individual journey for that person. It is then that supportive action by the family and friends can begin, improved relationships can begin, and family recovery can begin.

This path to recovery starts with understanding that sobriety is the responsibility of the addicted individual. The family has its own recovery cycle: that of recovering from the feelings of being responsible for the chemical addiction. Knowledge of addiction and sobriety cycles can free family members and friends of the chemically dependent loved one to rightfully assume responsibility for their own lives only.

THE SOS MEETING

Purpose

SOS groups provide a regular coming together of people with similar problems and concerns in a nonjudgmental and safe atmosphere. The members of such a group are free to work out its structure and the format of its meetings. Meetings usually include a free-thought forum for the exchange of information, experiences, and ideas. This exchange is always done in ways that are not threatening to the members and which help validate to the person in pain the realness of his or her experience. The meeting sometimes becomes the one anchor in the new member's current stormy existence.

Self-Help

SOS groups are also "self-help" groups in that they operate nonprofessionally, offering no medical advice or psychotherapy. Instead, the members share their own experiences and understandings, their personal failures and victories. In time, the new member begins to discover what is needed to fit their particular situation. In general, the goal of each group is to support its

members while they learn to cope with frustration, despair, and the isolation that brought most of them to the group initially. In addition, each group may want to define its own specific goals and emphasis, if any—always with sobriety as the priority. Unless sobriety is the priority for alcoholics, no amount of personal growth in other areas of life is likely to bring the needed recovery.

Group Variations

SOS groups, originally intended for alcoholics, have been extremely flexible in accommodating family members and friends of alcoholics and addicts, compulsive overeaters, gamblers, and those addicted to drugs other than alcohol. Some groups of family members are beginning to meet separately now (as SOS support groups) and other groups are in the making. SOS has begun to explore the open versus special interest group meetings. There are many possibilities. Groups could expand to include all those harmed by dysfunctional families or relationships, regardless of the initial cause of the problem. SOS groups can also be formed wherever a secular alternative is needed for compulsive overeaters, smokers, addicts of a specific drug or of drugs in general, compulsive gamblers, people with sexual obsessions, adult children of alcoholics (or from dysfunctional homes in general), or any other group needing to meet for mutual support. Adults may want to start SOS meetings for teenagers or younger children using drugs or living in dysfunctional homes. The only requirement for an SOS group is that the environment be secular (i.e., have no religious or spiritual requirements) and promote total abstinence.

Secular Distinction

The word that distinguishes our groups from other widely available groups is the word "secular." There are many groups that fit into the category of self-help support groups and that offer roads to recovery from a multitude of problems, but most of these groups imply strongly (and sometimes directly state) that true recovery without dependence on supernatural help is simply not possible. There is usually an insistence that their programs are "spiritual" rather than "religious," but in the final analysis, many secular people end up feeling alienated by these meetings and find recovery in these groups very difficult, if not impossible.

Needless to say, it should never be necessary to compromise integrity in the search for recovery. Nor should anybody be asked to pay lip service to beliefs or rituals that are alien to that person just to find acceptance and help.

SOS was founded to provide a neutral ground where the alcoholic or addict can safely explore an individual path to recovery. While many of us are atheists, agnostics, and secular humanists, many others are theists of one form or another who simply want a secular recovery environment—separation of church and recovery. There is no reason why religion should ever become a main topic of discussion in SOS meetings; such discussions are potentially offensive and generally not productive. The focus is recovery, as a separate issue.

STUDIES OF SOS MEMBERSHIP

At least two academic studies of SOS members have been completed. London et al. (5) surveyed SOS members in 1988 and 1989 and found that most respondents were white, college-educated nontheists. Most respondents had undergone professional treatment for alcoholism, and almost half (47%) had been told by a treatment professional that long-term sobriety is impossible unless he or she "turned your life over to a higher power." Almost all respondents had attended AA, and most (76%) reported having been told by a member of AA that it would be impossible to remain sober without reliance upon a higher power. Several respondents who had been told by their treatment professional that sobriety required reliance on a higher power remarked that they considered the treatment harmful rather than beneficial. Fifty percent of the respondents who indicated that they had been told by fellow AA members that "it would be impossible to stay sober unless they turned their lives over to a higher power" remarked that participation in AA was harmful rather than beneficial.

Almost all (97%) of the respondents indicated that they had abused alcohol. Of this group, 4% reported having used at least once since attending SOS, and 3% reported having used problematically since attending SOS. Respondents reported being alcohol and drug free for 31.8 months on average, with the longest period of abstinence 168 months (14 years).

More recently, Connors and Dermen (6) surveyed 158 SOS members from 22 states. The questionnaires were distributed at regular SOS meetings throughout the country. Respondents were 73% male, 27% female, and 56% of the respondents had obtained a college degree or higher. Many (83.5%) of respondents had a religious affiliation as children; only 29.7% indicated that they currently had a religious affiliation. A majority (70%) described themselves as atheists or agnostics.

Respondents to the Connors study indicated that most (70%) were currently abstinent and had been abstinent an average of 6.3 years. The average length of time respondents had been drinking problematically is 14 years. About half (49%) had sought professional help from a private therapist, 42% had undergone inpatient treatment, 39% had undergone outpatient treatment, and 26% had undergone medical detoxification.

Almost all (96%) of the respondents had an AA background prior to attending SOS. Sixty-one percent of respondents indicated that they do not plan to attend AA in the future; 85% found SOS to be helpful in maintaining their sobriety, whereas 56% found AA helpful; 23% found AA to be neither helpful nor harmful; and 19% found AA attendance to be harmful to their sobriety.

Typical comments from respondents indicate that what they like least about AA are the religious or spiritual components, and what they like best are the people and social interactions. Most respondents liked SOS for its lack of religion or dogma, the lack of rigid rules or procedures, and openness and/or comfortable environment. The most common complaint about SOS was that there were not as many meetings available.

CASE STUDIES IN SOBRIETY

Many SOS members have shared their experiences over the years in the *SOS International Newsletter*. The following letter emphasizes the tolerance members feel to pursue their sobriety in the best way possible for them:

I celebrated my fourth month of sobriety July 4th. When I first went to an SOS meeting I was impressed by the lack of "musts," spoken or unspoken, in more typical 12-step meetings. The only real and very sensible "must" I remember from my first SOS meeting was "just don't drink *no matter what.*" Making sobriety the top priority in my life is the SOS method. Everything else having to do with the quality of my life is external to this Sobriety Priority.

It really works. I sometimes feel that my use of the Sobriety Priority keeps my sobriety locked in a good strong safe—fireproof, bombproof, drunkproof.

I attend groups other than SOS for the fellowship, the sharing of experiences, and the wisdom of other people who share this disease. When it comes to it, though, I feel most comfortable in SOS.

I've put together what I call an Alcoholic's Toolkit. It's made up of literature, tapes, thoughts, things I've seen or heard about the disease and experience of alcoholism. I use it when wanted or needed to help me keep my sobriety. It's an eclectic toolkit—a little from here, a little from there. It's my way of staying sober, using whatever is necessary at any given time.

Nobody at SOS has told me I won't stay sober with my Alcoholic's Toolkit and the Sobriety Priority. Nobody in SOS has told me that I should attend only SOS meetings or read only certain chosen literature pertinent to alcoholism.

The feeling I have at SOS meetings is one of freedom. I don't have to walk or talk in any way but my own way in order to be sober, as long as I remember that I have a killer disease that can never be forgotten and must be acknowledged daily.

Sobriety through SOS is a reality I can understand. Sobriety comes from *me* with a little help from my friends.

Since 1987, SOS has provided recovery materials to prison personnel and inmates who start SOS meetings. This letter to SOS is representative of correspondence from incarcerated persons seeking options in their recovery:

I am an inmate. I am also a hard-core drunk and have been for most of my adult life. I have been drunk and in trouble with the law since 1972.

I am attending the prison's AA group and just received my certificate for attending. It has not been easy for me because I am not a believer in God, or a higher power.

My mother has sent me articles about SOS and the book *How to Stay Sober*. Sometimes after our meetings I am so frustrated I have to come back to my cell and read your book. Our group is very religious in orientation. I try to question their ways but am always shot down.

The leader of our group is a part-time preacher and counselor. He has told me at least twenty times that "if you don't believe in a Higher Power you are doomed," and also "you will come around sooner or later." I have few friends and am mostly shunned because of my realist views. His AA group is "the only store in town." I have no choice but to attend.

There are two or three men here who back me and are not afraid to challenge the majority. I also have my family supporting me in sharing my views.

The AA leader said last night that there are no people that have sober lives without "H.P." He is wrong.

References

1. Christopher J. Sobriety without superstition. Free Inquiry 1985;5(3):53.
2. Christopher J. How to stay sober. Recovery without religion. Buffalo, NY: Prometheus Books, 1988.
3. Christopher J. Unhooked. Staying sober and drug free. Buffalo, NY: Prometheus Books, 1989.
4. Christopher J. SOS sobriety: the proven alternative to 12-step programs. Buffalo, NY: Prometheus Books, 1992.
5. London WM, Courchaine KE, Yoho DL. Recovery experiences of SOS members. Preliminary findings. In: Christopher J, ed. SOS sobriety: the proven alternative to 12-step programs. Buffalo, NY: Prometheus Books, 1992:45–59.
6. Connors G, Derman K. Characteristics of participants in Secular Organizations for Sobriety (SOS). Am J Drug Alcohol Abuse 1996;22(2):281–295.

40   THE THERAPEUTIC COMMUNITY

William B. O'Brien and Charles J. Devlin

Despite constantly shrinking resources, today's Therapeutic Community (TC) has responded to an ever increasing volume and complexity of service requirements, all without compromising the integrity of its unique model of treatment. It has grown from a home-spun response to the problem of drug addiction into a sophisticated institution concerned with issues regarding credentialing, managed care, the needs of special populations, and the demands of multiple contractors and the criminal justice system.

The TC today is represented by a national professional association, Therapeutic Communities of America, Inc., which represents 400 sites across the United States. These sites have a total treatment capacity of 100,000 (1).

The TC has evolved to meet the needs of its target population by developing many specialized programs, both within its mainstream programs and through specialized facilities. These programs address the needs of these special populations: women; the HIV positive or at high risk for HIV; pregnant teenagers; the homeless; the terminally ill; the mentally ill chemical abuser; veterans suffering from post-traumatic stress syndrome; the incarcerated, probated, paroled and alternative-to-incarceration client; and siblings and parents of substance abusers.

OVERVIEW

The TC is founded on a social learning model that fosters behavioral and attitudinal change as a result of the client's membership in a community. Through this intensive, peer-based approach, the client learns pro-social values and addresses self-destructive, anti-social behavioral patterns. Whether in a traditional residential setting or a community-based ambulatory setting, most TCs offer individual and group counseling, family services, medical and mental health services, and vocational and educational services. In the residential and daycare setting, the client also attends "morning meetings," "encounter groups," "static groups," "request groups," and "seminars." In addition, the client must learn and use pro-social skills and assume responsibilities to help maintain the treatment community. As the client progresses in treatment, he or she earns more challenging and responsible assignments and a higher level of concomitant status. The TC is a powerful concept designed to provide its clients with the tools for growth on an emotional, spiritual, and intellectual plane (2).

Throughout its history, the TC has remained a leader in the field of addiction services by gauging the developing needs of its target population and offering therapies that respond to those needs. The demographic characteristics of the TC have changed markedly since its inception. In the 1960s, clients were largely heroin addicts; today, crack cocaine has become the overwhelming, primary drug of choice for adult TC residents. In 1995, *Daytop Village* and *Phoenix House Foundation* in New York reported that 75–80% of their adult populations report cocaine as their drug of choice, while only 10–15% of their respective populations were primarily heroin users (3). In contrast, only 22% of Daytop's adolescent admissions preferred cocaine, while 78% preferred marihuana and/or alcohol. Despite these figures, which indicate a lesser adolescent involvement with "hard" drugs, the TC has had to accommodate a dramatic influx of adolescents aged 12–16 years who exhibit serious dysfunction in school, family, and society. The TC has also experienced a great influx of women clients. Philadelphia, for example, experienced a 300% increase in female admissions from 1979 to 1989.

Perhaps connected to the shift in primary drugs, the TC population has exhibited a pattern of increased psychopathology (4), with increased incidents of psychosis, depression, and lower IQ scores. Likewise, with the advent of HIV and tuberculosis (TB), as well as increased incidents of sexually transmitted diseases (STDs), anemia, liver dysfunction, and pelvic inflammatory disease, the TC has needed to respond with extensive prevention and medical treatment initiatives. Parental substance abuse has also risen markedly as a coexisting factor for adult and adolescent residents. Upon admission, 49% of Daytop's adolescents report that immediate family members abuse alcohol and 43% of their parents abuse illegal substances (5). *Odyssey House* of New York reports that 70% of its clients are second-generation substance abusers. Cognizant of the role that families play in the client's substance abuse and of the future implications for children of substance abusers, the TC has expanded its services to families through parent and sibling support groups, programs for children and pregnant or postpartum women, and increasingly accessible adult outpatient services (whose clients often have children in adolescent programs). Finally, although the TC has historically serviced substance abusers in the criminal justice system, today close to half of Daytop's admissions arrive with a legal condition that they accept treatment.

TC INITIATIVES AND SPECIAL POPULATIONS

Mothers in Recovery Program

The TC model was originally applied to male addicts only (6). Substance abusing women have been traditionally under-served (7), while the need and demand for treatment has markedly increased. In New York City, between 1985 and 1990, the number of women using cocaine during pregnancy quadrupled. Some research indicates that, during the 1980s, the increase of cocaine use during pregnancy was 3000% for Los Angeles and 500% for New York (8). A nationwide survey indicates that 16% of all newborns tested positive for cocaine. According to the General Accounting Office, between 10 and 30% of such infants will be placed in foster-care at an average cost of $15,000 per year and an average stay of 4–5 years (although placement of an HIV-positive child may cost as much as $500,000 per year and the average annual cost of frequently necessary special education is $17,000 per year over twelve years).

In response to demand, an increasing number of women's TC initiatives began to emerge during the late 1980s and early 1990s. TCs became aware that women often avoided residential treatment for fear of separation from their children and were unable to attend outpatient treatment because of a lack of child care. In addition, many programs offered no services to pregnant women.

Despite difficulties in licensing and funding, residential pregnant women, mothers, and children programs have been implemented by many TCs. These programs allow women to receive residential treatment without being separated from their children. For example, in 1993, *APPLE* on New York's Long Island began its Mother-and-Child-Program for pregnant women. The 20-bed TC houses both the mother and her children, provides prenatal and pediatric care, and uses all the TC tools, including individual, group and family counseling, and vocational/educational training. The women receive instruction in Lamaze, infant care, and parenting skills. Children are supervised by certified child care workers while the women participate in therapeutic activities. *Operation PAR* in Florida has fashioned another approach to providing residential treatment for women. It transports their children to the facility three times per week for an after-school program, dinner with their parent, and support groups (9).

In light of the difficulty of locating bed space for pregnant and postpartum women and their children, *AMITY* of Arizona has begun Las Madres, which provides a wide variety of treatment and educational services to mothers and children for a three-month period or until appropriate placement in long-term treatment. *Marathon* of New England has also begun offering workshops to treatment providers throughout Vermont on how to treat pregnant substance abusers.

Daytop operates its Mothers In Recovery (MIR) program through funding from the New York City Child Welfare Administration. Daytop's MIR program is a voluntary, outpatient program, serving pregnant and postpartum women. It combines drug-free substance abuse treatment with medical, educational, and vocational services. Individual treatment plans take into account each woman's needs and schedule. Certified child care workers attend to the infants during their mother's treatment sessions. The program provides health education, prenatal, Lamaze childbirth education and parenting classes. The clients also attend health awareness seminars to educate them about HIV, AIDS, and STDs; specialized groups meet to discuss partner and family issues, sexual abuse, codependency, bereavement, and infant massage. Many of these groups invite the client's significant others to participate.

Daytop's highly successful MIR program has been in existence since 1989. In its first five years, it has serviced a total population of 1380 women; approximately 126 children were born drug-free following the treatment of their mothers. Of these women, 48% had 2–3 children at the time of treatment and 30% had four or more children; which indicates the number of lives positively affected and foster care monies saved due to the availability of treatment for these women (10).

Dual Diagnosis Clients

The combination of substance abuse and psychiatric disorders has become increasingly prevalent among TC clients and those seeking admission to the TC. Among hospitalized psychiatric patients, prevalence rates for a coexisting substance abuse problem range from 25 to 50% (11). Among substance abuse treatment admissions, studies have indicated that, depending on the treatment modality, 50–90% of substance abusers admitted to outpatient, inpatient, hospitals, methadone maintenance, and residential TCs have dual diagnosis (14), "although frank psychosis is the exception" (12).

Commonly found dual disorders include major depression with cocaine addiction, alcoholism with panic disorder, and poly-drug addiction with borderline personality disorder. The trend is toward "increased psychological disturbance" among TC clients (13).

According to the Center for Substance Abuse Treatment, coexisting psychiatric disorders may inhibit the client's full integration into the TC:

For example, patients with anxiety and phobias may fear and resist . . . group meetings. Depressed people may be too unmotivated and lethargic to participate in treatment. Patients with psychotic or manic symptoms may exhibit bizarre behavior and poor interpersonal relations during treatment, especially during group activities. Such behavior may be misinterpreted as signs of treatment resistance or symptoms of addiction relapse. (14, p. 3)

While maintaining the TC concept, many programs have therefore developed modified TC modalities which respond to the needs of the mentally ill chemical abuser (MICA). At some TC-MICA programs, modifications include shorter duration of meetings and activities; more meetings led by staff rather than clients; greater amount of time spent in group and individual discussion groups; a greater emphasis on staff role modeling for instruction and assistance; more individualized, non-hierarchical determination of work assignments; more "time-out" provided; and more immediate individual counseling.

Odyssey Residential Care Center for Adults in New York specializes in treatment of the homeless who have psychiatric disabilities and a substance abuse problem. It is a structured, long-term, modified TC offering psychiatric services, substance abuse treatment, assistance in daily living, basic and remedial education, and work-skills training. These basic elements are deemed vital to the client's return to independent living. *Aurora* of Queens, New York, also has a MICA program, specializing in the treatment of adolescents. New York's *Project Return* uses a "mainstream" approach, which mixes dual-diagnosed clients with the general population.

Adolescent Services

Adolescent populations have presented the TC with many significant questions with regard to how, if at all, adolescent treatment should differ from traditionally adult TC treatment:

- The TC's response to delinquency apart from substance abuse
- Dysfunctional family systems
- Educational difficulties
- Lack of motivation and denial
- The use of external systems such as criminal justice and family pressure to induce retention in treatment
- Marihuana and alcohol use (the drugs of preference for most adolescents)
- Coed versus single-sex treatment
- Appropriate duration of stay

TC tools and procedures are sometimes called into question where the treatment of adolescents is concerned: What level of confrontation is appropriate? What hierarchical job functions should adolescents assume in support of the community?

Nationwide, it is estimated that one in five TC clients are adolescents between the ages of 12 and 21. Most TCs have developed entirely separate treatment tracks and facilities for adolescents. Although it is economically advantageous to mix the populations, as adult residents perform better as "surrogate staff" than adolescents, the mixing of populations may lead to the "turning out" of a younger client by more experienced, heavier drug-using, and more seriously criminally involved adults. In fact, this phenomenon has been experienced even within adolescent programs that mix under 16-year-old clients with those age 17–21. At Daytop, if at all possible, the younger client receives residential treatment in a short-term facility and is then returned to family and ambulatory treatment. Most of the clients age 18–21 have a more extensive history of substance abuse and criminality, which calls for treatment in Daytop's long-term residential facility, a re-entry period and, often, participation in its Independent-Living Program. Therefore, a natural age segregation generally occurs. Although Daytop continues to provide coed treatment, experience has also shown the difficulties of providing such treatment to divergent age groups in a residential setting.

Daytop has enhanced substance abuse treatment, intervention, prevention, and education services to adolescents. It has emphasized a holistic approach to drug-free care, using an interdisciplinary, professional staff, proven drug-free clients and family members to provide a wide variety of services to accommodate the influx of adolescents and their special needs. Since 1972, Daytop New York has established seven community-based outreach centers and three residential units, providing a full continuum of adolescent-specific substance abuse treatment, prevention, education, and family services. Residential and daycare members attend school on-site and participate in groups, individual counseling, and other therapeutic activities or, if needing a lower level of intervention, attend an after-school program of group and individual counseling. Daytop's adolescent residential facilities include a 30-day assessment and treatment center, a short-term facility (1–6 months), a long-term facility (8–12 months), as well as Re-Entry and Independent Living Program. All Daytop facilities offer full high school and GED programs, family therapy, parent support groups, and sibling support groups (for Daytop clients' siblings age 8–16), as well as medical and mental health services as needed.

Daycare members participate 5 half-days per week in a highly-structured family environment, emphasizing positive peer support and self-help role modeling as catalysts for change. Accordingly, Daycare members take on facility chores to foster responsible attitudes, participate in daily morning meetings to discuss house issues and plans, participate in recreational activities, deal with confrontations and peer interaction issues, and learn to plan and account for their free-time activities when they are away from the Outreach Center.

Youth assessed as appropriate for residential care are admitted to Daytop's Adolescent Diagnostic Unit for 30 days. The program conducts a thorough diagnostic evaluation that includes medical, psychological, and educational testing. During this period, the youth receives individual and group counseling, family therapy, and a full school program. Client data are gleaned from a series of interviews with staff in the various disciplines, i.e., social work, educational, family, vocational/educational, psychological, and alcohol counseling. The information is then compiled and a comprehensive treatment plan is designed to meet the individual's needs. The particulars of this plan are presented to the individual's parents or guardians for consultation. Family sessions and participation are of primary importance to the evaluation.

Upon completion of the 30-day period, a youngster will be rotated to an Outreach Center or a residential facility in Millbrook, New York, for 1–6 months of short-term treatment or the Fox Run facility in Rhinebeck, New York, for 8–12 months of long-term residential treatment. A client's age, degree of prior substance abuse, and family support are key factors in determining whether to rotate the resident to outpatient or to short-term or long-term residential treatment.

For clients who complete short-term treatment at Millbrook, rotation to an Outreach Center follows. For clients who complete long-term treatment, rotation to the Adolescent Re-Entry Unit at Far Rockaway, Queens, follows. In Re-Entry, youngsters prepare for re-entering the community in a sheltered, supportive environment. Upon completion of the re-entry phase, youngsters may then participate in aftercare groups at an Outreach Center to continue to work on readjustment issues. Daytop also offers an Independent Living Program designed for youth age 16–21 who cannot return home, as an interim step toward self-reliance and independent living. This program teaches youth the skills necessary to live independently and responsibly while providing them with safe, hospitable, independent housing on Daytop's Far Rockaway property. The time frame for the Independent Living Program is determined by the youth's individual needs.

For the adolescent with a history of limited drug-use who is still functioning at school, Daytop's after-school/after-work program offers weekly individual counseling and group counseling twice a week on an early evening and/or weekend schedule.

Family therapy is an integral part of adolescent treatment. Daytop's experience indicates that family therapy and overall family participation has a direct impact upon adolescent client retention and success (15). Studies support this widely held view within the TC treatment field (16). Daytop uses a "solution focused approach" to family therapy, which views the family as part of the solution rather than the problem. During regularly scheduled family therapy sessions, family members are engaged in a mutual support system, where they gain a better understanding of their roles in the treatment process, develop healthy interpersonal relationships, and learn positive communication patterns. The Daytop Family Association provides weekly sibling groups for prevention, education, and support services for siblings age 8–16 of youth in treatment.

The Family Association offers weekly parent support groups to families whose children are now in, have been in, or have refused to accept treatment at Daytop. These support groups encourage individual growth and teach parents how to provide discipline and a structured environment, demanding responsibility from their troubled child.

As previously mentioned, divergent approaches to adolescent treatment have emerged within the TC movement. Some TCs have significantly modified the traditional, hierarchical, peer-based TC model by increasing reliance on adult professional staff; others retain a stricter adherence to the traditional TC concept. The former approach is exemplified by the programs of *Abraxas* in Pennsylvania and the latter approach by Daytop, especially its peer education program. Both approaches have proven successful, although more research may be required.

The Abraxas approach modifies the traditional tools of the TC for use in its adolescent facilities. For instance, Abraxas no longer uses a confrontational approach and conducts "issue groups" rather than encounter groups. They do not use a hierarchy of jobs corresponding to status, nor does any adolescent have authority over any other adolescent. However, they do have three levels of status depending on behavior, which have corresponding levels of privileges.

In contrast, the traditional TC modality is implemented more in Daytop treatment, including the assignment of resident responsibility for house chores, the reward of corresponding status as the resident progresses in treatment and job functions, resident leadership of seminars and morning meetings, and the use of peer-based role-modeling as incentives for change.

In addition, Daytop has recently developed a pilot project, the peer education program. While improving and preserving the TC model's integrity,

the project seeks to address the following problems that the TC has experienced in treating adolescents:

- The lack of same-age staff to serve as role models rather than parental figures.
- The lack of vocational opportunities for adolescents after treatment, leading to a sense of hopelessness in the later stages of treatment.
- The difficulties that adolescents experience during the re-entry phase of treatment in remaining committed to their personal development in the face of negative peer and family pressure.
- The lack of a continuing opportunity to do service for others as an integral part of their lives, as well as a lack of opportunity to do meaningful, paid work.
- Less than optimal retention rates in adolescent day treatment.

The peer education program has significantly enhanced peer-based role-modeling by placing a group of about six adolescents on stipend from various re-entry and ambulatory sites into a central ambulatory facility to function as mentors and counselors four days a week. In addition, it provides for an intensive didactic training and personal development group, once a week in another facility.

To date, five adolescents have successfully completed the training program. Three have become salaried counselors within Daytop's adolescent program, one continues to work as a peer educator pending his high school graduation (at which point he will be hired) and one, who is only 15 years old, has returned to high school and continues in the second stage of treatment. Initial evaluation indicates a 94% increase in overall client retention at the peer education site during the course of the program.

In sum, it is Daytop's position that the more the staff assume the TC roles traditionally reserved for residents, the further removed they become from the strength of the TC model. Becoming a service-delivery model limits the adolescent's personal investment, responsibility, self-actualization, and many of the ideals that the TC seeks to foster. One great success has been the realization that "doing to" and "doing for" fails to work. The core-benefit of the TC comes when the resident grows, unfolds, and blossoms into an individual who can "do it" for himself or herself. While Abraxas retains much of this philosophy, its decreased emphasis on hierarchy and confrontation remains a ripe topic for debate and investigation.

To address the issue of adolescent delinquency apart from substance abuse, Abraxas developed a "Drug-Sellers Program," which has gained national attention. It is interesting that Abraxas found that those referred by the criminal justice system as "non–drug using" drug-sellers actually had as much history of drug usage as the substance abuse referrals. Among both populations, alcohol and marihuana are the primary drugs of choice, a factor which often misleads judicial personnel to conclude that drugs are not a factor in the criminality. Thus the "Drug-Sellers Program" may be a necessary tool to induce judges to make alternative-to-incarceration referrals for adolescents that they would not otherwise consider. Daytop has noted a similar problem in trying to dismantle parental denial about the seriousness of a child's alcohol or marihuana problem. Such denial must often be countered with an emphasis on truancy, incorrigibility, and other behavioral problems before the parents will support the child's treatment.

Daytop and Phoenix House have recently proposed the beginning of programs for "drug-involved" youthful offenders, which will base admission on drug-related criminality rather than substance abuse levels. This proposed project will be discussed below in the context of alternative-to-incarceration programming. However, at this juncture, there is an overwhelming need for societal recognition of alcohol and marihuana abuse and drug-dealing as critical problems for today's youth.

Alternative-To-Incarceration and the Therapeutic Community

There can be no doubt as to the urgent need for substance abuse treatment for the offender population, whether provided in prison, in the form of an alternative-to-incarceration (ATI) or in a recidivism-reduction program. Approximately 80% of parolees, probationers, and criminal offenders have a substance abuse problem, which had an impact on their criminal history (17). Approximately 74% of New York State's inmate population has been identified as drug users. The National Institute of Drug Abuse (NIDA) estimates that 60–75% of prisoners with a background of heroin or cocaine use do not receive treatment and resume drug use within three months of release (18). Studies have shown that each dollar invested in treatment returns 2–20 dollars to society by reducing recidivism.

ATI programming is not a new concept for the TC. In 1963, Daytop pioneered the first court-diversion program as an ATI when it established an experimental project in Staten Island, New York, to treat 25 addict-probationers. In the ensuing years, TCs often worked with judges, defense lawyers, and district attorneys to arrange for treatment when the only other alternative would have been prison.

Formal ATI programs flourished in the 1990s. In October of 1990, the Kings County (NY) District Attorney's Office began a program, Drug Treatment Alternative-to-Prison (DTAP), which diverts predicate-felon/drug offenders from prison to residential TCs. DTAP offers eligible defendants 15–24 months of residential TC treatment in Daytop Village and Samaritan Village. The district attorney defers prosecution for participants in the program and the charges are reduced or dismissed if they successfully complete treatment. Because the defendants otherwise face mandatory incarceration, they are motivated to remain in treatment, and their retention-rate has been very high. The Kings County DTAP program has become a prototype for other district attorney-based ATIs.

In October of 1990, the Brooklyn Treatment Alternative to Street Crime (TASC) program assessed, advocated for, and placed into TC treatment its first predicate-felon. Funded by the New York City Department of Probation, as of 1996 this program has placed 521 predicate felons in treatment. Directed by a TC graduate and employing a preponderance of TC graduate staff, the program serves as a deferred sentencing intervention on behalf of defendants who have at least one prior felony conviction and are presently indicted on a felony. TASC screens, assesses, and matches the defendant to the appropriate treatment program.

The residential, ATI client referred by DTAP or TASC receives traditional TC treatment, which uses the self-help approach and relies on the use of program graduates as counselors and role models. The program is highly-structured and residents progress through stages; acquiring more responsibility and personal freedom in each new stage. Residents receive group, individual, and family therapy, as well as vocational and educational training. The re-entry phase focuses on preparing the residents for return to the community. Residents must have employment and housing plans in place before they can complete DTAP or TASC.

In an outpatient modality, Daytop and other TCs, such as Marathon in Vermont and Samaritan House in New York, have attempted to address the problem of moving clients from the criminal justice system and into treatment in a coherent and cost-effective way. These efforts may be more aptly characterized as recidivism reduction programs, since they generally treat the client during a term of probation or parole. Thus, treatment serves as a supplement to a term of imprisonment or probation and not as an alternative to such sanctions. In the present political climate, which emphasizes toughness on criminals, it is likely that the criminal justice system will increase use of this modality.

Daytop and other TCs have devised specific outpatient programs for clients referred from departments of parole and probation. At Daytop, clients are seen under contractual agreement with the referring departments. The design of these programs calls for group and individual sessions for each client, urinalysis at each visit, and psychiatric evaluations for those clients who are in need of that intervention. Clients agree to allow the program to divulge information to their parole or probation officers regarding attendance, results of urinalysis, progress in treatment, cooperation in treatment, and prognosis.

Clients serviced in Daytop's probation and parole projects fall into three basic categories: those whose full treatment will be the outpatient regime, who can and will successfully stay drug free in that modality; those who will not be able to stay drug free as an outpatient and will be geared toward residential treatment; and those who are not going to make it in either modality. Although the last category includes a small percentage of clients referred to

psychiatric or mental health settings or who opt for methadone treatment, the vast majority of these clients are simply unable to be reached by treatment and will, in most cases, be incarcerated, remain on probation, or become parole violators.

Clients in the second category, those being geared towards residential treatment, also need a period of outpatient treatment. Daytop's programs are specifically designed to help these clients change their perception of residential treatment as being punitive. The client who has been incarcerated is loathe to go directly into another restrictive environment. Often, the program will allow clients time to demonstrate to themselves that they are not making it as outpatients and then offers residential treatment as a solution to their overwhelming problems. If staff can build rapport, they can convince the client that treatment is preferable to incarceration. In this case, the TC graduate is the best person to advocate and offer outreach for residential referrals.

The most glowing successes in recidivism reduction programming are those clients who can be treated successfully as outpatients. Outpatient treatment is very cost-effective. Successful outpatients easily save the contractor the cost of the program. Even factoring in the client who eventually requires residential treatment (which is also lower in cost than incarceration) and the client who reduces drug use and commits fewer crimes, the overall benefits to society and government budgets is no small consideration.

In addition to the aforementioned programs, both Daytop and Phoenix House propose to begin programs for juvenile offenders through funding from the newly created New York State Department of Probation and Correctional Alternatives. These structured TC day-programs are characterized by the funding agency as graduated sanctions programs. The TC is called upon to provide treatment, to sanction, and to monitor as a supervisory arm of the criminal justice system. However distasteful this may seem, research indicates that court pressure may be the most effective, external motivator for the adolescent population (19).

Daytop's proposed project would service 50 drug-involved and/or substance-abusing youth in existing adolescent Daycare programs, located in community-based Outreach Centers. The target population is comprised of youthful offenders on felony probation that would otherwise be incarcerated due to a second drug-related felony offense. The project would include a collaboration with New York City TASC, which will identify members of the targeted population, provide representation in court and an escort to the program (often an insurmountable hurdle for the recalcitrant and frightened adolescent).

Through an intensive, peer-based TC approach, the proposed project will provide structured day treatment to address anti-social, self-destructive behavior patterns, including drug and alcohol use, drug dealing, nonviolent criminal behaviors, and attraction to a negative peer group. Participation will range from 9 to 12 months, depending on individual progress (although the adolescent will be urged to continue in Daytop aftercare upon completion of the court mandate). The project will seek to teach participants to cope with the complex problems confronting urban adolescents and to help them develop a positive peer network to mitigate pressures of tempting criminal lifestyle, which pervades their home communities. It will meet the educational needs of these youth who are often unable to function or are unwelcome in their community schools. It seeks to address the entire family of the adolescent and respond to parental substance abuse, as well as other intrafamilial dysfunction that contributes to the youngster's anti-social behaviors. It is hoped that, as a result of Daytop's comprehensive approach, participants will adopt positive, normative values, emphasizing a drug-free and law-abiding lifestyle. It is estimated that the New York State Department of Corrections will save over $1.2 million during each year of the project's operation.

The challenge to all of these modalities is for the TC to maintain its integrity and independence in making treatment decisions and servicing the client, while satisfying the needs of the criminal justice system. Most ATI clients see only certain punishment from a system that has always, in their view, attempted to crush their desires. The challenge and the question becomes, therefore, what role can the TC play in helping the ATI client?

First and foremost, the program must help the client recognize that it is substance abuse and not the threat of incarceration that is the most real and present danger to his or her well-being. Herein lies the power of the TC to assist in this process. In the case of the adolescent population, the counselor, who is both a TC graduate and a peer educator, is uniquely qualified to help the client confront his or her fears, because they themselves have confronted those fears. They have been able to see treatment as ultimately beneficial, not as another form of incarceration or punishment. It is this self-help model of the TC that provides the edge in engaging resistant clients in treatment.

SPECIAL CHALLENGES OF THE ATI POPULATION

Despite the TC's role as the best hope for addressing the problem of criminality related to substance abuse, ATI programming raises a number of difficulties.

Control of Treatment Plan

The TC has grappled with the problem of who controls the client, i.e., who controls assessment and who controls treatment planning. The decision as to the mandated course of treatment is made by the district attorney and/or presiding judge, and is determined by the crime committed rather than the level of substance abuse and coexisting clinical factors. District attorneys often attempt to take control of intake evaluation of potential clients and decisions regarding their amenability to treatment despite their lack of knowledge regarding clinical matters.

Conflicts of Interest

The TC also must struggle with gaining the client's trust *and* keeping the criminal justice contractor or referral agency informed regarding treatment progress. Daytop has found that retention of this recalcitrant population often depends on a good working relationship with the probation or parole officer who will "encourage" the client to comply with the demands of treatment. The counselor, therefore, has the difficult task of establishing a solid relationship with the client that fosters self-disclosure despite the risk of legal consequences.

More Complex Client History

The ATI clientele have the most serious personal, social, and medical problems associated with drug abuse. The experience of Daytop and Samaritan House in working with this population is that these individuals have a vast array of problems that are far more complex that their non-ATI counterparts in residential treatment. While the TC has successfully demonstrated that it can address all aspects of a person's rehabilitation, the TC model had to be enhanced and additional resources provided to fill the gaps and address the issues that were revealed during the pilot phase of these programs:

- **Homelessness:** 22% of DTAP clients had moved from place to place and 7% were homeless when arrested. Nearly one-third (31%) of those with a permanent address had resided at that address for less than six months. The average time that the homeless defendant had been without housing was 20 months.
- **Dysfunctional Family History:** Over half (53%) were from families where there was a history of alcoholism, drug abuse, or both, while 12% had immediate family members that were involved in criminal activity.
- **Severe Education and Employment Deficiencies:** 67% of DTAP clients had neither completed high school nor obtained a GED; over one-third (36%) had not completed more than 9th grade. Among the TASC population, 74% neither completed high school nor obtained a GED At the time of arrest, 82% of DTAP clients had no legal employment, 15% were employed full-time, and 3% had part-time employment; 51% had been employed full or part-time for some portion of the preceding 12 months; the most common jobs being construction laborer, factory worker, and clerical staff. The average weekly net wages of full-time workers was $245. Obtaining and holding gratifying and remunerative employment is the key to leading a stable, drug-free life. Since most ATI clients have poor work histories, few job skills, and little education, a more focused and intense vocational preparation and training program has been required to insure their successful reintegration into society.

- **Medical History:** Nearly two-thirds (63%) of DTAP participants reported that they were regularly affected by one or more health problems. The most common ailments were lung disorders such as asthma, emphysema, bronchitis, or TB (25%); gunshot or stab wounds (17%); heart disease, including high blood pressure (12%); and HIV-positive status (9%). Other ailments were STDs, gastrointestinal disorders, diabetes, and seizure disorders.

While two-thirds of this population are regularly afflicted with health problems, the difficulty is compounded because many clients have received no prior health care or poor health care. A primary concern has been the lack of specific medical information provided prior to admission. Over 90% of the information received is nonspecific to diagnosis and medical conditions. Frequently, TC staff must repeatedly submit requests before receiving the required detailed information. The client is often infected with TB and/or an HIV-related illness and also requires long-term dental care.

Gang Rivalry Issues

Resulting from the "buy-and-bust" concept, two-thirds of the DTAP enrollees are gang members. Rival gang members are often found within the same treatment facility, creating facility management issues. Also, the same gang members have formed cliques and, thus, do not respond to treatment. Separating these individuals within the TC's limited number of facilities has been difficult.

Reimbursement Issues

The funding of ATI services poses a substantial issue for the TC; its long-term orientation conflicts directly with the trend toward managed care. The criminal justice system requires long-term treatment so that the criminal does not "get off easy" and that society is protected from the offender for a year or more. Generally, the client's drug history and other clinical issues would warrant long-term treatment in any event. However, it may eventually prove difficult to access Medicaid reimbursement for this population. Even in cases when the referring criminal justice agency pays for treatment, pursuant to a contractual relationship with the TC, it normally expects the treatment provider to access third-party reimbursements to supplement treatment costs. In effect, although it is clearly less expensive to provide treatment rather than incarceration, the criminal justice system contractor rids itself of a portion of its costs by placing the burden on welfare and Medicaid. Eventually, despite the fact that the overall governmental expense is reduced due to ATI programs, the separate welfare and Medicaid systems may demand that they not be called upon to supplement the criminal justice system's costs.

Regardless of the aforementioned funding quagmire, the TCs have an excellent outcome in treating the ATI population. During the first 30 months of DTAP operations, 308 defendants entered the program and 20 graduated. The one-year rate of retention in treatment was 65%. As to Brooklyn TASC clients, 127 predicate felons were placed in treatment in 1991. As of January 1994, of the 90 clients in the study group, 70% successfully completed treatment and only 7% of the program graduates were re-arrested.

THE FUTURE OF THE TC

The most important factor in determining the future outcome of the TC may be the managed care movement. Managed care is growing and now controls almost 50% of the health care market; in the next few years, it will control approximately 85%.

Historically, many managed care organizations have thwarted access to treatment for people dependent on alcohol and/or other drugs. These managed care organizations have instituted arbitrary limits on the number of days a person can be in treatment and sometimes influence the type of treatment that person receives. Additionally, managed care often requires that people with alcohol and/or other drug problems be precertified before they begin the treatment process. This can constitute a long and arduous process, which may deter the client from pursuing treatment.

Statistics indicate that only 10–15% of people with alcohol and/or other drug problems seek treatment. Managed care organizations discourage access to substance abuse treatment; thereby resulting in other health care issues; such as AIDS, TB, and hepatitis; this will eventually increase the already high cost of health care. These managed care organizations, if involved in Medicaid reimbursement, require stringent guidelines, including expensive (and presently unfunded) administrative requirements of new computer hardware and software purchases, extensive staff training, and dedication of substantial person hours. Long-term ambulatory and residential treatment will be eliminated, and performance capitation incentives will be implemented based on utilization and efficiency.

With the current fiscal crises in New York State and elsewhere, the acceleration of managed care enrollment can be anticipated to negatively affect funding for substance abuse treatment. This impact will be seen on the insurance funding side of treatment stays and Medicaid funding of ancillary treatment services. It is also possible that substance abuse treatment administrative agencies, such as New York's Office of Alcohol and Substance Abuse Services, will adopt a managed care approach and begin to designate substance abuse treatment as a medical service within the same constraints as managed care organizations.

It may be that two entirely separate treatment tracks will develop: long-term treatment for ATI populations and women at risk of losing parental rights, and short-term or no treatment for anyone else. More and more, the TC's clinical decisions regarding appropriate treatment will be determined by contractors and managed care providers, without regard for actual client needs. Therefore, the Treatment Communities of America has endorsed a managed care treatment model, which allows for the option of 18 months in a residential TC, 40 days per year in an intensive outpatient TC, 60 days per year in outpatient treatment, and an additional 60 outpatient days of relapse prevention and aftercare, all without a lifetime cap.

In New York, it is estimated that the social costs of untreated substance abuse already exceed $12-billion annually (20). If the TC's economically sound and effective brand of treatment continues to be abandoned in favor of managed care realignments, the costs to the United States can only escalate to higher levels.

References

1. World Federation of Therapeutic Communities. International directory of substance abuse services. New York: World Federation of Therapeutic Communities, 1993.
2. McDermott N, Matthews S, eds. Residential treatment guidelines—January. A collaboration of ten therapeutic communities. New York: Therapeutic Communities of New York, 1994.
3. Drug Treatment Alternative to Prison (DTAP) of the Kings County District Attorney. Fifth annual report of operations, October 15, 1994–October 15, 1995.
4. Jainchill N. The relationship between psychiatric disorder, retention in treatment and client progress among admissions to a residential drug free modality. New York: New York University, 1989. Dissertation.
5. Daytop Village. Annual report 1993–1994. New York: Daytop Village, 1994.
6. Rom-Rymer J. An empirical assessment of Mowrer's theory of psychopathology applied to a therapeutic community. Gainesville: Florida State University, 1981. Dissertation.
7. Beschner G, Thompson P. Women and drug abuse treatment: needs and services. NIDA Res Monogr. USDHHS Publication 81-1057. Washington, DC: U.S. Government Printing Office.
8. Stevens S, Arbiter N, Glider P. Women residents: expanding their role to increase treatment effectiveness in substance abuse programs. Int J Addictions 1989;24(5):425–434.
9. Hughes PH, Coletti SD, Neri RL, Sicilian DM, Urmann CFMA. Planning conference: evaluating PAR Village Demonstration Project for cocaine abusing women, their children. New York: Therapeutic Communities of America, 1992.
10. Mothers In Recovery Outcome Study. New York Community Trust, Parent Education Research Project. Final report, June 30, 1995.
11. De Leon G, Sacks S. Modified therapeutic community for homeless mentally ill chemical abusers. Paper presented at the National Institute on Drug Abuse, April, 1996.
12. Jainchill N, De Leon G. Therapeutic community research. Recent studies of psychopathology. In: Bluhringer G, Platt JJ, eds. Drug abuse treatment research: German and American perspectives. Malabar, FL: Krieger Publishers, 1992.
13. Center for Substance Abuse Treatment (CSAT). Approaches in the treatment of adolescents with emotional, substance abuse problems. Technical Assistance Publication Series 1993;1:21.
14. Center for Substance Abuse Treatment (CSAT). Assessment, treatment of patients with coexisting mental illness and alcohol and other drug abuse. Treatment Improvement Protocol Series 1994;9:2–3.
15. Biase DV. Adolescent heroin abusers in a therapeutic community: use of MAACL to assess emotional traits and splitting from treatment. J Psychedelic Drugs 1971;4:145–147.
16. Pompi K. Adolescents in therapeutic communities: retention and posttreatment outcome. NIDA Res Monogr 1994;144:128–160.
17. State of New York, Department of Correctional Services. Drug offenders committed to state prison. Albany, NY: Division of Program Planning, Research and Evaluation, 1991.
18. Lipton DS, Wexler HK. The drug-crime connection: rehabilitation shows promise. Corrections Today 1988;50(5):144–147.
19. Heit DS, Pompi KF. Hypothetical client retention factors in residential treatment. Addict Ther 1977;2:1–3.
20. Newsletter of the Therapeutic Communities Association of New York 1993;1(1):1–12.

41 METHADONE MAINTENANCE

*Joyce H. Lowinson, J. Thomas Payte, Edwin Salsitz,
Herman Joseph, Ira J. Marion, and Vincent P. Dole*

Methadone maintenance as a treatment modality for opiate addiction and the events leading to its development are chronicled in this chapter. In the field of medicine, the use of medications as maintenance for the control or suppression of chronic illness and metabolic deficiencies is not unusual. Although opiate addiction is generally recognized as a chronic disease, many would apply different standards to its treatment.

In 1972, the United States Food and Drug Administration (FDA) approved the use of methadone hydrochloride for the treatment of narcotic addiction (23). Until 1985, when naltrexone hydrochloride received the same approval, methadone was the only drug approved for such use. Worldwide, it remains the major modality for the treatment of opioid dependency. It has been researched thoroughly and evaluated carefully for three decades (6). Methadone maintenance treatment does not represent a radical departure from previous approaches used to help addicted persons. Despite its proven effectiveness, it remains a controversial approach among substance abuse treatment providers, public officials, policy makers, the medical profession, and the public at large (13). This controversy has persisted for almost three decades and has particular importance, at present, because of the relationship between the epidemic of (illness related to) human immunodeficiency virus (HIV) and intravenous drug abuse. Recent studies have documented that methadone treatment has had a significant impact on the rate of HIV infection of patients in continuous treatment and that it is also a critical focal point for risk reduction and patient education, as well as counseling, testing, and treatment for HIV disorders (6).

In 1993, approval was given to introduce LAAM (L-acetyl methadol) a longer acting agonist methadone substitute. Patients taking it would only have to come to clinic three days a week. LAAM is described in further detail by Greenstein et al. in Chapter 42 and by Marion (63).

Despite ideological battles that persist and controversy that is impervious to considerable scientific evidence, almost every nation with a significant narcotics addiction problem has adopted methadone maintenance as the major treatment modality. About 200,000 people are currently in treatment throughout the world, of whom more than half are treated in the United States. However, not a single protocol for the use of methadone is followed consistently, and this, coupled with the persistent ideological issues, has resulted in "methadone programs" and "clinics" of varying quality and methods. It is therefore important to differentiate between the appropriate clinical use of methadone hydrochloride in maintenance treatment and that of the actual practices within "methadone programs" (78). Despite these differences, methadone maintenance treatment programs have remained an important part of health and human services for a population that is generally disenfranchised, difficult to treat, and now at risk for HIV infection. However, these programs have endured and succeeded despite controversy, inadequate funding, and a lack of public and community support, thus helping tens of thousands of former heroin addicts to live normal and productive lives.

HISTORICAL PERSPECTIVE

The Harrison Act, a revenue law passed to honor the United States' international commitment to the 1912 Hague convention to control narcotics, made the sale or transfer of all narcotic drugs a matter of record and subject to taxes and fees. At that time, many patent and prescription medications contained "narcotic" drugs, including cocaine, heroin, and morphine, and addiction was not uncommon (15). Physicians, faced with persons addicted to narcotic drugs, prescribed them. However, the United States Treasury Department viewed addiction as a criminal and moral problem rather than a medical concern. The Harrison Act was used as the legal basis to systematically prosecute these physicians, known as the "Doctor Cases" (see Chapter 1). Most significant among these cases was *Linder vs. the United States,* because it established that physicians could provide "good faith" treatment for addicts (26). Despite this favorable decision, physicians continued to be harassed and increasingly often refused to treat narcotic addicts.

By 1918, clinics dispensing morphine and other drugs were established in 14 cities in an effort either to maintain or withdraw addicts from addictive drugs. The two most famous of these clinics were in New York City and Shreveport, Louisiana. By 1923, however, the active campaign by the United States government ended this form of clinical intervention until methadone maintenance treatment research began in the mid 1960s (16).

Once the United States narcotics clinics were closed, treatment for addiction became largely unavailable until 1935, when the United States Public Health Service opened a hospital for this purpose in Lexington, Kentucky. This facility and another in Fort Worth, Texas, which opened in 1938, operated much like a prison, treating both involuntary criminal and volunteer addicts. They remained the only two public facilities treating addiction until the mid 1950s, when Riverside Hospital opened in New York City. Treatment consisted of detoxification with a goal of abstinence. However, a follow-up study of patients discharged from Riverside showed that more than 90% relapsed to heroin use (1).

The first renewed attempt of organized medicine to advocate treatment and medical research for narcotics addiction came in 1955 when the New York Academy of Medicine strongly objected to federal regulations that "prohibited physicians from prescribing a narcotic drug to keep comfortable a confirmed addict who refuses withdrawal, but who might, under regulated dosage, lead a useful life and later might agree to withdrawal" (66). The Academy report observed that the early morphine maintenance clinics opened after World War I were closed in 1923, not because they had failed, but because their goals were not in accordance with the prevailing philosophy of a punitive approach to the so-called "criminal problem." This report led to a renewed debate on narcotic maintenance at a time when the number of young heroin addicts in urban ghettos was increasing and concern over rising overdose deaths and drug-related crime was escalating. As a result, a position paper was generated by the Joint Committee of the American Bar Association and the American Medical Association in 1959, calling for a softening of penalties and the establishment of an experimental outpatient clinic for the treatment of drug addicts (11).

In 1962, the Medical Society of the County of New York recognized the need for systematic clinical investigation of medical maintenance treatment programs and ruled that "physicians who participate in a properly controlled and supervised clinical research project for addicts on a noninstitutional basis would be deemed to be practicing ethical medicine" (11). By 1963, the available treatment for narcotics addicts in New York City, where half of the nation's addicts lived, consisted of detoxification in Manhattan General Hospital and Metropolitan Hospital. Also that year, New York's first therapeutic community (Daytop Lodge) opened on Staten Island, New York, modeled on the Synanon program that had been operating in California since 1958. This program used a "self-help" concept that had its origins in Alcoholics Anonymous. Synanon and Daytop used recovering addicts as counselors and role models; evolved treatment principles of encounter groups, peer support, and therapy; and stressed total abstinence from drugs. However, the modern therapeutic community has developed into a far more sophisticated model, using the best techniques from many different approaches (see Chapter 40).

With the medical and legal professions calling for a reevaluation of American narcotics policies, the climate became more favorable for a maintenance approach to treating addiction in outpatient clinics. In 1963, the New York Academy of Medicine recommended again that clinics be established in affiliation with hospitals to dispense narcotics to addicts. The same year, President Kennedy's Advisory Committee on Narcotics and Drug Abuse made similar recommendations (11). At that time, heroin-related mortality was the leading cause of death for young adults between the ages of 15 and 35. Serum hepatitis cases related to injection of narcotics with contaminated needles were increasing markedly. A record number of addicts were being arrested for drug-related crimes (possession, sale of narcotics, property crimes) and jails were becoming overcrowded (42).

DEVELOPMENT OF METHADONE MAINTENANCE TREATMENT

In 1963, in response to the growing concern over the spread of heroin addiction, the New York City Health Research Council, viewing narcotic addiction as a chronic illness, recommended research in this area. Rockefeller Institute (now University) took up the challenge and asked Dr. Vincent Dole, a senior physician and researcher, to undertake research in this area. Dr. Marie Nyswander, a psychiatrist with extensive experience in narcotic addiction, joined him in this endeavor. As a result of her experience in Lexington, Kentucky, and in her private psychoanalytic practice in New York City, Dr. Nyswander became convinced that traditional psychiatric approaches alone could not help addicts to discontinue their use of narcotics. In fact, it was observed that "a careful search of the literature failed to disclose a single report in which withdrawal of drug and psychotherapy have enabled a significant fraction of the patients to return to the community and to live as normal individuals" (73). Recognizing that relapse in most cases was related to persistent or recurring craving, Dole and Nyswander theorized that control of this craving would be an important first step. Since their primary goal was rehabilitation rather than abstinence, this opened the door to the use of a narcotic medication as a means of controlling drug use and thereby making an addict accessible to rehabilitation. To test their theory, they admitted six "hard-core" heroin addicts to the hospital at Rockefeller Institute. An initial attempt to stabilize them on morphine proved unsuccessful because the patients alternated between being "high" and being "sick." Then, because its duration of action was longer, methadone was tried. Dole and Nyswander observed, in addition, that methadone administered in sufficiently high doses could be given orally once daily. As a result, peaks and troughs were eliminated and patients could function normally. A daily maintenance dose of 80–120 mg produced a pharmacological cross-tolerance, or "blockade," so that patients would not feel any narcotic or euphoric effects if they were to self-administer a normal dose of a short-acting narcotic (e.g., 25 mg of heroin). Finally, methadone appeared to be safe and nontoxic, with only minimal side effects. For Dole and Nyswander, the question was "whether a narcotic medicine prescribed by a physician as part of a treatment program could assist in the return of addicts to normal society" (20).

With the support of Dr. Ray Trussell, the New York City Commissioner of Hospitals opened a pilot program with 120 patients conducted at Manhattan General Hospital, which later became affiliated with the Beth Israel Medical Center (58). In 1967, 107 patients remained in treatment, of whom 71% were employed in steady jobs, attending school, or both. Dole and Nyswander stated: "To date we have seen no indication to remove the blockade from any patient in the treatment program since all of them are still in the process of rehabilitation and no patient has been limited by intolerance of the medication" (20). The support of the Columbia University School of Public Health was enlisted to conduct an independent evaluation of the project. With Dr. Frances Rowe Gearing as chairperson, these evaluations continued for the first 10 years of methadone maintenance treatment and yielded consistently positive outcomes for the entire period of time. Criteria were : (a) a decrease in antisocial behavior measured by arrest and/or incarceration; (b) an increase in social productivity measured by employment and/or schooling or vocational training; (c) clinical impression of freedom from heroin "hunger" confirmed by negative urine specimens after stabilization on methadone; and (d) a recognition of, and willingness to accept help for, psychiatric and other problems, including those related to excessive use of alcohol or other drugs. Based on these evaluations, further expansion of the program was recommended (24). Methadone maintenance treatment programs were opened in many urban areas throughout the United States. Reports of their success were published in the medical literature. Annual methadone conferences at Rockefeller University were held, giving an opportunity for in-depth discussion of this new modality. Some of the programs followed the protocol described by Dole and Nyswander (19) in their article "A Medical Treatment for Diacetyl-morphine (Heroin) Addiction" and applied the concept of narcotic blockade described by Dole, Nyswander, and Kreek (20). Others used methadone medication but developed programs with divergent goals and objectives including abstinence, low-dose therapy, and combinations of residential, outpatient, mental health, and other modalities (28, 41). In 1971, President Nixon appointed Dr. Jerome Jaffe to lead the White House Special Action Office for Drug Abuse Prevention. Dr. Jaffe, by expanding the methadone treatment system, played a major role in stemming the rise of heroin addiction in the United States.

By 1969 there were 2,000 patients enrolled in methadone maintenance programs in New York City alone, and 10,000 applicants were awaiting admission. The New York Academy of Medicine termed the situation a crisis. Although they recognized that treatment of heroin addiction with methadone, a long-acting narcotic, might be a lifelong affair, they felt that "no other regimen currently available offers as much to the chronic addict" (67). Legislators in New York State responded by appropriating $10 million for the establishment of additional methadone maintenance programs. In 1970 the Bureau of Narcotics and Dangerous Drugs, in a joint statement with the FDA, approved the use of methadone as an investigational drug for "experimental" maintenance programs and interdicted further research except in accordance with guidelines to be promulgated by regulations. Other established uses of methadone were complicated when it was removed from retail pharmacies and made available only through hospital pharmacies subject to specific restrictions. Emphasis continued to focus on eventual abstinence.

USE OF METHADONE AS A MEDICATION

Methadone is a synthetic narcotic analgesic compound developed in Germany at the end of World War II (29). After the war, it was studied at Lexington, Kentucky, and was found to have effects similar to those of morphine but longer in duration. These initial studies led to the use of methadone for analgesia and for withdrawal treatment of heroin addiction. Although methadone continues to be used for these purposes, its unique pharmacologic properties lend themselves to its use for maintenance (39, 40).

As a maintenance medication, methadone has distinct advantages. When administered in adequate oral doses, a single dose in a stabilized patient lasts between 24 and 36 hours, without creating euphoria, sedation, or analgesia. Therefore, the patient can function normally and can perform any mental or physical tasks without impairment. Patients continue to experience normal physical pain and emotional reactions. Most importantly, methadone relieves the persistent narcotic craving or hunger that is believed to be the major reason for relapse.

Narcotic cross-tolerance, or "blockade," is another important property of the medication. In sufficient doses, methadone "blocks" the narcotic effects of normal street doses of short-acting narcotics such as heroin and can lessen the likelihood of overdose, should the drugs be self-administered. Because tolerance to methadone remains steady, patients can be maintained indefinitely (e.g., in some cases more than 20 years) on the same dose.

Finally, methadone is a medically safe treatment medication, with minimal side effects (28, 41, 47). Much has been said about the importance of appropriate and adequate dosages of methadone. Since its early development, many practitioners have deviated from the original Dole-Nyswander protocol with the desire to conduct research to determine the most effective approach to treatment and detoxification. However, others, because of preconceived notions that abstinence was an achievable goal for the majority of addicts and that lower doses were less toxic, believed that less diversion would occur if doses were lower. They also assumed incorrectly that it would be easier to withdraw patients from low doses of methadone. Patients, themselves, continued to resist adequate dosages based on mythologies that methadone "rots the bones," decreases libido, and is more difficult to "kick" than heroin (27, 75).

Nevertheless, scientific knowledge is now available to suggest that the original dosage protocol works best and that lower doses (less than 60 mg) are appropriate for only a limited number of patients. A series of large-scale studies has emerged showing that patients maintained on doses of 60 mg/day or more had better treatment outcomes than those maintained on lower doses. Hartel reports data based on 2400 patients enrolled over a 15-year period. She observed that those patients maintained on a daily dose of 60 mg or more had longer retention in treatment, less use of heroin and other drugs, including cocaine, and a lower incidence of HIV infection and AIDS. The effectiveness of methadone was even greater for patients on a 70 mg dose and was still more pronounced for patients on 80 mg/day or more (34–36). Ball and Ross (6) reported on a 3-year study of six methadone programs in three Northeastern cities. They showed that patients reduced their use of intravenous heroin by 71% when compared with the preadmission level. Most importantly, this study revealed that opiate use was directly related to methadone dose levels. In patients on doses above 71 mg/day, no heroin use was detected, whereas those patients on doses below 46 mg were 5.16 times more likely to use heroin than those receiving higher doses (6). Similar results were found by Caplehorn and Bell (12), who reported on methadone treatment doses in Australia and found that patients on higher doses remained in treatment longer. Finally, in a review of 24 methadone treatment programs throughout the nation, the United States General Accounting Office (78) concluded that "sixty milligrams of methadone is the lowest effective dose to stop heroin use and low dose maintenance (20 to 40 milligrams) is inappropriate."

Kreek (47, 51) used blood plasma levels to establish doses and stated that whatever method is used, methadone dosages should never be used for social rewards or punishment (47, 51). Also, all doses must be determined individually, because of differences in metabolism, body weight, and maintenance of appropriate methadone blood levels throughout the 24-hour period.

These studies confirm that dosages below 60 mg appear inadequate for most patients. This is especially important at the beginning of treatment, when patients may experiment with heroin to test the effectiveness of the medication. These studies also confirm that medical decisions should not be based on public biases but on scientific knowledge and clinical evaluation. Low doses of methadone are rarely therapeutic; in fact, they prevent the effective treatment of narcotic addiction.

Physicians in Austria and Sweden have been determining methadone dose by measuring plasma levels of methadone at peak (2–4 hours) and at 24 hours after dosing, attempting to raise the methadone dose until a stable plasma level is reached (8). This method is often used in maintenance programs. It is important to refine this technology in methadone treatment so that dose levels have a scientific as well as a clinical basis.

CLINICAL APPLICATIONS: METHADONE MAINTENANCE PHARMACOTHERAPY

Goals for pharmacotherapy for addiction (52):

- Prevent or reduce withdrawal symptoms
- Prevent or reduce drug craving
- Prevent relapse to use of addictive drug
- Restore to or towards normalcy any physiological functions disrupted by drug abuse

For ease of discussion methadone *dosing* can be divided into simple phases as described in Table 41.1. Elsewhere in this chapter there is a separate discussion of methadone *treatment* phases looking at treatment in a broader context. Despite the apparent simplicity of these practice guidelines the need for emphasis of these principles is based on persistence of inadequate dosing practices in many programs and the apparent compulsion on the part of regulators and policy makers to determine methadone dose practices. The benefits of *adequate individualized methadone dosing* are well documented as are the problems associated with inadequate dosing levels (6, 12, 14, 17). This section focuses on how to ensure adequate dosing rather than why. Terms such as "high dose" and "low dose" are set aside to encourage the concept of individually determined *adequate* dose.

Initial Dose

The initial dose of methadone is most commonly given at a time when the patient is having both signs and symptoms of opioid withdrawal. The immediate purpose is to relieve the withdrawal that is present and also to establish a dose reference point upon which future dose adjustments can be made. Table 41.2 summarizes initial dose.

Michael Gossop and colleagues have reported experiences that fail to support the accepted view that dose is the major determinant of withdrawal severity (32). Clinical experience of three of the authors (JHL, JTP, VPD) supports this observation.

Patients present in varying stages of withdrawal. The presence or appearance of more severe withdrawal does not necessarily mean a high level of physical dependence or tolerance, or a higher initial or maintenance dose of methadone.

Early Induction

As indicated in Table 41.1 the purpose of the early induction is to bring the methadone dose to approximate the established opioid tolerance in a prompt but safe manner. To enable the patient to abstain from heroin or other opioids it is essential to relieve the withdrawal and to reduce the craving or drug hunger. If this process is too slow the patient may continue to "use"; if the process is too ambitious some degree of overdose may result. Induction overdoses can result from exaggeration of tolerance by the addict patient, overestimation on the part of the clinician, and the failure to consider basic steady-state pharmacology.

Methadone has a half-life of 24–36 hours. Twenty-four hours after the initial dose about half remains upon which the second dose is added. The result is a significant increase in mean methadone levels with no increase in dose. This accumulation process continues until steady-state is achieved at some 4–5 half lives. The important clinical lesson is that the effect of the medication will increase in the absence of a dose increase, that relief of withdrawal may require more time, not more medication. Both the clinician and the patient should be alert to any sedation or "getting loaded" on day one or two as subsequent days may bring over medication.

After oral administration of methadone the peak blood levels occur between 2 and 4 hours. During early induction when signs and symptoms of withdrawal persist it is prudent to wait at least 3 hours before additional doses of 5–10 mg are provided (38, 74).

Late Induction

Once the initial relief has been achieved a more gradual dose adjustment may be indicated to establish an adequate maintenance dose to ensure realization of the goals listed earlier. An example would be the patient who has an initial elimination of withdrawal and craving at 50 mg per day but who is exposed to opportunistic use suggesting the need to establish a "blockade" level of cross-tolerance, usually requiring doses of 80 mg or more. In other situations the late induction may involve a gradual reduction to find the lowest *effective* dose.

Maintenance and Stabilization

Once the stabilization dose is achieved, its indefinite administration should ensure continued maintenance of the desired effects. This stability is presumed to result from a steady-state occupation of the appropriate opiate receptors. Patients may remain on a stable dose for decades while others may require some adjustment at times. Both patients and clinicians should avoid the tendency to lower the dose simply because the patient is stable and doing well.

Maintenance to Abstinence

Medically supervised withdrawal should be attempted only when strongly desired by the rehabilitated patient with adequate supervision and support. Staff should carefully explore the motivation for withdrawal. In many cases the motivation is based on external pressures or regulatory or program policies that result in continued disruption of any efforts to achieve a normal, stable lifestyle. In consideration of the high rate of relapse to intravenous drug use and the substantial risks associated with relapse, patients who have withdrawn and who are withdrawing should be carefully monitored in a clinical setting. In the event of relapse or impending relapse appropriate intervention should be initiated including rapid resumption of maintenance pharmacotherapy (2).

The method of withdrawal usually involves a gradual reduction in dose

Table 41.2   Initial Dose

Degree of tolerance	Dose range
Nontolerant	10 mg +/−5
Unknown tolerance	20 mg +/−5
Known tolerance	20–40 mg

Reproduced with permission from Payte JT. Adequate dose lecture series. Paper presented at the Albert Einstein College of Medicine, Division of Substance Abuse, New York, November 26, 1996.

Table 41.1   Principles of Methadone Dosing

Phase	Purpose	Range in Mg /Comments
Initial Dose	Relieve abstinence symptoms	20–40 mg
Early Induction	Reach established tolerance level	Plus or minus 5–10 mg q 3–24 h
Late Induction	Establish *adequate* dose (desired effects)	Plus or minus 5–10 mg q 5–10 days
Maintenance/ Stabilization	Maintain desired effects (steady-state occupation of opiate receptors)	Ideally 60–120 mg May be more than 120 mg or less than 60 mg
Maintenance to Abstinence	Medically supervised withdrawal	As individually tolerated, up to 10% reduction q 5–10 days
Medical Maintenance	Indefinite maintenance of rehabilitated patient in a medical setting	Adequate dose with 2–4 weeks' medication at a time

Reproduced with permission from Payte JT, Khuri ET. Principles of methadone dose determination. In: State methadone treatment guidelines. Rockville, MD: Center for Substance Abuse Treatment, Treatment Improvement Protocol Series 1993;1:47–58.

over time. The schedule must be carefully individualized. Many patients will tolerate up to a 10% reduction in current dose at intervals of 5–10 days. (See Chapter 36 for a discussion of detoxification.)

Use of Plasma Levels of Methadone

In recent years reliable determination of methadone levels have become more available and affordable (10). Adequate dosing can be based on clinical findings in the majority of the cases. Blood levels may be considered in the following situations:

- To clarify a clinical picture that does not correspond to the dose of methadone
- To confirm suspected drug interactions (Table 41.3)
- To ensure adequacy of a given dose
- To document or justify the need for a particular dose or schedule
- To determine the need for and the effectiveness of split dose practices

Levels of 150–200 ng/ml are adequate to prevent most craving and withdrawal (22, 56). It is felt that adequate cross tolerance or "blockade" is achieved at levels at or above 400 ng/ml (57). The rate of change is critical and can be determined by calculating a peak to trough ratio. Ideally this ratio should be 2 or less. Higher ratios indicate rapid metabolism and the possible need for a split dose. Split dose induction is facilitated by giving the full customary dose on Day One followed in about 12 hours with one half the anticipated total daily dose. This "half-dose" is then continued twice daily.

Tolerance to the narcotic properties of methadone (sedation, analgesia) develops within a period of about 4–6 weeks. However, tolerance to the autonomic effects, most commonly constipation and sweating, develops at slower rates. Therefore, it is important to monitor the stabilization process carefully to minimize narcotic effects and withdrawal symptoms (28, 33).

Kreek has demonstrated that methadone prescribed in high doses on a long-term basis has no toxic effects and minimal side effects for adult patients maintained in treatment for up to 14 years and for adolescent patients treated for up to 5 years (36, 49). Medical complications identified among methadone patients include worsening of illnesses that existed prior to treatment. Methadone patients can develop illnesses such as chronic hypertension, diabetes, alcoholism and multiple substance abuse, HIV infection and acquired immune deficiency syndrome (AIDS), chronic liver disease and cirrhosis, asthma, tuberculosis, syphilis, endo-

carditis, and other infectious diseases. However, following entry into treatment, health status usually improves with access to medical care, elimination of injections with contaminated needles, and improved quality of life.

As noted previously, the major side effects during methadone maintenance treatment occur during the initial stabilization process. Although these effects are minor and usually subside over time, they can also be reduced or eliminated by an appropriate dose adjustment. In addition to constipation and sweating, the most frequently reported side effects are transient skin rash, weight gain, and water retention. Some of these are complicated by co-existing alcoholism, multiple substance abuse, smoking, advanced age, and lifestyle (54). Life-threatening interactions of methadone with other drugs have not been identified.

Methadone maintenance, itself, does not impair the normal functioning of patients. Psychomotor performance tests that measure skills such as reaction time, driving ability, intelligence, attention span, and other important abilities were administered to methadone patients, volunteers, and normal college students with no drug history. The performance of methadone patients did not differ from those of normal volunteers or college students. Studies of patients' driving records in both Texas and New York found that the driving records of methadone patients did not differ significantly from those of the driving population at large (5). On the Wechsler Adult Intelligence Scale, the mean IQ of methadone patients at the time of entry into treatment was slightly higher than the general population. Ten years later, the same patients showed even higher scores, possibly due to improved quality of life. Based on these studies, it can be concluded that methadone maintenance does not impair normal functioning or intellectual capacity (3, 9, 30, 31, 65).

METHADONE PROGRAMS

Methadone maintenance programs are controlled and regulated by federal and state agencies to an extent not found in any other form of medical treatment. In many states, the original Dole-Nyswander protocol has been altered to make abstinence the priority. In 1972, in order to establish minimal standards and quality, the FDA promulgated regulations governing the use of methadone; the Drug Enforcement Administration (DEA) oversees the security and dispensing of the medication. These minimum standards regulate admissions, staffing patterns, record keeping, treatment planning, service provision, storage, facility standards, frequency of visits and of urine testing, and dose limitations. Eight states totally interdict the practice of methadone maintenance. Some states place a ceiling on the maximum dose, making it impossible to produce a narcotic blockade or to remove narcotic craving. Some prohibit take-home medication, and others place a limit on time in treatment before a patient must be withdrawn from methadone. Such restrictions present physicians with serious dilemmas. Instead of being able to rely on their professional judgment and clinical experience, they are often forced to make medical decisions that are independent of the needs of the patients. The consequence of those factors is a reduced effectiveness of this treatment modality. In some cases individual programs may exceed FDA and state regulations compromising effective treatment even further.

For admission to methadone treatment, federal standards mandate a minimum of 1 year of addiction to opiates as well as current evidence of addiction, although they allow for exceptions such as recent discharge from a chronic care institution or prison. The minimum age for admission is 18 (under 18 with parental or legal guardian consent). Applicants under age 18 must have at least two prior documented treatment episodes, either short-term detoxification or drug-free treatment, before they can be considered for methadone maintenance. Pregnant women are routinely accepted for methadone treatment and can now be admitted without a 1-year addiction history because it is recognized that methadone maintenance treatment greatly improves the pregnancy outcome for the woman and her unborn child (see Chapter 54). Applicants with major medical conditions such as AIDS are eligible and should be routinely accepted for methadone treatment (71).

Table 41.3 Common Methadone-Drug Interactions

Drug	Mechanism	Effects/Remarks	Reference
Rifampin	Induction CYP-450 enzyme activity	Withdrawal Symptoms	48
Phenytoin	Induction CYP-450 enzyme activity	Withdrawal Symptoms	77
Ethyl Alcohol	Induction CYP-450 enzyme activity	Acute and chronic effects may differ	41, 50
Barbiturates	Induction CYP-450 enzyme activity	Acute and chronic effects may differ	55
Carbamazepine	Induction CYP-450 enzyme activity	Acute and chronic effects may differ	53
Opioid Agonist/ Antagonists	Opioid displaced from receptor sites	Withdrawal, usually inadvertent	74, 81

Reproduced with permission from Payte JT, Khuri ET. Principles of methadone dose determination. In: State methadone treatment guidelines. Rockville, MD: Center for Substance Abuse Treatment, Treatment Improvement Protocol Series 1993;1:47–58.

In the United States, methadone treatment has evolved into three phases (not to be confused with "dosing" phases previously discussed) during the past two decades. The first phase consists of a stabilization period that can last for about 3 months, during which patients adjust to the medication, receive their first annual physical examination, and are oriented to program regulations, expectations, routines, and services offered. Treatment planning begins with a thorough psychosocial history and assessment. Emergency situations and entitlements are addressed. Referrals are made to appropriate medical and social service agencies. New patients must report to the program daily (6 or 7 days per week) during this initial period. During the second phase, the treatment plan is reviewed and revised if necessary. This often involves implementing vocational goals such as job training or employment and providing ongoing medical and mental health treatment. For patients with serious medical problems such as HIV infection or AIDS or those with serious alcohol or multiple drug problems, this phase of treatment can be extended as long as necessary. Many patients profit relatively quickly from the relevant services that are provided and are able to improve family relationships, find employment, attend school, and function productively. During this phase patients may receive take-home medication, depending on their progress and adjustment to treatment. The third and final phase of treatment consists of continued methadone maintenance but a minimum of other services. These patients most often are employed and no longer require the intensive services provided in other phases but still require ongoing methadone maintenance. They continue to submit urine specimens for drug screening and ingest a dose of methadone under observation of a nurse, and they can consult with program staff if necessary. Many patients visit only once a week at this time. However, a limited number of experimental projects are currently operating that allow patients to visit even less frequently. These projects should be expanded for addicts seeking help.

The modern urban methadone treatment program is a full-scale medical and human service agency attempting to address major social and medical problems using a variety of techniques. During the past decade, patient characteristics have changed markedly due to increases in HIV infection among intravenous drug abusers, the epidemic of cocaine and crack, and homelessness (see Chapter 73). These problems and their sequelae require methadone providers to create and enhance services to meet these needs. These programs require expanded and more sophisticated physical facilities for an expanding population, better trained staff, and greater funding. However, public funding has not kept pace with program needs, and a pervasive downsizing and reform agendas in welfare and Medicaid managed care at the time of this writing does not allow for much hope in this area (for more information, see Chapter 87). However, providing primary care to substance abusers treated in methadone maintenance clinics could reduce the demand placed on emergency rooms and the need for hospitalization and thereby drastically cut the overall cost of their care.

Methadone maintenance treatment programs can be established in a variety of health care and social service settings. Whether located in a hospital, a primary care clinic, or a social service agency, methadone programs should be organized and managed to ensure optimal outcomes for patients in an environment conducive to health, safety, and good treatment.

In organizing and operating a program, concerns about how space is allocated and used can be critical to operations. Clinics operating in cramped or inadequate quarters cannot provide the kind of care or privacy needed for physical examinations or effective counseling and casework.

A quality program should have clear, cogent, consistent, and humanistic policies and procedures that are known and understood by both patients and staff. There should be a multidisciplinary approach that is flexible in order to provide individualized treatment planning and implementation based on assessed patient needs (59, 60).

A well-organized methadone maintenance treatment program must have enough space to allow staff to function in a professional manner consistent with good medical and mental health standards. Most states require programs to meet some degree of facility standards, and the federal government requires that facilities receiving federal funds provide unrestricted access for disabled persons. Over and above the minimum federal and state standards, programs should provide a clean, safe, and attractive environment that is friendly, cheerful, and accommodating.

Although it is difficult to estimate the optimal size of an adequate program, between 15 and 20 square feet for each patient in treatment should be allotted, based on a patient census of 300.

Each clinic should be organized around the services it provides, and services should flow into each other easily. There must be a methadone dispensing area that is easily accessible to the patients it will serve. Ideally, a nurses' station or dispensing area is constructed adjacent to a comfortable patient waiting area. The nurses' station should be well lighted and should allow for easy communication between nurse or dispenser and patient, as this interaction is the most frequent contact the patient has with staff. It allows the nurse to assess the patient and note any changes in appearance and demeanor, as well as to ensure that the patient ingests his or her medication. Generally, the medication is stored in a safe equipped for this purpose (the DEA currently requires a General Services Administration Class 5 safe within or adjacent to the nurses' station).

With the current concern about HIV infection and other health issues, the waiting room can be used to impart information about the program and its services, HIV education, prenatal care, and parenting skills as well as other important information. Through the creative use of videotapes that can run continuously while patients are waiting, a clinic can impart important information to its patients. Because patients often bring young children with them to the clinic, the area should be safe for young children and out of sight of the actual dispensing area.

The medical suite should be organized to ensure privacy and encourage patients to meet with the physician and other medical staff. The examination room must be well equipped and comfortable and there should be an adjacent office for staff to consult with patients. This area, as well as the entire clinic, should be equipped with adequate air exchange to prevent, as much as possible, airborne infections. Ultraviolet lighting and hepafiltration systems can also be helpful. Patient records should be stored in a secure area but should be easily accessible to those who must use them frequently. Programs should also provide offices for individual staff members rooms to hold patient groups and staff meetings, and a staff lounge.

The space should encourage patient and staff interaction, ensure privacy, and provide access to the services the program provides. This can best be accomplished by eliminating barriers between the patient and staff areas and by establishing an effective communications system that allows staff to communicate freely with each other whenever necessary.

Appropriate bathrooms are crucial, as programs must collect urine specimens from patients to clinically monitor whether patients continue to take methadone and remain free from other drugs. The bathrooms should also be clean and neat and allow for privacy. Some clinics turn off the hot water in patient bathrooms to prevent the warming of urine specimens brought from elsewhere. The bathrooms should also be located where staff can monitor use.

Clinics should be decorated in a friendly and inviting style to prevent a drab and institutional look. Bulletin boards should be hung in the waiting area and elsewhere to provide current information to patients.

Where space and funding allows, programs can experiment with recreation areas, classrooms, skills training (such as typing or word processing), or other methods to prevent patients from congregating directly outside the clinic or in the neighboring community.

Programs with clear, cogent policies, procedures, goals, and objectives that are familiar to both staff and patients and consistent with state of the art knowledge will provide the best outcomes. Programs must be operated humanistically but with clear rules against violence or threats of violence. Patients must see the clinic site as distinct from the hostile environments where they formerly used heroin and understand that different rules apply inside the clinic. However, the methods used to communicate these basics and the program's policies and procedures often can facilitate making the distinction. Patients must always be treated with compassion, dignity, and respect.

The dispensing of methadone is an important aspect of the treatment process, and the relationship between the patient and the nurse is very important. Program directors should endeavor to make this a therapeutic process. Therefore, the collection of clinic fees, urine specimens, or other clinic matters should be handled apart from the dispensing process to allow patients to view the dispensing of methadone in a therapeutic manner.

Because patient motivation is high upon entry into treatment, it is important that the entire treatment team engage the patient early. The medical history, physical examination, laboratory tests, psychosocial history, and medical, mental health, and social assessments should be accomplished during the first weeks of treatment. Most important in this process is staff-patient contact and the initial orientation. The initial physician-patient contact gives the doctor an opportunity to establish a relationship of trust, to explain the effectiveness and pharmacology of methadone, and to treat acute medical problems. Patients must come to see methadone as a medication and not a drug and to understand how it is used, its effects and its side effects, how the maintenance dose will be achieved, how to request a dosage change, and how to store methadone safely, if take-home doses are dispensed. Patients must understand how the program functions and be introduced to the program staff. The patient should participate in the development of an individualized treatment plan and clearly understand the goals and objectives the program has for his or her treatment and what the program expects. Most treatment plans are based on a triage concept, dealing with critical needs first. Housing, financial assistance, health care, and pending court cases are of primary importance. Later, vocational and educational goals can be pursued. Patients should know the services to which they entitled, what services are provided at the program and, if necessary, by referral to cooperating agencies.

Despite the poor prognosis indicated in early studies of methadone to abstinence (14, 61), many patients who progress well desire to withdraw from methadone after a successful period of maintenance. Programs must advise patients of the benefits and risks of tapering the dose and provide service and support for those who elect to undergo withdrawal. Service should continue after zero dose is achieved and should involve individual, family, and group treatment. Because craving may invariably return, the patient should be provided with tools and support in this area, including possible return to maintenance treatment without delay, if this becomes necessary.

Some methadone treatment programs have taken advantage of the fact that patients visit regularly and remain in treatment to offer needed services that are usually difficult to obtain. This model, "one-stop shopping," provides HIV-related services, services for children and families (see Chapter 64), services for pregnant and postpartum women (see Chapter 54), vocational and educational services, primary medical care, mental health services, and an array of substance abuse treatment services to deal with those who continue to abuse drugs and/or alcohol. Counseling and casework, relapse prevention techniques, 12-step and other self-help groups, and other modalities are offered to patients with these problems.

A methadone maintenance treatment program is a complex system of health care and service delivery that requires careful organization and a great many skills to operate. Clearly, health concerns dictate a sanitary environment. Medical and psychiatric care, nursing, counseling, casework, finance, public and community relations, pharmacy, administration, medical records management, clerical, housekeeping, security, communications systems, safety, biohazard disposal, and other skills and disciplines must all play a role in a successful and well-run program.

METHADONE TREATMENT AND HIV INFECTION

Several studies have confirmed that continuous methadone treatment is associated with a reduced risk of contracting HIV and may prevent infection of those patients not yet exposed to the virus. Infection rates among intravenous drug abusers in New York are estimated at 50%. Yet, studies in New York and Sweden examined patients in continuous treatment during the years when HIV exposure increased markedly (1983 was the pivotal year when HIV infection rates soared in both New York and Sweden). Infection rates for these groups of patients were extremely low (3% in Sweden; less than 10% in New York) compared with those for newly admitted patients and active addicts, leading investigators in these locations to conclude that continuous methadone treatment was associated with reduced risk of contracting HIV (8, 34). A study of 58 long-term socially rehabilitated patients showed that all were seronegative for HIV. These patients were enrolled in

treatment for more than 16 years and were maintained on a median dose of 60 mg/day (range, 5–100 mg/day). Prior to entry into treatment, these patients had used heroin by injection for an average of 10.3 years and engaged in high-risk behavior for contracting HIV, including sharing needles and "works," using "shooting galleries," and having unprotected sexual contacts. Successful methadone treatment was the major factor associated with the absence of HIV infection (70). Because of the relationship among HIV infection, AIDS, and methadone treatment, many programs have developed research and service delivery systems to deal with the high numbers of infected patients. Staff with special training in HIV spectrum disease provide risk reduction education, distribute condoms, and assist with referrals to infectious disease clinics. Primary medical care, including T cell monitoring and prescriptions for zidovudine (AZT) and other HIV medications, is provided along with prophylaxis for *Pneumocystis carinii* pneumonia and other opportunistic infections. An increase in tuberculosis, especially treatment-resistant tuberculosis, among this group has resulted in tuberculosis case management projects and the provision of medications for prophylaxis and treatment (18, 46). Some hospitals have developed specific methadone programs for HIV infection. At St. Clare's Hospital in New York City, for example, a special methadone clinic specifically designed for patients with HIV disease has been developed to ensure appropriate medical and social treatment (79). At Montefiore Medical Center in the Bronx, research into the natural history of HIV disease among intravenous drug abusers has been ongoing (see Chapter 59).

EFFICACY OF METHADONE MAINTENANCE TREATMENT

Despite the differences in goals and policies among programs, methadone maintenance treatment has yielded consistently positive evaluations since it was implemented in 1964. To fully understand methadone treatment, the program goals ". . . to reduce illicit drug consumption and other criminal behavior and secondarily to improve productive social behavior and psychological well being" must be considered (25). The primary goal of methadone treatment is to reduce or eliminate heroin use that is related most closely to the dosage level of methadone. As stated previously, when appropriate doses are provided, heroin use is markedly decreased or eliminated in most patients.

Cocaine (crack and cocaine hydrochloride) has become the major drug of abuse among methadone maintenance patients since the early 1980s. With this increase in use, programs have begun investigating 12-step models, self-help programs, pharmacotherapies, and other modalities to address this serious problem. In its review of methadone treatment programs, the General Accounting Office reported that in 1989, 14% of the patients in the programs surveyed had problems with cocaine or crack. In eight of the programs, up to 40% of the patients used the drug, while in 16 programs cocaine was used by 0–15% of the patients (78). In New York State, in 1990, 51% of the 14,282 admissions to methadone treatment admitted to a problem with a history of current cocaine or crack use, and 72% reported having administered cocaine by injection, thus further increasing the risk of HIV infection (68). This increase in cocaine abuse has led policy makers to criticize methadone maintenance treatment for failing to reduce these numbers. Yet, studies suggest that the level of cocaine use decreases from time of admission. Magura reports a decrease in cocaine use from 84% at admission to 66% after 6 months in treatment (62); Hartel et al. (35) report that prevalence of cocaine use is lower for those patients receiving more than 70 mg/day of methadone (51).

Prior to the increase in cocaine use and HIV infection, alcohol and the medical complications of alcoholism were the most serious problem found among methadone patients, affecting about 20–25% of the patients (7, 44). Before 1986, medical conditions related to alcoholism were the major cause of mortality in methadone maintenance treatment. Studies also suggest that when patients leave methadone treatment, their drinking behavior increases, possibly to obtain relief from symptoms of narcotic craving without relapsing to the use of heroin. However, many patients used alcohol in conjunction with heroin prior to entering treatment (44). Also, since patients with alcohol and other drug problems were routinely admitted into methadone treatment, these problems had program implications and decreased positive treatment response.

Many studies have documented a substantial reduction in criminal behavior from pretreatment levels. Like most other treatment variables, reduction in criminal behavior increases with length of time in treatment. These trends have been consistent throughout the more than two decades of methadone treatment and in a variety of settings. In Hong Kong, after methadone was introduced in 1976, there was an 85% reduction in the number of heroin addicts sent to prisons during a 4-year period (45). In the study conducted in three Northeastern cities, Ball and Ross (6) reported a 79% decrease in the number of crimes committed by patients during their first 6 months of treatment.

Socially productive behavior as measured by employment, schooling, or homemaking also improves with length of time in treatment. During the first 15 years of methadone treatment in New York, employment rates were just below 60%. During the 1980s, when the employment market changed, cocaine and crack use increased, and homelessness and HIV infection rates increased, social productivity and employment levels in New York declined to less than 40% in 1990 (4). A study of those socially productive methadone patients in New York showed that they held positions across the spectrum of the job market, including lawyer, architect, musician, film producer, housewife, chef, construction worker, social worker, secretary, laborer, and doorman. There was no relationship between the nature of employment and dose or number of treatment episodes. Many of these successful patients had attempted to become abstinent, relapsed, and subsequently returned to methadone treatment in order to maintain their employment. For the majority of inner-city patients, lack of education and job skills, child care, unemployment, and poverty continue to have an adverse impact on socially productive behavior and treatment response.

Recent research has concluded that program characteristics are the critical factor in successful outcomes. In their study, Ball and Ross (6) opened what they call the "black box" of treatment, indicating that the major factor in outcome is the length of time in treatment. Factors that influence longer retention are adequate dose, well-trained staff, trusting and confidential relationships between the patients and program staff, clear policies and procedures, low staff turnover and high morale, flexible take-home policies, and other pertinent program characteristics. Although many clinicians consider abstinence as a critical treatment goal, it is problematic and difficult to attain for most patients. There is a high degree of consistency in the results of studies of patients who leave treatment. The majority of discharged patients revert to use of heroin, other illicit narcotics, and/or alcohol. Ball and Ross (6, p. 82) found that 82% of the patients had relapsed to intravenous drug use after having been out of treatment for 10 months, or more, with almost half (45.5%) relapsing after having been out of treatment for 1–3 months. Dole and Joseph (21) found that relapse occurred independently of patient variables such as ethnicity, gender, or education level. Older patients may substitute heavy alcohol use for heroin, and favorable outcome is associated with shorter duration of heroin use, longer duration of treatment, employment, and an absence of behavioral problems while in treatment. Withdrawal from treatment may have fatal consequences. Dole and Joseph (21) found that death rates for discharged persons were more than twice those of patients still in treatment. The major difference in the causes of death between treatment and posttreatment is the sharp increase in narcotics-related deaths after leaving treatment. No evidence was found of narcotics-related deaths among properly stabilized patients during methadone treatment (43). However, this study was completed prior to the advent of the HIV epidemic. By 1986, AIDS had become the major cause of death among methadone patients in New York City programs (44).

Methadone maintenance treatment is cost effective and beneficial to society. Rufener and colleagues (76) studied the cost effectiveness of methadone maintenance and other treatment modalities and yielded a benefit/cost ratio of 4.4:1. The most comprehensive examination of economic benefits and costs was performed on data from the Treatment Outcome Prospective Study (TOPS) (37). After examining the average cost of a treatment day, detailed measurements of rates of criminal activities, and the costs to society of various crimes, the study yielded a final benefit/cost ratio of 4:1. Using any of the studies, it is clear that methadone maintenance pays for itself on the first day it is delivered and that posttreatment effects are an economic bonus. These benefits accrue not only to the patient but to society in general.

SPECIAL ISSUES AND NEW TREATMENT APPROACHES

The current methadone maintenance system faces many problems as it approaches the final years of this century. Numerous programs are publicly funded and have been subject to apathy and hostility, decreasing funding, deteriorating physical facilities, high staff turnover, and community opposition to the opening and/or continued operation of clinics, caused by concerns about patient loitering and diversion of take-home supplies of methadone. Program plans must be developed to address these critical issues. Programs must develop services to meet new needs as well as policies and procedures to address loitering, diversion, and community concerns.

Funding, always problematic, needs to be secured for physical facilities as well as for ongoing operations. Programs have developed strategies to secure additional funding from agencies that did not traditionally fund drug treatment, such as HIV and AIDS service systems and social services agencies. New models of treatment and service delivery should be developed and piloted to supplement existing program models. Service providers and funding and regulatory agencies must work cooperatively to improve treatment and seek solutions to existing problems. Provider coalitions on a state, national, and international basis can provide a forum for this to occur. Broad-based conferences can also serve to discuss, debate, and resolve concerns while serving as vehicles for the transfer of technology from researchers to clinicians.

To enhance the traditional outpatient methadone clinic, changing patient needs dictate that new and innovative approaches be piloted. Since the 1980s, several such efforts have been implemented. Some were developed specifically in response to HIV spectrum disease, whereas others sought to provide innovative ways to expand or enhance programs.

To address homelessness and abuse of cocaine and other drugs, residential short-stay methadone treatment was developed by the Lower East Side Service Center in New York for patients who were not functioning well. A similar program was established in Boston. These programs provide methadone maintenance and residential treatment while endeavoring to resolve the difficulties that interfered with adjustment to outpatient treatment. The program is usually 3–6 months in duration and the patient is returned to his or her outpatient clinic after completion. Methadone dose is maintained throughout the program. Although other residential programs provide methadone, most require tapering the dose over a 6-month period. Residential methadone maintenance originally was piloted in 1973 at the Albert Einstein College of Medicine, under the direction of Dr. Joyce Lowinson, but the program was closed because of lack of funding at the time.

In the New York City prison system, the Key Extended Entry Program (KEEP) offers methadone maintenance treatment to addict inmates who request treatment for heroin addiction upon incarceration. Eligible inmates are misdemeanor offenders with short sentences who otherwise comply with admission standards. They are maintained while in jail and are referred to a community clinic where they are guaranteed continued treatment. This program involves the cooperation of the New York City Department of Corrections, the prison health services, and a network of community-based methadone treatment providers (80). The Beth Israel Medical Center in New York City operated an "interim" clinic in 1989 as a research project. The purpose of interim maintenance was to provide immediate methadone treatment to eligible applicants on a waiting list for comprehensive methadone treatment in order to reduce HIV risk behaviors. The clinic provided an appropriate dose of methadone, AIDS education, and physical examinations. Casework and counseling were limited. A study of the 301 patients showed that heroin use was reduced from 63% at admission to 29% after 1 month. Cocaine use was not significantly reduced. The controls on the waiting list showed no reduction in the use of either substance. In 1989 the FDA originally proposed "interim methadone maintenance," prompting a rather strong reaction on the part of policy makers and providers (80). Much of the reaction did not support the concept of "interim methadone maintenance." The provision for interim methadone maintenance was ultimately approved but with very restrictive conditions that prevented any serious implementation of interim maintenance. The proposal for interim methadone maintenance heightened the debate concerning the appropriate use of methadone. Advocates for interim maintenance argued that it would take many years to adequately expand methadone treatment and that tens of thousands of addicts would be denied treatment. Opponents believed that those entering methadone maintenance treatment in the 1990s were most in need of comprehensive services. They believed that the interim clinic as an inexpensive substitute would jeopardize funding for comprehensive treatment programs. Opponents of interim treatment referred to a study at the Veterans Administration Medical Center in Philadelphia that showed that minimal or low-threshold treatment did not reduce illicit drug use significantly (64).

Medical Maintenance

Medical maintenance is the complete integration of socially rehabilitated methadone patients into general medical practice. They are not isolated in special clinics, as are regular maintenance and aftercare patients, but are treated by internists or other primary care physicians in a private practice setting, indistinguishable from other patients. In 1985, Drs. Dole and Nyswander transferred 25 stable long term methadone patients into the general medical practice of a group of internists (22). This was done as a continuation of a research study, under FDA auspices. At the present time approximately 120 patients are enrolled in this ongoing study.

All patients have met stringent entry criteria (22). They are seen on a monthly basis at which time: (a) a urine toxicology is obtained, (b) a 28-day supply of methadone diskets or tablets is dispensed, (c) a dose of methadone is taken, (d) any medical problems are treated, (e) other problems or issues are discussed.

A mutually convenient return appointment and any payments are made. The fee includes the office visit, the urinalysis, and the methadone. The methadone prescription is filled by the participating pharmacy and dispensed by the physician.

Medical maintenance is the essential "next phase" of methadone treatment for socially rehabilitated patients. The methadone clinic system, with its controls, prevents patients from developing their potentials. These controls may be appropriate at the beginning of treatment but they generally become obstacles to further rehabilitating experiences, such as business ventures, job-related travel, confidentiality issues, or need to quickly change an appointment. The stringent controls tend to infantilize the rehabilitated patient, giving the message that he or she is unworthy or too immature to be trusted.

The medical maintenance patient is removed from the nonrehabilitated patients in the clinic environment. In general, rehabilitated patients do not like the clinic atmosphere, which tends to reinforce the stigma they all share. The rehabilitated methadone patient fits nicely into an internal medicine practice. The personality profiles of medical maintenance patients are no different than patients with other chronic medical conditions.

Methadone patients are highly stigmatized by the general public. Entering into medical maintenance reduces the stigma and facilitates confidentiality. Since they are treated like any other patient with a chronic disorder their self-respect increases.

A follow-up study (72) reported a high retention rate and a low incidence of substance abuse or lost medication. These trends continued with approximately 6% of patients returned to their methadone clinic due to violation of the protocol, with cocaine abuse being the most common. An additional 5% of patients have electively withdrawn from methadone. In 1988, 58 medical maintenance patients were tested for HIV seropositivity (71). All had entered methadone treatment before the start of the HIV epidemic, all were HIV negative, and none have seroconverted.

A survey of 80 medical maintenance patients treated by one of the authors (ES) revealed 55% of patients have undergraduate or graduate degrees. Average family income was $62,000 (range, $12,000–$400,000), mean duration of methadone treatment was 22 years (range, 8–30 years) and mean dose was 60 mg (range, 5–100 mg). There was no correlation between dose level, job description, or income level.

Medical maintenance is a proven method of methadone treatment. Physicians must be properly trained and not labor under the many and pervasive methadone myths. Physicians must be flexible and sensitive to the patients' needs for confidentiality and changes of appointments. When referrals are made, contact must be made with the consulting physician or dentist to dispel misinformation and clarify issues about methadone.

Working in medical maintenance is extraordinarily gratifying and fulfilling. It is often the first time a patient feels self-respect and pride about his or her accomplishment in overcoming the severe disease of opiate addiction. Medical maintenance has been established in New York, Baltimore, and Chicago (69).

In an effort to provide specialized services for HIV-infected patients, clinics have developed special primary medical care services for patients with HIV infection and AIDS. These clinics provide a significant portion of the medical care for their patients and maintain linkages with infectious disease clinics and hospitals. Drug therapy, T cell monitoring, counseling and testing, prophylaxis for treatment of opportunistic infections, clinical trials, and counseling are part of routine care. Clinics providing these specialized services are now operating in San Francisco, New York, and Miami, and this model is being replicated elsewhere.

Several other models for innovative approaches have also been proposed or are being developed. At the Albert Einstein College of Medicine in the Bronx, two such models are now being developed. One will attempt to provide culturally sensitive, family-centered treatment. The other model involves "front-loading" services to newly admitted patients, in an effort to mobilize intensive resources at the time of greatest need and to integrate the patient more fully into the treatment system. These models are examples of ways to enhance or expand treatment to meet current needs. At present, methadone treatment programs in the United States treat approximately 15% of narcotics addicts at any given time.

The human and financial cost to society of from 400,000 to possibly 700,000 or even more untreated narcotics addicts is difficult to comprehend. That the expansion of treatment *and* enhancing the quality of care provided would result in savings of billions of dollars annually is simply not relevant. One might wonder just how long we, as a society, can afford do little or nothing to address this problem.

Effective methods to expand treatment must be developed in order to reach out to those either not yet in treatment or not motivated to seek it. With expansion of treatment the many barriers and obstacles to treatment must be addressed. Why are so few even motivated to seek treatment? At the same time, efforts to overcome community concerns and opposition to the location of new clinics must be made, if meaningful expansion is to be accomplished. Community and political leaders must be educated to understand the public health value of expansion. Effective outreach strategies must be employed to motivate those addicts in shelters and on the street to accept methadone treatment. Methadone treatment must be made more acceptable. Mobile vans have been used in the Netherlands and in Boston to reach addicts where it has not been possible to establish permanent clinic sites. Such a strategy could be used to introduce treatment to shelters and other social service agencies directly serving addicted people.

In the last few years federal and state governments have embarked on many reforms of the public health and welfare system, putting limits on entitlements and moving away from a fee for service system to one based on capitation, giving rise to the concept of managed care. As a long-term treatment of a chronic problem, methadone maintenance does not fit easily with these changes. As a result, some states have "carved out" methadone treatment, while others have ignored or incorporated it into their managed care plans. These changes represent an additional challenge to providers but many present an opportunity for outcome based, individualized care. Only time will tell.

SUMMARY AND CONCLUSION

Methadone maintenance treatment programs originally were developed to deal with the problem of heroin addiction. Methadone as a medication is unique in its capacity to reduce or eliminate the craving for narcotics and to provide a pharmacologic blockade against heroin. When the Dole-Nyswander protocol and philosophy has been followed, this modality has proved extremely effective. However, since the early years of methadone maintenance, many new social and health problems have emerged. Many of these have had an adverse effect on methadone patients and the programs that treat them. HIV infection and AIDS have placed methadone programs in the position of assuming ever-wider responsibilities. The high retention and attendance by patients give programs the opportunity and the responsibility of providing the medical and social care that a chronic, debilitating, and potentially terminal illness requires. These factors also provide the opportunity to educate and treat patients, to reduce transmission of HIV and other communicable illnesses such as tuberculosis, and to greatly improve the quality of life for infected patients. These programs are now moving in the direction of becoming primary care clinics for substance abusers.

In summary, a quality methadone maintenance treatment program is one that continuously evaluates and assesses the changing needs of its patients and seeks to meet them to the best of its ability. Today, most methadone maintenance treatment programs face their greatest challenge. The recession of the 1990s has made it mandatory for programs to seek new and creative funding support while patients fight HIV infection, epidemic cocaine and crack use, poverty, homelessness, and other social ills. Programs that seek to innovate, to meet most patient needs within the treatment setting, to develop new methodologies, or to replicate successful efforts of other programs can better meet present and future challenges. At the same time, the public demands programs that are cost effective and produce documented results they can understand. It is critical that all programs develop evaluation capability, document their productivity and that of their patients, and most of all, publicize their successes.

References

1. Alksne H, Trussel RE, Elinson J, Patrick S. A follow-up study of treated adolescent narcotics users [mimeographed report]. New York: Columbia University School of Public Health and Administrative Medicine, 1959.
2. American Society of Addiction Medicine (ASAM). American Society of Addiction Medicine policy statement on methadone treatment. Washington, DC: ASAM, 1991.
3. Appel PW, Gordon NB. Digit-symbol performance in methadone-treated ex-heroin addicts. Am J Psychiatry 1976;133:1337–1340.
4. Armstrong G. Methadone programs: a snapshot. Report prepared for the New York State Division of Substance Abuse Services, 1990.
5. Babst DV, Newman S, Gordon NB, Warner A. Driving records of methadone maintained patients in New York State. New York State Narcotic Control Commission, 1973.
6. Ball JC, Ross A. The effectiveness of methadone maintenance treatment. New York: Springer-Verlag, 1991.
7. Bickel WK, Marion I, Lowinson J. The treatment of alcoholic methadone patients: a review. J Subst Abuse Treat 1987;4:15–19.
8. Blix O, Gronbladh L. AIDS and IV heroin addicts: the preventive effect of methadone maintenance in Sweden. In: Programs and abstracts of the Fourth International Conference on AIDS, June 12–16, 1988, Stockholm, Sweden.
9. Blumberg RD, Pruesser DF. Drug abuse and driving performance. Final Report Control DOT-HS-009-1-184. Washington, DC: U.S. Department of Transportation, 1972.
10. Borg L, Ho A, Peters JE, Kreek MJ. Availability of reliable serum methadone determination for management of symptomatic patients. J Addict Dis 1995;14(3):83–96.
11. Brecher EM. Licit and illicit drugs: Consumers Union report on narcotics, stimulants, depressants, inhalants, hallucinogens, and marijuana. Boston: Little Brown and Company, 1972.
12. Caplehorn JRM, Bell J. Methadone dosage and retention of patients in maintenance treatment. Med J Aust 1991;154:195–199.
13. Cooper JB. Methadone treatment in the United States. In: Awni A, Westmermeyer J, eds. Methadone in the management of opioid dependence: programs and policies around the world. Geneva, Switzerland: World Health Organization, 1988.
14. Cooper JR. Ineffective use of psychoactive drugs—methadone treatment is no exception. JAMA 1992;267(2):281–282.
15. Courtwright DT. Dark paradise: opiate addiction in America before 1940. Cambridge, MA: Harvard University Press, 1982.
16. Courtwright DT, Joseph H, Des Jarlais D. Addicts who survived: an oral history of narcotic use in America, 1923–1965. Knoxville: University of Tennessee Press, 1989.
17. D'Aunno T, Vaughn TE. Variations in methadone treatment practices result from a national study. JAMA 1992:267(2):253–258.
18. Division of Substance Abuse of the Albert Einstein College of Medicine of Yeshiva University, New York City. Annual report, 1989.
19. Dole VP, Nyswander ME. A medical treatment for diacetyl-morphine (heroin) addiction. JAMA 1965;193:646.
20. Dole VP, Nyswander ME, Kreek MJ. Narcotic blockade. Arch Intern Med 1966;118:304–309.
21. Dole VP, Joseph H. Long term outcome of patients treated with methadone maintenance. Ann N Y Acad Sci 1978;311:181–189.
22. Dole VP. Implications of methadone maintenance for theories of narcotic addiction. JAMA 1988;260:3025–3029.
23. Federal Register, December 15, 1972;37:16790.
24. Gearing FR, Schweitzer MD. An epidemiological evaluation of long-term methadone maintenance treatment for heroin addiction. Am J Epidemiol 1974;100:101–112.
25. Committee for the Substance Abuse Coverage Study, Division of Health Care Services, Institute of Medicine. The effectiveness of treatment. In: Gerstein DR, Harwood HJ, eds. Treating drug problems. Washington, DC: National Academy Press, 1990;1:132–199.
26. Gewirtz PD. Notes and comments: methadone maintenance for heroin addicts. Yale Law J 1969;78:1175–1211.
27. Goldsmith DS, Hunt DE, Lipton DS, Strug DL. Methadone folklore: beliefs about side effects and their impact on treatment. Human Organization 1984;43(4):330–340.
28. Goldstein A. Blind dosage comparisons and other studies in a large methadone program. J Psychedelic Drugs 1971;4:177–181.
29. Goldstein A, Aronow L, Kalman S. Principles of drug action: the clinical basis of pharmacology. 2nd edition. New York: John Wiley & Sons, 1974.
30. Gordon NB. Influence of narcotic drugs on highway safety. Accid Anal Prev 1976;8:3–7.
31. Gordon NB, Lipset JS. Intellectual and functional status of methadone patients after nearly ten years of treatment. Internal report. The Rockefeller University and New York State Office of Drug Services. Presented at the 85th annual convention of the American Psychological Association, Washington, DC, September 5, 1976.
32. Gossop M, Bradley B, Phillips GT. An investigation of withdrawal symptoms shown by opiate addicts during and subsequent to a 21-day inpatient methadone detoxification procedure. Addict Behav 1987;12:1–6.
33. Gotsis CA. Personal communication, 1991.
34. Hartel D, Selwyn PA, Schoenbaum EE, et al. Methadone maintenance treatment and reduced risk of AIDS and AIDS-specific mortality in intravenous drug users [abstract 8526]. Paper presented at the Fourth International Conference on AIDS, Stockholm, Sweden, June, 1988.
35. Hartel D, Schoenbaum EE, Selwyn PA, et al. Temporal patterns of cocaine use and AIDS in intravenous drug users in methadone maintenance [abstract]. Paper presented at the Fifth International Conference on AIDS, Montreal, Canada, June, 1989.
36. Hartel D. Cocaine use, inadequate methadone dose increase risk of AIDS for IV drug users in treatment. NIDA Notes 1989/1990;5(1).
37. Harwood HJ, Hubbard RL, Collins JJ, Rachal JV. The costs of crime and the benefits of drug abuse treatment: a cost-benefit analysis using TOPS data. NIDA Res Monogr 1988;86:209–235.
38. Institute of Medicine. Treatment standards and optimal treatment. In: Rettig RA, Yarmolinsky A, eds. Federal regulation of methadone treatment. Washington DC: National Academy Press, 1995:185–216.
39. Isbell H. Methods and results of studying experimental human addiction to the newer synthetic analgesics. Ann N Y Acad Sci 1948;51:108.
40. Isbell H, Vogel V. The addiction liability of methadone (Amidone, Dolophine, 10820) and its use in the treatment of the morphine abstinence syndrome. Am J Psychiatry 1949;105:909.
41. Jaffe JH. Further experience with methadone in the treatment of narcotic users. Int J Addict 1970;5:375–389.
42. Joseph H, Dole VP. Methadone patients on probation and parole. Federal Probation 1970 (June):42–48.
43. Joseph H, Des Jarlais D. Methadone patients in conventional society. Treatment issues report 32. Bureau of Research and Evaluation, New York State Division of Substance Abuse Services, March, 1983.
44. Joseph H, Appel P. Alcoholism and methadone treatment: consequences for the patient and the program. Am J Drug Alcohol Issues 1985;11(1 & 2):37–53.
45. Joseph H. The criminal justice system and opiate addiction: a historical perspective. NIDA Res Monogr 1988;86:106–125.
46. Joseph H, Springer E. Methadone maintenance treatment and the AIDS epidemic. In: Platt JJ, Kaplan CD, McKim PJ, eds. The effectiveness of drug abuse treatment: Dutch and American perspectives. Malabar, FL: Robert E. Krieger, 1990:261–274.

47. Kreek MJ. Plasma and urine levels of methadone. N Y State J Med 1973;73:2773–2777.
48. Kreek MJ. Drug interactions with methadone. Ann N Y Acad Sci 1976;281:350–371.
49. Kreek MJ. Medical complications in methadone patients. Ann N Y Acad Sci 1978;311:29, 110–134.
50. Kreek MJ. Opiate-ethanol interactions: implications for the biological basis of treatment of combined addictive diseases. NIDA Res Monogr 1987;81:428–439.
51. Kreek MJ. Methadone maintenance for harm reduction. Paper presented at the International Symposium on Addiction and AIDS, Vienna, Austria, February, 1991.
52. Kreek MJ. Rationale for maintenance pharmacotherapy of opiate dependence. In: O'Brien CP, Jaffe JH, eds. Addictive states. Research publications: Association for Research in Nervous and Mental Disease. New York: Raven Press, 1992;70:210.
53. Kuhn KL, Halikas JA, Kemp KD. Carbamazepine treatment of cocaine dependence in methadone maintenance patients with dual opiate-cocaine addiction. NIDA Res Monogr 1989; 95:316–317.
54. Langrod J, Lowinson J, Ruiz P. Methadone treatment and physical complaints: a clinical analysis. Int J Addict 1981;16(5):947–952.
55. Liu SJ, Wang RI. Case report of barbiturate-induced enhancement of methadone metabolism and withdrawal syndrome. Am J Psychiatry 1988;141:1287–1288.
56. Loimer N, Schmid R. The use of plasma levels to optimize methadone maintenance treatment. Drug Alcohol Depend 1992;30(3):241.
57. Loimer N, Schmid R, Grunberger J, Jagsch R, Linzmayer L, Presslich O. Psychophysiological reactions in methadone maintenance patients do not correlate with methadone plasma levels. Psychopharmacology (Berl) 1991;103(4):538.
58. Lowinson JH. The methadone maintenance research program. In: Rehabilitating the narcotic addict. Report of Institute on New Developments in the Rehabilitation of the Narcotic Addict, Fort Worth, TX, February 16–18, 1966. Sponsored jointly by the Division of Hospitals of the United States Public Health Service, Vocational Rehabilitation Administration, and Texas Christian University. Washington, DC: United States Government Printing Office, 1967:271–284.
59. Lowinson JH. Commonly asked clinical questions about methadone maintenance. Int J Addict 1977;12:821.
60. Lowinson JH, Millman RB. Clinical aspects of methadone maintenance treatment. In: Dupont R, Goldstein A, O'Donnell J, eds. Handbook on drug abuse. Washington, DC: National Institute on Drug Abuse, 1979:49–56.
61. Lowinson JH. Methadone maintenance in perspective. In: Lowinson JH, Ruiz P, eds. Substance abuse: clinical problems and perspectives. Baltimore: Williams & Wilkins, 1981: 344–354.
62. Magura S, Siddiqi Q, Freeman R, Lipton DS. Changes in cocaine use after entry to methadone treatment [mimeographed report]. New York: Narcotic and Drug Research, Inc., 1991.
63. Marion IJ. LAAM in the treatment of opiate addiction treatment improvement protocol 22. Rockville, MD: U.S. Department of Health and Human Services, 1995.
64. McLellan AT, Woody GE, Luborsky L, Goehl L. Is the counselor an "active ingredient" in substance abuse rehabilitation? An examination of treatment success among four counselors. J Nerv Ment Dis 1988;176:423–430.
65. Moskowitz H, Sharma S. Skills performance in methadone patients and ex-addicts. Paper presented at the annual meeting of the American Psychological Association, New York City, September 5, 1979.
66. New York Academy of Medicine, Committee on Public Health, Subcommittee on Drug Addiction. Bull N Y Acad Med 1955;31:592.
67. New York Academy of Science, Committee on Public Health. Methadone management of heroin addiction. Bull N Y Acad Med 1990; 46:391.
68. New York State Division of Substance Abuse Services. Management information systems, client characteristics on admission from 1/1/90 to 12/31/90. Albany, New York, 1991.
69. Novick DM, Pascarelli EF, Joseph H, Salsitz EA, et al. Methadone maintenance patients in general medical practice: a preliminary report. JAMA 1988;259:3299–3302.
70. Novick DM, Ochshorn M, Ghail V, et al. Natural killer activity and lymphocyte subsets in parenteral heroin abusers and long term methadone maintenance patients. J Pharmacol Exp Ther 1989;250:606–610.
71. Novick DM, Joseph H, Croxson TS, Salsitz EA, et al. Absence of antibody to human immunodeficiency virus in long term, socially rehabilitated methadone maintenance patients. Arch Intern Med 1990;150:97–99.
72. Novick DM, Joseph H, Salsitz EA, et al. Outcomes of treatment of socially rehabilitated methadone maintenance patients in physicians' offices (medical maintenance): follow-up at three and a half to nine and a fourth years. J Gen Intern Med 1994;9(3):127–130.
73. Nyswander ME. The drug addict as a patient. New York: Grune & Stratton, 1956.
74. Payte JT, Khuri ET. Principles of methadone dose determination. In: State methadone treatment guidelines. Center for Substance Abuse Treatment, Treatment Improvement Protocol Series 1991;1:47–58.
75. Rosenblum AR, Magura S, Joseph H. Ambivalence towards methadone treatment among intravenous drug users. J Psychoactive Drugs 1991;23(1):21–27.
76. Rufener BL, Rachal JV, Cruze AM. Management effectiveness measures for NIDA drug abuse treatment programs. Cost benefit analysis. DHEW publication no. (ADM) 77–423. Rockville, MD: National Institute on Drug Abuse, 1977.
77. Tong TG, Pond SM, Kreek MJ, Jaffery NF, Benowitz NL. Phenytoin-induced methadone withdrawal. Ann Intern Med 1981;94(3): 349–351.
78. U.S. General Accounting Office. Methadone maintenance: some treatment programs are not effective. Greater federal oversight needed. Publication no. GAO/HRD-90–104, 1990. Washington DC: U.S. Government Printing Office, 1990.
79. Wilkinson W, Williams S. Personal communication, St. Clare's Hospital, New York City, 1991.
80. Yancovitz SR, Des Jarlais DC, Peyser NP, et al. A randomized trial of an "interim" methadone maintenance clinic. Am J Public Health 1991; 81(9):1185–1200.
81. Zweben JE, Payte JT. Methadone maintenance in the treatment of opioid dependence: a current perspective. West J Med 1990;152(5):588–599.

Suggested Readings

Cushman P. Ten years of methadone maintenance treatment: some clinical observations. Am J Drug Alcohol Abuse 1977;4:543–553.
Federal Register, June 11, 1970;35:9013.
Federal Register 21 CFR, part 21. Washington, DC: Food and Drug Administration, March 2, 1989.
Kreek MJ. Presentation at 1988 meeting of the Committee on Problems of Drug Dependence. Summarized in NIDA Notes, Fall, 1988, pp. 12, 25.
Stimmel B, Goldberg J, Rotkopf E. Ability to remain abstinent after methadone maintenance detoxification. A six year study. JAMA 1977;237:1216–1220.

42 ALTERNATIVE PHARMACOTHERAPIES FOR OPIATE ADDICTION

Robert A. Greenstein, Paul J. Fudala, and Charles P. O'Brien

The development of methadone maintenance by Dole and Nyswander in the mid 1960s (1) ushered in the modern era of pharmacological treatment for opiate dependence. Previously, except for a brief period of legalized opiate maintenance in several U.S. cities in the early 1900s, abrupt discontinuation of opiates or substitution of decreasing doses of methadone or shorter-acting legally prescribed opiates for patients' drugs of choice were used to detoxify opiate addicts. However, detoxification alone is a generally unsuccessful treatment for opiate dependence because relapse occurs shortly after the patient leaves the hospital (2). Detoxification followed by incarceration or inpatient or outpatient treatment has a somewhat better outcome but is highly influenced by patient selection and by availability of drugs in the community. Opioid substitution using methadone or levo-alpha-acetyl-methadol (LAAM), with or without adjunctive therapy such as counseling or vocational rehabilitation, enables many patients to reduce or stop use of illicit opiates and stabilize their lives. Nonetheless, methadone-maintained patients also have a high rate of relapse following discontinuation of the medication. Hence, many addicts require recurrent or extended courses of treatment.

Although social and physiological factors are involved in the vulnerability to relapse, including lability of mood and stress intolerance associated with the protracted abstinence syndrome (3), drug-related stimuli alone may elicit conditioned withdrawal effects in the absence of pharmacologically induced changes (4). Hence, addicts may experience physical symptoms similar to those related to the withdrawal of opiates when they are exposed to environmental cues or settings previously associated with drug use. Addicts may be more vulnerable to conditioned withdrawal effects during the period of autonomic instability known as protracted withdrawal, and they may resume drug use to relieve these symptoms. Methadone or LAAM maintenance reduces craving for opiates (5) but may prolong physical dependence.

Psychopharmacologists have searched for nonaddicting analgesics and treatments for opiate dependence for decades. Although methadone maintenance has helped thousands of opiate addicts in the United States during the past 30 years, there remain considerable philosophical objections to its use. This has given added impetus to the development of alternative pharmacological treatments that would not prolong physical dependence on opioids, thus enabling addicts to recover without months or years of treatment with methadone, and without the high rate of relapse that follows most drug-free treatments for substance dependence. This effort has led to the development of new therapeutic options for those patients who prefer a nonmethadone treatment or who respond less well to methadone.

Many addicts begin experimenting with or abusing drugs in adolescence and progress over a period of months or years to dependence. As dependence continues, addicts spend more of their time and energy securing drugs, which leads to disruption of interpersonal and family relationships, and diminished educational and vocational achievement. This results in increasing antisocial behavior and criminality, and high emotional and economic costs for sustaining dependence. Nonetheless, even individuals professing a strong desire to interrupt the addiction cycle are often ambivalent about achieving abstinence. Most have not learned to manage stress without opiates and look to drugs for immediate symptom relief. For any treatment, whether pharmacologically based or not, to produce significant benefit, the natural course of the opiate dependence process, the presence of concurrent psychiatric illness, and the abuse of other drugs or alcohol must be recognized and addressed. Additionally, treatment goals themselves may vary. For example, if a patient is early in the course of addiction or an older patient near the end of an addiction cycle, then total abstinence may be a realistic goal. Conversely, if a patient is in the throes of his or her addiction, a decrease in the amount and/or frequency of illicit drug abuse may be a more attainable and realistic goal than immediate abstinence.

Experience has taught us that interrupting the powerfully reinforcing effects of opiates and drug-seeking behavior requires a concerted effort by therapists, patients, and their families to permanently overcome addiction. This is particularly true once an addiction is established as a chronic condition, when most patients will require multiple interventions. During the past 30 years, much research has focused on three classes of treatment medications: nonopiates that alleviate withdrawal symptomatology; opiate agonists other than methadone; and opiate antagonists, partial agonists, and mixed agonists/antagonists, which can block or competitively inhibit opiates at their receptors. This chapter reviews the literature on alternative pharmacotherapies to methadone and discusses strategies for developing more effective treatments for opiate dependence.

NONOPIOID TREATMENT ALTERNATIVES: CLONIDINE AND LOFEXIDINE

The acute opioid withdrawal syndrome is a time-limited phenomenon, generally of brief duration. Following the abrupt termination of short-acting opioids such as heroin, morphine, or hydromorphone, withdrawal signs and symptoms usually subside by the second or third opioid-free day. Although uncomfortable for the addict, the opioid withdrawal syndrome, in contrast to the syndrome associated with the withdrawal of other drugs such as benzodiazepines and alcohol, does not pose a medical risk to the individual. Thus, there is a particular appeal for treating this syndrome symptomatically, especially with medications that do not themselves produce physical dependence.

Clonidine is an alpha-2 adrenergic agonist indicated for the treatment of hypertension and has been given orphan drug status for epidural use as an analgesic in selected cancer patients. Clonidine has shown utility in the medical detoxification of patients from methadone (6–8), as well as commonly abused opioids such as heroin (9, 10) morphine (11) propoxyphene (12), and meperidine (13). In particular, it has been shown to be useful in preparing individuals for stabilization onto the opioid antagonist naltrexone (14–17). Clonidine has also been reported to be useful in decreasing withdrawal signs and symptoms associated with the cessation of alcohol (18, 19) and tobacco (20–23) use.

The capacity of clonidine to ameliorate withdrawal-associated effects (e.g., lacrimation and rhinorrhea) has been linked to its modulation of noradrenergic hyperactivity in the locus ceruleus (24–27). Additionally, clonidine may affect central serotonergic (28), cholinergic (29), and purinergic systems (30). It seems to be most effective in suppressing certain opioid withdrawal signs and symptoms such as restlessness and diaphoresis. However, clonidine is not well accepted by addicts because it does not produce morphine-like subjective effects or relieve certain types of withdrawal distress, such as anxiety (11). Sedation and hypotension also limit its utility. No fixed dosing guidelines are currently available and dosages are generally individualized to each patient based on therapeutic response and side effect limitations.

Secondary to an effort to identify an agent with less sedating and hypotensive effects than clonidine, a number of other alpha-2-adrenergic agonists have been evaluated for their ability to moderate the opioid withdrawal syndrome. Of these, lofexidine, a clonidine analog licensed in the United Kingdom for opioid detoxification treatment, has been the subject of much clinical evaluation. Although lofexidine has not been as extensively studied as clonidine, available data indicate that it may be effective in suppressing some of the signs and symptoms of opioid withdrawal (31–34). The conduct of double-blind, placebo-controlled trials would aid in evaluating whether lofexidine may provide an improved therapeutic profile compared to clonidine. Some data relevant to the potential effectiveness of guanabenz (35, 36) and guanfacine (37–40) are available, but further studies are required to assess their potential utility.

LAAM: AN OPIOID AGONIST ALTERNATIVE TO METHADONE

LAAM (levo-alpha-acetylmethadol; levomethadyl acetate) is a derivative of methadone, and like methadone, is a synthetic mu-opioid agonist. LAAM was approved in the United States for the management of opioid dependence in 1993. It was initially developed in the late 1940s by chemists in Germany seeking an analgesic substitute for morphine. Subsequent studies indicated that LAAM would be unsuitable for the treatment of acute pain given its slow onset of effect and extended duration of action (41, 42). Further investigations indicated that orally administered LAAM produced a more rapid onset of effect than when it was given intravenously or subcutaneously (43–44). While it was noted that LAAM could alleviate the signs and symptoms of opioid withdrawal following the termination of morphine administration, it was also observed that giving LAAM on a daily basis could lead to signs indicative of opioid toxicity, such as severe nausea and vomiting and respiratory depression.

The use of methadone to treat opioid-dependent individuals, which began in the mid 1960s, provided a new and important therapeutic option for managing opioid addiction. Methadone, which has a plasma half-life of about 30 hours (45–47), requires administration on a daily basis to be optimally effective. There were concerns related to the potential diversion of this medication to illicit channels when it was dispensed to patients for consumption outside of the clinic environment. The opioid effects produced by

LAAM and its active metabolites, along with the potential for administering the parent drug on alternate days or on a three times weekly schedule (thus eliminating the need for "take-home" doses), fostered interest in its potential use as an alternative to methadone. LAAM had already been shown to produce effects that were qualitatively similar to morphine and methadone. Also, LAAM is converted to two pharmacologically active compounds by N-demethylation (nor-LAAM and dinor-LAAM) in addition to inactive compounds (48–50). The long half-lives of the nor-LAAM and dinor-LAAM metabolites, 48 and 96 hours, respectively, contribute to the extended duration of activity of LAAM (51).

Numerous studies (52–62) have provided evidence for the effectiveness of LAAM as an opioid-dependence treatment agent. Most of these investigations compared LAAM to methadone, since the latter has been considered the standard for opioid-addiction treatment. Outcome measures most often assessed in these studies included the amount of time individuals remained in treatment, patients' illicit use of opioids and other drugs during the course of treatment, various elements related to individuals' social functioning (such as employment history and interactions with legal system), and general medical and psychiatric parameters, including adverse events potentially related to the treatment medication.

Three phase III, multi-center clinical studies were considered pivotal with respect to the approval of LAAM by the Food and Drug Administration. Two of these (63, 64) were conducted in the 1970s and involved 25 clinical sites and approximately 1100 individuals, of which 470 received LAAM. The first study (63) used a randomized, double-blind, parallel-group design and compared one targeted dosage regimen of LAAM (80 mg given on Mondays, Wednesdays, and Fridays) to two regimens of methadone (50 or 100 mg daily). Overall, the group that received LAAM was associated with results similar to the one given methadone 100 mg with respect to safety assessments and various measures of efficacy. The second study (64) was open-label in design and used dosages of methadone and LAAM that were titrated by the site investigators to the clinical response of the study participants. The primary purpose of this study was to gain additional clinical experience with LAAM, with particular emphasis on accumulating safety data. Again, few differences were noted between LAAM-treated and methadone-treated groups with respect to measures of efficacy and safety.

The third pivotal trial (65, 66, 98) was just recently completed. Its primary purpose was to assess the adequacy of the prototype product labeling and treatment regulations which had been developed to guide clinicians in the use of LAAM as an opioid-dependence treatment. The study was also conducted to generate additional safety data regarding LAAM. Six-hundred twenty-three individuals who had been using opioids illicitly or receiving methadone in a dependence-treatment program received LAAM during the course of the 52-week, 26-site study. In contrast to previous trials of LAAM safety and efficacy that generally excluded women, the subject population of this study was 33% female. Additionally, issues related to the human immunodeficiency virus and the use of "crack" cocaine, which were not relevant to earlier evaluations, were considered in this study. Data from this trial confirmed previous observations regarding the general safety of LAAM in a "current" population of opioid-dependent individuals.

Since LAAM may be administered on alternate days or three times weekly, it may provide advantages over methadone for some patients (67). Some individuals, due to the distance of their place of residence or employment from the treatment program, may find it difficult to receive their methadone doses on a daily basis. Take-home doses of methadone may provide an alternative; however, methadone is sometimes diverted for illicit sale and street use. The use of LAAM eliminates the need for a schedule of daily medication administration and also much of the risk for diversion, since take-home doses are not permitted by current federal regulations.

As with the use of any opioid-dependence treatment medication, patients must be carefully evaluated prior to the initiation of therapy. Close monitoring is especially important during the first few weeks following the beginning of LAAM therapy while a pharmacokinetic steady state is being attained. Although alcohol and illicit drug use should be discouraged throughout the entire course of treatment, this is especially important during the first few weeks of LAAM therapy when the potential for cumulative tox-

icity with other agents may be particularly difficult to predict. Additionally, due to the nature of LAAM's metabolism, microsomal enzyme inducers such as phenobarbital and rifampin, and inhibitors such as cimetidine or ketoconazole, may have variable effects on the apparent activity or duration of action of LAAM.

LAAM, like methadone, may not be an appropriate or effective substitution pharmacotherapy for every opioid-addicted individual. However, LAAM will provide both patients and clinicians with an additional therapeutic alternative. It is hoped that with the recent approval of LAAM more individuals will be attracted into treatment.

OPIATE ANTAGONISTS, PARTIAL AGONISTS, AND MIXED AGONIST/ANTAGONISTS

Antagonists help addicts to avoid relapse by occupying opiate receptor sites and blocking the effects of agonists at the cellular level (68). Partial agonists and mixed agonist/antagonists may produce a broad spectrum of effects, from receptor blockade or activation to an apparent combination of activation and blockade. Their observed effects may depend on their relative agonist and/or antagonist potency, their specific affinity for various opiate receptors, and the amount and type of exogenous opiate a patient has self-administered.

Relatively pure opiate antagonists, such as naltrexone, are not in themselves addicting and do not have the pharmacologically reinforcing effects of agonists. However, if an individual stabilized on naltrexone administers an opiate agonist, the effects of that drug are effectively blocked. Partial agonists such as buprenorphine may block or enhance the effects of other opiates and may have an abuse potential of their own.

Among the opiate antagonists, naltrexone has emerged as the most extensively studied agent. Despite its relatively pure antagonist activity and minimal side effects, naltrexone has not been widely accepted by addicts. This may be due to several factors, including the risk of precipitating a withdrawal syndrome during naltrexone induction and the absence of reinforcing opiate effects, such as feelings of well-being and euphoria. Many addicts stop taking naltrexone before they have learned new methods for controlling anxiety or depression, or before they can recognize cues that can trigger withdrawal symptoms and the urge to use illicit drugs.

Pharmacology of Opiate Antagonists

Opiate antagonists are substances that bind to opiate receptors but do not produce morphine-like effects. Therefore, they compete with both exogenous (e.g., morphine) and endogenous (e.g., endorphins) opiate agonists. When an antagonist is given in sufficient quantities, drugs such as heroin are prevented from interacting with their receptors. Hence, they will have little or no effect and readdiction is prevented. This "neutralization" of an agonist by an antagonist may be contrasted to the activity of a metabolic inhibitor such as disulfiram used in the treatment of alcoholism. Rather than directly blocking the effects of alcohol, disulfiram blocks an enzyme in the pathway of alcohol metabolism leading to accumulation of a noxious metabolite (69). The resulting unpleasant effects may deter further alcohol use.

Opiate antagonists with high receptor affinity can also displace agonists from receptor sites, thus reversing agonist effects. This is the basis for using naloxone to treat opiate overdoses. In this regard, antagonists can also be used to assess physical dependence, since they will precipitate a withdrawal syndrome in chronic opiate users (70). However, some withdrawal symptoms can also be produced after a single opiate use under certain conditions (71). It is also possible that some individuals may feign a withdrawal response if they have a reason to want to appear dependent. Nonetheless, failure to respond to an opiate antagonist can be regarded as strong evidence against current opiate dependence.

There are at least three types of opiate receptors called mu, kappa, and delta with opiates and opioids varying in their affinity for each (72, 73). The first clinically useful antagonist was nalorphine, which reduced the effects of morphine, but it also produced some direct or agonist effects (74, 75). Because of the potential for increasing rather than decreasing respiratory depression, nalorphine has been replaced by naloxone, which has no agonist effects over a reasonable range of doses and is, therefore, considered to be a "pure" mu-opiate antagonist (76).

A "pure" mu-opiate antagonist would seem preferable for preventing readdiction, since it would block the effects of opiates such as heroin without producing direct effects of its own. Even with a pure antagonist, however, there is potential for creating untoward effects. Opiate antagonists could interfere with normal central pain inhibitory systems, although consistent experimental evidence of this effect has not been produced. Volavka and colleagues (77) have reported acute rises in adrenocorticotropic hormone and cortisol after naloxone injections, and Mendelson and coworkers (78) reported increases in luteinizing hormone and delayed rises in testosterone after oral ingestion of naltrexone.

Naloxone has limited utility as a maintenance agent because it is poorly absorbed and has a duration of only a few hours following oral administration (79, 80). Naltrexone, an analog of naloxone synthesized in 1963 (81), also has a very high affinity for opiate receptors but is well-absorbed by the gastrointestinal tract and has antagonist activity in humans for up to 72 hours after oral ingestion (82). Weak opiate agonist activity has been reported for naltrexone (83), but this has not been shown to be clinically significant. Patients have been maintained on effective blocking doses of naltrexone for up to 10 years, and large-scale studies including several thousand patients have failed to show evidence of naltrexone toxicity in humans after chronic administration. There has been no reported evidence of clinical problems related to the acute endocrine effects reported after naloxone injection.

Clinical Studies of Naltrexone

While the plasma half life of naltrexone is about four hours and that of its active metabolite, beta naltrexol, is 10–12 hours, the duration of naltrexone's blockade of opiate receptors is much longer. A single 50 mg dose was found to produce 80% inhibition of binding of the C^{11}-labeled mu ligand, carfentanil to brain receptors, at 72 hours (84).

The first human studies showing the potential of naltrexone blockade of opiate abuse were conducted in the early 1970s at the Addiction Research Center in Lexington, Kentucky. Martin and coworkers found that 30–50 mg of naltrexone administered orally blocked certain subjective effects of morphine for up to 24 hours (85). Subsequently, other investigators demonstrated that 150–200 mg of naltrexone attenuated the effects of heroin or hydromorphone for 72 hours, although some patients did report a "rush" or brief high (82).

It was also observed that recently detoxified patients, and particularly those discontinuing methadone maintenance, needed to be opiate free for at least 7–14 days to avoid the precipitation of a withdrawal syndrome following the first dose of naltrexone (86, 87). As an added precaution, it has been advocated that an intravenous or subcutaneous "challenge" of 0.4–0.8 mg naloxone be given prior to the administration of naltrexone to ensure that withdrawal signs and symptoms are not produced.

A naloxone challenge can prevent difficulties during naltrexone induction (88). If the challenge is negative, patients are usually asymptomatic during the induction. If it is positive (e.g., producing a short episode of yawning, abdominal cramps, irritability, anxiety, chills, etc.), the first dose of naltrexone given shortly thereafter would also precipitate a withdrawal syndrome, but of longer duration. After a negative naloxone challenge, patients are given graduated doses of naltrexone, beginning with a 25 mg test dose, followed by 50, 75, and 100 mg on subsequent days. If patients tolerate 100 mg without side effects, most can then be maintained on 100 mg of naltrexone on Mondays and Wednesdays and 150 mg on Fridays.

Generally, previously detoxified patients are more easily inducted onto naltrexone and remain in treatment longer. "Street addicts" and methadone maintenance patients are less likely to accept the concept of antagonist treatment and to complete detoxification. Patients involved in meaningful relationships with nonaddict mates, employed full time, or attending school and living with family members are most likely to benefit from this treatment (89).

Naltrexone treatment has a very high early dropout rate. In fact, only about 20–30% of street heroin addicts successfully complete opiate detoxi-

fication, remain opiate free for 7–14 days, "pass" a naloxone challenge, and begin naltrexone. Of those who begin naltrexone, 40% leave treatment before completing the first month. Only 10–20% take naltrexone for 6 months or longer, although addicted professionals (90) and former prisoners on probation (91) have significantly higher rates of accepting this treatment and remaining on the program. In a recent report acknowledging the difficulty in recruiting inner-city patients, only 15 of 300 (5%) offered naltrexone agreed to take it, and only three continued on naltrexone for more than 2 months (92). In contrast, Cornish and coworkers observed a retention rate of more than 50% in a group of federal probationers with a history of heroin addiction randomly assigned to naltrexone compared to controls with a similar history (93).

Almost 20% of naltrexone patients have more than one treatment episode (94). During treatment with naltrexone, about one third of patients will test its blockade at least once, although most urine samples collected during treatment are negative for opiates. If, however, patients show a pattern of missing naltrexone doses and using opiates, they invariably discontinue naltrexone and relapse to opiate use. No evidence indicates that patients switch to the use of nonopiate drugs while maintained on naltrexone, but those with a history of abuse of cocaine or other drugs may continue while taking naltrexone. Follow-ups of naltrexone-treated patients show 30–40% are opiate free for 6 months after terminating treatment (81); however, results depend on the population studied and the length of time that they remained on naltrexone.

It is obvious that a major problem with opiate antagonist treatment is the high initial dropout rate. Naltrexone has no reinforcing properties of its own and is perceived as a subjectively "neutral" drug that prevents a former addict from getting "high." As a result, many patients choose very early to return or switch to methadone maintenance. Various external reinforcers such as money have been used with some success to induce patients to remain longer on naltrexone, although their use has obvious practical limitations (95).

PATIENTS SUITED FOR TREATMENT WITH OPIATE ANTAGONISTS

Gonzalez and Brogden published a comprehensive review of therapeutic trials of naltrexone in 1988 (96). Because naltrexone is the most thoroughly studied of the opiate antagonists and the one currently available to physicians, the following discussion details the patient populations best suited for naltrexone treatment.

Physicians and Others in the Health Sciences

The best results with naltrexone treatment have been reported in studies of physicians and other medical professionals. Washton et al. (90) found that 74% of physicians completed at least 6 months of treatment with naltrexone and were opiate free and practicing medicine at 1 year follow-up. Ling and Wesson (97) treated 60 health care professionals for an average of 8 months. Forty-seven were rated as "much" or "moderately" improved at follow-up. Both studies involved comprehensive treatment programs that included full medical evaluations, detoxification, psychiatric and family evaluations with provisions for therapy, as well as confirmation of naltrexone ingestion. Ongoing therapy usually included both marital and individual components. Using this approach, physicians could be back at work within 2 weeks of beginning naltrexone. Although therapy, including naltrexone, may continue for several years, disruption of medical practice is minimized.

Middle Class or Suburban Addicts

In any treatment program, patients with the greatest material and psychological assets tend to have the best outcomes in treatment. Hence, patients with a history of recent employment and a good educational background often do well on naltrexone. Some of these patients prefer not to be maintained on methadone because it ties them to daily clinic visits, whereas there is greater flexibility with naltrexone. These patients can be strongly motivated to be drug free but are still susceptible to impulsive drug use. The idea of using naltrexone as "insurance" is often appealing to them.

Another reason for the successful use of naltrexone in this population is that it can be prescribed by any licensed physician. It does not have to be used in a special addiction treatment program. However, it is recommended that it be prescribed by physicians familiar with the psychodynamics and behavior patterns of addicted persons.

Tennant et al. (35) described a group of suburban practitioners in southern California treating opiate addicts from a wide range of socioeconomic groups. They reported on 160 patients with an average history of opiate use of 10.5 years. The majority (64%) were employed and all expressed a desire for abstinence-oriented treatment. The program was conducted on an outpatient basis beginning with detoxification and a naloxone challenge test. In addition to naltrexone administered three times per week, patients received counseling, and drug and alcohol testing using breath and urine tests. Patients paid a fee if the treatment was not covered by insurance. Although these individuals remained in treatment for a mean of 51 days with a range of up to 635 days, the majority were short-term patients, with only 27 (17%) remaining more than 90 days. Only 1–3% of tests for illicit drug and alcohol use were positive. The authors considered the program to be successful; however, they pointed out that despite long remissions on naltrexone, relapse to opiate use can still occur after naltrexone is stopped.

Another study of middle class patients from a higher socioeconomic group also reported good results with naltrexone. Washton and colleagues (90) treated 114 business executives addicted for at least 2 years to heroin, methadone, or prescription opiates. Most of these individuals were white males, about 30 years of age, with an average income of $42,000 per year. A critical feature of this group was that there was considerable external pressure for them to accept treatment and almost half were in jeopardy of losing their jobs or suffering legal consequences if they did not.

This program was oriented toward complete abstinence. It began with 4–10 weeks of inpatient treatment, during which time detoxification and induction onto naltrexone were accomplished. Intensive psychotherapy, including both individual therapy and self-help groups, was used. The importance of the post-hospital phase was stressed, and all patients signed a contract for aftercare treatment. All 114 patients succeeded in completing naltrexone induction, and 61% remained on naltrexone for at least 6 months with no missed clinic visits or positive urine samples. Twenty-eight percent took naltrexone for less than 6 months but remained in the program with drug-free urine samples. Of the entire group, 64% were opiate-free at the 12–18 month follow-ups. Those who were under pressure from their employers did significantly better than those who were not.

Probationers and Parolees

A large proportion of prison inmates throughout the country have been convicted of drug-related crimes. Relapse to drug use and crime is common among these individuals after they are released. One way to reduce recidivism and perhaps also to alleviate some prison overcrowding is to use naltrexone treatment for recently released former opiate addicts. A pioneering model of such a program has been in existence in Nassau County, Long Island, since 1972 (91). Treatment is part of a work-release program in which members live in transitional housing outside the prison and obtain employment in the community. Prior to the introduction of naltrexone, former opiate addicts did poorly in this type of program because of high rates of relapse to opiate use.

Inmates who volunteer for the program are first stabilized on an opiate antagonist; naltrexone has been used since 1974. Random urine tests are used to monitor the participants for illicit drug use. Uncashed paychecks must be turned in as proof that attendance at work has been regular, and a portion of the salary is applied to the cost of room and board. Individuals are given supervision and counseling during this reentry period. They are also offered the opportunity to continue in treatment after their sentences have been served.

Whereas former addicts had been unable to participate in work release programs in the past, after the introduction of naltrexone, the success record of former addicts has been equal to that of inmates without a drug history. Follow-up data suggest that after completing their terms and leaving the program, naltrexone-treated individuals had fewer drug arrests than those who did not receive naltrexone treatment.

Street Heroin Addicts

Theoretically, any individual detoxified from opiates can be treated with naltrexone. Unfortunately, many street addicts who assert that they want to stop using drugs have not thought through the treatment process. They often change their minds when they find themselves on medication that makes it impossible for them to "get high." In treatment programs with large numbers of street addicts, only 10% of individuals may express an interest in naltrexone, and, of these, only a small number will stabilize on the medication and stay in treatment for 4 or more weeks (94).

NALTREXONE AS PART OF A COMPREHENSIVE DRUG TREATMENT PROGRAM

Detoxification

Any abstinence-oriented program must begin with detoxification from the state of opiate dependence. A complete medical workup, as well as individual psychological and family evaluations, may also be performed during this time. There are several pharmacological options for detoxification. Methadone treatment can be started and then gradually tapered to block opiate withdrawal symptoms. Alternatively, a rapid detoxification using clonidine to reduce withdrawal symptoms may enable the patient to begin naltrexone treatment within 48 hours of having been opiate-dependent. The choice of therapies depends on the type of opiate the patient was using (short versus long-acting), the patient's level of motivation, and the speed desired for returning the patient to a protected drug-free state.

Naloxone Challenge Testing

Before a patient is started on an opiate antagonist, it is important that he or she not be physically dependent on opiate agonists. If a patient has been using a long-acting opiate such as methadone, it may be necessary to wait 7–10 days following the last dose before beginning naltrexone. With shorter-acting drugs such as heroin or hydromorphone, the time between detoxification and initiation of naltrexone treatment can be much briefer. If naltrexone is started too quickly, precipitated withdrawal effects may occur. Even if these effects are very mild, consisting only of stomach cramps or periods of nausea, it may be enough to discourage patients from further treatment.

Many clinicians have found it helpful to perform a naloxone challenge test to assess physical dependence on opiates prior to the first dose of naltrexone. Naloxone usually is given intramuscularly or intravenously in doses of 0.2–0.8 mg (70, 99–102). A positive test, indicative of physical dependence, would consist of typical signs and symptoms of opiate withdrawal. These signs and symptoms often last only 30–60 minutes and indicate that the patient should not be given naltrexone for at least 24 hours.

Some clinicians prefer to use a small dose of naltrexone to assess physical dependence. However, if even a mild withdrawal syndrome is precipitated by naltrexone, the duration will be relatively long (approximately several hours) and more likely to discourage a patient from further treatment. It is usually better to wait a longer period of time between the end of detoxification and the beginning of naltrexone treatment so as to avoid precipitating withdrawal symptoms. This time interval is critical because the patient is vulnerable to relapse until protected by the antagonist. Thus, the clinician must exercise judgment in balancing the benefits of rapid transition to naltrexone against the risks of discouraging the patient because of precipitated withdrawal symptoms. A procedure using intravenous midazolam and naloxone to shorten the transition time from methadone to naltrexone maintenance was reported (103). This allows patients to receive therapeutic doses of naltrexone within hours of beginning the rapid detoxification procedure. Highly motivated patients may be willing to tolerate rapid opiate withdrawal, enabling them to return quickly to their jobs or a more normal lifestyle.

Naltrexone Maintenance

Following a negative naloxone challenge, naltrexone treatment can be started. It is critical that psychotherapy sessions be initiated early in treatment and that these involve family members and other significant individuals in the patient's life. Compliance with the regular ingestion of naltrexone should be confirmed rather than left entirely up to the patient. Confirmed dosing can be accomplished in the clinic, but it is usually disruptive to a patient's rehabilitation to be required to come to the clinic for every dose. For this reason, significant people in the patient's life may be involved successfully to observe the ingestion of naltrexone and report periodically to the therapist. For example, in the case of physicians, this may involve a colleague (e.g., chief of staff or the chairperson of the patient's department) who has already helped the patient confront his or her problem and who may have directed the patient into therapy. It may also be a family member or coworker who can be enlisted after determining that the person has a constructive relationship with the patient.

When treatment is progressing well as determined by engagement in psychotherapy, performance on the job, and absence of illicit drug use confirmed by urinalysis, naltrexone dosing can be reduced to twice per week. This reduces the patient's dependence on the therapist and decreases interference with the patient's life. Although the degree of pharmacological blockade is reduced, the patient is unlikely at this stage to test it.

Side Effects

Properly prescribed naltrexone therapy is associated with few side effects, and many patients report none at all. A variety of side effects have been reported including nausea, abdominal pain, headache, and mild increases in blood pressure (85, 94). Many of these probably were related to the precipitation of a withdrawal syndrome. These side effects have become much less common since it has been recognized how potent naltrexone is at precipitating withdrawal in recently detoxified patients.

Naltrexone may block the effects of endogenous opioids in addition to those that are exogenously administered, and changes in endocrine systems have been reported. Mendelson and colleagues (78) reported a prompt rise in luteinizing hormone and a delayed rise in testosterone after naltrexone administration. They also noted affective changes in normal volunteers who ingested 50 mg of naltrexone on a single occasion. Some individuals reported inappropriate penile erections; dysphoria was also reported in that study and in others (105, 106). In contrast, a subsequent study did not indicate significant alterations in mood in nonaddicted, healthy individuals given naltrexone 100 mg twice daily (107).

Most former opiate-dependent patients do not report subjective effects that can be related directly to naltrexone. However, years of chronic opiate use potentially altered their endocrine patterns, libido, mood, and pain thresholds, and they could be expected to experience some rebound effects when opiate use was stopped. Some patients and their spouses report increased sex drive, a finding that has been related to opiate antagonists in rodents (108). Some report decreased appetite, while others tend to gain weight. Some effects attributed to naltrexone may be confused with those of protracted opiate withdrawal. Even in patients who have been maintained on naltrexone for several years, consistent reports of subjective effects have been lacking. Certainly, the fear that long-term blockade of opiate receptors will lead to problems such as depression has not been realized.

Although addicts generally are unhealthy to begin with, studies performed in addiction treatment programs have not indicated significant laboratory abnormalities in more than 2000 patients participating in clinical trials with naltrexone. Results from liver function tests in particular are a matter of great concern because of the high frequency of hepatitis among addicts. As many as 70–80% of addicts in methadone treatment programs have some abnormality usually ascribed to past or present hepatitis. Studies of nonaddict groups treated with high doses of naltrexone have shown dose-related increases in transaminase levels that were reversible when the medication was stopped. These patients generally received 300 mg of naltrexone per day, or about six times the therapeutic dose used in opiate-dependence treatment (109). Although this finding raises concerns for addiction treatment, in practice, these elevations have not been observed at lower naltrexone dosages.

It is currently recommended that opiate addicts in hepatic failure should not be treated with naltrexone, although those with minor abnormalities in liver function tests may receive the medication. Baseline laboratory tests should include a full battery of liver function studies, and monthly retesting should occur during the first 3 months. If there is no evidence of hepatic toxicity, the tests can then be repeated at intervals of 3–6 months.

NALMEFENE: A LONG-ACTING OPIOID ANTAGONIST

Nalmefene is an opioid antagonist that has recently been approved for use in the management of opioid overdose and for the reversal of opioid drug effects. It is an orally active analog of naltrexone (80) with a terminal phase plasma half-life of approximately 8–9 hours (111), in contrast to the poor oral bioavailability and approximately 1–2 hour half life of naloxone (112, 113).

Numerous clinical pharmacology and efficacy studies have assessed the antagonist properties of nalmefene in human subjects. A single oral dose of nalmefene 50 mg administered to healthy volunteers has been shown to block for 48–72 hours the respiratory depression, analgesia, and subjective effects (e.g., drowsiness, nausea, itching) secondary to intravenously administered fentanyl, 2 μg/kg (114). A subsequent study confirmed the ability of nalmefene to antagonize respiratory depression induced by multiple fentanyl challenges (115). Results also indicated that intravenous dose of nalmefene (0.4 mg/70 kg) was comparable to a four times greater dose of naloxone in reversing morphine-induced respiratory depression, and that nalmefene had a longer duration of action (116). In contrast, it was later reported that nalmefene and naloxone were equipotent in reversing fentanyl-induced respiratory depression following a single, intravenous dose of the antagonist (117). Other studies have shown nalmefene to be more effective or potent in reversing opioid-induced respiratory sedation (118) and to be effective in the emergency management of opioid overdosage (119).

Nalmefene has generally been reported to be well tolerated in healthy volunteers. In one study, lightheadedness was the most commonly reported subjective-effect following the administration of both single oral nalmefene doses of 50–300 mg, and 20 mg doses given twice daily for seven days (120). Similarly, the parenteral administration of nalmefene in doses up to 24 mg was also well tolerated, with lightheadedness, dizziness, and mental fatigue being reported. In a study using individuals with a history of opioid abuse, a somewhat different effect profile was reported when nalmefene in single oral doses up to 100 mg was compared to morphine and placebo (121). Side effects reported only after nalmefene administration included agitation and irritability, muscle tension, abdominal cramps, and a "hungover feeling." Drowsiness or sleepiness was the most common effect reported following each of the treatments. These effects did not appear to be dose related and nalmefene did not produce typical morphine-like effects.

Nalmefene, like naltrexone (122), apparently does not produce morphine-like subjective effects that could be considered desirable by opioid-dependent or abusing individuals. Additionally, as noted previously, nalmefene may produce effects that could limit its use in the abstinence treatment of individuals previously dependent on opioids. However, naltrexone, which has some utility in the maintenance treatment of certain patient populations, has also been reported to produce dysphoria, depressed mood, and other untoward effects in individuals not currently dependent on opioids (105, 106). The successful use of nalmefene, like naltrexone, as an adjunctive treatment for the maintenance of opioid abstinence will probably require highly motivated patients.

CURRENT STATUS OF ANTAGONIST TREATMENT

At present, the only opiate antagonist in clinical use for addiction treatment is naltrexone. In large, multimodal programs, only 5–10% of opiate addicts show an interest in naltrexone at any given time (94). Nonetheless, since new patients continually enter treatment and many methadone maintenance patients discontinue treatment after a period of several years, a fairly significant number will try naltrexone at least once. The difficulty in inducting patients onto naltrexone, along with high early dropout rates, may be discouraging to many clinicians. However, even patients who drop out early often show improvement. Thirty to forty percent of those who take the medication for 3 months or longer are opiate free 6 months after stopping treatment. Thus, naltrexone may be satisfying an important treatment need for many who take it. Opiate antagonist treatment is unlikely to become a popular method as compared with methadone maintenance. However, antagonists may be the best choice for patients who wish to remain opiate free, and clinicians generally agree that they are an important option to have available.

Why focus on the use of opiate antagonists? Some patients, albeit a small percentage of the total addict population, want and need a nonaddicting pharmacological agent as part of their total treatment. Addicted physicians, nurses, pharmacists, and other health care professionals appear to be best suited to antagonist treatment. Additionally, patients who have done well on low doses of methadone in maintenance programs may desire the "protection" afforded by an antagonist during the first several weeks or months following methadone discontinuation. Likewise, some patients leaving drug-free therapeutic communities may elect to receive an antagonist during their reentry into the community when the risk of relapse is high.

NALTREXONE IN THE TREATMENT OF ALCOHOLISM

Opiate antagonists have been used in numerous animal models to study the effects of specific blockade of opiate receptors. Some of these models involved rodents or monkeys given a choice of drinking either alcohol or water. In certain situations or in strains of animals, alcohol is preferred, but naloxone or naltrexone blocks this preference (104). Because of these animal studies, Volpicelli and colleagues conducted placebo controlled trials in human alcoholics who were also receiving standard outpatient rehabilitation (110, 123). This work was later replicated by O'Malley et al. (124) and this paved the way for Food and Drug Administration approval and marketing of naltrexone for alcoholism in 1995. The combined animal and human data suggest that alcohol activates endogenous opioid systems, particularly in susceptible alcoholics, but further research is needed to identify alcoholics most likely to be helped by this treatment.

BUPRENORPHINE: A PARTIAL OPIOID AGONIST

Unlike methadone and LAAM, which can be described as full mu-opioid agonists, buprenorphine may be described as a partial agonist. That is, buprenorphine produces submaximal effects relative to those produced by full mu-opioid agonists when a maximally effective dose of buprenorphine is given. While this description does not detail the molecular mechanisms involved in the drug's actions, it does provide a basis for understanding the potential utility and limitations of using buprenorphine as an opioid-dependence treatment medication.

Buprenorphine is currently marketed in the United States as an analgesic for parenteral use and is approximately 25–50 times more potent than morphine in this regard (125–127). Typically, 0.3 mg of buprenorphine is considered to produce analgesia approximately equivalent to 10 mg of morphine when both medications are given parenterally. Buprenorphine has poor oral bioavailability (128), less than 10% compared to that when given subcutaneously. It has also been demonstrated to be a kappa-opioid receptor antagonist (129). There are a number of opioid partial-agonist or agonist-antagonist medications, discussed later in this chapter, that are currently available commercially. However, buprenorphine is the only one generally considered to be a potentially useful opioid-dependence treatment agent.

The results of a clinical study published in 1978 by Jasinski and his coworkers (130) fostered interest in, and suggested the utility of, buprenorphine for the treatment of opioid dependence. Subsequent studies generally confirmed the initial observations regarding the potential effectiveness of buprenorphine by providing evidence for its patient acceptability, ability to substitute for and block the effects of other opioids, safety, and its utility in maintaining individuals in treatment.

It is obvious that a medication must be acceptable to the targeted treatment population if it is to be effective, and studies assessing the utility of buprenorphine as a treatment agent for opioid dependence have provided evidence of its acceptability. Subjects have reported "liking" buprenorphine and have reported opioid-like effects following its administration (131–135). These "positive" subjective effects may be important for initi-

ating and maintaining individuals on buprenorphine. However, as is true for methadone and LAAM, buprenorphine should be considered to have a potential for abuse. Reports of buprenorphine abuse have come from various countries (136–139), although its relative availability and the availability of licit and illicit alternatives needs to be taken into account when interpreting these reports. In a controlled clinical trial, intravenously administered buprenorphine was associated with positive subjective effects in individuals not dependent on opioids (140). This investigation also indicated that the effects of buprenorphine were not consistently dose-related, consonant with buprenorphine's partial agonist profile. Results from other studies (141–143) that assessed the effects of buprenorphine in methadone-maintained patients suggest that buprenorphine would have a limited potential for abuse in these individuals, and that the time of buprenorphine administration relative to that of the last methadone dose may be an important determinant of buprenorphine's subjective effects.

Findings from a number of studies have indicated that buprenorphine can substitute for other opioids and decrease illicit opioid use. In one of the first clinical pharmacology investigations, Mello and her colleagues (132) reported the results from an inpatient study in which individuals maintained on placebo or buprenorphine could make operant responses to earn money or receive intravenous heroin—those receiving buprenorphine took significantly less heroin. Over the next 15 years, numerous clinical laboratory and treatment-research studies, conducted in a variety of settings over varying periods of time and using various schedules of buprenorphine administration, have provided evidence that buprenorphine can be used effectively and safely as an opioid-substitution pharmacotherapy (for reviews, see 144–147).

While buprenorphine has been used effectively to substitute for other opioids and suppress the development of opioid withdrawal signs and symptoms, its partial agonist properties are also responsible for its potential to precipitate an opioid withdrawal syndrome under certain conditions. This precipitated withdrawal phenomenon has been observed or suggested by both preclinical (148) and clinical studies (149, 150). It may not always be clear in clinical situations, however, whether withdrawal symptomatology is due to an insufficient or excessive dosage of buprenorphine being administered. Further, for patients being maintained on high dosages of methadone or LAAM, or addicts using large amounts of heroin or other opioids, there may not be a dosage of buprenorphine that will fully substitute for the other opioid drug. The administration of buprenorphine to these individuals may result in the production of significant opioid withdrawal effects.

Of particular interest with respect to substitution therapy with buprenorphine has been its long duration of action, which has been ascribed to the slow dissociation of buprenorphine from the opioid receptor (151, 152). It was reported in some of the initial studies that, at sufficient doses, buprenorphine could be effectively administered once daily (133, 135, 153). Later studies indicated that even less frequent dosing could be possible. The potential for alternate-day dosing was first examined in an inpatient trial in which the maintenance dose (8 mg daily given sublingually) was administered every other day (135). The results were encouraging, but suggested that a higher alternate-day dose might be required in a clinical treatment setting, since study participants who received buprenorphine every other day reported less medication effect and increased withdrawal symptoms than did those who received it daily. Subsequent outpatient trials provided evidence that administering double the daily maintenance dose on alternate days was both safe and effective (154–156), and that even tripling the maintenance dose (157) could be a viable method of manipulating the dosage regimen to provide a more flexible and potentially cost-effective way of administering buprenorphine, thus expanding treatment options in some of the same ways suggested for LAAM.

The use of buprenorphine has not been associated with an adverse effect profile that would appear to limit its utility as an opioid-dependence pharmacotherapy. Adverse effects reported following the administration of buprenorphine for opioid dependence treatment have included primarily sedation, drowsiness, and constipation (132, 158), and other effects typical of mu-opioid agonists in general. Tolerance to these effects can be expected to develop during continued buprenorphine therapy. The safety of buprenorphine is, like its pharmacodynamic profile, related to its partial agonist properties. In particular, the potential for severe drug-induced respiratory depression, a concern for medications such as methadone and LAAM, as well as drugs primarily used illicitly such as heroin, does not appear to be a relevant concern for buprenorphine. Even 32 mg of buprenorphine administered sublingually (approximately 70 times higher, corrected for differences in bioavailability, than a 0.3 mg analgesic dose given intramuscularly) produced only marginal effects on respiratory function in individuals not dependent on opioids (159).

Most of the clinical trials conducted to date have used buprenorphine formulations for sublingual administration using a vehicle consisting of water and ethanol. Use of these formulations was necessitated due to the limited aqueous solubility of buprenorphine and its poor bioavailability when given by the oral route. When formulated in this way, sublingually administered buprenorphine has been found to be two-thirds as potent as buprenorphine given subcutaneously (160). However, the potential commercial application of a buprenorphine solution for sublingual administration could be associated with manufacturing and marketing limitations, as well as problems associated with its facile use in typical, clinical environments. As mentioned previously, such a formulation may also have the potential for abuse.

In an effort to develop a suitable dosage form for general use, a combination product containing buprenorphine and naloxone for sublingual administration is currently under development (161). Such a product would be expected to be undesirable for parenteral abuse by opioid-dependent individuals (due to the presence of the opioid antagonist naloxone), but safe and effective when used as an opioid-dependence treatment agent because of the limited sublingual bioavailability of naloxone. The parenteral effects of a combination of buprenorphine and naloxone at dose ratios ranging from 8:1 to 1:2 have been investigated in both opioid-dependent and nondependent individuals (162–165). The data showed dose-dependent opioid antagonist effects, with higher ratios of naloxone in the combination being associated with greater antagonist effects in dependent individuals. However, the combination appeared to be as effective as buprenorphine alone in buprenorphine-maintained subjects. If further clinical trials confirm the effectiveness of the buprenorphine-naloxone combination, it will provide both clinicians and patients with a treatment alternative to methadone and LAAM.

OTHER PARTIAL AGONISTS AND AGONIST/ANTAGONISTS

In addition to buprenorphine described earlier, there are four other opioid analgesics (butorphanol, dezocine, nalbuphine, and pentazocine) currently available for use in the United States. These medications exhibit different degrees of activity at various opioid receptors, most notably the mu, kappa, and delta (166, 167), and function as partial agonists or agonists at one type of opioid receptor and as antagonists at others. For example, with respect to their reported mu-opioid-like effects in human subjects, dezocine has been described as a partial agonist (168), nalbuphine as a partial agonist or an antagonist (169, 170), pentazocine as an antagonist (171, 172), and butorphanol as an agent with little or no activity (170). These descriptions, however, are not always adequate or consistent, due to the complex profile of drug effects observed, and the various paradigms and subject populations studied. Whether any of these medications may eventually find utility in the treatment of opioid dependence has yet to be determined.

SUMMARY

Various types of pharmacotherapies with different modes of action have been used and continue to be evaluated as treatments for opiate addiction. Because no single medication is appropriate for every individual, it is important that clinicians have a variety of therapeutic agents available to them. Additionally, pharmacotherapy is not a treatment end in itself; other adjuncts to successful treatment may include psychotherapy, social rehabilitation, vocational training, and others. Intraindividual treatment may also change over time as patients cycle through periods of abstinence and addiction. Rational medication therapy begins with an understanding of not only the disease state generally, but also of the specific dynamics of the addiction process that affect the overall success of treatment.

References

1. Dole VP, Nyswander M. A medical treatment for diacetylmorphine (heroin) addiction. A clinical trial with methadone hydrochloride. JAMA 1965;193:80–84.
2. Kreek MJ. Multiple drug abuse patterns and medical consequences. In: Meltzer HY, ed. Psychopharmacology: the third generation of progress. New York: Raven Press, 1987:1597–1604.
3. Martin WR, Jasinski DR. Physical parameters of morphine dependence in man: tolerance, early abstinence, protracted abstinence. J Psychiatr Res 1969;7:9–17.
4. Wikler A. Dynamics of drug dependence: implication of a conditioning theory for research and treatment. Arch Gen Psychiatry 1973;28:611–616.
5. Childress AR, McClellan AT, O'Brien CP. Abstinent opiate abusers exhibit conditioned craving, conditioned withdrawal and reductions in both through extinction. Br J Addict 1986;81:655–660.
6. Gold MS, Pottash ALC, Extein I. Clonidine in acute opiate withdrawal. N Engl J Med 1980;302:1421–1422.
7. Kleber HD, Gold MS, Riordan CE. The use of clonidine in detoxification from opiates. Bull Narc 1980;32:1–10.
8. Washton AM, Resnick RB. Clonidine for opiate detoxification: Outpatient clinical trials. Am J Psychiatry 1980;137:1121–1122.
9. Spencer L, Gregory M. Clonidine transdermal patches for use in outpatient opiate withdrawal. J Subst Abuse Treat 1989;6:113–117.
10. Cuthill JD, Beroniade V, Salvatori VA, Viguie

F. Evaluation of clonidine suppression of opiate withdrawal reactions: A multidisciplinary approach. Can J Psychiatry 1990;35:377–382.
11. Jasinski DR, Johnson RE, Kocher TE. Clonidine in morphine withdrawal. Differential effects on signs and symptoms. Arch Gen Psychiatry 1985;42:1063–1066.
12. Johnson DA, Bohan ME. Propoxyphene withdrawal with clonidine. Am J Psychiatry 1983;140:1217–1218.
13. Haggerty JJ, Slakoff S. Clonidine therapy and meperidine withdrawal. Am J Psychiatry 1981;131:698.
14. Charney DS, Riordan CE, Kleber HD, et al. Clonidine and naltrexone. A safe, effective, and rapid treatment of abrupt withdrawal from methadone therapy. Arch Gen Psychiatry 1982;39:1327–1332.
15. Charney DS, Heninger GR, Kleber HD. The combined use of clonidine and naltrexone as a rapid, safe and effective treatment of abrupt withdrawal from methadone. Am J Psychiatry 1986;143:831–837.
16. Kleber HD, Topazian M, Gaspari J, Riordan CE, Kosten T. Clonidine and naltrexone in the outpatient treatment of heroin withdrawal. Am J Drug Alcohol Abuse 1987;13:1–17.
17. Vining E, Kosten TR, Kleber HD. Clinical utility of rapid clonidine-naltrexone detoxification for opioid abusers. Br J Addict 1988;83:567–575.
18. Bjorkqvist SE. Clonidine in alcohol withdrawal. Acta Psychiatr Scand 1975;52:256–263.
19. Wilkins AJ, Jenkins WJ, Steiner JA. Efficacy of clonidine in treatment of the alcohol withdrawal state. Psychopharmacology 1983;81:78–80.
20. Glasman AH, Jackson WK, Walsh BT, et al.

Cigarette craving, smoking, withdrawal and clonidine. Science 1984;226:864–866.
21. Glassman AH, Steiner F, Walsh BT, et al. Heavy smokers, smoking cessation, and clonidine. JAMA 1988;259:2863–2866.
22. Ornish SA, Zisook S, McAdams LA. Effects of transdermal clonidine treatment on withdrawal symptoms associated with smoking cessation. Arch Intern Med 1988;148:2027–2031.
23. Wei H, Young D. Effect of clonidine on cigarette cessation and in the alleviation of withdrawal symptoms. Br J Addict 1988;83:1221–1226.
24. Aghajanian GK. Tolerance of locus ceruleus neurons to morphine and suppression of withdrawal response by clonidine. Nature 1978;276:186–188.
25. Crawley JN, Laverty R, Roth RH. Clonidine reversal of increased norepinephrine metabolites during morphine withdrawal. Eur J Pharmacol 1979;57:247–250.
26. Aghajanian GK. Central noradrenergic neurons: a locus for the functional interplay between alpha-2 adrenoceptors and opiate receptors. J Clin Psychiatry 1982;43:20–24.
27. Roth RH, Elsworth JD, Redmond DE. Clonidine suppression of noradrenergic hyperactivity during morphine withdrawal by clonidine: Biochemical studies in rodents and primates. J Clin Psychiatry 1982;43:42–46.
28. Gothert M, Huth H. Alpha-adrenoceptor-mediated modulation of 5-hydroxytryptamine release from rat brain cortex slices. Naunyn Schmiedebergs Arch Pharmacol 1980;313:21–26.
29. Buccafusco JJ, Spector S. Influence of clonidine on experimental hypertension induced by cholinergic stimulation. Experientia 1980;36:671–673.

30. Katsuragi T, Ushijima I, Furukawa T. The cloni-dine-induced self-injurious behavior of mice involves purinergic mechanisms. Pharmacol Biochem Behav 1984;83:550–552.
31. Gold MS, Pottash AC, Sweeney DR, Extein I, Annitto WJ. Opiate detoxification with lofexidine. Drug Alcohol Depend 1981;8:307–315.
32. Washton AM, Resnick RB, Perzel JF, et al. Opiate detoxification using lofexidine. NIDA Res Monogr 1982;41:261–263.
33. Washton AM, Resnick RB. Lofexidine in abrupt methadone withdrawal. Psychopharmacol Bull 1982;18:220–221.
34. Washton AM, Resnick RB, Geyer G. Opiate withdrawal using lofexidine, a clonidine analogue with fewer side effects. J Clin Psychiatry 1983;44:335–337.
35. Tennant FS Jr, Rawson RA, Cohen AJ, Mann A. Clinical experience with naltrexone in suburban opioid addicts. J Clin Psychiatry 1984;45:42–45.
36. Levadi DI. Use of guanabenz in methadone withdrawal. Am J Psychiatry 1985;142:1128–1129.
37. Schubert H, Fleischhacker WW, Meise U, Theohar C. Preliminary results of guanfacine treatment of acute opiate withdrawal. Am J Psychiatry 1984;141:1271–1273.
38. Soler Insa PA, Bedate Villar J, Theohar C, Yotis A. Treatment of heroin withdrawal with guanfacine; an open clinical investigation. Can J Psychiatry 1987;32:679–682.
39. San L, Cami J, Peri JM, Mata R, Porta M. Efficacy of clonidine, guanfacine, and methadone in the rapid detoxification of heroin addicts: a controlled clinical trial. Br J Addict 1990;85:141–147.
40. San L, Fernandez T, Cami J, Gossop M. Efficacy of methadone versus methadone and guanfacine in the detoxification of heroin-addicted patients. J Subst Abuse Treat 1994;11:463–469.
41. Keats AS, Beecher HK. Analgesic activity and toxic effects of acetylmethadol isomers in man. J Pharmacol Exp Ther 1952;105:210–215.
42. David NA, Semler HJ, Burgner PR. Control of chronic pain by dl-alpha-acetylmethadol. JAMA 1956;161:599–603.
43. Fraser HF, Isbell H. Actions and addiction liabilities of alpha-acetyl-methadols in man. J Pharmacol Exp Ther 1952;105:458–465.
44. Isbell H, Fraser, HF. Addictive properties of methadone derivatives. J Pharmacol Exp Ther 1954;13:369.
45. Inturrisi CE, Verebely K. The levels of methadone in the plasma in methadone maintenance. Clin Pharmacol Ther 1972;13:633–637.
46. Sawe J. High dose morphine and methadone in cancer patients. Clinical pharmacokinetic considerations or oral treatment. Clin Pharmacokinet 1986;11:87–106.
47. Inturrisi CE, Colburn WA, Kaiko RF, Houde RW, Foley KM. Pharmacokinetics and pharmacodynamics of methadone in patients with chronic pain. Clin Pharmacol Ther 1987;41:392–401.
48. Leimbach DG, Eddy NB. Synthetic analgesics. III. Methadols, isomethadols and their acyl derivatives. J Pharmacol Exp Ther 1954;110:135–147.
49. McMahon RE, Calp HW, Marshal FJ. The metabolism of alpha-dl-acetyl methadol in the rat: the identification of a probable active metabolite. J Pharmacol Exp Ther 1965;149:436–445.
50. Billings RE, Booker R, Smits S, Pehland A, McMahon RE. Metabolism of acetyl methadol. A sensitive assay for nor-acetyl methadol and the identification of a new active metabolite. J Med Chem 1973;16:305–306.
51. ORLAAM Product Labeling. Roxane Laboratories, Inc., Columbus, OH.
52. Jaffe JH, Schuster CR, Smith BB, Blachly P. Comparison of dl alpha acetylmethadol and methadone in the treatment of narcotics addicts. Pharmacologist 1969;11:256.
53. Jaffe JH, Schuster CR, Smith BB, Blachly PH. Comparison of acetylmethadol and methadone in the treatment of long-term heroin users. JAMA 1970;211:1834–1836.
54. Jaffe JH, Senay EC, Schuster CR, Renault PR, Smith B, DiMenza S. Methadyl acetate vs methadone. A double-blind study in heroin users. JAMA 1972;222:437–442.
55. Jaffe JH, Senay EC. Methadone and l-methadylacetate. Use in management of narcotics addicts. JAMA 1971;216:1303–1305.
56. Zaks A, Fink M, Freedman AM. Levomethadyl in maintenance treatment of opiate dependence. JAMA 1972;220:811–813.
57. Levine R, Zaks A, Fink M, Freedman AM. Levomethadyl acetate. Prolonged duration of opioid effects, including cross tolerance to heroin, in man. JAMA 1973;226:316–318.
58. Savage C, Karp E, Curran SA. A methadone/alpha-acetylmethadol (LAAM) maintenance study. Compr Psychiatry 1976;17:415–424.
59. Whysner JA. Phase III clinical study of levoalpha-acetylmethadol. NIDA Res Monogr 1976;8:109–111.
60. Judson BA, Goldstein A. Levo-alpha-acetylmethadol (LAAM) in the treatment of heroin addicts. I. Dosage schedule for induction and stabilization. Drug Alcohol Depend 1979;4:461–466.
61. Freedman RR, Czertko G. A comparison of thrice weekly LAAM and daily methadone in employed heroin addicts. Drug Alcohol Depend 1981;8:215–222.
62. Marcovici M, O'Brien C, McClellan T, Kacian J. A clinical controlled study of l-alpha-acetylmethadol in the treatment of narcotic addiction. Am J Psychiatry 1981;138:234–236.
63. Ling W, Charuvastra C, Kaim SC, Klett CJ. Methadyl acetate and methadone as maintenance treatments for heroin addicts. Arch Gen Psychiatry 1976;33:709–720.
64. Ling W, Klett CJ, Gillis RD. A cooperative clinical study of methadyl acetate. Arch Gen Psychiatry 1978;35:345–353.
65. Fudala PJ, Montgomery A, Herbert S, Mojsiak J, Rosenberg S, Vocci F. A multicenter, labelling assessment study of levo-alpha-acetylmethadol (LAAM) for the maintenance treatment of opiate addicts. NIDA Res Monogr 1994;141:145.
66. Herbert S, Montgomery A, Fudala P, et al. LAAM labeling assessment study: retention, dosing, and side effects in a 64-week study. NIDA Res Monogr 1995;153:259.
67. Fudala PJ. LAAM—Pharmacology, pharmacokinetics, developmental history, and therapeutic considerations. Subst Abuse 1996;17:127–132.
68. O'Brien C, Greenstein R, Ternes J, Woody G. Clinical pharmacology of narcotic antagonists. Ann N Y Acad Sci 1978;311:232–240.
69. Haley TJ. Disulfiram (tetraethylthioperoxydicarbonic diamide): a reappraisal of its toxicity and therapeutic application. Drug Metab Rev 1979;9:319–335.
70. Blachly PH. Naloxone for diagnosis in methadone programs. JAMA 1973;224:334–335.
71. Heishman SJ, Stitzer ML, Bigelow GE, Liebson IA. Acute opioid physical dependence in postaddict humans: naloxone dose effects after brief morphine exposure. J Pharmacol Exp Ther 1989;248:127–134.
72. Martin WR. Opiate antagonists. Pharmacol Rev 1967;19:463–521.
73. Gilbert PE, Martin WR. The effects of morphine- and nalorphine-like drugs in the nondependent and morphine-dependent and cyclazocine-dependent chronic spinal dog. J Pharmacol Exp Ther 1976;198:66–82.
74. Fraser HF. Human pharmacology and clinical uses of nalorphine (N-allylnormorphine). Med Clin North Am 1957;23:1–11.
75. Jasinski DR. Human pharmacology of narcotic antagonists. Br J Pharmacol 1979;7:287S–290S.
76. Jasinski DR, Martin WR, Haertzen CA. The human pharmacology and abuse potential of N-allylnoroxymorphone (naloxone). J Pharmacol Exp Ther 1967;143:157–164.
77. Volavka J, Cho D, Mallya A, Bauman J. Naloxone increases ACTH and cortisol in man. N Engl J Med 1979;300:1056.
78. Mendelson JH, Ellingboe J, Kuehnle J, Mello N. Heroin and naltrexone effects on pituitary-gonadal hormones in man: tolerance and supersensitivity. NIDA Res Monogr 1979;27:302–308.
79. Fishman J, Roffwarg H, Hellman L. Disposition of naloxone in normal and narcotic-dependent men. J Pharmacol Exp Ther 1973;187:575–580.
80. Hahn EF, Fishman J, Heilman RD. Narcotic antagonists. 4. Carbon-6 derivatives of N-substituted noroxymorphones as narcotic antagonists. J Med Chem 1975;18:259–262.
81. Resnick RB, Washton AM, Thomas MA, Kestenbaum RS. Naltrexone in the treatment of opiate dependence. NIDA Res Monogr 1978;19:321–332.
82. Resnick R, Volavka J, Freedman AM, Thomas M. Studies of EN-1639A (naltrexone): a new narcotic antagonist. Am J Psychiatry 1974;131:646–650.
83. Verebey K, Volavka J, Mule SJ, Resnick R. Naltrexone: disposition, metabolism and effects after acute and chronic dosing. Clin Pharmacol Ther 1976;20:315–328.
84. Lee MC, Wagner HN, Tanada S, Frost JJ, Bice AN, Dannals RF. Duration of occupancy of opiate receptors by naltrexone. J Nucl Med 1988;29(7):1207–1211.
85. Martin WR, Jasinski D, Mansky P. Naltrexone, an antagonist for the treatment of heroin dependence. Arch Gen Psychiatry 1973;28:784–791.
86. Bradford HA, Kaim S. National Institute on Drug Abuse studies evaluating the safety of the narcotic antagonist naltrexone. Washington, DC: Biometric Research Institute, Inc., 1977.
87. Hollister L. Clinical evaluation of naltrexone treatment of opiate-dependent individuals. Report of the National Research Council Committee on Clinical Evaluation of Narcotic Antagonists. Arch Gen Psychiatry 1978;35:335–344.
88. Greenstein RA, O'Brien CP, Mintz J, Woody G, Hanna N. Clinical experience with naltrexone in a behavioral research study. NIDA Res Monogr 1976;9:141–149.
89. Resnick R, Schuyten-Resnick E, Washton AM. Narcotic antagonists in the treatment of opioid dependence: review and commentary. Compr Psychiatry 1979;20:116–125.
90. Washton AM, Pottash AC, Gold MS. Naltrexone in addicted business executives and physicians. J Clin Psychiatry 1984;45:39–41.
91. Brahen LS, Henderson RK, Capone T, Kordal N. Naltrexone treatment in a jail work-release program. J Clin Psychiatry 1984;45:49–52.
92. Fram DH, Marmo J, Holden R. Naltrexone treatment—the problem of patient acceptance. J Subst Abuse Treat 1989;6:119–122.

93. Metzger DS, Cornish J, Woody GE, McClellan AT, Druley P, O'Brien CP. Naltrexone in federal probationers. NIDA Res Monogr 1990;95: 465–466.

94. Greenstein RA, Arndt IC, McClellan AT, O'Brien CP, Evans B. Naltrexone: a clinical perspective. J Clin Psychiatry 1984;45:25–28.

95. Grabowski J, O'Brien CP, Greenstein RA, Long M, Steinberg-Donato S, Ternes J. Effects of contingent payment on compliance with a naltrexone regimen. Am J Drug Alcohol Abuse 1979;6:355–365.

96. Gonzalez JP, Brogden RN. Naltrexone. A review of its pharmacodynamic and pharmacokinetic properties and therapeutic efficacy in the management of opioid dependence. Drugs 1988;35:192–213.

97. Ling W, Wesson DR. Naltrexone treatment for addicted health-care professionals: a collaborative private practice experience. J Clin Psychiatry 1984;45:46–48.

98. Fudala PJ, Vocci F, Montgomery A, Trachtenberg AI, and the LAAM Collaborative Study Group. Levo-alpha-acetylmethadol (LAAM) for the treatment of opioid dependence: a multisite, open-label study of LAAM safety and an evaluation of the product labeling and treatment regulations. J Maint Addict (submitted for publication).

99. Wang RIH, Wiesen RL, Lamid S, Roh BL. Rating, the presence and severity of opiate dependence. Clin Pharmacol Ther 1974;16: 653–658.

100. Zilm DH, Sellers EM. The quantitative assessment of physical dependence on opiates. Drug Alcohol Depend 1978;3:419–428.

101. Judson BA, Himmelberger DU, Goldstein A. The naloxone test for opiate dependence. Clin Pharmacol Ther 1980;27:492–501.

102. Peachey JE, Lei H. Assessment of opioid dependence with naloxone. Br J Addict 1988;83: 193–201.

103. Loimer N, Lenz K, Schmid R, Presslich O. Technique for greatly shortening the transition from methadone to naltrexone maintenance of patients addicted to opiates. Am J Psychiatry 1991;148:933–935.

104. Ulm RR, Volpicelli JR, Volpicelli LA. Opiates and alcohol self-administration in animals. J Clin Psychiatry 1995;56(suppl 7):5–14.

105. Hollister LE, Johnson K, Boukhabza D, Gillespie HK. Aversive effects of naltrexone in subjects not dependent on opiates. Drug Alcohol Depend 1981;8:37–41.

106. Crowley TJ, Wagner JE, Zerbe G, Macdonald M. Naltrexone-induced dysphoria in former opioid addicts. Am J Psychiatry 1985;142: 1081–1085.

107. Malcolm R, O'Neil PM, Von JM, Dickerson PC. Naltrexone and dysphoria: a double-blind placebo controlled trial. Biol Psychiatry 1987; 22:710–716.

108. Christian MS. Reproductive toxicity and teratology evaluations of naltrexone. J Clin Psychiatry 1984;45:7–10.

109. Maggio CA, Presta E, Bracco EF, et al. Naltrexone and human eating behavior; a dose-ranging inpatient trial in moderately obese men. Brain Res Bull 1985;14:657–661.

110. Volpicelli JR, O'Brien CP, Alterman AJ, et al. Naltrexone and the treatment of alcohol dependence: initial observations. In: Reid LD, ed. Opioids, bulimia, and alcohol abuse and alcoholism. New York: Springer-Verlag 1990: 195–214.

111. Dixon R, Howes J, Gentile J, et al. Nalmefene: intravenous safety and kinetics of a new opioid antagonist. Clin Pharmacol Ther 1986;39: 49–53.

112. Ngai SH, Berkowitz BA, Yang JC, et al. Pharmacokinetics of naloxone in rats and man: Basis for its potency and short duration of action in man. Anesthesiol 1976;44:398–401.

113. Aitkenhead AR, Derbyshire DR, Pinnock CA, Achola K, Smith G. Pharmacokinetics of intravenous naloxone in healthy volunteers. Anesthesiol 1984;61:A381.

114. Gal TJ, DiFazio CA, Dixon R. Prolonged blockade of opioid effect with oral nalmefene. Clin Pharmacol Ther 1986;40:537–542.

115. Moore LRC, Bikhazi GB, Tuttle RR, Weidler DJ. Antagonism of fentanyl-induced respiratory depression with nalmefene. Methods Find Exp Clin Pharmacol 1990;12:29–35.

116. Konieczko KM, Jones JG, Barrowcliffe MP, Jordan C, Altman DG. Antagonism of morphine-induced respiratory depression with nalmefene. Br J Anaesth 1988;61:318–323.

117. Glass PSA, Jhaveri RM, Smith LR. Comparison of potency and duration of action nalmefene and naloxone. Anesth Analg 1994;78: 536–541.

118. Barsan WG, Seger D, Danzl DF, et al. Duration of antagonistic effects of nalmefene and naloxone in opiate-induced sedation for emergency department procedures. Am J Emerg Med 1989;7:155–161.

119. Kaplan JL, Marx JA. Effectiveness and safety of intravenous nalmefene for emergency department patients with suspected narcotic overdose: a pilot study. Ann Intern Med 1993;22: 187–190.

120. Dixon R, Gentile J, Hsu HB, et al. Nalmefene: safety and kinetics after single and multiple oral doses of a new opioid antagonist. J Clin Pharmacol 1987;27:233–239.

121. Fudala PJ, Heishman SJ, Henningfield JE, Johnson RE. Human pharmacology and abuse potential of nalmefene. Clin Pharmacol Ther 1991;49:300–306.

122. Kleber HD. Naltrexone. J Subst Abuse Treat 1985;2:117–122.

123. Volpicelli JR, Alterman AI, Hayashida M, et al. Naltrexone in the treatment of alcohol dependence. Arch Gen Psychiatry 1992;49: 876–880.

124. O'Malley, SS, Jaffe AJ, Chang G, et al. Naltrexone and copying skills therapy for alcohol dependence: a controlled study. Arch Gen Psychiatry 1992;49:881–887.

125. Cowan A, Doxey JC, Harry EJR. The animal pharmacology of buprenorphine, an oripavine analgesic agent. Br J Pharmacol 1977;60: 547–554.

126. Cowan A, Lewis JW, Macfarlane IR. Agonist and antagonist properties of buprenorphine, a new antinociceptive agent. Br J Pharmacol 1977;60:537–545.

127. Houde RW. Analgesic effectiveness of the narcotic agonist-antagonists. Br J Clin Pharmacol 1979;7:297S–308S.

128. Jasinski DR, Haertzen CA, Henningfield JE, Johnson RE, Makhzoumi HM, Miyasato K. Progress report of the NIDA Addiction Research Center. NIDA Res Monogr 1981;41: 45–52.

129. Leander JD. Buprenorphine has potent kappa opioid receptor antagonist activity. Neuropharmacol 1987;26:1445–1447.

130. Jasinski DR, Pevnick JS, Griffith JD. Human pharmacology and abuse potential of the analgesic buprenorphine. Arch Gen Psychiatry 1978;35:501–516.

131. Mello NK, Mendelson JH. Buprenorphine suppresses heroin use by heroin addicts. Science 1980;207:657–659.

132. Mello NK, Mendelson JH, Kuehnle JC. Buprenorphine effects on human heroin self-administration: an operant analysis. J Pharmacol Exp Ther 1982;223:30–39.

133. Bickel WK, Stitzer ML, Bigelow GE, Liebson IA, Jasinski DR, Johnson RE. A clinical trial with buprenorphine: Comparison with methadone in the detoxification of heroin addicts. Clin Pharmacol Ther 1988;43:72–78.

134. Johnson RE, Cone EJ, Henningfield JE, Fudala PJ. Use of buprenorphine in the treatment of opiate addiction. I. Physiologic and behavioral effects during a rapid dose induction. Clin Pharmacol Ther 1989;46:335–343.

135. Fudala PJ, Jaffe JH, Dax EM, Johnson RE. Use of buprenorphine in the treatment of opioid addiction. II. Physiologic and behavioral effects of daily and alternate-day administration and abrupt withdrawal. Clin Pharmacol Ther 1990; 47:525–534.

136. Quigley AJ, Bredemeyer DE, Seow SS. A case of buprenorphine abuse. Med J Aust 1984; 140:425–426.

137. Rainey HB. Abuse of buprenorphine. N Z Med J 1986;99:72.

138. Gray RF, Ferry A, Jauhar P. Emergence of buprenorphine dependence. Br J Addict 1989; 84:1373–1374.

139. Hammersley R, Lavelle T, Forsyth A. Buprenorphine and temazepam abuse. Br J Addict 1990;85:301–303.

140. Pickworth WB, Johnson RE, Holicky BA, Cone EJ. Subjective and physiologic effects of intravenous buprenorphine in humans. Clin Pharmacol Ther 1993;53:570–576.

141. Walsh SL, June HL, Schuh KJ, Preston KL, Bigelow GE, Stitzer ML. Effects of buprenorphine and methadone in methadone-maintained subjects. Psychopharmacology 1995; 119:268–276.

142. Strain EC, Preston KL, Liebson IA, Bigelow GE. Acute effects of buprenorphine, hydromorphone, and naloxone in methadone-maintained volunteers. J Pharmacol Exp Ther 1992; 261:985–993.

143. Strain EC, Preston KL, Liebson IA, Bigelow GE. Buprenorphine effects in methadone-maintained volunteers: effects at two hours after methadone. J Pharmacol Exp Ther 1995; 272:428–438.

144. Johnson RE, Fudala, PJ. Development of buprenorphine for the treatment of opioid dependence. NIDA Res Monogr 1992;121: 120–141.

145. Mello NK, Mendelson JH, Lukas SE, Gastfriend DR, Teoh SK, Holman BL. Buprenorphine treatment of opiate and cocaine abuse: clinical and preclinical studies. Harvard Rev Psychiatry 1993;1:168–183.

146. Fudala PJ, Johnson RE. Clinical efficacy studies of buprenorphine for the treatment of opiate dependence. In: Cowan A, Lewis JW, eds. Buprenorphine: combatting drug abuse with a unique opioid. New York: Wiley-Liss, 1995; 213–239.

147. Bickel WK, Amass L. Buprenorphine treatment of opioid dependence: a review. Exp Clin Psychopharmacol 1995;3:477–489.

148. Aceto MD. Characterization of prototypical opioid antagonists, agonist-antagonists, and agonists in the morphine-dependent rhesus monkey. Neuropeptides 1984;5:15–18.

149. Kosten TR, Kleber HD. Buprenorphine detoxification from opioid dependence; a pilot study. Life Sci 1988;42:635–641.

150. Walsh SL, June HL, Schuh KJ, Preston KL, Bigelow GE, Stitzer ME. Effects of buprenorphine and methadone in methadone-maintained subjects. Psychopharmacology 1995; 119:268–276.

151. Dum J, Blasig J, Herz A. Buprenorphine: demonstration of physical dependence liability. Eur J Pharmacol 1981;70:293–300.

152. Lewis JW, Rance MJ, Sanger DJ. The pharmacology and abuse potential of buprenorphine: a new antagonist analgesic. In: Mello NK, ed. Advances in substance abuse. Greenwich, CT: JAI Press, 1983:103–154.

153. Bickel WK, Stitzer ML, Bigelow GE, Liebson IA, Jasinski DR, Johnson RE. Buprenorphine. Dose-related blockade of opioid challenge effects in opioid dependent humans. J Pharmacol Exp Ther 1988;247:47–53.

154. Amass L, Bickel WK, Higgins ST, Hughes JR, Peterson T. Detectability of buprenorphine dose alterations in opioid-dependent humans. NIDA Res Monogr 1993;132:335.

155. Amass L, Bickel WK, Higgins ST, Badger GJ. Alternate-day dosing during buprenorphine treatment of opioid dependence. Life Sci 1994; 54:1215–1228.

156. Johnson RE, Eissenberg T, Stitzer ML, Strain EC, Liebson IA, Bigelow GE. Buprenorphine treatment of opioid dependence: clinical trial of daily of versus alternate-day dosing. Drug Alcohol Depend 1995;40:27–35.

157. Bickel WK, Amass L, Crean JP, Higgins ST. Triple buprenorphine maintenance doses maintain opioid-dependent outpatients for 72 hours with minimal withdrawal. NIDA Res Monogr 1995;153:161.

158. Lange WR, Fudala PJ, Dax EM, Johnson RE. Safety and side-effects of buprenorphine in the clinical management of heroin addiction. Drug Alcohol Depend 1990;26:19–28.

159. Walsh SL, Preston KL, Stitzer ML, Cone EJ, Bigelow GE. Clinical pharmacology of buprenorphine: Ceiling effects at high doses. Clin Pharmacol Ther 1994;55:569–580.

160. Jasinski DR, Fudala PJ, Johnson RE. Sublingual versus subcutaneous buprenorphine in opiate abusers. Clin Pharmacol Ther 1989;45: 513–519.

161. Hawks R, Chiang CN. Buprenorphine-naloxone combination drug for the treatment of drug addiction. NIDA Res Monogr 1995; 153:165.

162. Preston KL, Bigelow GE, Liebson IA. Buprenorphine and naloxone alone and in combination in opioid-dependent humans. Psychopharmacol 1988;94:484–490.

163. Weinhold LL, Preston KL, Farre M, Liebson IA, Bigelow GE. Buprenorphine alone and in combination with naloxone in non-dependent humans. Drug Alcohol Depend 1992;30: 263–274.

164. Fudala PJ, Yu E, Macfadden W, Kampman K, Cornish J. Evaluation of the effects of naloxone and buprenorphine in morphine-stabilized opiate addicts. Clin Pharmacol Ther 1996; 59:210.

165. Jones RT, Mendelson J. Effects of buprenorphine and naloxone combination in opiate-dependent volunteers. NIDA Res Monogr 1996;162:344.

166. Martin WR. Pharmacology of opioids. Pharmacol Rev 1984;35:283–323.

167. Chen JC, Smith ER, Cahill M, Cohen R, Fishman JB. The opioid receptor binding of dezocine, morphine, fentanyl, morphine, butorphanol, and nalbuphine. Life Sci 1993;52: 389–398.

168. O'Brien JJ, Benfield P. Dezocine. A preliminary review of its pharmacodynamic and pharmacokinetic properties, and therapeutic efficacy. Drugs 1989;38:226–248.

169. Jasinski DR, Mansky PA. Evaluation of nalbuphine for abuse potential. Clin Pharmacol Ther 1972;13:78–90.

170. Preston KL, Bigelow GE, Bickel WR, Liebson IA. Drug discrimination in human postaddicts: Agonist-antagonist opioids. J Pharmacol Exp Ther 1989;250:184–196.

171. Keats AS, Telford J. Studies of analgesic drugs. VIII. A narcotic antagonist analgesic without psychotomimetic effects. J Pharmacol Exp Ther 1964;143:157–164.

172. Jasinski DR, Martin WR, Hoeldke RD. Effects of short- and long-term administration of pentazocine in man. Clin Pharmacol Ther 1970; 11:385–403.

43 COMPREHENSIVE TREATMENT PROGRAMS

Anne Geller

Addiction treatment is changing quickly, as managed care influences not only access to treatment but the level, intensity, duration, and sometimes the kind of treatment that can be provided. This chapter is intended to provide an overview of treatment options available and a summary of current clinical and health services research findings.

The treatment system is complex, and patients are heterogeneous with different treatment needs (1). Outcomes can be measured in many different ways, e.g., abstinence, reduction in days of drug or alcohol use, employment, arrests, improved marital functioning, or reduction in medical visits. Treatment services delivered by one program may be very different from those delivered by another even when the descriptions of the programs appear similar (2).

Outcome studies for substance abusers show abstinence rates declining over time after treatment so that at one year approximately one third will have sustained abstinence (3–6) with an additional 15–30% showing use without problems or reduction over pretreatment use. An important variable in treating addictions as in treating any chronic illness is patient compliance with treatment recommendations. Psychiatric comorbidity, lack of social and family supports, and low socioeconomic status all affect compliance adversely so that the outcomes of treatment will vary with the population being studied. In spite of these variables methodologically adequate studies over the years with different populations and different treatment approaches have consistently shown significant changes following treatment in drug or alcohol use and in other areas of functioning. A selection of comprehensive reviews is listed in the references (3–6). Although random assignment to a nontreatment condition is neither ethical nor practical, waiting-list patients (5) or out-of-treatment groups (7) show increases over time in drug and other problem severity compared to the decreases in treated groups.

In spite of the overall positive results of treatment, these results are not uniform and there is substantial variability in posttreatment patient outcomes. For example, in the Rand report (8) while 31% of patients had sustained abstinence for one year after treatment, 40% were drinking and 19% had been treated again during this period. To analyze the possible factors involved in these outcomes, it is necessary to go beyond general studies of treatment and to look at treatment in greater detail. This chapter considers the following six aspects in reviewing treatment outcome studies: the setting of treatment; the model or philosophy of the program; the areas in which services are being provided; the specific treatment techniques being used; the background and training of providers; and the intensity (or dose) of treatment.

SETTING

The setting refers to the place where treatment occurs. It can be hospital-based inpatient, day hospital, outpatient, free-standing clinic, free-standing residential, or halfway house. There has been much debate in the last 15 years over the virtues of inpatient versus outpatient settings with no differences in outcome in most studies, but considerable differences in cost (9). However, it is clear that locations cannot meaningfully be considered without also addressing the actual services being provided and the severity of illness of the participants.

MODELS OR PHILOSOPHY

Different models or treatment philosophies have been developed over the years, sometimes attached to a specific setting or technique. Such models include the Minnesota model (10); the therapeutic community model (see Chapter 40); the outpatient drug-free cognitive behavioral model; the community reinforcement model; and the California social model. An excellent description of treatment models is found in Miller and Hester (11). While research findings have been only slowly incorporated into clinical treatment (6) and the anonymous self-help movement has been difficult for research to address, there has nonetheless been a considerable hybridization of techniques; e.g., relapse prevention training is widely used in Minnesota model programs and some introduction to Alcoholics Anonymous, Cocaine Anonymous, or Narcotics Anonymous may be provided in outpatient drug-free programs.

SERVICES

Programs may claim that specific service elements are included, but when examined many programs seem to deliver a standard mixture of educational lectures, group therapy, individual counseling, and exposure to self-help. The actual services provided can, however, be considered quite independently of the program philosophy or the techniques of treatment being used. McLellan (12–14) has been a pioneer in this area, looking at specific services, drug and alcohol counseling, medical and psychiatric services, employment counseling and services, marital and family counseling, and services dealing with legal problems. Programs differ remarkably in the number of services they actually provide in each area. Outcomes vary as a function of the services provided; for example, for the population as a whole, overall psychiatric outcomes are better when psychiatric services are provided and individual patients with job problems do best when matched with a job placement program.

TECHNIQUES OR MODALITIES

Within each treatment program several different treatment techniques may be used. The techniques selected may be dictated by the program or individual therapist philosophy, by the availability of a particular person skilled in that technique, or by research findings. Examples of such techniques are acupuncture, aversion therapy, behavioral marital therapy, cognitive behavioral therapies, coping skills training, educational lectures, exercise, group psychotherapy, meditation, motivational enhancement, pharmacotherapies, and self-help meetings. These techniques will be considered in more detail later.

PROVIDER CHARACTERISTICS

Treatment is provided by people with different training, skills, attitudes and abilities, gender, ethnicity, and socioeconomic status, all of which might affect patient outcome. Recovery status of the therapist has been studied and does not appear to affect outcome (15). Most studies that have looked at therapists' interactive style with patients conclude that therapist empathy or general level of interpersonal functioning is related to patient outcomes at one and two years (16). Confrontational styles have been associated with poor results (17).

INTENSITY OR DOSE

The usual way of looking at intensity of treatment by setting (inpatient versus outpatient) or length of stay uncovers little effect (18–19). However, in looking at "psychosocial dose response curve," it is more reasonable to look at units of service and days of delivery as a more specific measure of dose. Using these measures, there does appear to be an association between dose and outcome (20–21).

PATIENT TREATMENT MATCHING

Global approaches to treatment, as stated, ignore the fact that addicted patients are not homogeneous. Not only do they vary in terms of severity of the illness and any medical or psychiatric comorbidities, but they also differ in their social supports, living environments, readiness to change, and personality characteristics. Patients need to be matched to the appropriate treatment based on these factors. Treatment matching studies have shown that patients do better if their needs are addressed (14) but much more research is needed in this area. Meanwhile, the American Society of Addiction Medicine

(ASAM) has developed a consensus document, the Patient Placement Criteria, last revised in 1996 (22). It considers six domains in which patients can be assessed and provides a set of criteria by which patients can be matched to the appropriate level of treatment. The six domains are (a) acute intoxication and withdrawal, (b) biomedical condition, (c) emotional behavioral conditions, (d) acceptance of treatment, (e) relapse potential, and (f) recovery environment. There are also patient placement criteria for adolescents (22, 23).

The Patient Placement Criteria provide an approach in which the least intensive level of care is initially recommended and the patient is stepped up if the response is poor. The levels of care range from outpatient once weekly groups to intensive outpatient day or evening programs to inpatient hospital-based detoxification. The ASAM criteria have as yet no outcome data to support them and require research validation but remain a useful working tool.

The matching of patients to specific treatment techniques is currently the focus of a large multisite study sponsored by the National Institute on Alcohol Abuse and Alcoholism (24). An interesting earlier finding by Kadden (25) subsequently confirmed by follow-up (26) compared coping skills training and interactional group therapy given by random assignment following residential treatment. Both modalities produced improvements in abstinence and psychosocial adjustment. However, for patients with higher levels of sociopathy, coping skills training was more effective whereas for patients low in sociopathy, interactional therapy produced better outcomes.

EFFICACY EFFECTIVENESS AND COST EFFECTIVENESS

Before examining treatment techniques in more detail, the concepts of treatment efficacy, treatment effectiveness, and cost effectiveness should be understood.

Treatment efficacy refers to the effects of treatment in a randomized clinical trial under ideal conditions: homogeneous patients, specifically trained therapists and monitored, manual-driven therapy. Treatment that is efficacious under these conditions may not be effective in the real world of heterogeneous patients, randomly skilled therapists, and unmonitored application of a treatment technique. Treatment effectiveness deals with outcomes of treatment applied in real world clinical settings.

A treatment may show efficacy and effectiveness but its cost may be so high that a less effective, but much less costly, treatment may be preferable; that is, it is not cost effective. Cost effectiveness generally refers to the cost of achieving a given outcome, e.g., treatment A may produce a 50% abstention rate after 12 months and cost $25,000 per patient, whereas treatment B results in a 30% abstention rate but costs only $2,000 per patient. Treatment A costs $50,000 per abstaining patient whereas treatment B costs $6,667 per abstainer. Treatment B is more cost effective but treatment A is more effective. Decisions at this point require a complex analysis of resources and consequences. Another consideration is cost offset. For example, treating patients for alcoholism in Holder's 1986 study (27) resulted in declining general health care costs beginning after treatment and continuing over several years—a medical cost offset.

Cost offsets, however, can be complicated and very tricky to apply. Willard Manning (28), for example, has shown that premature deaths from cigarette smoking result in a net financial gain to society in savings from pensions and expected health care costs entailed by a longer life compared with losses in productivity and health care costs due to the premature death, among many factors considered. This leads to the conclusion that it is economically advantageous not to treat nicotine addiction. Cost offset arguments alone obviously should not determine policy.

TREATMENT TECHNIQUES AND MODALITIES

Miller (11, 29) has provided excellent reviews of the studies to date on the efficacy of various treatment modalities. Miller and others have observed that those treatments which are most efficacious are not the ones favored by treatment providers whereas some which have been untested or insufficiently studied are widely adopted, e.g., meditation or acupuncture. Also widely used are educational lectures and films, which have been shown ineffective in changing behavior in 18 of 21 controlled trials. There is also thus far no evidence for the efficacy of family systems therapy used in many treatment programs; on the other hand, behavioral marital therapy, which is little used outside of research settings, has been efficacious in 23 controlled trials (11).

The gold standard of treatment efficacy is the randomized controlled trial. In addiction research one treatment is usually compared with another rather than a no-treatment condition; therefore, it is necessary to know the strength of the comparison treatment in order to assess the results. Agosti (30) performed a meta analysis of 15 studies in the alcohol literature in which measures of abstinence were obtained using a laboratory report and/or significant other report, had a control group and randomized patients to treatments. Of these only three studies had an odds ratio of more than 2; that is, the experimental group was at least twice as likely to be abstinent as the control group. In the first of these three studies, O'Malley (31) found that the group given naltrexone with coping-skills training was three times more likely to be abstinent than those in the control conditions. In the Walsh (32) study, mandatory inpatient treatment was twice as successful as mandatory Alcoholics Anonymous meetings or freedom of choice. Bowers (33) found that patients receiving group couples therapy aimed at enhancing marital communication skills were twice as likely to be abstinent as patients receiving conventional individual counseling.

Nevertheless, in looking not at odds ratios but at treatments which have been shown to be more efficacious than control groups, particular treatments stand out. They are coping skills training, a variety of cognitive behavioral approaches including relapse prevention, behavioral self-control training, behavioral contracting, the reinforcement approach, and behavioral marital therapy.

Coping skills training covers a number of skills training aiming at improving general life functioning. Social skills training focuses on teaching more effective communication skills and improving interpersonal functioning. Though not aimed directly at the addictive behaviors, use of these techniques has consistently resulted in better treatment outcomes (34) when compared with supportive counseling, brief interventions, or when added to traditional treatment.

Relapse prevention therapies have had generally positive outcomes particularly when used with coping skills training. Behavior contracting, setting goals, and reinforcing successes has had good outcomes in four of four studies. Behavioral self-control training, which is a set of self-management strategies used with either an abstinence or moderation goal, has had both positive and negative results (29). The provision of self-help manuals using behavioral self-control has been shown to improve outcome.

The community reinforcement approach (35) is a comprehensive stand-alone treatment which combines a number of cognitive behavioral techniques. This approach has had consistently positive outcome studies (36–37) compared with "traditional" programs, with outcomes measured by employment and social adjustment as well as abstinence. The approach includes monitored disulfiram, behavioral marital therapy, job finding, and social reinforcement.

Cue Exposure

Exposure to drug-related cues result in changes in a number of physiological measures such as salivation, heart rate, galvanic skin response, reaction time, and other signs of general physiological arousal. This cue reactivity is associated with reported urges to use the substance (38–39). Theoretically, the repeated exposure to drug cues without reinforcement should result in gradual abatement of the conditional responses and eventually extinction. In time, the extinction of these physiological responses and their accompanying urges should improve abstinence rates. Cue reactivity has been repeatedly demonstrated as has its reduction with nonreinforcement. However, improvement in abstinence rates has been less robust (40). Combining cue exposure with coping skills training is a promising approach (41).

Aversion

Aversion therapies based on classical conditioning when tested have had predominantly negative results; however, aversion therapies used routinely in special residential treatment settings (42) in which alcohol is paired with nausea produced by an emetic agent have been effective.

Group Therapy

Group therapy can be used with a wide range of treatment modalities and so is meaningless unless further specified. Insight-oriented group psychotherapy has not been shown to be helpful for substance abusers. The type of group therapy used in traditional "Minnesota model" treatment programs has not really been tested as an element separate from the overall program. Outcomes for group treatment in general are equivalent to those for individual treatment (43); therefore, since group therapy is less costly, it is to be preferred.

Alcoholics Anonymous (AA)

AA is not a treatment, as its literature expressly states; however, it is often regarded as one by some courts and employee assistance programs. In spite of the fact that coercion is against basic AA beliefs, people have been mandated into AA by the courts, employee assistance programs, and some physician disciplinary programs. Not surprisingly, the outcomes of compulsory AA attendance have been negative (32). Voluntary involvement with AA, on the other hand, has been associated with reduction in total drinking days (44). This is, of course, nonrandom and may reflect advantageous characteristics of the type of clients who are able to affiliate with AA after treatment rather than the benefits of the AA program itself.

Brief Intervention

This review of efficacy would not be complete without a mention of brief interventions, even though they occur mainly in the primary-care setting and less in specialized addiction treatment settings. Brief interventions of 1–4 sessions have been shown to be more efficacious than no treatment and sometimes as good as more extended treatments (45). These brief interventions are thought to raise the level of motivation and to shift the client towards the direction of making changes. Motivational interviewing which is structured, brief counseling, specifically designed toward increasing the level of motivation for change, has been tested and found effective in eight trials. Motivational interviewing should be a useful technique for specialist as well as primary programs since many patients enter these programs unwillingly or at best with motivation to deal with the immediate crisis and placate those responsible for getting them into treatment.

Combined Use of Pharmacotherapy with Other Modalities of Treatment

The development of medication to improve outcomes in addiction treatment is an exciting and busy area of research. Detoxification, maintenance medication, and the treatment of medical and psychiatric comorbidities are dealt with elsewhere. This section will be limited to those medications which have been shown to be efficacious or are extremely promising when used in conjunction with verbal therapies in ongoing addiction treatment.

Disulfiram is a drug which is much misunderstood and improperly used (46). It is both a psychological and a pharmacological treatment. It enables patients to practice coping skills when exposed to alcohol cues since the drinking response is prevented. Disulfiram works best when its use is supervised and when it is a part of a comprehensive program. Studies of supervised disulfiram from 1976 to 1992 (47, 48) have been uniformly positive. The supervision can be by a family member as well as by professionals who observe ingestion of the dissolved disulfiram. Some training of the observer in the techniques of evasion which the patient may use is desirable. Most patients (76% in one study) (49) will not risk drinking on disulfiram. Of the 24% who do, 50% will not get much of a reaction on the standard 250 mg dose. Brewer (46) suggests the following: For those patients in whom an early relapse, though undesirable, would not be disastrous, an initial dose of 200–300 mg daily is appropriate. If the patient drinks and there is no reaction the dose should be increased to 400 or 500 mg if necessary. Brewer has published a comprehensive review of the mechanism of action and adverse effects (46).

In spite of its impressive record of positive studies, supervised disulfiram is underused. Instead, it is most generally prescribed for the "well-motivated" alcoholic to use by himself or herself. Since well-motivated patients generally do well and since its efficacy has not been studied in this group, nothing much can be said about this method of use except that if a patient wishes to use it and says that it is helpful then certainly this is an appropriate use.

Naltrexone

As was mentioned earlier in this chapter, naltrexone in combination with coping skills has been the most efficacious modality of treatment for alcoholism tested thus far (31). Naltrexone added to treatment reduced drinking days, relapses, and craving for alcohol. Studies to determine which patients are more likely to respond to naltrexone have begun with initial results suggesting that those patients with high craving and high levels of somatic distress are more responsive (50). Naltrexone is given daily at a dose of 50 mg.

Naltrexone with behavior therapy has been shown to be more effective than naltrexone alone for the treatment of heroin addiction as has naltrexone with multiple family therapy (51) for heroin addicts. Supervised naltrexone is used for physicians addicted to opiates but has not been formally studied.

As with disulfiram, patients on naltrexone, whether for alcohol or opiate addiction, do best when the pharmacological treatment is combined with psychological interventions. This suggests that pharmacotherapy is best used as an adjunct to a psychosocial program in the initial stages of treatment. Pharmacotherapy alone may be useful in some patients to sustain abstinence and prevent relapse during crises once that treatment is completed.

FROM EFFICACY TO EFFECTIVENESS

Efficacious treatments do not always result in effective treatments. Linking the two are the aspects of the treatment process such as the characteristics of the patient, the treatment program, the individual therapist, the therapeutic alliance, the treatment actually provided, and the patient involvement in treatment. Process outcome research studies these aspects in relation to immediate outcomes (retention in treatment) as well as ultimate outcomes (reduction in drug use). Understanding the processes involved allows treatment to be used in a flexible and responsive fashion rather than being applied mechanically (52). To illustrate the importance of process a few studies will be cited. Using the National Drug Abuse Treatment System Survey, McCaughrin and Price (53) found that the provision of aftercare services and smaller client-staff ratios were associated with improved outcome as measured by the proportion of clients who were not abusing drugs and alcohol at follow-up. Moos (54) has developed two scales to measure treatment program environments, the Ward Atmosphere Scale and the Community-Oriented Program Environment Scale (COPES). A study using the COPES (55) looked at three therapeutic community programs. After two years residents from the two programs showed improved outcomes over a no-treatment group but in the third program there was a high attrition rate with no evidence of improvement. This program was characterized by a lack of clarity regarding rules and expectations, low staff control, and an emphasis on patient expression of anger and aggression.

Using the Treatment Services Review to access the quantity and breath of services, McLellan (14) examined treatment outcomes for patients receiving minimum methadone service, standard services, and enhanced services. Outcomes were in the expected direction (more services, better outcomes) for six of the seven target areas.

Process outcome research can also provide a test of treatment theory by looking at proximal outcomes. Cognitive behavioral programs focus on teaching skills to improve the effectiveness of responses in high-risk situations. The proximal question is, Does the training actually improve effectiveness? The ultimate question is, Does improved effectiveness in coping result in less drinking?

Monti (56) has developed a roleplaying test to assess patient skills in dealing with social situations or with adverse mood states (coping skills). Patients treated with communication skills training improved more on the rated effectiveness of the response than those treated in a mood management group. In general, patients who exhibited more effective responses had more abstinent days.

Morgenstern (57) looked at treatment theory and proximal outcomes in a traditional "Minnesota model" chemical dependency inpatient treatment program. Acknowledgment of powerlessness over substance use, belief in a higher power, commitment to AA or Narcotics Anonymous, acknowledgment of having a disease, and the belief that a slip will lead to a full-blown relapse have been identified as core processes in this model. These increased significantly during treatment but were not associated with avoiding relapse during the first month after treatment. Processes considered to be common to other treatment approaches as well as the traditional Minnesota model were commitment to lifetime abstinence and intentions to avoid high-risk situations. Scores on those measures were high on entering treatment but did not increase significantly during treatment. These scores were associated with treatment outcome. The result does call into question the relevance of process goals central to the theory of the Minnesota model.

TOWARDS AN IDEAL TREATMENT PROGRAM

An ideal program should be comprehensive; that is, it should provide a range of levels and intensities of treatment targeted to severity of illness as well as a range of specific services targeted to individual patients' needs. Assessment should be standardized (e.g., by the Addiction Severity Index) and should be ongoing so that patients are moved from one level of treatment to another based on an assessment of their current condition. Level of treatment should be determined according to generally accepted criteria (e.g., ASAM Patient Placement Criteria). Specific services, e.g., psychiatric services and marital counseling, should be provided in accordance with the specific problems generated in the assessment. Treatment modalities should be selected on the basis of proven effectiveness. Consideration should always be given to combining pharmacological with psychological treatments. Treatment shown to be ineffective in repeated trials should be discarded. When possible, staff should be retrained to use a more effective modality.

Staff and patients need clarity regarding treatment goals as well as the criteria to be met for particular levels and intensities of treatment; program length in general will not be fixed, even though a given number of sessions may be required to complete the basics, e.g., relapse prevention or coping skills training.

Attention should be paid to the general ambience of the program, the ease of transition from one level to another, and its user friendliness. Empathy should be encouraged and confrontational approaches discouraged. However, program regulations and expectations should be clear, consistent and reinforced.

Finally, the program should have ongoing methods for evaluating itself on a number of dimensions, including patient retention and outcomes.

References

1. Institute of Medicine. Prevention, treatment of alcohol-related problems. Research opportunities. Washington, DC: Institute of Medicine, 1989.
2. McLellan AT, Alterman AI, Woody GE, Metzger D. A quantitative measure of substance abuse treatments: the treatment service review. J Nerv Ment Dis 1992;180:101–110.
3. Gerstein D, Harwood H, eds. Treating drug problems. Volume I. Washington, DC: National Academy Press, 1990.
4. Moos RH, Finney JW, Cronkite RC. Alcoholism treatment, context, process and outcome. New York: Oxford University Press, 1990.
5. McLellan AT, Metzger D, Alterman AI, Cornish J, Urschel H. How effective is substance abuse treatment—Compared to what? In: O'Brien CP, Jaffe J, eds. Advances in understanding the addictive states. New York: Raven Press, 1992.
6. Hubbard RL, Marsden ME, Rachel JV, Harwood HJ, Cavanaugh ER, Ginzberg, HM. Drug abuse treatment: a national study of effectiveness. Chapel Hill: University of North Carolina Press, 1989.
7. Metzger DS, Woody GE, McLellan AT, Druley P, De Phillipis D, O'Brien C, et al. H.I.V. zero conversion among in and out of treatment intravenous drug users. An 18 month prospective follow-up. AIDS 1993;6(9):1049–1056.
8. Armor DJ, Polich JM, Stambul HB. Alcoholism treatment. Santa Monica, CA: Rand Corp Press, 1976.
9. Holder HD, Longabaugh R, Miller WR, Rubo-

nis AV. The cost effectiveness of treatment for alcoholism. A first approximation. J Stud Alcohol 1991;52:517–540.

10. Cook CH. The Minnesota model in the management of alcohol and drug dependency: miracle, method or myth. Part I. Br J Addict 1988; 83:625–634.

11. Hester RK, Miller WR, eds. Handbook of alcoholism treatment approaches: effective alternatives. New York: Allyn and Bacon, 1995.

12. McLellan AT, Alterman AI, Woody GE, Metzger DA. Quantitative measure of substance abuse treatments. The treatment services review. J Nerv Ment Dis 1992;180:101–110.

13. McLellan AT, Grissom G, Alterman AI, Brill P, O'Brien CP. Private substance abuse treatments: are some programs more effective than others? J Subst Abuse Treat 1993;10: 243–254.

14. McLellan AT, Arndt IO, Woody GE, Metzger, D. Psychosocial services in substance abuse treatment. A dose ranging study of psychosocial services. JAMA 1993;269(15):1953–1959.

15. McLellan AT, Woody GE, Luborsky L, Goehl L. Is the counselor an active ingredient in substance abuse rehabilitation? An examination of treatment success among four counselors. J Nerv Ment Dis 1988;176:423–430.

16. Valle SK. Interpersonal functioning of alcoholism counselors and treatment outcome. J Stud Alcohol 1981;42:783–790.

17. Miller WR, Benefield RG, Tonigan JS. Enhancing motivation for change in problem drinking: a controlled comparison of two therapist styles. J Consult Clin Psychol 1993;61:455–461.

18. Longabaugh R, McCrady B, Fink E, Stout R, McAuley T, Doyle C, McNeill D. Cost effectiveness of alcoholism treatment in partial vs. inpatient settings: six months outcomes. J Stud Alcohol 1983;44(6):1049–1071.

19. McKay JR, Alterman AI, McLellan AT, Snider EC, O'Brien CP. Effect of random versus nonrandom assignment in a comparison of inpatient and day hospital rehabilitation for male alcoholics. J Consult Psychol 1995;63(1):70–78.

20. Hoffman JA, Caudill BD, Koman JJ, Luckey JW, Flynn PM, Mayo DW. Psychosocial treatments for cocaine abuse. Treatment intensity as a predictor of long-term clinical outcomes. In: Harris LS, ed. Problems of drug dependence 1994. Proceedings of the 56th annual scientific meeting. Rockville, MD: National Institute of Drug Abuse, 1995;152(1):72–73.

21. McLellan AT. Dose Response Studies of Psychosocial Services During Substance Abuse Treatment. In: Harris LS, ed. Problems of drug dependence 1994. Proceedings of the 56th annual scientific meeting. Rockville, MD: National Institute of Drug Abuse, 1995; 152(1):73.

22. Patient placement criteria for the treatment of substance related disorders (ASAM PPC-2). 2nd edition. Chevy Chase, MD: American Society of Addiction Medicine, 1996.

23. Babor TF, DelBoca FK, McLaney MA, Jacobi B, Higgins-Biddle J, Hass W. Just say Y.E.S.: matching adolescents to appropriate interventions for alcohol and drug related problems. Alcohol Health and Research World 1991;15(1): 77–86.

24. Project MATCH (matching alcoholism treatment to client heterogeneity): rationale and methods for a multi-site clinical trial matching patients to alcoholism treatment. Alcohol Clin Exp Res 1993:17(6):1130–1145.

25. Kadden RM, Cooney NL, Getter H, Litt MD. Matching alcoholics to coping skills or interactional therapies. Post-treatment results. J Consult Clin Psychol 1989;57:678–704.

26. Cooney NL, Kadden RM, Litt MD, Getter H. Matching alcoholics to coping skills or interactional therapies. Two-year follow-up results. J Consult Clin Psychol 1991;59:598–601.

27. Holder HD, Blose JO. Alcoholism treatment and total health care to utilization and costs. A four-year longitudinal analysis of federal employees. JAMA 1986;256:1456–1460.

28. Manning WG, Keeler EB, Newhouse JP, Sloss EM, Wasserman J. The taxes of sin: do smokers and drinkers pay their way? JAMA 1989;261: 1604–1609.

29. Miller WR. The effectiveness of treatment for substance abuse. Reasons for optimism. J Subst Abuse Treat 1992;9:93–102.

30. Agosti V. The efficacy of controlled trials of alcohol misuse treatment in maintaining abstinence: a meta-analysis. Int J Addict 1994;29(6): 759–769.

31. O'Malley SS, Jaffe JJ, Chang G, Scottenfeld RS, Meyer R, Rounsaville B. Naltrexone, coping skills therapy for alcohol dependence. A controlled study. Arch Gen Psychiatry 1992;49: 881–887.

32. Walsh DC, Hingson RW, Merrigan DM, Levenson SM, Cupples LA, Heeren T, et al. A randomized trial of treatment options for alcohol-abusing workers. N Engl J Med 1991;325(11): 775–782.

33. Bowers TG, Al Redha MR. A comparison of outcome with group-marital and standard individual therapies with alcoholics. J Stud Alcohol 1990;51(4):301–330.

34. Monti PM, Rohsenow DJ, Colby SM, Abrams DB. Coping, social skills training. In: Hester RK, Miller WR, eds. Handbook of alcoholism treatment approaches. Effective alternatives. 2nd edition. New York: Allyn & Bacon, 1995: 221–241.

35. Mayers RJ, Smith JE. Treating alcohol abuse. The community reinforcement approach. New York: Guilford Press, 1995.

36. Azrin NH. Improvements in the community reinforcement approach to alcoholism. Behav Res Ther 1976;14:339–348.

37. Azrin NH, Sisson RW, Meyers R, Godley M. Alcoholism treatment by disulfiram and community reinforcement therapy. J Behav Ther Exp Psychiatry 1982;15:105–112.

38. Rohsenow DJ, Monti PM, Rubonis AV, Sirota AD, Niaura RS, Colby SM, et al. Cue reactivity as a predictor of drinking among male alcoholics. J Consult Clin Psychol 1994;62(3): 620–626.

39. Childress AR, Ehrman RN, McLellan AT, MacRae J, Natale M, O'Brien CP. Can induced moods trigger drug-related responses in opiate abuse patients? J Subst Abuse Treat 1994; 11(1):17–23.

40. Childress AR, Hole AV, Ehrman RN, Robbins SJ, McLellan AT, O'Brien CP. Cue reactivity and cue reactivity interventions in drug dependence. NIDA Res Monogr 1993;137:73–95.

41. Abrams DB. Cue exposure with coping skills treatment for male alcoholics: a preliminary investigation. J Consult Clin Psychol 1993;61(6): 101–109.

42. Smith JW, Frawley PJ, Polissar L. Six, twelve month abstinence rates in in-patient alcoholics treated with aversion therapy compared with matched inpatients from a treatment registry. Alcohol Clin Exp Res 1991;15:862–870.

43. Miller WR, Taylor CA, West JC. Focused versus broad spectrum behavior therapy for problem drinkers. J Consult Clin Psychol 1980; 48:590–601.

44. Emrick CD, Tonigan JS, Montgomery H, Little L. Alcoholics anonymous: what is currently known? In: McCrady BS, Miller WR, eds. Research on alcoholics anonymous opportunities and alternatives. New Brunswick, NJ: Rutgers Center of Alcohol Studies, 1993.

45. Bien TH, Miller WR, Tonigan JS. Brief interventions for alcohol problems. A review. Addiction 1993;88:315–336.

46. Brewer C. Recent developments in disulfiram treatment. Alcohol Alcohol 1995;28:383–395.

47. Azrin NH. Improvements in the community reinforcement approach to alcoholism. Behav Res Ther 1976;14:339–348.

48. Chick J, Gough K, Falkowski W, Kershaw P, Hore B, Mehta B, et al. Disulfiram treatment of alcoholism. Br J Psychiatry 1992;161:84–89.

49. Brewer C. Patterns of compliance and evasion in treatment programs which include supervised disulfiram. Alcohol Alcohol 1986;21:385–388.

50. Volpicelli JR, Clay KL, Watson NT, O'Brien CP. Naltrexone in the treatment of alcoholism: predicting response to naltrexone. J Clin Psychiatry 1995;56(suppl 7):39–44.

51. O'Malley SS. Integration of opioid antagonists and psychosocial therapy in the treatment of narcotic and alcohol dependence. J Clin Psychiatry 1995;56(suppl 7):30–38.

52. Leipsey MW. Theory as method: small theories of treatment. In: Sechrest LB, Scott AG, eds. Understanding causes and generalizing about them. New direction for program evaluation 57. San Francisco: Jossey-Bass, 1993.

53. McCaughrin WC, Price RH. Effective outpatient drug misuse treatment organizations. Program features and selection effects. Int J Addict 1992;27:1335–1338.

54. Moos RH. Community oriented programs environment scale manual. 2nd edition. Palo Alto, CA: Consulting Psychologists Press, 1988.

55. Bale RN, Zarcone VP, Van Stone WW, Kuldan JM, Engelsing TMJ, Elashoff RM. Three therapeutic communities. A prospective controlled study of narcotic addiction treatment. Arch Gen Psychiatry 1984;4:185–191.

56. Monti PM, Abrams DB, Binkoff JA, Zwick WR, Liepman, MR, Nirenberg TD, et al. Communication skills training, communication skills training with family and cognitive behavioral mood management training for alcoholics. J Stud Alcohol 1990;51:263–270.

57. Morgenstern J, Frey RM, McCrady BS, Labouvie E, Neighbors CJ. Examining mediators in change in traditional clinical dependence treatment. J Stud Alcohol 1996;57:53–64.

44 INDIVIDUAL PSYCHOTHERAPY

Bruce J. Rounsaville and Kathleen M. Carroll

Given that this is but one chapter in a comprehensive textbook that describes a variety of therapeutic approaches that can be used on an individual basis (e.g., coping skills training, behavioral therapy), this chapter will focus on those aspects of individual therapy that are unique to the one-to-one format of treatment delivery. In addition, this chapter focuses on individual therapy as applied to nonalcoholic drugs of abuse, as the extensive literature on this and other forms of treatment for alcoholics has been reviewed elsewhere (1–3).

HISTORY

The history of individual psychotherapy for drug abusers has been one of importation of methods first developed to treat other conditions. Thus, when psychoanalytic and psychodynamic therapies were the predominant modality for treating most mental disorders, published descriptions of dynamics of drug abuse or of therapeutic strategies arose from using this established general modality to treat the special population of drug abusers (4). Likewise, with the development of behavioral techniques, client-centered therapies, and cognitive behavioral treatments, earlier descriptions based on other types of patients were followed by discussions of the special modifications needed to treat drug abusers. Those types of psychosocial treatment approaches that have originated with treating substance abusers, such as Alcoholics Anonymous (AA) and therapeutic communities, have emphasized large-and small-group treatment settings.

Although always present as a treatment option, individual psychotherapy has not been the predominant treatment modality for drug abusers since the 1960s, when inpatient 12-step informed milieu therapy, group treatments, methadone maintenance, and therapeutic community approaches came to be the fixtures of substance abuse treatment programs. In fact, these newer modalities derived their popularity from the failures of dynamically informed ambulatory individual psychotherapy when it was used as the sole treatment for drug abusers. The problems reported for this form of treatment were premature termination, reaction to anxiety-arousing interpretations with resumption of drug use, erratic attendance at sessions, difficulties posed by attending sessions while intoxicated, and failure to pay fees because money was spent on drugs (5, 6).

Given these difficulties, it is a wonder that this approach has not been abandoned entirely. However, some inspection of what went wrong with outpatient dynamic therapy when applied to drug abusers may suggest the modifications that are needed when attempting to deliver individual treatment to drug abusers. Briefly, dynamic psychotherapy is based on an overall conception that explains all symptoms as arising from underlying psychological conflicts that are at least partly beyond the patient's awareness (unconscious). The major goal of this therapy is to help the patient become aware of these conflicts and to seek healthier methods of achieving wishes and aims that previously have been disavowed. According to this view of psychopathology, the actual symptom choice (e.g., depression, phobia, drug abuse) is less the focus of treatment because symptom substitution is likely to take place if the presenting symptom is removed without resolution of the underlying conflict. The process of the therapy relies heavily on discovering one's conflicts through an unstructured, exploratory, and anxiety-arousing procedure of attempting to say everything that comes to mind (free association). A major strategy for discovering unconscious conflicts is the analysis of transference, a process by which the patient begins to develop thoughts and feelings about the therapist that are derived from those originally experienced in other, formative relationships outside of the therapy. To facilitate this exploratory process and development of transference, the therapist typically assumes a neutral, passive stance and provides a minimum in the way of advice, support, or instruction (7, 8).

There are several reasons why this approach was poorly suited to the needs of drug abusers when it was offered as the sole ambulatory treatment. First, the lack of emphasis on symptom control and the lack of structure in the therapist's typical stance allowed the patient's continued drug abuse to undermine the treatment. Therapists did not develop methods for addressing the patient's needs for coping skills because this removal of symptoms was seen as palliative and likely to result in symptom substitution. As a result, substance use often continued unabated while the treatment focused on underlying dynamics. Limit setting by the therapist was to be avoided so as to maintain neutrality, and no clear guidelines were provided for dealing with intoxication during sessions. Dropout was a likely outcome because patients believed that their primary, presenting problem was not being addressed and because little progress could be made in the exploratory dynamic goals of treatment if drug abuse was not first brought under control. The major strategy that is now common to all currently practiced psychotherapies for drug abusers is to place primary emphasis on controlling or reducing drug use, while pursuing other goals only after drug use has been at least partly controlled. This means that either (*a*) the individual therapist employs techniques designed to help the patient stop illicit drug use as a central part of the treatment or (*b*) the therapy is practiced in the context of a comprehensive treatment program in which other aspects of the treatment curtail the patient's use of drugs (e.g., methadone maintenance, disulfiram for alcoholics, residential treatment). A second major misfit between individual dynamic therapy and drug abusers is its anxiety-arousing nature coupled with the lack of structure provided by the neutral therapist. Because substance abusers frequently react to increased anxiety or other dysphoric affects by resuming substance use, it is important to introduce anxiety-arousing aspects of treatment only after a strong therapeutic alliance has been developed or within the context of other supportive structures (e.g., inpatient unit, strong social support network, methadone maintenance) that guard against relapse to drug use when the patient experiences heightened anxiety and dysphoria in the context of therapeutic exploration.

Individual psychotherapy had a resurgence in use starting in the 1980s that continues today as the limitations of other modalities have become apparent (e.g., methadone maintenance without ancillary services) (9, 10), and necessary modifications in technique have been made to address the factors underlying earlier failures. As is reviewed in this chapter, growing evidence indicates that individual psychotherapy can be an effective modality with drug abusers, and a series of studies has been conducted with the aim of guiding the context and timing for delivery of individual therapy to drug abusers.

POPULATION SERVED

To address the issue of when and with whom individual psychotherapy might best be used, it is useful to consider first when psychotherapy appears to be indicated, and second, the conditions that are best suited for an individual form of treatment.

When Is Psychotherapy Indicated?

Is psychotherapy necessary in the treatment of drug abuse? What are the alternatives to psychotherapy? Of course, many, if not most, individuals who use psychoactive substances either do not become abusers of these substances or eventually stop or limit their substance use without formal treatment (11–14). Most of those who seek treatment do so only after numerous unsuccessful attempts to stop or reduce drug use on their own (14). For those who seek treatment, the alternatives to some form of psychotherapy are either structural (e.g., sequestration from access to drugs in a residential setting) or pharmacological. Removal from the drug-using setting is a useful and, sometimes, necessary part of drug treatment but is seldom sufficient, as is shown by the high relapse rates typically seen from residential detoxification programs or incarceration during the year following the patient's return to his or her community (15–18).

Psychotherapy and Pharmacotherapy

The most powerful and commonly used pharmacological approaches to drug abuse are maintenance on an agonist that has an action similar to that of the abused drug (e.g., methadone for opioid addicts, nicotine gum for cigarette smokers), use of an antagonist that blocks the effect of the abused drug (e.g., naltrexone for opioid addicts), and the use of an aversive agent that provides a powerful negative reinforcement if the drug is used (e.g., disulfiram for alcoholics). Although all of these agents are widely used, they are seldom used without the provision of adjunctive psychotherapy, because naltrexone maintenance alone is plagued by high rates of premature dropout (19, 20), and disulfiram use without adjunctive psychotherapy has not been shown to be superior to placebo (21, 22). In particular, the large body of literature on the effectiveness of methadone maintenance points to the success of methadone maintenance in retaining opioid addicts in treatment and reducing their illicit opioid use and illegal activity (10). However, there is a great deal of variability in the success across different methadone maintenance programs, which is in part due to wide variability in provision and quality of psychosocial services (10, 23).

The shortcomings of even powerful pharmacotherapies delivered without psychotherapy were convincingly demonstrated by McLellan and colleagues at the Philadelphia VA medical center (24). Ninety-two opiate addicts were randomly assigned to receive either (*a*) methadone maintenance alone, without psychosocial services; (*b*) methadone maintenance with standard psychosocial services, which included regular individual meetings with a counselor; or (*c*) enhanced methadone maintenance, which included regular counseling plus access to onsite psychiatric, medical, employment, and family therapy, in a 24-week trial. In terms of drug use and psychosocial outcomes, best outcomes were seen in the enhanced methadone maintenance condition, with intermediate outcomes for the standard methadone services condition, and poorest outcomes for the methadone alone condition. Although a few patients did reasonably well in the methadone alone condition, 69% had to be transferred out of that condition within 3 months of the study inception because their substance use did not improve or even worsened, or because they experienced significant medical or psychiatric problems that required a more intensive level of care. Results from this study suggest that although methadone maintenance alone may be sufficient for a small subgroup of patients, the majority will not benefit from a purely pharmacological approach and best outcomes are associated with higher levels of psychosocial treatments.

Even when the principal treatment is seen as pharmacological, psychotherapeutic interventions are needed to complement the pharmacotherapy by (*a*) enhancing the motivation to stop drug use by taking the prescribed medications, (*b*) providing guidance for use of prescribed medications and management of side effects, (*c*) maintaining motivation to continue taking the prescribed medication after the patient achieves an initial period of abstinence, (*d*) providing relationship elements to prevent premature termination, and (*e*) helping the patient to develop the skills to adjust to a life without drug use. These elements that psychotherapy can offer to complement pharmacological approaches are likely to be needed even if "perfect" pharmacotherapies are available. This is because the effectiveness of even the most powerful pharmacotherapies is limited by the patient's willingness to comply with them, and the strategies found to enhance compliance with pharmacotherapy (monitoring, support, encouragement, education) are inherently psychosocial. Moreover, the provision of a clearly articulated and consistently delivered psychosocial treatment in the context of a primarily pharmacological treatment is an important strategy for reducing noncompliance and attrition, thereby enhancing outcome in clinical research and clinical treatment (25).

Moreover, the importance of psychotherapy and psychosocial treatments is reinforced by recognition that the repertoire of pharmacotherapies available for treatment of drug abusers is limited to a handful, with the most effective agents limited in their utility to treatment of opioid abuse (26–28). Effective pharmacotherapies for abuse of cocaine, marihuana, hallucinogens, sedative-hypnotics, and stimulants have not yet been developed and talking therapies remain the principal approaches for the treatment of these classes of drug abuse (29–33).

GROUP VERSUS INDIVIDUAL THERAPY

If psychotherapy is necessary for at least a substantial number of treatment-seeking drug abusers, when is individual therapy a superior choice over other modalities such as family therapy or group therapy? Because group therapy has become the modal format for psychotherapy of drug abusers, evaluation of the role of individual therapy should take the strengths and weaknesses of group therapy as its starting point.

A central advantage of group over individual psychotherapy is economy, which is a major consideration in an era of generally skyrocketing health care costs and increasingly curtailed third-party payments for substance abuse treatment. Groups typically have a minimum of six members and a maximum of two therapists, yielding at least a threefold increase in the number of patients treated per therapist hour. Although the efficacy of group versus individual therapy has not been systematically studied with drug abusers, there is no evidence from other populations that individual psychotherapy yields superior benefits (34). Moreover, nearly all major schools of individual psychotherapy have been adapted to a group format.

In addition to the general concept that group therapy may be just as good as but less expensive than individual therapy, there are aspects of group therapy that can be argued to make this modality more effective than individual treatment of drug abusers. For example, given the social stigma attached to having lost control of drug use, the presence of other group members who acknowledge having similar problems can provide comfort. Related to this, other group members who are farther along in their recovery from addiction can act as models to illustrate that attempting to stop drug use is not a futile effort. These more advanced group members can offer a wide variety of coping strategies that may go beyond the repertoire known even by the most skilled individual therapist. Moreover, group members frequently can act as "buddies" who offer continued support outside of the group sessions in a way that most professional therapists do not. Finally, the "public" nature of group therapy with its attendant aspects of confession and forgiveness coupled with the pressure to publicly confess future slips and transgressions provides a powerful incentive to avoid relapse. Being able to publicly declare the number of days sober and the fear of having to publicly admit to "falling off the wagon" are strong forces pushing a drug abuser toward recovery. This public affirmation or shaming may be all the more crucial in combating a disorder that is characterized by a failure of internalized mechanisms of control. Drug abusers have been characterized as having poorly functioning internal self-control mechanisms (35–38), and the group process with many eyes watching provides a robust source of external control. Moreover, because the group is composed of recovering drug abusers, members may be more able to detect each other's attempts to conceal relapse or early warning signals for relapse than would an individual therapist who may not have a history of drug abuse.

Given these strengths of group therapy, what are the unique advantages of individual therapy that may justify its greater expense? First, a key advantage for individual therapy is that it provides privacy. Although self-help groups such as AA attempt to protect the confidentiality of group members by asking for first names only and routine group therapy procedures involve instructions to members to keep identities and content of sessions confidential, group therapy always breaches confidentiality, especially in small communities. Although publicly admitting to one's need for help may be a key element of the recovery process, it is a step that is very difficult to take, particularly when the problems associated with substance abuse have not yet become severe. Public knowledge of drug abuse problems can still be the ruin of careers and reputations despite the more widespread acknowledgment of the prevalence of these disorders that occurred in the 1970s and 1980s. Second, the individualized pace of individual therapy allows the therapist more flexibility to address the patient's problems as they arise, whereas group therapy may be out of sync with some members while suiting the needs of the majority. This is particularly an issue for open groups that add new members throughout the life of the group, necessitating repetition of many therapeutic elements so as to acquaint new members with the group's history and to address the needs of individuals who have just begun treatment. Third, from the patient's point of view, individual therapy allows a much higher percentage of therapy time concentrating on issues that are uniquely relevant to that individual. Members of therapy groups usually have the experience of spending many hours discussing issues that are not problems for them, and the individual tailoring of therapy sessions to fit particular needs ultimately may be more efficient. Fourth, logistical issues make individual therapy more practical in many settings. Given the decentralization of much mental health service delivery and the continued predominance of the individual practitioner system, individual therapy is most feasible for many mental health professionals or medical practitioners, who may not have a caseload of substance abusers that is large enough to conduct group treatment. If group therapy is to be started with a new group, it may be many weeks before enough members are screened to be entered into a new group, resulting in patients' discouragement and high dropout rates while awaiting the onset of treatment. If group therapy involves addition to an ongoing group, this can present formidable obstacles to joining. Also, unless group therapy is offered in the context of a large clinic or practice with many ongoing groups, scheduling may be very difficult for those patients whose employer is not apprised of the need for treatment. Fifth, the process and structure of individual therapy may confer unique advantages for dealing with some kinds of problems presented by patients. For example, individual therapy may be more conducive to the development of a deepening relationship between the patient and therapist over time, which may allow exploration of relationship elements not possible in group therapy. Alternatively, patients with particular personality disorders, such as schizoid patients, may be unable to get involved with other group members, as may avoidant patients, who are so shy that they cannot bring themselves to attend group sessions.

TREATMENT METHODS

Most schools of therapy, with widely varying rationales and strategies, have been adapted for potential use with substance abusers in an individual format, and separate chapters in this volume detail the theory and methods associated with some of the most widely used current approaches, including behavioral therapy and relapse prevention strategies (Chapter 48). Rather than duplicate the explication of these methods here, this chapter focuses on two topics that can guide the individual therapy of drug abusers within a variety of different schools: (*a*) specialized knowledge needed to apply individual psychotherapy to drug abusers, and (*b*) common goals and strategies that must be addressed by individual psychotherapists.

Areas of Specialized Knowledge About Drug Abusers

This section bases its recommendations on the supposition that most individual psychotherapists who attempt to work with drug abusers obtained their first psychotherapy experience and training with other groups of patients, such as those typically seen at inpatient or outpatient general psychiatric clinics. This supposition is based on the status of substance abuse treatment as a subspecialty placement within training programs for the major professional groups practicing psychotherapy, such as psychologists, psychiatrists, and social workers. Thus, to treat drug abusers, the task for the typical psychotherapist is to acquire necessary new knowledge and modify already learned skills.

The principal areas of knowledge to be mastered by the beginning therapist are the pharmacology, use patterns, consequences, and course of addiction for the major types of abused drugs. For therapy to be effective, it is useful not only to obtain the textbook knowledge about frequently abused

substances but also to also become familiar with street knowledge about drugs (e.g., slang names, favored routes of administration, prices, availability) and the clinical presentation of individuals when they are intoxicated or experiencing withdrawal from the different abused drugs. This knowledge has many important uses in the course of individual therapy with drug abusers.

First, it fosters a therapeutic alliance by allowing the therapist to convey an understanding of the addict's problems and the world in which the addict lives. This is an especially important issue when the therapist is from a different racial or social background from the drug-abusing patient. In engaging the patient into treatment, it is important to emphasize that the patient's primary presenting complaint is likely to be drug abuse, even if many other issues are also likely to be amenable to psychotherapeutic interventions. Hence, if the therapist is not comfortable and familiar with the nuances of problematic drug use, it may be difficult to forge an initial working alliance. Moreover, by knowing the natural history of drug use and the course of drug effects, the clinician can be guided in helping the patient anticipate problems that will arise in the course of initiating abstinence. For example, knowing the typical type and duration of withdrawal symptoms can help the addict recognize their transient nature and to develop a plan for successfully completing an ambulatory detoxification.

Second, knowledge of drug actions and withdrawal states is crucial for diagnosing coexistent psychopathology and for helping the addict to understand and manage dysphoric affects. It has been observed in clinical situations and demonstrated in laboratory conditions (39–42) that most abused drugs such as opioids or cocaine are capable of producing constellations of symptoms that mimic psychiatric syndromes such as depression, mania, anxiety disorders, or paranoia. Many of these symptomatic states are completely drug-induced and resolve spontaneously when substance abuse is stopped. It is frequently the therapist's job to determine whether or not presenting symptoms are part of an enduring, underlying psychiatric condition or a transient, drug-induced state. If the former, then simultaneous treatment of the psychiatric disorder is appropriate; if the latter, reassurance and encouragement to maintain abstinence are usually the better course.

This need to distinguish transient drug-induced affects from enduring attitudes and traits is also an important psychotherapy task. Affective states have been shown to be linked closely with cognitive distortions, as Beck and colleagues have demonstrated in their delineation of the cognitive distortions associated with depression (43, 44). While experiencing depressive symptoms, a patient is likely to have a profoundly different view about himself or herself, the future, the satisfactions available in life, and his or her important interpersonal relationships. These views are likely to change radically with remission of depressive symptoms, even if the remission of symptoms was induced by pharmacotherapy and not by psychotherapy or actual improvement in life circumstances (45). Because of this tendency for drug-related affective states to greatly color the patient's view of self and the world, it is important for the therapist to be able to recognize these states so that the associated distorted thoughts can be recognized as such rather than being taken at face value. Moreover, it is important that the patient also be taught to distinguish between sober and drug-affected conditions and to recognize when, in the colloquial phrase, it is "the alcohol talking" and not the person's more enduring sentiments.

Third, learning about drug actions is important for detecting when drug abusers have relapsed or have come to sessions intoxicated. It is seldom useful to conduct psychotherapy sessions when the patient is intoxicated, and when this happens the session should be rescheduled for a time when the patient can participate while sober. For alcoholics, noticing the smell of alcohol or using a breathalyzer is a useful technique for detecting intoxication, but such immediate aids are not available for other drugs of abuse. The clinician must then rely on his or her own clinical skills to determine whether or not the patient is drug free and able to participate fully in the psychotherapy.

A second area of knowledge to be mastered by the psychotherapist is an overview of treatment philosophies and techniques for the other treatments and self-help groups that are available to drug-abusing patients. As noted earlier, the early experience of attempting individual psychotherapy as the sole treatment of the more severe types of drug abuse was marked by failure and early dropout. Hence, for many drug abusers, individual psychotherapy is best conceived of as a component in a multifaceted program of treatment to help drug abusers overcome a chronic, relapsing condition. In fact, one function of individual psychotherapy can be to help the patient choose which additional therapies to take advantage of in his or her attempt to cease drug abuse. Thus, even when the therapist is a solo practitioner, he or she should know when detoxification is necessary, when inpatient treatment is appropriate, and what pharmacotherapies are available.

Another major function of knowing about the major alternative treatment modalities for drug abusers is to be alert to the possibility that different treatments may provide contradictory recommendations that may confuse the patient or foster the patient's attempts to sabotage treatment. Unlike a practitioner whose treatment is likely to be sufficient, the individual psychotherapist does not have the option of simply instructing the patient to curtail other treatments or self-help groups while individual treatment is taking place. Rather, it is vital that the therapist attempt to adjust his or her own work in order to bring the psychotherapy in line with the other treatments. A common set of conflicts arises between the treatment goals and methods employed by professional therapists and the predominant 12-step, self-help movements such as AA, Cocaine Anonymous, and Narcotics Anonymous. For example, the recovery goal for many who espouse a 12-step approach is a life with complete abstinence from psychotropic medications. This can come into conflict with professional advice when the therapist recommends use of psychopharmacological treatment for patients with coexistent psychiatric disorders such as depression, mania, or anxiety disorders. In the face of disapproval from fellow members of self-help groups, patients may prematurely discontinue psychotropic medications and experience relapse of psychological symptoms, with consequent return to drug abuse. To avoid this occurrence, it is important, when psychotropic medications are recommended or prescribed, to warn the patient about the apparently contradictory messages that he or she may receive between the 12-step admonition to lead a drug-free life and the clinician's support of the use of prescribed psychotropic medications. One way of describing this issue is to describe the psychiatric condition for which the medications are prescribed as a separate disease from the substance abuse and impress upon the patient that medications are as necessary for the treatment of this separate condition as insulin would be for diabetes. The fact that the medications are intended to affect brain functioning and attendant mental symptoms while insulin affects other parts of the body is less important than the concept that two diseases are present and not one. A second common area of conflict between some forms of psychotherapy and the 12-step philosophy is the role played by family members. The Al-Anon approach tends to suggest that family members get out of the business of attempting to control the drug abuser's use of drugs, and separate meetings are held for dealing with family members' and drug abusers' issues. In contrast, many therapists encourage involvement of family members in dealing with family dynamics that may foster drug use and/or in acting as adjunctive therapists (46, 47). As with the use of psychotropic medications, the major way of preventing a patient's confusion is to anticipate the areas of contradictory advice and to provide a convincing rationale for the therapist's recommendations. In doing so, it is advisable to acknowledge that different strategies appear to work for different individuals and that alternative approaches might be employed sequentially if the initial plan fails.

Common Issues and Strategies for Psychotherapy with Drug Abusers

This section reviews issues presented by drug abusers that must be addressed, if not emphasized, by any type of individual psychotherapy that is to be effective. As noted in reviewing the difficulties encountered by early psychodynamic practitioners, the central modification that is required of psychotherapists is always to be aware that the patient being treated is a drug abuser. Hence, even when attempting to explore other issues in depth, the therapist should devote at least a small part of every session to monitoring the patient's most recent successes and failures at controlling or curtailing substance use and being willing to interrupt other work to address slips and relapses when they occur.

Implicit in the need to remain focused on the patient's drug use is the requirement that psychotherapy with drug abusers entails a more active therapist stance than does treatment of patients with other psychiatric disorders such as depression or anxiety disorders. This is related to the fact that the principal symptom of drug abusers, compulsive drug use, is at least initially gratifying, and it is the long-term consequences of drug use that induce pain and the desire to stop. In contrast, the principal symptoms of depression or anxiety disorders are inherently painful and alien. Because of this key difference, psychotherapy with drug abusers typically requires both empathy and structured limit setting, while the need for limit setting is less marked in psychotherapy with depressed or anxious patients. Beyond these key elements, this section also elaborates on the following set of psychotherapy tasks: setting the resolve to stop drug use, teaching coping skills, changing reinforcement contingencies, fostering management of painful affects, and improving interpersonal functioning. Although different schools of thought about therapeutic action and behavior change may vary in the degree to which emphasis is placed on these different tasks, some attention to these areas is likely to be involved in any successful treatment.

SETTING THE RESOLVE TO STOP

Cummings (48) has noted that drug abusers most often enter treatment not with the goal to stop but to return to the days when drug abuse was enjoyable. The natural history of drug abuse (14) typically is characterized by an initial period of episodic use lasting months to years in which drug-related consequences are minimal and drug use is perceived as beneficial. Even at the time of treatment-seeking, which usually occurs only after drug-related problems have become severe, drug abusers usually can identify many ways in which they want or feel the need for drugs and have difficulty developing a clear picture of what life without drugs might be like. To be able to achieve and maintain abstinence or controlled use, drug abusers need a clear conception of their treatment goals. Several investigators (49, 50) have postulated stages in the development of drug abusers' thinking about stopping use, beginning with precontemplation, moving through contemplation, and culminating with determination as the ideal cognitive set with which to get the most out of treatment.

Regardless of the treatment type, an early task for psychotherapists is to gauge the patient's level of motivation to stop drug use by exploring his or her treatment goals. In doing this, it is important to challenge overly quick or glib assertions that the patient's goal is to stop using drugs. One way to approach the patient's likely ambivalence about treatment goals is to attempt an exploration of the patient's perceived benefits from drugs or perceived needs for them. To obtain a clear report of the patient's positive attitudes toward drug use, it may be necessary to elicit details of the patient's early involvement with drugs. When the therapist has obtained a clear picture of the patient's perceived needs and desires for drugs, it is important to counter these exploring advantages of a drug-free life.

As noted previously, while virtually all types of psychotherapy for drug abusers address the issue of motivation and goal setting to some extent, motivational therapy or interviewing (51, 52) makes this the sole initial focus of treatment. Motivational approaches, which are usually quite brief (e.g., 2–4 sessions), are based on principles of motivational psychology and are designed to produce rapid, internally motivated change by seeking to maximize patients' motivational resources and commitment to abstinence. Active ingredients of these approaches are hypothesized to include objective feedback of personal risk or impairment, emphasis on personal responsibility for change, clear advice to change, a menu of alternative change options, therapist empathy, and facilitation of patient self-efficacy (52). Motivational approaches have substantial empirical evidence supporting their effectiveness with alcoholics (3, 53) but have not yet been widely applied or evaluated for drug-abusing populations. These approaches are intuitively appealing, however, given that patients' commitment to abstinence has been found to be a predictor of treatment success in cocaine abusers (54).

One major controversy in this area is whether controlled use can be an acceptable alternative treatment goal to abstinence from all psychoactive drugs (55, 56). Many, if not most, patients enter treatment with a goal of controlled use, especially of alcohol (57), and failure to address the patient's presenting goal may result in failure to engage the patient. At the heart of the issue is whether or not drug abuse is seen as a categorical disease, for which the only treatment is abstinence, or a set of habitual dysfunctional behaviors that are aligned along a continuum of severity (58). For illicit drugs of abuse (e.g., cocaine, heroin), it is unwise for a professional therapist to take a position that advocates any continued use of illicit drugs, because such a stance allies the therapist with illegal and antisocial behavior. Even advocates of controlled use as an acceptable treatment goal usually acknowledge that drug abusers with more severe dependence should seek an abstinence goal. In practice, the therapist cannot force the patient to seek any goal that the patient does not choose. The process of arriving at an appropriate treatment goal frequently involves allowing the patient to make several failed attempts to achieve a goal of controlled substance use. This initial process may be needed to convince the patient that an abstinence goal is more appropriate.

TEACHING COPING SKILLS

The challenge of treating drug abusers is to help the patient avoid relapse after achieving an initial period of abstinence (59). A general tactic for avoiding relapse is to identify sets of circumstances that increase an individual's likelihood of resuming drug use and to help the patient anticipate and practice strategies (e.g., refusal skills, recognizing and avoiding cues for craving) for coping with these high-risk situations. Examples of approaches that emphasize the development of coping skills include cognitive-behavioral approaches such as relapse prevention (59, 60), where systematic effort is made to identify high-risk situations and master alternative behaviors, and coping skills intended to help the patient avoid drug use when these situations arise. A postulate of this approach is that proficiency in a variety of coping skills that are generalizable to a variety of problem areas will help foster durable change. Evidence is emerging that points to the durability and in some cases the delayed emergence of effects from coping skills treatments for substance abusers (61, 62). For other approaches, enumeration of risky situations and development of coping skills is less structured (63, 64) and embedded in a more general exploration of patients' wishes and fears.

CHANGING REINFORCEMENT CONTINGENCIES

Edwards and colleagues (58, 65, 66) have noted that a key element of deepening dependence on drugs is the rise of drug-using behavior to the top of an individual's list of priorities. As drug abuse worsens, it can take precedence over concerns about work, family, friends, possessions, and health. As compulsive drug use becomes a part of everyday life, previously valued relationships or activities may be given up so that the rewards available in daily life are narrowed progressively to those derived from drug use. When drug use is brought to a halt, its absence may leave the patient with the need to fill the time that had been spent using drugs and to find rewards that can substitute for those derived from drug use. The ease with which the patient can rearrange priorities is related to the level of achievement prior to the person's becoming a drug abuser and the degree to which drug abuse has destroyed or replaced valued relationships, jobs, or hobbies. Since the typical course of illicit drug abuse entails initiation of compulsive use between the ages of 12 and 25 (14), many drug abusers come to treatment never having achieved satisfactory adult relationships or vocational skills. In such cases, achieving a drug-free life may require a lengthy process of vocational rehabilitation and development of meaningful relationships. Individual psychotherapy can be important in the process by helping maintain the patient's motivation throughout the recovery process and exploring factors that have interfered with achievement of rewarding ties to others.

An example of an approach that actively changes reinforcement contingencies is the approach developed by Steve Higgins and his colleagues (67, 68), which incorporates positive incentives for abstinence into a Community Reinforcement Approach (69) approach. The Higgins' strategy has four organizing features grounded in principles of behavioral pharmacology: (*a*) drug use and abstinence must be swiftly and accurately detected, (*b*) abstinence is positively reinforced, (*c*) drug use results in loss of reinforcement, and (*d*) emphasis remains on the development of competing reinforcers to drug use (68).

FOSTERING MANAGEMENT OF PAINFUL AFFECTS

Marlatt and colleagues (70) have demonstrated that dysphoric affects are the most commonly cited precipitant for relapse, and many psychodynamic clinicians (36, 38) have suggested that failure of affect regulation is a central dynamic underlying the development of compulsive drug use. Moreover, surveys of psychiatric disorders in treatment-seeking drug abusers concur in demonstrating high rates of depressive disorders (71–73). A key element in developing ways to handle powerful dysphoric affects is learning to recognize and identify the probable cause of these feelings. This difficulty in differentiating among negative emotional states has been identified as a common characteristic among drug abusers (36, 38). Moreover, a process of stimulus generalization has been posited, whereby all negative affects are attributed to derive from drug withdrawal, with the attendant conclusion that relief is to be sought by drug use (74). To foster the development of mastery over dysphoric affects, most psychotherapies include techniques for eliciting strong affects within a protected therapeutic setting and then enhancing the patient's ability to identify, tolerate, and respond appropriately to them. Given the demonstrated efficacy of pharmacological treatments for affective and anxiety disorders (75) and the high rates of these disorders seen in treatment-seeking drug abusers, the individual psychotherapist should be alert to the possibility that the patient may benefit from combined treatment with psychotherapy and medications. Furthermore, as recent evidence points to the difficulty many substance users face in articulating strong affect (76), which may have an impact of treatment response (77), clinicians should be alert to the need to assess and address difficulties in expression of affect and cognition when working with substance abusers in psychotherapy.

IMPROVING INTERPERSONAL FUNCTIONING AND ENHANCING SOCIAL SUPPORTS

A consistent finding in the literature on relapse to drug abuse is the protective influence of an adequate network of social supports (59, 78). Gratifying friendships and intimate relationships provide a powerful source of rewards to replace those obtained by drug use, and the threat of losing these relationships can furnish a strong incentive to maintain abstinence. Typical issues presented by drug abusers are loss of or damage to valued relationships occurring when using drugs was the principal priority, failure to have achieved satisfactory relationships even prior to having initiated drug use, and inability to identify friends or intimates who are not, themselves, drug abusers. For some types of psychotherapy, working on relationship issues is the central focus of the work (e.g., interpersonal therapy, supportive-expressive treatment), while for others, this aspect is implied as a part of other therapeutic activities such as identifying risky and protective situations (59). A major potential limitation of individual psychotherapy as the sole treatment for drug abusers is its failure to provide adequate social supports for those patients who lack a supportive social network of people who are not drug abusers. Individual psychotherapy can fill only one to several hours per week of a patient's time.

Again, while most approaches address these issues to some degree in the course of treatment, approaches that strongly emphasize the development of social supports are traditional counseling and 12-step facilitation (79). Self-help groups offer a fully developed social network of welcoming individuals who are understanding and, themselves, committed to leading a drug-free life (56). Moreover, in most urban and suburban settings, self-help meetings are held daily or several times weekly, and a sponsor system is available to provide the recovering drug abuser with individual guidance and support on a 24-hour basis, if necessary. For psychotherapists working with drug abusers, encouraging the patient to become involved in a self-help group can provide a powerful source of social support that can protect the patient from relapse while the work of therapy progresses.

REVIEW OF LITERATURE

As noted earlier, early efforts to engage and treat drug users with dynamically oriented individual psychotherapy as the sole treatment were marked by failure. This has led researchers to focus increasingly on the evaluation of psychotherapy for drug users in terms of the context in which individual psychotherapy is delivered most effectively as well as the types of drug users most likely to benefit from individual psychotherapy. Hence, the following section reviews empirical evidence for the effectiveness of individual psychotherapy by treatment setting and with special emphasis on identifying those types of drug users who may respond to this form of treatment. In this section, we emphasize findings from the comparatively few studies that have used rigorous methodologies associated with the technology model of psychotherapy research (80, 81). These methodological features include random assignment to treatment conditions, specification of treatments in manuals, selection of well-trained therapists committed to the type of approach they conduct in the trial, extensive training of therapists, ongoing monitoring of therapy implementation, multidimensional ratings of outcome by independent evaluators blind to the study treatment received by the patient, and adequate sample sizes.

Opiate Addicts

OUTPATIENT DRUG-FREE TREATMENT

As noted in an earlier review (82), outpatient drug-free treatment (OPDFT) is a catch-all term for heterogeneous programs, defined only by their not offering pharmacological treatments and their reliance on psychotherapy or counseling as the core of treatment. To date, large-scale naturalistic evaluations have suggested that OPDFT may be as effective as other forms of treatment, such as methadone maintenance and therapeutic communities (15, 83, 84). However, interpretation of findings from these studies is confounded by their numerous methodological limitations, most importantly, substantial selection biases, since less severely addicted patients tended to be seen in the OPDFT programs evaluated and the more severely and chronically addicted individuals were treated in methadone maintenance programs or therapeutic communities. Furthermore, because the type of psychotherapy or counseling administered in the various OPDFT settings evaluated rarely was specified, these studies offer little guidance regarding the effectiveness of particular psychotherapeutic treatments in OPDFT settings or the types of addicts for whom they may be most appropriate. Finally, because the OPDFT programs evaluated were typically multimodality programs (comprised of individual, group, and/or family therapy, often in combination with self-help groups, vocational counseling, and the like), the unique contribution of individual psychotherapy to outcome in these programs was difficult to determine.

NARCOTIC ANTAGONIST PROGRAMS

Individual psychotherapy offered in the context of narcotic antagonist programs has been found to have a positive effect on the most significant drawback associated with this approach, that of very high dropout rates during the induction and stabilization phases (85). In the only published randomized clinical trial evaluating individual psychotherapy in the context of naltrexone treatment, Resnick et al. (86) randomly assigned 66 addicts to intensive weekly individual therapy (described as supportive and insight oriented) or to low-intervention case management. Sixty-three percent of subjects receiving counseling were successfully inducted into naltrexone treatment, as compared with 48% of the noncounseled addicts, a nonsignificant difference. Significant differences between the treatment groups emerged during the stabilization phase, however; of 37 subjects successfully inducted, 77% (17/22) of the group receiving counseling remained in treatment through 1 month, in contrast to 33% (5/15) of the controls.

The Resnick et al. (86) study also demonstrated differential responsiveness to psychotherapy by different types of addicts. The Resnick study included two types of addicts: those coming to treatment from the street, and those entering treatment after having been maintained on a methadone program. When results were analyzed by subjects' treatment history (street versus postmethadone), for the postmethadone maintenance group, the provision of psychotherapy had little effect; whereas for the street addicts, the addition of psychotherapy significantly increased rates of successful naltrexone induction (45% versus 12%) and stabilization.

METHADONE MAINTENANCE

A number of investigations have examined the value of individual counseling in the context of methadone maintenance programs. Notwithstanding the methodological flaws inherent in many of them (including nonrandom assignment to treatments, poorly defined outcome measures, vaguely defined study treatments, and failures to protect treatment integrity), these studies consistently suggest that the provision of counseling within methadone maintenance programs can be of benefit in reducing attrition and improving compliance with treatment. In a naturalistic study, Janke (87) found that switching from a primarily "medical model" methadone program to a more "heavily psychotherapeutic" program resulted in higher rates of successful program completion in two very large (n = 887) samples of methadone-maintained addicts, but few changes in other indicators of outcome were seen. Studies by Ramer and colleagues (88) as well as Senay and colleagues (89) compared outcome for addicts who received full-service methadone maintenance (which included individual counseling) to outcome for addicts assigned to methadone only, where staff was instructed to withhold psychological support. In both studies power to detect group differences was undercut by the staff's tendency to offer counseling on demand to subjects in the methadone-only group. In the Senay (89) study, the counseled group was found to have better program attendance than the methadone-only group, although differences in illicit drug use, employment, and illegal activity were not seen. In the Ramer (88) study, less attrition was found among the addicts who made use of counseling and other ancillary services; it was also noted that subjects making most use of these services tended to be those with higher levels of psychopathology.

Only a few well-designed randomized clinical trials have evaluated professional psychotherapy as an adjunct to standard full-service methadone maintenance. In one of the first, which has become the classic study of the benefits of individual psychotherapy in the context of methadone maintenance, Woody et al. (90) randomly assigned 110 patients entering a methadone maintenance program to a 6-month course of one of three treatments: drug counseling alone, drug counseling plus supportive-expressive psychotherapy (SE), or drug counseling plus cognitive-behavioral psychotherapy (CB). Although the SE and CB groups did not differ significantly from each other on most measures of outcome, subjects who received either form of professional psychotherapy evidenced greater improvement in more outcome domains than did the subjects who received drug counseling alone. Furthermore, gains made by the subjects who received professional psychotherapy were sustained over a 12-month follow-up, while subjects receiving drug counseling alone evidenced some attrition of gains (91, 92). Differential responsiveness to treatment by both presence and type of addict's psychopathology was found: addicts with low levels of psychopathology tended to show significant improvement regardless of treatment received, but those with higher levels of psychopathology were likely to improve only if they received professional psychotherapy (93). Addicts with antisocial personality disorder tended not to benefit from treatment, while those with concurrent depressive disorders showed improvements in all areas assessed (94).

In a recent replication of this study with psychiatrically impaired patients in community methadone maintenance programs, Woody and colleagues (95) evaluated SE psychotherapy versus supplemental drug counseling for 84 methadone-maintained subjects who were interviewed at one and six-months following a 24 week course of therapy. Patients assigned to the SE condition had significantly lower doses of methadone and fewer cocaine-positive urines, but no significant differences in the proportion of opiate-positive urines during treatment. No significant differences between the groups was seen at the 1-month follow-up, although patients in both conditions maintained the gains they made during treatment. However, at the 6-month follow-up, diminishment of gains was seen for subjects receiving drug counseling only, and several significant differences favoring the SE therapy emerged. These findings point to the durability of the effects of psychotherapy, particularly for psychiatrically impaired methadone-maintained opiate addicts. These findings also suggest that the benefits of psychotherapy are generalizable to community drug treatment programs and are not limited to treatment settings in academic centers.

Rounsaville and colleagues (96) randomly assigned addicts who had been maintained on methadone for at least 6 weeks to either weekly interpersonal psychotherapy (IPT) or a low-contact condition, in which the patient met with a therapist for one 20-minute session per month. The study was marked by low rates of patient recruitment (less than 5% of all eligible subjects opted to participate) and poor treatment retention. Although subjects in both conditions showed significant improvements over baseline levels on most measures of outcome, significant differences between treatment groups were not found. Furthermore, differential treatment responsiveness by depressed versus nondepressed subjects was not seen in this investigation. Rounsaville and Kleber (82) noted that, in contrast to the Woody et al. (90) study, there were important differences in implementation of the study treatments that may have accounted for the failure to demonstrate a psychotherapy effect. These included several factors: (a) the option to participate in psychotherapy was offered at least 6 weeks after patients enrolled in the methadone program, providing ample time for resolution of depressive symptoms as well as opportunity to become fully engaged with program staff and ongoing group therapy, both of which may have undercut patients' motivation to become involved in individual psychotherapy; and (b) the provision of psychotherapy was not well-integrated into the existing methadone program, and subjects were seen for psychotherapy at a site physically separated from the methadone program. This resulted in a low recruitment rate for the study, which in turn may have resulted in a preponderance of poor prognosis patients entering the study (e.g., as a "last resort" before being administratively discharged).

Cocaine Abusers

Although a variety of individual psychotherapeutic approaches to the treatment of cocaine abuse have been described (97–99), clinical trials evaluating their effectiveness thus far have been rare. In a pilot study evaluating the efficacy of purely psychotherapeutic treatments for ambulatory cocaine abusers, Carroll et al. (100) randomly assigned 42 subjects to either relapse prevention, a CB approach, or IPT adapted for cocaine abusers. Rates of attrition were significantly higher in IPT than relapse prevention, with 62% of those in IPT failing to complete a 12-week course of treatment, versus 33% of those in relapse prevention. On most measures of outcome, significant differences by treatment type were not seen but did emerge when subjects were stratified according to pretreatment severity of cocaine abuse. Among the subgroup of more severe users, subjects who received relapse prevention were significantly more likely to achieve abstinence (54% versus 9%) than were subjects in IPT, whereas subjects with lower levels of abuse improved regardless of treatment received.

These findings were replicated by our group in a more recent study evaluating both psychotherapy (CB relapse prevention or clinical management, a psychotherapy control condition) and pharmacotherapy (desipramine or placebo) in a 2 × 2 factorial design for 139 cocaine abusers in a 12-week abstinence initiation trial (101). After 12 weeks of treatment, all groups showed significant reductions in cocaine use, but significant main effects for medication or psychotherapy condition were not found for treatment retention, reduction in cocaine use, or other outcomes. However, exploratory analyses suggested a disordinal interaction of baseline severity with psychotherapy, which was consistent with that found in the earlier (100) study: Higher severity patients had significantly better outcomes including fewer urine toxicology screens positive for cocaine when treated with relapse prevention compared with supportive clinical management (28% versus 47% of screens). Subsequent exploratory analyses also suggested better retention and cocaine outcomes for depressed subjects treated with relapse prevention over clinical management (102).

Finally, 1-year follow-up of subjects in this study indicated possible "sleeper effects" for relapse prevention (61). That is, significant continuing improvement across time for cocaine outcomes (days of use, ASI composite scores) was seen for subjects who had received relapse prevention compared with clinical management. These findings suggest delayed emergence of effects for CB relapse prevention, which may reflect subjects' implementation of the generalizable coping skills learned during treatment. Moreover, these data underline the importance of conducting follow-up studies of substance abusers and other groups, as delayed effects may occur after cessation of acute treatments.

While not strictly an individual psychotherapy approach, some of the most exciting findings pertaining to the power of psychosocial treatments have been the recent reports of Higgins and colleagues (67, 103) of the effectiveness of a program incorporating positive incentives for abstinence, reciprocal relationship counseling, and disulfiram into a Community Reinforcement Approach (69). In this program, urine specimens are required three times weekly. Abstinence, assessed through drug-free urine screens, is reinforced through a voucher system where patients receive points redeemable for items consistent with a drug-free lifestyle, such as movie tickets, sporting goods, and the like, but patients never receive money directly. To encourage longer periods of consecutive abstinence, the value of the points earned by the patients increase with each successive clean urine specimen, and the value of the points is reset when the patient produces a drug-positive urine screen. In a series of well-controlled clinical trials, Higgins has demonstrated (a) high acceptance, retention, and rates of abstinence for patients randomized to this approach (85% completing a 12-week course of treatment; 65% achieving 6 or more weeks of abstinence) relative to standard-oriented substance abuse counseling (67, 104); (b) rates of abstinence do not decline when less valuable incentives, such as lottery tickets, were substituted for the voucher system (104); and (c) the value of the voucher system itself (as opposed to other program elements) in producing good outcomes by comparing the behavioral system with and without the vouchers (103).

Summary of Literature Review

The available empirical evidence suggests the following

1. To date, most studies suggest that individual psychotherapy is superior to control conditions as treatment for drug abusers. This is consistent with the bulk of findings from psychotherapy efficacy research in areas other than substance use, which suggests that the effects of many psychotherapies are clinically and statistically significant and are superior to no treatment and placebo conditions (105).

2. No specific type of individual psychotherapy has been shown consistently to be superior as treatment for drug abusers or for other types of patients as well (34). However, behavioral and CB therapies may show particular promise (105).

3. The studies examining the differential effectiveness of psychotherapy on those drug abusers with and without coexistent psychopathology (94, 100, 102) indicate with some consistency that those therapies shown to be generally effective were differentially more effective with patients who presented with high levels of general psychopathology or depression (93–95, 100, 102).

4. The effects of even comparatively brief psychotherapies appear to be durable among substance users (91) as they are among other populations (105). Recent evidence suggests that while the benefits of individual psychotherapy may not be immediately apparent with respect to control or treatment-as-usual conditions, meaningful gains may emerge after the termination of treatment (61, 62, 95), perhaps as patients have more time to implement or practice the skills acquired during treatment. Further research is needed to determine whether delayed benefits of individual psychotherapy in drug abusers are specific to the forms of treatment where this effect has so far been identified (coping skills treatment with cocaine abusers in the Carroll et al. study [100], and SE therapy with methadone-maintained opiate addicts in the Woody et al. study [90]) or is a more general effect of psychotherapy.

THE PLACE FOR INDIVIDUAL PSYCHOTHERAPY IN TREATING DRUG ABUSERS

The empirical literature clearly offers only the most general sort of guidance regarding which individual psychotherapy is likely to be useful for which type of drug abuser at what point in the course of treatment. Hence, the following recommendations are made on the basis of clinical experience rather than empirical evidence. With this caveat, it is suggested that individual psychotherapy may have the following uses: (a) to introduce a drug abuser into treatment, (b) to treat patients with low levels of drug dependence, (c) to treat failures of other modalities, (d) to complement other on-going treatment modalities for selected patients, and (e) to help the patient solidify gains following achievement of stable abstinence.

Psychotherapy as Introduction to Treatment

As noted previously, a key advantage of individual therapy is the privacy and confidentiality that it affords. This aspect may make individual therapy or counseling an ideal setting to clarify the treatment needs of patients who are in early stages (i.e., contemplation, precontemplation) of thinking about changing their drug use habits (50). For individuals with severe dependence or severe drug-related problems who deny the seriousness of their drug involvement, a course of individual therapy in which the patient is guided to a clear recognition of the problem may be an essential first step toward more intensive approaches such as residential treatment or methadone maintenance. An important part of this process may involve allowing the patient to fail one or more times at strategies that have a low probability of success, such as attempting to cut down on drug use without stopping or attempting outpatient detoxification. A general principle underlying this process is the successive use of treatments that involve greater expense and/or patient involvement only after less intensive approaches have been shown to fail. Hence, brief individual treatment can serve a cost-effective triage function.

Psychotherapy for Mildly or Moderately Dependent Drug Abusers

Although less studied with nonalcoholic drug abusers, the drug dependence syndrome concept (66) has received considerable attention in the study of alcoholism. This concept, first described by Edwards et al. (58), suggests that drug dependence is best understood as a constellation of cognitions, behaviors, and physical symptoms that underlie a pattern of progressively diminished control over drug use. This dependence syndrome is conceived of as aligned along a continuum of severity, with higher levels of severity associated with poorer prognosis and the need for more intensive treatment, and lower levels of severity requiring less intensive interventions. The dependence syndrome construct has generated a large empirical literature suggesting its validity with alcoholics (65). Moreover, several scales have been developed for gauging severity of alcohol dependence (106–108), although similar instruments are not yet available for other drugs of abuse. Generally, however, measures of quantity and frequency of alcohol use show high correlation with dependence severity, and similar quantity/frequency indices for other drugs of abuse may be an adequate gauge of dependence severity. Evidence from studies of individuals who are mildly to moderately dependent on alcohol have indicated that a brief course of psychotherapy is sufficient for many to achieve substantial reduction of or abstinence from drinking (1, 3, 57, 65). Although these findings have yet to be replicated with other types of substance abusers, they are likely to be generalizable.

Failures from Other Modalities

Although numerous predictors of treatment outcome for drug abusers have been identified (109–112), few are robust, and still fewer have been evaluated regarding the issue of matching patients to treatments (113). As a result, choice of treatments often involves some trial and error. Each type of treatment has its strengths and weaknesses that may prove a better or worse fit for particular patients. For example, individual therapy is more expensive but more private than group therapy, more enduring and less disruptive to normal routine than residential treatment, and less troubled by side effects and medical contraindications than pharmacotherapies. Each of these advantages may be crucial for a patient who has responded poorly to alternative treatments.

Psychotherapy as Ancillary Treatment

In considering psychotherapy as part of an ongoing comprehensive program of treatment, it is useful to distinguish between treatment of opi-oid addicts, for which powerful pharmacological approaches are available, and treatment of other drugs of abuse, for which strong alternatives to psychosocial treatments are still unavailable (29). For opioid abusers, the modal approach is methadone maintenance, which is used with the majority of those in treatment, while an alternative pharmacotherapy, naltrexone, can be highly potent for the minority who choose this approach. Because of their powerful and specific pharmacological effects either to satisfy the need for opioids or to prevent illicit opioids from yielding their desired effect, these agents, provided that they are delivered with at least minimal counseling, may be sufficient for many opioid addicts (111). The choice of those who might benefit from additional individual psychotherapy can be guided by the unique but robust empirical findings of Woody et al. (93, 94) and McLellan et al. (113), which suggest that psychotherapy is most likely to be of benefit for those opioid addicts with high levels of psychiatric symptoms as measured by the Addiction Severity Index (ASI) (114) or with a diagnosis of major depression as defined in DSM-III-R (115) or DSM-IV. Because benefits of psychotherapy may be maximized when instituted relatively soon after admission to treatment, screening instruments such as the ASI (114) or the Beck Depression Inventory (116) could be used to quickly identify those with psychopathology or depression, alerting staff to the need to refer the client for psychotherapy.

For nonopioid drugs of abuse, an active search for effective pharmacotherapies is currently under way. The mainstay of treatment for nonopioid drugs of abuse remains some form of psychosocial treatment offered in a group, family, residential, or individual setting. For cocaine use, forms of treatment that have empirical support at this time include behavioral and CB treatment (101, 103). Some evidence suggests that these forms of treatment may be of particular benefit to cocaine abusers who are higher in severity of cocaine dependence (101), have substantial depressive symptoms (102), or who have substantial family support (117). However, there is at this point no strong empirical evidence as to the optimal duration of treatment nor are there clear guidelines for matching patients to treatment. For other types of drug abuse, in the absence of empirically validated guidelines, the choice of an individual form of psychotherapy for this population can then be based on such factors as expense, logistical considerations, patient preference, or the clinical "fit" between the patient's presenting picture and the treatment modality (e.g., family therapy is ruled out for those without families).

Psychotherapy Following Achievement of Sustained Abstinence

As noted earlier, a drug abuser who is experiencing frequent relapses or who is only tenuously holding onto abstinence may be a poor candidate for certain types of psychotherapy, particularly those that involve bringing into focus painful and anxiety-provoking clinical material as an inevitable part of helping the patient master dysphoric affects or avoid recurrent failures in establishing enduring intimate relationships. In fact, some arousal of anxiety or frustration can occur with most types of psychotherapy, even those that are conceived of as being primarily supportive. Because of this, individual psychotherapy may be most effective for many individuals only after they have achieved abstinence using some other method such as residential treatment, methadone maintenance, or group therapy. Given the vulnerability to relapse, which can extend over a lifetime, and the frequency with which dysphoric affects or interpersonal conflict are noted as precipitants of relapse (70), individual psychotherapy may be especially indicated for those whose psychopathology or disturbed interpersonal functioning is found to endure following the achievement of abstinence. Given findings pointing to the delayed emergence of effects of individual psychotherapy for both cocaine (61) and opioid (95) addicts, psychotherapy aimed at these enduring issues can be helpful not only for these problems independent of their relationship to drug use but also as a form of insurance against the likelihood that these continuing problems will eventually lead to relapse of drug abuse.

References

1. Miller WE, Heather N, eds. Treating addictive behaviors. New York: Plenum Press, 1986.
2. Institute of Medicine. Broadening the base of treatment for alcohol problems. Washington, DC: National Academy Press, 1990.
3. Babor TF. Avoiding the horrid and beastly sin of drunkenness: does dissuasion make a difference? J Consult Clin Psychol 1994;62:1127–1140.
4. Blatt S, McDonald C, Sugarman A, Wilber C. Psychodynamic theories of opiate addiction: new directions for research. Clin Psychol Rev 1984;4:159–189.
5. Brill L. The treatment of drug abuse: evolution of a perspective. Am J Psychiatry 1977;134:157–160.
6. Nyswander M, Winick C, Bernstein A, Brill I, Kauger G. The treatment of drug addicts as voluntary outpatients: a progress report. Am J Orthopsychiatry 1958;28:714–727.
7. Bibring E. Psychoanalysis and the dynamic psychotherapies. J Am Psychoanal Assoc 1954;2:745–770.
8. Alexander F, French T. Psychoanalytic therapy: principles and applications. New York: Ronald Press, 1946.
9. Dole VP, Nyswander ME, Warner A. Methadone maintenance treatment: a ten-year perspective. JAMA 1976;235:2117–2119.
10. Ball JC, Ross A. The effectiveness of methadone maintenance treatment. New York: Springer-Verlag, 1991.
11. Brunswick AF. Black youth and drug use behavior. In: Beschner GM, Friedman AS, eds. Youth drug abuse. Lexington, MA: Lexington Books, 1979:52–66.
12. O'Donnell JA, Voss HL, Clayton RR, Slatin GT, Room RGW. Young men and drugs—a nationwide survey. NIDA Res Monogr 1976;5:i–xiv, 1–144.
13. Robins LN, Davis DH. How permanent was Vietnam drug addiction? Am J Public Health 1974;64(suppl):38–43.
14. Robins LN. Addicts' careers. In: Dupont RI, Goldstein A, O'Donnell J, Brown B, eds. Handbook on drug abuse. Rockville, MD: National Institute on Drug Abuse, 1979.
15. Hubbard RL, Rachal JV, Craddock SG, Cavanaugh ER. Treatment Outcome Prospective Study (TOPS): client characteristics and behaviors before, during, and after treatment. NIDA Res Monogr 1984;51:42–68.
16. O'Donnell JA. Narcotic addicts in Kentucky. Public Health Service publication 1981. Washington, DC: U.S. Government Printing Office, 1969.
17. Simpson DD, Joe GW, Bracy SA. Six-year follow-up of opioid addicts after admission to treatment. Arch Gen Psychiatry 1982;39:1318–1326.
18. Valliant GE. Twelve-year follow-up of New York addicts. Am J Psychiatry 1966;122:727–737.
19. Kleber HD, Kosten TR. Naltrexone induction: psychologic and pharmacologic strategies. J Clin Psychiatry 1984;45:29.
20. Rounsaville BJ. Can psychotherapy rescue naltrexone treatment of opioid addiction? NIDA Res Monogr 1995;105:37–52.
21. Fuller R, Branchey L, Brightwell D, et al. Disulfiram treatment of alcoholism: a Veteran's Administration cooperative study. JAMA 1986;256:1449–1455.
22. Allen JP, Litten RZ. Techniques to enhance compliance with disulfiram. Alcohol Clin Exp Res 1992;16:1035–1041.
23. Corty E, Ball JC. Admissions to methadone maintenance: comparisons between programs and implications for treatment. J Subst Abuse Treat 1987;4:181–187.
24. McLellan AT, Arndt IO, Metzger DS, Woody GE, O'Brien CP. The effects of psychosocial services in substance abuse treatment. JAMA 1993;269:1953–1959.
25. Carroll KM. Manual-guided psychosocial treatment: a new virtual requirement for pharmacotherapy trials? Arch Gen Psychiatry (in press).
26. Senay E. Methadone maintenance. In: Karasu TB, ed. Treatments of psychiatric disorders. Washington, DC: American Psychiatric Press, 1989:1341–1358.
27. Jaffe JH, Kleber HD. Opioids: general issues and detoxification. In: Karasu TB, ed. Treatment of psychiatric disorders. Washington, DC: American Psychiatric Press, 1989:1309–1331.
28. O'Brien CP, Woody GE. Antagonist treatment: naltrexone. In: Karasu TB, ed. Treatments of psychiatric disorders. Washington, DC: American Psychiatric Press, 1989:1332–1340.
29. Kosten TR, McCance-Katz E. New pharmacotherapies. In: Oldham JM, Riba MB, eds. American Psychiatric Press review of psychiatry. Washington, DC: American Psychiatric Press, 1995;14:105–126.
30. McCance-Katz E, Kosten TR. Overview of potential treatment medications for cocaine dependence. NIDA Res Monogr (in press).
31. Meyer RE. New pharmacotherapies for cocaine dependence . . . revisited. Arch Gen Psychiatry 1992;49:900–904.
32. Kleber HD. Psychoactive substance use disorders (not alcohol). In: Karasu TB, ed. Treatments of psychiatric disorders. Washington, DC: American Psychiatric Press, 1989:1183–1484.
33. Kosten TR. Pharmacotherapeutic interventions for cocaine abuse: matching patients to treatments. J Nerv Ment Dis 1989;177:379–389.
34. Smith M, Glass C, Miller T. The benefits of psychotherapy. Baltimore: Johns Hopkins University Press, 1980.
35. Khantzian EJ. The ego, the self and opiate addiction: theoretical and treatment considerations. Int Rev Psychoanal 1978;5:189–198.
36. Khantzian EJ. The self-medication hypothesis of addictive disorders: focus on heroin and cocaine dependence. Am J Psychiatry 1985;142:1259–1264.
37. Khantzian EJ, Schneider RJ. Treatment implications of a psychodynamic understanding of opioid addicts. In: Meyer RE, ed. Psychopathology and addictive disorders. New York: Guilford Press, 1986.
38. Wurmser L. The hidden dimension: psychopathology of compulsive drug use. New York: Jason Aronson, 1979.
39. Mendelson JH, Mello NK. Experimental analysis of drinking behavior in chronic alcoholics. Ann N Y Acad Sci 1966;133:828–845.
40. Mirin SR, Meyer RE, McNamme B. Psychopathology and mood duration in heroin use: acute and chronic effects. Arch Gen Psychiatry 1980;33:1503–1508.
41. Nathan PE, O'Brien JS. An experimental analysis of the behaviour of alcoholics and nonalcoholics during prolonged experimental drinking: a necessary precursor of behaviour therapy? Behav Ther 1971;2:455–476.
42. Gawin FH, Ellinwood EH. Stimulants: actions, abuse, and treatment. N Engl J Med 1988;318:1173–1183.
43. Beck AT. Depression: clinical, experimental and theoretical aspects. New York: Hoeber, 1967. (Republished as Depression: causes and treatment. Philadelphia: University of Pennsylvania Press, 1972).
44. Beck AT, Rush AJ, Shaw BF, Emery G. Cognitive therapy of depression. New York: Guilford Press, 1979.
45. Simons AD, Garfield SL, Murphy GE. The process of change in cognitive therapy and pharmacotherapy for depression. Arch Gen Psychiatry 1984;41:45–51.
46. Anton RF, Hogan I, Jalali B, et al. Multiple family therapy and naltrexone in the treatment of opioid dependence. Drug Alcohol Depend 1981;8:157–168.
47. Stanton MD, Todd TC, eds. The family therapy of drug abuse and addiction. New York: Guilford Press, 1982;393–402.
48. Cummings N. Turning bread into stones: our modern anti-miracle. Am Psychol 1979;34:1119–1129.
49. DiClemente CC, Prochaska JO, Gibertini M. Self-efficacy and the stages of self-change of smoking. Cognitive Ther Res 1985;9(2):181–200.
50. Prochaska JO, DiClemente C. Toward a comprehensive model of change. In: Miller WR, Heather N, eds. Treating addictive behaviors: processes of change. New York: Plenum Press, 1986:3–27.
51. Miller WR, Rollnick S. Motivational interviewing: preparing people to change addictive behavior. New York: Guilford Press, 1991.
52. Miller WR, Zweben A, DiClemente CC, Rychtarik RG. Motivational enhancement therapy manual: a clinical research guide for therapists treating individuals with alcohol abuse and dependence. NIAAA Project MATCH Monograph Series Volume 2, DHHS Publication No. (ADM) 92–1894. Rockville, MD: National Institute on Alcohol Abuse and Alcoholism, 1992.
53. Holder HD, Longabaugh R, Miller WR, Rubonis AV. The cost effectiveness of treatment for alcohol problems: a first approximation. J Stud Alcohol 1991;52:517–540.
54. Hall SM, Havassy BE, Wasserman DA. Effects of commitment to abstinence, positive moods, stress, and coping on relapse to cocaine use. J Consult Clin Psychol 1991;59:526–532.
55. Douglas DB. Alcoholism as an addiction: the disease concept reconsidered. J Subst Abuse Treat 1986;3:115–120.
56. Cook CCH. The Minnesota model in the management of drug and alcohol dependency: miracle, method or myth? Part I. The philosophy and the programme. Br J Addict 1988;83:625–634.
57. Sanchez-Craig M, Wilkinson DA. Treating problem drinkers who are not severely dependent on alcohol. Drugs Soc 1986/1987;1(2/3):39–67.
58. Edwards G, Gross MM. Alcohol dependence: provisional description of a clinical syndrome. Br Med J 1976;1:1058–1061.
59. Marlatt GA, Gordon J, eds. Relapse prevention. New York: Guilford Press, 1985.
60. Kadden R, Carroll KM, Donovan D, Cooney N, Monti P, Abrams D, et al. Cognitive-behavioral coping skills therapy manual: A clinical research guide for therapists treating individuals with alcohol abuse and dependence. NIAAA Project MATCH Monograph Series Volume 3, DHHS Publication No. (ADM) 92–1895. Rockville, MD: National Institute on Alcohol Abuse and Alcoholism, 1992.
61. Carroll KM, Rounsaville BJ, Nich C, Gordon LT, Wirtz PW, Gawin FH. One year follow-up of psychotherapy and pharmacotherapy for cocaine dependence: Delayed emergence of psy-

chotherapy effects. Arch Gen Psychiatry 1994; 51:989–997.

62. O'Malley SS, Jaffe AJ, Chang G, Rode S, Schottenfeld R, Meyer RE, Rounsaville BJ. Six-month follow-up of naltrexone and psychotherapy for alcohol dependence. Arch Gen Psychiatry 1996; 53:217–224.

63. Luborsky L. Principles of psychoanalytic psychotherapy: a manual for supportive-expressive (SE) treatment. New York: Basic Books, 1984.

64. Rounsaville BJ, Gawin FH, Kleber HD. Interpersonal psychotherapy (IPT) adapted for ambulatory cocaine abusers. Am J Drug Alcohol Abuse 1985;11:171–191.

65. Edwards G. The alcohol dependence syndrome: a concept as stimulus to enquiry. Br J Addict 1986;81:171–183.

66. Edwards G, Arif A, Hodgson R. Nomenclature and classification of drug and alcohol related problems. Bull WHO 1981;59:225–242.

67. Higgins ST, Delaney DD, Budney AJ, Bickel WK, Hughes JR, Foerg F, et al. A behavioral approach to achieving initial cocaine abstinence. Am J Psychiatry 1991;148:1218–1224.

68. Higgins ST, Budney AJ. Treatment of cocaine dependence through the principles of behavior analysis and behavioral pharmacology. NIDA Res Monogr Series 1993;137:97–121.

69. Sisson RW, Azrin NH. The community reinforcement approach. In: Hester RK, Miller WR, eds. Handbook of alcoholism treatment approaches. New York: Pergamon, 1989:242–258.

70. Marlatt GA, Gordon GR. Determinants of relapse: implications for the maintenance of behavior change. In: Davidson PO, Davidson SM, eds. Behavioral medicine: changing health lifestyles. New York: Brunner/Mazel, 1980:410–452.

71. Hesselbrock MN, Meyer RE, Keener JJ. Psychopathology in hospitalized alcoholics. Arch Gen Psychiatry 1985;42:1050–1055.

72. Khantzian EJ, Treece C. DSM-III psychiatric diagnosis of narcotic addicts. Arch Gen Psychiatry 1985;42:1067–1071.

73. Rounsaville BJ, Weissman M, Kleber HD, et al. Heterogeneity of psychiatric diagnosis in treated opiate addicts. Arch Gen Psychiatry 1982;39: 161–166.

74. Wikler A. Opioid dependence: mechanisms and treatment. New York: Plenum Press, 1980.

75. Beckman EE, Leber WR. Handbook of depression: treatment, assessment and research. Homewood, IL: Dorsey Press, 1985.

76. Keller DS, Carroll KM, Nich C, Rounsaville BJ. Differential treatment response in alexithymic cocaine abusers: findings from a randomized clinical trial of psychotherapy and pharmacotherapy. Am J Addict 1995;4:234–244.

77. Taylor GJ, Parker JD, Bagby RM. A preliminary investigation of alexithymia in men with psychoactive substance dependence. Am J Psychiatry 1990;147:1228–1230.

78. Tims F, Leukfeld C, eds. RAUS—relapse and recovery in drug abuse. NIDA Res Monogr 1986;86.

79. Nowinski J, Baker S, Carroll KM. Twelve-step facilitation therapy manual: a clinical research guide for therapists treating individuals with alcohol abuse and dependence. NIAAA Project MATCH Monograph Series Volume 1, DHHS Publication No. (ADM) 92–1893. Rockville, MD: National Institute on Alcohol Abuse and Alcoholism, 1992.

80. Waskow IE. Specification of the technique variable in the NIMH Treatment of Depression Collaborative Research Program. In: Williams JBW, Spitzer RL, eds. Psychotherapy research: where are we and where should we go. New York: Guilford Press, 1984.

81. Carroll KM, Rounsaville BJ. Can a technology model be applied to psychotherapy research in cocaine abuse treatment? NIDA Res Monogr 1991;104:91–104.

82. Rounsaville BJ, Kleber HD. Psychotherapy/counseling for opiate addicts: strategies for use in different treatment settings. Int J Addict 1985;20:869–896.

83. Simpson DD, Savage LJ, Lloyd MR. Followup evaluation of treatment of drug abuse during 1969 to 1972. Arch Gen Psychiatry 1979;36: 772–780.

84. Hubbard RL, Marsden ME, Rachal JV, Harwood JH, Cavanaugh ER, Ginzburg HM. Drug abuse treatment: a national study of effectiveness. Chapel Hill, NC: University of North Carolina Press, 1989.

85. Kosten TR, Kleber HD. Strategies to improve compliance with narcotic antagonists. Am J Drug Alcohol Abuse 1984;10:249–266.

86. Resnick RB, Washton AM, Stone-Washton N. Psychotherapy and naltrexone in opioid dependence. NIDA Res Monogr 1981;34:109–115.

87. Janke P. Differential effects on completion of treatment in a medical versus psychotherapeutic model for methadone maintenance. Paper presented to the Third National Drug Abuse Conference. New York, March 25–29, 1976.

88. Ramer BS, Zaslove MO, Langan J. Is methadone enough? The use of ancillary treatment during methadone maintenance. Am J Psychiatry 1971;127:1040–1044.

89. Senay EC, Jaffe JH, DiMenza S, et al. A 48-week study of methadone, methadylacetate, and minimal services. Psychopharmacol Bull 1973;9:37.

90. Woody GE, Luborsky L, McLellan AT, et al. Psychotherapy for opiate addicts: does it help? Arch Gen Psychiatry 1983;40:639–645.

91. Woody GE, McLellan AT, Luborsky L, O'Brien CP. Twelve-month follow-up of psychotherapy for opiate dependence. Am J Psychiatry 1987;144:590–596.

92. Woody GE, McLellan AT, Luborsky L, O'Brien CP. Sociopathy and psychotherapy outcome. Arch Gen Psychiatry 1985;42: 1081–1086.

93. Woody GE, McLellan AT, Luborsky L, et al. Severity of psychiatric symptoms as a prediction of benefits from psychotherapy: the Veterans Administration-Penn study. Am J Psychiatry 1984;141:1172–1177.

94. Woody GE, McLellan AT, Luborsky L, et al. Sociopathy and psychotherapy outcome. Arch Gen Psychiatry 1985;42:1081–1086.

95. Woody GE, McLellan AT, Luborsky L, O'Brien CP. Psychotherapy in community methadone programs: a validation study. Am J Psychiatry 1995;152:1302–1308.

96. Rounsaville BJ, Glazer W, Wilber CH, et al. Short-term interpersonal psychotherapy in methadone-maintained opiate addicts. Arch Gen Psychiatry 1983;40:629–636.

97. Anker AL, Crowley TJ. Use of contingency contracts in specialty clinics for cocaine abuse. NIDA Res Monogr 1982;41:452–459.

98. Galanter M. Social network therapy for cocaine dependence. Adv Alcohol Subst Abuse 1986;12:159–175.

99. Schiffer F. Psychotherapy of nine successfully treated cocaine abusers: techniques and dynamics. J Subst Abuse Treat 1988;1:131–137.

100. Carroll KM, Rounsaville BJ, Gawin FH. A comparative trial of psychotherapies for ambulatory cocaine abusers: relapse prevention and interpersonal psychotherapy. Am J Drug Alcohol Abuse 1991;17:229–247.

101. Carroll KM, Rounsaville BJ, Gordon LT, Nich C, Jatlow PM, Bisighini RM, Gawin FH. Psychotherapy and pharmacotherapy for ambulatory cocaine abusers. Arch Gen Psychiatry 1994;51:177–187.

102. Carroll KM, Nich C, Rounsaville BJ. Differential symptom reduction in depressed cocaine abusers treated with psychotherapy and pharmacotherapy. J Nerv Ment Dis 1995;183:251–259.

103. Higgins ST, Budney AJ, Bickel WK, Foerg FE, Donham R, Badger GJ. Incentives improve outcome in outpatient behavioral treatment of cocaine dependence. Arch Gen Psychiatry 1994;51:568–576.

104. Higgins ST, Budney AJ, Bickel WK, Hughes JR. Achieving cocaine abstinence with a behavioral approach. Am J Psychiatry 1993;150: 763–769.

105. Lambert MJ, Bergin AE. The effectiveness of psychotherapy. In: Bergin AE, Garfield SL, eds. Handbook of psychotherapy and behavior change. 4th edition. New York: John Wiley & Sons, 1994:143–189.

106. Skinner HA. Primary syndromes of alcohol abuse: their management and correlates. Br J Addict 1981;76:63–76.

107. Stockwell T, Hodgson R, Edwards G, et al. The development of a questionnaire to measure severity of alcohol dependence. Br J Addict 1979;74:79–87.

108. Chick J. Alcohol dependence: methodological issues in its measurement: reliability of the criteria. Br J Addict 1980;75:175–186.

109. Luborsky L, McLellan AT. Our surprising inability to predict the outcomes of psychological treatments with special reference to treatments for drug abuse. Am J Drug Alcohol Abuse 1978;5:387–398.

110. McLellan AT. Patient characteristics associated with outcome. In: Cooper JR, Altman F, Brown BS, eds. Research on the treatment of narcotic addiction: state of the art. Publication no. ADM 83–1281. Rockville, MD: Department of Health and Human Services, 1983.

111. McLellan AT, Alterman AI, Metzger DS, Grissom GR, Woody GE, Luborsky L, O'Brien CP. Similarity of outcome predictors across opiate, cocaine, and alcohol treatments: role of treatment services. J Consult Clin Psychol 1994; 62:1141–1158.

112. Carroll KM, Powers MD, Bryant KJ, Rounsaville BJ. One-year follow-up status of treatment-seeking cocaine abusers: psychopathology and dependence severity as predictors of outcome. J Nerv Ment Dis 1993;181:71–79.

113. McLellan AT, O'Brien CP, Kron R, et al. Matching substance abuse patients to appropriate treatments. Drug Alcohol Depend 1980;5: 189–195.

114. McLellan AT, Luborsky L, O'Brien CP, et al. An improved diagnostic evaluation instrument for substance abuse patients: the Addiction Severity Index. J Nerv Ment Dis 1980;168: 26–33.

115. American Psychiatric Association. Diagnostic and statistical manual of mental disorders. 3rd edition, revised. Washington, DC: American Psychiatric Association, 1987.

116. Beck AT, Ward CH, Mendelson M. An inventory for measuring depression. Arch Gen Psychiatry 1970;4:461–471.

117. Higgins ST, Budney AJ, Bickel WK, Badger GJ. Participation of significant others in outpatient behavioral treatment predicts greater cocaine abstinence. Am J Drug Alcohol Abuse 1994;20:47–56.

45 STRUCTURED OUTPATIENT GROUP THERAPY

Arnold M. Washton

This chapter discusses outpatient group therapy for alcohol and substance abusers within the context of a structured chemical dependency treatment program. Although group therapy is the focus of this chapter, it is by no means the optimal form of treatment for all addicts who seek professional help. The field has come to realize, especially in recent years, that a combination of different treatment interventions (e.g., group, individual, and family counseling) is often required to meet the needs of this diverse patient population and that careful patient-treatment matching is essential. Group therapy is presented here not as a stand-alone modality but as part of a structured, comprehensive treatment program (1, 2) that simultaneously provides individual counseling, supervised urine testing, family counseling, educational sessions, and encouragement to participate in self-help recovery meetings.

Specific clinical techniques and practical considerations for conducting successful group work with outpatient addicts are discussed at length in this chapter, including (*a*) the unique advantages of group therapy; (*b*) techniques for establishing and managing outpatient recovery groups; and (*c*) goals of group therapy. The material and recommendations presented here are based largely on the author's 20-plus years of clinical experience treating an extremely diverse population of chemical abusers in a variety of treatment (mostly outpatient) settings. No attempt is made here to review the existing literature on group therapy with addicted populations, and the interested reader is referred to several recent publications for additional information (3–6).

For our purposes, group therapy is defined as an assembly of chemically dependent patients, usually 5–10 in number, who meet regularly (usually at least once a week) under the guidance of a professional leader (usually a professional therapist or addiction counselor) for the purpose of promoting abstinence from all mood-altering chemicals and recovery from addiction. Therapy groups are usually goal-oriented, time-limited experiences. The group leader is simultaneously a participant, observer, and manager of the group's activities who assumes responsibility for a variety of "executive" or group management tasks (3), including (*a*) defining and maintaining adherence to group rules, (*b*) screening and selecting new members as well as removing those who disrupt the group's functioning, (*c*) formulating specific treatment goals, and (*d*) guiding the group through sequential stages of the treatment and recovery process. These features distinguish group therapy from self-help meetings such as Alcoholics Anonymous and other 12-step programs. Unlike therapy groups, self-help meetings are characterized by peer rather than professional leadership, the absence of screening or exclusion criteria, unlimited size of membership, and unlimited length of participation, which may extend over the full duration of a participant's life. A detailed comparison of group therapy versus self-help is presented by Spitz (3).

UNIQUE ADVANTAGES OF GROUP THERAPY

Group therapy is uniquely powerful for addressing the problems of addicts. Groups supply an unparalleled mixture of therapeutic forces not available in any other single modality of treatment (7). These forces include mutual identification, acceptance, role modeling, and confrontation; reality testing and immediate feedback; positive peer pressure; affiliation, cohesiveness, and social support; structure, discipline, and limit setting; experiential learning and exchange of factual information; and instillation of optimism and hope. The gathering together of people who share a common problem often creates a common bond between them, stemming from a sense of belonging and an expectation of being intuitively understood. This is critically important in counteracting the intense feelings of isolation, shame, and guilt of addicts appearing for treatment.

The social stigma of addiction and the humiliation of having lost control over one's behavior makes rapid acceptance into a peer group all the more important. The group instills hope by giving the newcomer a chance to make contact with others who are getting better and by instantly supplying him or her with a positive support network committed to the pursuit of healthy, shared ideals. Groups provide invaluable opportunities for experiential learning and role modeling through watching other group members who are struggling with and successfully solving personal problems. Group members have a unique opportunity to correct distorted self-concepts and resulting maladaptive behaviors through honest, consistent feedback from others. Groups provide a broad power base for positive reinforcement (approval) of adaptive behaviors and negative reinforcement (disapproval) of maladaptive behaviors. Because groups typically place high value on self-disclosure, active participation, compliance with group norms (e.g., abstinence, punctuality, attendance, honesty, etc.), a spirit of cooperation among group members, and facing rather than avoiding problems, it is difficult for resistant or noninteractive patients to "hide out" in small groups, as they sometimes do in large self-help meetings, since every member is subjected regularly to the scrutiny of the group.

Acceptance by other group members is often based on a member's openness, sincerity, and demonstrated efforts to make positive behavioral change. Lying, "lip service," superficial involvement, and other signs of ambivalence rarely go by unnoticed and are actively discouraged. Common themes emerge in the group that serve as the focal point for group interaction, peer identification, and problem resolution. Advice, suggestions, and feedback provided by group leaders and other members help patients develop self-monitoring and coping skills as alternatives to drug use. Groups can be shaped to meet the differing needs of patients who are at different stages of recovery as well as those who are grappling with special types of problems. Senior group members share with newcomers advice and strategies that were helpful at an earlier point in their own recovery. Similarly, newcomers provide the senior members with a chance to reflect on their own progress and at the same time supply helpful reminders about the chronic, insidious nature of addiction. Groups are an excellent way to orient and inform new patients about the treatment program, to establish emotional equilibrium in early recovery, to facilitate program retention and compliance as a by-product of bonding among members, and to counteract roadblocks to recovery including unhelpful myths and misconceptions about drugs and the people who use them.

From the standpoint of the therapist or program, group as compared with individual therapy is much more time-efficient and cost-effective. This is an important consideration when the treatment program otherwise might not be able to meet an overwhelming demand for its services. Moreover, group therapy allows the therapist who sees the same patient in both group and individual counseling (an optimal arrangement, in most cases) to gain access to a much wider range of the patient's behavior given the larger social context of the group. The therapist has an invaluable opportunity to observe "in the flesh" how others respond to the patient, how the patient responds to others, and perhaps even more importantly, how the patient's actual behavior compares with his or her self-perceived and self-reported behavior. Groups also provide an excellent training ground for student therapists, who can be brought in as co-leaders to actually observe and role model their teachers in action. Last, but not least, groups are professionally stimulating and rewarding. They provide a continuous source of learning and stimulation even for the most seasoned clinician.

GROUP STRUCTURE AND MANAGEMENT ISSUES

Heterogeneous versus Homogeneous Groups

There is no pat formula for choosing the best mixture of patients for each group, but as a general rule the composition of the group should be neither too heterogeneous nor too homogeneous. The principle of "maximum tolerable heterogeneity" (8) in selecting group members is based on the notion that groups function best when there is diversity in terms of age, gender, race, socioeconomic status, educational level, defensive style, and the like. But although heterogeneity holds the potentially positive benefits of enhancing the richness of the group experience and making it possible to integrate a wider variety of new members into the group, heterogeneity also has important limitations that must be respected so as to engender group cohesiveness and integrity. In general, newcomers find it easiest to integrate themselves into a group in which they can identify readily with at least one other member. Thus, single "outliers" (8) who differ substantially in one or more important respects from existing members (e.g., one cocaine addict among all alcoholics, one woman among all men, one gay among all heterosexuals, one seriously impaired patient among all highly functional people) feel out of place when thrust into groups in which they have no one to identify with, and they often drop out. In some cases, the clinician can facilitate the successful integration of a new and different member into the group by preparing both the individual and the group for the newcomer's entry and by looking for every possible opportunity to emphasize similarities rather than differences in order to promote group cohesiveness.

A question often raised about group work with addicts is whether to mix patients with different drugs of choice in the same group. For example, should alcoholics or cocaine addicts be treated separately from other patients, or should the drug of choice be ignored totally when placing addicts in groups? The rationale often used to justify separating patients by drug of choice is that the unique characteristics associated with different classes of drugs and the people who use them necessitate drug-specific treatment approaches. The opposing view held by many addiction counselors stems from the notion that "a drug is a drug is a drug" and that treatment should, therefore, address the patient's addictive disease irrespective of his or her chosen drug. From a purely practical standpoint, however, these opposing arguments may be purely academic in many cases because of the extremely high incidence of polysubstance abuse and cross-addiction among addicts currently appearing for treatment. For example, it is often impossible to tell whether a given patient is addicted primarily to cocaine or to alcohol, since so many report long histories of progressively destructive use of both substances. Nonetheless, even when the patient's primary addiction is clear-cut, there is much to be said in favor of treating together those suffering with different primary addictions as long as the program incorporates essential drug-specific treatment modifications and the clinically important differences among patients with different primary addictions are not accidentally overlooked or actively ignored (9). For example, a large percentage of cocaine-addicted males show compulsive sexuality associated with their cocaine use, and this issue must be addressed immediately to prevent unnecessary relapse precipitated by sexual triggers (10). A traditional alcoholism treatment program that overlooks this issue because it refuses to treat cocaine addicts as "special" (i.e., any differently from alcoholics) is making a serious therapeutic blunder that will diminish treatment success rates with these patients. There is potential therapeutic value in giving patients the opportunity to realize that different drugs can all lead to the same self-defeating patterns of compulsive use and that the way out of the problem in all cases requires fundamental changes in one's characteristic ways of thinking, feeling, and behaving no matter what one's drug of choice may have been. But this should not be done at the expense of using drug-specific treatment interventions within the group for patients who are addicted to different drugs. It is highly preferable to have mixed rather than segregated groups that are conducted in a manner that reliably anticipates and deals with drug-specific treatment issues in each and every one of its individual members.

Another question frequently raised about recovery groups is whether men and women should be treated separately. Many patients state that in mixed-gender groups they do not feel comfortable discussing highly personal issues such as sexual behavior, sexual inadequacy, relationship problems, and attitudes toward members of the opposite sex. On the other hand, these very same patients often simultaneously express a desire to have the group more closely parallel real-life situations and are very curious about how those of the opposite sex view their behavior. Realizing that drug addiction is often closely associated with difficulties in interpersonal relation-

ships, many patients strongly prefer a mixed-gender group that gives them an opportunity to explore their interaction with members of the opposite sex in the safety of the group setting. Although mixed-gender groups would appear to be preferable in most cases, it is sometimes necessary to create single-gender groups to facilitate entry into treatment for highly treatment-resistant men and women and especially for dual-diagnosis patients who suffer with a coexisting psychiatric disorder that creates highly charged, anxiety-laden issues related to the opposite sex. There are also instances in which time-limited, single-gender groups are very useful for working through special issues that present serious obstacles to recovery. For example, female addicts who are struggling with guilt over having been promiscuous or having exchanged sexual favors for drugs may be unable to talk about these issues in the company of men. Similarly, male addicts who have problems with sexual inadequacy may be too embarrassed to mention these problems in the company of women.

Closed versus Open Membership

The choice of open versus closed (fixed) membership is often decided on purely practical grounds. Without open membership it may be impossible to maintain adequate group size, because some members inevitably drop out of the group before successfully completing the program. Optimal group size is 8–12 members, and new members are added as others complete treatment or drop out. When group census falls below approximately five patients, it often stimulates fears among group members that the group is on the verge of dissolution and it becomes difficult to maintain sufficient morale and commitment to keep the group work moving at an acceptable pace.

The addition of new members unavoidably alters the dynamics of a group and interrupts continuing group themes. Usually, some initial discomfort and readjustment are created by the entry of new members, but with proper management by the group leader the potential benefits of adding new members usually outweigh any temporary setbacks. New members add new points of view, new problems, new ideas, and a new set of life experiences, all of which can broaden the scope and effectiveness of the group experience for its members (3). Because newcomers are typically at an earlier stage of recovery than established members, they often stimulate anxiety and even overt expressions of anger in established members by reminding them of early struggles to stop using drugs and the difficulties of accepting that one has lost control. Harsh, negative reactions to newcomers often signal how extremely vulnerable to relapse established group members still feel. In this regard, newcomers serve as catalysts for exposing incomplete recognition or acceptance by other group members of their own continuing vulnerability and potential for relapse. On the other hand, newcomers are often welcomed by established members, who experience a renewed sense of accomplishment when exposed to those who are just starting out. Additionally, newcomers give established group members a chance to express altruism by taking a fledgling "under their wing" and helping him or her to assimilate into the group. Listening to newcomers helps established group members keep their memory "green" by reminding them of how unmanageable their lives had become and why they came to treatment in the first place. This can counteract the common problems in established group members of overconfidence in one's ability to resist temptation, selective forgetting of drug-related consequences, and lingering fantasies about returning to controlled use. Certainly, from the standpoint of the newcomer, having immediate access to a ready-made group of recovering peers who are eager to share knowledge and lend emotional support is decidedly positive.

Stages of Group Treatment

Another issue concerning group membership is whether patients should remain in the same group throughout the entire course of treatment or move through a progression of different groups that focus on issues relevant to a particular stage of the recovery process, i.e., early abstinence, relapse prevention, and long-term recovery. In the author's outpatient program (1, 2), we have found a sequential stages model to be very useful and have experimented with several different ways of dividing the program into stages in terms of both the number and length of different stages. Originally, the program was divided into three distinct stages represented by three separate treatment groups: early abstinence group (8 weeks), relapse prevention group (12 weeks), and advanced recovery/continuing care group (open-ended). The major problem with this format was high dropout rates that typically occurred when patients moved from one group cohort to the next and one group leader to the next. This was especially true when patients left their early abstinence group (to which they had become strongly attached) to enter a relapse prevention group consisting of different patients and sometimes different group leaders as well. In addition to the negative impact of losing contact with a familiar "home" group, the frequency of group sessions dropped from four times a week during the early abstinence stage to twice a week during the relapse prevention stage. Many patients reported that they did not feel ready to deal with this sharp drop in support after only 8 weeks of treatment, and despite attending more self-help meetings, they experienced a good deal of fear and anxiety about having too much unstructured time on their hands. Some patients had not yet achieved enough stability after 8 weeks to fit comfortably into a relapse prevention group, which usually was less tolerant of continued slips and other typical "beginner" problems. Additional problems with this format stemmed from the fact that the early abstinence group often lacked sufficiently abstinent role models to assist newcomers, since everyone in the group was, by definition, a beginner. On the basis of this experience, we decided to eliminate what appeared to be a somewhat arbitrary and unhelpful division between early abstinence and relapse prevention groups and have now opted for a program format that appears to foster greater intensity and continuity of care. The current format consists of an intensive treatment group that meets four times a week throughout the first 12 weeks of the program. During the subsequent 4 weeks, patients attend only two of these four groups each week, but they do not switch groups or group leaders—they simply come less often to the same group. Patients who complete this 16-week intensive program are encouraged to enter an advanced recovery/continuing care group to solidify their commitment to recovery and address psychological issues (e.g., self-esteem, sexuality, relationships) in order to reduce the potential for relapse.

Urine Testing

Urine testing is an essential, nonnegotiable component of outpatient group therapy with substances abusers. It helps to create a safe environment for the patient, enhance trust between the clinician and patient, and provide an objective measure of treatment progress. The purpose of urine testing is not to catch patients in lies but to instill greater confidence in the treatment. Addicts usually appreciate mandatory urine testing because it helps them counteract their impulses to use and to hide their use. Not being able to hoodwink the therapist or the group can keep a patient from devaluing his or her treatment. And with accurate urine surveillance, family members and employers can breathe a little easier and be more supportive of the recovering outpatient when they no longer feel the need to scrutinize his or her every move for signs of possible drug use. To maximize the clinical value of urine testing: (a) All samples should be "supervised" (witnessed) in order to prevent falsification. The practical problem of having sufficient staff to supervise urine samples can be overcome, for example, by use of a "buddy" system in which patients give urine samples under the rotating supervision of a same-sex group member who signs for having monitored that sample. (b) Urine samples should be taken routinely at least every 3–4 days so as not to exceed the sensitivity limits of standard laboratory testing methods. (c) Samples should be tested by enzyme-immunoassay (EIA) or radioimmunoassay (RIA) methods to ensure accuracy, and all positive results should be confirmed by a second test (11). (d) The samples should be tested routinely for all commonly abused drugs including cocaine, amphetamines, opiates, marihuana, benzodiazepines, and barbiturates. (e) Patients should be tested throughout the entire treatment program and not be taken off urine testing until solidly in recovery. Even then, occasional testing can be helpful.

Leadership Roles and Styles

Group leaders face many challenging tasks that determine the fate and effectiveness of the group. Among the leaders' most important functions are

(a) to establish and enforce group rules in a caring, consistent, nonpunitive manner to protect the group's integrity and progress; (b) to screen, prepare, and orient potential group members to ensure suitability and proper placement in the group; (c) to keep group discussions focused on important issues and to do so in a way that maximizes the therapeutic benefit of these discussions to all members; (d) to emphasize, promote, and maintain group cohesiveness and reduce feelings of personal alienation, wherever possible; (e) to create and maintain a caring, nonjudgmental, therapeutic climate in the group that both counteracts self-defeating attitudes and promotes self-awareness, expression of feelings, honest self-disclosure, adaptive alternatives to drug use, and patterns of drug-free living; (f) to handle problem members who are disruptive to the group in a timely and consistent manner to protect the membership and integrity of the group; and (g) to educate patients about selected aspects of drug use, addiction, and recovery, in order to foster recovery and stimulate meaningful group discussion.

Leadership style is determined by many factors, not the least of which are the leader's personality, theoretic orientation, and experience in running groups. Irrespective of these factors, effective leadership of an outpatient recovery group demands that the leader adopt a certain posture in the group that differs significantly from that in traditional psychotherapy groups, particularly in the early stages of recovery. In psychotherapy groups, the therapist gently guides and focuses the attention of group members on matters pertaining to group process, group dynamics, and the complicated interpersonal interaction among group members. With the exception of carefully timed comments, the therapist may remain passive, quiet, and nondirective in the customary mode of traditional psychotherapy. By contrast, in early abstinence groups the therapist must be very active in keeping the group focused on concrete here-and-now issues that pertain directly to drug-related matters. The therapist plays a very active and directive leadership role that includes questioning, confronting, advising, and educating group members on relevant issues. The therapist keeps the group task-oriented and reality-based, and serves as the major catalyst for group discussion. Addressing addiction-related issues is always the number-one priority of the group, and the therapist must be sure always to keep the group focused on this task.

Single versus Co-leadership

Single leadership of recovery groups can be stressful, difficult, and not nearly as effective as team or co-leadership (3). Co-leadership has numerous advantages, including shared responsibility by the two leaders for the supportive, confrontational, and administrative (management) tasks involved in running the group. With dual leadership, group members receive clinical input from two leaders rather than only one. The presence of a second leader expands the options for interaction in the group and usually accelerates group progress. It also helps to diffuse intense anger and other negative feelings (transference reactions) that patients may develop toward one or the other leader. It is more difficult to rationalize that both leaders are all wrong.

However, co-leadership, unless well coordinated, can cause serious problems in the workings of a group. Trouble is likely to ensue when group leaders are unfamiliar with one another, overly competitive with one another, have clashing personalities and/or clinical styles, or disagree fundamentally about how the group should be run. Obviously, co-leaders must assess carefully their compatibility with one another and work out the details of their collaborative group roles before ever joining forces in a group. Their efforts in the group must be complementary, synergistic, and cooperative. They must agree fundamentally with one another on the rules, purpose, goals, and membership criteria for the group. Poor coordination and communication between co-leaders provides negative role modeling that can be very upsetting and countertherapeutic to group members. However, this is not to suggest that it is either necessary or desirable for co-leaders to agree with one another on each and every issue that comes up in the group. Differences in point of view, theoretical orientation, interpretation, and suggestions, when handled constructively, can substantially broaden the options made available to patients and greatly enhance the therapeutic power of the group. It can be very instructive and therapeutic for patients to see group leaders handling their own differences constructively.

To maximize their collaborative functioning, group leaders should meet with one another regularly to discuss progress and problems of the group. They should allocate time, if possible, to debrief one another after each group session and discuss strategies for the next session. They must also communicate information to one another from contact with members that takes place outside group meetings, as in telephone calls and individual therapy sessions, that may be relevant to the patient's participation in the group.

Screening New Members

A vital function of the group leader is to serve as the "gatekeeper" of the group—to evaluate and screen prospective group members for suitability and placement in a group. The leader must protect the group's integrity, its goals, and its membership in order to maintain an atmosphere of safety, consistency, and therapeutic focus. Leaders who permit patients to enter the group without adequate prescreening may find the group demoralized as the result of one or more problem members among them: people who are not "team players," who do not fit in well with the rest of the group, or who, because of disruptive behavior or lack of motivation, do not belong in the group at all.

Not all addicts entering treatment are appropriate for group therapy. Some are too severely disturbed or anxiety-ridden to tolerate group treatment. Those who suffer from extreme anxiety, paranoia, emotional lability, or other serious psychiatric problems should not be pressured to accept group treatment. Any such attempt could exacerbate these preexisting problems and lead to further deterioration in the patient's functioning—and damage the group as well. Some of these patients can be phased gradually into groups as a goal of early treatment, but only with intensive preparation on an individual basis.

Apart from the presence of serious functional impairment or psychiatric illness, it is often difficult to predict which patients will do well in group therapy. The patient's actual behavior in early group sessions usually indicates to what extent he or she can accept or be accepted by the group. Early sessions are best seen as an extension of the evaluation process. Newcomers who consistently exhibit destructive or disruptive behavior and those who are inordinately stressed or overwhelmed by the group generally should be removed as quickly as possible from the group to prevent harm both to themselves and to the integrity of the group.

Some patients who might otherwise be clinically appropriate for group treatment raise serious objections or flatly refuse to enter a group. Common objections are "I don't see any benefit in talking with a group of strangers about my personal problems or sitting there listening to their problems" or "I'm a private person, I'm concerned about confidentiality, and I'd rather just talk to you alone in individual sessions." Among those most likely to resist entering a group are patients with a history of negative experiences (such as harsh confrontation) in previous group therapy. In addition, patients with criminal backgrounds as well as those with high-level executive or professional jobs often have grave concerns about confidentiality and strongly balk at the idea of entering a group. Hesitant patients who are deemed clinically appropriate for group treatment should be encouraged to try it for at least a week before making a final decision. Usually, their fears are dispelled if they are placed carefully in a group in which they have a distinct opportunity to identify with established group members. Once the newcomer forms an initial bond with at least one other group member, the chances that he or she will elect to continue in the group are increased greatly. Patients who are extremely unmotivated to accept treatment, to the point at which they are unwilling to agree with the most fundamental group rules (e.g., to achieve total abstinence, to show up on time, etc.), should not be put into groups, even temporarily. They tend to anger and demoralize other group members and derive little benefit from the experience. If the integrity of the group is to be preserved, group membership for newcomers must be regarded as a privilege, not a right.

Preparing New Members for Group Entry

Preparing new patients for group entry involves not only orienting them to group rules but also clarifying realistic goals and expectations. Before admitting new patients into the group, it is generally a good idea for the group leader to meet individually with the newcomer for at least one or two private sessions to assess motivation, clarify myths and misconceptions about group therapy, and address any resistances to group participation. Many patients have stereotyped images of groups as places where they will be confronted harshly, humiliated, and punished for "bad" behavior. The patient is educated about the purpose, goals, expectations, rules, composition, content, and format of the group as well as the respective roles of group members and group leaders. One useful strategy for countering initial resistances and fears about entering group treatment is to arrange a one-to-one meeting between a prospective new group member and an established group member (preferably one of the more stable and senior members) who is willing to share his or her group experiences and answer questions in the hopes of overcoming the newcomer's hesitations.

A vital prerequisite to entering an early recovery (beginner's) group is for prospective new members to achieve at least several days of total abstinence immediately before attending their first group meeting. Not only does this give patients time to recover from the acute aftereffects of drug use, but it also concretizes their motivation to become drug free and screens out those who may unwilling or unable to achieve initial abstinence as a starting place. Established group members are understandably intolerant of newcomers who are still actively using drugs and are only hours away from their last high—they usually react with a mixture of disgust and jealousy. Active users are likely to spark intense cravings and hostile reactions in other group members. Before newcomers attend a first group meeting they must agree in writing to adhere to the group rules (1) without exception. Patients are notified from the outset that violation of these rules is potential grounds for immediate termination from the group and possibly from the program as well.

Group Rules

1. You are expected to come to group sessions completely "straight," not under the influence of any mood-altering chemicals whatsoever.
2. You are expected to abstain from the use of alcohol and all other mood-altering chemicals during your participation in the group. In the event of relapse you must notify your counselor before attending the next group session, and you must bring up the relapse episode for discussion at the beginning of that next group session. "Slips" will be viewed as potential learning experiences, but you will not be able to continue in the group if you show a regular pattern of slips, since this is destructive for you and for your fellow group members. If you are removed from the group due to slips, you will be given the option, where appropriate, of receiving three-times-a-week individual counseling to help you reestablish at least 2 consecutive weeks of uninterrupted abstinence as a prerequisite to applying for reentry into the group.
3. You agree to attend all scheduled sessions and to arrive on time without fail. This may require you to rearrange other obligations and perhaps even postpone vacations and out-of-town trips while participating in the group.
4. You agree to preserve the anonymity and confidentiality of all group members. You must not divulge the identity of any group member nor the content of any group discussions to persons outside the group.
5. You agree to remain in the group until you have completed the program. If you have an impulse or desire to leave the group prematurely, you will raise this issue for discussion in the group before acting on these feelings.
6. You agree to refrain throughout your participation in the program from becoming involved romantically, sexually, or financially with other group members.
7. You agree to accept immediate termination from the program if you offer drugs or alcohol to any member of the group or use these substances together with another group member.
8. You agree to have your telephone number(s) added to the contact list distributed to all group members.
9. You agree to give a supervised urine sample at least twice a week and whenever the group leader may request it.
10. You agree to raise for discussion in the group any issue that threatens your own or another member's recovery. You will not keep secrets regarding another member's drug use or other destructive behavior.

Managing Peer Confrontation

Peer confrontation by fellow group members can be extremely effective in helping patients achieve a more realistic assessment of their maladaptive attitudes and behaviors. But heavy-handed, excessive, and poorly timed confrontation can be countertherapeutic and even damaging. Some patients enter groups with the mistaken idea that humiliation and aggressive confrontation are acceptable ways to force resistant members of the group to face reality. Sometimes harsh confrontations are rationalized as attempts to be "truly honest" with members who violate group expectations and norms. Group members typically have less tolerance for negative attitudes and "B.S." than do group leaders, especially when these attitudes are reminiscent of their own. Likely targets for attack are members who relapse repeatedly, who remain defiant, superficial, or insincere, and who minimize their problem and fail to affiliate genuinely with other members of the group.

Sometimes group leaders feel ambivalent about stopping attacks on group members who have thorny problems that have been overlooked and are long overdue for being addressed. The group leader must never allow unpopular, frustrating, resistant, or severely troubled group members to be scapegoated and bludgeoned by their peers, even when the content of what is being said is entirely accurate. Harsh or excessive confrontation must not be used as a means to push selected members out of the group and to discourage them from coming back.

It is often the style rather than content of peer confrontation that determines its impact on the designated group member. The main goal of confrontation is to make the person more receptive to change without eliciting defensiveness or destructive acting-out behavior. Presenting group members with the following guidelines for therapeutic confrontation (1) can be helpful.

GUIDELINES FOR EFFECTIVE CONFRONTATION

1. Confrontation is defined as giving someone realistic feedback about their behavior as you see it—it is a process by which you attempt to "hold up a mirror" to let a person know how he or she appears to others—it is not an attempt at "character assassination."
2. Confrontation is most useful when spoken with empathy, concern, and caring in a respectful tone of voice.
3. Confrontation is descriptive of what you have observed, giving examples of the behavior in question: it excludes guesses, explanations, interpretations, advice, and criticisms about the person's behavior.
4. Confrontation includes a statement of your concern about the person's dangerous, self-defeating behavior and, if possible, an example of similar self-defeating behavior from your own experience.

Managing Problematic Group Members

Certain group members may cause serious problems that disrupt the functioning of the group. For example, some members are chronically antagonistic, argumentative, volatile, and sarcastic. Even those who emphatically state how much they need the group may nonetheless take every opportunity to devalue the group, complain about how poorly it is run, point out even the most minor inconsistencies, and categorically reject advice or suggestions. Problem patients may attempt to monopolize group sessions, feeling resentful or disrespectful of the time devoted to other members' problems and believing that not enough time is devoted to their own problems. Some problem patients are just the opposite: they sit silently in groups, glad to have the focus of attention always be on someone else. Silent members are often hiding intense feelings of ambivalence, resentment, anger, and fear. Often, patients who have slipped or run into serious or embarrassing problems, even if they were previously talkative in groups, may suddenly become silent and unresponsive—a clear outgrowth of addictive thinking that says "if there's a problem, ignore it, pretend that it doesn't exist." Patients who are chronically depressed and noninteractive in groups may also cause problems by casting a shadow of gloom and hopelessness over the group that stalls its movement. They may evoke uncomfortable feelings of pity and sorrow in other members, who then avoid paying attention to them or act as if they do not exist in the group.

Patients who come to groups while actively intoxicated or "crashing" from drugs (a very rare occurrence, since being in a group session is probably the last place someone in either state would want to be) can cause havoc in the group, and on all such occasions the intoxicated patient must be asked to leave the session immediately. The leader must vigilantly monitor and manage the behavior of problem group members and their impact on the rest of the group. Sometimes the content of what patients say in group is less important than the way in which it is said. The leader must attend continuously to patients' affect and communication style. Sarcastic and aggressive statements should not be ignored or overlooked. Monopolistic patients should not be allowed to go on indefinitely with tirades or intellectualized monologues. When this occurs, the leader should ask other group members why they are permitting one member to take up so much of the group's time without interruption. Do they not have any important issues of their own to discuss? If not, why not?

Silent members must also be confronted with their nonparticipation in the group. They must be helped to see how they are using their silence to avoid facing important issues and how silence is an enemy of their recovery. Similarly, severely depressed patients who are unable to interact in groups may require psychotropic medication or even hospitalization in serious, unremitting cases.

A special issue in managing problem patients is the formation of subgroups that undermine the group and sometimes threaten its very survival. Divisive members may work behind the scenes, chipping away at group cohesiveness, while simultaneously maintaining a facade of cooperativeness in the group. They form ties with certain group members that purposefully exclude other members, causing a build-up of tension and hostility among different "factions" in the group. These subgroups can quickly strangle group interaction, bring the therapeutic movement of the group to a grinding halt, and precipitate dropouts. Certain members who had been active in the group may suddenly fall sullen and silent. There may be a total absence of meaningful dialogue in group sessions. The leader is often the last to find out about the existence of these subgroups, since most members want to avoid being the person who "spills the beans." Dangerously divisive group members who threaten the recovery of other members or the survival of the group itself should be expelled from the program immediately, as in the case of one patient who was secretly pressuring other group members to leave the treatment program and form a peer group under his leadership that would meet every week at his home. When he failed to show up at a group meeting, one of the patients he was pressuring to leave the group blurted out the sabotage plan. Group members then talked openly about their conflicting feelings and how these feelings were stimulating intense cravings for drugs and fantasies about quitting treatment. Shortly thereafter, the divisive group member dropped out of treatment, much to the relief of other group members. Whenever problem patients seriously disrupt or stall the therapeutic movement of the group and remain chronically unresponsive to interventions by the group leader and fellow group members, they should be removed from the group— either temporarily or permanently. Sometimes temporary suspension from the group coupled with intensive individual therapy during an interim period can help to resolve some of the intense feelings and/or crises that may have been contributing to a patient's difficulty in the group. Group members usually are more relieved than upset when the leader takes decisive action with problem patients to preserve the safety and integrity of the group.

Coordinating Group and Individual Therapy

Although group therapy is the preferred modality of treatment for many addicts, it is usually insufficient by itself to address the full range of issues and problems experienced by all who enter treatment. A combination of individual and group therapy is optimal for many patients, preferably when the same therapist delivers both forms of treatment. When the patient's group leader also serves as his or her individual therapist, the inevitable problems in coordinating two different methods of treatment are eliminated. The dual role of the therapist provides an opportunity to observe directly a wider range of the patient's behavior firsthand and to use information obtained about the patient in one treatment context to maximize the effectiveness of interventions used in the other. For example, when patients actually display certain problems in group sessions that have been identified previously and discussed in individual sessions, the therapist has a unique opportunity to draw connections between the two. This type of interplay between individual and group therapy can have very potent synergistic effects that accelerate the patient's therapeutic progress. Issues raised in group sessions often serve as catalysts for discussions in individual sessions, and vice versa.

Individual therapy also gives patients an opportunity to address certain sensitive or embarrassing issues such as those involving intimate relationships, sexual functioning, self-esteem problems, and others that they are willing to discuss only in private. The therapist should not insist rigidly that patients discuss any and all personal matters in the group. Similarly, the therapist must guard against violating the patient's confidentiality on certain defined issues during groups. It is essential that the patient and therapist clarify with one another exactly which issues discussed in individual therapy sessions are not to be mentioned in groups. However, issues directly involving the patient's drug use must be excluded categorically from any such agreement: the therapist's hands cannot be tied when it comes to dealing with drug-related issues in the group, and there can be no secrets about drug use among group members.

When patients are referred for group treatment by an outside therapist who plans to continue seeing the patient in individual psychotherapy, the group leader must obtain the patient's permission to communicate with the individual therapist. When the two therapists communicate regularly and agree on a coordinated treatment plan, the two treatments can work well together. Both therapists must guard against the splitting defense of some patients (particularly those with narcissistic and/or borderline personality disorders), i.e., the patient's tendency to pit one therapist against the other in a way that deflects his or her personal responsibility for making change.

Fostering Outside Contact Between Group Members

Group members are actively encouraged to maintain contact with one another outside the group. (Again, this is very different from traditional psychotherapy, in which outside contact between group members is usually viewed as an undesirable "contamination" of the group's therapeutic environment.) A list of telephone numbers of all group members is updated routinely when newcomers enter the group and is distributed to all members. Newcomers are asked to call at least one group member every day during their first 2 weeks in the group to promote their rapid induction into the network of existing members and to foster group cohesiveness. Members are encouraged to plan social activities together, to go with one another to self-help meetings, and to call one another in time of need. One of the most important functions of the group, especially for newcomers, is as a support network to interrupt cravings and urges to use drugs. Patients are expected to report any contact they have had with one another between group sessions at the next meeting.

Dealing with Attendance, Lateness, and Fees

Consistency and predictability are essential to group treatment. Members must attend regularly, the only exception being truly unavoidable or extreme circumstances. Since most patients have histories of being generally irresponsible and unreliable and of failing to show up for scheduled meetings during their active addiction, they must not be allowed to continue this behavior in the group. The group leader must begin and end all group sessions on time. Members who are chronically late or absent and fail to change this behavior despite warnings from the leader and pressure from other group members may have to be expelled from the group. Chronic lateness and absenteeism indicates ambivalence about being in treatment that may be connected to the patient's denial about whether or not he or she is really addicted to the drug and whether the problem is really serious enough to warrant treatment in the first place. If fees are charged, they must be paid on time. Patients who are allowed to build up large outstanding balances of unpaid fees are prime candidates for dropping out of treatment precipitously.

A well-organized and well-run group serves as an example to patients of how planning and consistent follow-through are essential to achieving desired goals. From their experiences in a well-run group patients are able to extrapolate how to better organize and run their own lives—an essential goal of treatment. The group becomes a "learning laboratory" for acquiring basic life management skills, including planning one's time, avoiding procrastination, dealing with unanticipated problems, and paying attention to the needs of others.

Managing Early Resistance

An issue that often occupies a great deal of the group's attention is the ambivalence of certain members about making the initial behavioral and lifestyle changes needed to support abstinence. For example, newcomers often struggle with the idea of discontinuing all contact with fellow drug users and/or dealers, especially those they have known for a long time. They might be similarly reluctant to categorically avoid parties, bars, and other "hangouts" where the temptation to use alcohol and drugs is ever-present. Often these obstacles to early recovery stem from the patient's difficulty in accepting the identity of "addict" (i.e., that controlled use is no longer possible) and the fact that personal resolve and willpower are not good defenses against relapse. Established group members are likely to respond by assaulting the newcomer's defenses with vehement arguments that such self-defeating attitudes are indicative of the newcomer's extreme "denial" about being an addict. The group leader must intervene so as not to allow such discussions to get out of hand. Resistance is to be expected, and prematurely or excessively confronting it may do more harm than good by raising rather than lowering the patient's defenses and by actually driving him or her out of treatment (2). Furthermore, such discussions should not be allowed to dominate the group's attention in a way that consistently prevents other important issues from being addressed. When group sessions repeatedly focus on the problems of only one or two seriously problematic patients, the more established and stable group members may at first welcome having the focus taken off themselves but eventually become resentful and lose interest as their needs remain consistently unmet.

Successful group treatment relies heavily on the active leadership, direction, and education supplied by the group leader, who must continually emphasize the importance of retaining new members in the group. It is equally important to emphasize that working through a person's initial resistance to change is a process, not an instantaneous event, that requires time, patience, sustained commitment, and a willingness to tolerate temporary setbacks in oneself and others. The tone of the early abstinence group must convey caring, concern, nonjudgmental acceptance, and flexibility within a clearly defined structure. Limit setting, although very important, is too often carried to an extreme with addicts and becomes an end unto itself rather than a therapeutic tool. There is no clinical justification for taking a "tough guy" stance that assaults the patient's defenses and relies on harsh confrontation, domination, and control in an effort to blast through the patient's denial and foster compliance. Group leaders working with resistant early abstinence patients must be especially mindful of their own control fantasies and other negative countertransference reactions that are destructive to the therapeutic work of the group.

Getting locked into combative power struggles with poorly motivated group members will surely drive these patients out of treatment and confirm a self-fulfilling prophecy that every patient must "hit bottom" before they get serious about recovery. This is a serious therapeutic mistake—a failure to "start where the patient is." Forming a good working relationship with each and every group member is the most reliable way to positively influence his or her behavior. Giving patients permission to resist and to be ambivalent fosters openness and a willingness to take personal responsibility for their own actions. When the group leader takes an unreasonably "tough" stance on relapse, patients become very reluctant to share their drug fantasies in the group and are likely to *act* out rather *talk* out their secret impulses to get high. But the leader who instead joins with group members around shared goals and conveys understanding, empathy, and respect is often better able to engage even highly resistant patients in the process of honestly exploring their true attachment to drugs. A patient's inability or unwillingness to accept that he or she has a problem may not be evidence of intractable denial; it may just mean that the person is in a very early stage of change and that it will take time and a good bit of respectful coaxing by the group to move him or her forward into the next stage of change. These concepts can help the group leader maintain the perspective needed to avoid unnecessary frustration and negative group counseling techniques.

Responding to "Slips"

It is preferable to deal with "slips" experienced by group members as mistakes and motivational crises rather than tragic failures or willful noncompliance, should they occur (12). Slips can be valuable learning experiences that convince resistant patients of the need for total abstinence and more strenuous efforts to protect their abstinence. But many group leaders adopt inflexible, "get tough" attitudes about patients who slip. It is common practice to summarily terminate patients who fail to maintain perfect abstinence within the first few days or weeks of outpatient treatment. The patient who has one or more slips is often labeled an outpatient "failure" and told to go into a residential program. Although it is a delicate balancing act to avoid being an enabler on the one hand, and a hard-liner on the other, it hardly seems appropriate to terminate the patient for engaging in the very behavior that brought him or her to treatment in the first place. Saying that the patient is simply "unmotivated" or "noncompliant" is an inadequate explanation. Since most dropouts usually occur within the first 60 days, retaining patients through this difficult start-up period, despite initial slips and relapses, can markedly improve the chances of successful outcome.

Total abstinence from all mood-altering chemicals is a nonnegotiable treatment goal for all group members. The purpose for establishing and enforcing this group norm is to help create a therapeutic structure for the group that promotes positive changes in behavior and contains destructive impulses. Realistically, however, not all group members will remain entirely drug and alcohol free throughout their entire tenure in the group. When group members report that they have used drugs since the last session or their urine test indicates that this is so, the group must give priority to addressing this issue and the group leader must maintain a leadership style that models clear, consistent, and nonpunitive behavior. Group members usually have strong feelings in response to another member's use of drugs that must be expressed and put into proper perspective. The leader's task is to help the group use the occurrence of drug use by one of its members as an opportunity to learn something useful.

Suggested guidelines for discussing a member's slip in the group are as follows: (a) The member who has slipped is asked to provide the group with a detailed account of the sequence of feelings, events, and circumstances that led up to the slip. (b) Other group members are encouraged by the leader to further question the drug-using member, in a nonjudgmental way, about early warning signs, self-sabotage, and other factors that may have preceded the drug use. (c) The group leader summarizes and restates the relapse chain that appears to have led up to the patient's drug use. (d) Group members are asked to share any suggestions or feedback they can offer to the drug-using member about his or her slip and how to prevent it from happening again. They are also asked to share their feelings about the slip, but the group leader reminds them to avoid any tendency they may have to scapegoat the drug-using member or to act out feelings of anger and frustration on them. (e) With the participation of the drug-using member, a list of suggested strategies and behavioral changes is developed to guard against the possibility of further drug use. (f) The member who has slipped is asked to share thoughts and feelings about what was learned as a result of the slip and describe his or her willingness to take action to reduce the chances of using drugs again.

Although most group members respond supportively to another member's slip, there is an unspecified limit as to how often drug-using members can expect this type of supportive response. When members have slips repeatedly or regularly and show little or no evidence of utilizing the advice and suggestions offered by the group, others become intolerant and begin to feel that the group is enabling its drug-using member(s). This can happen after two slips, three slips, four slips, or more, depending on the overall attitude and behavior of the drug-using member and the nature of his or her relationships with others in the group. Peer confrontation can become very intense, and it is essential that the group leader guard against the group's tendency to scapegoat or ostracize the member who has slipped. The decision to temporarily suspend a drug-using member from the group usually develops out of the collective feelings and attitudes expressed by group members in combination with the clinical judgment of the group's leaders. This type of decision-making process is preferable to specifying in advance exactly how many slips patients are allowed before they are suspended from the group. If, for example, patients were told at the outset that three slips would result in suspension, this would be tantamount to giving them permission to have up to two slips—a distinctly countertherapeutic message!

TREATMENT GOALS IN GROUP THERAPY

Establishing Abstinence

The first goal of treatment is the cessation of all drug use and rapid integration of the patient into the group. To break the addictive cycle, the patient's habitual drug use must be replaced with habitual attendance at the group. This process is greatly facilitated by placing the newcomer into an intensive group that meets at least four or five times a week for at least several consecutive weeks. The consistent structure, discipline, and support provided by frequent group meetings assists patients in exercising greater self-control over their impulses to use and gives them a sense of safety and optimism about being able to change their behavior successfully. Frequent group meetings promote rapid induction into the group and rapid bonding with other group members. Because outpatient treatment can be effective only if patients actually show up, integrating newcomers into the group quickly is absolutely critical. This process is facilitated by asking one or more established group members to maintain daily contact with the newcomer outside the group, including escorting him or her to local self-help meetings. Newcomers must be helped to see as quickly as possible that their punctual attendance at all group sessions is essential to their recovery and to healthy functioning of the group. When patients miss a group session, it is critical that group members and the group leader call to express concern and communicate that his or her presence definitely was missed. One such phone call may go a long way toward preventing precipitous dropout in a relapsed patient who is ashamed to face the group and who assumes, incorrectly, that "no one really cares."

Newcomers who are attempting to establish or maintain initial abstinence usually need very specific guidance and instructions from the group on fundamental issues (13) such as (a) discarding all drug supplies and paraphernalia; (b) avoiding contact with dealers, users, parties, bars, and other high-risk situations; (c) learning how to recognize self-sabotaging behaviors and other "setups" for drug or alcohol use; and (d) learning how to manage urges and cravings. At times, a good deal of the group's work is devoted to formulating, implementing, reviewing, and continuously updating each group member's day-to-day plan for maintaining abstinence.

Establishing Stable Functioning

Once initial abstinence is established, the focus predictably shifts to stabilization of the individual's functioning. Often, a profound sense of disappointment emerges in the newly abstinent patient soon after he or she realizes that life is still fraught with problems despite having given up drugs. This realization may lead the patient to question seriously whether the struggle of staying abstinent is really worthwhile, especially in the face of delayed consequences of previous drug use such as financial, legal, and relationship problems that may begin to surface, seemingly "out of the blue." Support and advice from established group members who have dealt successfully with these types of problems are extremely helpful at this point to counteract the newcomer's tendency to impulsively "self-medicate" intense fears and anxiety about facing problems of daily living. Group members must also be helped to deal with a variety of other critically important issues and potential treatment obstacles that predictably surface during the first few weeks or months of group therapy, such as (a) negative feelings and negative mood states in the absence of drug use, (b) repeated "slips," (c) euphoric recall and recurrent fantasies about returning to controlled drug or alcohol use, (d) impulses to drop out of treatment, (e) resistance to attending self-help meetings, (*f*) unrealistic expectations of family members and significant others, and (*g*) making permanent lifestyle changes to support and protect continuing abstinence.

Preventing Relapse

The basic tasks of this stage are to solidify the patient's commitment to abstinence, work through residual ambivalence about or resistance to giving up alcohol and drugs, pinpoint environmental and psychological forces that insidiously move an individual toward relapse, and teach cognitive-behavioral coping skills to counteract reliably and deal adaptively with these negative forces.

Relapses that occur after solid abstinence has been firmly established usually are caused not as much by environmental triggers (which is more typical during early abstinence) as by failure of the patient to cope adequately with problems of daily living, especially stress and negative emotions. Recovering addicts often find it difficult to identify and deal with even mildly unpleasant feelings after the chemical blanket of chronic drug use has been removed. Frequently, it is this impaired ability to cope in combination with the resurfacing of important unresolved problems (sexual, relationship, self-esteem, psychological, financial, etc.) that precipitates relapse. In addition, the delayed consequences of drug use often catch up with people before they have acquired the adaptive coping skills to deal with these consequences. Perhaps the most important part of relapse prevention is making sure that treatment includes a programmatic attempt to teach patients how to respond adaptively to the demands of everyday living (including unanticipated problems) without resorting to drug and alcohol use (14, 15). Research on the relapse process (12) indicates that the major precipitants of relapse are negative mood states, interpersonal conflict, and social pressures to use drugs. Identifying the specific areas of vulnerability in each patient allows the group leader to prioritize which issues warrant current attention in the group. Among the many topics that must be addressed are how to identify negative feelings, how to manage anger, how to avoid impulsive decision-making, how to relax and have fun without drugs, how to give and receive constructive criticism, how to be assertive without being aggressive, and how to deal with the give-and-take of interpersonal relationships.

In addition to providing coping skills training, it is equally important to sensitize patients to relapse warning signs so that appropriate measures can be taken to "short-circuit" what is often a progressive backsliding in attitude and behavior. Explaining the relapse dynamic (16) as a progressive, identifiable process that is set in motion long before returning to drug use empowers group members to formulate plans to interrupt this relapse dynamic. Moreover, group members must be alerted to the possibility that flare-ups can occur even many months after stopping alcohol and drug use. For example, holidays, anniversaries, celebrations, and other such "trigger" events are often times of markedly increased relapse potential. In preparation for these events, it is generally wise to devote at least two or three group sessions to formulating strategies that will help group members successfully anticipate, avoid, and deal with potential dangers.

Addressing Psychological Issues

This stage overlaps the previous ones but focuses more specifically on identifying and working through long-standing problems that may have

been obscured or aggravated by drug and alcohol use (17). This stage of treatment addresses psychodynamic issues that go beyond the basic cognitive and behavioral factors that promote relapse. It explores in detail the inner emotional life of each group member and his or her relationship patterns that reliably give rise to the compulsive desire to "self-medicate" (5). Patients with long, destructive histories of drug or alcohol use often lack the ability to identify, regulate, tolerate, and appropriately express feelings (5). The ultimate goal here is not merely the acquisition of self-knowledge and insight but fundamental change in the individual's characteristically maladaptive patterns of thinking, feeling, behaving, and interacting. For example, learning how to tolerate unpleasant feelings instead of impulsively obliterating them with chemicals is an essential part of group treatment at this stage. At an appropriate time the group should also address long-standing, deep-seated problems that may stem from parental alcoholism, physical or sexual abuse, or other developmental and life traumas. Coordination between individual and group therapy is especially vital here. Moreover, whenever such sensitive, highly charged issues are being discussed, the group leader must be especially mindful of the possibility that group members may be at increased risk of relapse. Even when in-depth exploration of difficult issues appears to be well tolerated, patients should always be alerted to the possibility of relapse as an attempt to avoid painful material. It is essential that the group leader make a special effort to end each session with some closure and on a reasonably positive, optimistic note so as to prevent group members from leaving the session feeling overwhelmed by negative emotions. A good sense of timing on the part of the group leader is critical throughout this stage of treatment, i.e., knowing when to press harder on certain issues versus backing off, knowing when to be confrontational versus being supportive, etc.

MANAGED CARE CONSIDERATIONS

Consistent with demands of managed care, group therapy is an efficient, highly cost-effective form of treatment. As compared to individual therapy, for example, it makes treatment available to substantially larger numbers of patients at lower fees. It also an excellent vehicle for delivering programmatic services that are geared toward achieving realistic, clearly defined goals within a specified time frame. Managed care wants briefer, more clinically effective care at lower cost. Toward this end, specialized, focused groups can be developed to address specific patient needs within limitations of the patient's insurance benefits. At Washton Institute, for example, there are special time-limited groups for patients who need "readiness" or motivational counseling. These groups are separate and apart from early abstinence and relapse prevention groups for those who are ready and willing to work toward making the necessary behavioral changes to achieve or maintain abstinence.

Providers of chemical dependency treatment who wish to survive and hopefully thrive in the emerging managed care environment must be willing to challenge and if need be discard many of their long-held assumptions about the goals and length of treatment (18). Perhaps a new model of treatment delivery will consist of several relatively brief outpatient treatment episodes (e.g., 2–6 weeks each) interspersed over longer periods of time (e.g., 1–5 years). Each episode would focus on achieving specific goals and no single episode would be expected to initiate life-long recovery.

References

1. Washton AM. Cocaine addiction: treatment, recovery, and relapse prevention. New York: WW Norton, 1989.
2. Washton AM, Stone-Washton N. Abstinence and relapse in outpatient cocaine addicts. J Psychoactive Drugs 1990;22:135–148.
3. Spitz HI. Cocaine abuse: therapeutic group approaches. In: Spitz HI, Rosecan JS, eds. Cocaine abuse: new directions in treatment and research. New York: Bruner/Mazel, 1987: 156–201.
4. Flores PJ. Group psychotherapy with addicted populations. New York: Haworth Press, 1988.
5. Khantzian EJ, Halliday KS, McAuliffe WE. Addiction and the valuable self: modified group therapy for substance abusers. New York: Guilford Press, 1990.
6. Yalom I. Group psychotherapy and alcoholism. Ann N Y Acad Sci 1985;233:85–103.
7. Yalom I. The theory and practice of group psychotherapy. New York: Basic Books, 1985.
8. Vannicelli M. Group psychotherapy with adult children of alcoholics. New York: Guilford Press, 1990.
9. Washton AM. Structured outpatient treatment of alcohol vs. drug dependencies. In: Galanter M, ed. Recent developments in alcoholism. New York: Plenum, 1990:285–304.
10. Washton AM. Cocaine abuse and compulsive sexuality. Med Aspects Hum Sexuality 1989(9 December):32–39.
11. Verebey K. Drug detection by laboratory methods. In: Washton AM, Gold MS, eds. Cocaine: a clinician's handbook. New York: Guilford Press, 1987:214–228.
12. Marlatt GA, Gordon J. Relapse prevention. New York: Guilford Press, 1985.
13. Washton AM. Quitting cocaine: the first thirty days. Center City, MN: Hazelden, 1990.

14. Washton AM. Staying off cocaine: slips, relapses, and other drugs. Cocaine recovery workbooks. Center City, MN: Hazelden, 1990.
15. Monti PM, Abrams DB, Kadden RM, Cooney NL. Treating alcohol dependence. New York: Guilford Press, 1989.
16. Gorski T, Miller M. Staying sober: a guide for relapse prevention. Independence, MO: Independence Press, 1986.
17. Zweben J. Recovery-oriented psychotherapy. J Subst Abuse Treat 1986;3:255–262.
18. Washton AM, ed. Psychotherapy and substance abuse: a practitioner's handbook. New York: Guilford Press, 1995.

46 FAMILY AND MARITAL THERAPY

M. Duncan Stanton and Anthony W. Heath

For many years, substance abusers, especially drug addicts, were viewed as "loners"—people cut off from primary relationships and living a kind of "alley cat" existence. It was not until researchers began inquiring about addicts' living arrangements and familial contacts that the picture began to shift. The realization began to emerge that most substance abusers are closely tied to their families or the people that raised them:

- Vaillant (77), in a follow-up of New York narcotic addicts returning from the federal narcotics rehabilitation hospital in Kentucky, found that 90% of the 22-year-olds whose mothers were still alive went to live with them, while 59% of the 30-year-olds with living mothers either resided with them or with another female blood relative such as a grandmother or a sister.
- Perzel and Lamon (45) found that among a group of New Jersey heroin addicts and polydrug abusers (age range, 18–53; mean, 30 years; 48% female) 45% of the former and 42% of the latter lived with a parent—figures that were substantially higher than the 7% reported by a normal comparison group. Further, 64% of heroin addicts and 51% of polydrug abusers were in daily telephone contact with a parent, compared to 9% of normals.
- Douglas (15) compared matched groups of (male) opiate addicts, cocaine-dependent individuals and non–drug abusers, aged 20–40 (n = 90), and found opiate abusers were in face-to-face or telephone contact with their parents twice as often, and cocaine abusers three times as often (i.e., averaging 4 times per week) as the non–drug-using controls.
- In a study of 50 male opiate-cocaine abusers aged 30–42 years old, Bekir et al. (3) found 82% to be "in constant contact with their family of origin by phone or visiting" (p. 628). Further, 5 of the 12 married patients and their spouses each lived with their own families of origin and only "visited" each other.

It should be noted that this is not a strictly North American phenomenon. Reports from other countries have arrived at the following percentages of drug addicts who reside in the same households as their parents: England, 62%; Italy, 80%; Puerto Rico, 67%; Thailand, 80% (59).

Whether or not drug abusers actually live with their parents, the accumulated evidence indicates that most of them are in frequent contact with their families—usually one or both parents or parent surrogates. A recent review of this topic (62) found that 26 of 28 reports attested to the regularity of this contact.

Interestingly, questions of family-of-origin contact have apparently not been investigated with alcoholics. We have been unable to locate a single study that examines such patterns with this patient population. This, despite what the first author has observed during 30 years of treating alcoholics: A male drinker's wife typically voices this type of complaint: "I don't see him on weeknights because he's in the bars, and I don't see him on the weekend because he's over at his mother's putting up storm windows or something." In other words, present-day perception of this phenomenon among professionals and researchers is analogous to that which existed in the drug abuse field 30 years ago: Nobody asked, so nobody knew. Consequently, this author and colleagues (65) undertook a study of 111 consecutive admissions (ages 20–59; mean, 36.2 years; 44% female) in three different alcoholism programs in two cities; all were diagnosed alcohol dependent. Seventy-one percent of the subjects reported being in touch with one or both parents at least 2–3 times per month, while for 56% the contact was at least weekly. When the analysis was limited to those who had at least one living parent (i.e., 82.2% of the sample), the frequency of contact percentages rose to 87% and 68%, respectively. Thus we see a pattern very similar to that observed with drug abusers.

Of course, living with or regularly contacting parents is not in and of itself pathognomonic. In fact, such practices are the rule in some ethnic groups. We have emphasized such patterns of connectedness here because (a) they are often overlooked by treatment programs, and (b) they underscore that family members are important to substance abusers, and substance abusers are important to their families. Further, as discussed in a later section, "Treatment Engagement," family members can be a tremendous resource toward getting reluctant substance abusers to seek help (20).

SOME RELEVANT FAMILY DYNAMICS

There is an extensive body of literature, covered by a number of reviews (29, 38, 55, 73, 74), on the family and marital aspects of substance abuse. While most of this literature lies beyond the scope of the present chapter, some of it independently corroborates the family contact studies already noted:

- Madanes et al. (39) administered the Family Hierarchy Test (in which stick figures representing family members are moved about on a board) to families with an addict, a schizophrenic patient, or a high-achieving normal. The families of addicts were four times as likely as those with a schizophrenic disorder, and five times as likely as the normals, to place figures on the board so that they actually touched or overlapped. Over half of these instances for addict families were cross-generational (i.e., between a parent and child) as opposed to being close connections between those in the same generation, such as spouses and siblings. The implication is of alliances between an offspring and one parent against the other parental figure—a finding that also emerged in a study of families of alcoholics by Preli and Protinsky (47). Madanes et al. conclude that their data add to the accumulating evidence that addicts "are enmeshed in dependent relationships with their families of origin or parental surrogates" (39, p. 889).
- While there has sometimes been a tendency for the public to view parents of substance abusers in negative terms, that does not necessarily jibe with the views of the abusers themselves. In a Chicago study by Ben-Yehuda and Schindell (4), 70.2% of male and female methadone patients rated their family as warm, 61.7% said they had a good childhood, and 70.2% felt they had a satisfactory relationship with their parents.

A number of family factors have direct bearing on the remediation of addiction. For instance: (a) onset of drug abuse and overdoses may be precipitated by family disruptions, stresses and losses (16, 33, 40); (b) parental modeling of drug and alcohol taking is important (21); (c) the substance abuse may help to maintain family homeostasis or even serve as a means for getting the drug abuser's parents into treatment (see illustration later under "Overall Treatment Compliance" and 29, 72); and (d) family members can engage in "enabling" behaviors which perpetuate the substance abuse of a member (13). Indeed, recognition of such variables led Craig, in an overview of contemporary trends in substance abuse, to conclude that, "The need to address family issues in a comprehensive treatment program is now widely recognized in drug abuse treatment" (13, p. 185).

PRELIMINARY FAMILY AND MARITAL TREATMENT CONSIDERATIONS

About Family and Marital Treatment

Family therapy was foreshadowed in the work of psychoanalysts Sigmund Freud (the "Little Hans" case), Alfred Adler, and Harry Stack Sullivan, but the movement began when an eclectic bunch of maverick researchers, theorists, and psychotherapists, unknown to one another at the time, began to interview families together, usually in order to further understand the problems manifested by one member. Soon treatment began to shift from the intrapsychic experiences of the patient to the relational dynamics among the family members, with an eye to the psychological growth of all. Eventually, human problems became conceptualized as existing between (or among) people, rather than within (or only within) them, and the whole family became the "patient."

In 40 years the family therapy field has shown a good deal of fluidity, simultaneously growing, regressing, and advancing in various quarters around the world. Today, family and marital therapy is both an independent mental health profession (with a separate scholarly literature, over a dozen influential theories, separate licensing in most American states, and separate accreditation for its master's degree and doctoral programs), and a field of inquiry and practice that cuts across traditional professional boundaries.

Fundamentally, family therapy is *a way of thinking about human problems* that suggests certain actions for their alleviation (61), rather than a modality of treatment per se. Family therapists generally convene whole families of two or more generations when the presenting problem concerns a child or adolescent, and see couples or individuals, consulting with other family members, when there is an adult complaint. On the other hand, depending on his or her theoretical orientation and more practical constraints, a family therapist may conduct therapy with (*a*) only the person with the most apparent problem or only the person most concerned with the problem, (*b*) the whole family network (including friends, neighbors, other therapists, and social agents), or even (*c*) systems external to the family. In addition, family therapists commonly work with a wide range of family forms, including single-parent families and gay and lesbian families.

Expanding on the thinking of a number of authors, Stanton (61) has defined the approach as follows:

Family therapy—perhaps more appropriately, "systems" therapy—is an approach in which a therapist (or a team of therapists), working with varying combinations and configurations of people, devises and introduces *interventions* designed to *alter the interaction* (process, workings) *of the interpersonal system and context* within which one or more psychiatric/behavioral/human problems are imbedded, and thereby also alters the functioning of the individuals within the system, with the *goal of alleviating or eliminating the problems* (p. 9; emphasis added).

The term "systems therapy" actually is preferred by many family therapists, but most agree that it is too late to change the tag. Indeed, it is the systemic (relational, interactional) manner of their thought and interventions that defines the approach, not the attention to the social unit called a "family." Family therapists work with families because the family is one of the systems in which human problems can be most easily understood, and because families often provide a significant resource for solving problems.

Treating Families with a Chemical Dependency Problem

Substance abusers are not the family members most likely to seek the services of a therapist. In fact, the most characteristic feature of substance abuse may be the abuser's denial that the use of the substance is a problem at all.

Conversely, in many instances the substance abuse is overlooked by some family members; it may even be overtly or covertly encouraged. Recognizing this fact, family therapists offer their services to *anyone* who wants to discuss the substance abuse. Like Al-Anon and related self-help programs, family therapists generally believe that every family member can be helped to survive the abuse, whether the substance abuser stops drinking and/or "drugging" or not.

The case can be made that family therapy is appropriate and helpful throughout the process of recovery. This includes when the problem is initially identified by a family member or a therapist; when the family is mustering its forces to convince the abuser of the extent of the problem and the need for change; during any residential treatment for the substance abuse; and while the family learns new ways to go on in life without chemicals.

Indeed, it is our experience that a lack of some form of family-oriented services in substance abuse treatment can at times have even calamitous consequences. As Liepman, White, and Nirenberg (37) said in the conclusion to their review of the research on treatment of children of alcoholics, "Without family therapy, most families would suffer serious 'side effects' if the alcoholic were to stop drinking" (p. 53). Indeed, without concurrent treatment for non-abusing members, families have been known (in order to preserve the familiar and avoid the illumination of other problems) to attempt to sabotage treatment efforts, when those efforts begin to succeed (56). Examples of this have been commonly reported in the literature; they range from a spouse slipping beer to a recovering alcoholic, to the parents who refuse to work together in maintaining rules for their out-of-control adolescent. On the other hand, Steinglass et al. (74) have asserted, at least regarding alcohol treatment, that the evidence is compelling that "involvement of a nonalcoholic spouse in a treatment program significantly improves the likelihood that the alcoholic individual will participate in treatment as well" (pp. 331–332).

Families also can provide a significant positive influence in recovery. For example, Eldred and Washington (17) found that heroin addicts rated their families of origin or their in-laws as most likely to be helpful to them in their attempts to give up drugs; their second choice was their opposite-sex partner. Similarly, Levy (34) found that in a 5-year follow-up of narcotics addicts, patients who successfully overcame drug abuse most often had family support.

Although few family therapists believe that attendance at AA, Al-Anon, or other self-help groups is necessary for healthy recovery in *every* case, most would agree with this statement by Davis (14):

As a therapist, I operate according to the same presuppositions that operate in self-help groups: that every patient/client already has the resources or the capacity to develop the resources needed, that experts don't have all the answers, and that we are ultimately responsible for our own behaviors. (pp. 138–139)

Furthermore, in those instances when substance abusers and their families are adamantly opposed to involvement in 12-step groups, family therapy may offer a satisfactory alternative (24).

Over 20 books have been written specifically about family and marital therapy with substance abusers. Similarly, many different modalities of family treatment have been described, including: marital therapy; group therapy for parents or relatives; concurrent parent and index patient therapy; therapy with individual families, both inpatient and outpatient; sibling-oriented therapy; multiple-family therapy; social network therapy; and family therapy with one person. Readers interested in studying this area further are referred to the synopses by Heath and Atkinson (24) and Stanton (60).

STAGES OF FAMILY TREATMENT

In this section we will describe a selective, integrative model of the stages of family therapy with substance abusers. The model synthesizes literature on family therapy both with alcoholic adults (e.g., 5–9, 14, 41–43, 74), and with drug-abusing adolescents and adults (e.g., 18, 28, 32, 35, 36, 46, 63, 71, 72, 75, 76). It emphasizes the consensus among these various authors, and offers a rich collection of the clear and specific family therapy methods they have developed.

Stage 1: Defining the Problem and Negotiating a Contract

Therapists must convene enough of the family to gain adequate leverage to initiate change in family interaction. This may involve 1, 2, or 30 family members, and may include other members of the substance abuser's social network (19, 26, 36, 63). One generally starts by working with the most motivated family member or members, convening other family members when needed (Berenson, cited in 57).

Family therapists next attempt to identify and define the problem. When substance abuse is suspected, many begin by asking simple questions, such as "Who drinks?" or "What medications are used in your family?" We ask our clients these "loaded" questions as a matter of course. We work hard to avoid becoming involved in a debate over whether substance abuse is really "addiction" or "alcoholism" (e.g., 14). Like Davis, we believe:

> This is not the time to fight over the presence of an "ism." It is enough to establish that there is a serious problem that needs treatment. The drinker and family members can make up their own minds after some success with AA and family therapy as to whether they have been dealing with alcoholism. (14, p. 53)

Once the problem is defined, the therapist and family identify and prioritize their goals for treatment, starting with the primary goal of helping the substance abuser become "clean" and/or "sober," and directly relating each subsequent goal to this primary one. When family members bring up additional issues, the therapist may ask the family to justify them as relevant to the main goal of sobriety (71).

Other principles are also helpful:

- *Establish alliances with senior family members.* In the case of an adolescent or young adult, especially, treatment is unlikely to succeed or hold up unless parental figures and even grandparents are involved (26, 28, 36, 46, 72, 75).
- *Assume a nonblaming stance toward the entire family* (68). Indeed this tack is usually to be taken even further, so as to "ascribe noble intentions" to family members' actions (71).
- *The substance abuse should be labeled a family problem.* As Steinglass et al. (74) put it, the therapist must, in the first session, "get across to the family that there is no issue more important at this stage of the work than the cessation of drinking, and that the family and the therapist must mobilize all resources toward that goal and that goal alone" (p. 354).
- *Use of a genetic, disease interpretation of addiction helps to reduce guilt, blame, and shame.* This explanation should, of course, be respected as such and not allowed—due to the immutability of genes—to immobilize the therapist or family. Instead, all participants need to understand that, through working together, the disease's symptoms can be overcome and that the ostensible "destiny" can be reversed so that people can lead chemical-free lives.

There are, of course, clients who reject the genetic and disease explanations for addiction. And they may be justified, since there is no genetic evidence for most drug abusers or for a high proportion of alcoholics (53). But genetics or no genetics, addicted people can learn to live responsibly. They, too, can work together with their families to overcome their problems.

Stage 2: Establishing the Context for a Chemical-Free Life

Once substance abuse is defined as a problem, and a therapeutic contract is negotiated, family therapy enters a second phase in which a context for sobriety is established. Berenson has stated that this stage involves "management of an ongoing, serious drinking problem and setting up a context so that the alcoholic will stop drinking" (7, p. 33).

Most family therapists consider the cessation of substance abuse to be a prerequisite for further treatment (e.g., 5). Furthermore, many believe that therapists must consistently insist on abstinence over the course of therapy (e.g., 14). In the words of Steinglass et al. (74):

Meaningful therapy with an Alcoholic Family cannot proceed if the therapist adopts a laissez-faire attitude about drinking behavior and acquiesces in a decision to allow the identified alcoholic to continue drinking. The therapist must take a firm stand on this issue at the start of therapy, while at the same time acknowledging that it may not be an easy task and that there may be a number of slips before abstinence is achieved. (p. 343)

Other principles are also important at this stage:

- *Refer family members to 12-step programs* (e.g., Al-Anon, Nar-Anon, Cocaine Anonymous) and related self-help programs (5, 11, 14).
- *With couples, incorporate behavioral couples' techniques* (18, 41–43).
- *Use spouse support groups* whenever possible (Berenson, in 57).
- *Have no expectation that the change will occur.* The therapist must remain more skeptical than optimistic. This protects the therapist from pursuing family members unnecessarily and also protects her or him from becoming too deeply inducted into the system (Berenson, in 57).
- *Be prepared to deal with issues of unexpected deaths and unresolved losses at this stage* (12, 22, 48, 49, 54). If ignored, such issues can erode gains made with the presenting problem.

Stage 3: Ceasing Substance Abuse

In the family therapy of substance abuse there always comes a moment of truth. As a result of the changes in their family members' behavior, and the consistent position of the therapist, the abusers suddenly realize that they are going to have to choose between their families and their chemicals. When confronted (or abandoned) by parents, spouses, children, friends, employers, and perhaps even by recovering people in self-help groups and/or a therapist, substance abusers often "hit bottom." Sometimes they turn to the therapist for help in changing their ways.

Steinglass et al. (74) suggest that there are basically three possible ways to proceed at this juncture:

- *Arrange inpatient detoxification for the addicted substance abuser if this is indicated.* A therapist who knows there to be physical dependence on alcohol or drugs should refuse to continue therapy unless this option is selected, since without medical intervention the addict's independent withdrawal is unlikely, if not dangerous.
- *Agree to let the family attempt detoxification with the abuser on an outpatient basis.* Proceed on the condition that if there has been no meaningful progress made toward detoxification within 2 weeks, then inpatient treatment will be pursued.
- *Allow outpatient recovery using the family as the "treatment team,"* if the physical complications from withdrawal are minimal or well controlled. This approach, labeled "home detoxification," has been elaborated by Scott and Van Deusen (52) and Stanton and Todd (70). It involves setting up a round-the-clock monitoring or "watch" schedule—involving as many adult family members as possible—accompanied by medical back-up. Considerable effort is devoted ahead of time to anticipating slip-ups. A contract is also commonly negotiated to go through the process a second time, should the first attempt fail. Overall, the approach appears to be quite cost-effective (64, 66).

Whichever course of action is selected, it is essential to keep all family members involved in the change process, so that later they can accept some responsibility for the success of the treatment (58, 71). When treatment gets left to the "professionals," family members often fail to realize their responsibility for change. Then later, should the recovery process go awry, they may blame the setback on the treatment program.

Stage 4: Managing the Crisis and Stabilizing the Family

Once the substance abuser becomes "clean and sober," family therapists are prepared for a new set of problems. Stunned by the unfamiliar behavior of the "new" family member, and often terribly frightened, family members have been known to make seemingly irrational statements such as "I liked you better when you were drinking." One client we know actually gave a bottle of bourbon to her recently sober husband for his birthday. The potential for relapse is understandably high in this stage.

Steinglass et al. (74) have named an analogous stage in the treatment of alcoholic families "the emotional desert." Families that have been organized around alcohol, especially over many years, experience profound emptiness when the drinking stops. These families "have the sensation of having been cut adrift, loosened from their familiar moorings, lost in a desert without any landmarks upon which to focus to regain their bearings" (74, p. 344). Instead of experiencing joy over the newfound sobriety, the family members feel empty and sad. Thus the members of a family with a newly sober member tend to interact in more or less the same ways that they did while that member was abusing drugs or alcohol.

Family therapists disagree over how quickly to move to resolve family problems during this phase. Berenson has suggested that it is usually advisable to begin the stage with a hiatus from therapy while things calm down; thus he does not schedule regular appointments, but tells clients, "Get back to me in a month or so" (57). Instead, he encourages his clients to continue their AA or Al-Anon activities, with the understanding that if this state of distress continues beyond 6–12 months, family therapy will resume on a more regular basis. After a period of sobriety, Berenson returns to a more orthodox therapy schedule. Others (e.g., 5, 74) believe that regularly scheduled family therapy sessions can be very helpful at these times, especially if they focus on solving the series of problems that hound the families and wear them down.

Stage 5: Family Reorganization and Recovery

Although some families restabilize before reaching this phase and remain organized around alcohol or drug issues (e.g., "dry alcoholic" families), for others the previous stages of therapy culminate in a serious family crisis. This crisis then leads to disorganization and ultimately to a fundamentally different organizational pattern—a pattern which develops, albeit slowly, in Stage 5 of therapy.

In this stage, family therapists are concerned with helping families to move away from interaction focused on substance abuse issues and toward fundamentally better relationships. Here the substance abuser is stabilized and "clean and sober." The therapy now focuses on developing a better marriage, establishing more satisfactory parent-child relationships, and perhaps confronting long-standing family-of-origin and codependence issues. Steinglass et al. (74) have called this process "family reorganization" (p. 344).

In their couples-oriented family approach, Bepko and Krestan (5) enumerate the following goals in their analogue for this stage—a stage they call "rebalancing" (p. 135–136):

- **Shift extremes of reciprocal role behavior** from rigid complementarity (one person "up," the other "down") to greater symmetry (balance) or more flexible complementarity.
- **Help the couple or family to resolve issues of power and control.**
- **Directly address the pride structures of both partners** so that new forms of role behavior are permitted without the need for alcohol.
- **Help the couple to achieve whatever level of closeness and intimacy is desirable for them.**

With young addicts, this stage of the therapy evolves beyond crisis management and toward other issues, such as finding gainful employment and possibly a place to live away from home (68). Parents are often involved in these "launchings," so they can feel part of the addict's eventual success. Over time, it becomes increasingly possible to shift the parents' attention to other siblings, grandchildren, or retirement planning, thereby allowing both the parents and the recovering addict to let go. When marital issues surface, as they often do, family therapists work to prevent addicts from getting involved in their parents' marriages.

Stage 6: Termination

Ideally, treatment comes to an end when clients and therapist(s) mutually agree to stop meeting regularly. Family therapists agree to stop when they believe that serious structural and functional problems that have maintained

substance abuse have been replaced with new family rules, roles, and interactional patterns. Optimally, substance abuse has not been replaced with other addictive behaviors; however, sometimes socially acceptable "addictions," (e.g. "workaholism") are tolerated by family therapists when they are tolerated by family members.

Therapy's length and the specific definition of successful treatment vary widely among models of therapy and among individual families. Stanton and Todd (68), in describing their brief therapy model for treating drug addicts, have broadly stated that therapy is appropriately concluded when "adequate change has occurred and been maintained long enough for the family to feel a sense of real accomplishment" (p. 64). Adherents of other models would not attempt to reorganize family structure in the ways prescribed in our Stage 5. Instead, they may be content to conclude treatment when family members feel satisfied that their problems have been resolved (e.g., 23, 25).

Therapy need not be thought of as an event or as a process with a distinct end point. In fact, clients often seek subsequent counsel from the same therapist on new, unrelated issues.

SPECIAL ISSUES

Treatment Engagement

IDENTIFIED PATIENT

In a given year only 5–10% of people who are actively addicted actually become engaged either in treatment or in self-help groups (20, 31). This shocking finding underscores the need to find new and better ways to get help for these individuals. Family members can be a major source of energy and motivation for addressing this problem.

A number of approaches, such as the Johnson Institute's "Intervention," have been developed to help families enlist a substance-abusing member in treatment (see 62 for a review of these methods). Most recently, Garrett and associates (20) have developed a three-stage model for this endeavor. Entitled "ARISE," it delineates procedures for handling the first call from a "concerned other" about a substance abuser. That call is used to mobilize the natural system to organize, its specific goal being the abuser's enrollment in treatment. Guidelines are provided on how to plan and conduct meetings with the family and network (a second stage) if the initial, usually less ambitious, attempt is unsuccessful. The third stage is a modified Johnson Intervention. The advantage of the ARISE approach is that it maximizes the probability of patient recruitment, while minimizing the amount of time and energy required of staff.

FAMILY MEMBERS

Sometimes it is difficult to convene the whole family of a substance abuser for therapy (62, 69). Fathers of substance-abusing young people, in particular, often appear threatened by treatment and defensive about their contributions to the problem. Because many have drinking problems themselves, they may also fear discovery, being blamed for the problem, or that their own addiction will be challenged.

Recognizing such hesitancies, family therapists reach out to recruit families into therapy. Sometimes they ask other family members to help with recruiting, but they are cognizant that this approach may not be sufficient. Thus they extend personal invitations to the reluctant members. In less seriously disturbed families, one telephone call may enable a therapist to reassure family members that their contributions are important to the solution of the substance abuse. In more disturbed families, it may be necessary to meet family members on "neutral turf" (such as at a restaurant), or to write multiple letters, or even to pay family members for participation in treatment (67, 69).

Involving Parents in Decisions

Parents must be involved in all decisions about treatment when a substance abuser is an adolescent or a young adult. Thus parents should be involved in decisions about hospitalization, medication, and drug tests. Family therapists make the parents part of the treatment team because it helps to get the couple working together and because the responsibility for the resolution of the problem is correctly theirs. When the parents of a young abuser are divorced or unmarried, the same holds true; adult caretakers must be encouraged to work together to help their children.

Codependence

"Codependence" is a word that is often (and loosely) used to describe the process underlying many problems in the families of substance abusers. There is little consensus about how the term should be defined, but according to Schaef (50), one of the chemical dependency field's most respected authors, codependence is a disease that parallels the alcoholic disease process and has specific and characteristic symptoms (e.g., external referencing, caretaking, self-centeredness, control issues, dishonesty, frozen feelings, perfectionism, and fear). Codependence has generally replaced the concept of "enabling" and focused attention on the suffering of those who live with, or have lived with, a chemically dependent person.

Family therapists have learned a great deal about addiction and its treatment from Schaef (50), Beattie (2), and Wegscheider (78), who have bridged the fields of family therapy and chemical dependency counseling. They have learned, for example, to address the individual fears and difficulties of the parents, spouses, children, and grown children of alcoholics. They have learned to recommend self-help groups and books on codependence for codependents. They have also learned to recognize addictive processes at work in families when individuals express any of the hallmark symptoms of codependence. They already know that the pain of addiction affects everyone in and around these families, often for generations.

We are cautious in the use of the term "codependence," because it has been disproportionately and pejoratively applied to women in our society. Clearly caretaking, supporting, and selflessness—often considered feminine characteristics or responsibilities—can be admirable and socially necessary. The word "codependence" must be applied to both sexes, linked to the underfunctioning that may describe other family members' behavior, and reserved for extreme and clearly harmful situations.

Overall Treatment Compliance: Family Factors and Techniques in Fostering It

THE SUBSTANCE ABUSER'S INTERPERSONAL CONTEXT

Substance abusers often evoke irritation in medical and other helping professionals. The destructiveness of their habits, the reluctance with which they relinquish these habits, or the rapidity with which they can return to them, can test the patience of even the most composed professional.

One reason for this reaction is that the professional sees the abuser as a separate and autonomous individual. However, as has been pointed out earlier, substance abusers are rarely located within such isolated circumstance. Thus if an abuser attempts to unilaterally make as consequential a change as ceasing chemical abuse, she or he knows there will be reactions from others within the interpersonal system.

An example of this is the "family addiction cycle" (29, 72). A cyclical, homeostatic pattern has been described with families of addicts in which, when the addict improves in some way, the parents begin to fight and to separate from each other. When the addict "fails," such as by taking drugs or losing a job, the parents shift attention from their couple problem and address the addict's problem. Thus they become, in a sense, "unified." In this way the addict's behavior serves a purpose of at least temporarily keeping the family together. Further, from this viewpoint the chemical taking is simply one event within an interpersonal sequence of behavior. It is not an independent phenomenon occurring in a vacuum, but a response to a series of others' behaviors which precede (and succeed) it. That is the reason for the term *family* addiction cycle.

Professionals who are not attuned to these kinds of sequences taking place in a client's life put themselves at a disadvantage. They run the risk of being constantly mystified by onset and cessation of chemical taking. By not appreciating the plight both of the addict and his or her family members, they also risk losing their client's trust. Thus the tension between, for instance, doctor and patient, is increased.

COMPLIANCE-ENGENDERING TECHNIQUES

Substance abusers have a lot in common with people who manifest other behavioral health problems, such as asthma, diabetes, obesity and, of course, smoking. The typical interpersonal pattern attending each of these health problems (e.g., between "patient" and family member, or patient and health professional) is that one person says, "You must take care of yourself," and the other replies, "I don't want to," "Not yet," or "I can't." In spite of the fact that both parties in such standoffs usually have good intentions, the disagreement characteristically escalates—sometimes into a veritable shouting match. And the more this conflict intensifies, the more both parties tend to become entrenched in their positions: the helper "helps" more in the same way, the resister resists more, also in the same way, and an equilibrium results. Thus change doesn't occur.

Family therapists generally accept that individuals (and families) have the power to resist the changes demanded by others, even when resistance is "irrational." This resistance to change, by the way, is as true for helpers as for the substance abuser. So family therapists have asked, "If behavioral health problems are to be ameliorated, and compliance with a plan for health increased, what can be done to avoid or reverse these interpersonal standoffs?" The answer usually includes the following courses of action:

- *Assessment of customership.* Family therapists distinguish between those who are customers for therapy and those who are not. Customers desire what the therapist has to offer; non-customers want nothing to do with it. In families with substance abusers, it is commonly the others—spouses, partners, parents, offspring—who initially request help. Thus the family therapist starts with them, offering help in dealing with the substance abuser. Since customers will more probably comply with the therapist's suggestions, family change can commence from this starting point.
- *Listening.* Family therapists try to hear what every client has to say about his or her experience. Questions such as, "Why do you drink?" and "Who would be upset if you stopped?" are commonly asked. These questions convey an earnest curiosity and reflect an understanding that addiction is an interpersonal process. They also help a therapist understand what motivates each client. When clients feel heard, they are more likely to cooperate toward the benefit of their own health.
- *Avoiding lectures.* Generally, family therapists prefer not to teach substance abusers or their families about the actions of drugs or the disease process. Part of the reason is that assuming an authoritative, teacher role can make clients feel put down. Thus, to avoid the unhelpful responses (including noncompliance) that teaching may evoke, the family therapist seeks, instead, to learn. In other words, clients' questions are respectfully answered, but the use of information as a strategic tool of behavior change is avoided.
- *Developing contracts.* As noted earlier, family therapists attempt to engage their clients in agreements about the direction of treatment. With substance abusers, consensus goals help to promote compliance. The initial goals of substance abusers are rarely those of the family or therapist, but a cooperative effort—and process—toward any objective fosters trust and respect among all. Such an atmosphere can therefore engender the kind of context where beneficial change can flourish.
- *Candor.* Many family therapists opt for frank honesty with their clients. They tell clients what they think, framing it as opinion rather than fact. This forthright approach seems to startle—or even scare—many substance abusers and families, possibly because it is unfamiliar to them. A therapist's commitment to candor, however, tends to improve compliance with a health plan.

Through these techniques or principles of action, the family therapist attempts to enlist cooperation of the substance abuser and family, and to facilitate more healthy choices of conduct. When abusers are released from the insistence that they *must* change, they often tend, paradoxically, to move towards health.

Competition Among Programs and Families

In 1980, Schwartzman and Bokos (51) published a paper on a competitive process they observed taking place among drug treatment programs in a large city. Patients would appear at, say, "Program D" requesting admission and complaining about prior treatment they had received at "Program C." The staff person at the new program would then commiserate with the client, disparage Program C, and give assurance that no such problems would crop up at Program D, where "we treat our clients *right*." Thus an interpersonal triangle would be established, with two of its parties (the client and Program D) joined in opposition to the third (Program C). This process has been termed "triangulation." It is common, to at least some degree, in most interpersonal systems. (Schwartzman and Bokos also noted, incidentally, that in many cases the client would eventually become disenchanted with Program D and would defect either back to Program C, or to a new program, thus setting up a new triangle and repeating the process.)

Likewise, staff in addiction programs have been known to fall into the trap of triangulation vis à vis a client's parents or family members. This is a particular risk for individual-oriented approaches to therapy. Campbell (10) performed a content analysis of therapists' writings regarding their patients' family members and found that 90% of the time family members were referred to in negative terms. In a description of an effort to expand their drug treatment program to be more inclusive of parents and families, Balaban and Melchionda (1) reported that staff often got into awkward and destructive triangles in which they would compete with a client's family over the client—at times reaching the point of open disparagement of the parents or even fostering defection from the family.

When binds of this sort occur, they can put tremendous pressure on clients. Torn between their loyalties to parents or family members versus treatment staff, clients may choose an option that relieves the pressure: aborting treatment. For this reason, substance abuse professionals must be particularly wary of getting caught in patterns of triangulation.

RESEARCH

In 1974 the National Institute on Alcohol Abuse and Alcoholism recognized family therapy as "one of the outstanding current advances in the area of psychotherapy" for alcoholism (30, p. 116). Subsequently, a number of reviews have found "overwhelmingly favorable" (74, p. 331) evidence in support of the use of family therapy methods for substance abuse (e.g., 27, 41, 42, 44, 56, 64, 73). More specifically, the most updated reviews of the research on marital and family treatment for alcoholism (41, 42) have concluded that family and marital treatment produces better marital and drinking outcomes than non-family methods.

In terms of the effectiveness of family and couples treatment for drug abuse, Stanton and Shadish (64) have recently performed a review and meta-analysis across 15 outcome studies. All were controlled studies—using random assignment—and compared at least two treatment conditions, one of which was some form of family or couples therapy. Some of the major conclusions from this review are:

1. Overall, the studies' design quality was good.
2. Compared to the non-family modalities of individual counseling or therapy, group therapy, and treatment-as-usual, family and couples therapy showed superior results, with effect sizes of .55, .51, and .38, respectively. This was not meant to imply that the non-family approaches are not effective, for most of them are, but rather that either (*a*) their results can be improved by the addition of family or couples therapy—such as to methadone maintenance, or (*b*) family and couples therapy presents a more effective and/or cost-effective alternative.
3. Comparisons between family therapy and other forms of family intervention gave an edge to family therapy over family psychoeducation (effect size, .66), but equivalent effects for relatives' groups.
4. These findings hold for both adolescent and adult drug abusers.
5. Comparisons between different "schools" of family therapy are not conclusive. One reason is that many of these schools have not been involved in outcome research with this population. Secondly, most of the approaches that *have* submitted themselves to testing share many commonalities with each other, so that differences among them in effectiveness, if such differences exist, are difficult to tease out.
6. Compared with other studies and approaches to psychotherapy with drug abusers, family therapy conditions have attained relatively high rates of engagement and retention in treatment.
7. Differences between different treatment conditions as to their early dropout rates pose apotential problem. All too commonly, such dropouts have been excluded from outcome analyses. When, in this meta-analytic review, dropouts were reintroduced as treatment failures into the data analysis, it became apparent that family treatment, which was likely to have fewer dropouts, had, in the original analyses, been modestly penalized relative to other modalities.

In sum, the evidence is accumulating that family and marital treatments for substance abuse are both efficacious and cost effective. That they are being increasingly adopted by treatment programs seems therefore justified.

Acknowledgments. *Portions of this chapter are adapted with permission from Heath AW, Stanton MD. Family therapy. In: Frances RJ, Miller SI, eds. Clinical textbook of addictive disorders. New York: Guilford Press, 1991:406–430; Stanton MD, Heath AW. Family treatment of alcohol and drug abuse. In: Mikesell RH, Lusterman D, McDaniel SH, eds. Integrating family therapy: handbook of family psychology and systems theory. Washington, DC: American Psychological Association, 1995:529–541.*

References

1. Balaban BJ, Melchionda R. Outreach redefined: the impact on staff attitudes of a family education project. Int J Addict 1979;14(6):833–846.
2. Beattie M. Codependent no more. Center City, MN: Hazelden Educational Materials, 1987.
3. Bekir P, McLellan T, Childress AR, Gariti P. Role reversals in families of substance misusers: a transgenerational phenomenon. Int J Addict 1993;28(7):613–630.
4. Ben-Yehuda N, Schindell BJ. The addict's family of origin: an empirical survey analysis. Int J Addict 1981;16(3):505–525.
5. Bepko C, Krestan J. The responsibility trap. New York: Free Press, 1985.
6. Berenson D. A family approach to alcoholism. Psychiatric Opinion 1976;13:1–18.
7. Berenson D. Alcohol and the family system. In: Guerin P, ed. Family therapy: theory and practice. New York: Gardner Press, 1976:284–297.
8. Berenson D. The therapist's relationship with couples with an alcoholic member. In: Kaufman E, Kaufmann P, eds. The family therapy of drug and alcohol abuse. New York: Gardner Press, 1979:233–242.
9. Berenson D. The family treatment of alcoholism. Family Therapy Today 1986;1:1–2,6–7.
10. Campbell TW. Therapeutic relationships and iatrogenic outcomes: the blame-and-change maneuver in psychotherapy. Psychotherapy 1992;29(3):474–480.
11. Christopher J. How to stay sober: recovery without religion. Buffalo, NY: Prometheus Books, 1988.
12. Coleman S, Kaplan J, Downing R. Life cycle and loss: the spiritual vacuum of heroin addiction. Fam Process 1986;25(1):5–23.
13. Craig RJ. Contemporary trends in substance abuse. Professional Psychology: Research and Practice 1993;24:182–189.
14. Davis D. Alcoholism treatment: an integrative family and individual approach. New York: Gardner Press, 1987.
15. Douglas LJ. Perceived family dynamics of cocaine abusers, as compared to opiate abusers and non-drug abusers. Gainesville: University of Florida, 1987. Doctoral dissertation.
16. Duncan DF. Family stress and the initiation of adolescent drug abuse: a retrospective study. Corrective and Social Psychiatry 1978;24(3):111–114.
17. Eldred C, Washington M. Interpersonal relationships in heroin use by men and women and their role in treatment outcome. Int J Addict 1976;11:117–130.
18. Fals-Stewart W, Birchler GR, O'Farrell TJ. Behavioral couples therapy for male substance-abusing patients: effects on relationship adjustment and drug-using behavior. J Consult Clin Psychol (in press).
19. Galanter M. Network therapy for substance abuse: a clinical trial. Psychotherapy 1993;30(2):251–258.
20. Garrett J, Landau-Stanton J, Stanton MD, Stellato-Kabat J, Stellato-Kabat D. ARISE: a method for engaging reluctant alcohol- and drug-dependent individuals in treatment. J Subst Abuse Treat (in press).
21. Gorsuch RL, Butler MC. Initial drug abuse: a review of predisposing social psychological factors. Psychol Bull 1976;83(1):120–137.
22. Heard D. Death as a motivator: using crisis induction to break through the denial system. In: Stanton MD, Todd TC, eds. The family therapy

of drug abuse and addiction. New York: Guilford Press, 1982:203–234.

23. Heath A. Some new directions in ending family therapy. In: Breunlin D, ed. Stages: patterns of change over time. Rockville, MD: Aspen Systems, 1985:33–40.

24. Heath A, Atkinson B. Systemic treatment of substance abuse: a graduate course. J Marital Fam Ther 1988;14:411–418.

25. Heath A, Ayers T. MRI brief therapy with adolescent substance abusers. In: Todd T, Seleckman M, eds. Family therapy approaches with adolescent substance abusers. Boston: Allyn & Bacon, 1991:49–69.

26. Henggeler S, Borduin C, Melton G, Mann B, Smith L, Hall J, et al. Effects of multisystemic therapy on drug use and abuse in serious juvenile offenders: a progress report from two outcome studies. Fam Dynamics Addic Q 1991; 1(3):40–51.

27. Janzen C. Families in the treatment of alcoholism. J Stud Alcohol 1977;38:114–130.

28. Joanning H, Thomas F, Quinn W, Mullen R. Treating adolescent drug abuse: a comparison of family systems therapy, group therapy, and family drug education. J Marital Fam Ther 1992; 18(4):345–356.

29. Kaufman E. Family systems and family therapy of substance abuse: an overview of two decades of research and clinical experience. Int J Addict 1985;20(6&7):897–916.

30. Keller M. Trends in the treatment of alcoholism. In: Keller M, ed. Second special report to the U.S. Congress on alcohol and health. (DHEW: ADM 75–212). Washington, DC: U.S. Government Printing Office, 1974:111–127.

31. Kessler RC, McGonagle KA, Zhao S, Nelson CB, Hughes M, Eshleman S, et al. Lifetime and 12-month prevalence of DSM-III-R psychiatric disorders in the United States: results from the National Comorbidity Survey. Arch Gen Psychiatry 1994;51:8–19.

32. Kosten T, Jalali B, Kleber H. Complementary marital roles of male heroin addicts: evolution and intervention tactics. Am J Drug Alcohol Abuse 1982/1983;9(2):155–169.

33. Krueger DW. Stressful life events and the return to heroin use. J Human Stress 1981;7(2):3–8.

34. Levy B. Five years later: a follow-up of 50 narcotic addicts. Am J Psychiatry 1972;7:102–106.

35. Lewis R, Piercy F, Sprenkle D, Trepper T. Family-based interventions and community networking for helping drug abusing adolescents: The impact of near and far environments. J Adolesc Res 1990;5:82–95.

36. Liddle H, Dakof G, Parker K, Diamond G, Garcia R, Barrett K, Hurwitz S. Effectiveness of family therapy versus multi-family therapy and group therapy: results of the adolescents and families project—a randomized clinical trial. Paper presented at the Society of Psychotherapy Research Meeting, Pittsburgh, PA, June, 1993.

37. Liepman M, White W, Nirenberg T. Children of alcoholic families. In: Lewis D, Williams C, eds. Providing care for children of alcoholics: clinical and research perspectives. Pompano Beach, FL: Health Communications, 1986:39–64.

38. Mackenson G, Cottone RR. Family structural issues and chemical dependency: a review of the literature from 1985 to 1991. Am J Fam Ther 1992;20(3):227–241.

39. Madanes C, Dukes J, Haley J. Family ties of heroin addicts. Arch Gen Psychiatry 1977;37: 889–894.

40. Noone RJ. Drug abuse behavior in relation to change in the family structure. In: McCullough PG, Carolin JC, eds. Pittsburgh Family Systems Symposia: collection of papers. Pittsburgh, PA: Western Psychiatric Institute and Clinic, 1979–1980:174–186.

41. O'Farrell TJ. Marital and family therapy in alcoholism treatment. J Subst Abuse Treat 1989; 6(1):23–29.

42. O'Farrell TJ. Families and alcohol problems: an overview of treatment research. J Fam Psychol 1992;5:339–359.

43. O'Farrell TJ. Conclusions and future directions in practice and research on marital and family therapy in alcoholism treatment. In: O'Farrell TJ, ed. Treating alcohol problems: marital and family interventions. New York: Guilford Press, 1993:403–434.

44. Olson D, Russell C, Sprenkle D. Marital and family therapy: a decade review. J Marriage Family 1980;42(4):973–993.

45. Perzel JF, Lamon S. Enmeshment within families of polydrug abusers. Paper presented at the National Drug Abuse Conference, New Orleans, August, 1979.

46. Piercy F, Frankel B. The evolution of an integrative family therapy for substance-abusing adolescents: toward the mutual enhancement of research and practice. J Fam Psychol 1989;3: 5–25.

47. Preli R, Protinsky H. Aspects of family structures in alcoholic, recovered, and nonalcoholic families. J Marital Fam Ther 1988;14(3): 311–314.

48. Reilly D. Family factors in the etiology and treatment of youthful drug abuse. Fam Ther 1976;2:149–171.

49. Rosenbaum M, Richman J. Family dynamics and drug overdoses. Suicide and Life-Threatening Behavior 1972;2:19–25.

50. Schaef A. Codependence misunderstood/mistreated. New York: Harper & Row, 1986.

51. Schwartzman J, Bokos P. Methadone maintenance: the addict's family recreated. Int J Fam Ther 1979;4:338–355.

52. Scott S, Van Deusen J. Detoxification at home: a family approach. In: Stanton MD, Todd TC, eds. The family therapy of drug abuse and addiction. New York: Guilford Press, 1982: 310–334.

53. Searles J. The genetics of alcoholism: impact on family and sociological models of addiction. Fam Dynamics Addict Q 1991;1:8–21.

54. Stanton MD. The addict as savior: heroin, death and the family. Fam Process 1977;16:191–197.

55. Stanton MD. Drugs and the family: a review of the recent literature. Marriage Fam Rev 1979;2: 1–10.

56. Stanton MD. Family treatment approaches to drug abuse problems: A review. Fam Process 1979;18:251–280.

57. Stanton MD. Strategic approaches to family therapy. In: Gurman A, Kniskern D, eds. Handbook of family therapy. New York: Brunner/Mazel, 1981:361–402.

58. Stanton MD. Who should get credit for change which occurs in therapy? In: Gurman AS, ed. Questions and answers in the practice of family therapy. New York: Brunner/Mazel, 1981: 519–522.

59. Stanton MD. Appendix A: review of reports on drug abusers' family living arrangements and frequency of family contact. In: Stanton MD, Todd TC, eds. The family therapy of drug abuse and addiction. New York: Guilford Press, 1982.

60. Stanton MD. Coursework and self-study in the family treatment of alcohol and drug abuse: expanding Heath and Atkinson's curriculum. J Marital Fam Ther 1988;14(4):419–427.

61. Stanton MD. The Lobster Quadrille: issues and dilemmas for family therapy research. In: Wynne LC, ed. State of the art in family therapy research. New York: Family Process Press, 1988.

62. Stanton MD. The role of family and significant others in the engagement and retention of drug dependent individuals. NIDA Res Monogr (in press).

63. Stanton MD, Landau-Stanton J. Therapy with families of adolescent substance abusers. In: Milkman H, Sederer L, eds. Treatment choices in substance abuse. Lexington, MA: Lexington Books, 1990:329–339.

64. Stanton MD, Shadish WR. Outcome, attrition and family/couples treatment for drug abuse: a meta-analysis and review of the controlled, comparative studies. Psychol Bull (in press).

65. Stanton MD, Shea R, Garrett J. Family-of-origin contacts of alcoholics: an overlooked phenomenon. Rochester, NY: University of Rochester Medical Center. Unpublished manuscript.

66. Stanton MD, Steier F, Cook L, Todd TE. Narcotic detoxification in a family and home context: Final report 1980–1983 (Grant No. 5R01 DA 03097). Rockville, MD: National Institute on Drug Abuse, Treatment Research Branch, 1984.

67. Stanton MD, Steier F, Todd TC. Paying families for attending sessions: counteracting the dropout problem. J Marital Fam Ther 1982;8:371–373.

68. Stanton MD, Todd TC. Structural therapy with drug addicts. In: Kaufman E, Kaufmann P, eds. Family therapy of drug and alcohol abuse. New York: Gardner Press, 1979:55–69.

69. Stanton MD, Todd TC. Engaging resistant families in treatment. II: principles and techniques in recruitment. Fam Process 1981;20(3): 261–280.

70. Stanton MD, Todd TC. The therapy model. In: Stanton MD, Todd TC, eds. The family therapy of drug abuse and addiction. New York: Guilford Press, 1982:109–153.

71. Stanton MD, Todd TC. Structural-strategic family therapy with drug addicts. In: Kaufman E, Kaufmann P, eds. Family therapy of drug and alcohol abuse. 2nd edition. Needham Heights, MA: Allyn & Bacon, 1992:46–62.

72. Stanton MD, Todd TC, et al. The family therapy of drug abuse and addiction. New York: Guilford Press, 1982.

73. Steinglass P. Experimenting with family treatment approaches to alcoholism, 1950–1975: a review. Fam Process 1976;15:97–123.

74. Steinglass P, Bennett L, Wolin S, Reiss D. The alcoholic family. New York: Basic Books, 1987.

75. Szapocznik J, Kurtines WM, et al. Breakthroughs in family therapy with drug abusing and problem youth. New York: Springer-Verlag, 1989.

76. Trepper T, Piercy F, Lewis R, Volk R, Sprenkle D. Family therapy for adolescent substance abuse. In: O'Farrell TJ, ed. Treating alcohol problems: marital and family interventions. New York: Guilford Press, 1993:261–278.

77. Vaillant GE. A 12-year follow-up of New York narcotic addicts: III. Some social and psychiatric characteristics. Arch Gen Psychiatry 1966;15: 599–609.

78. Wegscheider S. Another chance: hope and health for the alcoholic family. Palo Alto, CA: Science and Behavior Books, 1981.

47 TREATMENT IN PRISONS AND JAILS

Nancy Mahon

As the incarceration rate in the United States continues to grow and the commitment to the so-called War on Drugs becomes more entrenched, imprisonment will be an increasingly common experience for certain communities, particularly drug users who are African-American or Hispanic. Today, over 1.5 million people are in prison or jail (1) and an additional 3.6 million are on probation or parole (2). Thus, over 5 million people—almost 3% of the country's adult population—are under some form of correctional supervision (2). African-Americans are incarcerated at a rate seven times higher than whites (1). Additionally, Hispanics are the fastest growing minority group in prison; they make-up 17.6% of federal and state prisoners in comparison to African-Americans, who represent 44.1%, and whites, who make-up 35.8% of the prison population (1).

Available statistics underestimate the number of drug users in prisons and jails because they are unable to accurately measure prisoners' behavior. Some of these data measure symptoms of drug use, such as the number of drug and drug-related offenses or results of urinalysis at the time of arrest. Other data, which attempt to address the issue of prisoners' behavior, rely on self-reporting from prisoners to correctional officials (3) about largely illegal drug use which prisoners have little impetus to report. Nevertheless, the number of *known* drug users behind bars is staggering. For instance, drug offenders represented 26% of all state and federal inmates in 1993, up from 8% in 1980 (1). Additionally, in 1991 (the most recent year for which data are available) half of state prisoners stated that they had taken illegal drugs in the month prior to arrest (3).

If piecing together such baseline data is difficult, understanding the relationship between incarceration and drug use is even more complex. Simply stated, the prevailing law enforcement theory in the United States asserts that through incapacitation, incarceration will decrease crime generally, drug-related crime in particular, and drug use overall. Critics and proponents of this theory abound, each marshaling a different set of statistics on crime trends from various time periods and localities (and often ignoring other statistics) to bolster their arguments. Despite this active debate, many questions about how incarceration affects drug use for individuals and populations remain largely unexamined. For instance, one survey of jail inmates in 1989 found that of inmates who reported that they regularly used drugs, 55% had not done so until after their first arrest (3). The role that incarceration plays in initiation into drug use and the health-related circumstances around such initiation needs to be explored. Additionally, other questions, such as the possible relationship between mental illness and drug use by prisoners and former prisoners, should also be examined further (4).

Until such issues are fully explored, the impact of incarceration on an individual's health and relationship to drugs and alcohol will be identified and addressed only by the individual, his or her family, and his or her health care providers. Also, as the United States becomes increasingly "correctionalized" by multiplying the numbers of people cycling in and out of correctional facilities, the experiences and conditions that individuals confront in prisons and jails will become more and more of a factor in health care and drug and alcohol treatment.

This chapter will provide background information on issues related to drug use and treatment in prisons and jails and identify drug-related issues of which health-care providers should be mindful in working with individuals who are currently, or may have previously been, incarcerated. Although much press is given to the notion that incarceration has been accepted as a common experience within some communities, there is still a stigma surrounding imprisonment for many former prisoners, particularly female ex-offenders. Individuals, therefore, may feel they need to be silent about their experience in the criminal justice system.

Epidemiological trends indicating high rates of tuberculosis, human immunodeficiency virus (HIV), hepatitis B and C, and sexually transmitted diseases in prison and jail populations highlight that creating an open and accepting environment for prisoners and former prisoners to discuss their experiences behind bars is a difficult, yet necessary, task for health care and drug treatment providers (5, 6). Providers should also speak openly with clients about whether the clients have had sexual or drug-related contact with former prisoners (7).

DRUG USE AND SEXUAL ACTIVITY IN PRISONS AND JAILS

Until recently in the United States, drug use and sexual activity behind bars was corrections' best kept secret. Prisoners and their advocates have known for some time, however, that sex and drug use is a daily aspect of prisoners' lives, and institutional denial of these behaviors exposes prisoners to HIV transmission and other dangers. There are some signs that correctional mythology is currently under siege. In a ground-breaking series of front-page articles on drug use behind bars, *The New York Times* recently referred to prisons as "warehouses of addiction" (8–10).

There has also been a slow trickle of studies on the rate of HIV transmission in correctional facilities (11, 12, which at least confirm in part the reality of high-risk behaviors in prisons and jails. The most current of these studies found a 21% conversion rate in a group of Florida state inmates (13). A study of prisoners' sex and drug use in New York State prisons and City jails detailed desperate acts among prisoners and between prisoners and correctional staff including sharing syringes, using make-shift syringes made from light bulbs and pens, and offering sex in exchange for drugs (14). As in the community, drug use behind bars is linked with sexual behavior because of prostitution and the possibility of HIV transmission between injection drug users (IDUs) and sex partners of IDUs.

No domestic research has been performed on the incidence and prevalence of drug use and sexual activity in prisons and jails; however, data from abroad indicate that such high-risk behaviors are prevalent (15–18). Studies in England and Scotland have shown that between 23 and 33% of IDUs inject while in custody (18) and between 66 and 75% of those prisoners who inject drugs while in custody share syringes (18). Regarding sexual behavior, a study in New South Wales, Australia, found that one-twelfth of their sample engaged in anal or oral sex in prison (19) while other data from South Australian prisons indicate that 12% of prisoners sampled engaged in anal sex while incarcerated (20).

International literature also suggests that correctional facilities present unique circumstances which increase the risk of HIV transmission. For instance, while no comparative data are available on the issue, Swiss public health officials infer that seroprevalence is higher among IDUs behind bars than IDUs on the street because inmates tend to be longer term drug users (21). Moreover, a study in Australian prisons found that HIV-positive IDUs were significantly more likely to inject in prison than IDUs that were HIV-negative or who did not know their HIV status (22). Lastly, the risk of HIV-negative IDUs becoming HIV-infected appears to be higher for those in custody because sterile syringes are less available than they are on the street, thus increasing the likelihood of sharing equipment and of sharing with a greater number of users (22).

In focusing on the role of incarceration in promoting risk behaviors, an Australian study has found that incarceration may contribute to the initiation of some users into injection drug use and of some IDUs into sharing works (15). This research has also shown that some previously active drug users abstain from use while incarcerated but intend to "pick up" after they are released into the community (15, 23). This group of abstainers could be an important target population for treatment programs in correctional facilities. However, unless and until such programs honestly confront the reality that drug users have a choice of whether to use drugs in prisons and jails, this potential treatment opportunity will be lost.

HARM REDUCTION IN PRISONS AND JAILS

For those prisoners who choose to engage in high-risk sex and drugs or for whom drug treatment is not available, models for responsive HIV prevention and harm reduction programs in prisons and jails also exist outside the United States. Currently, 6 nations have methadone programs, 12 distribute condoms and dental dams, 12 distribute bleach, 2 have pilot needle exchange programs, and 1 has a pilot heroin prescription program (19). By comparison, only six jurisdictions within the United States distribute condoms to male prisoners and two distribute them to female prisoners. No jurisdiction distributes bleach or any other form of drug-related harm reduction tools, and only one jail system, New York City, has a methadone detoxification and treatment program, KEEP, which is explained in detail later in this chapter.

In an era when chain gangs and other highly punitive measures against prisoners are gaining public support, arguments in favor of expanding harm reduction for prisoners may seem politically far afield of the public debate on prisons and jails. But sound public health practices and politics are often strangers, particularly when minority populations are involved. A full consideration of issues surrounding the implementation of harm reduction programs in United States correctional facilities exceed the scope of this chapter. Briefly stated, however, the opposition to such programs comes largely from correctional officials who assert that such programs would create security risks and would be seen as an implicit acceptance of sexual and drug-related behaviors that correctional regulations explicitly prohibit.

Regarding the first issue, to date, none of the domestic distribution programs of latex barriers for prisoners have had incidences of drug smuggling or other security-related problems. As for clean needle distribution for reduction of drug-related harms, pilot programs in Swiss prisons have found that clean needles which are used and then properly disposed of by inmates, pose far less of a security and health risk to prisoners and guards than makeshift items that are used for syringes and dirty syringes, conditions which already exist in correctional populations (24). Lastly, prisoner-participants in a domestic study on sex and drug use in prisons and jails indicated that they would not view harm reduction programs as an official imprimatur of prohibited behavior, but rather as disease control (14). Here the participants emphasized that if they were found to be in violation of correctional regulations that they should be punished under the regulations rather than by being exposed to illness (14).

Drug use in prisons and jails clearly raises drug enforcement issues for correctional officials. Drug trafficking appears to be endemic behind bars. Drugs enter the facilities through the mail, visitors, and staff. Anecdotal evidence and media reports indicate that individual personnel, and in some instances, smuggling rings and organized crime are involved in drug-trafficking (21) and that staff involvement may be widespread. Between 1990 and March 1995, for instance, 26 correctional employees were charged with smuggling drugs into Rikers Island jail complex in New York City (25). As in the community, it is clear that where there is a demand for drugs, there is also a supply. In the future, one would hope that funds are neither solely nor primarily invested in drug interdiction efforts, but in harm reduction and treatment programs for prisoners.

DRUG TREATMENT IN PRISONS AND JAILS

Prisons and jails provide an important opportunity for delivering substance abuse treatment for inmates who want to manage their opiate addiction with methadone or stop using drugs. Although politicians frequently cite the need for such services and call for their expansion (26), too few service and evaluation dollars find their way to such programs. To borrow from an old saying, if there was a dollar of funding for every time a politician pledged

support for such programs, there would be many, many more drug treatment programs in jails and prisons than exist today.

Indeed, drug treatment programs in correctional facilities are largely unavailable, underutilized, or not able to realize their full potential for a variety of reasons which will be briefly explored here. Before embarking on such an explanation, it is important to clarify one institutional difference between jails and prisons. The typical length of stay in a jail is shorter than in a prison. Jails are operated by cities or counties and detain people who have been arrested and are waiting to appear before a judge to be formally charged with an offense, people who are being detained prior to or during their trial, and inmates serving less than a year sentence which is sometimes referred to as "City Time," or in the case of a county jail, "County Time." These shorter lengths of stay make operating drug treatment and any other service program a challenge. Whether the facility is a jail or a prison, however, it is important to remember that the primary job of corrections is locking people up, not rehabilitating them.

Drug treatment is the exception rather than the rule in prisons and jails. For instance, one study which collected data from 1987 to 1989 from close to 17,000 IDUs who were not in treatment, found that 83% of the participants had been incarcerated but 81% had never been in a formal drug treatment program while they were imprisoned (27). A government report further found that in 1991 only 1% of inmates in federal prisons who had moderate to severe drug abuse problems had received appropriate treatment and, yet, at the same time, less than 50% of the treatment slots available to these inmates were filled (28). In a similar inquiry focusing on state prisons, another federal report found that less than 20% of state inmates who had a history of drug abuse were receiving treatment (29).

Regarding local correctional facilities, a recent survey of jails found that only 6.7% of the average inmate population were enrolled in a drug treatment program. Significantly, the study also found that only 20% of jails provided detoxification services (30).

Beyond head counting, it is also important to examine the substance and structure of drug treatment-related services that a particular correctional facility or system may call a "program." Many of these services would not be classified as a drug treatment program by those in the substance abuse field. By way of example, 34% of jails that stated that they provided drug treatment programs in the study mentioned above, in fact, only offered volunteer-based services, which generally consisted of allowing community volunteers from Alcoholics and Narcotics Anonymous to conduct meetings in the facilities on an occasional basis (30).

In addition to the numerical paucity of drug treatment programs behind bars, those programs that do exist are often not as effective as they might be because of a variety of issues, including lack of a comprehensive treatment model within the criminal justice system that would follow inmates through the criminal justice pipeline from the courthouse to correctional facilities to community-based aftercare programs, lack of standards for staffing and delivery of treatment programs, and lack of adequate evaluation data (31, 32).

Each of these issues is complex in its own right and merits considerable thought and discussion among the public, correctional officials, legislators, funders, and drug treatment professionals, and other health care providers. Such a discussion far exceeds the scope of this chapter, but it is worth noting that each of these issues raises perennial questions in both the drug treatment and correctional fields. For instance, with regard to staffing, one major question is, given corrections' primary mission of custody and control and its prohibition of drug use behind bars, should correctional personnel staff drug treatment programs or should they be staffed by outside community-based organizations? Additionally, on the program evaluation front, there are also weighty considerations about what criteria should be used to evaluate the success of a drug treatment program for prisoners. Should it be program completion, relapse, re-arrest, or perhaps other markers of post-release self-sufficiency, such as locating housing and community-based services? Or should it be a combination of all of these factors?

Unfortunately, many, if not most, drug treatment programs in corrections do not ever confront these outcome-related questions because the programs live and die without ever being evaluated. The average life of programs based on the prevailing model of substance abuse treatment in corrections, the therapeutic community, is 6.5 years (32). Significantly, when these programs are forced to shut their doors, the causes are largely administrative or fiscal issues such as loss of staffing, budget cuts, prison overcrowding and the like, rather than because of any problem to the treatment model (32).

On the issue of target populations, similar to community-based services, substance abuse programs in prisons and jails include programs with a range of target communities such as women, men, juveniles, as well as subpopulations defined by the security level of the facility, crime of commitment, drug of choice, and other criteria. Each of these populations and subpopulations is a study in and of itself. In general, correctional substance abuse treatment would benefit greatly if the distinct challenges of delivering a service dependent upon self-revelation in a coercive atmosphere were recognized and more explicitly confronted within the correctional substance abuse treatment community, and if the larger substance abuse treatment community more readily and completely welcomed their correctional colleagues into the larger substance abuse treatment community.

MODEL PROGRAMS

Examining a few model programs in greater detail may crystallize the issues addressed thus far and more fully convey the impact of the correctional setting on the delivery of substance abuse services. This section will explore a prison-based treatment program based on the therapeutic community (TC) model, Stay'n Out, and a jail-based methadone program, The Key Extended Entry Program (KEEP).

Stay'n Out

As mentioned earlier, the TC model is the prevailing treatment model in corrections. The Stay'n Out program belongs to the first generation of such programs and has received a fair amount of notoriety due to an early, laudatory evaluation of the program. Stay'n Out opened in 1977 at Arthurkill Correctional Facility, a state prison for men in Staten Island, New York. A year later, the program expanded to Bayview Correctional Facility in New York City, which houses women. Currently, Stay'n Out includes three 35-bed units at Arthurkill and one 40-bed unit at Bayview (32). To be eligible for the program an inmate must: (*a*) have a history of substance abuse; (*b*) have participated in other correctional programs during the prior 6 months; (*c*) desire to join the program; (*d*) be within 2 years of appearing in front of the Parole Board; (*e*) have no history of violence within the correctional system during the prior 8 months, and (*f*) have no history of mental illness, sex crimes, or attempts at escape (33).

As is true for all TCs, Stay'n Out is a highly structured program in which participants live apart from the general prison population. Staff members are generally people in recovery from substance abuse and thus serve as role models. Group counseling sessions and peer pressure enforce a sense of community order and inmates are responsible for maintaining the unit through work chores. When an inmate acts in a manner which is viewed as positive by the program, the inmate is rewarded with a higher level job with more status and responsibilities (34). Participants are encouraged to enroll in community-based TCs after release, and approximately half of them do so (32).

In 1984, under a grant from the National Institute on Drug Abuse, the program underwent a rigorous outcome evaluation study. In an example of how the correctional substance abuse field can add to the larger substance abuse knowledge-base, the evaluation not only evaluated the effectiveness of a prison-based TC in comparison to two other forms of in-prison treatment, but also tested the efficacy of what was termed the "time-in-program" hypothesis. This hypothesis posited that the effect of community-based TCs was severely limited by the high dropout rate of participants prior to completing three months of the program (34). The study concluded that Stay'n Out reduced recidivism rates, the Stay'n Out TC model was more effective in reducing recidivism rates than either non-TC based residential treatment or individual counseling alone, and that the more time that participants remained enrolled in Stay'n Out, the more successful they were in establishing crime-free and healthy lives (34).

Business Week has estimated that a Stay'n Out bed costs $8 day more than a regular prison bed (35). If participation in Stay'n Out and similar prison-based TCs continues to lead to the reduction in recidivism found in the 1989, however, then the $8 is wisely spent.

KEEP

Established in 1987, KEEP is located on Rikers Island jail complex in New York City and it is the only methadone treatment and detoxification program for incarcerated heroin addicts in the United States (36). As is true for most innovative services for prisoners, the program came about through a combination of the vision and persistence of several dedicated front-line service providers as well as historical factors which made correctional officials more receptive to innovation. In 1987, New York was experiencing jail overcrowding and unrest, which was caused at least in part by surging rates of heroin and other drug-related arrests (36). The HIV infection rate in the jail population was also multiplying. Lastly, prior to KEEP's inception, a successful methadone detoxification program had existed. Indeed, providers in the latter program performed 16,000 detoxifications on the 80,000 admissions to Rikers in 1986, the year prior to KEEP's establishment (37).

Against this backdrop, the Montefiore Rikers Island Health Services, which contracts with the New York City Health and Hospitals Corporation to provide medical and mental health care to prisoners on Rikers Island, allied with the City Department of Corrections and the State Division of Substance Abuse Services to establish the program. KEEP was only implemented, however, after substantial philosophical and operational opposition from the Department of Corrections (36).

KEEP's primary aim is to provide opiate-dependent inmates who will be detained for a relatively short amount of time with methadone treatment during the period of incarceration and a guaranteed place in a community-based methadone program after release. To be eligible, an inmate must be diagnosed as opiate dependent by medical staff, and his or her pending charges must be either a misdemeanor or low-level felony or the crime of conviction must be for a misdemeanor. This latter criteria is in place to exclude from the program inmates who may be transferred to state prisons where methadone treatment is not available. KEEP participants who were abusing illegal opiates at the time of arrest are maintained on 30 milligrams of methadone, whereas participants who have verifiably participated in a community-based methadone program are maintained on 40 milligrams of methadone regardless of the dosage they received in the community. Recently, there has been controversy over the dosage amounts for participants to the effect that dosages for both groups were too low when compared to dosages used in the community. Program coordinators are seeking to change the dosage policy so that dosing for prisoners is more in line with the standards in the community and participants enrolled in community-based programs at the time of arrest are maintained on Rikers on the dose that they received at the community program (36).

A federally funded evaluation of the program in 1989 found that KEEP had many successes but that it was not fulfilling its full potential due to staffing and funding shortages, and lack of counseling and other pre- and post release support services for participants. KEEP received additional funding in 1992 to enable the program to provide prerelease support services such as relapse prevention, discharge planning, individual counseling, and placement in alternative-to-incarceration programs and drug-free treatment programs in the community.

In 1994, KEEP treated 3700 inmates, approximately one quarter of whom were women. The daily census that year was 400 in the KEEP program and 300 in the detoxification program. The fact that the program has not been replicated is in part attributable to the controversial nature of methadone within the larger community, the lack of prioritization of programs for prisoners, and perhaps the relative decrease since 1987 of the use of heroin in comparison to crack cocaine and other drugs. With the recent increase of the use of heroin, replication of KEEP should be seriously considered.

CONCLUSION

For too many years, drug treatment in prisons and jails has occupied a small corner of the treatment world and has solely been the concern of the small number of correctional personnel and community-based organizations that delivered the services. Substance abuse treatment providers on both sides of the prison and jail walls along with legislators, correctional officials, and community leaders must work together to ensure that adequate, continuous drug treatment is delivered to individuals before, during, and after periods of incarceration. Ironically, it may be the incarceration of increasing numbers of drug users that finally brings together all these players to begin this important task. In addressing this issue, one would hope that we could all employ some of the hard lessons that managed care is teaching the community about the structure of substance abuse treatment, namely, that a cheaper per slot cost bears little relationship to the long-term effectiveness and thus ultimate economic and humanitarian value of substance abuse treatment.

References

1. Prisoners in 1994. U.S. Department of Justice, Bureau of Justice Statistics, August 1995. NCJ-151654.
2. The nation's correctional population tops 5 million [press release]. U.S. Department of Justice, Bureau of Justice Statistics, August 27, 1995.
3. Drugs, Crime, Facts, 1994. U.S. Department of Justice, Bureau of Justice Statistics, June 1995. NCJ-154043.
4. Steadman HJ, Morris SM, Dennis DL. The diversion of mentally ill persons from jails to community based services: a profile of programs. Am J Pub Health 1995;85:1630–1635.
5. Berkman A. Prison health: the breaking point. Am J Pub Health 1995;85:1616–1618.
6. Mahon N. Where medical care is criminal. New York Times 1994(July 2):A24.
7. Mahon N. Lockdown: living with AIDS/HIV behind bars. In: LIFEBeat Urban AID, The Music Industry Fights AIDS [concert program]. Concert presented at Madison Square Garden, New York, City, October 5, 1995.
8. Verhovek SM. A change in governors stalls model drug program in Texas. New York Times 1995(July 4):A1.
9. Treaster JB. Drug therapy: powerful tool reaching few inside prisons. New York Times 1995 (July 3):A1.
10. Purdy M. Bars don't stop the flow of drugs into the prisons. New York Times 1995(July 2):A1.
11. Castro K, Shansky R, Scardino V, Narkunas J, Coe J, Hammett T. HIV transmission in correctional facilities. Paper presented at Seventh International Conference on AIDS, Florence, Italy, 1991.
12. Horsburgh RC, Jarvis JQ, McArthur T, Ignacio RN, Stock P. Seroconversion to human immunodeficiency virus in prison inmates. Am J Pub Health 1990;80:209–210.
13. Mutter RC, Grimes RM, Labarthe D. Evidence of intraprison spread of HIV infection. Arch Intern Med 1994;4:793–795.

14. Mahon N. High risk behavior for HIV transmission in New York State prisons and city jails. Am J Public Health 1996;86:1211–1215.
15. Crofts N, Thompson S, Wale E, Hernberger F. Risk behaviors for blood-borne viruses in a Victorian prison.(in press).
16. Dolan K, Wodak A, Hall W, Gaughwin M, Rae F. HIV risk behavior before, during and after imprisonment in New South Wales. Addictions Research (in press).
17. Michels II. Prevention, education and support strategies (in Germany). Paper presented at IXth International Conference on AIDS, Roundtable 14, Berlin, Germany, June 10, 1993.
18. Turnbull P, Stimson GV, Stillwell G. Drug use in prison. West Sussex, England: The Centre for Research on Drugs and Health Behavior, 1994:3.
19. Dolan K, Hall W, Wodak A. Bleach availability and risk behaviors in prison in New South Wales. Sydney, Australia: National Drug and Alcohol Research Centre, 1994(July):14.
20. Gaughwin MD, Douglas RM, Liew CY, et al. HIV prevalence and risk behaviors for HIV transmission in South Australia prison. AIDS 1991;5:845–851.
21. HIV prevention in Switzerland. Liebefeld/Bern, Switzerland: Federal Office of Public Health and National AIDS Commission, 1993:138.
22. Dolan KA, Donoghoe M, Stimson G. Drug injecting and syringe sharing in custody and in the community. The Howard Journal 1990;29:177–186.
23. Berger. 10 guards are charged in smuggling. New York Times 1994(April 21):B1.
24. Project-Pilote de prevention du SIDA dans les etablissements penitentiaires de Hindelbank. Berne, Switzerland: L'Office Federal de la Sante Publique; 1995 Sept; Feinkonzept fur die Strafanstalt Kanton Solothurn. Solothurn, Switzerland: Kontrollierte Opiatobgabe in der Strafanstalt, 1995 May.
25. Purdy M. Rikers officers are arrested in a drug sting. New York Times 1995(March 21):Metro.

26. McCaffrey B. The drug czar's agenda [letter to the editor]. Washington Post 1996(March 25): A16.
27. Risk behavior for HIV transmission among intravenous drug uses not in treatment—United States, 1987–89. MMWR 1990;39:273–276.
28. Drug treatment. Despite new strategy, few federal inmates receive treatment. Report to the Committee on Government Operations, House of Representatives (GAO/HRD-92–116). Washington, DC: U.S. General Accounting Office, 1991.
29. Drug treatment. State prisons face challenges in providing services. Report to the Committee on Government Operations, House of Representatives (GAO/HRD-91–128). Washington, DC: U.S. General Accounting Office, 1991.
30. Peters RH, May RL, Kearns WD. Drug treatment in jails: results of a nationwide survey. J Crim Justice 1992;20:283–295.
31. Peters RH, Kearns WD, Murrin MR, Dolente AS, May RL. Examining the effectiveness of in-jail substance abuse treatment. J Offender Rehab 1993;19:1–39.
32. Leukefeld CG, Tims FM. The challenge of drug abuse treatment in prisons and jails. NIDA Res Monogr 1992;118:1–7.
33. Stay'n Out [program brochure]. New York: New York Therapeutic Communities, Inc., undated.
34. Wexler HK, Falkin GP, Lipton DS. Outcome evaluation of a prison therapeutic community for substance abuse treatment. Crim Just Behav 1990;17:71–90.
35. A real chance for a turnaround. Business Week 1989(November 27):192.
36. Tomasino VJ, Nolan JG. Key Extended Entry Program (KEEP): a multi-modality addiction services program. Montefiore Rikers Island Health Services Mental Health Department Report, 1995:1–3.
37. Magura S, Rosenblum A, Joseph H. Evaluation of in-jail methadone maintenance: preliminary results. NIDA Res Monogr 1992;118:192–210.

48 Relapse Prevention

Dennis C. Daley and G. Alan Marlatt

Individuals with substance use disorders face the possibility of relapse once they have initiated cessation of alcohol or other drug use. As a result of the problem of relapse, increasing emphasis has been placed on the maintenance stage of the change process for individuals with all types and combinations of substance use disorders. A number of relapse prevention (RP) approaches have been developed to help clinicians address relapse (8, 9, 16, 28, 44, 68, 89, 90). Initially developed for individuals with alcohol and drug problems, the principles and concepts of RP have been adapted to other addictive disorders and problems of impulse control, including smoking (93, 97), compulsive overeating (14, 103), sexual offenses (61), violence (42), and dual diagnosis—substance abuse combined with psychiatric illness (31, 82).

The purpose of this chapter is to review RP strategies that can be used in helping the individual with a substance use disorder. Before specific RP intervention strategies are reviewed, definitions of recovery, lapse, and relapse are provided, treatment outcome studies are summarized, common relapse precipitants are delineated, and models of RP are reviewed briefly. The cognitive and behavioral interventions discussed represent the common issues or themes espoused in the various RP treatment models. This chapter is based on a review of the literature on RP and the authors' experience developing and conducting RP programs aimed at helping clients maintain change and address common problems and issues associated with relapse.

OVERVIEW OF RECOVERY AND RELAPSE

Recovery

Recovery from a substance use disorder is the process of initiating abstinence from alcohol or other drug use as well as making intrapersonal and interpersonal changes to maintain this change over time. Specific changes vary among people with substance use disorders and occur in any of the following areas of functioning: physical, psychological, behavioral, interpersonal, family, social, spiritual, and financial (26, 29). It is generally accepted that recovery tasks are contingent on the stage or phase of recovery the individual is in (13, 114). Recovery is mediated by the severity and degree of damage caused by the substance use disorder, the presence of a comorbid psychiatric or medical illness, and the individual's perception, motivation, gender, ethnic background, and support system. Although some individuals may achieve full recovery, others achieve a partial recovery (44). The latter may experience multiple relapses over time.

Recovering from a substance use disorder involves gaining information, increasing self-awareness, developing skills for sober living, and following a program of change. The program of change may involve professional treatment, participation in self-help programs (Alcoholics Anonymous (AA), Narcotics Anonymous (NA), or Cocaine Anonymous (CA), Rational Recovery, SMART Recovery, Men or Women for Sobriety, Dual Recovery Anonymous) and self-management approaches. In the earlier phases of recovery, the individual typically relies more on external support and help from professionals, sponsors, or other members of support groups. As recovery progresses, more reliance is placed on oneself to handle problems and the challenges of living a sober lifestyle. The information and skills learned as part of RP offer an excellent mechanism to prepare for the maintenance phase of recovery.

Lapse and Relapse

The term *lapse* refers to the initial episode of alcohol or other drug use following a period of abstinence (68), whereas the term *relapse* refers to failure to maintain behavior change over time (8). Relapse can be viewed not only as the *event* of resumption of a pattern of substance abuse or dependency but also as a *process* in which indicators or warning signs appear prior to the individual's actual substance use (24).

A lapse may end quickly or lead to a relapse of varying proportions. Shiffman (97), for example, reported that 63% of lapsers who called his Stay-Quit line were smoking 2 weeks later. Thirty-seven percent were able to stop their lapses. The effects of the initial lapse are mediated by the person's affective and cognitive reactions. A full-blown relapse is more likely with the individual who has a strong perception of violating the abstinence rule (64). Although some individuals experience a full-blown relapse and return to pretreatment levels of substance abuse, others use alcohol and drugs problematically but do not return to previous levels of abuse and suffer less harmful effects as a result. Relapsers vary in the quantity and frequency of substance use as well as the medical and psychosocial sequelae that accompany a relapse.

TREATMENT OUTCOME STUDIES

Numerous reviews of the treatment outcome literature as well as studies of specific clinical populations receiving treatment generally have documented high rates of relapse among alcoholics, smokers, and drug abusers. Miller and Hester (76) reviewed more than 500 alcoholism outcome studies and reported that more than three-quarters of subjects relapsed within 1 year of treatment. Emrick (37) reviewed 384 studies of psychologically oriented alcoholism treatment and also reported that most treated clients relapsed. After review by Catalano et al. of numerous alcoholism treatment outcome studies, they similarly reported high rates of relapse (19). They also reviewed studies of relapse rates for opioid addicts and found relapse rates ranging from 25% to 97%. Relapse rates were lowest among opiate addicts who graduated from a therapeutic community in which they resided for a minimum of 18–24 months. Catalano and colleagues' review of tobacco de-

pendence interventions found relapse rates within 1 year to be in the 75–80% range. Hunt et al. (53) reported that 65–70% of alcoholics, heroin addicts, and smokers relapsed within the first year of treatment, most within the first 90 days. Simpson and colleagues (100) followed a group of 405 opioid addicts 12 years after admission to drug abuse treatment programs. At year 12, 26% were using opioids on a daily basis, 39% were using some opioids, 61% were using marihuana, 47% were using other drugs, and 27% were drinking more than 4 ounces of alcohol per day. However, there was a significant reduction in daily opioid use, from 47% at year 1 to 26% at year 12. Hoffmann and Harrison (50) followed 1957 adult clients with alcohol and/or drug problems who were treated in five different treatment centers in the St. Paul, Minnesota, area. They reported that approximately 50% of clients were abstinent for the entire 2-year period. The Comprehensive Assessment and Treatment Outcome Research (CATOR) group, an independent evaluation service for the substance abuse field, followed 8087 patients from 38 inpatient programs and 1663 patients from 19 different programs for 1 year (52). Sobriety rates at 1 year were 60% for inpatient and 68% for outpatient subjects successfully contacted at 6 and 12 months. Even when these rates are adjusted and assume a 70% relapse rate for missing cases, sobriety rates at 1 year are 44% and 52% for the inpatient and outpatient cohorts. This research shows that in addition to stopping or reducing substance use, clients receiving substance abuse treatment evidence significant decreases in posttreatment medical care for expensive hospital services, work problems including absenteeism, working under the influence, traffic violations, and other arrests. In a recent analysis of the alcohol treatment outcome literature, Miller and colleagues (78) reported that there was a "significant" treatment effect on at least one alcohol measure for at least one follow-up point" for 146 of 211 studies (69%) (p. 17). Despite relapse rates, many studies show that treatment of substance use disorders has positive effects on multiple domains of functioning.

The reader is cautioned about making generalizations regarding the effectiveness of treatment based on outcome studies or based on the sole criterion of resumption of substance use. Many methodological deficiencies have been noted in outcome studies (1, 41, 78, 96). These include lack of standardized measures of relapse or definition of successful outcome, problems with sample selection, small sample size, attrition, and length of follow-up interval (6, 16, 19, 51).

Individuals who relapse do not always return to pretreatment levels of substance use. The actual quantity and frequency of use may vary dramatically. A cocaine or heroin addict who injected large quantities of drugs on a daily basis for years may return to substance use after treatment. Yet this individual may not return to daily use, and the quantity of drugs used may be significantly less than the pretreatment level. Since drug and alcohol use is only one outcome measure, an individual may show improvement in other areas of life functioning despite an actual lapse or relapse to substance use.

Inpatient vs. Outpatient Treatment

Managed care has challenged drug and alcohol service providers to demonstrate that the treatment they offer is both clinically and cost effective. As a result, there is a movement away from more intensive and expensive inpatient, residential treatment programs toward less expensive, short-term outpatient programs. Most of the literature supports the use of less costly outpatient treatment. For example, Annis (6) reviewed six well-controlled randomized trials of longer versus shorter periods of inpatient alcoholism treatment and found no advantage for prolonged hospitalization. She also reviewed two well-controlled randomized trials comparing inpatient treatment with day treatment or partial hospitalization and found no advantage for inpatient care. Miller and Hester's (76) review of uncontrolled studies and 26 controlled studies similarly showed no overall advantage for inpatient over outpatient treatment or for more intensive over less intensive interventions for alcohol abuse. They believe that more intensive treatment is beneficial for more severely deteriorated and less socially stable individuals (77). Nace (81), on the other hand, suggests that negative reports on inpatient treatment are biased and based on studies that are flawed. He makes a case for the efficacy of inpatient treatment and delineates a number of advantages over outpatient treatment, particularly for clients with severe alcohol dependence or extensive social, psychiatric, or medical comorbidity.

Studies by McLellan and colleagues (71) showed that the effectiveness of substance abuse treatment increased significantly when clients were "matched" with the most appropriate level of treatment prospectively. Miller (75) also makes a strong case for matching clients with the appropriate interventions and points out numerous benefits.

RELAPSE PRECIPITANTS

Research by Marlatt and colleagues led to classifying relapse for alcoholics, smokers, heroin addicts, gamblers, and overeaters in two broad categories, intrapersonal and interpersonal determinants (68). This classification scheme has been found useful in other countries also (94). Intrapersonal determinants contributing to relapse include negative emotional states, negative physical states, positive emotional states, testing of personal control, and urges and temptations. According to this research, the category that most frequently affected relapse of alcoholics, smokers, and heroin addicts was negative emotional states. Thirty-eight percent of alcoholics, 37% of smokers, and 19% of heroin addicts relapsed in response to a negative affective state. Shiffman (97) reported that negative affect or stress was a factor in 52% of relapses of smokers who called his Stay-Quit line. In a study examining the posttreatment relationship between panic/phobic symptoms and substance use, LaBounty and colleagues (60) found that significantly more anxious clients reported relapsing to cope with depression, anxiety, and anger compared to matched controls without anxiety problems.

Interpersonal precipitants of relapse include relationship conflict, social pressure to use substances, and positive emotional states associated with some type of interaction with others (68, 95, 106). Social pressure to use drugs was identified by 36% of heroin addicts, 32% of smokers, and 18% of alcoholics as contributing to their relapses (68). Havassy and colleagues (49) reported that greater social support and spousal support predicted a lower risk of relapse among alcoholics, opiate users, and cigarette smokers completing treatment.

Catalano et al. (19) published an extensive review of rates and determinants of relapse. They investigated the strength of evidence for factors associated with relapse to alcohol, tobacco, and opiate use according to pretreatment, treatment, and posttreatment variables. For opiate addicts, the variables most strongly associated with relapse were degree of impairment caused by drug use, psychiatric impairment, length and modality of treatment, involvement in crime, lack of family and peer support, negative emotional states, and skill deficits. For alcoholics, the factors strongly associated with relapse were lack of family or peer support, negative emotional states, skill deficits, and negative life events. For smokers, the variables most strongly associated with relapse were negative emotional states and problems in family or peer relationships. Many other pretreatment, treatment, and posttreatment factors either had "some" association with relapse or were found to have an equivocal effect on outcome.

A review of the literature by Daley has led to a modification of Marlatt's categories of relapse precipitants (26–28). Relapse can be understood as resulting from an interaction of client-, family-, social-, and treatment-related factors (10, 21, 38, 55, 57, 73–75, 95, 101, 105, 106, 108). These include affective variables (e.g., negative or positive mood states), behavioral variables (e.g., coping skills or social skill deficits; impulsivity), cognitive variables (e.g., attitudes toward recovery, self-perception of ability to cope with high-risk situations, and level of cognitive functioning), environmental and interpersonal variables (e.g., lack of social or family stability, social pressures to use substances, lack of productive work or school roles, and lack of involvement in leisure or recreational interests), physiological variables (e.g., cravings, protracted withdrawal symptoms, chronic illness or physical pain, or response to medications used for medical or psychiatric disorders), psychiatric variables (e.g., presence of a comorbid psychiatric illness, sexual trauma, a higher global rating of psychiatric severity), spiritual variables (e.g., excessive guilt and shame, feelings of emptiness, a sense that life lacks meaning), and treatment-related variables (e.g., negative attitudes of caregivers; inadequate aftercare services following rehabilitation programs; lack of integrated services for dual diagnosis clients).

OVERVIEW OF RELAPSE PREVENTION

RP emerged as a way of helping the individual with a substance use disorder maintain change over time. Factors associated with achieving initial change (i.e., abstinence) differ from those associated with the maintenance of change over time (63). RP generally refers to two types of treatment strategies. First, RP may be incorporated in any treatment aimed at helping an individual with a substance use problem maintain abstinence once substances are stopped. In a general sense, all psychosocial treatments (e.g., drug counseling or 12-step counseling, supportive-expressive psychotherapy, coping skills training, cue exposure, contingency contracting, cognitive, behavioral, or cognitive-behavioral therapies) and pharmacological treatments (e.g., Trexan, ReVia, Antabuse) aim to help the client remain substance free and prevent relapse. Second, specific coping skills-oriented treatments incorporating the major tenets and interventions or approach discussed in the section below may comprise a specific program referred to as relapse prevention. The focus of RP is to reduce the relapse risk by addressing potential precipitants of relapse and high-risk factors.

A variety of models of RP are described in the literature. The more common approaches include (a) Marlatt and Gordon's cognitive-behavioral approach, which has been adapted for other clinical populations such as sex offenders, overeaters, and individuals with problems controlling sexual behaviors; (b) Annis' cognitive-behavioral approach, which incorporates concepts of Marlatt's model with Bandura's self-efficacy theory; (c) Daley's psychoeducational approach; (d) Gorski's neurological impairment model; and (e) Zackon, McAuliffe, and Ch'ien's addict aftercare model. A more complete description of these and other RP models is available elsewhere (26–28, 35, 104, 112).

Many inpatient and outpatient treatment programs have incorporated various aspects of these RP approaches. Some programs offer specific "relapse tracks" that are geared specifically for clients who have relapsed following a period of sustained recovery. The focus of these programs is primarily on problems and issues associated with relapse (28). Despite their differences, these RP approaches have many components in common. They focus on the need for individuals with a substance use disorder to develop new coping skills for handling high-risk situations and relapse warning signs; to make lifestyle changes to decrease the need for alcohol, drugs, or tobacco; to increase healthy activities; to prepare for interrupting lapses so that they do not end in a full-blown relapse; and to prepare for managing relapses so that adverse consequences may be minimized. All RP approaches emphasize the need to have a broad repertoire of behavioral, cognitive, and interpersonal coping strategies to help prevent a relapse. Most are time-limited or brief, making them more feasible in the current climate of managed care.

Empirical Studies of Relapse Prevention

There is evidence that RP does help improve recovery and reduce relapse rates (6, 8, 9, 16, 113). However, it should be noted that to date there is no superior treatment approach for substance use disorders. Carroll and colleagues (17) conducted a study of outpatient cocaine abusers in which they compared RP to interpersonal psychotherapy (IPT). RP was more effective than IPT for patients with more severe cocaine problems and, to some extent, for those with higher psychiatric severity. In another study of outpatient cocaine abusers, Carroll and colleagues (18) compared the outcomes of 12 weeks of treatment in which patients were randomized to psychotherapy (cognitive-behavioral RP or an operationalized clinical management condition) and pharmacotherapy (desipramine hydrochloride or placebo) in a 2 × 2 design. Patients were followed for 1 year and the research team found a significant psychotherapy-by-time effect, indicating a delayed improved response to treatment for patients who received RP.

In a study of 60 men with problem drinking, subjects receiving a relapse program returned to problematic alcohol use at a rate 4–7 times less rapidly than subjects in a discussion control group (95). A study of inpatient alcoholic veterans conducted by Chaney and colleagues (20) reported that results consistently favored clients receiving RP over those receiving a discussion group (DG). Clients in the RP group drank less, had fewer episodes of intoxication, experienced less severe lapses for shorter periods of time, and stopped drinking significantly sooner after a relapse compared to clients in the DG. A study of alcoholics receiving inpatient treatment, conducted by Koski-Jannes (57), found that there was greater treatment adherence and satisfaction, reduced lengths of inpatient treatment, and fewer alcohol-related arrests among clients receiving RP compared to clients receiving other treatment modalities. A study of hospitalized male alcoholics (54) found that clients receiving RP compared to interpersonal process therapy (IP) drank on fewer days, drank less alcohol, completed more aftercare, and had a slightly higher rate of continuous abstinence at 6-month follow-up.

Other studies have demonstrated RP to be effective in reducing substance abuse but not more effective than a comparison condition. For example, Stephens et al. (102) randomly assigned 161 men and 51 women seeking help for marihuana dependence to a RP or social support (SSP) discussion intervention. Twelve-month posttreatment data indicate substantial reductions in frequency of marihuana use and associated problems but no significant differences between these two interventions on measures of days of use, related problems, or abstinence rates. A study by Wells and colleagues (111) of outpatient cocaine abusers comparing RP and 12-step counseling (TSC) found that subjects in both treatment conditions reduced their use of cocaine, marihuana, and alcohol use at 6 months posttreatment. However, subjects in the TSC condition showed greater improvement in alcohol use compared to those receiving RP at the 6-month follow-up period.

Carroll (16) recently reviewed 24 randomized controlled trials on the effectiveness of RP among smokers (12 studies), alcohol abusers (6 studies), marihuana abusers (1 study), cocaine abusers (3 studies), the opiate addicted (1 study), and other drug abusers (1 study). Carroll reported that the strongest evidence for efficacy of RP is with smokers and concluded that "there is good evidence for RP approaches compared with no-treatment controls . . . [and that] outcomes where RP may hold greater promise include reducing severity of relapses when they occur, durability of effects after cessation, and patient-treatment matching" (p. 53). Clients with higher levels of impairment along dimensions such as psychiatric severity and addiction severity appear to benefit most from RP compared to those with less severe levels of impairment. Thus, RP may be especially helpful for dual diagnosis clients.

Several studies have included spouses in the RP intervention. A study of the first relapse episodes and reasons for terminating relapses of men with alcoholism who were treated with their spouses found that the relapses of clients receiving RP in addition to behavioral marital therapy (BMT) were shorter than those of clients not receiving the RP (62). In a study of married alcoholics, O'Farrell (84) found that in couples assessed to be "high distress," abstinence rates were highest for those who received BMT in combination with RP. Alcoholics who received RP after completing BMT had more days abstinence, fewer days drinking, and improved marriages compared to those who received only BMT (85).

There are several limitations to studies on RP (16, 34). First, some studies have used RP as the single treatment intervention for cessation of drinking rather than for maintenance of change once drinking was stopped. Second, studies usually do not differentiate between subjects who are motivated to change substance use behavior and those who have little or no motivation to change. Third, in some studies, sample sizes are small and there is not enough power to detect statistical differences between experimental and control conditions. Fourth, studies do not always use random assignment or operationalize the therapy being compared against RP, making it difficult to determine what factors contribute to treatment effects. And last, the follow-up period is often short-term (6 months or less). Despite these limitations, however, there is empirical evidence that RP strategies enhance the recovery of individuals with substance use disorders.

COGNITIVE AND BEHAVIORAL INTERVENTIONS

This section reviews a variety of practical RP interventions that can be used in multiple treatment contexts. These interventions reflect the approaches of numerous clinicians and researchers who have developed specific models of RP and/or written client-oriented RP recovery materials and the authors' experience with alcoholics and drugs addicts, including clients with comorbid psychiatric conditions. The interventions discussed herein include cognitive and behavioral ones. Whereas some of these interventions can be used by the client as part of a self-management recovery program, other interventions involve eliciting support or help from family or significant others. The literature emphasizes individualizing RP strategies, taking into account the client's level of motivation, severity of substance use, gender, ego functioning, and sociocultural environment.

The use of experiential learning (e.g., role-playing, fantasy, behavioral rehearsal, monodramas, psychodrama, bibliotherapy, use of workbooks, interactive videos, and homework assignments) is highly recommended to make learning an active experience for the client. Such techniques enhance self-awareness, decrease defensiveness, and encourage behavioral change (27). In treatment groups, action techniques provide numerous opportunities for the clinician to elicit feedback and support for individual clients, identify common themes and issues related to RP, and practice specific interpersonal skills.

The use of a daily inventory is also recommended (23, 46). A daily inventory aims to get clients to continuously monitor their lives so as to identify relapse risk factors, relapse warning signs, or significant life problems that could contribute to a relapse.

Summary of Key Themes in Relapse Prevention

1. Help Clients Identify Their High-Risk Relapse Factors and Develop Strategies to Deal With Them. The need to recognize the risk of relapse and high-risk factors is an essential component of RP. High-risk factors, or critical incidents, typically are those situations in which clients used alcohol or other drugs prior to treatment. High-risk factors usually involve intrapersonal and interpersonal situations (68). Annis (5) suggests that the situations in which the client used substances during the year preceding treatment represent high-risk situations following cessation of substance use.

Numerous clinical aids have been developed by researchers and clinicians to help clients identify and prioritize their individual high-risk situations and develop coping strategies to aid in their recovery. These include Annis' *Inventory of Drinking Situations* (3) and *Inventory of Drug-Taking Situations* (4), Daley's "Identifying High Risk Situations" inventory (23), Carroll's *Substance Abuse Problem Checklist* (15), Zackon, McAuliffe, and Ch'ien's "Your Dangerous Situations" worksheet (113), Gorski's "High Risk Situation List" and "High Risk Situations Worksheet" (46), and Washton's *Staying Off Cocaine* workbook (110).

For some clients, identifying high-risk factors and developing new coping strategies for each are inadequate, since they may identify large numbers of risk factors. Such clients need help in taking a more global approach to recovery and may need to learn specific problem-solving skills. Marlatt (65), for example, suggests that in addition to teaching clients "specific" RP skills to deal with high-risk factors, the clinician should also utilize "global" approaches such as skill training strategies (e.g., behavioral rehearsal, covert modeling, assertiveness training), cognitive reframing (e.g., coping imagery, reframing reactions to lapse or relapse), and lifestyle interventions (e.g., meditation, exercise, relaxation). Numerous skill training and stress management approaches have been found to increase the effectiveness of treatment (see, for example, Refs. 1, 18, 20, 38, and 80). Figure 48.1 summarizes one paradigm for conceptualizing high-risk factors.

2. Help Clients Understand Relapse as a Process and as an Event. Clients are better prepared for the challenges of recovery if they are cognizant of the fact that relapse occurs within a context and that clues or warning signs typically precede an actual lapse or relapse to substance use. Although a relapse may be the result of an impulsive act on the part of the recovering individual, more often than not, attitudinal, emotional, cognitive, and/or behavioral changes usually manifest themselves prior to the actual ingestion of substances (24, 72). An individual's clues or warning signs can be conceptualized as links in a relapse chain (14, 68). Many relapsers reported to the authors that their warning signs appeared days, weeks, or even longer before they ingested substances (Fig. 48.2).

Clients in treatment for the first time can benefit from reviewing common relapse warning signs identified by others in recovery. The authors have

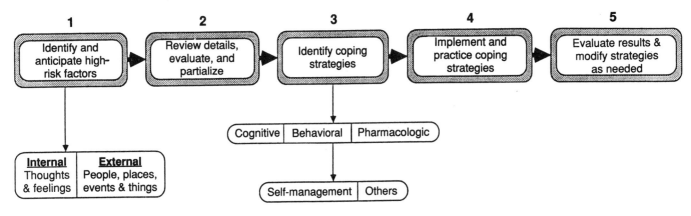

Figure 48.1. High-risk factors.

found it helpful to have relapsers review their experiences in great detail so that they can learn the connections among thoughts, feelings, events or situations, and relapse to substance use. An evaluation of the authors' psychoeducational model of RP and a workbook used in conjunction with this program by 511 clients found that "Understanding the Relapse Process" was the topic rated as most useful (27).

3. Help Clients Understand and Deal With Alcohol or Drug Cues as Well as Cravings. There is a growing body of research suggesting that alcoholics', drug addicts', and smokers' desire or craving for alcohol or other drugs can be triggered by exposure to environmental cues associated with prior use. Cues such as the sight or smell of the substance of abuse may trigger cravings that become evident in cognitive (e.g., increased thoughts of using) and physiological (e.g., anxiety) changes.

The advice given in AA, NA, and CA for alcoholics and addicts to "avoid people, places, and things" associated with their substance abuse was developed as a way of minimizing exposure to cues that trigger cravings that can be so overwhelming that they contribute to a relapse. A practical suggestion is to encourage clients to remove from their homes substances as well as paraphernalia (pipes, mirrors, needles, etc.) used for taking drugs. This may be more difficult for smokers, however, since most relapse crises occur in association with food or alcohol consumption (97).

Cue exposure treatment is one method used to help reduce the intensity of the client's reactions to cues. This treatment involves exposing the client to specific cues associated with substance use. Cue exposure also aims to enhance coping skills as well as the client's confidence in his or her ability to resist the desire to use.

Because it is impossible for clients to avoid all cues that are associated with substance use, the clinician can teach the client a variety of practical techniques to manage cravings (23, 45, 58, 66, 98, 110). Clients should learn information about cues and how they trigger cravings for alcohol or other drugs. Monitoring and recording cravings, associated thoughts, and out-

comes can help clients become more vigilant and prepared to cope with them. Helpful cognitive interventions for managing cravings include changing thoughts about the craving or desire to use, challenging euphoric recall, talking oneself through the craving, thinking beyond the high by identifying negative consequences of using (immediate and delayed) and positive benefits of not using, using AA/NA/CA recovery slogans and delaying the decision to use. Behavioral interventions include avoiding, leaving, or changing situations that trigger or worsen a craving, redirecting activities or getting involved in pleasant activities, getting help or support from others by admitting and talking about cravings and hearing how others have survived them, attending self-help support group meetings, or taking medications such as disulfiram or naltrexone (for alcoholics). Shiffman and colleagues (98) recommend that ex-smokers carry a menu card that lists various ways to cope with a craving to smoke, a strategy that can also address alcohol or other drug cravings.

Figure 48.3 represents a paradigm that the authors have found useful when helping clients understand and manage cravings.

4. Help Clients Understand and Deal With Social Pressures to Use Substances. A variety of direct and indirect social pressures can contribute to a relapse. Social pressures often lead to increased thoughts and desires to use substances, as well as anxiety regarding one's ability to refuse offers to drink alcohol or use other drugs.

Figure 48.4 outlines one method of helping clients understand and deal with social pressures. The first step is to identify high-risk relationships (e.g., living with or dating an active drug abuser or alcoholic) and situations or events in which the client may be exposed to or offered substances (e.g., social gatherings where people smoke cigarettes or drink alcohol). The next step is to assess the effects of these social pressures on the thoughts, feelings, and behaviors of the client. Planning, practicing, and implementing coping strategies is the next step. These coping strategies include avoidance and the use of verbal, cognitive, or behavioral skills. Utilizing role-playing to rehearse ways to refuse offers of drug or alcohol is one very practical and easy-to-use intervention. The final step of this process involves teaching the client to evaluate the results of a given coping strategy and to modify it as needed.

In many instances, pressures to use alcohol or other drugs result from relationships with active drug users or alcoholics. The client needs to assess his or her social network and learn ways to limit or end relationships that represent a high risk for relapse (113).

5. Help Clients Develop and Enhance a Supportive Social Network. Several authors have addressed RP from a broader perspective that involves the family or significant others. Daley (24, 26) has concluded that family involvement in RP is beneficial to both the addict and the family. McGrady (70) has modified Marlatt's cognitive-behavioral model of RP and applied it to couples in recovery. Gorski's model of RP (46) places strong emphasis on the need for relapse-prone people to involve significant individuals in their lives in a RP network. O'Farrell (84) and O'Farrell and colleagues (85) developed a RP protocol for use in combination with behavioral marital therapy (BMT). Maisto and colleagues (62) found that alcoholics who were

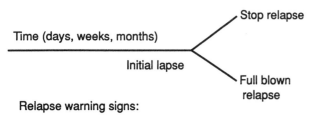

Figure 48.2. Relapse process.

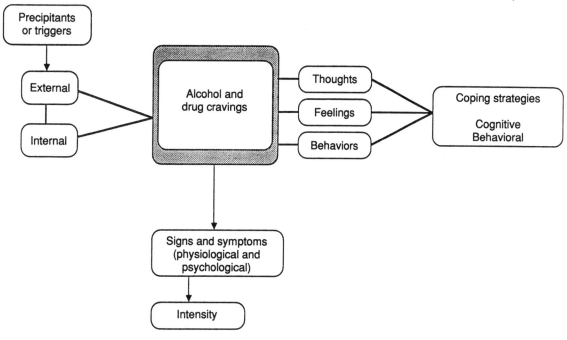

Figure 48.3. Cravings.

treated with their spouses with RP in addition to marital therapy had shorter and less severe relapses than clients not receiving RP.

Numerous studies have substantiated a positive correlation between abstinence from alcohol, drugs, and tobacco and the presence of family and social supports. Families are more likely to support recovery if they are involved in the process and have an opportunity to heal from the emotional pain they experienced. This is more likely to occur if the member with the substance use disorder understands the impact of substance abuse on the family and makes amends for some of the adverse effects on the family.

Involvement of immediate families or significant others in the recovery process provides them with an opportunity to deal with the impact of substance use on their lives as well as their own issues (e.g., enabling behaviors, preoccupation, feelings of anger, shame, and guilt). Families are then in a much better position to support the recovering member. The authors have seen family members sabotage the recovery of the addicted member in a multiplicity of overt and covert ways. Such behavior usually is an indication that they have not had an opportunity to deal with their own issues or heal from their emotional pain.

In addition to family or significant other involvement, clients can be encouraged to get involved in AA, Smokers Anonymous, Nicotine Anonymous, or other support groups. Sponsors, other recovery and personal friends, and employers may become part of an individual's RP network (10, 87). Clients generally should not try to recover in isolation, particularly during the early stages of recovery.

Following are some suggested steps for helping clients develop a RP network. First, the client needs to identify whom to involve in or exclude from this network. Others who abuse substances, harbor extremely strong negative feelings toward the recovering person, or generally are not supportive of recovery usually should be excluded.

The client should then determine how and when to ask for support or help. Behavioral rehearsal can help the client practice ways to make specific requests for support. Rehearsal also helps increase confidence as well as clarify thoughts and feelings regarding reaching out for help. Many clients, for example, feel guilty or shameful and question whether or not they deserve support from others. Yet others have such strong pride that the thought of asking others for support is very difficult to accept. Rehearsal may also

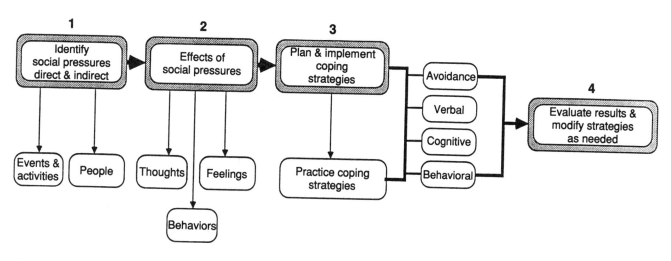

Figure 48.4. Social pressures.

clarify the client's ambivalence regarding ongoing recovery, and it helps better understand how the person being asked for support may respond. This prepares the client for dealing with potential negative responses from others. Clients should be advised to emphasize that recovery is ultimately their responsibility.

An action plan can then be devised, practiced, implemented, and modified as needed. Some clients find it helpful to put their action plan in writing so that all of those involved have a specific document to refer to. The action plan can address the following issues: how to communicate about and deal with relapse warning signs and high-risk situations; how to interrupt a lapse; how to intervene if a relapse occurs; and the importance of exploring all the details of a lapse or relapse after the client is stable so that it can be used as a learning experience. Having a plan can make both the recovering person and family feel more in control even if faced with the possibility of an actual relapse. Additionally, it helps everyone take a proactive approach to recovery rather than sit back passively and wait for problems to occur. The authors' clinical experience has been that clients and families who are involved in such discussions are much more likely to intervene earlier in the relapse process than those not involved in these discussions.

6. Help Clients Develop Methods of Coping With Negative Emotional States. Negative affective states are associated with relapse across a range of addictions (22). Several investigators reported that depression and anxiety were major factors in a substantial number of relapses (48, 60, 88). Zackon (112) believes that addicts frequently relapse as a result of joylessness in their lives. Shiffman and colleagues (98) found that coping responses for high-risk situations were less effective for smokers who were depressed. Other negative affective states associated with relapse include anger, anxiety, and boredom (23, 91, 92). The acronym "HALT" used in AA and NA (which stands for, "Don't get too *H*ungry, *A*ngry, *L*onely, or *T*ired") speaks to the importance of the recovering alcoholic's or drug addict's not allowing himself or herself to get too angry or lonely (2). These two emotional states are seen as high-risk factors for many.

Interventions for helping clients develop appropriate coping skills for managing negative emotional states vary, depending on the sources, manifestation, and consequences of these emotions. For example, strategies for dealing with depression that accompanies the realization that addiction caused havoc in one's life may vary from those for dealing with depression that is part of a bipolar or major depressive illness that becomes manifest after the client is substance-free and creates significant personal distress.

Interventions to help the client who occasionally gets angry and seeks solace in drugs, tobacco, or alcohol vary from those needed to help the client who is chronically angry at self and others. The former may need help in expressing anger appropriately rather than in suppressing it. The chronically angry individual, on the other hand, may need to learn how not to express anger, since it is often expressed impulsively and inappropriately and often is not even justified. With this type of individual, cognitive techniques that teach the individual to challenge and change angry thoughts that are not justified are helpful. The chronically angry person may also benefit from seeing his or her angry disposition as a "character defect." Psychotherapy and/or use of the 12-step program of AA and NA are appropriate interventions to help modify such an ingrained character trait.

Interventions for clients who report feelings of chronic boredom, emptiness, or joylessness similarly depend on the specific nature of the emotional state. The client may need help in learning how to use free time or how to have fun without chemicals. Or, the client may need help in developing new values and new relationships or in finding new activities that provide a sense of meaning in one's life. Many clients need to alter their beliefs regarding fun, excitement, and what is important in life. The authors have encountered many cocaine addicts who reported that being drug-free was boring compared with the high provided by the drug or behaviors associated with getting the drug or "living on the edge." In such a case, the client needs to change not only behaviors but also beliefs and attitudes.

7. Assess Clients for Psychiatric Disorders and Facilitate Treatment if Needed. Numerous studies of community samples, psychiatric treatment populations, and substance abuse treatment populations evidence high rates of dual diagnoses (substance use plus psychiatric disorder) (32). Dual diag-

nosis clients are at higher risk for substance use relapse than those with only a substance use diagnosis resulting from the effect of psychiatric symptomology on motivation, judgment, and functioning. In addition, dual diagnosis clients who resume substance use frequently fail to adhere to psychiatric treatment and comply poorly with pharmacotherapy, psychotherapy, and/or self-help program attendance. In a quality assurance/improvement study conducted by one of the authors' of 25 substance abusers with mood disorders and 25 substance abusers with schizophrenia who were rehospitalized as a result of significant worsening of psychiatric condition, it was found that alcohol and drug abuse relapse played a significant role in 60% of these psychiatric relapses.

RP strategies can be adapted and tailored to the specific problems and symptoms of the client's psychiatric disorder. Monitoring target moods or behaviors, participating in pleasant activities, developing routine and structure in daily life, learning to cope with persistent psychiatric symptoms associated with chronic or recurrent forms of psychiatric illness, and identifying early warning signs of psychiatric relapse and developing appropriate coping strategies are helpful interventions for dual diagnosis clients (30, 31).

Negative mood states that are part of an affective disorder (major depression, bipolar disease, etc.) or anxiety disorder (phobia, panic, etc.) may require pharmacotherapy in addition to psychotherapy and involvement in self-help programs. Clients on medications for these or other psychiatric disorders may also benefit from developing strategies for dealing with well-meaning members of self-help programs who encourage them to stop their medications because it is perceived as detrimental to recovery from their substance use disorder.

8. For Clients Completing Residential or Hospital-Based Treatment, Facilitate the Transition to Follow-up Outpatient or Aftercare Treatment (33). Many clients make significant gains in structured, hospital-based or residential substance abuse treatment programs only to have these negated due to failure to adhere to ongoing outpatient or aftercare treatment. Interventions used to enhance treatment entry and adherence that lower the risk of relapse include the provision of a single session of motivational therapy prior to discharge from inpatient treatment, the use of telephone or mail reminders of initial treatment appointments, and providing reinforcers for appropriate participation in treatment activities or for providing drug-free urines (56, 69, 79). In a pilot study conducted in one of the authors' treatment programs, a single motivational therapy session provided to hospitalized cocaine addicts with comorbid depressive illness led to a nearly 2-fold increase in the show rate for the initial outpatient appointment. Clients who show for their initial appointment and successfully "enter" outpatient treatment have a reduced risk of treatment dropout and subsequent psychiatric and/or substance use relapse.

9. Help Clients Learn Methods to Cope With Cognitive Distortions. Cognitive distortions or errors in thinking are associated with a wide range of mental health and substance use disorders (11, 12, 36). These distortions have also been implicated in relapse to substance use as well (26, 66). Twelve-step programs refer to cognitive distortions as "stinking thinking" and suggest that recovering individuals need to alter their thinking if they are to remain alcohol- and drug-free.

Teaching clients to identify their cognitive errors (e.g., black-and-white thinking, "awfulizing," overgeneralizing, selective abstraction, catastrophizing, or jumping to conclusions) and evaluate how these affect the relapse process is often very helpful. Clients can then be taught to use counter-thoughts to challenge their faulty beliefs or specific negative thoughts. The authors provide clients with a sample worksheet to help them learn to change and challenge relapse thoughts. This worksheet has three directives: (*a*) list the relapse-related thought; (*b*) state what's wrong with it; and (*c*) create new statements. A list of seven specific thoughts commonly associated with relapse is used to prompt clients in completing this therapeutic task. These examples include: "relapse can't happen to me"; "I'll never use alcohol or drugs again"; "I can control my use of alcohol or other drugs"; "a few drinks, tokes, pills, lines won't hurt"; "recovery isn't happening fast enough"; "I need alcohol or other drugs to have fun"; and "my problem is cured." Clients seldom have difficulty coming up with additional examples of specific thoughts that can contribute to a relapse.

Many of the AA and NA slogans were devised to help alcoholics and drug addicts alter their thinking and survive desires to use substances. Slogans such as "this, too, will pass," "let go and let God," and "one day at a time" often help the chemically dependent individual work through thoughts of using.

10. Help Clients Work Toward a Balanced Lifestyle. In addition to identifying and managing high-risk relapse factors, recovering individuals often need to make more global changes to restore or achieve a balance in their lifestyle (40, 67, 109). Development of a healthy lifestyle is seen as important in reducing stress that makes one more vulnerable to relapse.

The client's lifestyle can be assessed by evaluating patterns of daily activities, sources of stress, stressful life events, daily hassles and uplifts, balance between wants (activities engaged in for pleasure or self-fulfillment) and shoulds (external demands), health and exercise patterns, relaxation patterns, interpersonal activities, and religious beliefs (67). Helping clients develop positive habits or substitute indulgences (e.g., jogging, meditation, relaxation, exercise, hobbies, or creative tasks) for substance abuse can help to balance their lifestyle (39, 67, 83). Clients with needs for greater adventure or action may get involved in activities such as racing, skydiving, skiing, or contact sports (25, 40).

11. Consider the Use of a Pharmacological Intervention as an Adjunct to Psychosocial Treatment (7, 43, 99, 107). Some clients benefit from pharmacological interventions to attenuate or reduce cravings for alcohol or other drugs, enhance motivation to stay sober, and increase confidence in their ability to resist relapse. Several recent studies provide preliminary evidence that naltrexone (ReVia), for example, is helpful for alcoholics. Volpicelli and colleagues' study (107) of 70 male alcohol-dependent clients participating in a 12-week, double-blind, placebo-controlled trial of naltrexone found that 23% of subjects taking naltrexone met criteria for relapse compared with 54% of placebo treatment subjects. The primary effect of naltrexone was that subjects were much less likely to continue drinking following the initial use of alcohol compared to control subjects. In a study of naltrexone combined with coping skills and/or RP training (N+RP) or supportive therapy (N+ST), O'Malley and colleagues (86) found that N+RP subjects who returned to drinking were less likely to experience a relapse to heavy drinking compared to N+ST subjects.

As we mentioned in the previous discussion on dual diagnosis, treatment of psychiatric symptoms with appropriate medications has important implications for recovery. Kranzler and colleagues (59) conducted a randomized, 12-week, placebo-controlled trial of buspirone in 61 anxious alcoholics who also received weekly RP therapy. Clients receiving buspirone showed greater retention in treatment at 12 weeks, reduced anxiety, a slower return to heavy alcohol use, and fewer drinking days compared to those receiving placebo. In a randomized, controlled, double-blind clinical trial of 100 alcoholic patients, Gottlieb and colleagues (47) found that, among the 57 high-risk patients reporting cravings for alcohol at baseline, relapse rates were 90% for patients receiving placebo compared with 65% for those receiving atenolol, a β-adrenergic blocker. This study also found that poor levels of treatment adherence were strongly associated with adverse outcomes.

12. Help Clients Develop a Plan to Manage a Lapse or Relapse. The outcome literature shows that most alcoholics, smokers, and drug addicts lapse or relapse at one time or another. Therefore, it is highly recommended that clients have an emergency plan to follow if they lapse, so that a full-blown relapse can be avoided. If a full-blown relapse occurs, however, the client needs to have strategies to stop it. The specific intervention strategies should be based on the severity of the client's lapse or relapse, coping mechanisms, and prior history of relapse.

Helpful interventions include getting clients to use self-talk or behavioral procedures to stop a lapse or relapse, asking family, AA/NA/SA sponsors, friends, or professionals for help, carrying an *emergency card* with names and phone numbers of others who can be called on for support, or carrying a *reminder card* that gives specific instructions on what to do if a lapse or relapse occurs (23, 66). Marlatt recommends developing a relapse contract with clients that outlines specific steps to take in the event of a future relapse. The aim of this contract is to formalize or reinforce the client's commitment to change.

Analyzing lapses or relapses is a valuable process that can aid ongoing recovery. This helps to reframe a "failure" as a "learning" experience and can help the individual prepare for future high-risk situations.

CONCLUSION

A variety of RP clinical treatment models and specialized programs have been developed for clients with alcohol, tobacco, or other drug problems. Many of the cognitive and behavioral interventions described in these RP approaches can be adapted for use with clients who have additional problems, such as other compulsive disorders, impulse control disorders, or comorbid psychiatric illnesses. RP interventions aim to help clients maintain change over time and address the most common issues and problems raising vulnerability to relapse. Studies indicate that RP has efficacy in reducing both relapse rates and the severity of lapses or relapses. RP strategies can be used throughout the continuum of care in primary rehabilitation programs, halfway houses, or therapeutic community programs, as well as in outpatient and aftercare programs. In addition, family members can be included in educational and therapy sessions and involved in the development of RP plans for members with substance use disorders.

Many of the RP approaches described in the literature can be considered short-term or brief treatments and can be provided in individual or group sessions, making them attractive and cost effective. Most clinical models of RP are supported by user-friendly, interactive recovery materials such as books, workbooks, videos, and audiotapes. These supplemental materials provide additional information and support to clients who can learn to use self-management techniques of RP on their own, following completion of formal treatment.

References

1. Abrams D, Niaura R, Carey K, Monti P, Binkoff J. Understanding relapse and recovery in alcohol abuse. Ann Behav Med 1986;8(2–3):27–32.
2. Alcoholics Anonymous (big book). 3rd ed. New York: AA World Services, 1976.
3. Annis H. Inventory of drinking situations. Toronto: Addiction Research Foundation, 1982.
4. Annis H. Inventory of drug-taking situations. Toronto: Addiction Research Foundation, 1985.
5. Annis H. A relapse prevention model for treatment of alcoholics. In: Miller W, Heather N, eds. Treating addictive behaviors: process of change. New York: Plenum, 1986.
6. Annis H. Effective treatment for drug and alcohol problems: what do we know? Paper presented at the annual meeting of the Institute of Medicine, National Academy of Sciences, Washington, DC, 1987.
7. Annis H. A cognitive-social learning approach to relapse: pharmacotherapy and relapse prevention counseling. Alcohol Alcohol 1991;(suppl 1):527–530.
8. Annis H, Davis C. Self-efficacy and the prevention of alcoholic relapse: initial findings from a treatment trial. In: Baker T, Cannon D, eds. Addictive disorders. New York: Praeger, 1987.
9. Annis H, Davis C. Relapse prevention training. A cognitive-behavioral approach based on self-efficacy theory. J Chem Depend Treat 1989;2: 2,81–104.
10. Barber JG, Crisp BR. Social support and prevention of relapse following treatment for alcohol abuse. Res Soc Work Pract 1995;5(3):283–296.
11. Beck A. Cognitive therapy and the emotional disorders. New York: New American Library, 1976.
12. Beck A, Wright F, Liese B. Cognitive therapy of substance abuse. New York: Guilford, 1994.
13. Brown S. Treating the alcoholic: a developmental model of recovery. 2nd ed. New York: John Wiley, 1995.
14. Brownell K, Rodin J. The weight maintenance survival guide. Dallas, TX: LEARN Education Center, 1990.
15. Carroll J. Substance abuse problem checklist. Eagleville, PA: Eagleville Hospital, 1983.
16. Carroll KM. Relapse prevention as a psychosocial treatment: a review of controlled clinical trials. Exp Clin Psychopharmacol 1996;4(1): 46–54.
17. Carroll KM, Rounsaville BJ, Gawin FH. A comparative trial of psychotherapies for ambulatory cocaine abusers: relapse prevention and interpersonal psychotherapy. Am J Drug Alcohol Abuse 1991;17(3):229–247.
18. Carroll KM, Rounsaville BJ, Nich C, Gordon LT, Wirtz PW, Gawin F. One-year follow-up of psychotherapy and pharmacotherapy for cocaine

dependence. Delayed emergence of psychotherapy effects. Arch Gen Psychiatry 1994;51(12):989–997.

19. Catalano R, Howard M, Hawkins J, Wells E. Relapse in the addictions: rates, determinants, and promising prevention strategies. In: 1988 Surgeon General's report on health consequences of smoking. Washington, DC: Office of Smoking and Health, Government Printing Office, 1988.

20. Chaney E, O'Leary M. Skill training with alcoholics. J Consult Clin Psychol 1978;46(5):1092–1104.

21. Cuffel BJ, Chase P. Remission and relapse of substance use disorders in schizophrenia: results from a one-year prospective study. J Nerv Ment Dis 1994;182(6):342–348.

22. Cummings C, Gordon J, Marlatt G. Relapse: prevention and prediction. In: Miller W, ed. Addictive behaviors: treatment of alcoholism, drug abuse, smoking and obesity. New York: Pergamon Press, 1980.

23. Daley D. Relapse prevention workbook for recovering alcoholics and drug dependent persons. Holmes Beach, FL: Learning Publications, 1986.

24. Daley D. Relapse prevention with substance abusers: clinical issues and myths. Soc Work 1987;45(2):38–42.

25. Daley D. Relapse: a guide for successful recovery. Bradenton, FL: Human Services Institute, 1987.

26. Daley D. Relapse prevention: treatment alternatives and counseling AIDS. Bradenton, FL: Human Services Institute, 1988.

27. Daley D. Five perspectives on relapse in chemical dependency. J Chem Depend Treat 1989;2:2,3–26.

28. Daley D, ed. Relapse. Conceptual, research and clinical perspectives. New York: Haworth, 1989.

29. Daley D. Surviving addiction workbook. Holmes Beach, FL: Learning Publications, 1990.

30. Daley D. Preventing relapse. Dual Diagnosis Workbook Series. Center City, MN: Hazelden, 1994.

31. Daley D, Lis J. Relapse prevention: intervention strategies for mental health clients with comorbid addictive disorders. In: Washton A, ed. Psychotherapy and substance abuse: a practitioner's handbook. New York: Guilford Press, 1995:243–263.

32. Daley D, Moss H, Campbell F. Dual disorders: counseling clients with chemical dependency and mental illness. Center City, MN: Hazelden, 1987.

33. deLeon G. Aftercare in therapeutic communities. Special issue: relapse prevention in substance misuse. Int J Addict 1990–1991;25(9A–10A):1225–1237.

34. Dimeff LA, Marlatt GA. Relapse prevention. In: Hester R, Miller W, eds. Handbook of alcoholism treatment approaches. 2nd ed. Boston: Allyn and Bacon, 1995:176–194.

35. Donovan D, Chaney E. Alcoholic relapse prevention and intervention: models and methods. In: Marlatt GA, Gordon J, eds. Relapse prevention: maintenance strategies in the treatment of addictive behaviors. New York: Guilford, 1985:351–416.

36. Ellis A, McInerney J, DiGiuseppe R, Yeager R. Rational-emotive therapy with alcoholics and substance abusers. New York: Pergamon Press, 1988.

37. Emrick C. A review of psychologically oriented treatment of alcoholism. J Stud Alcohol 1974;35:523–549.

38. Eriksen L, Bjornstad S, Gotestam KG. Social skills training in groups for alcoholics: one-year treatment outcome for groups and individuals. Addict Behav 1986;11:309–329.

39. Gelderloos P, Walton KG, Orme-Johnson DW, Alexander CN. Effectiveness of the transcendental meditation program in preventing and treating substance misuse: a review. Int J Addict 1991;26(3):293–325.

40. George W. Marlatt, Gordon's relapse prevention model. J Chem Depend Treat 1989;3:2,125–152.

41. Goldstein MS, Surber M, Wilner DM. Outcome evaluations in substance abuse: a comparison of alcoholism, drug abuse, and other mental health interventions. Int J Addict 1984;19(5):479–502.

42. Gondolf E. Staying stopped: a gender based approach to preventing violence. Unpublished manuscript, 1988.

43. Gorelick DA. Overview of pharmacologic treatment approaches for alcohol and other drug addiction. Intoxication, withdrawal, and relapse prevention 1993;16(1):141–156.

44. Gorski T. Relapse prevention planning: a new recovery tool. Alcohol Health Res World 1986;Fall:6–11.

45. Gorski T. Managing cocaine craving. Center City, MN: Hazelden, 1990.

46. Gorski T, Miller M. Staying sober workbook. Independence, MO: Independence Press, 1988.

47. Gottlieb LD, Horwitz RI, Kraus ML, Segal SR, Viscoli CM. Randomized controlled trial in alcohol relapse prevention: role of atenolol, alcohol craving, and treatment adherence. J Subst Abuse Treat 1994;11(3):253–258.

48. Hatsukami D, Pickins R, Svikis D. Post-treatment depressive symptoms and relapse to drug use in different age groups of an alcohol and other drug abuse population. Drug Alcohol Depend 1981;8(4):271–277.

49. Havassy BE, Hall SM, Wasserman DA. Social support and relapse: commonalities among alcoholics, opiate users, and cigarette smokers. Addict Behav 1991;16(5):235–246.

50. Hoffmann N, Harrison P. CATOR 1986 report: findings two years after treatment. St Paul, MN: CATOR, 1986.

51. Hoffmann N, Harrison P. Relapse: conceptual and methodological issues. J Chem Depend Treat 1989;2:2,27–52.

52. Hoffmann NG, Miller NS. Treatment outcomes for abstinence-based programs. Psychiatr Ann 1992;22(8):402–408.

53. Hunt W, Barnett L, Branch L. Relapse rates in addiction programs. J Clin Psychol 1971;27:455–456.

54. Ito JR, Donovan DM, Hall JJ. Relapse prevention and alcohol aftercare: effects on drinking outcome, change process, and aftercare attendance. Br J Addict 1988;83:171–181.

55. Johnson E, Herringer LG. A note on the utilization of common support activities and relapse following substance abuse treatment. J Psychol 1993;127(1):73–77.

56. Kadden RM, Mauriello IJ. Enhancing participation in substance abuse treatment using an incentive system. J Subst Abuse Treat 1991;8:133–144.

57. Koski-Jannes A. Alcohol addiction and self-regulation: a controlled trial of relapse prevention program for Finnish inpatient alcoholics. Finland: Finnish Foundation for Alcohol Studies, 1992.

58. Kosten TR. Can cocaine craving be a medication development outcome? Drug craving and relapse in opioid and cocaine dependence. Am J Addict 1992;1(3):230–239.

59. Kranzler HR, Burleson JA, Del Boca FK, Babor TF, Korner P, Brown J, Bohn MJ. Buspirone treatment of anxious alcoholics. A placebo-controlled trial. Arch Gen Psychiatry 1994;51(9):720–731.

60. LaBounty LP, Hatsukami D, Morgan SF, Nelson L. Relapse among alcoholics with phobic and panic symptoms. Addict Behav 1992;17(1):9–15.

61. Laws R, ed. Relapse prevention with sex offenders. New York: Guilford, 1989.

62. Maisto SA, McKay JR, O'Farrell TJ. Relapse precipitants and behavioral marital therapy. Addict Behav 1995;20(3):383–393.

63. Marlatt GA. Relapse prevention: theoretical rationale and overview of the model. In: Marlatt GA, Gordon J, eds. Relapse prevention: a self-control strategy in the maintenance of behavior change. New York: Guilford, 1985:3–70.

64. Marlatt GA. Situational determinants of relapse and skill-training interventions. In: Marlatt GA, Gordon J, eds. Relapse prevention: a self-control strategy for the maintenance of behavior change. New York: Guilford, 1985:71–127.

65. Marlatt GA. Cognitive factors in the relapse process. In: Marlatt GA, Gordon J, eds. Relapse prevention: a self-control strategy for the maintenance of behavior change. New York: Guilford, 1985:128–200.

66. Marlatt GA. Cognitive assessment and intervention procedures for relapse prevention. In: Marlatt GA, Gordon J, eds. Relapse prevention: a self-control strategy for the maintenance of behavior change. New York: Guilford, 1985:201–279.

67. Marlatt GA. Lifestyle modification. In: Marlatt GA, Gordon J, eds. Relapse prevention: a self-control strategy for the maintenance of behavior change. New York: Guilford, 1985:280–350.

68. Marlatt GA, Gordon J, eds. Relapse prevention: a self-control strategy for the maintenance of behavior change. New York: Guilford, 1985.

69. Meichenbaum D, Turk DC. Facilitating treatment adherence: a practitioner's guidebook. New York: Plenum, 1987.

70. McGrady B. Extending relapse prevention to couples. Addict Behav 1989;14:69–74.

71. McLellan A, Woody G, Luborsky L, O'Brien C, Druly K. Increased effectiveness of substance abuse treatment: a prospective study of patient-treatment matching. J Nerv Ment Dis 1983;171:597–605.

72. McKay JR, Rutherford MJ, Alterman AI, Cacciola JS. An examination of the cocaine relapse process. Drug Alcohol Depend 1995;38(1):35–43.

73. Miller L. Predicting relapse and recovery in alcoholism and addiction: neuropsychology, personality, and cognitive style. J Subst Abuse Treat 1991;8(4):277–291.

74. Miller NS, Gold MS. Dissociation of "conscious desire" (craving) from and relapse in alcohol and cocaine dependence. Ann Clin Psychiatry 1994;6(2):99–106.

75. Miller W. Matching individuals with interventions. In: Hester RK, Miller WR, eds. Handbook of alcoholism treatment approaches. New York: Pergamon Press, 1990:261–272.

76. Miller W, Hester R. Treating the problem drinker: modern approaches. In: The addictive behaviors: treatment of alcoholism, drug abuse, smoking and obesity. New York: Pergamon Press, 1980.

77. Miller W, Hester R. Inpatient alcoholism treatment: who benefits? Am Psychol 1986;41:794–805.

78. Miller WR, Brown JM, Simpson TL, Handmaker NS, Bien TH, Luckie LF, Montgomery HA, Hester RK, Tonigan JS. What works? A

methodological analysis of the alcohol treatment outcome literature. In: Hester R, Miller W, eds. Handbook of alcoholism treatment approaches. 2nd ed. Boston: Allyn and Bacon, 1995:12–44.

79. Miller WR, Rollnick S. Motivational interviewing: preparing people to change addictive behavior. New York: Guilford, 1991.

80. Monti P, Adams D, Kadden R, Cooney N. Treating alcohol dependence. New York: Guilford, 1989.

81. Nace EP. Inpatient treatment of alcoholism: a necessary part of the therapeutic armamentarium. Psychiatr Hosp 1990;21:1,9–12.

82. Nigam R, Schottenfeld R, Kosten TR. Treatment of dual diagnosis patients: a relapse prevention group approach. J Subst Abuse Treat 1992;9(4):305–309.

83. O'Connell DF. The use of transcendental meditation in relapse prevention counseling. Alcohol Treat Q 1991;8(1):53–68.

84. O'Farrell TJ. Couples relapse prevention sessions after a behavioral marital therapy couples group program. In: O'Farrell TJ, ed. Treating alcohol problems: marital and family interventions. New York: Guilford, 1993:305–326.

85. O'Farrell TJ, Choquette KA, Cutter HS, Brown ED, McCourt WF. Behavioral martial therapy with and without additional couples relapse prevention sessions for alcoholics and their wives. J Stud Alcohol 1993;54(6):652–666.

86. O'Malley SS, Jaffe AJ, Chang G, Schottenfeld RS, Meyer RE, Rounsaville B. Naltrexone and coping skills therapy for alcohol dependence. Arch Gen Psychiatry 1992;49:881–887.

87. Peters RH, Witty TE, O'Brien JK. The importance of the work family with structured work and relapse prevention. J Appl Rehab Counsel 1993;24(3):3–5.

88. Pickens R, Hatsukami D, Spicer J, Svikis D. Relapse by alcohol abusers. Alcohol Clin Exp Res 1985;9(3):244–247.

89. Rawson RA, Obert JL, McCann MJ, Marinelli CP. Relapse prevention models for substance abuse treatment. Special issue: psychotherapy for the addictions. Psychotherapy 1993;30(2):284–298.

90. Rawson RA, Obert JL, McCann MJ, Marinelli CP. Relapse prevention strategies in outpatient substance abuse treatment. Special series: psychosocial treatment of the addictions. Psychol Addict Behav 1993;7(2):85–95.

91. Rosellini G, Worden M. Of course you're angry. Center City, MN: Hazelden, 1985.

92. Rosellini G, Worden M. Of course you're anxious. Center City, MN: Hazelden, 1989.

93. Rustin TA. Quit and stay quit: medical treatment program for smokers. Houston, TX: Discovery Publishing, 1990.

94. Sandahl C. Determinants of relapse among alcoholics: a cross-cultural replication study. Int J Addict 1984;19(8):833–848.

95. Saunders B, Allsop S. Alcohol problems and relapse: can the clinic combat the community? J Community Appl Soc Psychol 1991;1(3):213–221.

96. Saxe L, Dougherty D, Esty J, Fine M. The effectiveness and costs of alcoholism treatment. Health technology case study 22. Washington, DC: Office of Technology Assessment, 1983.

97. Shiffman S. Relapse following smoking cessation: a situational analysis. J Consult Clin Psychol 1982;50:71–86.

98. Shiffman S, Read L, Maltese J, Rapkin D, Jarvik M. Preventing relapse in ex-smokers: a self-management approach. In: Marlatt GA, Gordon J, eds. Relapse prevention: a self-control strategy for the maintenance of behavior change. New York: Guilford, 1985:472–520.

99. Smith JW, Frawley PJ. Treatment outcome of 600 chemically dependent patients treated in a multimodal inpatient program including aversion therapy and pentothal interviews. J Subst Abuse Treat 1993;10(4):359–369.

100. Simpson DD, Joe GW, Lehman WE, Sells SB. Addiction careers: etiology, treatment and 12-year follow-up outcomes. J Drug Issues 1986;12:107–123.

101. Stanislav SW, Sommi RW, Watson WA. A longitudinal analysis of factors associated with morbidity in cocaine abusers with psychiatric illness. Pharmacotherapy 1992;12(2):114–118.

102. Stephens RS, Roffman RA, Simpson EE. Treatment adult marijuana dependence: a test of the relapse prevention model. J Consult Clin Psychol 1994;62(1):92–99.

103. Sternberg B. Relapse in weight control: definitions, processes and prevention strategies. In: Marlatt GA, Gordon J, eds. Relapse prevention: a self-control strategy for the maintenance of behavior change. New York: Guilford, 1985:521–545.

104. Tims F, Leukefeld C, eds. Relapse and recovery in drug abuse. NIDA research monograph no. 72. Rockville, MD: NIDA, 1987.

105. Tracy JI. Assessing the relationship between craving and relapse. Drug Alcohol Rev 1994;13(1):71–77.

106. Tucker JA, Vuchinich RE, Gladsjo JA. Environmental influences on relapse in substance use disorders. Special issues: environmental factors in substance misuse and its treatment. Int J Addict 1990–91;25(7A-8A):1017–1050.

107. Volpicelli JR, Alterman AI, Hayashida M, O'Brien CP. Naltrexone in the treatment of alcohol dependence. Arch Gen Psychiatry 1992;49:876–880.

108. Wadsworth R, Spampneto AM, Halbrook BM. The role of sexual trauma in the treatment of chemically dependent women: addressing the relapse issue. J Counsel Dev 1995;73(4):401–406.

109. Wanigaratne S. Relapse prevention for addictive behaviors. London: Blackwell Scientific Publications, 1990.

110. Washton A. Staying off cocaine: cravings, other drugs and slips. Center City, MN: Hazelden 1990:1990.

111. Wells EA, Peterson PL, Gainey RR, Hawkins JD, et al. Outpatient treatment for cocaine abuse: a controlled comparison of relapse prevention and twelve-step approaches. Am J Drug Alcohol Abuse 1994;20(1):1–17.

112. Zackon F. Relapse, "re-joyment" observations and reflections. J Chem Depend Treat 1989;2(2):67–80.

113. Zackon F, McAuliffe W, Ch'ien J. Addict aftercare: recovery training and self-help. DHHS publication no. (ADM) 85–1341. Rockville, MD: NIDA, 1985.

114. Zinberg S, Wallace J, Blume S, eds. Practical approaches to alcoholism psychotherapy. 2nd ed. New York: Plenum, 1985.

Suggested Client Educational Videotapes

Living sober. Skokie, IL: Gerald T Rogers Production [(800) 227–9100], 1994. This is an interactive video series that focuses on the most common relapse issues such as resisting social pressures, coping with cravings, managing feelings, dealing with family and interpersonal conflict, building a recovery network and sponsorship, and coping with relapse warning signs.

49 COGNITIVE AND BEHAVIORAL THERAPIES

Bruce S. Liese and Lisa M. Najavits

Psychotherapies that focus primarily on individuals' thoughts and behaviors are generally known as cognitive-behavioral therapies. There have been many different cognitive-behavioral therapies; some have attended mostly to cognitive processes, some have attended mostly to behavioral processes, while others have been equally attentive to both. Cognitive-behavioral therapies have typically been active, structured, directive, focused, and present-oriented. Dobson and Block (1) review the historical and philosophical bases of cognitive-behavioral therapy. They credit Ellis (2) and Beck (3) with introducing the first cognitive-behavioral therapies (Rational Emotive Therapy and Cognitive Therapy, respectively), and they cite other important early contributors to cognitive-behavioral therapy (4–11).

Early applications of cognitive-behavioral therapy were to depression (12), anxiety (13), and various other problems including anger, stress, somatic disorders, sexual dysfunction, and pain (14, 15). More recently, cognitive-behavioral therapies have been applied to such complex problems as personality disorders (16–18), schizophrenia (19, 20), crises (21, 22), and suicidal behavior (23). Consistent with this focus on more complex problems, cognitive-behavioral therapies have increasingly been applied to substance abuse (24–30). In fact, two recent multi-site, randomized, controlled studies of alcohol and substance abuse have included cognitive-behavioral therapies as main treatment conditions. In Project MATCH (31), funded by the National Institute on Alcohol Abuse and Alcoholism, the cognitive-behavioral treatment developed by Kadden and colleagues (26) is based on a manual by Monti and colleagues (29). In the Collaborative Cocaine Treatment study (32), funded by the National Institute on Drug Abuse, the cognitive-behavioral treatment was developed by Beck and colleagues (24).

In this chapter two major cognitive-behavioral theories of substance abuse are reviewed, principles of treatment are discussed, and specific techniques are described. To illustrate the use of cognitive-behavioral therapy for substance abuse, the case example of "Carla" is used throughout the chapter. Carla, a 32-year-old woman, enters psychotherapy for depression, including crying spells, sleep problems, weight gain, and poor concentration. She reports that she has always had difficulties with intense feelings like anger, loneliness, and boredom. She admits that she has no friends because "people always stab you in the back." She states: "I've seen over a dozen therapists, and they've all given up on me." When the therapist asks Carla how she copes with her problems, she admits, "I smoke pot every day." Carla explains that smoking marihuana helps her "relax and enjoy life." She has tried to reduce her marihuana use, but says, "I can't fall asleep at night without smoking a joint." She recently quit her job as a child care worker after learning that her employer had implemented random drug screening. The therapist concludes that Carla's depression is at least partly related to her marihuana use. Carla reluctantly agrees: "Marihuana *might* be contributing to some of my problems."

COGNITIVE-BEHAVIORAL THEORIES OF SUBSTANCE ABUSE

The application of cognitive-behavioral theories to substance abuse is a relatively recent occurrence. Indeed, for most of this century up until the mid 1980s, the field of psychotherapy largely ignored substance abuse, viewing it as a superficial symptom of more important underlying problems. However, as substance abuse has become more widely recognized, interest in developing effective treatments has increased among both cognitive-behavioral and psychodynamic theorists (33).

In this section, two major cognitive-behavioral theories of substance abuse are described: relapse prevention (27) and cognitive therapy (24). These theories provide the conceptual foundation for treatment strategies discussed later in this chapter. Both of these cognitive-behavioral theories make the following assumptions:

1. Substance abuse is mediated by complex cognitive and behavioral processes.

2. Substance abuse and associated cognitive-behavioral processes are, to a large extent, learned.

3. Substance abuse and associated cognitive-behavioral processes can be modified, particularly by means of cognitive-behavioral treatment.

4. A major goal of cognitive-behavioral substance abuse treatment is to facilitate the acquisition of specific skills for resisting substance use and general coping skills for reducing the problems associated with substance abuse.

5. Cognitive-behavioral therapies require comprehensive case conceptualizations that serve as the basis for selecting specific cognitive-behavioral techniques.

6. In order to be effective, cognitive-behavioral therapies must be provided in the context of warm, supportive, collaborative therapeutic relationships.

Relapse Prevention: Marlatt and Gordon

Most cognitive-behavioral treatments are derived at least in part from the ground-breaking work of Marlatt and Gordon (27). Their relapse prevention model is important for several reasons: it was the first major cognitive-behavioral approach to substance abuse; it provides practical, flexible interventions that can be applied by a wide range of clinicians; it can be used adjunctively with other treatments; and, it provides a straightforward conceptual model for understanding substance abuse. Their sensitive descriptions of substance abusers' subjective experiences, as well as their clear articulation of a theoretical model and specific interventions, have contributed to making Marlatt and Gordon's text the seminal cognitive-behavioral work on substance abuse (34, 35). Some popular relapse prevention concepts and techniques have included the identification and avoidance of high-risk situations, exploration of the decision chain leading to drug use, lifestyle modification (e.g., choosing friends who do not use), and learning from "slips" in order to prevent future relapses. Originally developed for addictive behaviors, relapse prevention has since been adapted for a wide variety of psychological and behavioral problems (36, 37).

Marlatt and Gordon's (27) cognitive-behavioral model is illustrated in Figure 49.1. According to their model, the potential for relapse begins with a high-risk situation, defined as any circumstance "that poses a threat to the individual's sense of control and increases the risk of potential relapse" (38, p. 37). The most common high-risk situations are negative emotional states, interpersonal conflicts, and social pressure (39). Individuals with effective coping re-

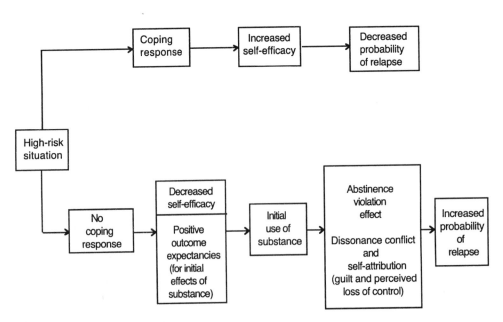

Figure 49.1.   A cognitive-behavioral model of the relapse process. (Reprinted by permission from Marlatt GA. Relapse prevention: theoretical rationale and overview of the model. In: Marlatt GA, Gordon JR, eds. Relapse prevention: maintenance strategies in the treatment of addictive behavior. New York: Guilford Press, 1985:38. Copyright 1985 by Guilford Press.)

sponses (e.g., alcohol and drug refusal skills) are most likely to develop self-efficacious beliefs (i.e., self-confidence) about their abilities to refrain from substance use. Self-efficacy, in turn, decreases their probability of relapse.

In contrast to individuals with effective coping responses, those without effective coping responses have decreased self-efficacy regarding their abilities to resist substance use. They are more likely to expect positive effects from initial substance use. Decreased self-efficacy and positive outcome expectancies lead to initial substance use (i.e., a "slip"), which may lead to the abstinence violation effect (AVE). The AVE is a form of cognitive dissonance that results from the discrepancy between a commitment to abstinence and subsequent use (e.g., "I've violated my abstinence, so I might as well give up on recovery."). The AVE, characterized by feelings of guilt and a perceived loss of control, increases the probability of relapse.

Carla's high-risk situations usually involve negative emotions. She lacks constructive cognitive and behavioral strategies for regulating these emotions and therefore she believes that she must smoke marihuana to feel good. She has attempted to quit many times, but she views even a single "hit" as complete failure (the AVE). Thus, each use leads to a downward spiral of extended marihuana use. To reduce her dependence on marihuana it will be essential for Carla to develop more effective cognitive and behavioral coping strategies.

Cognitive Therapy of Substance Abuse: Beck and Colleagues

The cognitive therapy of substance abuse, developed by Beck, Liese, and colleagues (24, 40–43), is based on the same basic principles as cognitive therapy for other problems, such as depression (12), anxiety (13), and personality disorders (16). Like other cognitive-behavioral substance abuse therapies, cognitive therapy has been substantially influenced by the work of Marlatt and Gordon (27).

Cognitive therapy is based on the premise that substance abuse involves numerous complex behaviors driven largely by drug-related beliefs, automatic thoughts, and facilitating beliefs. Complex behaviors involve the acquisition and consumption of substances as well as actions to avoid the negative consequences of substance abuse (e.g., lying about drinking to avoid conflicts with a spouse). Drug-related beliefs involve positive ("anticipatory") beliefs about the effects of substance use (e.g., "Nothing feels as great as getting stoned!"), as well as negative ("relief-oriented") beliefs about the effects of refraining from substance use (e.g., "If I quit now, I'll get the

shakes."). Automatic thoughts are brief, abbreviated ideas that spontaneously flash across a person's mind. Some automatic thoughts manifest themselves as sharp visual images, like frozen frames from a movie (e.g., the image of taking a gulp of ice-cold beer on a hot summer's day). Facilitating beliefs involve permission to use despite prior commitments to stop using.

The cognitive model is presented in Figure 49.2. Based on the work of Marlatt and Gordon (27), this model views substance use as being triggered by activating stimuli (synonymous with "high-risk situations"). Activating stimuli are categorized according to whether they occur internally or externally. For example, internal cues may include negative feelings (e.g., anxiety, boredom), positive feelings (e.g., joy, excitement), memories (e.g., flashbacks of being abused), and physiological sensations (e.g., cravings, pain). Examples of external cues include interpersonal conflicts, sights and sounds (e.g., seeing or hearing a beer can popped open), other substance users, problems at school or work, and celebration times (e.g., parties, holidays).

In response to internal and external cues, people use psychoactive substances because they believe they will either increase positive feelings (i.e., pleasure), or they will alleviate negative feelings (i.e., pain). These anticipatory and relief-oriented beliefs lead to automatic thoughts and images (e.g., "I need a drink!" "I want a hit!"), that result in craving for the substance. Following these cravings, individuals may give themselves permission to use (e.g., "I'll quit soon." "Just one won't hurt me."). Permissive beliefs lead to action plans, which eventually lead to continued use or relapse.

Carla's depression activates a string of thoughts and beliefs: "No one likes me and that's why I'm alone. Life sucks. Only pot makes me feel better." As Carla imagines herself smoking a joint her cravings grow so strong that she starts to believe, "I'll never quit." She tries to resist her cravings, but after a few minutes she gives herself permission to smoke: "Just a few tokes won't hurt me." Her cravings grow even stronger as she searches her closet for marihuana and imagines herself getting high. After just one hit Carla says to herself, "I've blown it again; I'm nothing but a damn addict!" (and she continues smoking). This vicious cycle recurs each time she smokes: depressed feelings, drug-related beliefs, automatic thoughts, strong cravings, permission to use, marihuana use, and the exacerbation of her depressed feelings.

Recently, Liese and Franz (42) have proposed a model for the development of substance abuse. As shown in Figure 49.3, individuals are more likely to abuse substances if they have had difficult or traumatic early life experiences. Such experiences contribute to basic beliefs about their own unlovability and inadequacy (e.g., "My situation will never improve"), which in turn increase the likelihood of experimentation with drugs and alcohol. As substance use continues, positive substance-related beliefs become increasingly salient.

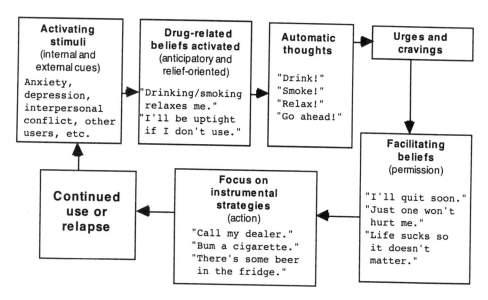

Figure 49.2. Cognitive therapy model of substance abuse. (Reprinted by permission from Liese BS, Franz RA. Treating substance use disorders with cognitive therapy: lessons learned and implications for the future. In: Salkovskis P, ed. Frontiers of cognitive therapy. New York: Guilford Press, 1996:477. Copyright 1996 by Guilford Press.)

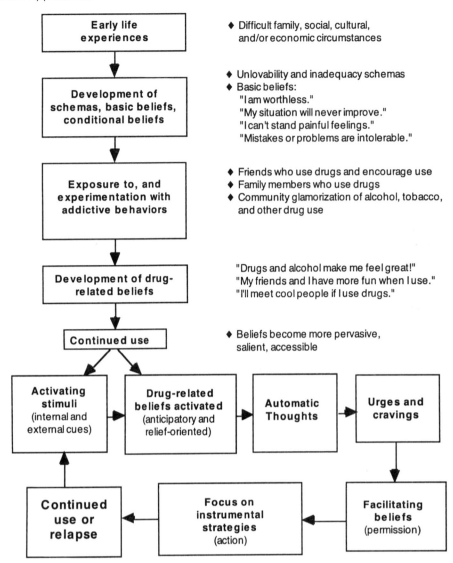

Figure 49.3. A cognitive-developmental model of substance abuse. (Reprinted by permission from Liese BS, Franz RA. Treating substance use disorders with cognitive therapy: lessons learned and implications for the future. In: Salkovskis P, ed. Frontiers of cognitive therapy. New York: Guilford Press, 1996:482. Copyright 1996 by Guilford Press.)

As a child, Carla was subjected to relentless verbal abuse by her parents. Her mother tended to criticize her appearance (e.g., "You look fat in that dress!") and her father tended to criticize her academic performance (e.g., "You're so stupid. I don't know why you even bother with school!"). These messages contributed to Carla's beliefs that she was "basically ugly and stupid." By the time Carla entered middle school, she hated herself. She became increasingly involved with other troubled kids, who seemed to accept her. By seventh grade Carla was smoking cigarettes, in eighth grade she began drinking alcohol, and in ninth grade she started smoking marihuana. With each new substance, Carla strengthened her belief that drugs could make her feel good. In eleventh grade, she dropped out of school. By that time she was smoking marihuana heavily. More than any other drug, marihuana provided the "numbing" effects she desired.

BASIC PRINCIPLES

Regardless of the specific therapeutic techniques selected, certain basic principles are important to all cognitive-behavioral substance abuse treatments. These principles include collaboration, case conceptualization, structure, and psychoeducation.

Collaboration

Carla has never fully trusted people. Unfortunately, some of her substance abuse treatment experiences reinforced her mistrust. She dropped out of one treatment center that made her feel humiliated by continually telling her that her *only* important problem was her addiction. Carla's counselor in that program would steer her away from her depression or other problems. When Carla would cry her therapist would say, "You're giving in to your addiction. You can't let it beat you down. You've got to fight back."

Cognitive-behavioral therapies for substance abuse are highly collaborative, supportive, and empathetic (24, 40–46). Collaboration is important because it creates a trusting atmosphere that supports the difficult work of changing addictive behaviors.

Substance abusers tend to evoke more negative responses in therapists than many other patient populations (47, 48). Some therapists feel frustrated, angry, or helpless because they are unable to stop patients from substance use. Many find that they cannot compete with substances that provide more intense and immediate effects than therapy. Some therapists feel frustrated because they cannot relate to the chronically impaired lives of such patients.

Cognitive-behavioral therapists are strongly encouraged to directly confront their prejudiced thoughts about patients who abuse substances (41, 42). For example, rather than thinking "This drug addict will never change," therapists are taught to think, "If I am patient, this person may eventually make some important changes." Therapists are also encouraged to use effective communication skills with patients. For example, they are discouraged from lecturing and cajoling patients; instead, active listening and roleplaying are recommended. When patients want to discuss non–substance-related problems, therapists are encouraged to spend appropriate time discussing, rather than minimizing, these problems. Therapists are also encouraged to regularly elicit feedback about patients' responses to therapy by asking such questions as, "What was most and least helpful about our talk today?" and "How will you implement the things we've talked about?"

At the very least, collaboration is important for retaining patients in treatment (41). When Carla first entered cognitive-behavioral therapy she was guarded and suspicious. To her surprise, Carla's therapist listened in a warm, caring, and nonjudgmental manner. By having such a therapist, Carla was helped to draw her own conclusions about her substance use. At first Carla was skeptical. However, she began to trust her therapist and she continued treatment. Though her progress was extremely slow (she was still smoking marihuana after 9 months of treatment), her therapist maintained a warm, accepting attitude.

Cognitive-behavioral substance abuse treatments emphasize the importance of adapting treatment to individuals, rather than expecting individuals to adapt to treatment. For example, some treatments make therapy more engaging by using inspirational quotations and stories, simplified cognitive-be-havioral therapy forms, and summary session handouts (46), others use reward systems (49, 50), while others call patients at home when they miss sessions (24).

Case Conceptualization

Substance use patients comprise an extremely heterogeneous group. Some have no coexisting psychiatric problems while others have one or more psychiatric syndromes (e.g., depression, anxiety, posttraumatic stress disorder [PTSD], schizophrenia, bipolar illness, or personality disorders). Some are highly motivated to change while others deny that they have serious problems. Some have major coexisting life problems, such as AIDS or homelessness, while others are stable and high-functioning.

The case conceptualization involves the process of assessing patients' backgrounds, presenting problems, psychiatric diagnoses, developmental profiles, and cognitive-behavioral profiles (24, 40, 42). This process may be facilitated by the use of standardized assessment instruments. Sobell, Toneatto, and Sobell (51) provide an excellent review of clinical instruments useful for the conceptualization of patients with substance use problems. Additionally, Beck (52) has developed a case conceptualization diagram (Fig. 49.4) that can be used effectively with patients who abuse substances. This diagram enables therapists to organize information about the development and maintenance of patients' substance use, as well as other problems.

Carla's case conceptualization diagram is presented in Figure 49.4. Her presenting problems include daily marihuana use and depressive symptoms.

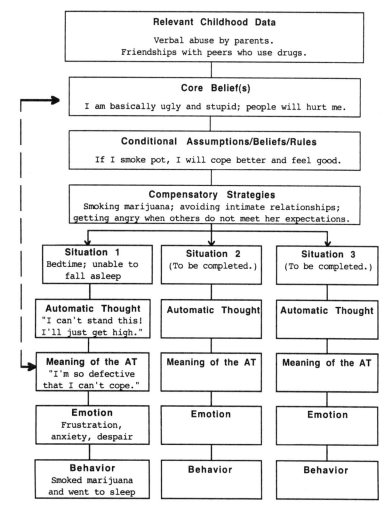

Figure 49.4. Cognitive Conceptualization Diagram. (Reprinted by permission from Beck JS. Cognitive therapy: basics and beyond. New York: Guilford Press, 1995:139. Copyright 1993 by Judith S. Beck.)

Her Axis I psychiatric diagnoses include marihuana dependence and major depression. On Axis II she has some borderline personality features (e.g., affective instability, intense interpersonal relationships, impulsivity, chronic feelings of boredom and emptiness). As previously discussed, relevant childhood data include parents that were verbally abusive and friends that used drugs. Carla's core beliefs are "I am basically ugly and stupid" and "People will hurt me." Important conditional beliefs involve the use of marihuana to reduce pain ("If I smoke pot, I will cope better and feel good." and "If I try to cope without smoking marihuana, I will fail.") Carla's most salient compensatory strategy is to smoke marihuana. For example at bedtime, when Carla is unable to fall asleep, she thinks: "I can't stand this! I'll just get high" (and she does).

The case conceptualization would be incomplete without an assessment of motivation to change. Prochaska, DiClemente, and Norcross (53, 54) have developed a system for assessing individuals' readiness to change. Substance abusers who believe that they have no problems are considered to be in the precontemplation stage. Those who believe that they may have problems are in the contemplation stage. Those taking steps to get ready for change are in the preparation stage. Those who have changed for at least 24 hours are in the action stage. And those who have endured change for at least 6 months are in the maintenance stage.

Like most other substance abusers, Carla has experienced dramatic fluctuations in her readiness to change. Upon entering cognitive-behavioral therapy she was highly motivated to reduce her depression, but only minimally motivated to reduce her marihuana use. As her therapist elicited background information from Carla, her ambivalence about change became apparent. Carla's therapist was able to use this information to "meet Carla where she was at" in the change process. At no time did Carla's cognitive-behavioral therapist demand that she stop using marihuana or threaten to end treatment if she continued to use.

Research on the stages of change model has consistently shown evidence of a relationship between readiness to change and treatment outcome (53). Hence, cognitive-behavioral therapists are encouraged to carefully assess individuals' thoughts and behaviors regarding change and choose therapeutic interventions accordingly. For example, those who are precontemplators are unlikely to benefit from interventions that are heavy-handed and focus on specific methods of changing. Instead, precontemplators are likely to positively respond to discussions in which they are listened to openly and empathetically and encouraged to discuss ambivalence.

Structure

Most cognitive-behavioral therapies, with their standardized techniques and procedures, are relatively structured. In the cognitive therapy of substance abuse (24, 40, 42), for example, the structure includes setting the agenda, checking the patient's mood, bridging from the last visit (including a review of substance use, urges, cravings, and upcoming triggers), discussion of problems (including potential coping strategies and skill-building activities), frequent summaries, the assignment and review of homework, and feedback from the patient about the session.

Similarly, in Project MATCH (31) each cognitive-behavioral session is highly structured. In session 1, for example, therapists spend the first 45 minutes building rapport and collecting data with such questions as "Tell me about yourself." and "How serious do you think your substance use problem is?" and "Why are you seeking treatment now?" Next, therapists spend 5 minutes "conceptualizing treatment" and providing a cognitive-behavioral explanation of alcohol abuse. Following this, therapists spend 15 minutes teaching patients to assess high-risk situations, they spend 5 minutes attempting to boost motivation, they spend 10 minutes discussing the contract and ground rules, and finally they spend 5 minutes assigning homework. Therapists are encouraged to probe for patients' understanding throughout sessions. Structure is further provided by written forms and schedules that are completed in sessions and as homework (26).

Cognitive-behavioral therapies for substance abuse are also offered in group settings. For example, in a new cognitive-behavioral treatment group for substance abuse and PTSD (46), there are eight behavioral sessions, eight cognitive sessions, and eight interpersonal sessions. Each session contains the following (46, p. 16): a review of group members' use since the last session; a tally of group members' attendance, abstinence, and homework completion; reading of a brief inspirational quotation; an introduction to the agenda by the leader; discussion of the agenda topic (with opportunities to practice new skills); homework review, and closure.

Early in therapy Carla became irritated with her therapist because she viewed the structure of cognitive-behavioral therapy as "controlling." At one point she said to her therapist, "You remind me of my parents!" As time progressed, however, she grew to appreciate the consistency provided by structured therapy and understand how structure facilitates the accomplishment of goals.

Psychoeducation

Cognitive-behavioral therapies usually incorporate significant psychoeducational efforts, particularly early in treatment. The complexity of biological, behavioral, cognitive, and spiritual problems associated with substance abuse requires that cognitive-behavioral therapists be well informed about these areas.

Psychoeducation is a delicate process. Just as individuals vary in their readiness to change, they also vary in their readiness to attend to educational interventions. Both timing and style of delivery determine the value of psychoeducational presentations. Rather than randomly lecturing patients, cognitive-behavioral therapists elicit knowledge from patients in areas relevant to their circumstances and needs. When patients expose knowledge deficits, therapists offer opportunities for patients to learn more by means of brief lectures, written materials, videotapes, or workbooks on a variety of topics. Obviously, long lectures are inappropriate. ("Too long" is defined as the point at which patients become bored or distracted). Areas for education might include specific strategies for managing cravings, general coping skills, physiological effects of particular substances, high-risk behaviors, the impact of substance use on the family, dual diagnosis, and psychological models for understanding substance abuse. Information in these areas may be found in cognitive-behavioral treatment manuals or they may be obtained free from extensive resource libraries, for example the National Clearinghouse for Alcohol and Drug Information (800-729-6686).

Carla was in treatment for only a short time when her therapist became confident that her marihuana use was contributing to her depression. When the therapist thought Carla might benefit from learning about the relationship between depression and chronic marihuana use, he asked Carla: "What do you know about the relationship between depression and marihuana use?" She replied, "You're not going to give me a big lecture now, are you?" The therapist replied, "You seem turned off by the idea," and Carla agreed that she was. The therapist dropped the subject until some time later when Carla said, "I'm forgetting a lot of things lately. I feel like I'm getting Alzheimer's disease or something." Carla's therapist responded by asking, "Would you like to hear about the effects of marihuana on memory?" At this time, Carla seemed receptive to such a discussion, and her therapist gave her a brief lecture and some written materials. Carla seemed genuinely interested at this time.

SPECIFIC TREATMENTS AND TECHNIQUES

Cognitive-behavioral therapies for substance abuse comprise a wide range of specific treatments and techniques (55, 56). Tables 49.1–49.3 list a sampling of cognitive-behavioral therapies for substance abuse. Most listed treatments have full-length manuals, and most have undergone or are currently undergoing empirical validation. While the list is not exhaustive, it provides a view of the variety of treatments available.

Despite their diversity, there are several strategies common to most cognitive-behavioral treatments of substance abuse. These strategies include monitoring substance use, motivational interviewing, identifying the cognitive-behavioral chain of events, management of cravings, case management, referral to self-help groups, reinforcement contingencies, focus on retention, attention to coexisting psychiatric disorders, emphasis on harm reduction, enhancement of social support, and lifestyle change. Each of these strategies is briefly described in this section.

Table 49.1 A Sampling of Cognitive Behavioral Therapies (CBTs) for Substance Abuse: General Models

Population	Treatment	Authors	Notes
General	Relapse prevention	Marlatt and Gordon (27)	First comprehensive CBT developed for substance abuse; ground-breaking theoretical and practical model.
General	Cognitive therapy	Beck et al. (24)	Cognitive therapy applied to substance abuse.
General	Contingency management	Anker and Crowley (57)	Community reinforcement approach with contingency management as central theme.
General	Behavior therapy	Higgins et al. (50)	Behavioral model emphasizing positive reinforcement (e.g., payment for clean urine screens; social reinforcement).
General	Cue exposure	Childress et al. (58)	A behavioral extinction model to eliminate response to drug-related cues.
General	Aversion therapy	Holder et al. (59)	Aversion methods used to create conditioned negative response to drug cues.
General	Network therapy	Galanter (60)	Use of the patient's social network to provide social reinforcement and monitoring of substance use.

Treatments are included in this table if a treatment manual has been developed and is being (or has been) subjected to empirical testing. Treatments are included if they address alcohol or major psychoactive drugs of abuse (i.e., not nicotine or caffeine). The table is selective, not comprehensive.

Table 49.2 A Sampling of Cognitive Behavioral Therapies (CBTs) for Substance Abuse: Specific Substances of Abuse

Substance	Treatment	Authors	Notes
Cocaine	Relapse prevention	Carroll et al. (61)	Adaptation of relapse prevention for cocaine abuse.
Cocaine	Neuro-behavioral	Rawson et al. (62)	Integrates relapse prevention with biological stage model.
Crack cocaine	Relapse prevention	Wallace et al. (63)	Adaptation of relapse prevention for crack cocaine abuse.
Cocaine	Intensive outpatient	Washton (64)	A blend of relapse prevention and Stages of Change models.
Alcohol	Relapse prevention	Monti et al. (29) Kadden et al. (26)	Original CBT manual for alcohol dependence and adapted version for Project MATCH (the largest study of CBT and other treatments for alcoholism).
Marihuana	Relapse prevention	Roffman et al. (65)	Adaptation of relapse prevention for marihuana abuse.
Opioids	Recovery training/self-help	McAuliffe and Ch'ien (66)	A hybrid of relapse prevention plus guided self-help.
Alcohol	Guided self-change	Sobell and Sobell (30)	Combined CBT and motivational approach for nonsevere problem drinkers.
Alcohol	Relapse prevention	Annis (67)	Emphasis on teaching patients to identify and cope with high-risk situations.

Treatments are included in this table if a treatment manual has been developed and is being (or has been) subjected to empirical testing. Treatments are included if they address alcohol or major psychoactive drugs of abuse (i.e., not nicotine or caffeine). The table is selective, not comprehensive.

Table 49.3 A Sampling of Cognitive Behavioral Therapies (CBTs) for Substance Abuse: Dual Diagnosis

Disorder	Treatment	Authors	Notes
Schizophrenia	Relapse prevention	Ziedonis and Fisher (68)	Uses the stages of change model and CBT to treat schizophrenics with substance abuse.
PTSD	CBT	Najavits et al. (46)	Adapts CBT to the themes and problems of patients with PTSD and substance abuse.
Bipolar disorder	Relapse prevention	Weiss et al. (69)	Adapts relapse prevention to bipolar disorder, with emphasis on medication compliance.
Borderline personality disorder	Dialectical behavior therapy	Linehan (70)	Dialectical behavior therapy applied to substance abuse.

Treatments are included in this table if a treatment manual has been developed and is being (or has been) subjected to empirical testing. Treatments are included if they address alcohol or major psychoactive drugs of abuse (i.e., not nicotine or caffeine). The table is selective, not comprehensive. Each of these models is currently undergoing empirical testing; and all were funded by the NIDA Behavioral Therapies Development Program.

Monitoring Substance Use

Cognitive-behavioral therapists actively monitor the types, quantities, and routes of recent substance use at each treatment session. By doing so, they assess their patients' current substance use status and estimate the impact of therapy. There are various methods for monitoring substance use (51). While self-report is the most common, urine and breathalyzer tests provide more objective data. Some forms of urine and breathalyzer testing are relatively easy to implement and some insurance companies will pay for this type of monitoring. Some patients report that they have been helped by substance use monitoring, despite initial resistance to it. For example, Carla initially resisted drug testing; however, when her therapist urged Carla to submit to drug testing she agreed, stating: "I'd like to see how long it takes to get pot out of my system."

One of the most commonly used self-report instruments for monitoring substance use is the *Timeline Followback* (TLFB) (71). Originally developed for alcohol use, the TLFB facilitates patients' recall of their substance use patterns over specified periods of time. This method has demonstrated reliability, especially when memory aids are used to facilitate recollection of substance use (51).

A relatively new self-report battery for assessing substance use is Form 90 (72), developed for project MATCH. Form 90 is a calendar-based structured interview that offers measures of alcohol consumption and related variables (72). Another method for assessing substance use is the widely used Addiction Severity Index (73). These instruments can be augmented with collateral data from family members, probation officers, or other persons who have knowledge of patients' substance use. Regardless of the method chosen, asking patients about substance use at each session is an essential component of cognitive-behavioral treatment and the accuracy of self-reports is enhanced when confidentiality is assured (51).

Motivational Interviewing

Motivational interviewing (44) refers to the process of communicating with patients in ways that facilitate their readiness to change substance use behaviors. Motivational interviewing is designed to address ambivalence and move patients from one stage of motivation to the next. There are five principles underlying motivational interviewing (44, p. 5): (*a*) express em-

	Abstinence	**Continued smoking**
Advantages	• Less depressed • Maybe feel better about myself • My kids won't have a mother who has a drug problem • Save money • Good for my health	• Fall asleep easier • Helps me deal with my problems • Easier than quitting
Disadvantages	• I have no other method for feeling better • I'll have trouble falling asleep • Can't forget my problems	• Depression • Spend money • Could get into legal problems • Bad for my health

Figure 49.5. Advantages-Disadvantages Analysis. (Reprinted by permission from Beck AT, Wright FD, Newman CF, Liese BS. Cognitive therapy of substance abuse. New York: Guilford Press, 1993:138. Copyright 1993 by Guilford Press.)

pathy, (*b*) help patients to see discrepancies in their lives, (*c*) avoid argumentation, (*d*) roll with resistance, and (*e*) support patients' development of self-efficacy.

A standard cognitive therapy technique for motivating patients is the advantages-disadvantages (A-D) analysis (24, 40, 42). In the A-D analysis, a four-cell matrix is drawn (Fig. 49.5) and patients are helped to list and evaluate the advantages and disadvantages of using versus not using substances. Carla's A-D analysis is presented in Figure 49.5. By completing this analysis, Carla and her therapist gain a greater appreciation for her ambivalence about marihuana use. The therapist, of course, focuses her attention on the disadvantages of using and the advantages of abstinence. But, moreover, Carla's therapist helps her imagine how she might achieve some of the advantages of smoking marihuana (e.g., falling asleep at night and dealing with her problems) without actually smoking it. For example, Carla's therapist teaches her relaxation techniques to help her fall asleep at night.

Identifying the Cognitive-Behavioral Chain of Events

The chain of events (i.e., precursors) associated with substance use include particular circumstances, feelings, beliefs, thoughts, and actions. Virtually all cognitive-behavioral treatments attempt to identify precursors that trigger substance use. An important assumption of cognitive-behavioral therapies is that patients can learn to manage these precursors (and thereby manage their substance use) after learning how they operate in their lives.

Liese and Franz (42) have developed a worksheet for identifying the cognitive-behavioral events leading to substance use (Fig. 49.6). This worksheet, which is actually a blank version of the cognitive model in Figure 49.2, provides a standardized form for collecting data while simultaneously teaching patients about the cognitive-behavioral dynamics of their substance use.

When Carla revealed that she had smoked marihuana on the day before one of her sessions, her therapist asked the following questions: "What led

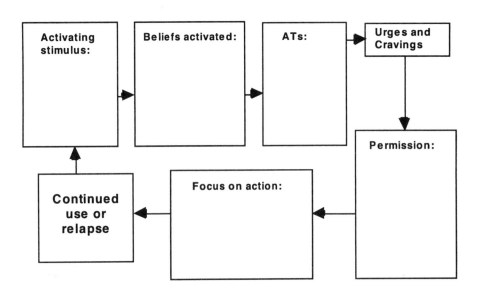

Figure 49.6. Cognitive Model Worksheet (completed with patient). (Reprinted by permission from Liese BS, Franz RA. Treating substance use disorders with cognitive therapy: lessons learned and implications for the future. In: Salkovskis P, ed. Frontiers of cognitive therapy. New York: Guilford Press, 1996:490. Copyright 1996 by Guilford Press.)

to your smoking? What were you doing prior to the time you began to smoke? What was going on around you? What were you feeling? What were your beliefs? Your automatic thoughts? How did you give yourself permission?" To facilitate this process, Carla's therapist said, "Imagine that you're watching a videotape replay of the scene and let's figure out what triggered you to smoke."

Annis' (67) relapse prevention approach places substantial emphasis on high-risk situations in the cognitive-behavioral chain of events. In fact, she has developed several standardized measures for assessing and monitoring such situations: the Inventory of Drinking Situations (74), the Inventory of Drug-Taking Situations (75) and the Situational Confidence Questionnaire (76). After identifying triggers, patients are taught to avoid them when possible and cope with them when they are unavoidable. Most cognitive-behavioral therapies identify craving as an important high-risk link in the cognitive-behavioral chain and most offer skills for managing cravings.

Management of Cravings

As patients attempt to overcome substance abuse, cravings are inevitable. There are numerous cognitive-behavioral strategies for managing cravings. Perhaps the most parsimonious are the distraction techniques. In one behavioral technique, patients snap rubber bands worn on their wrists to distract themselves from cravings. The cognitive version of this technique is thought-stopping wherein patients silently shout "stop!" (to themselves) when experiencing cravings. Cognitive-behavioral therapists can also use cognitive strategies such as flash cards, imagery, advantages-disadvantages analyses, and daily thought records to reinforce beliefs and thoughts that reduce cravings. For other examples of cognitive techniques, see McMullin (77).

Most cognitive techniques for managing cravings involve distinguishing between "addictive beliefs" (beliefs that promote substance use) and "control beliefs" (beliefs that promote abstinence). Beck and colleagues (24, p. 312) provide a list of addictive beliefs associated with craving, including the following:

"Craving can drive you crazy."
"I don't have any control over the craving."
"I can't stand the physical symptoms I have while craving."
"The craving makes me so nervous, I can't stand it."
"When I'm really craving drugs, I can't function."
"Either I'm craving drugs or I'm not; there's nothing in between."
"When craving drugs it's okay to use alcohol."
"The craving is stronger than my will power."

In one of her first sessions, Carla described herself as struggling with most of these addictive beliefs. Carla's therapist asked her to respond to each belief with control beliefs that would contradict these addictive beliefs. For example, in response to the first belief, "Craving can drive you crazy," Carla responded with such control beliefs as, "The cravings won't drive me crazy," and "The cravings will eventually go away." She also generated some humorous responses like, "I'm already crazy so I can't get any crazier!" and "What the hell, it's fun to be crazy!" Carla wrote these responses on index cards, which served as anti-craving flash cards. In fact, at a later date, Carla explained that, "the humorous cards were the ones that really helped me."

Case Management

Substance abusers typically suffer from variety of serious life problems, including health, legal, employment, family, and housing problems. In some cases these are the sequelae of substance use (e.g., a heroin abuser who has contracted HIV by sharing needles). In other cases these life problems may have led to substance abuse (e.g., a teenage girl who uses alcohol to cope with ongoing sexual abuse). Actively addressing these real life issues is considered a necessary component of cognitive-behavioral therapy.

There are numerous opportunities for cognitive-behavioral therapists to provide case management services. For example, they might refer patients for specialized assistance (e.g., medical, legal, or vocational counseling), give patients listings of sober houses, help patients fill out welfare forms, re-view newspaper job listings during sessions, monitor patients' important visits to their physicians, help patients complete domestic abuse restraining orders, or call detoxification hospital units to determine whether beds are available. Thus, therapists must be familiar with community resources, including legal services, detoxification centers, HIV testing sites, and self-help groups.

Referral to Self-Help Groups

It is important for cognitive-behavioral therapists to be familiar with self-help groups and make appropriate referrals to these groups. Such groups may include Alcoholics Anonymous (78) and other 12-step programs (Cocaine Anonymous, Narcotics Anonymous; Al-Anon for family members; Codependents Anonymous, Gamblers Anonymous, Overeaters Anonymous). In addition to the more traditional self-help groups, a new generation of self-help groups has recently arisen, based on cognitive-behavioral principles. These groups include Rational Recovery (79) and Moderation Management (80). It is important for cognitive-behavioral therapists to become familiar with these groups and make appropriate referrals. However, it is not considered beneficial to proselytize or coerce patients to attend such groups (81).

Providing basic information about the process and content of self-help groups is important in the treatment of substance abuse. Ideally, therapists might attend several groups in order to personally observe them. At the very least, cognitive-behavioral therapists should provide patients with lists of self-help groups, encourage them to attend, and follow-up with questions about groups. There are numerous issues that may be addressed in therapy relating to self-help groups. For example, therapists may address how patients feel about going to first group meetings; how they manage anxiety about speaking at such groups or socializing with others; how they find the right group for them; how they distinguish between more and less helpful aspects of groups; and how they respond to others in groups who do not believe in psychotherapy or medication. In short, self-help groups may be important adjuncts to cognitive-behavioral substance abuse treatment and they may even occasionally become the focus of therapy.

Reinforcement Contingencies

All cognitive-behavioral models implement reinforcement of some kind. Such reinforcement is usually positive (e.g., praise, payment vouchers), though some programs have investigated negative contingencies (e.g., inducing nausea). In some treatments (e.g., behavior therapy), positive reinforcement is the central mechanism of treatment (49, 50). Formal systems are devised, such as paying patients for clean urines with increasing rates of pay for longer periods of abstinence (e.g., $1.50 for the first urine; $3.00 for the third). In some programs, patients are provided with vouchers for items such as sports equipment and movie passes.

Another version of contingency management involves the use of social reinforcement contracts. Social reinforcement is a central technique in some behavior therapies and in network therapy (60) in particular. In negative reinforcement models, the patient agrees to have some aversive experience that will aid in diminishing substance use. Extinction models (58) in contrast, rely on eliminating responses to drug cues. Even in cognitive-behavioral treatments that do not formally provide rewards for behavior change, reinforcement manifests itself as session-by-session monitoring of goals, with therapist praise for successive approximations of abstinence.

Focus on Retention

Substance abuse patients have notoriously high treatment dropout rates (82). Thus, it is important to explicitly discuss retention with substance-abusing patients, especially when sessions are missed. In short, therapists are encouraged to do "whatever is reasonable" to retain patients in therapy. Some therapists, particularly in the past, believed in ejecting patients from treatment if they used substances. However, in cognitive-behavioral therapies, this approach is virtually never indicated.

Techniques for maximizing retention include general psychotherapeutic strategies such as cultivating rapport, collaboration, and alliance, as well as specific cognitive techniques such as the exploration of cognitions associated with missed sessions (41). In addition, behavioral strategies are encouraged, including the provision of transportation and onsite babysitting, incentives (e.g., snacks and coffee in the waiting-room), writing patients' appointment times on cards, and confirming appointments via telephone prior to each session.

Attention to Coexisting Psychiatric Disorders

Psychiatric disorders, including depression, anxiety, PTSD, bipolar disorder, and personality disorders tend to coexist with substance abuse (83). Such comorbidity presents significant treatment challenges, since these disorders are intricately bound to substance abuse in complex cyclical patterns. Abstinence from substances may either decrease or increase psychological symptoms. For example, Carla's anxiety and sleep problems increase when she stops using marihuana and most of her depressive symptoms decrease only after extended periods of abstinence.

The etiologies of dual diagnoses are typically complex and multifactorial. While psychiatric disorders might lead some people to "self-medicate," resulting in alcohol or drug problems, substance abuse might lead others to develop psychiatric problems (e.g., cocaine addicts who develop secondary anxiety disorders and depression). Comorbid disorders are known to affect treatment outcome, as seen in a classic study by Woody and colleagues (84), in which psychiatric severity predicted differential response to psychotherapy, including cognitive-behavioral therapy.

In treating dually diagnosed patients, the most important step is the initial assessment (i.e., conceptualization) and monitoring of symptoms throughout treatment. In monitoring it is important to understand the relationships between psychiatric symptoms and drug use, cravings, and withdrawal (85). Following initial assessment, patients with coping skills deficits are taught general coping skills for managing their lives. While previously many patients were told to first become abstinent before comorbid disorders could be addressed (e.g., "First get clean, and then we'll talk about your depression"), most cognitive-behavioral models support more integrated treatments (i.e., treatments that simultaneously address multiple disorders). For example, the cognitive-behavioral dual diagnosis models listed in Table 49.3 take such an approach. In cases where clinicians cannot directly provide dual diagnosis treatment, referral to adjunctive treatments is recommended. Thus, Carla was treated for depression and marihuana dependence with cognitive-behavioral therapy and antidepressants (for depression). She was also encouraged to attend 12-step and relapse prevention groups (though she rarely did so).

Emphasis on Harm Reduction

While abstinence is still widely regarded as the ultimate treatment goal, harm reduction is increasingly recognized as an important transitional goal by many cognitive-behavioral therapists (86, 87). Rather than take an "all-or-none" stance, cognitive-behavioral therapists are likely to accept that some patients elect to reduce their substance use. Indeed, for a subsample of patients, harm reduction (rather than abstinence) may be the most appropriate goal.

Examples of harm reduction strategies include conducting "experiments" to see what abstinence feels like; praising patients for the achievement of transitional goals; and, the replacement of one drug (e.g., heroin) with another drug (e.g., methadone). The most important feature of harm reduction is therapists' attitudes of basic respect for patients and a willingness to accept their decisions and goals.

Enhancement of Social Support

Substance abuse may be associated with extreme impairment of family and social functioning. In fact, the behaviors of some substance abusers results in their experience of "hitting bottom" (e.g., losing their jobs, being evicted from their homes, legal problems, medical problems, and so forth). Many cognitive-behavioral treatments involve family members in an effort to promote social support and compliance with treatment.

Several of the therapies listed in Tables 49.1–49.3 directly involve patients' social networks. In network therapy (60) and behavior therapy (50), for example, family or close friends are invited to attend sessions with patients and actively become involved in treatment contracting. In other treatments, such as cognitive therapy (24), family sessions are provided to enable family members to learn about the treatment and to help secure support for patients' efforts.

Lifestyle Change and Associated Coping Skills

The reduction of substance use is a necessary but not sufficient criterion for treatment success. The lure of substances is likely to remain powerful unless lifestyle change is facilitated in therapy. Virtually every cognitive-behavioral treatment encourages some degree of lifestyle change. This may range from informal discussions of lifestyle options to formal planning of, and participation in activities together (66). Other techniques include contracting for engaging in new activities, referring patients to external resources to develop alternative pursuits (e.g., helping patients sign up for volunteer work), and conducting inventories to identify healthy activities.

In cognitive-behavioral therapy, patients are taught such essential coping skills as communication and mood regulation. To a large extent, these skills are necessary to support any substantial lifestyle changes. Communication skills are taught mostly by means of roleplaying and didactic instruction. Mood regulation is taught by means of cognitive-behavioral techniques (e.g., daily thought records).

SUMMARY AND CONCLUSIONS

Over the past decade, numerous cognitive-behavioral therapies of substance abuse have been developed. These structured, focused, collaborative approaches have been based on the assumption that substance abuse is mediated by complex cognitive-behavioral processes. In this chapter, an overview of cognitive-behavioral substance abuse theories and techniques has been presented. According to Rotgers, these approaches "have been among the most productive of the last quarter century with respect to the advancement of empirically validated knowledge of the origins and treatment of psychoactive substance use disorders" (56, p. 198).

Recently Liese and Franz (42) have described 10 lessons learned from applying cognitive therapy to substance abuse. Specifically, cognitive-behavioral therapists should (a) be knowledgeable about a wide variety of psychoactive drugs, addictive behaviors, and traditional treatment modalities; (b) communicate and collaborate with other addiction treatment personnel; (c) understand and address the role of drugs in mood regulation; (d) conceptualize and treat coexisting psychopathology; (e) explore the development of all patients' drug use problems; (f) address therapeutic relationship issues; (g) confront patients appropriately and effectively; (h) stay focused in sessions; (i) use techniques appropriately and sparingly; and (j) never give up on addicted patients. It is assumed that many more lessons will be learned as cognitive-behavioral therapies continue to be applied to substance abuse.

References

1. Dobson KS, Block L. Historical and philosophical bases of the cognitive-behavioral therapies. In: Dobson KS, ed. Handbook of cognitive-behavioral therapies. New York: Guilford Press, 1988:3–38.
2. Ellis A. Reason and emotion in psychotherapy. Secaucus, NJ: The Citadel Press, 1962.
3. Beck AT. Thinking and depression: 1. Idiosyncratic content and cognitive distortions. Arch Gen Psychiatry 1963;9:36–46.
4. D'Zurilla TJ, Goldfried MR. Problem-solving and behavior modification. J Abnorm Psychol 1971;78:107–126.
5. Goldfried MR, Decenteceo ET, Weinberg L. Systematic rational restructuring as a self-control technique. Behav Ther 1974;5:247–254.
6. Guidano VF, Liotti G. Cognitive processes and emotional disorders: a structural approach to psychotherapy. New York: Guilford Press, 1983.
7. Mahoney MJ. Cognition and behavior modification. Cambridge, MA: Ballinger, 1974.
8. Maultsby MC. Rational behavior therapy. Englewood Cliffs, NJ: Prentice-Hall, 1984.
9. Meichenbaum DH. Cognitive behavior modification. New York: Plenum, 1977.
10. Rehm L. A self-control model of depression. Behav Ther 1977;8:787–804.

11. Spivack G, Platt JJ, Shure MB. The problem-solving approach to adjustment. San Francisco: Jossey-Bass, 1976.

12. Beck AT, Rush AJ, Shaw BF, Emery G. Cognitive therapy of depression. New York: Guilford Press, 1979.

13. Beck AT, Emery G, Greenberg RL. Anxiety disorders and phobias: a cognitive perspective. New York: Basic Books, 1985.

14. Foreyt JP, Rathjen DP, eds. Cognitive behavior therapy: research and application. New York: Plenum, 1978.

15. Kendall PC, Hollon SD, eds. Cognitive-behavioral interventions: theory, research, and procedures. New York: Academic Press, 1979.

16. Beck AT, Freeman A, et al. Cognitive therapy of personality disorders. New York: Guilford Press, 1990.

17. Layden MA, Newman CF, Freeman A, Morse SB. Cognitive therapy of borderline personality disorder. Boston: Allyn and Bacon, 1993.

18. Linehan MM. Cognitive-behavioral treatment of borderline personality disorder. New York: Guilford Press, 1993.

19. Kingdon DG, Turkington D. Cognitive-behavioral therapy of schizophrenia. New York: Guilford Press, 1994.

20. Perris C. Cognitive therapy with schizophrenic patients. New York: Guilford Press, 1989.

21. Dattilio FM, Freeman A, eds. Cognitive-behavioral strategies in crisis intervention. New York: Guilford Press, 1994.

22. Roberts AR, ed. Crisis intervention and time-limited cognitive treatment. Thousand Oaks, CA: Sage, 1995.

23. Freeman A, Reinecke MA. Cognitive therapy of suicidal behavior: a manual for treatment. New York: Springer, 1993.

24. Beck AT, Wright FD, Newman CF, Liese BS. Cognitive therapy of substance abuse. New York: Guilford Press, 1993.

25. Ellis A, Velten E. Rational steps to quitting alcohol. Fort Lee, NJ: Barricade Books, 1992.

26. Kadden R, Carroll K, Donovan D, Cooney N, Monti P, Abrams D, et al. Cognitive-behavioral coping skills therapy manual: a clinical research guide for therapists treating individuals with alcohol abuse and dependence. NIAAA Project MATCH Monograph Series, Volume 3. Washington, DC: U.S. Department of Health and Human Services, 1995.

27. Marlatt GA, Gordon JR. Relapse prevention: maintenance strategies in the treatment of addictive behavior. New York: Guilford Press, 1985.

28. Miller WR, Munoz RF. How to control your drinking. Englewood Cliffs, NJ: Prentice-Hall, 1976.

29. Monti PM, Abrams DB, Kadden RM, Cooney NL. Treating alcohol dependence: a coping skills training guide. New York: Guilford Press, 1989.

30. Sobell MB, Sobell LC. Problem drinkers: guided self-change treatment. New York: Guilford Press, 1993.

31. Project MATCH Research Group. 1993 Project MATCH: rationale and methods for a multisite clinical trial matching patients to alcoholism treatment. Alcohol Clin Exp Res 1993;17:1130–1145.

32. Crits-Christoph P, Siqueland L, Blaine J, et al. The NIDA Collaborative Cocaine Treatment Study: rationale and methods. Arch Gen Psychiatry (in press).

33. Najavits LM, Weiss RD. The role of psychotherapy in the treatment of substance use disorders. Harvard Rev Psychiatry 1994;2:84–96.

34. Rawson RA, Obert JL, McCann MJ, Marinelli-Casey P. Relapse prevention models for substance abuse treatment. Psychotherapy 1993a; 30:284–298.

35. Rawson RA, Obert JL, McCann MJ, Marinelli-Casey P. Relapse prevention strategies in outpatient substance abuse treatment. Psychol Addict Behav 1993b;7:85–95.

36. Brownell KD, Marlatt GA, Lichtenstein E, Wilson GT. Understanding and preventing relapse. Am Psychol 1986;41:765–782.

37. Wilson PH. Principles and practice of relapse prevention. New York: Guilford Press, 1992.

38. Marlatt GA. Relapse prevention: theoretical rationale and overview of the model. In: Marlatt GA, Gordon JR, eds. Relapse prevention: maintenance strategies in the treatment of addictive behavior. New York: Guilford Press, 1985:3–70.

39. Cummings C, Gordon JR, Marlatt GA. Relapse. Prevention and prediction. In: Miller WR, ed. The addictive behaviors: treatment of alcoholism, drug abuse, smoking, and obesity. Oxford, England: Pergamon Press, 1980:291–321.

40. Liese BS. Brief therapy, crisis intervention, and the cognitive therapy of substance abuse. Crisis Intervention and Time-Limited Treatment 1994; 1:11–29.

41. Liese BS, Beck AT. Back to basics: fundamental cognitive therapy skills for keeping drug-dependent individuals in treatment. NIDA Res Monogr (in press).

42. Liese BS, Franz RA. Treating substance use disorders with cognitive therapy: lessons learned and implications for the future. In: Salkovskis P, ed. Frontiers of cognitive therapy. New York: Guilford Press, 1996:470–508.

43. Wright FD, Beck AT, Newman CF, Liese BS. Cognitive therapy of substance abuse: theoretical rationale. NIDA Res Monogr 1992;137: 123–146.

44. Miller WR, Rollnick S. Motivational interviewing: preparing people to change addictive behavior. New York: Guilford Press, 1991.

45. Najavits LM, Weiss RD. Variations in therapist effectiveness in the treatment of patients with substance use disorders: an empirical review. Addiction 1994;89:679–688.

46. Najavits LM, Weiss RD, Liese BS. Group cognitive-behavioral therapy for women with PTSD and substance use disorder. J Subst Abuse Treat 1996;13:13–22.

47. Imhof J. Countertransference issues in alcoholism and drug addiction. Psychiatr Ann 1991; 21:292–306.

48. Najavits LM, Griffin ML, Luborsky L, et al. Therapists' emotional reactions to substance abusers: a new questionnaire and initial findings. Psychotherapy 1995;32:669–677.

49. Higgins ST, Budney AJ, Bickel WK, Foerg FE, Donham R, Badger GJ. Incentives improve outcome in outpatient behavioral treatment of cocaine dependence. Arch Gen Psychiatry 1994; 51:568–576.

50. Higgins ST, Delaney DD, Budney AJ, et al. A behavioral approach to achieving initial cocaine abstinence. Am J Psychiatry 1991;148:1218–1224.

51. Sobell LC, Toneatto T, Sobell MB. Behavioral assessment and treatment planning for alcohol, tobacco, and other drug problems: current status with an emphasis on clinical applications. Behav Ther 1994;25:533–580.

52. Beck JS. Cognitive therapy: basics and beyond. New York: Guilford Press, 1995.

53. Prochaska JO, DiClemente CC, Norcross JC. In search of how people change: applications to addictive behaviors. Am Psychol 1992;47:1102–1114.

54. Prochaska JO, Norcross JC, DiClemente CC. Changing for good. New York: William Morrow and Co., 1994.

55. Morgan TJ. Behavior treatment techniques for psychoactive substance use disorders. In: Rotgers F, Keller DS, Morganstern J, eds. Treating substance abuse: theory and technique. New York: Guilford Press, 1996:202–240.

56. Rotgers F. Behavioral theory of substance abuse treatment: bringing science to bear on practice. In: Rotgers F, Keller DS, Morganstern J, eds. Treating substance abuse: theory and technique. New York: Guilford Press, 1996:174–201.

57. Anker A, Crowley T. Use of contingency contracts in specialty clinics for cocaine abuse. NIDA Res Monogr 1982;41:452–459.

58. Childress A, Ehrman R, McLellan A, O'Brien C. Update on behavioral treatments for substance abuse. NIDA Res Monogr 1988;90:183–192.

59. Holder H, Longabaugh R, Miller W, Rubonis A. The cost effectiveness of treatment for alcoholism: a first approximation. J Stud Alcohol 1991;52:517–540.

60. Galanter M. Network therapy for addiction: a model for office practice. Am J Psychiatry 1993; 150:28–36.

61. Carroll KM, Rounsaville BJ, Keller DS. Relapse prevention strategies for the treatment of cocaine abuse. Am J Drug Alcohol Abuse 1991; 17:249–265.

62. Rawson RA, Obert JL, McCann MJ, Smith DP, Scheffey E. The neurobehavioral treatment manual: a therapist manual for outpatient cocaine addiction treatment. Beverly Hills, CA: Matrix Center, 1989.

63. Wallace BC. Crack cocaine. New York: Brunner/Mazel, 1991.

64. Washton AM. Cocaine addiction: treatment, recovery, and relapse prevention. New York: WW Norton, 1989.

65. Roffman RA, Stephens RS, Simpson EE, Whitaker DL. Treatment of marijuana dependencies: preliminary results. J Psychoactive Drugs 1990;22:129–137.

66. McAuliffe WE, Ch'ien JMN. Recovery training and self-help: a relapse prevention program for treated opiate addicts. J Subst Abuse Treat 1986; 3:9–20.

67. Annis HM. A relapse prevention model for the treatment of alcoholics. In: Miller WR, Heather N, eds. Treating addictive behaviors: process of change. New York: Plenum, 1986:407–433.

68. Ziedonis D, Fisher W. Motivation-based assessment and treatment of substance abuse in patients with schizophrenia. Directions in Psychiatry 16. New York: Hartherleigh Co., 1996.

69. Weiss RD, Greenfield SF, Najavits LM. Integrating psychological and pharmacological treatment of dually diagnosed patients. NIDA Res Monogr 1995;150:110–128.

70. Linehan MM. Dialectical behavior therapy for treatment of borderline personality disorder: Implications for the treatment of substance abuse. NIDA Res Monogr 1993;137:201–216.

71. Sobell LC, Sobell MB. Timeline Followback. A technique for assessing self-reported alcohol consumption. In: Litten RZ, Allen J, eds. Measuring alcohol consumption: psychosocial and biological methods. Totowa, NJ: Humana Press, 1992:41–72.

72. Miller WR. Form 90: a structured assessment interview for drinking and related behaviors. NIAAA Project MATCH Monograph Series, Volume 5. Washington, DC: U.S. Department of Health and Human Services, 1996.

73. McLellan T, Kushner H, Metzger D, et al. The fifth edition of the Addiction Severity Index. J Subst Abuse Treat 1992;9:199–213.

74. Annis HM, Graham JM, Davis CS. Inventory of Drinking Situations (IDS): users guide. Toronto: Addiction Research Foundation, 1987.
75. Annis HM, Martin G, Graham JM. Inventory of Drug-Taking Situations: Users guide. Toronto: Addiction Research Foundation, 1988.
76. Annis HM, Graham JM. Situational Confidence Questionnaire SCQ 39: Users guide. Toronto: Addiction Research Foundation, 1988.
77. McMullin RE. Handbook of cognitive therapy techniques. New York: WW Norton, 1986.
78. Alcoholics Anonymous World Services. Alcoholics Anonymous. 3rd edition. New York: Alcoholics Anonymous World Services, 1976.
79. Trimpey J. Rational recovery from alcoholism: the small book. 3rd edition. Lotus, CA: Lotus Press, 1989.
80. Kishline A. Moderate drinking: the new option for problem drinkers. Tucson, AZ: See Sharp Press, 1994.
81. Weiss RD, Najavits LM. Overview of treatment modalities and settings: Pharmacotherapy, psychotherapy, twelve-step programs. In: Kranzler HR, Rounsaville BJ, eds. Dual diagnosis: substance abuse and comorbid medical and psychiatric disorders (in press).
82. Crits-Christoph P, Siqueland L. Psychosocial treatment for drug abuse: selected review and recommendations for national health care. Arch Gen Psychiatry 1996;53:749–756.
83. Regier DA, Farmer ME, Rae DS, Locke BZ, Keith SJ, Judd LL, Goodwin FK. Comorbidity of mental disorders with alcohol an other drug abuse: results from the Epidemiological Catchment Area ECA study. JAMA 1990;264:2511–2518.
84. Woody GE, Luborsky LL, McLellan AT, et al. Psychotherapy for opiate addicts: Does it help? Arch Gen Psychiatry 1983;40:639–645.
85. Mirin SM, Weiss RD. Substance abuse and mental illness. In: Frances RJ, Miller SI, eds. Clinical textbook of addictive disorders. New York: Guilford Press, 1991:271–298.
86. Marlatt GA, Larimer ME, Baer JS, Quigley LA. Harm reduction for alcohol problems: moving beyond the controlled drinking controversy. Behav Ther 1993;24:461–504.
87. Marlatt GA, Tapert SF. Harm reduction: Reducing the risks of addictive behaviors. In: Baer J, Marlatt G, McMahon R, eds. Addictive behaviors across the lifespan. Newbury Park, CA: Sage Publications, 1993:243–273.

50   NETWORK THERAPY

Marc Galanter

There is a need for innovative techniques to enhance the effectiveness of psychotherapy with abusers of alcohol and other drugs in the office treatment setting in individual practice. Augmentation of treatment by group and family therapy in the multimodality clinic setting has led to considerably more success (1, 2), and in the clinic, these therapies may be supplemented by a variety of social rehabilitation techniques. Groups such as AA also offer invaluable adjunctive support. Nonetheless, a model for enhancing therapeutic intervention in the context of insight-oriented individual therapy would be of considerable value, given the potential role of the individual practitioner as primary therapist for many patients with addictive problems.

A LEARNING THEORY APPROACH

Classical Conditioning of Addiction Stimuli

An important explanatory model of drug dependence was elaborated by Wikler (3) based on his clinical investigations. In an attempt to explain the spontaneous appearance of drug craving in the absence of physiological withdrawal, Wikler looked to certain stimuli that may have been conditioned to evoke withdrawal phenomena. He pointed out that addictive drugs produce counteradaptive responses in the central nervous system (CNS) at the same time that their direct pharmacological effects are felt, and that these are reflected in certain physiological events. With alcohol, for example, electroencephalogram (EEG) evoked response changes characteristic of withdrawal may be observed in the initial phases of intoxication under certain circumstances (4). With opiates, administration of a narcotic antagonist to an addict who is "high" will precipitate a withdrawal reaction, which may be said to have been present in a latent form. Such responses are overridden by the direct effect of the drug and generally are observed only after the cessation of a prolonged period of administration, when they are perceived as physiological withdrawal feelings or craving.

Hence, the drug euphoria inevitably is followed by the counteradaptive responses that occur on a physiological level, shortly after the initial drug administration. The pairing of this administration with stimuli from the environment or with internal subjective stimuli in a consistent manner causes these stimuli to elicit the central counteradaptive response in the absence of prior drug administration. Wikler primarily discussed conditioning or a psychophysiological response. With regard to the issues presented here, however, it should be pointed out that the conditioned stimulus of the drug or the affective state may lead directly to the behavioral response before the addict consciously experiences withdrawal feelings. The addict may therefore automatically act to seek out drugs by virtue of this conditioning upon entry into his or her old neighborhood, or upon experiencing anxiety or depression, all of which may have become conditioned stimuli. O'Brien and associates (5) have demonstrated the conditioning of addicts of opiate withdrawal responses to neutral stimuli, such as sound and odor. This conditioning, produced in a laboratory setting, provided experimental corroboration of Wikler's hypothesis. Ludwig and associates (6) have demonstrated the direct behavioral correlates of such conditioned stimuli in relation to alcohol administration. They found that, for the alcoholic, the alcohol dose itself might serve as a conditioned stimulus for enhancing craving, as could the appropriate drinking context.

The following example illustrates the precipitation of drug-seeking by a stimulus previously conditioned through its association with drug-taking behavior. Two conditioned stimuli, a subjective anxiety state and the visual cue of the bottle, both combined to precipitate a relapse into drug-seeking behavior without intermediate steps of deliberation, and without the intervening sensation of craving.

> A 41-year-old recovered alcoholic had been abstinent for 6 years. She was a regular, if infrequent, attender at Alcoholics Anonymous (AA) meetings and had no interest in resuming drinking. One day, her 10-year-old daughter had not returned home from school. The daughter was sufficiently late so that the mother called the homes of her daughter's friends and then the police to find out whether there had been any reports of her whereabouts. The mother was sitting in her living room near the telephone awaiting a possible call and was quite anxious. At one point, she glanced over at a liquor cabinet and her attention was caught by a bottle of gin, which had been her preferred alcoholic beverage before achieving sobriety. The liquor cabinet was placed in the open because of her confidence and that of her family in the reliability of her maintaining abstinence. Without thinking, she went over to the bottle and poured a drink. This information was obtained from her in an interview by a detoxification service, some 6 months later; her drinking had increased to the point that she required hospital admission. The particular incident had been forgotten and was elicited only after a lengthy guided interview.

It should be noted that the initial dose of alcohol described here itself served as a conditioned stimulus for further alcohol seeking. As noted already, the enhancement of craving by an initial alcohol dose has been demonstrated in an experimental context. It is by this mechanism that a small amount of the addictive agent has been observed to precipitate "loss of control", i.e., unmoderated alcohol or drug use.

Learning Theory and the Treatment of Addiction

Mello (7) describes systematic research on behavioral variables during intoxication by studying ethanol self-administration among alcoholics. With colleagues, she investigated effects of a number of variables, including altering the amount of effort necessary to obtain ethanol. Nathan and colleagues (8) have undertaken the use of within-subject experimental manipulations to study psychological factors such as socialization versus isolation and affective state. Such studies gradually have led to a better understanding of the possibility for manipulating an alcoholic's drinking patterns. Further elaboration has been undertaken by behavioral researchers for the therapy of alcoholism (9).

This experimental work is cited to illustrate a perspective for defining and modifying drinking behavior. Certain conditioned drinking behaviors may be extinguished if the appropriate extinguishing stimulus is interposed in a systematic way. This may be done by using noxious stimuli or by reinforcing constructive behavior patterns.

Cognitive Labeling

The question may then be raised as to what would serve as a minimally noxious aversive stimulus that would be both specific for the conditioned stimulus and unlikely to be generalized, thereby yielding a maximal positive learning experience. To answer this, we may look at Wikler's initial conception of the implications of this conditioning theory. He pointed out (10) that

The user would become entangled in an interlocking web of self-perpetuating reinforcers, which perhaps explain the persistence of drug abuse, despite disastrous consequences for the user, and his imperviousness to psychotherapy which does not take such conditioning factors into account, because neither the subject nor the therapist is aware of their existence.

In addition, Ludwig et al. point out that the conditioned stimuli can be cognitively labeled so as to manipulate their role in precipitating craving and drug-seeking behavior (6). That is to say, by tagging the stimulus with some perceived label, the effect of the stimulus itself can be manipulated.

Because of the unconscious nature of the conditioned response of drug-seeking, the patient's attempt to alter the course of the stimulus-response sequence is generally not viable, even with the aid of a therapist. Neither party is aware that a conditioned sequence is taking place. However, sufficient exploration may reveal the relevant stimuli and their ultimate effect through conditioned sequences of drug-seeking behavior. By means of guided recall in a psychotherapeutic context, the alcoholic or addict can become aware of the sequence of action of conditioned stimuli. He or she can then label those stimuli. The therapeutic maneuver consists of applying an aversive stimulus to conditioned responses that are to be extinguished.

At this point, the patient's own distress at the course of the addictive process, generated by his or her own motivation for escaping the addictive pattern, may be mobilized. This motivational distress then serves as the aversive stimulus. The implicit assumption behind this therapeutic approach is that the patient in question wants to alter his or her pattern of drug use and that the recognition of a particular stimulus as a conditioned component of addiction will allow the patient, in effect, to initiate the extinction process. If a patient is committed to achieving abstinence from an addictive drug such as alcohol or cocaine but is in jeopardy of occasional slips, cognitive labeling can facilitate consolidation of an abstinent adaptation. Such an approach is less valuable in the context of: (a) inadequate motivation for abstinence, (b) fragile social supports, or (c) compulsive substance abuse unmanageable by the patient in his or her usual social settings. Hospitalization or replacement therapy (e.g., methadone) may be necessary here, since ambulatory stabilization through psychotherapeutic support is often not feasible. Under any circumstances, cognitive labeling is an adjunct to psychotherapy and not a replacement for group supports such as AA, family counseling, or outpatient therapeutic community programs, where applicable.

The following clinical examples may be helpful in illustrating this approach.

A 30-year-old amphetamine addict had been taking pills on binges for 10 years, with very few periods of abstinence longer than a few weeks. Early in the process of insight treatment, the various cues and behavior patterns associated with the initiation of binges were explored. After a 1-month period of abstinence the patient was encouraged to recall the particulars surrounding a relapse into drug taking that had occurred 3 days before. The drug taking began after a disappointment concerning her boyfriend. She reported going to a physician who supplied pills to abusers (under the nominal excuse of dieting) the day after her disappointment. She related a lengthy tale of going through the entire acquisition procedure, obtaining the pills, and ultimately taking them after a series of evasive arrangements to avoid her roommate's attention. When specifically asked, she said that all this occurred without her specific awareness of an intent to take the pills. Only after working on the guided recall was it clear to her that her actions were undertaken so as to assure that she could ingest the pills that day. The trip to the physician had been rationalized by saying it would make her feel more comfortable to have pills "in the house." By repeatedly examining such behaviors, she could ascertain each sequential stimulus that triggered an ensuing one. This allowed her to label these events and the feelings associated with them. After 9 months of such treatment she was able to terminate the episodes of amphetamine binging and remain abstinent over the course of psychotherapy for an ensuing 2 years.

Emphasis was placed on bringing into awareness each behavior from the initial conditioned stimulus to the final addictive act. Behaviors were labeled according to associated feelings and their role in the sequence.

Adjunctive support, such as disulfiram treatment and/or AA, is indicated for someone who is truly alcohol dependent. At such times, cognitive labeling may also play a role in the therapy.

A 40-year-old writer-publicist had been drinking heavily since his late teens, at least a pint daily for the past 10 years. He was referred to consultation by his child's therapist. This and a recent work-related crisis led him to appreciate the extensive damage caused by his drinking. He agreed to seek abstinence and to take disulfiram, but refused to attend AA. Although drinking presented a problem during only one subsequent episode, conditioned drinking cues emerged as an issue in therapy. These were illustrated by three contexts previously associated with drinking in which the patient experienced malaise and restlessness. All three were examined in depth in terms of the drinking antecedents as well as the patient's contemporaneous feelings. This allowed him to understand his malaise and consciously mobilize himself to deal with the craving he felt in these situations. The first setting was when he stayed up late at night, as was his habit, to do his writing; he had regularly drunk heavily at these times to allay anxiety aroused by his conflicts over his creative work. Second, he suffered from a mild phobia of airplane flights and would drink heavily before flying. Third, before major speeches out-of-town, he would spend the evening in a bar, sometimes to the point of affecting his ability to present his material the next day. Addressing the symptoms experienced at these times served as a basis for understanding the patient's conflicts and helped to bolster his commitment to abstinence.

Altogether, these examples illustrate enhanced means for approaching psychotherapy with the alcohol and drug abuser. They may provide the therapist with another tool to assist the patient at a time when more traditional therapeutic maneuvers may be less successful.

THE NETWORK THERAPY TECHNIQUE

This approach can be useful in addressing a broad range of addicted patients characterized by the following clinical hallmarks of addictive illness. When they initiate consumption of their addictive agent, be it alcohol, cocaine, opiates, or depressant drugs, they frequently cannot limit that consumption to a reasonable and predictable level; this phenomenon has been termed "loss of control" by clinicians who treat persons dependent on alcohol or drugs (11). Second, they have consistently demonstrated relapse to the agent of abuse; that is, they have attempted to stop using the drug for varying periods of time but have returned to it, despite a specific intent to avoid it.

This treatment approach is not necessary for those abusers who can, in fact, learn to set limits on their use of alcohol or drugs; their abuse may be treated as a behavioral symptom in a more traditional psychotherapeutic fashion. Nor is it directed at those patients for whom the addictive pattern is most unmanageable, such as addicted people with unusual destabilizing circumstances such as homelessness, severe character pathology, or psychosis.

These patients may need special supportive care such as inpatient detoxification or long-term residential treatment.

Key Elements

Three key elements are introduced into the Network Therapy technique. The first is a cognitive behavioral approach to relapse prevention, independently reported to be valuable in addiction treatment (12). Emphasis in this approach is placed on triggers to relapse and behavioral techniques for avoiding them, in preference to exploring underlying psychodynamic issues.

Second, support of the patient's natural social network is engaged in treatment. Peer support in AA has long been shown to be an effective vehicle for promoting abstinence, and the idea of the therapist's intervening with family and friends in starting treatment was employed in one of the early ambulatory techniques specific to addiction (13). The involvement of spouses (14) has since been shown to be effective in enhancing the outcome of professional therapy.

Third, the orchestration of resources to provide community reinforcement suggests a more robust treatment intervention by providing a support for drug-free rehabilitation (15). In this relation, Khantzian points to the "primary care therapist" as one who functions in direct coordinating and monitoring roles in order to combine psychotherapeutic and self-help elements (16). It is this overall management role over circumstances outside as well as inside the office session which is presented to trainees, in order to maximize the effectiveness of the intervention.

Initial Encounter: Starting a Social Network

The patient should be asked to bring his or her spouse or a close friend to the first session. Alcoholic patients often dislike certain things they hear when they first come for treatment and may deny or rationalize even if they have voluntarily sought help. Because of their denial of the problem, a significant other is essential to both history-taking and to implementing a viable treatment plan. A close relative or spouse can often cut through the denial in a way that an unfamiliar therapist cannot and can therefore be invaluable in setting a standard of realism in dealing with the addiction.

Some patients make clear that they wish to come to the initial session on their own. This is often associated with their desire to preserve the option of continued substance abuse and is born out of the fear that an alliance will be established independent of them to prevent this. Although a delay may be tolerated for a session or two, it should be stated unambiguously at the outset that effective treatment can be undertaken only on the basis of a therapeutic alliance built around the addiction issue that includes the support of significant others and that it is expected that a network of close friends and/or relatives will be brought in within a session or two at the most.

The weight of clinical experience supports the view that abstinence is the most practical goal to propose to the addicted person for his or her rehabilitation (17, 18), although as Pattison has pointed out (19), patients may sometimes achieve an outcome of limited drinking. For abstinence to be expected, however, the therapist should assure the provision of necessary social supports for the patient. Let us consider how a long-term support network is initiated for this purpose, beginning with availability of the therapist, significant others, and a self-help group.

In the first place, the therapist should be available for consultation on the phone and should indicate to the patient that he or she wants to be called if problems arise. This makes the therapist's commitment clear and sets the tone for a "team effort." It begins to undercut one reason for relapse, the patient's sense of being on his or her own if unable to manage the situation. The astute therapist, however, will assure that he or she does not spend excessive time on the telephone or in emergency sessions. The patient will therefore develop a support network that can handle the majority of problems involved in day-to-day assistance. This generally will leave the therapist to respond only to occasional questions of interpreting the terms of the understanding among himself or herself, the patient, and support network members. If there is a question about the ability of the patient and network to manage the period between the initial sessions, the first few scheduled sessions may be arranged at intervals of only 1–3 days. In any case, frequent appointments

should be scheduled at the outset if a pharmacological detoxification with benzodiazepines is indicated, so that the patient need never manage more than a few days' medication at a time.

What is most essential, though, is that the network be forged into a working group to provide necessary support for the patient between the initial sessions. Membership ranges from one to several persons close to the patient. Larger networks have been used by Speck (20) in treating schizophrenic patients. Contacts between network members at this stage typically include telephone calls (at the therapist's or patient's initiative), dinner arrangements, and social encounters and should be preplanned to a fair extent during the joint session. These encounters are most often undertaken at the time when alcohol or drug use is likely to occur. In planning together, however, it should be made clear to network members that relatively little unusual effort will be required for the long term, and that after the patient is stabilized, their participation will amount to little more than attendance at infrequent meetings with the patient and therapist. This is reassuring to those network members who are unable to make a major time commitment to the patient as well as to those patients who do not want to be placed in a dependent position.

Defining the Network's Membership

Once the patient has come for an appointment, establishing a network is a task undertaken with active collaboration of patient and therapist. The two, aided by those parties who join the network initially, must search for the right balance of members. The therapist must carefully promote the choice of appropriate network members, however, just as the platoon leader selects those who will go into combat. The network will be crucial in determining the balance of the therapy. This process is not without problems, and the therapist must think in a strategic fashion of the interactions that may take place among network members. The following case illustrates the nature of their task.

A 25-year-old graduate student had been abusing cocaine since high school, in part drawing from funds from his affluent family, who lived in a remote city. At two points in the process of establishing his support network, the reactions of his live-in girlfriend, who worked with us from the outset, were particularly important. Both he and she agreed to bring in his 19-year-old sister, a freshman at a nearby college. He then mentioned a "friend" of his, apparently a woman whom he had apparently found attractive, even though there was no history of an overt romantic involvement. The expression on his girlfriend's face suggested that she did not like this idea, although she offered no rationale for excluding this potential rival. However, the idea of having to rely for assistance solely on two women who might see each other as competitors was unappealing. I therefore finessed the idea of the "friend," and we moved on to evaluating the patient's uncle, whom he initially preferred to exclude, despite the fact that his girlfriend thought him appropriate. It later turned out (as I had expected) that the uncle was perceived as a potentially disapproving representative of the parental generation. I encouraged the patient to accept the uncle as a network member nonetheless, so as to round out the range of relationships within the group, and did spell out my rationale for his inclusion. The uncle did turn out to be caring and supportive, particularly after he was helped to understand the nature of the addictive process.

Defining the Network's Task

As conceived here, the therapist's relationship to the network is like that of a task-oriented team leader, rather than that of a family therapist oriented toward insight. The network is established to implement a straightforward task, that of aiding the therapist in sustaining the patient's abstinence. It must be directed with the same clarity of purpose that a task force is directed in any effective organization. Competing and alternative goals must be suppressed, or at least prevented from interfering with the primary task.

Unlike family members involved in traditional family therapy, network members are not led to expect symptom relief for themselves or self-realization. This prevents the development of competing goals for the network's meetings. It also assures the members protection from having their own motives scrutinized and thereby supports their continuing involvement without the threat of an assault on their psychological defenses. Because network members have—kindly—volunteered to participate, their motives must not be impugned. Their constructive behavior should be commended. It is useful to acknowledge appreciation for the contribution they are making to the therapy. There is always a counterproductive tendency on their part to minimize the value of their contribution.

The network must, therefore, be structured as an effective working group with high morale. This is not always easy:

A 45-year-old single woman served as an executive in a large family-held business—except when her alcohol problem led her into protracted binges. Her father, brother, and sister were prepared to banish her from the business but decided first to seek consultation. Because they had initiated the contact, they were included in the initial network and indeed were very helpful in stabilizing the patient. Unfortunately, however, the father was a domineering figure who intruded in all aspects of the business, evoking angry outbursts from his children. The children typically reacted with petulance, provoking him in return. The situation came to a head when both of the patient's siblings angrily petitioned me to exclude the father from the network, 2 months into the treatment. This presented a problem because the father's control over the business made his involvement important to securing the patient's compliance. The patient's relapse was still a real possibility. This potentially coercive role, however, was an issue that the group could not easily deal with. I decided to support the father's membership in the group, pointing out the constructive role he had played in getting the therapy started. It seemed necessary to support the earnestness of his concern for his daughter, rather than the children's dismay at their father's (very real) obstinacy. It was clear to me that the father could not deal with a situation in which he was not accorded sufficient respect and that there was no real place in this network for addressing the father's character pathology directly. The hubbub did, in fact, quiet down with time. The children became less provocative themselves, as the group responded to my pleas for civil behavior.

The Use of AA

Use of self-help modalities is desirable whenever possible. For the alcoholic, certainly, participation in AA is strongly encouraged. Groups such as Narcotics Anonymous, Pills Anonymous, and Cocaine Anonymous are modeled after AA and play a similarly useful role for drug abusers. One approach is to tell the patient that he or she is expected to attend at least two AA meetings a week for at least 1 month so as to become familiar with the program. If after a month the patient is quite reluctant to continue, and other aspects of the treatment are going well, his or her nonparticipation may have to be accepted.

Some patients are more easily convinced to attend AA meetings. Others may be less compliant. The therapist should mobilize the support network as appropriate, so as to continue pressure for the patient's involvement with AA for a reasonable trial. It may take a considerable period of time, but ultimately a patient may experience something of a conversion, wherein he or she adopts the group ethos and expresses a deep commitment to abstinence, a measure of commitment rarely observed in patients who undergo psychotherapy alone. When this occurs, the therapist may assume a more passive role in monitoring the patient's abstinence and keep an eye on his or her ongoing involvement in AA.

Use of Pharmacotherapy in the Network Format

For the alcoholic, disulfiram may be of marginal use in assuring abstinence when used in a traditional counseling context (21) but becomes much more valuable when carefully integrated into work with the patient and network, particularly when the drug is taken under observation. It is a good idea to use the initial telephone contact to engage the patient's agreement to abstain from alcohol for the day immediately prior to the first session. The therapist then has the option of prescribing or administering disulfiram at that time. For a patient who is earnest about seeking assistance for alcoholism, this is often not difficult, if some time is spent on the phone making plans to avoid a drinking context during that period. If it is not feasible to undertake this on the phone, it may be addressed in the first session. Such planning with the patient almost always involves organizing time with significant others and therefore serves as a basis for developing the patient's support network.

The administration of disulfiram under observation is a treatment op-

tion that is easily adapted to work with social networks. A patient who takes disulfiram cannot drink; a patient who agrees to be observed by a responsible party while taking disulfiram will not miss his or her dose without the observer's knowing. This may take a measure of persuasion and, above all, the therapist's commitment that such an approach can be reasonable and helpful.

Disulfiram typically is initiated with a dose of 500 mg, and then reduced to 250 mg daily. It is taken every morning, when the urge to drink is generally least. Particulars of administration in the context of treatment should be reviewed (22).

As noted previously, individual therapists traditionally have seen the abuser as a patient with poor prognosis. This is largely because in the context of traditional psychotherapy, there are no behavioral controls to prevent the recurrence of drug use, and resources are not available for behavioral intervention if a recurrence takes place—which it usually does. A system of impediments to the emergence of relapse, resting heavily on the actual or symbolic role of the network, must therefore be established. The therapist must have assistance in addressing any minor episode of drinking so that this ever-present problem does not lead to an unmanageable relapse or an unsuccessful termination of therapy.

How can the support network be used to deal with recurrences of drug use, when in fact the patient's prior association with these same persons did not prevent him or her from using alcohol or drugs? The following example illustrates how this may be done when social resources are limited. In this case, a specific format was defined with the network to monitor a patient's compliance with a disulfiram regimen:

A 33-year-old public relations executive had moved to New York from a remote city 3 years before coming to treatment. She had no long-standing close relationships in the city, a circumstance not uncommon for a single alcoholic in a setting removed from her origins. She presented with a 10-year history of heavy drinking that had increased in severity since her arrival, no doubt associated with her social isolation. Although she consumed a bottle of wine each night and additional hard liquor, she was able to get to work regularly. Six months before the outset of treatment, she attended AA meetings for 2 weeks and had been abstinent during that time. She had then relapsed, though, and became disillusioned about the possibility of maintaining abstinence. At the outset of treatment, it was necessary to reassure her that prior relapse was in large part a function of not having established sufficient outside supports (including more sound relationships within AA) and of having seen herself as failed after only one slip. However, there was basis for real concern as to whether she would do any better now, if the same formula was reinstituted in the absence of sufficient, reliable supports, which she did not seem to have. Together we came up with the idea of bringing in an old friend whom she saw occasionally and whom she felt she could trust. We made the following arrangement with her friend. The patient came to sessions twice a week. She would see her friend once each weekend. On each of these thrice-weekly occasions, she would be observed taking disulfiram, so that even if she missed a daily dose in between, it would not be possible for her to resume drinking on a regular basis, undetected. The interpersonal support inherent in this arrangement, bolstered by conjoint meetings with her and her friend, also allowed her to return to AA with a sense of confidence in her ability to maintain abstinence.

The following case history illustrates the implementation of a regimen designed to secure the use of pharmacotherapy in an unstable patient with better access to a social network:

A 24-year-old college dropout, involved in the arts, came for treatment after she had been using heroin intranasally daily, and drinking heavily for 7 days. This was a relapse to her previous longstanding pattern of drug dependence, as she had been hospitalized twice for heroin addiction in the previous two years. Her last hospitalization, 6 months before, had been followed by episodic heroin insufflation and bouts of heavy drinking. Her polysubstance abuse as well as her promiscuity and rebellious behavior dated back to her early teens. One month prior to presenting, while living in a rural area, she had been abducted by a man whom she had befriended at an AA meeting, and managed to escape after being held captive in a motel for a week. She was now living alternately with a friend in the city where she presented for treatment, and with her parents who lived 200 miles away; she commuted by train. She had not admitted to her parents that she had relapsed to heroin use. As the patient's history unfolded in her first session, it was clear that she had a long history of major problems of social and residential instability, as well as clear evidences of poor judgment since her hospitalization. Nonetheless, she wanted to escape from her self-destructiveness and her pattern of drug use.

The preliminary structure of a network was established in the second session with her and with the friend with whom she was staying some of the time. The patient, however, acknowledged she was still using heroin intermittently in this session. In the third session, her parents were added, having them participate via speaker-phone. This arrangement allowed for simultaneous planning along with the parties on whom her current life was rooted. Given her previous exposure to addiction treatment and AA, she was willing to accept a concrete plan for achieving abstinence from both alcohol and heroin as an appropriate course of action. She agreed to undergo detoxification from heroin while staying in her parents' home with the aid of clonidine, and to then continue with naltrexone and disulfiram treatment. The former was for opiate blockade and for alcohol craving, and the latter was for securing alcohol abstinence. These medications were to be taken under observation, using the format developed within the Network Therapy regimen as described below.

The patient was initially concerned that her parents would be upset if she told them that she had relapsed to heroin use after her last hospitalization. The therapist pointed out that it was important for them to be told in order for them to serve as properly informed members of the network. It was agreed in an individual session that this need not be done until the patient's abstinence was stabilized over two weeks of use of the medications. The patient's concern was discussed in light of the judgmental and highly critical attitude of her mother, which had been influential over the course of the patient's adolescence, and had contributed greatly to her rebellious use of drugs. On a few occasions during the initial weeks, the mother became angry when the patient, while staying at home, had not attended AA meetings as planned.

It was therefore important for the sake of the network's stability to make clear that the principal role of network members is to participate with the patient and therapist in discussing opportunities for abstinence and stabilization, and not to scrutinize all aspects of the patient's behavior. Problems in compliance with the regimen of medication observation or AA meetings are discussed in network and individual sessions, and not policed by network members. Thus, if the patient misses a pill, the therapist was to be called and the patient not confronted. This removes network members from the role of independent enforcers, although their perspective and assistance may be solicited by mutual agreement with the patient. In this way, it is the implicit social pressure from members of the network for compliance that is most directed at stabilizing of the treatment. Two more of the patient's friends were added to the network after the initial month of stabilization. This helped dilute the role of her parents in the network, and added additional practical resources, perspective, and support for recovery. The patient herself continued to take the medications under the observation of either her father or her friend, depending on where she was residing.

This patient's circumstances illustrate the value of drawing supportive figures into the treatment early on, and using this network resource in combination with the observation of ingestion of a blocking agent or an antidipsotropic. (Both were used in this case.) The fact that the patient was taking these two medications on any given day undercut her craving and left her prepared to be compliant with the medication regimen the next day, as well as with the overall treatment plan. In practice, patients experience less craving when such medications are integrated into the treatment regimen, because they know that opiates or alcohol, respectively, are not available to them for the next few days after ingestion of the medication.

Format for Medication Observation by the Network

1. Take the medication every morning in front of a network member.
2. Take the pill so that that person can observe you swallowing them.
3. Have the observer write down the time of day the pills were taken on a list prepared by the therapist.
4. The observer brings the list in to the therapist's office at each network session.
5. The observer leaves a message on the therapist's answering machine on any day in which the patient had not taken the pills in a way that ingestion was not clearly observed.

Meeting Arrangements

At the outset of therapy, it is important to see the patient with the group on a weekly basis, for at least the first month. Unstable circumstances demand more frequent contacts with the network. Sessions can be tapered off to biweekly and then monthly intervals after a time.

To sustain the continuing commitment of the group, particularly that between the therapist and the network members, network sessions should be held every 3 months or so for the duration of the individual therapy. Once the patient has stabilized, the meetings tend less to address day-to-day issues. They may begin with the patient's recounting of the drug situation. Reflections on the patient's progress and goals, or sometimes on relations among the network members, then may be discussed. In any case, it is essential that network members contact the therapist if they are concerned about the patient's possible use of alcohol or drugs, and that the therapist contact the network members if he or she becomes concerned over a potential relapse.

Adapting Individual Therapy to the Network Treatment

As noted previously, network sessions are scheduled on a weekly basis at the outset of treatment. This is likely to compromise the number of individual contacts. Indeed, if sessions are held once a week, the patient may not be seen individually for a period of time. The patient may perceive this as a deprivation unless the individual therapy is presented as an opportunity for further growth *predicated* on achieving stable abstinence assured through work with the network.

When the individual therapy does begin, the traditional objectives of therapy must be arranged so as to accommodate the goals of the substance abuse treatment. For insight-oriented therapy, clarification of unconscious motivations is a primary objective; for supportive therapy, the bolstering of established constructive defenses is primary. In the therapeutic context that is described here, however, the following objectives are given precedence.

Of first importance is the need to address exposure to substances of abuse or exposure to cues that might precipitate alcohol or drug use (23). Both patient and therapist should be sensitive to this matter and explore these situations as they arise. Second, a stable social context in an appropriate social environment—one conducive to abstinence with minimal disruption of life circumstances—should be supported. Considerations of minor disruptions in place of residence, friends, or job need not be a primary issue for the patient with character disorder or neurosis, but they cannot go untended here. For a considerable period of time, the substance abuser is highly vulnerable to exacerbations of the addictive illness and in some respects must be viewed with the considerable caution with which one treats the recently compensated psychotic.

Finally, after these priorities have been attended to, psychological conflicts that the patient must resolve, relative to his or her own growth, are considered. As the therapy continues, these come to assume a more prominent role. In the earlier phases, they are likely to reflect directly issues associated with previous drug use. Later, however, as the issue of addiction becomes less compelling from day to day, the context of the treatment increasingly will come to resemble the traditional psychotherapeutic context. Given the optimism generated by an initial victory over the addictive process, the patient will be in an excellent position to move forward in therapy with a positive view of his or her future.

RECENT RESEARCH ON THE NETWORK TECHNIQUE

Pilot Study

A retrospective study was conducted on 60 sequential patients who presented for treatment of alcohol and drug dependence in an office practice. The findings demonstrated the mode of operation and the outcome of this approach. Fifty-five of the 60 patients were treated with at least one other network member, and the average network had 2.3 members. Of the 55 so treated, 16 had a parent in the network, 13 a sibling, 28 a peer, 34 a spouse or mate, and 4 a child of their own. Using DSM criteria, 46 experienced major or full improvement, and those using disulfiram under observation of a network member showed the best outcome (24).

Standardization of the Treatment

A Network Therapy Rating Scale was used to rate videotape segments of addiction therapy sessions. Half the segments illustrated the Network format, and the remainder were of systemic family therapy. The Scale was first applied by medical school teaching faculty expert in the Network approach, and later by psychiatric residents who had received a seminar course on Network Therapy. The internal consistency of responses distinguishing between the two therapy techniques was high for both populations, with that of the faculty significantly higher than that of the residents (25). These scores reflected an acceptable level of integrity and differentiability of the Network Therapy modality, a greater level of expertise among the faculty who would be providing supervision for the trainees, and the ability of trainees to distinguish network therapy techniques from those of non-network approaches.

Study on Training Naive Therapists

A course of training for psychiatric residents naive to addiction and ambulatory treatments was undertaken over a period of two academic years. Before beginning treatment, the residents were given a structured treatment manual for network therapy and participated in a 13-session seminar on application of the Network Therapy technique. Cocaine-abusing patients were eligible for treatment in this study if they could come for evaluation with a friend or family member who could participate in their treatment. In all, 22 patients were enrolled. The treating psychiatric residents were able to establish requisite networks for 20 of these patients, that is to say, a network with at least one member. The networks had an average of 2.3 members, and the most typical configuration included family members and friends. Supervisors' evaluation of videotapes of the network sessions employing standardized instruments indicated good adherence to the manualized treatment, with effective use of network therapy techniques. The outcome of treatment, to be reported shortly by M. Galanter, D. Keller, and H. Dermatis, reflected retention and abstinence rates as good as, or better than, comparable ambulatory care carried out by therapists experienced in addiction treatment. The study demonstrated the feasibility of teaching the network technique to therapists naive to addiction treatment.

PRINCIPLES OF NETWORK TREATMENT

This section's summary material defines the Network Technique, as adapted from the principal text on its application (26).

Start a Network as Soon as Possible

1. It is important to see the alcohol or drug abuser promptly, as the window of opportunity for openness to treatment is generally brief. A week's delay can result in a person's reverting back to drunkenness or losing motivation.
2. If the person is married, engage the spouse early on, preferably at the time of the first phone call. Point out that addiction is a family problem. For most drugs, you can enlist the spouse in assuring that the patient arrives at your office with a day's sobriety.
3. In the initial interview, frame the exchange so that a good case is built for the grave consequences of the patient's addiction, and do this before the patient can introduce his or her system of denial. That way you are not putting the spouse or other network members in the awkward position of having to contradict a close relation.
4. Then make clear that the patient needs to be abstinent, starting now. (A tapered detoxification may be necessary sometimes, as with depressant pills.)
5. When seeing an alcoholic patient for the first time, start him or her on disulfiram treatment as soon as possible, in the office if you can. Have the patient continue taking disulfiram under observation of a network member.
6. Start arranging for a network to be assembled at the first session, generally involving a number of the patient's family or close friends.
7. From the very first meeting you should consider how to ensure sobriety till the next meeting, and plan that with the network. Initially, their immediate company, a plan for daily AA attendance, and planned activities may all be necessary.

Manage the Network with Care

1. Include people who are close to the patient, have a longstanding relationship with him or her, and are trusted. Avoid members with substance problems, as they will let you down when you need their unbiased support. Avoid superiors and subordinates at work, as they have an overriding relationship with the patient independent of friendship.
2. Get a balanced group. Avoid a network composed solely of the parental generation, or of younger people, or of people of the opposite sex. Sometimes a nascent network selects itself for a consultation if the patient is reluctant to address his or her own problem. Such a group will later supportively engage the patient in the network, with your careful guidance.
3. Make sure that the mood of meetings is trusting and free of recrimination. Avoid letting the patient or the network members be made to feel guilty or angry in meetings. Explain issues of conflict in terms of the problems presented by addiction—do not get into personality conflicts.
4. The tone should be directive. That is to say, give explicit instructions to support and ensure abstinence. A feeling of teamwork should be promoted, with no psychologizing or impugning members' motives.
5. Meet as frequently as necessary to ensure abstinence, perhaps once a week for a month, every other week for the next few months, and every month or two by the end of a year.
6. The network should have no agenda other than to support the patient's abstinence. But as abstinence is stabilized, the network can help the patient plan for a new drug-free adaptation. It is not there to work on family relations or help other members with their problems, although it may do this indirectly.

Keep the Network's Agenda Focused

1. Maintaining abstinence. The patient and the network members should report at the outset of each session any exposure of the patient to alcohol and drugs. The patient and network members should be instructed on the nature of relapse and plan with the therapist how to sustain abstinence. Cues to conditioned drug-seeking should be examined.
2. Supporting the network's integrity. Everyone has a role in this. The patient is expected to make sure that network members keep their meeting appointments and stay involved with the treatment. The therapist sets meeting times and summons the network for any emergency, such as relapse; the therapist does whatever is necessary to secure stability of the membership if the patient is having trouble doing so. Network members' responsibility is to attend network sessions, although they may be asked to undertake other supportive activity with the patient.
3. Securing future behavior. The therapist should combine any and all modalities necessary to ensure the patient's stability, such as a stable, drug-free residence; the avoidance of substance abusing friends; attendance at 12-step meetings; medications like disulfiram or blocking agents; observed urinalysis; and ancillary psychiatric care. Written agreements may be handy, such as a mutually acceptable contingency contract with penalties for violation of understandings.

Make Use of AA and Other Self-Help Groups

1. Patients should be expected to go to meetings of AA or related groups at least two to three times, with follow-up discussion in therapy.
2. If patients have reservations about these meetings try to help them understand how to deal with them. Issues like social anxiety should be explored if they make a patient reluctant to participate. Generally, resistance to AA can be related to other areas of inhibition in a person's life, as well as to the denial of addiction.
3. As with other spiritual involvements, do not probe the patients' motivation or commitment to AA once engaged. Allow them to work out things on their own, but be prepared to listen.

Acknowledgments. *This chapter was adapted in part from articles previously published by the author (24, 26–28).*

References

1. Institute of Medicine. Broadening the base of treatment for alcohol problems. Washington, DC: National Academy Press, 1990.
2. Galanter M, Castaneda R. Alcoholism and substance abuse: psychotherapy. In: Bellack AS, Hersen M, eds. Comparative handbook of treatment for adult disorders. New York: John Wiley and Sons, 1990:463–478.
3. Wikler A. Dynamics of drug dependence. Arch Gen Psychiatry 1973;28:611–616.
4. Begleiter H, Porjesz B. Persistence of a subacute withdrawal syndrome following chronic ethanol intake. Drug Alcohol Depend 1979;4:353–357.
5. O'Brien CP, Testa T, O'Brien TJ, et al. Conditioned narcotic withdrawal in humans. Science 1977;195:1000–1002.
6. Ludwig AM, Wikler A, Stark LM. The first drink. Arch Gen Psychiatry 1974;30:539–547.
7. Mello NK. Behavioral studies of alcoholism. In: Kissin B, Begleiter H, eds. The biology of alcoholism. New York: Plenum, 1972;2:219–292.
8. Nathan P, Titler N, Lowison L, et al. Behavioral analysis of chronic alcoholism. Arch Gen Psychiatry 1970;22:419–430.
9. Miller WE, Heather N, eds. Treating addictive behaviors. New York: Plenum, 1986.
10. Wikler A. Some implications of conditioning theory for problems of drug abuse. Behav Sci 1971;16:92–97.
11. Jellinek EM. The disease concept of alcoholism. New Haven, CT: Hillhouse, 1963.
12. Marlatt GA, Gordon J. Relapse prevention: maintenance strategies in the treatment of addictive behaviors. New York: Guilford Press, 1985.
13. Johnson VE. Intervention: how to help someone who doesn't want help. Minneapolis: Johnson Institute, 1986.
14. McCrady BS, Stout R, Noel N, Abrams D, Fisher-Nelson H. Effectiveness of three types of spouse-involved behavioral alcoholism treatment. Br J Addict 1991;86:1415–1424.
15. Azrin NH, Sisson RW, Meyers R. Alcoholism treatment by disulfiram and community reinforcement therapy. J Behav Ther Psychiatry 1982;13:105–112.
16. Khantzian EJ. The primary care therapist and patient needs in substance abuse treatment. Am J Drug Alcohol Abuse 1988;14(2):159–167.
17. Helzer JE, Robins LN, Taylor JR, et al. The extent of long-term drinking among alcoholics discharged from medical and psychiatric facilities. N Engl J Med 1985;312:1678–1682.
18. Gitlow SE, Peyser HS, eds. Alcoholism: a practical treatment guide. New York: Grune & Stratton, 1980.
19. Pattison EM. Non-abstinent drinking goals in the treatment of alcoholism: a clinical typology. Arch Gen Psychiatry 1976;33:923–930.
20. Speck R. Psychotherapy of the social network of a schizophrenic family. Fam Process 1967; 6:208.
21. Fuller R, Branchey L, Brightwell DR, et al. Disulfiram treatment of alcoholism. A Veterans Administration cooperative study. JAMA 1986; 256:1449–1455.
22. Gallant DM. Alcoholism: a guide to programs, intervention and treatment. New York: Norton, 1987.
23. Galanter M. Network therapy for addiction: a model for office practice. Am J Psychiatry 1993; 150:28–36.
24. Galanter M. Psychotherapy for alcohol and drug abuse: an approach based on learning theory. J Psychiatr Treat Eval 1983;5:551–556.
25. Keller D, Galanter M, Weinberg S. Standardization of network therapy: systematic use of peer and family support in addiction treatment. J Drug Alcohol Abuse 1997;23:115–127.
26. Galanter M. Network therapy for alcohol and drug abuse: a new approach in practice. New York: Basic Books, 1993.
27. Galanter M. Social network therapy for cocaine dependence. Adv Alcohol Subst Abuse 1987;6: 159–175.
28. Galanter M. Management of the alcoholic in psychiatric practice. Psychiatr Ann 1989;19: 226–270.

51 ACUPUNCTURE

Michael O. Smith, Vincent Brewington, Patricia D. Culliton, Lorenz K. Y. Ng, Hsiang-lai Wen, and Joyce H. Lowinson

Acupuncture (derived from the words "acus," meaning a sharp point, and "punctura," meaning puncturing), as its name implies, consists of stimulating certain points on or near the surface of the body by insertion of needles. As an ancient Oriental therapeutic art, it has been practiced in China for more than 5000 years. The wide publicity given the successful use of acupuncture as a method of anesthesia in surgery in the People's Republic of China, after President Nixon's trip to that country in 1972, generated considerable interest in the layman as well as in the medical profession in this particular modality.

Besides its reported effectiveness in the production of analgesia, acupuncture seems to have other potentially useful clinical and research applications (1, 2). Its use in the treatment of drug addiction represents a relatively recent application of a very old treatment technique. There are a number of practical and theoretical considerations that prompt a closer look at the use of acupuncture in the treatment of drug-dependent individuals. Available evidence (3, 4) indicates that there may be a close relationship in terms of neurochemical mechanisms between analgesia and the development of tolerance and physical dependence. Attempts to dissociate the analgesic effects of narcotics and opiates from their addictive liability have been rather unsuccessful, despite several decades of intensive research efforts. This and the recent findings from research on endorphins suggest that the neuropsychobiological factors involved in the development of narcotic dependency may be intimately related to the processes involved in the production of analgesia. Thus, a modality that can produce analgesia may have potential value for modifying the processes involved in narcotic dependence. A nonchemical modality such as acupuncture seems particularly intriguing, especially because it is safe and relatively easy to use and would appeal to individuals who are trying to rid themselves of chemical dependency.

In practice, the application of acupuncture in the treatment of narcotic addiction derives from a serendipitous observation made by Dr. H. L. Wen of Hong Kong in 1972. Here is a brief description by Dr. Wen of how this incident came about:

In early November 1972, a 50-year-old man was admitted to the Neurosurgical Unit of the Kwong Wah Hospital, Tung Wah Group of Hospitals, Kowloon, in Hong Kong, because of cerebral concussion. He was a known opium addict of five years' duration. While in the ward, he was given tincture of opium to relieve his withdrawal syndrome. After the cerebral concussion had improved, the patient was asked whether he would agree to cingulotomy (5) to relieve his drug abuse problem. He agreed. He was scheduled for surgery on the 9th of November, 1972. During the operation for surgery, instead of local anesthesia being injected under the scalp (where the incisions were to be made), acupuncture anesthesia (analgesia) was used.

Four needles were inserted into the right hand, using the following acupuncture points: Hoku = LI-4; Houshi = SI-3, and in the arm at Hsimen = EH-4; Szutu = TB-9. Another two needles were inserted into the right ear at the "brain-stem" and "god's door" points. Stimulation with an electrical stimulator, BT-701 (made in China), was carried out for ½ hour. At that time, our interest was in discovering whether the patient obtained analgesia in the scalp prior to surgery. During stimulation, 15 to 30 minutes later, the patient voluntarily stated that his withdrawal symptoms had completely cleared up. We examined him and found that he was free of withdrawal symptoms. The operation was canceled and the patient returned to the ward with advice to the nursing staff that the doctor should be informed if the patient showed withdrawal symptoms again. At 9:00 p.m., that night, I [HLW] was informed that the patient had had another withdrawal syndrome. Again, acupuncture and electrical stimulation was carried out in a similar manner to the method earlier in the day. After half an hour of acupuncture and electrical stimulation (AES), the withdrawal symptoms again disappeared. Encouraged by this, the next day we saw two other patients from the orthopedic wards of the same hospital, who were both opium abusers. One was suffering from a chronic leg ulcer and the other, from a fracture of the head of the femur. When we explained how we wanted to treat their withdrawal symptoms, both agreed to the procedure. Both responded well to the half hour of AES and their withdrawal symptoms stopped.

After the above observations, Dr. Wen and his colleague, Dr. Cheung, of the Kwong Wah Hospital, subsequently reported that, in a study of 40 heroin and opium addicts, acupuncture combined with electrical stimulation was effective in relieving the symptoms of narcotic withdrawal (6).

ELECTROACUPUNCTURE: TREATMENT METHODS

Acupuncture with electrical stimulation is used as a method of intervention to reduce the symptoms of withdrawal. The patient receives needling in the concha of both ears. Disposable needles, provided in convenient sterile packages, about 1/2 inch long and 32 gauge are used. After the ears have been cleansed with alcohol swabs, the sterile needle is inserted into each concha subcutaneously at the "lung" point for about 0.5 cm. The needles are then connected to a constant current electrical stimulator that has a total voltage of 12 volts and a built-in frequency of 1–125 cycles per second. It is difficult to predict the voltage or amperage that will suit a particular patient. The patient is asked to control the stimulus parameters as determined by his or her level of comfort and preference. The average voltage used is usually between 4 and 5 volts and about 3 milliamperes. If the patient has pain in the back and abdomen, extra needles can be inserted, using the same frequency. For backache, bladder points B-24 to B-54, B-57, and B-60 can be used. For anxiety and insomnia, large intestine—LI-4, heart—H-5 or H-6, or the ear points Shen Men are used.

EFFECTS OF ELECTROACUPUNCTURE STIMULATION

It has been observed that symptoms presented by the patients gradually improve after about 15 minutes' treatment and usually disappear almost entirely after 30 minutes. Signs and symptoms of lacrimation, runny nose, aching bones, wheezing, cramps in the stomach, cold feeling, and irritability usually disappear after 10–15 minutes of stimulation. Often it has been noted that patients have a desire to urinate and also that they feel thirsty and ask for water. After treatment, patients often seem less drowsy, are more talkative, and involve themselves more with their surroundings, beginning to do more for themselves in the wards. Also during stimulation, the patient's craving for the narcotic drug seems to diminish. The observed improvement in withdrawal signs and symptoms often lasts in the order of several hours (6–8). However, no systematic studies have yet been done to compare the effects of different acupuncture treatment techniques with that of placebo controls in the same setting.

Side Effects

It goes without saying that sterile techniques must be employed. In qualified hands, this procedure is remarkably free of side effects. Although there are no studies to support the concern that acupuncture may induce premature labor, the World Health Organization recommends that it should be carried out cautiously in pregnant women. Some patients may complain of dizziness and headaches when the current is increased beyond limits of comfort. These can be prevented by limiting the amount of current used. Syncope may occur when and if the needles are wrongly placed in the concha and also in anxious or nervous patients, but this can be avoided if patients are treated lying down during the initial stages. Acute gastric distention may occur if prolonged and continuous stimulation is given. However, the symptom usually subsides once the stimulation is stopped, and this complication has been observed only rarely.

Advantages

One advantage of electrical acupuncture is that it is easy to administer. Also it is inexpensive and economical in terms of the technique itself and in terms of expenses for drugs such as methadone, which can be quite costly in developing countries. Another advantage is that this is a nonchemical technique that may appeal to certain individuals who are trying to rid themselves of a chemical dependency, and there is no danger of addiction.

SOME SEQUELS TO THE INITIAL OBSERVATIONS

Since the initial report of Wen and Cheung, a number of investigators, both in this country and abroad, employing variations of this basic acupuncture paradigm, have reported beneficial effects on the narcotic withdrawal syndrome and on the clinical opiate detoxification process. However, the various acupuncture procedures that have been used are quite varied and diverse. Variations of this basic paradigm employ varying numbers of acupuncture points and various stimulation techniques. These include the use of needles with manual or electrical stimulation (9–17), use of staple puncture with electrical stimulation (13–18), as well as the stimulation of "acupuncture points" with surface electrodes without needles (19–21). These techniques have also been used in the treatment of alcoholism (3, 16, 24–23), cocaine (24–26), cigarette smoking (3, 7, 27, 28), and obesity (27).

PHYSIOLOGICAL MECHANISMS OF ACTION

There have been many efforts to determine the underlying physiological mechanisms of acupuncture. Some of the efforts were based on the misleading assumption that acupuncture is primarily a treatment for pain relief. Many acupuncture functions, such as autonomic and gastrointestinal effects, are independent of any aspect which relates to pain.

Acupuncture charts have a superficial resemblance to Western neuroanatomical charts. The functions of the meridian channels on acupuncture charts differ substantially, however, from those of nearby peripheral nerve trunks. Ear acupuncture is a particularly clear example in this regard. The acupuncture chart of the external ear identifies more than a hundred separate acupuncture points. These points relate primarily to different body locations and to various organic functions. One can easily verify some of these correlations by noting that the " shoulder point" on the ear shows abnormally low electrical resistance in patients with shoulder injuries, as does the ureter point in patients who are passing a kidney stone. The simple innervation pattern of the external ear cannot be used to explain these effects.

Researchers have noted the following variety of specific physiological effects associated with acupuncture as cited in Brewington (34). It has been reported that acupuncture at traditional points produced dramatic effects in EEG, galvanic skin response, blood flow, and breathing rate, while stimulation by needle placement in placebo points produced no appreciable effects. Various studies have linked acupuncture to the production of endogenous opiate peptides, such as beta-endorphin and met-enkephalins, and this has been speculated as a physiological mechanism behind the treatment's effects on withdrawal discomfort. Acupuncture has also been related to changes regarding other neurotransmitters, including serotonin, norepinephrine, ACTH, and cortisol levels.

It should be noted that certain medications—namely, methadone, corticosteroids, and benzodiazepines—seem to suppress part of the acupuncture effect. Patients taking these medications in substantial quantity have clearly less relaxation effect during treatment and seem to have a slower response to treatment. Nevertheless, acupuncture is an effective treatment for secondary addiction in high-dose methadone patients. Acupuncture is also widely used to treat adrenal suppressed patients who need to be weaned off corticosteroid medication. This may suggest that part of the initial relaxation response is endorphin and steroid dependent but that the more important mechanisms relate to a different type of process.

DETOXIFICATION USING ACUPUNCTURE

Inpatient

Treatment of the abstinence syndrome of drug addiction by AES in an inpatient setting was first reported in 1973 (6). In the inpatient setting, treatment can be carried out two or three times or more a day for optimum effect.

The periods of hospitalization vary in individuals but, on average, last about 7 days. This method is somewhat cumbersome, treatments have to be given frequently, and it takes an average of 7–8 days to detoxify the patients.

Outpatient

The technique of AES has also been used on an outpatient basis in detoxification programs. Of the 300 cases reported by Wen (28), it was observed that a total of 10% of the patients can be detoxified during a 14-day program. Another program where outpatient acupuncture treatment has been available is the detoxification project of the Haight-Ashbury Free Medical Clinic in San Francisco (9). Clients could choose between the acupuncture modality and the project's traditional medication modality on a voluntary basis. Although client retention in the acupuncture modality tended to be poor, it was found that about 37% of those clients who began the acupuncture modality persisted long enough to derive real benefits from the program.

Small though this proportion is, it seems to compare respectably with the proportion of drug-dependent clients judged clean at the time of termination from the project's conventional detoxification modality. This portion averaged about 17% over the 1975–1977 period.

Rapid Detoxification Using Naloxone and Electrical Acupuncture

The successful use of naloxone as a means of rapid detoxification of addicts from narcotic drugs has previously been reported by Resnick (14, 29) and Blachly (30, 31). These investigators have shown that naloxone-precipitated withdrawal, administered under proper supervision, is neither physically nor psychologically harmful to medically healthy individuals who elect this method of detoxification.

More recently, this rapid detoxification technique has been used combining naloxone with AES (32). With this particular technique, the patient is first primed for ½ hour with AES, before naloxone hydrochloride is injected in increasing doses until 0.8 (2 ml) is administered. Of the 50 cases that have been treated with this technique, 41 were successfully detoxified. The patients stated that the symptoms produced by naloxone could be better tolerated when AES was given but not when the current was decreased or stopped. It was also noted that patients seemed to suffer more if the current of the stimulator was not maintained. Symptoms tended to decrease when the current was increased slightly after a short interval. It was reported that the patients were detoxified within 3 hours and that the abstinence syndrome produced by naloxone was much milder and more tolerable and the time and dosage schedule were also well tolerated by the patients. Unfortunately, no controls were included in this study to compare the relative efficacy of electrical acupuncture on the naloxone-induced withdrawal syndrome. Because the naloxone-induced withdrawal symptoms are essentially self-limiting and manageable by conservative methods, there still remains the need to conduct research on the effectiveness of electroacupuncture in detoxification from narcotics or the attenuation of the withdrawal syndrome. More extensive studies have been conducted on the treatment of alcohol and cocaine dependence and are described here.

ALCOHOL DEPENDENCE

Directors of acupuncture detoxification in a social setting conducted in Marysville, Washington, estimate a yearly saving of $148,000 due to less frequent referrals to hospitals. Inpatient alcohol detoxification units typically combine acupuncture and herbal "sleep mix" with a tapering benzodiazepine protocol. Patients report few withdrawal symptoms and better sleep. Their vital signs indicate stability; hence, there is much less use of benzodiazepines.

Retention of patients being detoxified from alcohol has been reported to increase by 50% when acupuncture is added to conventional settings. Some alcoholics who receive acupuncture report an aversion to alcohol. Woodhull Hospital in Brooklyn reported a 94% abstinence rate in an acupuncture treated group compared to 43% of a control group who received only conventional outpatient treatment. The widely quoted control study by Bullock

(33) showed a 57% retention of acupuncture treated alcoholics compared to 2% of those treated with sham acupuncture.

LINCOLN HOSPITAL PROTOCOL

Acupuncture treatment for drug and alcohol problems was originally introduced in 1974 at Lincoln Hospital (LH), a city-owned facility in the impoverished South Bronx, for the treatment of drug and alcohol problems. The Substance Abuse Division at LH is a state-licensed treatment program that has provided more than 500,000 acupuncture treatments in the past 20 years. Dr. Yoshiaki Omura was the consultant who began the program (35). Initially, in 1974, Lincoln used Dr. H. L. Wen's method, applying electrical stimulation to the lung point in the ear (19). LH was a methadone detoxification program at that time; therefore, acupuncture was used as an adjunctive treatment for prolonged withdrawal symptoms after the 10 day detoxification cycle. Patients reported less malaise and better relaxation in symptom surveys. Subsequently, twice daily acupuncture was used concurrently with tapering methadone doses. Reduction in opiate withdrawal symptoms and higher retention rates were noted.

It was serendipitously discovered that electrical stimulation was not necessary to produce symptomatic relief. In fact, simple manual needling produced a more prolonged effect. Patients were able to use acupuncture only one time a day and still experience a suppression of their withdrawal symptoms. A reduction in craving for alcohol and heroin was described for the first time. This observation corresponds to the general rule in acupuncture that strong stimulation has primarily a symptom-suppression or "sedation" effect and that more gentle stimulation has preventive or "tonification" effect of longer duration.

Gradually the acupuncture protocol was expanded by adding the "Shen Men" (spirit gate), a point which is well known for producing relaxation. Other ear points were tried on the basis of lower resistance, pain sensitivity, and clinical indication during a several-year developmental process. Dr. Michael Smith of LH added the "sympathetic," "kidney," and "liver" points to create a basic five-point formula. Numerous other point formulas using body acupuncture points were tried on an individual basis without any significant improvement. Some programs omit the "sympathetic" point in pregnant patients although there is no basis in acupuncture studies for this precaution.

The standard formula seemed to be equally effective for different drugs of abuse and at different stages of treatment. Patients responded better when acupuncture treatment was administered quickly without a self-conscious, diagnostic prelude. Since acupuncture produces a homeostatic response, it was not necessary to adjust the formula for mood swings, agitation, or anergy.

A group setting enhances the acupuncture effect. A group size of less than six members seems to diminish symptom relief and retention significantly. Patients receiving acupuncture in an individual setting are often self-conscious and easily distracted. These problems are more evident in the management of new patients. In general acupuncture treatment sessions need to last 20–25 minutes. Because of chemical dependency patients are more resistant and dysfunctional; they should be instructed to remain in the acupuncture group setting for 40–45 minutes so that a full effect is obtained.

The atmosphere of the treatment room should be adjusted to fit varying clinical circumstances. Programs with a significant number of new intakes and/or socially isolated patients should use a well-lighted room and allow a moderate amount of conversation to minimize alienation and encourage social bonding. On the other hand, programs with relatively fixed clientele who relate to each other frequently in other group settings should dim the lights and not allow any conversation to minimize distracting cross talk. Background music is often used in the latter circumstance.

The location of ear points and the technique of insertion can be taught effectively in a 70-hour apprenticeship program so that most acupuncture components can be staffed by a wide range of substance abuse clinicians. Training must include a clinical apprenticeship because coping with the individual distractions and group process is more important and more difficult than the technical skill of repetitive needle insertion. Each clinician can provide about 15 treatments per hour in a group setting. General supervision should be provided by licensed or certified acupuncturists. This arrangement allows for acupuncture to be integrated with existing services in a flexible and cost-effective manner. Lincoln Hospital has trained more than 2000 clinicians in the past 7 years. The National Acupuncture Detoxification Association (NADA) was established in 1985 to increase the use of the LH model and to maintain quality and responsibility in the field.

Dr. Smith developed an herbal formula known as "sleep mix," which is used in most acupuncture for addiction settings and many other health care settings as well. The formula includes chamomile, peppermint, yarrow, scullcap, hops, and catnip. These are inexpensive herbs, traditionally used in Europe, which are reputed to calm and soothe the nervous system and tend to stimulate circulation and the elimination of waste products. The herb formula is taken as a tea on a nightly basis or frequently during the day as symptoms indicate. Sleep mix can be used for the treatment of conventional stress and insomnia as well as providing an adjunctive support in addiction treatment settings. Sleep mix is particularly appropriate for the management of alcohol withdrawal symptoms. Patients receiving conventional benzodiazepine treatment will often voluntarily refuse this medication if sleep mix is available.

CONTROLLED RESEARCH

Results from available placebo-design studies support the conclusion that acupuncture's effectiveness in facilitating abstinence with alcohol, opiate, and cocaine abusers is not due to a simple placebo effect (34). Seven published studies involving animal subjects (i.e., mice or rats) indicate that electroacupuncture reduces opiate withdrawal symptoms with morphine-addicted subjects. In these studies, experimental and control animals show behavioral differences regarding rodent opiate withdrawal symptoms, such as hyperactivity, "wet dog" shakes, and teeth chattering. Each of these studies note significantly less withdrawal symptoms with subjects receiving electroacupuncture relative to controls. Significantly different hormonal and beta endorphin levels post-electroacupuncture are noted between experimental and control subjects in several of these studies.

A number of controlled studies have been conducted on human subjects using various modified versions of the Lincoln Hospital ear point formula. Washburn (36) reported that opiate addicted individuals receiving correct site acupuncture showed significantly better program attendance relative to subjects receiving acupuncture on placebo sites. Two placebo-design studies provide strong support regarding acupuncture treatment for alcoholics. Bullock (37) studied 54 chronic alcohol abusers randomly assigned to receive acupuncture either at points related to addiction or at nearby point locations not specifically related to addiction. Subjects were treated in an inpatient setting but were free to leave the program each day. Throughout the study, experimental subjects showed significantly better outcomes regarding attendance and self-reported "desire to drink." Bullock (33) reported on 80 patients followed for 6 months. Eight weeks after treatment ended, of 40 patients in the experimental group, 21 were drug free as compared to only one in the control group (Table 51.l).

Subjects in the placebo group self-reported over twice the number of drinking episodes as reported by those in the experimental group. Placebo subjects were also readmitted to the local hospital alcohol detoxification unit at over twice the rate of experimental subjects during the follow-up period.

Worner (38) examined outpatient treatment outcomes for a sample (n = 56) of alcoholics subjects assigned to one of three conditions: acupuncture (n = 19), sham transdermal stimulation (n = 21), and control (standard care) (n = 16). Acupuncture involved both ear and body points, provided only three times weekly over a 3-month period. Subjects exposed to sham transdermal stimulation had electrocardiogram pads attached to their arms and legs, and were told that the procedure was a "needleless" form of acupuncture. No significant between-group differences were noted on outcome measures (e.g., retention, Alcoholics Anonymous [AA] attendance, alcohol relapse). It was concluded that the effectiveness of acupuncture in treating alcohol withdrawal might be a placebo effect, and that their results were "at variance" with Bullock (37). While statistically significant effects were not observed, it should be noted that the acupuncture group showed the best outcomes on seven of eight measures reported. Given this trend, it seems probable that results might have reached statistical significance if a larger sample were used.

Konefal (39) examined the efficacy of different acupuncture point protocol with patients with various substance abuse problems. Subjects (n = 321) were randomly assigned to one of three groups: a one-needle auricular treatment protocol using the Shen Men point; the five needle Lincoln protocol; or the five-needle Lincoln protocol plus selected body points for self-reported symptoms. All groups showed an increase in the proportion of drug-free urine tests over the course of treatment.

During the trial and error search for a more effective ear acupuncture formula for addiction treatment it was clear that a large number of points had some effect on acute withdrawal symptoms. Ear acupuncture charts indicate that all areas on the anterior surface of the ear are identified as active treatment locations. Using a "placebo" or "sham" acupuncture technique is actually an effort to use relatively ineffective points in contrast to the conventional use of totally ineffective sugar pills in pharmaceutical trials. "Sham" points are usually located on the external helix or rim of the ear, although there is no consensus about the level of effectiveness of this procedure. Bullock's alcoholism studies used highly failure-prone subjects and hence may have revealed the difference between active and "sham" points more effectively.

CLINICAL APPLICATIONS

Acupuncture is being used in numerous diverse treatment settings. Outcome reports have been published only to a limited degree because of an emphasis on placebo controlled studies. Unless otherwise noted these outcomes are based on clinical experiences at Lincoln Hospital or personal observation of other programs made by Smith.

Cocaine

Cocaine addiction has provided the most important challenge for acupuncture treatment because there are no significant pharmacological agents for this condition. Acupuncture patients report more calmness and reduced craving for cocaine even after the first treatment. The acute psychological symptoms of cocaine toxicity are visibly reduced during the treatment session. This improvement is sustained for a variable length of time after the first acupuncture treatment. After 3–7 sequential treatments the anticraving effect is more or less continuous as long as acupuncture is received on a regular basis.

Researchers from the substance abuse treatment unit at Yale describe 32 cocaine-dependent, methadone-maintained patients who received an 8-week course of auricular acupuncture for the treatment of cocaine dependence. Fifty percent completed treatment; 88% of study completers attained abstinence, defined as providing cocaine-free urine samples for the last 2 weeks of the study, yielding an overall abstinence rate of 44%. Abstainers reported decreased depression, a shift in self-definition, decreased craving, and increased aversion to cocaine-related cues. Post-hoc comparisons to pharmacotherapy with desipramine (DMI), amantadine (AMA), and placebo revealed a higher abstinence rate for acupuncture (44%) than for AMA (15%) or placebo (13%), but not significantly higher than for DMI (26%) (25).

Urinalysis outcomes were examined for Lincoln Hospital patients with cocaine or crack who had more than 20 treatment visits and were active during the 1-week study period in March, 1991. Patients typically provide urine samples for testing during each visit. Of the entire study group of 226 patients, 149 had more than 80% negative tests during their entire treatment involvement. Of the remaining patients, 39 had at least 80% negative tests during the 2 weeks prior to data collection (Table 51.2).

Table 51.1 Complete Rates in Hennepin Study

Treatment	Group	Control	p Value
Phase I (daily acupuncture for 2 weeks)	37 (92%)	21 (52%)	0.001
Phase II (3 times a week for 4 weeks)	26 (65%)	3 (7%)	0.001
Phase III (twice a week for 2 weeks)	21 (52%)	1 (2.1%)	0.001

Compiled from Bullock ML, Culliton PD, Olander RT. Controlled trial of acupuncture for severe recidivist alcoholism. Lancet 1989;1(8652):1435–1439.

Table 51.2   Effects of Acupuncture as Measured by Urinalysis

Urinalysis	Number	%
More than 80% negative (during entire involvement with program)	149	65
Recent 80% negative (during previous 2 weeks)	39	17
Recent relapse	26	12
30% to 70% positive	5	3
More than 80% positive	7	3

Methamphetamine

Methamphetamine abuse patients experience similar increases in treatment retention. Hooper Foundation, the public detoxification hospital in Portland, Oregon, reported 5% retention of methamphetamine users prior to the use of acupuncture and 90% retention after adding acupuncture to their protocol. Increased psychological stability and decreased craving were observed.

Methadone

Methadone maintenance patients receive acupuncture in a number of different settings. Patients report a decrease in secondary symptoms of methadone use such as constipation, sweating, and sleep problems. Typically there is a substantial drop in requests for symptomatic medication. Clinic staff usually notice decreased hostility and increased compliance in methadone patients receiving acupuncture. The most important effect of acupuncture in methadone maintenance programs is reduction of secondary substance abuse, primarily alcohol and cocaine, even in patients with minimal motivation (25). Reductions in secondary alcohol use are also frequently described. Acupuncture is effective with patients on any dosage level of methadone.

Lincoln Hospital used methadone and acupuncture together from 1974 to 1978. Several hundred methadone maintenance patients were detoxified during that period using tapered doses of methadone and acupuncture. Based on our previous non-acupuncture experience, we observed that patients were much more comfortable and confident in the acupuncture setting. Even though patients regularly complained about withdrawal symptoms, there were very few requests for dosage increase. The large majority of patients completed the entire detoxification process and provided at least one negative toxicology after the cessation of methadone. Methadone dosage was decreased 5–10 mg per week with a slower schedule during the final 10 mg. Starting levels of methadone ranged from 20 to 90 mg with a median of 60 mg. Acupuncture was provided 6 days per week and continued up to 2 months after the last methadone dose. Although many of these patients had been referred for administrative or mandatory detoxification due to secondary drug use, toxicologies were usually drug free after the first 2–3 weeks of treatment.

Methadone withdrawal is notable for unpredictable variations in symptoms and significant post-withdrawal malaise. Symptoms such as depression, anergy, and atypical insomnia are quite difficult to manage without acupuncture. Patients are usually fearful and have considerable difficulty participating in psychosocial therapy during the detoxification period. Acupuncture is particularly valuable in the methadone-to-abstinence setting, because the patient's future well-being depends on the ability to use psychosocial support.

Marihuana

At Lincoln, we have had a significant number of primary marihuana abusers seeking care. These patients usually report a rapid reduction in craving and improved mental well-being. Secondary marihuana use is usually eliminated along with the detoxification of the primary drug (e.g., cocaine).

Acupuncture treatment is generally made available to patients 5–6 days per week. LH offers treatment during an 8-hour period, but many smaller programs offer acupuncture during 1–2 hour periods each day. Morning treatment hours seem to be more beneficial. Active patients will receive treatment 3–6 times per week. Initially acupuncture should be defined as a required part of the program. If one describes acupuncture as a voluntary or optional part of the program, this description is not useful to a crisis-ridden addicted person. Such a person cannot handle choice and ambivalence effectively. Initially patients need direction and clarity. They should be asked to sit in the treatment room without needles if they are unsure about receiving acupuncture. New patients will learn about acupuncture from other more experienced patients and they will observe the process of treatment on a first hand basis. Sometimes a patient will be willing to try just one or two needles at first. Eventually a high percentage of patients will be active participants.

The duration of acupuncture treatment depends on many factors. Inpatient programs will stress acupuncture for detoxification and stabilization at the outset of treatment and for separation anxiety prior to discharge. Outpatients in a drug-free setting typically receive acupuncture for 1–3 months on an active basis. About 10% of these outpatients will choose to take acupuncture for more than one year if possible. Such patients usually have relatively great difficulties bonding on a psychosocial basis.

Acupuncture is not primarily a dose-related phenomenon as is pharmacological treatment. Acupuncture more appropriately represents a qualitative service comparable to a schoolroom class or psychotherapy session.

Patients who are using acupuncture appropriately should be allowed to choose how often they receive acupuncture treatment. Duration of the effect of each individual treatment increases as the patient becomes more stable. Since this treatment is a private personal process, it should come under the patient's control as soon as possible. Some patients will discontinue acupuncture too quickly, but they should be able to learn from the resultant loss of well being to make better decisions in the future. Participation in acupuncture is a different kind of decision than participation in group or individual psychotherapy. Relapsing patients are often able to continue to benefit from acupuncture even though they are no longer involved in psychotherapy. Acupuncture patients do not tend to "burn their bridges" as quickly; hence, retention and eventual success are increased in the acupuncture-based program.

A wide range of patients can be accepted for the initial stage of treatment because there is no verbal motivational requirement. Also, acupuncture is effective for most drugs and a wide range of psychological states. A low threshold, easily staffed program can be established for new patients. Ambivalent street-wise patients find the acupuncture setting almost impossible to manipulate. The setting is so soothing and self-protective that even extremely antisocial people can be included.. Problems relating to language and cultural differences are diminished. For new patients, frequent acupuncture treatment permits the gradual completion of assessment on a more accurate basis. Patients can be evaluated and triaged according to their daily response to treatment and testing rather than merely on the basis of an interview.

The tolerant, nonverbal aspect of acupuncture facilitates retention during periods when the patient would otherwise be ambivalent, fearful, or resentful within a more intense verbal interpersonal setting. Ear acupuncture makes it easy to provide outpatient treatment on demand, without appointments, while the patients are being acclimated to the interpersonal treatment setting.

Patients are often willing to be tested even when they know that their toxicology result is positive, thereby showing respect for the standard values of the overall treatment process. Those same patients may be unable or willing to share their crisis and failure verbally until they have time to reach more solid ground. In the acupuncture setting, time is on our side.

Acupuncture has many characteristics in common with 12-step programs such as AA and NA. It uses group process in a tolerant, supportive, and present-time oriented manner. Participation is independent of diagnosis and level of recovery. Both approaches are simple, reinforcing, nurturing and conveniently available. The emphasis on self-responsibility is common to both systems. In practice acupuncture provides an excellent foundation for 12-step recovery. Patients seem less fearful and more receptive when they first enter the meetings. The traditional advice "listen to learn and learn to listen" fits this model well. Acupuncture reduces "white knuckle sobriety" considerably. There is less guarding and greater ability to support each other warmly. The increased ability to use 12-step meetings provides more stable support for continuing treatment on an outpatient basis.

MATERNAL SUBSTANCE ABUSE

The use of acupuncture has led to a considerable expansion of treatment services for women using cocaine and crack. LH has been treating more than 100 pregnant cocaine users each year since 1987. These patients have regular visits with a nurse-midwife and receive specific education and counseling relative to pregnancy and child care. The LH program was cited as a model innovative program for prenatal care in a monograph, "Hospital and Community Partnership" issued by the American Hospital Association in 1991.

The average birth weight for babies at LH with more than 10 maternal visits is 6 pounds 10 ounces. The average birth weight for less than 10 visits is 4 pounds 8 ounces, which is typical of high-risk cocaine mothers. There is a high correlation between negative toxicologies, retention in the clinic program, and higher birth weights. Many (76%) of our pregnant intakes are retained in long-term treatment and give birth to nontoxic infants.

Female patients are often trapped in destructive and exploitative relationships and therefore will have special difficulty with any therapeutic relationship. A consistently tolerant and nonconfrontational approach prepares the way to establish a trauma survivor support service for patients at an early sobriety stage of recovery. The supportive atmosphere makes it relatively easy for patients to keep children with them during treatment activities. The acupuncture point formula used for substance abuse is also specific for the kind of emotional and muscular guarding associated with early sexual trauma. These patients will suffer intermittent crises and experience profound challenges to their physical and spiritual identity. All of their relationships will be strained and transformed. Acupuncture is a very appropriate adjunct to trauma survivors' support work.

PSYCHOSOCIAL MECHANISMS OF ACTION

It is essential to understand acupuncture's psychological and social mechanisms of action to use this modality effectively. Acupuncture has an impact on the patients's thoughts and feelings that is different from conventional pharmacological treatments. Subsequently we will discuss how the use of acupuncture has a valuable and profound effect on the dynamics of the treatment processes as a whole. We should emphasize that acupuncture for substance abuse is provided in a group setting. The new acupuncture patient is immediately introduced to a calm and supportive group process. Patients describe acupuncture as a unique kind of balancing experience. "I was relaxed but alert." "I was able to relax without losing control." Patients who are depressed or tired say that they feel more energetic. This encouraging and balancing group experience becomes a critically important basis for the entire process of substance abuse treatment.

Addiction is about trading present experience for past and future realities. Patients hang onto the present because the past and future seem to offer nothing but pain. Unfortunately conventional treatment efforts tend to focus on assessment of past activities and planning for the future. Patients are obsessed by present sensation and problems. They often feel alienated and resentful that they cannot focus on their immediate needs. Acupuncture allows treatment staff to respond to a patient's immediate needs without using addicting drugs. We can meet the patient in the present-time reality—validating their needs and providing substantial relief. Once a comfortable day-to-day reality support is established, we can approach past and future issues with a better alliance with the patient.

The nature of recovery from addiction is that patients often have quickly changing needs for crisis relief and wellness treatment. Many persons in recovery have relatively high levels of "wellness" functioning. Even so, a crisis of craving or past association may reappear at any time, Conventional treatment settings have trouble coping with such intense and confusing behavioral swings. Often merely the fear of a possible crisis can sabotage clinical progress. Acupuncture provides either crisis or wellness treatment using the same ear point formula. The nonverbal, present-time aspects of the treatment make it easy to respond to a patient in whatever stage of crisis or denial that may exist.

Patients readily accept that it is possible to improve their acute addictive status. They seek external help to provide hospitalization and medication for withdrawal symptoms. The challenge develops when they encounter the necessity for internal change. Addicts perceive themselves as being unable to change from within. Their whole life revolves around powerful external change agents. Each addict remembers countless examples of weakness, poor choices, and overwhelming circumstances, which lead to the conclusion that they cannot help themselves become drug free. Indeed, many influential members of society agree that "once an addict, always an addict."

Many of the complicating factors in our patients' lives echo this challenge of past internal failure. Persons leaving prison are confronted with a bleak uncaring world. Their own feelings of inadequacy frequently become so overwhelming that a return to prior drug and alcohol use may occur within hours of release. When patients learn that they are HIV positive, their self-esteem drops precipitously. Drug-abusing seropositive individuals typically feel punished for past weaknesses by their HIV status. How can such individuals have the confidence to seek out internal personal strength in the future?

We describe acupuncture as a foundation for psychosocial rehabilitation. In the beginning of treatment, building a proper foundation is very important. If we are building on a weak "sandy" personality, work on the foundation may take many months or years before it is strong enough to support any significant psychosocial treatment efforts. However, once a foundation is established, then the focus of treatment should shift away from acupuncture toward building a "house " of psychosocial recovery on that foundation. When one of our patients testified at city council hearings, she described how important it was to attend daily NA meetings and barely mentioned acupuncture. For a patient with 3-months' sobriety, this emphasis was appropriate. Of course, during her first 2 weeks in our program, she was quite angry, ambivalent, and was only able to relate to the acupuncture component of the program.

Addiction patients often cannot tolerate intense interpersonal relationships. Using a conventional one-to-one approach often creates a brittle therapeutic connection. It is easily broken by events or any stress. Patients have difficulty trusting a counselor's words when they can hardly trust themselves. Even after confiding to a counselor during an intake session, a patient may feel frightened and confused about expanding that relationship. Many of their concerns are so complex and troublesome that talking honestly about their lives could be difficult in the best of circumstances. The ambivalence typical of addicts makes it easy to develop misunderstandings. All of these factors support the usefulness of nonverbal techniques during early and critical relapse phases of treatment and critical periods of relapse.

Acupuncture helps a program develop an underlying environment of acceptance, tolerance, and patience. There is ample space for the ambivalence and temporary setbacks that are a necessary part of any transformation. Patients can have a "quiet day" by attending the program and receiving acupuncture without having to discuss their status with a therapeutic authority figure.

CRITIQUE

Although the array of favorable reports that have been published are quite impressive, the claims of the effectiveness of acupuncture on withdrawal symptoms or detoxification outcome seem to be based upon clinical observations that lack adequate controls and standardized procedures, thus making comparisons of techniques and results of outcome difficult. In none of these studies reported to date has there been an attempt to determine whether the observed effectiveness of the acupuncture treatment derives from "placebo" (i.e., nonspecific) factors or from certain specific stimulus components of the treatment procedure that make up the acupuncture treatment paradigm. For example, because so many seemingly different techniques seem to be effective, what are the basic elements that may be responsible for therapeutic efficacy? How crucial is the role of expectation that the therapist and the patient bring to the treatment process? Is the ritual (i.e., the administration of a reputedly potent treatment modality) a critical part of the paradigm? Can one isolate different components in the ritual itself that are responsible for particular biological effects? Is the needle insertion a critical component or is the stimulation itself the important component? Is the combination of needle with electrical stimulation more effective than use of either stimulation alone without needles or needles alone? How critical and specific are the so-called "acupuncture" points? Is specific localization of these points vital, or is the sensory modulation produced by stimulation of particular sensory distributions the critical variable? Obviously, these questions will require much intensive research conducted through properly controlled studies before they can be adequately answered.

IMPLICATIONS FOR RESEARCH

At the present time, the possible mechanisms by which electrical acupuncture produces alleviation of the narcotic withdrawal syndrome are highly conjectural. In animal studies using an experimental model for auricular electroacupuncture, Ng et al. (40, 41) found that electrical stimulation of the conchae of morphine-dependent rats produced significant attenuation of the naloxone-precipitated withdrawal syndrome, as manifested by diminished hyperactivity in the electrical acupuncture-treated rats, coupled with lower "wet dog" and teeth chattering scores, as well as a diminished rise in plasma catecholamines compared with untreated abstinent rats. More recently, auricular electroacupuncture in mice has also been found to be successful in reducing the naloxone-precipitated withdrawal symptoms of morphine-addicted mice, accompanied by a diminished rise in plasma adrenocorticotropin (41) and an elevation of brain "opiate-like activity" (42). These findings suggest that electroacupuncture stimulation may cause the release of a substance with morphine-like properties and are consistent with observations in humans (27) and in animals (43) that show that naloxone injection can abolish the analgesia produced by acupuncture stimulation (manual as well as electrical). Various studies have supported the hypothesis that acupuncture leads to the production of endogenous opiate peptides, such as beta-endorphin and met-enkephalin as well as changes in serotonin and norepinephrine. Hypophysectomy has also been found to abolish most of the acupuncture-induced analgesic effects (44). The somewhat slow induction period and the long lasting effects of acupuncture implicate a neurohumoral mechanism. These observations have led to the hypothesis that needling in appropriate points can stimulate sensory nerves to activate the pituitary or brain stem to release endorphin, which may at least in part mediate some of the acupuncture-induced effects (18, 33).

It should be pointed out that, although there is preliminary evidence to suggest that manual or electrical stimulation may activate certain somatosensory pathways (45, 46), including perhaps certain central neurohumoral mechanisms (47, 48) and possibly the endorphin system (18, 27, 33, 40–44), it is still far from clear whether any or all or which of the components embodied in the acupuncture paradigm are causally responsible for initiating such responses. It is premature to attribute a causal relationship between the observed improvement in subjective symptoms in addicts undergoing withdrawal to a particular treatment technique used or to a specific neurochemical effect observed. However, in a treatment modality as complex as that inherent in the acupuncture paradigm, the difficulty encountered in trying to isolate causal factors in such a complex set of relationships should not detract from the possible therapeutic uses of such a modality. There is clearly a great need for better controlled studies to help us develop our understanding of the mechanisms of action of acupuncture.

Although we may not understand how acupuncture works, it would be erroneous to equate acupuncture with hypnosis or placebo or conditioning as though these are all one homogeneous or unitary phenomenon (49). It is quite possible, and perhaps even likely, that the extremely complex phenomena of hypnosis, placebo response, the bedside manner of the attending physician and the autogenic suggestion of the patient are but some of the pieces in the jigsaw puzzle of acupuncture. It would be far too simplistic to label all acupuncture-induced phenomena as hypnosis or conditioning or placebo or autosuggestion, because in fact we know little of how these various modalities work. By equating acupuncture with hypnosis or placebo or conditioning or autosuggestion, we are labeling, in effect, X with Y, when we do not really know what X or Y is. From a research standpoint, it would be far more helpful to try to determine the commonalities and differences that may exist among these various modalities and to try to ask questions of manageable proportions, such as: What specifiable processes underlie acupuncture? Just as, what specifiable processes underlie hypnosis or placebo or conditioning? What are their similarities and what are their differences?

What clinical states can be induced with acupuncture? With hypnosis? With placebo? What are the optimal stimulus parameters? And how do these vary with and interact with the intervening variables and with the psychobiological program of the organism?

Because these various modalities in a clinical context are all complex, it may be more useful to shift from single cause to multifactorial models and to focus attention on the nature of interactions that can produce sufficient conditions for effective outcomes rather than to confine ourselves to the search for single causal effects. It would seem that an interactive conceptual model would be more appropriate and applicable to our understanding of complex and multifactorial modalities such as acupuncture, hypnosis, placebo, etc., in which therapeutic outcomes are understandably the result of interaction of many factors. A conceptual scheme for such an interactive model for acupuncture and other multifactorial phenomena is presented in Figure 51.1.

At one end, we can specify the input (independent) variables, as shown in Box I—Stimulus. These may be pharmacological (drugs) or nonpharmacological. The latter includes modalities using one or more sensory inputs, e.g., somatosensory (acupuncture, transcutaneous nerve stimulation), propriokinesthetic (biofeedback, massage), audiovisual (hypnosis). At the other end, we can look at the output (dependent) variables (Box V—Identifiable Response). These may include induced effects such as alterations in autonomic function, motor function, sensory perception, emotions, consciousness, cognition, or behavior. It is clear that the input can interact with many possible intervening variables to result in a particular observed effect (output). These intervening variables include the psychobiological program of the patient (Box II—genetic, learning, environmental factors), the motivation and expectation of the patient (Box III—Interacting Variables), and the interoceptive factors (Box IV—Internal Biological Events). These all may interact with each other and with the stimulus input (Box I—Stimulus) to produce a particular end effect (Box V—Identifiable Response). Even in the case of pharmacological agents with known specific effects, the end effects also can vary depending on the set and setting under which the agent is administered. Similarly, different individuals may respond to the same agent differently on the basis of certain genetic predispositions ("pharmacogenetics") or because of different learning, conditioning, or motivational factors. Also, the doctor-patient interaction may be critically important in determining the final outcome or induced effects.

This interaction model is presented as a framework that can be used to analyze and understand the multifactorial nature of complex modalities, such as acupuncture, hypnosis, biofeedback, etc., as applied in a treatment setting, in which the therapeutic outcome is the result of interaction of many factors. The needle in the acupuncture paradigm may be a necessary condition (if one defines acupuncture as a "puncturing with a sharp instrument") but not in and of itself a sufficient condition for successful therapeutic effects. If it is the sensory stimulation that should prove to be the critical variable in producing a desired effect, then the needle in the acupuncture paradigm would merely serve as a vehicle for sensory modulation, using manual or electrical stimulation.

There is increasing evidence to suggest that, in fact, acupuncture shares many similarities with transcutaneous electrical nerve stimulation (TENS) (43, 44, 46) and that it is the stimulation that is the important or critical variable. In this perspective, electrical acupuncture should be described more appropriately as "percutaneous electrical nerve stimulation" (PENS), and the so-called "acupuncture points" should be viewed in a relative sense as providing clues for sites of stimulation, rather than in absolute terms as requiring specific localization, because with electrical stimulation one would obviously be stimulating a field or a particular segmental distribution rather than a unique point. It should be pointed out that acupuncture stimulation (i.e., stimulation delivered through the skin with a needle) does offer certain advantages under certain situations. It allows for a more localized delivery of the stimulus to a greater depth than would be possible with surface (or transcutaneous) stimulation; also, by piercing the skin with a needle, the large resistance of the skin is overcome so that a much smaller amount of current is needed for stimulation.

It is our view that electrical acupuncture is a form of percutaneous

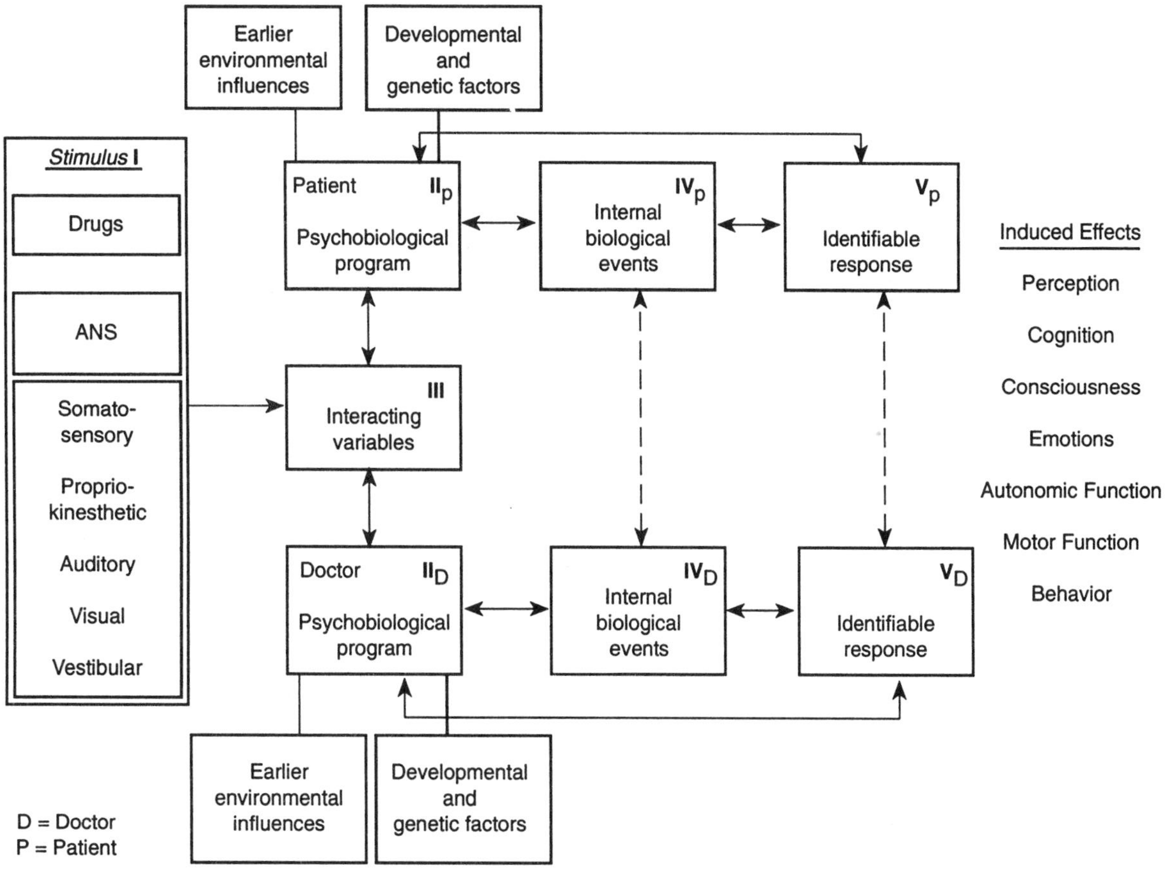

Figure 51.1. Interaction model for ANS and related sensory-induced phenomena.

nerve stimulation similar to the transcutaneous electrical stimulation that is gaining increasing acceptance in the West. As such, electrical acupuncture provides a simple, nonchemical means of stimulating or modulating certain neural pathways, and the needle merely provides a useful vehicle for sensory modulation using electrical current. Obviously, further research will be needed to allow us to determine the extent to which the physical stimulus components of the treatment paradigm contribute to the biological effects and to the clinical outcome. From the standpoint of an in-teractive model, it is understandable that sufficient conditions for effective outcome may be achieved from permutations derived from one or more of the different categories shown in Figure 51.1. The hierarchy of effects that can be produced by these permutations under appropriately controlled conditions remains a challenging area for further investigation. Much remains to be learned, and much careful research will be required before proper conclusions can be reached in regard to the many important questions that are being raised.

References

1. Kao F. Acupuncture therapeutics. New Haven, CT: Eastern Press, 1973.
2. Mann F. The treatment of disease by acupuncture. London: Heinemann Medical Books, 1972.
3. Low SA. Acupuncture and nicotine withdrawal. Med J Aust 1977;2:687.
4. Stein L. Reward transmitters: catecholamines and opioid peptide. In: Lipton MA, DiMascio A, Killam KF, eds. Pharmacology: a generation of progress. New York: Raven Press, 1978.
5. Foltz EL, White LE Jr. Experimental cingulumotomy and modification of morphine withdrawal. J Neurosurg 1957;14:655.
6. Leibeskind JC, Guilbaud G, Besson JM, Oliveras JL. Analgesia from electrical stimulation of the periaqueductal gray matter in the cat: behavioral observations and inhibitory effects upon spinal cord interneurons. Brain Res 1973;50: 441–446.
7. Chen JYP. Treatment of cigarette smoking by auricular acupuncture: a report of 184 cases. Paper presented at the National Symposia of Acupuncture and Moxibustion and Acupuncture Anesthesia, Beijing, China, January 1–5, 1979.
8. LeBars D, Dickenson AH, Besson JM. Diffuse noxious inhibitory controls (DNIC): effects on dorsal horn convergent neurons in the rat. Pain 1979;6:283–304.
9. Blum K, Newmeyer JA, Whitehead C. Acupuncture as a common mode of treatment for drug dependence: possible neurochemical mechanisms. J Psychedelic Drugs 1978;10:105.
10. Bradshaw J. The use of acupuncture in the treatment of heroin addicts. Paper presented at the 31st International Congress on Alcoholism and Drug Dependence, Bangkok, Thailand, February 23–28, 1975.
11. Chen CS, Hung LF, Su CY, Line CS, Lin BS, Wa YM. Preliminary clinical report on the treatment of narcotic addiction by using acupuncture and electrical stimulation. Paper presented at the International Congress on Acupuncture, Taipei, Taiwan, 1976.
12. Kao AH, Ly YC. Acupuncture procedure for treating drug addiction. Am J Acupuncture 1974;2:201.
13. Nathan PW. Acupuncture analgesia. Trends Neurosci 1978;1:21–23.
14. Han JS, Terenius L. Neurochemical basis of acupuncture analgesia. Ann Rev Pharmacol Toxicol 1982;22:193–220.
15. Takagi H. Critical review of pain relieving procedures including acupuncture. Advances in pharmacology and therapeutics. II. CNS pharmacology. Neuropeptides 1982;1:79–92.
16. Field J, Magoun HW, Hall VE. Handbook Physiol 1959;1:75.
17. Xuan YT, Shi ZF, Zhou F, Jan JS. Studies on the mesolimbic loop of antinociception. II. A serotonin enkephalin interaction in the nucleus accumbens. Neuroscience 1986;19(2):403–409.
18. Dymond AM, Coger RW, Serafetinides EA. Intracerebral current levels in man during electrosleep therapy. Biol Psychiatry 1975;10: 101–104.
19. Wen HL, Cheung SYC. Treatment of drug addiction by acupuncture and electrical stimulation. Asian J Med 1973;9:138–143.
20. Gomez E, Mikhail A. Treatment of methadone withdrawal with cerebral electrotherapy (elec-

trosleep). Presented at the annual meeting of the American Psychiatric Association, Detroit, MI, May 6–10, 1974.

21. Smith MO, Khan I. An acupuncture program for the treatment of drug addicted persons. Bull Narc 1988;15(1):35–41.
22. Deleted in proof.
23. Smith RB, O'Neil LO. Electrosleep in the management of alcoholism. Biol Psychiatry 1975; 10(B):675–680.
24. Lipton DS, Brewington V, Smith MO. Acupuncture for crack-cocaine detoxification: experimental evaluation of efficacy. J Subst Abuse Treat 1994;11(3):205–215.
25. Margolin A, Avants KS, Chang P, Kosten TR. Acupuncture for the treatment of cocaine dependence in methadone-maintained patients. Am J Addict 1993;2(3):194–201.
26. Mitchell ER. Fighting drug abuse with acupuncture. Berkeley CA: Pacific View Press, 1995.
27. Lau MP. Acupuncture and addiction: an overview. Addict Dis 1976;2:449.
28. Parker LN, Mole MS. The use of acupuncture for smoking withdrawal. Am J Acupuncture 1977;5:363.
29. Han JS, Tsang J, Ren MF, Zhou ZF, Fan SG, Qui X. Role of central neurotransmitters in acupuncture analgesia. In: Zhang X, Chang HT, eds. Research on acupuncture, moxibustion, and acupuncture anesthesia. Beijing: Science Press, 1986:241–266.
30. Blachly P. Naloxone in opiate addiction. In: Masserman J, ed. Current psychiatric therapies. Vol. 16. New York: Grune and Stratton, 1976.
31. Blachly P, et al. Rapid detoxification from heroin and methadone using naloxone. In: Senay EC, et al., eds. Developments in the field of drug abuse. Cambridge, MA: Schenkman, 1975: 327–335.
32. Ng LKY, Douthitt TC, Thoa NB, Albert CA. Modification of morphine withdrawal syndrome

in rats following transauricular electrostimulation: an experimental paradigm for auricular electroacupuncture. Biol Psychiatry 1975;10: 575–580.
33. Bullock ML, Culliton PD, Olander RT. Controlled trial of acupuncture for severe recidivist alcoholism. Lancet 1989;1(8652):1435–1439.
34. Brewington V, Smith M, Lipton D. Acupuncture as a detoxification treatment: an analysis of controlled research. J Subst Abuse Treat 1994; 11(4):289–307.
35. Omura Y, Smith M, Wong F, Apfel F, Taft R, Mintz T. Electroacupuncture for drug addiction withdrawal. Acupuncture and Eletro-Therapeutics Research International Journal 1975;1: 231–233.
36. Washburn AM, Fullilove RE, Fullilove MT, Keenan PA, McGee B, Morris KA, et al. Acupuncture heroin detoxification: a single-blind clinical trial. J Subst Abuse Treat 1993;10: 345–351.
37. Bullock ML, Umen AJ, Culliton PD, Olander RT. Acupuncture treatment of alcoholic recidivism: a pilot study. Alcohol Clin Exp Res 1987; 11(3):292–295.
38. Worner TM, Zeller B, Schwartz H, Zwas F, Lyon D. Acupuncture fails to improve treatment outcomes in alcoholics. Drug Alcohol Depend 1992;30:169–173.
39. Konefal J, Duncan R, Clemence C. Comparison of three levels of auricular acupuncture in an outpatient substance abuse treatment program. Alternative Medicine Journal 1995; 2(5):Sept.
40. Malizia E, Andreucci G, Cerbo R, Colombo G. Effect of naloxone on the acupuncture-elicited analgesia in addicts. Adv Biochem Psychopharmacol 1978;18:361–362.
41. Choy YM, Tso WW, Fung KP, Leung KC, Tsang YF, Lee CY, et al. Suppression of narcotic withdrawals and plasma ACTH by auricu-

lar electro-acupuncture. Biochem Biophys Res Commun 1978;82:305.
42. Ho WKK, Wen HL, Lam S, Ma LK. The influence of electro-acupuncture on naloxone-induced morphine withdrawal in mice: elevation of brain opiate-like activity. Eur J Pharmacol 1978;49:197.
43. Fox EJ, Melzack R. Comparison of transcutaneous electrical stimulation and acupuncture in the treatment of chronic pain. In: Bonica JJ, Albe-Fessard D, eds. Advances in pain research and therapy. Vol. 1. New York: Raven Press, 1976.
44. Chapman CR, Wilson ME, Gehrig JD. Comparative effects of acupuncture and transcutaneous stimulation on the perception of painful dental stimuli. Pain 1976;2:265.
45. Chaing CY, Chang CT, Chud HL, Yang LF. Peripheral afferent pathway for acupuncture analgesia. Sci Sin 1975;16:210.
46. Loeser JD. Nonpharmacologic approaches to pain relief. In: Ng LKY, Bonica JJ, eds. Proceedings of conference on pain, discomfort, and humanitarian care, held at the National Institutes of Health, February 15–16, 1979. Developments in neurology. Vol. 4. New York: Elsevier-North Holland, 1980;4:275–292.
47. Acupuncture Anesthesia Research Group, Hunan Medical College, Changsha, China. Relation between acupuncture analgesia and neurotransmitters in rabbit brain. Chinese Med J 1975;8:478.
48. Han CS, Tang J, Jen MF, et al. The role of central neurotransmitters in acupunctive analgesia. A brief report of the Research Group of Acupuncture Anesthesia, Beijing Medical College. Tidsskr Nor Laegeforen 1982;102(6):359–361.
49. Kroger WS. Acupunctural analgesia: its explanation by conditioning theory, autogenic training, and hypnosis. Am J Psychiatry 1973; 130:855.

52 RELIGION

John Muffler, John G. Langrod, James T. Richardson, and Pedro Ruiz

The complex quest for appropriate means of treating substance abuse must be informed by a knowledge of pharmacology, an understanding of psychosocial theories of human growth and development, principles of sound psychological and therapeutic practice, and, finally, an awareness and appreciation of the cultural context of the individual seeking treatment. This latter element, awareness of cultural context, can prove to be an important guide to providing effective treatment in a variety of cases, borne out by the increasing number of practitioners and programs placing a higher premium on cultural sensitivity toward the clients they serve. A comprehensive discussion of cultural context is presented in Chapter 10.

Unlike other established approaches to treating substance abuse, both conventional and unconventional, religiously oriented programs continue to be neglected in the professional literature (28, 45, 46). Characteristics such as *religious commitment, religious affiliation,* and *religiosity* most frequently are analyzed for their "behavior predictive" value, rather than being examined as significant elements potentiating recovery, maintaining sobriety, and encouraging social reaffiliation. At the extremes, there appears to be a not-so-benign neglect of religious treatment modalities on the part of "secular" psychotherapeutic professionals and an equally self-righteous distancing from "secular" approaches by religiously oriented practitioners. The di-

chotomy is further exacerbated by division within the religious community itself over theological grounding and methodological considerations in providing care for substance abusers. The increasing visibility of "ethnic" or "folk" religious practices, such as Santeria and Espiritismo, coupled with the growing awareness of and, in some quarters, uneasiness with the emergence of new religious movements (NRMs) has helped compound the confusion.

Clearly, not all substance abusers can be reached, much less successfully treated, by way of religiously oriented programs. This approach merits serious consideration, however, since for individuals with a high degree of religious motivation it has produced positive results comparable to those of other accepted forms of treatment. For these women and men, it is often the treatment of choice (16, 28, 29, 44, 56). The present chapter focuses on one much neglected element of that context, the religious milieu and the relative importance of religiously oriented programs for certain women and men seeking relief for their addictions.

RELIGIOUS MILIEU

Religion remains an almost universal attribute of our culture (33). The late Abraham Joshua Heschel, theologian and philosopher of the modern human condition, has suggested that religion is more than simply a mood or feeling. The pivotal role of the religious milieu is the simultaneous discovery and rediscovery of the sensitivity to ultimate questions while urging the individual on in his or her search for the answers to those questions. For Heschel (30), religious thinking is "an intellectual endeavor out of the depths of reason. It is a source of cognitive insight into the ultimate issues of human existence."

Viewed from this perspective, religion's major effort must be placed in the service of reversing technological society's seeming tendency to trivialize human existence while assisting man and woman's search for meaning and purpose. Religious traditions remind us that humanity is quite willing to endure sacrifice, discipline, and moral and spiritual exaltation in pursuit of an ultimate commitment to freedom and dignity. We also are reminded that, in the name of human freedom and dignity, we are accountable for our choices and actions and, as such, that people are capable of forgiving and being forgiven, of starting anew (30).

Religion, always comprising a system of beliefs and rituals, is a universal phenomenon that obviously answers some very fundamental human needs. The religious milieu, as understood here, is communal in nature, queries ultimate reality, and emphasizes a belief in the dominance of good over evil.

The concept of religion as a category separate from other aspects of social life is one that emerged with the Judeo-Christian tradition. Some small nonindustrialized societies do not recognize this dichotomy. There are also many characteristics of Western religions that are not necessarily associated with religion in other societies: an anthropomorphic divinity, a sharp distinction between natural and supernatural, a set of ethical principles, and the relation of earthly behavior to an afterlife (73).

H. Richard Niebuhr (53) suggests that the religious milieu, particularly as manifested in American Christianity, transcends ethical programs and doctrinal creeds, important though they are. It is not so much an organization as the organic movement of men and women who have been "called and sent forth." Christianity institutionalized, as it appears in various denominations and congregations, in liberal programs and conservative creeds, is a resting place in life's movement toward an infinite and eternal God. Still, the religious milieu for most Western women and men is almost exclusively understood and identified within the boundaries of formal denominations and organized congregations. It is within these denominations and congregations that religion seems to take form and find concrete, day-to-day expression.

It is important, therefore, to explain some key distinctions within the diverse world of American Christianity. This diversity is complex. There is a dynamism that encourages a blurring of the boundaries among Evangelical, Pentecostal, Charismatic, and mainline Christians. The emergence of NRMs also contributes to this complexity. The following discussion is presented with this in mind.

VARIETIES OF RELIGIOUS EXPERIENCE

The term *mainline church* generally refers to the members of the major Protestant denominations that were formed as a result of the Reformation in the sixteenth and seventeenth centuries. The Episcopalian, Lutheran, Presbyterian, Methodist, United Church of Christ, and Reformed churches are examples of mainline denominations. For a variety of historical reasons, today such churches tend to have less literal interpretations of Scripture, more progressive theologies and social agendas, and an appreciation of modern science and biblical scholarship. To the degree that contemporary Catholicism shares these characteristics, without compromising its particular theological history and ecclesiology, the Catholic Church is considered here as a mainline denomination. One must be aware, however, that there are Evangelical and Charismatic elements within these churches. Their presence reflects the same theological tensions within the denominations that exist between the mainline churches and Evangelical and Charismatic churches.

The term *Evangelical,* derived from the Greek word meaning "gospel," has become the common designation for the revival movements that swept through Europe and the Americas during the eighteenth and nineteenth centuries. Proclamation of Christ's saving work through His death on the cross and the absolute necessity of personally trusting in Christ for eternal salvation

constitute the pivotal beliefs (50). Evangelicals generally believe that a spiritual rebirth, a "born again" experience during which the individual acknowledges personal sinfulness and Christ's atonement, is required in order to be saved. When faced with the challenge of Darwin and more sophisticated forms of biblical critical scholarship, Evangelicals, who already embraced a literal interpretation of the Bible, began to emphasize its inerrant nature (4).

Evangelicalism today cuts across denominational identity. It includes any Christian willing to affirm these traditional tenets of faith: (*a*) the real historical character of God's saving work as recorded in the Bible; (*b*) salvation to eternal life based solely on the redemptive work of Christ; (*c*) the importance of a spiritually transformed life; (*d*) the centrality of evangelism and mission in the life of the church; and (*e*) the Reformation doctrine of the final authority of Scripture. Evangelicalism, then, includes an amazingly diverse membership: Holiness churches, Pentecostals, traditional Methodists, the various Baptist Conventions, elements of Presbyterian, Episcopalian, Reformed, and Lutheran churches, Anabaptists such as Mennonites, as well as Hispanic and African-American churches within all of these traditions. Recent surveys suggest that nearly 50 million Americans identify themselves as Evangelical Christians (4, 50, 78).

"Pentecostals" comprise another segment of evangelicalism. Growing out of the holiness movement of the nineteenth century and the emotion-laden Pentecostal revivals of the early twentieth century, Pentecostals take their name from this latter ecstatic religious phenomenon. In addition to the tenets of faith described above, Pentecostals believe that the gifts of the Holy Spirit bestowed on the church of the apostles, as recounted by Luke in the New Testament's *Acts of the Apostles,* are available to modern-day believers. They insist that a spiritual experience of baptism, a "filling by the Holy Spirit," constitutes the mark of the truly authentic Christian. The "gifts of the Spirit" include speaking in tongues and interpreting the message thus presented, the ability to discern the needs and spiritual condition of the brothers and sisters, and divine healing. Holiness in one's personal life is stressed. Secular activities such as social dancing, smoking, and social drinking are discouraged. Worship is characterized by singing, clapping, and the spontaneous participation of the congregation. "Fellowship" among members, both within and away from church, is highly valued and highly evident in Pentecostal churches. The Church of God in Christ and the Assemblies of God are two of the more familiar Pentecostal denominations (4, 44).

"Charismatics" form still another branch of the conservative evangelical family tree. Closely related to the Pentecostals in theology and style of worship, they also emphasize the availability of the gifts of the Holy Spirit. Charismatics generally are more dramatic, demonstrative, and emotive in worship and spirituality. The term *Charismatic,* however, usually refers to those Christians who are not affiliated with the traditional Pentecostal denominations. Cutting across all the major denominations, Charismatic Christians are especially well-represented within the ranks of the more liturgical denominations, such as the Catholic and Episcopalian churches (4, 50).

Although church attendance reportedly is declining in modern, industrialized societies, this is not true in the United States. Growth in this country has been especially noticeable among the Evangelical, Pentecostal, and Charismatic churches, as well as in the emergent NRMs. Although this growth is experienced across class and socioeconomic boundaries, these three churches' expressions of Christianity are especially well-represented among disadvantaged and low-income people. In cities, particularly, large numbers of Hispanic and African-American Christians are active members of Pentecostal and Charismatic churches (50, 56, 78).

RELIGION AND REHABILITATION

Fifty years of Gallup poll results indicate that, on average, 96% of Americans surveyed reported a belief in God (24). A study among Hispanic Americans in San Antonio by Desmond and Maddux (16) suggests that Pentecostal-type programs may prove effective in treating chronic opioid dependence. Research conducted by Larson et al. (45), utilizing data from the Epidemiologic Catchment Area Program of the National Institute of Mental Health, found surprisingly positive results for frequent use of religious providers by persons with alcohol and drug abuse disorders classified in the American Psychiatric Association's *Diagnostic and Statistical Manual of Mental Disorders.*

This chapter turns now to a closer examination of religion and rehabilitation. It presents a summary of mainline and Evangelical/Pentecostal Christian involvement with women and men seeking relief from their addictions, followed by an analysis of Teen Challenge, Espiritismo, and the New Religious Movement.

Mainline Christianity

Most of the early church-related programs were Protestant. Although they stressed religious values and the importance of faith in a God who delivers people from their afflictions, these mainline churches tended to adopt a more secular professional approach to treatment. In essence, they became ecclesiastical social service delivery systems. Religious belief provided the basis and framework for the involvement of these churches, though it was not necessarily emphasized in treating the individual (51).

The contemporary religious scene is quite a bit different today. The Catholic Church has become increasingly involved in providing treatment and rehabilitation services to substance-abusing women and men since the late 1960s. Both Protestant and Catholic efforts have been institutionalized and coordinated at the denominational and diocesan or presbyterial levels through organizations such as Catholic Charities or Lutheran Social Services, based primarily in hospitals and other community satellite centers. For the most part, the participation of local congregations is confined to providing sponsorship and meeting space in church facilities for Alcoholics Anonymous and Narcotics Anonymous. Some congregations offer a broader range of social services and referrals in conjunction with ministries to the homeless. Others have joined forces with neighboring churches and formally incorporated themselves into community not-for-profit organizations, such as Harlem Churches for Community Improvement in New York City and Newark Fighting Back in Newark, New Jersey (51).

Evangelical and Pentecostal Approaches

The Evangelical and Pentecostal churches traveled a different road. Programs such as Teen Challenge use religious conversion as the primary step to begin to combat addiction. It is primarily believed in these programs that there is no other effective way to overcome heroin or cocaine addiction, alcoholism, and other "deviant" behaviors. It is essential, according to this belief, that the troubled person, having sinned, be "born again" by accepting Jesus Christ as "personal savior." Ideally, the born-again person will then exhibit a change in personality and lifestyle that is consistent with the values and behaviors described in Scripture. Ultimately, the converted sinner is brought into the church as a brother or sister in a strong fellowship characterized by love and concern.

Those who come seeking "treatment" are taught to pray and to depend on God's assistance with all their personal problems, including addiction. Ideally, they are entirely freed from the mistakes of the former life. The desire to continue the old, evil ways will also fade with the passage of time. Interests become largely spiritual rather than "worldly" as the individual relates to a larger reality outside of himself or herself and his or her world view and value system become much less egocentric. Clearly, for Evangelical and Pentecostal Christians, faith is both the starting and end point of recovery. It is the healing power of Jesus Christ, in the Church, and not the intervention of behavioral science that brings about and maintains the individual's rehabilitation.

Teen Challenge

Teen Challenge is a drug-free religious residential program for drug abusers. Describing itself as a Christ-centered organization, it is a ministry for people who have "life-controlling problems and are without the necessary resources and opportunities to live productively" (76). Teen Challenge sees its mission as "helping people become mentally sound, emotionally balanced, socially adjusted, physically well, and spiritually alive," a haven for youth trapped in a world defined by drug and alcohol dependence and immorality" (77). Founded in 1961 by the Rev. David Wilkerson, a minister

in the Assemblies of God denomination, the original program was located in the Williamsburg section of Brooklyn, New York City. In 1989, a second Teen Challenge Center opened in Amityville, Long Island, founded by Jimmy and Miriam Jack, both Teen Challenge graduates. In 1990, the City Church was established to meet the spiritual needs of Teen Challenge students and their families. The Ladies Crisis Center, located in Long Island's Suffolk County, welcomed its first 12 women in May of 1995 (77).

Having spent 3 years in the slums of East Harlem, David Wilkerson judged narcotics addiction to be the greatest challenge facing the people of that community. He sensed that a reality more powerful, attractive, and rewarding than the needle was needed. He believed that new reality could be brought about only by religious conversion. Most young people who came to the Teen Challenge Center were addicts seeking help. In 1964, Rev. Don Wilkerson, David's brother, assumed the directorship of the Center, presiding over its transition to an induction and detoxification center. The group also established a Training Center on a 200-acre farm in Rehrersburg, Pennsylvania, far away from the temptations of the city.

As described above, Teen Challenge has grown rapidly during the intervening years. Prizing independence, the program does not accept government money or assistance. Referrals and financial contributions come through a vast network of individuals, churches, and other religious organizations. Today, there is a Teen Challenge Induction Center in most large cities in the United States, Canada, Puerto Rico, Europe, and Australia. Each local program remains autonomous and is only loosely affiliated with the others.

Teen Challenge accepts anyone who has been using drugs and is willing to abide by its rules and practices. However, the program is not prepared to provide services to the "mentally ill." It serves adolescents and some adults of all races and ethnic groups. The racial and ethnic makeup of the program generally reflects the locale. In New York, for example, two-thirds of the participants are Puerto Rican. This may reflect, in part, Rev. Wilkerson's previous involvement with Puerto Rican gang members. Two-thirds of the group come from low-income ghetto backgrounds, while one-third are middle class. There are facilities for both males and females. The majority, however, are male (6). This still appears to be the case, although the lack of data remains problematic.

According to Teen Challenge philosophy, individuals using drugs cannot be helped until they reach the desperation stage. They must admit to having a problem and actively seek help (76). The Teen Challenge induction centers are crisis centers, accepting people off the streets for immediate help or counseling 24 hours a day. If the individual wishes to enter the residential program, he or she goes through an intake interview to determine whether the program is suitable for the overall needs of the candidate.

From a research perspective, many of the participants select themselves into the program. Sometimes, however, candidates are referred by a judge, probation officer, minister, or counselor. Others find their way to Teen Challenge through street evangelization efforts or at the urging of relatives and recovering addict friends already in the program.

Four outcome studies have been done on Teen Challenge: one by Calof (6), an internal evaluation reported by Langrod et al. (44), a study of the program in northern California and Nevada by Glasscote et al. (27), and one by Hess (31, 32). The Hess study, as the most recent, bears summarizing.

Catherine B. Hess, M.D., M.P.H., was formerly Assistant Commissioner of Health for New York City. She also served as special consultant to Teen Challenge. Her 7-year follow-up study was on selected individuals who entered the program in Brooklyn in 1968. She divided the eligible respondents into three groups. Those designated "P1" are those who dropped out during the induction period (N = 70); those designated "P2," those who dropped out at the Training Center phase (N = 52); and those designated "P3," Training Center graduates (N = 64). Dr. Hess did not give selection criteria. She found that 60 of 186 applicants (32%) dropped out of the program in the first 4 weeks. Reasons given included: could not relate to concept; violated rules; too sick; urge to use drugs too great; too much religion; family needs. Contrary to the popular perception, not all program dropouts were asked to leave Teen Challenge. Approximately 5% were asked to leave the program. The remaining 27% left voluntarily (32).

Among the members of the total population, 83% were high-school dropouts. After leaving Teen Challenge, 96 (52%) of the subjects (P1, P2, and P3) "pursued more education." Nineteen received high-school equivalency diplomas, 2 received college degrees, 48 attended Bible schools with 25 completing the curriculum, and 14 became ministers (1 from P1, 3 from P2, and 10 from P3). At the time of the study, 56% of all the participants reported being employed: 47% among Induction Center dropouts, 52% among Training Center dropouts, and 70% among graduates (32).

In terms of continued drug use, 24% of the population for which this information was available reported never using narcotics after their Teen Challenge experience. Seventy-six percent did return to heroin use. Five percent of this group were drug-free at the time of follow-up, having been treated in other programs or having detoxified on their own.

The Hess study places the Teen Challenge graduation rate at 18.3%. This rate is somewhat higher than the 15% reported by Smart (35) in a review of outcome studies of therapeutic communities. This also appears consistent with later findings by Anglin and Hser (1), DeLeon (10–13), DeLeon and Rosenthal (14, 15), and Falkin (19).

Teen Challenge certainly has been successful in reorienting the lives of some young drug users. Future research would do well to examine issues of cost effectiveness, success rates compared with those of the traditional secular treatment programs, and an analysis of who would appear to benefit from treatment involving full or partial participation in this type of program. Further study would benefit Teen Challenge and other religious programs, as well as the larger drug treatment community.

Espiritismo

Espiritismo, often referred to as spiritism, is a belief system among Puerto Rican and other Hispanic cultures that transcends both socioeconomic status and national borders. At its core lies the assumption that spirits are able to influence and affect the lives of people existing here, in the material and tangible world. Spiritists believe that spirits have the ability to make people physically and mentally ill, including using drugs and other substances of abuse, as well as the power to cure them (69).

Various authors estimate that as many as 80% of Puerto Ricans believe in spiritism to some degree. Curet and Langrod (9) noted that 65% of their Puerto Rican patients reported utilizing Espiritismo at some time during their lives. Only one study has examined Espiritismo and substance abuse, and that study focused on alcohol abuse. Many Western mental health practitioners, however, tend to view such alternative healing systems as maladaptive or even pathological. Thus, this animosity (both real and perceived) toward a strongly held cultural belief system acts as a deterrent, discouraging the individual from seeking modern medical and mental health assistance (9, 25).

Espiritismo, in addition to its comforting familiarity, has other attractive qualities lacking in the common practice of modern health care. The atmosphere in which the medium, i.e. folk healer, works is one of warmth and relaxation rather than cold, sterile efficiency. The patient usually does not have to wait endlessly for her or his name to be called. The medium is concerned not simply with the entire person, but with the patient's entire family, living and dead. Family and friends frequently are present to lend support. They are not seen as "getting in the way" (69).

Perhaps the most significant reason many people seek out folk healing of any type is that it taps into one's reservoir of faith, and that faith, whether in a spirit, God, or oneself can heal. It is within this latter context that Espiritismo has proven to be an effective support system in substance abuse treatment programs. This practice, of course, has been subject to abuse and must be used with caution, in accordance with the patient's religious belief system. The clinician must be thoroughly conversant with Espiritista principles, as well as with the parallels, psychological dynamics, and the culture as a whole. The following two case studies illustrate how Espiritismo has assisted patients in methadone maintenance (9).

Case 1

S. G. is a 26-year-old woman of Puerto Rican descent who was doing well in methadone treatment. On learning that her husband was murdered in prison, however, she developed what appeared to be a reactive depression. The patient started coming late to the clinic. She was disheveled and did not want to leave the house. She complained that she had an impulse to jump under a subway train or throw herself out of the window. Further inquiry revealed that this suicidal ideation was related to her belief that her husband wanted her to join him in the spirit world. The clinician, knowledgeable about her belief system, asked whether she lit a candle in honor of her husband and where she did so. She said she did it at home. The clinician knew that, according to Espiritista principles, a newly departed spirit had difficulty in separating from the material plane and that lighting a candle would attract his spirit. The clinician interpreted this to the patient. He suggested that if she wanted to honor her husband's memory, she could light a candle at the local church and, at the same time, become involved with a responsible Espiritista center with which the clinician was acquainted. This strategy had a 2-fold purpose. One was to mobilize the patient to get her out of the house and engaged in constructive activity. The second was to ameliorate the patient's potentially harmful contact with her deceased husband by preventing his spirit from coming into the house. The patient did, in fact, become more constructively engaged. The depression eventually remitted, and she resumed treatment.

Case 2

R. L. is a 31-year-old Puerto Rican woman and practitioner of Espiritismo who was diagnosed with schizophrenia. Knowledgeable Espiritistas differentiate illnesses and other problems in terms of either material or spiritual causation. This patient ceased taking her newly prescribed neuroleptic medication because voices were telling her that she was being poisoned. The clinician, in collaboration with the Espiritista, convinced this patient that the voices telling her not to take the medication were trying to create material problems for her by not allowing her illness to be treated. Accepting this interpretation, the patient resumed taking her medication. She averted a complete decompensation and possible rehospitalization.

The above cases demonstrate that a collaborative effort can exist between responsible clinicians, who represent the material world, and trained Espiritistas, who are able to distinguish spiritual causation from the material. If this collaboration had not existed in the cases cited above, these patients' belief systems might have been labeled as pathological, and the patients lost to treatment.

New Religious Movements

Since the very beginning of public consciousness about what have come to be called "new religious movements" (NRMs) about three decades ago, there has been controversy about the relationship of these phenomena to drugs. Initially, it seemed to many that drugs and new religions were inextricably intertwined and that those involved in new religions were also often involved in drug use. We now know that such a view is overly simplified, but the apparent concurrence of religious experimentation and drug use made assumptions about the relationship too easy to make.

We also know now that *both* drug use and religious experimentation are anathema to some people (including some professionals), which contributes to misunderstandings about the relationship of drug use and religious experimentation among America's youth. Some commentators fail to recognize significant differences between these two types of countercultural behavior patterns and, instead, lump them together for purposes of treatment and public policy development. The assumption of some seems to be that religious participation is as bad as drug use, and that both require intervention (7, 71).

Considerable research relevant to explaining the relationship between participation in new religions and drug use has accumulated since NRMs first burst onto the scene. There has been, for instance, a large outpouring of research on personality assessment of participants and the effects of participation on psychological well-being (59, 60), as well as discussion of many specific therapeutic effects of participation in NRMs (41, 67). This brief section cannot summarize all of that work but does trace some themes that derive from the research that has been done. Specifically, it focuses on the relationship of drug use and participation. Hopefully, this will shed light on the way that drugs and religion have related to each other within the experience of a generation of youth in our society.

PREVALENCE OF HEAVY PRIOR DRUG USE

One major theme derived from early research on NRMs was that many of those participating had also been involved in the drug subculture and had personal histories of considerable drug use. Virtually all research done on various of the controversial new religions revealed that participants had been heavily into drugs, as the following sampling of research reports shows.

Downton's detailed study of the Divine Light Mission uses a number of case studies, selected to be representative of those involved (17). All spoke at length about their heavy drug usage. Nordquist's study (54) of Ananda Cooperative Village in Grass Valley, California, revealed heavy drug use among participants, with 68% of his respondents admitting drug use before becoming a member and 63% of those saying the use was "often." Johnson's study of the Hare Krishna in California as well as other work on this group showed heavy previous drug involvement for members (37, 65). Richardson, Stewart, and Simmonds' research on a major Jesus Movement organization (62, 64) showed that 90% of participants had used drugs, with 72% of those admitting to using hard drugs and 75% saying that they had used drugs "all the time" (42%) or "fairly often" (33%). This study also revealed quite high frequencies of alcohol and tobacco use before joining.

One major, but sometimes overlooked, explanation for these findings is that recreational drug use itself has been quite widespread over the past several decades among America's youth (38). Wuthnow's data on increases in drug use nationwide and in the San Francisco Bay Area show remarkable growth in drug use from the 1960s to 1970s, especially among college youth (79). Thus, any claim of an association or *causal* relationship between drug use and NRM participation is subject to question, since it cannot be clearly demonstrated that the relationship is not an artifact of both increased drug use and interest in new forms of religion among certain demographic categories arising from common social contextual factors.

Another of Wuthnow's studies (80) offers interesting data that speaks to this relationship. He reports results of a 1000-person sample from the San Francisco Bay Area designed to reveal information about knowledge of and interest in new religions. He classifies NRMs into one of three categories—"counter cultural," "personal-growth," and "neo-Christian"—and compares the values of those from the sample who are attracted to each of the types on a number of issues, including a few measures of drug-related values and experiences. Wuthnow's study shows that those attracted to "counter cultural" groups (such as TM, Yoga, Zen, Hare Krishna, and Satanism) do, at least for this sample, have a higher propensity toward having the experience of being "high" on drugs and favoring the legalization of marihuana than those attracted to either "personal-growth" groups (*est,* Scientology, Synanon) or "neo-Christian" groups (Christian World Liberation Front, Children of God, Jews for Jesus, and Campus Crusade). "Personal-growth" attractees also usually ranked higher than "neo-Christian" attractees on these two measures. There was a fairly consistent pattern on the drug-related questions among this sample, suggesting that at least some more radical religious groups might be more attractive to those more actively involved with drugs. Other studies have shown a marked relationship between earlier history of drug use and involvement in Eastern-oriented religions (18, 41, 52). These studies, however, were not controlled studies comparing participants and nonparticipants on the matter of drug use and values, so care must be taken in making claims about the basic relationship between NRM participation and drug use.

DRUG USE AS CATALYST FOR SPIRITUAL SEEKING

The huge controversy over the relationship of new religions and drugs has been fostered, in no small part, because of the claim that use of certain drugs such as LSD and other psychedelics actually contribute to a person's spiritual development. This claim, made by some prominent scholars and researchers in the 1960s and 1970s, deeply offended some in our society who apparently viewed the drug subculture as the farthest thing imaginable from a meaningful and worthwhile lifestyle. The widely publicized claims and research of such people as Timothy Leary (47, 48) and Walter Houston Clark (8) gave credence to the belief that the new religions must somehow be causally related to the drug subculture, resulting for some in the inescapable conclusion that NRMs should be controlled.

Clark discussed, for instance, the famous "Good Friday" experiment done by Walter Pahnke (55). The double-blind experiment using Protestant seminary students as subjects and controls resulted in strong differences in tendency to have mystical experiences. Nine of the ten receiving the drug (psilocybin) experienced significant mystical experiences, while nine of the ten who received the placebo reported no experiences. Clark said (p. 78), "in proper circumstances and in certain people properly prepared, the psychedelic drugs have a strong tendency to release mystical experience."

These claims may have possibly contributed to large numbers of young people experimenting with drugs. Regrettably, not all found god, and some became addicted to the substances being used as vehicles in their search for meaning. However, it now seems clear that some who tried drugs because of religious motivation did, indeed, have experiences they defined as religious and valuable. If we give credence to accounts reported by scholars such as Downton, Johnson, and Nordquist, there also appears to be a fairly common pattern for people to become more interested in religion *because of* their prior experience with certain drugs. Not everyone who embraced NRMs did so via the drug route, but many apparently did.

NRMs AS HALFWAY HOUSES: AN ALTERNATIVE PERSPECTIVE

New religions, including some of the most controversial, have shown a remarkable and usually unheralded ability to relieve psychiatric symptoms and psychological distress, including drug dependency. Detractors make many claims of damage caused by NRMs, suggesting that they "brainwash" people into joining, "destroy families," and create psychological and psychiatric problems (7, 61, 71, 72). A growing body of contrary research, however, points out the problematic nature of these claims, implying, for some, that such claims are self-serving (40, 41).

One counterargument that has been made, for example, is that NRMs often serve a valuable "halfway house" function. Sociologist Tom Robbins and psychologist Dick Anthony develop this theme in research reports on participation in Meher Baba groups, positing the rubric of the "reintegration hypothesis" (66–68). They show that at least some NRMs assisted the reintegration of a number of youth who had left their normal social locations back into "mainstream" society. Richardson and his fellow researchers also have presented supporting data for the idea that NRMs reintegrate participants into a more normal existence; while at the same time teaching useful skills increasing the probability of surviving in ordinary society (63, 64).

Another perspective on the reintegrative hypothesis was offered by Kilbourne and Richardson (43) who presented a social psychological model of healing based on similarities between communal new religions and therapy situations. It was assumed that many participants chose to participate in either (or even both) for reasons that could be broadly defined as seeking healing of one sort or another, including healing of drug dependencies. They noted that many religious groups as well as many therapies involve a common role of healer, a common role of healee, and an underlying "deep structure" focused on healing. McGuire in her analysis of religion and healing (49) suggested a similar idea that much of the interest in NRMs and alternative therapies derives from a deep desire to be healed. Psychiatrist Marc Galanter, as a result of doing several important studies of the effects of participation in controversial NRMs (21–23), posited a "relief effect" brought on by participation, as he attempts to explain what it is about NRMs that caused dramatic change, including in relief of psychiatric symptoms and dependencies on drugs and alcohol (20).

It seems clear that many NRMs served a crucial "halfway house" function for large numbers of participants (72). This important role, needed by many young people so disconnected from society that they were unable to access usual modes of social support, is often unappreciated and ignored. Some have countered that NRM participants are simply exchanging one form of dependency (drugs) for another (religion) (26, 57, 70) when they decide to embrace an NRM. Even if there is a grain of truth to this assertion, most people would tend to agree that religious affiliation usually is more acceptable than drug addiction. One might further argue that adopting such a position reveals a negative view of religious solutions to personal difficulties, a position not unknown among psychotherapeutic professionals, but one definitely at odds with the findings of the Gallup poll cited in this chapter.

NRMs AS A CRUCIAL SUPPORT COMMUNITY

Many people who join NRMs do so because their usual social supports are unavailable, either because they have left them voluntarily or because some external agent has alienated those relationships (39, 40). Individuals may be seeking a surrogate family or simply need food and shelter. Thus we saw in the 1960s and 1970s a move toward "communalization of religious experience" for many youth (42), as they explored alternatives to a normal lifestyle, even for short periods of time.

Religious communal organizations assisted large numbers of young people who were, temporarily at least, "shaken loose" from their usual social locations. This communal experience would seem most useful for participants who want to change their lifestyles. The group typically shares a belief system and an ethic built on the religious ideology of the group, and members support each other in the acting out of the new beliefs and values. Behavior deemed deviant and negatively sanctioned in previous reference groups may be accepted and encouraged in the new environment of a religious group (74). As Galanter has noted (20), the relief effect comes from participation in a human group that is accepting and personal. Participants are often helped with their problems, including problems of drug dependency.

One major reason for the apparent dramatic success record for alleviating problems such as drug addiction is the reality of *self-selection*. There is no denying that considerable self-selection is taking place by people who have decided that they want to change their lives. Research demonstrates that treatment for any dependency is more successful if the person wants to change and takes actions to facilitate that personal change. Many participants in NRMs are making a valiant effort to change themselves. Clearly *these* men and women are not, as is sometimes claimed by opponents to NRMs, passive zombies tricked into joining by using so-called "brainwashing" and trapped into staying through the use of sophisticated "mind control" methods (67). The key to NRM success at drug rehabilitation is *volition*, being exercised by people who want to use the groups as vehicles of change (39, 58, 75).

NRM groups, as with other religiously oriented programs, are not for everyone, as evidenced by their extremely high attrition rates and small size. Many people who experiment with these groups as possible personal vehicles for change reject them for a variety of reasons (74). For some, the often quite rigorous and lengthy resocialization methods are simply too difficult to accept. Others find the belief system too strange to accept as a center for one's life. Still others may be repulsed by the actions of some group members or leaders, actions perhaps regarded as unethical or illegal (3, 18).

Many leave NRMs voluntarily after a relatively short time, having used the experience to get themselves straightened out and reoriented. They "move back" to more normal types of existence, often establishing families, getting and holding jobs, and/or returning to school. For the individual, the NRM has provided a valuable halfway house function. In assisting participants to rid themselves of drugs or other problematic behaviors, they have been afforded an opportunity to recoup and regroup. The community at large benefits from the groups' capacity to act as a vehicle for reintegration—reinserting individuals into society after having assisted many of them.

FINAL THOUGHTS

This rather positive analysis of participation in NRMs requires some defense and qualification. The defense is required because of the negative attention focused on NRMs, often referred to pejoratively as "cults" in the media

and by many in positions of authority, and to acknowledge that the issues involved are, in fact, complex. A significant body of research by competent psychologists, psychiatrists, sociologists, and others include data supporting the view that NRMs serve a valuable role for many in stopping substance abuse of various kinds. It is important to identify and better understand the essential characteristics of these groups that are critical to producing positive outcomes.

A few caveats are also in order. Obviously, participation in NRMs is not for everyone. Most who do participate apparently agree with that assertion, as evidenced by the high attrition rates from these essentially volunteer organizations mentioned above. Many people who try out NRMs as vehicles of personal growth do not find them acceptable and simply leave. Not all NRMs qualify for the positive treatment presented here, although research results on some of the more controversial NRMs have been presented. Dick Anthony and his colleagues have noted that not all "spiritual choices" are equal (2). Some NRMs may not foster personal growth and do not seek to be vehicles of personal change for participants. Tragedies like those involving the People's Temple and the Branch Davidians (neither of which was a typical NRM) do occur. Sometimes, participation in NRMs has not been a positive experience for all involved (3).

Tragedies and "atrocity tales" should not mask the overall finding that participation in NRMs can lead to positive outcomes for many, if not most, of those involved. To ignore this broadly based finding from years of research would be a disservice, not only to those in the helping professions but also to those individuals needing help dealing with substance abuse, as well as to many NRMs. Needless to say, our larger society would also stand to suffer.

CONCLUSION

Synthesizing the extensive sociocultural analyses of Dean Hoge and David Roozen (34, 35), Margaret Poloma (56) has concluded that a major dichotomy exists in contemporary American culture. This dichotomy may be best expressed as a clash between the religious and secular humanist milieu. She rightly observes that the sense of meaning and purpose that grounds the lives of individual women and men is derived from one or the other or from some combination of these apparently competing world views. However, when professional practitioners search for appropriate drug use treatment programs for those who have placed themselves in their care, whether mental health professional, physician, or pastor, must these world views necessarily be in conflict?

The 1985 Gallup poll cited at the beginning of this chapter, indicating that 96% percent of Americans express a belief in God, also reveals a range of only 40–45% of mental health professionals reporting a belief in God. When mental health specializations are taken into consideration, 25–40% of each group report having abandoned the faith of their youth, opting for atheism or agnosticism (24). Clearly, there is discontinuity between the secular world view of mental health caregivers and the religious beliefs of those seeking care.

Religiously oriented treatment is not suitable for everyone. For those men and women who can accept the creeds, rituals, and commitments required of such programs, there seem to be advantages. The idea of being "born again" can be quite liberating, for the recovering addict is provided with a "clean slate" and a "clean life." He or she is free to substitute a new lifestyle based on faith, hope, and love for one that was characterized by fear, despair, and hate. The central life interest is no longer using drugs. Within a new reference group, the recovering drug user is surrounded by significant others who can serve as role models for behavior appropriate to his or her new social identity. The person is now guided by newly acquired values and normative expectations that are constantly reinforced through membership in the religious community and belief in God as the ultimate authority.

Another core religious belief is conversion. *Conversion* has its root meaning in the Greek word *metanoia*, literally, "to turn over." More idiomatically, it conveys the image of having a change of heart or turning over a new leaf. The religious community's idea of conversion does share with that of the secular community the reality that one must first accept drug use as life destroying, and then choose to discard it in favor of behavior that is life building, before rehabilitation can begin.

Clinicians providing services within ethnic communities need to be culturally attuned to their clients; particularly to the significance of faith and religious expression among Hispanic women and men. Neglect or derision of traditions that do not derive from Western constructs of science frequently result in individuals being lost to treatment, even among those acknowledging the need for both "professional" intervention and "spiritual" healing.

From the discussion presented in this chapter, one may conclude that religious commitment and religiously oriented treatment programs can be significant factors that merit consideration and inclusion when planning a mix of appropriate treatment alternatives. There remains a great need for additional rigorous research examining the significance of religious commitment and affiliation, experienced within mainline, ethnic, and NRM communities, in treatment readiness and outcome studies. Researchers also need to reduce emphasis on seeking predictive indicators of delinquency and deviance, steering analysis toward issues of social reintegration, potentiating recovery, and maintaining sobriety, particularly in the posttreatment milieu. Finally, religious practitioners and researchers can and should begin to work collaboratively with their secular professional mental health counterparts. At the very least, serious and open communication needs to be attempted.

This research was supported in part by the National Institute on Drug Abuse grant for "Behavioral Sciences Training in Drug Abuse Research" (5 T32 DA07233–12). Additional support was provided by the National Development and Research Institutes, Inc. The points of view and opinions expressed in this paper do not necessarily represent the official positions of the United States Government, the University of Nevada, or the National Development and Research Institutes, Inc.

References

1. Anglin MD, Hser YI. Treatment of drug abuse. In: Tonry M, Wilson JQ, eds. Drugs and crime. Chicago: University of Chicago Press, 1990.
2. Anthony D, Ecker B, Wilber K. Spiritual choices: the problem of recognizing authentic paths to inner transformation. New York: Paragon, 1987.
3. Balch R. Money and power in utopia. In: Richardson J, ed. Money and power in the new religions. Lewiston, NY: Edwin Mellen Press, 1988.
4. Balmer R. Mine eyes have seen the glory: a journey into the evangelical subculture in America. New York: Oxford University Press, 1989.
5. Breakey WR, Fischer P, Nestadt G, Romanoski A, Royall R, Ross A. Health and mental health problems of homeless men and women in Baltimore. JAMA 1989;262:1352–1357.
6. Calof J. A study of four voluntary treatment and rehabilitation programs for New York City's narcotic addicts. New York: Community Service Society of New York, 1967.
7. Clark J. Problems in referral of cult members. J Natl Assoc Private Psychiatr Hosp 1978;9:19–21.
8. Clark WH. Chemical ecstasy: psychedelic drugs and religion. New York: Sheed and Ward, 1969.
9. Curet E, Langrod J. Espiritismo as a support system in substance abuse treatment. New York: mimeographed report, 1997.
10. DeLeon G. Therapeutic community treatment research facts: what we know. Ther Communities Am Treat Newsletter Fall 1988.
11. DeLeon G. The therapeutic community perspective and approach for adolescent drug abusers. In: Feinstein SC, ed. Adolescent psychiatry development and clinical studies. Vol 15. Chicago: University of Chicago Press, 1988.
12. DeLeon G. The therapeutic community: status and evolution. Int J Addict 1985;20:823–844.
13. DeLeon G. The therapeutic community: study of effectiveness. Treatment research monograph series (ADM) 84–1286. Washington, DC: National Institute on Drug Abuse, 1984.
14. DeLeon G, Rosenthal MS. Treatment in residential therapeutic communities. In: Karasu TB, ed. Treatment of psychiatric disorders. Vol II. New York: American Psychiatric Press, 1989.
15. DeLeon G, Rosenthal MS. Therapeutic communities. In: Dupont R, Goldstein A, O'Donnell J, eds. Handbook on drug abuse. Washington, DC: Government Printing Office, 1979.
16. Desmond D, Maddux J. Religious programs and careers of chronic heroin users. Am J Drug Alcohol Abuse 1981;8(1):71–83.
17. Downton JV. Sacred journeys: conversion of young Americans to Divine Light Mission. New York: Columbia University Press, 1979.
18. Deutsch A. Psychiatric perspectives on an Eastern-style cult. In: Halperin D, ed. Psychodynamic perspectives on religion, sect, and cult. Boston: John Wright, 1983.
19. Falkin GP. Policy development report on residential drug treatment programs. Report to the New York State Division of Substance Abuse Services 1991. Albany, NY: mimeographed report, 1991.
20. Galanter M. The "relief effect": a sociobiological model for neurotic distress and large-group therapy. Am J Psychiatry 1978;135:588–591.
21. Galanter M. Cults. Faith, healing, and coercion. New York: Oxford University Press, 1989.
22. Galanter M, Buckley P. Evangelical religion and meditation: psychotherapeutic effects. J Nerv Ment Dis 1978;166:685–691.
23. Galanter M, Rabkin R, Rabkin F. The "Moonies": a psychological study of conversion and membership in a contemporary religious sect. Am J Psychiatry 1979;136:165–169.
24. Gallup G. Religion in America–50 years: 1935–1985. The Gallup report. Princeton, NJ: Princeton Religious Research Center, 1985.
25. Garrison V. Support systems of schizophrenic and nonschizophrenic Puerto Rican migrant women in New York City. Schizophr Bull 1978; 4:561.
26. Gerlach L. Pentecostalism. Revolution or counter-revolution? In: Zaretsky I, Leone M, eds. Religious movements in contemporary America. Princeton, NJ: Princeton University Press, 1984.
27. Glasscote R, Sussex J, Jaffe J, Ball J, Brill L. The treatment of drug abuse: programs, problems, prospects. Washington, DC: Joint Information Service of the American Psychiatric Association and the National Association for Mental Health, 1972.
28. Gorsuch R. Religious aspects of substance abuse and recovery. J Soc Issues 1995;51(2):65–83.
29. Hathaway W, Pargament K. Intrinsic religiousness, religious coping, and psychosocial competence: a covariance structure analysis. J Sci Stud Religion 1990;20(4):423–441.
30. Heschel AJ. The abiding challenge of religion. Center Mag 1958;March/April:43–51 (reprinted 1973).
31. Hess CB. A seven year follow-up study of 186 males in a religious therapeutic community. In: Schecter A, Alksne H, Kaufman E, eds. Critical concerns in the field of drug abuse. New York: Marcel Dekker, 1977.
32. Hess CB. Teen Challenge Training Center, research summation. Rehrersburg, PA: Teen Challenge, 1975.
33. Hoebel EA. Anthropology: the study of man. New York: McGraw-Hill, 1972.
34. Hoge DR. Division in the Protestant house: the basic reasons behind intra-church conflicts. Philadelphia: Westminster Press, 1976.
35. Hoge D, Roozen D. Understanding church growth and decline. New York: Pilgrim Press, 1980.
36. Deleted in proof.
37. Johnson G. The Hare Krishna in San Francisco. In: Glock C, Bellah R, eds. The new religious consciousness. Berkeley: University of California Press, 1976.
38. Keniston K. Drug use and student values. In: Needleman J, Bierman AK, Gould J, eds. Religion for a new generation. New York: Macmillan, 1973.
39. Kilbourne B. Equity or exploitation: the case of the Unification Church. Rev Religious Res 1986;28:143–150.
40. Kilbourne B, Richardson J. Cults versus families: a case of misattribution of cause? Marriage Fam Rev 1981;4:81–100.
41. Kilbourne B, Richardson J. Psychotherapy and new religion in a pluralistic society. Am Psychol 1984;39(3):237–251.
42. Kilbourne B, Richardson J. Communalization of religious experience in contemporary religious groups. J Community Psychol 1986;14: 206–213.
43. Kilbourne B, Richardson J. A social psychological analysis of healing. J Integrative Eclectic Psychother 1988;7(1):20–34.
44. Langrod J, Joseph H, Valdes K. The role of religion in the treatment of opiate addictions. In: Brill L, Lieberman L, eds. Major modalities in the treatment of drug abuse. New York: Behavioral Publications, 1972.
45. Larson D, Hohmann A, Kessler L, Meador K, Boyd J, McSherry E. The couch and the cloth: the need for linkage. Hosp Community Psychiatry 1988;39(10):1064–1069.
46. Larson D, Pattison M, Blazer D, Omran A, Kaplan B. Systematic analysis of research on religious variables in four major psychiatric journals. Am J Psychiatry 1986;143(3):329–334.
47. Leary T. High priest. New York: World Publishing, 1968.
48. Leary T. The politics of ecstasy. New York: GP Putnam, 1968.
49. McGuire M. Religion, healing. In: Hammond P, ed. The sacred in a secular age. Berkeley: University of California Press, 1985.
50. Marsden GM. Understanding fundamentalism and evangelicalism. Grand Rapids, MI: William B Eerdmans Publishing, 1991.
51. Muffler J. Church Lady Meets Wolfman: towards a paradigm of salvation, stigmatization, and the urban church's involvement with drug abusers and people with AIDS. New York: Society for the Study of Social Problems, 1995.
52. Needleman J. The new religions. Garden City, NY: Doubleday, 1970.
53. Niebuhr HR. The kingdom of God in America. New York: Harper & Row, 1937.

54. Nordquist T. Ananda Cooperative Village. A study in the beliefs, values, and attitudes of a New Age religious community. Uppsala: Borgstroms Tryckeri AB, 1978.

55. Pahnke WN. Drugs and mysticism: an analysis of the relationship between psychedelic drugs and mystical consciousness. Cambridge, MA: Harvard University doctoral dissertation, 1964.

56. Poloma M. Spiritual healing in social context: the effects of beliefs and practices on well being. Unpublished manuscript, 1990.

57. Rebhan J. The drug rehabilitation program: cults in formation? In: Halperin D, ed. Psychodynamic perspectives on religion, sect, and cult. Boston: John Wright, 1983.

58. Richardson J. The active versus passive convert: paradigm conflict in conversion/recruitment research. J Sci Study Religion 1985;24:163–179.

59. Richardson J. Clinical and personality assessment of participants in new religions. Int J Psychol Religion 1996;5(3):145–170.

60. Richardson J. Psychological and psychiatric studies of new religions. In: Brown LB, ed. Advances in the psychology of religion. New York: Pergamon Press, 1985.

61. Richardson J. Two steps forward, one back: psychiatry, psychology, and the new religions. Int J Psychol Religion 1996;5(3):181–186.

62. Richardson J, Davis R. Experiential fundamentalism: revisions of orthodoxy in the Jesus Movement. J Am Acad Religion 1983;LI(3): 397–425.

63. Richardson J, Reidy MTV. Form and fluidity in two contemporary glossolalic movements. Ann Rev Soc Sci Religion 1980;4:183–220.

64. Richardson J, Stewart M, Simmonds R. Organized miracles: a study of a contemporary, youth, communal, fundamentalist organization. New Brunswick, NJ: Transaction Books, 1979.

65. Rochford B. Hare Krishna in America. New Brunswick, NJ: Rutgers University Press, 1985.

66. Robbins T, Anthony D. Getting straight with Meher Baba: a study of drug rehabilitation, mysticism, and post-adolescent role conflict. J Sci Study Religion 1972;11(2):122–140.

67. Robbins T, Anthony D. Deprogramming, brainwashing, and the medicalization of deviant religious groups. Soc Probl 1982;29:283–297.

68. Robbins T, Anthony D, Curtis T. Youth culture religious movements: evaluating the integrative hypothesis. Sociol Q 1975(16(1):48–64.

69. Ruiz P, Langrod J. Cultural issues in the mental health of Hispanics in the United States. Am J Soc Psychiatry 1982;2(2)35–38.

70. Simmonds R. Conversion or addiction: consequences of joining a Jesus Movement group. In: Richardson J, ed. Conversion careers: in and out of the new religions. Beverly Hills, CA: Sage, 1980.

71. Singer M. Therapy with ex-cult members. J Natl Assoc Private Psychiatr Hosp 1978;9:14–18.

72. Smart R. Outcome studies of therapeutic community and halfway house treatment for addicts. Int J Addict 1976;11:143.

73. Smith H. The religions of man. New York: Harper & Row, 1964 (reprinted 1986).

74. Stark R. Psychopathology and religious commitment. Rev Religious Res 1971;12:165–176.

75. Straus R. Religious conversion as a personal and collective accomplishment. Sociol Analysis 1979;40:158–165.

76. Teen Challenge. The New York challenge. Brooklyn, NY: Teen Challenge, 1981.

77. Teen Challenge. Long Island Teen Challenge. Babylon, NY: Teen Challenge, 1996.

78. Wuthnow R. The struggle for America's soul: evangelicals, liberals, and secularism. Grand Rapids, MI: William B Eerdmans Publishing, 1989.

79. Wuthnow R. The consciousness reformation. Berkeley: University of California Press, 1976.

80. Wuthnow R. The new religions in social context. In: Glock C, Bellah R, eds. The new religious consciousness. Berkeley: University of California Press, 1976.

53 EVALUATION AND OUTCOME OF TREATMENT

Robert L. Hubbard

Various treatments for both alcohol and drug abuse have been available since the turn of the century. However, only in the late 1960s and early 1970s did both alcohol and drug abuse treatment become major parts of the public health system in the United States. Much of what we know about treatment and current clinical approaches to treatment was developed during these years. In the early 1990s, a number of studies have been initiated to update and expand this knowledge base. This knowledge will be especially important in shaping treatment in the rapidly changing cost containment environment of the late 1990s.

The alcohol treatment system emerged in the late 1960s in an effort to establish community-based alcohol treatment centers throughout many parts of the United States. Combined with this public approach was the proliferation of proprietary inpatient programs based on the "Minnesota model" treatment protocol (1, 2). These short-term inpatient regimens helped guide alcohol abusers through the first phases of the Twelve Steps of the Alcoholics Anonymous recovery process. Treatment for drug abuse, particularly cocaine, began to be provided in these chemical dependency programs originally designed for alcoholism. With increasing concerns about costs, the length of inpatient stays has been dramatically reduced and the chemical dependency model shifted largely to outpatient environments.

The rapid escalation of heroin addiction in communities in the late 1960s, coupled with the high rates of addiction among returning Vietnam veterans, led to the establishment of a national system of drug abuse treatment programs to deal with the increasing rates of addiction and associated crime (3). Since these early years there have been far-reaching changes in the drug abuse treatment system. The three major "modalities," or types of treatment, developed and under public funding in the United States have been the outpatient methadone clinics, therapeutic communities, and outpatient drug-free programs. Outpatient methadone programs treat opioid abusers, most of whom use heroin intravenously. After stabilization with medically prescribed doses of methadone, clients receive a variety of counseling and other services to help them resume productive lives. Therapeutic communities use group counseling with all types of drug abusers over long stays in a 24-hour community environment. Outpatient drug-free programs tend to be oriented toward nonopioid users, emphasizing counseling, often in community mental health center settings. Among these modalities, there are great variations in program size, setting, organization, philosophy, structure, therapeutic approach, services, and funding. Although existing in their original form, the three traditional modalities have faced a rapidly changing environment and reduced resources.

A rich database, including three national multiprogram studies, was developed to describe the effectiveness of these modalities and approaches. In addition, a number of studies of individual programs using quasi-experimental and clinical trial designs have been conducted. The overwhelming weight of the evidence from these studies and carefully designed epidemiologic outcome studies is that treatment contributes significantly to change in client behavior during and after treatment. Many of these data were summarized in major literature reviews and deliberation of expert panels at the Institute of Medicine (IOM) (4–6). These major reviews have concluded that treatment is effective. A more limited number of studies indicate that the benefits of these changes considerably outweigh the costs of the treatment. Because of the lack of studies of elements of treatment or of alternative strategies for reducing demand and supply, the comparative cost effectiveness of different treatment components or treatment versus prevention or enforcement is not known. The need for such studies has become even more important as concern has risen over containing health care costs during the 1990s.

Thus, questions continue to be raised about the overall effectiveness of treatment, the comparative effects of different treatment approaches, and the benefits of particular components of treatment. Despite the wealth of data, these questions are valid. Extensive, systematic research has not yet focused on the many components of treatment in typical programs in community settings. Further, the treatment system and the client population have changed since the late 1970s. Very limited information exists for the programs and approaches in operation during the 1980s. Major new research and data collection efforts are only beginning for the treatment system of the 1990s and beyond. These efforts must not only confirm or revise previous findings but also anticipate questions that will emerge in a rapidly changing environment.

The treatment system in the United States in the 1990s includes a broader array of public and private program types. The proportion of privately funded alcohol and drug abuse treatment programs increased during the 1980s, but by 1987 utilization rates in many areas were only 50% of capacity (5). Drug abuse treatment is now delivered in a wider variety of settings, including chemical dependency programs (formerly exclusive alcohol treatment programs) and community mental health centers, as well as treatment programs designed primarily for alcohol. The administration of the public treatment system has shifted from the federal government to states under the Omnibus Budget Reconciliation Act of 1981 and has entered an era of managed care in the 1990s. The distinction between publicly funded and private treatment has become blurred. The treatment of many clients in the traditional public treatment modalities is not fully supported by public funds. Clients pay for all or part of treatment through third-party reimbursements or their own resources, and costs are closely monitored by managed care organizations.

In recognition of the paucity of up-to-date information, major new research and demonstration efforts have been launched for the 1990s including two new multisite evaluation studies and a large scale clinical trial. While we await updated effectiveness and benefit-cost studies and more detailed studies of treatment components, we can have confidence that treatment is an effective and cost-effective strategy. However, more fundamental questions need to be addressed in analysis of treatment. Although various treatments have been shown to have an aggregate effect and a favorable benefit-cost ratio, many factors limit the effectiveness of treatment. Many drug abusers do not enter treatment. Many do not stay a sufficient time to receive the full benefits of treatment. Services to deal with increasingly complex problems of clients need to be expanded in quantity and enhanced in quality. Even after extensive treatment experience, many clients relapse and renew their treatment careers. It is also critical to determine whether the positive outcomes of previous studies can be confirmed during periods of reduced resources and cost containment.

Clearly, previous studies have shown that the full potential of treatment is not being realized. Questioning the aggregate effectiveness diverts research from a more fundamental issue of how to improve the many types of treatment currently available to clients with diverse backgrounds and impairments. The basic question facing us is how to maximize the return on each hour and dollar of resources invested in treatment.

This chapter attempts to accomplish two goals. First, it reviews and updates major findings on treatment effectiveness. Second, it outlines two major issues, client differences and treatment variations, that require extensive conceptual and empiric examination particularly when the environment is rapidly changing. To address these issues, the chapter broadens the reader's understanding of clients and treatment and their potential contribution to a more comprehensive investigation of the effectiveness of treatment. A broader perspective on client differences includes consideration of impairments and functioning of clients across multiple domains, exposure to many types and durations of programs during a treatment career, and dynamic, complex patterns of drug abuse. The development of a model of treatment structure and process components needs to include multilevel consideration of program structure, client-counselor interaction, and the process of service delivery and client change as well as the health and social system in which treatment is funded and delivered. In-depth investigation of these issues should build upon existing research to provide a more complete understanding of effectiveness of treatment and the factors that contribute to it. This chapter focuses primarily on prospective epidemiologic multiprogram studies. These studies provide the breadth of information necessary to identify the nature and range of client and treatment variables and their relative contribution to treatment outcomes.

EFFECTIVENESS

The effectiveness of both alcohol and drug abuse treatment has been continually questioned. One of the major reasons why is the difficulty of conducting broad-based epidemiologic outcome studies or controlled clinical trials of sufficient scope to answer the central questions about treatment. Prior to 1990, only one national study of alcohol treatment and two of drug abuse treatment have been mounted successfully in the prior 30 years. Clinical trials based on unblinded random assignment have often failed because of the limited compliance (7) and retention (8) for sufficiently long periods of time to demonstrate the efficacy of any particular treatment approach. Despite these limitations, IOM panels (5, 9) and individual reviewers (4, 6, 10, 11) have concluded that treatment does have positive effects. Since 1990 two major national epidemiologic outcome studies on drug abuse treatment and one clinical trial of alcohol treatment have been launched. The analysis of data bases from these studies are published in early stages. Where applicable, early results are included to broaden the base of knowledge presented in this chapter.

Epidemiologic outcome studies do indicate positive effects. The major clinical epidemiologic study of alcohol treatment was conducted in the early 1970s with a sample of 593 clients followed 18 and 48 months after treatment (12, 13). After 4 years, 21% were abstinent for at least 1 year before the follow-up. A positive correlation was reported between those clients receiving five or more outpatient visits and those with more than 7 days' inpatient visits. Using a cost-offset framework in an analysis of health insurance data, Holder and Blose (14) attributed substantial savings to alcohol treatment in health care costs. Other follow-up studies of proprietary programs reviewed in 1989 by the IOM Committee to Identify Research Effectiveness in the Prevention and Treatment of Alcohol-Related Problems (15) find abstinence rates between 40 and 60% in the first year after treatment. Similar results were found in studies of state programs (16) and private programs (17). Because of the often low rates of response to follow-up, the method of obtaining reports, and imprecise measurement of treatment process, including continuing care and other methodological considerations, these rates of abstinence likely exaggerate the positive effects of treatment.

In contrast to these findings and those for drug abuse treatment reported later in this section, the IOM committee found little evidence supporting longer-term treatment for alcohol abuse. Reviews (18–20) and a series of random assignment studies have found that neither length of treatment nor intensity (inpatient versus outpatient) influenced outcome. In such unblinded research, however, the levels of severity of client problems likely interact with selection bias from compliance and attrition to confound the interpretation of results. Further, most alcohol treatment protocols tested, typically less than 3 months, may not be of sufficient duration or intensity to produce demonstrable effects. Controlled studies of alcohol treatment may need to focus more on comparison of different continuums of care to examine how inpatient and outpatient programs can contribute to long-term compliance with aftercare and relapse prevention. A major multisite clinical trial was initiated in 1989 to examine patient matching hypotheses in both outpatient settings and for patients receiving aftercare following inpatient treatment (21). Initial results are due to be published in 1997.

A series of studies of drug abuse treatment conducted primarily over the past two decades has demonstrated the effectiveness of the publicly funded methadone maintenance and therapeutic community approaches (22, 23). Use of most drugs declines during and after treatment (24–28). Criminal activity is reduced among program clients, particularly during treatment (29–32).

To conclusively demonstrate effectiveness, results must be replicated across different client populations and diverse programs. Three multisite national prospective studies have been undertaken to demonstrate effectiveness and to consider the multiple factors that contribute to treatment outcome. Beginning with the Drug Abuse Reporting Program (DARP) admission cohorts in 1969–1973, followed by the Treatment Outcome Prospective Study (TOPS) cohorts in 1979–1981, and continuing with the Drug Abuse Treatment Outcome Study (DATOS) cohorts in 1991–1993, each of the studies has built upon its predecessor. Fundamental to such studies is the most comprehensive assessment of clients and treatments feasible across multiple programs and large client samples. Applying the advances in instrument design, improvement in interviewer training, and enhancement of conceptual models of client characteristics and treatment, the DATOS research will contain comprehensive client and treatment measurement in a sample of 99 programs for an estimated 10,000 clients. Until DATOS findings are fully available, much of our current knowledge about effectiveness of the broad range of community-based program clients, treatments, and their relationship to outcomes must be based on TOPS and a limited number of other individual program studies.

The previous clinical epidemiologic study of drug abuse treatment, TOPS, assessed client characteristics, treatment, and outcomes for 10,000 clients in 40 methadone, residential, and outpatient drug-free programs. Although less comprehensive than DATOS, TOPS has resulted in a substantial body of important knowledge about drug abuse treatment and treatment effectiveness. Major findings from TOPS, summarized later in this chapter, are reported in the book-length manuscript (33) that considers the substantive findings of TOPS within an explicit policy and clinical context. These findings are being updated and replicated within the DATOS studies.

Characteristics of Clients in Different Types of Treatment

The client populations of outpatient methadone, residential, and outpatient drug-free programs participating in TOPS in 1979–1981 had many common features but differed on many sociodemographic and background characteristics (34). Although high percentages of the clients in each modality had similar characteristics (i.e., young adult males are the predominant type of client), large numbers of clients in each modality also had special needs. Thirty percent of clients, for example, were women, 25% of residential and outpatient drug-free clients were under 21 years of age, and large numbers were members of racial and ethnic minorities. Similar ethnic differences were found in DATOS programs in 1991–1993 but clients were older and more likely to be female (33). These special populations suggest the need for targeted treatment services to provide effective treatment and to retain such groups in treatment for a significant length of time.

The analyses briefly described in the following paragraphs emphasize the need to consider client characteristics carefully, especially drug use patterns, extent of impairment, and experience with treatment and criminal justice systems, in the assessment of outcomes across modalities and in studies examining matching of clients to treatment. What type of treatment works best for a particular kind of client is still an unanswered question. The range of modalities and types of programs available may be part of the reason for the success of drug abuse treatment. The opportunity for a client or a referral source to choose may lead to an appropriate match of client and type of treatment. The high rates of self-referrals to methadone and criminal justice referrals to residential and outpatient drug-free treatment (3 in 10 in TOPS and 4 in 10 in DATOS) suggest differences in client motivations for seeking treatment and, consequently, differences in retention, services received, and outcomes (35).

DRUG USE PATTERNS

Drug use by treatment clients frequently is described in terms of the major drug of abuse upon entering treatment. However, the exclusive use of the traditional primary drug of abuse diagnosis or a focus on a particular drug such as heroin or cocaine obscures the extensive nature of abuse of multiple drugs by clients entering treatment in 1979–1981 (35). Some index or typology is needed to better describe and categorize the complex patterns of use by clients. These patterns need to capture lifetime pretreatment and posttreatment use.

One approach developed for clients entering the TOPS programs was a hierarchical seven-category drug use pattern summarizing the nature of drug use. The patterns are heroin/other narcotics, heroin, other narcotics, multiple nonnarcotics, single nonnarcotics, alcohol/marihuana, and minimal drug use. The categories were based on an extensive examination of the patterns of use of 20 drugs (including alcohol) combining statistical cluster analysis and clinical judgment. The procedures used to develop various typologic and quantitative measures of overall severity of drug use are described in Hubbard et al. (36) and Bray et al. (37).

The drug abuse pattern index used for TOPS reveals the differential concentration of types of drug abusers across the major modalities. Methadone clients were primarily (52%) traditional heroin users who used only cocaine, marihuana, and alcohol in addition to heroin. However, one in five methadone clients used heroin and other narcotics as well as a variety of nonnarcotic drugs. The remaining quarter of methadone clients were classified as former daily users who had histories of regular use but did not use heroin weekly or daily in the year before treatment. Residential clients were distributed more evenly among the patterns, and the majority of outpatient drug-free clients were alcohol and/or marihuana users (36%) or single nonnarcotics users (22%).

The seven-category drug use pattern captures the complex multiple patterns of drug use of clients entering drug abuse treatment in TOPS and may be used as one indicator of multiple drug use. However, this index needs to be reevaluated as a descriptor of drug abuse patterns, particularly in light of the increased use of cocaine in the 1980s. One advantage of the hierarchical typologic approach is its flexibility for emphasizing the importance of specific drugs. For example, the seven-category pattern emphasizes heroin use because of its prominence in the 1970s. For the 1990s in DATOS cocaine was used to create an alternate hierarchical typology. Two thirds of long-term residential, and 40% of methadone and outpatient drug-free programs used cocaine at least once a week. Generally, this cocaine use was combined with marihuana or alcohol. Use of other nonnarcotic drugs was much lower in 1991–1993 than in 1979–1981 (33).

IMPAIRMENT

A critical issue in evaluation of effectiveness of treatment is the severity of impairment of clients. Work with the Addiction Severity Index (ASI) and assessment of the extent of alcohol and other drug-dependent and psychiatric comorbidities of clients suggest different expectations for clients with more or less severe impairments. Although more limited in-depth and clinical expertise is available in multiprogram studies than in clinically based research studies, the former have included some key indicators of impairment. The TOPS data set was one of nine data sets used by a consortium of researchers (38) to examine the drug-dependence syndrome (DDS) concept (39). The goals were to determine the DDS patterning in clinic samples of opioid and alcohol-dependent persons, the generalizability of DDS to diverse cultural settings, the relation of DDS to certain antecedent and concurrent mediating variables, and the value of DDS as a predictor of treatment outcome. The results indicated that (a) almost all of the provisional DDS elements can be measured reliably in samples of alcoholics and opioid users (40–42); (b) summary measures of alcohol dependence before treatment predict reinstatement of alcohol dependence among relapsed alcoholics following a period of posttreatment abstinence (38); and (c) summary measures of drug dependence do not consistently predict reinstatement among opioid users (38).

Psychiatric impairment was a major interest at the inception of TOPS in 1975, but assessment instruments appropriate for use in multiprogram studies were not available when the TOPS instruments were designed. However, a brief hierarchy of indicators of depression was included to provide basic data on depressive and suicidal symptoms (43). Depression indicators were reported very commonly by clients entering drug abuse treatment programs (44, 45). Overall, about 60% of TOPS clients reported at least one item of a three-item scale at intake: nearly 75% of women under 21 years of age reported one or more depression indicators. A history of mental health treatment was predictive of depressive symptoms; however, prior drug abuse treatment was unrelated to signs of depression. Clients who used multiple nonnarcotics weekly or daily were more likely to report signs of depression than those in other drug abuse categories.

The residential clients were significantly more likely to report multiple use of drugs, more drug-related problems, suicidal thoughts and attempts, heavy drinking, predatory crimes, and less full-time employment than were methadone clients with similar backgrounds and demographic characteristics. Outpatient drug-free clients were more likely than similar methadone clients to report drug-related problems, suicidal thoughts or attempts, predatory crimes, and heavy drinking but were less likely than comparable residential clients to use multiple drugs. Those results demonstrate that each modality does serve very different and important segments of the drug-abusing population. In DATOS prevalence rates of DSM-III-R antisocial personality and other comorbid disorders could be assessed with modules for substance dependence and for antisocial personality, depressive, and anxiety disorders from the Composite International Diagnostic Interview and the Diagnostic Interview Schedule (46). Prevalence rates were 39.3% antisocial personality and 13.9% lifetime Axis I disorders. These rates differed by drug use pattern, age, gender, and race/ethnicity. Clients dependent on heroin, cocaine, and alcohol had higher rates of disorders compared with clients dependent on only a single drug or on alcohol.

TREATMENT EXPERIENCE AND CRIMINAL JUSTICE INVOLVEMENT

Detailed data on number of admissions and on weeks of treatment obtained in TOPS (47) were used to describe the drug abuse treatment career and to model the effects of the career on treatment outcomes. Drug abuse treatment is a recurrent phenomenon in the lives of drug abusers. Other results indicate that the duration of regular drug use and the number of prior treatment episodes are important indicators of the effectiveness of any single treatment episode; those with lengthy drug abuse or drug treatment histories have poorer prognoses. On average, clients began regular drug use at age 16 and entered drug abuse treatment for the first time at age 24. They averaged five treatment admissions and 70 weeks in treatment during their treatment careers. Most have been in several modalities, implying changes during the life span in the nature and severity of drug abuse. About one in five had also been in alcohol treatment, and one in four in mental health treatment during their lives. About 40% returned to treatment in the year after the TOPS episode. The time between treatment episodes averaged about 13 weeks. Basic analyses of the contributions of numbers of admissions or total weeks in treatment need to be developed further to investigate the effects of treatment experience. More refined assessment and analysis of patterns of treatment history should help determine the effects of treatment career on outcomes.

The results of the analyses of the treatment–criminal justice system link (48, 49) support the basic belief that criminal justice clients do as well as or better than other clients in drug abuse treatment. Treatment Alternatives to Street Crimes (TASC) programs and other formal or informal criminal justice system mechanisms appear to refer individuals who had not been treated previously and many who were not yet heavily involved in drug use. Criminal justice system involvement also helps retain clients in treatment. The estimated 6–7 additional weeks of retention for TASC referrals provided programs with considerably more time for rehabilitation efforts (50). There also seemed to be more substantial changes in behavior during treatment for criminal justice clients.

One major finding in both TOPS and DATOS research is that few clients referred from the criminal justice system entered outpatient methadone programs (33, 48). The reasons for the low numbers in methadone programs need to be explored. There appear to be many heroin addicts in the criminal justice system who could benefit from methadone treatment to reduce their criminal behavior. A second finding is that criminal justice system clients in outpatient drug-free programs received fewer services than did other clients in the same program. Although criminal justice system clients reported fewer drug-related problems than did clients with no legal involvement, they still reported a wide array of problems. The reasons for differential services were unclear.

Treatment Programs

Drug abuse treatment programs vary in the nature and intensity of treatment services provided, types of therapists and therapies provided, average length of stay, and inclusion of aftercare (51). The limited detailed research on the treatment process (52–54) suggests that the nature and intensity of treatment services are important determinants of treatment outcome. A description of variation in the nature of treatment across treatment settings can provide useful information about current drug abuse treatment. In addition, information about aspects of the course of treatment, together with information about treatment outcomes, can help identify the most effective types of treatment. A particular concern is how the treatment received in traditional treatment modalities compares with the treatments in new chemical dependency programs that treat drug abuse as well as alcohol abuse.

The study of the treatment process (52) in TOPS programs focused on the structure, nature, duration, and intensity of drug abuse treatment. Descriptions of aspects of the treatment process were developed from client self-reports of treatment service needs, services received, and satisfaction, combined with abstractions of clinical/medical records and descriptions of programs by counselors and directors. The characteristics of TOPS clinics were compared with those in the National Drug and Alcohol Treatment Utilization Survey. TOPS clinics were found to be larger and more urban than the national norms for each modality. In 1980 the outpatient methadone and outpatient drug-free treatment programs had budgets per client of approximately $2000 per year. Therapeutic communities had an average expenditure of $6135 per bed. TOPS clinics appeared to reflect the continued national trend toward employing fewer ex-addicts and more counselors with advanced degrees (master's degrees and above). The overall philosophy of the clinic directors was that abstinence was an appropriate goal.

The number of services (medical, psychological, family, legal, educational, vocational, and financial) available during the years 1979–1981 varied. Fewer services appeared to be available in the later years of the study. The proportion of clients receiving family, educational, and vocational services decreased noticeably in residential treatment programs during the 3-year period. During this same period, client demand for services increased. However, similar proportions of treatment clients continued to receive services during the study period. Fewer received aftercare services in 1981 than in 1979. In outpatient drug-free program clinical/medical records, mention of aftercare services decreased from 26% in 1979 to 5% in 1981.

Findings from DATOS document a further decline in the resources available for drug abuse treatment and the services being provided to clients in community-based drug abuse treatment programs (55). A marked decrease over the intervening decade in the number and variety of services to clients was reported. There was also a large increase in self-reported unmet service needs in DATOS. Clients reported having received at least some sessions of drug abuse counseling during treatment and the level of satisfaction with treatment and services was generally high across modalities, although drug abuse counseling alone did not address their wider ranging service needs. Methadone had the lowest level of drug abuse counseling and services/programs among the four modalities studied.

Programs in TOPS appeared to focus on the client's primary drug of abuse rather than addressing the client's multiple drug use, drug-related problems, and social and economic functioning. Programs in DATOS having considerably fewer resources provided an even more restricted range of services. For heroin abusers, low-dose methadone (69% of admissions initially were treated with less than 30 mg oral methadone daily) was the most common pattern of methadone treatment in the programs participating in TOPS. Forty percent of clients in methadone treatment for at least 3 months received 30 mg of methadone or less daily; 26% received more than 50 mg. In DATOS all participating programs reported higher methadone doses. Take-home privileges were common, but policies determining the qualification for the privilege and the number of doses varied greatly among the methadone treatment programs (56).

Treatment Outcomes

Many studies have demonstrated that community-based methadone, residential, and outpatient drug-free treatment helped reduce drug dependence of clients entering treatment in the early 1970s (57–59).

In TOPS, multiple measures of treatment outcome have been necessary to describe changes in the client's ability to function in society after treatment. The duration of abstinence, the predictors of relapse, the nature of posttreatment drug use patterns, the reinstatement of dependence, and treatment reentry are central indicators of the impact of treatment. Severity of medical, social, and psychological problems directly related to drug use, as well as other indicators of functioning such as alcohol use, employment, family stability, health, and psychological well-being, are also important evaluation measures considered.

Extensive descriptive and multivariate analyses of posttreatment drug use indicators (60), depression (44), and criminal behavior (51) were conducted using the TOPS data. In general, clients remaining in treatment for at least 3 months have more positive posttreatment outcomes (61), but the major changes in behavior are seen only for those who stay in treatment for more than 12 months (34). These findings are being replicated in other national studies such as the National Treatment Improvement Evaluation Study (NTIES) conducted from 1993 to 1995 with a sample of 6593 clients in 78 treatment units (62) as well as studies in individual states such as California (63).

Combined with results from other research, the findings described in this section provide comprehensive and convincing evidence that long-term treatment is effective. Several studies, however, including experiments with random assignment (64) and evaluation of abrupt closures of methadone programs (65), provide evidence that programs do produce effects independent of client motivation to remain in treatment. Further, the multivariate analyses and the research design used in the author's study carefully considered alternative assumptions about measurement validity and took into account potential indicators of client motivation, including previous treatment and reasons for entering treatment (33).

DRUG USE

Analyses of the TOPS data show that the posttreatment rate of daily heroin, cocaine, and psychotherapeutic drug use of clients who spent at least 3 months in treatment was half the pretreatment rate. The posttreatment rates of weekly or more frequent use for clients who stayed in treatment for at least 3 months were 10–15% lower than the rates for short-term clients.

Despite these major reductions in rates of use, many clients in each modality reported posttreatment use of at least one drug other than marihuana or alcohol: 40% of methadone, 30% of residential, and 20% of outpatient drug-free clients who stayed in treatment for at least 3 months reported weekly or daily use after treatment. One of the most disappointing findings of the TOPS follow-up was the continuation of pretreatment levels of marihuana and heavy alcohol use in the years after treatment. These data indicated that, despite the success of treatment, much work is still needed to maximize treatment effectiveness.

Multivariate log linear regression analyses were conducted to investigate the effects of client characteristics and treatment factors on treatment outcomes (60). Demographic factors (sex, age, race), treatment history, source of referral, and pretreatment drug use patterns were included as control variables. Three regression analyses (one for each modality) were used to describe the effect of different categories of time in treatment on the odds of being a weekly or more frequent drug user during the year after treatment. The results showed that time spent in treatment was among the most important predictors of most treatment outcomes. Stays of 1 year or more in residential or methadone treatment, or continuing methadone maintenance, produced significant decreases in the odds of using heroin in the follow-up period. These findings contrasted with those of prior research that suggested that shorter stays can produce significant differences in positive treatment outcomes.

DEPRESSION INDICATORS

TOPS clients reported a substantial decrease in depression indicators during the years after treatment (44, 45). Multivariate analysis using the logistic regression procedure revealed that, aside from pretreatment depression indicators, very few factors were significant predictors of posttreatment suicidal thoughts or attempts. Among methadone clients, race was found to be significantly related to posttreatment suicidal indicators. Among residen-

tial clients, gender, retention, and a history of prior drug abuse treatment were significant. In outpatient drug-free programs, source of referral and prior drug abuse treatment emerged as significant. In all cases, however, the relationships were weak and, although statistically significant, their clinical utility is doubtful. The use of detailed clinical assessments of depression in the DATOS research may help clarify the effect of treatment on depression.

CRIMINAL BEHAVIOR

Analyses of the effects of treatment on criminal behavior have focused on reduction in predatory crime and costs associated with crime. Although treatment itself reduces predatory crime (33), those referred by the criminal justice system do not show a greater reduction in predatory illegal acts after treatment than do those who were not involved with the criminal justice system (48). A more complex model such as path analysis would be a more appropriate way to demonstrate the overall impact of criminal justice involvement. The assessment of the benefit-cost ratio indicates that substantial benefits in reduction of crime-related costs are obtained regardless of the measures used or the time period for which benefits are calculated (66).

POSTTREATMENT SUPPORT

Conceptual models (67) and recent empiric findings (58, 68) stress the key role of posttreatment experiences in long-term recovery. Procedures for reducing relapse (69) and standard aftercare protocols have been developed for alcohol treatment (21, 40). DARP (58) analyses reveal that the positive effect of longer retention in a particular program diminishes over time. Treatment, employment, and other behaviors co-occurring with outcomes during a given year are hypothesized to be more important factors than prior treatment.

Benefit-Cost Studies and Cost Effectiveness

Benefit-cost studies of drug abuse treatment are needed to meet the increasing concerns about cost containment in both the public and private sectors. Most current benefit-cost studies are limited to the cost effectiveness of alcohol abuse treatment and merely calculate the difference between treatment costs and the savings in health care expenditures following treatment (14, 70). To date, no study has rigorously assessed all economic benefits from drug abuse treatment. The assessment of the crime reduction effects of drug abuse treatment by Harwood and colleagues (66) is the first step in building a benefit-cost framework. That assessment used information on the societal costs of crime and drug treatment to estimate the economic benefits of drug abuse treatment.

The economic costs imposed by drug abusers' criminal activities before, during, and after admission to residential, outpatient methadone, and outpatient drug-free programs were calculated in a secondary analysis of TOPS data. Using the framework from the Harwood social cost study (66), values were calculated for costs to victims, costs to the criminal justice system, and criminal career/productivity losses. Two alternative summary cost measures were defined: economic costs to society and economic costs to law-abiding citizens. The analysis demonstrated that drug abuse treatment significantly reduced the economic costs associated with criminal activity of drug abusers, and treatment produced a positive benefit-cost ratio within the first year after completing treatment regardless of the cost measures employed. A replication of this method in a study of California programs in 1992 indicated an overall return of $7 for each dollar invested and savings of $1.5 billion mostly due to crime reduction (63).

NEW QUESTIONS

New research must build upon and expand the knowledge generated by previous research on treatment effectiveness and ongoing clinic-based research programs. We need to expand our substantive knowledge about drug abuse treatment effectiveness and refine theory about treatment itself as well as recovery and relapse. National prospective studies such as the DARP study conducted on clients entering treatment during the late 1960s and early 1970s (27,

57) and TOPS studies conducted with clients entering drug abuse treatment between 1979 and 1981 (34, 35) provide rich data bases that have been used to answer many of the basic questions about treatment effectiveness. These answers are guiding current and future research such as DATOS and NTIES.

Several events, however, necessitate broader perspectives in studies of drug abuse treatment and treatment effectiveness. Major changes occurred in the nation's drug-abusing population and treatment system in the 1980s and 1990s and will likely continue to occur. New research questions have arisen because of these changes and because of the lessons learned from prior research. The prior research, however, has several inherent limitations. Finally, the acquired immune deficiency syndrome (AIDS) crisis has intensified interest in drug abuse treatment as a strategy to reduce exposure to the cause of AIDS, the human immunodeficiency virus (HIV). It is therefore necessary to update information to reexamine what we have learned about treatment effectiveness and to augment the types of available data to examine new issues about the nature, effectiveness, and costs of current treatment approaches.

Changes in Treatment Clients and the Treatment System

Although many attempts have been made to control drug abuse during the past century, the problem has persisted and the nature and extent of abuse has changed dramatically during the past decade. Opioid dependence has persisted for the past century (3, 71–74) and accounted for two thirds of the estimated $60 billion social cost of drug abuse in 1980 (75). Extensive use of multiple drugs by young adults in the general population (76) as well as by drug abusers entering treatment (36) was common in the 1980s. By 1980, too, many of those for whom heroin was the primary drug of abuse were using a greater variety of drugs (36, 77). Data from the National Household Survey on Drug Abuse show that the proportion of young adults (18–25 years of age) who had used marihuana increased from 48% in 1972 to 64% in 1982. Cocaine use tripled, and nonmedical use of stimulants, sedatives, and tranquilizers doubled (78). However, by 1985, the percentage of young adults who had used marihuana had decreased slightly, to 60%, and the prevalence of cocaine use was 25% (79). Clients entering treatment in the 1990s likely will reflect the trend in *multiple* drug use in the general population and will have a greater variety of problems and comorbidities (35, 61, 80), particularly psychiatric (81), than did drug abuse clients in the 1970s.

The TOPS and DATOS data confirmed the impression that drug use patterns and problems of clients coming into community-based drug abuse treatment changed dramatically during the 1970s (35) and the 1990s (33). The TOPS clients entering treatment between 1979 and 1981 were much more likely to use multiple drugs than were DARP clients entering treatment between 1969 and 1973. Whereas the drug use pattern of about half of DARP methadone clients was described as "daily opioid use only," only one in five TOPS methadone clients reported this use pattern. Daily opioid use was much more common for DARP residential (63%) and outpatient drug-free (35%) clients than for TOPS residential (30%) and outpatient drug-free (10%) clients. In TOPS, use of nonopioids was reported much more frequently in all modalities than in DARP and was the modal pattern for residential and outpatient drug-free clients. In DATOS cocaine use became the primary drug of interest.

The far-reaching changes in the drug abuse treatment system since studies of the DARP and TOPS admission cohorts require reconsideration of these studies. The DARP and TOPS samples were composed primarily of publicly funded outpatient methadone, residential, and outpatient drug-free programs. Privately funded drug abuse programs increased (81) during the 1980s and decreased in the 1990s, in part because concerns about costs and the introduction of managed care and cost containment were not included in DARP or TOPS. The role of state funding and oversight has not been reexamined (82). The distinction between publicly funded (state or local) and private (self-pay or insurance) treatment has become blurred. The treatment of many clients in traditional "public" treatment modalities is not supported by public funds. Fee-for-service is now more common (83), and long waiting lists for publicly funded treatment slots are reported in many areas.

Based on an assessment of the outpatient treatment system, some researchers hypothesize that changes in the drug abuse treatment environment will affect the way services are delivered and ultimately may influence treatment efficiency and effectiveness (84, 85). With the increase in concern about cost containment there is greater concern for the cost effectiveness of publicly delivered services. Cost issues were raised when Diagnostic Related Group costs for an episode of alcohol and drug abuse treatment were proposed in the Medicare system. It is assumed that the example set by Medicare may be followed by other public programs and private insurance companies. Although longer stays are related to more successful outcomes (24, 34, 57), cost constraints and public and client preference for short-term chemical dependency and methadone detoxification programs may pressure traditional programs to consider shorter treatment and more effective aftercare and relapse prevention efforts in place of long-term retention (69).

These changes in the drug abuse treatment population and in treatment itself suggest that existing information may no longer be adequate to describe treatment. Although the three major modalities remain, treatment is now provided in a broader range of settings to a more diverse clientele. DATOS will provide important new information about the nature of drug abuse, the treatment system, and treatment effectiveness.

New Research Questions

Knowledge is cumulative and new questions have been asked about drug treatment effectiveness since the last national multiprogram study was conducted. These include the role of psychiatric severity and depression in treatment outcomes; the effectiveness of the components of drug abuse treatment such as psychological services, family therapy, and aftercare; the process of client change during and after treatment; the role of posttreatment experiences in relapse and recovery; how clients and programs can best be matched to improve the effectiveness of treatment; the predictive role of drug use histories and dependence; and the chronicity of drug treatment episodes in the effectiveness of specific treatment episodes. Further, as discussed more fully later, the potential effect of drug abuse treatment on the AIDS epidemic has received increased attention. These new questions have not yet been investigated over a broad array of program types and across multiple sites.

Although the overall effectiveness of the major modalities has been examined in a number of studies, including DARP, TOPS, DATOS, and NTIES, the effectiveness of certain components of treatment—such as counseling and other types of services or of aftercare—has not been examined in detail. In recent years the perception of the need to evaluate the impact of treatment components has grown, but the complexity of the client process of change and the treatment factors involved have stalled the completion of such a study. Several studies have examined the role of relapse prevention and aftercare services in treatment outcome (69, 86), cognitive factors have received more attention in research in therapeutic communities (87, 88), and the TOPS researchers have investigated the role of the number and intensity of treatment services in treatment outcomes (51). The TOPS research, for instance, suggests that more positive treatment outcomes result from more intense services and that service intensity may compensate for the trend toward shorter stays in treatment.

Coupled with these concerns about what occurs during treatment is a greater recognition that posttreatment experiences such as social support and life events can also significantly influence treatment outcomes. Conceptual models (67) and recent empiric findings (62, 89) stress the role of posttreatment experiences in long-term recovery. As with treatment components, however, the study of the impact of posttreatment factors has received little attention because of the complexity of the issues involved. Posttreatment experiences such as social support and life events need to be developed and evaluated based on models of posttreatment recovery and relapse.

Research literature has found that some types of treatment are more effective for some types of client than others (90, 91), and that problem severity may require attention to matching of clients and therapists (92). Yet, there has been little research on matching, in part because of the complex statistical and methodologic issues involved in an appropriate study. However, several authors have developed models of client-treatment matching and reviewed the conceptual and methodologic issues (90, 93). The careful measurement of both clients and treatments should provide data that better inform researchers and clinicians about key factors to consider in controlled clinical studies such as project MATCH (21).

Potential of Drug Abuse Treatment in the AIDS Epidemic

Because of the central role of intravenous drug use in the spread of HIV infection, drug abuse treatment has been mentioned increasingly as an effective strategy. Drug abuse treatment not only can reduce intravenous drug use but, through its impact on reducing the number of drug users per se, it can reduce the transmission of HIV that is facilitated by the weakened immune systems of drug abusers (10, 60). Further, the treatment program provides a most appropriate site for educational messages on the prevention of HIV transmission.

The National Commission on AIDS has recommended doubling treatment capacity (94). Yet, few data are available to suggest where and how these resources can be directed most effectively. Reports of intravenous cocaine use by large numbers of abusers without a history of heroin use are a new and troubling phenomenon. Traditional publicly funded programs for intravenous drug abusers did not reduce cocaine use effectively (60). Treatment effectiveness for individuals entering programs because they fear AIDS or greater criminal sanctions (95) should continue to be carefully examined.

Broadened Economic Perspectives

The major types of publicly funded drug abuse treatment have been shown to be effective, and positive benefit-cost ratios have been obtained for outpatient methadone, long-term residential, and outpatient drug-free modalities. Such results justify the overall investment in treatment but provide little insight into ways to improve effectiveness and increase benefit-cost ratios.

If the investment in treatment is to produce a maximum return and guide payment justification for longer or more intense services, multiple approaches and improvements must be considered in resource allocation. Broader recruitment, more comprehensive assessment, improved services, matching of clients with services, increased retention, and an expanded continuum of care must be considered in terms of their contribution to outcomes. New frameworks need to include consideration of several factors:

1. Stage in the treatment career of clients
2. Components of treatment structure and process
3. Typology of client impairment
4. Complex patterns of alcohol and drug abuse

Such disaggregation of the entity of "treatment" and its appropriate application to clients of different types is essential. The specific elements and client-treatment matches can then be allocated costs and benefits, which should suggest ways to invest prudently new monies for demand reduction.

CLINICAL IMPLICATIONS OF CLIENT DIFFERENCES

Detailed consideration only recently has been given to how elements such as client characteristics and specific aspects of treatment affect treatment success (96) and to how client characteristics may interact with treatment type to affect treatment success (93, 97). Client characteristics are important because they define treatment populations across treatment types and can contribute to differential treatment effectiveness. Description of pretreatment behaviors provides the baseline against which treatment effectiveness may be assessed.

Treatment needs and prospects for successful outcomes differ by basic demographic characteristics such as gender (98), age (99, 100), and ethnicity (101, 102). Many aspects of a client's past and current treatment experience, such as prior treatment (34, 47, 89), the source of referral (48–50), method of paying for treatment (83), and sensitivity to client needs (103–105), could influence the course and outcome of a particular treatment episode.

Thus, assessment of the nature of client characteristics is essential for accounting for the level of effectiveness of drug abuse treatment for any particular client. Different types of clients benefit differentially from the treatment experience.

Differences in the types of clients entering a particular type of treatment program are also critical to the design, implementation, and outcome of the regimen. The major types of programs have been explicitly and implicitly designed to deal with specific types of drug abusers. Outpatient methadone programs admit only clients with documented histories of opioid addiction. Although residential and outpatient drug-free programs also serve opioid addicts, the use patterns of their clientele are more diverse (35). The broad-based orientation of residential treatment programs (106) attracts clients with a wide range of drug use patterns, often coupled with psychological disturbance and social dysfunction. Knowledge about the nature of client populations across modalities, including client characteristics, psychiatric severity, and social and economic functioning, is therefore essential for planning purposes.

Impairment

Indicators of both drug use patterns and impairment levels across an array of areas of function must be developed. The various components of each concept (i.e., types of drugs or types of impairment) must be considered as well as overall summary measures. For such complex concepts, both qualitative and typologic indices will be useful.

A major issue that emerged during the 1980s concerns the impact of impairment, particularly psychopathology, on treatment outcomes. Although the DARP study concluded that there were few differences in overall treatment outcomes for opioid abusers across treatment modalities, more recent work by McLellan and his colleagues suggests that psychological problems significantly detract from the treatment process (107, 108). Jaffe (81) argues that opioid abusers with severe psychological problems do poorly in the confrontational context of a therapeutic community but may function better in a methadone program. On the other hand, Woody et al. (109) found that methadone clients with antisocial personality and depression showed substantial improvement on multiple outcomes. A similar finding was reported for adolescents (110). Data to examine this issue are largely unavailable outside programs closely linked with clinical research centers.

Serious depression can affect the course of treatment and jeopardize successful outcomes (111, 112). The prevalence and course of depressive symptoms among clients in drug abuse treatment is, therefore, a topic of major concern among analysts of treatment effectiveness (24, 44, 45, 113, 114), and treatment requires more careful attention to the multiple problems of clients, particularly psychiatric severity (81).

Drug Use Patterns

The TOPS results (36, 37, 115) indicate that programs and researchers should move beyond the traditional diagnosis of primary drug of abuse or single drug use to consider patterns of multiple drug use. Using only basic single drug measures obscures the extensive nature of multiple abuse and may lead to similar treatments for clients with very different abuse patterns. In addition to a primary diagnosis of drug use, many clients entering drug abuse treatment programs appear to need treatment for alcohol abuse as well. Thus, problems related to alcohol abuse must also be assessed and treated. Programs also should consider how the general treatment regimen will affect multiple drug and alcohol use (116, 117). Separate intensive therapies focusing on cocaine, marihuana, and alcohol use for clients with multiple drug use patterns may be needed to supplement the basic treatment regimen for the primary drug of abuse. Even in the treatment of primary heroin or cocaine users, the abuse of other drugs, especially marihuana and alcohol, should be assessed and treated. In order to plan for appropriate treatment, multiple drug use patterns *and* use of particular types of drugs within these multiple use patterns must be considered.

Treatment Experience

The recognition that drug abuse treatment admissions—as with drug abuse episodes—recur, and that improvement may be incremental through a number of treatment episodes (47, 89, 118, 119), argues for closer consideration of the role in treatment outcomes of the client's treatment history. That is, is the client entering treatment for the first time, following a brief period of addiction, or has the client had multiple episodes of treatment? Research from the TOPS study has shown that drug abuse treatment clients are, in general, repeat clients; more than 40% of clients entering treatment had prior treatment experiences, and more than 30% reentered treatment in the year after leaving the TOPS program. Other analyses of the TOPS data (34) found that treatment outcomes are related to treatment history; those with no or few prior treatment episodes had more positive treatment outcomes than did those with many such episodes. The integration of this life history perspective with measures of motivation and readiness for treatment (87) can suggest ways to enhance retention, particularly during the key first weeks of treatment. The role of a particular treatment episode in the treatment career or recovery process must be identified. Thus, such an episode need not be an isolated event but part of a continuum of care.

Multidimensional Client Assessment

A variety of serious medical and mental health problems, serious family disruption, and employment problems are closely associated with drug and alcohol abuse, and the severity of these problems also varies across modalities. These "addiction-related" problems are theoretically and clinically important (108). It is generally agreed that assisting clients to cope with these problems should be a major goal of treatment and that, to be successful, treatment must be oriented to a variety of client needs and provide services to meet those needs effectively. Analyses of the TOPS data described previously indicate that clients entering each of the modalities had very different patterns of drug-related problems (35, 61).

There are two basic approaches to assessing problems. The nosologic approach is designed to categorize individuals as to the presence or absence of specific disorders—for example, using standard diagnostic criteria, such as those of the American Psychiatric Association's *Diagnostic and Statistical Manual of Mental Disorders*. The other type of assessment approach is dimensional rather than categoric. This approach focuses more on symptom severity and the relative importance of different types of problems. For efficiency and cost effectiveness, the nosologic and dimensional approaches could be combined by using a dimensional instrument as a screening scale to choose individuals for a follow-up interview by a clinician using an instrument with a nosologic approach.

In addition to psychiatric impairment, various other aspects of impairment that each can have a major influence on the response to treatment and on subsequent outcomes must be considered. Treatment history, criminal involvement, drug dependence, drug-related problems, health status, and employment all must be considered as elements of impairment and can also be considered as descriptors of client types.

The nature and extent of the multiple problems can have important implications for service needs for clients and potential outcomes. The ASI was developed by McLellan and colleagues for use in a clinical setting to evaluate the severity of problems in seven areas: drug abuse, alcohol abuse, medical, employment/support, family/social, legal, and psychological (108).

The psychological problems or psychiatric subscale of the ASI was found to be the best predictor of treatment outcome across all types of programs, and the appropriate matching of substance abusers with inpatient and outpatient programs was suggested (120). The TOPS interviews designed for field surveys collect similar data on most of the ASI problem areas. As in the ASI studies (108), analyses of the TOPS data indicate that the multiple problems reported by clients are not related (Table 53.1).

The results from both TOPS and the ASI suggest that a quantitative composite measure of severity does not effectively summarize the nature and extent of multiple problems. A typology may be a more appropriate and clinically useful method of describing and summarizing multiple problems. The categories in Table 53.1 represent the combinations of problem areas reported by clients in each modality. To simplify the construction of the typology, employment was deleted.

These results show that there are many combinations of problems among drug abusers. Multiple problems are most common among residential

Table 53.1   Typology of Multiple Problems in the Year Before Admission

Type of Problem	Methadone (%) (n = 4184)	Residential (%) (n = 2891)	Outpatient Drug-Free (%) (n = 2914)
Drug abuse only	35.9	13.6	24.3
Drug abuse and one other problem	33.1	29.2	31.7
Three or more drug-related problems	(13.4)	(11.2)	(11.6)
Suicidal indicators	(7.6)	(5.6)	(11.6)
Predatory crime	(12.1)	(12.4)	(8.5)
Multiple problems	30.6	57.6	44.7
Suicide and problems	(9.2)	(10.2)	(16.4)
Crime and problems	(9.7)	(19.4)	(8.3)
Crime and suicide	(3.8)	(5.5)	(6.1)
Crime, suicide, and problems	(7.9)	(22.5)	(13.9)

clients. It should also be noted that within each category of the typology, alcohol abuse accompanies drug abuse for 20–40% of the clients.

CLINICAL IMPLICATIONS OF TREATMENT STRUCTURE AND PROCESS

Program administrators, researchers, and policymakers are in general agreement that community-based drug abuse treatment "has been instrumental in the rehabilitation of significant numbers of drug-dependent individuals" (22). There is no question that treatment works, but little is known about how and why treatment works. In general, treatment outcomes have not been linked with the nature of treatment that clients have received (26). Variables in the diverse approaches that comprise drug abuse treatment must be better specified and their role in producing positive treatment outcomes better understood for methadone (96, 121), residential (106, 122), and outpatient treatment (123).

Treatment as currently rendered is a complex, multifaceted process delivered in a variety of contexts and environments to clients undergoing behavioral and cognitive changes at different rates. Thus, general descriptive information alone is not sufficient to examine specific hypotheses regarding the nature of the drug abuse treatment process.

Developing a typology of drug abuse treatment program structure or descriptions of approaches assumes that there is an agreed-upon definition of treatment, that the dimensions of treatment have been identified, and that there is a fair degree of consistency within treatment types. However, there is no consensus on what constitutes nonmedical psychological, mental health, alcohol, or drug "treatments." Similarly, the treatment process is poorly defined. It is useful, however, to regard treatment as a specific set of procedures, approaches, therapies, or services that are designed to achieve certain goals. Treatment process that can be thought of as the steps or the dynamic movement from addiction to recovery is also poorly defined. In the context of drug abuse, this process typically involves changes in one or more areas of a client's life.

Approach to Assessing Structure and Process

Research from both DARP and TOPS provides guidance for future consideration of treatment structure and process. One of the most comprehensive attempts to explore the issue of the interactive relationship of client and program typologies was initiated in the DARP studies. The early development of a treatment typology was based on client bimonthly status reports and program site visits (124). With this approach, it was possible to classify clients' treatment according to the services they received during the "majority" of each period covered by the status report. A second phase of the classification took into account "treatment objectives and rationales, program structure, staffing, and other program aspects within or between treatment categories" (125) that were assumed to be correlated with treatment outcome.

In TOPS, researchers described the overall structure and functioning of the major modalities based on director and counselor surveys (51) and examined the type and number of services received at the client level based on record abstractions and client self-reports. Although the treatment process was not fully elaborated, TOPS examined the relationship among treatment outcomes and treatment services, client characteristics, and the duration of treatment.

Client-Counselor Service Interaction

Though the DARP and TOPS treatment process studies showed that it is possible to assess the main elements of treatment, drug abuse treatment has a complex, multifaceted structure and dynamic process. To identify and quantify types of services or counseling, the client-counselor/staff interaction must be considered. Both within and across counseling sessions, many services may be provided, none necessarily as an independently structured service. Thus, any quantitative analysis may not be able to capture fully the complete dynamics of treatment. Encouraging findings on the relationship of the psychotherapy process to outcome (126) indicate that some of the key components and processes of drug abuse treatment can be described. Recent findings on counselor effects by McLellan et al. (52) are further confirmation that research can lead to better understanding of why some types of programs work or some types of clients succeed.

A second general point underscores the importance of systematic evaluation of program, client, and therapist interaction variables. For example, researchers and policymakers often appear to assume that the different types of modalities or environments could serve the total population of individuals with drug abuse problems equally well (8).

Finding variation among modalities and among clinics of different programs within modalities was not surprising. However, contrary to most expectations, in TOPS (34, 51, 56) extensive variation was found not only among clinics, but even within units of the same treatment program. This implies that, despite policies and plans at a general administrative level, distinctiveness of the counseling and services within clinics must be taken into account.

Psychotherapy Process Research

Although the modalities of psychotherapy are better defined than those of drug abuse treatment, the general approach to the study of psychotherapy process can help guide the current research. The research in psychotherapy also has a longer history. Kiesler (127) summarized some of the early work in process research. Greenberg and Pinsof (128) build upon this conceptual and methodological base to develop a more comprehensive assessment of psychotherapeutic process. They cite major emerging trends that will help advance the field:

1. Integration of process and outcome studies
2. Theory of process
3. Involvement of clients
4. Analysis of context, patterns, and change
5. Quality instrumentation to measure process

They believe that the study of treatment process should emphasize a system in addition to an individual perspective. They define process research as the study of interaction between the client and therapist in order to identify the factors contributing to change within and outside of the system.

In addition to conceptual and theoretical advances, new analysis approaches have been recommended that assess the counseling sequence and pattern process (129). These approaches (130) must be consistent with the general model of events listing analysis that has received increased attention in the sociologic literature. The analysis plan for the treatment process study includes consideration of these techniques to link process with outcome. Orlinsky and Howard (126) review a range of variables that must be considered in the assessment of the process and outcome in psychotherapy and a conceptual framework for their interaction. These variables and models can be adapted for drug abuse treatment.

A Conceptual Model for Treatment Process and Structure

A number of researchers have examined elements of drug abuse treatment and treatment process at the aggregate program level (124, 125, 131, 132). D'Aunno and Price (85) examined the organizational environment of drug abuse treatment but include no client-level data on treatment process. Magura (133) assessed participative decision making by clients in methadone clinics and its effects on process and outcomes. DeLeon (122) outlined the levels of the therapeutic approach as structure, elements, and process. Holland (25, 54) included organizational, client, and process variables as predictors of planned duration. Allison et al. (51) focused on service for clients in the programs. Aiken, Losciuto, and colleagues (134) concentrated on the counselor characteristics and the progress of clients in terms of behavioral change, as have McLellan et al. (52). Biase and colleagues (88, 135) focus more on the progress of the client through treatment in terms of cognitive development of self-concept. Joe et al. (136, 137) conducted secondary analysis of TOPS to examine the process of services received and behaviors during treatment.

None of these studies has fully integrated the many elements of treatment structure and treatment process. A framework is proposed in Figure 53.1, drawn in part from psychotherapy models. This framework suggests that three levels of variables and the factors influencing each level must be considered:

1. The program (the administrative structures, policies and procedures, staff-to-client ratios, staff training, and other objective, clearly identifiable characteristics of the program environment)
2. The counseling and services (availability, nature, and quality)
3. The client (receipt of service and satisfaction with perceived need for services)

At the client level, it is also suggested that the process of individual change during the course of treatment be considered. This dynamic element of treatment process has often been neglected.

At the *counseling and service level* one should be more interested in functional aspects of different program components, including the more objective features such as years of training and experience as well as personal qualities such as warmth, sensitivity, and empathy.

Most programs implicitly or explicitly plan progression through treatment, either as a 12-step model, a methadone to abstinence or maintenance regimen, or stages in a therapeutic community. Research has seldom, if ever, examined the nature and rate of this progression as either a dependent or predictor variable. The indicators of progression can include elements such as:

1. Readiness to progress
2. Relapse potential
3. Behavioral level or pattern of change (i.e., improvement or worsening)
4. Cognitive change (i.e., overcoming denial, commitment to recovery)
5. Changes in social functioning
6. Changes in psychological functioning

A major limitation of past drug abuse treatment research is a failure to fully examine changes in attitudes, motivation, knowledge, and skills associated with participation in treatment. These alterations include changes in beliefs, attitudes, and knowledge about dependence and recovery as well as behavioral changes during treatment (138–140). The application of psychological learning theory to the study of relapse (141) has led to the development of specific treatment techniques designed to prevent relapse and minimize the effects of brief lapses (142, 143). Studies of coping strategies in response to stressful life events and high-risk situations during the crucial transitional period after the termination of treatment have provided a scientific basis for these new approaches.

To fully understand treatment process and link process with outcome after treatment, we must understand the external factors contributing to client change as well as the program and service/counseling level components.

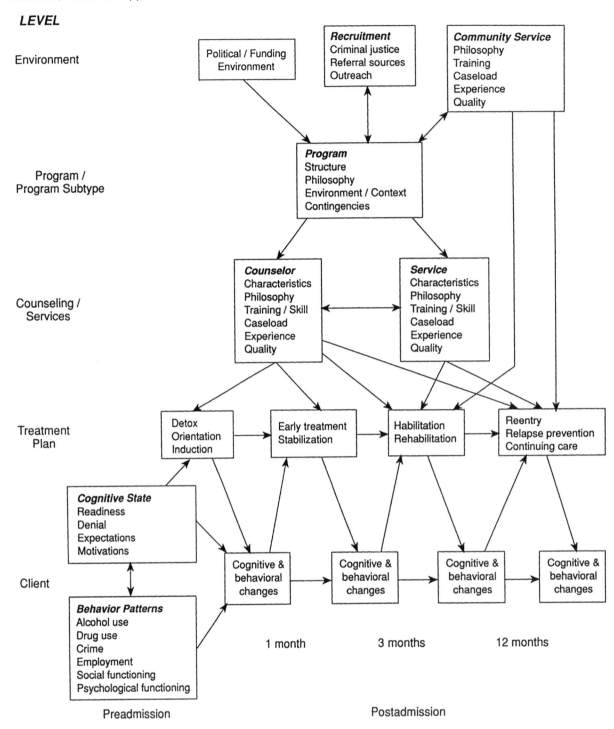

Figure 53.1. Conceptual model of treatment process.

SUMMARY

During the 1990s outcome and effectiveness have become major public concerns. A variety of individual clinical studies, multiprogram evaluations, and research reviews have substantiated the effectiveness of drug abuse treatment in reducing drug use and improving functioning. Further analyses have demonstrated that the benefits derived from drug abuse treatment considerably outweigh the cost of the treatment. Despite these positive conclusions, treatment can and should be improved. Further, effectiveness studies of individual programs and services are required to justify costs.

In order to identify the areas in which treatment should be supported and

can be improved, new conceptual models and empiric studies are needed that focus on client and treatment. By augmenting our understanding of the various domains of client impairment and functioning, the patterns of multiple drug abuse, and the diverse experiences with treatment and criminal justice systems, it should be possible to develop better treatment plans and services. By increasing our knowledge of treatment structure and process, including program organization and operation, client-counselor service interaction, and the dynamics of service delivery and client change, more appropriate and effective treatment programs and components can be designed and implemented.

A new generation of treatment research is being developed for the 1990s that builds upon prior multiprogram and clinically based research. These studies are focusing on improved assessment of clients and more refined measures of treatment. The results of this research should provide the foundation of knowledge to help improve drug abuse treatment into the next decade. This research conducted over three decades can identify the findings that remain constant despite rapidly changing environments. The studies can also identify the ways environment changes may affect outcomes.

References

1. Laundergan JC. Easy does it: alcoholism treatment outcomes: Hazelden and the Minnesota model. Duluth, MN: Hazelden Foundation, 1982.
2. Cook CCH. The Minnesota model in the management of drug and alcohol dependency: miracle, method, or myth? Part I. The philosophy and the programme. Br J Addict 1988;83:625–634.
3. Jaffe JH. The swinging pendulum: the treatment of drug users in America. In: DuPont RL, Goldstein A, O'Donnell J, eds. Handbook on drug use. Washington, DC: U.S. Government Printing Office, 1979:3–16.
4. Anglin MD, Hser Y. Treatment of drug abuse. In: Tonry M, Wilson JQ, eds. Drugs and crime. Chicago: University of Chicago Press, 1990: 393–460.
5. Gerstein DR, Harwood HJ, eds. Treating drug problems. Washington, DC: National Academy Press, 1990.
6. Sisk JE, Hatziandren EJ, Hughes R. The effectiveness of drug abuse treatment: implication for controlling AIDS/HIV infection. Washington DC: Office of Technology Assessment, 1990.
7. Fuller RK, Branchey L, Brightwell DR, et al. Disulfiram treatment of alcoholism. JAMA 1986;245:1449–1455.
8. Bale RN, Van Stone WW, Kuldau JM, Engelsing TMJ, Elashoff RM, Zarcone VP. Therapeutic communities vs. methadone maintenance. Arch Gen Psychiatry 1980;37:179–193.
9. Committee for the Study and Treatment and Rehabilitation Services for Alcoholism and Alcohol Abuse. Broadening the base of treatment for alcohol problems. Washington, DC: National Academy of Science, 1990.
10. Hubbard RL, Des Jarlais DC. Alcohol and drug abuse. In: Holland EE, Petels R, Knox G, eds. Oxford textbook of public health. 2nd edition. Vol. 3. London: Oxford University Press, 1991.
11. Landry MJ. Overview of addiction treatment effectiveness. Rockville, MD: Substance Abuse and Mental Health Administration, 1996.
12. Armor DJ, Polich JM, Stambul HB. Alcoholism and treatment. New York: Wiley, 1978.
13. Polich JM, Armor DJ, Braiker HB. The course of alcoholism: four years after treatment. New York: Wiley, 1981.
14. Holder HD, Blose JO. Alcoholism treatment and total health care utilization and costs: a four-year longitudinal analysis of federal employees. JAMA 1986;256:1456–1460.
15. Institute of Medicine, Committee to Identify Research Effectiveness in the Prevention and Treatment of Alcohol Related Problems. Prevention and treatment of alcohol problems. Washington, DC: National Academy Press, 1989.
16. Hubbard RL, Anderson J. A followup study of individuals receiving alcoholism treatment. Research Triangle Park, NC: Research Triangle Institute, 1988.
17. Hoffmann N, Harrison P. A 2 year followup of inpatient outpatient treatment. St. Paul, MN: Chemical Abuse Treatment Outcome Registry, 1987.
18. Saxe L, Dougherty D, Esty K, Fine M. Health technology case study 22: the effectiveness and costs of alcoholism treatment. Washington, DC: Office of Technology Assessment, 1983.

19. Annis HM. Is inpatient rehabilitation of the alcoholic cost effective? Con position. Adv Alcohol Subst Abuse 1986;5:175–190.
20. Miller WR, Hester RK. Inpatient alcoholism treatment: who benefits? Am Psychol 1986;41: 794–805.
21. Project MATCH Research Group. Project MATCH: rationale and methods for a multisite clinical trial matching patients to alcoholism treatment. Alcohol Clin Exp Res 1993;17: 1130–1145.
22. Tims FM. Effectiveness of drug abuse treatment programs. Treatment research report. DHHS publication no. (ADM) 84–1143. Rockville, MD: National Institute on Drug Abuse, 1981.
23. Tims FM, Ludford JP, eds. Drug abuse treatment evaluation: strategies, progress, and prospects. DHHS publication no. (ADM) 88–1329. Research monograph series 51. Rockville, MD: National Institute on Drug Abuse, 1984.
24. DeLeon G. The therapeutic community: study of effectiveness. DHHS publication no. (ADM) 84–1286. Rockville, MD: National Institute on Drug Abuse, 1984.
25. Holland S. Residential drug-free programs for substance abusers: the effect of planned duration on treatment. Chicago: Gateway Houses, 1982.
26. Sells SB. Treatment effectiveness. In: DuPont RL, Goldstein A, O'Donnell J, eds. Handbook on drug use. Washington, DC: Government Printing Office, 1979:105–118.
27. Sells SB, Simpson D. The effectiveness of drug abuse treatment. Vols. 1–5. Cambridge, MA: Ballinger Publishing Company, 1976.
28. Smart RG. Outcome studies of therapeutic community and halfway house treatment for addicts. Int J Addict 1976;11:143–159.
29. Dole VP, Joseph H. Long-term outcome of patients treated with methadone maintenance. Ann N Y Acad Sci 1978;311:181–189.
30. Gorsuch RL, Abbamonte M, Sells SB. Evaluation of treatments for drug users in the DARP: 1971–1972 admissions. In: Sells SB, Simpson DD, eds. The effectiveness of drug abuse treatment: evaluation of treatment outcomes for the 1971–1972 admission cohort. Cambridge, MA: Ballinger Publishing Company, 1976;4: 210–251.
31. Nash G. An analysis of twelve studies of the impact of drug abuse treatment upon criminality. In: Drug use and crime: report of the panel on use and criminal behavior [appendix]. Research Triangle Park, NC: Research Triangle Institute, 1976.
32. McGlothlin WH, Anglin MD. Long-term follow-up of clients of high- and low-dose methadone programs. Arch Gen Psychiatry 1981;38: 1055–1063.
33. Craddock SG, Rounds-Bryant JL, Flynn PM, Hubbard RL. Characteristics and pretreatment behaviors of clients entering drug abuse treatment 1969 to 1993. Am J Drug Abuse, 1997; 23:43–59.
34. Hubbard RL, Marsden ME, Rachal JV, Harwood HJ, Cavanaugh ER, Ginzburg HM. Drug abuse treatment: a national study of effectiveness. Chapel Hill, NC: University of North Carolina Press, 1989.
35. Hubbard RL, Cavanaugh ER, Craddock SG, et al. Drug abuse treatment client characteristics and pretreatment behavior: Treatment Outcome Prospective Study (TOPS), 1979–1981. Rock-

ville, MD: National Institute on Drug Abuse, 1986.
36. Hubbard RL, Bray RM, Craddock SG. Issues in the assessment of multiple drug use among drug treatment clients. NIDA Res Monogr 1986; 68:15–40.
37. Bray RM, Schlenger WE, Craddock SG, Hubbard RL, Rachal JV. Approaches to the assessment of drug use in the Treatment Outcome Prospective Study. Report no. RTI/ 1901,01–05S. Research Triangle Park, NC: Research Triangle Institute, 1982.
38. Babor T, Cooney N, Hubbard R, Jaffe J, et al. The syndrome concept of alcohol and drug dependence: results of the secondary analysis project. NIDA Res Monogr 1988;81:33–39.
39. Edwards G, Arif A, Hodgson R. Nomenclature and classification of drug- and alcohol-related problems: a WHO memorandum. Bull World Health Organ 1981;59:225–242.
40. Babor TF, Cooney NL, Lauerman RJ. The drug dependence syndrome concept as a psychological theory of relapse behavior: an empirical evaluation. Br J Addict 1987;82:393–405.
41. Kosten TR, Rounsaville BJ, Babor T, Spitzer RL, Williams JBW. Substance use disorders in DSM-III-R: the dependence syndrome across different psychoactive substances. Br J Psychiatry 1987;151:834–843.
42. Skinner HA, Goldberg AE. Evidence for a drug dependence syndrome among narcotic users. Br J Addict 1987;81:479–484.
43. Allison M, Hubbard RL, Ginzburg HM, Rachal JR. Validation of a three-item measure of depressive and suicidal symptoms. Hosp Community Psychiatry 1986;37:738–740.
44. Allison M, Hubbard RL, Ginzburg HM. Indicators of suicide and depression among drug abusers. Research monograph 68. DHHS publication no. (ADM) 85–1411. Rockville, MD: National Institute on Drug Abuse, 1985.
45. Magruder-Habib K, Hubbard RL, Ginzburg HM. Effects of drug abuse treatment on symptoms of depression and suicide. Int J Addict 1992; 27:1036–1065.
46. Flynn PM, Craddock SG, Luckey JW, Hubbard RL. Comorbidity of antisocial and mood disorders among psychoactive substance-dependent treatment clients. J Pers Disorders 1996;10: 56–67.
47. Marsden ME, Hubbard RL, Bailey SL. Treatment histories of drug abusers. Research Triangle Park, NC: Research Triangle Institute, 1988.
48. Hubbard RL, Collins JJ, Rachal JV, Cavanaugh ER. The criminal justice client in drug abuse treatment. NIDA Res Monogr 1988;86:57–80.
49. Collins JJ, Hubbard RL, Rachal JV, Cavanaugh E. Effects of legal coercion on drug abuse treatment. In: Anglin MD, ed. Compulsory treatment of opiate dependence. New York: Haworth Press, 1988.
50. Collins JJ, Allison M. Legal coercion and retention in drug abuse treatment. Hosp Community Psychiatry 1983;34:1145–1149.
51. Allison M, Hubbard RL, Rachal JV. Treatment process in methadone, residential, and outpatient drug free abuse treatment programs. Rockville, MD: National Institute on Drug Abuse, 1985.
52. McLellan AT, Woody GE, Luborsky L, Goehl L. Is the counselor an "active ingredient" in substance abuse rehabilitation? An examination of

treatment success among four counselors. J Nerv Ment Dis 1988;176:423–430.

53. Allison M, Hubbard RL. Drug abuse treatment process: a review of the literature. Int J Addict 1985;20:1321–1345.

54. Holland S. Measuring process in drug abuse treatment research. In: DeLeon G, Ziegenfuss JT, eds. Therapeutic communities for addictions: readings in theory, research and practice. Springfield, IL: Charles C Thomas, 1986.

55. Etheridge RM, Craddock SG, Dunteman GH, Hubbard RL. Treatment services in two national studies of community-based drug abuse treatment programs. J Subs Abuse 1995;7:9–26.

56. Hubbard RL, Allison M, Bray RM, Craddock SG, Rachal JV, Ginzburg HM. An overview of client characteristics, treatment services, and during treatment outcomes for outpatient methadone clinics in the Treatment Outcome Prospective Study (TOPS). In: Cooper JR, Altman F, Brown BS, Czechowicz D, eds. Research on the treatment of narcotic addiction: state of the art. Treatment research monograph series. DHHS publication no. (ADM) 83–1281. Rockville, MD: National Institute on Drug Abuse, 1983:714–751.

57. Simpson DD, Sells SB. Evaluation of drug abuse treatment effectiveness: summary of the DARP followup research. Rockville, MD: National Institute on Drug Abuse, 1982.

58. Simpson DD, Savage LJ, Sells SB. Evaluation of outcomes in the first year after drug abuse treatment: a replication study based on 1972–73 DARP admissions. IBR report no. 80–8. Fort Worth: Texas Christian University, 1980.

59. Burt Associates. Drug treatment in New York City and Washington, DC: followup studies. Rockville, MD: National Institute on Drug Abuse, 1977.

60. Hubbard RL, Marsden ME, Cavanaugh ER, Rachal JV, Ginzburg HM. Role of drug abuse treatment in limiting the spread of AIDS. Rev Infect Dis 1988;10:377–384.

61. Hubbard RL, Rachal JV, Craddock SG, Cavanaugh ER. Treatment Outcome Prospective Study (TOPS): client characteristics and behaviors before, during, and after treatment. NIDA Res Monogr 1984;51:42–68.

62. Center for Substance Abuse Treatment. The persistent effects of substance abuse treatment—one year later. Rockville, MD: Center for Substance Abuse Treatment, 1996.

63. Gerstein DR, Johnson RA, Harwood HJ, Sater N, Malloy K. Evaluating recovery services: The California drug and alcohol treatment assessment. Sacramento: California Department of Alcohol and Drug Programs, 1994.

64. Newman RG, Whitehill WB. Double-blind comparison of methadone and placebo maintenance treatments of narcotic addicts in Hong Kong. Lancet 1979;8:485–489.

65. McGlothlin WH, Anglin MD. Long-term follow-up of clients of high- and low-dose methadone programs. Arch Gen Psychiatry 1981;38:1055–1063.

66. Harwood HJ, Hubbard RL, Collins JJ, Rachal JV. The costs of crime and the benefits of drug abuse treatment: a cost-benefit analysis using TOPS data. NIDA Res Monogr 1988;86:209–235.

67. Cronkite RC, Moos RH. Determinants of the posttreatment functioning of alcoholic patients: a conceptual framework. J Consult Clin Psychol 1980;48:305–316.

68. Moos RH, Finney JW. The expanding scope of alcoholism treatment evaluation. Am Psychol 1983;38:1036–1044.

69. Tims FM, Leukefeld CG, eds. Relapse and recovery in drug abuse. DHHS publication no. (ADM) 86–1473. Research monograph series 72. Rockville, MD: National Institute on Drug Abuse, 1986.

70. Jones KR, Vischi TR. Impact of alcohol, drug abuse, and mental health treatment on medical care utilization. Med Care 1979;79:1–82.

71. Musto DF. The American disease. New Haven: Yale University Press, 1973.

72. Musto DF. The American disease. Expanded ed. New York: Oxford University Press, 1988.

73. Courtwright DT. Dark paradise: opiate addiction in America before 1940. Cambridge, MA: Harvard University Press, 1982.

74. Jaffe JH. Footnotes in the evolution of the American national response: some little known aspects of the first American strategy for drug abuse and drug traffic prevention [the Inaugural Thomas Okey Memorial Lecture]. Br J Addict 1987;82:587–600.

75. Harwood HJ, Napolitano DM, Kristiansen PL, Collins JJ. Economic costs to society of alcohol and drug abuse and mental illness: 1980. Report no. RTI/2734/00–01FR. Research Triangle Park, NC: Research Triangle Institute, 1984.

76. Clayton RR. Cocaine use in the United States: in a blizzard or just being snowed? NIDA Res Monogr 1985;61:8–34.

77. Des Jarlais DC. "Free" needles for intravenous drug users at risk for AIDS: current developments in New York City [letter]. N Engl J Med 1985;313:1476.

78. Miller JD, Cisin IH, Gardner-Keaton H, et al. National Household Survey on Drug Abuse: main findings 1982. Rockville, MD: National Institute on Drug Abuse, 1983.

79. National Institute on Drug Abuse. National Household Survey on Drug Abuse: main findings 1985. Rockville, MD: National Institute on Drug Abuse, 1987.

80. National Institute on Drug Abuse. Demographic characteristics and patterns of drug use of clients admitted to drug abuse treatment programs in selected states. Rockville, MD: U.S. Government Printing Office, 1988.

81. Jaffe JH. Evaluating drug abuse treatment: a comment on the state of the art. NIDA Res Monogr 1984;51:13–28.

82. Tims FM. Introduction. NIDA Res Monogr 1984;51:9–12.

83. Rosenbaum M, Murphy S, Beck J. Money for methadone: preliminary findings from a study of Alameda County's new maintenance policy. J Psychoactive Drugs 1987;19:13–19.

84. Price RH, Burke AC, D'Aunno T, et al. Outpatient drug abuse treatment services, 1988: results of a national survey. NIDA Res Monogr 1991;106:63–92.

85. D'Aunno T, Price RH. Organizational adaptation to changing environments: community mental health and drug abuse services. Am Behav Scientist 1985;28:669–683.

86. Marlatt GA, Gordon JR. Relapse prevention: maintenance strategies in addictive behavior change. New York: Guilford Press, 1984.

87. DeLeon G, Jainchill N. Circumstance, motivation, readiness, and suitability as correlates of treatment tenure. J Psychoactive Drugs 1986;18:203–208.

88. Biase DV, Sullivan AP, Wheeler B. Daytop Miniversity—phase 2—college training in a therapeutic community: development of self concept among drug free addict/abusers. In: DeLeon G, Ziegenfuss JT, eds. Therapeutic communities for addictions: readings in theory, research and practice. Springfield, IL: Charles C Thomas, 1986.

89. Simpson DD, Sells SB, eds. Opioid addiction and treatment: a 12-year followup. Malabar, FL: Krieger Publishing, 1990.

90. Glaser FB. Anybody got a match? Treatment research and the matching hypothesis. In: Edwards G, Grant M, eds. Alcoholism treatment in transition. Baltimore: University Park Press, 1980:178–196.

91. McLellan AT, Luborsky L, Woody GE, O'Brien CP, Druley KA. Predicting response to alcohol and drug abuse treatments. Arch Gen Psychiatry 1983;40:620–625.

92. Rounsaville BJ, Kleber HD. Psychiatric disorders in white addicts: Preliminary findings on the course and interaction with program types. In: Meyer R, ed. Psychopathy and addictive disorders. New York: Guilford Press, 1986.

93. Finney JW, Moos RH. Matching patients with treatments: conceptual and methodological issues. J Stud Alcohol 1986;47:122–134.

94. Watkins JD, et al. Report of the Presidential Commission on the Human Immunodeficiency Virus Epidemic. Washington, DC: U.S. Government Printing Office, 1988.

95. Leukefeld CG, Tims FM. An introduction to compulsory treatment for drug abuse: clinical practice and research. NIDA Res Monogr 1988;86:1–7.

96. Meyer R. Introduction: factors affecting the outcome of methadone treatment. In: Cooper JR, Altman F, Brown BS, Czechowicz D, eds. Research on the treatment of narcotic addiction: state of the art. DHHS publication no. (ADM) 83–1281. Rockville, MD: U.S. Government Printing Office, 1983:495–499.

97. Skinner HA. Profiles of treatment-seeking populations. In: Edwards G, Grant M, eds. Alcohol treatment in transition. Baltimore: University Park Press, 1981.

98. Beschner G, Thompson P. Women and drug abuse treatment: needs and services. DHHS publication no. (ADM) 81–1057. Washington, DC: U.S. Government Printing Office, 1981.

99. Finnegan LP. Women in treatment. In: DuPont RL, Goldstein A, O'Donnell J, eds. Handbook on drug abuse. Washington, DC: U.S. Government Printing Office, 1979:121–131.

100. Friedman AS, Beschner GM, eds. Treatment services for adolescent substance abusers. DHHS publication no. (ADM) 85–1342. Rockville, MD: National Institute on Drug Abuse, 1985.

101. Austin GA, Johnson BD, Carroll EE, Lettieri DJ, eds. Drugs and minorities. DHEW publication no. (ADM) 78–507. Research issues 21. Rockville, MD: National Institute on Drug Abuse, 1977.

102. Espada F. The drug abuse industry and the "minority" communities: time for change. In: Dupont RL, Goldstein A, O'Donnell J, eds. Handbook on drug abuse. Washington, DC: U.S. Government Printing Office, 1979:293–300.

103. Rosenbaum M, Murphy S. Not the picture of health: women on methadone. J Psychoactive Drugs 1987;19:217–226.

104. Reed BG. Developing women-sensitive drug dependence treatment services: why so difficult? J Psychoactive Drugs 1987;19:151–164.

105. Anglin MD, Hser Y, Booth MW. Sex differences in addict careers: treatment. Am J Drug Alcohol Abuse 1987;13:253–280.

106. DeLeon G, Rosenthal MS. Therapeutic communities. In: DuPont RL, Goldstein A, O'Donnell J, eds. Handbook on drug abuse. Washington, DC: U.S. Government Printing Office, 1979:39–47.

107. McLellan AT, Childress AR, Griffith J, Woody

GE. The psychiatrically severe drug abuse patient: methadone maintenance or therapeutic community? Am J Drug Alcohol Abuse 1984; 10:77–95.

108. McLellan AT, Luborsky L, Cacciola J, Griffith J, McGahan P, O'Brien CP. Guide to the Addiction Severity Index: background, administration, and field testing results. DHHS publication no. (ADM) 85–1419. Rockville, MD: National Institute on Drug Abuse, 1985.

109. Woody GE, McLellan AT, Luborsky L, O'Brien CP. Sociopathy and psychotherapy outcome. Arch Gen Psychiatry 1985;42:1081–1086.

110. Friedman AS, Glickman NW. Effects of psychiatric symptomatology on treatment outcome for adolescent male drug abusers. J Nerv Ment Dis 1987;175:1–6.

111. Dorus W, Senay EC. Depression, demographic dimensions, and drug abuse. Am J Psychiatry 1980;137:699–704.

112. Woody GE, Blaine J. Depression in narcotic addicts: quite possibly more than a chance association. In: DuPont RL, Goldstein A, O'Donnell J, eds. Handbook on drug abuse. Washington, DC: U.S. Government Printing Office, 1979: 277–285.

113. DeLeon G. Phoenix House: psychopathological signs among male and female drug-free residents. Addict Dis 1974;1:135–151.

114. Weissman MM, Slobetz F, Prusoff B, Mezritz M, Howard P. Clinical depression among narcotic addicts maintained on methadone in the community. Am J Psychiatry 1976;133:1434–1438.

115. Craddock SG, Bray RM, Hubbard RL. Drug use before and during drug abuse treatment: 1979–1981 TOPS admission cohorts. Rockville, MD: National Institute on Drug Abuse, 1985.

116. Hubbard RL, Marsden ME. Relapse to use of heroin, cocaine, and other drugs in the first year after treatment. NIDA Res Monogr 1986;72: 157–166.

117. Hubbard RL. Treating combined alcohol and drug abuse in community-based programs. In: Galanter M, ed. Recent developments in alcoholism. New York: Plenum Press, 1990;8: 273–283.

118. McLellan AT, Druley KA. A comparative study of response to treatment in court-referred and voluntary drug patients [brief reports].

Hosp Community Psychiatry 1977;28: 241–245.

119. Senay EC, Dorus W, Showalter C. Methadone detoxification: self versus physician regulation. Am J Drug Alcohol Abuse 1984; 10:361–374.

120. McLellan AT, Woody GE, Luborsky L, O'Brien CP, Druley KA. Increased effectiveness of substance abuse treatment: a prospective study of patient-treatment "matching." J Nerv Ment Dis 1983;171:597–605.

121. Lowinson JH, Millman RB. Clinical aspects of methadone maintenance treatment. In: DuPont RL, Goldstein A, O'Donnell J, eds. Handbook on drug abuse. Washington, DC: U.S. Government Printing Office, 1979:49–56.

122. DeLeon G. The therapeutic community for substance abuse: perspective and approach. In: DeLeon G, Ziegenfuss JT, eds. Therapeutic communities for addictions: readings in theory, research and practice. Springfield, IL: Charles C Thomas, 1986.

123. Kleber HD, Slobetz F. Outpatient drug-free treatment. In: DuPont RL, Goldstein A, O'Donnell J, eds. Handbook on drug abuse. Washington, DC: U.S. Government Printing Office, 1979:31–38.

124. Watson DD, Simpson DD, Spiegel DK. Development of a treatment typology for drug use in the DARP: 1969–1971 admissions. In: Sells SB, ed. The effectiveness of drug abuse treatment: research on patients, treatments and outcomes. Vol. 2. Cambridge, MA: Ballinger Publishing Company, 1974.

125. Cole SG, James LR. A revised treatment typology based on the DARP. Am J Drug Alcohol Abuse 1974;2:37–49.

126. Orlinsky DE, Howard KI. Process and outcome in psychotherapy. In: Garfield SL, Bergin AE, eds. Handbook of psychotherapy and behavior change. New York: Wiley, 1986.

127. Kiesler DJ. The process of psychotherapy. Chicago: Aldine, 1983.

128. Greenberg LS, Pinsof WM, eds. The psychotherapeutic process: a research handbook. New York: Guilford Press, 1986.

129. Lichtenberg JW, Heck EJ. Analysis of sequence and pattern in process research. J Counseling Psychol 1986;33:170–181.

130. Highlen PS. Analyzing patterns and sequence in counseling: reactions of a counseling process researcher. J Counseling Psychol 1986;33: 186–189.

131. Ball JC. A schema for evaluating methadone maintenance programs. In: Harris LS, ed. Problems of drug dependence 1989: proceedings of the 51st annual scientific meeting: the Committee on Problems of Drug Dependence, Inc. Research monograph series 95. Washington, DC: U.S. Government Printing Office, 1990:74–77.

132. Ball JC, Lange R, Myers P, Friedman SR. Reducing the risk of AIDS through methadone maintenance treatment. J Health Soc Behav 1988;29:214–226.

133. Magura S, Goldsmith DS, Casriel C, et al. Patient-staff governance in methadone maintenance treatment: a study in participative decision making. Int J Addict 1988;23: 253–278.

134. Aiken LS, LoSciuto LA, Ausetts MA, Brown BS. Paraprofessional versus professional drug counselors: the progress of clients in treatment. Int J Addict 1984;19:383–401.

135. Wheeler BL, Biase DV, Sullivan AP. Changes in self-concept during therapeutic community treatment: a comparison of male and female drug abusers. J Drug Educ 1986;16:191–196.

136. Joe GW, Simpson DD, Hubbard RL. Treatment predictors of time in methadone maintenance. J Subst Abuse 1991;3:73–84.

137. Joe GW, Simpson DD, Hubbard RL. Unmet service needs in methadone treatment. Int J Addict 1991;26:1–22.

138. Havassy BE, Tschann JM. Client initiative, inertia, and demographics: more powerful than treatment interventions in methadone maintenance. Int J Addict 1983;18:617–631.

139. Hunt DE, Lipton DS, Goldsmith DS, Strug DL. Problems in methadone treatment: the influence of reference groups. NIDA Res Monogr 1984;46:8–22.

140. McCrady B, Sher K. Treatment variables. NIDA Res Monogr 1985;15:48–62.

141. Marlatt GA, George WH. Relapse prevention: introduction and overview of the model. Br J Addict 1984;79:261–274.

142. Sorensen JL, Acampora A, Trier M, Gold M. From maintenance to abstinence in a therapeutic community: follow-up outcomes. J Psychoactive Drugs 1987;19:345–351.

143. McAuliffe WE, Ch'ien JMN. Recovery training and self-help: a relapse-prevention program for treated opiate addicts. J Subst Abuse Treat 1986;3:9–20.

54 MATERNAL AND NEONATAL EFFECTS OF ALCOHOL AND DRUGS

Loretta P. Finnegan and Stephen R. Kandall

Despite the acknowledgment that the use of licit and illicit substances by women in our country is increasing, the exact magnitude of the problem has been difficult to determine. It has not been widely publicized that, historically, women made up as many as two-thirds of America's opiate addicts and a significant percentage of users of cocaine, sedatives, and marihuana between 1850 and 1900 (133). Although the percentage of females in the addict population fell to about 20% during the Classic Era of drug repression (1914–1950s), it is now estimated that women represent about one-third of the drug abusers in the United States. This number would certainly be significantly higher if addiction to legal prescription medications were included, since women are overrepresented in that group of drug-dependent patients. Although "crack" cocaine use has recently declined from its peak in the late 1980s, the use of other "old" drugs such as heroin, now smoked as well as injected, and "new" drugs such as methamphetamine has increased.

Although their numbers are not exactly known, the fact that many drug-using women are of childbearing age means that large numbers of infants are being born following intrauterine drug exposure. The use of questionable epidemiological methodologies was highlighted by Dicker and Leighton (62), who found a huge disparity in "official" estimates of drug-exposed newborns born between 1979 and 1987, ranging from a low of about 13,000 to a high of about 700,000. In the late 1980s, Chasnoff (28) surveyed 36 hospitals throughout the United States and found an overall incidence of substance abuse in pregnancy, excluding alcohol, to be 11%, with an interhospital range of 0.4–27%. In his 1989 Pinellas County, Florida study, Chasnoff et al. (34) found that about 15% of the 715 urine samples screened during pregnancy were positive for illicit substances, including alcohol (1%). That study found similar rates of drug usage between "public" and "private" patients and between black and white women. Combining 27 reports published in the 1980s with existing National Institute on Drug Abuse (NIDA) data, Gomby and Shiono (98) estimated that about 2–3% of babies (75,000/year) may have been exposed to opiates during the intrauterine period, compared with 4.5% of babies (158,000/year) exposed to cocaine and 17% (611,000) to marihuana, all far less than the 73% (2.6 million) with possible exposure to alcohol.

At its 1994 conference, Drug Addiction Research and the Health of Women, NIDA presented the results of its National Pregnancy and Health Survey. Generating a probability sample of 2613 women in 52 metropolitan and nonmetropolitan hospitals, the survey estimated that 5.5%, or 222,000 of the 4 million women who give birth annually, used some illicit drug during their pregnancy. Highest estimates were found for marihuana (119,000; 2.9%) and for cocaine (45,000; 1.1%). The survey also found that estimated rates of drug use were higher for African-American women (11.3%) than for either Hispanic (4.5%) or Caucasian women (4.4%).

During the past decade, therefore, large numbers of pregnant drug-dependent women have been presenting themselves to medical facilities, some to receive ongoing prenatal care but others only to deliver their babies without the benefit of prenatal attention. Unfortunately, the threat of confrontations with legal and child protection authorities, often with punitive out-

comes, as well as the general unavailability of women-oriented treatment programs has kept many drug-dependent women from seeking general medical and prenatal care. Failure of such women to receive comprehensive health care during pregnancy is a known cause of increased morbidity and mortality in both the mother and her infant.

This chapter reviews the current literature, as well as the experiences of the authors, with regard to the sociomedical characteristics of pregnant drug-dependent women. In addition, the effects of substances of abuse on the pregnant woman, the fetus, and the newborn on immediate and long-term morbidity and mortality, and recommendations for management of both the mother and her infant are presented. Readers may refer to the recent Treatment Improvement Protocols published by the Center for Substance Abuse Treatment (CSAT) for guidelines related to management of pregnant substance-using women (176) and drug-exposed infants (132), as well as to CSAT's 1994 publication, *Practical Approaches in the Treatment of Women Who Abuse Alcohol and Other Drugs* (199). Other useful, more targeted monographs include the NIDA monographs, *Methodological Issues in Controlled Studies on Effects of Prenatal Exposure to Drug Abuse* (142) and *Methodological Issues in Epidemiological, Prevention, and Treatment Research on Drug-Exposed Women and their Children* (143), and *Medication Development for the Treatment of Pregnant Addicts and Their Infants* (41).

Throughout this discussion, because of the high incidence of polysubstance use, it is essential to remember the inherent difficulties involved in ascribing a specific perinatal effect to one specific substance. This chapter deals first with opiates (primarily heroin and methadone) and then stimulants (primarily cocaine and amphetamines). In addition, some brief comments about perinatal effects of alcohol are offered.

SOCIAL AND MEDICAL CHARACTERISTICS OF THE PREGNANT DRUG-DEPENDENT WOMAN THAT INFLUENCE THE INTRAUTERINE MILIEU

The lives of many drug-dependent women are chaotic and subject to influences that adversely affect their health and well-being. Because of preexisting conditions and ongoing active drug use, the drug-dependent woman frequently suffers from chronic anxiety and depression. Lacking self-confidence and hope for the future, these women often have interpersonal heterosexual difficulties and become victims of abuse and battering. Serious social stresses such as poverty, homelessness, and the need to engage in prostitution or other crimes to support a drug habit may overwhelm coping mechanisms and lead to involvement with the criminal justice system. Finnegan, Hagan, and Kaltenbach (82) found that 83% of addicted women coming into treatment were raised in households marked by parental chemical abuse; 67% of those women had been sexually assaulted, 60% had been physically assaulted, and almost all of the women wished that they were someone else as they were growing up. Chavkin and coworkers (38) similarly found that almost 60% of drug-dependent women in New York City had been homeless within the past 2 years, half had experienced at least one forced sexual en-

Table 54.1   Medical Complications Encountered in Pregnant Intravenous Addicts

Anemia
Bacteremia, septicemia
Cardiac disease, especially endocarditis
Cellulitis
Poor dental hygiene
Edema
Hepatitis—acute and chronic
HIV infection
Hypertension
Phlebitis
Pneumonia
Sexually transmitted diseases
Tetanus
Tuberculosis
Urinary tract infection—cystitis, urethritis, pyelonephritis

counter, and two-thirds gave histories of drug or alcohol abuse in their upbringing. Placed in the context of these serious and often crippling problems, the treatment and possible resolution of the superimposed addiction are usually complicated and require skill, understanding, compassion and patience. Addiction is a chronic, progressive, relapsing disease, and one cannot expect a smooth and rapid recovery. It should not be surprising, therefore, that the lifestyle of the pregnant user of illegal drugs has a profound influence on her psychological, social, and physiological well-being.

It is well known that medical complications compromise many drug-involved pregnancies (Table 54.1). Sexually transmitted diseases have played an increasingly important role in this spectrum of diseases. Of most concern is the fact that human immunodeficiency virus (HIV) disease has been significantly linked to drug use. The practices of sharing contaminated needles to inject drugs, engaging in prostitution to buy drugs, or conducting direct sex-for-drugs transactions associated with "crack" smoking have all contributed to this serious international health crisis. Currently, the spread of HIV disease is linked less to homosexual than to heterosexual transmission. Although the exact risk of an infected mother's passing the disease to her offspring during the perinatal period is not precisely known, it is estimated that approximately 25–30% of infants exposed in this fashion will actually contract the acquired immune deficiency syndrome (AIDS). A landmark study from April 1991 to June 1994 by the National Institute of Allergy and Infectious Diseases (ACTG 076) showed that administration of zidovudine (AZT) to the woman beginning at 14–34 weeks of pregnancy and to the infant for 6 weeks after birth reduced the risk of perinatal HIV transmission by about two-thirds. In addition to AIDS prevention counseling, therefore, retention of women in prenatal care provides the matrix in which services must be offered to pregnant substance-abusing women or women involved in close relationships with addicted men.

The drug-dependent pregnant woman may develop a range of nutritional deficiencies as a result of either preoccupation with drug seeking at the expense of food intake, inhibition of the central mechanism that controls appetite and hunger, or toxic interference with the absorption or utilization of ingested nutrients. Abnormalities of nutrient absorption are common in drug addicts because of the high incidence of lesions of the intestine, liver, and pancreas. Hepatitis, a frequent complication of abuse of injectable drugs, is nutritionally depleting because it causes a loss of protein, vitamins, minerals, and trace elements. Iron and folic acid deficiencies may be seen, and peripheral neuritis resulting from thiamine, vitamin B_6, pantothenic acid, or nicotinic acid depletion may occur. Hypoglycemia, vitamin B_6 deficiency, thiamine depletion, or magnesium deficiency may cause seizures in both alcoholics and drug addicts. Intensive dietary therapy is therefore desirable in drug and alcohol addiction, and parenteral therapy may be necessary to correct fluid, mineral, and vitamin deficits in acutely ill patients.

Chronic heroin addicts have been said to show frequent endocrine aberrations, including amenorrhea, anovulation, and infertility, possibly through depression of adrenocorticotropic hormone (ACTH) release and adrenal function, as well as ovulation. The women themselves believe that amenor-

rhea and infertility always occur when they are using substantial amounts of heroin. Wallach et al. (260), however, found that women maintained on methadone have regular menstruation, ovulation, and apparently normal pregnancies. Other investigators also support the use of methadone to normalize the mother's endocrinological status and to promote more normal pregnancies (50, 51, 57, 80, 110, 134, 186, 244, 245). When it occurs, severe dysmenorrhea is most likely due to pelvic inflammatory disease.

In addition to these many potential medical problems, the lifestyle of the addict is also detrimental to herself and to society. To meet the high cost of maintaining a drug habit, the pregnant drug-dependent woman must often indulge in criminal activities such as the sale of drugs, prostitution, robbery, or forgery. Because most of her day is consumed by the two activities of either obtaining drugs or using drugs, she spends most of her time unable to function in the usual activities of daily living. The opiate addict will have intermittent periods of normal alertness and well-being, but for most of the day she will either be "high" or "sick." The "high," or euphoric state, will keep her sedated or tranquilized, absorbed in herself, and incapable of fulfilling familial responsibility. The "sick" stage, or the periods during which she is going through abstinence symptoms, generally is characterized by craving for narcotics accompanied by malaise, nausea, lacrimation, perspiration, tremors, vomiting, diarrhea, and cramps. The cocaine user may go on "binges" of drug use, resulting in lack of sleep, poor nutrition, and potentially acute life-threatening complications such as hypertensive crises, cerebrovascular accidents, and seizures.

Because of her lifestyle and because she may fear calling attention to her drug habit, the pregnant addict often does not seek prenatal care. The physician or nurse should be able to determine that the woman is drug-addicted by taking a thorough history and conducting a careful physical examination. There may be no experiences of prenatal care, either in a hospital setting or in a private physician's office. A history of sexually transmitted diseases may be obtained. Tattoos or self-scarring of the body to disguise needle marks may be evident. Because of diminished pain perception when smoking while "high," burns of the fingertips and cigarette burns of the clothes may be found. The use of poorly cleaned needles or shared needles predisposes these women to serum hepatitis evidenced by jaundiced skin or sclera.

Additional history taking may reveal that she may have several other children who are currently not living with her but instead with a relative or in placement. Housing situations frequently are chaotic, and plans for the impending birth of the child often have not been considered. Drug-dependent women frequently are intelligent, although in a Philadelphia series at Family Center the average level of high school achievement was the 11th grade (104). Chavkin et al. (38) also found that the average number of educational years among their female addicts was 11.5.

Drug dependence in the pregnant woman is not only detrimental to her own physical condition but is also potentially dangerous to that of the fetus and eventually to the newborn infant. Obstetrical complications that are associated with heroin addiction are listed in Table 54.2. Most of these pregnancy-related problems can be diagnosed and treated antenatally, reinforcing the importance of enlisting and retaining drug-dependent women in prenatal care throughout the pregnancy (176).

Table 54.2   Obstetrical Complications Associated With Heroin Addiction[a]

Abortion (spontaneous early loss)
Amnionitis
Intrauterine death (late)
Intrauterine growth retardation
Placental insufficiency
Postpartum hemorrhage
Preeclampsia, eclampsia
Premature labor
Premature rupture of membranes
Septic thrombophlebitis

[a]Adapted from Finnegan LP, ed. Drug dependence in pregnancy: clinical management of mother and child. A manual for medical professionals and paraprofessionals prepared for the National Institute on Drug Abuse, Services Research Branch, Rockville, MD. Washington, DC: Government Printing Office, 1978.

NORMALIZING THE INTRAUTERINE MILIEU

Since pregnant drug-abusing women are afflicted with numerous and potentially overwhelming problems, most experts advocate the provision of a comprehensive approach that will specifically meet the various needs of these women (176, 199). It should also be acknowledged, however, that some women might find this approach overwhelming and thus prefer a more targeted strategy aimed at solving specific lifestyle problems.

The primary focus of a program of comprehensive care for the pregnant drug abuser should be addiction treatment in a setting in which medical, obstetrical, and psychosocial treatment and long-term planning for the mother and her newborn infant are provided. The underlying assumptions regarding drug treatment during pregnancy have changed, however, over the past 25 years. In 1972, the American Medical Association's Council on Mental Health and the Committee on Alcoholism and Drug Dependence recommended that a pregnant drug-dependent woman should undergo withdrawal prior to delivery. If there was insufficient time to accomplish withdrawal before delivery, the woman could be maintained on opiates during labor and then withdrawn after the delivery process (254). Current recommendations acknowledge that achieving the drug-free state is probably impossible for the large majority of opiate-addicted women. Most experts, therefore, have come to advocate methadone maintenance as a way of reducing illegal drug use, removing the woman from a drug-seeking environment, preventing fluctuations of drug levels throughout the day, improving maternal nutrition, increasing the likelihood of prenatal care, enhancing the woman's ability to prepare for the birth of her baby, reducing obstetrical complications, and offering the pregnant heroin addict an opportunity to restructure her life with a goal to continued stabilization after pregnancy (176). Although methadone maintenance as a treatment modality in and of itself has been extremely beneficial in the treatment of addiction during pregnancy, investigators stress that provision of psychosocial support in a structured treatment setting is extremely important (50, 57, 80, 111).

Although methadone maintenance during pregnancy is clearly the treatment of choice, a small number of highly motivated women or those facing logistical or geographic barriers to methadone maintenance may be candidates for medical withdrawal during pregnancy. The CSAT Consensus Panel recommended that undertaking a medical withdrawal regimen could be most safely accomplished during the second trimester with careful monitoring of fetal welfare by perinatal experts (176). The panel advised that opiate withdrawal was best accomplished through stabilization with methadone followed by gradual reduction of the methadone dosage by 2–2.5 mg every 7–10 days. At Beth Israel Medical Center in New York, between April 1993 and December 1995, 264 women were admitted for medical drug withdrawal during pregnancy. Of that group, 50 women were heroin users, 37 used both heroin and cocaine, and 11 were considered heavy users of heroin, cocaine, and alcohol. Using a multidisciplinary approach including obstetrical and neonatal consultation, substance abuse treatment and counseling, and a women's support group, the Beth Israel staff has found that medical withdrawal, although not usually recommended, can be safely accomplished.

A substantial experience with methadone maintenance during pregnancy has now been accumulated. In 1972, Statzer and Wardell (242) developed a specialized program of prenatal care for the high-risk mother at the Hutzel Hospital in Detroit. In addition to receiving regular prenatal care, patients were seen by a nutritionist, social worker, public health nurse, and staff with specialized training in the psychological needs of the heroin user. From that program's experience, Strauss et al. (245) concluded that low-dose methadone maintenance in conjunction with comprehensive prenatal care reduced obstetrical risk to a level comparable to that of nonaddicted women of similar socioeconomic circumstances.

Working at Beth Israel Medical Center in New York City, Blinick et al. (19, 20) found that methadone maintenance eliminated maternal mortality and reduced complication rates of pregnancy and fetal wastage in 105 women. Although one-third of the infants were low birth weight, no serious effects attributable to methadone in the neonatal period were reported; follow-up of a small number of the infants revealed normal growth and development. Harper et al. (111) organized the Family and Maternity Care Program for pregnant addicts, their spouses, and their newborn infants at the State University of New York Downstate Medical Center in Brooklyn. Low-dose methadone maintenance coupled with intense psychosocial support appeared to alleviate many of the common problems associated with addiction in pregnancy. Although the regimen failed to prevent withdrawal in the newborn infant, the withdrawal was not associated with an increase in mortality or prolonged morbidity.

Kandall et al. (134), working in conjunction with the Bronx State Methadone Program, studied 230 infants born to drug-dependent women and 33 infants born to ex-addicts between 1971 and 1974. Compared with heroin use, methadone maintenance was associated with more consistent prenatal care, more normal fetal growth, and reduced fetal mortality. Meconium staining of amniotic fluid was more common in infants exposed to heroin and heroin-methadone, but not in those infants in the well-controlled methadone group. In this program, neonatal withdrawal from methadone seemed to be more severe than that from heroin, but severity of the withdrawal did not correlate with late pregnancy maternal methadone dosage. In New York City as a whole, Newman (186) reported an extraordinarily high retention rate (95%) in the city's methadone treatment programs after delivery.

In Philadelphia, Connaughton et al. (50) developed Family Center, a comprehensive approach that has been used through the present time to care for more than 2500 pregnant addicted women. Combining methadone maintenance with consultations with obstetricians, medical consultants, psychiatric social workers, public health nurses, community workers, and psychiatrists, management of addiction is individualized to the patient's needs. Although most patients have chosen methadone maintenance, some patients have become drug-free, whereas others have been placed on a regimen of medical withdrawal from methadone, if deemed medically safe. Those patients who are to be methadone-maintained are hospitalized and started on 10 mg of methadone daily, and the dose is titrated upward to prevent withdrawal symptomatology. Depending on the length of the woman's addiction, the duration of time in methadone treatment, the concomitant use of other drugs, and her own metabolic state, homeostasis can usually be achieved with doses from 35 to 80 mg daily. Recently, however, an increasing number of women have required higher doses of methadone for stabilization. Family Center's multidisciplinary approach, combining outreach services with individual and interpersonal interventions to comprehensively address biological/physiological issues, psychological/behavioral/cognitive function, sociocultural demographic issues, mother-infant interaction, and early childhood development, has significantly reduced the maternal and infant morbidity that previously have been associated with pregnancies complicated by opiate addiction.

METHADONE MAINTENANCE

Although methadone therapy has been used during pregnancy for about 30 years, no randomized trials comparing dosing regimens have been published on which to base specific therapeutic recommendations. In general, clinicians have tended to use doses that are individually determined and will keep the woman and fetus subjectively and objectively comfortable and medically stable. Although the health and comfort of the pregnant substance-using woman remain paramount considerations, higher doses of methadone (50–150 mg/day) early in pregnancy have been reported to be associated with more normal fetal growth (135). Data on the relationship between maternal methadone doses, especially late in pregnancy, and subsequent severity of neonatal abstinence have been contradictory (see section on abstinence).

Plasma methadone levels during pregnancy show marked intrapatient and interpatient variability and usually are somewhat lower than those prior to pregnancy (198). This decrease can be explained by an increased fluid space, a large tissue reservoir (69), and altered drug metabolism by the placenta and fetus. These data suggest that pregnant women may need increasing methadone doses during gestation and that lowering the dosage in an attempt to minimize complications of the therapy would be medically inappropriate. Treatment with other drugs, such as tranquilizers, are strictly avoided unless the patient is addicted to these medications. In case of such addiction, the patient is transferred to a special detoxification ward where she can be safely weaned from drugs potentially more dangerous than opiates.

Regardless of the dosing regimen, every woman should receive a detailed health history, comprehensive physical examination, and a family psychosocial, medical, and substance-using history (on the father also) (176). An initial laboratory evaluation includes drug screening and blood work (blood group, Rh factor, and antibody screen; rubella immune status; serological test for syphilis; hepatitis B surface antigen screen; complete blood count; baseline liver function tests; baseline renal function tests). Other indicated tests include cervical cytology, cervical culture for gonorrhea, and chlamydia screen; hemoglobin electrophoresis, as indicated; tuberculin testing; and baseline sonogram. Optional studies, such as HTLV-1 testing, diabetic screening, maternal serum α-fetoprotein, and TORCH studies, may also be considered. HIV education and counseling are essential, and maternal testing should be strongly advised as part of a campaign to achieve universal voluntary testing. The patient should meet with other professionals involved in the program, including the neonatologist, public health nurse, community worker, obstetrician, and social worker, all of whom may be interacting with the patient during her hospital stay.

During labor, the patient is generally managed like any other parturient. Physicians in charge of the labor floor are made aware of her drug use, and an effort is made to start conduction anesthesia as early as possible to avoid the use of narcotic analgesics. The last dose of methadone is recorded, and, if necessary, methadone is given to the patient for analgesia and prevention of withdrawal symptoms. Since administration of Narcan (naloxone) or any other narcotic antagonist to an opiate-dependent woman in labor may result in stillbirth from fetal withdrawal, as well as more severe neonatal symptomatology immediately after birth, its use is contraindicated except as a last resort to reverse severe narcotic overdose.

IMPACT OF MATERNAL NARCOTIC USE ON FETAL WELFARE

Because of the obvious lack of quality control seen in street narcotics, the pregnant woman frequently may experience repeated episodes of withdrawal and overdose. Maternal narcotic withdrawal has been associated with the occurrence of stillbirth (51, 212). Severe maternal withdrawal is associated with increased muscular activity, metabolic rate, and oxygen consumption. At the same time, fetal activity also increases, and the increased oxygen needs of the fetus may not be met if labor contractions coincide with abstinence symptoms in the mother. As the pregnancy proceeds, the fetal metabolic rate and oxygen consumption increase; therefore, a pregnant woman undergoing severe abstinence symptoms during the latter part of pregnancy would be less likely to supply the withdrawing fetus with the oxygen it needs than would an addict in the first trimester of pregnancy (212).

Fetal Growth. Abundant animal laboratory evidence suggests that heroin directly causes fetal growth retardation; this observation is well supported by human data (80, 91, 113, 186, 272). Although earlier reports did not differentiate between premature infants and term infants who were small for gestational age, it is now evident that many of these low-birth-weight infants were, in fact, small for gestational age. Naeye et al. (181) found that infants born to heroin addicts were, as a group, growth-retarded, with all of their organs affected. Naeye observed that the small size of many of these organs in infants exposed to heroin was mainly due to a subnormal number of cells; this finding could not be explained by maternal undernutrition. Nearly 60% of the mothers or their newborn infants, most of whom delivered prematurely, showed evidence of acute infection. The placentas of the heroin-exposed infants commonly revealed meconium histiocytosis, suggesting that episodes of distress had occurred during fetal life.

In an analysis of 338 neonates, Kandall et al. (135) found that the mean birth weight of infants born to mothers using heroin during the pregnancy was 2490 g, an effect primarily due to intrauterine growth retardation. Low mean birth weight was also seen both in infants born to mothers who had used heroin only prior to this pregnancy (2615 g) and mothers who had used both heroin and methadone during the pregnancy (2535 g). Infants born to mothers on methadone maintenance during the pregnancy, however, had sig-

nificantly higher mean birth weights (2961 g), although they remained lower than those of the control group (3176 g). A highly linear significant relationship accounting for 27% of the variance was observed between maternal methadone dosage in the first trimester and birth weight. This study thus suggested that methadone administration to opiate-addicted mothers may promote fetal growth in a dose-related fashion.

In a subsequent study of 150 drug-exposed mother-infant pairs and 150 controls, Doberczak et al. (68) found that the mean birth weight of the drug-dependent infants was 2800 g, significantly less than the 3248 g mean birth weight of the controls. Low birth weight was primarily due to intrauterine growth retardation (20% in drug-exposed group versus 4% in controls); mean gestational age did not differ between the two groups. In addition, mean head circumference of the drug-exposed group was 32.6 cm, significantly less than the 33.8 cm mean head circumference of controls. This study thus documented a pattern of symmetric or proportional growth retardation in a large series of drug-exposed infants.

Various other parameters to assess fetal welfare have been studied in the drug-abusing pregnant woman: prostaglandin levels, corticosteroid production, estriol excretion, heat-stable alkaline phosphatase enzyme levels, liver function studies, serum immunoglobulin M (IgM) levels, and lecithin/sphingomyelin ratios in amniotic fluid. Singh and Zuspan (236) found no significant differences in the levels of amniotic fluid prostaglandins in normal, diabetic, and drug-associated human pregnancies. Glass et al. (94) found that addicted mothers had significantly lower corticosteroid concentrations than nonaddicted mothers; serum cortisol levels were comparable in both drug-exposed and control infants, however, perhaps because of a decreased responsiveness of the fetal pituitary to heroin or a relative insensitivity of the fetal adrenal cortex to fluctuations in ACTH secretion. Studies by Northrop et al. (187) on estriol excretion profiles and by Harper et al. (111) on heat-stable alkaline phosphatase have suggested that chronic narcotic administration may affect the maternal-placental-fetal unit in more subtle ways than have previously been considered. In a study of one pregnant methadone-maintained woman, Zuspan et al. (277) found that methadone detoxification during the second trimester of pregnancy was associated with a marked fetal response of the adrenal gland (increase in epinephrine) and sympathetic nervous system (increase in norepinephrine) that was blunted when the methadone dose was increased. These investigators concluded that detoxification during pregnancy was not recommended unless the fetus could be carefully monitored biochemically.

Amniotic fluid lecithin/sphingomyelin (L/S) ratios as a marker of fetal lung maturity were found to be increased in 10 narcotic-addicted pregnancies compared with controls (95). This finding may correlate with animal studies by Roloff et al. (217) and Taeusch et al. (251) that demonstrated accelerated lung maturation in narcotic-exposed fetuses, as well as a reduction in prematurity-related lung disease clinically observed by Glass et al. (93).

Laboratory and animal studies have shown that narcotics may have an inhibitory effect on enzymes of oxidative metabolism and oxygen-carrying cytochromes. Narcotics also alter fetal-placental perfusion by constricting the umbilical vessels and decreasing fetal brain oxygenation. These metabolic side effects may cause a decrease in oxygen availability to and utilization by the fetus, resulting in fetal hypoxia or acidosis. Chang et al. (27) reported that nalorphine, pethidine, morphine, and heroin each caused a decrease in pH and an increase in pCO_2 in the maternal blood and an independent decrease in pH and base excess in the fetal scalp blood. This was thought to be due to the respiratory depressant effect of the drugs, supporting the suggestion that narcotic agents may have subtle adverse metabolic effects on the fetus.

Archie et al. (5) found a significant decrease in fetal movements and cardiac accelerations on nonstress testing following administration of a methadone dose (mean dose 26 mg) to 30 women at a mean time of 34 weeks gestation. Richardson et al. (215), in a study of 6 methadone-maintained patients at between 28 and 40 weeks gestation, found that fetal breathing movements were decreased both before and after maternal methadone administration compared to controls; fetal respiratory responses were also blunted after administration of 5% carbon dioxide to the mothers.

The authors suggested that this blunted response may be predictive of subsequent respiratory regulatory abnormalities such as SIDS. Wittman et al. (269) found that a single dose of methadone averaging 40 mg (range 30–75 mg) significantly reduced fetal activity and respiratory activity and increased periods of inactivity 1 hour after administration of the medication. Split dosing every 12 hours, however, was associated with an insignificant change in parameters monitored. These studies suggest that certain women might benefit from split-dosing of daily methadone in achieving more optimal fetal stability.

Little information is available regarding the intrapartum course of opiate-using women. Silver et al. (233) reported that the duration of the first, second, and third stages of labor was similar in 112 drug-dependent women and 224 controls. The rate of cesarean sections and complications of labor also did not differ between the groups. Drug-dependent women, however, received more analgesia and anesthesia, specifically epidural anesthesia, which the authors speculated might have reduced perineal sensation and maternal bearing down, accounting for an increase in forceps deliveries.

Transition from intrauterine to extrauterine life usually proceeds smoothly in the opiate-exposed infant. As a measure of this transition, Apgar scores are usually normal. Kandall et al. (134) reported that meconium staining is seen more commonly in the setting of maternal heroin abuse than with methadone maintenance, reflecting the more stable intrauterine milieu in the latter. Airway toilet and mechanical aspiration of meconium and secretions from the infant's airway should be carried out with equipment that protects the resuscitator's mouth from blood and secretions. Universal precautions for handling of all newborn infants should be stressed in this population because of the increased risk of hepatitis B and HIV transmission.

Abrams (1), in a study of 34 pregnant addicts who used heroin and methadone, concluded that infants exposed predominantly to heroin in utero showed a significant increase in the frequency of chromosomal aberrations (dicentrics and rings) in their peripheral blood compared with controls, whereas infants exposed predominantly to methadone in utero did not. Adverse environmental factors that may have contributed to the abnormal cytogenetic findings in the heroin-exposed infants, however, were less prominent in the methadone-exposed infants. Amarose and Norusis (4) found chromosomal abnormalities in about 10% of the 27,907 cells scored in 80 methadone-managed and heroin-addicted pregnant women and their newborn infants. Chromosome damage was random, affected all chromosomes, and was mainly of the acentric fragment type. The percentage of hypodiploidy was significantly higher than the percentage of hyperdiploidy. In the mothers, no significant relationship was found between infant chromosome damage and maternal variables such as dose and duration of methadone treatment and years of heroin abuse. Dar et al. (55) found an increased frequency of abnormal palmar creases in a variety of at-risk groups (prematurity, intrauterine growth delay, pregnancy complications, and methadone exposure), as well as an apparent association of interrupted transverse creases with intrauterine methadone exposure. Based on such studies, concern has been raised that drug abuse may produce irreversible fetal chromosome damage. Considering the many high-risk variables frequently associated with drug-involved pregnancies, and most notably in the absence of any specific teratology in drug-exposed infants, it has thus far been impossible to link either methadone or heroin with clinically evident genetic damage.

Rementeria et al. (211) reported that multiple births in a small series of 126 drug-addicted women occurred at a threefold greater rate than that seen in the general population. The authors postulated that methadone and heroin may directly affect the ovary to stimulate the release of extra follicles. Although confirmatory studies regarding twinnings have not been published, Milstein et al. (173) reported that drug addicts using heroin for more than 2 years show increased mitotic indices and chromosomal replications in their peripheral lymphocytes; heroin may act directly on the ovaries in a similar manner. The pharmacological effect of these narcotics, however, may also be indirect, through stimulation of the pituitary by way of the hypothalamus, to release gonadotropins (as in the case of clomiphene), which, in turn, will cause the release of multiple ova.

ACUTE MORBIDITY AND MORTALITY IN THE INFANT BORN TO THE NARCOTIC-DEPENDENT WOMAN

Many of the medical complications seen in the neonates of heroin-dependent women are secondary to low birth weight and prematurity. Therefore, in addition to the neonatal abstinence syndrome, conditions such as asphyxia neonatorum, intracranial hemorrhage, nutritional deprivation, hypoglycemia, hypocalcemia, septicemia, and hyperbilirubinemia should be anticipated in opiate-exposed low-birth-weight babies. Because infants born to women who receive methadone maintenance are more apt to have higher birth weights and a decreased incidence of premature birth, medical complications in that group of infants generally reflect (a) the amount of prenatal care that the mother has received, (b) whether she has suffered particular obstetrical or medical complications, such as hypertension or toxemia of pregnancy, placental accidents, or infection, and, most importantly, (c) multiple drug use that may produce an unstable intrauterine milieu complicated by withdrawal and overdose.

Connaughton et al. (51), working at Family Center in Philadelphia, found that morbidity in infants born to drug-dependent women was dependent on the amount of prenatal care as well as the kind of dependence (heroin versus methadone). More than three-quarters of infants born to heroin addicts without prenatal care, as well as those born to methadone-maintained women with suboptimal prenatal care, suffered neonatal morbidity. This morbidity was somewhat decreased in infants born to methadone-maintained women who had received adequate prenatal care. Mean duration of hospitalization was 17 days for infants of methadone-maintained mothers and 27 days for infants of heroin-addicted mothers.

At that same program, data on 278 infants born to drug-dependent women and 1586 control infants from the general population delivering at the same hospital revealed an increased incidence of low birth weight and neonatal mortality in the infants of drug-dependent women (86). A study of infants born to heroin- and methadone-dependent mothers (the latter a stratified group of women having inadequate and adequate prenatal care) revealed an overall mortality incidence of 5.4% compared with 1.6% in controls. In low-birth-weight infants, mortality in the drug-dependent population reached 13.3%, compared with 10% in the controls. Within the methadone-dependent group, better outcomes were achieved with adequate prenatal care. Overall mortality in the methadone/inadequate care group was 10%, compared with 3% in the methadone/adequate prenatal care group and 4.8% in the heroin-dependent group. The same trend was found in the mortality rates seen in the low-birth-weight infants. These data confirmed that comprehensive care for pregnant drug-dependent women significantly reduced the morbidity and mortality in both the mother and the infant.

Detailed neuropathological studies were performed following death of 10 of the infants in the previous study (218). Eight categories of lesions were found, three of which were thought to bear some specific relationship to maternal drug dependence. These lesions included gliosis (5), foci of old infarction (4), and developmental retardation of the brain (3). In addition, minor microscopic brain malformations were found in three cases. Other lesions identified included those common to high-risk neonates: germinal plate hemorrhage (7), acute brain necrosis with and without hemorrhage (5), germinal plate cysts (4), and focal subarachnoid hemorrhages (3). Although the majority of the findings may be due to nonspecific secondary gestational complications, these neuropathological findings suggest primary and specific effects of addictive drugs on the developing nervous system. Further studies, including those that utilize an animal model, are necessary to define further the possible relationship of maternal addiction to neuropathological injury in the neonate.

NEONATAL NARCOTIC ABSTINENCE SYNDROME
Description of Symptomatology

During the 1950s and 1960s, numerous reports in the medical literature described the symptoms of heroin abstinence in the newborn (45, 99, 115, 152, 238). Since that time, increasing numbers of reports have described the neonatal abstinence syndrome resulting from combinations of heroin and methadone dependence exposure during pregnancy (61, 76, 134, 192, 209, 223, 271).

Table 54.3   Pharmacological Agents That May Cause Abstinence Symptoms in the Neonate

Alcohol
Amphetamines
Barbiturates
Bromides
Chlordiazepoxide (Librium)
Diazepam (Valium)
Diphenhydramine hydrochloride (Benadryl)
Ethchlorvynol (Placidyl)
Glutethimide (Doriden)
Hydroxyzine hydrochloride (Atarax)
Imipramine (Pertofrane)
Opioids—opium, meperidine, methadone, morphine
Pentazocine (Talwin)
Propoxyphene hydrochloride (Darvon)

Table 54.4   Abstinence Symptoms in the Neonatal Period: Frequency Seen in 138 Newborns at Family Center Program in Philadelphia

Symptoms	Frequency (%)
Tremors	
Mild/disturbed	96
Mild/undisturbed	95
Marked/disturbed	77
Marked/undisturbed	67
High-pitched cry	95
Continuous high-pitched cry	54
Sneezing	83
Increased muscle tone	82
Frantic sucking of fists	79
Regurgitation	74
Sleeps < 3 hours after feeding	65
Sleeps < 2 hours after feeding	66
Sleeps < 1 hour after feeding	58
Respiratory rate > 60/minute	66
Poor feeding	65
Hyperactive Moro reflex	62
Loose stools	51
Sweating	49
Excoriation	43
Mottling	33
Nasal stuffiness	33
Frequent yawning	30
Fever < 101° F	29
Respiratory rate > 60/minute, retractions	28
Markedly hyperactive Moro reflex	15
Projectile vomiting	12
Watery stools	12
Fever > 101° F	3
Dehydration	1
Generalized convulsions	1

Clear delineation of narcotic-related abstinence has been made more difficult by the recognition that a number of nonnarcotic drugs are capable of causing fetal dependence and subsequent neonatal abstinence (Table 54.3). In addition to the barbiturates (21, 60), certain sedatives, minor tranquilizers, and stimulants have been incriminated, including amphetamines, bromide, chlordiazepoxide (Librium), diazepam (Valium), diphenhydramine hydrochloride (Benadryl), ethchlorvynol (Placidyl), glutethimide (Doriden), hydroxyzine hydrochloride (Atarax), imipramine (Pertofrane), pentazocine (Talwin), and propoxyphene hydrochloride (Darvon) (6, 59, 72, 73, 96, 189, 200–202, 207, 210, 213, 224, 256). Alcohol (49, 197) has also been reported to produce neonatal withdrawal symptomatology. A study of 60 drug-dependent infants randomly chosen from 275 consecutive births in the Philadelphia comprehensive care methadone maintenance program between 1975 and 1979 indicated that changing patterns of polydrug abuse markedly increased the duration of pharmacotherapy needed for control of neonatal abstinence associated with maternal methadone administration (85).

Neonatal narcotic abstinence syndrome is described as a generalized disorder characterized by signs and symptoms of central nervous system hyper-irritability, gastrointestinal dysfunction, respiratory distress, and autonomic symptoms that include yawning, sneezing, mottling, and fever (Table 54.4).

Central Nervous System. Opiate-exposed infants tend initially to develop mild high-frequency, low-amplitude tremors that progress in severity if untreated. High-pitched cry, increased muscle tone, irritability, increased deep tendon reflexes, and an exaggerated Moro reflex are all characteristic of neonatal abstinence. These infants show an exaggerated rooting reflex and a voracious appetite manifested as sucking of fists or thumbs, yet when feedings are administered, the infants may have extreme difficulty because of an ineffectual sucking reflex and incoordination of the suck-swallow mechanism. Feeding may be so impaired that formula may have to be "milked" into the infant. Kron et al. (151) found that both heroin-exposed and methadone-exposed infants showed reductions in sucking rates and pressures, disordered sucking organization, and reduction in amounts of nutrients consumed.

Seizures may occur as the most dramatic drug-associated central nervous system abnormality. Reported incidences of seizures vary among published series, perhaps because these seizures may be subtle. In addition, recommended treatment for neonatal abstinence often calls for tightly swaddling the infant in a darkened room, exactly those conditions that could lead to failure to note seizure movements. Zelson et al. (271, 272) found that seizures were seen more frequently in infants of methadone-dependent mothers compared to heroin-exposed infants. Finnegan (79) found that 1% of infants who had withdrawn from heroin and/or methadone had evidenced generalized seizures. Davis et al. (56) observed myoclonic jerks in 7 of 49 methadone-exposed babies and tonic-clonic seizures in 5 others, whereas they observed myoclonic jerks in 2 of 21 heroin-exposed infants and tonic-clonic seizures in 1 additional infant.

The most extensive report on abstinence-associated seizures was published by Herzlinger et al. (114). Among 302 neonates passively exposed to narcotics during pregnancy, 18 (5.9%) had seizures that were attributed to withdrawal. Of these 18 infants, 10 were among the 127 infants (7.8%) exposed to methadone, 4 were among the 78 (5.1%) exposed to methadone and heroin, and 3 were among the 14 (21.4%) exposed to "other" drugs taken during pregnancy. There was no apparent relationship between maternal methadone dose (10–100 mg/day) and the frequency or severity of seizures, and no correlations were found between seizures and birth weight, gestational age, occurrence of other withdrawal symptoms, day of onset of withdrawal symptoms, or the need for specific pharmacological treatment. All infants with seizures manifested other withdrawal symptoms prior to the initial seizure. Only 2 of 48 infants initially treated for withdrawal with paregoric subsequently developed seizures, compared with 5 of the 12 infants initially treated with diazepam. Seizures occurred at a mean age of 10 days, with a range of 3–34 days. Generalized motor seizures or rhythmic myoclonic jerks, each of which occurred in 7 infants, were the principal seizure manifestations. In some, however, seizure manifestations were complex, and 3 of the 18 had refractory seizure activity. Paregoric was more effective than diazepam in controlling both initial and subsequent seizure episodes. Six EEGs were normal after clinical seizures had ceased. Of 7 EEGs obtained during the acute withdrawal stage, 1 was normal, 2 had clinical seizures associated with extensive movement artifacts, 3 showed either unifocal or multifocal discharges preceding and accompanying clinical seizures, and 1 showed a persistent right central sharp wave focus associated with a bifrontal slow dysrhythmia, which returned to normal after cessation of clinical seizures. Although some reports have indicated uncertainty with regard to the mechanism of neonatal myoclonic jerks in the neonatal abstinence syndrome (111, 127, 157), the report by Herzlinger et al. (114) suggests that such movements are true seizures.

In a subsequent study, Kandall et al. (136) studied 153 infants born following intrauterine opiate exposure. Twelve (7.8%) of those 153 infants demonstrated neonatal seizures that could not be otherwise explained. Seizures were unrelated to maternal age, parity, last methadone dosage, length of drug use, degree of polydrug use, gender, gestational age, 1-minute Apgar score, time of initial treatment, or severity of abstinence. However, the seizure group did have lower 5-minute Apgar scores, suggesting that mild asphyxia may potentiate abstinence-associated seizures. Mean time of seizure onset was 9.7 days, with a range of 5–26 days. Noteworthy was the observation that none of the 49 infants treated with paregoric developed seizures, while 7 of the 62 phenobarbital-treated infants developed seizures. The authors postulated that phenobarbital doses used to control abstinence (see below) were not adequate to provide antiseizure prophylaxis in the face of enhanced methadone clearance induced by phenobarbital.

The only follow-up of infants with abstinence-associated seizures was published by Doberczak et al. (66). Despite abnormal neurological examinations in 8 of 12 infants early in life, all neurological examinations and EEG tracings normalized during the first year of life. Infant assessment remained normal during the first year of life and did not differ either from passively addicted infants without seizures or from published norms. This short-term favorable prognosis suggests that the pathophysiological mechanism of these seizures differs from that associated with more ominous types of neonatal seizures.

In a study of ten narcotic-exposed infants, Sisson et al. (237) found that narcotics obliterate rapid eye movement (REM) sleep in the neonate, that withdrawal prevents normal adequate periods of deep sleep in such infants, that proper therapy causes the return of REM and deep sleep cycles, and that the maintenance of therapy can be best regulated by interpretation of polygraphic recordings rather than reliance on the observed absence of more gross signs and symptoms of withdrawal. Schulman (229) reported the absence of quiet sleep and a significant decrease in REM sleep in eight full-term, heroin-exposed infants who had evidence of mild withdrawal but did not require medication. Pasto et al. (196) studied serial cerebral sonographic characteristics of methadone-exposed infants at birth, 1 month, and 6 months of age. Methadone-exposed infants showed significantly increased incidences of slit-like ventricles at all three examinations. Although the pathophysiology of this abnormality is not clear, neither cerebral edema nor increased intracranial pressure could be demonstrated.

Gastrointestinal Tract. Regurgitation, projectile vomiting, and loose stools may be seen in the course of neonatal abstinence. Dehydration resulting from poor intake, coupled with increased losses from the gastrointestinal tract, may cause excessive weight loss, electrolyte imbalance, shock, coma, and death. Weinberger et al. (264) found that drug-exposed newborns who developed mild abstinence not requiring specific pharmacotherapy lost an average of only 4% of birth weight, reached a weight nadir on day 3 and regained birth weight by day 7 of life. Newborns displaying more severe abstinence lost more weight and did not regain birth weight until an average of 2 weeks of age. These data suggest that timely and appropriate pharmacological control of abstinence, as well as provision of extra fluids and calories to offset both clinically apparent and insensible losses, are important in the management of neonatal abstinence.

Respiratory System. The opiate abstinence syndrome may include excessive secretions, nasal stuffiness, sometimes accompanied by retractions, intermittent cyanosis, and apnea (78). Severe respiratory distress occurs most often when the infant regurgitates, aspirates, and develops aspiration pneumonia. Infants with acute heroin withdrawal show increased respiratory rates, leading to hypocapnia and an increase in blood pH during the first week of life (92). This respiratory alkalosis may play a beneficial role in the binding of indirect serum bilirubin to albumin, but it can also decrease the levels of ionized calcium and lead to tetany. As noted previously, the incidence of idiopathic respiratory distress syndrome is decreased in heroin-exposed infants, because of either chronic intrauterine stress, accelerated heroin-mediated maturation of lung function, or perhaps both. Newborn infants have decreased levels of 2,3-diphosphoglycerate (DPG) and, therefore, cannot unload oxygen effectively at the tissue level. In one study (88), mean values of P_{50} in the cord blood and total 2,3-DPG in red blood cells were increased in the opiate-addicted infants compared with normal controls.

Autonomic Nervous System. Behrendt and Green (12) found that 8 of 20 low-birth-weight infants of heroin-addicted mothers had spontaneous generalized sweating compared to that in only 2 of 108 healthy low-birth-weight babies. In addition, the pharmacological threshold for sweating was decreased in the drug-exposed infants. Other autonomic nervous system signs seen during abstinence include hyperpyrexia and lacrimation, both of which increase water loss.

Other Effects. Nathenson et al. (182) found a lack of significant jaundice among infants of heroin-addicted mothers. Further investigation demonstrated increased bilirubin glucuronide transferase activity in morphine-addicted mice and an electron microscopic increase in the smooth endoplasmic reticulum of their liver cells. The significance of increased hepatic bilirubin glucuronide transferase activity by opiates may extend beyond the metabolism of bilirubin to enhanced excretion of other biological substances requiring glucuronidation or to induction of other enzyme systems within and beyond the liver.

Burstein et al. (23) found a significant thrombocytosis in 33 prospectively studied methadone-exposed infants. Platelet counts rose during the second week of life, peaked at about 10 weeks of life, and returned to normal slowly during the next 8 months. Platelet levels exceeding 1 million/mm^3 were found in 7 infants. Fifteen of the studied patients had increased circulating platelet aggregates. Despite this abnormal platelet pattern, other hematological parameters, including hemoglobin concentration and white cell count, were normal.

Jhaveri et al. (126), in a study of 14 methadone-exposed infants, found increased levels of T3 on days 2 and 7 and increased levels of T4 on days 2, 3, and 7 compared with control infants. Although maternal drug-taking was not limited to methadone and despite a range of gestational ages in the infants, the authors speculated that this biochemical evidence of hyperthyroidism was related to either altered autonomic function or increased metabolic activity associated with neonatal withdrawal.

Determinants and Patterns of Neonatal Abstinence

Confirmation of fetal drug exposure has classically been documented through urine toxicological assay. These assays have been performed first with a screening method such as immunoassay and have been confirmed with a more specific testing procedure such as gas chromatography-mass spectroscopy. Confirmation is considered an essential part of drug testing because of the legal and social service implications of a positive test.

It should be recognized that the criteria for obtaining a urine toxicology and the actions that flow from a positive result vary widely from state to state and even within the same state. At Beth Israel Medical Center, a urine toxicology is obtained from the mother only when a drug history cannot be reliably obtained or when a discrepancy exists between clinical findings and the substance thought to be ingested. Informed consent is obtained, and a positive toxicology usually leads to referral for drug treatment and social work consultation. The major criterion for ordering a urine toxicology on an infant is usually signs of drug abstinence or toxicity, but it may include maternal factors such as lack of documented prenatal care.

Increasing interest has been shown recently in the use of meconium for toxicological testing. Throughout gestation, drugs are metabolized by the fetal liver and excreted into the urine or bile. Since the fetus does not usually pass stool in utero, meconium, containing its drug metabolites, represents a waste product that accumulates throughout the gestation. Meconium testing, therefore, represents a much wider window of drug exposure than does urine testing. Ostrea et al. (191) showed in both human and animal studies that meconium represented an excellent source from which metabolites of illicit drugs could be retrieved. In a subsequent study of over 3000 neonates at Hutzel Hospital in Detroit, Ostrea et al. (190) found that meconium drug testing yielded almost twice the number of positive drug tests compared with urine and 4 times that found by maternal self-report.

Not all infants born to drug-dependent mothers show withdrawal symptomatology. Several investigators have reported that between 60% and 90% of infants show symptoms (45, 55, 115, 134, 272). Because the biochemical and physiological processes governing withdrawal are still poorly understood and because polydrug abuse, erratic drug-taking, and vague and inaccurate maternal histories complicate accurate data-gathering, it is not surprising to find differing descriptions and experiences in reports from different centers.

Time of onset of abstinence symptoms varies. Once the infant is delivered, serum and tissue levels of the drug or drugs used by the mother begin to fall. The newborn infant continues to metabolize and excrete the drug, and signs of abstinence occur when critically low tissue levels have been reached. Rosen and Pippenger (222) could not demonstrate a relationship between maternal methadone dose and neonatal abstinence, but they found that abstinence was most closely correlated with the rate of excretion of methadone by the drug-exposed neonate. The authors found that plasma levels of 0.06 μg/ml protected the infant from abstinence; levels falling below that point were associated with the onset of abstinence. Recovery from the abstinence syndrome is gradual and occurs as the infant's metabolism is reprogrammed to adjust to the absence of the dependence-producing agent.

Immediately after birth, if the mother has continued her drug use, most passively dependent infants, whether born to heroin-addicted or methadone-dependent women, seem physically and behaviorally normal. Heroin is not stored by the fetus to any appreciable extent; if the mother has been on heroin alone, the majority (80%) of infants will develop clinical signs of withdrawal between 4 and 24 hours of age. Methadone, however, is stored by the fetus, primarily in the lung, liver, and spleen (69, 198). If the mother has been on methadone alone, the baby's symptoms usually appear within the first 24–72 hours but may appear somewhat later. Several methadone-exposed babies have had their onset of major withdrawal after the first or second week of life (139).

The type and amount of the drug or drugs used by the mother, timing of her dose before delivery, and the presence or absence of intrinsic disease in the infant, which may affect drug metabolism and excretion, may all play a role in determining the time of onset in the individual infant. Withdrawal may be mild and transient, delayed in onset, have a stepwise increase in severity, be intermittently present, or have a biphasic course that includes acute neonatal withdrawal followed by improvement and then an exacerbation of acute withdrawal.

In an early study, Blinick (17) reported mild to moderate withdrawal symptoms in approximately half of 19 infants exposed to methadone; none of the infants developed severe symptoms. Rajegowda et al. (204) found a higher incidence and more prolonged duration of withdrawal symptoms in methadone-exposed infants than in those exposed to heroin. However, mothers in Rajegowda's study were on higher doses of methadone (80–160 mg/day) than were Blinick's patients (60–120 mg/day). Zelson et al. (272) found an increase in severity of withdrawal and a higher number of seizures among 34 infants born to mothers who had used methadone alone or in combination with heroin compared with the number of seizures in 24 infants born to mothers who used heroin only. Davis et al. (57) found that 80% of infants born to women maintained on low doses of methadone (mean 45 mg/day) had evidence of withdrawal, but fewer than one-third showed signs that were severe enough to require therapy.

In a study of 196 drug-exposed infants at Hutzel Hospital in Detroit, Ostrea et al. (192) found that the severity of neonatal withdrawal did not correlate with the infant's gestational age, sex, race, or Apgar score, with maternal age, parity, or duration of heroin intake, or with the level of morphine measured in the infant's urine or blood. Reduction in the amount of illumination and noise in a study nursery also did not lower the incidence of severe withdrawal in the infants. A significant correlation between the severity of withdrawal in the infant and the maternal methadone dose prompted the recommendation that mothers on methadone treatment should be put on a low dose of drug (less than 20 mg/day) as soon as it is safely possible. Similar conclusions were reached by Madden et al. (162), who suggested a reduction of methadone to less than 20 mg daily in late pregnancy. A study at Philadelphia General Hospital (51) involving 260 pregnant addicts treated with methadone and street addicts on heroin showed a reduced incidence of severe withdrawal (12.5%) associated with low-dose methadone, compared with the incidence (25%) among infants of mothers on heroin only.

Doberczak et al. (64) found that more term infants (145 of 178) required treatment for abstinence than did the preterm infants (20 of 34). The authors also demonstrated that abstinence severity correlated with gestational age;

less mature infants showed lesser abstinence. This less severe abstinence in preterm infants may be due to either (a) developmental immaturity of the preterm nervous system, (b) reduced total drug exposure in shortened gestations, or (c) insensitivity of the testing instrument to gestational age and neurological development of neonates.

A number of studies have attempted to correlate drug levels in various body fluids to neonatal outcome. Blinick et al. (18) could not establish a simple relationship between the concentration of methadone in maternal plasma and urine of pregnant women on methadone and levels of amniotic fluid, cord blood, fetal urine, and breast milk or the intensity of the neonatal withdrawal syndrome. Harper et al. (110) found that the severity of neonatal abstinence correlated positively with the total amount of methadone ingested by the mother during the last 12 weeks of pregnancy, the maternal dose of methadone at the time of delivery, and the intrapartum maternal serum methadone level, suggesting that a strategy of reducing the methadone dose during pregnancy might constitute optimal management. Doberczak et al. (65) found an association between maternal methadone dosage at delivery and maternal plasma methadone level drawn 16 hours after delivery; the latter correlated significantly with the neonatal plasma methadone level on day 1 of life. The authors also found that severity of neonatal abstinence correlated with the rate of decline of neonatal plasma methadone level from day 1 to day 4. These data support those of Rosen and Pippenger (222) in suggesting that the rate of disposition of methadone from tissue or plasma influences the onset and severity of neonatal abstinence.

Because of the variable severity of the withdrawal, the duration of symptoms may last anywhere from 6 days to 8 weeks. Although the infants are discharged from the hospital after drug therapy is stopped, their symptoms or irritability may persist for more than 3 or 4 months (266). Although prolonged and untreated abstinence carries a risk of death, earlier recognition of the problem, more accurate laboratory diagnosis, and prompt treatment have essentially eliminated the mortality attributed to abstinence per se.

Behavioral Studies in the Neonatal Period

Many animal studies have demonstrated developmental, neuroendocrine, and behavioral effects of opiate exposure in young offspring. These effects include, among many others, an impaired ability to learn a condition suppression response (240), differences in reflex development (170), and altered response to stress (273).

In human neonates, the Brazelton Neonatal Assessment Scale has been used extensively to evaluate newborn behavior. This instrument assesses habituation to stimuli such as the light and bell, responsivity to animate and inanimate stimuli (face, voice, bell, rattle), state (sleep to alertness to crying), and the requirements of state change (such as irritability and consolability) and neurological and motor development. Soule et al. (241) compared 19 methadone-exposed babies who had received no pharmacological treatment prior to the first examination with 41 babies who were subjects of an unrelated developmental study. Group differences in scores on the Brazelton Neonatal Assessment Scale at 48 and 72 hours of age indicated that methadone-exposed babies were restless, tended to be in a neurologically irritable condition, cried more often, and were state-labile. The infants were also more tremulous and hypertonic and manifested less motor maturity than did the control group. In addition, although quite available and responsive auditorially, the methadone-exposed babies responded poorly to visual stimuli.

Strauss et al. (246) also found that addicted infants were less able to be maintained in an alert state and less able to orient to auditory and visual stimuli, signs that were most pronounced at 48 hours of age. Despite increased irritability, drug-exposed infants were as capable of self-quieting and responding to soothing intervention as were normal neonates. These findings have substantial implications for caregivers' perceptions of infants and thus may have long-term impact on the development of infant-caregiver interaction patterns. These implications have been further developed by Kaltenbach and Finnegan (129), who found that infants born to methadone-maintained women showed deficiencies in their attention and social responsiveness during the first few days of life; these abnormalities persisted during the infants' course of abstinence and treatment. Fitzgerald et al. (89) found that the interaction of drug-dependent mothers and their infants showed abnormalities on measures of social engagement; this dyadic interaction was explained by less maternal positive affect and attachment as well as infant behavior impeding social involvement. Many of these interactive abnormalities normalized by 4 months of age, but the need for "parenting training" is obvious.

Lodge et al. (160) noted that infants born to mothers on varying doses of methadone showed withdrawal-associated heightened auditory responsiveness and orientation, lowered overall alertness, and poor attentiveness to a visual stimulus compared to controls. Electroencephalographic recordings revealed high-frequency dyssynchronous activity suggestive of central nervous system irritability, as well as low arousal responses to visual stimulation.

Drug-exposed infants show an uncoordinated and ineffectual sucking reflex as a major manifestation of abstinence. Kron et al. (151) measured the sucking rate, pressure, and organization of sucking, as well as nutrient consumption, in drug-exposed neonates. Sucking rates and pressure parameters were felt to be most sensitive in distinguishing between the control and the drug-exposed populations. Paregoric-treated infants tended to suck more vigorously than infants treated with sedatives such as phenobarbital and were even superior to those who received no therapy at all. Diazepam-treated infants were found to be depressed in feeding behavior. These studies provide support for a pharmacotherapeutic approach to the treatment of neonatal abstinence.

Most recently, a neurodevelopmental follow-up battery of tests has been developed to assess substance-exposed infants as part of a multicenter prospective study in the National Institute of Child Health and Human Development (NICHD) Neonatal Research Network in conjunction with NIDA. This battery, called the Neonatal Network Neurobehavioral Scale (NNNS), developed by Lester, Tronick, Mayes, and Zuckerman, is being used to assess developmental constructs at eight time-points from 1 to 36 months of age (255).

Assessment and Management of Neonatal Narcotic Abstinence

It is important to stress that unrecognized and untreated neonatal opiate abstinence may result in death from factors such as excess fluid losses, hyperpyrexia, seizures, respiratory instability, aspiration, and apnea. With proper management, the neonate's prognosis for recovery from the acute phase of abstinence should be excellent. It should also be stressed that because of the nonspecific nature of signs of neonatal abstinence, other potentially serious illnesses such as bacterial sepsis and/or meningitis, intracranial hemorrhage, and metabolic disorders such as hypoglycemia, hyponatremia, or hypernatremia, which may mimic abstinence, should also be considered in symptomatic opiate-exposed newborns.

Because not all infants born to drug-dependent women develop abstinence, prophylactic drug therapy is not recommended. The asymptomatic narcotic-exposed infant should be observed in the hospital for at least 4 days. Even if the infant is still symptom-free at the time and evaluation of home and mothering capability has been adequate to permit discharge, observation at close intervals must be continued. A disrupted social situation or polydrug abuse may mandate a longer period of observation in the hospital. In any case, a home visit or return appointment should be made within a few days after discharge and the mother should be alerted to the possibility of late onset of withdrawal signs (139) that might necessitate readmission.

When signs of abstinence do appear, simple nonspecific measures should be instituted. At Beth Israel Medical Center in New York, an individualized treatment program (PANDA; Parent and Newborn Development and Assessment) has used supportive techniques to ameliorate the abstinence in opiate-exposed babies. These techniques include reducing noxious environmental stimuli, positioning that encourages flexion rather than extension, and individualized handling procedures based on the infant's level of tolerance. Gentle swaddling should be used to reinforce flexion and infant comfort. Demand feeding, sometimes as frequently as every 2 hours, has been found to reduce irritability.

Indications for specific pharmacotherapy, dose schedules, and duration of treatment courses have varied widely. Some of this variation is undoubtedly due to observer difference in judging severity of symptoms. To improve the objectivity of these judgments, a neonatal abstinence scoring system is strongly recommended. Although other scales have been proposed (102, 156), the 21-symptom rating scale of Finnegan has been most widely used as a research tool and treatment guide (Table 54.5). All infants born to drug-dependent mothers are assessed for withdrawal symptomatology by using this dynamic scoring scale at 2-hour intervals for the first 48 hours of life, then every 4 hours thereafter. If at any point the infant's score is 8 or greater (regardless of age), every 2-hour scoring is initiated and continued for 24 hours from the last total score of 8 or greater. If the 2-hour scores continue to be 7 or less for 24 hours, then 4-hour scoring intervals are resumed. The need for pharmacological intervention is indicated when the total abstinence score is 8 or greater for three consecutive scorings or when the average of any three consecutive scores is 8 or greater. The total abstinence score also dictates the dose of the pharmacotherapeutic agent (i.e., the dose is titrated against the total abstinence score). The specific details of the use of the scoring system have been reported elsewhere (79, 83).

Both a replacement opiate such as paregoric (camphorated tincture of opium) or a nonspecific central nervous system depressant such as phenobarbital appear to be effective in treating neonatal opiate abstinence (132). Generally, doses of medication must be regulated so that the infant's symptoms are minimized without excessive sedation. Paregoric treatment begins with an oral dose of 0.2 cc every 3 hours. If symptoms are not controlled based on the severity scale, doses are increased by 0.05 cc to a maximum of 0.4 cc every 3 hours. The stabilizing dose is maintained for 5 days, following which the dosage is slowly reduced by 0.05 cc every other day, maintaining a dosing regimen of every 3 hours.

Although opiate addiction is best treated with paregoric, polydrug abuse in which nonopiate use is suspected or confirmed is probably better treated taking advantage of the wider therapeutic spectrum of phenobarbital (87, 132). After a loading dose of 5 mg/kg of phenobarbital intramuscularly or intravenously, a maintenance dose of between 3 and 5 mg/kg per day should be started. Using the severity scale, phenobarbital dosages can be increased by 1 mg/kg to a stabilizing dose that generally should not exceed 10 mg/kg per day. Others have recommended much higher loading doses (110), but use of higher dosing carries the risk of excessive sedation and poor infant feeding.

Few controlled studies exist comparing the efficacy of these two therapies. Kandall et al. (136) found that control of abstinence appeared equally effective in 49 infants treated with paregoric and 62 infants treated with phenobarbital; however, seizures developed only in the phenobarbital-treated group. The superiority of higher-dose paregoric over phenobarbital treatment was also demonstrated by Finnegan and Ehrlich (81) in a study of 300 neonates. In that study, paregoric-treated infants were brought under therapeutic control more rapidly and required a shorter treatment period than phenobarbital-treated infants. An additional finding of interest was provided by the studies of Kron et al. (151), which demonstrated more rapid normalization of sucking reflexes during paregoric treatment compared to phenobarbital treatment.

The use of other agents, such as chlorpromazine or diazepam, to treat neonatal opiate abstinence should be discouraged. In addition, methadone has been used very infrequently because its pharmacology in the human neonate has not been studied adequately.

LATER SEQUELAE OF INTRAUTERINE OPIATE EXPOSURE

Delayed Presentation of Abstinence. Late presentation of neonatal abstinence symptoms in newborns was reported by Kandall and Gartner (139). Significant symptoms, primarily irritability and tremulousness, first occurred in seven infants between 2 and 4 weeks of age. Seizures occurred in three infants, while a fourth infant showed progression of symptoms and died at 3 weeks of age. The delayed onset of symptoms may be explained by the accumulation of methadone in the lung, liver, kidney, and spleen, its gradual accumulation, and its subsequent slow excretion (69, 198).

Table 54.5   Neonatal Abstinence Scoring System[a]

System	Signs and Symptoms	Score	AM	PM	Comments
Central Nervous System Disturbances	Excessive high-pitched (or other) cry	2			Daily Weight:
	Continuous high-pitched (or other) cry	3			
	Sleeps < 1 hour after feeding	3			
	Sleeps < 2 hours after feeding	2			
	Sleeps < 3 hours after feeding	1			
	Hyperactive Moro reflex	2			
	Markedly hyperactive Moro reflex	3			
	Mild tremors disturbed	1			
	Moderate-severe tremors disturbed	2			
	Mild tremors undisturbed	3			
	Moderate-severe tremors undisturbed	4			
	Increased muscle tone	2			
	Excoriation (specific area)	1			
	Myoclonic jerks	3			
	Generalized convulsions	5			
Metabolic Vasomotor Respiratory Disturbances	Sweating	1			
	Fever < 101° (99–100.8°F or 37.2–38.2° C)	1			
	Fever > 101° (38.4°C and higher)	2			
	Frequent yawning (> 3–4 times/interval)	1			
	Mottling	1			
	Nasal stuffiness	1			
	Sneezing (> 3–4 times/interval)	1			
	Nasal flaring	2			
	Respiratory rate > 60/minute	1			
	Respiratory rate > 60/minute with retractions	2			
Gastrointestinal disturbances	Excessive sucking	1			
	Poor feeding	2			
	Regurgitation	2			
	Projectile vomiting	3			
	Loose stools	2			
	Watery stools	3			
	Total Score				
	Initials of scorer				

[a]From Finnegan LP. Neonatal abstinence syndrome: assessment and pharmacotherapy. In: Rubaltelli FF, Granati B, eds. Neonatal therapy: an update. Amsterdam: Excerpta Medica, 1986:136.

Sudden Infant Death Syndrome. Sudden infant death syndrome (SIDS) is defined as the sudden and unexpected death of an infant between 1 week and 1 year of age whose death remains unexplained after a complete autopsy examination, full history, and death site investigation. Compared with an incidence of approximately 1.5 per 1000 live births in the general population, opiate-exposed infants appear to have an increased risk of SIDS. Anecdotal and small population studies (36, 77, 109, 127, 205, 221) have all found increased rates of SIDS in opiate-exposed infants.

The first large population study linking SIDS to maternal drug use was published by Ward et al. (262). Using a Los Angeles County database from 1986 and 1987, the authors found an unadjusted SIDS rate of 8.87 per 1000 births, with the highest rate seen with maternal opiate use. The most extensive study has been done by Kandall et al. (137), who studied SIDS rates in 1.21 million births in New York City from 1979 to 1989. The authors identified 90 SIDS deaths among 16,409 drug-exposed infants (5.48/1000 births), about 4 times the rate in the general population. Maternal opiate use increased the risk of SIDS about sixfold; after control for high-risk variables including race/ethnicity, young maternal age, parity, maternal smoking, and low birth weight, the risk of SIDS was still 3 times that of the general population. Al-

though the etiology of SIDS in either the general population or drug-exposed infants is not well understood, Olsen and Lees (188) and Richardson et al. (215) suggested that the mechanism in methadone-exposed infants lay in a reduced ventilatory arousal response to hypercapnia. The same mechanism has been subsequently postulated in relation to cocaine exposure (see the section entitled "Cocaine"). An extensive review of maternal drug use and subsequent SIDS has been published by Kandall and Gaines (138).

LONG-TERM OUTCOME OF CHILDREN EXPOSED IN UTERO TO NARCOTIC AGENTS

Once in-hospital pharmacological and supportive therapy have been discontinued, a paramount concern becomes appropriate discharge planning that will assure the infant's optimal growth and development. Because there is no standard method by which the disposition of these infants is decided, some infants may be discharged home with their mothers, some may be placed with relatives, and others may be placed in the custody of a state agency or voluntarily released by the mother to private agencies for temporary or permanent placement.

National pressure recommending separation of infants from their addicted mothers has been growing. This solution may not be practical in cities where social services and courts are already understaffed and overworked. Appropriate foster care is expensive and hard to find. Pediatricians basically feel that the mother-infant association should not be dissolved except when clearly indicated. Aside from intensive drug rehabilitation and medical treatment, drug-dependent women need extensive educational and job training so that they will become productive citizens and loving mothers who will positively influence the development and socialization of their children. Supportive outpatient care or residential treatment may help to eliminate many of the medical and social problems experienced by drug-dependent women and their children.

At Family Center of Thomas Jefferson University in Philadelphia, all mothers in recovery are given their infants when they are ready for discharge unless a team consisting of a nursery nurse, pediatrician, psychiatric social worker, obstetrician, and public health nurse finds that the mother cannot care for her infant adequately with the supportive services available to her. With strong support from this team providing intensive psychosocial services during her pregnancy and immediately after delivery, she usually is prepared to cope more realistically with motherhood. However, if the team believes that she neither wishes nor is able to assume this responsibility, arrangements are made for temporary foster placement or for a relative to accept the major caretaking duties.

Despite the fact that a drug-exposed newborn may be free of physical, behavioral, or neurological deficits at the time of birth, one cannot assume that no adverse effect has occurred. It is generally accepted that the effects of pharmacological agents may not become apparent for many months or years. Although heroin abuse during pregnancy has been recognized for more than 40 years and methadone treatment has been employed for more than 20 years, follow-up studies of opiate-exposed infants are notably fragmentary. Among the issues encountered in long-term follow-up assessment of this population are inability to document fully a mother's drug intake, the difficulty in differentiating a drug's organic effects from high-risk obstetric and neonatal variables, problems in maintaining a cohort of infants for study, and the need to isolate a specific drug effect from the profound impact of parenting and the home environment.

In 1973, Wilson et al. (266) reported on the growth and development of 30 heroin-exposed infants who were observed from 3 to 34 months. Eighty percent had shown signs of neonatal withdrawal, and 60% continued to have subacute withdrawal signs for 3–6 months. Behavioral disturbances, predominantly hyperactivity, brief attention span, and temper outbursts, were identified in 7 of 14 infants observed for 1 year or longer; 2 had neurological abnormalities. These disturbances seemed to be unrelated to subsequent environmental factors. Despite behavioral abnormalities, infants performed at age-appropriate levels on Gesell adaptive and motor testing. In 1979, Wilson et al. (268) compared the 3–6-year outcomes of 20 heroin-exposed infants to those of 55 infants at "high-risk" for suboptimal neurobehavioral outcomes for other reasons. Although overall testing of the heroin-exposed children fell within the normal range, those infants displayed significant deficits in behavioral adjustment, perceptual measures, and specific subtests related to the process of organization that require attention, concentration, short-term memory, and the internal manipulation of symbols. Wilson et al. (267) found that at 1 year of age, methadone-exposed infants showed excessive crying and delay in establishing quiet sleep patterns and showed deficits in fine motor coordination and attention despite testing within the normal range on Bayley mental scores. In a later study from the same medical center, Lifschitz et al. (154) found that despite overall testing that fell within the normal range, heroin-and methadone-exposed infants were overrepresented in the group of infants showing low-average and mildly retarded intellectual performance at 3–6 years of age.

Ramer and Lodge (208) studied 35 infants who were born to 32 mothers registered in a San Francisco city-operated methadone maintenance treatment program. Sixty percent of the infants demonstrated mild or no symptoms, and 40% developed moderate or severe symptoms of withdrawal. The infants whose symptoms were most severe were born to mothers who had documented histories of polydrug abuse. Although many infants were slow to gain

weight in the neonatal period, thereafter growth and development remained generally within the normal range. Bayley Scales of Infant Mental and Motor Development revealed that the older infants (up to 3 years of age) showed age-appropriate development in the area of vocalization and language, but that performance on perceptual motor tasks was somewhat less adequate.

In 1976, Strauss et al. (248) evaluated 60 infants born to narcotic-addicted women enrolled in the Hutzel Hospital's perinatal methadone treatment program and 53 control infants. Psychological development of a subset of the addicted infants (n = 25), using the Bayley Scales of Infant Development at 3, 6, and 12 months of age, fell within the normal range, but psychomotor development scores of these children declined through the first year from 119 to 103. Strauss et al. (247) found no difference between 5-year-old drug-exposed and control infants, using the McCarthy Scales of Children's Abilities; the mean General Cognitive Index was 86.8 for the narcotic-exposed children and 86.2 for controls.

Rosen and Johnson (219) reported follow-up to 18 months of age of 45 methadone-exposed infants and 25 comparison infants. The drug-exposed group displayed both hypertonia and hypotonia, as well as delays in sitting, transfer ability, fine motor coordination, and language acquisition. Although both study and control infants scored within the normal range on the Bayley Mental Developmental Index (MDI) and Physical Development Index (PDI) scales, scores for methadone-exposed infants were lower; differences were statistically significant at both 12- and 18-month examinations. A later study (220) by the same authors of methadone-exposed children found increased activity, attention deficits, poor fine and gross motor coordination, and speech and language delays at 7 years of age.

Hans (107) assessed 30 methadone-exposed infants and 44 control infants at 2 years of age. Although mean scores for drug-exposed and control infants fell well within the normal range, study infants evidenced deficient fine and gross motor coordination and greater body tension and lagged behind control infants by about 2 months of motor development.

At Family Center in Philadelphia between 1977 and 1979, Kaltenbach et al. (130) studied 43 infants (26 1-year-olds and 17 2-year-olds) exposed to methadone in utero and 51 control infants randomly selected from a population of children with comparable socioeconomic, racial, and medical backgrounds. Using the Bayley Mental Scale of Infant Development, they found that although both groups tested within the normal range, scores at 1 year of age were lower in the methadone-exposed group (103.4) than in controls (109.4). At 2 years of age, scores were lower but did not differ between the drug-exposed infants (90.9) and controls (94.6). The same group performed 4-year assessments on 25 study children born to women who received prenatal care and methadone maintenance during pregnancy (128). Children were assessed by neurological examination, the Wechsler Preschool and Primary Scale of Intelligence, the Test of Language Development, Imitation of Gestures, and the Motor-Free Visual Perception Test. Differences between children born to women maintained on methadone and controls were not statistically significant for either the subscales or the full-scale IQs; both groups performed better on the verbal scale than on the performance scale. Imitation of Gestures, the Test of Language Development, and the Motor-Free Visual Perception Test also showed no differences between the groups. All neurological findings were within the normal range, and there was no relationship between severity of neonatal withdrawal and the IQ scores. At 3½ to 4½ years of age, no intergroup differences were found, with use of the McCarthy Scales of Children's Abilities. Scores for the methadone-exposed population and controls averaged 106.5 and 106, respectively.

More and more studies have proposed multifactorial models to assess infant outcome following intrauterine drug exposure. One such postnatal influence involves maternal-infant interaction. Drug-exposed infants are often irritable and dysrhythmic and may display increased extensor tone when handled. On the other hand, arousal from sleep may be difficult. Both behaviors may be interpreted by the mother as "rejecting" behavior, leading to inappropriate maternal caretaking and possible neglect of the infant. Finnegan et al. (82) found that infants born to methadone-maintained women showed deficient social responsiveness after birth, that this deficient mother-infant interaction persisted until the infant's treatment was completed, and that maternal drug dose may affect that interaction.

Based on extremely limited data, therefore, children born to heroin-using women or women maintained on methadone appear to function within the normal range of mental and motor development at 5–6 years of age. Some data offer the tentative possibility that selected (but varying among studies) differences in behavioral, adaptive, and perceptual skills may exist between these children and those of comparable backgrounds whose mothers were not involved with drugs. Positive and reinforcing environmental influences can significantly improve infant outcome; women who show a caring concern for their infants are most likely to pursue follow-up pediatric care and cooperate in neurobehavioral follow-up studies. The lack of both a large database and long follow-up well into the school years points to an obvious need for comprehensive studies assessing the development of larger populations of opiate-exposed infants. Useful data should be shortly forthcoming from the Maternal Lifestyles Study of the NICHD Neonatal Research Network.

Cocaine

In contrast to opiate use, which remained relatively constant in the United States during the 1980s and began to rise again in the mid 1990s, cocaine use, especially that of "crack," rose rapidly during the 1980s. The number of babies reportedly exposed to drugs (much of it cocaine) in New York City rose from 7.9 per 1000 births in 1983 to 20.3 per 1000 births in 1987; more than 5000 drug-exposed babies were born in New York City in 1989. Of some consolation was the report of a 7% drop in New York City positive neonatology toxicology reports between 1989 and 1990, one of the first reports to demonstrate that this latest epidemic of cocaine use had peaked in the late 1980s.

Significant cocaine use persists, however, especially in urban ghettos. Some hospitals in these communities reported in the late 1980s that 20–30% of all newborn infants were testing positive for illegal drugs in their urine, with 80–90% of those being cocaine. Other cities such as Dallas, Denver, Oakland, Philadelphia, and Houston have reported threefold to fourfold increases in drug-exposed infants between 1985 and 1988. Nationwide, studies in the 1980s estimated that about 4.5% of newborns in the United States may have been exposed to cocaine in utero (98). A 1990 Ohio study (178) of more than 1800 neonates from 25 hospitals revealed a cocaine exposure rate of 2.0%; the adjusted prevalence rate was 7.2% for infants born to black mothers and 0.3% for infants born to white mothers. In 1991, Schutzman et al. (230) reported an incidence of 11.8% intrauterine cocaine exposure (6.3% of privately insured mothers and 26.9% of mothers with Medicaid or no insurance) in a suburban Philadelphia setting. Vega et al. (259), in a study of over 29,000 California births in mid 1992, documented maternal cocaine use in 1.1% of pregnancies; ethnic differences ranged from a low of 0.06% in Asians to almost 8% in blacks. A recent study in Rochester, New York, found that 5.5% of 1201 mother-infant pairs tested positive for cocaine (226). As noted earlier, the National Pregnancy and Health Survey reported in 1994 that slightly over 1% of the surveyed pregnancies were complicated by cocaine use.

Cocaine has been used medicinally and recreationally in this country since the 1870s (133). During that time, in the course of a number of epidemics of cocaine use, many adverse effects of cocaine on the adult user became well known; these include acute myocardial infarction, cardiac arrhythmias, rupture of the ascending aorta, cerebrovascular accidents, hyperpyrexia, seizures, and infections, as well as a range of psychiatric disorders such as dysphoric agitation (53). Much less has been reported regarding cocaine use during pregnancy and its effect on the mother, fetus, and newborn infant. The recent "crack" epidemic, however, stimulated research regarding cocaine's effects during the perinatal period (84). Although much of this research is still preliminary, controversial, and even contradictory, it has nonetheless revealed a wide variety of specific risks of great concern (Table 54.6).

PHYSIOLOGY AND PHARMACOLOGY

Cocaine (benzoylmethylecgonine hydrochloride) is an alkaloid derived from the leaves of coca plants, most prominently *Erythroxylon coca*. The first extraction process yields a coca paste, a raw and generally impure product consumed primarily in South America. Further extraction with hy-

Table 54.6 Possible Maternal and Neonatal Effects From Cocaine Use During Pregnancy[a]

Exhibit 5. Possible Complications of Maternal and Neonatal Effects of Cocaine Use That May Occur in Pregnancy

Maternal complications
  Poor nutritional status
  Increased risk for infections
  Hypertension/tachycardia/arrhythmias/myocardial infarctions
  Central nervous system hemorrhage
  Depression and low self-esteem
  Increased tendency to engage in risk behaviors for HIV

Pregnancy, labor, and delivery complications
  Spontaneous abortion
  Poor weight gain
  Abruptio placentae
  Fetal demise
  Precipitous delivery

Neonatal complications
  Intrauterine growth retardation
  Microcephaly or reduced head circumference
  Prematurity
  Congenital malformations/vascular disruption
  Congenital infections
  Cardiovascular dysfunction/arrhythmias
  Feeding difficulties/necrotizing enterocolitis
  Central nervous system hemorrhage-ischemic lesions
  Neurobehavioral dysfunction
  Seizure activity
  Sudden infant death syndrome (SIDS)
  Increased possibility of HIV involvement

[a]From Kandall SR, ed. Improving treatment for drug-exposed infants. Rockville, MD: U.S. Department of Health and Human Services (Center for Substance Abuse Treatment), 1993:16.

drochloric acid yields cocaine hydrochloride, which is usually diluted and either snorted or used intravenously. If the hydrochloride salt is treated with a base such as sodium bicarbonate and then reextracted with a solvent such as ether, the freebase form, also called "crack," is produced (75).

Cocaine displays varied pharmacokinetics based on its specific preparation and route of administration (124). Because cocaine is a very potent vasoconstrictor, it retards its own absorption when applied to mucous membranes, such as the nasal mucosa when snorted or gastrointestinal mucosa when ingested. This vasoconstriction leads to relatively slow achievement of peak levels of cocaine in the blood and brain. Cocaine plasma levels peak in about 15–60 minutes following snorting and in about 45–90 minutes after ingestion (75). Peak levels of cocaine are reached more rapidly following smoking or intravenous use. This more rapid absorption causes an intense euphoria and severe posteuphoria "crash" that leads to an intense craving and potentially rapid development of dependence on the drug.

Once absorbed, cocaine is metabolized by serum and hepatic cholinesterases to water-soluble inactive compounds, primarily benzoylecgonine, norcaine, and ecgonine methyl ester (75). Cocaine may be detectable in blood or urine for less than 12 hours, but its water-soluble products may be recovered from urine for up to 1 week, depending on the sensitivity of testing methodology. Usual toxicological testing involves the use of either an enzyme-multiplied immunoassay technique (EMIT) or radial immunodiffusion, with confirmation by either gas chromatography or high-performance liquid chromatography. Recent articles advocate the use of meconium testing for cocaine metabolites to enhance diagnostic accuracy regarding drug exposure over a longer gestational period. Using meconium analysis, Ostrea et al. (191) found a much higher yield of positive cocaine assays compared to urine drug testing, findings which were confirmed in a larger series of over 3000 infants by the same author (190). In that series, just over 30% of the infants tested for cocaine. The applicability of this finding was extended when cocaine was found in the intestines of three human fetuses, one as early as 17 weeks gestation (193). Ryan et al. (226) also reported that meconium testing for cocaine metabolites resulted in the detection of an additional 33% of cocaine-exposed neonates, compared to urine testing. Other researchers have suggested that hair analysis for cocaine metabolites gives a better estimate of gestational exposure to cocaine (24, 101). Another diagnostic possibility was offered by

Jain et al. (125), who detected the presence of cocaine metabolites in 74% of amniotic fluid samples of known cocaine users compared with recovery rates of 61% in maternal urine and only 35% in neonatal urine.

EFFECTS ON PREGNANCY AND UTEROPLACENTAL FUNCTION

Assessment of the organic impact of cocaine on the human pregnancy must consider confounding drug use-associated variables such as poverty, homelessness, inadequate prenatal and postnatal care, deficient nutrition, varying types of cocaine use, multiple drug use, sexually transmitted diseases, and the possible presence of toxic adulterants that are mixed with or used to process cocaine. Animal studies can limit the number of such variables, but extrapolation of animal data to human subjects should always be undertaken cautiously.

Maternal appetite suppression and cocaine "binging" with inadequate nutritional intake is well recognized. Many cocaine users admitted for treatment may have at least one vitamin deficiency (B_1, B_6, C). Correction of these vitamin deficiencies is particularly necessary during pregnancy to promote the biosynthesis of essential neurotransmitters.

Cocaine's low molecular weight and high solubility in both water and lipids allow it to cross the placenta easily and enter fetal compartments (265, 270). This transplacental passage is enhanced with intravenous or freebase use of cocaine. In addition, the relatively low pH of fetal blood (cocaine is a weak base) and the low fetal level of plasma esterases, which usually metabolize this drug, may lead to accumulation of cocaine in the fetus. Furthermore, the "binge" pattern commonly associated with adult cocaine use may lead to even higher levels of cocaine in the fetus. Transfer of cocaine appears to be greatest in the first and third trimesters of pregnancy. Because cocaine has such potent vasoconstrictive properties, the constriction of uterine, placental, and umbilical vessels may retard the transfer of cocaine from mother to fetus. A deleterious effect of this vasoconstriction, however, is a concomitant fetal deprivation of essential gas and nutrient exchange, resulting in fetal hypoxia (270). Studies in sheep have also shown that maternal cocaine administration results in a dose-dependent catecholamine-mediated increase in maternal blood pressure and a decrease in uterine blood flow, as well as significant reduction in uterine blood flow for at least 15 minutes (10, 177). In addition to an acute hypoxic insult, cocaine use of long duration may produce a chronic decrease in transplacental nutrient and oxygen flow, leading to intrauterine growth retardation. Although the relationship of cocaine use to congenital malformations is still controversial, a decrease in fetal blood supply during critical periods of morphogenesis and growth may be expected to result in organ malformations (see the section entitled "Teratogenic Effects").

The course of labor may also be affected by maternal cocaine use. Intravenous administration of a local anesthetic such as cocaine may cause a direct increase in uterine muscle tone. "Crack" also appears to directly increase uterine contractility and may thus precipitate the onset of premature labor. A higher rate of early pregnancy losses appears to be a major complication of maternal cocaine use (2, 15, 29, 103, 159). In addition, an increased frequency of abruptio placentae (29, 32, 106, 159, 161) and of placenta previa (106) has been reported. Livesay et al. (159) also found that the cocaine-using women had a higher rate of emergency cesarean sections (10.8%) than did the noncocaine drug-dependent group (3.6%) or the drug-free group (3.2%). The highest incidence of meconium staining also occurred in the cocaine-exposed group, a finding confirmed by Hadeed and Siegel (103). It is currently postulated that increased levels of catecholamines, increased blood pressure, and increased body temperature may play etiological roles in early fetal loss and later abruptio placentae. Wang and Schnoll (261) recently have suggested that cocaine-induced downregulation of placental β-adrenergic receptor sites may be linked with release of endogenous opiate peptides.

A cocaine-mediated increase in norepinephrine levels, as noted, is believed to increase uterine contractility with an increase in the incidence of preterm and precipitous labor. This theoretical underpinning supports the general consensus that maternal cocaine use leads to both shortened gestation and restriction of fetal growth. Although the mechanism for reduced fetal growth is not established, it is generally assumed to be mediated through reduced fetal nutritional support secondary to cocaine-mediated uteroplacental vasoconstriction. An early study by Chasnoff et al. (29) found no increased rate of prematurity, but their later report found a ninefold increase in preterm births; a decrease in mean birth weight and an increase in low birth weight and intrauterine growth retardation was seen when cocaine was used during the entire pregnancy (32). Cherukuri (40), Chouteau (42), and Livesay (159) all found significantly increased rates of prematurity following maternal cocaine use, as well as decreases in mean birth weights. MacGregor et al. (161) also reported lower birth weight, lower gestational age at delivery, higher incidences of preterm labor (21.4% versus 1.4%), and premature delivery (24.3% versus 2.9%) in a cocaine-exposed group compared with an appropriately matched control group. Others have reported increases in cocaine-associated fetal growth retardation without reductions in gestational length (91, 103, 274). In the metropolitan Chicago area with a database of over 17,000 deliveries, Handler at al. (106) found that maternal cocaine use was associated with higher rates of low birth weight (risk ratio (RR) 2.8), prematurity (RR 2.4), and intrauterine growth retardation in non-cigarette smokers (RR 3.4). Using both univariate and multivariate analysis, Kliegman et al. (145) found that cocaine use was a significant predictor of prematurity (odds ratio 13.4) and low birth weight (odds ratio 9.9). Racine et al. (203) found that the rate of low-birth-weight infants among cocaine users could be positively impacted by the provision of at least four prenatal visits. Zuckerman and Frank (276), commenting on the discrepancies in the literature, pointed out the need to use adequate statistical power, if cocaine's effect on birth weight and gestation turns out to be small, and the need to control for concurrent use of other substances (drug combinations, amounts, accuracy of measurements, etc.) and a range of medical and sociodemographic factors.

Although Chasnoff originally reported no decrease in head circumference in cocaine-exposed newborns compared with controls (29), his subsequent data did reveal smaller head size if cocaine was used throughout the pregnancy (32). Decreases in neonatal head circumference in cocaine-exposed newborns have been confirmed by other workers also (40, 91, 103, 274). These various data sets suggest, therefore, that maternal cocaine use is associated with a symmetric growth retardation in offspring, with reductions in both birth weight and head circumference. This pattern appears to be similar to that described in opiate-exposed newborns by Doberczak and Kandall (68), although the mechanism in the latter case appears as a result of reduced organ cell number.

TERATOGENIC EFFECTS

Representative animal studies suggest that cocaine has major teratogenic potential. Mahalik et al. (164) found a higher resorption ratio as well as a higher incidence of soft tissue abnormalities (especially skeletal anomalies) in mice exposed to cocaine compared with controls. Fantel and MacPhail (74) noted a significant decrease in maternal and fetal weights in rats given high-dose intraperitoneal cocaine, as well as fetal edema and higher resorption frequencies, but no increase in congenital malformations.

Preliminary data on the relationship of cocaine to human malformations can be characterized as inconsistent. Bingol et al. (15) found a 10% rate of congenital malformations among cocaine users compared with 4.5% among polydrug users and 2% in controls; malformations included cardiac, skeletal, and skull abnormalities. After their report of one infant with prune belly syndrome (a complex of signs including major malformations of the genitourinary tract, bilateral hydronephrosis, and bilateral cryptorchidism) and another infant with hypospadias born to a cocaine-abusing woman, Chasnoff et al. (30) then reported a higher incidence of genitourinary malformations in 50 infants born to cocaine-abusing women compared with 30 control infants. Lipshultz et al. (155) found a fourfold increase in cardiac malformations in cocaine-exposed infants compared with controls; lesions included peripheral pulmonary stenosis, patent ductus arteriosus, and ventricular and atrial septal defects. Isolated reports have linked intrauterine cocaine exposure with midline central nervous system abnormalities (113), craniosynostosis (11), a range of facial abnormalities (90), ankyloglossia (tongue tie) (112), and sirenomelia (fused legs) (228).

A unifying hypothesis linking cocaine with congenital anomalies has been suggested by Hoyme et al. (119). The authors present a range of malformations under the umbrella term *fetal vascular disruption;* these anomalies include growth deficiency, nonduodenal intestinal atresia, limb reduction defects, renal anomalies, and aplasia cutis congenita. Martin et al. (165), however, did not find an increase in congenital malformations attributable to vascular disruption between 1986 and 1989, based on data from the Metropolitan Atlanta Congenital Defects Program. The authors concluded that if cocaine is a teratogen, its teratogenicity is weak or perhaps associated with a small subset of births that needed further delineation. Rajegowda et al. (206) also found no increase in congenital urogenital abnormalities in 1324 cocaine-exposed infants when compared with 18,028 reportedly drug-free controls. In addition, ultrasound examinations were performed on 127 cocaine-exposed infants, with one abnormality found. The same lack of association was found by Hadeed and Siegel (103) and Zuckerman et al. (274). Koren et al., working in the Motherisk program in Toronto, found that although cocaine exposure early in pregnancy was not associated with an increased risk of teratogenesis (147), physicians' perception of a high risk of cocaine teratogenicity resulted in termination of many otherwise wanted pregnancies (146). Counseling of pregnant women as to actual teratogenic risk resulted in a decrease in risk perception and a decreased tendency to terminate the pregnancy (146). At the present time, therefore, mothers should be apprised that cocaine use *may* increase the risk of congenital malformations in their fetuses.

NEONATAL COMPLICATIONS

Cocaine-associated neurotoxicity during the newborn period has been clarified through recent publications. Early reports by Madden et al. (163) in a series of eight cocaine-exposed newborns and by Hadeed and Siegel (103) in a larger series of 56 babies described no obvious cocaine-related neurotoxicity. Chasnoff et al. (29), however, reported an increased degree of irritability, tremulousness, and state lability on the Brazelton Neonatal Behavioral Assessment Scale in 52 cocaine-exposed infants compared with 73 infants born to non-cocaine-using methadone-maintained women. Additionally, cluster analysis in the study by Chasnoff et al. revealed that cocaine-exposed infants showed a greater deficiency in state control than did infants not exposed to cocaine, which interfered with the ability of the caretaker to establish an appropriate relationship with the infant. Ryan et al. (225) found that symptoms of abstinence were less marked in a group of neonates exposed to cocaine and methadone than in those exposed to methadone alone. These findings are consistent with those found in adults by Kosten (148), who noted that cocaine attenuated the severity of naloxone-precipitated opioid withdrawal.

Doberczak et al. (67) confirmed the presence of hypertonia, brisk tendon reflexes, irritability, and tremors in 34 of 39 cocaine-exposed babies. In those 34 infants, neurological abnormalities were transient, lasting only a few days, and did not require specific treatment. No correlation could be found between neurotoxicity and specific perinatal variables such as route or quantity of maternal cocaine administration, gestational age, or birth weight. Oro and Dixon (189) also found significant neurological and physiological alterations in most cocaine- or amphetamine-exposed neonates (n = 46), including abnormal sleep patterns (81%), tremors (71%), poor feeding (58%), hypotonia, vomiting, and fever. These babies tended to spend long periods of time in a dull-alert state with eyes open and demonstrated poor visual processing of faces and objects. The greatest morbidity was seen with cocaine plus narcotic exposure, despite the theoretic possibility of antagonism between the stimulant and depressive effects of these two drugs.

Eisen et al. (71) found that within the first week of life on the Brazelton Neonatal Behavioral Assessment Scale, cocaine-exposed infants needed more trials to habituate to a presented stimulus, compared to controls. Coles et al. (48) compared 50 infants born to cocaine-using mothers (although alcohol, marihuana, and cigarettes were also used) to controls at 48–72 hours, 14 days, and 28 days. Although scores were generally normal, cocaine-exposed infants appeared to show minimal and transient autonomic depression. Mayes et al. (168) also found that cocaine-exposed infants (n = 56) showed

impaired habituation on the Brazelton score; persistence of abnormalities in habituation at a 3-month assessment was found by the same group (167).

Although the mechanism for these neurobehavioral abnormalities is not completely understood, increasing attention has been focused on cocaine-associated derangements in dopaminergic and serotonergic systems (166). Mirochnick et al. (175) postulated that neonatal neurobehavioral disturbances were related to an increase in catecholamine activity in cocaine-exposed infants. Needleman et al. (183) demonstrated a reduction in cerebrospinal fluid homovanillic acid, the principal metabolite of dopamine, in cocaine-exposed neonates.

In addition to neurobehavioral abnormalities, Doberczak et al. (67) found that despite the absence of clinical seizures, electroencephalograms (EEGs) were abnormal in 17 of 38 cocaine-exposed infants during the first week of life. EEG abnormalities were characterized as showing cerebral irritation with bursts of sharp waves and spikes and features of discontinuity. These abnormalities were unpredictable and did not correlate with variables such as maternal drug use, neonatal characteristics, or severity of neurological dysfunction. All abnormal EEGs reverted to normal when followed over a 3- to 12-month period, but the longer-term impact of these changes is not known. Although others have not noted the presence of clinical seizures in cocaine-exposed neonates, Chasnoff et al. (32) observed seizures in 6 of 52 infants born to mothers after cocaine use throughout the pregnancy; 2 of those 6 infants were reported to have abnormal EEGs. In addition, Kramer et al. (149) described 16 cocaine-exposed infants who developed seizures after birth. All seizures occurred within 36 hours after delivery and were either subtle (10), focal (1), tonic (2), or clonic (3). Many of the seizures responded poorly to therapeutic levels of anticonvulsant medications.

In addition to clinical neurological and electroencephalographic changes, a series of echoencephalographic abnormalities in neonates exposed to stimulants (cocaine and methamphetamine) and opiates was published by Dixon and Bejar (63). Thirty-five percent of the neonates had abnormal echoencephalographic studies, with the highest incidence in the stimulant subgroup. Lesions suggestive of prior hemorrhagic or ischemic injury with cavitation, located anterior and inferior to the lateral ventricles, in the frontal lobes and basal ganglia were found in 8% of the infants. Intraventricular hemorrhage was found in 12% of those drug-exposed babies; subependymal hemorrhage, in 11%; subarachnoid hemorrhage, in 14%; and ventricular dilatation suggesting diffuse atrophy, in 10%. Cerebral infarction was evident in two of the cocaine-exposed infants. Despite these impressive ECHO studies, infants with abnormal findings did not display identifiable neurobehavioral abnormalities during the newborn period. This is not totally surprising, since the location of the lesions may indicate damage that would be detectable when the infant is older and challenged with more complicated cognitive tasks.

Van de Bor et al. (258) demonstrated increased cerebral flow and increased mean arterial pressures on the first day of life in cocaine-exposed neonates and suggested that this cerebral hemodynamic abnormality may increase the risk of intracranial hemorrhage. In fact, Chasnoff et al. (32) had previously reported two infants who suffered perinatal cerebral infarction, which he ascribed to maternal cocaine use. Heier et al. (113) also found a higher rate of cortical infarctions (17%) in cocaine-exposed neonates than in the control population (only 2%). In a group of 39 term and near-term cocaine-exposed neonates, King et al. (144) found no increase in mild degrees of intraventricular hemorrhage and no instances of more severe hemorrhage, cystic periventricular leukomalacia, or stroke. Cocaine-exposed infants, however, showed an increase in anterior cerebral arterial blood flow velocity from day 1 to day 2; this change in vessel resistance may have been due to declining cocaine levels postnatally. Specifically in very-low-birth-weight infants (less than 1500 g), Singer et al. (235) found that cocaine-exposed infants had a higher incidence of mild intraventricular hemorrhages, as well as lower Bayley developmental scores and a higher incidence of developmental delay. In contrast, Dusick et al. (70) found no difference in the incidence of mild or severe intraventricular hemorrhage or of periventricular leukomalacia in cocaine-exposed infants of less than 1500 g than in controls.

Recent studies have expanded the spectrum of neonatal neurological abnormalities attributed to maternal cocaine use during pregnancy. Salamy et al. (227) found that intrauterine cocaine exposure was associated with prolonged auditory brainstem response (ABR) latencies and brainstem transmission time. Although these physiological parameters normalized by 3–6 months of age, transient abnormalities may have been caused by disturbed myelin synthesis or reduced number of oligodendrocites. Shih et al. (232) also demonstrated abnormal brainstem conduction time manifested as prolonged interpeak latencies and prolonged absolute latencies in ABR testing of 18 cocaine-exposed neonates. Carzoli et al. (25), however, found no differences in interpeak latencies of waveforms between cocaine-exposed infants and controls. Corwin et al. (52) found that the cry of cocaine-exposed infants (n = 404) differed from that of control infants (n = 364) in having fewer cry utterances, more short cries, and less crying in the hyperphonation mode, suggesting a pattern of underaroused neurobehavioral function. Abnormal eye findings following cocaine exposure that have been reported include a picture of "retinopathy of prematurity-like fundus and persistent hyperplastic primary vitreous" (253) and dilated and tortuous iris vessels (122).

Intrauterine exposure to cocaine has also been linked, usually through case reports, to neonatal problems involving other organ systems. These complications include necrotizing enterocolitis (252), bowel perforation (105), arterial thrombosis and hypertension (214), decreased cardiac output on day 1 of life (257), transient myocardial ischemia (171), and persistent hypertension (118).

FOLLOW-UP STUDIES

Sudden Infant Death Syndrome (SIDS).
Although as noted previously, the incidence of SIDS following intrauterine opiate exposure appears to be increased, the precise risk of SIDS in cocaine-exposed infants is not known. Discrepancies in the literature may be ascribed, in part, to confounding variables, such as low birth weight, racial-ethnic considerations, polysubstance use, and cigarette smoking, which are known to increase the incidence of SIDS. Chasnoff (29) anecdotally suggested that the risk of SIDS may be high, and subsequently reported that 15% of 66 infants exposed to cocaine in utero subsequently died of SIDS (22). In support of this alleged association, Chasnoff reported that cardiorespiratory patterns (pneumograms) in 32 cocaine-exposed infants at 8–14 days of age were abnormal in all 5 cocaine-exposed infants presenting with apnea of infancy and in 7 of the remaining 27 asymptomatic cocaine-exposed infants. All infants showing an abnormal pneumogram were treated with theophylline, with normalization of the repeat pneumogram 2 weeks later. No infant died of SIDS on follow-up. Silvestri et al. (234) found that cocaine-exposed infants showed longer pneumogram-confirmed apnea durations and bradycardia compared to controls; 2 of the 41 cocaine-exposed infants died of SIDS. Chen et al. (39) showed that facial airstream stimulation could bring out subtle respiratory abnormalities in cocaine-exposed infants. Data from Ward et al. (263) suggested that infants born to cocaine-using mothers, a large number of whom were polydrug users, showed blunted ventilatory responses to hypoxia, increased amount of periodic breathing, higher heart rates, and reduced response to hypercapnia before arousal. It is important to remember, however, that the links between "abnormal" cardiorespiratory tracings, apnea, and SIDS are still very tenuous.

In contrast to these findings, Bauchner et al. (9) found no increased incidence of SIDS in cocaine-exposed infants (1/174, 5.6/1000) compared with controls (4/821, 4.9/1000), although both incidences were increased over nationwide rates in their low socioeconomic Boston population. Kandall et al. (137) reviewed 41 cocaine-associated SIDS cases in a population of about 1.21 million births in New York City between 1979 and 1989. Once other high-risk variables (ethnicity, low maternal age, socioeconomic status, maternal cigarette smoking, low birth weight) were controlled, cocaine exposure resulted in only a very modest increase in the rate of SIDS (RR 1.3). Even when only the latter part of the decade (the "crack" years) was considered, the RR increased only slightly to 1.6, far lower than the risk of SIDS following maternal opiate use.

Postnatal Exposure.
Postnatal exposure to cocaine represents another potential source of toxicity for children. Given cocaine's lipophilic properties, which render it easily able to cross biological membranes, ready passage of the drug into breast milk has been established. Chasnoff (35) described a 2-week-old infant with signs of acute cocaine intoxication following exposure to cocaine in her mother's breast milk. Toxicity included irritability, vomiting, diarrhea, increased sucking reflex, hyperactive Moro reflex, increased symmetric deep tendon reflexes, and a marked lability of mood, as well as elevations of the infant's blood pressure, heart rate, and respiratory rate. All symptoms gradually waned over the next 72 hours. Chaney et al. (26) reported severe apnea and seizures in an 11-day-old infant following acute cocaine exposure while breastfeeding. It is also important to remember that a significant portion of drug-using patients may be HIV-positive. Until the precise risk of HIV transmission through breast milk is clarified, this concern forms another reason for discouraging breastfeeding in cocaine-using women.

Environmental Hazards.
Recent reports indicate that cocaine exposure may occur in young infants even after they leave the hospital. Shannon et al. (231) surveyed 1680 consecutive urine samples from 1120 pediatric patients in a children's hospital. Of the total sample, 52 (4.6%) had specimens positive for cocaine or a cocaine metabolite. Similar findings were reported by Kharasch et al. (141), who found that 2.4% of urine assays performed on 250 children ages 2 weeks to 5 years seen in a Boston hospital emergency department were positive for cocaine metabolites.

Case reports also support these surveys. Rivkin and Gilmore (216) described a 9-month-old infant who developed refractory seizures, apnea, and cyanosis following reported ingestion of cocaine left over from an adult party the night before. Bateman and Heagarty (8) described 4 infants ranging in age from 3´ months to almost 4 years admitted to a New York City municipal hospital with abnormal neurological findings ascribed circumstantially to passive "crack" inhalation. Two of the infants presented with seizures and two infants showed abnormal neurological signs, such as drowsiness and unsteady gait. Mirchandani et al. (174) reported 16 infant deaths at ages between 1 month and 5.5 months from the Philadelphia Medical Examiner's Office between 1987 and 1989 in which cocaine and/or its metabolite was found. Mott et al. (179) reported on 41 cocaine-exposed children between the ages of 2 months and 18 years, 19 of whom had abnormal neurological findings. These case descriptions should reinforce the need to rule out environmental toxins before labeling an infant death as SIDS.

Developmental Outcome.
Based on multiple biological and environmental risk factors, much concern has been voiced regarding the ultimate neurobehavioral prognosis of infants following intrauterine exposure to cocaine. The parents may be of poor socioeconomic status, culturally deprived, or lacking appropriate parenting models. The mother may be poorly nourished, may have medical and sexually transmitted diseases, including AIDS, and may have received little or no prenatal care. The infants frequently show suboptimal body and head growth during the intrauterine period. Uterine flow may be compromised as a result of cocaine-induced vasoconstriction, leading to acute or chronic fetal hypoxia. Central nervous system anomalies may be present. After birth, neurologic, neurobehavioral, electroencephalographic and echoencephalographic abnormalities have been documented. Stimulation for intellectual growth may be lacking because of prolonged hospital stays, infrequent and inappropriate parental contact, placement in a congregate care facility, or discharge to a home in which intellectual nurturing is lacking.

In spite of these valid concerns, long-term follow-up studies of large numbers of cocaine-exposed babies at present are lacking. Even before critically reviewed articles were published, the lay press began to report anecdotal experiences with the first cohort of 3- to 5-year-old children born in this "crack" epidemic (140). Cocaine-exposed babies were characterized as being "genetic inferiors" (150) and as showing significant deficits in environmental interactions such as play groups and nursery schools (54). These babies were also described as showing less representational play, decreased fantasy play and curious exploration, and lesser quality of play. Others described these children as "joyless," unable to participate fully in either structured or unstructured play situations, with attention deficits and flat, apathetic moods (16). Mothers were angrily accused of being uncaring and having lost their maternal instinct (13, 116). The coalescence of these reports fueled a groundswell of national anger directed at drug-using mothers, which led, among other things, to prosecution of many mothers for drug-related activities during pregnancy (133, 195). To counter press reports, experienced researchers and clinicians cautioned against a "rush to judgment" regarding cocaine-exposed infants (131, 153, 169, 180, 184, 275).

In fact, very little was actually known about the growth and development of cocaine-exposed babies (185). Alessandri et al. (3) found that cocaine-exposed infants at 4–8 months of age showed a decrease in arousal, less interest and joy in learning and less anger and sadness during extinction, and reduced response to stimuli when learning demand was reinstated. Chasnoff et al. (31) studied the 2-year growth and development of 106 infants following intrauterine exposure to cocaine and other drugs including marihuana, alcohol, and tobacco. Compared to a control group of infants, cocaine-exposed infants and infants exposed to alcohol and marihuana showed persistence of reduced head size on follow-up. Although Bayley developmental scores did not differ among the three groups, an increased number of drug-exposed infants scored more than 1 standard deviation below the mean. Cocaine exposure was the best predictor of reduced head size, and across all groups head size correlated well with developmental outcome. Azuma and Chasnoff (7) studied 3-year outcome data on 92 children exposed to "cocaine and other drugs" by path analysis, a multivariate method to determine the goodness-of-fit of hypotheses to actual generated data. The authors concluded that intrauterine drug exposure had both a direct and indirect (head circumference, home environment, and level of perseverance at a task) effect on cognitive ability at 3 years of age.

As more data are published, we may come to view this epidemic of cocaine use as having a very serious negative impact on a very large number of America's young children. It is important, however, to view these infants as medically and socially vulnerable not because of cocaine alone, but because of the wide array of adverse influences to which these children are subjected. An extremely useful paradigm has been formulated by Lester and Tronick (153). These researchers have conceptualized the mutual regulation that exists between the infant and its mother and other caretakers. The infant is impacted by the organic effects of the drug and other potentially adverse influences mediated through the prenatal environment. Environmental regulators affect the prenatal environment as well as maternal lifestyle. The mother or caretaker is additionally affected by substance abuse directly and those personality traits that led to her addiction. All of these factors impinge on the mutually regulatory process between infant and caretaker that is so essential for normal infant development. In this broader context, these parents and children should receive the comprehensive medical and social services that they so obviously need.

Amphetamines

Only a scanty literature exists describing the effects of amphetamines on the fetus, neonate, and young infant. This may soon change, since a smokable form of methamphetamine, called "ice" or "crystal," is reported to be widely used in Hawaii and has made its recent appearance in the United States.

Amphetamine (racemic (β-phenylisopropyl)amine) has powerful central nervous system stimulant actions and causes increased wakefulness, alertness, mood elevation, elation, and euphoria similar to cocaine. These effects are caused by stimulation of the release and blocking of reuptake of the neurotransmitters dopamine, norepinephrine, or serotonin. Acute neuropsychiatric effects of amphetamine overuse include agitation, tremors, hyperreflexia, irritability, confusion, aggressiveness, and panic states, among others. This is usually followed by fatigue and depression. Addiction and tolerance to amphetamine often occur. Methamphetamine is structurally similar to amphetamine but has relatively greater central effects and less prominent peripheral actions.

Animal studies assessing the impact of prenatal amphetamine administration on neonatal brain physiology and behavior have been summarized by Middaugh (172). Animal evidence indicates that maternal amphetamine administration reduces norepinephrine levels in the brains of newborn mice, which might affect neurotransmitter synthesis and function. Behaviorally, prenatal amphetamine administration leads to changes in motor activity and reduced performance on specific performance testing in offspring.

Since cocaine and amphetamines have similar central physiological effects, their impact on pregnancies should be similar. Both agents cause vasoconstriction and hypertension, which may result in acute or chronic fetal hypoxia. Eriksson et al. (72) described the perinatal course in 23 patients who were chronic amphetamine users, 6 of whom reportedly stopped amphetamine abuse during the pregnancy. Amphetamine use was associated with reduced prenatal care and an increased incidence of low-birth-weight babies. Neurological abnormalities consisted of unexplained seizures in one infant and drowsiness and inability to feed in two others. Eriksson et al. (73) later studied 69 amphetamine-using women, 52 of whom took amphetamine throughout the entire pregnancy. Although a concurrent control group was not compared, the authors reported a high perinatal mortality rate, high incidence of obstetric and pregnancy-related complications, an increased number of congenital malformations, and a high rate of neonatal neurological abnormalities in the drug-exposed group.

In a more recent study, Oro and Dixon (189) reported on 46 infants born to mothers who took cocaine and/or methamphetamine during their pregnancies. Comparison among the stimulant groups showed no difference in selected perinatal variables or in the number of neurological and physiological abnormalities in the infants. Use of stimulants led to an increase in placental abruptions and reductions in gestational age, birth weight, length, and head circumference compared with controls. After birth, stimulant-exposed infants showed abnormal weight change patterns, losing more weight and subsequently gaining weight more slowly. Neurologically, the infants' abnormalities included disordered sleep patterns, tremors, poor feeding, hyperactive reflexes, abnormal cry, and state disorganization. The authors noted that lethargy and poor feeding followed the hyperirritable stage in some methamphetamine-exposed infants. Recently, Billing et al. (14) studied 65 children to age 8 following intrauterine exposure to amphetamines. The authors found a significant correlation between the extent of exposure and subsequent poor psychometric testing, including aggressive behavior and problems of adjustment.

At the present time, although there is a clear need for more data on amphetamine exposure, cautious concern regarding developmental outcome seems appropriate.

Alcohol

A complete discussion of the effects of alcohol on pregnancy, fetal welfare, neonatal adaptation, and ultimate infant development is well beyond the scope of this chapter. It is critical to acknowledge, however, that alcohol abuse forms a prominent part in many, if not most, drug users' lives. As previously noted, many addicted women have been raised in alcoholic and abusive settings, and their own alcoholism may have roots in genetics, environmental influences, and predisposing psychosocial characteristics. Because alcohol is now known to represent a substance with enormous potential for human devastation in the perinatal period, inclusion of these comments seems warranted.

Similar to opiates and stimulants, estimates of intrauterine exposure to alcohol vary. A past estimate of approximately 2.6 million infants born annually following significant intrauterine alcohol exposure is considerably higher than that of 757,000 offered by the National Pregnancy and Health Survey. The most notable postnatal adverse effect of significant alcohol exposure is the fetal alcohol syndrome (FAS), which was first described by Lemoine in 1968 and by Jones and Smith in 1973. This syndrome can be identified in approximately 1 in 300 to 1 in 1000 births; a lesser degree of damage, termed fetal alcohol effects (FAE), may occur in 1 in 100 live births. Varying estimates of prevalence are based to some degree on the failure by health professionals to make the definitive diagnosis (158). Although the amount of alcohol that must be consumed to cause fetal damage is not known and must certainly be determined to some extent by individual variability, it is generally believed that consumption of more than 3 ounces of absolute alcohol daily, especially in conjunction with "binge drinking," poses special risk to the fetus. Because subtle effects may go unnoticed, no safe level of alcohol intake during pregnancy has been established.

Three series of findings define FAS:

1. One of the most constant features of FAS is fetal growth retardation; weight, length, and head circumference generally fall below the 10th percentile for gestational age (58, 97, 123, 158, 194, 239).
2. A nearly constant feature of FAS is the characteristic facial dysmorphism of short palpebral fissures, hypoplastic maxillae, short upturned nose, hypoplastic philtrum, thinned upper vermilion border, and micrognathia or retrognathia. Less common associated features include ptosis, strabismus, epicanthal folds, microphthalmia, posteriorly rotated ears, and cleft lip or palate. Other common somatic abnormalities include structural cardiac defects, cutaneous hemangiomas, aberrant palmar creases, and pectus excavatum; less common features include hypospadias, renal abnormalities, joint malformations, and hernias of the diaphragm, umbilicus, and abdominal wall (58, 100, 108, 121, 194, 239).
3. The most devastating aspect of FAS is severe alcohol-induced central nervous system dysfunction (47). Irritability, tremulousness, poor sucking, inconsolable crying, and hypertonia have been noted in many infants (49). Pierog et al. (197), in a small series of six neonates undergoing "alcohol withdrawal," noted the occurrence of tonic-clonic seizures. Ioffe et al. (120) found that maternal alcohol ingestion during pregnancy was associated with hypersynchrony of the neonatal EEG. Cerebral malformations, neurological heterotopia, and interruptions of neuronal migration have also been described (44). Holzman et al. (117) found that low-birth-weight babies of less than 31 weeks gestation born to mothers with moderate-to-high alcohol consumption during pregnancy were at increased risk for perinatal brain injuries such as isolated brain hemorrhage (odds ratio 5.5), any brain hemorrhage (odds ratio 6.7), and white matter damage (odds ratio 9.5).

Follow-up examinations tend to reveal mild cerebellar deficits, hypotonicity, hyperactivity, hearing deficits, speech and language problems, sleep disturbances, and behavioral disorders (43, 121, 243). The most serious neurological outcome attributed to alcohol exposure is mental retardation, which occurs in about 85% of FAS children. FAS is now believed to be the leading known cause of mental retardation in the United States. Although IQ scores vary, children with full-blown FAS rarely show normal mental ability. Golden et al. (97) studied 12 alcohol-affected infants at between 6 and 20 months. Significant developmental delay was observed in the study group compared to controls in both the Bayley mental development quotient (86 versus 105) and motor development quotient (90 versus 110). Iosub et al. (121) found that in 63 children aged 1 day to 23 years who were diagnosed with FAS, IQs ranged between 50 and 97. Most patients tended to cluster between 65 and 70, and mental retardation was found in 14 of 30 patients older than 3 years of age. Prominent neurobehavioral problems included irritability, hyperactivity in about three-quarters of patients, and speech and language deficits in about 80% of patients. Coles and her group at Emory University in Atlanta (22, 46) studied 25 school-age children born to mothers who drank regularly during pregnancy. The study group was found to show deficits in areas of intellectual functioning such as sequential processing, overall mental processing, and premath and reading skills, as well as attentional and behavioral problems in structured learning situations.

A landmark study on sequelae of FAS in adolescents and adults was published by Streissguth et al. (249). The authors studied 61 patients with FAS at 12 years of age or older (range 12–40 years). Seventy-four percent of the sample were Native American, 21% were black, and 5% were white. Physical examination showed that reduced height and head circumference were still apparent but that weight deficiency was less marked. The characteristic facial dysmorphology of FAS became less distinctive with increasing age. Most importantly, the average IQ score for the combined FAS-FAE group was 68, representing significant reduction in intellectual function. IQs ranged from 20 to 105, and 58% of the patients had an IQ below 70. In terms of academic and adaptive functionings, only 6% were in regular classes; the remainder required special education or were not in school or working. All patients showed maladaptive behaviors. This study documents that alcohol-induced deficits persist for as long as FAS patients have been studied. In this regard, the fiscal impact of alcohol-associated damage is estimated to be greater than $320 million dollars annually in the United States. The human impact is incalculable.

CONCLUSIONS AND RECOMMENDATIONS

Despite the influx of newer drugs of abuse, opiate and stimulant use, often in conjunction with alcohol abuse, continue to be major American societal problems. The ratio of women to men in the addicted population has increased since the 1920s and even more so since the mid-1980s. Although the history of women and addiction dates back over 150 years in the United States (133), controversy still exists on how best to prevent and treat the adverse sequelae of addiction. That many of these women are in the childbearing age group helps to explain the large numbers of drug-exposed infants that have recently been documented epidemiologically. Numerous investigators have reported extremely high incidences of obstetrical and medical complications among street addicts. Evidence as to increased morbidity and mortality among their newborn infants and preliminary data suggesting long-term developmental complications, especially related to alcohol exposure, has also reached a point of consensus.

It does seem clear that providing comprehensive multidisciplinary prenatal care for addicts offers an opportunity to significantly reduce morbidity and mortality in both drug-dependent mothers and their infants. The major impact of comprehensive care coupled with methadone maintenance for narcotic-dependent women has been to reduce perinatal morbidity and mortality, largely attributable to reduction of rates of low birth weight in offspring. Aside from problems arising from direct adverse effects of drugs, low-birth-weight infants are overrepresented in the population of infants who eventually show mental subnormality as well as those who will have great difficulty in school because they are "poor learners." These handicapped individuals will be unable to compete fully in our increasingly complex society.

Based on this conclusion, we strongly advise that the pregnant woman who abuses drugs must be designated as "high risk" and warrants specialized care in a perinatal center where she can be provided with comprehensive medical and obstetrical care, as well as addiction and psychosocial counseling. Care must be provided in a supportive, proactive, and nonjudgmental fashion. Women must know that sharing of confidential information with health care providers will *not* render them liable to criminal prosecution.

After an initial in-hospital assessment, treatment of addiction may take place in an inpatient or outpatient setting. Opiate-dependent women are best treated with methadone maintenance, although medical withdrawal using tapering doses of methadone (with close obstetric and medical supervision) may be offered in selected cases. Medical withdrawal, if requested or necessary, preferably should take place between the 16th and the 32nd week of gestation and should be carried out slowly (5 mg reduction every 2 weeks). The pregnant woman addicted to barbiturates or major tranquilizers along with opiates should be detoxified during her second trimester in a specialized detoxification center.

Psychosocial counseling should be provided by experienced social workers who are aware of the medical needs, as well as the social and psychological needs, of this population. Services should include, but not be limited to, provision of housing, nutritional advice, child care, legal services, and counseling about interpersonal relations.

Maternal-infant attachment, both antenatally and postpartum, should be strongly encouraged. Special emphasis should be placed on enhancing parenting skills of these women in an effort to decrease the anticipated increase in child neglect in this population.

Social and medical support should not end with the hospitalization; an outreach program, incorporating public health nurses and community workers, should be established. The ability of the mother to care for the infant after discharge from the hospital should be assessed by frequent observations in the home and clinic settings.

Clinicians working in this field must continue to strive for excellence in the care of pregnant drug-dependent women and their children. Government agencies on all levels must recognize their specific responsibility to these women and children and should provide adequate funding for much-needed comprehensive services. Only if clinicians and government funding officials make this comprehensive care a societal priority will we be able to cope with the pathophysiological and behavioral effects of drug use on pregnant women and their children.

Society's Approach to Maternal Drug Use

Frustration in the United States over its ability to deal effectively with its latest cocaine epidemic has created a very punitive mood in dealing with drug-using women (37, 133, 195). At the present time, a number of states have instituted criminal action against pregnant drug-using women despite those states' inability or reluctance to provide treatment and counseling specifically designed for substance-using pregnant women. A punitive rather than rehabilitative approach runs counter to medical and judicial precedent and may drive "hard to reach" women further from the health care system. Failure to provide family-based rehabilitation, when possible, places children in already overburdened and stressed child welfare and foster care systems. Drug-using women, frequently battered and abused as children and adults, need comprehensive medical, obstetrical, psychiatric, and drug counseling treatment. Our goals of promoting healthy mothers and children can best be met by providing such comprehensive services rather than abandoning these unfortunate women in a time of great need.

References

1. Abrams CAL. Cytogenic risks to the offspring of pregnant addicts. Addict Dis 1975;2:63–77.
2. Acker D, Sachs BP, Tracy KJ, Wise WE. Abruptio placentae associated with cocaine use. Am J Obstet Gynecol 1983;146:220–221.
3. Alessandri SM, Sullivan MW, Imaizumi S, Lewis M. Learning and emotional responsivity in cocaine exposed infants. Dev Psychol 1993; 29:989–997.
4. Amarose AP, Norusis MJ. Cytogenetics of methadone-managed and heroin-addicted pregnant women and their newborn infants. Am J Obstet Gynecol 1976;124:635–640.
5. Archie CL, Lee MI, Sokol RJ, Norman G. The effects of methadone treatment on the reactivity of the nonstress test. Obstet Gynecol 1989;74: 254–255.
6. Athinarayanan P, Pierog SH, Nigam SK, Glass L. Chlordiazepoxide withdrawal in the neonate. Am J Obstet Gynecol 1976;124:212–213.
7. Azuma SD, Chasnoff IJ. Outcome of children prenatally exposed to cocaine and other drugs: a path analysis of three-year data. Pediatrics 1993; 92:396–402.
8. Bateman DA, Heagarty MD. Passive freebase cocaine ("crack") inhalation by infants and toddlers. Am J Dis Child 1989;143:25–27.
9. Bauchner H, Zuckerman B, McClain M, Frank D, Fried LE, Kayne H. Risk of sudden infant death syndrome among infants with in utero exposure to cocaine. J Pediatr 1988;113:831–834.
10. Baxi LV, Petrie RH. Pharmacologic effects on labor: effect of drugs on dystocia, labor and uterine activity. Clin Obstet Gynecol 1987;30:19–32.
11. Beeram MR, Abedin M, Shoroye A, Jayam-Trouth A, Young M, Reid Y. Occurrence of craniosynostosis in neonates exposed to cocaine and tobacco in utero. J Natl Med Assoc 1993; 85:865–868.
12. Behrendt H, Green M. Nature of the sweating deficit of prematurely born neonates. N Engl J Med 1972;286:1376–1379.
13. Besharov DJ. Crack babies: the worst threat is mom herself. Washington Post August 6, 1989.
14. Billing L, Eriksson M, Jonsson B, Steneroth G, Zetterstrom R. The influence of environmental factors on behavioral problems in 8 year old children exposed to amphetamine during fetal life. Child Abuse Neglect 1994;18:3–9.
15. Bingol N, Fuchs M, Diaz V, Stone RK, Gromisch DS. Teratogenicity of cocaine in humans. J Pediatr 1987;110:93–96.
16. Blakeslee S. Crack's toll among babies: a joyless view, even of toys. New York Times September 17, 1989.
17. Blinick G. Fertility of narcotic addicts and effects of addiction on the offspring. Soc Biol 1971;18(suppl):34–39.
18. Blinick G, Inturrisi CE, Jerez E, Wallach RC. Methadone assays in pregnant women and progeny. Am J Obstet Gynecol 1975;121:617–621.

19. Blinick G, Jerez E, Wallach RC. Methadone maintenance, pregnancy and progeny. JAMA 1973;225:477–479.
20. Blinick G, Wallach RC, Jerez E. Pregnancy in narcotic addicts treated by medical withdrawal. Am J Obstet Gynecol 1969;105:997–1003.
21. Blumenthal I, Lindsay S. Neonatal barbiturate withdrawal. Postgrad Med J 1977;53:157–158.
22. Brown RT, Coles CD, Smith IE, et al. Effects of prenatal alcohol exposure at school age. II. Attention and behavior. Neurotoxicol Teratol 1991;13:369–376.
23. Burstein Y, Giardina PJV, Rausen AR, Kandall SR, Siljestrom K, Peterson CM. Thrombocytosis and increased circulating platelet aggregates in newborn infants of polydrug users. J Pediatr 1979;94:895–899.
24. Callahan CM, Grant TM, Phipps P, et al. Measurement of gestational cocaine exposure: sensitivity of infants' hair, meconium, and urine. J Pediatr 1992;120:763–768.
25. Carzoli RP, Murphy SP, Hammer-Knisely J, Houy J. Evaluation of auditory brain-stem response in full-term infants of cocaine-abusing mothers. Am J Dis Child 1991;145:1013–1016.
26. Chaney NE, Franke J, Wadlington WB. Cocaine convulsions in a breast-feeding baby. J Pediatr 1988;112:134–135.
27. Chang A, Wood C, Humphrey M, Gilbert M, Wagstaff C. The effects of narcotics on fetal acid base status. Br J Obstet Gynaecol 1976;83:56–61.
28. Chasnoff IJ. Drug use and women: establishing a standard of care. In: Hutchings DE, ed. Prenatal abuse of licit and illicit drugs. Ann N Y Acad Sci 1989;562:208–210.
29. Chasnoff IJ, Burns WJ, Schnoll SH, Burns KA. Cocaine use in pregnancy. N Engl J Med 1985; 313:666–669.
30. Chasnoff IJ, Chisum GM, Kaplan WE. Maternal cocaine use and genitourinary malformations. Teratology 1988;37:201–204.
31. Chasnoff IJ, Griffith DR, Freier C, Murray J. Cocaine/polydrug use in pregnancy: two-year follow-up. Pediatrics 1992;89:284–289.
32. Chasnoff IJ, Griffith DR, MacGregor S, Dirkes K, Burns KA. Temporal patterns of cocaine use in pregnancy. JAMA 1989;261:1741–1744.
33. Chasnoff IJ, Hunt CE, Kletter R, Kaplan D. Prenatal cocaine exposure is associated with respiratory pattern abnormalities. Am J Dis Child 1989;143:583–587.
34. Chasnoff IJ, Landress HJ, Barrett ME. The prevalence of illicit-drug or alcohol use during pregnancy and discrepancies in mandatory reporting in Pinellas County, Florida. N Engl J Med 1990;322:1202–1206.
35. Chasnoff IJ, Lewis DE, Squires L. Cocaine intoxication in a breast-fed infant. Pediatrics 1987; 80:836–838.
36. Chavez CJ, Ostrea EM, Stryker JC, Smialek Z. Sudden infant death syndrome among infants of drug-dependent mothers. J Pediatr 1979;95: 407–409.

37. Chavkin W, Kandall SR. Between a "rock" and a hard place: perinatal drug abuse. Pediatrics 1990;85:223–225.
38. Chavkin W, Paone D, Friedmann P, Wilets I. Psychiatric histories of drug using mothers: treatment implications. J Subst Abuse Treat 1993;10:445–448.
39. Chen C, Duara S, Neto GS, et al. Respiratory instability in neonates with in utero exposure to cocaine. J Pediatr 1991;119:111–113.
40. Cherukuri P, Minkoff H, Feldman J, Parekh A, Glass L. A cohort study of alkaloidal cocaine ("crack") in pregnancy. Obstet Gynecol 1988; 72:147–151.
41. Chiang CN, Finnegan LP, eds. Medication development for the treatment of pregnant addicts and their infants. NIDA research monograph no. 149, NIH publication no. 95–3891. Rockville, MD: National Institute on Drug Addiction, 1995.
42. Chouteau M, Namerow PB, Leppert P. The effect of cocaine abuse on birth weight and gestational age. Obstet Gynecol 1988;72:351–354.
43. Church MW, Gerkin KP. Hearing disorders in children with fetal alcohol syndrome: findings from case reports. Pediatrics 1988;82:147–154.
44. Clarren SK, Alvord EC, Sumi M, Streissguth AP, Smith DW. Brain malformations related to prenatal exposure to ethanol. J Pediatr 1978;92: 64–67.
45. Cobrinik RW, Hood TR, Chusid E. The effect of maternal narcotic addiction on the newborn infant; review of the literature and report of 22 cases. Pediatrics 1959;24:288–304.
46. Coles CD, Brown RT, Smith IE, Platzman KA, Erickson S, Falek A. Effects of prenatal alcohol exposure at school age. I. Physical and cognitive development. Neurotoxicol Teratol 1991;13: 357–367.
47. Coles CD, Platzman KA. Fetal alcohol effects in preschool children: research, prevention, and intervention. In: Identifying the needs of drug-affected children: public policy issues. OSAP prevention monograph no. 11. Rockville, MD: U.S. Department of Health and Human Services, 1992:59–86.
48. Coles CD, Platzman KA, Smith I, James ME, Falek A. Effects of cocaine and alcohol use in pregnancy on neonatal growth and neurobehavioral status. Neurotoxicol Teratol 1992;14: 23–33.
49. Coles CD, Smith IE, Fernhoff PM, Falek A. Neonatal ethanol withdrawal: characteristics in clinically normal, nondysmorphic neonates. J Pediatr 1984;105:445–451.
50. Connaughton JF, Finnegan LP, Schut J, Emich JP. Current concepts in the management of the pregnant opiate addict. Addict Dis 1975;2: 21–35.
51. Connaughton JF, Reeser D, Schut J, Finnegan LP. Perinatal addiction: outcome and management. Am J Obstet Gynecol 1977;129:679–686.
52. Corwin MJ, Lester BM, Sepkoski C, McLaugh-

lin S, Kayne H, Golub HL. Effects of in utero cocaine exposure on newborn acoustical cry characteristics. Pediatrics 1992;89:1199–1203.

53. Cregler LL, Mark H. Medical complications of cocaine abuse. N Engl J Med 1986;315:1495–1500.

54. Daley S. Born on crack and coping with kindergarten. New York Times February 7, 1991.

55. Dar H, Schmidt R, Nitowsky HM. Palmar creases and their clinical significance: a study of newborns at risk. Pediatr Res 1977;11:103–108.

56. Davis MM, Brown BS, Glendinning ST. Neonatal effects of heroin addiction and methadone-treated pregnancies. Preliminary report on 70 live births. In: Proceedings of the Fifth National Conference on Methadone Treatment. New York: National Association for the Prevention of Addiction to Narcotics, 1973:1153–1164.

57. Davis RC, Chappel JN, Mejia-Zelaya A, Madden J. Clinical observations on methadone-maintained pregnancies. In: Harbison RD, ed. Perinatal addiction. New York: Spectrum, 1975: 101–112.

58. Day NL, Jasperse D, Richardson G, et al. Prenatal exposure to alcohol: effect on infant growth and morphologic characteristics. Pediatrics 1989;84:536–541.

59. Debooy VD, Seshia MMK, Tennenbein M, Casiro OG. Intravenous pentazocine and methylphenidate abuse during pregnancy. Am J Dis Child 1993;147:1062–1065.

60. Desmond MM, Schwanecke RP, Wilson GS, Yasunaga S, Burgdorff I. Maternal barbiturate utilization and neonatal withdrawal symptomatology. J Pediatr 1972;80:190–197.

61. Desmond MM, Wilson GS. Neonatal abstinence syndrome: recognition and diagnosis. Addict Dis 1975;2:113–121.

62. Dicker M, Leighton EA. Trends in diagnosed drug problems among newborns: United States, 1979–1987. Drug Alcohol Depend 1991;28: 151–165.

63. Dixon SD, Bejar R. Echoencephalographic findings in neonates associated with maternal cocaine and methamphetamine use: incidence and clinical correlates. J Pediatr 1989;115:770–778.

64. Doberczak TM, Kandall SR, Wilets I. Neonatal opiate abstinence syndrome in term and preterm infants. J Pediatr 1991;118:933–937.

65. Doberczak TM, Kandall SR, Friedmann P. Relationships between maternal methadone dosage, maternal-neonatal methadone levels, and neonatal withdrawal. Obstet Gynecol 1993; 81:936–940.

66. Doberczak TM, Shanzer S, Cutler R, Senie RT, Loucopoulos JA, Kandall SR. One-year follow-up of infants with abstinence-associated seizures. Arch Neurol 1988;45:649–653.

67. Doberczak TM, Shanzer S, Senie RT, Kandall SR. Neonatal neurologic and encephalographic effects of intrauterine cocaine exposure. J Pediatr 1988;113:354–358.

68. Doberczak TM, Thornton JC, Bernstein J, Kandall SR. Impact of maternal drug dependency on birth weight and head circumference of offspring. Am J Dis Child 1987;141:1163–1167.

69. Dole VP, Kreek MJ. Methadone plasma level: sustained by a reservoir of drug in tissue. Proc Natl Acad Sci U S A 1973;70:10.

70. Dusick AM, Covert RF, Schreiber MD, et al. Risk of intracranial hemorrhage and other adverse outcomes after cocaine exposure in a cohort of 323 very low birth weight infants. J Pediatr 1993;122:438–445.

71. Eisen LN, Field TM, Bandstra ES, et al. Perinatal cocaine effects on neonatal stress behavior and performance on the Brazelton scale. Pediatrics 1991;88:477–480.

72. Eriksson M, Larsson G, Winbladh B, Zetterstrom R. The influence of amphetamine addiction on pregnancy and the newborn infant. Acta Pediatr Scand 1978;67:95–99.

73. Eriksson M, Larsson G, Zetterstrom R. Amphetamine addiction and pregnancy. Acta Obstet Gynecol Scand 1981;60:253–259.

74. Fantel AG, MacPhail BJ. The teratogenicity of cocaine. Teratology 1982;26:17–19.

75. Farrar HC, Kearns GL. Cocaine: clinical pharmacology and toxicology. J Pediatr 1989;115: 665–675.

76. Finnegan LP, ed. Drug dependence in pregnancy: clinical management of mother and child. A manual for medical professionals and paraprofessionals prepared for the National Institute on Drug Abuse, Services Research Branch, Rockville, MD. Washington, DC: Government Printing Office, 1978.

77. Finnegan LP. In utero opiate dependence and sudden infant death syndrome. Clin Perinatol 1979;6:163–180.

78. Finnegan LP. Pulmonary problems encountered by the infant of the drug-dependent mother. Clin Chest Med 1980;1:311–325.

79. Finnegan LP. Neonatal abstinence syndrome: assessment and pharmacotherapy. In: Rubaltelli FF, Granati B, eds. Neonatal therapy: an update. New York: Elsevier, 1986:122–146.

80. Finnegan LP, Connaughton JF, Emich JP, Wieland WF. Comprehensive care of the pregnant addict and its effect on maternal and infant outcome. Contemp Drug Probl 1972;1: 795–809.

81. Finnegan LP, Ehrlich SM. Maternal drug abuse during pregnancy: evaluation and pharmacotherapy for neonatal abstinence. Mod Methods Pharmacol Testing Eval Drugs Abuse 1990; 6:255–263.

82. Finnegan LP, Hagan T, Kaltenbach KA. Scientific foundation of clinical practice: opiate use in pregnant women. Bull N Y Acad Med 1991; 67:223–239.

83. Finnegan LP, Kaltenbach K. Neonatal abstinence syndrome. In: Hoekelman RA, Friedman SB, Nelson N, Seidel HM, eds. Primary pediatric care. St. Louis: CV Mosby, 1992:1367–1378.

84. Finnegan LP, Mellott JM, Ryan LM, Wapner RJ. Perinatal exposure to cocaine: human studies. In: Lakoski JM, Galloway MP, White J, eds. Cocaine: pharmacology, physiology, and clinical strategies. Boca Raton, FL: CRC Press, 1992:391–409.

85. Finnegan LP, Reeser DS. Maternal drug abuse patterns: effect upon the duration of neonatal abstinence. Pediatr Res 1979;13:368.

86. Finnegan LP, Reeser DS, Connaughton JF. The effects of maternal drug dependence on neonatal mortality. Drug Alcohol Depend 1977;2: 131–140.

87. Finnegan LP, Reeser DS, Kaltenbach K, Mac-New BA. Phenobarbital loading dose method for treatment of neonatal abstinence: effect upon infant development. Pediatr Res 1979; 13:331.

88. Finnegan LP, Shouraie Z, Emich JP, Connaughton JF, Schut J, Deli024-Papadopoulos M. Alternatives of the oxygen hemoglobin equilibrium curve and red cell 2,3-diphosphoglycerate (2,3-DPG) in cord blood of infants born to narcotic addicted mothers. Pediatr Res 1974; 8:344.

89. Fitzgerald E, Kaltenbach K, Finnegan LP. Patterns of interaction among drug-dependent women and their infants. Pediatr Res 1990;27:44.

90. Fries MH, Kuller JA, Norton ME, et al. Facial features of infants exposed prenatally to cocaine. Teratology 1993;48:413–420.

91. Fulroth R, Phillips B, Durand DJ. Perinatal outcome of infants exposed to cocaine and/or heroin in utero. Am J Dis Child 1989;143: 905–910.

92. Glass L, Rajegowda BK, Kahn EJ, Floyd MV. Effect of heroin on respiratory rate and acid-base status in the newborn. N Engl J Med 1972; 286:746–748.

93. Glass L, Rajegowda BK, Evans HE. Absence of respiratory distress syndrome in premature infants of heroin addicted mothers. Lancet 1971;2:685–686.

94. Glass L, Rajegowda BK, Mukherjee TK, Roth MM, Evans HE. Effect of heroin on corticosteroid production in pregnant addicts and their fetuses. Am J Obstet Gynecol 1973;117: 416–418.

95. Gluck R, Kulovich MV. Lecithin/sphingomyelin ratios in amniotic fluid in normal and abnormal pregnancy. Am J Obstet Gynecol 1973;115:539–546.

96. Goetz RL, Bain RV. Neonatal withdrawal symptoms associated with maternal use of pentazocine. J Pediatr 1974;84:887–888.

97. Golden NL, Sokol RJ, Kuhnert BR, Bottoms S. Maternal alcohol use and infant development. Pediatrics 1982;70:931–934.

98. Gomby DS, Shiono PH. Estimating the number of substance-exposed infants. In: The future of children. Los Altos, CA: Center for the Future of Children, 1991;1:17–25.

99. Goodfriend MJ, Shey IA, Klein MD. The effects of maternal narcotic addiction on the newborn. Am J Obstet Gynecol 1956;71:29–36.

100. Graham JM, Hanson JW, Darby BL, Barr HM, Streissguth AP. Independent dysmorphology evaluations at birth and 4 years of age for children exposed to varying amounts of alcohol in utero. Pediatrics 1988;81:772–778.

101. Graham K, Koren G, Klein J, Schneiderman J, Greenwald M. Determination of gestational cocaine exposure by hair analysis. JAMA 1989;262:3328–3330.

102. Green M, Suffet F. The neonatal narcotic withdrawal index: a device for the improvement of care in the abstinence syndrome. Am J Drug Alcohol Abuse 1981;8:203–213.

103. Hadeed AJ, Siegel SR. Maternal cocaine use during pregnancy: effect on the newborn infant. Pediatrics 1989;84:205–210.

104. Hagan TA. A retrospective search for the etiology of drug abuse: a background comparison of a drug-addicted population of women and a control group of non-addicted women. NIDA Res Monogr 1988;81:254–261.

105. Hall TR, Zaninovic A, Lewin D, Barrett C, Boechat MI. Neonatal intestinal ischemia with bowel perforation: an in utero complication of maternal cocaine abuse. AJR Am J Roentgenol 1992;158:1303–1304.

106. Handler A, Kistin N, Davis F, Ferre C. Cocaine use during pregnancy: perinatal outcomes. Am J Epidemiol 1991;133:818–825.

107. Hans SL. Developmental consequences of prenatal exposure to methadone. Ann N Y Acad Sci 1989;562:195–207.

108. Hanson JW, Streissguth AP, Smith DW. The effects of moderate alcohol consumption during pregnancy on fetal growth and morphogenesis. J Pediatr 1978;92:457–460.

109. Harper R, Concepcion GS, Blenman S. Observations on the sudden death of infants born to addicted mothers. In: Proceedings of the Fifth National Conference on Methadone Treatment. New York: National Association for the Pre-

vention of Addiction to Narcotics, 1973:1122–1127.

110. Harper RG, Solish G, Feingold E, Gersten-Woolf NA, Sokal MM. Maternal ingested methadone, body fluid methadone and the neonatal withdrawal syndrome. Am J Obstet Gynecol 1977;129:417–424.

111. Harper RG, Solish GI, Purow HM, Sang E, Panepinto WC. The effect of a methadone treatment program upon pregnant heroin addicts and their newborn infants. Pediatrics 1974;54:300–305.

112. Harris EF, Friend GW, Tolley EA. Enhanced prevalence of ankyloglossia with maternal cocaine use. Cleft Palate Craniofac J 1992;29:72–76.

113. Heier LA, Carpanzano CR, Mast J, Brill PW, Winchester P, Deck MDF. Maternal cocaine use: the spectrum of radiologic abnormalities in the neonatal CNS. Am J Neuroradiol 1991;12:951–956.

114. Herzlinger RA, Kandall SR, Vaughan HG. Neonatal seizures associated with narcotic withdrawal. J Pediatr 1977;91:638–641.

115. Hill RM, Desmond MM. Management of the narcotic withdrawal syndrome in the neonate. Pediatr Clin North Am 1963;10:67–86.

116. Hinds M deC. The instincts of parenthood become part of crack's toll. New York Times March 17, 1990.

117. Holzman C, Paneth N, Little R, et al. Perinatal brain injury in premature infants born to mothers using alcohol in pregnancy. Pediatrics 1995;95:66–73.

118. Horn PT. Persistent hypertension after prenatal cocaine exposure. J Pediatr 1992;121:288–291.

119. Hoyme HE, Jones KL, Dixon SD, et al. Prenatal cocaine exposure and fetal vascular disruption. Pediatrics 1990;85:743–747.

120. Ioffe S, Childiaeva R, Chernick V. Prolonged effects of maternal alcohol ingestion on the neonatal electroencephalogram. Pediatrics 1984;74:330–335.

121. Iosub S, Fuchs M, Bingol N, Gromisch DS. Fetal alcohol syndrome revisited. Pediatrics 1981;68:475–479.

122. Isenberg SJ, Spierer A, Inkelis SH. Ocular signs of cocaine intoxication in neonates. Am J Ophthalmol 1987;103:211–214.

123. Jacobson JL, Jacobson SW, Sokol RJ, Martier SS, Ager JW, Shankaran S. Effects of alcohol use, smoking, and illicit drug use on fetal growth in black infants. J Pediatr 1994;124:757–764.

124. Jaffe JH, Martin WR. Opioid analgesics and antagonists. In: Gilman AG, Goodman LS, Rall TW, Murad F, eds. Goodman and Gilman's the pharmacological basis of therapeutics. 7th ed. New York: Macmillan, 1985:518.

125. Jain L, Meyer W, Moore C, Tebbett I, Gauthier D, Vidyasagar D. Detection of fetal cocaine exposure by analysis of amniotic fluid. Obstet Gynecol 1993;81:787–790.

126. Jhaveri RC, Glass L, Evans HE, et al. Effects of methadone on thyroid function in mother, fetus, and newborn. Pediatrics 1980;65:557–561.

127. Kahn EJ, Neumann LL, Polk G. The course of the heroin withdrawal syndrome in newborn infants treated with phenobarbital or chlorpromazine. J Pediatr 1969;75:495–500.

128. Kaltenbach K, Finnegan LP. Children exposed to methadone in utero: assessment of developmental and cognitive ability. Ann N Y Acad Sci 1989;562:360–362.

129. Kaltenbach K, Finnegan LP. The influence of the neonatal abstinence syndrome on mother-infant interaction. In: Anthony EJ, Chiland C, eds. The child in his family: perilous development: child raising and identity formation under stress. New York: Wiley-Interscience, 1988:223–230.

130. Kaltenbach K, Graziani LJ, Finnegan LP. Methadone exposure in utero: developmental status at one and two years of age. Pharmacol Biochem Behav 1979;11(suppl):15–17.

131. Kandall S. Don't call them "crack babies." Newsday April 18, 1991.

132. Kandall SR, Consensus Panel Chair. Improving treatment for drug-exposed infants. Rockville, MD: U.S. Department of Health and Human Services (Center for Substance Abuse Treatment), 1993.

133. Kandall SR. Substance and shadow: women and addiction in the United States. Cambridge, MA: Harvard University Press, 1996.

134. Kandall SR, Albin S, Gartner LM, Lee K, Eidelman A, Lowinson J. The narcotic dependent mother: fetal and neonatal consequences. Early Hum Dev 1977;1:159–169.

135. Kandall SR, Albin S, Lowinson J, Berle B, Eidelman AI, Gartner LM. Differential effects of maternal heroin and methadone use on birth weight. Pediatrics 1976;58:681–685.

136. Kandall SR, Doberczak TM, Mauer KR, Strashun RH, Korts DC. Opiate v CNS depressant therapy in neonatal drug abstinence syndrome. Am J Dis Child 1983;137:378–382.

137. Kandall SR, Gaines J, Habel L, Davidson G, Jessop D. Relationship of maternal substance abuse to sudden infant death syndrome in offspring. J Pediatr 1993;123:120–126.

138. Kandall SR, Gaines J. Maternal substance use and subsequent sudden infant death syndrome (SIDS) in offspring. Neurotoxicol Teratol 1991;13:235–241.

139. Kandall SR, Gartner LM. Late presentation of drug withdrawal symptoms in newborns. Am J Dis Child 1972;127:58–61.

140. Kantrowitz B. The crack children. Newsweek 1990;February 12:62.

141. Kharasch SJ, Glotzer D, Vinci R, Weitzman M, Sargent J. Unsuspected cocaine exposure in young children. Am J Dis Child 1991;145:204–206.

142. Kilbey MM, Asghar A, eds. Methodological issues in controlled studies on effects of prenatal exposure to drug abuse. NIDA research monograph no. 114, DHHS publication no. (ADM) 91–1837. Rockville, MD: U.S. Department of Health and Human Services, 1991.

143. Kilbey MM, Asghar A, eds. Methodological issues in epidemiological, prevention, and treatment research on drug-exposed women and their children. NIDA research monograph no. 117, DHHS publication no. (ADM)92–1881. Rockville, MD: U.S. Department of Health and Human Services, 1991.

144. King TA, Perlman JM, Laptook AR, Rollins N, Jackson G, Little B. Neurologic manifestations of in utero cocaine exposure in near-term and term infants. Pediatrics 1995;96:259–264.

145. Kliegman RM, Madura D, Kiwi R, Eisenberg I, Yamashita T. Relation of maternal cocaine use to the risks of prematurity and low birth weight. J Pediatr 1994;124:751–756.

146. Koren G, Gladstone D, Robeson C, Robieux I. The perception of teratogenic risk of cocaine. Teratology 1992;46:567–571.

147. Koren G, Graham K, Feigenbaum A, Einarson T. Evaluation and counseling of teratogenic risk: the Motherisk approach. J Clin Pharmacol 1993;33:405–411.

148. Kosten TA. Cocaine attenuates the severity of naloxone-precipitated opioid withdrawal. Life Sci 1990;47:1617–1623.

149. Kramer LD, Locke GE, Ogunyemi A, Nelson L. Neonatal cocaine-related seizures. J Child Neurol 1990;5:60–64.

150. Krauthammer C. Crack babies: genetic inferiors. New York Daily News July 31, 1989.

151. Kron RE, Litt M, Phoenix MD, Finnegan LP. Neonatal narcotic abstinence: effects of pharmacotherapeutic agents and maternal drug usage on nutritive sucking behavior. J Pediatr 1976;88:637–641.

152. Kunstadter RH, Klein RI, Lundeen EC, Witz W, Morrison M. Narcotic withdrawal symptoms in newborn infants. JAMA 1958;168:1008–1110.

153. Lester BM, Tronick EZ. The effects of prenatal cocaine exposure and child outcome. Infant Ment Health J 1994;15:107–120.

154. Lifschitz MH, Wilson GS, Smith EO, Desmond MM. Factors affecting head growth and intellectual function in children of drug addicts. Pediatrics 1985;75:269–274.

155. Lipshultz SE, Frassica JJ, Orav EJ. Cardiovascular abnormalities in infants prenatally exposed to cocaine. J Pediatr 1991;118:44–51.

156. Lipsitz PJ. A proposed narcotic withdrawal score for use with newborn infants. Clin Pediatr 1975;14:592–594.

157. Lipsitz PJ, Blatman S. Newborn infants of mothers on methadone maintenance. N Y State J Med 1974;74:994–999.

158. Little BB, Snell LM, Rosenfeld CR, Gilstrap LC, Gant NF. Failure to recognize fetal alcohol syndrome in newborn infants. Am J Dis Child 1990;144:1142–1146.

159. Livesay S, Ehrlich S, Finnegan L. Cocaine and pregnancy: maternal and infant outcome. Pediatr Res 1987;21:387.

160. Lodge A, Marcus MM, Ramer CM. Neonatal addiction: a two-year-study. Part II. Behavioral and electrophysiological characteristics of the addicted neonate. Addict Dis 1975;2:235–255.

161. MacGregor SN, Keith LG, Chasnoff IJ, et al. Cocaine use during pregnancy: adverse perinatal outcome. Am J Obstet Gynecol 1987;157:686–690.

162. Madden JD, Chappel JN, Zuspan F, Gumpel J, Mejia A, Davis R. Observation and treatment of neonatal narcotic withdrawal. Am J Obstet Gynecol 1977;127:199–201.

163. Madden JD, Payne TF, Miller S. Maternal cocaine abuse and effect on the newborn. Pediatrics 1986;77:209–211.

164. Mahalik MP, Gautein RF, Mann DE. Teratogenic potential of cocaine hydrochloride in CF-1 mice. J Pharm Sci 1980;69:703–706.

165. Martin ML, Khoury MJ, Cordero JF, Waters GD. Trends in rates of multiple vascular disruption defects, Atlanta, 1968–1989: is there evidence of a cocaine teratogenic epidemic? Teratology 1992;45:647–653.

166. Mayes LC. Neurobiology of prenatal cocaine exposure effect on developing monoamine systems. Infant Ment Health J 1994;15:121–133.

167. Mayes LC, Bornstein MH, Chawarska K, Granger RH. Information processing and developmental assessments in 3-month-old infants exposed prenatally to cocaine. Pediatrics 1995;95:539–545.

168. Mayes LC, Granger RH, Frank MA, Schottenfeld R, Bornstein MH. Neurobehavioral profiles of neonates exposed to cocaine prenatally. Pediatrics 1993;91:778–783.

169. Mayes LC, Granger RH, Bornstein MH, Zuckerman B. The problem of prenatal cocaine ex-

posure: a rush to judgment. JAMA 1992;267: 406–408.

170. McGinty JF, Ford DH. The effects of maternal morphine or methadone intake on the growth, reflex development and maze behavior of rat offspring. In: Ford CH, Clouet DH, eds. Tissue responses to addictive drugs. New York: Spectrum, 1976:611–629.

171. Mehta SK, Finkelhor RS, Anderson RL, Harcar-Sevcik RA, Wasser TE, Bahler RC. Transient myocardial ischemia in infants prenatally exposed to cocaine. J Pediatr 1993;122: 945–949.

172. Middaugh LD. Prenatal amphetamine effects on behavior: possible medication by brain monoamines. Ann N Y Acad Sci 1989;562: 308–318.

173. Milstein M, Morishima A, Cohen MI, Litt IF. Effects of opium alkaloids on mitosis and DNA synthesis. Pediatr Res 1974;8:392.

174. Mirchandani HG, Mirchandani IH, Hellman F, English-Rider R, Rosen S, Laposata EA. Passive inhalation of free-base cocaine ('crack') smoke by infants. Arch Pathol Lab Med 1991; 115:494–498.

175. Mirochnick M, Meyer J, Cole J, Herren T, Zuckerman B. Circulating catecholamine concentrations in cocaine-exposed neonates: a pilot study. Pediatrics 1991;88:481–485.

176. Mitchell JL, Consensus Panel Chair. Pregnant, substance-using women. Rockville, MD: U.S. Department of Health and Human Services (Center for Substance Abuse Treatment), 1993.

177. Moore TR, Sorg J, Miller L, Key TC, Resnik R. Hemodynamic effects of intravenous cocaine on the pregnant ewe and fetus. Am J Obstet Gynecol 1986;155:883–888.

178. Moser JM, Jones VH, Kuthy ML. Use of cocaine during the immediate prepartum period by childbearing women in Ohio. Am J Prev Med 1993;9:85–91.

179. Mott SH, Packer RJ, Soldin SJ. Neurologic manifestations of cocaine exposure in childhood. Pediatrics 1994;93:557–560.

180. Myers BJ, Olson HC, Kaltenbach K. Cocaine-exposed infants: myths and misunderstandings. Zero To Three 1992;13:1–5.

181. Naeye RL, Blanc W, Leblanc W, Khatamee MA. Fetal complications of maternal heroin addiction: abnormal growth infections, and episodes of stress. J Pediatr 1973;83:1055–1061.

182. Nathenson G, Cohen MI, Litt IF, McNamara H. The effect of maternal heroin addiction on neonatal jaundice. J Pediatr 1972;81:899–903.

183. Needlman R, Zuckerman B, Anderson GM, Mirochnick M, Cohen DJ. Cerebrospinal fluid monoamine precursors and metabolities in human neonates following in utero cocaine exposure: a preliminary study. Pediatrics 1993; 92:55–60.

184. Neuspiel DR. On perjorative labeling of cocaine exposed children. J Subst Abuse Treat 1993;10:407.

185. Neuspiel DR, Hamel SC. Cocaine and infant behavior. Dev Behav Pediatr 1991;12:55–64.

186. Newman RG. Pregnancies of methadone patients. N Y State J Med 1974;1:52–54.

187. Northrop G, Ditzler J, Ryan WG, Wilbanks GD. Estriol excretion profiles in narcotic addicted women. Am J Obstet Gynecol 1972; 112:704–712.

188. Olsen GD, Lees MH. Ventilatory response to carbon dioxide of infants following prenatal methadone exposure. J Pediatr 1980;96: 983–989.

189. Oro AS, Dixon SD. Perinatal cocaine and methamphetamine exposure: maternal and neonatal correlates. J Pediatr 1987;111: 571–578.

190. Ostrea EM, Brady M, Gause S, Raymundo AL, Stevens M. Drug screening of newborns by meconium analysis: a large-scale, prospective, epidemiologic study. Pediatrics 1992;89: 107–113.

191. Ostrea EM, Brady MJ, Parks PM, Asensio DC, Naluz A. Drug screening of meconium in infants of drug-dependent mothers: an alternative to urine testing. J Pediatr 1989;115:474–477.

192. Ostrea EM, Chavez CJ, Strauss ME. A study of factors that influence the severity of neonatal narcotic withdrawal. J Pediatr 1976;88: 642–645.

193. Ostrea EM, Romero A, Knapp DK, Ostrea AR, Lucena JE, Utarnachitt RB. Postmortem drug analysis of meconium in early-gestation human fetuses exposed to cocaine: clinical implications. J Pediatr 1994;124:477–479.

194. Ouellette EM, Rosett HL, Rosman NP, Weiner L. Adverse effects on offspring of maternal alcohol abuse during pregnancy. N Engl J Med 1977;297:528–530.

195. Paltrow L. When becoming pregnant is a crime. Criminal Justice Ethics 1990;winter/spring:41–47.

196. Pasto ME, Graziani LJ, Tunis SL, et al. Ventricular configuration and cerebral growth in infants born to drug-dependent mothers. Pediatr Radiol 1985;15:77–81.

197. Pierog S, Chandavasu O, Wexler I. Withdrawal symptoms in infants with the fetal alcohol syndrome. J Pediatr 1977;90:630–633.

198. Pond SM, Kreek MJ, Tong TG, et al. Altered methadone pharmacokinetics in methadone-maintained pregnant women. J Pharmacol Exper Ther 1985;233:1–6.

199. Practical approaches in the treatment of women who abuse alcohol and other drugs. Rockville, MD: U.S. Department of Health and Human Services (Center for Substance Abuse Treatment), 1994.

200. Prenner BM. Neonatal withdrawal syndrome associated with hydroxyzine hydrochloride. Am J Dis Child 1977;131:529–530.

201. Preis O, Choi SJ, Rudolph N. Pentazocine withdrawal syndrome in the newborn infant. Am J Obstet Gynecol 1977;127:205–206.

202. Quillian WW II, Dunn CA. Neonatal drug withdrawal from propoxyphene. JAMA 1976; 235:2128.

203. Racine A, Joyce T, Anderson R. The association between prenatal care and birth weight among women exposed to cocaine in New York City. JAMA 1993;270:1581–1586.

204. Rajegowda BK, Glass L, Evans HE, Maso G, Swartz DP, Leblanc W. Methadone withdrawal in newborn infants. J Pediatr 1972;81: 532–534.

205. Rajegowda BK, Kandall SR, Falciglia H. Sudden unexpected death in infants of narcotic dependent mothers. Early Hum Dev 1978; 2/3:219–225.

206. Rajegowda B, Lala R, Nagaraj A, et al. Does cocaine (CO) increase congenital urogenital abnormalities (CUGA) in newborns? Pediatr Res 1991;29:71A.

207. Ramer CM. The case history of an infant born to an amphetamine-addicted mother. Clin Pediatr 1974;1:596–597.

208. Ramer CM, Lodge A. Neonatal addiction: a two-year study. Part I. Clinical and developmental characteristics of infants of mothers on methadone maintenance. Addict Dis 1975;2: 227–234.

209. Reddy AM, Harper RG, Stern G. Observation on heroin and methadone withdrawal in the newborn. Pediatrics 1971;48:353–357.

210. Rementeria JL, Bhatt K. Withdrawal symptoms in neonates from intrauterine exposure to diazepam. J Pediatr 1977;90:123–126.

211. Rementeria JL, Janakammal S, Hollander M. Multiple births in drug-addicted women. Am J Obstet Gynecol 1975;122:958–960.

212. Rementeria JL, Nunag NN. Narcotic withdrawal in pregnancy: stillbirth incidence with a case report. Am J Obstet Gynecol 1973;116: 1152–1156.

213. Reveri M, Pyati SP, Pildes R. Neonatal withdrawal symptoms associated with glutethimide (Doriden) addiction in the mother during pregnancy. Clin Pediatr 1977;16:424–425.

214. Reznik VM, Anderson J, Griswold WR, Segall ML, Murphy JL, Mendoza SA. Successful fibrinolytic treatment of arterial thrombosis and hypertension in a cocaine-exposed neonate. Pediatrics 1989;84:735–738.

215. Richardson BS, O'Grady JP, Olsen GD. Fetal breathing movements and the response to carbon dioxide in patients on methadone maintenance. Am J Obstet Gynecol 1984;150: 400–405.

216. Rivkin M, Gilmore HE. Generalized seizures in an infant due to environmentally acquired cocaine. Pediatrics 1989;84:1100–1102.

217. Roloff DW, Howatt WF, Kanto WP Jr, Borer RL Jr. The effect of long-term maternal morphine administration on the growth and lung development of fetal rabbits. In: Morselli PL, Garattini S, Serini F, eds. Basic and therapeutic aspects of perinatal pharmacology. New York: Raven Press, 1975.

218. Rorke LB, Reeser DS, Finnegan LP. Nervous system lesions in infants of opiate dependent mothers. Pediatr Res 1977;11:565.

219. Rosen TS, Johnson HL. Children of methadone-maintained mothers: follow-up to 18 months of age. J Pediatr 1982;101:192–196.

220. Rosen TS, Johnson HL. Long-term effects of prenatal methadone maintenance. NIDA Res Monogr 1985;59:73–83.

221. Rosen TS, Johnson HL. Drug-addicted mothers, their infants, and SIDS. Ann N Y Acad Sci 1988;533:89–95.

222. Rosen TS, Pippenger CE. Pharmacologic observations on the neonatal withdrawal syndrome. J Pediatr 1976;88:1044–1048.

223. Rothstein P, Gould JB. Born with a habit: infants of drug-addicted mothers. Pediatr Clin North Am 1974;21:307–321.

224. Rumack BH, Walravens PA. Neonatal withdrawal following maternal ingestion of ethchlorvynol (Placidyl). Pediatrics 1973;52: 714–716.

225. Ryan L, Ehrlich S, Finnegan L. Cocaine abuse in pregnancy: effects on the fetus and newborn. Neurotoxicol Teratol 1987;9:295–299.

226. Ryan RM, Wagner CL, Schutz JM, et al. Meconium analysis for improved identification of infants exposed to cocaine in utero. J Pediatr 1994;125:435–440.

227. Salamy A, Eldredge L, Anderson J, Bull D. Brain-stem transmission time in infants exposed to cocaine in utero. J Pediatr 1990; 117:627–629.

228. Sarpong S, Headings V. Sirenomelia accompanying exposure of the embryo to cocaine. South Med J 1992;85:545–547.

229. Schulman CA. Alterations of the sleep cycle in heroin addicted and "suspected" newborns. Neuropediatrics 1969;1:89–100.

230. Schutzman DL, Frankenfield-Chernicoff M,

Clatterbaugh HE, Singer J. Incidence of intrauterine cocaine exposure in a suburban setting. Pediatrics 1991;88:825–827.

231. Shannon M, Lacouture PG, Roa J, Woolf A. Cocaine exposure among children seen at a pediatric hospital. Pediatrics 1989;83:337–342.

232. Shih L, Cone-Wesson B, Reddix B. Effects of maternal cocaine abuse on the neonatal auditory system. Int J Pediatr Otorhinolaryngol 1988;15:245–251.

233. Silver H, Wapner R, Loriz-Vega M, Finnegan LP. Addiction in pregnancy: high risk intrapartum management and outcome. J Perinatol 1987;7:178–181.

234. Silvestri JM, Long JM, Weese-Mayer DE, Barkov GA. Effect of prenatal cocaine on respiration, heart rate, and sudden infant death syndrome. Pediatr Pulmonol 1991;11:328–334.

235. Singer LT, Yamashita TS, Hawkins S, Cairns D, Baley J, Kliegman R. Increased incidence of intraventricular hemorrhage and developmental delay in cocaine-exposed, very low birth weight infants. J Pediatr 1994;124:765–771.

236. Singh EJ, Zuspan FP. Content of amniotic fluid prostaglandins in normal, diabetic and drug-abuse human pregnancy. Am J Obstet Gynecol 1974;118:358–361.

237. Sisson TRC, Wickler M, Tsai P, Rao IP. Effect of narcotic withdrawal on neonatal sleep patterns. Pediatr Res 1974;8:451.

238. Slobody LB, Cobrinick R. Neonatal narcotic addiction. Q Rev Pediatr 1959;14:169–171.

239. Smith DW. The fetal alcohol syndrome. Hosp Pract 1979;14:121–128.

240. Sonderegger T. Persistent effects of neonatal narcotic addiction in the rat. In: Ford DH, Clouet DH, eds. Tissue responses to addictive drugs. New York: Spectrum, 1976:589–609.

241. Soule AB III, Standley K, Copans SA, Davis M. Clinical uses of the Brazelton Neonatal Scale. Pediatrics 1974;54:583–586.

242. Statzer DE, Wardell JN. Heroin addiction during pregnancy. Am J Obstet Gynecol 1972;113:273–278.

243. Steinhausen HD, Nestler V, Spohr HL. Development of psychopathology of children with the fetal alcohol syndrome. J Dev Behav Pediatr 1982;3:49–54.

244. Stimmel B, Adamsons K. Narcotic dependency in pregnancy: methadone maintenance compared to use of street drugs. JAMA 1976;235:1121–1124.

245. Strauss ME, Andresko MA, Stryker JC, Wardell JN, Dunkel CA. Methadone maintenance during pregnancy: pregnancy, birth and neonate characteristics. Am J Obstet Gynecol 1974;120:895–900.

246. Strauss ME, Lessen-Firestone JK, Chavez CJ, Stryker C. Children of methadone-treated women at five years of age. Pharmacol Biochem Behav 1979;11(suppl):3–6.

247. Strauss ME, Lessen-Firestone JK, Starr RH Jr, Ostrea EM. Behavior of narcotics addicted newborns. Child Dev 1975;46:887–893.

248. Strauss ME, Starr RH, Ostrea EM, Chavez CJ, Stryker JC. Behavioral concomitants of prenatal addiction to narcotics. J Pediatr 1976;89:842–846.

249. Streissguth AP, Aase JM, Clarren SK, Randels SP, LaDue RA, Smith DF. Fetal alcohol syndrome in adolescents and adults. JAMA 1991;265:1961–1967.

250. Sussman S. Narcotic and methamphetamine use during pregnancy: effect on newborn infants. Am J Dis Child 1963;106:325–330.

251. Taeusch HW Jr, Carson SH, Wang NS, Avery ME. Heroin induction of lung maturation and growth retardation in fetal rabbits. J Pediatr 1973;82:869–875.

252. Telsey AM, Merritt TA, Dixon SD. Cocaine exposure in a term neonate: necrotizing enterocolitis as a complication. Clin Pediatr 1988;27:547–550.

253. Teske MP, Trese MT. Retinopathy of prematurity-like fundus and persistent hyperplastic primary vitreous associated with maternal cocaine use. Am J Ophthalmol 1987;103:719–720.

254. Treatment of morphine-type dependency by withdrawal methods [Editorial]. JAMA 1972;219:1611.

255. Tronick EZ, Lester BM, eds. NICU network neurobehavioral scale (NNNS): refinements in a comprehensive assessment examination of the substance-exposed and high-risk infant. NIDA Res Monogr, 1996;166:198–204.

256. Tyson HK. Neonatal withdrawal symptoms associated with maternal use of propoxyphene hydrochloride (Darvon). J Pediatr 1974;85:684–685.

257. van de Bor M, Walther FJ, Ebrahimi M. Decreased cardiac output in infants of mothers who abused cocaine. Pediatrics 1990;85:30–32.

258. van de Bor M, Walther FJ, Sims ME. Increased cerebral blood flow velocity in infants of mothers who abuse cocaine. Pediatrics 1990;85:733–736.

259. Vega WA, Kolody B, Hwang J, Noble A. Prevalence and magnitude of perinatal substance exposures in California. N Engl J Med 1993;329:850–854.

260. Wallach RC, Jerez E, Blinick G. Pregnancy and menstrual function in narcotic addicts treated with methadone. Am J Obstet Gynecol 1969;105:1226–1229.

261. Wang CH, Schnoll SH. Prenatal cocaine use associated with down regulation of receptors in human placenta. Neurotoxicol Teratol 1987;9:301–304.

262. Ward SLD, Bautista D, Chan L, et al. Sudden infant death syndrome in infants of substance-abusing mothers. J Pediatr 1990;117:876–881.

263. Ward SLD, Bautista DB, Woo MS, et al. Responses to hypoxia and hypercapnia in infants of substance-abusing mothers. J Pediatr 1992;121:704–709.

264. Weinberger SM, Kandall SR, Doberczak TM, Thornton JC, Bernstein J. Early weight-change patterns in neonatal abstinence. Am J Dis Child 1986;140:829–832.

265. Wiggins RC. Pharmacokinetics of cocaine in pregnancy and effects on fetal maturation. Clin Pharmacokinet 1992;22:85–93.

266. Wilson GS, Desmond MM, Verniaud WM. Early development of infants of heroin addicted mothers. Am J Dis Child 1973;126:457–462.

267. Wilson GS, Desmond MM, Wait RB. Follow-up of methadone-treated and untreated narcotic-dependent women and their infants: health, developmental, and social implications. J Pediatr 1981;98:716–722.

268. Wilson GS, McCreary R, Kean J, Baxter JC. The development of preschool children of heroin-addicted mothers: a controlled study. Pediatrics 1979;63:135–141.

269. Wittmann BK, Segal S. A comparison of the effects of single- and split-dose methadone administration on the fetus: ultrasound evaluation. Int J Addict 1991;26:213–218.

270. Woods JR, Plessinger MA, Clark KE. Effect of cocaine on uterine blood flow and fetal oxygenation. JAMA 1987;257:957–961.

271. Zelson C. Infant of the addicted mother. N Engl J Med 1973;288:1393–1395.

272. Zelson C, Rubio E, Wasserman E. Neonatal narcotic addiction: 10-year observation. Pediatrics 1971;48:178–189.

273. Zimmerberg B, Charap AD, Glick SD. Behavioural effects of in utero administration of morphine. Nature 1974;247:376–377.

274. Zuckerman B, Frank D, Hingson R, et al. Effects of maternal marijuana and cocaine use on fetal growth. N Engl J Med 1989;320:762–768.

275. Zuckerman B, Frank DA. "Crack kids:" not broken. Pediatrics 1992;89:337–339.

276. Zuckerman B, Frank DA. Prenatal cocaine exposure: nine years later. J Pediatr 1994;124:731–733.

277. Zuspan FP, Gumpel JA, Mejia-Zelaya A, Madden J, Davis R. Fetal stress from methadone withdrawal. Am J Obstet Gynecol 1975;122:43–46.

55   THE MEDICALLY ILL SUBSTANCE ABUSER

David M. Novick, Harry W. Haverkos, and Douglas W. Teller

Medical illnesses frequently occur in substance abusers. Most of these are direct sequelae of the substance abuse, but the entire spectrum of human disease may be encountered. Substance abusers, no less than other patients, should receive the highest standard of medical care. Proper care of such patients consists not only of attention to the medical complications but also of evaluation of the underlying substance abuse and any associated social or psychiatric problems (1). Providing such care can be extraordinarily complex and usually requires a multidisciplinary approach. Excellent medical care for substance abusers is of value in its own right and also as a vehicle to bring substance abusers into treatment for their addiction.

In this chapter, the role of the physician in caring for substance abusers is discussed, and guidelines for medical and surgical care of patients on methadone maintenance are provided. The major medical complications of parenteral substance abuse and of cocaine use are reviewed. The complications of human immunodeficiency virus (HIV) infection, including acquired immune deficiency syndrome (AIDS), are reviewed in Chapter 59.

THE PHYSICIAN AND SUBSTANCE ABUSE TREATMENT

Substance abusers with medical complications requiring hospitalization are usually admitted to general inpatient services rather than to specialized units for substance abuse (1). The medical care provided on these services should include diagnosis and treatment plans for the substance abuse as well as the medical complications. The medical history should include data on all drugs of abuse, including alcohol, with details on the onset and duration of use, pattern (binge, daily, weekends, etc.), amount, and route of administration; past and present withdrawal syndromes; previous medical complications; and previous substance abuse treatments such as detoxification, rehabilitation programs, therapeutic communities, methadone maintenance, pharmacological adjuncts such as disulfiram (Antabuse) or naltrexone, and self-help programs such as Alcoholics Anonymous. The treatment plan should include detoxification (1) and referrals for ongoing substance abuse treatment. The disease concept, in which substance abuse is viewed as a medical disorder rather than a moral or psychological problem (2–4), helps both the physicians and patients to direct attention to therapeutic measures for the substance abuse itself rather then various personal problems or stresses, which may be perceived as having caused the substance abuse. Denial, a defense mechanism used by substance abusers, is often manifested by preoccupation with such "underlying causes," and the physician can help by shifting the focus to substance abuse as a disease requiring specific treatment. Counseling for personal problems may proceed during substance abuse treatment and may enhance its efficacy (5).

The relationship between the substance abuse and the medical complications should be emphasized to the patient. It is not uncommon that basic concepts, such as ability of alcohol to damage the liver, are not known by patients. Such discussions should use terminology that the patient can understand and should be nonjudgmental.

Interactions between physicians and patients with substance abuse can be enhanced by techniques that have been formulated to promote behavior change, such as motivational interviewing (6, 7). This is summarized by the acronym FRAMES, *feedback* of personal risk or impairment, emphasis on personal *responsibility* for change, clear *advice* to change, a *menu* of alternative change options, physician *empathy,* and facilitation of patient *self-efficacy* or optimism (6). Each element can in turn be adapted to most appropriately support the stage of change with which the patient is identified. Also important to this process is a realization that behavior change for substance abuse may evolve over a continuum or even recycle through stages as patients grapple with modifications in substance use or with abstinence (7).

Too often, physicians exhibit pejorative attitudes towards patients with substance abuse problems or believe that there is nothing they can contribute toward treating such patients (8–10). There are many reasons for this (see also Chapter 78). The high relapse rate of substance abuse problems leads to a belief that substance abuse cannot be treated successfully; the low expectations engendered by this attitude reduce the chances of success, creating a self-fulfilling prophecy (8). The contact of most physicians with substance abusers is limited to medically ill hospitalized patients, a disproportionate number of whom have frequent relapses of substance abuse and poor compliance with medical treatments. Pejorative attitudes also derive from belief that substance abusers are responsible for their addiction and hence their medical problems (4, 10, 11). Other factors include a lack of training and experience with substance abusers (10), difficult interactions between physicians and other disciplines involved in substance abuse treatment (4), hostile or manipulative behavior by patients in the hospital, their presumed criminal behavior outside the hospital, and their unkempt appearance (10). Pejorative slang terminology used by some physicians tends to propagate these attitudes.

Nevertheless, almost all physicians will encounter patients with substance abuse problems, and when they do they are obligated to provide the highest possible standard of medical care. A careful diagnostic approach and an effective therapeutic effort can be applied to chemical dependency problems as well as to the medical complications (12). This can be facilitated by recognition that substance abuse can be treated successfully; that substance abuse is best regarded as a disease that may have metabolic basis (8) rather than a moral weakness; and that negative attitudes contribute to treatment failure (4). Recent data suggest that a physician's warning against abuse of alcohol is associated with improved outcome two years later (13). Blaming patients for their disease is not helpful, and patients with other disease resulting in part from their behavior (examples include lung cancer, emphysema, obesity, and skin cancer) are not denied treatment. All physicians can be reasonably expected to treat all patients professionally, to increase their knowledge of substance abuse treatment through continuing education, and to maintain an awareness of resources in the community to which patients with substance abuse problems can be referred.

CARE OF METHADONE MAINTENANCE PATIENTS WITH MEDICAL OR SURGICAL PROBLEMS

Methadone maintenance is an effective treatment for hard-core heroin addicts (defined as patients with several uses per day for more than one year). The effectiveness of methadone results from its pharmacology: it is effective orally and has a long half-life and stable plasma levels over the 24-hour dosing interval, thus preventing both narcotic withdrawal and craving when used in proper doses (14). Methadone maintenance treatment is associated with high voluntary retention rates, reduction or elimination of heroin abuse, and reduction in needle sharing and other behavioral factors which predispose to HIV infection (15, 16). Many methadone maintenance patients are successfully rehabilitated in that they are employed, do not use illicit drugs, do not engage in criminal behavior, and have no social ties to active narcotic abusers (17–19). Methadone maintenance treatment, including "medical maintenance," a program in which socially rehabilitated methadone patients are treated in a physician's office rather than in a clinic, is discussed more fully in Chapter 41.

Methadone maintenance patients commonly undergo hospitalization for medical or surgical problems. In general, the management should be no different from that of other patients. Attention to the following points will lead to optimal care for methadone maintenance patients.

When a methadone-maintained patient is hospitalized, the usual maintenance dose of methadone should be given each day throughout the hospital stay. If the methadone dose cannot be verified by the patient's program, no more than 40 mg should be given. This dose will prevent severe withdrawal, even in a patient maintained on higher dose. Once the patient's dose is verified, it should be continued.

Methadone should be given intramuscularly when the patient cannot receive anything by mouth, as on the day of a surgical procedure and in the early postoperative period (20). In this situation the methadone dose should not be routinely reduced; rather, intramuscular administration of maintenance doses of 40 mg or higher should be given in two divided doses 12 hours apart. Doses of methadone under 40 mg may be given as a single intramuscular injection. Full doses of oral methadone should be reinstated when oral intake is possible. Although pharmacokinetic studies in cancer patients showed that parenteral methadone is about twice as potent as the oral form (21), methadone maintenance patients generally do not become oversedated from parenteral methadone because of the high degree of tolerance to opiates that has developed during heroin addiction and methadone maintenance treatment.

Postoperative patients, including those on methadone maintenance, frequently experience pain. Because of the development of tolerance to opiates, the daily dose of methadone will not serve as an analgesic for pain caused by a surgical procedure or an illness (22). Full therapeutic doses of analgesic drugs should therefore be given to methadone maintenance patients for painful conditions. Methadone maintenance patients also have cross-tolerance to other narcotics, and some such patients will need higher doses of analgesics and more frequent dosing intervals for pain control. Short-acting narcotic analgesics such as meperidine (Demerol) in doses that can exceed the patient's tolerance level are often indicated. Pentazocine (Talwin) and other mixed agonist-antagonist agents must not be given to methadone maintenance patients because they displace methadone from opiate receptors, leading to severe narcotic withdrawal. For this reason, methadone maintenance patients often state that they are "allergic to Talwin."

MEDICAL COMPLICATIONS OF INTRAVENOUS DRUG USE

Many medical complications result from the injection of heroin, cocaine, amphetamines, or other substances. Table 55.1 lists these medical complications. The next several sections review the most important of these. Features of diseases that are specific to substance abusers will be emphasized, and general medical texts should be consulted for additional details. Studies carried out before the onset of the epidemic of infection with HIV, the cause of AIDS, showed that intravenous drug abusers had higher age-adjusted mortality rates than expected (23, 24). Although infections were the single most common category of diseases leading to death, a very wide variety of illnesses have been observed (25). The medical complications of HIV infection and AIDS are discussed in chapter 59. In addition to opportunistic infections and malignancies, the HIV epidemic has been associated with marked increases (26) in the mortality from bacterial pneumonia, infective endocarditis, and tuberculosis, complications which have long been common in drug abusers. In the presence of HIV infection, more intensive antimicrobial therapy may be needed for these and other infections.

Table 55.1   Medical Complications in Parenteral Drug Abuse

Infectious	Renal failure
Arthritis, septic	Rhabdomyolysis
Aspergillosis	
Botulism	**Cardiovascular**
Candidiasis	Arrhythmia
Cellulitis	Mycotic aneurysm
Central nervous system infections	Thrombophlebitis
Chorioretinitis	
Endocarditis	**Pulmonary**
Endophthalmitis	Pulmonary edema
Episcleritis	Pneumothorax
Fasciitis, "flesh-eating" infections	Pneumomediastinum
Gastroenteritis	Pulmonary fibrosis
Hepatitis	Pulmonary hypertension
HTLV-I and HTLV-II infections	
Infected pseudoaneurysms	**Gastrointestinal**
Leishmaniasis	Motility disorders
Louse-borne infections	Constipation
Malaria	
Mucormycosis	**Neuromuscular**
Nocardiosis	Stroke
Osteomyelitis	Epidural abscess
Peptic ulcer disease	Subdural abscess
Pneumonia	Brain abscess
Pyomyositis	Transverse myelitis
Sexually transmitted diseases, i.e.,	Anoxic encephalopathy
chancroid, gonorrhea, HIV,	Peripheral neuropathy
syphilis	Horner's syndrome
Sinusitis	Myositis
Tetanus	
Tick-borne infections	**Miscellaneous**
Tuberculosis	Overdose
	Allergic reaction
Hepatic	Pyrogenic reaction
Acute hepatitis	Trauma
Fulminant hepatic failure	Needle embolus
Chronic hepatitis	Necrotizing angiitis
Cirrhosis	Amenorrhea
	Hormonal abnormalities
	Thrombocytopenia
Renal	Osteosclerosis
Nephrotic syndrome	
Glomerulonephritis	

Infectious Diseases

Infectious diseases are common among drug abusers (26–29). Some infections result when "dirty" or nonsterile paraphernalia or drugs are used for injection, and/or the skin is not cleaned adequately before injection (i.e., endocarditis, sepsis, soft tissue infections, bone and joint infections, tetanus). Some occur when equipment is shared and infected blood of others is directly inoculated (i.e., hepatitis B and C viruses, HIV, human T-cell lymphotropic viruses types I and II, and malaria). Other infections are transmitted from person to person via aerial droplets (i.e., tuberculosis). Several result from casual sexual relationships, common in the drug use scene (hepatitis B, HIV, syphilis, gonorrhea, chancroid). Pneumonias of various etiologies are also common among drug users. We will not attempt to review each and every possible infectious complication of drug abuse, but will review several of the more common, more life-threatening, and/or "newer" ones.

AIDS/HIV

Concomitant with the initial case reports of AIDS among homosexual men in the United States was a report of *Pneumocystis carinii* pneumonia among men who denied homosexuality but admitted intravenous drug use (30). Between June, 1981, and June 30, 1995, 476,899 cases of AIDS in the United States were reported to the Centers for Disease Control and Prevention (CDC). About 200 new cases are reported to the CDC each day. Approximately 28% of the new AIDS cases are among injecting drug users (31). In addition, many of the heterosexual-contact and pediatric AIDS cases in the United States can be directly linked to injection drug use in a sexual partner or mother.

The number of AIDS cases, however, does not adequately describe the extent of the problem. Because of the long latency period from infection to diagnosis of AIDS and the persistence of infectivity of HIV-infected individuals, the number of infected individuals is considered to be a better measure of the extent of the epidemic among intravenous drug users. The HIV seroprevalence among such patients in the United States varies widely from low rates to as much as 65%. The highest rates have been observed among African-Americans and Hispanics who abuse cocaine in urban areas in or near New York City and in Puerto Rico. Rates are consistently higher for those drug abusers not currently enrolled in drug abuse treatment compared to those in drug abuse treatment. New infections are occurring in many study sites (32–34).

All illicit drug users evaluated by a health care provider should be tested for HIV antibodies. Although a cure for AIDS has not yet been discovered, several antiviral agents have been documented to improve immunological function and/or prolong survival. The art of prescribing and combining antiretroviral therapies is evolving most rapidly (35). A multiagency treatise to aid physicians in preventing the opportunistic infections associated with HIV infection is available. This prevention document details effective measures to avoid exposure to organisms causing opportunistic infections in AIDS patients, antibiotic prophylactic and treatment regimens, and lists recommended vaccines (36). Hospitalizations of AIDS patients becomes more common as the disease progresses. For further details on HIV infection and AIDS, please see Chapters 58–61.

All HIV-infected pregnant women should be offered zidovudine therapy, which has been shown to reduce mother to infant HIV transmission rates from 25% of newborns of nontreated mothers to 8% of children of treated mothers. The regimen consists of zidovudine therapy to the mother antepartum and intrapartum and to the newborn for the first six weeks of life (37).

INFECTIVE ENDOCARDITIS

Endocarditis is a life-threatening infection that frequently occurs among injecting drug users. Although endocarditis is not a reportable disease, individual studies report that it represented 8–16% of hospital admissions for intravenous drug users and for 1.9–8% of all deaths among such patients in New York City in the 1960s and 1970s (38, 39). In a more recent series, infective endocarditis represented 13% of febrile injecting drug users admitted to a New Jersey hospital (40).

Outbreaks of endocarditis among injecting drug users have been episodically reported in various parts of the country, often associated with specific drugs of abuse and/or specific organisms (41–46). The national cocaine epidemic has resulted in an increased frequency of endocarditis in some areas (41).

The organisms responsible for drug abuse related endocarditis can be introduced from several sources. Organisms colonizing the skin appear to be particularly important, since the majority of addicts make no attempt to cleanse their skin before injection. Other potential sources of bacteria or fungi include the drugs, adulterants, glass packaging, and solutions, such as tap water and saliva, which are used to clean equipment and dissolve drugs. Tuazon and colleagues have shown that the organisms found in heroin are less likely to be the bacteremic agent than colonizers of skin (47). Significant collections of bacteria at injection sites, such as occur in cellulitis and phlebitis, may lead to seeding of heart valves.

Endocarditis among intravenous drug users is more likely to occur on the right side of the heart. In one study, 76% of drug-related endocarditis occurred on the right side compared with 9% among nonaddicts (41, 48). Mechanisms hypothesized for the increased right-sided pathology include drug-induced pulmonary hypertension causing valve dysfunction, and direct damage to the valve leaflets or endothelium by drugs or adulterants. It does not appear that the organisms involved are unique to the drug abusing community. Staphylococcus aureus is the most common pathogen in surveys of drug users and others, HIV positives and HIV negatives.

Endocarditis can be difficult to diagnose in the emergency department. In one study, only 4 of 12 addicts suspected of having endocarditis in the emergency department proved to have such a diagnosis, and 8 of 30 addicts admitted with other diagnoses ultimately were diagnosed with endocarditis (49). Therefore, all febrile intravenous drug users should be hospitalized to evaluate for endocarditis. Although the rates of fever, chills, and arthralgia occur as commonly in right-sided as in left-sided endocarditis, other manifestations, such as petechiae, hemorrhage, central nervous system emboli, and heart failure occur much less often in right-sided endocarditis. Chest pain and cough occur more commonly in right-sided endocarditis.

A number of therapeutic questions remain concerning duration of antibiotic therapy and indications for and timing of surgery. Intravenous drug users with "poor veins" present a challenge for parenteral therapy, and antibiotic selection is often difficult in the presence of multiple drug resistance. Recurrences of endocarditis are common in the drug-abusing population and represent reinfection in most cases. Indiscriminate use of prophylactic antibiotics among addicts is common (50) and may lead to more resistant causative organisms. HIV infection per se does not negatively influence outcomes due to endocarditis; however, those with symptomatic HIV disease and/or lower CD4 counts ($< 200/mm^3$) do worse than those HIV-infected patients with CD4 counts over $500/mm^3$ (51–53).

GONORRHEA

The rate of gonorrhea has continued to decline since 1975. In 1994, 418,068 cases of gonorrhea were reported in the United States, making it the most commonly reported infectious disease (54–56).

Gonorrhea is caused by a bacteria, *Neisseria gonorrhoeae,* and predominantly affects the mucous membranes of the lower genitourinary tract and less frequently the rectum, oropharynx, and conjunctivae. Gonorrhea usually presents as purulent penile discharge in men and as urethritis or cervicitis in women. The incubation period is 2–8 days. Asymptomatic carriers occur in both sexes, but are more common in females.

A rapid and reliable test for gonorrhea in men is Gram's stain of urethral discharge that shows intracellular gram-negative diplococci. (Gram's stain of urethral or cervical discharge in women is unreliable due to the presence of nonpathogenic *Neisseria* species.) Cultures for *N. gonorrhoeae* should be plated immediately on warm chocolate agar or Thayer-Martin medium and incubated in a carbon dioxide incubator.

The currently recommended regimen to treat uncomplicated urethral, endocervical, and rectal gonorrhea is ceftriaxone 250 mg intramuscularly (one dose only) and doxycycline 100 mg orally 2 times a day for 7 days. Doxy-

cycline is used to treat coexisting chlamydial infection, which is documented in up to 45% of gonorrhea patients (28).

HTLV-I AND HTLV-II INFECTIONS

Human T-lymphotropic viruses (HTLV) I and II are retroviruses which immortalize human T-cells and induce cell proliferation, in contrast to HIV, which is associated with cell destruction. All three of these human retroviruses appear to be transmitted by sexual, parenteral, and vertical transmission routes, although at varying efficiencies (57).

Although it is difficult to completely distinguish HTLV-I from HTLV-II infection by serologic methods, HTLV-II infection appears to be more common among intravenous drug users (58). However, HTLV-II's clinical consequences are less clearly understood than that of HTLV-I infection. HTLV-II infection is believed to be involved in the pathogenesis of atypical hairy cell leukemia. HTLV-II infections among intravenous drug users have also been associated with soft tissue infections, particularly deep-seeded staphylococcal infections. HTLV-I infection appears to be rare among intravenous drug users, although it is associated with several disorders, including tropical spastic paraparesis and adult T-cell leukemia/lymphoma (ATL) (59–61). Both HTLV-I and HTLV-II infections are lifelong infections with latency periods from infection to disease of several years to decades (57).

PNEUMONIA

Among parenteral drug abusers, pneumonia is the most common reason for admission to the hospital, accounting for 38% of hospitalizations in one recent survey (49). Contributing factors include depression of the gag reflex by alcohol and drugs, leading to aspiration of oropharyngeal and gastric secretions (1). Aspiration may also occur during seizures caused by withdrawal or sedative-hypnotic withdrawal. Cigarette smoking is almost universal among substance abusers, leading to impaired pulmonary function. Smoking marihuana and "crack" cocaine probably have similar effects on pulmonary function. Malnutrition and trauma frequently are associated with substance abuse, and may result in interference with ventilation and normal cough mechanisms. HIV-infected drug users have an increased incidence of bacterial pneumonia and increased mortality compared to HIV-negative counterparts (39, 62, 63). In fact, recurrent bacterial pneumonias among HIV-infected individuals is currently defined as AIDS.

Pneumonia generally presents with fever, cough, chest pain, and dyspnea. It can be difficult to differentiate from endocarditis (49). On physical examination, localized dullness to percussion or rales are helpful signs when present, but in some patients with pneumonia the physical examination is unremarkable.

Pneumococcal pneumonia is the most common bacterial pneumonia in substance abusers, as in the general population. An acute presentation with a single shaking chill is typical. *Hemophilus influenzae* pneumonia is not uncommon in smokers with chronic obstructive pulmonary disease. *Klebsiella pneumoniae* pneumonia should be suspected in alcoholics with fever, chills, and a lobar pneumonia. Patients with HIV infection frequently develop *Pneumocystis carinii* pneumonia. Fever and dyspnea are prominent features, and cough is often nonproductive. Symptoms may have been present for several weeks. Hypoxia and bilateral pulmonary infiltrates are characteristic of *P. carinii* pneumonia, but the clinical spectrum of presentations of this opportunistic infection is broad. Also, bacterial pneumonia may occur concomitantly with *P. carinii* pneumonia. Mixed infections including anaerobic organisms are associated with aspiration; foul-smelling sputum may be a clue. Pulmonary tuberculosis should always be suspected and included in the differential diagnosis in intravenous drug users with pneumonia. Tuberculosis occurs all too commonly in HIV-infected patients in whom the characteristic upper-lobe cavity lesions are less frequent. Mycobacterium-avium complex infections are also in the differential diagnosis, especially among HIV-infected patients.

The initial evaluation consists of chest roentgenograms, sputum Gram stain, culture, and evaluation for acid-fast organisms, blood cultures, arterial blood gases, and in some patients, sputum cytology for *P. carinii*. Intravenous antibiotics are begun promptly after collection of the above. Pneumococcal vaccine and annual influenza vaccines should be considered to prevent subsequent hospitalizations (1).

SKIN AND SOFT TISSUE INFECTIONS

Skin and soft tissue infections are common among intravenous drug users. At a university hospital in inner city Newark, New Jersey, about 25% of such patients admitted to the hospital had evidence of cellulitis, phlebitis, or other soft tissue infections. Suppurative and noninfectious thrombophlebitis, abscesses, and fistulae are common. As addicts age and veins sclerose, more dangerous injection sites are selected, such as femoral, axillary, jugular, and penile veins (64). Pubic symphysis osteomyelitis, jugular venous thrombosis, and penile gangrene have been reported following such injections. Pyomyositis, gas gangrene, and synergistic anaerobic myonecrosis, sometimes referred to as "flesh-eating" infections, are occasionally diagnosed among intravenous drug users.

The drug itself may contain a number of irritants, such as talc powder, lactate, and quinine. Staphylococcal and streptococcal infections predominate, but many other organisms have been reported. There is an increase in anecdotal reports of anaerobic infections among cocaine compared with heroin injectors. With HIV epidemic, clinicians have seen an increase in mycobacterial and nocardial soft tissue infections. Response to antibiotic therapy is especially poor for drug users who abuse alcohol, have poor nutrition, or have HIV infection.

SYPHILIS

In 1994, 20,627 cases of primary and secondary syphilis were reported to the CDC. This is the fewest cases reported since 1977. The highest rates in the country were reported in the Southern states (54).

Syphilis is a chronic systemic infection caused by a bacterium, *Treponema pallidum*. The disease may present in a variety of ways. The "classical" presentations are as a chancre at the inoculation site (primary syphilis), a disseminated form, which commonly includes a maculopapular rash and nontender lymphadenopathy (secondary syphilis), and aortitis and/or inflammation of the central nervous system (tertiary syphilis). The incubation period for the primary lesion is usually 2–6 weeks; secondary syphilis usually occurs 2–12 weeks later. Tertiary syphilis may appear within a few years of infection or remain latent and then appear several decades later.

Serologic testing is the most common method of diagnosis. Two types of serologic tests are employed. Nontreponemal tests, i.e., Venereal Disease Research Laboratory (VDRL), rapid plasma reagin (RPR), are used for initial screening and during follow-up. Treponemal tests, i.e., fluorescent treponemal antibody-absorption (FTA-ABS), *T. pallidum* hemagglutination assay (MHA-TP or TPHA), are specific and distinguish false-positive from true-positive nontreponemal tests. Once positive, the treponemal tests generally remain positive for life. Diagnosis of primary and secondary lesions can also be made by dark-field microscopy; however, this is difficult in outpatient settings unless an experienced microscopist is available.

Therapy for syphilis varies by stage of illness. Benzathine penicillin G, 2.4 million units intramuscularly (1.2 million units in each hip), in one dose, is recommended for primary and secondary syphilis and early latent syphilis of less than one year's duration. For latent syphilis of more than one year's duration and for cardiovascular syphilis (with normal lumbar puncture exam), benzathine penicillin G, 2.4 million units intramuscular weekly for 3 successive weeks, is recommended. The optimal treatment for neurosyphilis or syphilis of more than one year's duration is less well established. Concomitant HIV disease and syphilis are common. Some investigators recommend that all patients with HIV infection and syphilis receive treatment adequate for neurosyphilis (55, 56).

TUBERCULOSIS

One of the most troublesome aspects of the drug abuse and HIV epidemics is the effects on tuberculosis in the United States and throughout the world. Tuberculosis decreased in the United States every year since 1953

when reporting began (approximately 84,000 cases) through 1985 (22,201 cases), only to increase for the first time in 1986 (22,575 cases). The incidence continued to increase each year between 1986 and 1992 (26,673 cases). In 1993 and 1994, the incidence has decreased; 24,361 tuberculosis cases were reported in 1994 (65). There is much less optimism about controlling tuberculosis in the developing world due to increases in active tuberculosis fostered by immunosuppression associated with the ravages of the HIV pandemic and the already fragile public health infrastructure in many countries.

Tuberculosis is a chronic bacterial infection caused by *Mycobacterium tuberculosis*. *M. tuberculosis* is spread from person to person through airborne particles. These particles are coughed by untreated clinically active cases of pulmonary tuberculosis. After a susceptible individual inhales the bacilli, the organism reaches the alveoli of lungs and multiplies. Approximately 10% of individuals with *M. tuberculosis* infection develop active tuberculosis during their lifetime (about half of the clinically active cases develop disease within 2 years of inhalation). Progression of infection to clinically active tuberculosis is more common among debilitated and immunocompromised persons, i.e., alcoholics, drug abusers, and HIV/AIDS patients, than the general population. An investigation in a New York methadone maintenance program showed that 15% of HIV-infected, tuberculin-positive intravenous drug users developed active tuberculosis during follow-up (approximately 2 years), whereas none of the tuberculin positives who were HIV-negative developed active tuberculosis during the same follow-up period (66). Transmission of tuberculosis to health care workers has been documented. Health care workers who care for AIDS patients are at increased risk of acquiring tuberculosis.

All drug users should be screened for *M. tuberculosis* infection with a tuberculin skin test with purified protein derivative (PPD). All drug users infected with HIV or whose HIV status is unknown and whose TB skin test is five or more millimeters of induration should receive isoniazid preventive therapy for 12 months regardless of age. HIV-negative patients with skin tests ten or more millimeters of induration should receive prophylaxis for six months regardless of age (67, 68). Drug abuse treatment programs may be ideal sites to oversee prophylactic isoniazid therapy, which is given orally 300 mg daily (6 months for HIV-negative individuals and 12 months for HIV-positive ones). All patients with clinically active disease will require hospitalization (including respiratory isolation for pulmonary disease) and therapy with multiple antibacterial agents. Clinical activity can be assessed by chest x-ray and cultures of various body fluids for tuberculosis.

Multidrug-resistant tuberculosis is on the increase in the United States. All isolates of *M. tuberculosis* should be sent for sensitivity testing. An initial four-drug regimen (isoniazid, rifampin, pyrazinamide, and ethambutol or streptomycin) is recommended before sensitivity results are available. Compliance with self-administered therapy is poor in many areas and represents the major reason for increases in drug-resistant disease. All patients should receive directly observed therapy that includes patient incentives and the potential for enforcement of therapy (69, 70).

Methadone maintenance patients who are treated with rifampin may experience narcotic withdrawal symptoms. Rifampin lowers plasma methadone levels as a result of its enhancement of microsomal drug metabolizing activity. This may necessitate an increase in methadone maintenance dosing during treatment for tuberculosis (71).

Viral Hepatitis and Liver Disease

Viral hepatitis and acute and chronic liver disease are extremely common among parenteral drug abusers. From 41–48% of such patients have a history of acute hepatitis (16, 72) and about two-thirds display abnormalities in liver transaminases (73). Serologic evidence of hepatitis B virus (HBV) infection is found in 72–89% of unselected parenteral drug abusers (74–75) and in 98% of those with sufficient evidence of chronic liver disease to warrant liver biopsy (76). These high prevalences may be declining in some communities due to AIDS prevention efforts. Numerous factors, including alcoholism and at least five viral agents, cause acute and chronic liver disease in parenteral drug abusers (Table 55.2). In a series of 151 consecutive

Table 55.2 Causes of Liver Disease in Parenteral Drug Abusers

Alcoholism
Hepatitis A virus
Hepatitis B virus
Hepatitis C virus
Hepatitis D virus[a]
Hepatitis G virus
Cocaine [b]
Adulterants of illicit, injectable drugs

[a] Only in association with Hepatitis B virus infection
[b] Only in acute intoxications

hospitalized drug abusers with acute viral hepatitis, hepatitis A was seen in 13 (9%), hepatitis B in 101 (67%), non-A, non-B hepatitis in 35 (23%), and cytomegalovirus in one (1%); one patient was unclassified due to insufficient serum (77).

Hepatotoxicity can result from substances of use or abuse. Alcohol is directly hepatotoxic, and parenteral drug abusers who also abuse alcohol may display clinical and histologic evidence of alcoholic liver disease (25, 72). Many alcoholism treatment units are seeing increasing numbers of former parenteral drug users who now use only alcohol; careful and repeated interviews are often necessary to obtain this history (78). Cocaine is hepatotoxic in animal models and can cause hepatic necrosis in humans after acute intoxications (79). Cocaine-induced hepatic injury is often associated with rhabdomyolysis, hypotension, and renal failure. Several studies have shown that ethanol enhances the hepatotoxicity of cocaine when it is consumed either before cocaine or simultaneously with cocaine (80). This may be related to the formation of a unique metabolite of cocaine, cocaethylene, which is formed in the liver only in the presence of cocaine and ethanol (81). Cocaethylene has euphoric and reinforcing effects which exceed those of cocaine, and in animal studies, it is considerably more toxic than cocaine (81). These effects may explain the frequent use of alcohol with cocaine. In two studies, nonparenteral cocaine use without acute intoxication was not associated with liver disease (82, 83).

Methadone is not hepatotoxic (72, 84). Naltrexone, an orally administered opioid antagonist used in the treatment of alcohol abusers or drug-free former narcotic users, can cause dose-related hepatocellular injury. Elevated liver tests with naltrexone have been described mainly with doses higher than those currently recommended, but the drug should be used with caution in patients with active liver disease. It is contraindicated in acute hepatitis or liver failure. Nucleoside analog antiretroviral drugs such as zidovudine or didanosine can rarely cause severe hepatic steatosis with hepatomegaly, lactic acidosis, and liver failure (85). Many other medications used in HIV-infected patients are potentially hepatotoxic.

Hepatitis A

The hepatitis A virus (HAV) is a small, non-enveloped RNA virus in the picornavirus family (86). Unlike other hepatitis viruses associated with substance abuse, HAV is spread by the fecal-oral route. The incubation period is 2–6 weeks. HAV reaches its highest concentration in the stools during the late incubation period. By the onset of jaundice, which occurs 1–2 weeks after the onset of symptoms, the stools rapidly become noninfectious. A brief period of viremia precedes the liver disease. HAV does not cause chronic liver disease, and there is no carrier state. A safe and effective formalin-inactivated hepatitis A vaccine is now available (87, 88).

HAV infection is associated with sporadic or epidemic spread. Poor sanitation, overcrowding, and fecal contamination of food or water supply contribute to the high worldwide prevalence of HAV. In the United States, HAV infection occurs in homosexual men, travelers to less developed countries, contacts of persons with hepatitis, and children and staff of day-care centers.

Several outbreaks of HAV infection have been reported in substance abusers, initially in Sweden (89) and subsequently in the United States (90, 91). These outbreaks have been associated with parenteral use of heroin, cocaine, or amphetamines, although some cases of HAV infection have occurred in users of marihuana only. Possible explanations for the transmission of HAV among substance abusers include tasting the drug to assess its quality; direct contamination of drugs with fecal material at the cultivation site or during smuggling in rectum-carried condoms or baby diapers; sexual contacts; and poor personal hygiene and living conditions. Percutaneous transmission of HAV through needle sharing is less likely since the viremia is brief and transfusion-associated HAV infection, although reported (92), is rare.

Hepatitis B

The hepatitis B virus (HBV) is a 42 nm DNA virus. It consists of an outer envelope, which contains hepatitis B surface antigen (HBsAg), and a core which contains double-stranded circular DNA, the hepatitis B core antigen, and an endogenous viral DNA polymerase. The hepatitis B e antigen (HBeAg) is a serum protein which correlates with HBV replication. It is synthesized from the pre-C region of the HBV genome, adjacent to the C gene that encodes for the hepatitis B core antigen.

The outcome of HBV infection is variable. About 65% of patients will have a subclinical infection, another 5–10% will develop a chronic infection in which they remain HBsAg-positive, and the remainder manifest typical acute hepatitis (93). In acute HBV infection, HBsAg is cleared from the blood during convalescence, 1–5 months after the onset; following clearance of HBsAg, hepatitis B surface antibody (anti-HBs) appears. Anti-HBs confers immunity to hepatitis B. Antibody to hepatitis B core antigen (anti-HBc) appears shortly after HBsAg, remains detectable after HBsAg disappears, and, like anti-HBs, persists in the serum long after recovery from acute type B hepatitis.

There are two phases of chronic HBV infection (93, 94). Initially, HBeAg is detectable, HBV replication continues, hepatic inflammation is active, serum transaminases are elevated, and the patient is infectious. The second phase begins with seroconversion from HBeAg to hepatitis B e antibody (anti-HBe). Although HBsAg remains positive, during the anti-HBe-positive phase hepatic histology reveals reduced inflammatory activity, serum transaminases tend to normalize, markers of HBV replication disappear, and the infectivity is reduced (but cannot be assumed to be absent). Exceptions to these serologic relationships exist, as in the mutant form of HBV in which, despite the lack of HBeAg production due to a mutation in the pre-C region of the HBV genome, active viral replication as reflected by serum HBV-DNA is evident (95). In chronic HBV infection, a spectrum of hepatic histology may be seen, including mild, moderate, and severe chronic hepatitis and cirrhosis. Hepatocellular carcinoma is a consequence of prolonged HBV infection.

As noted earlier, most parenteral drug abusers have serologic evidence of HBV infection (74–76). Similar to other populations, about 5–10% of parenteral drug abusers become chronic HBsAg carriers (74–76, 84). In comparison to homosexual men, who also have a high prevalence of HBV infection, parenteral drug abusers clear HBeAg more rapidly (96). Exposure to HBV occurs soon after the onset of parenteral drug abuse in most patients. In one series, more than 80% with hepatitis had used drugs for less than one year (97). In most studies, the prevalence of HBV infection is associated with increasing duration of parenteral drug use; other risk factors for HBV infection in parenteral drug abusers vary with the population under study (98). Parenteral drug abusers with HBV infection may transmit this disease to non–drug users through sexual contact (99). Sexual transmission is also suspected in a group of crack cocaine users who developed fulminant HBV infection in a six-month period (100). All denied parenteral drug abuse.

HBV is not directly cytopathic (101). The marked variability in clinical features of patients with HBV infection is believed to reflect differences in the cellular immune response of the host. In HBV infection, the cytotoxic T-cells of the host will recognize viral markers on the surface of hepatocytes and will initiate lysis of the hepatocytes, leading to liver cell necrosis. Viral and genetic factors may also influence the course of HBV infection (101).

Since HIV infection is associated with cellular immune deficiency, it might be expected to reduce the severity of HBV-induced liver disease. Several studies suggest that this occurs despite enhanced HBV replication. Among chronic HBsAg carriers, HIV-infected homosexual men had less severe injury in liver biopsies than those not infected with HIV (102). Levels of DNA polymerase, an index of HBV replication, were higher in the HIV-seropositive patients. In another study of homosexual men (103), HBsAg carriers with HIV infection were significantly less likely to spontaneously clear HBV-DNA, another marker of viral replication, than those without HIV infection. Liver disease activity, as assessed by transaminase levels, was significantly reduced in HIV-infected patients despite the more frequent persistence of HBV-DNA. Among parenteral drug abusers with chronic HBV infection, detectable HBV-DNA was significantly more common in HIV-seropositive patients (104).

If HIV-infected persons who are susceptible to HBV infection become infected with HBV, they are more likely to develop the HBsAg carrier state. In a study of homosexual men with acute hepatitis B, 20% of 41 HIV-seropositive versus 6% of 151 HIV-seronegative patients became HBsAg carriers (105). Among parenteral drug abusers, this difference was even more pronounced. Only 2% of 57 anti-HIV-negative patients, but 89% of 9 anti-HIV-positive patients, became HBsAg carriers (106).

The hepatitis B vaccine is immunogenic, effective, and safe (94). Parenteral drug abusers who are susceptible to HBV infection have responded well to the hepatitis B vaccine in some (107) but not all (108) studies. Compliance with hepatitis B vaccination among drug users can be high within treatment programs which offer the vaccine (107, 109) but will be lower among such patients not regularly attending treatment facilities (110). More rapid vaccination schedules (0, 1, 2, and 12 months) should be considered when poor compliance is expected (111). Among recipients of the hepatitis B vaccine, HIV-infected patients develop anti-HBs less often and in lower titer than those without HIV infection (112). Recently, some methadone maintenance programs in New York City have noted that a majority of patients entering treatment since 1993 were seronegative for HBV (109). This increase in HBV seronegativity is probably due to AIDS risk-reduction efforts, and these findings suggest that greater efforts to vaccinate drug users may be warranted. Vaccination of the entire population during infancy and/or early adolescence, as is now recommended (113, 114), will eventually reduce the incidence of HBV infection, but full implementation of these recommendations will take considerable time. All staff of drug treatment programs who are susceptible to HBV infection should receive hepatitis B vaccine, which also effectively prevents hepatitis D (delta) virus infection (see later section).

Hepatitis C

During the 1970s and 1980s it became apparent that intravenous drug users could have multiple attacks of hepatitis (115) and that many episodes of acute and chronic hepatitis in these patients were not caused by HAV or HBV. One or more agents of "non-A, non-B" hepatitis were therefore postulated. In 1989, hepatitis C virus (HCV) was isolated and was quickly established as the cause of most cases of non-A, non-B hepatitis in intravenous drug users and transfusion recipients, and many patients with community-acquired hepatitis (116).

HCV is a 55 nm, single-stranded RNA virus which is related to flaviviruses and pestiviruses (117). There is significant sequence variation in the HCV-RNA, leading to the identification of six major genotypes of HCV (118). The prevalence of HCV genotypes varies with geographic location, and specific genotypes may be associated with different degrees of severity of HCV infection and response to interferon therapy. Further studies are needed to determine the relationship of these features of genotypes to HCV viremia, as reflected by HCV-RNA levels. A variety of HCV genotypes have been reported in intravenous drug users, and spread of drug use may introduce new genotypes into the population (119–120). Coinfections with more than one genotype have been reported (121). In a recent study, intravenous drug users had a variety of HCV genotypes in similar proportions to those of the total group of 438 patients from tertiary referral centers in the United States (122). Of 100 intravenous drug users, 73 had HCV type 1.

In addition to the HCV genotypes, HCV can mutate within an infected individual to form several distinct yet closely related sequences called quasispecies (117). These may contribute to chronic infection, since mutants develop which escape the host immune response of neutralizing antibodies and cytotoxic T-cells (117). The development of quasispecies could also explain the multiple attacks of acute HCV in some patients and the lack of protective immunity in HCV-infected chimpanzees after reinfection (123).

Chronic HCV infection is one of the most common liver diseases in the United States. Up to 3.5 million Americans, more than 1% of the population, are infected. Transfusions have virtually been eliminated as a cause of HCV infection now that donors are screened for hepatitis C antibody (anti-HCV). Intravenous drug users accounted for 42% of community-acquired HCV infection in a study by the CDC (124). Seropositivity rates for anti-HCV among intravenous drug users have ranged from 64 to 90% (125–129). In patients injecting drugs for 10 or more years, a prevalence of 94% has been reported (130). Among intravenous drug users with chronic liver disease, 98% had serologic evidence of HCV infection (131). HCV is usually acquired in the early period of a patient's drug use (130) and often after only a few injections. About 40% of patients with HCV have no known risk factor, and many of these are from lower socioeconomic groups (132). Sexual transmission of HCV is inefficient but can occur (132). However, coinfection with HCV and HIV is associated with increased sexual transmission of HCV to heterosexual partners in populations of intravenous drug users (133) and hemophiliacs (134).

There is usually no acute illness with HCV infection. In the first few months, anti-HCV may not be detectable and HCV-RNA is the only marker (135). Levels of serum aminotransferases are generally lower in acute and chronic HCV infection than in other forms of viral hepatitis. In chronic HCV, these levels often fluctuate considerably and may be normal, occasionally for prolonged time periods (116). The levels of aminotransferases are poor predictors of liver histology in chronic HCV infection, and liver biopsy is often indicated (136). Intravenous drug users with chronic HCV may have less severe histologic changes than those who acquired HCV via transfusion (137). Chronic infection occurs in 60–80% of patients infected with HCV, and spontaneous resolution is rare. Cirrhosis develops in 10–20% of patients with chronic HCV, usually after many years of mild or subclinical disease. Although a few patients with chronic HCV have a rapidly progressive course to end-stage liver disease, a long-term study of transfusion recipients showed no increase in overall mortality after non-A, non-B hepatitis (138).

HCV infection is diagnosed using the second-generation enzyme-linked immunosorbent assay (ELISA). This method, which uses three HCV-specific proteins as antigens, has increased sensitivity and specificity compared with earlier versions (139). Supplemental testing with recombinant immunoblot assay (RIBA) or direct measurement of HCV viremia by HCV-RNA should be considered to increase the accuracy of the diagnosis, especially if antiviral therapy is being considered.

Many studies of patients with alcoholic liver disease have shown an increased frequency of anti-HCV and an increased severity of liver disease in those with both HCV infection and alcohol abuse (140, 141). In some but not all studies, most of the alcohol users with HCV had parenteral risk factors, either drug use or transfusion (141). Several studies show that patients with alcoholic liver disease and HCV infection have more severe liver disease than those with either one alone (141). HCV infection is associated with more advanced alcoholic liver disease at a younger age (142). Among alcohol users with HCV infection, habitual drinkers have higher HCV-RNA levels than non-habitual drinkers (143). Alcoholic liver disease with HCV infection is associated with more severe histologic findings and decreased survival (144). These studies are consistent with work done a decade earlier showing a higher frequency of cirrhosis in abusers of alcohol and intravenous drugs compared with patients with either factor alone (72, 145).

Hepatitis D

The hepatitis D (delta) virus (HDV) is an atypical virus which requires a helper function of HBV (146). HDV is a 36 nm hybrid particle, consisting of a circular single-stranded RNA and the delta antigen, both of which are encapsidated by an HBsAg coat. The genome of HDV is smaller than that of any other animal virus. The small size, the need for a helper function, and the circular RNA genome, which lacks messenger RNA activity, are features of HDV which are markedly different from human viruses but resemble a group of subviral microorganisms of plants classified as viroids and circular satellites (147, 148).

HDV has an obligatory association with HBV, and the duration of HDV infection is determined by that of HBV (146). There are two mechanisms of HDV infection: coinfection with HBV, and superinfection of HBsAg carriers. In coinfection, HBV and HDV are acquired together. The usual outcome is acute hepatitis with recovery, and the replicative potential of HDV is limited by the short duration of HBV infection. Coinfection causes an increased frequency of fulminant hepatitis (149). There is, however, no increased risk of developing the HBsAg carrier state when HDV is acquired along with HBV. In superinfection, a chronic HBsAg carrier is infected with HDV. Most such patients develop chronic HDV infection, in which the chronic liver disease is more severe and more rapidly progressive than with HBV infection alone (150, 151). As in coinfection, superinfection of HBsAg carriers by HDV can precipitate fulminant hepatitis. HDV infection should be strongly considered when a stable HBsAg carrier has an exacerbation of chronic liver disease or an episode resembling acute hepatitis B. Diagnostic difficulty may result when the HBsAg status of a patient is unknown; IgM anti-HBc, a marker of recent HBV infection, will usually be positive in HDV coinfection and negative in superinfection (152).

Many serologic tests for HDV, including delta antigen (HDAg), delta antibody (anti-HD), and delta RNA (HDV-RNA), have been developed (146, 153). Total anti-HD, consisting mostly of IgG antibody, is most widely available. Anti-HD does not confer protection. In acute coinfection with HDV and HBV, total anti-HD is usually (but not always) detectable. Its appearance is often delayed until convalescence from the acute hepatitis, and repeated testing may be needed to diagnose HDV coinfection. IgM anti-HD and HDV-RNA are detectable earlier. In HDV superinfection, high titers of anti-HD appear promptly and persist during the course of chronic HDV infection. HDV-RNA is almost always detectable initially and persists for 5 years in about 80% (151).

As in HCV infection, HDV undergoes changes in viral sequence within an infected patient, and this may facilitate chronicity (154). Genotypes of HDV have been described which are associated with differences in disease severity and outcome (155).

Because of its association with HBV, HDV infection is transmitted parenterally. It is endemic in the Mediterranean region and in parts of Asia, Africa, and South America. HDV infection appears to have been spread to nonendemic areas such as the United States and Northern Europe by parenteral drug abusers (156). Outbreaks of severe and fulminant hepatitis primarily due to coinfection with HDV and HBV have been reported in parenteral drug abusers and their sexual contacts (149). The prevalence of anti-HD in chronic HBsAg-positive parenteral drug abusers is 71–80% (104, 156, 157). In a comparison of HDV infection in drug addicts and nonaddicts, evidence of more rapid histological deterioration was found in addicts (158). Serologic evidence of HDV infection among HBsAg carrier parenteral drug abusers is independent of HIV infection (104, 159), reflecting the high prevalence of HDV infection in such patients as well as differences in transmissibility between HDV and HIV. HIV infection facilitates the appearance of serum HDAg (75), a marker of HDV infection which is otherwise rarely detected.

Since transmission of HDV requires a helper function of HBV, vaccination against HBV will also prevent HDV infection.

Hepatitis G and Other Hepatitis Viruses

There are episodes of viral hepatitis that cannot be accounted for by hepatitis A, B, C, and D virus infections. These include about 10% of post-transfusion hepatitis and many cases of fulminant hepatitis (160). In 1995, a new flavivirus, distantly related to HCV, was identified and provisionally termed hepatitis G virus (HGV). In a preliminary study, 46% of intravenous drug users had HGV-RNA in serum (160). Other investigators have discovered two other possible agents of viral hepatitis (160), and one of these was seen in 24% of intravenous drug users with HCV-associated chronic liver disease in Japan (161). It is likely that the list of parenterally transmitted hepatitis viruses will continue to increase.

Chronic Liver Disease

A majority of parenteral drug abusers have chronic liver disease (73). The entire spectrum of histologic changes of chronic viral hepatitis from mild chronic hepatitis to cirrhosis, and alcoholic liver disease from fatty infiltration to alcoholic hepatitis to cirrhosis, can be seen in parenteral drug abusers (72). In the absence of alcohol abuse, most chronic liver disease in parenteral drug abusers is mild, probably because of the predominant role of HCV infection. In a comparison of liver biopsies in chronic HBV infection, severe histologic damage was more common in homosexual men than in parenteral drug abusers, unless HDV infection was present (96). The combination of alcohol and parenteral drug abuse leads to severe liver disease (72, 145). Cirrhosis, which usually occurs in the fifth or sixth decades in the United States, has been observed frequently in younger patients (ages 24–34) who have abused both alcohol and parenteral drugs (145). Among 204 liver biopsies in substance abusers with chronic liver disease, cirrhosis was found in 3 (9%) of 34 with parenteral drug abuse only, 7 (30%) of 23 with alcohol abuse only, and 76 (52%) of 147 with both alcohol and parenteral drug abuse (72). Cirrhosis was also significantly more common in alcohol-abusing former parenteral drug abusers than in simultaneous abusers of alcohol and parenteral drugs (72). These observations probably reflect a synergistic effect of alcohol and HCV infection, which leads to severe liver injury. In alcohol and parenteral drug abusers with severe chronic liver disease and hyperglobulinemia, false-positive enzyme-linked immunosorbent assay (ELISA) tests for HIV have been reported (162).

Hepatic amyloidosis has recently been reported in patients with a history of intravenous and subcutaneous drug use (163). As with renal amyloidosis in parenteral drug users, these patients have chronic skin ulcers. Also, some had HIV infection and/or pulmonary tuberculosis.

Liver disease causes abnormal disposition of many drugs, especially those metabolized by oxidative pathways. Although methadone is metabolized in the liver by oxidative biotransformation (71), studies of methadone disposition in moderate (164) and severe (165) chronic liver disease showed that most pharmacokinetic parameters were unchanged. It may be that damage to hepatic drug-metabolizing enzyme systems in severe liver disease is offset by damage to capacity of the liver to store and release unchanged methadone (164–166). The usual methadone maintenance dose can be continued in patients with stable chronic liver disease, including those with advanced cirrhosis. In acute liver disease, close clinical observation for signs of narcotic overdose or withdrawal is mandatory, and a modest reduction in the methadone dose may be indicated in some patients.

Recombinant alpha interferon is useful in the treatment of chronic HBV, HCV, and HDV infections (167–169). In chronic HBV infection, approximately one third of patients respond to 5–10 million units daily or thrice weekly with a sustained loss of HBV-DNA and HBeAg. HIV infection is associated with a poor response rate. In chronic HCV infection, about half will respond to 3 million units thrice weekly for six months with normalization of serum transaminase levels, but a majority of responders will relapse after the interferon is stopped. Increasing the duration of treatment appears to improve efficacy. In chronic HDV infection, a higher interferon dose (9 million units three times a week for 48 weeks) led to normalization of aminotransferases and loss of HDV-RNA in half, but HDV-RNA often reappears during follow-up. Side effects of interferon include flu-like symptoms, bone marrow suppression, mental depression, and autoimmune thyroid disorders.

Orthotopic liver transplantation has been successfully used in end-stage alcoholic cirrhosis (170, 171). Experience from many centers indicates that patient and graft survival are as good or better in alcoholic cirrhosis compared with transplant recipients with other liver diseases. For example, the one-year survival in 73 such patients at the University of Pittsburgh was 74%, a result which did not differ from control nonalcoholic patients receiving liver transplants at the same institution. Only 6 (11.5%) of these 73 have resumed consumption of any amount of alcohol, and none relapsed to daily drinking (170). Even when alcohol use has recurred, compliance with the immunosuppressive drug regimen has been good, and little serious alcoholic liver disease has been seen (172). Although further data are needed on liver transplantation in end-stage alcoholic liver disease, alcoholism per se should not be a reason for exclusion from this life-saving procedure. Therapeutic decisions about individual patients should be made on medical rather than moral grounds (170, 171). The same considerations should apply to former parenteral drug abusers, including those receiving methadone maintenance treatment.

Renal Diseases

A variety of renal lesions have been reported in intravenous drug abusers. These include nephrotic syndrome (173–175), glomerulonephritis secondary to infective endocarditis (176) or hepatitis B (177), and acute renal failure due to nontraumatic rhabdomyolysis (178). These disorders cause significant morbidity and mortality but are uncommon. It has been estimated that less than 1% of heroin addicts develop nephrotic syndrome (173). In a study from Buffalo, only 23 intravenous drug abusers with nephrotic syndrome or renal insufficiency were seen in a 10-year period (174). In the 1990s, nephrotic syndrome in intravenous drug users has virtually disappeared from a major medical center (179). The authors speculate that this may be due to an increase in the purity of street heroin, associated with reduced quantities of adulterants which may be nephrotoxic (179).

Nephrotic syndrome in intravenous drug abusers may present with asymptomatic proteinuria detected on routine urinalysis, or with clinical evidence of renal failure or anasarca (173). Renal biopsies in intravenous drug abusers with heavy proteinuria usually reveal either focal and segmental glomerulosclerosis (often referred to as "heroin nephropathy") or amyloidosis (175). Intravenous drug abusers with focal glomerulosclerosis are predominantly black (174, 180) and may have used needles for as little as one year (173, 175). Those with renal amyloidosis almost always have active or healed suppurative skin lesions (175, 181), and many have had extensive drug use by the subcutaneous route. In comparison with heroin addicts with focal glomerulosclerosis, those with amyloidosis are older and have longer durations of intravenous drug abuse (175). Little is known about the pathogenesis of either focal glomerulosclerosis or amyloidosis in heroin addicts, but both progress relentlessly to end-stage renal failure. There are case reports of addicts with renal amyloidosis who had marked reduction of proteinuria with colchicine treatment (182) or remission of nephrotic syndrome following cessation of intravenous drug use for six years (183), but these events are rare.

HIV infection is associated with a variety of renal lesions (184–186). In some series (184), the majority of patients have had a syndrome of HIV-associated nephropathy characterized by nephrotic-range proteinuria, focal and segmental glomerulosclerosis, and rapid progression to end-stage renal disease. This clinical syndrome is seen mainly in black parenteral drug abusers and is very infrequent in homosexual men with HIV infection. However, it has been observed in patients without parenteral drug abuse, including children with perinatal AIDS (184). As noted previously, parenteral drug abuse leads to focal glomerulosclerosis independently of HIV infection (173–175); it is uncertain whether HIV infection accelerates this process, the pathogenesis of which is unknown, or causes focal glomerulosclerosis by a separate mechanism. In some cities, HIV-associated focal and segmental glomerulosclerosis has been infrequent (186).

Glomerulonephritis resulting from infective endocarditis in parenteral drug abusers may be focal or diffuse (176). Immunologic mechanisms, including deposition of immune complexes in glomeruli and complement activation, are probably important in both types. Focal glomerulonephritis in this setting is clinically mild. Diffuse glomerulonephritis is associated with azotemia and microscopic hematuria and proteinuria, and it may progress to advanced renal failure (176). Casts, especially red blood cell casts, are helpful diagnostically when present. Hypocomplementemia is frequently observed. In most patients, the clinical manifestations resolve with effective antimicrobial therapy; a few patients are left with chronic renal failure despite cure of the acute infection.

Methadone maintenance treatment can be safely continued in the presence of chronic renal disease (187). Methadone is minimally removed by peritoneal dialysis or hemodialysis, and it does not accumulate in patients with renal failure. In anuric patients, methadone elimination by the fecal route may be increased (187).

Immunologic Abnormalities

Several immunologic abnormalities have been observed in parenteral drug abusers not infected with HIV (Table 55.3) (188). Generalized lymphadenopathy was reported in both clinical and autopsy studies in the 1960s and 1970s (189, 190). Although histology usually reveals reactive hyperplasia, occasionally a definitive diagnosis such as tuberculosis or malignant lymphoma is made. Elevated levels of serum immunoglobulins, particularly IgG and IgM, have been reported in parenteral heroin abusers by several groups (84, 191, 192). Use of heroin by the nasal route was associated with a lower frequency of IgM elevations than parenteral use (193). In prospective studies (191), mean IgM levels decreased during the first year of methadone maintenance treatment, and the number of patients with normal IgM levels increased from 24% to 48%. In successful long-term methadone maintenance patients (11–21 years in treatment with no parenteral drug abuse in at least 10 years), mean IgM levels did not differ from those of healthy volunteers; IgG levels remained elevated and did not differ significantly from those in parenteral heroin abusers (194). Levels of other serum proteins (73), including the immune activation markers, beta$_2$-microglobulin (195) and neopterin (196), are also elevated in HIV-seronegative parenteral drug abusers. Neopterin levels decreased during methadone maintenance treatment regardless of HIV infection or ongoing drug use (196).

False-positive results on a variety of serologic tests were found in parenteral heroin abusers in 1960s and 1970s. These include false-positive tests for syphilis (85, 192, 197), rheumatoid factor (192, 198), febrile agglutinins (199), and complement fixation tests for infectious agents (200). These false-positive reactions do not correlate with other immunologic abnormalities and are nonspecific (198, 199). Prospective studies of heroin addicts with false-positive tests for syphilis (197) or rheumatoid factor (198) showed a reduction in the frequency of these reactions after one or more years of methadone maintenance treatment.

Abnormalities in cellular immunity are also seen in HIV-seronegative heroin addicts. Lymphocytosis was observed in early studies (201). A decrease in total T lymphocytes, as assessed by the ability to rosette sheep red blood cells in vitro, and an increase in null lymphocytes, have been reported (202). Naloxone reversed these changes, suggesting that opioid receptors may be present on T lymphocytes. In the same study, less marked abnormalities were seen in patients after 8 years of methadone maintenance treatment (202). In more recent studies using monoclonal antibodies to cell surface markers (194, 195), HIV-seronegative parenteral heroin abusers had elevated numbers of total T lymphocytes (CD2- and CD3-positive), helper T lymphocytes (CD4-positive), and suppressor T lymphocytes (CD8-positive). Long-term, stable methadone maintenance patients, in contrast, had numbers of these cells which were significantly lower than those of the heroin abusers but similar to those of healthy volunteers (194). In studies of lymphocyte function, reduced responsiveness of lymphocytes from parenteral drug abusers to mitogens in short-term culture has been observed (192). Natural killer cell activity is reduced in HIV-seronegative heroin addicts, but long-term, stable methadone maintenance patients had levels similar to those of healthy volunteers (194). Administration of methadone (203) or naloxone (204) in vitro to lymphocytes from healthy volunteers or methadone-maintained patients caused no changes in natural killer activity except at concentrations greatly exceeding those ever attained clinically. In another study, peripheral blood mononuclear cells from methadone maintenance patients had an impaired ability to generate

Table 55.3 Immunologic Abnormalities in HIV-Seronegative Parenteral Drug Abusers

Generalized lymphadenopathy
Elevated serum immunoglobulins
False-positive serologic tests
Lymphocytosis
Increased lymphocyte subset cell numbers
Reduced responsiveness of lymphocytes to mitogens
Reduced natural killer cell activity

superoxide anion, but there is no evidence that this alteration is clinically significant (205).

Several factors may contribute to the development of these immunologic abnormalities in parenteral heroin addicts (188). Heroin, morphine, and other opioid drugs of abuse, as well as methadone, as used in the treatment of narcotic addiction, could act directly on the cells of the immune system either at specific opiate receptors or at other sites (188). The existence of specific opiate receptors in the immune system has been strongly suggested by several studies (202, 205) but has not been proven (207). Opioid drugs could also modulate immune function as a result of neuroendocrine effects such as alterations in the release of cortisol, ACTH, and beta-endorphin (188) (see Chapter 13). Factors related to the lifestyle of the heroin addict can contribute to immunologic abnormalities; these include stress, poor nutrition, and altered sleep-wake cycles, alcoholism, polydrug abuse, and the infectious complications of parenteral drug abuse. The numerous adulterants of street heroin may serve as antigens.

The relative contributions of these factors to the development of immunologic abnormalities is unknown. However, the observations that methadone maintenance treatment is associated with normalization of natural killer cell activity, numbers of lymphocytes, T lymphocytes, T helper and T suppressor lymphocytes, and serum IgM levels (188, 194), suggest that direct effects of opiates are of lesser importance. Also, the exposure to opiates

during methadone maintenance treatment is greater than during parenteral heroin abuse (188). The neuroendocrine and lifestyle effects of narcotic addiction are reduced or eliminated by effective methadone maintenance treatment, and these factors may therefore be primarily responsible for the immunologic abnormalities that resolve concomitantly during treatment.

COCAINE

The use of cocaine increased dramatically in the 1980s, and more potent formulations of the drug, freebase cocaine and crack cocaine, became widely available (208). As a result, the medical complications of cocaine use have increased in scope and frequency (209, 210). The neurobiological and clinical aspects of cocaine are described in Chapters 15 and 16. Table 55.4 lists the medical complications of cocaine abuse.

In contrast to heroin addiction, the complications of which result primarily from unsterile injection techniques, adulterants, and lifestyle, many of the complications of cocaine use are consequences of the pharmacologic actions of the drug. These actions may be associated with increased risk of significant toxicity in the setting of decreased ability to metabolize the drug, i.e., decreased plasma cholinesterase activity (211–213). Cocaine abusers may also develop complications associated with the three main routes of use: intranasal, intravenous, and inhalation. In addition to the systemic ef-

Table 55.4 Medical Complications of Cocaine Abuse

Head, Eyes, Ears, Nose, Throat
Madarosis
Corneal epithelial defects
Microbial keratitis
Iritis
Central retinal artery/vein occlusion
Chronic rhinitis
Epistaxis
Diminished olfaction
Atrophy nasal mucosa
Perforation septum and hard palate
Aspiration septum
CSF rhinorrhea
Midline granuloma
Osteolytic sinusitis
Optic neuropathy
Pott's puffy tumor
Brain abscess
Staphylococcal sepsis
Botulism
"Cracked" lips
Dental erosions
Periodontal disease
Pharyngeal ulcers and burns

Pulmonary
Dyspnea
Cough
Sputum production
Hemoptysis/pulmonary hemorrhage
Pleuritic chest pain
Airway burns
Exacerbation asthma
Carbonaceous material deposition
Bronchitis
"Crack" lung/eosinophilic lung disease
Bronchiolitis obliterans organizing pneumonia
Interstitial pneumonia
Decreased diffusing capacity
Pulmonary edema
Pulmonary infarction
Pulmonary hypertension
Pneumothorax
Pneumomediastinum

Rheum/Renal
Callus
Scleroderma
Muscle weakness
Rhabdomyolysis

Dermatomyonecrosis
Acute renal failure
Renal infarction
Renal artery thrombosis

Cardiovascular
Chest pain
Atherosclerosis
Coronary thrombosis
Coronary vasospasm
Coronary dissection
Myocardial ischemia/infarction
Left ventricular hypertrophy
Cardiomyopathy
Myocarditis
Arrhythmias
Pneumopericardium
Hypertension
Aortic dissection/rupture
Paget-Schroetter syndrome
Endocarditis

Neurologic
Headache
CNS ischemia/infarction
CNS hemorrhage
Cerebral vasculitis
Cerebral atrophy
Dystonic reactions
Exacerbation of Tourette's
Hyperthermia/neuroleptic malignant syndrome
Seizures
Cerebritis
Delirium

Psychiatric
Decreased concentration
Memory deficits
Personality changes
Kleptomania
Apathy
Psychomotor retardation
Depression
Suicidal ideation
Irritability
Anxiety
Panic disorder
Hallucinations
Psychosis/paranoia
Catatonia

Endocrine/Reproductive
Hypoprolactinemia
Hyperprolactinemia
ACTH secretion
LH secretion
Sexual dysfunction
Priapism/paraphimosis

Obstetric/Neonatal
Adverse maternal outcomes
Abruptio placentae
Premature rupture of membranes
Spontaneous abortion
Hypertension
Precipitate delivery
Adverse neonatal outcomes
Low birth weight
Intrauterine growth retardation
Prematurity
Congenital anomalies
Cerebral infarction
Neurobehavioral abnormalities
Respiratory pattern abnormalities
Sudden infant death syndrome
Postnatal exposure

Gastrointestinal
Perforated gastroduodenal ulcers
Intestinal ischemia
Colitis
Body packers/stuffers
Obstruction
Rupture

Hepatic
Hepatotoxicity

Hematopoietic
Thrombocytopenia
Hemolytic-uremia syndrome
Splenic infarction
Splenic hematoma

Miscellaneous
STDs/HIV
Tuberculosis
Violent/fatal injuries
Sudden death

fects of the drug, intranasal cocaine use can have devastating local effects on the nasal mucosa and its anatomic extensions (214–225). Cocaine use by intravenous drug abusers has been identified as a specific risk factor in the development of infectious complications (47, 226, 227), possibly because of an increased frequency of injection, increased needle sharing, and increased sexual activity. Also, cocaine-specific injecting practices may play a role in pathogen transmission. An example is "booting" (228), an injection technique in which blood is repeatedly aspirated into the syringe during cocaine delivery. Furthermore, complications may result from the use of cocaine in combination with other drugs (229, 230). Cocaethylene (81, 231, 232), i.e., ethanol-derived metabolite or benzoylecgonine ethyl-ester, is an example of a combination which has similar euphorigenic properties to cocaine but produces significantly more toxicity, especially cardiovascular (233–235).

Patients who use cocaine are being seen in increasing numbers by physicians in private practice who are not affiliated with chemical dependency treatment programs (236). The increase is particularly marked in emergency department settings where it is thought that 5–10% of visits nationwide are related to cocaine use (237). Patients seeking medical care for cocaine-related medical problems most commonly demonstrate cardiopulmonary, i.e., chest pain, dyspnea and palpitations, or neuropsychiatric, i.e., altered mental status, dizziness and headache, symptoms (238–240). In a multisite study of patients seen in emergency departments for chest pain, 17% had positive urines for cocaine (241). This included a 7% prevalence at a suburban site and 20% prevalence at the urban sites. Cocaine-positive urines were higher than expected in patients 41–50 years old at 18% and in patients 51–60 years old at 3%. The authors concluded that cocaine use is not uncommon in patients up to 60 years of age presenting with chest pain, and that asking about use should be routine and, perhaps, confirmed by objective testing given the unreliability of self-report and potential to alter treatment decisions. Another study (242) identified a prevalence rate of 1.1% of patients admitted to an urban, tertiary-care, teaching hospital with positive urine drug screens for cocaine. The authors retrospectively profiled physicians' responses to positive urine drug screens and found that medical history was "often incomplete, and counseling and substance abuse referrals occur in the minority of patients" (242).

Management of Acute Cocaine Toxicity

Acute presentations of cocaine toxicity are protean in form and complexity (see Table 55.4). The majority of users are presumed to experience the drug's effects and either avoid further use or continue casual use for some time without significant consequences. However, past uncomplicated use does not guarantee freedom from subsequent, unpredictable disaster. The simple headache that resolved without intervention previously may now prove to be the harbinger of an intracerebral event (243–245). The slight elevation in creatine kinase may eventually play out as severe rhabdomyolysis with myoglobinuric renal failure, hepatic dysfunction, and disseminated intravascular coagulation (79, 246–249). The sought-after euphoria and accompanying pleasurable anxiety may become an uncontrolled, agitated delirium with hyperthermia, seizure, respiratory depression, and sudden death (250–252). All are distinct possibilities with one use too many and should call attending physicians to consider the need for specific intervention.

A specific antidote for acute cocaine toxicity or prophylaxis against cocaine craving has been an area of active investigation characterized in general by breakthroughs unable to stand the test of time. Promises for the future are heightened by a keener understanding of central neurotransmitter effects in general and cocaine's role in particular. Perhaps this will lead to the development of a well-defined, well-tolerated blockade of the reinforcing effects of cocaine, i.e., antagonist model, provide a similar euphorigen to satiate desire, i.e., agonist model, or, possibly, intercept the drug's ability to access the central nervous system (253). Pharmacologic intervention of acute cocaine toxicity on the other hand, although without absolute consensus, has significant support for a variety of interventions, some of which are detailed here.

CARDIOVASCULAR COMPLICATIONS

Hypertension

Consider oxygenation and sedation as first line supplemented by pure alpha-blockade, i.e., phentolamine, or direct vasodilators, i.e., nitroglycerin/nitroprusside (254–257). Beta-blockade should be avoided because of the risk of unopposed stimulation of alpha-adrenergic receptors (254, 257–259). This includes the use of labetalol whose ratio of effect is skewed toward beta-blockage (254, 257, 260). The appropriate use of calcium channel blockers is still unclear (254, 257, 261, 262). Hydralazine may be substituted in cocaine-associated hypertension during pregnancy (254).

Arrhythmias

Supraventricular tachyarrhythmias are managed via dampening of central sympathomimetic effect with benzodiazepines along with cautious supplementation of calcium channel blockers (254, 257, 263). Beta-blocker use is controversial (254, 257–259). Similarly, benzodiazepines are the primary treatment of cocaine-induced ventricular arrhythmias as they too are manifestations of catecholamine excess (254). Correction of acidosis with sodium bicarbonate is important since acidosis sensitizes the heart to catecholamines (257, 263–265). Phenytoin (266) and calcium channel blockers (267) have also been suggested. Animal studies have yielded conflicting data in regard to the safe use of lidocaine in cocaine-induced arrhythmias (268, 269). Clinical concern has existed regarding the use of lidocaine because both lidocaine and cocaine share proconvulsant properties mediated by sodium-channel blockade. However, subsequent human data suggest that cautious use of lidocaine to treat ventricular arrhythmias that do not immediately follow cocaine use is reasonable (257, 270). Cardioversion and defibrillation remain part of established protocols (271).

Myocardial Ischemia or Infarction

Noncardiac sources of chest pain, especially of pulmonary origin, may mimic primary cardiac etiologies (272–274). The typical patient with cocaine-related myocardial infarction is a male in his mid-thirties with a history of chronic tobacco and repetitive cocaine use (257, 275). Neither symptoms nor the time from the last cocaine use can reliably predict actual injury since ischemia has been found to occur in early abstinence as well as while active metabolites are present (275–278). Electrocardiographic interpretation is difficult in that some cocaine users with myocardial ischemia or infarction have normal patterns (275–279). Also, creatine kinase elevation (with or without the MB fraction) can occur even without infarction (279–280), suggesting the need for more specific markers (280). Acute management includes standard monitoring, supplemental oxygen, nitrates and cautious use of thrombolytic therapy as indicated (257, 263, 281). In the event of cardiovascular collapse fluid resuscitation and pressors would be employed as per non-cocaine related cases (266). In one study (282), a twelve hour observation period appeared to be adequate to rule out patients for late complications. Since the incidence of late myocardial infarction is only 1% (283), further cardiac evaluation may not be needed when infarction is ruled out. However, given the known atherogenic effects of cocaine (284–286) and the more common catheterization evidence of coronary disease underlying coronary spasm (287), the role of non-invasive nuclear or echocardiographic stress testing remains controversial. Further studies are needed (257, 288). Aspirin may be useful for prophylaxis (257) along with obvious need to refrain from further cocaine and tobacco use.

NEUROLOGIC COMPLICATIONS

Seizures

Benzodiazepines are the first-line treatment. Intravenous diazepam or lorazepam are recommended (289). Barbiturates (254, 290) are also effective and phenytoin (266, 290) or valproic acid (291) can be considered as third-line drugs. Adequate ventilation and oxygenation are essential adjuncts to therapy. Refractory seizures are dealt with similar to non–cocaine-related events with mechanical respiratory support, neuromuscular blockade (pancuronium), and general anesthesia (254, 266).

Cerebrovascular Accidents

Imaging studies are essential when neurologic signs are present in cocaine users, and 80% of such patients will have abnormalities, with hemorrhage more common than ischemia (245). Management is similar to non–cocaine-related stroke while keeping in mind the specific cardiovascular interventions necessary in cocaine-related cases, especially in regard to blood pressure management. Magnesium may have a role in settling cocaine-induced cerebral vasospasm (292).

Hyperthermia

This poor prognostic sign should be aggressively treated with rapid cooling via ice water bath and fanning (254) supplemented by benzodiazepines for agitation. Dantrolene has no demonstrated efficacy (293) and haloperidol (D_2 receptor antagonist) may worsen matters by decreasing the hypothalamic response to heat dissipation (294, 295).

Delirium

"Agitated delirium" (250–252, 295) is generally a part of a complex clinical syndrome that demands prompt attention to cardiopulmonary support. Physical restraints should be applied until chemical restraints, i.e., benzodiazepines, can take effect. Detailed steps in treating the patient with cocaine-induced delirium have been described (295).

RHEUMATOLOGIC AND RENAL COMPLICATIONS
Rhabdomyolysis

In the event of cocaine-related muscle injury as evidenced by elevated serum creatine kinase, one should screen for myoglobinuria. Treatment includes hydration, alkalinization when indicated, and maintenance of adequate urine output (266). A classification system to predict the severity of cocaine-associated rhabdomyolysis has been suggested (248).

PULMONARY COMPLICATIONS
Respiratory Depression

Respiratory depression appears to be closely linked to seizure as a preterminal event (296). Aggressive ventilatory support may prevent death in patients presenting with seizures especially if instituted early (291).

GASTROINTESTINAL COMPLICATIONS
Body Packers

This refers to ingestion of packets of cocaine in order to smuggle the drug across international borders (297, 298). Body packers, or "mules," generally swallow carefully prepared packages containing large quantities of cocaine (266). Three types of cocaine packages have been described: Type 1—condoms, toy balloons, or finger cots (extremely susceptible to breakage and thus very dangerous); Type 2—five to seven layers of latex tubing; Type 3—smaller packets of cocaine paste in aluminum foil and then wrapped in three to five layers of latex (299). Rupture of even one cocaine package can cause

death; obstruction may also occur (297). A good history is important, but cocaine body packers are often uncooperative and unreliable. Abdominal x-rays are always indicated and will usually visualize Type 1 and 2 packets, but not Type 3 (299). Urine drug screening should also be done.

Interventions commonly employed in other foreign body obstructions of the gastrointestinal tract can be harmful in cocaine body packers. Rectal examination should be done cautiously; and digital rectal or endoscopic removal should be avoided as these could cause packet rupture (297, 298). Laxatives, ipecac, and enemas should similarly be avoided. Surgical removal should be performed in patients with Type 1 packets, broken packets, symptoms of cocaine toxicity, intestinal obstruction, or a time lapse of 24–48 hours since ingestion (297, 298). Activated charcoal may be a helpful adjunct, although its efficacy in humans is unproven (300). Asymptomatic patients with Types 2 and 3 packets may be closely monitored (297–299).

Body Stuffers

These are users or dealers of cocaine who rapidly swallow the drug to avoid being apprehended by the police (266). The cocaine may be ingested alone or within unsealed, quickly prepared packets of varying efficiency. Other drugs are frequently ingested along with the cocaine. Body stuffers ingest smaller quantities of cocaine than do body packers. Given these smaller amounts with less careful packaging, abdominal x-rays are less frequently useful (266). The packages can begin to leak immediately after ingestion, and thus surgery is rarely helpful.

Management of cocaine body stuffers has not been studied carefully. Ipecac has been suggested if ingestion is acute, the patient has a clear sensorium, and no seizure activity is documented (266). Whole-bowel irrigation with polyethylene glycol-electrolyte solutions at 1.5–2 L/hr along with activated charcoal are often used (266). Surgical consultation is indicated if bowel obstruction or mesenteric ischemia are possible.

Acute Cocaine Toxicity Conclusions

In summary, acute cocaine toxicity can involve multiple organ systems simultaneously or sequentially. Management must keep in mind the inextricable link between the cardiovascular and neurologic effects of cocaine (254), namely, that both are mediated centrally and manifested by increased sympathetic tone. Sedation with benzodiazepines had demonstrated a "conjoint therapy" effect, i.e., using a single drug for therapy of more than one organ system (266). This is supplemented by interventions that take into account cocaine-specific pharmacologic actions as well as general support for the clinical syndromes encountered.

ALCOHOLISM

Alcoholism is a common medical disorder that causes a vast array of significant medical complications. These are not discussed because of space limitations, but excellent reviews are available (301, 302).

Acknowledgments. *The authors thank Lisa Borg, M.D., and George Kim, M.D., for reviewing portions of the manuscript, and Sandra C. O'Neill for preparing the manuscript. This work was supported by National Institute on Drug Abuse Treatment Research Center No. P50-DA05130 and a grant from the Herbert and Nell Singer Philanthropic Fund of the Jewish Communal Fund. Support was also provided by the Department of Medical Education, Kettering Medical Center, Kettering, Ohio. We thank the staff of the Medical Library of Kettering Medical Center for help in literature searching.*

References

1. Novick DM. Major medical problems and detoxification treatment of parenteral drug-abusing alcoholics. Adv Alcohol Subst Abuse 1984;3:87–105.
2. Dole VP. In the course of professional practice. N Y State J Med 1965;65:927–931.
3. Jellinek EM. The disease concept of alcoholism. New Haven: Millhouse Press, 1960.
4. Chappel JN, Schnoll SH. Physician attitudes: effect on the treatment of chemically dependent patients. JAMA 1977;237:2318–2319.
5. McLellan AT, Arndt IO, Metzger DS, Woody GE, O'Brien CP. The effects of psychosocial services in substance abuse treatment. JAMA 1993;269:1953–1959.
6. Miller WR, Rollnick S. Motivational interviewing: preparing people to change addictive behavior. New York: Guilford Press 1991: 32–35.
7. Prochaska JO, DiClemente CC. Towards a comprehensive model of change. In: Miller WR, Heather N, eds. Treating addictive behaviors: processes of change. New York: Plenum Press, 1986:3–27.
8. Dole VP, Nyswander ME. Heroin addiction—a metabolic disease. Arch Intern Med 1967;120: 19–24.

9. Levine C, Novick DM. Expanding the role of physicians in drug abuse treatment: problems and perspectives. J Clin Ethics 1990;1:152–156.

10. Clark WD. Alcoholism: blocks to diagnosis and treatment. Am J Med 1981;71:275–286.

11. Stimmel B. Unlimited entitlement to health care: the dilemma of narcotic dependency. Mt Sinai J Med (N Y) 1989;56:176–179.

12. Gitlow SE. Considerations on the evaluation and treatment of substance dependency. J Subst Abuse Treat 1985;2:175–179.

13. Walsh DC, Hingson RW, Merrigan DM, et al. The impact of a physician's warning on recovery after alcoholism treatment. JAMA 1992; 267:663–667.

14. Kreek MJ. Rationale for maintenance pharmacotherapy of opiate dependence. In: O'Brien CP, Jaffe JH, eds. Addictive states. New York: Raven Press, 1992:205–230.

15. Cooper JR. Methadone treatment and acquired immunodeficiency syndrome. JAMA 1989;262: 1664–1668.

16. Novick DM, Joseph H, Croxson TS, et al. Absence of antibody to human immunodeficiency virus in long-term, socially rehabilitated methadone maintenance patients. Arch Intern Med 1990;150:97–99.

17. Novick DM, Pascarelli EF, Joseph H, et al. Methadone maintenance patients in general medical practice: a preliminary report. JAMA 1988;259:3299–3302.

18. Novick DM, Joseph H. Medical maintenance: the treatment of chronic opiate dependence in general medical practice. J Subst Abuse Treat 1991;8:233–239.

19. Novick DM, Joseph H, Salsitz EA, et al. Outcomes of treatment of socially rehabilitated methadone maintenance patients in physicians' offices (medical maintenance): follow-up at three and a half to nine and a fourth years. J Gen Intern Med 1994;9:127–130.

20. Rubenstein RB, Spira I, Wolff WI. Management of surgical problems in patients on methadone maintenance. Am J Surg 1976;131:566–569.

21. Beaver WT, Wallenstein SL, Houde RW, Rogers A. A clinical comparison of the analgesic effects of methadone and morphine administered intramuscularly and of orally and parenterally administered methadone. Clin Pharmacol Ther 1967;8:415–426.

22. Ho A, Dole VP. Pain perception in drug-free and in methadone-maintained human ex-addicts. Proc Soc Exp Biol Med 1979;162:392–395.

23. Concool B, Smith H, Stimmel B. Mortality rates of persons entering methadone maintenance: a seven-year study. Am J Drug Alcohol Abuse 1979;6:345–353.

24. Barr HL, Antes D, Ottenberg DJ, Rosen A. Mortality of treated alcoholics and drug addicts: the benefits of abstinence. J Stud Alcohol 1984;45: 440–452.

25. Sapira JD, Ball JC, Penn H. Causes of death among institutionalized narcotic addicts. J Chronic Dis 1970;22:733–742.

26. O'Connor PG, Selwyn PA, Schottenfeld RS. Medical care for injection-drug users with human immunodeficiency virus infection. N Engl J Med 1994;331:450–459.

27. Cherubin CE, Sapira JD. The medical complications of drug addiction and the medical assessment of the intravenous drug user: 25 years later. Ann Intern Med 1993;119:1017–1028.

28. Haverkos HW, Lange WR. Serious infections other than human immunodeficiency virus among intravenous drug abusers. J Infect Dis 1990;161:894–902.

29. Haverkos HW. Infectious diseases and drug abuse: prevention and treatment in the drug abuse treatment system. J Subst Abuse Treat 1991;8:269–275.

30. Masur H, Michelis MA, Greene JB, et al. An outbreak of community-acquired Pneumocystis carinii pneumonia: initial manifestation of cellular immune dysfunction. N Engl J Med 1981; 305:1431–1438.

31. Centers for Disease Control and Prevention. HIV/AIDS Surveillance Report 1995;7:1–34.

32. Hahn RA, Onorato IM, Jones TS, Dougherty J. Prevalence of HIV infection among intravenous drug users in the United States. JAMA 1989; 261:2677–2684.

33. Holmberg SD. Estimated HIV prevalence and incidence in 96 large metropolitan areas in the United States. Am J Public Health 1996;86: 642–654.

34. Rosenberg PS. Scope of the AIDS epidemic in the United States. Science 1995;270:1372–1375.

35. Abramowicz M. Drugs for AIDS and associated infections. Med Lett Drug Ther 1995;37: 87–94.

36. Kaplan JE, Masur H, Holmes KK. Prevention of opportunistic infections in persons infected with human immunodeficiency virus. Clin Infect Dis 1995;21(suppl 1):S1–S141.

37. Connor EM, Sperling RS, Gelber R, et al. Reduction of maternal-infant transmission of HIV type 1 with zidovudine therapy. N Engl J Med 1994;331:1173–1180.

38. Rho YM. Infections as fatal complications of narcotism. N Y State J Med 1972;72:823–830.

39. Stoneburner RL, Des Jarlais DC, Benezra D, et al. A larger spectrum of severe HIV-1-related disease in intravenous drug users in New York City. Science 1988;242:916–919.

40. Weisse AB, Heller DR, Schimenti RJ, Montgomery RL, Kapila R. The febrile parenteral drug user: a prospective study in 121 patients. Am J Med 1993;94:274–280.

41. Chambers HF, Morris DL, Tauber MG, Modin G. Cocaine use and the risk for endocarditis in intravenous drug users. Ann Intern Med 1987; 106:833–836.

42. Shekar R, Rice TW, Zierdt CH, Kallick CA. Outbreak of endocarditis caused by Pseudomonas aeruginosa serotype 011 among pentazocine and tripelennamine abusers in Chicago. J Infect Dis 1985;151:203–204.

43. Mills J, Drew D. Serratia marcescens endocarditis: a regional illness associated with intravenous drug abuse. Ann Intern Med 1976;84: 29–35.

44. Reiner NE, Gopalakrishna KV, Lerner PI. Enterococcal endocarditis in heroin addicts. JAMA 1976;235:1681–1683.

45. Noriega ER, Rubinstein E, Simberkoff MS, Rachal JJ. Subacute and acute endocarditis due to Pseudomonas cepacia in heroin addicts. Am J Med 1975;59:29–36.

46. Crane LR, Levine DP, Zervos MJ, Cummings G. Bacteremia in narcotic addicts at the Detroit Medical Center. I. Microbiology, epidemiology, risk factors and empiric therapy. Rev Infect Dis 1986;8:364–373.

47. Tuazon CU, Hill R, Sheagren JN. Microbiologic study of street heroin and injection paraphernalia. J Infect Dis 1974;129:327–329.

48. Chambers HF, Korzeniowski OM, Sande MA, and the National Endocarditis Study Group. Staphylococcus aureus endocarditis: clinical manifestations in addicts and nonaddicts. Medicine 1983;62:170–177.

49. Marantz PR, Linzer M, Feiner CJ, Feinstein SA, Kozin AM, Friedland GH. Inability to predict diagnosis in febrile intravenous drug abusers. Ann Intern Med 1987;106:823–828.

50. Novick DM, Ness GL. Abuse of antibiotics by abusers of parenteral heroin or cocaine. South Med J 1984;77:302–303.

51. Pulvirenti JJ, Kerns E, Benson C, Lisowski J, Demaris P, Weinstein RA. Infective endocarditis in injection drug users: importance of HIV serostatus and degree of immunosuppression. Clin Infect Dis 1996;22:40–44.

52. Nahass RG, Weinstein MP, Bartels J, Gocke DJ. Infective endocarditis in intravenous drug users: a comparison of human immunodeficiency virus type 1-negative and -positive patients. J Infect Dis 1990;162:967–970.

53. Sandre RM, Shafran SD. Infective endocarditis: review of 135 cases over 9 years. Clin Infect Dis 1996;22:276–286.

54. Centers for Disease Control and Prevention. Sexually transmitted disease surveillance, 1994. 1995:1–100.

55. Centers for Disease Control and Prevention. Sexually transmitted diseases guidelines. MMWR 1993;42(RR-14):1–102.

56. Abramowicz M. Drugs for sexually transmitted diseases. Med Lett Drug Ther 1995;37:117–122.

57. Trachtenberg AI, Gaudino JA, Hanson CV. Human T-cell lymphotropic virus in California's injection drug users. J Psychoactive Drugs 1991; 23:225–232.

58. Briggs NC, Battjes RJ, Cantor KP, et al. Seroprevalence of human T-cell lymphotropic virus type II infection, with or without HIV-I coinfection among intravenous drug users. J Infect Dis 1995;172:51–58.

59. Bhagavati S, Ehrlich G, Kula R, et al. Detection of human T-cell lymphoma/leukemia virus-type I (HTLV-1) in the spinal fluid and blood of cases of chronic progressive myelopathy and a clinical, radiological and electrophysiological profile of HTLV-1 associated myelopathy. N Engl J Med 1988;318:1141–1147.

60. Robert-Guroff M, Nakao Y, Notake K, Ito Y, Sliski A, Gallo RC. Natural antibodies to human retrovirus HTLV in a cluster of Japanese patients with adult T-cell leukemia. Science 1982; 215:975–978.

61. Poiesz B, Ruscetti F, Gazdar A, Bunn P, Minna J, Gallo R. Detection and continuous production of type-C retrovirus particles from fresh and cultured lymphocytes of a patient with cutaneous T-cell lymphoma. Proc Natl Acad Sci U S A 1980;77:7415–7419.

62. Selwyn PA, Feingold A, Hartel D, et al. Increased risk of bacterial pneumonia in HIV-infected intravenous drug users without AIDS. AIDS 1988;2:267–272.

63. Selwyn PA, Hartel D, Wasserman W, Drucker E. Impact of the AIDS epidemic on morbidity and mortality among intravenous drug users in a New York City methadone maintenance program. Am J Public Health 1989;79:1358–1362.

64. Myers EM, Kirkland LS, Mickey R. The head and neck sequelae of cervical intravenous drug abuse. Laryngoscope 1988;98:213–218.

65. Centers for Disease Control and Prevention. Reported tuberculosis in the United States, 1994. 1995:1–55.

66. Selwyn PA, Hartel D, Lewis VA, et al. A prospective study of the risk of tuberculosis among intravenous drug users with human immunodeficiency virus infection. N Engl J Med 1989; 320:545–550.

67. Centers for Disease Control and Prevention. A strategic plan for the elimination of tuberculosis in the United States. MMWR 1989;38(suppl 3):1–25.

68. Centers for Disease Control and Prevention. Tuberculosis and human immunodeficiency virus infection: a statement by the Advisory Committee for Elimination of Tuberculosis. MMWR 1989;38:236–250.

69. Barnes PF, Barrows SA. Tuberculosis in the 1990s. Ann Intern Med 1993;119:400–410.

70. Iseman MD, Cohn DL, Sbarbaro JA. Directly observed treatment of tuberculosis—we can't afford not to try. N Engl J Med 1993;328:576.

71. Kreek MJ, Gutjahr CL, Garfield JW, Bowen DV, Field FH. Drug interactions with methadone. Ann N Y Acad Sci 1976;281:350–371.

72. Novick DM, Stenger RJ, Gelb AM, Most J, Yancovitz SR, Kreek MJ. Chronic liver disease in abusers of alcohol and parenteral drugs: a report of 204 consecutive biopsy-proven cases. Alcoholism (NY) 1986;10:500–505.

73. Kreek MJ. Medical complications in methadone patients. Ann N Y Acad Sci 1978;311:110–134.

74. Weller IVD, Cohn D, Sierralta A, et al. Clinical, biochemical, serological, histological, and ultrastructural features of liver disease in drug abusers. Gut 1984;25:417–423.

75. Kreek MJ, Des Jarlais DC, Trepo CL, Novick DM, Abdul-Quader A, Raghunath J. Contrasting prevalence of delta hepatitis markers in parenteral drug abusers with and without AIDS. J Infect Dis 1990;162:538–541.

76. Novick DM, Gelb AM, Stenger RJ, et al. Hepatitis B serologic studies in narcotic users with chronic liver disease. Am J Gastroenterol 1981; 75:111–115.

77. Bortolotti F, Bertaggia A, Cadrobbi P, Crevellaro C, Pornaro E, Realdi G. Epidemiological aspects of acute viral hepatitis in drug abusers. Infection 1982;10:277–279.

78. Jiang JI, Dubois F, Driss F, et al. Clinical impact of drug addiction in alcoholics. Alcohol Alcohol 1995;30:55–60.

79. Silva MO, Roth D, Reddy KR, Fernandez JA, Albores-Saavedra J, Schiff ER. Hepatic dysfunction accompanying acute cocaine intoxication. J Hepatol 1991;12:312–315.

80. Odeleye OE, Watson RR, Eskelson CD, Earnest D. Enhancement of cocaine-induced hepatotoxicity by ethanol. Drug Alcohol Depend 1993;31: 253–263.

81. Randall T. Cocaine, alcohol mix in body to form even longer lasting, more lethal drug. JAMA 1992;267:1043–1044.

82. Tabasco-Minguillan J, Novick DM, Kreek MJ. Liver function tests in non-parenteral cocaine users. Drug Alcohol Depend 1990;26:169–174.

83. Kothur R, Marsh F, Posner G. Liver function tests in nonparenteral cocaine users. Arch Intern Med 1991;151:1126–1128.

84. Kreek MJ, Dodes L, Kane S, Knobler J, Martin R. Long-term methadone maintenance therapy: effects on liver function. Ann Intern Med 1972; 77:598–602.

85. Fortgang IS, Belitsos PC, Chiasson RE, Moore RD. Hepatomegaly and steatosis in HIV-infected patients receiving nucleoside analog antiretroviral therapy. Am J Gastroenterol 1995;90:1433–1436.

86. Lemon SM. HAV: current concepts of the molecular virology, immunobiology and approaches to vaccine development. Rev Med Virol 1992;2: 73–87.

87. Werzberger A, Mensch B, Kuter B, et al. A controlled trial of a formalin-inactivated hepatitis A vaccine in healthy children. N Engl J Med 1992; 327:453–457.

88. Margolis HS, Alter MJ. Will hepatitis A become a vaccine-preventable disease? Ann Intern Med 1995;122:464–465.

89. Widell A, Hansson BG, Moestrup T, Nordenfelt E. Increased occurrence of hepatitis A with cyclic outbreaks among drug addicts in a Swedish community. Infection 1983;11: 198–200.

90. Centers for Disease Control and Prevention. Hepatitis A among drug abusers. MMWR 1988;37:297–305.

91. Harkness J, Gildon B, Istre GR. Outbreaks of hepatitis A among illicit drug users, Oklahoma, 1984–87. Am J Public Health 1989;79: 463–466.

92. Hollinger FB, Khan NC, Oefinger PE, et al. Posttransfusion hepatitis type A. JAMA 1983; 250:2313–2317.

93. Hoofnagle JH, Schafer DF. Serologic markers of hepatitis B virus infection. Semin Liver Dis 1986;6:1–10.

94. Thomas HC, Novick DM. Chronic hepatitis B virus infection: treatment and prevention. In: Oriel JD, Harris JRW, eds. Recent advances in sexually transmitted diseases 3. Edinburgh: Churchhill Livingstone, 1986:157–174.

95. Foster GR, Corman WF, Thomas HC. Replication of hepatitis B and delta viruses: appearance of viral mutants. Semin Liver Dis 1991;11:121–127.

96. Moestrup T, Hansson BG, Widell A, Nordenfelt E, Hagerstrand I. Long term follow up of chronic hepatitis B virus infection in intravenous drug abusers and homosexual men. Br Med J 1986;292:854–857.

97. Cherubin CE, Hargrove RL, Prince AM. The serum hepatitis related antigen (SH) in illicit drug users. Am J Epidemiol 1970;91:510–517.

98. Levine OS, Vlahov D, Nelson KE. Epidemiology of hepatitis B virus infections among injecting drug users: seroprevalence, risk factors, and viral interactions. Epidemiol Rev 1994;16: 418–436.

99. Kelly DA, Carroll D, Shattock AG, O'Connor E, Weir DG. A secondary outbreak of hepatitis B among contacts of drug-abusers in Dublin. Ir J Med Sci 1983;76:205–208.

100. Comer GM, Mittal MK, Donelson SS, Lee TP. Cluster of fulminant hepatitis B in crack users. Am J Gastroenterol 1991;86:331–334.

101. Moradpour D, Wands JR. Understanding hepatitis B virus infection. N Engl J Med 1995; 332:1092–1093.

102. Perrillo RP, Regenstein FG, Roodman ST. Chronic hepatitis B in asymptomatic homosexual men with antibody to human immunodeficiency virus. Ann Intern Med 1986;105: 382–383.

103. Krogsgaard K, Lindhardt BO, Neilsen JO, et al. The influence of HTLV-III infection on the natural history of hepatitis B virus infection in male homosexual HBsAg carriers. Hepatology 1987;7:37–41.

104. Novick DM, Farci P, Croxson TS, et al. Hepatitis D virus and human immunodeficiency virus antibodies in parenteral drug abusers who are hepatitis B surface antigen positive. J Infect Dis 1988;158:795–803.

105. Taylor PE, Stevens CE, Rodriguez De Cordoba S, Rubinstein P. Hepatitis B virus and human immunodeficiency virus: possible interactions. In: Zuckerman AJ, ed. Viral hepatitis and liver disease. New York: Alan R. Liss, 1988: 198–200.

106. Monno L, Angarano G, Lo Caputo S, et al. Unfavorable outcome of acute hepatitis B in anti-HIV-positive drug addicts. In: Zuckerman AJ, ed. Viral hepatitis and liver disease. New York: Alan R. Liss, 1988:205–206.

107. Mezzelani P, Venturini L, Turrina G, Lugoboni F, Des Jarlais DC. High compliance with a hepatitis B virus vaccination program among intravenous drug users. J Infect Dis 1991; 163:923.

108. Rumi M, Colombo M, Romeo R, et al. Suboptimal response to hepatitis B vaccine in drug users. Arch Intern Med 1991;151:574–578.

109. Borg L, Khuri E, Wells A, et al. Hepatitis B vaccination of methadone maintained former heroin addicts is effective [abstract]. Hepatology 1995;22:324A.

110. Margolis HS, Alter MJ, Hadler SC. Hepatitis B: evolving epidemiology and implications for control. Semin Liver Dis 1991;11:84–92.

111. Jilg W, Schmidt M, Deinhardt F. Vaccination against hepatitis B: comparison of three different vaccination schedules. J Infect Dis 1989; 160:766–769.

112. Collier AC, Corey L, Murphy VL, Handsfield HH. Antibody to human immunodeficiency virus (HIV) and suboptimal response to hepatitis B vaccination. Ann Intern Med 1988;109: 101–105.

113. Centers for Disease Control and Prevention. Hepatitis B virus: a comprehensive strategy for eliminating transmission in the United States through universal childhood vaccination: recommendations of the Immunization Practices Advisory Committee (ACIP). MMWR 1991; 40(RR-13):1–25.

114. Francis DP. The public's health unprotected: reversing a decade of underutilization of hepatitis B vaccine. JAMA 1995;274:1242–1243.

115. Norkrans G, Frosner G, Hermodsson S, Iwarson S. Multiple hepatitis attacks in drug addicts. JAMA 1980;243:1056–1058.

116. Sherlock S. Chronic hepatitis C. Disease-a-Month 1994;40:122–196.

117. Bukh J, Miller RH, Purcell RH. Genetic heterogeneity of hepatitis C virus: quasispecies and genotypes. Semin Liver Dis 1995;15: 41–63.

118. Dusheiko G, Simmonds P. Sequence variability of hepatitis C virus and its clinical relevance. J Viral Hepatitis 1994;1:3–15.

119. Apichartpiyakul C, Chittivudikarn C, Miyajima H, Homma M, Hotta H. Analysis of hepatitis C virus isolates among healthy blood donors and drug addicts in Chiang Mai, Thailand. J Clin Microbiol 1994;32:2276–2279.

120. Silini E, Bono F, Cividini A, et al. Molecular epidemiology of hepatitis C virus infection among intravenous drug users. J Hepatol 1995; 22:691–695.

121. Soriano V, Nedjar S, Garcia-Samaniego J, et al. High rate of coinfection with different hepatitis C virus subtypes in HIV-infected intravenous drug addicts in Spain. J Hepatol 1995; 22:598–599.

122. Lau JYN, Davis GL, Prescott LE, et al. Distribution of hepatitis C genotypes determined by line probe assay in patients with chronic hepatitis C seen at tertiary referral centers in the United States. Ann Intern Med 1996;124: 868–876.

123. Farci P, Alter HJ, Govindarajan S, et al. Lack of protective immunity against reinfection with hepatitis C virus. Science 1992;258:135–140.

124. Alter M. Epidemiology of community-acquired hepatitis C. In: Hollinger FB, Lemon SM, Margolis HS, eds. Viral hepatitis and liver disease. Baltimore: Williams & Wilkins, 1991: 410–413.

125. Donahue JG, Nelson KE, Munoz A, et al. Antibody to hepatitis C virus among cardiac surgery patients, homosexual men, and intra-

venous drug users in Baltimore, Maryland. Am J Epidemiol 1991;134:1206–1211.

126. Esteban JI, Esteban R, Viladomiu L, et al. Hepatitis C virus antibodies among risk groups in Spain. Lancet 1989;2:294–296.

127. Kelen GD, Green GB, Purcell RH, et al. Hepatitis B and C in emergency department patients. N Engl J Med 1992;326:1399–1404.

128. Osmond DH, Padian NS, Sheppard HW, Glass S, Shiboski SC, Reingold A. Risk factors for hepatitis C seropositivity in heterosexual couples. JAMA 1993;269:361–365.

129. Woodfield DG, Harness M, Rix-Trott K. Hepatitis C virus infections in oral and injectable drug users. N Z J Med 1993;106:332–334.

130. Thomas DL, Vlahov D, Solomon L, et al. Correlates of hepatitis C virus infections among injection drug users. Medicine (Baltimore) 1995;74:212–220.

131. Novick DM, Reagan KJ, Croxson TS, Gelb AM, Stenger RJ, Kreek MJ. Hepatitis C virus serology in parenteral drug users with chronic liver disease. Addiction 1997;92:167–171.

132. Alter MJ. Epidemiology of hepatitis C in the West. Semin Liver Dis 1995;15:5–14.

133. Gabrielli C, Zannini A, Corradini R, Gafa S. Spread of hepatitis C virus among sexual partners of HCVAb positive intravenous drug users. J Infect 1994;29:17–22.

134. Eyster ME, Alter HJ, Aledort LM, Quan S, Hatzakis A, Goedert JJ. Heterosexual co-transmission of hepatitis C virus (HCV) and human immunodeficiency virus (HIV). Ann Intern Med 1991;115:764–768.

135. Farci P, Alter HJ, Wong D, et al. A long-term study of hepatitis C virus replication in non-A, non-B hepatitis. N Engl J Med 1991;325:98–104.

136. Haber MM, West AB, Haber AD, Reuben A. Relationship of aminotransferases to liver histological status in chronic hepatitis C. Am J Gastroenterol 1995;90:1250–1257.

137. Gordon SC, Elloway RS, Long JC, Dmuchowski CF. The pathology of hepatitis C as a function of mode of transmission: blood transfusion vs. intravenous drug use. Hepatology 1993;18:1338–1343.

138. Seeff LB, Buskell-Bales Z, Wright EC, et al. Long-term mortality after transfusion-associated non-A, non-B hepatitis. N Engl J Med 1992;327:1906–1911.

139. de Medina M, Schiff ER. Hepatitis C: diagnostic assays. Semin Liver Dis 1995;15:33–40.

140. McFarlane IG. Hepatitis C and alcoholic liver disease. Am J Gastroenterol 1993;88:982–988.

141. Koff RS, Dienstag JL. Extrahepatic manifestations of hepatitis C and the association with alcoholic liver disease. Semin Liver Dis 1995;15:101–109.

142. Caldwell SH, Li X, Rourk RM, et al. Hepatitis C infection by polymerase chain reaction in alcoholics: false-positive ELISA results and the influence of infection on a clinical prognostic score. Am J Gastroenterol 1993;88:1016–1021.

143. Oshita M, Hayashi N, Kasahara A, et al. Increased serum hepatitis C virus RNA levels among alcoholic patients with chronic hepatitis C. Hepatology 1994;20:1115–1120.

144. Mendenhall CL, Seeff L, Diehl AM, et al. Antibodies to hepatitis B virus and hepatitis C virus in alcoholic hepatitis and cirrhosis: their prevalence and clinical relevance. Hepatology 1991;14:581–589.

145. Novick DM, Enlow RW, Gelb AM, et al. Hepatic cirrhosis in young adults: association

with adolescent onset of alcohol and parenteral heroin abuse. Gut 1985;26:8–13.

146. Smedile A, Rizzetto M, Gerin JL. Advances in hepatitis D virus biology and disease. Prog Liver Dis 1994;12:157–175.

147. Diener TO. Viroids. Sci Am 1981;244:66–73.

148. Branch AD, Levine BJ, Robertson HD. The brotherhood of circular RNA pathogens: viroids, circular satellites, and the delta agent. Semin Virol 1990;1:143–152.

149. Lettau LA, McCarthy JG, Smith MH, et al. Outbreak of severe hepatitis due to delta and hepatitis B viruses in parenteral drug abusers and their contacts. N Engl J Med 1989;317:1256–1262.

150. Saracco G, Rosina F, Brunetto MR, et al. Rapidly progressive HBsAg-positive hepatitis in Italy: the role of hepatitis delta virus infection. J Hepatol 1987;5:274–281.

151. Wu JC, Chen TZ, Huang YS, et al. Natural history of hepatitis D superinfection: significance of viremia detected by polymerase chain reaction. Gastroenterology 1995;108:762–802.

152. Farci P, Smedile A, Lavarini C, et al. Delta hepatitis in inapparent carriers of hepatitis B surface antigen: a disease simulating acute hepatitis B progressive to chronicity. Gastroenterology 1983;85:669–673.

153. Di Bisceglie AM, Negro F. Diagnosis of hepatitis delta virus infection. Hepatology 1989;10:1014–1016.

154. Chao YC, Tang HS, Hsu CT. Evolution rate of hepatitis delta virus RNA isolated in Taiwan. J Med Virol 1994;43:397–403.

155. Wu JC, Choo KB, Chen CM, Chen TZ, Huo T, Lee SD. Genotyping of hepatitis D virus by restriction-fragment length polymorphism and relation to outcome in hepatitis D. Lancet 1995;346:939–941.

156. Hansson BG, Moestrup T, Widell A, Nordenfelt E. Infection with delta agent in Sweden: introduction of a new hepatitis agent. J Infect Dis 1982;142:472–478.

157. Navascues CA, Rodriguez M, Sotorrio NG, et al. Epidemiology of hepatitis D virus infection: changes in the last 14 years. Am J Gastroenterol 1995;90:1981–1984.

158. Buti M, Mas A, Sanchez-Tapias JM, et al. Chronic hepatitis D in intravenous drug addicts and non-addicts: a comparative clinicopathological study. J Hepatol 1988;7:169–174.

159. De Cock KM, Niland JC, Lu HP, et al. Experience with human immunodeficiency virus infection in patients with hepatitis B virus and hepatitis delta virus infections in Los Angeles, 1977–1985. Am J Epidemiol 1988;127:1250–1260.

160. Di Bisceglie AM. New hepatitis viruses: adding to the alphabet soup. Viral Hepatitis Rev 1995;1:3–5.

161. Aikawa T, Sugai Y, Okamoto H. Hepatitis G infection in drug users with chronic hepatitis C. N Engl J Med 1996;334:195–196.

162. Novick DM, Des Jarlais DC, Kreek MJ, et al. Specificity of antibody tests for human immunodeficiency virus in alcohol and parenteral drug abusers with chronic liver disease. Alcoholism (NY) 1988;12:687–690.

163. Osick LA, Lee TP, Pedemonte MB, et al. Hepatic amyloidosis in intravenous drug users and AIDS patients. J Hepatol 1993;19:79–84.

164. Novick DM, Kreek MJ, Fanizza AM, Yancovitz SR, Gelb AM, Stenger RJ. Methadone disposition in patients with chronic liver disease. Clin Pharmacol Ther 1981;30:353–362.

165. Novick DM, Kreek MJ, Arns PA, Lau LL, Yancovitz SR, Gelb AM. Effect of severe alco-

holic liver disease on the disposition of methadone in maintenance patients. Alcoholism (NY) 1985;9:349–354.

166. Kreek MJ, Oratz M, Rothschild MA. Hepatic extraction of long- and short-acting narcotics in the isolated perfused rabbit liver. Gastroenterology 1978;75:88–94.

167. Perrillo RP. Antiviral therapy of chronic hepatitis B: past, present, and future. J Hepatol 1993;17(suppl):S56–S63.

168. Fried MW, Hoofnagle JH. Therapy of hepatitis C. Semin Liver Dis 1995;15:82–91.

169. Farci P, Mandas A, Coiana A, et al. Treatment of chronic hepatitis D with interferon alfa-2a. N Engl J Med 1994;330:88–94.

170. Kumar S, Stauber RF, Gavaler JS, et al. Orthotopic liver transplantation for alcoholic liver disease. Hepatology 1990;11:159–164.

171. Osorio RW, Lake JR. Liver transplantation for alcoholic liver disease. Semin Gastrointest Dis 1993;4:165–169.

172. Lucey MR, Beresford TP. Can we triage alcoholics with end-stage liver disease? Am J Gastroenterol 1993;88:1314–1315.

173. Friedman EA, Rao TKS, Nicastri AD. Heroin-associated nephropathy. Nephron 1974;13:421–426.

174. Cunningham EE, Brentjens JR, Zielezny MA, Andres GA, Venuto RC. Heroin nephropathy: a clinicopathologic and epidemiologic study. Am J Med 1980;68:47–53.

175. Dubrow A, Mittman N, Ghali V, Flamenbaum W. The changing spectrum of heroin-associated nephropathy. Am J Kidney Dis 1985;5:36–41.

176. Neugarten J, Baldwin DS. Glomerulonephritis in bacterial endocarditis. Am J Med 1984;77:297–304.

177. Johnson RJ, Couser WG. Hepatitis B infection and renal disease: clinical, immunopathogenetic and therapeutic consideration. Kidney Int 1990;37:663–676.

178. Koffler A, Friedler RM, Massry SG. Acute renal failure due to nontraumatic rhabdomyolysis. Ann Intern Med 1976;85:23–28.

179. Friedman EA, Rao TKS. Disappearance of uremia due to heroin-associated nephropathy. Am J Kidney Dis 1995;25:689–693.

180. Haskell LP, Glicklich D, Senitzer D. HLA associations in heroin-associated nephropathy. Am J Kidney Dis 1988;12:45–50.

181. Novick DM, Yancovitz SR, Weinberg PG. Amyloidosis in parenteral drug abusers. Mt Sinai J Med (N Y) 1979;46:163–167.

182. Tan AU, Cohen AH, Levine BS. Renal amyloidosis in a drug abuser. J Am Soc Nephrol 1995;5:1653–1658.

183. Crowley S, Feinfeld DA, Janis R. Resolution of nephrotic syndrome and lack of progression of heroin-associated renal amyloidosis. Am J Kidney Dis 1989;13:333–335.

184. Bourgoignie JJ. Renal complications of human immunodeficiency virus type I. Kidney Int 1990;37:1571–1584.

185. Glassock RJ, Cohen AH, Danovitch G, Parsa KP. Human immunodeficiency virus (HIV) infection and the kidney. Ann Intern Med 1990;112:35–49.

186. Seney FD, Burns DK, Silva FG. Acquired immunodeficiency syndrome and the kidney. Am J Kidney Dis 1990;16:1–13.

187. Kreek MJ, Schecter AJ, Gutjahr CL, Hecht M. Methadone use in patients with chronic renal disease. Drug Alcohol Depend 1980;5:197–205.

188. Novick DM, Ochshorn M, Kreek MJ. In vivo and in vitro studies of opiates and cellular im-

munity in narcotic addicts. In: Friedman H, Specter S, Klein TW, eds. Drugs of abuse, immunity, and immunodeficiency. New York: Plenum Press 1991:159–170.

189. Helpern M, Rho YM. Deaths from narcotism in New York City: incidence, circumstances, and postmortem findings. N Y State J Med 1966; 66:2391–2408.

190. Geller SA, Stimmel B. Diagnostic confusion from lymphatic lesions in heroin addicts. Ann Intern Med 1973;78:703–705.

191. Cushman P, Grieco MH. Hyperimmunoglobulinemia associated with narcotic addiction: effects of methadone maintenance treatment. Am J Med 1973;54:320–326.

192. Brown SM, Stimmel B, Taub RN, Kochwa S, Rosenfield RE. Immunologic dysfunction in heroin addicts. Arch Intern Med 1974;134: 1001–1006.

193. Cushman P. Hyperimmunoglobulinemia in heroin addiction: some epidemiologic observations, including some possible effects of route of administration and multiple drug abuse. Am J Epidemiol 1974;99:218–224.

194. Novick DM, Ochshorn M, Ghali V, et al. Natural killer cell activity and lymphocyte subsets in parenteral heroin abusers and long-term methadone maintenance patients. J Pharmacol Exp Ther 1989;250:606–610.

195. Zolla-Pazner S, Des Jarlais DC, Friedman S, et al. Nonrandom development of immunologic abnormalities after infection with human immunodeficiency virus: implications for immunologic classification of the disease. Proc Natl Acad Sci U S A 1987;84:5404–5408.

196. DiFranco MJ, Marlink R, Hunter DJ, Tosteson T, Mayer K, Essex M. Association of immune activation with intravenous heroin use and methadone treatment in HIV-1 seropositive and seronegative subjects. J AIDS 1993;6: 1297–1300.

197. Cushman P, Sherman C. Biologic false-positive reactions in serologic tests for syphilis in narcotic addiction. Am J Clin Pathol 1974; 61:346–351.

198. Spiera H, Oreskes I, Stimmel B. Rheumatoid factor activity in heroin addicts on methadone maintenance. Ann Rheum Dis 1974;33: 153–156.

199. Vogel H, Cherubin CE, Millian SJ. Febrile agglutinins in narcotic addicts. Am J Clin Pathol 1970;53:932–935.

200. Cherubin CE, Millian SJ. Serologic investigations in narcotic addicts I. Syphilis, lymphogranuloma venereum, herpes simplex, and Q fever. Ann Intern Med 1968;69:739–742.

201. Kreek MJ. Medical safety and side effects of methadone in tolerant individuals. JAMA 1973;223:665–668.

202. McDonough RJ, Madden JJ, Falek A, et al. Alteration of T and null lymphocytes in the peripheral blood of human opiate addicts; in vivo evidence for opiate receptor sites on T lymphocytes. J Immunol 1980;125:2539–2543.

203. Ochshorn M, Novick DM, Kreek MJ. In vitro studies of methadone effect on natural killer (NK) cell activity. Isr J Med Sci 1990;26: 421–425.

204. Ochshorn-Adelson M, Novick DM, Khuri E, Albeck H, Hahn EF, Kreek MJ. Effects of the opioid antagonist naloxone on human natural killer cell activity in vitro. Isr J Med Sci 1994; 30:679–684.

205. Peterson PK, Gekker G, Brummitt C, et al. Suppression of human peripheral blood mononuclear cell function by methadone and morphine. J Infect Dis 1989;159:480–487.

206. Madden JJ, Donahoe RM, Zwemer-Collins J, Shafer DA, Falek A. Binding of naloxone to human T lymphocytes. Biochem Pharmacol 1987;36:4103–4109.

207. Sibinga NES, Goldstein A. Opioid peptides and opioid receptors in cells of the immune system. Ann Rev Immunol 1988;6:219–249.

208. National Institute on Drug Abuse. National Household Survey on Drug Abuse: population estimates 1991. Rev. ed [DHHS publication no. (ADM) 92–1887]. Washington, DC: U.S. Department of health and Human Services, 1992.

209. Cregler LL, Mark H. Medical complications of cocaine abuse. N Engl J Med 1986;315:1495–1500.

210. Warner EA. Cocaine abuse. Ann Intern Med 1993;119:226–235.

211. Jatlow P, Barash PG, Van Dyke C, Radding J, Byck R. Cocaine and succinylcholine sensitivity: a new caution. Anesth Analg 1979;58:235–238.

212. Devenyi P. Cocaine complications and pseudocholinesterase. Ann Intern Med 1989;110: 167–168.

213. Hoffman RS, Henry GC, Howland MA, Weisman RS, Weil L, Goldfrank LR. Association between life-threatening cocaine toxicity and plasma cholinesterase activity. Ann Emerg Med 1992;21:247–253.

214. Schwartz RH, Estroff T, Fairbanks DNF, Hoffmann NG. Nasal symptoms associated with cocaine abuse during adolescence. Arch Otolaryngol Head Neck Surg 1989;115:63–64.

215. Chaudhry RM, Abadir AR, Ginautienne K, et al. Effect of cocaine abuse on nasal mucosa, septum and turbinates. Proc West Pharmacol Soc 1990;33:249–251.

216. Gordon AS, Moran DT, Jafek BW, Eller PM, Strahan RC. The effect of chronic cocaine abuse on human olfaction. Arch Otolaryngol Head Neck Surg 1990;116:1415–1418.

217. Vilensky W. Illicit and licit drugs causing perforation of the nasal septum. J Forensic Sci 1982;27:958–962.

218. Mattson-Gates G, Jabs AD, Hugo NE. Perforation of the hard palate associated with cocaine abuse. Ann Plastic Surg 1991;26:466–468.

219. Libby DM, Klein L, Altorki NK. Aspiration of the nasal septum: a new complication of cocaine abuse. Ann Intern Med 1992;116: 567–568.

220. Sawicka EH, Trosser A. Cerebrospinal fluid rhinorrhea after cocaine sniffing. Br Med J 1983;286:1476–1477.

221. Becker GD. Midline granuloma due to illicit cocaine use. Arch Otolaryngol Head Neck Surg 1988;114:90–91.

222. Newman NM, DiLoreto DA, Ho JT, Klein JC, Birnbaum NS. Bilateral optic neuropathy and osteolytic sinusitis: complications of cocaine abuse. JAMA 1988;259:72–74.

223. Goldberg RA, Weisman JS, McFarland JE, Krauss HR, Hepler RS, Shorr N. Orbital inflammation and optic neuropathies associated with chronic sinusitis of intranasal cocaine abuse: possible role of contiguous inflammation. Arch Ophthalmol 1989;107:831–835.

224. Noskin GA, Kalish SB. Pott's puffy tumor: a complication of intranasal cocaine abuse. Rev Infect Dis 1991;13:606–608.

225. Rao AN. Brain abscess: a complication of cocaine inhalation. N Y State J Med 1988;88: 548–550.

226. Chaisson RE, Bacchetti P, Osmond D, Brodie B, Sande MA, Moss AR. Cocaine use and HIV infection in intravenous drug users in San Francisco. JAMA 1989;261:561–565.

227. Novick DM, Trigg HL, Des Jarlais DC, Friedman SR, Vlahov D, Kreek MJ. Cocaine injection and ethnicity in parenteral drug users during the early years of the human immunodeficiency virus (HIV) epidemic in New York City. J Med Virol 1989;29:181–185.

228. Chambers HF, Chaisson RE. Cocaine abuse and endocarditis: in response. Ann Intern Med 1988;109:82–83.

229. Grant BF, Harford TC. Concurrent and simultaneous use of alcohol with cocaine: results of a national survey. Drug Alcohol Depend 1990;25:97–104.

230. National Institute on Drug Abuse. Drug Abuse Warning Network: annual emergency room data 1991 [DHHS publication no. (ADM) 91–1839]. Washington, DC: U.S. Department of Health and Human Services, 1991.

231. Jatlow P. Cocaethylene: what is it? Am J Clin Pathol 1995;104:120–121.

232. Jatlow P, Elsworth JD, Bradberry CW, et al. Cocaethylene: a neuropharmacologically active metabolite associated with concurrent cocaine-ethanol ingestion. Life Sci 1991;48:1787–1794.

233. Foltin RW, Fischman MW. Ethanol and cocaine interactions in humans: cardiovascular consequences. Pharmacol Biochem Behav 1988;31:877–883.

234. Uszenski RT, Gillis RA, Schaer GL, Analouei AR, Kuhn FE. Additive myocardial depressant effects of cocaine and ethanol. Am Heart J 1992;124:1276–1283.

235. Pirwitz MJ, Willard JE, Landau C, et al. Influence of cocaine, ethanol, or their combination on epicardial arterial dimensions in humans. Arch Intern Med 1995;155:1186–1191.

236. Weinstein SP, Gottheil E, Sterling RC. Cocaine users in medical practice: a five-year follow-up. Am J Drug Alcohol Abuse 1992;18: 157–166.

237. Lange RA, Willard JE. The cardiovascular effects of cocaine. Heart Dis Stroke 1993;2: 136–141.

238. Derlet RW, Albertson TE. Emergency department presentation of cocaine intoxication. Ann Emerg Med 1989;18:182–186.

239. Brody SL, Slovis CM, Wrenn KD. Cocaine-related medical problems: consecutive series of 233 patients. Am J Med 1990;88:325–331.

240. Rich JA, Singer DE. Cocaine-related symptoms in patients presenting to an urban emergency department. Ann Emerg Med 1991;20: 616–621.

241. Hollander JE, Todd KH, Green G, Heilpern KL, Karras DJ, Singer AJ, et al. Chest pain associated with cocaine: an assessment of prevalence in suburban and urban emergency departments. Ann Emerg Med 1995;26:671–676.

242. Warner EA, Flores RM, Robinson BE. A profile of hospitalized cocaine users: patient characteristics, diagnoses, and physician responses. Substance Abuse 1995;16:205–212.

243. Levine SR, Brust JCM, Futrell N, et al. Cerebrovascular complications of the use of the "crack" form of alkaloidal cocaine. N Engl J Med 1990;323:699–704.

244. Spivey WH, Euerle B. Neurologic complications of cocaine abuse. Ann Emerg Med 1990; 19:1422–1428.

245. Brown E, Prager J, Lee HY, Ramsey RG. CNS complications of cocaine abuse: prevalence, pathophysiology, and neuroradiology. AJR 1992;159:137–147.

246. Warrian WG, Halikas JA, Crosby RD, Carlson GA, Crea F. Observations on increased CPK levels in "asymptomatic" cocaine abusers. J Addict Dis 1992;11:83–95.

247. Roth D, Alarcon FJ, Fernandez JA, Preston RA, Bourgoignie JJ. Acute rhabdomyolysis associated with cocaine intoxication. N Engl J Med 1988;319:673–677.

248. Brody SL, Wrenn KD, Wilber MM, Slovis CM. Predicting the severity of cocaine-associated rhabdomyolysis. Ann Emerg Med 1990; 19:1137–1143.

249. Welch RD, Todd K, Krause GS. Incidence of cocaine-associated rhabdomyolysis. Ann Emerg Med 1991;20:154–157.

250. Wetli CV, Fishbain DA. Cocaine-induced psychosis and sudden death in recreational cocaine users. J Forensic Sci 1985;30:873–880.

251. Mittleman RE, Wetli CV. Cocaine and sudden "natural" death. J Forensic Sci 1987;32:11–19.

252. Raval MP, Wetli CV. Sudden death from cocaine-induced excited delirium: an analysis of 45 cases [abstract]. Am J Clin Path 1995; 104:329.

253. Mendelson JH, Mello NK. Management of cocaine abuse and dependence. N Engl J Med 1996;334:965–972.

254. Goldfrank LR, Hoffman RS. The cardiovascular effects of cocaine. Ann Emerg Med 1991; 20:165–175.

255. Lange RA, Cigarroa RG, Yancy CW, et al. Cocaine-induced coronary artery vasoconstriction. N Engl J Med 1989;321:1557–1562.

256. Hollander JE, Carter WA, Hoffman RS. Use of phentolamine for cocaine-induced myocardial ischemia. N Engl J Med 1992;327:361.

257. Hollander JE. The management of cocaine-associated myocardial ischemia. N Engl J Med 1995;333:1267–1272.

258. Ramoska E, Sacchetti AD. Propranolol-induced hypertension in treatment of cocaine intoxication. Ann Emerg Med 1985;14: 112–113.

259. Lange RA, Cigarroa RG, Flores ED, et al. Potentiation of cocaine-induced coronary vasoconstriction by beta-adrenergic blockage. Ann Intern Med 1990;112:897–903.

260. Boehrer JD, Moliterno DJ, Willard JE, Hillis LD, Lange RA. Influence of labetalol on cocaine-induced coronary vasoconstriction in humans. Am J Med 1993;94:608–610.

261. Negus BH, Willard JE, Hillis LD, et al. Alleviation of cocaine-induced coronary vasoconstriction with intravenous verapamil. Am J Cardiol 1994;73:510–513.

262. Derlet RW, Albertson TE. Potentiation of cocaine toxicity with calcium channel blockers. Am J Emerg Med 1989;7:464–468.

263. Nelson L, Hoffman RS. How to manage acute MI when cocaine is the cause: why diazepam may be preferable to beta-blockade. J Crit Illness 1995;10:39–43.

264. Beckman KJ, Parker RB, Hariman RJ, Gallastegni JL, Javaid JI, Bauman JL. Hemodynamic and electrophysiological actions of cocaine: effect of sodium bicarbonate as an antidote in dogs. Circulation 1991;83:1799–1807.

265. Jonsson S, O'Meara M, Young JB. Acute cocaine poisoning: importance of treating seizures and acidosis. Am J Med 1983;75: 1061–1064.

266. Pollack CV Jr, Biggers DW, Carlton FB Jr, et al. Two crack cocaine body stuffers. Ann Emerg Med 1992;21:1370–1380.

267. Billman GE, Hoskins RS. Cocaine induced ventricular fibrillation: protection afforded by the calcium antagonist verapamil. FASEB J 1988;2:2990–2995.

268. Derlet RW, Albertson TE, Tharratt RS. Lidocaine potentiation of cocaine toxicity. Ann Emerg Med 1991;20:135–138.

269. Heit J, Hoffman RS. Lidocaine is protective against cocaine lethality in mice. Vet Hum Toxicol 1992;34:345.

270. Shih RD, Hollander JE, Burstein JL, Nelson LS, Hoffman RS, Quick AM. Cocaine-Associated Myocardial Infarction Study Group. Ann Emerg Med 1995;26:702–706.

271. Emergency Cardiac Care Committee and Subcommittees, American Heart Association. Guidelines for cardiopulmonary resuscitation and emergency care. III: adult advanced cardiac life support. JAMA 1992;268:2199–2241.

272. Shesser R, Davis C, Edelstein S. Pneumomediastinum and pneumothorax after inhaling alkaloidal cocaine. Ann Emerg Med 1981;10: 213–215.

273. Wiener MD, Putnam CE. Pain in the chest in a user of cocaine. JAMA 1987;258:2087–2088.

274. Savador SJ, Omori M, Martinez CR. Pneumothorax, pneumomediastinum and pneumopericardium: complications of cocaine smoking. J Fla Med Assoc 1988;75:151–152.

275. Hollander JE, Hoffman RS. Cocaine-induced myocardial infarction: an analysis and review of the literature. J Emerg Med 1992;10: 169–177.

276. Hollander JE, Hoffman RS, Gennis P, et al. Prospective multicenter evaluation of cocaine associated chest pain. Acad Emerg Med 1994;1:330–339.

277. Amin M, Gabelman G, Karpel J, Buttrick P. Acute myocardial infarction and chest pain syndromes after cocaine use. Am J Cardiol 1990;66:1434–1437.

278. Nademanee K, Gorelick DA, Josephson MP, Ryan MA, Wilkins JN, Robertson HA, et al. Myocardial ischemia during cocaine withdrawal. Ann Intern Med 1989;111:876–880.

279. Tokarski GF, Paganussi P, Urbanski R, Carden D, Foreback C, Tomlanovich MC. An evaluation of cocaine-induced chest pain. Ann Emerg Med 1990;19:1088–1092.

280. McLaurin MD, Henry TD, Apple FS, Sharkey SW. Cardiac troponin I, T and CK-MB in patients with cocaine related chest pain [abstract]. Circulation 1994;90:I-278.

281. Hollander JE, Burstein JL, Hoffman RS, Shih RD, Wilson LD. Cocaine-Associated Myocardial Infarction (CAMI) Study Group. Cocaine-associated myocardial infarction: clinical safety of thrombolytic therapy. Chest 1995; 107:1237–1241.

282. Hollander JE, Hoffman RS, Burstein JL, Shih RD, Thode HC Jr. Cocaine-Associated Myocardial Infarction (CAMI) Study Group. Cocaine-associated myocardial infarction: mortality and complications. Arch Intern Med 1995;155:1081–1086.

283. Hollander JE, Hoffman RS, Gennis P, et al. Cocaine associated chest pain: one year follow-up. Acad Emerg Med 1995;2:179–184.

284. Dressler FA, Malekzadeh S, Roberts WC. Quantitative analysis of amounts of coronary arterial narrowing in cocaine addicts. Am J Cardiol 1990;65:303–308.

285. Kolodgie FD, Virmani R, Cornhill JF, Henderick EE, Smialek J. Increase in atherosclerosis and adventitial mast cells in cocaine abusers: an alternative mechanism of cocaine associated coronary vasospasm and thrombosis. J Am Coll Cardiol 1991;17:1553–1560.

286. Eichhorn EJ, Peacock E, Grayburn PA, et al. Chronic cocaine abuse is associated with accelerated atherosclerosis in human coronary arteries [abstract]. J Am Coll Cardiol 1992;19 (suppl):105A.

287. Flores ED, Lange RA, Cigarroa RG, Hillis LD. Effect of cocaine on coronary artery dimensions in atherosclerotic coronary artery disease: enhanced vasoconstriction at sites of significant stenoses. J Am Coll Cardiol 1990;16: 74–79.

288. Gioia G, Manuel M, Russell J, Heo J, Iskandrian AS. Myocardial perfusion pattern in patients with cocaine-induced chest pain. Am J Cardiol 1995;75:396–398.

289. Acute reactions to drugs of abuse. Med Lett Drug Ther 1996;38:43–46.

290. Boushey HA, Warnock DG, Smith LH. Neurologic aspects of cocaine abuse. West J Med 1988;149:442–448.

291. Tseng CC, Derlet RW, Albertson TE. Cocaine-induced respiratory depression and seizures are synergistic mechanisms of cocaine-induced death in rats. Ann Emerg Med 1992;21: 486–493.

292. Huang QF, Gebrewold A, Altura BT, Altura BM. Cocaine-induced cerebral vascular damage can be ameliorated by Mg^{2+} in rat brain. Neurosci Lett 1990;109:113–116.

293. Fox AW. More on rhabdomyolysis associated with cocaine intoxication. N Engl J Med 1989; 321:1271.

294. Witkin JM, Goldberg SR, Katz JL. Lethal effects of cocaine are reduced by the dopamine-1 receptor antagonist SCH 23390 but not by haloperidol. Life Sci 1989;44:1285–1291.

295. Hoffman RS. An effective strategy for managing cocaine-induced agitated delirium: which therapies improve survival? which are counterproductive? J Crit Illness 1994;9:139–149.

296. Lathers CM, Tyau LSY, Spino MM, Agarwal I. Cocaine-induced seizures, arrhythmias and sudden death. J Clin Pharmacol 1988;28: 584–593.

297. Webb WA. Management of foreign bodies of the upper gastrointestinal tract. Gastroenterology 1988;94:204–216.

298. Pouagare M, Brady PG. New techniques for the endoscopic removal of foreign bodies. In: Barkin JS, O'Phelan CA, eds. Advanced therapeutic endoscopy. 2nd edition. New York: Raven Press, 1994:165–174.

299. McCarron MM, Wood JD. The cocaine "body packer" syndrome. JAMA 1983;250:1417–1420.

300. Tomaszewski C, McKinney P, Phillips S, Brent J, Kulig K. Prevention of toxicity from oral cocaine by activated charcoal in mice. Ann Emerg Med 1993;22:1804–1806.

301. Leiber CS. Medical disorders of alcoholism. N Engl J Med 1995;333:1058–1065.

302. U.S. Department of Health and Human Services. Eighth special report to the U.S. Congress on alcohol and health [DHHS publication (ADM) 94–3699]. Rockville, MD: National Institutes of Health, 1994.

56 PATIENTS WITH PSYCHOPATHOLOGY
Ann Bordwine Beeder and Robert B. Millman

INTRODUCTION

Drug taking may be at once a cause and a result of psychopathology. It is often difficult to determine whether the psychopathology noted is a result of the drug use or represents sequelae of the agonist effects of the drugs or withdrawal phenomena. Treatment providers increasingly note both sizeable psychiatric populations have comorbid drug use and substance abuse populations also demonstrate a significant prevalence of often unappreciated comorbid psychopathology. Terms initially used to describe these populations include *dual diagnosis,* developed in programs devoted primarily to the treatment of substance abusers to identify the patients with psychopathology. *Mentally ill chemical abuser* (MICA) was developed by programs informed by psychiatric perspectives to identify drug abusers within their population. Increasing interest and thought given to the interaction between substance abuse and psychopathology throughout the 1990s has generated numerous terms to describe various populations including MICAA (mentally ill, chemical abusers, and addicted), MISA (mentally ill substance abuser), MIDAA (mental illness, drug addiction and alcoholism), and CAMI (chemical abusing mentally ill) (1). Although this terminology is not particularly felicitous, it is used to describe patients who have coexisting psychopathology and substance abuse or dependence.

The etiology of dual diagnosis conditions has been described by four hypotheses: primary mental illness with subsequent substance abuse; primary substance abuse with psychopathological sequelae; dual primary diagnosis; and situations in which there is a common etiology, that is, one common factor causing both diseases (2). In every patient, one or more of these hypothetical models may pertain. In 1994, 435 consecutively admitted "dually diagnosed" inpatients from an inner-city population were studied and found to be predominately psychiatric patients with current substance abuse disorders (55.9%). Approximately half (53.6%) of those studied had psychiatric symptoms related to substance abuse without an independent history of prior psychiatric illness (3). Individuals with dual diagnoses fall into numerous subgroups that vary according to primary psychiatric disorder, types and patterns of substances used, and treatment history.

Treatment strategies described in this chapter are based primarily on clinical experience. Treatment approaches might be determined through outcome studies aimed at systematically defining effective protocols for substance abusers with psychopathology. Until recently, the confluence of this small literature surprisingly suggests that factors intuitively associated with poor treatment results, such as severity of psychopathology and intensity of symptomatology, do not necessarily affect outcome. Clearly, this is a difficult population to treat, though we must attempt to evaluate outcome (4, 5). In some patients severe Axis I psychopathology that can be treated is a better prognostic sign than character disorders that elude treatment efforts.

It has become evident that appropriate treatment depends upon the integration of various treatment models and an appreciation of the fluidity of multiple variables interacting at fluctuating intensities for each individual over time. Many problems presented to clinicians can be treated directly and monitored for change over time in a linear fashion, but treatment of dual diagnosis patients differs in that the clinician must be able to treat the state of the chemical dependence or abuse, treat the symptoms of the psychopathology, and monitor the possible interactions between the two problems (6). For example, substance abuse patients who present with symptoms consistent with an anxiety disorder require treatment for the drug use and evaluation of whether the anxiety symptoms are a premorbid entity, a result of the patient's decreasing or possibly increasing chemical use, or both, and possibly treatment of the debilitating effects of the anxiety. Therefore, in all patients careful evaluation of the presenting symptomatology, the characteristics of the pharmacology and sequelae of the drug use, the relationship of the drugs, and the psychopathology must be performed (7). It is necessary to assess the meaning of the drug taking at the particular stage of the patient's comorbid psychiatric illness. This meaning will vary over the course of the patient's disease (8).

Prevalence

The extent and characteristics of comorbidity of mental illness and substance abuse disorders is increasingly perceived to be significant. The prevalence of this comorbidity varies remarkably depending upon the perspectives of the assessment team, the clinical situation in which the evaluation takes place, the severity of the disorders, and the patient's perspective. An overview of a portion of these data may be useful, although these sometimes bewildering estimates should not be regarded as definitive.

Two large studies have concluded that the prevalence of comorbid psychiatric illness and substance abuse disorders is high with respect to the general population. Data from the latest phase of the Epidemiologic Catchment Area (ECA) Study, a survey of 20,291 people from five sites using the National Institute of Mental Health Diagnostic Interview Schedule (DIS), suggest that more than half of people who abuse drugs other than alcohol have at least one comorbid mental illness, with cocaine abusers demonstrating an additional psychiatric illness in 76% of cases. People with a psychiatric disorder reported a substance abuse disorder 15.7% in the past month, 19.5% in the past six months, and 32.7% in a lifetime history (9).

Results from the National Comorbidity Survey (NCS) in 1994 suggested that 48% of 8098 people between the ages of 15 and 54 reported a substance abuse disorder or psychiatric illness during their lifetime; 26.6% reported a history of a substance abuse disorder, approximately half endorsing an alcohol disorder. Affective disorders and anxiety disorders (19.3% and 24.9%) represented the most significant psychiatric disorders. Kessler suggested that the instrument used for the NCS, a modified Composite International Diagnostic Interview (CIDI) may have preferentially selected for endorsing these categories (10).

According to a psychiatric perspective, the prevalence of coexisting substance abuse, dependency, and psychopathology is remarkably high. Of the 22.5% of the United States population who have a diagnosed mental illness, approximately 29% had a lifetime history of either drug abuse or dependence. People diagnosed with anxiety disorders, including generalized anxiety disorder, panic attacks, and obsessive compulsive disorder, have a lifetime prevalence rate of alcohol dependence of 13.3% (6). In another study, approximately 25% of those with an anxiety disorder were diagnosed as having a substance abuse disorder. A lifetime prevalence of 8–16% for panic disorder patients and 3–55% for lifetime prevalence of phobia patients have been so diagnosed (11, 12).

Prevalence rates for psychiatric disorders for those in substance abuse treatment were generally double the rates for those who were not in treatment.

Even higher rates of psychopathology have been found in opiate abusers. The most common diagnoses seen in treatment seeking opiate dependent patients were major depression (lifetime 53.9%, current 23.8%), phobias (lifetime 9.6%, current 9.2%), and alcoholism (lifetime 34.5%, current 13.7%). When mood disorders such as intermittent depression and cyclothymic personality were considered, the rates of depressive disorders were particularly high. The lifetime rate for affective disorders was 74.3% (15). It is possible that being in a depressive episode may provide some of the impetus for seeking treatment; higher rates of current depression are seen in treatment seeking versus non–treatment seeking opioid addicts (16).

In the Veterans Administration health care system the percentage of substance abuse patients with a comorbid psychiatric disorder was reported to have increased to approximately 35% by 1994. This may be due in part to better diagnostic procedures and increased psychiatric sophistication in both the inpatient and outpatient programs. The proportion of programs offering speciality services for dual diagnosis patients increased to 44% of the inpatient programs and 47% of the outpatient programs. The number of psychiatrists working in the programs more than doubled between 1990 and 1994, and a much larger number of patients received psychiatric medication (17).

There are significant problems inherent in many of the studies reporting on the incidence of comorbidity. In studies of clinical populations, patients are often diagnosed while they are under the influence of drugs or soon thereafter. Studies done in treatment programs report on only the most severely afflicted patients. Follow-up studies after significant periods of abstinence generally have not been done.

A significant flaw in the ECA data is the reliance on the DIS. According to a study by Ford (18) in Cincinnati, the DIS made many diagnoses not made by clinicians, including posttraumatic stress disorder, obsessive-compulsive disorder, panic disorder, and generalized anxiety. In addition, several of the clinical diagnoses could not be made by the DIS, including schizoaffective and personality disorders other than antisocial. Thus there were low levels of concordance between the clinical interviews and diagnoses made by the DIS. Clients were willing to admit to problems of chemical dependency and abuse but not to problems of mental illness. The DIS includes only antisocial personality, whereas clinical interviews assessed a wider variety of personality disorders. The interview is too long, and the decision tree employed may make the DIS inaccurate. It is clear that a combination of a comprehensive clinical assessment augmented by structured data collection instruments is necessary to determine the prevalence of these disorders (18).

Gerstley et al. suggested that the reliance on behavioral criteria and the failure to require that antisocial behaviors occur independently of substance abuse tend to unduly increase the number of substance abusers labeled as antisocial personality disorders (19). Cleckley in 1941 emphasized dynamics in defining a psychopathic personality type. He suggested that these people were unable to experience guilt or remorse, anxiety, and loyalty, unable to form meaningful relationships, and tended to manipulate others to serve their own ends (20). In part because of the subjective and complex nature of the judgments required to make this diagnosis and that of other personality disorders, criteria in DSM-III-R have been based upon behavioral characteristics, and it has not been necessary to require that antisocial behaviors be independent of substance abuse. In many studies, then, the diagnosis of antisocial personality disorder may be based upon tautological reasoning. It does seem as if there is marked heterogeneity in these so-called antisocial personalities; there are the true psychopaths similar to the formulation of Cleckley ("when you've met one you know it") and these seem to be quite different from the majority of patients so diagnosed. Perhaps the majority of substance abusers who meet the criteria for antisocial personality should be thought of as situational psychopaths since they do experience guilt and loyalty and can form meaningful relationships with therapists and others. This is a critical issue in that the labels we affix to our patients influence our procedures and therapeutic zeal; antisocial personalities are often dismissed as incurable or unworthy.

It should be noted that a large number of clinicians view the problem of the coexistence of chemical dependence and psychopathology quite differently. In their view, the incidence of psychopathology in their substance-abusing populations in treatment is considered to be no higher, or perhaps no more than slightly higher, than that of the general population. According to this perspective, which holds sway in the majority of inpatient rehabilitation programs in the country, the psychopathology noted is most often a result of the drug taking and the symptoms will decrease markedly or disappear with time and abstinence. These programs generally are informed by a chemical dependency model; that is, the drug or alcohol use is perceived as a disease characterized by a profound inability to control drug use; chemically dependent patients are believed to handle the drugs quite differently from those who are able to control use. Chemical dependency is viewed as a life-long affliction, and often psychopathology, even those symptoms that preceded

drug use, are viewed as part of the disease process. Many of these programs provide excellent care for the disease as it is perceived; they recognize the existence of dual diagnosis patients though they perceive them as few in number (21).

Dual diagnosis patients often represent approximately one half of all patients seen in psychiatric emergency rooms and present with severe symptoms that are difficult to assess because of the complex and changing relationship of the drug and the perceived psychopathology (22).

General Treatment Strategies

Members of the treatment team often view the abuse or dependency and the psychopathology according to the model in which they were trained. It is often difficult for staff members to appreciate the influence of other determinants on the drug-taking behavior (23).

For example, whereas recovering physicians and other staff are often crucial to the treatment process because of their knowledge of the behaviors and ability to identify with patients, it is often difficult for them to recognize the presence or influence of psychopathology. Their tendency is to see all symptomatology as a function of the chemical dependency and all symptoms as being expected to subside with abstinence over time. This may be, in part, a function of their denial of the influence of their own personality or psychopathology on their own drug-taking behaviors. It is surprising how well-trained clinicians in programs informed by chemical dependency perspectives often miss or mistreat psychopathology.

Conversely, workers trained according to psychiatric perspectives are often unable to appreciate the ethos, meaning, and phenomenology of the drug-taking experience. They may view all drug abuse as generic and not appreciate individual drug abuse patterns. For example, as noted previously, the overdiagnosis of antisocial personality disorders in drug-taking, crime-committing populations is high (9, 19). They may also not be able to recognize the significance of spirituality and the 12-step approach in the treatment of these patients. There is a tendency for these people, most often physicians, to prematurely institute pharmacotherapy. It is as if they are seeking a purely technological answer to a complex array of psychosocial and cultural determinants. Patients presenting with dual diagnosis problems therefore are often viewed as difficult and recalcitrant to treatment, and, as with other drug-dependent patients, adversarial relationships often develop between the patient and the treatment team. Frequently, these patients are perceived as noncompliant, and they often demand to leave treatment prematurely. Crowe et al. found irregular discharge in 57% of 117 chemically dependent patients consecutively admitted to a Veterans Administration psychiatric ward (24).

In the treatment of dual diagnosis, or MICA, patients, in essence, the choice offered to the patient is whether the patient should take his or her drug in order to experience fleeting moments of joy and escape, a worsening level of overall function, and possibly a worse outcome from the sequelae of increasingly severe psychopathology, or whether the patient should accept prescribed treatments that might include "our drugs" such as neuroleptics or antidepressants, which provide little joy, ineffective escape, though better function and possibly a better outcome. It is not surprising that many patients elect to take "their" drugs to feel better or obtain release, even though the relief may be evanescent. Patients also often seek a sense of control over their symptoms, a predictability, even though the symptoms may worsen.

Evaluation and Early Treatment

Evaluative procedures should continue throughout the initial treatment stages whether the setting is inpatient or outpatient. A careful and complete drug and psychiatric history, including a careful mental status examination for current symptomatology, must be performed (25). Clinicians should be particularly sensitive to the possibility of psychosis, depression, anxiety, panic attacks, suicidality, homicidality, cognitive impairment, and character problems.

Assessing the nature of the comorbid psychopathology is often relevant to the phenomenology of a patient's drug use. Kleinman et al. examined 76 cocaine and crack abusers and divided them into three groups: users with no psychopathology except for substance use, users with Axis II diagnoses, and users with Axis I diagnoses. Participants were given the symptom checklist SCL-90 and Beck Inventory to measure depressive disorder. The data suggested that the most depressed users, those with Axis I pathology, had a greater intensity and longer duration of cocaine and all other drug use (14).

A careful drug use history should examine five areas. These include precipitating events leading to treatment, onset of drug use, duration and pattern of use, the subjective and objective effects the drug has on the patient and his or her symptomatology, and, finally, an exploration of the meaning the chosen drug has for an individual patient at the current moment. A history of the patient's drug use should also include an understanding of the changing pattern of the patient's drug use, withdrawal symptomatology, and medical sequelae. Characterization of the extent of loss or social deteriorations associated with drug use is necessary to appreciate the interpersonal, legal, educational, medical, and employment consequences the patient currently faces. The determination of premorbid psychopathology is often enhanced by assessing the choice of drugs, pattern of use, and positive and negative effects the drugs have had on the patient. For example, a borderline patient may take drugs in a disorganized, chaotic pattern whereas an obsessive-compulsive physician will take fentanyl or alcohol at carefully prescribed intervals. Since these patients are often poor historians because of denial or deliberate obfuscation, corroboration of information with outside sources, such as family members, employers, and probation officers, is imperative (26). If the people interacting with the patient are not included in the evaluation and treatment process, clinicians may reinforce negative and defensive behaviors such as isolation, denial, and compartmentalization.

A thorough physical examination, including a detailed neurologic examination, is essential. Given the increasing impact of the acquired immune deficiency syndrome (AIDS), careful consideration of this diagnosis insofar as it might produce psychiatric symptomatology should be made. Whereas mandatory testing of patients upon admission might discourage patients from completing the admission procedures and entering treatment programs, at varying points in the treatment process, sensitive counseling of patients should be implemented with a view toward encouraging human immunodeficiency virus (HIV) testing in almost all high-risk treatment populations (27). Procedures should be in place for pretest and posttest counseling in all programs. Cooperative ties should be established with testing and treatment agencies if they are not immediately at hand.

As noted elsewhere in this volume, treatment of withdrawal symptoms should be provided concurrently with treatment of severe psychiatric symptomatology that might interfere with early treatment compliance. Clinical judgment is required as to how vigorous the psychiatric intervention should be. In most cases, acute psychiatric symptomatology will decrease in importance when withdrawal symptoms are adequately treated in a supportive and safe environment. It should also be appreciated that just as the agonist effects of the drugs vary in each patient depending upon the personality, expectations, and milieu of the user, so do the severity and characteristics of withdrawal phenomena from each of the drugs.

As noted, continued observation of the patient in the early phases of treatment is essential to permit differentiation of the agonist effects of the drugs and their psychiatric sequelae from the premorbid psychopathology the drugs may have been used to self-medicate. If the psychiatric symptoms are well tolerated, and there is evidence to suggest that they are decreasing or related to the drug use, the psychopathology should not be instituted for at least 2 weeks post admission. This issue deserves special consideration, since the symptoms of the comorbid psychopathology may be sufficiently pressing that treatment must be provided presumptively or the patient will be unable to tolerate the program or the loss of the drug. There need not be a defined psychiatric disorder; personality factors and psychological symptoms should inform and help to individualize treatments where appropriate.

In order to provide a comprehensive assessment there are a variety of different instruments and strategies that might be implemented. For example, self-reported instruments may be used to secure staff time; these might be completed when patients are waiting to be seen. Whereas self-reported instruments may yield inadequate information because of patients' poor comprehension, denial, or purposeful omissions of data, some of these problems can be avoided if the clinician reviews the answers with the patient after completion. For example, the Beck Depression Inventory or the Michigan Alcoholism Screening Test may be useful (28). Many clinical investigators in the field advocate structured interviews with the view that these efficiently elicit a reliable history and diagnose psychopathology. These are thought to ensure uniformity in the areas assessed, the ways in which questions are asked, and the precision with which the diagnosis is made. Unstructured interviews performed by skilled clinicians may, however, provide greater depth as well as information and attitudes that may be more clinically useful. An empathic, imaginative, but thorough interview may also enhance the possibility of the development of a therapeutic alliance and might even improve early retention though this has not been studied. In our experience, the specific diagnostic categories of DSM-IV are often less useful than an appreciation of the severity of symptoms and how these symptoms influence behavior and performance. The most widely used structure interview systems for diagnosing the psychiatric disorders in these populations include (a) the Schedule for Affective Disorders and Schizophrenia (SADS), (b) the DIS, (c) the Diagnostic Interview Schedule (SCID), (d) the CIDI, and (e) the Addiction Severity Index (ASI). The SADS and SCID require trained clinicians; the DIS, the CIDI and the ASI do not require trained clinicians.

The ASI was developed (29) to provide a structured evaluation system that elicits information about a drug abuser's problems in six areas: drug use, medical, psychological, legal, social, and occupational. It may be administered by paraprofessionals in 30–45 minutes and provides reliable ratings that appear to be correlated with treatment and care. As with other screening instruments, such as the Beck, a more thorough diagnostic evaluation can be performed on those whose ratings in the area of psychopathology were high (29).

Treatment of concurrent psychiatric illness must include both short- and long-term procedures. Certainly, in the short term, severe acute symptomatology such as psychosis or severe depression or anxiety must be identified and treated aggressively so as to maximize the patient's ability to participate in chemical dependency treatment programs.

Treatment Facilities and Organizations

Inpatient institutionalization may be indicated according to the following criteria:

1. Psychiatric or medical conditions that require close observations and treatment, such as psychotic states, severe depressive symptoms, suicidal or homicidal ideation, severe debilitation, and severe withdrawal phenomena
2. The inability to cease drug use despite appropriate outpatient maneuvers
3. The absence of adequate psychosocial supports that might be mobilized to facilitate the cessation of drug use
4. The necessity to interrupt a living situation that reinforces continued drug use
5. The need to enhance motivation or break through denial

In recent years as a result of the cost containment policies of managed care programs, it has become more difficult to provide inpatient care for psychiatric patients whether or not they have a drug abuse problem, and the lengths of stay are stringently limited. For example, in this climate, it might not be possible to admit a patient on the basis of the latter four criteria. Severe withdrawal phenomenon, an element in the first group of admission criteria, is increasingly being denied as a reason for institutionalization; outpatient detoxification regimens are much preferred by managed care organizations because of their low cost and are likely to be encouraged in the next few years.

Dual diagnosis patients are often difficult to place in programs; their drug taking may render them less attractive to psychiatric facilities and their psychopathology may disqualify them for admission to drug treatment programs including therapeutic communities or rehabilitation programs. Inpatient options include general psychiatric or medical hospitals, rehabilitation programs, and therapeutic communities (30).

The characteristics of these programs vary depending on the particular institution; yet, some generalizations can be made. If the psychopathology is of significant severity to require skilled psychiatric care and close observation, a general psychiatric unit becomes necessary. Psychiatric facilities often lack an organized drug treatment program and may be insensitive to the needs of drug abuse patients. As noted, adversarial relationships often develop between staff and these patients over stylistic or control issues, particularly those patients with character disorders. There may be insufficient structure, and patients often break the rules. On balance, therapeutic communities and rehabilitation programs may lack the psychiatric expertise to diagnose and treat these patients, and they are often too confrontational for severely disturbed patients (30a).

It should be appreciated that there are few data on which programs are most effective for which patients, and referrals often must be made on relatively tenuous grounds. At the same time, a new generation of inpatient facilities that are able to provide treatments that incorporate aspects of each of the conventional inpatient models is being developed. For example, rehabilitation programs with good psychiatric backup and the ability to provide individualized treatments for severely disturbed patients are now available. Similarly, psychiatric hospitals increasingly are providing discrete drug treatment programs and dual diagnosis units within their confines. A new generation of outpatient programs based upon chemical dependency treatment models that provide integrated psychiatric evaluation and treatment is being developed, though the few existing programs clearly are inadequate to the needs of this population.

After evaluation and initial treatment has been accomplished, the attempt should be made to integrate these patients into a chemical dependency program model. Twelve-step programs, peer support, group therapy, and structured activities that help the patient to make the necessary behavioral and cognitive changes should be provided as appropriate. Whenever possible, family members should be included in the treatment process. Rounsaville et al. examined the prevalence of psychiatric disorders in family members of opiate addicts. Their work revealed elevated rates of depression, anxiety disorders, antisocial personality disorders, and alcoholism in relatives of opiate addicts, with particularly elevated rates of these disorders in depressed addicts (15). From a clinical perspective, involvement of the family in the treatment process may help the patient to address problems that reinforce drug abuse behaviors and that inevitably influence the treatment process. Confidentiality is an issue that should be raised with patients early in treatment. It should be made clear that strict laws govern the release of information about a patient's drug use and treatment and that therapists will not release information without the written consent of the patient or a court order, or unless there is a medical emergency, a child custody case, or a federal inspector's review of records. Laws governing minors vary from state to state and should be understood by the treatment team. Open discussion of the issue of confidentiality and appreciation of the patient's concerns in this area enhance the therapeutic alliance (31).

Well-run centralized intake service with case management offer promise in patients who are dually diagnosed, but there are significant problems with this mode of organization. A centralized intake program can develop a cadre of trained evaluators who can do reasonably reliable and consistent evaluations, develop a standardized database and refer patients to programs that have openings and that provide the appropriate level of care. To develop an effective system the centralized intake service should have a good sense of what each treatment resource can and must do, who it is best for, and what are its flaws. Site visits and regular mailings between central intake personnel and providers are essential to the development of a smoothly working system. Programs that are unfamiliar, lack knowledge or even judgment about these patients would not refer these patients; rather, they would be referred to programs that can demonstrate some integration of mental health and substance abuse programs or that demonstrate an organized ability to attract them to treatment and retain them. Case management should follow these patients throughout the process to assess whether they got to treatment, stayed, completed the treatment, and achieved abstinence. This system has been developed in New York City as part of the Target Cities Program funded by the Center for Substance Abuse Treatment. The evidence and clinical experience suggests that centralized intake, good data collection, appropriate referral, coordination, and delivery of all services to the patient enhance the quality of life. Simplified process and outcome studies are essential if we are to learn from our mistakes and those of the provider programs.

The efficacy or lack thereof of case management techniques in the treatment of the chronically mentally ill with or without substance abuse problems continues to be difficult to document. The inconsistency of the studies and the rhetoric becomes understandable when it is appreciated that the definition of case management varies widely. For example, Mondersheid and Henderson define case management as the "identification, coordination and delivery of all necessary services for keeping the patient in the community and enhancing the quality of life" (32). It is reasonable to assume that private sector managed mental behavioral health care organizations would see case management as resource control, identification of available services, and a focused attempt to provide lowest cost care that is appropriate. Those organizations are likely to merely provide only "intake and referral." Coordination and delivery of services are beyond the scope of these programs. Not surprisingly, a smaller percentage of patients actually got to treatment in a program that included centralized intake and referral (27%), compared to other programs providing more follow-up (33).

Problems with the system include the tendency on the part of centralized intake counselors, despite intensive training, to refer to programs that reflect their belief systems, rather than to the programs that can accept patients immediately. Programs that most frequently have openings may often also have the poorest retention rates. The system refers in the direction of least resistance. Then too, it is often difficult to persuade even the most heroic, well-meaning community programs that accurate records of retention, discharge, work histories, and abstinence must be kept. Optimally, provider programs with poor early or late retention rates or low abstinence rates might benefit from the ongoing scrutiny by CES, and by means of technical assistance schemes improve procedures and personnel.

Relapse prevention strategies should be made available for patients on an individualized basis and should target the particular needs of various diagnostic groups. It may be necessary to develop well-organized, concrete courses for severely disturbed patients; patients must often be painstakingly helped to develop new routes to work, new associations, and alternative recreational pursuits.

As in the treatment of other populations, the importance of empowering the patient to take responsibility for his or her own behavior and treatment cannot be overemphasized. It is often quite liberating for patients to be tactfully and gently apprised of their psychopathology; family and friends have often denied the problem or attempted to protect the patient from what he or she has long been aware of. Patients should be encouraged to examine their behavior and the effects drug use and psychopathology have had on their lives. Issues in treatment such as rule breaking and lack of engagement or sharing with others should be considered, as should issues related to patients' attempting to maintain control over their symptomatology, thoughts, or feelings by means of self-medication. Severely disturbed patients often benefit from repetition of concrete rules for safe behavior.

Chemical dependency treatment strategies depend to a large extent on peer support and group process. At the same time, the treatment of psychopathology often requires individualized attention, which can distract patients and clinicians from group process. The group setting often inhibits patients from discussing psychiatric symptomatology because of fears of stigmatization or feelings of shame, particularly in regard to psychotic symptoms, sexual deviance, and antisocial behaviors. A reasonably well-organized, yet flexible, curriculum that includes psychoeducation about the mode of action of drugs, the nature of psychopathology, issues related to stigmatization, the ethos of drug taking, and medical and psychiatric effects of drug use is essential. Patients must also be seen individually at frequent intervals to assess and treat psychiatric symptomatology, including the administration of medication and dose regulation. Patients should be encouraged to participate in professionally run group therapy and self-help groups. The chemical dependency model should be carefully integrated with individualized treatment of psychopathology.

Twelve-step programs may be an essential element of programs for dually diagnosed patients. At the same time, many of these patients are loath to participate in these groups because of their psychopathology and sense of isolation, or because of unpleasant experiences in the past. It has proved useful to attempt carefully to teach these patients how the groups work, what they must do to participate, and how they should act in various situations. Some programs provide special 12-step programs for patients with psychopathology ("double trouble" groups) to encourage their involvement in the fellowships. Well-prepared patients, even those with severe psychopathology, can then be slowly integrated into regular 12-step programs (34).

Some patients are unable to tolerate group treatment. Ideally, programs should tailor treatment plans to meet individual needs. Sensitivity, tact, and considerable delicacy are required to maintain a therapeutic milieu with useful structure and at the same time exempt certain patients from particular therapeutic activities. Although it appears that formal structure is essential, flexibility with certain patients is required for treatment to be effective. For example, it may be disruptive to both the patient or the group for some severe borderline or psychotic patients to be forced to participate.

TREATMENT STRATEGIES FOR SPECIFIC PSYCHOPATHOLOGIC DISORDERS

Schizophrenia and Psychotic Illnesses

The prevalence of drug use and dependence in association with psychotic states is quite significant, though the relationship between these disorders may be complex (35). It is necessary to attempt to determine whether the psychotic disorder was caused or precipitated by the drug use or whether the drugs are being used to self-medicate a preexisting psychopathologic state, although this may be difficult. It is likely that in many people both situations obtain: there is a preexisting psychopathology and the drug used as self-medication may in turn contribute significantly to that psychopathology. Acute and chronic psychotic disorders may be precipitated in predisposed individuals by the use of cocaine, marihuana, and the hallucinogens as well as by severe withdrawal states.

As noted earlier, the treatment of psychotic states requires the careful integration of chemical dependency and psychiatric models. Patients suffering from chronic or acute psychotic illnesses relate poorly to others, may be paranoid, and usually have impaired attention and concentration. Unlike traditional chemical dependency treatment models, group treatment should be highly supportive, less intense, and less confrontational. Certainly, the severity and characteristics of the psychotic process require careful attention to conventional treatment strategies. Pharmacotherapy with neuroleptics generally is necessary. As with all patients maintained on neuroleptics, the goal should be to use the smallest possible dose with the fewest side effects. Patients respond idiosyncratically to different classes of neuroleptics, and the clinician should be aware of the efficacy of different neuroleptics as well as the different side effect profiles of each class. For example, nonagitated young patients may benefit from an initial trial of a low-dose, high-potency neuroleptic such as haloperidol or fluphenazine. These medications are associated with significantly less sedation and orthostasis, though side effects such as dystonia, akathisia, and extrapyramidal symptoms that mimic parkinsonism and cogwheeling occur frequently and must be treated (36). Treatment may require the addition of anticholinergic medicines such as benztropine or trihexiphenidyl, or antihistaminic medications such as diphenhydramine. Although these medications are useful for the treatment of uncomfortable side effects, they are also subject to abuse on rare occasions. In agitated patients or those who develop severe side effects to high-potency neuroleptics, low-potency neuroleptics can be used. Neuroleptics such as chlorpromazine and thioridazine reduce psychotic symptoms and may calm agitated patients. Side effects similar to those with haloperidol do occur, though usually they are lower in frequency and intensity. In addition, patients on low-potency neuroleptics are subject to sedation and orthostasis, which may result in syncope. Consequently, careful observation of the patient's vital signs and the subjective experience of the medication may help the clinician titrate the dose most effectively. Long-term use of all neuroleptics is associated with the possibility of transient or permanent movement disorders denoting tardive dyskinesia. Clinicians must be sensitive to symptoms, such as tongue undulation, repetitive rhythmic movement of the extremities, and orofacial movement, so that appropriate intervention, including cessation of neuroleptic administration, can be made.

As already discussed, patients may prefer the euphoria of *their* drugs to the emotionally impoverished but more functional state allowed by many of *our* psychotropic medications. Relapse may commence when patients begin to abuse anticholinergic medication used to treat neuroleptic side effects in order to achieve a sense of more feeling, although the common drugs of abuse are more often used. Whereas the patient may experience transient highs or relief when the nonmedical use of drugs begins, it is likely that the reemergence or exacerbation of psychotic or other severe symptoms will soon follow. The complex and changing interaction among psychotic symptoms, the antipsychotic effects of medications and their side effects, and the sought-after effects of the drugs of abuse must be monitored carefully. Whenever possible, patients should be educated with regard to these interactions to prevent the emergence or exacerbation of both psychiatric symptoms and drug-taking sequelae.

Given the frequent contacts necessary with these patients and their unwillingness to take the medication, it is useful to incorporate administration of the neuroleptic into the routine of each visit. Consideration of the use of longer-lasting depot medicine is also indicated. By integrating the administration of the medicine into the chemical dependency treatment routine, compliance may be enhanced and relapse liability reduced. Relapse frequently is secondary to drug noncompliance, which ensues as the side effect profile of the neuroleptics is experienced; some patients say the drugs make them feel "dead inside." Kalakowska et al. found that the response of patients to a course of care of the conventional antipsychotic was a good prediction of the response to another (37).

Acute psychotic symptomatology may be caused by sympathomimetics such as cocaine or the amphetamines or precipitated by marihuana, by the hallucinogens such as lysergic acid diethylamide (LSD), phencyclidine (PCP), or psilocybin ("magic mushrooms"). These reactions may also be precipitated by withdrawal states from opiates, sedative depressants, or alcohol. Initial treatment should be supportive, with the patient provided with a warm, safe environment with frequent reassurance that the feelings and thoughts experienced are a function of the drug use and will pass ("talking down"). Anxiolytic drugs such as the benzodiazepine tranquilizers should be administered as necessary to allay anxiety; neuroleptics may exacerbate psychotic symptoms or even cause delirium through their anticholinergic side effects and should be reserved for later stages of treatment. If the psychotic process persists after several days of abstinence, the symptomatology should be treated as similar to functional psychotic disorders. It is likely that persistent psychotic symptomatology is a function of premorbid psychopathology or vulnerability. A crucial question that remains to be addressed is whether the psychotic reactions precipitated by heavy drug use in normal individuals may render that individual more vulnerable to subsequent psychotic episodes at a reduced threshold or to prolonged psychotic disorders. Clinical experience suggests that whereas all individuals are vulnerable to the development of psychotic episodes from various drugs at different dose and frequency intervals, a psychotic episode renders that individual more susceptible to subsequent ones. It has been suggested that the psychotic symptomatology of some of the so-called "young adult chronic patients" so often seen in homeless and inner city populations may be a function of chronic psychotomimetic drug use. A critical area for research is the relationship of drug use to these chronic states.

Schizophrenic patients who use illicit drugs are often attempting to self-medicate their illness, to reduce the intensity of their psychotic symptoms, or to alleviate the dysphoria integral to these disorders. Certainly, heroin and other opiates have been shown to be powerful antipsychotic agents, although alcohol and sedative depressants may also reduce the intensity or discomfort of psychotic symptomatology (38). Interestingly, many psychotic patients also use cannabis and cocaine, although these are psychotomimetic and can exacerbate their symptomatology (38a, 38b). Dynamically, this may represent the patient's attempt to take control of the hallucinatory or delusional symptoms by using substances that create or enhance them or to distance themselves from their symptoms. Even though the outcome is negative, the patient has determined it. The drug use may also represent an attempt at rationalization of psychopathology.

Additionally, patients' drug use is determined by availability, and they will often use the drug that is available even if it means feeling worse. Severely disturbed patients are often unable to go through the necessary machinations to obtain expensive, illicit drugs such as heroin. Hence alcohol and even inhalants may be used more frequently than heroin or depressants by some psychotic patients.

Affective Disorders

In patients with major depression, dysthymia, or related disorders, it is often difficult to determine whether the mood states noted are the cause or the sequelae of protracted drug use. Are they representative of a separate and distinct illness, a result of the agonist effects of the drugs such as depressants or opiates, part of an abstinence syndrome as from cocaine or opiates, or a combination of factors? A careful history is essential, including the assessment of mood pathology that antedated the drug use, along with a determination of whether the drugs were used as self-medication for the observed symptomatology. Patients may be attempting to alleviate uncomfortable symptoms such as depression or agitation or to enhance a desirable mood state such as hypomania or mania. Symptoms that persisted during abstinent periods also should be determined. Information also should be obtained from family and friends.

Whenever possible, patients should be withdrawn from their drugs of abuse using appropriate medication and then carefully observed for extended periods on no medication. In most patients, severe drug-related affective symptomatology wanes within 1–4 weeks. In these patients, whether or not there is evidence for premorbid psychopathology, the attempt should be made to help the patient relate the internal mood state to adverse drug effects. Carefully educating the patient individually and in group situations with respect to how cocaine and alcohol, for example, exacerbated depressive symptoms that may or may not have preceded the drug use is often useful. Discussion of the opiate withdrawal syndrome with its depressive signs and symptoms may help the patient separate the drug use from psychopathology. If the patient can identify depressed feelings and attempt to cope with these using nonpharmacologic interventions, relapse may be prevented.

After several weeks to months of observation and treatment with no reduction or worsening of symptomatology, pharmacotherapy is indicated. In addition, when the depressive symptomatology is sufficiently severe that sobriety is threatened, or when repeated relapses have occurred, it is necessary to presumptively institute a trial of antidepressant medication. The choice of drugs will depend upon the psychopathology of the patient, although certain generalizations can be made. Certainly, medications subject to abuse or misuse with unduly reinforcing properties should be avoided if possible. For example, amitriptyline with its profound sedating properties should be avoided in depressant abusers. A tricyclic antidepressant with less sedation such as nortriptyline or desipramine should be tried initially. Since the tricyclic antidepressants such as desipramine have been shown to decrease cocaine craving and prevent relapse, administration of these drugs for this dual indication may be indicated (7, 30). Whereas monoamine oxidase inhibitors have proved useful in some patients, the severe hypertensive crisis that may occur in patients who might ingest tyramine-containing foods, certain wines such as Chianti, or analeptic drugs such as cocaine or amphetamines limit its usefulness (39). It should be noted that it is possible that some of the salutary effects of the antidepressants or other medications are less specific than have been noted previously. Perhaps in some of these patients who have sought rapid, predictable change in their feelings from their nonmedical drug taking, the pharmacotherapeutic medications provide this same sort of change and sense of control (40).

Anxiety Disorders

Anxiety symptoms may be due to a premorbid generalized anxiety disorder or panic attacks, or secondary to drug or alcohol use. Controversy persists relative to the relationship of anxiety symptoms to drug use (41). Vaillant maintained that in alcoholics, most psychopathology occurs secondary to the alcohol use itself (42). Others contend that primary psychopathology spawns drug use as an attempt at self-medication of debilitating symptoms (43). It is likely that the relationship is more complex and is often marked by a vacillating interaction of many variables, including the drugs and the anxiety in different situations and over time (44). Kushner reviewed family studies, epidemiologic surveys, and field studies and found that alcohol was often used as self-medication for agoraphobia and social phobia. Interestingly, panic attacks and generalized anxiety disorder were most likely to follow the compulsive consumption of alcohol (45). The exacerbation of anxiety symptoms may be a result of acute or protracted abstinence syndromes, particularly from alcohol, sedative depressant drugs, and the opiates. Long-term cocaine use has been implicated in producing chronic anxiety symptoms as well, as is discussed later in this chapter.

Szuster examined the pattern of marihuana use in patients known to have panic attacks. He found that these patients experienced significantly more anxiety with marihuana use than did matched controls. He also found that users with panic attacks rarely continued use over a prolonged period of time (46).

Patients often use a variety of drugs to self-medicate discomfort, including alcohol, benzodiazepines, tranquilizers, and narcotics. Initially, some patients may start out with a high level of anxiety or panic attacks and begin by using drugs to treat these symptoms (47). Over time, the anxiety symptoms may not be perceived as such but they become the conditioned stimuli for drug craving, which abets these patients' continued drug use (41).

In recent years, following the initial work of Martin et al. in Lexington, Kentucky, with opiate addicts (48), there has been enhanced appreciation of the existence of a protracted abstinence syndrome in many patients marked by psychological and physical symptoms. This area needs study, but clearly some people who become abstinent from alcohol, narcotics, analeptics, and sedative-hypnotics develop persistent anxiety or affective symptoms or other sequelae that may not have been present prior to drug use. Though it is not clear why the development of persistent psychological symptoms is so variable, one might postulate that it is determined in part by premorbid psychopathology as well as by the character and extent of drug use. Certainly, acute withdrawal symptoms may represent psychophysiologic stress that can precipitate a variety of psychiatric symptoms in predisposed individuals, including psychosis and affective and anxiety disorders. Yet, protracted abstinence symptoms may also occur in individuals who do not necessarily have severe psychiatric sequelae in the acute phase of abstinence from drugs.

Because anxiety symptoms can be so debilitating, it is essential to carefully evaluate their determinants and treat patients in a timely fashion. After detoxification, a period of observation with supportive counseling or psychotherapy and peer support is essential. Employment of behavioral treatments such as biofeedback, hypnosis, or cognitive psychotherapy can be useful. Cognitive labeling can be an effective treatment strategy used with these patients to break this cycle. In chemically dependent patients the experience of anxiety, whatever the etiology, is often associated with the experience of withdrawal and/or drug craving. During periods of abstinence, carefully and in an organized fashion, encouraging patients to identify symptoms of anxiety separate from drug withdrawal and drug craving is often useful. The experience of anxiety may be separated from drug craving and the tendency to relapse (49). If the anxiety symptoms persist or threaten abstinence, tricyclic antidepressants can be useful, in carefully controlled dose regimens. Benzodiazepines are to be avoided because of their reinforcing properties and abuse liability (50). In rare cases, minor tranquilizers with low reinforcing properties such as chlordiazepoxide may be indicated. Though not well studied to date, acupuncture or electroacupuncture appear to offer a possible treatment for acute and perhaps chronic anxiety, particularly that associated with withdrawal states.

Personality Disorders

Personality disorders or chronic maladaptive styles and behaviors frequently are diagnosed in chronic drug users, although as noted earlier, these entities are fraught with considerable diagnostic problems. Most importantly, the criteria necessary to make the diagnoses often are not clear, depend upon the perspective of the therapist, and change with time and changing situations. For example, in programs informed by psychiatric perspectives, the diagnosis of borderline, antisocial, or narcissistic personality disorder is made with alarming frequency. In other centers, these diagnoses rarely are made and are perceived to be less than useful, as they often carry with them a poor prognosis and hinder therapeutic zeal. At the same time, the effort to continue to define these character problems is important, and patients so diagnosed should be carefully followed.

Patients with narcissistic, borderline, and antisocial personality disorders often present as recalcitrant and difficult. Although the tendency may be to rely on individual psychotherapy to address the characteristics and perceived severity of the dysfunction, results are often poor with these patients. Chemical dependency treatments informed by the disease model and based on tight structure, peer support, and confrontation that addresses the significant denial of these patients appears to be more useful. Group process with formal structure may improve the ability of these patients to learn new and more appropriate behaviors and perceptions that may help them in their ability to relate to others. Further, conventional treatment strategies relying on group process serve to diffuse the inevitable transference issues that can undermine treatment in an individualized setting.

As noted earlier, antisocial personality disorder is often overdiagnosed secondary to the precipitating events that lead to treatment such as legal problems, interpersonal violence, and dissembling. This sort of labeling often creates a level of hopelessness in the treatment team that can inhibit effective treatment. It should be stressed that diagnosis of antisocial personality disorder is often based on the substance abuse and dependence and the related behaviors rather than lifelong personality patterns (51). It would appear that the diagnosis of antisocial personality should be made only when the characteristic behaviors precede the drug use and seem to be independent of it.

Chronic drug use may create personality changes and even psychiatric illness incident to the pharmacologic actions of the drugs and the associated denial and marginal thinking, particularly when it occurs in the context of societal norms that tend to reject drug use and users and consider the behavior abnormal or shameful (52, 53). Drug users may develop character dysfunction marked by feelings of isolation, poor ability to relate to others, a sense of unreality associated with the drug effects, and compulsive lying in attempts to conform to societal expectations (54). Chronic users may become inappropriately impulsive and manipulative over time, to their attempts to control their feelings through the drug experience and perhaps in an attempt to defend themselves against chronic feelings of inadequacy. The disorganization and even chaos that they encourage or precipitate in others may be integral to their attempts to gain control over situations that feel out of control, as in a hospital setting.

Dulit examined the prevalence of substance abuse in 137 patients given a diagnosis of borderline personality disorder. When substance abuse was not part of the diagnostic criteria, 32 (23%) of the patients no longer met criteria for borderline personality disorder. In this subgroup, symptoms were less severe and the course of the illness was more favorable than for the other group (55). This work adds weight to the possibility that the drug abuse was an important factor in the development and diagnosis of the personality disorders observed in these patients.

Patients with histrionic, passive-aggressive, and self-defeating personality disorders present with other concerns. Often healthier than the group previously discussed, these patients tend to sabotage their treatment in subtle ways that can lead to relapse. Psychotherapeutic strategies, both group and individual, should target behaviors that undermine the treatment as it progresses. Frequently, insight can benefit these generally less impaired patients. The psychopathology in these patients is significant though more subtle than in more impaired patients, and it can be minimized or even overlooked by the treatment team. Consequently, these diagnoses must be considered in any patient who begins to lose ground in treatment secondary to self-defeating behavior. Future study is needed in this area.

No definitive psychopharmacologic treatment exists for personality disordered patients. Yet, medication can be beneficial for particular patients if used to treat symptoms that threaten sobriety. Treatment should focus on particular symptoms most prominently related to relapse and interpersonal dysfunction. For example, patients with severe mood lability have been known to benefit from mood stabilizing agents such as lithium. Affective panic or depressive symptoms may respond to selective serotonin re-uptake inhibitors. The use of non–dependency-producing anxiolytics such as bus-

pirone or low-dose neuroleptics such as perphenazine and carbamazepine should be considered. Use of agents that are subject to abuse, such as the minor tranquilizers, or antidepressants with sedative effects, such as amitriptyline, generally is unwarranted, though even these may be considered in the context of repeated relapses.

Minimal Brain Dysfunction

Treatment strategies for patients who present with drug use and attention deficit disorders (ADD) or minimal brain dysfunction (MBD) have not been well studied. This population presents with varying and often subtle symptomatology, including inability to concentrate, decreased attention span, disorganization, and impulsiveness. Symptoms often are not sufficiently well defined. These disorders generally are diagnosed in children; only recently has it been recognized that ADD or MBD children grow up and often continue to have some level of brain dysfunction. It has been found that these patients tend to self-medicate with illicit drugs and alcohol to allay their symptoms.

Mirin et al. suggested that patients with MBD preferred to self-medicate with stimulants such as cocaine and amphetamines. These drugs often help patients organize and concentrate better. This mimics the use of methylphenidate hydrochloride and amphetamines in children with ADD. Less well recognized is the widespread use of alcohol, sedative-hypnotics, and tranquilizers in patients with MBD. Patients often report a lessening of impulsivity and, surprisingly, better concentration with the use of both depressants and stimulants (56).

Nonpharmacologic interventions should be attempted initially, particularly conventional, well-structured chemical dependency procedures. Many of these patients, even those functioning at a relatively high level, feel "out of control," and treatment procedures should be focused on helping them gain a sense of control. This can be accomplished through implementation of relapse prevention techniques, peer support, and individualized psychotherapy. Use of tricyclic antidepressants, particularly desipramine, which has a palatable side-effect profile, might be beneficial for these patients in regard to concentration difficulty and impulsivity. Fluoxetine has not been studied in this population, although its analeptic and antidepressant properties make it an intriguing possibility for this patient group. For patients who either do not respond to a tricyclic antidepressant or have particular problems with impulsivity and disorganization, low-dose neuroleptic medication may prove effective. Low doses of haloperidol or perphenazine at bedtime may contribute significantly to these patients' ability to function and sense of well-being. The neuroleptic dose should be kept as low as possible and increased slowly as necessary. The side-effect profiles of these medications should be clear to the clinician, particularly the signs of tardive dyskinesia.

Triple Diagnosis

As the spread of HIV increases in the drug-abusing population, the psychopathology noted may be a result of AIDS or may be influenced by central nervous system AIDS. Cognitive impairment, including short-term memory loss and emotional lability, may be early signs of central nervous system AIDS.

Treatment strategies for these "triple diagnosis" patients have been described by Batki, who found improved outcome in patients whose management was informed by intensified interdisciplinary communication and treatment procedures. These include the medical treatment of complications of HIV disease, abstinence-based treatment for drug use, and access to psychiatric services as needed for evaluation and treatment of psychiatric illness and neuropsychiatric syndromes associated with AIDS (57). Well-organized case management strategies, most usefully based in the chemical dependency treatment program, represent the cornerstone to this approach. Frequent communication among clinicians and programs provides better care and serves to reassure patients that treatment is integrated and consistent, thus lessening anxiety and potential noncompliance (58). Perry examined treatment strategies in patients with organic mental disorders caused by HIV. He found that the mental status examination alone was not adequate for diagnosing cognitive impairment and that close observation and more extensive evaluative procedures were indicated. He suggested the use of psycho-stimulants to benefit those patients who experience dysphoria and apathy though this strategy may be problematic in substance abusers, and found that increased incidence of the neuroleptic malignant syndrome is seen when these patients are treated with high-potency neuroleptics (59).

Weddington examined the impact of seropositivity on a group of cocaine users versus seronegative controls. He found that although distress was significantly increased in the early phase of treatment, no difference in outcome was noted (60). Whereas controversy persists about HIV testing in the early stages of recovery, our experience suggests that if the need for the test is presented in a tactful, empathic manner, outcome is not affected adversely and patients do not leave treatment prematurely. According to a public health perspective, widespread testing should be strongly encouraged in these high-risk populations reasonably early in the treatment course.

In our experience, making the diagnosis of HIV or AIDS early has helped some patients to mobilize their resources and become abstinent and responsible. It creates a paradigm for the patient to recognize the need to take control of his or her own life and remain "straight" in order to live. Increased vigilance relative to the complications of the disease, and perhaps earlier treatment with zidovudine, pentamidine, and other antibiotics may be life saving in some patients. In rare cases, the diagnosis may serve to accelerate a patient's drug use and increase needle sharing and unsafe sex, thus putting others at risk (61). Psychiatric and general medical evaluation should attempt to assess patients' mood, including suicidality, and specialized treatment should be available, particularly for issues related to grief and loss. Opponents of widespread testing note these adverse reactions and decry the currently inadequate treatment systems and the bias often directed at these patients when they are identified.

TREATMENT OF INTOXICATION WITHDRAWAL AND DRUG CRAVING

As noted earlier, the agonist effects of the drugs and withdrawal symptoms may mimic a variety of psychiatric symptoms. Although it is obvious that management of these discrete sequelae are crucial to good clinical management, almost invariably the majority of patients presenting for treatment are using more than one drug. Therefore, it is imperative that the clinician take a careful history, obtain a urine or blood specimen for toxicology, and perform a physical examination. The clinician should be reasonably familiar with the pharmacology of the various drug classes so as to be able to treat presumptively patients who may be intoxicated, since some patients are unable to remember what they have taken and others are loath to reveal their drug intake. The sequelae, both sought and unwanted, and withdrawal characteristics of the nine separate classes of substances, including the barbiturates or similarly acting sedative-hypnotics, amphetamines or similarly acting sympathomimetics, opioids, cannabis, cocaine, PCP, or similarly acting arylcyclohexylamines, and the hallucinogens should be well understood (62). Corroboration of the patient's history with significant others or with previously obtained medical data often proves useful. Careful monitoring of treatment response is essential.

Alcohol

Alcohol intoxication and withdrawal syndromes can produce profound alterations in behavior and cognition (63). Although this information is covered in other chapters, an overview of these phenomena according to psychiatric perspectives may be useful. Alcohol intoxication may produce mood lability, depression, agitation, disinhibition, and impaired judgment. Alcohol withdrawal syndromes include uncomplicated alcohol withdrawal, alcohol withdrawal delirium, alcohol hallucinosis, alcohol amnestic disorder, and dementia associated with alcohol.

Withdrawal symptoms may occur between 4 and 6 hours after the last drink or as a result of a reduction in alcohol intake in chronic drinkers and peak at 48–72 hours. Symptoms may persist for days and include agitation, tremulousness, increased pulse and blood pressure, sweating, and insomnia. These symptoms may be diagnosed as anxiety states and remain untreated.

Generalized seizures may occur during withdrawal or during drinking episodes, though they usually occur between 7 and 48 hours after the last drink. A past history of seizures and photophobia can serve as predictors for possible future seizures. Hypomagnesemia, hypoglycemia, and respiratory alkalosis have been associated with these seizures.

Symptoms may subside without treatment or progress to delirium tremens, depending on the individual's state of health and history of use. Delirium tremens is marked by autonomic hyperactivity, including hyperpyrexia, fluctuation in levels of consciousness from agitation to somnolence, disorientation, and hallucinations. These symptoms may be confused with psychosis, particularly in previously diagnosed schizophrenics. Mortality rates may be significant, particularly in patients with concomitant medical illness, including infection.

The alcohol hallucinosis syndrome occurs rarely and is marked by a clear sensorium and hallucinations. These hallucinations can be visual, tactile, or auditory and may last 1–2 weeks or more after withdrawal. It is likely that the syndrome is in part a function of premorbid psychopathology.

Previously described as Wernicke's encephalopathy and Korsakoff's psychosis, the alcohol amnestic syndrome can occur with varying intensity in the chronic alcoholic. Thought to be spawned by nutritional deficiency in the context of long-term alcohol use, symptoms include paralysis of lateral gaze or nystagmus, ataxia, and confusion. Within 1–6 hours of intravenous thiamine replacement, reversal of some of these symptoms can occur. Cognitive deficits, including severe problems with short-term memory and confabulation, may persist indefinitely (64).

As discussed elsewhere in this volume, alcohol and sedative-hypnotic withdrawal symptomatology require systematic treatment with barbiturates or long-acting benzodiazepines such as chlordiazepoxide or diazepam, although short-acting benzodiazepines are used in some programs. Where liver disease is a consideration, oxazepam can be used to prevent build-up of methylated benzodiazepine metabolites produced by other drugs in this group. Vitamins (including thiamine, folacin, and multivitamins), rest, and adequate nutrition are essential.

Chronic alcohol use and dependence are associated with depression and anxiety states, due to the pharmacologic effects of the drug and the demoralization attendant to alcohol dependence and its psychosocial implications. Whereas most patients do well in conventional chemical dependency treatment programs, evidence is accumulating that antidepressants such as the tricyclics may be useful in some patients.

Disulfiram may be particularly useful in alcohol-dependent patients with psychopathology. Since relapse may result from impulsive behavior due to transient experiences of exacerbated psychotic symptoms, depressed mood, or anxiety symptoms, this medication can prove useful in dual diagnosis patients (2). When provided as a routine part of treatment, and administered during regular program contacts, disulfiram can reduce impulsive alcohol use in patients with schizophrenia, anxiety, and affective and severe personality disorders. In essence, disulfiram places patients in a situation where alcohol is perceived as unavailable and may reduce the conditioned associations between psychiatric symptoms and drug craving. The drug may also enhance the patient's sense of control. In some patients with minimal psychopathology, disulfiram can be used intermittently when they may be feeling vulnerable to relapse. Caution should be used in patients whose judgment is so impaired that they are unable to make the connection between taking the disulfiram and experiencing the severe reactions that may occur upon intake of alcohol.

Clinical experience suggests that unless patients are persistently encouraged to continue taking disulfiram, most cease taking the drug due to a loss of momentum and the feeling that they can remain abstinent without it, or due to a recurrence of alcohol craving.

Opiates

A small population of opiate addicts with psychotic or borderline characteristics abuse these drugs for their well-described antipsychotic properties. Methadone has been used in a well-controlled trial with refractory schizophrenic patients based upon these actions. Whereas acutely there is a marked diminution in psychotic symptoms, tolerance seems to occur with chronic use, although additional work is warranted (65, 66). Others self-medicate a variety of psychiatric disorders with the opiates. In most patients, in part determined by premorbid psychopathology, chronic use of these drugs produces dysphoria, depression, or anxiety. Clinical observation suggests that chronic use of the opiates may also produce character pathology that is often thought to have preceded the drug use (53). It is as if the euphoric release and the unreality induced by the opiates reinforce narcissistic or antisocial personality organization.

It is often misunderstood that the central features of narcotic withdrawal are profound anxiety or depression, although the vegetative signs such as fixed, dilated pupils, mydriasis, itching, yawning, nausea, vomiting, or diarrhea are noted most often in the literature. Though the withdrawal syndrome is often described as "flu-like" and not life-threatening, the psychiatric symptoms may be perceived as intolerable or even life-threatening and may precipitate suicidal ideation or attempts. Withdrawal may also precipitate psychotic symptoms in predisposed individuals. Detoxification with decreasing doses of methadone usually alleviates these symptoms. In treatment settings in which methadone is not available, clonidine may be used to reduce these withdrawal symptoms. Procedures are described elsewhere in this volume. Clonidine is less useful for patients with severe psychopathology, since it does not allay the full range of abstinence symptomatology, although it can be used in a supportive, well-structured setting.

Acute narcotic withdrawal is a time-limited experience, yet, the relapse rate after detoxification is high. Traditionally, it had been thought that relapse was due to the persistence of premorbid psychopathology or to the persistence of the disease of chemical dependency. Dole and others postulated that derangement of the endogenous ligand-narcotic receptor system by high-dose chronic use of exogenous opiates, perhaps via a neurohormonal feedback mechanism, may result in chronic suppression or alteration of the endogenous opioid neurotransmitter system, resulting in a profound metabolic deficit and chronic drug craving. Perhaps protracted abstinence symptoms based upon this mechanism are responsible for the remarkably high relapse rate after opiate detoxification (67). It is also possible that this metabolic derangement or neurochemical deficit produce chronic depressive or anxiety symptoms. Though this protracted abstinence syndrome is not well studied, clinical experience suggests that it is quite variable and depends on the premorbid psychopathology of the individual patient. Methadone maintenance, the most widely used treatment for opiate addicts, thus may not only allay drug craving and block or lessen the effects of administered opiates but also may represent effective treatment for debilitating psychiatric symptoms based on the hypothesized neurochemical deficit and the associated protracted abstinence syndrome.

Cocaine

Early and experimental use of cocaine is marked by feelings of euphoria, energy, and hyperalertness, though some agitation may be noted. With chronic use at high doses, agitation, anxiety, and paranoia are noted, which increase with continued use in susceptible individuals. It might be noted that any drug that induces hyperalertness, such as cocaine or the amphetamines, also leads inevitably to paranoia; in fact, hyperalertness, the inappropriate attention to outside stimuli, may be visualized as on a continuum with paranoia.

Increased use of cocaine in high doses leads to intense anxiety and paranoia in most people and psychotic symptoms in a variable percentage. The psychotomimetic effects appear to depend upon the premorbid psychopathology and personality of the user, though at high enough doses at frequent intervals, psychotic reactions appear to be inevitable. Clinical reports suggest that chronic users develop increasingly severe anxiety and paranoid reactions with continued use, often at lower doses than were necessary to precipitate these reactions at earlier stages, suggesting a process of kindling and sensitization as posited by Post (68). Continued use of cocaine with its inevitable adverse sequelae generally mandates the use of other depressant drugs such as sedative depressants, opioids, or alcohol to allay the dysphoric effects of the cocaine. Patients state that with continued cocaine use their anxiety symptoms, paranoia, and even psychotic symptoms occur at more frequent intervals and at lower cocaine doses than previously. There may be a natural history of cocaine use in some people that has not been appreciated, marked by increasing use initially, the development of adverse sequelae, and the increased use of other drugs to reduce the associated dysphoria. Subsequently, decreased use of cocaine occurs because of the side effects of anxiety and paranoia, though the alcohol or other drug use may continue or escalate. It has been noted that some patients develop chronic anxiety disorders and panic attacks, and even psychotic symptoms, that seem to persist after cessation of cocaine use. The possibility that cocaine may produce these reactions de novo in individuals with no significant premorbid psychopathology must be studied. Rounsaville et al. studied 298 cocaine abusers seeking treatment and found that 55.7% met current and 73.5% met lifetime criteria for another psychiatric disorder. They found that affective disorders usually preceded cocaine use, whereas anxiety disorders, attention deficit disorders, and antisocial personality disorders usually followed use (69).

Acutely, the symptoms of agitation and paranoia can be overwhelming and require treatment. Patients may benefit from short-term benzodiazepine treatment to reduce symptomatology. Acute psychotic symptoms, paranoia, or agitation that is clearly related to the cocaine use should be treated with benzodiazepines and supportive care. If symptoms persist beyond several days or are unmanageable, neuroleptics such as haloperidol are indicated. Treatment resistance or poorly tolerated side effects of conventional neuroleptics necessitate a trial of the atypical neuroleptics such as clozapine, risperidone, and olanzapine (36).

Cessation of the drug use may lead to depressed or anhedonic states with or without anxiety symptoms, often for protracted periods. It should be appreciated that treatment of these disorders depends upon the stage of drug use and the symptoms that are most prominent or that threaten abstinence. Whereas Gawin et al. described a specific withdrawal syndrome for cocaine, much controversy exists as to its uniformity; in the authors' experience the withdrawal symptomatology is quite variable, often not severe, and depends strongly on set and setting. Certainly, post use symptoms can include an acute "crash" marked by apathy, depression, and somnolence, and these symptoms may persist over a protracted period (70).

Despite the remarkable amount of attention and research funds devoted to the development of pharmacotherapies for cocaine use, in general, medications have not proved particularly effective. Pharmacotherapies aimed at reducing symptoms of cocaine withdrawal and craving are considered elsewhere and include use of dopamine agonists such as tricyclic antidepressants, amantadine, bromocriptine, and the anticonvulsant carbamazepine. These agents have varying effects depending on the individual and the situation. Persistent psychopathology should be treated with appropriate medication. Neuroleptics or lithium are indicated as needed. Anxiety or depression that threatens abstinence or people who have had multiple relapses should be treated with the tricyclic antidepressants, fluoxetine or carbamazepine, which may also allay the drug craving and improve treatment retention. In some patients, it has been found that dopaminergic agents can exacerbate symptoms of anxiety and paranoia, suggesting that these agents should be used with great caution.

Amphetamines

Methamphetamine abuse by smoking or insufflation has sharply increased in areas of the country. The agonist effects and sequelae of the amphetamines are similar to those of cocaine. Because of the longer duration of action and their potentially higher potency, amphetamines may be associated with more prolonged adverse effects. Agitation, anxiety, or acute psychotic episodes should be treated with benzodiazepines. Persistent psychotic reactions may require neuroleptics such as haloperidol or risperidone. When chronic amphetamine users are withdrawn from the drugs, there is often a period of profound depression, hypersomnolence, and hyperphagia. Treatment of these withdrawal symptoms generally does not require medication. Long-term users, when abstinent, often report chronically decreased energy and motivation and an inability to function. Group process and supportive psychotherapy should be instituted, although in extreme cases a trial of antidepressant medication should be considered.

Cannabis

Acute adverse effects of marihuana use can include anxiety, panic attacks, and even psychotic episodes. Anxiety and panic attacks often occur in first-time users or when cannabis is smoked in an unfamiliar setting. The characteristics of prolonged or chronic psychotic episodes precipitated by the drug cannot be distinguished from functional disorders, suggesting that these relatively rare episodes are a function of premorbid vulnerability. It is probable, though not documented, that cannabis and other psychedelic or hallucinogenic drugs such as LSD or PCP may have precipitated chronic psychotic states that would not have occurred otherwise (71, 72). Treatment of the acute episodes includes reassurance in a safe, supportive environment, with constant reminders that the effects are drug related. Benzodiazepines may be indicated in severe cases. Prolonged psychotic reactions should be treated similarly to functional psychotic episodes with neuroleptics.

It has been well documented that in schizophrenic patients, marihuana use is a significant determinant of general noncompliance with medical regimens, failure to take prescribed medication, and increased severity of psychotic symptoms. The drug has been associated with a return to the hospital in a large number of patients. As noted earlier, the drug may be used by severely ill patients to distance themselves from painful symptoms or perceptions and to achieve a measure of control over these symptoms even if they worsen predictably. It has been used to reduce the feeling of deadness or emptiness patients describe that is associated with schizophrenia, particularly the negative symptoms, and with neuroleptic treatment. If possible, schizophrenic patients should be concretely and tactfully helped to understand the adverse effects of marihuana that they, in particular, are likely to experience, and they should be helped to develop alternative means to add joy or meaning to their lives. Groups are indicated for those who can tolerate them, and procedures should be in place to help patients to make use of 12-step meetings (72).

The so-called amotivational syndrome associated with chronic cannabis use has been described in the Middle East, the Orient, and the United States. This syndrome is characterized by apathy, diminished interest in activities and goals, and an inability to master new challenges (73). The syndrome has been used to explain poor job performance, deterioration in school, and unconventional prioritization, such as adolescents focusing intense concentration on a particular rock group instead of school. It has been postulated that the amotivational syndrome might better be termed *aberrant motivational syndrome* and is a product of the complex interactions among drug pharmacology and social and psychological factors. The impact of the drug's pharmacology on motivation and performance varies remarkably according to individual personality patterns and the social milieu. It has been difficult to distinguish drug effects from the influence of set and setting. A variety of studies have shown that heavy use of cannabis is associated with reduced function of the attentional executive system, decreased mental flexibility, and increased perseveration (74). Reduced memory function has been described but this deficit may be related to impaired concentration. In some users, cannabis clearly causes decreased motivation, significant difficulty in adapting to intellectual and interpersonal tasks, and decreased energy levels. It should be appreciated that in some young people the drug may profoundly derail them from accomplishing the tasks of living and growth and may be associated with depression, anxiety, and demoralization.

Programs based upon the Twelve Steps are useful for some of these young people. Many others are reluctant to involve themselves in these programs; they are repelled by the language and mores of these fellowships. In fact, it may not be appropriate to insist that a 15-year-old girl identify herself as having the disease of chemical dependency and plan to remain abstinent from alcohol or other drugs for the rest of her life. In young people, the drug use and dependence may be situational and time limited, and, with time and support, they can be expected to distance themselves from drugs. Supportive psychotherapy and identification with a healthy and/or recovering group has been useful. Ancillary services such as tutoring, educational and vocational counseling may be critical to the process of helping these people get back on track.

Hallucinogens

The terms *hallucinogen* or *psychedelic* are used to describe approximately a dozen naturally occurring and about a hundred synthetic compounds that induce alterations in perception, emotion, or cognition. These are primarily derivatives of indoles or phenylalkylamines and include LSD, psilocybin, peyote, PCP, and ketamine (75).

Whereas this class of drugs induces perceptual distortions, frank hallucinations are uncommon. As with cannabis, these drugs acutely may produce anxiety, panic, paranoia, and, rarely, psychotic symptoms, depending in part on premorbid psychopathology and the setting in which the drugs are taken. Treatment requires supportive, calm reassurance in a safe atmosphere. Benzodiazepines are indicated in situations marked by intense anxiety. Acute psychotic or anxiety reactions induced by PCP should also be noted with supportive reassurance and medication when necessary. The much-abused sensory deprivation should be reserved for situations marked by neuromuscular hyperactivity and disorientation. Prolonged psychotic reactions are indistinguishable from functional psychotic states and should be treated as such. It is likely that these chronic states are a function of premorbid psychopathology. It is not known whether chronic psychotic states can be precipitated de novo in individuals without a premorbid vulnerability.

In some patients, low-level psychotic symptoms persist, including perceptual distortions such as "trailing," depersonalization, and derealization. Reassurance, a trial of benzodiazepines and, if necessary, low-dose neuroleptics may be indicated in these patients. Confrontational techniques such as those associated with particular therapeutic modalities are not indicated and may exacerbate the symptomatology.

ATTITUDES OF THE TREATMENT TEAM

Patients with coexisting psychopathology and substance abuse or dependence often are considered untreatable, inappropriate for most treatment programs, and not worth the efforts of the treatment team since they seem to be unwilling to help themselves. These attitudes on the part of therapists may be a serious obstacle to the painstaking treatment process that is often required to effect improvement in psychiatric symptomatology and abstinence from the drugs of abuse. According to psychiatric perspectives, the feelings that the therapist or the treatment team develop toward these patients are termed *countertransference* and are believed to be an inevitable result of the therapist's past experiences or current feelings. In treating this group of patients, these countertransferential reactions must be well understood and perhaps discussed so that, rather than being an obstacle to treatment, they may be used to enhance the treatment process. Similarly, the transferential reactions of the patients (their thoughts and feelings based upon previous experiences) to the program or to the therapist must be appreciated and become an integral part of the treatment process.

Patients often do well early on, abetting the therapist's sense of effectiveness and validity; the almost inevitable relapses that occur may change these emotions to feelings of hopelessness and even anger. Well-trained counselors or therapists given adequate supervision may be able to anticipate and understand these reactions and use them for the benefit of the patient (76).

For example, chronic relapses may reinforce the therapist's feelings of impotence and lack of control. A well-trained treatment team must be sensitive to these feelings and reinforce the energy and commitment of each member of the group. Extensive training with respect to these issues, although often rare in drug abuse treatment programs, is essential to prevent the feelings of negativity or "burnout" that are so common in front-line counselors. Counselors in drug treatment programs are often well-meaning, caring individuals who take the failures of their patients personally and, with time, often develop hostile and unsympathetic attitudes to protect themselves. It is often as if extensive training, although not providing particularly powerful therapeutic interventions, aids the counselor to understand that although the patient is not doing so well, the therapist's own incompetence or inadequacy is not the cause.

Patients, no matter how psychiatrically disabled, often deny the existence or the extent of drug use for weeks or months while the therapist is laboring under the belief that the treatment is going well. When the drug use is discovered, it is not unusual for the therapist or the counselor to become angry and punitive towards the patient (76a). It should be understood that despite the therapist's most intensive efforts and appropriate organizational structuring, patients must bear important responsibilities for their own recovery. Dual diagnosis patients often seem to be unable to accept this responsibility, though when given adequate support, they are often able to demonstrate significant improvement.

It is not unusual for therapists to identify with their patients' lack of discipline or control and even unconsciously encourage the perceived Dionysian lifestyle of the clients. This tendency to encourage drug use and antisocial behaviors must be well understood and controlled (76).

RATIONALIZATION

As noted previously, patients and families and even rehabilitation counselors often minimize psychopathology and focus attention on drug use to explain all problems. Performance and behavioral problems are reduced to the issue of chemical dependency. This frequently occurs in disturbed young people who involve themselves heavily in the drug abuse subculture: "I'm not crazy, I'm a pothead" or "I'm a coke freak." Many patients prefer to view themselves as drug addicts rather than as mentally ill; there is more honor in drug dependence than in psychiatric disorders for many people. Programs informed by chemical dependency models that utilize 12-step programs often encourage this tendency to deny or reduce psychopathology and attribute symptoms to the disease of chemical dependency. Patients and families are more willing to accept this formulation as well. Collusion among patients, families, and even treatment programs can result in the minimization of psychopathology such that patients remain untreated and vulnerable to relapse.

Interestingly, this process also works in a reverse manner for the patient and family demoralized by drug treatment failures and relapse. By rationalizing, they seek to emphasize the possibility that psychopathology is the primary etiologic factor, which, if treated, may reduce or eliminate the drug use and dependence. This is well-illustrated by Drake, who studied alcoholic schizophrenics and found that their alcohol disorders were missed approximately 75% of the time during hospitalization (77). These patients and their families often are unwilling to accept referral to a chemical dependency treatment program and seek psychiatric care that may not sufficiently address the problem.

TREATMENT OUTCOME

Treatment outcome studies have recently attempted to characterize factors associated with prolonged abstinence. Studies have measured length of stay, treatment modality, and personality traits to length of abstinence in various populations. Conclusions generally confirm that longer lengths of stay (78, 79), intense treatment models such as community residential care programs (80, 81), personal resources such as coping skills (82), family support, higher levels of education, likability, and ability to relate improve outcome.

Evidence suggests that the particular diagnosis is less important in predicting outcome than the severity of the symptoms and the related disability.

In recent years, in part determined by the necessity for third-party payers, an increased number of studies reporting on the outcome of systematic treatment of drug users with psychopathology have been done. Adequate outcome studies are difficult to do because of the varying definitions of outcome, the difficulty of following these patients and the significant expense. Current treatment strategies continue to be based primarily on clinical experience though outcome studies are beginning to have an impact on clinical practice.

Dropout rates from substance abuse treatment programs vary considerably depending on the characteristics of the patient as well as of the program, though rates of 50% or more are commonly reported (83, 84). Premature withdrawal from treatment is a critical issue since data from a number of sources have demonstrated that the longer a patient remains in treatment, in essence the duration of the treatment dose, the more likely he or she will do well. Whereas prior history of criminal activity, socioeconomic factors, or history of previous treatment has not been shown to identify patients more or less likely to drop out, increased severity of drug and alcohol use, particularly drug use that occurs immediately prior to drug treatment, has been shown to increase the likelihood of premature termination (85). Comorbid psychopathology has also been shown to increase the likelihood of dropout though the evidence is conflictual (33, 86). Little and Robinson (87) reported that personality disorders and elevated psychopathic deviant scores on the Minnesota Multiphasic Personality Inventory, MMPI, were more common in dropouts than in treatment completers. The attempt to use psychometric assessment instruments to preemptively identify on entry those patients more likely to drop out has not been able to distinguish treatment completers from dropouts on a consistent basis (84).

Factors that anecdotally appear to affect treatment outcome favorably are the presence of family support, higher levels of education, likability, and ability to relate to others. Evidence suggests that the particular diagnosis is less important in predicting outcome than the severity of the symptoms and the related disability.

CONCLUSION

In view of the remarkable prevalence and complex relationships between drug abuse and dependence and psychopathology, much work remains to be done. Innovative treatment models with particular groups of patients must be developed and evaluated. Which patients do well in which treatment programs and what are the effective and essential elements in the treatment of dual diagnosis patients remain questions that we must attempt to answer. At the same time, the study of the interaction of the drugs of abuse with people of diverse psychological characteristics is fascinating and promises to shed light on both the addictive processes and the nature of psychopathology. Finally, we should appreciate that effective treatments, appropriately delivered, can effect remarkable change in the lives of these severely disabled people.

References

1. Sciacca K. An integrated treatment approach for the severely mentally ill individuals with substance disorders. New directions for mental health services. San Francisco: Jossey-Bass, 1991:50.
2. Lehman AF, Myers CP, Corty EC. Assessment and classification of patients with psychiatric and substance abuse syndromes. Hosp Community Psychiatry 1989;40:1019–1030.
3. Lehman AF, Myers CP, Corty EC, Thompson JW. Prevalence and patterns of "dual diagnosis" among psychiatric inpatients. Compr Psychiatry 1994;35(2):106–112.
4. McLellan AT, Luborsky L, Woody GE, O'Brien CP, Druley KA. Predicting response to alcohol and drug abuse treatments. Arch Gen Psychiatry 1983;40:620–625.

5. Case N. The dual diagnosis patient in a psychiatric day treatment program: a treatment failure. J Subst Abuse Treat 1991;8:69–73.
6. Miller NS, Millman RB, Keskinen BA. Outcome at six to twelve month post inpatient treatment for cocaine and alcohol dependence. Adv Alcohol Subst Abuse 1990;9:101–119.
7. Zweben JE. Recovery-oriented psychotherapy: facilitating the use of 12 step programs. J Psychoactive Drugs 1987;19:243–251.
8. Millman RB. Considerations on the psychotherapy of the substance abuser. J Subst Abuse Treat 1986;3:103–109.
9. Helzer JE, Pryzbeck TR. The co-occurrence of alcoholism with other psychiatric disorders in the general population and its impact in treatment. J Stud Alcohol 1988;49:219–224.
10. Kessler RC, McGonagle KA, Zhao S, et al. Lifetime and 12-month prevalence of DSM-III-R

psychiatric disorders in the United States: results from the National Comorbidity Survey. Arch Gen Psychiatry 1994;51:8–19.
11. Hesselbrock MN, Meyer RE, Keener JJ. Psychopathology in hospitalized alcoholics. Arch Gen Psychiatry 1985;42:1050–1055.
12. Schuckit MA. The clinical implications of alcoholism and affective disorder. Arch Gen Psychiatry 1985;42:1081–1086.
13. Deleted in proof.
14. Kleinman PH, Miller AB, Millman RB, et al. Psychopathology among cocaine abusers entering treatment. J Nerv Ment Dis 1990;178:442–447.
15. Rounsaville B, Weissman M, Kleber H, et al. Heterogeneity of psychiatric diagnosis in treated opiate addicts. Arch Gen Psychiatry 1982;39:161–166.
16. Rounsaville BJ, Kleber HD. Inherited opiate ad-

dicts: how do they differ from those seeking treatment? Arch Gen Psychiatry 1985;42:1072–1077.

17. Humphreys K, Moos RH, Hamilton FG. Psychiatric services in VA substance abuse programs. Psychiatr Serv 1996;47:1203.

18. Ford J, Hillard JR, Giesler LJ, Lassen KL, Thomas H. Substance abuse/mental illness; diagnostic issues. Am J Drug Alcohol Abuse 1989;15:297–308.

19. Gerstley LJ, Alterman AI, McLellan AT, Woody GE. Antisocial personality disorders in patients with substance abuse disorders: a problematic diagnosis. Am J Psychiatry 1990;147:173–178.

20. Cleckley HM. The mask of sanity. St. Louis: CV Mosby, 1941.

21. Nace EP, Davis CW, Gaspari JP. Axis II comorbidity in substance abusers. Am J Psychiatry 1991;148:118–120.

22. Osher FL, Kofoed L. Treatment of patients with psychiatric and psychoactive substance abuse disorders. Hosp Community Psychiatry 1989; 40:1025–1030.

23. Minkoff K. An integrated treatment model for dual diagnosis of psychosis and addiction. Hosp Community Psychiatry 1989;40:1031–1036.

24. Crowe DB, Rosse RB, Sheridan MJ, Deutsch SI. Substance use diagnoses and discharge patterns among psychiatric inpatients. Hosp Community Psychiatry 1991;42:403–405.

25. Schuckit MA. The clinical implications of primary diagnostic groups among alcoholics. Arch Gen Psychiatry 1985;42:1043–1049.

26. Schuckit MA. Evaluating the dual diagnosis patient. Drug Abuse Alcohol Newsletter 1988; 17:1–4.

27. Des Jarlais DC, Friedman S. HIV infection among intravenous drug users: epidemiology and risk reduction. AIDS 1987;1:67–76.

28. Rounsaville BJ, Weissman MM, Wilbur EH, Kleber HD. Identifying alcoholism in treated opiate addicts. Am J Psychiatry 1983;140(6): 764–766.

29. McLellan AT, Luborsky L, O'Brien CP, et al. An improved diagnostic instrument for substance abuse patients: the Addiction Severity Index. J Nerv Ment Dis 1980;168:26–33.

30. Millman RB. Evaluation and clinical management of cocaine abusers. J Clin Psychiatry 1988; 49(suppl 2):27–33.

30a. Bell CM, Khantzian EJ. Contemporary psychodynamic perspectives and the disease concept of addiction: complementary or competing models? Psychiatr Ann 1991;21:273–281.

31. Senay EC. Diagnostic interview and mental status examination. In: Lowinson JH, Ruiz P, Millman RB, Langrod JG, eds. Substance abuse: a comprehensive textbook. 2nd edition. Baltimore: Williams & Wilkins, 1992.

32. Mondersheid RW, Henderson MJ. Federal and state legislative and program directors for managed care: implications for case management. Rockville, MD: Medical Center for Mental Health Services, Division of State and Community Systems Development, October 1995.

33. Rohren JE, Vaughan MS, Codoret RJ, Carswell C, Patterson A, Zwick J. Effect of centralized intake on outcomes of substance abuse treatment. Psychiatr Serv 1996;47:1233–1238.

34. Woody GE, McLellan AT, O'Brien CP, Luborsky L. Addressing psychiatric comorbidity. NIDA Res Monogr 1991;106:152–166.

35. Ross HE, Glaser FB, Germanson T. The prevalence of psychiatric disorders in patients with alcohol and other drug problems. Arch Gen Psychiatry 1988;45:1023–1031.

36. Van Patten T, Mander SR, Mintz J, et al. Haloperidol plasma levels and clinical response: a therapeutic window relationship. Am J Psychiatry 1992;149:500–505.

37. Kolakowska T, Williams AO, Ardan M, et al. Schizophrenia with good and poor outcome. I: Early clinical features, response to neuroleptics and signs of organic dysfunction. Br J Psychiatry 1985;146:229–239.

38. Millman RB. The provision of opioid therapy to the mentally ill; conceptual and practical considerations. In: Verebey K, ed. Opioids in mental illness: theories, clinical observations and treatment possibilities. New York: New York Academy of Sciences, 1982:178–185.

38a. Castaneda R, Galanter M, Lifshutz H, France H. Effect of drugs of abuse on psychiatric symptoms among hospitalized schizophrenics. Am J Alcohol Abuse 1991;17:313–336.

38b. Vardy MM, Kay SR. LSD psychosis or LSD-induced schizophrenia? A multimethod inquiry. Arch Gen Psychiatry 1983;40:877–883.

39. Greenberg R. The patient with cardiovascular disease. In: Jarvik L, ed. Treatments of psychiatric disorders. Washington, DC: American Psychiatric Association, 1989:913–914.

40. Gawin FH, Kleber HD. Pharmacologic treatment of cocaine abuse. Psychiatr Clinic North Am 1986;9(suppl 3):573–583.

41. Linnoila MI. Anxiety and alcoholism. J Clin Psychiatry 1989;50(suppl 11):26–29.

42. Vaillant G. The national history of alcoholism. Cambridge, MA: Harvard University Press, 1983.

43. Quitkin FM, Rifkin A, Kaplan J, et al. Phobic anxiety syndrome complicated by drug dependence and relevance. Br J Psychiatry 1979; 135:565–573.

44. Kranzler HR, Liebowitz NR. Anxiety and depression in substance abuse: clinical implications. Med Clin North Am 1988;72:867–885.

45. Kushner MG, Sher KJ, Beitman BD. The relationship between alcohol problems and the anxiety disorders. Am J Psychiatry 1990;147: 685–694.

46. Szuster RR, Pontius EB, Campos PE. Marijuana, sensitivity and panic anxiety. J Clin Psychiatry 1988;49:427–429.

47. Johannessen DJ, Cowley DS, Walker RD, Jensen CF, Parker LP. Prevalence, onset and clinical recognition of panic states in hospitalized male alcoholics. Am J Psychiatry 1989; 146:1201–1203.

48. Martin WR, Jasinki DR. Physiological parameters of morphine dependence in man—tolerance, early abstinence, protracted abstinence. J Psychiatr Res 1969;7:9–17.

49. Galanter M. Office management of the substance abuser: the use of learning theory and social networks. In: Lowinson JH, Ruiz P, Millman RB, Langrod JG, eds. Substance abuse: a comprehensive textbook. 2nd edition. Baltimore: Williams & Wilkins, 1992.

50. Roth M. Anxiety disorders and the use and abuse of drugs. J Clin Psychiatry 1989;50(suppl 11):30–42.

51. Grande TP, Wolf AW, Schubert DS, Patterson MB, Brocco K. Associations among alcoholism, drug abuse and antisocial personality: a review of literature. Psychol Rep 1984;55:455–474.

52. McLellan AT, Woody GE, O'Brien CP. Development of psychiatric illness in drug abusers. N Engl J Med 1979;301:1310–1314.

53. Zinberg NE. Addiction and ego function. In: Eissler RS, Freud A, Kris M, Solnit AJ, eds. The psychoanalytic study of the child. New Haven, CT: Yale University Press, 1975.

54. Bean-Bayog M. Psychopathology produced by alcoholism. In: Meyer RE, ed. Psychopathology and addictive disorders. New York: Guilford Press, 1986:334–345.

55. Dulit RA, Fyer MR, Haas GL, Sullivan T, Frances AJ. Substance use in borderline personality disorder. Psychiatry 1990;147:1002–1004.

56. Mirin SM, Weiss RD. Substance abuse and mental illness. In: Frances RJ, Miller SI, eds. Clinical textbook of addictive disorders. New York: Guilford Press, 1991:271–298.

57. Batki SL. Drug abuse, psychiatric disorders and AIDS, dual and triple diagnosis. West J Med 1990;152:547–552.

58. Smith D. The role of substance abuse professionals in the AIDS epidemic. Adv Alcohol Subst Abuse 1989;7:175–195.

59. Perry S, Jacobson P. Neuropsychiatric manifestations of AIDS-spectrum disorders. Hosp Community Psychiatry 1986;37:135–142.

60. Weddington WW, Haertzen CA, Hess JM, Brown BS. Psychologic reactions and retention by cocaine addicts during treatment according to HIV-serostatus: a matched control study. Am J Drug Alcohol Abuse 1991;17:355–368.

61. Rothenberg R, Woefel M, Stoneburner R, Milberg J, Parker R, Truman B. Survival with the acquired immunodeficiency syndrome. N Engl J Med 1987;317:1297–1302.

62. Millman RB. General principles of diagnosis and treatment. In: American Psychiatric Association annual review. Washington, DC: American Psychiatric Press, 1985:122–211.

63. Schuckit MA. Goals of treatment. In: Treatments of psychiatric disorders, section 12. Washington, DC: American Psychiatric Association, 1989:1072–1075.

64. Nace EP, Isbell PG. Alcohol. In: Frances RJ, Miller SI, eds. Clinical textbook of addictive disorders. New York: Guilford Press, 1991: 43–68.

65. Millman RB. The provision of opioid therapy to the mentally ill: conceptual and practical considerations. In: Verebey K, ed. Opioids in mental illness: theories, clinical observations, and treatment possibilities. New York: New York Academy of Sciences, 1982:178–185.

66. Brizer DA, Hartman N, Sweeney J, Millman RB. Effects of methadone plus neuroleptics in treatment-resistant chronic paranoid schizophrenia. Am J Psychiatry 1985;142(9):1106–1107.

67. Dole VP. Implications of methadone maintenance for theories of narcotic addiction. JAMA 1988;260:3025–3029.

68. Post RM, Kopanda RT. Cocaine, kindling, and psychosis. Am J Psychiatry 1976;133:627–634.

69. Rounsaville BJ, Anton SF, Carroll K, Budde D, Prusoff BA, Gawin F. Psychiatric diagnoses of treatment-seeking cocaine abusers. Arch Gen Psychiatry 1991;48:43–51.

70. Gawin FH, Kleber HD. Abstinence symptomatology and psychiatric diagnosis in cocaine abusers. Arch Gen Psychiatry 1986;43:107–113.

71. Millman RB, Sbriglio R. Patterns of use and psychopathology in chronic marijuana users. Psychiatr Clin North Am 1986;9:533–545.

72. Millman RB. Cannabis abuse and dependence. In: American Psychiatric Association Task Force on treatments of psychiatric disorders. Washington, DC: American Psychiatric Association, 1989;2:1241–1260.

73. Grinspoon L, Bakalar JB. Marihuana. In: Lowinson JL, Ruiz P, eds. Substance abuse: clinical problems and perspectives. Baltimore: Williams & Wilkins, 1981.

74. Pope HG Jr, Yurgelun-Todd DA. The residual cognitive effects of heavy marijuana use in college students. JAMA 1996;275(7):521–527.
75. Weiss CJ, Millman RB. Hallucinogens, phencyclidine, marijuana, inhalants. In: Frances RJ, Miller SI, eds. Clinical textbook of addictive disorders. New York: Guilford Press, 1991: 146–170.
76. Imhof JE. Countertransference issues in alcoholism and drug addition. Psychiatr Ann 1991; 21:292–296.
76a. Imhof J, Hirsch R, Terenzi RE. Countertransferential and attitudinal considerations in the treatment of drug abuse and addiction. Int J Addict 1983;18:491–510.
77. Drake RE. Psychiatric patients have high rate of concurrent addictive disorders. Psychiatric Times 1990(May):18–19.
78. Charuvastra VC, Dalali, ID, Cassuci M, Ling W. Outcome study: comparison of short-term vs long-term treatment in a residential community. Int J Addict 1992;27(1):15–23.
79. Bleiberg JL, Devlin P, Croan J, Briscoe R. Relationship between treatment length and outcome in a therapeutic community. Int J Addict 1994; 29(6):729–740.
80. Moos RH, Pettit B, Gruber V. Characteristics and outcomes of three models of community residential care for abuse patients. J Subst Abuse 1995;7(1):99–116.
81. Moos RH. Why do some people recover from alcohol dependence, whereas others continue to drink and become worse over time. Addiction 1994;89(1):31–34.
82. Moos RH, Pettit B, Gruber V. Longer episodes of community residential care reduce substance abuse patients' readmission rates. J Stud Alcohol 1995;56(4):433–443.
83. Bakelund F, Lundwoll L. Dropping out of treatment: an annual review. Psychol Bull 1975; 82:738–783.
84. Stark MJ. Dropping out of substance abuse treatment: a clinically oriented review. Clin Psychol Rev 1992;12:93–116.
85. Stark MJ, Campbell BK. Personality, drug use, and early attrition from substance abuse treatment. Am J Drug Alcohol Abuse 1988;14:475–485.
86. Jerrell JM, Ridgley MS. Evaluating images in symptoms and functioning of dually diagnosed clients in specialized treatment. Psychiatr Serv 1995;46:233–235.
87. Little GL, Robinson KD. One-day dropouts from correctional drug treatment. II. Psychol Rep 1987;60(2):454.

57 ACUTE AND CHRONIC PAIN

Russell K. Portenoy and Richard Payne

An interesting paradox can be discerned in the perception of opioid compounds by various sectors of the medical community: some consider these drugs to be a major cause of abuse, associated with dire consequences to the individual and society at large, whereas others view them as essential medications, capable of mediating one of the highest goals of medicine, the relief of pain and suffering. Generally, specialists in addiction focus on the former characterization and pain specialists project the latter. Given the antithetical nature of these perspectives, it is not surprising that historically there has been little communication between these two groups.

The lack of interaction between pain and addiction specialists in the past is unfortunate, since the knowledge gained by each could enhance the other's ability to apprehend clinical phenomena and formulate questions for research. The potential for opioid addiction is a constant consideration in the management of acute and chronic pain, but most clinicians have little understanding of the criteria that define this outcome or the factors that may contribute to it. Conversely, specialists in addiction have developed the terminology of dependence and discuss the attendant risks, but they usually fail to address the impact of this potential in patients treated with analgesics for painful medical disease.

This chapter brings together these two perspectives through an examination of the issues raised by each of two situations commonly encountered in clinical practice: the management of pain in patients with a history of opioid abuse, and the risk of opioid abuse in patients with no such history who are administered opioid drugs for medical purposes. Throughout, an effort is made to balance the clinical imperative to provide adequate relief of pain with legitimate concerns about the consequences of opioid abuse. Opioids are the focus of this discussion because they have a unique position as both major analgesics and drugs of abuse, and thereby encourage a comprehensive examination of the issues. It should be noted, however, that many of the topics explored herein apply equally to other drug classes, such as the benzodiazepines (1, 2).

TERMINOLOGY OF ABUSE AND CLASSIFICATION OF SUBSTANCE ABUSERS

The relationship between the medical use and abuse of opioid drugs cannot be clarified without a precise characterization of terms, including *tolerance, dependence, abuse,* and *addiction.* The application of inappropriate definitions, such as the use of the term *addict* to describe patients who are physically dependent, unnecessarily stigmatizes the patient and may have adverse effects on the therapy. Conversely, lack of clarity about those characteristics that truly constitute addiction may delay recognition of the syndrome when it does occur in the clinical setting.

Terminology of Abuse

The terminology of substance abuse, as discussed elsewhere in this volume, has been developed by specialists in addiction, whose frame of reference is the addict rather than the medical patient receiving opioids for pain. It is necessary to clarify this terminology when applying it to the assessment of medical patients (3, 4).

TOLERANCE

Tolerance is a pharmacologic property of opioid drugs defined by the need for increasing doses to maintain effects (5–7). Tolerance to virtually all opioid effects can be induced reliably in animal models (8), and it is commonly believed that tolerance develops similarly during long-term exposure to opioids in humans (9). Indeed, loss of analgesic efficacy due to the development of tolerance typically is perceived to be a major impediment to the clinical use of opioid drugs. The development of tolerance to the reinforcing effects of opioids, and the consequent need to increase doses to regain these effects, has also been speculated to be an important element in the pathogenesis of addiction, notwithstanding the generally accepted belief that tolerance may or may not exist in the addicted patient (10).

There is a compelling need to reevaluate the concept of tolerance as it pertains to the long-term use of opioid drugs for patients with chronic pain (11, 12). The view that tolerance to analgesic effects routinely interferes with the clinical efficacy of opioids is not credible given numerous surveys that demonstrated relatively stable dose requirements for prolonged periods in diverse populations. In the cancer population, for example, the need for dose escalation typically occurs only in the setting of a progressive, painful lesion (13–17). Likewise, cancer patients who self-administer morphine for several weeks to control mucositis pain following bone marrow transplantation do not increase the dose after an initial rapid titration (18). Surveys of patients with nonmalignant pain treated with opioids for prolonged periods also fail to demonstrate the need for increasing doses to maintain effects (19–24). Despite the demonstrable development of tolerance to some of the side effects of the opioids, such as cognitive impairment (25), tolerance to the favorable clinical effects of these drugs seldom compromises the efficacy of treatment.

PHYSICAL DEPENDENCE

Similar to tolerance, physical dependence is a pharmacologic property of opioid drugs. It is defined solely by the occurrence of an abstinence syndrome (withdrawal) following abrupt dose reduction or administration of an antagonist (5–7, 26). Because some degree of physical dependence can be produced with very little opioid exposure (27), and neither the dose nor duration of administration required to produce clinically significant physical dependence in humans is known, most practitioners assume that the potential for an abstinence syndrome exists after opioids have been administered repeatedly for only a few days.

There is great confusion among clinicians about the differences between physical dependence and addiction. This continues despite the widespread acceptance among addiction specialists of the critical distinctions between these phenomena. Although physical dependence, like tolerance, has been suggested to be a component of addiction (28, 29), and the avoidance of withdrawal (the sine qua non of physical dependence) has been postulated to create behavioral contingencies that reinforce drug-seeking behavior (30), most experts define addiction in a manner that fully distinguishes it from physical dependence (6, 31, 32). Physical dependence alone does not preclude the uncomplicated discontinuation of opioids in the medical setting, as amply demonstrated by the success of opioid detoxification by multidisciplinary pain programs (33) and the routine cessation of opioids in cancer patients who become fully analgesic following a pain-relieving neurolytic procedure. Indirect evidence for this distinction between physical dependence and addiction is even provided by animal models of opioid self-administration, which have demonstrated that persistent drug-taking behavior can be maintained in the absence of physical dependence (34).

Use of the term *addiction* to describe patients who are merely physically dependent reinforces the stigma associated with opioid therapy and should be abandoned. If the clinician wishes to describe a patient who is believed to have the capacity for abstinence, the term physical dependence must be used. Labeling the patient as *dependent* also should be discouraged, since it fosters confusion between physical dependence and psychological dependence. The latter is an accepted component of the addiction syndrome (as described later in this chapter) and is unrelated to the occurrence of physical dependence. For the same reason, use of the term *habituation* should be eschewed; in the clinical setting, this term is often used indiscriminately to refer to tolerance, physical dependence, or psychological dependence.

ADDICTION

Current definitions applied to the assessment of addiction, which have been developed by addiction specialists, characterize it as a psychological and behavioral syndrome in which there is drug craving, compulsive use, and a strong tendency to relapse after withdrawal (6, 10, 29, 30). In addition to craving, the psychological component, or psychological dependence, often involves rumination about the drug and an intense desire to secure its supply. Compulsive use, as it is observed in the addict population, is indicated by persistent or escalating consumption of the drug despite physical, psychological, or social harm to the user. The latter behavior has also been used to define *abuse* (28), a term that has been applied additionally to any drug use that is outside accepted societal and cultural standards (6).

Thus, there is substantial, but not complete, overlap between the terms *addiction* and *abuse*. An individual who uses an illicit drug could be considered an abuser even if the compulsive quality of use that characterizes the addict is absent; similarly, an individual could be psychologically dependent on a licit drug, such as a prescription opioid, but theoretically have enough controls established that abuse behaviors do not occur. These considerations may be important in assessing the medical patient who receives opioids for pain.

As discussed, the foregoing definitions have been developed by experts in addiction whose frame of reference is the individual who develops addiction outside of the medical context and has no disease for which the drug or drugs may be indicated. This nomenclature must be interpreted cautiously when applied to patients who are seeking a legitimate therapy for pain. For example, a reference to "relapse after withdrawal" (6) may be difficult to interpret if the drug is prescribed for a medical indication, and reference to tolerance and physical dependence (29), which are expected phenomena when opioids are medically administered for prolonged periods, have no relevance to clinical populations.

According to a task force of the American Medical Association, addiction is a chronic disorder characterized by "the compulsive use of a substance resulting in physical, psychological or social harm to the user and continued use despite that harm." (31). This definition focuses on the quality and consequences of drug-taking, is sufficiently broad to be applied to patients who develop addiction while receiving a licit opioid drug for a painful medical condition, and avoids the inappropriate inclusion of phenomena related to tolerance and physical dependence. Like other definitions, it emphasizes that addiction is a psychological and behavioral syndrome that is characterized fundamentally by (a) loss of control over drug use, (b) compulsive drug use, and (c) continued use despite harm.

This type of definition is appropriate, but has limited clinical utility unless operationalized for a clinical setting, in which patients with painful disorders are prescribed an opioid for an appropriate indication. To do so, a concept that may be labeled "aberrant drug-related behavior" is needed. Patients who receive an opioid for legitimate medical purposes have the potential to engage in a broad range of behaviors that are conventionally perceived by prescribers as problematic (Table 57.1). The routine evaluation of patients who receive opioids or other potentially abusable drugs must include monitoring for the development of these behaviors. Should they occur, the assessment must yield information that would support a specific diagnosis and facilitate an appropriate therapeutic response.

Aberrant drug-related behaviors in the clinical setting have a "differential diagnosis." In some cases, the behaviors are sufficiently extreme (for example, injection of an oral formulation) to immediately suggest the diagnosis of an addiction disorder. In other cases, however, the behaviors are less egregious and could reflect other processes, including impulsive behavior driven by unrelieved pain, a psychiatric disorder other than an addiction, or mild encephalopathy with confusion about drug intake. Occasionally, aberrant behaviors indicate criminal intent.

The importance of this differential diagnosis for aberrant drug-related behavior has been highlighted in the population with cancer pain through acceptance of the term, "pseudoaddiction" (35). Pseudoaddiction refers to the drug-seeking behavior that is occasionally observed in the setting of uncontrolled cancer pain and disappears when analgesic interventions, often including increased doses of an opioid, become effective. Clinical experience

---

Table 57.1   Aberrant Drug-Related Behaviors

Behaviors More Suggestive of an Addiction Disorder
Selling prescription drugs
Prescription forgery
Stealing or "borrowing" drugs from others
Injecting oral formulations
Obtaining prescription drugs from nonmedical sources
Concurrent abuse of alcohol or illicit drugs
Multiple dose escalations or other noncompliance with therapy despite warnings
Multiple episodes of prescription "loss"
Repeatedly seeking prescriptions from other clinicians or from emergency rooms without informing prescriber or after warnings to desist
Evidence of deterioration in the ability to function at work, in the family, or socially that appear to be related to drug use
Repeated resistance to changes in therapy despite clear evidence of adverse physical or psychological effects from the drug

Behaviors Less Suggestive of an Addiction Disorder
Aggressive complaining about the need for more drug
Drug hoarding during periods of reduced symptoms
Requesting specific drugs
Openly acquiring similar drugs from other medical sources
Unsanctioned dose escalation or other noncompliance with therapy on one or two occasions
Unapproved use of the drug to treat another symptom
Reporting psychic effects not intended by the clinician
Resistance to a change in therapy associated with "tolerable" adverse effects with expressions of anxiety related to the return of severe symptoms

indicates that similar dynamics are sometimes encountered in populations with nonmalignant disease. Clearly, the diagnosis of addiction is not tenable if pain control eliminates behaviors that would otherwise be considered to reflect loss of control, compulsive use, and continued use despite harm.

The extraordinary heterogeneity of the population with painful disorders that presents to physicians further complicates the assessment of the individual's degree of control over drug use, and the pattern and consequences of this use. The clinician must recognize that some addicts without pain may feign illness to obtain drugs for diversion or personal use (36), and some with a bona fide medical illness seek opioids or other drugs primarily for their psychic effects. In contrast, some patients engage in behaviors that would be strong evidence of addiction in the absence of the painful disorder, but are best understood as an alternative process in the context of the disease and the psychosocial condition of the individual.

Thus, the assessment of addiction in the setting of opioid treatment for a painful disorder requires a detailed understanding of the drug-related behaviors, pain syndrome, medical and psychological status, social situation, and true impediments to adequate relief. If the patient engages in behaviors that could be fairly labeled as aberrant, the clinician must determine if the problem is likely to be transitory, perhaps an impulsive action related to a flare of unrelieved symptoms, or more serious and abiding. This may require observation over time. Although evidence of abuse, and the likelihood of addiction, is clear when patients engage in behaviors that involve illicit drugs or illegal acts, the meaning of other behaviors may be far more difficult to interpret (see Table 57.1). For example, the patient with unrelieved pain who deliberately increases the dose of the opioid by one third, but no more, and fails to contact the physician until an early refill is needed has doubtless engaged in aberrant behavior, which could be considered abuse and a potential indication of addiction. Perhaps, however, the patient had not been apprised of the clinician's expectations for therapy. Although standards of drug-taking behavior are tacitly acknowledged by most patients and require no reinforcement, noncompliance with all types of therapy is common and some patients require an explicit statement of these expectations. If the same unsanctioned dose escalation occurs after this discussion, the clinician may be more concerned that this behavior indicates a problem with the drug. Even if this occurs, however, the degree of this inappropriate behavior (that is, dose escalation by one third without prior communication with the clinician) continues to be very modest, and in the setting of unrelieved pain and associated psychological distress, the implications of this noncompliance again may be difficult to assess.

The potential for mislabeling behaviors as addiction is particularly great in the patient with a remote or current history of substance abuse. Although opioids may be clearly indicated, any evidence of aberrant drug-related behavior may generate great concern that relapse, rather than symptom control, is driving the therapy. This concern is well placed if the aberrant behaviors are egregious (e.g., prescription forgery), but the more common scenario, which involves behaviors that are unlike the norm but do not themselves constitute abuse, is more difficult to interpret. Pain complaints may be voluble and disproportionate to the degree of nociception. The patient may appear to require unusually high doses or may request injections instead of oral administration. Interactions with the medical staff may be perceived to have a manipulative quality, in which the patient appears to be unusually knowledgeable about opioid treatment and presents a posture of negotiation about therapy.

Again, it is extremely important that the clinicians caring for these patients recognize that such behaviors may or may not reflect the aberrant psychological and behavioral states that characterize addiction. Complaints that are perceived to be excessive for the degree of nociception clearly should not alone be labeled addiction. Many chronic pain patients with no history of substance abuse present such complaints, which after careful assessment may be determined to have a prominent psychological contribution. Likewise, knowledge about opioids and negotiation about treatment cannot themselves be construed as addiction. The challenge of the assessment is to determine the nature of the patient's behavior and thereby provide the information necessary to respond appropriately.

Categories of Substance Abusers

Patients with a history of opioid abuse can be divided into categories that may predict some of the problems encountered during pain treatment. These categories comprise (a) patients with a remote history of opioid substance, (b) patients with a history of opioid abuse who are currently in methadone maintenance treatment, and (c) patients actively abusing opioid drugs (14). To this scheme, it may be reasonable to add other groups, such as patients with a remote or present history of addiction to alcohol, nonopioid illicit drugs (e.g., cocaine), or nonopioid prescription drugs (e.g., benzodiazepines). These distinctions help to identify patients at risk for management problems, and this in turn may facilitate the assessment process and suggest approaches to therapy.

Unfortunately, there have been no adequate studies that specifically assess the needs and problems posed by these patient types during therapy for pain. Case reports have been helpful in defining the range of concerns, and have been particularly useful in highlighting the observation that even a remote history of abuse can stigmatize a patient and complicate pain treatment (37). Nonetheless, generalizations developed from clinical experience may fail to prepare the clinician for the vagaries of practice, where the experience of pain itself, or other facets of the disease causing the pain, may alter responses in an unpredictable way. They cannot substitute for a comprehensive assessment of each case.

PRINCIPLES OF PAIN ASSESSMENT

An optimal approach to therapy depends on a comprehensive assessment that clarifies the organic and psychological contributions to the pain and characterizes associated problems that may also require treatment. These associated problems may themselves be medical, psychological (including disorders of personality or affect, or profound behavioral disturbances), social, or familial. A history of substance abuse is one such consideration.

Categories of Patients with Pain

Patients with pain can be categorized in several clinically meaningful ways. Some distinctions are particularly relevant to the selection of treatment approaches.

ACUTE MONOPHASIC PAIN

The most common pains are acute and self-limited. Most are never evaluated by physicians and demand no therapy beyond simple measures taken by the individual. Some are severe or associated with serious underlying pathology, however, and require clinical intervention. The latter include pains associated with surgery, major trauma, and burns. Notwithstanding substantial data documenting the frequent undertreatment of these syndromes (38, 39), the short-term administration of opioid drugs is widely considered to be medically appropriate treatment for acute severe pains.

RECURRENT ACUTE PAINS

Recurrent acute pains are also extremely prevalent. They, too, range in severity and need for clinical intervention. These pains include headache, dysmenorrhea, sickle cell anemia, inflammatory bowel disease, and some arthritides or musculoskeletal disorders (e.g., hemophilic arthropathy). Although opioids commonly are considered to be accepted treatment of the management of acute pain, the decision to use these drugs may become more complicated if episodes of acute pain recur frequently or are expected to recur indefinitely. In this setting, there may be greater concern about the logistics of management (in the home, emergency ward, or hospital), risk of adverse pharmacologic reactions, and abuse potential.

CHRONIC PAIN ASSOCIATED WITH CANCER

Opioid therapy is considered to be the major therapeutic approach to patients with cancer pain (40–51). It can be speculated that the acceptance of opioid therapy in this setting relates primarily to humane considerations that alter the perceived risk-to-benefit ratio for the treatment such that the risks believed to exist, whether supported by the evidence or not (discussed in length later in this chapter), diminish in importance relative to the desire to provide comfort. Although the scientific underpinning of this perception is tenuous, the general acceptance of opioid treatment for cancer pain during the past decade has provided the opportunity to observe large numbers of patients during long-term therapy. As discussed in later sections, this experience has both confirmed the favorable outcomes associated with this approach and led to a desire for a critical reappraisal of conventional thinking about the risks associated with opioid administration to other patient types. Moreover, the acceptance of opioid therapy for cancer pain indicates that optimal management of the substance abuser with cancer requires both expertise in opioid pharmacotherapy and appreciation for the specific problems presented by this population.

CHRONIC PAIN ASSOCIATED WITH PROGRESSIVE NONMALIGNANT MEDICAL DISEASES

Like pain due to cancer, other pain syndromes are related to progressive medical illness associated with poor prognosis. A recent study, for example, demonstrated striking similarities between cancer and the acquired immunodeficiency syndrome (AIDS) in the prevalence, characteristics, and impact of pain (52, 53). In this study, the factor that most distinctly separated the population with AIDS-related pain from the cancer pain population was the degree of undertreatment with opioid drugs (54). Other progressive diseases are also characterized by a high prevalence of pain, including sickle cell anemia, hemophilia, and some connective tissue diseases. Although psychosocial disturbances are extremely important determinants of the presentation and management of these conditions, as they are in pain due to cancer, the pain in most patients usually is assumed to be explained adequately by the organic lesion. Many clinicians also perceive a connection between cancer and these conditions and would be inclined to offer chronic opioid therapy, if this approach would be helpful. As discussed later, a history of substance abuse clearly influences this therapeutic inclination.

CHRONIC PAIN ASSOCIATED WITH A NONPROGRESSIVE ORGANIC LESION

Many patients have an overtly painful organic lesion that is not life threatening but is presumed to be adequate to explain the pain. Although psychological processes again can have a profound impact on symptoms and associated functional disturbances, the pain is perceived to be commensurate with the underlying organic condition. In contrast to the previous groups, however, the prognosis for a long survival is good. Included in this category are numerous musculoskeletal pain syndromes (e.g., osteoporosis and spondylolisthesis) and neuropathic pain syndromes (e.g., postherpetic neuralgia, painful polyneuropathy, central pain, or reflex sympathetic dystrophy). Although opioid therapy of these patients continues to be highly controversial, the existence of a clear-cut organic process may encourage some physicians to consider this approach, at least in patients with no overt psychiatric disorder and no prior history of substance abuse.

CHRONIC NONMALIGNANT PAIN SYNDROME

A large group of patients experience pain or associated disability that is perceived by the clinician to be excessive for the degree of organic pathology extant. These pains have been termed *idiopathic* (55). In many patients, a careful assessment may suggest the importance of a psychological or behavioral pathogenesis to the pain. However, only a small proportion have no identifiable organic lesion and fulfill criteria for discrete psychiatric disorders, such as psychogenic pain or somatization disorder (56). Depending on the locus of the pain complaint, some of these syndromes have received other appellations, including atypical facial pain, failed low back syndrome, chronic tension headache, and chronic pelvic pain of unknown etiology. To a large extent, the multidisciplinary approach to pain management, which is now considered to be the state of the art in the treatment of these patients, evolved in response to the recognition that the complex organic and psycho-

logical interactions that resulted in chronic pain and disability could not be managed effectively without a multimodality approach to therapy undertaken by professionals of diverse disciplines. As discussed later, the use of opioid drugs in this group of patients is particularly controversial.

COMPREHENSIVE PAIN ASSESSMENT

Regardless of the category of pain patient, it is useful clinically to conceptualize the goal of assessment as the development of a pain-oriented problem list. In addition to pain itself, this list prioritizes other physical and psychosocial problems that may influence pain therapy or be amenable to primary treatment. The development of a pain-oriented problem list requires an appropriate history, a physical examination, and, often, confirmatory laboratory and radiographic procedures.

The patient should be asked to characterize the pain in terms of its temporal features (onset, course, and daily pattern), location, severity, quality, and factors that provoke or relieve it. Other relevant information includes medical and surgical disorders (related or unrelated to the pain), prior history of persistent pain, past pain treatments, and previous use of licit drugs (including alcohol, tobacco, and both over-the-counter and prescription medicines) and illicit drugs. The patient's level of physical functioning should be detailed and important concurrent symptoms, such as level of energy (or, conversely, level of fatigue), sleep disturbance, appetite and weight, should be elicited. A psychosocial history is essential and should determine premorbid psychiatric disease or personality disorder, coping styles demonstrated during earlier episodes of physical disease or psychological stress, work and education history, current level of function and psychological state (particularly anxiety, depression, and changes that had occurred in role functioning), issues related to family cohesion and status of intimate relationships (including changes in the relationship with spouse), and current resources (social, familial, and financial). The patient's activities during the day should be enumerated to help clarify the degree of physical inactivity and social isolation.

In patients with a known history of substance abuse, the interview must clarify both the specific pattern of addictive behaviors (e.g., drug or drugs, routes, frequency of administration, means of acquisition, and means of financing) and the relationship between these behaviors and the pain. It is important to determine whether or not the patient perceives that pain precipitated or perpetuates the addiction, and similarly, whether or not the patient perceives that drugs that are abused are treating the pain.

A careful history will occasionally elicit evidence of misuse or abuse of a drug in a patient with no previously known substance abuse. This evidence may be recent use of an illicit drug or aberrant involvement with a licit drug. In all cases, the clinician must determine the specific behaviors that have occurred and the extent, quality, and impact of the cognitions and feelings that relate to the drug. This assessment may be very complicated in patients with chronic pain, whose use of psychotropic and analgesic drugs may be monitored by physicians and closely tied to the experience of symptoms.

The physical examination of patients with chronic pain attempts to determine the existence of an underlying organic contribution to the pain. In most cases, the information obtained from the history and examination guides the selection of appropriate laboratory and imaging procedures that may provide confirmatory evidence of this organic lesion. It must be emphasized again, however, that the discovery of a lesion does not indicate that the predominating pathogenesis for the pain is organic, and the failure to identify a lesion does not confirm that the pain is primarily determined by psychological factors. The assessment should attempt to characterize potentially treatable organic conditions and clarify other factors that may be contributing to the patient's pain and disability.

From the detailed information obtained in this manner, specific clinically relevant aspects of the pain can be highlighted. The most salient considerations include the following features.

Temporal Features

One of the most important considerations in the clinical management of pain is the distinction between acute and chronic pain. The phenomenology of pain varies with these temporal features (Table 57.2), and treatment deci-

Table 57.2 Clinical Characteristics of Acute and Chronic Pain

	Acute	Chronic
Onset	Rapid, discrete, recalled	May be rapid (acute pain becomes chronic), but may be insidious
Duration	Brief (typically within weeks) or anticipated to be brief	Prolonged (typically months) or anticipated to be prolonged
Pattern	Variable, but usually most intense soon after onset, then waning	Variable, but usually continuous, or mostly continuous, with fluctuation or periods of acute exacerbation
Associated psychological disturbances	Anxiety may be present	Variable; depression common, but anxiety and personality disorders encountered
Associated features	Signs of sympathetic hyperactivity may be present soon after onset; need to rest and immobilize the painful part	Sometimes vegetative signs, with sleep disturbance most common; often disturbances in ability to work and function physically or socially
Biologic role	Adaptive	Not adaptive

sions are strongly influenced by these characteristics and the anticipated duration of the pain. As noted, clinical distinctions are also drawn between those with monophasic acute pain syndromes, such as postoperative pain, and those with recurrent acute pains. Among patients with chronic pain, different temporal profiles also occur. Most patients with continuous pain, for example, experience episodes of acute exacerbation that may be far more disabling than the baseline pain itself. In a survey of patients with cancer, for example, almost two thirds experienced transitory flares of pain (57).

Pathophysiologic Features

In recent years, increasing attention has focused on the importance of putative pain mechanisms in determining the phenomenology of pain syndromes and their response to therapy. In general, pain syndromes can be divided broadly into those that are believed to have a predominating organic pathogenesis, those that are believed to have a predominating psychological pathogenesis, and those that are unclassifiable (including patients with idiopathic pain). Based on clinical observation, pains with a predominating organic contribution have been described as either nociceptive or neuropathic (55, 58, 59). Nociceptive pain is presumed to be commensurate with the degree of ongoing activation of afferent nerves subserving pain perception. Although this judgment obviously oversimplifies complex neurophysiologic and psychological processes, it is nevertheless useful clinically. Pain classified in this way (e.g., related to cancer or arthritis) usually can be reduced through interventions that improve the peripheral nociceptive lesion. For example, radiotherapy often can eliminate pain from a bony metastasis, and severe joint pain from arthritis usually can be alleviated by joint replacement.

Neuropathic pain is related to aberrant somatosensory processes induced by an injury to the peripheral or central nervous system (58). The pains are often dysesthetic (abnormal pain, unfamiliar to the patient) and disproportionate to any nociceptive lesion identified during the evaluation. The latter factor may complicate the clinical distinction between these pains and pains that are predominantly determined by psychological factors, which are also disproportionate to any identifiable tissue injury. The diagnosis of a neuropathic pain may suggest the use of selected types of analgesic drugs (60) or other analgesic interventions.

Syndromic Features

Syndrome identification is extremely useful in pain assessment, since it may provide information about underlying organic processes, suggest an efficient evaluation, guide the selection of treatments, and indicate prognosis. To further this process, the International Association for the Study of Pain has developed a taxonomy of pain, the goal of which is to establish criteria for the diagnosis of specific pain syndromes (59). The importance of syndrome identification in the assessment of an underlying organic etiology for the pain has been particularly well established in cancer (61, 62). A recent survey, for example, observed that an unrecognized organic lesion could be discovered in 64% of cancer patients with pain who underwent consultation by a pain service, and that this diagnosis led to the use of primary therapy, either antineoplastic drugs or antibiotic, in almost 20% of the patients (63). In a similar way, recognition of discrete neuropathic pain syndromes may lead to specific interventions that would not be considered otherwise, such as sympathetic nerve blocks for suspected sympathetically maintained pains or neurectomy for painful neuroma.

The utility of these distinctions, and, indeed, of the pain-oriented problem list itself, derives from the availability of diverse pain therapies. Although most patients with acute pain and many with chronic pain can be managed appropriately by a single clinician who expertly administers one or more treatments, many patients, particularly those with complex chronic nonmalignant pain problems, benefit from the involvement of specialists in various disciplines, who together implement a sophisticated multimodality approach to therapy. A specialist in substance abuse can be considered to be an appropriate member of a multidisciplinary pain management team in selected patients with substance abuse and chronic pain.

MANAGEMENT OF PAIN IN THE SUBSTANCE ABUSER

Regardless of the population in question, there are important differences between the relatively brief use of opioids to manage acute pain and the chronic administration of these drugs to patients with persistent pain. The therapeutic use of opioids in the patient with a history of substance abuse raises additional issues in both clinical settings.

Chronic Pain

As noted previously, the role of opioid therapy in patients with a history of substance abuse and chronic pain has traditionally varied with the distinction between cancer pain and nonmalignant pain. Opioids are accepted treatment in cancer pain, and management of this condition in patients with a history of substance abuse requires pharmacologic expertise equal to that applied to similar patients without this history. Opioids have generally been discouraged in other populations with chronic pain, and particularly so when pain is complicated by a history of substance abuse.

From a critical perspective, this distinction between cancer pain and nonmalignant pain may be difficult to rationalize. Nonmalignant pain syndromes are extraordinarily diverse and, as discussed previously, even a simple classification identifies other large groups of patients with chronic severe pain due to progressive medical disorders that are similar to cancer in terms of prognosis and functional outcomes, but are not neoplastic. It is particularly difficult to justify the view that opioids are the first-line drug for cancer pain but are relatively contraindicated in these latter pain syndromes, which include AIDS, sickle cell anemia, hemophilia, inflammatory bowel disease, and others. Similar concerns may arise in attempting to discern the medical rationale for the conventional rejection of opioid drugs in other chronic pain populations, some of which may, like the cancer population, experience pain as a consequence of tissue injury or neuropathic lesions, or experience chronic pain without the development of psychiatric comorbidity or disability.

The implications of a critical reassessment of the conventional "last resort" positioning of opioid drugs in all chronic pain syndromes that are not cancer-related are discussed further later. The overriding implication, however, has direct relevance to the management of acute or chronic pain in patients with a history of substance abuse. It may be quite appropriate to position opioid therapy differently when defining a general approach to pain therapy in populations that usually vary, but this positioning should be based on specific characteristics of the patients or pain syndromes (which may or may not be manifest by an individual patient in the population), and not on the mere designation as "not cancer." A substance abuse history may be an important factor in defining the role of opioid therapy in any population.

Chronic Cancer Pain

Cancer pain is the model for the first-line use of opioid pharmacotherapy in the treatment of pain related to medical illness. Pain is experienced by more than one third of cancer patients undergoing active antineoplastic therapy and up to 90% of those with advanced disease (61). Cancer pain specialists have accumulated an enormous clinical experience that strongly supports the view that opioid drugs should be considered the mainstay therapeutic approach to this problem (40–51, 64–66). Surveys suggest that opioids can provide adequate control to more than three quarters of these patients (40–46, 64). Although a history of substance abuse influences the approach to opioid therapy, the general approach to cancer pain is similar to the management of cancer pain in patients without this history (Table 57.3).

Although the need for opioid therapy in patients with cancer pain and a history of substance abuse is widely accepted, the practical management of these patients generates profound concerns about the potential for inappropriate use of prescribed drugs or concurrent abuse of illicit drugs. These concerns highlight the conflict between the clinician's humane desire to provide an opioid at whatever quantity is necessary for pain relief and the fear that this therapy is ill-advised and legally suspect when it appears to feed only the addiction. In these cases, compassionate care must be balanced by recognition of the special needs and requirements of the substance abuser.

The complexity of these issues underscores the need for a comprehensive assessment as a first step in the management of pain patients with a history of substance abuse. Ironically, it often appears that a history of substance abuse tempers enthusiasm for such an evaluation, particularly in patients who are actively abusing drugs or have striking psychological disturbances. This inclination to perform a limited evaluation cannot be condoned. Given the high likelihood of an underlying neoplastic cause for the pain in cancer patients and the multitude of diagnostic and therapeutic problems associated with the history of drug abuse, a comprehensive clinical assessment of the pain and related physical and psychosocial impairments is essential.

A history of substance abuse may also encourage misdiagnosis should the assessment fail to identify a structural lesion capable of explaining the pain. An actual or suspected substance abuse history may increase the tendency to ascribe the pain in this setting to psychological factors, including needs related to an addiction or substance abuse history, even in the absence of any positive evidence for these factors. This potential for an actual or sus-pected substance abuse history to distort interpretation of clinical findings has also been observed in other medically ill populations. For example, patients with sickle cell anemia and frequent painful episodes that are not clearly related to vaso-occlusion are often suspected of being substance abusers, even in the absence of any other evidence of this disorder. This attribution may be especially prominent when pain becomes associated with multiple emergency room visits. Regardless of the population, there is a need for circumspection in assuming that pain-related behaviors are determined primarily by an aberrant response to the drug. The risks of misdiagnosis in the setting of medical illness include compromise of the therapeutic alliance during a progressive illness, selection of less effective therapies, and inappropriate refusal to assess the patient further.

USE OF PRIMARY THERAPY

The first consideration in the management of cancer pain is the feasibility of primary therapy directed against the underlying nociceptive lesion that exists in most of these patients. Radiotherapy to tumors associated with pain can provide relief to more than half the patients treated (67–69). Other primary antineoplastic therapies, including surgical resection of neoplastic lesions (70–72) and chemotherapy (72–75), can also have analgesic consequences, but rarely are attempted for pain palliation alone. Occasional patients may also be candidates for primary therapies that are not antineoplastic. For example, empirical antibiotic therapy has been found to have profound analgesic effects in some patients (76). This response, which presumably indicates that occult infection contributes to the pain, suggests that a trial of an antibiotic may be indicated in patients with refractory or progressive pain who are predisposed to the development of local infection.

The importance of primary therapy in the management of cancer pain is affirmed by similar observations in other painful medical illnesses. Indeed, the potential for such quality of life outcomes appears to drive research into disease-modifying therapies for many disorders. For example, anti-inflammatory therapies can be profoundly analgesic in a destructive inflammatory disorder, and primary therapies for treatment of the sickling disorder are actively being sought for sickle cell anemia. In the latter disorder, the identification of primary therapies would be particularly attractive, because the use of chronic opioids are often resisted by clinicians and biases surrounding the potential for drug-seeking will be difficult to alter. Unfortunately, research in this area remains disappointing. For example, a recent controlled trial of oxygen therapy in the treatment of acute pain in sickle cell diseases did not result in a reduction of the duration of vaso-occlusive crises when compared to breathing room air (77). Recent studies suggest that hydroxyurea therapy may be a promising approach to the primary therapy of this disorder (78).

SELECTING A PHARMACOLOGIC APPROACH

The pharmacologic management of cancer pain requires expertise in the use of three broad groups of analgesics: nonsteroidal anti-inflammatory drugs (NSAIDs), opioid analgesics, and the so-called adjuvant analgesics. The latter are a diverse group of unrelated agents that have other primary indications but may be analgesic in selected circumstances.

An approach to the selection of these drugs has been developed by the Cancer Pain Relief and Palliative Care Program of the World Health Organization (47). Known as the "analgesic ladder," this approach employs stepwise selection of analgesics based on the usual severity of pain (Fig. 57.1). Patients with mild to moderate pain are first treated with a NSAID. This drug is combined with one or more adjuvant drugs if a specific indication for one exists. These adjuvant drugs include those selected to treat a side effect of the analgesic (e.g., a laxative) and those with analgesic effects (the so-called adjuvant analgesics). Patients who present with moderate to severe pain, or who fail to achieve adequate relief after a trial of a NSAID, are treated with an opioid conventionally used for pain of this severity, which typically is combined with a NSAID and may be co-administered with an adjuvant, if indicated. Patients who present with severe pain or fail to achieve adequate relief following appropriate administration of drugs on the second rung of the analgesic ladder should receive an opioid conventionally selected for severe

---

Table 57.3 Guidelines for the Management of Chronic Cancer Pain in the Known or Suspected Opioid Addict

1. Perform a comprehensive assessment that includes detailed evaluation of current and past drug use. Obtain all medical records. As needed, contact other health care providers, family, and pharmacies to assess drug-taking behavior; use urine drug screening to identify misuse or abuse.
2. Distinguish among the patient with a remote history of drug abuse, the patient receiving methadone maintenance, and the patient who is actively abusing drugs and use this information to clarify the nature of the treatment team, the likely issues that will arise during therapy, the system for monitoring drug use, and the type of education that will be needed by patient and staff.
3. Consider the use of primary therapy directed at the underlying structural cause of the pain (e.g., radiotherapy).
4. Select and administer an appropriate pharmacologic approach using standard guidelines for cancer pain management (see text).
5. Create requirements for continued drug administration that provide a degree of control and monitoring appropriate to the history and recent behaviors of the patient. Frequent visits, written contracts with little flexibility, and repeated drug screens may be appropriate for the actively abusing patient and very inappropriate for others. Adjust requirements over time as experience is gained with the patient. Maintain contact with drug abuse treatment program or methadone maintenance program if patient continues with this therapy.
6. Consider adjunctive approaches, including those that are anesthetic, neurosurgical, physiatric, psychological, and neurostimulatory.
7. If drug abuse behaviors occur, require appropriate change in behavior and initiate new controls as needed.
8. Provide early consultation to psychiatric and substance abuse services, or pain service (if available).

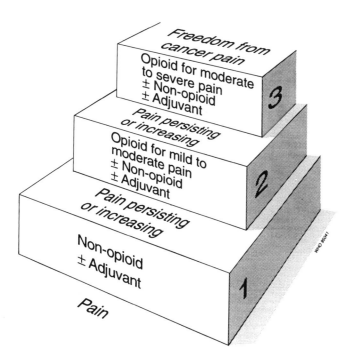

Figure 57.1. World Health Organization's analgesic ladder approach to the selection of drugs for the management of cancer pain. (Reproduced with permission from World Health Organization. Cancer pain relief, with a guide to opioid availability. 2nd edition. Geneva: World Health Organization, 1996.)

pain. This treatment may also be combined with a NSAID or an adjuvant drug, as indicated.

The drugs on the second and third rungs of the analgesic ladder were previously termed "weak" and "strong" opioids, respectively. This designation misrepresented the pharmacology of this distinction and is no longer used. The drugs that are typically used on the second rung of the analgesic ladder are pure agonists and have no ceiling dose, a phenomenon that would justify the weak vs. strong dichotomy on pharmacologic grounds. Rather, these drugs are generally used for moderate pain in convenient formulations in which the opioid is mixed with a nonopioid analgesic (aspirin or acetaminophen). Upward dose titration is usually limited by the toxicity associated with high doses of the nonopioid co-analgesic. The limited dose range permits the use of these drugs in patients with limited opioid exposure and moderate pain.

Simple guidelines for drug administration applied to the analgesic ladder model yields an approach to the management of cancer pain that has gained widespread acceptance (49–51). Trials of this analgesic approach suggest that 70–90% of patients can achieve adequate relief of cancer pain without additional treatments (40–46).

CANCER PHARMACOTHERAPY: NONSTEROIDAL ANTI-INFLAMMATORY DRUGS AND ACETAMINOPHEN

The NSAIDs (Table 57.4) and acetaminophen are characterized by a ceiling dose and analgesia that is additive to that of the opioids (79, 80). The ceiling dose implies that there is a dose beyond which additional increments in dose fail to yield any further analgesia. Anecdotal data suggest that these agents have particular efficacy in malignant bone pain and relatively little effect in neuropathic pain (81). Thus, NSAIDs may be ineffective because pain is too severe or has a pathogenesis that renders it unresponsive to these drugs.

NSAIDs should be used cautiously in patients with renal disease, history of peptic ulceration, history of a bleeding diathesis, congestive heart failure or volume overload of any other cause, and encephalopathy. Significant renal disease, active upper gastrointestinal ulceration, and coagulopathy usu-

ally are absolute contraindications. Acetaminophen is contraindicated in the setting of severe hepatic dysfunction, and recent data suggest that this drug should also be used cautiously in patients with renal disease (82).

The selection of an NSAID should be based on an understanding of differential toxicity, pharmacokinetics, and prior experience with these drugs. Consideration of these factors may improve compliance with therapy or the likelihood of a favorable response. However, it should be recognized that there is great intraindividual variability in the response to different NSAIDs. The practitioner should be familiar with several agents in different subclasses (see Table 57.4) and be prepared to switch from one drug to another if desired effects are not achieved.

Differential toxicity can guide the selection of specific drugs. The pyrazole class, specifically phenylbutazone, has a substantially greater risk of toxicity and has been supplanted by newer drugs. Acetaminophen is widely regarded to be the safest nonopioid analgesic, but this drug has minimal peripheral anti-inflammatory effects and, therefore, may have a narrower spectrum of uses. The salicylates, such as choline magnesium trisalicylate and salsalate, differ from other NSAIDs in that they have less platelet toxicity and ulcerogenic effects at usually prescribed doses (83–86). These characteristics suggest that these agents may have special utility in patients who are predisposed to bleeding or ulcer formation. The risk of gastrointestinal toxicity has also been studied in numerous epidemiologic surveys (87, 88). These surveys vary in the specific drugs and endpoints evaluated, and, consequently, definitive conclusions about relative risks are not possible. In general, they support the view that ibuprofen is relatively safer than aspirin and piroxicam is relatively less safe. Some studies suggest that diclofenac and nabumetone are relatively less likely to cause serious gastrointestinal toxicity and that ketorolac and some of the older NSAIDs, such as mefenamic acid, are relatively more so. Both ketorolac and mefenamic acid are recommended for short-term use only because of the cumulative risk of gastrointestinal toxicity (see Table 57.4).

Pharmacokinetics may also be useful to consider in selecting an NSAID. A patient with demonstrably poor compliance may be more likely to use a drug that has a relatively long half-life and therefore requires once-daily (nabumetone, oxaprozin, or piroxicam) or twice-daily (sulindac, naproxen, and many others) dosing. Conversely, patients with intermittent pain may prefer to use a short half-life drug that can be effective with "as needed" dosing, such as aspirin, acetaminophen, or ibuprofen.

Given the lack of information about the dose-response relationship for any of the NSAIDs in patients with cancer, it is prudent to begin with a relatively low dose. Upward dose titration can then be implemented to identify a minimal effective dose, the ceiling dose, and dose-related toxicity. The dose should be increased, usually on a weekly basis, until side effects develop, no further analgesia occurs with an increment in dose, or an arbitrary limit of approximately 1½–2 times the usual starting dose is reached. This recommendation is derived from clinical experience and is based on the assumption that exploration of the dose-response relationship is the safest and most efficient way of determining the potential benefit of these drugs in a population of patients for whom customary doses may be too high or, conceivably, too low.

CANCER PHARMACOTHERAPY: OPIOID ANALGESICS

Opioid analgesics are needed in a large majority of patients with cancer pain. Guidelines for the selection and administration of these drugs derive from knowledge of opioid pharmacology and clinical experience (4, 13, 14, 47–51). Some of the key principles follow:

Select an Appropriate Drug

Several factors should be considered in the decision to use one opioid drug rather than another. First is the distinction between the pure agonist subclass and the agonist-antagonist subclass (Table 57.5). The pure agonist opioids bind to one or more of the opioid receptors and demonstrate no antagonist activity. Morphine is the prototypic drug in this class, but numerous others are available in the United States, including hydromorphone, oxy-

Table 57.4 Nonsteroidal Anti-inflammatory Drugs

Chemical class	Generic name	Approximate half-life (hr)	Dosing schedule	Recommended starting dose (mg/day)[a]	Maximum recommended dose (mg/day)	Comment
p-aminophenol	acetaminophen[b]	2–4	q 4–6h	2600	6000	Overdosage produces hepatic toxicity. Not anti-inflammatory and therefore not preferred as first-line analgesic or coanalgesic for bone pain. Lack of GI and platelet toxicity may be important.
Salicylates	aspirin[b]	3–12[c]	q 4–6h	2600	6000	Standard for comparison. May not be tolerated as well as some of the newer NSAIDs.[d]
	diflunisal[b]	8–12	q 12 h	1000 × 1 then 500 q 12 h	1500	Less GI toxicity than aspirin.[d]
	choline magnesium trisalicylate[b]	8–12	q 12 h	1500 × 1 then 1000 q12h	4000	Unlike other NSAIDs, choline Mg trisalicylate and salsalate have minimal GI toxicity and no effect on platelet aggregation, despite potent anti-inflammatory effects. May therefore be particularly useful in some cancer patients.[d]
	salsalate	8–12	q 12 h	1500 × 1 then 1000 q 12 h	4000	
Propionic acids	ibuprofen[b]	3–4	q 4–8h	1600	4200	Available over-the-counter.[d]
	naproxen[b]	13	q 12 h	500	1500	Available over-the-counter and as a suspension.[d]
	naproxen sodium[b]	13	q 12h	550	1375	[d]
	fenoprofen	2–3	q 6h	800	3200	[d]
	ketoprofen	2–3	q 6–8 h	100	300	Available over-the-counter[d]
	flurbiprofen[b]	5–6	q 8–12 h	100	300	Experience too limited to evaluate higher doses, though it is likely that some patients would benefit.[d]
Acetic Acids	oxaprozin	40	q 24 h	600	1800	[d]
	indomethacin	4–5	q 8–12 h	75	200	Available in sustained-release and rectal formulations. Higher incidence of side effects, particularly GI and CNS, than propionic acids.[d]
	tolmetin	1	q 6–8 h	600	2000	[d]
	sulindac	14	q 12 h	300	400	[d]
	diclofenac	2	q 6 h	75	200	[d]
	ketorolac (IM)	4–7	q 4–6 h	120	120	Parenteral formulation available. Long-term use not recommended[d]
	etodolac	7	q 8h	600	1200	[d]
Oxicams	piroxicam	45	q 24 h	20	40	Administration of 40 mg for > 3 weeks is associated with a high incidence of peptic ulcer, particularly in the elderly.[d]
Naphthyl-alkanones	nabumetone	24	q 24 h	1000	1000–2000	Appears to have a relatively low risk of GI toxicity.
Fenamates	mefenamic acid[b]	2	q 6 h	500 × 1 then 250 q6h	1000	Not recommended for use longer than one week and therefore not indicated in cancer pain therapy.[d]
	meclofenamic acid	2–4	q 6–8h	150	400	[d]
Pyrazoles	phenylbutazone	50–100	q 6–8 h	300	400	Not a first-line drug due to risk of serious bone marrow toxicity. Not preferred for cancer pain therapy.

[a]Starting dose should be one-half to two-thirds recommended dose in the elderly, those on multiple drugs, and those with renal insufficiency. Doses must be individualized. Low initial doses should be titrated upward if tolerated and clinical effect is inadequate. Doses can be incremented weekly. Studies of NSAIDs in the cancer population are meager; dosing guidelines are thus empiric.
[b]Pain is approved indication.
[c]Half-life of aspirin increases with dose.
[d]At high doses, stool guaiac, liver function tests, BUN, creatinine, and urinalysis should be checked periodically.

codone, levorphanol, and methadone. The agonist-antagonist opioids comprise two subtypes, a mixed agonist-antagonist type (e.g., pentazocine, nalbuphine, butorphanol, and dezocine) and a partial agonist type (e.g., buprenorphine). Although these two subclasses can be distinguished by differences in specific receptor interactions, all are characterized by potential antagonism of one or more opioid receptors, a ceiling effect for analgesia, and the capacity to reverse favorable effects and precipitate an abstinence syndrome in patients who are physically dependent on pure agonist opioids (89, 90). Most also have an incidence of psychotomimetic effects substantially greater than that of the agonist drugs. Together, these properties indicate that the agonist-antagonist opioids are not generally useful in the management of chronic pain, including cancer pain.

The agonist-antagonist opioids do appear to have less abuse potential than the pure agonist drugs. Although this characteristic could potentially be important in a population with a prior or current history of substance abuse, it is generally regarded to be an insignificant benefit in cancer patients without a history of substance abuse, who only rarely develop addiction or abuse de novo during medical therapy with an opioid. Among those with a history of substance abuse, the risk of aberrant drug-taking behavior during medical therapy may be greater, and it could be conjectured that the use of agonist-

antagonists in this population may present some advantages. Neither data nor substantial clinical experience support this view, however, and most pain specialists employ pure agonist drugs even in those with a history of substance abuse. Should the clinician choose an agonist-antagonist drug, it must be used early, before physical dependence on a pure agonist drug has developed or there is a need for effects greater than those associated with the ceiling dose of these agents. An agonist-antagonist drug should not be administered to a patient with a history of substance abuse who may be physically dependent on opioids before pain treatment is begun, including those receiving methadone maintenance and those actively abusing opioids.

A second consideration in the selection of an opioid drug relates to the distinction between "weak" vs. "strong" opioids, which has been incorporated into the "analgesic ladder." As noted previously, this designation is fundamentally operational rather than pharmacologic. "Weak" opioids are those that are conventionally used orally for moderate pain, whereas the so-called "strong" opioids are conventionally selected for severe pain. In the United States, the "weak" opioids include codeine and oxycodone (administered with acetaminophen or aspirin in a combination product), hydrocodone and dihydrocodeine (only available with acetaminophen in a combination product), and propoxyphene (either alone or in combination products). Other

Table 57.5 Opioid Analgesics

	Equianalgesic Doses[a]	Half-life (hr)	Peak Effect(hr)	Duration (hr)	Toxicity	Comments
Morphine-like Agonists						
Morphine	10 IM	2–3	0.5–1	3–6	Constipation, nausea, sedation most common; respiratory depression rare in cancer patients.	Standard comparison for opioids; multiple routes available
	20–60 p.o.[b]	2–3	1.5–2	4–7		
Controlled-release morphine	20–60 p.o.[b]	2–3	3–4	8–12		
Sustained-release morphine	20–60 p.o.[b]	2–3	4–6	24		Once-a-day morphine recently approved in the U.S.
Hydromorphone	1.5 IM	2–3	0.5–1	3–4	Same as morphine	Used for multiple routes
	7.5 p.o.	2–3	1–2	3–4		
Oxycodone	20–30 p.o.	2–3	1	3–6	Same as morphine	Combined with aspirin or acetaminophen, for moderate pain; available orally without coanalgesic for severe pain
Controlled-release oxycodone	20–30 p.o.	2–3	3–4	8–12		
Oxymorphone	1 IM	—	0.5–1	3–6	Same as morphine	No oral formulation
	10 p.r.	—	1.5–3	4–6		
Meperidine	75 IM	2–3	0.5–1	3–4	Same as morphine + CNS excitation; contraindicated in those on MAO inhibitors	Not preferred for cancer pain due to potential toxicity
	300 p.o.	2–3	1–2	3–6		
Heroin	5 IM	0.5	0.5–1	4–5	Same as morphine	Analgesic action due to metabolites, predominantly morphine; not available in U.S.
Levorphanol	2 IM	12–15	0.5–1	3–6	Same as morphine	With long half-life, accumulation occurs after beginning or increasing dose
	4 p.o.					
Methadone	10 IM	12–>150	0.5–1.5	4–8	Same as morphine	Risk of delayed toxicity due to accumulation; useful to start dosing on p.r.n. basis, with close monitoring
	20 p.o.					
Codeine	130 IM	2–3	1.5–2	3–6	Same as morphine	Usually combined with nonopioid
	200 p.o.					
Propoxyphene HCl	—	12	1.5–2	3–6	Same as morphine plus seizures with overdose	Toxic metabolite accumulates but not significant at doses used clinically; often combined with nonopioid
Propoxyphene napsylate	—	12	1.5–2	3–6	Same as hydrochloride	Same as hydrochloride
Hydrocodone	—	2–4	0.5–1	3–4	Same as morphine	Only available combined with acetaminophen
Dihydrocodeine	2–4	0.5–1	3–4	Same as morphine		Only available combined with acetaminophen or aspirin
Partial Agonists						
Buprenorphine	0.4 IM	2–5	0.5–1	4–6	Same as morphine, except less risk of respiratory depression	Can produce withdrawal in opioid-dependent patients; has ceiling for analgesia; sublingual tablet not available in U.S.
	0.8 s.l.		2–3	5–6		
Mixed Agonist-Antagonists						
Pentazocine	60 IM	2–3	0.5–1	3–6	Same profile of effects as buprenorphine, except for greater risk of psychotomimetic effects	Produces withdrawal in opioid-dependent patients; oral formulation combined with naloxone or nonopioid in the U.S.; ceiling doses and side-effect profile limits role in cancer pain
	180 p.o.	2–3	1–2	3–6		
Nalbuphine	10 IM	4–6	0.5–1	3–6	Same as buprenorphine, except for greater risk of psychotomimetic effects, which is lower than that of pentazocine	Produces withdrawal in opioid-dependent patients; no oral formulation; not preferred for cancer pain therapy
Butorphanol	2 IM	2–3	0.5–1	3–4	Same profile of effects as nalbuphine	Produces withdrawal in opioid-dependent patients; no oral formulation, not preferred for cancer pain therapy
Dezocine	10 IM[c]	1.2–7.4	0.5–1	3–4	Same profile of effects as nalbuphine, but purported to have fewer psychotomimetic effects	Produces withdrawal in opioid-dependent patients; no oral formulation; not preferred for cancer pain therapy

[a]Dose that provides analgesia equivalent to 10 mg IM morphine. These ratios are useful guides when switching drugs or routes of administration. When switching drugs, reduce the equianalgesic dose of the new drug by 25–50% to account for incomplete cross-tolerance. The only exception to this is methadone, which appears to manifest a greater degree of incomplete cross-tolerance than other opioids; when switching to methadone, reduce the equianalgesic dose by 90%.
[b]Extensive survey data suggest that the relative potency of IM:p.o. morphine of 1:6 changes to 1:2–3 with chronic dosing.
[c]Approximate equianalgesic dose suggested from meta-analysis of available comparative studies.

drugs, such as oral pentazocine and meperidine, are also occasionally employed in this setting.

The most common approach to the second "rung" of the analgesic ladder in the United States involves the administration of a combination product containing acetaminophen or aspirin plus either codeine or oxycodone. The dose of this drug is increased as needed until the maximum safe dose of the aspirin or acetaminophen is reached, usually 4 grams (sometimes as high as 6 grams) per day. Should pain persist, the patient is usually then switched to one of the so-called "strong" opioids.

The pure agonist drugs available in the United States that are customarily employed at the third "rung" of the analgesic ladder include morphine, hydromorphone, oxycodone (when not combined with a co-analgesic), levorphanol, and methadone. Fentanyl recently has become available in a formulation for transdermal administration, and oxymorphone is available in a rectal formulation. Morphine is currently considered the preferred drug, based on extensive clinical experience, relative ease of oral titration, and availability of numerous formulations, including a controlled release form that allows dosing at 12-hour intervals (91).

Although morphine generally is used as the first-line drug, it is essential to recognize that individual differences in the response to different opioids are great, and a patient may find treatment with another to be more salutary (92). Furthermore, morphine may not be the best choice in some patients. Recent studies have established the existence of an active metabolite of morphine, morphine 6-glucuronide, that accumulates in patients with renal insufficiency and has been associated with toxicity in some renally impaired patients (93–98). A recent survey suggests that the impact of the metabolite in the cancer population overall is insufficient to recommend a change in routine dosing guidelines (99); nonetheless, occasional patients who develop morphine toxicity in the setting of renal insufficiency should be offered a trial of an alternative opioid, such as hydromorphone or fentanyl, in the hope that lesser metabolite accumulation may contribute to a better response.

The selection of a pure agonist drug as an alternative to morphine is largely empiric, but some guidelines can be proffered based on the pharmacology of these agents. For example, meperidine appears to have substantially greater toxicity than the others and is not preferred in cancer pain management. This toxicity relates to the appearance of a metabolite, normeperidine, which may produce dysphoria, tremulousness, hyperreflexia, and seizures (100).

Some constraints are also appropriate in the use of the two drugs currently available in the United States that have considerably longer half-lives than other opioids, namely levorphanol and methadone. Since four or five half-lives must pass before steady state is approached after dosing is begun or altered, use of these drugs is associated with a relatively long period following each dose adjustment during which close monitoring is required to avoid unanticipated delayed toxicity. This need for monitoring is most critical in patients predisposed to opioid side effects, including those with advanced age or major organ failure (encephalopathy or disturbances in pulmonary, hepatic, or renal function). Clinically, most problems appear to develop with methadone, which has a highly variable half-life that ranges from less than 24 hours in some patients to more than 150 hours in others (101). These observations suggest that levorphanol and methadone should be considered second-line drugs for those who are difficult to monitor (e.g., noncompliant patients or those who live alone or at a distance) and those predisposed to opioid side effects.

Confusion about the role of methadone therapy in cancer pain management is often exaggerated in the patient with a history of substance abuse. In contrast to the once-daily administration that is adequate in the treatment of addiction, the use of methadone as an analgesic typically requires multiple doses per day (102). Although occasional patients can maintain continuous analgesic effects with twice-daily dosing, clinical experience indicates that most require doses four times daily, and a few need a dosing interval of only 4 hours. Furthermore, the use of methadone as an analgesic necessitates dose titration based on the report of pain. Thus, patients receiving methadone maintenance who develop cancer pain can be given methadone for pain, but both dose and dosing interval must be adjusted to the new indication, using the guidelines described later.

Select the Route of Administration

The oral route is preferred for chronic opioid therapy due to its simplicity, economy, and acceptability. A substantial proportion of patients, however, will require an alternative route at some point during the course of the disease (65). A large number of alternative routes are available (Table 57.6), of which the transdermal (103–105), the subcutaneous (by chronic infusion using an ambulatory pump) (106, 107), and intraspinal (epidural and intrathecal) (108–111) represent the most important recent advances. Other routes, including intravenous (112) and rectal (113), are also used commonly. New routes continue in development, including oral transmucosal and transdermal iontophoresis, and will offer further options for therapy.

Table 57.6   Routes of Administration

Route	Comment
Oral	Preferred in cancer pain management.
Buccal	Supporting data meager, and the method is generally impracticable.
Sublingual	Buprenorphine effective but not available in U.S. Efficacy of morphine controversial. No clinical studies of other drugs.
Rectal	Available for morphine, oxymorphone, and hydromorphone. Although few studies available, customarily used as if dose is equianalgesic to oral dose. Absorption is variable, however, and relative potency may be higher than expected depending on the degree of nonportal absorption.
Transdermal	Available for fentanyl citrate, with patches delivering 25, 50, 75, and 100μg/hr. Can provide analgesia for 2–3 day period per dose and is indicated for patients who are unable to use oral drug, are noncompliant with repetitive dosing, or have failed other opioids and could potentially benefit from a trial of fentanyl. Although not confirmed empirically, quality of life advantage over oral dosing is experienced by some patients.
Intranasal	Available for butorphanol, a mixed agonist-antagonist not preferred for chronic pain management.
Oral transmucosal	Formulation using fentanyl currently undergoing trials for breakthrough pain.

Subcutaneous
  Repetitive bolus
  Continuous infusion
  Continuous infusion with patient-controlled analgesia (PCA)
	Ambulatory infusion pumps can provide continuous infusion with any parenteral opioid formulation. More advanced pumps can also provide PCA. Clearest indication is inability to tolerate oral route.

Intravenous
  Repetitive bolus
  Continuous infusion
  Continuous infusion with patient-controlled analgesia (PCA)
	Continuous infusion possible if permanent venous access device available.

Epidural
  Repetitive bolus
  Continuous infusion
  Continuous infusion using percutaneous or implanted system
	Clearest indication is pain in lower half of body and dose-limiting side effects from systemic opioid. Often co-administered with local anesthetic.

Intrathecal	Usually administered via a totally implanted infusion pump. May be cost-effective for those patients with clear indication for intraspinal therapy and long life expectancy.
Intracerebroventricular	Rarely indicated. Experience is limited.

Apply Appropriate Dosing Guidelines

The successful treatment of cancer pain derives less from the selection of the drug and route than from the clinical protocols used in initiating and altering the dose (4, 13, 14, 47, 49, 51). Specific dosing guidelines can be summarized as follows:

Dose "By the Clock." Because it is generally agreed that it is more effective to prevent the recurrence of severe pain than abort it once it appears, "by the clock" dosing has replaced "as needed" dosing in the treatment of continuous or frequently recurring pain using opioid drugs. "As needed" dosing still plays a role, however, and should be considered in the nontolerant patient during the initiation of therapy (given the risk of gradual accumulation, methadone is often started with 1–2 weeks of "as needed" dosing), in the patient with rapidly changing pain (such as may follow radiotherapy to a painful bony lesion), and in patients with intermittent pains separated by pain-free intervals. Additionally, clinical experience strongly supports the use of an "as needed" dose (so-called "rescue dose") in combination with a fixed dosing schedule to treat "breakthrough" pains (57).

Titrate the Dose. Once an opioid and route of administration are selected, the dose should be increased until adequate analgesia occurs or intolerable and unmanageable side effects supervene. There is no ceiling effect to the analgesia provided by the pure agonist opioid drugs and the maximal dose is immaterial as long as the patient attains a favorable balance between analgesia and side effects. This implies that the opioid responsiveness of a specific pain can only by ascertained by dose escalation to limiting side effects. In clinical practice, the range of opioid doses required by patients is enormous. Doses equivalent to more than 35 g morphine per day have been reported in highly tolerant patients with refractory cancer pain (65).

Although doses typically stabilize for prolonged periods during long-term management, dose escalation is usually required at intervals to maintain analgesia. In the patient with pain due to medical illness, the need for a dose increase usually can be explained by some change in clinical status, typically worsening of a pain-producing structural lesion. The changing opioid requirement over time underscores the need for repeated assessment and dose adjustment, which is always guided by the effort to gradually increase the dose until adequate analgesia occurs or the development of intolerable and unmanageable side effects indicates that the pain will not be satisfactorily controlled with the drug. Given the inherently subjective nature of the critical endpoints "adequate analgesia" and "intolerable side effects," careful patient assessment is essential.

Use Appropriate Dosing Intervals. With the exception of controlled release morphine preparations (administered every 8–12 hours), sustained-release oral morphine formulations (administered every 24 hours), transdermal fentanyl system (administered every 48–72 hours), and methadone (usually, but not always, effective with dosing every 6–8 hours), all other pure agonist opioid drugs must be administered every 3–4 hours to provide continuous analgesia.

Be Aware of Relative Potencies. Using morphine as a standard, relative potencies have been determined for most pure agonist drugs in single-dose analgesic assays (114) (see Table 57.5). Relative potency tables (also known as equianalgesic dose tables) should be consulted when switching from one drug or route of administration to another. These estimates should be viewed as broad guidelines, the use of which must be tempered by clinical judgment. A switch from one drug to another should be accompanied by a reduction in the equianalgesic dose of at least one third, in recognition that incomplete cross-tolerance between opioids may result in a potency greater than anticipated for the newly initiated drug. The equianalgesic dose should be further reduced (up to 90%) when patients are predisposed to opioid side effects (e.g., in the elderly or those with encephalopathy) and when the new drug is methadone. For reasons that are not yet known, the degree of incomplete cross-tolerance is greater when a switch is made to methadone than to other opioids. In the case of morphine, there is evidence that the oral:intramuscular relative potency with chronic administration is 2 to 3:1, rather than the 6:1 ratio suggested by controlled single-dose studies.

Treat Side Effects. Treatment of opioid-induced side effects is an integral part of cancer pain management (115). Successful amelioration of symptoms both enhances patients' comfort and allows continued upward dose titration of the opioid drug. Although respiratory depression fosters the greatest concern, tolerance to this adverse effect develops quickly and it is rarely a problem in the management of cancer pain. The most common and persistent side effect is unquestionably constipation (116). Although less prevalent, sedation often limits dose escalation. Recent experience suggests that a relatively small dose of a psychostimulant, such as methylphenidate or dextroamphetamine (usually 5–20 mg in the morning, possibly with a repeat dose at lunchtime), can reverse this effect as well as potentially provide co-analgesic effects (117). Nausea is common but usually can be managed with one or another of a large number of drugs with antiemetic effects. If nausea occurs, it is often wise to administer an antiemetic on an around-the-clock basis for several weeks, since this may markedly reduce this adverse experience during the time required for the patient to develop tolerance to the effect. Psychotomimetic effects, when marked, usually require a switch to a different opioid drug, although some patients improve with the addition of a neuroleptic, such as haloperidol. Other side effects, such as itch, dry mouth, and urinary retention, rarely are a problem, although occasional patients will require other treatments as a result of these effects. In all cases, unmanageable side effects necessitate a trial of an alternative analgesic approach. One such approach is a trial of an alternative opioid, since the pattern of side effects produced by one drug does not reliably predict the response to another (92, 118).

CANCER PHARMACOTHERAPY: ADJUVANT ANALGESICS

Adjuvant analgesics are drugs that have primary indications other than pain but can be analgesic in selected circumstances. This category is extremely diverse, representing numerous drugs in many classes (119) (Table 57.7). These drugs are now used commonly in the treatment of many malignant and nonmalignant pain syndromes. When used in the management of cancer pain, they are typically added to an optimally titrated opioid regimen. Some, such as the tricyclic antidepressants, are used as primary analgesics for specific nonmalignant pain syndromes.

Some adjuvant analgesics are particularly important in patients with cancer pain. Corticosteroids, for example, are used for bone pain, neuropathic pain, headache due to intracranial hypertension, pain related to bowel obstruction and other indications (120, 121). Dexamethasone is the steroid most often selected, but there have been no comparative trials among the different agents, and, as yet, the best drug and dosing regimen remain uncertain and the durability of effects is unknown. The chronic administration of these agents usually is reserved for those with far-advanced disease.

The largest number of adjuvant analgesics are used in the setting of neuropathic pain. These syndromes are believed to be relatively less responsive to opioid drugs than pain syndromes sustained by persistent injury to pain-sensitive tissues (nociceptive pain) (122). Antidepressants, anticonvulsants, oral local anesthetics, and others are commonly administered to patients who continue to experience inadequate analgesia despite opioid dose titration.

OTHER ANALGESIC APPROACHES IN CANCER PAIN MANAGEMENT

The use of an adjuvant analgesic may be conceptualized as one alternative among many for the management of patients who fail to achieve a favorable balance between analgesia and side effects during opioid dose titration (Table 57.8). A switch to an alternative opioid is another technique that has recently gained wide acceptance. Still other approaches use nonpharmacological interventions to reduce or even eliminate the opioid requirement.

Neurostimulatory approaches, most commonly transcutaneous electrical nerve stimulation, typically are implemented in patients with refractory neuropathic pains and those with more acute, transient pains. Experience is limited in cancer patients. The anecdotal impression is that many patients respond initially, but long-term benefit is rarely achieved with this technology. Other types of neurostimulatory approaches include counterirritation (brisk rubbing of the painful part), acupuncture, percutaneous electrical nerve stimulation, dorsal column stimulation, and deep brain stimulation. Although the invasive approaches have been applied in cancer pain (123), the noninvasive techniques are preferred.

Table 57.7   Adjuvant Analgesics

Drug Class		Examples
Multipurpose analgesics	Antidepressants Tricyclic antidepressants	amitriptyline doxepin imipramine nortriptyline desipramine
	"Newer" antidepressants	trazodone maprotiline fluoxetine paroxetine
	MAO inhibitors	phenelzine
	Alpha-2 adrenergic agonists	clonidine
	Corticosteroids	prednisone dexamethasone
	Neuroleptics	methotrimeprazine pimozide
Drugs used for neuropathic pain	Anticonvulsants	carbamazepine phenytoin valproate clonazepam gabapentin
	Oral local anesthetics	mexiletine tocainide
	N-methyl-D-aspartate blockers	dextromethorphan ketamine
	Sympatholytic drugs	prazosin phenoxybenzamine phentolamine beta blockers
	Topical agents	local anesthetic capsaicin
	Miscellaneous	baclofen calcitonin
Drugs used for musculoskeletal pain	"Muscle relaxants"	orphenadrine carisoprodol methocarbamol chlorzoxazone cyclobenzaprine
	Benzodiazepine	diazepam
Drugs used for cancer pain	Drugs for bone pain	calcitonin bisphosphonates strontium-89
	Drugs for bowel obstruction	scopolamine octreotide
Drugs used for headache	Beta blockers	propranolol nadolol
	Calcium channel blockers	verapamil nifedipine

Table 57.8   Alternative Analgesic Approaches for Cancer Patients who Fail a Conventional Oral Opioid Therapy

Approach	Therapeutic Options	Examples
Pharmacologic techniques to reduce systemic opioid requirement	Use of adjuvant analgesics	See text
	Use of spinal opioids	—
Identifying an opioid with a more favorable balance between analgesia and side effects	Sequential opioid trials	—
Improving the tolerability of the opioid	Better side effect management	Stimulant drug for opioid-induced sedation
Nonpharmacological techniques to reduce systemic opioid requirement	Anesthetic approaches	Nerve blocks
	Surgical approaches	Cordotomy
	Rehabilitative approaches	Bracing
	Psychologic approaches	

The analgesic potential of physiatric techniques is poorly appreciated. Patients with painful musculoskeletal complications of cancer may benefit from physical or occupational therapy, and the use of orthoses or prostheses may have analgesic consequences in other situations. For example, a surgical corset may benefit patients with back pain on movement caused by neoplastic infiltration of the spine.

Anesthetic approaches include the use of nitrous oxide for pain in far-advanced disease (124), myofascial trigger point injection, and a large variety of nerve block procedures that employ either local anesthetics or neurolytic solutions (125–127). The technique of continuous epidural local anesthetic is a recent innovation capable of providing a long-standing neural blockade without inflicting permanent damage on nerves (128). With the exception of trigger point injections, the implementation of anesthetic procedures should be undertaken only by trained personnel.

Similar to the neurolytic anesthetic procedures, surgical neuroablative procedures are designed to isolate the painful part from the central nervous system (127, 129–131). The most widely used procedure, cordotomy, usually can be performed percutaneously in the awake patient. In selected patients, this technique has an extremely high likelihood of success and a low risk of complications. Surgical approaches should be undertaken only by those trained in the assessment and treatment of pain.

Psychological approaches are underutilized in cancer pain management. There is a strong association between mood disturbance and persistent pain (132) and all patients with cancer pain benefit from the support provided by a concerned and experienced staff. Those with evidence of psychiatric disorders should be appropriately referred and treated (133–135). Some patients may benefit from specific cognitive approaches that have been found useful to reduce pain intensity, including relaxation training, distraction, hypnosis, and others (134, 136–141). Behavioral approaches are occasionally useful to optimize function and thereby improve quality of life.

OTHER CONSIDERATIONS IN THE SUBSTANCE ABUSER WITH CANCER PAIN

Although the basic approach to the management of cancer pain should apply equally to all patients, including substance abusers, it is nonetheless true that problems may be encountered in the latter population that distinguish it from others. As noted previously, clinical experience suggests that there may be salient differences among those with remote history of addiction, those currently treated in methadone maintenance programs, and those actively abusing opioids or other drugs. A small retrospective study (142) suggested that all three groups were at relatively high risk for inadequate pain management, but only those who were actively abusing could not reliably achieve adequate symptom control once they were treated aggressively by pain service personnel. The major issues encountered during the treatment of each of these groups can be summarized as follows:

PATIENTS WITH A REMOTE HISTORY OF SUBSTANCE ABUSE

Although clinical experience suggests that patients with a remote history of substance abuse respond appropriately to opioids, the empirical data in support of this conclusion are meager. From a theoretical perspective, it could be speculated that the same genetic, psychological, and situational factors that predisposed to the addiction syndrome initially could increase the risk of aberrant drug-taking behavior in patients administered opioids for therapeutic purposes. The failure to observe these outcomes in practice suggests that the factors that ultimately combined to eliminate the abuse behaviors, combined with the situational changes associated with the diagnosis and treatment of the cancer, may reduce the likelihood of iatrogenic addiction.

It has been observed clinically that some cancer patients with a remote history of substance abuse are poorly compliant with opioid therapy due to a persistent fear of these drugs. Like the staff surrounding them, these patients fear loss of control over drug use (37). An example of such a patient is depicted in Figure 57.2, which demonstrates the opioid use of a 47-year-old man with severe bone pain from metastatic lung cancer and a history of polysubstance abuse that ended more than 17 years ago. While home, he experienced unrelieved pain and was advised repeatedly by pain service personnel

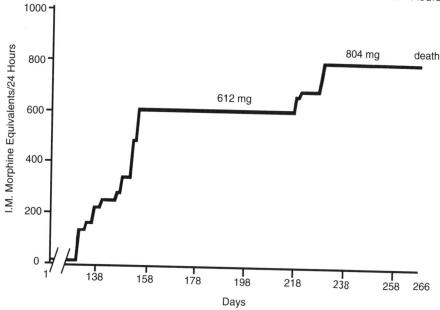

Figure 57.2. Opioid requirements in a 47-year-old man with a remote history of drug abuse who developed severe pain due to progressive lung cancer. Fear of readdiction caused the patient to resist escalation of opioid doses. While at home, he continued on stable doses, despite unrelieved pain and the wishes of his physicians that he continue upward dose titration; doses were increased only after he was admitted to the hospital. (Reproduced with permission from Gonzales GR, Coyle N. Treatment of cancer pain in a former opioid abuser: fears of the patient and staff and their influence on care. J Pain Symptom Manage 1992;7(4):246–249.)

to escalate the dose of his opioid. He refused to do so. Ironically, his opioid doses increased rapidly in the hospital, where medical staff insisted on the use of higher doses to treat severe unrelieved pain.

Thus, the optimal management of the patient with cancer pain and remote history of addiction must incorporate careful, ongoing assessment of drug-taking behavior and the recognition that successful treatment may be compromised both by the attitudes of practitioners, whose overconcern about addiction can distort analgesic management, and the attitudes of the patient, whose behavior may implicitly or explicitly endorse the concerns of the staff or result directly in undertreatment. Education of the staff and the patient may limit the adverse consequence of these attitudes and thereby improve pain management.

PATIENTS IN METHADONE MAINTENANCE PROGRAMS

Like those who have a remote history of substance abuse, patients receiving methadone maintenance are at high risk for undertreatment of cancer pain. In this population, negative attitudes held by the medical staff may combine with some degree of tolerance to opioid analgesics to limit the efficacy of therapy. If persistent pain reports are interpreted as a manipulative attempt to obtain opioids for purposes other than analgesia, the therapeutic relationship will become conflicted and the clinician's goals for analgesia will be superseded by the desire to prevent drug abuse. This concern is, of course, legitimate if the patient does develop a return of aberrant drug-taking behaviors. If "drug-seeking" reflects only the need for pain relief, however, undertreatment will result from the failure to respond.

It may also be speculated that patient noncompliance also can undermine therapy in this population. Like those with a remote history of abuse, some of these patients have achieved a measure of personal and social success as a consequence of a stable methadone regimen and may fear a loss of control with the therapeutic use of opioids.

The failure to recognize the need for higher starting doses may lead to initial problems with the management of cancer pain in methadone-treated patients. Patients who have not received an opioid for pain before, but have been receiving methadone for some time, may require starting doses substantially higher than those conventionally used at the initiation of cancer pain therapy. In a rather typical scenario, a patient administered an opioid at a dose perceived by the clinician to be effective gains no relief and voices a complaint; the persistence of pain, perhaps now combined with a sense of

mistrust or acrimony, is interpreted as evidence of addiction, and the patient is managed by the further withholding of opioids, rather than by aggressive upward dose titration. This, of course, further undermines the therapeutic alliance and reduces the likelihood of successful treatment.

Although the foregoing scenario has been observed anecdotally, it must be stated that there are no data that confirm this effect of methadone treatment on the efficacy of conventional opioid doses at the start of therapy. Indeed, a retrospective study that compared a control group with 25 hospitalized methadone maintenance patients who required opioids for the management of acute nonmalignant pain suggested that "standard" doses of opioids could be used to treat these patients and that the administration of therapeutic opioids for a brief period did not induce a need for a higher methadone dose subsequently (143). Although the finding that routine doses of opioids were effective for acute pain in this population supported the results of an earlier survey (144), neither of these studies directly assessed pain relief, and consequently, neither they nor any other studies have adequately evaluated the role of tolerance in the clinical setting.

It is a common misconception that the use of methadone as an analgesic for pain can mirror its use in the therapy of opioid addiction. In pain management, doses must be titrated according to patient response; there is no predefined appropriate dose range. Equally important, the single daily dose that is sufficient for the management of addiction is almost never adequate to sustain analgesia throughout the day. Extensive clinical experience indicates that analgesia usually requires at least three doses per day (145). Many patients actually achieve more stable analgesia with four or six doses per day, an observation supported by studies that demonstrate a duration of analgesia that is typically much briefer than would be expected from the half-life of this drug (102, 146–148).

ACTIVE DRUG ABUSERS

The sanguine view of opioid therapy in patients with a remote history of drug abuse and those in methadone maintenance is not applicable to the small number of patients who develop cancer pain while actively abusing opioids or other drugs. Anecdotally, pain management in many of these patients is complicated by substantial psychopathology and adverse situational factors. The degree of psychopathology may be severe enough that a useful therapeutic alliance is impossible, and both the veracity of the complaints and compliance with prescribed therapies become major problems.

Careful assessment is again critical to appropriate management. Clear-cut abuse behaviors, including continued use of illicit drugs, must be distinguished from other behaviors, such as frequent emergency room visits, that may be more difficult to interpret. Although both types of behaviors may reflect inadequacy of pain treatment as well as psychological dependence on the drug, the former is clear-cut abuse, which cannot be condoned, whereas the latter potentially may indicate a lesser degree of psychopathology and a desire to remain in the medical setting for the treatment of a pain problem. The specific psychopathology of these patients must be carefully evaluated. Sociopathy is relatively common among the addict population (149, 150), and to the extent possible, the clinician should attempt to determine whether sociopathic behaviors have been characteristic of the patient prior to the diagnosis of cancer. Straightforward questioning about illegal practices may yield surprisingly frank answers, from which an assessment of these behaviors can be made. Although it must be emphasized that the studies needed to clarify these issues have not been performed, it is likely that the risk of management problems during analgesic therapy correlates generally with the degree of psychopathology, and more specifically with the severity of sociopathic proclivities.

In some cases, efforts to implement a simple and effective pharmacologic regimen for pain may have to be sacrificed in lieu of interventions designed to maintain therapeutic control. Virtually all patients require greater frequency of monitoring and more strict attention to the assessment of efficacy, side effects, and drug-taking behavior. Occasional patients require the use of a written contract that is kept in the medical record and both defines the medication regimen and explicitly states the responsibilities of both the patient and clinician. These guidelines should include specific reference to the methods that will be used to renew prescriptions and the response that a report of lost or stolen drugs will generate. It may be useful to establish a rule that lost or stolen drugs must be reported to the police and that documentation of this must be provided. The use of drugs with relatively low street value, such as methadone, may be more appropriate when such considerations arise than the use of others, such as hydromorphone, for which there is greater demand among street addicts.

For some patients, the cardinal principle of opioid dose titration simply cannot be accommodated due to demands that are perceived to be inappropriate. Limits must be set based on the clinician's assessment of the risks and benefits in this difficult situation. Likewise, the occurrence of management problems may preclude the use of some techniques commonly employed in cancer pain management, such as long-term continuous subcutaneous infusion. In rare cases, the persistence of severe pain in the setting of intractable management problems suggests the immediate use of some approaches, such as neurolytic techniques, that generally are considered only after an optimal opioid therapy fails.

In all of this decision-making, the dictates of humane and compassionate care should support a bias that patients generally are to be believed. Factitious pain complaints and malingering are extraordinarily rare among patients who are not actively abusing drugs (including those with a remote history of addiction) and probably are uncommon among active abusers who develop cancer. Rather, most substance abusers are like other patients with pain, whose symptoms reflect some combination of ongoing nociception and psychological distress. Unless the evidence in support of malingering is compelling, the clinician is better served by avoiding an argument about the "reality" of the pain and focusing instead on the possibility that pain may be profoundly influenced by psychological factors, possibly including psychological dependence on opioids. It is more productive simply to believe the patient's complaint and thoughtfully assess the degree to which it can be explained by physical and psychological determinants. In keeping with this view, it may be postulated that the premorbid psychopathology of the addict predisposes to a greater psychological contribution to pain than is usually observed in the cancer population. This, too, must be evaluated in future research.

Chronic Nonmalignant Pain

As discussed previously, chronic nonmalignant pain comprises an extremely diverse group of syndromes that vary remarkably in phenomenology, pathogenesis, and impact. Physical and psychological factors contribute to the pain and associated disability in virtually all patients, but the characteristics of these factors and their respective prominence are highly variable, both across syndromes and among patients with the same diagnosis.

Some principles of clinical management apply to all patients with chronic nonmalignant pain. The need for a comprehensive assessment is one such principle. This assessment must first determine the potential for primary therapy directed against any treatable organic contribution to the pain. For example, joint replacement may be an effective primary therapy in some patients with chronic pain due to arthritis, and resection of a neuroma may relieve some patients with painful traumatic mononeuropathy. There is no definitive primary therapy for most chronic pain patients, however, and the assessment must also provide the information necessary to develop a multimodality approach to symptomatic therapy that can improve comfort and enhance physical and psychosocial function.

The various analgesic modalities have been discussed previously in the context of cancer pain. The broad approaches can be categorized as pharmacologic, anesthetic, neurostimulatory, physiatric, surgical, and psychological. The number of approaches selected in the management of any patient and the specific therapies within each approach vary according to the needs of the patient. The emphasis can differ markedly among patient types. For example, the chronic pains associated with progressive rheumatoid arthritis or disabling multiple sclerosis require a different set of treatments than do the pains and profound disability that characterize the patient with long-standing low back pain or chronic tension headache. Whereas drug therapy may be very prominent in the former patients, pharmacologic interventions may be minimized in lieu of intensive psychological and physical therapies in the latter.

During the past two decades, a great deal of attention has focused on the development of multidisciplinary pain programs as a system for the delivery of multimodality treatment for chronic pain. These programs were an innovation that evolved from the recognition that the complex problems posed by some patients with chronic pain exceeded the clinical capabilities of any one practitioner (151). Thousands of such programs now exist, and they are widely considered to be the state of the art in the management of patients with intractable pain associated with a high level of disability (152).

Multidisciplinary pain programs best address the needs of a specific subpopulation of pain patients. Although many of the patients referred to these programs have histories that include misuse of prescribed drugs, it is not clear that the structure of these programs is optimal for patients with other patterns of substance abuse, including abuse of illicit drugs, alcoholism, polysubstance abuse, or severe addiction. At the present time, it should not be assumed that the traditional multidisciplinary pain management program contains the expertise necessary to manage these clinical problems. Unfortunately, it is similarly doubtful that most substance abuse programs provide optimal assessment or management of pain. Further efforts are needed to foster communication between the disciplines of addiction medicine and pain management and define appropriate therapeutic strategies for those challenging patients who develop both pain and substance abuse. The individual practitioner should acknowledge that these disciplines possess differing insights into the clinical needs of this population and that a treatment team that includes specialists in both areas may be needed in some cases.

Although the chronic pain patients referred to multidisciplinary pain management programs represent an enormous drain on medical and societal resources, they are a small minority of those who experience chronic pain (153–155). Certainly, most patients with cancer pain do not need this approach to obtain symptom relief (156), and it is unlikely that most patients with other types of chronic pain, specifically those whose pain is not strongly determined by psychological factors or complicated by severe disability, would have a substantially different outcome if care were managed by a single knowledgeable practitioner who devised a multimodality therapeutic approach.

The long-term treatment of chronic pain with opioid drugs continues to be controversial. As discussed in the following sections, the conventional rejection of this approach in pain patients with no prior history of substance abuse is gradually evolving to a more balanced perspective. In populations with pain and substance abuse, however, there is neither a large and reassuring clinical experience nor empirical data that confirm the safety and efficacy of opioid therapy. Consequently, clinicians must exercise caution in considering opioid trials in such patients. Treatment guidelines must be clearly established if long-term therapy is undertaken. Generally, the use of opioid therapy for chronic pain should not be initiated if the patient has a current history of substance abuse, and such treatment should be offered those with a remote history of addiction only by experienced clinicians who can provide skilled assessment and management over time.

Acute Pain

Acute pain is, by definition, self-limited (or anticipated to be so) and usually is readily associated with a specific tissue injury, related to either trauma, surgery, or a disease process. The management of acute pain in the addict is not a trivial issue, since addicts experience traumatic injuries (157) and a myriad of medical disorders (158) at a disproportionately higher rate than does the general population. There is no reason to believe that the complex physiologic, behavioral, and psychological phenomena that are associated with drug addiction or abuse protect the individual from painful experiences; to the contrary, some have suggested that addicts may have a relatively low tolerance for pain (159).

Pains associated with recent tissue injury may be associated with signs of sympathetic nervous system stimulation, including diaphoresis, pupillary dilation, hypertension, tachycardia, and even nausea. Although the physiologic basis for this sympathetic hyperactivity is not known in humans, animal models of experimental inflammatory arthritis simulating rheumatoid arthritis (160), peripheral nerve injury simulating causalgia (161), and visceral tissue injury (162) have all demonstrated that co-activation of efferent sympathetic fibers occurs with the afferent volley induced by the lesion. Autonomic signs often render the patient's pain complaint more "believable" to the clinician and reassure the physician about the appropriateness of opioid analgesics for the management of the pain.

The interpretation of symptoms and signs in the opioid addict may be difficult, however, and this may contribute to difficulties encountered by these patients in the medical setting. With the knowledge that very diverse symptoms and signs can result either from a direct effect of a drug or from drug withdrawal, clinicians may express doubts about the nature of the pain or about medical comorbidity. For example, the objective physical signs associated with acute pain may also be produced by opioid withdrawal. Even obtundation with visual and auditory hallucinations, which can certainly be caused by opioids or other drugs of abuse, has been reported as a rare consequence of opioid withdrawal (163); this syndrome was speculated to be related to the withdrawal of morphine from non-mu receptors.

Although the management of acute pain in the addict may be difficult for even the most experienced clinician, it is nonetheless possible to develop guidelines that ensure a careful and fair assessment of the acute pain complaint and provide the best chance of achieving satisfactory pain relief in these

Table 57.9 Guidelines for Management of Acute Pain in the Known or Suspected Opioid Addict

1. Define the pain syndrome and provide treatment for the underlying disorder.
2. Distinguish among the patient with a remote history of drug abuse, the patient receiving methadone maintenance, and the patient who is actively abusing drugs.
3. Apply appropriate pharmacological principles of opioid use:
   a. Use the appropriate opioid.
   b. Use adequate doses and dosing intervals.
   c. Use appropriate route of administration.
4. Provide concomitant nonopioid therapies when appropriate:
   a. Use nonopioid analgesics.
   b. Use nonpharmacological therapies.
5. Recognize specific drug abuse behaviors.
6. Avoid excessive negotiations over specific drugs and doses.
7. Provide early consultation to appropriate services:
   a. Psychiatry and substance abuse service.
   b. Pain service (if available).
8. Anticipate problems associated with opioid prescription renewals if outpatient treatment is required.

circumstances (Table 57.9). The guidelines that follow should be considered complementary to those applied to the management of chronic cancer pain.

DEFINE THE PAIN SYNDROME AND PROVIDE PRIMARY TREATMENT

Acute pain almost always has an identifiable etiology, the characterization of which is an essential aspect to the assessment. This may allow specific primary therapy, which can have analgesic consequences. For example, specific orthopedic treatments and surgical debridement may be indicated as the single best method of acute pain relief for traumatic injuries involving fractures or burns, respectively. In the case of acute pain complicating medical disorders such as hemophilia, sickle cell anemia, or cancer, specific therapies directed at the underlying disorder may also be possible. For example, red cell transfusion may be indicated in patients with sickle cell disease as the initial treatment for acute "crisis" pain complicated by infection, lung disease, or stroke (164); this approach is combined with symptomatic opioid treatment (138). As mentioned previously, other primary disease-modifying approaches for sickle cell anemia are in clinical trials, each of which evaluates pain as one important endpoint (77, 78). Regardless of the disorder, the appropriate management of the underlying etiology for the pain often will decrease the opioid requirement.

DISTINGUISH AMONG TYPES OF ABUSERS

As discussed previously, the management of pain in the patient with a history of opioid abuse may be facilitated by distinguishing addicts who are actively abusing at the time of treatment from those with a remote history of drug abuse and those in methadone maintenance. Although the implications of these distinctions have not been clearly substantiated in prospective clinical studies, it is common practice to apply them in the setting of acute pain management (166).

Patients who are actively abusing either licit or illicit opioids, and those on methadone maintenance, may be assumed to have some degree of tolerance, which may be reflected in a need for relatively higher starting doses and shorter dosing intervals than generally are recommended for acute pain in the nonaddicted population. Furthermore, patients who are actively abusing drugs often manifest psychological disorders that can influence pain perception (such as anxiety and depression) and may require intervention.

As discussed previously, patients who are actively abusing drugs present a range of concerns related to difficulties in assessing subjective phenomena and the relatively high likelihood that aberrant drug-related behaviors will occur during opioid therapy for acute pain. Although it can also be postulated that medically ill patients who have abused drugs in the past or who are participating in methadone maintenance programs may be at increased risk of abuse behaviors following treatment for pain, in part related to the stress of the illness, this possibility has not been confirmed clinically and must be evaluated further.

APPLY APPROPRIATE PHARMACOLOGIC PRINCIPLES OF OPIOID USE

The use of opioid agonist-antagonist compounds for the management of acute pain in known or suspected opioid addicts generally is not preferred. These drugs have analgesic ceiling effects and may consequently be ineffective for severe pain, and their antagonist properties may precipitate withdrawal and increase pain in physically dependent patients. As in the treatment of cancer pain, pure agonist opioids usually are administered for the management of acute pain in these patients.

As noted, patients who are actively abusing opioids or who are participating in methadone maintenance may demonstrate a need for higher doses or shorter dosing intervals due to the development of tolerance. Tolerance to opioid analgesics decreases the duration of effective analgesia following a dose (167). For example, morphine, which has an average duration of analgesia of 3–4 hours, may produce only 1–2 hours of pain relief in a tolerant opioid addict.

Clinical experience in the nonaddict population has suggested that some patients with acute severe pain require rapid escalation of opioid doses. This may be facilitated by the use of intravenous administration, such as a continuous infusion supplemented by additional bolus doses (168). Patient-controlled analgesia (PCA), in which the patient self-administers an opioid intravenously, is being used with increasing frequency in this setting. PCA provides a means to rapidly titrate the opioid dose without the time delays inherent in physician or nurse administration of the drug (169). In the population without a history of substance abuse, studies indicate that PCA does not lead to excessive self-administration of the opioid. Indeed, even prolonged morphine PCA (for weeks) did not result in overmedication or addiction when administered to cancer patients with acute mucositis pain following bone marrow transplantation (18); in these patients, PCA actually decreased the requirements for morphine by 53% in comparison with standard intravenous infusion (170).

Despite this favorable impression and the lack of empiric data demonstrating different responses among those with and without a history of opioid abuse, many experts believe that the use of PCA in opioid addicts is problematic. Addicts may report a euphoric feeling or "high" that is coincident with an intravenous injection of an opioid, which presumably reinforces the self-administration of the drug; this phenomenon may increase the risk of aberrant use of the PCA device. Others believe, however, that intravenous opioids, including those administered via PCA, can be used effectively in this population if appropriate guidelines are followed. If PCA is employed, it must be implemented with due regard for the possibility that the patient with a history of abuse may be opioid tolerant. Unless appropriately large bolus doses and/or brief "lock-out" periods (i.e., the minimum interval allowed between doses) are selected, the tolerant patient may not receive an effective dose and may experience poor pain relief as a result. This, in turn, may precipitate frequent requests for additional drug doses that can be misinterpreted by the clinician as evidence of addiction, rather than the search for pain relief.

Although methadone is seldom administered for acute pain, it may be reasonable to consider its use in patients maintained on this drug for addiction. The use of methadone for the treatment of acute pain may facilitate the process by which the patient is tapered back to the baseline maintenance dose once the painful episode has been treated. However, this potential advantage must be weighed against several problems. Most methadone maintenance programs do not have the flexibility to allow increases in the daily methadone dose or dosing frequency. Thus, the treatment of pain with methadone usually must take place outside of the typical maintenance program. Equally important, the clinician must be knowledgeable about the use of methadone as an analgesic and the ways in which this varies from its role in addiction. Oral methadone is about half as potent as parenteral methadone (114), and as discussed previously, there is a large disparity between the plasma half-life of this drug, which ranges from less than a day to many days (101), and the duration of analgesia after a dose. Although one study suggested that the duration of action of methadone was as long as 12 hours in opioid-naive postoperative patients (171), a more recent controlled trial in cancer patients determined that the analgesic duration of both methadone and morphine was about 4 hours (102). The latter estimation is likely to apply to patients who previously have received methadone maintenance, since some degree of opioid tolerance characterizes this group and potentially reduces the duration of analgesic effect.

PROVIDE CONCOMITANT NONOPIOID THERAPIES WHEN APPROPRIATE

Nonopioid analgesics may be highly efficacious in specific acute pain syndromes, and their use may minimize the need for opioids in some situations. For example, a controlled clinical study has demonstrated that the NSAID ketoprofen, administered orally, may have significant efficacy in labor and postoperative pain (172). Ketorolac is available as a parenteral formulation in the United States and can be very effective in the management of acute pain; when this drug is administered in doses ranging from 30 to 90 mg, there is a reported analgesic potency equal to that of 6–12 mg morphine or 50–100 mg meperidine (147). Recent anecdotal experience with ketorolac in patients with acute pain from sickle cell anemia suggests that it may

provide enough analgesia to allow a substantial reduction in morphine doses, thereby improving dose-related constipation and sedation.

Although NSAIDs that have high analgesic efficacy may be useful even for severe acute pain in some patients, they are most often helpful in combination with opioids when the latter are causing dose-limiting opioid side effects. An NSAID should not be considered an opioid "substitute," and the desire to withhold opioids from suspected or known substance abusers with acute pain should not be viewed as an indication for these drugs.

Other types of nonopioid therapies may be useful in selected cases. For acute focal pain syndromes, regional anesthetic approaches, such as somatic or sympathetic nerve blocks, should be considered. It is well-accepted that anesthetic procedures may be more efficacious than systemic opioids in some types of acute pain, such as acute reflex sympathetic dystrophy (for which sympathetic blockade is indicated). These approaches must be implemented by experienced clinicians who can appropriately assess the risks and benefits for the patient.

Rarely, other nonpharmacological methods are useful adjuncts in acute pain management. For example, although recent studies have reported that transcutaneous electrical nerve stimulation cannot be distinguished from placebo in the treatment of chronic back pain (174) or acute postoperative pain (175), a plethora of earlier reports, many uncontrolled, suggested that this approach may be useful in a variety of pain syndromes (176). Because this technique is almost devoid of adverse effects, it is reasonable to consider a trial in the management of focal acute pain syndromes.

Psychological methods of pain control, such as relaxation and biofeedback (177), and other cognitive-behavioral approaches to pain management (178) have been most extensively employed in chronic pain management. These approaches may be helpful in providing coping strategies and skills to selected patients with acute pain associated with overwhelming anxiety or overtly maladaptive behaviors.

RECOGNIZE AND PREVENT SPECIFIC DRUG ABUSE BEHAVIORS

Patients who are actively abusing opioids may not set limits on drug-seeking behavior during pain treatment, even if opioids are provided liberally. In the hospital setting, some of these patients may engage in highly aberrant behaviors, such as tampering with drug infusion devices or dissolving tablets to inject the residue intravenously. Such behavior obviously cannot be tolerated. In many cases, efforts to control behavior are best implemented as part of a formal drug abuse program that is initiated coincident with medical and pain treatments. This goal clearly may be difficult, if not impossible, to accomplish.

Some measures can be recommended that may allow the continuation of opioid use for acute severe pain despite the potential for ongoing abuse behaviors. First, it is essential to engage the patient in a frank discussion that clearly defines the expectations for therapy and the limits of acceptable and unacceptable behavior. Second, simple security measures are advisable, such as the use of drug infusion pumps with locks that prevent changes in the settings; routine nursing policies in the hospital call for such rigorous supervision of the storage and dispensing of opioids. If oral opioid analgesics have been abused, the patient should be told that ingestions will be witnessed and that room searches for hidden pills or signs of hoarding will be done.

Although acute severe pain in a known opioid addict is seldom treated in the outpatient setting, additional guidelines should be followed if this circumstance arises. Guidelines should be written, given to the patient, and filed in the patient's medical record. They should state the absolute requirement that only one physician prescribe opioid medications and should provide procedures for prescription renewals and the response to lost or stolen prescriptions or drugs. As noted previously, it is generally prudent to require patients to report lost or stolen prescriptions or drugs to the police; drugs should be renewed only after a document that confirms this is obtained.

Prescription theft or forgery cannot be tolerated, and if either occurs when opioids are still indicated medically, therapy can be continued only if rigid guidelines are implemented. In some cases, patients should be admitted to the hospital to allow drug use to stabilize in a controlled environment.

If opioid therapy is no longer required, the drug should be withdrawn and the patient referred to an appropriate drug treatment program. Outpatients with a history of opioid abuse who are receiving opioid analgesics should be seen frequently, even daily if necessary, and a limited quantity of the drug should be prescribed at any one time. In some states, such as California, the prescription of opioids to a patient known to be a "habitual user" or addict must be reported to state regulatory agencies (179).

AVOID EXCESSIVE NEGOTIATION ABOUT SPECIFIC DRUGS AND DOSES

The management of acute pain should be approached systematically, and although the treatment approach should be discussed with the patient, the physician must assume responsibility for specific orders establishing the drug, doses, and route and frequency of administration. In the absence of known hypersensitivity to a specific drug, it is just as inappropriate for a patient to demand a specific opioid, dose, or route of administration for acute pain as it would be for the same patient to demand a specific antibiotic for management of an acute infection. This (or a similar) analogy should be discussed with the patient. Although there are obviously major differences between the management of an inherently subjective condition, such as pain, and other medical conditions, it is useful to consider the process of treatment from a similar medical orientation.

PROVIDE EARLY CONSULTATION WITH APPROPRIATE SERVICES

Many patients with acute pain and substance abuse disorders require interdisciplinary assessment and care. These patients are not well managed by the traditional medical model of acute care, since a unified approach to pain management and drug abuse may be beyond the competence of a single physician or clinical service. Indeed, without the benefit of expert consultation, a unified approach may appear to be impossible, since the fundamental goals of pain treatment and substance abuse treatment can conflict directly. Increased cooperation between pain specialists and addiction specialists must be encouraged during the treatment of these patients, and clinical research is needed to develop a new medical model that will provide flexibility in traditional concepts of substance abuse and pain management.

CHRONIC OPIOID THERAPY IN PATIENTS WITHOUT SUBSTANCE ABUSE

In most cultures, the fear of opioid addiction is etched deeply into the consciousness of both health care providers and the public at large. This fear may contribute to the undertreatment of both acute pain and chronic cancer-related pain in populations with no prior history of substance abuse, notwithstanding wide support for the first-line use of these drugs for these types of pain (18, 30, 47–49, 180–183). Undertreatment is most likely in two clinical settings: (a) postoperative patients whose pain intensity or duration exceeds that considered to be the norm (38), and (b) cancer patients with pain associated with early or limited disease who appear relatively well and function at nearly a normal level (184). Efforts to define the true risks involved in the therapeutic use of opioid drugs and debunk inappropriate attitudes about these drugs will likely benefit the management of these groups of patients most dramatically.

In the setting of chronic nonmalignant pain, the traditional view holds that opioid therapy is inappropriate because of the potential for addiction, the inevitability of side effects, and the likelihood that analgesic tolerance will compromise long-term efficacy. During the past 10 years, however, advances in pain research, burgeoning experience in the clinical management of pain, and greater recognition of the defining characteristics of addiction have suggested the need to critically evaluate this view (3, 24, 185–196).

Three major issues must be considered to assess the role of opioid therapy in chronic nonmalignant pain: (a) potential efficacy, (b) the possibility of adverse pharmacologic outcomes, and (c) the risk of addiction. These issues are themselves complex, and various aspects of each must be addressed independently to provide a comprehensive assessment of this approach (Table 57.10).

Table 57.10 Issues Relevant to the Evaluation of Chronic Opioid Therapy for Nonmalignant Pain

Critical Issues
Efficacy
    Responsiveness of nonmalignant pain syndromes to opioids
    Waning efficacy due to tolerance
    Effects on goals of therapy other than pain relief
Adverse pharmacologic outcomes
    Persistent side effects
    Long-term toxicity
    Subtle neuropsychological impairment
Drug dependence
    Terminology
    Role of physical dependence
    Risks of addiction

Related Issues
    Undertreatment of pain as a result of attitudes toward opioids
    Limited availability of opioids for bona fide medical uses
    Effects on medical practice from perceived risk of sanctions

---

Efficacy

The most relevant information about the potential efficacy of chronic opioid therapy for nonmalignant pain is provided by published reports (16, 19–24, 197–218) that specifically describe this approach. There are a limited number of controlled trials. Most describe one or two weeks of treatment, and although largely (204–208), but not uniformly (209), favorable to the treatment, their relevance to long-term management is dubious. None demonstrated the development of abuse behaviors during this brief therapy. One controlled trial had an open-label extension phase, during which treatment benefit was maintained (204). The most relevant study to date compared titrated doses of oral morphine against an active placebo (benztropine) in patients with chronic musculoskeletal pain using a crossover design that included 6-week treatment periods (203); there was a significant reduction in pain during morphine therapy, no change in physical or psychological functioning, and no evidence of psychological dependence (measured on a "drug liking" scale) or aberrant drug-related behavior.

Most of the empirical data have been provided by surveys. Older surveys, which originated from multidisciplinary pain management programs, portrayed opioid therapy as problematic, associated with relatively worse pain, more functional impairment and psychological distress, aberrant drug-related behaviors, and cognitive impairment (210–218). More recent surveys, however, suggest favorable outcomes. For example, a survey of 100 patients with mixed diagnoses who received various opioid drugs for many months reported good analgesia in more than one-half, with improved performance status associated with pain relief, and no serious toxicity or aberrant drug-related behaviors (24). Another survey of 124 patients with mixed pain diagnoses who were treated for 2–60 months with methadone recorded good pain control in almost 90%, improved psychological status on a validated questionnaire, and no reported morbidity (202).

These surveys suggest a spectrum of outcomes associated with opioid therapy. Although treatment can evidently become a problem in some disabled patients, there appears to be a subpopulation of patients with chronic nonmalignant pain who attains at least partial relief from opioid drugs for a prolonged period, without the development of opioid toxicity, clinically significant tolerance, or abuse behaviors. Although some patients who experience relief of pain demonstrate improvement in functional status, others do not. Abuse behaviors can develop, but appear to be very uncommon in the populations who were not surveyed in the setting of a multidisciplinary pain management program.

There is no evidence in these surveys that the type of chronic pain or degree of functional impairment at the start of therapy predicts the failure of opioid therapy. Although it is clear that opioid responsiveness can vary with characteristics of the patient or pain syndrome (223, 224), there is no evidence that any subgroup of patients with chronic pain is inherently resistant to this therapy. The example of neuropathic pain is illustrative. Although an inferred neuropathic mechanism for pain has been associated with a relatively lower likelihood of successful opioid therapy (55, 223–227), the potential for a favorable response in any individual case is unquestionable (21, 22, 24, 122, 202). Thus, the diagnosis of neuropathic pain may raise concerns about the ultimate outcome of opioid therapy but does not reliably predict its failure. Neither it nor other diagnoses of this type should be used as rationales for the withholding of therapy.

The issues surrounding this therapeutic approach are also illuminated by several surveys of chronic opioid therapy in nonpainful conditions. Long-term treatment with codeine, dihydrocodeine, propoxyphene, or methadone has been described in restless legs syndrome (219, 220), neuroleptic-induced dyskinesias (221), and intractable dyspnea (222). The long-term efficacy of the opioid administered in each of these conditions only rarely was compromised by the development of tolerance, and psychological dependence on the drugs did not occur.

The large number of opioid-treated patients with chronic pain described in the medical literature do not resolve many questions: How large is the group of patients who may benefit from chronic opioid therapy and how might they be identified? Is it the drug itself, the physician-patient relationship, the therapeutic context, the additional therapies provided within that context, or some combination of these factors that leads to the benefits and low prevalence of adverse consequences in these patients? Is the specific drug, method of dosing, or absolute dose important? If, as suggested by some of the surveys, enhanced comfort is not followed by improved function, are the benefits of therapy ever greater than the possible risks? What is the value of this treatment approach compared with others, even in the highly selected group of patients described?

DEVELOPMENT OF TOLERANCE

The possibility that opioid drugs potentially could provide some degree of pain relief to patients with chronic nonmalignant pain is perhaps less controversial than the observation that this relief may persist for a prolonged period of time. The concern that opioid analgesia inevitably wanes over time due to the development of pharmacologic tolerance is a critical element in the assessment of this therapeutic approach. It is apparent that chronic opioid therapy for nonmalignant pain would not be viable if pharmacologic tolerance to analgesia developed at such a rate that effective pain relief was brief or could be maintained only by rapid escalation of doses to unacceptable levels.

As discussed previously, a diminution in salutary opioid effects with prolonged administration is seldom observed in surveys of cancer patients and patients with chronic nonmalignant pain (11–24). In a study of three nonmalignant pain patients treated with meperidine for 3–12 months, the minimal effective analgesic plasma drug concentrations remained constant over time (228). Taken together, these data suggest that pharmacologic tolerance to analgesic effects is seldom the driving force for dose escalation in the clinical setting. Concern about waning analgesic efficacy due primarily to tolerance is overstated.

GOALS OF PAIN THERAPY

It has become widely accepted that the management of chronic nonmalignant pain must consider two goals simultaneously: improved comfort and functional gains. Opioid therapy would rarely be considered acceptable if it causes function to decline, even if patients report additional comfort. If function remains stable during therapy, however, the assessment of the approach is less straightforward. Although it is reasonable to propose that opioid therapy should be judged solely by the relief of pain, this is fundamentally a philosophic position. Some pain specialists, especially those who work within a multidisciplinary pain management program, assess the overall utility of treatment according to its effects on physical and psychosocial functioning. Continued efforts to resolve the controversy about this approach will require clear statements about the criteria by which it is evaluated.

As discussed previously, published surveys of opioid therapy for nonmalignant pain describe disparate outcomes. Some patients improved function during therapy and others did not. Surveys originating from pain clinics have demonstrated a relationship between opioid use on admission to the

treatment program and a greater number of prior hospitalizations and operations, more physical impairment, worse psychological disturbance, potential misuse of analgesic drugs, and poorer outcome of therapy (210–218).

Unfortunately, all these associations suffer from the usual problems inherent in surveys of highly selected patient populations. Just as clinicians inclined to use opioid therapy choose patients likely to benefit, many patients are referred to pain clinics because they have already demonstrated a problem with prescription drugs. Furthermore, the relationships derived from these data are correlative and do not determine causality. Thus, both opioid use and its reported adverse outcomes actually may result from a third factor, such as a more severe pain syndrome or a more aggressive, help-seeking personality. Similarly, patients who appear to benefit from opioid administration may, in fact, improve as a result of the relationship with a committed physician or associated treatments, rather than use of the drug itself. Finally, many of these surveys are compromised by methodological flaws, most notably the lack of long-term follow-up (229–231), and some surveys of pain clinic patients that purport to demonstrate adverse effects of opioids use definitions for drug-related behavior that do not conform to current standards (32).

Given the conflicting survey data, the most reasonable hypothesis is that opioids by themselves neither substantially improve nor damage function. For some patients, access to an opioid can contribute to globally impaired function or a tendency to drug abuse, whereas for others, the availability of a strong analgesic allows a degree of function that would otherwise be impossible. The drug has an important role in determining the overall outcome, but the nature of the outcome cannot be attributed to the pharmacology of the drug. Further studies are needed to evaluate this hypothesis and clarify those characteristics of the patient or treatment setting that will probably be more useful in predicting clinical response.

Adverse Pharmacologic Outcomes

The issue of potential adverse consequences due to the long-term administration of opioid drugs to patients with chronic nonmalignant pain must address two major considerations: the risk of major organ dysfunction and the incidence of persistent side effects. Among the most important of the potential side effects is subtle neuropsychological impairment, which could undermine concurrent rehabilitative efforts.

RISK OF MAJOR ORGAN DYSFUNCTION

Major organ toxicity following exposure to opioid drugs has not been observed among cancer patients or those on methadone maintenance (232–234). In a study of patients receiving methadone, hepatic dysfunction did not occur in the absence of viral hepatitis or alcoholism (235). Pulmonary edema has been reported in several dying cancer patients who were receiving high doses of an opioid (236), but this phenomenon is not relevant to the routine treatment setting. A variety of dysimmune effects have been reported in animal models (237–243), but human data are minimal and there is no evidence at the present time that opioids produce clinically relevant impairment of immune function.

PERSISTENT SIDE EFFECTS

In addition to well-known alterations in the central nervous system function, acute administration of an opioid produces changes in the hypothalamic-pituitary axis, peripheral vasculature, gastrointestinal tract, urinary tract, skin, and immune system (244, 245). Many of these effects are not experienced overtly by the patient, while some produce aversive phenomena, such as nausea, constipation, or confusion. With chronic administration, tolerance develops at different rates to each effect. The evaluation of long-term safety, therefore, depends on the prevalence of sustained opioid effects and the risks associated with each, whether experienced by the patient or not.

The most detailed assessment of this issue has been done in the methadone maintenance population. Studies of these patients have demonstrated persistent constipation, insomnia, and decreased sexual function in 10–20% of patients and the complaint of excessive sweating in a somewhat higher proportion (232–234). Elevated plasma proteins often persist, and occasionally, sustained abnormalities of hypothalamic-pituitary regulation, particularly abnormalities in the level and fluctuation of prolactin, are observed. Although some of the clinical effects can be troubling to the patient, none of the biochemical abnormalities has ever been associated with symptomatic disease. In the cancer population, clinical experience suggests that constipation is the most common opioid effect for which tolerance develops so slowly that persistent problems ensue.

Although cognitive impairment and disturbances in psychomotor functioning are commonly observed following acute administration of opioids to nontolerant patients or dose escalation in those on chronic therapy, these effects typically wane with stable long-term therapy (246). In opioid-treated patients with cancer pain, small impairments in reaction time have been observed (247, 248), but the clinical significance of this finding is not clear. A recent study of cancer patients receiving long-term morphine therapy revealed only minimal effects on cognitive and psychomotor functions related to driving (249). Another study of cancer patients suggested that tolerance to adverse neuropsychological effects that occur immediately after opioid dose escalation develops within two weeks (25). In patients without cancer, data are somewhat more conflicting. Surveys of patients admitted to pain programs who are dependent on opioids and other prescription drugs, as well as surveys of heroin addicts and methadone maintenance patients, have demonstrated clinically evident sedation or abnormalities on neuropsychological testing (213, 215, 216, 250–253). All these populations were subject to selection bias, however. Another survey of methadone maintenance patients did not reveal the problems reported by others (254), and none of the surveys controlled for the concurrent use of other drugs (particularly sedative-hypnotics), premorbid cognitive deficits, or history of head trauma. A small study in which pain patients who were chronically receiving opioids alone were compared with patients using benzodiazepines and no opioids noted substantial cognitive deficits only in the latter group (255). Equally reassuring, surveys of driving records performed in methadone maintained populations have not reveal a increased rate of infractions or accidents (256, 257).

These observations suggest that cognitive deficits could occur in patients with chronic nonmalignant pain who are administered long-term opioid therapy, but the prevalence and severity of these deficits, and their clinical significance, is probably less than commonly believed. Additional investigations are needed to clarify this issue, and the potential for cognitive impairment must be evaluated when opioids are employed in the clinical setting.

RISK OF ADDICTION

The potential for addiction or abuse is the most salient issue to address in the assessment of chronic opioid therapy for nonmalignant pain. This concern is ubiquitous in all clinical settings but historically has had the greatest impact on the management of this population.

The use of inappropriate nomenclature has been an ongoing concern in the assessment of addiction liability (32). As discussed previously, confusion between physical dependence and addiction is common in clinical settings. Misuse of the term "addiction" to describe the potential for withdrawal (physical dependence) can undermine efforts to evaluate opioid therapy in the individual patient and the population overall. Although the impact of physical dependence is certainly an appropriate issue to consider in the overall assessment of opioid therapy, withdrawal can be easily prevented and does not appear to preclude the uneventful discontinuation of treatment when this is required. Concern about physical dependence is thus minor in comparison with the possibility of iatrogenic addiction from the therapeutic use of opioid drugs.

The perception that opioid consumption may lead to the development of addiction derives largely from clinical experience with street addicts. The observed reactions of addicts following exposure to opioids are often assumed to be merely a more extreme expression of the experience of patients administered these agents for pain. Implicit in this view is the belief that such powerful reinforcements attend the use of these drugs that administration to otherwise normal individuals for appropriate medical reasons may be sufficient to produce addiction. If this were true, chronic opioid therapy for non-malignant pain should certainly be rejected, except perhaps in patients with life-threatening diseases.

Several types of data support the potentially reinforcing qualities of opioids. For example, some of these drugs are highly reinforcing in animals, and conditioned responses that perpetuate opioid consumption and increase the likelihood of use after detoxification have been well demonstrated in nonhuman experimentation (34, 258, 259). In humans, the high recidivism rate in detoxified addicts appears to support the existence of similar reinforcing properties (260, 261). Moreover, although physical dependence is now considered to be distinct from addiction, it has been postulated that the need to avoid the aversive experience of abstinence may also impel drug-seeking behavior. This classical conditioning theory of addiction views abstinence as an unconditioned response that can lead to a conditioned abstinence syndrome, which contributes to continued opioid-seeking (30). Because the potential for physical dependence is inherent in opioid pharmacology, this theory lends further support to the view that the risk of addiction may be an intrinsic property of the drug.

This conclusion is contradicted by extensive experience with pain patients, predominantly those with cancer pain, and numerous clinical investigations. For example, although it is widely believed that opioids produce the reinforcing experience of euphoria, surveys of cancer patients, postoperative patients, and normal volunteers indicate that elation is uncommon following administration of an opioid; dysphoria is observed more typically, especially in those who receive meperidine (100, 262, 263). The rarity of euphoria, the "high" or "rush" of the street addict, in patients suggests that there may be fundamental distinctions between opioid addicts and those without addiction who receive these drugs for pain.

The lack of euphoria does not, of course, exclude the possibility that other powerful reinforcements inhere in opioid pharmacology and impart a substantial risk of iatrogenic addiction. This possibility was suggested by early surveys of addicts, which noted that a relatively large proportion began their addiction as medical patients administered opioid drugs for pain (264–266). The most influential of these surveys recorded a pain history from 27% of white male addicts and 1.2% of black male addicts (266).

Surveys of addict populations, however, do not provide a valid measure of the addiction liability associated with the use of prescribed opioid drugs in various nonmalignant pain populations. Patient surveys are needed to define this risk. The Boston Collaborative Drug Surveillance Project evaluated 11,882 inpatients who had no prior history of addiction and were administered an opioid while hospitalized; only four cases of psychological dependence could be identified subsequently (267). A national survey of burn centers could find no cases of addiction in a sample of more than 10,000 patients without prior drug abuse history who were administered opioids for pain (39), and a survey of a large headache clinic identified opioid abuse in only three of 2369 patients admitted for treatment, most of whom had access to opioids (268). Cancer patients allowed to self-administer morphine for several weeks during an episode of painful mucositis do not demonstrate escalating use, which could indicate either tolerance or addiction (18, 269). The latter finding is consistent with clinical experience, which indicates that addiction is an exceedingly rare outcome during long-term opioid treatment of cancer pain.

These surveys of patients with pain are reassuring, but should not be assumed to be fully representative of the varied populations who seek treatment for chronic nonmalignant pain. As mentioned previously, data collected by multidisciplinary pain management programs suggest that abuse behaviors may be quite common among the patients referred to this setting (270). The latter surveys have numerous deficiencies, however, including selection bias, limited assessment, and the use of questionable criteria for the diagnosis of abuse or addiction (270). Moreover, the interpretation of all survey data require comparison to United States population prevalence rates for alcoholism (3–16%) and other forms of substance abuse (5–6%) (271).

Overall, these surveys provide evidence that the outcomes of drug abuse and addiction do not commonly occur among patients with no history of abuse who receive opioids for medical indications. Other epidemiologic data similarly contradict the notion that exposure to opioid drugs reliably leads to escalating use and recidivism after detoxification. The existence of so-called "chippers," individuals who use heroin recreationally on a periodic basis (272), belies the inevitability of the full addiction syndrome, even in those who consume the drugs for purposes other than pain control. More interesting, perhaps, is the evidence that a large proportion of soldiers who abused heroin in Vietnam stopped this activity abruptly on return to the United States, then demonstrated a low rate of relapse subsequently (273).

Addiction also associates with a number of factors that may be etiologically important and are uncommon in populations of chronic pain patients. These include specific personality disorders, such as psychopathy (149, 150), and a variety of situational and social factors never experienced by the typical medical patient. There is even some direct evidence that a genetic factor may be important in the genesis of addiction (274). A genetic predisposition has been demonstrated convincingly in alcoholism (275), and it has been postulated that the development of alcoholism in a small minority of those who imbibe is a parallel process to that determining opioid addiction in a small proportion of those administered these drugs (276).

These correlations, like the aforementioned surveys, suggest that opioid exposure by itself is not sufficient to produce abuse or addiction. The reinforcing properties of opioid drugs may be experienced differently by the individual predisposed to addiction than by the typical patient with chronic nonmalignant pain. Although correlations do not demonstrate causality, and it is conceivable that the characteristics of the street addict, like psychopathy, develop as a result of the addiction or relate to drug abuse through some other unknown factor, a reasonable hypothesis is that addiction results from the interaction between the reinforcing properties of opioid drugs and any number of characteristics that are specific to the individual. These characteristics, such as the capacity for euphoria from an opioid and psychopathy, appear to be rare among pain patients.

In sum, the existing data suggest that patients without a prior history of substance abuse are unlikely to become addicted during long-term opioid treatment of chronic pain. The risk should not be assumed to be nil, however, and the data also suggest that the risk may vary with specific characteristics of the patient. Unfortunately, little is known about the nature of these characteristics or their predictive value, and all impressions must be applied cautiously in practice. On the basis of clinical experience, it may be surmised that the risk of iatrogenic addiction during long-term opioid therapy is probably greater among those with a prior history of substance abuse, those with severe character pathology characterized by impulsivity, and those with a chaotic home environment; the risk is probably relatively lower among older than younger patients, even if drug-related problems have never occurred. Additional studies are needed to confirm this low risk of addiction or abuse overall and clarify the predictive value of specific patient characteristics.

OTHER OBSERVATIONS

As noted, the three critical issues most salient in assessing the potential utility of chronic opioid therapy in nonmalignant pain reflect basic medical concerns, the perceived benefits and risks to the individual patient. Other observations in this clinical setting may be useful in further clarifying the tension that exists between the licit medical use of opioid drugs and the concerns raised by their potential for abuse.

One such observation, which is also relevant to the chronic treatment of cancer pain, relates to the inadequate availability of oral opioids for long-term outpatient use. Although it is now widely accepted that the precepts of effective and humane medical care mandate unimpeded access to opioid drugs, at least by patients with some types of pain, the unfortunate reality is that these analgesics are not readily available in most parts of the world (47). In the United States, a number of opioids are available commercially, but prescribing is hampered by the failure of pharmacies to maintain a supply (277), strict limits in the quantities dispensed, and the burden of record-keeping. Although the factors that impede the ready access to opioid drugs for therapeutic purposes have not been assessed systematically, it is reasonable to presume that the fear of abuse plays a major role.

More compelling, perhaps, is the potential influence on prescribing practices of the intense efforts to reduce prescription drug abuse (278, 279). Physicians, pharmacists, and other professionals who administer opioids to patients may be aware of rare reports of legal action against physicians who have prescribed opioids, particularly those who have provided these drugs to patients with nonmalignant pain (280, 281). Other, often unverified cases are considered common knowledge, discussed among practitioners. This word-of-mouth transfer of information from physician to physician is a cardinal element of medical education and has been held responsible for the perpetuation of a number of misconceptions about the appropriate use of opioids (282). Although physicians generally agree with the need for careful monitoring of opioid prescription, and probably none would fault the identification and punishment of professionals engaged in criminal behavior (283), it may be speculated that the net effect of all these perceptions is to suggest that a degree of personal risk attends the administration of opioid drugs to patients.

Although controversial, it may be possible to infer the impact of prescription drug regulation on the licit use of opioids by evaluating the effects of the multiple copy prescription program. At the present time, nine states have implemented a program in which a copy of every prescription written for an opioid is sent to state regulators. In each of these states, the initiation of this program was followed by a greater than 50% reduction in the statewide prescribing of opioid drugs (284). This large reduction has been attributed to a decline in diversion and misuse by those in the regulatory and law enforcement communities, who favor multiple copy prescription programs as a useful method for "point of sale" monitoring (285, 286). Although reduced diversion and misuse in fact may occur, pain specialists believe that this change also reflects reduced prescribing by legitimate physicians, which worsens undertreatment (278, 279, 287–291).

Multiple copy prescription programs may reduce licit prescribing by reminding physicians about the scrutiny that accompanies opioid prescribing. The impact of this perception is likely to be greatest in the use of these drugs for patients with nonmalignant pain. This therapy remains controversial and prescribers cannot be assured that those in the regulatory community will not initiate an investigation, or even issue a sanction, because of bias against the approach and without regard for the details of the case. The concern that those in the regulatory community may make these judgments without adequate knowledge of either the medical or legal issues involved was recently piqued by a nationwide survey of members of boards of medical examiners (292). This survey revealed that a substantial proportion of these regulators had misconceptions about the laws and regulations governing opioid prescribing for nonmalignant pain and would initiate investigations of prescribers solely in response to knowledge that this therapy was taking place.

Medical decision-making may be unduly influenced by regulatory policies or fear of regulatory scrutiny. On the basis of this observation, it is reasonable to hypothesize that both the rejection of opioid therapy for nonmalignant pain and the tendency to undertreat acute pain and chronic cancer pain relate to a perceived risk of personal sanctions that is induced by these factors. Inasmuch as it is agreed that the factors responsible for the undertreatment of acute pain and cancer pain with opioid drugs should be reversed, and that decisions about chronic opioid therapy for nonmalignant pain should be made in response to medical considerations rather than the fear of sanctions, the influence of perceived risk on prescribing practices should be approached as an independent problem in medical care. In support of this view, some states have recently adopted statutes designed to reassure physicians of their autonomy in selecting patients for chronic opioid therapy and rendering medical judgments about appropriate administration of these drugs (278, 293).

Clinical Implications

It has been suggested that a selected subgroup of patients with chronic nonmalignant pain may be able to obtain sustained improvement in comfort from opioid drugs, without the development of significant toxicity or evidence of addiction. There is now general agreement among pain specialists that the doctrinaire rejection of this approach that was the norm must be replaced by a more balanced perspective that respects the complexity of the medical and pharmacologic issues, and a growing clinical experience with opioid therapy.

Table 57.11 Proposed Guidelines in the Management of Chronic Opioid Therapy for Nonmalignant Pain

1. Should be considered only after all other reasonable attempts at analgesia have failed.
2. A history of substance abuse, severe character pathology and chaotic home environment should be viewed as strong relative contraindications.
3. A single clinician should take primary responsibility for treatment. This practitioner should review all medical records.
4. Patients should give informed consent before the start of therapy and the consent discussion should be documented in the medical record. This discussion should cover recognition of the low risk of true addiction as an outcome, potential for cognitive impairment with the drug alone and in combination with sedative/hypnotics, likelihood that physical dependence will occur (abstinence possible with acute discontinuation), and understanding by female patients that children born when the mother is on opioid maintenance therapy will likely be physically dependent at birth.
5. After drug selection, doses should be given on an around-the-clock basis; several weeks should be agreed upon as the period of initial dose titration, and although improvement in function should be continually stressed, meaningful partial analgesia should be accepted as the appropriate goal of therapy.
6. Failure to achieve at least partial analgesia at relatively low initial doses in the patient with no substantial prior opioid exposure raises questions about the potential treatability of the pain syndrome with opioids; such an occurrence should lead to reassessment of the pain syndrome.
7. Emphasis should be given to attempts to capitalize on improved analgesia by gains in physical and social function. Opioid therapy should be considered complementary to other analgesic and rehabilitative approaches.
8. In addition to the daily dose determined initially, patients should be permitted access to additional analgesic on days of increased pain; two methods are acceptable: (a) Prescription of an additional 4–6 "rescue doses" to be taken as needed during the month; (b) Instruction that one or two extra doses may be taken on any day, but must be followed by an equal reduction of dose on subsequent days.
9. Initially, patients must be seen and drugs prescribed at least monthly. When stable, less frequent visits may be acceptable.
10. Exacerbations of pain may occur and, following a careful assessment, the clinician may decide to increase the stable dose. This change in therapy should be stated clearly for the patient and documented in the medical record. If repeated dose escalation is needed to maintain pain control, the clinician should consider admitting the patient to the hospital, where reassessment and dose adjustment can be accomplished in a controlled environment, a decision regarding continuation of therapy can be made with close observation of the patient, and additional analgesic techniques can be implemented.
11. Evidence of drug hoarding, acquisition of drugs from other physicians, uncontrolled dose escalation, or other aberrant behaviors must be carefully assessed. In some cases, tapering and discontinuation of opioid therapy will be necessary. Other patients may appropriately continue therapy within rigid guidelines. Consideration should be given to consultation with an addiction medicine specialist.
12. At each visit, assessment should specifically address: (a) Comfort (degree of analgesia); (b) Opioid-related side effects; (c) Functional status (physical and psychosocial); (d) Existence of aberrant drug-related behaviors.
13. Use of self-report instruments may be helpful but should not be required.
14. Documentation is essential and the medical record should specifically address comfort, function, side effects and the occurrence of aberrant behaviors repeatedly during the course of therapy.

Chronic opioid therapy should not be considered an approach to replace current pain management techniques. Rather, opioid therapy, like other primary analgesic treatments, may be best conceived as a useful element in a multimodality approach for chronic pain management. Indeed, it is even possible that opioid therapy could be complementary to the range of interventions offered in traditional multidisciplinary pain management programs (20). A large proportion of patients in these programs continue to experience severe pain and it would be valuable to provide more comfort, if this could be done without restraining rehabilitative efforts. Also, the failure and dropout rates from these programs are substantial (231, 294, 295), and it is interesting to consider whether access to better analgesic therapy could have a positive impact on these figures.

Guidelines based on clinical experience have been proposed for the management of opioid therapy in patients with nonmalignant pain (3) (Table 57.11). These guidelines attempt to capture the potential for salutary effects from opioid therapy without losing sight of the possibility of serious morbidity (pharmacological or functional) associated with this treatment approach. Additional data from prospective clinical series and controlled trials will likely lead to an evolution of therapeutic guidelines that will better optimize benefits and minimize risk.

The guidelines have several important implications. First, they indicate that patient selection is empirical at the present time. Opioid therapy is not considered a first-line approach, but might be evaluated against other therapies in terms of its risk:benefit ratio. As discussed previously, some patient characteristics, such as a prior history of substance abuse, should be viewed as strong relative contraindications given current experience. A recent survey suggests that some patients with a history of substance abuse may be able to maintain effective stable therapy, but the challenge of treating this population suggests that it should be undertaken only by experienced clinicians (296).

Second, the guidelines suggest the potential utility of a therapeutic opioid trial. Because opioid therapy can almost always be discontinued without difficulty after short-term administration, a therapeutic trial can be initiated like any other reversible analgesic approach. During a defined trial period, the dose can be adjusted while clinically relevant endpoints are monitored. These endpoints should include pain relief, opioid-related side effects, functional status (including the willingness to engage in other components of therapy), and the development of aberrant drug-related behaviors. A trial that produces benefits that exceed any evident disadvantage can be stabilized into a pattern of long-term administration, during which the same endpoints can be followed on a regular basis.

Third, the guidelines highlight the importance of patient consent. Some clinicians have adopted formal written consent as standard practice (297). Others obtain verbal consent, which is documented in the medical record. Regardless, a consent discussion is needed, which provides a useful opportunity to educate patients about the nature of the therapy and the need for responsible drug-taking behavior.

Fourth, the guidelines imply that long-term opioid therapy for nonmalignant pain must be based on a working knowledge of the widely accepted pharmacologic techniques described previously for cancer pain. Although some clinicians advocate specific approaches for the population with nonmalignant pain, such as the sole use of long-acting drugs or the avoidance of any "as needed" dosing, any such recommendation remains supported only by anecdote. In the absence of data from controlled trials, rigid adherence to any specific recommendation of this type is not warranted.

Although the extrapolation of dosing principles from the cancer pain population to the nonmalignant pain population can be recommended on theoretical grounds, the practical application can be problematic in some cases. As discussed previously, the absolute dose required to identify a favorable balance between analgesia and side effects is widely considered to be immaterial when treating the patient with cancer pain. In nonmalignant pain populations, however, the need for repeated dose adjustments can raise concerns. An intense focus on dose titration could possibly foster an unrealistic view of the treatment and divert attention from rehabilitative pursuits. Furthermore, high doses may increase the discomfort of the clinician, both in terms of appropriate medical considerations and the potential for increased regulatory scrutiny that may accompany this approach. If the clinician perceives any interference with other goals of treatment, this should be directly discussed with the patient. A careful reassessment is needed whenever pain worsens sufficiently to suggest the need for dose escalation. This reassessment should clarify the nature of the pain (including the status of its physical and psychological determinants), record side effects, determine functional status (both physical and psychosocial), and affirm the lack of aberrant drug-related behaviors.

Concern about regulatory scrutiny is understandable, and it is likely that dose escalation is sometimes withheld solely in response to a perceived risk of sanctions. When these concerns arise, it useful to seek additional consultations from specialists in pain management or take a strong stance by proactively informing local authorities of the treatment plan.

Finally, the guidelines note the importance of a clearly defined strategy for the management of aberrant drug-related behaviors, should they occur during therapy. Many clinicians have a stereotyped response to these behaviors based on a perception that they invariably represent addiction. This type of inflexibility is not justified given the diversity of these behaviors and the multiple meanings they may reflect. As discussed previously, the assessment of aberrant behavior in patients receiving an abusable drug for an appropriate clinical indication is a complex process that must distinguish the development of an addiction disorder from many other possible determinants.

Aberrant drug-related behavior requires a comprehensive assessment. In some cases, this assessment can be facilitated by consultation with a specialist in addiction medicine. It may include telephone calls to other physicians or local pharmacies, or a request to bring all medications and used bottles from home. A urine drug screen can be a very helpful aspect. On the basis of this assessment, some episodes of aberrant opioid use are best characterized as symptomatic of addiction, a diagnosis that suggests a targeted therapeutic approach best organized with the assistance of a specialist in addiction medicine. In other cases, a comprehensive assessment suggests that the diagnosis of addiction would not be appropriate. The clinician may wish to continue therapy while instituting a highly structured approach, which may include new instructions for dosing, more frequent visits, and smaller prescriptions. A written contract is sometimes useful and repeated urine drug screens can again be helpful.

The clinician who takes responsibility for opioid pharmacotherapy cannot confuse therapeutic support with tacit acceptance of questionable behavior. The demand for responsible drug-taking behavior should never be viewed as patient abandonment or an unjustified diversion from the goals of analgesia and function. The clinician must assess the patient over time, arrive at an appropriate diagnosis, and institute whatever controls are necessary to re-establish appropriate drug use. If the patient cannot comply with the requirements of therapy, the risks are too great to continue prescribing.

CONCLUSION

Principles of opioid therapy for the treatment of pain are well established and generally are believed to provide the capability for adequate pain control in the great majority of patients with acute and chronic pain. Concerns about opioid addiction or abuse imbue all aspects of management. Patients with a history of opioid abuse who are evaluated carefully and are determined to be appropriate candidates for opioid therapy, either brief or long-term, require ongoing assessment and the skillful adaptation of pharmacologic principles that have proved essential in the optimal management of pain in patients with no such history. The available data suggest that inadequate management of these patients is common and relates to some combination of reticence to prescribe on the part of physicians and noncompliance with therapy on the part of the patient. In the much larger population with no prior history of substance abuse, the potential for opioid addiction contributes substantially to the pervasive undertreatment of acute pain and chronic cancer pain and is the major issue that must be confronted in the chronic administration of opioid drugs to patients with nonmalignant pain.

Very few clinical investigations have been designed to address the relationship between the licit medical use of opioid drugs and their potential for illicit use. Studies are needed to clarify the range of responses of patients with a history of substance abuse who require treatment for severe pain and determine the true risk associated with the long-term use of opioids in patients with chronic nonmalignant pain. There is a need to replace anecdotal observations with scientific findings and maintain the balance between needed regulation of prescription drugs and their availability for clinical use. Physicians should be reassured that aggressive opioid management of acute pain and chronic cancer pain is fully acceptable, and those physicians who choose to employ opioids in the management of chronic nonmalignant pain should not fear reprisals for this decision if it is undertaken with the care that such controversial therapy warrants. All of these objectives will be more likely to occur if an active dialogue develops between pain specialists and addiction specialists.

References

1. Uhlenhuth EH, DeWit H, Balter MB, Johanson CE, Mellinger GD. Risks and benefits of long-term benzodiazepine use. J Clin Psychopharmacol 1988;8:161–167.
2. Woods JH, Katz JL, Winger G. Use and abuse of benzodiazepines. Issues relevant to prescribing. JAMA 1988;260:3476–3480.
3. Portenoy RK. Opioid therapy for chronic nonmalignant pain: current status. In: Fields HL, Liebeskind JC, eds. Progress in Pain Research and management. Pharmacological approaches to the treatment of chronic pain: new concepts and critical issues. Seattle: IASP Press, 1994; 1:247–288.
4. Portenoy RK. Opioid analgesics. In: Portenoy RK, Kanner RM, eds. Pain management: theory and practice. Philadelphia: FA Davis, 1996: 248–276.
5. Dole VP. Narcotic addiction, physical dependence and relapse. N Engl J Med 1972;286: 988–992.
6. Jaffe JH. Drug addiction and drug abuse. In: Gilman AG, Goodman LS, Rall TW, Murad F, eds. The pharmacological basis of therapeutics. 7th edition. New York: Macmillan, 1985:532–581.
7. Martin WR, Jasinski DR. Physiological parameters of morphine dependence in man—tolerance, early abstinence, protracted abstinence. J Psychiatr Res 1969;7:9–17.
8. Ling GSF, Paul D, Simantov R, Pasternak GW. Differential development of acute tolerance to analgesia, respiratory depression, gastrointestinal transit and hormone release in a morphine infusion model. Life Sci 1989;45:1627–1636.

9. Ling W, Wesson DR. Drugs of abuse—opiates. West J Med 1990;152:565–572.
10. World Health Organization. Technical report no. 407: Expert Committee on Drug Dependence, 16th report. Geneva: World Health Organization, 1969.
11. Portenoy RK. Opioid tolerance and efficacy: basic research and clinical observations. In: Gebhardt G, Hammond D, Jensen T, eds. Proceedings of the VII World Congress on Pain. Progress in pain research and management. Seattle: IASP Press, 1994;2:595–619.
12. Foley KM. Clinical tolerance to opioids. In: Basbaum AI, Besson J-M, eds. Towards a new pharmacotherapy of pain. Chichester: John Wiley, 1991:181–204.
13. Twycross RG, Lack SA. Therapeutics in terminal cancer. 2nd edition. Edinburgh. Churchill Livingstone, 1990.
14. Foley KM. The treatment of cancer pain. N Engl J Med 1985;313:84–95.
15. Twycross RG. Clinical experience with diamorphine in advanced malignant disease. Int J Clin Pharmacol Ther Toxicol 1974;9:184–198.
16. Kanner RM, Foley KM. Patterns of narcotic drug use in a cancer pain clinic. Ann N Y Acad Sci 1981;362:161–172.
17. Gourlay GK, Cherry DA, Cousins MJ. A comparative study of the efficacy and pharmacokinetics of oral methadone and morphine in the treatment of severe pain in patients with cancer. Pain 1986;25:297–312.
18. Chapman CR, Hill HF. Prolonged morphine self-administration and addiction liability: evaluation of two theories in a bone marrow transplant unit. Cancer 1989;63:1636–1644.

19. Taub A. Opioid analgesics in the treatment of chronic intractable pain of non-neoplastic origin. In: Kitahata LM, Collins D, eds. Narcotic analgesics in anesthesiology. Baltimore: Williams & Wilkins, 1982:199–208.
20. France RD, Urban BJ, Keefe FJ. Long-term use of narcotic analgesics in chronic pain. Soc Sci Med 1984;19:1379–1382.
21. Portenoy RK, Foley KM. Chronic use of opioid analgesics in non-malignant pain: report of 38 cases. Pain 1986;25:171–186.
22. Urban BJ, France RD, Steinberger DL, Scott DL, Maltbie AA. Long-term use of narcotic-antidepressant medication in the management of phantom limb pain. Pain 1986;24:191–197.
23. Portenoy RK. Opioid therapy in the management of chronic back pain. In: Tollison CD, ed. Interdisciplinary rehabilitation of low back pain. Baltimore: Williams & Wilkins, 1989:137–158.
24. Zenz M, Strumpf M, Tryba M. Long-term opioid therapy in patients with chronic nonmalignant pain. J Pain Symptom Manage 1992;7: 69–77.
25. Bruera E, Macmillan K, Hanson JA, MacDonald RN. The cognitive effects of the administration of narcotic analgesics in patients with cancer pain. Pain 1989;39:13–16.
26. Redmond DE, Krystal JH. Multiple mechanisms of withdrawal from opioid drugs. Ann Rev Neurosci 1984;7:443–478.
27. Heishman SJ, Stitzer ML, Bigelow GE, Liebson IA. Acute opioid physical dependence in humans: effect of varying the morphine-naloxone intervals. J Pharmacol Exp Ther 1989;250: 485–491.
28. World Health Organization. Technical report

no. 516: youth and drugs. Geneva: World Health Organization, 1973.

29. American Psychiatric Association. Diagnostic and statistical manual of mental disorders. 4th edition. Washington, DC. American Psychiatric Association, 1994.

30. Wikler A. Opioid dependence: mechanisms and treatment. New York: Plenum Press, 1980.

31. Rinaldi RC, Steindler EM, Wilford BB, Goodwin D. Clarification and standardization of substance abuse terminology. JAMA 1988;259:555–557.

32. Sees KL, Clark HW. Opioid use in the treatment of of chronic pain: assessment of addiction. J Pain Symptom Manage 1993;8:257–264.

33. Halpern LM, Robinson J. Prescribing practices for pain in drug dependence: a lesson in ignorance. Adv Alcohol Subst Abuse 1985/1986;5:184–197.

34. Dai S, Corrigal WA, Coen KM, Kalant H. Heroin self-administration by rats: influence of dose and physical dependence. Pharmacol Biochem Behav 1989;32:1009–1015.

35. Weissman DE, Haddox JD. Opioid pseudoaddiction—an iatrogenic syndrome. Pain 1989;36:363–366.

36. Wilford BB. Abuse of prescription drugs. West J Med 1990;152:609–612.

37. Gonzales GR, Coyle N. Treatment of cancer pain in a former opioid abuser: fears of the patient and staff and their influence on care. J Pain Symptom Manage 1992;7(4):246–249.

38. Edwards WT. Optimizing opioid treatment of postoperative pain. J Pain Symptom Manage 1990;5:S24–S36.

39. Perry S, Heidrich G. Management of pain during débridement: a survey of U.S. burn units. Pain 1982;13:267–280.

40. Jorgensen L, Mortensen M-J, Jensen N-H, Eriksen J. Treatment of cancer pain patients in a multidisciplinary pain clinic. The Pain Clinic 1990;3:83–89.

41. Moulin DE, Foley KM. Review of a hospital-based pain service. In: Foley KM, Bonica JJ, Ventafridda V, eds. Advances in pain research and therapy. Second International Congress on Cancer Pain. New York: Raven Press, 1990;16:413–427.

42. Schug SA, Zech D, Dorr U. Cancer pain mangement according to WHO analgesic guidelines. J Pain Symptom Manage 1990;5:27–32.

43. Schug SA, Zech D, Grond S, Jung H, Meurser T, Stobbe B. A long-term survey of morphine in cancer pain patients. J Pain Symptom Manage 1992;7:259–266.

44. Ventafridda V, Tamburini M, DeConno F. Comprehensive treatment in cancer pain. In: Fields HL, Dubner R, Cervero F, eds. Advances in pain research and therapy. Proceedings of the Fouth World Congress on Pain. New York: Raven Press, 1985;9:617–628.

45. Ventafridda V, Tamburini M, Caraceni A, et al. A validation study of the WHO method for cancer pain relief. Cancer 1990;59:850–856.

46. Walker VA, Hoskin PJ, Hanks GW, White ID. Evaluation of WHO analgesic guidelines for cancer pain in a hospital-based palliative care unit. J Pain Symptom Manage 1988;3:145–149.

47. World Health Organization. Cancer pain relief, with a guide to opioid availability. 2nd edition. Geneva: World Health Organization, 1996.

48. Health and Public Policy Committee, American College of Physicians. Drug therapy for severe chronic pain in terminal illness. Ann Intern Med 1983;99:870–873.

49. Agency for Health Care Policy and Research, U.S. Dept. of Health and Human Services. Clinical practice guideline number 9: management of cancer pain. Washington, DC: U.S. Department of Health and Human Services, 1994.

50. Ad Hoc Committee on Cancer Pain, American Society of Clinical Oncology. Cancer pain assessment and treatment curriculum guidelines. J Clin Oncol 1992;10:1976–1982.

51. American Pain Society. Principles of analgesic use in the treatment of acute pain and cancer pain. Skokie, IL : American Pain Society, 1992.

52. Breitbart W, McDonald MV, Rosenfeld B, Passik SD, Hewitt D, Thaler H, Portenoy RK. Pain in ambulatory AIDS patients. I. Pain characteristics and medical correlates. Pain (in press).

53. Rosenfeld B, Breitbart W, McDonald MV, Passik SD, Thaler H, Portenoy RK. Pain in ambulatory AIDS patients. II. Impact of pain on psychological functioning and quality of life. Pain (in press).

54. Breitbart W, Rosenfeld BD, Passik SD, McDonald MV, Thaler H, Portenoy RK. The undertreatment of pain in ambulatory AIDS patients. Pain 1996;65:239–245.

55. Arner S, Myerson BA. Lack of analgesic effects of opioids on neuropathic and idiopathic forms of pain. Pain 1988;33:11–23.

56. American Psychiatric Association. Diagnostic and statistical manual of mental disorders. 4th edition. Washington, DC: American Psychiatric Association, 1994.

57. Portenoy RK, Hagen NA. Breakthrough pain: definition, prevalence and characteristics. Pain 1990;41:273–282.

58. Portenoy RK. Issues in the management of neuropathic pain. In: Basbaum A, Besson J-M, eds. Towards a new pharmacology of pain. New York: John Wiley, 1991:393–416.

59. Merskey H, Bogduk N. Classification of chronic pain. 2nd edition. Seattle: IASP Press, 1994.

60. Hegarty A, Portenoy RK. Pharmacotherapy of neuropathic pain. Semin Neurol 1994;14:213–224.

61. Portenoy RK. Cancer pain: epidemiology and syndromes. Cancer 1989;63:2298–2307.

62. Foley KM. Pain syndromes in patients with cancer. In: Portenoy RK, Kanner RM, eds. Pain management: theory and practice. Philadelphia: FA Davis, 1996:191–216.

63. Gonzales GR, Elliot KJ, Portenoy RK, Foley KM. The impact of a comprehensive evaluation in the management of cancer pain. Pain 1991;47:141–144.

64. Takeda F. Results of field-testing in Japan of WHO draft interim guidelines on relief of cancer pain. Pain Clin 1986;1:83–89.

65. Coyle N, Adlehardt J, Foley KM, Portenoy RK. Character of terminal illness in the advanced cancer patient: pain and other symptoms in the last 4 weeks of life. J Pain Symptom Manage 1990;5:83–93.

66. Cherny NI, Portenoy RK. Systemic drugs for cancer pain. Pain Digest 1995;5:245–263.

67. Salazar OM, Rubin P, Hendrickson FR, et al. Single-dose half-body irradiation for palliation of multiple bone metastases from solid tumors. Final Radiation Therapy Oncology Group report. Cancer 1986;58:29–36.

68. Tong D, Gillick L, Hendrickson FR. The palliation of symptomatic osseous metastases: final results of the study by the Radiation Therapy Oncology Group. Cancer 1982;50:893–899.

69. Gilbert HA, Kagan AR, Nussbaum H, et al. Evaluation of radiation therapy for bone metastases: pain relief and quality of life. AJR 1977;129:1095–1096.

70. Siegal T, Tiqva P, Siegal T. Vertebral body resection for epidural compression by malignant tumors. Results of forty-seven consecutive operative procedures. J Bone Joint Surg 1985;67A:375–382.

71. Sundaresan N, DiGiacinto GV. Antitumor and antinociceptive approaches to control cancer pain. Med Clin North Am 1987;71:329–348.

72. MacDonald N. The role of medical and surgical oncology in the management of cancer pain. In: Foley KM, Bonica JJ, Ventafridda V, eds. Advances in pain research and therapy. New York: Raven Press, 1990;16:27–40.

73. Bonadonna G, Molinari R. Role and limits of anticancer drugs in the treatment of advanced pain. In: Bonica JJ, Ventafridda V, eds. Advances in pain research and therapy. New York: Raven Press, 1979;2:131–138.

74. Brule G. Role and limits of oncologic chemotherapy of advanced cancer pain. In: Bonica JJ, Ventafridda V, eds. Advances in pain research and therapy. New York: Raven Press, 1979;2:139–144.

75. Tannock IF, Osoba D, Stockler MR, et al. Chemotherapy with mitoxantrone plus prednisone or prednisone alone for symptomatic hormone-resistant prostate cancer: a Canadian randomized trial with palliative endpoints. J Clin Oncol 1996;14:1756–1764.

76. Bruera E, MacDonald RN. Intractable pain in patients with advanced head and neck tumors: a possible role of local infection. Cancer Treat Rep 1986;70:691–692.

77. Zipursky A, Brown EJ, O'Brodovich H, Coppes MJ, Oliveri NF. Oxygen therapy in sickle cell disease. Am J Pediatr Hematol Oncol 1992;14(3):222–228.

78. Charache S, Terrin ML, Moore RD, et al. Effect of hydroxyurea on the frequency of painful crises in sickle cell anemia. Investigators of the Multicenter Study of Hydroxyurea in Sickle Cell Anemia. N Engl J Med 1995;332(20):1317–1322.

79. Sunshine A, Olson NZ. Nonnarcotic analgesics. In: Wall PD, Melzack R, eds. Textbook of pain. 3rd edition. Edinburgh: Churchill Livingstone, 1994:923–942.

80. Portenoy RK, Kanner RM. Nonopioid and adjuvant analgesics. In: Portenoy RK, Kanner RM, eds. Pain management: theory and practice. Philadelphia: FA Davis, 1996:219–247.

81. Ventafridda V, Fochi C, DeConno F, Sganzerla E. Use of nonsteroidal anti-inflammatory drugs in the treatment of pain in cancer. Br J Clin Pharmacol 1980;10:343–346.

82. Sandler DP, Smith JC, Weinberg CR, et al. Analgesic use and chronic renal disease. N Engl J Med 1989;320:1238–1243.

83. Cohen A, Thomas GB, Coen EE. Serum concentration, safety and tolerance of oral doses of choline magnesium trisalicylate. Curr Ther Res 1978;23:358–364.

84. Porro GB, Petrillo M, Ardizzone S. Salsalate in the treatment of rheumatoid arthritis: a double-blind clinical and gastroscopic trial versus piroxicam. II. Endoscopic evaluation. J Int Med Res 1989;17:320–323.

85. Danesh BJZ, Saniabadi AR, Russell RI, Lowe GDO. Therapeutic potential of choline magnesium trisalicylate as an alternative to aspirin for patients with bleeding tendencies. Scot Med J 1987;32:167–168.

86. Montrone F, Caruso I, Cazzola M. Salsalate in the treatment of rheumatoid arthritis in a double-blind clinical and gastroscopic trial versus piroxicam. I. Clinical trial. J Int Med Res 1989;17:316–319.

87. Langman MJS, Well J, Wainwright P, et al. Risks of bleeding peptic ulcer associated with individual nonsteroidal anti-inflammatory drugs. Lancet 1994;343:1075–1078.

88. Savage RL, Moller PW, Ballantyne CL, et al. Variation in the risk of peptic ulcer complications with nonsteroidal anti-inflammatory drug therapy. Arthritis Rheum 1993;36:84–90.

89. Houde RW. Analgesic effectiveness of the narcotic agonist-antagonists. Br J Clin Pharmacol 1979;7:297S–308S.

90. Hoskin PJ, Hanks GW. Opioid agonist-antagonist drugs in acute and chronic pain patients. Drugs 1991;41:329–344.

91. Portenoy RK, Maldonado M, Fitzmartin R, Kaiko R, Kanner R. Controlled-release morphine sulfate: analgesic efficacy and side-effects of a 100 mg tablet in cancer pain patients. Cancer 1989;63:2284–2288.

92. Galer BS, Coyle N, Pasternak GW, Portenoy RK. Individual variability in the response to different opioids. Report of five cases. Pain 1992;49:87–91.

93. Hanna MH, Peat SJ, Woodham M, Knibb A, Fung C. Analgesic efficacy and CSF pharmacokinetics of intrathecal morphine-6-glucuronide: comparison with morphine. Br J Anaesth 1990;64:547–550.

94. Peterson GM, Randall CTC, Paterson J. Plasma levels of morphine and morphine glucuronides in the treatment of cancer pain: relationship to renal function and route of administration. Eur J Clin Pharmacol 1990;38:121–124.

95. Osborne JR, Joel SP, Slevin ML. Morphine intoxication in renal failure: the role of morphine-6-glucuronide. Br Med J 1986;292:1548–1549.

96. Hagen NA, Foley KM, Cerbone DJ, Portenoy RK, Inturrisi CE. Chronic nausea and morphine-6-glucuronide. J Pain Symptom Manage 1991;6:125–128.

97. Portenoy RK, Thaler HT, Inturrisi CE, et al. The metabolite, morphine-6-glucuronide, contributes to the analgesia produced by morphine infusion in pain patients with normal renal function. Clin Pharmacol Ther 1992;51:422–431.

98. Sjogren P. Clinical implications of morphine metabolites. In: Portenoy RK, Bruera EB, eds. Topics in palliative care. Vol 1. New York: Oxford University Press (in press).

99. Tiseo PJ, Thaler HT, Lapin J, et al. Morphine-6-glucuronide concentrations and opioid-related side effects: a survey in cancer patients. Pain 1995;61:47–54.

100. Kaiko RF, Foley KM, Grabinski PY, et al. Central nervous system excitatory effects of meperidine in cancer patients. Ann Neurol 1983;13:180–185.

101. Plummer JL, Gourlay GK, Cherry DA, Cousins MJ. Estimation of methadone clearance: application in the management of cancer pain. Pain 1988;33:313–322.

102. Gorchow L, Sheidler V, Grossman S, Green L, Enterline J. Does intravenous methadone provide longer lasting analgesia than intravenous morphine? A randomized, double blind study. Pain 1989;38:151–157.

103. Korte W, de Stoutz N, Morant R. Day-to-day titration to initiate transdermal fentanyl in patients with cancer pain: short- and long-term experiences in a prospective survey of 39 patients. J Pain Symptom Manage 1996;11:146.

104. Donner B, Zenz M, Tryba M, Strumpf M. Direct conversion from oral morphine to transdermal fentanyl: a multicenter study in patients with cancer pain. Pain 1996;64:527–534.

105. Portenoy RK, Southam M, Gupta SK, et al. Transdermal fentanyl for cancer pain: repeated dose pharmacokinetics. Anesthesiology 1993; 28:36–43.

106. Bruera E, Brenneis C, MacDonald RN. Continuous sc infusion of narcotics for the treatment of cancer pain: an update. Cancer Treat Rep 1987;71:953.

107. Swanson G, Smith J, Bulich R, et al. Patient-controlled analgesia for chronic cancer pain in the ambulatory setting: a report of 117 cases. J Clin Oncol 1989;7:1903–1906.

108. Cousins MJ, Mather LE. Intrathecal and epidural administration of opioids. Anesthesiology 1984;61:276–310.

109. Arner S, Rawal N, Gustafson LL. Clinical experience of long-term treatment with epidural and intrathecal opioids: a nationwide survey. Acta Anaesthesiol Scan 1988;32:253–259.

110. Plummer JL, Cherry DA, Cousins MJ, et al. Long-term spinal administration of morphine in cancer and non-cancer pain: a retrospective study. Pain 1991;44:215–220.

111. Payne R. Role of epidural and intrathecal narcotics and peptides in the management of cancer pain. Med Clin North Am 1987;71:313–328.

112. Portenoy RK, Moulin DE, Rogers A, Inturrisi CE, Foley KM. Continuous intravenous infusion of opioids in cancer pain: review of 46 cases and guidelines for use. Cancer Treat Rep 1986;70:575–581.

113. Cole L, Hanning CD. Review of the rectal use of opioids. J Pain Symptom Manage 1990;5:118–126.

114. Houde RW. Misinformation: side effects and drug interactions. In: Hill CS, Fields WS, eds. Advances in pain research and therapy. New York: Raven Press, 1989;11:145–161.

115. Portenoy RK. Management of opioid side effects. Singapore Med J 1994;23:160–170.

116. Derby S, Portenoy RK. Assessment and management of constipation. In: Portenoy RK, Bruera EB, eds. Topics in palliative care. Vol 1. New York: Oxford University Press (in press).

117. Bruera E, Brenneis C, Paterson AH, MacDonald RN. Use of methylphenidate as an adjuvant to narcotic analgesics in patients with advanced cancer. J Pain Symptom Manage 1989; 4:3–6.

118. De Stoutz ND, Bruera E, Suarez-Almazor M. Opioid rotation for toxicity reduction in terminal cancer patients. J Pain Symptom Manage 1995;10:378–384.

119. Portenoy RK. Adjuvant analgesics. In: Cherny NI, Foley KM, eds. Hematology/oncology clinics of North America pain and palliative care. Philadelphia: WB Saunders, 1996:103–119.

120. Ettinger AB, Portenoy RK. Use of corticosteroids in the treatment of symptoms associated with cancer. J Pain Symptom Manage 1988;3:99–104.

121. Bruera E, Roca E, Cedaro L, Carraro S, Chacon R. Action of oral methylprednisolone in terminal cancer patients: a prospective randomized double-blind study. Cancer Treat Rep 1985; 69:751–754.

122. Portenoy RK, Foley KM, Inturrisi CE. The nature of opioid responsiveness and its implications for neuropathic pain: new hypotheses derived from studies of opioid infusions. Pain 1990;43:273–286.

123. Young RF, Brechner T. Electrical stimulation of the brain for relief of intractable pain due to cancer. Cancer 1986;57:1266–1272.

124. Fosburg MT, Crone RK. Nitrous oxide analgesia for refractory pain in the terminally ill. JAMA 1983;250:511–513.

125. Raj PP. Prognostic and therapeutic local anesthetic block. In: Cousins MJ, Bridenbaugh PO, eds. Neural blockade in clinical anesthesia and management of pain. 2nd edition. Philadelphia: JB Lippincott, 1988:899–933.

126. Cousins MJ, Dwyer B, Gibb D. Chronic pain and neurolytic neural blockade. In: Cousins MJ, Bridenbaugh PO, eds. Neural blockade in clinical anesthesia and management of pain. 2nd edition. Philadelphia: JB Lippincott, 1988: 1053–1084.

127. Cherny NI, Arbit E, Jain S. Invasive techniques in the management of cancer pain. In: Cherny NI, Foley KM, eds. Hematology/oncology clinics of North America pain and palliative care. Philadelphia: WB Saunders, 1996: 121–138.

128. Nitescu P, Applegren L, Linder LE, Sjoberg M, Hultman E, Curelaru I. Epidural versus intrathecal morphine-bupivacaine: assessment of consecutive treatments in advanced cancer pain. J Pain Symptom Manage 1990;5:18–26.

129. Gybels JM, Sweet WH. Neurosurgical treatment of persistent pain. Basel: Karger, 1989.

130. Pagni CA. Role of neurosurgery in cancer pain: re-evaluation of old methods and new trends. In: Benedetti C, Chapman CR, Moricca G, eds. Advances in pain research and therapy. New York: Raven Press, 1984;7:603–629.

131. Arbit E, ed. Surgical treatment of cancer-related pain. New York: Futura, 1993.

132. Glover J, Dibble S, Dodd MJ, Miaskowski C. Mood state of oncology outpatients: does pain make a difference? J Pain Symptom Manage 1995;10:120–128.

133. Massie MJ, Holland JC. The cancer patient with pain: psychiatric complications and their management. Med Clin North Am 1987;71:243–258.

134. Loscalzo M. Psychological approaches to the management of pain in patients with cancer. In: Cherny NI, Foley KM, eds. Hematology/oncology clinics of North America pain and palliative care. Philadelphia: WB Saunders, 1996:139–155.

135. Breitbart W. Psycho-oncology: depression, anxiety, delirium. Semin Oncol 1994;21:754–769.

136. Cleeland CS, Tearnan BH. Behavioral control of cancer pain. In: Holzman AD, Turk DC, eds. Pain management. New York: Pergamon Press, 1986.

137. Fishman B, Loscalzo M. Cognitive-behavioral interventions in the management of cancer pain: principles and applications. Med Clin North Am 1987;71:271–289.

138. Cagnello VW. The use of hypnotic suggestion for relief of malignant disease. Int J Clin Exp Hypn 1961;9:17–22.

139. Fotopoulos SS, Graham C, Cook MR. Psychophysiologic control of cancer pain. In: Bonica JJ, Ventafridda V, eds. Advances in pain research and therapy. New York: Raven Press, 1979;2:231–243.

140. Simonton O, Matthews-Simonton S, Sparks T. Psychological intervention in the treatment of cancer. Psychosomatics 1980;21:226–233.

141. Fleming U. Relaxation therapy for far-advanced cancer. Practitioner 1985;229:471–475.

142. Macaluso C, Weinberg D, Foley KM. Opioid abuse and misuse in a cancer pain population [abstract]. J Pain Symptom Manage 1988; 3:S24.

143. Kantor TG, Cantor R, Tom E. A study of hospitalized surgical patients on methadone maintenance. Drug Alcohol Depend 1980;6:163–173.

144. Rubenstein R, Spiro I, Wolff WI. Management of surgical problems in patients on methadone maintenance. Am J Surg 1976;131:566–569.

145. Sawe J, Hansen J, Ginman C, et al. A patient-controlled dose regimen of methadone in chronic cancer pain. Br Med J 1981;282:771–773.

146. Inturrisi CE, Colburn WA, Kaiko RF, Houde RW, Foley KM. Pharmacokinetics and pharmacodynamics of methadone in patients with chronic pain. Clin Pharmacol Ther 1987;41:392–401.

147. Hansen J, Ginman C, Hartvig P, et al. Clinical evaluation of oral methadone in treatment of cancer pain. Acta Anaesth Scand Suppl 1982;74:124–127.

148. Beaver WT, Wallenstein SL, Houde RW, Rogers A. A clinical comparison of the analgesic effects of methadone and morphine administered intramuscularly, and of orally and parenterally administered methadone. Clin Pharmacol Ther 1967;8:415–426.

149. Hill HE, Haertzen CA, Davis H. An MMPI factor analytic study of alcoholics narcotic addicts and criminals. Q J Stud Alcohol 1962;23:411–431.

150. Hill HE, Haertzen CA, Glaser R. Personality characteristics of narcotic addicts as indicated by the MMPI. J Gen Psychol 1960;62:127–139.

151. Bonica JJ. Evolution and current status of pain programs. J Pain Symptom Manage 1990;5:368–374.

152. Loeser JD, Egan KJ. Managing the chronic pain patient: theory and practice at the University of Washington multidisciplinary pain center. New York: Raven Press, 1989.

153. Von Korff M. Epidemiology of temporomandibular disorders. II. TMD pain compared to other common pain sites. In: Dubner R, Gebhart GF, Bond RM, eds. Proceedings of the Fifth World Congress on Pain. Amsterdam: Elsevier, 1988:506–511.

154. Nuprin Pain Report. New York: Louis Harris and Associates, 1985.

155. Crook J, Rideout E, Browne G. The prevalence of pain complaints in a general population. Pain 1984;18:299–314.

156. Portenoy RK, Coyle N. Controversies in the long-term management of analgesic therapy in patients with advanced cancer. J Pain Symptom Manage 1990;5:307–319.

157. Cameron AJ. Heroin addicts in a casualty department. Br Med J 1964;1:594.

158. Sapiro JD. The narcotic addict as a medical patient. Am J Med 1968;45:555–588.

159. Ho A, Dole VP. Pain perception in drug-free and in methadone-maintained human ex-addicts. Proc Soc Exp Biol Med 1979;162:392–395.

160. Levine JD, Coderre TJ, Basbaum AI. The peripheral nervous system and the inflammatory process. In: Dubner R, Gebhart GF, Bond MR, eds. Proceedings of the Fifth World Congress on Pain. Pain research and clinical management. Amsterdam: Elsevier, 1988;3:33–43.

161. Janig W. Pathophysiology of nerve following mechanical injury. In: Dubner R, Gebhart GF, Bond MR, eds. Proceedings of the Fifth World Congress on Pain. Pain research and clinical management. Amsterdam: Elsevier, 1988;3:89–108.

162. Cervero F, Morrison JFB, eds. Progress in brain research. Visceral sensation. Vol. 67. Amsterdam: Elsevier, 1986.

163. Kumor KM, Grochow LB, Hausheer F. Unusual opioid withdrawal syndrome. A case-report. Lancet 1987;1:720–721.

164. Charache S, Lubin B, Reid CD, eds. Management and therapy of sickle cell disease. Washington, DC: U.S. Dept. of Health and Human Services, NIH publication no. 89–2117, revised 1989.

165. Payne R. Pain management in sickle cell disease: rationale and techniques. Ann N Y Acad Sci 1989;565:189–206.

166. Fultz JM. Guidelines for the management of hospitalized narcotic addicts. Ann Intern Med 1975;82:815–818.

167. Houde RW. The use and misuse of narcotics in the treatment of chronic pain. In: Bonica JJ, ed. Advances in neurology. International symposium on pain. New York: Raven Press, 1974;4:527–536.

168. Portenoy RK. Continuous intravenous infusion of opioid drugs. Med Clin North Am 1987;71:233–241.

169. White PF. Use of patient-controlled analgesia for management of acute pain. JAMA 1988;259:243–247.

170. Hill HF, Chapman CR, Kornell JA, Sullivan KM, Saeger LC, Benedetti C. Self-administration of morphine in bone marrow transplant patients reduces drug requirement. Pain 1990;40:121–129.

171. Gourlay GK, Willis RJ, Lamberty J. Double-blind comparison of the efficacy of methadone and morphine in post-operative pain. Anesthesiology 1986;64:322–327.

172. Sunshine A, Olson NZ. Analgesic efficacy of ketoprofen in postpartum, general surgery, and chronic cancer pain. J Clin Pharmacol 1988;28:S47–S54.

173. Buckley MM-T, Brogen RN. Ketorolac: a review of its pharmacodynamic and pharmacokinetic properties, and therapeutic potential. Drugs 1990;39:86–109.

174. Deyo RA, Walsh NE, Martin DC, Schoenfeld LS, Rammamurthy S. A controlled trial of transcutaneous electrical nerve stimulation (TENS) and exercise for chronic low back pain. N Engl J Med 1990;332:1627–1634.

175. McCallum MID, Glynn CJ, Moore RA, Lammer P, Phillips AM. Transcutaneous electrical nerve stimulation in the management of acute postoperative pain. Br J Anaesth 1988;61:308–312.

176. Woolf CJ. Segmental afferent fibre-induced analgesia: transcutaneous electrical nerve stimulation (TENS) and vibration. In: Wall PD, Melzack R, eds. Textbook of pain. 2nd edition. Edinburgh: Churchill Livingstone, 1989:884–896.

177. Jessup BA. Relaxation and biofeedback. In: Wall PD, Melzack R, eds. Textbook of pain. 2nd edition. Edinburgh: Churchill Livingstone, 1989:989–999.

178. Turk DC, Meichenbaum DH. A cognitive-behavioral approach to pain management. In: Wall PD, Melzack R, eds. Textbook of pain. 2nd edition. Edinburgh: Churchill Livingstone, 1989:1001–1020.

179. Tennant FS, Uelmen GF. Prescribing narcotics to habitual and addicted narcotics users. West J Med 1989;133:539–545.

180. Ward SE, Goldberg N, Miller-McCauley V, et al. Patient-related barriers to management of cancer pain. Pain 1993;52:319–324.

181. Donovan M, Dillon P, McGuire L. Incidence and characteristics of pain in a sample of medical-surgical inpatients. Pain 1987;30:69–78.

182. Cohen F. Postsurgical pain relief: patients' status and nurses' medication choices. Pain 1980;9:265–274.

183. Marks RM, Sachar EJ. Undertreatment of medical inpatients with narcotic analgesics. Ann Intern Med 1973;78:173–181.

184. Von Roenn JH, Cleeland CS, Gonin R, Hatfield A, Pandy K. Physician's attitudes and practice in cancer pain management: a survey from the Eastern Cooperative Oncology Group. Ann Intern Med 1993;119:121–126.

185. Brena SF, Sanders SH. Opioids in nonmalignant pain: questions in search of answers. Clin J Pain 1991;7:342–345.

186. Chabal C, Jacobson L, Chaney EF, Mariano AJ. Narcotics for chronic pain: yes or no? A useless dichotomy. APS Journal 1992;1:276–281.

187. Chabal C, Jacobson L, Chaney EF, Mariano AJ. The psychosocial impact of opioid treatment. APS Journal 1992;1:289–291.

188. Clark HW, Sees KL. Opioids, chronic pain and the law. J Pain Symptom Manage 1993;8:297–305.

189. Glynn CJ, McQuay H, Jadad AR, Carroll D. Opioids in nonmalignant pain: questions in search of answers. Clin J Pain 1991;7:346.

190. Gourlay GK, Cherry DA. Can opioids be successfully used to treat severe pain in nonlignant conditions? Clin J Pain 1991;7:347–349.

191. Merry AF, Schug SA, Richards EG, Large RG. Opioids in chronic pain of nonmalignant origin: state of the debate in New Zealand. Eur J Pain 1992;13:39–43.

192. Schofferman J. Long-term use of opioid analgesics for the treatment of chronic pain of nonmalignant origin. J Pain Symptom Manage 1993;8:279–288.

193. Schug SA, Merry AF, Acland RH. Treatment principles for the use of opioids in pain of nonmalignant origin. Drugs 1991;42:228–239.

194. Savage SR. Long-term opioid therapy: assessment of consequences. J Pain Symptom Manage 1996;11:274–286.

195. Hagen N, Flynne P, Hays H, MacDonald RN. Guidelines for managing chronic nonmalignant pain: opioids and other agents. Can Fam Physician 1995;11:49–53.

196. Jamison RN. Comprehensive pretreatment and outcome assessment for chronic opioid therapy for nonmalignant pain. J Pain Symptom Manage 1996;11:231–241.

197. Gardner-Nix JS. Oral methadone for managing chronic nonmalignant pain. J Pain Symptom Manage 1996;11:321–328.

198. Green J, Coyle M. Methadone use in the control of nonmalignant chronic pain. Pain Management 1989;(Sept/Oct):241–246.

199. Tennant FS, Uelman GF. Narcotic maintenance for chronic pain: medical and legal guidelines. Postgrad Med 1983;73:81–94.

200. Tennant FS, Robinson D, Sagherian A, Seecof R. Chronic opioid treatment of intractable nonmalignant pain. Pain Management 1988;(Jan/Feb):18–36.

201. Wan Lu C, Urban B, France RD. Long-term narcotic therapy in chronic pain. Presented at the Canadian Pain Society and American Pain Society joint meeting, Toronto, Canada, November 10–13, 1988.

202. Kell MJ. Long-term methadone maintenance for intractable, nonmalignant pain: pain control and plasma methadone levels. Am J Pain Manage 1994;4:10–16.

203. Moulin DE, Iezzi A, Amireh R, Sharpe WKJ, Boyd D, Merskey H. Randomised trial of oral morphine for chronic non-cancer pain. Lancet 1996;347:143–147.

204. Arkinstall W, Sandler A, Goughnour B, Babul N, Harsanyi Z, Darke AC. Efficacy of controlled-release codeine in chronic non-malig-

nant pain: a randomized, placebo-controlled clinical trial. Pain 1995;62:169–178.

205. Boissier C, Perpoint B, Laport-Simitsidis S, et al. Acceptability and efficacy of two associations of paracetamol with a central analgesic (dextro-propoxyphene or codeine): comparison in osteoarthritis. J Clin Pharmacol 1992; 32:990–995.

206. Lloyd RS, Costello F, Eves MJ, James IG, Miller AJ. The efficacy and tolerability of controlled-release dihydrocodeine tablets and combination dextro-propoxyphene paracetamol tablets in patients with severe osteoarthritis of the hips. Curr Med Res Opin 1992;13:37–48.

207. Thurel C, Bardin T, Boccard E. Analgesic efficacy of an association of 500 mg paracetamol plus 30 mg codeine versus 400 mg paracetamol plus 30 mg dextropropoxyphene in repeated doses for chronic lower back pain. Curr Ther Res 1991;50:463–473.

208. Vlok GJ, Van Vuren JP. Comparison of a standard ibuprofen treatment regimen with a new ibuprofen/paracetamol/codeine combination in chronic osteoarthritis. S Afr Med J 1987;suppl 1:1–6.

209. Kjaersgaard-Andersen P, Nafei A, Skov O, et al. Codeine plus paracetamol versus paracetamol in longer-term treatment of chronic pain due to osteoarthritis of the hip. A randomised double-blind, multi-centre study. Pain 1990; 43:309–318.

210. Buckley FP, Sizemore WA, Charlton JE. Medication management in patients with chronic non-malignant pain. A review of the use of a drug withdrawal protocol. Pain 1986;26: 153–166.

211. Finlayson RE, Maruta T, Morse RM. Substance dependence and chronic pain: profile of 50 patients treated in an alcohol and drug dependence unit. Pain 1986;26:167–174.

212. Finlayson RE, Maruta T, Morse RM, Martin MA. Substance dependence and chronic pain: experience with treatment and follow-up results. Pain 1986;26:175–180.

213. Maruta T. Prescription drug-induced organic brain syndrome. Am J Psychiatry 1978;135: 376–377.

214. Maruta T, Swanson DW, Finlayson RE. Drug abuse and dependency in patients with chronic pain. Mayo Clin Proc 1979;54:241–244.

215. Maruta T, Swanson DW. Problems with the use of oxycodone compound in patients with chronic pain. Pain 1981;11:389–396.

216. McNairy SL, Maruta T, Ivnik RJ, Swanson DW, Ilstrup DM. Prescription medication dependence and neuropsychologic function. Pain 1984;18:169–177.

217. Ready LB, Sarkis E, Turner JA. Self-reported vs. actual use of medications in chronic pain patients. Pain 1982;12:285–294.

218. Turner JA, Calsyn DA, Fordyce WE, Ready LB. Drug utilization pattern in chronic pain patients. Pain 1982;12:357–363.

219. Hening WA, Walthers A, Kavey N, Gidro-Frank S, Cote L, Fahn S. Dyskinesias while awake and periodic movements in sleep in restless legs syndrome: treatment with opioids. Neurology 1986;36:1363–1366.

220. Sandyk R, Bamford CR. Efficacy of an opiate-benzodiazepine combination in the restless legs syndrome. Neurology 1987;37(suppl 1): 105.

221. Walters A, Hening W, Chokroverty S, Fahn S. Opioid responsiveness in patients with neuroleptic-induced akathisia. Mov Disord 1986; 1:119–127.

222. Bar-Or D, Marx JA, Good J. Breathlessness, alcohol, and opiates [letter]. N Engl J Med 1982;306:1363–1364.

223. Mercadante S, Maddaloni S, Roccella S, Salvaggio L. Predictive factors in advanced cancer pain treated only by analgesics. Pain 1992;50: 151–155.

224. Bruera E, Schoeller T, Wenk R, et al. A prospective multi-center assessment of the Edmonton Staging System for Cancer Pain. J Pain Symptom Manage 1995;10:348–355.

225. McQuay HJ, Jadad AR, Carroll D, et al. Opioid sensitivity of chronic pain: a patient-controlled analgesia method. Anaesthesia 1992;47: 757–767.

226. Jadad AR, Carroll D, Glynn CJ, Moore RA, McQuay HJ. Morphine responsiveness of chronic pain: double-blind randomised crossover study with patient-controlled analgesia. Lancet 1992;339:1367–1371.

227. Cherny NI, Thaler HT, Friedlander-Klar H, et al. Opioid responsiveness of cancer pain syndromes caused by neuropathic or nociceptive mechanisms: a combined analysis of controlled, single-dose studies. Neurology 1994;44: 857–861.

228. Glynn CJ, Mather LE. Clinical pharmacokinetics applied to patients with intractable pain: studies with pethidine. Pain 1982;13:237–246.

229. Aronoff GM, Evans WO, Enders PL. A review of follow-up studies of multidisciplinary pain units. Pain 1983;16:1–11.

230. Turner JA, Romano JM. Evaluating psychologic interventions for chronic pain: issues and recent developments. In: Benedetti C, Chapman CR, Moricca G, eds. Advances in pain research and therapy. New York: Raven Press, 1984;7:257–298.

231. Turk DC, Rudy TE. Neglected topics in the treatment of chronic pain patients—relapse, noncompliance and adherence enhancement. Pain 1991;44:5–28.

232. Kreek MJ. Tolerance and dependence: implications for the pharmacological treatment of addiction. NIDA Res Monogr 1987;76:53–62.

233. Kreek MJ. Medical safety and side effects of methadone in tolerant individuals. JAMA 1973;223:665–668.

234. Kreek MJ. Medical complications in methadone patients. Ann N Y Acad Sci 1978;311: 110–134.

235. Kreek MJ, Dodes S, Kne S, et al. Long-term methadone maintenance therapy: effects on liver function. Ann Intern Med 1972;77: 598–602.

236. Bruera E, Miller MJ. Non-cardiogenic pulmonary edema after narcotic treatment for cancer pain. Pain 1989;39:297–300.

237. Arora PK, Fride E, Petitto J, Waggie K, Skolnick P. Morphine-induced immune alterations in vivo. Cell Immunol 1990;126:343–353.

238. Donohoe RM, Falek A. Neuroimmunomodulation by opiates and other drugs of abuse: relationship to HIV infection and AIDS. Adv Biochem Psychopharmacol 1988;44:145–158.

239. Einstein TK, Meissler JJ, Geller EB, Adler MW. Immunosuppression to tetanus toxoid induced by implanted morphine pellets. Ann N Y Acad Sci 1990;594:377–379.

240. Molitor TW, Morilla A, Risdahl JM, et al. Chronic morphine administration impairs cell-mediated immune responses in swine. J Pharmacol Exp Ther 1992;260:581–586.

241. Peterson PK, Sharp B, Gekker G, Brummit C, Keane WF. Opioid-mediated suppression of interferon-Î production by cultured peripheral blood mononuclear cells. J Clin Invest 1987; 80:824–831.

242. Shavit Y, Lewis JW, Terman WG, Gale RP, Liebeskind JC. Opioid peptides mediate the suppressive effect of stress on natural killer cell cytotoxicity. Science 1984;223:188–190.

243. Weber RJ, Ikejiri B, Rice KC, Pert A, Hagan AA. Opiate receptor mediated regulation of the immune response in vivo. NIDA Res Monogr 1987;76:341–348.

244. Jaffe JH, Martin WR. Opioid analgesics and antagonists. In: Gilman AG, Goodman LS, Rall TW, Murad F, eds. Goodman and Gilman's the pharmacological basis of therapeutics. 7th edition. New York: Macmillan, 1985;491–531.

245. Ferrante FM. Principles of opioid pharmacotherapy: practical implications of basic mechanisms. J Pain Symptom Manage 1996; 11:265–273.

246. Zacny JP. A review of the effects of opioids on psychomotor and cognitive functioning in humans. Exp Clin Psychpharmacol 1995;3: 432–466.

247. Sjogren P, Banning A. Pain, sedation and reaction time during long-term treatment of cancer patients with oral and epidural opioids. Pain 1989;39:5–12.

248. Banning A, Sjogren P. Cerebral effects of long-term oral opioids in cancer patients measured by continuous reaction time. Clin J Pain 1990; 6:91–95.

249. Vainio A, Ollila J, Matikainen E, Rosenberg P, Kalso E. Driving ability in cancer patients receiving long-term morphine analgesia. Lancet 1995;346:667–670.

250. Rounsaville BH, Novelly RA, Kleber HD, Jones C. Neuropsychological impairment in opiate addicts: risk factors. Ann N Y Acad Sci 1981;362:79–90.

251. Martin WR, Jasinski DR, Haertzen CA, et al. Methadone—a reevaluation. Arch Gen Psychiatry 1973;28:286–295.

252. Gritz ER, Shiffman SM, Jarvik ME, et al. Physiological and psychological effects of methadone in man. Arch Gen Psychiatry 1975;32: 237–242.

253. Haertzen CA, Hooks NT. Changes in personality and subjective experience associated with the chronic administration and withdrawal of opiates. J Nerv Ment Dis 1969;148:606–614.

254. Lombardo WK, Lombardo B, Goldstein A. Cognitive functioning under moderate and low dose methadone maintenance. Int J Addict 1976;11:389–401.

255. Hendler N, Cimini C, Ma T, Long D. A comparison of cognitive impairment due to benzodiazepines and to narcotics. Am J Psychiatry 1980;137:828–830.

256. Gordon NB. Influence of narcotic drugs on highway safety. Accid Ann Prev 1976;8:3–7.

257. Babst DV, Newman S, Gordon NB, Warner A. Driving records of methadone maintained patients in New York State. Albany, NY: New York: State Narcotic Control Commission, 1973.

258. Koob GF. Neural substrates of opioid tolerance and dependence. NIDA Res Monogr 1987;76: 46–52.

259. Lynch JJ, Stein EA, Fertziger AP. An analysis of 70 years of morphine classical conditioning: implications for clinical treatment of narcotic addiction. J Nerv Ment Dis 1976;163:47–58.

260. Simpson DD, Savage LJ, Lloyd MR. Follow-up evaluation of treatment of drug abuse during 1969 to 1972. Arch Gen Psychiatry 1979;36: 772–780.

261. Vaillant GE. A 20-year follow-up of New York: narcotic addicts. Arch Gen Psychiatry 1973;29:237–241.

262. Jarvik LF, Simpson JH, Guthrie D, Liston EH. Morphine, experimental pain and psychological reaction. Psychopharmacology 1981;75:124–131.

263. Jaffe JH. Misinformation: euphoria and addiction. In: Hill CS, Fields WS, eds. Advances in pain research and therapy. New York: Raven Press, 1989;11:163–174.

264. Kolb L. Types and characteristics of drug addicts. Mental Hygiene 1925;9:300.

265. Pescor MJ. The Kolb classification of drug addicts. Public Health Rep Suppl 1939;155.

266. Rayport M. Experience in the management of patients medically addicted to narcotics. JAMA 1954;156:684–691.

267. Porter J, Jick H. Addiction rare in patients treated with narcotics. N Engl J Med 1980;302:123.

268. Medina JL, Diamond S. Drug dependency in patients with chronic headache. Headache 1977;17:12–14.

269. Chapman CR. Giving, the patient control of opioid analgesic administration. In: Hill CS, Fields WS, eds. Advances in pain research and therapy. New York: Raven Press, 1989;11:339–352.

270. Fishbain DA, Rosomoff HL, Rosomoff RS. Drug abuse, dependence, and addiction in chronic pain patients. Clin J Pain 1992;8:77–85.

271. Regier DA, Meyers JK, Dramer M, et al. The NIMH epidemiologic catchment area program. Arch Gen Psychiatry 1984;41:934–958.

272. Graeven DB, Folmer W. Experimental heroin users: an epidemiologic and psychosocial approach. Am J Drug Alcohol Abuse 1977;4:365–375.

273. Robins LN, Davis DH, Nurco DN. How permanent was Vietnam drug addiction? Am J Public Health 1974;64:38–43.

274. Grove WM, Eckert ED, Heston L, Bouchard TJ, Segal N, Lykken DT. Heritability of substance abuse and antisocial behavior: a study of monozygotic twins reared apart. Biol Psychiatry 1990;27:1293–1304.

275. Goodwin DW, Schulsinger F, Moller N, Hermansen L, Winokur G, Guze SB. Drinking problems in adopted and nonadopted sons of alcoholics. Arch Gen Psychiatry 1974;31:164–169.

276. Newman RG. The need to redefine addiction. N Engl J Med 1983;18:1096–1098.

277. Kanner RM, Portenoy RK. Unavailability of narcotic analgesic for ambulatory cancer patients in New York City. J Pain Symptom Manage 1986;1:87–90.

278. Hill CS. Government regulatory influences on opioid prescribing and their impact on the treatment of pain of nonmalignant origin. J Pain Symptom Manage 1996;11:287–298.

279. Cooper JR, Czechowicz DJ, Petersen RC, Molinari SP. Prescription drug diversion control and medical practice. JAMA 1992;268:1306–1310.

280. Rose HL. Letter to the editor. Pain 1987:29:261–262.

281. Kofoed L, Bloom JD, Williams MH, Rhyne C, Resnick M. Physicians investigated for inappropriate prescribing by the Oregon Board of Medical Examiners. West J Med 1989;150:597–601.

282. Morgan JP. American opiophobia: customary underutilization of opioid analgesics. Adv Alcohol Subst Abuse 1985;5:163–173.

283. Berina LF, Guernsey BG, Hokanson JA, Doutre WH, Fuller LE. Physician perception of a triplicate prescription law. Am J Hosp Pharm 1985;42:857–859.

284. United States Department of Justice, Drug Enforcement Administration. Multiple copy prescription program resource guide. Washington, DC: U.S. Government Printing Office, 1987.

285. Haislip GR. Impact of drug abuse on legitimate drug use. In: Hill CS, Fields WS, eds. Advances in pain research and therapy. New York: Raven Press, 1989;11:205–211.

286. Gitchel GT. Existing methods to identify retail drug diversion. NIDA Res Monogr 1993;131:132–140.

287. Sigler KA, Guernsey BG, Ingim MB, et al. Effects of a triplicate prescription law on prescribing of Schedule II drugs. Am J Hosp Pharm 1984;41:108–111.

288. Jacob TR. Multiple copy prescription regulation and drug abuse: evidence from the DAWN network. In: Wilford BB, ed. Balancing the response to prescription drug abuse. Chicago: American Medical Association, 1990:205–217.

289. Reidenberg MM. Effect of the requirement for triplicate prescriptions for benzodiazepines in New York State. Clin Pharm Ther 1991;50:129–131.

290. Weintraub M, Singh S, Byrne L, Maharaj K, Guttmacher L. Consequences of the 1989 New York State triplicate benzodiazepine prescription regulations. JAMA 1991;266:2392–2397.

291. Angarola RT, Wray SD. Legal impediments to cancer pain treatment. In: Hill CS, Fields WS, eds. Advances in pain research and therapy. New York: Raven Press, 1989;11:213–231.

292. Joranson DE, Cleeland CS, Weissman DE, Gilson AM. Opioids for chronic cancer and non-cancer pain: a survey of state medical board members. Fed Bulletin 1992;415–449.

293. Senate Bill 20, 71st legislature, 1st called session, State of Texas, July 18, 1989.

294. Parris WCV, Jamison RN, Vasterling JJ. Follow-up study of a multidisciplinary pain center. J Pain Symptom Manage 1987;2:145–154.

295. Duckro PN, Margolis RB, Tait RC, Korytnyk N. Long-term follow-up of chronic pain patients: a preliminary study. Int J Psychol Med 1985;15:283–292.

296. Dunbar SA, Katz NP. Chronic opioid therapy for nonmalignant pain in patients with a history of substance abuse: report of 20 cases. J Pain Symptom Manage 1996;11:163–171.

297. Burchman SL, Pagel PS. Implementation of a formal treatment agreement for outpatient management of chronic nonmalignant pain with opioid analgesics. J Pain Symptom Manag 1995;10:556–563.

SECTION VIII. HIV INFECTION AND AIDS
58 EPIDEMIOLOGY AND EMERGING PUBLIC HEALTH PERSPECTIVES

Don C. Des Jarlais, Holly Hagan, and Samuel R. Friedman

THE GLOBAL EPIDEMIC OF ILLICIT DRUG INJECTION

The injection of illicit psychoactive drugs has been reported in 121 different countries (1). There are now an estimated 5 million persons throughout the world who inject illicit drugs (2), and this number is probably growing rapidly. While there is still much to be learned about the international diffusion of illicit drug injection, the following factors appear to be important:

1. There has been substantial international growth in the use of "licit" psychoactive drugs. Use of nicotine and alcohol has spread to many areas of the world where these psychoactive drugs are not part of the traditional culture (3–5). Nonmedical psychoactive drug use as a whole, and not simply illicit psychoactive drug use, has been increasing over the last several decades.
2. The globalization of the world economy. Improvements in communication and transportation and reductions in trade barriers have led to great increases in international trade. These same developments also facilitate international trade in illicit drugs.
3. Economies of scale in illicit drug production. The very large profit margins possible in the sale of illicit addicting substances also means that substantial profits can be made selling these drugs, even to "poor" people. The large profit margins from selling illicit drugs in industrialized countries can be used to underwrite the development of new markets in developing countries. The economics of the international distribution of illicit drugs particularly facilitate the development of domestic drug markets in producing and transit countries.
4. Injecting produces a strong drug effect due to the rapid increase in the concentration of the drug in the brain. Injecting is also highly cost-efficient in that almost all of the drug is actually delivered to the brain. On these grounds, intravenous injection can be considered a technologically superior method of psychoactive drug administration. Inexpensive technological advances tend to disperse widely and are very difficult (though not impossible) to reverse (6).

While it is probably possible to improve current efforts to reduce the supplies of illicit psychoactive drugs, the effectiveness of such efforts is likely to vary across time and place, so that public health officials should plan in terms of further worldwide increases in illicit psychoactive drug injection, with the potential for severe public health consequences, including transmission of blood-borne pathogens such as HIV.

HIV INFECTION AMONG INJECTING DRUG USERS

HIV has been reported among injecting drug users (IDUs) in 80 countries (1). This is a substantial increase over the 59 countries with HIV infection among IDUs in 1989 (7). In some European countries such as Spain and Italy, injecting drug use has long been the most common risk factor for HIV infection and AIDS (8). In the United States, injecting drug use has been associated with approximately one third of the cumulative cases of AIDS (9). Over half of the United States heterosexual transmission cases have involved transmission from an injecting drug user, and over half of the perinatal transmission cases have occurred in women who injected drugs themselves or were the sexual partners of IDUs. In the most recent estimate of new HIV infections in the United States, approximately half of all new infections in the country are occurring among IDUs (10).

HIV may be introduced into a local population of IDUs through a "bridge population" such as men who both have sex with men and inject drugs. This appears to be the way in which HIV was first introduced into the IDU population in New York City (11), which was also probably the introduction of HIV into the IDU population in the United States. Travel by IDUs may also serve to introduce HIV into local populations. Contrary to popular stereotypes, many drug injectors do travel, including internationally (12). International "drug tourism" (13) has been noted, though not yet well studied. Additionally, incarceration of IDUs from different geographic areas may also contribute to spread of blood-borne viruses among IDUs (14).

OUTCOMES OF HIV INFECTION AMONG IDUs

In sharp contrast to HIV infection among homosexual or bisexual men, HIV infection among IDUs leads to a wider variety of illnesses than the original opportunistic infections that were used to define AIDS. HIV infection has been associated with increased morbidity and/or increased mortality for tuberculosis, bacterial pneumonias, endocarditis (15), and cervical cancer (through a possible interaction with human papilloma virus) (16). The 1987 and 1993 revisions of the Centers for Disease Control and Prevention surveillance definition for AIDS were based in part on the studies of the wider spectrum of HIV-related illnesses among IDUs. Prior to these revisions, many IDUs were dying from HIV-related illnesses without ever being classified as having AIDS (15).

The mechanisms through which HIV infection leads to this wider spectrum of illnesses have not yet been identified. Tuberculosis infection is controlled primary through cell-mediated immunity, so that one would expect HIV infection to lead to increased reactivation of latent TB infection and increased susceptibility to TB infection. HIV infection can also affect humoral immune functioning (17), so that resistance to many infectious agents may be compromised. The lifestyle of many IDUs may also put them at greater risk for exposure to a wide variety of pathogens, and reduce immune functioning through mechanisms such as poor nutrition.

Whether continued use of psychoactive drugs influences the course of HIV infection among IDUs has been an important question since AIDS was first noticed among IDUs. A wide variety of psychoactive substances have at least some in vitro effects on components of the immune system. Studies comparing progression of HIV infection among IDUs and among men infected through male-with-male sex, however, have generally shown no differences in the rate of CD4 cell count loss or development of AIDS (18). At present, it does not appear that continued use of psychoactive drugs per se has any strong effect on the course of HIV infection among IDUs. Immune system activation, however, may increase replication of HIV (19), so that very high frequencies of nonsterile injections, or development of other infections such as bacterial pneumonias, may increase progression of HIV infection.

RAPID TRANSMISSION OF HIV AMONG IDUs

In many areas, HIV has spread extremely rapidly among IDUs, with the HIV seroprevalence rate (the percentage of IDUs infected with HIV) increasing from less than 10% to 40% or greater within a period of one to two years (20). Several factors have been associated with extremely rapid transmission of HIV among IDUs: (*a*) lack of awareness of HIV and AIDS as a local threat; (*b*) restrictions on the availability and use of new injection equipment; and (*c*) mechanisms for rapid, efficient mixing within the local IDU population. Without an awareness of AIDS as a local threat, IDUs are likely to use each other's equipment very frequently. Indeed, prior to an awareness of HIV and AIDS, providing previously used equipment to another IDU is likely to be seen as an act of solidarity among IDUs, or as a service for which one may legitimately charge a small fee.

There are various types of legal restrictions that can reduce the availability of sterile injection equipment and thus lead to increased multi-person use ("sharing") of drug injection equipment. In some jurisdictions, medical prescriptions are required for the purchase of needles and syringes. Possession of needles and syringes can also be criminalized as "drug paraphernalia," putting users at risk of arrest if needles and syringes are found in their possession. In some jurisdictions drug users have also been prosecuted for possession of drugs based on the minute quantities of drugs that remain in a needle and syringe after it has been used to inject drugs. In addition the possible legal restrictions on the availability of sterile injection equipment, the actual practices of pharmacists and police can create important limits. Even if laws permit sales of needles and syringes without prescriptions, pharmacists may choose not to sell without prescriptions, or not to sell to anyone who "looks like a drug user." Similarly, police may harass drug users found carrying injection equipment even if there are no laws criminalizing the possession of narcotics paraphernalia.

"Shooting galleries" (places where IDUs can rent injection equipment, which is then returned to the gallery owner for rental to other IDUs) and "dealer's works" (injection equipment kept by a drug seller, which can be lent to successive drug purchasers) are examples of situations that provide rapid, efficient mixing within an IDU population. The "mixing" is rapid in that many IDUs may use the gallery or the dealer's injection equipment within very short periods of time. Several studies have indicated that the infectiousness of HIV is many times greater in the 2–3 month period after initial infection compared to the long "latency" period between initial infection and the development of severe immunosuppression (21). Thus, the concentration of new infections in these settings may synergistically interact with continued mixing and lead to highly infectious IDUs transmitting HIV to large numbers of other drug injectors. "Efficient" mixing refers to the "sharing" of drug injection equipment with few restrictions upon who shares with whom. Thus efficient mixing serves to spread HIV across potential social boundaries, such as friendship groups, which otherwise might have served to limit transmission.

HIV AND AIDS PREVENTION FOR IDUs
Early Studies

The common stereotype that IDUs are not at all concerned about health led to initial expectations that they would not change their behavior because of AIDS. In sharp contrast to these expectations, reductions in risk behavior were observed among IDU participants in a wide variety of early prevention programs, including outreach/bleach distribution (22, 23), "education only" (24, 25), drug abuse treatment (26), syringe exchange (27), increased over-the-counter sales of injection equipment (28, 29), and HIV counseling and testing (30, 31).

It is also important to note that there is evidence that IDUs will reduce HIV risk behavior in the absence of any specific prevention program. IDUs in New York City reported risk reduction prior to the implementation of any formal HIV prevention programs (32, 33). IDUs had learned about AIDS through the mass media and the oral-communication networks within the drug-injecting population (32, 33) and the illicit market in sterile injection equipment had expanded to provide additional equipment (34).

Rather than having to overcome indifference to AIDS among IDUs, the scientific problem became one of understanding and quantifying the change processes. The differences in research design and measurement instruments in these early studies have generally precluded any comparisons regarding the differential effectiveness of the different HIV prevention programs. It was

also difficult to determine how a specific prevention program might be contributing to behavior change processes, and the effects of the behavior change on the rate of new HIV infections among IDUs and their sexual partners.

While the early studies did indicate that IDUs were very likely to change their behavior in response to the threat of AIDS, there also were important limitations of these studies. The studies were implemented in a rapidly changing historical context and there was very little consistency in the measurement of behavior change among the studies. Thus, it was not possible to compare the amount of behavior change associated with different HIV prevention programs. These two problems in the interpretation of behavior change data generally persist.

Possible "social desirability" effects were also an important potential problem in interpreting the early behavior change studies. It was clear that subjects were reporting reduced risk behavior, but this might have been that the subjects simply learned what the researchers wanted to hear, and were providing the socially desirable responses without any meaningful changes in risk behavior. There is now evidence that self-reported AIDS risk reduction is associated with a lower probability of HIV infection (35, 36), though social desirability effects still must be considered in any research on highly stigmatized behaviors such as injecting drug use and the "sharing" of drug injection equipment.

Finally, even if the behavior change reported by subjects in the early studies did represent real reductions in risk behavior, there was the final problem of attempting to translate the reduced levels of risk behavior into the rate of new HIV infections (incidence).

Behavior Change and HIV Incidence Studies

Over the last five years, sufficient data has been accumulated to provide reasonable estimates of the likely HIV incidence after implementation of two types of prevention programs—street outreach and syringe exchange. The National AIDS Demonstration Research/AIDS Targeted Outreach Model (NADR/ATOM) program was begun in the United States in 1987, and eventually included 41 projects in nearly 50 different cities (37). In all of the cities, the NADR/ATOM project involved street outreach to IDUs not in treatment programs. The eligibility requirements for subjects to be enrolled in the research component of the NADR/ATOM projects required that the person must have injected illicit drugs in the previous 6 months and must not have been in drug abuse treatment in the preceding month. Approximately 40% of the more than 30,000 subjects enrolled in the NADR/ATOM projects reported that they had never been in drug abuse treatment.

Many of the NADR/ATOM projects used experimental designs to test psychological theories of health behavior change. All subjects were provided with a "standard" intervention to reduce HIV risk behavior, which included information about HIV and AIDS, a baseline risk assessment, and the option of HIV counseling and testing. Some of these subjects were then randomly assigned to an "enhanced" condition, that typically involved several additional hours of counseling, education, and skill training, which incorporated components of the psychological theories of health behavior. Subjects were followed at 6-month intervals to assess changes in HIV risk behaviors and the incidence of new HIV infections.

The NADR/ATOM projects provided a wealth of data about HIV risk behaviors among IDUs not in drug treatment programs. With respect to changes in HIV risk behaviors, there were two strong and very consistent findings. First, almost all of the NADR/ATOM projects showed substantial reductions in injection risk behavior from the baseline assessment to the follow-up interviews, with the percentage of IDUs reporting that they did not "always use a sterile needle" declining from 64% to 41%, while those reporting ever sharing needles declined from 54% to 23% (38).

The second consistent finding was that almost none of the different projects showed significant differences in risk reduction between the "standard" intervention and the "enhanced" interview. The general lack of differences between the "standard" and the "enhanced" interventions should not be interpreted as meaning that the psychological theories of health behavior are not relevant to HIV risk reduction among IDUs. Rather, these results suggest two other possible explanations. First, after the provision of basic information about AIDS (as in the standard intervention), 2–6 hours of additional education and counseling does little to further "strengthen" anti-AIDS attitudes, perceptions, and intentions.

A second explanation is that risk reduction among IDUs, again, after basic HIV and AIDS education, is primarily a function of social processes rather than the characteristics of individual IDUs. Thus, information about HIV and AIDS, new attitudes towards risk behaviors, and skills in practicing new behaviors would have been transmitted among active IDUs, influencing persons who had not participated in the "enhanced" conditions.

The NADR/ATOM studies included follow-up of the participants with repeated HIV counseling and testing to detect new HIV infections. Table 58.1 presents data on new HIV infections among participants in the NADR/ATOM projects for which these outcome data are available (39). (The cities are not identified individually, because researchers in those cities are preparing individual research reports.)

There are two clear findings from the NADR/ATOM HIV incidence (new infection) studies. First, the new infection rates are substantially lower in the cities where the initial (background) HIV seroprevalence rates were low. Second, both background HIV seroprevalence and the new infection rates are generally much lower in areas that permit over-the-counter sales of sterile injection equipment (i.e., do not have prescription requirements for the sale of injection equipment).

The higher new infection rates in areas with higher HIV seroprevalence are easily understood in epidemiologic terms. An uninfected person who engages in risk behavior ("sharing" of drug injection equipment or unprotected sexual intercourse) is more likely to encounter an HIV-infected risk partner. Indeed, even within the low seroprevalence cities, in the NADR/ATOM seroincidence data, there was a direct relationship between higher background seroprevalence and higher incidence (39).

The overall incidence rate was also much lower in areas with legal-over-the-counter sales of injection equipment (0.79 per 100 person-years at risk) than in areas that had prescription requirements for sale of injection equipment (1.99 per 100 person-years at risk) (39). Current HIV seroprevalence is the product of past seroincidence (plus changes in the composition of the IDU population), and the presence of over-the-counter sales was also strongly linked with current seroprevalence (so strongly that multivariate analyses were not possible).

However, given the difficulties in establishing factors accounting for current HIV seroprevalence in United States cities where over-the-counter sales

of injection equipment are legal, one must be cautious in drawing conclusions about causal relationships between such sales and lower rates of HIV incidence. The data in Table 58.1, however, strongly suggest that over-the-counter sales may be one factor in facilitating safer injection among IDUs. Studies from France (28, 40), Glasgow, Scotland (29), and Connecticut (41) all show HIV risk reduction associated with over-the-counter sales, supporting the interpretation of a causal role for over-the-counter sales in reducing HIV transmission among IDUs.

In addition to the NADR/ATOM outreach/bleach distribution program data presented in Table 58.1, one such program deserves additional consideration. The NADR program in Chicago not only had one of the strongest theoretical bases, but the Chicago research group was able to collect four years of HIV incidence data in the cohort of IDUs who participated in the program (42). There was a dramatic drop in injection risk behavior over the four-year period, from 95% of the subjects reporting recent injection risk behavior at the start of the project to only 15% reporting injection risk behavior in the fourth year. HIV incidence in the cohort fell from approximately 9 per 100 person-years at risk during the first year of the cohort follow-up to approximately 2 per 100 person-years at risk for the rest of the follow-up period. Most importantly, there was a strong relationship between self-reported injection risk behavior and actual HIV seroconversion: all of the subjects who became infected with HIV were from among those who reported current injection risk behavior. All subjects who reported that they stopped injection risk behavior avoided HIV infection. The study did not include a comparison group, so that caution is needed in making causal inferences. Nevertheless, the dramatic drop in reported injection risk behavior and the strong association between HIV incidence and reported injection risk behavior suggests that this project did lead to a substantial reduction in HIV transmission among IDUs in the study.

Many of the NADR/ATOM programs distributed small bottles of bleach to IDUs for disinfection of used injection equipment. Bleach is a relatively strong viricide, but there is some doubt as to whether the bleach disinfection as practiced by IDUs in the field actually protects against HIV infection. Studies from Baltimore (43) and New York City (44) failed to show any relationship between self-reported use of bleach to disinfect injection equipment and protection from infection with HIV. (A third study from Miami, however, did find a significant protective effect against HIV incidence (C. McCoy, personal communication).) There are, of course, numerous difficulties in attempting to find such a relationship. Reporting on the frequency and circumstances of using bleach may not be very accurate. Drug users may not now how to "properly" use bleach to disinfect injection equipment. (The current recommendation is for 30 seconds of contact time of full strength (not diluted) bleach in the needle and syringe.) Even if the drug injectors know how to properly use bleach, they may not be using it properly under "field conditions" (45).

Thus, the effectiveness of the outreach/bleach distribution programs in lowering rates of new HIV infections among IDUs may be a result of participants obtaining more sterile injection equipment (from pharmacies or on the illicit market), rather than resulting from the actual use of bleach to disinfect used injection equipment.

Table 58.2 presents HIV incidence data among participants in syringe exchange programs. First, as with the outreach/bleach distribution programs, HIV incidence is quite low in areas with low background HIV prevalence. HIV incidence is, among other factors, related to the probability of a seronegative IDU "sharing" equipment with a seropositive IDU. Because of this, it may be that almost any HIV prevention program will appear to be effective in a low seroprevalence area. Conversely, the presence of syringe exchange programs (or other good access to sterile injection equipment) may itself be an important reason why HIV seroprevalence and HIV incidence has remained low in many populations of IDUs.

IDUs from the Montreal exchange have an HIV incidence rate notably above that of the other cities in Table 58.2. The Montreal program appears to attract a subgroup of IDUs with extremely high initial risk levels (46, 47), including high rates of cocaine injection and high levels of unprotected commercial sex work. Still, additional data are needed to fully explain the Montreal incidence rate, and new studies are presently being initiated in Montreal (C. Hankins, personal communication).

Table 58.1 HIV Seroprevalence and HIV Seroconversions Among Injecting Drug Users in 14 Localities by Legal Status of Over-the-Counter Syringe Sales

Locality[a]	HIV-negative	HIV-positive	% HIV-positive	Sero-conversions	Person-years at risk[b]	Sero-conversions per 100 person-years at risk
Localities where over-the-counter sales are illegal						
A	288	311	51.9	4	49.3	8.11
B	1088	908	45.5	6	146.1	4.10
C	855	589	40.8	3	81.9	3.66
D	669	194	22.5	17	262.8	6.47
E	1222	76	5.9	2	956.1	0.21
F	787	14	1.7	0	109.0	0.00
Localities where over-the-counter sales are legal						
G	1760	138	7.3	7	184.0	3.80
H	652	43	6.2	5	187.0	2.67
I	1968	61	3.0	8	732.5	1.09
J	651	17	2.5	0	225.3	0.00
K	2099	31	1.5	2	765.1	0.26
L	891	13	1.4	3	983.4	0.31
M	372	4	1.1	0	18.0	0.00
N	514	5	1.0	0	53.7	0.00

[a]The Principal Investigators of specific sites are preparing detailed analyses of their data on seroconversion rates. Data are publicly available (with locality identifiers removed) through Nova Research Company, Bethesda, Maryland.
[b]Numbers presented for person-years at risk by locality do not add up to those for the summary table due to rounding error.

Table 58.2   Recent Studies of HIV Incidence Among Syringe Exchange Participants

City	HIV Prevalence[a]	Measured HIV Seroconversions[b]	Estimated HIV Seroconversions[c]	Reference
Lund	low	0		70
Glasgow	low		0–1 (2)	12
Sydney	low		0–1 (2)	12
Toronto	low	102 (1)		12
England and Wales (except London)	low		0–1(1)	71
Kathmandu	low	0		72
Tacoma, WA	low	< 1		73
Portland, OR	low	<1		74
Montreal	moderate	5–13		47
London	moderate		1–2 (3)	71
Amsterdam	high	4		Van den Hoek, personal communication
Chicago, IL	high	3		Wiebel, personal communication
New York, NY	very high	1.5		49
New Haven, CT	very high		3 (4)	75

[a]low, 0–5%; moderate, 6–20%; high, 21–40%; very high, > 40%.
[b]Cohort study and/or repeated testing of participants in per 100 person-years at risk.
[c]Estimated from: (1) stable, very low <2% seroprevalence in area; (2) self-reports of previous seronegative test and a current HIV blood/saliva test; (3) stable or declining seroprevalence; (4) from HIV testing of syringes collected at exchange per 100 person-years at risk.

The HIV incidence data from the three United States high HIV seroprevalence cities (New Haven, Chicago, and New York) with syringe exchange programs must be considered extremely encouraging with respect to reducing HIV transmission in high seroprevalence areas. The data from New Haven are generally consistent with the previously developed mathematical model to assess the effectiveness of the New Haven syringe exchange program (48).

A major difficulty in interpreting the HIV incidence studies of syringe exchange participants is the lack of meaningful comparison groups. In almost all of the areas, IDUs who do not use the syringe exchanges purchase sterile injection equipment from pharmacies, e.g., in the United Kingdom, Sydney, and Amsterdam. In the New York City study, however, only the IDUs who used the syringe exchanges had legal access to sterile injection equipment, as New York has a prescription law requirement. The New York City study did show a significantly higher HIV incidence rate among IDUs who did not use the syringe exchanges—5.3 per 100 person-years at risk (49). The New York City study is the first to show a difference in HIV incidence between IDUs who had full legal access to sterile injection equipment for injecting illicit drugs versus IDUs who used illegal sources for obtaining their injection equipment.

A study of incident hepatitis B and hepatitis C infection among IDUs in Tacoma, Washington, also provides support for the effectiveness of syringe exchange programs on reducing transmission of blood-borne viruses (50). Tacoma/Pierce County is one of the four counties in the U.S. Centers for Disease Control Hepatitis Surveillance System, and thus has among the best data on hepatitis incidence in the United States. A case-control design was used. Cases of hepatitis B and hepatitis C among IDUs were identified through the surveillance reporting system. Controls were identified among IDUs attending the drug treatment and HIV counseling clinics in the county. (Sera is collected at both clinics, and could thus be tested to identify IDUs who were seronegative for hepatitis.) Demographic data, drug injection history data, and whether the subject had ever used the local syringe exchange program were abstracted from the clinics' records.

Multiple logistic regression analyses were used to identify statistically independent factors differentiating the incident IDU hepatitis cases from the controls. Failure to use the local syringe exchange was strongly associated with both incident hepatitis B and incident hepatitis C. After statistical control for age, gender, race/ethnicity, and duration of injection, the odds ratio for acute infection with hepatitis B among IDUs who had never used the ex-

change compared to any use of the exchange was over 5 for hepatitis C, the adjusted odds ratio also was over 5 for "never" versus "ever" using the exchange. One of the possible reasons for the strength of these associations is that the local syringe exchange program is the primary HIV prevention program in the area. While pharmacies in the area are legally permitted to sell injection equipment without a prescription, many pharmacists choose not to sell to persons suspected of being IDUs.

Of course, the HIV seroincidence data in Table 58.2 and the hepatitis data from the Tacoma study are far from constituting "experimental proof" of the effectiveness of syringe exchange programs in reducing transmission of blood-borne viruses. Nevertheless, these data clearly indicate that IDUs will use syringe exchange programs to successfully protect themselves against infection with blood-borne viruses.

INTEGRATING MULTIPLE PREVENTION PROGRAMS

While assisting drug injectors to practice safer injection and providing drug abuse treatment to reduce drug injection per se are often perceived as contradictory strategies, in practice they have been complementary strategies. One of the most important lessons of the early outreach programs was that the process of teaching drug injectors how to practice safer injection uncovered previously hidden demand for entry into drug abuse treatment. This unexpected demand for drug abuse treatment led to a program in which New Jersey outreach workers distributed vouchers that could be redeemed for no-cost detoxification treatment (24). Over 95% of the vouchers were redeemed by drug users entering treatment, many of whom had never before been in drug abuse treatment.

The NADR/ATOM projects also uncovered previously hidden demand for treatment, and were able to successfully refer many people into treatment (51). The limiting factor in the ability of these programs to place drug users into treatment was usually the lack of available treatment capacity in the different cities.

There are also examples of syringe exchange programs that have become important sources of referral to drug-misuse treatment programs. For example, the New Haven program reports 33% of the first 569 participants were referred to drug treatment (48). The Tacoma syringe exchange program has become the leading source of referrals to the local drug treatment program (52). The "harm reduction" philosophy used in many outreach/bleach distribution programs and in most syringe exchange programs emphasizes reducing drug injection as a preferred method for reducing the risk of HIV infection, as soon as the individual drug user believes that he or she is ready for such treatment. The "user-friendly" staff attitude that has been adopted in most syringe exchanges also emphasizes providing a variety of services to IDUs, including referrals to other health and social services, particularly to drug abuse treatment. The capacity of outreach/bleach distribution programs and syringe exchange programs to make effective referrals to drug treatment programs may depend primarily upon the availability of treatment in the local area, and whether the programs can afford the appropriate staff to make and follow through on referrals.

While much progress has been made in providing referrals from outreach/bleach distribution programs to drug abuse treatment programs, HIV prevention efforts in the United States are still hampered by a lack of "referrals" from drug abuse treatment programs to bleach distribution and syringe exchange programs. While drug abuse treatment programs lead to substantial and well-documented reductions in illicit drug use (53), it would be unrealistic to expect that all IDUs who enter treatment programs will abstain from further illicit drug injection. Indeed, the majority are likely to fail to complete treatment and/or to use illicit drugs while in treatment. Some United States drug treatment programs currently include information about the locations and hours of operation of local bleach distribution and syringe exchange programs as part of the "AIDS education" provided to all entrants into treatment. (Many European drug treatment programs actually provide syringe exchange services on site.) In general, however, United States drug treatment programs have not yet developed strategies for reducing the likelihood that persons who relapse back to drug injection will not become infected with HIV through sharing of drug injection equipment.

CURRENT PROBLEMATIC ISSUES IN PREVENTING HIV INFECTION AMONG IDUs

Much has been learned in the last decade of research on prevention of HIV infection among IDUs. Most importantly, all studies to date have shown that the large majority of IDUs will modify their behavior to reduce the chances of becoming infected with HIV. The theoretical bases for HIV prevention efforts have expanded from "factual education" to psychological and social-change theories. Prevention programs are increasingly providing the means for behavior change (for safer injection and, less frequently, for reducing drug injection).

Despite the progress in terms of research findings, increasing sophistication of prevention programs, and actual reduction in HIV transmission, there still are a number of problem areas with respect to prevention of new HIV infections among IDUs in some industrialized countries—the United States in particular—and in many developing countries.

Provision of Prevention Services

The biggest single problem may simply be the scarcity of HIV prevention services for IDUs in the nation. In the United States, the Presidential Commission on the HIV Epidemic recommended in 1988 that drug abuse treatment be provided to all persons who desire it. The U.S. National Commission on AIDS made the same recommendation in 1991 (54). The National Commission on AIDS also recommended the removal of "legal barriers to the purchase and possession" of sterile injection equipment. Although there has been some expansion of syringe exchange services in the United States in the last several years, the Commission's recommendations would appear as valid today as when they were initially made.

In many developing countries, drug addiction is not seen as a health problem, and there are few resources to provide either HIV prevention or drug abuse treatment for IDUs.

Sexual Transmission of HIV

While there is highly consistent evidence that IDUs will make large changes in their injection risk behavior in response to concerns about AIDS, changes in sexual behavior appear to be much more modest. All studies that have compared changes in injection risk behavior with changes in sexual risk behavior found greater changes in injection risk behavior (55). In general, IDUs appear more likely to make risk-reduction efforts (reduced numbers of partners, increased use of condoms) for "casual" sexual relationships rather than in "primary" sexual relationships (55).

The reasons for the difficulties in changing the sexual behavior of IDUs have not been fully clarified, but the problem appears in many different cultural settings, including IDUs in Asia, Europe, and South America, as well as in the United States (12). To place the problem in perspective, however, IDUs have undoubtedly changed their sexual risk behavior more than noninjecting heterosexuals in the United States as a whole (56).

One factor that appears to be important in increasing condom use among IDUs is an altruistic desire to avoid transmitting HIV to a non-injecting sexual partner. In both Bangkok (57) and New York City (58), IDUs who know (or have reason to suspect) that they are HIV-positive are particularly likely to use condoms in relationships with sexual partners who do not inject illicit drugs. Most programs that have urged IDUs to use condoms thus far have focused on the self-protective effects of condom usage. Appealing to altruistic feelings of protecting others from HIV infection may be an untapped source of motivation for increasing condom use.

Heterosexual transmission from IDUs to their sexual partners who do not inject drugs has occurred in the United States since the first heterosexual IDUs were infected with HIV. The use of crack cocaine is often associated with high frequencies of unsafe sexual behaviors. In cities like New York and Miami, where there are large numbers of HIV-infected IDUs who also use crack cocaine, the use of crack without injection drug use has itself become an important risk factor for infection with HIV (59). While intervening in the nexus of injection drug use, crack use, and unsafe sex will be quite difficult, one strategy that might be used is to provide prompt treatment for genital ulcerative sexually transmitted diseases such as syphilis. The presence of these ulcerative sexually transmitted diseases appears to greatly increase the likelihood of HIV transmission (60).

It is also worth noting that additional strategies are needed for increasing safer sex among IDUs who engage in male-with-male sexual activities. IDUs who also engage in male-with-male sex can act as a bridge population between non–drug-injecting men who engage in male-with-male sex and the larger IDU population. In many areas of the United States, HIV seroprevalence among men who engage in male-with-male sex is substantially higher than among exclusively heterosexual IDUs (60). There are indications of "slippage" back to high-risk sexual behavior among men who have sex with men in San Francisco (61, 62) and Amsterdam (63). If slippage back to unsafe sex should occur among men who have sex with men in the United States as a whole, this could lead to more HIV infection among IDU men who engage in male-with-male sex, followed by more transmission from these men to other IDUs.

Role of Voluntary HIV Counseling and Testing

Voluntary HIV counseling and testing receives more federal funding than any other type of prevention activity. The use of voluntary HIV counseling and testing as an HIV prevention strategy has recently been reviewed by the U.S. Centers for Disease Control and Prevention (64). HIV counseling and testing can be considered as a standard part of health care. Anyone at any risk of being infected with HIV should have the right to learn his or her HIV status. HIV counseling and testing may also be an important gateway for engaging HIV-infected persons into full treatment for HIV infection, which would both improve the quality and length of their own lives and reduce the chances that they will transmit HIV to others. This requires, however, that counseling and testing services reach persons who are likely to be infected with HIV. Unfortunately, the present alternative-site counseling and testing system in the United States generally does not reach persons at high risk for HIV infection. IDUs in particular are not likely to use the present HIV counseling and testing sites.

It is also unclear how counseling and testing affects the risk behavior of persons who receive these services. While there are studies showing reductions in risk behavior among persons who have been counseled and tested (for a review, see 31), there are also concerns about (a) the stress associated with learning that one is infected with HIV and (b) the possibility that some persons who test negative might see this result as an indication that they will not become infected, despite their risk behavior.

The role of voluntary counseling and testing is undergoing some revision in HIV prevention. Rather than being seen as a method of "primary" prevention, voluntary counseling and testing is now being viewed as a method for engaging HIV infected persons, providing them with access to medical treatment, and facilitating behavior change so that they do not transmit HIV to others.

HIV Prevention in High Seroprevalence Areas

Current prevention programs for IDUs in low seroprevalence areas appear capable of achieving control over HIV transmission (31). These programs cannot prevent all new HIV infections, but it does appear that they can maintain low seroprevalence indefinitely. In these low HIV seroprevalence areas, almost all of the remaining risk behavior among IDUs occurs among persons who are HIV-seronegative, and therefore without transmission of the virus. In high HIV seroprevalence areas, however, even moderate levels of injection risk behavior are likely to involve persons of different HIV serostatus and thus lead to transmission of the virus. Recent analyses conducted by Holmberg of the CDC (64) suggest that transmission of HIV among IDUs in high seroprevalence areas may account for the plurality of new HIV infections in the United States.

A new generation of HIV prevention programs may thus be needed for IDUs in high HIV seroprevalence areas. In addition to more intensive programs focusing on safer injection, there is a need for programs to reduce the numbers of persons injecting illicit drugs in high seroprevalence areas. Massive expansion of drug abuse treatment could lead to large reductions in the numbers of persons who are injecting illicit drugs. Programs to reduce initiation into drug injection would also be very useful for high seroprevalence areas, as these would also lead to a reduction over time in the numbers of IDUs (65).

HARM REDUCTION

The worldwide epidemic of HIV infection among IDUs has led to important conceptual developments on injecting drug use as a health problem. HIV and AIDS have dramatically increased the adverse health consequences of injecting drug use, and thus have led to seeing psychoactive drug use as more of a health problem and not just a criminal justice problem. At the same time, HIV infection can be prevented without requiring the cessation of injecting drug use. This potential separation of a severe adverse potential consequence of drug use from the drug use itself has encouraged analysis of other areas in which adverse consequences of drug use might be reduced without requiring cessation of drug use.

The ability of many IDUs to modify their behavior to reduce the chances of HIV infection has also led to consideration of drug addicts as both concerned about their health and as capable of acting on that concern (without denying the compulsive nature of drug dependence).

These ideas have formed much of the basis for what has been termed the "harm reduction" perspective on psychoactive drug use (66–69). This perspective emphasizes the pragmatic need to reduce harmful consequences of psychoactive drug use while acknowledging that eliminating psychoactive drug use and misuse is not likely to be feasible in the foreseeable future. One of the major strengths of the harm-reduction perspective is its applicability to both licit (alcohol, nicotine) as well as illicit psychoactive drugs.

Acknowledgments. *Sections of this chapter were originally prepared as reports to the United Kingdom Department of Health and for the United States Congress Office of Technology Assessment.*

References

1. Des Jarlais DC, et al. Emerging infectious diseases and the injection of illicit psychoactive drugs. Current Issues in Public Health 1996; 2:130–137.
2. Mann J, Tarantola J, Netter T. AIDS in the world. Cambridge, MA: Harvard University, 1992:407–411.
3. Peto R. Smoking and death: the past 40 years and the next 40. Br Med J 1994;309:937–939.
4. Mackay JL. The fight against tobacco in developing countries. Tuber Lung Dis 1994;75:8–24.
5. Ambler CH. Drunks, brewers and chiefs: alcohol regulation in colonial Kenya 1900–1939. In: Barrow S, Room R, eds. Drinking behaviour and belief in modern history. Berkeley, CA: University of California Press, 1991.
6. Rogers E. Diffusion of innovations. Vol. 3. New York: The Free Press, 1982.
7. Des Jarlais DC, Friedman SR. AIDS and IV drug use. Science 1989;245:578–579.
8. First Quarterly Report 1966. WHO-EC Collaborating Centre on AIDS, 1966.
9. U.S. Centers for Disease Control and Prevention. HIV/AIDS Surveillance Report 1995;7(2).
10. Holmberg S. The estimated prevalence and incidence of HIV in 96 large US metropolitan areas. Am J Public Health 1996;86(5):642–654.
11. Des Jarlais DC, Friedman SR, Novick DM, Sotheran JL, Thomas P, Yancovitz SR, et al. HIV-1 infection among intravenous drug users in Manhattan, New York City, from 1977 through 1987. JAMA 1989;261:1008–1012.
12. Ball A, et al. Multi-centre study on drug injecting and risk of HIV infection. Geneva: World Health Organization, Programme on Substance Abuse, 1994.
13. Simons M. Drug tourism in Europe. New York Times 1994(April 20):A8.
14. Wright NH, Vanichseni S, Akarasewi P, Wasi C, Choopanya K. Was the 1988 HIV epidemic among Bangkok's injecting drug users a common source outbreak? AIDS 1994;8:529–532.
15. Stoneburner RL, Des Jarlais DC, Benezra D, Gorelkin L, Sotheran JL, Friedman SR, et al. A larger spectrum of severe HIV-1-related disease in intravenous drug users in New York City. Science 1988;242:916–919.
16. Vermund SH, Kelley KF, Klein RS, Feingold AR, Schreiber K, Munk G, et al. High risk of human papillomavirus infection and cervical squamous intraepithelial lesions among women with symptomatic human immunodeficiency virus infection. Am J Obstet Gynecol 1991;165:392–400.
17. Zolla-Pazner S, Des Jarlais DC, Friedman SR, Spira TJ, Marmor M, Holzman R, et al. Nonrandom development of immunologic abnormalities after infection with human immunodeficiency virus: Implications for immunologic classification of the disease. Proc Natl Acad Sci U S A 1987;84:5404–5408.
18. Margolick JB, Munoz A, Vlahov D, Astemborski J, Solomon L, He XY, et al. Direct comparison of the relationship between clinical outcome and change in CD4+ lymphocytes in human immunodeficiency virus-positive homosexual men and injecting drug users. Arch Intern Med 1994;154(8):869–875.
19. Zagury D, Bernard J, Leonard R, Cheynier R, Feldman M, Sarin PS, et al. Long-term cultures of HTLV-III-infected T cells: a model of cytopathology of T-cell depletion in AIDS. Science 1986;231:850–853.
20. Des Jarlais DC, Friedman SR, Choopanya K, Vanichseni S, Ward TP. International epidemiology of HIV and AIDS among injecting drug users. AIDS 1992;6:1053–1068.
21. Jacquez JA, Koopman JS, Simon CP, Longini IM Jr. Role of the primary infection in epidemic HIV infection of gay cohorts. J Acquir Immune Defic Syndr 1994;7:1169–1184.
22. Thompson PI, et al. Promoting HIV prevention outreach activities via community-based organizations. Paper presented at Sixth International Conference on AIDS, San Francisco, CA, June 1990.
23. Wiebel W, Chene D, Johnson W. Adoption of bleach use in a cohort of street intravenous drug users in Chicago. Paper presented at Sixth International Conference on AIDS, San Francisco, CA, June 1990.
24. Jackson J, Rotkiewicz L. A coupon program: AIDS education and drug treatment. Paper presented at Third International Conference on AIDS, Washington, DC, 1987.
25. Ostrow DG. AIDS prevention through effective education. Daedalus 1989;118:29–254.
26. Blix O, Gronbladh L. AIDS and IV heroin addicts: The preventive effect of methadone maintenance in Sweden. Paper presented at Fourth International Conference on AIDS, Stockholm, Sweden, 1988.
27. Buning EC, et al. The evaluation of the needle/syringe exchange in Amsterdam. Paper presented at Fourth International Conference on AIDS, Stockholm, Sweden, 1988.
28. Espinoza P, et al. Has the open sale of syringes modified the syringe exchanging habits of drug addicts? Paper presented at Fourth International Conference on AIDS, Stockholm, Sweden, 1988.
29. Goldberg D, et al. Pharmacy supply of needles and syringes—the effect on spread of HIV in intravenous drug misusers. Paper presented at Fourth International Conference on AIDS, Stockholm, Sweden, 1988.
30. Cartter ML, Petersen LR, Savage RB, Donagher J, Hadler JL. Providing HIV counseling and testing services in methadone maintenance programs. AIDS 1990;4(5):463–465.
31. Higgins DL, Galavotti C, O'Reilly KR, Schnell DJ, Moore M, Rugg DL, et al. Evidence for the effects of HIV antibody counseling and testing on risk behaviors. JAMA 1991;266:2419–2429.
32. Friedman SR, Des Jarlais DC, Sotheran JL, Garber J, Cohen H, Smith D. AIDS and self-organization among intravenous drug users. Int J Addict 1987;22:201–219.
33. Selwyn PA, Feiner C, Cox CP, Lipshutz C, Cohen RL. Knowledge about AIDS and high-risk behavior among intravenous drug abusers in New York City. AIDS (England) 1987;1:247–254.
34. Des Jarlais DC, Friedman SR, Hopkins W. Risk reduction for the acquired immunodeficiency syndrome among intravenous drug users. Ann Intern Med 1985;103:755–759.
35. Des Jarlais DC, Choopanya K, Vanichseni S, Plangsringarm K, Sonchai W, Carballo M, et al. AIDS risk reduction and reduced HIV seroconversion among injection drug users in Bangkok. Am J Public Health 1994;84(3):452–455.
36. Des Jarlais DC, et al. HIV/AIDS-related behavior change among injecting drug users in different national settings. Am J Public Health (in press).
37. Brown BS, Beschner GM, eds. Handbook on risk of AIDS: injection drug users and sexual partners. Westport, CT: Greenwood Press, 1993.
38. Stephens RC, et al. Comparative effectiveness of NADR interventions. In: Brown BS, Beschner GM, eds. Handbook on risk of AIDS. Westport, CT: Greenwood Press, 1993.
39. Friedman SR, Jose B, Deren S, Des Jarlais DC, Neaigus A. Risk factors for human immunodeficiency virus seroconversion among out-of-treatment drug injectors in high and low seroprevalence cities. Am J Epidemiol 1995;142(8):864–874.
40. Ingold FR, Ingold S. The effects of the liberalization of syringe sales on the behavior of intravenous drug users in France. Bull Narc 1989;41:67–81.
41. Groseclose SL, Weinstein B, Jones TS, Valleroy LA, Fehrs LJ, Kassler WJ. Impact of increased legal access to needles and syringes on practices of injecting-drug users and police officers—

Connecticut, 1992–1993. J Acquir Immune Defic Syndr Hum Retrovirol 1995;10(1):82–89.

42. Wiebel W, et al. Positive effect on HIV seroconversion of street outreach intervention with IDU in Chicago, 1988–1992. Paper presented at Ninth International Conference on AIDS, Berlin, 1993.

43. Vlahov D, Astemborski J, Solomon L, Nelson KE. Field effectiveness of needle disinfection among injecting drug users. J Acquir Immune Defic Syndr 1994;7:760–766.

44. Titus S, Marmor M, Des Jarlais D, Kim M, Wolfe H, Beatrice S. Bleach use and HIV seroconversion among New York City injection drug users. J Acquir Immune Defic Syndr 1994;7:700–704.

45. Gleghorn AA, Jones TS, Doherty MC, Celentano DD, Vlahov D. Acquisition and use of needles and syringes by injecting drug users in Baltimore, Maryland. J Acquir Immune Defic Syndr Hum Retrovirol 1995;10(1):97–103.

46. Lamothe F, et al. Risk factors for HIV seroconversion among injecting drug users in Montreal: the Saint-Luc cohort experience. Paper presented at Tenth International Conference on AIDS, Yokohama, Japan, 1994.

47. Hankins C, Gendron S, Tran T. Montreal needle exchange attenders versus non-attenders: what's the difference? Paper presented at Tenth International Conference on AIDS, Yokohama, Japan, 1994.

48. O'Keefe E, Kaplan E, Khoshnood K. Preliminary report. New Haven, CT: City of New Haven Needle Exchange Program, Office of Mayor John C. Daniels, 1991.

49. Des Jarlais DC, et al. HIV incidence among syringe exchange participants in New York City. Lancet 1996;348:987–991.

50. Hagan H, Jarlais DC, Friedman SR, Purchase D, Alter MJ. Reduced risk of hepatitis B and hepatitis C among injecting drug users participating in the Tacoma Syringe exchange program. Am J Public Health 1995;85(11):1531–1537.

51. Ashery RS, et al. Entry into treatment of IDUs based on the association of outreach workers with treatment programs. In: Brown BS, Beschner GM, eds. Handbook on risk of AIDS. Westport, CT: Greenwood Press, 1993:386–395.

52. Hagan H, et al. Risk of human immunodeficiency virus and hepatitis B virus in users of the Tacoma syringe exchange program. In: Proceedings of the National Academy of Sciences Workshop on Needle Exchange and Bleach Distribution Programs. Washington, DC: National Academy Press, 1994.

53. Hubbard RL, Marsden ME, Rachal JV, Harwood HJ Cavanaugh ER, Ginzburg HM, eds. Drug abuse treatment: a national study of effectiveness. Chapel Hill, NC: University of North Carolina Press, 1989.

54. National Commission on AIDS. The twin epidemics of substance use and HIV. Washington, DC: National Commission on AIDS, 1991.

55. Friedman SR, Des Jarlais DC, Ward TP. Overview of the history of the HIV epidemic among drug injectors. In: Brown BS, Beschner GM, eds. Handbook on risk of AIDS. Westport, CT: Greenwood Press, 1993:3–15.

56. Laumann EO, et al. The social organization of sexuality: sexual practices in the United States. Chicago: University of Chicago Press, 1994.

57. Vanichseni S, Des Jarlais DC, Choopanya K, Friedmann P, Wenston J, Sonchai W, et al. Condom use with primary partners among injecting drug users in Bangkok, Thailand and New York City, United States. AIDS 1993;7:887–891.

58. Friedman SR, Jose B, Neaigus A, Goldstein M, Curtis R, Ildefonso G, et al. Consistent condom use in relationships between seropositive injecting drug users and sex partners who do not inject drugs. AIDS 1994;8:357–361.

59. Edlin BR, Irwin KL, Faruque S. Intersecting epidemics: crack cocaine use and HIV infection among inner-city young adults. N Engl J Med 1994;331:1422–1427.

60. Chiasson MA, Stoneburner RL, Hildebrandt DS, Ewing WE, Telzak EE, Jaffe HW. Heterosexual transmission of HIV-1 associated with the use of smokable freebase cocaine (crack). AIDS 1991;5:1121–1126.

61. Ekstrand ML, Coates TJ. Maintenance of safer sexual behaviors and predictors of risky sex: the San Francisco Men's Health Study. Am J Public Health 1990;80:973–977.

62. Stall R, Ekstrand M, Pollack L, McKusick L, Coates TJ. Relapse from safer sex: The next challenge for AIDS prevention efforts. J Acquir Immune Defic Syndr 1990;3:1181–1187.

63. de Wit JB, de Vroome EM, Sandfort TG, van Griensven GJ, Coutinho RA, Tielman RA. Safe sexual practices not reliably maintained by homosexual men [letter]. Am J Public Health 1992;82(4):615–616.

64. Holmberg S. The estimated prevalence and incidence of HIV in 96 large U.S. metropolitan areas. Am J Public Health 1996;86:642–654.

65. Des Jarlais DC, Casriel C, Friedman SR, Rosenblum A. AIDS and the transition to illicit drug injection: results of a randomized trial prevention program. Br J Addict 1992;87:493–498.

66. Brettle RP. HIV and harm reduction for injection drug users. AIDS 1991;5:125–136.

67. Des Jarlais DC, Friedman SR, Ward TP. Harm reduction: a public health response to the AIDS epidemic among injecting drug users. Annu Rev Public Health 1993;14:413–450.

68. Des Jarlais DC. Harm reduction—a framework for incorporating science into drug policy [editorial]. Am J Public Health 1995;85(1):10–12.

69. Heather N, et al., eds. Psychoactive drugs and harm reduction: from faith to science. London: Whurr Publishers, 1993.

70. Ljungberg B, Christensson B, Tunving K, Andersson B, Landvall B, Lundberg M, et al. HIV prevention among injecting drug users: three years of experience from a syringe exchange program in Sweden. J Acquir Immune Defic Syndr 1991;4:890–895.

71. Stimson GV. AIDS and injecting drug use in the United Kingdom, 1987–1993; the policy response and the prevention of the epidemic. Soc Sci Med 1995;41(5):699–716.

72. Maharjan SH, et al. Declining risk for HIV among IDUs in Kathmandu: impact of a harm reduction programme. Paper presented at Tenth International Conference on AIDS, Yokohama, Japan, 1994.

73. Hagan H, Des Jarlais DC, Purchase D, Reid T, Friedman SR. The Tacoma Syringe Exchange. J Addict Dis 1991;10(4):81–88.

74. Oliver K, et al., eds. Behavioral and community impact of the Portland Syringe Exchange Program. Proceedings of the Workshop in Needle Exchange and Bleach Distribution Programs. Washington, DC: National Academy of Sciences, 1994:35–39.

75. Kaplan EH, Heimer R. HIV incidence among needle exchange participants: estimates from syringe tracking and testing data. J Acquir Immune Defic Syndr 1994;7:182–189.

59 MEDICAL COMPLICATIONS AND TREATMENT

Peter A. Selwyn and Fernando L. Merino

The advent of the epidemic of the acquired immune deficiency syndrome (AIDS) has posed new challenges for the field of substance abuse treatment. Although the first cases of AIDS in the United States were reported in 1981 in homosexual or bisexual men (1, 2), cases were soon identified in injection drug users (3). Since the early 1980s, the extent and nature of the AIDS epidemic, and the dynamics of transmission of human immunodeficiency virus (HIV)—the retrovirus which causes AIDS—have been closely linked with the phenomenon of injection drug use (3–7). Injection drug users now account for growing numbers of AIDS cases not only in North America but also in Europe (4, 8–10). In certain regions in the northeastern United States and parts of southern Europe, drug users represent the largest proportion of current or newly reported AIDS cases (8–11). As of the end of 1995, 36% of all cases of AIDS reported to the U.S. Centers for Disease Control and Prevention (CDC) were directly or indirectly associated with injection drug use (12). The presence of HIV infection has been documented among drug users in Australia and parts of Latin America; the recent sudden spread of HIV infection has also been described among injecting drug users in Bangkok and in Myanmar (formerly called Burma), and may be anticipated in other areas as well (13–15). HIV infection has also been noted at increasing levels among drug users in the United States outside of the northeastern states, although the geographic distribution remains concentrated there at present (12). Despite the increasing use of nonparenteral routes for drugs commonly used by injection, injection drug users thus continue to represent a growing percentage of HIV infection and AIDS cases, both in industrialized and developing countries (15, 16).

In addition to reported cases among drug users themselves, the role of injection drug use in the epidemic is reflected in AIDS cases involving heterosexual and perinatal transmission, in which the predominant number in the United States represents sexual contacts of injecting drug users or children born to drug users or their sexual partners (5, 16). With more than two thirds of all AIDS cases among women in the United States involving drug-using women or the female sexual partners of male drug users (5, 16), it is clear that, especially among women, AIDS and drug use are virtually inseparable. This phenomenon has had important clinical and social implications, which are discussed in more detail later in this chapter.

Another feature of the AIDS epidemic among drug users in the United States is the concentration of cases among black and Hispanic populations (8, 17). Studies of HIV seroprevalence among drug users have also generally found an increased likelihood of HIV infection among blacks and Hispanics (18–21). It has been suggested that this may be due to the concentration of injection drug use in poor, inner-city areas, and perhaps to other behavioral or environmental factors that would place these populations at greater risk for drug use–related transmission of HIV (18). A recent study showed that the predominant exposure category for HIV infection among Hispanic men and women born in Puerto Rico was injection drug use. The study showed significant differences in exposure category among women of Hispanic ethnicity according to their place of birth, race, and other categories (22). The importance of heterosexual transmission of HIV in Hispanic women linked to sexual contact with drug users is also represented in those studies. Regardless of the underlying explanation for this phenomenon, the observed pattern of cases indicates the need for preventive and therapeutic interventions that are comprehensive, accessible, and culturally appropriate for at-risk populations of drug users.

As well as having distinct demographic and geographic characteristics, the epidemic of HIV infection among injecting drug users in the United States has also had certain clinical and epidemiologic features that differ from those seen in other populations. The infrequent occurrence of Kaposi's sarcoma among drug users, for example, as compared with homosexual men with AIDS (23), or the increased risk of tuberculosis and severe bacterial infections seen in HIV-infected drug users (24–37), are epidemiologic observations that have immediate clinical relevance. Further, the need for ongoing management of HIV-infected drug users with chronic medical therapies, often involving multiple medications or other interventions, raises important issues concerning patient compliance, coexisting substance abuse, and the relationship between primary medical care and substance abuse treatment in different treatment settings (38–46). These issues have become even more critical with the recent introduction of new therapeutic agents to treat HIV infection, which have shown great promise but which also require close follow-up and medical monitoring to be used effectively (47).

The role of injecting drug use in the framework of HIV transmission behaviors has been defined largely by the importance of shared, contaminated injection equipment as a vector for the spread of HIV among drug-using populations (18–21, 45, 48, 49). This in itself would pose a challenge to the drug abuse treatment field, to address issues of risk behavior involving ongoing drug use, needle use, and needle sharing among injecting drug users. In addition, however, important links have been made as well between nonparenteral substance use and other behaviors associated with transmission of HIV, e.g., the relationship among cocaine use, prostitution, and sexually transmitted diseases in general, or between drug or alcohol use and unsafe sexual behavior—among both homosexuals and heterosexuals—due to these substances' disinhibiting effects on such behavior (50–57). The question has also been raised whether ongoing injecting or other drug use may accelerate the rate of progression to AIDS in HIV-infected persons, although existing data regarding this possibility are equivocal (58–62). It should be noted, however, that injection drug users who continue to share injection equipment may be exposed to potentially more virulent or resistant strains of the virus, strains that may have undergone multiple mutations after being exposed to different antiretroviral medications.

These issues highlight the complex and wide-ranging issues involving HIV infection and its clinical and programmatic implications for drug abuse treatment.

AIDS AND HIV INFECTION: DEFINITIONS

The first portion of this chapter addresses basic issues regarding HIV infection and AIDS, including case definitions and certain clinical topics of general importance. The remaining sections of the chapter focus on clinical themes more specifically related to the management of drug users with HIV infection. This chapter is not intended to serve as a comprehensive review of the treatment for HIV infection or of the full range of AIDS-associated opportunistic infections and malignancies, for which the reader is referred to a number of excellent sources (47, 63–66). Rather, the intention is to establish the basic framework for understanding the clinical dimensions of HIV infection, with special reference to the manifestations and treatment of HIV infection among drug users.

Diagnosis of HIV Infection

Human immunodeficiency virus type I (HIV-I, or, hereafter in this chapter, HIV) is now accepted as the causative infectious agent of the acquired immune deficiency syndrome (67). Previously referred to as human T lymphotrophic virus type III (HTLV-III) (68), lymphadenopathy-associated virus (LAV) (69), or AIDS-associated retrovirus (ARV) (70), the virus is now denoted as HIV or HIV-1 in the current standard nomenclature (71).

Following exposure to HIV through sexual contact or blood-borne transmission, persons infected with HIV develop a characteristic serum antibody response. It is estimated that among those infected with HIV, HIV serum antibody typically is detectable within 1–4 months following primary infection, and 95% of infected individuals would be expected to demonstrate a positive antibody test within 6 months following exposure, if not sooner (72–75). It has also been suggested that delayed seroconversion—up to almost 3 years—may occur in certain individuals, and even that HIV infection may not result in the production of serum antibody to HIV in some cases—but these have not been common or consistent findings (72–75). Because of the potentially variable time course of seroconversion, it is prudent to consider repeating the HIV antibody test, if initially negative, several times during a 12-month follow-up period, for patients whose presumed exposure to HIV may have occurred proximate to the time of the first antibody test. The standard procedure for HIV serum antibody testing involves a two-step process including a screening test for HIV antibody (e.g., enzyme-linked immunosorbent assay, or ELISA) followed by a confirmatory test performed on the same specimen (e.g., Western blot immunoblot; immunofluorescence assay, or IFA). The ELISA must be reactive and the Western blot or IFA positive for the test to be considered positive for HIV antibody (76).

Recent research interest has been devoted to the development of reliable virologic markers of HIV activity or disease progression. Among those are tests for HIV serum antigen (p24) (77), viral culture (78), and, most recently, commercially available assays ("viral load" tests) that measure quantitative plasma HIV RNA using molecular genetic techniques, including either genome amplification or signal amplification (79).

The HIV antigen assays, while specific for HIV infection, generally are not sensitive enough to warrant their use in routine testing for HIV, especially since levels of p24 antigen appear to vary over the natural history of HIV infection (77, 78). Viral culture remains primarily a research tool at the present time, and viral load measurements should not be used for the actual diagnosis of HIV infection. Thus, as of late 1996, the standard clinical test for detecting HIV infection in adults remains the HIV antibody test.

Diagnosis of AIDS

Since the first AIDS cases were reported in 1981 (1, 2), several classification systems have been developed for surveillance and clinical purposes, in order to establish case definitions for AIDS and to provide a framework for categorizing different manifestations of HIV infection (3, 80–83) (Table 59.1). The original CDC AIDS case definition was promulgated primarily for epidemiologic surveillance (3) and was restricted to a series of 10 opportunistic infections (expanded to 12 in an early revision) and two malignancies, which, when reliably diagnosed and in the absence of known causes of immunodeficiency, were considered indicators of AIDS. In 1987,

Table 59.1 Center for Disease Control's Revised Clinical Staging System for HIV Infection and Disease

CD4+ T-Lymphocyte Categories

1. Category 1: > 500 cells/mm^3
2. Category 2: 200–499 cells/mm^3
3. Category 3:^{a} < 200 cells/mm^3

Clinical Categories

1. Clinical Category A
   At least one of the conditions listed below with documented HIV infection, and none of the conditions listed in categories B and C.
   - Asymptomatic HIV infection
   - Persistent generalized lymphadenopathy (PGL)
   - Acute or history of acute HIV infection
2. Clinical Category B
   Conditions not included in either category A or C and that meet the following criteria:
   (a) The conditions are attributed to HIV infection or to a cellular immunity defect;
   (b) Clinical course or management of these conditions is complicated by HIV infection. Examples (list is not exhaustive):
      - Oral hairy leukoplakia
      - Oropharyngeal candidiasis
      - Persistent vulvovaginal candidiasis
      - Cervical dysplasia or cervical carcinoma *in situ*
      - Pelvic inflammatory disease (PID)
      - Constitutional symptoms^b
      - Herpes zoster involving > 1 dermatome or episode
      - Idiopathic thrombocytopenic purpura (ITP)
      - Peripheral neuropathy
      - Bacillary angiomatosis
3. Clinical Category C
   Conditions listed in the AIDS surveillance case definition. Once a category C condition has occurred, the person will remain in category C.
      - Upper/lower respiratory tract candidiasis
      - Esophageal candidiasis
      - Invasive cervical cancer
      - Disseminated coccidioidomycosis
      - Extrapulmonary cryptococcosis
      - Chronic intestinal cryptosporidiosis
      - Cytomegalovirus disease (except liver/spleen/nodal involvement)
      - HIV-related encephalopathy
      - Herpes simplex: chronic ulcers or respiratory/esophageal disease
      - Disseminated histoplasmosis
      - Chronic intestinal isosporiasis
      - Kaposi's sarcoma
      - Lymphoma; Burkitt's immunoblastic or CNS lymphoma
      - Disseminated *Mycobacterium avium* complex or *M. Kansasii*
      - Mycobacterium tuberculosis, any site
      - Disseminated *Mycobacterium* disease (species not included above)
      - *Pneumocystis carinii* pneumonia
      - Progressive multifocal leukoencephalopathy
      - Recurrent *Salmonella* septicemia
      - CNS toxoplasmosis
      - HIV-related wasting syndrome

CD4+ T-cell categories (cells/mm^3)	A Asymptomatic, acute HIV infection or PGL	B Symptomatic, not A or C condition	C AIDS-indicator conditions
1: > 500	A1	B1	C1
2: 200–499	A2	B2	C2
3: > 200	A3	B3	C3

Adapted from U.S. Centers for Disease Control and Prevention. 1993 revised classification system for HIV infection and expanded surveillance case definition for AIDS among adolescents and adults. MMWR 1992;41(RR-17):1–19.
^{a}Note that *all* patients with CD4+ cell counts < 200/mm^3 are classified as having AIDS under the CDC's 1993 Classification System, regardless of their clinical category.
^{b}Includes fever (38.5° C) or diarrhea lasting > 1 month.

the CDC issued a revised AIDS case definition, which expanded the number of AIDS-qualifying diagnoses, relying more explicitly on the use of laboratory tests for HIV, and permitting the inclusion of certain presumptively diagnosed indicator diseases as AIDS-qualifying in the presence of a positive HIV antibody test (or other laboratory tests confirming HIV infection) (82). The introduction of the revised AIDS surveillance case definition in 1987 resulted in a disproportionate increase in reported cases among injecting drug users, women, and minorities (84, 85); more than 40% of AIDS cases among injecting drug users reported in 1988 in the United States met only the revised case definition criteria, compared with 23% of all other cases. This phenomenon may reflect both the inclusion in the revised case definition of certain opportunistic infections (e.g., extrapulmonary tuberculosis) (33), which in developed countries most commonly affect drug users with HIV infection, and the possibility that drug users' lack of access to or

avoidance of medical care may result in a decreased likelihood of definitive diagnoses being made.

The CDC has issued a new HIV clinical classification, the 1993 Classification System for HIV Infection and Expanded Surveillance Case Definition for AIDS among Adolescents and Adults (83). It includes pulmonary tuberculosis, recurrent pneumonia, and invasive cervical cancer in the expanded AIDS surveillance case definition. As in previous revisions (84), the introduction of the new surveillance classification has resulted in a disproportionately larger increment of new cases in injecting drug users (86, 87). This fact reflects the systematic under-reporting of cases of HIV infection and AIDS which had previously been noted in drug injectors, since early in the epidemic (88).

In addition to the AIDS case definition, the CDC's 1993 classification and other systems have been developed to help characterize the broader range and spectrum of HIV infection, to include less severe conditions that are not AIDS-qualifying but that are manifestations of the natural history of HIV infection. Given the current estimate that the mean time from HIV infection to the development of AIDS is between 7 and 10 years (89)—not accounting for any potential treatment effect in delaying AIDS incidence (90)—it is not surprising that there are many clinical conditions and complications that may present in the period prior to the actual development of AIDS in HIV-infected patients. Especially in primary medical care settings (91), with growing trends toward early treatment intervention in HIV infection (92–95), it has been increasingly important for practitioners to recognize the early and sometimes varied manifestations of HIV-related illness, both for therapeutic reasons and to assist in diagnostic and prognostic evaluation.

The CDC's 1993 Revised Classification System for HIV Infection establishes a staging system that includes three clinical categories of infection, each including a variety of specific conditions. In addition, it relies on the use of CD4+ T-lymphocyte count to incorporate a laboratory marker related to immune function, which helps enhance the prognostic value of this classification scheme (see Table 59.1).

Since early in the AIDS epidemic, the disease was associated with cellular immune dysfunction and a reversal of normal T lymphocyte helper-to-suppressor ratios (2). More recently, the CD4+ or T4 molecule has been identified as the HIV receptor on the membrane surface of T lymphocytes in the helper or inducer subset (96, 97). Although previously referred to as T4 lymphocytes, T4 helper/inducer cells, or by other terms, CD4 antigen-positive T lymphocytes are now designated as CD4+ T cells or simply as CD4+ cells in standard clinical parlance. HIV directly infects and ultimately leads to the destruction of CD4+ T lymphocytes, and much (though not all) of the immunopathogenesis of AIDS may be explained based on the selective depletion of this lymphocyte subset. Studies of the natural history of HIV infection have indicated that CD4+ cell levels tend to decline over time following initial HIV infection, and that the absolute number and percentage of CD4+ T lymphocytes are important predictors of the likelihood of disease progression and the development of AIDS (98–102). Since the late 1980s, the use of diagnostic tests such as total CD4+ T lymphocyte counts and percentages has been a routine component of HIV-related clinical care, in which decisions to initiate certain therapies or prophylactic interventions, even among asymptomatic individuals, were increasingly linked with determinations of CD4+ cell levels (95, 103).

More recently, the introduction of laboratory methods that determine the concentration of virus in blood, or total viral load (HIV-RNA test), has given a new dimension to laboratory markers as predictors of progression of disease and risk of death (104). Recent studies have suggested that the total viral load in plasma soon after HIV infection is a good independent predictor of risk for AIDS (105). Most recent studies suggest that plasma viral load may be a better predictor of progression to AIDS and death, at any stage, than the CD4+ T-lymphocyte count, particularly in asymptomatic patients with higher CD4+ counts (104). Indeed, viral load tests may increasingly be used as a stronger indication than CD4+ counts in decisions regarding therapy initiation and monitoring, although CD4+ counts will remain important in the determination of patients' current levels of immunodeficiency.

The role played by lymphatic tissue in the establishment of HIV infection, viral replication, and progression of disease is the focus of intense research. Within 1–2 months after acute infection, the number of viral particles in blood is dramatically decreased, an event that reflects the initial response by the immune system. What follows is a long period of clinical latency (up to 10 years) characterized by a great turnover of HIV replication: half of the virus population is turned over within hours, and it is estimated that several billions of virions and similar numbers of CD4+ cells are produced and destroyed every day, while the patient remains clinically asymptomatic (47, 106). In the early asymptomatic stage, HIV RNA can be detected in high concentration in lymph nodes and lymphoid tissue, and up to one third of CD4+ cells in lymphoid tissue are infected (106). Potentially, studies of lymph node tissue may be used in the future to assess the complex host-virus interaction at any given time during the course of the disease and to assist in the choice of the appropriate therapy (107). These observations highlight the fact that, even during the clinically latent phase of HIV infection, there is no virologic latency, and early treatment to control virologic replication may have important long-term benefits.

These developments have signaled a shift over time in HIV-associated medical care from the late-stage or inpatient focus of the first years of the epidemic, toward a new and ascendant emphasis on early intervention, outpatient evaluation and treatment, and management of HIV infection by primary care practitioners. These trends have posed both challenges and opportunities for drug treatment programs and other settings in which drug users with HIV infection are likely to be found.

SPECTRUM OF HIV-RELATED DISEASE IN INJECTING DRUG USERS

Comparative epidemiologic studies have indicated that the expression of HIV-related disease and AIDS may vary substantially in different geographic regions. For example, it has been observed that *Pneumocystis carinii* pneumonia (PCP), the most common AIDS-defining opportunistic infection in the United States and Europe (108–110), is seen only infrequently in AIDS cases in Central Africa, where esophageal candidiasis, tuberculosis, toxoplasmosis, cryptococcosis, enteric infections, and wasting syndromes are more common findings (111–113). In addition, it has been noted that even within a single geographic area, the spectrum of HIV-related illness may differ by risk group, with divergent patterns of illness observed in drug users as compared with homosexual men. For example, it has been a consistent finding that Kaposi's sarcoma, though commonly seen in homosex-ual men, rarely is noted in drug users with HIV infection (23). A recently identified human herpes virus, Kaposi's sarcoma-associated herpesvirus (KSAHV), could play an etiologic role in the pathophysiology of Kaposi's sarcoma, as suggested in recent studies. KSAHV is thought to be transmitted sexually; if the epidemiology of this virus were more limited to sexual transmission through male same-sex contact, this would explain the observation of the low incidence of Kaposi's sarcoma in injection drug users (23, 114). Table 59.2 summarizes the major conditions seen in HIV-infected drug users more commonly than in other populations with HIV infection.

Bacterial Infections

It has been reported, since early in the AIDS epidemic, that drug users with HIV infection may be at risk for developing serious bacterial infections, especially bacterial pneumonia, endocarditis, and bacterial sepsis (24, 36, 37, 115–117). This phenomenon was first described in New York City, where mortality data analyzed by investigators at the New York City De-

Table 59.2 Spectrum of HIV-related Disease in Injection Drug Users[a]

Pyogenic Bacterial Infections
    Pneumonia
        Streptococcus pneumoniae
        Haemophilus influenzae
        Endocarditis or sepsis
Tuberculosis
    Pulmonary
    Extrapulmonary
Sexually Transmitted Disease
    Syphilis
    Human papillomavirus
Neurologic Disease
    Central
    Peripheral
Hepatitis
    Infectious hepatitis A, B, C, D (delta)
    Alcoholic hepatitis
Other Retroviral Infections
    Human T-cell lymphotrophic virus types I, II or both
Cancer
    Lung
    Cervix
    Other (e.g., oropharynx or larynx)

Adapted from O'Connor P, Selwyn PA, Schottenfeld RS. Medical management of injection drug users with HIV infection. N Engl J Med 1994;331:450–459.
[a]These are common complications of HIV infection, drug use, or both, which may occur more commonly among injection drug users with HIV infection.

partment of Health showed a steady increase in deaths from pneumonia and other bacterial infections among injecting drug users beginning in the early 1980s (24). Further analysis indicated that a disproportionate number of these cases showed suggestive or confirmatory evidence of the presence of HIV infection, even after excluding those that would meet criteria for the surveillance case definition of AIDS (24). This observation, along with additional population-based data, led to the suggestion that the burden of HIV-related morbidity and mortality among drug users may be underestimated by focusing attention on AIDS cases alone, an effect that has implications not only for clinical care but also for health policy and planning (24, 118).

Subsequent analyses in different populations of drug users have further corroborated the association between HIV infection and serious bacterial infections in injecting drug users, although this has not been reported consistently in all geographic areas (25, 35–37, 115–121). Although pneumonia, endocarditis, and other bacterial infections historically were noted to occur with high frequency in injecting drug users well before the AIDS epidemic (122, 123), evidence has accumulated to suggest that these infections may occur more commonly among drug users in the setting of HIV infection (24, 25, 35, 115, 116, 118, 119). One study determined yearly rates of bacterial pneumonia hospitalizations among HIV-seropositive and seronegative drug users enrolled in a prospective study of HIV infection at a New York City methadone maintenance program (115). Even after controlling for demographic variables and for current drug, alcohol, and tobacco use, the HIV-seropositive group showed a fourfold increased risk of bacterial pneumonia compared with the seronegative group. It has also been suggested in a more recent study, however, that smoking illicit drugs may be a risk factor for bacterial pneumonia (124), including marihuana and smoked cocaine. This suggests that HIV-infected drug users may be at even greater risk of bacterial pneumonia than otherwise if they continue to smoke illicit drugs.

In all published investigations examining bacterial pneumonia in drug users and other HIV-infected patients, the predominant pathogenic organisms have been encapsulated bacteria such as *Streptococcus pneumoniae* and *Haemophilus influenzae;* less frequently identified have been *Staphylococcus aureus,* Gram-negative enteric organisms, and other miscellaneous bacterial pathogens (115–117, 125–129).

A number of characteristics have been described to explain the increased risk of bacterial infections in drug-using populations. In summary, these are (*a*) increased rates of mucocutaneous and upper respiratory carriage of pathogenic organisms, particularly strains of *Staphylococci* and *Streptococci;* (*b*) improper injection technique, that does not include sterilization of skin and favors the breakdown of natural barriers and the transfer of bacteria from mucocutaneous surfaces into the bloodstream; (*c*) use of contaminated injection equipment or injecting substances with viral, bacterial, and parasitic microorganisms that may have originated in body fluids, particularly residual blood, or different fluids used as drug solvents or for rinsing the injection equipment; (*d*) altered immune response from underlying medical conditions (including AIDS) or from the effect of the drugs used; (*e*) factors related to the oropharynx, namely poor dental hygiene, periodontal and soft tissue disease, and impairment of gag and cough reflexes by the use of drugs; (*f*) change in normal microbial flora promoted by prior use of antibiotics; (*g*) low socioeconomic status and its associated risk of exposure to pathogens like *Mycobacterium tuberculosis;* (*h*) behavioral aspects associated with injection drug use, particularly use of multiple substances and the excessive use of alcohol and tobacco; (*i*) poor utilization or limited access to primary health care services, with resultant low levels of immunization and prophylaxis and the lack of timely diagnosis and treatment of infections (130).

It has been suggested that bacterial infections not only occur more commonly in HIV-infected drug users than in their HIV-seronegative counterparts, but also that they may be more severe as well, with higher case fatality rates and more lengthy hospitalizations (115). Several case control studies have suggested that bacterial endocarditis in HIV-infected drug users may be more complicated and difficult to treat than endocarditis in HIV-seronegative drug users, although the magnitude of this alleged effect is uncertain (131, 132), and some studies have indicated no difference in outcome (133). A potentially life-threatening infection at any stage of HIV infection, the microbiology of bacterial endocarditis in injection drug users reflects unsterile injection techniques that favor the transfer of bacteria from the skin and mucous membranes into the bloodstream. *Staphylococcus aureus,* an organism commonly found in nares, upper respiratory system, and skin, is the most common etiologic organism of bacterial endocarditis in drug injectors. Streptococci and enterococci are also commonly isolated. Finally, Gram-negative bacilli like *Pseudomonas* species and *Serratia* marcescens are not uncommon etiologic agents in this patient population (134). Management of endocarditis in drug injectors requires prompt institution of intravenous antibiotic therapy after blood cultures have been obtained. The empiric use of specific antibiotic regimens will depend on the local geographic incidence of specific pathogens, and particular emphasis should be placed on the clinical suspicion of methicillin-resistant *Staphylococcus aureus* (MRSA) (135–137) and vancomycin-resistant *enterococci* (VRE) (138, 139). The prognosis will depend on the degree of valve damage, the use of adequate antimicrobial therapy, and general medical condition. The importance of completion of therapy and the negative effect of continued injection drug use should be addressed with each patient individually.

The occurrence of bacterial pneumonia has been viewed as a sentinel event or harbinger of subsequent HIV-related disease in drug users, who may often present with bacterial infections as the first sign of HIV-related illness (115, 140). Indeed, unlike the major opportunistic infections that constitute a diagnosis of AIDS, bacterial pneumonias tend first to occur earlier in the course of HIV infection, before the later stages of immunosuppression marked by severe CD4 lymphocyte depletion (115, 121, 124, 141). Although bacterial infections may occur in the latter setting as well, as a first presentation they usually are seen in HIV-infected patients who have not yet shown evidence of major opportunistic infections (115, 124, 141).

The finding of an increased likelihood of bacterial infections in HIV-infected drug users has a number of implications for epidemiologic surveillance, clinical management, and preventive strategies. As noted previously, there may be certain behavioral, demographic, or environmental factors that put HIV-infected drug users at risk for bacterial infections. More specifically, the pathophysiologic mechanism resulting in an increased risk of bacterial infections in HIV-infected drug users has not been elucidated; however, it has been hypothesized that this may relate to the known deleterious effects of HIV on B cell function as well on T cell function, which would result in an inability to respond effectively to encapsulated bacterial pathogens (115, 125–127, 129, 142–144). The depletion of CD4+ cells characterizes the immunopathogenesis of AIDS. The CD4+ T lymphocyte plays a central role in most immunologic functions, not just those that affect cellular immunity. Persons with AIDS have significant abnormalities in B-cell function, characterized by polyclonal activation, hypergammaglobulinemia, and circulating immunocomplexes and auto-antibodies, and those abnormalities are manifested clinically as increased susceptibility to certain pyogenic bacteria (100). A good clinical example of this observation is represented by the Gram-negative bacillus *Pseudomonas aeruginosa,* a very rare pathogen in immunocompetent patients presenting with community-acquired infections. Multiple clinical studies have come to recognize the increased incidence of *P. aeruginosa* infection in HIV-infected patients, particularly bronchopulmonary infections, recognized both as an indolent relapsing pathogen in the outpatient setting and as an agent causing fulminant pneumonia and bacteremia in the hospitalized patient (145–148). Prolonged survival in AIDS patients with associated severe immunosuppression has been proposed as a risk factor for *P. aeruginosa* infections (145). A higher index of suspicion is required for some bacterial pathogens like *P. aeruginosa* that are rare community-acquired pathogens for non–HIV-infected individuals.

The recognition of the increased susceptibility of HIV-infected patients for bacterial pathogens has led to the inclusion of recurrent pneumonia in the CDC's 1993 expanded AIDS surveillance case definition (83). It has also been proposed that surveillance for pneumococcal pneumonia or bacteremia in young adult populations may be used as a surrogate marker for drug abuse or to help detect trends in HIV infection in certain geographic areas, where drug use and HIV infection are concentrated (149, 150). For clinicians, the importance of bacterial infections in this population highlights the need for precise microbiologic diagnosis of pathogenic organisms in pneumonia cases among HIV-infected drug users. The specificity and positive predictive value of the standard criteria for presumptive diagnosis of PCP (82)—

i.e., exertional dyspnea, arterial hypoxemia, and diffuse bilateral interstitial infiltrates on chest roentgenogram or a positive gallium citrate lung scan—may well be diminished in a population at risk for pneumonia syndromes of different etiology.

Therefore, sputum Gram stain, sputum and blood cultures, sputum induction, and/or bronchoscopy are often necessary before an appropriate diagnosis can be made in drug users presenting with pneumonia. The practice of treating pneumonias in HIV-infected patients presumptively with trimethoprim-sulfamethoxazole (TMP-SMX), under the rationale that such treatment would be effective both for PCP and/or common bacterial pathogens, may indeed yield good empiric results in many cases. However, the high likelihood of adverse reactions to TMP-SMX in HIV-infected patients (151) often requires a change of therapy to pentamidine, the other principal agent for treating PCP, which is not effective against bacterial pathogens. In such cases, in which a precise microbiologic diagnosis has not been made, and in which TMP-SMX therapy has been initiated presumptively, one then may be faced with a partly treated bacterial infection that may be difficult to diagnose by culture and therefore difficult to treat definitively.

Given the increased risk of bacterial infections among HIV-infected drug users, the possibility for preventive interventions in this area is of strategic importance. Since most series indicate that pneumococcal pneumonia is one of the most common entities seen in HIV-seropositive patients with bacterial infections (115, 125, 129), it has been suggested that pneumococcal polysaccharide vaccine be considered for drug users and other individuals with HIV infection. In fact, current guidelines published by the CDC recommend that all persons with known HIV infection be offered antipneumococcal vaccine (152). Although there have been reports of pneumococcal vaccine failure in patients with AIDS, presumably due to underlying immunosuppression and the inability to respond adequately to vaccine antigens (126, 144, 153), several studies have indicated at least a moderate antibody response to this vaccine in both homosexual men and drug users with HIV infection (154, 155). In these studies, a post-vaccine rise in specific antipneumococcal antibody titers, to levels that would be considered protective, generally was seen only in patients in the earlier stages of HIV infection who were not profoundly immunosuppressed. However, vaccination has not been deemed to be harmful in patients with AIDS and at times may result in an appropriate antibody response in such patients; therefore, the recommendation has been that all patients with HIV infection be considered eligible to receive pneumococcal vaccine (152). Some clinicians have also recommended the use of conjugate *Haemophilus influenzae* vaccine for HIV-infected adults, although data to support this practice are less available than for pneumococcal vaccine. Despite its generalized use in the pediatric non–HIV-infected population, routine use of *Haemophilus influenzae* type b (Hib) vaccine in the adult HIV-infected patient is not standard care at present. (It has also been recommended that patients with AIDS receive yearly influenza vaccine, which is discussed later.)

An additional preventive intervention, more in the behavioral arena, was suggested by a study from San Francisco in which active drug users who used alcohol to clean skin injection sites prior to injecting drugs were found to be at lower risk of soft tissue bacterial infections and endocarditis compared with drug users who did not use such techniques (156). Another recent study from Baltimore yielded similar findings on the possible protective effect of skin cleaning on bacterial infections (157). Although this intervention has not been prospectively demonstrated to be effective in preventing bacterial pneumonias in the setting of HIV infection—for which the pathogenesis does not appear to depend upon bacteremia resulting from drug injection—it is plausible that this intervention may indeed help prevent certain other serious bacterial infections in drug users and therefore should be promoted in active drug users who are unable to cease drug injection behavior.

Of special significance is the recognition and increasing number of reports from systematic surveillance studies of penicillin-resistant strains of *Streptococcus pneumoniae*. Although it appears that those strains are no more virulent than the fully sensitive ones, management problems associated with them are related to the delay in diagnosis and timely institution of appropriate therapy. The increased mortality and morbidity associated with delayed treatment can be prevented with an increased clinical suspicion in the

treatment of patients more susceptible to harbor resistant strains of *S. pneumoniae* and also by reducing the incidence of pneumococcal infection, broadening the indications for the use of the available 23-valent pneumococcal vaccine and targeting the appropriate population, that should include all HIV-infected individuals and all injection drug users, as discussed earlier. Although not fully explained to date, the emergence of penicillin-resistant strains of *S. pneumoniae* is thought to be due to two main factors: the misuse of beta-lactam antibiotics, and the poor compliance with full therapeutic courses. Both characteristics are well described in the injection drug–using population, and therefore preventive measures directed at reducing the incidence of infections caused by this organism should be applied with particular emphasis to this group of patients (158, 159).

Infections of skin and soft tissue are more directly related than pneumonia to the behavioral aspects of drug injection as well as to the use of contaminated injection equipment, and are the most common bacterial infections among injection drug users (130, 157). The spectrum of infections is broad and ranges from localized cellulitis originated at the site of injection to rapidly spreading fasciitis, local abscess formation, and metastatic complications: thrombophlebitis, septic emboli, endocarditis, and visceral abscess formation. The pathogens found in these infections are normally not found in the equipment used when it is cultured, but rather are pathogens carried in the skin, either common skin or nasopharyngeal flora (Staphylococci, Streptococci, P. acnes, Diphtheroids, etc.) or more aggressive organisms that are able to grow at the site of prior soft tissue injury favored by the use of solvents, contaminants, and substance adulterants commonly used by drug injectors. Additionally, injection drug users may be at increased risk for becoming carriers of potentially aggressive organisms that are associated with antibiotic use or hospital exposure, such as MRSA (135–137) and VRE (138, 139). This raises the further possibility of person-to-person spread of these agents between drug users, which could lead to local outbreaks of these difficult-to-treat infections.

Tuberculosis

Another important condition that has been noted among certain HIV-infected populations, particularly among drug users, is tuberculosis. Tuberculosis in the setting of coexistent HIV infection has been reported with increasing frequency in a variety of geographic settings, including not only industrialized countries but also, of particular importance, countries in the Caribbean and Central Africa, where both HIV infection and tuberculosis are concentrated (24, 29–32, 34, 160–165). Reports from sub-Saharan Africa describe a dual epidemic of alarming magnitude, in which millions of individuals may be co-infected with *Mycobacterium tuberculosis* and HIV (111, 161, 166, 167). This combination has important and grave implications for tuberculosis control and public health, and it has been suggested that many of the historical gains in tuberculosis control may be lost due to a resurgence of HIV-associated tuberculosis.

HIV infection is considered to be the strongest risk factor for the progression of latent tuberculosis infection to active disease (168–170), and an estimated six million people worldwide are thought to have HIV and *M. tuberculosis* co-infection (171). Extrapulmonary tuberculosis was included as an AIDS-defining illness in the 1987 CDC revised AIDS surveillance case definition (82). Any anatomic site of tuberculosis involvement, however, constitutes an AIDS-defining illness in the CDC's 1993 Classification System for HIV Infection and Expanded Surveillance Case Definition (83).

Until recently, it was believed that the development of active tuberculosis in patients with HIV infection was almost always due to the reactivation of latent tuberculosis infection in the setting of HIV-induced immunosuppression, in patients previously exposed to *M. tuberculosis* (30, 31, 164, 172, 173). This phenomenon remains important; however, more recently, primary infection with rapid disease progression has been identified as another important mechanism. Recent molecular genetic techniques, namely restriction fragment length polymorphism (RFLP) and polymerase chain reaction (PCR)-based methods, permit the identification of identical strains of *M. tuberculosis*, allowing investigators to identify transmission patterns in a specific geographic area. These methods have been very useful in studies of local tuberculosis outbreaks, and recent reports have documented, both in outbreak studies and in broader epidemiological analysis, that HIV-infected patients may acquire primary infection with *M. tuberculosis* and progress rapidly to active disease (174–178). This phenomenon has been documented for both drug-sensitive and drug-resistant strains of *M. tuberculosis* (179–181). HIV-infected patients may be at high risk of acquiring tuberculosis infection from other HIV-infected patients, and then progressing themselves to disease, thus continuing the chain of transmission in a potentially explosive manner.

In the United States, tuberculosis in HIV-infected patients is concentrated primarily among injecting drug users and minority populations (30, 164, 165, 172, 182). The association between the two infections has been shown most strikingly in certain cities in the northeastern and southeastern United States, where HIV seroprevalence studies have found levels of HIV infection as high as 40% among patients treated at tuberculosis clinics (183). Tuberculosis traditionally was recognized as a common condition among drug users well before the AIDS epidemic (184). Levels of latent tuberculous infection among drug-using populations—as demonstrated by positive tuberculin skin tests—have been found to be as high as 25% (34, 172, 184). Given this background of risk, the introduction of HIV infection into these populations could well be expected to amplify the expression of tuberculosis in the setting of HIV-induced immunosuppression. One study performed at a methadone maintenance program in New York City prospectively followed a cohort of 520 injecting drug users with known HIV antibody and tuberculin skin test status over approximately 2 years of follow-up (172). This study found a rate of 7.9 cases of active tuberculosis per 100 person-years among HIV-seropositive patients with prior positive tuberculin skin tests, compared with zero cases among HIV-seropositive patients without prior positive tuberculin tests. HIV-seropositive patients with positive tuberculin skin tests were 24 times more likely to develop active tuberculosis in this study than were HIV-seropositive patients without evidence of prior exposure to tuberculosis. None of the patients in this study who had received isoniazid prophylaxis for a positive purified protein derivative (PPD) test developed active tuberculosis during the study period (172). Although not designed as a clinical trial of the efficacy of isoniazid prophylaxis in this population, this study's results support recommendations for aggressive identification and treatment of patients with dual HIV and *M. tuberculosis* infection (165). Several other studies, from Zambia, Haiti, and Spain, have all documented tuberculosis incidence rates of 6–12 per 100 person-years in HIV-infected patients with prior positive tuberculin tests (185–187).

Numerous studies and surveillance reports have examined the temporal relationship between the diagnoses of pulmonary tuberculosis and AIDS in individuals ultimately diagnosed with both conditions. In such cases the diagnoses tend to cluster together, with tuberculosis usually diagnosed several months prior to an AIDS-defining illness in HIV-infected patients, although variations on this sequence are not uncommon (30–32, 172). The relationship between tuberculosis and CD4+ lymphocyte count has been examined in different studies (188–190). It has been found that HIV-infected patients with tuberculosis tend to be less immunocompromised than those diagnosed with other AIDS-defining conditions. The approximate range of CD4+ count most commonly observed for patients with HIV infection and pulmonary tuberculosis is 150–400 cells/mm^3 (191). Remarkably, a recent study showed a higher risk for opportunistic infections and death in HIV-infected patients who are co-infected with *M. tuberculosis* (192), and another study suggested that treatment of latent tuberculosis infection in HIV-infected persons actually reduces their risk of HIV disease progression (185). It has also been noted that extrapulmonary involvement occurs most commonly with increasing degree of immunosuppression, with disseminated disease and lymphadenitis as the most common diagnoses (190, 191, 193). Most series of tuberculosis cases in HIV-infected patients have consisted of a majority of pulmonary cases but have included a greater percentage of extrapulmonary cases—between 25 and 70%—than would be seen in -non–HIV-infected patients with tuberculosis (33, 34, 164, 172, 173, 190).

Most analyses of the treatment of tuberculosis in HIV-infected patients have suggested that, as in non–HIV-infected patients, tuberculosis usually responds well to appropriate chemotherapy (33, 164, 166, 173, 182, 190,

194). However, certain clinical features of these cases may differ from those seen in classic cases of tuberculosis, especially when tuberculosis is diagnosed in HIV-infected patients in the later stages of immunosuppression. For example, the typical findings of upper lobe lung involvement and cavitation seen in classic pulmonary tuberculosis are relatively uncommon in HIV-associated cases, and it has been reported that sputum smears for acid-fast bacilli may be less frequently positive in HIV-associated pulmonary tuberculosis, even in the presence of ultimately positive sputum cultures (164, 172, 182, 194–196). In addition, the presentations of extrapulmonary tuberculosis can be varied and, at times, nonspecific, ranging from meningitis, peritonitis, and localized involvement of bone or soft tissues, to vague constitutional symptoms, fever, or malaise. It is therefore important for clinicians treating patients at risk for HIV infection and tuberculosis to have a high index of suspicion for unusual presentations of tuberculosis; diagnosis may depend on mycobacterial blood cultures, bone marrow aspiration or biopsy, liver biopsy, or CSF examination and culture, in addition to the standard procedures of chest roentgenogram and sputum smear and culture, which would be used routinely for suspected pulmonary cases (164).

Once a provisional diagnosis of tuberculosis has been made—usually with the finding of acid-fast bacilli on smears of sputum or other body fluids—therapy should be initiated (164, 165). A biopsy specimen showing caseating granulomas, in the right clinical setting, should be considered diagnostic for tuberculosis.

Given the possibility that acid-fast smears may be negative in HIV-infected patients, empiric therapy should also be considered in patients with negative smears when the diagnosis of tuberculosis is strongly suspected (164). Current recommendations published by the American Thoracic Society and the CDC for initial therapy of tuberculosis in HIV-infected persons do not differ from those for non–HIV-infected patients and are for the oral use of isoniazid 300 mg per day, rifampin 600 mg per day (or 450 mg for patients weighing less than 50 kg), and pyrazinamide 20–30 mg/kg per day, with the addition of ethambutol (15–25 mg/kg per day) in cases of disseminated tuberculosis or when isoniazid resistance is suspected, for 2 months followed by same doses of isoniazid and rifampin for 4 months (197, 198). An acceptable alternative for patients who cannot take pyrazinamide is a 9-month course of isoniazid and rifampin, adding ethambutol until culture results are available. Drug susceptibility testing should be performed routinely on all isolates of *M. tuberculosis* (164, 165). In the event of drug resistance, the treatment regimen may need to be revised accordingly to ensure efficacy. Current CDC recommendations suggest that treatment should be continued for a minimum of 6 months as noted here, although treatment may need to be more prolonged for disseminated disease, when specific sites of disease are involved (prostatic, osteoarticular, meningeal, miliary disease), or in cases in which either isoniazid or rifampin cannot be included in the treatment regimen (197). Longer therapeutic courses should be given serious consideration in cases of delayed clinical response, slow radiographic improvement, or slow conversion to negative culture.

Recently, the phenomenon of reinfection has also been identified in HIV-infected patients with tuberculosis, based on molecular genetic analyses which have documented new disease from different strains of *M. tuberculosis* in patients who have already been successfully treated for prior active tuberculosis (177). Of great concern has also been the significant number of cases of multiple drug-resistant tuberculosis (MDR-TB) reported in the early 1990s in urban areas in the United States with substantial levels of poverty, drug use, and HIV co-infection. HIV-infected drug users with tuberculosis, in the absence of effective community-based treatment programs, may be unlikely to comply fully with medical treatment. It is believed that poor compliance with medications results in subsequent subtherapeutic blood levels of antituberculosis drugs and plays a key role in the development of drug-resistant patterns in MDR-TB strains. Studies of MDR-TB diagnosed in San Francisco, Miami, and New York City in recent years confirm this trend (199, 200).

Directly observed therapy (DOT) should be considered the standard for all patients with tuberculosis, especially when there is evidence or suspicion for medication nonadherence (201, 202). Directly observed preventive therapy (DOPT) for recent tuberculin skin test converters should also be considered in selected cases. Methadone (203) and other drug treatment programs as well as other sites including prisons, primary care centers, and medical outreach programs (e.g., mobile vans) are among the appropriate settings where this intervention can be made (40, 41, 43, 203–205).

The potential for developing tuberculosis with MDR-TB strains in the drug-using population has high relevance in clinical practice both for the treatment of the individual patient and for the potential for dissemination of resistant strains in the community. The realization that the emergence of multidrug-resistant strains of *Mycobacterium tuberculosis* was directly associated with suboptimal adherence to therapy spurred the implementation of DOT programs by public health authorities with great success in reducing the number of cases of tuberculosis, particularly in northeastern American urban communities (178, 200, 206). The full implementation of these programs in HIV-infected patients is a key intervention in the management of tuberculosis. The costs associated with these programs are by far offset by the therapeutic benefits and the avoidance of health care costs that would represent the cases being prevented (207). DOT can safely be implemented with twice or thrice weekly regimens with equal therapeutic success. DOPT is also associated with a higher success in treating tuberculosis infection (i.e., positive PPD test in a patient without evidence of disease). Given the large numbers of people with positive tuberculin skin tests, the full implementation of DOPT could represent an unbearable increase in health care costs. It has been proposed, though, that HIV-infected individuals with a positive tuberculin test should be considered candidates for DOPT and in some states departments of public health and other agencies and institutions are already offering DOPT to this population.

Concerning tuberculosis infection, not active tuberculosis disease, current recommendations suggest that all patients with HIV infection and positive tuberculin skin tests be offered isoniazid chemoprophylaxis (300 mg daily by mouth) for at least 12 months, regardless of age or the recency of skin test conversion (165). These recommendations are critical given the extremely high risk of reactivation and the development of active tuberculosis in HIV-infected patients co-infected with *M. tuberculosis* (162, 172, 185–187, 208). While a 12-month course is the accepted minimum effective regimen at present, there has been a debate concerning whether isoniazid should be continued indefinitely in such patients (164, 165, 209), and some clinicians have adopted the practice of continuing prophylaxis beyond 12 months as long as it is well tolerated by the patient. This may be important in certain patients who are severely immunosuppressed, even though, as noted previously, tuberculosis can also occur in patients without signs of immune dysfunction or severe CD4+ cell depletion. As in drug users without HIV infection, it is important to monitor patients closely for signs of hepatotoxicity while on isoniazid, given the high frequency of underlying liver disease and regular alcohol use among drug-using patients (210–212). For patients on methadone maintenance, experience suggests that isoniazid prophylaxis—as well as multidrug chemotherapy—can be given effectively and with excellent compliance within the setting of a methadone treatment program, by administering antituberculous medication along with patients' daily methadone doses (172, 184, 203).

Routine admission medical screening for all drug treatment program entrants should include tuberculin skin testing (Mantoux), with intradermal administration of 5 tuberculin units (TU) of PPD. This test should be repeated at least annually among skin test-negative patients. Given the possibility of the increasing spread of tuberculosis in the setting of the AIDS epidemic, it may be prudent to consider retesting every 6 months in high-risk settings, if feasible. (The latter recommendation applies to staff as well as to patients [213].) Because HIV-infected patients may be unable to react appropriately to skin test antigens because of immunosuppression, it has also been recommended that a PPD reading greater than or equal to 5 mm be considered a positive result in such patients, unlike the standard of greater than or equal to 10 mm that normally defines a positive skin test (165). Indeed, since many HIV-infected patients may have complete cutaneous anergy as a result of immune dysfunction (100)—generally but not exclusively seen in patients with advanced symptomatic HIV disease (172)—it is important to assess whether patients are, in fact, capable of demonstrating an appropriate response to skin test antigens. In this way, one can determine whether a negative PPD test is

truly negative or merely reflects an inability to demonstrate the normal delayed-type hypersensitivity response. Traditionally, delayed-type hypersensitivity skin testing has involved the separate intradermal administration of one or more antigens (e.g., mumps, *Candida, Trichophyton*) (214).

More recently, the technology has been developed for simultaneous multiple-antigen skin testing, using a multipuncture tine device (Multitest CMI, Merieux, Lyon, France). This type of device has been used successfully in a drug treatment setting (172) and is appealing for its simplicity and safety, as compared with nursing staff's having to handle up to three separate needles when administering several different intradermal injections. It may also offer greater sensitivity and specificity than the traditional method (214, 215), although one study among patients in a methadone program suggested that the multiple-antigen test (Multitest CMI) and a single intradermal *Candida* antigen test were comparable in their performance (216). Regardless of which techniques are used, it should be stressed that tuberculin skin testing in drug users with or at risk for HIV infection should be accompanied by an assessment of patients' ability to respond to skin test antigens, in order to avoid the under-detection of latent tuberculous infection in HIV-infected individuals with falsely negative PPD tests (172, 217, 218). For patients who are tuberculin negative and anergic, the initial routine evaluation should include a chest roentgenogram, and, if any signs or symptoms suggest pulmonary disease, then sputum should be obtained for acid-fast smear and culture. HIV-infected patients who are anergic and at highest risk for tuberculosis (e.g., those with household or other close contact with a known case of active tuberculosis) should be considered for isoniazid prophylaxis even in the absence of demonstrable tuberculous infection (219). The irregular performance of available skin antigens used in anergy panels has been noted and may be due to a combination of factors, namely lack of standardization, different injection techniques, and lack of agreement on what constitutes a positive skin reaction (220).

However, it has been found that, despite its variability, anergy in HIV-infected persons, particularly in tuberculosis-endemic areas, may be important not only in the interpretation of tuberculin skin tests but also as a risk factor for the development of active tuberculosis (186, 208, 221). For these reasons, CDC recommendations currently suggest that isoniazid prophylaxis be considered for HIV-infected patients who are anergic in areas where the population prevalence of latent tuberculosis infection is estimated to be greater than or equal to 10% (219). In a Bronx methadone program in which the previous rate of active tuberculosis was approximately 6 cases per 100 person-years in HIV-seropositive anergic patients (208), the rate of active disease fell to zero after the initiation of routine isoniazid prophylaxis for 12 months in this high-risk subgroup (M. Gourevitch, personal communication).

In addition to the risk of tuberculosis for HIV-infected patients, a rising incidence of active tuberculosis cases poses public health risks for non–HIV-infected persons as well. With a greater density of HIV infection and tuberculosis cases, and hence growing numbers of infectious individuals, the risk of transmission to household members, health care providers, and other close but not necessarily intimate contacts would be expected to increase. Whereas the occupational risk of HIV transmission is estimated in general to be low—approximately a 0.3% likelihood of transmission following a parenteral exposure (222)—the risk of acquiring tuberculosis would be expected to be substantially higher in certain health care settings. In addition, the possibility of MDR-TB has become a growing concern as larger numbers of patients are treated for active disease and the likelihood of poor compliance with chemotherapy increases, especially among populations of injecting drug users (181, 223–229). Indeed, a recent report from Florida described nosocomial transmission of multiple drug-resistant tuberculosis to health care workers and patients in the setting of an inpatient AIDS unit, which highlights the importance of this issue in medical care settings (230). In drug treatment programs, where tuberculosis and HIV infection are likely to be concentrated, it is critical for public health considerations and workplace safety to consider such interventions as (*a*) semiannual as opposed to annual PPD testing for patients and staff, with testing for anergy as appropriate; (*b*) inspection and evaluation of the adequacy of clinic ventilation systems; (*c*) installation of ultraviolet light fixtures to assist in air disinfection; and (*d*) supervised chemotherapy for all patients with active disease, with strict sanctions for noncompliance (165, 213, 230–232). Additionally, because of the risk of household transmission, screening and follow-up of at-risk household members should be offered to drug-using patients diagnosed with tuberculosis as well.

Sexually Transmitted Diseases

HIV infection frequently has been associated with the presence of other coexisting sexually transmitted diseases in a variety of patient populations (53, 56, 233). This may result in part simply from the common co-occurrence of such disease in persons whose behavior may tend to expose them to sexually transmitted infection. In addition, however, the presence of anal and genital ulcerations has been found to be a strong independent risk factor for HIV infection in both men and women, presumably through the facilitation of viral transmission via non-intact mucosal or dermal layers (56, 234). Injecting drug users historically have been found to be at increased risk of sexually transmitted disease, presumably related both to sexual behaviors associated with drug use and to the engagement in prostitution as a means of supporting the costs of addiction (235). In the context of the AIDS epidemic, it has been reported in multiple studies that although drug users have, in fact, adopted safer drug-using practices in some instances to reduce the risk of HIV transmission, such changes have not, in general, been noted in the realm of sexual behavior (118, 236, 237). Further, the recently described relationship between cocaine use and sexually transmitted diseases—either through a drug-specific disinhibition of sexual behavior or the more formal exchange of sex for drugs or money—underscores the importance of addressing sexually transmitted diseases in the care of drug users with or at risk for HIV infection (50–55, 57, 238).

Initial assessment of drug-using patients with known or suspected HIV infection should include a thorough history regarding other sexually transmitted diseases. Certain of these other infections (e.g., herpes simplex virus) may reactivate and become more severe or more difficult to treat in immunosuppressed individuals than in patients with normal immune systems. Indeed, chronic mucocutaneous herpes simplex virus infection is an AIDS-defining illness when it is severe, non-healing, and lasts for longer than 1 month (81, 82). Other common sexually transmitted infections may be altered in their presentation or expression in the setting of HIV infection; syphilis is the most important example in this regard (239–244). Syphilis has been reported to be both accelerated and aberrant in its course, and at times refractory to standard therapy, in certain patients with HIV infection; this is discussed in more detail later (239–244). In addition, human papillomavirus (HPV) infection, which may cause oral, anogenital, and common skin warts—and, less commonly, genital tract malignancies—in non–HIV-infected persons, has been found to occur with increased frequency in HIV-infected patients (245–249). In such patients, HPV may cause extensive or recurrent genital or oral warts that may be difficult to treat. Further, HPV infection has been strongly linked with an increased risk of cervical cytologic abnormalities in HIV-infected women, including dysplasia and frank carcinoma (245–248); the degree of malignant cytologic change appears to increase as women become more immunosuppressed in the course of their HIV infection (245–248, 250). A recent report also described an increased risk of anal cancer in immunosuppressed HIV-infected homosexual men with coexistent HPV infection, further indicating the importance of the latter virus as a potential cause of malignancies in HIV-infected patients (251).

In addition to eliciting a history of sexually transmitted diseases from HIV-infected drug users, baseline assessment should also incorporate screening and assessment for the most commonly found co-infections or their sequelae. Specifically, this assessment should include (a) physical examination for the presence of genital ulcers, warts, or other lesions; (b) routine serologic tests for syphilis including both nontreponemal tests (e.g., Venereal Disease Research Laboratory [VDRL]; serologic test for syphilis [STS]; rapid plasma reagin [RPR]) and treponemal tests (e.g., fluorescent treponemal antibody absorption [FTA-ABS]; microhemagglutinating antibody to *Treponema pallidum* [MHA-TP]); (c) cervical Papanicolaou smear for female patients, with consideration of a rectal cytologic smear for homosexual or bisexual men; and (d) cultures or assays for gonorrhea, *Chlamy-*

dia, and, as appropriate, herpes simplex virus. Depending upon the findings on initial evaluation, further diagnostic tests may be appropriate, e.g., *Haemophilus ducreyi* cultures or empiric therapy for chancroid in patients with painful, exudative genital ulcers, or referral for colposcopy for HIV-infected women with abnormal cervical cytology.

Regarding the management of sexually transmitted diseases in the setting of HIV infection, it must be noted, as suggested earlier, that both the natural history and response to treatment of certain of these infections may differ in HIV-infected patients from the accepted standards in other patient populations. Therefore, clinicians may need both to have a high index of suspicion of certain sexually transmitted diseases in HIV-infected patients and to be prepared to treat such diseases more aggressively and/or for longer periods of time. The instance of greatest relevance in this regard is that of syphilis, in which there is both evidence that the disease's manifestations may be altered by coexistent HIV infection and that the response to standard therapy in HIV-infected patients may be suboptimal (239–244, 252). However, substantial uncertainty still exists regarding the extent to which HIV does, in fact, modify the expression of syphilis, beyond what has been described in a series of case reports, and also concerning the appropriate standard for diagnosis and treatment of HIV-infected patients with syphilis. Indeed, one study in a methadone program found that, when followed prospectively, HIV-infected drug users were not at significantly increased risk of showing unusual manifestations of syphilis when compared to their HIV-seropositive counterparts, even though in this same population syphilis was a risk factor for HIV infection (253, 254). Case reports have suggested that certain HIV-infected patients with early syphilis may not be cured by standard single-dose therapy with benzathine penicillin, and that such patients may be at risk for symptomatic or asymptomatic neurosyphilis even after standard therapy (239–244). Therefore, certain authorities have recommended that all HIV-infected patients with syphilis undergo lumbar puncture and cerebrospinal fluid (CSF) examination to rule out neurosyphilis (243); some clinicians have elected to treat all HIV-infected patients with syphilis with high-dose regimens adequate for neurosyphilis, regardless of the observed clinical stage at presentation (242–244). However, it has also been noted that the CSF VDRL may be negative in a substantial percentage of HIV-infected patients with early syphilis involving the central nervous system (CNS), and that nonspecific CSF abnormalities are common in HIV-infected patients (241–243). Consequently, lumbar puncture may be nondiagnostic in HIV-infected patients with syphilis. Therefore, one is often confronted with the prospect of either treating all HIV-infected patients with syphilis in whom CNS involvement cannot be excluded with at least 10 days of high-dose parenteral penicillin, or using less aggressive outpatient regimens that may be inadequate for CNS infection. If outpatient treatment is pursued, clinicians must ensure close follow-up and have a low threshold for inpatient referral for definitive treatment if serologic titers fail to decline appropriately or in the presence of neurologic signs or symptoms. A recent study showed that HIV-positive patients with syphilis are less likely to experience serologic improvement after appropriate therapy has been instituted (255). Close follow-up is therefore recommended also for all HIV-infected patients who have completed a course of standard therapy for syphilis.

Diagnosis and treatment of syphilis in HIV-infected patients may be further complicated by the possibility of an abnormal serologic response to syphilis in such patients, an effect most likely related either to HIV-induced polyclonal B cell activation or to the failure of the normal antibody response to infection; these factors may result either in abnormally high titers, in falsely negative titers, or in other unusual serologic patterns (242, 243, 256–258). Notwithstanding these reported abnormalities, it is believed that most HIV-infected patients with syphilis are indeed able to demonstrate appropriate antibody responses (242, 243, 257, 258). It should be noted, however, that the serologic response to syphilis in HIV-infected populations of drug users has not been studied adequately. Given the well-documented phenomenon of false-positive nontreponemal serologic tests for syphilis in injecting drug users (122, 235), it is particularly important to define the patterns of syphilis serology in this population in the setting of HIV infection.

Current CDC recommendations for the treatment of syphilis in HIV-infected patients attempt to highlight some of these uncertainties, while stressing the importance of close follow-up and the potential need for aggressive treatment of syphilis in patients with both infections (259, 260). These guidelines include the following points, all relevant for clinicians caring for drug users with HIV infection: (a) when clinical findings suggest syphilis but serologic tests are negative, dark-field microscopy or direct fluorescent antibody tests for *T. pallidum* (DFA-TP) on lesion exudate or biopsy tissue should be performed; (b) laboratories performing syphilis serologic tests should titrate nontreponemal tests to a final endpoint, rather than reporting results as greater than an arbitrary cutoff point (e.g., greater than 1:512), to enable detection of unusual serologic responses to syphilis and to monitor the response to therapy; (c) quantitative nontreponemal tests should be repeated at 1, 2, and 3 months following therapy and at 3-month intervals thereafter, until a satisfactory serologic response to treatment occurs. If a two-dilution decrease in titer is not seen in 3 months for primary syphilis or in 6 months for secondary syphilis, or if an increase in titer of two dilutions or greater occurs, then patients should undergo CSF examination; (d) CSF examination should be performed in HIV-infected patients with latent syphilis of greater than 1 year's or of unknown duration; if this is not possible, patients should be treated with a regimen adequate for presumed neurosyphilis, e.g., aqueous crystalline penicillin G, 2–4 million units intravenously every 4 hours (a total of 12–24 million units daily) for at least 10 days; or aqueous procaine penicillin G, 2.4 million units intramuscularly daily plus probenecid, 500 mg orally four times daily, for 10 days; and (e) neurosyphilis should be considered in the differential diagnosis of all patients with HIV infection and neurologic disease (259, 260).

The CDC guidelines also note, however, that there is disagreement regarding how aggressive clinicians must be in treating HIV-infected patients with syphilis, and that indeed at present no change in standard therapy is officially recommended for HIV patients co-infected with early syphilis. However, one more recent review concluded that, based on existing data, the minimum accepted treatment for early syphilis in HIV-infected patients should be three consecutive weekly injections of benzathine penicillin, 2.4 million units each (243), and indeed this approach has been adopted increasingly in clinical practice. There is also much current interest in the possibility of oral or parenteral outpatient regimens effective against neurosyphilis, which clearly would help resolve the logistic problems posed by the prospect of undertaking lumbar puncture, CSF examination, and prolonged inpatient management for a potentially large population of injecting drug users co-infected with HIV and syphilis. Such regimens, which have not yet been recommended formally by CDC, include high-dose amoxicillin (2 g with probenecid 500 mg orally, three times daily for 14 days), doxycycline (200 mg orally, two times daily for 21 days), and ceftriaxone (1 g intramuscularly daily for 14 days) (242–244).

A recent study showed that HIV-infected patients may be more likely to present during the secondary stage of syphilis, and they are more likely to have persistent chancres at this stage than non–HIV-infected individuals (261).This is an important observation, since, as mentioned already, sexual transmission is enhanced by ulcerative genital lesions and therefore appropriate prevention strategies (i.e., use of condoms) should be encouraged with even more emphasis.

Another important sexually transmitted agent that may coexist with the HIV is HPV, which may cause oral and genital warts and has been associated with cervical dysplasia and neoplasia, cancer of the vulva, vagina, and penis, and anal cancer in homosexual and bisexual men (245–249, 251). Health maintenance for HIV-infected women should include at least annual and perhaps semiannual Papanicolaou (Pap) smears, with referral for colposcopy and/or further diagnostic evaluation as appropriate based on Pap smear results. (Viral culture and molecular genetic techniques to detect HPV are not available in clinical settings, and, at present, indirect measures of the virus' activity—i.e., cervical cytologic smears and colposcopic biopsy—comprise the standard for screening and diagnosis.) High-risk men should also be offered annual rectal Pap smears for cytologic evaluation (262). The observation that HPV-associated neoplastic changes are often most severe in patients with advanced HIV-related disease suggests that clinicians' level of suspicion for cervical malignancies in women and anal cancer in homosexual or bisexual men should be higher for patients in the later stages of HIV

infection (245, 249, 250). However, HPV and the associated cervical dysplasia and neoplasia have also been found in HIV-infected women who are not severely immunosuppressed (245, 246, 249, 263).

It has also been suggested that HIV-infected women may be at increased risk of severe or refractory pelvic inflammatory disease (264), yet the evidence to support this suggestion has remained largely anecdotal; prospective studies of the gynecologic manifestations of HIV infection are urgently needed to help address this and related issues among women with HIV infection. Although population-based studies have not clearly identified an increased risk of severe pelvic inflammatory disease associated with HIV infection, this diagnosis certainly should be considered in drug-using women presenting with abdominal pain syndromes, especially in cases in which patients are known to be at high risk for sexually transmitted diseases.

Neurologic Disease

HIV infection has been shown to have a wide range of effects on the central and peripheral nervous systems, some of which are the consequence of specific opportunistic infections and malignancies and others apparently the result of HIV infection itself or the host response that it evokes (265, 266). Among drug users with HIV, an important challenge for clinicians is the distinction between HIV-associated neurologic disease and that which results from acute or chronic substance abuse and its effects on the nervous system. This distinction is particularly important since many of the neurologic syndromes seen in HIV-infected patients may be treatable, but successful treatment depends on an accurate identification and differentiation of the underlying and immediate problems. It has not been uncommon, for example, for clinicians in drug treatment settings who are unfamiliar with HIV disease to assume that patients' cognitive or behavioral disturbances reflect a resumption of alcohol or drug use behavior, when in fact these findings may indicate a CNS opportunistic infection or HIV-associated dementia or encephalopathy. Similarly, clinicians in inpatient AIDS treatment units may respond to a patient who develops lethargy, dysarthria, and pinpoint pupils by performing an emergent computed tomographic (CT) brain scan and lumbar puncture, when, in fact, a simple urine toxicology screen would have detected evidence of illicit intramural opiate use. A complete discussion of the myriad effects of HIV infection and its sequelae on the nervous system is beyond the scope of this chapter, and the reader is referred to several excellent sources on this subject (265, 267, 268). In the present context it may be useful, however, to focus on certain neurologic aspects of HIV disease of particular relevance to drug-using populations, especially with respect to differential diagnosis.

The most important CNS manifestation of HIV infection is an entity that has been denoted as the AIDS dementia complex (ADC), also described as subacute encephalitis or AIDS encephalopathy (265, 267–269). This clinical syndrome is believed to result either from the direct effects of HIV and/or from additional factors related to the local response of the CNS to HIV infection (266, 268). Clinical features of this syndrome range from mild cognitive deficits, memory loss, and subtle findings on neurologic examination to full-blown dementia with mutism, incontinence, and inanition (267–271). Associated behavioral and affective changes may also vary greatly and can include apathy and social withdrawal, abulia, emotional lability, pronounced personality changes, and organic psychosis (267–269). An important distinguishing feature of ADC, which differentiates it from acute drug use effects, is the relative preservation of a normal level of consciousness and alertness even until the later stages of severe cognitive dysfunction (268, 269). Specific neurologic findings that may be associated with ADC include psychomotor retardation, hypertonia, pyramidal tract signs, frontal release signs, tremor, ataxia, apraxia, and myoclonus, in varying degrees of severity (267–269). CT scans of the brain in patients with ADC often demonstrate widespread cortical atrophy with ventricular dilation and enlarged sulci, although the degree of clinical dysfunction may not always correlate closely with radiographic findings (267–269). Cranial magnetic resonance imaging (MRI) in patients with ADC often shows diffuse white matter hyperintensity, especially in the frontal regions (268); it has been suggested that MRI is superior to CT in the evaluation and detection of brain lesions in patients with HIV infection (272).

Lumbar puncture and CSF examination generally are nonspecific in patients with ADC; results may show mononuclear pleocytosis and/or a slightly elevated protein concentration (268, 269). Recent studies suggest that the ADC may respond clinically to antiretroviral therapy (e.g., zidovudine), which may also be of benefit in preventing its emergence (270, 271, 273).

The ADC is often a diagnosis of exclusion, being made once other possible HIV-related CNS diseases are ruled out. The most common of these, all of which qualify as AIDS-defining illnesses, are cryptococcal meningitis, cerebral toxoplasmosis, CNS lymphoma, and progressive multifocal leukoencephalopathy (80, 82, 83, 267). In addition, tuberculous meningitis and neurosyphilis are both seen in HIV-infected patients and may be more likely to occur in drug users than in certain other populations with AIDS, given the increased likelihood of coexisting tuberculosis and syphilis among HIV-infected drug users, as noted earlier. These varied entities may present with mental status changes, headache, focal neurologic deficits, seizures, fever, behavioral or personality changes, or other evidence of CNS involvement. Compared with these opportunistic infections and malignancies of the CNS, the ADC tends to be more indolent in onset and without localizing (267–269); however, the time course and presentation of ADC may be variable, and certain of these other entities also may present with relatively gradual onset and nonspecific signs such as weakness, apathy, or a decreased level of consciousness. In addition to the ADC and the specific AIDS-related infections and malignancies, an increased incidence of stroke and cerebrovascular disease in HIV-infected patients has also been described recently; this phenomenon, if it is indeed substantiated, is of uncertain etiology, but it has been hypothesized that it may result from a direct effect of HIV on vascular tissue or from immune-mediated vasculitis with antigen-antibody deposition on vascular endothelium (274).

The basic diagnostic evaluation of HIV-infected patients with CNS disease should incorporate a full neurologic examination, including a mental status examination, a CT scan of the brain, lumbar puncture, and CSF examination and culture. These diagnostic tests will help to identify the AIDS-related meningitides and will provide at least presumptive diagnoses of most of the mass or focal brain lesions. For certain of the focal brain lesions, involving specific opportunistic infections and malignancies, biopsy of the brain is the only means for definitive diagnosis. However, a common practice is often to initiate empiric therapy for the suspected clinical entity, e.g., cerebral toxoplasmosis, and to reserve brain biopsy for cases that are either atypical or else do not respond to a brief trial of empiric therapy (267).

For drug users with HIV infection, the same diagnostic guidelines should be followed as outlined already, although here the possibility of drug use-related CNS effects becomes relevant. Drug intoxication commonly may present with apathy, lethargy, and diminished level of consciousness, as can certain of the CNS opportunistic infections, which may not at first be accompanied by localizing signs. Drug or alcohol withdrawal may also be accompanied by tremulousness, seizures, hallucinosis, other mental status changes, mood swings, or nonspecific findings including inability to concentrate, dysphoria, anhedonia, insomnia, and other vegetative signs (218). Clearly, some or all of these findings may also be seen in ADC or in certain of the HIV-related CNS syndromes. In addition, drug users historically have been known to be at risk for certain CNS infections related to drug injection, e.g., pyogenic or fungal brain abscess, meningitis, spinal or epidural abscess, and endophthalmitis (122, 275, 276). Several reports have described an increased incidence of stroke associated with the use of cocaine, including ischemic, thrombotic, and, especially, hemorrhagic stroke (277–279).

Because some of the CNS manifestations of drug use and its sequelae may mimic or overlap those related to HIV infection, it is critical for successful diagnosis and treatment to consider all these possibilities in the assessment of HIV-infected drug users with CNS disease. In this regard, accurate and complete history-taking is essential, for which it is often helpful to seek corroboration from patients' families or close contacts. This will help to define the temporal course and pattern of the development of symptoms—often an important feature in distinguishing ADC from opportunistic infections or drug-related effects—and will also help in the formulation of an accurate history regarding recent use of drugs and alcohol. The timely use of urine toxicology testing is also critical to the assessment of HIV-infected patients presenting with CNS disease in whom substance abuse is suspected. When urine toxicology testing is not performed in such situations, as is often the case, the opportunity may be lost to make a specific diagnosis of certain drug-related conditions that may be treatable.

In addition to these simple diagnostic tools, which can help in the detection of substance abuse problems, it must also be stressed that the use of CT scan of the brain, lumbar puncture, and CSF examination should be equally routine in the assessment of known substance users presenting with HIV-related CNS disease. The not uncommon failure to diagnose substance abuse problems in AIDS patients should not be paralleled by a failure to diagnose HIV-related CNS infections and malignancies in substance users with HIV infection. In addition, the possibility of non–HIV-related medical complications of drug injection or drug use on the CNS—e.g., pyogenic or fungal brain abscess, cocaine-induced cerebrovascular disease—must also be considered in drug users with HIV infection.

Aside from CNS disease, patients with HIV infection have also been found to have peripheral nervous system (PNS) dysfunction related to HIV itself, in addition to the PNS effects of specific AIDS-related infectious syndromes (e.g., herpes zoster radiculitis). The most well-described entities affecting the PNS in such patients are chronic inflammatory demyelinating polyneuropathy, distal symmetric polyneuropathy, mononeuropathy multiplex, and progressive polyradiculopathy (265, 267, 280). The most common of these is the distal symmetric polyneuropathy, which is a predominantly sensory neuropathy usually affecting the distal lower extremities, occurring most often among patients in the later stages of HIV-related disease. This syndrome is characterized by marked paresthesia or dysesthesia, areflexia, and mild, if any, muscle weakness; in some patients this syndrome may be a source of great discomfort. Diagnosis may be made via neurologic examination, nerve conduction studies, electromyography, and, in some cases, nerve biopsy.

Treatment is supportive, with analgesics and anti-inflammatory agents; tricyclic antidepressants (e.g., amitriptyline) and clonazepam have also been used with variable success. While several preliminary reports suggested that zidovudine might also be helpful in the treatment of certain HIV-related peripheral neuropathies (281, 282), this has not been borne out in clinical practice.

Of importance with regard to drug-using patients is that HIV-related peripheral neuropathies may mimic or coexist with the known complications of drug and alcohol use involving the peripheral nervous system, e.g., distal symmetric polyneuropathy associated with chronic alcohol use or nutritional deficiencies, compression neuropathy resulting from limb compression during periods of drug-induced somnolence, or traumatic neuropathy involving direct injury to peripheral nerves from inaccurate or errant drug injection attempts (283). Further, it should be noted that certain of the standard and newer therapies for HIV infection and its sequelae—e.g., isoniazid, didanosine (ddI), zalcitabine (ddC), stavudine (d4T), and, to a much lesser extent, lamivudine (3TC)—may cause symptomatic and severe peripheral neuropathy (284–286). Indeed, in the case of ddI, the second antiretroviral dideoxynucleoside analogue to be developed for clinical use after zidovudine, the development of peripheral neuropathy is one of the more serious side effects and may even be treatment-limiting at higher dose levels (285, 286). It is not known whether the combination of HIV, certain of these prescribed medications, and drug or alcohol use may have an augmented toxic effect on the PNS, but the possibility of multiple and combined etiologies for PNS disease should be considered by clinicians caring for HIV-infected drug users.

The newer classes of antiretroviral medications, namely the non-nucleoside reverse transcriptase inhibitors and the protease inhibitors, have not been associated with PNS dysfunction to date. A recent study of the temporal trends in the incidence of HIV-related neurologic diseases, part of a larger prospective cohort study of homosexual men, concluded that, over the course of follow-up, neurological complications have remained frequent, and that peripheral neuropathy showed an increasing incidence (273). This may have particular relevance to drug users as well: this population, as noted, may be at higher baseline risk for PNS disease, which may be compounded by the toxic effects of antiretroviral and other medications, and which may also pose management problems involving the use of narcotic analgesics for the often severe pain syndromes seen in peripheral nerve disease.

Other Human T Lymphotrophic Retroviruses

HIV-1, previously known as human T lymphotrophic retrovirus type III (HTLV-III), is one of three HTLVs identified since the late 1970s. Human T lymphotrophic retrovirus type I (HTLV-I) was the first virus in this group to be discovered and was identified as the causal agent in adult T cell leukemia/lymphoma, first described in Japan in 1977 (287–289). HTLV-I infection has since been associated with chronic degenerative neurologic diseases designated as tropical spastic paraparesis and HTLV-I-associated myelopathy (290, 291). It has also been found to have a restricted geographic distribution, with endemic regions in Japan, the Caribbean basin, Africa, South America, and parts of the southeastern and southwestern United States (289, 292, 293). Human T lymphotrophic retrovirus type II (HTLV-II), though originally isolated from a patient with hairy cell leukemia, has not consistently been identified as an etiologic agent for specific disease, nor has it been found to have a particular geographic distribution (293).

The routes of transmission of HTLV-I are believed to be similar to those of HIV, though perhaps less efficient, involving sexual contact, parenteral exposure to blood through transfusion or use of contaminated injection equipment, and mother-to-infant transmission either perinatally or through breast-feeding (293). Serologic tests now exist to identify antibodies to HTLV-I and HTLV-II, both of which are readily distinguished from serum antibodies to HIV-I. However, current serologic tests do not distinguish between HTLV-I and HTLV-II, which has complicated efforts to determine the pathogenicity, if any, of HTLV-II (293, 294). Because of the lack of specificity of current assays, seropositivity to HTLV-I is often referred to as seropositivity to HTLV-I and HTLV-II. It is believed that there is a long latency period from infection to disease in HTLV-I–infected persons (293), although a recent report described rapid development of myelopathy following transfusion-acquired HTLV-I infection in a patient who had undergone cardiac transplantation (295).

Although HTLV-I and HTLV-II are not believed to be endemic infections in most of the United States, it is noteworthy that the presence of these HTLVs in the United States has been strongly associated with injection drug use; among drug users, these viruses have been found mostly among blacks (21, 292, 296–298). Seroprevalence studies have indicated that HTLV-I and/or HTLV-II were present in up to one third or more of drug users sampled in the New York metropolitan area in the mid 1980s, and other reports have documented HTLV-I and HTLV-II infection among drug users in areas in the southeastern and western United States as well (21, 292, 296, 297). In fact, in some United States samples, levels of HTLV-I infection exceeded those of HIV infection among populations of drug users in certain geographic areas (299, 300).

These data suggest that clinical disease related to HTLV-I infection may begin to be expressed in certain populations of drug users or their sexual contacts. However, this generally has not been the finding, even in settings where such groups have been prospectively monitored. This may reflect, in part, the long latency period or indolent course of HTLV-I infection; it is also not known whether other cofactors may be involved in the expression of HTLV-I-related disease; it is also possible that at least some of the populations studied may have more predominant HTLV-II than HTLV-I infection. Nevertheless, a cluster of adult T cell leukemia/lymphoma (ATL) cases associated with HTLV-I in New York City has been described, and a report documented a case of ATL in a California patient co-infected with HIV and HTLV-I (301, 302). Further, prospective studies among drug users in New Jersey and Florida have suggested that HTLV-I co-infection may accelerate the rate of progression to AIDS in HIV-infected patients (303, 304). These considerations should prompt concern and raise diagnostic suspicion of HTLV-I infection among HIV-infected drug users with degenerative neurologic disease, T cell leukemias, or, perhaps, with rapid HIV disease progression; serologic testing for antibody to HTLV-I and HTLV-II will help to corroborate the diagnosis in such cases.

Hepatitis B Virus and Hepatitis Delta Virus

Injecting drug users historically have been known to be at high risk for hepatitis B virus (HBV) infection, since long before the AIDS epidemic (212, 235, 305–307). Seroprevalence studies have demonstrated that more than 50% of chronic drug users in most samples show evidence of prior hepatitis B exposure (305–307); most such patients are seropositive for antibody to hepatitis B surface antigen and/or antibody to hepatitis B core antigen, with a small percentage (usually less than 10%) exhibiting chronic hepatitis B surface antigenemia. HBV infection is believed generally to be an early event in the injection career of injecting drug users, usually occurring within the first 1 or 2 years after the initiation of drug injection (307–309). Given these considerations, it is probable that in most populations of chronic injecting drug users into which HIV is introduced, HBV infection is likely to have been a prior event, with serologic evidence of immunity to HBV in most cases.

New developments in the field of therapeutics have shown combined benefits in the treatment of both HIV infection and hepatitis B: a preliminary trial reported that the use of one of the new antiretrovirals, lamivudine (3TC), is associated with a significant reduction in the total viral load of HBV when treating chronic hepatitis B (310). Additionally, interferon alpha, an agent used in the treatment of chronic hepatitis B, was found to be an acceptable alternative in the treatment of zidovudine-refractory, HIV-related thrombocytopenia (311). The long-term implication of both studies is still unknown.

There has not been consistent evidence that the natural history and clinical course of HBV infection in drug users are altered by concomitant HIV infection, due perhaps in part to the abovementioned factors by which de novo HBV infection is unlikely to occur in HIV-infected drug users, at least in the populations studied to date. There is also little evidence that quiescent HBV infection is likely to reactivate in patients with HIV-induced immunosuppression. In fact, several studies have indicated that the extent of histologic injury from HBV may be milder in HIV-infected patients with chronic HBV-associated hepatitis than in those patients with hepatitis from HBV who do not have coexisting HIV infection (312, 313). However, it has also been documented that levels of hepatitis B surface antigenemia may be higher and the temporal duration of antigenemia and viral replication increased in HBV-infected patients with concomitant HIV infection, when compared with patients not infected with HIV (314–316). In addition, a case report has described a case of fulminant, fatal hepatitis B infection in an injecting drug user co-infected with HIV and suggested that HIV may have contributed to the patient's rapidly fatal course (317). These data would support the use of hepatitis B vaccine for susceptible injecting drug users and medical personnel providing care to such patients, both as a clinical intervention and to help minimize occupational acquisition of HBV from patients who may show greater or more prolonged infectivity with HBV due to a greater burden of circulating virus.

Several studies have examined the association between hepatitis delta virus (HDV) infection and HIV in injecting drug users, and have found that such patients exhibit delayed clearance of HDV, increased HDV replication, and accelerated loss of HDV antibody (318–320). Although existing data do not clearly suggest an increased severity of HDV infection in patients co-infected with HIV (321), the findings of increased and persistent HDV antigenemia in HIV-infected patients adds further support to the promotion of HBV vaccine among susceptible patients and medical staff (318), since immunity to HBV in effect precludes infection with HDV (322).

Hepatitis C Virus

Only recently identified as an etiologic agent of what was formerly known as non-A, non-B hepatitis, hepatitis C virus is transmitted by the parenteral route in an overwhelming majority of cases (> 90%) (323, 324). Its epidemiology has not been fully elucidated; however, low level sexual transmission, probably facilitated by HIV co-infection, has been identified (although its infectivity by this route is much lower than that for hepatitis B infection), and cases of perinatal and household transmission have also been reported (325–328). Given the new, more comprehensive and effective methods that blood banks have implemented to screen blood donations, the epidemiological importance of injection drug use as a vehicle of hepatitis C transmission is enhanced. High seroprevalence rates for hepatitis C infection among illicit drug users have been consistently reported, much higher than in all other HIV risk groups except hemophiliacs in the pre blood-screening era (329, 330). A recent retrospective study found a seroprevalence rate of 76.9% and 64.7% for those who had injected for one year of less (309).

An estimated 60% of patients with hepatitis C infection develop chronic hepatitis and approximately 20% of them develop cirrhosis within 2 years of infection (324). At present, liver failure secondary to hepatitis C infection is one of the leading indications for liver transplant; however, active substance abuse and HIV infection are absolute contraindications for liver transplant. Extrahepatic manifestations associated with chronic hepatitis C infection include essential mixed cryoglobulinemia, membranoproliferative glomerulonephritis, and porphyria cutanea tarda (211, 324).

Despite encouraging early reports regarding the use of alpha-interferon in the treatment of hepatitis C infection, later studies reported a disappointing low cure rate (around 10%) and a high relapse rate (50%) among those who respond after treatment was stopped.

Hepatitis B and C co-infection is common in drug-using patients with HIV infection, particularly in those who continue to practice unsafe injection techniques. The common occurrence of underlying hepatic disease in injection drug users, in whom high incidence of infection, toxic, and alcoholic hepatitis has been reported, may complicate the course of hepatitis C. Some of the medications commonly used in the HIV infection with high potential for hepatotoxicity include zidovudine, didanosine, TMP-SMX, pentamidine, dapsone, rifampin, and isoniazid. Thus, drug users are at high risk for liver disease from a variety of causes which may converge to produce potentially severe liver damage or may complicate HIV medical management with hepatotoxic medications.

Hepatitis C infection is a complex disease with potential for multiorgan involvement and also associated risk for developing hepatocellular carcinoma; its morbidity and overall prognosis in the HIV-infected population have not been fully determined in appropriate longitudinal studies, although an increase in morbidity and possibly mortality has been suggested (210, 330).

Outreach, education, and other interventions including needle exchange and instruction in safe injection technique could significantly decrease morbidity and mortality from hepatitis C in drug users, as already demonstrated for both hepatitis B and C in studies for needle exchange programs (308, 331–334).

Malignancies

As noted, heterosexual drug users with HIV infection have been found to be at low risk for Kaposi's sarcoma as compared with homosexual men (23, 335). However, case reports and hospital-based series from the United States and Europe have documented the occurrence of malignant lymphomas among HIV-infected drug users (336–338). Certain of these lymphomas are AIDS-defining (80–83). Further, a recent review of malignant neoplasms reported among HIV-infected injecting drug users in Italy described the occurrence of a variety of non–AIDS-defining solid tumors, primarily involving the lung, testis, brain, skin, rectum, and oropharynx (339). Another study among drug users in a Bronx methadone program found an increased risk of lung and other cancers in HIV-infected versus HIV-seronegative cohorts (340). Although such malignancies remain rare, and even though it is not possible from this report to confirm an etiologic relationship with HIV infection, these data suggest that clinicians who care for HIV-infected drug users should be alert to the possibility of neoplasms not formally recognized as AIDS-related in existing HIV classification systems.

Reported cases of lymphoma among HIV-infected drug users have included Hodgkin's and non-Hodgkin's types, with a wide variety of phenotypes, showing a high incidence of extranodal involvement and generally poor prognosis. Compared with AIDS-related opportunistic infections, such malignancies are infrequent, and it is not clear that they are more common among drug users than among other HIV-infected groups. However, the possibility of such diagnoses highlights the importance of definitive diagnosis of suspect lesions involving the CNS, in order to avoid mistaken presumptive diagnosis of entities such as cerebral toxoplasmosis. Similarly, although persistent generalized lymphadenopathy is a frequent finding in HIV infection (81)—usually consisting of soft, movable, nontender lymph nodes less

than 2 cm in diameter—and although palpable lymphadenopathy due to skin abscesses and local soft tissue infection has long been known to be common among injecting drug users (235), the presence of large, firm, or rapidly growing lymph nodes should prompt consideration of a diagnosis of lymphoma with appropriate diagnostic interventions.

In addition, as already mentioned, the common occurrence of HPV co-infection in HIV-infected drug-using women requires clinical vigilance for cervical dysplasia and carcinoma in such patients, and similarly, in male homosexual or bisexual drug users the possibility of HPV-induced anal carcinoma should also be considered (245–248, 250, 262, 339, 341). Finally, as discussed previously, the documented presence of HTLV-I/II infection in certain populations of drug users (21, 292–294, 296, 299, 300) indicates that adult T cell leukemia/lymphoma may become an increasingly recognized problem in such patients, although this entity had not yet been noted with any regularity among drug users by the middle of the second decade of the AIDS epidemic in 1996.

Effects of Drug Use versus Effects of HIV

As is apparent from the preceding review, it is important for clinicians who care for HIV-infected drug users to attempt to distinguish in such patients between the manifestations of HIV infection and the effects of drug use and its acute and chronic sequelae. As noted, certain infectious diseases commonly seen among injecting drug users may be more frequent or severe in the setting of HIV infection. In addition, certain infectious complications of injection drug use may be mistaken for manifestations of HIV infection, and vice versa. The possibility of coexisting morbidity both from HIV disease and the medical complications of drug use must also be considered in many instances (Table 59.3). These factors serve to emphasize the importance of obtaining accurate and relevant information concerning the nature and extent of drug use practices in substance users with HIV infection.

Table 59.3 Medical Complications of Substance Abuse That Affect the Differential Diagnosis in Injection Drug Users with HIV Infection

Symptoms	Possible Diagnoses	
	HIV-related	Substance abuse–related
Constitutional Anorexia Weight loss Fever Night sweats Diarrhea	HIV infection, *M. Avium* complex, cytomegalovirus, tuberculosis	Cocaine use, injection-related bacterial infections, heroin withdrawal
Pulmonary Chest pain Cough Dyspnea	Bacterial pneumonia, *P. carinii* pneumonia, tuberculosis	Cocaine (crack) use, tobacco use, aspiration pneumonia
Neurologic Altered mental status Psychosis Seizures Focal deficits Peripheral neuropathy alcoholic polyneuropathy	HIV infection, toxoplasmosis, cryptococcosis, cytomegalovirus infection, progressive multifocal leuko-encephalopathy, HTLV-1, medication toxicity	Intoxication with and withdrawal from heroin, cocaine, alcohol, or benzodiazepines; drug-related chronic encephalopathy; pyogenic central nervous system infection, trauma
Dermatologic Pruritus Rash Purpura	HIV-related dermatitis, HIV-related thrombocytopenia, medication allergy	Drug-related pruritus, chronic hepatitis, cellulitis, alcohol or heroin-induced thrombocytopenia, lymphedema
Miscellaneous Lymphadenopathy Uremia	HIV-related lymphadenopathy, HIV-related nephropathy	Localized infection, heroin nephropathy

Adapted from O'Connor P, Selwyn PA, Schottenfeld RS. Medical management of injection drug users with HIV infection. N Engl J Med 1994;33:450–459.

Aside from infectious complications and other related syndromes, there are a number of constitutional symptoms often seen in HIV-infected patients that may overlap with symptoms due to acute or chronic drug use. These include fever, weight loss, fatigue, malaise, and diarrhea (86) and are believed to be a consequence of HIV infection itself, apart from the symptomatology that may accompany specific infectious syndromes. Indeed, the definition of HIV-related wasting syndrome, which qualifies as an AIDS-equivalent diagnosis in the CDC's 1993 revised AIDS case definition (83) includes several of these symptoms as necessary criteria for this diagnosis. It is important, therefore, to attempt to differentiate between the overlapping symptomatology of HIV infection per se and that of chronic drug use or withdrawal. Among active injecting drug users, fever, fatigue, malaise, and diarrhea are not uncommon (the latter particularly among opiate addicts, who alternately experience constipation and diarrhea as they fluctuate between narcotic intoxication and withdrawal) (235, 342). Weight loss is also a common finding among street addicts, especially among cocaine users, in whom anorexia and a hypermetabolic state are related directly to the pharmacologic effects of the drug (235, 342).

Substance dependent patients may often be malnourished due to disorganized lifestyle and lack of self-care, making it difficult to differentiate the effects specifically related to poor nutrition, drug use, or HIV-infection and its sequelae.

Further, the recent escalation in smoked freebase cocaine or crack use has been associated with pulmonary edema, barotrauma, bronchospasm, and other pulmonary manifestations (343–345), and dyspnea on exertion or at rest is often reported by such patients. Since dyspnea without a productive cough or other obvious signs of pneumonia is also one of the most common symptoms to herald the onset of PCP in HIV-infected patients (109), it is important for clinicians to be aware of the different potential causes of such pulmonary symptoms in injecting drug users. In addition to crack use, these also include heavy cigarette smoking, a widespread practice among illicit drug users (346), which may produce similar symptoms. Patients and clinicians may often mistakenly attribute cough or dyspnea simply to excessive smoking—especially in the absence of fever or other signs of pneumonia—when, in fact, these symptoms may indicate the gradual onset of PCP. Interestingly, anecdotal clinical experience suggests that among HIV-infected drug users who smoke tobacco, abrupt smoking cessation due to perceived worsening shortness of breath can be an indirect indicator of the development of PCP (P. Selwyn, unpublished data).

Finally, the presence of generalized lymphadenopathy, often found in HIV-infected patients (81), may at times be confused with the finding of multiple palpable lymph nodes due to lymphatic drainage from sites of drug injection, localized soft tissue infection, oral pathology, or other conditions commonly seen in injecting drug users (235). For this reason, it has been suggested that, among drug users, the sites most specific for HIV-related lymphadenopathy are the posterior cervical chains, which, in the absence of scalp lesions, are the sites least likely to reflect lymph node enlargement due merely to local skin and soft tissue pathology.

SPECIFIC CLINICAL ISSUES IN THE CARE OF DRUG USERS WITH HIV INFECTION

In addition to the particular spectrum of HIV disease in injecting drug users and the need to distinguish between the manifestations of HIV infection and the effects of drug use and its sequelae, several issues are of clinical relevance to the care of HIV-infected drug users, which are discussed briefly here.

Pain Management

Frequently, patients with HIV infection require analgesia for pain syndromes resulting from specific opportunistic infections or their complications. Although clinicians may express appropriate concern about the possibility of drug-seeking behavior or manipulation on the part of drug users attempting to obtain narcotics or other psychotropic medications, this concern may result at times in the inappropriate withholding or underuse of strong analgesics in settings in which they are medically indicated. A com-

mon misconception, although one presumably not widespread among readers of this volume, is that patients maintained on methadone do not require additional narcotics for analgesia, or that analgesia can be achieved, if necessary, simply by increasing patients' daily methadone doses. In fact, patients on methadone maintenance quickly develop tolerance to the drug's analgesic effects and have not been found to have a blunted perception of noxious stimuli (347, 348). Indeed, because of their tolerance to narcotic drugs, such patients require at least the standard and at times higher-than-standard doses of short-acting narcotic analgesics (e.g., oxycodone, hydromorphone, meperidine, codeine) when indicated for pain relief. In addition, these drugs often must be administered on a more frequent dosing schedule than when used for nontolerant patients, because of their rapid elimination in narcotic addicts (348). Although drug users certainly are not the only category of patients in whom the inadequate clinical use of strong analgesics is common, such under-medication predictably results in a typical pattern of confrontation and acting out among such patients, with the frequent result of poor patient outcomes and increasing frustration and/or dissatisfaction among medical staff. The judicious and appropriate use of strong narcotic analgesics, when indicated, can help prevent this undesirable chain of events (348, 349). Clearly, however, when such drugs are used, clinicians must remain mindful of the possibility of abuse—e.g., by providing small quantities at a time for outpatients, and by renewing prescriptions on a fixed schedule—and should taper such medications gradually before discontinuation.

Drug Interactions

Several potential drug interactions have been identified that are of specific relevance to the care of HIV-infected opiate addicts, especially those on methadone maintenance. The most important of these is the interaction between rifampin and methadone, described by Kreek et al. in 1976 (350). Given the common occurrence of tuberculosis in HIV-infected drug users, as noted earlier, the concurrent use of methadone and rifampin has become increasingly frequent in the AIDS era. Rifampin has been shown to increase the elimination of methadone and to reduce methadone plasma levels, an effect believed to be due to enhanced hepatic microsomal enzyme activity resulting from rifampin administration (350). This effect results clinically in the onset of typical opiate withdrawal symptoms, at times severe, within several days of the initiation of rifampin therapy in methadone-maintained patients (350). This phenomenon may be prevented in most cases by increasing patients' daily methadone doses, usually by 10 mg every 1–2 days, beginning on the day that rifampin is introduced. At times, the final maintenance dose arrived at may be at least 50% greater than the original maintenance dose before the patient reaches a new stable steady state. Patients should be monitored closely during these rapid methadone increases, with increased dose levels titrated to oversedation, although this seldom occurs when rifampin therapy is introduced. Occasionally, rifampin-induced withdrawal may be lessened by dividing the daily methadone dose on a twice-daily schedule—e.g., two thirds in the morning, one third in the evening—although this practice may not always be possible in the outpatient setting, within the constraints of dispensing regulations for methadone maintenance treatment programs (MMTPs). In addition, it should be noted that patients may, at times, resist or attempt to evade the daily ingestion of rifampin, especially in MMTP settings where methadone and rifampin are often co-administered, because of the feared or perceived noxious effects of the latter drug. This possibility must be considered carefully by clinicians who supervise the care of such patients to ensure both the effective management of tuberculosis and to avoid the potential for methadone overdose in patients who have surreptitiously minimized their rifampin intake after having had their methadone doses increased to compensate for the anticipated rifampin-induced effects on methadone metabolism. (One simple measure to monitor whether patients in drug treatment settings are, indeed, ingesting rifampin as ordered is to instruct nursing staff to inspect patients' routine urine toxicology specimens for the presence of the typically bright red-orange color that is typically noted in urine and other body fluids among patients on rifampin therapy) (351). When rifampin is discontinued, following completion of tuberculosis therapy or for other reasons, it is advisable gradually to reduce patients' daily methadone doses accordingly, although the final level arrived at in such cases may be higher than the starting level before rifampin therapy was introduced. Rifabutin, an antimicrobial regularly used in the treatment and prevention of disseminated Mycobacterium avium complex and closely related in structure to rifampin, also reduces the methadone levels by enhancing the hepatic microsomal enzymatic activity (352). To date, there has been only one clinical study of this interaction, which showed equivocal results (352); clinicians must be aware of the possibility of increased dosing requirements for methadone and other opioids, although this effect is neither as well documented nor as predictable as that of rifampin.

In another small study, the antifungal agent fluconazole was found to increase the plasma levels of methadone (353), although the magnitude of this effect had uncertain clinical implications. No information is available at this time regarding the potential interaction between methadone and the new class of antiretroviral agents, the protease inhibitors. Further studies are needed before firm recommendations regarding dose adjustments can be made.

Another medication frequently used in the care of HIV-infected drug users is phenytoin, since seizures may occur as a common complication of certain HIV-related CNS infections or malignancies. Phenytoin has been shown to have an effect on methadone metabolism similar to that of rifampin, presumably through a comparable effect involving the hepatic microsomal enzyme system, although in the case of phenytoin the effect is less dramatic and usually occurs more slowly, often over the course of several weeks as opposed to the first few days following initiation of therapy (354). Accordingly, although methadone dose increases are often necessary to prevent opiate withdrawal in patients on methadone maintenance who are placed on phenytoin, these increases generally need not be as great or as rapid as in the case of rifampin.

The introduction of antiretroviral agents for the treatment of HIV infection has raised the question of whether these agents may exhibit pharmacologic interactions with methadone or other drugs that might commonly be used among HIV-infected drug users. Zidovudine's interaction with methadone has been studied since its introduction as an antiretroviral agent. Earlier reports suggested that zidovudine levels are increased in patients taking opiates (355, 356). Recent data confirm those reports (357), although the clinical implications of this observation are unknown, and at present there is no recommendation to change the dose of zidovudine in patients taking methadone. Additionally, it does not appear that zidovudine therapy affects the metabolism of methadone, and there is no biologic or pharmacologic evidence to suggest that methadone doses must be modified in patients initiating zidovudine therapy. Interestingly, however, it has been found that among certain methadone-maintained patients who begin taking zidovudine, the side effects of insomnia, malaise, gastrointestinal distress, or headache that may be seen among patients started on zidovudine (358) may be attributed mistakenly to methadone withdrawal. Indeed, informal street lore in certain areas has come to support the mistaken belief that zidovudine interferes with methadone's effects, although, as noted, there is no scientific evidence at present on which to base this assertion.

Among the most recently introduced antiretroviral agents, the protease inhibitors ritonavir and indinavir have been noted to have certain drug interactions that deserve a brief discussion. Ritonavir can increase the serum levels of the opiates fentanyl, meperidine, and propoxyphene, as the serum level of amphetamine (359).

The concomitant use of rifampin, rifabutin, phenytoin, or phenobarbital results in decreased plasma concentrations of ritonavir, indinavir, and saquinavir. Among multiple other drug interactions, ritonavir increases the plasma levels of desipramine and saquinavir, and reduces levels of theophylline, all of which require dose adjustment. The antifungal agent ketoconazole can increase plasma levels of indinavir, and a dosage reduction of the latter drug should be considered (360).

Self-Medication

The use of nonprescribed antibiotics available through the street drug market, or "antibiotic abuse," has been described among injecting drug users independent of the AIDS epidemic (361, 362). This phenomenon appears to

be common and was identified in one large study from Detroit as a risk factor for MRSA infection among drug users hospitalized for bacterial endocarditis (362). This practice is of particular relevance to the management of HIV-infected drug users, who may thereby present with acute illness due to partly treated bacterial infections, which may make it difficult to diagnose or treat such infections effectively. Consequently, eliciting a specific history for street antibiotic use is critical for the assessment of drug users presenting with suspected bacterial infections, since such information may not be volunteered by patients who would not consider nonprescribed antibiotic use to be pertinent to their medical or drug abuse histories. Anecdotal evidence now suggests that certain AIDS-related medications (e.g., zidovudine, acyclovir, ketoconazole), in addition to standard antibiotics, are also available on the street, and that such medications may be taken sporadically in an unsupervised manner as a form of self-treatment (363). In the case of zidovudine, this may result in the periodic ingestion of large amounts of zidovudine following episodes of needle sharing or other unsafe practices, in an attempt at self-prophylaxis against HIV infection. Although there has been no documentation of serious medical consequences as a result of such behavior among drug users, several case reports have described instances of intentional zidovudine overdose among injecting drug users as a form of suicide attempt (363, 364). These findings suggest both that clinicians who care for drug users at risk for HIV infection should consider the possibility of unsupervised self-medication with AIDS-related therapeutic agents in such patients, and that an assessment of patients' reliability, responsibility, and expected compliance should inform the decision to initiate such medication regimens.

The use of prescription medications that potentiate or modify the effect of common street drugs has always been a source of experimentation among drug addicts. Commonly used medications with psychotropic effect can be found in the street market with relative ease and their effect when combined with illegal drugs is well recognized and described elsewhere in this text.

Different medical devices may also have an impact in the market of illegal drugs, like the case of aerosol devices intended to deliver bronchodilators and their use by cocaine smokers to enhance the pulmonary absorption of their drug. Further, as outpatient medicine becomes more sophisticated and procedures and techniques traditionally reserved for hospital use become widely available in outpatient settings and private homes, an impact is also noted in the drug-using population. Of special note is the increasing use of permanent indwelling intravenous devices for multiple medical indications (e.g., prolonged courses of antibiotics, chemotherapy, dialysis) often indicated in patients with HIV infection, which may also be used as a means of injecting illicit drugs (365).

PRIMARY MEDICAL CARE FOR DRUG USERS WITH HIV INFECTION

During the first decade of the AIDS epidemic, there was a gradual shift in the clinical care of HIV-infected patients, involving earlier medical intervention and a growing emphasis on outpatient care (91, 93–95). This trend emerged as specific antiretroviral therapy became available—with the introduction of zidovudine in 1987 (366)—and as prophylactic regimens against PCP gained acceptance soon afterward (103). As a result of this trend, medical therapies began to be offered to patients even in the asymptomatic stages of HIV infection, whereas earlier in the epidemic the clinical approach to HIV had been limited largely to the treatment of specific opportunistic infections and malignancies among patients in the later phases of HIV disease and AIDS. Consequently, the population of HIV-infected patients now considered eligible for specific medical interventions—offered in the hope of prolonging the asymptomatic state and reducing the risk of opportunistic infections and death in the short-term—has grown steadily in parallel with the growth in preventive interventions (91, 93–95). (Table 59.4) Because asymptomatic individuals, or those who have not yet progressed to AIDS, would be expected to comprise the largest proportion of an HIV-infected population at any one point in time (367)—especially in the early phases of the epidemic—the prospect of early medical intervention for HIV infection has had major implications for health planning and policy (47, 91–95). These

Table 59.4   Primary Care Interventions in HIV Infection

Agent/Dose	Absolute CD4+ T-Lymphocyte count/mm³			
	0–75	76–200	201–500	>500
Antiretroviral therapy[a]	Therapy recommended for all patients. In patients with CD4 + >350/mm³ and asymptomatic and/or stable HIV disease, observation may be considered.			Therapy recommended only for patients with high viral load (> 30,000 HIV-RNA copies/ml), rapidly decreasing CD4 + T-cell count, or other signs of HIV disease progression.[b]
AZT + Didanosine ± Protease inhibitor				
AZT + Zalcitabine ± Protease inhibitor				
AZT + Lamivudine ± Protease inhibitor				
Didanosine monotherapy				
Prophylaxis against opportunistic infections				
PCP TMP-SMZ 1DS PO QD[c]	Indicated		Indicated if oropharyngeal candidiasis or unexplained fever for > 2 weeks, or as suppressive therapy after first episode.	
or				
TMP-SMZ 1DS PO 3 per week				
or				
TMP-SMZ 1 SS PO QD[d]				
or				
Dapsone 50 or 100 mg PO QD				
or				
Dapsone 50 or 100 mg PO QD +				
Pyrimethamine 50 mg PO q week +				
Leukovorin 25 mg PO q week				
or				
Dapsone 200 mg PO q week +				
Pyrimethamine 50 mg PO q week +				
Leukovorin 25 mg PO q week				
or				
aerosolized Pentamidine 300 mg q month				
Mycobacterium avium complex (MAC) Clarithromycin 500 mg PO BID	Recommended	Uncertain benefit	Not recommended	
or				
Azithromycin 1200 mg PO q week				
or				
Rifabutin 300 mg PO QD				
Tuberculosis Isoniazid 300 mg PO + Pyridoxine 50 mg PO QD × 12 mo	Indicated for PPD skin reaction of ≥ 5 mm or contact with active case or prior positive PPD test without treatment, or for anergic HIV-positive patients in areas of high prevalence of tuberculosis infection.			
or				
Isoniazid 900 mg PO + Pyridoxine 50 mg PO biw × 12 mo[d,e]				
Toxoplasmosis TMP-SMZ 1DS PO QD[c]	Indicated for patients with positive IgG serum antibody against Toxoplasma gondii, and CD4 + count < 100/mm³. Lifelong suppressive therapy after disease.			
or				
TMP-SMZ 1DS PO 3 per week				
or				
TMP-SMZ 1 SS PO QD[d]				
or				
Dapsone 50–100 mg PO QD +				
Pyrimethamine 50 mg PO q week +				
Leukovorin 25 mg PO q week				
or				
Dapsone 200 mg PO q week +				
Pyrimethamine 50 mg PO q week +				
Leukovorin 25 mg PO q week				
Candida infections Fluconazole[f]	Indicated only in selected patients.			
Cryptococcosis Fluconazole	Indicated only in selected patients. Lifelong suppressive therapy after disease.			
or				
Itraconazole				
or				
Amphotericin B[f]				
Histoplasmosis as above	as above			
Coccidioidomycosis as above	as above			
Cytomegalovirus (CMV)	No prophylaxis recommended to date. Lifelong suppressive therapy after retinitis.			
Herpes simplex virus	Suppressive therapy only for recurrent infections.			
Acyclovir[f]				
or				
Famciclovir[f]				
or				
Valacyclovir[f]				
Varicella-Zoster Virus as above	Suppressive as above. Varicella-Zoster immune globulin (VZIG) recommended after documented exposure.			
Immunizations				
Influenza Whole or split virus	Recommended for all patients.			
Diphtheria/Tetanus	Recommended for all patients if not received < 10 years.			
Hepatitis B Recombinant Hepatitis B vaccine	Recommended for all non-immune patients.			
Pneumovax 23-valent Pneumococcal vaccine	Recommended for all patients.			
Hemophilus influenza type B Hib poly-saccharide vaccine	May be considered for use in patients with recurrent bacterial pneumonia.			

[a]Other combinations of antiretrovirals being tested at present. Decision regarding therapy should be individualized. Refer to text for appropriate dosing schedule.
[b]Recurrent candidiasis, oral hairy leukoplakia, chronic unexplained fever, constitutional symptoms.
[c]First choice.
[d]Alternative choices.
[e]Alternative regimens needed for resistant strains.
[f]Dosing schedule should be individualized.
Adapted from U.S. Centers for Disease Control and Prevention. USPHS/IDSA guidelines for prevention of opportunistic infections in persons infected with human immunodeficiency virus: a summary. MMWR 1995;44(RR-8):1–34; and Carpenter CCJ, Fischl M, Hammer SM, et al. Antiretroviral therapy for HIV infection in 1996. JAMA 1996;276:146–154.

trends have only intensified with the recent introduction of more effective HIV treatment regimens and the desirability of reducing HIV viral load even during the long period of clinical latency.

Current management of HIV infection with different combinations of recently introduced antiretroviral drugs will predictably prolong the lifespan of HIV-infected patients. This will have a particularly noticeable impact in patients with later stages of the disease, where immune reconstitution is no longer achievable (at least with the present knowledge we have of the immune response) and the potential for severe opportunistic infections is high. This population with later-stage disease is expected to increase markedly within the foreseeable future, and will require enhanced sources and treatment options in both outpatient and inpatient setting.

Among injecting drug users, the finding of HIV seroprevalence levels exceeding 30% in certain heavily affected geographic areas in the United States (368) suggests that a substantial number of such individuals would now be considered eligible for early medical intervention. This has posed both a great challenge and a great opportunity for the drug abuse treatment system, which is now faced with a growing number of patients for whom the delivery of primary medical care services has become an urgent priority. Indeed, there are few other areas of the health care system in which individuals at such high risk for HIV infection are likely to be concentrated. This has meant that drug abuse treatment programs and other related facilities have had to respond to the growing needs of HIV-infected patients, often in the setting of limited resources and considerable marginalization within the medical care system. Fortunately, however, there have been certain successes in different areas as attempts have been made to link drug abuse treatment with primary medical care for HIV infection (43, 44, 46, 369, 370). Although no single model of linkage or integration would be expected to be successful in all settings, it is encouraging that these first efforts may become part of the more comprehensive integration of drug abuse treatment into mainstream medical care, a process that may be spurred in coming years by the needs of drug-using patients with HIV infection.

For clinicians who care for HIV-infected drug users, regardless of the clinical context, certain basic elements are central to the comprehensive primary care of such patients. The following sections briefly outline some of the medical and psychosocial issues that are of key importance for the evaluation and care of HIV-infected drug users in the outpatient setting.

Baseline Medical Assessment of Drug Users with HIV Infection

First, as in most other medical evaluations, eliciting a thorough history is a central component of the baseline assessment of patients presenting with a diagnosis of HIV infection. The history should focus on drug use and sexual behavior, especially within the preceding 5–10 years. This information can be helpful both to assess the likelihood of ongoing risk behavior—particularly important in terms of the current risk of other sexually transmitted diseases or of infections due to continuing drug use practices—and, at times, to help identify when patients are likely first to have become infected with HIV. The latter information most often is not known and at best can only be estimated, but in certain cases the cumulative history of risk behavior can be instructive (e.g., patients who report long-standing abstinence following episodes of high-risk behavior in the distant past, or who describe temporally limited high-risk practices such as "shooting gallery" injection or street prostitution in HIV-endemic areas).

In addition to behavioral information, the history should focus on medical data such as hospitalizations for pneumonia, endocarditis, or tuberculosis—suggestive, though not always diagnostic, of HIV infection among drug users—and on any other known or suspected HIV-related illnesses. These include not only the specific illnesses and conditions that qualify for a diagnosis of AIDS (80, 82, 83) but also (and more commonly) certain HIV-related conditions such as oral candidiasis (thrush), herpes zoster, chronic fungal skin infections, seborrheic dermatitis and psoriasis, and generalized lymphadenopathy. A thorough inquiry should be made into patients' histories of tuberculosis, regarding results of prior skin tests and possible tuberculosis exposure, with documentation of the date of the first positive PPD

test or any known exposure to tuberculosis (e.g., household contact with an active tuberculosis case). Complete information should be elicited regarding the dates and length of past treatment or prophylaxis for tuberculosis. A history of hepatitis B exposure, disease, or vaccination should also be elicited. For patients in whom a specific date or time period for acquisition of HIV is strongly suspected, it may be useful to attempt to elicit a history of the acute retroviral syndrome, an entity that has been described in certain patient populations with documented primary HIV infection and seroconversion for HIV antibody (371–373). This syndrome is self-limited, lasting not more than several weeks, characterized generally by fever, malaise, lymphadenopathy, rash, myalgias, pharyngitis, and/or other nonspecific manifestations that may be easily confused with mononucleosis or a flu-like syndrome. It is uncertain how often this syndrome occurs among individuals newly infected with HIV, and it is likely that many individuals become infected with no clinical symptoms to accompany seroconversion. In addition, this syndrome has not been described consistently among drug users, which may reflect the low likelihood that drug users would commonly seek medical attention for what is generally a mild, self-limited illness, and/or the possibility that the background level of medical symptoms among such patients would be likely to obscure a nonspecific syndrome that would be more noticeable among healthy nonaddicted individuals. Nevertheless, for patients in whom a specific time period for primary HIV infection is known or suspected, it may be useful to corroborate this with a history of acute retroviral syndrome, if present. One should also attempt to elicit a baseline history of HIV-related constitutional symptoms—e.g., fever, weight loss, fatigue, diarrhea—although, as noted, it is important among drug users to attempt to distinguish these symptoms from those due to the effects of acute or chronic drug use.

The baseline physical examination for HIV-infected drug users should incorporate a standard complete examination with special emphasis on the detection of HIV-related conditions. With particular relevance to the latter, the examination should include measurement of height and weight (with calculation of ideal body weight); a complete examination of the oral cavity (374) (examining for oral candidiasis, oral hairy leukoplakia, Kaposi's sarcoma, aphthous or other oral ulcers, and HIV-related periodontal disease); palpation for all accessible lymph nodes with notation of size, consistency, tenderness, and location; complete inspection of the skin and nails (375) (examining for fungal dermatoses, onychomycosis, seborrheic dermatitis or psoriasis, xerosis, verrucous lesions, molluscum contagiosum, folliculitis, Kaposi's sarcoma, active or healed zosteriform eruptions, as well as fresh or old injection marks); and evaluation for hepatosplenomegaly. Female patients should be given a complete pelvic examination with Pap smear for cervical cytology and cultures or assays for gonorrhea, *Chlamydia*, and, if indicated by symptoms or history, herpes simplex virus. Both males and females should receive a genital and rectal exam with inspection for genital or anal ulcers. As previously indicated, it may be prudent to obtain a rectal Pap smear for cytologic examination in males with a history of homosexual contact.

Baseline laboratory tests should include the following: complete blood count with differential and platelet count; serum electrolytes, chemistries, and liver function tests; lymphocyte subset studies, including determination of total lymphocytes, number and percentage of CD4+ T lymphocytes, CD8 number and percentage, and CD4/CD8 ratio; serologic testing for syphilis, including both nontreponemal (e.g., VDRL, STS, RPR) and treponemal (e.g., FTA-ABS, MHA-TP) tests; complete HBV serology, including hepatitis B surface antigen (HBsAg), hepatitis B surface antibody (HBsAb), and antibody to hepatitis B core antigen (HBcAb); hepatitis C antibody; and a baseline serum anti-*Toxoplasma gondii* antibody assay.

As already noted, the absolute number and/or percent of CD4+ T lymphocytes was until recently the most useful laboratory marker indicating short-term prognosis and risk for disease progression in HIV-infected individuals (98–102, 121, 376–379). Additional laboratory markers such as serum p24 antigen, beta-2-microglobulin, and neopterin have also been studied and found to be somewhat predictive of HIV disease progression and prognosis in certain HIV-infected populations (77, 341, 377, 378, 380). However, less is known about the performance of these indicators in populations of drug users, and indeed, at least in the case of beta-2-microglobulin, current data suggest that among drug users this may be a relatively non-specific marker that does not reliably predict disease progression and that may be elevated even in HIV-seronegative drug users who are actively using drugs (121, 381–383). Additionally, p24 antigen, although more readily interpretable as a marker for disease progression, is present only infrequently in asymptomatic individuals and would not be considered sufficiently sensitive to warrant its use as a screening test (77, 380).

Thus, until very recently it had been standard practice to limit routine screening for prognostic markers among HIV-infected drug users to the performance of T lymphocyte subset determinations. However, the recent introduction of quantitative methods to measure the HIV RNA-HIV in plasma ("viral load") has already resulted in a dramatic change in the assessment of prognosis and eligibility on response to therapy to perform as a very sensitive indicator of disease stage and progression (79, 104, 105, 384). Quantitative viral load testing has been used as an outcome measure in most recent studies of the efficacy of antiretroviral therapies and it is expected to become standard practice in monitoring disease progression and response to therapy in individual patients, together with the CD4+ T lymphocyte count (47, 64, 106, 385–389). Specific questions still to be addressed regarding viral load testing include the optimal timing and frequency of the test, and the prognostic significance of different threshold plasma levels of virus. Nevertheless, even the few studies completed to date have shown convincingly that there is a stepwise relationship between increasing viral load levels and increasing risk of death or disease progression, much more powerful in its prognostic ability than the CD4+ count.

As an additional component of routine HIV primary care, all patients without a well-documented prior positive PPD or history of previously diagnosed tuberculosis should receive an intradermal 5 TU PPD (Mantoux) along with an assessment for cutaneous anergy using either a multiple-antigen skin test delivery system (e.g., Multitest CMI), or single intradermal injections of appropriately prepared antigens (e.g., *Candida,* mumps, *Trichophyton*) (214). It is also advisable for all patients to have a baseline chest x-ray, something that is especially critical for any patient found to be anergic or to have a positive PPD test by history or examination.

Recommendations regarding routine immunizations in HIV-infected patients have been re-evaluated recently, since certain studies demonstrated a transient effect of in vivo immunization on the expression of HIV, causing an increase in total viral load and also an increase in the in vitro susceptibility to infection from peripheral blood mononuclear cells from uninfected persons (390, 391). The relevance of this observation, however, remains to be determined, since this effect is transient, and its translation into clinical practice is unclear. Current consensus is that vaccines which would be routinely considered for HIV-infected patients should still be used, since the potential risk of the preventable illness is greater than the small theoretical risk of vaccination (63, 392). It is judicious in general, however, to withhold the administration of any vaccine in patients showing signs of active progression of disease or those at very advanced stages of disease, since such patients are generally unable to respond effectively to vaccines.

Current recommendations support the routine use of four vaccines in the HIV-infected patient: (*a*) influenza vaccine yearly, at the appropriate time and season (393); (*b*) hepatitis B vaccine for patients seronegative for all HBV markers (394), given in a three-dose series following standard recommendations for non–HIV-infected individuals to be repeated if no appropriate response is documented; (*c*) tetanus toxoid if not given with the prior 10 years; (*d*) the 23-valent pneumococcal polysaccharide vaccine, to be offered on a one-time basis, although some authorities recommend a repeated dose every 5–6 years (152). Although there is no formal recommendation to use *Haemophilus influenzae* type b (Hib) vaccine in HIV-infected adults, some clinicians have considered this especially for injection drug users at risk for recurrent bacterial pneumonia.

Treatment of HIV Infection

The introduction of zidovudine (AZT) in 1987 was followed by a long period in which monotherapy was the only possible therapeutic approach. Since 1993, the rapid development and subsequent FDA approval of new classes of antiretroviral agents, with different and in some instances complementary mechanisms of action, has brought new hope into the field of pharmacologic treatment of HIV disease (47). Eradication or cure of HIV infection, although the final conceivable goal of all efforts in the development of new therapeutic strategies, is not achievable at this moment. However, this possibility has recently been raised for the first time, and the use in combination of the new available antiretroviral agents signifies a dramatic therapeutic breakthrough in HIV management. Most ongoing studies have reported a sustained reduction in the total HIV viral load with the use of at least two agents (47, 64, 387–389, 395). If such an effect persists, a slower rate of progression of disease would be expected, potentially allowing the immune system to generate a partial recovery.

The addition of new drugs to the already complex daily medication regimens of many patients also brings to light the issue of new drug interactions (as discussed previously) and important concerns about adherence with chronic medication regimens in patients who may be actively using illicit drugs.

What follows is a brief description of the main pharmacologic properties, accepted uses, and interactions of the antiretroviral drugs available as of late 1996.

REVERSE TRANSCRIPTASE INHIBITORS: NUCLEOSIDE ANALOGUES

Zidovudine

By the early 1990s, existing recommendations and clinical practice concerning the use of zidovudine (ZDV, AZT) (Retrovir) suggested that zidovudine was clearly indicated for HIV-infected patients in the following categories: AIDS or advanced HIV-related disease (e.g., oral candidiasis with persistent constitutional symptoms); patients with CD4+ counts lower than 200/mm^3, regardless of symptoms; patients with HIV-related neurologic disease or thrombocytopenia; and those with milder symptomatic HIV disease with CD4+ T lymphocyte counts between 200 and 500/mm^3 (95, 270, 281, 366, 396–398). The persistent use of this agent as monotherapy favored the development of resistant strains of the HIV, a well-described effect directly related to the distinctive ability of the virus to undergo multiple mutations, especially after prolonged therapy of 12 months or more (306, 307). Most recent data from unpublished clinical trials tend to discourage the use of zidovudine monotherapy based on reduced mortality with combination therapy and a substantial reduction in development of resistant strains. Zidovudine monotherapy is now considered suboptimal therapy for HIV infection (47).

The currently recommended dose of zidovudine is 200 mg orally every 8 hours (a total daily dose of 600 mg) (47, 95, 399). Higher doses may be required when there is CNS involvement. It is available in both oral and intravenous formulations (the latter used to prevent HIV transmission to infants in the peripartum period). The most serious toxicities of zidovudine are hematologic: anemia, leukopenia, and granulocytopenia, generally reversible upon discontinuation of the drug. These effects are less common with the current recommended dose than with the regimens in earlier use that involved up to 1200 mg zidovudine daily (358, 396–399). Other reported side effects include headache, nausea, gastrointestinal upset, malaise, and insomnia (358, 398, 399), most of which tend to resolve over time with continuation of therapy or with symptomatic interventions. Zidovudine-related hepatotoxicity has also been described (400–402), as well as myopathy, marked by proximal muscle weakness and elevations in serum creatine kinase (CK), believed to be due to a direct toxic effect on muscle mitochondria, most common in patients taking zidovudine for 12 months or longer and readily reversible upon discontinuation of the drug (402). Baseline serum CK determinations and liver function tests should be obtained and repeated every few months during therapy. Despite its potential hepatotoxicity, the use of acetaminophen in moderation should not be avoided in patients on zidovudine therapy since serum levels of zidovudine and its glucuronidated metabolite are not increased by acetaminophen administration (403). Another common side effect, reported in up to 60% of cases, is headache, which also seems to be dose-related and reversible upon discontinuation of the drug. Other documented side effects are nausea, anorexia, xerostomia, hepatomegaly, cardiomyopathy, pigmentation of the nails, and leukocytoclastic vasculitis.

Didanosine

Didanosine (ddI) (Videx) was the second reverse transcriptase inhibitor to receive FDA approval for use in the treatment of patients with HIV infection. Initially recommended for use only in combination with zidovudine, it has proven to be a good agent for use as monotherapy and also in combination with other classes of antiretrovirals (404–406).

Available only on oral formulation, its accepted dosage is 200 mg every 12 hours (tablet or powder), with lower doses based on patient weight. It should be taken on an empty stomach. Most notable adverse effects are peripheral neuropathy (up to 20%) and pancreatitis (up to 6%, the most common reason for discontinuation of the drug). It should be used with caution in diabetics and alcoholics. Other documented side effects include nausea, diarrhea, abdominal pain, fever, headache, hepatomegaly, and a number of laboratory abnormalities: anemia, leukopenia, thrombocytopenia, hyperuricemia, hypertriglyceridemia, and elevation of liver function tests.

Zalcitabine

Similar in most respects to didanosine, zalcitabine (ddC) (HIVID) has a better toxicity profile, but the disadvantage of a three-times daily schedule. It has been tested in different trials and has been found to be an efficacious agent in combination therapy, most recently with zidovudine in triple combination therapy with a protease inhibitor (389). The recommended dose schedule is 0.75 mg every 8 hours, with lower doses based on weight.

Its major adverse effect is peripheral neuropathy (up to 35%). The incidence of pancreatitis (< 1%) is much lower than that for didanosine. Other side effects include oral ulcers (up to 13%), abdominal pain, dysphagia, skin rash, headache, myalgia, and laboratory abnormalities: anemia, leukopenia, thrombocytopenia, and elevation of liver function tests.

Stavudine

Similar to didanosine and zalcitabine, stavudine (d4T) (Zerit) has a much better toxicity profile with only a significant incidence of peripheral neuropathy (21%), and a very low incidence of pancreatitis and gastrointestinal side effects: nausea, vomiting, diarrhea, abdominal pain. An effective agent in monotherapy, it also appears to be a very promising agent in different two and three drug combinations (395). Given its ease of administration (40 mg twice daily) and favorable toxicity profile, it is associated with one of the best compliance rates, and therefore should be strongly considered as a potentially useful agent in populations with suspected poor adherence with therapy, in whom a two-pill per day regimen may be more realistic than the more demanding, albeit probably more effective, multiple combination regimens.

Lamivudine

A very well-tolerated agent, lamivudine (3TC) (Epivir) is not approved for use as monotherapy given the rapid development of viral resistance. Preliminary data from ongoing clinical trials, however, suggest that lamivudine may be one of the most effective agents in promoting a reduction in the total viral load when used in double and triple drug combinations (385, 395). As discussed previously, lamivudine is now also being tested as an efficient agent in the management of chronic hepatitis B. If further studies confirm this observation, it would have special significance for the drug-injecting population, with high levels of hepatitis B co-infection, in whom lamivudine used in combination with other agents may have added benefit. Like stavudine (d4T), lamivudine is generally well tolerated—diarrhea is the major side effect, and uncommon—and this medication involves only a two pill per day regimen, which makes it attractive in combination regimens, especially with AZT (47).

REVERSE TRANSCRIPTASE INHIBITORS: NON-NUCLEOSIDE ANALOGUES

The non-nucleoside analogues reverse transcriptase inhibitors nevirapine (Virimune) and delavirdine have not been yet fully tested in clinical trials, although it appears that their efficacy will be limited to use in combination therapy, given the rapid development or viral resistance reported in vitro as well as in early clinical trials. Their main toxicity reported to date is skin rash and fever, as well as laboratory abnormalities: thrombocytopenia and elevated liver function tests. Preliminary data suggest promising efficacy of these agents in combination with other reverse transcriptase inhibitors (407, 408).

PROTEASE INHIBITORS

The new generation of antiretroviral agents, the protease inhibitors, Saquinavir (Invirase), Ritonavir (Norvir), and Indinavir (Crixivan), are associated with the most potent antiviral effect achieved so far, both in vitro and in the different clinical trials that have shown a dramatic reduction in the total viral load (47, 64, 387–389). HIV-1 protease is an essential viral enzyme that acts late in the viral life cycle promoting the assembly of infectious virions (409). The complete inhibition of this enzyme results in the formation of non-infectious particles (410). While the protease inhibitors have shown impressive preliminary results, their use may be problematic in practice, especially in drug users, due to side effects, toxicity, the sheer number of pills which must be ingested—over 12 per day in most combination regimens—drug interactions, and the requirements for rigorous adherence to complex medication schedules. Thus, the enthusiasm for these new therapies which has emerged from clinical trials must be tempered by the challenges which are posed to their effective use by the real-world circumstances of many patients who might benefit from them (411).

Saquinavir, the first agent of this group to receive FDA approval (412), has very poor bioavailability (4% in phase I studies) (413), which results in very low plasma concentrations with a subsequently reduced antiviral effect and a higher risk for development of viral resistance. It is, however, well tolerated and has a very low toxicity profile. Ritonavir has the advantage of a twice-daily administration schedule (as opposed to three times daily for the other two agents), but the liquid form of the drug is unpalatable and the capsules need to be kept refrigerated prior to their administration. Ritonavir's good bioavailability (388) is offset by the high incidence of gastrointestinal side effects (nausea, dyspepsia, diarrhea) as well as hypertriglyceridemia, elevated liver function tests, and circumoral paresthesia. Indinavir, the latest addition to this class of drugs, seems to have the most favorable profile, with good bioavailability and a low incidence of side effects, mostly gastrointestinal intolerance, indirect hyperbilirubinemia, and nephrolithiasis (observed in up to 4% of the cases) (360).

Importantly, this class of medications is associated with significant drug interactions that affect medications commonly used by HIV-infected patients, and possibly illicit drugs as well. All three of these protease inhibitors demonstrate a significant reduction in blood levels when used in combination with medications that activate the cytochrome p-450 liver enzyme system: rifampin, rifabutin, phenytoin, phenobarbital, and H-2 receptor blockers (359, 360). Indinavir and ritonavir will increase the drug levels of most benzodiazepines, and the serum levels of amphetamine will increase with concomitant use of ritonavir (Table 59.5). The interactions of the protease inhibitors with opioid drugs, particularly with methadone in chronic dosing regimens, are not fully elucidated.

Treatment Strategies

The introduction of agents that inhibit different steps in the viral replicative cycle allows clinicians to use a therapeutic strategy that will predictably be associated with more significant and sustained reductions of total viral load and increases in CD4+ and T-lymphocyte counts. The duration of this beneficial effect will only be determined in adequate longitudinal studies.

Although no official guidelines have yet been published, what follows is a summary of current (1996) recommendations by an international panel of experts (47) and a review of major clinical trials (64).

The decision regarding initiation of antiretroviral therapy has to be individualized. A number of variables will affect that decision, and the most important ones are the patient's symptoms, and disease stages prior treatment history, CD4+ lymphocyte count, and total viral load (plasma HIV RNA). Treatment should be initiated before the damage to the immune system is irreversible, as estimated by the stage of disease and progression. While no single optimal treatment strategy has been defined, current accepted practice is to initiate ther-

Table 59.5 Potential Pharmacologic Interactions of Importance in the Management of HIV-Infected Drug Users

Drug	Antiretroviral Agents	Antimicrobial Agents	Central Nervous System Agents
Opioids			
Methadone	zidovudine (357, 471) ↑ zidovudine serum level	**rifabutin**[a] (352) ↓ methadone serum level **rifampin**[a] (350) ↓ methadone serum level fluconazole[b] (472) ↑ methadone serum level	**fluvoxamine**[b](473) ↑ methadone serum level phenytoin[a] (354) ↓ methadone serum level
Fentanyl	**ritonavir**[b] (359) ↑fentanyl serum level nevirapine[a] (474) ↓ fentanyl serum level		
Meperidine	**ritonavir(C)**[b] (359) ↑ meperidine serum level		**MAO inhibitors(C)** (478) hyperpyrexia, hypertension, coma phenytoin[a] (477) ↓ meperidine serum level
Propoxyphene	**ritonavir(C)**[b] (359) ↑ propoxyphene serum level		
Benzodiazepines Alprazolam, Clorazepate, Diazepam, Estazolam, Flurazepam, Midazolam, Triazolam	**ritonavir(C)**[b] (359) ↑ listed benzodiazepines' serum levels **indinavir(C)**[b] (475) ↑ midazolam, triazolam serum levels nevirapine[a] (474) ↓ midazolam, triazolam serum levels	itraconazole and ketoconazole (481) ↑ midazolam, triazolam serum levels	**fluvoxamine**[b] (476) ↑ alprazolam, diazepam, triazolam serum levels fluoxetine[a] (478) ↑ alprazolam serum level carbamazepine[b] (482) ↓ alprazolam serum level phenytoin with concurrent diazepam (480) ↑ or ↓ phenytoin serum level
Amphetamines	**ritonavir**[b] (359) ↑ methamphetamine serum level		**MAO inhibitors(C)** (478) hypertensive crisis tricyclic antidepressants (479) ↑ amphetamine effect neuroleptics (479) ↑ seizure activity, ↓ neuroleptic effect

Table prepared by Carolyn Skowronski, Pharm. D., Yale AIDS Program, Yale-New Haven Hospital.
Interactions with agents in **bold** print have the greatest potential for clinical significance **(C)**, concurrent therapy is contraindicated; numbers in parentheses indicate references.
[a] Induces hepatic drug metabolizing enzymes.
[b] Inhibits hepatic drug metabolizing enzymes.

apy in asymptomatic patients when the CD4+ count is below 500/mm³. There are studies, however, that support initiation of therapy at higher CD4+ counts (92), particularly if the patient has a high viral load (e.g., > 30,000 viral copies/ml) (47, 104, 105). As a general rule, antiretroviral therapy should be given to all symptomatic patients regardless of their stage (47, 92).

INITIAL ANTIRETROVIRAL REGIMENS

The first question confronted by clinicians when initiating therapy is whether to choose the most potent therapy available first or to treat patients according to their stage, viral load, and signs of progression of disease, deferring the use of the most potent combinations for later stages, or after the failure of initial therapy. One paradox of the current state of knowledge is that it may be that the patients who are in the earlier stages of HIV infection—i.e., those who might do well in the short term regardless of treatment—are also those who may benefit the most from therapy if it is started early.

Didanosine is the only agent accepted for use as monotherapy. Stavudine, a promising agent for use both as monotherapy and in combination with other agents, has not been adequately tested as a single agent in clinical trials to date.

There are three combinations that are widely accepted as standard therapy: zidovudine plus didanosine, zidovudine plus zalcitabine, and zidovudine plus lamivudine. Each of these combinations may also be used together with a protease inhibitor (47). It has been generally accepted that the lower one is able to reduce HIV viral load, the better the outcome, and that the more drugs one uses, the better the likelihood of reducing viral load and preventing or delaying the emergence of resistance. The difficulty, however, is that increasing efficacy is achieved at the price of increasing toxicity and complexity, which poses significant management dilemmas in the care of HIV-infected drug users. Further, due to the predictable development of resistant HIV in the setting of suboptimal or erratic use of antiretroviral therapy, the additional concern arises that poorly compliant drug-using patients,

receiving infrequent and poorly supervised therapy, may be a factor in the selection of multiple drug-resistant HIV which will not be able to be treated with currently available medications, similar to what transpired in the early 1990s, when injection drug use was an important risk factor in the development of multiple drug-resistant tuberculosis in New York City (199).

WHEN TO CHANGE THERAPY

Given our current understanding of HIV infection and disease and the incorporation of viral load measurement as a sensitive marker of disease, it can be anticipated that patients may not remain on their first combination of antiretroviral agents for a prolonged period. There are three reasons at present contemplated to support a change in instituted therapy: (a) treatment failure, defined as increased viral load, decreased CD4+ count, or progression of disease; (b) drug-related factors, namely toxicity, drug intolerance and nonadherence (commonly observed in patients with substance abuse problems) to the prescribed regimen, which often requires change in therapeutic approach; (c) current use of suboptimal regimens, as in the case of zidovudine monotherapy.

The choice of a new therapeutic regimen should be guided by the reason that prompted the change in therapy. Avoidance of drug toxicity of closely related agents, the addition of new agents in combination with proven benefit in clinical trials, likely resistance and cross-resistance patterns, and the choice of agents likely to be associated with improved adherence on the part of the patient (e.g., one pill twice daily versus three pills three times daily) are all factors to consider when making a change in therapy.

Prophylaxis for Opportunistic Infections in HIV Infection

In addition to the use of agents with specific antiretroviral activity, the other area in which the management of HIV infection has undergone a significant expansion is that of prophylaxis for opportunistic infections. PCP was the first opportunistic infection for which survival benefit was found when prophylaxis with TMP-SMX was instituted in patients taking zidovudine (414). Following the implementation of different prophylactic regimens, it was found that effective prophylaxis against PCP is associated with a delay in progression of HIV disease, prolongation of life, and decreased morbidity, with an associated reduction in health care costs (415, 416).

The overwhelming evidence supporting the use of primary and secondary prophylactic strategies against PCP highlighted the importance of developing similar strategies against other opportunistic pathogens commonly seen in HIV infection, and since then, the study of prophylactic regimens against opportunistic infections has become an area of intense research and a rapidly evolving field in therapeutics.

Efficacy is the primary consideration for prophylaxis. Safety and tolerability of the medications chosen, given the prolonged courses that will be required, are imperative. Ease of administration and frequency, drug interactions, and overall costs are also important considerations (63). What follows is an overview of the present recommendations in the field of prophylaxis.

PCP

PCP is the most common of the major AIDS-defining opportunistic infections seen in HIV-infected patients in the United States and Europe, occurring in 60% or more of patients presenting with an AIDS diagnosis (108–110). Prospective data have indicated that the risk of PCP is particularly elevated for patients with CD4+ lymphocyte counts lower than 200/mm^3, with one prospective study in a cohort of homosexual men indicating that, even including asymptomatic individuals with baseline CD4+ counts in this category, the risk of developing PCP during a 12-month period approached 20% (103, 417). Accordingly, clinical recommendations have been developed to help prevent the common occurrence of PCP in high-risk individuals through the use of several prophylactic regimens. Current guidelines and recommendations, as of early 1996, suggest that PCP prophylaxis should be offered to patients in the following categories: AIDS (especially, but not limited to, patients who already have had an episode of PCP), advanced HIV-related disease, and asymptomatic HIV-infected individuals with CD4+ counts lower than 200/mm^3 (66, 241, 417). Several regimens for PCP prophylaxis have been adopted for clinical use, including oral TMP-SMX, aerosolized pentamidine, and oral dapsone. These are discussed briefly in turn.

TMP-SMX, also used in both parenteral and oral forms for the acute treatment of PCP (109), is the preferred agent for PCP prophylaxis (66). The currently approved dose for this indication is TMP (160 mg) and SMX (800 mg) once daily by mouth (103), although a three-times-a-week regimen is also used with equal efficacy. The most common side effects of TMP-SMX include rash, pruritus, fever, leukopenia, neutropenia, thrombocytopenia, and liver function abnormalities (109, 418). These toxicities have been observed to occur more frequently in HIV-infected patients than in non–HIV-infected individuals (151, 419–421), although many of these effects appear to be dose dependent and, although seen at the relatively low dose levels employed for PCP prophylaxis, generally are less common with low-dose TMP-SMX than is the case with the higher doses used for acute treatment of PCP (e.g., 15–20 mg/kg trimethoprim per day) (109, 418, 422, 423). In addition, certain of these toxicities—particularly rash, pruritus, and fever—often may be managed symptomatically when they occur and need not be treatment-limiting, though one must be mindful of certain more uncommon but potentially serious toxicities such as exfoliative dermatitis and the Stevens-Johnson syndrome (109, 418, 423). Patients receiving chronic PCP prophylaxis with TMP-SMX—many of whom would also be likely to be on zidovudine therapy, which requires its own periodic monitoring, as noted earlier—should undergo routine monitoring of hematologic parameters, serum chemistries, and liver function tests as well.

Pentamidine isethionate has long been used for the treatment of PCP (424), and remains one of the standard medications for treating PCP in patients with AIDS (109). For treatment purposes, in patients diagnosed with PCP, pentamidine generally is given in a daily intravenous or intramuscular dose (4 mg/kg) for a total of 14–21 days. For prophylaxis against PCP in patients who do not actually have the pneumonia but are deemed to be at high risk of developing it—the patient groups noted already—pentamidine is given in a standard 300 mg aerosolized dose once a month delivered via a nebulizer system (e.g., the Respirgard II nebulizer system, Marquest Medical Products, Englewood, Colorado) (103, 109, 418). (This dose and the nebulizer system are considered the current standard for the use of aerosolized pentamidine for PCP prophylaxis, approved by the FDA for this purpose.) Side effects of parenterally administered pentamidine include hypotension, hypo- and hyperglycemia, renal insufficiency, leukopenia, pancreatitis, and liver function abnormalities (109). Such toxicities are unlikely following aerosolized pentamidine administration, since systemic absorption of the drug is minimal, although isolated occurrences of hypotension, hypoglycemia, cutaneous eruptions, and pancreatitis have been reported following aerosolized pentamidine use (418, 425–427). However, the aerosolized use of pentamidine does result commonly in cough and/or bronchospasm, due to the irritant effects of the drug on the respiratory tract; patients may also report an unpleasant metallic taste following pentamidine inhalation (418, 428, 429). The former symptoms often may be minimized or prevented through pretreatment with an inhaled bronchodilator immediately prior to pentamidine administration (418, 428).

The phenomenon of extrapulmonary pneumocystosis has also been described in HIV-infected patients receiving aerosolized pentamidine; case reports have documented pneumocystosis affecting most commonly the spleen, liver, gastrointestinal tract, and lymph nodes, with one recent report describing a case of fulminant disseminated disease in which thromboemboli containing *P. carinii* were identified in the peripheral vasculature (109, 418, 430, 431). This phenomenon has prompted the concern that perhaps a systemic prophylactic agent against *P. carinii* might be preferable to one whose coverage is limited to the lung, although extrapulmonary pneumocystosis has also been well-described in AIDS patients not receiving aerosolized pentamidine (430, 432, 433), and the overall frequency of this occurrence is believed to be low. Of greater clinical concern has been the finding that, due to relative under-penetration of the upper lobes of the lung with pentamidine during aerosolized administration, PCP limited to the apices or upper lobes may be more likely to occur in such patients (418, 434–437).

The third currently available prophylactic regimen to prevent PCP is oral dapsone, which, like TMP-SMZ, offers the potential advantage of a systemic agent while posing the concomitant risk of drug-related toxicity. Dapsone has been used effectively in conjunction with TMP as a combined oral regimen for the treatment of mild-to-moderate PCP, for which the standard doses have been 100 mg dapsone and 20 mg/kg TMP daily in four divided doses (438). For prophylaxis, dapsone alone has been used in doses from 50 to 100 mg daily, with results suggesting acceptable efficacy and similar toxicity compared with oral TMP-SMZ (439, 440). The currently recommended dose for prophylaxis is 100 mg daily. Dapsone generally is well tolerated, and the principal reported toxicities include rash, anorexia, nausea, and gastrointestinal distress, varying degrees of hemolysis, anemia, and methemoglobinemia (418, 438, 441). Significant hemolysis and anemia are most common in, but not restricted to, patients receiving high-dose dapsone who have preexisting bone marrow suppression or a glucose-6-phosphate dehydrogenase deficiency (351, 441). Screening of patients for glucose-6-phosphate dehydrogenase deficiency has been advised prior to the initiation of dapsone therapy for pneumocystosis (438), especially given the possibility of coexisting anemia or other disorders of red cell production in HIV-infected patients. Though dapsone is a member of the sulfone class of drugs, chemically related to the sulfonamides, AIDS patients with histories of allergy to TMP-SMZ have been reported to tolerate dapsone therapy for PCP prophylaxis (439, 440).

TMP-SMZ has been proved to be the best agent for secondary prophylaxis of PCP (416). Given its added effect as a prophylactic agent against toxoplasmosis and as an antibacterial agent which may reduce the incidence of common bacterial infections in HIV disease, it should be considered the agent of choice when PCP prophylaxis is indicated. Patients with intolerance to TMP-SMZ, commonly presenting as severe skin rashes, should be considered for a trial of desensitization, which is generally a safe and effective procedure (442).

Atovaquone, a new agent with anti-PCP activity, has received FDA approval for use in the treatment of mild cases of PCP. Promising also in preventing PCP, its efficacy as a prophylactic agent is currently being tested in clinical trials (443).

MYCOBACTERIUM AVIUM COMPLEX (MAC)

Disseminated MAC infection is the most common systemic bacterial infection in late stages of HIV disease, with an estimated incidence of up to 40% in patients who do not take any form of prophylaxis against it (444). The disseminated form of the disease, very uncommon in patients with a CD4 count of more than 100, but increasingly common as the CD4+ count drops below 50/mm³ (445), frequently presents as a multisystem disease, with bacteremia, constitutional symptoms, and typical involvement of the gastrointestinal tract, bone marrow, liver, and lungs. As in the case of *M. tuberculosis,* multiple other sites of involvement are well documented. The need for prophylaxis against disseminated disease has been a subject of debate until very recently, given the toxicity profile and unfavorable drug interactions associated with the regimens most commonly used in the recent past, and the effectiveness of the available regimens to treat mycobacterial disease once it occurred. Disseminated MAC, however, has been associated with a decrease in survival, and its negative impact on quality of life is unequivocal. MAC prophylaxis is now recommended for consideration for all HIV-infected patients with a CD4 count less than 75 (63, 66). Currently accepted prophylactic regimens include the use of daily rifabutin (300 mg), or the macrobide antibiotics, clarithromycin (500 mg twice a day), or weekly azithromycin (1200 mg). The latter two drugs show comparable efficacy in reducing incidence of disseminated MAC disease and providing a survival benefit, and are at least as effective as rifabutin without the toxicity and drug interactions seen with the former drug (446, 447).

TOXOPLASMA GONDII ENCEPHALITIS

Prophylaxis against T. gondii is recommended for all HIV-infected patients with a CD4 count of less than 100 cells/mm³ and a positive IgG antibody to *toxoplasma,* since an estimated 20–47% of HIV-infected patients with latent *T. gondii* infection will develop cerebral toxoplasmosis (448). Secondary prophylaxis for life is indicated after an episode of toxoplasmic encephalitis (63, 66). Standard regimens for primary prophylaxis include TMP-SMX, one double strength daily or three times weekly (this choice provides adequate prophylaxis for both PCP and toxoplasma encephalitis), and dapsone 200 mg plus pyrimethamine 50 mg weekly (63, 449). Daily dapsone (100 mg) plus weekly pyrimethamine (50 mg) may also help provide prophylaxis against PCP as well as toxoplasmosis (439).

PSYCHOSOCIAL AND DRUG TREATMENT ISSUES

The psychiatric, psychosocial, and drug treatment issues relevant to the care of HIV-infected drug users are addressed elsewhere in this volume. However, it is important before concluding a chapter on medical management of such patients to stress the central importance of these issues to the effective, comprehensive care of drug users with or at risk for HIV infection.

From the overview of therapeutic management of HIV infection presented here, it is readily understood that later stages of HIV infection are inevitably associated with the use of multiple medications, some of them with complex interactions, and some of them with specific requirements in regards of meal schedule or avoidance of specific foods. Didanosine, for example, has to be taken on an empty stomach. Ritonavir and saquinavir should be taken with food. Indinavir requires an empty stomach for better absorption, and increased fluid intake is needed to avoid the formation of kidney stones. Atovaquone requires food with high fat content for optimal absorption. It is clear that therapeutic goals cannot be achieved without a high level of engagement and adherence on the side of the patient. Despite enhanced access to primary care provided to HIV-infected individuals in many communities, the complex issues of social isolation, use of illegal substances, problems with the criminal justice system, and a resulting low self-esteem in many instances, contribute to the fact that many injection drug users still do not have an identifiable source of primary care (65% in one study) (369).

Active drug use, unstable household and social situations that preclude regular attendance to primary care centers, and resumption of prior drug or alcohol habits are all factors that interfere with appropriate adherence to medical advice and plans. It has been shown, however, that drug addicts exhibit good compliance with medical therapy when it is delivered in the appropriate context given their personal situation, whether drug treatment clinics, HIV clinics, other outpatient settings, or prisons (42, 43, 46, 365, 450). Despite those observations, drug users have been forced to be less likely to receive HIV primary care and/or specific HIV therapy with antiretroviral drugs compared to other groups (451–454).

The frequent co-occurrence of psychiatric disorders and HIV infection has been described in drug-using populations—in which the background prevalence of psychopathology is already likely to be elevated—and the need for psychiatric intervention is often compelling in many cases (38, 39, 365, 455, 456). In addition, since HIV infection is so clearly a condition that affects family units, attention to the needs and concerns of the family as a whole is an essential part of effective care. For those in young adult heterosexual populations, as are most drug users with HIV infection, issues of childbearing, child support, and custody, and the growing phenomenon of orphanhood, are major themes that often require an intense and coordinated effort to help families respond to the potentially devastating effects of HIV (457, 458). These issues often require involvement not only of medical and psychiatric staff but also, and at times more importantly, of social service staff, legal services, pastoral and religious services, peer support groups, extended family members, and other community-based networks of care (459–465). Social and legal services are of particular importance with regard to child custody arrangements, entitlements, living wills, and other instruments that can help empower patients to make important decisions concerning their medical care, family and institutional arrangements, and financial affairs. The multiplicity of services and disciplines—medical, psychiatric, social, spiritual, legal—often involved in the care of HIV-infected patients and families requires that effective case management systems be developed to ensure coordination of care and to avoid fragmentation or duplication of services. The concept of case management received increasing recognition as an important approach to the care of patients with HIV infection during the first decade of the AIDS epidemic (459–465) and will continue to hold relevance for this multifaceted endeavor during the coming years.

Regarding drug abuse treatment, a discussion of the various treatment modalities and strategies is beyond the scope of this chapter, and indeed these issues are addressed in great detail in other sections of this volume. For HIV-infected drug users, as for other drug-using individuals, treatment options to help diminish or cease drug use behavior should be available and accessible as indicated. Clearly, from a public health standpoint, drug abuse treatment should be expected to play an important role in strategies attempting to reduce the risk of transmission of HIV within a given population (466, 467). On clinical grounds, there has also been ongoing interest in whether active ongoing drug abuse may accelerate the rate of progression to AIDS in HIV-infected individuals (58–62, 118). Although certain authors have suggested that alcohol and/or drugs of abuse may, in fact, exert adverse effects on lymphocyte function or on different elements of the immune system, other studies have found no association between drug or alcohol use per se and aggravation of immunosuppression in HIV-infected patients (58–62, 118). Regardless of whether there may be specific biologic effects, however, it is evident that active drug use is likely eventually to interfere with efforts to provide ongoing primary medical care and that compliance with often-complicated medical regimens is likely to be diminished in HIV-infected patients who remain heavily involved in the drug-using milieu (40). For the latter reasons, at the very least, it is important to address the possibility of ongoing drug and/or alcohol abuse in the assessment and monitoring of HIV-infected drug users and to provide or arrange for appropriate drug abuse treatment as indicated. In addition, because it may be expected that the risk for relapse to drug or alcohol abuse can be heightened in some patients at various points during the course of HIV infection (39, 468–470) (e.g., upon disclosure of HIV seropositivity or the development of symptoms or serious signs of immunosuppression, or after the death of a friend or family member from AIDS-related illnesses), it is important for medical staff to be aware of and indeed to anticipate these possibilities. Nevertheless, it must also be noted that certain patients may respond to their illness or to their identification as being HIV-infected with great inner resources and strength and indeed embrace a spiritual or transcendent outlook that in fact can promote abstinence from alcohol and drugs.

CONCLUSION

The preceding discussion has highlighted some of the salient themes concerning the epidemiology, clinical manifestations, and medical management of drug users with HIV infection. This is clearly a rapidly changing field, with the likely and welcome emergence of new medications and therapeutic strategies that would be expected to alter or expand certain of the approaches outlined here. However, one theme that is likely to remain central to the care of HIV-infected drug users is that the manifestations and treatment of HIV infection in such patients cannot meaningfully be considered without an assessment and understanding of substance abuse and its sequelae, and that effective substance abuse treatment in the AIDS era cannot be undertaken without an appreciation of the profound changes that the HIV epidemic has brought to the field. In closing, one can only hope that all the disciplines relevant to this endeavor may be broad enough in their outlook and perspective to permit and encourage the development of comprehensive approaches to the twin challenges of AIDS and drug addiction in the 1990s and beyond.

Acknowledgments. *The authors would like to acknowledge the invaluable assistance of Carolyn Skowronski, Pharm.D., with the table of drug interactions, and Ernestine Jones with manuscript preparation.*

References

1. U.S. Centers for Disease Control and Prevention. *Pneumocystis* pneumonia—Los Angeles. MMWR 1981;30:250–252.
2. Gottlieb MS, Schroff R, Schanker HM, et al. *Pneumocystis carinii* pneumonia and mucosal candidiasis in previously healthy homosexual men. N Engl J Med 1981;305:1425–1431.
3. Selik RM, Haverkos HW, Curran FW. Acquired immune deficiency syndrome (AIDS) trends in the United States, 1978–1982. Am J Med 1984;38:229–236.
4. U.S. Centers for Disease Control and Prevention. Update: acquired immune deficiency syndrome (AIDS) in the United States, 1981–1988. MMWR 1989;38:229–236.
5. Haverkos HW, Edelman R. The epidemiology of acquired immunodeficiency syndrome among heterosexuals. JAMA 1988;260:1922–1929.
6. Des Jarlais DC, Friedman SR, Stoneburner RL. HIV infection and intravenous drug use: critical issues in transmission dynamics, infection outcomes, and prevention. Rev Infect Dis 1988;10:151–158.
7. Brickner PW, Torres RA, Barnes M, et al. Recommendations for control and prevention of human immunodeficiency (HIV) infection in intravenous drug users. Ann Intern Med 1989;110:833–837.
8. U.S. Centers for Disease Control and Prevention. First 100,000 cases of acquired immunodeficiency syndrome—United States. MMWR 1989;39:561–563.
9. Downs AM, Ancelle-Park RA, Costagliola DC, Rigaut JP, Brunet JB. Monitoring and short-term forecasting of AIDS in Europe [abstract F.C.220]. Paper presented at the Sixth International Conference on AIDS, San Francisco, June, 1990.
10. Moss AR. Epidemiology of AIDS in developed countries. Br Med Bull 1988;44:56–67.
11. Department of Health, State of New Jersey. AIDS surveillance report 1990;October 31.
12. U.S. Centers for Disease Control and Prevention. AIDS associated with injecting-drug use—United States, 1995. MMWR 1996;45(19):392–398.
13. Sato PA, Chin J, Mann JM. Review of AIDS and HIV infection: global epidemiology and statistics. AIDS 1989;3(suppl 1):S301–S307.
14. Wodak A, Dolan K, Imrie A, et al. Antibodies to the human immunodeficiency virus in needles and syringes used by intravenous drug abusers. Med J Aust 1987;147:275–276.
15. Des Jarlais DC, Friedman SR, Choopanya K, Vanichseni S, Ward TP. International epidemiology of HIV and AIDS among injecting drug users. AIDS 1992;6:1053–1068.

16. Nwanyanwu OC, Chu SY, Green TA, Buehler JW, Berkelman RL. Acquired immunodeficiency syndrome in the United States associated with injection drug use, 1981–1991. Am J Drug Alcohol Abuse 1993;19(4):399–408.
17. Selik RM, Castro KG, Pappaioanou M. Racial/ethnic differences in the risk of AIDS in the United States. Am J Public Health 1988;78:1539–1545.
18. Schoenbaum EE, Hartel D, Selwyn PA, et al. Risk factors for human immunodeficiency virus infection in intravenous drug users. N Engl J Med 1989;321:874–879.
19. Lange WR, Snyder FR, Lozovsky D, et al. HIV infection in Baltimore: antibody seroprevalence rates among parenteral drug abusers and prostitutes. Md Med J 1987;36:757–761.
20. Chaisson RE, Moss AR, Onishi R, Osmond D, Carlson JR. Human immunodeficiency virus infection in heterosexual drug users in San Francisco. Am J Public Health 1987;77:757–761.
21. Robert-Guroff M, Weiss SH, Giron JA, et al. Prevalence of antibodies to HTLV-I, -II and -III in intravenous drug abusers from a AIDS-endemic region. JAMA 1986;255:3133–3137.
22. Diaz T, Buehler JW, Castro KG, Ward JW. AIDS trends among Hispanics in the United States. Am J Public Health 1993;83(4):504–509.
23. Haverkos HW, Drotman DP, Morgan M. Prevalence of Kaposi's sarcoma among patients with AIDS. N Engl J Med 1985;312:1518.
24. Stoneburner RC, Des Jarlais DC, Benezra D, et al. A larger spectrum of severe HIV-1 related disease in intravenous drug users in New York City. Science 1988;242:916–919.
25. Farizo KM, Buehler JW, Chamberland ME, et al. Spectrum of disease in persons with human immunodeficiency virus infection in the United States. JAMA 1992;267:1798–1805.
26. Garcia-Leoni ME, Moreno S, Rodeno P, Cerecenado E, Vicente T, Bouza E. Pneumococcal pneumonia in adult hospitalized patients infected with the human immunodeficiency virus. Arch Intern Med 1992;152:1808–1812.
27. U.S. Centers for Disease Control and Prevention. Crack cocaine use among persons with tuberculosis—Contra Costa County, California, 1987–1990. MMWR 1991;40:485–489.
28. Barnes PF, Bloch AB, Davidson PT, Snider DE Jr. Tuberculosis in patients with human immunodeficiency virus infection. N Engl J Med 1991;324:1644–1650.
29. U.S. Centers for Disease Control and Prevention. Tuberculosis—United States, 1985—and the possible impact of human T-lymphotropic virus type III/lymphadenopathy-associated virus infection. MMWR 1986;35:74–76.
30. U.S. Centers for Disease Control and Prevention. Tuberculosis and acquired immunodefi-

ciency syndrome—New York City. MMWR 1987;36:785–795.
31. U.S. Centers for Disease Control and Prevention. Tuberculosis and acquired immunodeficiency syndrome—Florida. MMWR 1986;35:587–590.
32. U.S. Centers for Disease Control and Prevention. Tuberculosis and AIDS—Connecticut. MMWR 1987;36:133–135.
33. Casabona J, Bosch A, Salas T, Sanchez E, Segura A. The effect of tuberculosis as a new AIDS definition criteria in epidemiological surveillance data from a South European area. J Acquir Immune Defic Syndr 1990;3:272–277.
34. Friedman LN, Sullivan GM, Bevilaqua RP, Loscos R. Tuberculosis screening in alcoholics and drug addicts. Am Rev Respir Dis 1987;136:1188–1192.
35. Hirschtick RE, Glassroth J, Jordan MC, et al. Bacterial pneumonia in persons infected with the human immunodeficiency virus. N Engl J Med 1995;333:845–851.
36. Mientjes GH, van Ameijden EJ, van den Hoek AJAR, Coutinho RA. Increasing morbidity without rise in non-AIDS mortality among HIV-infected intravenous drug users in Amsterdam. AIDS 1992;6:207–212.
37. Willocks L, Cowan F, Brettle RP, Emmanuel FXS, Flegg PJ, Burns S. The spectrum of chest infections in HIV positive patients in Edinburgh. J Infect 1992;24:37–42.
38. Batki S. Drug abuse, psychiatric disorders, and AIDS: dual and triple diagnosis. West J Med 1990;152:547–552.
39. Sorensen JL, Constantini MF, London JA. Coping with AIDS: strategies for patients and staff in drug abuse treatment programs. J Psychoactive Drugs 1989;21:435–440.
40. Selwyn PA, Feingold AR, Iezza A, et al. Primary care for patients with human immunodeficiency virus (HIV) infection in a methadone maintenance treatment program. Ann Intern Med 1989;111:761–763.
41. O'Connor PG, Molde S, Henry S, Shockcor WT, Schottenfeld RS. Human immunodeficiency virus infection in intravenous drug users: a model for primary care. Am J Med 1992;93:382–386.
42. Samet JH, Libman H, Steger KA, et al. Compliance with zidovudine therapy in patients infected with human immunodeficiency virus, type 1: a cross-sectional study in a municipal hospital clinic. Am J Med 1992;92:495–501.
43. Selwyn PA, Budner NS, Wasserman WC, Arno PS. Utilization of on-site primary care services by HIV-seropositive and seronegative drug users in a methadone maintenance program. Public Health Rep 1993;108:492–500.
44. Samuels JE, Hendrix J, Hilton M, Marantz PR,

Sloan V, Small CB. Zidovudine therapy in an inner city population. J Acquir Immune Defic Syndr 1990;3:877–883.

45. Friedland GJ, Harris C, Butkus-Small C, et al. Intravenous drug users and the acquired immunodeficiency syndrome (AIDS): demographic, drug use, and needle-sharing patterns. Arch Intern Med 1985;145:1414–1417.

46. Selwyn PA. The impact of the HIV/AIDS epidemic on medical services and drug abuse treatment programs: problems, prospects, and policy. J Subst Abuse Treat (in press).

47. Carpenter CCJ, Fischl M, Hammer SM, et al. Antiretroviral therapy for HIV infection in 1996. JAMA 1996;276:146–154.

48. Marmor M, Des Jarlais DC, Cohen H, et al. Risk factors for infection with human immunodeficiency virus among intravenous drug abusers in New York City. AIDS 1987;1:39–44.

49. Vlahov D, Munoz A, Anthony JC, et al. Association of drug infection patterns with antibody to human immunodeficiency virus type 1 among intravenous drug users in Baltimore, Maryland. Am J Epidemiol 1990;132:847–856.

50. Rolfs RT, Goldberg M, Sharrar RG. Risk factors for syphilis: cocaine use and prostitution. Am J Public Health 1990;80:853–857.

51. U.S. Centers for Disease Control and Prevention. Relationship of syphilis to drug use and prostitution—Connecticut and Philadelphia. MMWR 1988;37:755–764.

52. Fullilove RE, Fullilove MT, Bowser BP, Gross SA. Risk of sexually transmitted disease among black adolescent crack users in Oakland and San Francisco, California. JAMA 1990;263:851–855.

53. Cates WJ. Acquired immunodeficiency syndrome, sexually transmitted disease, and epidemiology. Am J Epidemiol 1990;131:749–758.

54. Goldsmith MF. Sex tied to drugs = STD spread [news]. JAMA 1988;260:2009.

55. Stall R, McKusick L, Wiley J, Coates TJ, Ostrow DG. Alcohol and drug use during sexual activity and compliance with safe sex guidelines for AIDS: the AIDS Behavioral Research Project. Health Educ Q 1986;13:359–371.

56. Mertens TE, Hayes RJ, Smith PG. Epidemiologic methods to study the interaction between HIV infection and other sexually transmitted disease. AIDS 1990;4:57–65.

57. Coates TJ, Stall RD, Catanca JA, Kegeles SM. Behavioral factors in the spread of HIV infection. AIDS 1988;2(suppl 1):S239–S246.

58. Ginzburg HM, Weiss SH, MacDonald MC, Hubbard RL. HTLV-III exposure among drug users. Cancer Res 1985;45(suppl):4605–4608.

59. Des Jarlais DC, Friedman SR, Marmor M, et al. HTLV-III/LAV-associated disease progression and co-factors in a cohort of IV drug users. AIDS 1987;1:111–125.

60. Kaslow RA, Blackwelder WC, Ostrow DG, et al. No evidence for a role of alcohol or other psychoactive drugs in accelerating immunodeficiency in HIV-1-positive individuals. JAMA 1989;261:3424–3429.

61. Psychoactive drug use and AIDS [letter]. JAMA 1990;263:371–373.

62. Rezza G, Lazzarin A, Angarano G, et al. The natural history of HIV infection in intravenous drug users: risk of disease progression in a cohort of seroconvertors. AIDS 1989;3:87–90.

63. Gallant JE, Moore RD, Chaisson RE. Prophylaxis for opportunistic infections in patients with HIV infection. Ann Intern Med 1994;120:932–944.

64. Spooner KM, Lane HC, Masur H. Guide to major clinical trials of antiretroviral therapy administered to patients infected with human immunodeficiency virus. Clin Infect Dis 1996;23:15–27.

65. Branson BM. Early intervention for persons infected with human immunodeficiency virus. Clin Infect Dis 1995;20(1):S3–S22.

66. U.S. Centers for Disease Control and Prevention. USPHS/IDSA guidelines for the prevention of opportunistic infections in persons infected with human immunodeficiency virus: a summary. MMWR 1995;44(RR8):1–34.

67. Mitsuya H, Yarchoan R, Broder S. Molecular targets for AIDS therapy. Science 1990;249:1533–1544.

68. Gallo RC, Salahuddin SZ, Popovic M, et al. Frequent detection and isolation of cytopathic retroviruses (HTLV-III) from patients with AIDS and at risk for AIDS. Science 1984;224:500–503.

69. Barre-Sinoussi F, Chermann JC, Rey F, et al. Isolation of a T-lymphotropic retrovirus from a patient at risk for acquired immune deficiency syndrome (AIDS). Science 1983;220:868–871.

70. Levy JA, Hoffman AD, Kramer SM, et al. Isolation of lymphocytopathic retroviruses from San Francisco patients with AIDS. Science 1984;225:840–842.

71. Coffin J, Haase A, Levy JA, et al. Human immunodeficiency viruses. Science 1986;232:697.

72. Horsburgh CRJ, Ou CY, Jason J, et al. Duration of human immunodeficiency virus infection before detection of antibody. Lancet 1989;2(8664):637–640.

73. Salahuddin SZ, Groopman JE, Markham PD, et al. HTLV-III symptom-free seronegative persons. Lancet 1984;2(8417–18):1418–1420.

74. Ranki A, Valle SL, Krohn M, et al. Long latency precedes overt seroconversion in sexually transmitted human immunodeficiency virus infection. Lancet 1987;2(8559):589–593.

75. Haseltine WA. Silent HIV infections. N Engl J Med 1989;320:1487–1489.

76. Hjelle B, Busch M. Direct methods for detection of HIV-I infection. Arch Pathol Lab Med 1989;113:975–980.

77. Goudsmit J, de Wolf F, Paul DA, Epstein LG, Lange JM, Krone WJ, et al. Expression of human immunodeficiency virus antigen (HIV-Ag) in serum and cerebrospinal fluid during acute and chronic infection. Lancet 1986;2(8500):177–180.

78. Popovic M, Sarnagadharan MG, Read E, Gallo RC. Detection, isolation, and continuous production of cytopathic retroviruses (HTLV-III) from patients with AIDS and pre-AIDS. Science 1984;224:497–500.

79. Volberding PA. HIV quantification: clinical applications. Lancet 1996;347:71–72.

80. World Health Organization. WHO/CDC case definition for AIDS. Wkly Epidem Rec 1986;61:69–73.

81. U.S. Centers for Disease Control and Prevention. Classification system for human T-lymphotropic virus type III/lymphadenopathy-associated virus infection. MMWR 1986;35:334–339.

82. U.S. Centers for Disease Control and Prevention. Revision of the CDC surveillance case definition for acquired immunodeficiency syndrome. MMWR 1987;36(suppl 1S):1S–18S.

83. U.S. Centers for Disease Control and Prevention. 1993 revised classification system for HIV infection and expanded surveillance case definition for AIDS among adults and adolescents. MMWR 1992;41(No. RR-17):1–19.

84. Selik RM, Buehler JW, Karan JM, Chamberland ME, Berkelman RL. Impact of the 1987 revision of the case definition of acquired immune deficiency syndrome in the United States. J Acquir Immune Defic Syndr 1990;3:73–82.

85. Payne SF, Rutherford GW, Lemp GF, Clevenger AC. Effect of the revised AIDS case definition on AIDS reporting in San Francisco: evidence of increased reporting in intravenous drug users. AIDS 1990;4:335–339.

86. Chaisson RE, Stanton DL, Gallant JE, Rucker S, Bartlett JG, Moore RD. Impact of the 1993 revision of the AIDS case definition on the prevalence of AIDS in a clinical setting. AIDS 1993;7:857–862.

87. Des Jarlais DC, Wenston J, Friedman SR, et al. Implications of the revised surveillance definition: AIDS among New York City drug users. Am J Public Health 1992;82:1531–1533.

88. Alcabes P, Friedland G. Injection drug use and human immunodeficiency virus infection. Clin Infect Dis 1995;20:1467–1479.

89. Lui K-J, Darrow WW, Rutherford GW III. A model-based estimate of the mean incubation period for AIDS in homosexual men. Science 1988;240:1333–1335.

90. Gail MH, Rosenberg PS, Goedert JJ. Therapy may explain recent deficits in AIDS incidence. J Acquir Immune Defic Syndr 1990;3:296–306.

91. Northfelt DW, Hayward RA, Shapiro MF. The acquired immunodeficiency syndrome is a primary care disease. Ann Intern Med 1988;109:773–775.

92. Ho DD. Time to hit HIV, early and hard. N Engl J Med 1995:450–451.

93. Arno PS, Shenson D, Siegal NF, Franks P, Lee PR. Economic and policy implications of early intervention in HIV disease. JAMA 1989;262:1493–1498.

94. Francis DP, Anderson RE, Gorman ME, et al. Targeting AIDS prevention and treatment toward HIV-1 infected persons: the concept of early intervention. JAMA 1989;262:2572–2576.

95. Friedland GH. Early treatment for HIV: the time has come. N Engl J Med 1990;322:1000–1002.

96. Dalgleish AG, Beverly PCL, Clapham PR, et al. The CD4 (T4) antigen is an essential component of the receptor for human retrovirus LAV. Nature 1984;321:767–768.

97. McDougal JS, Kennedy MS, Sligh JM, et al. Binding of HTLV-III/LAV to T4+ T cells by a complex of the 110K viral protein and the T4 molecule. Science 1986;231:382–385.

98. Lang W, Perkins H, Anderson RE, et al. Patterns of T lymphocyte changes with human immunodeficiency virus infection: from seroconversion to the development of AIDS. J Acquir Immune Defic Syndr 1989;2:63–69.

99. Brinchmann JE, Vardtal F, Thorsby E. T lymphocyte changes in human immunodeficiency virus infection. J Acquir Immune Defic Syndr 1989;2:398–403.

100. Fauci AS. The human immunodeficiency virus: infectivity and mechanisms of pathogenesis. Science 1988;239:617–622.

101. Goedert JJ, Biggar RJ, Melbye M, et al. Effect of T4 count and cofactors on the incidence of AIDS in homosexual men infected with human immunodeficiency virus. JAMA 1987;257:331–334.

102. Polk BF, Fox R, Brookmeyer R, et al. Predictors of the acquired immunodeficiency syndrome developing in a cohort of seropositive homosexual men. N Engl J Med 1987;316:61–66.

103. U.S. Centers for Disease Control and Prevention. Guidelines for prophylaxis against Pneumocystis carinii pneumonia for persons infected with human immunodeficiency virus. MMWR 1989;38(suppl S-5):1–9.

104. Mellors JW, Rinaldo CR Jr, Gupta P, White RM, Todd JA, Kingsley LA. Prognosis in HIV-1 infection predicted by the quantity of virus in plasma. Science 1996;272:1167–1170.

105. Mellors JW, Kingsley LA, Rinaldo CR, et al. Quantitation of HIV-1 RNA in plasma predicts outcome after seroconversion. Ann Intern Med 1995;122:573–579.

106. Havlir DV, Richman DD. Viral Dynamics of HIV: Implications for drug development and therapeutic strategies. Ann Intern Med 1996;124:984–994.

107. Pantaleo G, Graziosi C, Demarest JF, Butini L, et al. HIV infection is active and progressive in lymphoid tissue during the clinically latent stage of disease. Nature 1993;362:355–358.

108. U.S. Centers for Disease Control and Prevention. Update: acquired immunodeficiency syndrome—United States. MMWR 1986;35:17–21.

109. Glatt AE, Chirgwin K. *Pneumocystis carinii* pneumonia in human immunodeficiency virus-infected patients. Arch Intern Med 1990;150:271–279.

110. World Health Organization. Acquired immunodeficiency syndrome (AIDS): WHO European region—update to 30 September 1990. Wkly Epidemiol Rec 1991;66:33–38.

111. Fleming AF. Opportunistic infections in AIDS in developed and developing countries. Trans R Soc Trop Med Hyg 1990;84(suppl 1):1–6.

112. Sewankambo NK, Mugerwa RD, Goodgame R, et al. Enteropathic AIDS in Uganda: an endoscopic, histological, and microbiological study. AIDS 1987;1:9–13.

113. Serwadda D, Mugerwa RD, Sewankambo NK, et al. Slim disease: a new disease in Uganda and its association with HTLV-III infection. Lancet 1985;2(8460):849–852.

114. Gessain A, Sudaka A, Briere J, et al. Kaposi sarcoma-associated herpes-like virus (human herpes virus type 8) DNA sequences in multicentric Castleman's disease: is there any relevant association in non-human immunodeficiency virus-infected patients? Blood 1996;87(1):414–416.

115. Selwyn PA, Feingold AR, Hartel D, et al. Increased risk of bacterial pneumonia in HIV-infected intravenous users without AIDS. AIDS 1988;2:267–272.

116. Mouton Y, Chidiac C, Senneville E. Pneumonies bacteriennes et virales au cours du SIDA chez les utilizateurs de drogue par voie intraveineuse [abstract Th.B.O.13]. Paper presented at the Fifth International Conference on AIDS, Montreal, June, 1989.

117. Dobkin J, Mandell W, Sethi N. Bacteremic pneumococcal disease as the first manifestation of HIV infection in adults [abstract M.B.P.71]. Paper presented at the Fifth International Conference on AIDS, Montreal, June, 1989.

118. Des Jarlais DC, Friedman SR. HIV and intravenous drug use. AIDS 1988;2(suppl 1):S65–S69.

119. Selwyn PA, Hartel D, Wasserman W, Drucker E. Impact of the AIDS epidemic on morbidity and mortality among intravenous drug users in a New York City methadone maintenance program. Am J Public Health 1989;79:1358–1362.

120. Galli M, Codini G, Carito M, et al. Causes of death in a large cohort of IV drug users in Milan: an update [abstract W.A.P.30]. Paper presented at the Fifth International Conference on AIDS, Montreal, June, 1989.

121. Selwyn PA, Alcabes P, Hartel D, et al. Clinical manifestations and predictors of disease progression in drug users with human immunodeficiency virus infection. N Engl J Med 1992;327:1697–1703.

122. Cherubin C. The medical sequelae of narcotic addiction. Ann Intern Med 1967;67:23–33.

123. Rho YM. Infections as fatal complications of narcotism. N Y State J Med 1972;72:823–830.

124. Caiaffa WT, Graham NMH, Vlahov D. Bacterial pneumonia in adult populations with human immunodeficiency virus (HIV) infection. Am J Epidemiol 1993;138:909–922.

125. Witt DJ, Craven DE, McCabe WR. Bacterial infections in adult patients with the acquired immune deficiency syndrome (AIDS) and AIDS-related complex. Am J Med 1987;82:900–906.

126. Simberkoff MS, El-Sadr W, Schiffman G, Rahal JJJ. Streptococcus pneumoniae infections and bacteremia in patients with acquired immune deficiency syndrome, with a report of pneumococcal vaccine failure. Am Rev Respir Dis 1984;103:1174–1176.

127. Polsky B, Gold JWM, Whimbey E, et al. Bacterial pneumonia in patients with the acquired immunodeficiency syndrome. Ann Intern Med 1986;104:38–41.

128. Gilks CF, Brindle RJ, Otieno LS, et al. Life-threatening bacteremia in HIV-1 seropositive adults admitted to hospital in Nairobi, Kenya. Lancet 1990;336:545–549.

129. Schrager LK. Bacterial infections in AIDS patients. AIDS 1988;2(suppl 1):S183–S189.

130. Friedland GH, Selwyn PA. Infections in injection drug users (excluding AIDS). In: Isselbacher KE, Braunwald E, et al., eds. Harrison's principles of internal medicine. New York: McGraw-Hill, 1994.

131. Slim J, Boghassian J, Perez G, Johnson E. Comparative analysis of bacterial endocarditis in HIV+ and HIV- intravenous drug abusers [abstract 8027]. Paper presented at the Fourth International Conference on AIDS, Stockholm, June, 1988.

132. Poblete R, Sone C, Fishchl M. Staphylococcus aureus endocarditis in HIV+ and HIV-intravenous drug abusers [abstract Th.A.O.24]. Paper presented at the Fifth International Conference on AIDS, Montreal, June, 1989.

133. Weisse AB, Heller DR, Schimenti RJ, Montgomery RL, Kapila R. The febrile parenteral drug user: a prospective study in 121 patients. Am J Med 1993;94(3):274–280.

134. Sheagren JN. Endocarditis complicating parenteral drug abuse. In: Remington JS, Swartz MN, eds. Current clinical topics in infectious diseases. New York: McGraw-Hill, 1981:211–233.

135. Pujol M, Pena C, Pallares R, Ariza J, Dominguez MA, Gudiol F. Nosocomial Staphylococcus aureus bacteremia among nasal carriers of methicillin-resistant and methicillin-susceptible strains. Am J Med 1996;100(5):509–516.

136. Jernigan JA, Titus MG, Groschel DH, Getchell-White S, Farr BM. The effectiveness of contact isolation during a hospital outbreak of methicillin-resistant Staphylococcus aureus. Am J Epidemiol 1996;143(5):496–504.

137. Moreno F, Crisp C, Jorgensen JH, Patterson JE. Methicillin-resistant Staphylococcus aureus as a community organism. Clin Infect Dis 1995;21(5):1308–1312.

138. Wells CL, Juni BA, Cameron SB, et al. Stool carriage, clinical isolation, and mortality during an outbreak of vancomycin-resistant enterococci in hospitalized medical and/or surgical patients. Clin Infect Dis 1995;21(1):45–50.

139. Shay DK, Maloney SA, Montecalvo M, et al. Epidemiology and mortality risk of vancomycin-resistant enterococcal bloodstream infections. Clin Infect Dis 1995;172(4):993–1000.

140. Chirurgi VA, Edelstein H, McCabe R. Pneumococcal bacteremia as a marker for human immunodeficiency virus infection in patients without AIDS. Southern Med J 1990;83:895–899.

141. Hopewell PC. Prevention of lung infections associated with human immunodeficiency virus infection. Thorax 1989;44:1038–1044.

142. Lane CH, Masur H, Edgar LC, et al. Abnormalities of B-cell activation and immunoregulation in patients with the acquired immunodeficiency syndrome. N Engl J Med 1983;309:453–458.

143. Pahwa SG, Quilop MTJ, Lange M, et al. Defective B-lymphocyte function in homosexual men in relation to the acquired immunodeficiency syndrome. Ann Intern Med 1984;101:757–763.

144. Ammann AJ, Schiffman G, Abrams D, et al. B-cell immunodeficiency in acquired immune deficiency syndrome. JAMA 1094;251:1447–1449.

145. Baron AD, Hollander H. Pseudomonas aeruginosa bronchopulmonary infection in late human immunodeficiency virus disease. Am Rev Respir Dis 1993;148:992–996.

146. Kielhofner M, Atmar RL, Hamill RJ, Musher DM. Life-threatening Pseudomonas aeruginosa infections in patients with human immunodeficiency virus infection. Clin Infect Dis 1992;14:403–411.

147. Mendelson MH, Gurtman A, Szabo S, et al. Pseudomonas aeruginosa bacteremia in patients with AIDS. Clin Infect Dis 1994;18:886–895.

148. Fichtenbaum CJ, Woeltje KF, Powderly WG. Serious Pseudomonas aeruginosa infections in patients with human immunodeficiency syndrome virus: a case-control study. Clin Infect Dis 1994;19:417–422.

149. Schuchat A, Broome CV, Hightower A, Costa SJ, Parkin W. Use of surveillance for invasive pneumococcal disease to estimate the size of the immunosuppressed HIV-infected population. JAMA 1991;265(24):3275–3279.

150. Haverkos HW, Lange WR. Serious infections other than human immunodeficiency virus among intravenous drug users. J Infect Dis 1990;161:894–902.

151. Gordin FM, Simon GL, Wofsy CD, Mills J. Adverse reactions to trimethoprim-sulfamethoxazole in patients with AIDS. Ann Intern Med 1984;100:495–499.

152. U.S. Centers for Disease Control and Prevention. Pneumococcal polysaccharide vaccine. MMWR 1989;38:64–76.

153. Ballet JJ, Sulcebe G, Couderc LJ, et al. Impaired antipneumococcal antibody response in patients with AIDS-related generalized lymphadenopathy. Clin Exp Immunol 1987;68:479–487.

154. Huang KL, Ruben FL, Rinaldo CRJ, et al. Antibody responses after influenza and pneumococcal immunization in HIV-infected homosexual men. JAMA 1987;257:2047–2050.

155. Klein RS, Selwyn PA, Maude D, et al. Response to pneumococcal vaccine among asymptomatic heterosexual partners of persons with AIDS and intravenous drug users infected with human immunodeficiency virus. J Infect Dis 1989;160:826–831.

156. Herb F, Watters JK, Case P, Petitti D. Endocarditis, subcutaneous abscesses, and other

bacterial infections in intravenous drug users and their association with skin-cleaning at drug injection sites [abstract Th:D.0.4]. Paper presented at the Fifth International Conference on AIDS, Montreal, June, 1989.

157. Vlahov D, Sullivan M, Astemborski J, Nelson KE. Bacterial infections and skin cleaning prior to injection among intravenous drug users. Public Health Rep 1992;107:595–598.

158. Hoffman J, Cetron MS, Farley MM, et al. The prevalence of drug-resistant Streptococcus pneumoniae in Atlanta. N Engl J Med 1995; 333:481–486.

159. Appelbaum PC. Antimicrobial resistance in Streptococcus pneumoniae: an overview. Clin Infect Dis 1992;15:77–83.

160. Braun MM, Truman BI, Maguire B, et al. Increasing incidence of tuberculosis in a prison inmate population: association with HIV infection. JAMA 1989;261:393–397.

161. Africa's tuberculosis burden and chemoprophylaxis [editorial]. Lancet 1990;335:1249–1250.

162. Selwyn PA, Hartel D, Lewis VA, et al. A prospective study of the risk of tuberculosis among intravenous drug users with HIV infection. N Engl J Med 1989;320:545–550.

163. Hopewell PC. Impact of human immunodeficiency virus infection on the epidemiology, clinical features, management, and control of tuberculosis. Clin Infect Dis 1992;15:540–547.

164. Chaisson RE, Slutkin G. Tuberculosis and human immunodeficiency virus infection. J Infect Dis 1989;159:96–100.

165. U.S. Centers for Disease Control and Prevention. Tuberculosis and human immunodeficiency virus infection: recommendations of the advisory committee for the elimination of tuberculosis (ACET). MMWR 1989;38:236–250.

166. Harries AD. Tuberculosis and human immunodeficiency virus infection in developing countries. Lancet 1990;335:387–390.

167. Pitchenik AE. Tuberculosis control and the AIDS epidemic in developing countries. Ann Intern Med 1990;113:89–90.

168. Rieder HL, Cauthen GM, Kelly GD, et al. Tuberculosis in the United States. JAMA 1989; 262:385–389.

169. Barnes PF, Bloch AB, Davidson PT, Snider DE Jr. Tuberculosis in patients with human immunodeficiency virus infection. N Engl J Med 1991;324:1644–1650.

170. Hopewell PC. Impact of human immunodeficiency virus infection on the epidemiology, clinical features, management, and control of tuberculosis. Clin Infect Dis 1992;15:540–547.

171. Dolin PJ, Raviglione MC, Kochi A. Global tuberculosis incidence and mortality during 1990–2000. Bull World Health Organ 1994: 72:213–220.

172. Selwyn PA, Hartel D, Lewis VA, et al. A prospective study of the risk of tuberculosis among intravenous drug users with HIV infection. N Engl J Med 1989;320:545–550.

173. Pitchenik AE, Cole C, Russell BW, et al. Tuberculosis, atypical mycobacteriosis, and the acquired immunodeficiency syndrome among Haitian and non-Haitian patients in south Florida. Ann Intern Med 1984;101:641–645.

174. Daley CL, Small PM, Schecter GF, Schoolnik GK. An outbreak of tuberculosis with accelerated progression among persons infected with the human immunodeficiency virus. N Engl J Med 1992;326:231–235.

175. Small PM, Hopewell PC, Singh SP, Paz A. The epidemiology of tuberculosis in San Francisco. N Engl J Med 1994;330:1703–1709.

176. Alland DA, Kalkut GE, Moss AR, McAdam RA, et al. Transmission of tuberculosis in New York City. N Engl J Med 1994;330:1710–1716.

177. Small PM, Shafer RW, Hopewell PC, Singh SP, Murphy MJ. Exogenous reinfection with multidrug-resistant Mycobacterium tuberculosis in patients with advanced HIV infection. N Engl J Med 1993;328:1137–1144.

178. Shafer RW, Edlin BR. Tuberculosis in patients infected with human immunodeficiency virus: perspective on the past decade. Clin Infect Dis 1996;22:683–704.

179. Valway SE, Greifinger RB, Papania M, Kilburn JO, Woodley C. Multidrug-resistant tuberculosis in the New York State prison system, 1990–1991. J Infect Dis 1994;170:151–156.

180. Valway SE, Richards SB, Kovacovich J, Greifinger RB, et al. Outbreak of multidrug-resistant tuberculosis in a New York State prison, 1991. Am J Epidemiol 1994;140(2):113–122.

181. Friedman CR, Stoeckle MY, Kreiswirth BN, Johnson WD, et al. Transmission of multidrug-resistant tuberculosis in a large urban setting. Am J Respir Crit Care Med 1995;152:355–359.

182. Sunderam G, McDonald RJ, Maniatis T, et al. Tuberculosis as a manifestation of the acquired immunodeficiency syndrome (AIDS). JAMA 1986;256:362–366.

183. U.S. Centers for Disease Control and Prevention. National seroprevalence surveys, 1992. Washington, DC: U.S. Government Printing Office, 1993.

184. Reichman LB, Felton CP, Edsall JR. Drug dependence a possible new risk factor for tuberculosis disease. Arch Intern Med 1979;139:337–339.

185. Pape JW, Simone SJ, Ho JL, Hafner A, Johnson WD Jr. Effect of isoniazid prophylaxis on incidence of active tuberculosis and progression of HIV infection. Lancet 1993;342:268–272.

186. Moreno S, Baraia-Extaburu J, Bouza E, et al. Risk for developing tuberculosis among anergic patients infected with HIV. Ann Intern Med 1993;119:194–198.

187. Wadhawan D, Hira S, Mwansa N, Tembo G, Perine PL. Isoniazid prophylaxis among patients with HIV-1 infection [abstract Th.B.510]. Paper presented at the Sixth International Conference on AIDS, San Francisco, June, 1990.

188. Nunn P, Mungai M, Nyamwaya J. The effect of human immunodeficiency virus type-1 on the infectiousness of tuberculosis. Tuber Lung Dis 1994;75:25–32.

189. Jones BE, Young SMM, Antoniskis D, Davidson PT, Kramer F, Barnes PF. Relationship of the manifestations of tuberculosis to CD4 cell counts in patients with human immunodeficiency virus infection. Am Rev Respir Dis 1993;148:1292–1297.

190. Theuer CP, Hopewell PC, Elias D, et al. Human immunodeficiency virus infection in tuberculosis patients. J Infect Dis 1990;162:8–12.

191. De Cock KM, Soro B, Coulibaly IM, Lucas SB. Tuberculosis and HIV infection in Sub-Saharan Africa. JAMA 1992;268:1581–1587.

192. Whalen C, Horsburgh CR, Hom D, Lahart C, Simberkoff M, Ellner J. Accelerated course of human immunodeficiency virus infection after tuberculosis. Am J Respir Crit Care Med 1995; 151:129–135.

193. Shafer RW, Goldberg R, Sierra M, Glatt AE. Frequency of Mycobacterium tuberculosis bacteremia in patients with tuberculosis in an area endemic for AIDS. Am Rev Respir Dis 1989;140:1611–1613.

194. Louie E, Rice LB, Holzman RS. Tuberculosis in non-Haitian patients with acquired immunodeficiency syndrome. Chest 1986;90:542–545.

195. Pitchenik AE, Burr J, Suarez M, et al. Human T-cell lymphotropic virus-III (HTLV-III) seropositivity and related disease among 71 consecutive patients in whom tuberculosis was diagnosed: a prospective study. Am Rev Respir Dis 1987;135:875–879.

196. Pitchenik AE, Rubinson HA. The radiographic appearance of tuberculosis in patients with the acquired immune deficiency syndrome (AIDS) and pre-AIDS. Am Rev Respir Dis 1985; 131:393–396.

197. American Thoracic Society, U.S. Centers for Disease Control and Prevention. Treatment of tuberculosis and tuberculosis infection in adults and children. Clin Infect Dis 1995; 21:9–27.

198. U.S. Centers for Disease Control and Prevention. Initial therapy for tuberculosis in the era of multidrug resistance. Recommendations of the Advisory Council for the Elimination of Tuberculosis. MMWR 1993;42(RR-7):1–8.

199. Frieden TR, Sterling T, Pablos-Mendez A, et al. The emergence of drug-resistant tuberculosis in New York City. N Engl J Med 1993; 328:521.

200. Frieden TR, Fujiwara PI, Washko RM, Hamburg MA. Tuberculosis in New York City—turning the tide. N Engl J Med 1995;333:229–233.

201. U.S. Centers for Disease Control and Prevention. National action plan to combat multidrug-resistant tuberculosis; meeting the challenge of multidrug-resistant tuberculosis; summary of a conference; management of persons exposed to multidrug-resistant tuberculosis. MMWR 1992;41(RR-11):5–48.

202. U.S. Centers for Disease Control and Prevention. Prevention and control of tuberculosis in U.S. communities with at-risk minority populations: recommendations of the Advisory Council for the Elimination of Tuberculosis and Prevention and control of tuberculosis among homeless persons: recommendations of the Advisory Council for the Elimination of Tuberculosis. MMWR 1992;41(RR-5):1–11.

203. Gourevitch MN, Wasserman W, Panero MS, Selwyn PA. Successful adherence to observed prophylaxis and treatment of tuberculosis among drug users in a methadone program. J Addict Dis 1996;15(1):93–104.

204. Altice FL, Fleck EM, Selwyn PA, et al. Provisions of health care and HIV counseling and testing for clients of the New Haven Needle Exchange Program [abstract PO-D17–3927]. Paper presented at the Ninth International Conference on AIDS, Berlin, June, 1993.

205. Altice F, Tanguay S, Hunt D, Blanchette EA, Selwyn PA. Demographics of HIV infection and utilization of medical services among IDU's in a women's prison [abstract PoC4358]. Paper presented at the Eighth International Conference on AIDS, Amsterdam, June, 1992.

206. Chaulk CP, Moore-Rice K, Rizzo R, Chaisson RE. Eleven years of community-based directly observed therapy for tuberculosis. JAMA 1995;274:945–951.

207. Iseman MD, Cohn DL, Sbarbaro JA. Directly observed treatment of tuberculosis: we can't

afford not to try it. N Engl J Med 1993;328: 576–578.

208. Selwyn PA, Sckell BM, Alcabes P, Friedland GH, Klein RS, Schoenbaum EE. High risk of active tuberculosis in HIV-infected drug users with cutaneous anergy. JAMA 1992;268: 504–509.

209. Iseman MD. Is standard chemotherapy adequate in tuberculosis patients infected with the HIV? Am Rev Respir Dis 1987;136:1326.

210. Eyster ME, Fried MW, Di Bisceglie AM, Goerdert JJ. Increasing hepatitis C virus RNA levels in hemophiliacs: relationship to human immunodeficiency virus infection and liver disease. Multicenter Hemophilia Cohort Study. Blood 1994;84(4):1020–1023.

211. Gumber SC, Chopra S. Hepatitis C: a multifaceted disease. Review of extrahepatic manifestations. Ann Intern Med 1995;123(8):615–620.

212. Kreek MJ. Medical safety and side effects of methadone in tolerant individuals. JAMA 1973;223:665–668.

213. U.S. Centers for Disease Control and Prevention. Screening for tuberculosis and tuberculous infection in high-risk populations; and the use of preventive therapy for tuberculous infection in the United States: recommendations of the Advisory Committee for Elimination of Tuberculosis. MMWR 1990;39(RR-8):1–12.

214. Ahmed AR, Blose DA. Delayed type hypersensitivity skin testing: a review. Arch Dermatol 1983;119:934–945.

215. Dobozin BS, Judson FN, Cohn DL, et al. The relationship of abnormalities of cellular immunity to antibodies to HTLV-III in homosexual men. Cell Immunol 1986;98:156–171.

216. Neshin S, Bishburg E. Comparison of two skin test systems for anergy in intravenous drug users on methadone maintenance [abstract S.B.541]. Paper presented at the Sixth International Conference on AIDS, San Francisco, June, 1990.

217. Robert CF, Hirschel B, Rochat T, Deglon JJ. Tuberculin skin reactivity in HIV-seropositive intravenous drug addicts. N Engl J Med 1989; 321:1268.

218. U.S. Centers for Disease Control and Prevention. Tuberculin reactions in apparently healthy HIV-seropositive and HIV-seronegative women—Uganda. MMWR 1990;39:638–646.

219. U.S. Centers for Disease Control and Prevention. Purified protein derivative (PPD)-tuberculin anergy and HIV infection: guidelines for anergy testing and management of anergic persons at risk of tuberculosis. MMWR 1991; 40(RR-5):27–33.

220. Janis EM, Allen DW, Glesby MJ, et al. Tuberculin skin test reactivity, anergy, and HIV infection in hospitalized patients. Am J Med 1996;100:186–192.

221. U.S. Centers for Disease Control and Prevention. Guidelines for preventing the transmission of mycobacterium tuberculosis in healthcare facilities [abstract]. Federal Register 1994;59:54242–54250.

222. Klein RS, Friedland GH. Transmission of human immunodeficiency virus type 1(HIV-1) by exposure to blood: defining the risk. Ann Intern Med 1990;113:729–730.

223. Pitchenik AE, Bun J, Laufer M, et al. Outbreaks of drug-resistant tuberculosis to health-care workers and HIV-infected patients in an urban hospital—Florida. MMWR 1990;39:718–722.

224. U.S. Centers for Disease Control and Prevention. Mycobacterium tuberculosis transmission in a health clinic—Florida, 1988. MMWR 1989;38:256–264.

225. U.S. Centers for Disease Control and Prevention. Tuberculosis outbreak among persons in a residential facility for HIV-infected persons—San Francisco. MMWR 1991;40:649–652.

226. U.S. Centers for Disease Control and Prevention. Nosocomial transmission of multidrug-resistant tuberculosis among HIV-infected persons—Florida and New York: 1988–1991. MMWR 1991;40:585–591.

227. DiPerri G, Cruciani M, Danzi MC, et al. Nosocomial epidemic of active tuberculosis among HIV-infected patients. Lancet 1989;2(8678–8679):1502–1504.

228. U.S. Centers for Disease Control and Prevention. Transmission of multidrug-resistant tuberculosis from an HIV-positive client in a residential substance-abuse treatment facility—Michigan. MMWR 1991;40:129–131.

229. Shafer RW, Chirgwin KD, Glatt AE, Dahdouh MA, Landesman SH, Suster B. HIV prevalence, immunosuppression, and drug resistance in patients with tuberculosis in an area endemic for AIDS. AIDS 1991;5:399–405.

230. U.S. Centers for Disease Control and Prevention. Nosocomial transmission of multidrug-resistant tuberculosis to health care workers and HIV-infected patients in an urban hospital—Florida. MMWR 1989;39:425–441.

231. U.S. Centers for Disease Control and Prevention. A strategic plan for the elimination of tuberculosis in the United States. MMWR 1989; 38(S-3):1–25.

232. Nardell EA. Dodging droplet nuclei: reducing the probability of nosocomial tuberculosis transmission in the AIDS era. Am Rev Respir Dis 1990;142:501–503.

233. Quinn TC, Glasser D, Cannon RD, et al. Human immunodeficiency virus infection among patients attending clinics for sexually transmitted diseases. N Engl J Med 1987;318:197–203.

234. Stamm WE, Handsfield HA, Rompalo AM, et al. The association between genital ulcer disease and acquisition of HIV infection in homosexual men. JAMA 1988;260:1429–1433.

235. Sapira JD. The narcotic addict as a medical patient. Am J Med 1968;45:555–588.

236. Des Jarlais DC, Friedman SR. HIV infection among intravenous drug users: epidemiology and risk reduction. AIDS 1987;1:67–76.

237. Office of Technology Assessment. How effective is AIDS education? Washington, DC: Office of Technology Education, 1988.

238. McCusker J, Westenhouse J, Stoddard AM, et al. Use of drugs and alcohol by homosexually active men in relation to sexual practices. J Acquir Immune Defic Syndr 1990;3:729–736.

239. Johns DR, Tierney M, Felsenstein D. Alteration in the natural history of neurosyphilis by concurrent infection with the human immunodeficiency virus. N Engl J Med 1987;316:1569–1572.

240. Berry CD, Hooton TM, Collier AC, Lukehart SA. Neurologic relapse after benzathine penicillin therapy for secondary syphilis in a patient with HIV infection. N Engl J Med 1987;316: 1587–1589.

241. Lukehart SA, Hook EWI, Baker-Zander SA, et al. Invasion of the central nervous system by Treponema pallidum: implications for diagnosis and therapy. Ann Intern Med 1988;109: 855–862.

242. Hook EW III. Syphilis and HIV infection. J Infect Dis 1989;160:530–534.

243. Musher DM, Hamill RJ, Baughn RE. Effect of human immunodeficiency virus infection on the course of syphilis and on the response to treatment. Ann Intern Med 1990;113:872–881.

244. Tramont EC. Syphilis in the AIDS era. N Engl J Med 1987;316:1600–1601.

245. Feingold AR, Vermund SH, Burke RD, et al. Cervical cytologic abnormalities and papillomavirus in women infected with human immunodeficiency virus. J Acquir Immune Defic Syndr 1990;3:896–903.

246. Byrne MA, Taylor-Robinson D, Munday PE, Harris JRW. The common occurrence of human papillomavirus infection and intraepithelial neoplasia in women infected by HIV. AIDS 1989;3:379–382.

247. Henry MJ, Stanley MW, Cruikeshank S, Carson L. Association of human immunodeficiency virus-induced immunosuppression with human papillomavirus infection and cervical intraepithelial neoplasia. Am J Obstet Gynecol 1989;160:352–353.

248. Greenspan D, de Viliers EM, Greenspan JS, De Souza YG, zur Hausen H. Unusual HPV types in oral warts in association with HIV infection. J Oral Pathol 1988;17:482–487.

249. Friedmann W, Schafer A, Schwartlander B. Cervical neoplasia in HIV-infected women [abstract W.C.P.53]. Paper presented at the Fifth International Conference on AIDS, Montreal, June, 1989.

250. Wright TC Jr, Ellerbrock TV, Chiasson MA, Devanter NV, Sun X-W. Cervical intraepithelial neoplasia in women infected with human immunodeficiency virus: prevalence, risk factors, and validity of Papanicolaou smears. Obstet Gynecol 1994;84:591–597.

251. Palefsky JM, Gonzales J, Greenblatt R, Ahn DK, Hollander H. Anal intraepithelial neoplasia and anal papillomavirus infection among homosexual males with group IV HIV disease. JAMA 1990;263:2911–2916.

252. U.S. Centers for Disease Control and Prevention. Recommendations for diagnosing and treating syphilis in HIV-infected patients. MMWR 1988;37:601–608.

253. Gourevitch MN, Hartel D, Schoenbaum EE, et al. A prospective study of syphilis and HIV infection among injection drug users receiving methadone in the Bronx, N.Y. Am J Public Health 1996;86:1112–1115.

254. Gourevitch MN, Selwyn PA, Davenny K, et al. Effects of HIV infection on the serologic manifestations and response to treatment of syphilis in intravenous drug users. Ann Intern Med 1993;118:350–355.

255. Yinnon AM, Coury-Doniger P, Polito R, Reichman RC. Serologic response to treatment of syphilis in patients with HIV infection. Arch Intern Med 1996;156(3):321–325.

256. Hicks CB, Benson PM, Lupton GP, Tramont EC. Seronegative secondary syphilis in a patient infected with the human immunodeficiency virus (HIV) with Kaposi sarcoma: a diagnostic dilemma. Ann Intern Med 1987;107: 492–495.

257. Matlow AG, Rachlis AR. Syphilis serology in human immunodeficiency virus infected patients with symptomatic neurosyphilis: case report and review. Rev Infect Dis 1990;12: 703–706.

258. Haas JS, Bolan G, Larsen SA, et al. Sensitivity of treponemal tests for detecting prior treated syphilis during human immunodeficiency virus infection. J Infect Dis 1990;162:862–866.

259. Rolfs RT. Treatment of syphilis. Clin Infect Dis 1995;20(1):S23–S38.

260. U.S. Centers for Disease Control and Prevention. 1993 sexually transmitted diseases treatment guidelines. MMWR 1993;42(RR-14): 1–100.

261. Hutchinson CM, Hook EW, Sheperd M, Verley J, Rompalo AM. Altered clinical presentation of early syphilis in patients with human immunodeficiency virus infection. Ann Intern Med 1994;121:94–99.

262. Palefsky JM, Holly EA, Gonzales J, Berline J, Ahn DK, Greenspan JS. Detection of human papillomavirus DNA in anal intraepithelial neoplasia and anal cancer. Cancer Res 1991; 51:1014–1019.

263. U.S. Centers for Disease Control and Prevention. Risk for cervical disease in HIV-infected women—N.Y.C. MMWR 1990;39:846–849.

264. Hoegsberg B, Abulafia O, Sedlis A, et al. Sexually transmitted diseases and human immunodeficiency virus infection among women with pelvic inflammatory disease. Am J Obstet Gynecol 1990;163:1135–1139.

265. Dalakas M, Wichman A, Sever J. AIDS and the nervous system. JAMA 1989;261:2396–2399.

266. Guilian D, Vaca K, Noonan CA. Secretion of neurotoxins by mononuclear phagocytes infected with HIV-1. Science 1990;250: 1593–1596.

267. Levy RM, Bredesen DE, Rosenblum ML. Neurologic complications of HIV infection. Am Fam Physician 1990;41:517–536.

268. Ho DD, Bredesen DE, Vinters HV, Daar ES. The acquired immunodeficiency syndrome (AIDS) dementia complex. Ann Intern Med 1989;111:400–410.

269. Navia BA, Jordan BD, Price RW. The AIDS dementia complex: I. Clinical features. Ann Neurol 1986;19:517–524.

270. Portegies P, Enting RH, de Gans J, et al. Presentation and course of AIDS dementia complex: 10 years of follow-up in Amsterdam, The Netherlands. AIDS 1993;7:669–675.

271. Portegies P. Review of antiretroviral therapy in the prevention of HIV-related AID dementia complex. Drugs 1995;49(suppl 1):25–31.

272. Levy RM, Mills CM, Posin JP, et al. The efficacy and clinical impact of brain imaging in neurologically symptomatic AIDS patients: a prospective CT/MRI study. J Acquir Immune Defic Syndr 1990;3:461–471.

273. Bacellar H, Munoz A, Miller EN, et al. Temporal trends in the incidence of HIV-1-related neurologic diseases: Multicenter AIDS Cohort Study, 1985–1992. Neurol 1994;44(10):1892–1900.

274. Engstorm JW, Lowenstein DH, Bredesen DE. Cerebral infarctions and transient neurologic deficits associated with acquired immunodeficiency syndrome. Am J Med 1989;86: 528–532.

275. Amine ARC. Neurosurgical complications of heroin addiction: brain abscess and mycotic aneurysm. Surg Neurol 1977;7:385–386.

276. Elliott JH, O'Day DM, Gutow GS, Podgorski SF, Akrabawi P. Mycotic endophthalmitis in drug abusers. Am J Ophthalmol 1979;88: 66–72.

277. Rowbotham MC. Neurologic aspects of cocaine abuse. West J Med 1988;149:442–449.

278. Levine SR, Brust JCM, Futrell N, et al. Cerebrovascular complications of the use of the "crack" from alkaloidal cocaine. N Engl J Med 1990;323:699–704.

279. Kaku DA, Lowenstein DH. Emergence of recreational drug use as a major risk factor for stroke in young adults. Ann Intern Med 1990; 113:821–827.

280. Wiley CA. Neuromuscular disease of AIDS. FASEB J 1989;3:2503–2511.

281. Yarchoan R, Berg G, Prouwers P, et al. Response of human immunodeficiency virus-associated neurological disease to 3'-azido-2',3'-dideoxythymidine. Lancet 1987;1(8525): 132–134.

282. Dalakas MC, Yarchoan R, Spitzer R, Sever JL. Treatment of HIV-related polyneuropathy with 3'-azido-2,3',-dideoxythymidine (AZT). Ann Neurol 1988;23(suppl):92–94.

283. Rubin AR. Neurologic complications of intravenous drug abuse. Hosp Pract [Off] 1987; 22:279–288.

284. Yarchoan R, Perno CF, Thomas RV, et al. Phase I studies of 2',3'-dideoxycytidine in severe human immunodeficiency virus infection as a single agent and alternating with zidovudine (AZT). Lancet 1988;1(8577):76–81.

285. Lambert JS, Seidlin M, Reichman RC, et al. 2',3'-dideoxyinosine (ddI) in patients with the acquired immunodeficiency syndrome or AIDS-related complex. N Engl J Med 1990; 332:1333–1340.

286. Cooley TP, Kunches LM, Saunders CA, et al. Once-daily administration of 2',3'-dideoxyinosine in patients with the acquired immunodeficiency syndrome or AIDS-related complex. N Engl J Med 1990;322:1340–1345.

287. Takatsuki K, Uchiyama J, Sagawa K, et al. Adult T-cell leukemia in Japan. In: Seno S, Takaku F, Irino S, eds. Topics in hematology. Amsterdam: Exerpta Medica, 1977:73–77.

288. Poiesz BJ, Ruscetti FW, Gazdar AF, et al. Detection and isolation of type-C retrovirus particles from fresh and cultured lymphocytes of a patient with cutaneous T-cell lymphoma. Proc Natl Acad Sci U S A 1980;77:7415–7419.

289. Blattner W, Takatsuki K, Gallo RC. Human T-cell leukemia-lymphoma virus and adult T-cell leukemia. JAMA 1983;250:1074–1082.

290. Osame M, Usuku K, Izumo S, et al. HTLV-I associated myelopathy, a new clinical entity. Lancet 1986;i:1031–1032.

291. Jacobson S, Raine CS, Mingiolio ES, McFarlin DE. Isolation of the HTLV-I-like retrovirus from patients with tropical spastic paraparesis. Nature 1988;331:540–543.

292. Williams AE, Fang CT, Slaman DJ, et al. Seroprevalence and epidemiological correlates of HTLV-I infection in U.S. blood donors. Science 1988;240:643–646.

293. Blattner W. Human T-lymphotropic viruses and diseases of long latency. Ann Intern Med 1989;111:4–6.

294. U.S. Centers for Disease Control and Prevention. Human T-lymphotropic virus type I screening in volunteer blood donors—United States. MMWR 1990;39:915–924.

295. Gout O, Baulac M, Gessain A, et al. Rapid development of myelopathy after HTLV-I infection acquired by transfusion during cardiac transplantation. N Engl J Med 1990;322: 383–388.

296. Lee H, Sawson P, Shorty V, et al. High rate of HTLV-II infection in seropositive IV drug abusers in New Orleans. Science 1989;244: 471–475.

297. Khabbaz RF, Onorato IM, Cannon RO, et al. Seroprevalence in HTLV-I and HTLV-II among intravenous drug users and persons in clinics for sexually transmitted diseases. N Engl J Med 1992;326:375–380.

298. Khabbaz RF, Hartel D, Lairmore M, et al. Human T-lymphotropic virus type II infection in a cohort of New York: intravenous drug users: an old infection? J Infect Dis 1991;163: 252–256.

299. Lentino JR, Pachucki CT, Schaaff D, et al. Prevalence of HTLV-I/HIV-I infection among male intravenous drug abusers and their sexual partners in Chicago [abstract Th.A.P.1]. Paper presented at the Fifth International Conference on AIDS, Montreal, June, 1989.

300. Feigal EG, Murphy E, Drummond J, et al. HTLV-I infection in intravenous drug addicts and gay men in San Francisco [abstract Th.A.P.24]. Paper presented at the Fifth International Conference on AIDS, Montreal, June, 1989.

301. Dosik A, Anandarkrishnan A, Denic S. Adult T-cell leukemia/lymphoma: a cluster in Brooklyn, a new endemic area? Blood 1985;66(suppl 1):187a.

302. Shibata D, Brynes RK, Rabinowitz A, et al. Human T-cell lymphotropic virus type I (HTLV-I)-associated adult T-cell leukemia-lymphoma in a patient infected with HIV-I. Ann Intern Med 1989;111:871–875.

303. Page JB, Lai S, Chitwood DD, et al. HTLV-I/II seropositivity and death from AIDS among HIV-1 seropositive intravenous drug users. Lancet 1990;335:1439–1441.

304. Weiss SH, Klein C, French J, et al. Mortality associated with human T-cell lymphotropic virus type 2 (HTLV-2) infection in intravenous drug abusers [abstract Th.C.101]. Paper presented at the Seventh International Conference on AIDS, Florence, Italy, June, 1991.

305. Stimmel B, Vernace S, Schaffner F. Hepatitis B surface antigen and antibody in asymptomatic drug users. JAMA 1975;243:1135–1138.

306. Mangia JL, Kim YM, Brown MR, et al. HB-Ag and HB-Ab in asymptomatic drug addicts. Am J Gastroenterol 1976;65:121–126.

307. Minichiello L, Rettia R. Trends in intravenous drug abuse as reflected in national hepatitis reporting. Am J Public Health 1976;66:872–877.

308. Levine OS, Vlahov D, Brookmeyer R, Cohn S, Nelson KE. Difference in the incidence of hepatitis B and human immunodeficiency virus among injection drug users. J Infect Dis 1996;173(3):579–583.

309. Garfein RS, Vlahov D, Galai N, Doherty MC, Nelson KE. Viral infections in short-term injection drug users: the prevalence of the hepatitis C, hepatitis B, human immunodeficiency, and human T-lymphotropic viruses. Am J Public Health 1996;86(5):655–661.

310. Dienstag JL, Perrillo RP, Schiff ER, Bartholomew M, Vicary C, Rubin M. A preliminary trial of lamivudine for chronic hepatitis B infection. N Engl J Med 1995;333: 1657–1661.

311. Marroni M, Gresele P, Landonio G, et al. Interferon-alpha is effective in the treatment of HIV-1-related, severe, Zidovudine-resistant thrombocytopenia. Ann Intern Med 1994;121: 423–429.

312. Perrillo RP, Regenstein FG, Roodman ST. Chronic hepatitis B in asymptomatic homosexual men with antibody to the human immunodeficiency virus. Ann Intern Med 1986;105: 382–383.

313. Glasgow BJ, Anders K, Layfield LJ, et al. Clinical and pathologic findings of the liver in the acquired immunodeficiency syndrome. Am J Clin Path 1985;83:582–588.

314. Krogsgaard K, Lindhardt BO, Nielson JO, et al. The influence of HTLV-III infection on the natural history of hepatitis B virus infection in male homosexual HBs Ag carriers. Hepatology 1987;7:36–41.

315. Rossol S, Voth R, Meyer zum Buschenfelde KH, Hess G. Modulation of viral hepatitis in HIV-I infection [abstract M.B.P.220]. Paper presented at the Fifth International Conference on AIDS, Montreal, June, 1989.

316. Bodsworth N, Donovan B. The effect of HIV on chronic hepatitis: a study of 150 homosexual men [abstract M.B.P.222]. Paper presented at the Fifth International Conference on AIDS, Montreal, June, 1989.

317. Lange WR, Moore JD, Cibull ML, Brutsche RL. Human immunodeficiency virus as a possible cofactor in the development of fulminant hepatitis B in intravenous drug abusers. J Med 1988;19:203–212.

318. Kreek MJ, Des Jarlais DC, Trepo C, et al. Hepatitis delta antigenemia in intravenous drug abusers with AIDS: potential risk for health care workers [abstract Th.P.216]. Paper presented at the Third International Conference on AIDS, Washington, DC, June, 1987.

319. Lake-Baharr G, Chat K, Goundarajan S. HIV infection and delta hepatitis in intravenous drug addicts [abstract M.B.P.218]. Paper presented at the Fifth International Conference on AIDS, Montreal, June, 1989.

320. Castillo I, Bartolome J, Martinez MA, et al. Influence of HIV infection in hepatitis delta chronic carriers [abstract M.B.P.221]. Paper presented at the Fifth International Conference on AIDS, Montreal, June, 1989.

321. Novick DM, Farci P, Croxsan TS, et al. Hepatitis D virus and human immunodeficiency virus antibodies in parenteral drug abusers who are hepatitis B surface antigen positive. J Infect Dis 1988;158:795–803.

322. Rizzetto M. The delta agent. Hepatology 1983; 3:729–737.

323. Esteban JI, Esteban R, Viladomiu L, et al. Hepatitis C virus antibodies among risk groups in Spain. Lancet 1989;2(8658):294–297.

324. Alter MJ, Margolis HS, Krawczynski K, et al. The natural history of community-acquired hepatitis C in the United States. The sentinel counties chronic non-A, non-B hepatitis study team. N Engl J Med 1992;327:1899–1905.

325. Iwarson S, Norkrans G, Wejstal R. Hepatitis C: natural history of a unique infection. Clin Infect Dis 1995;20:1361–1370.

326. Resti M, Azzari CC, Lega L, et al. Mother-to-infant transmission of hepatitis C virus. Acta Paediatr 1995;84:251–255.

327. Thomas DL, Zenilman JM, Alter HJ, et al. Sexual transmission of hepatitis C virus among patients attending transmission diseases clinics in Baltimore: an analysis of 309 sex partnerships. J Infect Dis 1995;171:768–775.

328. Zanetti AR, Tanzi E, Paccagnini S, et al. Mother-to-infant transmission of hepatitis C virus. Lombardy Study Group on Vertical HCV Transmission. Lancet 1995;345: 289–291.

329. Donahue JG, Nelson KE, Munoz A, et al. Antibody to hepatitis C virus among cardiac surgery patients, homosexual men, and intravenous drug users in Baltimore, Maryland. Am J Epidemiol 1991;134:1206–1211.

330. Eyster ME, Diamondstone LS, Lien JM, Ehmann WC, Quan S, Goedert JJ. Natural history of hepatitis C virus infection in multitransfused hemophiliacs: effect of coinfection with human immunodeficiency virus. The Multicenter Hemophilia Cohort Study J Acquir Immune Defic Syndr 1993;6:602–610.

331. Stryker J, Smith MD. Needle exchange. Menlo Park, CA: The Kaiser Forums, 1993.

332. Workshop on Needle Exchange and Bleach Distribution Programs. Washington, DC: National Academy Press, 1994.

333. Heimer R, Khoshnood K, Jariwala-Freeman B, Duncan B, Harima Y. Hepatitis in used syringes: the limits of sensitivity of techniques to detect hepatitis B virus (HBV) DNA, hepatitis C virus (HCV) RNA, and antibodies to HCV core antigens. J Infect Dis 1996;173(4): 997–1000.

334. Hagan H, Des Jarlais DC, Friedman SR, Purchase D, Alter MJ. Reduced risk of hepatitis B and hepatitis C among injection drug users in the Tacoma syringe exchange program. Am J Public Health 1995;85(11):1531–1537.

335. Beral V, Peterman TA, Berkelman RL, Jaffe HW. Kaposi's sarcoma among persons with AIDS: a sexually transmitted infection? Lancet 1990;335:123–128.

336. Barbieri D, Gualandi M, Tassinari MC, et al. B-cell lymphomas in two HIV-seropositive heroin addicts. Lancet 1986;ii:1039.

337. Tirelli U, Rezza G, Lazzarin A, et al. Malignant lymphoma related to HIV infection in Italy: a report of 46 cases. JAMA 1987;258:2064.

338. Vazquez M, Rotterdam H, Sidhu G. Malignant neoplasms in surgical specimens of different AIDS risk groups [abstract M.B.P.293]. Paper presented at the Fifth International Conference on AIDS, Montreal, June, 1989.

339. Monfardini S, Vaccher E, Pizzocaro G, et al. Unusual malignant tumors in 49 patients with HIV infection. AIDS 1989;3:449–452.

340. Gachupin-Garcia A, Selwyn PA, Budner NS. Population-based study of malignancies and HIV infection among injecting drug users in a New York City methadone treatment program, 1985–1991. AIDS 1992;6:843–848.

341. Lange JMA, Paul DA, Huisman HG, et al. Persistent HIV antigenaemia and decline of HIV core antibodies associated with transition to AIDS. Br Med J 1986;293:1459–1462.

342. Jaffe JH. Drug addiction and drug abuse. In: Gilman AG, Rall TW, Nies AS, Taylor P, eds. The pharmacological basis of therapeutics. 8th edition. New York: Pergamon Press, 1990: 522–573.

343. Leitman BS, Greengart A, Wasser HJ. Pneumomediastinum and pneumopericardium after cocaine abuse. AJR 1988;151:614.

344. Kissner DG, Lawrence DW, Selis JE, Flint A. Crack lung: pulmonary disease caused by cocaine abuse. Am Rev Respir Dis 1987; 136:1250–1252.

345. Hoffman CK, Goodman PC. Pulmonary edema in cocaine smokers. Radiology 1989;172: 463–465.

346. Joseph AM, Nichol KL, Willenbring ML, Korn JE, Lysaght LS. Beneficial effects of treatment of nicotine dependence during an inpatient substance abuse treatment program. JAMA 1990;263:3043–3046.

347. Ho A, Dole VP. Pain perception in drug-free and in methadone-maintained human ex-addicts. Pro Soc Exp Biol Med 1979;162: 392–395.

348. Kreek MJ. Health consequences associated with the use of methadone. In: Cooper JR, Altman F, Brown BS, Czechowicz D, eds. Research on the treatment of narcotic addiction. Rockville, MD: National Institute on Drug Abuse, 1983:456–482.

349. Nyswander ME, Dole VP. The treatment of chronic pain. N Engl J Med 1984;310:599.

350. Kreek MJ, Garfield JW, Gutjahr CL, Giusti LM. Rifampin-induced methadone withdrawal. N Engl J Med 1976;294:1104–1106.

351. Mandel GL, Sande MA. Antimicrobial agents: drugs used in the chemotherapy of tuberculosis and leprosy. In: Gilman AG, Rall TW, Nies AS, Taylor P, eds. The pharmacological basis of therapeutics. 8th edition. New York: Pergamon Press, 1990:1146–1164.

352. Sawyer RC, Brown LS, Narong PK, Li R. Evaluation of a possible pharmacologic interaction between rifabutin and methadone in HIV-seropositive injecting drug users [abstract PO-B30–2197]. Paper presented at the Ninth International Conference on AIDS, Berlin, June, 1993.

353. Cobb M, Desal J, Brown LS, et al. The effect of fluconazole on the clinical pharmacokinetics of methadone [abstract Mo.B1196]. Paper presented at the Eleventh International Conference on AIDS, Vancouver, June, 1996.

354. Tong TG, Pond SM, Kreek MJ, et al. Phenytoin induced methadone withdrawal. Ann Intern Med 1981;94:349–351.

355. Schwartz EL, Brechbuhl AB, Kahl P, et al. Pharmacokinetics interactions of zidovudine and methadone in intravenous drug-using patient with HIV infection. J Acquir Immune Defic Syndr 1992;5:619–626.

356. Brettle RP, Jones GA, Gingham J, et al. Pharmacokinetics of zidovudine in injection drug use-related HIV infection [abstract W.B.O.3]. Paper presented at the Fifth International Conference on AIDS, Montreal, June, 1989.

357. McCance EF, Jatlow P, Rainey PM, et al. Methadone increases zidovudine exposure in HIV-infected injection drug users (ACTG 262). Paper presented at the Third Conference on Retroviruses and Opportunistic Infections, Washington, DC, 1996.

358. Richman DD, Fischl MA, Grieco MH, et al. The toxicity of azidothymine (AZT) in the treatment of patients with AIDS and AIDS-related complex. N Engl J Med 1987;317: 192–197.

359. Abbott laboratories. Norvir (Ritonavir) product information, February, 1996.

360. Merck and Co. Inc. Crixivan (Indinavir) product information, 1996.

361. Novick DM, Ness GL. Abuse of antibiotics by abusers of parenteral heroin or cocaine. Southern Med J 1984;77:302–303.

362. Crane LR, Levine DP, Zervos MJ, Cummings G. Bacteremia in narcotic addicts at the Detroit Medical Center I. Microbiology, epidemiology, risk factors, and empiric therapy. Rev Infect Dis 1986;8:364–373.

363. Selwyn PA, Iezza A. Zidovudine overdose in an intravenous drug user. AIDS 1990;4:822–824.

364. Terragna A, Mazzarello G, Auselmo A, Canessa A, Rossi E. Suicidal attempts with zidovudine. AIDS 1990;4:88.

365. O'Connor P, Selwyn PA, Schottenfeld R. Medical management of injection drug users with HIV infection. N Engl J Med 1994;331: 450–459.

366. Fischl MA, Richman DD, Grieco MH, et al. The efficacy of 3′-azido-2′,3′-deoxythymidine (azidothymidine) in the treatment of patients with AIDS and AIDS-related complex: a double-blind placebo-controlled trial. N Engl J Med 1987;317:185–191.

367. U.S. Centers for Disease Control and Prevention. HIV prevalence estimates and AIDS case projections for the United States: report based upon a workshop. MMWR 1990;39(RR-16): 1–31.

368. Hahn RA, Onorato IM, Jones TS, Dougherty J. Prevalence of HIV infection among intravenous drug users in the United States. JAMA 1989;261:2677–2684.

369. O'Connor PG, Molde S, Henry S, Shockcor WT, Schottenfeld RS. Human immunodeficiency virus infection in intravenous drug users: a model for primary care. Am J Med 1992;93:382–386.

370. Samet JH, Libman H, Steger KA, et al. Compliance with Zidovudine therapy in patients infected with human immunodeficiency virus, type 1: a cross sectional study in a municipal hospital clinic. Am J Med 1992;92:495–502.

371. Cooper DA, Gold J, Maclean P, et al. Acute AIDS retrovirus infection: definition of a clinical illness associated with seroconversion. Lancet 1985;i:537–540.

372. Ho DD, Sarngadharan MG, Resnick L, et al. Primary human T-lymphotropic virus type III infection. Ann Intern Med 1985;103:880–883.

373. Needlestick transmission of HTLV-III from a patient infected in Africa [editorial]. Lancet 1984;ii:1376–1377.

374. Robertson PB, Greenspan JS. Perspectives on oral manifestations of AIDS. Littleton, MA: PSG Publishing, 1988.

375. Penneys NS. Skin manifestations of AIDS. Philadelphia: JB Lippincott, 1989.

376. Taylor JMG, Fahey JL, Detels R, Giorgi JV. CD4 percentage, CD4 number, and CD4: CD8 ratio in HIV infection: which to choose and how to use. J Acquir Immune Defic Syndr 1989;2:114–124.

377. Fahey JL, Taylor JMG, Detels R, et al. The prognostic value of cellular and serologic markers in infection with human immunodeficiency virus type I. N Engl J Med 1990; 322:166–172.

378. Moss AR, Bacchetti P, Osmond D, et al. Seropositivity for HIV and the development of AIDS or AIDS related condition: three year follow up of the San Francisco General Hospital cohort. Br Med J 1988;296:745–750.

379. Graham NMH, Piantadosi S, Park LP, et al. CD4+ lymphocyte response to zidovudine as a predictor of AIDS-free time and survival time. J Acquir Immune Defic Syndr 1993;6:1258–1266.

380. Allain JP, Laurian Y, Paul DA, et al. Serological markers in early stages of human immunodeficiency virus infection in hemophiliacs. Lancet 1986;ii:1233–1236.

381. Alcabes P, Selwyn PA, Davenny K, et al. Laboratory markers and the risk of developing HIV-1 disease among injecting drug users. AIDS 1994;8:107–115.

382. Munoz A, Vlahov D, Solomon L, et al. Prognostic indicators for development of AIDS among intravenous drug users. J Acquir Immune Defic Syndr 1992;5:694–700.

383. Davenny K, Buono D, Schoenbaum EE, Friedland GH. Baseline health status of intravenous drug users with and without HIV infection [abstract F.B.430]. Paper presented at the Sixth International Conference on AIDS, San Francisco, June, 1990.

384. Ho D. Viral counts count in HIV infection. Science 1996;272:1124–1125.

385. Eron JJ, Benoit SL, Jemsek J, et al. Treatment with Lamivudine, Zidovudine, or both in HIV-positive patients with 200 to 500 CD4+ cells per cubic millimeter. N Engl J Med 1995;333:1662–1669.

386. Fauci AS, Pantaleo G, Stanley SS, Weissman D. Immunopathogenic mechanisms of HIV infection. Ann Intern Med 1996;124:654–663.

387. Danner SA, Carr A, Leonard JM, et al. A short-term study of the safety pharmacokinetics and efficacy of Ritonavir, an inhibitor of HIV-1 protease. N Engl J Med 1995;333:1528–1533.

388. Markowitz J, Saag M, Powderly WG, et al. A preliminary study of ritonavir, an inhibitor of HIV-1 protease, to treat HIV-1 infection. N Engl J Med 1995;333:1534–1539.

389. Collier AC, Coombs RW, Schoenfeld DA, et al. Treatment of human immunodeficiency virus infection with saquinavir, zidovudine, and zalcitabine. N Engl J Med 1996;334:1011–1017.

390. Stanley SK, Ostrowski MA, Justement JS, et al. Effect of immunization with a common recall antigen on viral expression in patients infected with human immunodeficiency virus type I. N Engl J Med 1996;334:1222–1230.

391. Stanley SK, Ostrowski MA, Justement JS, Gantt K, et al. Effects of immunization with a common recall antigen on viral expression in patients infected with human immunodeficiency virus type I. N Engl J Med 1996; 334:1222–1230.

392. Fauci AA. Multifactorial value of HIV disease: implications for therapy. Science 1993;262:1011–1018.

393. U.S. Centers for Disease Control and Prevention. Prevention and control of influenza. MMWR 1988;37:361–373.

394. U.S. Centers for Disease Control and Prevention. Update on hepatitis B prevention [abstract]. MMWR 1987:353–366.

395. Merrill DP, Moonis M, Chou T, Hirsch MS. Lamivudine or stavudine in two- and three-drug combinations against human immunodeficiency virus type 1 replication in vitro. J Infect Dis 1996;173:355–364.

396. Schmitt FA, Bigley JW, McKinnis R, et al. Neuropsychological outcome of zidovudine for the treatment of patients with AIDS and AIDS-related complex. N Engl J Med 1988; 319:1573–1578.

397. The Swiss Group for Clinical Studies on the Acquired Immunodeficiency Syndrome. Zidovudine for the treatment of thrombocytopenia associated with human immunodeficiency virus. A prospective study. Ann Intern Med 1988;109:718–721.

398. Fischl MA, Richman DD, Hansen N, et al. The safety and efficacy of zidovudine (AZT) in the treatment of subjects with mildly symptomatic human immunodeficiency virus type 1 infection. Ann Intern Med 1990;112:727–737.

399. Volberding PA, Lagakos SW, Koch MA, et al. Zidovudine in asymptomatic human immunodeficiency virus infection: a controlled trial in persons with fewer than 500 CD4-positive cells per cubic millimeter. N Engl J Med 1990; 322:941–949.

400. Dubin G, Braffman MN. Zidovudine-induced hepatoxicity. Ann Intern Med 1989;110:85–86.

401. Melamed AJ, Muller RJ, Gold JWM, et al. Possible zidovudine-induced hepatoxicity. JAMA 1987;258:2063.

402. Dalakas MC, Illa I, Pezeshkpour GH, et al. Mitochondrial myopathy caused by long-term zidovudine therapy. N Engl J Med 1990;322:1098–1105.

403. Steffe EM, King JH, Inciardi FJ, et al. The effect of acetaminophen on zidovudine metabolism in HIV-infected patients. J Acquir Immune Defic Syndr 1990;3:691–694.

404. Spruance SL, Pavia AT, Peterson D, Berry A, et al. Didanosine compared with continuation of zidovudine in HIV-infected patients with signs of clinical deterioration while receiving zidovudine. A randomized, double-blind clinical trial. Ann Intern Med 1994;120:360–368.

405. Kahn JO, Lagakos SW, Richman DD, et al. A control trial comparing continued zidovudine with didanosine in human immunodeficiency virus infection. N Engl J Med 1992;327:581–587.

406. Montaner JSG, Schechter MT, Rachlis A, et al. Didanosine compared with continued zidovudine therapy for HIV-infected patients with 200 to 500 CD4 cells/mm3: a double blind, randomized controlled trial. Ann Intern Med 1995;123:561–571.

407. Myers MW, Montaner JG, The Incas Study Group. A randomized double-blinded comparative trial of the effects of zidovudine, didanosine and nevirapine combinations in antiviral naive, AIDS-free, HIV-infected patients with CD4 counts 200–600/mm^3 [abstract]. Paper presented at the Eleventh International Conference on AIDS, Vancouver, June, 1996.

408. D'Aquila RT, Hughes MD, Johnson VA, et al. Nevirapine, zidovudine, and didanosine compared with zidovudine and Didanosine in patients with HIV-1 infection. Ann Intern Med 1996;124:1019–1029.

409. Kramer RA, Schaber MD, Skalka AM, Ganguly K, Wong-Staal F, Reddy EP. HTLV-III gag protein is processed in yeast cells by the virus pol-protease. Science 1986;231:1580–1584.

410. Lambert DM, Petteway SR Jr, McDanal CE, et al. Human immunodeficiency type I protease inhibitors irreversibly block infectivity of purified virions from chronically infected cells. Antimicrob Agents Chemother 1992;32:982–988.

411. Selwyn PA. HIV therapy in the real world. AIDS 1996;10:1591–1593.

412. Vella S. HIV therapy advances: update on a protease inhibitor. AIDS 1994;8(suppl):S25–S29.

413. Kitchen VS, Skinner C, Ariyoshi K, et al. Safety in activity of saquinavir in HIV infection. Lancet 1995;345:952–955.

414. Fischl MA, Dickinson GM, La voie L. Safety and efficacy of sulfamethoxazole and trimethoprim chemoprophylaxis for *Pneumocystis carinii* pneumonia in AIDS. JAMA 1988;259:1185–1189.

415. Graham NMH, Zeger SL, Park LP, et al. Effect of zidovudine and *Pneumocystis carinii* pneumonia prophylaxis on progression of HIV-1 infection to AIDS. Lancet 1991;338:265–269.

416. Hardy WD, Feinberg J, Finkelstein DM, Power ME, He W, et al. A controlled trial of trimethoprim-sulfamethoxazole or aerosolized pentamidine for secondary prophylaxis of *Pneumocystis carinii* pneumonia in patients with the acquired immunodeficiency syndrome. N Engl J Med 1992;327:1842–1848.

417. Phair J, Munoz A, Detels R, et al. The risk of *Pneumocystis carinii* pneumonia among men infected with human immunodeficiency virus type 1. N Engl J Med 1990;322:161–165.

418. Klein RS. Prophylaxis of opportunistic infections in individuals infected with HIV. AIDS 1989;3(suppl 1):S161–S173.

419. Kovacs JA, Hiemenz JW, Macher AM, et al. *Pneumocystis carinii* pneumonia: a comparison between patients with the acquired immunodeficiency syndrome and patients with other immunodeficiencies. Ann Intern Med 1984; 100:663–671.

420. Small CB, Harris CA, Friedland GH, Klein RS. The treatment of *Pneumocystis carinii* pneumonia in the acquired immunodeficiency syndrome. Arch Intern Med 1985;145:837–840.

421. Murray JF, Felton CP, Garay JM, et al. Pulmonary complications of the acquired immunodeficiency syndrome: report of a National Heart, Lung and Blood Institute Workshop. N Engl J Med 1984;312:1682–1688.

422. Shafer RW, Seitzman PA, Tapper ML. Successful prophylaxis of *Pneumocystis carinii* pneumonia with trimethoprim sulfamethoxazole in AIDS patients with previous allergic reactions. J Acquir Immune Defic Syndr 1989;2:389–393.

423. Sattler FR, Cowan R, Nielsen DM, Ruskin J. Trimethoprim sulfamethoxazole compared with pentamidine for treatment of *Pneumocystis carinii* pneumonia in the acquired immunodeficiency syndrome. A prospective, noncrossover study. Ann Intern Med 1988;109: 280–287.

424. Ivady G, Paldy L, Koltay M, et al. *Pneumocystis carinii* pneumonia. Lancet 1967;i:616–617.

425. Karboski JA, Bodley PJ. Inhaled pentamidine and hypoglycemia. Ann Intern Med 1988; 108:490.

426. Herer B, Chinet T, Labrune S, et al. Pancreatitis associated with pentamidine by aerosol. Br Med J 1989;298:605.

427. Berger TG, Tappero JW, Leoung GS, Jacobsen MA. Aerosolized pentamidine and cutaneous eruptions. Ann Intern Med 1989;110:1035–1036.

428. Smith DE, Herd D, Guzzard BG. Reversible bronchoconstriction with nebulized pentamidine. Lancet 1988;ii:905.

429. Girard PM, Gaudebout C, Lottin P, et al. Prevention of *Pneumocystis carinii* pneumonia relapse by pentamidine aerosol in zidovudine-treated AIDS patients. Lancet 1988;i:1348–1353.

430. Telzak EE, Cote RJ, Gold JWM, Campbell SW, Armstrong D. Extrapulmonary *Pneumocystis carinii* infections. Rev Infect Dis 1990; 12:380–386.

431. Davey RT, Margolis D, Kleiner D, Deyton L, Travis W. Digital necrosis and disseminated *Pneumocystis carinii* infection after aerosolized pentamidine prophylaxis. Ann Intern Med 1989;111:681–692.

432. Schinella RA, Breda SD, Hammerschlag PE. Optic infection due to *Pneumocystis carinii* infection in an apparently healthy man with antibody to human immunodeficiency virus. Ann Intern Med 1987;106:399.

433. Macher AM, Bardenstein DS, Zimmerman LE, et al. *Pneumocystis carinii* choroiditis in a male homosexual with AIDS and disseminated pulmonary and extrapulmonary *P. carinii* infection. N Engl J Med 1987;316:1092.

434. Jules-Elysee KM, Stover DE, Zaman MB, Bernard EM, White DA. Aerosolized pentamidine: effect on diagnosis and presentation of *Pneumocystis carinii* pneumonia. Ann Intern Med 1990;112:750–757.

435. Abd AG, Weitman DM, Ilowite JS, et al. Bilateral upper lobe *Pneumocystis carinii* pneumonia in a patient receiving inhaled pentamidine prophylaxis. Chest 1988;94:329–331.

436. Golden JA, Hollander H, Chernorff D, et al. Prevention of *Pneumocystis carinii* pneumonia by inhaled pentamidine. Lancet 1989;i: 654–657.

437. Bradburne RM, Ettensohn DB, Opal SM, McCool FD. Relapse of *Pneumocystis carinii* pneumonia in the upper lobes during aerosol pentamidine prophylaxis. Thorax 1989;44: 591–593.

438. Medina I, Mills J, Leoung G, et al. Oral therapy for *Pneumocystis carinii* pneumonia in the acquired immunodeficiency syndrome: a controlled trial of trimethoprim-sulfamethoxazole versus trimethoprim-dapsone. N Engl J Med 1990;323:776–782.

439. Blum RN, Miller LA, Gaggini LC, Cohn DL. Comparative trial of dapsone versus trimethoprim/sulfamethoxazole for primary prophylaxis of *Pneumocystis carinii* pneumonia. J Acquir Immune Defic Syndr 1992;5:341–347.

440. Podzamczer D, Salazar A, Jiminez J, et al. Intermittent trimethoprim-sulfamethoxazole compared with dapsone-pyrimethamine for the simultaneous primary prophylaxis of *Pneumocystis* pneumonia and toxoplasmosis in patients infected with HIV. Ann Intern Med 1995;122:755–761.

441. Pengelly CDR. Dapsone-induced hemolysis. Br Med J 1963;2:662–664.

442. Absar N, Daneshvar H, Beall G. Desensitization to trimethoprim-sulfamethoxazole in HIV-infected patients. J Allergy Clin Immunol 1994;96(3):1001–1005.

443. Hughes WT. The role of atovaquone tablets in treating *Pneumocystis carinii* pneumonia. J Acquir Immune Defic Syndr 1995;8(3): 247–252.

444. Chaisson RE, Benson CA, Dube MP. Clarithromycin therapy for bacteremic Mycobacterium avium complex disease: a randomized, double blind, dose ranging study in patients with AIDS. Ann Intern Med 1994;121: 905–911.

445. Nightingale SD, Cameron DW, Gordin FM, Sullam PM, et al. Two controlled trials of rifabutin prophylaxis against Mycobacterium avium complex infections in AIDS [abstract]. N Engl J Med 1993;329:828–833.

446. Havlir DV, Dube MP, Sattler FR, Forthal DN, et al. Prophylaxis against disseminated Mycobacterium avium complex with weekly azithromycin, daily rifabutin or both. N Engl J Med 1996;335:392–398.

447. Pierce M, Crampton S, Henry D, Heifets L, LaMarca A, et al. A randomized trial of clarithromycin as prophylaxis against disseminated Mycobacterium avium complex infection in patients with advanced acquired immunodeficiency syndrome. N Engl J Med 1996;335:384–391.

448. Grant IH, Gold JW, Rosenblum M, Niedzwiecki D, Armstrong D. Toxoplasma gondii serology in HIV-infected patients: the development of central nervous system toxoplasmosis in AIDS. AIDS 1990;4:519–521.

449. Opravil M, Hirschel B, Lazzarin A, et al. Once-weekly administration of dapsone/pyrimethamine vs. aerosolized pentamidine as combined prophylaxis for *Pneumocystis carinii* pneumonia and toxoplasmic encephalitis in human immunodeficiency virus-infected patients. Clin Infect Dis 1995;20:531–541.

450. O'Connor PG, Waugh ME, Schottenfeld RS, Diakogiannis IA, Rousaville BJ. Ambulatory opiate detoxification and primary care: A role for the primary care physician. J Gen Intern Med 1992;7:532–534.

451. Piette JD, Mor V, Mayer K, Zierler S, Wachtel T. The effects of immune status and race on health service use among people with HIV disease. Am J Public Health 1993;83:510–514.

452. Piette JD, Fleishman JA, Stein MD, Mor V, Mayer K. Perceived needs and unmet needs for formal services among people with HIV disease. J Community Health 1993;18:11–23.

453. Moore RD, Hidalgo J, Bareta JC, Chaisson RE. Zidovudine therapy and health resource utilization in AIDS. J Acquir Immune Defic Syndr 1994;7:349–354.

454. Rosenberg PS, Gail MH, Schrager LK, et al. National AIDS incidence trends and the extent of zidovudine therapy in selected demographic and transmission groups. J Acquir Immune Defic Syndr 1991;4:392–401.

455. Ross HE, Glaser FB, Germanson T. The prevalence of psychiatric disorders in patients with alcohol and other drug problems. Arch Gen Psych 1988;45:1023–1031.

456. Silberstein CH, McKegney FP, O'Dowd MA, et al. A prospective longitudinal study of neuropsychological and psychosocial factors in asymptomatic individuals at risk for HTLV-III/LAV infection in a methadone program: preliminary findings. Int J Neurosci 1987; 32:676–699.

457. American Academy of Pediatrics TFA. Infants and children with acquired immune deficiency syndrome: placement in adoption and foster care. Pediatrics 1989;83:609–612.

458. Falloon J, Eddy J, Wiener L, Pizzo PA. Human immunodeficiency virus infection in children. J Pediatr 1989;114:1–30.

459. Pinching AJ. Models of clinical care. AIDS 1989;3(suppl 1):S209–S213.

460. Shelp EE, DuBose ER, Sunderland RH. The infrastructure of religious communities: a neglected resource for care of people with AIDS. Am J Public Health 1990;80:970–972.

461. Ostrow DG, Gayle T. Psychosocial and ethical issues of AIDS health care programs. QRB 1986;12:284–294.

462. Boyd L, Kuehnert P, Sherer R. Serving hope, humor and compassion: implementation of a widely diverse volunteer support program for persons with AIDS/HIV infection at Cook County Hospital, Chicago [abstract S.D.804]. Paper presented at the Sixth International Conference on AIDS, San Francisco, June 1990.

463. Herb A, LaGamma D. Legal services for persons with AIDS of predominantly heterosexual, poor, minority background [abstract Th.F.O.2]. Paper presented at the Fifth International Conference on AIDS, Montreal, June, 1989.

464. Goeren W, Wade K, Rodriguez L. Case management of families with HIV infection [abstract S.D.803]. Paper presented at the Sixth International Conference on AIDS, San Francisco, June 1990.

465. Eric K, Drucker E, Worth D, Chabon B. The Women's Center: a model peer support program for IV drug and crack-using women in the Bronx [abstract Th.D.P.7]. Paper presented at the Fifth International Conference on AIDS, Montreal, June, 1989.

466. Ball JC, Lange WR, Myers CP, Friedman SR. Reducing the risk of AIDS through methadone maintenance treatment. J Health Soc Behav 1988;29:214–226.

467. Ball JC, Lange WR, Myers CP, Friedman SR. Reducing the risk of AIDS through methadone maintenance treatment. J Health Soc Behav 1988;29:214–226.

468. Wolcott DL, Fawzy FI, Pasnau RO. Acquired immune deficiency syndrome (AIDS) and consultation-liaison psychiatry. Gen Hosp Psychiatry 1985;7:280–292.

469. Miller D. HIV and social psychiatry. Br Med Bull 1988;44:130–148.

470. Karan LD. Primary care for AIDS and chemical dependence. West J Med 1990;152: 538–542.

471. Schwartz EL, Brechluhl AB, Kahl P, Miller MH, Selwyn PA, Friedland GH. Pharmacokinetic interactions of zidovudine and methadone in intravenous drug-using patients with HIV infection. J Acquir Immune Defic Syndr 1992; 5:619–626.

472. Cobb M, Desai J, Brown LS, et al. The effect of fluconazole on the clinical pharmacokinetics of methadone [abstract Mo.B.1196]. Paper presented at the Eleventh International Conference on AIDS, Vancouver, June, 1996.

473. Bertschy G, Baumann P, Eap CB, Baettig D. Probable metabolic interaction between metha-

done and fluvoxamine in addict patients. Ther Drug Monit 1994;16(1):42–45.

474. Roxane Laboratories, Inc. Viramune (nevirapine) product information, June 1996.

475. Merck, Co., Inc. Crixivan (indinavir) product information, March 1996.

476. Solvay Pharmaceuticals, Inc. Luvox (fluvoxamine) product information, January 1995.

477. Pond SM, Kretschzmar KM. Effect of phenytoin on meperidine clearance and normeperi-

dine formation. Clin Pharmacol Ther 1981;30: 680–686.

478. Hess AJ, Rumack BH, eds. Drug-Reax system. Micromedex, Inc., Englewood, Colorado, September, 1996.

479. Hansen PD, Horn JR. Drug interactions. Philadelphia: Lea & Febiger, 1989.

480. Gelman CR, Rumack BH, Hess AJ, eds. Drugdex system. Micromedex, Inc., Englewood, Colorado, September, 1996.

481. Olkkola KT, Backman JT, Neunonen PJ. Midazolam should be avoided in patients receiving the systemic antimycotics ketoconazole or itraconazole. Clin Pharmacol Ther 1994;55: 481–485.

482. Arans GW, Epstein S, Molloy M, et al. Carbamazepine-induced reduction of plasma alprazolam concentrations: a clinical case report. J Clin Psychiatry 1988;49:448–449.

60 NEUROPSYCHIATRIC COMPLICATIONS

Francisco Fernandez, Jorge Maldonado, and Pedro Ruiz

Human immunodeficiency virus type 1 (HIV-1) infection is currently the leading cause of death in adults ages 25–44 (1). Homosexual and heterosexual unprotected intercourse, injecting drug use (IDU) and contaminated blood and blood products transfusion are well known mechanisms of HIV-1 transmission. Crack-cocaine in women (2) and other non-IDU in homosexuals are well-determined risk factors for HIV-1 infection, (3) with marihuana and volatile nitrites ("poppers") increasing the likelihood of HIV-1 infection for any given exposure in the male homosexual population (3, 4). The emotional distress caused by HIV seroconversion, as well as the psychiatric disorders due to medical conditions (both direct effect of the virus and secondary opportunistic infections and brain tumors) and neurologic syndromes, may drive patients to the psychiatrist for evaluation and treatment. This might be complicated by previous psychopathology and substance-induced psychiatric disorders (illicit and prescribed drugs). In an attempt to make clinicians aware and more capable of managing these complex and challenging patients, this chapter reviews the neuropsychologic symptomatology, its neuropathology, and the treatments of neuropsychiatric disorders associated with the HIV-1 infection.

NEUROPATHOLOGY IN HIV-1 INFECTION

The HIV-1 penetrates the blood-brain barrier (BBB) early in the course of the infection and is replicated in brain tissue using monocytes and multinucleated macrophages as hosts (5). In patients with acquired immunodeficiency syndrome (AIDS) the virus may be recovered in the cerebrospinal fluid (CSF) (6) or in brain tissue, which quantitatively contains more virus than other organs in the body (7, 8).

The mechanisms whereby HIV-1 penetrates the nervous system are not completely understood. It may enter the brain through endothelial gaps in brain capillaries (9), via the choroid plexus (6), or as a proviral form contained in a latently infected cell—a monocyte—which once inside the central nervous system (CNS) differentiates into a macrophage converting to a productively infected cell (7). The virus is known to invade and destroy subcortical areas such as the basal ganglia and temporolimbic areas, as well as support cells such as astrocytes, which share similar CD4 receptors with their well-known lymphocyte host (10). It also affects cortical areas as demonstrated by quantitative measurements of neuronal numbers in various cortical regions (11) and MRI measurement in patients with HIV-1 dementia (12).

Direct effect of the HIV-1 might be responsible for the development of neuropathology; however, this is not completely understood, and immunohistochemical and in situ hybridization studies have indicated that only macrophages/microglia are significantly infected in the CNS (13). Other forms of neurotoxicity have been studied and there is evidence now that the surface glycoprotein gp 120 may potentiate the neurotoxicity of endogenous excitatory amino acid neurotransmitters (glutamate and aspartate) by sensitizing the N-Methyl D-Aspartate (NMDA) receptor either directly or through release of arachidonic acid via activation of phospholipase A2 (14, 15). This induces an increase in levels of intracellular calcium (16, 17), which triggers a series of neurotoxic events leading to cellular necrosis or apoptosis (18–20), a common pathway in other neurological diseases (21). Other neurotoxins secreted by HIV-1–infected macrophages/microglia might be involved in the pathogenesis of neuronal damage as well. These include tumor necrosis factor-alpha (TNF-α) (22), tumor necrosis factor-receptor (TNF-R) (23), quinolinic acid (24), platelet activating factor, cysteine, interleukin-1B (IL-1B), nitric oxide, and superoxide anion (18).

Different steps in this complex cascade have been the target of many attempts to prevent its neurotoxicity. Removal of glutamate by glutamate dehydrogenase (16), and glutamate receptor antagonists (16) have been ineffective in preventing neurotoxicity. NMDA receptor antagonists, memantine, and MK-801 (dizocilpine), prevent the injury engendered by the glycoprotein gp 120 without significantly altering the release of arachidonic acid (14, 25). Calcium channels blockers have had different responses according to specific drugs (16, 18) in preventing early rise in calcium concentration and delayed neuronal injury, with nimodipine and nifedipine being the most effective, and with verapamil potentiating HIV-1 replication in lymphoid cells (26). Dantrolene and extracellular calcium removal with bis-(o-aminophenoxy)-ethane-N,N,N′,N′-tetra-acetic acid (16) have also been effective in neurotoxicity prevention. Investigation to discover a clinically tolerated drug that will prevent the neurotoxic effects continues.

Clinically, patients suffer from a wide spectrum of cognitive impairment, personality change, and motor dysfunction, which goes from subclinical symptoms without impairment of work or activities of daily living to severe dementia with paraplegia and double incontinence (27). This syndrome is known as HIV-1 associated cognitive-motor complex (28), and its severity is related to the degree of inflammatory response in the brain (29). In patients with moderate to severe dementia, multinucleated giant cells (MNGC) are found, and are now considered essential for the diagnosis and pathognomonic of HIV-1 infection in the CNS (30). However, the finding of MNGC in the CNS of patients with HIV-1 infection is only noted in 25–50% of patients with dementia. Nonetheless, in MNGC-negative brains of mildly demented AIDS patients, the viral CNS burden as measured by in situ hybridization or polymerase chain reaction for viral nucleic acids is reportedly higher than in nondemented patients (31). Microglial and glial changes, and MNGC, can be found in any part of the CNS, but are more common in deep white matter of the cerebral hemispheres, basal ganglia, and brainstem (30). White matter pallor with astrogliosis, diffuse or focal vacuolation that can be associated with axonal or myelin loss (32), and cortical atrophy (11, 33) are changes less commonly observed. Rather than a true demyelination process of the oligodendritic myelin sheath, the pallor is due to an increase in interstitial water content most likely caused by a leaky BBB.

PERIPHERAL NERVOUS SYSTEM PATHOLOGY AND MYOPATHY IN HIV-1 INFECTION

Patients with HIV-1 infection may present with a wide variety of symptoms involving the peripheral nervous system (PNS) (34–36), as well as the skeletal muscles (34, 37). It has been hypothesized that similar mechanisms are involved in the pathogenesis of CNS and PNS dysfunction (13). PNS pathology has been reported between 9 and 38% (13, 34), and it is thought that its incidence is underestimated due to the variability in the severity of the symptoms (34) and due to the fact that the patients present with other severe and life-threatening illnesses (35).

Distal symmetric peripheral neuropathy (DSPN) is the most common presentation among patients with generalized neuropathies (34, 36, 38, 39). Initial symptoms include trophic changes in lower extremities, paresthesias, edema, and weakness; they progress slowly to centripetally spread weakness and sensory loss. Chronic inflammatory demyelinating polyradiculopathy (CIDP) presents as subacute or chronic weakness in upper and lower extremities, decreased to absent deep tendon reflexes, and mild sensory abnormalities. Cranial nerves may also be involved (34, 36). Mononeuritis multiplex (MM) presents usually as an abrupt onset mononeuropathy with periodical additional abrupt mononeuropathies in other distributions. It may present with sensory or motor manifestation and may involve cranial nerves as well (34, 39–42). Pain may be present in any of the abovementioned neuropathies and may be severe and incapacitating (13, 34, 38, 39).

Less common presentations of PNS dysfunction are progressive polyneuroradiculopathy (34) with early impairment of bladder and rectal sphincter control, and autonomic neuropathy with postural hypotension, diarrhea, and sudden arrhythmias with the risk of death (38, 43, 44).

The PNS may be affected at any time during the course of the disease and may be the presenting problem during the acute retroviral infection (40, 41). Neuropathies are most commonly related directly to the HIV-1 infection, but in about one third of the patients these complications are caused by secondary pathogens or by medications used for other complications of the HIV-1 infection (34, 38).

Treatment of neuropathies involves pain management with capsaicin cream, amitriptyline, desipramine, anticonvulsants, or narcotics (38, 39); however, pain control is often difficult. Corticosteroids, plasmapheresis, and IV immunoglobulin have been used with success for DSPN, CIDP, and MM (34, 39, 45). Hypotension in the case of autonomic neuropathy may be controlled with fludrocortisone (39).

Myopathy associated with HIV-1 infection has three different histologic findings: polymyositis, necrotizing myopathy without inflammatory infiltrates, and nemaline rod myopathy (46, 47). Clinically, patients present with painless progressive weakness involving the shoulder and pelvic girdle muscles, elevated creatinine kinase (CK) and electromyographic (EMG) abnormalities. Treatment with prednisone alone or in combination with plasmapheresis is usually effective (34, 39). The most important and common myopathy in HIV-1–infected patients is that related to zidovudine (AZT), which usually develops after 9–12 months' treatment and is manifest with wasting of the buttocks muscles and leg weakness (34, 37–39). Symptom reversal may be complete with cessation or reduction of therapy. Patients taking AZT must be monitored regularly to detect early increments of CK (34, 38, 39).

DIAGNOSIS AND MANAGEMENT OF HIV-1 SECONDARY NEUROLOGIC COMPLICATIONS

HIV-1 CNS involvement may occur at any time with or without indications of quantifiable immune compromise. Opportunistic infections and HIV-1–related malignancies affecting the nervous system are usually a late manifestation of the HIV-1 infection (45) occurring in patients with less than 200 CD4 cells/mm. Table 60.1 indicates the possible range of nervous pathologies (35, 48) that are likely to attack the CNS as a result of HIV-1 infection. No significant differences in the incidence of neurological disease between IDUs and non-IDUs have been reported (49).

Toxoplasma gondii infection is the most prevalent (50) and the most frequent cause of focal intracerebral lesions in patients with AIDS (35, 51, 52). Pri-

Table 60.1 Neuropsychiatric Infections/Malignancies Associated with HIV

Atypical aseptic meningitis
CMV encephalitis
Herpes simplex virus encephalitis
Progressive multifocal leukoencephalopathy
Subacute encephalitis
Varicella zoster virus encephalitis or vasculitis

Aspergillus
Candidiasis
Coccidioidomycosis
Cryptococcus neoformans
Toxoplasma gondii

Atypical mycobacteria
Mycobacterium tuberculosis

Kaposi's sarcoma
Primary or secondary CNS lymphoma

Adapted from Bredesen DE, Levy RM, Rosenblum ML. The neurology of human immunodeficiency virus infection. Q J Med 1988;68:665–667. By permission of Oxford University Press.

mary infection is usually asymptomatic. Fever and headache is the most common presentation, along with a subacute onset of focal neurologic abnormalities. Seizures affect one third of the patients (53). Empirical therapy when neuroradiologic studies suggest toxoplasmosis is almost a universal practice; however, neuroimaging studies have a low sensitivity, especially when patients have nonfocal symptoms (22–74%) (54); and, when serum immunoglobulin G (IgG) is negative or the patient fails to improve, a brain biopsy is necessary for a definitive diagnosis (53, 54). Treatment with pyrimethamine and sulfadiazine or clindamycin is usually effective, and maintenance treatment, as well as primary prophylaxis, are now recommended (55).

Cryptococcus neoformans is the most common cause of meningitis and the most important CNS fungal infection in patients with AIDS (45, 50). Typically the clinical presentation is one of an insidious onset of fever, headache, nausea, vomiting, and altered mental status in a patient with a CD4 count of less than 100/mm. If untreated this is a fatal disorder (48), but mortality can be reduced to 17–20% (56) with amphotericin-B, either alone or in combination with flucytosine or with fluconazole therapy (57). Again, maintenance therapy with fluconazole is recommended indefinitely (50).

Other secondary neurologic infections associated with HIV-1 include progressive multifocal leukoencephalopathy (PML) secondary to papovavirus infection (45, 58), cytomegalovirus (CMV) encephalitis and polyradiculopathy (39, 59), herpes simplex virus (HSV) encephalitis (60), neurosyphilis (40, 46, 61), mycobacterial and other fungal infections. PML is an increasingly important source of neurologic complications in HIV-1 disease, and although there is not proven therapy for PML, cytosine arabinoside has been suggested as an efficacious alternative (61). Ganciclovir and foscarnet are effective in the treatment of CMV infection and maintenance therapy. HSV encephalitis is a rare but life-threatening complication of HSV infection, especially in patients with advanced HIV-1 infection and other opportunistic infections of the CNS. Brain biopsy is often required for a definitive diagnosis, and intravenous acyclovir, foscarnet, or vidarabine may be used for its treatment. Neurosyphilis has a more aggressive course in patients with AIDS and its diagnosis may be difficult (45, 60). Fortunately intravenous penicillin is a highly effective and definitive treatment. Herpes zoster, mycobacterial, and fungal infections also produce CNS complications among HIV-1–infected individuals and generally respond well to multimodal treatment.

Non-Hodgkin's lymphoma is a complication of advanced HIV-1 disease that is present in 8% of the AIDS population (62). It may involve the CNS-causing neurologic as well as neuropsychiatric complications including delirium, seizures, and cognitive impairment (48). A diagnosis can be made via neuroimaging, but a brain biopsy and/or evidence of malignant cells in the CSF is usually required prior to initiation of treatment. Multiagent chemotherapeutic treatment induces complete response in 54% of patients (63), but these responses are usually of short duration and the median survival time is 4–7 months after the diagnosis (64). AIDS patients are 100 times more likely than controls to suffer strokes (48, 65), sometimes resulting in a clinical syndrome of multi-infarct dementia (66).

PNS may also be affected by secondary complications, such as herpes zoster neuropathy and cytomegalovirus polyradiculopathy. Toxic neuropathies caused by nucleotides (ddI, ddC) may appear in late phases of the HIV-1 infection with a CD4 count of less than 200/mm (45). A reversible myopathy secondary to AZT may also affect these patients (34, 37–39).

NEUROBIOLOGICAL EVALUATION IN HIV-1 INFECTION

Mental Status and Neuropsychological Assessment

Learning about the pathogenicity of HIV-1 is a key factor in its management. Needless to say, we have recently gained much insight and knowledge in this respect. The HIV-1–associated cognitive/motor complex consists of a combination of cognitive, motor, behavioral, and affective disturbances (29, 67) that may be severe and sufficient for the diagnosis of AIDS, and may be the presenting manifestation of HIV-1 infection (68); or may cause mild

symptoms and not be associated with a significant impairment in the social or occupational level of functioning of these patients. Several investigators have found that asymptomatic HIV-1 positive patients have an elevated rate of cognitive dysfunction when compared to HIV-1 negative controls (69–75). These are usually subtle impairments that are unrelated to the level of immunosuppression or to depression (73, 74, 76, 77), and are most evident in individuals with lower cognitive reserve (78). Although controversy still exists as to whether the cognitive functioning of asymptomatic patients is distinguishable from that of controls (79, 80), it is generally accepted by clinicians that HIV-1–related cognitive impairment can occur at any time during the course of the disease. It has also been shown that cognitive abnormalities in asymptomatic patients are related to increased risk of mortality (81) and work disability (82, 83). While varying psychological tests have been used to determine or evaluate the earlier signs of HIV-1 effects on mental function (84, 85), no definitive test can be used, either alone or in combination with others, to establish a diagnosis of HIV-1–associated cognitive/motor complex. Taking a careful cognitive history can be an extremely useful adjunct in the differential diagnosis of etiologies of cognitive

Table 60.2   HIV Cognitive History

Name
Age and birthday
Handedness
First language at home
Educational background
       Best subjects, grades
       Worst subjects
Occupational background
       How long
Medical history
       Childhood diseases or injuries
       Head injuries with loss of consciousness
       Strokes
       High fevers
       Toxin exposure
       Major illness, injuries, or surgeries
       Medicines: prescription, non-prescription
Duration of diagnosis of HIV infection; AIDS
Current problem
       Change in thinking functions: how long, or, over what period of time
Any change in ability to concentrate
Any periods of confusion or mental "fuzziness"
       When talking with people, or on the phone, watching TV or a movie, reading
Any problem with following the train of thought
Any difficulties with handwriting
Any word-finding problems, difficulties with slurring or stammering
Any slowing of thinking or understanding, trouble with mental arithmetic, like making change or balancing checkbook
Wear glasses
Any blurring vision, double vision, or flashing lights in eyes
Any change in understanding what is seen; do things look right in their relation to each other?
Overlook things when right in front of you
Hearing any unusual sounds; see unusual things; have any strange feelings?
Any changes in any other senses:
       Decreased hearing, ringing, or buzzing sounds
       Change in smell or taste
       Any numbness, "pins or needles," loss of feeling, tingling, or burning feelings
       Any severe pain
Memory:
       Any areas of memory that are better or worse
       Memory for recent information?
       Information from way back in life
       Any difference in memory for *situations* versus rote facts and figures
       Kinds of things most easily forgotten: names, addresses, directions, reading
       How long can things be remembered, more notes written than used to
       Any lapses noted
       Any getting lost or forgetting where one is
Any new difficulties with thinking through problems or solving them, decision making, staying organized—on job, at home
How is sleep: any trouble getting to sleep, night versus daytime, any awakenings from which one cannot immediately return to sleep
Any inability to move any parts of the body
Muscle weakness, twitching, spasms, trouble walking, coordination problems, tremors or shakiness, problems with dropping things, feeling like moving more
       slowly, difficulty using tools or household utensils, getting dressed, telling right from left
Headaches or dizziness, instances thought to be seizures (staring off into space for a long time, uncontrollable movements, periods where one seemed to
       "lose" time, incontinence)
Changes in mood, feelings, ideas
       Mood swings, loss of patience or change in temper, increase in irritability, change in amount of worry, sense of panic
(Continue with Hamilton Depression and Anxiety Scales)

Adapted from Levy JK, Fernandez F. HIV infection of the CNS: Implications for neuropsychiatry. In: Yudofsky SC, Hales RE, eds. The American Psychiatric Press textbook of neuropsychiatry. Third edition. Washington, DC: American Psychiatric Press, in press.

dysfunction in HIV-1–infected patients with cognitive complaints. This is most important when there is no formal capacity for neuropsychological testing. The essentials of this interactive interview are listed in Table 60.2. We have found that the answers to these questions can help match the individual patient complaints to the criterional system for defining HIV-1–associated cognitive disorder and dementia such as that proposed by the American Academy of Neurology (28). The cognitive history must also include a mental status examination. A standard examination, such as the Mini-Mental State Examination, may miss the types of memory and attention/concentration problems often associated with CNS HIV-1 infection, and a more formal evaluation with neuropsychological testing is required.

The most significant signs of cognitive impairment related to HIV-1 infection include mild problems with abstraction, learning, language, verbal memory, and psychomotor speed during the early phases, which progress to more serious difficulties with attention and concentration, slowing of information processing, slowed psychomotor speed, impaired cognitive flexibility, impairment in nonverbal abilities of problem solving, visuospatial integration and construction, and nonverbal memory in the late phases of the infection (73, 84). Most affected in the early stages of cognitive impairment associated with HIV-1 are psychomotor tasks, such as the Wechsler Adult Intelligence Scale digit symbol and block design, and the trail making test part B from the Halstead-Reitan Neuropsychological Battery; memory tasks, such as the delayed visual reproduction subtest from the Wechsler memory scale; and the delayed recall of the Rey-Osterrieth complex figure (84). Psychomotor and neuromotor tasks may reveal HIV-1–related cognitive dysfunction and are also sensitive measures for the early detection of HIV-1–related cognitive impairment.

The neuropsychological tests used for assessment of dementia generally appraise functions, such as aphasia, apraxia, and other complex language-associated functioning; higher level cognitive functions of verbal and nonverbal abstract reasoning and problem solving; and perceptual functioning of the different sensory modalities. However, as more was learned about the HIV-1–associated cognitive/motor complex, it became apparent that these neuropsychological assessments were not reliably sensitive for the necessary early detection of HIV-1 minor cognitive/motor disorders (86, 87). These neuropsychological batteries are most useful for detecting areas of mental dysfunction related to focal disturbances in the CNS, such as abscess created by an HIV-1–related opportunistic infection or tumor, but they are not useful for detecting the often subtle impairments of the early stages of HIV-1's effects on the CNS. Table 60.3 shows the neuropsychological battery recommended by the NIMH for use in these patients; however, modifications according to the patient's cognitive status may be more useful than a full evaluation.

With the aid of these more sensitive testing procedures, it became clear that cognitive dysfunction of sufficient severity to disrupt the patient's normal daily activities may occur at any time during the course of the infectious process with HIV-1. Navia and colleagues characterized these disabilities and established a scale for the clinical staging of the fully developed HIV-1–associated dementia (HAD) (67, 88) (Table 60.4). The staging system is specific for the HAD, ranking cognitive, behavioral, and neurologic/motoric functioning commensurate with the stages of progression within the AIDS diagnosis. However, because we are aware of the possibility of early cognitive impairment before the diagnosis of HAD, a means of ranking cognitive functioning needs to be developed to define cognitive disabilities at earlier stages of infection. The Global Deterioration Scale of Reisberg and colleagues (89) is useful in this respect because of its use in characterizing cognitive functioning in activities of daily living and dementia of the Alzheimer's type, as well as other neurodegenerative dementias (Table 60.5). Application of the Global Deterioration Scale to a sample of HIV-1–infected patients (90) determined that 21% of the patients at the earlier stage of symptomatic infection, such as progressive generalized lymphadenopathy, had Global Deterioration Scale stage 1, or normal, and that 42% of the sample had cognitive

---

Table 60.3 NIMH Neuropsychological Battery

A. Indication of premorbid intelligence
1. Vocabulary (WAIS-R)
2. National adult reading test (NART)
B. Attention
1. Digit span (WMS-R)
2. Visual span (WMS-R)
C. Speed of processing
1. Sternberg search task
2. Simple and choice reaction time
3. Paced serial addition test (PASAT)
D. Memory
1. California verbal test (CVLT)
2. Memory working test
3. Modified visual reproduction test
E. Abstraction
1. Category test
2. Trail making test, parts A and B
F. Language
1. Boston naming test
2. Letter and category fluency test
G. Visuospatial
1. Embedded figures test
2. Money's standardized road-map test of direction sense
3. Digit symbol substitution
H. Construction abilities
1. Block design test
2. Tactual performance test
I. Motor abilities
1. Grooved pegboard
2. Finger tapping test
3. Grip strength
J. Psychiatric assessment
1. Diagnostic interview schedule (DIS)
2. Hamilton depression scale
3. State-trait anxiety scale
4. Mini-mental state examination

Adapted from Butters N, Grant I, Haxby J, et al. Assessment of AIDS-related cognitive changes: recommendations of the NIMH Workgroup on Neuropsychological Assessment Approaches. J Clin Exp Neuropsychol 1990;12:963–978.

Table 60.4 Clinical Staging System for HIV-1–associated Dementia Complex

Stage 0 (normal)	Normal mental and motor function. Neurologic signs are within the normal age-appropriate spectrum.
Stage 0.5 (subclinical)	Minimal or equivocal symptoms without impairment of work or capacity to perform activities of daily living (ADL). Mildly abnormal signs may include reflex changes (e.g., generalized increase in deep tendon reflexes with active jaw jerk, snout or glabellar sign) or mildly slowed ocular/limb movements, but without clear loss of strength (must be differentiated from fatigue).
Stage 1 (mild)	Able to perform all but the more demanding aspects of work or ADL but with unequivocal evidence (symptoms or signs including performance on neuropsychological testing) of intellectual or motor impairment. The abnormal clinical motor signs usually include slow or clumsy movements of extremities, but the patient can walk without assistance.
Stage 2 (moderate)	Able to perform basic activities of self-care at home but cannot work or maintain more demanding aspects of daily life (e.g., maintain finances, read text more complex than newspaper). Ambulatory but may require single prop (e.g., cane).
Stage 3 (severe)	Major incapacity in intellectual capacity (cannot follow news or personal events, cannot sustain conversation of any complexity, considerable slowing of all output) and motor ability (cannot walk unassisted, requiring walker or personal support, usually with slowing and clumsiness of arms as well).
Stage 4 (end stage)	Nearly vegetative. Intellectual and social comprehension and output limited to rudimentary understanding. Nearly or absolutely mute. Paraparetic or plegic with double incontinence.

Adapted from Brew BJ, Sidtis JJ, Petito CK, Price RW. The neurologic complications of AIDS and human immunodeficiency virus infection. In: Plum F, ed. Advances in contemporary neurology. Philadelphia: FA Davis, 1988:1–49.

Table 60.5   Global Deterioration Scale (GDS) for Age-Associated Cognitive Decline

GDS Stage	Clinical Phase	Clinical Characteristics
1 No cognitive decline	Normal	No subjective complaints of memory deficit. No memory deficit evident on clinical interview.
2 Very mild cognitive decline	Forgetfulness	Subjective complaints of mild memory deficit, most frequently in following cognitive areas: (a) forgetting where one has placed familiar objects; (b) forgetting names one formerly knew well. No objective evidence of memory deficit on clinical interview. No objective deficits in employment or social situations. Appropriate concern with respect to symptomatology.
3 Mild cognitive decline	Early confusional	Earliest clear-cut deficits. Manifestations in more than one of the following areas: (a) patient may have gotten lost when traveling to an unfamiliar location; (b) co-workers become aware of patient's relatively poor performance; (c) word- and name-finding deficits become evident to intimates; (d) patient may read a passage or a book and retain relatively little material; (e) patient may demonstrate decreased facility in remembering names upon introduction to new people; (f) patient may have lost or misplaced an object of value; (g) concentration deficit may be evident on clinical testing.
4 Moderate cognitive decline	Late confusional	Clear-cut deficit on careful clinical interview. Deficit manifested in following areas: (a) decreased knowledge of current and recent events; (b) possibly some deficit in memory of one's personal history; (c) concentration deficit elicited on serial subtractions; (d) decreased ability to travel, handle finances, etc. Frequently, no deficit in following areas: (a) orientation to time and person; (b) recognition of familiar persons and faces; (c) ability to travel to familiar locations. Inability to perform complex tasks. Denial is dominant defense mechanism. Flattening of affect and withdrawal from challenging situations occur.
5 Moderately severe cognitive decline	Early dementia	Patients can no longer survive without some assistance. Patients are unable during interview to recall a major relevant aspect of their current lives: e.g., their address or telephone number of many years, the names of close member of their family, the name of the high school or college from which they graduated. Frequently some disorientation to time (date, day of week, season, etc.) or to place. An educated person may have difficulty counting back from 40 by 4s or from 20 by 2s. Persons at this stage retain knowledge of many major facts regarding themselves and others. They invariably know the name of their significant others. They require no assistance with toileting or eating but may have some difficulty choosing the proper clothing to wear.
6 Severe cognitive decline	Middle dementia	May occasionally forget the name of significant others upon whom they are entirely dependent for survival. Will be largely unaware of recent events and experiences in their lives. Retain some knowledge of their past lives, but this is very sketchy. Generally aware of their surrounding, the year, the season, etc. May have difficulty counting from 10, both backward and sometimes forward. Will require some assistance with activities of daily living, e.g., may become incontinent, will require travel assistance but occasionally will display ability to travel to familiar locations. Diurnal rhythm frequently disturbed. Almost always recall their own name. Frequently continue to be able to distinguish familiar from unfamiliar persons in their environment. Personality and emotional changes occur. These are quite variable and include: (a) delusional behavior, e.g., patients may accuse their significant others of being an impostor, may talk to imaginary figures in the environment or to their own reflection in the mirror; (b) obsessive symptoms, e.g., person may continually repeat simple cleaning activities; (c) anxiety symptoms, agitation, and even previously nonexistent violent behavior may occur; (d) cognitive abulia, i.e., loss of will power because an individual cannot carry a thought long enough to determine a purposeful course of action.
7 Very severe cognitive decline	Late dementia	All verbal abilities are lost. Frequently, there is no speech at all—only grunting. Incontinent of urine; requires assistance toileting and feeding. Loses basic psychomotor skills, e.g., ability to walk. The brain appears no longer to be able to tell the body what to do. Generalized and cortical neurological signs and symptoms.

Adapted from Reisberg B, Ferris SH, de Leon MJ, et al. The global deterioration scale (GDS): an instrument for the assessment of primary degenerative dementia (PDD). Am J Psychiatry 1982;139:1136–1139.

impairment ranging from forgetfulness to early dementia. As HIV-1 disease progressed, such as with AIDS-related complex, 27% of these patients were shown to have forgetfulness, and almost 30% qualified for classification of early, middle, or late dementia. Therefore, the Global Deterioration Scale has proved to provide the necessary information for successfully assessing the decline of cognitive function clinically as it relates to an HIV-1–infected person's performance of daily activities, even before the patient fulfills the diagnostic criteria for the HIV-1–associated cognitive/motor complex. The Global Deterioration Scale is also of benefit to research and planning investigations because it is capable of comparing the cognitive impairment associated with HIV-1 infection with the cognitive impairment found in dementias unrelated to HIV-1. When we see the similarities and differences between them, we are better able to foresee, and adequately plan for, the predicted course of the patient's progressive cognitive decline.

Neuroimaging

Although computed tomography (CT) and magnetic resonance imaging (MRI) are most useful in the diagnosis of secondary infections and brain tumors, primary CNS HIV-1 infection can be associated with characteristic imaging features, including cortical atrophy, ventricular enlargement, diffuse or patchy white matter abnormalities particularly in periventricular areas (91, 92), and in children calcification of the basal ganglia and delayed myelination (93, 94). MRI changes correlate with neuropsychological testing (95) and is more sensitive than CT scan in detecting white matter changes (96). However, both are useful as diagnostic tools and may also have utility in assessing prognosis of these patients (97).

Neuroimaging reflecting physiologic functioning of the CNS via positron emission computed tomography (PET) reveals regional metabolic abnormalities with hypermetabolism in the basal ganglia, thalamus, and parietal and temporal lobes early in nondemented patients with HIV-1 infection, and regional and then general hypometabolism as the HIV-1 CNS involvement progresses and is clinically associated with dementia (98–100). Single-photon emission computed tomography (SPECT) has shown cortical and subcortical perfusion defects in early phases of the HIV-1–related cognitive impairment that become more pronounced in the later stages (101–103). PET and SPECT are more sensitive than CT and MRI in detecting early changes in asymptomatic patients, and may even detect changes before cognitive impairment is apparent in neuropsychological testing (100–103). The therapeutic effects of antiviral treatment may also be monitored by PET, that shows reversal of the previously described abnormalities in glucose metabolism after treatment of the HIV-1–associated cognitive/motor complex with AZT (98). This improvement correlated with neurologic improvement and possibly recovery of relevant neuropsychological functioning after treatment with AZT.

Electrophysiology

The role of electrophysiology in cognitive and neurologic conditions is a key factor in early detection and understanding of these conditions. The percentage of patients with abnormal electroencephalograms appears to increase as the systemic disease progresses, and a low amplitude pattern may be found in advanced dementia and atrophy on CT scan (104). In asymptomatic patients, studies have found conflicting results, with some finding no abnormalities in asymptomatic patients (105), and others finding frontotemporal theta slowing as a predominant finding (106). Computerized electroencephalography may be more sensitive in detecting early changes and may predict subsequent development of HIV-1–related neurological disease (106).

Evoked potential studies have also been useful to detect abnormalities in neurologically and physically asymptomatic HIV-1 seropositive patients (107, 108). When compared with controls, these patients showed significant delays in latency of response to the brainstem auditory evoked potential, somatosensory evoked potentials from tibial nerve stimulation, and visual evoked potentials. Thus, evoked potentials may represent a preliminary direct indicator of neurologic involvement in HIV-1 disease even before the HIV-1–associated cognitive/motor complex becomes clinically apparent.

Cerebrospinal Fluid Studies

The CSF reflects changes consistent with HIV-1 infection, including HIV-1 virions, abnormally elevated IgG levels, HIV-1 specific antibodies, mononuclear cells, and oligoclonal bands (6, 109–115). Although the amount of the intrathecal virus and antibody has not been found to correlate with either the severity of neurological disease or cognitive dysfunction (110), CSF beta-2-microglobulin has shown a high correlation between its concentration and both the severity of the dementia and the level of systemic disease (111–112). Elevation in the myelin basic protein and its degradation was found in patients with HIV-1–associated cognitive/motor complex and with PML, this was not seen in patients with other opportunistic infections (116). An abnormally low CD4+/CD8+ ratio was found in the CSF and preceded the one in blood (117); this may have importance for treatment considerations.

TREATMENT OF HIV-1 CENTRAL NERVOUS SYSTEM INFECTION

It is currently a well-known fact that brain infection is the most common cause of cognitive impairment of any person suffering with HIV-1 infection. Most of the histopathologic changes and HIV-1 viral antigens are localized in subcortical areas (7, 8), comparable with the predominant clinical presentation of the HIV-1–associated cognitive/motor complex (118, 119). Because these studies so clearly implicate direct HIV-1 brain infections, the rationale for treating the HIV-1–associated cognitive/motor complex with antiviral agents appears obvious. Given that the CNS can serve as a sanctuary for HIV-1 itself, further rationale exists for the antiviral approach to treatment. Antiviral medication that penetrates the BBB and blood-CSF barrier is clearly necessary.

Various drugs are now effective against the HIV-1 and approved by the Food and Drug Administration for clinical use (120, 121). The most widely used and the initial drug of choice for patients who have not received any prior anti-HIV-1 therapy is AZT. In vitro results of its capacity to inhibit retroviral replication have been confirmed in human studies that indicate that AZT is effective in reducing the morbidity and mortality of AIDS patients and of asymptomatic patients with fewer than 500 CD4 cells/mm (122), but not in those with more than 500 CD4 cells/mm (123). Is also suggested that therapy with AZT during the primary infection may improve the subsequent clinical course and increase the CD4 cell count (124). Studies also show that AZT improves cognitive functioning in patients with minor cognitive changes who are otherwise asymptomatic (125) and reduces the neurocognitive deficits when used long-term, therefore reducing the risk of HIV-1–associated dementia (126, 127). The optimum dose of AZT for the treatment of cognitive impairment is not known. Low doses (300 mg/day) have been associated with improvement in cognitive function tests, but systematic evaluation of low doses in the treatment of HIV-1 dementia has not been completed. Experimental data show that AZT penetrates the brain at a level half of which can be recovered from CSF (128). Furthermore, the findings of Sidtis and colleagues (129) that significant gains in cognition occurred with AZT doses of 2000 mg/day are consistent with this brain parenchymal bioavailability characteristic. Another nucleoside, didanosine (ddI), is now used in the treatment of AIDS and has also been effective in improving HIV-1–associated cognitive impairment in a small number of cases (130). However, controlled studies confirming ddI's efficacy in improving cognitive function or preventing further decline are yet to be conducted. Other nucleosides, zalcitabine (ddC), stavudine (D4T) and lamivudine (3TC), and the nonnucleoside reverse transcriptase inhibitors (derivatives of tetrahydroimidazobenzodiazepin, dipyridodiazepine, pyridinone, and bis(heteroaryl) piperazines) have efficacy alone or in combination, in the treatment of AIDS (120), but no reports have been made about their effect in the neurocognitive decline of HIV-1–infected persons. Additionally, the new protease inhibitors that prevent maturation of HIV-1 particles (131) are showing promise in proposed combination therapy with the reverse transcriptase agents in ameliorating the cognitive effects of CNS HIV-1 infection.

Side effects of the nucleoside drugs include mania (132, 133), delirium (134), and myopathy (34, 37–39) for AZT, mania (135, 136) and peripheral neuropathies for ddI, and peripheral neuropathies for ddC (120). Less commonly, confusion, insomnia or somnolence, and anxiety or nervousness may be bothersome for patients on nucleoside therapy (137). Other systemic side effects may mandate dose modification to reduce risks. Therapy with vitamin B12 to reduce risk of hematologic toxicity with AZT (137) may be also used.

Other biological interventions specific for CNS HIV-1 infection include peptide-T (138), which is capable of blocking the binding of gp120 to CD4 receptors in the CNS. It appears to be less toxic than the antivirals and is reported to reverse, as well as prevent, neurocognitive impairments. As mentioned earlier, calcium channel blockers such as nimodipine are being used to regulate CNS injury secondary to intracellular calcium increases caused by HIV-1 infection. Other agents also being tested provide a rational approach to the treatment of the pathophysiology presumed to be related to HAD.

NEUROPSYCHIATRIC SYMPTOMATOLOGY OF HIV-1 INFECTION

Mental disorders secondary to medical conditions such as delirium, dementia, mood disorders, and anxiety disorders are the most common neuropsychiatric conditions associated with HIV-1 infection (139, 140). Personality change with significant variation in the MMPI (141), psychotic disorders due to general medical condition, and substance-induced disorders may also be seen. One of the most perplexing aspects of these presentations is that HIV-1–related neuropsychiatric manifestations so closely resemble other primary psychiatric (functional) disorders. Like syphilis, HIV-1 infection often confounds precise diagnostic criteria due to its characteristic as a "great imitator."

Delirium

Delirium is the most common mental disorder observed in general medical conditions associated with HIV-1 infection. It is estimated that as many as 30% of hospitalized medical/surgical patients may have an undetected delirium process (142). Delirium may also be the most frequently undiagnosed of all organic disorders in the outpatient setting. As the treatment of most HIV-1 complications has become more sophisticated, it has also become more simple. Patients are treated more aggressively in either an ambulatory clinic (such as cancer chemotherapy settings) or at home with infusion therapy for infections and malignancies associated with HIV-1 infection. Undiagnosed delirium in the ambulatory setting poses a particular danger because of the lost opportunity to diagnose and treat a potentially reversible complication of a medical disorder or its treatment.

Delirium reflects diffuse cerebral cellular metabolic dysfunction (143). A common prodromal phase involves patients' complaints of difficulty in thinking, restlessness, irritability, insomnia, or interrupted short periods of sleep containing vivid nightmares. Evidence of this prodromal phase should be regarded seriously and generate a search for the underlying cause of the delirium process. A brief mental status examination should focus on arousal, attention, short-term memory, and orientation. Diurnal variations in the delirium process are common with symptoms typically worsening at night. Motor abnormalities, including tremor, picking at clothing, multifocal myoclonus, and asterixis, can also be found.

There are diverse suggestions for the etiology of HIV-1–related delirium (134, 142). However, it is important to attempt to determine the particular etiology for each individual patient because certain frequent causes are life-threatening or may lead to permanent brain damage. These conditions include Wernicke's encephalopathy, hypoglycemia, hyperglycemia, hypoxemia, hemodynamic instability with cerebral hypoperfusion, infections, metabolic disturbances, and electrolyte imbalances (142). Herpes and *Toxoplasma gondii* encephalitis, cryptococcal meningitis, space-occupying lesions from cerebral tumors, progressive multifocal leukoencephalopathy, and neurotoxicities from antiviral agents should be included in the differential diagnosis of delirium in HIV-1 patients (142). In the substance abuse population, the detection of alcohol and nonalcohol intoxication or withdrawal is extremely important in the differential diagnostic considerations for the etiology of delirium in HIV-1 disease.

Prompt pharmacologic interventions may help remediate the various behavioral abnormalities associated with the delirium process. High-potency neuroleptics may be used prudently for the control of delirium in HIV-1–infected patients (134, 144–148). Haloperidol, especially by oral or intramuscular administration, has been successful in the management of delirium in HIV-1–infected patients, but not without significant treatment-emergent side effects. At low doses, haloperidol and chlorpromazine—a low potency neuroleptic—have been used effectively and with few side effects in the treatment of delirium in hospitalized AIDS patients (149).

Intravenous haloperidol, either alone or in combination with lorazepam and/or hydromorphone, appears to be both safe and effective for use with agitated delirious HIV-1 patients (134, 146–148). A continuous intravenous infusion of haloperidol may be considered to achieve full control of refractory cases of delirium associated with severe agitation as has been described for cancer patients (148). Although the possibility of treatment-related adverse effects, even with intravenous neuroleptics (150–153), must be weighed against the dangers of the delirium, the use of intravenous haloperidol, either alone or in combination with other agents, can be safe and effective. Although intravenous haloperidol is not specifically approved by the Food and Drug Administration, it can be approved for compassionate use with permission from one's institutional review board or hospital pharmacy committee.

Molindone has also been reported as an efficacious and safer alternative for the treatment of delirious patients who can take oral medications and are sensitive to side effects with high-potency neuroleptics (154). Risperidone has been reported as useful in the treatment of hypoactive delirious HIV-1–infected patients with hallucinations (155).

Lorazepam is useful in the management of agitated delirious HIV-1–infected patients when used in combination with haloperidol; however, lorazepam alone appears to be ineffective and associated with treatment-limiting side effects (149).

Due to the fact that HIV-1–infected patients are often more sensitive to neuroleptics, a lower dose than that administered to other medically ill delirious patients (134) may accomplish the desired clinical effects while limiting side effects. However, in cases where there is an imperative and urgent need to control severe agitation that threatens the patient's or the medical staff's well-being, high doses of intravenous neuroleptics may be warranted. Extrapyramidal side effects have been noted to be significantly more frequent if the patient has delirium with a coexisting organic mental disorder (134). Intravenous neuroleptic therapy has not been reported to aggravate concurrent seizure cases. Likewise, intravenous haloperidol did not worsen the hemodynamic state of delirious HIV-1–in-

fected patients when they were not hypovolemic at the initiation of therapy (134). Moreover, no instances of neuroleptic malignant syndrome have been reported with the intravenous route of administration as opposed to others (153).

Dementia

Among the neuropsychiatric complications of HIV-1 infection, dementia is commonly seen. It is characterized as an acquired intellectual impairment resulting in persistent deficits in many areas, including memory, language, cognition, visuospatial skills, personality, or emotional functioning. Dementia differs from delirium in that its related deficits persist over time. Table 60.6 lists the formal evaluation of an HIV-1 demented patient. HIV-1–associated cognitive disorders involve a subcortical degenerative or dementing process, and it is estimated that approximately 70% of persons infected with HIV-1 will develop an organic cognitive or mental disorder sometime during the course of their illness. Basic functions such as alertness, arousal, memory, and normal rates of information processing are impaired by HIV-1 involvement of the white matter in the CNS. Thus, HIV-1–associated dementia has been characterized as a "subcortical" dementing process

Table 60.6 Evaluation of Dementia in HIV Disease

History

GDS Stage[a]	Clinical Stage
1	Normal—no cognitive decline
2	Forgetfulness—subjective complaints
3	Early confusional—mild cognitive decline
4	Late confusional—moderate cognitive decline
5	Early dementia—moderately severe cognitive decline
6	Middle dementia—severe cognitive decline
7	Late dementia—global deterioration

Physical and neurologic examination (for the psychiatrist)

(1)	State of consciousness—level, variability
(2)	Pattern of breathing
(3)	Size and reactivity of pupils
(4)	Eye movements and vestibular response
(5)	Motor responses (including psychomotor)

Psychiatric (mental status)

(1)	Cognitive—attention, concentration, memory, abstraction
(2)	Affective—apathy, irritability, startle, lability
(3)	Perceptual—hypersensitivity, illusions, hallucinations
(4)	Physiologic—sleep-wake, headache, weakness
(5)	Behavioral—impulsivity, tact, activities of daily living

Clinical laboratory assessment

Recommended tests	Additional tests
CBC	T4, T3 uptake, TSH
BUN, creatinine	Magnesium, zinc
FBS	Toxic screen
VDRL	B12, folate
CMV, EBV, *Toxoplasma,*	
Candida, herpes, and	
cryptococcal serologies	
Electrolytes	
Liver function tests	
Serum cortisol levels	
Urinalysis	
Blood gases	
CT scan—brain	
Chest x-ray	
Liver enzymes, bilirubin, ammonia	
Ca, P, Alkaline phosphatase	
Electroencephalogram	
CSF	

Adapted from Fernandez F, Levy JK. Adjuvant treatment of HIV dementia with psychostimulants. In: Ostrow D, ed. Behavioral aspects of AIDS and other sexually transmitted diseases. New York: Plenum Publishing, 1990:279–286.
[a] Global Deterioration Scale from Reisberg B, Ferris SH, de Leon MJ, et al. The global deterioration scale (GDS): an instrument for the assessment of primary degenerative dementia (PDD). Am J Psychiatry 1982;139:1136–1139.

Table 60.7 Criteria for Clinical Diagnosis of HIV-1–Associated Minor Cognitive/Motor Disorder

1. Cognitive/motor/behavioral abnormalities (each of the following)
   a. At least two of the following present for at least one month
      (1) Impaired attention or concentration
      (2) Mental slowing
      (3) Impaired memory
      (4) Slowed movements
      (5) Incoordination
      (6) Personality change, irritability, or emotional lability
   b. Acquired cognitive/motor abnormality verified by clinical neurologic examination or neuropsychological testing (e.g., fine motor speed, manual dexterity, perceptual motor skills, attention/concentration, speed of processing information, abstraction/reasoning, visuospatial skills, memory/learning, or speech/language).
2. Disturbance from # 1 causes mild impairment of work or activities of daily living.
3. Does not meet criteria for HIV-1–associated dementia complex or HIV-1–associated myelopathy (see Table 60.8).
4. No evidence of another etiology, including active CNS opportunistic infection or malignancy, severe systemic illness, active alcohol or substance use, acute or chronic substance withdrawal, adjustment disorder, or other psychiatric disorders.
5. HIV seropositivity (ELISA test confirmed by Western blot, polymerase chain reaction, or culture).

Adapted from Janssen RS, Saykin AJ, Cannon L, et al. American Academy of Neurology AIDS Task Force. Nomenclature and research case definitions for neurologic manifestations of human immunodeficiency virus-type-1 (HIV-1) infection. Neurology 1991;41: 778–785.

Table 60.8 Criteria for Clinical Diagnosis of HIV-1–Associated Cognitive/Motor Complex

A. HIV-1–associated dementia complex

Each of the following:

1. Acquired abnormality in at least two of the following cognitive abilities for at least one month: attention/concentration, speed of processing information, abstraction/reasoning, visuospatial skills, memory/learning, and speech/language. Cognitive dysfunction causing impairment of work or activities of daily living should not be attributable solely to severe systemic illness.
2. At least one of the following:
   (a) Acquired abnormality in motor function or performance verified by clinical examination, neuropsychological testing or both.
   (b) Decline in motivation or emotional control or change in social behavior.
3. Absence of clouding of consciousness during a period long enough to establish the presence of # 1
4. No evidence of another etiology, including active CNS opportunistic infection or malignancy, other psychiatric disorders (e.g., depression), active alcohol or substance use, or acute or chronic substance withdrawal.
5. HIV seropositivity (ELISA test confirmed by Western blot, polymerase chain reaction, or culture).

B. HIV-1–associated myelopathy

Each of the following:

1. Acquired abnormality in lower-extremity neurologic function disproportionate to upper-extremity abnormality verified by reliable history and neurologic examination.
2. Myelopathic disturbance is severe enough to require constant unilateral support for walking.
3. Criteria for HIV-1–associated dementia complex are not fulfilled.
4. No evidence of another etiology, including neoplasm, compressive lesion, or multiple sclerosis.
5. HIV seropositivity (ELISA test confirmed by Western blot, polymerase chain reaction, or culture).

Adapted from Janssen RS, Saykin AJ, Cannon L, et al. American Academy of Neurology AIDS Task Force. Nomenclature and research case definitions for neurologic manifestations of human immunodeficiency virus-type-1 (HIV-1) infection. Neurology 1991;41: 778–785.

(119). Symptoms closely associated with subcortical disorders, such as Parkinson's disease, progressive supranuclear palsy, and multiple sclerosis, are also seen with HIV-1 CNS involvement and the HIV-1–associated cognitive/motor complex. In the early stages, neuropsychological tests for HIV-1 cognitive impairment should reflect memory registration, storage, and retrieval; psychomotor speed; information processing rate; and fine motor function, which reflects the characterization of HIV-1 cognitive impairment as a subcortical process (119, 139). In the later stages of HIV-1 disease, other traditionally cortical syndromes such as aphasia, agnosia, apraxia, and other sensory-perceptual functions are also manifested, perhaps as a result of some focal opportunistic infection or neoplastic invasion of the CNS or HIV-1 infection itself.

Diagnostic criteria for the HIV-1–associated minor cognitive/motor disorder that manifest early in the course of the HIV-1 infection are found in Table 60.7. Because the early signs of cognitive impairment are often mild, they often go undiagnosed or misdiagnosed as a systemic or psychosocial reaction to HIV-1 infection. Complaints such as forgetfulness, inattention and difficulty concentrating, mental slowing, and loss of interest or pleasure in everyday activities often may be misinterpreted as an understandable reaction to having contracted the virtually always fatal HIV-1 disease. Many patients will be able to recognize and report their own mental, physical, and mood symptoms, even with the cognitive impairment of early HIV-1 disease. Diagnostic criteria for the HIV-1–associated cognitive/motor complex encountered late in the course of the dementia are found in Table 60.8. Moderate to severe cognitive deficits, confusion, psychomotor slowing, and seizures may develop as the course of the dementia advances. Patients may appear mute and catatonic. Socially inappropriate behavior, psychosis, mania, and marked motor abnormalities, including ataxia, spasticity, hyperreflexia, hypertonia and incontinence of bladder and bowel, can occur.

Besides antiviral therapy to recover and prevent cognitive decline associated with HIV-1 infection, improvement of affective and cognitive symptoms has been described with the use of methylphenidate in doses ranging from 10 to 90 mg/day in divided doses (155–157). Medications that prevent the toxicity caused by the HIV-1 through the NMDA receptor are currently under investigation; they include calcium-channel blockers such as nimodipine or nifedipine, and NMDA-receptor antagonists such as memantine and nitroglycerin (158). These may prevent the development of cognitive symptoms associated with the toxicity caused by the HIV-1. However, no controlled studies have been reported that confirm this hypothesis.

Mood Disorders

Mood disorders associated with HIV-1 infection are most frequently depressive, but manic and hypomanic disturbances have also been described (159, 160). Close to 85% of HIV-1 seropositive individuals will exhibit some evidence of mood disturbance (161). The diagnostic process for evaluating mood disorders is complex, requiring careful consideration of the interaction of medical conditions, substances and behavioral factors. A reliable diagnosis ensures that prompt and effective therapeutic intervention will be undertaken.

Depression is commonly observed in patients with HIV-1–related disorders. A wide spectrum of mood disorders may be classified as depression. Patients may report mood disturbances that range from normal sadness to major affective disorder, as well as mood disorder due to a general medical condition or substance induced. It is very difficult, therefore, to arrive at a universally appropriate description of HIV-1–related depression. Formulating an accurate diagnosis of depression in HIV-1 disease is so difficult because many of the usual diagnostic indicators of depression are also common to both HIV-1 systemic disease and to HIV-1–related neurologic impairment (162). Although it has been suggested that clinicians rely on psychological rather than somatic symptoms of depression to fulfill diagnostic criteria for depression in the medically ill (163), an all-inclusive approach is often the simplest and most clinically effective. If all symptoms are counted toward a diagnosis of depression (regardless of the etiology), then symptoms of questionable physical or psychological origin will nonetheless be considered valid diagnostic indicators. Depression in all medically ill patients is both underdiagnosed and undertreated (164), and this is particularly true of HIV-1–infected persons, who suffer an increased incidence of depression when compared with other medically ill patients or the general population. This correlation has led some to postulate that there are certain features of HIV-1 infection that contribute to a depressive syndrome.

Suicidal thoughts are almost always a symptom of depression, and patients need to be assessed carefully. Definite risk factors include social isolation, perceived lack of social support, adjustment disorder, personality disorder, alcohol abuse, HIV-1–related interpersonal or occupational problems, and a past history of depression; possible risk factors include current major depression, previous suicide attempt and history of alcohol abuse (165). One should never blithely consider the notion of "rational suicide" (166) as an understandable reaction to patients' devastating and socially stigmatized disease. Due to impaired decision-making capacities and likely cognitive inefficiencies associated with HIV-1 disease, it is vital that clinicians respond promptly to any and all reports of suicidal ideation. A thorough assessment of the patient includes a realistic appraisal of the psychosocial situation and of the motivation for completing the suicide, along with a comprehensive neurodiagnostic assessment to rule out a potentially reversible organic mental disorder.

Still today, the treatment of depressed HIV-1–infected patients often comes down to a matter of the clinician's intuition being based on his or her own relevant clinical experience. The area of pharmacotherapy, in particular, lends itself to individual interpretation of risk and benefit for any given treatment regimen. The specific choice of medication and dose should draw from the physician's knowledge of the pharmacologic side effects of antidepressants (167) and take into consideration the unusual vulnerability of HIV-1–infected patients with respect to their likely excessive disability from drug therapy. One such consideration is that antidepressants with greater affinity for the central muscarinic receptor should be avoided for symptomatic HIV-1–infected patients because of their anticholinergic effects, which can mask or aggravate HIV-1–related cognitive impairment or precipitate delirium. Another adverse side effect of these agents is the possibility of excessive drying of the mucous membranes, which introduces the possibility of oral candidiasis, which is often refractory to treatment in HIV-1–infected patients. Antidepressants that have been preferable for HIV-1–infected individuals are the tricyclic antidepressants with low anticholinergic affinity, second generation antidepressants, such as the serotonin selective reuptake inhibitors (SSRIs), bupropion, and the psychomotor stimulants. Newer antidepressants such as as venlafaxine and nefazodone are probably also well tolerated and as effective, and therefore need to be considered as well; however, their use has not been reported in the HIV-1 population.

Generally, the tricyclic antidepressants are chosen to initiate pharmacotherapy with asymptomatic HIV-1–infected patients (168). That is to say, patients who are not medically or immunologically compromised are the best candidate for this form of therapy. Beginning with a low dose of 10–25 mg at bedtime, the dose is then increased by 10–25 mg every 1–2 days until symptom response is achieved. The physician should always keep in mind that, as with other medically ill patients, it is quite common for depressed HIV-1–infected patients to show a positive therapeutic response to a tricyclic antidepressant at much lower doses, ranging from 25 to 100 mg, than the ones usually required in otherwise healthy, depressed patients. After this response is achieved, pharmacotherapy is continued at this optimal dose for 4–6 months longer, after which time the dose is gradually lowered until finally it is discontinued. Having noted the preference for tricyclic antidepressants in asymptomatic HIV-1–infected patients, the question arises as to which particular tricyclic agent might be used for the most successful outcome. As with other medically ill patients (169), the tricyclic antidepressants with sedating effects, such as amitriptyline, trimipramine, imipramine, or doxepin are beneficial to those depressed HIV-1–infected patients who suffer from agitation or severe insomnia. On the other hand, patients with psychomotor slowing benefit from the use of compounds that have the least sedating effects, such as the secondary amines protriptyline and desipramine. Whenever an effective therapeutic response cannot be achieved or where side effects have outweighed the benefits, one of the second generation antidepressants, such as trazodone, the SSRIs, or bupropion, may be tried. Fluoxetine may also be an effective alternative to some of the second generation agents with varying antihistaminic and anticholinergic effects (168). Sertraline was also effective and well tolerated in a small sample (170), whereas fluvoxamine was effective but poorly tolerated due to its side effects (171). However, for sertraline, fluvoxamine, and paroxetine, randomized placebo-

controlled trials with larger samples are needed to confirm their efficacy and safety in the HIV-1 population. Bupropion (168, 172) has an activating effect that may be useful for withdrawn or anhedonic HIV-1–infected patients. Thus it may be an effective alternative to the use of psychostimulants, if the clinician is appropriately cautious in administering bupropion to patients with significant CNS pathology and in whom underlying seizure disorder may be precipitated or aggravated (168). In cases in which the patient is unable to take oral medication, intravenous administration of amitriptyline and imipramine has proved to be effective (173, 174). Despite the fact that the Food and Drug Administration has not yet approved the intravenous use of antidepressants, investigational use of these agents has had safe and effective results. In many instances, it would be prudent to seek approval for the compassionate use of intravenous antidepressants through one's pharmacy or institutional review board. The principal drawback of this practice is that in medically ill HIV-1–infected patients, intravenously administered imipramine and amitriptyline can increase the risk of hypotensive crisis and anticholinergic delirium. Therefore, it would be advisable to begin using the lowest dose possible and infusing it slowly and precisely over 90 minutes (175).

Patients who are being treated with lithium carbonate or monoamine oxidase inhibitors (MAOIs) prior to their diagnosis with HIV-1 disease usually should continue to take it. Increased vigilance in toxicity monitoring with a concomitant dosage alteration may be necessary as HIV-1 disease progresses (176), especially when infectious complications cause severe diarrhea, or in those patients suffering any other form of fluid loss, as rapid nephrotoxicity and neurotoxicity may ensue. The presence of mania secondary to AZT (132, 133), ddI (135), ganciclovir, or antidepressants (160), may also respond to lithium. Likewise, MAOIs may be continued for patients who had depression prior to their diagnosis with HIV-1 disease and who previously responded well to these agents. However, it is usually wise to treat a depression that arises after HIV-1 seropositivity with agents other than MAOIs, because the associated dietary restriction of tyramine-containing foods may exacerbate the nutritional problems associated with advanced HIV-1 disease and MAOIs theoretically are incompatible with AZT therapy, which is reported to have catechol-o-methyl-transferase inhibiting effects (168).

Psychostimulants (methylphenidate and dextroamphetamine) may be tried (157, 177–179) with depressed patients who are symptomatic of HIV-1 infection; with those in whom tricyclic antidepressants are contraindicated or have proved ineffective; and, especially, with those depressed patients who are cognitively impaired or who suffer from both depression and dementia. Methylphenidate has been found to be an especially safe and effective treatment for depression. Response usually occurs within hours of the first administration, providing psychomotor activation, appetite stimulation, and qualitative as well as quantitative improvement in higher cortical functions. The initial administration of methylphenidate is usually 5–10 mg by mouth, feeding tube, or suppository. Its equivalent dose in dextroamphetamine could also be used. After gradually raising the dose to 20 mg or less three times a day, a favorable response is usually achieved. Adequate therapeutic response usually takes less than 30 mg daily (although in unusual circumstances, up to 90 mg a day may be required). These stimulants are useful in treating depression from various etiologies and can be continued safely up to several months after the patient's symptoms remit. Special care should be taken in using dextroamphetamine, which has been noted to unmask or aggravate abnormal involuntary movements in AIDS dementia patients (178). The use of psychostimulants in managing depressive or cognitive symptomatology in drug-abusing patients is questionable. Further research is needed in this subgroup of patients to establish the place for psychostimulant use in the management of depressed or cognitively impaired drug-abusing HIV-1 patients with advanced disease.

SUMMARY

HIV-1 infection has become one of the major health and social issues of our time, with drug abuse, unprotected sexual intercourse, and transfusion of contaminated products being well-determined risk factors. As the prevalence of HIV-1–infected individuals continues to rise, the neuropsychiatric complications are found more often, and their understanding and treatment continues to improve. Signs of neuropsychiatric disorders are now detected earlier, allowing a prompt and aggressive management of these potentially devastating complications of the HIV-1 infection. The overall prognosis of these patients at the moment of seroconversion continues to improve, as well as the quality of their lives; and the contribution of neuropsychiatry is of great importance as we attend to the neurobehavioral aspects of HIV-1 disease in these individuals.

References

1. Selik RM, Chu SY, Bueler JW. HIV infection as leading cause of death among young adults in US cities and states. JAMA 1993;269(26): 2991–2994.

2. Buehler JW, Petersen LR, Jaffe HW. Current trends in the epidemiology of HIV/AIDS. In: Sande MA, Volberding PA, eds. The medical management of AIDS. 4th edition. Philadelphia: WB Saunders, 1995:3–21.

3. Ostrow AG. Substance abuse and HIV infection. Psychiatr Clin North Am 1994;17(1):69–89.

4. Seage GR, Mayer KH, Horsburgh CR, et al. The relation between nitrite inhalants, unprotected receptive anal intercourse and the risk of HIV infection. Am J Epidemiol 1992;135:1–11.

5. Koeing S, Gendelman HE, Orenstein JM, et al. Detection of AIDS virus in macrophages in brain tissue from AIDS with encephalopathy. Science 1986;233:1089–1093.

6. Falangola MF, Hanly A, Galvao-Castro B, Petito CK. HIV infection of human choroid plexus: a possible mechanism of viral entry into the CNS. J Neuropathol Exp Neurol 1995;54(4):497–503.

7. Wiley CA. Pathology of neurologic disease in AIDS. Psychiatr Clin North Am 1994;17(1): 1–15.

8. Shaw GM, Harper ME, Hahn BH, et al. HTLV-III infection in brains of children and adults with AIDS encephalopathy. Science 1985;227: 177–182.

9. Gyorkey F, Melnick JL, Gyorkey P. Human immunodeficiency virus in brain biopsies of patients with AIDS and progressive encephalopathy. J Infect Dis 1987;155:870–876.

10. Hill JM, Farrar WL, Pert CB. Autoradiographic localization of T4 antigen, the HIV receptor in human brain. Int J Neurosci 1987;32:687–693.

11. Wiley CA, Masliah E, Morey M, et al. Neocortical damage during HIV infection. Ann Neurol 1991;29(6):651–657.

12. Aylward EH, Brettschneider PD, McArthur JC, et al. Magnetic resonance imaging measurement of gray matter volume reductions in HIV dementia. Am J Psychiatry 1995;152(7):987–994.

13. Tyor WR, Wesselingh SL, Griffin JW, et al. Unifying hypothesis for the pathogenesis of HIV-associated dementia complex, vacuolar myelopathy, and sensory neuropathy. J Acquir Immune Defic Syndr Hum Retrovirol 1995; 9:379–388.

14. Ushijima H, Nishio O, Klocking R, et al. Exposure to gp 120 of HIV-1 induces an increased release of arachidonic acid in rat primary neuronal cell culture followed by NMDA receptor-mediated neurotoxicity. Eur J Neurosci 1995;7: 1353–1359.

15. Barks JDE, Sun R, Malinak C, et al. gp 120, an HIV-1 protein, increases susceptibility to hypoglycemic and ischemic brain injury in perinatal rats. Exp Neurol 1995;132:123–133.

16. Nath A, Padua RA, Geiger JD. HIV-1 coat protein gp120-induced increases in levels of intrasynaptosomal calcium. Brain Res 1995;678: 200–206.

17. Codazzi F, Menegon A, Zacchetti D, et al. HIV-1 gp120 glycoprotein induces (Ca^{2+})i responses not only in type-2 but also type-1 astrocytes and oligodendrocytes of the rat cerebellum. Eur J Neurosci 1995;7:1333–1341.

18. Lipton SA. Ca^{2+}, N-Methyl-D-Aspartate receptors, and AIDS-related neuronal injury. Int Rev Neurobiol 1994;36:1–27.

19. Adle-Biassette H, Colombel LM, Poron F, et al. Neuronal apoptosis in HIV infection in adults. Neuropathol Appl Neurobiol 1995;21:218–227.

20. Petito CK, Roberts B. Evidence of apoptotic cell death in HIV encephalitis. Am J Pathol 1995; 146(5):1121–1130.

21. Cohen JJ. Apoptosis. Immunol Today 1993; 14(3):126–130.

22. Nakamura S, Nagano I, Yoshioka M, et al. Detection of tumor necrosis factor-α positive cells in cerebrospinal fluid of patients with HTLV-I-associated myelopathy. J Neuroimmunol 1993; 42:127–130.

23. Puccioni-Sohler M, Rieckmann P, Kitze B, et al. A soluble form of tumour necrosis factor receptor in cerebrospinal fluid and serum of HTLV-I-associated myelopathy and other neurological diseases. J Neurol 1995;242:239–242.

24. Heyes MP, Rubinow D, Lane C, et al. Cerebrospinal fluid quinolinic acid concentrations are increased in acquired immune deficiency syndrome. Ann Neurol 1989;236:275–277.

25. Lipton SA. Memantine prevents HIV coat protein-induced neuronal injury in vitro. Neurology 1992;42:1403–1405.

26. Harbison MA, Kim S, Gillis JM, Hammer SM. Effect of the calcium channel blocker verapamil on human immunodeficiency virus type 1 replication in lymphoid cells. J Infect Dis 1991; 164:53–60.

27. Price RW, Brew BJ. The AIDS dementia complex. J Infect Dis 1988;158:1079–1083.

28. Janssen RS, Saykin AJ, Cannon L, et al. American Academy of Neurology AIDS Task Force. Nomenclature and research case definitions for neurologic manifestations of human immunodeficiency virus-type 1 (HIV-1) infection. Neurology 1991;41:778–785.

29. Everall I, Luthert P, Lantos P. A review of neuronal damage in human immunodeficiency virus infection: Its assessment, possible mechanism and relationship to dementia. J Neuropathol Exp Neurol 1993;52:561–566.

30. Sharer LR. Pathology of HIV-1 infection of the central nervous system. A review. J Neuropathol Exp Neurol 1992;51:3–11.

31. Wiley CA, Achim C. Human immunodeficiency virus encephalitis is the pathological correlate of dementia in acquired immunodeficiency syndrome. Ann Neurol 1994;36:673–676.

32. Smith TW, DeGirolami U, Hénin D, et al. Human immunodeficiency virus (HIV) leukoencephalopathy and the microcirculation. J Neuropathol Exp Neurol 1990;49:357–370.

33. de la Monte SM, Ho DD, Schooley RT, et al. Subacute encephalomyelitis of AIDS and its relation to HTLV-III infection. Neurology 1987; 37:562–569.

34. Miller RG. Neuropathies and myopathies complicating HIV infection. J Clin Apheresis 1991; 6:110–121.

35. Levy RL, Bredesen DE, Rosenblum ML. Neurological manifestation of the acquired immunodeficiency syndrome (AIDS): experience at UCSF and review of the literature. J Neurosurg 1985;62:475–495.

36. Cornblath DR, McArthur JC. Predominantly sensory neuropathy in patients with AIDS and AIDS-related complex. Neurology 1988;38: 794–796.

37. Authier FJ, De Grissac N, Degos JD, et al. Transient myasthenia gravis during HIV infection. Muscle Nerve 1995;18(8):914–916.

38. Brew BJ. HIV-1-related neurological disease. J Acquir Immune Defic Syndr 1993;6(suppl 1): s10–s15.

39. Brew BJ. Central and peripheral nervous system abnormalities. Med Clin North Am 1992; 76(1):63–81.

40. Krasner CG, Cohen SH. Bilateral Bell's palsy and aseptic meningitis in a patient with acute human immunodeficiency virus seroconversion. West J Med 1993;159(5):604–605.

41. Grimaldi LM, Luzi L, Martino GV, et al. Bilateral eight cranial nerve neuropathy in human immunodeficiency virus infection. J Neurol 1993; 240(6):363–366.

42. Sweeney BJ, Manji H, Gilson RJ, et al. Optic neuritis and HIV-1 infection. J Neurol Neurosurg Psychiatry 1993;56(6):705–707.

43. Freeman R, Roberts M, Friedman LS, et al. Autonomic function and human immunodeficiency virus infection. Neurology 1990;40:575–580.

44. Craddock C, Pasvol G, Bull R, et al. Cardiorespiratory arrest and autonomic neuropathy in AIDS. Lancet 1987;2:16–18.

45. Price RW, Worley JM. Management of neurologic complications of HIV-1 infection and AIDS In: Sande MA, Volberding PA, eds. The medical management of AIDS. 4th edition. Philadelphia: WB Saunders, 1995:261–288.

46. Maytal J, Horowitz S, Lipper S, et al. Progressive nemaline rod myopathy in a woman coinfected with HIV-1 and HTLV-2. Mt Sinai J Med 1993;60(3):242–246.

47. Seidman R, Peress NS, Nuovo GJ. In situ detection of polymerase chain reaction-amplified HIV-1 nucleic acids in skeletal muscle in patients with myopathy. Mod Pathol 1994;7(3): 369–375.

48. Bredesen DE, Levy RM, Rosenblum ML. The neurology of human immunodeficiency virus infection. Q J Med 1988;68:665–667.

49. Malouf R, Jacquette G, Dobkin J, et al. Neurologic disease in human immunodeficiency virus-infected drug abusers. Arch Neurol 1990;47: 1002–1007.

50. Saag MS. Cryptococcosis and other fungal infections (histoplasmosis, coccidioidomycosis). In: Sande MA, Volberding PA, eds. The medical management of AIDS. 4th edition. Philadelphia: WB Saunders, 1995:437–459.

51. Moller A, Backmund H. CT findings in different stages of HIV infection: a prospective study. J Neurol 1990;237:94–97.

52. Mehren M, Burns PJ, Mamani MD, et al. Toxoplasmic myelitis mimicking intramedullary cord tumor. Neurology 1988;38:1648–1650.

53. Pedrol E, Gonzalez-Clemente J, Gatell JM, et al. Central nervous system toxoplasmosis in AIDS patients: efficacy of an intermittent maintenance therapy. AIDS 1990;4:511–517.

54. Wong SY, Israelski DM, Remington JS. AIDS-associated toxoplasmosis. In: Sande MA, Volberding PA, eds. The medical management of AIDS. 4th edition. Philadelphia: WB Saunders, 1995:460–493.

55. Mallolas J, Zamora L, Gatell JM, et al. Primary prophylaxis for Pneumocystis carinii pneumo-

nia: a randomized trial comparing cotrimoxazole, aerosolized pentamidine and dapsone, plus pyrimethamine. AIDS 1993;7:59–64.

56. Saag MS, Powderly WG, Cloud GA, et al. Comparison of amphotericin B with fluconazole in the treatment of acute AIDS-associated cryptococcal meningitis. N Engl J Med 1992;326:83–89.

57. Stern JJ, Hartmen BJ, Sharkey P, et al. Oral fluconazole therapy for patients with acquired immunodeficiency syndrome and cryptococcal meningitis: experience with 22 patients. Am J Med 1988;85:477–480.

58. Berger JR, Kaszovitz B, Post MJ, et al. Progressive multifocal leukoencephalopathy associated with human immunodeficiency virus infection. A review of the literature with a report of sixteen cases. Ann Intern Med 1987;107:78–87.

59. Drew WL, Buhles W, Erlich KS. Management of herpes virus infection (CMV, HSV, VZV). In: Sande MA, Volberding PA, eds. The medical management of AIDS. 4th edition. Philadelphia: WB Saunders, 1995:512–536.

60. Bolan G. Management of syphilis in HIV-infected persons. In: Sande MA, Volberding PA, eds. The medical management of AIDS. 4th edition. Philadelphia: WB Saunders, 1995: 537–554.

61. Portegies P, Algra PR, Hollak CEM, et al. Response to cytarabine in progressive multifocal leukoencephalopathy in AIDS. Lancet 1991;1: 680–681.

62. Hamilton-Dutoit SF, Pallesen G, Franzman MB, et al. AIDS-related lymphoma: Histopathology, immunophenotype and association with Epstein-Barr virus as demonstrated by in situ nucleic acid hybridization. Am J Pathol 1991;138: 147–163.

63. Kaplan LD, Abrams DI, Feigal E, et al. AIDS-associated non-Hodgkin's lymphoma in San Francisco. JAMA 1989;261:719–724.

64. Kaplan LD, Northfelt DW. Malignancies associated with AIDS. In: Sande MA, Volberding PA, eds. The medical management of AIDS. 4th edition. Philadelphia: WB Saunders, 1995:555–590.

65. Engstrom JW, Lowenstein DH, Bredesen DE. Cerebral infarctions and transient neurologic deficits associated with acquired immunodeficiency syndrome. Am J Med 1989;86:528–532.

66. Frank Y, Lin W, Kahn E, et al. Multiple ischemic infarcts in a child with AIDS, varicella zoster infection, and cerebral vasculitis. Pediatr Neurol 1989;5:64–67.

67. Navia BA, Jordan BD, Price RW. The AIDS dementia complex: I. Clinical features. Ann Neurol 1986;19:517–524.

68. Navia BA, Price RW. The acquired immunodeficiency syndrome dementia complex as the presenting or sole manifestation of human immunodeficiency virus infection. Arch Neurol 1987; 44:65–69.

69. Grant I, Atkinson JH, Hesselink JR, et al. Evidence for early central nevous system involvement in the immunodeficiency syndrome (AIDS) and other human immunodeficiency virus (HIV) infections: studies with neuropsychological testing and magnetic resonance imaging. Ann Intern Med 1987;107:828–836.

70. Stern Y, Marder K, Bell K, et al. Multidisciplinary baseline assessment of homosexual men with and without human immunodeficiency virus infection. Arch Gen Psychiatry 1991;48: 131–138.

71. Lunn S, Skydsbjerg M, Schulsinger H, et al. A preliminary report on the neuropsychologic sequelae of human immunodeficiency virus. Arch Gen Psychiatry 1991;48:139–142.

72. Heaton R, Kirson D, Velin RA, et al. The utility of clinical ratings for detecting cognitive change in HIV infection. In: Grant I, Martin A, eds. Neuropsychology of HIV infection. Oxford, England: Oxford University Press, 1994:188–206.

73. Bornstein RA, Nasrallah HA, Para MF, Whitacre CC, Rosenberger P, Fass RJ. Neuropsychological performance in symptomatic and asymptomatic HIV infection. AIDS 1993; 7:519–524.

74. Wilkie FL, Morgan R, Fletcher MA, et al. Cognition and immune function in HIV-1 infection. AIDS 1992;6:977–981.

75. Martin EM, Robertson LC, Edelstein HE, et al. Performance of patients with early HIV-1 infection on the Stroop Task. J Clin Exp Neuropsychol 1992;14:857–868.

76. Podraza AM, Bornstein RA, Whitacre CC, et al. Neuropsychological performance and CD4 levels in HIV-1 asymptomatic infection. J Clin Exp Neuropsychol 1994;16:777–783.

77. Beason-Hazen S, Nasrallah HA, Bornstein RA. Self-report of symptoms and neuropsychological performance in asymptomatic HIV-positive individuals. J Neuropsychiatry Clin Neurosci 1994;6:43–49.

78. Stern RA, Silva SG, Chaisson N, Evans DL. Influence of cognitive reserve on neuropsychological functioning in asymptomatic human immunodeficiency virus-1 infection. Arch Neurol 1996;53:148–153.

79. Riccio M, Pugh K, Jadresic D, et al. Neuropsychiatric aspects of HIV-1 infection in gay men: controlled investigation of psychiatric, neuropsychological and neurological status. J Psychosom Res 1993;37:819–830.

80. Goethe KE, Mitchell JE, Marshall DW, et al. Neuropsychological and neurological function of human immunodeficiency virus seropositive asymptomatic individuals. Arch Neurol 1989; 46:129–133.

81. Mayeux R, Stern Y, Tang M-X, et al. Mortality risks in gay men with human immunodeficiency virus infection and cognitive impairment. Neurology 1993;43:176–182.

82. Albert SM, Marder K, Dooneief G, et al. Neuropsychologic impairment in early HIV infection. Arch Neurol 1995;52:525–530.

83. Heaton RK, Velin RA, McCutchan JA, et al. Neuropsychological impairment in human immunodeficiency virus-infection: implications for employment. HNRC group. HIV neurobehavioral research center. Psychosom Med 1994; 56:8–17.

84. Van Gorp WG, Miller E, Satz P, Visscher B. Neuropsychological performance in HIV-1 immunocompromised patients. J Clin Exp Neuropsychol 1989;11:35.

85. Selnes OA, Miller EN. Development of a screening battery for HIV-related cognitive impairment: The MACS experience. In: Grant I, Martin A, eds. Neuropsychology of HIV infection. Oxford, England: Oxford University Press, 1994:176–185.

86. Stern Y. Neuropsychological evaluation of the HIV patient. Psychiatr Clin North Am 1994; 17:125–134.

87. Atkinson JH, Grant I. Natural history of neuropsychiatric manifestation of HIV disease. Psychiatr Clin North Am 1994;17:17–33.

88. Navia BA, Cho E-S, Petito CK, Price RW. The AIDS dementia complex: II. Neuropathology Ann Neurol 1986;19:525–535.

89. Reisberg B, Ferris SH, de Leon MJ, et al. The global deterioration scale (GDS): an instrument for the assessment of primary degenerative dementia (PDD). Am J Psychiatry 1982;139: 1136–1139.

90. Fernandez F, Levy JK. Adjuvant treatment of HIV dementia with psychostimulants. In: Ostrow D, ed. Behavioral aspects of AIDS and other sexually transmitted diseases. New York: Plenum Publishing, 1990:279–286.

91. Syndulko K, Singer EJ, Nogales-Gaete J, Conrad A, Schmid P, Tourtellote WW. Laboratory evaluations in HIV-1-associated cognitive/motor complex. Psychiatr Clin North Am 1994; 17:91–123.

92. Chrysikopoulos HS, Press GA, Grafe MR, Hessenlik JR, Wiley CA. Encephalitis caused by human immunodeficiency virus: CT and MR imaging manifestations with clinical and pathologic correlation. Radiology 1990;175: 185–191.

93. Chamberlain MC. Pediatric AIDS: a longitudinal comparative MRI and CT brain imaging study. J Child Neurol 1993;8:175–181.

94. DeCarli C, Civitello LA, Brouwers P, Pizzo PA. The prevalence of computed tomographic abnormalities of the cerebrum in 100 consecutive children symptomatic with the human immune deficiency virus. Ann Neurol 1993; 34:198–205.

95. Hestad K, McArthur JH, Dal Pan GJ, et al. Regional brain atrophy in HIV-1 infection: association with specific neuropsychological test performance. Acta Neurol Scand 1993;88: 112–118.

96. Portegies P, Enting RH, de Gans J, et al. Presentation and course of AIDS dementia complex: 10 years of follow-up in Amsterdam, The Netherlands. AIDS 1993;7:669–675.

97. Mundinger A, Adam T, Ott D, et al. CT and MRI: prognostic tools in patients with AIDS and neurological deficits. Neuroradiology 1992;35:75–78.

98. Brunetti A, Berg G, DiChiro G, et al. Reversal of brain metabolic abnormalities following treatment of AIDS dementia complex with 3′-azido-2′,3′-dideoxythymidine (AZT, zidovudine): a PET-FDG study. J Nucl Med 1989;30:581–590.

99. van Gorp WG, Mandelkern MA, Gee M, et al. Cerebral metabolic dysfunction in AIDS: Findings in a sample with and without dementia. J Neuropsychiatry Clin Neurosci 1992;4: 280–287.

100. Hinkin CH, van Gorp WG, Mandelkern MA, et al. Cerebral metabolic change in patients with AIDS: Report of a six-month follow-up using positron emission tomography. J Neuropsychiatry Clin Neurosci 1995;7:180–187.

101. Ajmani A, Habte-Gabr E, Zarr M, Jayabalan V, Dandala S. Cerebral blood flow SPECT with Tc-99m exametazine correlates in AIDS dementia complex stages. A preliminary report. Clin Nucl Med 1991;16:656–659.

102. Sacktor N, Prohovnik I, Van Heertun RL, et al. Cerebral single-photon emission computed tomography abnormalities in human immunodeficiency virus type 1-infected gay men without cognitive impairment. Arch Neurol 1995;52: 607–611.

103. Masdeu JC, Van Heertum RL, Abdel-Dayem H. Viral infections of the brain. J Neuroimaging 1995;5(suppl 1):s40–s44.

104. Harden CL, Daras M, Tuchman AJ, Koppel BS. Low amplitude EEGs in demented AIDS patients. Electroencephalogr Clin Neurophysiol 1993;87:54–56.

105. Tinuper P, de Carolis P, Galeotti M, et al. Electroencephalography and HIV infection (letter). Lancet 1989;1:554.

106. Parisi A, Strosselli M, DiPerri G, et al. Electroencephalography in the early diagnosis of

HIV-related subacute encephalitis: analysis of 185 patients. Clin Electroencephalogr 1989; 20:1–5.

107. Smith T, Jakobsen J, Gaub J, et al. Clinical and electrophysiological studies of human immunodeficiency virus-seropositive men with AIDS. Ann Neurol 1988;23:295–297.

108. Malessa R, Agelink MW, Diener HC. Dysfunction of visual pathways in HIV-1 infection. J Neurol Sci 1995;130:82–87.

109. Marshall DW, Brey RL, Cahill WT, et al. Spectrum of cerebrospinal fluid findings in various stages of human immunodeficiency virus infection. Arch Neurol 1988;45:954–958.

110. Reboul J, Schuller E, Pailoux G, et al. Immunoglobulins and complement components in 27 patients infected by HIV-II virus: comparison on general (systemic) and intrathecal immunity. J Neurol Sci 1989;89:243–252.

111. Brew BH, Bhalla RB, Fleisher M, et al. Cerebrospinal fluid 2 microglobulin in patients infected with human immunodeficiency virus. Neurology 1989;39:830–834.

112. Portegies P, Epstein LG, Hung STA, et al. Human immunodeficiency virus type 1 antigen in cerebrospinal fluid. Correlation with clinical neurologic status. Arch Neurol 1989;46: 261–264.

113. McArthur JC, Sipos E, Cornblath DR, et al. Identification of mononuclear cells in CSF of patients with HIV infection. Neurology 1989; 39:66–70.

114. Chiodi F, Keys B, Albert J, et al. Human immunodeficiency virus type 1 is present in the cerebrospinal fluid of a majority of infected individuals. J Clin Microbiol 1992;30:1768–1771.

115. Buffet R, Agut H, Chieze F, et al. Virological markers in the cerebrospinal fluid from HIV-1-infected individuals. AIDS 1991;5:1419–1424.

116. Luizzi GM, Mastroianni CM, Fanelli M, et al. Myelin degrading activity in the CSF of HIV-1-infected patients with neurological diseases. Neuroreport 1994;6:157–160.

117. Elovaara I, Muller KM. Cytoimmunological abnormalities in cerebrospinal fluid in early stages of HIV-1 infection often precede changes in blood. J Neuroimmunol 1993;44: 199–204.

118. Pumarola-Sune T, Navia BA, Cordon-Cardo C, et al. HIV antigen in the brains of patients with the AIDS dementia complex. Ann Neurol 1987;21:490–496.

119. Becker JT, Caldararo R, Lopez OL, Dew MA, Dorst SK, Banks G. Qualitative features of the memory deficit associated with HIV infection and AIDS: cross-validation of a discriminant function classification scheme. J Clin Exp Neuropsychol 1995;17:134–142.

120. Fischl MA. Treatment of HIV infection. In: Sande MA, Volberding PA, eds. The medical management of AIDS. 4th edition. Philadelphia: WB Saunders, 1995:141–160.

121. Clercq ED. Toward improved anti-HIV chemotherapy: Therapeutic strategies for intervention with HIV infections. J Med Chem 1995;38:2491–2517.

122. Fischl MA, Richmann DD, Grieco MH, et al. The efficacy of azidothymidine (AZT) in the treatment of patients with AIDS and AIDS-related complex; a double blind, placebo-controlled study. N Engl J Med 1987;317: 185–191.

123. Volberding PA, Lagakos SW, Grimes JM, et al. A comparison of immediate with deferred zidovudine therapy for asymptomatic HIV-infected adults with CD4 cell counts of 500 or more per cubic millimeter. N Engl J Med 1995; 333:401–407.

124. Kinloch-De Loes S, Hirschel BJ, Hoen B, et al. A controlled trial of zidovudine in primary human immunodeficiency virus infection. N Engl J Med 1995;333:408–413.

125. Elovaara I, Poutiainen E, Lahdevirta J, et al. Zidovudine reduces intrathecal immunoactivation in patients with early human immunodeficiency virus type I infection. Arch Neurol 1994;51:943–950.

126. Schmitt FA, Bigley JW, McKinnis R, et al. Neuropsychological outcome of zidovudine (AZT) treatment of patients with AIDS and AIDS-related complex. N Engl J Med 1988; 319:1573–1578.

127. Baldeweg T, Catalan J, Lovett E, Gruzelier J, Riccio M, Hawkins D. Long-term zidovudine reduces neurocognitive deficits in HIV-1 infection. AIDS 1995;9:589–596.

128. Wong SL, Wang Y, Sawchuk RJ. Analysis of zidovudine distribution to specific regions in rabbit brain using microdialysis. Pharmaceut Res 1992;9:332–338.

129. Sidtis JJ, Gatsonic C, Price RW, et al. Zidovudine treatment of the AIDS dementia complex: results of a placebo-controlled trial. AIDS clinical trials group. Ann Neurol 1993;33: 343–349.

130. Yarchoan R, Pluda JM, Thomas RV, et al. Long-term toxicity/activity profile of 2',3'-dideoxyinosine in AIDS or AIDS-related complex. Lancet 1990;336:526–529.

131. Neuzil KM. Pharmacologic therapy for human immunodeficiency virus infection: a review. Am J Med Sci 1994;307:368–373.

132. Maxwell S, Scheftner WA, Kessler HA, Busch K. Manic syndrome associated with zidovudine treatment. JAMA 1988;259:3406–3407.

133. O'Dowd MA, McKegney FP. Manic syndrome associated with zidovudine. JAMA 1988;260: 3587–3588.

134. Fernandez F, Levy JK, Mansell PWA. Management of delirium in terminally ill AIDS patients. Int J Psychiatry 1989;19:165–172.

135. Brouillette MJ, Chouinard G, Lalonde R. Didanosine-induced mania in HIV infection. Am J Psychiatry 1994;151:1839–1840.

136. Katz MH. Effect of HIV treatment on cognition, behavior, and emotion. Psychiatr Clin North Am 1994;17:227–230.

137. Richman DD, Fischl MA, Grieco MH, et al. The toxicity of azidothymidine (AZT) in the treatment of patients with AIDS and AIDS-related complex: a double-blind, placebo controlled trial. N Engl J Med 1987;317:192–197.

138. Julander I, Alexius B, Britton S, et al. Treatment of HIV-1 infected patients with peptide T. Antiviral Chem Chemother 1990;1: 349–354.

139. Perry SW. Organic mental disorders caused by HIV: update on early diagnosis and treatment. Am J Psychiatry 1990;147:696–710.

140. American Psychiatric Association. Diagnostic and statistical manual of mental disorders. 4th edition. Washington, DC: American Psychiatric Press, 1994:165–174.

141. Ayers MR, Abrams DI, Newell TG, Friedrich F. Performance of individuals with AIDS on the Luria-Nebraska neuropsychological battery. Int J Clin Neuropsychol 1987;3:101–105.

142. Fernandez D, Holmes VF, Levy JK, Ruiz P. Consultation-liaison psychiatry and HIV-related disorders. Hosp Community Psychiatry 1989;40:146–153.

143. Lipowski ZJ. Delirium (acute confusional states). JAMA 1987;258:1789–1792.

144. Ayd FF Jr. Haloperidol: twenty years' clinical experience. J Clin Psychiatry 1978;39:807–814.

145. Tesar GE, Murray GB, Cassem NH. Use of high-dose intravenous haloperidol in the treatment of agitated cardiac patients. J Clin Psychopharmacol 1985;5:344–347.

146. Adams F, Fernandez F, Anderson BS. Emergency pharmacotherapy and delirium in the critically ill cancer patient: intravenous combination drug approach. Psychosomatics 1986; 27(suppl 1):33–37.

147. Adams F. Emergency intravenous sedation of the delirious medically ill patient. J Clin Psychiatry 1988;49(suppl):22–26.

148. Fernandez F, Holmes VF, Adams F, Kavanaugh JJ. Treatment of severe, refractory agitation with a haloperidol drip. J Clin Psychiatry 1988;49:239–241.

149. Breitbart W, Marotta R, Platt MM, et al. A double-blind trial of haloperidol, chlorpromazine and lorazepam in the treatment of delirium in hospitalized AIDS patients. Am J Psychiatry 1996;153:231–237.

150. Konikoff F, Kuritzky A, Jerushalmi Y, et al. Neuroleptic malignant syndrome induced by a single injection of haloperidol. Br Med J 1984; 289:1228–1229.

151. O'Brien PJ. Prevalence of neuroleptic malignant syndrome. Am J Psychiatry 1987;144: 1371.

152. Huyse F, Van Schijndel RS. Haloperidol and cardiac arrest. Lancet 1988;2:568–569.

153. Breitbart W, Marotta RF, Call P. AIDS and neuroleptic malignant syndrome. Lancet 1988; 2:1488–1489.

154. Fernandez F, Levy JK. The use of molindone in the treatment of psychotic and delirious patients infected with the human immunodeficiency virus. Gen Hosp Psychiatry 1993;15: 31–35.

155. Levy JK, Fernandez F. HIV infection of the CNS: implications for neuropsychiatry. In: Yudofsky SC, Hales RE, eds. Textbook of neuropsychiatry. 3rd edition. Washington, DC: American Psychiatric Press (in press).

156. Brown G. The use of methylphenidate for cognitive decline associated with HIV disease. Int J Psychiatry Med 1995;25:21–37.

157. Fernandez F, Adams F, Levy JK, Holmes VF, Neidhart M, Mansell PWA. Cognitive impairment due to AIDS-related complex and its response to psychostimulants. Psychosomatics 1988;29:38–46.

158. Lipton SA, Gendelman HE. Dementia associated with the acquired immunodeficiency syndrome. N Engl J Med 1995;332:934–940.

159. Lyketsos CG, Hanson AL, Fishman M, Rosenblatt A, McHugh PR, Treisman GJ. Manic syndrome early and late in the course of HIV. Am J Psychiatry 1993;150:326–327.

160. Holmes VF, Fricchione GL. Hypomania in an AIDS patient receiving amitriptyline for neuropathic pain. Neurology 1989;39:305.

161. Perry SW, Tross S. Psychiatric problems of AIDS inpatients at the New York Hospital: preliminary report. Public Health Rep 1984; 99:200–205.

162. Ostrow D, Grant I, Atkinson H. Assessment and management of the AIDS patient with neuropsychiatric disturbances. J Clin Psychiatry 1988;49(suppl):14–22.

163. Cavanaugh S, Clark DC, Gibbons RD. Diagnosing depression in the hospitalized medically ill. Psychosomatics 1983;24:809–815.

164. Maldonado JL, Fernandez J, Fernandez F. Depresion en el paciente con enfermedades medicas. Medico Interamericano 1996;1:353–357.

165. Rundell JR, Kyle KM, Brown GR, Thomason JL. Risk factors for suicide attempts in a human immunodeficiency virus screening program. Psychosomatics 1992;33:24–27.

166. Siegel K. Psychosocial aspects of rational suicide. Am J Psychother 1986;3:405–418.

167. Richelson E. Pharmacology of antidepressants—characteristic of the ideal drug. Mayo Clin Proc 1994;69:1069–1081.

168. Fernandez F, Levy JK. Psychopharmacotherapy of psychiatric syndromes in asymptomatic and symptomatic HIV infection. Psychiatry Med 1991;9(3):377–394.

169. Massie MJ, Holland J. The cancer patient with pain: psychiatric complications and their management. Med Clin North Am 1987;71:243–248.

170. Rabkin JG, Wagner G, Rabkin R. Effects of sertraline on mood and immune status in patients with major depression and HIV illness: an open trial. J Clin Psychiatry 1994;55:433–439.

171. Grassi B, Gambini O, Scarone S. Notes on the use of fluvoxamine as treatment of depression in HIV-1-infected subjects. Pharmacopsychiatry 1995;28:93–94.

172. Golden RN, Rudofer MV, Sherer MA, et al. Bupropion in depression. I. Biochemical effects and clinical responses. Arch Gen Psychiatry 1988;45:139–143.

173. Bloomingdale LM, Bressler B. Rapid intramuscular administration of tricyclic antidepressants. Am J Psychiatry 1979;136:8.

174. Dorfman W. Can parenteral intramuscular amitriptyline avoid ECT? Psychosomatics 1967;8:131–132.

175. Adams F. Use of intravenous amitriptyline in cancer patients. Paper presented at the Twelfth Annual Education and Scientific Symposium of the Society of Critical Care Medicine, New Orleans, May 1983.

176. Fernandez F, Levy JK. Psychopharmacology in HIV spectrum disorders. Psychiatr Clin North Am 1994;17:135–148.

177. Fernandez F, Levy JK, Sampley HR. Effects of methylphenidate in HIV-related depression: a comparative trial with desipramine. Int J Psychiatry Med 1995;25:53–67.

178. Fernandez F, Levy JK, Galizzi H. Response of HIV-related depression to psychostimulants: case reports. Hosp Community Psychiatry 1988;39:628–631.

179. Holmes VF, Fernandez F, Levy JK. Psychostimulant response in AIDS-related complex patients. J Clin Psychiatry 1989;50:5–8.

61 PSYCHOSOCIAL SEQUELAE

James L. Sorensen and Steven L. Batki

The continuing expansion of the acquired immune deficiency syndrome (AIDS) epidemic among injection drug users has ushered in a new set of problems—how to provide drug abuse treatment to patients who have symptomatic human immunodeficiency virus (HIV) infection. Drug abuse treatment of patients with HIV disease is complicated but can be a key factor in both prevention and treatment of AIDS. Drug abuse treatment for the HIV-infected drug user is, in itself, a form of AIDS prevention because it reduces the needle use of its patients and the associated needle sharing that spreads HIV. Drug abuse treatment programs also provide a setting to deliver other services needed by HIV-infected patients, such as medical treatment, psychiatric care, and social services. However, the needs of these patients with symptomatic HIV infection challenge the resources of drug abuse treatment programs and require the creation of new systems of care that cross the boundaries of psychiatry, psychology, social work, and medicine.

This chapter is about the psychological and social difficulties that accompany the drug abuse treatment of injection drug users and how substance abuse professionals can manage these problems. Other chapters explained how to manage the medical and neuropsychiatric deficits of these patients, so this chapter does not discuss medical and neuropsychiatric issues except as they affect the patients' psychosocial well-being. After a brief introduction, the chapter discusses the psychological problems of drug users with HIV infection. It then suggests several approaches for the management of psychological problems in the setting of drug abuse treatment clinics, including both assessment strategies and treatment techniques. Recognizing that the problems of HIV-infected patients are social as well as psychological, the next two sections of the chapter discuss the psychosocial problems of these patients and strategies for managing them in drug abuse clinics. The need for an integrated approach that reaches beyond medical or psychological care and into the community is stressed. HIV infection has also presented a number of problems for staff who work in drug abuse treatment programs; the subsequent section explains what these programs are and how to manage them. Finally, the chapter concludes by considering these issues in the context of comprehensive care of substance users.

PSYCHOLOGICAL PROBLEMS OF DRUG USERS WITH HIV INFECTION

The drug user who has AIDS is subject to numerous psychological problems (1). Even without the added difficulties of HIV disease, opiate-dependent patients have very high rates of psychiatric disorders (2). These problems include depression, anxiety, and cognitive impairment, which are the topics of earlier chapters. Such problems tend to be exacerbated among HIV-infected patients, as the preceding chapter illustrates.

Four common psychological problems have been depicted in opiate users with HIV disease who are enrolled in substance abuse treatment (2): denial, anger (with antisocial behavior), depression, and isolation. Denial is well recognized as a defense mechanism in substance abuse generally, and it is often exacerbated with the problems that accompany HIV disease. Patients may deny having HIV and refuse to reveal it to their family members and friends. Denial may also contribute to reluctance or refusal to accept medical treatment for HIV disease. Anger also appears. Patients may displace anger about HIV, directing it at their counselors, at their drug treatment, or at their AIDS treatment regimen. They can express this anger by refusing to comply with the prescribed treatment regimen or missing appointments at the AIDS clinic. More overtly, antisocial aspects of anger can also be seen among drug users. These can include continued drug abuse, the selling of medications, or threats of violence. Depression, already common among drug users, may be nearly universal among those with AIDS. A final common problem is isolation. Drug users with HIV disease can feel doubly isolated: as drug users they already feel ostracized from mainstream society, and HIV may serve to isolate them even from fellow drug users.

PSYCHOLOGICAL TREATMENT APPROACHES FOR DRUG USERS WITH HIV DISEASE

This section describes treatment approaches, based on the authors' experience at the Outpatient Substance Abuse Services, San Francisco General Hospital (SFGH). The treatment programs of Outpatient Substance Abuse Services include a 300-patient methadone maintenance clinic, where drug users with symptomatic HIV infection have received highest priority for admission since 1985. Concomitant with this policy, a special treatment program has been developed for these patients (3) and has had its efficacy evaluated (4). As a result of this admission policy, most of the patients in the treatment program are those with HIV infection, and the treatment program has developed expertise in both assessment and management of their care.

Assessment

Diagnosis of HIV-related problems rests on the same basic elements as any other area of medicine—laboratory tests, history, and physical examination. The first step in addressing the psychosocial sequelae of HIV disease in drug users is, of course, to make the diagnosis of HIV infection. In general, injection drug users are strongly encouraged to obtain HIV antibody testing. Any patient who shows signs or symptoms of HIV disease is aggressively counseled about the need for immediate testing because results have a real impact on changing the medical interventions to be applied, e.g., the use of zidovudine (ZDV). Laboratory testing results can also provide direct evidence of drug use, as in the use of urine drug screens.

A complete history is crucial and should include asking patients in a nondiscriminatory, interested, and empathetic manner about their needle use. Questions can include basics such as drugs most often used and duration, frequency, and amount of use. It is important to ask about the route of administration of drugs and patterns of drug use, to get at such issues as frequenting "shooting galleries" and sharing needles with people from casual acquaintances to intimate partners.

The authors also recommend gathering corroborative information from another source, such as a family member or another health care provider, because drug users often tend to minimize or deny their problems with drugs. Drug users may hold back information about family members, but when asked, they often have close family ties (5). Information about the close contacts of drug users must focus on essential areas such as drug use and sexual behaviors, with the aim of reducing risk behavior and the threat of infecting others. Physicians need to be aware of policies that may require informing the partners of HIV-infected drug users if the identified patient will not cooperate with recommendations about safe sex or safer needle use. Consequently, it is important to obtain consent and clearly delineate the confidentiality vs. disclosure issues before broaching issues about family members or significant others.

The physical examination also has an important role. When the physical examination is conducted, the physical stigmata of drug use will often be apparent, such as injection marks or signs of liver disease. A mental status evaluation should pay particularly close attention to the presence of any psychiatric symptoms, as explained in the preceding chapter.

Management

Drug abuse treatment of patients with HIV disease requires much more flexibility than is customary in traditional substance abuse programs (6). These patients generally have more psychological problems than other drug users. Their psychological distress is notable for severe depression. For example, among HIV-infected patients in treatment at SFGH's Substance Abuse Services, 13% reported attempting suicide in the month before they began treatment (7). Depression and hopelessness can erode motivation for drug abuse treatment. Consequently, these patients may need more assistance than others to discontinue their drug use.

In addition, it has become necessary to be more flexible about treatment duration. Even after planned withdrawal from methadone maintenance, the risk of relapse to heroin use is high, and for HIV-infected patients the public health costs of discontinuing methadone treatment are great. Therefore, the authors have been tolerant of program violations in these patients, believing that it is important to keep them in methadone treatment. This approach stems from a harm-reduction philosophy. It applies different standards of care for patients with varying levels of HIV severity and psychosocial functioning (8). This approach also encompasses different expectations of patients regarding substance abuse treatment outcome; a sicker patient, for example, may need to be given more opportunities to achieve a decrease in substance use than does a more functional patient. Even HIV-infected patients must occasionally be discharged, however, if continuing their treatment is harmful to the program as a whole or dangerous to staff or other patients.

Counseling about AIDS issues is a necessary part of the treatment plan. Such counseling is different from typical drug abuse treatment in several ways. It may be necessary to assist patients' families in coping with the impact of HIV. In addition, interventions to help with grief and loss can be very important for the patients themselves, who may be particularly vulnerable when their friends or family members die.

It has been found that appeals to altruism and self-interest are two counseling strategies that can help in motivating these patients. The message "don't use drugs because you may spread HIV" can be powerful, especially if it is paired with the opportunity for patients to become involved in self-help or service organizations.

PSYCHOSOCIAL PROBLEMS INFLUENCING RISK BEHAVIORS

The problems that accompany HIV infection are social, not just psychological. As a group, injection drug users with AIDS have few economic or educational resources. These factors make it difficult for a treatment program to help them build the self-confidence and skills needed to make good use of drug abuse treatment.

It is a mistake to think that all drug users are alike; there is considerable diversity among these patients, and treatment professionals need to understand the variations in culture, ethnicity, and sexual orientation that are so integral to understanding AIDS among drug users. First, African-Americans and Hispanics are dramatically overrepresented among AIDS cases (9). In addition, men who report both injection drug use and homosexual/bisexual contact make up 6% of AIDS cases (10). Consequently, it is crucial to develop treatment programs that are culturally sensitive—tolerant of diversity and understanding of how ethnicity and gender identification intertwine with HIV risks.

In addition, HIV-infected injection drug users have far greater needs for social services than do "healthy" addicts. Drug abuse treatment programs traditionally have had few resources to provide anything but minimal social services. The minimum is not enough, however, when drug users have AIDS. These patients have difficulties making and keeping the numerous appointments with health care and social service providers. Consequently, the burden of care often falls on the drug treatment program.

PSYCHOSOCIAL MANAGEMENT APPROACHES TO SLOWING THE SPREAD OF HIV

Education about AIDS and drug abuse is an important part of managing HIV infection in drug treatment programs. A "levels of defense" approach has been used to prevent the spread of HIV, which emphasizes both drug use and sexual behavior (11) (Fig. 61.1). Regarding drug use, the successively more risky behaviors are, respectively, abstinence, not using needles, not sharing needles, and always cleaning needles between users. They are portrayed in the figure by increasingly permeable lines between the HIV-infected drug user and that person's drug-sharing partner. Regarding sexual activities, the successively more risky levels of defense include abstinence, mutual monogamy, and always using condoms/spermicides.

We must caution that new research has indicated that needle-cleaning is less effective than we once hoped. In the 1980s, research established bleach to be the best of the commonly available disinfectants, like alcohol and hydrogen peroxide, against HIV. Across the country guidelines were written informing drug users, first, not to use drugs, second, not to share equipment, then, if they had to use drugs and share equipment, to use bleach to clean their syringes and needles. Small bottles of bleach, handed out on the streets, carried labels with instructions to flush twice with the bleach, and then with fresh water. These recommendations were based on early research comparing disinfectants against the virus in cell-free media (12). HIV in nature, however, is rarely found unprotected by cell walls or serum. It is often mixed in blood in injection drug users. New studies show that bleach can work, but only if syringes and needles are thoroughly cleaned of blood and clots. Then the equipment must be exposed to bleach at full strength for prolonged periods of time.

In 1993, much of the new research was presented at a meeting cosponsored by the National Institute on Drug Abuse, Centers for Disease Control, and the Center for Substance Abuse Treatment, and it resulted in a widely distributed community alert (13). The new research later appeared in a six-article special feature of the *Journal of Acquired Immune Deficiency Syndromes* (14). One study found that drug users who reported disinfecting their

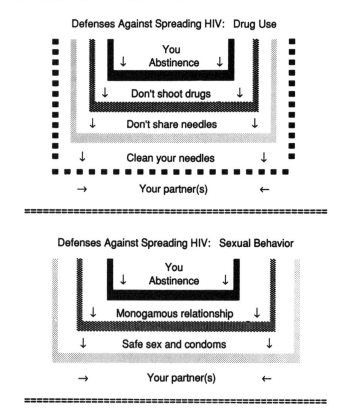

Defenses Against Spreading HIV: Drug Use

You
Abstinence

Don't shoot drugs

Don't share needles

Clean your needles

→ Your partner(s) ←

Defenses Against Spreading HIV: Sexual Behavior

You
Abstinence

Monogamous relationship

Safe sex and condoms

→ Your partner(s) ←

Figure 61.1. For the drug user who is infected with HIV, there are several lines of defense against spreading the virus.

needles every time were only slightly less likely to acquire HIV infection than a matched group who never cleaned needles (15). Another study found that the concentration of bleach and the time of exposure were critical and that killing HIV in clotted blood in a syringe required using undiluted bleach for at least 30 seconds of exposure time (16). In another study, drug injectors were videotaped cleaning their needles. The researchers observed that observed cleaning times were only half as long as drug users estimated and only 20% had bleach inside the syringe for 30 seconds (17). Another study indicated that the "compliance" of drug users with bleach-cleaning procedures decreased as the instructions became more complex (18).

Another caution is that a mutually monogamous relationship provides *no protection* for the partner of the seropositive drug user, but only for others who might otherwise be exposed if the drug user had more sexual partners. Within the context of this model, education can aim at promoting two "bottom line" messages: always use clean needles, and always use condoms.

Encouraging safe sex involves more than simply handing out condoms. Drug users with HIV infection need counseling about the risks of having sex at all, as well as advice about how to introduce condoms into intimate relationships and the mechanics of using condoms and spermicides. Educational approaches may have greater potential if they include instruction that actually demonstrates proper condom use.

Several research teams have had some success with small-group psychoeducational AIDS prevention interventions totaling anywhere from 6 to 20 hours (19–21). This group approach fits well with the tradition of drug abuse treatment programs, and it is an efficient way to share information. In addition, the small-group atmosphere gives a chance for drug users to build social support for changing their drug use and sexual behaviors.

Drug treatment programs also face a growing responsibility to assist disabled patients with social services. These include making referrals for food, shelter, and general assistance. In some geographic areas, stand-alone clinics for AIDS patients may be available to those in methadone treatment. However, drug abuse treatment staff may, at times, need to be the case man-

agers and advocates for their patients, to help them gain access to these services. In some communities, drug treatment programs may need to become the primary health care providers for their patients because of the shortage of these services in the community.

NEED FOR INTEGRATED APPROACH

The widespread problems of these patients do not sort neatly within the lines of professional disciplines, and they militate for interdisciplinary solutions. A patient in methadone treatment who is living in a run-down hotel, for example, may need to be hospitalized, and while in the hospital all of the person's belongings and identifications may be stolen. When discharged from the hospital, the person will need to reestablish his or her identity and benefits, plus attend follow-up medical care and the methadone treatment program.

Managing the various medical, psychiatric, and social problems seen in HIV-infected drug users involves different levels of intervention. The most basic of these is providing material supports. Assisting patients with housing, meals, welfare funds, transportation, and health care can help to reduce the patients' many difficulties and anxiety about them. Another level of intervention is providing information to reduce patients' feelings of helplessness. Self-help groups can be quite important in reducing isolation. Supportive psychotherapy can help to bolster the coping abilities of patients. Pharmacological intervention may also be needed to treat serious anxiety and mood disorders or psychosis. Safety is the keystone of pharmacological management of HIV-infected drug users. The physician must not allow the use of medications to increase morbidity by adding adverse effects to the problems of AIDS and drug use. Furthermore, drug users may not be capable of handling psychoactive (potentially abusable) medications responsibly. All of these strategies can be used on an outpatient basis.

When outpatient strategies fall short, the concerned professional can seek more intensive interventions in the form of day treatment or halfway houses. If these are insufficient, the patient may need to be hospitalized to protect himself or herself, to protect others, or to provide basic self-care.

The increasing severity of these patients' problems, together with their wide variety, points out the need for developing integrated approaches to care. The clinical case management concept has been successful with psychiatric patients (22) and is a promising approach to employ with drug users who have AIDS. Similarly, a peer advocacy model has been attempted with AIDS-diagnosed patients who were homeless (23). These approaches allow the case manager to cut across agency boundaries in bringing these patients to the appropriate services.

Another approach is to *bring the services to the patients* by building the capability of drug treatment programs to provide a variety of supportive services. For example, the SFGH's Substance Abuse Services program has created strong links with other human service agencies. The program is able to provide screening and prophylaxis for tuberculosis to its HIV-infected patients and also provides care for their medical problems. The commencement of this primary care model quickly resulted in a 37% increase in the number of medical visits provided to HIV-infected drug users (24). Models of integrated care such as these warrant serious consideration as the toll of AIDS cases continues to mount in drug treatment programs.

STAFF PROBLEMS AND MANAGEMENT APPROACHES

In planning for the management of the psychosocial sequelae of HIV infection, it is extremely important to consider how to take care of the needs of staff. AIDS has created a psychological crisis for staff in drug treatment programs. They are being asked to attend to the physical, psychological, and social stressors of HIV infection among their patients, while their program policies and practices may be counterproductive for coping with AIDS. In addition, they need to cope with their own fears of infection and feelings about death. This combination of professional stressors and personal helplessness creates a situation that is ripe for professional burnout. Drug abuse treatment staff may be poorly prepared to cope with the stresses of death among their patients. Many of the staff in drug abuse treatment programs are paraprofessionals, non-degreed former drug users working in a clinical capacity. Paraprofessionals carry an additional burden because they are working with patients from a lifestyle they experienced. Paraprofessional caregivers are at greater risk for burnout than degreed professionals (25–27) and more vulnerable to occupational stress because of their limited training (28). As SFGH's program developed an increasing concentration of AIDS cases, several problems were observed to emerge among its staff (29).

Fear of Infection

When a drug abuse treatment program begins to treat AIDS, a concern is likely to arise about staff becoming infected with HIV. Program staff may be concerned that they will be exposed to HIV by drawing blood (which clearly is risky), and they may have other concerns at different levels of certitude about the safety of collecting samples for urinalysis, dispensing medications, and simply being near so many HIV-infected patients. At the SFGH program these were frontally expressed concerns, but the fear of infection came up in other ways: One staff member considered increasing the amount of a life insurance policy, while another had troubling dreams about a doctor's informing them that they were HIV-infected.

Programs can manage these concerns by developing guidelines and providing training. It is important to apply clear infection control guidelines derived from universal hospital precautions for handling potentially infectious body fluids (30). Staff group support sessions and in-service training sessions are helpful.

Confidentiality Dilemmas

Staff can be perplexed by the ethical binds that are posed by unclear and changing confidentiality regulations. For example, should they inform a patient's needle-sharing partner about a patient's HIV infection if the patient refuses to do so and continues to share needles? Similarly, lack of clarity may exist about how much information staff should share with other drug abuse or AIDS treatment providers. Different localities have different requirements about reporting of HIV infection.

There are no perfect solutions to these dilemmas. Drug abuse treatment programs must keep up to date with confidentiality laws and guidelines and make use of outside experts. Until the judicial and legislative systems promulgate a consistent set of local, state, and federal regulations, confidentiality will remain a confusing problem for drug treatment staff who have patients with HIV infection.

CONCLUSION

This chapter has provided information about the psychosocial problems that occur for an HIV-infected drug user who enters drug abuse treatment. The problems are serious, and they challenge the substance abuse professional who intends to provide comprehensive care. Further, these problems are symptomatic of larger dilemmas that go beyond the scope of this chapter. Only a small minority of drug users are in treatment programs, and their HIV-related problems may be largely beyond the reach of most human services. The need to be flexible in approaching this problem has been stressed, as well as the desirability of developing new service models to cope with HIV infection in drug treatment programs.

Other chapters in this volume round out the broad view that is needed to manage effectively the psychosocial sequelae of HIV infection. The field will be more successful if it better understands the determinants of substance abuse and how to intervene early enough to prevent youth from advancing to injection drug use. As treatment approaches are improved, they will provide more effective tools for intervening with patients, including those who are HIV-infected. The suggestions of the chapters dealing with medically ill substance users and substance users with psychopathology also complement the advice provided here, and the chapters on gay and lesbian issues, staff training, and policies can help the reader to better design programs that are sensitive to patient, staff, and community needs.

In closing, the authors want to emphasize the importance of the extremely difficult tasks of providing drug abuse treatment to patients with HIV infection. Treatment is difficult, for both patients and staff members. However, it can be extremely effective in decreasing the destructive drug abuse of HIV-infected addicts, stabilizing the medical problems, and blunting the spread of HIV to other drug users, their sexual partners, and their progeny.

Acknowledgments. *The authors are grateful for the collaboration of the staff and patients of Substance Abuse Services at SFGH. This chapter was supported in part by grants from the National Institute of Drug Abuse (NIDA) (grant numbers R18DA06097, R01DA08753, P50DA09235, R01DA08526, and DA01696).*

References

1. Batki SL, Sorensen JL, Faltz B, Madover S. AIDS among intravenous drug users: psychiatric aspects of treatment. J Hosp Community Psychiatry 1988;39:439–441.
2. Rounsaville BJ, Weissman MM, Kleber HD, Wilber C. Heterogeneity of psychiatric disorders in treated opiate addicts. Arch Gen Psychiatry 1982;39:439–441.
3. Sorensen JL, Batki SL, Good P, Wilkinson K. Methadone maintenance program for AIDS-affected opiate addicts. J Subst Abuse Treat 1989; 6:87–94.
4. Batki SL, Sorensen JL, Gibson DR, Maude-Griffin P. HIV-infected drug users in methadone treatment: outcome and psychological correlates—a preliminary report. NIDA Res Monogr 1989;95:405–406.
5. Cervantes OF, Sorensen JL, Wermuth L, Fernandez L, Menicucci L. Family ties of drug abusers. Psychol Addict Behav 1988;2:34–39.
6. Batki SL. Drug abuse, psychiatric disorders, and AIDS: dual and triple diagnosis. West J Med 1990;152:547–552.
7. Batki SL, Sorensen JL, Coates C, et al. Methadone maintenance for AIDS-affected IV drug users: treatment outcome and psychiatric factors after three months. In: Harris LS, ed. Problems of drug dependence 1988. Proceedings of the 50th Annual Meeting of the Committee on the Problems of Drug Dependence.

NIDA research monograph no. 90. Washington, DC: Government Printing Office, 1989:343.
8. Selwyn P, Batki SL, Consensus Panel Co-Chairs. Treatment for HIV-infected alcohol and other drug users. DHHS publication no. (SMA) 95–3038. Washington, DC: U.S. Government Printing Office (Center for Substance Abuse Treatment), 1995.
9. Brown LS Jr, Primm BJ. A perspective on the spread of AIDS among minority intravenous drug abusers. In: National Institute on Drug Abuse. AIDS and intravenous drug abuse among minorities. Washington, DC: U.S. Government Printing Office, 1986:3–23.
10. Centers for Disease Control and Prevention. HIV/AIDS Surveillance Rep 1995;7(1):1–8.
11. Sorensen JL, Heitzmann C, Guydish J. Community psychology, drug use, and AIDS. J Community Psychol 1990;18:347–353.
12. Resnick L, Veren K, Salahuddin Z, Tondreau S, Markham PD. Stability and inactivation of HTLV-III/LAV under clinical and laboratory environments. JAMA 1986;255:1887–1991.
13. Millstein RA. NIDA community alert bulletin. Rockville, MD: National Institute on Drug Abuse, March 25, 1993.
14. Haverkos HW, Jones TS. HIV, drug use paraphernalia, and bleach. J Acquir Immune Defic Syndr 1994;7:741–742.
15. Vlahov D, Astemborski J, Solomon L, Nelson KE. Field effectiveness of needle disinfection

among injecting drug users. J Acquir Immune Defic Syndr 1994;7:760–766.
16. Shapshak P, McCoy CB, Shah SM, Page JB, Rivers JE, Weatherby NL, Chitwood DD, Mash DC. Preliminary laboratory studies of inactivation of HIV-1 in needles and syringes containing infected blood using undiluted household bleach. J Acquir Immune Defic Syndr 1994; 7:754–759.
17. Gleghorn AA, Doherty MC, Vlahov D, Celentano DD, Jones TS. Inadequate bleach contact times during syringe cleaning among injection drug users. J Acquir Immune Defic Syndr 1994; 7:767–772.
18. McCoy CB, Rivers JE, McCoy HV, Shapshak P, Weatherby NL, Chitwood DD, Page JB, Inciardi JA, McBride DC. Compliance to bleach disinfection protocols among injecting drug users in Miami. J Acquir Immune Defic Syndr 1994;7: 773–776.
19. Magura S, Shapiro JL, Grossman JI, Lipton DS. Education/support groups for AIDS prevention with at-risk clients. Soc Casework 1989;70: 10–20.
20. Schilling RF, El-Bassel N, Schinke SP, Gordon K, Nichols S. Building skills of recovering women drug users to reduce heterosexual AIDS transmission. Public Health Rep 1991;106: 297–304.
21. Sorensen JL, London J, Morales ES. Group counseling. In: Sorensen JL, Wermuth L, Gibson DR, Choi K, Guydish J, Batki SL, eds. Pre-

venting AIDS with drug users and their sexual partners. New York: Guilford Press, 1991: 99–115.

22. Kanter J. Clinical case management: definition, principles, components. Hosp Community Psychiatry 1989;30:361–368.

23. Froner G. AIDS and homelessness. J Psychoactive Drugs 1988;20:197–202.

24. Batki SL, London J, Goosby E, et al. Medical care for intravenous drug users with AIDS and ARC: delivering services at a methadone treatment program [abstract ThD60]. Paper presented at the 6th International Conference on AIDS, San Francisco, 1990.

25. Broadhead RS, Fox KJ. Occupational health risks of harm reduction work: combatting AIDS among injection drug users. In: Albrecht GL, Zimmerman RS, eds. The social and behavioral aspects of AIDS. Greenwich, CT: Jai Press, 1993:123–142.

26. Niehoff MS. Burnout and alcoholic treatment counselors. Counseling Values 1984;29(1): 67–69.

27. Rubington E. Staff burnout in a detox center: an exploratory study. Alcohol Treat Q 1984; 1(2):61–71.

28. Coyle A, Soodin M. Training, workload and stress among HIV counsellors. AIDS Care 1992; 4(2):217–221.

29. Sorensen JL, Costantini MF, London JA. Coping with AIDS: strategies for patients and staff in drug abuse treatment programs. J Psychoactive Drugs 1989;21:435–440.

30. Body substance precautions handbook. San Francisco: San Francisco General Hospital, 1988.

62 WOMEN: CLINICAL ASPECTS

Sheila B. Blume

WHY A SPECIAL FOCUS ON WOMEN'S PROBLEMS?

Western society has a long history of interest in the use of psychoactive substances by women. Dating as far back as the Law of Hammurabi, cultures which have permitted the use of alcohol and other drugs have prescribed different rules for use by men and women (1). These "double standards" have been based on culturally transmitted theories of how women react to the substances (2). The theories, in turn, have led to deeply ingrained stereotypes about the nature and behavior of chemically dependent women. Negative stereotypes underlie the intense stigma suffered by these women in contemporary society, a stigma which at once acts as a barrier to treatment and encourages the victimization of chemically dependent women (3). (See "Sociocultural Factors" section). Yet in spite of the tradition of strong feelings about women's alcohol and drug use, little research was focused on the physiological, psychological, or sociological aspects of women's use of alcohol and other drugs until the mid 1970s. At that time, as part of the renewed interest in women's lives prompted by the women's liberation movement, the National Council on Alcoholism and Drug Dependence (NCADD) and the National Institute on Alcohol Abuse and Alcoholism (NIAAA) led a nationwide effort to focus scientific and public attention on this subject. NCADD established an office on women and a women's committee that coordinated a network of state and local task forces on women. In 1978 the NIAAA sponsored a comprehensive review of the literature about women and alcohol, and convened a conference aimed at evaluating research to date and pointing to promising new directions (4). A second review and conference, which for the first time included a discussion of public policy issues, followed in 1984 (5). The National Institute of Drug Abuse (NIDA) has also been active in sponsoring research in this area, and has published several monographs on women and drugs (6). The Center for Substance Abuse Treatment (CSAT) has also issued several treatment-oriented publications (7, 8).

In spite of these efforts, however, knowledge of women's problems has lagged, and the special prevention, intervention, and treatment needs of chemically dependent women are still largely unmet (9, 10). As late as 1990, sex bias in addictions research was still evident. Studies using exclusively male populations were still common, with results automatically generalized to both sexes (11). This chapter will attempt to review important knowledge about alcohol and other drug problems in women, to highlight some of these women's special needs, and to suggest practical strategies for clinicians and policy makers interested in improving the present situation.

PHARMACOLOGY OF PSYCHOACTIVE DRUGS IN WOMEN

Early studies of the pharmacology of alcohol and other psychoactive drugs were performed on male subjects, with the assumption that the findings would apply to women as well. It was not until the 1970s and 1980s that researchers began to realize that there were significant sex differences in alcohol absorption and blood levels. Jones and Jones (12) found that single doses of ethanol, under standard conditions, produced higher peak blood alcohol concentrations (BACs) in women than in men given equal doses of ethanol per pound of body weight. This may be explained, in part, by the higher average content of body water in men (65% $\pm$ 2%), than women (51% $\pm$ 2%) (13). Since ethanol is distributed in total body water, a standard dose will be less diluted in a woman. However, the body water content difference did not fully account for differences in peak BACs, nor could it account for the observation that sex differences were much greater after oral than intravenous ethanol administration. Frezza et al. (14) subsequently offered an explanation in their finding of a substantial first-pass metabolism of ethanol in the human gastric mucosa, through oxidation by alcohol dehydrogenase (ADH). Normal women were found to have much lower levels of gastric ADH and to metabolize only about a quarter as much alcohol as normal men under standard conditions, thus absorbing significantly more of the alcohol consumed. Alcoholic subjects of both sexes in the study had less gastric ADH, but among alcoholic women the level was extremely low and virtually all of the alcohol consumed was absorbed.

Other sex differences in alcohol pharmacology have been described. Unlike the predictable and reproducible peak BACs in men, day-to-day variability, with higher peaks in the premenstrual phase, has been observed in women by some investigators (12) but not others (15). Increased BAC variability (16), faster ethanol metabolism (17), and less marked acute alcohol tolerance have also been reported in women compared to men (16). In practical terms, this means that a woman will both react more intensely to a given dose of alcohol and be less able than a man to predict the effects of any given amount of beverage alcohol she might consume.

Chemically dependent women in treatment frequently relate their substance use to their menstrual cycles. Women who meet diagnostic criteria for premenstrual syndrome have been found to drink more heavily than controls (18) and to have a high rate of alcohol abuse and dependence (19). In normally cycling nonalcoholic women, Sutker et al. (20) found significantly more negative moods, more drinking to relieve tension or depression, and more solitary drinking during the menstrual period itself, rather than the premenstruum, while Russell and Czarnecki (21) found a correlation between heavy drinking and self-reported menstrual distress. Mello's 1986 review (21a) of research on the relationship between the menstrual cycle and the quantity and frequency of alcohol and marihuana consumption concludes that increased use in the premenstrual period correlates with premenstrual dysphoria rather than the menstrual cycle itself.

Sex differences in the proportions of body fat and water which influence BAC differences also have an effect on the pharmacology of other psychoactive drugs. Lipid-soluble substances such as diazepam, oxazepam (and perhaps some of the barbiturates and phenothiazines as well) have longer half-lives in women (22). As women age, there is a further increase in the body ratio of fat to water, exaggerating this trend (23).

INFLUENCES OF ALCOHOL CONSUMPTION ON WOMEN'S HEALTH

Heavy drinking has a uniformly negative effect on women's health. There is some evidence, however, for an association between low to moderate levels of alcohol consumption and decreased risk of coronary artery disease (24) and ischemic stroke. On the other hand, however, the same intake is associated with elevated risk for subarachnoid hemorrhage (25). Alcohol intake is directly related both to the risk for hypertension (26) and to overall cardiovascular mortality in women (27).

Evidence of a relationship between alcohol consumption and breast cancer has accumulated over a number of years (28). Several large studies have demonstrated a dose-response relationship between alcohol intake and risk in women (29, 30) and another yielded evidence for a weak association at best (31). However, because breast cancer is a major cause of premature death in women, this association and the possibility of an etiological relationship deserves further study.

The role of addictive disorders in the spread of sexually transmitted diseases has been highlighted by the AIDS epidemic. The vast majority of HIV-positive women are between the ages of 13 and 39 (32). Half are injection drug users, while an additional 15% are non–drug-using partners of male users (33).

Prolonged heavy drinking is also known to be an etiologic factor in many diseases of the gastrointestinal, neuromuscular, cardiovascular, and other body systems (34). There is growing evidence that women may develop many of these pathological effects of alcohol more rapidly than men. For example, fatty liver, hypertension, anemia, malnutrition, gastrointestinal hemorrhage, and peptic ulcer requiring surgery have been shown to differ in natural history in alcoholic women compared to men (35). Similarly, several studies have demonstrated the development of liver cirrhosis at lower levels of alcohol intake (even accounting for differences in body weight) and for shorter periods of time, when compared to men (36–38). A recent study from Spain found evidence that alcoholic women develop both myopathy and cardiomyopathy at lower rates of alcohol intake than men and suffered greater declines in cardiac function (39). These differences in sensitivity to alcohol's toxic effects may well be related to the more complete absorption of alcohol in alcoholic women (absence of first-pass metabolism) demonstrated by Frezza et al. (14). In any case, such findings should reinforce our resolve to accomplish early case finding and intervention with female problem drinkers.

EFFECTS OF DRINKING ON SEXUAL FUNCTIONING AND REPRODUCTION IN WOMEN

The effects of drinking on women's sexuality and reproduction are complex and not completely understood. Single doses of alcohol seem to have little effect on levels of female sex hormones. However, inhibition of ovulation, decrease in gonadal mass, infertility, and a wide variety of obstetrical, gynecological, and sexual dysfunctions have been reported in association with chronic heavy drinking (40–42).

The effects of drinking on sexuality in both sexes involve a complicated interaction of socially determined expectations and pharmacological actions (43). Experiments that use special techniques to separate the influences of expectation and pharmacology have found differences between men and women in the effects of single doses of alcohol on sexual arousal (44). Women, unlike men, experience a dissociation between subjective feelings of arousal and physiological responses. Women who thought they had received an alcoholic beverage said they felt more aroused by sexual stimuli under experimental conditions, whether or not they actually consumed alcohol. This expectation effect was similar to that of men. However, their bodies reacted differently. Actual alcohol consumption had a negative linear relationship to measured physiological arousal in women. Thus, although the women *said* they felt more aroused, their physical responses were depressed when they consumed alcohol. The same dissociation between subjective feelings of sexual arousal and actual physical arousal was found in a study on female orgasm, which was depressed by alcohol consumption in a dose-response relationship (45). In another study, normal young women kept diaries of their drinking and sexual behavior. Although drinking was associated with initiating *fewer* sexual activities, the subjects believed that alcohol *enhanced* their sexual desire and activity (46).

Likewise, women suffering from alcoholism also report that they expect greater desire and enjoyment of sex after drinking, while at the same time they report a variety of sexual dysfunctions (47). Recovering alcoholic women have been reported to avoid sex in early sobriety (48). Treatment professionals can be of great help to recovering women by explaining that, contrary to their expectations, alcohol actually depresses their physical responsiveness to sexual stimuli. Thus they should not fear that abstinence will diminish their sexuality. In a loving relationship, they will be likely to find sex far more enjoyable than they did when their disease was active. A study of 58 recovering alcoholic women who had a regular sexual partner revealed significant improvement in sexual desire, arousal, and ability to achieve orgasm with alcohol abstinence (49).

Women who drink and use other drugs during pregnancy risk significant harm to their offspring (50). The fetal alcohol syndrome has a current estimated incidence of between one and three cases per 1000 live births, making it one of the three most frequent causes of birth defects associated with mental retardation, along with Down's syndrome and spina bifida. Fetal alcohol syndrome includes prenatal and postnatal growth retardation, central nervous system abnormalities, usually with mental retardation, a characteristic facial dysmorphism, and an array of other birth defects. Although full-blown fetal alcohol syndrome is seen almost exclusively in the offspring of alcoholic women, other fetal alcohol effects such as spontaneous abortion, reduced birth weight, and behavior changes have been associated with lower levels of alcohol intake (51). The use of other drugs of abuse during pregnancy is also associated with fetal growth retardation and birth defects (50). In addition, untreated chemical dependency in the mother, even if the infant is spared physical damage, may interfere with maternal-infant bonding and adequate parenting. Pregnancy is therefore a critical time for the identification and treatment of chemical dependency in women (8).

Since no safe level of alcohol use during pregnancy has been established, all women should be counseled to refrain from drinking while pregnant. This abstinence should continue throughout the nursing period. Although in the past lactating women were often advised to drink beer or ale, this practice is unwise (52). A study of 400 infants born to members of a health maintenance organization discovered a significant difference in motor development at one year of age between infants breast-fed by mothers who drank during lactation and infants of mothers who were abstinent. There was a dose-response relationship between ethanol exposure in breast milk and decreased psychomotor development scores (53). Although the effect was relatively small, it was significant.

EPIDEMIOLOGY OF ALCOHOL AND OTHER DRUG USE IN WOMEN

Since detailed discussion of epidemiology will be found elsewhere in this volume, this chapter will discuss only a few issues of particular relevance to women. Surveys of drinking and drug use have uniformly found that women drink and use illegal drugs less than men, whereas women are more frequent users of prescribed psychoactive drugs. Cigarette use has historically been more prevalent among males, but more recently smoking by teenage girls has equalled that of boys (54, 55).

Women's alcohol use has increased over the last half century, as have their alcohol problems. Clinicians have reported an additional increase in the number of alcoholic women appearing for treatment during the past ten years, particularly among younger women. This perceived increase in the incidence of female heavy drinking or alcoholism has been difficult to document in population studies, but has been found in some areas of the country (56). There is also evidence from a number of sources that younger cohorts of women may be showing higher rates of heavy, frequent drinking than the generations of women who preceded them. Engs and Hanson (57) have shown an increase in both heavy drinking (from 4.4 to 11.5%), and in various alcohol-related problems in college women, when comparing a 1982 survey with data obtained in 1974. Thus younger women may constitute an especially high risk group.

In the early 1980s, a national survey of male and female drinking practices was conducted by Wilsnack and her colleagues. Women who drank heavily (the top 20% in intake), were oversampled so that their behavior could be studied. Several aspects of the study's findings have been reported (58). The researchers found the highest rates of alcohol-related problems in the youngest age group included in the study (age 21–34), while the highest proportion of heavier drinkers was found in the 35–49 age group. Married women had the lowest overall problem rates, while those cohabiting in "common law" had the highest. The demographic characteristics of women with the highest rates of alcohol-related problems varied strongly with age (59). In the women aged 21–34, those described as "role-less" (never married, no children, not employed full time) were most likely to have problems. In the women aged 35–49, women characterized as "lost role" (separated or divorced, unemployed, their children not living at home) had the highest problem rates. In their oldest cohort, aged 50–64, the women characterized by "role entrapment" (married, children not living at home, not working outside the home) had the most alcohol problems. This last group seems to resemble the so-called "empty nest" syndrome (60). Wilsnack also noted a strong correlation between the drinking patterns of women and their "significant others," more so than for men. Thus clinicians should carefully evaluate the drinking and drug use patterns of the wives of their male chemically dependent patients, rather than just make the assumption that she is "the non-drinker or non-user of the pair."

Estimates of the prevalence of alcohol problems, based on an earlier general population survey and updated to account for population changes, were prepared by Grant (61). Using DSM-IV criteria, this author estimated that there were 2,068,000 adult women (age 18 and above) in the United States who could be diagnosed as suffering from alcohol abuse and 1,950,000 from alcohol dependence during the previous 12 months, for a total of 4,018,000 women affected. This compares with 11,167,000 adult men suffering from alcohol abuse or dependence.

A review of gender-related trends in the epidemiology of other psychoactive substance use may be found in the article by Clayton et al. (54). Data about the use of these substances is collected regularly in national household surveys sponsored by the Substance Abuse and Mental Health Services Administration (62). Data from the 1993 survey indicate that approximately 4.1% of American women (aged 12 years old and older) admitted some illicit drug use (including nonmedical use of a prescription drug) during the month prior to the survey. Among women of childbearing age the prevalence was higher: 8.1% for age 18–25, and 5.9% for age 26–34. For nonmedical use of psychotherapeutic drugs the overall rate of use in the past month was 1.2%, with age 18–25 reporting 2.1% and age 26–34 reporting 1.6%. Regular use, defined as once a week or more, was reported as follows: Marihuana: overall, 1.4%; age 18–25, 2.6%; age 26–34, 2.1%. Cocaine: overall, 0.1%, age 18–25, 0.4%; age 26–34, 0.1%. Alcohol: overall, 10.6%; ages 18–25, 12.3% and 26–34, 14.1%.

It is important to note that these surveys, by their nature, exclude men and women not living in households. This means that homeless people or transients and people living in institutional settings such as the military, college dormitories, or treatment centers are not represented. Since these populations are likely to include a disproportion of regular alcohol and other drug users, the data above must be considered very conservative estimates.

Nicotine dependence is a special problem for women. The mortality for lung cancer in women, after rising steadily since the 1960s, in 1986 surpassed breast cancer mortality as the most common cause of death from cancer in American women. While the prevalence of smoking in men has continued to fall since its peak in the mid 1960s, the rate in women has remained essentially unchanged. Today more new smokers are female than male (55, 63). In 1993, 22.3% of American women aged 12 and over reported smoking cigarettes in the past month (62). Girls and young women should be a priority target for smoking prevention.

FACTORS INFLUENCING ALCOHOLISM AND OTHER DRUG DEPENDENCE IN WOMEN
Genetic Factors

Research investigating the existence of a genetic predisposition to some types of alcoholism is discussed elsewhere in this volume. Here it is sufficient to note that studies which have involved both men and women show differences in hereditary patterns between the sexes. There is evidence that inherited risk factors in women are also strongly influenced by environment (64).

Studies comparing identical twins (who share nearly 100% of their genes) with fraternal twins (who share about 50% of their genes) have been used to yield evidence of genetic and environmental effects on various behaviors and problems. Studies performed on male pairs have generally demonstrated a genetic influence on drinking practices as well as on the development of alcoholism. A recent review of female twin studies by Kendler et al. (65) demonstrates both specific genetic influences for alcoholism and

interplay of genetic and environmental influences in the causation of both alcoholism and psychiatric comorbidity in women.

Studies seeking genetic markers that would identify individuals who carry a predisposition for alcoholism have focused primarily on males (66). However, Lex and colleagues (67) compared a small number of nonalcoholic young women with and without first degree relatives suffering from alcoholism. The groups did not differ in blood alcohol levels attained after a measured dose of ethanol, nor were the rates of ethanol disappearance from the blood different. However, the higher risk women made fewer errors on a cognitive motor task and had less body sway under the influence of alcohol.

These findings were comparable to those observed in male samples. They point to the possibility that genetically predisposed individuals are less responsive to alcohol and less able to judge their level of intoxication.

Psychological Factors

There is a great deal of uncertainty about the role of psychological factors in the etiology of addictive disease in general. Studies utilizing clinical populations of chemically dependent patients regularly demonstrate high levels of psychopathology. Female patients characteristically have higher levels of anxiety and depressive symptoms and lower self-esteem (68, 69) as well as higher levels of shame and guilt (70), while male patients display more antisocial trends. Distinguishing preexisting pathology from that caused by the substance dependence itself has been difficult, but a number of approaches have yielded important and clinically helpful information.

The first approach has been the use of longitudinal studies that follow subjects over many years. Unfortunately, only two of these studies have included female subjects. The Oakland Growth Study identified general feelings of low self-esteem and impaired ability to cope at the junior-high-school and high-school levels in girls who later became problem drinkers (71), a finding that contrasted with the male data (72). The small number of female problem drinkers in the study constrained the interpretation of the study's results. Both abstaining women (many from alcoholic families), and problem drinking women showed similar predisposing psychological traits.

Fillmore et al. (73) conducted a 27-year follow-up study of the drinking status of American adults who had taken part in an earlier survey of college drinking practices. College women who had scored highest on a "feeling adjustment" scale, which contained items such as drinking to relieve shyness, drinking to get high, drinking to be gay, and drinking to get along better on dates, had the highest level of later drinking problems.

These two studies underscore the wisdom of focusing prevention efforts in school and college age women on a broad audience, rather than limiting the programs to girls already in trouble with alcohol.

Several researchers using retrospective data collection methods have studied the occurrence of traumatic events that might predispose to later addictive disease. Miller and her colleagues (74) have studied the experiences of alcoholic women as victims. Their studies compared 45 alcohol dependent women recruited from Alcoholics Anonymous and a treatment program with 40 matched controls from a community sample. Sixty-seven percent of the alcoholic women reported that they had been the victims of sexual abuse by an older person during childhood. Only 28% of the matched community control group reported such abuse, a significant difference. The alcoholic women were not only more likely to have one such experience, but reported more frequent experiences over longer periods of time, especially if they were daughters of alcoholic parents. In these families, the father was not usually the aggressor. Rather, there was a lack of protection for the child, who was abused by others.

These findings were reinforced in a much larger general population sample, derived from the National Institute of Mental Health Epidemiological Catchment Area study (75). The lifetime prevalence of alcohol abuse or dependence was more than three times greater, and the prevalence of other drug abuse or dependence more than four times greater in women who reported a history of sexual assault.

A third approach to understanding the relationship between addictive disorders and other psychopathology is the study of dual diagnosis (the co-occurrence of psychoactive substance dependence and other psychiatric diagnoses). Several studies have found the lifetime prevalence of dual diagnosis higher among women than men in the general population (76), and in clinical caseloads (77). Evidence for preexisting psychiatric disorder was obtained by separating the primary diagnosis (defined as the diagnosis that appears first in time) from the secondary diagnosis (defined as that which becomes symptomatic after criteria for another psychiatric diagnosis have been met). In the general population sample, 19% of the women who fulfilled diagnostic criteria for alcohol abuse or dependence at some time during their lifetime also fulfilled criteria for a lifetime diagnosis of major depression (compared to 5% of men). This rate of lifetime diagnosis of major depression in alcoholic women was nearly three times the general population rate for women, of 7%. Comparing men and women with both alcohol abuse/dependence and major depression, Helzer and Pryzbeck reported that depression was primary in 66% of women, but only 22% of the men. Likewise, in the clinical population (77), women outnumbered men in prevalence of most psychiatric diagnoses. Fifty-two percent of the alcoholic women satisfied a lifetime diagnosis of major depression (compared to 32% of the men). In 66% of these female patients, the major depression was primary (compared to 41% of the males). In both studies, major depression was the most common additional diagnosis to accompany psychoactive substance use disorders in women.

Although equivalent studies in primary versus secondary major depression in women suffering from other drug dependencies are not available, clinical populations of opiate addicts (78, 79) have shown significant rates of affective disorder, and higher rates in female than male addicts.

In further exploration of the relationship between depression and alcohol problems in women, longitudinal surveys of drinking patterns demonstrate that depressive symptoms in women at the time of an earlier survey predict quantity of alcohol consumed by the same subjects in a second survey several years later, while quantity of alcohol consumed at the earlier point also predicts later depressive symptoms (80). In a follow-up of the survey of women's drinking cited above, Wilsnack et al. (58) found that both sexual dysfunction and depression predicted chronicity of drinking problems five years later (81).

The significant prevalence of preexistent depression in women with chemical dependence raises important questions about the relationship of the two disorders. The nature of this relationship and its possible link to the high rate of sexual abuse in these women is not yet understood. A study of alcoholic patients in treatment found women more likely than men to crave alcohol in response to dysphoric mood (82). In any case, the frequency of this co-occurrence underscores the importance of accurate diagnosis and treatment planning for women with primary affective disorder and secondary chemical dependence. Both disorders must be evaluated and treated. Patients should be alerted to the possibility of recurrence of depression during recovery from chemical dependence. Such recurrences should be recognized and treated immediately while special measures to maintain abstinence from alcohol and other drugs are taken. Vigorous intervention can avoid a relapse of the chemical dependence while the depression is being treated. Other psychiatric diagnoses found in chemically dependent or abusing women include anxiety and sexual disorders (83) bulimia (83, 84), and borderline personality disorder (85, 86). Men outnumber women in only two diagnostic categories: antisocial personality (77, 79, 83), and pathological gambling (87). However, women do develop these disorders as well. Accurate diagnosis of coexistent psychiatric disorders is critical for both short and long term treatment.

In summary, women who suffer from chemical dependence are likely to suffer from a variety of other emotional problems, especially depression, both before and after the onset of chemical abuse. Whether or not any of these are specific predisposing factors is unclear, but they are of utmost importance for treatment planning.

Sociocultural Factors

There is little doubt that sociocultural factors significantly influence the drinking and drug use patterns of women, including their patterns of abuse and dependence. Societal norms and attitudes are a double-edged sword. On one hand they are a major determinant of our current difficulties in case finding, diagnosis, and access to treatment. Social stigma and inaccurate stereotypes about chemically dependent women also encourage their victimization (3). On the other hand, drinking norms which dictate lower quantities and frequencies of alcohol use for women may also be protective.

Chemically dependent women are triply stigmatized in contemporary society. First, they are victims of the same stigma applied to alcoholic and addicted males, which either attributes their condition to a moral deficiency, or, if the disease concept is accepted, considers the illness "self-inflicted." Second, since women are generally held to a higher moral standard than men, the shame involved in their "fall from grace" is more intense. This idea of a relationship between a higher moral standard and the prevalence of alcoholism in women has a long history in Western thought, and was expressed by Immanuel Kant in 1798 (88). Behavior that is acceptable for men, as Kant pointed out, may be considered scandalous for women. Consider the expression "drunk as a lord." Now consider its female counterpart, "drunk as a lady."

The third and most pernicious aspect of the stigma dates back at least as far as the ancient Romans (2) and Israelites (89). This is the sexual stigma: the idea that alcohol makes women promiscuous. Although a large general population study of nearly 1000 women failed to find substantial evidence that alcohol has such an effect (58), the stereotype of the promiscuous drinking woman is deeply ingrained in contemporary thought (3).

In the Klassen and Wilsnack (58) study women were asked to complete a questionnaire about their sexual experience and drinking in an atmosphere that maximized privacy. Among women who used alcohol to some extent, only 8% said they had ever become less particular in their choice of sexual partner when they had been drinking. This proportion differed only slightly between lighter and heavier drinkers. On the other hand, 60% of the women surveyed said that someone else who was drinking had become sexually aggressive toward them. The percentage was constant for light drinkers, moderate drinkers, and heavier drinkers. Thus the stereotype of women made promiscuous by alcohol is not merely inaccurate. It results in promoting the sexual victimization of drinking women.

Other researchers have explored aspects of victimization of women who drink. Fillmore (89a), in a study of social victimization related to drinking by another person, found that unlike men, women who drink in bars (that is, who are exposed to others while drinking) are far more likely to be victimized, even if they are not themselves heavy or problem drinkers. In the Miller et al. study (74) cited earlier, women suffering from alcoholism were significantly more likely to have been the victim of a violent crime (38% versus 18% of matched controls), including rape (16% versus none of the control women). These women were victimized not only by outsiders, but also by their own spouses. The alcoholic women had significantly more experience of spousal violence of every kind from verbal abuse (insult, swearing) to serious assaults with fists or weapons (90). Society tends to blame the victim of a rape if she is under the influence of alcohol at the time of the assault, while intoxication by the rapist tends to reduce society's perception of his responsibility for the crime (91).

The practical result of this intense social stigma applied to alcoholic and drug dependent women is to keep them in hiding. Since the chemically dependent woman grows up in the same society as the rest of us, she applies these stereotypes to herself. She reacts to her problem with guilt and shame. She tends to drink and take other drugs alone, often in the privacy of her kitchen or bedroom. For example, 84% of 116 alcoholic women studied in depth by Corrigan (68) did their drinking at home. Married women, employed women, and upper socioeconomic status women were most likely to drink alone. Partly for this reason, the nature and extent of the chemically dependent woman's drinking or other drug use is often not appreciated by her family and friends until she has reached an advanced state of her disease. In addition, although she may seek medical help repeatedly because of numerous physical problems, nervousness, and insomnia, the stereotype of the alcoholic and addicted female as a "fallen woman" makes health professionals unlikely to suspect these diagnoses in their well-dressed, socially competent female patients. A study from Johns Hopkins Medical School examined the prevalence of alcoholism among patients admitted to the university hospital. Although alcoholic patients were under recognized on all but the psychiatric services, the study found that the alcoholic patients least likely to be correctly identified were those with private insurance, higher incomes, and educations, and those who were female (92).

The failure to identify alcohol and drug problems in women early in their development has many destructive implications. Women of childbearing age may produce offspring with serious birth defects if their illness is unrecognized. Physicians who do not diagnose their chemical dependency are likely to treat these women symptomatically for the wide variety of physical and emotional manifestations of the dependence, often with prescription sedatives and minor tranquilizers. These in turn may create an additional drug dependence without interrupting the underlying disease process. Finally, a delay in diagnosis often allows the patient to develop later stage physical, mental, and social complications, making definitive treatment more difficult and less successful.

As already mentioned, sociocultural factors can also be protective to women. Cloninger et al. (93), using data obtained by family history studies, demonstrated that differences in the prevalence of alcoholism between men and women are predominantly due to extrafamilial environmental factors. Protective social factors for women are likely to include less social pressure to drink, different drinking customs, for example drinking primarily in mixed groups (whereas men drink in both mixed and all-male groups), and the relatively limited range of occasions in women's lives in which drinking is expected.

In an ethnographic case study (94) of the wives of heavy drinking men who became unemployed, protective factors in women who did not develop alcohol problems included role modeling by these women's mothers, the belief that "partying" is acceptable for a woman only in teen and young adult years but not after she becomes a mother, the acceptance of drinking by men as part of male social networks, and the custom of women's drinking restricted to special occasions.

CLINICAL FEATURES OF CHEMICAL DEPENDENCY IN WOMEN

Although the basic nature of the addictive process is probably the same in both sexes, physiological, sociocultural, and psychological factors continue to produce sex differences in the course and symptom pattern of addictive diseases (68, 69, 89, 95, 96). Such differences include the following:

1. Alcoholic women start drinking and begin their pattern of alcohol abuse at later ages but appear for treatment at about the same age as male alcoholics and with the same severity of alcohol dependence. This points to a more rapid development or "telescoping" of the course of the illness in women (68). Telescoping has been noted by Smith and Cloninger (97) to be particularly characteristic of women who suffer from depressive illness before the onset of their alcohol dependence. In contrast to both alcoholic and opiate-addicted women, Griffin et al. (96) found that cocaine dependent women began using the drug earlier and came to treatment at a younger age than their male counterparts. This finding needs confirmation.

2. Alcoholic women drink significantly less than alcoholic men. For example, in a study of 11,500 men and 2,600 women accepted for treatment in NIAAA-sponsored alcoholism programs, women's intake averaged 4.5 ounces of absolute alcohol per day (about 9 drinks) compared to the male average of 8.2 ounces (about 16½ drinks), although men and women had the same degree of impairment (98). In addition to sex differences in absorption and body water, differences in the use of other sedatives may also help explain this disparity. The equivalent of the male alcoholic's morning drink may be a morning diazepam (Valium) for an alcoholic woman. Her "nightcap" may contain less alcohol and more sedative drug. Thus alcoholism should not be diagnosed as a function of quantity of intake alone (4). As the alcoholic woman ages, her tolerance for both alcohol and other drugs falls and she will drink even less than before, while still experiencing adverse health and social consequences from her drinking.

3. Women entering addiction treatment are more likely to be married to or living with an alcoholic or addicted sexual partner, or to be divorced or separated, while men entering treatment are more likely to be married to a nonaddicted spouse (96, 99).

4. Alcoholic women are more likely than alcoholic men to date the onset of pathological drinking to a particular stressful event. This is true of cocaine dependent women as well (96).

5. As mentioned previously, chemically dependent women are more likely to report both psychiatric symptoms and dual diagnosis. Depression is especially common, and not unlike depression in nonaddicted women. Turnbull and Gomberg (100) have analyzed and compared the symptoms of depression in 301 alcoholic and 137 nonalcoholic women. They found no differences in the structure of depression in the two groups. They further noted that 88% of the alcoholic women attributed their entry into treatment to "feeling very low and depressed."

6. A history of suicide attempts is also more frequent in female than male chemically dependent patients. Suicide attempts in alcoholic women were found to be 4 times more frequent than in other women, and twice as frequent at ages 20–29 as at ages 40–49. This age difference was not seen in nonalcoholic women who had attempted suicide (101).

7. Chemically dependent women are more likely to be motivated to enter treatment by health (including mental health) and family problems, whereas for the male, job and legal problems, particularly arrests for driving while intoxicated, are more prevalent.

8. Alcoholic women are more likely to reach treatment with histories of other substance abuse along with their alcoholism, particularly tranquilizers, sedatives, and amphetamines, although they are less likely to be abusers of illicit drugs. The drugs these women abuse have usually been prescribed by their physicians.

9. Women who commit homicide have a much higher prevalence of alcohol abuse and dependence than the general population of women, and are particularly likely to meet diagnostic criteria for both alcoholism and personality disorder (102).

IDENTIFICATION OF CHEMICALLY DEPENDENT WOMEN

Women tend to be under represented in chemical dependence treatment. Women are kept in hiding by stigma, which creates shame and denial in these women and their families. However, these are not the only reasons for the under representation of women in treatment. The most common systematic case finding methods in use today, including Employee Assistance Programs, Public Inebriate Programs, and especially Drinking Driver Programs, are very strongly male oriented (4).

Women are most often motivated to seek treatment by problems with health (both physical and emotional) and family. Sensitivity to this fact can lead to the development of new and improved case finding systems for women. Both alcoholic and drug dependent women may be reached through systematic screening in the doctor's office, in hospitals and in medical clinics. Examples of such case finding in medical practice may be found in the literature (19, 92, 103, 104).

Women's special problems with alcohol (including effects on pregnancy and the rapid progression of the late stage physical complications of alcoholism in women), coupled with women's strong representation in medical facilities, reinforce the need for effective systematic screening, diagnosis, and referral of women with alcohol and drug problems in the health care system (105). Screening instruments that have been used for case finding among women include the Michigan Alcohol Screening Test (MAST), its short version (SMAST), and the four CAGE questions. In addition, a simple self-test meant to be completed in the physician's waiting room was designed by Russell for the New York State Fetal Alcohol Syndrome prevention campaign in 1979 (106). The questionnaire has subsequently been slightly adjusted to include several drug-related questions (107).

In screening for high risk drinking in obstetric patients, Sokol et al. (108) developed four questions which follow the mnemonic T-A-C-E. *Tolerance* (an answer of more than 2 to the question, "How many drinks does it take to make you feel high?") scores 2 points. One point is given for a positive response to "Have people *Annoyed* you by criticizing your drinking?", "Have you felt you ought to *Cut down* on your drinking?" and "Have you ever had a drink first thing in the morning to steady your nerves or get rid of a hangover (*Eye-opener*)?" A score of 2 or more was highly correlated with "risk-drinking" during pregnancy. In light of the high rate of prescription drug use in alcoholic women, the eye-opener question might better be worded "Have you had a drink *or medication of some kind* first thing in the morning to steady your nerves or get rid of a hangover?" for general screening of female populations. In a related study of women who drank heavily early in pregnancy, those most likely to continue throughout their pregnancies were those with longer drinking histories, greater alcohol tolerance and alcohol-related illness, and those who were daughters of alcoholic mothers (but not fathers) (109).

Laboratory testing can also be helpful in screening. Dahlgren (110) analyzed the records of 100 women undergoing their first episode of alcoholism treatment in the city of Stockholm. It was found that increased mean corpuscular volume of the red blood cells (MCV) was present in 48% of these women, and an increase in the enzyme gamma glutamyl transferase (GGT) in 42%. If *either* an elevated MCV *or* an elevated GGT was used as the screening criterion, 67% of the alcoholic women were correctly identified. Both tests were also indicators of heavy drinking and birth defects in an obstetric population (111).

Urine testing for drugs of abuse may be an aid in screening for other drug dependence. However, it must be stressed that any positive screening must be followed by a careful diagnostic assessment. A positive urine test should not be equated with a diagnosis.

TREATMENT OF CHEMICAL DEPENDENCY IN WOMEN

There is little research to indicate the best way to treat alcoholism and other drug dependence in women. However, clinicians agree that sensitivity to women's special needs and problems is critical to treatment success (112, 113). Among these needs are the following:

1. Special attention should be given to a history of physical and sexual abuse. Abuse may be missed in routine history-taking because of the deep feeling of shame attached to these events, or because the memory of these episodes may be repressed. It is therefore imperative that gentle approaches to the subject of incest and abuse be made repeatedly throughout the treatment process.
2. Careful physical and psychiatric diagnosis are critical for treatment success. Since women develop late stage physical damage more rapidly and have a higher prevalence of psychiatric dual diagnosis, special care should be taken in making a comprehensive diagnostic assessment. Screening for prescription drug abuse and nicotine dependence is especially important, so that the treatment plan can address all of the relevant problems.
3. Evaluation and treatment of family members is also of special value in women patients. Their spouses are more likely to have alcohol/drug problems, and their children may show fetal alcohol or drug effects and/or other sequelae of growing up in a dysfunctional family (66, 114).
4. Education about alcohol and other drugs should include information about the effects of these drugs during pregnancy, about birth control, and about the prevention of AIDS and other infectious diseases transmitted through blood and body fluids.
5. Parenting education may be particularly important for chemically dependent women, who are often single parents. Furthermore, these women are often offspring of alcoholic parents and have had little experience with adequate parental role models in their own childhood.
6. Child care services are a critical factor in allowing many chemically dependent women to participate in treatment. Residential facilities than can accommodate the female patient along with her children are particularly helpful (115, 116), but few such programs are currently available. The lack of adequate child care has been identified as a major barrier to treatment for women (9).
7. Couples' and family therapies have been useful in some cases, as an adjunct to self help and/or other counseling which focus on the chemically dependent woman herself.
8. Female role-models, in the form of female treatment staff and recovering alcoholic and other drug dependent women, are helpful in treatment.

Self-help groups such as Alcoholics Anonymous, Narcotics Anonymous, and Women for Sobriety (117) are an important source of ongoing support. Female sponsorship should be sought to help the newcomer understand and participate in these self-help fellowships. This role modelling can be supplemented by recommending that the patient read biographies and autobiographies of recovering women (118–121).

9. The low self-esteem of the chemically dependent woman should be addressed in treatment. Special techniques such as assertiveness training have been employed.
10. Sexism and its consequences (for example, unequal societal roles, undervaluation of women's contributions to societal and family functioning, underemployment, and inadequate pay) should be explored in relationship to the experience of the chemically dependent women. It is important that the treating professional not measure success only in terms of adjustment to the societal stereotype of the female role, because in doing so he or she may avoid helping the patient confront her feelings about individuality and independence, and thereby miss the best possible opportunity to enlarge the range of conscious choices about her life. This narrow "adjustment" goal may also fail to raise self-esteem and may reinforce dependent, childlike, or seductive behavior toward the therapist, rather than encouraging straightforward, aboveboard communication. Since the responsibility for her recovery must continue to rest squarely on the shoulders of the woman in treatment, dependence in the therapeutic interaction becomes a threat to that sobriety. Should the patient relapse during therapy, care must be taken not to reinforce this behavior by oversolicitousness or a level of interest not accorded her in the sober state.
11. Special care must be taken to avoid creating iatrogenic drug dependence. Benzodiazepines, other sedative drugs, and dependence-producing analgesics should be avoided wherever possible. When these medications are absolutely necessary, their use should be closely monitored and the drug should be discontinued as soon as possible.
12. Special populations of chemically dependent women need focused attention. Minority women have special needs (122, 123) and may suffer from particularly intense stigmatization. Lesbian women are believed to have a high prevalence of alcohol and other drug problems and may profit from treatment in specially oriented groups (124–127). In some areas of the country gay and lesbian AA groups are available. These have been of great help to many.
13. Chemically dependent women in the criminal justice system are often overlooked, although their need for specific treatment is no less than that of men (128).

There is no consensus about the comparative efficacy of individual versus group therapy for women or the value of all-women groups or facilities as opposed to mixed-sex treatment. If the female patient is treated in a facility that serves both sexes, it is important that she has adequate opportunity to explore issues that she may find hard to discuss with male patients. This may be accomplished either in individual counseling sessions or in an all-female group.

Coed residential facilities should be managed so as to avoid role assignments based on societal stereotyping. Men and women should share equally in meal preparation, housekeeping, fiscal management, building maintenance, and other tasks. Both sexes should take advantage of the opportunity to learn new and unfamiliar skills. Likewise, vocational training opportunities for women in treatment should not be limited to traditionally female job categories. Staff training and ongoing supervision will be needed to institute and perpetuate a nonsexist attitude in chemical dependency treatment.

TREATMENT OUTCOME

The literature on chemical dependency treatment has little to offer in outcome studies of treatment designed specifically for women. However, a number of studies have reported outcome data by sex. These studies have concluded that adult males and females treated together for alcoholism in the same programs do about equally well (129, 130). Less work has been done comparing the sexes in treatment for other drug dependence. Rounsaville et al. (131) found that among opiate addicts, women had a higher treatment retention rate and experienced less legal problems at follow-up, while McLellan et al. (132) did not find sex differences in their study of three different populations of alcoholics and other drug abusers. The McLellan study found that the psychiatric severity scale of the Addiction Severity Index (ASI), a global measure of pretreatment psychiatric problems, was the best predictor of outcome for all groups. Looking at specific psychopathology, Rounsaville et al. (133) followed alcoholic men and women for one year after treatment. They found that those with the dual diagnosis of antisocial personality and alcoholism, whether male or female, had a poor outcome. However, women with the dual diagnoses of alcoholism and major depression did slightly better than average.

Other studies have sought social factors that might influence treatment outcome. MacDonald (134) followed 93 alcoholic women for one year after inpatient treatment. He found that the number of life problems and the number of supportive relationships were the best predictors of favorable outcome. Being married was less important as a predictor than the supportive quality of the patient's marriage. Similar results were found by Havassy et al. (135), who found a relationship between social support and time abstinent after detoxification from alcohol, methadone, and tobacco. They also found that their female subjects experienced less social support than males.

Wilsnack et al. (136) looked at factors that predicted remission of problem drinking in their general population sample of women reinterviewed 5 years after their original survey. Women who experienced remission of their drinking problems were more likely to be under 35 or over 50 years old, divorced or separated, traditional in feminine traits and moral standards, free of sexual dysfunction, and not reporting heavy-drinking friends.

Taking a broad look at the outcome literature, two major factors emerge: psychopathology on one hand and sociocultural factors on the other, particularly support by a social network that does not encourage alcohol and drug use by women. Both prevention and treatment efforts aimed at women will be more effective if they focus on these areas.

Women suffering from alcoholism experience a high rate of mortality, both when compared to the general population of women and to rates of excess mortality in alcoholic men (137). For example, Lindberg and Agren (138) followed nearly 4,000 male and 1,000 female patients over a period ranging from 2 to 22 years following hospital treatment for alcoholism. The excess mortality was higher for the alcoholic women (5.2 times the expected rate) than for the men (3 times the expected rate). Smith et al. (139) found a mortality rate 4.5 times higher than expected among 103 alcoholic women followed for 11 years after inpatient treatment. These women lost an average of 15 years of expected life span. These data on mortality rates for alcoholic women reinforce the need for better systems of case finding intervention and treatment for women.

PREVENTION AND POLICY ISSUES

Having reviewed some of the factors involved in the development, perpetuation, and treatment of alcohol and other drug problems in women, what can be applied to improve prevention strategies? While stigma and stereotypes keep the chemically dependent woman from receiving help and serve to promote the victimization of women, cultural expectations that encourage lower alcohol intake for women are protective. At present, per capita alcohol consumption in American women is less than half as much as that of American men (61). Because of their lower body weight, greater sensitivity to alcohol and special risk during pregnancy, if women were ever expected to match "drink for drink" with men, they would be likely to have more alcohol problems than men instead of less. Unfortunately, drinking customs in contemporary American society are changing. The advertising and marketing of alcoholic beverages sends messages that can, and do, change cultural norms. Manufacturers of these beverages see women today as a "growth market." Because market research indicates that women drink much less than men but make a significant proportion of the purchases of beverage alcohol, women are being increasingly targeted by alcoholic beverage advertising (140). Beverage manufacturers and retailers, who used to cater primarily to a male market with advertisements emphasizing the masculinity of drinking, are now portraying the genteel refinement of feminine drinking

(141). Thus the cultural norms that have served as protection for women are in danger of vanishing.

To accomplish the goal of prevention of alcohol problems in women we must simultaneously work to combat stigma and to preserve the custom of abstinence or moderation for women. Our best strategy would seem to be widespread education about the special sensitivity to alcohol in women, the teratogenicity of alcohol, the risk involved in using alcohol to medicate feelings of inadequacy or other emotional states, the risk of mixing alcohol and sedatives, and other relevant issues (142).

The importance of sociocultural factors in causing and shaping women's problems with alcohol and other drugs also highlights the necessity to explore and utilize the ethnic or subcultural background of the addicted woman in treatment. For example, Carter (122) points to the importance of the mother-daughter relationship in preserving the health and strength of the African-American family, and the role of this relationship in black women's recovery from chemical dependency. Similarly, an understanding of the "corporate" culture for a female executive (143) and the values and expectations of the health professional's milieu, the military (144), and the campus can be helpful in prevention, just as an understanding of specific Native American and Hispanic American cultures is necessary for preventing problems in these groups.

Women can be helped to develop self-esteem and coping skills through stressful periods of transition without the "help" of alcohol or other drugs. Special treatment methods (145) and nonprofessional self-help groups such as Alateen (146) have been developed to help children of alcoholics and others from dysfunctional families. Part of all such programs is education about the increased familial risk for chemical dependency and the development of healthy social support networks.

Little research has been conducted to evaluate the efficacy of these approaches. A single controlled study of an ambulatory program for alcoholic women in Stockholm found a better outcome in the single-sex program than in a control "traditional" outpatient treatment (110).

Policy issues with special relevance for alcoholism in women have been reviewed (105). These include the marketing of alcoholic beverages to women, highway safety, prevention of fetal alcohol syndrome and fetal alcohol effects, child abuse and neglect, custody and child care, and support for outreach, treatment, and research about women.

One of the important roles of government is the removal of barriers that keep chemically dependent people from obtaining the treatment they need. For women, a major barrier is the lack of child care. Many alcoholic and drug dependent women are single parents, or, if married, lack the resources to provide adequate care for their children. In a multi-city survey of services for alcoholic women conducted by the Woman to Woman program of the Association of Junior Leagues, the most frequently mentioned institutional barrier to treatment was the lack of child care services for women needing residential care (9).

Another major barrier to treatment is lack of third party payment for care. Many women in need of chemical dependency treatment are single or divorced and unemployed or underemployed, leaving them without adequate health insurance coverage. This is particularly true for black women (147).

Legal definitions of child abuse and neglect may create additional treatment barriers, especially for women. In many states the habitual or addictive use of alcohol or drugs by a parent makes that parent a child abuser or neglector by definition. This definition becomes a barrier, particularly for disadvantaged and single mothers who must rely on public social service agencies for child care in order to enter treatment. Asking for help in such a situation puts them in real jeopardy of losing custody of their children. Paradoxically, continuing their chemical dependency without seeking help does not, in general, have this effect. Child abuse laws can be altered in their language, not only to remove this barrier, but to provide an incentive for the alcoholic or addicted parent to accept treatment. The State of New York has revised its definitions so that an addicted parent who is participating in a program of recovery is no longer presumed to be guilty of abuse or neglect without additional evidence (105).

Unfortunately, a recent public policy trend, which began in the late 1980s, threatens to erect new barriers to discourage chemically dependent women from seeking the treatment they need (148). This policy directly opposes the rights of the unborn fetus against those of the pregnant alcoholic or drug abuser, by defining her behavior as "prenatal child abuse." Such policies can be used to punish pregnant women for alcohol or other drug use through loss of custody, or through arrest, prosecution, and incarceration (149).

It should be clear from this review of scientific knowledge and societal attitudes in relation to women's use of alcohol and other drugs that the relationship continues to be a troubled one in American society. Until more and better knowledge improves our ability to understand and intervene in chemical dependency in women, and until adequate screening and treatment systems are in place, public policy will continue to reflect the debate between punitive and humane approaches to these problems. However, even at our present state of knowledge, society could be far more effective in dealing with alcohol and other drug problems in women. Simply by applying what we know, devoting adequate societal resources, and maintaining an attitude of concern, our nation could do a great deal more to help the women of today as well as the generations to come.

References

1. Heath AC, Jardine R, Martin NG. Interactive effects of genotype and social environment on alcohol consumption in female twins. J Stud Alcohol 1989;50:38–48.
2. McKinlay AP. The Roman attitude toward women's drinking. In: McCarthy RG, ed. Drinking and intoxication. Glencoe, IL: The Free Press, 1959:58–61.
3. Blume SB. Sexuality and stigma: the alcoholic woman. Alcohol Health and Research World 1991;15:139–146.
4. Blume SB. Researches on women and alcohol. In: Alcohol and women. Research monograph no. 1. DHEW publication no. (ADM)80–835. Washington, DC: U.S. Department of Health, Education and Welfare, 1980:121–151.
5. Blume SB. Women and alcohol: public policy issues. In: Women and alcohol: health-related issues. Research monograph no. 16. DHEW publication no. (ADM)86–1139. Washington, DC: U.S. Department of Health and Human Services, 1986:294–311.
6. Ray BA, Braude MC. Women and drugs. a new era for research. NIDA Res Monogr 1986;65.
7. Center for Substance Abuse Treatment (CSAT). Practical approaches in the treatment of women who abuse alcohol and other drugs. Rockville, MD: U.S. Department of Health and Human Services, Public Health Service, 1994.
8. Center for Substance Abuse Treatment (CSAT). Pregnant, substance-using women: treatment improvement protocol (TIP) series. DHHS publication no. (SMA) 1993:93–1998.
9. Association of Junior Leagues. Highlights of the women to women survey: findings from 38 communities in the U.S. and Mexico. New York: Association of Junior Leagues, 1987.
10. National Council on Alcoholism and Drug Dependence. A federal response to a hidden epidemic: alcohol and other drug problems among women. New York: National Council on Alcoholism and Drug Dependence, 1987.
11. Brett PJ, Graham K, Smythe C. An analysis of specialty journals on alcohol, drugs and addictive behaviors for sex bias in research methods and reporting. J Stud Alcohol 1995; 56:24–34.
12. Jones BM, Jones MK. Women and alcohol: intoxication, metabolism, and the menstrual cycle. In: Greenblatt M, Schuckit MA, eds. Alcohol problems in women and children. New York: Grune & Stratton, 1976:103–136.
13. Van Thiel DH, Tarter RE, Rosenblum E, et al. Ethanol, its metabolism and gonadal effects: does sex make a difference? Adv Alcohol Subst Abuse 1988:3–4:131–169.
14. Frezza M, DiPadova C, Pozzato G, Terpin M, Baroona E, Lieber CS. High blood alcohol levels in women: the role of decreased gastric alcohol dehydrogenase activity and first-pass metabolism. N Engl J Med 1990;322:95–99.
15. Hay WH, Nathan PE, Heermans HW, Frankenstein W. Menstrual cycle, tolerance and blood alcohol level discriminating ability. Addict Behav 1984;9:67–77.
16. Wilson JR, Nogoshi CT. One-month repeatability of alcohol metabolism, sensitivity and acute tolerance. J Stud Alcohol 1987;48:437–442.
17. Cole-Harding S, Wilson JR. Ethanol metabolism in men and women. J Stud Alcohol 1987; 48:380–387.
18. Tobin MB, Schmidt MD, Rubinow DR. Reported alcohol use in women with premenstrual syndrome. Am J Psychiatry 1994;151:1503–1504.
19. Halliday A, Bush B, Cleary P, et al. Alcohol abuse in women seeking gynecologic care. Obstet Gynecol 1986;68:322–326.
20. Sutker PB, Libet JM, Allain AN, Randall CL. Alcohol use, negative mood states, and menstrual cycle phases. Alcohol Clin Exp Res 1983; 3:327–331.
21. Russell M, Czarnecki D. Alcohol use and menstrual problems [abstract]. Alcohol Clin Exp Res 1986;10:99.
21a. Mello NK. Drug use patterns and premenstrual dysphoria. NIDA Res Monogr 1986;65:31–48.
22. Barry PP. Gender as a factor in treating the elderly. NIDA Res Monogr 1986;65:65–69.
23. Braude MC. Drugs and drug interaction in the elderly women. NIDA Res Monogr 1986;65: 58–64.
24. Fuchs CS, Stampfer MJ, Colditz GA, et al. Alcohol consumption and mortality among women. N Engl J Med 1995;332:1245–1250.
25. Stamper MJ, Colditz GA, Willett WC, Speizer FE, Hennekens CH. A prospective study of moderate alcohol consumption and the risk of coronary disease and stroke in women. N Engl J Med 1988;319:267–273.
26. Witterman JCM, Willett WC, Stampfer MJ, et al. Relation of moderate alcohol consumption and risk of systemic hypertension in women. Am J Cardiol 1990;65:633–637.
27. Hanna E, Dufour MC, Elliott S, et al. Dying to be equal: women, alcohol, and cardiovascular disease. Br J Addict 1992;87:1593–1597.
28. Longnecker MP, Berlin JA, Orza MJ, Chalmers TC. A meta-analysis of alcohol consumption in relation to risk of breast cancer. JAMA 1988; 260:652–656.
29. Schatzkin A, Jones DY, Hoover RN, et al. Alcohol consumption and breast cancer in the epidemiologic follow-up of the first national health and nutrition examination survey. N Engl J Med 1987;16:1169–1173.
30. Willett WC, Stampfer MJ, Colditz GA, Rosner BA, Hennekens CH, Speizer FE. Moderate alcohol consumption and the risk of breast cancer. N Engl J Med 1987;316:1174–1179.
31. Harris RE, Wynder EL. Breast cancer and alcohol consumption: a study in weak associations. JAMA 1988;259:2867–2871.
32. Campbell CA. Women and AIDS. Soc Sci Med 1990;30:407–415.
33. Cohen JB, Hauer LB, Wofsy DB. Women and IV drugs. J Drug Issues 1989;19:39–56.
34. U.S. Department of the Treasury and U.S. Department of Health and Human Services. Report to the President and the Congress on health hazards associated with alcohol and methods to inform the general public of these hazards. Washington, DC: Department of the Treasury, 1980.
35. Ashley MJ, Olin JS, leRiche WH, et al. Morbidity in alcoholics: evidence for accelerated development of physical disease in women. Arch Intern Med 1977;137:883–887.
36. Wilkinson P. Sex differences in morbidity of alcoholics. In: Kalant OJ, ed. Research advances in alcohol and drug problems in women. New York: Plenum Press, 1980:331–364.
37. Gavaler JS. Sex-related differences in ethanol-induced liver disease: artifactual or real? Alcohol Clin Exp Res 1982:186–196.
38. Hislop WS, Bouchier IAD, Allan JG, et al. Alcoholic liver disease in Scotland and Northeastern England; presenting features in 510 patients. Q J Med 1983;52:232–243.
39. Urbano-Marquez A, Estruch R, Fernandez-Sola J, et al. The greater risk of alcoholic cardiomyopathy and myopathy in women compared with men. JAMA 1995;274:149–154.
40. Van Thiel DH, Gavaler JS. The adverse effects of ethanol upon hypothalamic-pituitary-gonadal function in males and females compared and contrasted. Alcohol Clin Exp Res 1982;6: 179–185.
41. Mello NK. Some behavioral and biological aspects of alcohol problems in women. In: Kalant OJ, ed. Alcohol and drug problems in women. New York: Plenum Press, 1980:263–298.
42. Gavaler JS. Effects of alcohol on endocrine function in postmenopausal women: a review. J Stud Alcohol 1985;46:495–516.
43. Wilsnack SC. Drinking, sexuality and sexual dysfunction in women. In: Wilsnack SC, Beckman LJ, eds. Alcohol problems in women. New York: Plenum Press, 1980:263–298.
44. Wilson GT, Lawson DM. Effects of alcohol on sexual arousal in women. J Abnorm Psychol 1976;85:489–497.
45. Malatesta VJ, Pollack RH, Crotty TD, Peacock LJ. Acute alcohol intoxication and female orgasmic response. J Sex Res 1982;18:1–17.
46. Harvey SM, Beckman LJ. Alcohol consumption, female sexual behavior and contraceptive use. J Stud Alcohol 1986;47:327–332.
47. Beckman LJ. Reported effects of alcohol on the sexual feelings and behavior of women alcoholics and nonalcoholics. J Stud Alcohol 1979; 40:272–282.
48. Apter-Marsh M. The sexual behavior of alcoholic women while drinking and during sobriety [dissertation]. San Francisco: Institute for Advanced Study of Human Sexuality, 1982.
49. Gavaler JS, Rizzo A, Rossaro L, et al. Sexuality of alcoholic women with menstrual cycle function: effects of duration of alcohol abstinence. Alcohol Clin Exp Res 1993;17:778–781.
50. Hoegerman G, Wilson CA, Thurmond E, et al. Drug-exposed neonates. In: Addiction medicine [special issue]. Western J Med 1990;152: 559–564.

51. Institute of Medicine. Fetal alcohol syndrome: research base for diagnostic criteria, epidemiology, prevention, and treatment. Washington, DC: National Academy Press, 1995.

52. Blume SB. Beer and the breast-feeding mom. JAMA 1987;258:2126.

53. Little RE, Anderson KW, Ervin CH, Worthington-Roberts B, Clarren SK. Maternal alcohol use during breast-feeding and infant mental and motor development at one year. N Engl J Med 1989;321:425–430.

54. Clayton RC, Voss HL, Robbins C, et al. Gender differences in drug use: an epidemiological perspective. NIDA Res Monogr 1986;65:80–99.

55. Gritz ER. Which women smoke and why? In: Not far enough: women vs. smoking. National Institute of Health Publication no. 87–2942. Washington, DC: Department of Health and Human Services, 1987:15–19.

56. Hilton ME, Clark WB. Changes in American drinking patterns and problems 1967–1984. J Stud Alcohol 1987;48:515–522.

57. Engs RC, Hanson DJ. Drinking patterns and problems of college students. J Alcohol Drug Educ 1985;31:65–83.

58. Wilsnack SC, Wilsnack RW, Klassen AD. Epidemiological research on women's drinking, 1978–1984. In: Women and alcohol: health-related issues. National Institute on Alcohol Abuse and Alcoholism. Research monograph no.16. Publication no. (ADM)86–1139. Washington, DC: Department of Health and Human Services, 1986:1–68.

59. Wilsnack RW, Cheloha R. Women's roles and problem drinking across the life span. Soc Probl 1987;34:231–248.

60. Curlee J. Alcohol and the "empty nest." Bull Menninger Clin 1969;33:165–171.

61. Grant B. Alcohol consumption, alcohol abuse and alcohol dependence: the United States as an example. Addiction 1994;89:1357–1365.

62. Substance Abuse and Mental Health Services Administration. National household survey on drug abuse: population estimates 1993. Rockville, MD: DHHS Publication No (SMA), 1994:94–3017.

63. American Medical Women's Association. Position paper on tobacco. Alexandria, VA: American Medical Women's Association, undated.

64. Cloninger RJ, Sigvardsson S, Gilligan SB, et al. Genetic heterogeneity and the classification of alcoholism. Adv Alcohol Subst Abuse 1988;3/4:3–16.

65. Kendler KS, Walters MS, Neale MC, et al. The structure of the genetic and environmental risk factors for six major psychiatric disorders in women. Arch Gen Psychiatry 1995;52:374–383.

66. Russell M, Henderson C, Blume SB. Children of alcoholics: a review of the literature. New York: Children of Alcoholics Foundation, 1985.

67. Lex BW, Lukas SE, Greenwald NE. Alcohol-induced changes in body sway in women at risk for alcoholism: a pilot study. J Stud Alcohol 1988;49:346–356.

68. Corrigan EM. Alcoholic women in treatment. New York: Oxford University Press, 1980.

69. Beckman LJ. Self-esteem of women alcoholics. J Stud Alcohol 1978;39:491–498.

70. O'Connor LE, Berry JW, Inaba D, et al. Shame, guilt, and depression in men and women in recovery from addiction. J Subst Abuse Treat 1994;11:503–510.

71. Jones MC. Personality antecedents and correlates of drinking patterns in women. J Consult Clin Psychol 1971;36:61–69.

72. Jones MC. Personality correlates and antecedents of drinking patterns in adult males. J Consult Clin Psychology 1968;32:2–12.

73. Fillmore KM, Bacon SD, Hyman M. The 27 year longitudinal panel study of drinking by students in college. Report 1979 to National Institute of Alcoholism and Alcohol Abuse. Contract No: ADM 281–76-0015. Washington DC, 1979.

74. Miller BA, Downs WR. Conflict and violence among alcoholic women as compared to a random household sample. Paper presented at the 38th annual meeting of the American Society of Criminology, Atlanta, GA, 1986.

75. Winfield I, George LK, Swartz M, Blazer DG. Sexual assault and psychiatric disorders among a community sample of women. Am J Psychiatry 1990;147:335–341.

76. Helzer JE, Pryzbeck TR. The co-occurrence of alcoholism with other psychiatric disorders in the general population and its impact on treatment. J Stud Alcohol 1988;49:219–224.

77. Hesselbrock MN, Meyer RE, Keener JJ. Psychopathology in hospitalized alcoholics. Arch Gen Psychiatry 1985;42:1050–1055.

78. Khantzian EJ, Treece C. DSM-III psychiatric diagnosis of narcotic addicts. Arch Gen Psychiatry 1985;42:1067–1071.

79. Rounsaville BJ, Kleber HD. Untreated opiate addicts: how do they differ from those seeking treatment? Arch Gen Psychiatry 1985;42: 1072–1077.

80. Hartka E, Johnstone B, Leino EV, et al. A meta-analysis of expressive symptomatology and alcohol consumption over time. Br J Addict 1991;86:1283–1298.

81. Wilsnack SC, Klassen AD, Schur BE, et al. Predicting onset and chronicity of women's problem drinking: a 5-year longitudinal analysis. Am J Pub Health 1991;81:305–318.

82. Rubonis AV, Colby SM, Monti PM, et al. Alcohol cue reactivity and mood induction in male and female alcoholics. J Stud Alcohol 1994;55:487–494.

83. Ross HE, Glaser FB, Stiasny S. Sex differences in the prevalence of psychiatric disorder in patients with alcohol and drug problems. Br J Addict 1988;83:1179–1192.

84. Bulik CM. Drug and alcohol abuse by bulimic women and their families. Am J Psychiatry 1987;144:1604–1606.

85. Vaglum S, Vaglum P. Borderline and other mental disorders in alcoholic female psychiatric patients: a case control study. Psychopathology 1985;18:50–60.

86. Nace EP, Saxon JJ, Shore N, et al. Borderline personality disorder and alcoholism treatment: a one-year follow-up study. J Stud Alcohol 1986; 47:196–200.

87. Lesieur HR, Blume SB, Zoppa RM. Alcoholism, drug abuse, and gambling. Alcohol Clin Exp Res 1986;10:33–38.

88. Jellinek EM. Immanuel Kant on drinking. Q J Stud Alcohol 1941;1:777–778.

89. Gomberg ESL. Women and alcoholism: psychosocial issues. In: Women and alcohol: health-related issues. Research monograph no. 16. Publication No. (ADM)86–1139. Washington, DC: Department of Health and Human Services, 1986:78–120.

89a. Fillmore KM. The social victims of drinking. Br J Addict 1985;80:307–314.

90. Miller BA, Downs WR, Gondoli DM. Spousal violence among alcoholic women as compared to a random household sample of women. J Stud Alcohol 1989;50:533–540.

91. Richardson D, Campbell J. The effect of alcohol on attribution of blame for rape. Pers Soc Psych Bull 1982;8:468–476.

92. Moore RD, Bone LR, Geller G, Mamon JA,

Stokes EJ, Levine DM. Prevalence, detection and treatment of alcoholism in hospitalized patients. JAMA 1989;261:403–408.

93. Cloninger RC, Christiansen KO, Reich T, et al. Implications of sex differences in the prevalence of antisocial personality, alcoholism, and criminality for familial transmission. Arch Gen Psychiatry 1978;35:941–951.

94. Klee L, Ames G. Reevaluating risk factors for women's drinking: a study of blue collar wives. Am J Prev Med 1987;3:31–41.

95. Schmidt G, Klee L, Ames G. Review and analysis of literature on indicators of womens' problems. Br J Addict 1990;85:179–192.

96. Griffin ML, Weiss RL, Mirin SM, et al. A comparison of male and female cocaine abusers. Arch Gen Psychiatry 1989;46:122–126.

97. Smith EM, Cloninger CR. Alcoholic females: mortality at twelve-year follow-up. Focus on Women 1981;2:1–13.

98. Armor DJ, Polich JM, Stambul HB. Alcoholism and treatment. New York: John Wiley, 1978.

99. Jacob T, Bremer DA. Assortative mating among men and women alcoholics. J Stud Alcohol 1986;47:219–222.

100. Turnbull JE, Gomberg ESL. The structure of depression in alcoholic women. J Stud Alcohol 1990;51:148–155.

101. Gomberg ES. Suicide risk among women with alcohol problems. Am J Public Health 1989; 79(10):1363–1365.

102. Eronen M. Mental disorders and homicidal behavior in female subjects. Am J Psychiatry 1995;152:8:1216–1218.

103. Cyr MG, Wartman SA. The effectiveness of routine screening questions in the detection of alcoholism. JAMA 1988;259:51–54.

104. Cleary PD, Miller M, Bush BT, Warburg MM, Delbanco TL, Aronson MD. Prevalence and recognition of alcohol abuse in a primary care population. Am J Med 1988;85:466–471.

105. Blume SB. Women and alcohol: a review. JAMA 1986;256:1467–1470.

106. Blume SB. Drinking and pregnancy, preventing fetal alcohol syndrome. N Y State J Med 1981;81:95–98.

107. Blume SB, Russell M. Alcohol and substance abuse in the practice of obstetrics and gynecology. In: Stewart DE, Stotland NL, eds. Psychological aspects of women's health care: the interface between psychiatry and obstetrics and gynecology. Washington, DC: American Psychiatric Press, 1993:391–409.

108. Sokol RJ, Martier SS, Ager JW. The T-ACE questions: practical prenatal detection of risk-drinking. Am J Obstet Gynecol 1989;160: 863–870.

109. Smith IE, Lancaster JS, Moss-Wells S, Coles CD, Falek A. Identifying high-risk pregnant drinkers: biological and behavioral correlates of continuous heavy drinking during pregnancy. J Stud Alcohol 1987;48:304–309.

110. Dahlgren L, Willander A. Are special treatment facilities for female alcoholics needed? A controlled 2-year follow-up study from a specialized female unit (EWA) versus a mixed male/female treatment facility. Alcohol Clin Exp Res 1989;13:499–504.

111. Ylikorkala O, Stenman U, Halmesmaki E. Gammaglutamyl transferase and mean cell volume reveal maternal alcohol abuse and fetal alcohol effects. Am J Obstet Gynecol 1987;157:344–348.

112. Corse SJ, McHugh MK, Gordon SM. Enhancing provider effectiveness in treating pregnant women with addictions. J Subst Abuse Treat 1995;12:3–12.

113. Schliebner CT. Gender-sensitive therapy: an alternative for women in substance abuse treatment. J Subst Abuse Treat 1994;11:511–515.

114. Deren S. Children of substance abusers: a review of the literature. J Subst Abuse Treat 1986;3:77–94.

115. Reckmon LW, Babcock P, O'Bryan T. Meeting the child care needs of the female alcoholic. Child Welfare Leagues of America 1984;63: 541–546.

116. Davis TS, Hagood LA. In-home support for recovering alcoholic mothers and their families. J Stud Alcohol 1979;40:313–317.

117. Kirkpatrick J. Turnabout: help for a new life. New York: Doubleday, 1978.

118. Ford BB. Betty: a glad awakening. New York: Doubleday, 1978.

119. Robertson N. Getting better inside AA. New York: William Morrow and Co., 1988.

120. Meryman R. Broken promises, mended dreams. New York: Little Brown, 1984.

121. Allen C. I'm black and I'm sober. Minnesota: Comp Care, 1978.

122. Carter CS. Treatment of the chemically dependent black female: a cultural perspective. Counselor 1987;5:16–18.

123. Fernandez-Pal B, Bluestone H, Missouri C, Morales G, Mizruchi MS. Drinking patterns of inner-city black Americans and Puerto Ricans. J Stud Alcohol 1986;47:156–160.

124. Weathers B. Alcoholism and the lesbian community. In: Eddy CC, Ford JL, eds. Alcoholism in women. Dubuque, IA: Kendall/Hunt, 1980.

125. Diamond DL, Wilsnack SC. Alcohol abuse among lesbians: a descriptive study. J Homosexuality 1978;4:123–142.

126. Anderson SC, Henderson DC. Working with lesbian alcoholics. Soc Work 1985;30:518–525.

127. Schaefer S, Evans S, Coleman E. Sexual orientation concerns among chemically dependent individuals. J Chem Depend Treat 1987;1:121–140.

128. Miller BA. Drugs and crime interrelationships among women in detention. J Psychoactive Drugs 1981;13:289–295.

129. Annis HM, Leban CB. Alcoholism in women: treatment modalities and outcomes. In: Kalant OJ, ed. Research advances in alcohol and drug problems. New York: Plenum Press, 1980: 385–422.

130. Vannicelli M. Treatment considerations. In: Women and alcohol: health-related issues. Research monograph no. 16. Publication no. (ADM) 86–1139. Washington DC: Dept. of Health and Human Services, 1986:130–153.

131. Rounsaville BJ, Tierney T, Crits-Christoph K, Weissman MM, Kleber HD. Predictors of outcome in treatment of opiate addicts. Compr Psychiatry 1982;23:462–478.

132. McLellan AT, Luborsky L, O'Brien CP, et al. Alcohol and drug abuse treatment in three different populations: is there improvement and is it predictable? Am J Drug Alcohol Abuse 1986;12:101–120.

133. Rounsaville BJ, Dolinsky ZS, Babor TF, Meyer RE. Psychopathology as a predictor of treatment outcome in alcoholics. Arch Gen Psychiatry 1987;44:505–513.

134. MacDonald JG. Predictors of treatment outcome for alcoholic women. Int J Addict 1987; 22:235–248.

135. Havassy BE, Hall SM, Tschann JM. Social support and relapse to tobacco, alcohol, and opiates: preliminary findings. NIDA Res Monogr 1987;76:207–213.

136. Wilsnack SC, Wilsnack RW, Klassen AD. Women's drinking problems. A U.S. national longitudinal survey. Paper presented at the American Public Health Association annual meeting, 1989.

137. Hill SY. Physiological effects of alcohol in women. In: Women and alcohol: health-related issues. Research monograph no. 16. Publication no. (ADM)86–1139. Washington, DC: Department of Health and Human Services, 1986.

138. Lindberg S, Agren G. Mortality among male and female hospitalized alcoholics in Stockholm 1962–1983. Br J Addict 1988:83:1193–1200.

139. Smith EM, Cloninger CR, Bradford S. Predictors of mortality in alcoholic women: a prospective follow-up study. Alcohol Clin Exp Res 1983;7:237–243.

140. Jacobson M, Hacker G, Atkins R. The booze merchants. Washington, DC: CSPI Books, 1983.

141. Marsteller P, Karnchanopee K. The use of women in the advertising of distilled spirits. J Psychedelic Drugs 1980;12:1–12.

142. Shore ER. Outcomes of a primary prevention project for business and professional women. J Stud Alcohol 1994;55:657–659.

143. Cahill MH, Volicer BJ, Neuburger E. Female referral to employees assistance programs: the impact of specialized intervention. Drug Alcohol Depend 1982;10:223–233.

144. Jeffer EK, Baranick M. Drug abuse and the U.S. Army in Europe: women and substance abuse. Int J Addict 1983;18:133–138.

145. Vannicelli M. Group psychotherapy with adult children of alcoholics. New York: Guilford Press, 1989.

146. Al-Anon Family Groups. Alateen: hope for children of alcoholics. New York: Al-Anon Family Groups, 1973.

147. Amaro H, Beckman LJ, Mays VM. A comparison of black and white women entering alcoholism treatment. J Stud Alcohol 1987;48: 220–228.

148. Poland ML, Dombrowski MP, Ager JW, et al. Punishing pregnant drug users: enhancing the flight from care. Drug Alcohol Depend 1993; 31:199–203.

149. Blume SB. Women and alcohol: issues in social policy. In: Gender and alcohol. New Brunswick, NJ: Rutgers Center of Alcohol Studies (in press).

63 WOMEN: RESEARCH AND POLICY

Marsha Rosenbaum

The vast majority of women in the United States use some type of drug on a regular basis. We use prescription and over-the-counter drugs to help us sleep, stay awake, alleviate pain, cope with depression, etc. We drink coffee and tea, we eat chocolate, all of which contain caffeine. We consume alcoholic beverages. Yet when we think of "women and drugs" what comes to mind are users of *illegal* drugs, although in reality less than 5% of us use such substances on a regular basis (1).

What is known about women and drugs is influenced by scientific research, information dissemination, and the perspective of the scientist/writer(s). Formal research is limited largely by what our government sanctions as "significant," or having the potential to contribute to the solution of an already defined problem. Whether protocols utilize quantitative methodologies, qualitative methodologies, surveys, clinical trials, or field studies, researchers with a conventional perspective generally collect and analyze data and ultimately produce information. Most have a covert investment in the status quo, the preservation of traditional values (including gender roles), and prevailing (prohibitionist) policy toward drugs.

The decision to publish research findings is political. Conventional scientific journals have ultimate decision-making power about which "findings" constitute serious scholarship, often defined as that which is government-sanctioned (and funded). The other major source of information, the popular media, is motivated to define drug use as problematic when it contains sensational stories. Historically, women's drug use has been defined as problematic when their traditional gender roles were violated or abandoned, therefore jeopardized. Details about women ingesting drugs during pregnancy and violating that most sacred role as caretaker and mother sells papers.

In sum, our knowledge of women and drugs is limited to that which is government-funded and published in scholarly journals and/or the popular media. This information does not represent the experience of the majority of women drug users. It does not even represent the majority of women who use illegal drugs, because most use drugs in controlled ways and without serious consequence. We know very little about how they manage and control their use because prohibitionist rhetoric dismisses such use as impossible, therefore research funding is difficult if not impossible to obtain.

Instead, most conventional research focuses on a relatively small group of women whose drug use becomes visible, therefore problematic. They use illegal means to earn enough money to buy (expensive) drugs. As a result of their illegal activities they come into contact with the criminal justice system. They are often poor, underskilled, undereducated, and supported by public assistance. They have difficulty taking care of their children and as part of the welfare system, come to the attention of social service agencies designed to protect children. Some have no real home and as a result much of their existence takes place "on the street." Most important, they incite fear because they deviate from sexual norms and in general violate traditional gender role expectations with regard to pregnancy and parenting.

Since women "emerged from the shadows" in the 1970s (2), patterns of drug use and problems associated with it have shifted. The focus of research on women and drugs mirrors societal concerns and has also changed. This chapter will examine some of the salient issues related to women and drugs, with primary attention given to research areas that have dominated the literature with special attention to research on pregnancy and drug treatment.

Societal responses to women who use (illegal) drugs has also shifted over the past 25 years. During the 1970s treatment expanded with the hope that rehabilitation would address the problem. By the late 1980s, with AIDS, the crack "epidemic" and a powerful war on drugs, a more punitive climate prevailed. Women drug users were being held responsible for many of society's ills and actively prosecuted for deviating from conventional gender roles.

This chapter will use research findings to examine shifting trends in and societal responses to women's (illegal, problematic) drug use during the 1970s and 1980s. It concludes with the 1990s and a discussion of feminist analyses of violence, treatment, and the implications of the War on Drugs. Finally policy recommendations are made for reducing drug-related harm.

THE 1970s

The early feminist movement of the late 1960s and early 1970s called attention to and encouraged women's participation in many activities in which they had been absent or invisible. It also opened a range of occupations that had been the exclusive or nearly exclusive domain of men. Among these occupations was illegal drug use, particularly heroin addiction. Research began with assessments of prevalence, in an effort to determine just how many women used illegal drugs (3–6). Epidemiological studies compared women with men, among themselves on the basis of race, with other drug users, and longitudinally (7–13). Several other studies focused on gender-specific aspects of women's participation in the drug world, including prostitution (14–17).

Another set of studies looked at the etiology of women's criminality (18–20, 27, 29). Women drug users had begun to participate in property (though not violent) crime such as burglary, larceny, and forgery. Their representation in large-scale money-making enterprises such as drug distribution was minimal, although many served as assistants to male dealers (17, 21, 30). Research on women heroin addicts revealed that a sizable proportion prostituted, at least occasionally, to earn money to support their heroin habits (8, 15, 16, 19, 20, 22–34).

By far, during the 1970s the bulk of research focused on a major concern regarding women's deviation from traditional gender roles, pregnancy, and motherhood. Drug treatment was another research area that dominated the 1970s.

Pregnancy and Heroin Use

Early studies of pregnancy and heroin use focused on physiological problems associated with addiction. During pregnancy, heroin addiction was thought to be connected with such problems as premature rupture of membranes, impaired fetal growth, diminished birth weight, preterm delivery, maternal infections, meconium staining, stillbirths, toxemia, and infant withdrawal (35–48).

At that time there was a dearth of information about pregnant women and heroin-addicted mothers. Rosenbaum and Murphy (17) first studied the career of the woman heroin addict addiction in 1977 by interviewing 100 women, 70% of whom were mothers. This sociological and ethnographic study produced findings that differed from, but often complemented, the more medically oriented publications appearing at about the same time (35–48). The discovery of pregnancy was problematic, as many women had stopped menstruating while they were addicted. By the time they were certain (often because they were "showing") they were in the fourth or fifth

month and too far along for an abortion. It was also too late to stop using drugs, the rationale being that (a) most of heroin's most deleterious effects would have occurred during the first trimester, and (b) withdrawal in later stages of pregnancy was too dangerous to the fetus. Birth and delivery, according to the study participants, was often physiologically as well as psychologically difficult. Many of the women had suffered from such ailments as toxemia as a result of addiction as well as little prenatal care. As a result, birth could be a dangerous and fearful experience. In addition, hospital staff familiar with the women's addiction were less than supportive and often abusive. The last thing the women wanted to do was to return to such an unpleasant environment, and many never came back. To compound feelings of disdain they received at the hospital, women often went home with an irritable and difficult to placate infant. This combination had the potential to send them into motherhood with feelings of failure and a need to use heroin to relieve their suffering (17).

Drug Treatment

The establishment of National Institute of Drug Abuse's Program for Women's Concerns in 1974 opened treatment options for women heroin addicts. These included inpatient detoxification, outpatient detoxification, Narcotics Anonymous, methadone maintenance, and therapeutic communities. Despite these advances, women drug users had felt the stigma of being defined as socially as well as psychopathologically more deviant than their nonaddicted sisters or their male counterparts, and as a result, many hid their addiction, making it difficult to recruit them for treatment (49).

When women did decide to go to treatment, they found that many programs were incompatible with their needs and obligations as mothers (50, 51, 104). As a result most women were limited to outpatient detoxification and methadone maintenance.

The increasing recognition of women as a "special" population of addicts due to their childbearing and childrearing roles occurred simultaneous to the expansion of methadone maintenance treatment (MMT). At that time, research on MMT and pregnancy focused on medical issues pertaining to the fetus and newborn and the management of the pregnant addict (40, 48, 52–69, 112). Research findings, while in general supportive of methadone as a tool to reduce drug-related harm, were inconsistent in terms of fetal health and severity of withdrawal symptoms. Still, for a pregnant addict who found it impossible to quit the use of heroin, maintenance was one of few viable options, and, by the end of the 1970s, women occupied nearly one third of new MMT slots (70).

The rehabilitative orientation of 1970s resulted in the proliferation of treatment, with methadone maintenance the single largest modality available (71). A subsequent study by Rosenbaum (72) focused on the methadone experience for women, which found MMT to be a "presence" in the heroin world for the 100 women on MMT interviewed for the study. Women had to confront the possibility of getting on methadone, whether or not they chose to enroll in a program. A major impetus for women to enlist in a methadone program was pregnancy (72). Many women who became pregnant opted for the control methadone provided. Their lives were necessarily stabilized due to (a) the highly structured clinic routine, and (b) the elimination of the need to participate in criminal activities for the purpose of buying heroin. Women's lives became as routinized as possible, enabling them to work around their addiction, provide a home for their baby, eat well, and learn skills in preparation for motherhood.

Despite enlisting in drug treatment and stabilizing their lives, women reported that when they went to the hospital to give birth, they were faced with the stigma of being "just a junkie." The guilt which may have been suppressed during pregnancy surfaced very quickly—often brought back by the attitude of the hospital staff, which was most often neither knowledgeable nor sympathetic.

The guilt experienced by women on methadone extended from birth and continued throughout the baby's childhood. It began in the hospital, but did not end there. They felt responsible for the baby's withdrawal, although there was no way to predict severity of withdrawal, or even whether it would happen at all (47, 62, 73–76).

Motherhood often began badly for women on methadone, and there were more problems when the baby came home from the hospital. Just as with heroin, babies in withdrawal could be extremely irritable (74, 75), with "postpartum depression" accentuated and extended for addicted mothers. The guilt experienced by mothers on methadone haunted them, and never seemed to end. First they looked for signs their babies were addicted. Later women wondered if their children's problems might be attributable to their own use of heroin or methadone. The guilt and fear could extend through life, and every ailment was suspect.

Despite an increase in treatment options for women in the 1970s, there were not enough programs, and the quality of treatment was questionable at best. Women often found the structure of treatment, including long waiting lists, difficult to negotiate. Some women expressed little respect for counselors, especially those who were ex-addicts. Women on methadone often experienced physiological problems. Many women were dissatisfied due to the male orientation and their own lesser position within the treatment world, regardless of the particular modality. In the early years it was not uncommon for programs to limit their acceptance of women to the wives or girlfriends of male clients as an incentive for men to enroll. Women heroin addicts in treatment were defined as "sicker" and more deviant than their male counterparts (7, 23, 77–78). When they enlisted in drug treatment, they discovered they were treated as more pathological than male addicts, and experienced discrimination and sexism as a result (79–81). The major obstacles women faced in accessing and utilizing treatment effectively were (*a*) the lack of facilities for children and (*b*) the failure of institutions to acknowledge the difficulties they faced in attempting to fulfill their mothering obligations while following a treatment regimen.

THE 1980s

The study of women and drugs was altered radically in the 1980s. The AIDS epidemic and its relation to drug use, the introduction of "crack" to the drug scene, and an unprecedented escalation in the war on drugs changed the drug experience for women.

AIDS

Intravenous drug use accounts for half of all AIDS in women (82). Epidemiological and etiological studies have found that women injection drug users (IDUs) were vulnerable to the disease through both needle sharing and unsafe sexual contact (83–93). Women's risk through unsafe needle sharing had much to do with their inequitable power relationship to men (94–98). Researchers found that women were much more likely than men to obtain drugs through their (male sexual) partners; that men often controlled the level of intake of drugs for their women partners; and women tended to be "fixed" by someone else more often than men, increasing their chances of being "hit" by a previously used needle (17, 97–99).

Prostitution, or "sex work," as it was called by the 1980s, contributed greatly to women's HIV risk and sexually transmitted diseases. Still, women had fewer economic resources and conventional job skills than their male counterparts (100–103), and as result of a reduction in programs for the poor, fewer resources than they had in the 1970s. This wanting economic situation rendered them desperate, forcing them to engage in sex work to earn enough money to support their basic needs as well as their drug habits. Women's need to support themselves through sex work created an insidious cycle. Women remained in sex work because they had few, if any, other ways to make a living. But in order to cope with the distasteful nature of prostitution, they used drugs to block their feelings. They were therefore unable to separate themselves from the drug world, which was in turn tied to prostitution (16, 105–107).

Drugs and prostitution added up to a tangled package creating increased HIV risk for women through both needle-sharing and sexual contact (108–110). Drug-dependent women in withdrawal and in desperate need of money were vulnerable to the demands of a "trick" who did not want to use a condom (117). Furthermore, incest, economic hardship, physical abuse, and cultural influences such as perception of control over one's own life shaped women's use of contraceptive technologies, including condoms (111). Nu-

merous studies were completed documenting cultural and racial factors that contributed to risky sexual behaviors (85, 113–124).

Crack

By the mid 1980s, cocaine had replaced heroin as the most dangerous drug. A number of cross-sectional surveys had documented the dramatic rise in incidence and prevalence of cocaine use and related problems (125–128). Drug use among women in general seemed to be increasing (129), with use among women of childbearing age in particular increasing as well (130). Researchers compared women and men (103, 131); looked at sexuality (133–134); "sex for crack" exchanges and implications for the spread of HIV and other sexually transmitted diseases (132, 135–141, 185); women's participation in the cocaine-selling economy (142–146); and pregnancy, fetal development, and neonatal behavior (147–148).

In a qualitative study of 100 women who used crack cocaine (151), Murphy found that women crack users' impoverished early lives set the stage for what would occur later:

> Early in life, many were trapped by childhoods in violent, fragmented, or drug-involved households; teenage pregnancies; truncated educations and lack of skills; poverty that was worsened by diversion of resources to drugs; oppressive relationships with men; and eventually by the demeaning social world surrounding crack cocaine (149).

Murphy also found that victimization characterized these women's perspectives; they had little hope for a better future. Parenting concerns were central in women's lives.

Motherhood, Pregnancy, and Crack

The majority of Murphy's (151) study participants (68%) were mothers, and parenting and pregnancy issues were of paramount concern to them. Women's viewpoints on pregnancy had much to do with their (non) use of birth control, believing themselves to be controlled by sex rather than sex being controllable by *them*. Many believed babies, rather than a chosen responsibility, came "from God." Fertility was a "distant issue" rather than a present reality and distinct possibility. Unforeseen sexual experiences were attributed to youth, lack of knowledge, powerlessness, carelessness, or ambivalence. As a consequence of women's beliefs and unforeseen experiences, most became pregnant unexpectedly (149). Most women in the study population wanted to be mothers at some point in their lives, even if they did not themselves determine *when* this would occur. Lacking the opportunity to assume other viable social roles involving occupational success, motherhood remained as one of few conventional, respectable life options.

Crack-using women in this study population were not at all like the "monsters" portrayed in the popular media at that time (150–152). On the contrary, they felt a strong responsibility for their children, as well as deep pride. As mothers, they expressed their goals as nurturing and modeling. The use of crack cocaine presented mothering problems: a drain on attention to children's needs, finances, and role modeling. Women found themselves in a downward spiral, as the use of crack served to alleviate mothering concerns and ultimately worsened the situation. Nonetheless, women attempted to carve out various strategies involving "defensive compensation" and the effort to maintain mothering standards while using crack. They separated drug use and parental roles, budgeted money, tried to get away from the crack scene. As a very last resort they reluctantly but voluntarily relinquished their children "for their own good" to a more responsible party. When custody was lost, the downward slide escalated and women often used even more crack, claiming, "they took my self" (150–151).

Paradoxically, along with well-meaning action, an insidious force was working with regard to pregnancy, motherhood, and drug use: the Reagan-Bush version of the War on Drugs. It was fueled by the crack cocaine "epidemic" and the American need for swift, punitive action. Ira Chasnoff, in his 1989 article citing 375,000 "crack babies," set off an hysterical panic about the out-of-control epidemic of pregnancy and cocaine use (153). The popular press seized this story, claiming the needs of babies who were exposed to drugs in utero "will present an overwhelming challenge to schools, future employers and society" (154); "crack cocaine can overwhelm one of the strongest forces in nature, the parental instinct" (155–156); and drug use during pregnancy was "interfering with the central core of what it is to be human" (154). Negative media attention on drugs peaked with the phenomenon of the "crack baby." When preliminary research findings indicated crack use during pregnancy might be associated with fetal morbidity, the popular press quickly ran a series of alarmist stories. Journalists reported that mothers addicted to crack cocaine lost basic parenting instincts (154) and had utter disregard for their children (155–156); maternal crack cocaine use robbed children of "the central core of what it is to be human" (154), and crack made a mother "indifferent to her child or abusive when its cries irritate her" (157). The use of drugs and even more specifically the use of crack during pregnancy was the equivalent of abusive parenting, and crack severed "that deepest and most sacred of bond: that between a mother and child" (158).

According to media representations, the problems of maternal drug use extended beyond the mother-child unit. News stories linked this phenomenon to a collection of social problems by asserting that pregnancy and drug use was draining public drug treatment funds and medical resources (155, 156, 159–162) and threatening the nation's school and criminal justice systems (154, 163–168).

The Criminalization of Pregnancy

By the late 1980s the fetal rights movement had combined with the War on Drugs (169). As a result of the scientific "crack baby" literature and subsequent media attention, pregnant drug users were increasingly stigmatized and further marginalized. At this point the United States government stepped in to take action, with prosecutors in nearly half the states in the United States hoping to solve the problem by punishing pregnant drug users through prosecution (170–175). As a consequence, a drug-using pregnant woman could be arrested and incarcerated for "delivering drugs to a minor" (176). A woman who tested positive for drugs during delivery could immediately lose custody of her newborn. Although by 1991 the association between fetal harm and cocaine use had been seriously questioned by medical research (177–182), hundreds of infants and children continued to be removed from their mother's custody, overloading the child welfare system, and jeopardizing women's control of their own bodies. As Boyd (183) notes:

> Feminists conclude that the criminalization of pregnancy, and emerging fetal rights (171, 184), have culminated in a situation where the well-being and security of women's bodies is legally and physically challenged (186–187).

Class and racial bias in these prosecutions were obvious (188). Although the use of illegal substances was distributed fairly evenly throughout the population in terms of class and race, all of the women who were prosecuted were not only poor but non-white (189–191), with Jennifer Johnson's case perhaps the most famous (2).

The social conditions characterizing crack-users' lives were far more deleterious to the health, well-being, and safety of mother and child than drugs. The media and political focus on drugs was not only oversimplified but purposeful. Crack mothers were being scapegoated, diverting attention from (a) the realities of the failed, post-Reagan social experiment with cutbacks of needed social programs and (b) complex social conditions that would require major political change (152, 174, 192, 193). As Lisa Maher wrote:

> The criminalization of "crack pregnancies" facilitates the punishment of those who blatantly violate established social mores. It provides a way of striking out simultaneously at minorities, druggies, and women who fail to conform to engendered cultural expectations. At the same time, Middle America can vent its moral indignation by using the rhetoric of compassion for those "poor little [black] babies. . . ." [W]omen who use crack cocaine provide an attractive place for Middle America to circle its wagons, and crack pregnancies provide an ideal opportunity for projecting deep-seated cultural anxieties about the urban minority poor and about drugging, crime, and female sexuality. (194, pp. 123–124)

The increase in prosecutions suggested that more information was needed to intervene in the misdirected, unjust, and downright harmful direction of persecution, prosecution, and punishment of pregnant drug users. The

prevalence of drug use during pregnancy was not subsiding (195) and low birth weight, small head circumference, irritability, SIDS, and malformation among babies born to addicted mothers continued to be commonly reported (196). Others had discovered that the pregnant addict was less likely to attend prenatal care appointments, more likely to live in poor conditions, more likely to have a host of confounding problems such as sexually transmitted infections, more likely to experience higher rates of violence than non–drug users, but no more "pathological" than women in the general population (197–199). With all the research that had been conducted, the perspective of pregnant women themselves was rarely the focus. There was a need to present a "human" view of the pregnant drug user while attempting to humanize her treatment.

The author and Sheila Murphy learned that the crack-using pregnant women studied were stigmatized and consumed by guilt. They expressed great concern about the levels of drug-related harm that occurred during their pregnancies, their evaluations varying according to the particular drug(s) they were using, and often based on what they had heard or read through the media. Contrary to popular myth, study participants cared very much about the outcomes of their pregnancies and used a variety of strategies to reduce drug-related harm. They tried to lower their intake, switched from "harder" to "softer" drugs such as marihuana which would help them eat and sleep, and ingested health-promoting substances such as vitamins (200). Perhaps most problematic in this potpourri of methods was prenatal care (201). The crack-using women in the author's study population, 82% of whom were African-American, were well aware that because they were black, as soon as they entered a clinical setting they would automatically be suspect of illegal drug use. They would be targeted for drug testing, which could lead to punitive social service and criminal justice interventions such as incarceration and removal of their children (175, 189, 202). Quite simply, despite their intent to reduce drug-related harm through contact with medical institutions, if they believed custody would be jeopardized, they made the difficult decision to stay away. Chavkin summarized the problem:

> Attempts to criminalize drug use during pregnancy may further deter [pregnant women] from seeking care or from giving accurate information to health care providers. Anecdotal reports suggest that efforts to detect maternal drug use by means of urine toxicology testing of the newborn may even frighten some women away from delivering in hospital (203).

THE 1990s

By the 1990s feminist scholars questioned basic assumptions about gender roles and the way women and drugs had been viewed (151, 204–206). The ways in which abuse, violence, drug treatment, and the War on Drugs have shaped women's experience have become central concerns in this last decade of the twentieth century.

Abuse and Violence

Researchers have consistently found high levels of past and present abuse in the lives of women drug users (144, 197, 207, 209, 210). Many have suggested that there is a relationship, if not absolutely causal, between violence experienced by women and drug use (211–228).

In one study of pregnancy and drug use (208), 70% (n = 120) of the study participants reported they had been in one or more relationships in which they had been physically battered by a male partner. Of the 84 women who had been assaulted by their partners, nearly half (45%) reported being battered during their current or most recent pregnancy. Twenty-five of the 84 women (30%) who had been victims of partner violence were in a battering relationship at the time of the interview. In addition to the violence they endured within their homes, the neighborhoods these women grew up in were, in many instances, veritable "combat zones." Between gang warfare, police raids, random shootings, and drug dealing, fear became a way of life for the overwhelming majority of the women who participated in this study. These findings concur with other studies that indicate a link between childhood experiences of violence, sexual abuse, physical abuse, and the increased likelihood that a woman will develop drug and alcohol problems later in life

(224). For many of the study participants, drug use was a way of numbing themselves to the violence that engulfed them.

In a recent study of methadone maintenance (117), 51% of the 108 women (n = 55) reported some form of past or present violence in their lives. Forty percent (n = 22) of the women who experienced abuse reported surviving multiple abuse patterns, such as a combination of child abuse, rape, *and* domestic violence. Some violent partners prohibited women from seeking or continuing treatment. In addition, women's limited economic resources meant they had few options for ending violent relationships. The implications of such violence, although difficult to determine in a tangible way, did affect women's perceptions of their treatment progress. The study found that violence provided a catalyst to self-medicate (230, 231). In addition, women's sense of self-worth, importance, competence, and control was eroded with the accumulation of violent and abusive experiences (214, 232). As such, each of these experiences formed a link with women's problems in treatment and acted as a barrier to successful MMT in the following ways. First, psychological turmoil from violent episodes drove women to initiate or continue to use heroin for self-medication and escape. Secondly, the effects of past violence, if not sufficiently addressed in counseling and therapy, could continue to haunt the women and propel them towards using heroin for escape and, ironically, control (205).

Drug Treatment

Recent studies of drug treatment have focused on themes of violence, male dominance, dependence, motherhood issues and depression (233, 234), pregnancy (235); retention and relapse (236–239), ethnic and gender differences (240), treatment in a criminal justice setting (210, 241, 243), and treatment of women with HIV (244).

In Rosenbaum et al.'s recent study of MMT (117), the women's primary reason for entering a program was to reduce drug-related harm to themselves and their children. They experienced barriers to treatment also faced by men (such as prohibitive clinic fees and waiting lists), but also had to contend with women-specific barriers that discouraged and sometimes prevented some from entering and others from fully engaging in treatment.

Although both men and women shared many similar motivations for treatment, such as avoiding the criminal justice system, burning out on "the life," and desire to change their lives, women spoke specifically of their relationships and family responsibilities as reasons for entering treatment programs. They sought MMT when their partners influenced them to use heroin and/or other drugs and to share injection equipment in an unsafe way, and when they were in abusive relationships. Occasionally these women could not initiate the treatment process until they had ended these relationships.

As has been the case for decades, many of the women in the study population (117) viewed pregnancy as a motivation for entering treatment. They wanted to "clean up for the baby," and saw the pregnancy as an opportunity to make other positive changes in their lives. In addition, women's desire to improve their capacity for parenting was a motivation for treatment. Both pregnant women and women with children experienced tremendous feelings of guilt over drug use and its potential detrimental effects on their children. This guilt often translated into efforts to seek treatment.

The data revealed at least three substantial barriers to treatment for women: (*a*) family responsibilities, (*b*) interpersonal and sexual violence, and (*c*) sex work. Either alone or in interaction with other factors, these barriers often effectively deterred and possibly prevented women from seeking treatment. Ironically, for those women in treatment, occasionally clinic policies converted motivations into barriers that may have prevented them from maximizing the therapeutic benefits that MMT had to offer (117).

The familial barriers fell into two categories: sexual partners and children. It was not uncommon for women to experience resistance from their partners in seeking treatment. Sometimes this resistance was subtle, such as in cases when they received no help with child care from their partners while they were trying to meet clinic demands. At other times resistance was more overt, such as when a partner's violence was meant to prevent a woman from seeking treatment. These women wanted MMT and all the benefits of stabilization, but they often faced resistance from those closest to them, their partners.

Although pregnancy and children were motivations for treatment, both also served as barriers to treatment. Some programs were hesitant to take pregnant women because of the extra resources they required. Even when they did present for treatment during pregnancy, many experienced discrimination at the hands of health care and social service workers within the clinic setting. So although pregnancy was a primary motivation for women to seek MMT, it also deterred them from getting help for their drug dependency. This effect had negative health consequences for both the women and their children, since adequate health care was not received.

A final barrier to treatment specific to women was their working situations. Sex work, in particular, made it difficult for women to fully engage in treatment, since the social worlds of sex work and drug use are closely intertwined. Many of the women found it economically necessary to continue with sex work, as they had few job skills and little social or economic support. In addition, many of the women in the Rosenbaum et al. study had criminal records. They reported that it was next to impossible to find conventional work after serving time. Although men, too, frequently struggled to find legal work after a jail or prison term, the women we interviewed believed it was especially difficult for them because of what they saw as greater social stigma attached to jail terms for women. With few or no legitimate work possibilities, women continued to find economic support in occupations such as sex work, which as noted earlier, increased their risk of HIV infection (117).

Implications of the War on Drugs for Women

The Reagan-Bush drug war was overt in its emphasis on interdiction and enforcement. The rhetoric of the Clinton war initially suggested a public health orientation, with proposed funding reversing to 70% for prevention, education, and treatment and 30% for enforcement. Ultimately, however, Clinton's drug control strategy allocated 64% of the budget to enforcement (245). The result has been that more drug users than ever before have been arrested and incarcerated.

For women, the war on drugs has been devastating, and for African-American women it has been a catastrophe. Drug *arrests* for women have escalated, and according to Wellisch, Anglin, and Prendergast, "From 1982 to 1991 the number of women arrested for drug offenses, including possession, manufacturing and sale, increased 89%, a rate almost twice that for men during the same period." (210). *Incarceration* rates have also soared. From 1980, the beginning of the escalation of the War on Drugs, to 1992, when Clinton took office, the female prison population increased by 276%, compared with "just" 163% for men (242, 247). Mandatory minimums had a tremendous impact on sentencing for women. In 1986, when the "mandatories" were instituted, one woman in eight was incarcerated in prison for a drug-related crime, and by 1991 that figure had increased to one in three, an increase of 433% (compared with a 283% increase for men). Drug offenders accounted for over half (55%) of the national increase during this period (248).

Women have been arrested and incarcerated at escalating rates, not because their criminality has increased or that they are more violent and threatening. Owen and Bloom found quite the opposite:

> Whereas the increasing population of imprisoned women implies an increased criminality among women, we disagree. Both our data and the research literature on imprisoned women stress the prominent role played by substance abuse, physical and sexual abuse, and poverty and underemployment in the role of female offenders. Our survey data also support the contention that a significant proportion of female offenders are not dangerous, are not career criminals, and thus do not represent a serious threat to the community. The impact of the huge increase in drug-related offenses is seen in the state and federal surveys as well as in the California data. We suggest that the criminality of women has not increased; instead, the legal response to drug-related behavior has become increasingly punitive, resulting in a flood of less serious offenders into the state and federal prison. (249)

African-American women have experienced even more dramatic increases in arrest and incarceration rates. Between 1986 and 1991 there was an 828% increase in the number of black women incarcerated for drug-related offenses, which was nearly double that of black men (242). This increase is due to conservative fiscal policies that reduced not only economic options but government support for the poor, as well as an escalation in criminal justice sanctions as part of the War on Drugs. The crack economy provided those without economic options the opportunity to earn money at the cost of the incarceration of nearly one in four young black Americans.

The punishment of women extends far beyond themselves and into their families and communities. When women go to prison, their absence is felt by the 125,000 children under 18 they leave behind, whose lives are disrupted emotionally, psychologically, and physically. One wonders who is actually being punished:

> Children of incarcerated mothers suffer disproportionate disruption in their lives. In 1992 about 90% of fathers in state prisons reported that their children were living with the children's mothers. Only a quarter of female inmates had similar support from a father. Ten percent of mothers said their children were living in foster homes, children's agencies or institutions. For children of women who are imprisoned more than once, the situation is even worse. Children are shuttled from home to home, relative to relative, institution to institution, returning to their mothers only to be separated. (250)

Alternatives to prison, such as treatment, for drug-related, nonviolent crimes, have not been realized. Despite a "treatment on demand" rhetoric emanating from Clinton's first drug czar, Lee Brown, Americans seem to be much more willing to spend shrinking funds on prisons than options such as drug treatment, which cost a fraction. Despite evidence that women are overwhelmingly arrested and incarcerated on (nonviolent) drug charges, the vast majority have not, for a variety of reasons, been exposed to drug treatment (242, 249, 251, 252).

Finally, the War on Drugs has contributed directly to increased AIDS risk for women, their sexual partners, and their children. The government has gone beyond refusing to support and endorse needle exchange. Recently the Clinton administration actively suppressed important evidence demonstrating the HIV-reducing efficacy (without increased drug use) of syringe exchange programs.

RECOMMENDATIONS

In the early 1970s, Nixon's War on Drugs began primarily to combat rising drug-related crime. This war had a heavy medical-rehabilitative orientation in which deviance was seen as illness. For example, it was during the early 1970s that MMT became institutionalized (71). Simultaneously (and not coincidentally) increased federal funds for drug research became available. Drug-using women were seen as victims, "sicker" than their male counterparts. When the Reagan-Bush War on Drugs escalated in the 1980s, users of illegal drugs were no longer seen as ill but bad, and culpable for their drug-related problems. Women bore the brunt of drug scapegoating, defined as epidemiologically dangerous and responsible for the spread of HIV to the heterosexual community. By the late 1980s, women drug users had become the less-than-human "crack moms" who were blamed and punished for creating a generation of permanently impaired children.

The increasing size and scope of the problem of women's substance abuse has been exacerbated, if not caused, by two national trends. First, poverty, homelessness, substandard education, and health care have increased since 1980 (253). As members of America's ever-growing "underclass," drug users' lives have become more chaotic, risky, dangerous, and violent (254). Second, for addicts without financial resources, access to drug treatment has become increasingly problematic due to a decline in federal funding of programs since 1976 (255). Although the Office of National Drug Control Policy advocates a shift in funding from enforcement to prevention and treatment, thus far drug users have experienced little change in access (256, 257). Ironically, if monies and availability *were* increased, it seems unlikely that even the best form of drug treatment could reverse the deleterious effects of the social and political policies of the 1980s and 1990s. Lacking a chance at the American Dream and a "stake in conventional life," drug abusers will continue to relieve their suffering through the use of pain-killing and euphoria-producing substances (258, 259).

The "drug problem" has more to do with social conditions than drugs, and this chapter's recommendations are in agreement with Canadian Susan Boyd's recommendations about pregnancy and drug use:

> Exposure to toxic environments, malnutrition, lack of housing, lack of income or poor antenatal care have adverse effects on pregnancy outcomes. If pregnancy outcomes were truly a "health issue" Canadians might consider eliminating the social environmental variables affecting pregnancy rather than stigmatizing a generation of children and their mothers. (183, p. 188)

In addition to these "environmental" factors, a wholly revamped society that is truly open and receptive to a range of life options available to all would also help relieve these problems. In the meantime, drug treatment should be expanded and embellished and a policy of harm reduction toward drugs instituted immediately.

Treatment

In general, more treatment slots are needed for both men and women drug users. Under the current inadequately-funded system, there are long waiting lists and "treatment on demand" is anything but a reality, resulting in an underserved population of women (242, 249, 260). The lack of treatment slots is particularly glaring for pregnant women. In 1990, Wendy Chavkin conducted a survey of drug treatment facilities throughout New York City and found:

> The general shortage of treatment slots is aggravated by the unwillingness of many drug programs to include pregnant women. A recent survey in New York by the author revealed that 54% of treatment programs categorically excluded the pregnant. Effective availability was further limited by restrictions on method of payment or specific substance of abuse. Sixty-seven percent of the programs rejected pregnant Medicaid patients and only 13% accepted pregnant Medicaid patients addicted to crack. (261, p. 485)

Another survey conducted in the same year found of the approximately 675,000 pregnant women in need of drug treatment nationwide, less than 11% received it (173, p.28). Most treatment facilities are unprepared and inadequate to the multiplicity of needs of pregnant women. Separate clinics or clinics within clinics must be instituted.

Current treatment models are male-oriented and not prepared to address women's multiple needs (17, 50, 81, 224, 262–267). For 25 years, since the expansion of drug treatment, women have been motivated to enlist themselves in programs, primarily to get out of "the life" and better fulfill their mothering roles. Currently, a majority of inpatient treatment programs require a minimum 30-day commitment and some are as long as one year. For a woman with young children, this can be an insurmountable obstacle (268, 269). In 1981, the author wrote the following:

> [L]ive-in treatment facilities—either equipped for detoxification or opiate-free—work better than other modalities (outpatient detox or methadone maintenance). For a woman addict, live-in treatment is currently possible if she has no commitments; to the 70 per cent of the women in this sample who were mothers, treatment facilities without accommodations for children are of no use. (17, p. 126)

Little has changed in the ensuing 15 years. Women who have substance abuse problems are still unable, for the most part, to find inpatient services that will accommodate their children. Those women who need outpatient services are also in need of assistance with their child care responsibilities, such as supervised play areas for children within the treatment facility. In the context of counseling, programs also should be sensitive to women's privacy needs (17, 264, 265, 270).

All treatment modalities that serve women must be sensitive to their special needs, including counseling, family therapy, and ancillary services such as transportation, child care, children's health services, housing, legal assistance, and job or vocational training. They must also be sensitive to women's diverse cultural needs. Ideally, alternatives to the current system might include women-only treatment programs, inpatient programs that accept children, expansion (and in some areas of the country, creation) of clinics for pregnant women, special job training programs for women and long-term commitment of funding for after care.

Both women drug users and treatment professionals must participate in the institutionalization of advocacy groups which could influence the formulation of treatment policy. Such organizations would go a long way in combating the depression, isolation, and low self-esteem that persists among women in treatment (262, 264, 265, 270, 271). Treatment providers also need the support provided by gender-specific and in-service training in order to decrease burnout and increase program efficacy (272). Finally, public policy makers (e.g., legislators) need to be educated by treatment professionals as well as clients to the needs of this population (208).

Treatment facilities also need to acknowledge the devastating impact of HIV on women drug users, and incorporate AIDS education into their programs. HIV-positive women need special attention. Drug treatment facilities must alter their admission criteria and treatment methods to accommodate this population. They should include comprehensive services, including parenting and employment skills, workshops, and access to health care, and incorporate research and evaluation components with planned dissemination of results (273).

A Policy of Harm Reduction

Drug use has been with us for centuries and is part of our cultural, and perhaps biological heritage (274, 275). Given current social and economic policies that limit life options, the sale and use of intoxicating substances is not likely to disappear, despite our most fervent efforts at "zero tolerance." Americans do not like to admit failure, although the task of eliminating illegal drug use was impossible from the outset. Instead, we should look seriously at the adoption of "harm reduction" strategies instead of futile attempts to eliminate drug use completely. Harm reduction is a set of principles that defines abstinence from drug use as just one of several means of reducing drug-related problems. It is a simple concept, not a camouflage for radical change in drug policy, first implemented in Europe and Australia and used primarily to deal with the AIDS crisis. Those who subscribe to a harm reduction perspective deplore, yet accept, the inevitability of drug abuse. They advocate working *with* users to minimize the harms brought about by abuse, even if drug use itself cannot be stopped (246). Harm reduction shifts the focus away from idealistic long-term goals, such as abstinence from all drug use, toward more attainable short-term goals such as safer behaviors.

As noted earlier, women studied by the author, whether pregnant and using drugs, or enrolled in treatment, attempted to reduce drug-related harm for themselves and their offspring. These efforts should be encouraged and facilitated. Women should have better information so their efforts are more effective. Those who intervene should stop punishing pregnant women and instead facilitate their harm reduction efforts. Women should have access to health care without the risk of losing their baby to social services or humiliation. They should have access to treatment that does not require total abstinence. Finally, professionals in research and treatment must learn to settle for less, because insisting on absolute perfection may exacerbate the problem.

Motherhood is at the core of many drug-using women's identities. They love and care very much about their children, who often provide the impetus for harm reduction through exiting "the life" or instituting safer behaviors. Since American society is currently consumed with "family values," drug-using women should derive some of the benefits of this perspective. To begin, they should have the resources to raise children in this country—to feed, house, clothe, and educate them. On the meager, subsistence level provided by our government (which is currently being reduced), paying the rent, providing food, and buying clothes and school supplies are nearly impossible. When women take refuge from this depressing, hopeless, and seemingly endless existence through drugs, social service agencies threaten to take away their most precious "possession." Their children are placed in foster care or with relatives, where they may "bounce around" for years. Loss of custody results in a further spiraling into drug abuse and the commitment on

the part of women to have another "replacement" baby in order to regain "one's ideal image of oneself as a competent mother" (276, p. 149). Obviously we should weigh levels of harm and rethink social service policies. Rather than removal of custody, we should provide women with the resources needed to raise children.

Treatment, as noted in earlier sections of this chapter, should be expanded and sensitized to women's needs. In addition, a harm reduction perspective within the context of drug treatment should be instituted. Women often enlist in programs when their drug careers are at the height of risk and chaos. The recovery process is slow, and requires an extended period of time during which the woman is not always abstinent from drugs. Treatment should be seen as a *process* of harm reduction, during which deleterious behaviors are gradually eliminated. For example, if a woman enters treatment with a 365-day "habit" and after a month reduces her drug use to weekends, this should be seen not as failure but as progress. The very last action taken by a treatment program should be to terminate the woman from the program. Instead, she should be encouraged to stay in treatment and further reduce the harms related to her drug use.

Alternatives to incarceration that reduce harm should be explored and instituted. Teresa Albor argues:

> In an immediate and practical sense, it is time to recognize that there are forms of punishment for women that are more effective, less expensive and cause less disruption to families. These include small model programs in which mothers live with their children while serving sentences, community correction or restitution and home-based confinement using electronic monitoring. Instead of building more prisons for women, we should use scarce resources for prison-based reproductive health counseling, education, vocational training and post-release programs, which provide former inmates with continued access to alcohol and drug treatment and other emotional support. And if mothers must be in prison, it is essential that they be able to get together with their children for weekend retreats, or that transportation be provided for the children so they can visit their mothers.
>
> It is time to raise the more radical question of whether most women offenders should be incarcerated at all. Most female prisoners don't belong in prison and are harmed by the experience. Most are women whom society has failed. When we lock them up, separate them from their children, provide inadequate health care and rehabilitative services and treat them as loathsome and irresponsible criminals, that failure is amplified. Removing women from their families perpetuates cycles of criminality and dysfunction by both the mothers and their children. The ultimate cost to society is far greater than if these families had not been torn apart. (277, p. 237)

Needle exchange programs have been shown to reduce syringe-related HIV risk in the general population of IDUs and for women in particular (278). The Clinton Administration should stop suppressing evidence of the efficacy of syringe exchange and make this harm-reducing program fully accessible to both women and men.

The United States has been slow in adopting harm reduction strategies (246, 279, 280). A notable exception is MMT which has been used, but not without controversy, for some 30 years (71). This is largely due to fear on the part of policy-makers that a harm reduction message will encourage increased drug use among current users and lead to the initiation of new users (281). In fact, there is no evidence to suggest that harm reduction strategies such as safe drug-using messages, needle exchange programs, and greater access to treatment increase drug use (280, 282–284). We can only hope the continued failure of criminal justice/interdiction strategies will eventually enlighten Americans to the only pragmatic course regarding women (and men) who use drugs, the institutionalization of harm reduction as policy.

References

1. NIDA Household Survey. Preliminary estimates from the 1994 National Household Survey on Drug Abuse. Washington, DC: U.S. Department of Health and Human Services, 1995:77.
2. Kandall SR. Substance and shadow: women and addiction in the United States. Cambridge, MA: Harvard University Press, 1996.
3. Hunt LG, Chambers CD. The heroin epidemics. New York: Spectrum, 1976.
4. Hunt LG. Prevalence of active heroin use in the United States. NIDA Res Monogr 1977;16:61–86.
5. Walter PV, Sheridan BK, Chambers CD. Methadone diversion: a study of illicit availability. In: Chambers CD, Brill L, eds. Methadone: experiences and issues. New York: Behavioral Publications, 1973:171–176.
6. Cuskey WR, Wathey RB. Female addiction. Lexington, MA: Lexington Books, 1982.
7. DeLeon G. Phoenix House: psychopathological signs among male and female drug-free residents. Addict Dis 1974;1:135.

8. Ellinwood EH, Smith WG, Vaillant GE. Narcotic addiction in males and females: a comparison. Int J Addict 1966;(1):33.

9. Miller JS. Value patterns of drug addicts as a function of race and sex. Int J Addict 1973;8:4.

10. Waldorf D. Careers in dope. Englewood Cliffs, NJ: Prentice-Hall, 1973.

11. Cuskey WR, Moffet AD, Clifford HB. A comparison of female opiate addicts admitted to Lexington Hospital in 1961 and 1967. In: Cohen CS, Roningson S, Smart E, eds. Psychotherapy and drug addiction. I: diagnosis and treatment. New York: MSS Information, 1974:89–103.

12. Baldinger R, Goldsmith BM, Capel WG. Pot smokers, junkies and squares: a comparative study of female values. Int J Addict 1972;7:153.

13. Climent CE. Epidemiological studies of female prisoners: biological, psychological, and social correlates of drug addiction. Int J Addict 1974; 9:345.

14. Adler F, Simon R. The criminology of deviant women. Boston: Houghton Mifflin, 1979.

15. James J. Prostitution and addiction: an interdisciplinary approach. Addict Dis 1976;2:601–618.

16. Goldstein P. Prostitution and drugs. Lexington, MA: Lexington Books, 1979.

17. Rosenbaum M. Women on heroin. New Brunswick, NJ: Rutgers University Press, 1981.

18. d'Orban PT. Heroin dependency and delinquency in women—a study of heroin addicts in Holloway Prison. Br J Addict 1970;65:67.

19. File KN, McCahill TW, Savitz LD. Narcotics involvements and female criminality. Addict Dis 1974;1:177.

20. Weissman JC, File KN. Criminal behavior patterns of female addicts: a comparison of findings in two cities. Int J Addict 1976;11:6.

21. Klein D, Kress J. Any woman's blues: a critical overview of women, crime and the criminal justice system. Crime Soc Justice 1976;5:34–30.

22. Ball R, Lilly JR. Female delinquency in an urban country. Criminology 1976;14:279–281.

23. Chambers C, Hinesley RK, Moldstad M. Narcotic addiction in females: a race comparison. Int J Addict 1970;5:257.

24. Cuskey WR. Survey of opiate addiction among females in the United States between 1850 and 1970. Public Health Rev 1972;1:8–39.

25. Densen-Gerber J, Weiner M, Hochstedler R. Sexual behavior, abortion, and birth control in heroin addicts: legal and psychiatric considerations. Contemp Drug Probl 1972;1:783.

26. Eldred CA, Washington MM. Female heroin addicts in a city treatment program: the forgotten minority. Psychiatry 1975;38:75.

27. Chambers C, Inciardi J. Some aspects of the criminal careers of female narcotics addicts. Paper presented to the Southern Sociological Society, Miami Beach, FL, 1971.

28. Fiddle S. Sequences in addiction. Addict Dis 1976;2:553–567.

29. James J. Female addiction and criminal involvement. Paper presented to the Pacific Sociological Association, Victoria, British Columbia, 1975.

30. Steffensmeier DJ. Contemporary patterns of female criminality. Paper presented at the 39th annual meeting of the American Society of Criminology, Montreal, November, 1987.

31. Rosenbaum M. Sex roles among deviants: the woman addict. Int J Addict 1981;16(3):859–877.

32. Sutter A. The world of the righteous dope fiend. Issues Criminol 1966;2:177–182.

33. Yablonsky L. Synanon: the tunnel back. New York: Macmillan, 1965.

34. Zahn M, Ball J. Patterns and causes of drug addiction among Puerto Rican females. Addict Dis 1974;1:203–214.

35. Blinick G. Fertility of narcotics addicts and effects of addiction on the offspring. Soc Biol 1971;18:S34–S39.

36. Blinick G, Wallach C, Jerez EM. Pregnancy in narcotics addicts treated by medical withdrawal. Am J Obstet Gynecol 1969;105:997–1003.

37. Finnegan LP. Narcotics dependence in pregnancy. J Psychedelic Drugs 1975;7(July–September):3.

38. Finnegan LP. Women in treatment. In: Dupont R, Goldstein A, O'Donnell J, eds. Handbook on drug abuse. Rockville, MD: National Institute on Drug Abuse, 1979.

39. Glass L. Narcotic withdrawal in the newborn infant. J Natl Med Assoc 1974;6:117–118.

40. Kandall SR, Albin S, Lowinson J, Berle B, Eidelman AI, Gartner LM. Differential effects of maternal heroin and methadone use on birthweight. Pediatrics 1976;58:681–685.

41. Naeye RL, Blanc W, Leblanc W, Khatamee MA. Fetal complications of maternal heroin addiction: abnormal growth, infection and episodes of stress. J Pediatr 1973;83:1055–1061.

42. Naeye RL, Ladis B, Drage JS. Sudden infant death syndrome. A prospective study. Am J Dis Child 1976;130:1207–1210.

43. Ostrea EM, Chavez CJ, Strauss ME. A study of factors that influence the severity of neonatal narcotic withdrawal. J Pediatr 1976;88:642–645.

44. Rementeria JL, Nunag NN. Narcotic withdrawal in pregnancy. Am J Obstet Gynecol 1973;116: 1052–1056.

45. Stone ML, Salerna LJ, Green M. Narcotic addiction in pregnancy. Am J Obstet Gynecol 1971;109:716.

46. Wilson G, McCreary K, Kean J, Baxter J. The development of preschool children of heroin-addicted mothers: a controlled study. Pediatrics 1979;63:135–141.

47. Zelson C. Infant of the addicted mother. N Engl J Med 1973;288:26.

48. Zuspan F, Gumpel J, Mejia-Zelaya A, et al. Fetal stress from methadone withdrawal. Am J Obstet Gynecol 1975;2:43–48.

49. Blume S. Chemical dependency in women: important issues. Am J Drug Alcohol Abuse 1990;16(3,4):297–309.

50. Cuskey WR, Berger L, Densen-Gerber J. Issues in the treatment of female addiction: a review and critique of the literature. Contemp Drug Probl 1977;6:307–371.

51. Rosenbaum M, Murphy S. Getting the treatment: recycling women addicts. J Psychoactive Drugs 1981;13(1):1–13.

52. Blinick G, Jerez E, Wallach RC. Methadone maintenance, pregnancy and progeny. JAMA 1973;225:447–449.

53. Blinick G, Inturrisi C, Jerez E. Methadone assays in pregnant women and progeny. Am J Obstet Gynecol 1975;1:617–619.

54. Clark D, Keith L, Pildes R. Drug dependent obstetric patients. J Obstet Gynecol Nurs 1974;3: 17–20.

55. Cohen SN, Neumann LL. Methadone maintenance during pregnancy. Am J Dis Child 1973; 6:445–446.

56. Connaughton JF, Finnegan LP, Schut J, Emich JP. Current concepts in the management of the pregnant opiate addict. Addict Dis 1975;2:21–35.

57. Connaughton JF, Reeser D, Schut J, Finnegan LP. Perinatal addiction: outcome and management. Am J Obstet Gynecol 1977;9:679–686.

58. Finnegan LP. Drug dependence in pregnancy: clinical management of mother and child. A manual for medical professionals and paraprofessionals prepared for the National Institute on Drug Abuse, Services Research Branch. Washington, DC: U.S. Government Printing Office, 1978.

59. Finnegan LP, Connaughton JF, Emich JP. Comprehensive care of the pregnant addict and its effect on maternal and infant outcome. Contemp Drug Probl 1972;1:795.

60. Harper RG, Solish GI, Purow HM, Sand E, Panepinto WC. The effect of a methadone treatment program upon pregnant heroin addicts and their newborn infants. Pediatrics 1974;54: 300–305.

61. Newman RG. Pregnancies of methadone patients. N Y State J Med 1974;1:52–54.

62. Rajegowda BK, Glass L, Evans HE, Maso G, Swartz DP, LeBlanc W. Methadone withdrawal in newborn infants. J Pediatr 1972;81(3): 532–534.

63. Ramer CM, Lodge A. Clinical and developmental characteristics of infants of mothers on methadone maintenance. Addict Dis 1975;2:227–233.

64. Statzer DE, Wardell JN. Heroin addiction during pregnancy. Am J Obstet Gynecol 1966;94: 253–257.

65. Sullivan RD, Fischbach AL, Hornick FW. Treatment of a pregnant opiate addict with oral methadone. Arizona Med 1972;29:30.

66. Waldeman H. Psychiatric emergencies during pregnancy and in the puerperium. Munch Med Wochenschr 1973;115:1039–1043.

67. Wallach RC, Jerez E, Blinick G. Pregnancy and menstrual function in narcotics addicts treated with methadone, the Methadone Maintenance Treatment Program. Am J Obstet Gynecol 1969; 105(8):1226–1229.

68. Zelson C, Lee SJ, Casalino M. Neonatal narcotic addiction: comparative effects of maternal intake of heroin and methadone. N Engl J Med 1973;289(23):16–20.

69. Zelson C. Infant of the addicted mother. N Engl J Med 1973;288:1393–1395.

70. Arif A, Westermeyer J. Methadone in the management of opioid dependence: programs and policies around the world. Geneva: World Health Organization, 1988.

71. Rosenbaum M. The demedicalization of methadone maintenance. J Psychoactive Drugs 1995;27(2):145–149.

72. Rosenbaum M. Getting on methadone. Contemp Drug Probl Law Q 1982;spring:113–143.

73. Finnegan LP, Connaughton JF, Emich JP. Abstinence Score in the treatment of infants of drug dependent mothers. Pediatr Res 1973;7:319.

74. Lodge A, Marcus MM, Ramer CM. Behavioral and electro-physiological characteristics of the addicted neonate. Addict Dis Int J 1975;2: 235–255.

75. Mondanaro J. Women: pregnancy, children and addiction. J Psychedelic Drugs 1977;9(1): 59–68.

76. Reddy AM, Harper RG, Stern G. Observation on heroin and methadone withdrawal in the newborn. J Pediatr 1971;48:353–358.

77. Glaser F. Narcotic addiction in the pain-prone female patient. Int J Addict 1966;1:2.

78. Chein I, Gerard DL, Lee RS, Rosenfeld E. The road to H. New York: Basic Books, 1964.

79. Soler E, Ponser L, Abod J. Women in treatment: client self-report. In: Bauman A, et al, eds. Women in treatment: issues and approaches. Arlington, VA: National Drug Abuse Center for Training and Resource Development, 1976.

80. White L. It isn't easy being gay. In: Bauman A, et al, eds. Women in treatment: issues and approaches. Arlington, VA: National Drug Abuse Center for Training and Resource Development, 1976.

81. Levy SJ, Doyle KM. Attitudes toward women in

a drug treatment program. J Drug Issues 1974;4:423–434.

82. Centers for Disease Control. HIV/AIDS Surveillance Rep 1994;6(2):12.

83. Kane S. HIV, heroin, and heterosexual relations. Soc Sci Med 1991;32(9):1037–1050.

84. Campbell CA. Women and AIDS. Soc Sci Med 1990;30:407–415.

85. Carpenter CCJ, Mayer KH, Stein MD, Leibman BD, Fisher A, Fiore TC. Human immunodeficiency virus infection in North American women: experience with 200 cases and a review of the literature. Medicine 1991; 70(5):307–325.

86. Cohen JB, Haver LB, Wofsy CB. Women and intravenous drugs: parenteral and heterosexual transmission of human immunodeficiency virus. J Drug Issues 1989;19:39–56.

87. Feucht TE, Stephens RC, Roman SW. The sexual behavior of intravenous drug users: assessing the risk of sexual transmission of HIV. J Drug Issues 1990;20(2):195–213.

88. Klee H, Faugier J, Hayes C, Boulton T, Morris J. Sexual partners of injecting drug users: the risk for HIV infection. Br J Addict 1990; 85:413–418.

89. McCoy HV, Inciardi JA. Women and AIDS: social determinants of sex-related activities. Women Health 1993;20(1):69–86.

90. Mondanaro J. Strategies for AIDS prevention: motivating health behavior in drug-dependent women. J Psychoactive Drugs 1987;19(2): 143–149.

91. Project MENU (Methods Estimating Needle Users At Risk for AIDS). Section three: what percentage of drug injectors are women? An analysis of gender-by-age interactions of drug injectors on three reporting systems in three cities. Unpublished report, 1989.

92. Schilling RF, El-Bassel N, Schinke SP, Nichols SE, Botvin GJ, Orlandi MA. Sexual behavior, attitudes towards safer sex, and gender among a cohort of 244 recovering IV drug users. Int J Addict 1991;26:865–883.

93. Weiss SH, Weston CB, Quirinale J. Safe sex? Misconceptions, gender differences and barriers among injection drug users: a focus group approach. AIDS Educ Prev 1993;5(4): 279–293.

94. Amaro H. Love, sex, and power: considering women's realities in HIV prevention. Am Psychol 1995;50:437–447.

95. Brown V, Weissman G. Women and men injecting drug users: an updated look at gender differences and risk factors. In: Brown B, Beschner F, eds. At risk for AIDS: injection drug users and their partners. Westport, CT: Greenwood Press, 1994.

96. Murphy DL. Heterosexual contacts of intravenous drug abusers: implications for the next spread of the AIDS epidemic. Adv Alcohol Subst Abuse 1987;7:89–97.

97. Murphy S. Intravenous drug use and AIDS: notes on the social economy of needle sharing. Contemp Drug Probl 1987;14:373–395.

98. Wayment H, Newcomb MD, Hannemann VL. Female and male intravenous drug users not-in-treatment: are they at differential risk for AIDS? Sex Roles 1993;28(1,2):111–125.

99. Rosenbaum M. Women addicts' experience of the heroin world: risk, chaos, and inundation. Urban Life 1981;10(1):65–91.

100. Argeriou M, McCarty D, Potter D, Holt L. Characteristics of men and women arrested for driving under the influence of liquor. Alcohol Treat Q 1986;3:127–137.

101. Brady KT, Grice DE, Dustan L, Randall C. Gender differences in substance use disorders. Am J Psychiatry 1993;150:1707–1711.

102. Ferrence R, Whitehead P. Sex differences in psychoactive drug use: recent epidemiology. In: Kalant OJ, ed. Research advances and drug problems: vol 5. Alcohol and drug problems in women. New York: Plenum, 1980:125–201.

103. Griffin ML, Weiss RD, Mirin SM, Lange U. A comparison of male and female cocaine abusers. Arch Gen Psychiatry 1989;46:122–126.

104. Ruzek SK. Report to the California State Office of Narcotics and Drug Abuse. Prevention and treatment of female drug dependency. Sacramento, CA, 1974.

105. Kuhns JB, Heide KM, Silverman I. Substance use/misuse among female prostitutes and female arrestees. Int J Addict 1992;27(11):1283–1292.

106. Marshall N, Hendtlass J. Drugs and prostitution. J Drug Issues 1986;16:237–248.

107. Plant ML, Plant MA, Peck DF, Setters J. The sex industry, alcohol, and illicit drugs: implications for the spread of HIV infection. Br J Addict 1989;84(1):53–59.

108. McKeganey NP. Prostitution and HIV: what do we know and where might research be targeted in the future. AIDS 1994;8:1215–1226.

109. Cohen JB, Alexander P, Wofsy C. Prostitutes and AIDS: public policy issues. AIDS Public Policy 1988;3(2):16–22.

110. Dorfman LE, Derish PA, Cohen JB. Hey girlfriend: an evaluation of AIDS prevention among women in the sex industry. Health Educ Q 1992;19(1):25–40.

111. Worth D. Sexual decision-making and AIDS: why condom promotion among vulnerable women is likely to fail. Stud Fam Planning 1989;20(6):297–307.

112. Davis RC, Chappel JN. Pregnancy in the context of narcotic addiction and methadone maintenance. Paper presented at the Fifth National Conference on Methadone Treatment, Washington, DC, March, 1973.

113. Corby NH, Wolitski RJ, Thornton-Johnson S, Tanner WM. AIDS knowledge, perception of risk, and behaviors among female sex partners of injection drug users. AIDS Educ Prev 1991; 3(4):353–366.

114. Kim MY, Marmor M, Dubin N, Wolfe H. HIV risk-related sexual behaviors among heterosexuals in New York City: associations with race, sex, and intravenous drug use. AIDS 1993;7: 409–414.

115. Lewis DK, Watters JK. Human immunodeficiency virus seroprevalence in female intravenous drug users: the puzzle of black women's risk. Soc Sci Med 1989;29:1071–1076.

116. Lewis DK, Watters JK. Sexual risk behavior among heterosexual intravenous drug users: ethnic and gender variations. AIDS 1991;5: 67–73.

117. Rosenbaum M, Washburn A, Knight KR, Kelley M, Irwin J. Methadone maintenance: treatment as harm reduction, policy as harm maximization. Final Report to the National Institute on Drug Abuse, Grant #1 R01 DA08982, 1995.

118. Mays VM, Cochran SD. Issues in the perception of AIDS risk and risk reduction activities by black and Hispanic/Latina women. Am Psychol 1988;43(1):949–957.

119. Nyamathi A, Vasquez R. Impact of poverty, homelessness, and drugs on Hispanic women at risk for HIV infection. Hispanic J Behav Sci 1989;11(4):299–314.

120. Nyamathi A, Shin DM. Designing a culturally sensitive AIDS educational program for black and Hispanic women of childbearing age.

NAACOGS Clin Issues Perinat Wom Nurs 1990;1(1):86–98.

121. Nyamathi A. Comparative study of factors relating to HIV risk level of black homeless women. J Acquir Immune Defic Syndr 1992;5: 222–228.

122. Nyamathi A, Flaskerud J. A community-based inventory of current concerns of impoverished homeless and drug-addicted women. Res Nurs Health 1992;15:121–129.

123. Pivnick A. HIV infection and the meaning of condoms. Cult Med Psychiatry 1993;17: 431–453.

124. Grella C, Annon J, Anglin MD. Ethnic differences in HIV risk behaviors, self-perceptions, and treatment outcomes among women in methadone maintenance treatment. J Psychoactive Drugs 1995;27(4):421–433.

125. Abelson HI, Miller JD. A decade of trends in cocaine use in the household population. NIDA Res Monogr 1985;61:35–49.

126. Adams EH, Durell J. Cocaine: a growing public health problem. NIDA Res Monogr 1984; 50:9–14.

127. Inciardi J. The war on drugs: heroin, cocaine, crime and public policy. Palo Alto, CA: Mayfield Publishing, 1986.

128. Johnston LD, Bachman JG, O'Malley PM. Highlights from student drug use in America, 1975–1984. Washington, DC: National Institute on Drug Abuse, U.S. Department of Health and Human Services, 1984.

129. National Institute on Drug Abuse. Highlights: 1985 National Household Survey on Drug Abuse. Washington, DC: U.S. Government Printing Office, 1987.

130. Clayton R, Voss H, Robbins C, Skinner W. Gender preferences in drug use: an epidemiological perspective. NIDA Res Monogr 1986; 65:80–99.

131. Erickson PG, Murray GF. Sex differences in cocaine use and experience: a double standard revived? Am J Drug Alcohol Abuse 1989; 15(2):135–152.

132. Inciardi JA. 1991. Kingrats, chicken heads, slow necks, freaks, and bloodsuckers: a glimpse at the Miami sex for crack market. Paper presented at the Annual Meeting of the Society for Applied Anthropology, Charleston, SC, March 13–17, 1991.

133. Siegel RK. Cocaine and sexual dysfunction: the curse of mama coca. J Psychoactive Drugs 1982;14(1,2):71–74.

134. Smith DE, Wesson DR, Apter-Marsh M. Cocaine and alcohol induced sexual dysfunction in patients with addictive disease. J Psychoactive Drugs 1984;16:359–361.

135. Inciardi JA, Lockwood D, Pottieger AE. Crack dependent women and sexuality: implications for STD acquisition and transmission. Addict Recovery 1991;2:25–28.

136. McCoy HV, Miles C, Inciardi J. Survival sex: inner-city women and crack cocaine. In: Inciardi J, McElrath K, eds. The American drug scene: an anthology. Los Angeles: Roxbury, 1995.

137. Siegal HA, Carlson RG, Falck R, Forney MA, Wang J, Li L. High risk behaviors for transmission of syphilis and human immunodeficiency virus among crack cocaine-using women: a case study from the Midwest. Sex Transm Dis 1992;19(5):266–271.

138. Fullilove MT, Fullilove RE. Black teen crack use and sexually transmitted diseases. J Am Med Wom Assoc 1989;44(5):146–147, 151–153.

139. Bowser B. Crack and AIDS: an ethnographic impression. J Natl Med Assoc 1989;81: 538–540.

140. Chitwood D. Epidemiology of crack use among injection drug users and partners of injection drug users. In: Brown BS, Beschner GM, eds. Handbook on risk for AIDS: injection drug users and sexual partners. Westport, CT: Greenwood Press, 1993.

141. Centers for Disease Control and Prevention. Update: AIDS among women—United States, 1994. MMWR Morb Mortal Wkly Rep 1995; 44(5):81–84.

142. Adler P. Wheeling and dealing: an ethnography of an upper-level drug dealing and smuggling community. New York: Columbia University Press, 1985.

143. Bourgois P. In search of Horatio Alger: culture and ideology in the crack economy. Contemp Drug Probl 1989;16:619–650.

144. Fagan J. Women and drugs revisited: female participation in the cocaine economy. J Drug Issues 1994;24(2):175–225.

145. Morningstar PJ, Chitwood DD. How women and men get cocaine: sex-role stereotypes and acquisition patterns. J Psychoactive Drugs 1987;19(2):135–142.

146. Murphy S, Rosenbaum M. Women who use cocaine too much: smoking crack vs. snorting cocaine. J Psychoactive Drugs 1992;24(4): 381–388.

147. Acker D, Sachs BP, Tracey KJ, Wise WE. Abruptio placentae associated with cocaine use. Am J Obstet Gynecol 1983;146(2):220–221.

148. Newald I. Cocaine infants. Hospitals 1986; 60:76.

149. Kearney MH, Murphy S, Rosenbaum M. Learning by losing: sex and fertility on crack cocaine. Qualitat Health Res 1994;4(2):147.

150. Kearney MH, Murphy S, Rosenbaum M. Mothering on crack cocaine: a grounded theory analysis. Soc Sci Med 1994;38(2): 351–361.

151. Murphy S. It takes your womanhood: women and crack cocaine. Philadelphia: Temple University Press (in press).

152. Rosenbaum M, Murphy S, Irwin J, Watson L. Women and crack: what's the real story? In: Trebach A, Zeese K, eds. Drug prohibition and the conscience of nations. Washington, DC: Drug Policy Foundation, 1990.

153. Chasnoff IJ. Drug use and women: establishing a standard of care. Ann N Y Acad Sci 1989; 562:2008–2010.

154. Blakeslee S. Crack's toll among babies: a joyless view, even of toys. New York Times 1989;September 17(sect 1):1.

155. The instincts of parenthood become part of crack's toll. New York Times 1990;March 17.

156. Study of addicted babies hints vast cost. New York Times 1990;March 17(sect 1):8.

157. Crack babies. Economist 1989;April 1:28.

158. Gillman D. The children of crack. Washington Post 1989;July 31(sect D):3.

159. Kadaba LS. Crack's costly legacy. Boston Globe 1990;July 1(sect B):19.

160. Crack babies: the numbers mount. Los Angeles Times 1990;March17.

161. Crack's smallest, costliest victims. New York Times 1989;August(sect A):14.

162. Crack mothers, crack babies and hope. New York Times 1989;December 31(sect 4):10.

163. 'Crack babies' in Gainesville schools foreseen. Atlanta Constitution 1990;March 19(sect C):3.

164. Will area schools be ready to rehabilitate crack babies? Atlanta Journal 1990;April 16:8(sect A).

165. Dorris M. A desperate crack legacy. Newsweek 1990;June 25.

166. Milloy C. A time bomb in cocaine babies. Washington Post 1989;September 17(sect B):3.

167. Crack babies turn 5, and schools brace. New York Times 1990;May 25(sect 1):1.

168. Sanchez R. Addicts' children a new challenge to schools. Washington Post 1990;November 14(sect D):1.

169. Beckett K. Fetal rights and 'crack moms': pregnant women in the war on drugs. Contemp Drug Probl 1995;22(4):587–612.

170. Balisy SS. Maternal substance abuse: the need to provide legal protection for the fetus. South Calif Law Rev 1987;60:1209–1238.

171. Maher L. Punishment and welfare: crack cocaine and the regulation of mothering. In: Feinman C, ed. The criminalization of a woman's body. New York: Haworth Press, 1992.

172. Norton-Hawk MA. How social policies make matters worse: the case of maternal substance abuse. J Drug Issues 1994;24(3):517–526.

173. Paltrow L. Criminal prosecutions against pregnant women. National update and overview. Reproductive Freedom Project, American Civil Liberties Union Foundation, 1992;April.

174. Siegel L. The criminalization of pregnant and child-rearing drug users. Drug Law Rep 1990; 2(15):169–176.

175. Vega W, Kolody B, Noble A, Hwang J, Porter P, Bole A, Dimas J. Profile of alcohol and drug use during pregnancy in California, 1992; Final Report: State of California, Health and Welfare Agency, Department of Alcohol and Drug Programs, contract no. 91–00252. 1993.

176. Paltrow L. Winning strategies: defending the rights of pregnant addicts. Champion 1993;August.

177. Coles CD, Platzman KA, Smith I, James ME, Falek A. Effects of cocaine and alcohol use in pregnancy and neonatal growth and neurobehavioral status. Neurotoxicol Teratol 1992;14: 23–33.

178. Hepburn M. Drug use in pregnancy. Br J Hosp Med 1993;49(1):51–55.

179. Lutiger B, Graham K, Einarson TR, Koren G. Relationship between gestational cocaine use and pregnancy outcome: a meta-analysis. Teratology 1991;44(4):405–414.

180. Mathias R. Developmental effects of prenatal drug exposure may be overcome by postnatal environment. NIDA Notes 1992;7(1):14–17.

181. Woodhouse BB. Poor mothers, poor babies: law, medicine, and crack. In: Humm SR, et al, eds. Child, parent and state: law and policy reader. Philadelphia: Temple University Press, 1994.

182. Zuckerman B. Drug exposed infants: understanding the medical risk. Future Child 1991; 1(1):26–35.

183. Boyd S. Women and illicit drug use. Int J Drug Policy 1994;5(3):185–189.

184. Humphries D, Dawson J, Cronin V, Keating P, Wisniewski C, Eichfeld J. Mothers and children, drugs and crack: reactions to maternal drug dependency. In: Feinman C, ed. The criminalization of a woman's body. New York: Haworth Press, 1992:203–221.

185. Weissman G, Sowder B, Young P. The relationship between crack cocaine use and other risk factors among women in a national AIDS prevention program. Poster session presented at the Sixth International Conference on AIDS, San Francisco, June 10–24, 1990.

186. Oakley A. The captured womb. Oxford: Basil Blackwell, 1984.

187. Gallagher J. Fetus as patient. In: Cohen S, Taub N, eds. Reproductive laws for the 1990s. Totowa, NJ: Humana Press, 1989:185–235.

188. Roberts DE. Punishing drug addicts who have babies: women of color, equality, and right of privacy. Harvard Law Rev 1991;194:1419–1482.

189. Chasnoff IJ, Landress HJ, Barrett ME. The prevalence of illicit-drug or alcohol use during pregnancy and discrepancies in mandatory reporting in Pinellas County, Florida. N Engl J Med 1990;322(17):1202–1206.

190. Moss K, Crockett J. Testimony on children of substance abusers. Reproductive Freedom Project, American Civil Liberties Union. New York, 1990.

191. Bader EJ. Pregnant drug users face jail. New Directions Wom 1990;19:2.

192. Reinarman C, Levine HG. The crack attack: politics and media in America's latest drug scare. In: Best J, ed. Images and issues: typifying contemporary social problems. New York: Aldine De Gruyter, 1989.

193. Trebach A, Zeese K, eds. Drug prohibition and the conscience of nations. Washington, DC: Drug Policy Foundation, 1990.

194. Maher L. Criminalizing pregnancy: the downside of a kinder, gentler nation? Soc Justice 1990;17(3):111–135.

195. Gomby DS, Shiono PH. Estimating the number of drug exposed infants. Future Child 1991; 1(1):17–25.

196. Zuckerman BS, Frank DA, Hingson R, Amaro H, Levenson SM, Hayne H, et al. Effect of maternal marijuana and cocaine use on fetal growth. N Engl J Med 1989;320:762–768.

197. Amaro H, Fried L, Cabral H, Zuckerman B. Violence during pregnancy: the relationship to drug use among women and their partners. Am J Public Health 1990;80(5):575–579.

198. Robins L, Mills N. Effects of in utero exposure to street drugs. Am J Public Health 1993; 83(suppl):9–13.

199. Stranz I, Welch S. Postpartum women in outpatient drug abuse treatment: correlates of retention/completion. J Psychoactive Drugs 1995;27(4):357–373.

200. Irwin K. Ideology, pregnancy and drugs: differences between crack-cocaine, heroin and methamphetamine users. Contemp Drug Probl 1995;22(4):613–638.

201. Kearney MH. Damned if you do, damned if you don't: crack cocaine users and prenatal care. Contemp Drug Probl 1995;22(4): 639–662.

202. Vega WA, Kolody B, Hwang J, Noble A. Prevalence and magnitude of perinatal substance exposures in California. N Engl J Med 1993;329(12):850–854.

203. Chavkin W, Allen M, Oberman M. Drug abuse and pregnancy: some questions on public policy, clinical management, and maternal and fetal rights. Birth 1991;18(2):107–112.

204. Friedman J, Alicea M. Women and heroin: the path of resistance and its consequences. Gender Society 1994;9(4):432–449.

205. Ettorre E. Women and substance use. New Brunswick, NJ: Rutgers University Press, 1992.

206. Taylor A. Women drug users. Oxford: Clarendon Press, 1993.

207. Dunlap E, Johnson BD. Aggression, violence, and family life in crack seller/abuser households. Paper presented at the American Sociological Association annual meeting, Los Angeles, CA, August, 1994.

208. Rosenbaum M, Murphy S. An ethnographic study of pregnancy and drug use. Final Report to the National Institute on Drug Abuse, Grant #R01 DA 06832, 1995:229.

209. Regan D, O'Malley LB, Finnegan LP. The incidence of violence in the lives of pregnant

drug-dependent women. Pediatr Res 1982; 16:77, 330.

210. Wellisch J, Anglin MD, Prendergast ML. Numbers and characteristics of drug-using women in the criminal justice system: implications for treatment. J Drug Issues 1993;23(1): 7–30.

211. Boyd CJ. The antecedents of women's crack cocaine abuse: family substance abuse, sexual abuse, depression and illicit drug use. J Subst Abuse Treat 1993;10:433–438.

212. Dobash RE, Dobash RP. Women, violence, and social change. New York: Routledge, 1992.

213. Finkelhor D. The sexual abuse of children: current research reviewed. Psychiatr Ann 1987; 17:233–241.

214. Hagan TA, Finnegan LP, Nelson-Zlupko L. Impediments to comprehensive treatment models for substance-dependent women: treatment and research questions. J Psychoactive Drugs 1994;26(2):163–171.

215. Hagan TA, Kaltenback K. Women and drug dependency: a developmental approach to recovery. Unpublished paper, 1994.

216. James J, Meyerding J. Early sexual experience and prostitution. Am J Psychiatry 1977; 134(12):1381–1385.

217. Ladwig G, Andersen M. Substance abuse in women: relationship between chemical dependency of women and past reports of physical and/or sexual abuse. Int J Addict 1989; 24(8):739–754.

218. Lowrance N. Domestic violence. In: Eng RC, ed. Women: alcohol and other drugs. Dubuque, IA: Kendall/Hunt, 1990.

219. Miller BA. The interrelationship between alcohol and drug and family violence. NIDA Res Monogr 1990;103:177–207.

220. Miller BA, Downs WR, Gondoli DM. Spousal violence among alcoholic women as compared to a random household sample of women. J Stud Alcohol 1989;50(6):533–540.

221. Pagelow M. Family violence. New York: Prager, 1992.

222. Power R, Kutash I. Alcohol, drugs, and partner abuse. In: Roy M, ed. The abusive partner, an analysis of domestic battering. New York: Van Nostrand Reinhold, 1990.

223. Quinby PM, Graham AV. Substance abuse among women. Prim Care 1993;20(1): 131–140.

224. Reed BG. Linkages, battering, sexual assault, incest, child sexual abuse, teen pregnancy, dropping out of school, and the alcohol and drug connection. In: Roth P, ed. Alcohol and drugs are women's issues. Metuchen, NJ: Women's Action Alliance and Scarecrow Press, 1991.

225. Root MPP. Treatment failures: the role of sexual victimization in women's addictive behavior. Am J Orthopsychiatry 1989;59(4):542–549.

226. Russel S, Wilsnack S. Adult survivors of childhood sexual abuse: substance abuse and other consequences. In: Roth P, ed. Alcohol and drugs are women's issues. Metuchen, NJ: Women's Action Alliance and Scarecrow Press, 1991.

227. Van Den Bergh N. Having bitten the apple: a feminist perspective on addiction. In: Van Den Bergh N, ed. Feminist perspectives on addictions. New York: Springer, 1991.

228. Zierler S, Feingold L, Laufer D, Velentgas P, Kantrowitz-Gordon I, Mayer K. Adult survivors of childhood sexual abuse and subsequent risk of HIV infection. Am J Public Health 1991;81(5):572–575.

229. Theidon K. Taking a hit: pregnant drug users and violence. Contemp Drug Probl 1995; 22(4):663–686.

230. Bollerud K. A model for the treatment of trauma-related syndromes among chemically dependent inpatient women. J Subst Abuse Treat 1990;7:83–87.

231. Coleman E. Child physical and sexual abuse among chemically dependent individuals. J Chem Depend Treat 1987;1:27–29.

232. Reed B, Moise R. Implications for treatment and future research. In: Beschner GH, ed. Addicted women: family dynamics, self-perceptions, and support systems. DHEW publ. no. (ADM) 80–762. Rockville, MD: National Institute on Drug Abuse, 1979.

233. Amaro H, Hardy-Fanta C. Gender relations in addiction and recovery. J Psychoactive Drugs 1995:27(4):325–337.

234. Woodhouse LD. Women with jagged edges: voices from a culture of substance abuse. Qualitat Health Res 1992;2(3):262–281.

235. Chang G, Carroll KM, Behr HM, Kosten TR. Improving treatment outcome in pregnant opiate-dependent women. J Subst Abuse Treat 1992;9:327–330.

236. Haller D, Dawson K, Knisely J, Elswick RK, Schnoll S. Retention as a function of psychopathology. In: Harris LS, ed. Problems of drug dependence, 1993. NIDA research monograph no. 141. Rockville, MD: National Institute on Drug Abuse, 1993.

237. Knisely JS, Haller D, Dawson K, Elswick R, Schnoll S. Factors associated with retention in two intensive outpatient substance abuse programs. In: Harris LS, ed. Problems of drug dependence, 1993. NIDA research monograph no. 141. Rockville, MD: National Institute on Drug Abuse, 1993.

238. Ingersoll KS, Lu IL, Haller DL. Predictors of in-treatment relapse in perinatal substance abusers and impact on treatment retention: a prospective study. J Psychoactive Drugs 1995: 27(4):375–387.

239. Copeland J, Hall W. A comparison of predictors of treatment drop-out of women seeking drug and alcohol treatment in a specialist women's and two traditional mixed-sex treatment services. Br J Addict 1992;87:883–890.

240. Longshore D, Hsieh S, Anglin MD. Ethnic and gender differences in drug users' perceived need for treatment. Int J Addict 1993;28(6): 539–558.

241. Baldwin DM, Brecht ML, Monahan G, Annon K, Wellisch J, Anglin MD. Perceived need for treatment among pregnant and non-pregnant women arrestees. J Psychoactive Drugs 1995: 27(4):389–399.

242. Huling T. African American women and the war on drugs. Paper presented to the American Society of Criminology, Boston, 1995.

243. Wellisch J, Anglin MD, Prendergast ML. Treatment strategies for drug-abusing women offenders. In: Inciardi J, ed. Drug treatment in criminal justice settings. Thousand Oaks, CA: Sage Publications, 1993.

244. Weissman G, Melchoir L, Huba F, Smerek F, Needle R, McCarthy S, et al. Women living with drug abuse and HIV disease: drug abuse treatment access and secondary prevention issues. J Psychoactive Drugs 1995;27(4): 401–411.

245. Office of National Drug Control Policy. National drug control strategy: executive summary. Washington, DC: Executive Office of the President, 1995;April:39.

246. Nadelmann E, Cohen P, Locher U, Stimson G,

Wodak A, Drucker E. The harm reduction approach to drug control: international progress. Unpublished manuscript, 1995.

247. Mauer M, Hurling T. Young black Americans and the justice system: five years later. Washington, DC: Sentencing Project, 1995:October.

248. Bureau of Justice Statistics. Special report: women in prison. Washington, DC: U.S. Department of Justice, 1994.

249. Owen B, Bloom B. Profiling women prisoners: findings from national surveys and a California sample. Prison J 1995;75(2):181–182.

250. Gage B. The kids get pain. Nation 1995;February 20:237.

251. Women, babies, drugs. Family-centered treatment options. In: Network briefs. National Conference of State Legislatures Women's Network, July, 1990.

252. Implications of the drug use forecasting data for TASC programs: female arrestees. Washington, DC: Bureau of Justice Assistance, 1991.

253. Phillips MD. Courts, jails, and drug treatment in a California county. Unpublished manuscript, 1990.

254. Currie E. Reckoning: drugs, the cities, and the American future. New York: Hill and Wang, 1993.

255. Gerstein DR, Harwood HJ, eds. Treating drug problems. Washington, DC: National Academy Press, 1990;1.

256. Office of National Drug Control Policy. National drug control strategy: executive summary. Washington, DC: Executive Office of the President, 1995;April.

257. Wenger L, Rosenbaum M. Drug treatment on demand—not. J Psychoactive Drugs 1994; 26(1):1–11.

258. Rosenbaum M. Just say what? An alternative view on solving America's drug problem. San Francisco: National Council on Crime and Delinquency, 1989.

259. Waldorf D, Reinarman C, Murphy S. Cocaine changes: the experience of using and quitting. Philadelphia: Temple University Press, 1991.

260. Prendergast ML, Wellisch J, Falkin GP. Assessment of and service for substance-abusing women offenders in community and correctional settings. Prison J 1995;75(2).

261. Chavkin W. Drug addiction and pregnancy: policy crossroads. Am J Public Health 1990; 80(4):483–487.

262. Michaels B, Noonan M, Hoffman S, Brennan R. A treatment model of nursing care for pregnant chemical abusers. In: Chasnoff I, ed. Drugs, alcohol, pregnancy and parenting. Boston: Kluwer Academic Publishers, 1988.

263. Mondanaro J, Wedenoja M, Densen-Gerber J, Elahi J, Mason M, Redmond AC. Sexuality and fear of intimacy as barriers to recovery for drug dependent women. In: Treatment services for drug-dependent women. NIDA (ADM) 82–1219. Rockville, MD: National Institute on Drug Abuse, 1982;2:303–378.

264. Murphy S, Rosenbaum M. Women and substance abuse. Introduction [special edition]. J Psychoactive Drugs 1987:20(4).

265. Reed BG. Developing women-sensitive drug dependence treatment services: why so difficult? Int J Addict 1987;20(1):13–62.

266. Rosenbaum M, Murphy S. Not the picture of health: women on methadone. J Psychoactive Drugs 1987;19(2):217–255.

267. Wellisch J, Prendergast ML, Anglin MD. Drug-abusing women offenders: results of a national survey. Washingtton, DC: National Institute of Justice, 1994.

268. Daghestani A. Psychosocial characteristics of pregnant women addicts in treatment. In: Chasnoff I, ed. Drugs, alcohol, pregnancy and parenting. Boston: Kluwer Academic Publishers, 1988.

269. Jessop M, Green J. Treatment of the pregnant alcohol dependent woman. J Psychoactive Drugs 1987;19:193–203.

270. Mondanaro J. Treating drug dependent women. Springfield, IL: Lexington Books, 1988.

271. Beckman L. The self-esteem of women alcoholics. J Stud Alcohol 1978;39:491–498.

272. Zweben J, Sorenson J. Misunderstandings about methadone. J Psychoactive Drugs 1988; 20(3):275–281.

273. Wells DVB, Jackson JF. HIV and chemically dependent women: recommendations for appropriate health care and drug treatment services. Int J Addict 1992;27(5):571–585.

274. Siegel R. Intoxication: life in pursuit of artificial paradise. New York: EP Dutton, 1989.

275. Weil A. The natural mind. Boston: Houghton Mifflin, 1972.

276. Raskin VD. Maternal bereavement in the perinatal substance abuser. J Subst Abuse Treat 1992;9:149–152.

277. Albor T. The women get chains. Nation 1995 (February 20).

278. Paone D, Caloir S, Shi Q, Des Jarlais D. Sex, drugs, and syringe exchange in New York City: women's experiences. J Am Med Wom Assoc 1995;50(3,4):109–114.

279. O'Hare PA, Newcombe R, Matthews A, Buning EC, Drucker E. The reduction of drug-related harm. London: Routledge, 1992.

280. Ward J, Shane D, Hall H, Mattick R. Methadone maintenance and the human immunodeficiency virus: current issues in treatment and research. Br J Addict 1992;87: 447–453.

281. Stevenson R. Harm reduction, rational addiction and the optimal prescribing of illegal drugs. Contemp Economic Policy 1994;12: 101–108.

282. Des Jarlais DC, Friedman SR, Ward TP. Harm reduction: a public health response to the AIDS epidemic among injecting drug users. Annu Rev Public Health 1993;14: 413–450.

283. Watters JK, Estilo MJ, Clark GL, Lorvick J. Syringe and needle exchange as HIV/AIDS prevention for injection drug users. JAMA 1994;271:115–120.

284. Wodak A. HIV infection and injecting drug use in Australia: responding to a crisis. J Drug Issues 1992;22(3):549–562.

64 CHILDREN OF SUBSTANCE ABUSING PARENTS

Patti Juliana and Carolyn Goodman

The problem of substance abuse in the United States has continued unabated through the last several decades, giving rise to a host of political, social, and health problems. The view of health experts has been uniform and consistent: "Evidence is overwhelming that alcoholism and drug abuse are inextricably linked to the most pernicious social, health and economic problems facing Americans today. These problems include family violence and child abuse, increased health care costs, AIDS transmission and decreased learning in school, among others" (1).

In 1975, it was estimated that a quarter-million children up to age 18 had mothers who were addicted to heroin (2). A little more than a decade later, an estimated 375,000 infants a year were exposed to illicit drugs (3). The 1991 National Household Survey indicates that, of the approximately 59.2 million women of childbearing age (15–44), over 4.5 million are estimated to have used illicit drugs during the previous month (4). The public became aware of the special needs and problems of childhood and adolescence in the early 1960s. The children's rights movement gained momentum when the United Nations General Assembly adopted the Declaration of the Human Rights of the Child in 1959. In 1979, the United States Congress passed the Child Welfare Reform Act, which promoted public and professional concern for children. Then, as cocaine use peaked and indicators of heroin use reappeared, the large numbers of infants born with symptoms of drug withdrawal and human immunodeficiency virus (HIV) infection dramatized the need for treatment and prevention for the entire family.

The proliferation of the substance abuse problem and the heightened attention to the needs of children and youth generated recognition that there was a distinct population, the children of substance abusers (hereafter referred to as COSAs), who were thought to have unique characteristics that demanded attention. It was also apparent that an addicted woman with children required help for herself, her children, and her family. It is now well documented that the children of untreated drug and alcohol–using parents are at risk for serious educational, medical, and emotional problems and have the potential for abusing illicit drugs themselves. Physical and developmental disabilities, compounded by the risk of HIV infection and the acquired immune deficiency syndrome (AIDS), have created a generation of children in crisis.

This chapter focuses on young children from birth to early adolescence. It describes the scope of the problem and presents a review of the literature concerning the characteristics of this special population of mothers and children. The chapter discusses treatment approaches, treatment models, and special problems that are associated with the ever-growing numbers of COSAs. The chapter concludes with recommendations in the interest of prevention and treatment of drug-exposed children and families.

SCOPE OF THE PROBLEM

In June 1990, Dr. Louis W. Sullivan, Secretary of Health and Human Services, in his testimony before the United States Committee on Finance, reported that 5 million women of childbearing age abuse illicit drugs. He added that "7.15% of all births in four selected major cities involved drug use by the mother" (5). This is an underestimation of at-risk children born to drug-using women, many of whom do not seek prenatal care; some of whom do not give birth in hospitals, and others who continue drug use during pregnancy. Other patients may cease drug use during pregnancy and then resume subsequent to the birth. There is also a sizeable group of drug-using women who are not reported by their physicians. For these and other social and economic reasons, figures vary on the numbers of women drug users of childbearing age.

Although the estimated number of women using illicit drugs increased from 3 million in 1985 to 28 million in 1988 according to some national indicators, the proportion of women, including those of childbearing age, who tested positive for drugs rose from 25% in 1972 to 40% in 1988 (6), consistent with epidemiological studies of substance abuse during the 1980s that reflect a sharp rise in the incidence of births of drug-exposed infants (7). Assessment of cocaine-exposed infants based upon observation alone may not detect mild withdrawal symptoms or signs that may appear only after discharge from the hospital. Self-reports and observation often result in low recorded incidence; when more vigorous detection methods are used, the incidence is substantially higher.

Given the trend toward abuse of licit and illicit substances, the likelihood of children being born to addicted women will increase during the next decade. This is a growing population of children who may experience impairment and disability, the extent of which is as yet unknown. It is expected that the children will be further affected by health and welfare reform as "reform will drive many [substance] abusers and their children into the streets" (8).

REVIEW OF THE LITERATURE

A review of the literature from the end of the nineteenth century reflected a concern about the passage of drugs through the human placenta and through the breast milk of the drug-using mother. As early as 1888 the possibility of long-term effects of fetal opioid exposure was addressed (9). The increasing concern about COSAs during the 1970s resulted in a significant number of studies of maternal heroin or methadone use and its effect on the neonate.

Much of the literature on COSAs is focused on the impact of medical complications of the neonate. Finnegan has reported that the effects of maternal heroin or methadone use on infants are influenced by the adequacy of prenatal care, obstetrical complications, and maternal polydrug use (10) (see also Chapter 54). She has well documented the characteristics of neonatal abstinence syndrome describing infants born to heroin-addicted mothers as small for gestational age, often experiencing withdrawal symptoms beginning shortly after birth (11), as irritable and difficult to parent (12, 13). There is some agreement that the neonatal behavioral and developmental effects of maternal heroin use include irritability, feeding disturbances, sleeplessness, deficits in attention span, and impaired mother-child communications (14, 15).

There have been discrepancies in the research literature that identify and describe cocaine-exposed babies. This is in part due to confounding factors of poverty, lack of prenatal care, family instability, and polydrug abuse. Kandall noted that studies have not controlled for specific drug use patterns or psychosocial variables (7). Although the long-term effects of maternal crack use are expected to vary, given the neurotoxicity of cocaine COSAs may suffer from learning disabilities and other neurologic deficits that may become manifest in later years. The neonatal effects range from severely premature to full-term infants with no apparent effects (6).

During the postnatal period, children may be inconsolable and tax the tolerance of the parents. Development of effective maternal-infant communication is impaired as the infant experiencing withdrawal rejects the mother's attempts at consolation; insufficient feedback makes it difficult for the mother to understand her child's needs (16). The behavior patterns of the neonate reduce the caregiver's responsiveness to the infant and exacerbate the low self-esteem often seen in drug-using parents (17–19).

A review of the literature since the previous edition of this book reflects the publication of over 135 studies related to maternal substance abuse or families and addiction. Of those articles, 55 were related to infancy and fetal drug exposure, and the balance were related to treatment of families with a substance-abusing member. Research on childhood effects of parental substance use remains sparse and continues to suggest biological and psychosocial impacts as described in earlier studies.

Among the problems found in COSAs are increased vulnerability to visual problems, inadequate fine motor coordination, heightened levels of motor activity, and attention deficits, particularly in structured interactions (20). It was found that children exposed to heroin in utero scored lower on perceptual tests than did their peers and were less able to concentrate on tasks (16, 21–23). Although some of these studies are inconclusive, they suggest that these children are at high risk for developmental disabilities.

Assessment of older children of heroin-addicted and formerly addicted parents reveal that they suffer from emotional and cognitive problems; they express feelings of anxiety and insecurity and are characterized by shorter attention spans than their peers (20). More than half of these children have poor prognoses for school success and age-appropriate socioemotional development. The 8- to 17-year-old children of drug-using parents are characterized by increased problems in school and behavioral and adjustment problems at a greater rate than a comparison group of their peers. These problems may be related to parental substance abuse at home, compromised communications within families, unstable home lives, and impacts of HIV/AIDS on families, among other sequelae of drug use.

Teenaged children of addicted parents also show increased incidence of behavioral problems at home and with their peers and are more likely to be involved in delinquent activities and drug and alcohol use (20). These findings are consonant with problems expressed by a similar group of children during early childhood; unsuccessful completion of developmental tasks can result in attention deficits, poor impulse control, and impaired attachment to others, which are risk factors and predictors for later drug and alcohol use (22, 23). When strong familial bonds exist, the likelihood of attachment to drug-using peers decreases; however, the homes of drug-using adolescents reflect poor family management, parental antisocial behavior, and parental substance abuse (23).

Similarly, the family histories of the drug-using parents reflect a high incidence of disruption, conflict, loss of parental figures, and lack of strong, affectionate parent-child bonds (24). Studies of addicted women reveal feelings of low self-esteem, anxiety, depression, and serious problems in their families of origin such as addiction and physical abuse (18, 25). The childhood experiences of drug-abusing women can be characterized by maternal deprivation, lack of supportive family networks, and maltreatment (26). As parents who were deprived of age-appropriate experiences in childhood, they approach parenthood with minimal bonding experience, unrealistic expectations, and without having learned adequate parenting skills. They may require more assistance in parenting as the interpersonal and environmental impact of substance abuse compound the effects of in utero drug exposure. Substance abuse is not only the problem of the individual but must be considered in the context of family and social systems.

APPROACHES TO THE TREATMENT OF ADDICTED WOMEN AND COSAs

Treatment of Children

When a substance-abusing parent has children, it is critical to remedy those problems that have occurred as a result of parental drug use. The symptoms of COSAs can manifest as health, behavioral, or learning difficulties; developmental assessments identify lags in individual children. However, these children are least likely to receive developmental screening and early intervention, especially if their parents are actively addicted, overwhelmed by their recovery efforts, confounding health, environmental, and psychosocial stressors (26).

Assessment and treatment of the needs of children must be coordinated so as to offer the full range of services that may be necessary. Collaboration among medical and social services is particularly critical to facilitate recovery, family stability, improved parent-child interactions, and access to appropriate care for the children involved.

Low self-esteem, anxiety, and depression associated with being raised in an addicted family may be treated as primary symptoms. Children of substance abusing parents often lack basic trust and ability to become attached as they hope for parental love and nurturance; as parents live in continually shifting states of intoxication and abstinence, the child learns self-care that interrupts development of intimacy and results in isolation and depression (27). Positive, supportive, trusting relationships are helpful in improving a child's self-image. In such relationships a child can be helped to recognize and appropriately express feelings, to understand the disease concept of addiction, and to develop coping mechanisms. Every child requires the security of order and consistency; it is particularly important that these needs be addressed when working with COSAs, whose surroundings are often characterized by repeated disruption and uncertainty.

Play groups have been effective in developing the cognitive, emotional, social, and physical development of younger children; group interaction provides stimulation of cognitive and language functions (28). Early childhood programs, in general, promote optimal development of children, and early intervention is critical for children with developmental delays. Groups benefit older children and adolescents, providing support and reducing isolation. Such groups help children identify and recognize their experiences, ventilate feelings, and participate in a corrective "family" environment. Further retrospective and prospective studies on the long-term effects of parental drug use are essential to plan and develop more effective interventions for older COSAs.

Treatment of the Parents

Studies reveal a direct relationship between the emotional and cognitive difficulties of the mothers and those of their children (27, 28). The mother's attitude and behavior often have negative effects on the growth and development of her child. She may be ambivalent, loving, and resentful at the same time (29, 30). She may be authoritarian and over involved and yet have great difficulty in recognizing the needs of her children (31, 32). The parents, often maternally deprived themselves, may have difficulty responding to their children. Women face multiple obstacles to seeking treatment for substance abuse including child care, financial constraints, and lack of support systems. They must contend with increased stigma as social mores stereotype female addicts as weak-willed, irresponsible, and promiscuous, and they often experience resistance from their partners and children who resent the treatment that disrupts homeostasis (33). Single parents are further stressed as they often neglect their own well-being, choosing to meet their children's needs at the expense of their own (34).

Research suggests that drug treatment programs providing ancillary services designed to meet the particular needs of parents, such as child care, and those involving other family members and significant others hold the greatest promise for women with drug and alcohol problems (35). Assisting parents in their recovery is the optimal means of treating their children. Parenting skills can be reinforced in drug treatment settings. Parents are best assisted individually, in combination with family intervention, support groups, and parenting skills training.

Family Treatment

There is general agreement that in planning programs for drug-abusing parents and their children, an approach that involves the family unit is most effective. Family therapy combined with drug treatment has been found to be effective in treatment of substance abusing families (36) and has been recognized as an essential approach to treating the full range of addictive problems in families (37). Some of the principles that guide family therapy include a pragmatic approach to treatment with an eye toward what works, emphasis on the present rather than a historical perspective, interruption of behavior patterns, focus on process rather than on content, and restructuring of families (38).

Systems theory assumes that all people in the family unit play a part in the way family members function in relation to each other and in the way the symptom of addiction finally erupts (39). This theory focuses on functional facts of relationships and provides a framework for conceptualizing chemical dependency; systems therapy can be used to alleviate the symptom as it addresses familial interactions. Minuchin's structural family therapy focuses on patterns of family interactions and communications; within this approach, the therapist reinforces generational boundaries between parents and children (40). Stanton and Todd combine structural techniques with Haley's strategic model; with a view of symptoms as attempts at changing family difficulties they emphasize a specific treatment plan, external events, changes in the symptom, and collaboration among treatment systems (41). A detailed application of family therapy techniques in substance abuse treatment can be found in Chapter 46 of this text.

Parent Support Groups

Parent support networks are critical components of treatment and prevention programs for addicted parents and their children. The goal of the support group is to improve the parents' interactions with their children by developing viable peer networks. Within this context, the parents are able to consider their children's feelings, to understand their behaviors in the context of developmental stages, and to become aware of the dynamics of their interactions with their children. The group eventually becomes an independent mutual support network that helps its members develop self-esteem and empathy.

The task of empowering the parents is a three-stage process: bonding, facilitation, and separation. For these tasks to be accomplished, the staff must be understanding, accessible, and nurturing. The first stage of connecting parents with helpers is the most challenging; for parents who experienced rejection and loss in childhood, the process of forming relationships does not come easily. The parents must be able to learn that they will not be rejected by their "family" even when their behavior is provocative or excessively demanding. The development of trust in a continued relationship with a counselor or health professional who can provide understanding, acceptance, and support has been found to be critical in improving the lifestyle of drug-addicted persons (42).

In the second stage, when a relationship of trust is established, the counselor or helper role becomes one of facilitation and advocacy. Parents are mobilized to act on their own behalf, and staff encourage self-exploration and development of self-awareness. When intervention fosters input, feedback, decision making, and networking, these behaviors flourish. Parents learn about the purpose of their children's behaviors and gain insight into effective interactions. They begin to see a link between their childhood experiences and their behaviors and feelings toward their children.

With the development of sensitivity to and understanding of their children, unrealistic expectations diminish. Parents are able to assume a more positive and consistent role in the growth of their children. Additionally, as they experience the acceptance of the facilitator and peers and recognize they are not isolated in their struggles, the parents articulate a sense of relief and a growth of self-tolerance.

In the third stage, separation, the parents are ready to rely upon other resources and support systems. The helper's role becomes that of a resource for the parents, and the group becomes an independent mutual support network that strengthens its members' self-esteem and increases empathic interactions. They are able to rely upon each other.

Parenting Skills Groups

Men and women who are addicted to drugs often have not experienced positive parenting models; many feel inadequate as parents. More than most caregivers, they need to experience self-esteem by being accepted, respected, and educated in the skills of parenting. Although they have difficulties coping with their children, they want to be "good" mothers and fathers (24). This motivation can be tapped and used to engage parents in skills groups.

Parenting skills training is didactic in format. Three approaches that have been found effective in working with parents and COSAs are behavior management, relationship therapy, and child development theory. The principles of each approach focus on different aspects of understanding, but ideas borrowed from all three may guide the groups.

Behavior management is based on the concepts of reinforcement and modeling behaviors (43–45). Reinforcement emphasizes those actions of the parent that encourage approved behaviors and extinguish disapproved behaviors in the child. Parents are taught to understand and use appropriate rewards to shape and strengthen desirable behaviors in their children and withhold rewards for undesirable behaviors. Modeling is based on the principle that children tend to imitate and then internalize the behaviors, ideas, and attitudes of their parents.

Relationship therapy uses the insights of Rogers (46) and Axline (47). Parents are taught to empathize with their children and to understand that children often express feelings through their actions rather than words. They learn how to listen and respond through physical expressions of warmth and caring. Because of the dangerous environment in which many families typically reside, parents are taught how to create safe and secure settings and seek alternative approaches to the management of multiple stressors.

Child development theory assists parents in understanding each developmental level to establish reasonable expectations and cope with the normal frustrations of particular age groups. When parents understand the meaning of their children's behavior, the frustration of unrealistic demands can be avoided. As parents are helped to understand their children's development and gain insight into their interactions, the problems of being socialized in an addicted family may be corrected. Studies have documented that the self-esteem of women who participated in parenting skills groups was substantially raised, and this, in turn, resulted in the improved development of their children (48, 49).

Treatment Models Designed for Addicted Mothers and Their Children

A broad range of psychosocial services may be required to address the needs of children whose parents abuse substances and to meet the needs of the parents in recovery (7). Whether services are provided onsite or through linkages with community-based organizations, service needs include medical care for parents and children alike, chemical dependency treatment, legal services, education and job training, child care, developmental assessments, parenting education, mental health services, housing assistance, transportation, and case management services (7); availability and accessibility of a range of services can minimize stress and promote the relationship between the addicted parent and the treatment facility. Outreach efforts can facilitate engagement of drug-dependent persons into treatment as indigenous workers encourage women, especially, to use available medical and social services (50).

One of the pioneer programs designed to treat addicted women as part of a family unit was PACE (Parent and Child Education) (51). PACE began in 1968 as a program for mentally ill mothers and their children. When it became known that increasing numbers of mothers were also substance abusers, the program design was modified to meet the needs of this special population of women and their children. PACE was a comprehensive intervention program that served mothers, children from birth through 5 years of age, fathers, and other available family members. The staff was a team of mental health clinicians and teachers, some of whom resided in the communities where the families lived.

The unique approach of the PACE program was the inclusion of family members as active participants in the treatment team. The underlying concept was that an informed, competent parent is in a favorable position to promote the development of his or her young child. To achieve this goal, a mother must be involved in trying to understand herself and, in many instances, in changing her self-concept from one of passive powerlessness to one of active mastery. The mother at PACE became both teacher and student as she engaged in the process of empowering herself and her child. The thrust of the PACE program was the development of parenting skills and self-esteem that could enable the mother to deal with the physical and psychological needs of her young child.

At PACE, mother and child attended an education center several days a week, where they spent part of the time together in a classroom setting. At other times, parents participated in parent education, treatment, and social recreation groups with other mothers while their children were in the classroom with teachers. This arrangement allowed mother and child to interact with each other and also to develop and learn in keeping with age-appropriate tasks. To facilitate the growth of the children, the physical arrangement of the classroom where they spent all their time was designed to create a structured, secure, and consistent setting where order and routine prevailed; the room was arranged for maximum interaction between mother and child.

The children's education program at PACE varied with developmental age and was based on four major areas of growth: muscular, cognitive, language, and creative skills. Within clearly defined limits, children were encouraged to explore their bodies and their environment through activities such as storytelling and dramatization. When mothers were in the classroom, they not only learned to interact with their children but had the opportunity to enjoy educational experiences they had been deprived of in their own childhood.

When not in the classroom, mothers were involved with a number of group activities in which they learned child development concepts and health care, took part in group and family therapy, and had opportunities to socialize and engage in recreational pursuits with other mothers. All the groups—educational, treatment, social and recreational—served to promote support networks and initiate friendships. Mothers realized they could call on each other for help in emergencies as well as find companionship and relaxation. Changes in behavior, attitude, and self-perception took place in an atmosphere in which the mothers found parenting models and support networks they had never experienced before. The staff at PACE, themselves part of a support network, became a nurturing family until the mothers were able to shape their own family systems.

Another program that approaches the problems of women substance abusers and COSAs is incorporated into the Department of Psychiatry's Division of Substance Abuse at the Albert Einstein College of Medicine (AECOM). The Division of Substance Abuse (DoSA) treats more than 3600 former heroin addicts in nine community-based clinics. Most patients suffer from many stresses of living with poverty, unemployment, inadequate housing or homelessness, chaotic home lives, broken families, inferior schools, and discrimination.

Since its inception, the philosophy of DoSA has been to provide a diversified approach to meet the broad range of medical, social, and psychological problems presented by narcotic addicts entering treatment. As the perception of addiction broadened, the program sought to prevent the residual effects associated with being raised in an addicted family and to treat those problems that had already occurred. A state-funded demonstration project for children was developed at AECOM to study the children and to assist in designing programs for parents who were patients and their at-risk children. Identification, evaluation, and referral services for the children were integrated into the regular division services to include parent education, staff training, advocacy, and liaison with children's services in the surrounding community.

The program provides a point of entry to medical and social services for the children of patients who are traditionally disenfranchised and alienated from these services. Staff work cooperatively with parents and children individually and with parent-child dyads to improve family life and break the cycle of substance abuse and other intergenerational problems. Staff training for this population addresses special needs and issues that confront children and families. Liaison services operate among the DoSA program, school-based intervention and prevention services, and other health, welfare, and education resources. These services are accessible to all program staff.

With the increased incidence of maternal substance abuse, attention has shifted to focus on pregnant women. State funding has provided a wide range of specialized comprehensive and coordinated services. Drug treatment, obstetric, pediatric, HIV-related, and social services for pregnant substance abusers have been designed to minimize drug use, reduce the incidence of neonatal abstinence syndrome, improve the well-being of neonates, and facilitate early bonding among family members. Caseworkers trained in maternity services work in conjunction with the clinic treatment team to address the range of drug treatment, medical, and psychosocial needs of pregnant addicted women. Prenatal education and individual counseling services are coordinated with health and welfare services to provide a continuum of treatment services.

As COSAs enter the school system in increasing numbers, there are rising demands for special education services to deal with language and cognitive delays, and behavior problems. More children are showing deficits in problem solving, concentration, and behavioral controls, characteristic of COSAs. Their special educational needs resonate in the school system. It will be important to accommodate these needs to forestall school failure and dropout. Critical collaborative efforts include provision of full developmental assessments and services through linkage with the Rose F. Kennedy Children's Evaluation and Rehabilitation Center. Provision of onsite services has improved parental compliance with completion of evaluations as it minimizes fears of being judged as inadequate parents and reduces apprehensions about breach of confidentiality (26).

When blinded HIV seroprevalence studies revealed that 32% of patients enrolled in the Division's programs were positive, extensive HIV services components were developed for patients with a family approach. Currently, the Division offers a continuum of HIV services beginning with pretest counseling and HIV testing. Ongoing support for seropositive patients includes counseling, health and risk reduction counseling and education, tuberculosis screening, prophylaxis and treatment, and a full spectrum of medical and mental health services. Additional support is provided to patients who are parents and for seropositive pregnant women.

Children who face the loss of a parent face fears of who will care for them. Children of parents with AIDS are often placed into foster care upon their parent's final hospitalization by child protective services or by the parent's appointed caretaker; in many cases, the parents, by virtue of their illness and multiple problems, have not had opportunity or ability to plan for the care of their children upon their death. These children lose the support of significant family and friends who might otherwise ease the child's resolution of the loss of their parent. The depth of emotional reactions is often overwhelming and cannot be overstated. Guilt, powerlessness, and recurrent anxiety are the debilitating feeling left to these children. Their sense of isolation is exacerbated and their fears of abandonment are not addressed as children are often forgotten by grieving adults. Therefore, the AECOM-DoSA addresses the concerns of HIV-affected families by assisting the parents in planning for permanent homes for their children. The aim of family services in any drug treatment is to enhance the quality of life for the entire family.

Other treatment approaches include the Pregnant Addicts and Addicted Mothers program (PAAM) of New York Medical College's Center for Comprehensive Health Practice. Initiated in 1975 under a grant from the National Institute on Drug Abuse, the program is open to any woman who is pregnant and addicted to opiates, or who was addicted while pregnant and gave birth within the previous year. The goals of PAAM are to have the pregnant addict achieve a normal pregnancy, deliver a healthy baby, find satisfaction in the parenting role, and have her child develop normally, both physically and psychologically. PAAM services include medical care (obstetric, pediatric, psychiatric, and general), methadone maintenance and detoxification, counseling, preschool groups, and parenting skills training in the home and in program groups (52).

Odyssey House, a residential drug-free therapeutic community, serves clients with chemical dependency problems. This 12–14 month program integrates cognitive behavioral techniques with a self-help model of recovery. Its Family Center, which began in 1971, provides special services for pregnant substance abusers as well as parents and their young children. While parents receive a broad range of clinical services, children up to age 5 are cared for in an on-site professional day-care center. The program provides a nurturing environment that meets the children's physical, emotional, and developmental needs while parents attend their scheduled therapy groups and other aspects of their individualized treatment plan. Parents at the Family Center receive parenting skills instruction as well as supervised mother-child interaction time. Odyssey House emphasizes the relationship between child and caregiver, since it is through this relationship that the child learns about self and the world (53).

In summary, program development around services for children in drug treatment settings may include:

1. *identification and orientation* of staff who will implement family services
2. *reinforcement* or development of linkages with referral resources, including notification of service agencies and meetings with personnel of key agencies to introduce treatment services and solidify work plans
3. *training* of program and referral resource staff on addiction, families and relevant cultural issues
4. *development* of outreach strategies

Core family services activities may include

1. *identification* and referral of children and patients who might benefit from the services
2. *initial family evaluation* to be conducted (within 30 days) on each family referred to the project. This may include:
   a. review of presenting circumstances, including who referred the patient
   b. assessment of the family and children's strengths and problems
   c. family history and family background, deaths, illnesses
   d. assessment of family relations
   e. assessment of social relations
   f. identification of service needs
3. *psychosocial evaluation of each child* completed to identify possible problems
   a. family relations—child's response to parental guidance, behavior expressed towards the family, child's perception of his or her role in family, child's perception of current circumstances
   b. social relations—child's behavior in social settings, towards peers, towards authority, self-sufficiency, and stability
   c. educational status—cognitive, perceptual and motor abilities, behavior in school, academic performance
   d. life skills—ability to care for his or her needs, constructive leisure, function independently congruent with age
   e. health—including developmental history, current health status and immunization record

4. An *initial service plan* may be compiled upon completion of the family assessment. This plan will include identification of service needs and a plan of action.

SPECIAL PROBLEMS ASSOCIATED WITH COSAs AND THEIR FAMILIES

It has been indicated that prenatal drug exposure and drug-abusing families are placing increasing demands on social welfare systems; in addition to concerns about the safety and care of drug-exposed infants, programs must also address the needs of the many children who also have long-term learning and developmental disabilities. Without intervention, academic problems and high dropout rates can be anticipated. The cost of helping these children overcome the effects of drug exposure varies with the severity of disability. "Drug exposed infants need medical and social services that will cost billions of dollars in the years to come. One estimate of the cost of services for a drug-exposed infant who is significantly impaired is $750,000 for the first eighteen years of life" (6).

The tragedy of substance abuse is compounded by the failure of substance abuse treatment facilities to provide services that are sensitive to the needs of women, particularly those who are pregnant or have young children. Because few treatment programs address parenting issues or other needs of women, there is a growing population of addicted mothers and drug-exposed children with few resources for assistance, and the rise in the number of drug-exposed children has placed an onerous burden on child welfare and health and education systems.

Child Welfare

Child maltreatment is not a recent phenomenon, nor is it unique to substance-abusing parents. Some would argue that the use of illicit substances does not automatically constitute child abuse or neglect. However, some jurisdictions are now proceeding with criminal cases against pregnant mothers who use drugs, charging them with drug delivery in utero.

A number of surveys and reports indicate a 38% increase in the death toll of children of substance abusers since 1985 (54). In a sample of 734 parents and children, Sowder and Burt determined that the rate of abuse and neglect among addicted families was "15.9 times higher than the rate reported for the United States" (20), and according to the New York City's Mayor's Task Force on Child Abuse and Neglect, the increase in number and severity of these cases between 1985 and 1988 occurred primarily among COSAs (55).

Approximately 675,000 children are mistreated every year by alcoholic or drug-abusing caretakers (56), and the child protective system is taxed beyond its capacity as the increasing use of substances has added substantially to the numbers of cases reported to child protective services and those separated from their families (50). Human and institutional resources for prevention and treatment of abuse and neglect are often incapable of handling these problems. Assessment of risk factors for children whose parents may be difficult to locate or engage into a preliminary working relationship presents special difficulties for child protective service workers. If one is able to engage the parents into treatment on behalf of their children, treatment services are not readily available, and the rehabilitation period may be protracted.

The federal Administration for Children and Families launched the Child Welfare Initiative in 1991, which sought to improve the effectiveness of child welfare and related services to children and families, particularly those affected by substance abuse (50). Funding generated the development of crisis nurseries, specialized foster care services for drug-exposed infants, support services designed to prevent child maltreatment among children whose parents are actively using drugs and cross-disciplinary training projects.

Of these efforts, it seems the most critical may be the training of child protective service workers and foster parents in the needs of children and their parents who abuse substances, specialized care of HIV or drug-affected infants, ethnic and cultural issues and values, attitudes and behaviors regarding use of drugs and alcohol, given the barriers that lack of knowledge, nonsupportive or hostile attitudes of caregivers, and stigma associated with drug use present for women, in particular (7). Similarly, training of staff needs to involve agency policies and philosophy as well as issues of countertransference. Some workers may reject the mother because they believe the child is simply a victim of the mother's abuse. Others show greater interest in seeing the mother as victim as well and either overlook maltreatment for fear of alienating the mother or seek to keep the family intact, sometimes against better judgment. Ultimately, preservation of families must be central to child welfare efforts with families affected by substance abuse.

Health Services

The health care system reports that an increased number of pediatric beds are occupied by drug-exposed babies. Prematurity and low birth weight of crack-exposed babies is not uncommon. Many mothers receive no prenatal care, and infants are often born with complications that require extended hospital stays, which further disrupts fragile maternal-infant bonding. The public health care system is suffering from the strain of increasing numbers of drug-exposed infants and "boarder babies."

The incidence of sexually transmitted diseases such as gonorrhea, chlamydia, and herpes is rising among infants of substance abusing women. There has been a dramatic rise in the incidence of HIV infection among infants and very young children of addicted parents. The majority of children with HIV infection acquire it perinatally from their mothers. As of June, 1996, there were 7296 reported AIDS cases in the United States involving children under the age of 13; reported cases of pediatric AIDS underestimates the scope of the problem as one can expect that for every child who has AIDS, another two to ten children are HIV infected.

It has been determined that provision of comprehensive drug treatment benefits family members affected by substance abuse besides assisting the recovery of the patient. Although the substance abuse treatment community recognizes that the health of family members may be compromised by substance abuse, Spear and Mason found a significant decrease in insurance claims following the family member's completion of treatment, thus suggesting a relationship between the chemical dependency of one family member and the health of the other members (57).

PAUCITY OF TREATMENT RESOURCES

In 1986 it was reported that close to 500,000 COSAs younger than 6 years of age were living with adult substance abusers who were not receiving treatment (24). The National Association of State Alcohol and Drug Abuse Directors estimated that only 30,000 of 250,000 pregnant substance-abusing women were being treated; these findings represented only 31 states and Washington, DC (58). The lack of substance abuse programs for pregnant women is compounded by the unavailability of prevention and treatment resources for COSAs and the resistance of some substance abuse treatment facilities to provide these services to pregnant women (59).

RECOMMENDATIONS

In summary, the children of substance abusers suffer from the addiction of their parents; they are at risk for social, psychological, educational, and medical disabilities that require system-wide policies at all levels of government. Guidelines for prevention, education, treatment, and research programs that focus on the unique situation of COSAs and begin to address the needs of drug-using pregnant women and their children are of paramount importance.

A sweeping review and redefinition of system policies and procedures is necessary to ensure that parents are evaluated not only in terms of their addiction but also as members of a family. This holds particularly true for pregnant women and mothers, who are vulnerable to prosecution as a result of their addiction. Epidemiologic studies and family research have amply demonstrated that thousands of addicted mothers are not receiving prenatal,

parenting, or medical care or treatment for substance abuse. Very few programs exist for substance-abusing women who are pregnant and/or parents, and fewer still for child care and child development services.

Creative approaches that assure confidentiality, protection from punitive interventions, and development of parenting skills are needed. The problems of COSAs are often preventable, and the effects of parental addiction can be minimized. Legislation, regulation, and adequate funding are critical to protecting the health and well-being of addicted families.

Coordination

COSAs, their families, and their caretakers present so complex an array of problems and needs that no one system or institution could adequately handle a single family. Nevertheless, substance abuse affects the entire family, and all its members have a right to obtain help. The importance of interagency coordination is well-recognized; without provisions for case management, families as well as staff can become lost in the service labyrinth.

As problems of COSAs confront a variety of local, state, and federal agencies, the structure and bureaucratic policies of these agencies hamper provision of coordinated services. Although different agencies, by virtue of their structure and function, are accustomed to working in their respective fields, the nature of the needs of these children is such that it is crucial that services for them and their families be coordinated rather than fragmented and duplicated. Linkages among systems must be developed. Families may be involved with a variety of services simultaneously, and appointments with each may conflict. The overlap of scheduling creates stress and confusion. The goal for agencies should be to assist addicted mothers in organizing and simplifying their lives so their children can be raised with less stress and confusion.

Staff Training

Programs for substance-abusing pregnant women and parents and their children are relatively new in the field of human services. Staff in drug treatment clinics and other agencies are more familiar with traditional approaches that focus on the drug user. As the idea of prevention and treatment for mothers and children grows, training programs are essential for the diverse array of people involved in these endeavors. There now exists a broad spectrum of providers in drug prevention and treatment agencies and others in social and medical services who lack information about families of drug users and cultural issues surrounding substance abuse. Cultural issues are addressed in Chapters 68 and 69. The complexity of the problems presented by COSAs and their families requires skilled interdisciplinary teams that can recognize, assess, and treat drug-exposed children and substance-abusing families.

CONCLUSION

At this writing, although reported data suggest that we are confronting an issue of substantial proportions, the full impact of drug-exposed children on the mental health, educational, and juvenile justice systems is still unknown. However, drug-exposed children and their families present a problem that has reached such vast proportions that we cannot deny its impact on the future. Comprehensive drug treatment services must include services for parents as patients and must address the special needs of the children of patients. Services sensitive to the needs of parents must attend to day care, perinatal services, and parenting skills training. Medical services should become familiar with the social and psychological factors associated with drug and alcohol use, and children's services including schools need to be aware of indicators of family drug or alcohol use. Although these measures may be costly, they will be far less so than institutional hospital-based treatment of complications of perinatal drug use and rehabilitative or custodial care of the children.

References

1. New York State Anti-Drug Abuse Council. The case for drug and alcohol treatment. State alcohol and drug abuse profile report, 1989.

2. Carr JN. Drug patterns among drug-addicted mothers—incidence, variance in use, and effects on children. Pediatr Ann 1975;4:408–417.

3. United States House of Representatives, Committee on Ways and Means, Subcommittee on Human Resources. The enemy within: crack-cocaine and America's families. June 12, 1990. Washington, DC: U.S. Government Printing Office, 1990.

4. National Household Survey USDHHS, National Institute on Drug Abuse, 1991.

5. Bowsher CA. Drug-exposed infants: a generation at risk. Statement before the United States Senate Committee on Finance. June 28, 1990.

6. Feig L. Drug exposed infants: service needs and policy questions. USDHHS, Office of Assistant Secretary for Policy and Evaluation, January 1990.

7. Kandall S. Improving treatment for drug-exposed infants. USDHHS. Substance Abuse and Mental Health Services Administration. Center for Substance Abuse. Treatment Improvement Protocol No. 5. Rockville, MD, 1993.

8. Califano J. New York Times 1996(August 24).

9. Zagon IS. Opioids and development: new lessons from old problems. NIDA Res Monogr 1985;60:58–77.

10. Finnegan LP. Effects of maternal opiate abuse on the newborn. Fed Proc 1985;44:2315–2318.

11. Finnegan LP. Management of the drug dependent pregnancy and effects on neonatal outcome. In: Bescher G, Brotman R, eds. Proceedings of the NIDA symposium on comprehensive health care for addicted families and their children. DHEW publication no. 017–024-00598–3. Washington, DC: U.S. Government Printing Office, 1976:59–66.

12. Escamilla-Mondanaro J. Women: pregnancy, children and addiction. J Psychedelic Drugs 1977;9:59–68.

13. Householder J, Hatcher R, Burn W, Chasnoff I. Infants born to narcotic-addicted mothers. Psychol Bull 1982;92:453–468.

14. Kandall SR, Albin S, Lowinson J, Berle B, Eidelman A, Gartner LM. Differential effects of maternal heroin and methadone use on birthweight. Pediatrics 1976;58:681–685.

15. Kron RE, Kaplan SL, Phoenix MD, Finnegan LP. Behavior of infants born to drug-dependent mothers: effects of prenatal and postnatal drugs. In: Rementeria JL, ed. Drug abuse in pregnancy and neonatal effects. St. Louis: CV Mosby, 1977:129–144.

16. Strauss ME, Lessen-Firestone JK, Starr RH, Ostrea EM. Behavior of narcotic-addicted newborns. Child Dev 1975;46:887–893.

17. Colten ME. A comparison of heroin-addicted and non-addicted mothers: their attitudes, beliefs, and parenting experiences. NIDA services research report. Heroin addicted parents and their children: two reports. DHHS publication no. (ADM) 81–1028. Washington, DC: U.S. Government Printing Office, 1980.

18. NIDA Services Research Monograph Series. Addicted women: family dynamics, self-perceptions and support systems. USDHEW publication No. 80–762, Washington, DC: U.S. Government Printing Office, 1979.

19. Wilson GS, McCreary R, Kean J, Baxter JC. The development of preschool children of heroin-addicted mothers: a controlled study. Pediatrics 1979;63(1):135–141.

20. Sowder BJ, Burt MR. Children of heroin addicts: an assessment of health, learning, behavioral and adjustment problems. New York: Praeger, 1980.

21. Herjanic BM, Barreto VH, Herjanic M, Tomleri CJ. Children of heroin addicts. Int J Addict 1979;14:919–931.

22. Greenspan SI. The development of psychopathology and risk for drug abuse. In: Jones CL, Battjes RJ, eds. Etiology of drug abuse: implications for prevention. National Institute on Drug Abuse monograph no. 56. Washington, DC: Government Printing Office, 1985.

23. Hawkins JD, Lishner DM, Catalano RF. Childhood predictors and the prevention of adolescent substance abuse. Presented at the National Institute on Drug Abuse research analysis and utilization system meeting, etiology of drug abuse: implications for prevention, April, 1984.

24. Deren S. Children of substance abusers: a review of the literature. J Subst Abuse Treat 1986;3(2):77–94.

25. Cuskey WR, Wathey B. Female addiction. Lexington, MA: Lexington Books, 1982.

26. Shapira S. Developmental outreach. Project summary report. September, 1996.

27. Rivinus TM, ed. Children of chemically dependent parents. New York: Bruner-Mazel, 1991.

28. Lief N. Some measures of parenting behavior for addicted and nonaddicted mothers. Paper presented at the Symposium on Comprehensive Health Care for Addicted Families and Their Children, New York, May, 1976. NIDA services research report. Washington, DC: U.S. Government Printing Office, 1977.

29. Singer A. Mothering practices in the heroin addict. Am J Nursing 1974;74:77–82.

30. Nichtern S. The children of drug users. J Am Acad Child Psychiatry 1973;12:24–31.

31. Wellisch DK, Steinberg MR. Parenting attitudes of addicted mothers. Int J Addict 1980;15(6):809–819.

32. Fiks KB, Johnson HL, Rosen TS. Methadone-maintained mothers: 3-year follow-up of parental functioning. Int J Addict 1985;20(5):651–660.

33. Kane-Cavaiola C, Rullo-Cooney D. Addicted women: their families' effect on treatment outcome. J Chem Depend 1992;4(1):111–119.

34. Finkelstein N, Derman L. Single-parent women: What a mother can do. In: Roth P, ed. Alcohol and drugs are women's issues: Vol. One. A review of issues. Metuchen, NJ: Scarecrow Press, 1991.

35. Marsh JC, Miller NA. Female clients in substance abuse treatment. Int J Addict 1985;20(6–7):995–1019.

36. Stanton MD, Todd TC. The family therapy of drug abuse and addiction. New York: Guilford Press, 1982.

37. Heath AW, Stanton MD. Family Therapy. In: Frances RJ, Miller SI, eds. Clinical textbook of addictive disorders. New York: Guilford Press, 1991.

38. Todd TC, Stanton MD, Calway J. Treatment manual of marital and family therapy [special adaptation for treatment of cocaine dependence]. Unpublished manuscript, 1985.

39. Bowen M. Alcoholism as viewed through family systems theory and family psychotherapy. Family Dynamics of Addiction Quarterly 1991;1(1):94–102.

40. Minuchin S. Families and family therapy. Cambridge, MA: Harvard University Press, 1974.

41. Stanton MD, Todd TC. Structural-strategic family therapy with drug addicts. In: Kaufman E, Kaufman P, eds. Family therapy of drug and alcohol abuse. 2nd edition. Boston: Allyn and Bacon, 1992.

42. Beschner G, Thompson P. Women and drug abuse treatment: needs and services. NIDA service research monograph series. USDHHS publication no. 81–1057. Washington, DC: U.S. Government Printing Office, 1981.

43. Bandura A. Social learning theory. Englewood Cliffs, NJ: Prentice-Hall, 1977.

44. Dodson J. Dare to discipline. New York: Bantam Books, 1970.

45. Ginott H. Between parent and child. New York: Macmillan, 1965.

46. Rogers C. On becoming a person. New York: Houghton-Mifflin, 1970.

47. Axline VM. Play therapy. New York: Ballantine Books, 1974.

48. Glaser YIM. A unit for mothers and babies in a psychiatric hospital. J Child Psychology 1962;3:53–60.

49. Grunebaum H, Weiss J. Psychotic mothers and their children: joint admission to an adult psychiatric hospital. Psychiatry 1963;26:36–53.

50. Maternal drug abuse, drug exposed children. Understanding the problem. USDHHS publication no. (ADM) 92–1949. September 1992.

51. Goodman C. The PACE family treatment and education program: a public health approach to parental competence and promotion of mental health. In: Cohler B, Musick J, eds. Intervention with psychiatrically disabled parents and their young children. New dimensions for mental health services, no. 24. San Francisco: Jossey-Bass, 1984.

52. Hutson D. New York Medical College, Center for Comprehensive Health Practice, Pregnant Addicts and Addicted Mothers Program. Telephone interview, July 1991.

53. Walker B. Odyssey House. Telephone interview, July 1991.

54. Besharov D. Crack children in foster care: reexamining the balance between children's rights and parent's rights. Children Today 1990;Vol 19(4).

55. Kusserov C. Crack babies—selected model practices. June 1990.

56. United States House of Representatives, Committee on Ways and Means, Subcommittee on Human Resources. The impact of crack/cocaine on the child welfare system. April 1990.

57. Spear SF, Mason M. Impact of chemical dependency on family health status. Addict Behav 1991;26(2):179–187.

58. Mitchell J. Pregnant substance abusing women. Treatment Improvement Protocol No. 2. Rockville, MD: Substance Abuse and Mental Health Services Administration, Center for Substance Abuse Treatment, 1993.

59. Chavkin W, Kandall S. Between a rock and a hard place—perinatal drug abuse. Pediatrics 1990;85(2):223–225.

65 Co-dependence, Addictions, and Related Disorders

Charles L. Whitfield

Co-dependence is a disease of lost selfhood and can be defined as *any suffering and/or dysfunction that is associated with or results from focusing on the needs and behavior of others*. Co-dependents become so preoccupied with other people in their lives that they neglect the healthy needs of their *true self*—who they really are. Table 65.1 lists seven recent definitions of co-dependence. The common elements are synthesized into the first definition, which will act as the guiding definition for this chapter's discussion.

Co-dependence is the most common addiction people develop. It comes from focusing so much outside of ourselves that we lose touch with what is inside of us. Inside are our internal cues that assist us in countless ways: our beliefs, thoughts, feelings, decisions, choices, experiences, memories, wants, needs, sensations, intuitions, unconscious factors, and some indications of our physical functioning, such as heart rate and respirations. These and more are part of an exquisite feedback system called the *inner life* (Fig. 65.1) (1).

Co-dependence is *addiction to looking elsewhere*. We believe that something outside of our self (i.e., outside of our true self) can give us happiness and fulfillment. But has it ever done so in any lasting way? Whether the "elsewhere" is people, places, things, behaviors, or experiences, we neglect our own self for it, so that we get a payoff of some sort from focusing outward. The payoff is most often a reduction in painful feelings, although it may at times be a *temporary* increase in joyful feelings. But this feeling or *mood alteration* is predicated principally on the other—the something else outside of us—and not on our healthy wants and needs. It is not based on our own internal cues.

What we need is a healthy balance of awareness of our inner and our outer lives. This balance has nothing to do with what others may try to construe as being "normal," "proper," or "required." Rather, it has to do with what *is*—what is happening precisely in the eternal now of our own individual consciousness. To have such a healthy balance does not come automatically, given our current world where most people are co-dependent much of the time. In fact, we learn to be co-dependent from others around us. In this sense it is a *contagious* or acquired illness. From the time we are born, it is modeled and taught to us by a seemingly endless string of important people in our life: parents, teachers, siblings, friends, heroes, and heroines. Co-dependence is reinforced by the media, government, organized religion, and the helping professions.

Co-dependence comes from our trying to protect our delicate true self (the child within) from what may appear to be insurmountable forces outside ourselves (1, 8, 9). But our true self is a paradox. Not only is it sensitive, delicate, and vulnerable, but it is also powerful. In fact, it is so powerful, that, in a *full recovery program* for co-dependence, it heals through a process of self-responsibility and creativity that often is awesome to behold.

When our alive true self *goes into hiding*—to please its parent figures, to lessen the nearly overwhelming pain, and thus *to survive*—a false, co-dependent self emerges to take its place. We thus lose our awareness of our true self to such an extent that we *lose awareness of its existence*. We lose contact with who we really are. Gradually, we begin to get used to that false self. Then it becomes a habit, and finally an addiction.

Co-dependence is not only the most common addiction, it is the *base* out of which all our addictions and compulsions emerge. Underneath nearly every addiction and compulsion lies co-dependence. What generates and maintains them is a sense of shame that our true self, our child within, is somehow defective or inadequate, combined with the innate and healthy drive of our true self to realize and express itself. Whichever form it may take, the addiction or compulsion becomes the manifestation of the erroneous notion that something outside ourselves can make us happy and fulfilled.

A BRIEF HISTORY OF CO-DEPENDENCE

Exactly where, when, and from whom the idea of co-dependence first emerged has not been identified. But the idea and dynamics of family members and others close to alcoholics, other chemical dependents, and other dysfunctional people began around the end of the nineteenth century, as shown in Table 65.2.

Throughout the decades, clinicians, theorists, writers, and groups have built on the contributions of their predecessors and have made their own special contributions, adding another part of the puzzle describing the human condition, psyche, and relationships. Each of these and others contributed to the background from which the concepts of co-dependence and the adult children of dysfunctional families emerged. Around 1980 the concept of co-dependence emerged. While a few have criticized it, of all the important concepts discovered and developed throughout the twentieth century, co-dependence appears to offer among the most practical solutions to helping people recover from a variety of disorders. The following sequence of events, principles, and dynamics may be helpful in clarifying some of the developments in the continuing emergence of the concept of co-dependence (1).

1. Observers who deliver therapy for and who research, write, and teach about the adult child condition and co-dependence come from diverse backgrounds and professions, (e.g., medicine, psychiatry, counseling, social work, nursing, and the recovering community).

2. For practical purposes of therapy and recovery, the adult child condition and co-dependence can be viewed as one condition and can be called by either name, some other name, or simply the "human condition."

3. Many of its characteristics and dynamics were partially described before it was given these names. These descriptions come from many sources, including:

- Ancient legends and myths
- Freud's trauma/seduction theory
- Theory and practice of working with the human unconscious
- Jung's and others' expanded psychology
- Object relations and self psychology's differentiation of the true and false self
- Study of traumatic stress disorders
- Family therapy dynamics
- Humanistic and transpersonal psychology
- Addictions dynamics and recovery experience
- 12-step self-help groups

4. After Johnson described *co-alcoholism* about 1973, several observers around 1980 began to expand and describe the condition as *co-dependence* (10). At first it was associated with living with or being close to an active alcoholic or other chemical dependent person. Then it was shown to be also associated with living with or being close to *any* dysfunctional person or persons.

5. It originates primarily from having grown up in a troubled, unhealthy, or dysfunctional family and society. Therefore it is clinically useful to describe many of its features as part of a condition that can be called co-dependence, which is a major manifestation of the adult child syndrome.

Table 65.1 Some Definitions of Co-dependence

1. A multidimensional (physical, mental, emotional, and spiritual) condition manifested by any suffering and dysfunction that is associated with or due to focusing on the needs and behavior of others. It may be mild to severe, and most people have it. It can mimic, be associated with, and aggravate many physical, psychological, and spiritual conditions; it develops from turning the responsibility for our life and happiness over to our ego (false self) and to others. It is treatable, and recovery is possible (1).
2. An emotional, psychological, and behavioral pattern of coping that develops as a result of an individual's prolonged exposure to, and practice of, a set of oppressive rules—rules which prevent the open expression of feeling, as well as the direct discussion of personal and interpersonal problems (2).
3. A personality disorder based on a need to control in the face of serious adverse consequences; neglecting one's own needs; boundary distortions around intimacy and separation; enmeshment with certain dysfunctional people; and other manifestations such as denial, constricted feelings, depression, and stress-related medical illness (3).
4. A stress-induced preoccupation with another's life, leading to maladaptive behavior (4).
5. A dysfunctional pattern of symptoms of adult children of living which emerges from our family of origin as well as our culture, producing arrested identity development, and resulting in an over-reaction to things outside of us and an under-reaction to things inside of us. Left untreated, it can deteriorate into an addiction (5).
6. (A disease wherein a person has difficulty:) (6)
   a. Experiencing appropriate levels of self-esteem
   b. Setting functional boundaries
   c. Owning and expressing their own reality
   d. Taking care of their adult needs and wants
   e. Experiencing and expressing their reality moderately
7. A pattern of painful dependence on compulsive behaviors and on approval from others in an attempt to find safety, self-worth, and a sense of identity. Recovery is possible (7).

Reproduced with permission from Whitfield CL. Co-dependence: healing the human condition—the new paradigm for helping professionals and people in recovery. Deerfield Beach, FL: Health Communications, 1991.

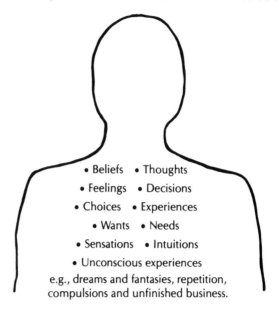

- Beliefs • Thoughts
- Feelings • Decisions
- Choices • Experiences
- Wants • Needs
- Sensations • Intuitions
- Unconscious experiences

e.g., dreams and fantasies, repetition, compulsions and unfinished business.

Figure 65.1. My inner life. (Reproduced with permission from Whitfield CL. Co-dependence: healing the human condition—the new paradigm for helping professionals and people in recovery. Deerfield Beach, FL: Health Communications, 1991.)

6. Throughout the 1980s its characteristics and dynamics were clarified and described in more detail.
7. Central to this concept was the observation that the "child within," mentioned by many writers, teachers, and 12-step groups, was the true self that others had begun to describe decades earlier (1, 9, 24).
8. The cause of co-dependence is a wounding of the true self to such an extent that to survive, it had to go into hiding most of the time, with the subsequent running of its life by the false or co-dependent self (19, 22, 24, 40).
9. The above insights gave many people with various disorders—physical, mental, emotional, and spiritual (which are either manifestations of or aggravated by this wounding)—certain advantages in their healing:

- The term *child within* gave them an easier understanding of their true self.
- *Co-dependent self* gave them an easier understanding of their false self or negative ego.
- *Co-dependence* and *adult child* gave them a clearer description of the dynamics and manifestations of their woundedness and its relationship to any stage-0 conditions (Table 65.3) and to everyday life. It has spoken to the deep malaise found in our society today (11).

10. This approach frees the person from the stifling and self-esteem–damaging idea that they are somehow inferior or defective—that is, that they are bad, sick, crazy, or stupid. Instead they learn in recovery that they are none of these. They are simply wounded.
11. This wounding is learned, and what is learned can be unlearned. Unlearning happens during the healing and recovery process.

IDENTIFYING CO-DEPENDENCE

Recognition and Diagnosis

Co-dependence may be present in any one or a combination of the following ways: (*a*) *persistent* stress-related or functional illness or complaints; (*b*) stress-related illness that is *unresponsive* or only *partially re-*

sponsive to conventional therapy; (*c*) *relapse* of addictions or compulsions; (*d*) many *medical* or *psychological conditions;* and (*e*) many *problems in living.* While co-dependence is not the only causal factor for each of these categories or conditions, it can be helpful therapeutically to view co-dependence as a major underlying condition and dynamic in the genesis of these conditions.

To assist in making the diagnosis, one may use the various definitions of co-dependence in Table 65.1. While there appears to be no diagnostic survey instruments for co-dependence equivalent to the Michigan Alcoholism Screening Test, there are several survey tests that, if needed, the clinician may consider using:

- A Co-dependence Test (12)
- Co-dependent Assessment Inventory (12)
- Co-dependency Assessment Inventory (13)
- Acquaintance Description Form (14)
- Co-dependent Relationship Questionnaire (15)
- The Original Laundry List: The Problem and the Solution (16)
- Relationship Addiction (17)
- Sexual Addiction (17)
- Family Drinking Survey (8)
- Checklist from Co-dependents Anonymous (18)

To further assist in making the diagnosis, one may apply the appropriate manifestations and cardinal characteristics described below. While making the diagnosis of co-dependence is useful at any time, it appears to be most useful in late stage-1 recovery and in relapses or exacerbations of any disorders (stage-0 conditions), and in stage-2 recovery (Table 65.3).

Cardinal Characteristics

In addition to those presented in Table 65.1, co-dependence has at least 12 cardinal characteristics. It (*a*) is learned and acquired; (*b*) is developmental; (*c*) is outer focused; (*d*) is a disease of lost selfhood; (*e*) has personal boundary distortions; (*f*) is a feeling disorder; (*g*) manifests especially by emptiness, low self-esteem, shame, fear, anger, confusion, and numbness; and (*h*) produces relationship difficulties with self and with others. Co-dependence is also (*i*) primary, (*j*) chronic, (*k*) progressive, (*l*) malignant, and (*m*) treatable.

Table 65.2   Recent Historical Overview of the Family, Adult Child, and Co-dependence Continuum

Approximate Year	Theoretical and Clinical Events	Formation of Self-Help Group
1896	Groddeck and others: Unconscious	
	Freud: Unconscious forces from personal and historical experience	
	Jung: Relationships and collective unconscious; letter to Bill W. (in 1930s)	
	Adler: Birth order, sibling relationships and rivalry	
	Sullivan: Interpersonal and intrapsychic dynamics	
	Moreno: Psychodrama	
	Horney: Importance of Real Self in relationships; the "neurosis of our time"	
	Klein: Importance of relationships and projective identification	
1935	Mahler: Early childhood development	Alcoholics Anonymous
	Object relations theorists, e.g., Winicott (True Self in relationships) and self psychologists	
	Miscellaneous observations of spouses of alcoholics (e.g., Rado, etc.)	
	Cork: *The Forgotten Children*	
	Studies of loss and post-traumatic stress begin	
1950	Satir and others: Begin generic family therapy movement	Al-Anon
1960	Bateson; Jackson; Haley: Double bind, etc.	
	Bowen: Systems theory; reciprocal relationship, etc.	
1970	Johnson: Family dynamics and intervention; co-alcoholism	
1975	Minuchin: Structural family therapy; Philadelphia Child Guidance Clinic	ACoA
	Booz-Allen study (NIAAA): Children of alcoholics	
	Berenson: Integration of family therapy with mainstream recovery	
	Wegscheider: Adapts and expands Satir's family roles and dynamics to alcoholic families	
	Steinglass, et al.: Research, theory	
1978	First CoA conference (NIAAA)	
	First AC therapy group (Brown et al.)	
1980	Residential programs add family treatment	
	Miller and Masson: Clarify child mistreatment and abuse, expanding trauma theory	
1983	Many conferences begin	(NACoA)
	First Adult Child focused intensive residential treatment	ACA
	Co-dependence theory and recovery intensifies	ACoDF
1987	Child within (True Self) healing techniques expanding	CoDA
	Books proliferate	
	Spirituality importance expands	
	Co-dependence and adult child recovery importance in relapse prevention, therapy, and serenity	
	Criticisms aired more often	
1989	Co-dependence and adult child approaches begin to be integrated into general mental health treatment	
1990	The decade of psychological and spiritual growth for increasing numbers of people	
1992–present	Continued spread to other specialties and disciplines	
	Anti-recovery backlash escalates (45)	

Expanded in 1996 with permission from Whitfield CL. Co-dependence: healing the human condition—the new paradigm for helping professionals and people in recovery. Deerfield Beach, FL: Health Communications, 1991.

Learned and Acquired

Co-dependence develops unconsciously and involuntarily. In its primary form, it begins with mistreatment, abuse, or both to a vulnerable and innocent child by its environment, especially its family of origin, and eventually by its culture or society. In contrast to addictions, co-dependence does not appear to have a genetic transmission. Rather, it appears to come about by the process of *wounding*. This description of the wounding process uses terms from self psychology, object relations theory, and from the recovery literature (1, 8, 9, 19–22). Like most psychologic wounding, this process is largely unconscious. What appears to happen is the following.

1. Wounded themselves, the child's parents feel inadequate, bad, and unfulfilled.
2. They project this feeling onto others, especially their spouse and their vulnerable children. They may also project grandiosity. They look outside themselves to feel whole.
3. In a need to stabilize the parent and to survive, the child denies that the parents are inadequate and mistreat or abuse, and internalizes (takes in, introjects, and accepts) the parents' projected inadequacy and badness, plus a common fantasy (e.g., that "If I'm really good and perfect, they will love me, and they won't reject or abandon me"). The child idealizes the parents.
4. As a result, the child's vulnerable true self (lost heart of the self, libidinal ego) is wounded so often that, to protect its true self, it defensively submerges ("splits off") itself deep within the unconscious part of its psyche. The child goes into hiding.
5. The child takes in whatever else it is told—both verbally and nonver-

bally—about others, and stores it in its unconscious (mostly) and its conscious mind (sometimes and to some degree).

6. The child takes in messages from important relationships. The mental representations of these relationships are called "objects" by the object relations theorists. These representations are laden with feelings and tend to occur in "part-objects" (e.g., good parent, bad parent, aggressive child, and shy child).
7. The more self-destructive messages are deposited most often in the false self (internal saboteur, antilibidinal ego, negative ego, or the internalized or introjected, rejecting or otherwise mistreating parent).
8. A tension builds. The true self strives to come alive and to evolve. At the same time, the negative (antilibidinal) ego attacks the true self, thus forcing it to stay submerged, keeping self-esteem low. Also, the child's grieving of its losses and traumas is not supported. This resulting "psychopathology" or "lesion" has been called a schizoid compromise by Guntrip, multiplicity of repressed egos by Fairbairn, and a splitting off of the true self by Winnicott (19). The outcome can be developmental delay, arrest, or failure.
9. Some results include chronic emptiness, sadness, and confusion and often periodic explosions of self-destructive and other destructive behavior—both impulsive and compulsive—that allows for some release of the tension and a glimpse of the true self.
10. The consequences of the continued emptiness, repeated destructive behavior, or both keep the true self stifled or submerged. The person maintains a low self-esteem, remains unhappy, yet wishes and seeks fulfillment. Compulsions and addictions ("repetition compulsions") can provide temporary fulfillment, can lead to more suffering, and ultimately block fulfillment and serenity. What results from this wounding process

Table 65.3 Tasks in Human Development^a (reading from bottom to top)

Tasks	Approximate Age in First Cycle	Realm of Being	Stage in Recovery
Be	Later in life, usually second half, when have a sense of self that can let go of its ego	Spiritual	3
Co-create			
Extend love			
Transcend ego			
Self-realize			
Recycle	19		
Evolve and grow	13	Emotional	
Regenerate (heal)			
Evaluate	6		
Develop morals, skills, and values			
Create (make)			
Master	4		2
Cooperate	3		
Think		Mental	
Separate	2		
Initiate			
Explore			
Trust	1		1
Feel		Physical	0
Love			
Connect			
Be	0		

Reproduced with permission from Whitfield CL: Co-dependence: healing the human condition—the new paradigm for helping professionals and people in recovery. Deerfield Beach, FL: Health Communications, 1991.
^aWe recycle these tasks throughout our lives. Healthy adolescents repeat the first 14–16 tasks. Parents usually cycle in parallel with their children.

is co-dependence in its primary form. Several decades ago Karen Horney called it "the neurosis of our time" (40, 46), and today we can also call it the adult child syndrome or condition.

11. Recovery and growth is discovering and gently unearthing the true self (child within) so that it can exist and express itself in a healthy way, day to day, and restructuring the ego to become a more flexible assistant (positive ego) to the true self. Some other results are aliveness, creativity, and growth.

12. Such self-discovery and recovery is most effectively accomplished gradually and in the presence of safe, compassionate, skilled, and supportive people. With commitment to and active participation in recovery, this healing process usually takes from 3 to 5 years or more.

Developmental

While many of the definitions of co-dependence (see Table 65.1) suggest or imply a developmental factor, several address it directly. In their definition, Friel and Friel (5) include "arrested identity development," and Subby elaborates on some of the developmental defects of co-dependence in *Lost in the Shuffle* (2).

If the mistreatment, abuse, or both that begins the wounding process continues, it interrupts, damages, and blocks normal human development and growth. Described in several ways by authors such as Erikson, Piaget, Levin, Levinson, and Greenspan, these stages involve learning to explore, connect, love, feel, trust, explore, initiate, separate, think, cooperate, master, create, develop, evaluate, regenerate, recycle, evolve, and grow—all crucial for healthy human life (see Table 65.3). Any form of blocking of these developmental stages paralyzes healthy growth and threatens survival. In a survival mode, the person focuses more outside of his or her self, neglecting their inner life. They gradually become more and more distant and eventually alienated from their true self in all its dimensions, including these developmental points of growth. This leaves them deficient in whichever crucial inner life functioning ability has been blocked.

Because of our society's emphasis on thinking and doing, most people can generally function intellectually and do various tasks. But in their relationship with their true self and with others, they often have difficulty in their inner life with connecting, mastering, and loving.

Outer Focused

This characteristic is addressed throughout the definitions and dynamics of co-dependence. There is nothing harmful or wrong with a person looking outside of self. In fact, doing so is useful not only in everyday life, but to our survival. However, co-dependents overdo it by focusing outward so much that they neglect their inner lives to an extent that they suffer inordinately and unnecessarily. This suffering often leads to dysfunction.

A Disease of Lost Selfhood

Whether it is called our true or real self, child within, consciousness, ego ideal, mind, or identity, this being appears to be who we really are. This, our true identity, is mostly lost in co-dependence. Not knowing how to handle the pain of living in a mistreating, abusing, or otherwise dysfunctional environment, our true self feels overwhelmed and goes into hiding. The false self, ego, or co-dependent self then comes in to assist us in surviving and functioning. This absence of the self brings about a feeling of *emptiness*, which we then may try to fill with things outside of our self. But doing so doesn't fill us in a lasting and fulfilling way. It is only after experiencing the repeated pain and frustration of the consequences of addictions, compulsions, and/or other disorders—combined with the ongoing feeling of emptiness—that we are often forced to look within, into our true self and then eventually and experientially to connect to our Higher Power. Thus we can begin to recover and to feel more fulfilled (1, 23).

Personal Boundary Distortions

A boundary is a personally initiated and maintained dynamic that protects the well-being and integrity of the true self (9, 24). In co-dependence there are numerous boundary distortions, and boundary distortions are implied throughout the definitions of co-dependence (see Table 65.1). Co-dependence cannot develop without distortions in personal boundaries, and it appears that a person cannot recover from any disorder, including co-dependence, without forming healthy boundaries.

A Feeling Disorder

In co-dependence the person loses touch with their crucial inner life, which especially includes their feelings. They become alienated from their feelings. Yet these feelings do not disappear. They continue to surface, most commonly as emptiness, low self-esteem, and shame, fear, anger, confusion, and numbness (1, 8, 9). These feelings are usually masked in other disguises, since actively co-dependent people have difficulty recognizing and dealing directly with their feelings. In recovery, the person learns experientially what these and other feelings are, how to recognize them, and how to use them in their everyday life.

Relationship Difficulties

Co-dependent people have difficulty relating to themselves, to others, and to their Higher Power. These relationship difficulties are reflected throughout their lives, including their core recovery issues.

An *issue* is any conflict, concern, or potential problem—whether conscious or unconscious—that is incomplete for us or that needs action or change. A *core issue* is one that comes up repeatedly for many of us. There are at least 15 core issues. These include the following:

- Control
- Trust
- Being real
- Feelings
- Low self-esteem
- Dependence
- Grieving ungrieved losses
- Fear of abandonment
- All-or-none thinking and behaving
- High tolerance for inappropriate behavior

- Over-responsibility for others
- Neglecting one's own needs
- Difficulty resolving conflict, giving love, and receiving love

Core issues reflect some of our areas of conflict as healthy human beings. They show up for us in our day-to-day lives in *countless ways,* including some of the following areas of our recovery and life:

- *Relationships* of any kind with others, self, and our Higher Power
- Doing experiential recovery work throughout our healing
- *Feedback* given by therapy group members, therapists, sponsors, friends, and others
- *Insight* from reading, listening, reflecting upon, or working through conflict

Recognizing and working through these issues are an integral part of recovery from co-dependence (1, 8, 9, 26, 45).

Primary

Most co-dependence is primary in that it occurs from childhood. *Primary* also means that no other disorder causes it, although one or more disorders—including addictions—may exist concomitantly and be a factor in aggravating it. Figure 65.2 illustrates any of these disorders that may *exist with* co-dependence as "stage-0 disorders or conditions." In this view, the stage-0 disorder or condition represents the tip of the iceberg, with much of the bulk of the iceberg being co-dependence with all of its multiple dimensions and dynamics. Depending on genetic, familial, and environmental factors, each person will likely manifest a different disorder (stage-0 condition) or set of disorders.

If the person obtains specific treatment for the stage-0 condition, I call that *stage-1 recovery,* which usually takes a few months to a few years to stabilize (Table 65.4). Here, any addiction, compulsion, or related disorder may be addressed. Once stabilized, the person may wish to address their co-dependence, which in perhaps 95% of people with co-dependence is the same as the adult child syndrome or condition. This *stage-2 recovery* process usually takes from 3 to 5 years or longer in the best full-recovery program (9). In *stage-3 recovery* the person is more able to address their spirituality successfully (26).

Table 65.4 Recovery and Duration According to Stages[a]

Recovery Stage	Condition	Focus of Recovery	Approximate Duration
3	Human/spiritual	Spirituality	Ongoing
2	Adult child	Adult child specific Full recovery program	3–5 years
1	Stage-0 disorder	Basic-illness specific Full recovery program	6 months to 3 years
0	Active illness	Addiction, compulsion, disorder, woundedness	Indefinite

Reproduced with permission from Whitfield CL: Co-dependence: healing the human condition—the new paradigm for helping professionals and people in recovery. Deerfield Beach, FL: Health Communications, 1991.
[a]The time to focus on stages 2 and 3 recovery usually depends on the person's prior healing and present condition.

Secondary

Co-dependence *may* occur in a person who grew up in a healthy family when they enter into a close or important relationship with an actively addicted, disordered, or otherwise dysfunctional person. Frequently associated DSM-IV diagnoses for secondary co-dependence may include adjustment disorder (309.28), dysthymic disorder (300.40), or anxiety disorder (300.00). A difference is that *secondary* co-dependence is often milder and easier to treat. With appropriate treatment, some persons may make a successful recovery in a matter of a few months, and most can do so in less than a year. This is because they have a healthier self and therefore healthier ego defenses and coping mechanisms.

Distracting Co-dependence

"Distracting co-dependence" can be recognized when a person comes in requesting assistance in doing adult child oriented or childhood trauma recovery work, yet they are too distracted to do the necessary and appropriate amount of introspection and family of origin work. The distraction is often due to their being in a close relationship with an actively addicted or other actively dysfunctional person. In addition they themselves may have an active addiction or other disorder that distracts them from the trauma recovery work.

Chronic

Co-dependence is chronic. Until the person works appropriately and for a sufficient duration in a specific recovery program that addresses whatever stage-0 disorder(s) they may have (in a stage-1 recovery program), including co-dependence (stage-2 recovery), it is unlikely that they will make a successful recovery.

Progressive

Without specific and appropriate treatment and recovery, co-dependence usually gets worse over the course of time. While partial treatment interventions—such as psychoactive medication, psychotherapy that does not address the core of co-dependence and the childhood trauma, and behavior therapy—may offer some brief periods of relief, it is unlikely that the person will make a successful ongoing and long-term recovery.

Malignant

At times, co-dependence takes a malignant course. It may do so in the form of overt or covert suicide, homicide, relapses of addictions, and possibly medical illnesses such as cancer.

Treatable

Co-dependence is treatable. With sufficient motivation by the patient and appropriate treatment interventions by the helping professional and with long-term treatment, the co-dependent person is likely to make a successful

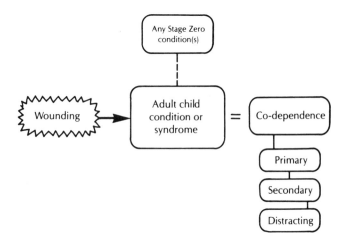

Figure 65.2. Interrelationships among the adult child syndrome, co-dependence, child mistreatment/abuse, and medical and psychological disorders. (Reproduced with permission from Whitfield CL. Co-dependence: healing the human condition—the new paradigm for helping professionals and people in recovery. Deerfield Beach, FL: Health Communications, 1991.)

recovery. This usually also depends on the nature and response of any stage-0 disorders to any specific stage-1 treatment prior to the person's recovery work from co-dependence.

Some Manifestations

Among the dimensions of co-dependence are at least 12 manifestations that may present as various guises of personality. These illustrate the many ways that co-dependence can disguise itself and present to helping professionals. While many patients already in recovery may be familiar with these terms in varying degrees, referring to them at selected times during the recovery process can be therapeutically helpful. Any individual may present with any one or a combination of the following.

RESCUER AND FIXER

In trying to rescue, fix, or help others to the neglect of being fully aware of, attending to, and helping his or her self, the person loses identity in others. Helping professionals are among those who are at high risk for manifesting co-dependence in this way.

PEOPLE PLEASER

Not knowing one's self fully and thus not having healthy personal boundaries and limits (9, 24), one would rather acquiesce and comply with others than to express one's own healthy wants and needs. These people have a hard time saying no to others. Part of their recovery includes learning to say no. People pleasing is a subtle form of manipulation and control.

OVERACHIEVER

Feeling empty from the loss of their true self, these people try to fill the emptiness with one and usually more achievements. But because the emptiness was not due to lack of achievement, it tends not to be relieved for very long with each achievement. The "family hero" is among those who are at especially high risk for this manifestation (27).

THE INADEQUATE ONE OR "FAILURE"

Still empty, similar to the overachiever, this seeming opposite to the overachiever is another common way that co-dependence can show itself. Associated with low self-esteem and a feeling of shame, the person feels imperfect, incomplete, inadequate, not good enough, bad, rotten, and flawed at their core. Rather than being the exact opposite of the overachiever, this dynamic is what actually *underlies* and *runs* the overachiever's drive to overachieve. It also underlies and is a major dynamic in all the other manifestations and consequences of co-dependence.

In recovery, the co-dependent person discovers that, rather than *being* rotten at their core, this sense of shame was only a *shell,* similar to the outer layers of an onion, that covered and blocked their true self from fully knowing and expressing itself (1, 8).

VICTIM

The victim can present as the sick one—with chronic illness—or as the bad one—the delinquent or scapegoat who is always getting into trouble. The victim admits and expresses self-pity and feels they are misunderstood, often whining while telling their story of woe. Although they may toy with getting help, they rarely commit to it or follow through with any actions. They admittedly run from taking responsibility for self-improvement. They often lure rescuers, fixers, and helping professionals to try to help them, so that they can shame or otherwise punish them for not really helping; a common response is "In fact, you've made it worse . . ."

Living mostly in the past with an endless string of "if onlys," the victim knows and admits that they are a loser and asks others to feel sorry for them. Until the person begins to take responsibility for being a victim, their prognosis with any treatment is poor at worse and guarded at best. Even so, they tend to be one step ahead of the martyr.

MARTYR

The martyr is more difficult to treat than the victim because they deny most of what the victim admits, such as their self-pity and feeling misunderstood, unappreciated, hopeless, and burdened, although they may manifest these feelings by their actions and their treatment of others (i.e., their behavior speaks louder than their words). Often sighing, they refuse all suggestions or help, and say that they "already know all of these solutions and have tried them anyway."

The martyr's victimhood is more difficult to recognize because they can look so good on the surface. They do not take responsibility for their life, often feel they have "too much" responsibility, and may disguise themselves as a rescuer or fixer. Both martyr and victim want another person to take responsibility for them and want to see the other person struggle and suffer.

Living mostly in the future, pretending to be done with the past, they also may be overly religious. While the victim admits he is a loser, the martyr will not—and does not even know it. Both martyr and victim refuse to face and feel their pain (48). The martyr is one of the most difficult to help of all co-dependent patients.

ADDICTED ONE

The author's 20 years of clinical, full-time work with alcoholics and other chemical-dependent people has yet to uncover a patient with these disorders that was not also co-dependent. Also, each of these patients grew up in a dysfunctional family and thus had primary co-dependence. Of course, the addiction with which a person may present can also be to other people, places, things, behaviors, or experiences than alcohol or drugs. Common ones are eating disorders, sex addiction, workaholism or work addiction, money-related addictions such as compulsive spending or shopping, compulsive or pathological gambling, and relationship addiction, which is another guise of co-dependence.

COMPULSIVE ONE

Similar to and on the same spectrum as the addictions, compulsions are another manifestation of co-dependence, and some have already been listed. While it may be difficult to differentiate some compulsions from addictions, one important difference is that compulsions tend to have less severe consequences. Because of this, people with mild or socially acceptable compulsions, such as compulsive neatness, may not be identified as easily by their family and friends or helping professionals.

GRANDIOSE ONE

This person may present as overconfident and even grandiose. Men may be "macho" and woman may have overexaggerated femininity—may be fragile or frail—or they may also appear overconfident and express a grandiose self-image. Related to ego inflation, this guise is the opposite of the healthy characteristic in recovery described as *humility,* which does not take the form of groveling or acting like a doormat, but rather of being open to learning about one's self, others, and one's Higher Power.

BULLY OR ABUSER

So insecure about and alienated from their true selves, both the bully and the abuser may lash out at others to feel stronger and more in control. When accused, some child molesters may react by attacking the person who disclosed their abusive behavior or a helping professional who may assist their victims in recovery (45).

LOST CHILD

Often the third-born or later child in a dysfunctional family, the lost child feels so overwhelmed by trying to get appropriate attention and to have needs met in competition with his or her older first-born siblings (often the hero or overachiever) and the second-born (often the delinquent, bully, or bad one), that the child gives up and withdraws (27). It may become a victim or martyr in an attempt to handle its frequent psychosomatic illness.

In recovery, co-dependent persons may draw on any of these less desirable traits as they transform them into healthier ones. For example, the bully can learn to be assertive in a healthy way, and the martyr or victim can learn to be more sensitive to their inner life and take responsibility for making their life a success.

PHYSICAL ILLNESS FROM CO-DEPENDENCE

Somewhere from the middle to an advanced stage of co-dependence, physical illness may develop. In one possible development, unresolved stress becomes *distress,* which often develops into stress-related illness. Much of medical practice is spent treating stress-related illnesses (26, 28, 29). In an attempt to avoid the pain of short-term stress or "eustress" (that which is usually easier to deal with), co-dependents bury their feelings and attempt to please others. Such avoidance usually produces long-term stress, which is called distress.

Another way that physical illness may develop—and which is probably intimately related to the stress model—is through disallowed or repressed grieving. From birth we are taught dysfunctional family rules, the incorporation of which is part of the genesis of co-dependence. Some of these rules include the following (2):

1. It's not OK to talk about problems or to talk about or express feelings openly.
2. Communicate indirectly—that is, through another person rather than to the one you need to talk to.
3. Don't be selfish.
4. Always be strong, good, perfect, and happy.
5. It's *not* OK to be playful and have fun.
6. Don't rock the boat.

These kinds of rules may serve to protect us from short-term conflict and pain, but they set the stage for hiding our true self, including its needs, wants, and feelings.

With the inevitable repeated losses in our lives, these rules tend to prevent us from grieving our losses in a healthy way. What we do not *grieve* healthily, we tend to *act out* (re-enact or repeat) in physical, mental, emotional, or behavioral ways, which are often problematic. For example, unexpressed and unprocessed *anger* may be manifest in numerous ways, including depression, compulsion, and addiction; family and child abuse; and perhaps even a lowering of the body's immune response, which is a major factor in our ability to fight off infection and cancer.

Unexpressed *fear* can result in anxiety and panic disorders, insomnia, heart arrhythmias, sexual dysfunction, and other stress-related illness. Unexpressed guilt may lead to self-neglect, compulsion and addiction, other self-destructive behavior, and other chronic conditions. Unexpressed *shame* can result in self-neglect, compulsion and addiction, other self-destructive behavior, sexual dysfunction, and other chronic conditions. Feelings are not just "mental" occurrences; they are complex *physiological* interactions within the true self's sophisticated system of internal cues (1, 8).

Preliminary studies suggest that writing and sharing feelings strengthens the body's immune response, as shown by the following. Twenty-five adults kept a diary of disturbing life events for 5 days and wrote how they felt about each of them. Another 25 adults kept a diary about superficial life events only. When their immune response was measured at 6 weeks and then 6 months later, as compared with their baseline, the former group had improved immune response, whereas the latter group had no change (30, 31). Studies like these, as well as clinical observations (32), indicate that when we do not grieve in a healthy way—that is, when we do not let our true self experience and express itself—we often become ill (8). The author has observed more than 1100 co-dependent patients in close to 30 years of medical practice. There exists a pattern of chronic functional, psychosomatic, or physical illnesses in these people, covering a spectrum of illnesses from asthma to migraine headaches to arthritis to hearing loss, all of which tended to improve or clear with treatment that was specific for their co-dependence.

The concept of co-dependence will in some important way eventually have an impact on the practice of medicine and psychiatry. Is it possible that co-dependence is a co-factor in the pathogenesis of cancer? How might co-dependence affect the development of cardiovascular disease and many other medical and surgical conditions, including AIDS? Others are writing on the important and often crucial effect of the mind and spirit on the body (28, 29, 33), but none has related it to co-dependence.

PSYCHOLOGICAL ILLNESS

Since its beginning, the mental health field has been helping people with co-dependence but used other terms to describe it. For a while it was called *neurosis, undifferentiation, passive aggressive, locus of control,* and *other directed;* simpler terms were also used, such as *victim, martyr,* and *stress.* Mental health professionals helped these people get to know themselves better and take more responsibility for their lives. What is new and more helpful about an understanding of co-dependence includes a reframing and broadening of the dynamics of the disorders and conditions long observed and a more precise and sophisticated way of helping people who suffer from them (1). Two questions become readily apparent: How does co-dependence impinge on or fit in with the various psychological disorders, and how useful will it be to describe co-dependence as an independent disorder or disease entity?

For those helping professionals who are *aware* of and treat people with co-dependence, describing it as a discreet disorder is useful. In whatever guise it may first present, it is helpful to know that it either lies at the base of or is associated in some important way with co-dependence. The original trauma(s) that led to the co-dependence may even be causal in the person's difficulties or suffering. This is practical because co-dependence is such an imminently understandable and treatable condition for both the recovering person and the therapist. There are effective treatment approaches and techniques available for co-dependence as a specific disorder. It is likely that these will be progressively refined with time and experience and that additional treatment approaches and techniques will be developed.

When co-dependence is described as a specific disorder, how broad should the description be? Will it be most useful to fit it into a *category* of disorders? Cermak describes it under the category of personality disorders—suggesting it is specifically most like mixed personality disorder (3). But describing it as a personality disorder alone is limiting to both the patient and the clinician. This approach has advantages and disadvantages. Advantages include the availability of current discrete diagnostic criteria for those who may be less familiar with co-dependence. Hence, the diagnosis potentially may be more available to the general mental health professional, as well as to the public. However, co-dependence is currently not fully understood or accepted by the mainstream of mental health professionals. For example, as late as 1995 some critics said that it "holds women partly responsible for perpetuating the alcoholism and addiction of their male partners" (47). While thoughtful, this criticism lacks a complete understanding of co-dependence, since it has no gender or situational limitations. Co-dependence is so basic and so pervasive among humans that it likely affects not just those who come for psychotherapy or counseling, but *most people.*

Since co-dependence is so far not accepted as a diagnosis in DSM-IV or ICD-9-CM, insurance companies are not aware of its existence and therefore will not pay for its treatment (35). Therefore, the patient or client's history must yield an acceptable additional diagnosis if they are to be considered for reimbursement for treatment, as they are entitled to be when they are covered by health insurance. While any disorder may be a manifestation of or associated with co-dependence, the following frequently are:

Avoidant personality disorder (301.82)
Dependent personality disorder (301.60)
Obsessive-compulsive personality disorder (301.4)
Mixed personality disorder (now called personality disorder not otherwise specified) (301.90)
Dysthymic disorder (300.40)
Anxiety disorder (not otherwise specified) (300.00)
Posttraumatic stress disorder (309.81)
Various addictive disorders

Less frequently, other DSM diagnoses may be appropriate, such as:

Histrionic personality disorder (301.50)
Borderline personality disorder (301.83)
Paranoid personality disorder (301.00)
Bipolar disorder (296.6)
Major depression (296.2)

While co-dependence may play a part in the genesis and the relapse of other psychotic disorders, we are just beginning to explore whether and where co-dependence and trauma recovery based treatment may help in their total management. People with some disorders, such as narcissistic personality disorder and antisocial personality disorder, are not usually interested in or responsive to treatment for co-dependence or past trauma.

We can consider co-dependence as lying *within* a diagnostic category (e.g., of personality disorders), *and* we can view it (probably more accurately) as such a general and pervasive part of the painful side of the human condition that it is itself a category under which many, if not most, conditions can be subsumed and clarified.

Personality disorders are said to be less treatable than other conditions. However, with a specific and full recovery program (1, 3, 8, 9), co-dependence is usually treatable. While recovery is generally slow and varies from person to person, when approached from the dynamic of co-dependence, the same person—who otherwise might have been diagnosed as having a personality disorder and therefore "less treatable"—would now have a greater chance for recovery—that is, a better prognosis. The latter would depend, of course, on whether the therapist had specific training and skills in treating co-dependence and its past trauma and in recognizing and treating (or referring) other major and treatable psychological disorders.

The disadvantages of classifying co-dependence as a distinct diagnostic entity include the possibility that it may cease to be recognized as a general and pervasive part of the painful side of the human condition (36) and thus as a focal point from which any number of patients can begin treatment. In addition, because it is as much a category as a distinct disorder, there is the potential that counselors and therapists may diagnose it alone and neglect or miss other important or treatable conditions.

Another concern is when co-dependence or co-dependent are used to describe a certain symptom, sign, behavior, or dynamic, when it would be more appropriate, accurate, or helpful to use a more precise word or phrase or a more elaborate description. This is one of the criticisms that some people make about these terms (34). There are other words in the mental health field that have been and are still being so misused, such as "schizophrenic," "depression," "borderline," and "stress."

SPIRITUAL ILLNESS

Spirituality is another way that understanding co-dependence assists in expanding and eventually transcending a more constricting psychology. Spirituality concerns relationship with our self, others, and the Universe (i.e., a Higher Power). Spirituality has certain characteristics, such as its being subtle, yet powerful, and thus paradoxical; personal, practical, and experiential; inclusive, supportive, and nurturing, yet also transcending the physical and psychological realms of human existence (1, 26).

People learn to heal the wounds of the true self out of the constriction felt from the co-dependent self. We learn and heal in three of our states of being: when we are alone (i.e., with our true self), with others (especially close and safe others), and with our Higher Power. These three states eventually merge as we heal.

William James described alcoholics as being "frustrated mystics." A mystic is someone who wants to experience everything fully, including nonordinary realms of awareness or consciousness and especially their relationship with God/Goddess/All-That-Is. Co-dependent people are also frustrated mystics. Thus, rather than being simply an *escape* from reality, co-dependence (e.g., compulsion, addiction, and co-addiction) is also a *search*. It starts out as a search for happiness and fulfillment *outside* one's self. After the repeated frustration of being unable to do so, it ultimately becomes a search for *inner* wholeness and completion.

One way to describe this spiritual journey is to use a model from a modern book of spiritual or transpersonal psychology, a modern holy book that

increasing numbers of recovering people are examining called *A Course in Miracles* (37). The book describes the co-dependent or addicted relationship (which it calls a "special relationship") by at least 10 characteristics. While the concept of the special relationship is complex and is spread throughout the course, here are 10 of its major characteristics.

Special (Co-dependent) Relationship

1. Denies the need for relationship with or assistance from Higher Power.
2. Is based on self-hate from guilt and shame.
3. Hides this shame and guilt under the guise of love of another.
4. Thus places the answer to our shame/guilt outside of us.
5. Assumes that something is lacking in us and that we need it to be happy.
6. Fixes expectations on the other (i.e., the special relationship). By so doing, it denies the other's true identity in a Higher Power (i.e., that they are a part of God).
7. Is based on the "scarcity principle," that there is only a limited amount of love to go around.
8. Becomes the focus of our anger and resentments.
9. Shifts responsibility for our happiness to the other (i.e., the special relationship). For example, "If only you were or would be such and such, then I would be happy."
10. The ego (false or co-dependent self) uses the special relationship for attacking the other by projecting our shame and guilt onto the other and thus promising salvation (i.e., happiness and fulfillment).

This concept can be used as an expanded description of co-dependence. These characteristics are related to some of the core issues of co-dependence, such as denial, control, difficulty trusting, low self-esteem, difficulty handling conflict, and difficulty giving and receiving love (1, 9).

The characteristics described in *A Course in Miracles* and in the writings of Wapnick (38) may sound discouraged and even hopeless. If most relationships are this way, how can relationships ever work? The course's answer to the special relationship is that *we do not have to control* more by being something we are not (e.g., by doing more, better or different, which the ego would want). Rather, all we need is a "little willingness" to open ourselves to the healing power of God, which it refers to as "the awareness of Love's presence," among other terms. When we do so, a miracle happens. We shift our perception, and we heal.

We simply shift our way of thinking. We change our mind about our mind. What results is a *process* that continues as the course's answer to the special relationship, which it calls the Holy Relationship. I summarize its characteristics as follows:

Holy (Healthy) Relationship

1. Based on my love of Higher Power and true self/Higher Self.
2. I see this love in everyone.
3. I take responsibility for my suffering by looking within myself.
4. I address and release my shame, guilt, hurt, anger, and resentment through the forgiveness process.
5. I realize that there is only abundance of Love, and that the scarcity principle is only an illusion.
6. I know that there is nothing lacking in me, that I am a perfect child of God, and that my natural state is Serenity.
7. I respect my positive ego (48) and use it as an assistant in my growth.
8. To facilitate this experience, I use daily spiritual practices.
9. I live and relate in the present moment, the Now.
10. In relationships I am open and communicating, trusting, gentle, peaceful, joyful, and celebrating.

These characteristics are those of a healthy relationship, which includes a balance of healthy dependence and healthy independence (1). They are compatible with 12-step programs and with the core teachings of the world's great religious systems, both eastern and western.

Ancient and modern spiritual teachers and literature say that to realize serenity, we first have to discover who we are. The second of the Twelve

Steps says "Came to believe that a Power greater than ourselves could restore us to sanity," wherein sanity means wholeness or completeness. By so doing, we become progressively more aware of *all* parts of our self (who we are), including our *lower self* (physical, mental, and emotional), our Heart (or acceptance through conflict) level—which is the hub of our true self and is the bridge to our Higher Self (intuition, creativity, compassion, and God consciousness). We thus have within each of us a divine part, which means that Higher Power is in us, and that we are in Higher Power. Christ said, "The Kingdom of Heaven is within." When we so discover our whole self, we then begin to forgive it and love it. When we have done so, we are free—we realize serenity (26, 37).

TREATMENT OF CO-DEPENDENCE

The First Step of the fellowship of Co-Dependents Anonymous reads, "We admitted we were powerless over others—that our lives had become unmanageable." To treat and heal the suffering and dysfunction of co-dependence, we first realize that we are *powerless* over others. We are powerless over their beliefs, thoughts, feelings, decisions, choices, and behavior. But we discover we are *powerful* over *ourselves,* our *own* beliefs, thoughts, feelings, decisions, choices, and behaviors. We begin to reclaim our personal power through a process of increasing *awareness* and by taking *responsibility* for our well-being and functioning. A formula to use is Power = Awareness plus Responsibility (1).

Since co-dependence is a disease of lost selfhood, we can increase our awareness and responsibility by beginning to heal our true self. To rediscover our true self and heal our child within, we can begin a *process* that involves the following four actions (8).

1. Discover and practice being our *real self* (21, 39, 40).
2. Identify our ongoing physical, mental, emotional, and spiritual *needs*. Practice *getting* these needs *met* with safe and supportive people (20).
3. Identify, reexperience, and *grieve* the pain of our *ungrieved losses* or traumas in the presence of safe and supporting people (39, 42).
4. Identify and work through our *core issues* (1, 8, 20, 43).

These actions are closely related, although not listed in any particular order. Working on them and thereby healing our true self generally occurs in a circular fashion, with work and discovery in one area a link to another area. Vehicles, techniques, or methods to assist us in this healing and recovery include:

1. Regular and long attendance at:
   a. *Self-help* groups, such as Co-Dependents Anonymous (CoDA), Al-Anon, and Adult Children Anonymous, Adult Children of Alcoholics, or Adult Children of Dysfunctional Families
   b. *Group therapy* that is specific for either co-dependence or adult children of dysfunctional families or trauma (this may take from 3 to 5 years or more of recovery work) (1, 8)
2. As needed:
   a. *"Detoxification"* or *detachment* from whatever person, place, thing, behavior, or experience that may otherwise block the work of recovery from co-dependence
   b. *Individual* psychotherapy or counseling
   c. Inpatient or other *intensive* recovery experiences
   d. *Educational* experiences about co-dependence
3. An *ongoing* support system, which may include:
   a. Any of 1(a), 1(b), or 2(b)
   b. *Journaling,* or keeping a personal diary
   c. *Regular contact and sharing* with one or more trusted and safe friends
   d. *Continuing, conscious contact* in a relationship with our Higher Power

All of the above work better if the person has first handled, through detoxification or detachment in some way, any active primary addictions or compulsions (i.e., stage-0 disorders) that may block ongoing recovery from co-dependence. Sedative-hypnotic drugs, benzodiazepine antianxiety agents, and tranquilizers usually worsen co-dependence and are generally contraindicated. Buspirone (Buspar) and some antidepressant drugs may be helpful in selected patients.

Self-help Groups

Self-help groups that are oriented to assist co-dependents and adult children in their recoveries include the fellowships of Al-Anon or Nar-Anon, adult children self-help groups, and Co-dependents Anonymous (CoDA). Each uses the universal Twelve Steps and Twelve Traditions borrowed from Alcoholics Anonymous as the basis for their recovery "program." Meetings are free of charge, last about 1 hour, and the size consists of from two people (rarely) to 50 or more. A secretary usually reads a preamble and introduction, then there is sharing of personal stories, experiences, strength, and hope. People usually do not use their last names and in this way the meetings are more anonymous.

"Cross talk" or direct feedback during the meeting is generally and wisely discouraged; this differs from group therapy, in which the therapeutic aid of *feedback* is facilitated by the two group leaders and by observations and the recovery experience of the other group members. These 12-step programs have many uses, including sharing, identifying, fellowship, and program structure, guidance, and work. Table 65.5 describes and compares some characteristics of all three self-help programs, as well as group therapy, individual therapy, short-term intensive therapeutic experiences, and workshops, conferences, and educational groups.

The co-dependent person, with or without the suggestion of the therapist, may make use of any or a combination of these three self-help groups. The general focus of Al-Anon or Nar-Anon is getting free of the unnecessary pain and suffering from living with or being close in a relationship with an alcoholic or other drug-dependent person. For adult children self-help groups the general focus is on recognizing and sharing experiences around family-of-origin issues and getting free of unnecessary pain and suffering concerning these. For Co-dependents Anonymous the general focus is on getting free of unnecessary pain and suffering in *any* relationship, whether it be past or current.

It is useful to acquire a *sponsor* (usually of the same gender) who has had more recovery time than the newly recovering person and with whom they feel comfortable and to use them as an assistant in working the Twelve Steps.

Group Therapy

Group therapy is a crucial hub around which a person can heal their co-dependence. If a person has "distracting co-dependence," a combination of individual psychotherapy (usually supportive and directive at first) and weekly, short-term group therapy (e.g., 6 months to 1 year) focused on the distracting features of their co-dependence is recommended. The purpose of these two is to stabilize their early recovery so that they can then begin to work without being so distracted on the major causes of their co-dependence, which are usually their adult child issues (1, 8, 9, 20). Regular attendance at a 12-step self-help group strengthens this stabilization.

Not everyone with co-dependence will need this stabilization. Perhaps 20% or less will need it; the remaining 80% can enter directly into a full recovery program for adult children of a dysfunctional family.

The hub of the recovery program for those 80% of co-dependents (and for the 20% with distracting co-dependence, once stabilized) is adult child, trauma-specific group therapy. Many therapists who assist co-dependents and adult children in their recoveries have found that, for a number of reasons, group therapy is a helpful treatment aid and probably the treatment of choice for these conditions. The adult child specific therapy group:

1. is safe. While at times the person may get some feedback that is uncomfortable, it is highly unlikely that they will be mistreated. The group generally follows principles of being safe.
2. is confidential. Names and any identifying details of members and what goes on in the group stays in the group.
3. re-creates many aspects of each member's family of origin and thus provides a vehicle to work through much unfinished business, such as painful emotional ties, conflicts, and struggles (i.e., transference or projections) associated with their family of origin and past trauma.

Table 65.5 Characteristics of Recovery Methods for Adult Children of Dysfunctional Families and for Co-dependents

	Al-Anon	ACA Self-help	Co-Dependents Anonymous	Group Therapy (Interactional)	Individual Psychotherapy	Short-Term Intensive Treatment	Workshops, Conferences and Educational Groups	No Recovery Program
Potential for personal growth	1–2	2	2–3	1–4	1–3	2–3	1	0–1
Meeting size	2–100	2–100	2–100	7–10	2	10–30	Small to large	0
Length of meeting	1 hour	1 hour	1 hour	1¼–2 hours	30–50 minutes	Multiple and vary	Varies	0
Consistency of attendance by others	1–3	1–2	1–3	3–4	4	4 (short term only)	Varies	0
Frequency of meeting	Daily possible	Weekly to daily possible	Weekly or more	Weekly	As scheduled	Daily short term	Short term	0
Professional therapists	0	0	0	Yes	Yes	Yes	Varies	0
Supervision in overall recovery	1–2	1–2	1–2	3–4	1–3	2–3	0–1	0
Fee	0	0	0	Yes	Yes	Yes	Yes	0
Depth of shared feelings	1–2	2–3	2–3	2–4	1–4	2–4	0–2	0–1
Level of intimacy	1–2	1–3	1–3	2–4	1–3	2–4	1–2	0–1
Confidentiality	1–3	1–3	1–3	3–4	4	3–4	0–1	0–4
Healthy family modeled	1–2	1–3	1–3	3–4	1–2	3	1–2	0
Feedback	0–1	0–1	0–1	2–4	1–4	2–4	1–2	0
Suggested duration of attendance	Long term	Long term	Long term	3–5 years	As needed	Short-/long-term program needed	Short term	0
Commitment to attend	0	0	0	Long term	Varies	Yes	Varies	0
Availability of long-term support	As available	As available	As available	Yes	As scheduled	0	0	0
Comments: For guidelines on recovery, see Gravitz and Bowden (25), Whitfield (8, 9), Subby (2). Most experts agree that **group therapy** is the treatment of choice for adult children and for co-dependent people, supplemented by other methods shown here.	Focus: Relationships with alcoholics; teaches detachment and self-awareness	Focus: Family-of-origin work. Awareness and expression of feelings.	Focus: Relationships past and current and awareness of self.	Co-leaders' specific experience and personal recovery is important.	Specific experience and personal recovery of the therapist is crucial. Ask around and test your intuition and personal growth in the therapy.	Varies from residential 5–30 days to weekends to "reconstruction." Long-term recovery program is up to the individual and may be weak. Can be dangerous if used alone.	Useful for awakening and general information. Supplements other recovery methods. Frustrating if used alone long term.	Depends on individual. Full recovery rare, if ever. Can enter any recovery method at any time.

or

Useful for sharing, identifying, program structure and fellowship. Advice from others varies from excellent to poor. Get a sponsor. Work the program. Integrate these self-help group experiences with other methods as described here and elsewhere (see column to left), especially group therapy.

Reproduced with permission from Whitfield CL. A gift to myself: A personal workbook and guide to healing my child within. Deerfield Beach, FL: Health Communications, 1990.
Legend: 0, none; *1,* minimal or some; *4,* maximal or most.

---

4. provides each member with several "therapists," instead of just one, as in individual therapy.

5. models recovery in various stages. Especially motivating and healing is the ability to see people in beginning, middle, and sometimes advanced stages of recovery. Many make definitive and at times dramatic positive changes in their lives and in healing their true self.

6. with appropriately trained and skilled group leaders, the group is able to work on specific life issues that span the range of physical, mental, emotional, and spiritual recovery. Two co-leaders who are not only trained and skilled in group therapy, but who are advanced in healing their own wounds, work well in this situation.

7. provides supervision and guidance in overall adult child and co-dependence recovery and healing.

8. provides a safe place to use many of the experiential techniques described in the literature (9, 44).

9. provides the well-known advantages of group therapy in general, such as

the ability to obtain identification, validation, feedback, appropriate healing confrontation, support, and the many other useful factors and dynamics in group therapy.

The ideal size for such a therapy group is about eight or nine people. The weekly fees vary—ranging from a sliding scale based on the person's income or ability to pay (found usually only in a few funded agencies) to fees that are in keeping with community standards (most groups). Just like each individual group member, each group has its own individual personality.

Developing Recovery Goals

A useful tool in recovery is making and using specific goals and objectives. Each group member can be encouraged to establish recovery goals, which are updated every few months and are specific for their own needs and recovery. Some overall goals and guidelines for adult children and co-dependent people (1, 9) are listed in this section.

LONG-TERM RECOVERY GOALS FOR CO-DEPENDENTS AND ADULT CHILDREN

Self-Awareness

1. Discover, develop, and accept my personal and individual identity as separate from spouse or partner, parental or other authority figure, children, and institutions.
2. Identify my ongoing needs (physical, mental, emotional, and spiritual).

Self-Acceptance

3. Practice getting these needs met on my own and with safe people in healthy relationships.
4. Identify, trust, and process my internal cues (feelings, sensations, and experience from my inner life). If not comfortable, check my responses with someone I trust.
5. Assess my feelings, upsets, conflicts, and similar situations and handle them in a healthy way (alone, with safe others, and if I choose, with my Higher Power).
6. Learn to accept myself as an individual and unique child of God, with strengths and weaknesses.
7. Learn to like myself and eventually to love myself, as my Higher Power loves me.

Self-Responsibility

8. Identify, reexperience, and grieve the pain of my ungrieved losses, hurts, or mistreatment alone and with safe others.
9. Identify and work through my major core recovery issues.
10. Grieve the loss of my childhood while in group therapy (for adult children).
11. Develop and use an ongoing support system (at least three supports).

Self-Reflection

12. There is no hurry for me to accomplish these goals right away. I can take my time.
13. I don't have to reach every goal perfectly.
14. I do not have to work on these goals in exactly this order.
15. From these above goals I will—in my own time—make more specific and more personal goals for myself during my recovery.
16. I can accomplish these goals through techniques such as risking and telling my story to safe people, through prayer and meditation, keeping a journal and other experiential techniques.
17. When I use the above, I am caring for and healing my true self.

A person in recovery should be encouraged to begin thinking about specific problems or conditions in their life that they would like to improve or change. From listing these problems or conditions, they can create specific personal goals, or what they want to happen. And from these specific goals, they create a specific plan or method of just how they will reach these goals (9). The author finds these instructions helpful to patients at this stage: "It will be helpful now for you to share these goals with your therapist or group and ask them to support you as you work through them. You can also ask for feedback and suggestions. Keep a copy of your recovery plan handy and read it carefully every week or so. Every 3 or 4 months it is useful to review your plan and add to, subtract from, or change it in any way that you choose. Then review it with your group or therapist. It is especially healing to tell your group and/or your individual therapist, if you choose, about everything that comes up for you around all of this."

The recommended duration for assisting people in the complete healing of the co-dependence/adult child syndrome in group therapy is a minimum of about 3–5 years. The use of recovery goals helps speed the healing process and gives the patient, therapists, and group some useful markers as to when group therapy termination may be appropriate.

Other Group Experiences

Another tool is educational group experience. This may consist of several sessions in which didactic material on co-dependence or the adult child syndrome is presented by a therapist, counselor, or teacher. It may also include some experiential exercises and some brief group interactions. While these are not meant to be formal group therapy and while, alone, they are not sufficient to reach a complete recovery, they can be helpful in cognitive learning and in beginning to learn to heal with others, which can be of some assistance in recovery.

Individual Psychotherapy

Some indications for individual psychotherapy include:

- More time is needed for recovery work than the time available in group therapy.
- The person has issues to work on that they do not yet feel comfortable talking about in group therapy. For example, sexual issues, incest, extremely embarrassing issues, and the like.
- The person feels somehow blocked in group therapy and wants to explore that outside, as well as inside, the group.
- The person has a major psychological disorder that needs ongoing individual therapy.
- The person just wants to work on their recovery in individual therapy.

The individual therapist should speak frequently (ideally, at least every 3 or 4 months) with the patient's therapy group leader to share such information as the patient's needs, goals, and dynamics.

Intensive Residential or Weekend Experiences

Another recovery tool is intensive weekend or longer residential experiences. These can be helpful in several circumstances, including when the patient:

- has difficulty working and growing in adult child specific outpatient treatment, which ideally includes group therapy.
- has continued difficulty in identifying and expressing feelings in an adult child, trauma-specific recovery program.
- has worked well and grew initially and is now in a prolonged lull.
- has persistent minimizing or denying of family-of-origin issues.
- needs some more time to work than is available in group.
- is motivated and wants to have an intensive residential experience.
- has experienced a marked dysfunction or crisis that cannot be managed by adult child specific outpatient treatment. (Some people who are especially dysfunctional may benefit for up to 30 days or longer in a hospital or residential facility that uses an adult child, co-dependence, or trauma recovery focus. Some health insurance plans may pay for part or most of this treatment.)

CONCLUSION

Recovery from co-dependence, which is essentially the same as the adult child syndrome, is neither easy nor short. For most people, it takes a minimum of 3–5 years of a full recovery program. We have much to learn and to enjoy in our lives. Co-dependence and recovery from trauma can be our teachers.

References

1. Whitfield CL. Co-dependence: Healing the human condition—The new paradigm for helping professionals and people in recovery. Deerfield Beach, FL: Health Communications, 1991.
2. Subby R. Lost in the shuffle: the co-dependent reality. Deerfield Beach, FL: Health Communications, 1987.
3. Cermak TL. Diagnosing and treating co-dependence: A guide for professionals who work with chemical dependents, their spouses, and children. Minneapolis, MN: Johnson Institute, 1986.
4. Mendenhall W. Course on co-dependence. New Brunswick, NJ: Rutgers Summer School of Alcohol Studies, June 1987–1994.
5. Friel JC, Friel LD. Adult children: the secrets of

dysfunctional families. Deerfield Beach, FL: Health Communications, 1988.

6. Mellody P, et al. Facing codependence. San Francisco: Harper & Row, 1989.

7. *US Journal* preconference forum on co-dependence. Scottsdale, AZ, 1989.

8. Whitfield CL. Healing the child within: discovery and recovery for adult children of dysfunctional families. Deerfield Beach, FL: Health Communications, 1987.

9. Whitfield CL. A gift to myself: A personal workbook and guide to healing my child within. Deerfield Beach, FL: Health Communications , 1990. (Individual recovery plan booklets are available from 1-800-851–9100; ask for My Recovery Plan for Stage 2 recovery)

10. Johnson VE. I'll quit tomorrow. New York: Harper & Row, 1973.

11. Gravitz HL. Personal communication. October, 1990.

12. Kitchens JA. Understanding and treating co-dependence. Englewood Cliffs, NJ: Prentice-Hall, 1991.

13. Friel JC. Co-dependency assessment inventory: a preliminary research tool. Focus Family Chem Depend 1985;8:20–21.

14. Wright PH, Wright KD. Measuring co-dependents' close relationships: a preliminary study. J Subst Abuse 1990;2:335–344.

15. Kritsberg W. Am I in a co-dependent relationship? [booklet]. Deerfield Beach, FL: Health Communications, 1988, 1989.

16. Tony A, Dan F. The laundry list: the ACoA experience. Deerfield Beach, FL: Health Communications, 1990.

17. Black C. Double duty. New York: Ballantine, 1990.

18. Co-dependents Anonymous. Characteristics [brochure]. Phoenix, AZ: Co-dependents Anonymous, 1989.

19. Guntrip H. Psychoanalytical theory, therapy and the self: A basic guide to the human personality in Freud, Erickson, Klein, Sullivan, Fairbairn, Hartman, Jacobsen, and Winnicott. New York: Basic Books, 1973.

20. Brown S. Treating adult children of alcoholics: a developmental perspective. New York: John Wiley and Sons, 1988.

21. Kohut H. The analysis of the self. New York: International University Press, 1971.

22. Wood BL. Children of alcoholism: the struggle for self and intimacy in adult life. New York: New York University Press, 1987.

23. Whitfield CL. Co-alcoholism: recognizing a treatable illness. Family Commun Health 1984;7.

24. Whitfield CL. Boundaries and relationships: knowing, protecting and enjoying the self. Health Communications, Deerfield Beach, FL, 1993.

25. Gravitz HL, Bowden JD. Therapeutic issues of adult children of alcoholics. Alcohol Health Res World 1984;8(4):25–36.

26. Whitfield CL. Spirituality in recovery (formerly alcoholism and spirituality). Rutherford, NJ: Perrin & Treggett E. Rutherford, 1985 (800-321-7912).

27. Wegscheider S. Another chance: hope and health for the alcoholic family. Palo Alto, CA: Science and Behavior Books, 1981.

28. Dossey L. Beyond illness: discovering the experience of health. Boulder, CO: Shambhala, 1985.

29. Siegel BS. Love, medicine, and miracles: lessons learned about self-healing from a surgeon's experience with exceptional patients. New York: Harper & Row, 1986.

30. Pennebaker JW, et al. Disclosure of traumas and immune functions: health implications for psychotherapy. J Consult Clin Psychol 1988;56: 239–245.

31. Pennebaker JW. Opening up: the healing power of confiding in others. New York: Morrow Publishers, 1990.

32. Simos BG. A time to grieve: loss as a universal human experience. New York: Family Services Association of America, 1979.

33. Simonton OC, Matthews-Simonton S, Creighton J. Getting well again: a step-by-step, self-help guide to overcoming cancer for patients and

their families. New York: St. Martin's Books, 1978.

34. Wolin SJ, ed. Proceedings of National Working Conference on Co-dependence and the Adult Child Syndrome. Washington, DC: American Society of Addiction Medicine, 1992.

35. American Psychiatric Association. Diagnostic and statistical manual of mental disorders. 3rd edition. Washington, DC: American Psychiatric Press, 1987.

36. Schaef AW. Co-dependence. Misunderstood, mistreated. San Francisco: Harper/Winston, 1986.

37. A course in miracles. Tiburon, CA: Foundation for Inner Peace, 1976.

38. Wapnick K. Christian psychology in A Course in Miracles. Tiburon, CA: Foundation for Inner Peace, 1979.

39. Winnicott DW. The capacity to be alone. Int J Psychiatry 1958;39:416–440.

40. Horney K. Neurosis and human growth. New York: WW Norton, 1950.

41. Deleted in proof.

42. Bowlby J. Attachment and loss. Vol. I. Attachment. London: Hogarth, 1969.

43. Gravitz HL, Bowden JD. Guide to recovery: a book for adult children of alcoholics. New York: Simon & Schuster, 1985.

44. Vannicelli M. Group psychotherapy with adult children of alcoholics. In: Seligman M, Marshall LA, eds. Group psychotherapy: interventions with special populations. New York: Grune & Stratton, 1990.

45. Whitfield CL. Memory and abuse: remembering and healing the effects of trauma. Deerfield Beach, FL: Health Communications, 1995.

46. Horney K. The neurotic personality of our time. New York: WW Norton, 1952.

47. Babcock M, McKay C. Challenging codependency: feminist critiques. Toronto: University of Toronto Press, 1995.

48. Lazaris. Releasing negative ego and the crisis of martyrhood [taped talks]. Palm Beach, FL: Concept Synergy, 1986 (800-678-2356).

66 ADOLESCENTS

Sharon Hird, Elizabeth T. Khuri, Linda Dusenbury, and Robert B. Millman

The greatest risk for initiating substance abuse in the United States occurs during the late teenage years and early 20s (1). Many adolescents succumb to substance abuse, yielding an estimated 3 million adolescent problem drinkers in this country (2), 20% of the total problem drinkers (3), and 400,000 adolescents in need of substance abuse treatment (4). This data coupled with the anticipation that the year 2010 will have the largest numbers of teenagers recorded in history (5) demonstrates a clear need to improve our understanding of the phenomenon, and to provide effective prevention and treatment. Adolescents have unique treatment needs because of their stage of development (6). We cannot necessarily apply concepts used in adult models with the anticipation that they will yield desired results. As background, this chapter provides an examination of the developmental stage of adolescence, the characteristics of adolescent substance use, the progression of substance use behavior, and a theoretical orientation for conceptualizing the problem of adolescent substance abuse. The second part of this chapter examines approaches to prevention, assessment and treatments available for adolescent substance abusers; the problem of relapse is also addressed. In conclusion, recommendations are made for the treatment of the adolescent substance abuse and for considering the problem of adolescent substance more generally.

ADOLESCENCE

The developmental stage of adolescence is characterized by dramatic change and readjustment (7), which results in new stresses and anxieties and may increase vulnerability to peer pressure. In terms of intrapsychic development, it is a time of consolidating an identity (8) and practicing new roles. From early childhood, youngsters practice adult roles through pretend play (e.g., dressing up or playing house). But during adolescence, this practice of adult roles and behaviors shifts from pretend play to actual behavior. After 10 years of age the preadolescent begins experimenting with a range of new behaviors, and for many, regardless of culture or locale, cigarettes, alcohol, and other drugs have become a normal part of coming of age (8, 9).

Socially, adolescence is marked by increasing autonomy from parents and a corresponding increase in reliance on peers for validation and direction (10). Conformity to the peer group increases rapidly to its peak in pre- and early adolescence; it then gradually declines. Adolescents assess themselves and their behaviors through the reactions of their peers. Peers are vital to the teenager's emotional and psychological development, and acceptance by peers is critically important; more than at any other age, rejection can be devastating (7).

Puberty is characterized by striking and rapid physical changes, which can often produce a disruption of self-image and self-esteem. Moreover, these changes accompany an increasing interest in boy-girl relationships and a resultant changed status of peer group members.

Adolescence also involves a number of cognitive changes (11, 12). The final stage of intellectual development is reached during early adolescence when the adolescent shifts from concrete operational thinking to formal operational or abstract thinking, which is much more flexible (13). The adolescent is able to think hypothetically, and for the first time in development the young person can appreciate literary metaphors and is capable of complex mathematical operations. The younger child is more anchored in concrete reality and in what is immediately available to perception. When presented with a problem, the child will begin directly trying to solve the problem before considering all the possibilities. Given more sophisticated reasoning capabilities, the adolescent is able to consider many possibilities and can deal with proposition and theory. While remarkable and exciting, these cognitive shifts also can result in new tensions between adolescents and authority figures and institutions. Adolescents are able to begin questioning rules that had previously been taken for granted, and novel and alternative lifestyles are considered or experienced (7).

Thought becomes introspective during adolescence, but it remains egocentric relative to adults. Specifically, adolescents have developed to the point that they understand that other people have lives independent of them and that other people have internal thoughts of their own. But adolescents have more difficulty separating their own thoughts from the thoughts of others, and they often assume that others are as preoccupied with their behavior as they themselves are; their "imaginary audience" may help to explain the excruciating level of self-consciousness frequently observed in adolescents (8, 14).

Risk taking increases during adolescence, and while exploring any new behavior or role involves risk taking, adolescents also appear to engage in risk taking just for the exhilaration of the dare (15). Sensation seeking and risk taking appear to be related to hormone levels, particularly testosterone, and it may be that some risk taking is the result of the surging, poorly modulated hormones of puberty. In addition, however, cognitive changes may also contribute to increased risk taking. Adolescents want to impress their peers, but they are not yet adept at assessing risks. Hamburg (16) observes that adolescents frequently assume that, if they engage in a behavior several times without negative consequences, the perceived risk goes down. For example, if they have unprotected sex without getting pregnant, the chances of negative consequences diminish (9). There is also a tendency among adolescents to exaggerate based on immediate experience, which allows risks to be minimized. Finally, adolescents have a sense of invulnerability—an attitude of "it won't happen to me" (17, 18).

Adolescents may actually be making risk assessments, however. Adolescent thought is more anchored in the "here and now" than is adult thought, so that they are less concerned with the far off future. Given their immediate time orientation, immediate consequences may outweigh longer term risks. With smoking, for example, the potential long-term negative health consequences may seem less important than the short-term effects, which may actually be satisfying and pleasurable, fulfilling the adolescent's immediate needs. Also, some risks may have more salience than others. The norms of the peer group have a very strong influence over the individual adolescent, and affiliation with and acceptance by peers is paramount during this period. Thus, the risk of losing status with peers, being rejected or ridiculed, or of appearing immature or inexperienced may seem more dangerous or aversive than the possible risks of taking a drink or smoking a joint.

The general tasks of adolescence include adjusting to the physical changes of puberty, gaining independence from parents, establishing relationships with peers, and preparing for work (7). While these tasks are normal, they are also difficult and challenging (18). Struggling to cope with them can result in strong feelings of powerlessness, alienation, and rebellion. To accomplish these developmental tasks, the adolescent must develop a philosophy of life, including personal values, as well as a sense of meaning or purpose. Thus, adolescence is the most idealistic phase of development, a period when everything seems to be possible. Since it is also a time when health habits and future behaviors are still being formed and when many of the lifetime strategies for coping with stress and peer pressure are developed (19), adolescence is an important window of opportunity for intervention and prevention.

ADOLESCENT SUBSTANCE USE AND ABUSE

Because of the rapid changes they are experiencing, adolescents are at risk for developing substance abuse more quickly than adults (17, 20). The initiation of substance use and early stages of abuse have their roots in adolescence (21). Examining tobacco use alone, 85% of current smokers began smoking by the age of 21, and approximately 3000 children a day start using tobacco (22). Much evidence supports the theory that tobacco use is a gateway to alcohol and illicit drug use and abuse. The exact point along the use-abuse continuum at which use becomes abuse is arbitrary and may differ for subgroups. Psychiatric criteria established for defining abuse and dependence has largely grown out of studying adults. The DSM-IV criteria for abuse includes a substance use pattern that results in impaired function at work, school, home, or in relationships with continued use despite having these impairments, recurrent use in dangerous situations, and continued use despite negative consequences (23). Many experts believe that waiting to intervene until adolescents meet criteria would be irresponsible (20). DSM-IV criteria for substance dependence includes tolerance (need for increased amount to achieve desired effect; diminished effect with continued use of the same amount of substance) and withdrawal (a characteristic syndrome of withdrawal for the substance; taking the substance to avoid withdrawal) (23). As applied to adolescents, research supports the utility of DSM-IV construct of dependence, but that tolerance, withdrawal, and medical problems present differently in the adolescent population than in adult populations, suggesting limitations in the criteria for DSM-IV in adolescence (24).

Epidemiology

To a large extent, information about adolescent substance abuse is derived from the annual Monitoring the Future survey (25) which from 1975 to 1990 sampled over 15,000 high school seniors in 135 public and private schools across the country each year. In 1991, the survey expanded to include 8th and 10th grade students of similar sample size as the seniors. The study monitors prevalence, trends, and attitudes of substance use in this population. Although it is an invaluable resource, the study has been criticized for missing data on students who have dropped out and who were absent on the day of survey administration. In 8th, 10th, and 12th grades there is an absenteeism rate of 11%, 12% and 16%, respectively, and seniors have a 16% dropout rate. Investigators attached to the survey say that with the exception of heroin, crack, and PCP statistics, the influence of dropout and absence on day of administration rates does not significantly affect prevalence. Another debated weakness of the Monitoring the Future survey is that the data are collected from retrospective self-reports, which may result in under reporting since most drug use is illicit or disapproved of by teachers, parents, and peers (26). There are data, however, to support the validity of self-reporting in the adolescent population. Other sources of data on adolescent substance use include DAWN (emergency room reports), regional school studies, studies on treatment programs, arrest and death rates, and national household surveys.

The 1994 Monitoring the Future survey reports a lifetime prevalence of *any* illicit drug use for 8th graders to be 26%, 10th graders 37%, and high school seniors 46%. Marihuana and inhalant use are important contributors and significantly increase the prevalence. In general, a higher proportion of males than females are involved in illicit and licit drug use; overall, illicit drug use is similar among the United States regions for use in the past year as reported by seniors (Northeast 39%, North Central 37%, West 35%, and South 34%). For virtually all drugs, licit and illicit, African-American students have a lower reported lifetime and annual prevalence than those for whites and Hispanics; and Hispanics have the highest lifetime and annual prevalence rates for cocaine and crack. Trends in specific drug use will be addressed later in this chapter. Trends in perceived harmfulness, which may parallel or influence drug use and help predict upcoming use, show some important shifts. Perceived harmfulness of amphetamines and barbiturates used on a regular basis had been steady between 1975 and 1994 when perceived harmfulness began a downward trend. This holds true for LSD, which had steady rates until 1991 and then began a downward trend for views on regular use, and in 1992 for use of LSD once or twice. Perceived harmfulness of heroin use regularly and occasionally have remained steady, but showed more fluctuation of perceived harmfulness for use once or twice. Alcohol is perceived harmful with consistency at the 4–5 drinks/day and 5 or more drinks 1–2 times per weekend level, but perceived harmfulness of 1–2 drinks nearly every day reached its highest level between 1990 and 1991 and then began to decline, and trying 1–2 drinks have remained steady, but low, with 10% or less of students perceiving this type of use to be harmful. Smoking one or more packs of cigarettes per day significantly increased in perceived harmfulness between 1990 and present. Perhaps of equal importance is perceived availability of drugs, especially illicit drugs: the percentage of students stating that it is easy to obtain cocaine peaked in 1988; marihuana perceived availability has remained constant with 90% stating that it is easy to obtain; LSD shows a steady and dramatic rise in perceived availability from 1986 to 1994; and heroin shows an all-time high since 1975 with approximately 30% students believing that it is easy to get, starting in 1992. These trends in perceived availability may be important when evaluating peer pressure and assumed normative adolescent drug use by adolescents ("everyone smokes marihuana"). As already stated, drug use and potential abuse may be initiated prior to adolescence. This is supported by reports given by 8th grade students delineating 4th grade being the grade at which they first used many substances: alcohol 8.9%, cigarettes 9.5%, inhalants 4.1%, and marihuana 1.1%.

Tobacco use is associated with more than 400,000 deaths each year, which is more than alcohol, cocaine, heroin, homicide, suicide, car accidents, firearms, and AIDS combined; nearly 3 million teenagers and children smoke cigarettes (22). Much has been written about "gateway" drugs, and many consider tobacco a gateway drug to illicit substance abuse (22, 27–29). This may be particularly true for certain populations. A recent investigation looking at tobacco use in San Diego Hispanic junior high school students (30) found that in 7th to 9th grade, smoking change is highly predictive of subsequent alcohol use. Despite restrictions on sale of cigarettes to minors and aggressive campaigns to dissuade people from smoking, adolescents have access to and continue to use cigarettes. The daily prevalence of smoking half a pack or more of cigarettes are 4% of 8th graders, 8% of 10th graders, and 11% of high school seniors surveyed (25). In 1976 and 1977 a peak 30-day prevalence for smoking was reached at 38% then declined through 1981, halting until 1984 when use declined again; there was very little change between 1984 and 1992, but in 1993 both the 30-day and daily prevalence rate rose significantly (a 2.1 and 1.8 percentage point rise, respectively), and rose again in 1994. It is not clear whether this represents a decline in effectiveness of campaigns against smoking, an increase in effectiveness of marketing cigarettes to adolescents, or a change in availability.

Alcohol use by adolescents has changed very little over time and, in fact, has persisted as the number one drug problem (3). In addition to alcohol's known contribution to premature adolescent mortality through a variety of routes, there are reports of recent alcohol consumption associated with an increase of adolescents carrying a weapon for both males and females (31) and a positive association between alcohol use and sexually transmitted diseases in adolescent females (32). Reported daily use of alcohol in 8th graders is 1%, 1.7% for 10th graders, and 2.9% for high school seniors. Eighty percent of 12th grade students have tried alcohol by the time they reach this grade, 50% report using alcohol within a month of the Monitoring the Future survey, 12% report having 5 or more drinks in a row within 2 weeks of the survey, and 60% report using alcohol to the point of inebriation (25). The age of initiation of drinking has declined over the past 30 years (2). Many attribute the consistency of alcohol use to the rapid onset of affective change provided by alcohol, as well as the positive associations to role models.

Marihuana is the most frequently used illicit substance. It is potentially debilitating to adolescents because it can suppress motivation ("aberrant motivational syndrome" or "chronic cannabis syndrome") and lead to decline in academic performance, which can in turn lead to increased marihuana use to cope with anxiety about poor performance. The daily prevalence for marihuana use in high school seniors is 3.6%, 2.2% in 10th grade students, and 0.7% in 8th graders. Daily use in 1975 for 12th grade students was 6% with a rise to 11% in 1978, leveling in 1979 followed by a decline in use dropping to 1.9% in 1992; 1993 saw the first significant increase in use to 2.4%, and again in 1994 to 3.6%, which represents the highest rate since 1986.

Cocaine and especially *crack,* the smokeable from of cocaine, is one of the most reinforcing substances (26, 33). Its use peaked in the 1980s, and in 1987 and 1988, according to self-reports by students, began to decline to less than 2% reporting use in the previous month from 6.7% in 1985. The 1994 use in previous month reflects the same (1.5%, which is slightly up from 1.3% in 1992). Crack use appears to be following a similar downward trend: between 1986 and 1991 the annual prevalence declined from 4.1% to 1.5% but is starting to inch up again in 1994 after having been relatively stable. The decline in use can be attributed to increased perception of harmfulness by students, or more likely the school dropout rate associated with crack use. According to some experts, the statistical decline of crack use is not reflective of the problem in the adolescent population. They cite an increase in inner city use of cocaine and crack, an increase of violent crimes and arrests associated with its use, an increase of cocaine or crack–related emergency room visits and neonates testing positive for cocaine, and a decrease in the price of the substance (26).

Heroin shows a negative association with age, with 8th grade students reporting a higher lifetime prevalence (2%) than 10th grade (1.5%), or 12th grade students (1.2%). Trends of use showed a steady decline from 1975 (2.2% lifetime prevalence of high school seniors) to 1979 (1.1%), with the decline halting and statistics remaining constant to date. Again, this may reflect a higher dropout rate associated with heroin users with these adolescents unavailable at survey. It is important to consider international statistics on heroin use and production, as well as the natural history of epidemics before making conclusions about heroin use in the United States. The first heroin epidemic in the United States began after World War II with the highest incidence occurring in the late 1940s and early 1950s; the second epidemic began in the 1960s with peak incidence between 1971 and 1977 (34). As the purity of heroin began to decline and the prices to increase, the spread of heroin use slowed (34). However, there are concerns that spread of use will increase again due to introduction of high quality-low cost heroin, increased production of heroin by well-established cocaine distributors in South America, the increase in annual worldwide amount of heroin seized, and the increase in use trends in Europe (34).

Hallucinogens, especially LSD, are showing a renewed popularity among adolescents. From 1975 to 1984 use steadily declined, leveled through 1986, and again declined through 1988, leveling through 1992. In 1993 the United States experienced an increase in annual prevalence from 6.2% to 7.8% where it remains for 1994. LSD is one of the least expensive, longest-lasting highs available to adolescents, easy to carry and conceal, difficult to detect in urine toxicology, difficult to detect use by objective findings (expect for perhaps mydriasis, caused by anticholinergic effect), and has appeal to the stage of adolescent development that involves self-exploration and intellectual expansion (35). Fewer high school students perceive LSD as harmful when trying it once or twice. The 1990s may be in an LSD use cycle similar to the 1960s.

Other substances that are used with some frequency by high school and college students include amphetamines, tranquilizers, barbiturates, anabolic steroids, ketamine (Special K), Ecstasy, and new drugs including gamma hydroxybutyrate (GHB). GHB, a dopamine enhancer, has infiltrated the clubs and inner circles of the modeling industry. It is illegal in the United States, but used in Europe (especially Italy) to treat narcolepsy and alcohol abstinence syndrome. Recreationally, it causes a euphoria; in overdose it can cause electrolyte imbalance, decreased respiration, bradycardia, vomiting, hypotension, seizure-like activity, confusion, delirium, and death (Hird and Millman, unpublished data).

It seems that as use declines in one category of mood-altering substance there is a natural homeostasis to replace it with another. There is also a cyclical nature to use and an enculturation of substance use that supports the theory that some experimentation is normative. Prevention and treatment have to target these trends and at the very least stay abreast if not ahead of them.

Substance Use Progression

Substance abuse follows a fairly predictable developmental progression (27, 28) that begins with experimentation and recreational use of alcohol and cigarettes. Generally, cigarette use is sequentially followed by alcohol, marihuana, and other illicit drugs (22), especially cocaine or crack in the inner city population. The risk of using other illicit drugs is low without prior use of marihuana (29), perhaps with the exclusion of inhalants, which may be viewed as a "gateway" to other use. After initiation to drug use with a gateway substance individuals might progress to other illicit drugs such as opiates and hallucinogens. There may, however, be a distinct subgroup of adolescents who are vulnerable to early and rapid escalation of substance use progression.

During the stage of experimentation and recreational use, substances are associated with euphoria and pleasure and are not perceived to cause harm or have dangerous consequences. As use becomes more regular, a tolerance for the substance develops, a preoccupation with obtaining and using the substance ensues, and the individual may progress to daily use. It is at this stage that polysubstance use may begin. Functioning begins to decline and the reason for using the substance shifts; rather than using the substance for pleasure, the individual now uses the substance to alleviate and prevent negative affect. The prevention of withdrawal, either physical or psychological, becomes a focus of substance use, and attempts to discontinue use at this stage results in an abstinence syndrome.

Although we can predict a sequence of progression, it does not mean there is a causal relationship, and use of substances at one stage does not necessarily mean progression to another stage (29). Escalation of use is believed to occur from usage in 7th to 9th grade with a combination of factors associated with a high risk of occurrence: greater life stress, lower parental support, more parental substance abuse, maladaptive coping skills, low self-control ability, and a greater affiliation with substance-using peers (36). Experimentation with substances has become so prevalent and normative that some suggest that experimentation may represent psychologically healthier adolescents compared to those who have never experimented (37). This belief may be age related, with experimentation in later adolescence being more developmentally normative than experimentation in early or middle adolescence (36).

Risk for substance use (legal and illicit) peaks between 18 and 22 years of age, with the exception of cocaine use. There appears to be a decline of substance use, excluding cocaine and prescription psychoactive substances, after the age of 25. An explanation for this decline may be that conventional adult roles in marriage, family, and career are being assumed during this stage (38). Individuals who begin using substances before the age of 15 are at the greatest risk of developing long-lasting patterns of abuse and dependence (36, 39).

Risk Factors

In the medical model, the identification of risk factors leads to improved techniques in prevention and more efficacious treatments. In the adolescent substance-using population there is a complex multiplicity of risk factors that are not necessarily consistent across stages of development, ethnic subgroups, and determinants that are biological, psychiatric, behavioral, social, and perhaps even substance category-specific. This makes investigation of correlates and predictors of substance use both challenging and exciting. As with vulnerability to any disease, different combinations of risk factors and different pathways may all result in substance use (4). As the number of risk factors increase, so does the frequency and extent of substance use and abuse (40). It remains impossible to predict precisely how these risk factors may interact in an individual to produce a serious substance use problem. In fact, what is documented to be a risk factor in one group may act as a protective factor in another. Risk factors can be grouped into five general categories:

cognitive and attitudinal; personality; behavioral, social and environmental; and biologic or genetic (6, 27, 41–45).

COGNITIVE AND ATTITUDINAL

Adolescents who use substances are less likely to be aware of the negative consequences of use, have less negative attitudes about substances, and believe that substance use is normative (4, 46–48).

PERSONALITY

Personality characteristics that have been linked to substance use include low assertiveness (49), low self-efficacy or self-esteem, low self-confidence, low social confidence, and external locus of control (4, 50–53); additional characteristic include aggressiveness, unconventionality, problems with interpersonal relatedness, and precocious sexuality (54). A recent study discusses sensation seeking as a personality disposition, which can be measured in children between the ages of 6 and 9; this trait is consistent, and the underlying mechanism can influence adolescent risk-taking behaviors such as substance abuse (55). A recent longitudinal study looked at 6-year-old boys' individual characteristics and found an early onset disruptive behavior pattern was pivotal in the development of substance use (56). Additionally, substance users tend to be more anxious, impulsive, and rebellious; they are more impatient to appear grown up, and have a stronger need for approval (4, 42, 43, 57). They also tend to be more pessimistic (58) and to be more alienated from social values (4).

When discussing personality variables associated with substance use it is important to note that, despite contradictory findings, no data from prospective studies have clearly identified personality patterns specific to substance abusers, and there is no evidence of an "addictive personality type" (59–61). In addition, substance abuse is frequently associated with psychopathology. Several recent studies link psychiatric comorbidity with substance abuse. One study examined 165 adolescent psychiatric inpatients (62): findings suggest that conduct disorders and substance abuse disorders have a high comorbidity with other psychiatric disorders in this population; that two distinct groups of conduct disorder emerged, those without substance abuse and conduct disorder with substance abuse; that cluster B personality disorders were more often diagnosed in the groups with substance abuse alone and co-existing conduct and substance disorders than in the group with conduct disorders alone. While this study is biased toward the inpatient population and may not be generalizable to outpatient populations, it may help shape successful treatment approaches for this particular population. Another recent study (63) found that there was no significant association between early attention deficit behaviors and later substance use, but that early conduct problems were significantly associated with later substance use. Rohde et al. found that, in general, alcohol disorders followed rather than preceded the onset of other psychiatric disorders, and that more than 80% of adolescents with alcohol disorders had some other form of psychopathology (64). Overall, for the adolescent, the likelihood that substance use will be associated with psychopathology depends on how aberrant the adolescent's substance use is for his or her own social context (26).

Approximately 20% of adolescents are affected by mental and emotional disorders (11), and psychological distress and psychopathology may be involved in both the initiation and continuation of substance abuse patterns. Some postulate that early onset of substance use may promote the development of psychopathology (39). In addition, there is a small identifiable cohort of adolescent heroin addicts who use opiates to assuage the psychotic symptoms of an emerging thought disorder (65), and there is evidence of psychotic symptoms emerging when individuals are medically detoxified from methadone maintenance (66). While a relationship between substance use and psychopathology may exist, the most prudent course in treatment is to begin by treating the substance abuse.

BEHAVIORAL, SOCIAL, AND ENVIRONMENTAL

There are behavioral correlates to substance use, including antisocial behavior (4, 67–70) and poor academic performance (4). Of the most powerful predictors of substance use are social influences including behavior and attitudes of family and friends (46, 71–74). Family influences (67, 70, 75–77) such as parenting, parental substance use, permissive or tolerant attitudes of substance use by parents, and the quality of relationship between parents and adolescents have all been implicated in adolescent substance use (4, 20). Specific family management styles that appear to promote substance use (54) include inconsistent discipline, lack of maternal involvement in child's activities, use of guilt as a motivator, lack of praise for achievement, and unrealistic expectations. The most powerful of the social influences are peer influences, particularly in terms of initial experimentation with substances (20, 78) and reinforcement of use by continued association with groups who use substances. A recent longitudinal, multiracial, multiethnic study found peer factors to be a more powerful predictor of substance use than self-rejection or derogation (79).

Other social or environmental factors associated with substance use include deprivation (4), children who care for themselves after school if parents work (54), a low socioeconomic status (4, 70, 80, 81), a history of sexual abuse (40, 54), immigrant status (82), and employment during the school year (83).

BIOLOGIC AND GENETIC

Although genetic and biological factors in initiation and continuation of adolescent substance use have been the subject of much focus, they, are in general, in need of further delineation. Studies examining concordance rates in monozygotic versus dizygotic twins and adoption studies of twins reared apart (54, 84, 85) show heritability of alcohol use and abuse and differences in transmissibility between males and females. Some studies (54, 86) show a three to four-fold increase of alcohol disorders with a positive family history. Blum et al. (87) reported an allelic association of the dopamine D2 receptor gene with a susceptibility to alcohol disorders. Attempts to repeat the findings were unsuccessful. Influences of genetically determined metabolism, such as alcohol dehydrogenase deficiency found in Asians, have been well established and manipulated to create treatment approaches (disulfiram). Genetic predisposition, however, always interacts with environmental factors, so that genes probably determine vulnerabilities to environmental factors, rather firmly establishing substance abuse disorders (85).

PROTECTIVE FACTORS

While research is generally aimed at establishing clear-cut risk factors leading to substance use patterns and abuse disorders, less attention seems to be focused on factors that protect the adolescent from problematic substance use. Adolescents who have emotionally supportive parents with open communication styles, involvement in organized school activities, and the importance of academic achievement are related to lower risk for substance use (54). Involvement in organized sports activities can be both a risk factor and a protective factor. Certain athletic activities and sports in general have been associated with anabolic steroid use and dependence, which is further associated with other drug use (88, 89). While males who participate in athletics may be less at risk to use drugs and alcohol, they may be at increased risk for early sexual contacts (90).

THEORETICAL ORIENTATION

A number of theoretical models have been proposed for understanding the development of substance abuse (20). Two prominent theories, problem behavior and social learning theory, are described in this section.

Social Learning Theory

Social learning theory (91) suggests that individuals learn through a vicarious process of observing the behaviors of role models, particularly high-status role models. The consequences of behavior, especially the reinforcements that role models receive for behavior, are most salient to the observer, and behaviors that are observed to be rewarded are much more likely to be learned. Role models for the adolescent include parents, siblings, peers, and media figures. Peers and older peers have especially high status as role models. Role models who smoke, drink, or use other substances and who appear sophisticated, mature, sexy, cool, or macho may suggest to adolescents that these behaviors are not only acceptable, they may be necessary to achieving popularity or being attractive.

Expectancies regarding substance use are learned and appear more powerful than actual experience. Family influences are important in shaping expectations toward substance use, and parental drinking habits clearly have an impact on adolescent drinking and beliefs. For example, people who believe that drinking will ease social interaction or enhance performance are more likely to drink and to drink at a younger age (2).

The media in our society plays a powerful role in creating expectancies about substance use, particularly in the form of advertising for cigarettes and alcohol. Adolescents are struggling to conform and fit into adult society, which makes them easy targets for cigarette and alcohol advertising that suggests simple associations between using products and being happy, sexy, cool, or macho (26).

Problem Behavior Theory

Problem behavior theory derives from the work of Jessor and Jessor (42) and is based on an empirical integration of psychological, social, and biochemical factors that contribute to adolescent problem behaviors. "Problem behaviors" refer to those behaviors that are socially defined and recognized as "problems" by a group or culture, and they may be viewed as acceptable for one age group but problematic in another age group. For example, drinking is acceptable among adults in our society, but not among children or young adolescents. Adolescent problem behaviors include smoking, drinking, other substance use, premature sexual involvement and pregnancy, delinquency, and violence.

According to problem behavior theory, substance use is functional for the adolescent and may even be instrumental in achieving personal goals. For example, substance use may serve as a means of demonstrating alliance with and being accepted by peers. It may serve as a way of coping with anxiety, failure (real or anticipated), hopelessness, or boredom. Adolescents are preoccupied with and often anxious about sex, and alcohol and other substances may be used to reduce the anxiety attached to sex or to enhance sexual experience. Substance use may serve as a predictable source of pleasure. By engaging in adult behaviors such as smoking, drinking, and other substance use, adolescents may believe they appear more mature. Thus these behaviors are functional and effective for adolescents in achieving their goals.

It is a basic characteristic of human nature that, when a behavior is effective at achieving a desired outcome or objective, it will be difficult to eliminate the behavior, unless there are alternate ways of achieving the same outcomes. Moreover, objectives such as coping with anxiety, gaining entry into a peer group, and demonstrating independence from parents are normal and healthy (19), so that behaviors used to achieve these objectives are difficult to modify. The obvious implication for treatment is that unless adolescents have other ways of achieving their personal goals, substance use may be impossible to modify or extinguish.

Jessor's work on the issue of perceived life choices provides a useful way of conceptualizing this issue (92). Perceived life choices refer to adolescents' perceptions or beliefs about their future opportunities in terms of education, work, family, and friends. A measure of life choices asks adolescents how likely they believe it is that they will graduate from high school and college, own their own home, have a happy family life, and enjoy the respect of others. Jessor found that adolescents who believed they had positive life choices were more likely to engage in health promoting behavior, and adolescents who believed their life choices to be limited were more likely to engage in risk behavior (92). Adolescents with limited life choices and options are the ones at the greatest risk for substance abuse. Thus, the social context of the adolescent has a fundamental role in creating and regulating problem behaviors such as substance use (19). Poverty and powerlessness are substantial limiting factors in human experience. It is therefore crucial to note that 27% of adolescents between 10 and 18 years of age in the United States live near or below poverty level (11).

SCREENING, ASSESSMENT, AND PREVENTION

A basic understanding of the risks leading to substance use, a knowledge of current substances of abuse, and familiarity with normal adolescent development and behavior should prepare the clinician to adequately identify and refer, when necessary, to appropriate treatment settings the adolescent exhibiting problematic substance use. The limiting factor is the need to *ask* the individual about drug use.

Pediatricians are traditionally believed to be positioned to have an ongoing relationship with both the adolescent and the family and thus be able to detect changes over time. However, current studies indicate that pediatricians are failing to identify the at-risk adolescent user and family (93). A recent college survey of student health clinics reported only 37% of health care providers routinely screened all students for alcohol and other drugs of abuse who visited the clinic (94). This may be due to a discomfort with the issue of drug use, a lack of knowledge, insufficient time during a visit, and inadequate reimbursement for the service (93). Another important factor may be a change in the continuity of care. Urban clinics are often staffed by resident physicians who frequently rotate on and off service and cannot establish the traditional long-term relationship that permits detection of subtle changes that could signal substance use. In addition, medical attention may not be sought out unless an urgent or emergent situation arises, leading to emergency rooms centers acting as the primary care provider site. This situation further limits the establishment of a relationship and perhaps misses the adolescent at most risk for problematic substance use.

On routine visits most adolescents do not present with dramatic or overt signs and symptoms easily accounted for by the effects of alcohol or drug use. A basic knowledge of substance use related changes prove vital to screening (93): physical findings (such as weight loss, nasal irritation, chronic cough, needle tracks); personal habits (such as altered sleep pattern, new friends or interests, change in dress); academic performance (such as falling grades, truancy, suspension); and behavioral and psychological symptoms (such as affective dysregulation, risk taking, stealing). Effective evaluation, history-taking, and discussion with the adolescent should yield the desired information, and toxicological screening for substance use should be limited to emergency situations (overdose, trauma) (93). The American Academy of Pediatrics (AAP) advocates against involuntary testing in adolescents with decisional capacity, even if parental consent is given, unless there is strong medical or legal reasons to do so (95). Results of toxicological screens can have potentially damaging effects on the adolescent and not achieve the desired result of deterrence from use. When a clinician has suspicion of substance abuse, the AAP endorses referral to a qualified health care professional for comprehensive evaluation (95).

Prevention of adolescent substance abuse is multidimensional, complex, dynamic, and requires a great deal more than the slogans "just say no" and "just don't do it" imply. Preventive approaches are varied and differ in style and content. Prevention includes development life skills and resistance skills, fostering healthy self-esteem, appropriate decision making paradigms, stress management, communication skills, and assertiveness training; they are rooted in cognitive and affective systems and require cultural sensitivity (96). Programs also must be evaluated frequently and marketed successfully in order to maintain appropriate results. Perhaps most importantly, drug prevention programs must be aimed at and reach adolescents deemed at high risk for substance use disorders.

Often programs that target one layer of risk factors are limited and attract low risk participants. This theory is supported by a recent evaluation of a parent-targeted, school-based adolescent drug prevention program (97). This study suggests that parents who participate in a drug abuse prevention program already demonstrated better parenting skills and relations with their children than did nonparticipants, a factor known to be associated with a lower risk of substance abuse. More comprehensive programs include involvement at the school and community level and include parent participation, peer involvement, adequate training for adult and peer leaders, and attention to multiple risk factors associated with substance abuse as well as implementing life skills training. The Nebraska "Network of Drug-Free Youth" program (98) was designed to delay onset of substance use and to reduce or eliminate substance use among adolescents already using, by targeting 7th through 12th grade students, and to provide local, regional, and statewide support services. Study of the program reports it helped keep drug-free students from initiating use, and helped occasional users stop or reduce use. It also suggests that mixing high-risk students with low-risk students is an effective prevention strategy. However, students of both risk groups involved in the program self-selected to participate, which may be indicative of a high level of motivation to be drug free. Another comprehensive program, "Project Northland," targeting 6th, 7th, and 8th grade students in 24 school districts in northeastern Minnesota, was designed to test the efficacy of a multilevel, multiyear program addressing alcohol (99). Overall, students from participating districts appeared to benefit positively as compared to reference districts. However, the project seems to have been more successful with students who had not used alcohol at the start of 6th grade than with those who had initiated use, suggesting that alcohol use may be very difficult to reverse even as early as the start of 6th grade.

Evaluation of contemporary prevention programs suggests a need for earlier intervention than currently employed and a meaningful way to involve adolescents and preadolescents who are at high risk for problematic substance use.

TREATMENT

In general, adolescents who are seen in treatment are heavily involved in substance use and may drink or use drugs on a daily basis. At the time they present for treatment, adolescents have usually endured many negative consequences within a relatively brief time period, and functioning in school and family is suffering (20, 26).

There are a range and variety of treatment programs available to the adolescent substance abuser that can be organized into six major categories: detoxification (DT); methadone maintenance (MM); inpatient treatment; therapeutic communities (TC); outpatient programs (OP); and self-help (100). DT and MM derive from a biological or medical orientation, while TCs and drug-free OPs are based on an understanding of the interpersonal and intrapersonal factors involved in substance abuse. Matching adolescents to an appropriate treatment modality is based on considerations of age, gender, severity of problem, financial status, and legal mandates (101). Few programs are designed to treat the special needs of females, especially young pregnant females, minority groups, and medically compromised individuals such as those with AIDS.

Detoxification

The goal of detoxification is to terminate substance use and conduct the process of physiological withdrawal from the drug of abuse safely, with medical support and supervision. The earliest detoxification programs were inpatient programs in federal hospitals in Lexington, Kentucky, and Fort Worth, Texas, and were connected to the criminal justice system. The majority of detoxification programs today are conducted on an outpatient basis. While detoxification with brief outpatient follow-up used to be the most common procedure for treating substance abuse, the effectiveness of this approach has been questioned as simply a "revolving door" to relapse. Detoxification is currently viewed as appropriate only as the first step in a more comprehensive approach to treatment, involving longer-term counseling, support, and group work (100). This practice may reverse as managed care restricts the number of detoxification days paid for as well as the amount and type of follow-up.

Inpatient Programs

Inpatient programs are usually located in hospitals, are run by medical providers, drug counselors, therapists, and psychologists, and provide an expensive, highly structured therapeutic experience, beginning with a battery of assessments and evaluations. These programs are usually not limited to drug treatment but also address other aspects of the adolescent's experience through educational programs and family therapy. Inpatient programs provide psychiatric care, medical care, and counseling for the individual, group, and family (33a). Education about substance abuse and group therapy are emphasized (92a). Inpatient programs for adolescents use a strict, controlled environment complete with detailed daily activity schedules; the average length of stay is 30 days. Like detoxification and methadone maintenance approaches, most inpatient programs for adolescents are modeled after adult treatment programs, which view substance abuse as a disease, albeit more behavioral (92a). An increasing number of inpatient programs are targeting adolescents, and inpatient programs often have aggressive advertising campaigns. Without a standardization of admission criteria (104) a concern has been raised about potential misuse or overuse of these facilities, and in fact many have come under investigation.

Therapeutic Communities

Therapeutic communities were originally organized to help heroin addicts, although TCs now exist for virtually every substance including alcohol, marihuana, and pills (100). TCs are designed to isolate the substance abuser from the substance-using group and setting. They provide a drug-free environment in which new, drug-free ways of coping can be learned and resocialization for a drug-free life can occur. TCs are often based on a mutual help or self-help philosophy and are frequently staffed by recovering addicts. Although professionals originally helped to organize the TC movement, it is not uncommon to find resistance to involvement by professionals in this system.

TCs provide intensive therapy and counseling to build self-esteem, develop social skills, and educate and train the individual for work (33a, 100). Treatment usually lasts from 6 to 18 months in the TC, and the vast majority of people who enter TCs drop out before completing their course of treatment (20). TCs are set up to deal with substance misuse, developmental problems, and problems with relationships using education and individual, group and family counseling and therapy. Generally, one finds TCs falling into one of two philosophical camps that view substance dependence either as an incurable disease or as a behavior that can be extinguished (92a).

TCs originated in the 1960s in many ways in reaction to the simple detoxification treatment approach. The earliest TC was Synanon, and others which have developed national reputations include Daytop Village, Odyssey House, and Phoenix House (100). The early TCs emphasized communication and openness, as well as public criticism of self and others, and had very structured, strict codes of behaviors, with severe consequences for breaking with community norms and rules.

Currently, TCs have become more supportive, and it is less common for them to be as punitive or critical. The structure and approach of the TCs may be best suited for adolescents who are antisocial or delinquent (33a). Given the developmental stage of adolescence, a peer-oriented treatment milieu may be the most efficacious.

In addition to therapeutic communities, there are a variety of other residential programs (e.g., wilderness programs) that are designed to provide a drug-free environment as a way of getting the adolescent substance abuser out of the substance-using context, but these programs do not usually provide the strong group process and loyalty that is the essence of the therapeutic experience of the TC. The better residential programs do include some individual and family counseling (33a).

Outpatient Programs

The majority of substance abuse treatment programs are outpatient programs, which include everything that is not residential:

1. Substance abuse *counseling* to reduce substance use
2. *After care* following a TC or a residential community program
3. Structured *day treatment,* which is an alternative to inpatient care
4. *Family therapy* (92a)

Eight out of 10 adolescents who receive treatment for substance abuse receive it in outpatient programs (26a). To qualify for this approach, adolescents should be free of serious medical or psychiatric problems and should be motivated and cooperative with the treatment program. They should be willing to submit to random drug testing, and the family should also have a willing-

ness to be involved. Outpatient programs may involve any number of therapeutic interventions such as behavior therapy, hypnosis, acupuncture, or biofeedback, as well as crisis intervention programs such as telephone hotlines, walk-in centers, referral services, and emergency intervention (105).

Self-Help

The prototype for the self-help approach is Alcoholics Anonymous, and many drug programs, including TCs and inpatient and outpatient programs, are based on self-help and 12-step programs. Recovering addicts are important in the self-help and 12-step programs, where involvement of professionals tend to be resisted.

The 12-step model was developed with adults, and while many drug programs are based on its principles, it does not immediately lend itself successfully to the treatment of adolescent substance abusers. Importantly, self-help is based on the idea that an individual's participation is willing and voluntary, but treatment with adolescents is often not voluntary (11). In fact, most adolescents are brought into treatment by parents or school officials or through the criminal justice system. In addition, the 12-step model is based on an initial, fundamental first step of admitting helplessness and powerlessness to cope with substance abuse on one's own, but a major task of adolescence is to achieve independence. Therefore it may be difficult for the adolescent to humbly admit helplessness (17). Finally, because of their "here and now" time orientation, adolescents do not usually conceptualize substance use problems as chronic or as a disorder they may have for the rest of their lives. They usually have not "hit bottom," which is important in the 12-step program, although proponents of the self-help approach sometimes argue that with adolescents it may be appropriate to "raise the bottom." The 12-step model must be adapted when used with adolescents. Adolescents may need extra clarification of what powerlessness and willpower mean, and they may also need more time to accept the idea that they have a problem and to become a willing participant in the treatment process (17). More developmentally adapted 12-step programs are needed for adolescents. Despite their limitations, 12-step programs can be an effective treatment modality for adolescents in that they are free, are available in virtually every community across the country, and through sponsorship may establish a supportive "big brother" relationship (106).

Methadone Maintenance

Methadone maintenance was developed at Rockefeller University by Dole and Nyswander in 1964 as a treatment for narcotics addition (102). In methadone maintenance, the opiate drug of choice, generally heroin, is replaced with a synthetic opiate, methadone, that does not induce euphoria in proper doses, and blocks the euphoric effects of other opiates. The replacement drug is taken orally, lasts for 24–36 hours (6–8 times longer than most abused opiates) allowing the individual to lead a stable life, free from the burdens of obtaining the illegal drug. Tolerance to methadone dose does not occur, allowing patients to be steadily maintained over long periods. Methadone maintenance was originally conceptualized and continues to be the treatment of choice for narcotics addition. Outcome studies (103) have shown methadone maintenance is best combined in a program with comprehensive services including psychosocial support, counseling, group and vocational therapies, educational help, and medical and psychiatric diagnosis and treatment. The Adolescent Development Program in New York City is such a program, specialized in the treatment of youthful heroin addiction and other drug abuse. Most applicants for methadone treatment, however, must be above 18 years of age by federal regulations.

Evaluation of Treatment Programs

Substance abuse is one of the most urgent and serious problems facing society and increasing resources should be devoted to its treatment. However, there is a striking consensus in the literature that we do not yet know what treatment approaches are most effective or how to best match patients with treatment approaches (107–110). This is particularly true with adolescents. One of the problems is that evaluation of treatment programs is costly and difficult and is not routinely done (26, 111). However, evaluation not only validates effective approaches, it also provides information which is essential for improving or enhancing treatment strategies (26).

Two early major studies concerning the efficacy of treatment programs for substance abuse include the National Institute of Drug Abuse's (NIDA) National Follow-Up Study of Drug Abuse Treatment in the Drug Abuse Reporting Program (the DARP Study) which followed 4627 individuals who were in treatment with 34 treatment agencies 20 years ago; and NIDA's Treatment Outcome Prospective Study (TOPS) which followed 3389 individuals who were in treatment in 27 treatment centers between 1979 and 1981. A current NIDA study, the Center for Therapeutic Community Research (CTCR) aimed to study adolescent substance abusers in TCs, evaluate effectiveness of TCs for dually diagnosed adolescents, and to examine relationships between initial admission status, progress in treatment, and retention. Finally, another study in progress is the Drug Abuse Treatment Outcome Study-Adolescent (DATOS-A), which assesses client characteristics, treatment structure and process, and outcome evaluation of long-term residential TCs, drug-free outpatient, and short-term inpatient programs (109).

It is difficult to draw conclusions based on the literature, due in part to variations between studies in operational definitions and terminology, as well as in measures of outcome effectiveness (26, 26a). However, reviews in the field conclude that any treatment is better than no treatment (11, 108), and the best predictor of treatment outcome is the amount of time spent in treatment (100). Success also appears more likely when skills training is part of the treatment and when families participate (11), and attending aftercare, including self-help and support groups, favorably influence outcome (108).

It is interesting to note that the studies of treatment efficacy often focus on the characteristics of the individual who does well in treatment, as opposed to the characteristics of the treatment program that produces positive outcomes (26a), and quite a bit is known about which adolescents have the best prognosis. Factors that predict success in treatment include demographic characteristics, attendance in school or other educational programs, and an older age when substance use began. In addition, adolescents who are not involved in opiate or multiple substance use or criminal behavior and who have fewer problems to start with are more likely to have positive outcomes (11, 20, 26).

While it is difficult to say whether one approach is more successful than another, it does appear that different approaches may be better suited to different types of people. For example, the highly structured environment of the TC may work best for delinquent or antisocial youth. It appears that individuals engaged in outpatient programs are more likely to have been productive at some point in the past in education, or career, as compared to those in TCs, MMs, or DT (100) who are less likely to attend school or work and are more often involved in a chaotic lifestyle.

Relapse

Substance abuse, like most medical or psychological disorders, tend to be chronic. Most individuals who develop chemical dependence are likely to resume taking substances following attempt to quit, no matter what the mode of treatment (26). One third of those who relapse do so in the first month af-

ter treatment, and two thirds in the first six months. Contrary to adults who tend to relapse because of negative affect or personal distress, adolescents appear to relapse more often as a result of peer pressure; it is also more difficult to treat successfully the teen who believes substance use will help with social interaction (2).

Given the nature and stages of adolescent development and the chronicity of substance abuse disorders, perhaps treatment success would be better evaluated in terms of use reduction rather than total abstinence.

CONCLUSION

Substance abuse is a public health concern that has reached epidemic proportions; one out of ten adolescents in the United States has a problem with alcohol or other substances. While true addiction is the same in the adolescent and adult, the developmental stage of adolescence results in some unique characteristics of substance abuse and in special treatment needs, especially in terms of the role of peers and the importance of coping skills.

A variety of treatment approaches have been used with adolescents, including detoxification, methadone maintenance, therapeutic communities, inpatient, outpatient, and self-help programs. These approaches were originally designed for adults and require modification when used with adolescent populations. Adolescents need structured treatment strategies that are appropriate for various stages of recovery. To complete the treatment process, a combination of supportive community and outpatient services in the social, educational, and vocational, as well as medical and psychological treatment, may be necessary. Adolescents may need extra clarification of concepts; they may also need more time to accept the idea that they have a problem and to become a willing participant in the treatment process.

There are many more substance abusers than there are treatment slots available in this country, and treatment services for adolescents must be made more accessible and acceptable (11). Even so, many adolescents do not recognize they need help and may never reach treatment. While increasing treatment services may reduce the existing cases of substance abuse, it will not reduce the new cases. An important lesson from the field of public health is that no major epidemic, such as polio, smallpox, or measles, has ever been brought under control with efforts at treatment alone. All epidemics that have been controlled were controlled by prevention. An important aspect of the disease of addiction that sets it apart from other diseases that have reached epidemic proportion is that it involves a *product* that yields a *desired* effect. Thus, in addition to the biopsychosocial and developmental aspects of prevention, the concept of supply and demand has a role. Because of these complicated issues, perhaps a reexamination of the goal of prevention is required: is eradication a reasonable expectation?

Future focus on addiction should include at least the following: an improvement of the quality and consistency of undergraduate and graduate medical education in substance abuse and effective screening techniques and tools; a database of treatment facilities and specialists in substance abuse available to the primary care provider for appropriate referrals; improved targeting of prevention programs to high-risk adolescents; and expanded funding to include program creation (such as effective multidisciplinary treatment settings) and ongoing program evaluation.

References

1. U.S. Department of Health and Human Services. National High School Senior Survey. Press release, 1991.
2. Brown SA. Adolescent alcohol expectancies and risk for alcohol abuse. Addict Recovery 1990;10:16–19.
3. Morrison SF, Rogers PD, Thomas MH. Alcohol and adolescents. Pediatr Clin North Am 1995; 42(2):371–387.
4. Adger H. Problems of alcohol and other drug use and abuse in adolescence. Paper presented at the seventh Cornell University Medical College Conference on health policy, adolescents at risk:

Medical and social perspectives, February 21–22, 1991, New York.
5. Kolata G. Experts are at odds on how best to tackle rise in teenagers' drug use. New York Times 1996(September 18).
6. Newcomb MD, Bentler PM. Consequences of adolescent drug use: impact on the lives of young adults. New York: Sage, 1988.
7. Mussen PH, Conger JJ, Kagan J. Child development and personality. 5th edition. New York: Harper & Row, 1979.
8. Carnegie Corporation of New York: Adolescence: path to a productive life or a diminished future? Carnegie Q 1990;35:1–13.
9. Goleman D. Teenage risk-taking: rise in deaths

prompts new research effort. New York Times 1987(November 24).
10. Utech D, Hoving KL. Parents and peers as competing influences in the decisions on children of differing ages. J Soc Psych 1969;78:267–274.
11. U.S. Congress, Office of Technology Assessment. Adolescent health: summary and policy option. No. OTA-H-468. Vol. 1. Washington, DC: U.S. Government Printing Office, April, 1991.
12. Ginsburg H, Opper S. Piaget's theory of intellectual development. Englewood Cliffs, NJ: Prentice-Hall, 1978.
13. Piaget J. The moral judgment of the child. New York: Collier, 1962.

14. Elkind D. Understanding the young adolescent. Adolescence 1978;8:127–134.
15. Keyser-Smith J, Stoil MJ. And I will stand the hazard of the die: Risk-taking and alcohol use among Washington, DC adolescents. Alcohol Health Res World 1987;Summer:48–53.
16. Hamburg BS. Life skills training: preventive interventions for young adolescents—Report of the Life Skills Training Working Group. New York: Carnegie Council on Adolescent Development, 1990.
17. Dusenbury L, Botvin GJ. Competence enhancement and the prevention of adolescent problem behavior. In: Hurrelmann K, Losel F, eds. Health hazards in adolescence. Berlin: Walter de Gruyter, 1990:459–477.
18. Smith DD, Ehrlich P, Seymour RB. Current trends in adolescent drug use. Psychiatr Ann 1991;21:74–79.
19. Jessor R. Risk behavior in adolescence: a psychosocial framework for understanding an action. Paper presented at the seventh Cornell Health Policy Conference on adolescents at risk: Medical-social perspectives. Cornell University Medical College, New York, February 21–22, 1991.
20. Sernlitz L, Gold MS. Adolescent drug abuse: diagnosis, treatment and prevention. Psychiatr Clin North Am 1986;9:455–473.
21. Millman RB, Botvin GJ. Substance use, abuse and dependence. In: Levine MD, et al. eds. Developmental behavioral pediatrics. Philadelphia: WB Saunders, 1983:683–708.
22. Epps RP, Manley MW, Glynn TJ. Tobacco use among adolescents: strategies for prevention. Pediatr Clin North Am 1995;42(2):389–399.
23. Frances A. Diagnostic and statistical manual of mental disorders. 4th edition. Washington, DC. American Psychiatric Association, 1994.
24. Martin CS, Kaczynski NA, Bukstein OM, Moss HB. Patterns of DSM-IV alcohol abuse and dependence symptoms in adolescent drinkers. J Stud Alcohol 1995;56(6):672–680.
25. Johnston LD, O'Malley PM, Bachman JG. The Monitoring the Future Study, 1975–1994, Vol. 1. Rockville, MD: National Institute on Drug Abuse, 1995.
26. Cambor R, Millman RB. Alcohol and drug abuse in adolescents. In: Lewis M, ed. Child and adolescent psychiatry: a comprehensive textbook. Baltimore: Williams & Wilkins, 1991:736–755.
26a. Kaminer Y, Bukstein O. Adolescent chemical use and dependence; Current issues in epidemiology, treatment and prevention. Acta Psychiatr Scand 1989;79:415–424.
27. Kandel DB. Convergences in prospective longitudinal surveys of drug use in normal populations. In: Kandel DB, ed. Longitudinal research on drug use: empirical findings and methodological issues. Washington, DC: Hemisphere (Halsted-Wiley), 1978:3–38.
28. Hamburg BA, Braemer HC, Jahnke WA. Hierarchy of drug use in adolescence: behavioral and attitudinal correlates of substantial drug use. Am J Psych 1975;132:1155–1167.
29. Yamaguchi K, Kandel D. Patterns of drug use from adolescence to young adulthood. II. Sequences of progression. Am J Public Health 1984;74:668–672.
30. Parra-Medina DM, Talavera G, Elder JP, Woodruff SI. Role of cigarette smoking as a gateway drug to alcohol use in Hispanic junior high school students. J NCI Monogr 1995;18:83–86.
31. Dukarm CP, Byrd RS, Aunger P, Weitzman M. Illicit substance use, gender, and the risk of violent behavior among adolescents. Arch Pediatr Adolesc Med 1995;150(8):797–801.
32. Millstein SG, Moscicki AB. Sexually-transmitted disease in female adolescents: effects of psychosocial factors and high risk behaviors. J Adol Health 1995;17(2):83–90.
33. Czechowikz D. Adolescent alcohol and drug abuse and its consequences: an overview. Am J Drug Alcohol Abuse 1988;14:189–197.
33a. Beschner G, Friedman AS. Teen drug use. Lexington, MA: Lexington Books, 1986.
34. Hughes PH, Rieche O. Heroin epidemics revisited. Epidemiol Rev 1995;17(1):66–73.
35. Schwartz RH. LSD: its rise, fall, and renewed popularity among high school students. Pediatr Clin North Am 1995;42(2):403–413.
36. Wills TA, McNamara G, Vaccaro D, Hirky AE. Escalated substance: a longitudinal grouping analysis from early to middle adolescence. J Abnorm Psychol 1996;105(2):166–180.
37. Shedler J, Block J. Adolescent drug use and psychological health: a longitudinal inquiry. Am Psychol 1990;45:612–630.
38. Kandel DB, Logan JA. Patterns of drug use from adolescence to young adulthood. I. Periods of risk for initiation, continued use, and discontinuation. Am J Public Health 1984;74:660–666.
39. Robins LN, Przybeck TR. Age of onset of drug use as a factor in drug and other disorders. NIDA Res Monogr 1985;56:178–192.
40. Newcomb MD, Maddahian E, Bentler PM. Risk factors for drug use among adolescents. Am J Public Health 1986;76:525–531.
41. Blum R, Richards L. Youthful drug use. In: Dupont RI, Goldstein A, O'Donnell J, eds. Handbook on drug abuse (National Institute on Drug Abuse). Washington, DC: U.S. Government Printing Office, 1975:257–267.
42. Jessor R, Jessor SL. Problem behavior and psychosocial development: A longitudinal study of youth. New York: Academic Press, 1977:281.
43. Battjes RJ, Jones CL. Implications of etiological research for preventive interventions and future research. NIDA Res Monogr 1985;56:269–276.
44. Meyer RE, Mirin SM. The heroin stimulus: implications for a theory of addiction. New York: Plenum, 1979:276.
45. Wechsler H. Alcohol intoxication and drug use among teenagers. J Stud Alcohol 1976;37:1672–1677.
46. Krosnick JA, Judd CM. Transitions in social influence in adolescence: who induces cigarette smoking? Dev Psych 1982;18:359–368.
47. Smith GN, Fogg CP. Psychological predictors of early use, late use, and non-use of marijuana among teenage students. In: Kandel DB, ed. Longitudinal research on drug use: empirical findings and methodological issues. Washington, DC: Hemisphere, 1978.
48. Chassin L, Presson CC, Sherman SJ, Corty E, Olshavsky RW. Predicting the onset of cigarette smoking in adolescents: a longitudinal study. J Appl Soc Psychol 1984;14(3):224–243.
49. Jessor R. Critical issues in research on adolescent health promotion. In: Coates T, Petersen A, Perry C, eds. Promoting adolescent health: a dialogue on research and practice, New York: Academic Press, 1982:447–465.
50. Clarke JG, MacPherson, BV, Holmes DR. Cigarette smoking and external local of control among adolescents. J Health Soc Behav 1982;23:253–259.
51. Page RM. Shyness as a risk factor for adolescent substance use. J Sch Health 1989;59(10):432–435.
52. Dielman TE, Leech SL, Lorenger AT, Horvath WJ. Health locus of control and self-esteem as related to adolescent health behavior and intentions. Adolescence 1984;19:935–950.
53. Braucht GN, et al. Deviant drug use in adolescence: a review of psychosocial correlates. Psychol Bull 1973;79:92–106.
54. Patton LH. Adolescent substance abuse: risk factors and protective factors. Pediatr Clin North Am 1995;42(2):283–293.
55. Potts R, Martinez IG, Dedmon A. Childhood risk taking and injury: self-report and informant measures. J Pediatr Psych 1995;20(1):5–12.
56. Dobkin PL, Tremblay RE, Masse LC, Vitaro F. Individual and peer characteristics in predicting boys' early onset of substance abuse: a seven-year longitudinal study. Child Devel 1995;66:1198–1214.
57. Reeder LG. Sociocultural factors in the etiology of smoking behavior: an assessment. NIDA Res Monogr 1977;17:186–201.
58. Coan RW. Personality variables associated with cigarette smoking. J Pers Soc Psychol 1973;28:86–104.
59. Millman RB, Khuri ET. Determinants of compulsive substance abuse in adolescents. In: Lopez RI, ed. Adolescent medicine: topics. New York: John Wiley & Sons, 1980;2:5–20.
60. Millman RB, Khuri ET. Adolescent substance abuse. In: Lowinson JH, Ruiz R, eds. Substance abuse. Clinical problems and perspectives. Baltimore, MD: Williams & Wilkins, 1981:739–751.
61. Zinberg NE. Addiction and ego function. In: Eissler RS, et al., eds. The psychoanalytic study of the child. New Haven, CT: Yale University Press, 1975.
62. Grilo CM, Becker DF, Fehon DC, Edell WS, McGlashan TH. Conduct disorder. Substance use disorders, and coexisting conduct and substance use disorders in adolescent inpatients. Am J Psychiatry 1996;153(7):914–920.
63. Lynskey MT, Fergusson DM. Childhood conduct problems. Attention deficit behaviors, and adolescent alcohol, tobacco, and illicit drug use. J Abnorm Child Psychol 1995;23(3):281–302.
64. Rohde P, Lewinsohn PM, Seeley JR. Psychiatric comorbidity with problematic alcohol use in high school students. J Am Acad Child Adolesc Psychiatry 1996;35(1):101–109.
65. Vereby K. Opioids in mental illness: theories, clinical observations, and treatment possibilities. New York: New York Academy of Sciences, 1982:398.
66. Levinson I, Galynker II, Rosenthal RN. Methadone withdrawal psychosis. J Clin Psychiatry February 1995;56(2):73–76.
67. Demone HW. The nonuse and abuse of alcohol by the male adolescent. In: Chafetz M, ed: Proceedings of the second annual alcoholism conference. DHEW Publication No. HSM 73–9083. Washington, DC: U.S. Government Printing Office, 1973:24–32.
68. Jessor R, Collins MI, Jessor SL. On becoming a drinker: social-psychological aspects of an adolescent transition. Ann N Y Acad Sci 1972;197:199–213.
69. Newcomb MD, Bentler PM. Drug use, educational aspirations, and work force involvement: the transition from adolescence to young adulthood. Am J Community Psychol 1986;14(3):303–321.
70. Wechsler H, Thurn D. Alcohol and drug use among teenagers: a questionnaire study. In: Chefiz M, ed. Proceedings of the second annual alcoholism conference. DHEW Publication No. HSM 73–9083. Washington, DC: U.S. Government Printing Office, 1973.
71. Barnes GM, Welte JW. Patterns and predictors

of alcohol use among 7–12th grade students in New York State. J Stud Alcohol 1986;47:53–62.

72. Brown B, Clasen D, Eicher S. Perceptions of peer pressure, peer conformity dispositions, and self-reported behavior among adolescents. Dev Psychol 1986;22:521–530.

73. Gfroerer J. Correlation between drug use by teenagers and drug use by older family members. Am J Drug Alcohol Abuse 1987;13(1–2):95–108.

74. Kandel DB. On processes of peer influences in adolescent drug use: A developmental perspective. Adv Alcohol Substance Use 1985;4:139–163.

75. Bewley B, Bland J, Harris R. Factors associated with the starting of cigarette smoking by primary school children. Br J Prevent Soc Med 1974;28:37–44.

76. Borland BL, Rudolph JP. Relative effects of low socioeconomic status, parental smoking and poor scholastic performance on smoking among high school students. Soc Sci Med 1975;9:27–30.

77. Seldin NE. The family of the addict: a review of the literature. Int J Addict 1972;7:97–107.

78. Freeland JB, Cambell RS. The social context of first marijuana use. Int J Addict 1973;8:317–334.

79. Warheit GJ, Biafora FA, Zimmerman RS, Gil AG, Vega WA, Apospori E. Self-rejection/derogation. Peer factors, and alcohol, drug, and cigarette use among a sample of Hispanic, African-American, and white Non-Hispanic adolescents. Int J Addict 1995;30(2):97–116.

80. Gergen MK, Gergen KJ, Morse SM. Correlates of marijuana use among college students. J Appl Soc Psychol 1972;2:1–16.

81. U.S. Public Health Service. Teenage smoking, national patterns of cigarette smoking, ages 12 through 18, in 1972 and 1974. DHEW Publication No. NIH 76–931. Washington, DC: U.S. Government Printing Office, 1976.

82. Brindis C, Wolfe AL, McCarter V, Ball S, Starbuck-Morales S. The association between immigrant status and risk-behavior patterns in Latino adolescents. J Adolesc Health 1995;17(2):99–105.

83. Bernan DS. Risk factors leading to adolescent substance abuse. Adolescence 1995;30(117):201–208.

84. Murray RM, Clifford HMD. Twin and adoption studies: how good is the evidence for a genetic role? In: Galanter M, ed. Recent developments in alcoholism. Vol. 1. New York: Plenum Press, 1983.

85. Grove WM, Eckert ED, Heston L, Bouchard TJ, Segal N, Lykken DT. Heritability of substance abuse and antisocial behavior: a study of monozygotic twins reared apart. Biol Psychiatry 1990;27:1293–1304.

86. Schuckit MA, Smith TL. An 8-year follow-up of 450 sons of alcoholic and control subjects. Arch Gen Psychiatry 1996;53:202–210.

87. Blum K, Noble EP, Sheridan PJ, et al. Allelic association of human dopamine D2 receptor gene in alcoholism. JAMA 1990;263(15):2055–2060.

88. Yesalis CE. Epidemiology and patterns of anabolic-androgenic steroid use. Psychiatr Ann 1992;22(1):7–18.

89. DuRant RH, Escobedo LG, Heath GW. Anabolic-steroid use, strength training, and multiple drug use among adolescents in the United States. Pediatrics 1995;96(1):23–28.

90. Forman ES, Dekker AH, Javors JR, Davison DT. High-risk behaviors in teenage male athletes. Clin J Sport Med 1995;5(1):36–42.

91. Bandura A. Social learning theory. Englewood Cliffs, NJ: Prentice-Hall, 1977:247.

92. Jessor R, Donovan JE, Costa F. Personality, perceived life chances, and adolescent health behavior. In: Hurrelmann K, Losel F, eds. Health hazards in adolescence. New York: Walter de Gruyter, 1990:25–41.

92a. Schinke SP, Botvin GJ, Orlandi MA. Substance abuse in children and adolescents: Evaluation and intervention. In: Kazdin A, ed. Developmental clinical psychology and psychiatry. Newbury Park, CA: Sage Publications, 1991:22.

93. Fuller PG, Cavanaugh RM. Basic assessment and screening for substance abuse in the pediatrician's office. Pediatr Clin North Am 1995;42(2):295–306.

94. Rickman KJ, Mackey TA. Substance abuse screening in student health services. Subst Abuse 1995;16(2):99–108.

95. American Academy of Pediatrics Committee on Substance Abuse. Testing for drugs of abuse in children and adolescents. Pediatrics 1996;98(2 Pt 1):305–307.

96. Making the grade: a guide to school drug prevention programs. Washington, DC: Drug Strategies, 1996.

97. Cohen DA, Linton KLP. Parent participation in an adolescent drug abuse prevention program. J Drug Education 1996;25(2):159–169.

98. Nelson-Simley K, Erickson L. The Nebraska "Network of Drug-Free Youth" program. J School Health 1995;65(2):49–53.

99. Perry CL, Williams CL, Veblen-Mortenson S, et al. Project Northland: outcomes of a communitywide alcohol use prevention program during early adolescence. Am J Public Health 1996;86(7):956–965.

100. Polich JM, Ellickson PL, Reuter P, Kahan JP. Strategies for controlling adolescent drug use. Santa Monica, CA: The Rand Corporation, 1984.

101. Jenson JM, Howard MO, Yaffe J. Treatment of adolescent substance abusers: issues for practice and research. Soc Work Health Care 1995;21(2):1–18.

102. Dole VP, Nyswander ME, Kreek MJ. Narcotic blockade. Arch Int Med 1966;118:304–309.

103. Ball JC, Ross A. The effectiveness of methadone maintenance treatment. New York: Springer-Verlag, 1991.

104. More young patients being hospitalized. Clin Psychiatr News 1989;17:1, 12–13.

105. Smith HE, Margolis RD. Adolescent inpatient and outpatient chemical dependence treatment: an overview. Psychiatr Ann 1991;21:105–108.

106. Jaffee SL. Preventing relapse: guidelines for the pediatrician. Pediatr Clin North Am 1995;42(2):473–478.

107. Pickens RW, Fletcher BW: Overview of treatment issues. NIDA Res Monogr 1991;106:1–19.

108. Bergmann PE, Smith MB, Hoffmann NG. Adolescent treatment: implications for assessment, practice guidelines, and outcome management. Pediatr Clin North Am 1995;42(2):453–472.

109. Jainchill N, Bhattacharya G, Yagelka J. Therapeutic communities for adolescents. NIDA Res Monogr 1995;156:190–217.

110. Werner MJ. Principles of brief intervention for adolescent alcohol, tobacco, and other drug use. Pediatr Clin North Am 1995;42(2):335–349.

111. Milby JB. Addictive behavior and its treatment. New York: Springer, 1981.

67 THE ELDERLY

Steven R. Gambert

Few realize the true extent of substance abuse by the elderly. Although data vary depending on what community and substance are studied, it is currently estimated that the prevalence of alcoholism alone is between 3 and 15% in community-dwelling elderly (1) and as high as 18 to 44% in elderly general medical (2) and psychiatric (3) inpatients, respectively. In a study of 1155 men with a mean age of 73.7, 10.4% reported that they had been "heavy drinkers" at some time during their lives (4). Of even greater concern, however, is the large number of elderly using a variety of illicit drugs or prescription medications without proper physician direction. Although the problem is not a new one, new cases of abuse are compounded by the fact that substance abusers are living longer than ever before. A study in Canada reported a lifetime prevalence of drug abuse or dependence of 6.9% with a male:female ratio of 3:1. The most commonly used drug was cannabis, followed by amphetamines, opiates, barbiturates, hallucinogens, and cocaine. These authors also noted that 80.3% of those with a drug abuse or dependence diagnosis also had a lifetime diagnosis of another psychiatric disorder (5).

There are over 30 million Americans currently over 65 years of age, representing 12.5% of our nation's population. This number is expected to exceed the 50 million mark within the next few decades, with the fastest growing segment being those 85 years of age and older.

This chapter discusses certain unique characteristics of the aged population that may predispose it to the problem of substance abuse, modifying the physiological effects of abused substances and/or requiring altered treatment.

NORMAL AGING

We all age in two distinct ways, e.g., chronologically (based on date of birth) and physiologically (based on functional capacity). Both genetics and environment play significant roles in how "well" one will age. Although we are unable to retard or reverse the "normal" aging process at least as we know it today, we most certainly are capable of *accelerating* our physiological aging process. In general, these normal changes are progressive and result in a loss of reserve capacity. Although each change in itself results in little if no change in function, by the time one is in his or her ninth decade of life, the changes have often become additive and eventually synergistic. The end result is a decline in functional capacity and vulnerability. Any medication, illicit drug, or environmental stress may have a more dramatic effect in an elderly person as compared to a younger person.

A perfect example is alcohol ingestion. Alcohol is distributed in the fluid compartment of the human body. With normal aging, there is a decline in extra and intracellular fluid and an increase in the proportion of body fat. Although there appears to be no age-related change in liver detoxification of alcohol, there is a decreased volume of distribution for alcohol with age, resulting in a greater load reaching the central nervous system. Making things even worse is the age-related decline in the number of brain cells. This results in an even higher alcohol to brain cell ratio in the older person despite a similar amount of alcohol ingestion. Elderly persons are therefore particularly vulnerable to the side effects of alcohol, including altered cognition, behavior, and a tendency for falling. Medications such as morphine derivatives that may cause hypotension will also have more profound effects on the elderly merely as a result of the normal aging process. With age, there is a decreased sensitivity of the baroreceptors; the heart is less able to increase its rate when needed to increase cardiac output. Changes in peripheral blood vessels result in a decreased ability to constrict, and a pooling of blood in the extremities may further result in clinical problems. Hypotension may be more dramatic and more prolonged at this time of life. In addition, there is a normal age-related decline in brain, heart, and renal cell number. It is more likely that a hypotensive episode in the elderly will result in a dementia, stroke, myocardial infarction, or renal insufficiency. Age-related changes in body composition, brain cell number, renal and hepatic function, and physiologic responsiveness can affect medication use, particularly psychotropic agents; when used, extreme caution is advised. Whenever possible, drug levels should be obtained and above all, in prescribing "start slow and go slow."

Table 67.1 is a listing of normal age-related physiological changes (6). It becomes readily apparent that many of these changes result in an altered tolerance and increased morbidity with substance abuse.

Table 67.1   Normal Age-Related Physiological Changes Leading to Altered Tolerance and Increased Morbidity with Substance Abuse

System	Effect of Age	Consequences
Central nervous system	Decline in number of neurons and weight of brain	Do not impair function
	Reduced short-term memory	
	Takes longer to learn new information	
	Slowing of reaction time	
Spinal cord/peripheral nerves	Decline in nerve conduction velocity	Slowness of "righting" reflexes
	Diminished sensation	Diminished sensory awareness
	Decline in number of fibers in nerve trunks	Reduced vibratory sensation
Cardiovascular system	Reduced cardiac output (normal?)	Reduced exercise tolerance
	Valvular sclerosis of aortic valves common	
	Reduced ability to increase heartbeat rate in response to exercise	
Respiratory system	Decline in vital capacity	Diminished oxygen uptake during exercise
	Increased lung compliance	
	Reduced ciliary action	Reduced pulmonary ventilation on exercise
	Increased residual volume	
	Increased anteroposterior chest diameter	Increased risk of pulmonary infection
		Reduced exercise tolerance
Gastrointestinal tract	Decrease in number of taste buds	Reduced taste sensation
	Loss of dentition	Possible difficulty in mastication
	Reduced gastric acid secretion	Potential cause of iron deficiency anemia
	Reduced motility of large intestine	Constipation
Kidneys	Loss of nephrons	Decreased creatinine clearance
	Reduced glomerular filtration rate and tubular reabsorption	
	Change in renal threshold	Reduced renal reserve may lead to reduced glycosuria in the presence of diabetes mellitus
	Decreased concentrating ability	
Musculoskeletal system	Osteoarthritis	Poor mobility; pain
	Loss of bone density (normal?)	Decreased vertical height
		May predispose to fractures
		Change in posture
	Diminished lean muscle mass	Reduced strength
Endocrine/metabolism	Reduced basal metabolic rate (related to reduced muscle mass)	Reduced caloric requirements
	Impaired glucose tolerance	Must distinguish from true diabetes mellitus
Reproductive	*Men:* Delayed penile erection, infrequent orgasm, increased refractory period, decreased sperm motility, altered morphology	Diminished sexual response
		Decreased reproductive capacity
	Women: Decreased vasocongestion, delayed vaginal lubrication, diminished orgasm, ovarian atrophy	Increased wrinkling; senile purpura
		Difficulty in assessing dehydration
Skin	Loss of elastic tissue	Reduced sweating
	Atrophy of sweat glands	
	Hair loss	
Sensory		
Eye	Arcus senilis	
	Lenticular opacity	Increased risk of falls and fracture
	Decreased pupillary size	Poor vision
	Contraction of visual fields	Presbyopia
Ears	Atrophy of external auditory meatus	Presbycusis (loss of hearing of high frequencies)
	Atrophy of cochlear hair cells	
Taste	Reduced number of taste buds	Loss of interest in food
	Decreased size of taste buds	
Smell	Decline in the sensation of smell	Increased risk of gas poisoning; decreased appetite

Another aspect of aging and its losses relates to psychological well-being. An increasing number of elderly are outliving their spouses, friends, and even children. Loss of family and friends is further affected by loss of job, economic stability, and failing health. It has been reported that over 50% of elderly persons experience either depression or serious anxiety disorder. When coupled with a 10% prevalence of dementia in those over age 65 and 22–47.2% in those over 85 years of age (7), mental illness is a common occurrence.

It is not surprising then that elderly men who have recently lost their spouses have the highest rate of completed suicide and incidence of new alcoholism. "Closet drinkers" and abusers of either prescription or over-the-counter medications are not uncommon. This is further complicated by the all too often fragmented approach to health care for the elderly. Many physicians care for single problems in isolation from what is happening with the rest of the patient's medical care. This affords an opportunity for persons to obtain multiple prescriptions for the same medication through different physicians.

AGE-PREVALENT ILLNESS

Symptoms of substance abuse are often missed in elderly persons who tend to suffer more commonly from multiple pathological conditions. Changes in cognition, behavior, or physical functioning may be wrongly blamed on some underlying medical condition. In fact, both the substance abuse and illness may cause the same problem. In the case of alcoholism, it is readily apparent that alcohol abuse may result in both acute and chronic problems. Anemia, peripheral neuropathy, altered cognition, and liver abnormalities are just a few problems easily confused with other age-prevalent illnesses. Table 67.2 is a listing of common age-prevalent illnesses (6). It is clear that physicians must consider substance abuse in the differential diagnosis of all problems affecting the elderly. Since "economy of diagnosis" does not hold when trying to explain a sign or symptom in the older person, any number of causes must be considered and ruled out prior to making a definitive diagnosis.

ATYPICAL PRESENTATION OF ILLNESS IN THE ELDERLY

Many illnesses present atypically or nonspecifically during later life (6). This makes it even more necessary to consider all potential causes of a problem, including substance abuse. A patient with pneumonia may present with a change in behavior, appetite, or sleep-wake cycle, much like the symptoms of alcohol abuse or when other medications are taken in excess (Table 67.3).

It is important to remember that addiction to alcohol or some other substance may occur unknowingly. Certain over-the-counter medications contain potentially harmful and addicting amounts of alcohol (e.g., antitussive preparations). In addition, elderly persons commonly take unused medications belonging to family and/or friends. This may result from economic need or a feeling that no harm can be done as long as the "pill" was prescribed by a physician. As discussed previously, age, illness, or other medications may interact and cause undue effects.

ALCOHOL SPECIFIC PROBLEMS

Diagnostic Considerations

There appear to be two types of elderly alcohol abusers: those who have a lifelong pattern of drinking, individuals who were probably alcoholic all their lives and are now elderly, and those who become alcoholic in their drinking patterns for the first time late in life. While either group may drink openly, it is more common for drinking to occur in secrecy. Depression, loneliness, and lack of social support are the most frequently cited antecedents to drinking for both groups (8). Both will minimize their alcohol use. Several characteristic differences between early onset and late onset alcoholics are summarized in Table 67.4.

As with alcoholics of any age, there is a strong tendency for geriatric alcoholics to try to hide their illness. It is not possible to apply all of the usual diagnostic criteria of alcohol abuse to the elderly alcoholic. A useful sign that can be picked up during a routine history includes the daily use of alcohol. Although daily use may be denied, repeated efforts may elicit a history. The elderly may very well experience amnestic periods while drinking, but again this will almost always require a history from family or acquaintances. The alcoholic will often be unaware of the memory lapses or will adamantly deny them. Another strong indicator of alcohol abuse is continuation of drinking even after repeated warnings to stop for medical or cognitive reasons. In the presence of any of these signs, there should be a high index of suspicion of serious alcohol abuse. Some diagnostic signs of alcoholism in the elderly are summarized in Table 67.5.

Difficulty in recognizing substance abuse in older patients cannot be over emphasized (9, 10). In a study of 263 elderly persons with a history of substance abuse, only 3 of 88 problem users of benzodiazepines, 29 out of 76 smokers, and 33 out of 99 problem drinkers were correctly identified by medical staff (11). Patients presenting with symptoms of self-neglect, falls, cognitive and affective impairment, and social withdrawal should be carefully screened for substance abuse (12). Early identification that a substance abuse problem exists is mandatory if proper treatment is to be instituted.

Table 67.2   Age-Prevalent Diseases Possibly Coexisting with Substance Abuse

System	Disease
Central nervous system	Dementia
	Depression
	Parkinsonism
	Subdural hematoma
	Transient ischemic attack
	Trigeminal neuralgia
Eyes	Poor vision (cataract, macular degeneration)
Ears	Poor hearing
Cardiovascular system	Hypertension
	Ischemic heart disease
	Arrhythmia
	Cardiac failure
	Peripheral vascular disease
	Varicose veins
Respiratory system	Chronic obstructive pulmonary disease
	Pneumonia
	Pulmonary tuberculosis
Endocrine/metabolic	Diabetes mellitus
	Hypothyroidism
	Hypokalemia/hyponatremia
	Gout
Gastrointestinal tract	Hiatus hernia
	Dysphagia
	Constipation
	Fecal incontinence
	Diarrhea
	Malabsorption syndrome
	Ischemic colitis
	Irritable bowel syndrome
	Rectal prolapse
	Carcinoma of colon
Genitourinary system	Urinary tract infection
	Urinary incontinence
	Prostatism
	Renal insufficiency
	Prostatic carcinoma
Musculoskeletal system	Osteoporosis
	Osteoarthrosis
	Osteomalacia
	Polymyalgia rheumatica
	Paget's disease of bone
Hematological system	Anemia
	Multiple myeloma
	Myelofibrosis
Autonomic nervous system	Hypothermia
	Postural hypotension
Oral pharynx	Edentulous; periodontal disease
Miscellaneous	Dehydration
	Foot problems
	Fractures
	Immobility
	Iatrogenic illness
	Malnutrition
	Cancer
	Pressure sores

Table 67.3 Possible Atypical and/or Nonspecific Presentations of Disease in the Elderly, Confusing the Diagnosis and/or Treatment of Substance Abuse

Disease	Examples of Atypical/Nonspecific Presentation
Pneumonia	Anorexia Acute confusional state Normal pulse rate No elevation of body temperature No rise in white blood cell count Falls common
Pulmonary embolism	"Silent" embolism Nonspecific symptoms
Myocardial infarction	Anorexia Absence of chest pain General deterioration Falls Weakness Shortness of breath common
Congestive cardiac failure	Nonspecific symptoms
Acute abdomen	Absence of rigidity and tenderness
Urinary tract infection	Acute confusional state Absence of pyrexia No rise in white blood cell count Incontinence
Parkinsonism	General slowness
Transient ischemic attacks	Acute confusional state Falls
Polymyalgia rheumatica	Nonspecific symptoms Poor general health Aches/pains Lethargy
Hyperthyroidism	Angina Atrial fibrillation Heart failure Absence of eye signs No increase in appetite Appetite may be poor Goiter commonly not palpated Bowel movements rarely increased Depression
Hypothyroidism	Nonspecific deterioration Confusional state Depression Anemia Vaginal bleeding Sensory deficit
Depression	May mimic dementia Weight loss
Malignancy	Nonspecific symptoms
Diabetes mellitus	Incontinence Anorexia Delirium Depression Dementia Weight loss Nonspecific symptoms Falls Altered sleep-wake cycle

Table 67.4 Comparison and Contrast of Early Onset and Late Onset Alcoholism

	Early Onset Alcoholism	Late Onset Alcoholism
Family history of alcoholism	Very common (>80%)	Less common (40%)
Psychosocial functioning	Personality disorders common Greater prevalence of schizophrenia Commonly poor socioeconomic status Malnutrition History of multiple physical injuries	Stable early adjustment Rarely "skid row" alcoholics Likely to live with family Positive work history

While many argue that elderly persons would be less likely to respond to therapy, studies have demonstrated that the elderly were as likely as or more likely than their younger counterparts to make a treatment contact, remain in treatment, and to recover (13). Programs specially tailored to the older person's needs may have an even higher rate of success. In a study of 137 older alcoholic patients randomly assigned to either an "older alcoholic rehabilitation" program or a conventional program, those in a special program were 2.1 times more likely to report abstinence at one year (14).

Acute Alcohol Intoxication

Elderly persons are particularly prone to problems from acute alcohol intoxication. Although one's ability to detoxify alcohol in the liver is unaffected by age, age-related changes in body composition result in a significantly greater number of clinical problems following alcohol ingestion. With age there is a decline in total body water content, primarily due to a change in extracellular fluid volume. Alcohol is rapidly distributed in body water af-

ter ingestion. In the average individual, body water content, as a percentage of total composition, declines from 60% at age 25 to approximately 50% at age 70. This decrease in the available volume of distribution for alcohol results in an increase in the amount of alcohol reaching the central nervous system.

Clinically, the same amount of alcohol consumed in earlier years with impunity may now cause clinical symptoms such as slurred speech, instability, falls, and confusion. The elderly alcoholic may be mistakenly diagnosed with dementia or tumor rather than a subdural hematoma resulting from a fall during a bout of drinking or acute alcoholism. Some regions of the brain are more vulnerable to ethanol than others, which is particularly relevant in older alcoholics. The basal ganglion, hippocampus, reticular activating system, and neocortex undergo neuronal loss with aging at a faster rate than do other regions of the brain. These changes result in impaired cognition and motor skills. Even moderate drinking will take an additional toll on these processes. The performance of young social drinkers on abstracting and adaptation tests is correlated significantly and negatively with the amounts of alcohol consumed. This trend is similar in older drinkers but with an even greater detriment to their cognitive functioning. Performances on tests of abstracting, socialization, and concept formation are all proportionately impaired by drinking practices and age.

The nature of cognitive deficits associated with aging and those of alcohol abuse may mimic or magnify changes associated with the normal aging process. When evaluating an elderly patient, the clinician should be aware that a confused, disoriented older patient may be drunk, not demented.

Alcohol also has an acute effect on cardiac muscle, leading to increased cardiac rate and output. Systolic blood pressure may be increased and blood shunted from the splanchnic circulation to the periphery. This latter phenomenon results in cutaneous vasodilation and loss of body heat. When coupled with other age-related problems in maintaining thermoneutrality, the elderly person is at greater risk of developing hypothermia.

Alcohol increases acid production by the stomach's parietal cells. Since aging results in a reduction in parietal cell mass, a significant problem may not result unless an abnormal mucosal lining coexists. As the amount of alcohol consumed increases, there is greater risk of hyperemia, increased mucus production, and decreased acid secretion leading to acute gastritis. Resulting nausea and vomiting may lead to electrolyte and fluid imbalance earlier in the elderly person due to decreased physiologic reserve.

Although less common with age, alcohol may stimulate secretin production by the pancreas resulting in increased pancreatic enzyme output. These proteolytic enzymes may lead to autodigestion of pancreatic tissue with the potential for producing an acute pancreatitis. While the age-related decrease in parietal cell mass decreases the ability of alcohol to stimulate acid production and thus secretin stimulation, alcohol may cause the duodenum to be inflamed with resultant edema and spasm at the sphincter of Oddi obstructing pancreatic flow.

Acute alcohol ingestion may result in alcoholic ketoacidosis. Arterial blood ph is reduced with a high anion gap; test results for serum ketones are usually only weakly positive due to the predominant ketone being betahydroxybutyrate, which is not detected by standard tests for ketones. Patients

Table 67.5   Common Signs and Symptoms of Alcoholism in the Elderly

Daily use of alcohol
Amnestic periods while drinking
Continuation of drinking after warnings to stop
Physical stigmata of chronic alcohol use
Altered cognitive abilities
Anemia
Liver chemistry abnormalities
Frequent falls/fractures
New seizure activity

Table 67.6   Acute Alcohol Intoxication

Physiological Effects	Potential Consequences
Decreased volume of distribution	Increased serum levels
Increased heart rate and output	Increased blood pressure; flushing; congestive heart failure; angina
Increased stomach acid	Gastritis
Increased pancreatic secretion	Pancreatitis
Alcoholic ketoacidosis	Neurotoxicity; coma
Hypoglycemia	Neurotoxicity; falls; fractures
Inhibitors of ADH	Incontinence; dehydration; hyponatremia
Depression of CNS	Falls; dementia

may vary from being alert, but ill, to frankly comatose. Supportive care is necessary until such time as metabolic balance returns. Although administration of bicarbonate is rarely needed, acid-base balance must be followed closely.

The elderly are particularly prone to alcohol-induced hypoglycemia. Usually preceded by a period of starvation, glycogen stores are further impaired by alcohol's inhibition of hepatic gluconeogenesis (15). Since many diseases, both physical and psychological, affecting the elderly result in anorexia and reduced dietary intake, hypoglycemia will have a greater impact on older persons because they have less efficient counterregulatory mechanisms and fewer brain, cardiac, and renal cells. This decreased reserve may result in more significant tissue damage and altered functional status.

Alcohol's inhibition of antidiuretic hormone (ADH) secretion from the posterior pituitary gland leads to prompt water diuresis. This more frequently results in symptoms of urinary incontinence in the elderly. Neurologically, acute alcohol ingestion has a tendency to depress the central nervous system. Tendon reflexes may be hyperactive due to reduced inhibitory spinal motor neuronal activity (Table 67.6).

Effects of Chronic Alcohol Ingestion

Alcohol can affect almost every cell, organ, and tissue in the body. Changes in vitamin D metabolism may result from the inability of the cirrhotic liver to hydroxylate vitamin D3 at the 25 position to its more active form. This condition may be worsened by a diet deficient in vitamin D, malabsorption of fat, and/or concomitant use of either phenytoin or phenobarbital. The end result may be osteomalacia resulting in bone pain and fractures.

Since the liver is the main site of "binding globulin" production and catabolism of testosterone and conjugation of its metabolites with sulfuric or glucuronic acid, alcoholic changes may result in an increase in the ratio of physiologically free estrogen to free androgen. This may result in clinical manifestations including testicular atrophy, spider angiomata, palmar erythema, and gynecomastia.

An increased rate of conversion of adrenocortical steroid precursors to estrogen has also been reported (16, 17). This is thought to result from decreased uptake of androstenedione by the diseased liver with a resultant increase in estrone production (18).

Decreased concentrations of plasma testosterone, decreased testosterone production, increased testosterone clearance, and an altered hypothalamic-pituitary axis have all been noted following alcohol ingestion even in the absence of liver disease. This may result in impotence, often wrongly dismissed as a function of increasing age. Since decreasing alcohol consumption may reverse the problem, intervention is key.

Chronic alcohol ingestion has both a direct and indirect effect on the cardiovascular system. Care must be taken not to blame cardiomyopathy on atherosclerotic disease when, in fact, it is alcohol induced. Alcohol has been associated with cardiomegaly (19), cardiac fibrosis (20), microvascular infarcts and swelling (21, 22), and altered subcellular myocardial components, glycogen, and lipid deposition (23). Clinically, chronic alcoholism has been associated with reduced myocardial contractibility and output, and with tachycardia (19, 24).

Elderly persons who are chronic users of alcohol have higher rates of glossitis, stomatitis, and parotid gland enlargement (25, 26). In addition, they have an increased incidence of squamous cell carcinoma of the oral pharynx further exacerbated by chronic tobacco use.

Chronic gastritis may lead to an iron deficiency anemia. Anemia may also result from a deficiency in folate or vitamin B12 (25). Vitamin B12 absorption may decline due to a malfunctioning ileum, not a well-understood condition. Sideroblastic and hemolytic anemias are also more common. Anemia must never be attributed to the aging process and a thorough evaluation must be undertaken to delineate reversible causes, especially in the chronic alcohol abuser. Thrombocytopenia with or without granulocytopenia may also be noted (27). In fact, alcohol is the most common cause of thrombocytopenia; failure of these parameters to return to normal within one week of abstinence, however, usually indicates another etiological factor.

Perhaps the best-known complication of chronic alcohol abuse is liver toxicity. A spectrum of illness has been described ranging from fatty metamorphosis to cirrhosis (28). Consequences may include systemic complaints of fatigue, anorexia, and weight loss. Until jaundice is noted, these vague complaints may not be ascribed to alcoholic liver disease in elderly persons with other age-prevalent disorders. On examination, while patients may show typical clinical signs, including spider angiomata, icterus, ecchymoses, gynecomastia, testicular atrophy, muscle wasting, palmar erythema, and Dupuytren's contracture, these findings may be easily mistaken for other disorders or wrongly blamed on advanced age. Even laboratory testing may be misleading as normal liver function tests may be noted as the liver fails and production of hepatic enzymes is diminished. Doses of medications cleared through the liver must be adjusted; patients must abstain from alcohol while consuming sufficient calories and vitamins; severe disease will require protein and sodium restriction.

Nutritional deficiencies are common in elderly alcoholics and may include protein-calorie malnutrition, select vitamin deficiencies, hypomagnesemia, hypophosphatemia, and hypocalcemia (29, 30). Active forms of vitamin D may be diminished by alcoholic liver disease and reduced ability to hydroxylate D3 in the 25 position as stated previously.

The Wernicke and Korsakoff syndromes are associated abnormalities which result from a thiamine deficiency commonly found in alcoholics. The cognitive symptoms of Wernicke's syndrome can easily be mistaken as delirium or dementia when the patient's alcohol abuse is unrecognized. Typically, the patient will be someone who has been living alone, is admitted to the hospital for a medical problem, and has had no documented history of cognitive impairment. During the hospitalization, cognitive impairment is very obvious and thought to be a dementia of either acute onset or a delirium related to medications or unknown causes. Acutely, the patient with Wernicke's syndrome can have symptoms that are quite striking, but as the symptoms of amnesia and confabulation become apparent, the diagnosis of Wernicke's syndrome is more likely. In many cases the only evidence of Wernicke's syndrome is the clinical syndrome. Electroencephalograph tracings may show diffuse slowing or be normal, cerebrospinal fluid and laboratory profiles tend to be normal. With thiamine treatment these patients often improve relatively rapidly; however, all too often the memory deficits do not reverse. The effects of chronic alcohol ingestion are summarized in Table 67.7.

Use of alcohol is often encouraged by family and friends of older people to increase socialization and to improve appetite. Older individuals who use alcohol, as already described, either acutely or chronically may suffer from serious cognitive impairment, and after even one drink these impairments will be of sufficient severity to significantly interfere with any meaningful

Table 67.7 Effects of Chronic Alcohol Ingestion

Physiological Effects	Potential Consequences
Decreased hydroxylation of vitamin D	Osteomalacia
Increased estrogen ratio	Fractures
	Testicular atrophy
	Spider angiomata
	Gynecomastia
	Palmar erythema
Decreased testosterone	Impotence
Thiamine deficiency	Wernicke-Korsakoff syndrome (dementia)
Altered cardiovascular function	Arrhythmias
	Congestive heart failure
B_{12} malabsorption	Megaloblastic anemia
Gastritis	Atrophic gastritis
	Iron deficiency anemia
	Altered pharmacokinetics
Fatty and/or fibrotic liver	Hepatitis
	Cirrhosis
	Altered pharmacokinetics

dialogue. The older individual is very unlikely to be able to actively engage in conversation and almost certainly will have difficulty in recalling what is being discussed. Small amounts of alcohol may in fact stimulate appetite; unfortunately, the daily use of this "appetite stimulant" will generally lead to regular and increased use of alcohol as well as tolerance. The alcohol often becomes a substitute for good nutrition. The use of alcohol for either of these purposes is highly questionable, and, in any case, a meaningful and sincere dialogue without alcohol and with well-balanced nutritional dietary habits are vastly preferable to any type of alcohol use associated with socialization or eating.

Alcohol also is often used to help with sleeping problems, a common complaint among elderly patients. In normal aging, total sleep time decreases to an average of approximately six hours per night. The proportion of REM sleep decreases by nearly 25% and phase IV or deep sleep is significantly decreased in advanced age. Compared to younger adults, elderly individuals have an increased sleep latency, or length of time to fall asleep, and more frequent awakenings throughout the night. Regardless of the length of total time asleep, the decrease in deep sleep results in a less restful or effective sleep.

Alcohol does decrease sleep latency. A "nightcap" thus may help the elderly person fall asleep faster. This effect of alcohol can be subjectively perceived as a definite benefit. The other side of the coin, however, is that a significant alcohol- induced decrease in REM and delta sleep in the elderly alcoholic may result in practically no deep sleep at all. This loss of REM and especially phase IV sleep can lead to undesirable clinical consequences during waking hours. A lack of deep sleep can manifest itself in increased lethargy; REM sleep deprivation can lead to increased irritability. For these reasons the effects of alcohol on sleep in the elderly are very deleterious.

Treatment

Many elderly alcoholics are frankly unaware of the effects of aging on the dynamics of alcohol use and do not realize how greatly alcohol affects their cognition. Often a frank and direct discussion about the interaction of age and alcohol use can be extremely effective in limiting the use of alcohol by many older people. The goal of any treatment modality must include total and complete abstinence for the elderly individual.

For those patients whose alcohol use has resulted in dietary deficiencies and vitamin deficiencies, replacement of the vitamins and an adequate diet is essential. Medical support for those with alcohol-related medical illnesses is also of paramount importance.

More specific measures would include thiamine supplements of 100 mg daily for at least the first week of treatment. In addition, the patient may require hospitalization for the acute stages of detoxification.

Many elderly patients benefit from participation in Alcoholics Anonymous, although some will object that the members of many Alcoholics Anonymous groups are much younger than the patient.

Above all, the major objective of treatment of alcoholism in the elderly is clearly abstinence. As stated previously, programs specially tailored to the elderly appear to have a higher rate of success.

PROBLEMS SPECIFIC TO SUBSTANCE ABUSE: COCAINE, AMPHETAMINES, OPIATES, AND SEDATIVE-HYPNOTIC ABUSE

All forms of addiction know no age limitation. In fact, elderly persons are at particularly high risk for addiction due to their more frequent use of medications to treat a variety of acute and chronic medical conditions, to economic stability for the majority, and to a high prevalence of depression and anxiety disorders. Although data concerning the use of "illegal" drugs by the elderly are not readily available, one must remember that the use of any prescription medication in a manner other than that prescribed is illegal. In general, intravenous or subcutaneous use of illicit drugs is thought to be uncommon in the elderly. Young individuals who use these agents are at great risk for a shortened life span and thus few reach senescence. Those who do rarely use the same quantities as earlier in life. Vascular sclerosis may make it increasingly difficult for the long-term intravenous drug addict to achieve sufficient drug levels, essentially self-weaning themselves from the addicting agent. If an older person is known to be a user of intravenous drugs, extreme caution is advised to not blame any change in condition on another problem. A myriad of drug-related problems may occur at any age. These include dental problems such as root caries, advanced periodontal disease, and acute necrotizing ulcerative gingivitis; bacterial infections including abscess formation, cellulitis, septicemia, lymphangitis, and thrombophlebitis; endocarditis; tetanus; malaria; tuberculosis; osteomyelitis; septic arthritis; hepatitis; venereal disease; acquired immunodeficiency disease syndrome (AIDS); and pneumonitis.

Neurological disturbances are perhaps most frequently encountered. These may result from direct effects of the drugs themselves on the central nervous system or from infections or emboli. Drug use should be considered in all cases of stroke, seizure, altered behavior, or change in cognition.

Cocaine and amphetamine abuse, even in low dosage, has been associated with a higher rate of intracranial hemorrhage leading to a cerebral vascular accident. Tics, choreiform or athetoid movements, ataxia, and gait disturbances are also more commonly noted in frequent users of these agents. Heroin, when burned and inhaled, has been associated in the Netherlands (31) with spongiform leukoencephalopathy, presenting as a dementing illness. Elderly addicts are being treated in numerous methadone treatment programs throughout the country. Although little data are available regarding the exact number of elderly persons receiving such treatment, estimates place this figure between 0.5 and 1.1% of the total caseload (32).

Perhaps one of the most under reported problems affecting the elderly is the all too frequent use of sedative-hypnotics, particularly among women (33). Whether used for anxiety or to help induce sleep, these agents are addicting. The most commonly misused prescription drug classes among the elderly are sedative-hypnotics, antianxiety agents, and analgesics. Diazepam, codeine, meprobamate, and flurazepam are on top with 92% of those abusing these drugs doing so for more than five years. It should be noted that there is a high correlation between prescription drug abuse and previous or active alcohol abuse (34). Many elderly only know of their addiction when they discontinue or inadvertently run out of their medication. The use of triplicate prescriptions may reduce the use of these agents or at least help alert authorities to potential abuses. Unfortunately, these agents, especially those with longer half-lives, often result in unwanted side effects affecting functional capacity and cognition, placing the older person at greater risk of falling and institutionalization. Drug-related delirium or dementia may wrongly be labeled Alzheimer's disease. The elderly appear to be more sensitive to the effects of benzodiazepines, both because of changed pharmacodynamics with aging and because of altered postreceptor cerebral response (35). A thorough evaluation of all problems is essential when caring for the elderly. Failure to do so will undoubtedly increase the number of false diagnoses and limit the quality of patients' life.

SPECIAL PROBLEMS IN THE ELDERLY PREDISPOSING TO SUBSTANCE ABUSE

Chronic Medical Conditions

The elderly have a higher prevalence of physical ailments capable of limiting function. Arthritis, in fact, is the most commonly noted problem affecting the elderly, with approximately half of all persons over 65 years of age limited to some degree. Osteoporosis affects millions of elderly women and predisposes to fractures. In both conditions, the prospect of lifelong disability and potential pain is real. Chronic pain is a problem many elderly must face every day.

Other age-prevalent medical conditions that may predispose the older person to substance abuse include neuropathies, recurrent gout attacks, and cancer.

These problems clearly place the elderly person at a higher risk of substance abuse. Most elderly have ready access to prescription drugs because physicians are often quick to prescribe medication at this time of life. The elderly often feel frustrated and angry at being dependent, socially isolated, and even discriminated against. Associated feelings of depression, anxiety, low motivation, and self-esteem also predispose elderly people to substance abuse.

Visual and Hearing Disturbances

With increasing age, there is an ever greater number of persons who lose vital communication skills. Although many may deny the loss of these vital functions, depression, isolation, and loneliness are almost certain results. Alcohol, drugs, or both may become ways of dealing or forgetting the problem. Maximal treatment, ophthalmologic evaluation, hearing screening tests, and referral for hearing and visual aids must be complemented with psychosocial support.

Institutionalized Elderly

Currently, 2.5 million persons reside in nursing home settings. This number is expected to rise to 5 million within the next few decades. Although substance abuse is largely limited to a mishandling and/or inappropriate ordering of medications for most residents of skilled nursing facilities, access to street drugs and alcohol is not impossible. This is an even greater problem for residents of intermediate care or health-related facilities who are encouraged to frequent community settings. For many, this may involve a visit to the local bar or restaurant. The "visitor supplier" is another potential source not to be overlooked. Health professionals caring for the elderly must be familiar with warning signs of substance abuse and at least consider it in the differential diagnosis of any change in condition that may occur.

SUMMARY

Regardless of one's age, substance abuse must be considered a major cause of emotional and physical disability. Elderly persons have many unique characteristics that predispose them to higher rates of substance abuse, particularly alcohol and "prescribed" medications. A thorough understanding of what constitutes normal age-related changes, age-prevalent disease, and the atypical presentation of illness will hopefully enable the health professional to better recognize and successfully treat this problem. Past substance abusers, now elderly, may have accelerated their normal aging or have diseases they otherwise might never have developed. A clear understanding of the significant consequences of substance abuse will also help identify potential problems and help guide the clinician. Caution is advised to not blame all problems on aging. Increasing age and consequences of substance abuse may be additive, however. Unless substance abuse is stopped, treatment will be less than optimal at all stages.

There have been few studies of treatment options for substance abuse in the elderly. The negative feelings of many health professionals toward the elderly clearly may decrease potential referrals. Chronic pain problems are more common at this time of life, and while abuse is clearly not the answer, depriving the older person of treatment has moral, ethical, and practical considerations. As long as all alternative options have been tried and have failed, most health professionals would opt for a regulated and controlled addiction over a callous disregard for comfort and well-being. The goal of as high a quality of life as possible must be maintained throughout life. In the case of most substance abuse, however, the goal must be to stop the problem. Before treatment can start, however, the problem must be recognized. Even before that, those at potential risk must be identified and counseled, and predisposing factors eliminated.

As our population continues to age, we will undoubtedly face a growing number of persons seeking physical and psychological benefits from substance abuse. To some, this is a way to counteract the void created by a series of losses. To others, it is a way to escape from chronic, unrelenting pain and suffering. To still others, it is the result of a failure of the medical profession to properly evaluate and treat many of the problems of old age. Whatever the circumstances, health professionals must be more knowledgeable about and willing to care for the special needs and problems of the elderly, including substance abuse.

References

1. Myers JK, et al. Six month prevalence of psychiatric disorders in three communities. Arch Gen Psychiatry 1984;41:959.
2. McCusher J, Cherubin CE, Zimberg S. Prevalence of alcoholism in general municipal hospital population. N Y State J Med 1971;71:751.
3. Moore RA. The diagnosis of alcoholism in a psychiatric hospital: a trial of the Michigan Alcoholism Screening Test. Am J Psychiatry 1972; 128:1565.
4. Colsher PL, Wallace RB. Elderly men with histories of heavy drinking: correlates and consequences. J Stud Alcohol 1990;51:528–535.
5. Russell JM, Newman SC, Bland RC. Epidemiology of psychiatric disorders in Edmonton. Drug abuse and dependence. Acta Psychiatr Scand Suppl 1994;376:54–62.
6. Gambert S. Aging: an overview. In: Gambert SR, ed. Handbook of geriatrics. New York: Plenum, 1987.
7. Evans DA, et al. Prevalence of Alzheimer's disease in a community population of older persons. JAMA 1989;262:2551.
8. Schonfeld L, Dupree LW. Antecedents of drinking for early- and late-onset elderly alcohol abusers. J Stud Alcohol 1991;52:587–592.
9. D'Archangelo E. Substance abuse in later life. Can Fam Physician 1993;39:1986–1988, 1991.
10. McMahon AL. Substance abuse among the elderly. Nurse Pract Forum 1993;4:231–238.
11. McInnes E, Powell J. Drug and alcohol referrals: are elderly substance abuse diagnoses and referrals being missed? Br Med J 1994;308:444–446.
12. Thibault JM, Maly RC. Recognition and treatment of substance abuse in the elderly. Prim Care 1993;20:155–165.
13. Fitzgerald JL, Mulford HA. Elderly vs. younger problem drinker "treatment" and recovery experiences. Br J Addict 1992;87:1281–1291.
14. Kashner TM, Rodell DE, Ogden SR, Guggenheim FG, Karson CN. Outcomes and costs of two VA inpatient treatment programs for older alcoholic patients. Hosp Community Psychiatry 1992;43:985–989.
15. Levy LJ, Duga J, Girgis M, Gordon EE. Ketoacidosis associated with alcoholism and nondiabetic subjects. Ann Intern Med 1973;78:213.
16. Edman CD, MacDonald PC. Extraglandular production of estrogen in subjects with liver disease. Gastroenterology 1975;69:a-19, 819.
17. Olivo J, Gordon GG, Rafii F, Southren AL. Estrogen metabolism in hyperthyroidism and in cirrhosis of the liver. Steroids 1975;26:47–56.
18. Siiteri PK, MacDonald PC. Role of extraglandular estrogen in human endocrinology. In: Greep RO, ed. Handbook of physiology. Washington, DC: American Physiological Society, 1973;2: 615–629.
19. Bollinger O. Ueber die Haufigkeit und Ursachen der idiopathischen Herzhypertrophie in Munchen. Dtsch Med Wochenschr 1884;10:180–181.
20. Alexander CS. Alcoholic cardiomyopathy. Postgrad Med 1975;58:127–131.
21. Factor SM. Intramyocardial small vessel disease in chronic alcoholism. Am Heart J 1976;92: 561–575.
22. Pintar K, Wolanskyj BM, Buggay ER. Alcoholic cardiomyopathy. Can Med Assoc J 1965: 93:103–194.
23. Alexander CS. Electron-microscopic observations in alcoholic heart disease. Br Heart J 1967; 29:200–206.
24. Bode JD. Alcohol and the gastrointestinal tract. Ergeb Inn Med Kinderheilkd 1980;45:1–75.
25. Sullivan LW, Herbert V. Suppression of hematopoiesis by ethanol. J Clin Invest 1964; 43:2048–2062.
26. Van Thiel DH, Lipsitz HD, Porter LE, Schade RR, Gottlieb GP, Graham TO. Gastrointestinal and hepatic manifestations of chronic alcoholism. Gastroenterology 1981;81:594–615.
27. Cowan DH, Hines JD. Alcohol, vitamins and

platelets. In: Bimitrov NV, Nodine JH, eds. Drugs and hematologic reactions. New York: Grune and Stratton, 1973:282–295.

28. Sherlock S. Diseases of liver and biliary system. Oxford: Blackwell Scientific Publications, 1981.

29. Hurt RD, Higgins JA, Nelwon RA, Morse RM, Dickson ER. Nutritional status of a group of alcoholics before and after admission to an alcoholism treatment unit. Am J Clin Nutr 1981;34: 386–393.

30. Barboriak JJ, Rooney CB, Leitschuh TH, Anderson AJ. Alcohol and nutrient intake of elderly men. J Am Diet Assoc 1978;72(5): 493–495.

31. Walters EC, Stam FC, Lousberg RJ. Leucoencephalopathy after inhaling "heroin" pyrolysate. Lancet 1982;2:1233.

32. Pascarelli EF. Drug abuse and the elderly. In: Lowinson JH, Ruiz P, eds. Substance abuse: clinical issues and perspectives. Baltimore: Williams & Wilkins, 1981:752–757.

33. Farnsworth MG. Benzodiazepine abuse and dependence: misconceptions and facts. J Fam Pract 1990;31:393–400.

34. Jinks MJ, Raschko RR. A profile of alcohol and prescription drug abuse in a high-risk community-based elderly population. DICP 1990;24: 971–975.

35. Closser MH. Benzodiazepines and the elderly. A review of potential problems. J Subst Abuse Treat 1991;8:35–41.

68   African Americans: Epidemiologic, Prevention, and Treatment Issues

Stanley John, Lawrence S. Brown, Jr., and Beny J. Primm

Substance abuse continues to have a devastating impact in American communities. The prevalence of any illicit drug use in the general population has been alarming. According to the National Household Survey on Drug Abuse, as of 1993, some 77,022,000 youths 12 years and older have abused some illicit drug (1).

Although there have been increased efforts to study drug abuse in special populations since the passage of the Anti-Drug Abuse Act of 1986 (2), little is known about the relationships between race or ethnicity and illicit drug use and between race or ethnicity and drug abuse treatment effectiveness (3). There have been a number of thoughtful reviews of these relationships (2, 4); however, much necessary research remains to be done. That research needs to take into account certain study design issues.

First, how does one accurately and adequately describe this very important subpopulation of Americans? The African American subpopulations present a diverse multicultural community. Fundamentally there are at least three cultural subgroups:

1. African Americans who are descendants of African slaves and who were actually born in the United States.
2. African Americans who are descendants of African slaves of the Caribbean and who migrated to the United States.
3. African Americans who were born in Africa and migrated to the United States. Within this subgroup there are a multitude of different cultures depending on the originating African country.

Each of these subcultures has unique characteristics which easily differentiate one group from another. Such characteristics reflect aspects of their colonizing mother country and include dialect, traditional dress and festivities, and religion. The geographic distribution of African Americans subcultures vary considerably. For example in New York City, African Americans of Caribbean origin are concentrated in some Brooklyn neighborhoods, African Americans of American birth are more predominant in the Bushwick/Brownsville areas of Brooklyn, and African Americans of recent migration from Africa are localized predominately in the Harlem neighborhood of Manhattan.

The next major concern is how were subjects selected for participation? If not randomly chosen, how was the study population representative? If it is a comparative study, what was the evidence that there was no bias between the compared populations in the observation of important events (reporting drug use, actual drug use, reported adverse events, and actual adverse events)? Given the variety of African American subcultures, the method of population selection is of critical importance in making conclusions regarding African Americans.

Many surveys of substance abuse generally determine use of a psychoactive substance, whether it is alcohol or an illegal drug. For example, the National Household Survey and the High School Senior Survey assess use of various substances in the past year, month, or some other time period. Although this is useful epidemiological information, its clinical utility is limited. Substance abuse and dependence, which are more difficult to ascertain using survey methods, are of greater importance to clinical care and are correlated more closely with the medical and social consequences of psychoactive substance use.

The choice of outcome variables is also important. While the use of self-reporting is not uncommon in substance abuse, there are limitations. Drug abuse is an illegal act and along with alcohol abuse is stigmatized within society. Hence, participants may be reluctant to admit the true magnitude of their illegal drug or alcohol use. Even less is known about the extent to which this issue affects surveys of illicit drug use and alcohol use among African Americans. It is often argued that given the disproportionately greater arrests and incarceration rate for drug-related crimes in many African American communities, there may be more reluctance for many African Americans to respond reliably to large substance abuse surveys.

Recognizing the foregoing limitations in this chapter, we will confine our consideration to problems of substance abuse, focusing on the following questions: What is the existing knowledge concerning the prevalence, correlates, and adverse consequences of substance use and abuse in African Americans? What efforts exist to prevent substance use and abuse in this population? What is the nature and effectiveness of treatment for African American substance abusers?

SUBSTANCE USE AND ABUSE PREVALENCE

There are an estimated 3.2 million African Americans who used illicit drugs in the past year; 1.7 million African Americans used an illicit drug in the past month (1, 2). The 1993 National Household Survey, conducted by the Substance Abuse and Mental Health Services Administration, indicates that African American males between 12 and 35 years of age were much more likely to be users of an illicit substance compared to their white counterparts. This is particularly the case for cocaine use; 1.4% of African American males over 35 years of age had used cocaine in the past year, in contrast to 0.2% of whites. However, an equal percentage of African Americans and whites between the ages of 12 and 17 had used an illicit drug in their lifetime, in the past year, or past month (1). African American and Latino women were more likely than white women to have used crack cocaine, a form of cocaine which many believe to be especially virulent (5, 6). On the other hand, data from the National High School Senior Survey (6) indicates that the rate of drug use among African American high school seniors was lower for all drugs, except heroin and marihuana.

When considering the latter data, it is important to recognize that in using African American high school seniors to represent African American youths, the statistics may be biased because of the disproportionately greater high school dropout rate among African Americans as compared to their white counterparts. It is also important to keep in mind that, because surveys such as those described previously have not included such difficult groups as prisoners, runaways, or high school dropouts, the current estimates of illicit drug use in minority populations may underestimate the extent of the problem.

In one New York City study of African American youths, a survey was conducted among inner-city adolescents in jail (n = 427) to examine the correlates of cocaine/crack use. Twenty-three percent had used cocaine/crack in the month prior to arrest and 32% reported lifetime use. Interestingly, there was no correlation between the type of crime and cocaine/crack use (7).

DEVELOPMENT AND COURSE OF USE AND ABUSE

A small body of studies has attempted to characterize the development and course of substance use and abuse in African American individuals. These consist of studies of community citizens and studies of addicts.

In what appears to be the earliest systematic study of drug abuse in a African American population, Robins and Murphy (8) studied 235 African American men between the ages of 30 and 35 years who were living in the community. They reported that 50% had used some drug illegally and that 10% had been addicted to heroin. Marihuana had served as the introduction to drugs for most. The younger the age of initial marihuana use, the more likely the continuation to heroin use. Delinquency was a predictor of drug use and within this group, those without a father at home were more likely to be users.

Brunswick (9) studied 536 African American young adults (52% male) between the ages of 18 and 23 years who lived in the Harlem section of New York City. One third of the study sample had not completed high school. One third had jobs and, of these, approximately 75% maintained full-time employment. Four percent of the males were in jail when interviewed. About one fifth of the women were married, in contrast to 4% of the men. Fifty-two percent of the women and 28% of the men had at least one child, and incomes for the households of these subjects were quite low.

Brunswick found that the study sample had used heroin an average of 939 times in their lifetime, had used methadone 542 times, cocaine 278 times, marihuana 869 times, and psychedelics 190 times. The modal frequency (47%) of alcohol use for males was daily and/or several times a week. By the time of the interview, three quarters of the alcohol users had been using alcohol regularly for at least 5 years. Of the males, 68% used marihuana at least once or twice a week, and 77% used heroin at least one or two times weekly. Half of the men and 40% of the women had used two or more drugs in the past year.

Not unexpectedly, alcohol was the drug used earliest. By 14 years of age, half of male drinkers and almost that proportion of females had used alcohol. Indeed, 20% of the men had started alcohol use by age 10. The median age of onset of marihuana use was 14.8 years for males and 15.6 years for females. Therefore, the initiation of marihuana use occurred about 1 year after initial alcohol use. The median age of first use for heroin was approximately the same age as for marihuana use. The initial age of cocaine and psychedelics use for these individuals was about 17.5 years. The age of onset of alcohol use predicted use of illicit substances, and the early onset of illicit substance use was related to the subsequent frequency of substance use. In the study, 9% of the men and 7% of the women reported having been in heroin treatment at least once. The longer the period of heroin use, the greater the likelihood that the user would request treatment.

Sadly, Brunswick reported that initial use for all of the above drugs occurred most commonly while the subject was on the way to school. She found that the heroin user group differed from the rest of the sample on a number of characteristics. For example, they had the lowest educational achievement and were less often employed. Interestingly, if the individual had not initiated heroin use by age 18 years, he or she was not likely to do so thereafter. Brunswick (9) felt that the high use rates of the subjects studied were due to the marginality and ambiguity of the life situation of youth generally and the dubious access that the African American youth in the study had to society's opportunities.

Admittedly, the Brunswick study design does not allow one to make comparative statements between African Americans and other populations. Similarly, we cannot necessarily conclude that the cohort under investigation was representative of African Americans. Nonetheless, it does suggest that, at least in some poor African American communities, substance use and abuse begins at a relatively early age and can be found in a substantial proportion of individuals.

Halikas and his colleagues (10) reported findings on the early life and natural history of heroin addiction in a population of African American drug abusers. In this study, 192 addicts were examined, most of whom were in methadone maintenance treatment. The average age of the subjects studied was 28 years of age. The age of initial illegal drug use was found to be 14.4 years of age. Heroin use first occurred when the individual was slightly over 18 years of age, followed by addiction about 1.5 years later (group mean = 19.9). The first drug-related arrest took place about 6 months after the onset of addiction (age 20.4 years). The number of drugs tried by these individuals ranged from 3 to 35. Of this group of heroin addicts, 90% were truant from school beginning in the 7th grade and 95% acknowledged some non–school-related misbehavior by age 12 years.

In an earlier study of African American opiate-dependent subjects, Chambers and his colleagues (11) reported that 89% of their subjects were introduced to opiates by peers. Early termination of education and early arrest histories were consistent with the findings of Halikas et al. (10). A study by Craig (12) reported similar findings. That is, the African American, male, inner-city, heroin-dependent patients, treated in a Veterans' Administration facility, averaged 30 years of age, used or were dependent for about 8 years, and had made five attempts at drug detoxification without the benefit of a treatment program. The average patient was educationally impaired, had a poor work history, and had spent 3 years in prison for committing either crimes against property or other drug-related crimes. Craig found many of these patients to have character disorders, suffering either from sociopathy or a schizoid personality disorder.

In a large study of a methadone treatment population of over 500 African American and Latino patients by Alterman et al. (13), Latinos reported significantly more symptomatology in somatic complaints, anxiety, depression, alcohol problems, and suicidal ideation scales using the Personality Assessment Inventory (PAI). While the PAI may possess some limitations in its validity for lower socioeconomic groups and its ease of administration, it is a psychometric instrument found to have concurrent validity when compared with the Diagnostic Interview Schedule and the Addiction Severity Index (ASI). This finding of more reported symptomatology among Latinos when compared to African Americans was also reported by Kosten and colleagues (35). Unfortunately, there were an inadequate number of non-black, non-Hispanic patients in the Alterman and Kosten study populations to make appropriate comparisons between African American patients and white, non-Hispanic patients.

In the same study population investigated by Alterman et al., Brown and fellow researchers (14) reported differences between African American and Latino patients in their ASI scores. While African American patients had significantly more severe scores in the employment domain, Latinos scored more severely in the legal domain and in psychological problems. Depression, evaluated using the Beck Depression Inventory or the Diagnostic Interview Schedule, was especially more serious among Latino patients than among African American patients.

To summarize, education impairment, a poor work history, a history of arrests and imprisonment, and possibly psychiatric problems are found in many of the opiate-dependent African Americans evaluated in the studies just described. However, we must consider these findings with caution. As with the Brunswick study, the study designs generally do not allow comparisons of African Americans with other ethnic or racial groups. Also, these results may not have implications for all African Americans, as we cannot ascertain the degree to which there was bias in the selection of the African Americans in each study. Furthermore, retrospective studies, like the ones mentioned, have the danger of missing some influential factors (or cofactors) that may correlate better with the evolution of chemical dependency. Alternatively, the degree of justifiable (or drug-induced) memory impairment may lessen or strengthen the magnitude of effect of some of the self-reported information collected.

In an effort to reduce the obvious bias of the above mentioned studies, Lillie-Blanton et al. (15) investigated the use of psychoactive substances in African Americans from a different perspective. The objective of the study was to estimate the degree to which crack cocaine smoking is associated with personal factors specific to race or ethnicity. In the design, the social and environment risk factors were held at a constant because they potentially may have confounded the racial comparison. Respondents were poststratified into neighborhood risk sets. Subjects were selected using multistage area probability sampling of all residents aged 12 years and older. The results demonstrated that once respondents were grouped into neighborhood clusters the relative odds of crack use did not differ significantly for African American or for Latino Americans when compared with white Americans.

It must be mentioned that the study did not refute the analysis of previous studies, but simply provided evidence that prevalence estimates, unadjusted for social environment risk factors, may lead to misunderstanding about the role of race or ethnicity in the epidemiology of crack use. By extension, this may also be true for other illegal drugs and alcohol. The study recommended that future research should seek to identify which characteristics of the neighborhood's social environment are important modifiable determinants of drug use.

ADVERSE CONSEQUENCES OF DRUG USE AND ABUSE

Drug abuse has many adverse health-related consequences including fatal and nonfatal overdose, acquired immunodeficiency syndrome (AIDS), hepatitis B infection, increased risk for complications of pregnancy, and adverse birth outcomes. In addition, drug abuse may have negative effects on employment, school achievement, socioeconomic status, and family stability, although it is difficult to determine whether these are the cause or are the result of drug abuse (2). An important issue that needs to be considered is whether African Americans are at greater or lesser risk for these consequences. Van Hasselt et al. (16) pointed out not only that African Americans are at greater risk but familial and socioeconomic factors also contribute to the exceedingly high prevalence rates of drug abuse in African American children.

Medical examiner data on drug-related deaths are another source of information on adverse drug-related consequences. The total number of deaths reported is proportionally higher for African Americans than for either whites or Hispanics (2, 17). African American decedents accounted for 1999 (30%) of the 6756 drug abuse–related deaths reported by medical examiners to the Drug Abuse Warning Network (DAWN) in 1988; whereas African Americans constitute only 23% of the population in the cities surveyed by DAWN (2). Over 74% of the African American decedents were males, and 46% were age 30–39. Cocaine was the most frequently mentioned drug in DAWN medical examiner cases, followed by heroin or morphine (18). Drug-related deaths among African Americans and Hispanics were more likely to be attributed to accidental or unexpected circumstances, while those for whites were more likely to be attributed to suicide (2). The combined use of heroin with alcohol appeared to be associated with several drug-related epidemics with disproportionate numbers of African American deaths (2).

In New York City methadone maintenance treatment clinics, Brown and colleagues (19) assessed the range of medical disorders in calendar year 1987 among 1780 patients. Over 90% were African American or Latino and 40% were female. While this study used chart reviews as the source of data and therefore had potential ascertainment limitations, this study represented one of the few systematic reviews of drug abusers in an ambulatory setting. Histories of gonorrhea, hepatitis B infection, pneumonia, and anemia were found in 28%, 23%, 21%, and 21% of the patients, respectively. This study suggested that a considerable portion of African American heroin users sustain a considerable range of medical disorders during their lives.

AIDS and human immunodeficiency virus (HIV) infection is another complication of substance abuse which has received increasing public attention over the last two decades. African American and Hispanics comprise

54% of the reported cases of AIDS (20). Two thirds of these cases, or 34% of total AIDS cases, are found in African Americans alone. Injecting drug use is the behavior associated with the second greatest number of reported cases of AIDS and is the primary source of HIV infection in adult heterosexual and pediatric AIDS cases (21). African American and Hispanics comprise 44% of the total injecting drug use–related AIDS cases, and African Americans constitute 50% of the cases of AIDS among heterosexual injecting drug abusers (IDUs) (20). African Americans account for more than half of the AIDS cases who are heterosexual partners of IDUs (21), and African Americans account for 53% of pediatric AIDS cases. Over 60% are infected because their mothers were IDUs or had sex with an IDU (21). AIDS is spread among IDUs primarily by the sharing of drug injection equipment and by engaging in unprotected sex.

For African Americans, the foregoing information is especially sobering. African Americans are disproportionately over represented among total adult AIDS cases, among adult female AIDS cases, and among pediatric AIDS cases. This picture is largely due to the over representation of African Americans among IDUs.

HIV seropositive rates have been found to be higher in IDUs who also use cocaine (1, 22). Studies by many investigators have shown higher rates of HIV seropositivity in African Americans. The higher incidence of cocaine use among African American IDUs than in white IDUs suggests one basis for the higher rate of HIV infection in African American IDUs. This may also explain, in part, the greater rate among African American IDUs of human T-lymphotrophic virus type I, a member of the same retrovirus family in which the AIDS virus is a member.

PREVENTION

Having considered a variety of consequences associated with drug use and abuse, it should be emphasized that prevention encompasses several approaches. One such approach is the prevention of drug and alcohol use in youths, i.e., primary prevention. Reducing the number of retail outlets selling alcohol and prohibiting the use of illicit drugs are examples of primary prevention. Another very different strategy involves the prevention of the consequences of drug or alcohol use by reducing high-risk behaviors. This is a secondary prevention strategy. The provision of condoms or the use of needle-exchange programs represent two types of secondary prevention approaches for HIV transmission. A third and an equally important strategy is to prevent death or further morbidity in persons who have sustained at least one clinical consequence of alcohol use or illicit drug use. An example of this approach would be efforts to prevent the development of AIDS or disease progression in HIV-infected drug users or efforts to prevent end-stage renal disease in patients with illicit drug-induced renal disease.

Two key points are important in any commentary on the status of drug abuse prevention generally and prevention specifically in African Americans. First, given the American experience with Prohibition and efforts to reduce smoking, large-scale reduction of any addictive behavior is very difficult and complex. Any solution has to be both large scale and long term. Second, much less is known about how prevention should proceed than what is known about the prevalence and effects of drug use. Given this state of affairs, specifically with reference to prevention of drug abuse in African Americans, there is often more conjecture, opinion, and polemics in the literature than evidence of systematic work. This is not necessarily bad, if the former helps to bring about the latter.

Finally, there are many theories concerning the high incidence of drug use in poor African American communities. As indicated previously, Brunswick (9) concluded that the lack of access to the societal opportunity structure is one cause of the problem. Rappaport (23) provided a similar explanation in describing the lack of access to resources as causing problems of living. These explanations are consistent with the National Institute on Drug Abuse's (22) statement that most drug abusers use drugs as a substitute for a lack of fulfillment of basic human needs. This viewpoint suggests that the large-scale drug use and abuse by African American youths is as much the result of a societal problem as an individual problem. Tucker (24) states "that many ethnic minorities view drug abuse as an adaptive response to oppressive societal conditions." A number of workers in the field support the concept of the inherent ghetto culture as the cause of drug abuse. Indeed, Feldman (25) and Blumer (26) concluded that peer pressures for drug use in the ghetto environment were so great that they were amazed that anyone escapes the problem of drug addiction. The National Household Survey finding that African American children were most likely to disagree with the statement that "crack or cocaine can kill you" (2) appears to support this viewpoint. Also, Paton and Kandel's (27) finding that use in African American and Puerto Rican youths was not related to depressive mood and normalessness, in contrast to white youths, provides additional indication that the causes of drug use in African American youth may be somewhat different than those of whites. These findings are key in that they offer some suggestion for the design of prevention programs.

Preventing Drug Use and Abuse in Youths

Both Tucker (24) and Crisp (28) have concluded that prevention programs generally designed for middle-class whites are not appropriate for African Americans in lower socioeconomic groups. It is also not clear that these programs are useful for African Americans of any socioeconomic class. Crisp described a program designed by Ortiz (29) to counter these biases. Ortiz's systemic approach was based on the belief that oppressed people often have a hard time relating to present prevention models because these often fail to deal with their reasons of abusing drugs. This researcher felt that a "systemic" approach which focuses on racism, sexism, power, economic realities, and policy-making was necessary before the usual individual-based approaches can be applied.

Recently, more studies and perspective tend to counter these biases. Metsch et al. (30) designed a family-centered treatment program for substance-abusing mothers and their children. The program adapted a systemic approach and aimed to reduce reliance on social and health welfare. Improved functioning in specific life and vocational skills were encouraged. Providing instruction on parenting techniques and maternal/child relations for the mothers while providing prevention services for their children in a safe and supportive environment were all integral parts of this program. Funded by Center for Substance Abuse Treatment this 5-year demonstration grant has just recently concluded its implementation phase. The results of this approach are presently unclear.

Rouse (2) reviewed data from the annual National High School Senior Survey which indicated that drug education courses or lectures in school had a greater preventive impact on African American than white students. Slightly less than half of the whites students surveyed indicated that information provided in school about illicit drugs made them less interested in trying drugs, as compared with 75% of the African American students. However, fewer African Americans than whites reported that they had received such drug courses or lecturers. Rouse (2) therefore concluded that every effort should be made to make drug education available to African American students. While these findings are encouraging, it is important to emphasize that African American high school seniors are not entirely representative of African American youths who use and abuse drugs.

Based on our earlier discussion, it would appear that interventions designed to reach African American youth require tailoring to the beliefs, percepts, and needs of these individuals. Crisp (28) describes a number of levels of intervention indicated by Rappaport (23), none of which need be mutually exclusive—individual, group, organization, institutional, community, and societal. Although Crisp (28) criticized existing intervention approaches for not being innovative, he also failed to offer any alternative innovative strategies. Rowe and Grill (31) offered an alternative innovative strategy based on an appreciation of core beliefs. Key ontological and epistemological assumptions of rational clinical and counseling interventions are presented that highlight the difference between traditional goals and theories and the proposed alternative conceptual system and treatment strategies with the African centered approach proposed by Rowe and Grill. The difficulty with both the proposed intervention by Crisp and the approach proposed by Rowe and Grill is that there is no report or published evaluation of any existing prevention program based on these strategies.

Nuttall and his colleagues (32) developed an effective approach to drug abuse prevention intended for teenagers from an inner-city minority population. Through informal seminars, including films and discussion, youngsters were led to explore their feelings and goals for the future and the possible effects of drug use on these goals. Relatively little emphasis was given to education about drugs per se, but rather, the emphasis was on value clarification, learning to think about the future, and how actions in the present would affect that future. The program was designed by people from an African American inner-city background. Positive change was indicated by higher scores following the intervention for the "no drug condition" and lower scores for the "frequent drug use" condition. Boys showed positive changes, although the absolute amount of reported change was relatively small. Girls showed no change. The authors speculated that no changes were obtained for girls because the girls were already aware of the negative implications of drug use. This study demonstrates the difficulties of instituting and evaluating change in short-term programs, no matter how carefully designed.

Ghadivian (33) offered another innovative approach. The approach targeted the individual, the family, and society. The individual is helped to develop a sense of purpose, a feeling of self-esteem, and respect for others. This resulted in a state of maturity making possible an objective evaluation of circumstances and postponement of immediate gratification for a future goal, resulting in a feeling of responsibility and spiritual orientation. It was postulated that this can help the individual to develop positive attitudes toward himself or herself and the environment. Parents are encouraged to promote love and unity, as well as a drug-free lifestyle, so children are provided with positive health models. The family experience is also intended to help children to cope with stress and other problems of daily life. By means of education, society at large is encouraged to adopt positive attitudes toward health and to promote activities that lead to the elimination of isolation. While interesting, there does not exist a published report of an evaluation of a prevention program based on that approach.

Graham and his colleagues (34) evaluated the efficacy of a social skills and affect management curriculum for each of four major ethnic groups: Asian, African American, Hispanic, and white. The subjects were 7th graders when the intervention was introduced and 8th graders when the change was assessed. One group was exposed to a 12-session program, giving students social skills for resisting drug offers. Another group was administered an affect management program, and a third control group received no special drug prevention curriculum other than that offered by the schools. The outcome measures were composite indices based on lifetime and recent use items for cigarettes, alcohol, and marihuana. The results showed clear prevention effects for females, but not for males. Overall prevention effects were strongest for smoking and weakest for alcohol. The program appeared to be least effective for whites and most effective for Asians.

The findings from the Nuttall and Graham prevention studies are consistent with Rouse's (2) conclusion that prevention and intervention strategies demonstrate differential effects within various ethnic groups and socioeconomic populations. Still, it is unclear whether the results may or may not be expected in other African American subjects or communities. As Rouse (2) concluded, there is no one answer of how best to approach different ethnic or racial populations. Nonetheless, she wisely stressed the need for community-wide *and* school-based approaches.

The development of programs that would effectively reduce drug use in African American youth would represent a major advance. Clearly, it would be important for the program developer to make the program meaningful to the recipient audience. It would appear that the only way to do this would be to ensure ample input and participation from members of the relevant communities. Detailed descriptions of the interventions as well as a clearly defined evaluation process are essential components of any such effort.

CHANGING HIGH-RISK BEHAVIORS IN IDUs

It is extremely difficult to change health and sexual behaviors (2). This would seem to be particularly difficult for individuals with few psychosocial resources as is known to be the case with many African American drug-dependent persons (35, 36). Additionally, a significant portion of drug-dependent persons (African American and other ethnic groups) are known to suffer from additional psychopathology such as affective or anxiety disorders, antisocial personality disorder, schizophrenia, or other substance abuse disorders (35, 36), which may make them more resistant to substance abuse treatment (37). The high incidence of needle sharing and unsafe sex practices, such as prostitution among African American IDUs, highlights the great need for effective intervention programs for these individuals. There is evidence that IDUs testing positive for HIV are more likely to suffer from psychopathology, such as an antisocial personality disorder (38), suggesting that high-risk behaviors are more likely to be found in IDUs with greater psychopathology. If this is the case, it is very likely that such individuals will be more resistant to HIV prevention efforts.

Needle sharing appears to be, at least in some part, associated with a feeling of friendship and intimacy. The elimination of this behavior may possibly increase the degree of alienation and loneliness in a population badly in need of social supports. Use of safe sex practices may conflict with sociocultural values regarding sexual behavior, gender roles, and social structure. A good example of this conflict relates to condom use, which has always been viewed as suspicious or mistrustful by sex partners. Thus, there is very little to suggest how to bring about such change in our open society. Education in itself does not appear to be sufficient. The National Institute for Drug Abuse is supporting considerable research directed toward increasing knowledge and effecting change in this very critical area (2).

This point was reinforced by a review by Lanarme (39). This investigator pointed out that school drug abuse prevention programs represent an enormous education resource. Recent perception of an epidemic of drug abuse among the nation's youth have fueled the escalation in expenditures for drug prevention programming. An important question that needs to be addressed concerns whether broad-ranging drug education efforts directed at all public and private school students are efficient and effective uses of available resources. After a brief evaluation of drug education programming in the United States, Lanarme examines recent longitudinal research regarding the antecedents of drug abuse among young people. Based on this research, suggestions are made for a new approach to drug education programs which would direct intensive interventions at the minority of youth who are identifiable in early childhood as particularly susceptible to problems with drug abuse (40).

In a comprehensive review of existing published reports of prevention programs, which included African Americans and focused on preventing HIV transmission, Brown (41) made the following conclusions. While there are many theories of human behavior, the relevance of most to risky HIV-related behaviors has not been found and do not reflect the sociocultural or historical perspectives or male-female relationships of many African American communities. The existing published reports are flawed in at least one of the following ways:

1. Small study sample and unclear whether findings would be reproducible
2. Short period of observations and thus unclear that changes were not temporary
3. Study population selection bias
4. Focused on self-reports of behavior change
5. Few comparisons between African Americans and other ethnic or racial groups
6. Few comparisons between male and female subjects
7. Few studies with an appropriate control population

In Brown's review, he noted that among illicit drug users there were more studies that reported changes in drug-related behaviors than in sex-related behaviors.

TREATMENT

Data collected by the National Institute on Drug Abuse (40) indicate that African Americans and Hispanics are three times as likely as whites to be in treatment for substance abuse. Some writers have concluded that current theories and models of addiction and addiction treatment have been based on middle-class whites (28). It has also been argued that since the causes of ad-

diction are different for African Americans, the treatment needs of African Americans may be different from whites and other groups. (3, 24). The corollary question deriving from this viewpoint is whether there is a need for alternative treatment and prevention models which are sensitive to the needs of people of color.

The literature thus far does not support the viewpoint that African Americans do not benefit as much from existing treatments as other groups. On the other hand, there also does not exist unequivocal evidence that African Americans benefit equally as well as other ethnic or racial groups. Rouse (2) concluded that the existing large longitudinal studies of treatment outcomes have, with few exceptions, found that demographic variables such as race are significant predictors of treatment outcomes. However, a large-scale study of treatment outcomes in a number of treatment programs throughout the country conducted by Joe and his colleagues (42) found that the ethnic status of the patient was not as important in influencing outcome as the community structure surrounding the treatment. Pretreatment variables such as employment and type of treatment were more important (3).

In contrast, Brown et al. (43) cited several studies with opiate-dependent subjects which indicated that an ethnic group with at least a 75% majority in a program was likely to do better in that program than the other ethnic groups represented in the program. However, their own research provided, at most, limited support for this conclusion. They compared three kinds of programs: methadone maintenance, residential drug-free, and outpatient drug-free. Evidence consistent with their hypothesis was revealed for only the outpatient drug-free programs. The limited evidence that exist for this study indicates that the program attempted to adapt to the nature of their patient constituency.

Phillips and Phin (44), for example, found that counselors were usually of the same ethnicity as their clients. Minority group members tended to be clustered in a few programs rather than being dispersed throughout the treatment network. They concluded that "it seems that a minority treatment network does exist which recognizes the need for cultural sensitivity and uses a shared staff/client cultural identity to attract individuals to treatment." Pentz also mentioned this when he described future directions for drug abuse prevention, the overarching perspective of interfusing basic and social science research approaches (45).

Despite the foregoing, it is likely that African Americans as well as other ethnic subgroups have specific needs for which particular treatment forms may be more effective. It is important to increase our knowledge concerning similarities and differences in the characteristics and treatment responses of different ethnic subgroups. For example, an important treatment question that has not been addressed adequately is whether African American patients respond more favorably—all other factors held equal—to a therapist of similar background. Lillie-Blanton and her colleagues attempted to address this aspect and concluded that ethnicity of the counselor or clinician may not be the dominant determining factor (15). A related question in need of further investigation concerns the sensitivity of various aspects of treatment programs to African American patients and how such sensitivities are expressed.

One of the problems in substance abuse treatment is that we have only limited knowledge and ability to objectively measure the actual treatment services that various individuals receive in treatment. Also, there is presently only limited knowledge concerning the amounts of and types of treatment that are most effective for particular substance abuse problems. For example, will the provision of primary medical care on-site in drug abuse treatment programs enhance drug abuse treatment outcome for African Americans? Once the necessary knowledge exists, is disseminated, and the appropriate tools are in place, it will be possible to more adequately address and answer some of the questions and issues that have been raised concerning the treatment of African American substance abusers. While these considerations may limit the precision of the findings that can be obtained presently, they should not preclude systematic investigation into these questions.

SUMMARY

In considering substance abuse epidemiology, prevention, and treatment as they relate to African Americans a number of complex issues arise. For one, Americans of African descent are heterogeneous in culture, language, geographic distribution, and other important factors. Consequently, any discussions must stress this important limitation in assigning any attributes to this group of Americans.

Secondly, the scientific basis for making observations on substance abuse concerning most Americans and especially Americans of African descent is extremely limited. While the data base is more plentiful epidemiologically, published rigorous reports of prevention or treatment studies are rare. Present studies are limited because of an insufficient number or description of the study population; bias in the selection of the study population; under ascertainment of hidden populations (such as the homeless and school dropouts) where substance abuse may be more prevalent; lack of an appropriate control or comparative population; a diverse range of selected outcomes, some of which present significant challenges in justifying their appropriateness (i.e., should the focus be use, abuse, or dependence); continuing concern about the validity of self-reporting in measuring the outcomes of interest; an inadequate description of the intervention(s) of other studies; and inadequate descriptions of the evaluation of prevention and treatment interventions.

With this background, this chapter has considered existing knowledge and discussed some of the questions and issues that have been raised concerning the prevalence and consequences of substance use among African Americans. The status and merits of published prevention and treatment efforts were also considered.

African Americans are over represented among Americans who use an illicit drug. This is not the case for all substances of abuse or for all age groups. While there are higher prevalence rates of cocaine and marihuana use in the past month among African Americans, the lifetime rates of marihuana and cocaine use are higher among whites. There are also differences between African Americans and whites in the ages at which illicit drug use is more prevalent.

Many factors have been reported to be associated with substance abuse among African Americans. These include under education, unemployment, under employment, hopelessness, dysfunctional families, and other indices of poverty. However, none of these factors has been unequivocally demonstrated to be causal, perhaps because of the fundamental and inseparable relationships between these factors. Indeed, there is also evidence that some, if not all, may also be consequences of substance abuse.

Whether predictors or consequences of substance abuse, these factors are over represented in many African American communities. These social dislocations are not the only consequences of substance abuse which have a devastating and disproportionately greater impact on African Americans. HIV/AIDS, other causes of excess morbidity, and substance abuse-related deaths are also overrepresented among African Americans.

In the context of this pervasive impact of substance abuse, prevention and treatment programs do provide services for African Americans. Most of these programs are neither described or evaluated in the published literature. The utilization by African Americans of prevention and treatment programs and the effectiveness of these programs is largely unknown.

While there is a clear sense that specialized prevention programs are badly needed, the existing knowledge base does not unequivocally support such an initiative and is not sufficient to direct program development. It will require creative and dedicated effort coupled with systematic evaluation to develop programs that work. It is also clear that there is a need to determine the specific needs of African Americans and other ethnic or racial populations, the nature and effectiveness of current treatments for these patients, and whether more effective treatments can be developed for African American communities.

Society has in recent years become increasingly aware of the problems of African American substance abusers. Studies of and programs for African American substance abusers designed to provide answers to some of the more pressing questions are receiving funding. More investigations, using a wide variety of methodological designs, are needed. The answers to these questions will require sustained funding and the development of long-standing programs of prevention and treatment. There must also be well-designed and adequately funded evaluation components of prevention and treatment programs.

Clearly, one of the reasons why so many substance abuse questions remain is the stigma of substance abuse in America. Among many Americans of African descent, the continuing existence of substance abuse in their communities is related, in part, to the stigma of discrimination. Nonetheless, the public health implications for answers to substance abuse problems are an imperative for all Americans. Individual dedication and a commitment of all Americans to open discussion and change will be tremendous assets to finding effective solutions to the undeniable and unrelenting impact of substance abuse.

References

1. National Institute on Drug Abuse. Drug use among racial/ethnic minorities. NIH publication no. 95–3888, 1995.
2. Rouse B. Drug abuse among racial/ethnic minorities: a special report. Rockville, MD: National Institute of Drug Abuse, 1989.
3. Hanson B. Drug treatment effectiveness: Case of racial and ethnic minorities in America—some research question and proposals. Int J Addict 1985;20:99–137.
4. Fort S. Family history and patterns of addiction in African American cocaine and alcohol dependent individuals [doctoral dissertation]. University of Iowa, 1990.
5. National Institute on Drug Abuse. National household survey on drug abuse: main findings 1985. DHHS Pub. No. (ADM) 88–1586. Washington, DC: U.S. Government Printing Office, 1988.
6. National Institute on Drug Abuse. Illicit drug use, smoking and drinking by America's high school students, college students, and young adults (1975–1987). DHHS Pub. No. (ADM) 89–1602. Washington, DC: U.S. Government Printing Office, 1988.
7. Kang S, Magura S, Shapiro JL. Correlates of cocaine/crack use among inner-city incarcerated adolescents. Am J Drug and Alcohol Abuse 1994;20(4):413–429.
8. Robins LN, Murphy GE. Drug use in a normal population of young Negro men. Am J Public Health 1967;57:1580–1596.
9. Brunswick AF. Black youths and drug use behavior. In: Beschner GM, Friedman AS, eds. Youth drug abuse: problems, issues, and treatment. Toronto: Lexington Books, 1979: 443–490.
10. Halikas JA, Darvish HS, Rimmer JD. The black addicts. I. Methodology, chronology of addiction, and overview of the population. Am J Drug Alcohol Abuse 1976;3:529–543.
11. Chambers CD, Moffett D, Jones JP. Demographic factors associated with Negro opiate addiction. Int J Addict 1968;3:329–543.
12. Craig RJ. Characteristics of inner city heroin addicts applying for treatment in a Veteran Administration hospital drug program (Chicago). Int J Addict 1980;15:409–418.
13. Alterman A, et al. Personality Assessment Inventory (PAI) scores of lower socioeconomic African-American and Latino methadone maintenance patients. Assessment 1995;2:91–100.
14. Brown LS, et al. Addiction severity index (SI) scores of four racial ethnic and gender groups of methadone maintenance patients. J Subst Abuse 1993;5:269–279.
15. Lillie-Blanton M, Anthony JC, Schuster CR. Probing the meaning of racial/ethnic group comparison in crack cocaine smoking. JAMA 1993; 269(8):993–997.
16. Van Hasselt NB, et al. Drug abuse prevention for high risk African American children and their families. Addict Behav 1993;18(2): 213–234.
17. National Institute on Drug Abuse. Data from the Drug Abuse Warning Network (DAWN)—annual data, 1985. Statistical Series, Report 1: 5, DHHS Publication No. (ADM)-86-1469, Washington, DC: U.S. Government Printing Office, 1986.
18. NIDA Capsules. Substance abuse among blacks in the U.S. Rockville, MD: National Institute on Drug Abuse, 1990.
19. Brown LS, et al. Medical disorders in a cohort of NYC drug abusers, much more than HIV diseases. J Addiction Dis 1993;12:11–27.
20. U.S. Centers for Disease Control and Prevention. First 500,000 AIDS cases—United States, 1995. MMWR Morb Mortal Wkly Rep 1995; 44(46):849–853.
21. U.S. Centers for Disease Control and Prevention. AIDS weekly surveillance report—United States AIDS program, Center for Infectious Disease, 6 February 1989.
22. National Institute on Drug Abuse. Can drug abuse be prevented in the black community? Rockville, MD: National Institute on Drug Abuse, 1977.
23. Rappaport J. Community psychology: values, research, and action. New York: Holt, Rinehart, & Winston, 1977.
24. Tucker MB. U.S. ethnic minorities and drug abuse: an assessment of the science and practice. Int J Addict 1985;20:1021–1047.

25. Feldman HW. Ideological supports to becoming and remaining a heroin addict. J Health Soc Behav 1968;9:131–139.

26. Blumer H. The world of youthful drug use. Berkeley, CA: University of California School of Criminology, 1967.

27. Paton SM, Kandel DB. Psychological factors and adolescent illicit drug use: ethnicity and sex differences. Adolescence 1978;13:187–200.

28. Crisp AD. Making substance abuse prevention relevant to low-income black neighborhoods. J Psychoactive Drugs 1980;12:13–19.

29. Ortiz C. NIDA workshop on drug abuse prevention for low income populations. Washington, DC, 1978.

30. Metsch LR, et al. Implementation of a family-centered treatment program for substance abusing women and their children. J Psychoactive Drugs 1995;27(1):73–83.

31. Rowe D, Grill C. African centered drug treatment, an alternative conceptual paradox for drug counseling with African American clients. J Psychoactive Drugs 1993;5(1):21–33.

32. Nuttall RL, Moreland ML, Hunter JB. Effects of an affective drug abuse prevention program on inner city black youth. In: Schechter AJ, ed. Drug dependence and alcoholism. Vol. 2. Social and behavioral issues. New York: Plenum Press, 1981.

33. Ghadivian AM. A Ba'hai perspective on drug abuse prevention. McGill University, Montreal, Canada, Bulletin on Narcotics.

34. Graham JW, Johnson CA, Hansen WB, Flay BR, Gee M. Drug use prevention programs, gender, and ethnicity: Evaluation of three seventh-grade project SMART cohorts. Prev Med 1990; 19:305–313.

35. Kosten T, Rounsaville BJ, Kleber HD. Ethnic and gender differences among opiate addicts. Int J Addict 1985;20:1143–1163.

36. Kosten T, Gawin FH, Rounsaville BJ, Kleber HD. Cocaine abuse among opioid addicts: demographic and diagnostic factors in treatment. Am J Drug Alcohol Abuse 1986;12:1–16.

37. Alterman A, Carciola J. The antisocial personality disorder diagnosis in substance abusers: problems and issuers. J Nerv Ment Dis (in press).

38. Brooner RK, Bigelow GE, Greenfield L, Strain EC, Schmidt CW. Intravenous drug abusers with antisocial personality disorder: high rate of HIV-1 infection. NIDA Res Monogr 1991;105:488–489.

39. Lanarme RJ. School drug education programming: in search of a new direction. J Drug Educ 1993;23(4):325–331.

40. National Institute on Drug Abuse. Data from the national drug and alcoholism treatment utilization survey (NDATUS), main findings for drug abuse treatment units. Statistical Series, Report F:10, DHHS Publication No. (ADM) 83–1284. Washington, DC: U.S. Government Printing Office, 1983.

41. Brown LS. Substance abuse and HIV/AIDS: Implications of prevention efforts for Americans of African descent. In: Amuleru-Marshall O, ed. Substance abuse treatment in the era of AIDS. Rockville, MD: National Institute on Drug Abuse, 1995:17–58.

42. Joe GW, Singh BK, Finklea D, Hudelburg R, Sells SB. Community factors, racial composition of treatment programs and outcomes. Services research report. Rockville, MD: National Institute on Drug Abuse, 1977.

43. Brown BS, Joe GW, Thompson P. Minority group status and treatment retention. Int J Addict 1985;20:319–335.

44. Phillips P, Phin J, ed. Drug dependence and alcoholism. Social and behavioral issues. New York: Plenum Press, 1981;2:22.

45. Pentz MA. Direction for future research in drug abuse prevention. Prev Med 1994;23(5): 646–652.

69   HISPANIC AMERICANS

Pedro Ruiz and John G. Langrod

Addiction to drugs and alcohol is a major problem among the different nationality groups of Hispanics who reside throughout the United States. Yet, our knowledge and understanding of the intimate link between addiction and its sociocultural context is seriously lacking. As a consequence, the treatment approaches offered to Hispanics are of limited relevance or of less than optimal quality. For instance, only a little more than half of Puerto Rican addicts in New York City become involved in some form of treatment, and, even more importantly, many of those who get involved in treatment drop out prematurely (1). In Miami, a similar pattern has been found with respect to Cuban addicts (2). The limited literature that does exist on this subject suggests that significant factors in the etiology of addiction among most Hispanics, primarily Puerto Ricans, are socioculturally related to a considerable extent. It is also apparent that treatment programs designed and operated by "Anglo" professionals have not developed adequate cultural components and sensitivity in programming to attract lower socioeconomic Hispanics. Among the problems related to the special needs of Hispanic patients in drug abuse and alcoholism programs are the low percentage of bilingual and bicultural professional staff who work in these programs. In most instances, non–Spanish-speaking staff presents difficulties in understanding the specific sociocultural issues faced by Hispanic addicts. It is definitely unrealistic to expect that Hispanic addicts could feel comfortable and be amenable to treatment efforts in the face of unfamiliar program settings and staff lacking in cultural sensitivity. Even when programs employ enough Hispanic staff and offer culturally sensitive treatment approaches, governmental regulations and policies may interfere with the acceptance of such programs by Hispanic populations. For instance, the requirement of compulsory urine testing in methadone maintenance programs with its implicit message of disbelief of the patient's word may offend the Hispanic's sense of dignity, which is highly relevant and firmly defended.

It is within this sociocultural context that, in this chapter, we will attempt to offer a unique perspective on the Hispanic substance abuser. In so doing, we plan to focus on (a) definition of the population; (b) current epidemio-logic trends of substance abuse among Hispanics; (c) sociocultural considerations relevant to their substance abuse patterns; (d) research and treatment outcomes; and most significantly (e) public policy formulations.

DEFINITION OF THE POPULATION

As depicted in Table 69.1 and according to the 1990 U.S. Census data (3), there are currently about 21.4 million Hispanics residing in this country, out of a total United States population of approximately 246 million. As one can deduct from the review of these sociodemographic characteristics, Hispanics confront major socioeconomic challenges in their quest for educational, career, and economic advancement. Moreover, these socioeconomic challenges could be translated into stressors which can lead, directly or indirectly, to the abuse of drugs. These differences between the varying Hispanic groups also suggest the need for special programming for each of these groups.

CURRENT EPIDEMIOLOGIC TRENDS

During the last decade, a major attempt has been made to scientifically measure the prevalence of drug use among the American household population. The National Institute on Drug Abuse and the Substance Abuse and Mental Health Services Administration have sponsored a series of national household surveys. These surveys have shed much light on the prevalence of substance abuse in the civilian and noninstitutionalized Hispanic population. In discussing current trends among this Hispanic population, we will focus primarily on the last of these surveys: The National Household Survey on Drug Abuse conducted in 1993 (4). This survey sampled 6894 Hispanics out of a total population of about 20.8 million. Table 69.2 summarizes the lifetime use of any illicit drug for the general population and for the subpopulations of Hispanics, African Americans, and whites. Hispanics have a lower rate of having ever used illicit drugs in comparison to the general population,

Table 69.1 Sociodemographic Characteristics

	Non-Hispanic whites	African Americans	Hispanics	Mexican Americans	Puerto Ricans	Cuban Americans	Central and South Americans
Population (in millions)	227.4	30.9	21.4	13.4	2.4	1.1	3.0
Median household income	$30,513	$18,676	$22,330	$22,439	$16,169	$25,900	$23,568
Percent of individuals below poverty level	12.1	31.9	28.1	28.1	40.6	16.9	25.4
Percentage of households with income of $50,000 or more	25.4	11.9	13.4	11.6	11.9	19.8	15.7
Percentage who completed high school	80.5	66.7	51.3	43.6	58.0	61.0	60.4
Percentage with four or more years of college	22.3	11.5	9.7	6.2	10.1	18.5	15.1
Percentage of female headed households	11.4	47.8	19.1	15.6	33.7	15.3	21.5
Home ownership	65.8	42.4	39.0	43.5	23.4	47.3	22.2

Adapted from U.S. Bureau of the Census: Current Population Reports. Series P-20, No. 449, 1991 (3).

with the exception of a slightly higher rate for having ever used crack and heroin. Further, Hispanics also have a slightly higher rate of cocaine, crack, and heroin use in comparison to the white population, and a higher rate of use of most drugs in contrast to the African American population, with the exception of marihuana, crack, cigarettes, and heroin.

In order to discuss the index of drug use among different Hispanic subgroups, we will first refer to the results of the Hispanic Health and Nutrition Examination Survey conducted between 1982 and 1984 (5). In this survey published in 1987, 8021 individuals between the ages of 12 and 74 years from Hispanic households were surveyed concerning their use of marihuana, cocaine, inhalants, and sedatives. In Table 69.3, we summarize the results of this survey. In general, Mexican Americans and Puerto Ricans were each more likely than Cuban Americans to have ever used marihuana and cocaine. Concerning marihuana, the percentages were quite similar among Mexican Americans and Puerto Ricans (41.6% versus 42.7%). Mexican Americans used inhalants slightly more than Puerto Ricans (6.4% versus 4.8%). However, Puerto Ricans were somewhat more likely to use sedatives than Mexican Americans (5.8% versus 5.0%). Regarding cocaine, Puerto Ricans were much more affected (21.5%) than either Mexican Americans (11.1%) or Cuban Americans (9.2%).

Concerning the use of alcohol, the Hispanic Health and Nutrition Examination Survey shows significant differences among these three Hispanic groups (6). As seen in Table 69.4, the highest percentage for each group were the abstainers, with females abstaining considerably more than males. Mexican Americans have the lowest percentage of abstainers (50.3%), while Puerto Ricans and Cuban Americans have similar percentages (59.6 and 59.8). However, in terms of heavy drinking, the differences are more notable, with Mexican Americans reporting a rate of 8.4% of heavy alcohol consumption, Puerto Ricans 6.7%, and Cuban Americans 3.8%.

SOCIOCULTURAL CONSIDERATIONS

The relationship between substance abuse and the addict's sociocultural context, particularly the ethnic minority addict, has already been well documented (7–10). At the heart of the problem is the fact that there is a dearth of Spanish speaking and/or bilingual and bicultural professional staff working in substance abuse treatment programs that service large numbers of Hispanic addicts. As a consequence, the unique sociocultural needs of these Hispanic addicts have not as yet been met. Furthermore, the rich sociocultural resources which could be utilized in the treatment of these patients have not been used to their maximum. On many occasions, these situations contribute to both treatment failure and dropout.

At times, stress related to migration add to these sociocultural factors. Take, for instance, the case of Puerto Ricans. Migrants from Puerto Rico to New York City and other parts of the continental United States are faced with the necessity of forging a new identity for themselves. However, they are also migrating from a society which itself is undergoing an identity cri-

sis. For instance, Puerto Ricans are United States citizens, which permits them to travel freely between the Island and the mainland. However, Puerto Ricans residing on the Island cannot vote to elect the President of the United States, or other federal officials, but they are subject to military service in this country. Puerto Rico is neither a State of the Union, nor is it an independent country. These situations create an artificial state of confusion, and thus an identity crisis. Furthermore, the socioeconomic and cultural milieus of Puerto Ricans are characterized by great discrepancies between rich and poor. Moreover, the poverty that exists in Puerto Rico is combined with a consumer mentality and a strong push toward assimilation into the majority "Anglo" culture. This compulsory assimilation and rapid urbanization have led to (a) a devaluation of the Puerto Rican culture, (b) a fragmentation of the extended family network system, and (c) an identity crisis. Undoubtedly, confusion, alienation, and loss of self-esteem are factors responsible for increases in substance abuse among Puerto Ricans. For instance, in the spring of 1986, a statewide household survey of substance abuse was conducted in New York State by the Division of Substance Abuse Services, Alcoholism and Alcohol Abuse (ll). This survey suggests certain cultural correlates of illicit substance use among Hispanics. For example, findings for Hispanics show that the stronger the ties to the Hispanic culture, the less likely the use of drugs is to occur; conversely, the stronger the ties to the American culture, the more likely the drug use. Fifty-three percent of Hispanics born in the United States reported using some illicit drugs during their lifetime, compared to only 25% of those born in Puerto Rico and 11% of Hispanics born in other Hispanic countries. Along the same lines, 45% of Hispanics who spoke only English or mostly English had used some illicit drugs during their lifetime, while only 8% of those Hispanics who spoke Spanish or mostly

Table 69.2 Percentage of Lifetime Illicit Drug Use

	USA population	African Americans	Hispanics	Whites
Any drug	37.2	33.5	31.2	38.9
Marihuana	33.7	30.7	28.1	35.6
Cocaine	11.3	9.4	9.5	12.0
Crack	1.8	3.4	2.0	1.6
Inhalants	5.3	2.9	4.9	5.8
Hallucinogens	8.7	3.0	5.9	10.1
Stimulants	6.0	3.0	3.9	6.9
Sedatives	3.4	2.2	2.2	3.6
Tranquilizers	4.6	2.3	2.8	5.2
Analgesics	5.8	3.5	3.9	6.3
Alcohol	83.6	75.2	77.0	86.4
Cigarettes	71.2	59.6	57.4	75.5
Phencyclidine (PCP)	4.1	1.9	3.2	4.5
Heroin	1.1	2.1	1.4	0.9

Adapted from National Household Survey on Drug Abuse: Population Estimates 1993. Substance Abuse and Mental Health Services Administration, DHHS Publication No. (SMA)94-3017, 1993 (4).

Table 69.3 Lifetime Percent Distribution of Drug Use (12–74 Years Old)

Drugs	Mexican American (n = 3394)			Puerto Rican (n = 1286)			Cuban American (n = 555)		
	Total	Male	Female	Total	Male	Female	Total	Male	Female
Marihuana	41.6	54.2	27.9	42.7	52.9	35.8	20.1	28.2	13.1
Cocaine	11.1	16.5	5.6	21.5	28.3	16.8	9.2	14.3	4.9
Inhalants	6.4	9.5	3.1	4.8	7.1	3.2	—	—	—
Sedatives	5.0	7.3	2.6	5.8	9.1	3.5	—	—	—

Adapted from Use of selected drugs among Hispanics: Mexican-Americans, Puerto Ricans, and Cuban-Americans. Findings from the Hispanic Health and Nutrition Examination Survey. Rockville, MD: National Institute of Drug Abuse, 1987:5.
Note: Inhalants and sedatives percentages for Cuban-Americans were unreliable, and thus not included.

Spanish did so. Additionally, Puerto Ricans—as well as Mexican Americans, Cuban Americans, and other Hispanics who have recently migrated to the United States—must confront the additional disadvantage of a language barrier. This language barrier further complicates the acculturation process and thus increases vulnerability to substance abuse.

To counteract these negative influences, Puerto Rican migrants who are older or have better economic resources frequently visit the Island and thus attempt to maintain their traditional values and customs. In contrast, however, younger Puerto Ricans identify more often with the "Anglo" mainland society and therefore are under greater pressure to reject their Hispanic culture in favor of the "Anglo" culture. Many of them, in fact, are caught between cultures, having given up or forgotten the traditions of the Island, while not as yet having developed a strong identification with the American way of life. This group is certainly very vulnerable to drug abuse. Indeed, the incidence of substance abuse among Hispanics, particularly Puerto Ricans, is higher among the youth.

In the case of Cuban Americans, there have been, so far, minimal opportunities to visit Cuba, a situation which has contributed to a stronger sense of survival within the United States. Fortunately for Cuban Americans, however, the process of acculturation has resulted in integration rather than assimilation, separation, or marginalization. This integration process has had a very positive impact insofar as substance abuse is concerned. Cuban Americans have developed a new ethnic identity while preserving their Cuban traditions and heritage. This has resulted in much less alienation and identity confusion among Cuban Americans than among other Hispanic subgroups who have migrated to the United States. Furthermore, in part, it has assisted Cuban Americans to achieve economic success and independence in the United States.

Table 69.4 Percent Distribution of Mexican American, Cuban American and Puerto Rican Drinking Levels According to Sex (1982–1984)

Ethnicity and Sex	Drinking Levels			
	Abstainer (%)	Light (%)	Moderate (%)	Heavier (%)
Mexican American (n = 4590)				
Male	32.3	26.1	26.4	15.3
Female	68.5	23.8	6.4	1.4
Total	50.3	24.9	16.4	8.4
Puerto Rican (n = 1821)				
Male	42.6	21.9	22.6	13.0
Female	71.2	19.9	6.5	2.3
Total	59.6	20.7	13.1	6.7
Cuban American (n = 1060)				
Male	37.8	30.6	23.6	7.9
Female	78.2	17.2	4.1	0.4
Total	59.8	23.4	13.1	3.8

Adapted from National Clearinghouse for Alcohol and Drug Information—Update. Office of Substance Abuse Prevention of the Alcohol, Drug Abuse and Mental Health Administration. January 1989, P.2. (16).
Note: Percentages were calculated with weighted data for persons 12 to 74 years of age.

The previously discussed sociocultural issues lead to a series of key questions concerning substance abuse among Hispanic populations. For instance, how do specific sociocultural factors common to all Hispanics affect types of drug use, patterns of abuse, and treatment needs? Despite the fact that all Hispanic subgroups have some common characteristics—such as the Spanish language, Catholic background, Indian and/or African traits, and an Iberian heritage—they differ in the incidence and type of substance abuse. How can we account for these differences? Do Hispanics born and raised in the mainland United States have different treatment outcomes than Hispanics born and raised outside of the United States and who later migrated to this country? If so, why? For instance, it has already been reported in the medical literature (12) that different ethnic groups, including Hispanics, vary in terms of response to drug dosages, side effects, and metabolism of certain psychotherapeutic medications. To what extent could this be physiologically caused and to what extent could this be culturally determined? These types of questions need to be researched further so that the answers could be incorporated into the health care and substance abuse treatment armamentarium.

Also of great importance—particularly from a prevention point of view—are gender differences in current substance abuse trends. For instance, substance abuse among young Hispanic women in Puerto Rico and in the United States is on the rise, particularly for certain substances. The factor of female emancipation must be considered in the analysis of these trends, as well as the unnecessary prejudice and discrimination which this emancipating process creates. Culturally determined family dynamics also could play a major role in this increased incidence of substance abuse among Hispanic women (13). Furthermore, a large number of Hispanic women in the United States are heads of households and therefore are forced to function in a variety of different social roles. Undoubtedly, these situations lead to additional stress and thus to increased vulnerability to substance abuse.

Along the same lines, we also must address the special treatment needs of Hispanic female addicts. First of all, they must be treated with equality and respect. Personal and sexual issues must be addressed sensitively and with understanding, particularly when the counselors and therapists are males. The employment of Hispanic female staff is certainly indicated in programs with a large Hispanic female clientele.

In addition, the involvement of the family in the treatment process is critically important. Hispanic families have excellent networking systems, and these systems can play a positive role both in the treatment process and in primary prevention. For instance, Hispanic families with no father figure present are said to be more vulnerable to addiction. In these cases, the individual roles of all family members must be understood, respected, and utilized appropriately in the treatment setting (14). Each member of the family plays a unique role in the dynamics of the family. For example, grandparents are respected for their wisdom, fathers for their authority, mothers for their devotion, children for their future role, and godparents ("padrinos") for their potential available support in times of need.

At times, however, cultural values and norms may militate in the fight against substance abuse. For instance, it is well known that fatalism is an important trait among Hispanics. "Que sea lo que Dios quiera" (God willing) is an attitude which frequently is taken by Hispanics (14). This posture can play a negative influence by leading an individual to not seek help or drop out of a treatment program. We must combat, educate, persuade, and break those negative attitudes that are caused by poverty, feelings of hopelessness, and powerlessness. Conversely, however, key Hispanic cultural values such as dignity, respect, and love (dignidad, respeto, y cariño), which represent the core triangle of the Hispanic culture, can all be positively used in both treatment and prevention (14). At times, migration can also play a negative role in the fight against substance abuse since it could lead to a breakdown of the family network system, thus making the members who migrate, as well as those who remain behind, very vulnerable to sociocultural stressors and therefore to addiction (11). Frequent visits to the native country, telephone calls, and correspondence among family members can all minimize these negative influences. In this respect, reinforcement of new networking systems, which could include treatment staff, should be maximized. This should be accomplished without fears of transferential and other related psychodynamic issues.

These problems can also be addressed through the use of group therapy approaches. Group discussions with a focus on historical and/or patriotic themes, when skillfully utilized, could lead to improvement of individual self-esteem. In this regard, the role of church affiliations—whether it be Catholic, Pentecostal, Jehovah's Witness, or other nonorthodox religious beliefs, such as Spiritism, Santeria, Brujeria, and Curanderism—could play a major positive role in the development of networking systems, treatment compliance, and primary prevention (15). On certain occasions, it is quite appropriate to develop linkages and liaisons between substance abuse treatment programs and religious institutions for the specific purpose of implementing preventive methods, whether primary, secondary, or tertiary (15). These approaches have already proven to be beneficial in other areas of health care (16), as well as mental health care (15, 17), and thus could also be applied in the field of substance abuse treatment and prevention. Along these same lines, it is important to recognize that Mexican Americans have a strong Indian heritage derived from the Aztec and Mayan cultures; thus, they share a widespread belief in Curanderism. Likewise, Cuban Americans and Puerto Ricans have been highly influenced by the European Spiritist philosophy of Alan Kardec. Moreover, Cuban Americans, in common with many other Hispanic Caribbean populations, also believe in Santeria and Brujeria. Santeria and Brujeria are syncretistic religious beliefs which were brought to the Caribbean from Africa during the period of slavery.

As previously discussed and documented, sociocultural factors could play a major role in the prevention and treatment of substance abuse among Hispanics, and are critically important to the development of comprehensive programs for the treatment of the substance abuser in the United States.

RESEARCH AND TREATMENT OUTCOMES

Unfortunately, there have not been enough well-conducted treatment outcome studies directed at the Hispanic substance abuse populations. However, some of the studies previously conducted deserve review and discussion. Maddux et al. (18) have reported in the medical literature that most Mexican Americans treated for substance abuse have returned to the use of heroin after hospital discharge. Furthermore, they have also reported that most of these Mexican American patients rejected nearly all posthospital social casework services except for crisis intervention. This occurred despite the fact that these services were provided within the geographical boundaries of the Hispanic barrio and were rendered by Mexican American caseworkers. In contrast, however, in another study Maddux and McDonald (19) reported that Mexican Americans do well in methadone maintenance programs, are very likely to be retained in treatment, and are also likely to be employed after one year of treatment. In another study, Savage and Simpson (20) compared posttreatment outcomes of African American, white, Mexican American, and Puerto Rican patients treated in a methadone maintenance program. They found that both Hispanic subgroups had the highest rates of dropout, expulsion, or both from their programs, as well as the lowest rates of treatment completion. Furthermore, Mexican Americans were found to show the smallest decrease in heroin use from pretreatment levels and a higher rate of posttreatment arrest and incarceration. However, Mexican Americans had the highest rate of employment when compared to the patients from the other ethnic subgroups. On the positive side, Langrod et al.

(21) have reported that in treating hard-core Puerto Rican addicts a positive response can be secured when placing a high degree of program emphasis on areas such as education, cultural sensitivity, and employment of bilingual/bicultural staff. In this regard, one of the most relevant treatment outcome studies was conducted by Nurco et al. (22). In this study, the authors reviewed 897 individual narcotic addiction treatment programs operating in 25 drug treatment centers in the states of Hawaii, Washington, Maryland, New Jersey, Connecticut, and New York. In the sample, 11.6% of subjects were Hispanics, 37.7% African Americans, and 49.6% whites. The focus of the research was to evaluate treatment outcome in relation to client/counselor congruence. Congruence was defined as agreement between client and counselor with regard to (a) appraisal of the client's problems and (b) the most effective approaches for dealing with them. The results of this study show that, for the entire sample, treatment outcome, in terms of compliance, improvement in quality of life, primary drug abuse problem, and primary nondrug problem were not significantly differentiated according to ethnicity or gender. The only exception, however, was that significant positive correlations were found between appropriateness of services congruence and a positive outcome for Hispanic males. Additionally, for Hispanic females congruence with respect to relative problem severity was related to positive outcomes for compliance with treatment. This type of research merits further exploration, with a particular focus on the different Hispanic subgroups living in the United States. Another important substance abuse treatment outcome study focusing on Cuban Americans was conducted by Szapocznik et al. (23). In this study, the authors presented evidence for the effectiveness of a strategy in engaging adolescent drug users and their families in therapy. The intervention method was based on strategic and structural systems concepts. To overcome resistances, the identified pattern of interactions that interfere with entry into treatment was restructured. Within the context of this study, strategic structural systems engagement is a planned and purposeful approach in diagnosing, joining, and restructuring a family—from the initial contact to the first therapy session. Theoretically, the family is conceptualized as a natural social system that establishes routine patterns of interactions among its members and within its environment. The behavior of the identified patient is perceived within the context of interactions of the entire family. Subjects involved in this study were engaged at a rate of 93%, in comparison to 42% for those not involved with this type of treatment approach. Furthermore, 77% of the patients in the study completed their treatment, in contrast to 25% of those treated with conventional treatment approaches.

Since the publishing of the last edition of this textbook in 1992 (24) several well-conceptualized research and treatment outcome studies were conducted. Among them, Longshore et al.'s (25) study involved 1170 drug-using subjects arrested in Los Angeles, California during the period April, 1988 to January, 1990, of which 35.9% were Hispanics. The perceived need for treatment among them was positively related to (a) self-reported drug dependence, (b) attitudes toward treatment for drug use, and (c) occurrence of drug-related problems other than dependence. Moreover, self-reported drug dependence was found to be higher among women drug users. Hispanics were found to be less likely to perceive a need for treatment among daily drug users (31.4%) in comparison to African Americans (37.9%) and whites (44.1%). These ethnic differences are not explained by self-reported drug dependence or any other predisposing factor. Likewise, positive attitude toward professional care was much lower among Hispanics (38.1%) than it was among African Americans (74.3%) or whites (75.2%). Concomitantly, heroin use among Hispanics was much higher (39.8%) than among African Americans (11.7%) or whites (18.5%).

In another interesting study (26), 4157 Mexican American and Mexican youths, between the ages of 11 and 19 years old, living along the U.S.-Mexico border were studied with respect to (a) their recent drug use, (b) problem drug use, (c) depressive symptomatology, and (d) their activity orientation. The results show that the Mexican youths had significantly lower rates of both recent and problematic drug use than their Mexican American counterparts on the U.S. side of the border. Moreover, while culturally related activity orientation carries a significantly increased risk for substance abuse, symptoms of distress/depression and specific sociodemographic factors exerted a stronger effect on these youths' use of substances.

Along the same lines, in another study (27), data from 144 Cuban American, 299 Puerto Rican, and 794 Mexican American adolescents included in the Hispanic Health and Nutrition Examination Survey (5) were analyzed to determine whether family structure is related to alcohol and drug use. The results of this study showed that family structure had a significant effect for alcohol abuse, drug use, and overall risk-taking behaviors among Mexican American adolescents, as well as overall risk-taking behaviors among Puerto Rican adolescents, but not among Cuban American adolescents. Mexican American adolescents living in female-headed households reported more drinking, drug use, and overall risk-taking behaviors than those living in two-parent households.

Additionally, Puerto Rican adolescents living in female-headed households had higher rates of overall risk-taking behaviors than those living with both parents. Moreover, family structure was unrelated to Cuban American adolescents' risk-taking behaviors. Also, males reported greater alcohol consumption than females in each of the three Hispanic subgroups. Of interest was the fact that Mexican Americans and Cuban Americans who were predominantly English speakers reported more drug use than those who were predominantly Spanish speakers. The same was true for Cuban Americans in relation to alcohol consumption. Also, Mexican Americans who lived in households with higher income reported more alcohol use than those who lived in lower income households.

In another youth study (13), 223 Hispanic youth age 12–17 were analyzed to determine parental and youth variables with regard to drug use. The results showed that parents' attitudes and use of licit and illicit drugs played an important role in their children's drug using behavior. Moreover, substance use was associated with having less educated mothers and more educated fathers, and with fathers having fewer children. Also, youths in one-parent households had higher rates of drug use than youths in two-parent households. Additionally, substance use by mothers highly correlated with substance use by children. However, fathers' substance use did not show a consistent pattern of correlation with youth substance use. Among Hispanic subgroups, Mexican Americans had the highest rate for use of drugs. Of interest was the fact that Hispanic children whose parents are more acculturated into the "American" society are at higher risk of using drugs, particularly females.

From another context, a series of research studies focusing on HIV/AIDS among Hispanics and other ethnic substance-abusing populations have recently been published. Schilling et al. (28) studied a sample of 91 African American and Hispanic/Latina women who were enrolled in five methadone maintenance clinics throughout New York City. Among the subjects in the study, there were 37.4% African American women and 62.6% Hispanic women. Of the Hispanic women, 96.6% described themselves as Puerto Rican, of whom 26.8% were born in Puerto Rico. The results of this study demonstrated that only 42.4% of these women reported that they had modified their sexual practices to reduce their risk of becoming HIV infected. Half of the women said that they had never used a condom before, and only 12.2% said that they used condoms every time they had sexual intercourse during the last three months. Similarly, only 4.4% had used spermicides. Also, 25% of the women said that they had sex during the last three months with a partner whose sexual history was not known to them. Moreover, condom use was unrelated to the number of sexual partners. Concerning frequency of drug use and sexual practices, those who reported using drugs more frequently also reported more sexual partners, more frequent sex relations with intravenous drug users, and less frequent use of condoms. No significant differences were found between African American and Hispanic women with respect to frequency of condom use during sexual intercourse. However, African American women felt more strongly that they could reduce or eliminate their risk of becoming HIV infected than their Hispanic counterparts. Likewise, Hispanic women felt more strongly than their African American counterparts that getting HIV/AIDS depends on luck. In general, single respondents used condoms more frequently than their non-single counterparts, and age was unrelated to frequency of condom use during sexual intercourse. Among the 56.3% who stated that they do not like to use condoms, 23.1% blamed the possibility of condoms' breaking, 25.9% blamed the reduced sexual sensation, 27.3% said that condoms spoil the

mood, and 13.2% are afraid about their partners becoming upset. Moreover, 32% of the sample said that they do not feel comfortable asking their partners to use a condom, 23% said that it is embarrassing for them to talk about sex with their sexual partners, and 46% said that they would have sex anyway if their sex partner refused to use a condom. Also of importance was the fact that the education of the subjects was inversely related to frequency of sex with intravenous drug users and frequency of sex with a partner whose sexual history was unknown. However, no significant relationships were found between level of education and frequency of condom use during sexual intercourse or number of sexual partners. Moreover, less educated women felt that they knew enough about HIV/AIDS.

In another similarly related study (29), questionnaire data from almost 12,000 street-recruited drug injectors in 19 cities were analyzed to determine racial differences that may affect HIV infection. The ethnic representation of the sample was 61% African American, 16% Hispanic, and 22% white. Also, 76% were male and 24% female. The results of this study showed that the percentage of sex acts in which a condom was used was similar for African American males, white males, and Puerto Rican males, and for African American females and white females in all city types. However, Puerto Rican females reported greater condom use than their African American counterparts. In contrast, however, Mexican American male and female drug injectors were least likely to report using condoms in multicultural cities. Additionally, white male drug injectors reported less unprotected vaginal sex than African American and Hispanic male drug injectors in multicultural and biracial cities. Also, African American drug users of both sexes were less likely than white or Hispanic drug users to report unprotected anal sex in multicultural cities.

In another study (30), 257 male intravenous drug abusers were studied to focus on their needle-sharing behavior with familiar individuals and with strangers. The ethnic representation of the sample was 21% African American, 20% Hispanic, and 59% white. Moreover, 42% of the subjects in the sample were HIV positive. The results of the study showed that the percentage of subjects who shared needles with familiar individuals was as follows: 46% never, 24% a few times, 24% sometimes, 17% most of the time, and 6% always. In contrast, however, the percentage of subjects who shared needles with strangers was as follows: 71% never, 18% a few times, 7% sometimes, 7% most of the time, and 4.2% always. Unfortunately, this study did not depict the results along ethnic lines.

Finally, Parra et al. (31) studied 50 Mexican American males from the Cornerstone methadone maintenance program in East Los Angeles and their 50 female sexual partners were examined to determine their risk behaviors, knowledge, and beliefs regarding HIV/AIDS. In the female sexual partners sample, 80% were Mexican American, and 100% were born in the United States. Also, 74% of the female sexual partners had a history of intravenous drug use, and 88% knew that their male counterparts were intravenous drug users. The results of the study showed that 73% of the females and 88% of the males were currently intravenous drug users and shared uncleaned needles. Concerning condom use, 76% of females and 84% of males never used a condom during the previous year, and about 20% of both sexes had more than one sexual partner. While 64% of females and 86% of males indicated that cleaning needles with bleach can kill the AIDS organism, only 42% of the females and 34% of males knew that using contaminated needles was the primary source of HIV infection among women.

Without question, the previously addressed research and treatment outcome studies have profound implications in the prevention and treatment of substance abuse among Hispanic populations, as well as other ethnic and non-ethnic populations. Undoubtedly, more research needs to be conducted with Hispanic populations if we ever intend to master the substance abuse problem faced by the different Hispanic subgroups who live in the United States.

PUBLIC POLICY FORMULATIONS

In discussing the subject of substance abuse among the different Hispanic populations residing in the United States, one must also address issues related to public policy development and implementation. To begin with, we must recommend and expect that Hispanics be directly involved, and fully participate in, the design and implementation of such policies. This type of involvement will ensure identification with these policies and, more importantly, compliance with them. Hispanic consumers must also be involved at all levels of this process since, after all, they will be the recipients of the impact of these policies. Hispanics tend to underutilize all types of mental health services, including substance abuse services (14, 16). If mental health and substance abuse programs were to be planned, designed, and implemented by Hispanic professionals and consumers, one would expect that these services will be more accepted and therefore utilized by Hispanic communities. Hispanics, based on their clinical skills and cultural knowledge, can better plan and design culturally sensitive program models geared to the treatment of Hispanic patients. In so doing, they can also serve as ideal role models for the future generations of Hispanic mental health professionals. For instance, the Eco-structural family therapy model seems to be quite effective with the Hispanic substance abuser (32). This model fits quite well the expectations, values, and traditions of the Hispanic family. This model is present oriented, and adapts itself effectively to the needs of the Hispanic family. Furthermore, it places emphasis on family interactions, as well as in the family ecological system rather than on the individual patient.

An important public policy issue has to do with the development of an appropriate national data base for Hispanics. So far, efforts in this regard have been rather rudimentary. The collection of reliable data at a national level will be a positive step towards its application to public policy development. It was only recently that Hispanics began to be classified according to their country of origin, and that attention was given to this very important issue. Reliable national data is very powerful in calling attention to public health problems, and thus leading to their solution.

Another issue which requires attention is the development of preventive and educational programs. While clinical care is important, efforts directed at prevention are also very important.

Unfortunately, with the introduction of managed care, the current national health care trends are focused largely on direct patient care rather than on prevention. The spiraling costs of health care in the nation has negatively affected prevention efforts. However, the most effective method of reducing health care costs is to prevent illnesses. In this respect, some very promising preventive models have recently been advanced in the field of substance abuse. For instance, it has been reported (33) that strained social relationships and a heightened sense of powerlessness and helplessness may induce adolescents to rely more heavily on substance use as a means of emotional self-regulation. This behavior requires lesser effort and ability, promises instant effects, and provides a sense of control. This model, which focuses on stress reduction, social learning, support networks, and is based on coping, acculturation, and informational network theories, is ideal for substance abuse prevention among adolescents. Along these lines, Fried (34) has also reported that the endemic stress among the socioeconomically disadvantaged serves to diminish the effective means of coping with acute stress, thereby increasing the vulnerability to pathology. This suggests that much of the phenomenology of life among the disadvantaged might be best understood as an attempt to adapt to chronic stress. Such an adaptation process can lead to a depressive orientation, a sense of helplessness and powerlessness and therefore vulnerability to substance use and abuse. In this context, public policy could advocate for a promotion of functional competency and thus advocate for programs with a clear emphasis on psychoeducational initiatives, and with a focus on the development of coping skills.

Besides models with a focus on stress reduction, we should also focus on socioeconomic models either independently or in conjunction with models focusing on stress reduction. For instance, migration is known to produce strains associated with economic status. Migration leads to immigrants entering the host nation at the lowest socioeconomic levels. This situation could lead to great stress among migrants. Furthermore, it is an accepted fact that the rates of all types of psychopathology in the lowest socioeconomic categories are about two and one-half times the rates of psychopathology in the highest socioeconomic categories (35). The prevailing explanation for this inverse relationship focuses on the distribution of stress across the socioeconomic system, with more stress tending to concentrate at the bottom of the system. In this context, public policies could address the socioeco-

nomic conditions of the Hispanic substance abuser and, in so doing, could also address the factors that affect their socioeconomic status such as unemployment, low education, and poor housing, among others. To ignore the relationship that exists between socioeconomic factors and substance abuse will undoubtedly lead to an inefficient public policy formulation. The impact of class-related socioeconomic strains is very strong among Hispanic migrants since they must also face acculturation and language barriers. Perhaps, the best example of the relationship between social class levels and psychopathology can be found in the research conducted among children and adolescents. For instance, Langner et al. (36) compared a large sample of welfare children with a nonwelfare children group. They found that the referral rates to health care services for the welfare group increased as their mother's level of education increased. They also noted that the children from the welfare group were more severely impaired in their health status than the children from the nonwelfare group. Similarly, Harrison et al. (37), while investigating the relationship between social classes and mental health care, found that children of professional or executive parents had twice as great a chance of being treated with intensive psychotherapy as the children of blue-collar parents. Furthermore, they also found that children of middle-class parents were more frequently diagnosed as suffering from neurotic disorders or as being normal, while children of lower-class parents were more often diagnosed as suffering from psychosis or personality disorders. Likewise, Rutter et al. (38), while studying elementary school children, observed that children's behavior changed according to the school they attended. Behavioral difficulties were more often found in schools with high rates of teacher and student turnover. Generally, larger turnovers were usually found in urban ghettos and in lower class neighborhoods.

Finally, we shall focus on the legal system in relation to public policy formulation. In this regard, drug legalization or decriminalization deserve consideration and attention. In analyzing legalization of drugs, we must focus on the pros and cons of drug prohibition policies. The total United States antidrug expenditure during 1990 was 9.5 billion dollars (39). Because legalization or decriminalization could lead to a reduction in the cost of the government's antidrug expenditures, it could also lead to a redistribution of expenditures in the direction of treatment, prevention, and education. Furthermore, because legalization or decriminalization would result in lowering the cost of illicit drugs, it would also result in a decrease in drug crime activities. This reduction in drug-related criminal activities could also further reduce the cost of the criminal justice system. In this regard, methadone maintenance programs represent a limited form of drug legalization and decriminalization. While the connection between drugs and crime could be seen as coincidental, it is nevertheless important. For instance, a survey conducted in 1986 among inmates of state prisons revealed that 43% were using illegal drugs on a daily basis (40). Furthermore, it is a well-accepted fact that some illicit drugs influence people to commit crimes by reducing inhibitions and increasing aggressiveness. Cocaine, for instance, is a drug that has gained this reputation in recent years (40). On the other hand, opponents of legalization or decriminalization claim that such measures would certainly increase drug availability, decrease their price, and remove the deterrent power of the criminal sanction, thus leading to an increase in drug use and abuse. However, the use of tobacco has decreased in recent years as a result of educative and prevention efforts.

Undoubtedly, legalization or decriminalization of illicit drugs contains some risks. However, our current laws and policies have not yet yielded much benefit. We must objectively evaluate all of our options, including legalization or decriminalization alternatives. Not to do so will help maintain the current status quo, and will further contribute to the deterioration in the living conditions of our minority ghetto populations, particularly Hispanics.

CONCLUSION

For decades, the substance abuse problem has been devastating for the Hispanic population residing in the United States. However, not enough attention has, so far, been given to this problem, particularly with respect to preventive approaches, epidemiological research, culturally sensitive clinical interventions, treatment outcome studies, and public policy formulations.

Furthermore, program development and financial allocations have not been commensurate with the size of these problems. Recently, however, the substance abuse and HIV epidemics have extended into the white population of this country. As a result of this shift, the government, particularly at the federal level, has been forced to pay more attention to the substance abuse problem. Hopefully, this new governmental emphasis will help to also focus attention on the ethnic minority substance abuser. Generally, traditional agencies and the government bureaucracy have overlooked the need for basic awareness of the characteristics, conditions, and circumstances surrounding the Hispanic substance abuser.

Unfortunately, most of the non-Hispanic staff currently employed in substance abuse treatment programs servicing Hispanics are unprepared in terms of (a) Spanish language ability, (b) comprehension of the Hispanic substance abuser's socioeconomic background, and (c) awareness of the Hispanic culture and heritage. Undoubtedly, these critical gaps have had a negative impact on service effectiveness, treatment outcome and, even more importantly, on prevention strategies. If Hispanic substance abusers are to be rehabilitated effectively, program designers and treatment staff must understand not only the values and norms inherent in the Hispanic culture, but also the circumstances which threaten that culture.

In this chapter, we have attempted to shed light upon these problems, and have presented data to support our assumptions. Hopefully, through research efforts and the appropriate financial support, we will eventually conquer this major tragedy facing the Hispanic family.

References

1. Langrod J, Ruiz P, Alksne L, Lowinson J. Understanding cultural conflict in community based treatment for the Hispanic addict. In: Schecter A, Alksne H, Kauffman E, eds. Drug abuse: modern trends, issues and perspectives. Proceedings of the Second National Drug Abuse Conference, New Orleans, Louisiana, 1975. New York: Marcel Dekker, 1978:837–848.
2. Szapocznik J, Scopetta MA. Innovative treatment models with Latins. In: Schecter A, Alksne H, Kauffman E, eds. Critical concerns in the field of drug abuse. Proceedings of the Third National Drug Abuse Conference. New York: Marcel Dekker, 1978:639–643.
3. U.S. Bureau of the Census. Current populations reports. Series P-20, No. 449, 1991.
4. Substance Abuse and Mental Health Services Administration. National Household Survey on Drug Abuse. Population estimates 1993. DHHS publication no. (SMA)94–3017, 1994.
5. Use of selected drugs among Hispanics, Mexican-American, Puerto Ricans, and Cuban-Americans. Findings from the National Health and Nutrition Examination Survey. National Institute of Drug Abuse, 1987.
6. National Clearinghouse for Alcohol and Drug Abuse Information. Update. Office for Substance Abuse Prevention of the Alcohol, Drug Abuse, and Mental Health Administration. January, 1989:2.
7. Gomez AG, Vega DM. The Hispanic addict. In: Lowinson JH, Ruiz P, eds. Substance abuse: clinical problems and perspectives. Baltimore: Williams & Wilkins, 1981:717–728.
8. Langrod J, Alksne L, Lowinson J, Ruiz P. Rehabilitation of the Puerto Rican addict: a cultural perspective. Int J Addict 1981;16(5):841–847.
9. Ruiz P, Langrod JG. Substance abuse among Hispanic-Americans: current issues and future perspectives. In: Lowinson JH, Ruiz P, Millman RB, eds. Substance abuse: a comprehensive textbook. 2nd edition. Baltimore: Williams & Wilkins, 1992:868–874.
10. Velez CN, Ungemack JA. Psychosocial correlates of drug use among Puerto Rican youth: generational status differences. Soc Sci Med 1995;40(1):91–103.
11. Statewide Household Survey of Substance Abuse, 1986. Illicit substance use among Hispanic adults in New York State. New York: State Division of Substance Abuse Services, 1988.
12. Marcos L, Cancro R. Pharmacotherapy of Hispanic depressed patients: clinical observations. Am J Psychotherapy 1982;26(4):505–512.
13. Gfroerer J, De La Rosa M. Protective and risks factors associated with drug use among Hispanic youth. j Addict Dis 1993;12(2):87–107.
14. Ruiz P. The Hispanic patient: sociocultural perspectives. In: Becerra RM, Karno M, Escobar JI, eds. Mental health and Hispanic Americans: clinical perspectives. New York: Grune & Stratton, 1982:17–27.
15. Ruiz P, Langrod J. Psychiatry and folk healing: a dichotomy? In: Mezzich JE, Berganza CE, eds. Culture and psychopathology. New York: Columbia University Press, 1984:470–475.
16. Ruiz P. Cultural barriers to effective medical care among Hispanic-American patients. Annu Rev Med 1985;36:63:71.
17. Koss JD. Expectations and outcomes for patients given mental health care or spiritist healing in Puerto Rico. Am J Psychiatry 1987; 144(1):56–61.
18. Maddux JF, Berlinger AK, Bates WB. Engaging opioid addicts in a continuum of services: a community-based study in the San Antonio Area. Fort Worth, TX: Texas Christian University Press, 1971.
19. Maddux JF, McDonald LK. Status of 100 San Antonio addicts one year after admission to methadone maintenance. Drug Forum 1973;2: 239–252.
20. Savage LJ, Simpson DD. Posttreatment outcomes of sex and ethnic groups treated in methadone maintenance during 1969–1972. J Psychedelic Drugs 1980;12:55–64.
21. Langrod J, Alksne L, Lowinson J, Ruiz P. Rehabilitation of the Puerto Rican addict: a cultural perspective. Int J Addict 1981; 16(5):841–845.
22. Nurco DN, Shaffer JW, Hanlon TE, Kinlock TW, Duszynski KR, Stephenson P. Relationships between client/counselor congruence and treatment outcome among narcotic addicts. Compr Psychiatry 1988;29(1):48–54.
23. Szapocznik J, Perez-Vidal A, Brickman AL, Foote FH, Santiesteban D, Hervis O, Kurtiness WM. Engaging adolescent drug abusers and their families in treatment: a strategic structural system approach. J Consult Clin Psychol 1988;56(4):552–557.
24. Lowinson JH, Ruiz P, Millman RB, eds. Substance abuse: a comprehensive textbook. 2nd edition. Baltimore: Williams & Wilkins, 1992.
25. Longshore D, Hsieh S, Anglin MD. Ethnic and gender differences in drug users' perceived need for treatment. Int J Addict 1993;28(6):539–558.
26. Pumariega AJ, Swanson JW, Holzer CE, Linskey AO, Quintero-Salinas R. Cultural context and substance abuse in Hispanic adolescents. J Child Fam Stud 1992;1(1):75–92.
27. Sokol-Katz JS, Ulbrich PM. Family structure and adolescent risk-taking behavior: a comparison of Mexican, Cuban, and Puerto Rican Americans. Int J Addict 1992;27(10):1197–1209.
28. Schilling RF, El-Bassel N, Gilbert L, Schnike SA. Correlates of drug use, sexual behavior, and attitudes toward safer sex among African-Americans and Hispanic women in methadone maintenance. J Drug Issues 1991;21(4):685–698.
29. Friedman SR, Young PA, Snyder FR, Shorty V, Jones A, Estrada AL. Racial differences in sexual behaviors related to AIDS in a nineteen-city sample of street-recruited drug injectors. AIDS Educ Prev 1993;5(3):196–211.
30. Brooks JS, Brooks DW, Whiteman M, Roberto J, Masci JR, De Catalogne J, Amundsen F. Psychosocial risk factors for HIV transmission in male drug abusers. Genet Soc Gen Psychol Monogr 1993;119(3):369–387.
31. Parra EO, Shapiro MF, Moreno CA, Linn L. AIDS-related risk behavior, knowledge, and beliefs among women and their Mexican-American sexual partners who used intravenous drugs. Arch Fam Med 1993;2(6):603–610.
32. Szapocznik J, Scopetta MA, King OE. Therapy and practice in matching treatment to the special characteristics and problems of Cuban immigrants. J Community Psychol 1978;6:112–122.
33. Labouvie EW. Alcohol and marijuana use in relation to adolescent stress. Int J Addict 1986;21: 333–345.
34. Fried M. Disadvantage, vulnerability, and mental illness. In: Parron DL, Solomon F, Jenkins CD, eds. Behavior, health risks and social disadvantage. Washington, DC: National Academy Press, 1982.
35. Dohrenwend BP, Dohrenwend BS, Gould MS, et al. Mental illness in the United States. New York: Praeger 1980:56.
36. Langner TS, Gersten J, Eisenberg J. Approaches to measurement and definition in the epidemiology of behavior disorders: ethnic background and child behavior. Int J Health Serv 1974;4: 483–501.
37. Harrison SI, McDermott JF, Wilson PT. Social class and mental illness in children: choice of treatment. Arch Gen Psychiatry 1965;13: 411–417.
38. Rutter M, Yule B, Quentin D, et al. Attainment and adjustment in two geographical areas: some factors accounting for area differences. Br J Psychiatry 1975;126:520–533.
39. U.S. News & World Report 1990(December 24):12.
40. Nadelmann EA. Drug prohibition in the United States: cost, consequences, and alternatives. Science 1989:245:939–946.

70 NATIVE AMERICANS, ASIANS, AND NEW IMMIGRANTS

Joseph Westermeyer

HISTORICAL AND CULTURAL BACKGROUND

Subsistence Groups

Subsistence groups consist of simple societies that produce most of their own food, clothing, housing, and tools. They need little from the outside world and export little to the outside. The environment limits the risk to alcohol abuse in these subsistence-based communities to a considerable extent. Fermentation of alcohol requires that a carbohydrate source (such as grain, fruit, vegetables, or milk) be present in sufficient quantities to meet dietary needs, with enough left over to produce alcohol. Each family often produces its own alcohol; this requires that adequate supplies, time, equipment, and skill be brought together for the production process. If alcohol is purchased, it tends to be relatively expensive in terms of the time and labor required to purchase it. These factors combine to limit the volume of alcohol produced and the occasions for consuming it. Few cultural limits to intoxication may exist, and infrequent but socially acceptable binge use may occur under the circumstances. In societies with simple technology (e.g., no cars or complex machinery), infrequent episodes of intoxication are relatively safe. This drinking pattern also provides episodic "time out" from social and cultural constraints (1, 2). Religious and cultural practices may even support this form of infrequent, heavy drinking (3, 4).

Given the constraints on carbohydrate supply, many such societies have employed other psychoactive substances for intoxication. In the Americas, leaves, barks, flowers, and fleshy cactus were harvested for their stimulant, relaxing, or hallucinogenic properties. Some were grown domestically, and others were harvested from the wild. Examples include coca leaf, tobacco leaf, and peyote plants. Perhaps due to their potent effects and potential for impairment, use of these more potent psychoactive substances was often restricted to religious, social, or laboring occasions. Particular climates and topographies favored production of certain psychoactive substances, so that some tribal and peasant peoples have specialized in the production and even export of these substances (5). Examples include the production of coca leaf and cannabis.

Although hundreds of psychoactive substances were used by the original Americans (6), Asians have employed a narrower selection of compounds. Tribal people and peasants have grown *Papaver sominiferum* poppy from the Middle East to South Asia, Southeast Asia, and Far Eastern Asia. For centuries, cannabis has also been widely used from Africa to the Orient, and only recently in Europe and North America. The stimulant compound betelareca continues to be favored in South Asia to Southeast Asia and in Oceania (7). In the Middle East, the stimulant leaf chat (also spelled *qat* or *khat*) is popular (8), whereas some Southeast Asians prefer kratom, another stimulant leaf. Alcohol is widely used by tribal and peasant peoples outside the Islamic areas of Asia. Buddhist monks are forbidden to drink alcohol and to use other psychoactive substances; some fervent Buddhist lay people may adhere to the same values. Many tribal and peasant peoples have been economically dependent on the production of these psychoactive compounds, particularly opium, but also betel-areca and chat (9).

Mercantile Communities

In larger, more highly organized mercantile communities, psychoactive substances are simply another commodity whose consumption is limited only by one's ability to purchase it (46). In this setting, frequent, daily, or even continuous intoxication with alcohol or other psychoactive substances becomes possible. On the other hand, heavy or binge use is inconsistent with most economic endeavors, which require careful eye-hand coordination,

cognition, memory, and judgment. Still, smaller but titrated doses are consistent with certain regular occupational functions. Moderate use or even abstinence is supported by many mercantile religions (e.g., Islam and latter-day Christian groups), cultures, and state governments. Intoxication while working in certain occupations can risk the public health (e.g., among sailors, military personnel, truck drivers, pilots, and health care workers).

These mercantile communities sometimes foster the production and distribution of psychoactive substances. Technology can be used to concentrate the substance, which can reduce storage and transport costs and may prolong "shelf life" (e.g., distillation of alcohol, extracting morphine or heroin from opium, and extracting cocaine from coca leaf). In addition to facilitating transportation, this may also favor smuggling if export is not legal. Areas with a surplus of a particular substance may gain economically from this process (e.g., Scotland and Scotch whiskey, Burma and opium, Peru and cocaine). Mercantile methods and concepts can permit a few people to make huge profits from mass production, transport, or distribution of alcohol or drugs.

Social and Cultural Change

The apposition of formerly disparate ethnic groups in North America has exposed its participants to new models of psychoactive substance use. European Americans, not schooled in the ceremonial use of tobacco, readily developed tobacco dependence along with its several medical diseases (e.g., lung cancer, coronary artery disease, Burger's disease, and emphysema). Likewise, many American Indian tribes with no social strictures on alcohol use and who were exposed to frontier drunkenness, adapted a "drink to get drunk" style of alcohol use (10). Some Hmong immigrants from Asia, with their social imperatives to drink on particular occasions and to provide alcohol to guests at their own expense, have chosen fundamentalist Christianity and its abstinence strictures (11). Thus, in a context of sociocultural change, old traditions of use can be abandoned as readily as new patterns of use can be taken up.

Several other aspects of sociocultural change also affected alcohol and drug use. New technology has made carbohydrate production—and thus alcohol production—less expensive. More rapid and less expensive modes of transport have reduced the cost and heightened the efficiency of drug distribution, whether licit or illicit. However, greater access to and use of high-speed vehicles (e.g., speedboats, planes, and fast cars), as well as expensive industrial machinery, make intoxication a risky proposition not only for the user, but for the society at large which bears the cost of vehicular and industrial accidents (5). As a consequence of these changes, alcohol, in particular, and other drugs, in general, have become virtually a scourge in the United States. Substance abuse and dependence are a major cause of child neglect, family violence, divorce, vehicular accidents, injury, and several causes of death. The latter include accidents, homicide, liver cirrhosis, and certain infections.

Cultural Diversity

Groups of Native Americans, Asian Americans, and new immigrants to the United States each differ greatly. This is also true of individuals within these groups. Some have remained strongly traditional, while others have assimilated to a considerable extent with "mainstream" American culture. Socioeconomic status of these groups and individuals in these groups also varies widely. For example, Japanese Americans and Hmong refugees from Laos, as groups, occupy virtually opposite ends of the economic spectrum.

In recent years, up to half of new immigrants to the United States have been refugees from Asia, Africa, and Latin America. Immigration laws no longer favor European immigrants, as once was the case. For example, from 1980 to 1990 the total Asia-Pacific population went from 3,723,440 to 7,273,662, due in large part to immigration (12). The percentage of foreign-born people in the United States has almost doubled in the last three decades. These new inhabitants manifest considerable ethnic diversity. For example, their religious affiliations include animism, Hinduism, and Buddhism. Given this great range, any general statements are apt to be inaccurate. Despite their smaller populations, these groups are fully as diverse as European Americans, African Americans, and Hispanics.

NATIVE AMERICANS

Models of Use

Even in pre-European days, certain Southwestern tribes and Mexican peoples prepared beverage alcohol from cactus (13). Various tribes employed intoxicants, as well as fasting and isolation, to obtain visions that were to guide one's life—the so-called Dream Quest (14). However, the Native American norm for alcohol is abstention, rather than use. To this day most tribes prefer reservation prohibition against the sale of alcohol (15). From 1802 to 1953, the United States government forbade the sale of alcohol to Native Americans (16); this fact, along with exposure to frontier drinking, may have fostered a norm for rapid drinking and episodic binges (17). For long periods of time (i.e., years or even decades), many Native Americans voluntarily choose abstinence. However, among those living in the majority societies of North America, moderate social drinking is a viable and popular alternative. As one might expect, the types of pathological use patterns differ among tribes just as they do among various European groups. For example, the "Pueblo model" involves regular controlled use (or "titer" drinking) and an effort to appear sober despite intoxication. The "Papago model" includes controlled use of a local cactus wine on ceremonial occasions in parallel with secular use of "American" alcoholic beverages, which can occur in an abusive fashion (13). The stereotypic "Indian" pattern of alcohol abuse includes relatively rapid drinking over a prolonged period, with drunkenness as the aim (10, 18). This drunkenness has an aspect of "time out" from cultural rules (1), so that the drinker may behave in ways that would ordinarily be considered taboo by the tribe (e.g., exhibiting violence towards others, participating in casual sexuality, or failing to put clan or tribal needs above one's own needs). This pattern may also result in a higher rate of alcohol-associated delirium and dementia, as compared to rates in other groups (19). Although a biological predisposition for this has been suggested, comparative studies have failed to show a consistent and significant difference in alcohol metabolism among Native Americans (20–22).

Populations at Risk

The risk for substance abuse differs considerably among various subgroups of Native Americans (23). For example, the five "eastern" tribes of Oklahoma—socially complex, agricultural societies, some with a tradition of literacy in their own language—had lower rates of alcohol-related problems compared to the warrior-hunter-gatherer tribes of the Great Plains (22). Motor vehicle crashes and injuries (often associated with intoxication) were considerably increased among some Western mountain tribes, even when rates are adjusted for the younger average age of Native Americans (24). Rates in one mountain tribe were seven times that of the general population (age-adjusted rate, four times) and three times those of other Native Americans. In a Northwestern tribe, lifetime rates of alcoholism were among the highest ever observed (25).

Native American children and adolescents in certain locales from Mexico to Canada have had epidemics of solvent-inhalant abuse (26), with high rates of mental retardation (27). Cannabis use and abuse has been widespread among some Native American adolescents (28), as has tobacco chewing (29). Suicide and homicide linked to alcohol and drugs have occurred among Native Americans of all ages with rates comparable to those in the white population and twice those in the African American populations (30). Homicide has been common among some tribes (31). Cirrhosis of the liver has occurred among women in high rates, with the expected result of fetal alcohol effect and fetal alcohol syndrome in certain areas (32). Since psychiatric services are seldom readily available in the rural and ghetto areas that are inhabited by many Native Americans, alcohol use may be a self-treatment for anxiety or affective disorders leading to a so-called dual disorder (33).

Treatment

Indigenous Native American healing methods for alcoholism have long been used by various tribes across North America, often with temporary benefit and occasionally with more permanent results (34–37). These methods include shaman ceremonies, community "sings," herbal medications, and sweat lodges. Syncretic religions and self-help groups have included the Native American Church (35), the Indian Shaker Church (36), the Handsome Lake Movement (37), evangelical Christian groups (34), and Indian Alcoholics Anonymous groups. Hospital units, detoxification centers, halfway houses, and outpatient programs for alcoholism have been funded by the Indian Health Service, the Office of Economic Opportunity, some state and county governments, and certain tribes (38). A key feature of these programs has been the inclusion of Native American staff members, who can serve as outreach workers and role models for recovering persons. Since over half of Native Americans (about 63%) now live away from traditional communities in multiethnic urban areas, their special needs must be considered in developing treatment programs (39).

Outcomes from these various treatment efforts, when they have been measured, have been modest, varying from virtually nil to the 15–20% improvement rates typical of "skid row" populations (33). This is not unexpected in a population that often comes to treatment at a late stage, bereft of family support, unemployed, and with few or no job skills. Still, an increasing number of recovered Native American persons compose a growing resource for their tribes and communities. An important factor lies in the recovering person's having a "stake" or advantage in sobriety (40)—not always an obvious or simple task for unemployed persons in rural areas. Some data suggest a leveling-off, and possibly even a decrease of alcoholism rates, among some groups (41).

Prevention

At times, prevention efforts have focused on identifying alcohol and other drugs as "the white man's evil." This is part truth, since European Americans have contributed greatly to the problem (17, 42). It is also part fiction because some pre-Columbian North Americans had access to alcohol and had legal and religious regulations against its abuse (43, 44). Nonetheless, this concept does support tribal pride and cultural revivalism, while choosing a strategy (i.e., total abstinence and prohibition) that is not part of the societal mainstreams of Canada, the United States, Mexico, and other North American countries (45).

This "alcohol-as-evil" approach to prevention finds its expression on reservations as prohibition (although at times the leaders who enforce legal prohibition have been the same people who profit from illegal bootlegging of alcohol). Perhaps a more effective measure has been religious affiliation with groups that forbid any use of alcohol or other recreational drugs. These religious groups fall into three different categories: aboriginal tribal religions; syncretic religions involving animistic and Christian principles and practices, such as the Native American Church; and fundamentalist Christian religions. The latter have an additional advantage over the traditional Christian religions on reservations (i.e., Catholicism and Anglicanism) in that Native Americans can more readily become lay leaders and even clergy in these fundamentalist groups.

ASIAN AMERICANS

National Origins

As with Native American tribes, Asian Americans differ greatly by culture and traditional substance use pattern, including alcohol use (46). Most numerous Asian groups include those from China, the Philippines, Japan, India, Korea, and Vietnam. Virtually all of the world's great religions are represented:

animism, Hinduism, Buddhism, Judaism, Christianity, and Islam. Although Moslem groups eschew alcohol use to various degrees as do some Hindus, Buddhists, and Christians (47), ritual drinking is a key element of many Asian cultures from the Mediterranean to the Pacific. Tribal "binge" drinking and mercantile "titer" drinking occur, with both ceremonial and secular use.

Perhaps in part due to religious strictures against alcohol and in part due to carbohydrate scarcity, drug production and use loom larger in Asia than in Europe (48). In this respect, Asians resemble their relatives in North America. Most of the world's opium, illicit as well as licit, is produced in Asia. Millions of Asian poppy farmers are engaged in producing opium for millions of opiate addicts and other opiate users. Betel-areca, tobacco, cannabis, and more local substances (such as chat and kratom) are sold in local markets across Asia and have accompanied Asian Americans to the United States. Some of these substances, such as opium, are now grown by Asian Americans in the United States (49). Other substances such as betel-areca and chat are imported. It has been argued that sedative drugs such as opium fit better with a common Asian theme of self-control, as compared to alcohol and its disinhibiting effects (50). The alcohol-induced "flushing response" found among an increased number of Asians may favor abstention or minimal use (51), although Sue et al. (52) failed to find a correlation between facial flushing and reported drinking patterns. Recent data have suggested that age might play a role, with older drinkers being more influenced by flushing than younger drinkers (53).

In recent decades substance use and abuse has changed dramatically in Asia (54). For example, as opium use has declined in areas of the Orient, alcohol abuse has increased (55). Manufactured sedatives and stimulants have spread across large areas of Asia. Opiate use, abuse, and dependence waxes and wanes, but continues in regular use in several countries of Asia from the Middle East to the China Sea (56). Especially as drugs (particularly opium) have become illegal in many Asian countries, alcohol abuse has increased in many areas. Secularism and urbanism may also have contributed to this change (57).

These changes in Asia parallel those observed among some Asian American groups (58). Heavier alcohol use has been reported by North Americans of Japanese, Filipino, and Korean origins, as compared with those of Chinese origin (46). Some recent Asian American immigrants have been involved in the illicit drug trade, either by producing drugs in the United States (e.g., opium) or by smuggling drugs into the country (e.g., refined opiates) (49). Some of the dependency-producing but less socially noxious drugs (e.g., betel-areca, chat) have been brought to the United States through licit channels, predominantly for use by Asian immigrants (59). With acculturation to the United States, some transition away from traditional alcohol-drinking patterns to American alcohol-drinking patterns has occurred in many Asian groups (60).

Treatment and Prevention

Certain special problems and advantages attend the care of substance-abusing Asians. Entry into treatment is apt to occur late, since a personal admission of loss of control of a substance's use runs against the ideal norm of many Asian cultures. Likewise, the awareness of living primarily for one's self and one's addiction, rather than for the family and community, is an insight unacceptable to many Asians raised to embody the opposite value. In addition to personal shame, family shame is also apt to delay confrontation of the patient and entry into treatment. Admission that the family cannot aid and control its own members involves a sense of family failure and, hence, inferiority. Predictably, such families often enable and rescue the patient repeatedly until the family can take no more. Then, at the point of the patient's entry into treatment, precisely when family support and involvement are most needed, the family may dump the patient on the treatment facility and exit the scene. Family abandonment at this juncture may further compromise treatment outcome.

On the positive side, Asian patients who are in treatment can be expected to comply reasonably well once a treatment relationship is established. If educated regarding the need for medication, they may be quite willing to take disulfiram or other medication for an associated psychiatric disorder. Social

retraining and religious affiliations during recovery are consistent with many Asian traditions, in which life-long education and self-development are fostered. Families can often be guided toward therapeutic support and away from enabling behaviors.

Certain treatment strategies may need to be modified or explained. Many Asian healing traditions support the notion of brief, magical cures and concurrent consultation with many healers. Long-term recovery strategies and persistence within a program may not be automatically understood. Public admission of private sins and family secrets, as in the usual self-help group or group therapy, may run against the patient's preference. In family therapy, the explicit family hierarchy will often hold sway, so that matriarchs and patriarchs are not confronted and have the final say.

Some traditional values from Asia may actually support heavy or binge drinking (61). Such attitudes, and the practices that attend them, may be conducive to more moderate drinking practices in some groups.

RECENT IMMIGRANTS

History and Epidemiology

A few decades ago the percentage of foreign-born inhabitants of the United States had fallen to an all-time low of 8%. It has since risen to 14% and is rising still. About half of recent immigrants are refugees from Asia, Latin America, Africa, and Eastern Europe. In addition, students, guest workers, and visitors reside in the country for various periods of time. For example, in the United States, there are about a million people from India, a million from Africa, several hundred thousand from Indochina, and perhaps 2 million migrants from Latin America. The United States admits more legal immigrants than the rest of the world's nations combined. Similarly, Canada accepts a very large percentage of immigrants each year. Mexico receives back a large number of repatriates each year, mostly from the United States (59, 62).

Psychopathology among migrants has been well studied for almost 60 years, beginning with Odegaard's study of Norwegian migrants to Minnesota (63). Low rates of psychopathology occur when migrants can maintain their language, dress, social status, customs, occupation, and ready access to their home country. Insofar as these conditions do not hold true, migrants are at increased risk for alcohol and drug problems. Substance abuse can occur soon after relocation, but risk appears to increase after several years in the new country (49, 64).

Types of Substance Abuse Among Immigrants

Two general types of substance abuse are apt to occur among immigrants: first, the types of substance abuse currently prevalent in the receiving community; and second, the type of substance abuse formerly current among immigrants in the country of origin. Thus, immigrants to the United States are at risk for secular alcohol use, tobacco dependence, cocaine abuse, and cannabis abuse, even though these substances may have been virtually nonexistent in the country of origin. These "American" forms of substance use and abuse are especially apt to occur among acculturating youth (65).

Immigrants may also manifest the substance abuse of their country of origin. Current examples are opium addiction and betel-areca dependence among Southeast Asian refugees in the United States. Economic factors may also adversely influence substance abuse among immigrants. For example, Caribbean and other Hispanic drinkers have used industrial volatile inhalants as intoxicants when unable to afford beverage alcohol (66, 67).

Special Problems

Self-treatment for psychiatric and medical symptoms with alcohol and other drugs of abuse can occur among immigrants who do not have effective access to health care, including mental health care. Culturally sensitive care must be available geographically and economically if this problem is to be avoided. Inclusion of immigrant staff in the health care system is a key tactic in this strategy, so that the indigenous immigrant network can interdigitate with the health care network (68).

Immigrant and refugee waves include criminals and candidates for criminal careers (59). The number of criminals can swell if opportunities for achievement are not available in the host country. Several factors can foster the development of criminality among immigrants and refugees. These include the following:

- Criminals may be forced out by new governments in the country of origin, which may be sweeping aside established traditions of corruption.
- The migrant minority may not perceive a loyalty to or identification with the new society.
- The behavior (e.g., poppy production or smuggling) may have been part and parcel of a former lifestyle, so that taboos do not exist against behaviors considered criminal by the host country.
- Migrants may have access to skills (e.g., bilingual fluency or smuggling), information (e.g., contacts with suppliers and distributors), and resources (e.g., modes of transportation) that put them in an excellent position to undertake a criminal career.
- Occupational failure of the migrant in licit activities may motivate some migrants to initiate a criminal career.
- Drug abuse, pathological gambling, or other expensive proclivities may motivate the migrant toward a profitable, but illicit occupation.

Among the various illicit activities practiced by migrants in North America (e.g., illegal gambling houses and protection rackets), the drug trade is a common one (62). Participation in this trade includes smuggling from Asia via the mail, smuggling directly from Latin America over land and air routes, growing poppy in the United States, and distribution of opium to users.

Treatment and Prevention

Members of the immigrant group should be represented on the treatment staff of programs serving alcoholic or addicted immigrants, especially if they occur in large numbers. Family members should be involved in treatment, although shame may impede their willingness to do so. In the event of patient reluctance to participate in treatment or repeated treatment failure, repatriation to the country of origin may be considered if the person is not yet a citizen. Some patients unable to recover in a foreign country do benefit from treatment rendered in their society of origin, in which family, relatives, and recovering role models may be more accessible (68).

Prevention among immigrants can be fostered by making culturally sensitive medical care available, as a means of preventing self-treatment with alcohol and dependence-producing drugs. Immigrating individuals and families can be educated to the early signs and symptoms of substance abuse and to methods of supportive confrontation and avoidance of enabling and rescuing behaviors. To reduce the availability of illicit drugs in large immigrant communities, expatriate police officers should be represented in local law enforcement. As with health care, the civil security network must be available to the expatriate networks. Non-citizen drug traffickers should be deported as rapidly as feasible, whether or not they are drug-dependent themselves. Leaders of the expatriate community should be actively involved in leading the community away from drug trafficking and use, if drug trafficking and use are present (59).

CONCLUSION

Minority and immigrant groups bring their own special histories and traditions to the societal mainstream of North America. In addition to their rich customs and values, they also bring their vulnerabilities to psychoactive substances, both traditional substances and new substances that are unfamiliar to them. They may bring new substances to the United States and drug trafficking skills that pose a risk to their own expatriate group and to the societal mainstream. American society and its institutions should recognize its contributions to the minority and immigrant use and abuse of substances and its responsibility in fostering prevention of and recovery from substance abuse. Treatment staff should include members of patients' ethnic groups to attract patients to treatment early and to maintain them in treatment. Prevention activities require the efforts of both the mainstream society and the ethnic subgroup.

References

1. Hill TW. Drunken comportment of urban Indians: time out behavior? J Anthropol Res 1978; 34:442–467.
2. Horton D. The functions of alcohol in primitive societies: alcohol, science and society. Q J Stud Alcohol 1945;6:153–177.
3. Klausner SZ. Sacred and profane meaning of blood and alcohol. J Soc Psychol 1964;64:27–43.
4. Westermeyer J. Use of alcohol and opium by the Meo of Laos. Am J Psychiatry 1971;127:1019–1023.
5. Westermeyer J. Cultural patterns of drug and alcohol use: an analysis of host and agent in the cultural environment. UN Bull Narcotics 1987;39:11–17.
6. Du Foit BM. Drugs, rituals, and altered states of consciousness. Rotterdam: Balkema, 1977.
7. Burton-Bradley BG. Some implications of betel chewing. Med J Aust 1977;2:744–746.
8. Getahun A, Krikorias AD. Chat. Coffee's rival from Harar, Ethiopia. Econ Botany 1973;27: 353–389.
9. Westermeyer J. Poppies, pipes and people: Opium and its use in Laos. Berkeley, CA: University of California, 1983.
10. Weisner TS, Weibel-Orlando: JC, Lang J. Seniors drinking, white man's drinking, and teetotaling: drinking levels and styles in an urban American Indian population. J Stud Alcohol 1984;45:237–250.
11. Westermeyer J. Hmong drinking practices in the United States: the influence of migration. In: Bennett L, Ames G, eds. The American experience with alcohol. New York: Plenum, 1985:373–391.

12. Committee on Cultural Psychiatry. Alcoholism in the United States: racial and ethnic considerations. Washington, DC: American Psychiatric Press, 1996.
13. Waddell JO, Everett ME, eds. Drinking behavior among Southwestern Indians: an anthropological perspective. Tucson, AZ: University of Arizona Press, 1980.
14. Carpenter E. Alcohol in the Iroquois dream quest. Am J Psychiatry 1959;116:148–151.
15. May PA. Alcohol beverage control: a survey of tribal alcohol statutes. Am Indian Law Rev 1977;5:217–228.
16. May P. Alcohol abuse and alcoholism among American Indians: an overview. In: Watts TD, Wright R, eds. Alcoholism in minority populations. Springfield, IL: Charles C Thomas, 1989: 95–119.
17. MacAndrew C, Edgerton RB. Drunken comportment: a sociological explanation. Chicago: Aldine, 1969.
18. Lurie NO. The world's oldest on-going protest demonstration. Pacific Historic Rev 1971;40: 311–332.
19. Westermeyer J. Substance disorder among 100 American Indian vs. 200 other patients. Alcohol Clin Exp Res 1994;18:692–694.
20. Bennion L, Li TK. Alcohol metabolism in American Indians and whites. N Engl J Med 1976;284:9–13.
21. Farris JJ, Jones BM. Ethanol metabolism in male American Indians and whites. Alcohol Clin Exp Res 1978;2:77–81.
22. Zeiner AR, Paredes A, Cowden L. Physiologic responses to ethanol among the Tarahumara Indians. Ann N Y Acad Sci 1976;273: 151–158.

23. Manson SM, Shore JH, Baron AE, Ackerson L, Neligh G. Alcohol abuse and dependence among American Indians. In: Helzer JE, Canino GJ, eds. Alcoholism in North America, Europe, and Asia. Oxford, England: Oxford University Press, 1992:113–130.
24. U.S. Centers for Disease Control and Prevention. Motor vehicle crashes and injuries in an Indian community—Arizona. JAMA 1989;262: 2205–2206.
25. Kinzie JD, Leung PK, Boehnlein J, et al. Psychiatric epidemiology of an Indian village: a 19-year replication study. J Nerv Mental Dis 1992; 180:33–39.
26. Kaufman A. Gasoline sniffing among children in a Pueblo Indian village. Pediatrics 1975;51: 1060–1065.
27. Beauvais F, Oetting ER, Edwards RW. Trends in drug use in Indian adolescents living on reservations: 1975–1983. Am J Drug Alcohol Abuse 1985:11:209–229.
28. Winfree LT, Griffiths CT. Youth at risk: marijuana use among Native American and Caucasian youths. Int J Addict 1983;18:53–70.
29. Hoover J, McDermott R, Harsfield T. The prevalence of smokeless tobacco use in Native children in northern Saskatchewan, Canada. Can J Public Health 1990;81:350–352.
30. Baker SP, O'Neill B, Karpf R. The injury fact book. Lexington, MA: Lexington Books, 1984.
31. Levy JE, Kunitz SJ, Everett MW. Navajo criminal homicide. Southwest J Anthropol 1969;25: 124–152.
32. May PA, Hymbaugh KJ, Aase M, Samet JM. Epidemiology of fetal alcohol syndrome among American Indians of the Southwest. Soc Biol 1983;30:374–387.

33. Westermeyer J, Peake E. A ten-year follow-up of alcoholic Native Americans in Minnesota. Am J Psychiatry 1983;140:189–194.

34. Kearny M. Drunkenness and religious conversion in a Mexican village. Q J Stud Alcohol 1970;31:248–249.

35. La Barre W. The peyote cult. New York: Schocken Books, 1969.

36. Slagel AL, Weibel-Orlando J. The Indian Shaker Church and Alcoholics Anonymous: revitalistic curing cults. Hum Organiz 1986;45:310–319.

37. Wallace AFC. The death and rebirth of the Seneca. New York: Alfred Knopf, 1970.

38. Weibel-Orlando J. Treatment and prevention of Native American alcoholism. In: Watts TD, Wright R, eds. Alcoholism in minority populations. Springfield, IL: Charles C Thomas, 1989:121–139.

39. U.S. Bureau of Census. A statistical profile of the American Indian population—1980 census. Washington, DC: Census Fact Sheet, 1984.

40. Ferguson FN. Stake theory as an explanatory device in Navajo alcohol treatment response. Hum Organiz 1976;35:65–77.

41. Becker TM, Wiggins CL, Key CR, Samet JM. Changing trends in mortality among New Mexico's American Indians, 1958–1987. Int J Epidemiol 1992;21:690–700.

42. Dailey RC. The role of alcohol among North American Indian tribes as reported in the Jesuit relations. Anthropologica 1968;10:45–57.

43. Parades A. Social control of drinking among the Aztec Indians of Mesoamerica. J Stud Alcohol 1975;36:1139–1153.

44. Anawalt PR, Berdan FF. The Codex Mendoza. Sci Am 1992;June:70–79.

45. Mail PD. Closing the circle: a prevention model for Indian communities with alcohol problems. IHS Primary Care Provider 1985;10:2–5.

46. Kitano HHL. Alcohol and the Asian American. In: Watts TD, Wright R, eds. Alcoholism in minority populations. Springfield, IL: Charles C Thomas, 1989:143–146.

47. Ratanakorn P. Asia and problems of alcoholism. Ann N Y Acad Sci 1976;273:33–38.

48. Baasher T. The use of drugs in the Islamic world. Br J Addict 1981;76:233–243.

49. Westermeyer J, Lyfoung T, Neider J. An epidemic of opium dependence among Asian refugees in the U.S.—Characteristics and causes. Br J Addict 1989;84:785–789.

50. Singer K. Choice of intoxicant among the Chinese. Br J Addict 1974;69:257–268.

51. Ewing JA, Rouse BA, Pelizzari ED. Alcohol sensitivity and ethnic background. Am J Psychiatry 1974;131:206.

52. Sue S, Zane N, Ito J. Reported alcohol patterns among Asian and Caucasian Americans. J Cross Cult Psychol 1979;10:43–56.

53. Nakawatase T, Yamamoto J, Sasao T. The association between fast flushing response and alcohol use among Japanese Americans. J Stud Alcohol 1993;55:48–53.

54. Arif A, Westermeyer J. A manual for drug and alcohol abuse: guidelines for teaching. New York: Plenum, 1988.

55. Sargent MJ. Changes in Japanese drinking patterns. Q J Stud Alcohol 1967;28:709–722.

56. Westermeyer J. National and international strategies to control drug abuse. Adv Alcohol Subst Abuse 1989;8:1–35. [Abridged version in Strategies to control the availability of drugs: economic, social and political issues. Subst Abuse 1989;10:48–69.]

57. Chafety ME. Consumption of alcohol in the Far and Middle East. N Engl J Med 1964;271:297–301.

58. Izuno T, Miyakawa M, Tsunoda T. Alcohol related problems encountered by Japanese, Caucasian, and Japanese Americans. Int J Addict 1992;27:1389–1400.

59. Westermeyer J. Mental health for refugees and other migrants. Springfield, IL: Charles C Thomas, 1989.

60. Bennett L, Ames G, eds. The American the experience with alcohol. New York: Plenum, 1985.

61. Cho YI, Faulkner WR. Conceptions of alcoholism among Koreans and Americans. Int J Addict 1993;28:681–694.

62. Westermeyer J. The psychiatric care of migrants: a clinical guide. Washington, DC: American Psychiatric Press, 1989.

63. Odegaard O. Emigration and insanity. Acta Psych Neurol Scand 1932;4:1–206.

64. Krupinski J, Stoller A, Wallace L. Psychiatric disorders in East European refugees now in Australia. Soc Sci Med 1973;7:31–49.

65. Westermeyer J. Substance use disorders among young minority refugees: common themes in a clinical sample. NIDA Res Monogr 1993;130:308–320.

66. Westermeyer J. The psychiatrist and solvent-inhalant abuse: recognition, assessment and treatment. Am J Psychiatry 1987;144:903–907.

67. Westermeyer J. Review of treatment approaches for volatile solvents/inhalant abuse. In: Arif A, Grant M, Narvaratnam V, eds. Abuse of volatile solvents/inhalants, World Health Organization report MNH/DAT/5.2. Malaysia: Universiti Sains Malaysia, 1988:302–325.

68. Williams C, Westermeyer J, eds. Refugee mental health in resettlement countries. New York: Hemisphere, 1986.

71 PERSONS WITH DISABILITIES

Allen W. Heinemann

RELATIONSHIPS BETWEEN ALCOHOL AND OTHER DRUG ABUSE AND DISABILITY

Substance abuse may be related to disability in several ways. First, it may contribute to the cause of the disability. Examples include becoming injured as a result of driving while intoxicated, a cocaine-induced stroke, frostbite leading to amputations in homeless persons, or gangrenous infection from heroin or cocaine injection. Chronic, heavy drinking may result in alcohol ataxia, neuropathy, and arthropathy. Bystanders to urban turf battles may sustain gunshot wounds. Second, alcohol and other drug abuse may adversely affect the rehabilitation process by causing behavioral alterations or by impairing cognition. Rehabilitation requires the capacity to learn; impairments in learning ability will limit rehabilitation benefits. Third, rehabilitation outcome may be affected by medical complications resulting from the use of substances, for example, chronic urinary tract infections or skin breakdown resulting from neglected self-care (1). Finally, substance abuse may disrupt vocational rehabilitation and reverse the cost-effectiveness of rehabilitation in persons who continue to abuse alcohol and other drugs.

One of the first studies to explore the extent of substance abuse among persons with disabilities was an investigation of vocational rehabilitation clients. Rasmussen and DeBoer (2) reported that 62% of 273 adults had serious problems with alcohol and that half of these met diagnostic criteria for alcoholism. More recently, a study of 227 applicants to a state rehabilitation system (3) found that 51% drank alcohol, 29% used cocaine at least once, 40% went to work or school intoxicated at least once while 17% went intoxicated 10 or more times, and 15% had trouble at work because of drinking. Clearly, the extent of alcohol and other drug abuse remains a concern in rehabilitation settings. What has changed in the past 15 years is the frequency with which these problems has been investigated and efforts to implement assessment, treatment, and prevention programs.

Substance abuse and dependence is sometimes concealed by rehabilitation clients and patients because they fear rejection and stigmatization by staff. Rehabilitation professionals may feel unprepared and awkward in dealing with issues of chemical abuse dependence. And, staff in substance abuse treatment programs may know little about the consequences of disabling conditions and feel unprepared to deal with clients who have sensory or mobility limitations. This chapter summarizes alcohol and other drug abuse issues as they affect persons with disabilities, describes new directions for treatment and prevention, and identifies emergent issues so as to enhance the professional competence of both rehabilitation and chemical dependence professionals.

FACTORS ASSOCIATED WITH ALCOHOL AND OTHER DRUG USE BY PERSONS WITH DISABILITIES

Depression, anxiety, social isolation, medical complications, and self-neglect are important factors to consider when alcohol and other drugs are used by persons who incur traumatic injury. The relationship of self-esteem and mood to rehabilitation outcome is critical. Fullerton and associates (4) found that 30% of their spinal cord injury (SCI) patients met diagnostic criteria for various depressive disorders. Psychiatric comorbidities, including substance abuse, among inpatients with traumatic brain injury (TBI) and SCI at a regional trauma center were associated with longer lengths of stay (5). Trieschmann (6) suggests that persons who incur injury are at risk for developing pathological coping strategies, including use of substances to relieve of chronic pain, depression, and anxiety. The use of alcohol and other drugs by persons with TBI can contribute to even greater impairment of cognitive and motor skills (7). In addition, the use of substances following TBI is potentially dangerous when combined with prescription medications and may increase the likelihood of seizures (8). Heinemann and associates (9) examined patterns of post-injury substance use following recent SCI; patients reported use for the 6 months before, and 6 and 18 months after injury. Use of alcohol and marihuana were particularly resilient after declining during the first 6 months after injury. Persons with SCI who used substances at abusive levels before injury appear to be at risk for use after injury. Use of alcohol and other drugs following SCI was associated with lower employment rates, lower levels of disability acceptance, and higher levels of depressive symptomatology (10). Kreutzer and associates (11) found that alcohol use may decrease following TBI compared to preinjury use, but that problem drinking and moderate to heavy drinking are likely to have a negative influence on rehabilitation outcomes.

A task force sponsored by the National Head Injury Foundation conducted a national survey of alcohol and drug abuse problems among TBI rehabilitants (12). About 40% of all patients had moderate to severe substance abuse problems before injury, with alcohol being the most frequently abused substance. Only half of the facilities providing post-acute rehabilitation services reported that substance abuse treatment services were available to clients. The task force concluded that substance abuse problems are extensive and inadequately addressed or overlooked in TBI rehabilitation facilities, and that structured treatment programs are needed to meet the needs of TBI patients.

Blindness and Visual Impairments

Few studies have examined the extent of alcohol and other drug abuse among persons with blindness and visual impairments (13, 14). Risk factors for substance abuse in this population identified by Nelipovich and Buss (15) include social isolation, an excess of unstructured time, and underemployment. While these risk factors are certainly not unique to persons with vision loss, they do reflect common age-related etiologies: cataracts, glaucoma, diabetes, and vascular disease. Hence, the risks for substance abuse in this population reflect issues shared with older adults generally. Persons whose vision loss is the result of trauma at a younger age or genetic etiology probably experience distinct risk factors. Special consideration should be given to even moderate drinking as it can exacerbate underlying health problems for persons whose vision loss is related to diabetes and glaucoma; impaired balance, mobility, and orientation are also special issues. Alcohol and other drug use which reflects efforts to cope with disability, or which reflects social isolation and negative self image, are issues shared in common with other disability groups. Treatment and prevention programs which use printed material should give consideration to the communication needs of persons with vision loss; talking books and Braille materials may be needed.

Deafness and Hearing Impairments

Etiology has a major influence on the nature and extent of communication problems and consequent social integration for persons with hearing loss. Hearing loss may be the result of a congenital disorder or be acquired later in life as the result of injury or disease. People with congenital deafness often form their own communities which gives rise to a unique culture. The fluency with which a person communicates with speech reading, vocal training, gesturing, or sign language affects acculturation within the hearing community. Insensitivity to communication needs by the general population contributes to social stigma, a major cause of social isolation.

The few studies examining the prevalence of substance abuse among persons with hearing loss and deafness suggest that it of roughly the same magnitude as in the general population. However, the limited ability of social service agencies, alcohol and drug abuse programs, school and work settings, and the legal system to communicate with persons who are deaf allow some people to avoid negative consequences of substance abuse (16). Boros (17) suggests that attempts by persons who are deaf to avoid the additional stigma of substance abuse contributes further to social isolation and difficulty accessing substance abuse services. McCrone (18) suggests the following program accessibility guidelines: use of telecommunication device (TDD) to communicate with service agencies, availability of certified sign language interpreters, teaching sign language to substance abuse counselors, co-counseling arrangements with deafness specialists and vocational rehabilitation specialists, outreach efforts to the deaf community, and contacts with professional organizations providing substance abuse services to the deaf community. A survey of deaf service providers and substance abuse service providers by Whitehouse, Sherman and Kozlowski (19) found that substance abuse services are generally inaccessible by telephone to clients who are deaf and that relatively few services are provided to persons who are deaf. Few programs contract for sign language interpreters; instead, family members, volunteers, and printed materials are used to communicate with patients who are deaf despite problems with confidentiality and violation of client rights. Their finding of no specialized services for persons who are deaf has been remedied in some communities by the founding of specialized substance abuse programs such as that provided by The Anixter Center in Chicago. This specialized program was designed for persons who are deaf and employs staff who are fluent in sign language.

Traumatic Brain Injury (TBI)

TBI is a major cause of disability; incidence estimates vary from 422,000 (20) to 1,255,000 annually (21). TBI is the major cause of death for persons younger than 35 years in the United States (22). Men are twice as likely as women to sustain TBI; persons age 15–24 are at greatest risk. Motor vehicle crashes account for about half of all injuries (23). Roughly half of persons who incur major TBI survive more than one month with permanent impairment (20); mild brain injury cases total about 375,500 cases per year (24). The cost of care for this group is estimated to be up to $4 billion annually (25), and the indirect costs are estimated to be $25 billion a year (26).

Factors that are strongly related to TBI outcome are gender, age, duration of coma, systemic injuries, and premorbid level of function (27). Head injury is two to three times more common in males than in females. Rimel and associates (28) studied 1248 patients, in whom the incidence of TBI among males was about twice that of females for most age categories; however, the greatest incidence differences were between males and females in the 15–24 year age group. Duration of coma is an excellent prognostic indicator. A University of Virginia study found that coma length was strongly related to mortality (29). Patients with moderately impaired scores of 9, 10, or 11 on the Glasgow Coma Scale (GCS) experienced a 6% mortality rate, whereas patients with mildly impaired scores of 12 or 13 had a mortality rate of 1%, while no patient with a score of 14 or 15 died. The influence of multiple trauma and systemic injuries compounds the severity of TBI and leads to poor rehabilitation outcome (30). Proper triage, which includes immediate attention to alcohol intoxication, provides the opportunity to manage systemic injuries and minimize trauma severity.

Estimates of intoxication at injury from emergency room and epidemiologic reports suggest that the rate ranges from 29 to 86% (31, 32). Alcohol is a causal factor in about half of all automobile crashes and is causally implicated in a majority of other types of etiologies. A study of TBI admissions to a regional trauma center found that substance use was suspected or documented in 49% of all cases and in 66% of cases which resulted from motor vehicle crashes (33). In a similar study reporting a larger sample admitted for head injury, alcohol was a major associated factor (34) with detectable levels of blood alcohol (BAL) found in 62% of the men and 27% of the women. Alcohol intoxication was a contributing factor more often for moderate than for mild brain injury in a study reported by Rimel and associates (28). Of 199 patients evaluated for moderate head injury, 73% were intoxicated, whereas 53% of 538 patients who sustained mild head injuries were intoxicated. In a sample of 623 patients admitted to an urban trauma center, the odds of brain injury were increased 1.4 times when serum ethanol was detected (32). While these studies provide valuable data, the mechanisms of brain injury due to alcohol use remain poorly described.

Jagger, Fife, Vernberg, and Jane (35) followed 257 adults with TBI and found that improvement of GCS scores was significantly related to BAL on admission: patients with the highest BAL showed the greatest cognitive improvement. Although a common myth is that alcohol protects against injury, Waller and associates (36) found that drinking drivers are more likely than sober drivers to sustain serious injury or death. The apparent improvement in GCS for persons who are intoxicated at injury onset may be misleading when mismatched to GCS of nonintoxicated patients. Alcohol consumption immediately before injury is likely to affect negatively later cognitive outcomes (37). Sparadeo and Gill (38) found that patients who were intoxicated at time of injury had longer hospitalizations, longer periods of agitation, and lower cognitive status at discharge. It remains unclear, however, to what extent the actual level of intoxication impairs cognitive outcomes and recovery of injured neurons and cerebral blood vessels. Basic neuroscience research is examining plasticity of the brain and its capacity to mediate recovery of function (26), as well as the role of high BALs that may contribute to brain tissue damage (39). Understanding the role of alcohol in brain injury and subsequent cognitive outcomes may help prevent the rapidly occurring toxic effects of injury and promote the regeneration of cells that are injured but have not died (40). Any additive effects of intoxication to TBI in affecting neuropsychological and functional recovery must be identified if we are to understand these more basic processes.

Spinal Cord Injury (SCI)

Alcohol and drug intoxication is a frequent contributor to SCI onset. Intoxication estimates for persons incurring traumatic injury range between 17 and 49% (4, 33, 34, 41, 42). Impaired judgment resulting from intoxication contributes to increased risk-taking that contributes to many injuries. Heinemann, Schnoll, Brandt, Maltz, and Keen (43) examined the rate of intoxication at injury onset in a sample of 88 cases at admission to an acute SCI center. BALs greater than 50 mg/dl were observed in 40% of the cases, followed by urine analysis evidence of cocaine (14%), cannabinoids (8%), benzodiazepines (5%), and opiates (4%). Across all cases, 35% had evidence of substances with abuse potential in their urine and 62% had either BAL greater than 50 mg/dl or a positive urine analysis. While these results cannot be interpreted as evidence of dependence, they do reveal a high level of abuse which is detectable with toxicology screens.

The prevalence of alcohol use and abuse following initial rehabilitation may also be high. In a sample of vocational rehabilitation and independent living center clients with SCI, Johnson (44) reported a rate of moderate and heavy drinking that was nearly twice the rate reported in the general population (46% versus 25%). Studies of alcoholic symptomatology in persons with recent SCI estimate rates from 49% (45) to 62% of vocational rehabilitation facility clients (2). Rates of drinking problems parallel age-related trends in the able-bodied population with adolescents and young adults more likely to drink heavily. Heinemann, Donohue, Keen, and Schnoll (45) examined the chronicity of substance use in a sample of 103 persons with recent SCI. By selection, age ranged between 13 and 65 years at injury, respondents with cognitive impairments which would limit self-report were excluded, injuries within one year of assessment, and all were English speaking. The sample's mean age was 28 years; the majority (75%) were men. Lifetime exposure to and recent use of several substances with abuse potential were compared with norms for a like-age national sample reported by the National Institute on Drug Abuse (46). Significantly greater exposure to am-

phetamines, marihuana, cocaine, and hallucinogens was reported by the SCI sample of young adults. The SCI also reported a significantly higher rate of recent alcohol, amphetamines, marihuana, cocaine, and hallucinogen use than did the like-aged national sample. In contrast, the SCI group which was 26 years of age and older reported significantly greater exposure to narcotic analgesics and tranquilizers than did the national sample, as well as recent use of tobacco, alcohol, amphetamines, and marihuana which exceeded the rate in the national sample by at least 10 percentage points. The young adults with SCI reported greater use of marihuana before injury and greater cocaine exposure than did the older group of adults with SCI, while the 26 years of age and older group reported greater tobacco exposure. Intoxication at time of injury served as a marker of preinjury substance use as the 39% who reported intoxication at injury reported greater exposure to tobacco, amphetamines, marihuana, hallucinogens, tranquilizers, and sedatives, and recent use of tobacco, alcohol, amphetamines, cocaine, and hallucinogens than did those denying intoxication at injury. Substance use and abuse is a concern in this population because it occurs frequently, increases the risk for medical complications, may complicate medical and vocational rehabilitation, and reduces the capacity for independent living. It is important to remember that substance use is not necessarily abuse nor dependence, nor does use necessarily result in specific problems. This fact makes it imperative that chemical dependence and rehabilitation professionals understand the context, expectancies, and motives for use. Substance use may serve as a means of engaging others socially, managing stress, or the beginning of a pattern which could escalate into addiction. Hence, it is important to routinely assess substance use and its consequences.

Health Implications of Substance Abuse for Persons with Disabilities

Alcohol and other drug abuse can affect the health of persons with disabilities in both direct and indirect ways (47). Direct effects of drugs include gout, increased spasticity, increased tolerance and potentiation of medication effects, and reduced coordination and concentration. These effects can have adverse consequence for persons with arthritis, SCI, and brain injury, among other conditions. Self-medication of chronic pain is a frequent reason for substance abuse, as it is for depression, anxiety, and adjustment disorders. Indirect effects result from neglected self-care. For persons with SCI, failure to relieve skin pressure regularly increases the risk of decubitus ulcers or pressure sores. The consequences of forgetting to take prescription medications as prescribed reflect the nature of the condition which is being treated. For example, a person who fails to take antihypertensive medication following a stroke increases the risk of recurrent stroke. Health professionals are encouraged to inquire about the reasons for missed appointments, recurring medical problems and injury; alcohol and other drug abuse is frequently a concealed cause of these problems.

ALCOHOL AND OTHER DRUG ABUSE TREATMENT ISSUES FOR PERSONS WITH DISABILITIES

Etiologic Considerations

A physical disability can either precede or follow the onset of substance abuse. Persons who are primary substance abusers are at increased risk of injury which may result in permanent disability. Moore and Li (3) note that risks faced by substance abusers which may limit rehabilitation outcomes include meager social resources, low socioeconomic status, and multiple disabilities. A useful distinction in the alcoholism treatment literature made by Cloninger, Bohman, Sigvardsson, and Von Knorring (48) is applicable when considering disability and substance abuse. They defined Type I alcoholism as characterized by minimal criminal records, late onset of drinking-related problems, and isolated or mild problems, and Type II alcoholism as affecting primarily men with severe alcohol-related problems and criminal histories, and an early onset of problems. Persons characterized by Type II alcoholism more frequently report an alcoholic father, suggesting that the type of an individual's alcoholism reflects familial alcoholism. Glass (13) made a similar distinction in highlighting the potential differences between persons with physical disabilities whose drinking problems predate injury, which he called Type A drinkers, and those whose drinking problems began after injury, which he called Type B drinkers. He expected Type A drinkers to have less favorable rehabilitation outcomes.

A study addressing these issues was reported by Heinemann, Doll, and Schnoll (49) who examined the rate of self-reported alcohol use, consequent problems, perceived need for treatment, and receipt of treatment in a sample of 75 persons with recent SCI. The mean age was 28 years; 75% were men. They reported alcohol use information across three time periods covering 6 months before injury to 18 months after injury. Drinking on three or more occasions was reported by 93% at one or more of the assessment periods and 71% reported one or more drinking problems. However, only 15% reported a need for alcohol abuse treatment and only 11% received treatment. The risk of postinjury alcohol abuse in persons for whom no preinjury abuse was reported was low: 65% reported drinking problems before injury while only 6% reported drinking problems for the first time after injury. Issues of dual disability in preinjury substance abusers who sustain spinal injury are clearly important topics for rehabilitation and chemical dependence programs.

Representative Treatment Approaches

SYSTEMATIC MOTIVATIONAL COUNSELING

A useful treatment model developed for adults undergoing inpatient treatment of alcohol abuse has been applied successfully to adults with TBI. Systematic Motivational Counseling (SMC) (50, 51) recognizes that, while substance use is fueled by complex biological, psychological, and environmental influences, the common route to use reflects individuals' motivation. Variables that affect alcohol and other drug use do so as they contribute to expectations of emotional change resulting from use. Consequently, on any occasion when a person decides to use or abstain from use, it is premised on the anticipation that the positive emotional consequences of using will outweigh those of not using.

The model describes major influences that affect people's motivation to use substances, and provides for varying contributions of each influence on decisions to use across individuals and within the same individual at different times. Consequently, decisions to use or abstain reflect the person's weighting of influences across time and situations depending on expectations of positive and negative emotional consequences of use. SMC seeks to enhance sources of emotional satisfaction that are incompatible with drug use so that the person decides not to use.

A person's current and past experiences are important influences on decisions about substance use, including history of use, the immediate environment, availability of alcohol and other drugs, and others' use. Also important are the person's goals that enhance positive emotions and negative incentives, and situations that intensify negative emotions. Both historical and current experiences evoke beliefs, thoughts, and perceptions about the effects of use. People expect that a drug will change their emotions through immediate, chemical action or through indirect effects on nonchemical incentives. Ultimately, the decision to use is made by judging whether the positive consequences of using outweigh those of not using. Persons who abuse alcohol and other drugs often fail to find emotional satisfaction through pursuit of nonchemical goals, or pursue positive goals which are unrealistic or inappropriate, or pursue goals which conflict with each other.

In SMC, counselors help clients to evaluate goals which may be inappropriate or unrealistic and their roles and commitments in relation to them; identify patterns of facilitation and interference among goals; resolve conflicts among interfering goals and disengage from inappropriate goals; identify nonchemical sources of emotional satisfaction; find new sources of self-esteem and eliminate sources of self-condemnation; shift from pursuing negative goals to positive goals; develop skills for reaching realistic long-range goals and identify subgoals; and formulate and practice assignments for reaching long-range goals and immediately gratifying activities.

The Motivational Structure Questionnaire (MSQ) (52) is used in SMC to assess clients' motivation to use alcohol and other drugs. Clients begin by listing their concerns in major life areas, then describe each of their concerns with a verb drawn from one of 12 verb classes, classified by their valence and goal striving (e.g., appetitive, aversive, agonistic, epistemic), and then indicate the relative strength of their positive and negative motivation. Clients next rate each concern on 10 dimensions which include their role in achieving the goal, that is, the degree to which they actively participate in goal striving and their commitment. They rate the amount of joy they would experience if the goal was attained and the amount of sorrow they would feel if the goal was not attained. Ambivalence is rated by gauging the amount of unhappiness they would imagine feeling when attaining each goal. Also rated are the expected probability of success in attaining each goal, the probability of success if no action is taken, the time that is available before action must be taken on each goal, how near they are to goal attainment, and the consequences that drug use will have on each goal. Ratings are used to construct a profile of motivational features based on norms of persons undergoing alcohol rehabilitation. This profile is discussed with clients in terms of the properties of their goals and the status of their goal pursuit so that motivational patterns that interfere with their finding satisfaction nonchemically can be identified.

SMC attempts to modify the motivational basis for alcohol and then to help clients develop a meaningful life without drugs. Activities within SMC include setting immediate and long-range goals, formulating plans for reaching goals, and regular review of clients' success in reaching goals. Goal ladders are constructed that use a series of hierarchical subgoals that are necessary to attain the ultimate final. Counselors and clients formulate activities for the client to undertake between counseling sessions that are immediately pleasurable and that are aimed at reaching subgoals that comprise the goal ladder. Counselors further help clients enhance their goal attainment by helping clients develop the skills needed to achieve subgoals, resolve conflicts among goals, disengage from inappropriate goals, identify new incentives, shift from an aversive to a goal-fulfilling lifestyle, and examine sources of self-esteem.

This treatment model was evaluated in 60 persons with TBI during a 12-week program (53) who were enrolled in Schwab Rehabilitation Hospital and Care Network-affiliated programs. The sample was composed primarily of men (81%) and African Americans (44%) of working age; 44% of the original sample completed treatment and was available for a one year follow-up. At follow-up, 40% maintained abstinence, 14% became abstinent, 38% continued using, and 8% began using. For the 33 clients for whom both use patterns and employment status were reported at one year follow-up, 42% were employed and working, 33% were unemployed and seeking a job, and 24% were unemployed and not seeking a job. Compared with a no treatment group of 72 adults with TBI, the number of concerns reported on the MSQ declined significantly for the SMC group from initial to one year follow-up assessment. Aversive motivation was greater in the no-treatment group than in the SMC group; assumption of a spectator role was greater in the SMC group than in the no-treatment group; and ambivalence declined more in the SMC group than in the no-treatment group. Lack of commitment was greater in persons who began using substances; ambivalence declined for SMC clients who remained abstinent and began using; composite emotional intensity declined for persons who began using substances; hopelessness was greatest in those who began using substances; and, goal distance declined for SMC clients who became abstinent and increased for no-treatment comparison group members who began using substances. Life satisfaction at one year follow-up in the SMC treatment group was significantly related to the MSQ ineffectiveness score at initial assessment and initial life satisfaction such that persons reporting greater satisfaction at recruitment and those with lower levels of ineffectiveness reported greater levels of satisfaction at follow-up. In summary, SMC proved to be a useful means of reducing substance use, though a longer treatment program was needed to maximize treatment benefits.

SKILLS-BASED SUBSTANCE ABUSE PREVENTION COUNSELING

Skills-Based Counseling (SBC) was developed specifically for persons who experience cognitive deficits resulting from brain injury (54, 55). The model uses a skill acquisition sequence in which clients are taught to recognize high-risk situations related to their preinjury lifestyle or the consequences of their brain injury. Strategies to improve problem solving and response flexibility in high-risk situations are rehearsed and practiced in clinic and then field settings. The client is taught to monitor and use feedback, and to apply skills automatically with minimal disruption by external influences across a variety of settings. When available, family members and others who provide support are taught to appreciate high-risk situations, anticipate problems, and support effective responses. The consequences of brain injury and alcohol use are viewed as closely related: each may exacerbate problems originating with the other, and each realm of problems may have contributions from either source. Efforts to reduce substance abuse must be integrated carefully with physical and cognitive rehabilitation because alcohol and other drugs can be used as both a means of coping with frustrations and as a reinforcer. SBC aims to develop an alternative lifestyle in which drinking and drug use is less central.

SBC includes four stages: (a) comprehensive evaluation, (b) motivational enhancement, (c) coping skill training, and (d) structured generalization. Multidisciplinary approaches are adopted and behavioral techniques employed within each stage while considering each client's neuropsychological strengths and limitations. A multidisciplinary approach is adopted and behavioral techniques are taught and rehearsed, taking into account clients' neuropsychological abilities and limitations.

Comprehensive evaluation uses the modified Adaptive Skills Battery (ASB) (55), a 12-item instrument designed to evaluate coping skillfulness in various situational categories that involve negative emotional states; anger, frustration, and conflict; social pressure to use; and cue-exposure to use alcohol or other drugs. Clients describe their responses to these situations and the counselor rates skillfulness of responses on a three-level scale. ASB items describe a situation that requires a solution to a problem which could result in drinking or drug using; the items were developed with behavior-analytic methodology (56) that identified ecologically relevant problem situations for substance abusers with brain injuries. These situations were chosen because effective responses have a low likelihood of occurring, automatic responses are unlikely to be effective, and new learning and problem solving are required. Clients respond to each situation by anticipating and describing their real-life response. Six situations are intrapersonal and six are interpersonal; six situations are alcohol-specific and six are not alcohol-specific. Specific situations involve feeling worthless, being alone and feeling bored on a Saturday afternoon, being unjustly criticized by a supervisor, dealing with an insistent friend who wants to drink, dealing with unemployment, craving alcohol, and passing a familiar liquor store.

An evaluation of SBC with a sample of 40 adults who sustained TBI was undertaken as part of a collaborative project funded by the National Institute on Disability and Rehabilitation Research (NIDRR), and involving Employment Resources, Inc., and Vocational Consulting Services of Madison, Wisconsin; Advocap, Inc. of Oshkosh, Wisconsin; Curative Rehabilitation Center of Green Bay, Wisconsin; and the Rehabilitation Institute of Chicago (53). All had sustained moderate to severe TBI and were receiving supported employment services. They completed the ASB as a prelude to their participation and again after program completion; a comparison group of 103 adults who received no treatment also completed the ASB and neuropsychological measures. The SBC sample was composed primarily of men (83%), Caucasians (97%), and working-age adults (mean age was 33 years). Motor vehicle crashes were the cause of injury for 73%. History of alcohol or other drug abuse was acknowledged by 56% of the SBC group. The proportion of cases that completed the 12-week counseling program and was available for one year follow-up was 75%. The SBC group significantly increased in ASB-measured skillfulness from initial to follow-up assessment while no change was observed in the no-treatment comparison group. The SBC group also changed their drinking patterns from before to one year after the commencement of counseling such that 24% became abstinent while only 9% of the no-treatment comparison group did so; in contrast 40% of the comparison group continued to drink while 21% of the SBC group did so. These results support the effectiveness of SBC and its utility for persons with TBI.

PREVENTION OF ALCOHOL AND OTHER DRUG ABUSE FOR PERSONS WITH DISABILITIES

Historically, rehabilitation professionals have not addressed the consequences of substance abuse. A number of reasons account for this failure. First, preservice training and accreditation standards do not exist. Rehabilitation specialists often feel unprepared to confront alcohol and other drug issues because they have little educational background on the subject. Few graduate programs address substance abuse as an integral part of rehabilitation specialists' training. Similarly, no accreditation standards for rehabilitation specialists address alcohol and other drug abuse prevention as an explicit area of required professional competence. As a result, there are no generally accepted standards of professional performance. Second, interdisciplinary training is lacking. Like professionals in other fields, rehabilitation specialists across physiatry, speech-language pathology, physical and occupational therapy, counseling, psychology, and others focus on what they have been trained to do and what they know, with a goal of achieving optimal physical, mental, or occupational outcomes for their clients. Because education programs and clinical training do not include substance abuse prevention for each rehabilitation discipline, individuals frequently fail to detect and consequently address these problems in their practice. As a result, teams of professionals may not act in a coordinated manner. For example, while a rehabilitation specialist attempts to address a problem with a client's substance abuse, the client's physician may inadvertently encourage abuse by failing to adequately monitor prescription drugs or excusing alcohol use as an acceptable coping mechanism. Third, an absence of quantifiable research data limits our knowledge about the extent and consequences of alcohol and other drug abuse problems. Some rehabilitation specialists argue that there is insufficient research data to support arguments concerning prevalence or to support the claim that improved rehabilitation outcomes will result from intervention efforts. Though the body of research data is growing, studies of substance abuse and disability are relatively few. Greer and colleagues noted in their synthesis of the literature (57) that there is little uniformity in sampling, data collection, and criteria. Similarly, there are few long-term evaluations of the relationship between alcohol and other drug use and rehabilitation outcomes. What evidence is available is consistent and compelling. Today, the vast majority of rehabilitation professionals have begun to recognize substance abuse as a clear and persisting problem for their clients—even though they may not feel qualified to address these problems.

Labeling alcohol and other drug abuse as a secondary disability may lead to a perception of it being less important than the primary disability or as a condition that can be addressed subsequent to medical rehabilitation and by another service provider. This attitude prevails even though substance abuse is frequently the cause of the disability, particularly in persons who sustain traumatic injuries that occur under the influence of alcohol or other drugs. Gaps in service delivery also contribute to a perpetuation of alcohol and other drug abuse problems. Since substance abuse intervention services are generally not reimbursable through private or government insurance, many rehabilitation programs ignore the problems in their patients or offer collateral services at patients' expense through an outside provider. Such practice perpetuates the view that substance abuse is someone else's rather than the rehabilitation team's problem. Unfortunately, the large gaps in community health delivery systems mean that most persons with disabilities never get treatment or prevention services. Finally, most substance abuse professionals are unaccustomed to working with persons with disabilities, so fully accessible programs are rare.

Knowledge, attitudes, and professional behaviors related to substance abuse prevention are changing throughout the rehabilitation community. A few recent examples suggest the scope of current interest in this issue:

1. Interdisciplinary models for rehabilitation and substance abuse prevention: Under grants from NIDRR and the J. M. Foundation, the Rehabilitation Institute of Chicago (RIC) developed a model approach for alcohol and other drug abuse prevention as an integral aspect of medical rehabilitation. RIC's model recognizes the potential role of all rehabilitation professionals and is interdisciplinary in structure and approach.

Similar interdisciplinary models were developed at the Medical College of Virginia for TBI patients, the Sister Kenny Institute, and other sites around the country.

2. Vocational rehabilitation training system: The Rehabilitation Services Administration (RSA) of the Department of Education awarded a contract to provide training on substance abuse issues to vocational rehabilitation counselors. This training addresses the special challenges posed by vocational rehabilitation clients with dual disabilities and was offered through RSA's Regional Rehabilitation Continuing Education Program.

3. National policy and leadership development symposium: In August, 1991, the Institute on Alcohol, Drugs and Disability brought together leaders to create action plans for implementing policies that were intended to improve access to prevention services for persons with disabilities. The Symposium Report (58) provides a strategy for addressing the scope and complexity of the issue of substance abuse and disability.

4. The Resource Center on Substance Abuse Prevention and Disability[a] was created in 1990 when Very Special Arts' Educational Services received a grant from the Federal Office for Substance Abuse Prevention. The Center attracted participation by the leading experts in the field, built a comprehensive library, developed and disseminated information, and formed coalitions between alcohol and drug prevention and rehabilitation as well as special education constituents. These national initiatives reflect growing attention to the issue of substance abuse and disability.

Preservice Education

Both rehabilitation and chemical dependency professionals play vital roles in understanding, recognizing, and addressing the alcohol and other drug abuse problems of people with disabilities. Training for these professionals regarding substance use problems among people with disabilities is a necessary step in remediating this significant rehabilitation problem. Information designed to change both attitudes and knowledge of professionals is likely to lead to a change in rehabilitation practices.

Rehabilitation educators have recognized the need for enhanced training on substance abuse issues by persons with physical disabilities and implemented innovative programs. For example, the Rehabilitation Counselor Education Program at New York University provides a specialty in chemical dependence counseling; the Hunter/City University of New York program in Rehabilitation Counseling provides a specialization in chemical dependence. To date, few disciplines outside of rehabilitation counseling offer such specialization.

Inservice Education

National needs for alcohol and other drug abuse education for rehabilitation professionals were investigated among members of the American Congress on Rehabilitation Medicine. Kiley and colleagues (59) conducted a survey that assessed members' knowledge of substance abuse, attitudes regarding patients' substance use, and referral practices for patients with substance abuse problems. The survey was completed by 37% of the eligible respondents (1211 professionals) after two follow-up attempts. Respondents suspected that 29% of their patients with traumatic injuries had substance problems. Routine screening for alcohol and drug problems at their facility was reported by only 30%. Substance abuse education for staff was reported by 50%; patient education regarding substance abuse was reported by 59%. While 79% reported that their facilities had referral procedures for patients with substance abuse problems, only 44% reported making referrals. Patients were referred most often to Alcoholics Anonymous. The results support the need for enhanced inservice education regarding substance abuse assessment and treatment, facility policies, and referral procedures.

An example of a substance abuse prevention education program for rehabilitation staff are the efforts made at the Rehabilitation Institute of Chicago (60). The initial program described a theoretical context within which staff could understand substance use problems, categorized abusable drugs, reviewed the epidemiology of alcohol and other drug abuse, presented basic science information about alcohol abuse, described the nature of attitudes toward chemical use, reviewed hospital policies and procedures, and defined assessment and referral procedures. The hour-long program was supplemented with printed materials. The effectiveness of the education program was evaluated with a questionnaire which was administered before and 6 months after the presentation to assess changes in staff knowledge, attitudes, and behavior. Knowledge about substance abuse issues, as reflected in the number of correct responses 6 months after education, was greater for both attendees and nonattendees than at the pretest. However, improvement in knowledge was greater for staff who attended the education program than for staff who did not attend. Staff who attended the presentation reported making more referrals before and 6 months after the program than did those who did not attend. Staff who made the most referrals after education were those who made more referrals before education, who suspected more patients of preinjury substance abuse, and who had less experience in rehabilitation. The results of this study suggest that substance abuse education should be provided to all rehabilitation team members in order to assure sufficient understanding of substance abuse issues, hospital policies and procedures related to patients' use of substances, and to improve the effectiveness of rehabilitation services.

Staff came to realize that issues of attitude change and program implementation required involvement of staff at all levels of the organization. These early inservice efforts were expanded to include a task force composed of consumer and rehabilitation staff members under the auspices of the Midwest Regional Head Injury Center for Rehabilitation and Prevention at RIC. These efforts were made in collaboration with the Illinois Prevention Resource Center and with funding provided by the J. M. Foundation for a project titled "Substance Abuse Prevention Programming for Patients Incurring Traumatic Injury." A major product of these efforts was a resource manual titled "Alcohol and Other Drug Abuse Prevention for People with Traumatic Brain and Spinal Cord Injuries" (61). It provides an overview of substance abuse prevention models, information about alcohol and other drugs and traumatic injury, skills training to identify alcohol and other drug problems, and skill development exercises for staff working with clients around coping issues. It employs a train-the-trainer model which empowers staff trainers to work within their own departments to enhance department members' skills in dealing with alcohol and other drug abuse issues. Examples of implementing basic prevention strategies, including ways of involving and training impactors, providing information, developing life skills, creating alternatives to substance abuse, and influencing policies are provided.

Consumer Education

A variety of organizations have emerged and resources developed in the past several years that address alcohol and other drug abuse issues for persons with disabilities. A resource guide for persons with SCI and their families was developed by John de Miranda titled "Inform Yourself: Alcohol, Drugs and Spinal Cord Injury" with funding provided by the Paralyzed Veterans of America.[b] The guide provides personal stories of addiction and recovery, a self-assessment tool, organizational contacts for additional information along with an extensive glossary and bibliography. Described as the "total resource for the wheelchair community" is Sam Maddox's "Spinal Network."[c] The book begins with a chapter by Barry Corbet and goes on to cover medical, sports and recreation, travel, media, technological, sex, disability rights, legal and financial issues, and resource information in the United States and Canada. Substance abuse issues are addressed in two sections of a "features page" chapter. For persons who have sustained traumatic brain injuries, Robert Karol and Frank Sparadeo's 1993 booklet "Alcohol,

---

[a] Resource Center on Substance Abuse Prevention and Disability, 1331 F Street NW, Suite 800, Washington, DC 20004. Voice: 202-737-2900, TDD: 202-737-0645, Fax: 202-628-3812.

[b] Available from Novation, Inc., 2165 Bunker Hill Drive, San Mateo, CA 94402; Voice/TDD/Fax: 415-578-8047.

[c] Available from Spinal Network, P.O. Box 4162, Boulder, CO 80306; 800-338-5412.

Drugs and Brain Injury" (62) published by the Vinland Center in Loretto, Minnesota, provides an overview of alcohol and other drug effects, reproduces assessment tools, and helps consumers create an action plan for dealing with substance use and urges to use. Also available for consumers is Ohio Valley Center for Head Injury Prevention and Rehabilitation's "User's Manual" that addresses the cumulative effects of substance abuse for persons with TBI. The 16-page pamphlet provides a short quiz about the effects of alcohol and other drug abuse on persons with brain injury and uses a computer analogy to explain how learning is impaired. Both the National SCI Association and the National Head Injury Foundation, among others, have included presentations for consumers about substance abuse at recent annual meetings.

Other Resource Materials

The Substance Abuse Prevention Project at the Rehabilitation Institute of Chicago produced a training manual for medical rehabilitation professionals working with patients who have sustained traumatic injuries. Materials are suitable for group or inservice education programs and include materials designed for family members and patients.[d]

The Substance Abuse Assessment and Education Kit was designed by the Rehabilitation Research and Training Center on Severe Traumatic Brain Injury for professionals working in brain injury rehabilitation. Contents include clinical materials designed for assessment, research information, and plans to develop education and prevention policies and procedures.[e]

The Center for Substance Abuse Prevention provides a Clearinghouse for Alcohol and Drug Information.[f] Materials describe a full array of prevention topics, including those relevant to persons with physical, sensory and developmental disabilities.

The Minnesota Chemical Dependence Program for Deaf and Hard of Hearing in Minneapolis developed a 105 minute videotape for professionals titled "Chemical Dependence—What Is It?" which is open captioned and sign language interpreted.

Available from Rochester Institute of Technology is a directory listing of 308 drug prevention and treatment programs for persons who are deaf. Program services include staff trained in American Sign Language and cultural issues, interpreters, closed captioned equipment, teletext equipment and accessible 12 step programs.[g]

Baylor College of Medicine produced a videotape titled "Substance Abuse in Rehabilitation Facilities—No Problem? Think Again" and a manual titled "Spinal Cord Injury: A Manual for Healthy Living" that focuses on ways to prevent complications.[h]

REHABILITATION SETTING ISSUES
Agency Policies

Rehabilitation agency policy issues regarding possession and use of alcohol and drugs as well as recreational or socialization programs that incorporate alcohol use need to be clearly formulated in light of studies examining controlled drinking outcomes. While moderate alcohol use is likely to pose few problems for many persons, those with histories of substance abuse are at risk of relapse by policies and programs that provide opportunities for alcohol consumption. Also at particular risk are persons with cognitive impairment resulting from brain trauma or other neurologic injury. Policies that

provide for monitoring of psychoactive prescription medications obtained during or after hospitalization should also be considered. In short, the opportunity for abuse of prescribed medications and histories of alcohol or illicit drug use requires case-by-case assessment of each patient's history as rehabilitation plans are made.

Staff Education

INSERVICE EDUCATION

The need for enhanced education on substance abuse issues has been urged by several educators (63–66) and rehabilitation practitioners (67–70). Several clinical issues have not been addressed sufficiently in medical rehabilitation settings. One of the most important is the risk of prescription medication misuse. While the specific drugs misused may vary across clinical populations and reflect specific medical complications, continued monitoring of long-term prescription use is important. Clinicians should attend to depression and poor psychological adjustment which may underlie medical complications. Physician, nursing, and allied health staff education should focus on recognizing prescription medication misuse and the reasons for misuse (71).

In addition to the inservice education materials listed above is "Substance Abuse and Adolescents with Disabilities" produced by the Region II Rehabilitation Continuing Education Program at the State University of New York at Buffalo (72). It provides a detailed curriculum, complete with materials suitable for use as transparencies with an overhead projector. Topics addressed include models of chemical dependence, family system issues, how disability affects developmental issues, and implications for vocational counseling. Available from Wright State University's Substance Abuse Disability and Vocational Rehabilitation is their Training Manual (73). It provides a compendium of educational materials for rehabilitation and chemical dependence professionals about substance abuse and disability.

RECOMMENDATIONS

Relatively few persons who sustain traumatic injury may believe that they need treatment for drinking or other drug problems. Such a perception may reflect individuals who are at relatively early stages of readiness for change (74). For some persons who are intoxicated at injury, the fact of injury may serve to illustrate the extent of their substance use problems and motivate them to initiate action, consistent with Marlatt and associates' model of substance use change (75). The belief that one does not need treatment, despite major trauma, can be understood as an aspect of denial or rationalization about the severity of drinking problems. The importance of external agents—employers, courts, family, and physicians—in encouraging treatment is evident in Heinemann, Doll, and Schnoll's (49) findings that these agents were most often cited as a reason for pursuing treatment. Clearly, the process of acknowledging drinking or other drug problems is developmental in nature. Major injury does no more to cure drinking problems for some persons than does job loss, divorce, or other forms of trauma.

Glass' (13) typology of problem drinkers is useful in planning prevention and treatment efforts. Knowing the etiology of substance abuse and whether it proceeded or followed disability is an important issue. It is important to assess drinking and illicit drug history along with coping skills in rehabilitation settings because of the evidence that pre-disability substance abuse places individuals at high risk for abuse after disability. Traumatic onset disability may provide an opportunity for some persons to recognize the seriousness of their substance abuse patterns and to make changes. While some persons may make changes on their own, others will continue to use and experience consequences of their use. The pernicious quality of addiction is illustrated by continued use after injury. It may be that some persons with preinjury drinking problems are representative of an early onset, Type II drinking or drug use pattern which reflects a genetic component. The success of rehabilitation interventions that consider familial and personal drinking histories are apt to be enhanced when interventions consider these factors.

Several implications for enhancing medical rehabilitation are evident. First, assessment of alcohol and other drug use should be a routine part of all

[d] Available from Rehabilitation Institute of Chicago, Education and Training Center, 345 East Superior, Chicago, IL 60611; 312-908-2859.

[e] Available from Rehabilitation Research and Training Center on Severe Traumatic Brain Injury, Box 434 MCV Station, Richmond, VA 23298–0434; 804-786-7290.

[f] P.O. Box 2345, Rockville, MD 20852; 800-729-6686.

[g] Available from Campus Connection Bookstore, 48 Lomb Memorial Drive, Rochester, NY 14623–5604; Voice: 716-475-2504; TTY: 716-475-7071; FAX: 716-475-6499.

[h] Available from Rehabilitation Research and Training Center on Community Integration in SCI, Baylor College of Medicine, 1333 Moursund Avenue B-107, Houston, TX 77030; 713-797-5945.

admissions to acute care and rehabilitation programs for persons incurring traumatic injury. Responsibility for this screening could be assumed by a variety of staff members including physicians, nurses, psychologists, and social workers. Second, training of team members to recognize alcohol and other drug abuse is critical to allow them to provide competent assessments. Substance abuse treatment program professionals should consult with physical medicine and rehabilitation providers to acquire this knowledge. Third, referral networks to alcohol treatment programs are necessary if a potential dual disability is to be identified and treated in a timely fashion. Adequate communication links must be established so that chemical dependence treatment programs and counselors learn about the special needs of persons with disabilities. Accessibility needs, functional abilities, and attitudes toward persons with disabling conditions are some of the topics that could be addressed in training programs for alcoholism treatment personnel. Chemical dependence treatment programs designed specifically for persons with physical disabilities are another treatment alternative (76–80).

CHEMICAL DEPENDENCE TREATMENT SETTING ISSUES

Chemical dependency professionals often are uninformed regarding the unique risks and needs of people with disabilities and consequently may be unprepared to offer appropriate treatment. Moreover, attitudes of professionals regarding what constitutes a primary and secondary disability influence the provision of treatment. If alcohol and other drug abuse is viewed as a secondary disability, then it may be viewed as less important than the primary disability; as a consequence, it may be left untreated. Both chemical dependency and rehabilitation professionals need to be appreciate the value of treating primary and secondary disabilities concurrently.

Implications of Americans with Disabilities Act

The Americans with Disabilities Act of 1990 (ADA, Public Law 101–336) is one of the major civil rights laws passed since 1964. It addresses the severe disadvantages persons with disabilities experience in their daily lives. These disadvantages include intentional exclusion, overly protective rules and policies, segregation, exclusionary standards, and architectural, transportation, and communication barriers. The ADA is important for alcohol and other drug prevention programs because public accommodations, along with other social service, health care, and education programs, must allow people with disabilities to participate fully.

Architectural Accessibility and Communication Issues

Accessibility of substance abuse services involves physical, programmatic, and administrative aspects. Physical accessibility is enhanced by architectural modifications such as ramps and Braille material. The use of sign language interpreters for persons with hearing impairments, staff training on disability issues, and modification of printed materials for persons with learning disabilities are examples of enhanced programmatic accessibility. Enhanced interagency coordination, advocacy for accessible transportation, and reduced attitudinal barriers are examples of administrative accessibility.

The New York State Office of Alcoholism and Substance Abuse Services' Ad Hoc Task Force Report on Acquired Physical Disability and Chemical Dependency (81) reported a study of services available to persons with disabilities at five New York City Health and Hospital Corporation hospitals. The report concluded that departments responsible for substance abuse services did not have standard policies and procedures in place to identify, treat, and refer to after care treatment persons who have physical disabilities and substance abuse problems. Efforts in all states are needed to assure not only ADA compliance, but equitable and effective services for persons with disabilities.

Attitudinal Barriers and Need for Inservice Education

As early as 1960, Wright (82) noted the power of language in conveying attitudes about persons with disabilities. Terms such as "handicapped," "afflicted with," "victim of," and "crippled" are often offensive to persons with disabilities and draw our attention to what is different about a person rather than their basic decency as a human being. "People first" language, such as "person with a spinal cord injury," "person who uses a wheelchair," and "person with mental retardation" emphasizes abilities rather than limitations. Inservice education should include discussions of how to increase sensitivity to language and attitudes that exclude persons with disabilities from appropriate services.

Paraprofessional Training

Nondegreed paraprofessionals in recovery have served important roles in chemical dependence treatment programs. Efforts to credential paraprofessionals include those of the New York Department of Employment which developed a certificate program for persons in recovery from substance abuse. However, disability awareness training has only recently been incorporated in these programs. In contrast, staff of independent living centers often have disabilities and use a peer role-modeling approaching in working with consumers. Consequently, they often emphasize disability rights, self-help, and self-advocacy in contrast with traditional substance abuse models which treat service recipients as patients. Federal support for consumer involvement in rehabilitation research and education activities are reflected in the National Institute on Disability and Rehabilitation Research's use of Participatory Action Research methods which promote relevance to consumers. Engaging persons with disabilities in the training and certification programs of paraprofessionals in chemical dependence could enhance the accessibility of these programs. Cross-training of consumer advocates in both chemical dependence issues and disability rights would serve to enhance their functioning.

Recommendations

The New York State Office of Alcoholism and Substance Abuse Services' Ad Hoc Task Force Report on Acquired Physical Disability and Chemical Dependency (81) made several specific training and accessibility recommendations which deserve repeating. Training recommendations included (a) helping rehabilitation staff to recognize chemical dependency problems in rehabilitation and disability service delivery systems, (b) training chemical dependency staff to recognize other disabilities, and (c) providing interdisciplinary education and training to staff working with people with acquired physical and chemical dependence disabilities. Accessibility recommendations included making chemical dependency treatment more architecturally, programmatically, and administratively accessible, developing guidelines and strategies in vocational rehabilitation agencies to enhance work with clients who have dual disabilities, developing prevention strategies for clients with dual disabilities, and developing community resources to serve clients with dual disabilities.

SUMMARY

Our knowledge about the extent of substance abuse problems and the consequences of substance abuse in persons with disabilities has grown markedly in the past decade. Promising treatment and prevention programs have been evaluated. Professional education and program accessibility has increased. Continuing efforts are required in the next decade to assure that alcohol and other drug abuse services are made available to persons with disabilities in both rehabilitation and chemical dependence settings.

References

1. Yarkony GM. Medical complications in rehabilitation. In: Heinemann AW, ed. Substance abuse and physical disability. New York: Haworth, 1993.

2. Rasmussen GA, DeBoer RP. Alcohol and drug use among clients at a residential vocational rehabilitation facility. Alcohol Health Res World 1980;5:48–56.

3. Moore D, Li L. Substance use among applicants for vocational rehabilitation services. J Rehabilitation 1994;60:48–53.

4. Fullerton DT, Harvey RF, Klein MH, Howell T. Psychiatric disorders in patients with spinal cord injuries. Arch Gen Psychiatry 1981;38:1369–1371.

5. Lyons J, Larson D, Burns B, Cope N, Wright S, Hammer J. Psychiatric co-morbidities and patients with head and spinal cord trauma. Gen Hosp Psychiatry 1988;10:292–297.

6. Trieschmann R. Spinal cord injuries: psychological, social and vocational adjustment. New York: Pergamon Press, 1980.

7. Wehman P, Kreutzer J, eds. Vocational rehabilitation after traumatic brain injury. Rockville, MD: Aspen Publishers, 1990.

8. Murray PK. Clinical pharmacology in rehabilitation. In Caplan B, ed. Rehabilitation psychology desk reference. Rockville, MD: Aspen Publishers, 1987:501–525.

9. Heinemann AW, Mamott BD, Schnoll S. Substance use by persons with recent spinal cord injuries. Rehabil Psychol 1990;35:217–228.

10. Kiley D, Heinemann AW. The relationship between employment, substance abuse and depression following spinal cord injury. Paper presented at the annual convention of the American Psychological Association, Boston, Massachusetts, 1990.

11. Kreutzer J, Harris J, Doherty K. Substance abuse patterns before and after traumatic brain injury. Paper presented at the 97th annual convention of the American Psychological Association, New Orleans, August, 1989.

12. National Head Injury Foundation. Substance abuse task force white paper. Southborough, MA: National Head Injury Foundation, 1988.

13. Glass E. Problem drinking among the blind and visually impaired. Alcohol Health Res World 1980/81;5:20–25.

14. Resource Center on Substance Abuse Prevention and Disability. A look at alcohol and other drug abuse prevention and blindness and visual impairments, 1992.

15. Nelipovich M, Buss E. Alcohol abuse and persons who are blind. Alcohol Health Res World 1989;13:128–131.

16. Resource Center on Substance Abuse Prevention and Disability. A look at alcohol and other drug abuse prevention and deafness and hearing loss, 1992.

17. Boros A. Activating solutions to alcoholism among the hearing impaired. In: Schecter AJ, ed. Drug dependence and alcoholism: social and behavioral issues. New York: Plenum, 1981.

18. McCrone WP. Serving the deaf substance abuser. J Psychoactive Drugs 1982;14:199–203.

19. Whitehouse A, Sherman RE, Kozlowski K. The needs of deaf substance abusers in Illinois. Am J Drug Alcohol Abuse 1991;17:101–113.

20. Kalsbeek W, McLaurin RL, Harris BSH, Miller JD. The national head and spinal cord injury survey: major findings. J Neurosurg 1980;53: S19–S31.

21. Caveness WF. Incidence of craniocerebral trauma in the United States in 1976 with trend from 1970 to 1975. Adv Neurol 1979;22:1–3.

22. Annegers JF, Kurland LT. The epidemiology of central nervous system trauma. In: Odom GL, ed. CNS Trauma Research Status Report, NINCDS, 1–8.

23. Anderson DW, McLaurin RL. The national head and spinal cord injury survey. J Neurosurg 1980;53:1–43.

24. Kraus JF, Nourjah P. The epidemiology of mild, uncomplicated brain injury. J Trauma 1988;28: 1637–1643.

25. Kraus JF, Black MA, Hessol N, et al. The incidence of acute brain injury and serious impairment in a defined population. Am J Epidemiol 1984;119:186–201.

26. Munsat TL. Statement of the American Academy of Neurology to the Interagency Head Injury Task Force. American Academy of Neurology, September 1988.

27. Miner ME, Wagner KA. Neurotrauma—treatment, rehabilitation and related issues. Boston: Butterworth, 1989.

28. Rimel RW, Giordani B, Barth JT, Jane JA. Moderate head injury: completing the clinical spectrum of brain trauma. Neurosurgery 1982;11: 344–351.

29. Rimel RW, Giordani B, Barth JT, Boll TJ, Jane JA. Disability caused by minor head injury. Neurosurgery 1981;11:344–351.

30. Stone JL, Lowe RJ, Jonasson O, Baker RJ, Barrett JA, Oldershaw JB, et al. Acute subdural hematoma: direct admission to a trauma center yields improved results. J Trauma 1986;26: 445–450.

31. Field JH. Epidemiology of head injuries in England and Wales. London: Her Majesty's Stationary Office, 1976.

32. Sloan E, Zalenski R, Smith R, Sheaff C, Chen E, Niko I, et al. Toxicology screening in urban trauma patients: drug prevalence and its relationship to trauma severity and management. J Trauma 1989;29:1647–1653.

33. Gale JL, Dikmen S, Wyler A, Temkin N, McClean A. Head injury in the Pacific Northwest. Neurosurgery 1983;12:487–491.

34. Galbraith S, Murray WR, Patel AR, Knitt-Jones R. The relationship between alcohol and head injury and its effects on the conscious level. Br J Surgery 1976;63:128–130.

35. Jagger J, Fife D, Vernberg K, Jane J. Effect of alcohol intoxication on the diagnosis and apparent severity of brain injury. Neurosurgery 1984;15:303–306.

36. Waller PF, Stewart JR, Hansen AR, Stutts JC, Popkin CL, Rodgman EA. The potentiating effects of alcohol on driver injury. JAMA 1986;256:1461–1466.

37. Brooks N, Campsie L, Symington C, Beattie A, McKinlay W. The effect of severe head injury on patient and relative within seven years of head injury. J Head Trauma Rehabil 1987;8: 1–30.

38. Sparadeo FR, Gill D. Effects of prior alcohol use on head injury recovery. J Head Trauma Rehabil 1989;4:75–82.

39. Albin MS, Bunegin L. An experimental study of craniocerebral trauma during ethanol intoxication. Crit Care Med 1986;14:841–846.

40. Stonnington HH. Traumatic brain injury rehabilitation. Am Rehabil 1987;13:4–20.

41. Frisbie J, Tun C. Drinking and spinal cord injury. J Am Paraplegia Soc 1984;7:71–73.

42. Heinemann AW, Goranson N, Ginsburg K, Schnoll S. Alcohol use and activity patterns following spinal cord injury. Rehabil Psychol 1989;34:191–206.

43. Heinemann AW, Schnoll S, Brandt M, Maltz R, Keen M. Toxicology screening in acute spinal cord injury. Alcohol Clin Exp Res 1988;12:815–819.

44. Johnson DC. Alcohol use by persons with disabilities. Wisconsin Department of Health and Social Services, 1985.

45. Heinemann AW, Donohue R, Keen M, Schnoll S. Alcohol use by persons with recent spinal cord injuries. Arch Phys Med Rehabil 1988;69: 619–624.

46. National Institute on Drug Abuse. National household survey on drug abuse: main findings 1988. Rockville, MD: U.S. Department of Health and Human Services, 1990.

47. Moore D, Polsgrove L. Disabilities, developmental handicaps and substance misuse: a review. Int J Addict 1991;26:65–90.

48. Cloninger CR, Bohman M, Sigvardsson S, Von Knorring AL. Psychopathology in adopted-out children of alcoholics: the Stockholm adoption study. Recent Dev Alcohol 1985;3:37–51.

49. Heinemann AW, Doll M, Schnoll S. Treatment of alcohol abuse in persons with recent spinal cord injuries. Alcohol Health Res World 1989;13:110–117.

50. Cox WM, Klinger E. A motivational model of alcohol use. J Abnorm Psychol 1988;97: 168–180.

51. Cox WM, Klinger E. Incentive motivation, affective change and alcohol use: a model. In: Cox WM, ed. Why people drink: parameters of alcohol as a reinforcer. New York: Gardener Press, 1990.

52. Cox WM, Klinger E, Blount JP. Alcohol use and goal hierarchies: systematic motivation counseling for alcoholics. In: Miller WR, Rollnick S, ed. Motivational interviewing: preparing people for change. New York: Guilford Press, 1991: 260–271.

53. Rehabilitation Institute of Chicago. Substance abuse as a barrier to employment following traumatic brain injury. Final report submitted to the National Institute on Disability and Rehabilitation Research for Research and Demonstration Project H133A10014–93, December 28, 1995.

54. Langley MJ. Prevention of substance abuse in persons with neurological disabilities. NeuroRehabilitation 1992;2:52–64.

55. Langley MJ, Ridgely MP. Skill-based substance abuse prevention counseling: behavioral interventions for clients with neurological disabilities. Unpublished manuscript, 1994. [Available from the first author at Clinical Psychology Associates, Waterford, Wisconsin 53185.]

56. Goldfriend MR, D'Zurilla TJ. A behavior analytic model for assessing competence. In: Spielberger CD, ed. Current topics in clinical and community psychology. New York: Academic Press, 1969;1:151–196.

57. Greer BG. Substance abuse among clients with other primary disabilities: curricular implications for rehabilitation education. Rehabil Educ 1990;4:33–34.

58. Cherry L. Summary report. Alcohol, drugs, disability. National Policy and Leadership Development Symposium. San Mateo, CA: Institute on Alcohol, Drugs and Disability, 1991.

59. Kiley D, Heinemann A, Doll M, Shade-Zeldow Y, Roth E, Yarkony G. Rehabilitation professionals' knowledge and attitudes about substance abuse issues. NeuroRehabilitation 1992;2:35–44.

60. Heinemann AW, Kiley D, Shade-Zeldow Y, Roth E, Doll M. Chemical dependence education for rehabilitation professionals. Paper presented at the annual meeting of the American Congress of Rehabilitation Medicine and the American Academy of Physical Medicine and Rehabilitation, Phoenix, AZ, October 22, 1990.

61. Midwest Regional Head Injury Center for Rehabilitation and Prevention, Rehabilitation Institute of Chicago, Illinois Prevention Resource Center. Alcohol and other drug abuse prevention for people with traumatic brain and spinal cord injuries: resource manual, 1996.

62. Karol R, Sparadeo FR. Alcohol, drugs and brain injury. Loretto, MN: Vinland Center, 1993.

63. Beck R, Marr K, Taricon P. Identifying and treating clients with physical disabilities who have substance abuse problems. Rehabil Educ 1991;5:131–13.

64. Greer BG. Alcohol and other drug abuse by the physically impaired: a challenge for rehabilitation educators. Alcohol Health Res World 1989;13:114–149.

65. Moore D, Siegal H. Double trouble: alcohol and other drug use among orthopedically impaired college students. Alcohol Health Res World 1989;13:118–123.

66. Prendergast M, Austin G, de Miranda J. Substance abuse among youth with disabilities. Prevention Research Update 1990:7.

67. Corrigan JD. Substance abuse as a mediating factor in outcome from traumatic brain injury. Arch Phys Med Rehabil 1995;76:302–309.

68. Corrigan JD, Lamb-Hart GL, Rust E. A programme of intervention for substance abuse following traumatic brain injury. Brain Inj 1995; 9:221–236.

69. Corrigan JD, Rust E, Lamb-Hart GL. The nature of extent of substance abuse problems in persons with traumatic brain injury. J Head Trauma Rehabil 1995;10:29–46.

70. Krause JS. Delivery of substance abuse services during spinal cord injury rehabilitation. NeuroRehabilitation 1992;2:45–51.

71. Heinemann AW, McGraw TE, Brandt MJ, Roth E, Dell'Oliver C, Schnoll S. Prescription medication misuse among persons with spinal cord injury. Int J Addict 1992;27:301–316.

72. Stewart E, Burganowski DF, Larson DM, Kauppi DR. Substance abuse and adolescents with disabilities. Region II. Rehabilitation continuing education program. Buffalo, NY: State University of New York at Buffalo, 1992.

73. Moore D, Ford J. Substance abuse disability and vocational rehabilitation issues training manual. Dayton, OH: Wright State University School of Medicine, SARDI Center, 1996. [Available from Department of Community Health, School of Medicine, Wright State University, Dayton, OH 45401; 513-259-1384.]

74. Prochaska JO, DiClemente CC. Stages and processes of self-change of smoking: toward an integrative model of change. J Consult Clin Psychol 1983;51:390–395.

75. Marlatt GA, Baer JS. Addictive behavior: etiology and treatment. Am Rev Psychol 1988;39:223–252.

76. Anderson P. Alcoholism and the spinal cord disabled: a model program. Alcohol Health Res World 1980/81;5:37–41.

77. Kiley D, Brandt M. Issues and controversies in chemical dependence services for persons with physical disabilities. In: Heinemann AW, ed. Substance abuse and physical disability. New York: Haworth, 1993.

78. Langley M, Kiley D. Prevention of substance abuse in persons with neurological disabilities. NeuroRehabilitation 1992;2:52–64.

79. Lowenthal A, Anderson P. Network development: linking the disabled community to alcoholism and drug abuse programs. Alcohol Health Res World 1980/81;5:16–17.

80. Sweeney TT, Foote JE. Treatment of drug and alcohol abuse in spinal cord injury veterans. Int J Addict 1982;17:897–904.

81. Chemical Dependency Research Working Group, Division of Vocational Rehabilitation Services. Acquired physical disability, chemical dependency, ad hoc task force report. New York: Office of Alcoholism, Substance Abuse Services, May, 1994.

82. Wright BA. Physical disability: a psychological approach. New York: Harper & Row, 1960.

72 Gays, Lesbians, and Bisexuals

Robert P. Cabaj

Substance abuse is expressed in various communities and populations at different rates and with differing incidences. Clinicians wishing to serve the needs of a particular ethnic or cultural group have learned that the particular community in question must be understood, respected, and consulted with, to make effective interventions. Gay men, lesbians, and bisexuals make up one of these populations with special needs, a population defined not by traditionally understood cultural and ethnic minority criteria, but, rather by having a different sexual orientation from the majority. This chapter discusses the nature of homosexuality and bisexuality; gay men, lesbians, and bisexuals themselves; the substance use and abuse concerns among these people; and, the specific treatment issues that need to be addressed in working with gay men, lesbians, and bisexual men and women.

There is no solid agreement about the amount of alcohol and other substances used or the incidence of substance abuse in the gay, lesbian, and bisexual population. Most studies (1–8), reports (9–10), or reviews of surveys (11–12) and the experiences of most clinicians working with gay men and lesbians (13–14) estimate an incidence of substance abuse of all types at approximately 30%—with ranges of 28–35%; this estimate contrasts with an incidence of 10–12% for the general population.

A careful review of each report, however, demonstrates significant and persistent methodological problems, ranging from poor or absent control groups, unrepresentative population samples (some studies gathered subjects only from gay and lesbian bars), to a failure to use uniform definitions of substance abuse or of homosexuality itself. Nonetheless, no matter where the sample was taken—urban or rural, various socioeconomic settings, in the United States or other countries—the rates are strikingly uniform, though there are some variations in use reported. For example, one study (15), using very simple screening questions, notes greater substance use but no greater alcohol use in gay men as compared to heterosexual men in San Francisco, whereas another (5) reports that heavy alcohol use was not greater for gay men and lesbians compared to heterosexuals sampled, but did note that there were fewer gay and lesbian alcohol abstainers and a greater number of gay and lesbian moderate alcohol users.

A few surveys have focused on lesbian substance abuse, most in the general population (16–18), and one in lesbian medical students (19). Both continue to indicate a high use of alcohol and other drugs in lesbians, and a higher concern over a problem with alcohol and drug use than in similar heterosexual populations. Currently, no study specifically focuses on the drug or alcohol use of bisexual men or women, though many such people are included in some of the studies already described. Most of the ideas in this chapter can apply to bisexuals, since the focus is on the effects of external and internalized homophobia.

Alcohol abuse has been the primary focus of most studies. No specific studies of injecting drug use (IDU) and the gay population are currently available. The quarterly Centers for Disease Control (CDC) report on acquired immunodeficiency syndrome (AIDS) and human immunodeficiency virus (HIV) infections clearly indicate a subgroup of IDU gay and bisexual men, and one of the routes of HIV infection for lesbians is via IDU (20). One survey (21) did review the use of all types of abusable substances among gay men and lesbians, noting a greater use of cigarettes, marihuana, and alcohol than in the general population.

Over the last several years, concerns about the epidemic of HIV-related conditions have led to increased studies of both gay and bisexual men and intravenous drug users. An explosive use of methamphetamine, known as "speed," "crystal," or "crank," by gay and bisexual men has become evident, and of grave concern. The primary route of use is intravenous (IV); combined with its disinhibiting effect and sexual stimulating effect, the IV gay male users of methamphetamine are at extremely high risk for HIV infection (22–23).

SEXUAL ORIENTATION IN GENERAL

Homosexuality, as a term, is subject to some controversy. It was first used by Krafft-Ebing and implied a clinical, pathological condition (24). Because of these associations—and the linking in this century of homosexuality and illness—attempts are being made to avoid using or even to eliminate this term. Dr. John Boswell traced homosexuality in history and reports the term *gay* has a long association with homosexual men (25). Since gay is less prejudicial, this chapter refers to gay men, lesbians, and bisexuals as people, and homosexuality and bisexuality in reference only to certain types of behavioral activities or orientations.

The understanding of certain terms is crucial to understanding homosexuality; failure to have clear definitions and understanding has led to much of the confusion in the literature about homosexuality and sexuality in general and certainly has contributed to some of the prejudicial feeling about homosexuality. It is important to recognize the difference between sexual orientation and sexual behavior, as well as the differences between sexual orientation, gender identity, and gender role. Sexual orientation refers to the desire for sex, love, and affection, and/or sexual fantasies from or with another person, whereas sexual behavior is strictly sexual activities and may not coincide with primary sexual orientation. Gender identity is the sense of self as male or female, with no reference to sexual orientation or gender role. Gender role, in turn, refers to behaviors and desires to behave that are viewed as masculine or feminine by a particular culture. Behavior that a particular culture may label as masculine or feminine is not necessarily a reflection of gender role or identity, but it is common to call behavior, styles, or interests shown by a male that are associated with women as "effeminate" (boys are often labeled "sissies") and the equivalent by a woman as "being like a man" or "butch" (girls are often labeled "tomboys").

Using both the pioneering scientific and psychological evidence collected by Dr. Evelyn Hooker that gay men were as psychologically healthy as matched heterosexuals (26) and subsequent research, the American Psychiatric Association (APA) in 1973 removed homosexuality per se as a mental illness from its list of disorders. This decision was challenged by some psychiatrists who mistakenly thought the removal was a response to political pressure, but the APA supported its scientifically based decision. There was, however, a "political" compromise, with the creation of a nonscientific diagnosis called "ego-dystonic homosexuality"; in 1987 the APA recognized this error and removed that label from the *Diagnostic and Statistical Manual of Mental Disorders,* third edition revised (DSM-III-R) (27–28). The current DSM-IV followed the same revisions (29). Efforts are in progress to remove all references to homosexuality in the World Health Organization's (WHO) *International Classification of Diseases,* tenth revision (ICD-10).

This nonjudgmental, nonprejudicial framework on homosexuality has led to new thinking and revisions on homosexual behavior and on gay men, lesbians, and bisexuals (12, 30–35). A new literature founded on work with gays in psychotherapy and substance abuse counseling continues to be generated (14, 36–44). American psychoanalytic thinking has been extremely persistent in trying to view homosexuality as pathological, but even some new psychoanalytical literature has been able to review and revise some traditional, conservative views on homosexuality (45–49). The literature also continues to increase for the non–mental health clinician working with gays and lesbians (50–53). Two journals focus on new and nonprejudicial scientific and clinical information on gays and lesbians, the *Journal of Homosexuality* and the *Journal of Gay and Lesbian Psychotherapy.* A forthcoming journal, the *Journal of Gay and Lesbian Health,* will be produced by the Gay and Lesbian Medical Association.

Through such new reviews and the efforts of many gay-sensitive clinicians and researchers, many of the myths and prejudices about gay people are being laid to rest. There have been persistent false beliefs about gay men and lesbians, including the following:

Myth: Gay men are promiscuous. *Fact:* Only a small segment of gay men fit this description and may more accurately reflect a trait of maleness in our society than of homosexuality (32).

Myth: Gay men cannot form relationships. *Fact:* A majority of gay men are in relationships of various types (32).

Myth: Gay men or lesbians only need one good heterosexual sexual experience to "straighten" them out; or gay men and lesbians try to "recruit" young people to "become" gay or lesbian. *Fact:* Sexual orientation is not due to a *lack* of an experience but is an internal desire for most people, shaped in expression by many factors (31).

Myth: Gays are child molesters. *Fact:* The vast majority of child molesters are heterosexual (37).

Myth: All gay men are "effeminate." *Fact:* Though some gay men have gender-discordant behavior as children, usually manifested as avoidance of rough and tumble play, the vast majority of adult men are not "effeminate" and there is no equation of homosexual orientation and effeminacy (32, 45–46).

HOMOSEXUAL BEHAVIOR AND BISEXUALITY

Homosexual Behavior

Besides the work of Dr. Hooker noted above (26), the now famous Kinsey report helped put homosexual behavior itself in perspective (54). Although dated, the extensive survey reported that 67% of American men have had at least one homosexual experience to orgasm after adolescence; 30% have had more than one experience; 5–7% have bisexual experiences but prefer homosexual ones; and 4–5% have homosexual experiences exclusively as adults. The often used estimate that 10% of the male population is primarily or exclusively homosexual in terms of sexual behavior is based on this data from 1948 (55). These data point out the widespread occurrence of male homosexual behavior, not necessarily the numbers of gay men, and has very broad implications for the spread of the HIV virus by the sexual route.

Gay and bisexual people and homosexual and bisexual behavior are found in almost all societies and cultures around the world and throughout history (56–60). Tolerance and acceptance has varied throughout history, and currently varies from country to country, culture to culture, and community to community. Since anyone may be gay, lesbian, or bisexual, gay and bisexual men and women do not have uniform ways of behaving nor live uniform lifestyles. There is, therefore, no such thing as a "gay community" per se (12, 32, 61), just gay, lesbian, and bisexual individuals. Gay people are found in all segments of society and in all minority and ethnic groups, may be of any age, and may have any occupation or career. Most gay people are not readily identifiable, in spite of some persistent stereotypes. Sexual behavior and sexual orientation itself are not necessarily fixed in an individual and may change over time. Intense homosexual longings in young adulthood or adolescence may change as one grows older; some heterosexuals may discover gay feelings later in life (62).

Bisexuality

Many people are clearly bisexual in behavior, being able to sexually function with either sex, but often prefer one sex over the other (46). The Kinsey report (54) devised the famous Kinsey scale to describe this range of behavior: 0 for exclusive heterosexual behavior ranging to 6 for exclusive homosexual behavior. This classification puts the majority of men in a bisexual range based on sexual experiences. As will be discussed, bisexuality and bisexual behavior are especially important in HIV infection prevention work, since many men have gay sexual experiences, without informing their spouses or other female partners; many lesbians have had and do have sex with men. For many minority populations, bisexuality, but not homosexuality per se, is acceptable, or at least admitted to, in surveys and interviews. In the 1989 CDC 8-year review of AIDS cases among gay or bisexual men, 54.2% of African Americans were reported as bisexual; 44.2% of Hispanics were reported as bisexual; and 11.3% of whites were reported as bisexual (63).

GAY SEXUAL ORIENTATION

Given the previous discussion, gay men and lesbians are remarkably like everyone else. There are three major differences, however, which may be of help in understanding the high incidence of substance abuse: (*a*) having a sexual orientation expressed by the desire to have affectional, sexual, sexual fantasy, and/or social needs met more often by a same sex partner than opposite sex partner; (*b*) negotiating a process of self-identity and self-recognition as a gay person, different from the majority, known as "coming out"; and, (*c*) confronting a widespread and insidious dislike, hatred, and/or fear of gay and lesbian people, homosexual activity, and homosexual feelings, known as "homophobia." This last factor forms the largest barrier to gays and lesbians obtaining quality health care and substance abuse treatment, and may be the primary factor in explaining the widespread incidence of substance abuse in gay populations. Homophobia is a result of societal heterosexism, that is, the perspective that the majority situation, heterosexuality, is preferable or better, if homosexuality is even considered at all. Homophobia is parallel to such societal forces as racism and sexism (64).

In trying to understand the nature of homosexuality, there have been new insights into sexuality, in general, and in the nature of gender identity. In looking at the etiology of homosexuality, most new research indicates that a homosexual orientation is not learned and not a result of any family or social patterns. The "classic" psychoanalytical description of a close, seductive mother and absent, distant father does not occur more frequently in the backgrounds of gay men and, in fact, may occur more often in heterosexuals (45, 46, 65). In fact, new research is pointing out familial patterns that may indicate a genetic component (46, 66–70) and/or biological and biochemical factors (71–72). Such knowledge and awareness about the origins of sexual orientation may help relieve both the patients who are having difficulty accepting their homosexuality and the families of patients who are gay or lesbian who may feel guilty, as if they had done something "wrong" to "cause" the sexual orientation.

Coming Out

Coming out is a long and complex process that may occur throughout the entire life cycle (73–77). The best way to conceptualize coming out is to view it as a series of steps that an individual negotiates at his or her own time and pace, with periodic steps forward and backward. The individual must first become aware of his or her own sexual orientation as "different" from that of the majority. The next step is to accept the awareness and begin to integrate it into a self-concept and grapple with the negative feelings associated with homosexuality. Next, the individual may choose to act on the feelings (although some gay people with strong gay feelings do not engage in sex with others of the same sex). Finally, the person makes a series of life-long decisions about whether to let others know and whom to let know, such as friends, family, work colleagues and peers, teachers, and medical providers. Some gay people only come out to selected people and not to everyone at once; some may come out, then deny it later or not continue to let new friends or people at new workplaces know. The bias and prejudice against people with AIDS and the mistaken association of AIDS and gay men, rather than the association of HIV infection and behaviors that may lead to infection, may lead some men to "return to the closet" or hesitate in continuing the coming out process.

Homophobia and Heterosexism

Homophobia, both internalized and externalized, combined with heterosexism, are the major forces that gays and bisexuals must deal with in our society (34, 78–80). All gay people have internalized homophobia, having been brought up in a homophobic society that tends to promote prejudicial myths about gay people or, from the heterosexist concentric point of view, to just ignore gay and bisexual people in general. The coming out process may be delayed or undergo great difficulties depending on the intensity of internalized homophobia (if the person believes homosexuality is a sin, an illness, unnatural, evil, or will only lead to sadness, loneliness, and isolation) and may well require the help of psychotherapy (45, 75, 81–82).

Externalized homophobia is found at every level in our society: legal, medical, scientific, religious, political, social, educational, and judicial. Many feel that the resistance to earlier governmental help with the AIDS crisis was a result of homophobia in the government, linking the routes of HIV infection and homosexuality (83). The ever increasing violent attacks on gays, from verbal threats to outright physical attacks and murder, are usually fueled by homophobia. Heterosexist thinking and homophobia and the fear of what others will do if they know an individual is gay or even think an individual is gay are major factors in the difficulty of getting accurate data about gays and lesbians for scientific investigations (33, 78).

Ostrow has reported that many men in both military recruit studies and college population surveys who were HIV-positive but denied any high-risk behaviors admitted to homosexual activities and, much less frequently, IV drug use, in extremely confidential interviews (84). Homophobia and the fear of reprisals explain these findings: the military will discharge known homosexuals; college students fear the reactions of peers, teachers, and family. Gays fear loss of insurance coverage if insurers discover sexual orientation no matter what the HIV status may be and hesitate to let health providers know this crucial information (all insurers will deny they cancel insurance for this reason, but many observations from the author's own practice and from the reports of colleagues refute this assertion). In surveys, gay and bisexual people hesitate to disclose sexual orientation, even with great assurances of confidentiality; gathering information on gay and bisexual people, therefore, is extremely difficult and contributes to the skewed samples, as already noted in the studies on substance abuse and the gay community.

Gay people also face many additional challenges that majority populations escape. There are many issues generated by two people of the same gender forming a relationship (85–86) such as finding comfortable and safe living quarters, financial concerns, legal battles over insurance and wills, or coping with a lover with AIDS. Since there is such a high incidence of substance abuse, there are many codependent relationships or relationships between two active substance abusers. Although everyone needs to relearn how to be safely sexual in this age of AIDS, some gay men are sexually compulsive (87) or have never had "sober sex" and will need special help and support. Married bisexual men face ever greater pressures, such as deciding about coming out to spouses and children, negotiating safe sex with a spouse not used to such behavior, and finding a community identity (88).

Gay and lesbian adolescents are a population of great and grave concern, since many studies indicate a much higher suicide attempt rate in these youth, a more volatile type of substance abuse than is seen in other adolescents, and hesitancy to follow HIV infection risk reduction guidelines (89–94). Older gays and lesbians face the same problems other elderly face, with added isolation, loneliness, and possible senses of hopelessness and resignation about substance abuse (95–96). The constant loss and bereavement gay men and women face with the widespread, continuous loss of loved gay friends due to AIDS is exacting a heavy toll, in addition to the general stress of being gay in our society (97).

Lesbian Issues

Lesbians have some specific issues that need to be highlighted. As described previously, the incidence of substance abuse is equally high among gay men and lesbians. In general, lesbians may have additional social struggles and concerns. Compared to gay men, they are more likely to have lower incomes (as do women in general, compared with men); lesbians are more likely to be parents (about one third of lesbians are biological parents); lesbians face the prejudices aimed at women as well as those for being gay, including the stronger reaction against and willingness to ignore female substance abusers; lesbians are more likely to come out later in life (about 28 years of age versus 18 years of age in men); and lesbians are more likely to have bisexual feelings or experiences, so that they are still at risk for HIV infection via a sexual route as well as possible IV drug use (16, 19, 32, 43, 52, 65).

According to several surveys, lesbians are a bit more likely to be in a long-term relationship than the comparable gay man (16, 32), so there needs to be a clear focus on relationships, parenting, and family concerns in working with lesbian substance abusers. Lesbians are also subject to the increase in violence, both verbal and physical, against gays; and as is true with anyone, they are subject to domestic violence. This latter fact is often ignored; since there are correlations with domestic violence and substance abuse, clinicians need to be aware of this possibility in working with lesbians (98).

A growing literature is developing on working with lesbians in psychotherapy and substance abuse work (99). There has been an overemphasis on male homosexuality in the psychiatric literature; only recently has female homosexuality been subject to similar examination and discussion.

Bisexuality

The study and understanding of bisexuality has grown exponentially in the last few years. Several published works focus on both the theoretical concepts involved in understanding bisexuality and the clinical issues that evolve for bisexuals (100–102). Bisexuality is increasingly understood to be another expression of human sexual orientation, and not an in-between or undecided state of sexual orientation expression. The Kinsey studies (54, 103), again, clearly documented the range of sexual behaviors in which men and women participate. There are no clear studies of bisexuals and substance abuse, though with the focus on men who have sex with men as a risk factor for HIV infections, more information will no doubt be forthcoming. The issues that face men and women who are bisexual, especially if relating more strongly to the homosexual longings, will be the same issues that men who identify as gay and women who identify as lesbian will face.

SUBSTANCE ABUSE AND GAY IDENTITY FORMATION

Many factors contribute to the prominent role of substance use and abuse in gay men, lesbians, and bisexuals. At one point, American psychoanalytic psychiatry, for years focused on the etiology of male homosexuality, even postulated that homosexuality was a cause of alcoholism (104). Since homosexuality, repressed or not, does not cause alcoholism (105)—indeed, alcoholism and substance abuse are not "caused" by any psychodynamic or personality factor alone—other factors must be examined, the two most important being genetic or biological contributions and the psychological effects of heterosexism and homophobia.

New research continues to support, in great part, genetic, biological, and biochemical origins for the diseases of alcoholism and substance abuse. As already noted, there is continuing and growing evidence that homosexual orientation may have—at least in part—genetic, biological, and biochemical components (46, 66–72). Such parallel contributions to both sexual orientation and substance abuse has led to some speculation of a possible chromosomal link between the genetic contributions to substance abuse and sexual orientation. Such a direct genetic link between sexual orientation and the propensity to substance abuse, however, is unlikely. The studies just cited indicate that male homosexuality and female homosexuality may be different phenomena, with differing familial patterns; substance abuse appears to have equal incidence among gay men and women.

Societal, cultural, and environmental factors, however, may lead to a greater expression of any genetic predisposition. By analogy, there has been an increase in the incidence of alcoholism in women since the beginning of the twentieth century (106). Though partially explained by better data collection, and awareness of the hidden homebound female alcoholic, the increase can also be explained by social factors. In the early 1900s, women were prohibited by societal pressures from drinking in public; as the social acceptability of drinking increased, more women drank, thus increasing the likelihood of exposure to alcohol, which is needed to trigger the genetic expression of alcoholism.

Gay men, lesbians, and bisexuals have faced great societal prohibitions, not only on the expression of their sexual feelings and behavior, but on their very existence. Societal homophobia could well have a parallel effect, leading to the higher degree of expressivity of the genetic potentials for substance abuse in gay men, lesbians, and bisexuals. Also, societies or cultures in turmoil or undergoing social change have higher rates of alcoholism (106–107).

For most of the twentieth century, societal pressures forced most gay people to remain "in the closet," hiding their sexual orientation or not acting on their feelings. Responding to societal expectations rather than personal desire, some gay, lesbian, and bisexual people may marry someone of the opposite sex and raise a family, creating a potentially stressful situation. Legal prohibitions on homosexual behavior, overt discrimination, and the failure of society to accept or even acknowledge gay people have limited the types of social outlets available to gay men and lesbians to bars, private homes, or clubs where alcohol and other drugs often played a prominent role. The role models for many young gay men and lesbians just coming out may be gay people using alcohol and other drugs, who are met at bars or parties. Continuing societal homophobia, as well as the impact of HIV on gay men, lesbians, and bisexuals, further add to the stress (108–109).

Some gay and bisexual men and women cannot imagine socializing without alcohol or other mood-altering substances. Gay men, lesbians, and bisexuals are brought up in a society that says they should not exist and certainly should not act on their feelings. Such homophobia is internalized. Many men and women have had their first homosexual sexual experiences while drinking or being drunk to overcome their internal fear, denial, anxi-

ety, or even revulsion about gay sex. For many men and women, this linking of substance use and sexual expression persists and may become part of coming out and the development of a personal and social identity. Many gay people continue to feel self-hatred; the use of mood-altering substances temporarily relieves, but then reinforces, this self-loathing in the drug withdrawal period. Alcohol and many other drugs can cause depression, leading to a worsening of self-esteem and the "erosion of spirit" so well described by many of the 12-step recovery programs.

Given the state of acceptance of homosexuality and bisexuality in our society at this time, the stages of developing a gay, lesbian, or bisexual identity, influenced by such societal reactions, may be intimately involved with substance abuse. Though some substance abusers appears to have a genetic predisposition to substance abuse—supporting an illness model with psychosocial manifestations—not all people with such a genetic predisposition develop alcoholism or substance abuse in their lifetimes. Intrapsychic, psychological, and psychodynamic factors, influenced by psychosocial and parental upbringing, may lead certain people to turn to substance use and, therefore, potentiate a genetic predisposition for substance abuse.

The link between the psychodynamic forces in developing a gay, lesbian, or bisexual identity and the use or abuse of substances becomes clear in examining the early development and progression through the life cycle for a gay person from the perspective of the work of Swiss psychoanalyst Alice Miller (110). Her description of how parents influence the emotional lives of their "talented" or different children has strong parallels with the development of a gay, lesbian, or bisexual identity. Parental reactions shape and validate expressions of children's needs and longings; parents reward what is familiar and acceptable to them and discourage or de-emphasize behavior or needs they do not value or understand. Harm of course occurs when a parent is too depressed, preoccupied, or narcissistic to respond to the *actual* child and the *actual* needs and wants of the child. Children eventually learn to behave the way parents expect to get rewards, and to hide or deny the longings or needs that are not rewarded.

Like Miller's examples, many gay and bisexual men and women are aware of being different early in life because they have affectional and sexual needs and longings that are different from others around them (111). Some male children who will grow up to be gay may desire a closer, more intimate relationship with father; this desire is not encouraged or even understood in our society (45). The prehomosexual child learns to hide such needs and longings, creating a false self. Real needs are often suppressed or repressed and rejected as wrong, bad, or sinful. Dissociation and denial, therefore, become major defenses to cope with internal feelings.

The studies of familial patterns (66–67) point out that gay men have a greater than normal chance of having an alcoholic father and a greater chance of having a mother with a major affective disorder and who is more likely to be unavailable. Newer clinical impressions from many clinicians working extensively with gays and lesbians indicate that sexual abuse in childhood is probably more common than once believed. The psychological, as well as genetic and emotional, backgrounds in the families of many gays and lesbians already predispose them to substance abuse.

The psychology of being different and learning to live in a society that does not accept difference readily shapes the sexual identity development as the child emerges from childhood and the latency period (112). With the rewards for the "false self," the child suppresses his more natural feelings. He or she has no clear role models about how to be gay or lesbian; teachers usually cannot reveal their sexual orientation and there is little positive media attention for gays and lesbians. In latency, children who will become gay or bisexual, especially boys who may be effeminate, may fear other children, feel very different, and become more isolated. In adolescence, the gay sexual feelings emerge with great urgency, but with little or no context or permission. Conformity is certainly encouraged, further supporting denial and suppression of gay feelings. Adolescents often reject and isolate those who are "different." The gay adolescent further develops dissociation and splitting off of affect and behavior. These factors may help explain the many problems facing gay youth (90). Gay youth are very subject to sexual abuse and violence and sometimes are introduced to sex via hustling or prostitution or get "used" sexually by others. The extreme difficulty many gay men and women have in coming out and integrating sexuality and personal identity makes sense from this perspective.

Substance use serves as an easy relief, can provide acceptance, and more importantly, mirrors the comforting dissociation developed in childhood. Alcohol and other drugs cause a dissociation of feelings, anxiety, and behavior and may mimic the emotional state many gay people had to develop in childhood to survive. The "symptom-relieving" aspects help fight the effects of homophobia; it can allow "forbidden" behavior, allow for social comfort in bars or other unfamiliar social settings, and again, provide comfort through the familiar experiences of dissociation and isolation.

The easy availability of alcohol and drugs at gay bars or parties and the limited social options other than those bars and parties certainly encourages the use of substances early in the coming out and gay or lesbian socialization process. For gay men especially, sex and intimacy are often split off—dissociated. Again, substance use allows for an acting on feelings long suppressed or denied, but also mirrors the dissociative experience and makes it harder to integrate intimacy and love. There is an easy relief of longings and needs, with sex and/or substance use, and the more challenging needs for love and intimacy may be ignored. Substances help many gay people brace themselves for rejection by others, either as a gay person coming out to friends or family or from potential dates and sexual partners. It allows for denial and even "blackouts" about sexual behavior. It can certainly make "living in the closet" with its built in need for denial and dissociation easier or even possible (the "I-was-so-drunk-I-didn't-know-what-I-did-last-night" scenario often used in high school and college). Since so many gay people are adult children of alcoholics, they are even more skilled at denying their own self and their own needs.

Finally, the internal state that accompanies internalized homophobia and that occurs with substance abuse are very similar—the "dual oppression" of homophobia and abuse (14). The following traits are seen in both: denial; fear, anxiety, and paranoia; anger and rage; guilt; self-pity; depression, with helplessness, hopelessness, and powerlessness; self-deception and development of a false self; passivity and the feeling of being a victim; inferiority and low self-esteem; self-loathing; isolation, alienation, and feeling alone, misunderstood, or unique; and fragmentation and confusion. These close similarities make it very difficult for gay men or lesbians who cannot accept their sexual orientation to recognize or successfully treat their substance abuse. Self acceptance of one's sexual orientation thus appears to be crucial to recovery from substance abuse.

The pervasive internal and social pressures to use mood-altering substances and the difficulty in creating or finding currently existing non–substance-using social situations certainly contributes to the marked expression of the alcohol and other drug-dependence potentials in gay men and women. One wonders if the rate of substance abuse in the general population would not be much greater if everyone in the United States was subject to such pressures. Possibly, there is no greater genetic predisposition to substance abuse in gays, but an increased potentiation of expression due to greater use and presence of such substances in gay society.

HOMOSEXUAL BEHAVIOR, SUBSTANCE ABUSE, AND HIV INFECTIONS AND AIDS

Men who have sex with men continues to be the largest "at-risk" group for current and new HIV-related infections and cases of AIDS in the United States, comprising 53% of all adult AIDS cases in the United States at the end of June, 1994 (113). Although most clinicians and researchers attribute the spread of HIV in this population to certain highly risky unsafe sexual practices, the role of IV drug use is significant. The same CDC report noted that 6% of all adult cases were men who had sex with men *and* IV drug users. Many men in the CDC statistics "IV-drug-users-only" category are also gay or bisexual, but fail to report this additional risk category for the reasons already discussed.

Besides the obvious potential spread of HIV through the IV drug–using segments of the gay population via dirty needle sharing, substance abuse plays a not so obvious role in spreading the virus through sexual practices. In most reviews of gay men and safer sex practices, men who were knowl-

edgeable about safer sex but failed to practice it uniformly report being under the influence of some substance, such as alcohol or other drugs, at the times they failed to follow the guidelines (92, 114–116). In addition, some very high-risk sexual activities such as "fisting" (inserting of fingers, hand, or forearm into the anus and rectum of a partner) very often are performed with the use of drugs such as amyl nitrite, known as "poppers," alcohol, marihuana, or a combination of these to help with relaxation of anal sphincter tone (117–120).

Judgment is clearly suspended or altered during even the moderate, let alone heavy, use of alcohol and other substances. There is definitely a higher risk for exposure to HIV with larger numbers of sexual partners, but the risk is also higher in any *one* particular encounter when safer sex guidelines are not followed, whether due to suspended judgment with substance use, pressure by the partner to not bother, or having highly charged sexual feelings. Furthermore, there is clear evidence that most abused substances alter the immune system, which may well compromise the immune system's initial reaction to exposure to HIV in men engaged in unsafe sexual practices under the influence of substances (121).

With the widespread use of such agents and such conditions in the gay community, it appears that substance use and abuse is a definite cofactor in the spread of HIV through sexual practices.

SPECIAL TREATMENT CONCERNS FOR GAY PEOPLE

Evaluation and Treatment Issues

Treatment must focus on recovery from substance abuse and from the consequences of homophobia. To reverse and treat the denial and dissociation, the patient will need to address his or her own acceptance of self as a gay or bisexual person. Although no one should be forced to come out to any one, self-acceptance appears to be crucial to recovery. Treatment needs to be at least gay-sensitive if not gay-affirmative, as will be discussed. To "recover" from an "Alice Miller" childhood, the patient, once in solid recovery, will need to deal with the grief and rage associated with mourning the loss of the "false self" and must learn how to get his or her own real needs met.

In the assessment of a gay man, lesbian, or bisexual person presenting for mental health services, clinicians need to be aware of the higher incidence of substance abuse in this population and, accordingly, routinely screen for symptoms of alcoholism or other substance abuse. In formulating a treatment plan for gay men, lesbians, or bisexuals determined to have a substance abuse problem, the personalized treatment plan needs to include the influences and effects of the following for each individual: the stage in the life cycle; the degree and impact of internalized homophobia; the stage in the coming out process and the experience of coming out; the support and social network available; current relationship, if any, including married spouses and the history of past relationships; the relationship with the family of origin; comfort with sexuality and expression of sexual feelings; career and economic status; and health factors, including HIV status.

Most clinicians working with the addictions recognize that psychotherapy alone will not treat or cure the substance abuse, and, in fact, may actually be harmful and not indicated (106). Individual psychotherapy can be isolating and lonely, and may create the false hope that understanding and insight will lead to recovery; often, the insights lead to an excuse to continue using substances. If a patient is already in therapy when recovery begins, the therapy need not stop, but the work will need to be much more supportive and focused on the here and now, while the emotional and neurological systems begin to heal. Once in solid recovery, the patient can deal with the grief and rage involved in mourning the loss of the "false self," and learn how to get his or her own real needs met. In most cases, a 12-step program such as Alcoholics Anonymous (AA) is a vital part of recovery and may well be essential for all substance-abusing patients in recovery who undertake psychotherapy.

Homophobia is the major consideration in meeting the treatment needs of gay men and lesbians with substance abuse problems, as well as the proper care and prevention of HIV-related infections. Few inpatient or outpatient detoxification and rehabilitation programs have knowledge about homosexuality and are often unaware that they have gay and lesbian patients, who may be too frightened to come out to the staff (122). There, attitudes of the staff and treating clinicians about homosexuality are crucial in the success of treatment for gays and lesbians. Many gay and lesbian staff are afraid to come out because of administrative reaction and are not able to either serve as role models or to provide a more open and relaxed treatment. More and more gay-sensitive programs, that is, programs that are aware of, knowledgeable about, and accepting of gay people in a non-prejudicial fashion, are opening up around the country; some current and well-established programs are training staff about gay concerns. There is currently only one program in the country, however, which is gay-affirmative—that is, actively promoting self-acceptance of a gay identity as a key part of recovery. This program, PRIDE Institute, released data showing a very successful treatment rate when sexual orientation is considered a key factor in recovery. At a 14-month follow-up with verified reports, 74% of all patients treated 5 or more days were continuously abstinent from alcohol use, and 67% abstinent from all drugs, as compared to four similar, sometimes gay-sensitive, but not gay affirmative programs with unverified reports taken at follow-ups ranging from 11 months to 24 months, with rates of 43%, 55%, 57%, and 63% (123). As these findings imply, substance abuse and sexual identity formation are often tightly woven together, and it is difficult to imagine much success in treating the gay or lesbian substance abuser without addressing sexual orientation and homophobia.

Aftercare may be a major problem. Twelve-step recovery programs and philosophies are the mainstays, of course, in recovery and in staying clean and sober. There may be no gay-sensitive therapists or counselors in the patients' communities. AA, although open to all, is still a group of people at any individual meeting that may reflect the perceptions and prejudices of the local community and not be open to or accepting of openly gay members (124–126). Many communities now have gay and lesbian AA, Narcotic Anonymous (NA), and Al-Anon meetings, and AA as an organization clearly embraces gays and lesbians, as it embraces anyone concerned about a substance abuse problem (127). However, some gay people in recovery may not have come out or may not feel comfortable in such meetings, especially if a discussion of sexual orientation was not part of the early recovery. Some groups parallel and similar to AA have formed to meet the needs of these gays and lesbians, such as Alcoholics Together, and many large cities sponsor "round-ups," large 3-day weekend gatherings focused on AA, NA, lectures, workshops, and drug- and alcohol-free socializing.

Although 12-step programs such as AA and NA recommend avoiding emotional stress and conflicts in the first 6 months of recovery, for the gay man, lesbian, or bisexual in such programs, relapse is almost certain if the gay or bisexual person cannot acknowledge and accept his or her sexual orientation. Discussion about the conflicts around acknowledging sexual orientation and ways to learn to live comfortably as a gay or bisexual person are essential for recovery, even if these topics are emotionally laden and stressful.

Many localities now have gay, lesbian, and bisexual health or mental health centers, almost all with a focus on recovery and substance abuse treatment. National organizations, such as the National Association of Lesbian and Gay Alcoholism Professionals, the National Gay and Lesbian Health Association, the Association of Gay and Lesbian Psychiatrists, the Gay and Lesbian Medical Association, the Association of Lesbian and Gay Psychologists, and the National Gay Social Workers, can help with appropriate referrals.

Some of the suggestions and guidelines of AA and NA and most treatment programs may be difficult for some gay men, lesbians, and bisexuals to follow; giving up or avoiding old friends, especially fellow substance users, may be difficult when the gay or bisexual person has limited contacts who relate to him as a gay person. Staying away from bars or parties may be difficult if they are the only social outlets; special help on how to not drink or use drugs in such settings may be necessary. Many gay people mistakenly link AA and religion; because many religious institutions denounce or condemn homosexuality, gay men, lesbians, and bisexuals may be resistant to trying AA or NA.

Specific Additional Factors to Consider

Gay men, lesbians, and, especially, bisexually identified people of color who abuse substances must deal with homophobia—often from within the same self-identified ethnic or cultural groups—in addition to possible racism and other prejudices in seeking recovery (128–131).

There is still a popular misconception linking gay men, and not risky sexual behavior, with HIV infections and AIDS. The fears surrounding HIV may also interfere with the comfortable and objective treatment of gay men who are not HIV-positive or who do not have AIDS. Treatment centers and programs may still be frightened to work with HIV-positive individuals, despite the clear CDC guidelines, or may resist talking about safer sex because it is uncomfortable to talk about such matters or it is viewed as detracting from recovery issues. All one needs to do is remember that AIDS prevention education is just as lifesaving an intervention for a substance abuser. There are many additional difficult clinical issues facing a substance-abusing gay man who is HIV-positive or who has AIDS, whether actively using substances or in recovery, such as suicidality, dementia, negotiating safer sex, and legal issues concerning wills and powers-of-attorney (132–134). Finding a treatment setting that will accept a gay, clean, and sober person with AIDS may be very difficult (13). Some communities now have AA groups with a special focus on HIV-positive individuals or people with AIDS, such as the Positively Sober groups.

Other factors affect the treatment of lesbians, gay men, and bisexuals. Many gay men, lesbians, and bisexuals are in long-term relationships, and treatment for these individuals must clearly focus on relationships, parenting, and family concerns. Lesbians, gay men, and bisexuals are also subject to an increase in violent attacks because of their sexual orientation, both verbal and physical (135); reaction to such an attack may include a relapse to drug or alcohol use in a person in recovery or an increase in use by someone currently using or abusing substances. In addition, many gay men, lesbians, and bisexuals are victims of domestic violence. This latter fact is often ignored by clinicians; however, because there are correlations with domestic violence and substance abuse, clinicians need to be aware of this possible combination (136).

A brief list of additional treatment issues facing all people in recovery—with special impact on gays and lesbians—beyond the scope of this brief review chapter includes learning how to have safer sex while clean and sober; learning how to adjust to clean and sober socializing, without the use of alcohol or drugs to hide social anxiety; dealing with employment problems and adjusting to the impact of being out as a gay person at work; working with the family of origin regarding their acceptance of the sexual orientation of their gay, lesbian, or bisexual child; helping couples adjust to the damaging effects substance use may have had over the years and embrace a recovery that will avoid the negative impact of codependent relationships; maintaining confidentiality in record keeping, especially around discussion in the medical record of sexual orientation or HIV status; dealing with child custody issues when necessary; diagnosing and treating additional medical problems; and coping with the effects of legal problems. Finnegan and McNally (14) address most of these concerns.

Clinicians and counselors must be aware of their own personal attitudes regarding homosexuality and HIV-related conditions. If a health care provider is homophobic and cannot get help in working out these attitudes with a supportive colleague or supervisor, the patient would be better off if he or she was referred to another staff member for help (36). Gay men and women facing recovery from substance abuse should not have to fight homophobia in a health care system to get quality care.

CONCLUSION

A growing literature on working with gay, lesbian, and bisexual substance abusers will help clinicians with the situations described in this chapter (14, 40–41, 44). Substance use, especially alcohol, is woven into the fabric of the lives of many gay men, lesbians, and bisexuals. The use of substances can be associated with identity formation, coming out, and self-acceptance processes for many gay men, lesbians, and bisexuals. The greater use and presence of alcohol and other drugs in settings where gay men, lesbians, and bisexuals socialize, combined with the dissociation and denial produced by the use of these substances, may help to explain a greater expression among gay people of a biological or genetic predisposition for substance abuse. Internalized homophobia and societal homophobia combine to reinforce the use of alcohol and drugs and may make the recognition and treatment of substance abuse in lesbians, gay men, and bisexuals more difficult. Extended recovery is more likely to happen—indeed, may only be possible—if a gay man, lesbian, or bisexual person is able to accept his or her sexual orientation, address internalized homophobia, and discover how to live clean and sober without fearing or hating his or her real self.

References

1. Beatty R. Alcoholism and adult gay male populations of Pennsylvania. Master's thesis. University Park: Pennsylvania State University, 1983.
2. Diamond DL, Wilsnack SC. Alcohol abuse among lesbians: a descriptive study. J Homosexuality 1978;4(2):123–142.
3. Lewis CE, Saghir MT, Robins E. Drinking patterns in homosexual and heterosexual women. J Clin Psychiatry 1982;43:277–279.
4. Lohrenz L, Connelly J, Coyne L, Spare K. Alcohol problems in several Midwestern homosexual communities. J Stud Alcohol 1978;39(11):1959–1963.
5. McKirman D, Peterson PL. Alcohol and drug abuse among homosexual men and women: epidemiology and population characteristics. Addict Behav 1989;14:545–553.
6. Mosbacher D. Lesbian alcohol and substance abuse. Psychiatr Ann 1988;18(1):47–50.
7. Pillard RC. Sexual orientation and mental disorder. Psychiatr Ann 1988;18(1):52–56.
8. Saghir M, Robins E. Male and female homosexuality. Baltimore: Williams & Wilkins, 1973.
9. Fifield L, De Crescenzo TA, Latham JD. Alcoholism and the gay community. Summary: on my way to nowhere: alienated, isolated, drunk—an analysis of gay alcohol abuse and evaluation of alcoholism rehabilitation services for Los Angeles County. Los Angeles: Los Angeles Gay Community Services Center, 1975.
10. Lesbian, gay and bisexual substance abuse needs assessment: a report. San Francisco: Lesbian and Gay Substance Abuse Planning Group, August, 1991.
11. Morales ES, Graves MA. Substance abuse: patterns and barriers to treatment for gay men and lesbians in San Francisco. San Francisco: San Francisco Prevention Resources Center, 1983.
12. Weinberg M, Williams C. Male homosexuals: their problems and adaptations. New York: Oxford University Press, 1974.
13. Cabaj RP. AIDS and chemical dependency: special issues and treatment barriers for gay and bisexual men. J Psychoactive Drugs 1989;21(4):387–393.
14. Finnegan DG, McNally EB. Dual identities: counseling chemically dependent gay men and lesbians. Center City, MN: Hazelden, 1987.
15. Stall R, Wiley J. A comparison of alcohol and drug use patterns of homosexual and heterosexual men: the San Francisco Men's Health Study. Drug Alcohol Depend 1988;22:63–73.
16. Bradford J, Ryan C. Mental health implications—national lesbian health care survey. Washington, DC: National Lesbian and Gay Health Foundation, 1987.
17. Hall JM. Lesbians and alcohol: patterns and paradoxes in medical notions and lesbians' beliefs. J Psychoactive Drugs 1993;25(2):109–119.
18. Bloomfield K. A comparison of alcohol consumption between lesbians and heterosexual women in an urban population. Drug Alcohol Depend 1993;33(3):257–269.
19. Mosbacher D. Alcohol and other drug use in female medical students: a comparison of lesbians and heterosexuals. J Gay Lesbian Psychotherapy 1993;2(1):37–48.
20. U.S. Centers for Disease Control and Prevention. HIV/AIDS Surveillance Report 1994;5:1–33.
21. Skinner WF. The prevalence and demographic predictors of illicit and licit drug use among lesbians and gay men. Am J Public Health 1994;84:1307–1310.
22. Gorman EM, Morgan P, Lambert EY. Qualitative research considerations and other issues in the study of methamphetamine use among men who have sex with other men. NIDA Res Monogr 1995;157:156–181.
23. Sadownick S. Kneeling at the crystal cathedral: the alarming new epidemic of methamphetamine abuse in the gay community. Genre, January, 1994:37–42.
24. Krafft-Ebing R. Psychopathia sexualis. (1898). Reprinted by Brooklyn Physicians and Surgeons Book Company, 1922.
25. Boswell J. Christianity, social tolerance, and homosexuality. Chicago: University of Chicago Press, 1980.
26. Hooker E. The adjustment of the male overt homosexual. J Projective Technique 1957;21(1):18–31.
27. American Psychiatric Association. Diagnostic and statistical manual of mental disorders. 3rd edition, revised (DSM-III-R). Washington, DC: American Psychiatric Press, 1987.
28. Bayer R. Homosexuality and American psychiatry. New York: Basic Books, 1987.
29. American Psychiatric Association. Diagnostic and statistical manual of mental disorders. 4th edition (DSM-IV). Washington DC: American Psychiatric Press, 1994.
30. Cabaj RP, ed. New thinking on sexuality and homosexuality. Psychiatr Ann 1988;18(1).
31. Marmor J, ed. Homosexual behavior: a modern reappraisal. New York: Basic Books, 1980.
32. Bell AP, Weinberg MS. Homosexualities: a study of diversities among men and women. New York: Simon & Schuster, 1978.
33. Morin SF. Heterosexual bias in psychological research on lesbianism and male homosexuality. Am Psychol 1977;32:629–636.
34. Weinberg G. Society and the healthy homosexual. New York: St. Martin's Press, 1983.
35. Cabaj RP, Stein TS, eds. Homosexuality and mental health: a comprehensive review. Washington DC: American Psychiatric Press, 1996.
36. Cabaj RP. Homosexuality and neurosis: considerations for psychotherapy. J Homosexuality 1988;15(1–2):13–23.
37. Ross MW, ed. Psychopathology and psychotherapy in homosexuality. New York: Haworth, 1988.
38. Coleman E, ed. Psychotherapy with homosexual men and woman: integrated identity approaches for clinical practice. J Homosexuality 1987;14(1–2).
39. Stein TS, Cohen CC, eds. Contemporary perspectives on psychotherapy with lesbians and gay men. New York: Plenum, 1986.
40. Gonsiorek JC, ed. A guide to psychotherapy with gay and lesbian clients. New York: Harrington Park Press, 1985.
41. Ziebold TO, Mongeon JE, eds. Gay and sober: directions for counseling and therapy. New York: Harrington Park Press, 1985.
42. Hetrick ES, Stein TS, eds. Innovations in psychotherapy with homosexuals. Washington, DC: American Psychiatric Press, 1984.
43. Hart JE, ed. Substance abuse treatment: Considerations for lesbians and gay men. The MART Series #2. Boston, MA: The Mobile AIDS Resource Team, 1991.
44. Cabaj RP. Substance abuse in gay men, lesbians, and bisexual individuals. In: Cabaj RP, Stein TS, eds. Homosexuality and mental health: a comprehensive review. Washington DC: American Psychiatric Press, 1996:783–799.
45. Isay RA. Being homosexual: Gay men and their development. New York: Farrar, Straus & Giroux, 1989.
46. Friedman RC. Male homosexuality: a contemporary psychoanalytic perspective. New Haven, CT: Yale University Press, 1988.
47. Lewes K. The psychoanalytic theory of male homosexuality. New York: Simon & Schuster, 1988.
48. Friedman RM. The psychoanalytic model of male homosexuality: a historical and theoretical critique. Psychoanal Rev 1986;73(4):483–519.
49. Friedman RC, Downey JI. Homosexuality. N Engl J Med 1994;331(14):923–930.
50. Owen WF. The clinical approaches to the male homosexual patient. Med Clin North Am 1986;70:499–535.
51. Owen WF. Gay and bisexual men and medical care. In: Cabaj RP, Stein TS, eds. Homosexuality and mental health: a comprehensive review. Washington DC: American Psychiatric Press, 1996:673–685.
52. Banks A, Gartrell NK. Lesbians in the medical setting. In: Cabaj RP, Stein TS, eds. Homosexuality and mental health: a comprehensive review. Washington DC: American Psychiatric Press, 1996:659–671.
53. Dardick L, Grady KE. Openness between gay persons and health professionals. Ann Intern Med 1980;93(1/Part 1):115–119.
54. Kinsey AC, Pomeroy WB, Martin CE. Sexual behavior in the human male. Philadelphia: WB Saunders, 1948.
55. Michaels S. Prevalence of homosexuality in the United States. In: Cabaj RP, Stein TS, eds. Homosexuality and mental health: a comprehensive review. Washington DC: American Psychiatric Press, 1996:43–63.
56. Greenberg DE. The construction of homosexuality. Chicago: University of Chicago Press, 1988.
57. Herdt G. Cross-cultural forms of homosexuality and the concept "gay." Psychiatr Ann 1988;18(1):29–32.
58. Mihalik GJ. Sexuality and gender: an evolutionary perspective. Psychiatr Ann 1988;18(1):40–42.
59. Whitam FL, Mathy RM. Male homosexuality in four societies. New York: Praeger, 1986.
60. Herdt G. Issues in the cross-cultural study of homosexuality. In: Cabaj RP, Stein TS, eds. Homosexuality and mental health: a comprehensive review. Washington DC: American Psychiatric Press, 1996:65–82.
61. Miller N. In search of gay America: women and men in a time of change. New York: Atlantic Monthly Press, 1989.
62. McWhirter DP, Sanders SA, Reinisch JM, eds. Homosexuality/heterosexuality: concepts of sexual orientation. New York: Oxford University Press, 1990.

63. U.S. Centers for Disease Control and Prevention. Update: acquired human immunodeficiency syndrome—United States, 1981–1988. MMWR 1989;38(14):1–28.

64. Herek GM. Heterosexism and homophobia. In: Cabaj RP, Stein TS, eds. Homosexuality and mental health: a comprehensive review. Washington DC: American Psychiatric Press, 1996: 101–113.

65. Bell AP, Weinberg MS, Hammersmith SK. Sexual preference: its development in men and women. Bloomington, IN: Indiana University Press, 1981.

66. Pillard RC, Weinrich JD. Evidence of familial nature of male sexuality. Arch Gen Psychiatry 1986;43:808–812.

67. Pillard RC, Poumadere J, Carretta RA. A family study of sexual orientation. Arch Sex Behav 1982;11(6):511–520.

68. Bailey JM, Pillard RC, Neale MC, Agyei Y. Heritable factors influence sexual orientation in women. Arch Gen Psychiatry 1993;50:217–223.

69. Bailey JM, Pillard RC. A genetic study of male sexual orientation. Arch Gen Psychiatry 1991; 48:1089–1096.

70. Pillard RC. Homosexuality from a familial and genetic perspective. In: Cabaj RP, Stein TS, eds. Homosexuality and mental health: a comprehensive review. Washington DC: American Psychiatric Press, 1996:115–128.

71. Byne W. Biology and homosexuality: implications of neuroendocrinological and neuroanatomical studies. In: Cabaj RP, Stein TS, eds. Homosexuality and mental health: a comprehensive review. Washington DC: American Psychiatric Press, 1996:129–146.

72. Imperato-McGinley JI, Peterson RE, Gautier T. The impact of androgens on the evolution of male gender identity. In: DeFries Z, Friedman RC, Corn R, eds. Sexuality: new perspectives. Westport, CT: Greenwood Press, 1981.

73. Hanley-Hackenbruck P. "Coming-out" and psychotherapy. Psychiatr Ann 1988;18(1):29–32.

74. McDonald G. Individual differences in the coming out process for gay men: implications for theoretical models. J Homosexuality 1982;8: 47–60.

75. de Monteflores C, Schultz SJ. Coming out: similarities and differences for lesbians and gay men. J Soc Issues 1978;34:59–73.

76. Coleman E. Developmental stages in the coming out process. J Homosexuality 1982;7:31–43.

77. Cass V. Sexual orientation identity formation: a Western phenomenon. In: Cabaj RP, Stein TS, eds. Homosexuality and mental health: a comprehensive review. Washington DC: American Psychiatric Press, 1996:227–251.

78. Forstein M. Homophobia: an overview. Psychiatr Ann 1988;18(1):33–36.

79. Cabaj RP. Homophobia: a hidden factor in psychotherapy. Contemp Psychiatry 1985;4(3): 135–137.

80. De Cecco JP, ed. Homophobia: an overview. New York: Haworth Press, 1984.

81. Maylon AK. Psychotherapeutic implications of internalized homophobia in gay men. In: Gonsiorek JC, ed. A guide to psychotherapy with gay and lesbian clients. New York: Harrington Park Press, 1985.

82. Stein TS, Cabaj RP. Psychotherapy with gay men. In: Cabaj RP, Stein TS, eds. Homosexuality and mental health: a comprehensive review. Washington DC: American Psychiatric Press, 1996:413–432.

83. Shilts R. And the band played on: politics, people, and the AIDS epidemic. New York: St. Martin's Press, 1987.

84. Ostrow DG, ed. Biobehavioral control of AIDS. New York: Irvington, 1987.

85. Cabaj RP, Klinger RL. Psychotherapeutic interventions with lesbian and gay couples. In: Cabaj RP, Stein TS, eds. Homosexuality and mental health: a comprehensive review. Washington DC: American Psychiatric Press, 1996:485–501.

86. Cabaj RP. Gay and lesbian couples: lessons on human intimacy. Psychiatr Ann 1988;18(1): 21–25.

87. Quadland MC, Shattles WD. AIDS, sexuality, and sexual control. J Homosexuality 1987; 14(1–2):277–298.

88. De Cecco JP, ed. Bisexual and homosexual identities: critical theoretical issues. J Homosexuality 1984;9(1–2).

89. Gibson P. Gay male and lesbian youth suicide. In: Sullivan LW, ed. Report of the Secretary of Health and Human Services' Task Force on Youth Suicide. Washington, DC: U.S. Government Printing Office, 1989;3:110–142.

90. Hetrick ES, Martin AD. Developmental issues and their resolution for gay and lesbian adolescents. J Homosexuality 1987;14(1–2):25–43.

91. Rotheram-Borus MJ, Rosario M, Reid H, Koopman C. Predicting patterns of sexual acts among homosexual and bisexual youth. Am J Psychiatry 1195;152(4):588–595.

92. Donovan C, McEwan R. A review of the literature examining the relationship between alcohol use and HIV-related sexual risk-taking in young people. Addiction 1995;90(3):319–328.

93. Savin-Williams RC. Verbal and physical abuse as stressors in the lives of lesbian, gay male, and bisexual youths: association with school problems, running away, substance abuse, prostitution, and suicide. J Consult Clin Psychol 1994;62(2):261–269.

94. Hartstein NB. Suicide risk in lesbian, gay, and bisexual youth. In: Cabaj RP, Stein TS, eds. Homosexuality and mental health: a comprehensive review. Washington DC: American Psychiatric Press, 1996:819–837.

95. Friend RA. The individual and social psychology of aging: clinical implications for lesbians and gay men. J Homosexuality 1987;14(1–2):307–331.

96. Berger RM, Kelly JJ. Gay men and lesbians grown older. In: Cabaj RP, Stein TS, eds. Homosexuality and mental health: a comprehensive review. Washington DC: American Psychiatric Press, 1996:305–316.

97. Jax J. How to survive gay stress. Christopher Street 1985;89:16–19.

98. Schilit R, Lie GY, Montagne M. Substance use as a correlate of violence in intimate lesbian relationships. J Homosexuality 1990;19(3):51–65.

99. Falco KL. Psychotherapy with lesbian clients: theory into practice. New York: Brunner/Mazel, 1991.

100. Weinberg MS, Williams CJ, Pryor DP. Dual attractions: understanding bisexuality. New York: Oxford University Press, 1994.

101. Fox RC. Bisexuality: an examination of theory and research. In: Cabaj RP, Stein TS, eds. Homosexuality and mental health: a comprehensive review. Washington DC: American Psychiatric Press, 1996:147–171.

102. Matteson DR. Psychotherapy with bisexual individuals. In: Cabaj RP, Stein TS, eds. Homosexuality and mental health: a comprehensive review. Washington DC: American Psychiatric Press, 1996:433–450.

103. Kinsey A, Pomeroy W, Martin C. Sexual behavior in the human female. Philadelphia: WB Saunders, 1954.

104. Israelstam S, Lambert S. Homosexuality as a cause of alcoholism: a historical review. Int J Addict 1983;18(8):1085–1107.

105. Israelstam S, Lambert S. Homosexuality and alcohol: observations and research after the psychoanalytic era. Int J Addict 1986; 21(4–5):509–537.

106. Vaillant GE. The natural history of alcoholism: causes, patterns, and paths to recovery. Cambridge, MA: Harvard University Press, 1983.

107. Cassel J. The contributions of the social environment to host resistance. Am J Epidemiol 1976;104:107–123.

108. Israelstam S, Lambert S. Homosexuals who indulge in excessive use of alcohol and drugs: psychosocial factors to be taken into account by community and intervention workers. J Alcohol Drug Educ 1989;34(3):54–69.

109. McKirman D, Peterson PL. Psychological and cultural factors in alcohol and drug abuse: an analysis of a homosexual community. Addict Behav 1989;14:555–563.

110. Miller A. The drama of the gifted child. New York: Basic Books, 1981.

111. Hanson G, Hartmann L. Latency development in prehomosexual boys. In: Cabaj RP, Stein TS, eds. Homosexuality and mental health: a comprehensive review. Washington DC: American Psychiatric Press, 1996:253–266.

112. de Monteflores C. Notes on the management of difference. In: Stein TS, Cohen CC, eds. Contemporary perspectives on psychotherapy with lesbians and gay men. New York: Plenum, 1986.

113. U.S. Centers for Disease Control and Prevention. HIV/AIDS Surveillance Report 1994; 6(1):1–27.

114. Stall R, McKusick L, Wiley J. Alcohol and drug use during sexual activity and compliance with safe sex guidelines for AIDS: The AIDS Behavior Research Project. Health Educ Q 1986;13:359–371.

115. Stall R. The prevention of HIV infection associated with drug and alcohol use during sexual activity. In: Siegel L, ed. AIDS and substance abuse. New York: Harrington Park Press, 1988.

116. Ostrow DG, Keslow RA, Fox R. Sexual and drug use behavior change in men at risk of AIDS [abstract no. 96]. Program and abstract of the 114th annual meeting of the American Public Health Association, 1986.

117. Cabaj RP. Working with male homosexual patients. I. GI problems in homosexual men. Practical Gastroenterology 1985;9(4):7–12.

118. Lange WR, Haetzen CA, Hickey JE. Nitrites inhalants: patterns of abuse in Baltimore and Washington, DC. Am J Drug Alcohol Abuse 1988;14(1):29–39.

119. Smith DE, Smith N, Buxton ME, Moser C. PCP and sexual dysfunction. In: Smith DE, ed. PCP: problems and prevention. Dubuque, IA: Kendal-Hunt, 1982.

120. Goode E, Troiden RR. Amyl nitrite use among homosexual men. Am J Psychiatry 1979; 136(8):1067–1069.

121. MacGregor RR. Alcohol and drugs as co-factors for AIDS. In: Siegel L, ed. AIDS and substance abuse. New York: Harrington Park Press, 1988.

122. Hellman RE, Stanton M, Lee J, Tytun A, Vachon R. Treatment of homosexual alcoholics in government-funded agencies: provider training and attitudes. Hosp Community Psychiatry 1989;40(11):1163–1168.

123. Ratner EF, Kosten T, McLellan A. Treatment outcome of PRIDE Institute patients: first

wave—patients admitted from September 1988 through February 1989. Eden Prairie, MN: PRIDE Institute, April, 1991.

124. McCormick K. A program evaluation of Operation Recovery: findings and recommendations regarding a gay and lesbian sample. Report for Operation Concern, San Francisco, 1994.

125. Hall JM. Lesbians recovering from alcohol problems: an ethnographic study of health care experiences. Nurs Res 1994;43(4):238–244.

126. Kus RJ. Sobriety, friends, and gay men. Arch Psychiatr Nurs 1991;5(3):171–177.

127. Kus RJ. Bibliotherapy and gay American men of Alcoholics Anonymous. J Gay Lesbian Psychotherapy 1989;1(2):73–86.

128. Jones BE, Hill MJ. African American lesbians, gay men, and bisexual individuals. In: Cabaj RP, Stein TS, eds. Homosexuality and mental health: a comprehensive review. Washington DC: American Psychiatric Press, 1996:549–561.

129. Nakajima GA, Chan YH, Lee K. Mental health issues for gay and lesbian Asian Americans. In: Cabaj RP, Stein TS, eds. Homosexuality and mental health: a comprehensive review. Washington DC: American Psychiatric Press, 1996:563–581.

130. Gonzalez FJ, Espin OM. Latino men, Latina women, and homosexuality. In: Cabaj RP, Stein TS, eds. Homosexuality and mental health: a comprehensive review. Washington DC: American Psychiatric Press, 1996: 583–601.

131. Tafoya TN. Native two-spirit people. In: Cabaj RP, Stein TS, eds. Homosexuality and mental health: a comprehensive review. Washington DC: American Psychiatric Press, 1996:603–617.

132. Cabaj RP. Assessing suicidality in the primary care setting. AIDS File: Focus on Management of Psychiatric Complications of HIV Disease 1994;8(2):7–9.

133. Flavin DK, Franklin JD, Frances RJ. The acquired immune deficiency syndrome (AIDS) and suicidal behavior in alcohol-dependent homosexual men. Am J Psychiatry 1986;143(11): 1440–1442.

134. Ostrow DG, Monjan A, Joseph J. HIV-related symptoms and psychological functioning in a cohort of homosexual men. Am J Psychiatry 1989;146(6):737–742.

135. Klinger RL, Stein TS. Impact of violence, childhood sexual abuse, and domestic violence and abuse on lesbians, bisexual individuals, and gay men. In: Cabaj RP, Stein TS, eds. Homosexuality and mental health: a comprehensive review. Washington DC: American Psychiatric Press, 1996:801–818.

136. Schilit R, Lie GY, Montagne M. Substance use as a correlate of violence in intimate lesbian relationships. J Homosexuality 1990;19(3): 51–65.

73 THE HOMELESS

Herman Joseph and Denise Paone

Chemical dependency cuts across all social classes, but in the inner cities of the United States poverty, unemployment, and homelessness shape not only the social context of substance abuse but also the spread of infections such as human immunodeficiency virus (HIV), tuberculosis (TB), and hepatitis.

The United States Department of Housing and Urban Development categorized persons as homeless if they lived at night in:

1. "Public or private emergency shelters which take a variety of forms—armories, school, church basements, government buildings, former firehouses and where temporary vouchers are provided by private and public agencies, even hotels, apartments or boarding homes"
2. "The streets, parks, subways, bus terminals, railroad stations, airports, under bridges or aqueducts, abandoned buildings without utilities, cars, trucks, or any of the public or private space that is not designed for shelter" (1)

The National Institute of Mental Health defined individuals as homeless if they lack "adequate shelter, resources and community ties" (2).

Homelessness for the purpose of this chapter encompasses persons without permanent housing who live on the streets or in public places such as parks, transportation terminals, subways, underground tunnels, abandoned buildings and transportation vehicles, depend on the shelters for living quarters, reside in low-priced hotels that cater to transients and welfare recipients, and live as squatters in apartments belonging to others. When homeless, it is difficult for chemically dependent persons to acquire and to apply knowledge with the accuracy, consistency, and hygienic measures necessary to protect themselves from becoming infected with and transmitting organisms associated with HIV, sexually transmitted diseases (STDs), TB, and hepatitis. This chapter will discuss some of the causes of homelessness and present studies comparing substance abuse and risk behaviors among the homeless to persons with stable living accommodations.

CAUSES OF HOMELESSNESS

The issue of homelessness is critical in the area of public health and treatment for chemical dependency. Causes of homelessness are interrelated. In 1995, the United States Conference of Mayors estimated that about 45% of the homeless have serious substance abuse problems. The lack of treatment for this group was cited as a major unmet need. Also, according to this report about 23% of the homeless nationwide could be considered mentally ill (3).

Other major causes identified as contributing to homelessness by surveys include lack of adequate affordable housing for persons with low incomes; major fires that destroy existing housing; a new job market requiring more technically skilled and educated workers than unskilled workers; chronic unemployment and high levels of poverty among those unable to find work in the new job market; decreases in government benefits; the deinstitutionalization of the mentally ill without adequate follow-up services that include housing; personal crises in families resulting in domestic violence and the breaking up of families with women and their children relying on shelters for housing; personal crisis in the lives of youths especially gays, lesbians, transsexuals, and cross dressers that result in their being thrown out of their homes; the "hidden homeless" or the "doubling up" of single persons and families in apartments belonging to friends, relatives, and others. The "hidden homeless" population is at great risk of finding themselves without housing if a crisis should occur in their lives or the lives of the primary tenants of the apartments. Also, at risk for homelessness are persons residing in congested substandard conditions whose low incomes either through work or benefits are insufficient to pay for adequate standard apartments (3–9).

Wilson is of the opinion that persistent unemployment in minority and poor communities is due primarily to the disappearance of jobs for persons without the necessary skills for employment in the modern global economy (10). One of his recommendations is for a WPA-type program that Franklin Roosevelt implemented during the Great Depression to meet current job training and placement needs of the chronically unemployed.

ESTIMATING THE NUMBER OF HOMELESS

It is difficult to estimate the number of homeless in the United States. Estimates from various sources on the number of homeless nationwide range from about 500,000 to 2,000,000 persons a year. One survey estimated that on any given night about 700,000 persons are homeless (5, 6, 11).

Disagreements about the number of homeless notwithstanding, in 1995 the United States Conference of Mayors reported that in a nationwide survey of 29 cities, requests for shelter increased in these cities by an average of 11% and requests for food increased about 9% over the requests recorded in

1994 (3). Within the 29 cities, the average length of time persons were homeless was about 6 months; the duration of episodes of homelessness increased over the previous year in about 62% of the cities. In 1995 about 19% of the requests for housing in the 29 surveyed cities were not met notwithstanding an increase over the past year of 3% in shelter beds within the 29 cities.

The United States Conference of Mayors expect increases in requests for food and shelter within the next few years with the passage of new welfare regulations in 1996. Under the new legislation signed by President Clinton on March 29, 1996 (P.L. 104–121) persons could be denied SSI or SSDI disability benefits and Medicaid if addiction is considered the contributing or major factor in the determination of their disability status. Effective January 1, 1997, it is possible that about 200,000 persons could find themselves without benefits unless their disability status is reclassified to another condition unrelated to their addiction. Also, effective in March of 1996, no additional persons can receive benefits if addiction is the major contributing factor in their disability. In order for any benefits to be continued, chemically dependent persons must be enrolled in treatment. However, chemical dependency itself is not a reason to remain unemployed. The Social Security Administration estimates that perhaps 40,000 persons will lose benefits under the new regulations, thus potentially adding to the number of homeless nationwide.

Furthermore, the new welfare reforms do not mandate states to provide treatment for chemical dependency. Therefore, benefits can be terminated within two years irrespective of whether or not recipients have children. Califano predicts that by 1998 women with chemical dependency problems and hundreds of thousands of their children will become more impoverished and therefore more likely to become homeless (12).

DESCRIBING THE POPULATION OF HOMELESS

Estimates from the 1995 survey of the United States Conference of Mayors show that single men account for approximately 46% of the homeless population followed by families headed by single women with children (36.5%), single women (14%), and unaccompanied minors (3.5%). Unaccompanied minors and children in homeless families account for about 25% of the homeless population (3).

Nationwide, minorities are over represented among the homeless: African Americans comprise an estimated 56% of the homeless population, followed by whites (29%), Hispanics (12%), Native Americans (2%), and Asians (1%). Within the homeless population, veterans account for an estimated 21% and employed persons unable to find affordable housing account for about 20% (3).

An analysis of data gathered from nine cities in the Health Care for the Homeless Program by Dr. James Wright in 1984 shows that the incidence of AIDS among the homeless was significantly higher than in the domiciled population (230 cases per 100,000 versus 144 cases per 100,000, respectively) (13). At the beginning of the AIDS epidemic, infected persons were subjected to discrimination in existing social and medical programs. Many were fearful of physical harm in shelters or denial of services if their HIV status became known. Therefore, they tended to conceal their illness or HIV status when applying for services (14). However, within the last decade special social service, medical, and housing programs have been developed for persons infected with HIV disease. Notwithstanding this development of special services, the United States Conference of Mayors reports that in 1994 and 1995 about 8% of the homeless in major cities nationwide had either AIDS or HIV-related illness (3).

PERCEPTION OF THE HOMELESS BY SERVICE PROVIDERS

Homeless people are perceived as difficult to service by social service agency and health providers in communities throughout the country. Reports from service providers indicate that the homeless are more desperate and harder to treat with wide-ranging, serious health, social, mental health, substance abuse, alcohol, and behavioral problems. No one social agency is able to service the needs of homeless people and families. Referrals must be made to a variety of agencies to solve all presenting problems. Special coordinated approaches and training are needed especially in treating clients with alcohol, drug, and mental health problems (15, 16).

Stigmatization of homeless persons is commonplace. They are placed on waiting lists for services; beds or treatment slots are not readily available. There are few appropriate providers who are able to service adequately this population. However, if services should be available, homeless people do not have money, and in many cases identification, to obtain the necessary benefits or services. Therefore they are placed at the bottom of waiting lists. They are also considered transient, hard to contact, and without access to transportation to keep appointments. As compared to domiciled clients, homeless people lack a stable, drug-free environment; lack support networks of family and friends; have more chronic problems; appear to have more endemic and comprehensive medical needs; and require a vast array of services that cover the spectrum of social and medical services in a community. A comment by a service provider summarizes the perception of the homeless—"They are at the absolute bottom when they get to us" (15, 16).

These perceptions by service providers reflect the perceptions of the homeless within the greater society not only in the United States but in countries throughout the world. For example, in 1996 homeless persons in Moscow were detained and transported to their villages of origin (17). In a 1994 study of homelessness in 49 cities across the United States, the National Law Center noted that services to help the homeless were inadequate despite the development of some exemplary programs (16). However, restrictive laws and antihomeless activities were commonplace. In summation, people are punished for being homeless, and banishment from cities is an option.

SUBSTANCE ABUSE IN A TRANSIENT POPULATION

In this section various surveys and studies are discussed that describe the type and extent of drug abuse within a transient population. In this context, a transient individual is one who lives in a shelter, single-room occupancy or welfare hotel; sleeps in parks, abandoned buildings, transportation terminals, or other public places; and/or is fed by a soup kitchen.

An Ethnographic Study of a Shelter

The first study is an ethnographic investigation of a men's shelter in Manhattan that provides sleeping accommodations to about 1000 persons daily. This study was conducted in April of 1988 by the Street Studies Unit of the Bureau of Applied Studies Research and Evaluation of the New York State Division of Substance Abuse Services (18). In this unit, former addicts and individuals with experience on the streets are trained in ethnographic research and participant observation techniques to obtain information which could not be collected through standard surveys. Although use of alcohol was widespread by residents, crack cocaine was the major drug used and sold in and around the shelter. The workers estimated that about half of the shelter residents smoked this form of cocaine. A large number of crack vials were discarded in the area around the shelter. Although, 78 (36.4%) of 214 residents canvassed in this study admitted injecting heroin either alone or in combination with cocaine, the researchers estimated conservatively that about 180–365 untreated heroin addicts reside in the shelter. Shooting galleries—places where addicts in the shelter use heroin intravenously, usually with shared, unsterile needles—were located in the immediate vicinity of the shelter.

One purpose of the study was to determine whether the residents in the shelter were in favor of an on-site methadone program. Of the 55 persons who responded to this inquiry, 34 (61.8%) were in favor of such a program. The majority of shelter residents who wanted an on-site methadone program were self-admitted heroin addicts, many of whom bought methadone on the streets.

Notwithstanding the verified problem of heroin addiction within the shelter and the need for an on-site methadone service, the community board refused to consider the implementation of a small pilot program to determine if the project were feasible. While rejecting on-site treatment of heroin addicts with methadone, the community board approved the establishment of an on-site alcohol detoxification program to treat alcoholics residing in the shelter.

An Ethnographic Study of a Welfare Hotel

Over a 3-month period—April–June, 1989—an ethnographic study of homeless mothers and their children was undertaken in New York City by Dr. Michele Schedlin under the auspices of the Medical and Health Research Association of New York City (19). In this study, 25 homeless African American and Hispanic women living in a welfare hotel with children under 5 years of age were interviewed. As in the New York City shelter, crack was the major drug of abuse. Teenage crack dealers were noted around the hotel, and drug paraphernalia were noted in the hallways. It was estimated by residents and the staff that perhaps 80–90% of the residents were involved with drugs—about 75–80% smoked crack and 10–15% injected heroin, cocaine, or both.

Some of the addicted women in the hotel supported their habits by selling drugs and preparing crack. Furthermore, they harbored myths about the nature of addiction—cocaine and heroin "work well together," cocaine takes heroin "out of the system," "they [cocaine and heroin] are not habit forming," and "crack is not addictive . . . it's boredom . . . it's all in your head." Although there is extensive use of drugs, the residents deny they are addicted and claim they do not need help. The constant use of crack may be a significant contributing factor to the neglectful and violent behavior which some of the drug-involved mothers directed towards their children. Child abuse, especially against children under the age of 5 years, was a major problem in the hotel.

The health problems of the children and adults were considerable. Outbreaks of meningitis, pinkeye, chicken pox, herpes, skin rashes, ear infections, and colds were noted during the 3-month research period. Asthma was the most commonly reported health condition, which may be caused by roach and rat droppings. A staff physician reported high rates of syphilis among the adolescents.

The women who were addicted continued using illegal drugs—crack and heroin—during pregnancy. They were of the opinion that crack shortens and eases labor. Many did not register for prenatal care when pregnant. However, if they did register, they registered late in their pregnancies and did not regularly attend clinic.

Study of Drug Users Within a Soup Kitchen Population

Schilling, El-Bassel, and Gilbert interviewed 148 current and former drug users in a Manhattan soup kitchen about drug use and AIDS risk behavior (20). Of the sample 12.8% advised that they were enrolled in outpatient treatment for drug addiction with about 7.4% enrolled in methadone maintenance programs. Only those who were involved in methadone maintenance participated in AIDS prevention programs. The subjects reported using at least one of the following drugs for long periods of average lifetime use: cocaine (11 years), crack (3.6 years), heroin (11 years), marihuana (16 years), and speedballs (9 years). Within 3 months of the interview 84.5% of the subjects admitted using at least one of the five drugs. About 51.4% of the sample admitted injecting drugs in the past and 12.3% within the past 3 months. For those who injected, about one third admitted sharing needles in the past. However, for those who injected drugs within 3 months of the interview, 85% indicated that they were sharing needles, 30% were sharing cookers, and 40% borrowed needles and syringes. Only 24.3% lived in their own apartments while the remainder lived in shelters (25.2%), the street (11.6%), "doubling up" in someone else's home (34.7%), and in other places (4.1%). The long durations of drug abuse among this population, the low level of enrollment in treatment, and the prevalence of high-risk behavior for contracting and transmitting HIV and other infections demonstrate the need for aggressive outreach in places where homeless drug users congregate.

Homelessness in Two Manhattan Parks

In 1993 the New York Community Trust sponsored a study of an outreach program to the homeless in two parks located respectively on the Upper East Side and Upper West side of Manhattan (21). The study attempted to investigate the extent of homelessness in the two parks, the destitution of those living in the parks and the disruption of the quality of life of the neighborhood residents. Homeless residents were linked to services in the community by outreach workers. The overall coordination of the outreach to the homeless and the linkages to community services were administered by the study group. Of the 283 homeless contacted in this study, an extremely high proportion—77% in one park and 95% in the other—were found to be abusing drugs (e.g., heroin, crack cocaine) and/or alcohol. Axis I mental illness was estimated to affect 15–18% of the homeless in one park and 28% in the other; personality disorder Axis I was estimated to be about 38% in one of the parks, but information was not available in the other.

Contact was made with 283 "unduplicated" homeless persons in the two parks: 89 were referred to 164 services including substance abuse treatment and detoxification, social entitlements, and temporary shelters. However, 24 clients were placed in permanent and transitional housing but only 4 of these housed clients were known to be residing "indoors" 6 months following placement. However, emphasis in this study was on the initial engagement of the client rather than emphasis on housing. The study was handicapped by a high turnover rate of outreach workers, demonstrating that retention of qualified outreach staff is a major issue. Finally, tracking of clients, collection of data, and analysis were critical for the effective management of resources and development of policy.

Prescription Drugs on the Streets of New York City

The Street Studies Unit of the New York State Office of Alcoholism and Substance Abuse Services has identified a street market for prescription drugs (22, 23). These legitimate medications find their way into the street market through physicians employed in Medicaid mills who prescribe them to patients who fill the prescriptions in pharmacies and then sell them to street middlemen. These middlemen then sell the drugs on the street or back to the druggists for prices that are below the wholesale level.

On the street these drugs are then sold for a variety of reasons to persons who may not have medical insurance, do not have ready access to physicians and clinics, or who treat their own symptoms without medical supervision. These persons include drug users and homeless people who may not have the identification papers to obtain medications through legal channels.

Further research is indicated that will combine ethnography with medical investigation and diagnosis to gain a better understanding of the dynamics of this market. Examples of licit street drugs include zidovudine (AZT) used in the treatment of AIDS, various antibiotics, medications to treat chronic and acute illness such as ulcers and stomach disorders, various antidepressants, benzodiazepines, and analgesics. They may also be used to help ward off withdrawal symptoms when heroin and methadone are not available. The price of prescription drugs respond to market prices. For example in the 1980s a large market existed for diazepam (Valium). When controls were instituted on the prescribing of Valium, a Valium panic ensued that resulted in higher street prices for the diminishing street supply.

Surveys of the Transient Population

The above-mentioned studies were implemented at single sites with populations known to be involved with drugs and alcohol. Therefore, while the results provide a contextual richness and descriptive quality, the conclusions cannot be generalized to the entire homeless population in shelters and single-room occupancy hotels. A more balanced perspective is found in the random sample surveys such as that conducted by the New York State Division of Substance Abuse Services and the Division of Alcoholism and Alcohol Abuse in 1986 (24). A random selection of residents of shelters and single-room occupancy hotels was interviewed and classified as the transient population of the state. Randomly selected state residents who lived in more stable conditions were also interviewed.

The transient population had the greatest proportion of individuals who used illicit drugs and were involved in drug-related risk behavior associated with contracting and spreading HIV. Table 73.1 shows that the overall proportion of transients who inject drugs, including heroin, in comparison with residents in more stable living conditions is about 15:1. Table 73.2 summarizes the drugs used by the transient population in comparison with the domiciled population for the 6-month period in 1986 prior to the survey. The proportion of drug users among the transient population far exceeds the

Table 73.1 Percentages of New York City Residents in Different Living Accommodations with Drug-using Risk Behaviors Associated with AIDS

Drug-Using Risk Behaviors Associated with AIDS	Living Accommodations	
	Shelters Single-Room Occupancy and Low-Priced Hotels (n = 270)	Other Accommodations (n = 2874)
Residents with any lifetime needle use	21%	1.5%
Residents with any lifetime needle use and use of heroin within last 5 years	12%	0.8%
Residents with any lifetime needle use and use of heroin within last 2 years	10%	0.6%

From the New York State Division of Substance Abuse Services, Bureau of Research and Evaluation: State household survey, 1986.

proportion of drug users among the domiciled population. The percentage of cocaine users among the transient population is over five times the percentage of cocaine users among domiciled residents, while the proportion of heroin users in the transient population is about 20 times the proportion within the domiciled population. These figures apply to the 3144 randomly selected residents in New York City who cooperated with the survey. A similar trend was obtained in the remaining part of New York State with smaller percentages (24).

Alcohol consumption among the state transient population showed the following major trends (25). The transient population has a greater rate of abstinence from alcohol than the domiciled population (39.8% versus 26.3%). However, the transient population's daily average consumption of alcohol is significantly greater than the consumption of the domiciled population (7.2 drinks/day versus 1.2 drinks/day, respectively). About 17% of the transient population drank more than 10 drinks per day (over 5 pure ounces of alcohol) as compared with 1.8% of the domiciled population. The percentage of transients who drank two or more drinks per day was correlated with their type of sleeping arrangements. For example, those who slept in public places had the highest percentage of such drinkers (48%), followed by those who slept in shelters (38%), and those who slept in single-room occupancy or welfare hotels (27%). The percentage of transient males who drank two or more drinks per day was higher than the percentage for females (39% versus 19%, respectively). Also, transient African Americans had the highest percentage of persons who drank two or more drinks per day, followed by transient Hispanics and transient whites (40%, 27%, and 25%, respectively).

Table 73.2 Use of Illicit Substances Among Adults 18 Years of Age and Older in New York City: Comparison of Transients and Household Residents in New York City During a 6-month Period in 1986 Prior to Survey

Drug	Living Accommodations	
	Shelters Single-Room Occupancy and Low-Priced Hotels (n = 270)	Other Accommodations (n = 2874)
Marihuana	40%	11%
Cocaine	27%	5%
Heroin	9%	*
PCP (angel dust)	4%	*
Inhalants (aerosol spray, solvents, amyl nitrite)	3%	*
Illicit methadone	3%	*
Hallucinogens (LSD, mescaline, psilocybin)	2%	*

From the New York State Division of Substance Abuse Services, Bureau of Research and Evaluation: State household survey, 1986.
* = less than 0.5% of survey respondents.

In a survey conducted in 1987 of 26 shelters in New York City, with a weighted sample equivalent to 1000 residents, Struening and Pittman found that 10.7% admitted using heroin within the 6-month period prior to the interview (14, 26). However, 18% admitted using heroin over 50 times during their lives, 36% admitted using cocaine more than 50 times, and 18% admitted smoking crack. This group includes daily users of drugs. Alcoholism is a major problem, with 12% of the men and 6% of the women having been hospitalized for this condition. The rates of hospitalizations for alcoholism were 24 hospitalizations per 100 women and 41 hospitalizations per 100 men.

The participants in the 1987 study were subdivided into categories based on a high degree of alcohol and/or substance abuse, mental illness (depression, psychotic episodes), and hospitalizations for these conditions (26). About one third of the residents were classified as a reference group. For the purpose of this study, the persons in the reference group were considered to have minimal or nonexistent conditions. Of the other two thirds, about 15% had mental disorders which were serious, 28% had substance abuse problems (e.g., with alcohol, heroin, and cocaine), and 21.3% had both serious substance abuse and mental health problems. However, about 50% of this group reported symptoms of mental illness, including depression (26).

A study of alcohol and drug use among randomly selected transients in shelters and single room occupancy hotels throughout New York State was completed during the period October, 1992 through September, 1995 (27). The transient population reported the higher rates of substance abuse as compared to other state residents. Transients were disproportionately minorities, reporting little or no employment and low incomes. Using questions from the DSM-III, over half (51.4%) were considered to be chemically dependent on one or more substances—13.5% on drugs only (marihuana, cocaine/crack, heroin, other drugs), 16.1% on alcohol alone, and 21.8% on alcohol and another drug. Alcohol and cocaine showed the highest rates for dependency. Except for opiates, rates for dependency were higher outside of New York City. This finding showed that the cocaine/crack epidemic with its epicenter in New York City in the 1980s had spread to the rest of the state. Rates of lifetime use were also very high among the transient population—marihuana (79%), cocaine/crack (65%), heroin (28%), other drugs such as PCP, LSD, barbiturates, pain killers, etc. (between 15 and 23% depending on the drug). Among recent users between 30 and 35% injected drugs such as heroin and cocaine and 82% smoked crack cocaine. About 49% of the transient population entered treatment at least once, and 60% of those who entered had at least two episodes of treatment for chemical dependency. Projecting the results of this survey on an estimated homeless/transient population of about 50,000 in New York State, about 25,000 transients are in need of treatment for chemical dependency and alcoholism. With an estimated 8,000 homeless in programs, 17,000 of the homeless/transient constitute an unmet need for treatment.

The high prevalence rates of alcohol, drug and mental disorders (ADM) within the homeless population age 18 and over are summarized in an analysis and review of 24 studies by Lehman and Cordray (28). In these studies homeless persons were not in environments specifically targeted to persons with ADM disorders. The following prevalence estimates were calculated: undifferentiated mental health problem Axis I (between .45 and .50), severe Axis I disorder (between .18 and .23), severe and persistent Axis I disorder (between .19 and .23), any Axis I substance use disorder (between .45 and .55), alcohol use disorders (between .40 and .50), drug use disorder (between .28 and .37), dual diagnosis of co-occurring mental health and substance use disorders (between .10 and .20). Important subgroups in this study could not be properly modeled because of sample limitations and the existence of a large number of variables between the studies.

Comparison of Domiciled and Undomiciled Users of a Needle Exchange Program in New York City

New York City has an estimated 200,000 injecting drug users (IDUs); about 50% are infected with HIV. New York State is one of the 44 states with statutes which place criminal penalties on the possession and distribution of syringes (drug paraphernalia laws), and is one of nine states that prohibit the sale of needles and syringes without a prescription (prescription laws) (29). However, New York State law also permits the Commissioner of the State

Table 73.3   Syringe Exchange Evaluation: Housing Status by Selected Sociodemographics

Demographics[a]	Mean age[b] (years)	Female[c] n (%)	Male[c] n (%)	Black[d] n (%)	Latino[d] n (%)	White[d] n (%)	Other[d] n (%)	Total n (%)
Not Homeless	37	718 (76)	1419 (65)	778 (69)	799 (70)	517 (63)	43 (72)	2137 (68)
Homeless	36	224 (24)	777 (35)	345 (31)	339 (30)	300 (37)	17 (28)	1001 (32)
Total	36.6	942 (100)	2196 (100)	1123 (36)	1138 (100)	817 (100)	60 (100)	3138 (100)

[a] Percent totals may not equal 100% due to rounding.
[b] Scheffe's test
[c] $p = .001$
[d] $p < .05$

Health Department to grant waivers to the paraphernalia and prescription laws for the purpose of protecting public health—in this case the operation of syringe exchange programs as an HIV prevention measure among active IDUs, their sexual partners, and the children born to them (30). Needle exchanges programs are important components of harm reduction strategies to lessen the transmission of infections such as HIV (see Chapter 4).

The first legal syringe exchange program in New York City was operated by the New York City Department of Health with a waiver to dispense legally needles and syringes from the New York State Department of Health from November 1988 to January 1990 (31). This controversial program operated from a single site located at the central offices of the New York City Department of Health located near the courts, jails, and police headquarters in lower Manhattan from November 1988 to January 1990. The location was chosen since the program was rejected by communities throughout New York City. Participants were enrolled through AIDS outreach organizations such as ADAPT. However, because of the location few participants enrolled. The program was closed after the election of a new mayor who was opposed to the program. Shortly thereafter, AIDS activists began several underground exchanges in New York. These programs did not have the appropriate waivers from the state Health Department. However, when some of the activists were arrested, they were subsequently found not guilty by reason of public health necessity (32). Subsequently, the American Foundation for AIDS Research funded a research project to test the efficacy of needle exchange programs to lessen the transmission of HIV. The findings validated that (a) HIV-positive seroconversions among participants were low and comparable to seroconversions in drug treatment programs (about 2%) and (b) needle exchange programs did not encourage new users to inject drugs. As of January, 1996, there were six authorized syringe exchange programs in New York City with approximately 27,000 registered participants (33, 34).

Syringe Exchange and Homelessness

Data were collected from five syringe exchange programs during October 1992 and January 1995 (33, 34). Subjects for interviewing were randomly selected from those attending the exchanges within a given week. To be eligible for inclusion in the study, subjects must (a) have been an active IDU, (b) have used syringe exchange on at least one occasion, and (c) have just exchanged syringes. Verbal informed consent is obtained in order to protect the subject's confidentiality.

For this analysis homeless was defined as living on the street, in a shelter, or in a welfare hotel during the 6 months before the interview. Using these criteria, 1001 (32%) of the total sample were classified as homeless, and 2137 (68%) were considered domiciled. The population was racially and ethnically diverse, composed of males (70%), females (30%), African Americans (36%), Latinos (36%), whites (26%), and others (2%). About 74% had been in prison during their lifetimes, 78% had previous histories of treatment for drug abuse, and 39% were currently enrolled in treatment.

Whites were more likely to be homeless than African Americans, Latinos, and others (37% versus 31%, 30%, and 28%, respectively). Also, males were more likely to be homeless than females (35% versus 24%). Those classified as homeless were more likely to have spent time in prison during their lifetime (86% versus 69%) and were less likely to be currently enrolled in treatment for drug abuse (33% versus 42%). See Tables 73.3 and 73.4.

Table 73.4   Syringe Exchange: Prison and Drug Treatment History by Housing Status

History	Total n (%)	Not Homeless n (%)	Homeless n (%)
Been in prison[a]	2326 (74)	1467 (69)	859 (86)
Been in drug treatment[b]	2463 (78)	1688 (79)	775 (77)
In treatment now[c]	1232 (39)	905 (42)	327 (33)

[a] $p = .001$
[b] $p < .05$
[c] $p = .319$

With regard to HIV risk behavior during the 30-day period prior to the interview, homeless participants were more likely to inject cocaine and were more likely to practice risky injection (injecting with a used syringe) than domiciled participants (13% versus 6%). Homeless persons were also less likely than domiciled participants to always use condoms with casual partners (47% versus 58%) and reported slightly higher rates of HIV-positive status (Table 73.5).

MAJOR HEALTH PROBLEMS OF THE HOMELESS SUBSTANCE ABUSER

Health conditions found with greater prevalence in the homeless, as compared to the general population, include vascular disease, trauma from accidents and violence, serious frostbite and infection at injection sites both resulting in amputation of affected limbs or digits, hypertension, poor dentition, gastrointestinal disorders, liver disease as a result of alcoholism and hepatitis, various types of hepatitis, neurological and seizure disorders, arthritis, generalized infections, HIV, drug-resistant mycobacterium tuberculosis infection and, especially because of the crack cocaine epidemic, STDs (35–43).

Recent studies of deaths among the homeless show that substance abuse has been a major factor in deaths either directly through overdose or in causes associated with substance abuse (41, 42). For example, in Atlanta, Georgia, about half of the deaths among the homeless were attributed to substance abuse, while in Philadelphia conditions associated with substance abuse were among the major causes of death: injuries, liver disease, and poisoning, rather than infections. Furthermore, in Philadelphia the homeless age-adjusted mortality rate was 3.5 times that of the general domiciled population; homeless nonwhites, whites, males, and females died younger and at higher rates than their domiciled counterparts. Homeless substance abusers and white males had the highest death rates. Among dead homeless whites males, substance abuse was more prevalent than among other homeless dead groups. Also it is hypothesized that homelessness among nonwhites may be more economically based while among white males a preexisting illness was usually present that may be a contributing factor to their homelessness. There is also the possibility that deaths of homeless white men were more likely to be recorded; although in this study, white males were also more likely to have information missing on certificates and in records.

Medical conditions among the homeless are straining the resources of drug treatment programs, hospitals, the criminal justice system, and social agencies that service the indigent. Homeless persons are a medically underserved group without access to primary care. This results in delays in diagnosing medical conditions, which can result in further complications and increased rates of mortality (42).

Table 73.5   Syringe Exchange Evaluation: Drug Risk Behavior[a]

	Total n (%)	Not Homeless n (%)	Homeless n (%)
Risky injection in last 30 days[b, c]	262	128 (6)	134 (13)
Use of condoms during last 30 days before interview			
With primary partner[d]	939	714 (100)	225 (100)
Always		252 (35)	69 (31)
Not always		462 (65)	156 (69)
With casual partner[e]	470	305 (100)	165 (100)
Always		176 (58)	78 (47)
Not always		129 (42)	87 (53)
Self-reported HIV status	1961	1332 (100)	609 (100)
HIV positive[e]		331 (25)	179 (29)
HIV negative[e]		1021 (75)	430 (71)

[a] Percent totals may not equal 100% due to rounding.
[b] Defined as any injection with a used dirty syringe.
[c] p = .001
[d] p = .202
[e] p < .05

In the early stages of the AIDS epidemic, homosexual men constituted the major group associated with the prevalence and incidence of the disease. However, by 1988 the greatest incidence of new cases was collectively among substance abusers, their sexual partners, and their children (43, 44).

Also, substance abuse plays a major role in the transmission of HIV among the homeless. In a study of 169 homeless men who sought medical help and agreed to be tested for HIV antibodies in a New York City shelter, 62% were seropositive. However, of the group testing positive for HIV antibody, 53% were IDUs, 8% were both IDUs and homosexual, and 23% were homosexual (45).

A study of AIDS risk behavior among 4824 IDUs completed in May of 1989 showed that the 879 homeless substance abusers were more likely to engage in high-risk behavior than those who lived in more stable conditions. In this study 55% of the homeless lived in shelters and 45% were on the streets (46). In the 6 months prior to the interview, a greater proportion of the homeless shared needles (71% versus 64%) and rented or borrowed needles (83% versus 74%) than IDUs with homes. However, a greater proportion of the domiciled users tended to clean their needles with bleach (32% versus 25%). Also, the proportion of homeless users who exchanged sex for drugs or money was greater than the proportion of domiciled users (males, 18% versus 11%; females, 46% versus 42%) (46).

Visits to shooting galleries, where needles are shared for injecting heroin and cocaine without proper sterilization, resulted in widespread HIV infection among IDUs. Because of the short duration of its effect, injection of cocaine requires a greater frequency of injection than heroin. Also, the heat generated by the pipe used to smoke crack is capable of producing lesions in and around the mouth. In crack houses, unprotected sex is exchanged for money or drugs; therefore numerous infections including HIV, syphilis, and hepatitis are transmitted.

Tuberculosis

With the rise of homelessness and the increase in HIV infection, TB has reemerged as a public health concern. In a study of 132 patients afflicted with mycobacterium tuberculosis in New York City in 1990, it was found that drug-resistant mycobacterium tuberculosis was found in 21% of the 53 homeless patients as compared to 8% of the 79 nonhomeless patients (38).

In 1985 the New York City Health Department began to collect data about the living conditions of patients who were diagnosed with active TB. In 1985, 150 patients, or about 8% of the diagnosed cases for the year, were identified as homeless or living in the shelter system. By 1988, 10% (or 240) of the active TB cases were classified as either homeless or in the shelter system (40). By 1988 admissions to a New York inner city hospital showed that TB was associated with medical and social conditions: one half were HIV

positive, two thirds were drug injectors or crack cocaine smokers, and two thirds were either homeless or poorly housed.

New York City, while having the greatest increase of TB cases in the country during the period of 1978–1993 (from 18 to 41 cases per 100,000 persons), was not the only urban center to report increases of TB in a homeless population. For example, the Health Department in Boston began to note an increase in active TB in 1983 among homeless, white, alcoholic males between the ages of 50 and 59 years old who were residents of the shelter system. However, by 1987 active TB was noted in a younger homeless shelter population of males between the ages of 30 and 39 years afflicted with substance abuse problems, alcoholism, and who were at risk for HIV infection (39).

Drug-resistant TB is associated with HIV-positive IDUs both those who are domiciled and homeless. However, because of the unstable living conditions associated with homelessness, the homeless TB patients are less compliant with medical procedures than the domiciled patients. The taking of medication for TB under supervision known as direct observational therapy had been successful in curbing the drug-resistant TB epidemic among methadone patients who are diagnosed with TB. Many receive their medication in methadone clinics that have the facilities to dispense TB medication and ingest the medication in front of a nurse.

Medical Management Problems of Homeless AIDS Patients

A study of 231 persons with AIDS conducted by Dr. Ramon A. Torres of the St. Vincent's Hospital in Manhattan underscores the serious medical and follow-up problems presented by homeless persons with AIDS (46). Although 36 (16%) of the 231 patients were intravenous substance abusers, 21 (70%) of the 30 homeless patients were intravenous substance abusers. Homeless patients were more difficult to manage. They had higher rates of being lost to follow-up, of signing out of the hospital against medical advice, of longer periods of hospitalization, of broken clinic appointments, of incomplete tests for diagnosis of and failure to comply with treatment for opportunistic infections, of lost prescriptions, and of TB.

Homeless Youth: A Group at High Risk for Contracting HIV

Homeless youth are a particular segment of the population at risk for HIV and other infections, especially those who inject drugs and are involved in prostitution. Homeless youth are unable to return to their homes for a variety of reasons. Some ran away because of conditions within the home; others, castaways, may have been thrown out because of crisis within the family because of their sexual orientations (especially if they were homosexual or transgender), poor relationships with other members of the family, and/or substance abuse. Others come from dysfunctional families where economic and emotional crises destroyed the family or where parents were chemically dependent or alcoholic and subjected the children to stress and violence. Many homeless youth also report that they were subjected as children to verbal, physical, and sexual abuse and, in some cases, incest (8, 9).

Clatts and Davis have reported that homeless youth, because of the trauma of their everyday lives, tend to mistrust and avoid institutions for health and social services (9). However, they do respond to outreach services which are provided outside of institutional settings. The outreach project functions as a bridge to mainstream services and institutions for these youth who may not have the skills to access these services. Youth contacted by outreach begin to discuss the issues which adversely affect their lives. Sympathetic outreach often results in higher than expected rates of compliance from homeless youth. They begin to discuss their health concerns, respond to AIDS counseling and testing, utilize a variety of drop-in center prevention services, seek health care, obtain treatment for STDs, and remain in contact with the outreach team.

To survive, runaway and homeless youth are forced into circumstances and behavior with high risks for contracting HIV. A study in 1985 in Los Angeles, California, comparing behavior and social characteristics of 110 homeless runaway youth with 655 other youth showed that the prevalence of behavior leading to the transmission of or exposure to HIV is greater among the homeless youth (47). For example, 34.5% of the homeless youth and about 3.7% of the other youth were IDUs. To support themselves and their drug habits, homeless youth participated in street prostitution more than 100 times the rate of other youth (26.4% versus 0.2%). Compared to other youth, runaways were more prone to engage in homosexual (7.3% versus 4.9%) and bisexual (9.1% versus 4.9%) behavior. The runaways also showed greater prevalence rates than other youth for mental health problems (18.2% versus 3.8%), depression (83.6% versus 24.0%), and pelvic inflammatory disease (4.4% versus 1.4%).

Between October of 1987 and June of 1989, a blinded study to determine the seroprevalence of HIV antibody in a population of 1840 runaway and street youth was conducted by Covenant House, a home for homeless youth in New York City. A total of 110 (6%) were seropositive. The rate of infection increased with age from about 2% for 15 year olds to approximately 10% for youth 20 years of age and older. The 1158 males had a higher rate of HIV than did the 682 females (6.3% versus 5.1%, respectively). Hispanic youth had the highest rate of HIV seroprevalence, followed by whites and African Americans (7.4%, 6.1%, and 5.1%, respectively) (48). The causes of HIV infection were not given in this study. Extrapolating from the research on runaway youth in San Francisco and the analysis of the AIDS data for teens and young adults in New York City, intravenous drug use and unprotected sexual activity with infected persons are the major vectors for transmitting the AIDS virus among the homeless youths.

The New York Peer AIDS Education Coalition counsels homeless youth who are gay, lesbian, transsexual, and cross dressers; most are or have been involved with street prostitution (8). These marginal homeless youths were usually asked to leave or were thrown out of their homes because of their sexual orientations and have remained estranged from their families. As children, many were subjected to physical and sexual abuse. The major drugs used by these youths are alcohol, marihuana, and crack cocaine. According to the clinical director, injection of heroin and cocaine is rare. However, drugs to facilitate sex changes such as estrogen are injected, and needles for injection of hormones have been shared. The clinic director estimates that over 50% of the youth who come for help in this program are HIV positive. They avoid applying for help or medical treatment from mainstream community institutions because of the rejection, hostility, and stigmatization they encounter in these institutions. For example, the youth in this group exchange needles at a particular program that tolerates their sexual orientation and behavior.

THE SPECIAL PROBLEMS OF HOMELESS WOMEN

Prostitution, Substance Abuse, and AIDS

Surveys of prostitutes throughout the world have shown primarily two basic types of behavior which result in either transmitting or contracting HIV: substance abuse (either intramuscular or intravenous use of drugs with shared needles and the smoking of crack) and the absence of condom use during sexual activity. Therefore, HIV infection is found among those prostitutes who use drugs and are not observant about the use of condoms. These prostitutes are mostly found in the lower income and streetwalking hierarchy of prostitution. They are usually poorly educated and of minority background, and many may be homeless. Upper- and middle-class prostitutes usually do not use drugs and may use condoms during sexual activity. Furthermore, escort services tend to hire more educated women than those who are engaged as streetwalkers. Also, patterns of sexual behavior and the use of condoms and drugs vary among different groups of prostitutes depending on geographic location or county, hierarchy in prostitution, and economic level (49–52).

In 1987, a study by the Centers for Disease Control of 564 prostitutes at seven sites in the eastern and western sections of the country showed that about 11% were seropositive for HIV (49). Inner-city African American and Latina prostitutes had significantly higher rates of infection then white, Native American, or Asian prostitutes.

A study conducted in 1989 by Dr. Joyce Wallace of the Foundation for Research on STDs of 950 streetwalking prostitutes in the five boroughs of New York City showed that 33.7% were infected with HIV (52). In one area of Manhattan the HIV rate doubled within a 2-year period from 8 to 15% among the prostitutes studied. In a subgroup of 13 male transvestites and 8 transsexuals, 10 out of the 21 were seropositive. There were no significant differences in rates of HIV infection between homeless and "domiciled" streetwalking prostitutes. Of the 189 streetwalkers who considered themselves homeless, 34.4% had positive test results for HIV as compared to the 32.5% infection rate among the 781 "domiciled" streetwalkers.

However, the chance of HIV infection is positively correlated with the level of education. Those streetwalkers who dropped out of school before the 8th grade had the highest rates of infection, followed by those who attended high school and college (43.1%, 32.1%, and 25%, respectively).

There were 60 streetwalkers who did not use drugs but claimed to use condoms consistently (52). In this group only four (6.7%) had positive test results. In summation, a higher level of education, use of condoms, and desisting from drug use were associated with a decreased risk of contracting HIV in this group of prostitutes. In this study, if a prostitute used drugs intravenously, she had a 58% chance of having a positive test result. If the prostitute did not use drugs intravenously, but her boyfriend either used drugs at the time or used drugs in the past, she had a 23.5% chance of a positive result. If the prostitute used cocaine or crack but was not an IDU, she had an 18.9% chance of testing positive. If a prostitute did not use drugs, there was a 6.25% chance she would test positive.

Drug Use, Homeless Women, and Effects on Child Care and Social Institutions

Women may be the fastest growing group among the homeless. As reported by the U.S. Conference of Mayors in 1995, female heads of families and their children constituted the second major group of homeless persons following undomiciled males. Single women, however, constituted another major group of homeless (3). Surveys in different cities showed that about 33–45% of the homeless women are substance abusers of crack cocaine and, to a lesser extent, heroin and alcohol.

A 2-year blind HIV seroprevalence study of homeless pregnant women was implemented in January of 1992 in two New York City shelters (53). Of the 356 women tested, 38 (10.67%) were seropositive for HIV. Women over 35 had the highest rate of infection (21.43%), followed by 25–29 year olds (13.45%), 20–24 year olds (10.28%) and 30–34 year olds (7.69%). No HIV was reported for women under 19. Hispanic women had the highest rate of infection (15%) followed by African Americans (10.32%).

The heroin, cocaine, crack, and AIDS epidemic in New York City has created a new group of homeless—the neonates or children of parents who are infected with HIV, who are drug users, who are the sexual partners of drug users, or any combination of these. Irresponsible behavior, drug use, HIV infection, and STDs have rendered thousands of parents incapable of providing adequate care for their children. The foster care placement of these children in institutions or with surrogates or relatives has become a major social policy issue. For the period 1980–1984 there was a reduction of 20% in the foster care caseload in New York City (20,000 children versus 16,000 children). However, because both the AIDS and crack cocaine epidemics affected the drug-using population during the period 1984–1989, foster care placements increased from 16,000 children to 24,000 children. An additional 10,000 children were being cared for by relatives, usually a maternal grandmother. In 1986 about 1325 infants were placed in foster care because of drug abuse by the parents. With the cresting of the crack and AIDS epidemics in 1988, 4263 infants were placed in foster care, an increase of 222% within a 2-year period (54). By 1990 an estimated 50,000 children of all ages were in foster care in New York City (54).

From 1982 through 1994, 1600 cases of AIDS in children under the age of 13 been reported in New York State. Of these cases, 1496 have been attributed to maternal transmission. About 74% of these children had mothers who were either involved with drugs or were the sexual partners of drug users. As of December of 1994 about 41% of the children diagnosed with

AIDS were known to have died; however, reporting was incomplete. About 87% of the mothers were either Hispanic or African American (53).

During the 9-year period 1980–1989 annual complaints of child abuse rose from 18,000 to 66,000, an increase of 266%. Serious aberrant behavior has been observed in compulsive crack users and those involved in the sale of the drug, including promiscuous sexual activities within crack houses; unwanted pregnancies and the birth of children exposed to crack cocaine in utero with possible neurological damage; the use of babies as collateral for crack cocaine; the neglect, battering, and abandoning of infants and children; and the paranoid ideation and accompanying violence. Some child welfare experts are of the opinion that circumstances surrounding compulsive crack use may destroy or impair the mother's ability to bond with the infant. This may lead to such dire consequences (54).

TREATING THE HOMELESS IN METHADONE AND RESIDENTIAL THERAPEUTIC COMMUNITIES

Homeless substance abusers and those who live in unstable living arrangements present specific problems to outpatient clinic programs. However, a program in New York City that treated homeless patients in a therapeutic community in which methadone is prescribed to opiate-dependent residents reported that the homeless patients cooperated and generally finished treatment. There were few if any noticeable differences in behavior or cooperation between the homeless and nonhomeless residents. However, the future housing needs of homeless residents must be addressed while they are in treatment so they can move into adequate housing after completing the program. In the outpatient division of Promesa a different picture emerged. Most of the homeless patients were unable to comply with daily reporting schedules and quickly dropped out of treatment. With the new welfare and SSI regulations, it is anticipated that the number of homeless will increase, and the program will have to intensify their efforts to find housing for homeless residents who complete the regimen (57, 58). Residential programs that prescribe methadone maintenance and that address the patient's health, social, vocational, housing, and psychological needs should be developed and expanded (55, 56).

The ideological bias against methadone maintenance is a widespread phenomenon among the homeless addicts as among the general public (57). The most common complaints are that methadone "eats or rots the bones," "methadone is too hard to kick," and serious effects such as bone cancer are attributed to methadone. Furthermore, few if any of the homeless addicts appear willing to commit themselves to long-term treatment for 2 or more years. This may be the result of their fears about methadone, unfortunate experiences with treatment programs, their desire to continue using heroin and other illegal substances, or a hope to become free of drug dependency. Considering their lengthy drug addiction and their histories—replete with cyclical episodes of compulsive use, treatment, arrests, incarcerations, and relapses—the hope for a "cure" appears to be elusive for the majority of the homeless substance abusers.

Since methadone is a longer acting drug than heroin, it is perceived by addicts as "harder to kick and more addicting" (57). However, mythologies about methadone persist in various guises and are responsible for shaping attitudes about the long-term use of methadone among the homeless and transient addicted population. Outreach programs to counteract mythologies about methadone not only among homeless addicts but among professionals and the community are indicated if the program is to be expanded as part of a public health endeavor (57).

Homeless Substance Abusers in Drug-Free Therapeutic Communities

A study comparing retention and treatment completion rates over a 2-year period of homeless and nonhomeless residents of 19 residential therapeutic communities in New York City and other parts of the state was completed in 1990 by the Bureau of Research and Evaluation of the New York State Division of Substance Abuse Services (58). Over 60% of the individuals admitted indicated that use of cocaine was their major problem, and over 70% of the

cocaine users admitted smoking cocaine in the form of crack. In the treatment year of 1987–1988, only about 5.9% of 1010 homeless residents and about 6.4% of the 4481 nonhomeless or regular residents completed treatment. For the year 1988–1989, about 8.0% of the 935 homeless and 6.6% of the 4696 regular residents completed treatment. The homeless also had higher annual retention rates in treatment for 1988–1989 than did regular residents (13.2% versus 8.0%). There was no follow-up to determine whether the residents were able to remain abstinent after a course of treatment.

APPROACHES TO REACH, EDUCATE, AND TREAT HOMELESS SUBSTANCE ABUSERS

Different approaches have been employed in the past few years to reach homeless substance abusers. The recent development of outreach was motivated by a desire to curtail the transmission of HIV. Several major concepts and programs of outreach and harm reduction originated in the Netherlands: treatment on demand in methadone maintenance and drug-free residential programs; the needle-exchange program; the organization of substance abusers into active government-recognized self-help and pressure groups known as *Junkiebunden;* the use of special vans or buses staffed by social service personnel to deliver methadone, needle exchange programs, psychotropic medication, and AIDS education pamphlets to street addicts and patients who cannot be treated in a regular clinic; and drop-in centers and special methadone programs where prostitutes can receive medical and personal care; the separation of drug policy into separate attitudes towards the use of marihuana ("soft drugs") and the use of heroin and cocaine ("hard drugs"). Some of these programs have been implemented in modified form by countries throughout the world. Other strategies to organize outreach to addicts were developed from programs organized by programs in the United States such as ACT-UP, the Gay Men's Health Crisis, ADAPT and, in Australia, the Prostitute's Collective (59–64). The National Alliance of Methadone Advocates (NAMA) is an internationally recognized group of methadone patients, their families, and professionals that is based in the United States (62). Currently approximately 60 groups from five countries are affiliated with NAMA. NAMA strives to liberalize methadone program policy (i.e., treatment on demand) while advocating for the rights and dignity of methadone patients.

Outreach programs have been developed in communities throughout the country to assist homeless substance abusers, to educate them about AIDS risk behavior, and to refer them to treatment programs, to social service agencies, and for HIV testing. The majority of these programs consist of professional ethnographers, sociologists, psychologists, social workers, administrators, and researchers working with ex-addicts in inner cities to develop lines of communication with active drug users and IDUs. The outreach programs are based on models developed in the Netherlands where addicts themselves developed organizations such as *Junkiebunden* to reach addicts with AIDS education and information about treatment and to develop needle exchange programs. The *Junkiebunden* are supported by the Dutch government and participate in the formation of policy for the treatment and social acceptance of drug users (59).

However, in the United States, programs to develop outreach, harm reduction, and communication links to the addict community are usually headed by professionally trained staff working with ex-addicts. The basic strategy is to transform attitudes and behavior within the addict community so that behavior that reduces the risk of contracting or transmitting HIV becomes normative (61). This is achieved by community-organizing techniques, group discussions, counseling, education (use of literature and video), and peer pressure.

Outreach strategies should also be targeted to specific groups. The cultural norms of communities are determinants of behavior. If the behavior is destructive, the norms of the group must be changed through education, peer pressure, social networks within a given community, and specialized services. Therefore, it is important to provide culturally relevant education so that the groups at risk for contracting or transmitting HIV are able to make meaningful responses. Hispanic males may require a different outreach strategy than runaway teenage gay youths or African-American women.

The outreach programs have shown that IDUs are willing and able to reduce high-risk AIDS-transmission behavior, especially when related to needle-cleaning and needle-sharing practices. About 60% of the IDUs in several studies made attempts to change needle-sharing practices by cleaning needles more often, entering treatment, and reducing or abstaining from intravenous drug use (63).

Vans have been used to reach homeless addicts on the streets in ghetto neighborhoods and in areas where addicts congregate. In New Jersey vans have been used to distribute vouchers for treatment. In Boston and Baltimore methadone clinics have been organized in vans, and patients report to selected sites for their medication. In New York City, the Manhattan Bowery Project operates a medical van that offers examinations and acute care at soup kitchens for homeless people, many of whom are using drugs. The shelters have also been used as sites for counseling homeless addicts about addiction, treatment, and high-risk behavior leading to transmission of HIV. Also, homeless addicts are referred to treatment from the shelters.

Homeless substance abusers—mainly those who used crack—organized a drug-free living zone in a Brooklyn shelter and developed a therapeutic community setting within the shelter. There are about 161 beds allocated to this program, known as the STAR project. The goal of the program is for the shelter resident to develop sufficient confidence and resources to leave the shelter and enter a community treatment program and to obtain housing, employment, or vocational training.

Therapeutic communities have traditionally adopted a drug-free philosophy. However, within the past decade, there have been examples of therapeutic communities such as the Short-Stay Program affiliated with the Lower Eastside Service Center in New York City that developed methadone programs for their residents. Short-Stay treats methadone patients who are either homeless or whose problems are so severe that they cannot be treated effectively in an outpatient clinic. Residents are referred by their clinics, are maintained on their daily dose of methadone in Short-Stay for 3–6 months, and return to their clinics after their problems are either resolved or effective outpatient treatment plans are developed.

Residence for homeless substance abusers with AIDS have been established in New York City. An example is Bailey House, a 41-bed residence with medical services. In New Jersey a 43-bed program was developed in selected therapeutic communities. In these institutions, homeless opiate dependent substance abusers with AIDS are maintained on methadone, if indicated, and receive basic medical care, nursing, lodging, and food. However, there is a dire shortage of facilities that cater to homeless substance abusers diagnosed with AIDS, and it is now believed that there is a "hidden population" on the streets and in the shelters that has not been reached.

By 1990 the AIDS Resource Center estimated that there may be as many as 10,000 homeless persons infected with HIV in New York City. Sufficient housing is not available to adequately house this group of ill and potentially ill people. Private groups have initiated housing and job-training programs for homeless substance abusers and people with AIDS. For example, the DOE Foundation sponsors the Ready, Willing, and Able program. In this project, homeless persons with drug abuse problems from the shelter help renovate abandoned buildings, receiving compensation and a place to live. Twelve-step and other programs are available if the participants needs help. Housing Works, another private voluntary initiative in New York City, locates apartments for homeless people with AIDS and ensures that entitlements are obtained for needed services.

Since there are long waiting lists to enter treatment, a possible approach to reaching homeless addicts would be the development of medical facilities in shelters or on vans which would also incorporate social services and appropriate medications. In one New York City shelter, a physician connected with St. Vincent's Hospital developed an on-site voluntary HIV counseling and testing program. AZT was successfully prescribed to eligible patients infected with HIV. However, the development of front-line medical programs may encounter community opposition, especially if methadone maintenance or methadone for detoxification is introduced.

Project Renewal in New York City is an example of a coordinated effort by the corporate world, private philanthropy, foundations, and government funding to create effective programs for the homeless including those who are mentally ill and chemically dependent. Their projects include the renovation of Holland House, formerly a squalid welfare hotel, into a model of permanent housing with case management, vocational assessment and GED programs, relapse prevention, recreational activities, psychiatric and social services for the homeless; a medical van that meets the acute needs of homeless people who live in shelters and frequent soup kitchens; creating programs for the treatment of alcoholism in shelters; establishing a therapeutic community for homeless substance abusers in a shelter; a mobile psychiatric van to assist treatment of the homeless mentally ill.

The National Demonstration Program

In cities throughout the country, exemplary programs have been implemented to meet the needs of the homeless. Although inadequate to the demand, good models for service delivery to homeless chemically dependent persons have been developed. Cities have developed coordinated programs along a continuum of care. The models usually starts with the immediate needs of shelter and food and proceeds with case management to mental health counseling and substance abuse treatment if available, attempts to provide transitional or permanent housing, counseling for entitlements, primary health care including attention to persons with disabilities, and prevention strategies.

The major federal source of funding for homeless programs in cities is through the Stewart B. McKinney Homeless Assistance Act passed by Congress in July of 1987. This comprehensive federal initiative targeted the needs of homeless people in the areas of most concern: "emergency food and shelter, health and mental health care, housing, educational programs, job training and other community services" (66). Demonstration projects by the National Institute on Alcohol Abuse and Alcoholism (NIAAA) in conjunction with the National Institute on Drug Abuse (NIDA) are authorized under section 613 of the Act to assist homeless persons affected by alcohol and drug abuse problems. In 1988 nine grants were approved in eight cities throughout the country: Anchorage, Boston, Los Angeles, Louisville, Minneapolis, New York, Oakland, and Philadelphia (two grants).

In establishing these projects, NIAAA and NIDA were aware that the targeted population presented many unique problems that cannot be addressed in regularly funded programs. Homeless clients are difficult to track and treat and often do not complete follow-up. Existing programs cannot address the many service needs these clients present (e.g., housing, unemployment, education, drug and alcohol problems, and health and mental care issues). Nor do existing programs have the resources to coordinate the community facilities and services which must be directed to the homeless client if treatment is to be effective. Finally, currently funded programs do not have the research capacity to evaluate their efforts.

The demonstration projects include outcome and evaluation studies of treatment with comparison groups and outreach or intervention programs. The projects use case management techniques and provide vocational education and housing assistance. Some of the programs provide alcohol-free housing and boarding homes to the participants, as well as treatment or referrals for treatment and other services.

Within the first 2 years of operation, the programs encountered community resistance. Community advisory boards have been established to reduce hostilities toward the target population and the service. Continuity of care is essential, and therefore case management methods that bring together disparate community services are essential. The demand for this service exceeds the original estimates. Applicants who enter the program realize they are in need of multiple services that traditional programs cannot offer. Based on the limited experience of the demonstration projects, more socially community-based orientations are needed for future planning (67).

The following are five conclusions from evaluations of the demonstration projects (67).

1. Addiction programs must also focus on housing needs, means of support and gainful employment.
2. Dropout rates in all programs were high. Programs must develop more user friendly programs that clients and patients can respond to and com-

mit themselves to upon admission. More intensive therapeutic measures can be gradually introduced.

3. Of those who remained in treatment, both subjects and controls improved significantly by the end of the treatment episode. Controls received minimal services as compared to the subjects. In some programs controls received as many services but of a different type including 12-step programs.

4. Positive posttreatment outcomes diminish over time suggesting the need for posttreatment interventions and after care programs.

5. Patients or clients with higher levels of education, lower levels of severe substance abuse, less criminal activity, and greater social integration have more positive outcomes than others who participated in the program.

CONCLUSION

This chapter presented many of the serious social, substance abuse, and medical problems which have afflicted the homeless and transient populations of the inner cities of the United States. Causes of homelessness are interrelated. The following have been reported as causes of homelessness in cities across the United States: lack of affordable housing, chronic unemployment, lack of job skills among the homeless in the current technologically oriented global job market, disappearance of blue collar and manufacturing jobs in the inner cities, substance abuse, alcoholism, mental illness and the break up of families leading to domestic violence, and the spectrum of HIV disease. Meaningful employment and affordable permanent housing are essential if young homeless drug users are to be helped. Therefore, treatment programs should include referrals for housing, vocational assessment, job training, and most important, job placement as an integral part of treatment. With the enactment of current SSI and SSD regulations and the lack of adequate subsidies for affordable housing, cities anticipate an increase in the number of homeless persons within the next few years.

Violence is part of the reality of life for persons who are homeless or whose life is enmeshed in street activities. For example, the homicide rates of young African American men aged 15–24 years increased from 60.6 deaths to 101.1 deaths per 100,000 during the years 1983 through 1988. The 1988 rate is about nine times greater than the homicide rate for white males in the same age range. Reasons given for the high homicide rates include the rise of gangs and drug trafficking, especially crack cocaine, alcohol and substance abuse, easy access to guns and firearms, poverty, homelessness, racial discrimination, unemployment, and an acceptance of violence as an alternative in urban life (68). Homeless chemically dependent people may be involved in street crime such as theft and burglary to support their addictions, but they also are victims of urban violence whether it is perpetrated on the streets, in shelters, or in places where transients congregate. However, in the 1990s in cities nationwide, a long-term trend was identified in the reduction of random murders, overall violent crimes, robbery, burglary, and thefts. Many factors have been attributed to this reduction, including the leveling off of the crack cocaine epidemic, the increase in the prison population, the deaths of persons involved with the drug trade and the use of drugs, the dismantling of drug and gun trafficker gangs, more aggressive and sophisticated police tactics, tougher gun control and possession strategies, the enactment of the Brady Law, which requires a five-day waiting period before the purchase of handguns, enrollment of active addicts into drug treatment, and a better economy (68, 69).

Since substance abuse is a primary generator of the spread of HIV, hep-

atitis, and STDs, it is essential that outreach in the form of concrete services such as housing, education, medical and social services be extended to the homeless population. However, recent welfare reforms contract needed benefits thus threatening efforts at harm reduction. Studies presented in this chapter show that the prevalence of high-risk behaviors resulting in the spread of HIV are highest in the population who live in substandard housing or who are homeless. Proper education, organizing substance abusers, and outreach has shown that norms of behavior can be changed and high-risk behavior for the transmission of HIV can be modified. However, housing must be provided if the changes are to be long lasting and effective for the large numbers of homeless people at risk for infection.

Studies have shown that needle-sharing practices are easier to modify since the shared use of needles is more an economic and availability problem than a deeply ingrained need. Safe sex procedures are more difficult to impart, and modification of sexual practices may require a greater degree of organizing, social networking, peer pressure, and counseling to change behavioral norms, such as the use of condoms. The negotiating of safe sex practice is a major issue for homeless women who may exchange sex for drugs or money or whose partners may threaten them with violence if they do not engage in high-risk sexual practices.

Front-line medicine and relevant social services should be established in the shelters with the use of methadone for the treatment of narcotic addiction and other medications for treating crack cocaine use and alcoholism. Services with fully developed referral networks should be organized within a given site or program since the needs of homeless people demand an array of integrated social and medical services. Testing for HIV and the administration of AZT and other approved AIDS medications can be prescribed in a shelter setting with proper controls. In New York City programs are being established within the family shelter system. On-site alcohol and drug treatment facilities will be developed in these programs.

Since the homeless tend to congregate in transportation terminals, programs which begin to address their medical and social needs should be established there. One such undertaking is the New York City Metropolitan Transit Authority Homeless Outreach Program, which involves cooperative planning among city agencies, including the New York City Health and Hospitals Corporation. Outreach programs to the homeless have been established throughout the public transit subway system, including the Grand Central Terminal at 42nd Street and the Pennsylvania Railroad Station at 34th Street in Manhattan. Access and referrals to employment, soup kitchens, shelters, residential facilities, treatment for alcoholism and substance abuse, social services, and medical and mental health services are provided (70).

Vans can be used to deliver medical and social services to people whose living conditions are so unstable that they are unable to comply with regulations to receive services. The type of delivery system that might be developed would entail the coordination and cooperation of several types of agencies and institutions—for instance, social service agencies, departments of health, substance abuse treatment, medical centers, and divisions within the criminal justice system.

Historically, programs have been developed that linked agencies with common concerns to create new programs and a more effective delivery of services. However, to meet the challenges of the current problems of the inner cities—chronic poverty, homelessness, unemployment, violence, high death rates, substance abuse, the transmission of HIV and other infections—demands an unprecedented coordination of public and private institutions.

References

1. U.S. Department of Housing and Urban Development. A report to the Secretary on the Homeless and Emergency Shelters, May 1984. Washington, DC: U.S. Department of Housing and Urban Development.
2. Levine IS. Homelessness: its implications for mental health policy and practice. Paper presented at the annual meeting of the American Psychological Association, Toronto, Canada, August 30, 1983.
3. U.S. Conference of Mayors. A status report on hunger and homelessness in America's cities: 1995. A 29-city survey. Washington DC: U.S. Conference of Mayors, 1995.
4. Wallace R. A synergism of plagues: planned shrinkage, contagious housing destruction and AIDS in the Bronx. Environ Res 1988;47:1–33.
5. Homelessness. A complex problem and the federal response. Report to the Chairman, Subcommittee on Intergovernmental Relations and Human Resources, Committee on Government Operations, House of Representatives. Pub. No.
GAO/HRP-85–40. Washington, DC: United States General Accounting Office, 1985.
6. Hopper K, Hamberg J. The making of America's homeless: from skid row to new poor. New York: Community Service Society of New York, 1984.
7. U.S. Department of Labor, Bureau of Labor Statistics. Handbook of labor statistics. Washington, DC: U.S. Department of Labor, 1989.
8. Springer E. Personal communication. New York Peer AIDS Education Coalition, 1996.
9. Clatts MC, Davis WR. The public health impact

of street outreach to homeless youth in New York City: implications for AIDS education and prevention. Paper presented at the Third Science Symposium on HIV Prevention Research: Current Status and Future Directions, Flagstaff, AZ, August 16, 1995. [Reprint available from Youth at Risk Project, National Development Research Institutes, Inc., 2 World Trade Center, New York City 10048.]

10. Wilson WJ. When work disappears: the world of new urban poor. New York: Alfred A Knopf, 1996.

11. Institute of Medicine, Gerstein D, Harwood H, eds. Treating drug problems: a study of the evolution, effectiveness and financing of public and private drug treatment systems. Washington DC: National Academy Press, 1990.

12. Califano JA. Welfare's drug connection. New York Times 1996(August 24):23.

13. Wright JD. The health of the homeless: evidence from the National Health Care for the Homeless Program. In: Brickner P, et al., eds. Under the safety net. New York: WW Norton, 1990:15–31.

14. Struening EL, Padgett D. Associations of physical health status with substance use, and mental disorder in homeless adults. J Soc Issues 1991; 46(4):65–81.

15. U.S. Department of Health and Human Services. Office of the Inspector General. Alcohol, drug and mental health services for homeless individuals. Washington, DC: U.S. Government Printing Office, 1992.

16. National Law Center on Homelessness and Poverty. No homeless people allowed. Washington DC: National Law Center on Homelessness and Poverty, 1994.

17. Swarns RL. Moscow sends homeless to faraway home towns. New York Times 1996(October 15):1.

18. Toledo R. The assessment of heroin abuse among residents of the 3rd Street Men's Shelter (Internal Report). New York: Bureau of Research and Evaluation, Ethnography Section, New York State Division of Substance Abuse Services, 1989.

19. Schedlin MG. The health care of homeless mothers and children: impact of a welfare hotel. New York: Medical and Health Research Association of New York City, 1989.

20. Schilling RF, El-Bassel N, Gilbert L. Drug use and AIDS risks in a soup kitchen population. Soc Work 1992;37(4):353–358.

21. Sheffer E, Meier J, Baker S. Evaluation of The Park Homeless Project. New York: New York Community Trust, August, 1995.

22. Bureau of Applied Studies, New York State of Office of Alcoholism and Substance Abuse Services. Availability of prescription drugs on the streets of New York City [internal report]. 1991.

23. Galea J. Personal communication. Chief of Ethnography Section. New York State Office of Alcoholism and Substance Abuse Services, October 24, 1996.

24. Bureau of Research and Evaluation, New York State Division of Substance Abuse Services. Household survey, 1986. New York: Bureau of Research and Evaluation, 1986.

25. Welte JW, Barnes GM. Drinking among the homeless in New York State [internal report]. New York: Research Institute on Alcoholism, New York State Division of Alcoholism, 1988.

26. Struening EL, Pittman J. Characteristics of residents of the New York City shelter system: executive summary. New York: New York State Psychiatric Institute, 1987.

27. Appel P. New York State final report on transient survey 10/1/92–9/30/95. New York: Bureau of Applied Studies, Office of Alcoholism and Substance Abuse Services, 1995.

28. Lehman AF, Cordray DSS. Prevalence of alcohol, drug, and mental disorders among the homeless: one more time. Report to National Institute of Mental Health Office on Programs for the Homeless, 1992.

29. Lurie P, Reingold AL, eds. The public impact of needle-exchange programs in the United States and abroad: summary, conclusions, and recommendations. San Francisco: University of California, San Francisco, Institute for Health Policy Studies, 1993.

30. New York State Department of Health/AIDS Institute. Annual report of the New York State Authorized Needle Exchange Programs, August 1, 1992–September 30, 1993.

31. Anderson W. The New York needle trail: the politics of public health in the age of AIDS. Am J Public Health 1991;81:1506–1517.

32. Bordowitz v. State of New York, 1991. Criminal Court of the City of New York: Docket no. 90N028424/3/5/6.

33. Paone D, Des Jarlais DC, Clark J, Shi Q, Orris A, Krim M, et al. Syringe exchange program—United States. MMWR 1994–1995;44(37): 685–691.

34. Paone D, Des Jarlais DC, Calior S, Friedman PB, Ness I, Friedman SR. New York City syringe exchange: an overview. In: Panel on Needle Exchange and Bleach Distribution Programs. Proceedings: Workshop on Needle Exchange and Bleach Distribution Programs. Washington DC: National Academy Press, 1994.

35. Torres RA, Lefkowitz P, Kales C, Brickner PW. Homelessness among hospitalized patients with acquired immunodeficiency syndrome in New York City. JAMA 1980;258:779–780.

36. Pablos-Mendez A, Raviglione MC, Battan R, Ramos-Zuniga R. Drug resistant tuberculosis among the homeless in New York City. N Y State J Med 1990;90(7):351–355.

37. New York City Department of Health. Tuberculosis and acquired immunodeficiency syndrome (AIDS) in New York City. City Health Inform 1988;7(3).

38. New York City Department of Health. Tuberculosis among the homeless. City Health Inform 1989;8(7).

39. McAdam J, Brickner P. TB in the homeless: a national perspective. In: Brickner P, et al., eds. Under the safety net. New York: WW Norton, 1990:234–249.

40. New York City Department of Health. Congenital syphilis. City Health Inform 1990;8(5).

41. Hibbs JR, Benner L, Klugman L, Spencer R, Macchia I, Mellinger AK, Fife D. Mortality in a cohort of homeless adults in Philadelphia. N Engl J Med 1994;331(5):304–309.

42. Redliner I. Healthcare for the homeless—lessons from the front line. N Engl J Med 1994; 331(5):327–328.

43. Joseph H, Roman-Nay H. The homeless intravenous drug abuser and the AIDS epidemic. NIDA Res Monogr 1990;93:210–253.

44. Raba JM, et al. Homelessness and AIDS. In: Brickner P. et al., eds. Under the safety net. New York: WW Norton, 1990:214–233.

45. Torres RA, Mani S, Altholz J, Brickner PW. HIV infection in homeless men in a New York City shelter. Paper presented at the Fifth International Conference on AIDS, Montreal, Canada, June 4, 1989.

46. Shuster CR. NADR/ATOM homeless data. Paper presented at NIDA-NIAAA meeting, Rockville, MD, July 7, 1990.

47. Yates G, Pennbridge MJ, Cohen E. A risk profile comparison of runaway and non-runaway youth. Am J Public Health 1988;78(9):668–673.

48. Kennedy JT, et al. Health care for families, runaway street kids. In: Brickner P, et al., eds. Under the safety net. New York: WW Norton, 1990:82–117.

49. U.S. Department of Health and Human Services, Public Health Service. Antibody to HIV in female prostitutes. MMWR 1987;36(11):157–161.

50. Padian NS. Prostitute women and AIDS: epidemiology. AIDS 1988;2:413–419.

51. Day S. Prostitute women and AIDS: anthropology. AIDS 1988;2:421–428.

52. Wallace GI. New York City streetwalker data, 1989. New York: Foundation for Research on Sexually Transmitted Disease, 1989.

53. New York State Department of Health. AIDS in New York State, 1994. Albany: New York State Department of Health, 1994.

54. New York City Department of Health. Maternal drug abuse—New York City. City Health Inform 1989;8(8).

55. Torres M, Director of Clinical Services, Director of Therapeutic Community, Promesa. Personal communication, 1990.

56. Deleted in proof.

57. Rosenblum A, Magura S, Joseph H. Ambivalence towards methadone treatment among intravenous drug users. Paper presented at the American Public Health meeting, New York City, 1990. [Available from NDRI, 11 Beach St., New York, NY 10013.]

58. Smith RB. Homeless services project assessment: characteristics of homeless admissions and client outcomes for 1987–88 and 1988–89. Treatment Issue Report No. 73. New York: New York State Division of Substance Abuse Services, Bureau of Research and Evaluation, 1990.

59. Kaplan C. Personal communication, 1986.

60. De Jong WM. The social organization of drug users in the Netherlands [doctoral thesis]. Rotterdam: Erasmus University, 1986.

61. Friedman SR, Serrano Y, Sufian M. Organizing drug injectors against AIDS. National AIDS Demonstration Research Network 1991;2(2): 6–9.

62. Woods J. Personal communication, National Alliance of Methadone Advocates, 1996.

63. Neaigus A, et al. Effects of outreach intervention on risk reduction among intravenous drug users. AIDS Educ Prev 1990;2(4):253–271.

64. Serrano Y. Personal communication, 1991.

65. Lubran B. Alcohol and drug abuse among the homeless population: a national response. Alcohol Treat Q 1990;7(1):11–23.

66. Stahler GJ, Stimmel B, eds. The effectiveness of social interventions for homeless substance abusers. New York: Haworth Press, 1995.

67. Mydans S. Homicide rate up for young blacks: a report from the Federal Center for Disease Control. New York Times 1990(December 7):A14.

68. Cooper M. Decline in random murders cuts overall rate to a 28 year low. New York Times 1996(December 29):25.

69. Kennedy R. FBI reports New York is safer than most cities. New York Times 1997(January 6):B3.

70. Mekos V, Assistant Director of Metropolitan Transit Authority Homeless Outreach Program. Personal communication, January 1997.

74 Physicians and Other Health Professionals

Karl V. Gallegos and G. Douglas Talbott

In the first half of this century medical doctors slowly and painstakingly acquired a special position in society as providers of health care services. Through a series of strategic efforts, the result was a profession that had gained autonomy, monopoly, and expertise over the practice of medicine (1). Physicians have the moral responsibility to care for their patients not only by direct care and precept, but also by the example of their lives and personal conduct. The misuse of alcohol and drugs by a member of the medical profession is an occupational, social, and personal problem that demands action to ensure early detection, treatment, and rehabilitation.

The majority of all health consumers are concerned about the effect alcohol and drug use by their physician could have on the quality of care they receive (2). Addiction to alcohol and other drugs of abuse has been a major concern of the profession ever since the initial American Medical Association (AMA) initiatives in the 1970s (3). The "sick doctor statute" (4) was a pioneering legislative effort to define the inability to practice medicine with reasonable skill and safety, and to revise grounds for professional discipline under the Medical Practice Acts of Florida. In 1973, the AMA Council on Mental Health published a landmark report, "The Sick Physician" (5). Two major recommendations were made by the Council in this report. First, state medical societies needed to establish programs or committees devoted to identifying and helping impaired physicians. The second proposal was that the AMA develop model legislation to amend state medical practice acts so that treatment, rather than punitive disciplinary measures, could be made available.

Prior to the Council's report, two national surveys were conducted by the AMA. One asked state medical societies if they had a committee to deal with physicians who were addicted or psychiatrically impaired. Only seven states had such committees. The second survey examined disciplinary actions by three state boards of medical examiners. The Council concluded that little was being done to address the problem of physician impairment.

Extensive information has accumulated over the past two decades regarding the excessive use of alcohol and other drugs of abuse by physicians (6–9). Organized medicine has carefully and systematically begun to evaluate the extent to which drug addiction, alcoholism, and psychiatric disorders among doctors affect professional performance. The conceptualization of standard performance as a medical rather than legal, moral, or ethical problem has led to the development of programs and policies that integrate medical rehabilitation with professional peer review (10).

This chapter will focus solely upon physician impairment caused by chemical dependency. The authors will identify assumptions underlying the concept of physician impairment; outline the characteristics of an impaired physician; describe the identification, intervention, treatment, rehabilitation, outcome monitoring, and the effectiveness of treatment; present the evolution, progress, and policies that links organized concern for sick doctors to social, legal, and political pressures of professional accountability; and document the practice of medical supervision of problem doctors in terms of its compatibilities with professional values and interests.

Today the nation's health care system is undergoing rapid and dramatic change, and a coming new century is shaping an irreversibly different style of medical practice. There is now increasing regulation for all levels of patient care, heightened peer review, changes imposed on the practice of medicine by managed care, and the emergence of the capability to micro-monitor financial and professional performance information on individual physicians' activities. This review of the impaired physicians' movement has been undertaken at a time when the assessment of the social and cultural components of professional self-governance needs careful re-evaluation. In terms of both prevalence and identification, a historical perspective is useful.

HISTORICAL PERSPECTIVE

The proneness to seclusion, the slight peculiarities amounting to eccentricities at times (which to his old friends in New York seemed more strange than to us) were the only outward traces of the daily battle through which this brave fellow lived for years. When we recommended him as full surgeon to the hospital in 1890, I believed, and Welch did too, that he was no longer addicted to morphia. He had worked so well and so energetically that it did not seem possible that he could take the drug and done so much.

About six months after the full position had been given, I saw him in severe chills, and this was the first information I had that he was still taking morphia. Subsequently, I had many talks about it and gained his full confidence. He had never been able to reduce the amount to less than three grains daily; on this, he could do his work comfortably and maintain his excellent physical vigor (for he was a very muscular fellow). I do not think that anyone suspected him, not even Welch. (11)

Professor William Oster had chronicled, in "The Inner History of the John Hopkins Hospital" in a small, locked black book not opened until 1969, his observation and concerns for his friend and colleague, Professor William Stewart Halsted. This excellent identification of an opiate-addicted physician is classic, yet rarely taught to students of medicine. The report by Paget (12) on the fate of 1000 medical students, the articles by Mattison (13), Partlow (14), DeQuincy (15), and others (16–19), could well be used by medical educators to begin the study of substance abuse prevention and occupational risk. Unfortunately, these writings instead have become a "beacon" for early public concern and scandal about pharmacologic excess by physicians.

After the Flexner report on medical education in the United States (20), state medical societies and legislatures began to regulate medical practice and to pass laws and regulations requiring that physicians and surgeons be free of vice, moral turpitude, and the intemperate use of alcohol and drugs. In 1906, the Congress passed the Pure Food and Drug Act. This act marks the beginning of federal drug regulations (21). The Harrison Narcotics Act began the process of classifying, regulating, and controlling drugs with potential for abuse (22). It criminalized the use of certain drugs and forbade drug maintenance treatment.

In 1920, the English Parliament passed the Dangerous Drug Control Act (23) in an attempt to control addiction by the registration of addicts. Nearly 25% of registered addicts were doctors, dentists, nurses, or veterinary surgeons. In the United States, with prohibition (24), the Marihuana Tax Acts (25), and the connection of drug use as a "Communist conspiracy" (during the McCarthy Era), there has been a gradual avoidance of alcoholism and addiction treatment by the medical profession. Until recently, many physicians have viewed addiction as a legal and social issue rather than a medical illness. There has also been a relative absence of teaching and research about alcohol and drug dependence in medical schools until the last two decades. Negative attitudes still permeate much of the health care system.

PREVALENCE

The literature from the United States related to physician alcohol and drug problems from the mid 1950s to the mid 1980s consistently documented an apparent excess prevalence of these disorders (26). Reports of physician substance abuse from Britain, Germany, Holland, France, and Canada (18, 27–35) from the same study period consistently revealed higher than expected rates of physician addiction. An excellent article by Brewster (33) reviewed the existing, mostly English, written literature to estimate the prevalence of drug and alcohol problems among physicians. She concluded that "extreme statements regarding the prevalence of physician problems with alcohol and other drugs have been made without firm empirical supports." The principal conclusion was that the prevalence of substance abuse problems among practicing physicians is unknown. She noted that when alcohol and other drugs are considered together, practicing physicians may not be unusually likely to have such problems, and the prevalence may be no higher than that of the general population.

Hughes et al. (34) used a mailed, anonymous, self-report survey on a sample of 9600 physicians, stratified by specialty and career stage and randomly selected by the AMA master file. He concluded that the higher prevalence of alcohol use among physician respondents was more likely due to their socioeconomic class than to their profession. He commented on the high rate of reported self-treatment with controlled substances by the study group. Because of inherent methodological issues of the study design, this investigation could not have overestimated the prevalence of substance use or chemical dependence in the total physician population.

Several major surveys in the United States and internationally have assessed the prevalence of substance abuse and dependence disorders within the general population. One of the largest surveys measuring psychiatric and substance use epidemiology is the National Institute of Mental Health Epidemiologic Catchment Area program (ECA) (35). Data from the ECA provide information regarding diagnoses of substance abuse and dependence according to criteria from the *Diagnostic and Statistical Manual of Mental Disorders,* third edition revised (36). The overall rates for alcohol disorders from the ECA survey data were 13.5% (37) for lifetime prevalence. The lifetime prevalence for men was found to be 23.8%, and for women it was 4.7% (38). The ECA surveys reported an overall lifetime prevalence of drug abuse and drug dependence of 6.2% (39). The lifetime prevalence for illicit drug disorders for men in the study population was 7.7% and for women was 4.8% (38).

Currently, there are more than 684,400 physicians in the United States. Women make up 19.5% of the total doctor population. Based on ECA data, an estimated 137,397 physicians (131,124 men and 6,273 women) will have alcohol disorders during their lifetime, and 48,829 medical doctors (42,423 men, and 6,406 women) will have drug disorders.

Physicians are believed to have essentially the same incidence and prevalence rates for alcohol/drug abuse and dependence disorders as the general population. There are no scientific studies published that measure the damage done by physician substance abuse and dependence. However, chemical dependency does appear to be the single most frequent disabling illness for the medical professional and poses a major problem for the profession (40) and society alike.

ETIOLOGY

There is no evidence to support the existence of a premorbid "professional" personality type that predisposes a physician to addiction. There is also no evidence that medicine selects those with special risk for addiction. Who then is at risk for becoming addicted? Vaillant (41) has reported psychological vulnerabilities including passivity and self-doubt, dependency, and pessimism. Physicians whose childhood and adolescence were unstable also appear to have excess risk for addiction. A narcissistic personality type (42), non-Jewish ancestry and a lack of religious affiliation (43), cigarette use of more than one pack per day, the regular use of alcohol, the history of alcohol-related difficulties, and a family history of alcoholism, substance dependence, and/or mental illness are risk factors (44). The authors have found that certain specialty groups and physicians in academic medicine appear to have excess risk for addiction (45). Hughes et al. (34) found by comparison with controls that physicians are five times more likely to take sedatives and minor tranquilizers without medical supervision, and Vaillant (46) has stated that self-prescribing (and self-treatment with prescription drugs) is a risk factor for chemical dependence.

McAuliffe (47) listed risk factors as: (*a*) access to pharmaceuticals, (*b*) family history of substance abuse, (*c*) emotional problems, (*d*) stress at work or at home, (*e*) thrill seeking, (*f*) self treatment of pain and emotional problems, and (*g*) chronic fatigue. Talbott et al. (48) reviewed the medical records of 1000 physicians with chemical dependence and concluded that

age, specialty, drug access, genetic predisposition, stress and poor coping skills, the lack of education regarding substance abuse, the absence of effective prevention and control strategies, drug availability in the context of a permissive professional and social environment, and denial are risk factors for physician substance abuse. Wright (6) postulated that physicians who have excess risk for addiction are those with a history of illicit substance use (including self-prescribing of controlled substances), those in high-risk specialties, those who have a pattern of overprescribing, those with an urge to succeed in an academic setting who overwork, and those who have the combined problems of grandiosity and excessive guilt.

Physicians may be no more at risk for addiction than the general population. No study has specially looked at the genetic predisposition, the psychobiology of craving, the relationship of classically conditioned factors, brain reward mechanisms, and psychodynamic factors, and sociocultural determinants of addiction in physicians by comparison with nonphysician peers.

IDENTIFICATION

Detection of the chemically dependent physician is often delayed by the ability of the physician-patient to protect job performance at the expense of every other dimension of their lives. Clinical studies (49, 50) suggest the order in which addiction-related injury occurs: family, community, finances, spiritual and emotional health, physical health, and finally, job performance. As with any potentially fatal illness, early detection is critical. Identification of the physicians who are afflicted with substance abuse and the disease of chemical dependence follow a sequential course. The family is affected first. The work arena, particularly the hospital, is the last place that drug use by the physician is apparent. Identifiable signs and symptoms can be listed as follows.

Family

1. Withdrawal from family activities, unexplained absences.
2. Spouse becomes a solicitous caretaker.
3. Fights, dysfunctional anger, spouse tries to control physician's substance abuse.
4. Disease of "spousaholics": isolated, angry physically and emotionally, unable to meet the demands of the addict's illness, the grieving loner.
5. Child abuse.
6. Children attempt to maintain normal family functioning.
7. Children develop abnormal, antisocial behavior (depression, promiscuity, runaways, substance abuse).
8. Sexual problems: impotence, extramarital affairs.
9. Spouse disengages, abuses drugs and alcohol, or enters recovery.

Community

1. Isolation and withdrawal from community activities, church, friends, leisure, hobbies, and peers.
2. Embarrassing behavior at clubs or parties.
3. DUIs, legal problems, role discordant behaviors.
4. Unreliable and unpredictable in community and social activities.
5. Unpredictable behavior: excessive spending, risk taking behaviors.

Staff and Employment Applications: Clues from Curriculum Vitae

If any three of these items are present on a job application, suspicion index is high.

1. Numerous job changes in past five years.
2. Relocated geographically, frequently, unexplained reasons.
3. Frequent hospitalizations.
4. Complicated and elaborate medical history.
5. Unexplained time lapse between jobs.
6. Indefinite or inappropriate medical references and vague letter of reference.

7. Working in an inappropriate job for individual's qualifications.
8. Decline of professional productivity.

Physical Status

1. Personal hygiene deteriorating.
2. Clothing and dressing habits deteriorate.
3. Multiple physical signs and complaints.
4. Numerous prescriptions and drugs.
5. Frequent hospitalizations.
6. Visits to physicians and dentists.
7. Accidents and trauma.
8. Serious emotional crisis.

Office

1. Appointment and schedule becomes disorganized, progressively late.
2. Behavior to staff and patients hostile, withdrawn, unreasonable.
3. "Locked door" syndrome.
4. Ordering excessive supply of drugs from local druggists or by mail order.
5. Patients begin to complain to staff about doctor's behavior.
6. Absence from office: unexplained or frequently sick.

Hospital

1. Making late rounds or inappropriate abnormal behavior.
2. Decreasing quality of performance in staff presentations, writing in charts, etc.
3. Inappropriate orders or overprescribing medications.
4. Nurses, secretaries, orderlies, LPNs reporting behavioral changes: "hospital gossip."
5. Involvement in malpractice suits and legal sanctions against the physician or hospital.
6. Emergency room staff reports: unavailability or inappropriate responses to telephone calls.
7. Failure or prolonged response to paging.
8. Reluctance to undergo immediate physical examination or do urine drug screens upon request.
9. Heavy drinking at staff functions.

Early identification and diagnosis are critical. Barriers to early diagnosis are the conspiracy of silence and denial by family, friends, peers, and even the patients. Often one hears such statements by the patient as "I'd rather have Doc Jones drunk as my physician than any other doc I know." Such barriers are products of lack of education concerning the true nature of the primary, psychosocial, biogenetic disease of addiction. They demonstrate lack of training in early diagnosis and detection of addiction in physicians. It is established that female physicians represent a significantly greater difficulty in identification and diagnosis (51, 52). Gender attitudes, female metabolism, and cultural factors concerning the female account for some of these difficulties. While the Georgia program has been involved with the identification of 3500 addicted physicians, there is an under-representation of female, African-American, Hispanic, Asian, and South Pacific physicians in the population treated. Further research is needed to understand what factors contribute to the under-representation of minority group physicians presenting for treatment.

INTERVENTION

Chemically dependent individuals rationalize their avoidance of treatment. Denial is an almost universal characteristic of the disease of addiction. Denial absolves the physician-patient of personal accountability. At the same time, denial (both the deliberate, conscious deception and the unconscious defense mechanism) fills the addicted physician with guilt, shame, and remorse so that most addicted physicians cannot reach out for help. It is the nature of the disease for the denial system to progress as the addiction gains control over the individual's functioning. This distortion of the truth is an unconscious defense mechanism that protects a damaged self-esteem and the addictive process. The denial system as well as the addictive process itself can prevent the physician-patient from wanting or even feeling the need for treatment.

Intervention is a procedure that is necessary when an individual is either unaware of their addiction or, because of denial, is psychologically unable to recognize the seriousness of his or her disease and seek treatment (53). Currently, intervention is utilized, initially, as a component of a comprehensive assessment. Once addiction is suspected by colleagues, intervention needs to be carefully planned and swiftly expedited. Intervention is an act of love and caring. It is a very serious experience that can prevent the addicted individual from hitting a personal bottom, but the authors have seen improperly done interventions result in death. Over the past two decades intervention has been refined into a science and an art. Successful intervention has several components.

Selection of the Intervention Team

The leader of the intervention team needs to select the most significant people in the physician-patient's life at the time. The best intervenors include family members, peers, supervisors, close friends, clergy, hospital administrators, medical society members, court officials, or members of the licensing board. Selection must exclude individuals who are resentful and/or hostile. The best intervenors are often individuals who are knowledgeable about the disease of addiction and are able to maintain objectivity yet express an attitude of caring and concern. Intervenors must be emotionally stable, believe in the progressive nature of chemical dependence, and understand that the illness is treatable. An intervention should never be done alone.

A Trained and Experienced Intervention Leader

Proper preparation for an intervention is essential. The interventionist must select individuals to do the intervention, train the intervenors to present relevant information to the physician-patient, set goals for the intervention, and expedite the prompt referral for recommended treatment.

Selection of the Intervention Site

The site of the intervention needs to be nonthreatening and quiet. Time and experience have taught that an early morning intervention prior to the intake of alcohol or other drugs by the physician is best accomplished in the patient's home with the cooperation of the spouse and children. Occasionally, guilt and shame are present to such a degree that intervention needs to be away from the home and can be at some neutral site. Some spouses believe that their participation in an intervention will result in divorce. If the spouse is not convinced that addiction is a progressive, potentially fatal, but treatable illness affecting the entire family, it may be wise to exclude them from the intervention. It is necessary that all members of the intervention team present a strong cohesive explanation of the problem.

Intervention Goals Must Be Established

This needs to be done in advance, understood and accepted by all intervention team members. Intervenors must decide what choices they will give the physician-patient and what they will commit to if the physician-patient refuses all offers of help. Frequently, the perception of reality is grossly distorted by the effects of alcohol and drugs on the brain. Intervenors need to review the pain and consequences they have experienced as a result of the addict's substance abuse. No intervention is a failure for the seed has been planted. The impaired physician may reject, refuse, or even elope from the intervention, but the health professional then recognizes that his or her support systems are aware and concerned about them.

Factual Data

It is critical that the data be factual and documented. Previous gossips or innuendos may reduce the chances of having a successful intervention. The intervention team members should write down and present to the physician-addict their experiences of the addiction-influenced behaviors. The addict should be told why the intervention is necessary along with the legal, social, personal, health-related, and professional implications of their illness. The team needs to also consider presenting advocacy/immunity regulations within the state, should the individual voluntarily seek the appropriate treatment as a result of the intervention.

Adequate Intervention Time

Intervention sometimes must be repeated. Extremely important is the fact that the individual not feel rushed during the intervention and adequate time is allowed. The doctor should not be intoxicated. An intervention done quickly after an addiction-precipitated crisis frequently is likely to be successful. If the physician-patient refuses recommended help, the interventionist may negotiate a behavioral contract, so that with the next relapse or crisis, another intervention can be swiftly initiated.

Rehearsals

Careful planning including rehearsal is critical. Each individual of the intervention team must know and practice their roles and what they will say during their intervention. Anticipation of the doctor-patient's reaction including hostility and flight needs to be anticipated and plans for this complication provided. No matter what the intervention outcome is, it is important that the intervention team regroup and process their feelings and thoughts about the intervention. Some interventions fail. A cohesive team can develop an action plan for the next time the addicted doctor is in an addiction-precipitated crisis.

At the conclusion of the successful intervention, the physician-patient will follow the recommended assessment, treatment, or both. Referral options, transportation, and an action plan should be in place before the intervention is begun. The authors have seen more than one intervention that seemed successful, but the doctor negotiated his or her own arrangements ("I'll go after getting business in order") that enabled suicide.

ASSESSMENT

Interventionists, most state medical society impaired physician committees, and many state licensing boards recommend a comprehensive assessment in a specified treatment facility for impaired physicians to determine the extent of illness and the individual's treatment needs. Physicians who voluntarily seek the recommended treatment after assessment, successfully complete their treatment, and enter into their state medical society–sponsored monitoring program frequently receive advocacy in lieu of punitive sanctions. Ideally, the recovering physician will allow the experienced treatment team to make the best choices about their recovery, rather than to treat themselves or undertreat their illness.

In the past decade many specialized treatment programs have evolved to meet the needs of the chemically dependent and/or psychiatrically impaired physician. The Georgia program has refined the 96-hour assessment. This process is used to evaluate the scope of illness and results in triage to the appropriate care (54) based on individualized needs. The assessment program is comprised of five teams that provide an interdisciplinary composite diagnostic score after which treatment recommendations are formulated. This interdisciplinary team approach has the following advantages (55): the best use of skills, coordination, flexibility, synergy, support, and communication. The five teams are listed as follows:

The Medical Team

This team is headed by a physician who is trained in addiction medicine. These individuals are certified, knowledgeable, and experienced in addiction medicine and are trained to identify and treat the medical consequences of alcohol and drug abuse. They perform a detailed history and physical examination and order the appropriate diagnostic and confirmatory laboratory, radiologic, and other needed examinations. Inherent in the functioning of the medical team is appropriate consultations for specific medical complications.

Addiction Medicine Team

This is headed by a certified addiction medicine specialist. Trained to diagnose and recommend a range of addiction medicine services, these individuals provide needed detoxification services after a comprehensive addictive disease assessment is obtained. They evaluate the psychological and behavioral effects of the drugs that have been used by the patient, assess the addiction severity from a biopsychosocial perspective, and collect and collate information from the individual support system members (including intervention team members) to validate the physician-patient's history. This rapid data acquisition effort followed by presentation of the information to the physician-patient and family is often critical for rapid decompression of the impaired physician's denial system.

Psychiatric Team

Recent years have made it apparent that the disciplines of addiction medicine and psychiatry must work in concert for the benefit of the addicted physician. Addicted patients frequently manifest multiple addictions and psychiatric problems at once (56). Consequently, a comprehensive psychiatric assessment is a critical component of any assessment of an alcoholic and/or drug-addicted individual. It is necessary to determine if a definitive psychiatric diagnosis is present or if there is a working differential diagnosis, contingent upon further evidence and re-evaluation. Treatment evaluation research has documented that untreated dual diagnosed patients are more likely to relapse after treatment then addictive patients without psychiatric comorbidity (57).

The Neuropsychological Team

The addicted physician may appear cognitively unimpaired, particularly if he or she has had training in psychiatry or psychology. However, neuropsychological testing will often reveal significant deficits in reasoning and memory (58). After a focused clinical interview, psychological testing should involve the Halstead-Reitan Neuropsychological Test Battery (HRNB), which includes the Booklet Category Test, Tactile Performance Test, Reitan-Indiana Aphasia Screening Test, the Trailmaking Test, Reitan-Klove Sensory Examination, and the Seashore Rhythm Test. Useful adjuncts to the HRNB include the Wechsler Adult Intelligence Scale (WAIS), Wechsler Memory Scale Revised (WMS-R), the Graham-Kendal Memory for Design Test, Minnesota Multiphasic Personality Inventory (MMPI), and the Rorschach Test. Often missed in standard evaluations or in less robust or specific psychological testing, neuropsychological deficits may become apparent with more sensitive evaluation techniques.

Family Therapy Team

The family is critical to the program's treatment and monitoring of the addicted patient. Interviews with the main significant other, children, parents, and siblings are diagnostically very helpful. Enlistment of these individuals in the treatment and recovery program is coordinated by the family therapists.

Assessments are done ideally in the hospital where close and constant observation allows documentation of withdrawal symptoms, medical symptoms, and complications. This method also allows detection of self medication by the physician-patients. Team members see the patient for testing and evaluation. Such assessments are done independently by each team member. The team then meets for discussion of diagnosis and treatment recommendations. Differences of diagnoses are discussed and resolved. It is in this forum that collateral information from other sources, particularly from the family therapist and the addiction medicine team member, becomes critical. Obviously, informed consent must be obtained from the patient to gain this information. Finally, a primary Axis I diagnosis, as well as subdiagnoses, are arrived at by the team members. A detailed plan of treatment is then recommended.

The team then meets with the patient. It is useful to have not only the main significant other, but often other family members present at the diagnostic and therapeutic recommendations of the assessment team. If inpatient treatment is indicated, a choice for treatment at several different facilities is offered to the patient. Adequate time should be provided for questions and answers from the patient and his or her family. Often the patient, and his or her family, is given a choice of two or three facilities for inpatient treatment. Likewise, various alternatives for treatment should be discussed, as well as the problems that may be anticipated if the patient refuses treatment. The assessment team is not in a position, and should not ever comment upon, the licensure or DEA consequences, as these will be left up to the appropriate organizations. The assessment and treatment team must present themselves as advocates for the physician-patient, not as prosecutors. Assurance of patient confidentiality is of the highest priority.

TREATMENT

The treatment of the impaired physician has many special features that combine the highest clinical standards and serve as a benchmark for the field of addiction medicine. Commonly accepted goals of treatment include (a) abstinence from alcohol and other psychoactive substances and (b) identification of the biopsychosocial treatment modality to which the patient's severity of illness will be matched. Treatment centers specialized in the care of chemically dependent physicians provide levels of care based on the American Society of Addiction Medicine (ASAM) patient placement criteria. These levels have been labeled to be more descriptive of the intensity of services provided: Level I—outpatient treatment; Level II—intensive outpatient/partial hospitalization; Level III—medically monitored inpatient treatment; and Level IV—medically managed inpatient treatment (54).

The outstanding treatment centers specializing in impaired physicians programs have learned that malignant denial is characteristic of this group of alcoholics and drug addicts. Defined as denial which is deeply inculcated in professional training, this type of denial can complicate early recovery. For addicted physicians, malignant denial appears to be a strong factor in the failure of outpatient treatment alone. While some impaired physicians have attained true sobriety with intense and focused long-term attendance in Alcoholics Anonymous (AA), the most successful programs in the past decade have been found to be residential outpatient programs with adequate time to work through such denial (see "Treatment Outcome"). Outpatient programs, by themselves without either long-term treatment or the residential component, have not been found to be very successful in either the Oklahoma (59) or the Oregon (60) experience. Successful treatment of the impaired physicians has revealed several significant elements.

Understanding and Acceptance of the Disease Concept

For the impaired physician to both understand and to accept that he or she has a primary biopsychosocial genetic disease has proven to be the most critical and elementary aspect of recovery. Acceptance of the disease concept can quickly begin the absolution of the guilt, shame, and fear which are the inevitable companion of the impaired physician. Initially, this is accomplished by education. Understanding of this disease of addiction dispels the shame. Compulsivity is a primary symptom of chemical dependence. The recovering physician must be carefully schooled in the neurobiochemistry of addiction and the medical and sociocultural consequences of their disease. Only then can they be taught that they are not responsible for their disease, but they are responsible for their recovery. Impaired physicians can understand the disease model intellectually, but to accept this concept in depth is a process requiring time and the proper environment. The impaired physician must be helped to understand their addictive disease and the fact that they can't think their way into sober living; they must live their way into sober thinking. Physicians, by training, wish to solve all their problems intellectually, but addiction is not an intellectual disease. This has been apparent, since a physician (Dr. Bob) and a stockbroker turned counselor (Bill W.) stated in June, 1935, that alcoholism was an illness of mind, body, and soul (61) and founded AA. Knowledge and acceptance of this disease has proved to be a primary element in recovery.

Identification of the Trigger Mechanisms

Appreciating that abuse plus the genetic predisposition will produce the disease, identification of triggers that produce abuse is critical to recovery. Research into the psychology of craving, the classically conditioned factors in addiction and brain reward mechanisms, has demonstrated that such triggers can involve a wide variety of emotional, personal, physical, and situational stresses. Each impaired physician must, over a period of time, with education and counseling identify his or her own triggers. With personal knowledge of triggers for alcohol and drug use, the physician-patient can begin to learn more about relapse thinking and behavior, and develop coping skills to prevent relapse.

Nonchemical Coping

Impaired physicians have become dependent on chemical coping skills. Basic to recovery is the need to develop and assume a nonchemical coping way of life. For example, one of the most widespread and troublesome symptoms of drug withdrawal is insomnia. Addicted physicians have to be taught that this common withdrawal symptom must be dealt with by nonchemical coping mechanisms. For example, nonchemical coping prescribed for insomnia includes (a) a quiet restful environment; (b) small, balanced, multiple feedings during the day; (c) abstinence from caffeine and nicotine, a diminution in salt, and high protein intake; (d) a prescribed time for trying to fall asleep and then 2-hour increments of planned insomnia time (pit) where planned activities are scheduled prior to going to sleep the evening before; (e) hot baths; (f) massage; (g) light reading; (h) counseling every evening as to anticipating the coming night and periods of activity during planned insomnia time; (i) charting the insomnia activities the night before trying to relate it to specific thought processes; and (j) reading books or tapes about insomnia, i.e., reference the self-help section of a local bookstore.

These simple nonchemical coping methods can be applied in a wide variety of emotional and situational conditions for each individual. Such nonchemical prescriptions then have to be taught to the impaired physician for anxiety, grief, guilt, depression, and situational crisis such as divorce, loss of job, death in the family, personal problems, or physical problems such as a heart attack, stroke, or accidents. The impaired physician, therefore, must develop a multitude of nonchemical coping skills, abilities, and capabilities to deal with stresses without chemicals. For all of their professional lives, physicians have been taught that drugs and chemicals are a powerful part of their therapeutic armamentarium, and this requires "extended unlearning" procedures and practices on their part.

Balance in Changing Priorities

Many impaired physicians by virtue of their selection of their life work and their training put their professional lives and their physician's work as a priority before everything else. Almost by definition, they are both workaholics and perfectionists. For many, this behavior becomes a major "trigger" where substance abuse is used to relieve their stress. If the biogenetic predisposition is there in the face of this abuse, then disease is likely to occur. Sixty years ago, addiction was defined as a multifactorial disease by the founders of AA (61). Recovery depends upon medical, emotional, and spiritual growth. A large asset in recovery is balance of these three elements. The impaired physician is taught that recovery and growth are first, family is second, and his or her profession is third. Leisure time and fun are critical to recovery, yet many impaired physicians have lost the ability to have fun and have forgotten how to play. They have lost the balance in their life. Therefore, balance must be restored between work, play, and a spiritual life, as well as a reordering of life's priorities. This tenet is essential to the recovery of the impaired physician.

Family Involvement

The family is critical in the diagnostic process as well as in the recovery and therapeutic process. Most often the family knows of the disease long before peers, friends, or individuals in the professional office or in the hospital.

If the family is involved initially in the recovery process they can be a powerful factor in recovery. The main significant other, as well as the children, parents, and the siblings suffer from the disease as they have the illness of "spousaholics," "childolics," "siblingolics," and "parentolics." Their pain and discomfort must be dealt with in a manner that shows them how to help the alcoholic and the addicted physician, as well as how to help themselves. Basic to this aid is their own family understanding and acceptance of the disease and specific suggestions as to how they can modify their own responses and behaviors towards the recovering physician who returns home after treatment.

Mutual Help Groups

Successful health professional programs have been based on 12-step programs. Traditional psychiatric individual counseling by itself has not been shown successful unless the patient has a dual diagnosis. The effectiveness of self-help programs like AA, when offered to hospitalized and treatment-based patients, depends on how well their ethos is integrated into the psychotherapeutic treatment program. Effectiveness may also depend on how well the self-help program is built into an extended structured aftercare process (62). The merit of the 12-step programs are that they are widely available, free, functioning at all times of the day and night, supportive, *and* they work!

Aftercare and Monitoring

While these will be discussed in a subsequent section, it is important to incorporate them into the therapeutic process. The planning of aftercare and monitoring should start from the first day of treatment and should involve the family and all other support systems of the impaired physician.

The treatment team should be experienced in dealing with impaired physicians and other health professionals. They need to be experienced in setting firm limits and boundaries, and they need to be experienced with the specific needs (both legal and professional) in treating the impaired physician. They should be familiar with the National Practitioner Data Bank, malpractice insurance, DEA certification, and issues of state medical licensures. These professionals also need to be experienced with specific drug therapies such as naltrexone and disulfiram. They need to be skilled at helping to solve re-entry problems once the patient gets back to work and be available for frequent consultation.

TREATMENT OUTCOME

The primary goal of treatment is to help the physician-patient achieve and maintain long-term remission of his or her addictive disease (62). Reported recovery rates vary considerably with complete abstinence from mood-altering substances ranging from 27% (63) to 92% (64). The interpretation of treatment outcomes, however, requires explanation.

Many methodological problems (65) exist when comparing different outcome studies of physicians who have been treated for chemical dependence. The following are some notable differences among investigations.

1. Patient selection bias: Some study populations include other health professionals including nurses, dentists, and medical students.
2. Significant differences in the types, intensity, and length of time of treatment given. (There is no standard way to retrospectively evaluate intensity, quantity, and quality of treatment.)
3. Authors rely on self-reports from physician-patients about abstinence versus relapse.
4. Positive urine drug test results are based on random urine drug screens to be done within 24 hours of the recovering physician's notification. (Alcohol and some drugs of abuse taken a day or two before notification might not be detected.)
5. Reliance on inadequate or incomplete diagnostic criteria in choosing subjects for study.
6. Failure to adequately account for treatment dropouts in the analysis of treatment outcome data.

7. Failure to follow patients for adequate lengths of time post treatment.
8. Failure to provide for adequate, multidimensional treatment outcome measures that map a full range of patient behavior.

These methodological differences have made meta-analysis impossible. However, there has been a steady progression in the cohesiveness of findings in all investigations published in the last decade. Physicians appear to have better treatment outcomes than the general population when long-term aftercare and monitoring is done. There are also sufficient data to conclude that most physicians can be successfully rehabilitated to re-enter medical practice with reasonable skill and safety to their patients.

Reading (66) reported that after two years of program involvement after formal treatment, New Jersey physicians had a recovery rate of 83.8% with no relapses, and 13.8% had one relapse. He concluded that the overall two-year success rate of 97.5% was related to the formal, frequent, and structured outpatient counseling. In addition, the structured urine monitoring program, 12-step participation, family involvement, validity checks by responses of other recovering physicians and/or physician monitors from the index physician's community, and monthly face to-face contacts with the Physicians Health Program Staff, are necessary components of an effective Physicians Health Program (PHP).

Gallegos et al. (67) studied 100 physicians who subsequently entered into a continuing care contract with the Georgia Impaired Physicians Program between July 1982 and June 1987. Seventy-seven physician-patients maintained documented abstinence from all mood-altering substances from 5 to 10 years after initiation of the continuing care contract. One physician was lost to follow-up, and 22 relapsed. Of those who relapsed, 1 died during relapse. One physician was involved in a pattern of continuous relapses and was unable to practice medicine. All but four of the remaining physicians who relapsed had at least two years of continuous sobriety since their last relapse.

Shore reported on 63 addicted or impaired physicians who had been put on probation with the Oregon Board of Medical Examiners. These physicians were followed for 8 years. This investigation allowed the evaluation of the effectiveness of monitored outpatient supervision by comparing monitored and unmonitored subgroups. There was a significant difference for the improvement rate for monitored subjects (96%) compared with the treated but unmonitored addicted physicians (64%). Shore concluded that "there is increasing evidence that random urine monitoring during a two to four year period is positively correlated with treatment outcome" (60).

Other studies demonstrate similar results. In the Oregon (60) experience, Shore reported a 96% "improved" rate in monitored physicians compared to a 64% "improved" rate in unmonitored physicians.

Smith and Smith (59) reported treatment outcomes of impaired physicians in the Oklahoma program. Physician-patients were categorized by length of time in treatment. Type I had treatment for 3–4 months in a program specializing in the care of health professionals. Type II had inpatient treatment for 4–6 weeks. Type III had other treatment modalities including: outpatient treatment, psychiatric or psychological therapy, and/or 12-step groups without prior chemical dependency treatment. Eighty-five percent of those with Type I treatment had a favorable outcome. Of those with Type II treatment, only 46% had a favorable outcome, compared to Type III physician-patients, of which only 38% had favorable outcomes.

Other studies demonstrate similar results. Gallegos and Norton (68) reported on 250 consecutive physicians who had completed a specialized impaired physicians program with a minimum of 4 months of supervised treatment. These were the first physicians who went through the Georgia program between 1974 and 1982. Complete abstinence was reported by 73.9% with a minimum of 2 years of follow-up. Twenty-nine (11%) of the 250 physicians were lost to follow-up and counted as treatment failures.

Morse et al. compared recovery rates of 73 physicians with 185 middle class patients treated for chemical dependence in a hospital-based program. In the physician group, 83% (compared to 62% of nonphysicians) who completed treatment had favorable outcomes one or more years after treatment (69). He concluded that close monitoring may account, in part, for the better prognosis for physicians.

Harrington et al. reported that 31 of 33 physicians who completed treatment (94%) had returned to full practice. Twenty-two (67%) had experienced no relapse, and 15% had a very brief period of relapse during follow-up, which lasted up to two years (70).

Johnson and Connelly evaluated and treated 50 physicians in a psychiatrically oriented, short-term addiction program. The criteria for a successful treatment outcome were abstinence and a return to effective job functioning. A "brief relapse" was not considered a treatment failure (71). Patients were followed from 9 months to 4.5 years. Thirty-two (64%) of the study population were sober and practicing medicine at the time of follow-up. Of significant concern, 4 (8%) were dead, 3 of suicide and 1 of subdural hematoma.

Kliner studied treatment outcomes of alcoholic physicians (72) with a multiple-choice questionnaire sent to each patient 1 year after discharge from an inpatient 30-day alcoholism treatment. Of the 85 patients, 10 had died, 4 never returned the questionnaire, 3 refused permission to be contacted, and 1 could not be located. Fifty-one (76%) reported abstinence since treatment, and 53 (79%) of those who responded to these questionnaires reported general improvement in their professional performance. The physician-patient response to treatment was more favorable than the general patient population (only 61% remained abstinent at one year).

Goby et al. identified 51 physician-patients who underwent treatment (between 1967 and 1977, with between 1 and 10 years of follow-up) for alcohol and/or chemical dependence (73). Only 43 were interviewed via phone. Of those not included for follow-up 1 was incarcerated and 7 were dead (only 1 of 7 dead were abstinent since treatment). Only 19 (44%) of those interviewed reported no use of alcohol since treatment.

Review of the treatment outcome studies above demonstrates that (*a*) treatment does work, (*b*) long-term abstinence and personal well-being correlates with strict aftercare monitoring and improved recovery surveillance techniques, (*c*) death is more prevalent among those who leave treatment prematurely and those who relapse, and (*d*) the majority of physicians who successfully complete treatment and participate in aftercare monitoring can successfully return to the practice of medicine.

AFTERCARE AND MONITORING

Since substance abuse is a chronic illness, treatment is but the beginning of recovery. Most treatment centers have developed structured aftercare programs so that patients can continue to work on issues identified during their treatment program. Initially, many recovering physicians regard aftercare as punitive, hostile, or intrusive. However, when he or she understands and accepts the relapsing nature of the disease, and when aftercare monitoring is presented as a legal and licensing advocacy issue, compliance, acceptance, and gratitude usually result.

Several state medical societies have selected full or part-time directors of their Physicians Health Programs (PHP). After treatment, physicians are expected to participate in their state medical society–sponsored PHP for monitoring, in addition to the aftercare provided by their treatment program. Many states, including Florida (74), New Jersey (66), Maryland (75), Oregon (76), Georgia (77), New Mexico (78), Alabama (79), Oklahoma (59), and others, provide recovering physicians who voluntarily seek treatment and monitoring "sanctuary" and advocacy from the state licensing agency. Physicians who are reported directly to the state board of medical examiners are required to have a formal relationship with the board.

Typically, PHPs provide the following low cost or no cost services to the physician:

1. Receive requests to investigate questions of specific impairment.
2. Provide training of intervention specialists and perform interventions.
3. Seek assistance for physicians who need financial aid during the treatment or rehabilitation process.
4. Establish a registry of the appropriate resources for treatment of alcoholism, other drug dependence, mental health, geriatrics, and other problems resulting in physician impairment.
5. Establish liaisons with hospitals, medical staffs, managed care organizations, and medical societies throughout the state.

6. Liaison with the directors of approved chemical dependency treatment programs.
7. Recommend appropriate treatment to physicians seeking help.
8. Monitor the progress of the licensee after treatment.
9. Collaborate with other State PHPs to improve standards of recovery monitoring, data collection, process refinements, and to plan research to evaluate effectiveness of treatment and monitoring.
10. Make reports to appropriate individuals, committees, or organizations, funding sources, and credentialing agencies regarding success of the monitoring program.
11. Several state PHPs also provide individual, group, and family therapy or counseling.
12. Conduct educational programs to educate physicians and their families, hospital staffs, county medical societies, medical auxiliaries, and other appropriate groups or agencies about physician impairment.

State medical society PHPs have an underlying premise that impaired physicians may be unable to seek help spontaneously due to the nature of their illness and, therefore, that their colleagues have a special obligation to take the initiative of encouraging voluntary treatment. After treatment, these programs have two main functions: to protect the public from impaired physicians and to rehabilitate addicted or mentally ill physicians. Most PHPs supervise physicians for a minimum of five (5) years.

Programs that are administered by state licensing boards appear to be punitive. It is believed that such programs may be less effective in reaching out to physicians who would voluntarily seek treatment and/or assistance, and do not have board actions. State medical society PHPs are programs of advocacy. It is believed that when physicians are not threatened with the potential for discovery by the medical board, they will voluntarily join PHPs at an earlier stage in their disease.

FACTORS THAT INFLUENCE RECOVERY

Close and careful monitoring by the state medical society PHP is believed necessary to follow physicians safely through the stages of recovery and to avoid "stuck points." Galanter et al. (80) studied 100 recovering physicians who were successfully treated in a program that combined professionally directed psychotherapeutic treatment and peer-led self-help. An average of 37.4 months after admission, they all reported being abstinent and rated AA as more important to their recovery than professionally directed modalities. Feelings of affiliation to AA, which were very high, were strong predictors of the respondents' perceived support for their recovery. These feelings, and the identification with the role of caregiver in addiction treatment, appeared to be central to their recovery. Twelve-step groups were ranked as the most potent element in their recovery followed by physician counseling, the desire to do well at work, family therapy, and urinalysis.

Gallegos (67) reported that all 100 of the physicians studied signed a continuing care contract that included witnessed urines, a primary care physician, attendance at five 12-step meetings and one Caduceus meeting a week, individual and family therapy when indicated, a spiritual program, physical fitness program, and a leisure activity program.

Those who relapsed within the first year were likely not to believe the disease concept, did not believe they needed the recommended help, and felt that they would not run into difficulties staying sober. Those who relapsed in the second year most often reported family and emotional issues as triggers for relapse. For the 22 physicians who relapsed, behavioral changes and denial of their condition elevated their stress, increased their isolation, and impaired their judgement. Each individual reported slowly stopping attendance at AA. They also felt that neither their fear of losing their license to practice medicine, nor any other legal, marital, or professional sanction could have inhibited the progression of their relapse or promoted recovery once substance use was re-initiated.

State PHPs attempt to provide quantitative documentation of individuals' progress in recovery by obtaining data from face-to-face interviews with the physician-patient. In the Georgia program, Talbott has postulated 16 factors which appear to have predictive value in assessing successful recovery (81):

1. The number of 12-step meetings attended per week.
2. A working relationship with a sponsor and frequent sponsor contact.
3. Random urine drug screens.
4. Monitoring milestones in each stage of recovery to help the physician avoid "stuck points" or emotional traps (i.e., anger, guilt, depression, anxiety, insomnia, etc.)
5. Monitor for the effects of the emergence of compulsive behaviors (sex, work, food, nicotine, gambling, etc.)
6. Evaluate the status of current therapies, treatments, and medications.
7. Assessment of family relationships.
8. Physical health status.
9. Number of leisure activities per week.
10. Compliance with all monitoring activities, and timely attendance at recommended therapies and 12-step meetings.
11. Amount of time spent exercising per week.
12. Evaluation of work-related stressors (professional status, job duties, and workplace attitudes).
13. Changes in financial status.
14. Additional training and/or continuing medical education.
15. Self-rated quality of recovery program.
16. The identification of "soft parts" of the physician-patient recovery program.

Data for surveillance of recovery are obtained by the PHP at regularly scheduled 2-week intervals in the first year after treatment. The evaluation schedule gradually lengthens to biannual monitoring and face-to-face interviews toward the end of five years. Aftercare monitoring of recovering physicians has become an essential part of promoting continued recovery.

Contingency contracting has also been found to be helpful in reducing the risk for relapse. State PHPs or a therapist obtain a license-surrendering letter from the physician being monitored. If the urine drug screen is positive, the letter is sent to the state licensing agency and professional sanctions will be issued by the licensing agency. Crowley (82) has reported on contingency contracting as a treatment modality that decreases physician drug use.

One common denominator for successful recovery seems to be the extent that the physician is able to internalize the treatment experience (83). Physician-patients who are most successful in their recovery avoid emotions such as anger, guilt, depression, and anxiety by using 12-step recovery program principles (84). They avoid compulsive behaviors and learn to become skillful in participating in important relationships (family, sponsor, spouse, parents, children, friends, etc).

Physicians who do the best in their recovery develop a profound and abiding attitude of gratitude. They learn to have open and honest communication with family members. They are regular in their attendance at AA (or other 12-step meetings), they communicate with their sponsor, and check out their behavior with other trusted family members and recovering friends. These behaviors must become part of the recovering physicians' normal life.

STAGES OF RECOVERY

The milestones in recovery from addiction are both similar to and different from the process of recovering from almost any chronic, life-threatening illness. Each individual has unique amounts of protective features, risk factors, and resilience for recovery. Treatment and aftercare ideally combine to improve outcome by changing a relapse-prone individual into a recovery-prone person.

The needs of every recovering physician change over time. Without appropriate problem-solving strategies, the willingness to reach out for help and respond appropriately to feedback, and the ability to successfully cope with "struck points" (85) and stressors, relapse is likely. A thorough recognition of the stages through which the recovering physician must pass and ways to overcome "stuck points" in the journey of recovery is essential.

Recovery is a process with clearly defined stages (86). It requires changes that are perceptible to those around the recovering physician. It is a long term process that requires:

1. Total abstinence from mood-altering substances.
2. A conscious decision to take those specific actions that increase the likelihood for success in recovery (including changes in values, perceptions, and behaviors).
3. Knowledge about the natural history of the illness (87) and its recovery.
4. Knowledge of the skills to begin and continue.
5. The ability to identify strengths and weaknesses in their current recovery program.
6. The willingness to accept feedback from others who are skilled at monitoring continued personal growth.
7. The ability not to deny and evade problems, stresses, and behaviors that (when unopposed) frequently lead to relapse.

Although the recovery time course is unique for each individual, Gorski (88) has defined these recovery stages:

1. Transition: Starts when the individual begins to believe they have a problem with alcohol or drugs. It ends when the individual becomes willing to reach out for help.
2. Stabilization: The patient completes the physical withdrawal and post-acute withdrawal. Both physical and emotional healing begin. The obsession from drug and/or alcohol use subsides. The physician-patient begins to feel hope and develop motivation for recovery.
3. Early Recovery: A time of internal change when the recovering physician begins to let go of painful feelings about his or her disease (guilt, shame, fear, resentment, etc). The compulsion to use alcohol and/or drugs vanishes. The reliance on nonchemical coping skills to address life problems and situations, that use to trigger chemical use, strengthens.
4. Middle Recovery: Balance begins to be restored. The wreckage of the past is cleaned up. Relationships are developed that positively reinforce learned skills that ensure continued personal growth.
5. Late Recovery: Resolution of painful events and issues related to growing up in a dysfunctional family must occur.
6. Maintenance: The recovering physician begins to practice the principles of successful recovery in all daily activities.

PHPs that are responsive to the changing needs of the recovering physician, monitor the stages of recovery thoroughly, and use every resource available to help each individual physician become recovery-prone may ultimately be the most successful.

PREVENTION

The AMA has provided leadership in the prevention of chemical dependence and early rehabilitation for physicians with addiction. Every state medical society now has a stated policy and a committee on physician impairment. The Federation of State Medical Boards has suggested guidelines for the relationship between the impaired physicians program (PHPs) and the regulatory entity (89).

The definitions of terms and language for effective communication between treatment providers have been documented (90). Standardization of diagnoses (36), the measurement of illness severity (91), and the levels of care and intensities of treatment have been established (92). The science of matching addicted patients to specific kinds of treatment and treatment outcome research that links process with outcome (93) is evolving. A computerized master file of physician characteristics for comparative, randomized, stratified, and/or case-control studies has been developed and refined (94).

Recently, a uniform mechanism of data collection and the development of a collaborative process of investigating physician impairment have been proposed (65). This research would build upon prior multiprogram, clinically based research. Information gleaned from such an investigation would provide the foundation to improve drug abuse treatment into the next century. This research would have broad implications in the development of strategic prevention initiatives for the medical profession, for high-risk specialities, and for the general public.

How would a prospective study of physician impairment be significant? Doll and Hill (95), in a 10-year prospective epidemiological study of British doctors, were able to show for the first time that there appears to be a dose, frequency, and duration causal effect for mortality in relation to smoking.

This finding resulted in more focused investigations that have been the formation of a strategic national prevention effort (96) and public health policy on tobacco use.

Investigating chemical dependence in physicians may lead to a better understanding of the strength of association, the dose-response effect, the consistency of findings, the biologic plausibility, coherence of evidence and the specificity of the association of previously investigated risk factors for the development of addiction. Information about physician addiction, risk factors for the disease, ability to seek help and recover, and the long-term health consequences of drug and alcohol use might be applicable to the general population.

What are the psychological and behavioral effects of the drug(s) being used by patients? What is the incidence of psychiatric comorbidity in addicted patients? What is the patient's temporal state of substance use, along the continuum of intoxication, withdrawal, cognitive impairment, abstinence and recovery? These questions can be best answered by a prospective study of physician impairment. Recovering chemically dependent physicians:

1. Understand the need for research and most often are willing to participate in an investigation (if confidentiality can be guaranteed).
2. Can give a good history of their substance abuse patterns and present information about dose, frequency, and duration of drug and alcohol use.
3. Are monitored by PHPs for a minimum of five years to obtain multidimensional outcome measures.
4. Are easily tracked because of licensing requirements.
5. Are a source for comparative analysis available through the AMA master file (94).

It is the responsibility of every physician to become involved in the prevention of alcohol, tobacco, and other drug problems. Recovering physicians have through the treatment of their own illness a heightened awareness of the disease of chemical dependence. Traditionally, physicians in recovery have had a primary role in prevention as practitioners, as educators, as consultants to policy makers, and as concerned citizens. Through their recovery, there is a positive "ripple effect" of prevention into their families, patients, colleagues, and within the communities they serve.

REGULATORY ISSUES AND ETHICAL CONSIDERATIONS

The Federation of State Medical Boards (FSMB) has proposed guidelines to promote uniformity in rules and regulations regarding impaired physicians. The goal of the Federation is to protect the public. Efforts to educate citizens and the dissemination of information to the public about physician impairment have been initiated. The Federation also communicates with the AMA, state medical boards, state medical societies, and administrators in medicine. When appropriate, the Federation pursues federal and state legislative initiatives to provide improved powers to state medical boards for the supervision of impaired physicians (97).

Monitoring of recovering physicians by PHPs provides a sensitive and specific mechanism for detecting relapsed chemically dependent physicians. There is concern that informed consent disclosure will compromise the privacy and employment rights of physicians and that rigorous monitoring should protect the welfare of patients (98). Others contend that when physicians who seek help are automatically sanctioned by regulatory agencies, there will be fewer referrals of chemically dependent physicians to PHPs. State medical societies and state medical boards often become distrustful of each other (99) and may work at cross purposes.

Talbott (100) expressed concern about the discrimination against recovering physicians by (a) licensing agencies, (b) managed care organizations, and (c) clinics, hospitals, or partnerships. Because of anecdotal reports made by physicians who have gone through treatment for chemical dependence and lack of documented information, careful consideration of each report and its relationship to the Americans With Disabilities Act (ADA) (101) and an "action response" were proposed.

The ADA is a federal civil rights law which states that:

No covered entity shall discriminate against a qualified individual with a disability because of the disability of such individual in regard to job application procedures, the hiring, advancement of employees, or discharge of employees, employee compensations, job training, and other terms, conditions and privileges of employment. (101)

The spirit of the ADA is a "case-by-case" assessment of risk and the evaluation of risk "must be based on the behavior of the particular disabled person, not merely on generalizations about the disability" (102). When recovering physicians are carefully and closely monitored by the appropriate means, there has so far been no documented risk or harm to a patient.

Recently, an organization of full and part-time medical directors of PHPs has gathered to form the Federation of State Physician Health Programs (FSPHP). "The Federation provides a forum for the exchange of information between State Physician Health Programs (PHPs) and promotes the safety and well-being of the public and the State Medical Associations' PHPs. The final goal of the Federation is to promote early identification prior to the illness impacting upon the care of patients" (97). The FSPHP is developing a closer relationship with the AMA and the FSMB. Encouragement has attended the formation of the FSPHP. A common ground can be established that links organized concern for sick doctors to social, legal, and political pressures of professional accountability. The medical profession has recognized alcoholism and drug addiction as a disease. The medical control of impaired physicians in terms of its compatibilities with professional values and interests has demonstrated that when conflicting, but overriding considerations are put into action, a partnership can form. This partnership is capable of meeting the demands of disparate forces ultimately resulting in improved safety to the public while maximizing the personal rights of recovering physicians.

CONCLUSION

Wright has stated that "Impaired physicians are to the rest of the profession as the canary was to the coal miners of another generation. Until we can determine the risk of addiction to drugs for a specific individual before the individual is exposed to them, we must rely on the experience of the most vulnerable individuals in our occupational cohort to learn how to protect ourselves from the chemical tools of our trade" (6).

In recent years, many stakeholders who guard public safety and the practice of medicine (the AMA, FSMBE, medical and specialty societies, ASAM, regulatory agencies, FSPHP and others) have joined forces to find solutions to the "challenging" issues of physician substance abuse. Changes in the landscape of health care delivery have diverted the attention of many practitioners away from the compassionate concern for colleagues who have become impaired by chemical dependence. In spite of significant improvements in identification, intervention, assessment, treatment, and aftercare and monitoring, much is still unknown about the nature of chemical dependence.

References

1. Starr P. The social transformation of American medicine. New York: Basic Books, 1982.
2. Harris L. Consumers perception of substance abuse by health care providers. Research abstracts presented at the AMA Eighth National Conference on Impaired Health Professionals. Chicago, 1987.
3. Steindler E. Physician impairment: past, present, and future. J Med Assoc GA 1974;73:741–743.
4. Nesbitt J. The sick doctor statute: a new approach to an old problem. Fed Bull 1970;70:266–279.
5. American Medical Association Council on Mental Health. The sick physician: impairment bypsychiatric disorders, including alcoholism and drug dependence. JAMA 1973;233:684–687.
6. Wright C. Physician addiction to pharmaceuticals: personal history, practice setting, access to drugs and recovery. MD Med J 1990;39:1021–1025.
7. Robinson J. Annotated bibliography on physician impairment and well-being. Chicago: American Medical Association. 1986.
8. American Medical Association. International Conference on Physician Health. Uncertain times: preventing illness, promoting wellness. Chandler, AZ, 1996.

9. Centrella M. Physician addiction and impairment—current thinking: a review. J Addict Dis 1994;13:91–105.

10. Watry A, Morgan D, Earley P, Gallegos K, et al. Georgia composite state board of medical examiners guidelines for problem physicians. Paper presented at the American Medical Association International Conference on Physician Health. Uncertain times: preventing illness, promoting wellness. Chandler, AZ, 1996.

11. Noland S. William S. Halsted: idiosyncrasies of a surgical legend. Harvard Med Alum Bull 1991;65:17–23.

12. Paget J. What becomes of medical students. St. Bartholomew's Hospital Rep 1869;5:238–242.

13. Mattison J. Morphinism in medical men. JAMA 1984;23:186–188.

14. Partlow WD. Alcoholism and drug addiction among physicians of Alabama. Trans Med Assoc AL 1914:685–691.

15. DeQuincy T. Confessions of an English opium eater. New York: Heritage Press, 1950:38–39.

16. Pescor MJ. Physician drug addicts. Dis Nerv Syst 1942;3:2–3.

17. Stimson G, Oppenheimer B, Stimson C. Drug abuse in the medical profession. Br J Addict 1984;79:395–402.

18. Ehrhardt H. Drug addiction in medical and allied professionals in Germany. Bull Narcotics 1959;11:18–26.

19. Modlin H, Montes A. Narcotic addiction in physicians. Am J Psychiatry 1964;121:358–363.

20. Flexner A. Medical education in the United States and Canada. Bulletin No. 4. New York: Carnegie Foundation for the Advancement of Teaching, 1910.

21. Musto D. The American disease: origins of narcotic control. New Haven, CT: Yale University Press, 1973.

22. Pub L No. 63–233. Approved December 7, 1914.

23. Stimson G, Oppenheimer B, Stimson C. Drug abuse in the medical profession. Br J Addict 1984;79:395–402.

24. Caston S. Prohibition: the lie of the land. New York: The Free Press, 1981.

25. Pub L No. 75–238. Approved, August 2, 1937.

26. Keeve J. Physicians at risk: some epidemiologic considerations of alcoholism, drug abuse, and suicide. J Occup Med 1984;26:503–508.

27. Wollot H, Lambert J. Drug addiction among Quebec physicians. Can Med Assoc J 1982;126:927–930.

28. East W. The British government report to the United Nations on the traffic of opium and other dangerous drugs. Br J Addict 1947;46:38–39.

29. Clatt M. Alcoholism and drug dependence in doctors and nurses. Br Med J 1968;1:380–381.

30. A'Brook M, Hailstone J, McLauchlan I. Psychiatric illness in the medical profession. Br J Psychiatry 1967;113:1013–1023.

31. Watterson D. Psychiatric illness in the medical profession: incidence in relation to sex and field of practice. Can Med Assoc J 1976;115:311–317.

32. Vincent MO, Robinson EA, Latt L. Physicians as patients: private psychiatric hospital experience. Can Med Assoc J 1969;100:403–412.

33. Brewster J. Prevalence of alcohol and other drug problems among physicians. JAMA 1986;255:1913–1920.

34. Hughes P, Brandenburg N, Baldwin D, et al. Prevalence of substance use among U.S. physicians. JAMA 1992;267:2333–2339.

35. Robins L, Regier D. Psychiatric disorders in America: the epidemiologic catchment area study. New York: The Free Press, 1991.

36. American Psychiatric Association. Diagnostic and statistical manual of mental disorders. 3rd edition revised. Washington, DC: American Psychiatric Association, 1987.

37. Regier D, et al. Co-morbidity of mental disorders with alcohol and other drug abuse: results of the epidemiologic catchment area (ECA) study. JAMA 1990;264:2511–2518.

38. Halzer J, Burnam A, McEvoy L. Alcohol abuse and dependence. In: Robins LN, Regier DA, eds. Psychiatric disorders in America: the epidemiologic catchment area study. New York: The Free Press, 1991:81–115.

39. Anthony J, Hetzer J. Syndrome of drug abuse and dependence. In: Robins LN, Regier DA, eds. Psychiatric disorders in America: the epidemiologic catchment area study. New York: The Free Press, 1991:116–154.

40. Talbott GD, Wright C. Chemical dependence in healthcare professionals. Occup Med 1987;2:581–591.

41. Vaillant GE, Soborale NC, McArthur C. Some psychologic vulnerabilities of physicians. N Engl J Med 1972;287:372–375.

42. Richman JA. Occupational stress, psychological vulnerability and alcohol-related problems over time in future physicians. Alcohol Clin Exp Res 1992;16(2):166–171.

43. Moore R. Youthful precursors of alcohol abuse in physicians. Am J Med 1990;88:332–336.

44. Gallegos K, Browne C, Veit F, Talbott G. Addiction in anesthesiologists: drug access and patterns of substance abuse. Quality Review Bull 1988:116–122.

45. Jex S, et al. Relations among stressors, strains, and substance use among resident physicians. Int J Addict 1992;27:479–494.

46. Vaillant G. Physician, cherish thyself: the hazards of self prescribing. JAMA 1992;267:2373–2374.

47. McAuliffe WE, Santangelo S, Magnuson E, Sobol A, Rohman M, Weissman J. Risk factors of drug impairment in random samples of physicians and medical students. Int J Addict 1987;22(9):825–841.

48. Talbott G, Gallegos K, Wilson P, Porter T. The medical association of Georgia's impaired physician program—review of the first 1,000 physicians: analysis of specialty. JAMA 1987;257:2927–2930.

49. Bissell L, Haberman P. Alcoholism in the professions. New York: Oxford University Press, 1984.

50. Vaillant G, Clark W, et al. Prospective study of alcoholism treatment. Am J Med 1983;75:455–463.

51. Bissell L, Skorina J. One hundred alcoholic women in medicine: an interview study. JAMA 1987;257:2939–2944.

52. Blume S. Women, alcohol, and drugs. In: Miller NS, ed. Comprehensive handbook of drug and alcohol addiction. New York: Marcel Dekker, 1991:147–177.

53. Talbott G, Gallegos K. Intervention with health professionals. Addict Recovery 1990;10(3):13–16.

54. Hoffman N, Halikas J, Mee-Lee D. Patient placement criteria for the treatment of psychoactive substance use disorders. 2nd edition. Washington, DC: American Society of Addiction Medicine, 1996.

55. Talbott G, Martin C. Treating impaired physicians: fourteen keys to success. VA Med J 1986;113:95–99.

56. Kosten T, Kleber H. Differential diagnoses of psychiatric comorbidity in substance abusers. J Subst Abuse Treat 1988;5:201–206.

57. Catalano R, Howard M, Hawkins J, Wells E. Relapse in the addictions: rates, determinants, and promising prevention strategies. In: 1988 Surgeon General's report on health consequences of smoking. Washington, DC: U.S. Government Printing Office, 1986.

58. Robinson E, Fitzgerald J, Gallegos K. Brain functioning and addiction: what neuropsychologic studies reveal. J Med Assoc GA 1985;73:74–79.

59. Smith P, Smith D. Treatment outcomes of impaired physicians in Oklahoma. J Oklahoma State Med Assoc 1991;84:599–603.

60. Shore J. The Oregon experience with impaired physicians on probation. JAMA 1987;257:2931–2934.

61. Alcoholics Anonymous. 2nd edition. New York: Alcoholics Anonymous World Services, 1972.

62. Gordis E. Relapse and craving. Alcohol Alert. Rockville, MD: U.S. Department of Health and Human Services, National Institute on Alcohol Abuse and Alcoholism, 1989;6:3.

63. Wall J. The results of hospital treatment of addiction in physicians. Fed Bull 1958;45:144–152.

64. Jones L. How 92% beat the dope habit. Bulletin of the Los Angeles County Medical Society 1958;19:37–40.

65. Gallegos K. The pilot impaired physicians epidemiologic surveillance system (PIPESS). MD Med J 1987;36:264–266.

66. Reading E. Nine years experience with chemically dependent physicians: the New Jersey experience. MD Med J 1992;41:325–329.

67. Gallegos K, Lubin B, Bowers C, Blevins J, et al. Relapse and recovery: five to ten year follow study of chemically dependent physicians—the Georgia experience. MD Med J 1992;41:315–319.

68. Gallegos K, Norton, M. Characterization of Georgia's impaired physicians program treatment population: data and statistics. J Med Assoc GA 1984;73:755–758.

69. Morse R, et al. Prognosis of physicians treated for alcoholism and drug dependence. JAMA 1984;251:743–746.

70. Harrington R, et al. Treating substance-use disorders among physicians. JAMA 1982:2253–2257.

71. Johnson R, Connelly, J. Addicted physicians: a closer look. JAMA 1981;245:253–257.

72. Kliner D, Spicer J, Barnett P. Treatment outcome of alcoholic physicians. J Stud Alcohol 1980;41:1217–1220.

73. Goby M, Bradley N, Bespalec D. Physicians treated for alcoholism: a follow-up study. Alcohol Clin Exp Res 1979;3:121–124.

74. Goetz R. Personal communication, June, 1996.

75. Alpern F, et al. A study of recovering Maryland physicians. MD Med J 1992;41:301–303.

76. Ulwelling J. The evolution of the Oregon program for impaired physicians. Am Coll Surg Bull 1991;76:18–21.

77. Gallegos K, Keppler J, Wilson P. Returning to work after rehabilitation: aftercare, follow-up and workplace reliability. Occup Med 1989;4:357–371.

78. Miscal B. Monitoring recovering physicians: the New Mexico experience. Am Coll Surg Bull 1991;76:22–40.

79. Summer G. Personal communication, June, 1996.

80. Galanter M, Talbott G, Gallegos K, Rubenstone E. Combined alcoholics anonymous and professional care for addicted physicians. Am J Psychiatry 1990;147:64–68.

81. Talbott G. Reducing relapse in health providers and professionals. Psychiatr Ann 1995;25:11:669–672.

82. Crowley T. Doctor's drug abuse reduced during contingency-contracting treatment. Alcohol Drug Res 1986;6:299–307.

83. Centrella M. Physician addiction and impairment—current thinking: a review. J Addict Dis 1994;13:91–105.

84. Kurtz E. Why AA works. J Stud Alcohol 1982; 43:38–80.

85. Gorski T. Staying sober: a guide for relapse prevention. Independence, MO: Independence Press, 1986.

86. Gorski T. The relapse and recovery grid. Center City, MN: Hazelden, 1989.

87. Valliant G. Natural history of alcoholism. Cambridge, MA: Harvard University Press, 1983.

88. Gorski T. Passages through recovery: an action plan for preventing relapse. Center City, MN: Hazelden, 1989.

89. Rasseth H, et al. Ad hoc committee on physician impairment [report]. Euless, TX: Federation of State Medical Boards, September, 1994.

90. Rinaldi RC, Steindler EM, Wilford BB, Goodwin D. Clarification and standardization of substance abuse terminology. JAMA 1988;259:555–557.

91. Mee-Lee D. An instrument for patient progress and treatment assignment: The Recovery Attitude and Treatment Evaluator (RAATE). J Subst Abuse Treat 1988;5:1883–1886.

92. Mee-Lee D. Patient placement criteria and patient-treatment matching. In: Principles of addiction medicine. Section IX, Chapter 3, Clinical overview of addiction treatment. Washington, DC: American Society of Addiction Medicine, 1974.

93. Filstead W, Parrella D, Ross A, Norton E. Key issues in outcomes research. In: Principles of addiction medicine. Section X, Chapter 5. Management of addiction treatment. Washington, DC: American Society of Addiction Medicine, 1994.

94. Robeck G, Randolph L, Mead D, et, al. Physician characteristics and distribution in the U.S. Chicago: American Medical Association, 1993.

95. Doll T, Hill S. Mortality in relation to smoking: ten years' observation of British doctors. Br Med J 1964;1:1399–1410, 1460–1467.

96. U.S. Department of Health and Human Services. Reducing the health consequence of smoking: 25 years of progress. A report of the surgeon general. Rockville, MD: Office of Smoking and Health, 1989.

97. Summer G. Personal communication, June 19, 1996.

98. Ackerman T. Chemically dependent physician and informal consent disclosure. J Addict Dis 1996;15:25–42.

99. Ikoda R, Pelton C. Diversion programs for impaired physicians. West J Med 1990;152: 617–621.

100. Talbott G. Personal communication, April, 1996.

101. Pub L No. 101–336, 104 Stat 327, 1990.

102. House of Representatives Rep. No 485, 101st Congress, 2nd Sec. (part 2) 56, (part 3) 46 (1990); Reprinted in US Code Cong Admin News,1990;4:338–469.

75 COMMUNITY ACTION PROGRAMS

Charles Winick and Mary Jo Larson

In the continuing debates over how to combat substance abuse in the United States, community action programs (CAPs), designed to mobilize local resources to reduce alcohol, tobacco, and other drug (ATOD) problems, have assumed growing significance. The initial focus of these programs (sometimes called community-wide or community-based coalitions) was primary prevention but many now include secondary prevention, treatment, law enforcement, and larger social change goals. Their targets have expanded from tobacco and alcohol to include illegal drugs, such as crack and heroin and from single to multiple substances. This chapter will examine the development of and rationale for CAPs, describe some examples, discuss three large national programs and collateral activities, and comment on the evaluation and future of CAPs. Programs that have a research or evaluation component will be the primary focus.

CAPs are designed to influence how community members think about and use ATOD. CAPs are more broad-based than focused interventions deriving from one entity like a health or educational institution (1). Nevertheless, CAPs typically include specific components, such as school-based educational efforts and drunk driving initiatives. Some programs focus on a single substance, such as alcohol. CAPs may emerge from the government or voluntary sectors and operate in a community that can be either a geopolitical entity (e.g., city or county), a geographic area (e.g., a neighborhood), or a specific ethnic group. The emergence of CAPs reflects concern about piecemeal approaches to substance abuse prevention and a belief that systemic changes will only result from community-wide policy and environmental changes.

The concept of community mobilization to deal with such problems is not new but it has been implemented on a major scale only over the last several decades, as there is growing realization that all elements in the community are affected by its substance abuse problems. CAPs, or similar initiatives, are found in many countries and settings (2–4). Whatever the venue, CAPs offer a way to reduce perceived overlap of services or policies and develop targeted and integrated ATOD programs.

DEVELOPMENT OF CAPs

Voluntary community action to address alcohol use in the United States first appeared in the 1830s as temperance societies (5). In England and Scandinavia, during the early twentieth century, a number of community programs developed as well to deal with alcohol problems (6, 7). Around the same time in America, CAPs were begun to provide and coordinate services that had become necessary because of large-scale immigration and industrialization. During the 1960s, contemporary models of community action became a central feature of the federal government's antipoverty program (8).

The health CAP era began in the 1970s, after an influential community cardiovascular disease prevention study conducted in three communities by Stanford University (9). One community received a media program, a second received media messages plus group interaction activities and a third acted as a control. After three years, the group interaction community was the most successful on behavioral measures that predicted future risk of cardiovascular disease. The original three-city study was later extended to five sites and other multiple component psychosocial community action prevention programs, designed to prevent the onset of cardiovascular disease, followed (10). Major risk factors for heart disease—smoking, high blood pressure, and poor diet—are so prevalent that comprehensive social influence interventions directed at the whole community were hypothesized to be more effective than targeting high-risk persons.

Some features of the cardiovascular trials were later adopted in community-based substance abuse programs. Community programs that seek to prevent either cardiovascular disease or ATOD abuse have common concerns: issues in community leadership, organization, time, resources, research design, scale, and behavioral objectives. Also important to both are the role of the mass media in setting agenda and the relationship between mass media and interpersonal communication (11–13). The first modern CAPs that targeted substance abuse addressed alcohol problems, because alcohol abuse was widely prevalent and because alcohol was subject to regulation (14). Many community-based alcohol initiatives conducted in the 1970s assessed their impact by collecting survey data and social indicators but typically did not collect information on factors such as community dynamics and the factors associated with substance abuse effects (15).

The early as well as more recent alcohol CAPs tend to have preintervention, intervention, and postintervention phases. They typically involve five tasks: conceptualization; community mobilization; intervention planning, development, and implementation; monitoring and assessment; and dissemination and application (16).

In the 1970s, an influential alcohol project was begun in three countries by the World Health Organization (WHO) (17). The Scottish project used a social planning model, the Mexican program emphasized locality development, and Zambia utilized a social action approach. The WHO study led to programs in Poland and other European countries (18).

A reflection of the vigorous activity in the field was the first international CAP symposium in Ontario, Canada, in 1989. Twenty community reports were presented, including nine from Canada and five from the United States. A second symposium, in 1992 in San Diego, heard reports from the United States (7), Canada (6), and other countries (8). Both meetings were cosponsored by the Addiction Research Foundation of Canada and the U.S. Center for Substance Abuse Prevention (CSAP) or its 1989 predecessor and dealt with the details and challenges of starting, operating, and evaluating CAPs. At both meetings, alcohol abuse was the primary focus, although other substance abuse problems were discussed (19, 20).

Probably the first effort to harness community energies to deal with drug abuse other than alcohol began in the 1970s with the American Social Health Association (ASHA). ASHA developed a format for organized community action and, by 1972, had formalized the approach into the United Drug Abuse Councils (UDAC). The UDAC model involved integration of community components dealing with prevention and education, treatment and rehabilitation, and control and law enforcement (21). The UDAC model was implemented in a number of Ohio and California communities.

AIDS problems became another focus of CAPs in the early 1980s (22). Since a special goal was reduction in the spread of AIDS associated with intravenous drug abuse, a number of cities created CAPs that attempted to minimize AIDS-related harm for intravenous drug abusers and their sexual partners and children.

The power of the CAP format could also be seen in the 1980s in another AIDS context when gay men in San Francisco, New York, and other cities created innovative community coalitions that successfully initiated a range of prevention, education, treatment, and political advocacy activities (23). The campaign for safer sex among gay men "may be the most intensive public health intervention ever" and influenced the whole social system (24).

RATIONALE OF CAPs

Approaches and theory drawn from several disciplines have been applied to an emerging rationale for the efforts to reduce demand for the target substances via CAPs: community development and organization, social learning, a diffusion-innovation model, social marketing, a communication-behavior-change model, social/structural analysis, stepping stone approaches to substance use, a distribution of consumption model, and behavior modification (25–33). CAPs draw on community development and health promotion, which emphasize public participation (34). For example, community development involves informed citizens evaluating needs, establishing priorities, and making policy (35).

These approaches hold in common a belief that the etiology of substance abuse is complex, with both individual and community-level risk factors. So, for example, communities with easy access to alcohol or greater availability of illegal drugs are presumed to place youth and other individuals at greater risk of exposure to ATOD problems. Community factors may be structural, environmental, or social, and one rationale for CAPs is that multiple strategy, community-wide initiatives are the best approach to changing these factors. The public health leadership, since the nineteenth century, has launched many community-oriented, rather than individual-focused, interventions for other infectious diseases and environmental conditions (36). ATOD models that rely on the public health model use multiple strategies designed to target all levels and change the host (behavior of individuals), the agent (availability or access), and the social environment as well as the manner in which these three interact. CAPs address attitudes, norms, and behavior and their interactions in peer, family, and community levels.

The universal premise underlying CAPs is that substance use is seldom restricted to any subgroup and is embedded in community norms and support systems. A CAP can address underlying structural, ecological, and cultural factors associated with substance abuse whereas traditional programs focus on individual pathology (37). A comprehensive CAP includes a multistrategy, multisystem range of program channels in order to increase intervention exposure, reinforce community support of substance abuse prevention practices and of a social norm for non-ATOD use, and provide means to resist pro-ATOD influences.

High-risk populations, hard to reach by traditional means, could be accessible to CAPs that are based in the general population rather than clients of social agencies (38). Single component stand-alone programs are less likely to be effective, especially for long-term effect maintenance, than multifaceted community activities at multiple levels of social organization, that address several levels of needs in a cost effective manner, coordinate resources to meet those needs, and contribute to increased involvement by community members (39, 40). Social capital, or the program's ability to implement access to social networks involving norms of cooperation, is an important element in achievement of CAP goals (41, 42). The mutual interest, investment of effort, and earned trust that represent social capital strengthen a community's ability to cope with its substance abuse problems.

Theoretical demand models can be translated into prevention programs to reduce alcoholism (43). In the community action framework against alcohol problems developed by Torjman, the person is discouraged from using alcohol, and interventions are directed at reducing harm (44). Environmental goals involve reducing the risks of alcohol use in specific contexts and dimensions of marketing like price and availability.

Programs directed to drug abuse other than alcohol often have a different rationale from those with an alcoholism focus. For example, the "communities that care" approach to drug abuse, adopted in a number of states, targets risk factors such as economic and social deprivation, low neighborhood attachment, community disorganization, transitions and mobility, community laws and norms, and drug availability (45). This approach also emphasizes protective factors that can contribute to a broad base of support for behavior change that is lasting, as resources are reallocated to reduce risk.

TWO EXAMPLES OF CAPs

Of the many CAPs, two that have reported significant achievements provide examples of programs that address different aspects of substance use. The Miami program focuses on use of illegal drugs in the whole community. The Midwest Prevention Project, in contrast, targets a defined population of young people in terms of primary and secondary prevention of their use of specific substances.

Miami

The Miami coalition against illegal drugs began in 1988 as a response to widespread crack use (46). Its board of directors has 110 business, civic, and private sector representatives. The coalition operates through specific task forces: neighborhood, international, law enforcement, religious, schools, treatment, and workplace. From 1990 through 1995, it was funded by CSAP.

Miami has expanded abuser intake, treatment, and reentry and mounted a comprehensive neighborhood and education campaign. Its Drug Court, the first in the country, diverts first-time drug possession felony offenders into treatment. Media coverage of drug matters has increased substantially and a student advisory board was developed. There has been extensive special training for ministers and other religious leaders. Miami has donated more local media resources to antidrug messages than any other city. Over 2000 crack houses were closed, and drug dealing areas have been reclaimed. There was a very sharp drop in the number of beginning cocaine and heroin users seeking help at ERs between 1990 and 1995, suggesting a decline in new users in the community (47).

Although the rest of the country showed an increase in 1993 drug use, as measured by the National Household Survey on Drug Abuse, compared with 1992, Miami had a decrease. Questions have been raised, however, about the possible effect of Hurricane Andrew in 1992, or other factors, on the national survey's sampling procedure and thus on the reported decrease (48).

Midwest Prevention Project

A long standing CAP demonstration, now in its tenth year, the Midwestern Prevention Project (MPP) targets tobacco, alcohol, and marihuana and, secondarily, use of "harder" drugs in adolescents (49, 50). The five program components were sequentially introduced into communities at the rate of six months to one year apart to minimize a drain on community resources and sustain interest (51). Media, school, and parent program components were directed at demand reduction; community organization and health policy changes sought supply reduction.

Changes in adolescent drug use are assumed by the researchers to represent an interaction among person, situation, and environmental factors. MPP results include significant reductions among target compared with control subjects in tobacco (25% versus 31%) and marihuana use (12% versus 20%) and equivalent reductions for youth at different levels of risk (52). There were no differences in alcohol use. In public and private schools in Indianapolis, the MPP multicomponent CAP was more effective in decreasing the prevalence rates of marihuana and tobacco use at all levels than standard school-based health education and drug prevention. There was a significant gain rather than the decay in effectiveness that has been reported by other studies by the third year of the follow-up. Some secondary prevention effects, especially on baseline alcohol and cigarette use, were reported (53, 54).

ALCOHOL-TARGETED CAPs

Alcohol-targeted CAPs have some unique strategies related to alcohol regulation, advertising, and distribution. The CAPs described below convey the elements of some representative programs.

In Rhode Island, alcoholic beverage servers and police were special foci of a program (55). Arrest rates increased in the intervention site in contrast to two comparison sites. Emergency room (ER) visit rates for assault injuries dropped by 21% in the intervention site, versus a 4% increase in the comparison sites, between 1986 and 1987. Vehicle crash injury visit rates at ERs declined 10%, versus a 12% increase for the companion sites.

In Massachusetts, the cities in the Saving Lives Program were compared, over five years, with the rest of the state (56). Programs included media and business information campaigns, drunk driving awareness days, telephone speed hotlines, police training, student chapters, alcohol-free prom nights, beer keg registrations, police checkpoints, crosswalk signs, liquor outlet surveillance, preschool education, and hospital staff training. The test communities spent approximately $1 per inhabitant annually for the program. Hingson and his colleagues (56) found that the program cities had 25% fewer crash fatalities, and 42% fewer alcohol-related crash fatalities, 5% fewer crash injuries, 17% more seat belt use, and a 43% greater decline in speeding than the rest of the state.

Successful outcomes were also reported by Minnesota's Project Northland, a three-year, multilevel, community-wide program targeting 6th grade students to prevent or reduce alcohol use (57). Innovative school and parent activities, ordinance enactment, community opinion leaders, theater, and substantial community task forces were involved. The baseline nonusers, at the end of the intervention, were significantly less likely to drink at all levels of use than students in comparison districts. Northland's facilitation of community participation multiplied the impact of its themes by targeting both young adolescents and their environments.

Control is sometimes the theme of alcohol-targeted CAPs and was the key goal of CAPs directed at the excesses of the heavy drinking spring break celebrations of college students (58, 59). In Fort Lauderdale and Daytona Beach in Florida and Cancun in Mexico, organized community programs achieved a sharp reduction in the violence, rowdiness, and other alcohol-related problems caused by the several hundred thousand students visiting each city in a concentrated time period.

Alcohol CAPs have been effective in nonurban settings, as in a program that addressed the problem of adolescent alcohol abuse on a Native American reservation in a western Plains state (60). The community action group engaged in alcohol- and drug-free events, skills development programs, public campaigns, and classes. Binge drinking and driving after drinking showed considerable declines in the reservation population, compared with control communities.

Outcome data are not yet available from Communities Mobilizing for Change on Alcohol (CMCA), a CAP directed at alcohol use among those under 21. Operating in 18 communities, CMCA employs a standardized mobilization model but permits each community to select whatever strategies are most relevant for its problems (61). Results will also be forthcoming from the three trial communities of the Prevention Research Center Project, which seeks to reduce alcohol-related accidents and fatalities and has five components: community mobilization; server training; retailer, parent, and community education; better Driving Under the Influence (DUI) enforcement; and better ordinance enforcement (62).

DRUG CONTROL PROGRAMS

Some CAPs have a control and law enforcement dimension but others concentrate on such issues. In Tampa, for example, the citywide Quick Attack on Drugs dealt with a major street crack-dealing problem (63). The police developed techniques for communicating with citizens without exposing them to retaliation and a response was guaranteed to every complaint. All city departments were involved in the monitoring of conditions. Dealers who could not be arrested were inconvenienced. High visibility conditions like poor lighting and abandoned buildings were promptly improved (the "broken windows" theory) to discourage use as drug sites. In a few years, the street drug trade was all but dead. As in the Massachusetts Saving Lives alcohol program, the broad community mobilization was more important to the program's success than any single feature of it.

Operation Push Out the Pusher (POP), a Miami neighborhood program in a high drug-crime neighborhood, helped to clear the streets of pushers, and provided job placement services and parent training. A study of POP and three comparable neighborhood efforts found that all the programs had significant positive effects (64).

In the Department of Justice's Community Responses to Drug Abuse (CRDA), the communities first developed an approach and then obtained funding to implement it over a three-year period, beginning in 1989 (65).

The CAPs in the 10 participating communities implemented public advocacy and community empowerment activities. In each case, the target area had a high rate of substance abuse, unemployment, and crime. The CRDA organization's strategies fell into five categories: organizing the community around drug issues, strengthening enforcement, protecting youth, treating drug users, and developing the community.

The CRDA organizations generally moved from law enforcement to broader strategies. A similar progression has characterized many other communities that began their programs by reclaiming neighborhoods from drug dealers and became much more broad-based. A success experience, like seeing crack houses closed, provide tangible achievement that encourages citizens to consider new dimensions of cooperative social action that are relevant to other aspects of ATOD problems.

NATIONAL EXPANSION OF CAPs

Two new national programs led to an enormous expansion of CAPs in the late 1980s, in terms of goals, number, innovations, support, length, and evaluation. In 1988, the Fighting Back (FB) program was announced by the Robert Wood Johnson Foundation (RWJF). The following year, the federal government's CSAP initiated the Community Partnership Demonstration Program (CPDP). Both organizations set ambitious goals and attacked the problems caused by ATOD by encouraging each community to develop its own action model, in contrast to the earlier cardiovascular and alcohol studies, in which researchers designed the intervention. In 1994, CSAP extended the Partnership idea in a third new program, the Community Prevention Coalitions Demonstration (CPCD).

Fighting Back (FB)

Fighting Back has the most ambitious goals and substantial support, over the longest period, of any CAP. The view that the effort to reduce demand had not been given a fair test became the basis for the FB program (66). RWJF had previously sponsored other notable innovative community action activities such as helping develop the 911 telephone emergency system, interfaith volunteer care giving, improving chronic health care, immunization monitoring, and comprehensive AIDS services. In addition to FB, other related drug abuse RWJF projects include Join Together, Community Anti-Drug Coalitions for America, the Partnership for a Drug-Free America, the Center on Addiction and Substance Abuse, Reducing Substance Abuse Among Native Americans, and Head Start Partnerships to Promote Substance-Free Communities.

FB had its National Program Office at the Vanderbilt University Medical School through 1996; the Office moved to Boston University early in 1997. The 14 communities that were selected after a national competitive process included portions of moderately large cities as well as smaller cities and counties (67). The goal is to demonstrate whether and how communities can reduce ATOD by coordinating and consolidating resources and strategies and creating a single community-wide system that reduces demand and harm by implementing prevention, early identification, treatment, and aftercare. The relatively lengthy planning phase encouraged broad participation and coalition formation.

A FB coalition is expected to be broad and deep and operates with a representative citizen task force that develops its own program. The coalition's aim, in addition to primary and secondary prevention, is to extend the continuum of care.

Five specific outcomes are targeted: a measurable and sustained reduction in the initiation of drug and alcohol use among children and adolescents; a reduction in drug and alcohol-related deaths and injuries, especially among children, adolescents, and young adults; a decline in the prevalence of health problems related to or exacerbated by drug and alcohol use; a reduction in on-the-job problems and injuries related to substance abuse; and a reduction in drug-related crime (68).

MINIMUM PROGRAM ELEMENTS

A FB community is intended to have a shared vision and link demand reduction programs and activities under an overall, unified strategy developed

Table 75.1   Fighting Back Grass Roots and Professional Community Initiated Strategies

Basis of Approach	Promote Neighborhood Cohesion	Change Social Environment/Social Norms	Strengthen Care Continuum for Individuals
Largely grassroots	Neighborhood cleanups	Community organizing for local problem identification, decision-making and action	Youth volunteer/community service programs, self-esteem leadership programs and conflict resolution
	Local economic development programs	Subcontracts to neighborhood groups	
			Alternative youth recreation, after school, summer opportunities
	Demolish abandoned buildings used by drug dealers	Clergy training and outreach	
		Billboard removals and code enforcement	Friendly visitors and peer counseling
	Restricting licenses for liquor outlets in certain areas	Gang prevention	Youth mentoring, peer counseling
	Renovating neighborhoods, including new housing	School culture and curriculum improvement	Services for recovering individuals, such as housing, job referrals, support groups, alternative recreational and social activities
	City beautification projects	Promoting drug-free college campuses	
		Workplace programs	
	Cultural arts programs	Public awareness materials and campaigns	Multiservice centers with ATOD assessments
	Street lighting near bars		Case management for ATOD clients
			Training for health professionals
			Parenting classes
			Youth academic assistance/dropout prevention
			Acupuncture
Largely professional			Diversion/ATOD treatment programs such as drug court and juvenile court

Adapted from Hallfors D. Fighting Back national evaluation: MIS. Waltham, MA: Brandeis University, unpublished manuscript.

by the citizens' task force. The strategy has at least four elements: a highly visible public awareness campaign to generate broad-based support; a multifaceted prevention effort for young people; a well-defined program, with training for professionals, of policies and procedures for the early identification, assessment, and initial referral into treatment of alcohol and drug users; and a broad range of accessible options for treatment and relapse prevention. All the sites have significant minority population and representative neighborhood organizations.

COMMUNITY STRATEGIES

Many communities adopted an early strategy that related to neighborhood redevelopment, public policy, and family support (69). Such initiatives are aimed at changing local systems' responses to alcohol and drug issues, closing gaps in prevention or treatment services, expanding youth prevention services, and building a sense of community. Two broad approaches to demand reduction have been adopted: (*a*) grassroots organizing, which empowers neighborhood residents, promotes cohesive neighborhoods, and facilitates communication between institutions and neighborhood residents; and (*b*) problem-solving approaches identified by prevention and treatment professionals (Table 75.1).

FB sites have supported grassroots initiatives that build neighborhood cohesion, empower residents to identify their own needs, and build an antidrug neighborhood identity. In New Haven, for example, neighborhood prevention initiatives were reorganized into neighborhood management teams comprised solely of residents. Each team serves as a link to police, religious institutions, city government, and social service and health care agencies. Its purpose is to create potent neighborhood resistance to substance abuse and advocate greater availability of meaningful alternative activities.

In Little Rock, identifying crack houses, breaking up gang violence, and organizing marches on property where drugs are sold are part of the work of the Neighborhood Alert Centers. Each Center has a neighborhood facilitator who surveys residents about problems and needs, and cooperates with relevant local officials. In Milwaukee, FB neighborhoods convinced companies to discontinue new billboard advertisements of tobacco and alcohol products as part of the community's Erase & Replace Campaign.

PROFESSIONAL-DRIVEN APPROACHES

Many program sites have relied upon professional networks, and others have successfully supported both grassroots and professional initiatives. Vallejo, California, has begun acupuncture services for people in aftercare and for those not yet in treatment; HMO physicians' groups meet with FB staff to identify current clinical practices.

Sites engage in a wide range of initiatives that promote a comprehensive, accessible treatment system (Table 75.2). These initiatives generally focus on one of three approaches: assessment or counseling services to high-risk individuals; system coordination, provider networking and training, strategies to address systemic access barriers; and advocacy that promotes treatment system expansions.

ASSESSMENT, COUNSELING, AND SYSTEMS COORDINATION

Some of the FB programs offer assessment and counseling services that link neighborhood residents with appropriate treatment. Concern about health care cost containment in Worcester, Massachusetts, for example, spawned a coalition of private insurance companies, Medicaid, managed care organizations, alcohol and drug treatment providers, and researchers.

Student participation in drug treatment programs tripled after the Little Rock FB started its Insure the Children program, which provided school-based substance abuse insurance for education, counseling, group therapy, and residential treatment for drug and alcohol problems for Little Rock's 26,000 students, for an average per pupil cost of about $12 a year (70).

In Kansas City, a referral tracking system for clients who had been linked with treatment facilities was started. FB in Santa Barbara trained police officers in substance abuse issues, which led to changes in the handling of substance abuse–related incidents. Some advocacy models lead to construction of new programs, while others seek expansion for existing treatment services. Marshall Heights in Washington, DC, with the highest levels of illegal drug use in the city, had no drug treatment. A FB task force brought drug treatment and social service programs into the neighborhood. In Vallejo, no resources were available for addicted pregnant women until FB facilitated a program, with counseling, support and training, and a halfway house. Both the Kansas City and the Little Rock

Table 75.2 Fighting Back Continuum of Care Initiatives

Assessment/Counseling Services	System Coordination/Training/Access Barriers	Service Expansion
Emergency Room (ER) counseling and early intervention by staff	Computer network system for treatment collaborative; catalogue community services	Establish recovery homes
Client follow-up and aftercare by neighborhood worker	Van service to treatment for pregnant women and children; co-location of services	Jail treatment groups established with matching funds from Sheriff (VA); advocacy for substance abuse (SA) counselors in ERs; Medicaid funding gained for services to students in schools
Medication compliance education for the elderly	Pilot of managed care program; managed care task force; link HMO and SA community providers	Funded to construct detox center
Criminal justice diversion/early intervention; Assessment and counseling for court-referred juvenile offenders	Coordinate treatment and ancillary services for Drug Court	Award grants to provide outreach and early intervention services and to treatment programs
Provision of acupuncture services	Insure the Children initiative to develop a specialized SA insurance program for adolescents	Housing authority persuaded to redevelop community nursing home for detox and treatment center
Student assistance; healthy lifestyles workshops; SA workshops in schools	Neighborhood Support Center which places clients into treatment	Develop Women's Treatment Center through CSAP grant submissions; gain funding for day care at treatment program
Abstinence counseling program, treatment program, and HIV counseling	Native American Treatment Task Force	Establish first neighborhood intake and counseling services site
Follow-up on people in recovery, job referrals, treatment referrals; resume development	New protocol to assess public inebriates for treatment	Advocacy to distribute ½ cent sales tax funds to treatment programs
Treatment group in jail	Develop continuum of care criteria Train ER to recognize SA; train minority applicants in counseling skills	

sites successfully advocated incremental sales tax increases (1/4% and 1/2%, respectively) with funds dedicated to treatment and prevention services.

EVALUATION

FB is being evaluated in a large quasi-experiment. Its goal is to assess the success of the national FB program, including what types of initiatives were implemented, whether or not there were measurable reductions in targeted outcomes, and any systemic change in civic infrastructure resulting from coalition activities (67). Data on the program's impact on substance abuse–related harm are being compared with data from two to three comparison communities in each of the FB site states. Systemic change in the treatment system is evaluated with ethnographic and site histories. Survey data on trends in treatment use and alcohol and drug use behaviors are collected. Rates of change in alcohol and other drug abuse deaths, arrest trends, traffic fatalities, homicides and other crimes, hospitalizations, and hospital discharges are among the social indicators being studied.

Community Partnership Demonstration Program (CPDP)

With authorization from the Anti-Drug Abuse Act of 1988, CSAP developed the CPDP and has awarded grants to 252 partnerships from Alaska to the Virgin Islands. Two cohorts received five-year grants: 95 in 1990 and 157 in 1991. All partnerships use creative methods to build public-private partnerships, take a systems approach, and rely upon needs assessment, planning, and coordination. CPDP is unique in being in so many and varied communities.

The CPDP theory is that prevention activities are more likely to be effective and sustained when key local institutions and citizen's groups together organize strategies (71). A coalition promotes a community learning about prevention strategies that work best for the large neighborhood. Community development is an essential ingredient in the change process that is not addressed in traditional single-focus prevention programs that might, for example, aim solely to change values (72). Coalitions revitalize neighborhood institutions, allow citizens to participate in change, and empower the community to take control.

COMMUNITY DEVELOPMENT

An "enabling system" CAP model in New Jersey stresses training and consultation, information and referral, networking and coalition development, communications, incentive grants and recognition, public information and social marketing, and research and evaluation (73). The multilevel enabling system involves strengthening of citywide leadership, professionals, neighborhood institutions, and resident leaders around substance abuse issues. Based on this model, one partnership had established links among 18 institutions in one community and a second program had integrated 97 institutions in its community. They started family resource centers, a health care enterprise zone to attract health-related businesses, job and health fairs, block and tenant organizing a youth leadership institute, community policing, and a community development corporation. Another variation is the "bottom-up" approach, which empowers neighborhood organizations to develop their own prevention strategies and establish linking mechanisms, as used by the Milwaukee Neighborhood Partners (74).

PREVENTION NETWORK BUILDING

In addition to community development, a second Partnership prevention approach focuses upon developing services, addressing community and individual risk factors, and building community and individual resiliency. The focus is prevention system change or new programs, strategies, power relations, systems, employee assistance programs, culturally-specific models and policies (75). Coalitions are engaged in network-building activities: public education, education and skills programs, alternative activities, and public policy changes (76).

One Winston-Salem coalition committee developed a strategic treatment plan and strategic prevention plan (77). It promoted alternatives to incarceration and a treatment education program at the county detention center. It also trained treatment agencies in assessment criteria, and supported local policy related to zoning for halfway houses and alternatives to incarceration. The District of Columbia Partnership sponsored workshops on HIV, women, drug abuse diagnosis, and case management training for providers.

Over two thirds of partnerships implemented substance abuse policy changes, such as drug testing policies, ordinances for local control of liquor licensing, and drug courts (78).

TWO PROGRAM ILLUSTRATIONS

The Milwaukee Neighborhood Partners Program (NPP) is an example of a grassroots, neighborhood organization empowerment approach (74). NPP sustains grassroots organizations working against ATOD problems via "bottom-up" empowerment strategies. By the third program year, 48 neighborhood-level partnerships had been established. Neighborhood groups began to see themselves as a composite force, cooperating on community-wide patrols, clearing out drug houses, and banding together to advocate policy changes.

The Wisconsin Dane County Partners in Prevention is county-wide and operates with a shared leadership approach rather than a strictly grassroots leadership approach. This Partnership's five communities have a county-wide focus. By its fifth year of program operation, the partnership successfully redefined its focus to include community organizing and prevention (79).

EVALUATION APPROACH

There is local evaluation of all Partnership programs, and a national evaluation of about two dozen communities. Key Partnership elements measured include organizational structure and dynamics and program activities. Key outcome measures include changes in risk and protective factors (e.g., attitudes, beliefs, school quality), service and program assessments (e.g., availability, record review), and successful mobilization (e.g., resources, fundraising, image, and activism). Impact is typically measured by alcohol and drug consumption; alcohol and drug–related incidents (e.g., arrests, DUI complaints, ER records); and economic indicators of alcohol and drug availability and prices (80). The national cross-site evaluation of the Partnership program is especially concerned with empowerment, or evaluation that fosters improvement and self-assessment (81).

Evaluation of 24 Partnerships and their matched comparison communities on adult rates of drug and alcohol use has not found statistically significant differences (82). However, the evaluators reported that rates were lower, as expected, in CAP areas even though not significantly so. Data from a 1996 survey will allow further test of the extent to which these differences persist.

Community Prevention Coalitions Demonstration (CPCD)

In 1994, CSAP launched the Community Prevention Coalitions Demonstration (CPCD) Grant Program, in 124 communities. Eligible communities must demonstrate that an effective community partnership is already in place and provide a rationale for expansion into a coalition, which includes at least two community partnerships. A community partnership is a formal group with no fewer than seven organizational members which are committed to reducing substance abuse and other community problems. A coalition can be formed by an existing partnership with other partnerships, or state-level models can address sub-state or state-wide areas (83).

Coalitions address policy and legislative changes, make structural changes in organizations and systems, and integrate substance abuse prevention activities into the health care services delivery system. Coalitions are also asked to consider how they will relate to developments of managed health care systems. The intended impact of coalitions of partnerships is more far-reaching and inclusive than that of partnerships. Coalitions cover a broader geographic area, combine a broader array of strategies, and may operate at the state and community level. Coalitions combine diverse cultural groups to work together on a common issue, or otherwise draw resources from heterogeneous communities that share a common interest. Long-term impact areas include reducing school-related problems, runaways, domestic violence, and related conditions including mental illness, injuries, and deaths.

CAP SUPPORT AND OTHER VOLUNTARY ORGANIZATIONS

There are two national support and resource centers—Join Together and Community Anti-Drug Coalitions of America—that provide a range of support, technical assistance, and organizational services to the several thousand ATOD CAPs. There is also a parallel but independent media campaign (Partnership for a Drug-Free America). Each of these is discussed here.

Such organizations are particularly important because of the lack of a single national voluntary agency that can perform the lobbying, hortatory, advisory, research, quality control, public relations, and similar traditional functions of such a group. There are, however, special interest groups like organizations of parents and mothers and students against drunk driving and special events like the Great American Smoke-Out that have helped to make the problems of ATOD more salient, offer support, sponsor special services like hotlines, and otherwise keep different publics involved and informed.

Join Together (JT)

JT is a Boston-based organization that supports the diverse community coalitions springing up across the country. Its periodic survey of over 1900 CAP programs, most recently in 1995, is the largest study of its kind (84).

The 1995 survey found that CAPs such as FB and the CSAP partnerships represent 24% of responding organizations. Others are school-sponsored or affiliated groups (15%), government executive agency (7%), government health agency (7%), nongovernmental health agency (2%), freestanding coalition (5%), other nonprofit organization (29%), or other (11%).

The activities of community coalitions are diverse. Over two thirds (78%) extensively engage in prevention, compared to 29% that do so in treatment, aftercare, or early identification. Alcohol use (67%) is slightly more likely to be extensively addressed than drug use (60%). Health and crime problems are extensively addressed by about one-quarter of coalitions.

Over one third report their involvement with public policy issues is increasing. Over half (54%) felt they had a direct impact on alcohol abuse, 48% a direct impact on illicit drug use, and 35% a direct impact on tobacco use. Some 34% had community school surveys on substance use; 14% had regular monitoring studies; 22% used official statistics to measure impact.

Community Anti-Drug Coalitions of America (CADCA)

CADCA supports a growing network of 3800 CAPs. Based in Alexandria, Virginia, it is membership-driven and provides technical assistance, promotes program development, and advocates national policies that will support drug prevention initiatives. Its mission is to promote comprehensive responses to the nation's drug-related problems. CADCA has published 19 manuals that provide step-by-step assistance on CAP topics. The manuals include three treatment related topics: services for Americans with disabilities who abuse ATOD, services for substance-using mothers and drug-exposed babies, and treatment-oriented drug courts (85–87).

The list of CAP activities that may be effective in reducing demand for alcohol and drugs is extensive and continually expanding. Because CAPs involve alliances across institutions and sectors, they lead to adoption of broad-based grassroots and professional-based initiatives. These initiatives build community capacity to sustain prevention and treatment efforts and create a neighborhood climate that is intolerant of alcohol and drug use that involves risk.

Partnership for a Drug-Free America

A unique antidrug advertising campaign has been conducted for 10 years by the Partnership for a Drug-Free America (88). The Partnership is a nonprofit coalition of communications professionals whose mission is to reduce demand for illicit drugs through media. In the largest public service advertising campaign in history and with advertising agencies working pro bono, the country's mass media have donated over $2.2 billion in broadcast time and print space for the Partnership's antidrug messages.

The messages are prevention oriented, target nonusers and occasional users, and appear in print, broadcast, outdoor, and nontraditional media. The messages are based on research-derived strategies. Independent studies have found statistically significant correlations between the degree of exposure to Partnership messages and changes in attitudes toward use of drugs (89). The decline in use of marihuana and cocaine was substantially greater in communities receiving a high volume of Partnership messages than in those receiving fewer messages.

EVALUATION OF CAPs

In recent years, there has been a surge in the range, quality, and quantity of CAP evaluations. Evaluation includes tracking the formation of CAPs and the processes by which they operate, as well as community-level and individual outcomes. The outcomes include individual behavior and attitudes as well as community indicators, like the number of substance abuse cases seen in an ER. Quantitative outcome measures tend to be prioritized over process and formative assessment (90).

There are many methodological issues in the evaluation of health-related CAPs (91). Such issues include the weaker effects in studies using randomized designs, not enough power to detect prevention outcomes because of too few communities assigned to experimental conditions, and differential attrition of users from experimental groups (92, 93). Another problem is that the proliferation of CAPs is decreasing the number of sites that are available for comparison purposes, or two separate programs may be operating in the same community, like the 8 of 14 FB sites that also have CSAP programs (Table 75.3). Of the 30 FB comparison sites, 8 get some funding from CSAP. A number of techniques have been developed to implement program evaluation based on single system designs, such as longitudinal designs, individual growth curve models, within-experimental control design, meta-analytical controls, multiple time series control methods, retrospective pretest design, and ethnographic approaches (94).

The recency of the application of newer research methodologies to assess the impact of alcohol CAPs may help to explain why only a small number of studies report program effects on behavior (95). Since significant long-term behavioral change in alcoholism projects has proven to be difficult to establish, we can expect challenges in documenting such change in programs directed against illegal drug use, the more unyielding elements of which are correlated with social distress and the larger political economy. Researchers have accepted the challenge of documenting the ways in which CAPs are directly tackling the institutional structure that supports illegal drug use and is deeply embedded in the society.

Another consideration is that the three-year program length frequently found in CAPs directed at relatively low-frequency behavior like alcohol or drug dependence may not be enough time to document program behavioral effects. The five-year period for FB, Partnership, and other broad-based CAPs also may not be enough for a longitudinal assessment of a complex community-wide program that addresses multiple substances and seeks ambitious long-term prevention, social change, and harm reduction goals, especially if the program has to devote substantial energy to seeking refunding.

In communities that are at high risk for drug abuse, the factors that elevate the risk, such as unemployment, insufficient social services, and high crime rates, can also slow the development of community-based action (96). Yet, there has to be enough time for synergy to develop among groups before they can set aside their territorial interests, cooperate in the continuing process of prioritizing and dealing cooperatively with problems, and build generalized social capital among the varied elements of the community. A program that lasts longer would require an evaluation that also would have to continue longer in order to develop and analyze endpoint data.

Evaluations increasingly are generating interactional models that reflect the complexities of substance abuse. The FB evaluation found a dynamic interrelationship between substance use and abuse and physical and interpersonal environments. Even controlling for individual risk factors, involvement in this substance abuse system predicted both alcohol and drug dependence. Programs directed at strategic points in the system could lead to reductions in substance use and abuse (97).

THE FUTURE OF CAPs

The ultimate decisions about CAPs will derive from their implementation and evaluation. Much remains to be learned about how they can be optimally implemented and their role in reducing the larger ATOD problem (98). We can expect that the future will bring significant data on the relative contribution to the success in CAPs of different approaches to format, target, scope, length, sponsorship, and setting.

In the first generation of alcoholism CAPs, the disjunction between program activity and impact could have resulted from a number of factors in addition to insufficient project length: divergent interests of participants, inappropriate foci, ineffective interventions, shortage of resources, not enough emphasis on behavior change, competing vested interests, politicalization of issues, or lack of a central strategy and action (99). Many of these problems are being addressed in the second generation of CAPs that target substances like cocaine and heroin.

Another matter that is being actively addressed is the extent to which survey data may indicate declining levels of cocaine and heroin use nationally but find no such trend among subgroups like inner-city residents, among whom use is higher, more chronic, and enduring and reflects structural strain, environmental enabling factors, and exacerbation of normal life stage risks (100). This difference between a generally downward trend and the higher rate of inner-city use is a challenge to the effectiveness of CAPs and is analogous to the problem that emerged in the evaluation of the Community Intervention Trial for Smoking Cessation (COMMIT), where light to moderate, but not heavy smokers, were significantly affected by the program (101).

Another lesson of the COMMIT trial was recognition of the importance of striking a balance between standardization of the defined intervention and allowance for flexibility in each community (102). An alternate approach might give more focus to the processes by which an intervention is developed and less attention to definition of the intervention and governance. Identifying the relative merit of different approaches can contribute to better methods for reaching the pockets of heightened prevalence of ATOD. The distinction between programs directed at such pockets and these concerned with the broader community could reflect different phases of CAP activity rather than distinctive approaches to it.

Comprehensive, long-term CAPs concerned with substances like alcohol, cocaine, and heroin differ from time-limited anti-smoking experiments, like COMMIT. The latter assess a participant at the end of the project as either a failure or success in quitting smoking. In communities with full-scale CAPs, however, there are additional contributors to evaluation, such as measurement of increases or decreases in the number of persons participating in some form of treatment. In the future, rates of entry and reentry into and retention in treatment, as manifestations of tertiary prevention, will be among the multiple contributors to understanding the dynamics of alcohol and drug use prevalence in a community. A long-term CAP could also be reporting significant change in social structure which would not occur in a short-term experiment. Demonstrating the impact of such a CAP on social structure and institutions that will help to sustain ATOD demand reduction is likely to require "taking the long view" (103).

In the future, we can anticipate that large multipurpose CAPs as well as more targeted interventions should be able to draw on future propositional inventories of "what works." Such findings can be found in independent policy-related research as well as CAP studies. Typical findings of this kind, for

Table 75.3 Locations of Fighting Back and Selected CSAP Programs

State	City
Arkansas	Little Rock
California	Santa Barbara[a]
	Vallejo[a]
	Oakland[a]
Connecticut	New Haven
Massachusetts	Worcester[a]
Missouri	Kansas City
New Mexico	Northwest NM, 3 counties[a]
New Jersey	Newark[a]
North Carolina	Charlotte
South Carolina	Columbia
Texas	San Antonio
Washington, DC	Washington, DC[a]
Wisconsin	Milwaukee[a]

[a]Locations which are also funded by the CSAP community partnership grant.
Note: Most sites are only selected districts or neighborhoods, and not the listed locations in their entirety.

example, are that active enforcement of the age 21 minimum drinking law reduces damaging consequences of youth alcohol use, or that compulsory training of alcohol servers leads to significant reductions in single-vehicle nighttime crashes (104, 105).

A recent review of community-based initiatives to deal with social problems concluded that up until recently, political barriers have hampered effective evaluation, persistent dilemmas have hindered community initiatives, and evaluation has had a limited role in determining the fate of the initiatives (106). The substance abuse problem, however, has become so salient that political barriers to CAPs are lessening, communities are better able to implement their ideas, and evaluation has a growing role.

The community battle against substance abuse partially derives from and can be compared to the very successful effort to achieve reductions in the prevalence of cardiovascular disease. Success in this effort required an extensive latency period and many program vehicles and channels, with only modest changes occurring per year. These changes gradually led to social movements and political action that, in turn, brought about additional long-term shifts in individual and group behavior (107). In society's efforts to reduce ATOD abuse, an analogous situation could exist in the manner in which CAPs are implementing an evolving research-driven procedure for using the community as both method and site for constructive change in reducing ATOD problems.

References

1. Edwards G, Anderson P, Babor TF, et al. Alcohol policy and the public good. New York: Oxford University Press, 1994:175–176.
2. Weiss S. Alcohol and drunkenness—an innovative curriculum for the Kibbutz movement in Israel: a model for adapting general prevention programs to specific populations. J Drug Educ 1988;18:267–274.
3. Lang E, Kickett M. A grassroots approach for reducing petrol sniffing among aboriginal youth: some problems and possible solutions. In: Giesbrecht N, Conley P, Denniston RW, eds. Research, action, and the community: Experiences in the prevention of alcohol and other drug problems. Rockville, MD: Office for Substance Abuse Prevention, 1989.
4. Pentz MA, Dwyer JH, Mackinnon DP, et al. A multi-community trial for primary prevention of adolescent drug use: effects on drug use prevalence. JAMA 1989;261:3259–3266.
5. Blocker JS. "Give to the winds thy fears": the women's temperance crusade 1873–1874. Westport, CT: Greenwood Press, 1985.
6. Catlin CEG. Liquor control. London: Thornton Butterworth, 1931.
7. Rosenquist P, Takala JP. Two experiences with lay boards: the emergence of compulsory treatment of alcoholics in Sweden and Finland. Contemp Drug Prob 1987;14:15–38.
8. Bloomberg W, Schmandt HJ. Urban poverty: its social and political dimensions. Beverly Hills, CA: Sage, 1978:280–370.
9. Farquhar JW. Changing cardiovascular risk factors in entire communities: the Stanford three-community project. In: Lauer RM, Shekelle RB, eds. Childhood prevention of atherosclerosis and hypertension. New York: Raven, 1980:435–440.
10. Farquhar JW, Fortmann SP, Flora JA, et al. Effects of community wide education on cardiovascular disease risk factors: the Stanford five-city project. JAMA 1990;264:359–365.
11. McCombs ME, Shaw DL. The agenda setting function of the mass media. Pub Opin Q 1972; 36:176–187.
12. Rogers EM, Shoemaker FF. Communication of innovations. New York: Macmillan, 1971.
13. Katz E, Lazarsfeld P. Personal influence: The part played by people in the flow of mass communications. Glencoe, IL: The Free Press, 1955.
14. Bacon S. The mobilization of community resources for the attack on alcoholism. Q J Stud Alcohol 1947;8:473–497.
15. Giesbrecht N, West P, Hyndman B. Community-based prevention research: will coordinated action make a difference? Prevention partnership demonstration project. Toronto: Addiction Research Foundation, 1994.
16. Giesbrecht N, Krempulec L, West P. Community-based prevention research to reduce alcohol-related problems. Alcohol Health Res World 1993;17:84–88.

17. Ritson EB. Community response to alcohol-related problems: review of an international study. Geneva: World Health Organization, 1985.
18. Moskalewicz J. Alcohol as an economic issue: recent Polish experience. Contemp Drug Prob 1991;18:407–415.
19. Giesbrecht N, Conley P, Denniston RW, et al, eds. Research, action and the community: experiences in the prevention of alcohol and other drug problems. Rockville, MD: Office for Substance Abuse Prevention, 1989.
20. Greenfield TK, Zimmerman R, eds. Experiences with community action projects: new research in the prevention of alcohol and other drug problems. Rockville, MD: Center for Substance Abuse Prevention, 1993.
21. American Social Health Association. Guidelines. A comprehensive community program to reduce drug abuse. I-V. New York: American Social Health Association, 1972.
22. Leukefeld CG, Battjes RJ, Amsel Z, eds. AIDS and intravenous drug use: future directions for community-based prevention research. Rockville, MD: National Institute on Drug Abuse, 1990.
23. Shilts R. And the band played on: people, politics, and the AIDS epidemic. New York: Viking Penguin, 1993.
24. Green J. Flirting with suicide. New York Times Magazine 1996(September 15):40.
25. Rothman J. Three models of community organization practice. In: Cox FM, Erlich JL, Rothman J, eds. Strategies of community organization. Itasca, IL: Peacock, 1970:20–36.
26. Shea S, Basch CE. A review of five major community-based cardiovascular disease prevention programs; Part 1: rationale, design and theoretical framework. Am J Health Promotion 1990; 4:203–213.
27. Rogers E. Diffusion of innovations. New York: The Free Press, 1962.
28. Kotler P, Zaltman G. Social marketing: an approach to planned social change. J Marketing 1971;35:3–12.
29. Flay B, diTecco D, Schlegal R. Mass media in health promotion: an analysis using an extended information processing model. Health Educ Q 1989;7:127–147.
30. Kokeny M, Gryarfas I, Makara P, et al. The role of health promotion in preventive policy against cardiovascular diseases in Hungary. Health Promotion 1986;1:85–92.
31. Kandel DB, Logan SA. Problems of drug use from adolescence to young adulthood. Am J Pub Health 1984;74:660–666.
32. Lederman S. Alcool, alcoolisme, alcoolisation. Vol. 2. Paris: Universitaires de France, 1964.
33. Andreasen AR. Marketing social change: changing behavior to promote health, social development and the environment. San Francisco: Jossey-Bass, 1995.
34. Hyndman B, Giesbrecht N, Bernardi DR, et al. Preventing substance abuse through multicomponent community action research projects:

Lessons from past experiences and challenges for future initiatives. Contemp Drug Prob 1992; 19:133–164.
35. Porter RA, Peters JA. An ecological framework for the integration of practice methods: community organization for the 80s. Soc Development Issues 1981;5:157–185.
36. Aguirre-Molina M, Gorman DM. Community-based approaches for the prevention of alcohol, tobacco, and other drug use. Annu Rev Public Health 1996;17:337–358.
37. Edwards G, Anderson P, Babor TF, et al. Alcohol policy and the public good. New York: Oxford University Press, 1994.
38. Johnson CA, Pentz MA, Weber MD, et al. Relative effectiveness of comprehensive community programming for drug abuse prevention with high-risk and low-risk adolescents. J Consult Clin Psychol 1990;53:447–456.
39. Schaps E. Prevention directions and issues. Paper presented at Robert Wood Johnson Substance Abuse Grantee Conference, Newark, NJ, December 2–3, 1993.
40. M'Tikulu D. Primary prevention, mutual support systems and the rationale for a community development type of intervention. In: Campfens H. ed. Rethinking community development in a changing society: Issues, concepts, and cases. Guelph, Ontario: Community Development Society, 1983:95–99.
41. Smith SR. Social capital, community coalitions, and the role of institutions. Durham NC: Duke University Institute of Policy Sciences and Public Affairs, 1996.
42. Putnam RD. The prosperous community: social capital and public life. Am Prospect 1993;13: 35–42.
43. Holder HD. Undertaking a community prevention trial to reduce alcohol problems: translating theoretical models into action. In: Holder HD, Howard HM, eds. Community prevention trials for alcohol problems. Westport, CT: Praeger, 1992:227–243.
44. Torjman SR. Prevention in the drug field. Monograph I: Essential concept and strategies. Toronto: Addiction Research Foundation, 1986.
45. Hawkins JD, Catalano RF, Associates. Communities that care: action for drug abuse prevention. San Francisco: Jossey-Bass, 1992.
46. Culp MW. The Miami coalition for a drug-free community. In: Community Epidemiology Work Group. Epidemiological trends in drug abuse: Proceedings, December 1991. Rockville, MD: National Institute on Drug Abuse, 1992: 523–533.
47. Hall JN, Michael GW. Drug use in Miami (Dade County), Florida. In: Community Epidemiology Work Group. Epidemiological trends in drug abuse: Proceedings, June 1995. Rockville, MD: National Institute on Drug Abuse, 1996:113–131.
48. Witt M, Guess L, Gfroerer J, et al. Estimates of drug use prevalence in Miami from the 1991–1994 National Household Survey on Drug

Abuse: methodological report. Rockville, MD: Substance Abuse and Mental Health Services Administration, 1996. Working Paper (July 15).

49. Pentz MA, Terbow EA, Hanson WB, et al. Effects of program implementation on adolescent drug use behavior: The Midwestern prevention project. Eval Rev 1990;14:264–289.

50. Johnson CA, Pentz MA, Weber MD, et al. Relative effectiveness of comprehensive community programming for drug abuse prevention with high-risk and low-risk adolescents. J Consult Clin Psychol 1990;58:447–456.

51. Pentz MA, Bonnie RJ, Shopland DR. Integrating supply and demand reduction strategies for drug abuse prevention. Am Behav Scient 1996; 39:897–910.

52. Pentz MA. Adaptive evaluation strategic for estimating effects of community-based drug abuse prevention programs. J Community Psychol 1974;Special:155–169.

53. Chou CP, Montgomery S, Pentz MA, et al. Effects of a community-based prevention program on decreasing drug use in high risk adolescents. Los Angeles: University of Southern California Institute of Prevention Research, 1996.

54. Pentz MA, Johnson CA, Glay BR. Longitudinal results of a randomized community-based trial for prevention of tobacco, alcohol, and other drug abuse. Los Angeles: University of Southern California Institute of Prevention Research, 1996.

55. Putnam SL, Rockett IRH, Campbell MK. Methodological issues in community-based alcohol-related injury prevention projects: attribution of program effects. In: Greenfield TK, Zimmerman R, eds. Experiences with community action projects: new research in the prevention of alcohol and other drug problems. Rockville, MD: Center for Substance Abuse Prevention, 1992:31–42.

56. Hingson R, McGovern T, Howland J, et al. Reducing alcohol-impaired driving in Massachusetts: the impact of the Saving Lives Program. Am J Public Health 1996;86:791–797.

57. Perry CL, Williams CL, Veblen-Mortenson S, et al. Project Northland: outcomes of a community-wide alcohol use prevention program during early adolescence. Am J Pub Health 1996; 86:956–965.

58. Ryan BE, Mosher JF. Spring break, alcohol promotions, and community responses. In: Greenfield TK, Zimmerman R, eds. Experiences with community action projects: new research in the prevention of alcohol and other drug problems. Rockville, MD: Center for Substance Abuse Prevention, 1992:189–195.

59. McDowell E. Cancun tells its spring-break visitors to behave themselves. New York Times 1996(March 11):A15.

60. Cheadle A, Pearson D, Wagner E, et al. A community-based approach to prevention of alcohol use among adolescents on an American Indian reservation. Public HealthRep 1995;110:439–447.

61. Wagenaar AC, Murray DM, Wolfson M, et al. Communities mobilizing for change on alcohol: Design of a randomized community trial. J Community Psychol 1994;Special:79–101.

62. Holder HD. Prevention of alcohol-related accidents in the community. Addiction 1993;88: 1003–1012.

63. Kennedy DM. Controlling the drug trade in Tampa, Florida. Washington, DC: National Institute of Justice, 1993.

64. Lurigio AJ, Davis RC. Taking the war on drugs to the streets: the perceptual impact of four neighborhood drug programs. Crime Delinquency 1992;38:522–538.

65. U.S. Department of Justice. Community responses to drug abuse. Washington, DC: U.S. Department of Justice, 1994.

66. Jellinek PS, Hearn RP. Fighting drug abuse at the local level. Issues Sci Technol 1991;(Summer):78–84.

67. Saxe L, Kadushin C, Beveridge A, et al. Fighting Back evaluation plan. New York: City University of New York Graduate School, 1995.

68. Robert Wood Johnson Foundation. Fighting Back: community initiatives to reduce demand for illegal drugs and alcohol. Call for proposals. Princeton, NJ: The Robert Wood Johnson Foundation, 1989.

69. Spickard WA, Dixon GL, Sarver FW. Fighting Back against America's public health enemy number one. Bull N Y Acad Med 1994;71: 111–135.

70. Join Together. World Wide Web site: http://www.jointogether.org. 1996.

71. Kaftarian SJ. National evaluation of the community partnership program. New Designs 1991;(Summer):34–36.

72. Chavis DM, Speer PW, Resnick I, et al. Building community capacity to address alcohol and drug abuse: getting to the heart of the problem. In: Davis RC, Lurigio AJ, Rosenbaum DP, eds. Drugs and the community: involving community residents in combating the sale of illegal drugs. Springfield, IL: Charles C Thomas, 1993: 251–284.

73. Chavis DM. Building community capacity to prevent violence through coalitions and partnerships. J Health Care for Poor and Underserved 1995;6:234–244.

74. Florence J, Moberg DP, Garcia V. Milwaukee neighborhood partners annual report. Madison: University of Wisconsin Medical School, Center for Health Policy and Program Evaluation, 1994.

75. Florence J, Moberg DP, Connor T. Dane County partners in prevention: annual report. Madison: University of Wisconsin Medical School, Center for Health Policy and Program Evaluation, 1995.

76. Cook R, Roehl J, Oros C, et al. Conceptual and methodological issues in the evaluation of community-based substance abuse prevention coalitions: Lessons learned from the national evaluation of the community partnership program. J Community Psychol 1994;Special:155–169.

77. Winston-Salem/Forsyth County Coalition on Alcohol, Drug Problems. Report of community partnership demonstration grant #3129. Winston-Salem, NC: Winston-Salem/Forsyth County Coalition on Alcohol, Drug Problems, 1995.

78. COSMOS Corporation. National evaluation of the community partnership demonstration program. Executive summary of the fourth annual report. Rockville, MD: Center for Substance Abuse Prevention, 1995.

79. Florence J, Moberg DP, Connor T. Dane County partners in prevention: Annual report. Madison: University of Wisconsin Medical School, Center for Health Policy and Program Evaluation, 1995.

80. Hansen WB, Kaftarian SJ. Strategies for comparing multiple-site evaluations under nonequivalent design conditions. J Community Psychol 1994;Special:170–187.

81. Yin RK, Kaftarian SJ, Jacobs NF. Empowerment evaluation at federal and local levels: dealing with quality. In: Fetterman DM, Kaftarian SJ, Wandersman A, eds. Empowerment evaluation: knowledge and tools for self-assessment and accountability. Thousand Oaks, CA: Sage Publications, 1996:188–207.

82. Kaftarian SJ. Executive summary of the fourth annual report: National evaluation of the Community Partnership Demonstration Program. Rockville, MD: Substance Abuse and Mental Health Services Administration, 1995.

83. Substance Abuse and Mental Health Services Administration. The community prevention coalitions demonstration grant program. Guidance for applicants no. SP95–03. Rockville, MD: Substance Abuse and Mental Health Services Administration, 1995.

84. Join Together. The third national Join Together survey of communities fighting substance abuse. Boston: Join Together, 1996.

85. Resource Center on Substance Abuse Prevention and Disability. Coalitions address Americans with disabilities. CADCA Strategizer 9. Alexandria, VA: Community Anti-Drug Coalitions of America, undated.

86. CADCA. Addressing drug-exposed babies and substance using mothers. CADCA Strategizer 9. Alexandria, VA: Community Anti-Drug Coalitions of America, undated.

87. CADCA. Treatment oriented drug courts. CADCA Strategizer 17. Alexandria, VA: Community Anti-Drug Coalitions of America, undated.

88. Partnership for a Drug-Free America. Partnership tracking study. New York: Partnership for a Drug-Free America, 1995.

89. American Association of Advertising Agencies. What we've learned about advertising from the media-advertising Partnership for a Drug-free America. New York: American Association of Advertising Agencies, 1990.

90. Casswell S. Issues of transfer and ownership: commentary and reflections on the day. In: Greenfield TK, Zimmerman R, eds. Experiences with community action projects: new research in the prevention of alcohol and other drug problems. Rockville, MD: Center for Substance Abuse Prevention, 1992:273–276.

91. Koepsell TD, et al. Selected methodological issues in evaluating community-based health-promotion and disease prevention programs. Annu Rev Public Health 1992;13:31–57.

92. National Research Council. Prevention of drug abuse: what do we know? Washington, DC: National Academy of Sciences Press, 1993.

93. Hansen WB, Tobler NS, Graham J. Attrition in substance abuse prevention research: a meta-analysis of 85 longitudinally-followed cohorts. Eval Rev 1990;14:677–685.

94. Kim S, Crutchfield C, Williams C, et al. An innovative and unconventional approach to program evaluating in the field of substance abuse prevention. J Community Psychol 1994;Special: 61–78.

95. Gorman DM, Speer PW. Preventing alcohol abuse and alcohol-related problems through community interventions: a review of evaluation studies. Psychol Health 1995;10:1–38.

96. Aquire-Molina M, Gorman DM. Community-based approaches for the prevention of alcohol, tobacco, and other drug use. Annu Rev Public Health 1996;17:337–358.

97. Kadushin C, Reber E, Saxe L, Livert D. The substance abuse system: social and neighborhood environments associated with substance use and misuse. Substance Use and Misuse (in press).

98. Johnson CA, Farquhar JW, Sussman S. Methodological and substantive issues in substance abuse prevention research: an integration. Am Behav Scient 1996;39:935–942.

99. Giesbrecht N, West P, Hyndman B. Community based prevention research: will coordinated ac-

tion make a difference? Paper presented at the International Council of Alcohol and Addictions, Krakow, Poland, June, 1993:7–11.

100. Brunswick A, Rier DA. Structural strain: Drug use among African-American youth. In: Taylor RL, ed. African-American youth: their social and economic status in the United States. Westport, CT: Praeger, 1995:225–246.

101. COMMIT Research Group. Community intervention trail for smoking cessation (COMMIT): I. Cohort results from a four-year community intervention. Am J Public Health 1995;85:183–191.

102. Fisher EB Jr. The results of the COMMIT trial [editorial]. Am J Public Health 1995;85: 159–160.

103. Saxe L, Reber E, Hallfors D, Stirratt MJ. Taking the long view: evaluating community-based efforts to reduce substance abuse. Waltham, MA: Brandeis University, 1996.

104. Wagenaar AC, Wolfson M. Deterring sales and provision of alcohol to minors: a study of enforcement in 295 counties in four states. Public Health Rep 1996;110:419–427.

105. Holder HD, Wagenaar AC. Mandated server training and reduced alcohol-involved traffic crashes: a time series analysis of the Oregon experience. Accid Anal Prev 1993;26: 89–97.

106. O'Connor A. Evaluating comprehensive community initiatives: A view from history. In: Connell JP, Kubisch AC, Scherr LB et al, eds. New approaches to evaluating community initiatives: Concepts, methods, and contexts. Washington: The Aspen Institute, 1995: 23–64.

107. Susser M. The tribulation of trials: intervention in communities [editorial]. Am J Public Health 1995;85:156–158.

76 SCHOOL-BASED PROGRAMS

Gilbert J. Botvin and Elizabeth M. Botvin

INTRODUCTION

The problem of substance abuse has been a source of concern to health professionals, parents, community leaders, and law enforcement agencies for more than two decades. During this time considerable effort and resources have been spent attempting to understand the causes of substance abuse and to identify potentially effective intervention strategies. Although progress has been made on both fronts, it has been painfully slow. Moreover, advances in understanding the etiology of substance abuse, the refinement of treatment approaches, and the identification of promising prevention programs have not yet translated into reductions in the prevalence of substance use. In fact, recent national survey data indicate that the problem of substance abuse is growing worse (1). The problem is particularly keen among youth where there has been a sharp increase in marihuana use among 8th, 10th, and 12th graders as well as an increase for all three grade levels in the use of cigarettes, stimulants, LSD, and inhalants. This upswing in substance use reverses a decade-long decline and has raised the specter of a new drug epidemic.

Prevalence and Current Trends

Data from the 1994 Monitoring the Future Study (1) found that among high school seniors, 31% had used illicit drugs in the last year and 42.9% had done so during their lifetime. The annual prevalence rate for marihuana use was 26% and the lifetime rate was 35.5%; the annual inhalant prevalence rate was 7% and the lifetime rate was 17.4%; the annual LSD prevalence rate was 6.8% and the lifetime rate was 10.3%; the annual stimulant prevalence rate was 8.4% and the lifetime rate was 15.1%; the annual alcohol rate was 76% and the lifetime rate was 87%. For cigarette smoking the lifetime rate was 61.9% and the 30-day rate was 29.9%. For marihuana and many other substances, adolescent use has increased each year for the past three years. This upward trend has been observed for a wide cross-section of individuals, including youth from different regions of the country, different social classes, and different ethnic and racial groups.

The Importance of Prevention

In view of the high levels of substance use among American youth and the disturbing upward trend noted in recent years as well as the continuing threat of contracting acquired immunodeficiency syndrome (AIDS) through injection drug use, new urgency now exists for the development of more effective intervention strategies. Added to this is the longstanding concern over the deleterious health, legal, social, and pharmacological effects of substance abuse.

Over the years the treatment of substance abuse has proven to both difficult, expensive, and labor-intensive. Moreover, even the most effective treatment modalities are plagued by high rates of recidivism. Clinicians are confronted by a disorder that more often than not proves to be refractory to change, by patients whose knowledge of drugs may be daunting to even the most experienced practitioner, and by a pathogenic environment that does its best to undermine any progress made by the patient through the ubiquity of drugs and a social network supportive of continued substance abuse.

Prevention is important because it offers a logical alternative to treatment. An underlying assumption of prevention efforts is that it is likely to be easier to prevent substance abuse than to treat such an insidious disorder once it has developed. However, the logical simplicity of prevention belies its difficulty. The development of effective prevention approaches has been far more difficult than was initially imagined. Indeed, most efforts to develop effective substance abuse prevention efforts have achieved only a limited degree of success, and many have failed completely. The first major breakthrough came at the end of the 1970s in the area of smoking prevention. That work stimulated more than two decades of prevention research and led to the development of several promising prevention approaches. During the 1980s and up to the present, mounting empirical evidence from a growing number of carefully designed and methodologically sophisticated research studies indicates that prevention works.

The School as the Site of Prevention Efforts

The development and testing of approaches for preventing adolescent substance abuse have largely focused on middle/junior high school students, with schools serving as the primary setting for prevention efforts. Despite their traditional educational mission, schools have been asked to assume responsibility for a variety of social and health problems. Many states mandate schools to provide their students with programs in health education and/or tobacco, alcohol, and drug education as well as teenage pregnancy and AIDS education. Although there has been considerable debate about whether schools should provide programs dealing with health and social problems, particularly at a time when there is renewed concern about academic standards, the simple truth is that schools offer the most efficient access to large numbers of adolescents. Moreover, many educators are gradually recognizing that problems such as drug abuse are a significant barrier to the achievement of educational objectives. The United States Department of Education, for example, has included "drug-free schools" as one of its goals for improving the quality of education in this country.

Chapter Overview

This chapter provides a summary of developments in the field of substance abuse prevention over the past two decades. It begins with a discussion of what is currently known about the etiology and developmental progression of substance use and the implications for prevention. Traditional and contemporary prevention approaches are described and the evidence for their effectiveness is summarized. A major emphasis of this chapter is on the current generation of substance abuse prevention approaches, the results of research testing their effectiveness, and recent work concerning the effectiveness of these approaches with ethnic minority youth. The final section concerns conclusions to be drawn from this body of research, directions for future research, and implications for public health policy.

ETIOLOGY AND IMPLICATIONS FOR PREVENTION

To provide a context for understanding existing substance abuse prevention efforts and for developing a prescription for the most effective preventive interventions possible, it is necessary to be familiar with the factors associated with the initiation and maintenance of tobacco, alcohol, and drug abuse. Furthermore, it is necessary to pinpoint as accurately as possible the initial period for substance use onset to determine the most appropriate point of intervention. It is also important to understand the developmental course of substance abuse—both the progression from nonuse to abuse and the general sequence of using specific psychoactive substances or classes of substances.

Etiological Determinants

Although some of this evidence is based on retrospective studies (which are regarded as the weakest source of such data), much of what is currently known about the causes of substance abuse comes from cross-sectional and longitudinal studies. The evidence that exists in the extant literature indicates that substance abuse results from the complex interaction of a number of different factors including cognitive, attitudinal, social, personality, pharmacological, and developmental factors (2–9).

SOCIAL FACTORS

Social factors are the most powerful influences promoting the initiation of tobacco, alcohol, and drug abuse. These include the behavior and attitudes of significant others such as parents, older siblings, and friends (10–14). They also include influences from the popular media portraying substance use as an important part of popularity, sophistication, success, sex appeal, and good times. Both the modeling of substance use behavior by media personalities and the messages communicated are powerful sources of influence that promote and support substance use (15, 16).

COGNITIVE AND ATTITUDINAL FACTORS

Individuals who are unaware of the adverse consequences of tobacco, alcohol, and drug use, as well as those who have positive attitudes toward substance use, are more likely to become substance users than those with either more knowledge or more negative attitudes toward substance use (14, 17). In addition, individuals who believe that substance use is "normal" and that most people smoke, drink, or use drugs are more likely to be substance users (18).

PERSONALITY FACTORS

Substance use has been found to be associated with a number of psychological characteristics. Substance users have been found to have lower self-esteem, self-confidence, self-satisfaction, social confidence, assertiveness, personal control, and self-efficacy than nonusers (19–21). Substance users have also been found to be more anxious, impulsive, rebellious, impatient to acquire adult status, and in need of more social approval than nonusers (5, 6). The clinical literature also suggests that individuals with a specific psychiatric condition (e.g., anxiety, depression) may use particular substances as a way of alleviating the symptoms associated with that condition (22). This has been referred to in the literature as the self-medication hypothesis. For example, through experimentation with different substances, highly anxious individuals may have found that alcohol or other depressants help them

to feel less anxious, and they might use those substances as a way of regulating their feelings of anxiety.

PHARMACOLOGIC FACTORS

The pharmacology of commonly abused substances varies considerably; however, virtually all of these substances produce effects that are highly reinforcing and dependency-producing. For tobacco, alcohol, and most illicit drugs, tolerance develops quickly, leading to increased dosages and an increased frequency of use. Once a pattern of dependent use has been established, termination of use produces dysphoric feelings and physical withdrawal symptoms.

BEHAVIORAL FACTORS

Substance abuse does not occur in a vacuum but rather appears to be part of a general syndrome or life-style reflecting a particular value orientation (23). Substance use has been found to be highly associated with a variety of health-compromising or problem behaviors. First, individuals who use one substance are more likely to use others. Second, individuals who smoke, drink, or use drugs tend to get lower grades in school, are not generally involved in adult-sanctioned activities such as sports and clubs, and are more likely than nonusers to exhibit antisocial patterns of behavior including aggressiveness, lying, stealing, and cheating (24–27). Finally, substance use has also been found to be related to premature sexual activity, truancy, and delinquency. The finding that different types of problem behaviors are part of a general syndrome or collection of highly associated behaviors suggests that they may have the same or highly similar causes. To the extent that this is true, it would have significant implications for prevention. The most important of these is that it may be possible to develop a single preventive intervention capable of having an impact on several associated behaviors at the same time.

Initiation and Developmental Course

For most individuals, experimentation with one or more psychoactive substances occurs during the adolescent years. Initial use of the "gateway" substances of tobacco, alcohol, and marihuana typically takes place during the early adolescent years. First use and intermittent experimentation generally occur within the context of social situations. In its initial stages, substance use is almost exclusively a social behavior. Since the 1960s, some degree of experimentation with drugs has become commonplace in contemporary American society. This is particularly true with respect to tobacco, alcohol, and marihuana, which are the most widely used and abused substances in our society. After a relatively brief period of experimentation, many individuals develop patterns of use characterized by both psychological and physiological dependence. The initial social and psychological motivations for using drugs eventually yield to one driven increasingly by pharmacological factors (8, 28).

Substance Use Progression

Data from several sources indicate that experimentation with one substance frequently leads to experimentation with others in a logical and generally predictable progression (7, 29). Most individuals begin by using alcohol and tobacco, progressing later to the use of marihuana. Some individuals may also use inhalants early in this sequence. This developmental progression corresponds exactly to the prevalence of these substances in our society, with alcohol and inhalants being the most widely used, followed by tobacco, which is followed by marihuana. For some individuals this progression may eventuate in the use of depressants, stimulants, hallucinogens, and other drugs. However, many individuals may either discontinue use after a short period of experimentation or may not progress from the use of one substance to the use of others. The likelihood of progressing from one point in the developmental sequence to another can best be understood in probabilistic terms, with an individual's risk of moving to greater involvement with drugs increasing at each additional step in the developmental progression.

Knowledge of the developmental progression of substance use is important because it has implications for the focus and timing of preventive interventions. Interventions targeted at the use of substances occurring towards the beginning of this progression have the potential of not only preventing the use of those substances, but also the potential for reducing or even eliminating altogether the risk of using other substances further along the progression.

Adolescence and Substance Abuse Risk

Adolescence is frequently characterized as a period of great physical and psychological change. During adolescence, individuals typically experiment with a wide range of behaviors and life-style patterns. This occurs as part of the natural process of separating from parents, developing a sense of autonomy and independence, establishing a personal identity, and acquiring the skills necessary for functioning effectively in an adult world.

Many of the developmental changes that are necessary prerequisites for becoming healthy adults increase an adolescent's risk of smoking, drinking, or using drugs. Adolescents who are impatient to assume adult roles and appear more grown-up may smoke, drink, or use drugs as a way of laying claim to adult status. Adolescents may also engage in substance use because it provides them with a means of establishing solidarity with a particular reference group, rebelling against parental authority, or establishing their own individual identity.

During adolescence, the influence of parents is typically supplanted by that of the peer group (30). As the result of normal cognitive development, adolescents shift from a "concrete operational" mode of thinking—which is characteristically rigid, literal, and grounded in the "here and now"—to a "formal operational" mode of thinking—which is more relative, abstract, and hypothetical (31). It has been suggested that these changes in the manner in which adolescents think may serve to undermine previously acquired knowledge relating to the potential risks of smoking, drinking, or using drugs. For example, the "formal operational" thinking of the adolescent facilitates the discovery of inconsistencies or logical flaws in arguments being advanced by adults concerning the health risk associated with substance use. Similarly, this new mode of thinking may enable adolescents to formulate counter-arguments to antidrug messages, which may in turn permit rationalizations for ignoring potential risks, particularly if substance use is perceived to have social or personal benefits.

Conformity needs and conformity behavior increase rapidly during preadolescence and early adolescence and decline steadily from middle to late adolescence (32). However, despite this general developmental trend toward increased conformity, an individual's susceptibility to conformity pressure may vary greatly, depending on values and a variety of psychological factors, as well as the relative importance of peer acceptance. Finally, because adolescents characteristically have a sense of immortality and invulnerability, they tend to minimize the risk associated with substance use and overestimate their ability to avoid personally destructive patterns of use.

PREVENTION STRATEGIES

In view of the adverse health, social, and legal consequences of substance abuse and the difficulty of achieving sustained abstinence once addictive patterns of use have developed, it is readily apparent that the most propitious approach to the problem of substance abuse is prevention. Prevention efforts have taken place on several different levels and have taken many forms. Prevention has been conceptualized in terms of supply and demand reduction models and as primary, secondary, and tertiary prevention. Each encompasses a different aspect of prevention, and has substantially different operational implications.

Supply and Demand Reduction

Supply reduction efforts are based on the fundamental assumption that substance use can be controlled by simply controlling the supply (i.e., availability). This has been the driving force behind the activities of law enforcement agencies, particularly with respect to the interdiction of drugs by governmental agencies such as the Drug Enforcement Administration (DEA), the Federal Bureau of Investigation (FBI), and local police departments. *Demand reduction* efforts, on the other hand, are conceptualized as those that attempt to dissuade, discourage, or deter individuals from either using drugs or desiring to use drugs. Demand reduction includes prevention, education, and treatment programs.

Types of Prevention

Consistent with usage in the field of public health, *primary prevention* interventions are designed to reach individuals before they have developed a specific disorder or disease. As such, they target a general population of individuals who, for the most part, have not yet begun using tobacco, alcohol, or other drugs. The goal of these approaches is to prevent substance use and abuse by intervening upon individual and/or environmental factors viewed as promoting or supporting this type of health-compromising behavior. *Secondary prevention* involves screening and early intervention. *Tertiary prevention* involves preventing the progression of a well-established disorder to the point of disability. The central focus of this chapter is on demand reduction and primary prevention.

Substance abuse prevention efforts can be divided into five general strategies:

- Information dissemination approaches
- Affective education approaches
- Alternatives approaches
- Social resistance skills approaches
- Broader competency enhancement approaches, which emphasize personal and social skills training

These prevention strategies are summarized in Table 76.1 and are discussed in the following sections.

Table 76.1   Overview of Major Preventive Approaches

Approach	Focus	Methods
Information Dissemination	Increase knowledge of drugs, their effects and consequences of use; promote antidrug use attitudes	Didactic instruction, discussion, audio/video presentations, displays of substances, posters, pamphlets, school assembly programs
Affective Education	Increase self-esteem, responsible decision-making, interpersonal growth; generally includes little or no information about drugs	Didactic instruction, discussion, experiential activities, group problem-solving exercises
Alternatives	Increase self-esteem, self-reliance; provide variable alternatives to drug use; reduce boredom and sense of alienation	Organization of youth centers, recreational activities; participation in community service projects; vocational training
Resistance Skills	Increase awareness of social influence to smoke, drink, or use drugs; develop skills for resisting substance use influences; increase knowledge of immediate negative consequences; establish non-substance use norms	Class discussion; resistance skills training; behavioral rehearsal; extended practice via behavioral "homework"; use of same-age or older peer leaders
Personal and Social Skills Training	Increase decision-making, personal behavior change, anxiety reduction, communication, social and assertive skills; application of generic skills to resist substance use influences	Class discussion; cognitive-behavioral skills training (instruction, demonstration, practice, feedback, reinforcement)

Information Dissemination

Ubiquitous on the prevention landscape are programs that rely on the dissemination of factual information. The hallmark of these programs is that the main focus is on the provision of factual information concerning pharmacology and the adverse consequences of use. Information dissemination approaches to substance abuse prevention are based on a rational model of human behavior. Substance abuse is seen as being the result of insufficient knowledge of the adverse consequences of using psychoactive drugs. The prescription for preventing substance abuse, according to this model, is to educate adolescents about the dangers of smoking, drinking, or using drugs. It is assumed that, once they are armed with this knowledge, they will act in a rational and logical way and simply choose not to become substance users. It has also been assumed that exposure to factual information about the dangers of using drugs will effectuate changes in attitudes which, in turn, will lead to non-substance use behavior. Within the context of the information dissemination approach, individuals are seen as being essentially passive recipients of factual information.

Information dissemination programs have taken the form of public information campaigns and school-based tobacco, alcohol, and drug education programs. Public information campaigns have involved the use of pamphlets, leaflets, posters, and public service announcements (PSAs) to increase public awareness of the problem of tobacco, alcohol, or drug abuse and alter societal norms concerning use. School programs have involved classroom curricula, assembly programs featuring guest speakers (frequently policemen or health professionals), and educational films.

Many informational approaches have been designed to deter substance use by emphasizing and even dramatizing the risks associated with substance use. The underlying assumption of *fear-arousal* approaches is that evoking fear is more effective than a simple exposition of the facts. These approaches go beyond a dispassionate presentation of information by providing a clear and unambiguous message that substance use is dangerous. In addition, many traditional prevention programs have focused on the immorality of substance use. Program providers not only teach the objective facts but "preach" to students about the evils of smoking, drinking, or using drugs and exhort them not to engage in those behaviors.

Examination of the empirical evidence concerning the effectiveness of the different approaches to tobacco, alcohol, and drug abuse prevention described above indicates quite clearly that these approaches are *not* effective (33–39). Studies testing information dissemination approaches to prevention have consistently found that they can increase knowledge and change attitudes toward substance use. These studies have rather consistently indicated that informational approaches do *not* reduce or prevent tobacco, alcohol, or drug use; they indicate quite clearly that increased knowledge has virtually no impact on substance use or on intentions to engage in tobacco, alcohol, or drug use in the near future. As such, the evaluation studies call into question the basic assumption of the information dissemination model—that increasing knowledge will result in attitude and behavior change. Some studies have even suggested that this approach may lead to increased usage, possibly because it may serve to stimulate adolescents' curiosity (40, 41).

Because fear arousal and moral appeals are typically used in conjunction with informational programs, no evidence exists concerning their independent effects if any on substance use. However, since virtually all of the evaluation studies conducted with information dissemination approaches have not found evidence of prevention effects on behavior, it is unlikely that either of these approaches would yield any effects if used independently.

Considering the complex etiology of substance abuse, it is not surprising that approaches which rely on the provision of factual information are ineffective. Information dissemination approaches are inadequate because they are too narrow in their focus and are based on an incomplete understanding of the factors promoting substance use and abuse. Although knowledge about the negative consequences of substance use is important, it is only one of many factors considered to play a role in the initiation of substance use among adolescents (42).

Affective Education

Substance abuse prevention efforts have also utilized "affective education," which was intended to promote affective development. Affective education approaches are based on a different set of assumptions than cognitive approaches. Less emphasis is placed on factual information about the adverse consequences of substance abuse, and more emphasis is placed on students' personal and social development.

Affective education approaches focus on increasing self-understanding and acceptance through activities such as values clarifications and responsible decision making; improving interpersonal relations by fostering effective communication, peer counseling, and assertiveness; and increasing students' abilities to fulfill their basic needs through existing social institutions (43). A common component of many affective education programs is the inclusion of norm-setting messages concerning responsible substance use.

The results of evaluation studies testing the effectiveness of affective education approaches have been as discouraging as evaluations of informational approaches. Although affective education approaches have, in some instances, been able to demonstrate an impact on one or more of the correlates of substance use, they have not been able to have an impact on substance use *behavior* (42, 44).

Alternatives

One method of preventing substance abuse which has been a part of both community-based and school-based interventions has been to restructure part of the adolescent's environment to provide them with alternatives to substance use and activities associated with substance use. However, while some alternatives may decrease substance use, some may also increase it (45). Some alternatives have little theoretical connection to substance abuse, whereas others may be health compromising in their own right. Several different alternative approaches have been developed and, in some cases, evaluated (45).

The original model for alternatives typically involved the establishment of youth centers providing a particular activity or set of activities in the community (e.g., community service, academic tutoring, sports, hobbies). It was assumed that if adolescents could be provided with real-life experiences that would be as appealing as substance use, their involvement in these activities would actually take the place of involvement with substance use. Another type of alternative approach is *Outward Bound* and similar programs. These activities were organized in the hope that they would alter the affective-cognitive state of an individual—that they would change the way individuals felt about themselves and others, and how they saw the world. These were healthy activities frequently designed to promote teamwork, self-confidence, and self-esteem.

A third type of alternatives approach is targeted more to specific individual needs. For example, the need for relaxation or more energy might be satisfied by exercise, participating in sports, or hiking; the desire for sensory stimulation might be satisfied through activities that enhance sensory awareness such as learning to appreciate the sensory aspects of music, art, and nature; and the need for peer acceptance might be satisfied through participation in sensitivity training or encounter groups.

In this context, it is important to recognize that, while some activities have been associated with non-substance use, others have consistently been found to be associated with substance abuse (45). For example, entertainment activities, participation in vocational activities, and participation in social activities have been found to be associated with more substance use. On the other hand, academic activities, involvement in religious activities, and participation in sports have generally been associated with less substance use. Consequently, it is conceivable that some alternatives programs could be counterproductive if the wrong type of activities were selected. At the same time, the activities that may be the most appropriate alternatives are likely to be those which would have the least interest for individuals at high risk for using drugs. None of the evaluations of alternatives approaches have found any impact on substance use behavior (37, 46).

Psychological Inoculation

The pioneering work of Evans and his colleagues at the University of Houston toward the end of the 1970s triggered a major departure from traditional approaches to tobacco, alcohol, and drug abuse prevention. Unlike previous approaches that focus on information dissemination, fear arousal, or moral suasion, the strategy developed initially by Evans and his colleagues (47, 48) focused on the social and psychological factors believed to be involved in the initiation of cigarette smoking.

Evans' work was strongly influenced by persuasive communications theory as formulated by McGuire (49, 50) and a concept called "psychological inoculation." Psychological inoculation is analogous to that of inoculation used in infectious disease prevention. Persuasive communications designed to alter attitudes, beliefs, and behavior are conceptualized as the psychosocial analogue of "germs." To prevent "infection" it is necessary to expose the individual to a weak dose of those "germs" in a way that facilitates the development of "antibodies" and thereby increases resistance to any future exposure to persuasive messages in their more virulent form.

The application of the concept of psychological inoculation as a smoking prevention strategy is fairly straightforward. Smoking is conceptualized as being the result of social influences (persuasive messages) to smoke from peers and the media which are either direct (offers to smoke from other adolescents or cigarette advertising) or indirect (exposure to high-status role models who smoke). If adolescents are likely to be called "chicken" for refusing to try cigarettes, they can be forewarned of the likelihood of encountering that kind of pressure and provided with the necessary skills for countering it. For example, they can be trained to reply: "If I smoke to prove to you that I'm not a chicken, all I'll really be showing is that I'm afraid not to do what you want me to do. I don't want to smoke; therefore I'm not going to." If adolescents are likely to see older youth posturing and acting "tough" by smoking, they can be taught to think to themselves: "If they were really tough, they wouldn't have to smoke to prove it."

The intervention initially developed by Evans consisted of a series of films designed to increase students' awareness of the various social pressures to smoke that they would be likely to encounter as they progressed through the critical junior high school period. Also included in these films were demonstrations of specific techniques that could be used to effectively resist various pressures to smoke. The prevention strategy developed by Evans also included two other important components: periodic assessment of smoking with feedback to students and information about the immediate physiological effects of smoking. Smoking was assessed by questionnaire on a biweekly basis and saliva samples were collected as an objective measure of smoking status. The rate of smoking in each classroom (which was considerably lower than most adolescents thought) was publicly announced to correct the misperception that cigarette smoking is a highly normative behavior (i.e., that everybody is doing it).

In the first major test of this prevention strategy, Evans compared students receiving assessment/feedback with those receiving monitoring/feedback plus inoculation against a control group (48). The students in the two treatment conditions exhibited smoking onset rates of about 50% lower than that observed in the control group. Although the inoculation intervention did not produce any additional reduction in smoking onset beyond that produced by the assessment/feedback intervention, the overall reduction in smoking onset was dramatic in view of the history of failed prevention efforts that preceded this study. The success of the study conducted by Evans triggered an explosion of prevention research and offered the first real evidence in more than two decades that preventive interventions could work.

Resistance Skills Training

Several variations on the prevention model originally developed by Evans have been subsequently tested over the years (51–61). Similar to Evans' model, these interventions were designed to increase students' awareness of the various social influences to engage in substance use. A distinctive feature of these prevention models is that they place more emphasis on teaching students specific skills for effectively resisting both peer and media pressures to smoke, drink, or use drugs.

This chapter refers to this type of prevention program as social "resistance skills training," since it captures two distinctive aspects of these programs: (a) the focus on increasing participants' resistance to negative social influences to engage in substance use and (b) the focus on skills training. They have also been referred to as "social influence" approaches (because they target the social influences promoting substance use) or "refusal skills training" approaches (because a central feature of these programs is that they teach how to say "No" to substance use offers).

The psychosocial prevention approaches that rely on resistance skills training are based on a conceptual model stressing the fundamental importance of social factors in promoting the initiation of substance use among adolescents. These influences come from the family (parents and older siblings), peers, and the mass media. Adolescents may be predisposed toward substance use because substance use behavior is modeled by parents or older siblings or because of the transmission of positive or ambiguous messages concerning the rectitude of substance use. Similarly, individuals who have friends who smoke, drink, or use drugs are more likely to become substance users themselves as a result of issues relating to modeling and the need for peer acceptance (as well as availability). Finally, on the larger societal level, high-status role models in the mass media may promote substance use, supported by the perception of positive norms and expectations with respect to substance use. Group norms are enforced by both implicit and explicit rules governing behavior, as well as perceived desirability. As Bandura (62) has indicated, all social influences are themselves a product of the interaction between individual learning histories and forces in both the community and the larger society.

On the individual level, influences related to specific behaviors arise from learned expectations and skills regarding those behaviors. For example, individuals may smoke because they expect relatively immediate positive outcomes such as increased alertness, relief from anxiety, or enhanced social status. Logically, it would appear reasonable that individuals would choose not to smoke if they did not expect to receive rewarding consequences or if they had the ability to resist specific social pressures to smoke. Expectations and skills are learned both from observation and from direct experience.

Resistance skills training approaches generally teach students how to recognize situations in which they will have a high likelihood of experiencing peer pressure to smoke, drink, or use drugs so that these high-risk situations can be avoided. In addition, students are taught how to handle situations in which they might experience peer pressure to engage in substance use. Typically, this includes teaching students not only what to say (i.e., the specific content of a refusal message), but also how to deliver it in the most effective way possible.

Another distinctive feature of these programs is the use of peer leaders as program providers. The peer leaders used in these interventions are typically older students (e.g., 10th graders might serve as peer leaders for 7th graders). Peer leaders could also be the same age as the participants and may even be from the same class. The rationale for using peer leaders is that peers generally have higher credibility with adolescents than do adults. Finally, students are generally provided with the opportunity to observe other students using these skills, as well as to practice these skills through the use of roleplaying in class (Table 76.2).

Material has also generally been included in these programs to combat the perception that substance use is widespread (i.e., "everybody's doing it") since research has indicated that adolescents typically overestimate the prevalence of smoking, drinking, and the use of certain drugs (63). This has been accomplished by simply providing students with the prevalence rates of substance use among their age-mates in terms of national survey data or conducting classroom or school-wide surveys, which are organized and directed by students participating in the program. Finally, these programs typically include a component designed to increase students' awareness of the techniques used by advertisers to promote the sale of tobacco products or alcoholic beverages and to teach techniques for formulating counter-arguments to the messages used by advertisers.

The effectiveness of social resistance skills prevention strategies has been documented in a number of studies. A review of these preventive interventions indicates that they are able to reduce the rate of smoking by be-

Table 76.2 Studies Testing Social and Resistance Skills Training Approaches

Reference	Subjects	Intervention Approach	Evaluation Design	Results
Adolescent Alcohol Prevention Trial (58, 66)	5th graders	Nine-session school-based program assessing the effectiveness of Resistance Skills Training, Normative Education, and drug education; 7th grade booster sessions; includes discussion, homework, and video	Pre- and posttest; 3-year follow-up; tested information only, Resistance Training, Normative Education, and Combined curricula	Resistance Training and Normative Education significantly increased the skills they targeted; only Normative Education positively affected substance use into 8th grade; Resistance Training only condition increased levels of substance abuse
Alcohol Misuse Prevention Study (65)	5th and 6th graders	Four-session resistance training curriculum, with three booster sessions; involves health education, coping strategies; uses positive reinforcement, roleplay, homework, and video	Pre- and posttest; 26-month follow-up; compares intervention, intervention plus boosters, and control	No treatment effect as a whole for alcohol use, or misuse; program effects found for alcohol misuse in the subgroups who had experienced drinking prior to implementation
Project ALERT (59)	7th graders; urban, suburban, and rural	Eight-session social influence and resistance skills training curriculum; three 8th grade booster sessions; utilized roleplay and discussion; conducted by classroom teachers and older teenagers	Pre- and posttest; follow-up (3-, 12- and 15-month); program tested on students in three levels of risk	Initial reductions in drinking for different risk levels; Project effects for marihuana and cigarette initiation for all risk levels; reductions in drinking not sustained after 7th grade
Project ALERT (78)	7th graders	Same as above	Pre- and posttest; 2-year follow-up	Effects on cognitive risk factors persist through 9th grade in teen-led condition; all effects on actual use decay after 2 years
Project ALERT (79)	7th graders	Same as above	Pre- and posttest; 6-year follow-up	Effects on substance use decay after intervention; some effects on cognitive risk factors persist until 10th grade
University of Vermont School and Mass Media Program (67)	4th, 5th, and 6th graders	Four-year mass media and school-based educational intervention; 4 sessions/year in grades 5–8, and 3 sessions/year in grades 9 and 10; includes decision-making, resistance training, and health information; mass media program included health information and resistance skills components	Pre- and posttest; follow-up (4 years annually); compares school-only and media-and-school interventions	Reductions in smoking and targeted mediating variables for media-and-school condition
Midwestern Prevention Project (69)	6th and 7th graders	Ten-session intervention program includes school, parent, mass media components; school-based intervention includes resistance training, normative education, and health education; reinforced by roleplay, problem solving, discussion and practice; taught by classroom teachers, using peer leaders; includes booster sessions	Pre- and posttest; 2-year follow-up	Proportion of smokers lower in experimental group for recent smoking and having smoked within one month; experimental group marginally lower in number of students who have ever smoked
Midwestern Prevention Project (71)	6th and 7th graders; high and low risk	Ten-session school-based social influences curriculum mentioned above	Pre- and posttest; 3-year follow-up	Experimental reductions in tobacco and marihuana use; equivalent reductions across risk levels; with marginal effect for lifetime smoking
Midwestern Prevention Project (113)	6th and 7th graders	Ten-session school-based social influences curriculum mentioned above	Pre- and posttest; 1-year follow-up	Experimental reductions in cigarette smoking, drinking, and marihuana use; positive effects on mediating variables, such as communication skills, and beliefs about friends' tolerance of drug use
Midwestern Prevention Project (68)	6th graders	Thirteen-session social influence school prevention curriculum similar to Pentz et al. (69), plus parent curriculum consisting of parent-child homework, parent training workshops, and community activities	Pre- and posttest; 18-month follow-up	73% of parents participated in at least one of the components; parent participation in program resulted in less cigarette use, and marginally associated with less alcohol use at follow-up
Minnesota Team (70)	7th graders	Five-year behavioral health and community education program; school-based component focuses on health education, resistance skills, normative beliefs, and peer and media influences;	Pre- and posttest; follow-up (7-year, annually)	Significant reductions in smoking prevalence and intensity at all subsequent test points through high school

Continued

Table 76.2   Studies Testing Social and Resistance Skills Training Approaches (*continued*)

Reference	Subjects	Intervention Approach	Evaluation Design	Results
		includes roleplay, discussion, and a public commitment to abstain; community smoking prevention in 7th grade		
Project SMART (72)	7th graders	Twelve-session social skills and drug resistance curriculum, and a 12-session affective education curriculum; utilized roleplay and discussion; conducted by health educators, with peer assistants	Pre- and posttest comparison of 2 program types within 6 subgroups (males, females, Asians, blacks, Hispanics, and whites); 1-year follow-up of 3 cohorts	Positive effects for females in both programs for cigarette smoking and alcohol consumption; significant sex by program interactions for cigarettes and marihuana use
Project TNT (Towards No Tobacco Use) (61)	7th graders	Three individual 10-session social influence curricula focusing on resistance skills, normative beliefs, health consequences and a combined curriculum; involves discussion, decision-making, video, and public commitment; taught by health educators	Pre- and posttest; 1-year follow-up; compares effects of 3 components of program: resistance skills, normative beliefs, and health consequences	The comprehensive, informational, and health education curricula were superior in reducing both trial and weekly use of tobacco compared to normative and control; all conditions except the informational condition were superior to control for reduction of smokeless tobacco use

tween 35 and 45% after the initial intervention. Most of these prevention studies have focused primarily on preventing the onset of cigarette smoking—that is, preventing the transition from nonsmoking to smoking. The results reported range from reductions of 33–39% in the proportion of individuals beginning to smoke (comparing the proportion of new smokers in the experimental group with that of the control group). Several studies have demonstrated reductions in the overall prevalence of cigarette smoking among the participating students both for experimental smoking (less than one cigarette per week) and for regular smoking (one or more cigarettes per week). In these studies, the impact on the prevalence of regular smoking has ranged from reductions of 43 to 47%. Similar reductions have been reported for alcohol and marihuana use (59, 64, 65). Although most studies assessing the impact of these prevention approaches on tobacco use have focused on cigarette smoking, recent research indicates that the social resistance skills training approach also reduces smokeless tobacco use (61)

Most of the research studies conducted with resistance skills training approaches have been targeted at junior high school students, generally beginning with 7th graders. Some studies have included students as young as 4th, 5th, and 6th graders (58, 65–67). The programs tested have been of varying lengths, ranging from as few as three or four sessions to as many as 11 or 12 sessions. Considerable variation also exists among the individuals responsible for implementing these programs. Some programs have been implemented by college students, others by members of the research project staff, and still others have used classroom teachers to implement the prevention programs. In addition to studies testing the effectiveness of social resistance skills training approaches in school settings, studies have also tested this intervention approach along with media (67), parent (68), or media and parent (69, 70) components. These studies indicate that the inclusion of additional intervention components produces stronger prevention effects than the school-based intervention alone.

To develop more effective interventions, it is necessary to identify the relative efficacy of program components and the most effective providers. For example, many social resistance skills approaches include a public commitment component; yet the results of a study conducted by Hurd and his collaborators (52) suggest that this component may not contribute to the effectiveness of these programs. Similarly, many of these programs have used films or videotapes similar to those initially developed by Evans and his colleagues (48). However, it is not yet clear what type of media material is the most effective or the extent to which it is necessary as a component. Finally, little is known concerning the optimal age (grade) of intervention, program length, program structure, or the characteristics of the individuals who are the most influenced by these programs. With respect to the latter, studies have attempted to examine the characteristics of the individuals who are af-

fected by interventions based on the social resistance skills prevention approach. Results have generally indicated that these prevention programs are effective with a broad range of adolescents including high and low risk individuals (71) and urban, suburban, and rural students (59). At least one study, however, found differential prevention effects by gender (72).

It has generally been assumed that peer leaders play an important role in social influence approaches. Same-age or older peer leaders have been included in nearly all of the studies testing social resistance skills training approaches. In general, evidence supports the use of peer leaders for this type of prevention strategy (51, 56). Although peer leaders have been used successfully to varying degrees in these programs, they usually assist adult program providers and have specific and well-defined roles. The primary providers in most of these studies have been either members of the research project staff or teachers. There is also evidence to suggest that peer-led programs may not be uniformly effective for all students. For example, the results of one study suggest that, while boys and girls may be equally affected by social influence programs when conducted by teachers, girls may be more influenced by peer-led programs than boys (73). Perhaps the best known application of the social resistance skills training model is Project DARE (Drug Abuse Resistance Education) which is being used in approximately 60% of the classrooms in America. A unique aspect of DARE and one that no doubt has contributed to its adoption by many schools is that it is conducted by police officers. Although DARE has been remarkably successful with respect to being adopted by a large number of schools and in promoting an awareness of drug abuse, the results of DARE have been disappointing. According to a major meta-analysis of studies evaluating the DARE program, it is less effective than other resistance skills training approaches and has produced only minimal effects (74).

Follow-up studies using school-based approaches indicate that the positive behavioral effects of these prevention approaches are evident for up to 3 years after the conclusion of these programs for cigarette smoking (55, 57, 61, 64) and multicomponent studies have found prevention effects for up to seven years (75). However, results from long-term follow-up studies of school-based approaches indicate that these prevention effects are typically not maintained (76–79). While this has led some to conclude that school-based prevention approaches may not be powerful enough to produce lasting prevention effects (80), others have argued that the prevention approaches tested in these studies may have deficiencies which undermined their long-term effectiveness.

For example, Resnicow and Botvin (81) make the case that the apparent failure of studies testing resistance skills training approaches to produce long-term prevention effects may have to do with factors related to either the type of intervention tested in these studies or the way these interventions were implemented. According to them, the absence of long-term prevention effects in these studies should not be taken as an indictment of school-based prevention. Durable prevention effects may not have been produced in several long-term follow-up studies because (*a*) the length of the intervention may have been too short (i.e., the prevention approach was effective, but the initial prevention "dosage" was to low to produce a long-term effect), (*b*) booster sessions were either inadequate or not included (i.e., the prevention approach was effective, but it eroded over time because of the absence or inadequacy of ongoing intervention), (*c*) the intervention was not implemented with enough fidelity to the intervention model (i.e., the correct prevention approach was used, but it was implemented incompletely, improperly, or both), and/or (*d*) the intervention was based on a faulty assumptions, was incomplete, or was otherwise deficient (i.e., the prevention approach was ineffective).

Based on the findings of more recently published research using the prevention approach described in the next section, it now appears that all four of these factors may have played a role in the negative findings of long-term follow-up studies with prevention approaches based on the resistance skills training model. It is also clear that it is possible to develop and implement school-based prevention approaches powerful enough to have a durable impact on adolescent substance use. However, to be effective, school-based interventions need to be more comprehensive, have a stronger initial dosage, include at least two additional years of (booster) intervention, and be implemented in a manner that is faithful to the underlying intervention model.

Personal and Social Skills Training

Since the end of the 1970s and up to the present, considerable prevention research has also been conducted with a prevention model which teaches general personal and social skills either alone (82) or in combination with components of the social resistance skills model (83–94). These approaches are more comprehensive than either traditional cognitive/affective approaches or the recently developed resistance skills model. Moreover, unlike affective education approaches which rely on experiential classroom activities, these approaches emphasize the use of proven cognitive/behavioral skills training methods. They are based on social learning theory (62) and problem behavior theory (5). Substance abuse is conceptualized as a socially learned and functional behavior, resulting from the interplay of social and personal factors. Substance use behavior is learned through modeling and reinforcement and is influenced by cognition, attitudes, and beliefs.

Personal and social skills training prevention approaches typically teach two or more of the following:

- General problem-solving and decision-making skills
- General cognitive skills for resisting interpersonal or media influences
- Skills for increasing self-control and self-esteem
- Adaptive coping strategies for relieving stress and anxiety through the use of cognitive coping skills or behavioral relaxation techniques
- General social skills
- General assertive skills

These skills are taught using a combination of instruction, demonstration, feedback, reinforcement, behavioral rehearsal (practice during class), and extended practice through behavioral homework assignments.

The intent of these programs is to teach the kind of generic skills for coping with life that will have a relatively broad application. This is in contrast to the resistance skills training approaches which are designed to teach skills with a *problem-specific* focus. Personal and social skills training programs emphasize the application of general skills to situations directly related to substance use and abuse (e.g., the application of general assertive skills to situations involving peer pressure to smoke, drink, or use drugs). These same skills can be used for dealing with many of the challenges confronting adolescents in their everyday lives, including but not limited to smoking, drinking, or drug abuse.

Although prevention approaches which emphasize the development of general personal and social skills are in sharp contrast to problem-specific approaches designed to teach skills for resisting social influences to use

drugs, the most effective prevention approaches appear to be those which combine the features of both. For example, evidence from one study suggests that broad-based competence enhancement approaches may not be effective unless they also contain some resistance skills training material. This may be necessary both because such material includes a focus on antidrug norms and helps students apply generic personal and social skills to situations related specifically to the prevention of substance abuse.

Most of the prevention studies on this approach that have been conducted thus far have focused on 7th graders. However, some studies have been conducted with 6th graders (95) and one was conducted with 8th, 9th, and 10th graders (83). Program length has ranged from as few as seven sessions to as many as 20 sessions. Some of these prevention programs were conducted at a rate of one class session per week, while others were conducted at a rate of two or more classes per week. Most of the studies conducted so far have used adults as the primary program providers. In some cases these adults were teachers; in other cases they were outside health professionals (i.e., project staff members, graduate students, social workers). Some studies have included booster sessions, although the majority have not.

Evaluation studies testing personal and social skills training approaches have demonstrated significant behavioral effects. Moreover, the magnitude of reported effects has typically been relatively large. In general, these studies have demonstrated that generic skills approaches to substance abuse prevention can produce reductions in new experimental smoking ranging from 42 to 75%. Data from two studies with a promising program called *Life Skills Training* (LST) (88, 96) demonstrated reductions ranging from 56 to 67% in the proportion of pretest nonsmokers becoming regular smokers at the 1-year follow-up without additional booster sessions. With booster sessions these reductions have been as high as 87% (88). Moreover, initial reductions of an equal magnitude have also been reported for regular smoking (87, 88, 96). Several studies also provide evidence for the efficacy of this approach, on the use of alcohol (85, 86, 89, 97, 98) and marihuana (86, 97, 99) (Table 76.3).

One of the most important issues regarding substance abuse prevention concerns long-term effectiveness, particularly in light of the generally negative findings of resistance skills training approaches. Long-term follow-up data (100) from one of the largest school-based substance abuse prevention studies ever conducted found reductions in smoking, alcohol, and marihuana use six years after the initial baseline assessment. This randomized, controlled field trial involved nearly 6000 7th graders from 56 public schools in New York State. After random assignment to prevention and control conditions, students in the prevention condition received the LST program during the 7th grade (15 prevention sessions) with booster sessions in the 8th grade (10 sessions) and 9th grade (5 sessions). No intervention was provided during grades 10–12. Follow-up data were collected by survey in class, by mail, and/or by telephone at the end of the 12th grade and beyond for those students not available for the school survey. The prevalence of cigarette smoking, alcohol use, and marihuana use for the students in the prevention condition was up to 44% lower than for controls. Significant reductions (relative to controls) of up to 66% were also found with respect to the prevalence of polydrug use (students using all three gateway drugs) during the past week.

Until recently, most of the research testing the effectiveness of contemporary substance abuse prevention approaches has been limited to predominantly white, suburban populations. While there is a paucity of high-quality data concerning the etiology of substance use among racial/ethnic minority populations, existing evidence suggests that there is substantial overlap in the factors promoting and maintaining substance use among different populations (101–106).

Studies testing the efficacy of the LST approach have shown that it has an impact on a broad range of students. According to the results of these studies, the LST approach is effective in preventing cigarette smoking among Hispanic youth (107, 108) and African-American youth (109, 110). Follow-up data with Hispanic youth have demonstrated the continued presence of lower levels of cigarette smoking up to the end of the 10th grade (111). Most of the research with minority youth has been directed at cigarette smoking. However, the results of several new studies show that school-based substance abuse prevention approaches such as the LST approach are also able to reduce alcohol and marihuana use (111, 112), and that tailoring

Table 76.3   Studies Testing Life Skills Training Approaches

Reference	Subjects	Intervention Approach	Evaluation Design	Results
Life Skills Training (Botvin et al., 1989)	7th graders; urban, African-American	12-session resistance and general life skills curriculum similar to Botvin et al. (97)	Pre- and posttest	Reductions in tobacco use; increased knowledge of consequences of smoking and normative expectations concerning adult and peer smoking
Life Skills Training (94)	7th graders, white, suburban	20-session intervention similar to Botvin et al. (97); 10 booster sessions in 8th grade	Pre- and posttest; 1-year follow-up; compares 5 interventions peer-led, peer-led with booster sessions, teacher-led, teacher-led with booster sessions, and control	Peer-led implementation with booster sessions resulted in reductions in tobacco, alcohol, and marihuana use; similar effects for females in teacher-led condition; program effects on mediating variables
Life Skills Training (97)	7th graders, white, suburban	15-session personal, social and resistance skills curriculum; 10 2nd- and 5 3rd-year booster sessions; sessions include decision making, assertiveness, self-esteem, stress management, media influences, drug knowledge, social skills, and communication skills; utilized discussion, homework, video, roleplay, behavioral rehearsal, and reinforcement; taught by classroom teachers	Pre- and posttest; 3-year follow-up; compares implementation with provider training workshops and consultations, videotaped training only, and information only control	Reductions in cigarette, marihuana, and alcohol use; program effects on mediating variables such as normative expectations, substance use knowledge, interpersonal and communication skills
Life Skills Training (111)	7th graders, minority, urban	Generic program same as above; culturally-focused program similar, but utilized multicultural myths and stories to model various skills; taught by outside providers and peer leaders	Pre- and posttest; 1-year follow-up; compares generic skills-training, culturally-focused, and information-only control	Both prevention programs show reductions in intentions to drink alcohol, and changes in mediating variables consistent with nondrug use; generic program also reduced intentions to use illicit drugs
Life Skills Training (112)	7th graders, minority, urban	Same as Botvin et al. (111)	Pre- and posttest; 2-year follow-up	Reductions in current alcohol use and intentions to drink alcohol. Effects on mediating variables consistent with nondrug use
Life Skills Training (100)	7th graders, white, suburban	Same as Botvin et al. (97)	Pre- and posttest; 6-year follow-up	Reductions in drug and polydrug use; strongest effects found for students who received a more complete version of the program
Positive Youth Development Program (82)	6th and 7th graders; urban and suburban	20-session program including: stress management, self-esteem, problem solving, substance and health information, assertiveness and social networks; involves discussion, roleplay, diaries, and video tapes; conducted by classroom teachers and health educators	Pre- and posttest	Increases in social adjustment and coping skills. Intentions to use substances remained the same for program students, while control students reported increased intentions at post assessment; positive effects on alcohol use, but no effects on reported drug use

the intervention to the culture of the target population can enhance its effectiveness (112).

A major strength of the evaluation studies conducted with the broader personal and social skills training approaches is that they have also a demonstrated impact on variables hypothesized to mediate the effect of the prevention programs in a direction consistent with non-substance use. These include significant changes in knowledge and attitudes, assertiveness, locus of control, social anxiety, self-satisfaction, decision-making, and problem-solving. Together, the results of these studies provide compelling evidence supporting the efficacy of broad-spectrum prevention strategies focusing on personal and social skills development. Thus, this prevention approach has been demonstrated to produce reductions in substance use (relative to controls) as well as changes on several hypothesized mediating variables in a direction consistent with reduced substance abuse risk.

SUMMARY AND CONCLUSION

A number of substance abuse prevention approaches have been developed and tested over the years. The most common approaches to tobacco, alcohol, and drug abuse prevention are those that focus on providing factual information about the adverse consequences of using these substances, with some approaches including a mix of scare tactics and moral messages. Other commonly used approaches to substance abuse prevention have utilized affective education and alternatives approaches. The existing evaluation literature shows rather conclusively that these are not effective prevention strategies when the standard of effectiveness concerns the ability to influence substance use behavior.

The only prevention approaches that have been demonstrated to have an effective impact on substance use behavior are those that teach junior high school students social resistance skills either alone or in combination with approaches designed to enhance general personal competence by teaching an array of personal and social life skills. Both approaches emphasize skills training and de-emphasize the provision of information concerning the adverse health consequences of substance use. These approaches utilize well-tested behavioral intervention techniques to facilitate the acquisition of skills for resisting social influences to engage in substance use.

Recognizing the critical importance of the early adolescent years, these preventive interventions have generally been implemented with middle and junior high school students. Despite generally impressive prevention effects, it is clear that, without booster sessions, these effects decay over time, thus arguing for ongoing prevention activities throughout early adolescent years and perhaps until the end of high school.

Although there has been considerable activity in the form of both the parents' movement and mass media campaigns, there is little evidence to indicate that such approaches are effective when used alone. However, community-based substance abuse prevention approaches based on principles derived from the most effective school-based prevention programs and successful community-based cardiovascular disease prevention studies appear to offer considerable promise.

Over the past decade, there have been a number of significant developments in the field of substance abuse prevention. Yet, despite the promise offered by these approaches, future research is needed to further refine current prevention models and to develop new ones. Given the urgency and importance of dealing with the problem of substance abuse, it seems prudent to proceed on two simultaneous tracks: one involving further prevention re-search and the other involving the dissemination of the most promising existing prevention approaches. This is particularly important in view of the fact that the most widely utilized prevention approaches continue to be those that have already been found either to be ineffective or to lack any scientifically defensible evidence of their efficacy.

The problem of substance abuse is still very prevalent. However, for the first time in the history of its prevention, evidence now exists from a number of rigorously designed evaluation studies that specific school-based and community-based prevention models are effective. It is now incumbent upon health care professionals, educators, community leaders, and policymakers to move expeditiously toward wide dissemination and utilization of these approaches. It is equally important for private and governmental agencies to provide adequate funding for the important research necessary to further refine existing prevention models and to increase our understanding of the causes of substance abuse.

References

1. Johnston LD, O'Malley PM, Bachman JD. National survey results on drug use from the Monitoring the Future Study, 1975–1994. Vol. 1 Secondary school students. National Institute on Drug Abuse, DHHS Pub. No (ADM) 95–4026. Washington, DC: U.S. Government Printing Office, 1995.
2. Newcomb MD, Bentler PM. Consequences of adolescent drug use: Impact on the lives of young adults. New York: Sage, 1988.
3. Baumrind D, Moselle KA. A developmental perspective on adolescent drug abuse. Alcohol Subst Use Adolesc 1985:45–65.
4. Blum R, Richards L. Youthful drug use. In: Dupont RI, Goldstein A, O'Donnell J, eds. Handbook on drug abuse (National Institute on Drug Abuse). Washington, DC: U.S. Government Printing Office, 1975:257–267.
5. Jessor R, Jessor SL. Problem behavior and psychosocial development: a longitudinal study of youth. New York: Academic Press, 1977.
6. Battjes RJ, Jones CL. Implications of etiological research for preventive interventions and future research. NIDA Res Monogr 1985;56:269–276.
7. Kandel DB. Convergences in prospective longitudinal surveys of drug use in normal populations. In: Kandel DB, ed. Longitudinal research on drug use: empirical findings and methodological issues. Washington, DC: Hemisphere (Halsted-Wiley), 1978:3–38.
8. Meyer RE, Mirin SM. The heroin stimulus: implications for a theory of addiction. New York: Plenum, 1979:276.
9. Wechsler H. Alcohol intoxication and drug use among teenagers. J Stud Alcohol 1976;37:1672–1677.
10. Barnes GM, Welte JW. Patterns and predictors of alcohol use among 7–12th grade students in New York State. J Stud Alcohol 1986;47:53–62.
11. Brown B, Clasen D, Eicher S. Perceptions of peer pressure, peer conformity dispositions, and self-reported behavior among adolescents. Dev Psychol 1986;22:521–530.
12. Gfroerer J. Correlation between drug use by teenagers and drug use by older family members. Am J Drug Alcohol Abuse 1987;13(1&2):95–108.
13. Kandel D. On processes of peer influences in adolescent drug use: a developmental perspective. Adv Alcohol Subst Abuse 1985;4(3,4):139–163.
14. Krosnick JA, Judd CM. Transitions in social influence in adolescence: who induces cigarette smoking? Dev Psychol 1982;18:359–368.
15. Whelan EM. A smoking gun: how the tobacco industry gets away with murder. Philadelphia: George F. Stickley Co., 1984.
16. Tye J, Warner K, Glantz S. Tobacco advertising and consumption: evidence of a causal relationship. J Public Health Policy 1987:492–507.
17. Smith GN, Fogg CP. Psychological predictors of early use, late use, and non-use of marijuana among teenage students. In: Kandel DB, ed. Longitudinal research on drug use: Empirical findings and methodological issues. Washington, DC: Hemisphere-Wiley, 1978.
18. Chassin L, Presson CC, Sherman SJ, Corty E, Olshavsky RW. Predicting the onset of cigarette smoking in adolescents: a longitudinal study. J Appl Soc Psychol 1984;14(3):224–243.
19. Clarke JG, MacPherson BV, Holmes DR. Cigarette smoking and external locus of control among adolescents. J Health Soc Behav 1982;23:253–259.
20. Page RM. Shyness as a risk factor for adolescent substance use. J Sch Health 1989;59(10):432–435.
21. Dielman TE, Leech SL, Lorenger AT, Horvath WJ. Health locus of control and self-esteem as related to adolescent health behavior and intentions. Adolescence 1984;19:935–950.
22. Millman RB, Botvin GJ. Substance use, abuse, and dependence. In: Levine MD, Carey WB, Crocker AC, Gross RT, eds. Developmental-behavioral pediatrics. Philadelphia: WB Saunders, 1983:683–708.
23. Jessor R. Critical issues in research on adolescent health promotion. In: Coates T, Petersen A, Perry C, eds. Promoting adolescent health: a dialogue on research and practice. New York: Academic Press, 1982:447–465.
24. Demone HW. The nonuse and abuse of alcohol by the male adolescent. In: Chafetz M, ed. Proceedings of the second annual Alcoholism Conference. (DHEW Publication No. HSM 73–9083.) Washington, DC: U.S. Government Printing Office, 1973:24–32.
25. Jessor R, Collins MI, Jessor SL. On becoming a drinker: social-psychological aspects of an adolescent transition. Ann N Y Acad Sci 1972;197:199–213.
26. Newcomb MD, Bentler PM. Drug use, educational aspirations and work force involvement: the transition from adolescence to young adulthood. Am J Community Psychol 1986;14(3):303–321.
27. Wechsler H, Thum D. Alcohol and drug use among teenagers: a questionnaire study. In: Chafetz M, ed. Proceedings of the second annual Alcoholism Conference. (DHEW Publication No. HSM 73–9083.) Washington, DC: U.S. Government Printing Office, 1973:33–46.
28. Ray OS. Drugs, society, and human behavior. St. Louis: CV Mosby, 1974.
29. Hamburg BA, Braemer HC, Jahnke WA. Hierarchy of drug use in adolescence: behavioral and attitudinal correlates of substantial drug use. Am J Psychiatry 1975;132:1155–1167.
30. Utech D, Hoving KL. Parents and peers as competing influences in the decisions on children of differing ages. J Soc Psychol 1969;78:267–274.
31. Piaget J. The moral judgment of the child. New York: Collier, 1962.
32. Mussen P, Conger J, Kagan J. Child development and personality. 4th edition. New York: Harper & Row, 1974.
33. Dorn N, Thompson A. Evaluation of drug education in the longer term is not an optional extra. Community Health 1976;7:154–161.
34. Goodstadt MS. Myths and methodology in drug education: a critical review of the research evidence. In: Goldstadt MS, ed. Research on methods and programs of drug education. Toronto: Addiction Research Foundation, 1974.
35. Kinder B, Pape N, Walfish S. Drug and alcohol education programs: a review of outcome studies. Int J Addict 1980;15:1035–1054.
36. Richards LG. Government programs and psychological principals in drug abuse education. Paper presented at the annual convention of the American Psychological Association, Washington, DC, 1969.
37. Schaps E, Bartolo RD, Moskowitz J, Palley CS, Churgin S. A review of 127 drug abuse prevention program evaluations. J Drug Issues 1981:17–43.
38. Schaps E, Moskowitz JM, Malvin J, Schaeffer G. Napa project summary. Unpublished report. Lafayette, CA: Pacific Institute for Research and Evaluation, 1983.
39. Swisher JD, Hoffman A. Information. The irrelevant variable in drug education. In: Corder BW, Smith RA, Swisher JD, eds. Drug abuse prevention: perspectives and approaches for educators. Dubuque, IA: William C. Brown, 1975:49–62.
40. Mason ML. Drug education effects. Dissert Abstr 1973;134(4-B):418.
41. Swisher JD, Crawford JL, Goldstein R, Yura M. Drug education: pushing or preventing? Peabody J Educ 1971;49:68–75.
42. Kearney AL, Hines MH. Evaluation of the effectiveness of a drug prevention education program. J Drug Educ 1980;10:127–134.
43. Swisher JD. Prevention issues. In: Dupont RI, Goldstein A, O'Donnell J, eds. Handbook on drug abuse. Washington, DC: National Institute on Drug Abuse, 1979:49–62.
44. Kim S. A short- and long-term evaluation of here's looking at you alcohol education program. J Drug Educ 1988;18(3):235–242.
45. Swisher JD, Hu TW. Alternatives to drug abuse: some are and some are not. NIDA Res Monogr 1983;47:141–153.

46. Schaps E, Moskowitz JM, Malvin JH, Scheffer GH. Evaluation of seven school-based prevention programs: a final report on the Napa Project. Int J Addict 1986;21:1081–1112.

47. Evans RI. Smoking in children: developing a social psychological strategy of deterrence. Prev Med 1976;5:122–127.

48. Evans RI, Rozelle RM, Mittlemark MB, Hansen WB, Bane AL, Havis J. Deterring the onset of smoking in children: knowledge of immediate physiological effects and coping with peer pressure, media pressure, and parent modeling. J Appl Soc Psychol 1978;8:126–135.

49. McGuire WJ. Inducing resistance to persuasion: some contemporary approaches. In: Berkowitz L, ed. Advances in experimental social psychology. New York: Academic Press, 1964:192–227.

50. McGuire WJ. The nature of attitudes and attitude change. In: Lindzey G, Aronson E, eds. Handbook of social psychology. Reading, MA: Addison-Wesley, 1968:136–314.

51. Arkin RM, Roemhild HJ, Johnson CA, Luepker RV, Murray DM. The Minnesota smoking prevention program: a seventh grade health curriculum supplement. J Sch Health 1981;51:616–661.

52. Hurd P, Johnson CA, Pechacek T, Bast CP, Jacobs D, Luepker R. Prevention of cigarette smoking in 7th grade students. J Behav Med 1980;3:15–28.

53. McAlister A, Perry C, Maccoby N. Adolescent smoking: onset and prevention. Pediatrics 1979; 63:650–658.

54. Murray DM, Johnson CA, Luepker RV, Pechacek TF, Jacobs DR. Issues in smoking prevention research. Paper presented at the American Psychological Association, Montreal, Canada, September, 1980.

55. Luepker RV, Johnson CA, Murray DM, Pechacek TF. Prevention of cigarette smoking: Three year follow-up of educational programs for youth. J Behav Med 1983;6:53–61.

56. Perry C, Killen J, Slinkard LA, McAlister AL. Peer teaching and smoking prevention among junior high students. Adolescence 1983;9: 277–281.

57. Telch MJ, Killen JD, McAlister AL, Perry CL, Maccoby N. Long-term follow-up of a pilot project on smoking prevention with adolescents. J Behav Med 1982;5:1–8.

58. Donaldson SI, Graham JW, Hansen WB. Testing the generalizability of intervening mechanism theories: understanding the effects of adolescent drug use prevention interventions. J Behav Med 1994;17:195–216.

59. Ellickson PL, Bell RM. Prospects for preventing drug abuse among young adolescents. Science 1990;247:1299–1305.

60. Snow DL, Tebes JK, Arthur MW, Tapasak RC. Two-year follow-up of a social cognitive intervention to prevent substance abuse. J Drug Educ 1992;22:101–114.

61. Sussman S, Dent CW, Stacy AW, Sun P. Project Towards No Tobacco Use: 1-year behavior outcomes. Am J Public Health 1993;83:1245–1250.

62. Bandura A. Social learning theory. Englewood Cliffs, NJ: Prentice-Hall, 1977.

63. Fishbein M. Consumer beliefs and behavior with respect to cigarette smoking: a critical analysis of the public literature. In: Federal Trade Commission Report to Congress pursuant to the Public Health Cigarette Smoking Act of 1976. Washington: DC: U.S. Government Printing Office, 1977.

64. McAlister A, Perry CL, Killen J, Slinkard LA, Maccoby N. Pilot study of smoking, alcohol, and drug abuse prevention. Am J Public Health 1980;70:719–721.

65. Shope JT, Dielman TE, Butchart AT, Campanelli PC, Kloska DD. An elementary school-based alcohol misuse prevention program: a follow-up evaluation. J Stud Alcohol 1992;53:106–121.

66. Donaldson SI, Graham JW, Piccinin AM, Hansen WB. Resistance-skills training and onset of alcohol use: evidence for beneficial and potentially harmful effects in public schools and in private Catholic schools. Health Psychol 1995;14:291–300.

67. Flynn BS, Worden JK, Secker-Walker S, Badger GJ, Geller BM, Costanza MC. Prevention of cigarette smoking through mass media intervention and school programs. Am J Public Health 1992;82:827–834.

68. Rohrbach LA, Hodgson CS, Broder BI, Montgomery SB. Parental participation in drug abuse prevention: results from the Midwestern Prevention Project. Special issue: preventing alcohol abuse among adolescents: preintervention and intervention research. J Res Adolesc 1994;4: 295–317.

69. Pentz MA, Dwyer JH, MacKinnon DP, et al. A multicommunity trial for primary prevention of adolescent drug abuse: effects on drug prevalence. JAMA 1989;261:3259–3266.

70. Perry CL, Kelder SH, Murray DM, Klepp KI. Community-wide smoking prevention: long-term outcomes of the Minnesota heart health program and the class of 1989 study. Am J Public Health 1992:82(9):1210–1216.

71. Johnson CA, Pentz MA, Weber MD, Dwyer JH, Baer N, MacKinnon DP, Hansen WB. Relative effectiveness of comprehensive community programming for drug abuse prevention with high-risk and low-risk adolescents. J Consult Clin Psychol 1990;58(4):447–456.

72. Graham JW, Johnson CA, Hansen WB, Flay BR, Gee M. Drug use prevention programs, gender, and ethnicity: evaluation of three seventh-grade project SMART cohorts. Prev Med 1990;19:305–313.

73. Fisher DA, Armstrong BK, de Kler NH. A randomized-controlled trial of education for prevention of smoking in 12 year-old children. Paper presented at the fifth World Conference on Smoking and Health, Winnipeg, Canada, 1983.

74. Ennett ST, Tobler NS, Ringwalt CL, Flewelling RL. How effective is drug abuse resistance education? A meta-analysis of project DARE outcome evaluations. Am J Public Health 1994; 84:1394–1401.

75. Perry CL, Kelder SH. Models for effective prevention. J Adolesc Health 1992;13:355–363.

76. Murray DM, Davis-Hearn M, Goldman AI, Pirie P, Luepker RV. Four and five year follow-up results from four seventh-grade smoking prevention strategies. J Behav Med 1988;11(4): 395–405.

77. Flay BR, Keopke D, Thomson SJ, Santi S, Best JA, Brown KS. Long-term follow-up of the first waterloo smoking prevention trial. Am J Public Health 1989;79(10):1371–1376.

78. Bell RM, Ellickson PL, Harrison ER. Do drug prevention effects persist into high school? Prev Med 1993;22:463–483.

79. Ellickson PL, Bell RM, McGuigan K. Preventing adolescent drug use: Long-term results of a junior high program. Am J Public Health 1993;83:856–861.

80. Dryfoos JG. Common components of successful interventions with high risk youth. In: Bell NJ, Bell RW eds. Adolescent risk taking. Newbury Park CA: Sage Publications, 1993:131–147.

81. Resnicow K, Botvin GJ. School-based substance use prevention programs: why do effects decay? Prev Med 1993;22:484–490.

82. Caplan M, Weissberg RP, Grober JS, Sive PJ, Grady K, Jacoby C. Social competence promotion with inner-city and suburban young adolescents: effects on social adjustment and alcohol use. J Consult Clin Psychol 1992;60:56–63.

83. Botvin GJ, Eng A, Williams CL. Preventing the onset of cigarette smoking through life skills training. Prev Med 1980;9:135–143.

84. Botvin GJ, Eng A. A comprehensive school-based smoking prevention program. J Sch Health 1980;50:209–213.

85. Botvin GJ, Baker E, Renick N, Filazzola AD, Botvin EM. A cognitive-behavioral approach to substance abuse prevention. Addict Behav 1984;9:137–147.

86. Botvin GJ, Baker E, Botvin EM, Filazzola AD, Millman RB. Alcohol abuse prevention through the development of personal and social competence: a pilot study. J Stud Alcohol 1984;45:550–552.

87. Botvin GJ, Baker E, Filazzola A, Botvin E, Danilo M, Dusenbury L. A cognitive-behavioral approach into substance abuse prevention: a one year follow-up. Paper presented at the 93rd annual meeting of the American Psychological Association, Los Angeles, August 23–27, 1985.

88. Botvin GJ, Renick N, Baker E. The effects of scheduling format and booster sessions on a broad-spectrum psychosocial approach to smoking prevention. J Behav Med 1983;6: 359–379.

89. Pentz MA. Prevention of adolescent substance abuse through social skill development. NIDA Res Monogr 1983;47:195–232.

90. Schinke SP, Gilchrist LD. Primary prevention of tobacco smoking. J Sch Health 1983;53: 416–419.

91. Schinke SP, Gilchrist LD. Preventing cigarette smoking with youth. J Prim Prev 1984;5: 48–56.

92. Gilchrist LD, Schinke SP. Self-control skills for smoking prevention. In: Engstrom PF, Anderson P, eds. Advances in cancer control. New York: Alan R. Liss, 1983.

93. Schinke SP. Preventing teenage pregnancy. In: Hersen M, Eisler RM, Miller PM, eds. Progress in behavior modification. New York: Academic Press, 1984:31–64.

94. Botvin GJ, Baker E, Filazzola A, Botvin EM. A cognitive-behavioral approach to substance abuse prevention: a one-year follow-up. Addict Behav 1990;15:47–63.

95. Kreutter KJ, Gewirtz H, Davenny JE, Love C. Drug and alcohol prevention project for sixth graders: first-year findings. Adolescence 1991; 26:287–293.

96. Botvin GJ, Eng A. The efficacy of a multicomponent approach to the prevention of cigarette smoking. Prev Med 1982;11:199–211.

97. Botvin GJ, Baker E, Dusenbury L, Tortu S, Botvin E. Preventing adolescent drug abuse through a multimodal cognitive-behavioral approach: results of a three-year study. J Consult Clin Psychol 1990;58:437–446.

98. Epstein JA, Botvin GJ, Diaz T, Schinke SP. The role of social factors and individual characteristics in promoting alcohol use among inner-city minority youths. J Stud Alcohol 1995;56:39–46.

99. Epstein JA, Botvin GJ, Diaz T, Toth V, Schinke SP. Social and personal factors in marijuana use and intentions to use drugs among inner-city minority youth. J Dev Behav Pediatrics 1995;16:14–20.

100. Botvin GJ, Baker E, Dusenbury L, Botvin EM, Diaz T. Long-term follow-up results of a ran-

domized drug abuse prevention trial in a white middle-class population. JAMA 1995; 273:1106–1112.

101. Bettes BA, Dusenbury L, Kerner J, James-Ortiz S, Botvin GJ. Ethnicity and psychosocial factors in alcohol and tobacco use in adolescence. Child Dev 1990;61:557–565.

102. Botvin GJ, Baker E, Botvin EM, Dusenbury L, Cardwell J, Diaz T. Factors promoting cigarette smoking among black youth: a causal modeling approach. Addict Behav 1993;18: 397–405.

103. Botvin GJ, Epstein JA, Schinke SP, Diaz T. Predictors of cigarette smoking among innercity youth. J Dev Behav Pediatrics 1994;15: 67–73.

104. Botvin GJ, Goldberg CJ, Botvin EM, Dusenbury L. Smoking behavior of adolescents exposed to cigarette advertising. Public Health Rep 1993;108:217–224.

105. Dusenbury L, Kerner JF, Baker E, Botvin GJ, James-Ortiz S, Zauber A. Predictors of smoking prevalence among New York Latino youth. Am J Public Health 1992;82:55–58.

106. Epstein JA, Dusenbury L, Botvin GJ, Diaz T, Schinke SP. Determinants of intentions of junior high school students to become sexually active and use condoms: implications for reduction and prevention of AIDS risk. Psychol Rep 1994;75:1043–1053.

107. Botvin GJ, Dusenbury L, Baker E, James-Ortiz S, Kerner J. A skills training approach to smoking prevention among Hispanic youth. J Behav Med 1989;12:279–296.

108. Botvin GJ, Dusenbury L, Baker E, James-Ortiz S, Botvin EM, Kerner J. Smoking prevention among urban minority youth: assessing effects on outcome and mediating variables. Health Psychol 1992;11:290–299.

109. Botvin GJ, Batson H, Witts-Vitale S, Bess V, Baker E, Dusenbury L. A psychosocial approach to smoking prevention for urban black youth. Public Health Rep 1989;104: 573–582.

110. Botvin GJ, Cardwell J. Primary prevention (smoking) of cancer in black populations. Grant contract number N01-CN-6508. Final report to the National Cancer Institute. Cornell University Medical College, 1992.

111. Botvin GJ, Schinke SP, Epstein JA, Diaz T. Effectiveness of culturally-focused and generic skills training approaches to alcohol and drug abuse prevention among minority youths. Psychol Addict Behav 1994;8:116–127.

112. Botvin GJ, Schinke SP, Epstein JA, Diaz T. Effectiveness of culturally-focused and generic skills training approaches to alcohol and drug abuse prevention among minority adolescents: Two-year follow-up results. Psychol Addict Behav 1995;9:183–194.

113. MacKinnon DP, Johnson CA, Pentz MA, Dwyer JH, Hansen WB, Flay BR, Wang EYI. Mediating mechanisms in a school-based drug prevention program: first-year effects of the midwestern prevention project. Hlth Psychol 1991;10(3):164–172.

77 PUBLIC HEALTH APPROACHES

Steven Jonas

AN HISTORICAL PERSPECTIVE ON DRUG POLICY DEVELOPMENT

Unfortunately, drug policy in the United States has changed little in the five years since the last edition of this textbook was published. Other than for tobacco use, both national drug politics and national drug policy have changed only marginally, at least in their major parameters. The "Drug War" against illicit drugs, conducted almost entirely in nonwhite neighborhoods, rages on, killing some, repressing others, and turning certain neighborhoods into war zones. This "war" has had no measurable impact upon drug use (1–7), largely because the majority of illicit drug use is found among whites (Table 77.1), whom the government has mostly ignored, and drug use has not been declining among the nonwhite population that has been targeted.

The two major drug scourges on the health and mortality of the American people, tobacco and alcohol (8), continue to be referred to by some not as "drug problems," but as "habits," "personal choices," "rights," and legitimate objects of commerce, to be subjected to only the most limited kind of "government interference." To be sure, in 1995 the Food and Drug Administration proposed to treat tobacco products as what they are: delivery systems of the drug nicotine (9). But there is strong political opposition to this initiative (10). Beyond that, there is still a failure to see tobacco use as what it is: a central part of the larger drug use picture rather than a problem standing separate and apart (to be discussed later in "Ignoring the Gateway Drug Effect").

Nor has much of the "drug policy reform" community, focused so closely on the legalization of the sale and use of the illicit drugs rather than drug use regulation and control for health, been able to see the drugs with which it is primarily concerned as part of the larger picture either (11). Since this chapter was first written in 1990, drug policy (non)development continues to be driven primarily by ideology, politics, and money, not by concern for the health of the people.

SOME DEFINITIONS

The use of any of the common "recreational" mood-altering drugs can lead to negative health, psychological, and social outcomes in at least some users. Several different definitions of the term "drug" are presented in this book. As the word is used in this chapter, a drug is "any substance other than food which by its chemical nature affects the structure or function of the living organism" (12). Building on the dictionary definition of recreation, a "recreational" mood-altering drug can be defined as one ingested, inhaled, or injected for the primary purpose of providing diversion, relaxation, heightened sensation, or other enjoyment and pleasure, by changing the user's state of mind (13). The word "drug" as used in this chapter should be taken to mean "recreational mood-altering drug." Since recreational drug use may produce habituation or addiction, the user may develop a secondary purpose for using: to avoid the negative effects associated with withdrawal and abstinence.

As the term is used in this chapter, the "drug problem" in the United States is, in sum: the negative effects of drug use in individuals; the negative effects on society caused by drug-induced behaviors occurring in some users, and the negative outcomes of the trade in the illicit drugs. The "Drug War" is that combination of measures based primarily in the criminal law supposedly designed to reduce and/or eliminate the use of certain recreational mood-altering drugs.

LEGAL STATUS OF DRUGS AND THEIR USE IN THE UNITED STATES

Central to any discussion of recreational drug use policy in the United States is an analysis and understanding of the "Drug War," the principal tool of government at all levels for dealing with the drug problem. The existence of the "Drug War" colors all other antidrug use efforts, both government and private. Therefore, before considering any alternatives, it must be reviewed.

As noted, the "Drug War" attempts to diminish or eliminate the use of certain drugs by application of the criminal law. It appears to make certain drugs "legal" while making certain others "illegal." However, this construction represents a false reality, and that fallacy is a central reason why United States drug policy works as poorly as it does. The fact is that *de jure* in the United States, with the exception of caffeine, there are virtually no "legal" drugs, in the sense that, for example, food is "legal." De facto, of course, there are major differences between them.

The fact is that the distribution, sale, and in certain instances use, of *all* recreational mood-altering drugs (other than caffeine) are illegal, at least for

Table 77.1 Illicit Drug Use in Past Month by Race and Drug, 1994

Drug	White		Black		Hispanic	
	Number (thousands)	%	Number (thousands)	%	Number (thousands)	%
Marihuana	7695	78	1386	14	791	8
Cocaine (including crack)	850	62	305	22	217	16
Heroin (use in past year)	113	41	116	41	51	18
Any illicit drug	9557	78	1716	14	1034	8
Psychotherapeutics	2167	85	201	8	184	7

Table from Substance Abuse and Mental Health Services Administration. National Household Survey on Drug Abuse: population estimates 1994. DHHS Pub. No. (SMA) 95-3063. Rockville, MD: U.S. Department of Health and Human Services, September, 1995:Tables 2, 3, 4, 8, 17.

certain people. Thus in the law, the propaganda of the "Drug War" to the contrary notwithstanding, there is no sharp "legal/illegal" dichotomy among the various drugs. In practice, it happens that most drugs are de facto legal for most of the people who sell and use them, regardless of their statutory categorization, because most drug laws are largely decriminalized and unenforced.

Drug Laws in Practice

The legal differences between the several recreational mood-altering drugs and the laws applied to their distribution, sale, possession, and use are defined by the following characteristics:

- For whom which drugs are illegal.
- Which drug laws are decriminalized, in which jurisdictions.
- Which drug laws are enforced, and against whom they are enforced.

In practice, only a narrow band of the drug laws are enforced, primarily against selected elements of the population. Nonwhites are selectively punished for violations for which the white user majority on the whole is not held either civilly or criminally accountable (14–16).

In practice, therefore, under the law drug categorization differs rather markedly from the commonly held but fallacious "legal/illegal" dichotomy. There are not, in practice, two artificial categories, but three real ones.

Category One represents tobacco and the alcoholic beverages, the so-called "legal drugs." The distribution, sale, and use of these drug carriers are illegal for persons under 18 or 21 (the age varying by state and drug). In practice, however, these laws are effectively decriminalized in most jurisdictions.

Category Two is the prescription psychoactive drugs. The distribution, sale, possession, and use of these drugs, on a nonprescription basis, are illegal for persons of all ages. These laws too are effectively decriminalized in most jurisdictions. Ironically, there are about 40% more regular users of the prescription psychoactives on a nonprescription basis than there are regular users of cocaine (17, Tables 4A, 8A).

Category Three is comprised of marihuana, heroin, cocaine, and the other "illicit" drugs. Like the Category Two drugs, their distribution, sale, possession, and use are illegal for persons of all ages. However, in most jurisdictions the laws concerning these drugs are enforced but selectively. For the most part, general enforcement occurs only in geographic areas in which sellers and users are found in open or otherwise easily accessible spaces, that is, poor, minority neighborhoods.

It is only when this reality is recognized that the questions, the answers to which will provide the basis for developing a workable and effective drug policy, can be usefully dealt with.

THE QUESTIONS

This textbook presents a variety of philosophies of and approaches to the problem of substance use and abuse in American society. The contributors to this book represent a broad spectrum of basic science, clinical medicine, public health, and political perspectives. But common to all of them is the goal of "doing something" about the problem. None looks at it and says, "Everything's fine—there's nothing to do." However, after agreeing on that point, the contributors have many disagreements on these significant questions, which lead to major differences in intervention policy:

- Just what is the "drug problem" or the "substance abuse problem" (18, 19, p. 8)? How do we define it? Is there a difference between "use" and "abuse"? For example, is substance abuse a disease and, if so, is it a disease in all abusers or only in some of them (20–22)? If "use" and "abuse" are different, what is the difference, and what are its implications for intervention policy?
- Is substance abuse—however it is defined pharmacologically and medically—a moral, legal, personal health, public health, or criminal problem, or some combination of two or more of those five categories?
- Is there a need for societal intervention in dealing with the problem? If so, what kind of intervention should it be and what goals should be established for it? At what stage of the development of the problem in individuals, communities, and society should intervention be employed?
- What should the interface between the law and substance use and abuse be?
- Assuming that the current substance abuse policy is not working satisfactorily (discussed later in "Defects in Current Policy"), what is wrong with it? Why doesn't it work? Does current policy make the drug problem worse in any way? Does the policy need to be repaired or totally replaced? For either alternative, just what should be done?

This chapter does not attempt to answer all of these questions in detail. Many of them are dealt with—to at least some extent—in other chapters in this book. However, this chapter does ask the reader to bear these questions in mind as she or he peruses this description of the public health approach to the prevention of substance abuse.

THE PUBLIC HEALTH APPROACH IN BRIEF

The Public Health Approach (PHA) to the prevention of substance abuse uses epidemiological, pharmacological, toxicological, and medical science to define the substance abuse problem. It does not use history, fashion, politics, or prejudice. It identifies the real causes of the drug problem and then develops interventions directed at those causes, not imaginary ones. Some of the interventions are of a classically "public health" nature, as they appear, for example, in the "Statement and Resolution on Tobacco and Health" of the Committee on Public Health of the New York Academy of Medicine (23). Others are drawn from a broader perspective.

The primary goal of the PHA is to:

Reduce the use and abuse of all the recreational mood-altering drugs, to provide, when, as, and if possible, for their safe, pleasurable use, consistent with centuries' old human experience, while minimizing to the greatest degree possible the harmful effects of their use on individuals, the family, and society as a whole.

Before considering the PHA in detail, the nature of the drug problem and then the major defects in current policy will first be analyzed.

MODELING THE DRUG PROBLEM

Disease/Medical Model

Some observers hold that substance abuse of any of the drugs in any of the three categories is primarily a disease (21, 24, 25). The focus of this approach is to organize medical treatment for "drug abusers" (22). This formulation, valid or not, is of little utility for the PHA, which focuses primarily on prevention.

Moral/Criminal Model

A most articulate spokesman for this model and the "Drug War" strategy based upon it was the first Director of the Bush Administration's National Drug Control Policy, Dr. William Bennett. In 1990 he said: "We identify the chief and seminal wrong here as drug use. Drug use, we say, is wrong" (26). His is a strong moralistic position, characterized by the judgmental word "wrong." He made it clear that his position applied only to the illicit drugs. Those who hold the view that the problem is primarily one of morality, and limit their moral purview to the illicit drugs, also tend to see law enforcement as the key to solving the problem. Dr. Bennett also said, "Those who use, sell, and traffic in drugs must be confronted, and must suffer consequences . . . . We must build more prisons. There must be more jails" (27).

The principal focus of Dr. Bennett's "War on Drugs" was thus not on even the minority of the recreational mood-altering drugs themselves that were ostensibly the "War's" targets, but on certain of those people who sold and took the specified drugs. It was on using the law to enforce one particular view of what is moral and what is not, and on punishment of individuals for transgressions against that view.

As defined by the Bush Administration's original National Drug Control Strategy (28, 29) and the Clinton Administration's version of it (30), this model is generally concerned only with Category Three drugs. This model defines the problem primarily in terms of the law and its violation, not health.

"It's Not a Problem" Model

For other observers, the principal focus is that substance abuse is not a disease, not a moral breach, not a crime, and *not* a public health problem. Rather, it is an adaptive behavior (31) or, according to the libertarians Milton Friedman and Thomas Szasz, the result (or should be the result) of a free choice (32). The holders of this view advocate that government should abdicate all responsibility and authority in the area.

Public Health Model

An alternative to the disease, moral/criminal, and "no problem" models is the public health model. It has the following major defining characteristics:

- Substance use or abuse of drugs in all three categories is seen as a far-reaching social, economic, and political problem (33) that is a unity, not a duality or tripartite phenomenon. The PHA considers the current "legal/illegal" duality to have been artificially created and not related either to health considerations (34, 35) or to science.
- The problem is viewed primarily as one of health and health deficits, not, as already noted, of morality, crime, or (other than in a limited number of cases) disease.
- The PHA recognizes that, while in most drug users, use is not a disease, in every drug user, use increases the risk, to a greater or lesser extent, of contracting one or more diseases or conditions damaging to one's health (36, pp. 109–265).
- It is recognized that tobacco is the one drug or drug carrier that, when used as intended, is harmful to most users (by significantly increasing organic disease risk), as well as to those in the user's vicinity (19, pp. 12–13, 32–33).[a]
- It is recognized that all of the other commonly used recreational mood-altering drugs are harmful in one way or another to some of those who use them (19, pp. 31–45). Any use of any drug thus increases the risk of harmful use later. However, the harm varies in degree and kind from person to person and even within the same person from time to time. Dr. Norman Zinberg has described the relevant variables as those of "drug, set, and setting" (37). In some cases this harm is the result of the action of the drug on the body, in some cases on the mind and the person's mental status. Drug use harms range from lung cancer to cirrhosis of the liver to chronic drug dependency to loss of job and family life to sudden death in a motor vehicle crash. However, it is important to understand that the only *certain* negative of recreational drug use, even of cigarettes, is an increase in the *risk, not* the certainty, of harm.

- Using neither the false "legal/illegal" dichotomy nor the present three-category division, the PHA categorizes drugs biologically by such characteristics as addictivity potential, long-term health risks, and potential social pathology.
- The PHA does not see the drug and drug-related crime problems as one and the same. Although they are of course interrelated, they have different solutions. The public health model necessarily invokes state power to solve problems of the public's health, but unlike the "Drug War," the law is used in ways known to be efficacious and cost-effective. (There is, of course, no societal consensus on the morality of substance use or abuse. For the PHA, therefore, dealing with the drug problem in any way as a moral one is considered inappropriate and counterproductive.)

DEFECTS IN CURRENT POLICY

Before considering the principles and components of the PHA to the prevention of substance use/abuse in detail, we must first answer the questions: Why is it necessary to develop and implement a new policy? What's wrong with the current national policy for dealing with substance abuse?[b] Looking more closely at these questions uncovers a number of defects in current policy.

Lack of Focus on the Real Drug Problems

Perhaps the most serious defect in current national policy is that it directs the bulk of its attention to the least of the drug-related health harms. For example, in 1990, there were about 500,000 deaths associated with the use of alcohol and tobacco (8). By 1994, it could be estimated that that figure had risen to at least 530,000 (19, Section 2). In 1994 there were only about 2.6 times as many regular cocaine *users* as there were alcohol and tobacco *deaths*. Yet the Office of National Drug Control Policy focuses almost exclusively on the former group (30).

By way of comparison, the illicit drugs are responsible for about 20,000 deaths, with about half of those the direct result of the "Drug War," not drug use (8). The total number of cocaine users about which all the fuss is being made, all the money on law enforcement being spent, in 1994 was less than 1.4 million, while the total number of heroin users was less than 300,000 (17, Table 4A)! Compare these numbers with over 110 million regular users of alcohol and about 60 million cigarette smokers (17, Tables 13A and 14A).

Artificial Bimodality and Lack of Comprehensiveness

As noted, national policy is based on the fallacious "legal/illegal" dichotomy, when the true picture is quite different. Further, even though it doesn't openly recognize the three true, functional drug categories, national policy addresses the Category One drugs in one way, the Category Three drugs in another, and the Category Two drugs hardly at all.

Conflict over the Role of Education

In current policy, there is a conflict over the role of education in dealing with the drug problem. For the Category One drugs the major emphasis of national policy is on education. De facto, the law plays a secondary role, e.g., banning cigarette smoking in many public places, cracking down on drunk drivers. There is no program of any kind for dealing with the Category Two drugs. For the Category Three drugs, while criminal law enforcement aimed at nonwhites is widely employed, some attempts at education are also made. However, there is a sharp disagreement on the value of education in dealing with the Category Three drugs. This is what Dr. Bennett had to say about school (illicit) drug education programs (38): "Should we have drug educa-

---

[a]The harm from cigarettes to the user and others is caused both by the contents of the smoke and the organic effects of nicotine, and occasionally by cigarette-caused fires, but not by the effect of the drug nicotine on the *behavior* of the user. This is distinguished from the use of drugs other than cigarettes, where the user's drug-induced behavior may also cause harm to some of those in the vicinity of the user.

[b]This chapter presents a highly critical view of current policy. However, it does *not* propose simple expansion of the present policy of decriminalization as a solution to the substance abuse problem. Broadening the present partial decriminalization of the illicit drugs, if properly implemented, could solve much of the drug-traffic-related crime problem. However, it would do nothing to solve the general substance abuse problem, especially that major part of it caused by tobacco and alcohol. In the view presented here, general decriminalization for any of the illicit drugs without first dealing comprehensively with the total substance abuse problem would be ill-advised.

tion programs or should we have tough policy? If I have a choice of only one, I will take policy every time because I know children. And you might say this is not a very romantic view of children, not a very rosy view of children. And I would say, 'You're right.'" National policy under President Clinton takes a more positive view of the power of education (30, Section III).

Contradiction in Goals

While the National Drug Control Strategy does not address the issue of the currently legal drugs, another federal document does. The Offices of the Assistant Secretary for Health and Human Services for Health and the Surgeon General produced *Promoting Health Preventing Disease: Year 2000 Objectives for the Nation* (39). In 1995, *Healthy People 2000: Midcourse Review and 1995 Revisions* was published (40). Between them, the two documents set goals for reduced prevalence for the use of the two major drugs as well as for marihuana and cocaine (40, pp. 171–186). There are also goals for significant reductions in alcohol- and tobacco-related negative health outcomes. Recognizing reality, "drug-free" is not on this national health agenda for any of the drugs.

However, the 1988 White House Conference for a Drug Free America, which laid the ground work for current Category Three drug policy, called for just that: "Drug Free" (41). The major national advertising campaign supporting the "drug-free" approach, for the illicit drugs only of course, is produced by the "Partnership for a Drug-Free America" (42). The Partnership is a creature of the American Association of Advertising Agencies. The latter is the trade organization for most of the companies which make their living promoting the use of tobacco and alcohol, especially to the young.

Thus the true goal of current national policy remains unclear. Is it drug-free, or drug use reduction? Or is it drug-free for certain users of the minor drugs, drug use reduction for all users of the major ones, tobacco and alcohol?

Discordance Between Means and Desired Ends

FUTILITY OF CRIMINAL LAW ENFORCEMENT AIMED AT SIMPLE USE

Studies have indicated that the perceived certainty and severity of punishment are insignificant factors in deterring use (43). In the late 1980s and early 1990s, what apparently was more important in reversing the trend of increasing illicit drug use that marked the 1970s was the growth in perceived harmfulness of the activity, which, in turn, likely augmented social disapproval of drug use behavior. Among users, in any weighing of legal and health risks of drug use, concerns about health predominate (43).

There are other indicators of the futility of criminal law enforcement. In the mid 1990s, regular cocaine use was remaining fairly stable among both whites and nonwhites, while both heroin and marihuana use were rising (5).

These events occurred in the context of rapidly rising imprisonment levels for drug-related crimes by nonwhites (15, 16, pp. 9–13). But if imprisonment or threat of it had a real impact on illicit drug use, one would expect it to be much lower among nonwhites than whites since the former are imprisoned for drug offenses at a much higher rate than are the latter (Table 77.2). But that is not the case (17).

Table 77.2   Admission to Correctional Institutions for Drug Offenses, by Race

Race	Jurisdiction			Total Population, Illicit Drug Users (%)
	Federal (%)	State (%)	Local (%)	
White	26	10	25	78
Black	74	74	48	14
Hispanic	—[a]	16	25	8
Other	—	—	2	—

Table data from Mauer M, Huling T. Young black Americans and the criminal justice system. Washington, DC: The Sentencing Project, October, 1995 (federal and state statistics); Bureau of Justice Statistics. Drugs and jail inmates, 1989. Washington, DC: Department of Justice, 1991 (local statistics).
[a] White percentage (26%) includes Hispanics.

In 1936 August Vollmer, a "prominent police administrator" of the time, said:

> Drug Addiction, like prostitution and like liquor, is not a police problem; it never has been and never can be solved by policemen. It is first and last a medical problem, and if there is a solution it will be discovered not by policemen, but by scientific and competently trained medical experts whose sole objective will be the reduction and possible eradication of this devastating appetite. There should be intelligent treatment of incurables in outpatient clinics, hospitalization of those not too far gone to respond to therapeutic measures, and application of the prophylactic principles which medicine applies to all scourges of mankind. (25)

Robert Stutman, retired in 1990 as the Special Agent in charge of the New York Office of the Drug Enforcement Administration, put it more succinctly (44): "Cops are not the answer to the drug problem. They're a short-term answer to clean up the streets. But the long-term answer is prevention."

Even if criminal law enforcement were effective and relevant, history shows that its use is not necessary to achieve reduction in substance use and abuse. Over a 25-year period, a limited national antismoking campaign led to a decline of almost 30% in the proportion of adults smoking (45), a decline of almost 40% in per capita cigarette consumption (19, pp. 12–13). This was accomplished with an educational program of modest proportions and some recent restrictions on smoking in public facilities, all in the face of much pro drug use advertising by the tobacco industry and government tobacco subsidies.

THE FUTILITY OF INTERDICTION

A major element in the "Drug War" strategy is the attempt to reduce or eliminate the supply of the illicit drugs imported from abroad, and/or to have a major impact upon prices. There is much evidence that neither objective is or can be achieved (4, 46).

Take for example, one of the "Drug War's" centerpieces, the elimination of the supply of cocaine coming from the Andean countries of South America. This is what a House of Representatives Government Operations Committee Report had to say about that effort:

> The Andean Initiative reflects a largely military and law enforcement response to deep-rooted and diverse economic problems. . . . Source-country supply reduction programs for eradication, interdiction and enforcement have been ineffective in reducing the cultivation of coca or the available supply of coca products for processing or export in the Andean region. . . . Source-country interdiction and enforcement efforts have also been largely unsuccessful in curbing the amount of coca or coca products available for processing and export. Interdiction strategies in 1989 resulted in the seizure of less than one percent of all coca paste and base produced in Peru, and only one-half of one percent of Bolivian coca products. . . . (47)

There is no evidence to indicate that the situation has changed as of the mid 1990s (57a). The Committee's investigation revealed little evidence to suggest that supply reduction programs in source countries affect the supply or use of cocaine in the United States. Compelling evidence was presented to the Committee that even successful source-country supply reduction efforts can have nothing more than a negligible impact on cocaine prices and consumption in the United States: the costs of producing cocaine are so low that even a 50% reduction in supply would add less than 3% to the retail price.

Implementing a Pseudo "Demand-Side" Strategy

In 1990, under Dr. Bennett, a law enforcement–based "demand reduction," "user accountability" strategy was introduced to national policy for illicit substances. Ostensibly, this strategy recognized the limitations of the traditional "supply-side" approach. However, it did not focus on the causes of demand, such as the Drug Culture and the Gateway Drug Effect (discussed later). It continued to give short shrift to education. Rather, it looked at demand in a totally simplistic way, simply targeting the "casual user" for the imposition of criminal sanctions. As if those "casual users," entirely on their own, were the major, indeed the only, factor in creating demand.

In a leap of faith supported by no evidence, it assumed that the "casual user" bears a major responsibility for maintaining the drug trade and recruiting new users. Also, supported by no evidence, it assumed that the threat of imprisonment for "casual use" would deter drug use in the general population. However, as Erickson has pointed out, studies "consistently indicate that the perceived certainty and severity of punishment are insignificant factors in deterring use" (43).

The doctrine of "user accountability" also ignored the evidence from the Alcohol, Drug Abuse, and Mental Health Administration that in the late 1980s at least 53% of drug abusers had a diagnosable mental disorder (48). As Cohen and Weiss stated, "Screening substance using patients for concurrent psychiatric diagnosis often reveals a dual diagnosis" (49, p. 289).

An apparent end result of the "Drug War" policy has been the imprisonment of significant numbers of mentally ill people. The others incarcerated were those seeking some pleasure from a drug other than tobacco or alcohol, those addicted to an illicit substance, and still others out to make a profit from the retail sale of recreational mood-altering drugs, just as the supermarkets, convenience stores, liquor stores, bars, and tobacconists do.

Failure to Acknowledge United States Drug Culture

Demand and demand creation are of course very important factors in the drug problem. In fact, the way the Category One drugs are promoted and sold has a major impact on their use. This impact is mediated through the drug culture and the gateway drug effect (discussed in the next section).

Current national policy fails to recognize that there is a drug culture in the United States which directly and indirectly promotes the use of all drugs. Gitlin has put it this way:

[I]n many ways American culture is a drug culture. Through its normal routines it promotes not only the high-intensity consumption of commodities but also the idea that the self is realized through consumption. It is addicted to acquisition. It cultivates the pursuit of thrills; it elevates the pursuit of private pleasure to high standing; and, as part of this ensemble, it promotes the use of licit chemicals for stimulation, intoxication, and fast relief. The widespread use of licit drugs in America can be understood as part of this larger set of values and activities. (50)

Consider that alcohol and tobacco advertising is associated with, for example, being a friend ("Gotta be Your Bud"); thinness in women (Virginia Slims, "You've come a long way, baby"); rugged individualism (the Marlboro Man, Red Dog beer); speed (Coors Light, the Silver Bullet); excitement (giant young people playing around in the Rockies with Coors beer); humor (the Budweiser frogs; the not-too-bright knock-hockey playing Hanson brothers); being "with it" (RJR Nabisco's "smooth Joe Camel"); crossdressing (the Bud Lite "ladies' night at the bar" and beach volleyball match); racing (the Budweiser sponsorship of auto and boat racing, Marlboro sponsorship of auto racing, Marlboro and Bud labels on model racing cars); sports (beer sales and advertising (51), Marlboro billboards in sports stadiums); what might be called "positive fraud" (the man who declares his love for his father, brother, putative girlfriend, a random beer truck driver, Charlton Heston, all in a transparent attempt to get a Bud Light); what might be called "positive bribery" (the ugly dog that wins the dog show award because it has a supply of Budweiser beer in its doghouse).

A particularly disturbing trend in pro drug use advertising using sports figures appeared first in 1990. The "Bud Bowl" is a several months' long promotion Anheuser-Busch stages on behalf of both Budweiser and Bud Light beer. It leads up to an "ad spectacular" seen during the telecast of the National Football League's championship game, the "Super Bowl."

Chris Berman is a well-respected sportscaster for the Entertainment Sports Network (ESPN). An authority figure to many sports fans, he appeared that year in the "build-up to the Bud Bowl" ads, promoting the sale and consumption of Anheuser-Busch beers. In the ads, Chris Berman appeared just as he does in real life, as a television sportscaster.

Keith Jackson is a college football play-by-play announcer for the ABC network. In a 1995 ad for Miller Lite beer he did a "telecast" of a rather energetic wedding between two athletes, with plenty of Miller Lite in the vicinity.

In both cases there is a cross-over between the broadcasters' real-life roles and their roles in the ads. The confusion of reality and role-playing may be either inadvertent or intentional, as may be the fact that when viewers see either Berman or Jackson doing their real jobs, they may think "Bud" or "Miller," respectively. Regardless, with ads like these is it not easy for anyone, especially youngsters, to get confused about roles, messages, and behaviors?

To compound the problem, "do drugs" messages of the drug culture extend well beyond the world of the recreational mood-altering drugs. Over-the-counter drugs are sold as instant problem solvers: if you have a headache, take this pill; if you overate, swallow this liquid; if you can't get to sleep, take this other pill. The message never is "to avoid feeling overstuffed from eating too much pizza, why not try not eating less pizza next time?" In the mid 1990s, an antacid called Pepcid AC was actually promoted as a medication to take before eating food known to give heartburn, so that the user can eat that food without suffering heartburn.

Vitamins are not drugs, but they come in pill form, and to many people look like drugs. In addition, they are sold as an easy, painless means of self-improvement, even for children: "We're the Flintstones kids—one million strong and growing." Is it any wonder that some of those children a few years later experiment with other pills that are promoted as easy, painless ways to a better you? Finally, in America, medicine is practiced with an inordinate emphasis on treatment using pharmaceutical drugs as contrasted to personal health promotion and disease prevention by life-style modification.

Ignoring the Gateway Drug Effect

Mid 1990s policy does not deal with the gateway drug effect, even though in its analysis of the drug problem it recognizes that gateway drugs exist (5, p. 33). In most substance abusers the problem starts in childhood or the early teenage years (45, 52). The Centers for Disease Control and Prevention have pointed out that 90% of new smokers begin before the age of 21 (53). For almost all youngsters it is the "OK" drugs, tobacco and alcohol, that form the "gateway" to the use of the "not-OK" drugs, which are all of the others (54–60). For example, a teenage user of marihuana is eight times more likely to also be a cigarette smoker than a teenager who does not use marihuana (61).

According to the Research Institute of the New York State Division of Alcoholism and Alcohol Abuse Statement on teenagers in New York State: "Unless alcohol is used first, there is very little use of any other drug, including cigarettes and over-the-counter drugs. New York State youth of every age and sex combination—as well as blacks, Hispanics and whites—follow a definite pattern of progression from alcohol to marihuana to hard drug use" (62).

Dr. Jack Henningfield, Chief of the Clinical Pharmacology Branch of the National Institute on Drug Abuse Addiction Research Center put the gateway focus on tobacco succinctly: "Reducing tobacco use is one of the most important elements in all long-range strategies for reducing drug addiction" (63).

But while permitting the enthusiastic promotion and widespread sale of the "OK" drugs, concerning the "non-OK" drugs current national policy says to young people, and primarily minority young people: "If you happen to follow the natural progression from the approved drugs to the unapproved ones and if we catch you, we'll lock you up."

Creating the "OK" Drugs and the "Not-OK" Drugs

The lack of comprehensiveness of policy, the discriminatory application of criminal sanctions to the sale and use of certain drugs but not others and by certain people but not others, the discordance between means and ends, and the failure to recognize and deal with the drug culture and the gateway drug effect, all artificially create in the mind of the public those two artificially defined groups of recreational mood-altering drugs: those which are "OK" and those which are "not OK."

Confounding the Drug Problem and the Crime Problem

Present policy confounds the illegal drug problem with the illegal drug–related crime problem (2). There is much crime directly related to drug use and abuse. These crimes, such as murder, rape, and vehicular homicide, are defined in our society as crimes, whether drug-related or not. The most dangerous drug in this regard is alcohol (64, 65). For example, up to one half of all persons convicted of violent crimes had been consuming alcohol at about the time the crime was committed, and about half of all deaths in motor vehicle accidents (in most of which at least one law has been broken) are associated with alcohol use (19, p. 35).

However, for the illicit drugs, the majority of the crime associated with their manufacture, distribution, sale, and use is a result solely of the fact that they are illegal: trafficking itself is criminal. Thus this whole class of crime is created not by the action of drugs on a user but by the law itself, in this case described by some observers as "criminogenic" (66).

A subset of drug traffic–related crime is that created by the illegality and unregulated nature of the market: street dealers killing each other over market share, unhappy users exacting the ultimate penalty for being supplied with poor-quality drugs, and bystanders being caught in the cross fire.

One study examined the 414 homicides that occurred in New York City between March 1 and October 31, 1988 (67). In this study, 218 (53%) of homicides were classified as "drug related." Of those, 188 were associated with one or more of the illegal drugs. Of that number, 159 (85%) were "systemic," that is related to "the normally aggressive patterns of interaction within the systems of drug use and distribution."

Assuming that none of these murders would have taken place if the drug trade were not illegal, New York City would have had 38% fewer murders during that period. Murder rates continued to rise in 1990: in the first 6 months of that year the murder rate in New York City rose by 25% (68). Nationally, it rose by 8% (69). In the argument so far put forth, if it were not for illegalization, the murder rate would be going down; however, it happened that in 1995, the national murder rate dropped sharply, by 12% in the first half of the year (70). Even more strikingly, it dropped by 31% in New York City and 19% in Chicago. What would account for this drop, given that the legal status of the drug trade had not changed? Alfred Blumstein, a professor at Carnegie-Mellon University in Pittsburgh, was quoted as saying: "In the big cities, [the falling murder rate] probably reflects the maturing of the drug markets. . . . Just like the Mafia markets matured years ago, [the drug markets] have found ways to settle disputes without so much lethal violence."

Focus on Young, Black Males

As noted, this complex set of circumstances leads to the selective punishment of nonwhites for violations of the law for which the white user majority is not held accountable (15). For example, about 75% of persons being held in jail for drug-related offenses are black, about 80% of all persons in state prison for drug-related offenses are nonwhite, and up to 90% of all federal prisoners serving time for drug-related offenses are nonwhite (16, 71–74) (see Table 77.2). It thus happens that the proportion by ethnicity of those imprisoned for drug-related crimes is the approximate reciprocal of the proportion by ethnicity of use rates (17).

A further example of the racism inherent in this policy is the disparity in sentencing for crack and powder cocaine–related offenses (16, p. 11, 75, 76). Sentences handed down for selling crack cocaine, primarily a black-related offense, are 100 times more severe than those for selling powdered cocaine, primarily a white-related offense.

It happens that young, black males are the only easily catchable "casual users" and retail illicit drug dealers. But the apparently racist nature of current policy goes beyond these contradictions. It also focuses public attention on this one group and makes people think that the "drug problem" is almost exclusively theirs—when of course it almost exclusively isn't. Making the problem a "black" one also makes it easy for current policy to pretend that the "illicit drug problem" is one of huge import epidemiologically, which it is not.

The negative outcomes of regular drug use, however, do appear to be more severe among those blacks who use drugs than among whites. This is probably due to the same reasons that blacks suffer more serious negative long-term effects from many health problems than do whites: poverty, lack of education, lack of routine preventive services, and lack of available and affordable disease treatment services (77).

Some of those who advocate continuing this apparently race-based policy, without ever studying the possibility of "legalization" (in reality extending current decriminalization policy to affect all United States citizens equally) (78), do so on the grounds that to study the problem would

necessarily lead to what they call "legalization," and that the latter, whatever it would prove to be in practice, would necessarily lead to an increase in use.

The former position means, in essence, "we don't want our long-held conclusory positions possibly confused by facts;" the latter that "we know the truth, so why study the matter at all." It happens that there is virtually no evidence to support the latter position, as demonstrated in the next section. But suppose studies would prove that the supporters of present policy are correct. The following question should then be considered. Is it appropriate to have a national policy that aims to reduce white suburban drug use by locking up inner-city blacks?

On Simple Availability and Drug Use

The most common argument against ending the "Drug War" is that to do so would lead directly to vastly increased use (79–81). First of all, it is not necessarily the case that a regulated, taxed supply of drugs, sold only through controlled retail outlets, would necessarily lead to any relative increase in supply: there is almost always an excess of supply over demand for any of the drugs, including the illicits (2, 30, p. 9). But more importantly, there is no historical evidence to support the notion that simple availability, without significant advertising and promotion, leads to use or that simple increase in availability leads to increase in use.

Since World War II the greatest success achieved in the United States in drug use reduction has been for cigarette smoking among adults (19, p. 29; 82). This was accomplished in the face of unlimited supply, low price, and extensive pro drug use advertising and promotion. The observed modest decline in per capita alcohol consumption during the 1980s (83) occurred in the same environment.

Before the gradual decline in adult cigarette use that began in the mid 1960s, it took 80 years after the invention of the automatic cigarette-making machine in the 1880s and 50 years after the perfection of the safety match in the early part of this century for per capita cigarette use, negligible at first, to top out, in the climate of a heavy promotional campaign and little negative publicity.

It took between 30 and 40 years following the end of Prohibition for per capita beer consumption to reach the level at which it stood in 1919 (84, 85). Cocaine is much more readily available in black than in white communities, yet the proportion of persons who have "ever used" the drug is over 45% higher among whites than blacks (17, Table 2). "Crank," an old, synthetic, Category Two street drug with a new name, was made widely available in the late 1980s, but it never caught on. The decline in the use of the illicit drugs that occurred from the late 1970s to the early 1990s (86, p. 30) took place in the context of a constant supply, sold at a fairly reasonable price, although somewhat higher than tobacco and alcohol.

Occasional experiments in decriminalization in the United States have generally not led to a rise in use. Professor Steven Duke (87) referred to the experience of 11 American states in which marihuana was fully or partially decriminalized (54, 88, p. 176; 89). Not only did consumption not rise; it actually continued down at approximately the same rate as elsewhere. (As Professor Duke also points out, marihuana use also did not increase in the Netherlands following full decriminalization.)

The laws regarding the street sale of cocaine and heroin were informally and partially decriminalized in New York City between 1989 and 1993. Both cocaine street sales and cocaine use went down during that period (90). Further, if simple availability had a direct effect on use, it should have been much higher among blacks than whites, which, as already noted, it is not.

Two national polls have considered the question of what would happen to the use of Category Three drugs should they become decriminalized as are the Category One and Two drugs, and as widely available (but not as heavily advertised and promoted as are the Category One drugs). The polls showed that among both adults and high school students there would be very little interest in using them (91, pp. 217–218; 92, footnote 28).

If the drug problem were caused simply by the presence of a drug or drugs, the Andean countries themselves would be awash in cocaine addicts. They are not. If it were, neither tobacco nor alcohol use would be declining in the United States, which they are. The drug problem is caused primarily by demand for drugs and those factors which create demand.

What, in addition to the drug culture, might those factors be? In a comprehensive study, the Department of Justice itself listed at length the factors considered to cause or lead towards drug use (86, pp. 20–23). Included are such factors as the desire to achieve the effects the drugs produce, such as pain relief, relaxation, or excitement; among persons with psychiatric disorders, the need or desire to self-medicate; and among youth especially, peer pressure, inadequate parent-child relationships, personality factors such as low self-esteem, orientation towards risk-taking, and poor school performance. Conspicuous by its absence from the Department of Justice's own list is simple availability.

In summary, tobacco and alcohol are the major killers, they are the causes of the major nonpunishment drug-related expenditures (19, pp. 15–17), and their use by children is almost entirely responsible for the subsequent use of the illicits by adults.

Still, national drug policy does not address the drug problem, per se. The major focus of national drug policy, the "Drug War," creates many very serious non–drug use-related problems for the nonwhite communities in which it is waged. National drug policy is standing on its head. It is time to put it on its feet. It is time to provide an alternative to present policy that addresses not only the drug traffic-related crime problem but more importantly the overall drug problem head on. It is for these objectives that the PHA has been developed.

PRINCIPLES OF THE PHA

The PHA attempts to create a comprehensive national policy and program for dealing with the use and abuse of all the commonly used recreational mood-altering drugs, regardless of category. It is based on tried and true public health principles. In its details it has a few new wrinkles here and there. However, it is constructed largely of ideas, programs, and recommendations that have been in the marketplace of ideas for some time now (23, 43, 93–96). As far back as 1913 Dr. Charles Terry "urged the [American Public Health] Association to take up the matter [of drug addiction] as a public health matter of importance" (43). Dr. Terry also noted that: "Narcotic drug addiction-disease will never be solved by forcible measures only . . . [P]olice measures to be successful must go hand in hand with intelligent medical services."

The PHA is based on several important principles, derived from knowledge of what works in public health and what does not work in present policy.

The Drug Problem Is a Unity, Not a Duality or a Trinity

The drug problem presents as a seamless web. The evidence of the interrelatedness of its various components is clear. It is fruitless, as present experience shows, to attempt to deal with only one part of the problem, or to deal with one part one way and another part another way. A drug is a drug, regardless of its current criminal justice system status. All drugs must be dealt with from the same public health, harm reduction perspective.

Single National Policy

Perhaps the most important element of the PHA is a single national policy for controlling the abuse of all the recreational mood-altering drugs. Among other things, this approach will end the current "OK"/"not-OK," drug/person dichotomies.

Substance Abuse Is a Problem with a Natural History

Having a substance abuse problem is not like having a common cold. It is not something a person catches one day that shows up in its clinical form the next. Furthermore, unlike the common cold, in adults substance abuse manifests itself differently in different persons over time and varies widely in breadth and depth from person to person and drug to drug (37). For example, most users of cigarettes are habituated to them, but a few are not. All cigarette smokers are at much higher risk for a number of serious diseases than are nonsmokers for the same diseases. But most cigarette smokers contract only one of those diseases, if they contract any at all. Most users of alcohol do not become alcoholics. There are about 75 different diseases and

negative health conditions for which regular alcohol use raises the risk (97), and the manifestations of the condition vary widely from person to person.

Most cocaine users do not become abusers (98). Some do. The PHA recognizes and provides for the reality that in adults substance abuse has no consistent natural history. The current selective decriminalization approach does not do so.

However, the PHA also recognizes that in children there is a common natural history: for most substance abusers the problem starts in childhood or the early teenage years, with the use of tobacco, alcohol, or both (53, 62). Thus, the PHA pays a great deal of attention to preventing the use of those two drugs by young people, as recommended by Dr. Henningfield (63).

The Universally Harmful Drug Form Is Tobacco

As noted previously, there is one drug form that since most users are addicted, when used as intended increases the risk of negative health outcomes for most users, as well as for all of those in the vicinity of use: tobacco. That fact, in addition to the centrality of tobacco to the gateway drug effect, makes tobacco use prevention in children central to the PHA.

The Spectrum of Harmfulness and the Concept of Safe Use

All of the commonly used recreational mood-altering drugs other than tobacco increase the risk of health harms for only some of those who use them and for only some of those in the vicinity of use. The primary risk incurred by the use of the drugs other than tobacco is that one might eventually use them to that level at which the risk of health harm appears. Thus, for the drugs other than tobacco, there is a "spectrum of harmfulness" from none to severe.

Some of these harms are due to the actions of the drugs on the body. Others are the result of drug-induced behaviors in the user. Of course, any use of any drug makes the user susceptible to the possibility of incurring health-harmful risk. But apparently for each commonly used drug other than tobacco, safe use is possible (99). For no recreational mood-altering drug has this spectrum yet been fully defined or clearly understood.

Law Enforcement Can Be Used Intelligently

History has taught us that criminal law enforcement works poorly to reinforce moral sanctions against personal behaviors such as the use of recreational mood-altering drugs (34, 35). However, selectively applied criminal and civil law enforcement has been an important tool in implementing many programs for improving the public's health.

Law enforcement can be effective, for example, when the health problem has been caused by a disease organism that infects individuals regardless of personal choice or by an economic behavior that damages the environment (e.g., isolation in tuberculosis control, mandatory vaccination, required automotive emissions control, regulated toxic waste disposal).

But to be broadly helpful, law enforcement must be applied in those situations in which it has been shown to be effective. Also, its use must be consistent with the beliefs of a large majority of the population. Thus, law enforcement has very important roles to play in the PHA: for example, reducing the sale of recreational mood-altering drugs to minors, controlling the operation of motor vehicles by intoxicated persons (96, 100), and enforcing drug taxation statutes.

In Great Britain since World War I, significant reductions in cirrhosis of the liver mortality have been achieved by modestly limiting availability and controlling price to favor beer and wine over spirits (101). This has been accomplished by curtailing the opening hours of pubs and liquor stores, by generally restricting liquor sales to those establishments, and by taxing hard liquor heavily as compared with beer and wine.

Legalization Is Not the Focus, Solving the Drug Problem Is

The PHA is neither for nor against what is called "legalization." However, it recognizes the great health harms the "Drug War" brings to the nonwhite communities in which it is waged, harms probably more injurious to the public's health that the use of the drug forms other than alcohol and tobacco itself. Thus it sees a direct and very important benefit of its own implementation, the opportunity to end the "Drug War."

The Place of Moral Suasion

The PHA respects the belief that the raising of moral considerations and the invocation of moral sanctions may be useful for some in diminishing drug use. At the same time, the PHA recognizes that in dealing with this kind of highly personal behavior, historical experience has demonstrated the futility and waste of attempting to invoke or reinforce the moral sanction through the use of the criminal law.

THE PUBLIC HEALTH APPROACH

In recommending the development of a "Public Health Response to the War on Drugs," in 1989 the American Public Health Association published the following statement. It is still valid in the mid 1990s (93):

Alcohol, tobacco, and other drug problems represent one of the most pressing public health issues in the United States today. Despite numerous assaults on these problems, including the current "War on Drugs," they remain intractable—continuing at epidemic levels and unresponsive to a variety of strategies and public policy initiatives. This intractability is in part a result of a fundamental misunderstanding of and a blindness to the nature of alcohol, tobacco, and other drug problems and the degree to which they are integrated into our society. The purpose of this position paper is to provide a blueprint for a comprehensive policy for addressing the nation's alcohol, tobacco, and other psychoactive drug problems. . . .

As stated at the beginning of this chapter, this approach to the prevention of substance abuse has a number of components. Some are of a classically "public health" nature. For example, they include improved school and public health education, strengthened regulatory approaches, such as limitations on the advertising and promotion of all recreational mood-altering drugs, and the legal prohibition of cigarette vending machines.

Other measures are political, such as shifting the national leadership emphasis of the substance abuse control program from one that focuses on punishment for bad behavior to one that focuses on health. All of these measures stress helping people to change their behavior in a positive way. Certainly not every element in the list presented here need be included in an effective PHA. In addition, there may be other elements inadvertently left off the list that should be added.

As stated at the beginning of the chapter, the primary goal of the PHA is to reduce the use and abuse of all the recreational mood-altering drugs to provide for their safe, pleasurable use, consistent with centuries' old human experience, while minimizing to the greatest degree possible their harmful effects on individuals, the family, and society as a whole.

National Policy Education Campaign

The top national political and health leadership will be called upon to educate the public on the new policy and stimulate their participation in and cooperation with it. The educational campaign will recognize the drug culture and the gateway drug effect as significant causes of the total substance abuse problem and thus will focus major emphasis on dealing with them. To be effective, this campaign must be very carefully thought out, since the American people have been trained by present national policy (which tolerates the promotion of recreational mood-altering drug use) to not think of alcohol and tobacco as "drugs." The 1995 Food and Drug Administration initiative to declare nicotine a drug and tobacco products drug delivery systems is a very important step in this direction.

Many of the PHA's messages will be new to many of the American people. While smokers may not object too strongly to being told that they are drug addicts (at least 80% of smokers want to quit at any one time, and many of them know that they are addicted to nicotine), many alcohol users, most of whom are not addicts, will object very strongly to the association. Thus it is vital that the public health messages be delivered by the top national po-

litical and health leadership. It would be very helpful if their counterparts at the state and local levels participated also.

Rational Drug Classification System

A rational system for classifying all of the recreational mood-altering drugs (including tobacco and alcohol) by their potential dangers and benefits would be developed. This system would be based upon at least these major criteria: addictive potential, short-term and long-term personal hazards, personal benefits (if any), and potential harmfulness to other individuals and society. Pharmacological, toxicological, pathological, medical, epidemiological, and sociological data would be used to develop the system.

Responsible or Safe Use

As part of this effort, the highly controversial "safe use" and "responsible use" issues would be dealt with. To define safe use and responsible use for each of the major recreational mood-altering drugs is no mean feat. But if any program to reduce and prevent abuse is to be created and successfully implemented, one must be developed.

CHILDREN

For children there is no such thing as responsible use of any drug. This is based on the fact that most regular and addictive drug use begins before the age of 21 years. A national campaign on this subject may be just beginning in the mid 1990s. Even the tobacco industry is ostensibly out to "discourage smoking by youngsters under 18, those most likely to take up the habit" (102). And the beer industry, with some irony considering what alcohol does to mental judgment, broadly promotes the slogan: "Drink responsibly; know when to say when."

ADULTS

There is responsible use of certain drugs for adults. For example, most users of alcohol in the United States are light to moderate users. The data indicate that the same may be true for the major illicit drugs (98). Certainly, any effective program to reduce the use and abuse of all recreational mood-altering drugs must deal with the reality of safe alcohol use by many American adults. At the same time, the majority of Americans appear to have recognized that there is no such thing as responsible use of cigarettes, at least in public. These accepted understandings must be built into the definition of responsible use if a broad-based policy is going to be politically viable and effective.

Regulated Sale Model

All drugs could, for example, be sold only in "Drug Stores," either state-run or licensed to private interests. Or there could be "Drug Sections" in general retail stores, with access permitted only for adults. The regulated sale model would be supported by the other elements of the PHA.

Rational Price and Tax Structure

A rational price structure and tax policy for all drugs would be implemented. It would be aimed both at raising funds to pay for the program and at reducing consumption. It could be modeled on the British approach to alcohol beverage taxation and availability control. To assist in the overall public health campaign against substance abuse, the taxes should not be referred to as "sin" taxes, but rather as "risk-reduction" taxes or some similar appellation.

Furthermore, drug tax revenues would not go to the general fund. They would not be used as a substitute for income, property, capital gains, or other progressive taxes. Following the example of the 1990 California antismoking advertising campaign (103), these revenues would be used only to fund the PHA. Such taxes would, of course, be gradually self-liquidating as drug use declined with the effectiveness of the programs the taxes supported.

This system would be designed to avoid the creation of an underpriced black market (which, although serious, is not as potentially dangerous as the overpriced one which exists now). Based on the experience with taxation of alcohol and tobacco in this country (104) and others, it appears that taxes on legal drugs could be raised significantly without incurring the risk of developing any significant underpriced black market. To avoid the bootlegging from low-tax to high-tax states that now occurs in the tobacco market, it is important that taxes on the recreational mood-altering drug be levied at the point of production.

Availability Controls

As already shown, there is a significant difference between "simple availability" versus "availability with promotion." There would be controls on the places and hours of availability and sale of all the currently legal recreational drugs, especially of the illegal sale to minors of those otherwise legal drugs. This could take a variety of forms. Former Secretary of Health and Human Services Louis Sullivan has proposed the licensing of cigarette sales places and the banning of cigarette vending machines (105). Historically, vending machines have significantly increased cigarette sales (104).

Measures such as the following could also be considered: (a) expanding the distance in which the sale of the legal drugs is banned in the vicinity of schools and (b) prohibiting the sale even of legal drugs on all government-owned premises.

Many other useful recommendations along these lines were made by the Surgeon General's Workshop on Drunk Driving (96).

Assault on the Drug Culture

A clear assault would be made on the drug culture. This is a critical part of the program. The public must be educated to understand the interrelatedness of the use and abuse of all the recreational mood-altering drugs. They must also be educated to understand that the atmosphere created by the promotion of legal drugs, over-the-counter medications, and vitamins, and the way medicine itself is practiced all contribute to the drug abuse problem. The political difficulties of implementing this policy must not be underestimated. Advertising policy is central to this effort.

Advertising Policy

Pro–drug use advertising has been analyzed in depth for tobacco by Dr. Kenneth Warner (106). First, in the PHA there would be no future expansion beyond that which is presently permitted: no reintroduction of radio and television cigarette advertising, no advertising of spirits on radio and television, and no advertising of any kind for any illicit drug for which the legal status might change in the future.

Second, a complete ban on pro–drug use advertising could be undertaken, as recommended, for example, by the Committee on Public Health of the New York Academy of Medicine (23). Significant constitutional questions would be raised by such legislation; however, there are strong arguments that it would be constitutional in the case of cigarettes (107). The same arguments might apply to the other drugs as well.

In summary, Polin's position is that:

Tobacco advertising is not commercial speech protected by the First Amendment because it is inherently misleading, if not fraudulent, and/or relates to criminal activity (i.e., the sale of tobacco to minors). Assuming, arguendo, that tobacco is protected commercial speech, . . . in recognition that tobacco is lawful only because of its exceptional [political and economic] background, that the substantial governmental interest at stake justifies extraordinary control of intended effect—promoting the use of a uniquely [and inherently] harmful product (107).

Furthermore, one might argue (108) that, if the State has the constitutional power to regulate the promotion, sale, and use of a substance, which it clearly does in the case of drugs, it also has the power to regulate or prohibit an activity designed solely for the purpose of increasing the sale and use of the same substance. Alternatively, a variety of restrictions on the advertising and promotion of drugs could be imposed, as recommended by former Surgeon General C. Everett Koop for alcohol (109).

If it were to be concluded that a complete advertising ban were not desirable or constitutional, pro–drug advertising could be taxed. A dollar tax for each advertising dollar spent would both reduce the amount of advertising and raise a significant amount of money for the PHA. A tax on pro–drug use advertising levied on the manufacturers, the advertising agencies, and the sellers of advertising time and space would be more equitable than increases in the taxes on sales, especially in the case of cigarettes. At any one time, 80% of smokers would like to be able to quit but cannot do so primarily because of the extraordinary addictivity of nicotine—is it equitable to tax an addiction?

Public Education Campaign

There would be a comprehensive public education campaign against drug use per se, beyond the national leadership education program outlined in the section on National Policy Education Campaign. It would be much more comprehensive than the modest anti–cigarette smoking program of the last 20 years. Also, much remains to be learned about what will constitute an effective campaign (110).

School Health Education

A comprehensive school health education program will deal with all of the recreational drugs in a unified manner, building on the successful experience of such programs as Project STAR in the Kansas Cities of Missouri and Kansas (111, 112). The introduction to the Project STAR curriculum states that: "Project STAR's goal is to reduce alcohol and other drug use among young people and to create an environment that supports and encourages youth to remain drug free."

By carefully studying prevention programs and related research, Project STAR identifies effective strategies and encourages communities to implement those strategies to help young people avoid alcohol and other drug use. One of the most effective strategies uses a curriculum taught by classroom teachers to help adolescents anticipate and resist social pressure.

Research shows that successful prevention programs must not only involve schools, but entire communities. As students develop refusal skills, their commitment to nonuse must be reinforced and supported by parents, churches, businesses, and community leaders. To sustain this commitment, community-wide changes in attitudes must be made. Only then will young people achieve the quality of life they want and deserve (113).

Treatment

Comprehensive treatment, rehabilitation, and job-training programs for those who are addicted to or are abusers of any of the recreational mood-altering drugs would be made available. The matters of the appropriateness of "on demand" treatment, the role of the law enforcement system in placing drug abusers in treatment, and who would pay for what would have to be worked out. (It must be remembered, however, that drug treatment programs, while vital for those persons already in need of them, will not solve the drug problem. Only prevention can do that.)

Termination of Drug Price Supports

Tobacco crop subsidy and price support systems (which do nothing but boost profits and keep marginal lands in the tobacco-growing business) (27) would be terminated. Subsidized tobacco crop allotments could be restricted either to reduce demand or increase price. Tax shelters for grape growing, tax incentives for Puerto Rican and Virgin Islands rum production, and similar measures would be ended.

Assistance for Displaced Drug Workers and Farmers

Subsidies, relocation assistance, and retraining opportunities for the tens of thousands of workers and small farmers who would be put out of work in the United States by a significant decline in the legal recreational drug trade and/or the ending of various crop subsidy programs would be provided.

National Domestic Spending

The very important programs of national domestic spending to deal with the identified political, economic, and social causes of the illegal drug trade in inner-city neighborhoods would be implemented. (At the same time it will be recognized and made clear that the drug problem is hardly the exclusive domain of the African-American and other minority communities.)

Liability Law Development

A medicolegal commission would be created to review the civil liability laws covering the purveyors of all recreational mood-altering drugs with the aim of strengthening the effectiveness of those laws in reducing harmful drug use. According to Mosher, this element holds promise (104). In the mid 1990s, liability challenges seemed to become more difficult for the tobacco industry to defend against. But given the political and economic power of the industry, the end of that process was anything but certain.

Focused Law Enforcement

The focus of drug-related law enforcement would be on punishing criminal behavior resulting from drug use, not simply punishing drug use, although the required effort to enforce the laws against traffic in illicit substances would of course be maintained. Current law enforcement efforts would be continued until the use and abuse of all recreational mood-altering drugs is significantly reduced.

However, the current emphasis on the incarceration of "casual users" (which sometimes leads to the jailing of people for being addicted to drugs—just imagine what would happen if that policy were applied to cigarette smoking) would be brought to an end as counterproductive and wasteful of law enforcement time, money, and manpower. The drug traffic focus would be returned to the major dealers, as well as corrupted law enforcement officials and "illegitimate" business activity, such as money laundering.

As the PHA implementation proceeded, law enforcement would focus on those areas in which it has some hope of success: controlling the violation of statutes governing the promotion, distribution, and sale of all the recreational drugs to persons of minor age; tax collection and evasion; and dealing with the antisocial behaviors associated with the abuse of all recreational drugs (e.g., driving while intoxicated, family violence). Current plans and proposals to build more jails, establish "reeducation camps" on closed military bases, employ the military in interdiction of foreign drug supplies, and use the military as domestic antidrug police further erode Fourth Amendment protections, and would be canceled.

The PHA might very well include an expansion in the federal court system so that current case calendars can become unclogged and civil cases can begin moving through it again. It would also reverse current policy, which inhibits legal representation of drug crime defendants.

SUMMARY

Solving the drug problem requires (a) recognizing that it is a continuum occupied by all three drug categories; (b) setting rational goals for its control—goals which are consistent with human experience with the mood-altering drugs, achievable by the methods to be used in the program, and separate from the goal of crime reduction; (c) clearly understanding that its causes in the United States go far beyond the simple availability of drugs upon which current policy focuses so much of its attention; (d) and, therefore, turning major attention from the supply side to the demand side, to the drug culture, the gateway drug effect, and the specific causes of the inner-city drug trade: unemployment, poor housing, poor education, and hopelessness.

This program would markedly reduce the use and abuse of all the recreational drugs; reduce the tremendous pressure on and corruption of the criminal justice and law enforcement systems created by the present approach, freeing them to focus on other criminal behaviors; and largely pay for itself through taxes on recreational drug sales, use, advertising, and profits. Its major political downside is that it requires a major assault on the tobacco and alcohol industries. But it can be done. Based on the record achieved by public health so far, it will meet with success.

References

1. Shannon E. A losing battle. Time 1990 (December 3):44.
2. Horowitz C. The no-win war. New York Magazine 1996 (February 5):23.
3. McNamara JD. The Los Angeles riots and the crisis in American policing. In: Trebach AS, Zeese KB, eds. Strategies for change. Washington, DC: The Drug Policy Foundation Press, 1992:13.
4. Nadelmann E. Drug prohibition in the United States: costs, consequences, and alternatives. Science 1989;245:939–947.
5. Office of National Drug Control Policy. Pulse check: national trends in drug abuse, Fall 1995. Washington, DC: Executive Office of the President, 1995.
6. Salerno R. A policeman's surveillance report. In: Trebach AS, Zeese KB, eds. The great issues of drug policy. Washington, DC: The Drug Policy Foundation, 1990:61.
7. Sweet RW. Admit that the drug war is not successful; abolish prohibition. In: Trebach AS, Zeese KB, eds. Drug prohibition and the conscience of nations. Washington, DC: The Drug Policy Foundation, 1990:205.
8. McGinnis JM, Foege WH. Actual causes of death in the United States. JAMA 1993;270:2207.
9. Coalition on Smoking or Health. FDA proposed rule on tobacco regulation. Washington, DC: Coalition on Smoking or Health, 1995.
10. Tobacco state legislators introduce bills to block FDA regulation of tobacco products. Tobacco on Trial 1995;7(December):13.
11. Nadelmann E. Legalisation or harm reduction: the debate continues. Int J Drug Policy 1992; 3(2):76–82.

12. National Commission on Marihuana and Drug Abuse. Second report: drug use in America—problem in perspective. Washington, DC: U.S. Government Printing Office, 1973.
13. Random House dictionary of the English language. New York: Random House, 1987.
14. Drug Policy Foundation. The drug war in black and white. Drug Policy Letter 1996;28:1(a).
15. Mauer M. The drug war's unequal justice. Drug Policy Letter 1996;28:11.
16. Mauer M, Huling T. Young black Americans and the criminal justice system. Washington, DC: The Sentencing Project, October, 1995:9–13.
17. Substance Abuse and Mental Health Services Administration. National Household Survey on Drug Abuse: population estimates 1994. DHHS Pub. No. (SMA) 95–3063. Rockville, MD: U.S. Department of Health and Human Services, September, 1995.
18. Rosenbaum M. Just say what? An alternative view on solving America's drug problem. 2nd edition. San Francisco, CA: National Council on Crime and Delinquency, 1990.
19. Institute for Health Policy, Brandeis University. Substance abuse. Princeton, NJ: Robert Wood Johnson Foundation, 1993.
20. Fingarette H. We should reject the disease concept of alcoholism. Harvard Med Sch Ment Health Lett 1990;6(8):4.
21. Kissin B. The disease concept of alcoholism. In: Smart RG, et al., eds. Research advances in alcohol and drug problems. New York: Plenum Press, 1983;7:93–126.
22. Vaillant GE. We should retain the disease concept of alcoholism. Harvard Med Sch Ment Health Lett 1990;6(9):4.
23. Committee on Public Health, New York Academy of Medicine. Statement and resolution on

tobacco and health. Bull N Y Acad Med 1986;62:1029–1033.
24. Jarvis CD. Cited in: Dropping acid. City Paper [New York], May 25, 1990:6.
25. Lindesmith AF. The addict and the law. New York: Vintage Press, 1965.
26. Weinraub B. President offers strategy. New York Times 1989(September 6):1, B7.
27. Massing M. The two William Bennetts. New York Review of Books, March 1, 1990:29.
28. Executive Office of the President. The national drug control strategy. Washington, DC: U.S. Government Printing Office, September 5, 1989.
29. Executive Office of the President. The national drug control strategy. Washington, DC: U.S. Government Printing Office, January 25, 1990.
30. Office of National Drug Control Policy. National Drug Control Strategy, Washington, DC: Executive Office of the President, February, 1994.
31. Schaler J. Drugs and free will. Soc Sci Modern Society, November/December 1990.
32. Trebach AS, Zeese KB. Milton Friedman and Thomas Szasz: on liberty and drugs. Washington, DC: The Drug Policy Foundation Press, 1992.
33. Cohen G, et al. Epidemiology of substance use. In: Friedman L, et al., eds. Source book of substance abuse. Baltimore: Williams & Wilkins, 1996.
34. Brecher E. Licit and illicit drugs. Boston: Little, Brown, 1972.
35. Musto DF. The American disease. New York: Oxford University Press, 1987.
36. Friedman L, et al., eds. Source book of substance abuse. Baltimore: Williams & Wilkins, 1996:109–265.
37. Zinberg N. Drug, set, and setting. New Haven, CT: Yale University Press, 1984.
38. Berke RL. Bennett asserts education isn't key. New York Times 1990(February 3).

39. Public Health Service. Promoting health/preventing disease: Year 2000 objectives for the nation. Draft for public review and comment. Washington, DC: U.S. Government Printing Office, September, 1989.

40. Public Health Service. Healthy People 2000: Midcourse review and 1995 revisions. Hyattsville, MD: National Center for Health Statistics, 1995.

41. White House Conference for a Drug Free America. Final report. Washington, DC: U.S. Government Printing Office, 1988.

42. Partnership for a Drug Free America. Read this page. New York Times 1992(October 26):A5.

43. Erickson PG. A public health approach to demand reduction. J Drug Issues 1990:20(3).

44. Lutz P. Drug fight stresses educational approach. New York Times 1989(June 11):1 (Long Island Section).

45. U.S. Department of Health and Human Services. Reducing the health consequences of smoking: 25 years of progress. DHHS Publication No. (CDC) 89–8411. Washington, DC: U.S. Government Printing Office, 1989.

46. Wisotsky S. Breaking the impasse in the war on drugs. New York: Greenwood Press, 1986.

47. Committee on Government Operations, House of Representatives. United anti-narcotics activities in the Andean region. Union Calendar No. 584. Washington, DC: U.S. Government Printing Office, 1990.

48. Regier DA, Farmer ME, Rae DS, Locke BZ, Keith SJ, Judd LL, et al. Comorbidity of mental disorders with alcohol and other drug abuse. JAMA 1990;264:2549–2550.

49. Cohen S, Weiss R. Substance abuse and mental illness. In: Friedman L, et al., eds. Source book of substance abuse. Baltimore: Williams & Wilkins, 1996.

50. Gitlin T. On drugs and mass media in America's consumer society. In: Resnik H, et al., eds. Youth and drugs: society's mixed messages. Rockville, MD: Office of Substance Abuse Prevention, 1990.

51. Johnson WO. Sports and suds. Sports Illustrated 1988 (August 8):68.

52. Johnson C. Prevention and control of drug abuse. In: Last JM, ed. Public health and preventive medicine. Norwalk, CT: Appleton-Century-Crofts, 1986.

53. U.S. Centers for Disease Control and Prevention. Survey of state and local laws on tobacco sales. MMWR 1990;39(21):349–352.

54. Johnston L. Ban cigarette advertising to reduce adolescent drug abuse. Drug Abuse Update June 1988;25:2.

55. Kandel DB. Issues of sequencing of adolescent drug use and other problem behaviors. J Drug Issues 1989;3:55–76.

56. Chen K, Kandel DB. The natural history of drug use. Am J Public Health 1995;85:41.

57. New York Division of Alcoholism and Alcohol Abuse. Alcohol: the gateway drug. Focus 1991; 6(1).

57a.Fratello D. Listening to cocaine. Drug Policy Letter 1994:(Fall):11.

58. Henningfield J. Smokeless tobacco: addictive and a gateway drug. Tobacco and Youth Reporter 1990;(Autumn):11.

59. Keegan A. Tobacco may provide gateway to drug, alcohol abuse. NIDA Notes 1991;(Summer/Fall):23.

60. National Institute of Drug Abuse. Tobacco as a gateway drug [chart]. New York: Smokefree Educational Services, 1993.

61. Stark F. The 2nd annual drug test for members of congress. Washington, DC: House of Representatives, 1989.

62. New York State Division of Alcoholism and Al-

cohol Abuse. Alcohol. The gateway to other drug use. Buffalo, NY: Research Institute on Alcoholism, 1989. [See this publication for a comprehensive bibliography on the gateway drug effect.]

63. More teens are smoking! Tobacco and Youth Reporter 1990;4(3).

64. Bradley AM. A capsule review of the state of the art: the sixth special report to the U.S. Congress on alcohol and health. Alcohol Health Res World 1987(Summer).

65. Stewart K. Use of alcohol contributes to costs of violence. Prevention Pipeline, 1995;(July/August):1.

66. Criminogenics: how the drug war causes crime. Cato Policy Forum 1994;16(3).

67. Goldstein P, et al. Most drug-related murders result from crack sales, not use. Drug Policy Letter 1990;2(2):6.

68. Greenberg J. All about crime. New York Times 1990(September 3):20.

69. Saul S. 90 expected to set record for murders. Newsday 1990(December 10):7.

70. Dramatic drop in U.S. murders: 12%. Newsday 1995(December 18).

71. Meddis S. Drug arrest rate is higher for blacks. USA Today 1989(December 20):A1[a].

72. Meddis S. Whites, not blacks, at the core of drug crisis. USA Today 1989(December 20):A1[a].

73. Beck A, et al. Survey of state prison inmates, 1991. Pub. no. NCJ-136949. Washington, DC: Department of Justice, 1993.

74. Bureau of Justice Statistics. Drugs and jail inmates, 1989. Washington, DC: Department of Justice, 1991.

75. Drug Policy Foundation. Voices. Drug Policy Letter 1996;28:14.

76. Morley J. White gram's burden. Drug Policy Letter 1996;28:17.

77. Rosenthal E. Health problems of inner city poor reach crisis point. New York Times 1990(December 24):1.

78. Rosenthal AM. Surrender on drugs? New York Times 1990(December 10).

79. Califano J. No, fight harder. New York Times 1993(December 15).

80. Center on Addiction and Substance Abuse. Legalization: panacea or pandora's box? New York: Center on Addiction and Substance Abuse, 1995.

81. Rosenthal AM. Dismantling the war. New York Times 1993(May 18):A21.

82. U.S. Centers for Disease Control and Prevention. Cigarette smoking among adults—United States, 1991. MMWR 1993;42(14):231.

83. Williams GD, et al. Surveillance report #23, apparent per capita alcohol consumption: national, state, and regional trends, 1977–1990. Washington, DC: National Institute of Alcohol Abuse and Alcoholism, December, 1992.

84. Lender ME, Martin JK. Drinking in America. A history. New York: The Free Press, 1982: 196–197.

85. Rorabaugh WJ. The alcoholic republic, an American tradition. New York: Oxford University Press, 1979:233, 290–293.

86. Department of Justice. Drugs, crime and the justice system. Pub. no. NCJ-133652. Washington, DC: Department of Justice, December, 1992.

87. Duke S. Drug prohibition: an unnatural disaster. Connecticut Law Review 1995;27(2):571–612.

88. Kleiman MAR. Marijuana. Costs of abuse, costs of control. New York: Greenwood Press, 1989.

89. Single EW. The impact of marijuana decriminalization: an update. J Public Health Policy 1989;10(4):456–466.

90. Treaster JB. Mayor's drug strategy: new plan for chronic problem. New York Times 1994(April 11).

91. Dennis R. The American people are starting to question the drug war. In: Trebach A, Zeese K, eds. Drug prohibition and the conscience of nations. Washington, DC: Drug Policy Foundation, 1990.

92. Nadelmann E. Thinking seriously about alternatives to drug prohibition. Daedelus 1992; 121: 85.

93. American Public Health Association. A public health response to the war on drugs: reducing alcohol, tobacco and other drug problems among the nation's youth. Res. 8817 (PP). Am J Public Health 1989;79:360–364.

94. Association of State and Territorial Health Officials (ASTHO). Guide to public health practice: state health agency tobacco prevention and control plans. NIH Pub. No. 90–1577. Washington, DC: U.S. Department of Health and Human Services, 1989.

95. Resnik H, et al. eds. Youth and drugs: society's mixed messages. Rockville, MD: Office of Substance Abuse Prevention, 1990.

96. U.S. Surgeon General. Proceedings. Workshop on drunk driving. Rockville, MD: US Department of Health and Human Services, 1989.

97. Rankin JG, Ashley MJ. Alcohol-related health problems and their prevention. In: Last JM, ed. Public health and preventive medicine. Norwalk, CT: Appleton-Century-Crofts, 1986.

98. National Institute of Drug Abuse Capsules. In: Population estimates of lifetime and current drug use, 1988. Rockville, MD: National Institute of Drug Abuse, 1989.

99. Office of National Drug Control Policy. Understanding drug treatment. Washington, DC: U.S. Government Printing Office, June 1990.

100. U.S. Centers for Disease Control and Prevention. Alcohol-related traffic fatalities—United States, 1982–1989. MMWR 1990;39(49):889–891.

101. Terris M. Epidemiology of cirrhosis of the liver: National mortality data. Am J Public Health 1967;57:2076.

102. Ramirez A. Tobacco campaign set to warn off teenagers. New York Times 1990(December 11):D1.

103. Mydans S. California uses tobacco tax for ads attacking smoking. New York Times 1990 (April 11):1.

104. Mosher J. Drug availability in a public health perspective. In: Resnick H, et al., eds. Youth and drugs: society's mixed messages. Rockville, MD: Office of Substance Abuse Prevention, 1990.

105. Sullivan LW. We're letting our kids kill themselves. Newsday 1990(June 13).

106. Warner K. Selling smoke: cigarette advertising and public health. Washington, DC: American Public Health Association, 1986.

107. Polin K. Argument for the ban of tobacco advertising: a First Amendment analysis. Hofstra Law Rev 1988;17:99–135.

108. Christoffel T. Personal communication, May 14, 1990.

109. Koop CE. Restrict alcohol advertising. Newsday 1989(June 1).

110. DeJong W, Winsten J. The use of mass media in substance abuse prevention. Health Affairs 1990;9(2):30–46.

111. Cormack CC, Daniels S. Project STAR research findings. Kansas City, MO: Project STAR, 1990.

112. Pentz MA, et al. A multicommunity trial for primary prevention of adolescent drug abuse. JAMA 1989;261:3259–3266.

113. Project STAR. Curriculum overview. Kansas City, MO: Project STAR, 1990.

78 MEDICAL EDUCATION: THE ACQUISITION OF KNOWLEDGE, ATTITUDES, AND SKILLS

John N. Chappel and David C. Lewis

"Physicians regularly miss the diagnosis of underlying substance abuse in patients because their training has not demanded that they develop the requisite attitudes, knowledge, and clinical skills."

Thomas H. Meikle, Jr., M.D. (1)

Medical education in substance abuse continues to make slow but steady progress. The best summary of this progress is contained in the proceedings of the Macy conference (1). Leaders from the primary care specialties and psychiatry participated in a conference which urged the specialties of family practice, internal medicine, pediatrics, and obstetrics and gynecology to "promptly respond to the need to improve the quality of care provided by physicians trained in these specialties to patients with alcohol and other drug problems" (p. 101). The conference also urged the certifying boards and Residency Review Committees to take specific actions to strengthen their requirements so that "the performance of residents in managing substance abuse patients is measurably improved." The progress displayed in these recommendations is all the more remarkable in view of the continued position in our culture that alcohol and drug abuse are moral and legal problems. This fact is reflected in the increasing number of individuals who are incarcerated for alcohol and drug–related offences.

Medical education has not been as successful in competing with cultural trends in the past. Historically the ravages of alcoholism and other drug addictions have been quite clear. While the gin epidemic raged in England between 1750 and 1800, Benjamin Rush, America's first Surgeon General and the father of American psychiatry, described alcoholism as a disease (2). In the latter part of the nineteenth century the United States experienced epidemics of cocaine and opiate abuse following the Civil War (3). Physicians tried a variety of approaches to deal with these addictions. In the meantime, political decisions were made to attack the problems through regulation and enforcement. The Harrison Act of 1914 (3) and the Prohibition Amendment (4) to the Constitution in 1919 appeared to have a major effect on medicine. During the 1920s, while some physicians were prosecuted for prescribing opioids to narcotic addicts, there was a gradual avoidance of narcotic and alcohol problems in medical practice and an absence of significant teaching about alcoholism and other drug addiction in medical schools. As a result several generations of physicians have had little or no training in the recognition and treatment of alcohol and other drug addictions.

HISTORY OF MODERN MEDICAL EDUCATION IN SUBSTANCE ABUSE

Despite the societal view that alcoholism and other drug addictions were moral and legal problems, physicians have always had to manage difficult detoxification and the medical complications of these disorders. There was no criticism as long as the underlying addiction was left alone. Following World War II a small group of physicians began to take an interest in the addictive disorders. In 1954 the New York Medical Society on Alcoholism was founded (5). This small group of physicians prompted the American Medical Association (AMA) in 1956 and in 1966 to declare that alcoholism was a medical illness (6). The intent was to get physicians to diagnose and treat the underlying conditions rather than the sequelae. Unfortunately these actions had little or no effect on medical school curricula.

In 1967 interest had spread sufficiently to form a national organization, the American Medical Society on Alcoholism (AMSA). Interest slowly grew amongst these physicians and expansion occurred in 1984 to include all drugs of abuse. The result was the American Medical Society on Alcoholism and Other Drug Dependencies (AMSAODD) which was the first national medical society representing all the addictions. In 1989 this organization became the American Society of Addiction Medicine (ASAM).

During the 1960s the development of methadone maintenance and therapeutic communities as treatment modalities began to stimulate more medical interest. This was probably augmented by the ferment over drug use amongst service men in Vietnam. In 1970 the National Council on Alcoholism held a conference (7). The American Medical Student Association, an active participant in that conference, surveyed students from 60 medical schools (8). Only 10% of the students reported a formal course or clerkship dealing with the treatment and rehabilitation of the alcoholic. The students concluded their report with the following statement:

If physicians and other medical personnel are to be trained to provide better treatment, rehabilitation, and prevention of alcoholism, they must have the opportunity for a coherent educational program in their medical school career. Only in this fashion can the great shortage of adequately trained professionals and the archaic attitudes of many practitioners be overcome. (Reprinted with permission from reference 8)

The AMA added its voice to the pressure for change, publishing a position statement which described the need for effective medical education on the use and abuse of drugs to have reached "a point of urgency" (9). In 1972 the Macy Foundation and Rockefeller University held a conference of medical educators which recommended a core curriculum for medical students, postgraduate courses, and integration of substance abuse teaching in basic science courses (10).

Governmental response to these developments was to initiate the Career Teacher program in Alcohol and Drug Abuse sponsored by the newly founded National Institute on Alcoholism and Alcohol Abuse (NIAAA) and National Institute on Drug Abuse (NIDA) (11). The goal of the Career Teacher program was to train established faculty to develop and implement substance abuse curricula in their medical schools. Over the 10-year period of its existence (1972–1981) career teachers were funded in 59 schools. The results were positive, but limited. An evaluation of the program concluded that the program had resulted in (12):

1. An average increase in curriculum hours, both required and elective, from 18.5 to 123.6 hours, of which almost all is attributed to career teachers.
2. Clinical substance abuse programs started in a number of medical schools.
3. A large number of curriculum materials and professional writings.

A study comparing a stratified random sample of 35 schools with and without career teachers concluded that the presence of a career teacher resulted in "notable improvements" in substance abuse teaching (13). This success is tempered by the fact that the percentage of required teaching time on alcoholism and drug abuse remained well under 1%.

The medical academic ferment begun by the Career Teacher program resulted in the formation of the Association for Medical Education and Research in Substance Abuse (AMERSA) in 1976 (14). This organization has grown to include not only medical school faculty, largely physicians and clinical psychologists, but other health professional faculty in nursing and social work. It holds an annual meeting and publishes a journal, *Substance Abuse,* which enables its members to share both support and stimulus for their often lonely work in attempting to expand and improve the substance abuse education provided by their schools.

The work begun by the career teachers and carried on by AMERSA has continued the slow growth of substance abuse education in medical schools. A recent study in curricular changes between 1986 and 1991 showed the mean number of required and elective curriculum units in substance abuse had increased from 3.5 to 7.2 (15). While the most teaching was done in departments of psychiatry, the increase was most marked in departments of family medicine. The percentage of medical school graduates interested in primary care who think they have received inadequate training in substance abuse treatment fell from 42% in 1976 to 31% in 1992. Although this progress is significant, Table 78.1 shows that there is still a long way to go in comparison with other key aspects of the medical school curriculum.

In 1989 a federal initiative began the Faculty Fellow training program in alcohol and drug abuse. This program provided modest part-time support for 3–5 faculty members from primary care departments and psychiatry (16). This program was a logical sequel to the career teacher program. It also extended support to schools of nursing, social work, and psychology. Unfortunately funding has been dramatically reduced and that promising program is in jeopardy.

In parallel with these developments in medical education there has been a major growth in the subspecialty of addiction medicine. In 1935 Alcoholics Anonymous (AA) developed out of the failure of medicine and psychiatry to help alcoholics achieve long-term stable sobriety (17). Since that time many alcohol and drug–dependent physicians have been helped by AA and NA (Narcotics Anonymous). The numbers of these physicians increased substantially with the development of impaired physician programs in every state (18). Many of these able and energetic recovering physicians decided to dedicate themselves to treating alcohol and drug dependency. In the 1970s and 1980s there was a marked increase in the number of substance abuse treatment programs within the health care system. This growth in treatment interest led to the continued growth of ASAM. In 1983 the first review course and certification examination for physicians was held by the California Society of Addiction Medicine (CSAM). This group of physicians had included other drug addictions in addition to alcoholism when it was formed in 1972. It provided the template for AMSA to include other drug addictions and become ASAM. In 1986 a national examination was held. This certification exam stimulated membership growth in ASAM from 719 in 1981 to over 4000 in 1990 (19). Over two thirds of ASAM's membership comes from internal medicine, family medicine, and psychiatry. The activities of this pool of experienced clinicians has led to the representation of addiction medicine in the AMA house of delegates and the designation of addiction

medicine as a subspecialty in medicine (ADM) along with 85 other self-designated practice specialties.

American medicine has officially left no doubt that training in the diagnosis and treatment of alcohol and other drug addictions should play an important role in medical education. The AMA's position statement in 1972 clearly recognized the need and urged medical educators to address the complex psychological, social, and biologic factors involved (9). In 1988 the AMA Council on Scientific Affairs republished its guidelines for physician involvement in the care of substance abusing patients and added this important statement:

> The AMA also believes it is important that all physicians consider the degree to which they are personally at risk for alcohol and other drug related problems, as well as their ethical obligation to intervene with a colleague who gives evidence of such impairment. Proficiency at this basic level may be considered a personal as well as a professional responsibility. (Reprinted with permission from reference 20)

Family medicine, internal medicine, pediatrics, emergency medicine, and psychiatry have all issued position statements emphasizing the importance of education within their specialties in addiction medicine.

Despite this interest there has been a considerable time lag in developing specific requirements for residency training. For example, in 1981 the American Psychiatric Association (APA) recognized that nearly 30% of the total mental health problems in the United States were due to alcohol and drug abuse problems. Comprehensive training about substance abuse was recommended for all psychiatry residency programs (21). It was not until 1987 that the Residency Review Committee (RRC) for psychiatry included the following requirement:

> Specific clinical experiences must include: supervised clinical management of patients with alcoholism and drug abuse, including detoxification and long term management in inpatient and/or outpatient settings and familiarity with self-help groups. (22)

Table 78.2 shows a comparison of RRC special requirements in substance abuse training for primary care specialties in medicine. It should be noted that only two of the four primary care specialties specify training in substance abuse. Family practice includes theirs as one section under human behavior and psychiatry. Internal medicine focuses entirely on physician impairment. The Macy conference was very clear in recommending to residency review committees and certifying boards that they take specific action to strengthen their requirements in addiction medicine (1). The participants at that conference concluded:

> We recommend that the specialties of Family Practice, Internal Medicine, Pediatrics, and Obstetrics-Gynecology promptly respond to the need to improve the quality of care provided by physicians trained in these specialties to patients with alcohol and other drug problems. These primary care specialties should require all residents to be trained to develop and to demonstrate those skills necessary to prevent, screen for and diagnose alcohol and other drug problems; to provide initial therapeutic interventions for patients with these problems; to refer these patients for additional care when necessary; and to deliver follow-up care for these patients and their families. The certifying boards and residency review committees of these specialties should expeditiously take specific actions to strengthen their requirements so that the performance of residents in managing substance abuse patients is measurably improved. (Reprinted with permission from reference 1)

PROBLEMS IN MEDICAL PRACTICE

There is a long and well-documented history of problems which are the sequelae of the historical events already described. In the 1950s Mendelson and Chafetz found that less than 1% of the alcoholics admitted to the emergency room at the Massachusetts General Hospital sought treatment in the hospital's outpatient program, although all were offered treatment (23). They found both personnel and institutional attitudinal problems accounting for this lack of success. The authors then studied the needs of the alcoholics appearing in the emergency room and developed a system whereby the residents and other staff were expected to treat the alcoholic patient with respect

Table 78.1   Proportion of U.S. Medical Schools Covering Special Topics in Required Courses

Topic	Percentage
Biostatistics	47
Ethical Problems in Medicine	40
Nutrition	32
Community Health	25
Human Sexuality	19
Geriatrics	13
Substance Abuse	8

Modified and reprinted with permission from Fleming M, Barry K, Davis A, Kropp S, Kahn R, Rivo M. Medical education about substance abuse: changes in curriculum and faculty between 1976 and 1992. Acad Med 1994;69:362.

Table 78.2 Comparison of RRC Special Requirements in Substance Abuse Training

Family Practice	Internal Medicine	Pediatrics	Ob/gyn
Human Behavior and Psychiatry • Substance Abuse	Physician Impairment • recognition and management of impairment including substance abuse, and other mental, emotional, and physical disorders as well as principles of active intervention	No specific substance abuse training required	No specific substance abuse training required

Reprinted with permission from Blank LL. Teaching and learning about substance abuse. Macy Conference Proceedings. New York: Josiah Macy Jr. Foundation, 1995:71–79.

and consideration. In addition they were to work at reducing frustrating situations and to gratify reasonable requests. Two hundred consecutive alcoholic patients admitted through the emergency room were randomly assigned to this experimental treatment approach or to a control group which had the usual approach. Following completion of the admission of the 200 patients both groups were followed for one year. An 89% follow-up rate was achieved in a group of men with high rates of homelessness, poverty, and characteristics "most often referred to as skid row alcoholics." (24). The response of the experimental group was both dramatic and significant (Table 78.3).

The authors concluded that this response "graphically documents the necessity of developing and applying new and imaginative variations of clinical skills to mental health problems." They described the differences and emphasis on action rather than words "placing the responsibility for achieving a therapeutic alliance on the caretaker rather than the patient." This approach could be considered to be a template for modern training in addiction medicine.

Research over the following decades continued to reveal clinical problems associated with negative attitudes. Westermeyer and his colleagues used the Michigan Alcoholism Screening Test (MAST) as a diagnostic screening device on the medical and surgical wards of the university teaching hospital (25). They concluded that physicians and nurses in this facility:

1. Did not take adequate alcohol and drug use histories.
2. Did not identify chemical dependency as a medical problem, even when they knew it was present.
3. Did not involve themselves in treatment or treatment recommendations even when the problem was identified.

Mannon, a sociologist, provided some help in understanding this behavior (26). After spending 270 hours of direct observation in the emergency room of a 600-bed hospital, he concluded that the alcoholic represented an exercise in futility for physicians specializing in treating the acutely ill and injured. They coped with this problem by defining the alcoholic as a management problem rather than a medical case to be diagnosed and treated. Successful outcome of a management problem was not defined by medical criteria but by holding the amount of staff time and resources to a minimum. These observations suggest that a process of cognitive restructuring enables the physician to dismiss the need for diagnosing and treating addictive disorders.

These negative attitudes which permeate our culture have resulted in a continuing medical education program, which trained 838 medical professionals in the 1970s, to conclude that "our trainees have touched many alcoholic livers but almost no alcoholic lives" (27). Pursch immersed these professionals in a treatment setting where their primary defenses could be

Table 78.3 Five or More Clinic Visits by Group (Percentages)

	Group	
	Experimental (n = 100)	Control (n = 93)
Yes	42.0	1.1
No	58.0	98.9
Total	100.0	100.0

Reprinted with permission from Chaftez ME, et. al. Establishing treatment relations with alcoholics. J Nerv Ment Dis 1962; 134(5):395–409.
$x^2 = 46.61$, 1 df, $P < .001$.

removed and where they could become aware of their own attitudes and lack of useful knowledge about addictions (27).

In the mid 1980s a study done at a New York teaching hospital involved 385 physicians (28). Psychiatrists, internists, and surgeons were studied. Some significant differences were found. Surgeons were more likely to refer alcoholic patients for both diagnosis and treatment. Internists were more likely to make the diagnosis and refer for treatment, while psychiatrists were more likely to both diagnose and treat their alcoholic patients ($p < .001$). Psychiatrists were found to also see alcoholic patients as more treatable than did either internists or surgeons ($p < .001$). Of importance to continuing medical education in this study was the finding that surgeons had the weakest background in alcoholism and the least desire to learn about treatment resources ($p < .05$). All three groups rejected reading, symposia, lectures, or consultation as methods of learning about alcoholism. These responses confirm the experience many medical educators have had. It is very difficult to attract practicing physicians to attend continuing medical education courses in addiction medicine.

A few years later Moore and his colleagues screened 2002 new adult inpatient admissions to Johns Hopkins Hospital (29). All the new admissions were screened with the CAGE and the MAST tests. Detection rates by house staff and attending physicians varied by departments. Their findings paralleled those of the New York study. In surgery with 23% of the patients screening positive for alcoholism, less than 25% of these were detected with one fifth receiving intervention. In medicine, with 25% of the patients screening positive about 25% were detected with one third of these receiving intervention. In psychiatry with 30% of the patients screening positive for alcoholism, 65% were detected and intervention was initiated in over half of these. In all cases the intervention consisted of presenting the diagnosis to the patient and recommending that they get help. These physician interventions correlated with the patient's reported decrease in the use of alcohol following discharge ($p < .01$). At the recent Macy Conference, Stimmel (30) concluded that physician attitudes have a major effect on physician behavior. He noted not only the effect on failure to diagnose, but also observed trends toward inadequate pain relief and over-prescription of benzodiazepines.

The continuing epidemic of alcohol and other drug addictions makes it imperative that medical education improve its track record and effectiveness in dealing with both physician attitudes and behaviors in diagnosing and treating the harmful effects of alcohol and drug use and addictive disorders. The training staff of one program in the 1970s concluded that 75% of the physicians they trained were unable to deal effectively with alcohol-troubled patients for the following reasons (27):

1. Inadequate training in addiction medicine
2. Unresolved addiction problems in their own families
3. Personal problems with addiction, including self-prescribing
4. Negative experiences with addicted patients
5. A rigid personality structure with inability to deal with patients on a feeling level
6. Fear of loss of collegial support and career advancement

THE KNOWLEDGE BASE OF ADDICTION MEDICINE

The explosion of knowledge and experience which have occurred since the AMA declared that alcoholism was a disease has done much to establish medical credibility for the field of addiction medicine (6). The dramatic increase in research findings has led ASAM and the National Council on Alcoholism and Drug Dependence to develop a new definition of alcoholism (31). The revised definition produced by a committee of 27 experts is as follows:

Alcoholism is a chronic, primary disease with genetic, psychosocial, and environmental factors influencing its development and manifestations. The disease is often progressive and fatal. It is characterized by continuous or periodic:

1. Impaired control over drinking
2. Preoccupation with the drug alcohol
3. Use of alcohol despite adverse consequences
4. Distortions in thinking, most notably denial

The ASAM definition appears to have had an influence on the DSM-IV definition which has reduced the number of criteria for alcohol and other drug dependencies from nine to seven. One of the major differences is the continued inclusion of tolerance and withdrawal in the DSM-IV (32). The remaining 5 criteria are very similar to those in the ASAM definition.

A major change in the last 5 years has been the development of competency definitions and practice guidelines, not only for addiction medicine specialists, but also for all physicians which will require mastery of the knowledge of addiction medicine. New initiatives to integrate substance abuse training with primary care physician training emphasize the similarities that primary care physicians face in the management of other common chronic conditions such as diabetes, cancer, coronary heart disease, and gout (33). In all of these conditions environmental and behavioral factors play a very large role in the rehabilitative potential and the outcome of treatment. Since lifestyle-related illness accounts for half the annual mortality rate in the United States and alcohol and drug problems account for half of these or 25% of annual deaths (34), there is an increasing imperative for primary care physicians to attend to drug and alcohol problems in the course of their day-to-day practice. More and more, the training of primary care physicians includes an emphasis on screening and brief interventions and the techniques of motivational interviewing (35–38).

At the Macy conference Fleming outlined nine recommended physician competencies, which are listed in Table 78.4. These can be contrasted with the conference on Alcohol, Drugs, and Primary Care Physician Education a decade earlier in 1985, which agreed that "at minimum, primary care physicians should demonstrate mastery of the following subject areas" (39):

1. Epidemiology, including knowledge of risk factors and the natural history of substance abuse
2. Physiology and biochemistry of dependence and addiction
3. Pharmacology, including knowledge of effects of commonly abused drugs and drug-drug interactions
4. Diagnosis, intervention, and referral
5. Case management, including short-term and long-term consequences of abuse and dependence
6. Prevention through health promotion, early identification, and patient education
7. Identification and assessment of their own personal and professional attitudes toward alcohol and drug use and abuse

As research and clinical experience grow, the conceptual models of chemical dependence are becoming more sophisticated (40). The role of neurotransmitter and receptor changes has given the field even stronger basic science roots. The application of knowledge to clinical skills is emphasized by the APA guidelines for the treatment of patients with substance use disorders, which has 481 references (41), and the briefer NIAAA physician's guide to helping patients with alcohol problems (42). A national initiative has begun, including NIAAA, ASAM, and AMERSA, with the intent of helping every physician in the country develop and practice skills in screening their patients for substance use disorders. Attending to the managed care environment, ASAM's initiative adopted in April, 1996, recommends that it is the fundamental responsibility of health care organizations to screen for alcohol use disorders.

Help in organizing the expanding knowledge base of addiction medicine is essential for medical educators. Along these lines Brown University has

Table 78.4 Recommended Physician Competencies for Treating Substance Abuse Disorders

1. **Screening** patients for alcohol and drug use
2. **Assessment** for problems related to alcohol and drug use
3. Office based **treatment**
4. **Pharmacology**
   a. Withdrawal
   b. Symptom relief post withdrawal
   c. Comorbid conditions
5. **Referral** to treatment programs
6. **Pain Management**
   a. Acute pain
   b. Chronic pain
7. **Drug Testing**
   a. Breath
   b. Urine
   c. Blood
8. Care of Affected **Family Members**
9. **Physician Impairment**
   a. Prevention
   b. Recognition
   c. Monitoring recovery

Reprinted with permission from Fleming M. Competencies for substance abuse training. Macy Conference Proceedings. New York: Josiah Macy Jr. Foundation, 1995:215.

developed Project ADEPT, an inexpensive core curriculum which is being used in many United States medical schools (43). This educational material, which emphasizes skill training, includes one volume of five core curriculum modules that require from 7–13 hours of curriculum time. Useful suggestions are contained in the module, which will help both the student and instructor review the knowledge base before a patient encounter. The patient encounters are then observed and rated by both instructor and other students. The subsequent discussion does much to promote integration of knowledge and the development of positive attitudes.

The models developed by the Institute of Medicine and modified by Skinner are depicted in Figures 78.1 and 78.2 (44, 45). These figures help physicians understand the continuum of substance use, abuse, and dependence. When the problems are initially noted brief interventions may be very valuable (46). As the addiction progresses more intensive treatment is needed and participation in a 12-step program, such as AA, may be life saving (47).

Recent epidemiological research has underlined the importance of the continuum. Kandel and Davies have recently reaffirmed the importance of parents, the peer group, and juvenile delinquent behavior in the development of illegal drug use (48). Vaillant, in reviewing the literature and the data from his monumental 50-year follow-up of a prospective study of alcoholism, has made the etiologic statement that "genetic loading is an important predictor of *whether* an individual develops alcoholism and that an unstable childhood environment is an important predictor of *when* an individual loses control of alcohol" (49, p. 101).

In dealing with the pressures of managed care, physicians working with addicted patients can benefit from some of the recent research findings. It has been found that length of stay in treatment improves treatment outcome (50). An increasing number of studies are also showing that treatment works. A 14-year study of 3729 alcoholics demonstrated that the post-treatment costs of treated alcoholics were 24% lower than comparable costs for untreated alcoholics (51).

In the first wave of managed care, substance abuse treatment benefits were organized by the creation of specialized "carve out" contracts which initially tended to fragment substance abuse intervention and treatment from core medical and surgical services and from the primary care delivery system. But as the managed care system has evolved, a reintegration of specialized behavioral care systems and primary care is occurring.

Textbooks reflect a body of knowledge, and a growing number of good ones exist in the field of addiction medicine. This book will serve as a text for specialty or fellowship training. Schuckit's book has proved popular enough to have been reissued in a fourth edition in 1994 and is a useful resource for medical students and residents (52). The World Health Organization has sponsored a textbook designed for use in medical training around the world (53). A notable addition to the field has been the ASAM *Princi-*

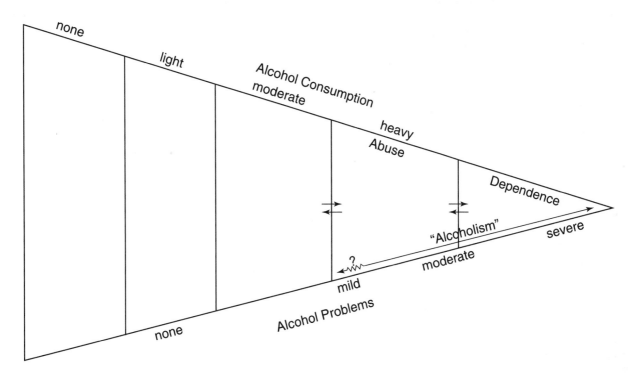

Figure 78.1. Relation between alcohol consumption patterns and level of alcohol problems. (Reprinted with permission from Skinner HA. Spectrum of drinkers and intervention opportunities. Can Med Assoc J 1990;143:1054.)

ples of Addiction Medicine (54). Anyone teaching at an undergraduate, postgraduate, or continuing medical education level can now find suitable textbooks in addiction medicine and addiction psychiatry.

A notable gap in the medical body of knowledge continues to be detailed

information on the 12-step programs, particularly AA. This nonprofessional program of recovery from alcoholism grew out of the failure of medicine and psychiatry to provide lasting help to chronic alcoholics, one of whom was a physician (17). The Twelve Steps, when worked with the help of a sponsor

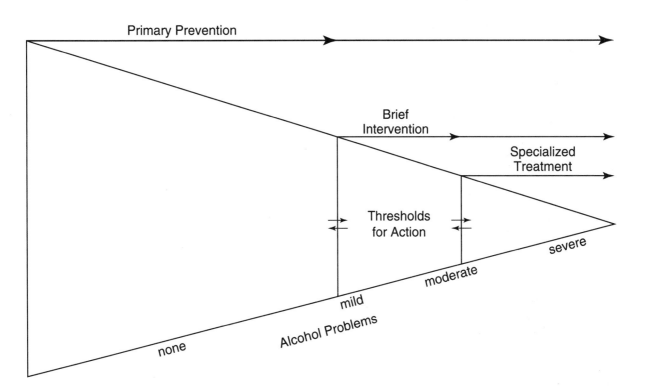

Figure 78.2. Relation between level of alcohol problems and type of intervention. (Reprinted with permission from Skinner HA. Spectrum of drinkers and intervention opportunities. Can Med Assoc J 1990;143:1054.)

Table 78.5 Stability of Abstinence (n = 56)

Length of Abstinence	Still abstinent	Relapsing that year	% eventually relapsing
2 years	56	9	41%
3 years	47	5	25%
4 years	42	0	25%
5 years	42	5	16%
6 years	37	1	7%[a]

Reprinted with permission from Vaillant GE. The natural history of alcoholism revisited. Cambridge, MA: Harvard University Press, 1995:235.
[a] These three relapsed after 8, 10, and 13 years of abstinence.

and home group, can make sobriety tolerable and even enjoyable. The program was hammered out over three years by the first 100 chronic hopeless alcoholics who were managing to stay sober. The product of this field research, which is described in the "Big Book" of AA (55), has continued to be the most effective long-term way of returning chronic addicts to productive life and stable sobriety. A number of references are useful for educating health professionals and patients about AA (56, 57).

Vaillant's new 50-year follow-up confirms the importance of AA in establishing stable sobriety for chronic alcoholics. He concluded that "after abstinence had been maintained for 5 years, relapse was rare. In contrast, return to controlled drinking without eventual relapse was unlikely" (58). The importance of long-term follow-up is shown in Table 78.5, which reflects the frequency of relapse following two years or more of sobriety. Research continues to support the importance of 12-step programs in maintaining sobriety. A manual has been developed for clinician use in supporting patients working a 12-step program recovery in AA or NA. This manual has been used in Project Match. A similar approach has been used with dual diagnosis patients with severe mental disorders (59). This study randomly assigned 132 dual diagnosis patients to a control group of 12-step recovery and to experimental groups of behavioral skills training and intensive case management. To the authors' great surprise there was very little difference in outcome over 18 months of treatment. This finding is of no surprise to clinicians who work with dual diagnosis patients and have found that 12-step recovery greatly aids the treatment of other mental disorders. Knowledge of the 12-step program is essential for any clinician working with alcohol or other drug–addicted patients.

ATTITUDES AND ATTITUDINAL CHANGE IN ADDICTION MEDICINE

Many of the problems in the health care system previously described stem from a combination of ignorance and negative attitudes on the part of health care professionals. Those involved in the practice of addiction medicine and addiction psychiatry have had experiences with physicians whose negative attitudes resulted either in the delay or in the absence of diagnosis, treatment, or referral of addicted patients (25, 60). One pregnant patient was turned away from the hospital of her choice when it was discovered that she was a former heroin addict currently on methadone maintenance. The result was a traumatic delivery in a taxi en route to another hospital. These experiences led to an early consensus among the career teachers that attitudes would be given a high priority in the planning and implementation of teaching at undergraduate, postgraduate, and continuing medical educational levels. The decision was easy to make but has been difficult to implement.

Part of the difficulty lies in the complex nature of attitudes. Social psychologists have had great interest in this area. Allport (61) reviewed over a hundred definitions of attitude and concluded that there was basic agreement that *an attitude is a learned predisposition to respond to an object or class of objects in a consistently favorable or unfavorable way.* A current textbook on social psychology elaborates on this definition, describing attitude as a shorthand way of saying that we have feelings and thoughts of like or dislike, approval or disapproval, attraction or repulsion, trust or distrust towards something or someone (62). These evaluative responses have cognitive, affective, experiential, and even physiologic components. To add to their complexity, most attitudes develop out of our life experience and are strongly influenced by the value systems of the family and culture in which we grew up.

As our life experience increases we may develop attitudes which are inconsistent or even contradictory with each other. For example, physicians with strong positive attitudes toward preserving life may find their behavior changing when they encounter patients who evoke negative attitudes in them. Sudnow noted that less than strenuous efforts were made by hospital physicians to resuscitate patients who were alcoholic (63). Even in other aspects of the medical treatment of the alcoholic, it appeared that these physicians believed that it was proper to have less concern about treatment than they had with other patients. The origins of these negative attitudes probably stemmed from the view of addiction as a moral and legal problem.

Another source of negative attitudes in medicine has come from psychoanalytic theory. Early psychoanalytic thought viewed alcohol and other drug addictions as symptoms of underlying conflict or developmental delay (64). This view had a profound influence on psychiatric education. Despite the large body of evidence that alcohol and other drug addictions are chronic primary diseases (31), there are still many practicing physicians and psychiatrists who share the early psychoanalytic view. Modern psychoanalytic thinking has moved away from these old ideas. Brickman has stated that viewing substance abuse as a secondary phenomenon to underlying psychopathology is a basic misconception (65). After reviewing the psychoanalytic and addiction literature he concludes that "the most effective treatment approach in most cases is informed by the concept that chemical dependency is a disease entity in its own right and must be treated as such." He concludes persuasively that psychoanalytic treatment can be extended through an integrated approach emphasizing abstinence and participation in AA for the patient. This approach is emphasized by two Harvard training analysts who describe AA as a "sophisticated psychosocial treatment for alcoholism" (66).

On the positive side, psychoanalytic theory has contributed greatly to our understanding of the negative attitudes which have characterized the health care system and alcohol and other drug addictions. Negative transference is ubiquitous when chemically dependent alcohol or drug–abusing patients approach health care professionals. The patients expect a moralistic lack of understanding accompanied by rejection and even mistreatment. The transference aspect of this reaction does not stem from childhood experience with parents but from an internal reaction originating from the patients' superego, where internalized parental and cultural values and standards react to the loss of control and compulsion to use alcohol and other drugs despite adverse consequences. The result is a traumatic loss of self-esteem, which has been well described by Bean-Bayog (67). This negative superego response, which contributes to the denial in alcohol and other drug addictions, is projected onto the physician.

Countertransference responses of the physician often reverberate in a synchronized manner with the negative transference reactions of the patient. The sources for these reactions have many similarities. The parental and cultural messages experienced in early life by the physician were similar to those experienced by the patient. Among these are disapproval of intoxication, antisocial behavior, and a recreational use of prescription drugs. Negative countertransference reactions are amplified if the physician has had a family member affected with alcohol or drug dependence. Available data suggest that about one third of medical students come from families with alcohol or drug–dependent members (68). The physician's personal use of dependence-producing substances may contribute to or modify countertransference reactions. The most common countertransference is a strong unconscious need or wish not to make a diagnosis of addiction. The intensity of this need is directly related to the negative reaction which would occur if the diagnosis were made. If the reaction is strong enough to remove the person from the patient role and to view him or her as no longer needing or deserving treatment, the physician will feel considerable discomfort. If the patient's use of alcohol or other drugs is similar to or less than the physician's use, then denial will be reinforced even though the patient may meet the criteria for dependence. A survey of 589 graduating seniors from 13 medical schools in the 4 major regions of the United States showed that nearly 90% used alcohol on a monthly basis and nearly 10% used alcohol almost daily (69). Medical student use of tranquilizers was significantly more (p < .05) then their same age cohort in the general population, while the use of cigarettes was significantly less (p < .001). Little is known about the contribution of personal alcohol and drug use to countertransference reactions in physicians. This is an area which deserves more research.

Perry has noted the difficulty in documenting countertransference in physicians (70). He describes fear of addiction, which leads to underprescribing of narcotic analgesics despite an absence of documentation that adequate narcotic analgesia for acute pain increases the risk of substance abuse or addiction. One source of this irrational response is the fear of formal or informal peer review criticism. He notes the generous prescribing of dependence-producing hypnotics, anxiolytics, and mild narcotic analgesics in the privacy of a physician's office. This contrasts with inadequate doses of potent opiate analgesics prescribed for acute pain in hospital settings when the indications and effectiveness of these medications are well known.

Whether due to transference or countertransference there has been extensive documentation of combinations of negative attitudes and negative behavior toward alcohol and drug addicts in the health care system. Musto has described the use of the Harrison Act during prohibition to persecute physicians who prescribed narcotic analgesics for opiate addicts (71). The enduring effects of attitudes generated by this experience have contributed to the irrational behavior of physicians who have wanted to provide relief for patients with acute pain but who have prescribed inadequate doses for several decades (30, 70).

Studies at Harvard in the 1950s and 1960s demonstrated that physicians behaved diagnostically as though alcoholics were derelicts (23, 24). These same physicians recognized that alcoholism can occur in other social groups, but they hesitated to make the indicated diagnosis in those cases because of this negative stereotype. A second attitudinal set in this group of senior medical and surgical residents was a focus on bodily symptoms and physical problems. These medical problems often would become the diagnosis rather than the alcoholism. This preference for a medical diagnosis has the effect of delayed treatment for alcoholism at a time when it might have beneficial effects.

If negative attitudes have such a profound effect on the health care professional's behavior, then how are we to understand those attitudes and how can they be changed? It is generally agreed that attitudes have three components (72):

1. Cognitive, involving belief and knowledge
2. Affective, involving feelings and emotion
3. Conative, involving decision and behavior

Each component may be positive or negative in varying degrees and influenced by other factors. Favorable attitudes are usually positive in all three components. Unfavorable attitudes are usually negative in all three components.

The logical but not sufficient place to start educational efforts to influence attitudes is in the cognitive area, which is conscious and responds to new knowledge and information. The affective component is equally, if not more, powerful. Affective experience is more difficult to arrange educationally. It usually occurs with direct patient experience and in response to the role models of attending physicians. Since feelings are less conscious and are viewed as subjective, they are less likely to be valued or expressed by health professional students. The conative component, involving the will and motivation to act, is not well understood. It may be influenced most by repeated practice of desired behaviors. In this way the physician may apply familiar diagnostic and treatment skills to patients he or she does not like.

Attitudinal formation begins at birth and is profoundly influenced by the family and culture in which we grow up. It is estimated that in the United States the average child, before turning 18 years old, will see 75,000 drinking scenes on television (73). Religious and political beliefs which develop early in life have also been shown to influence physician attitudes on issues like the legalization of marihuana use (74). Clinical experience also contributes to the development of negative attitudes. Vaillant notes that it is very easy to become pessimistic about treating alcoholics in some clinical settings. In a 6½ year study of 19,000 admissions of 5,000 persons to a detoxification clinic, 2,500 never returned. On the other hand 25 indelibly remembered patients returned 2,500 times. Thus 0.5% of the population "be-

came far more deeply etched in clinician's consciousness than did the 50% who never came back and who must have included the best outcomes" (47).

Brickman, a psychoanalyst, in his review of both the psychoanalytic and the addiction medicine literature traces the strongly held belief that alcohol and drug dependence are not the core problem but the symptoms of an underlying conflict or mental disorder (65). The repeated experience of poor treatment results has not resulted in a change in this belief for many practitioners. He notes that "the psychoanalytic literature is rich in psychodynamic formulations but unfortunately poor in favorable outcome studies." He believes that psychoanalysts fail to integrate the findings in the addiction medicine literature because their view with each patient is retrospective and they can find what appears to be a continuous chain of events leading to the alcohol or drug dependence. As Freud himself anticipated, prospective studies have failed to support this particular theory.

The complexity of attitudes makes them difficult to measure accurately. Attitudinal measurement in the medical literature has utilized primarily the semantic differential and agree-disagree statements. The semantic differential was developed by Osgood (75). It utilized polar opposite adjectives such as good-bad, clean-dirty, pleasant-unpleasant, and valuable-worthless. Each scale is separated by 7–10 points and the respondent marks the point between the two adjectives on the scale that best reflects his or her response to the concept, e.g., alcoholic, being tested. In more common use is the Likert Scale (76). An attitudinal statement is followed by a five-choice scale of strongly disagree, disagree, uncertain, agree, and strongly agree. The usual scoring is obtained by assigning the numbers one to five with the highest number assigned to strongly agree. Most surveys include a number of attitudinal statements. The results are factor analyzed. Statements, or items, loading positively or negatively on the main factors are retained in the final form of the survey. Items with negative loadings on a factor are reversed when developing a scoring for each factor.

A British test, the Alcohol and Alcohol Problems Perception Questionnaire (AAPPQ), measures an overall therapeutic attitude (77). One study using this test has shown that experience in treating alcoholics and the availability of collegial support are significantly associated with increases of therapeutic attitudes (Fig. 78.3). Experience, defined as treating alcoholics, and support, defined as availability of colleagues to help with treatment problems, taken together, explains 63% of the variance in the therapeutic attitudes.

The career teachers began developing a Substance Abuse Attitude Survey (SAAS) in 1977 (78). Over the years a 50-item questionnaire with five stable factors emerged. Two factors, treatment intervention and treatment optimism, significantly differentiated clinicians who met the criterion of at least 6 years experience with 10% or more of their patients being alcohol or drug dependent and who derive satisfaction and experience success treating these patients (Table 78.6). Improving scores on these two factors were set as educational objectives in a course in substance abuse for second year medical students (79). The instrument was well accepted in pre- and post-testing. The desired attitudinal change was only achieved when students met with patients, attended AA, worked patient management problems, and participated in small group discussions. A brief SAAS of 18 items, which differentiate recovering from nonrecovering physicians and which change most in response to education, has recently been developed but not validated (see Table 78.6).

A health care professional's personal experience with chemical dependence has a major effect on attitudes. A comparison was made between 307 physicians who reported a past alcohol or drug dependence problem, excluding nicotine, but no current problems, with 962 physicians who reported no or slight past and no current problems (80). The samples were obtained from continuing medical education courses on substance abuse. The recovering were significantly more (p < .0001) oriented toward abstinence during and after treatment. They were significantly more positive (p < .0001) toward early diagnosis, urine screening during treatment, group therapy, and family involvement in treatment. In Table 78.7 a standard score of 50, with 10 representing plus or minus one standard deviation, for each factor represents the mean scores of criterion clinicians who report both satisfaction and success in working with alcohol and drug dependent patients. As might be expected the recovering physicians were also significantly more (p < .0001) optimistic and accepting about treating alcohol and drug addicted patients.

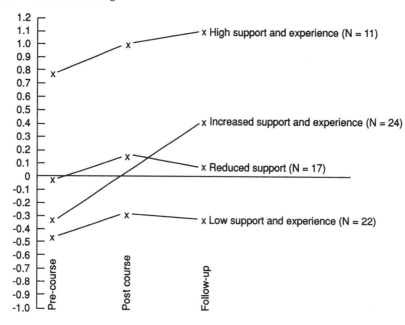

Figure 78.3. Comparison of therapeutic attitude scores of different groups of trainees at precourse, postcourse, and follow-up. (Reprinted with permission from Cartwright AKJ. The attitude of helping agents towards the alcoholic client: the influence of experience, support, training, and self-esteem. Br J Addict 1980;75:419.)

TEACHING FOR ATTITUDINAL CHANGE

One reason for the enduring resistance to additional change was revealed in a study of 177 health and welfare personnel (81). Over half of the respondents rated the alcoholic as unmotivated to recover. Typical statements were: "He did not have enough motivation to deal with the problem. I don't determine this, they do." "He didn't want to change." "They tell you they want to recover, but when you think they are going along just right, something happens, so I suppose they aren't sincere." This belief of poor motivation serves as "a convenient rationale for unwillingness to review and modify current policies and practices so as to encourage the alcoholic to seek treatment and stay with it."

Attitudes in the undergraduate years also show resistance to change. Medical education has been found to be accompanied by an increase in cynical attitudes (82) and in negative attitudes towards alcoholics (83). A review of the literature on attitude change during medical school concluded that the positive attitudinal change accompanying one course does not last (84). The author suggested that at least two years of exposure were needed. We suspect that stable attitudes, like stable sobriety, require 5 years or more of exposure (see Table 78.5).

Research at the University of Illinois College of Medicine confirmed the difficulties in maintaining attitudinal change in medical education (85). The entire third year class was given an examination after all of their clerkships had been completed. Working from a mock chart with clear data indicating a patient with peptic ulcer, major depression, and alcoholism, the students'

mean score for each condition was 3.64, 2.56, and 1.46 (p < .0001) for each condition. The authors noted that "A review of the curriculum shows that their education in addiction is comparable to that offered in most medical schools." They concluded that the deficiencies were not related to a lack of knowledge, "but to the inability to apply this knowledge in a clinical setting because of experiential or attitudinal traits developed in the clinical setting." This problem continues into residency training. One teacher commented, "I have had the experience of presenting well thought out and well received workshops on how to identify problem drinkers and what to do once you identify them, only to observe residents finish the seminar, meet with a patient shortly afterward, and miss virtually every clue that suggested a drinking problem" (86).

The social science and psychiatric literature suggests the following techniques of training for behavior that counteracts social norms (87, 88):

1. A message has more attitudinal impact if its *source has credibility and perceived expertise*. For medical students and physicians this means *role models* who are from their own clinical discipline. Effective training is hampered when there is a shortage of physician role models with expertise in alcohol and drug dependence. Frank (88) has emphasized the importance of supportive peers and faculty in helping attitude change persist.

Table 78.6 Comparative Attitudinal Scores

Factor	Nonclinicians (n = 268)	Noncriterion Clinicians (n = 312)	Criterion Clinicians (n = 108)	ANOVA F
Permissiveness	50.4	49.2	50.1	.91
Nonstereotype	51.5	51.0	50.0	.87
Treatment intervention	45.3	47.0	50.0	8.48[a]
Treatment optimism	44.6	45.2	50.1	11.19[a]
Nonmoralism	49.6	49.9	49.9	.11

Reprinted with permission from Chappel JN, Veach TL, Krug RS. The Substance Abuse Attitude Survey: an instrument for measuring attitudes. J Stud Alcohol 1985;46(1):51.
[a]P < .001

Table 78.7 SAAS Standardized Attitude Scores for Recovery and Nonrecovery Group Physicians

Scale	Recovery Group (n = 307)		Nonrecovery Group (n = 962)		P Value
	Mean	SD	Mean	SD	
Permissiveness	38.44	9.76	43.38	9.98	.0001
Nonstereotype	48.69	8.70	49.16	9.06	.5379
Treatment Intervention	54.60	10.55	50.17	9.99	.0001
Treatment Optimism	56.88	9.91	46.46	12.25	.0001
Nonmoralism	51.10	8.32	50.48	9.17	.3471

Reprinted with permission from Veach TL, Chappel JN. Physician attitudes in chemical dependency: the effects of personal experience and recovery. Subst Abuse 1990;11(2):99.

2. Yielding occurs when *the recipient agrees with the presented attitude.* Cognitive yielding probably precedes affective and conative yielding and may occur in classrooms settings in response to didactic presentations. However, the evidence suggests that this either does not happen often or is very difficult to achieve. Two reviews of the literature conclude that knowledge gain in substance abuse is easily demonstrated but the changes in attitudes and skills require something different than lectures in nonclinical settings (89, 90). Most reported programs were found lacking in any meaningful attitude or practice evaluation which could provide data for guidance in the design of future programs.

3. Retention is enhanced by *repetitions of experience over time.* The effects of short courses die quickly if reinforcement and support are not present (84). *Active participation in the learning experience and subsequent practice* contribute to the persistence of attitudinal changes (91). Improvisation by the learner, as one of the activities, appears to be important in consolidating and retaining new attitudes and behavior. This occurs with opportunities for independent research or practice while still in the training situation. As noted earlier, retention or attitude change is greatly enhanced by a supportive group of peers and faculty (77) (see Fig. 78.3).

4. *Overt behavior reflects the new positive attitudes.* Medical training has a huge advantage over social psychology's attempts to induce attitude change. We can require the behavior before any affective or conative yielding has occurred. Requiring the desired behavior *in conjunction with close supervision* usually results in maintenance of the behavior, especially if the position is to be examined on the same behavior later. Behavior itself may have a strong influence on attitudinal change. This likelihood of change is enhanced if the behavior is accompanied by favorable results such as a positive outcome.

One of the earliest demonstrations of significant changes in family medicine residents' attitudes and the frequency of diagnosis of alcoholism occurred in the 1970s (92). The changes were noted in response to a 14-hour course spread over 7 months. In the 1980s the Commonwealth Harvard Alcohol Research and Teaching (CHART) program demonstrated success with a similar program for internal medicine residents (93). The success of this seminar course resulted in five Boston teaching hospitals incorporating the course into their primary care residencies. The same group of teachers found that a 1-month rotation on an inpatient alcoholism unit in the first postgraduate year, followed by individual case by case supervision by several alcoholism experts throughout the remainder of residence training, resulted in even more significant changes in the clinical behavior of internal medicine residents with alcoholics (94). Supervised clinical training was by far the most powerful predictor of practice behavior. The authors were so impressed by this finding that they recommend using this teaching strategy rather than attempt to change attitudes or increase knowledge (Table 78.8).

There is little evidence that this practice has been incorporated into residency training even when addiction training is required. A study of 106 undergraduate and 169 psychiatry residency programs found great variation in alcohol and drug abuse education (95). A minority of the training programs provided clinical training in university affiliated hospitals. Courses oriented toward enhancing positive attitudes were rarely in evidence. Almost half of the programs did not expose residents to 12-step programs. The importance of training physicians in combining AA with professional care has been well demonstrated in current research (47, 96). These retrospective and prospective studies found AA to be an influence far more powerful than professionally directed modalities in recovery from addiction.

The need for educational planning in substance abuse education is emphasized by the evidence that current clinical training in medical school and residencies results in an increase in negative attitudes and behavior. There is some suggestion that the personal experience of the medical student with alcohol and other drugs, combined with family members' chemical dependencies, may contribute to this growth of negative attitudes. Therefore, in planning health care professional education it is recommended that attention be paid to the affective and conative components of attitudes, in addition to the cognitive. This has been most effectively done in clinical settings in which students and residents are involved in direct patient care under the supervi-

Table 78.8   Correlations Between Predictor Variables of 123 Responding Internal Medicine Residents and Practice Behavior Variables in Their Responses to Patients with Alcohol-Abuse Problems at Five Hospitals Affiliated with Harvard Medical School, Boston, Massachusetts

Predictor Variable	Perceived Prevalence of Alcoholism	Treatment by Resident	Referral by Resident
Age	−.17	.07	.07
Status (second or third year resident)	−.06	.03	.03
Residency (traditional or primary care)	.05	.17	.27
Hours of alcohol education	.10	.23[a]	.25[a]
Amount of supervised clinical experience	.34[c]	.32[c]	.46[c]
Medical knowledge	.03	.10	.00
Confidence in non-biomedical alcoholism management skills	.18	.30[b]	.41[b]
Negative attitudes toward alcoholism	−.01	−.05	−.05
Sense of responsibility for changing unhealthy behaviors	.04	.25	.17
Belief in disease concept of alcoholism	.20[a]	.11	.12

Reprinted with permission from Warburg MM, Cleary PO, Rohman M, Barnes HN, Aronson M, Delbanco TL. Residents' attitudes, knowledge, and behavior regarding diagnosis and treatment of alcoholism. J Med Educ 1987;62:501.

sion of role models who are expert in addiction medicine. Continued supervision in other clinical settings may be essential in maintaining positive attitudes and behavior. These training settings also need to provide supportive, understanding, nonpunitive environments for helping health care professionals deal with their own personal pain which arises in response to the training and clinical experiences. The educational research suggests that the best results, in terms of positive attitudes and skills, occur when residents rotate through addiction treatment units and are supervised by experts in addiction medicine, including supporting patients and families use of AA, NA, and Al-Anon.

TRAINING FOR SKILL DEVELOPMENT

Medical education excels in the development of skill acquisition. The process begins in the basic science years and continues throughout training and practice with continuing knowledge acquisition. Attitudes are acquired more often by example than by discussion. Skills are acquired over years of observation and practice. The old adage of "See one, do one, teach one" disappeared with the rotating internship prior to general practice. As the field of addiction medicine has matured there has developed a much greater clarity about the type of skills needed by any physician in this field. This section reviews the competencies listed in Table 78.4.

The first skill to be taught is that of *screening patients for alcohol and drug use.* This is part of basic medical interviewing and should be taught in the introduction to clinical medicine courses in the first two years of medical school. Reinforcement should occur in the clerkships. A key skill in the screening area is the ability to cover the history of the major areas of addicting drugs: tobacco, alcohol, prescription drugs, and illicit drugs used for recreational purposes. Once the history of use has been obtained some simple sets of questions can help the physician decide whether a more extensive assessment is needed. The CAGE is the best known of these sets of questions (42). One or two positive responses indicates a need for further assessment. The FOY is even simpler to use (54). It has the advantage of being very sensitive and will produce a number of false positives, but few false negatives.

Training for the development of *assessment skills* is diagnostic training. Here the medical student and resident acquire the skills necessary to diagnose substance abuse or substance dependence, sometimes known as early and established addiction, or problem drinking and alcoholism. For all physicians the focus should be on the area of heavy use associated with mild to moderate problems (see Fig. 78.1). The association of problems related to alcohol and drug use is the principal clinical skill to be developed by the medical student and resident. This not only includes skill in taking a history from the patient, but also includes acquiring information from other sources, including family members. Attention is paid to routine lab tests which reflect the effects of heavy alcohol or drug use. Specific tests are also ordered at this stage including the GGT and the testing of breath, urine, and blood. In medical training, competency in drug testing and interpreting the results of those tests would be included under diagnostic assessment. The chapter in this book devoted to diagnosis provides a good outline of the knowledge and skills needed in assessment training.

Treatment skills come later in medical training. These should begin in the clerkship years and should be found in each of the required clerkships. *Office based treatment* focuses on the development of brief intervention skills. These are often referred to as behavioral self-control training (46). Once alcohol and or drug abuse, including nicotine dependence, have been diagnosed, specific behavioral techniques have been shown to be effective when used by physicians. These include goal setting, self-monitoring, controlling the rate of consumption, self-reinforcement, and the learning of alternative behavioral competencies to substitute for the alcohol or drug use. An excellent practical summary of office based treatment for the primary care physician is contained in the *Physicians' Guide to Helping Patients with Alcohol Problems* (42). This guide is based on the findings of more than a decade of research and summarizes the best current knowledge for screening, assessing, and intervening in the primary care physician's office.

Referral to treatment programs should be done when there is evidence of alcohol dependence, especially when the patient continues to drink or use other drugs despite the physician's attempts at interventions. The NI-AAA guide recommends involving the patient in making referral decisions (42). This should include a discussion of available addiction treatment services in the community. Referral works best when a referral appointment is scheduled while the patient is in the office. A direct linkage to the referral source at the time increases patient compliance. The physician should be aware of treatment resources within his or her community. These resources should offer a multimodality, community-based treatment such as that described elsewhere in this book. The practice guidelines of the APA describe programs which provide detoxification and other pharmacologic treatments, educational services, cognitive behavioral and interpersonal therapies including groups and families, and active participation in 12-step programs such AA and/or NA (41). It is recommended that treatment take place in the least restrictive settings that are likely to be safe and effective. This may begin with hospitalization or residential treatment. It will usually continue into partial or day care and then into outpatient treatment. The duration of treatment is tailored to individual needs and may vary from a few months to several years. Good programs continue to monitor their patients for the first year or two following cessation of active treatment. This monitoring can be done cooperatively with the primary care physician. The NI-AAA physician's guide recommends monitoring the patients progress in much the same way that the physician would monitor other chronic medical problems such as hypertension or diabetes. We believe that monitoring the patient's progress should be added to this list of competencies in Table 78.4.

Pain management involves the judicious use of medications with addiction liability for the management of both acute and chronic pain. There is ample documentation that physicians underprescribe opioid analgesics for the management of acute pain. Perry believes that one source of this irrational response is the fear of formal or informal peer review criticism (70). He notes the irrational, almost phobic, response of physicians in prescribing adequate doses of narcotic analgesics despite an absence of documentation that adequate doses for the management of acute pain increase the risk of addiction. If narcotic analgesia is needed in a recovering alcoholic or other drug addict, this can usually be successfully done without precipitating a relapse if the patient's spouse, sponsor, and home group are aware of the need for the medication and the way in which it is prescribed (97). Rapid reduction in dose and termination of opioids when the acute pain subsides can usually be effectively done in these circumstances.

Chronic benign pain poses a very different problem. In most instances chronic pain should be managed without the use of addicting or controlled medication, if possible. This requires active work with the chronic pain patient and the intensive use of a variety of nonaddicting methods of pain relief. The details of this management are provided in other sections of this book and in the report of the Macy Conference (1).

Drug testing of breath, urine, and blood are listed as a separate competency because they are involved in so many areas. Their initial use will be in the screening and assessment of an individual patient. Drug testing can continue to have utility during treatment. This will often be done by the addiction treatment program. Drug testing continues to be useful in monitoring ongoing recovery. It is also very valuable in the management of chronic pain problems. The physician's knowledge of drug testing will also be useful in helping the patient deal with the increasing frequency with which drug testing is used in employment and legal settings.

The *care of affected family members* is particularly important for the primary care physician. Family physicians have been trained in this principle. It is also strongly recommended for all the other primary care disciplines and for psychiatry, when treating alcohol or other drug addicted patients. The active involvement of family members is a relatively recent addition to the specialized treatment of alcohol and other drug addictions. The primary care physician should be comfortable talking to and counseling the family members of their alcohol and other drug dependent patients. Of particular value in this aspect of patient care is a good working knowledge of Al-Anon, Al-Ateen, Al-Atot, and their counterparts in NA, if available.

The *prevention, recognition, and monitoring recovery of alcohol and other drug addicted physicians* is a relatively new competency in medical education. The currently existing system of State Medical Association's Physicians Assistance Committees was catalyzed by a landmark article in the *Journal of the American Medical Association* in 1973 (98). By 1980 every state had a Physician Assistance Committee which usually worked in cooperation with the State Board of Medical Examiners. Physicians are as vulnerable as the general population to alcohol abuse and dependence and have a much greater access to other addicting drugs. This topic is well covered in another chapter in this book. Every practicing physician should be aware of the fundamentals of physician impairment. This is especially important if the physician works in a group practice, practices in a hospital setting, or has a responsible position on the medical staff of a hospital or clinic.

The treatment of alcohol and other drug addicted physicians has developed rapidly in the last two decades. It is generally more intensive and longer than that used for the treatment of addictive disorders within the community. It should also be noted that recovering physicians are generally monitored for at least five years following treatment for addiction.

The tenth competency of monitoring a patient's progress in recovery should also include specific knowledge of the 12-step programs, particularly AA. The evidence is continuing to grow that this 12-step program of recovery is still the most effective method which has been developed for maintaining long-term stable sobriety. Vaillant in his 35-year follow-up of two groups of alcoholics found that attendance at AA accounted for 27% of the variance of good clinical outcome (47). His 50-year follow-up continues to document the same degree of efficacy of AA (49). The author notes that, over the long term in prospective studies, the effects of formal treatment for alcoholism become negligible. This fact has led Miller to conclude that in the short run there are many approaches that work well in addiction treatment. Over the long run, of years to lifetimes, only abstinence-oriented treatment associated with regular, continuous, and indefinite attendance at AA appears to work (99). Vaillant, in noting that some alcoholics achieve a stable sobriety without AA, recommended the following factors for all physicians in treating alcoholism (47, p. 367):

1. *Offering the patient a nonchemical substitute dependency* for alcohol and other addicting drugs. This means that the physician should help his or her patient find other ways of achieving the benefits which they obtained from alcohol or other addicting drugs.

2. *Reminding the patient ritually that even one drink can lead to pain and relapse.* The physician can help the patient deal with euphoric recall by providing frequent or continual reminders of the detrimental effects of the addicting drugs. This is much easier for the physician when there have been medical consequences associated with the patient's addiction.

3. *Repairing the social and medical damage* that the patient has experienced.

4. *Restoring the patient's self-esteem.*

Vaillant acknowledges that "providing all four components is not easy." He states the simplest way of doing this is through "self help groups, of which Alcoholics Anonymous is one model."

There is a tendency amongst even knowledgeable researchers such as Vaillant to lump the 12-step program of recovery developed by AA with many other "self help" groups such as Rational Recovery, Women for Sobriety, etc. The fact is that the available long-term research data only support working a 12-step program of recovery. The rest of the long-term approaches remain theoretical. The big difference between a 12-step program of recovery and medical treatment for chronic diseases is that the 12-step programs are not under physician control. This may account for the continued pejorative terminology used in the medical literature such as "cult," "adjunct," "zealous self-help," etc. It is our belief that every physician should become knowledgeable and comfortable in working with the 12-step programs of AA and NA. These programs are actively interested in working with any physician (100).

The physician competencies listed in Table 78.4 do not include primary prevention. These competencies can be reviewed as secondary prevention. The tasks of primary prevention have usually been left to the fields of education and community organization. However, it is clear that primary prevention work, in the sense of preventing new cases of alcohol or other drug abuse and addiction, is very appropriate for primary care physicians in the specialties of obstetrics, pediatrics, family medicine, and general internal medicine. Kandel and Davies (48) have noted that the developmental sequence of drug use by adolescents has not changed over the past 20 years. They note that "drug use by peers and delinquent participation emerge as the two most important factors that differentiate drug users from non drug users of particular classes of drugs at each state of the developmental sequence of drug use." They also note that "young people who become involved in drug use are alienated from two of the most important institutions in their lives, school and family." Decreased interest in school is important in the early stages preceding experimentation with illicit drugs. Detachment from parents is important in the progression of the use of illicit drugs, particularly including cocaine and crack, which are significantly associated with lower grades in school, delinquent behavior, and visits to doctors for emotional problems. These investigators also noted that parental alcohol use predicted initiation into legal drug use by adolescents. Parental use of prescribed psychotropic drugs predicted initiation into illicit drug use. The authors suggest that anything professionals can do to strengthen adolescents' commitment to schooling and education and their ties to their families might contribute to a reduction in the risk of initiating and persisting in the use of drugs. They note that any postponement of drug experimentation may in itself have positive public health consequences for a young person's well-being.

The development of clinical skills in addiction medicine requires building on the foundation begun in undergraduate medical education and continued into residency training. The magnitude of this task is illustrated by a study of addiction medicine teaching in psychiatry in 1989 (95). This was the year that the Psychiatry Residency Review Committee mandated that all psychiatry residencies offer a structured experience in addiction treatment (22). At that time 97% of undergraduate and 91% of residency programs offered curriculum units in substance abuse. It was noted, however, that almost half of the programs did not expose their students to 12-step programs, few taught chronic pain management, and little attention was paid to dual diagnosis patients. Two model programs in psychiatric addiction education have been developed at the University of California, San Diego (UCSD) and Texas Tech. At UCSD all second year residents in psychiatry rotate for a minimum of 8 weeks in the addiction treatment program (101). At Texas Tech the second year residents rotate for 4 months in addiction treatment. Each of these programs also has fellowships in addiction medicine for physicians who want to become "competent clinicians and consultants in this increasingly specialized field" (102) (see Table 78.8).

The best evidence for specific training in addiction medicine for primary care physicians has been developed at Harvard (94). They compared the training of residents by lectures and discussion meetings combined with consultation and teaching in the outpatient clinics with a one month rotation on an inpatient alcoholism unit, with exposure to AA, outpatient treatment, and individual case supervision by alcoholism experts. The results of this comparative training are shown in Table 78.8. The only training predictor which significantly (p < .001) predicted a perceived prevalence of alcoholism in patients, a willingness to initiate treatment, and a willingness to refer to specialized treatment, was the amount of supervised clinical experience which the resident had had. The authors concluded that "the most direct strategy to influence physician's skills and practice behavior appears to be the provision of clinical experience and training relevant to their practices rather than to change attitudes or increase knowledge." These data support the superiority of supervised clinical training in a specialized setting over a good course taught in a primary care setting where physicians participate in patient care. Clinical supervision in a specialized setting is a standard teaching strategy in most areas of medical training and should become standard in addiction medicine training.

TEACHING METHODS AND EVALUATION

Teaching methods are rarely addressed in the substance abuse literature. The lecture is the best known method of passing on the knowledge base. Lectures have little influence on attitudes or skills. For the faculty member who has been assigned the task of developing course material, Project ADEPT provides a useful outline and material for overhead transparencies (43). Recovering AA or NA members can also be very useful in the classroom, in small group discussion, and in taking medical students to open meetings. Even discussion of applicable literary works can have a profound impact on students (103).

In the clinical clerkship years students need exposure to addiction treatment programs. This experience has the greatest impact if there is continuity in following patients and exposure to residents working in these programs. In residency training supervised clinical experience on addiction treatment units appears to be essential for the development of positive attitudes and clinical skills. There should then be an opportunity for applying the knowledge, attitudes, and skills in both ambulatory and hospital settings.

Medical educators should know the difference between pedagogy and andragogy. Two articles describe the reasons for favoring an andragogical approach (104, 105). In pedagogy, "the relationship between teacher and learner is based on authoritative expertise." In andragogy "the teacher/ learner relationship is one of mutual participation. The teacher's role is to facilitate, promote, and encourage the learner's active involvement." Five conditions have been identified for optimal adult learning:

1. Motivation to change
2. Active involvement of a learner
3. Relevance to past experience
4. Feedback
5. An informal atmosphere

Supervised clinical experience with rapid feedback to the resident or physician who had responsibility for patient care comes closest to satisfying these conditions for learning.

Continuing medical education for physicians who have had little or no exposure to addiction medicine poses a major challenge. Pursch achieved some success with an immersion educational experience in the 1970s (27). Physicians were included in a treatment program for a 2-week period. Both the Hazelden and Betty Ford Center have more recently developed Professionals In Residence (PIR) training programs where physicians spend one week in the treatment program. Those who conduct these programs have reported impressive attitudinal changes as a result. Once physicians are in practice continuing medical education efforts in areas in which they have little or no interest are almost useless. Brown offered CME credits and money to a random sample consisting of 242 practicing family physicians and general internists. Only 39% agreed to participate in a diagnostic evaluation of a simulated patient on a computer program (106). Although the majority who participated consider the program more worthwhile than other CME experiences, there was no change in the number of alcoholism diagnoses made or attempts to treat alcoholism in the pretest to posttest periods. The author concluded from the data that a voluntary system of CME would probably not work in "areas of high public health concern and low physician competence and interest."

Expecting certain behavioral responses in the professional setting has the advantage of allowing the student or resident to separate these from his or her personal responses. Attempts to change personal values and opinions will usually be resisted. Failure to separate the professional from the personal may account for some of the difficulty which has been experienced in attaining attitudinal and behavioral educational objectives. The goal of developing physicians who are tolerant and open to alcoholic or addicted patients can be more easily attained in a medical setting. There the different values and behaviors can be understood in the context of medical problem solving and patient care without threatening the professional's personal values.

The Macy Conference emphasized the need for faculty role models (1). These are most likely to come from physicians who take fellowship training in addiction medicine. The Center for Medical Fellowships in Alcoholism and Drug Abuse was established in the 1980s (107). The center tracks all fellowship programs which have been established in residencies approved by the American Board of Medical Specialties. Most of these fellowships require completion of postgraduate training in an accredited specialty and last for one or two years. The center has developed an advisory group to enhance collaboration among fellowship training programs. The development of a certification exam by ASAM in 1986 and the Certificate of Added Qualification in Addiction Psychiatry by the American Board of Psychiatry and Neurology in 1993 has provided recognized roots for the development of a competent faculty and teaching clinicians. It is to be hoped that the other boards of medical specialties will accept the recommendation of the Macy Conference and add certificates of added qualification in Addiction Medicine.

Other countries are showing similar interests. In Great Britain a diploma in Addiction Behavior has been developed (108). Unfortunately, few physicians have taken the one year course. The ferment which is occurring in medical education in addiction medicine in the United States is occurring in other countries as well. At the beginning of the decade the Advisory Council on the Misuse of Drugs recommended that each speciality should define minimum standards for training in addiction medicine. An editorial commenting on this report noted that similar recommendations made 10 years ago have still not been implemented. The author noted that "it is time to move beyond platitudes and to see some good models of training and practice." (109). In Canada a national conference was held with representatives from the undergraduate and postgraduate sections of each Canadian medical school (110). The participants concluded that current training is both variable and inadequate particularly with regard to prevention training. It was also noted that many postgraduate programs had no alcohol-related curriculum. It was also noted that most medical schools were not using the clinical resources of treatment programs available to them.

EVALUATION

Medical education in substance abuse is most effective when clear objectives are stated for knowledge, attitudes, and skills (111). The ultimate objective of this training is improved patient care through early diagnosis, before tissue and social damage have occurred, followed by effective treatment intervention. Unfortunately, evaluation is an area for which medical education prepares us poorly, if at all. We are exposed to examinations of various kinds throughout our training but we take them far more often than we give them. There is little opportunity to construct good multiple choice questions, patient management problems, standardized clinical examinations, or attitudinal surveys. A survey of substance abuse training programs

for health professionals in English speaking countries concluded that "most reported programs are lacking in any meaningful evaluation that could provide data for evidence in the design of future programs." (89). A similar survey of medical school courses in England reported that there was no written component to the examinations given in 70% of the departments (108).

Knowledge examinations are the easiest to construct, but even these require so much work and analysis that no standardized examination exists. ASAM with the help of the National Board of Medical Examiners has developed a secure pool of questions which have been used in certification exams since 1986. Questions for this pool have been offered to the various boards of the American Board of Medical Specialties (1). It is tempting to believe that multiple choice questions (MCQ) test clinical skills, but there is no evidence to support this claim. The Psychiatry Residents In Training Examination (PRITE) develops a new pool of over 20 questions on addiction for use in this annual examination which is given to most of the psychiatry residents in the United States. Since these questions, with the appropriate references, are made available to residents following the annual administration of the examination, they have the potential of forming a pool of questions which could be used in evaluating courses in addiction medicine.

Attitudinal evaluation has been considered both important and difficult. Hanlon, after reviewing the literature on medical education in addiction medicine, concluded that it is important for educators to "clarify and specify the attitudes that they wish to enhance or change in their alcoholism training programs." (90). The career teachers in the 1970s gave a high priority to attitudinal change and its evaluation by developing the Substance Abuse Attitude Scale (SAAS) (78). The SAAS was validated with criterion clinicians experienced in treating substance abusers. However, it shares a problem with all attitudinal surveys in that it has no clearly defined relationship to clinical practice. The Harvard team concluded that helping physicians improve their attitudes was best achieved by providing relevant clinical experience in alcoholism treatment (94). Their experience does not obviate the need for assessing the achievement of attitudinal goals. It does confirm that experiential techniques are more effective than didactic ones in changing attitudes.

Skills assessment has posed a significant challenge to medical educators. Early attempts compare changes in frequency of diagnosing alcoholics in a patient population (92). Patient management problems or simulated patient encounters provide another means of assessing skills without the cost and inconvenience of direct practice observation. A new national project on the use of simulated patients in substance abuse medical education holds great promise. Sponsored by the Macy Foundation, this effort will provide scripts, evaluation, and techniques for the use of simulated patients (111). The use of standardized patients in Observed Standardized Clinical Examinations (OSCE) is expensive but very useful (112). Chart audits in clinical settings can also be used to evaluate the acquisition of physician skills. This technique, used in a family practice setting, confirmed the Harvard experience that a rotation on an addiction treatment unit significantly increased primary care resident recognition of alcoholism (p < .05) and chemical dependence (p < .001) (113).

A similar study, on an orthopedics ward in New Zealand, demonstrated significant improvement in diagnosis and intervention on alcoholism (114). The authors noted the "amazing plasticity" of junior doctors. They also noted how rapidly the gains disappeared when the teaching stopped. Sustained teaching and supervision are needed if clinical practice changes are to be maintained.

While evaluation of medical education to date continues to suggest that the educational experience in addiction medicine should be both extensive and intensive, interesting results have been obtained from less intensive educational activities. An intervention project sponsored by the World Health Organization (WHO) tested brief intervention protocols in 10 countries with diverse cultures and health care systems (115). Health care workers ranging from aides through nurse practitioners and physicians were trained to do brief interventions on patients who were heavy alcohol users. Patients who were identified as alcoholic were excluded from this study. A total of 1655 subjects were included in the 10 countries. The control group received a 20-minute health interview plus five minutes of advice on the importance of sensible drinking or abstinence. The experimental groups received an additional 15 minutes of counseling and a self-help manual, plus three follow-up meetings. Follow-up varied with a minimum of 6 months and an average of 9 months. The study was positive and demonstrated a significant reduction in alcohol use and binge drinking in the experimental groups.

Evaluation can be considered a form of educational research. Reporting the results can help the educator maintain academic viability. Such results are not always pleasant. Our students do not always apply what we think they have learned. Assistance from experts in evaluation can be very useful, when the feedback from students is negative or wounding. This assistance is particularly useful in shaping the feedback provided to faculty who participate in the educational process.

CONCLUSION

Alcohol and other drug addictions have shown no sign of decreasing. Medical education in addiction medicine is slowly emerging from a past which ignored the primary disease of addiction and focused on treating its medical sequelae. The results of this neglect are documented in this chapter and in other parts of this textbook. We echo the challenge the Macy Conference has made to the primary care specialties.

This chapter has outlined briefly some of the fundamentals that medical education in addiction must address. The importance of routine screening and intervention by all physicians is stressed, as is earlier diagnosis and treatment for addictive disorders. A solid and growing body of knowledge has been developed from both research and clinical practice supporting diagno-sis and treatment. Positive attitudes toward individuals with addictive disorders and optimism about treatment helps the physician transmit hope and retain a healthy curiosity about these baffling and powerful problems. Clinical skills have been identified and described in increasing detail. These skills appear to be best acquired in supervised clinical settings with continuing supervision for the resident. Evaluation methods have been developed which enable faculty to assess the effectiveness of education in three areas of knowledge, attitude, and skill.

At the present time there is an acute shortage of subspecialists in addiction medicine in each of the medical specialties. This means that clinical departments may have to look for teachers from other clinical specialties, e.g., psychiatry and family medicine, until they can develop their own.

In the United States managed care is pushing more addiction treatment into day care and outpatient settings. These clinical settings are particularly well suited for training primary care physicians. A national initiative involving ASAM, AMERSA, and NIAAA will have as its goal the development of screening competency for alcohol and other drug problems by every physician in the country. The last two decades have produced a cadre of experienced clinicians who can materially upgrade medical education in addiction medicine. Any medical school and/or residency training program in the country will be able to find experienced faculty by contacting ASAM (the American Society of Addiction Medicine), AMERSA (the Association for Medical Education and Research in Substance Abuse), or AAAP (the American Academy of Addiction Psychiatry).

References

1. Macy Conference Proceedings. Training about alcohol and substance abuse for all primary care physicians. New York: Josiah Macy Jr. Foundation, 1995.
2. Rush B. An inquiry into the effects of ardent spirits upon the human body and mind: with an account of the means of preventing and of the remedies for curing them. 8th edition. Springfield, MA: Merriam Webster, 1814.
3. Musto DF. The American disease: origins of narcotic control. New Haven, CT: Yale University Press, 1973:122.
4. Cashman SD. Prohibition: the lie of the land. New York: The Free Press, 1981.
5. American Medical Society on Alcoholism and Other Drug Dependencies (AMSAODD) [now American Society of Addiction Medicine (ASAM)]. 12 West 21st St., New York, NY 10010. Obtained from Directory of Information Resources Online (DIRLINE) National Library of Medicine database, Bethesda, MD: 1990. Telephone 1-(800)-638-8480.
6. Report of Officers. Hospitalization of patients with alcoholism. JAMA 1956;162:750; House of Delegates. Summary of action. JAMA 1966; 198:34.
7. Seixas FA, Sutton JY, eds. Professional training on alcoholism. Ann N Y Acad Sci 1971;178: 1–139.
8. American Medical Student Association. Appendix II: alcoholism education in American medical schools. Ann N Y Acad Sci 1971;178: 135–138.
9. AMA Council On Mental Health, Committee on Alcoholism and Drug Dependency. Medical school education on abuse of alcohol and other psychoactive drugs. JAMA 1972;219(13): 1746–1749.
10. Macy Foundation. Medical education and drug abuse: report of a Macy conference. New York: William P. Fell, 1973.
11. Labs SM. The Career Teacher Grant program: alcohol and drug abuse education for the health professions. J Med Educ 1981;56(3):202–204.
12. Ewan CE, Whaite A. Training health profes-sionals in substance abuse: a review. Int J Addict 1982;17(7):1211–1229.
13. Pokorney AD, Solomon J. A followup survey of drug abuse and alcoholism teaching in medical schools. J Med Educ 1983;58(4):316–321.
14. Lewis DC, Niven RG, Czechowicz D, Trumble JG. A review of medical education in alcohol and other drug abuse. JAMA 1987;257(21): 2945–2948.
15. Fleming M, Barry A, Davis A, Kropp S, Kahn R, Rivo M. Medical education about substance abuse: changes in curriculum and faculty between 1976 and 1992. Acad Med 1994;69:362–369.
16. U.S. Department of Health and Human Services. Clinical training grants for faculty development in alcohol and other drug abuse. RFA-AA-90–02. Catalog of Federal Domestic Assistance No. 13.214, Rockville, MD: U.S. Department of Health and Human Services, 1990.
17. Alcoholics Anonymous. The story of how many thousands of men and women have recovered from alcoholism. 3rd edition. New York: AA World Services, Inc., 1976. [AA literature may be obtained from General Service Office, Box 459, Grand Central Station, New York, NY 10163.]
18. Talbott GD, Gallegos KV, Wilson PO, Porter TL. The Medical Association of Georgia's impaired physician program: review of the first thousand physicians. JAMA 1987;257:2927–2930.
19. American Society of Addiction Medicine. Profile of ASAM members specialties. ASAM News 1990;5:7. See also AMSA News. Alcohol Clin Exp Res 1981;5:582.
20. Bowen OR, Sammons JH. The alcohol abusing patient: a challenge to the profession. JAMA 1988;260:2267–2270.
21. American Psychiatric Association. Position statement of substance abuse. Am J Psychiatry 1981;138(6):874–875.
22. American Psychiatric Association. Special essentials (requirements) for graduate education in psychiatry. Washington, DC: Residency Review Committee, November, 1989.
23. Mendelson JH, Chafetz ME. Alcoholism as an emergency ward problem. Q J Stud Alcohol 1959;20:270–275.
24. Chafetz ME, Blane HT, Abram HS, Golner J, Lacy E, McCourt WF, et al. Establishing treatment relations with alcoholics. J Nerv Ment Dis 1962;134(5):395–409.
25. Westermeyer J, Doheny S, Stone B. An assessment of hospital care for the alcoholic patient. Alcohol Clin Exp Res 1978;2(1):53–57.
26. Mannon JM. Defining and treating "problem patients" in a hospital emergency room. J Med Care 1976;14(12):1004–1013.
27. Pursch JA. Physicians' attitudinal changes in alcoholism. Alcohol Clin Exp Res 1978;2(4): 358–361.
28. Bander KW, Goldman DS, Schwartz MA, Rabinowitz E, English JT. Survey of attitudes among three specialists in a teaching hospital toward alcoholics. J Med Educ 1987;62(1):17–24.
29. Moore RD, Bone LR, Geller G, Masson JA, Stokes EJ, Levine DM. Prevalence, detection, and treatment of alcoholism in hospitalized patients. JAMA 1989;261(3):403–407.
30. Stimmel B. Appropriate training in alcohol and substance abuse for primary care physicians: defining the problem. Macy Conference Proceedings. New York: Macy Foundation, 1995: 249–274.
31. Morse RM, Flavin DK. The definition of alcoholism. JAMA 1992;268:1012–1014.
32. American Psychiatric Association. Diagnostic and statistical manual of mental disorders. 4th edition. Washington, DC: American Psychiatric Association, 1994.
33. Lewis DC. Comparison of alcohol and drug addiction to other diseases in the disease concept of alcoholism and drug addiction. Psychiatr Ann 1991;21:256–265.
34. McGinnis JM, Foege WH. Actual causes of death in the United States. JAMA 1993;270: 2202–2212.
35. Miller W, Rollnick S. Motivational interviewing: preparing people to change addictive behavior. New York: Guilford Press, 1991.
36. Babor TF, Grant M, Acuda W, et al. A randomized trial of brief interventions in primary care: summary of a WHO project. Addiction 1994; 89(6):657–660.
37. Babor T, Korner P, Wilber C. Screening and early intervention strategies for harmful

drinkers: Initial lessons learned from the AMETHYST Project. Aust Drug Alcohol Rev 1987;6:325–339.

38. Miller WR, Sovereign RG. The check-up: a model for early intervention in addictive behaviors. In: Loberg T, et al., eds. Addictive behaviors: prevention and early intervention. Amsterdam: Swets & Zeitlinger, 1989:219–231.

39. Alcohol, Drug Abuse, and Mental Health Administration. Consensus statement from the conference on alcohol, drugs and primary care physician education: issues, roles, responsibilities. November 12–15, 1985. Rancho Mirage, California. Rockville, MD: U.S. Department of Health and Human Services, 1985.

40. Giannini AJ, Miller NS. Drug abuse: a biopsychiatric model. Am Fam Pract 1989;40(5):173–182.

41. APA Work Group on Substance Use Disorders. Practice guidelines for the treatment of patients with substance use disorders: alcohol, cocaine, opioids. Am J Psychiatry 1995;152(11 Suppl):1–59.

42. National Institute on Alcohol Abuse and Alcoholism. The physician's guide to helping patients with alcohol problems. National Institutes of Health Pub. No. 95–3769. Rockville, MD: National Institute on Alcohol Abuse and Alcoholism, 1995.

43. Dube GE, Goldstein MD, Lewis DC, Myers ER, Zwick WR. Project ADEPT: curriculum for primary care physician training. Vol. 1. Core modules, 1989. Vol. 2. Special topics and videotape, 1990. Providence, RI: Brown University Center for Alcohol and Addiction Studies, 1989–1990.

44. Institute of Medicine. Broadening the case of treatment for alcohol problems. Washington DC: National Academy Press, 1989.

45. Skinner HA. Spectrum of drinkers and intervention opportunities. Can Med Assoc J 1990;143(10):1054–1059.

46. Babor TF. Brief intervention strategies for harmful drinkers: new directions for medical education. Can Med Assoc J 1990;143(10):1070–1076.

47. Vaillant GE. The natural history of alcoholism. Cambridge, MA: Harvard University Press, 1983.

48. Kandel DB, Davies M. High school students who use crack and other drugs. Arch Gen Psychiatry 1996;53(1):71–80.

49. Vaillant GE. The natural history of alcoholism revisited. Cambridge, MA: Harvard University Press, 1995.

50. Gottheil E, McLellan AT, Druley KA. Length of stay, patient severity, and treatment outcome: sample data from the field of alcoholism. J Stud Alcohol 1992;53(1):69–75.

51. Holder HD, Blose JD. The reduction of health care costs associated with alcoholism treatment: a 14 year longitudinal study. J Stud Alcohol 1992;53:293–302.

52. Schuckit MA. Drug and alcohol abuse: a clinical guide to diagnosis and treatment. 4th edition. New York: Plenum, 1994.

53. Arif A, Westermeyer J, eds. Manual of drug and alcohol abuse: guidelines for teaching in medical and health institutions. New York: Plenum, 1988.

54. Miller NS, ed. Principles of addiction medicine. Chevy Chase, MD: American Society of Addiction Medicine, 1994.

55. Kurtz E. Not-God. A history of Alcoholics Anonymous. Center City, MN: Hazelden, 1979.

56. Hamilton B. Getting started in AA. Center City, MN: Hazelden, 1995.

57. McGovern JT, DuPont RL. A bridge to recovery: an introduction to 12-step programs. Washington, DC: American Psychiatric Press, 1994.

58. Vaillant GE. A long-term follow up of male alcohol abuse. Arch Gen Psychiatry 1996;53:243–249.

59. Jerrell JM, Ridgely MS. Comparative effectiveness of three approaches to serving people with severe mental illness and substance abuse disorders. J Nerv Ment Dis 1995;183(9):566–576.

60. Chappel JN, Schnoll SH. Physician attitudes: effects on the treatment of chemically dependent patients. JAMA 1977;237(21):2318–2319.

61. Allport GW. Attitudes. In: Murchison CA, ed. A handbook of social psychology. Worcester, MA: Clark University Press, 1935:798–844.

62. Eiser JR. Social psychology: attitudes, cognition, and social behavior. New York: Cambridge University Press, 1986:11.

63. Sudnow D. Passing on: the social organization of dying. Englewood Cliffs, NJ: Prentice-Hall, 1967:104–109.

64. Rado S. The psychoanalysis of pharmacothymia (drug addiction). Psychoanal Q 1933;2:1–3.

65. Brickman B. Psychoanalysis and substance abuse: toward a more effective approach. J Am Acad Psychoanal 1988;16(3):359–379.

66. Khantzian EJ, Mack JE. Alcoholics Anonymous and contemporary psychodynamic theory. In: Galanter M, ed. Recent developments in alcoholism. New York: Plenum Press, 1989;7:67–89.

67. Bean-Bayog M. Psychopathology produced by alcoholism. In: Meyer R, ed. Psychopathology and addictive disorders. New York: Guilford Press, 1986.

68. Waller JA, Casey R. Teaching about substance abuse in medical school. Br J Addict 1990;85:1451–1455.

69. Conard S, Hughes P, Baldwin DC, Achenbach KE, Sheehan DV. Substance use by fourth year students at 13 U.S. medical schools. J Med Educ 1988;63(10):747–758.

70. Perry SW. Traditional attitudes toward addicts and narcotics. Bull N Y Acad Med 185;61(8):706–727.

71. Musto D. The American disease: origins of narcotic control. New Haven, CT: Yale University Press, 1973.

72. McGuire WJ. The nature of attitudes and attitude change. In: Lindzey G, Aronson E, eds. Handbook of social psychology. 2nd edition. Vol. 3. Reading, MA: Addison-Wesley, 1969.

73. Public Statement by T Radecki, Chairman of National Coalition on Television Violence, Champaign, IL, 1987. Reported in NCADD Fact Sheet, revised 6/90, 12 West 21st St., New York, NY 10010.

74. Linn LS, Yager J, Leake B. Physicians' attitudes toward the legalization of marijuana use. West J Med 1989;150(6):714–717.

75. Osgood CE, Suci GJ, Tannenbaum PH. Attitude measurement. In: Summers GF, ed. Attitude measurement. Chicago: Rand McNally, 1970:237. [Originally published in 1957.]

76. Likert R. A technique for the measurement of attitudes. In: Summers GF, ed. Attitude measurement. Chicago: Rand McNally, 1970:149–157. [Originally published in 1932.]

77. Cartwright AKJ. The attitudes of helping agents towards the alcoholic client: the influence of experience, support, training, and self-esteem. Br J Addict 1980;75:413–431.

78. Chappel JN, Veach TL, Krug RS. The substance abuse attitude survey: an instrument for measuring attitudes. J Stud Alcohol 1985;46(1):48–52.

79. Chappel JN, Veach TL. Effect of a course on students' attitudes toward substance abuse and its treatment. J Med Educ 1987;62(5):394–400.

80. Veach TL, Chappel JN. Physician attitudes in chemical dependency: the effects of personal experience and recovery. Subst Abuse 1990;11(2):97–101.

81. Sterne MW, Pittman DJ. The concept of motivation: a source of institutional and professional blockage in the treatment of alcoholics. Q J Stud Alcohol 1965;26:41–57.

82. Eron LD. The effect of medical education on attitudes: a follow up study. J Med Educ 1958;33(pt2):25–33.

83. Fisher JC, Mason RL, Keeley KA, Fisher JV. Physicians and alcoholics: the effect of medical training on attitudes toward alcoholics. J Stud Alcohol 1975;(7):949–955.

84. Rezler AG. Attitude changes during medical school: a review of the literature. J Med Educ 1974;49(11):1023–1030.

85. Flaherty JA, Flaherty EG. Medical students' performance in reporting alcohol related problems. J Stud Alcohol 1983;44(6):1083–1087.

86. Cooley FB. The attitudes of students and housestaff toward alcoholism [letter]. JAMA 1990;263(9):1197–1198.

87. Azjin I, Fishbein M. Understanding attitudes and predicting social behavior. Englewood Cliffs, NJ: Prentice-Hall, 1980.

88. Frank JD. Persuasion and healing: a comparative study of psychotherapy. Baltimore: Johns Hopkins University Press, 1973.

89. Evan CE, Whaite A. Training health professionals in substance abuse: a review. Int J Addict 1982;17(7):1211–1229.

90. Hanlon MJ. A review of the recent literature relating to the training of medical students in alcoholism. J Med Educ 1985;60(8):618–626.

91. Watts W. Relative persistence of opinion change induced by active compared to passive participation. J Pers Soc Psychol 1967;5:4–15.

92. Fisher JV, Fisher JC, Mason RL. Physicians and alcoholism: modifying behavior and attitudes of family practice residents. J Stud Alcohol 1976;37(11):1686–1693.

93. Barnes HN, O'Neill SF, Aronson MD, Delbanco TL. Early detection and outpatient management of alcoholism: a curriculum for medical residents. J Med Educ 1984;59:904–906.

94. Warburg MM, Cleary PD, Rohman M, Barnes HN, Aronson M, Delbanco TL. Residents' attitudes, knowledge, and behavior regarding diagnosis and treatment of alcoholism. J Med Educ 1987;62:497–503.

95. Galanter M, Kaufman E, Taintor Z, Robinowitz CB, Meyer RE, Halikas J. The current status of psychiatric education in alcoholism and drug abuse. Am J Psychiatry 1989;146(1):35–39.

96. Galanter M, Talbott D, Gallegos K, Rubenstone E. Combined alcoholics anonymous and professional care for addicted physicians. Am J Psychiatry 1990;147(1):64–68.

97. Chappel JN. Educational approaches to prescribing practices and substance abuse. J Psychoactive Drugs 1991;23(4):359–363.

98. AMA Council on Mental Health. The sick physician: impairment by psychiatric disorders, including alcoholism and drug dependence. JAMA 1973;223:684–687.

99. Miller NR. Treatment of the addictions: applications of outcome research for clinical management. New York: Haworth Press, 1995.

100. Chappel JN. Long term recovery from alcoholism. Psychiatr Clin North Am 1993;16(1):177–187.

101. Shuckit MA, Berger F. The integration of an

educational program into a treatment facility. Br J Addict 1989;84:191–195.

102. Arredondo R, Weddige RL, Pollard S, McCorkle AJ. Implementing a substance abuse curriculum in a medical school. Acad Psychiatry 1989;13:44–47.

103. Mueller T, Lewis DC. The short story in substance abuse education. Subst Abuse 1994; 15(1):47–51.

104. McCann DP, Blossom HJ. The physician as a patient educator: from theory to practice. West J Med 1990;153:44–49.

105. Soumerai SB, Avorn J. Principles of educational outreach (academic detailing) to improve clinical decision making. JAMA 1990; 263(4):549–556.

106. Brown RL, Carter WB, Gordon MJ. Diagnosis of alcoholism in a stimulated patient encounter by primary care physicians. J Fam Pract 1987;25(3):259–264.

107. Galanter M. Postgraduate medical fellowships in alcoholism and drug abuse. New York: Center for Medical Fellowships in Alcoholism and Drug Abuse, New York University School of Medicine, 1988.

108. Glass IB. Undergraduate training in substance abuse in the United Kingdom. Br J Addict 1989;84:197–202.

109. Farrell M. Beyond Platitudes: Problem Drug Use: A review of training. Br J Addict 1990; 85:1559–1562.

110. Brewster JM, Single E, Ashley MJ, Chow YC, Skinner HA, Rankin JG. Preventing alcohol problems: survey of Canadian medical schools. Can Med Assoc J 1990;143(10): 1076–1082.

111. AMERSA Committee on Substance Abuse Teaching Objectives. Physician education in substance abuse: curriculum objectives. In: Alcohol and drug abuse in medical education.

Pub. No. (ADM) 79–891. Washington, DC: U.S. Department of Health, Education and Welfare, 1980.

112. Stillman PL, et. al. Assessing clinical skills of resident with standardized patients. Ann Intern Med 1986;105:762–771.

113. Mulry JT, Brewer ML, Spencer DL. The effect of an inpatient chemical dependency rotation on residents clinical behavior. Fam Med 1987;19(4):276–280.

114. Hamilton MR, Menkes DB, Jeffery DK. Early intervention for alcohol misuse: encouraging doctors to take action. N Z Med J 1994; 107(989):454–456.

115. Saunders J, Aasland O, Amundsen A, Grant M. Alcohol consumption and related problems among primary health care patients: WHO collaborative project on early detection of persons with harmful alcohol consumption. Addiction 1993;88:349–362.

79 Education and Training of Clinical Personnel

David A. Deitch and Susie A. Carleton

The nonmedical clinical training of treatment personnel and ancillary practitioners in the field of substance abuse is filled with colorful characters, events, debate, and frequently confusion. Such training has occurred amid bias, zeal, occasional distorted information, chaos, and always with great passion. What is drug addiction? What is treatment? Who needs treatment? What kind of treatment works? How do we best train treatment personnel? Over the last decades, these questions have been answered in radically different ways. In an effort to sort through the bedlam that often accompanies the topic of training nurses, psychologists, child care workers, teachers, social workers, therapeutic community staff, drug rehabilitation counselors, and recovering addicts themselves, this chapter will begin with a review of treatment approaches in both the private and public sectors since the 1930s and the way in which those treatments have affected the training of nonmedical personnel. The second half of the chapter will focus on training philosophies and methods that, despite the great divergence of thinking in this field, have proved tried and true in countries throughout the world.

TREATMENT ISSUES

Trying to Reach a Consensus

Nonmedical personnel who come to be trained in the subject of substance abuse most likely arrive with a preconceived set of biases based on personal experience, varied expectations, previous training experiences, professional orientation, and beliefs about addiction itself. They may well feel very strongly that their "way" is the only way (1). Often, this strong bias or zealousness is a substitute for more complicated training. For example, one often finds new, relatively unsophisticated paraprofessionals following a faith-based system derived from their own treatment experience. They may carry this system into new and sometimes quite inflexible staff roles. Some believe that addiction is a medical symptom, episodic in nature, and that the way to deal with drug abuse is through detoxification. Others believe that denial is the largest stumbling block to recovery and that once denial is conquered, recovery is sure to follow. Those schooled in therapeutic community and 12-step models may find it difficult to open themselves to new ideas based on different paradigms. Those for whom religion, psychotherapy, methadone maintenance, chemotherapy, or the disease model form their beliefs about drug treatment may be quite resistant to other approaches. In addition, nonmedical health professionals may very well be grappling with some aversion

to the drug-abusing population. This aversion can take the form of hopelessness, helplessness, dislike, disgust, discomfort, and affective distancing (2).

Because of the strong convictions that both medical and nonmedical personnel bring to drug abuse training grounds, training in this field is especially sensitive. This sensitivity can be successfully negotiated by first presenting a historical overview in a training setting, including a review of some of the cultural, historical, political, and religious features of drug use. This history is best presented in terms of its effect on treatment choices. What do we know about both historical and current treatment responses to various types of drug use problems? What are the methods? What theories underlie these methods? What benefits do some methods have over others? What liabilities? What are the outcomes of various methods?

The Great History of Treatment Failure

Why treat drug abusers? This is a question that must come before treatment theories, practical interventions, or training approaches. Different groups will answer the question differently. For some, the aim is to help the individual overcome the use of drugs. For others, the aim is to help the individual live a better life. This generally means addressing social and psychological issues beyond the drug abuse. For some, social concerns are of the utmost importance, especially creating a safer environment for those not involved in drug abuse. For these people, criminal prosecution and punishment offer the best approach. Some other people take a more global view and believe that eradicating drug abuse creates a healthier world community.

Whatever the aim, drug abuse treatment has frustrated and perplexed people for decades. From the 1920s to the early 1940s, American society viewed the drug abuser as a person with weak character and morals. In response to that cultural belief, jail was the usual answer and the only treatment choice was to detoxify addicts based on a medical model. Invariably, however, detoxified people returned to drugs, giving rise to a conviction that "once an addict, always an addict." This myth grew along with an increase in the use of drugs and alcohol, and most medical practitioners were repulsed by having to face the "junkie" or "wino" in public hospitals. Those who suffered from drug addiction were not helped by the harrowing portrayals of such people in movies and the propaganda of Harry Anslinger, Director of the Federal Bureau of Narcotics from its inception in 1930 until 1962 (3). During this period, the Superintendent of the Federal Prison System in 1929 was prevailed upon to take addicts out of the federal prison systems, where they were both exposing nonusers to drug culture and being taught by criminals to become better at committing crimes, and to place them into a special system. These special systems became popularly known as "narcotic farms."

In a post-Depression eagerness to provide construction and other jobs for people in economically deprived areas, senators from two Southern sites volunteered to house these first detention "narcotic farms" for addicts. They were located in Lexington, Kentucky, and Fort Worth, Texas. Federal prisoners were removed from various settings and placed in one of these two centers. Eventually, other officials decided that addicts from around the country could be permitted to volunteer for these centers and that some addicts could be sent involuntarily for short stays in these "hospital 'narco-farm' jails," which were operated by the United States Public Health Service (PHS) with the presence of security personnel.

After World War II, with the first heroin epidemic in 1948, the problem slowly but steadily grew worse. Responding to it as we had for the previous 30 years meant an increase in criminal penalties for those found guilty of using drugs. At this point in history, although the criminal model remained entrenched, some people in the field began to believe that the addict (the morphine or heroin addict in particular) was not really a criminal first, but suffered instead from a problem of wanting drugs. Because those drugs were illegal, the addict would frequently commit crimes to obtain money for drugs.

In the early 1950s, after years of failure in other hospitals and jails, there were stirrings in the "narco-farms" of what might be considered a more enlightened response to the problem of drug addiction. This expressed itself in a attempt to treat addicts by using what little was known at the time about social case work, vocational training, and (as a result of work with war veterans) some aspects of "group therapy." The thinking was that if these activities kept the addict away from drugs long enough and, if the addict was restored to physical health and given the possibility of insight or job skills or social case work support, there was hope that the individual could or would return to the community, no longer requiring drugs.

Also during this period in the United States, there had been some efforts by psychiatrists in the public health system to conduct group work with addicts. The group model was made available on a voluntary basis for those who were interested. As it turned out, the addicts drawn to group therapy were by and large fairly verbal, either by dint of their middle class status or native verbal abilities. At the same time, social workers attempted an amalgam of counseling aimed at supporting these individuals, which included some of the prevailing social case work theories existing in the country at that time. No one realized, however, that a bridge would be necessary to ease these individuals back into society (4). This oversight resulted in failure and frustration on the part of social workers and psychologists working to heal the bumps and bruises that accompany the drug-abusing lifestyle. These workers had made sincere but patchwork efforts at rehabilitation. Consequently, despite this new work, there returned the ever-present dream that a miracle medicine could be found that would cure the problem once and for all.

Medical research was in progress at Lexington and Fort Worth in the continuing search for a "magic bullet" medication to handle the problem of drug abuse. Researchers had a powerful wish (as they do today) that just the right medicine would finally treat this multifaceted, mystifying problem.

By 1960, heroin use had expanded greatly and, with it, criminal behavior. Substance abuse professionals became discouraged again: It seemed that psychiatry had not paid off, social work had not paid off, jail in and of itself (even the PHS "narco-farm" model) had not paid off (in many instances it exacerbated the problem), and pure vocational training had not paid off. Furthermore, in the community and at large, there was little reimbursement to those professionals who had attempted to give birth to a theoretical body of thinking about addiction (5). In addition, the plethora of problems associated with trying to work with individuals whose conduct, thefts, and repeated failures gave little reward meant that these practitioners did not even experience the gratification of knowing that they were making an impact on the problem. While the more articulate addicts presented an intriguing and romantic challenge in their proclaimed desire to resist using drugs, the truth was that, regardless of interventions put into place, they continued to use drugs.

The problem grew worse. Finally, increased mandatory sentences, anger at the user, and self-hatred by users themselves resulted in a deadlocked, completely disheartened situation.

New Answers in the 1960s

Out of this discouragement came the first breakthroughs in the problem of drug abuse, breakthroughs that garnered much excited press coverage throughout the 1960s. As the scope of drug abuse threatened to overwhelm the United States, two major new paradigms came into being. One was the therapeutic community movement, which really began in 1959, but did not gain widespread recognition until 1963 or 1964 with the advent of Daytop in New York. The promulgation of that methodology now known as therapeutic community (TC) was an approach that held great promise and excitement. The TC approach was primarily conducted by people who had been afflicted with the problem, claiming that they alone, because of their affliction, could work successfully with this problem. In the opinion of these new thinkers, those who had not suffered from drug addiction were often too indulgent, too easily manipulated, and too easily conned by addicts. Cure could result, they felt, only in a more rigorously honest disclosure of self and a challenging demand for new behavior, conducted in large measure by those who knew the addict's world from the inside.

TCs offered the promise that, not only could they handle the addict where others had failed, but they could get people who were obsessive-compulsive drug users and criminals to stop behaving that way voluntarily. The climate at TCs was set up as one unswervingly opposed to drug use. This eliminated any cultural ambivalence, thus increasing the motivation that participants had to "stay clean." In these rigidly structured communities, there was a powerful social coercion for individuals to cooperate with treatment if they wanted to avoid something even worse, such as jail. TCs became the first model to be able to predictably effect the cure of heroin dependency (6, 7).

The second major breakthrough in the early 1960s came out of earlier research with the German-invented narcotic dolophine at the U.S. Public Health Hospital at Lexington: the development of methadone. This synthetic narcotic, as implemented by Vincent Dole at The Rockefeller University, seemed to hold the hope that methadone maintenance was the magic pill that could cure drug addiction. Indeed, high doses could, in fact, reduce craving and offset the preoccupation with the lifestyle of heroin addiction. Initially, methadone maintenance was resisted by those in drug enforcement, the mental health community, and by most workers in drug-free treatment communities. It slowly gained in use and credibility. Much of the credibility came from the drug's ability to demonstrate the fact that it could not meet the critical criteria of reducing criminal behavior in those who took it. Its use fit into the medical model, in that it was medication controlled by dosage. As such, it lent itself to a wide variety of studies in the academic and medical communities. These studies tended to verify its promise (8).

Within the drug treatment culture, Alcoholics Anonymous (AA) did exist, although no one considered it a breakthrough applicable to the special problems of addiction. Narcotics Anonymous (NA) was created as a way of engaging heroin users, but by and large it did not prove a successful approach at that time. Alcoholics and drug addicts frequently viewed each other with contempt and suspicion, and one would not be seen with the other. As a model, it simply did not prove engaging of addicts during the two decades.

The New "Professionals"
(Paraprofessionals and Others)

Despite the discovery of methadone's ability to inhibit some heroin use behaviors, it soon proved evident that the medication itself was not enough to "cure" drug addiction. Those people who, in the early 1960s, claimed that personal experience with addiction was a route toward successfully engaging users became more prominent. It became clear that this "been-there" approach had great merit (1). These ex-addicts became the first nonacademically trained, nonprofessional drug rehabilitation workers. They became known as "paraprofessionals" in the field, working either in separate freestanding settings (such as TCs) or in conjunction with some medical professionals who adjusted methadone doses and performed other medical diagnostic procedures. These paraprofessionals were, in fact, often seen as the first actual experts in the muddled world of substance abuse. They also saw themselves as experts, sometimes the only experts, and were often considered such by professionals and addicts alike (9). Their tough, pragmatic, sometimes brutally honest, empathetic approach to the problems of addiction, along with their intimate knowledge of the workings of an addict's life, gave the field a much-needed push in the direction of understanding and creating real change in lives that seemed hopeless.

The Middle Class Enters the Picture

The majority of treatments for drug addiction in the second half of the twentieth century were aimed at the bewildering problem of heroin addiction and its attendant criminal activity. However, the use of drugs of choice—such as heroin—did not remain static. During the late 1960s and early 1970s, while antidrug efforts were being mounted, there was a slow but ever-expanding use of other drugs, particularly marihuana and the "psychedelics." It is crucial to understand that, because these "new" drugs were used in large part by children of the middle class, some of the previous criminal sanctions surrounding drug abusers were called into question. Middle-class parents did not want their children to go to jail. Confusion reigned about how destructive these new drugs were, primarily because the many youthful users of these drugs seemed to demonstrate to their parents that they could use the drugs without problems, and whether criminal penalties for the possession and use of these drugs were out of proportion to any problems created by them.

As this elite class of drug users grew, so did cultural ambivalence. An aura of intrigue clung to the "psychedelic drug user." Across the country an almost religious response arose in people who did not necessarily use these psychedelics, but who wanted to rub elbows with those who did. These people often adopted the style of these users, if not the drug use itself, and wanted to become part of saving/helping groups that rapidly formed. However, some of these "helpers" did use psychedelics themselves. "Crash pads" and "psychedelic clinics" came into being all across the nation. Everyone wanted to get in on the act of treating a child with whom they could finally identify: mostly white and college educated. Many of these young people who asked for help had either overused a drug or had a bad experience with these particular drugs. Furthermore, an air of romance clung to these users, so much so that other youth with a variety of mental health problems claimed drug use as a way of getting some attention. Many of the helpers and some of the users were students in professional schools of psychology, social work, and psychiatry. Their approval to working with these youngsters was at times quite cavalier; at other times it was to use traditional models or those that were in professional vogue at the time (e.g., Gestalt, Sensitivity, Scream Therapy, Transactional Analysis). Much of the "helping" took place in hastily set up clinics, some on the street, and others associated with student counseling centers, mental health centers, and finally churches and dormitories.

The Government Steps In

By 1970 the matter of "training" became a viable topic in the field of drug abuse when, under Nixon's administration, the first "War on Drugs" began in the form of the Special Action Office for Drug Abuse Prevention (SAODAP). Shortly thereafter came the birth of the National Institute of Drug Abuse (NIDA). SAODAP, with the help of NIDA, mounted a national strategy meant to diminish the problem of drug abuse in America. The goal was to create a treatment system that could accomplish the following outcomes (in order of priority):

1. To reduce crime in the streets
2. To reduce tax-consumptive behavior (any activity that costs the public money such as welfare, unemployment, or public hospital stays)
3. To reduce illicit drug use
4. To increase tax-productive behavior (any activity that restores individuals to legitimate work and taxpaying)
5. To enhance personal well-being

At that point, one of the tasks of these new agencies was to develop a pool of person-power that could finally address the treatment of this pervasive problem on a national level. This indicated a clear switch, both in overt policy and in mentality. The addict would no longer be exclusively a criminal; instead, he or she was also to become a "patient." In light of this new view, "treatment systems" were the way to deal with the drug user, because treatment promised to show some positive outcome, however small, where incarceration in and of itself had not.

This new approach called for a network of national treatment agencies and experts who could devote the time and research necessary to become career practitioners and teachers in the field. Within NIDA, the Manpower Training Branch was created to train these practitioners. Its goals were as follows:

1. To train career teachers so that medical schools and other schools of professional training would commit people to teach others within their profession. To further this aim, grants were made available.
2. To offer grants to individual researchers in the field of drug abuse.
3. To train a large pool of practitioners around the country in a way that would positively affect their present treatment efforts in the field (10, 11).

While this expansion in treatment systems created fresh enthusiasm in the field, it also created a certain amount of chaos. How were we to track various treatments? How were we to verify efficacy? How could we figure out what was good treatment and what was bad? To answer these questions, systems of reporting, patient tracking, and program management were instituted. Also, as a result of quality-of-care concerns within the Division of Community Assistance under the leadership of Lee Dogoloff, the Clinical Review Board was created. Its goal was to study various treatment programs around the country and set standards for acceptable clinical care. The Board's overriding concern was to ensure that treatment centers show consideration for their "patients" and that they were not just caught up in the zeal and dizzying excitement of a new national policy.

The concerns created additional definite training needs:

1. How does one manage the bureaucratic needs of an expanding system and respond to funding agents' requests for data?
2. How does one become trained to implement the baseline requisite standards that would ensure that individuals in treatment receive high-quality care?

In response to these questions, the large number of paraprofessionals that came out of the 1960s received a series of trainings in compliance with these demands. These trainings covered various treatment approaches, assessment, establishing rapport, managing an environment, short-and long-term planning, and report writing.

Some Gains, Some Losses

This new national interest attracted many new professionals to the field because of their college experiences working with psychedelic drug users and the possibility of rewarding salaries and an increase in social status. They merged with the paraprofessionals who had already been working in the field. As a result of the merger, the traditional methodologies and counseling approaches taught in graduate schools were reignited in the national training systems. Short-term treatment planning and short-term counseling systems, more in line with conventional psychological counseling and social work counseling, took some precedence over TC approaches and work done by the earlier paraprofessionals who grew up in the treatment of heroin. Some crossover of approaches did occur, but there were definite demands on the paraprofessional treater to adopt many of the methods and approaches of the middle-class psychedelic treatment approach within the training system. While there were benefits for the street paraprofessionals and TCs in establishing treatment and tracking plans, some of the unique methodological breakthroughs, skills, and approaches pioneered by therapeutic communities and methadone maintenance were neglected.

Treatment systems across the country attempted to expand in light of the new public funds available and a resurgence of interest in the field. In the mid 1970s, however, during the Carter administration, these public funds were cut back, paradoxically, just as the field began to fully mount a national effort against drug abuse and just as these systems began to experience outcomes of positive significance in terms of treating and controlling the problem. The field lost career teachers, the more trained practitioners, and a large part of the infrastructure of NIDA (along with the accrued education and experience within that agency). Public funds and support eroded even further during the Reagan years, to a point at which the treatment and prevention field lost much of the national resources personnel already trained and educated to help mount the war on drugs.

During these same years of funding reductions, however, services grew in two quarters. The first quarter expansion was in public sector methadone maintenance programs and TCs, and the second quarter expansion included private for-profit insurance reimbursement approaches.

Within the public sector, heroin users continued to seek help from methadone maintenance clinics, especially as the threat of acquired immunodeficiency syndrome (AIDS) in intravenous drug users took root. TCs expanded to meet an increase in demand as well. The TC had already realized that the methods originally intended to aid heroin addicts were equally effective with multidrug users and ever-younger users. Both methadone clinics and TCs responded strongly during the years of government cutbacks, despite the decrease in public money available to them.

The second quarter expansion, which took place in the 1980s, was of privately funded, for-profit drug programs operating chiefly in hospitals. This new direction in treatment germinated from the incorporation of AA and 12-step programs into hospital settings, chiefly under the umbrella of doctors and other allied health providers. Because the first of these programs began at Willmar State Hospital in Minnesota and was further refined at Hazelden and the Johnson Institute in Minnesota, these programs are often referred to as the "Minnesota Model."

This model also became known as the "28-day program," as an outgrowth of the insurance industry placing limits on maximum hospital lengths of stay. They arrived at this figure coincidentally, based on a study made on the average length of inpatient stays early on at Hazelden. The populations studied at Hazelden—white, middle-class males between the ages of 25 and 40 years, most of whom had alcohol problems and all of whom had a reasonably successful work history—showed relatively good outcomes. Because the insurance industry was willing to fund this length of stay, hospitals across the country were eager to implement this "28-day model."

The Return of Stimulants: Cocaine

The national surge in cocaine use that occurred in the late 1970s supported the advent of these 28-day programs. As cocaine overuse worked its way down steadily from the upper and middle classes, both working and middle class youth began to get into trouble with this drug. Neither these groups nor their families seriously considered treatment in public sector programs (at least, not until their insurance funds were depleted). In response to the middle class' search for answers, hospitals expanded the base of the Minnesota Model and even the 28-day program, now calling themselves chemical dependency treatment programs (CDs). The private-sector, CD response to this burgeoning cocaine abuse was based on a trend of considering the problem as a disease. Borrowing from the rich history of AA, those who followed the disease model of drug abuse developed a set of approaches incorporating 12-step activities.

Two-Tier Treatment System

At the end of the 1980s, a two-tier response system existed, with the public nonprofit groups (stretched thin as a result of diminished public funding, with massive waiting lists) and the private for-profit groups competing with each other for clients. Both tiers required training to either respond to demand or improve the attractiveness of their services. Despite the multiplicity of these public and private sector programs that now exist in explicit response to drug abuse, training has not kept pace in its ability to prepare those who work in the field. A 1981 survey of graduate schools in psychology found a "disproportionately low" level of training in substance abuse issues

"relative to the magnitude of these problems" (12). A 1982 study reviewed a population in English-speaking countries and found four essential types of courses: those for practitioners and teachers of health professionals, those for medical students, those for nurses and nursing students, and those for allied health professionals. In spite of the apparent thoroughness of these curricula, the study found very little guidance for future program development (13). In light of these findings and bearing in mind the great effect of training on treatment, it is imperative to examine both the content and ideology of successful training programs for drug abuse workers.

TRAINING ISSUES

How Bias Affects Treatment and Training

Those who come to drug abuse training programs often do so with strong biases. These biases result from prior professional or lay education, as well as personal experience, and they have a significant impact on the way in which people approach training. Preconceived beliefs about substance abuse and what constitutes an appropriate response to substance abuse create a tunnel through which only some addicts can pass. If people are convinced that their treatment ideas are the "only" correct ideas, they tend to herd people through a rigid set of interventions that simply are not flexible enough to bend to individual needs. Cultural beliefs (be they national, regional, neighborhood, or association) further complicate these practitioner biases. Strongly held cultural views may dictate that only certain types of treatment are valid, meaningful, or useful. Some of the biases in basic thinking about substance abuse are as follows:

1. All drug dependence (both overuse and addiction) is a disease process.
2. Working with a client who is actively using drugs is "enabling."
3. If a client does not think of his or her drug use as an out-of-control disease, he or she is in denial.
4. If a client does admit to having a "disease," a 12-step program is the only concrete, long-lasting solution.
5. Psychotherapy is ineffective.
6. Psychotherapy is necessary to effect long-term recovery.
7. Medical intervention in the form of medication is destructive or impedes recovery.
8. The only real, cost-effective help lies in a medicopharmacological response.
9. Drug-dependent people most likely have substance-dependent parents.
10. The TC approach is the only long-lasting rehabilitation that is drug free.
11. TC approaches work with only a small segment of the drug-using population.
12. Regardless of original drug use patterns, all "recovering" people must abstain from any drug use (e.g., alcohol, medications) for the rest of their lives.

Obviously, these divergent convictions can create a chaos of misunderstanding in both treatment and training programs. No one approach is right. No one approach can be right, given the cultural, economic, experiential, and personality differences of substance abusers. The goal of drug abuse training should be to create an atmosphere in which people are actually able to openly listen to new ideas and to offer a range of care options broad enough to encompass many kinds of addicts, at many stages of addiction.

The Continuum of Care Model

Options are critical to handling the complex problem of providing help to drug abusers. A model that provides a continuum of care offers the greatest possibility of engaging a variety of people at different points in their lives, depending upon their needs and resources, the severity of their problem, and the context in which their problem takes place. The flexibility of such a continuum of care model is especially important because it has been shown that, not only will a single model be dysfunctional for some clients, but that this dysfunctionality will also impede treatment for others in the same setting for whom such a single model might actually be appropriate. Dr. Herbert Kleber states that "no known treatment is completely effective

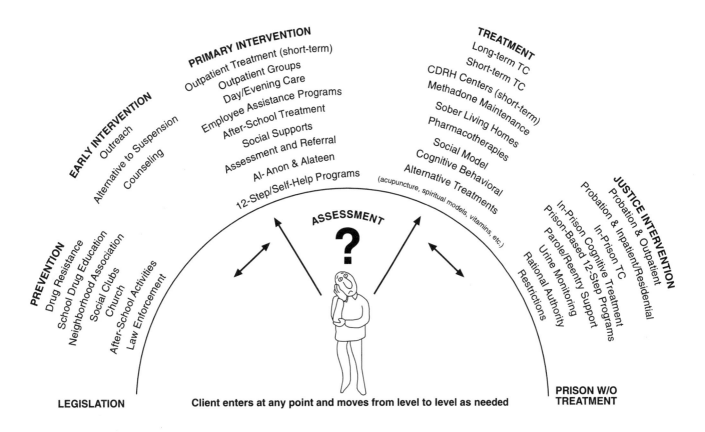

Figure 79.1. Continuum of care model. (Copyright 1990, D. A. Deitch, Ph.D.)

for all of its participants, nor is any existing program suitable for all kinds of drug-dependent individuals . . . at this time it seems unlikely that a 'technological fix' will provide a complete answer to the complex psychosocial-biologic condition known as narcotic addiction" (14). In an outpatient clinic, for example, much staff effort is taken up by the most severely affected people. Those clients with more modest problems may be ignored. Conversely, if the staff concentrates on those with modest problems, the most severely affected clients may be underserved.

A broad base of learning for practitioners dealing with substance abuse must therefore include an understanding and appreciation of the continuum of care available to any client. Figure 79.1 offers a schematic view of some of the possible responses available in a continuum of care approach. Curricula for substance abuse training programs should cover a broad spectrum, from law enforcement to prevention to education to intervention to after-school programs to day-care programs to family care programs. This information should cover the following topics: theories of drug dependence and addiction; historical, cultural, social, and biological implications; what types of treatment are available; the pros and cons of each type of treatment; how to care for clients without bias; and how to determine the most suitable treatment for each client. The Institute of Medicine of the National Academy of Science in its Substance Abuse Coverage study included a comprehensive list of treatment types available today (15). Aspects of this list (Table 79.1) can help serve as part of a basic overview curriculum for the content of substance abuse training.

What Kind of Training for What Kind of Treatment?

Many community and political leaders, as well as some treatment practitioners, believe that each new drug that makes its way through the culture means that there is a brand new problem with which to deal. According to this belief, cocaine treatment requires special skills, "ice" (smokable amphetamine) treatment requires special skills, PCP treatment requires special skills. If this were so, then a massive new approach would need to be created from scratch each time a new drug made its appearance—a draining, difficult endeavor.

Generally, however, it has been proven that the same skills and approaches are functionally applicable to any and all drug use (16). What is required is a familiarity with the particular language and nomenclature surrounding a particular drug, along with knowledge of the unique or sexual/romantic colorations associated with that drug. In addition, each drug does have short-lived, specific information regarding physiological responses. Those who treat drug abuse must be informed about these particulars, but it is erroneous to believe that a whole new industry must crop up to treat each new drug (17). As such, most existing treatment models and methodologies have proved effective with people who are in trouble with drugs, regardless of the particular drug. What is required, however, is sensitivity to social, cultural, and unique pharmacological issues related to each drug.

Basic Concepts of Training

Successful training in drug abuse is predicated on certain fundamental theories. These basic ideas permeate any and all specific parts of the curriculum. They serve the dual purpose of being both immediately applicable to the training setting and to the workplace.

1. Personal responsibility: Methods that help mobilize the individual impulse toward health, despite personal and environmental obstacles
2. Self-help: Technology whereby both individuals and groups can become effective in coping and problem solving on an ongoing basis
3. Social systems perspective: Information that stresses practitioners' awareness of the interdependence of individuals and their social environment and provides for richer assessments and increased alternatives for intervention

Table 79.1   Basic Overview Curriculum for the Content of Substance Abuse Training

Outpatient non-methadone treatment (OPNM)
  What is OPNM?
  Theories
  Private versus group practice
  How well does OPNM work?
  When and why does OPNM treatment fail?
  Costs and benefits
Detoxification (medical and social)
  History
  Process
  How well does detoxification work?
  When and why does detoxification fail?
  Costs and benefits
Other therapy models
  Psychotherapy
  Supportive counseling
  Rational emotive therapy
  Cognitive behavioral approaches such as relapse prevention
Chemical dependency treatment (CD)
  What is CD?
  How well does CD work?
  When and why does CD fail?
  Costs and benefits
Therapeutic communities (TCs)
  What is a TC?
  History, operating principles, and methodologies
  How well do TCs work?
  When and why do TCs fail?
  Costs and benefits
Methadone maintenance
  Theories
  How well does it work?
  When and why does it fail?
  Costs and benefits
Social Model
  What is the Social Model?
  History, operating principles, and methodologies
  How well does the Social Model work?
  When and why does the Social Model fail?
  Cost and benefits
Correctional treatment programs
  History
  Examples and models
  The California Civil Addict Program
  "Boot" camps
  A variety of therapeutic community in-prison programs (Stayin' Out, Phoenix House, Amity, etc.)
  General conclusions about prison treatment
Needs and issues of special populations
  Pregnant women
  Adolescents
  Parents and children
  Dual diagnosis
  HIV and AIDS patients
  Disabled patients
  Cultural sensitivity

4. Social support: Methods for creating and/or using helping networks that can enhance the functioning of individuals and help maintain change
5. Transdisciplinary practice: Skills and attitudes that prepare practitioners from different disciplines to collaborate in "whole person" responses in planning, goal setting, and problem solving
6. Systematic problem solving: Goal-oriented perspective that recognizes a common systemic and empirical process of stages and strategies that can be applied in assessing and treating problems at the individual, family, community, and societal levels
7. Interorganizational relations: Concepts and perspectives relevant to understanding the forces that shape service-delivery systems
8. Cooperative learning: Concepts and techniques to enhance self-esteem, acquisition of knowledge, and prevention of drug use (18, 19)

Skill Enhancement

While the inclusion of general information about the context of drug abuse treatment and models is essential to training, it must be accompanied by skill development—pragmatic techniques that help practitioners perform their jobs better. For those people fighting in the trenches of drug abuse treatment programs on a day-to-day basis, this necessity to do a better job becomes of the utmost importance. The job can be so challenging and difficult that many practitioners yearn for magic solutions—answers, theories, or step-by-step directions—that can make their job less trying and more effective. More often than not, clients act out, regress, misbehave, deny problems, try to run away from treatment, have crazy families, and act irresponsibly. Those who work with them often look for formula answers to reassure them and diminish understandable anxiety, as they also work in a climate that often makes the job harder by demands for excessive bureaucratic compliance to various funding agency monitor demands.

Because of these complex demands, skill enhancement for drug treatment personnel essentially can be divided into two categories. The first category concerns skills demanded by the funding and oversight agencies, who require ever more accurate and specific reporting mechanisms and management systems. Practitioners who are overloaded with paperwork simply cannot perform as effectively with clients. In light of this, many training candidates need specific organizational information, such as how to keep clinical records, how to track client activities, and how to track management activities. Mastery of these skills can prove a great relief to those in daily contact with drug addicts. This was true in 1979 and remains relevant in the 1990s (11).

The second category of skills needed by treatment personnel in the field includes the neglected art of specific case management skills, as well as treatment planning, case note making, and assessment skills. These skills are all part of the practitioner's main concern: How to improve one's ability to do the required paperwork and still successfully treat the client? Some of the ground that needs to be covered in this area of clinical skill enhancement includes answers to the following questions:

1. How do I engage the client on a personal level?
2. How do I interview a client?
3. What are the varying levels of resistance and how do I get through them?
4. How do I determine the severity of my client's symptoms and indications?
5. How do I assess my client's criminal background, social background, family background, psychological background, and academic background?
6. How do I assess my client's unique and special family, job, living, or environmental resources?
7. How do I interview the client's parent(s)?
8. What mode of treatment should I involve the client in (residential, day care, outpatient care, hospitalization, etc.)?
9. How do I enable the client to change his or her behavior?
10. How do I assist the family in understanding the client's problem?
11. How do I help the family change in ways that support the client's new behavior?
12. How do I get the client invested in his or her treatment and outcome?
13. How do the client and I set the orientation for treatment?
14. How do I confront the client?
15. What specific skills do I need to function in an induction group as opposed to a behavior change group, as opposed to a therapy group, as opposed to an individual counseling group?
16. How do I help my client identify short-term, achievable goals, while maintaining a long-term plan for recovery?
17. How can my client and I create enduring and meaningful behaviors that promote change?

Training Populations

Within any particular training model, there should also be unique program training approaches. These special programs must be relevant not only to emerging problems (such as AIDS, child abuse, needs of women with children, sexuality, and homelessness), but must accommodate those particular populations likely to seek training, such as workers in mental health, social welfare, drug and alcohol treatment, health, corrections, and education. Each of these populations needs basic substance abuse treatment information, as well as job unique information. Figure 79.2. below shows a basic curriculum with corresponding practitioner needs. In this updated matrix, motivational interviewing and cue extinction have been added, and additional curriculum items have been assigned to each group. In addition to this basic information, a curriculum for mental health practitioners (psychiatrists, psychologists, social workers, psychiatric nurses, and related mental health workers) should include material relating to chronic and acute mental illness, as well as developmentally disabled and brain-injured clients. Social welfare curriculum (for those practitioners in public social services and nonprofit voluntary agencies) should include information about child and family welfare, poverty, aging, community-based care, and community development. Health workers who directly address the emotional and living needs of people with serious medical and degenerative conditions (including AIDS, cancer, and Alzheimer's disease) require knowledge about death and dying, coping with chronic disabilities, maintaining extrainstitutional relationships, and providing opportunities for continuing social contributions.

CORE CURRICULUM
Who Should Receive What Training

CORE CURRICULUM	CORE ALLIED PROFESSIONALS	HEALTH PROFESSIONALS	SOCIAL WELFARE	EDUCATORS/CLASSROOM	FAMILY THERAPISTS	PSYCHOLOGISTS	MENTAL HEALTH PROFESSIONALS	CORRECTIONS OFFICERS	PARENTS	COMMUNITY MEMBERS
Contextual Issues										
History of Drug Abuse	X	X	X	X	X	X	X	X		
History of Treatment	X	X	X		X	X	X	X		
Cultural Issues	X	X	X	X	X	X	X	X		
Client Profiles	X	X	X	X	X	X	X	X		
Continuum of Care										
Treatment Models	X	X	X	X	X	X	X	X	X	X
Referral Systems	X	X	X	X	X	X	X	X		
Support Systems	X	X	X		X	X	X	X	X	X
Case Management										
Initial Evaluation	X	X	X		X		X			
Psychosocial Evaluation	X		X		X		X			
Treatment Planning	X		X		X	X	X			
Case Notes	X		X							
Skill Enhancement										
Interview Skills	X	X	X		X		X			
Motivational Interviewing	X	X	X		X		X			
Identifying Resistance	X	X			X	X	X	X		
Client Engagement	X	X	X	X	X	X	X	X		
Contingency Contracting	X		X	X	X	X	X	X		
Confrontation	X	X	X		X	X	X	X		
Supportive Coercion	X		X		X	X	X	X		
One-to-One Counseling	X	X	X		X		X			
Group Skills										
Behavior Change Groups	X		X		X	X	X	X	X	X
Orientation or Induction Groups	X		X		X	X	X			
Static Groups	X		X		X	X	X			
Gender Groups	X		X		X	X	X			
Marathon Groups	X		X		X	X				
Special Treatment Issues										
Relapse Prevention	X		X		X	X	X	X	X	X
Cue Extinction	X		X		X	X	X			
12-Step Programs (AA/ACOA/etc.)	X	X	X	X	X	X		X	X	X
AIDS	X	X	X	X	X	X	X	X	X	X
Pharmacology	X	X	X							
Dual Diagnosis	X				X		X			
ETOH Alcohol	X	X	X		X	X	X	X		
Psychiatric	X	X	X		X	X	X	X		
Physically Handicapped	X	X	X		X	X	X	X		
Family Treatment Issues										
Engagement	X		X	X	X	X	X	X		
Confronting Denial	X		X		X	X	X	X		
Eliciting Active Support	X	X	X	X	X	X	X	X	X	X
Systems Theory	X		X		X					
Transdisciplinary Teambuilding	X	X	X	X	X	X	X	X		
Prevention Skills										
Early Intervention	X	X	X	X	X	X		X	X	X
Alternative to Suspension	X		X	X			X			
Community Organization	X		X		X	X		X	X	X
Program Development	X		X		X	X		X	X	X

Figure 79.2. Core curriculum design.

Participants from public and private institutions that treat drug and alcohol abuse need material about engagement, recruitment, retention, assessment, inpatient and outpatient treatment, differentiation between adult and adolescent treatment, as well as school and community prevention programs.

Inasmuch as these drug and alcohol treatment practitioners often emanate from two uniquely different learning settings—academia or personal treatment experience—their curriculum also needs to emphasize exposure that provides a contrast to this background. As such, those from academic settings need exposure to the benefits of raw emotion and the expression of feeling. Equally, those from a treatment experience background need intel-lectual exposure to the benefits of understanding rationale and theory underlying their often emotional individual and group counseling experiences.

Competencies

Compare the Core Curriculum matrix (Fig. 79.2) with the Addiction Counselor Competencies (Fig. 79.3). These competencies were developed by the National Curriculum Review Committee of the federally funded Addiction Training Center Program with input from various national organizations, including NDAC, ICRC, and members of the APA Proficiency De-

Addiction Counselor Competencies

Highlights of the Addiction Counselor Competencies Developed by the Curriculum Review Committee of the Addiction Training Center Program

Foundations for Addiction Professionals
Understanding Addiction
Treatment Knowledge
Application to Practice
Professional Readiness

Clinical Evaluation
Screening
Assessment

Treatment Planning
Assessment Information and Findings
Client Needs and Readiness
Outcomes and Strategies
Treatment Matching
Treatment Plan Development and Reassessment

Referral
Assessment and Evaluation of Referral Resources
Self-Referral vs. Counselor Referral
Matching Referrals to Client Needs
Information Exchange

Case Management
Implementing the Treatment Plan
Consulting
Continuing Assessment and Treatment Planning
Counseling
   Individual Counseling
   Group Counseling
   Counseling for Families, Couples, and Intimate Dyads

Client, Family, and Community Education
Education Programs
Cultural Identification, Ethnicity, Age, and Gender Issues
Principles and Philosophies of Prevention, Treatment, Relapse, and Recovery
Health and Behavioral Problems
Basic Life Skills

Documentation
Client Record Management
Client Rights to Privacy and Confidentiality
Screening, Intake, and Assessment Reports
Treatment Plans and Progress Reports
Discharge Summary/Treatment Outcome Documentation

Professional and Ethical Responsibilities
Ethical Behaviors
Federal and State Laws, Agency Regulations
Counseling and Addictions Research
Individual Differences

Inquiries or requests for copies of the Competencies may be directed to:
California Addiction Training Center, 9500 Gilman Drive, Department 0980, La Jolla, California 92093-0980

Figure 79.3. Addiction Counselor Competencies

velopment Group. They describe the knowledge, skills, and attitudes that characterize competent and effective practice in addictions counseling and provide a comprehensive description of training outcomes that can be achieved through various educational strategies. The Foundations for Addiction Professionals include the knowledge and attitudes that form the basis of competent care across all health care disciplines. The competencies are divided among eight primary functions: Clinical Evaluation, Treatment Planning, Referral, Case Management, Client, Family, and Community Education, Documentation, and Professional and Ethical Responsibilities.

In the spring of 1995 Jerry Adams of the Northwest Frontier Addiction Training Center, with the assistance of treatment providers in the states of Oregon and Washington, conducted a study using the curriculum outline prepared by the National Curriculum Review Committee. An important aspect of the study was the ranking of competencies for entry level addiction counselors by agency supervisors.

The supervisors rated professional ethics as the most important competency. Two of the highest rated competencies dealt directly with ethics. The top ranked competency was, "Understand the addiction professional's obligation to adhere to generally accepted ethical and behavioral standards of conduct in the helping relationship." The competency ranked third was, "Demonstrate ethical behaviors by adhering to established professional codes of ethics that define the professional context within which the counselor works in order to maintain professional standards and safeguard the client." The protection of client privacy and confidentiality, which certainly has ethical implications, also ranked high in the list of competencies.

The second kind of competency rated high by agency supervisors described the basic professional-client relationship: "Establish a helping relationship with the client characterized by warmth, respect, genuineness, concreteness, and empathy." The ability to establish this necessary and fundamental relationship is not simply a matter of knowledge, but also a function of personal qualities. The same qualification applies to ethics as well.

Another highly rated competency was "Adhere to federal and state laws, and agency regulations, regarding AOD [alcohol and drug] treatment." Supervisors want entry level addiction counselors to know, understand, and follow governmental regulations regarding treatment of clients. This kind of knowledge is easily taught, but compliance with regulations lies with the personal qualities of the professional and the supervision of the agency.

The National Curriculum Review Committee is now presently at work developing the knowledge, skill, and attitude for every component of each competency. That book will be available next year and will be an important resource for educators, trainers, and consumers. Readers will understand what it is exactly that they need to learn, what skills they need to acquire, and what attitude they need to be most effective.

Clearly, curriculum priorities must be based on the actual work situation rather than on an academic conception of the domain knowledge defined by a professional role. While physiological knowledge is useful and relevant, courses for entry level addiction specialists who are already employed in the field should begin with ethics and the other areas of competency identified by the supervisors. This knowledge of highest priority would be applicable immediately and would have been taught regardless of whether or not a trainee took any more courses in the field (20).

TRAINING PHILOSOPHY
Training Adult Learners

Adults are a special group of learners, requiring special adult education concepts to maximize learning. They perceive of themselves as responsible, self-directing, independent persons. They demand that the instructor accept him or her as such. Resistance to learning solidifies under conditions that are not in keeping with this concept of self-direction. The best approach to teaching adults is to view training as a planned, sequential process designed to provide the self-awareness, skills, knowledge, and attitudes needed to perform particular tasks.

This is not to say that instructors will not make some decisions for trainees. Whenever possible, trainees should be responsible for suggestions regarding training content and design. This increases feelings of "owner-

ship" and fosters personal engagement with the training. The most effective training for adults is designed with the following points in mind:

1. A climate of mutual respect must exist between trainer and trainees.
2. An open, friendly, and casual atmosphere facilitates the exchange of differing viewpoints and ideas.
3. Trainees should be aided in diagnosing their own skills and growth needs, as well as in analyzing the specific training elements needed by their agency.
4. Adult learners learn best that which is relevant and useful to them. "Here and now" problems should be the focus of training. Whenever possible, training ideas should be applied to current work situations. The emphasis should always be on illustrating new concepts as they relate to the life and work experiences drawn from the trainees (21).

Creating a Receptive Training Climate

According to Goldstein, the "training process is defined as the systematic acquisition of skills, rules, concepts, or attitudes that result in improved performance in the work environment" (22). Successful training, however, is not possible unless learners are receptive to the skills, rules, concepts, and attitudes presented. There are several considerations that go into creating an open-minded, fruitful training setting: overall tone and climate, geographic location, and class composition.

To begin with, the tone and climate of training sessions are crucial. People hear information in different ways, at different points in their lives, depending on its relevance to their own experience. The first challenge of training is to elicit an investment in the training itself. This investment must come, not only from those undergoing training, but from the managers, directors, and administrators in the environments from which the trainees come. One way in which to elicit investment at the actual time of training is to discuss the many different perspectives among the trainees at the beginning of any training effort. Furthermore, it is useful to discuss the value of these differences in creative process and problem solving and to explain that the training will by necessity present the very divergent views of those attending. From this, it is possible to create a desire among attendees to think about the potential benefits of these differing perspectives heard from others. Finally, it is critical for these trainees to have a determining voice in what they want to learn more about.

From a training point of view, this early intellectual activity has the effect of engaging people in the training. Requiring early, active participation in the training increases the emotional readiness for new experiences and reduces anxiety so that hearing can occur. Much depends on the group itself—how they define what they need (based on their experiences) to improve their competence. In the larger sense, this activity, of course, models tactics and procedures that will be useful in treatment: negotiating differences, making an investment, and determining options. Learning is drastically increased when people feel that they have some control over what and how they learn (23).

Bandura's work in self-efficacy validates this practical notion that people will take in information in which they have a determining voice, information that they find useful, and information that they can successfully apply to their particular work situation (24). According to theories on sustaining new behaviors (e.g., Skinner, Bandura, and Newsome), people's beliefs about how much control they have in a setting determine how much effort they will mobilize for that activity, how long they will persevere in the face of difficulties and setbacks, whether their thoughts on the subject are positive or negative, and the amount of stress they experience in coping with the experience.

To foster an active learning atmosphere, work is done to establish the concept of sharing information, in terms of both talking and listening. Ensuring a balance between the receiving and giving of information permits learners to share what they know without fear of failure. It also increases their skills as both dispensers and collectors of information. With information flowing in both directions, no one can take a passive stance. This promotes a dynamic learning environment (23).

Trainers often quote the ancient Chinese folk proverb that if you hear something, you remember it. If you hear it and read it, you remember it a little longer, but if you hear it, read it, and practice it, you will retain it—providing it works for you. Because of this, arranging the curriculum so that students can hear, see, discuss, practice, and receive feedback throughout the training period has proved meaningful to trainees (25). An added benefit is that these activities ensure that any difficulties leading to potential failure will be identified and addressed early so that corrections can result in success.

One of the aspects of any teaching setting that can have a negative effect on outcome is resistance. The successful handling of such resistance is another facet in eliciting an investment in learning. Here again, there is a rich opportunity to demonstrate—both explicitly and implicitly—the handling of a problem within the training process that is a major concern of most attendees. Furthermore, by using concepts found in the short-term therapy systems literature, it is possible to very quickly call attention to many forms of unconscious resistance. Sifnos describes this use of active and explicit drawing of attention to resistances as it is used in short-term anxiety provoking therapy, as well as in the use of recapitulation and problem solving (26). Similarly, eliciting their own types of resistance from attendees makes them both aware of and alert to such resistance, and it models the types of resistance they will most likely encounter in their clients. In this case, the training process often illuminates content.

Logistics and Atmosphere

In any training plan, the site location—such as geography—can also have a surprising influence on outcome. For some, instruction seems to be most effective when it is done physically close to home or people's work site. For others, leaving the normal work environment and traveling to unfamiliar surroundings for training has a bracing effect. In the absence of supervisors and peers, these individuals may feel less inhibited about disclosing certain problems and questions and more free to receive new information and ideas. Needs assessment prior to training can help determine what might work for a particular trainee or group of trainees.

Finally, class composition is a determining factor in the creation of a successful training climate. There are advantages to both homogeneous and heterogeneous groupings. People from similar disciplines have the following advantages when training together:

1. They can practice skills relevant to their particular methodology, because they are familiar with the treatment model and its context.
2. They can offer relevant feedback and problem solving ideas appropriate to their unique setting.
3. If the trainees already work together every day, problems characteristic of their system can be addressed in training in ways that are impossible in a day-to-day setting.
4. People who already know and work with each other can study, practice skills, and work together as teams in ways that they can carry directly to the workplace.

Trainees from different backgrounds, on the other hand, can benefit greatly from a classroom situation in which people come from various disciplines, as follows:

1. They may feel freer to ask questions.
2. They may feel important because they can offer a unique perspective from their setting.
3. They can hear how others handle similar problems in different settings.
4. Work problems will not cloud their ability to learn.
5. They may bypass power struggles that often exist in a homogeneous group that works together from day to day.

Some recent realizations have occurred about how to mix groups in a training activity. An example of this is the distinctions of need and the distinctions of perception as held by people who work in non-profit community-based treatment versus for-profit commercial treatment versus providers from the public care sector. As we look at some of their unique needs for problem resolution and their interaction with community agencies, we recognize that content alone is not enough. Appreciation must be developed for different goals, different views of client care, and different views of what

support for the client is as mandated by law or as obligated in the transaction between the welfare recipient and the provider of welfare resources.

Specific Training Goals

While each trainer will have his or her curriculum—partially standardized to present the history of drug abuse treatments and partially tailored to the training population—all training programs should be constructed around the following training goals. These goals relate not to basic philosophical concepts but to pragmatic, specific outcomes of training.

1. Increased awareness on the part of trainees in regard to the particular values, attitudes, and emotions that influence their work behavior. This includes an awareness of how their behavior affects others and how the behavior of others affects them.
2. Increased understanding of the ethics, subculture, sexual, generational, and socioeconomic differences that influence their attitudes, values, and behaviors.
3. Increased verbal and nonverbal communications skills obtained through analysis of body language, the use of fantasy, and other innovative techniques.
4. A basic understanding of group dynamics. This includes the ability to function well in different types of groups (e.g., encounter groups, task groups, staff groups). It also includes a knowledge of appropriate and inappropriate group leader-member interactions and specific skills for working in a variety of group settings.
5. A broad base of knowledge about drug abuse prevention, treatment, and control. Trainees will be able to draw on this knowledge in their worksite planning, problem solving, in-house training, and consulting.

Successful Training Methods

It is important for training sessions to include a mix of training methods. This counters boredom and acknowledges the fact that different people learn in different ways. Some of the tried and true methods used in successful training are described here.

Critical to each of these training methods are written and/or oral commitments to action on the part of the trainees.

1. Didactic presentations. The history of drug abuse and treatment approaches is best presented in lecture format, as is theoretical and organizational material on groups, counseling principles, program planning, etc.
2. Small groups. The small group as a learning tool has as its theoretical underpinning the assumption that individuals learn best in a group structure that demands interdependence. This interdependence heightens self-awareness and awareness of others.
3. Large groups. Large groups are the most appropriate setting for brainstorming, process observations, daily training program evaluation, action planning, homework, reading, and practice.
4. Simulation and role playing. These theatrical techniques bring problems to life and demonstrate vividly how trainees can effectively respond in new and useful ways. They can be a dramatic means of revealing other people's points of view and of uncovering one's own misconceptions and misjudgments.
5. Task groups. The task group has as its purpose the completion of clearly defined work. The work at hand should be based on real tasks from the trainees' work sites. Some possible task group work may be identifying problems, solving problems, and collecting data.
6. Videotape. Videotape is an effective learning tool for isolating and identifying behaviors that trainees may be unaware of, in both individuals and group dynamics.

CONCLUSION: CONCERNS ON THE HORIZON

Certification Standards

Certifications and licensure vary from state to state; some states having multiple certifying bodies and other states having only one. Someone certified to practice as a drug abuse counselor in Florida may not be able to practice to the standard in Hawaii. Clearly, the coming challenge is the development of a minimum standard to which all states and certifying groups could ascribe. This could be best accomplished with the National Addiction Training Center system providing the guidance as they already have with the Addiction Counselor Competencies described earlier, and utilizing the Knowledge, Skills, and Attitudes (KSA) for Addiction Professionals the National Curriculum Review Committee is currently developing. This can then perhaps lead to the generation of a minimum evaluation process that could ensure some form of standardization throughout the country.

While there are many degreed people, the major core of treatment personnel continues to be people who arrived there as a result of their own treatment and recovery experience. The backbone of public care and its minimum cost—which is attractive to managed care—continues to rest on the back of the nondegreed person in recovery. These people need the opportunity to gain the training, sophistication, and broadening that will allow them to become better practitioners.

Finally, there will be increasing numbers of people who will seek certification both within the corrections system and within the public welfare service system. Certainly, what has also transpired is that each of the disciplines has come up with proficiencies related to their discipline; for example, the American Psychological Association now has a set of proficiencies. Social work is almost finished with theirs; marriage, family, and child counselors also are developing a set. There is no question that very separate disciplines are moving, even if on parallel paths (many of these paths are beginning to converge) to the benefit of the field. This movement will result in not only better practitioners but with certification that will allow them to remain competitive in a managed care climate. In response to the managed care company's need for licensure or certification, practitioners will bring the values and outcomes of the treatment models they represent as well as the economic considerations of a nation facing serious health costs crisis.

Managed Care

A major shift in how health care is being delivered has occurred with the rapid onset of managed care firms being asked to deliver care to public alcohol and drug populations. Practitioners must learn how to provide services within the context of demands from the managed care umbrella and their concern with ensuring close review of all patient services with preferences toward outpatient and short duration services.

International Cultural Concerns

Countries in transition—from communist socialist block to capitalist—are experiencing huge epidemics of amphetamine and heroin use. Some of the complications are found in terms of culture, ethnicity, and the need for sensitivity to these issues. This is especially true in the Balkans where people are migrating from one country to another with biases about their history, religions, and/or backgrounds. The impact on the providers in treating those people of different backgrounds has been enormous. Generic appreciation for diversity, culture, and the ability to be sensitive is recognized now as an important and discrete training event in addition to its integration in other training activities.

Treatment in the Prison Setting

Finally, we cannot overlook the national trend to both incarcerate drug users relevant to drug and other offenses and to incarcerate offenders for longer and longer periods of time. There is finally recognition that providing treatment in the prison setting reduces recidivism. This significant data—which is very promising about in-prison therapeutic community approaches in particular—and their outcomes are very important and significant, especially if the potential of continued care exists for at least 3–6 months in the community upon discharge.

As such we have created another category of training for practitioners in this field: the ability to work within the prison setting and to work with an increased number of antisocial personalities. The necessity to become familiar with the criteria for antisocial personality disorder and the possibility of engagement with psychopathic individuals has increased the need for clinical skills around diagnosis and assessment. It is also important to develop increased sensitivity to the different cultures present in a prison, both of the inmates and of the personnel that bring the prison's primary mission of safety and security to realization.

References

1. Deitch DA. The end of the beginning: dilemmas of the paraprofessional in current drug abuse treatment. J Community Altern 1974:August.
2. Minkoff K. Resistance of mental health professionals to working with the chronic mentally ill. In: Meyerson AT, ed. Barriers to treating the chronic mentally ill. San Francisco: Jossey-Bass, 1987.
3. Courtright D. A century of American narcotic policy. Vol. 2. Treating drug problems, papers to the Committee for the Substance Abuse Coverage Study, Institute of Medicine. Washington, DC: National Academy Press, 1990.
4. Schnick D. Ideal and reality in field education: provocatory dilemmas and practical solutions. Paper presented at the Annual Program Meeting of Council on Social Work Education, Atlanta, GA, March, 1988.
5. Kolb L. Drug addiction: a medical problem. Springfield, IL: Charles C Thomas, 1962.
6. Mower H. The mental health professional and mutual self-help programs: Co-option or collaboration. In: Garlner A, Riesman F, eds. Self help revolution. New York: Human Services Press, 1980.
7. De Leon G, Wexler HK, Jainchill N. The therapeutic community: success and improvement rate five years after treatment. Int J Addict 1982;17:703–747.
8. Dole VP, Nyswander MA. Medical treatment of diacetylmorphine (heroin) addiction. JAMA 1965;193:646.
9. De Leon G. Program-based evaluation research in therapeutic communities. NIDA Res Monogr 1984;51:69–87.
10. Deitch D, Casriel D. The role of the ex-addict in the treatment of addictions. Fed Probation 1967:December.
11. Denby RF. Developments in training. In: Dupont RL, Goldstein A, O'Donnel J, eds. Handbook on drug abuse. Rockville, MD: National Institute of Drug Abuse, 1979.
12. Selin JoA, Svanum S. Alcoholism and substance abuse training: a survey of graduate programs in clinical psychology. Yeshiva U Ferkauf Grad Sch Psychol 1981;12(6):717–721.
13. Ewan CE, Whaite A. Training health professionals in substance abuse: a review. Int J Addict 1982;17(7):1211–1229.
14. Kleber HD. Treatment of narcotic addicts. Psychiatr Med 1985;3(4):389–418.
15. Gerstein DR, Harwood H, eds. Treating drug problems. Washington, DC: Committee for the Substance Abuse Coverage Study, National Institute of Medicine, National Academy Press, 1990.
16. Hubbard RL, Rachal JV, Craddock SG, Cavanaugh ER. Treatment outcome perspectives study (TOPS): client characteristics and behavior before, during, and after treatment. NIDA Res Monogr 1984;51:42–68.
17. Sells SB, Simpson DD, Joe GW, Demaree RG, Savage LJ, Lloyd MR. A national follow-up study to evaluate the effectiveness of drug abuse treatment: a report on Cohort I of the DARP five years later. Am J Drug Alcohol Abuse 1976: 3(4):545–556.
18. Deitch D. Training material. Berkeley, CA: Daytop International Associates Training Institutes, 1989.
19. Knowles M, Malcom S. Innovations in teaching styles and approaches based upon adult learning. J Educ Soc Work 1972;8(2):32–39.
20. Skager R. An evaluation of dedicated courses for addiction counselors and recovery specialists. La Jolla, CA: California Addiction Training Center, 1995.
21. Kolb DA. Experiential learning: experience as the source of learning and development. Englewood Cliffs, NJ: Prentice-Hall, 1984.
22. Gillman IL, Goldstein P. Training systems in the year 2000. Am Psychol 1989;3:134.
23. Zenke R, Gundler J. Twenty-eight techniques for transforming training into practice. Training 1985; April:53.
24. Bandura A. Perceived self-efficacy: exercise self control through self belief. The Sixth Walter V. Clarke Memorial Lecture. Providence, RI: Brown University, November, 1985:18.
25. Edwards G. Reports to U.S. Department of Education, National Training Institute, NE Regional Training Center. Garden City, NY: Adelphi University, 1981:1988–1989.
26. Sifnos PE. Short-term dynamic psychotherapy evaluation and techniques. 2nd edition. New York: Plenum Press, 1987.

80 FORENSICS

Milton Earl Burglass

This chapter is intended as an introduction and practical guide to forensic practice for the specialist in addiction medicine. Because of the enormous breadth and depth of both the clinical and legal materials relevant to forensic practice, the following discussion is necessarily a synoptic overview, further limited in focus to criminal, rather than civil, legal proceedings. The effects of the specific intoxicants on cognition, emotion, and behavior are thoroughly presented elsewhere in this volume. A comprehensive analysis of the relevant legal rules, doctrines, and principles; the evolution of the insanity defense; a detailed medical-legal discussion of significant cases; and a comparative analysis of the relevant federal and state laws are clearly beyond the scope of this chapter. The urgent conceptual problems arising from the interaction between the law and addiction medicine are highlighted throughout the discussion. References to primary legal sources, textbooks, reviews, and commentaries are provided for the interested reader.

The first section summarizes the fundamental legal principles and procedures governing expert testimony about the "mental" elements in the criminal law. The second section examines the potential roles for the addiction expert in criminal proceedings. The third section discusses the relevance of the effects of intoxicant use on criminal responsibility—considering both defenses and mitigation based on intoxication, dependence, and withdrawal. (For heuristic purposes, unless otherwise qualified, the term "intoxicant" refers herein to "substances," i.e., drugs.)

The fourth section explores the issues raised by the "addictive processes," focusing on pathological gambling. The fifth section considers the grave problem of the credibility of the testimony of intoxicant involved witnesses. The final section discusses intoxicant-related issues in regulatory and administrative matters, emphasizing the implications of the problematic concept of "impairment" and the regulatory problems of long-term opioid therapy in private practice.

THE ADDICTION MEDICINE SPECIALIST AS A FORENSIC EXPERT

Clinical Experts in the Criminal Law

The participation of specialists in addiction medicine as experts in forensic matters (civil and criminal) is a comparatively recent development that reflects the development of the accredited specialty of addiction medicine over the past 10 years and the courts' longstanding disenchantment with the testimony of traditional mental health experts in these matters. Historically, psychiatrists, psychologists, and other mental health professionals have provided expert testimony about the mental and/or physical factors (including intoxicant use) affecting an individual's emotion, cognition, and behavior. Although these professionals continue to testify about the effects of intoxicant use, increasingly, attorneys are preferentially seeking specialists in addiction medicine for consultation and expert testimony in such cases. This change is the result of three factors: (*a*) the stormy and problematic relationship of psychiatry and the law; (*b*) the conceptual fragmentation and factionalism in the traditional mental health disciplines; and (*c*) the emergence of a body of "facts" in the specialty of addiction medicine, about which there is little or no difference of opinion in the field. Burglass and Shaffer have analyzed and critiqued the state of knowledge, including theory, research, and practice, in the addictions field (1–5).

Being Qualified as an Expert

Determining who should be an expert witness for "psychological" matters has been a difficult task for the courts. Although there are federal and state standards that govern expert testimony, there is little consistency between and within jurisdictions about the qualifications of expert witnesses. Often, decisions regarding who qualifies as an "expert" are made on pragmatic rather than jurisprudential grounds.

With rare exceptions, psychiatrists, physicians who specialize in mental (neurologic and psychologic) disorders, and doctoral level clinical psychologists are qualified as experts. However, some courts have permitted (or precluded) a wide range of individuals, including case workers (6, 7), police officers (8–10), and even lay witnesses (11, 12), to testify about a variety of psychological issues (including the question of sanity). Other courts have been unwilling to recognize the expertise of psychiatrists, physicians, psychologists, and others, and have refused to admit their testimony in selected matters. Examples include compulsive gambling (13, 14), the effects of drugs on witness credibility (15, 16), and satanic ritual murder (17). Although professional associations in psychiatry (18) and psychology (19) have developed guidelines for determining forensic expertise and practice, these criteria have not been adopted as authoritative by the courts. For the most part, courts have been reluctant to admit psychological evidence tending to favor an accused (20). For a comprehensive review of the determination and utilization of expertise in mental matters in the federal and state jurisdictions see Moriarty (21, §2:2–11).

Rationale for the Admission of Expert Testimony

Most states have a rule of evidence that parallels the Federal Rule of Evidence 702, which provides that "[I]f scientific, technical, or other specialized knowledge will assist the trier of fact [judge or jury] to understand the evidence or to determine a fact in issue, a witness qualified as an expert by knowledge, skill, experience, training, or education, may testify thereto in the form of an opinion or otherwise" (22). But a few states have adopted different and confusing rules on this point. The states also have tended to follow the Federal Rule of Evidence 704, which limits expert testimony to an explanation of the defendant's diagnosis and the characteristics of the disease or defect. This rule specifically precludes expert opinion on "whether the defendant did or did not have the mental state or condition constituting an element of the crime charged or of a defense thereto" (22). This question (referred to in the law as the "ultimate issue") is for the jury to decide. Despite the prevailing rules of evidence, the final decision regarding expertise and the admissibility of expert testimony is made by the trial judge (13, 14, 23–26).

In practice, if you can provide satisfactory evidence of knowledge, skill, experience, or training in the diagnosis and/or treatment (but *not* mere research) of intoxicant-involved patients, it is likely that you will be recognized by the court as an expert in the areas of addiction and the effects of intoxicants. Although qualified as an expert by the court, the admissibility of your testimony into evidence is a separate question to be argued by counsel. Ultimately, all decisions regarding the qualification of experts and the admissibility of their testimony are made at the discretion of the trial judge (27–31).

How the Law Views Expert Testimony

Under prevailing rules of evidence, the testimony of expert witnesses is presented to the court in the form of expert *opinion,* and as such it does not enjoy the same privileged status as "fact" testimony. It remains for the trier of fact (judge or jury) to evaluate the credibility, reliability, relevance, and applicability of any expert testimony introduced. What an expert in addiction medicine may know to be an accepted medical "fact" is nonetheless considered to be only "opinion" when expressed in expert testimony. As opinion, such information may be accepted, discounted, or rejected in whole or in part by the trier of fact. When testifying, any lapse of awareness of this crucial distinction may result in your being perceived as argumentative, defensive, sanctimonious, condescending, or hostile. This always compromises your credibility, undermines the power of your testimony as evidence, and may prove fatal to the client's case.

THE ROLE OF THE EXPERT IN ADDICTION MEDICINE

The following discussion may seem to express a defense bias, but bear in mind that it rarely serves the interest of the prosecution's case to introduce expert testimony in support of exculpating or mitigating mental defenses. Of course, the prosecution may call experts to rebut testimony introduced by defense experts. Although you are more likely to be engaged by the defense, you should be willing to appear for either side. Remember that as an expert witness you are not an advocate. Your professional mandate is to assist the court. You fulfill this responsibility by providing the judge and jury with information that is truthful, intelligible, and clear; and by offering opinions that are unbiased, carefully reasoned, and based on your understanding of the facts in evidence.

The Pretrial Phase

In the pretrial phase, the addiction specialist can assist the attorney by reviewing the initial discovery materials (e.g., police reports, arrest forms, affidavits of investigating agencies, waivers of rights, medical examiner reports, toxicology screens, statements of witnesses and/or the accused, confessions, the formal complaint, information, or indictment, etc.) to identify any immediate or potential issues related to intoxicants. Attorneys also may seek assistance in managing a difficult, compromised, or dangerous client. It may be necessary to immediately evaluate and refer the client for primary treatment or stabilization so that he or she can adequately assist counsel in the preparation of the case. Determination of competency to stand trial is a separate matter, both clinically and legally.

Once prospective witnesses have been identified, the addiction specialist should make a preliminary assessment of all available background materials to identify any possible clinical (i.e., medical, neuropsychiatric, or addiction) issues that require investigation. You can also help the attorney to prepare for depositions by (a) drafting specific questions to be posed, (b) doing content and psycholinguistic analyses of taped or written evidence (e.g., statements or depositions made by the defendant or witnesses), and (c) suggesting strategies and tactics for conducting interviews or depositions. It is often important to interview family members, friends, former teachers, or others who may have particular knowledge or a different perspective of the defendant or witness (32).

The cornerstone of your evaluation of the defendant is a comprehensive addiction history. You must aggressively inquire about every aspect of use and experience with intoxicants of all classes, and all of the addictive processes. You also must take a lifetime neuropsychiatric history, exploring every sign or symptom reported, suggested, implied, or suspected. Of course, complete medical (including *all* responses to prescription and over-the-counter medications), psychosocial, developmental, educational, relational, and vocational histories must be taken. History or indicia of psychological, sexual, or physical abuse also must be aggressively sought and explored.

During the pretrial phase you will work closely with the attorney. Your responsibility to the attorney is to identify, analyze, develop, and explain facts or issues relating to the use or effects of intoxicants. The attorney's responsibility to you is to analyze and explain the laws of the jurisdiction that (a) govern the nature and scope of admissible expert testimony, (b) define the required mental "elements of the offense" for the crime charged, and (c) determine the availability of defenses or mitigation based upon the use and/or effects of intoxicants. This interaction between the disciplines of law and medicine, unfettered by the legal rules of the courtroom, is invariably a stimulating and instructive experience for both the attorney and the addictionist. The collaboration will result in the formulation of potential clinical approaches to the defense of the case. In time, you and the attorney will agree upon a strategy for the clinical component of the defense and set the general contour of your testimony.

Once the clinical and legal issues are clarified and resolved, you should draft the actual questions that the attorney should ask you on direct examination. At the very least, you *must* frame the questions that establish your expertise and any questions required to elicit the predicate facts and issues to be introduced into evidence as the basis for your testimony and opinions. Although this is a tedious and time-consuming task, it cannot be done by the attorney. As the expert in addiction medicine, only you can fully appreciate the relevance and implications of the clinical subtleties and distinctions. Only you can identify and illuminate the clinical concepts likely to confuse the judge or jury. And only you can anticipate the pitfalls that loom on the narrow plateau of accommodation between the restrictive rules of legal discourse and the broad latitude required in complex clinical explanations. For an expert, there is no more frustrating or unsettling experience than being put or left in a compromised position on the witness stand as a result of having been asked ill-framed questions by an inadequately prepared attorney.

If the other side will be calling an addiction expert, you can assist your attorney by (a) evaluating that expert's credentials, (b) anticipating the nature of the testimony, (c) analyzing the strengths and weaknesses of both expert positions, and (d) drafting appropriate questions for your attorney to ask in cross-examination.

The Trial Phase

The two most common types of cases in which you will be engaged are those in which a person either is accused of having committed a crime while drug involved (i.e., while experiencing the acute, subacute, chronic, or residual effects of previous intoxicant use, dependence, or withdrawal), or is on trial as the result of statements made to law enforcement officers or testimony given by witnesses who themselves are or have been drug-involved. The first type of case typically requires testimony about the nature and effects of intoxicant use on the *defendant*. Common issues here include the impact of specific intoxicants on (a) the physical and mental ability to have committed the crime, (b) the state of mind required for the offense charged, or (c) the formation of the requisite intent. Other potential questions may involve the special issues of diminished capacity or insanity. The second type of case typically involves testimony about the effects of acute and/or chronic intoxicant use on cognition and memory, and how such use might affect the credibility of *witnesses*.

In some jurisdictions, the fact pattern of a specific case and/or the local rules may preclude an expert from commenting or offering an opinion on *any* aspect of the mental state of the defendant. Even in such circumstances, an addiction expert will usually be permitted to "assist the trier of fact" by giving the jury a basic education about the intoxicants involved in the case. Such a "mini-course" on intoxicants might include (a) general pharmacology; (b) modes, methods, patterns, and demographics of use; (c) interaction with antecedent or concurrent neuropsychiatric or medical conditions; and (d) specific effects on cognition, emotion, and behavior.

The Post-Conviction Phase

It is difficult to accept that defenses involving intoxicants usually do *not* prevail—even in cases where you believe that any colleague in the field would find the clinical evidence supportive of the defense position. It is always painful to lose a case in which you strongly believe. Longstanding biases in the criminal law, public opinion, and political factors often have greater influence on the outcome of a case than does the clinical evidence. Realize that most of your clients *will* be convicted. But also realize that, as the result of your testimony, the conviction may be for a lesser offense, which carries a lesser penalty. Try to remember that your testimony in every case *can* make a meaningful difference to what eventually happens to the defendant.

Often, your most valuable contribution to a case will be made in the post-conviction phase, that is, at sentencing. Most jurisdictions permit the defense to present evidence (including expert testimony) in support of mitigation during the sentencing process. The rules governing the nature, content, form, and scope of expert testimony are far more liberal at this phase than at trial. For example, at sentencing, an expert may be permitted to (a) discuss the defendant's entire intoxicant history, (b) comment on the influence of intoxicant use on the acts constituting the crime charged, (c) make prescriptive treatment recommendations, or (d) propose an alternative sentencing plan, e.g., providing for dispositions such as supervised release (probation), community control (home confinement), or community service. If you do offer sentencing recommendations to the judge, do not lose sight of the fact that, finally, the court has the awesome responsibility of striking "that delicate balance" between the needs of the community for protection and justice and those of the defendant for treatment and rehabilitation.

CRIMINAL RESPONSIBILITY AND INTOXICANTS

Although the connection between the use of intoxicants and crime has been universally recognized, the explosive increase in drug-related crime over the past two decades has had only minimal impact on substantive criminal law. The recognition (albeit equivocal) of addiction as a "disease" and the growth of a professional field and industry around it has had significant social and professional consequences (33, 34) and instructive (although surprisingly limited) effects on the legal rules (35).

Recent scientific research illuminating the distinction between mind and brain, mechanisms of cognition, the nature of rationality, the relationship between intention and action, mechanisms of emotional and behavioral control, and the distinctions between reaction, response, compulsion, and decision are of fundamental relevance to the criminal law. Yet, the law remains self-consciously nescient. Its reasoning remains grounded in long discarded models, disproved theories, and culturally dated assumptions about human rationality, intent (knowledge and volition), motivation, and the regulation of behavior (action). Moreover, although well understood in the addictions field, the specific effects of all classes of intoxicants on these complex processes have been essentially ignored by the law. Legal reasoning about intoxication continues to be informed by eighteenth and nineteenth century understanding of the effects of alcohol on behavior (36).

Conceptual Problems

DEFINITION, DESCRIPTION, AND THE PROBLEM OF DSM-IV

Because the criminal law has a long history of difficulty defining the concepts of "mental disease" and "mental defect," it is perhaps not surprising that the American Psychiatric Association's DSM-IV (37) has been adopted by the courts as a Rosetta Stone for recognizing a defendant's alleged "mental" problems as true diseases or defects. As clinicians, we know that DSM-IV is not and was never intended to be a textbook of neuropsychiatry or addiction medicine. Despite the very explicit caveat about its limitations stated in the Introduction (37, pp. xxiii–xxiv) and the Cautionary Statement about its validity and application in forensic contexts (37, p. xxvii), expect to see a copy of DSM-IV on counsel tables in every criminal case wherein a mental defense is anticipated. Also, you should expect to be examined and cross-examined about your findings and opinions in the constricting terminology of DSM-IV. As one prosecutor remarked, "If it's listed in DSM-IV, then it's a real mental illness; if it's not in DSM-IV, then it isn't a real disease and should be given no credence." To undermine the unwarranted authority this publication has accrued, you must make it clear that neither you, the psychiatric profession, nor the addiction medicine field recognizes DSM-IV as the "authoritative" text. After that, you will not be bound by its serious limitations, simplifications, and omissions. In preparing your testimony, it is vital that you anticipate and analyze all the ways that opposing counsel might use the language of DSM-IV to try to make your testimony appear unreliable, inconsistent, or contradictory. Next, you must formulate your strategy and tactics for thwarting this predictable assault on your credibility. Finally, you must make your attorney aware of all such potential problems so that he or she will be prepared to help you to be "rehabilitated" on redirect examination.

DISEASE, DISORDER, DEFECT, AND DYSFUNCTION

Moving beyond the hurdle of DSM-IV, you must be prepared to confront the distinctions between "disease," "disorder," and "dysfunction." These first two terms have long and tortuous histories in the law of every jurisdiction, while the concept of cerebral "dysfunction" has virtually none. And yet, it is precisely in terms of cognitive, emotional, and behavioral *dysfunction* that one can best explain (and even quantify) the effects of acute, subacute, and chronic intoxicant use. Most defendants seeking to avail themselves of an intoxicant-based defense will have grossly normal findings on such "recognized" neuropsychiatric diagnostic tests as the EEG, CAT scan, or MRI scan. Even when administered using the latest enhanced techniques, these modalities are of limited value in demonstrating cerebral dysfunction (38–40). Although the newer brain imaging technologies, such as the quantitative EEG (38), SPECT (39), and BEAM (40), promise considerable future utility, at present valid norms for these modalities are still in the earliest stages of development. Because the legal tests applied by the courts for the admissibility of scientific evidence based on "newer" technologies are strict and narrow (23, 24), historically, the courts have been slow to recognize the evidentiary validity of emerging scientific technologies.

The Utility of Neuropsychological Testing

Of far greater potential utility for the addiction medicine expert is descriptive neuropsychological testing (41–43). There are many validated neuropsychological tests that, when administered prescriptively, can precisely describe and quantify specific perceptual, cognitive, and emotional skills or behavioral controls that have been adversely affected by the client's use of intoxicants. Such test data may convincingly illuminate the impact of intoxicant use on the required elements of the crime charged. It can also help to answer critical, often bewildering, questions about how a defendant's cognitive, emotional, or behavioral function can be selectively and incompletely affected by intoxicants (44–46). For clients with long, extensive histories of single or multiple intoxicant use and/or histories of antecedent central nervous system insult (e.g., infections, head trauma, high fevers, poisoning) or disease (e.g., learning disabilities, attention deficit-hyperactivity disorder, or epilepsy), neuropsychological testing is essential (47). When working with a neuropsychologist, always ask that he or she assess temporal sequencing, as this is the higher cortical function that enables the discrimination of cause and effect. Do not rely on any of the standard descriptive neuropsychological test batteries, for instance, the Luria-Nebraska or the Halstead-Reitan, as these are not sufficiently specific for forensic purposes (48, 49).

The neuropsychologist will testify about the purpose, validity, and administration of the tests, and will explain the test results and neuropsychological implications thereof. But it is the addiction specialist, who, by drawing upon experience in diagnosing and treating intoxicant-involved patients, can best "bring it all home" in nontechnical language for the judge and jury. The addiction expert must (above all) be articulate and must have comprehensive knowledge about the *specific* effects of intoxicants, and a working knowledge of neuropsychological testing. Presenting this knowledge in analogical stories, examples, patient vignettes, and clinical anecdotes will help the jurors understand and relate such counterintuitive material to their personal life experiences. Every day in the criminal courts juries are expected to decide cases involving complex clinical material. The interests of justice are not well served unless the law permits jurors to be assisted in their deliberations by expert testimony.

The Elements of the Offense

Definitions of both common law and statutory crimes require the *voluntary* commission of a bad act or harmful omission (*actus reus*) in conjunction with a bad state of mind (*mens rea*). However, these fundamental concepts have resisted enduring definition. Most older common law crimes have been redefined in modern criminal statutes. Criminal codifications often use adverbial qualifiers such as "knowingly," "willfully," or "intentionally" to designate as voluntary an act performed consciously as the result of effort or determination (50).

THE EXCULPATORY DOCTRINE IN COMMON LAW

The early common law made no concession whatever because of impaired behavioral control. Justice Story, in an 1828 case involving alcohol intoxication, stressed the merit of "the law allowing not a man to avail himself of the excuse of his own gross vice and misconduct to shield himself from the legal consequences of such crime" (51).

Over time, scientific views of human behavior gradually supplanted moral ones. Concurrently, there was a substantial increase in the consumption of alcohol in all social and economic strata. In response to these societal changes, the common law evolved what came to be known as "the exculpatory doctrine." This doctrine permitted the presentation of evidence of specified mental conditions (including intoxication) in legal proceedings as a means of mitigating culpability, liability, or responsibility. Such evidence could be introduced in the form of an assertion of a defendant's insanity or lack of the "specific" intent required as an element of the offense charged. New and more difficult problems arose almost immediately.

THE ENDURING PROBLEMATIC CONCEPT OF "INTENT"

The early cases in which the exculpatory doctrine was applied involved alcohol intoxication. The courts gradually realized that "common sense" suggested that a distinction should be made between a crime committed by an intoxicated as opposed to a sober person. But traditional moral attitudes stigmatizing intoxication as a vice indicated the impropriety of complete exculpation. The criminal rules on "intent" provided an expedient, if inadequate, means of mediation.

These doctrines, which were the foundation for the exculpatory rule, imply that "specific intent" is distinguishable from "general intent." These also signify that certain crimes require only "general intent," whereas other offenses require certain "specific" intents. This dubious distinction persists at law, although neither the courts nor modern cognitive science has yet to formulate a reliable criterion or test for distinguishing "general" from "specific" intent. Today, "specific intent" most often refers to a "special" mental element which must be present in addition to the bad mental state required to accompany the bad act constituting the offense. For an analysis of the evolution and modern status of the legal premise of intent and its application to mental defenses (including intoxication) see LaFave and Scott (52, §3.5). When impulsive or compulsive behavior is involved, as in intoxicant use, this distinction is even more problematic.

The meaning of "intent" in the criminal law has always been obscure. Traditionally, intent was defined to include elements of both knowledge and volition. In the modern era, a statutory distinction generally is made between the mental states of knowledge and intent. Obviously, certain intoxicants, when used in certain ways by certain persons, affect certain cognitive, emotional, and behavioral functions in certain ways. Defining, distinguishing, and presenting these to the jury in nontechnical, readily intelligible language is the responsibility of the addiction expert. Successful communication of these clinical complexities to the jury by the expert is the cornerstone of a viable intoxicant-based defense.

Despite limited recognition by the courts and society that some degree of exculpation might be warranted in cases where an intoxicant-involved person commits a crime, neither the exculpatory doctrine of the common law nor modern statutory laws dealing with intoxication and related mental defenses has been even moderately satisfactory or equitable. One important reason for this is that both the exculpatory doctrine of the common law and our modern statutory laws were based upon very early medical observations and common lay experience with the effects of *alcohol*. Despite the wealth of scientific knowledge about the specific cognitive, emotional, and behavioral effects of all the intoxicants, the substantive criminal law in this area has evolved very little and still reflects its alcohol-informed heritage.

The implicit public policy in the prevailing law reflects society's historical vacillation and expedient compromises between the punishment of intoxicant-influenced offenders in complete disregard of their condition (i.e., viewing them as ordinary criminals), and the total exculpation often suggested by the clinical evidence (i.e., viewing them as patients).

Intoxication as a Defense

Today, the effect of intoxication on criminal responsibility is well established, but only precariously settled. At law, intoxication can be either (a) *in-voluntary,* where the intoxicant is ingested as the result of force or duress (53), deceit or trickery (54), medical advice (55), or lack of awareness of a susceptibility to a recognized atypical reaction to that substance (56), as in pathological intoxication; or (b) *voluntary,* where the intoxicant is ingested for effect, as in recreational drug use. Many jurisdictions have recognized involuntary intoxication as a complete defense to criminal behavior in appropriate circumstances, as already noted. Most jurisdictions, however, adhere to the view that *voluntary* intoxication does *not* excuse a criminal act unless the actor, because of his intoxication, could not form the intent required in the statutory definition of the crime. That is, voluntary intoxication may be raised to negative an element of an offense. Unfortunately, neither the distinctions between voluntary and involuntary intoxication nor those between general and specific intent are clear or consistent. See LaFave and Scott for a review of intoxication-based defenses (52, §4.10).

In cases involving the ingestion of intoxicants courts have consistently applied the same rules of analysis, mitigation, and exculpation derived from the common law and developed to deal with alcohol intoxication (57). One notable exception was expressed in the dissenting opinion in *State v. Hall* (58), which argued that drug and alcohol intoxication ought to be distinguished, and that "[o]ur intoxication rationale as applied to alcohol simply does not fit the use of modern hallucinatory drugs; and it was never meant to" (58, p. 213). Similarly, most legal commentators have not distinguished intoxication resulting from the ingestion of alcohol and the other classes of intoxicants (59, 60). In 1980, this problem was addressed in a remarkably comprehensive law review article (61). This scholarly commentary (a) examined in detail the specific effects of all of the intoxicants then in general use, (b) reviewed the traditional and prevailing legal reasoning on intoxication and intent, (c) discussed the resultant implications for intoxicant-based defenses against criminal responsibility, and (d) concluded with a recommendation that ". . . either the court or the legislatures must increase their expertise in these areas and respond to these potentially serious flaws in the criminal legal system" (61, p. 1145). Despite having been extensively cited in subsequent cases, its well-reasoned proposals have yet to be implemented. The criminal law continues to fail or refuse to recognize the fundamental differences between the effects of alcohol and other intoxicants (most importantly, cocaine) on human cognition, emotion, and behavior (62–66).

The law views alcohol as a neural depressant and disinhibitor which releases (cognitive and moral) inhibitions, thereby setting free ill-defined drives and putative "bad" impulses and traits, which are subsequently expressed in a criminal act. An analogy echoing through many judicial opinions regarding the mechanism of intoxication states: "drinking alcohol is like taking your foot off the brake [of a car]." Whereas this may not be an entirely ill-informed metaphor, it is surely an inadequate one, for it implicitly maintains that alcohol effects are stable, predictable, and consistent both across and within individuals. When applied to other intoxicants, this analogy is clearly out of touch with currently accepted principles of neuropsychopharmacology and the cognitive sciences. This disparity is most glaring for cocaine intoxication. After introducing the "removing the foot from the brake" analogy for alcohol intoxication for contrast, it is useful to explain to the jury that the effect of ingesting cocaine is better understood as being more like "stepping on the gas." The outcome may be the same: the metaphoric car moves forward, that is, the person commits a criminal act, but the mechanism is entirely different. It has been suggested that in a sense cocaine is that drug which supplies intent where otherwise there would have been none. Distinguishing the effects of cocaine (or other intoxicants) from those of alcohol is vital because it problematizes the legal concepts of intent and intoxication. This alone may lead the jury to find "reasonable doubt" about the defendant's having the required state of mind.

Consider, as an example, the conceptual problem posed for a jury in a case where a polydrug addict with a long history of robbing drugstores to get drugs (not money) now robs a drugstore while grossly intoxicated from high intravenous doses of PCP, heroin, and cocaine. Eyewitness testimony states that although he looked and acted as if intoxicated the defendant also appeared to have acted with purpose. His actions clearly demonstrated that he "knew" (at least) the following: (a) to rob a pharmacy (as opposed to, say, a grocery store) to get drugs; (b) which specific (desirably intoxicating) drugs to steal;

and (*c*) how to commit a robbery and get to the controlled substances in the safe. In this scenario, it would be nonetheless possible that the extent and specific effects of the polydrug intoxication had rendered the defendant incapable of forming the specific intent required as an element of the offense of robbery in that jurisdiction. To succeed in negativing the elements of the offense of robbery, the defense would have to introduce expert testimony to attempt to explain at least the following: (*a*) that his "intent" was to get drugs, not specifically to commit the crime of robbery; (*b*) that his intoxication precluded him from forming the specific intent required for robbery, but (*c*) that the intoxication did *not* affect his previously well-learned ("overlearned") knowledge about intoxicating drugs and about how to rob drugstores. For such expert testimony to be accepted by the jury, it would need to tie together (*a*) the defendant's intoxicant history, (*b*) the specific effects of each intoxicant influencing the defendant at the time of the robbery, (*c*) his prior experience in robbing drug stores, and (*d*) the specific facts of the instant case.

Dependence as a Defense

Dependence on an intoxicant, absent more, does not provide a complete defense in any jurisdiction (67, 68). The nature, course, and effects of dependence on specific substances on cognition, emotion, or behavior have not been recognized by the law.

Interestingly, opioid intoxication (but not dependence) may be of such extent as to negative the "knowingly" element of criminal intent. But neither opioid intoxication nor dependence has been held to negative the "willfully" element of criminal intent. Intoxication (but not dependence) induced by any substance may be sufficient to render a person incapable of the "deliberation" or "premeditation" required as an element of a specific degree of an offense, as in first degree murder. In no jurisdiction has dependence on specific intoxicants been differentiated from that of alcohol, thereby warranting special consideration.

Until recently, attempts to use dependence as a defense to criminal responsibility were couched in terms of insanity, by characterizing dependence or addiction as a mental disorder that rendered the defendant insane and therefore not criminally responsible. For the most part, these attempts have been unsuccessful. In 1984, *United States v. Lyons* held that henceforth no defendant could base any defense of insanity on the claim that he lacked substantial capacity to conform his conduct to the requirements of law, supporting that opinion by citing "the present murky state of medical knowledge" about human volition (69).

A novel defense of "medical necessity" proposed in 1985 by Uelmen and Tennant sought to present addiction not as a mental disorder but, by reason of its involving a putative endorphin deficiency, as a physical condition requiring medical treatment (70). Analogizing the situation of the addict to that of the diabetic, the defense of "medical necessity" sought to conform to the contours of the well-established defenses of duress or necessity. Uelmen and Tennant suggested that "[O]bviously, the legal profession is sleeping through the current revolution in Biochemistry" (70, p. 6). Although inconsistently successful in minor cases involving possession of small quantities of marihuana by persons using that substance to alleviate the symptoms of glaucoma (71), multiple sclerosis (72), or spasticity (73), the defense of "medical necessity" has otherwise been rejected by the courts. Many cases in which this novel defense was rejected relied upon the early case of *United States v. Moore*, which pointed to "the choice that each addict makes at the start as to whether or not he is going to take narcotics and run the risk of becoming addicted to them" (74).

Withdrawal as a Defense

Defenses based upon the argument that the criminal act at issue was the direct or indirect product of withdrawal from an intoxicant have not prevailed, except in the limited and infrequent circumstance where a defendant in withdrawal commits an act while semiconscious or unconscious. An action that, while purposive, is not spontaneous, and therefore is not voluntary, is defined at law as an "automatism" and does not incur criminal responsibility. See LaFave and Scott for a discussion of the utilization of automatism in a criminal defense (52, §4.9).

Intoxicant-Induced Insanity as a Defense

An insanity defense asserts that at the time the accused committed the act for which he is charged, a mental illness precluded him from having the required bad state of mind to be convicted of the act. The insanity defense has been a part of English and American jurisprudence for several hundred years. It reflects a shared belief that only those individuals who have *chosen* to commit wrongful acts should be punished, and that those without the capacity to appreciate the wrongfulness of their conduct should be absolved. The roots of the insanity defense are ultimately embedded in the Judeo-Christian tradition of linking moral responsibility with punishment and absolution.

The elements of the legal definition of insanity that predominates today was shaped primarily by two famous cases: the 1843 English case of Daniel M'Naghten (75) and the 1982 acquittal of John Hinckley (76), who had shot President Reagan. In both instances, the public outcry over the successful employment of the insanity defense as it existed at those times resulted in a substantial conceptual redefinition and limitation of the availability of the defense. Most notably, the federal 1984 Insanity Defense Reform Act (20) and the Comprehensive Crime Control Act of 1984 (77), which followed in the wake of Hinckley's successful defense based on a legal test for insanity then in wide use, eliminated many types of mental illness as bases for a defense and reinstated the strict cognitive test of insanity set forth in *M'Naghten* (75). Temporary insanity caused by voluntary intoxication does not meet the requirements of the 1984 Act, nor does intoxicant dependence, absent more (78). However, where the insanity caused by the chronic use of intoxicants endures beyond any period(s) of intoxication it may insulate a defendant, providing the resulting insanity otherwise conforms to the requirements of the 1984 Act (21, §3:13;52, §4.10(g)). Interestingly, neither intoxication nor dependence has been recognized as a uniquely aggravating factor to an antecedent or concurrent mental condition that by itself would not render a defendant insane as defined in the 1984 Act.

Insanity that arises from either acute or chronic intoxicant use has not been distinguished from insanity produced by other causes. Thus, whether temporary insanity caused by voluntary intoxication will be exculpatory largely depends on the legal test for insanity used in that jurisdiction. Several states have statutorily excluded this defense.

The Concept of Partial Responsibility

Partial responsibility, or diminished capacity, is a difficult and muddled concept in the law, with little coherence or consistency. Many courts appear to reject or not understand it.

Insanity of the legal type is considered a *complete* defense to criminal acts in most jurisdictions. A mental disorder that constitutes "something less than insanity" is not considered a complete defense to a crime, but is widely thought to lessen the degree of criminal responsibility, at least for crimes where there is a lesser degree of responsibility or severity available (as in murder, which might be reducible from first degree to second or a lesser degree). Today, mitigation, not exculpation, is the most common application of the concept of diminished capacity (21, §3:16).

Argument asserting diminished capacity can also be made when a defendant claims that a mental illness precluded him from having the mental elements required for the crime. That is, because of a mental disorder, the severity of which did not render the defendant insane as provided by the test for insanity employed in that jurisdiction, the defendant nonetheless was unable to have committed the crime as charged because his mental disorder prevented his having the statutorily required elements of the offense charged (e.g., acting with "malice" or "premeditation"). That the effects of specific intoxicants can reach this threshold may be an undisputed clinical "fact"; nonetheless, courts continue to resist its acceptance (79).

Many states have disallowed any evidence of diminished capacity to be admitted during trial. By public referendum, the California Penal Code eliminated diminished capacity as a defense, but retained its availability as a mitigating factor (80). In *Bethea v. United States,* the court expressed the now widely held view that embracing the concept of diminished responsibility would lead to an unacceptable "sliding scale of sanity in criminal responsibility" (81). Moriarty provides an elegant analysis of the concept and a comparison of the positions taken by the American Bar Association, the federal courts, and the various state courts (21, §§3:19–21).

Intoxicant Use and Effects as Mitigating Factors

Although many states now require judges to adhere to legislatively prescribed sentencing guidelines, in some jurisdictions judges have retained limited discretion to consider a convicted defendant's complete drug history (including intoxication and dependence) as a mitigating factor. However, it is a general rule that the nature, extent, and effects of the intoxicant history must be introduced into evidence before being eligible for consideration at sentencing. There are marked differences between jurisdictions regarding the type of evidence (expert testimony, corroborating witnesses, etc.) required or admissible to establish the extent and effects of intoxication in support of mitigation.

Under the current Revised Federal Sentencing Guidelines, a federal judge may exercise a downward departure from the legislated guidelines for sentencing based on "diminished capacity" except where it is the result of voluntary intoxication with any substance (82). Nonetheless, in some federal jurisdictions, "addiction" has been accepted as evidence of diminished capacity and therefore as a basis for granting a downward departure at sentencing. This is the exception, however, not the rule.

THE ADDICTIVE PROCESSES

The concept of behaviors involving addictive processes, rather than intoxicating substances, as in "compulsive" or "pathological" gambling, is of exceptional theoretical importance for the criminal law and the addictions field. The concept has required a re-examination of many fundamental legal postulates, precedents, and assumptions about criminal responsibility and intentionality. If viewed as *addictive* disorders (as in "compulsive gambling") in which no exogenous intoxicating substance is ingested, such processes raise profound questions about the paradigms that inform research, theory, and practice in the addictions field. If viewed as *impulse control* disorders (as in "pathological gambling"), these processes raise difficult questions about the causal and temporal relationships between a person's impulses and the acts issuing therefrom (35).

Pathological Gambling

Burglass has reviewed in depth the rationale, process, conceptual problems, and practical implications of introducing dysfunctional gambling behavior in defense or mitigation of criminal responsibility (35). One critical step toward the resolution of the conceptual problems would be for the field to formulate a classification of pathological gamblers and the situations relevant to their behavior(s) that would be defensible empirically and relevant to the issue of criminal responsibility. For example, pathological gamblers who commit crimes would be either normal or diseased, and their gambling behavior at the time of the commission of the crime charged would be pathological in various degrees (35). Unfortunately, no such classification schema has been proposed.

What we find in the fact patterns of cases involving pathological gambling is not a total or even substantial incapacity to carry out simple (or even complex) acts that can be reasonably attributed to the "disease." Nor do we find such a compromise of intellectual function as to entirely exclude purposeful conduct. Instead, we observe an apparent blunting of ethical sensitivity sufficient to destroy the understanding, appreciation, or regard for the moral quality of the criminal act, combined with a drastic, often protracted, lapse of inhibition. Rarely do we find a lapse of conscious awareness of the criminal act itself. Because pathological gambling is a chronic disorder with a recognizable natural history (83, 84), these mental elements typically can be identified before, during, and after the crime is committed. In this sense, the problem behavior seen in pathological gambling is more like a *process* than like a *state*. In its effects it more closely resembles "insanity" of both legally recognized varieties—the inability to distinguish right from wrong or the inability to resist an impulse—than it does any state of intoxication. Before being widely rejected, the "capacity to conform" test for an insanity defense highlighted the problem of defining a "mental disease or defect." The *Freeman* court held that "an abnormality manifested only by repeated criminal or otherwise anti-social conduct" was not a disease (78, p. 625).

CLINICAL AND FORENSIC DISTINCTIONS

It is recognized clinically that at least some compulsive gamblers who commit crimes are impaired physically and psychologically, and thus may be only partially responsible for their misconduct. In this sense, at law they resemble the inebriate, whose reason has been temporarily compromised; and for them the rules governing intoxication often seem more applicable than do those for insanity. Although they are only very rarely psychotic, and only a few may even be neurotic (83), they are nonetheless considered abnormal by many clinicians (84–89), albeit in ways of questionable relevance. Hence, for this subgroup of "impaired" compulsive gamblers, neither complete exculpation nor full responsibility seems appropriate. One might argue that as applied to pathological gamblers who commit crimes, the legal rules should be applied not in terms of lack of intent, but in terms of lack of understanding of the ethical quality of the act and/or the ability to control behavior. But the legal rules have not adopted this view. As noted by Strassman, "[t]he link between compulsive gambling and a criminal offense is too tenuous to permit the court to find that the defendant lacks substantial capacity to conform his behavior to the requirements of the law as a result of his compulsive gambling disorder" (90, p. 201).

It must be conceded that many (possibly most) compulsive gamblers accused of crimes are simply persons who gamble to excess, not helpless victims of a "disease" of gambling that drives them to crime; and that such individuals should be accountable for their actions and the consequences thereof.

In practice, rather than raising an insanity defense, counsel for a pathological gambler is more likely to attack the elements of the offense charged, arguing that the mental disorder of pathological gambling rendered the defendant incapable of forming the specific intent requisite to the crime. *Wilson v. Commissioner* held that the defendant did not act "willfully" in filing an inaccurate tax return because his mental disorder prevented his forming a specific intent to violate the tax laws (91). For a comprehensive review of mental defenses in federal tax cases, see Ritholz and Fink (92).

Most judges—unpersuaded by modern scientific knowledge—in exercising their broad discretion in evidentiary matters, hold many persons criminally liable even though they are clearly afflicted with recognized diseases. The general failure of pathological gambling as a defense in most criminal prosecutions reflects precisely this point of view. Currently governing case law in most, but not all, jurisdictions is based on *United States v. Shorter* (13).

THE IMPLICATIONS OF UNITED STATES V. SHORTER

In *Shorter,* Judge Greene clearly considered pathological gambling to be an addictive disorder. He correctly identified the conceptual problem that arises when the state of mind caused by such disorders exists over a long period, during which time the disordered person commits one or more crimes but otherwise manages to behave in a controlled and rational manner (13). In such cases the defense faces the daunting task of explaining how selected behaviors can be the substantially involuntary products of the intoxication or disorder, while other, relatively contemporaneous, behaviors need not be similarly affected. There is no satisfactory, unitary explanation for this. The elements of each offense must be analyzed in light of the facts of the case and the nature of the addictive process involved.

In *Shorter,* the judge also challenged the qualifications and legitimacy of clinicians specializing in compulsive gambling and refused to admit much of their testimony (13 [1985 p. 257]).

Sexual Addiction

In recent years, the diagnosis of "compulsive sexuality" or "sexual addiction" (93) has been offered as the basis for exculpation or mitigation in cases involving sexual as well as less obviously related offenses. Some few courts have admitted expert testimony about this controversial condition. In no jurisdiction has such a defense prevailed, absent more. A number of courts have admitted a defendant's alleged "sexual addiction" as a mitigating factor at sentencing. Limited treatment programs (most based on 12-step or other self-help principles) are available in the federal prison system and in that of most states.

Eating Disorders

There have been a few cases involving shoplifting and petty theft from groceries where an eating disorder (bulimia) was advanced as a defense. In none of these cases did the defense exculpate the accused. In two cases, after the defendants were convicted of the crimes charged, the sentencing judge recognized the eating disorder as a legitimate "mental disorder" which constituted a valid mitigating factor. Both defendants were sentenced to community supervision and service and to mandatory professional treatment instead of incarceration.

Compulsive Spending or Shopping

Recently, support groups based on 12-step principles and other self-help models have emerged for persons with the "diseases" of "compulsive spending" and "compulsive shopping." Advocates in these movements have adopted or endorsed addiction-derived explanations, language, and treatment approaches for these problems. The application of an addiction paradigm to these behaviors is of dubious validity, and neither problem has been widely recognized as an addictive disorder by professionals in the field (94, 95).

Criminal defenses based on the "diseases" of compulsive spending or shopping have been rejected by the courts. In a few cases involving petty theft and shoplifting, expert clinical testimony about these excessive behaviors, although admitted, had little mitigatory impact at sentencing. A very thought-provoking feminist analysis of kleptomania and "compulsive shopping" as *sexual* disorders diagnosed only in women has been advanced by Camhi (96).

THE EFFECTS OF INTOXICANTS ON MEMORY

Expert Testimony About the Memory of Witnesses

Human memory is a complex phenomenon. One would expect the literature on the effects of intoxicants on human cognition, particularly memory, to be extensive: it is not. In cases where the defendant has been accused by persons who are or have been drug involved, an expert must assess the potential impact of their intoxicant use on their credibility as witnesses. The focus must be on the effect of the relevant intoxicant(s) on memory and its constituent cognitive processes (38–40, 44–47). Although Federal Rule of Evidence 704(b) prohibits expert testimony on whether or not a defendant had the state of mind required for a particular crime (a decision reserved for the jury), it does not prohibit expert testimony about mental factors potentially affecting *witnesses* (22). To be an effective expert in this area, the addiction specialist requires a broad and deep understanding of human memory. Authoritative texts on research and theory about human memory written from both the clinical (41) and legal (21, Chap. 13) perspectives need to be studied closely.

Cocaine-Related Memory Dysfunction in Criminal Proceedings

Although any of the intoxicants can have potentially deleterious effects on selected memory functions, the effects of cocaine raise the most serious and frequent concerns (35, 39, 44–46, 62–65, 97, 98). A significant number of today's large scale cocaine trafficking cases are founded principally or solely on the testimony of alleged or self-styled co-conspirators, who, more often than not, were themselves using large amounts of cocaine (and usually other intoxicants as well) during the period about which they will testify in great detail as to time, place, person, sequence, and events. In evaluating the credibility of such witnesses, it is critical to look for any possible effects of intoxicant use on their memory functions. It is always important and often productive to look for predicates and indicia of (cocaine-induced) confabu-

lation that may taint their testimony. In order to establish the *possibility* that testimony may contain confabulated elements and therefore be subject to "reasonable doubt," it is necessary to assess the circumstances, frequency, extent, and detail of the witness's prior statements, depositions, narratives, or conferences with the authorities. Evidence of high-dose cocaine use, extensive "testimonial schooling" (21, §13:18), and progressively detailed and inclusive recall provides a sufficient predicate for an addiction medicine expert to consider reasonably and responsibly the *possibility* that confabulation is present (35). See Moriarty for a discussion of the legal issues, problems, and concerns associated with witness confabulation arising from all causes (21, §§13:17–19).

THE PHENOMENON OF CONFABULATION

Confabulation is a neuropsychiatric symptom characteristic of diffuse organic brain disease and/or dysfunction. It refers to the unconscious filling in of memory gaps by imagined experiences, fabricated stories, or grossly distorted accounts of recent or remote events. It is absolutely distinct from lying, which implies both motive and awareness of the distortion or untruth. Confabulatory recall is inconsistent; it may change from moment to moment; and it may be induced unwittingly by suggestion. Characteristically, isolated events and information from the past are retained in fragmented form, but are at times related without regard for the intervals that separated these or for their proper temporal sequence. Sometimes, in confabulating, a person will telescope events, compressing time, thereby linking as cause and effect events that were widely separated in time and causally unrelated. These memory fragments may be cued, intentionally or unintentionally, during conversation (*a*) by suggestion, (*b*) by presentation of selected data about recent or remote events as if it were unequivocal fact, or (*c*) by provision of a cogent, internally consistent narrative explanation of some situation or event. The dysfunctional brain, in an attempt to maintain consistency with this apparent "reality," may fill in any memory gaps with associative, derivative, or suggested data.

Confabulation is never a consistent finding in any clinical condition. It is most frequently seen in cases of severe, nutrition-deficient alcoholism, head trauma, cerebral hypoxia, certain heavy metal poisonings, certain infections of the central nervous system (e.g., herpes or HIV encephalitis), or high-dose psychostimulant use.

COCAINE-INDUCED CONFABULATION

Confabulation may be seen in two phases of high-dose cocaine use. During the acute intoxication phase, the profound confusion, grandiosity, emotional lability, false sense of mastery, illusions, delusions, and hallucinations occasionally can induce certain users to confabulate "in real time." During the convalescent phase, after a period of abstinence from cocaine, the person gradually recalls fragments of past experience (many of which may have been originally misperceived) in a distorted way. In an attempt to preserve logical consistency, these may be linked with confabulated material. The more often such confabulated material is ratified by the social setting and in particular by authority figures (e.g., physicians, attorneys, or law enforcement officers) the more likely it is to become a fully integrated and unquestioned part of that person's self-history. It even may go on to become the basis for future thoughts, conclusions, and actions.

Although the Sixth Circuit upheld the disallowance of such testimony in *United States v. Ramirez,* finding that such testimony went to the credibility, not the competence, of a witness (99), the exclusion of such testimony by a qualified addiction expert has been the rare exception, not the rule. A transcript of the direct and cross-examinations of the author about the effects of cocaine on the memory (confabulation) and credibility of a witness in a cocaine conspiracy case can be found in Moriarty (21, Appendix 3E).

REGULATORY AND ADMINISTRATIVE PROCEEDINGS

Members of licensed, regulated, or otherwise supervised professions (e.g., health care professionals, attorneys, airline pilots, interstate truckers) can find their licenses at risk for a number of reasons involving intoxicants.

Two, however, are of exceptional importance and will be discussed here: (a) allegations of "impairment" consequent to intoxicant use, and (b) for physicians, allegations of the "inappropriate" prescribing of opioids for the long-term management of chronic nonmalignant pain. In cases involving professional impairment, Burglass has identified two fundamental and very serious medical-legal issues: (a) the common presumption that "use equals abuse equals addiction equals impairment"; and (b) the fact that only a few regulatory agencies (e.g., the Federal Aviation Administration for pilots and the Department of Transportation for interstate truck drivers) have normative data defining the cognitive, sensory, or motor skills required of a normal, i.e., a "non-impaired" practitioner (100, 101). With the exception of the blood alcohol concentration, which, as a matter of public policy, has been adopted in every state as an objective, affirmative indicia of impairment for the operation of a motorized vehicle, there are no similarly established norms for any other intoxicants, nor for alcohol-mediated impairment in other contexts.

Characteristically, these investigations and prosecutions of professional impairment are undertaken in the name of public health and safety. However, the ill-specified nature of these causes and the zeal and fervor with which intoxicant regulatory activities are pursued have led some observers to characterize our present food and drug laws, all medical and scientific justifications aside, as ultimately religious in intent, purpose, and effect, as being in effect the dietary and liturgical laws of the modern secular religion of science (2).

Professional Impairment

In the assessment of professional impairment, regulatory policies do not reflect the clinically significant, specific differences between intoxicants in terms of their effects, patterns of use, routes of administration, nature of the dependence and/or withdrawal syndromes (if applicable), or resultant substance-related disabilities. Although there have been some few regulatory and legal cases where (limited) consideration has been given to these crucial distinctions, such deliberations are clearly the exception, not the rule.

All too often, the proverbial deck is stacked against the accused professional, who, upon being accused of even the mere *use* of an intoxicant, is presumed to be *impaired* consequent thereto. Contrary to the traditions of Anglo-American jurisprudence, the accused professional then has the *effective* burden of proving his or her "innocence" in the face of the presumption of guilt. These prosecutions are invariably legitimized and justified as necessary to protect patients or clients, institutions, or professions from the harmful actions of impaired practitioners. But in practice, the hearing panels are often biased, punitive, and easily influenced by professional or institutional interests and politics. Even the isolated or occasional use of an intoxicant is often conflated with impairment, and harsh sanctions are imposed. If the accused admits to any use of intoxicants, impairment is usually presumed. If the accused denies use of intoxicants, the conclusion that he or she is in "denial" will likely be drawn and considered as evidence of "addiction" and, consequently, of "impairment."

Of course, some intoxicant-involved professionals *are* impaired and in need of treatment until they are able to resume practicing with the skill and safety required in their profession. In recent years, a virtual industry for the diagnosis and treatment of "impaired" professionals has emerged. One can detect therein a disturbing propensity to conceptualize and treat professional "impairment" as if it were itself a distinct disease entity. *It is not* (100, 101). The determination of intoxicant-related impairment in professionals is a very complex assessment that requires extensive input from independent, *unbiased* addiction medicine specialists throughout the process. If injustices are to be avoided, specialists in addiction medicine must be willing to become involved in these unpopular and often unsavory cases. They need to offer expert testimony that (a) obligates the regulators (clinically, ethically, and legally) to recognize and consider all relevant intoxicant-specific distinctions, and (b) requires that they "prove" their case for impairment by *specifying* and *quantifying* the alleged deficiencies or disabilities of cognition, emotion, behavior, or professional skill that define the accused as impaired when measured against the standards of performance, skill, care, and safety required for professional practice in that jurisdiction or context.

As if this entire area were not already sufficiently troubling, an ominous trend toward requiring physicians who have been treated for chemical dependency to make informed consent disclosure to all patients has been identified by Ackerman (102).

Prescribing Opioids for Pain in Private Practice

Each year the prescribing profiles for controlled substances (Class II opioids, in particular) of thousands of physicians are routinely (often automatically) monitored, sampled or otherwise scanned, and evaluated by state regulatory bodies (103, 104). Despite the dubious ethics and questionable purposes/efficacy of such monitoring programs, these practices increasingly are being "justified" by state regulatory bodies in the name of public health and safety, which are (presumptively) privileged over issues of individual privacy and confidentiality. The legal authority for these actions and the regulation of opioid prescribing for pain is provided by health (medical) practice acts legislated at the state level and by federal and state acts governing the use of controlled substances. Hundreds of physicians whose prescribing profiles are deemed "questionable" are then more thoroughly investigated. Such investigations and prosecutions may be initiated by even the brief treatment of a single patient! Of course, there are physicians whose prescribing of opioids is clinically inappropriate and/or unethical. Some in this group simply lack adequate current knowledge about the indications for opioid analgesia and/or the rational choice of appropriate opioid agents. Others are motivated by simple greed or sexual interest. Others are innocently duped, manipulated, or otherwise pressured by cunning and/or demanding patients. Regulatory agencies, in the main, have adequate procedures and appropriate sanctions to deal with these groups of physicians. What the majority of the state regulatory agencies lack are provisions and procedures for dealing fairly with physicians whose prescribing of opioids is not inappropriate and/or unethical. Indeed, most of the standards of practice governing opioid use are based on myths, prejudice, and misinformation about opioids, and the unexamined belief that mere exposure to these drugs invariably results in addiction in all patients. The prevailing obsession of regulators with "police" activities intended to prevent diversion has blinded them to their coequal obligation to ensure adequate access to opioids for patients who require these drugs for legitimate medical purposes (104). Conscientious, compassionate physicians in the latter group face substantial forensic problems: (a) the investigatory process raises serious ethical questions of privacy and confidentiality for both physician and patient; and (b) the regulatory hearings not infrequently violate fundamental legal principles of due process. The language of most state medical practice acts is predominantly proscriptive in intent, overly broad and/or vague, and easily subject to misinterpretation (104). It is therefore not surprising that the majority of American physicians tend to be "opiophobic." As a consequence, many legitimate pain patients are undertreated, mistreated, or not treated at all (105, 106).

Although the use of opioids for the treatment of chronic nonmalignant pain remains the subject of sociopolitical controversy, clinical debate, and research (106, 107), the validity and utility of the modality have been recognized and conscientious clinical protocols have been developed and implemented (108–112). When such protocols are used by pain specialists based in prestigious academic medical centers or dedicated pain treatment programs, the legitimacy, knowledge, and competence of the prescribing physician(s) are presumed, and regulatory problems rarely arise. The situation in private practice, however, is markedly different. In the latter context, legitimacy, knowledge, and competence are not presumed. The physician in private practice who is charged with the "inappropriate" prescribing of opioids effectively bears the burden of establishing his or her "legitimacy" and proving that the questioned use of opioids was in fact clinically appropriate and/or otherwise in keeping with applicable standards of care and practice. Sadly, state regulators have little difficulty finding addiction medicine experts who do not hesitate to condemn the opioid prescribing practices of knowledgeable and ethical colleagues as "inappropriate" and/or "substandard."

Each year, dozens of well-informed, well-intentioned physicians are formally charged with violation(s) of a state medical practice act for having "inappropriately" prescribed opioid drugs to patients for chronic nonmalignant pain. They then must defend themselves (and their licenses) in a formal, adversarial hearing process, not unlike a criminal trial. Because such regulatory violations do not in themselves constitute acts of malpractice, medical malpractice insurance rarely provides counsel or funds the costs for the defense of such matters. The accused physician therefore must fund his or her own defense, the cost of which can easily exceed $100,000.

The two most frequent bases upon which regulators found allegations that a physician's use of long-term opioid therapy for chronic, nonmalignant pain is inappropriate are that such therapy "creates addicts" and that opioid therapy is contraindicated in any patient with a history of substance abuse. Both assertions are highly controversial, and the underlying assumptions, concerns, and issues of both have been comprehensively examined and challenged by specialists in pain management and addiction medicine (113–115). Although a 1992 review of the literature revealed reported prevalences of drug abuse, dependence, and addiction in chronic pain patients ranging from 3.2 to 18.9% (116), it has been suggested that the true prevalence of addictive disease in the chronic, *nonmalignant* pain population is unknown (117). In any event, every chronic pain patient being considered for long-term opioid therapy must undergo a comprehensive, multidimensional evaluation, which must include an analysis of their (*a*) pain (etiology, history, character); (*b*) prior experience with all modalities of pain management, including opioids; and (*c*) prior and current use of all classes of psychoactive drugs, prescribed or otherwise (117, 118). The clinician in the pain clinic, private practice, or other settings must make a conscious effort to identify prior or current addictive disease, and must also attempt to identify those patients who are in active recovery (117).

For even the most knowledgeable, best intentioned, and best prepared practitioner accused of opioid prescribing violations, exculpation is by no means assured, and ultimate vindication should never be assumed. However, documentation of the following material in the medical record often has proved to be *the* pivotal element in the successful defense of such cases:

1. A comprehensive evaluation and assessment of the etiology, history, and character of the patient's pain.
2. Clinical records or summaries from the specialists or subspecialists who have diagnosed and treated the primary medical or surgical conditions thought to be producing the patient's pain.
3. An appropriately executed (signed, witnessed, and notarized) document of the patient's "Informed Consent to Treatment with Opioid Drugs." Because the law on informed consent varies substantially from state to state and is subject to increasingly frequent review and revision (119), this critical document must be drafted in close consultation with an attorney who is experienced, and absolutely up-to-date in this area of the law. Moreover, the trend in the law of informed consent is in the direction of requiring increased specificity about alternatives and risks, broader comprehensivity, and clearer evidence of the patient's *practical* understanding of both the proposed treatment and the meaning of the signed document of consent.
4. Frequent multidimensional assessment and documentation of the efficacy of opioid therapy, the absence of drug toxicity, and the absence of indicia of "addiction" (including periodic urine toxicology screening). Multidimensional assessment of the frequency and distress illuminates the impact of symptoms and the efficacy of treatment on a patient's quality of life (120).
5. Annual (or more frequent if indicated) "Letters of Indemnification" from an appropriate surgical or medical specialist stating that he or she has reexamined the patient, found that the underlying medical or surgical condition is still present and/or unchanged, that there have been no treatment innovations or technological breakthroughs from which the patient might be expected to benefit, and that therefore continued management of the patient's pain is clinically justifiable.
6. If the physician prescribing the opioids is not a credentialed expert or specialist in either pain management or addiction medicine, letters of consultation from a specialist in both of these areas are essential. Moreover, even if the prescribing physician is an expert in one of these two areas, a consultation letter from an expert in the other area is critical. These

consultative reports should be updated at intervals appropriate to the patient's underlying diseases and/or reflective of the results of the regular multidimensional assessments described previously. Thus, patients who have exhibited behaviors that might be construed as "drug-seeking behavior" will need to be more frequently assessed by an addiction medicine specialist. Patients whose response to opioid therapy is untoward or inadequate (in terms of enhanced function and comfort) will require more frequent evaluation by a pain specialist.

Despite the application of scrupulous clinical "due diligence" and the maintenance of thorough, ongoing documentation, the use of long-term opioid therapy in patients with chronic nonmalignant pain is still fraught with potential pitfalls. Although articles in law reviews and clinical journals can provide insightful overviews of the policy and law governing the prescribing of opioids for pain (104, 121, 122), the interpretation and application of those laws by regulatory bodies changes substantially from one case to the next. *Therefore, for anyone who uses this treatment modality in private practice, knowledge of the current state of the law is absolutely essential!*

To date, the attempt to define and control this complex area of medical practice by substituting regulations for clinical judgement has failed—resulting in grievous injustices for many practitioners and patients. The problem is neither "bad regulations" nor "incompetent regulators," and the solution is neither the drafting of more enlightened regulations nor the revision of biased regulatory procedures. The fundamental problem is that *regulation* is an inappropriate strategy for shaping policy and practice in this area. Clearly, a different approach is needed. The interests and concerns of all parties can be met by the promulgation of practice guidelines—specific, yet broad and flexible. Appropriate guidelines cannot possibly be formulated by bureaucrats, politicians, administrators, third-party payers, or any of the other marginally educated and/or nonclinically trained "watchdogs" of medicine and public health. The task demands comprehensive clinical knowledge and broad patient experience in pain management and addiction medicine. It needs to be an interdisciplinary, collaborative project initiated and directed by *medical* specialists in the fields of pain management and addictive disease. *Fortunately, both fields are currently hard at work developing such guidelines.* Input from practitioners (both specialists and generalists), as well as from patients, is being actively solicited and is an indispensable element of the process.

Administrative Proceedings

The effects of intoxicants of different classes have not been differentiated in administrative hearings or other proceedings involving employment eligibility, benefits, restriction, discrimination, supervision, discipline, or termination. In these venues, as in professional regulatory contexts, the prevailing presumption reflects the false and dangerous syllogism that "use equals abuse equals addiction equals impairment" (100). Moreover, routine screening for intoxicant use in the workplace is technically problematic (123) as well as legally and ethically questionable (124). Well-established principles of administrative law procedure are often violated, and fundamental legal rights (e.g., due process) often ignored. Despite their being treated like criminal "defendants," the accused in these proceedings are neither guaranteed adequate legal representation nor provided with the funds and resources (e.g., expert witnesses) necessary to present an adequate defense. Data and conclusions from questionably valid screening protocols and dubious testing methods and procedures often go unchallenged. It is vital that an addiction medicine specialist (preferably one with added qualifications as a Medical Review Officer) (*a*) reviews all of the technical data, (*b*) examines the accused to assess the nature and extent of any intoxicant-related problems or disabilities that might be relevant to job performance, and (*c*) provides testimony to the administrative review body to explain the meaning, significance, and implications of the findings. There is no other way to assure fairness for all parties.

Given the cultural prejudices about intoxicant use and the pressures on employers to maintain a "drug-free workplace," an employee who is accused of intoxicant use cannot safely assume that he or she will get a fair hearing or receive an equitable disposition. Addiction medicine specialists must be aware of these prevailing inequities. The need and opportunities for professional involvement in intoxicant-related matters of administrative law are great.

CONCLUSION

There can be no doubt that there are many serious conceptual problems and resultant inequities in the modern criminal law. History has shown that "the engine of the law doth indeed grind slowly." Now more than ever, the practice of law and the science of jurisprudence are in need of consultation and collaboration with other professions, intellectual disciplines, and fields of knowledge. The challenge to the medical, biological, and cognitive sciences is clear. The response remains to be seen.

Doubtless, working in the forensic arena is not for everyone. For many addiction medicine professionals, the intense adversarial nature and constricting rules of criminal proceedings are personally offensive and professionally intolerable. For some others, ethical concerns, opinions and values, or personal experiences make them reluctant or unwilling to participate in what they perceive to be the shielding of an intoxicant user from the full consequences of his or her actions. For a few others, their understanding or personal history of addiction may lead them to interpret and condemn any such involvement as a form of professional "enabling" of a patient's addiction. But for those addictionists who do choose to participate in the judicial process, to make a contribution to the cause of justice, and to work to illuminate this vital medical-legal interface, the rewards from the intellectual challenge, professional enrichment, and personal fulfillment can be substantial.

References

1. Burglass ME, Shaffer H. The natural history of ideas in the addictions. In: Shaffer H, Burglass ME, eds. Classic contributions in the addictions. New York: Brunner/Mazel, 1981:xvii–xlii.
2. Burglass ME, Shaffer H. Diagnosis in the addictions I: Conceptual problems. Adv Alcohol Subst Abuse 1984;3(1&2):19–34.
3. Gambino B, Shaffer H. The concept of paradigm and the treatment of addiction. Prof Psychology 1979;10:207–233.
4. Shaffer H. Theories of addiction: in search of a paradigm. In: Shaffer H, ed. Myths and realities: a book about drug users. Boston: Zucker, 1977: 42–45.
5. Shaffer H, Gambino B. Addiction paradigms II: theory, research and practice. J Psychedelic Drugs 1979;11:299–304.
6. State v. Eldredge, 773 P.2d 29 (Utah 1989).
7. Commonwealth v. Baldwin, 502 A.2d. 253 (Pa. Super. Ct. 1985).
8. People v. Rogers, 800 P.2d 1327 (Colo. Ct. App. 1990).
9. State v. Peeler, 614 P.2d 335 (Ariz. Ct. App. 1980).
10. People v. Gallegos, 644 P.2d 920 (Colorado 1982).
11. United States v. Rea, 958 F.2d 1206 (2d Cir. 1992).
12. United States v. LeRoy, 944 F.2d 787 (10th Cir. 1991); aff'd. after remand, 984 F.2d 1095 (10th Cir. 1993).
13. United States v. Shorter, 608 F. Supp 871 (D. D.C. 1985); aff'd:,18 F. Supp 255 (D. D.C. 1987).
14. United States v. Davis, 772 F.2d 1339 (7th Cir. 1985).
15. United States v. Berrios-Rodriguez, 768 F. Supp 939 (D. Puerto Rico 1991).
16. United States v. Ramirez, 871 F.2d 582 (6th Cir. 1989).
17. Hall v. State, 568 So. 2d 882 (Fla. 1990).
18. Simon R. Clinical psychiatry and the law. 2nd edition. Washington, DC: American Psychiatric Press, 1992.
19. Golding SL, et al. Specialty guidelines for forensic psychologists. Law Hum Behav 1991;15: 655–665.
20. Insanity Defense Reform Act of 1984, 18 U.S.C. sec. 17.
21. Moriarty JC. Psychological and scientific evidence in criminal trials. New York: Clark Boardman Callaghan, 1996.
22. Federal Criminal Code and Rules, 18 U.S.C., 1996.
23. Frye v. United States, 293 F. 1013 (D.C. Cir. 1923).
24. Daubert v. Merrell Dow Pharmaceuticals, Inc., 113 S. Ct. 2786 (1993).
25. United States v. DiDomenico, 985 F.2d 1159, 1163 (2d Cir. 1993).

26. Arcoren v. United States, 929 F.2d 1235 (8th Cir.), cert. denied, 112 S. Ct. 312 (1991).
27. United States v. Rubio-Villareal, 927 F.2d 1495, 1502 (9th Cir. 1991).
28. United States v. Azure, 801 F.2d 336, 340 (8th Cir. 1986).
29. United States v. Schmidt, 711 F.2d 595, 598 (5th Cir. 1983).
30. United States v. Gilliss, 645 F.2d 1269, 1278 (8th Cir. 1981).
31. United States v. Zink, 612 F.2d 511, 514–515 (10th Cir. 1980).
32. Burglass ME. The role of the medical-psychiatric expert witness in drug-related cases. Inside Drug Law 1985;2(3):1–6.
33. Blume SB. Compulsive gambling and the medical model. J Gambling Behav 1988;3:237–247.
34. Scodel A. Inspirational group therapy: a study of Gamblers Anonymous. Am J Psychiatry 1964; 18:115–125.
35. Burglass ME. Pathological gambling: forensic update and commentary. In: Shaffer H, Cummins T, Gambino B, Stein S, Furstenberg M, eds. Compulsive gambling. Yesterday, today, and tomorrow. Lexington, MA: Lexington Books/DC Heath, 1981:205–222.
36. Nemerson SA. Alcoholism, intoxication, and the criminal law. Cardozo L Rev 1988;10:423.
37. American Psychiatric Association. Diagnostic and statistical manual of mental disorders. 4th edition. Washington, DC: American Psychiatric Association, 1994.
38. Roemer RA, Cornwell A, Dewart D, Jackson P, Ercegovac DV. Quantitative electroencephalographic analyses in cocaine-preferring polysubstance abusers during abstinence. Psychiatry Res 1995;58(3):247–257.
39. Strickland TL, Mena I, Villanueva-Meyer J, Miller BL, Cummings J, Mehringer CM, et al. Cerebral perfusion and neuropsychological consequences of chronic cocaine use. J Neuropsychiatry Clin Neurosci 1993;5(4):419–427.
40. Herning RI, Glover BJ, Koeppl B, Phillips RL, London ED. Cocaine-induced increases in EEG alpha and beta activity: evidence for reduced cortical processing. Neuropsychopharmacology 1994;11(1):1–9.
41. Lezak MD. Neuropsychological assessment. 3rd edition. New York: Oxford University Press, 1995.
42. Lezak MD. Domains of behavior from a neuropsychological perspective: the whole story. Nebr Symp Motiv 1994;41:23–55.
43. Bondy KN. Assessing cognitive function: a guide to neuropsychological testing. Rehabil Nurs 1994;19(1):24–30, 36.
44. Beatty WW, Katzung VM, Moreland VJ, Nixon SJ. Neuropsychological performance of recently abstinent alcoholics and cocaine abusers. Drug Alcohol Depend 1995;37(3):247–253.

45. Bernal B, Ardila A, Bateman JR. Cognitive impairments in adolescent drug-abusers. Int J Neurosci 1994;75(3–4):203–212.
46. Berry J, van Gorp WG, Herzberg DS, Hinkin C, Boone K, Steinman L, Wilkins JN. Neuropsychological deficits in abstinent cocaine abusers: preliminary findings after two weeks of abstinence. Drug Alcohol Depend 1993;32(3): 231–237.
47. Meek PS, Clark HW, Solana VL. Neurocognitive impairment: the unrecognized component of dual diagnosis in substance abuse treatment. J Psychoactive Drugs 1989;21(2):153–160.
48. Bryson GJ, Silverstein ML, Nathan A, Stephen L. Differential rate of neuropsychological dysfunction in psychiatric disorders: comparison between the Halstead-Reitan and Luria-Nebraska batteries. Percept Mot Skills 1993; 76(1):305–306.
49. Kane RL. Standardized and flexible batteries in neuropsychology: an assessment update. Neuropsychol Rev 1991;2(4):281–339.
50. Cook J. Act, intention, and motive in the criminal law. Yale Law J 1917;26:645–658.
51. United States v. Drew, 25 Fed. Cas. No. 14,993 (C. C. D. Mass. 1828).
52. LaFave WR, Scott AW. Substantive criminal law. St. Paul, MN: West, 1986, supp 1996.
53. Burrows v. State, 297 P. 1029 (Arizona 1931).
54. People v. Scott, 146 Cal. App.3d 823, 194 Cal. Rptr. 633 (1983).
55. City of Minneapolis v. Altimus, 306 Minn. 462, 238 N.W.2d 851 (1976).
56. Kane v. United States, 399 F.2d 730 (9th Cir. 1968).
57. Burke SB. The defense of voluntary intoxication: now you see it, now you don't. Ind L Rev 1986;19:147.
58. State v. Hall, 214 N.W.2d 205 (Iowa 1974).
59. Hall J. Intoxication and criminal responsibility. Harv L Rev 1944;57:1056.
60. Schabas PB. Intoxication and culpability: towards an offence of criminal intoxication. U T Fac L Rev 1984;42:147.
61. Benton EH, Bor A, Leech WH, Levy JA, Lipshie SD, Mitchell TB, Brown GM. Special project. Drugs and criminal responsibility. Vanderbilt L Rev 1980;33:1145–1218.
62. Foltin RW, Fischman MW, Pippen PA, Kelly TH. Behavioral effects of cocaine alone and in combination with ethanol or marijuana in humans. Drug Alcohol Depend 1993;32(2):93–106.
63. Higgins ST, Rush CR, Hughes JR, Bickel WK, Lynn M, Capeless MA. Effects of cocaine and alcohol, alone and in combination, on human learning and performance. J Exp Anal Behav 199;58(1):87–105.
64. Ardila A, Rosselli M, Strumwasser S. Neuropsychological deficits in chronic cocaine abusers. Int J Neurosci 1991;57(1–2):73–79.

65. Manschreck TC, Schneyer ML, Weisstein CC, Laughery J, Rosenthal J, Celada T, Berner J. Freebase cocaine and memory. Compr Psychiatry 1990;31(4):369–375.

66. Duffy JD. The neurology of alcoholic denial: implications for assessment and treatment. Can J Psychiatry 1995;40(5):257–263.

67. Evans v. State, 645 P.2d 155 (Alaska 1982).

68. Commonwealth v. Sheehan, 376 Mass. 765, 383 N.E.2d 1115 (1978).

69. United States v. Lyons, 731 F.2d 243 (5th Cir. 1984) (en banc).

70. Uelmen GF, Tennant FS. Endorphins, addiction and the defense of medical necessity. The Champion 1985;9:6–11.

71. United States v. Randall, 104 Wash. Daily L. Rep. 2249 (1976).

72. State v. Diania, 604 P.2d 1312 (Wash. App., 1979).

73. State v. Tate, 477 A.2d 462 (N.J. Ct. App., 1984).

74. United States v. Moore, 486 F.2d 1139 (D.C. Cir. 1973) (en banc).

75. M'Naghten's Case, 8 Eng. Rep. 718 (1843).

76. United States v. Hinckley [No opinion issued], (D. D.C.), 1982.

77. Comprehensive Crime Control Act of 1984 (18 U.S.C. sec 20), 1984.

78. United States v. Freeman, 804 F.2d 1574 (11th Cir. 1986).

79. Commonwealth v. Mello, 420 Mass. 375; 649 N.E.2d 1106 (Massachusetts 1995).

80. West's Ann. Cal. Penal Code § 28.

81. Bethea v. United States, 365 A.2d 64 (App. D.C. 1976).

82. United States Sentencing Commission. Federal sentencing guidelines manual, 1995–96 ed. St. Paul, MN: West Publishing Co., 1996.

83. Custer RL. Gambling and addiction. In: Craig RJ, Baker SL, eds. Drug dependent patients. Springfield, IL: Charles C Thomas, 1982: 367–381.

84. Lesieur HR. The chase career of the compulsive gambler. New York: Anchor Press/Doubleday, 1977.

85. Carlton PL, Manowitz P. Physiological factors as determinants of pathological gambling. J Gambling Behav 1988;3:274–285.

86. Goldstein L. Differential EEG activation and pathological gambling. Biol Psychiatry 1985; 20:1232–1234.

87. Milkman H, Sunderwirth S. Addictive processes. J Psychoactive Drugs 1982;14(3):177–192.

88. Moran E. An assessment of the report of the royal commission on gambling 1976–1978. Br J Add 1979:74:3–9.

89. Wray I, Dickerson MG. Cessation of high frequency gambling and "withdrawal" symptoms. Br J Addict 1981;76:401–405.

90. Strassman HD. Forensic issues in pathological gambling. In: Balski T, ed. The handbook of pathological gambling. Springfield, IL: Charles C Thomas, 1987:195–204.

91. Wilson. v. Commissioner, 76 TC 623 (1981).

92. Ritholz J, Fink R. New developments and dangers in the psychiatric defense to tax fraud. J Taxation 1970;32:322–330.

93. Carnes PJ. Don't call it love. New York: Bantam Books, 1991.

94. Christenson GA, Raber RJ, deZwann M, et al. Compulsive buying: descriptive characteristics and psychiatric comorbidity. J Clin Psychiatry 1994;55:5–11.

95. Bernik MA, Akerman D, Amaral JAMS, Braun RCDN. Cue exposure in compulsive buying [letter]. J Clin Psychiatry 1996;57:90.

96. Camhi L. Stealing femininity: department store kleptomania as sexual disorder. Differences 1993;5(1):26–50.

97. Withers NW, Pulvirenti L, Koob GF, Gillin JC. Cocaine abuse and dependence. J Clin Psychopharmacol 1995;15(1):63–78.

98. Teoh SK, et al. Pituitary volume in men with concurrent heroin and cocaine dependence. J Clin Endocrinol Metab 1993;76:1529–1532.

99. United States v. Ramirez, 871 F.2d 582 (6th Cir. 1989).

100. Burglass ME. Use equals abuse equals impairment: a false and dangerous syllogism [abstract]. Alcohol Clin Exp Res 1988;12(1):190.

101. Burglass ME. Chemical dependence and impairment: conceptual problems [abstract]. Alcohol Clin Exp Res 1989;13(1):147.

102. Ackerman TF. Chemically dependent physicians and informed consent disclosure. J Addict Dis 1996;15(2):25–42.

103. Portenoy RK. Therapeutic use of opioids: prescribing and control issues. NIDA Res Monogr 1993;131:35–50.

104. Hills S. Government regulatory influences on opioid prescribing and their impact on the treatment of pain of nonmalignant origin. J Pain Symptom Manage 1996;11(5):287–298.

105. Morgan J. American opiophobia: customary underutilization of opioid analgesics. Adv Alcohol Subst Abuse 1985;5:163.

106. Portenoy RK. Chronic opioid therapy for persistent noncancer pain: can we get past the bias? APS Bull 1991;1:4–5.

107. Reidenberg MM, Portenoy RK. The need for an open mind about the treatment of chronic non-malignant pain. Clin Pharmacol Ther 1994;55(4):367–369.

108. Portenoy RK, Foley KM. Chronic use of opioid analgesics in non-malignant pain: report of 38 cases. Pain 1986;25(2):171–186.

109. Portenoy RK. Chronic opioid therapy in non-malignant pain. J Pain Symptom Manage 1990;5(1 suppl):S46–62.

110. Savage SR. Long-term opioid therapy: assessment of consequences and risks. J Pain Symptom Manage 1996;11(5):274–286.

111. Schug S, Merry A, Acland R. Treatment principles for the use of opioids in pain of nonmalignant origin. Drugs 1991;42:228–232.

112. Schofferman J. Longterm use of opioid analgesia for the treatment of chronic pain of non-malignant origin. J Pain Symptom Manage 1993; 8:279–288.

113. Portenoy RK, Payne R. Acute and chronic pain. In: Lowinson JH, Ruiz P, Millman RB, Langrod JG, eds. Substance abuse: a comprehensive textbook. 2nd edition. Baltimore: Williams & Wilkins, 1992:691–721.

114. Wesson DR, Ling W, Smith DE. Prescription opioids for the treatment of pain in patients with addictive disease. J Pain Symptom Manage 1993;8:289–296.

115. Savage SR. Management of acute and chronic pain and cancer pain in the addicted patient. In: Miller NS, ed. Principles of addiction medicine. Chevy Chase, MD: American Society of Addiction Medicine, 1995;Sec VIII, Chap 1: 1–16.

116. Fishbain DA, Rosomoff HL, Rosomoff RS. Drug abuse, dependence, and addiction in chronic pain patients. Clin J Pain 1992;8: 77–85.

117. Savage SR. Addiction in the treatment of pain: significance, recognition, and management. J Pain Symptom Manage 1993;8(5):265–278.

118. Sees KL, Clark HW. Opioid use in the treatment of chronic pain: assessment of addiction. J Pain Symptom Manage 1993;8(5):257–264.

119. Faden R, Beauchamp T. A history and theory of informed consent. New York: Oxford University Press, 1986.

120. Portenoy RK, Thaler HT, Kornblith AB, Lepore JM, Friedlander-Klar H, Kiyasu E, et al. The Memorial Symptom Assessment Scale: an instrument for the evaluation of symptom prevalence, characteristics and distress. Eur J Cancer 1994;30A(9):1326–1336.

121. Tennant FS, Uelmen GF. Narcotic maintenance for chronic pain: medical and legal guidelines. Postgrad Med 1983;73:81–94.

122. Clark HW, Sees KL. Opioids, chronic pain, and the law. J Pain Symptom Manage 1993; 8(5):297–305.

123. Osterloh J, Becker C. Chemical dependency and drug testing in the workplace. West J Med 1990;152:506–513.

124. Burglass ME. Employee assistance and drug testing: striving for fairness [abstract]. Alcohol Clin Exp Res 1988;12(1):190.

81 THE ADDICT AS A PATIENT

Mary Jeanne Kreek and Marc Reisinger

UNITED STATES PERSPECTIVE

Introduction

The problems of drug addictions, and, in a broader sense, the general problems of chemical dependency, are increasingly recognized as a category of medical disorders and are increasingly accepted as such by health care providers including physicians, nurses, and all other professionals and paraprofessionals involved in the delivery of health care, as well as by policy makers and the lay public. This acceptance has been slow, but has been emerging gradually since the first identification of AIDS disease in 1981 (later found to be caused by HIV-1 infection), coupled with the recognition in 1983 of a linkage between intravenous drug abuse and AIDS, which added to the earlier recognition of linkage between intravenous drug use and hepatitis B, delta, non-A, non-B, and more recently, hepatitis C. This emergence of acceptance of the specific addictions as medical problems is occurring after many years when the addictions and chemical dependency were considered to be criminal behaviors, sociological phenomena, or personality and psychiatric disorders. Such formulations of the bases of these disorders were directly related both to federal and state laws in the United States which defined most types of drug abuse and addiction as criminal behaviors, and to the frustration of health care professionals in their earlier attempts to manage these disorders, about which very little was known on either a metabolic or behavioral basis at the time. There were, therefore, very few, if any, effective approaches to treatment.

Psychiatrists and other physicians who wanted to attempt to approach the treatment of addictions as medical problems were confronted with the fact that most psychiatrists, as a physician specialty group, had usually classified the addict as a psychopath or a sociopath, a diagnosis which usually implies a very poor or hopeless outcome in treatment of any type. Even now, further refinement of the diagnosis of antisocial personality type clearly remains needed, to differentiate those antisocial signs and symptoms displayed by the addict which are a result of drug use per se or related to the acquisition of funds and illegal drugs to support an addiction, from those signs and symptoms that characterize the defined antisocial personality disorder but which appeared before any drug abuse began (often as early as age 8–10).

Modest early attempts of pharmacotherapy for addictions, such as the use of heroin and other opiates to treat alcoholism, the use of cocaine to treat heroin addiction, and the use of opiates to treat cocaine dependency (similar self-therapeutic approaches are still being attempted by the street addict today), had failed, as had a few more thoughtful and research-based attempts to apply other types of pharmacotherapy or specific behavioral therapies to the management of addictions. Well-based fears on the part of many physicians and other health care professionals, that treatment of the addicts would be interpreted as illegal behaviors on their part, reinforced the general rejection of the addict as a patient. The magnitude of the problem of the specific addictions and other chemical dependency problems began to be increasingly recognized by many policy makers, as well as health care workers and academicians, including clinical and laboratory scientists, in the early 1960s. This led to many changes over the ensuing 30 years, especially over the last decade, in the setting of increasing recognition of both the epidemic of drug addiction and of AIDS. The obligatory role of the health care profession in managing addiction and other chemical dependencies is now being reconsidered. In this setting again, as was pleaded for by the late Dr. Marie Nyswander in her thoughtful 1956 book *The Drug Addict as a Patient,* the concept of treating the addict as a patient in a medical setting is increasingly accepted.

In the intervening years, when the addict was considered to be simply a criminal or a social deviant, possibly the one substantial ray of hope for future reconsideration of the medical concept of addiction was provided by Alcoholics Anonymous (AA), developed by Bill Wilson and friends. This original 12-step program, which has gone on to proliferate worldwide and to spawn development of similar 12-step programs and other self-help approaches for management of other specific chemical dependencies, recognized alcoholism as a medical disorder, though a disorder without a known metabolic, genetic, or behavioral definition. The program also accepted that alcoholism was probably a life-long chronic and often relapsing disorder, which required continuing treatment or management, even though the treatment available was one which involved no medication and no specific psychological or behavioral approaches.

The magnitude of the problem of chemical dependencies in the United States and worldwide is enormous (see the "European Perspective" later in this chapter). It is now estimated that over 2.7 million persons in the United States have used heroin at some time, that approximately one million use heroin regularly, and that approximately 500,000–1,000,000 are "hard-core" heroin addicts, persons who use multiple doses of illicitly obtained opiates each day, with the development of tolerance (that is, need for increasing dose of drugs to achieve the desired effects of analgesia or euphoria and to pre-

vent withdrawal); physical dependence (presentation of a cascade of easily measured signs and symptoms which occur following abrupt cessation of chronic use of opiates); and drug-seeking behavior. It has similarly been estimated by various federal and state surveys that approximately 22 million persons have used cocaine at some time, approximately 2 million have used cocaine with some regularity, and that approximately 700,000 are regular daily and/or intermittent binge users of cocaine. Similarly it is estimated that there are now over 11 million alcohol abusers or alcoholics.

These three addictions, opiate dependency, cocaine dependency, and alcoholism, constitute the major causes for emergency room visits directly related to drug abuse and chemical dependency and are also the three most common causes of death directly due to drug abuse and drug addiction as documented by medical examiners' offices. Other addictions, including chronic marihuana use, nicotine dependency, benzodiazepine dependency, barbiturate dependency, amphetamine dependency, as well as use of hallucinogens, are the other major chemical dependency problems. However, even with increasing recognition of the magnitude of the chemical dependency problem in the late 1950s and early 1960s, very little attention, outside of the United States Public Health Service Facility at Lexington, Kentucky, had been given to the clinical needs of chemically dependent persons and very limited research done to attempt to address scientifically, in basic clinical or laboratory research, the problems of addictions.

This chapter will offer the first author's reflections on her experiences as a physician-scientist in both the early research on the treatment of heroin addiction during the mid 1960s as well as in more recent basic laboratory and clinical research on the addictive diseases, research performed to provide information about the biological, including possibly genetic, bases of addictions. These reflections will be used to provide possible insights into what can be accomplished, both for the individual and for society, by the treatment of the addict as a patient, as well as to provide some perspective as to what may be hoped to be achieved in the future. When an original research team to study a possible new pharmacotherapeutic approach for heroin addiction was formed in late 1963 and brought together in the early months of 1964 at the then Rockefeller Institute for Medical Research and the Rockefeller Institute Hospital, the team was led by Professor Vincent P. Dole, an established laboratory and clinical scientist and Senior Member of the Institute, and included the late Dr. Marie Nyswander, a well-trained psychiatrist experienced in the area of treatment of addictions, and the first author, then a first-year resident (second-year house officer) in internal medicine at the New York Hospital-Cornell University Medical Center, sent as the first resident from that medical center to do a research elective at The Rockefeller Institute.

One of the most important early lessons the first author received was from the late Dr. Nyswander; she had worked for many often frustrating years attempting to treat addiction, through her early training at Bellevue Hospital, in her later work at the United States Public Health Services at Lexington, Kentucky, and then back on the streets of New York, under the partial guidance of many people including Dr. Beatrice Berle. Although it became quite clear to Dr. Nyswander that there was no established or effective approach for treatment of heroin dependency (just as there was no established and highly effective approach for treatment of alcoholism, other than AA), her constant and persuasive teaching was that the drug addict must be treated as a patient. This meant, and still means, that the addict must be treated with the same dignity and respect for individual needs, including the need for maintenance of confidentiality, and for rigorous addressing of specific medical and behavioral problems, as any other patient seeking treatment for any other disease would be treated. Having worked with many heroin addicts, as well as patients with other chemical dependencies for many years, Dr. Nyswander appreciated the failure of most health care professionals and medical institutions to ever treat the addict as a patient. She also was keenly aware of the origins of the frustrations, both legally imposed and due to lack of knowledge, with which physicians and other health care professionals were confronted when an addict would present himself or herself in an emergency room or in a clinic setting. Based on her experience, Dr. Nyswander brought to the original research team a very important lesson which, in fact, pertains to all new basic clinical research efforts, as well as to all excellent approaches to medical care for any patient: the investigator or the physician must listen, and listen carefully, to the patient at all times. Only by careful questioning and listening can one hope to learn things from a patient which one certainly needs to learn when a disease is not well understood and is being studied, or when a new treatment or type of management for such a disease is being attempted.

Dr. Dole brought to that original team the humanity of a basic clinical investigator as well as the quiet insight of the need for a deeply committed quest for more knowledge in this already stigmatized research area, riddled with atypical barriers, along with unexpected findings as in any field full of unknowns, a research situation which he had confronted many times in his earlier distinguished career as a laboratory and clinical investigator in the fields of lipid metabolism, obesity, and hypertension.

As the youngest member of the team, the first author brought simply an open mind, an intense desire to learn about the biology of addiction at the most fundamental level possible, and enthusiasm based in part on previous exciting and fulfilling research experiences, since the first author had already had the privilege of spending several college summers and medical school electives in both clinical and laboratory research at the National Institutes of Health and at the Columbia University College of Physicians and Surgeons.

In our initial research on the treatment of narcotic addiction in early 1964, we read and we taught each other, but primarily we learned from "hard-core," long-term heroin addicts who became our research patients, most with a history of narcotic addiction of over 15 years, each with at least three failures at detoxification and "drug-free" treatment and each with multiple arrests and incarcerations prior to admission to our research project. We learned from these addicts by treating them as research patients in the very special, quiet and supportive environment of the Rockefeller Institute Hospital.

In February 1964, after recapitulating negative studies of earlier workers, primarily those at the U.S. Public Health Service hospital at Lexington, Kentucky, to see if heroin addiction could be effectively managed by use of multiple shots of morphine and reconfirming earlier findings, including the need for constantly escalating doses of morphine because of rapidly developing tolerance, coupled with the problem that intermittent parenteral morphine treatment renders patients in either a euphoric or somnolent state or in a state of narcotic withdrawal, neither of which would ever permit achievement of a satisfactory level of stabilization needed for rehabilitation in most patients, studies of new therapeutic approaches were initiated.

Many factors contributed to the selection of the synthetic opiate methadone, to be administered orally, as the potential pharmacotherapeutic agent for study as a possible maintenance treatment for narcotic addiction: the extensive earlier clinical experiences of Dr. Marie Nyswander along with the first author's limited experiences gained while working as a medical student extern on the Columbia University service at Bellevue Hospital in New York, where the synthetic, orally effective opiate, methadone, had been used to some limited extent in short-term (10–14 days) detoxification treatment of heroin addiction; and voluminous anecdotal data obtained from dozens of interviews with heroin addicts on the street or attempting to enter some type of treatment program. Numerous heroin addicts had mentioned using "dollys," or Dolphine, the then Eli Lilly trade name of methadone hydrochloride, for self-detoxification or short-term self-maintenance treatment when heroin was not available on the streets or when the degree of tolerance became so high that heroin was no longer affordable.

Our research team decided on the fundamental requirements for a pharmacological treatment agent for heroin addiction: (a) an agent which would be orally effective, thus removing the addict forever from both the mystique and group behavior of using and sharing needles and related equipment for injection of an opiate drug, and therefore also from the many potential health hazards resulting from such needle-sharing, including infection with viruses causing hepatitis and other infectious diseases; and (b) an effective treatment agent with a slow onset (to avoid any opiate-like reinforcing effects) and a long-acting effect (thus providing steady blood levels and steady state perfusion of what, even in 1964, were hypothesized to be specific opiate receptors).

In 1964 there were no sufficiently sensitive and specific analytical chemical techniques, such as gas-liquid chromatography, high-performance liquid chromatography, or mass spectrometry, which would allow measurement of blood levels of any opiate drugs (or other related basic amine drugs)

with their characteristically low plasma levels, even after high-dose administration. Therefore, there was no pharmacokinetics or drug dispositional information available, nor could such information be generated concerning any narcotic medication. The pharmacokinetics of morphine and its man-made diacetylated derivative, heroin, as well as of the newer synthetic pharmacotherapeutic agents such as methadone, were not known. However, based, in part, on clinical observations made during use of methadone at the limited sites at which it was being used for "detoxification" treatment of heroin addicts, and also, in part, on the more careful clinical observations made in research studies of attempts to manage pain using methadone, it was discerned that methadone might be a long-acting opiate for at least some of its effects. In the pain studies, it had been shown that, although methadone had a time course of analgesic action very similar to morphine (4–6 hours), when repeated doses were administered over a 24-hour interval, apparent drug accumulation would occur, with resultant well-known adverse opiate effects, such as respiratory depression. This suggested a long terminal half-life of methadone, with sustained action at least at those sites at which opiates depress respiration.

It was by careful questioning, listening to, and observing the addict as a research patient that we were able to distinguish the profound differences in behavior, and, later, in signs and symptoms related to physiological changes, in these former heroin addicts when they were receiving methadone as contrasted to when they were self-administering heroin or when they had been given morphine in a research setting. In these early clinical research studies, methadone was administered orally only one time a day as a single dose. We chose to slowly escalate the daily dose of methadone from the selected initial doses of 30–40 mg/day (which had been used as the total daily doses in detoxification treatment of addiction), up to doses which we hypothesized would provide sufficient blood levels to prevent narcotic abstinence signs and symptoms over a 24-hour dosing interval, to prevent "drug hunger" and also, as we were to document in subsequent studies, to provide sufficient tolerance and therefore cross-tolerance to other opiates to prevent any perception of narcotic effects from any subsequent self-administration of illicit opiates, and thus, to discourage any further illicit narcotic use.

We then performed two series of 4-week studies of this so-called "narcotic blockade" after doses of methadone had been slowly increased over several weeks, from 30–40 mg up to 80–120 mg/day. These studies were performed using a double-blinded protocol in which, in random order, in a Latin square design, heroin, morphine, dihydromorphine (Dilaudid), methadone, or saline each were injected intravenously against a background of daily, single oral dosing with methadone. When the code was broken for each of these two 4-week sequences of studies using different research subjects, it was found that no narcotic-like effects were perceived or observed by the patient, or by the clinical research observer, and no objective indices changed after intravenous administration of what were comparable to analgesic doses or street-abuse doses of each of these short-acting opiates, methadone itself, or saline, superimposed on the daily administration of methadone. The only sensation that was perceived by the former addict was a feeling of "pins and needles" after morphine was injected, subsequently attributed to the abrupt release of histamine, a well-established phenomenon resulting from morphine injection. However, that "pins and needles" sensation was not followed by any "rush," "high," or euphoric feelings, nor by any somnolence, both of which would customarily accompany morphine self-administration by an addict. Thus the very high level of opiate tolerance provided by daily treatment with methadone, which we now know is a pharmacokinetically very long-acting opioid in humans (24-hour apparent terminal plasma half-life for the racemic dl (RS)-methadone; 48-hour plasma half-life for the active [R]-l enantiomer), and which acts primarily or exclusively at mu subtype opiate receptors, was sufficient to prevent any narcotic effect when modest to moderate amounts of any short-acting opiate were superimposed.

Subsequent single-blinded studies showed that an amount of heroin valued on the streets at over $200 in 1964 would be required to overcome the level of opiate cross-tolerance provided by 80–120 mg per day of methadone and then, but only then, could any narcotic effects of the possibly desired "euphoric type" be perceived by the research patient and observed by the investigator.[a]

In 1964, by careful clinical observations and discussions with the former addict, research patients, it was readily discerned that methadone neither rendered the patient "high" (that is, euphoric or somnolent) when appropriate doses of methadone were used and kept within the level of tolerance which had been developed by that individual, nor "sick" (that is, in a state of narcotic abstinence or withdrawal), even at the end of a 24-hour dosing interval in most patients. However, the amount of methadone to be administered in an oral daily dose needed, both to prevent withdrawal symptoms during early medication and to provide adequate cross-tolerance to prevent perception of narcotic effects from any superimposed heroin, must be adjusted upward if the purity of street heroin increases significantly as it has in 1995 and 1996 in some regions. Clearly treating the addict as a research patient was essential for this clinical research to be accomplished. When the first experimental work performed in 1964 and early 1965 at the Rockefeller University was then moved to the Manhattan General Hospital (a proprietary hospital later to become the Bernstein Institute, a not-for-profit, voluntary hospital of the Beth Israel Medical Center), to attempt to see whether methadone maintenance for heroin addiction would continue to be efficacious as pharmacological treatment for heroin addiction in a less sheltered and pleasant setting than the Rockefeller Institute Hospital provided, it became equally clear that the concept of continuously treating each addict as a patient should be the first lesson given to all medical staff and to all other persons who would interact with patients, both before entering treatment research and during treatment at all times.

After demonstrating the success of methadone maintenance treatment in the applied clinical research studies performed at the Manhattan General Hospital, Dr. Marie Nyswander and Dr. Vincent Dole with facilitation by Dr. Raymond Trussell, then Director of the Beth Israel Medical Center, and the help of Dr. Harold Trigg, a senior psychiatrist at Beth Israel, and Dr. Joyce Lowinson developed the first inpatient treatment facilities for methadone maintenance treatment patients at the Manhattan General Hospital, and subsequently at other hospitals under the auspices of the Beth Israel Medical Center. This program continued to develop in number of patients and scope and, under the leadership of Dr. Robert Newman who succeeded Dr. Trussell as the President of Beth Israel Medical Center, had become the largest network of methadone maintenance treatment programs in the world by the 1970s and continuing through the 1980s and 1990s. Dr. Herman Joseph, then working with the New York City Narcotics Unit of the Department of Probation, encountered many former prisoners who desperately needed treatment and began to work with Drs. Dole and Nyswander in 1967. He both referred patients to the methadone maintenance treatment programs at The Rockefeller University, at the Beth Israel Medical Center, and at the Van Etten Hospital; he also assisted Dr. Dole with special evaluation and follow-up studies from then on. Dr. Frances Gearing of the Columbia University School of Public Health initiated an independent evaluation of methadone maintenance treatment.

Dr. Joyce Lowinson, a psychiatry resident and student of Dr. Marie Nyswander, played an important role in further implementing and expanding the original methadone research project from The Rockefeller University to the Beth Israel Medical Center in collaboration with Drs. Dole and Nyswander. In 1966, Dr. Lowinson established a methadone maintenance

program for addicts with tuberculosis at the Van Etten Hospital, a city hospital affiliated with the Albert Einstein College of Medicine. In 1968, upon completion of her residency at the Albert Einstein College of Medicine, she established the first methadone maintenance treatment program which accepted dually diagnosed patients, that is, patients with specific psychiatric diagnoses as well as opiate addiction, at the Bronx State Hospital in affiliation with Albert Einstein College of Medicine. It has become the largest methadone maintenance programs in the United States under the direct auspices of a medical school. This program pioneered in the practice of offering diversified counseling services including both special vocational and educational programs to meet the various and changing needs of its patients. Also under Dr. Lowinson's direction, one of the first residential methadone therapeutic communities was later opened at the Bronx State Hospital with excellent treatment outcome.

In 1967 and 1968 Drs. Dole, Nyswander, and Kreek at The Rockefeller University Hospital pioneered an exclusively outpatient methadone maintenance treatment program with no inpatient treatment or induction component, a model which was soon to replace all initial inpatient methadone maintenance treatment because of fiscal constraints. Another physician who became actively involved in this area of work was a psychiatrist, Dr. Jerome Jaffe, who, after spending some time training at The Rockefeller University in 1967, established at the Albert Einstein College of Medicine an early methadone treatment and research program involving ambulatory stabilization. Subsequently, Dr. Jaffe went on to pioneer using methadone treatment in residential therapeutic communities at the Department of Psychiatry of the University of Chicago and the Illinois Drug Abuse Program. In the early 1970s, Dr. Jaffe was to become director of the President's Special Action Office on Drug Abuse Prevention, the precursor of the National Institute on Drug Abuse, and in that position become instrumental in promoting the expansion of methadone maintenance treatment throughout the nation.

Dr. Robert Millman, trained in both internal medicine and psychiatry at the New York Hospital Cornell University Medical Center, worked at The Rockefeller University with both Dr. Kreek and Dr. Dole in 1969 and 1970, both in the laboratories and in the clinics. With Dr. Dole, he assisted in conducting the first methadone detoxification treatment study within a New York City detention center. Dr. Elizabeth Khuri, trained in general medicine and adolescent medicine, came to The Rockefeller University in 1970 to work with Drs. Nyswander, Dole, and Kreek to train both in clinical care and research related to opiate addiction. In 1971 Dr. Millman and Dr. Khuri opened the first program for treatment of "hard-core," long-term (two years or more), adolescent heroin addicts, the Adolescent Development Program at the New York Hospital Cornell University Medical Center under the auspices of the Department of Public Health and Pediatrics. In 1973 a second clinic for treatment of older addicts, the Adult Clinic, was opened under the auspices of the Department of Medicine at the medical center, soon to come under the direction of Dr. Aaron Wells. All of these physicians, primarily devoted to clinical care and trained in diverse medical specialties including psychiatry, internal medicine, general medicine, adolescent medicine, and pediatrics, helped mold the concept of treating the addict as a medical patient.

Several investigators joined the early research team at The Rockefeller University, and by the end of 1964 the initial research team had expanded to include Drs. Ann Ho and Norman Gordon, both psychologists, and Dr. Edward Gordon, a psychiatrist. Each came to study various aspects of performance capacity of chronic methadone treated former heroin addicts, and each helped expand the concept of the former addict as a research patient. One of the greatest contributors in continuing to help develop and maintain this concept of the addict as a patient has been Dr. Enoch Gordis, who was already an accomplished biomedical scientist in a laboratory of Dr. Vincent Dole at The Rockefeller Institute in 1964 when the initial studies on narcotic addiction began. Within the next 10 years, Dr. Gordis went on to establish an outstanding research and treatment program to address the problems of another addiction, alcoholism, at the Elmhurst General Hospital of the Mount Sinai Medical Center, and in that role helped develop the concept of progressive needs of the alcoholic in recovery ranging from inpatient hospital care during detoxification and acute medical management up through halfway house care and finally into outpatient care deeply enriched by AA's

---

[a]This is a clinical and research issue that now must be revisited, since the purity of heroin on the streets in some regions of the United States such as New York City has dramatically increased, with analyses of street "heroin powder" performed by the United States Drug Enforcement Agency (DEA) in 1995 showing around 70% purity, as compared with less than 30% purity in recent years. Also, the cost of "heroin" has been constant or declined; thus, more milligrams of actual heroin are now purchased per dollar. This has led also to an increasing number of heroin overdose deaths. In 1995 in New York City, the DEA has found that the average cost of street heroin is one US dollar ($1) for 3–5 milligrams, whereas in the past the cost has been two to five times more than that (or around one U.S. dollar per milligram). Therefore, the level of tolerance of heroin addicts now entering methadone maintenance treatment may be greater than in the recent and more distant past. Also, the doses of methadone needed to prevent or "blockade" narcotic effects following superimposition of illicit heroin may be greater.

12-step programs. While directing the treatment and research programs, Dr. Gordis also pioneered in the treatment of dual addictions of alcoholism and narcotic addiction combining methadone maintenance treatment with drug-free treatment for alcoholism. Since 1986, he has been the Director of the National Institute on Alcoholism and Alcohol Abuse and in this leadership role continues to teach the needs for addressing all of the problems of the alcoholic, including dual addictions, in the most appropriate and effective manner within the state of the art. He has continued to be a leader in nurturing interaction between various types of treatment approaches while constantly demanding excellence in treatment and research efforts of all types.

The intrinsic need for humanity, which includes the respect and dignity that must be provided for any patient, was intuitively seen as an essential need from the time of our early research. Addressing this need, that is, providing appropriate management of the addict as a patient, yielded enormous benefits, not only for the patient, but society as a whole. Compliance in research, as well as compliance in treatment, was the most immediate positive response seen in the majority of former heroin addicts who were treated as patients in our early work at the Rockefeller University. However, even now, one cannot assume that all addicts seeking or in treatment, including clearly medically based treatment, such as pharmacological treatment of heroin addiction with the long-acting opioid methadone, will be automatically treated as patients. More often than not, we unfortunately still hear patients referred to as "junkies" or "dope fiends" or "sociopaths," rather than being referred to as patients with an addictive disease or chemical dependency problem, with or without some additionally diagnosed medical or psychiatric disorder.

As both epidemiologic data and both basic and applied clinical and laboratory research findings extend our knowledge about addiction and about the biological basis of addiction, we increasingly appreciate the role of host vulnerability in addiction. For instance, even a cursory look at the numerical estimates, based on findings from epidemiological surveys and studies, of those who become addicts after being once exposed to heroin, or the numbers who become regular or dependent users of cocaine after initial exposure to cocaine, suggests that between 1 in 4 down to 1 in 10 of those exposed to illicit drug will go on to develop addiction to heroin or cocaine respectively. The question of whether or not there is a genetic basis for this host vulnerability is currently under active research both at the laboratory and, most importantly, at a clinical research level at a number of research sites including our own, at this time. The current consensus of most experts working in this area is that there is a genetic vulnerability of some type for opiate addiction and cocaine dependency, just as research findings support a genetic vulnerability for alcoholism. A primary etiological role may be played by genetic factors in approximately 25% of alcoholics. It is the current consensus that although a single gene may be involved, it is more likely that multiple genes, either with abnormal or normal alleles, may form the genetic basis of the disease of alcoholism. The impact of environment remains important, since only through exposure to the addicting agent, alcohol, will the vulnerability be unmasked. Similarly, in around 75% of alcoholics, in whom it would appear on the basis of studies conducted to date that environmental factors play the primary etiological role, there still may be an inherent genetic vulnerability. Much less is known at this time about the potential genetic vulnerability, as well as other types of environmentally induced vulnerabilities, to the other addictions. It is appreciated also that the studies which are needed to elucidate these questions will be long and complex. Only imperfect laboratory animal models are available for such studies, although these may provide some clues of potential importance to the clinical situation. However, from either a humane or simply a completely selfish standpoint of society, unless the addict is treated as a patient, we will never have any hope of unraveling the genetic, as well as metabolic, toxicological, physiological, and environmental factors which form the basis of vulnerability to develop addictions in response to exposure to specific addicting drugs or other chemicals, or of understanding the requisite steps of becoming addicted to and also recovering from or being managed for such addictions.

Thus, it is both inherently appropriate to treat the addict as a patient and to abide by the same code of ethics which applies to physicians and other health care professionals in the management of all medical diseases, and also expedient, in terms of best serving society, for the addict to be treated as a

patient. Effective treatment of any addiction or chemical dependency will probably depend on such a humane approach. The early experience from 1964 to the present time with respect to human studies relating to: (*a*) opiate and also cocaine dependency; (*b*) related studies of the pharmacological and physiological effects of both illicit opiates and the long-acting opiate, methadone and also LAAM, its even longer-acting congener, as well as other agents which could be used in the management of heroin or other types of drug dependency; (*c*) the few clinical research studies of the physiological effects of other drugs of abuse (especially cocaine); and (*d*) studies of specific infectious diseases which usually result from use of shared and dirty needles and the atypical natural history of these diseases which may pertain in the setting of addiction, are referenced at the close of this chapter simply as examples of the diverse achievements which can be made when the addict is treated as a patient in an appropriate medically based, or medically linked, research or clinical treatment environment.

Types of Treatment for Chemical Dependency

There are two fundamentally different types of treatment for the chemically dependent patient (or client, as such persons are often unfortunately referred to by their care providers). One is a medical model of treatment and the other a nonmedically based, self-help model or behavioral modification approach of diverse types.

MEDICAL MODEL TREATMENT

Medical model treatment may involve primarily pharmacotherapy or use of a medication combined with behavioral therapy. The one major example of a pharmacotherapeutic approach which has proven to be both safe and efficacious in long-term studies is methadone maintenance treatment for opiate addiction. Other potential pharmacotherapies are currently under intensive investigation for the management of cocaine and nicotine dependencies. Also, since relatively small percentages of "hard-core" alcoholics respond on a sustained basis to AA or similar self-help programs, possible pharmacotherapeutic approaches for this disorder are also under study. The profound pressures imposed upon society, scientists, physicians, and other health care professionals by the fact that less than 10–30% of "hard-core" heroin addicts are able to be successfully treated by purely medication-free approaches, and that less than 30–50% of alcoholics or long-term cocaine dependent persons are able to be effectively treated on a long-term basis by abstinence approaches, even when coupled with the best of self-help groups, has led to increasing consideration and use of a medical model for treatment. Other medical model treatments are nonpharmacologically based, but use techniques of psychology and behavioral modification, such as deconditioning, or techniques of psychotherapy, such as using supportive-expressive, cognitive behavioral, or other formal manuals based on classical verbal psychiatric approaches to treatment.

NONMEDICAL TYPES OF TREATMENT

An even larger number of programs, but probably not larger in numbers of persons served in treatment, are the completely nonmedical programs, which rely on one of several philosophies, all of which include a concept of self-help. The best of these are very thoughtful conceptual approaches, which may include a philosophy involving spirituality, as well as personal insight and commitment in the recovering process.

Both the medical and nonmedical approaches to treatment may involve outpatient treatment, residential inpatient treatment, or "half-way house" type treatment, where a protected environment is offered as a residence, but where the patients are allowed to return to the "real world" for education or employment. Each of these approaches and treatment sites clearly has strong points; each also has weak points.

COMBINED MEDICAL AND NONMEDICAL TYPES OF TREATMENT

It becomes increasingly clear that the finest treatment approaches are a combination of medical treatment, usually involving a specific pharmacotherapy, behavioral and psychiatric care as needed, and primary health care, and a nonmedical model including 12-step or other self-help programs. Combined or "dual" addictions, that is concomitant addiction to two or more agents, are increasingly the most prevalent pattern of addictive disease and not just the exception. At this time, combinations of heroin addiction and alcoholism, heroin addiction and cocaine dependency, cocaine dependency and alcoholism, or all three of the above, with or without addition of one or more other agents used, are extremely common. Since we have only effective and specific pharmacotherapy for opiate addiction and possibly for alcoholism at this time, until more specific pharmacotherapies are developed for cocaine addiction, behavioral or nonmedical approaches must be relied upon. Pharmacotherapy for heroin addiction, including use of the agonists methadone and LAAM, the experimental partial agonist buprenorphine, and the antagonist naltrexone, has been used most effectively in combination with other medical-behavioral approaches and also with nonmedical approaches. With increasing numbers of homeless persons, as well as those who have been rejected by parents or spouse or children because of their chemical dependency, it is quite clear that we need more residential or partial residential resources for treatment at this time.

Novel combinations of such treatment approaches are desperately needed at this time; however, all of these approaches must assume that the addict will be treated as a patient with respect and dignity. This is unfortunately not always the case. In any one of these types of modalities, the addict may simply be treated as a criminal or a deviant. With the increasing recognition of specific, and often life threatening, medical problems, especially AIDS, hepatitis of various types, as well as tuberculosis and other devastating infectious diseases, in the chemically dependent person, a linkage with or in situ primary health care in the chemical dependency treatment programs is becoming essential. Possibly with the infusion of more health care providers from such fields such as infectious disease and hepatology, as well as from other specialties within the discipline of internal medicine and psychiatry as indicated, including physicians who may bring less pejorative attitudes towards the addicts, we may see a more natural acceptance of the addict as a patient. Previous experience would suggest that treatment of the addict as a patient, with all that implies, will help not only the addict and his or her family, but also society as a whole.

Primary and Specialized Health Care and Other Ancillary Services Related to the Treatment of Addiction

It is becoming increasingly apparent to policy makers and society as whole, as well to physicians and other health care providers, that many or most patients with addictive diseases have little or no access to primary health care. Alienation from the mainstream of society often has been most obvious in the attempts of the addict to intersect with the health care system. Often the primary motive for such intersection of the addict is to attempt to manipulate physicians or other health care providers into providing licit drugs for illicit self-medication of the addiction. Also the potential for the addict to display various criminal behaviors has made the active addict or chemically dependent person consistently unattractive to accept as a patient in a medical practice, clinic, or even in an emergency room setting, where such behaviors can be extremely disruptive. The chemically dependent person or the addict usually has no funds or medical insurance to pay for health care. Although many may be eligible for Medicaid or other types of partial or complete financial assistance for health care, more often than not a disrupted lifestyle has prevented them from following through the many and often tedious, frustrating, and difficult steps required to obtain Medicaid or similar health care financial support. Others, who have had jobs which included health care insurance, may be in the process of separating from their jobs and are not yet knowledgeable about the ways to continue active health care coverage. Some others may be working for cash in various types of licit or illicit employment with no access to health care insurance. These factors, coupled with many physicians' lack of knowledge about addiction and the paucity of specialized resources for the treatment of addiction, may lead the physician or other health care workers simply to reject addicts as potential patients, even though they may have presented themselves with bona fide medical problems in addition to their major untreated medical problem of addiction or chemical dependency. The emerging role of managed care may or may not help provide more extensive and widespread treatment of the addictions and may or may not appreciably change the chronic relapsing profiles of these diseases.

The multiple medical problems of the heroin addict were defined in the early studies from the 1960s, both at special resources such as the U.S. Public Health Service Hospital at Lexington, as well as our prospective studies at the Rockefeller Institute for Medical Research, later extended to several hospitals and clinical resources throughout New York City as part of the initial experiment on methadone maintenance for the treatment of narcotic addiction. Many of these medical complications were directly related to the use of shared needles, which were usually dirty or unsterilized; others were related to various aspects of the lifestyle of the addict. Some of the problems were also related to the pharmacological effects of the abused opiate drug itself, or the impact of the long-acting pharmacological agent used in treatment of opiate addiction on normal physiology. With the development of well-structured methadone maintenance treatment programs from 1964 to 1973, initially all in direct conjunction with university or community hospitals, and therefore with defined access to primary health care, and in some cases, with actual primary health care offered on site, for the first time the heroin addict had access to ongoing health care. This allowed for both improvement of the health care status of these patients, as well as recognition of some of the more subtle pharmacological and physiological effects, first of heroin, and later of methadone as used in maintenance in high-dose, long-term treatment of opiate dependency.

It is striking that up to this current time, almost all prospective studies and also most one point-in-time studies of any aspect of the medical problems of heroin addicts, persons with combined addictive diseases, or medical diseases which commonly afflict the addict on the street, such as AIDS, hepatitis B, hepatitis C, hepatitis delta, tuberculosis and sexually transmitted diseases, which may continue, since they are chronic medical diseases, during chronic methadone maintenance treatment, have been performed in methadone maintenance clinics, including studies of active heroin addicts at time of entry to treatment and former addicts during long-term methadone maintenance. This is because the patients are regularly seen in the methadone maintenance clinics, whether they are the "best clinics," with a great deal of humanity and caring, as well as insight and knowledge about the specific medical disorders as well as about the pharmacotherapy itself, or whether they are the "worst methadone maintenance clinics," which simply hand out methadone with no insight into the pharmacological or physiological effects of this agent and which provide no counseling or access to health care, and may even have negative staff attitudes towards patients. Both "good" and "bad" methadone maintenance programs are more efficacious in managing heroin addiction or opiate dependency than any other approach to the treatment of heroin addiction, with a 1–2 year retention in treatment of around 45–55% in the "worst" clinics and 60 to over 80% retention of all entrants in the "best" clinics. Thus, methadone maintenance treatment programs provide the one resource where clinical research studies can be performed.

They also offer a logical source to actually provide primary health care and even specialized care for those disorders which affect large numbers of patients. Several events have led to the recognition of the need to medically treat the active and former addicts in pharmacological or nonpharmacological treatment programs for opiate or parenteral cocaine dependency: the identification of AIDS in 1981, the discovery of the etiological retroviral agent HIV-1, the recognition that a significant risk group for HIV-1 infection is parenteral drug users, the recognition that HIV-1 infection or AIDS, by virtue of significantly altering immune function, may alter the natural history of other diseases, such as hepatitis B and delta in infected populations, and also the documentation that HIV-1 infection has increased the prevalence of typical and atypical tuberculosis as well as some other diseases. However, this recognition has come in the setting of an overall decrease in availability of health care services, because of both a decrease number of primary care physicians in urban areas of highest need, as well as decrease in funding or reimbursement of all kinds for health care delivery. Also this recognition comes in the setting of steady or decreasing funds available for treatment of chemical dependencies on a per patient basis.

It is obvious at this time that all treatment programs for chemical dependency, including the treatment programs for heroin addiction, cocaine dependency, alcoholism, and other addictions or chemical dependencies, both those designed to care for "hard-core" addicts defined by the current federal regulations governing use of methadone in maintenance treatment, since 1983, and LAAM since 1995, as at least one year or earlier for drug users, and including both treatment resources using a pharmacological approach when available or nonpharmacological approach, need to provide for their patients with access to primary health care delivery. At this time, direct linkages must be formed and whenever possible, primary health care and primary psychiatric and behavioral care must be placed within the chemical dependency clinics. Both the chemically dependent patient as well as society as a whole can be best served by this type of model. Those clinics which now have part or full-time general practitioners, internists, adolescent medicine specialists, and/or psychiatrists have been repeatedly shown to be able to offer more in terms of overall rehabilitation, as well as improving general health care status of former addicts in treatment. However, the numbers of programs with this kind of medical expertise in place are very few. In addition, a variety of counseling and rehabilitation efforts, including such diverse topics as AIDS risk reduction education, special counseling for avoidance of contacting other infectious diseases, special counseling and management of incipient or ongoing dual or multiple chemical dependencies, preparation for high school education equivalency certification, post-high school technical or college training, and employment training, are all highly desirable, and when present, contribute to increasing efficacy of treatments of all types. It has been repeatedly shown, however, that the best counseling, individual and group psychiatric therapy, and special rehabilitation efforts alone, without pharmacotherapy, are of only modest effectiveness (10–30%) in management of "hard-core" heroin addicts, and probably of similar degree of efficacy in long-term cocaine dependency or alcoholism. Therefore, it is quite clear that more fundamental laboratory research, basic clinical research, and applied clinical research are needed to develop specific pharmacotherapies for each of these additional specific addictive diseases.

Special Advantages and Rewards of Medical Care: Linked Treatment of Addiction

FUNDAMENTAL CLINICAL RESEARCH: OUR HYPOTHESIS ON THE BASIS OF ADDICTION

One of the major advantages of a medical care–linked chemical dependency treatment program in which the former addict is always treated as a patient, with respect, dignity, and observance of confidentiality, as well as with other ethical constraints of health care delivery and research, is the fact that these are ideal sites to conduct applied and sometimes basic clinical research. The fundamental research studies of former heroin addicts entering, and prospectively during, methadone maintenance treatment, as an example, has provided enormous insights into the effects of exogenous opiates on normal physiology. The research findings which defined the specific opiate effects beyond analgesia and production of euphoria or somnolence, coupled with the determination of the rates of development of tolerance to each of these exogenous opioid effects, provided considerable information as to what might be the expected side effects or adverse effects of chronic use of opiates in the treatment management of pain or chronic management of opiate dependency. Even more excitingly, these findings have provided a guide for predicting and then later determining what would be the modulating roles and also controlling roles in normal physiology of the endogenous opioids, once they were discovered.

In the earliest days of the research at The Rockefeller Institute and at the research hospital at Lexington, Kentucky, and as well as elsewhere, several investigators including Dole, Martin, Collier, and Goldstein had postulated the presence of specific opiate receptors, that is, sites at which the opiate drugs would act. It is now recognized that there are at least three types of opiate receptors, mu, delta, and kappa, each of which has one or more subtypes. However, the precise physiological roles of each of these opiate receptors and their subtypes are not yet fully appreciated. As soon as specific opiate receptors were definitively identified in 1973 independently by Snyder, Simon, and Terenius, following the earlier hypotheses and experimental work of Dole, Martin, and Goldstein, it was clear that these opiate receptors were binding sites coupled with functions, not for creating the effects of exogenous opioids, but for activation by some endogenous ligands. Thus the search for the endogenous opioids commenced, and culminated first in 1975 with the discovery of met- and leu-enkephalin by Kosterlitz and Hughes, followed by the discoveries of beta-endorphin and the dynorphin opioid peptides by Terenius and Goldstein respectively, as well as the findings of many other active endogenous opioid peptides by other workers. Three separate classes of endogenous opioids have now been defined, each of the three derived from a single separate gene and each yielding a single gene peptide product, which is in turn processed and converted to active opioid peptides. These peptides are then degraded to inactive peptide fragments. These three genes respectively code for: proopiomelanocortin, which yields beta endorphin as the sole opioid peptide, but also other biologically active peptides of considerable interest including ACTH, beta-MSH and beta-lipotropin; proenkephalin, which yields met- and leu-enkephalin, as well as several other active enkephalin related opioids; and prodynorphin, which yields dynorphin A 1–17 and dynorphin B, with further conversion to other active dynorphin-related opioid peptides. Recently, the genes for the three opioid receptors have been cloned, first for the delta opioid receptor cloned by Evans and Kieffer and then the mu and kappa opioid receptors by several laboratories including Yu, Uhl, Thompson, Akil and Watson, Bell and Reisine, Kieffer, Evans, and others.

Prospective studies of the effects of methadone as used in the maintenance treatment of addiction, as stated earlier, have provided a guide for study and ultimately elucidation of many of the physiological roles of the endogenous opioids, as well as some insights into which pathological conditions may involve excess activity of the endogenous opioids or their receptors. By use of specific opioid antagonists in humans, as well as in animal studies, the roles of the endogenous opioids in both normal physiology and pathological states have been further elucidated (Table 81.1).

With the initial discovery of the endogenous opioids, and the endogenous opioids (or "endorphins" as they are often still called incorrectly in lay terms), it was hoped that the metabolic and biological basis of narcotic addiction would soon be fully understood. Although we have much greater insights now about the interactions between exogenous opiates and endogenous opioids, and more recently from our laboratory and others, suggestions that cocaine also may profoundly perturb the endogenous opioid system, we still do not know precisely the role of the endogenous opioid system in the addictive diseases. However, based on clinical research findings we have been able to reject the earlier hypothesis that narcotic addiction is due to an intrinsic endogenous opioid or "endorphin" deficiency, and also to reject the hypothesis that narcotic addiction is due to an excessive production of endogenous endorphins but with failure of re-

Table 81.1 Some Human Pathological Conditions in Which Excessive Activity of the Endogenous Opioid System Has Been Inplicated

1. Secondary amenorrhea related to excessive activity or stress
2. Male hypogonadism with delayed onset of puberty
3. Gastrointestinal dysmotility disorders resulting in chronic constipation
4. Pruritus associated with primary biliary cirrhosis
5. Pruritus associated with specific dermatological disorders
6. Interstitial cystitis
7. Endotoxic "shock"
8. Necrotizing encephalomyelopathy
9. ?Acute and chronic sequelae of stroke
10. ?Acute and chronic sequelae of head injury
11. ?Acute and chronic sequelae of spinal cord injury
12. ?Sudden infant death syndrome
13. ?Specific arthritic and collagen vascular disorders
14. ?Specific neurological and neuromuscular disorders
15. ?Specific subtypes of obesity
16. ?Other specific endocrine disorders (e.g., hyperprolactinemia)

Adapted from Harris LS, ed. Problems of drug dependence, 1991; Proceedings of the 53rd Annual Scientific Meeting of the Committee on Problems of Drug Dependence. Rockville, MD; U.S. Dept. of Health and Human Services, Public Health Service, Alcohol, Drug Abuse, and Mental Health Administration, 1992.

ceptors to respond to these endorphins. We have increasing evidence that narcotic addiction, and possibly cocaine dependency, may be, at least in part, due to a dysregulation of the endogenous opioid system, with abnormalities in either the gene expression, production, processing, or release of one or more of the endogenous opioids, or abnormal density or activation of the opioid receptors, coupled with abnormal negative and also positive feedback control mechanisms and interactions between the endogenous opioids and other neuropeptide and neurotransmitter systems. We now know that the endogenous opioid system is extremely complex, with complex patterns of cross-reactivity between the endogenous opioids and the different opioid receptor subtypes. We also know that there are profound species and strain differences in the content, density, and affinity of the opioid receptors, as well as in the endogenous opioid ligands, with both differences in localization as well as amounts of each of these components, and possibly differences in the impact of exogenous opioids on the responses of the endogenous opioid system. For instance, we know that the acute effects of short-acting opiates such as morphine or heroin on the endogenous opioid system and on related neuroendocrine peptide and steroid components of the hypothalamic-pituitary-adrenal axis are profoundly different in the human as contrasted to the rat, the most commonly used laboratory animal. In turn we know that the rat is significantly different from the guinea pig with respect to specific aspects of the endogenous opioid system and its function in physiology and potentially also in pathological states. Therefore, although modern biology allows us to study both the molecular and cell biology of the endogenous opioid system, as well as related peptide and neurotransmitter systems, and integrated physiology along with pharmacology in animal models and in human subjects, we have not yet elucidated the full complexity of this endogenous opioid system. Nevertheless, through basic clinical research performed in parallel with laboratory research, we have already learned an enormous amount and have realistic hopes soon to more thoroughly understand the metabolic and biological basis of the addictive diseases through such studies.

Some of our most provocative studies at this time are related to one hypothesis of our laboratory that the addictive diseases may, in part, be due to an underlying (possibly genetically controlled) or drug-induced atypical responsivity, with abnormalities in the endogenous opioid system, to stress, including both environmental and emotional stress, with (a) potentially hyperresponsivity to stress, responding to use of opiate drugs yielding hyporesponsivity, and conversely with (b) euresponsivity or hyporesponsivity, responding with hyperresponsivity following cocaine or other stimulant use. In the setting of long-term methadone maintenance treatment, we have shown that normalization of the hypothalamic-pituitary-adrenal axis response occurs, including normal responsivity to stressors, at least with respect to the hypothalamic-pituitary-adrenal axis responses, and the levels, patterns of release, and responsivity components of the endogenous opioid system. This is achieved in a setting of steady long-term administration of moderate to high doses of methadone which results in sustained plasma opioid levels. In this setting, drug-seeking behavior and self-administration of illicit opiates are significantly reduced or cease in most patients. However, we have also shown that drug-free former heroin addicts and also recently abstinent cocaine addicts are not normal in their response to an experimentally induced stress.

APPLIED CLINICAL RESEARCH

In addition to fundamental clinical research which may lead to an understanding of the biological basis, including the genetic basis, of the addictions, applied clinical research may also be performed when chemical dependency programs are linked to the mainstream of medical care and provide primary health care delivery, including medical and behavioral care, either on site or by close linkages. This applied clinical research may include studies of potentially effective new pharmacotherapeutic agents, once the laboratory and basic clinical research studies have been completed, and also a wide variety of novel behavioral modification techniques, as well as other types of psychiatric, behavioral, or sociological approaches to the management of addiction.

OUTCOME EVALUATION

It is only through well-structured treatment programs, in which each addict is treated as a patient, that one can hope to perform the very long-term prospective studies which are mandatory for outcome evaluation in this field. Any treatment or any intervention that proclaims to be effective and yet cites data for only 2, 4, or 6 weeks, or even 6 months, must be viewed as only modestly successful at best. Since it is now increasingly recognized that each of the major addictions is a chronic relapsing disorder, long-term follow-up studies of 1–2 years minimally are essential before one can determine whether or not any intervention is really effective. Only through the availability of structured programs, and usually those which are closely or directly linked to academic or community-based health care centers, which have a tradition of performing applied and possibly also basic clinical research, can such evaluations and related research studies be appropriately performed and brought to completion. Literally millions of dollars have undoubtedly been spent by our federal, state, and local governments and by private sector agencies in attempting to perform research projects in or evaluations of programs which are so poorly constituted, and which often are so pejorative in their attitudes towards their patients (in fact, usually not treating their chemically dependent persons as patients), that one should not expect any kind of meaningful information to be derived from the research or evaluation. Thus, again, society and the individual may be best served if the addict is treated as a patient, and if this chemically dependent person, either a new patient or former addict in chronic treatment, is followed on a long-term basis, and in an appropriately structured treatment program, which is either intrinsically imbedded in, or closely linked to, a conventional health care facility.

Cost Effectiveness of Treatment of Chemical Dependency

As already alluded to, the funding for treatment of the addictive diseases and other chemical dependencies has stayed at a steady level or in most areas actually gone down over the past 32 years, despite the magnitude of the problem of the chemical dependencies and the increasingly recognized need to address these problems from a demand standpoint. Recently it was stated that the monies available for treatment of chemical dependency had doubled over the last year. This is somewhat frightening since other data have shown that only 10–20% of all chemically dependent persons are in any treatment program at this time. Treatment capacity, as well as improvement in the quality and humanity of treatment, are urgently needed at this time. Thus far more than the doubling of funding is necessary. In the specific case of methadone maintenance treatment programs in different geographical locations, the real dollars expended per patient have for most regions either kept at a steady level or in many areas have been significantly reduced over the past 20 years. Now in most locations, the per capita annual funding to treat a patient who must be seen in clinic from 1 to 7 times a week, receive methadone maintenance as a pharmacotherapy, and also receive counseling and hopefully at least referral to primary medical and psychiatric care as needed (although far better would be on site primary health care delivery) ranges from $1800 to $3500. This is in fact, in real dollars, less than that which was being provided in the early 1970s for similar treatment. Therefore, it is not surprising that the size and quality of staff, as well as knowledge of the staff about fundamental aspects of methadone maintenance treatment, including the need for use of adequate dose (usually 60–120 mg per day), is increasingly limited at this time.

In a rather simplistic medical economic evaluation of various models of treatment of addiction, as well as an evaluation of a few special treatment programs, it can be estimated that if the per capita annual funding in the methadone program were increased to approximately $6000–8000, group-oriented pharmacotherapy along with appropriate counseling, as well as on site referral or primary medical care, psychiatric care, and behavioral services could be offered, along with possibly even some chronic on-site health care, such as regular assistance in chronic chemotherapy for AIDS, tuberculosis, and disulfiram management of alcoholism. If the per capita funding could be increased to $8,000–10,000 a year, all primary health care delivery, including all screening for medical and psychiatric problems and chronic care of most of these problems (although not necessarily for isolated needs for specialist care) could be provided. These levels of existing and desirable potential funding could be sharply contrasted with the average annual cost of treatment in a drug-free residential community, which ranges from $12,000 to over $30,000 a year in most regions, for treatment in a private drug-free institution or hospital-type or other institutional-based program which range from $500 to over $1500 a day; or the costs for incarceration for one year in a municipal, state, or federal prison which range from $25,000 to $80,000 a year. The costs for effective treatment are also strikingly less than the estimated costs to society through theft of consumer goods, destruction of property, and other such actions by the chemically dependent person in their search for money for the acquisition of drugs, which is estimated to range from $50,000 to $200,000 per addict per year. It is also substantially less when compared with the estimated costs for managing a patient once HIV-1 infection has progressed to AIDS, the average costs for which are estimated as being from $30,000 to $200,000 a year.

Therefore, for one type of addiction, heroin dependency, clearly methadone maintenance, which can be provided to the "hard-core" heroin addict, is not only medically and societally effective, but cost effective, and methadone maintenance programs which would provide more services and therefore be likely to treat the addict more effectively and as a patient would in fact be far more cost effective.

However, it is also recognized that some patients do not respond to intensive counseling and rehabilitation efforts. Those patients should be able to be identified after three or more years of effort and possibly should be placed into a more purely pharmacologically based treatment program with exclusive on site administration of medication. Also, when highly specialized health care or psychiatric treatments are needed, it may become more cost effective to group patients accordingly.

Needs for Medical Education and Related Education of Health Care Professionals and Allied Personnel

Having discussed in a highly simplified manner the medical-economic view of the need for effective treatment of chemical dependency (and the need for "good" treatment for chemical dependency), that is, effective treatment for chemical dependency, it should be pointed out that even if appropriate funding were offered at this time, there would be inadequate staff of all types to carry out such programs. Even now the numbers of appropriately trained staff are deficient, but this is in part due to the failure to attract the best trained physicians, nurses, social workers, and other health care providers to the field of chemical dependency treatment. The failure to attract such highly qualified personnel is in part directly related to the disregard of the addict as a patient, and the failure for most medical institutions and academic centers to accept addiction as primarily a medical problem, and one that needs all of the academic, scientific, and humanistic approaches that are provided for other major medical disorders. An attitude change on part of institutions, as well as individual health care providers, is essential along with increased funding. There is ample evidence that attitudes are changing now and they are changing primarily because of the increased recognition by society of the magnitude of the chemical dependency problem and its widespread and pervasive negative effects. Increasingly frequent identification within the family structure or neighborhood area of chemical dependency problems coupled with the recognition of the linkage of these problems with such devastating diseases as AIDS, hepatitis B, hepatitis delta, and tuberculosis have led the lay public as well as the young medical student or nursing student to increasingly appreciate the importance of bringing the treatment of chemical dependency into the mainstream of our health care system. In addition, many of our most brilliant young scientists are recognizing the excitement and rewards of addressing some very fundamental laboratory and basic clinical research questions in the field of the addictive diseases and related areas of neurobiology. Molecular biologists are realizing the tremendous challenge and potential satisfaction which may reside in elucidating which abnormal genes, or specific combination of normal alleles of several genes, may contribute to the genetic vulnerability of people for specific addictions such as alcoholism or opiate dependency. All three opioid receptor genes have now been cloned and studies of their heterogeneity in humans, including those with defined addictive diseases, are in progress.

Therefore, it would seem that the time is ripe to effect policy changes which would bring research related to chemical dependency up to a very high priority status and into the mainstream of our academic medical institutions and research institutions, as well as bring treatment of chemical dependency into the mainstream of our health care delivery systems. Also, with the establishment of health maintenance organizations and managed care in many regions and the increasingly broad use of this approach to health provision by businesses and institutions, inclusion of long-term, effective, multifaceted health care including specific treatments for specific addictions for the numerous persons with drug and alcohol addictions will be essential. Clearly this would necessitate a significantly increased commitment to teaching about addictions and related areas at all educational levels to physicians, nurses, social workers, health care providers, ancillary workers and also additional teaching of potential scientists in various disciplines about the addictive diseases, including what is known and what is not known. Several private foundations as well as the federal government are now addressing the problem of medical education and related health care and scientific education in the areas of the pathophysiology, treatment, and research related to the addictive diseases and chemical dependencies. Two national institutes of health, the National Institute on Drug Abuse (NIDA) and the National Institute on Alcoholism and Alcohol Abuse (NIAAA) are devoted to biomedical research, from the most fundamental laboratory and basic clinical research, to applied clinical and epidemiologic research, to elucidate the mechanisms underlying the addictions, the various effects of the addicting agents, and to develop potential new pharmacotherapeutic treatment agents and other novel treatment approaches, as well as to study other related topics.

In addition to an enhanced educational effort, measures must be taken to assure that established health care institutions provide care for chemically dependent patients. At this time, it is unconscionable that many health care centers with multimillion dollar AIDS treatment and research clinics have no resource on site for treatment of chemical dependency. It is equally unconscionable that such institutions may have not a single professor involved in studies of the neurobiological basis or medical aspects of the addictions. All of these issues, however, can be addressed by a combination of public policy, appropriate funding, and public education. Again, all of these improvements will lead to an almost automatic acceptance of the addict as a patient.

Ethical Issues

Many ethicists, health care providers, and basic clinical and laboratory investigators, like our own group, have addressed the specific ethical issues concerning the addict, the other chemically dependent persons, as well as persons with diseases such as AIDS which afflict highly significant numbers of parenteral drug abusers. It is quite clear that part of treating an addict as a patient includes embracing all of the appropriate ethical constraints of health care delivery. Similarly when an active addict or former addict is involved in a research program, all of the appropriate ethical constraints of biomedical research must be employed. Possibly at the top of the list of ethical issues that are of very special and fundamental importance to this group of patients is the appropriate maintenance of confidentiality. Sometimes this maintenance of confidentiality may seem to preclude appropriate health care delivery in general, as well as appropriate treatment of chemical dependency, or use of a volunteer patient in a research project. Such a misinterpretation concerning maintenance confidentiality is due to lack of knowledge of how to appropriately maintain confidentiality while conducting appropriate health care delivery or research. This common problem needs to be addressed. Clearly, confidentiality must and can be maintained, both for the chemically dependent patient, as well as for AIDS patients. Similarly, confidentiality can and must be maintained in research efforts. Many techniques for maintaining confidentiality and assuring that it be preserved have been developed over the years and simply need to be taught to health care providers and clinical scientists.

The Demonstrated Successful Outcome of Managing the Addict as a Patient

It is quite clear that we must offer the best currently available treatments for each of the addictions and chemical dependency problems. We must enhance the numbers of programs and of trained staff to provide this treatment. We must link this treatment closely to or include it directly within the fabric of primary health care delivery, either by placing chemical dependency treatment directly in the setting of primary health care delivery, or alternatively putting primary health care delivery within the chemical dependency treatment programs. We must also nurture appropriate scientific endeavors of all types to elucidate the underlying mechanisms of the biology of addictive diseases and other chemical dependencies, as well as the various genetic, metabolic, toxicological, behavioral, and environmental factors which modify the vulnerability to, expression of, and persistence of these chronic relapsing disorders.

We have seen the one effective pharmacotherapeutic model, methadone maintenance treatment, currently available evolve over the years from an experimental treatment developed at a research institute to a large-scale worldwide treatment modality. However, we have unfortunately also very often seen that these methadone maintenance treatment programs are not well executed because of funding and staffing constraints and also because of the stigmatization of such treatment by society, which has been nurtured in part by unenlightened mass communications. At the same time we have seen some excellent programs develop and progress over a period of 30 years or more. In our own laboratory group, we have recently reported a study of patients in chronic methadone maintenance treatment for 10–27 years and have learned that even at that very long time on moderate to high dose treatment, no adverse medical consequences have resulted from treatment. At the same time, we have learned that the remarkable findings of early rehabilitation have pertained over long periods, with essentially an elimination of illicit opiate use in patients in long-term treatment and with a highly significant reduction of illicit use of other drugs or excessive use of alcohol in over 70% of all patients in chronic methadone maintenance treatment, coupled with a very high level of functioning of these patients as students, homemakers, and employees in a wide spectrum of occupations. We have learned that neuroendocrine function, which may be disrupted by the effects of a short-acting narcotic such as heroin, becomes normalized. Related to this, response to an induced stress becomes normal. We have learned that immune function, which may be directly impaired by short-acting opiates such as heroin, in addition to being impaired by the multiple diseases to which the heroin addict is constantly exposed to by use of dirty needless and by abnormal lifestyle, becomes normalized during chronic methadone maintenance treatment, probably related to the normalization of neuroendocrine function in this setting. We have learned that even gastrointestinal function, specifically slowing of gastrointestinal transit, which is the one opiate effect to which tolerance develops most slowly in humans, becomes normalized in over 80% of all chronic methadone maintained patients in treatment for three years or more.

We have also seen methadone maintenance begin to move into the mainstream of medical care, through the early applied clinical research efforts of the late Dr. Marie Nyswander and then later meticulously carried out by Dr. David Novick at the Beth Israel Hospital in New York, the late Mr. Richard Lane at Man Alive Clinic in Baltimore, and Dr. Edward Senay at the University of Chicago, as well as by other groups. In New York City, patients who have been successfully maintained in methadone treatment for 5 years or more, with no evidence of ongoing cocaine, alcohol, or other substance abuse and with a stable lifestyle, have been admitted on an experimental basis into a medical maintenance program. In these programs, daily doses of methadone are delivered once every 2–4 weeks for patients to take home and use daily as any other medication would be used, with clinic visits mandated at only 2, 3, or 4 week intervals, and not at the daily or as infrequently as once a week visits as in all other conventional clinics. This U.S. Food and Drug Administration Investigator Initiated "investigational new drug" (IND) approval based clinical research, which is still ongoing, has shown a very high level of compliance and continued success in over 95% of patients thus managed. A physician, either an internist, general practitioner, or a general psychiatrist, is the physician of record in these programs; each physician sees each patient not less often than once every 4 weeks. As with all physicians offering primary care, they are available to the patient at any time on a emergency basis, with appropriate coverage. Those few patients who have failed in this program, with failure defined as either recrudescence of some type of illicit use of drugs, inappropriate use of alcohol, or any type of antisocial behavior, may be returned to a more conventional methadone program. Through several years of follow-up studies, it has been shown that this medical maintenance form of treatment is highly successful for the well-rehabilitated, long-term, methadone-maintained patient. These findings are the direct result of the addicts being treated as patients and

usually having been treated as patients from the very beginning of entry to the methadone maintenance treatment program.

Accepting the addict as a patient is a critical first step in not only the medical but also social rehabilitation of the addict, to provide, in some cases, for the first time, a respect for the individual as a human being, thus sharing the concept of the dignity of the human being, a philosophy which has formed the fundamental basis of medicine since early civilization. This approach may in turn yield enormously positive results which help society as a whole. The findings which we were able to make in 1983–1984 were that of those heroin addicts who had entered an effective and humanely run methadone maintenance treatment program before the beginning of the HIV-1 infection and AIDS epidemic in New York City in 1978 (based on our research bank of blood specimens from 1969 onward which showed that HIV-1 infection hit street heroin addicts in New York City in that year), and then who remained in effective treatment until 1984, less than 10% were anti-HIV-1 positive then, at a time in 1983–1984, when 50–60% of all street addicts and those entering treatment were anti-HIV-1 positive up until 1993. From 1993 onward in New York City, there is some hopeful evidence that the prevalence of HIV-1 is decreasing due to AIDS risk reduction efforts. Thus society was incredibly well served from the public health standpoint, and the patients well served on an individual basis, by having offered humane treatment to a group of heroin addicts from the time they entered treatment and by treating each addict as a patient.

This model can and must be replicated to treat thousands of untreated addicts; similar models using different pharmacotherapeutic agents or other effective treatment approaches must be developed through biomedical research and put into the mainstream of medical care for different addictions and chemical dependencies, as knowledge, staff, and funds permit. All of this depends upon the respect given to each addict who comes into treatment, just as a physician or other health care professional would respect any other patient seeking health care. By these actions, we can and must attract the alienated thousands of as yet untreated addicts to come into treatment.

From the time of last publication of this chapter (1992), little progress has been made in the United States, either in increasing the numbers of available methadone maintenance treatment sites or in increasing the total number of patients who can be served by treatment. Also, little progress has been made in improving the quality of treatment in existing programs, with little to no expansion in resources for appropriate staffing, staff education, or physical environments. More erudite patient matching and progression to different resources, as treatment effectiveness is achieved, has not been implemented. The situation has been generally static. However, in contrast, with the recognition of the magnitude of the HIV-1 infection problem and the linkage of AIDS and with drug abuse, parenteral opiate abuse and addiction are now recognized as major medical problems in Europe, as well as in the United States. In response to this recognition, multiple approaches have been taken in Europe to address problems of heroin addiction, and effective approaches have been implemented to provide long-term methadone treatment.

EUROPEAN PERSPECTIVE

A review of opiate addiction treatment is essential to a review of maintenance or "substitution" (agonist or partial agonist treatment) treatment, since that form of treatment accounts for:

1. the highest demand from heroin addicts: 70% of heroin addicts are willing to undergo maintenance or substitution treatment versus 10% for drug-free (no pharmacotherapy) treatment.
2. the highest rate of retention in treatment: 70% of addicts stay in treatment versus 30% in drug-free treatment (after one year).
3. the recovery rate of maintenance or substitution treatment is: (70% x 70%) = 50% vs. (10% x 30%) = 3% for drug-free treatment (after one year).

Drug-free treatment of opiate addiction admits fewer patients and has a very high relapse rate.

A review of maintenance or substitution treatment in Europe must take account of: (*a*) a wide variety of public health and legal approaches for each European country; (*b*) rapid changes in the situation during the last few years (with an overall increase of maintenance or substitution treatment).

Table 81.2   Substitution Treatment in Europe

Country	Population (millions)	Opiate Addicts	MT Clinics	Office-based MT	MT Total	In MT/Total Addicts	Other Substitution Treatment	Number
A. Western Europe								
1. Austria	7.5	20,000	+	+	2,000	10%	Buprenorphine	
2. Belgium	10	30,000	20%	80%	5,000	16%	Buprenorphine	
3. Denmark	5	10,000	30%	70%	3,700	37%		
4. Finland	5	500	−	5	5	1%		
5. France	56	150,000	+	+	1,500	1%	Codeine	30,000
							Buprenorphine	500
							Morphin sulf.	
6. Germany	80	100,000	+		+15,000	15%	Codeine	20,000
7. Greece	10	40,000	300	−	300	0.7%	−	
8. Ireland	3.5	7,000	+	−	600	8%	Morphine sulf.	
9. Italy	57	150,000	+	−	30,000	20%	Buprenorphine	300
							Morphine	
							Codeine	
10. Luxenburg	0.3	1,500	+	−	50	3%		
11. Netherlands	15	22,000	80%	20%	14,000	63%		
12. Norway	4	3,000	85%	15%	100	2.5%	Buprenorphine	
							Morphine sulf.	
							Codeine	
13. Portugal	10	40,000	+	−	1,000	2.5%	LAAM	50
14. Spain	39	150,000	+	−	15,000	10%	Buprenorphine	
15. Sweden	8.5	5,000	+	−	450	9%		
16. Switzerland	6.5	30,000	+	+	12,000	40%	Heroin	400
							Buprenorphine	
17. United Kingdom	57	150,000	+	+	26,000	17%	Heroin	250
							Buprenorphine	
TOTAL	**375**	**909,000**		**126,705**	**14%**			
B. Central Europe								
18. Czech Republic	10	10,000	−	−	In project	0	Ethylmorphine	
18. Slovak Republic	5	10,000	−	−	0	0	Ethylmorphine	
							Codeine	
19. Poland	37.5	100,000 (Komp ot)	−	−	In project	0		
20. Hungary	10	?	−	−	0	0	−	
TOTAL	**62.5**							
C. Eastern Europe								
21. Bielorussia	10	?	−	−	0			
22. Estonia	1.5	?	−	−	0			
23. Latvia	2.5	?	0	0	0	0		
24. Lithuania	3.8	?	1	−	15 (9/95)	0		
25. Russia	150	?	−	−	0			
26. Ukraine	52	?	−	Illegal, but present	0			
TOTAL	**220**				**1**			
D. Ex-Yugoslavia								
27. Bosnia	4.5	?						
28. Croatia	5	?	+	+				
29. Serbia	10.5	?						
30. Slovenia	2	2–6,000	600	−	600	15–30%		
31. Macedonia	2	5,000			100	2%		
TOTAL	**24**	**?**						
E. Balkanic Countries								
32. Albania	3.5	−	−	−	−		pethidine	
33. Bulgaria	9	?	+	−	100			
34. Romania	23.5	?						
TOTAL	**36**	**?**						

Table from Narcotic Drugs, International Narcotics Control Board, Vienna, 1995.

In this section available data on the current situation are first presented, and then situations and trends in each country are classified.

A Survey of the Use of Methadone Maintenance Treatment ("Substitution" Therapy)

As seen in Table 81.2, there are now:

1. around 400 million population in Europe and 1 million opiate addicts (prevalence of opiate addiction: 1 in 400 compared with around 1 in 250 in the United States)
2. 125,000 opiate addicts are in methadone maintenance treatment in Europe
3. the percentage of opiate addicts in methadone maintenance treatment varies from country to country from 0.7% (Greece) to 63% (Netherlands)
4. more than 85% of opiate addicts out of methadone treatment
5. methadone is the main "official" maintenance or substitution treatment
6. codeine is the main "hidden" (that is, nonlegitimatized) "substitution" treatment
   a. *France:* Neocodion (codeine) is an over-the-counter medicine widely used by opiate addicts because of lack of official maintenance or substitution treatment until very recently (17,484 kg of codeine were used in 1993). Thirty thousand former heroin addicts probably use codeine daily, far more than the number of patients currently in methadone treatment (around 1000 in October 1995).
   b. *United Kingdom:* codeine (14,000 kg) and dihydrocodeine (5,000 kg) used in treatment of addiction.
   c. *Germany:* codeine (7,500 kg) and dihydrocodeine (3,500 kg) are prescribed by general practitioners as substitution treatment to as many persons as in methadone maintenance (around 30,000 patients).
   d. *Netherlands:* use of codeine (1,000 kg); methadone maintenance treatment is well developed; self-medication of opiate addiction, with codeine for instance, is less developed.
   e. *Italy*: no data are available.
7. *morphine sulfate* is used as substitution treatment in some countries such as France, Ireland, Italy, and Norway; consumption is high in United Kingdom (2,500 kg/year)
8. *dextropropoxyphene* is also used as substitution treatment in Sweden and Denmark; consumption is high and increasing in France and United Kingdom.
9. *buprenorphine* is prescribed as maintenance or substitution treatment in several countries: Belgium, Spain, Austria, Norway, France, Switzerland, Italy, and United Kingdom (a few hundred patients in each country and increasing).
10. *heroin* is also still used legally in management in the United Kingdom and for a few years in Switzerland.

Classification of Situations and Trends in Western Europe

The current use of methadone maintenance treatment in Western Europe (as shown in Table 81.3) is summarized as follows:

1. Only three countries admit more than 30% of opiate addicts into maintenance or substitution treatment.
2. Six countries admit less than 5%.
3. However, the example of cities where methadone maintenance treatment is available on demand shows that up to 70% of opiate addicts may be admitted for voluntary pharmacotherapeutic treatment (in Amsterdam, for example).

The estimated amounts of use of methadone in treatment, expressed as kilograms of methadone per million population, is shown in Figure 81.1:

Table 81.3 Methadone Treatment in Western Europe

Heroin Addicts In MT/Total #	Country	Increase Rate[a]
>30%	Denmark	18.2
	Switzerland	17.2
	Netherlands	8.5
	United Kingdom	6.5
	Austria	5.2
5–30%	Spain	3.6
	Belgium	3.3
	Ireland	2.9
	Italy	2.2
	Sweden	1.9
	Germany	1.7
	Portugal	0.9
	Norway	0.8
<5%	France	0.1
	Finland	0
	Greece	0
	Luxembourg	0

[a] Increase Rate = 1991–1994/1986–1993.

1. The differences are due to restriction of methadone maintenance treatment in most countries.
2. Maintenance or substitution treatment does not keep up with the demand.
3. Most European countries should increase the availability of maintenance or substitution treatment to meet the demand.

There is now a defined trend for a global increase of methadone consumption (Fig. 81.2). Global consumption of methadone during 1974–1993 shows a twofold increase in the last 10 years. There also is clearly an increase in methadone consumption in treatment in western Europe with a six fold increase in the last 10 years (Fig. 81.3).

Recognition of AIDS Linked with Intravenous Drug Abuse and Increase in Methadone Maintenance Treatment

Methadone consumption in treatment is clearly linked with the recognition of and concern about the AIDS epidemic in Europe (Fig. 81.4). Many studies show that addicts in methadone maintenance treatment have a reduced risk of HIV infection. In most countries during the period of penetration of HIV (1980–1985) the development of methadone maintenance treatment was insufficient to avoid an AIDS epidemic among drug addicts. Methadone consumption increase appears as a delayed response to AIDS progression among drug addicts. The fear of AIDS and its costs helped to overcome social resistances to methadone maintenance treatment (see below).

Methadone consumption in treatment has increased recently in each European country (Figs. 81.5–81.18). However, the rate and time of increase varies. Methadone consumption per million population in Europe when contrasted by individual countries suggests the following:

1. Development of methadone consumption in maintenance treatment still faces considerable opposition.
2. In spite of a rapid increase of methadone consumption in France, it is still very low, but this may represent in part a very recent official acceptance of methadone maintenance treatment (Fig. 81.19).

Recent increases in methadone maintenance treatment by country have been classified for three groups of countries as (a) above average, (b) under average, or (c) methadone treatment absent or undetectable (Table 81. 4).

Of interest, three countries with the highest percentage of heroin addicts in methadone maintenance treatment (>30%) still have an increasing methadone consumption in maintenance treatment: Denmark, Switzerland, and the Netherlands (see Table 81.4).

Also, all countries with a medium percentage of heroin addicts in methadone maintenance treatment (5–30%) have an increasing consumption of methadone in maintenance treatment, and most of them show a rapid increase (Table 81.5).

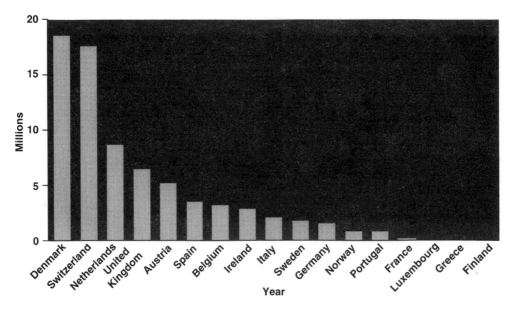

Figure 81.1. Kilograms methadone per million population (data from International Narcotics Control Board, Vienna).

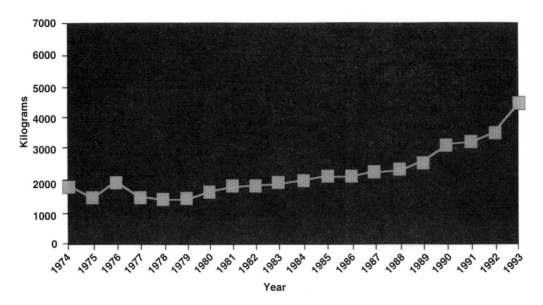

Figure 81.2. Global consumption of methadone, 1974–1993 (data from International Narcotics Control Board, Vienna).

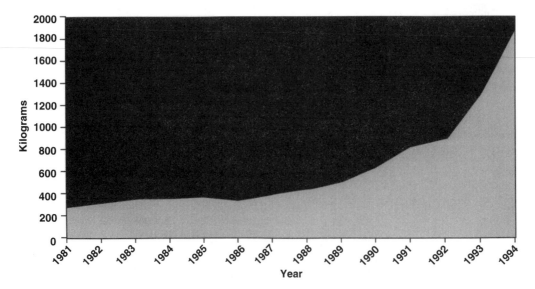

Figure 81.3. Methadone consumption in Western Europe (data from International Narcotics Control Board, Vienna).

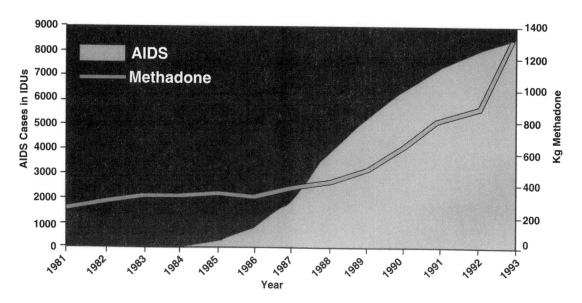

Figure 81.4. Methadone consumption and AIDS epidemics in Western Europe (data from International Narcotics Control Board, Vienna).

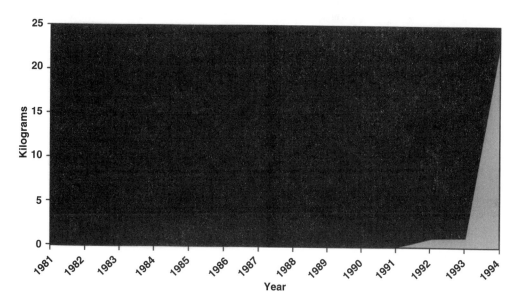

Figure 81.5. Methadone consumption in France (data from International Narcotics Control Board, Vienna).

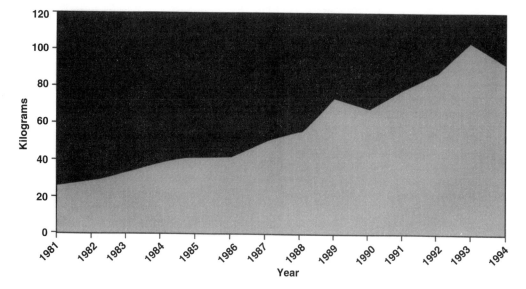

Figure 81.6. Methadone consumption in Denmark (data from International Narcotics Control Board, Vienna).

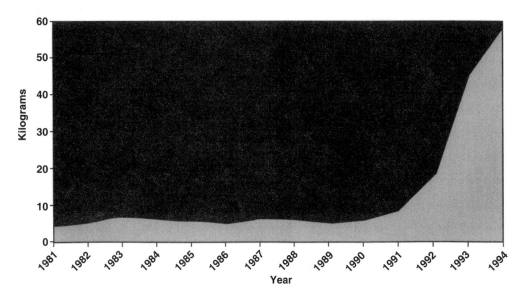

Figure 81.7. Methadone consumption in Belgium (data from International Narcotics Control Board, Vienna).

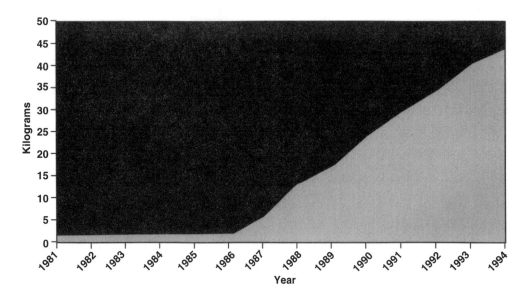

Figure 81.8. Methadone consumption in Austria (data from International Narcotics Control Board, Vienna).

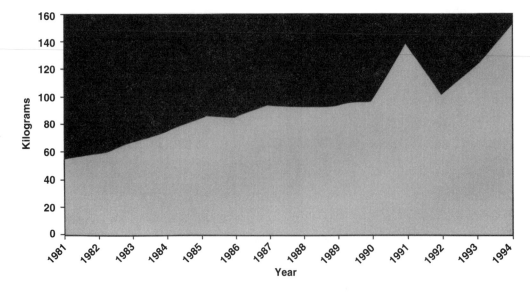

Figure 81.9. Methadone consumption in the Netherlands (data from International Narcotics Control Board, Vienna).

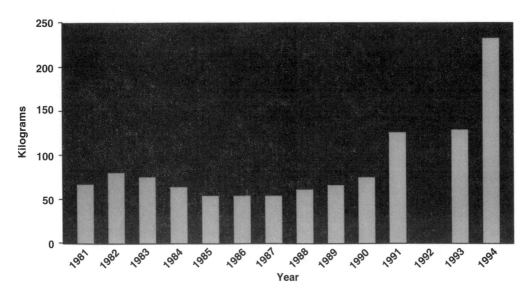

Figure 81.10. Methadone consumption in Italy (data from International Narcotics Control Board, Vienna).

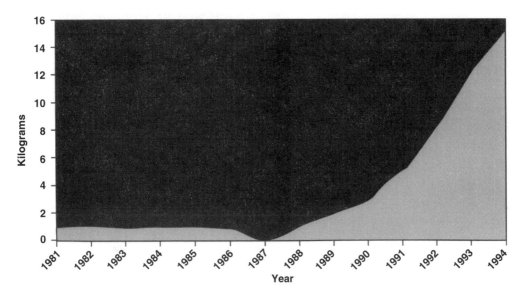

Figure 81.11. Methadone consumption in Ireland (data from International Narcotics Control Board, Vienna).

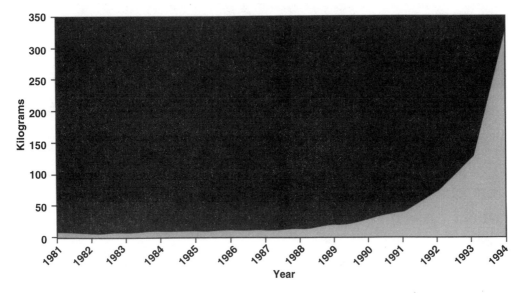

Figure 81.12. Methadone consumption in Germany (data from International Narcotics Control Board, Vienna).

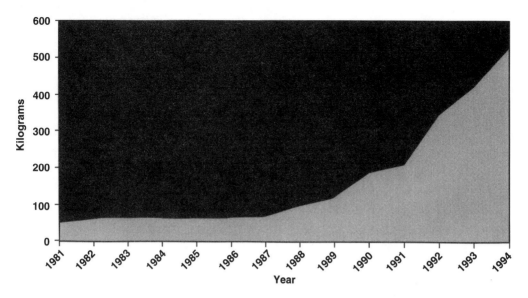

Figure 81.13. Methadone consumption in the United Kingdom (data from International Narcotics Control Board, Vienna).

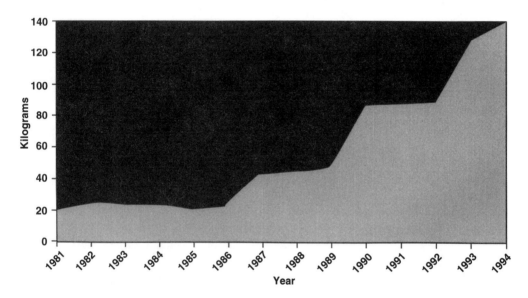

Figure 81.14. Methadone consumption in Switzerland (data from International Narcotics Control Board, Vienna).

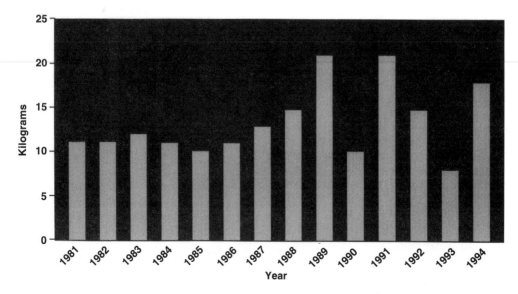

Figure 81.15. Methadone consumption in Sweden (data from International Narcotics Control Board, Vienna).

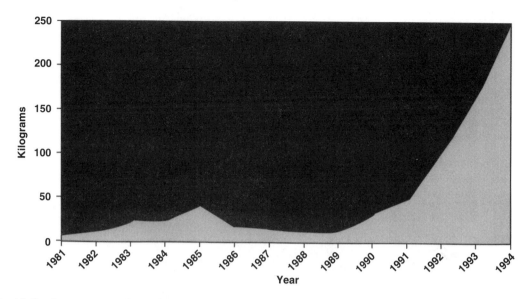

Figure 81.16. Methadone consumption in Spain (data from International Narcotics Control Board, Vienna).

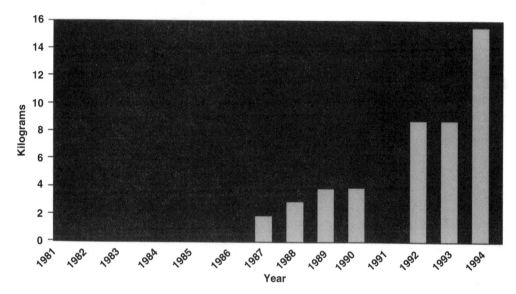

Figure 81.17. Methadone consumption in Portugal (data from International Narcotics Control Board, Vienna).

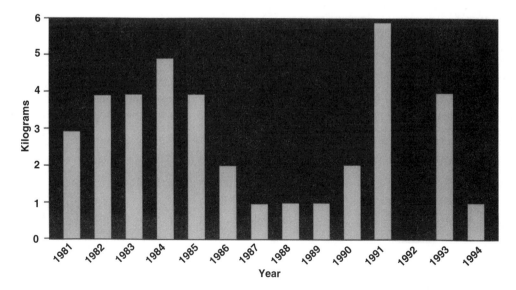

Figure 81.18. Methadone consumption in Norway (data from International Narcotics Control Board, Vienna).

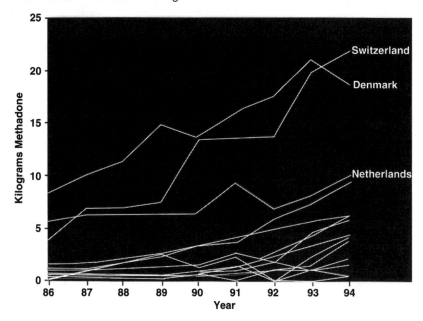

Figure 81.19. Methadone consumption per million population (data from International Narcotics Control Board, Vienna).

Countries with a low percentage of heroin addicts in methadone maintenance treatment may be divided into three groups:

1. High increase rate: France has the highest methadone consumption increase in Europe, reflecting recent official acceptance of methadone maintenance treatment (June 1995); Greece started methadone maintenance treatment very recently, in November 1995.
2. Low increase rate: Norway still imposes very strict criteria for admission to methadone maintenance treatment, although this is in transition very recently.
3. Methadone consumption undetectable: Luxembourg's and Finland's consumption do not appear in the statistics of the International Narcotics Control Board, which take account only of full kilograms of methadone.

Summary

Methadone maintenance and other "substitution" treatments show a rapid progression in Europe, but the availability of maintenance or substitution treatment is still largely inferior to the demand.

Maintenance or substitution treatments are limited both quantitatively and qualitatively. For example, in France only 52 patients were admitted in methadone treatment until 1993. Until recently, when there was a policy change, Norway limited methadone treatment to AIDS patients with less

than 200 T4 lymphocytes (except for 50 patients with more than 10 years of addiction); now, heroin addicts with a very long history of addiction without AIDS are being admitted in increased numbers.

The development of methadone maintenance or other "substitution" maintenance treatment (including buprenorphine treatment) is impeded by attitudes of resistance, in spite of its effectiveness on numerous factors: reduction of heroin consumption; intravenous injection; infectious risks (HIV, hepatitis); mortality; delinquency and prostitution; improvement in social rehabilitation.

To overcome such resistance, it is not enough to improve knowledge of maintenance or substitution treatments. It is also imperative to analyze the psychosocial mechanisms at the roots of these attitudes of resistance. We can not analyze them here in detail, but, in general, they can be explained as follows. We live in a society dominated by the values of the work ethic, competition, and autonomy. The existence of drug addicts seems to be dictated by values that are diametrically opposed to these: the pursuit of pleasure, passivity, and dependence. Thus, most of the time, drug addicts inspire attitudes of rejection and an absence of compassion. Drug addiction is perceived more as a vice than as an illness or a problem. This leads to the widespread refusal to provide care.

However, this vision of heroin addiction and its treatment is based on misconceptions; first, that the heroin addict experiences continuing pleasure while addicted. In fact, heroin consumption brings pleasure essentially only before the user becomes dependent on the drug. Subsequently, the accompanying problems far outweigh the pleasure, but the addict is compelled to continue using heroin in order not to be sick with acute or protracted abstinence symptoms.

Table 81.4 Methadone Utilization Increase (Treatment)

	Country	Increase Rate[a]
	France	24
	Germany	3.5
	Spain	2.8
A	Belgium	2.6
"high"	Ireland	2.5
	Portugal	2.2
	United Kingdom	2
	Austria	1.8
	Italy	1.7
	Switzerland	1.6
B	Denmark	1.3
	Norway	1.3
	Netherlands	1.2
	Sweden	1.1
	Finland	0
C	Greece	0
"low"	Luxembourg	0
	Average	1.9

[a]Increase Rate = 1991–1994/1986–1993.

Table 81.5 Classification by Recent Increases in Methadone Treatment in Countries with Moderate(> 30%), Medium (5–30%) and Low (< 5%) Rates of Heroin Addicts in Methadone Maintenance Treatment

Increase Rate in MT	A >2	B <2	C =0
>30%		Denmark Switzerland Netherlands	
5–30%	United Kingdom Spain Belgium Ireland Germany	Austria Sweden Italy	
<5%	France Portugal Greece	Norway	(Finland) (Luxembourg)

The second misconception behind the refusal to provide maintenance or substitution treatment is the belief that such treatment prolongs the drug addict's pleasure, that all they do is "replace one drug with another." In reality, patients undergoing maintenance or substitution treatment are in a perfectly normal state of awareness 24 hours a day with no euphoria or "high" and no withdrawal or "sick" periods.

In conclusion, the development of maintenance or substitution treatments (including methadone, LAAM and buprenorphine treatment) will require not only a better dissemination of the knowledge about these treatments, but also a demystification of the prejudices existing in all sectors of society: medical professions, politicians, journalists and the general population.

Acknowledgments. *The section "United States Perspective" was supported in part by the New York State Office of Alcohol and Substance Abuse Services; and by an HHS-NIH-NIDA Specialized Research Center Grant No. HHS-NIH-NIDA-P50-DA05130; by a Research Scientist Award from HHS-NIH-NIDA to Dr. Kreek KO5-DA-00049; by grants from the Herbert and Nell Singer Fund; and by grants from The Aaron Diamond Foundation.*

The first author acknowledges and is very grateful to Angela Daly for initial preparation of this manuscript and referencing, and Charlotte Kaiser, Jennifer Horne, Richard King, and Henrik Albert for their efforts of literature searches and referencing of the initial manuscript, along with Dr. Lisa Borg for additional literature searches for the updated version, Dr. Stefan Schlussman, Mr. Neil Maniar, Ms. Esperance Anne Kreek Schaefer for their assistance in revision of and additions to the revised version, and Ms. Jen Sudul for the preparation of the new and extended version.

References

I. METHADONE MAINTENANCE TREATMENT STUDIES

1. Himmelsbach CK. The morphine abstinence syndrome, its nature and treatment. Ann Intern Med 1941;15:829–839.
2. Pescor MJ. Follow-up study of treated narcotic drug addicts. Public Health Rep Suppl 1943; 170:1.
3. Isbell H, Eisenman AJ, Wikler A, Daingerfield M, Frank K. Treatment of the morphine abstinence syndrome with 10820 (4,4-diphenyl-6-dimethylamino-heptanone-3). Fed Proc 1947;6:340.
4. Isbell H, Eisenman AJ, Wikler A, Daingerfield M, Frank K. Experimental addiction to 10820 (4,4-diphenyl-6-dimethylamino-heptanone-3) in man. Fed Proc 1947;6:264.
5. Isbell H, Wikler A, Eddy NB, Wilson JL, Moran CF. Tolerance and addiction liability of 6-dimethylamino-4,4-diphenyl-heptanone-3(methadon). JAMA 1947;135:888.
6. Kirchhof AC, Uchiyama JK. Spasmolytic action of 6-dimethylamino-4-4-diphenyl-3-heptanone (Dolophine), a synthetic analgesic. Fed Proc 1947;6:345.
7. Bercel NA. Clinical trial of 10820, a new synthetic analgesic. Dis Nerv Sys 1948;9:15.
8. Isbell H, Eisenman AJ. Physical dependence liability of drugs of the methadon series and of 6-methyldihydromorphine. Fed Proc 1948;7:162.
9. Jenney EH, Pfeiffer CC. Comparative analgesic and toxic effects of the optical isomers of methadon and isomethadon. Fed Proc 1948; 7:231.
10. May EL, Mosettig E. Some reactions of amidone. J Org Chem 1948;13:459–464.
11. Popkin RJ. Experiences with a new synthetic analgesic, amidone. Its action on ischemic pain of occlusive arterial diseases. Am Heart J 1948;35:793.
12. Eddy NB, Touchberry CF, Lieberman JE. Synthetic analgesics: I. Methadone isomers and derivatives. J Pharmacol Exp Ther 1949;98:121–137.
13. Fraser HF, Isbell H. Addiction potentialities of isomers of 6-di-methylamino-4–4-diphenyl-3 acetyoxy-heptane (acetylmethadol). J Pharmacol Exp Ther 1951;101:12.
14. Fraser HF, Isbell H. Actions and addiction liabilities of alpha-acetylmethadols in man. J Pharmacol Exp Ther 1952;105:210–215.
15. Keats AS, Beecher HK. Analgesic activity and toxic effects of acetylmethadol isomers in man. J Pharmacol Exp Ther 1952;105:210–215.
16. Wikler A, Fraser HF, Isbell H. N-allylnormorphine: effects of single doses and precipitation of acute "abstinence syndromes" during addiction to morphine, methadone or heroin in man (post-addicts). J Pharmacol Exp Ther 1953;109:8–20.
17. Nyswander M. The drug addict as a patient. New York: Grune & Stratton, 1956.
18. Gruber CM, Baptisti A. Acceptability of morphine and noracymethadol. Clin Pharmacol Ther 1963;4:172–181.
19. Dole VP, Nyswander ME. A medical treatment for diacetylmorphine (heroin) addiction. JAMA 1965;193:646–650.
20. Dole VP, Nyswander ME. Rehabilitation of heroin addicts after blockade with methadone. N Y State J Med 1966;66:2011–2017.
21. Dole VP, Nyswander ME, Kreek MJ. Narcotic blockade. Arch Intern Med 1966;118:304–309.
22. Dole VP, Nyswander ME, Kreek MJ. Narcotic blockade: a medical technique for stopping heroin use by addicts. Trans Assoc Am Physicians 1966;79:122–136.
23. Vaillant GE. A twelve-year follow-up of New York narcotic addicts: I. The relation of treatment to outcome. Am J Psychiatry 1966;22(7):727–737.
24. Dole VP, Nyswander ME. Rehabilitation of the street addict. Arch Environ Health 1967;14:477–480.
25. Louria DB, Hensle T, Rose J. The major medical complications of heroin addiction. Ann Intern Med 1967;67:1–22.
26. Nyswander ME, Dole VP. The present status of methadone blockade treatment. Am J Psychiatry 1967;123:1441–1442.
27. Dole VP, Nyswander ME, Warner A. Successful treatment of 750 criminal addicts. JAMA 1968; 206:2708–2711.
28. Sapira JD. The narcotic addict as a medical patient. Am J Med 1968;45:555–588.
29. Dole VP, Robinson JW, Orraca J, Towns E, Searcy P, Caine E. Methadone treatment on randomly selected criminal addicts. N Engl J Med 1969;280:1372–1375.
30. Martin WR, Jasinski DR. Physiological parameters of morphine dependence in man—tolerance, early abstinence, protracted abstinence. J Psychiatr Res 1969;7:9–17.
31. Chambers CD, Babst DV, Warner A. Characteristics predicting long-term retention in a methadone maintenance program. In: Proceedings of the Third National Conference on Methadone Treatment. Washington, DC: U.S. Government Printing Office, 1970:140–143.
32. Dole VP. Biochemistry of addiction. Annu Rev Biochem 1970;39:821–840.
33. Gearing FR. Evaluation of methadone maintenance treatment programs. Int J Addict 1970;5:517–543.
34. Jaffe JH. Further experience with methadone in the treatment of narcotics users. Int J Addict 1970;5(3):375–389.
35. Jaffe JH, Schuster CR, Smith BB, Blachley PH. Comparison of acetylmethadol and methadone in the treatment of long-term heroin users. JAMA 1970;211:1834–1836.
36. Jaffe JH, Senay EC. Methadone and L-methadyl acetate: Use in management of narcotic addicts. JAMA 1971;216(8):1303–1305.
37. Jaffe JH, Senay EC, Schuster CR, Renault PR, Smith B, DiMenza S. Methadyl acetate v. methadone: A double-blind study in heroin users. JAMA 1972;222(4):437–442.
38. Maslansky R. Methadone maintenance programs in Minneapolis. Int J Addict 1970;5:391–405.
39. Babst DV, Chambers CD, Warner A. Patient characteristics associated with retention in a methadone maintenance program. Br J Addict 1971;66:195–204.
40. Dobbs WH. Methadone treatment of heroin addicts. JAMA 1971;218:1536–1541.
41. Goldstein A. Blind comparison of once-daily and twice-daily dosage schedules in a methadone program. Clin Pharmacol Ther 1971; 3(1):59–63.
42. Goldstein A, Lowney LT, Pal BK. Stereospecific and nonspecific interactions of the morphine congener levorphanol in subcellular fractions of mouse brain. Proc Nat Acad Sci U S A 1971;68:1742–1747.
43. Goldstein A. Heroin addiction and the role of methadone in its treatment. Arch Gen Psychiatry 1972;26:291–297.
44. Perkins ME, Bloch HI. A study of some failures in methadone treatment. Am J Psychiatry 1972; 128:47.
45. Zaks A, Fink M, Freedman AM. Levomethadyl in maintenance treatment of opiate dependence. JAMA 1972;220(6):811–813.
46. Dole VP. Detoxification of methadone patients and public policy. JAMA 1973;226:780–781.
47. Cushman P Jr, Dole VP. Detoxification of rehabilitation methadone-maintained patients. JAMA 1973;226:747–752.
48. Kreek MJ. Medical safety and side effects of methadone in tolerant individuals. JAMA 1973: 223:665–668.
49. Kreek MJ. Physiological implications of methadone treatment. In: Proceedings of the Fifth National Conference on Methadone Treatment. New York: National Association for the Prevention of Addiction to Narcotics, 1973;2:85–91.
50. Levine R, Zaks A, Fink M, Freedman AM. Levomethadyl acetate: prolonged duration of opioid effects, including cross tolerance to heroin in man. JAMA 1973;226(3):316–318.
51. Maddux JG, McDonald LK. Status of 100 San Antonio addicts one year after admission to methadone maintenance. Drug Forum 1973;2:239–252.
52. Martin WR, Jasinski DR, Haertzen CA, Kay DC, Jones BE, Mansky PA, et al. Methadone—a reevaluation. Arch Gen Psychiatry 1973;28:286–295.
53. Scott NR, Orzen W, Musillo C, et al. Methadone in the Southwest: a three-year follow-up of Chicano heroin addicts. Am J Orthopsychiatry 1973;45:355–361.

54. White AG. Medical disorders in drug addicts: 200 consecutive admissions. JAMA 1973;223:1469–1471.

55. Yaffe GJ, Strelinger RW, Parwatiker S. Physical symptom complaints of patients on methadone maintenance. In: Proceedings of the Fifth National Conference on Methadone Treatment. New York: National Association for the Prevention of Addiction to Narcotics, 1973;1:507–514.

56. Eddy NB. Morphine-like analgesic. J Pharm Assoc 1974;8:536.

57. Gearing FR, Schweitzer MD. An epidemiologic evaluation of long-term methadone maintenance treatment for heroin addiction. Am J Epidemiol 1974;100:101–112.

58. Stimmel B, Goldberg J, Rotkopf E, Cohen M. Ability to remain abstinent after methadone detoxification: a six-year study. JAMA 1974;237:1216–1220.

59. Betz TG. Facial edema, heroin and methadone. Am Fam Physician 1975;12:27.

60. Kreek MJ. Methadone maintenance treatment for chronic opiate addiction. In: Richter R, ed. Medical aspects of drug abuse. New York: Harper & Row, 1975:167–185.

61. Kreek MJ. Pharmacologic modalities of therapy: methadone maintenance and the use of narcotic antagonists. In: Stimmel B, ed. Heroin dependency: medical, economic and social aspects. New York: Stratton Intercontinental Medical Book Corp., 1975:232–290.

62. Kreek MJ, Khuri E, Joseph H. A new "heroin epidemic?" Ann Intern Med 1975;83:420–421.

63. Ling W, Charuvastra VC, Klett CJ. Current status of the evaluation of LAAM as a maintenance drug for heroin addicts. Am J Drug Alcohol Abuse 1975;2(3–4):307–315.

64. Schecter A, Kauders F. Methadone and L-alpha-acetylmethadol in a treatment program in Brooklyn. Am J Drug Alcohol Abuse 1975;2(3–4):331–339.

65. Stimmel B, Kreek MJ. Pharmacologic actions of heroin. In: Stimmel B, ed. Heroin dependency: medical, economic and social aspects. New York: Stratton Intercontinental Medical Book Corp., 1975:71–87.

66. Stimmel B, Kreek MJ. Dependence, tolerance and withdrawal. In: Stimmel B, ed. Heroin dependency: medical, economic and social aspects. New York: Stratton Intercontinental Medical Book Corp., 1975:88–97.

67. Woody GE, O'Brien CP, Rickels K. Depression and anxiety in heroin addicts: A placebo-controlled study of doxepin in combination with methadone. Am J Psychiatry 1975;132:447–450.

68. Blaine J, Renault P. Introduction. Roc: 3x/week LAAM: alternative to methadone. NIDA Res Monogr 1976;(8):1–9.

69. Cushman P Jr. Detoxification from methadone maintenance. JAMA 1976;235:2604.

70. Dole VP, Nyswander ME. Methadone maintenance treatment: a ten-year perspective. JAMA 1976;235:2117–2119.

71. Ling W, Charuvastra C, Kaim SC, Klett CJ. Methadyl acetate and methadone as maintenance treatments for heroin addicts: a Veterans Administration cooperative study. Arch Gen Psychiatry 1976;33(6):709–720.

72. Resnick RB, Orlin L, Geyer G, Schuyten-Resnick E, Kestenbaum RS, Freedman AM. L-alpha-acetylmethadol (LAAM): prognostic considerations. Am J Psychiatry 1976;133(7):814–819.

73. Dole VP, Joseph H. Where do the old addicts go? [abstract]. Clin Res 1977;25:513A.

74. Dole VP, Joseph JH. Methadone maintenance: outcome after termination. N Y State J Med 1977;77:1409–1412.

75. Resnick RB, Kestenbaum RS, Washton A, Poole D. Naloxone-precipitated withdrawal: a method for rapid induction onto naltrexone. Clin Pharmacol Ther 1977;21(4):409–413.

76. Senay EC, Dorus W, Goldberg F, Thornton W. Withdrawal from methadone maintenance. Arch Gen Psychiatry 1977;34:361–367.

77. Stimmel B, Rabin J. The ability to remain abstinent upon leaving methadone maintenance: a prospective study. Am J Drug Alcohol Abuse 1977;1:379–391.

78. Webster IW, Waddy N, Jenkins LV, Lai LYC. Health status of a group of narcotic addicts in a methadone treatment programme. Med J Aust 1977;64;2:485–487, 489.

79. Bahna G, Gordon NB. Rehabilitation experiences of women ex-addicts in methadone treatment. Int J Addict 1978;13:639–655.

80. Blaine JD, Renault P, Levine GL, Whysner JA. Clinical use of LAAM. Ann N Y Acad Sci 1978;311:214–231.

81. Dole VP, Joseph H. Long-term outcome of patients treated with methadone maintenance. Ann N Y Acad Sci 1978;311:181–189.

82. Kreek MJ. Medical complications in methadone patients. Ann N Y Acad Sci 1978;311:110–134.

83. Ling W, Klett CJ, Gillis RD. A cooperative clinical study of methadyl acetate I.3x/week regimen. Arch Gen Psych 1978;35(3):345–353.

84. Stimmel B, Goldberg J, Cohen M, Rotkopf E. Detoxification from methadone maintenance: Risk factors associated with relapse to narcotic use. Ann N Y Acad Sci 1978;311:173–180.

85. Jaffe JH, Schuster CR, Smith BB, Blachley PH. Comparison of acetylmethadol and methadone in the treatment of long-term heroin users. JAMA 1979:1834–1836.

86. Judson BA, Goldstein A. Levo-alpha-acetylmethadol (LAAM) in the treatment of heroin addicts I. Dosage schedule for induction and stabilization. Drug Alcohol Depend 1979;4(6):461–466.

87. Kreek MJ. Methadone in treatment: physiological and pharmacological issues. In: Dupont RL, Goldstein A, O'Donnell J, eds. Handbook on drug abuse. Washington, DC: National Institute on Drug Abuse, U.S. Dept. of Health, Education, and Welfare, 1979:57–86.

88. Oppenheimer E, Stimson GV, Thorley A. Seven-year follow-up of heroin addicts: abstinence and continued use compared. Br Med J 1979;2:627–630.

89. Dole VP, Joseph H. The long-term consequences of methadone maintenance treatment. In: Dupont RL, Goldstein A, O'Donnell J, eds. Handbook on drug abuse. Washington, DC: National Institute on Drug Abuse, U.S. Dept. of Health, Education, and Welfare, 1979.

90. Judson BA, Ortiz S, Crouse L, Carney TM, Goldstein A. A follow-up study of heroin addicts five years after first admission to a methadone treatment program. Drug Alcohol Depend 1980;6:295–313.

91. Kantor TG, Cantor R, Tom E. A study of hospitalized surgical patients on methadone maintenance. Drug Alcohol Depend 1980;6:163–173.

92. Ling W, Blakis M, Holmes ED, Klett CJ, Carter WE. Restabilization with methadone after methadyl acetate maintenance. Arch Gen Psychiatry 1980;37(2):194–196.

93. Blaine JD, Renault PR, Thomas DB, Whysner JA. Clinical status of methadyl acetate (LAAM). Ann N Y Acad Sci 1981;362:101–115.

94. Cushman P Jr. Detoxification after methadone maintenance treatment. Ann N Y Acad Sci 1981;362:217–230.

95. Des Jarlais DC, Joseph H, Dole VP. Long-term outcomes after termination from methadone maintenance treatment. Ann N Y Acad Sci 1981;362:231–238.

96. Gunne LM, Gronbladh L. The Swedish methadone maintenance program; a controlled study. Drug Alcohol Depend 1981;7:249–256.

97. Kreek MJ. Medical management of methadone-maintained patients. In: Lowinson JH, Ruiz P, eds. Substance abuse: clinical problems and perspectives. Baltimore: Williams & Wilkins, 1981:660–673.

98. Langrod J, Lowinson J, Ruiz P. Methadone treatment and physical complaints: a clinical analysis. Int J Addict 1981;16:947–952.

99. De Leon G, Waxler HK, Jainchill N. The therapeutic community: success and improvement rates 5 years after treatment. Int J Addict 1982;17:703–747.

100. Dole VP, Nyswander ME, DesJarlais D, Joseph H. Sounding board: performance-based rating of methadone maintenance programs. N Engl J Med 1982;306:169–172.

101. Judson BA, Goldstein A. Symptom complaints of patients maintained on methadone, LAAM (methadyl acetate), and naltrexone at different times in their addiction careers. Drug Alcohol Depend 1982;10(2–3):269–282.

102. McLellan AT, Luborsky L, O'Brien CP, Woody GE, Druley KA. Is treatment for substance abuse effective? JAMA 1982;247:1423–1428.

103. Sorensen JL, Hargreaves WA, Weinberg JA. Withdrawal from heroin in three or six weeks. Comparison of methadyl acetate and methadone. Arch Gen Psychiatry 1982;39(2):167–171.

104. Cooper JR, Altman F, Brown BS, Czechowicz D, eds. Research on the treatment of narcotic addiction: state of the art. Rockville, MD: U.S. Dept. of Health and Human Services, Public Health Service, Alcohol, Drug Abuse, and Mental Health Administration, National Institute on Drug Abuse, 1983.

105. DesJarlais DC, Joseph H, Dole VP, Schmeidler J. Predicting post-treatment narcotic use among patients terminating from methadone maintenance. Adv Alcohol Subst Abuse 1983;2:57–68.

106. Gunne LM. The case of the Swedish methadone maintenance treatment programme. Drug Alcohol Depend 1983;11:99–103.

107. Judson BA, Goldstein A, Inturrisi CE. Methadyl acetate (LAAM) in the treatment of heroin addicts II. Double-blind comparison of gradual and abrupt detoxification. Arch Gen Psychiatry 1983;40(8):834–840.

108. Kreek MJ. Health consequences associated with use of methadone. In: Cooper JR, Altman F, Brown BS, Czechowicz D, eds. Research on the treatment of narcotic addiction: state of the art. Rockville, MD: U.S. Dept. of Health and Human Services, Public Health Service, Alcohol, Drug Abuse, and Mental Health Administration, National Institute on Drug Abuse, 1983:456–482.

109. Kreek MJ. Discussion on clinical perinatal and developmental effects of methadone. In: Cooper JR, Altman F, Brown BS, Czechowicz D, eds. Research on the treatment of narcotic addiction: state of the art. Rockville, MD: U.S. Dept. of Health and Human Services, Public Health Service, Alcohol, Drug Abuse, and Mental Health Administration, National Institute on Drug Abuse, 1983:444–453.

110. McLellan AT, Luborsky L, Woody GE, O'Brien CP, Druley KA. Predicting response to alcohol and drug abuse treatments. Arch Gen Psychiatry 1983;40:620–625.

111. Gunne LM, Gronbladh L. The Swedish methadone maintenance program. In: Serban G, ed. Social and medical aspects of drug abuse. New York: Spectrum Publications, 1984:205–213.

112. Ling W, Dorus W, Hargreaves WA, Resnick R, Senay E, Tusson VB. Alternative induction and crossover schedules for methadyl acetate. Arch Gen Psychiatry 1984;41(2):193–199.

113. Kleber HD, Riordan CE, Rounsaville B, Kosten T, Charney D, Gaspari J, et al. Clonidine in outpatient detoxification from methadone maintenance. Arch Gen Psychiatry 1985;42:391–394.

114. Senay EC. Methadone maintenance treatment. Int J Addict 1985;20:803–821.

115. Singer B. Self-selection and performance-based ratings: a case study in program evaluation. In: Warren H, ed. Drawing inferences from self-selected samples. New York: Springer-Verlag, 1986:28–49.

116. Williams A. Primary care of parenteral substance abusers. Nurse Pract 1986;11:17, 20, 25, 29–32, 37.

117. Ball JC, Corty E, Petruski SP, et al. Treatment effectiveness: medical staff and services provided to 2394 patients at methadone programs in three states. NIDA Res Monogr 1987;76:175–181.

118. Novick DM, Senie RT, Kreek MJ, Yancovitz SR. Clinical and demographic features of patients admitted to a new chemical dependency program in New York City. Drug Alcohol Depend 1987;20:271–278.

119. Rounsaville BJ, Kosten TR, Kleber HD. The antecedents and benefits of achieving abstinence in opioid addicts: a 2.5 year follow-up study. Am J Drug Alcohol Abuse 1987;13:213–229.

120. Ball JC, Corty E. Basic issues pertaining to the effectiveness of methadone maintenance treatment. NIDA Res Monogr 1988;86:178–191.

121. Ball J, Corty E, Bond H, et al. The reduction of intravenous heroin use, non-opiate abuse, and crime during methadone maintenance treatment. NIDA Res Monogr 1988;81:224–230.

122. Dole VP. Implications of methadone maintenance for theories of narcotic addiction. JAMA 1988;260:3025–3029.

123. Himmelsbach C. Clinical studies of morphine addiction: Nathan B. Eddy memorial award lecture. NIDA Res Monogr 1988;81:8–18.

124. Novick DM, Pascarell EF, Joseph H, Salsitz EA, Richman BL, Des Jarlais DC, Anderson M, et al. Methadone maintenance patients in general medical practice: a preliminary report. JAMA 1988;259:3299–3302.

125. Novick DM, Joseph H, Dole VP. Methadone maintenance: response to article "Methadone maintenance patients in general medical practice." JAMA 1988;260:2835–2836.

126. Foy A, Drinkwater V, White A. A prospective clinical audit of methadone maintenance therapy at the Royal Newcastle Hospital. Med J Aust 1989;151:332–334.

127. Kosten TR, Krystal JH, Charney DS, Price LH, Morgan CH, Kleber HD. Letters to the editor: rapid detoxification from opioid dependence. Am J Psychiatry 1989;146(10):1349.

128. San L, Cami J, Peri JM, Mata R, Porta M. Success and failure at inpatient heroin detoxification. Br J Addict 1989;84:81–87.

129. Kreek MJ. Historical and medical aspects of methadone maintenance treatment: Effectiveness in treatment of heroin addiction and implications of such treatment in the setting of the AIDS epidemic. In: Adamsson C, Jansson B, Rydberg U, Westrin C, eds. Evaluation of different programmes for treatment of drug addicts. Stockholm: Medicinska Forskningsradet, 1990:61–76.

130. Kreek MJ. Methadone maintenance treatment for heroin addiction. In: Platt JJ, Kaplan CD, McKim PJ, eds. The effectiveness of drug abuse treatment: Dutch and American perspectives. Malabar, FL: Krieger Publishing Co., 1990:275–293.

131. Loimer N, Jagsch R, Linzmayer L, Grunberger J. Habituation of skin conductance response in a methadone population. Drug Alcohol Depend 1990;26:199–202.

132. Loimer N, Lenz K, Presslich O, Schmid R. Rapid transition from methadone maintenance to naltrexone. Lancet 1990;335:111.

133. Nolimal D, Crowley TJ. Difficulties in a clinical application of methadone-dose contingency contracting. J Subst Abuse Treat 1990;7:219–224.

134. San L, Cami J, Peri JM, Mata R, Porta M. Efficacy of clonidine, guanfacine and methadone in the rapid detoxification of heroin addicts: a controlled clinical trial. Br J Addict 1990;85:141–147.

135. Woody GE, McLellan TA, O'Brien CP. Clinical-behavioral observations of the long-term effects of drug abuse. NIDA Res Monogr 1990;101:71–85.

136. Zweben JE, Payte JT. Methadone maintenance in the treatment of opioid dependence: a current perspective. West J Med 1990;152:588–599.

137. Deleted in proof.

138. Ball JC, Ross A. The effectiveness of methadone maintenance treatment patients, programs, services and outcome. New York: Springer-Verlag, 1991.

139. Bocker FM. Treatment of drug dependent patients with methadone. Fortschr Med 1991;109(5):129–131.

140. Caplehorn JR, Bell J. Methadone dosage and retention of patients in maintenance. Med J Aust 1991;154:195–199.

141. Ennis M, Schneider C, Nehring E, Lorenz W. Histamine release induced by opioid analgesics: a comparative study using porcine mast cells. Agents Actions 1991;33(1–2):20–22.

142. Gossop M, Strang J. A comparison of the withdrawal responses of heroin and methadone addicts during detoxification. Br J Psychiatry 1991;158:697–699.

143. Joe GW, Simpson DD, Hubbard RL. Treatment predictors of tenure in methadone maintenance. J Subst Abuse 1991;3(1):74–84.

144. Kanof PD, Aronson MJ, Ness R, Cochrane KJ, Horvath TB, Handelsman L. Levels of opioid physical dependence in heroin addicts. Drug Alcohol Depend 1991;27(3):253–262.

145. Kosten TR, Morgan C, Kleber HD. Treatment of heroin addicts using buprenorphine. Am J Drug Alcohol Abuse 1991;17(2):119–128.

146. Kreek MJ. Multiple drug abuse patterns: recent trends and associated medical consequences. In: Mello NK, ed. Advances in substance abuse: behavioral and biological research. London: Jessica Kingsley Publishers, 1991;4:91–111.

147. Kreek MJ. Using methadone effectively: achieving goals by application of laboratory, clinical, and evaluation research and by development of innovative programs. NIDA Res Monogr 1991;106:245–266.

148. Kreek MJ. Methadone maintenance treatment for harm reduction approach to heroin addiction. In: Loimer N, Schmid R, Springer A, eds. Drug addiction and AIDS. New York: Springer-Verlag, 1991:153–177.

149. Loimer N, Lenz K, Schmid R, Presslich O. Technique for greatly shortening the transition from methadone to naltrexone maintenance of patients addicted to opiates. Am J Psychiatry 1991;148(7):933–935.

150. Martin J, Payte JT, Zweben JE. Methadone maintenance treatment: a primer for physicians. J Psychoactive Drugs 1991;23(2):165–176.

151. Novick DM, Joseph H. Medical maintenance: the treatment of chronic opiate dependence in general medical practice. J Subst Abuse Treat 1991;8:233–239.

152. Shaham Y, Shuffman EN, Scher J, Barel C, Zlotogorski Z, Cohen E. Methadone maintenance and clonidine detoxification in the treatment of opiate addicts in Israel: suggesting evidence for cultural differences in the effectiveness of treatment modalities for opiate addiction. Isr J Psychiatry Relat Sci 1991;28(3):45–57.

153. Stark MJ, Campbell BK. A psychoeducational approach to methadone maintenance treatment: a survey of client reactions. J Subst Abuse Treat 1991;8(3):125–131.

154. Bianchi E, Maremmani I, Meloni D, Tagliamonte A. Controlled use of heroin in patients on methadone maintenance treatment. J Subst Abuse Treat 1992;9(4):383–387.

155. Brooke D, Fudala PJ, Johnson RE. Weighing up the pros and cons: help-seeking by drug misusers in Baltimore USA. Drug Alcohol Depend 1992;31(1):37–43.

156. el-Bassel N, Schilling RF. 15-month follow-up of women methadone patients taught skills to reduce heterosexual HIV transmission. Public Health Rep 1992;107(5):500–504.

157. Follmann D, Wu M, Geller N. Issues in the analysis of clinical trials for opiate dependencies. NIDA Res Monogr 1992;178:97–115.

158. Jain RB. Analysis of clinical trials for treatment of opiate dependence: what are the possibilities? NIDA Res Monogr 1992;128:116–136.

159. Johnson RE, Fudala PJ. Background and design of a controlled clinical trial (ARC 090) for the treatment of opioid dependence. NIDA Res Monogr 1992;128:14–24.

160. Johnson RE, Jaffe JH, Fudala PJ. A controlled trial of buprenorphine treatment for opioid dependence. JAMA 1992;267(20):2750–2755.

161. Kanof PD, Handelsman L, Aronson MJ, Ness R, Cochrane KJ, Rubinstein KJ. Clinical characteristics of naloxone-precipitated withdrawal in human opioid-dependent subjects. J Pharmacol Exp Ther 1992;260(1):355–363.

162. Kreek MJ. Effects of opiates, opioid antagonists, and cocaine on the endogenous opioid system: clinical and laboratory studies. NIDA Res Monogr 1992;119:44–48.

163. Kreek MJ. Effects of drugs of abuse and treatment agents in women. NIDA Res Monogr 1992;119:106–110.

164. Kreek MJ. Epilogue. Medical maintenance treatment for heroin addiction, from a retrospective and prospective viewpoint. In: State Methadone Maintenance Treatment Guidelines. Rockville, MD: Office for Treatment Improvement, Division for State Assistance, 1992:255–272.

165. Kreek MJ. The addict as a patient. In: Lowinson JH, Ruiz P, Millman RB, Langrod JG, eds. Substance abuse: a comprehensive textbook. 2nd edition. Baltimore: Williams & Wilkins, 1992:997–1009.

166. Kreek MJ. Pharmacological treatment of opioid dependency. In: Buhringer G, Platt J, eds. Drug abuse and treatment: German and American perspectives. Malabar, FL: Krieger Publishing, 1992:398–406.

167. Mason B, Kreek MJ, Kocsis J, Melia D, Sweeney J. Psychiatric comorbidity in metha-

done maintained patients. NIDA Res Monogr 1992;119:230.

168. Murphy D. Opiate addiction in Iowa. Iowa Med 1992;82(11):455–457.

169. San L, Cami J, Fernandez T, Olle JM, Peri JM, Torrens M. Assessment and management of opioid withdrawal symptoms in buprenorphine-dependent subjects. Br J Addict 1992;87(1):55–62.

170. Silverstone PH, Attenburrow MJ, Robson P. The calcium channel antagonist nifedipine causes confusion when used to treat opiate withdrawal in morphine-dependent patients. Int Clin Psychopharmacol 1992;7(2):87–90.

171. Steels MD, Hamilton M, McLean PC. The consequences of a change in formulation of methadone prescribed in a drug clinic. Br J Addict 1992;87(11):1549–1554.

172. Stitzer ML, Iguchi MY, Felch LJ. Contingent take-home incentive: effects on drug use of methadone maintenance patients. J Consult Clin Psychol 1992;60(6):927–934.

173. Unnithan S, Gossop M, Strang J. Factors associated with relapse among opiate addicts in an out-patient detoxification programme. Br J Psychiatry 1992;161:654–657.

174. Bornemann R. Advantages and disadvantages of the alternatives of private practice, public health and clinic out patient department as dispensaries for methadone substitution of drug users. Forensic Sci Int 1993;62:57–61.

175. Brown LS Jr, Hickson MJ, Ajuluchukwu DC, Bailey J. Medical disorders in a cohort of New York City drug abusers: much more than HIV disease. J Addict Dis 1993;12(4):11–27.

176. Caplehorn JRM, McNeil DR, Kleinbaum DG. Clinic policy and retention in methadone maintenance. Int J Addict 1993;28(1):73–89.

177. Caplehorn JRM, Bell J, Kleinbaum DG, Gebski VJ. Methadone dose and heroin use during maintenance treatment. Addiction 1993; 88:119–124.

178. Kaplan JL, Marx JA. Effectiveness and safety of intravenous nalmefene for emergency department patients with suspected narcotic overdose: a pilot study. Ann Emerg Med 1993; 22(2):187–190.

179. Kreek MJ. Opioid agonists: use in treatment of opiate dependency. NIDA Res Monogr 1993; 132:84.

180. Kreek MJ. Pharmacotherapy of addictive diseases. NIDA Res Monogr 1993;132:83.

181. Lehmann F, Lauzon P, Amsel R. Methadone maintenance: predictors of outcome in a Canadian milieu. J Subst Abuse Treat 1993;10(1): 85–89.

182. McLellan AT, Arndt IO, Metzger DS, Woody GE, O'Brien CP. The effects of psychosocial services in substance abuse treatment. JAMA 1993;269(15):1953–1959.

183. Novick DM, Richman BL, Friedman JM, Friedman JE, Fried C, Wilson JP, et al. The medical status of methadone maintenance patients in treatment for 11–18 years. Drug Alcohol Depend 1993;33:235–245.

184. Saxon AJ, Calsyn DA, Kivlahan DR, Roszell DK. Outcome of contingency contracting for illicit drug use in a methadone maintenance program. Drug Alcohol Depend 1993;31(3): 205–214.

185. Strain EC, Stitzer ML, Liebson IA, Bigelow GE. Methadone dose and treatment outcome. Drug Alcohol Depend 1993;33:105–117.

186. Weinstein SP, Gottheil E, Sterling RC, DeMaria PA Jr. Long-term methadone maintenance treatment: some clinical examples. J Subst Abuse Treat 1993;10(3):277–281.

187. Wilson RS, DiGeorge WS. Methadone combined with clonidine versus clonidine alone in opiate detoxification. J Subst Abuse Treat 1993;10:529–536.

188. Abramowicz M. LAAM—a long-acting methadone for treatment of heroin addiction. Med Lett 1994;36(924):52.

189. Borg L, Ho A, Kreek MJ. Tuberculosis testing in an urban VA methadone clinic: compliance and results. NIDA Res Monogr 1994;141:180.

190. Caplehorn JR, Dalton MS, Cluff MC, Petrenas AM. Retention in methadone maintenance and heroin addicts' risk of death. Addiction 1994; 89:203–209.

191. Friedman P, Des Jarlais DC, Peyser NP, Nichols SE, Drew E, Newman RG. Retention of patients who entered methadone maintenance via an interim methadone clinic. J Psychoactive Drugs 1994;26:217–221.

192. Gallimberti L, Schifano F, Forza G, Miconi L, Ferrara SD. Clinical efficacy of gamma-hydroxybutyric acid in treatment of opiate withdrawal. Eur Arch Psychiatry Clin Neurosci 1994;244:113–114.

193. Ghodse H, Myles J, Smith SE. Clonidine is not a useful adjunct to methadone gradual detoxification in opioid addiction. Br J Psychiatry 1994;165:370–374.

194. Goldstein A. Addiction: from biology to drug policy. New York: WH Freeman, 1994.

195. Kreek MJ. Pharmacotherapy of opioid dependence: rationale and update. Regulatory Peptides: Proceedings of the 25th International Narcotics Research Conference (INRC). New York: Elsevier, 1994;S1:S255-S256.

196. Janiri L, Mannelli P, Persico AM, Serretti A, Tempesta E. Opiate detoxification of methadone maintenance patients using lefetamine, clonidine and buprenorphine. Drug Alcohol Depend 1994;36:139–145.

197. Kidorf M, Stizer ML, Brooner RK, Goldberg J. Contingent methadone take-home doses reinforce adjunct therapy attendance of methadone maintenance patients. Drug Alcohol Depend 1994;36:221–226.

198. Kreek MJ. Pharmacology and medical aspects of methadone treatment. In: Rettig RA, Yarmolinsky A, eds. Federal regulation of methadone treatment. Washington, DC: National Academy Press, 1994:37–60.

199. Deleted in proof.

200. Kreek MJ. Biological correlates of methadone maintenance pharmacotherapy. In: Christoforov B, ed. Ann. med interne: intérêts et limites des traitements de substitution dans la prise en charge des toxicomanes. Paris: Masson, 1994;145:9–14.

201. Novick DM, Joseph H, Salsitz EA, Kalin MF, Keefe JB, Miller EL, Richman BL. Outcomes of treatment of socially rehabilitated methadone maintenance patients in physicians' offices (medical maintenance): Follow-up at three and a half to nine and a fourth years. J Gen Intern Med 1994;9:127–130.

202. Rettig RA, Yarmolinsky A, eds. Federal regulation of methadone treatment. Washington, DC: National Academy Press, 1995.

203. San L, Fernandez T, Cami J, Gossop M. Efficacy of methadone versus methadone and guanfacine in the detoxification of heroin-addicted patients. J Subst Abuse Treat 1994;11:463–469.

204. Strain EC, Stitzer ML, Liebson IA, Bigelow GE. Outcome after methadone treatment: influence of prior treatment factors and current treatment status. Drug Alcohol Depend 1994;35:223–230.

205. Umbricht-Schneiter A, Ginn DH, Pabst KM, Bigelow GE. Providing medical care to methadone clinic patients: referral vs. on-site care. Am J Public Health 1994;84:207–210.

206. Wilson P, Watson R, Ralston GE. Methadone maintenance in general practice: patients, workload, and outcomes. BMJ 1994;309: 641–644.

207. Borg L, Broe DM, Ho A, Kreek MJ. Cocaine abuse is decreased with effective methadone maintenance treatment at an urban Department of Veterans Affairs (DVA) Program. NIDA Res Monogr 1995;153:17.

208. dePetrillo PB, Rice JM. Methadone dosing and pregnancy: impact on program compliance. Int J Addict 1995;30:207–217.

209. Des Jarlais DC, Paone D, Friedman SR, Peyser N, Newman RG. Regulating controversial programs for unpopular people: methadone maintenance and syringe exchange programs. Am J Public Health 1995;85:1577–1584.

210. Dole VP. On federal regulation of methadone treatment. JAMA 1995;274:1307.

211. Eklund C, Hilttmen AJ, Melin L, Borg S. Factors associated with successful withdrawal from methadone maintenance treatment in Sweden. Int J Addict 1995;30:1335–1353.

212. Finnegan LP, Sloboda Z, Haverkos HW, Mello NK, Kreek MJ, Cottler LB, Frank DA. Drug abuse and the health of women. NIDA Res Monogr 1995;152:45–48.

213. Ghodse II, Taylor DR, Greaves JL, Britten AJ, Lynch D. The opiate addiction test: a clinical evaluation of a quick test for physical dependence on opiate drugs. Br J Clin Pharmacol 1995;39:257–259.

214. Hilttmen AJ, Lafolie P, Martel J, Ottosson EC, Boreus LO, Beck O, et al. Subjective and objective symptoms in relation to plasma methadone concentration in methadone patients. Psychopharmacology 1995;118:122–126.

215. Kosten TR, Rayford BS. Effects of ethnicity on low-dose opiate stabilization. J Subst Abuse Treat 1995;12:111–116.

216. Kreek MJ, Simon E, Evans C, Uhl G, Wang JB, Johnson P, et al. Symposium for 20th anniversary of National Institute of Drug Abuse: update on opioid receptor cloning: implications for research on addiction. NIDA Res Monogr 1995;152:37–41.

217. Kreek MJ. Drug addiction and health. In: Hall NRS, Altman F, Blumenthal SJ, eds. Mind-body interactions and disease, proceedings of a conference on stress, immunity and health sponsored by the National Institute of Health. Orlando, FL: Health Dateline Press, 1995:87–94.

218. Kreek MJ. Pharmacological treatment of addiction: normalization of physiology and AIDS risk reduction. In: Tagliamonte A, Maremmani I, eds. Drug addiction and related clinical problems. New York: Springer-Verlag, 1995:165–173.

219. Newman RG. Methadone: prescribing maintenance, pursuing abstinence. Int J Addict 1995; 30:1303–1309.

220. Rosen MI, McMahon TJ, Margolin A, Gill TS, Woods SW, Pearsall HR, et al. Reliability of sequential naloxone challenge tests. Am J Drug Alcohol Abuse 1995;21:4:453–467.

221. Rosenbaum M. The demedicalization of methadone maintenance. J Psychoactive Drugs 1995;72:145–149.

222. Wells EA, Fleming C, Calsyn DA, Jackson TR, Saxon AJ. Users of free treatment slots at a community-based methadone maintenance clinic. J Subst Abuse Treat 1995;12:13–18.

223. Wilson P, Watson R, Ralston GE. Supporting problem drug users: improving methadone

maintenance in general practice. Br J Gen Pract 1995;45:454–455.

224. Adelson MO, Shiloney E, Mana S, Kreek MJ. Model treatment research unit patterned after most effective treatment facility following early experience in U.S.A. NIDA Res Monogr 1996;162:198.

225. Kreek MJ. Long-term pharmacotherapy for opiate (primarily heroin) addiction: opiate agonists. In: Schuster CR, Kuhar MJ, eds. Pharmacological aspects of drug dependence: toward an integrated neurobehavioral approach. Berlin: Springer-Verlag, 1996:487–541.

226. Kreek MJ. Long-term pharmacotherapy for opiate (primarily heroin) addiction: opiate antagonists and partial agonists. In: Schuster CR, Kuhar MJ, eds. Pharmacological aspects of drug dependence: toward an integrated neurobehavioral approach. Berlin: Springer-Verlag, 1996:563–592.

227. Kreek MJ. Treatment of addictions: biological correlates. In: Koslow SH, Murthy RS, Coelho GV, eds. Decade of the brain: India/USA research in mental health and neuroscience. Rockville, MD: U.S. Department of Health and Huaman Services, National Institutes of Medicine, 1996:145–159.

228. Kreek MJ. Opiates, opioids and addiction. Mol Psych 1996;1:232–254.

229. Rosen MI, McMahon TJ, Pearsall HR, Hameedi FA, Woods SW, Kosten TR, Kreek MJ. Correlations among measures of naloxone-precipitated opiate withdrawal. NIDA Res Monogr 1996;162:120.

II. DISPOSITION AND PHARMACOKINETICS OF METHADONE AS USED IN MAINTENANCE TREATMENT OF ADDICTION

230. Isbell H, Wikler A, Eisenman AJ, Frank K. Effect of single doses of 10820 (4,4-diphenyl-6-dimethylamino-heptanone-3) on man. Fed Proc 1947;6:341.

231. Bockmuhl M, Erhart G. Justus Liebigs. Ann Chem 1948;561:52–85.

232. Chen KK. Pharmacology of methadone and related compounds. Ann N Y Acad Sci 1948;51:83–97.

233. Finnegan JK, Haag HB, Larson PS, Dreyfuss ML. Observations on the comparative pharmacologic actions of 6-dimethylamino-4,4-diphenyl-heptanone-3 (amidone) and morphine. J Pharmacol Exp Ther 1948;92:269.

234. Isbell H, Eisenman AJ, Wikler A, Frank K. The effects of single doses of 6-dimethylamino-4-4-diphenyl-3-heptanone (amidone, methadone, or "10820") on human subjects. J Pharmacol Exp Ther 1948;92:83.

235. Pohland A, Marshall FJ, Carney TP. Optically active compounds related to methadon. NY Acad Med 1949;71:460–462.

236. Speeter ME, Byrd WM, Cheney LC, Binkley SB. Analgesic carbinols and esters related to amidone (Methadon). J Am Chem Soc 1949; 71:57–60.

237. Eddy NB, May EL, Mosettig E. Chemistry and pharmacology of the methadols and acetylmethadols. Comp Cl Bib 1952:321–326.

238. Sung C-Y, Way EL. The fate of the optical isomers of alpha-acetylmethadol. J Pharmacol Exp Ther 1954;110:260–270.

239. Dole VP, Kim WK, Eglitis J. Detection of narcotic drugs, tranquilizers, amphetamines, and barbiturates in urine. JAMA 1966;198:349–352.

240. Ingoglia NA, Dole VP. Localization of d and l-methadone after intraventricular injection into rat brain. J Pharmacol Exp Ther 1970;175:84–87.

241. Sullivan HR, Blake DA. Quantitative determination of methadone concentrations in human blood, plasma, and urine by gas chromatography. Res Commun Chem Pathol Pharmacol 1972;3(3):467–478.

242. Sullivan HR, Smits SE, Due SL, Booher RE, McMahon RE. Metabolism of d-methadone: isolation and identification of analgesically active metabolites. Life Sci 1972;11(1):1093–1104.

243. Inturrisi CE, Verebey K. A gas-liquid chromatographic method for the quantitative determination of methadone in human plasma and urine. J Chromatogr 1972;65:361–369.

244. Inturrisi CE, Verebey K. The levels of methadone in the plasma in methadone maintenance. Clin Pharmacol Ther 1972;13:633.

245. Dole VP, Kreek MJ. Methadone plasma level: Sustained by a reservoir of drug in tissue. Proc Natl Acad Sci U S A 1973;70:10.

246. Kreek MJ. Plasma and urine levels of methadone. NY State J Med 1973;73:2773–2777.

247. Sullivan HR, Due SL, McMahon RE. Metabolism of alpha-l-methadol. N-acetylation, a new metabolic pathway. Res Commun Chem Pathol Pharmacol 1973;6(3):1072–1078.

248. Anggard E, Gunne L-M, Holmstrand J, McMahon RE, Sandberg C-G, Sullivan HR. Disposition of methadone in methadone maintenance. Clin Pharmacol Ther 1974;17(3):258–266.

249. Billings RE, McMahon RE, Blake DA. L-acetylmethadol (LAAM) treatment of opiate dependence: plasma and urine levels of two pharmacologically active metabolites. Life Sci 1974;14(8):1437–1446.

250. Kreek MJ, Schecter A, Gutjahr CL, Bowen D, Field F, Queenan J, Merkatz I. Analyses of methadone and other drugs in maternal and neonatal body fluids: use in evaluation of symptoms in a neonate of mother maintained on methadone. Am J Drug Alcohol Abuse 1974;1(3):409–419.

251. Kaiko RF, Inturrisi CE. Disposition of acetylmethadol in relation to pharmacologic action. Clin Pharmacol Ther 1975;18(1):96–103.

252. Misra AL, Mule SJ. L-alpha-acetylmethadol (LAAM) pharmacokinetics and metabolism: Current status. Am J Drug Alcohol Abuse 1975;2(3–4):301–305.

253. Gerber N, Lynn RK. Excretion of methadone in semen from methadone addicts; comparison with blood levels. Life Sci 1976;19:787–792.

254. Hachey DL, Mattson DH, Kreek MJ. Quantitation of methadone in biological fluids using deuterium labeled internal standards. In: Klein ER, Klein PD, eds. Proceedings of the Second International Conference on Stable Isotopes. Springfield, VA: National Technical Information Source, U.S. Dept. of Commerce, 1976:518–523.

255. Henderson GL, Wilson K, Lau DHM. Plasma l-a-acetylmethadol (LAAM) after acute and chronic administration. Clin Pharmacol Ther 1976;21(1):16–25.

256. Kreek MJ. The role of qualitative and quantitative analysis of drugs and their metabolites in maternal-neonatal studies. In: National Institute on Drug Abuse Symposium on Comprehensive Health Care for Addicted Families and Their Children, Services Research Report (US-GPO), #017–024-00598-3, Washington, DC: U.S. Government Printing Office, 1976:67–73.

257. Hachey DL, Kreek MJ, Mattson DH. Quantitative analysis of methadone in biological fluids using deuterium-labelled methadone and GLC-chemical-ionization mass spectrometry. J Pharm Sci 1977;66:1579–1582.

258. Bowen DV, Smit ALC, Kreek MJ. Fecal excretion of methadone and its metabolites in man: application of GC-MS. In: Daly NR, ed. Advances in mass spectrometry. Philadelphia: Heyden & Son, 1978;7B:1634–1639.

259. Klein PD, Hachey DL, Kreek MJ, Schoeller DA. Stable isotopes: essential tools in biological and medical research. In: Baillie TA, ed. Stable isotopes: applications in pharmacology, toxicology and clinical research. Baltimore: University Park Press, 1978:3–14.

260. Kreek MJ, Gutjahr CL, Bowen DV, Field FH. Fecal excretion of methadone and its metabolites: a major pathway of elimination in man. In: Schecter A, Alksne H, Kaufman E, eds. Critical concerns in the field of drug abuse: proceedings of the Third National Drug Abuse Conference, New York, 1976. New York: Marcel Dekker, 1978:1206–1210.

261. Kreek MJ, Oratz M, Rothschild MA. Hepatic extraction of long- and short-acting narcotics in the isolated perfused rabbit liver. Gastroenterology 1978;75:88–94.

262. Rubenstein RB, Kreek MJ, Mbawa N, Wolff WI, Korn R, Gutjahr CL. Human spinal fluid methadone levels. Drug Alcohol Depend 1978; 3:103–106.

263. Blake DA, Chappel JN, Kreek MJ, Meyer KC, Neumann LL, Stimmel B, Stryker J. Drug dependence in pregnancy: clinical management in mother and child. NIDA Res Monogr 1979; 27:1–109.

264. Kreek MJ. Methadone disposition during the perinatal period in humans. Pharmacol Biochem Behav 1979;11, suppl:1–7.

265. Kreek MJ, Hachey DL, Klein PD. Stereoselective disposition of methadone in man. Life Sci 1979;24:925–932.

266. Kreek MJ, Bencsath FA, Field FH. Effects of liver disease on urinary excretion of methadone and metabolites in maintenance patients: quantitation by direct probe chemical ionization mass spectrometry. Biomed Mass Spectrom 1980;7:385–395.

267. Kreek MJ, Kalisman M, Irwin M, Jaffery NF, Scheflan M. Biliary secretion of methadone and methadone metabolites in man. Res Commun Chem Pathol Pharmacol 1980;29:67–78.

268. Kreek MJ, Schecter AJ, Gutjahr CL, Hecht M. Methadone use in patients with chronic renal disease. Drug Alcohol Depend 1980;5:197–205.

269. Nakamura K, Kreek MJ, Hachey DL, Irving CS, Klein PD. Studies on disposition of dl-methadone in former heroin addicts by the multiple deuterium labeling method. Proceedings of the Japanese Society for Medical Mass Spectrometry 1981;6:119–124.

270. Novick DM, Kreek MJ, Fanizza AM, Yancovitz SR, Gelb AM, Stenger RJ. Methadone disposition in patients with chronic liver disease. Clin Pharmacol Ther 1981;30:353–362.

271. Kreek MJ. Disposition of narcotics in the perinatal period. In: Publication of AMERSA and The Career Teacher Program in Alcohol and Drug Abuse 1981–82;3:7–10.

272. Finnegan LP, Chappel JN, Kreek MJ, Stimmel B, Stryker J. Narcotic addiction in pregnancy. In: Niebyl JR, ed. Drug use in pregnancy. Philadelphia: Lea & Febiger, 1982:163–184.

273. Hachey DL, Nakamura K, Kreek MJ, Klein PD. Analytical techniques for using multiple, simultaneous stable isotopic tracers. In: Schmidt HL, Forstel H, Heinzinger K, eds. Sta-

ble isotopes. Amsterdam: Elsevier Scientific Publishing Company, 1982:235–239.

274. Kreek MJ. Opioid disposition and effects during chronic exposure in the perinatal period in man. J Addict Dis 1982;1:21–53.

275. Nakamura K, Hachey DL, Kreek MJ, Irving CS, Klein PD. Quantitation of methadone enantiomers in humans using stable isotope-labeled [2H3]-[2H5]-, and[2H8] methadone. J Pharm Sci 1982;71:39–43.

276. Kreek MJ. Critique: clinical perinatal and developmental effects of methadone. In: Cooper JR, Altman F, Brown BS, Czechowicz D, eds. research on the treatment of narcotic addiction: state of the art. Rockville, MD: U.S. Dept. of Health and Human Services, Public Health Service, Alcohol, Drug Abuse, and Mental Health Administration, National Institute on Drug Abuse, 1983:444–453.

277. Kreek MJ, Bencsath FA, Fanizza A, Field FH. Effects of liver disease on fecal excretion of methadone and its unconjugated metabolites in maintenance patients: quantitation by direct probe chemical ionization mass spectrometry. Biomed Mass Spectrom 1983;10:544–549.

278. Pond SM, Kreek MJ, Tong TG, Raghunath J, Benowitz NL. Altered methadone pharmacokinetics in methadone-maintained pregnant women. J Pharmacol Exp Ther 1985;233:1–6.

279. Novick DM, Kreek MJ, Arns PA, Lau LL, Yancovitz SR, Gelb AM. Effect of severe alcoholic liver disease on the disposition of methadone in maintenance patients. Alcohol Clin Exp Res 1985;9:349–354.

280. Beck O, Boreus LO, Lafolie P, Jacobsson G. Chiral analysis of methadone in plasma by high-performance liquid chromatography. J Chromatogr 1991;570(1):198–202.

281. Bryant HU, Holaday JW. Opioids in immunologic processes. In: Herz A, ed. Handbook of experimental pharmacology: opioids II. Berlin: Springer-Verlag, 1991;104(II):361–392.

282. Loimer N, Schmid R, Grunberger J, Gagsch R, Linzmayer L, Presslich O. Psychophysiological reactions in methadone maintenance patients do not correlate with methadone plasma levels. Psychopharmacology 1991;103:538–540.

283. Wolff K, Hay A, Raistrick D. High-dose methadone and the need for drug measurements. Clin Chem 1991;37:1651–1654.

284. Wolff K, Hay A, Raistrick D, Calvert R, Feely M. Measuring compliance in methadone maintenance patients. Clin Pharmacol Ther 1991; 50:199–207.

285. Dristensen K, Angelo HR. Stereospecific gas chromatographic method for determination of methadone in serum. Chirality 1992;4(4):263–267.

286. Wolff K, Hay AW, Raistrick D. Plasma methadone measurements and their role in methadone maintenance detoxification programs. Clin Chem 1992;38(3):420–425.

287. Brewer C. Hair analysis as a tool for monitoring and managing patients on methadone maintenance. A discussion. Forensic Sci Int 1993; 63:277–283.

288. Schmidt N, Sittl R, Brune K, Geisslinger G. Rapid determination of methadone in plasma, cerebrospinal fluid, and urine by gas chromatography and its application to routine drug monitoring. Pharm Res 1993;10:441–444.

289. Simpson D, Greenwood J, Jarvie DR, Moore FM. Experience of a laboratory service for drug screening in urine. Scott Med J 1993; 38(1):20–26.

290. Wolff K, Hay AWM, Raistrick D, Calvert R. Steady-state pharmacokinetics of methadone in opioid addicts. Eur J Clin Pharmacol 1993; 44:189–194.

291. Wu D, Otton SV, Sproule BA, Busto U, Inaba T, Kalow W, Sellers EM. Inhibition of human cytochrome P450 2D6(CYP2D6) by methadone. Br J Clin Pharmacol 1993;35:30–34.

292. McCarthy J. Quantitative urine drug monitoring in methadone programs: potential clinical uses. J Psychoactive Drugs 1994;26:199–206.

293. Norris RL, Ravenscroft PJ, Pond SM. Sensitive high-performance liquid chromatographic assay with ultraviolet detection of methadone enantiomers in plasma. J Chromatogr B Biomed Appl 1994;661:346–350.

294. Borg L, Ho A, Peters JE, Kreek MJ. Availability of reliable serum methadone determination for management of symptomatic patients. J Addict Dis 1995;14:83–96.

295. Gomez E, Martinez-Jorda R, Suarez E, Garrido MJ, Calvo R. Altered methadone analgesia due to changes in plasma protein binding: role of the route of administration. Gen Pharmacol 1995;26:1273–1276.

296. Kell MJ. Utilization of plasma Na during methadone concentration measurements to limit narcotics use in methadone maintenance patients: II. Generation of plasma concentration response curves. J Addict Dis 1995;14:85–108.

III. DRUG AND ALCOHOL INTERACTIONS WITH METHADONE

297. Finelli PF. Phenytoin and methadone tolerance. N Engl J Med 1976;294:227.

298. Kreek MJ, Garfield JW, Gutjahr CL, et al. Rifampin-induced methadone withdrawal. N Engl J Med 1976;294:1104.

299. Kreek MJ, Gutjahr CL, Garfield JW, Bowen DV, Field FH. Drug interactions with methadone. Ann N Y Acad Sci 1976; 281:350–374.

300. Bending MR, Skacel PO. Rifampicin and methadone withdrawal. Lancet 1977;1:1211.

301. Cushman P Jr, Kreek MJ, Gordis E. Ethanol and methadone in man: a possible drug interaction. Drug Alcohol Depend 1978;3:35–42.

302. Kreek MJ. Effects of drugs and alcohol on opiate disposition and action. In: Adler ML, Manara L, Samanin R, eds. Factors affecting the action of narcotics. New York: Raven Press, 1978:717–739.

303. Tong TG, Benowitz NL, Kreek MJ. Methadone-disulfiram interaction during methadone maintenance. J Clin Pharma col 1980;20:506–513.

304. Kreek MJ. Metabolic interactions between opiates and alcohol. Ann N Y Acad Sci 1981; 362:36–49.

305. Pond SM, Kretzschmar KM. Effect of phenytoin on meperidine clearance and normeperidine formation. Clin Pharmacol Ther1981;30:680–686.

306. Tong TG, Pond SM, Kreek MJ, Jaffery NF, Benowitz NL. Phenytoin-induced methadone withdrawal. Ann Intern Med 1981;94: 349–351.

307. Donnelly B, Balkon J, Lasher C, Lynch VD, Bidanset JH, Blanco J. Evaluation of the methadone-alcohol interaction. I. Alterations of plasma concentration kinetics. J Anal Toxicol 1983;7:246–248.

308. Kreek MJ. Factors modifying the pharmacological effectiveness of methadone. In: Cooper JR, Altman F, Brown BS, Czechowicz D, eds. research on the treatment of narcotic addiction: state of the art. Rockville, MD: U.S. Dept. of Health and Human Services, Public Health Service, Alcohol, Drug Abuse, and Mental Health Administration, National Institute on Drug Abuse, 1983:95–107.

309. Baciewicz AM, Self TH. Rifampin drug interactions. Arch Intern Med 1984;144:1667–1671.

310. Kreek MJ. Drug interactions with methadone in humans. NIDA Res Monogr 1986;68: 193–225.

311. Kreek MJ. Exogenous opioids: drug-disease interactions. In: Foley KM, Inturrisi CE, eds. Advances in pain research and therapy. New York: Raven Press, 1986;8:201–210.

312. Preston KL, Griffiths RR, Cone EJ, Darwin WD, Gorodetzky CW. Diazepam and methadone blood levels following concurrent administration of diazepam and methadone. Drug Alcohol Depend 1986;18:195–202.

313. Baciewicz AM, Self TH, Bekemeyer WB. Update on rifampin drug interactions. Arch Intern Med 1987;147:565–568.

314. Kreek MJ. Opiate-ethanol interactions: implications for the biological basis and treatment of combined addictive diseases. NIDA Res Monogr 1988;81:428–439.

315. Saxon AJ, Whittaker S, Hawker CS. Valproic acid, unlike other anticonvulsants, has no effect on methadone metabolism: two cases. J Clin Psychiatry 1989;50:228–229.

316. Fraser AD. Clinical toxicology of drugs used in the treatment of opiate dependency. Clin Lab Med 1990;10:375–386.

317. Kreek MJ. Drug interactions in humans related to drug abuse and its treatment. Modern Methods in Pharmacology 1990;6:265–282.

318. Bertschy G, Baumann P, Eap CB, Baettig D. Probable metabolic interaction between methadone and fluvoxamine in addict patients. Ther Drug Monit 1994;16:42–45.

319. Borg L, Kreek MJ. Clinical problems associated with interactions between methadone pharmacotherapy and medications used in the treatment of HIV-positive and AIDS patients. Curr Opin Psychiatry 1995;8:199–202.

IV. TOXICITY AND MORTALITY RELATED TO OR CAUSED BY METHADONE

320. Helpern M, Rho Y-M. Deaths from narcotics in New York City: incidence, circumstances, and post-mortem findings. N Y State J Med 1966; 66:2391–2408.

321. Baden MM. Methadone related deaths in New York City. Int J Addict 1970;5:489–498.

322. Dole VP, Foldes FF, Trigg H, Robinson JW, Blatman S. Methadone poisoning: diagnosis and treatment. N Y State J Med 1971;71: 541–543.

323. Gay GR, Inaba DS. Treating acute heroin and methadone toxicity. Anesth Analg 1976;55: 607–610.

324. Kjeldgaard JM, Hahn GW, Heckenlively JR, Genton E. Methadone-induced pulmonary edema. JAMA 1971;218:882–883.

325. Frand UI, Shim CS, Williams MH Jr. Methadone-induced pulmonary edema. Ann Intern Med 1972;76:975–979.

326. Chabalko J, Larosa JC, Dupont RL. Death of methadone users in the District of Columbia. Int J Addict 1973;8:897–908.

327. Chappel J, Mays V, Senay E. Death and the treatment of drug addiction: a five year study of deaths occurring to members of the Illinois Drug Abuse Program. In: Proceedings of the Fifth National Conference on Methadone Treatment. New York: National Association for the Prevention of Addiction to Narcotics, 1973;1:530–537.

328. Greene MH, Dupont RL. Medical complica-

tions associated with the use of methadone: methadone related mortality. In: Proceedings of the Fifth National Conference on Methadone Treatment. New York: National Association for the Prevention of Addiction to Narcotics, 1973;2:811–823.

329. Presant S, Knight L, Klassen G. Methadone-induced pulmonary edema. Can Med Assoc J 1975;113:966–967.

330. Schecter A, Kauders F. Patient deaths in a narcotic antagonist (naltrexone) and L-alpha-acetylmethadol program. Am J Drug Alcohol Abuse 1975;2(3–4):443–449.

331. Spira IA, Rubenstein R, Wolff D, Wolff WI. Fecal impaction following methadone ingestion simulating acute intestinal obstruction. Ann Surg 1975;181:15–19.

332. Wilen SB, Ulreich S, Rabinowitz JG. Roentgenographic manifestations of methadone-induced pulmonary edema. Radiology 1975;114:51–55.

333. Persky VW, Goldfrank LR. Methadone overdoses in a New York City hospital. J Am Coll Emerg Med 1976;5:111–113.

334. Concool B, Smith H, Stimmel B. Mortality rates of persons entering methadone maintenance: a seven-year study. Am J Drug Alcohol Abuse 1979;6:345–353.

335. Bradberry JC, Raebel MA. Continuous infusion of naloxone in the treatment of narcotic overdose. Drug Intell Clin Pharm 1981;15:945–950.

336. Hartman N, Kreek MJ. Narcotic poisoning. In: Conn HF, ed. Current therapy. Philadelphia: WB Saunders, 1983:896–898.

337. Gronbladh L, Ohlund LS, Gunne LM. Mortality in heroin addiction: impact of methadone treatment. Acta Psychiatr Scand 1990;82:223–227.

338. Levine B, Wu SC, Dixon A, Sinialek JE. Site dependence of postmortem blood methadone concentrations. Am J Forensic Med Pathol 1995;16:97–100.

V. EFFECTS OF SHORT-ACTING (HEROIN) VERSUS LONG-ACTING (METHADONE) OPIOIDS IN HUMANS

A. Neuroendocrine

339. Eisenman AJ, Fraser HF, Sloan J, Isbell H. Urinary 17-ketosteroid excretion during a cycle of addiction to morphine. J Pharmacol Exp Ther 1958;124:305–311.

340. Eisenman AJ, Fraser HF, Brooks JW. Urinary excretion and plasma levels of 17-hydroxycorticosteroids during a cycle of addiction to morphine. J Pharmacol Exp Ther 1961;132:226–231.

341. Blinick G. Menstrual function and pregnancy in narcotic addicts treated with methadone. Nature 1968;219:180.

342. Shenkman L, Massie B, Mitsuma T, et al. Effects of chronic methadone administration on the hypothalamic-pituitary-thyroid axis. J Clin Endocrinol Metab 1972;35(1):169–170.

343. Eisenman AJ, Sloan JW, Martin WR, Jasinski DR, Brooks JW. Catecholamine and 17-hydroxycorticosteroid excretion during a cycle of morphine dependence in man. J Psychiatr Res 1969;7:19–28.

344. Cushman P Jr, Bordier B, Hilton JG. Hypothalamic-pituitary-adrenal axis in methadone-treated heroin addicts. J Clin Endocrinol Metab 1970;30:24–29.

345. Cushman P Jr. Growth hormone in narcotic addiction. J Clin Endocrinol Metab 1972;35:352–358.

346. Cushman P Jr. Studies on growth hormone in narcotic addiction. In: Proceedings of the Fourth National Conference on Methadone Treatment. New York: National Association for the Prevention of Addiction to Narcotics, 1972:421–423.

347. Kreek MJ. Medical safety, side effects and toxicity of methadone. In: Proceedings of the Fourth National Conference on Methadone Treatment. New York: National Association for the Prevention of Addiction to Narcotics, 1972:171–174.

348. Renault PF, Schuster CR, Heinrich RL, Van der Kolk B. Altered plasma cortisol response in patients on methadone maintenance. Clin Pharmacol Ther 1972;13:269–273.

349. Azizi F, Vagenakis AG, Longcope C, Ingbar SH, Braverman LE. Decreased serum testosterone concentration in male heroin and methadone addicts. Steroids 1973;22:467–472.

350. Cushman P Jr, Kreek MJ. Plasma testosterone in narcotic addiction. Am J Med 1973;55:452–458.

351. Espejo R, Hogben G, Stimmel B. Sexual performance of men on methadone maintenance. In: Proceedings of the Fifth National Conference on Methadone Treatment. New York: National Association for the Prevention of Addiction to Narcotics, 1973;1:490–493.

352. Santen RJ, Bardin CW. Episodic luteinizing hormone secretion in man, pulse analysis, clinical interpretation, physiologic mechanisms. J Clin Invest 1973;52:2617–2628.

353. Webster JB, Coupal JJ, Cushman P Jr. Increased serum thyroxine levels in euthyroid narcotic addicts. J Clin Endocrinol Metab 1973;37:928–934.

354. Azizi F, Vagenakis AG, Portnay GI, Braverman LE, Ingbar SH. Thyroxine transport and metabolism in methadone and heroin addicts. Ann Intern Med 1974;80:194–199.

355. Cushman P Jr, Kreek MJ. Methadone-maintained patients: effects of methadone on plasma testosterone, FSH, LH, and prolactin. N Y State J Med 1974;74:1970–1973.

356. Cushman P Jr, Kreek MJ. Some endocrinologic observations in narcotic addicts. In: Zimmermann E, George R, eds. Narcotics and the hypothalamus. New York: Raven Press, 1974:161–173.

357. Pelosi MA, Sama JC, Caterini H, Kaminetzky HA. Galactorrhea-amenorrhea syndrome associated with heroin addiction. Am J Obstet Gynecol 1974;118:966–970.

358. Santen RJ. How narcotics addiction affects reproductive function in women. Contemp Obstet Gynecol 1974;3.4:93–96.

359. Cicero TJ, Bell RD, Wiest WG, et al. Function of the male sex organs in heroin and methadone users. N Engl J Med 1975;292:822.

360. Hellman L, Fukushima DK, Roffwarg H, Fishman J. Changes in estradiol and cortisol production rates in men under the influence of narcotics. J Clin Endocrinol Metab 1975;41:1014–1019.

361. Mendelson JH, Mello NK. Plasma testosterone levels during chronic heroin use and protracted abstinence: a study of Hong Kong addicts. Clin Pharmacol Ther 1975;17:529–533.

362. Mendelson JH, Mendelson JE, Patch VD. Plasma testosterone levels in heroin addiction and during methadone maintenance. J Pharmacol Exp Ther 1975;192:211–217.

363. Mendelson JH, Meyer RE, Ellingboe J, Mirin SM, McDougle M. Effects of heroin and methadone on plasma cortisol and testosterone. J Pharmacol Exp Ther 1975;195:296–302.

364. Santen RJ, Sofsky J, Bilic N, Lippert R. Mechanism of action of narcotics in the production of menstrual dysfunction in women. Fertil Steril 1975;26:538–548.

365. Bastomsky CH, Dent RRM. Elevated serum concentrations of thyroxine-binding globulin and ceruloplasmin in methadone-maintained patients. Clin Res 1976;24:655A.

366. Mendelson JH, Inturrisi CE, Renault P, Senay EC. Effects of acetylmethadol on plasma testosterone. Clin Pharmacol Ther 1976;19(3):371–374.

367. Mirin SM, Mendelson JH, Ellingboe J, Meyer RE. Acute effects of heroin and naltrexone on testosterone and gonadotropin secretion: a pilot study. Psychoneuroendocrinology 1976;1:359–369.

368. Clement-Jones V, McLoughlin L, Lowry PJ, Besser GM, Rees LH. Acupuncture in heroin addicts; changes in met-enkephalin and B-endorphin in blood and cerebrospinal fluid. Lancet 1979;2(8139):380–383.

369. Deleted in proof.

370. Ho WKK, Wen HL, Ling N. Beta endorphin-like immunoactivity in the plasma of heroin addicts and normal subjects. Neuropharmacology 1980;19:117–120.

371. Mendelson JH, Ellingboe J, Kuehnle JC, Melb NK. Heroin and naltrexone effects on pituitary-gonadal hormones in man: interaction of steroid feedback effects, tolerance and supersensitivity. J Pharmacol Exp Ther 1980;214:503–506.

372. Holmstrand J, Gunne LM, Wahlstrom A. CSF-endorphins in heroin addicts during methadone maintenance and during withdrawal. Pharmakopsychiatria 1981;14:126–128.

373. Kreek MJ, Wardlaw SL, Friedman J, Schneider B, Frantz AG. Effects of chronic exogenous opioid administration on levels of one endogenous opioid (beta-endorphin) in man. In: Simon E, Takagi H, eds. Advances in endogenous and exogenous opioids. Tokyo: Kodansha, 1981:364–366.

374. Lafisca S, Bolelli G, Franceschetti F, Filicori M, Flamigini C, Marigo M. Hormone levels in methadone-treated drug addicts. Drug Alcohol Depend 1981;8:229–234.

375. Borg S, Kvande H, Rydberg U, Terenius L, Wahlstrom A. Endorphin levels in human cerebrospinal fluid during alcohol intoxication and withdrawal. Psychopharmacology 1982;78:101–103.

376. Kreek MJ, Hartman N. Chronic use of opioids and antipsychotic drugs: side effects, effects on endogenous opioids and toxicity. Ann N Y Acad Sci 1982;398:151–172.

377. Mendelson JH, Mello NK. Hormones and psycho-sexual development in young men following chronic heroin use. Neurobehav Toxicol Teratol 1982;4:441–444.

378. O'Brien CP, Terenius L, Wahlstrom A, McLellan AT, Krivoy W. Endorphin levels in opioid-dependent human subjects: a longitudinal study. Ann N Y Acad Sci 1982;398:377–387.

379. Smith DE, Moser C, Wesson DR, et al. A clinical guide to the diagnosis and treatment of heroin-related sexual dysfunction. J Psychoactive Drugs 1982;14:91–99.

380. Emrich HM, Nusselt L, Gramsch C, et al. Heroin addiction: beta endorphin immunoreactivity in plasma increases during withdrawal. Pharmakopsychiatria 1983;16:93–96.

381. Hargreaves WA, Tyler J, Weinberg JA, Benowitz N. [-]-alpha acetylmethadol effects on alcohol and diazepam use, sexual function

and cardiac function. Drug Alcohol Depend 1983;12(4):323–332.

382. Kreek MJ, Wardlaw SL, Hartman N, Raghunath J, Friedman J, Schneider B, Frantz AG. Circadian rhythms and levels of beta-endorphin, ACTH, and cortisol during chronic methadone maintenance treatment in humans. Life Sci Suppl I 1983;33:409–411.

383. Ziring B, Shepperd S, Kreek MJ. Reversed phase thin-layer chromatography for the separation of beta-endorphin, beta-lipotropin and enkephalins. Int J Peptide Protein res 1983; 22:32–38.

384. Facchinetti F, Grasso A, Petraglia F, Perrini D, Volpe A, Genazzani AR. Impaired circadian rhythmicity of beta-lipotropin, beta-endorphin and ACTH in heroin addicts. Acta-Endocrinologica 1984;105:149–155.

385. Kreek MJ, Raghunath J, Plevy S, Hamer D, Schneider B, Hartman N. ACTH, cortisol and beta-endorphin response to metyrapone testing during chronic methadone maintenance treatment in humans. Neuropeptides 1984;5: 277–278.

386. Mendelson JH, Ellingboe J, Judson BA, Goldstein A. Plasma testosterone and luteinizing hormone levels during levo-alpha-acetylmethadol maintenance and withdrawal. Clin Pharmacol Ther 1984;35:545–547.

387. Vescovi PP, Gerra G, Rastelli G, Ceda GP, Valenti G. Effect of methadone on TSH and thyroid hormone secretion. Horm Metab Res 1984;16:53–54.

388. Rittmaster RS, Cutler GB Jr, Sobel DO, Goldstein DS, Koppelman MCS, Lorraux DL, Chrousos GP. Morphine inhibits the pituitary adrenal response to ovine corticotropin-releasing hormone in normal subjects. J Clin Endocrinol Metab 1985;60:891–895.

389. Tagliaro F, Dorizzi R, Lafisca S, Maschio S, Marigo M. Calcitonin serum levels in heroin addicts: effects of methadone and clonidine detoxication treatments. Drug Alcohol Depend 1986;16:181–183.

390. Vescovi PP, Pezzarossa A, Ceresini G, Rastelli G, Valenti G, Gerra G. Effects of dopamine receptor stimulation on opiate-induced modifications of pituitary-gonadal function. Horm Res 1985;21:155–159.

391. Allolio B, Deuss U, Kaulen D, Leohardt U, Kallabis D, Hamel E, Winkelmann W. FK 33–824, a met-enkephalin analog, blocks corticotropin-releasing hormone-induced adrenocorticotropin secretion in normal subjects but not in patients with Cushing's disease. J Clin Endocrinol Metab 1986;63:1427–1431.

392. Kosten TR, Kreek MJ, Ragunath J, Kleber HD. Cortisol levels during chronic naltrexone maintenance treatment in ex-opiate addicts. Biol Psychiatry 1986;21:217–220.

393. Kosten TR, Kreek MJ, Ragunath J, Kleber HD. A preliminary study of beta-endorphin during chronic naltrexone maintenance treatment in ex-opiate addicts. Life Sci 1986;39:55–59.

394. Kreek MJ, Raghunath J, Spagnoli D, Mueller D, Stubbs V, Paris P. Possible age-related changes in levels of beta-endorphin in humans. Alcohol Drug Res 1986;6:117.

395. Tennant FS Jr, Rawson RA, Pumphrey E, et al. Clinical experiences with 959 opioid-dependent patients treated with levo-alpha-acetyl-methadol (LAAM). J Subst Abuse Treat 1986;3:195–202.

396. Allolio B, Schulte HM, Deub U, Kallabis D, Hamel E, Winkelmann W. Effect of oral morphine and naloxone on pituitary-adrenal response in man induced by human corti-

cotropin-releasing hormone. Acta Endocrinologica 1987;114:509–514.

397. Kosten TR, Kreek MJ, Swift C, Carney MK, Ferdinands L. Beta-endorphin levels in CSF during methadone maintenance. Life Sci 1987; 41:1071–1076.

398. Kreek MJ. Tolerance and dependence: implications for the pharmacological treatment of addiction. NIDA Res Monogr 1987;76:53–62.

399. Kreek MJ. Multiple drug abuse patterns and medical consequences. In: Meltzer HY, ed. Psychopharmacology: the third generation of progress. New York: Raven Press, 1987: 1597–1604.

400. Rastelli G, Gerra G, Mineo F, et al. Homeostasis of blood glucose and abuse of exogenous opiates: evaluation of fructosamine and glycosylated hemoglobin. Minerva Med 1987;78: 1291–1296.

401. Spagnolli W, DeVenuto G, Mattarei M, Dalri P, Miori R. Prolactin and thyrotropin pituitary response to thyrotropin releasing hormone in young female heroin addicts. Drug Alcohol Depend 1987;20:247–254.

402. O'Brien CP, Terenius LY, Nyberg F, McLellan AT, Eriksson AT. Endogenous opioids in cerebrospinal fluid of opioid-dependent humans. Biol Psychiatry 1988;24:649–662.

403. Ragni G, De-Lauretis L, Bestetti O, et al. Gonadal function in male heroin and methadone addicts. Int J Androl 1988;11:93–100.

404. Kennedy JA, Hartman N, Sbriglio R, Khuri E, Kreek MJ. Metyrapone-induced withdrawal symptoms. Br J Addict 1990;85:1133–1140.

405. Vescovi PP, Gerra G, Maninetti L, et al. Metyrapone effects on beta-endorphin, ACTH and cortisol levels after chronic opiate receptor stimulation in man. Neuropeptides 1990;15: 129–132.

406. Kreek MJ, Culpepper-Morgan J. Neuroendocrine (HPA) and gastrointestinal effects of opiate antagonists: possible therapeutic application. NIDA Res Monogr 1991;105:168–174.

407. Cami J, Gilabert M, San L, de la Toree R. Hypercortisolism after opioid discontinuation in rapid detoxification of heroin addicts. Br J Addict 1992;87(8):1145–1151.

408. Kosten TR, Morgan C, Kreek MJ. Beta-endorphin levels during heroin, methadone, buprenorphine and naloxone challenges: preliminary findings. Biol Psychiatry 1992;32:523–528.

409. Kreek MJ, Ho A, Borg L. Dynorphin A_{1-13} administration causes elevation of serum levels of prolactin in human subjects. NIDA Res Monogr 1994;141:108.

410. Rosen MI, McMahon TJ, Hameedi FA, Pearsall HR, Woods SW, Kreek MJ, Kosten TR. Effect of clonidine pretreatment on naloxone-precipitated opiate withdrawal. J Pharmacol Exp Ther 1996:276:1128–1135.

B. Gastrointestinal (GI)

411. Karr NW. Effects of 6-dimethylamino-4-4-diphenyl-3-heptanone (Dolophine) on intestinal motility. Fed Proc 1947;6:343.

412. Rubenstein RB, Wolff WI. Methadone ileus syndrome: report of a fatal case. Dis Colon Rectum 1976;19:357–359.

413. Hahn EF, Lahita R, Kreek MJ, Duma C, Inturrisi CE. Naloxone radioimmunoassay: an improved antiserum. J Pharm Pharmacol 1983;35: 833–836.

414. Kreek MJ, Schaefer RA, Hahn EF, Fishman J. Naloxone, a specific opioid antagonist, reverses chronic idiopathic constipation. Lancet 1983;1(8319):261–262.

415. Naloxone in chronic constipation [letter]. Lancet 1983;1(8327):758.

416. Kreek MJ, Marsh F, Albeck H, Kutscher J, Schmugler J, Connor B, Schaefer RA. Effects of opioid antagonist naloxone on fecal evacuation in patients with idiopathic chronic constipation, irritable bowel syndrome, and narcotic-induced constipation. Alcohol Drug Res 1986; 6:168.

417. Albeck H, Woodfield S, Kreek MJ. Quantitative and pharmacokinetic analysis of naloxone in plasma using high-performance liquid chromatography with electrochemical detection and solid phase extraction. J Chromatogr 1989; 488:435–445.

418. Culpepper-Morgan JA, Inturrisi C, Portnoy R, Kreek MJ. Oral naloxone treatment of narcotic induced constipation: dose response. NIDA res Monogr 1989;95:399–400.

419. Albeck H, Woodfield S, Wahlstrom A, Kreek MJ. Naloxone pharmacokinetics in man following an intravenous dose. NIDA Res Monogr 1991;105:408–409.

420. Culpepper-Morgan JA, Inturrisi CE, Portenoy RK, Foley K, Houde RW, Marsh F, Kreek MJ. Treatment of opioid induced constipation with oral naloxone: a pilot study. Clin Pharmacol Ther 1992;23:90–95.

421. Kreek MJ, Culpepper-Morgan JA. Constipation syndromes. In: Lewis JH, ed. A pharmacologic approach to gastrointestinal disorders. Baltimore: Williams & Wilkins, 1994:179–208.

C. Pulmonary (Resp)

422. Marks CE, Goldring RM. Chronic hypercapnia during methadone maintenance. Am Rev Respir Dis 1973;108:1088–1093.

423. Santiago TV, Pugliese AC, Edelman NH. Control of breathing during methadone addiction. Am J Med 1977;62:347–354.

424. Santiago TV, Goldblatt K, Winters K, Pugliese AC, Edelman NH. respiratory consequences of methadone: the response to added resistance to breathing. Am Rev Respir Dis 1980;122: 623–628.

425. Olsen GD, Wilson JE, Robertson GE. Respiratory and ventilatory effects of methadone in healthy women. Clin Pharmacol Ther 1981;29: 373–380.

D. Immunological

426. Cushman P Jr. Persistent increased immunoglobulin M in treated narcotic addiction: Association with liver disease and continuing heroin use. J Allergy Clin Immunol 1973;52: 122–128.

427. Cushman P Jr. Significance of hypermacroglobulinemia in methadone maintained and other narcotic addicts. In: Proceedings of the Fifth National Conference on Methadone Treatment. New York: National Association for the Prevention of Addiction to Narcotics, 1973;1:515–522.

428. Geller SA, Stimmel B. Diagnostic confusion from lymphatic lesions in heroin addicts. Ann Intern Med 1973;78:703–705.

429. Brown SM, Stimmel B, Taub RN, Kochwa S, Rosenfield RE. Immunologic dysfunction in heroin addicts. Arch Intern Med 1974;134: 1001–1006.

430. Cushman P Jr. Hyperimmunoglobulinemia in heroin addiction: some epidemiologic observations including some possible effects of route of administration and multiple drug abuse. Am J Epidemiol 1974;99:218–224.

431. Cushman P, Sherman C. Biologic false-positive reactions in serologic tests for syphilis in narcotic addiction. Am J Clin Pathol 1974;61:346.

432. Drusin LM, Litwin SD, Armstrong D, Webster BP. Waldenstrom's macroglobulinemia in a patient with a chronic biologic false-positive serologic test for syphilis. Am J Med 1974; 56:429–432.

433. Spiera H, Oreskes I, Stimmel B. Rheumatoid factor activity in heroin addicts on methadone maintenance. Ann Rheum Dis 1974;33: 153–156.

434. Cushman P Jr, Gupta S, Grieco MH. Immunological studies in methadone maintained patients. Int J Addict 1977;12:241–253.

435. Adham NF, Song MK, Eng BF. Hyper-alpha-2-macroglobulinemia in narcotic addicts. Ann Intern Med 1978;88:793–795.

436. Jacob H, Charytan C, Rascoff JM, Golden R, Janis R. Amyloidosis secondary to drug abuse and chronic skin suppuration. Arch Intern Med 1978;138:1150–1151.

437. Hazum E, Chang KJ, Cuatrecasas P. Specific nonopiate receptors for B-endorphin. Science 1979;205:1033–1035.

438. Wybran J, Appelboom T, Famaey J-P, Govaerts A. Suggestive evidence for receptors for morphine and methionine-enkephalin on normal human blood T-lymphocytes. J Immunol 1979;123:1068–1070.

439. Kay N, Allen J, Morley JE. Endorphins stimulate normal human peripheral blood lymphocyte natural killer activity. Life Sci 1984;35:53–59.

440. Lazzarin A, Mella L, Trombini M, Ubert-Foppa C, Franzetti F, Mazzoni G, Galli M. Immunological status in heroin addicts: effects of methadone maintenance treatment. Drug Alcohol Depend 1984;13:117–123.

441. Poli G, Introna M, Zanaboni F, Pen G, Carbonari M, Aiuti F, et al. Natural killer cells in intravenous drug abusers with lymphadenopathy syndrome. Clin Exp Immunol 1985;62: 128–135.

442. Donahoe RM, Nicholson JKA, Madden JJ, Donahoe F, Shafer DA, Gordan D, et al. Coordinate and independent effects of heroin, cocaine and alcohol abuse on T-cell E-rosette formation and antigenic marker expression. Clin Immunol Immunopath 1986;41:254–264.

443. Dyke CV, Stesin A, Jones R, Chuntharapai A, Seaman W. Cocaine increases natural killer cell activity. J Clin Invest 1986;77:1387–1390.

444. Falek A, Madden JJ, Shafer DA, Donahoe R. Individual differences in opiate-induced alterations at the cytogenetic DNA repair, and immunologic levels: opportunity for genetic assessment. NIDA Res Monogr 1986;66:11–24.

445. Nair NMP, Laing TJ, Schwartz SA. Decreased natural and antibody-dependent cellular cytotoxic activities in intravenous drug abuser. Clin Immunopathol 1986;38:68–78.

446. Novick DM, Brown DJC, Lok ASF, et al. Influence of sexual preference and chronic hepatitis B virus infection on T lymphocyte subsets, natural killer activity, and suppressor cell activity. J Hepatol 1986;3:363–370.

447. Novick DM, Tregenza GS, Solinas A, Newman RG, Ghodse AH, Thomas HC. T lymphocyte subsets in parenteral and non-parenteral heroin abusers in Britain. Br J Addict 1986;81: 679–683.

448. Donahoe RM, Bueso-Ramos C, Donahoe F, et al. Mechanistic implications of the finding that opiates and other drugs of abuse moderate T-cell surface receptors and antigenic markers. Ann N Y Acad Sci 1987;496:711–721.

449. Sharp BM, Tsukayama DT, Gekker G, Keane WF, Peterson PK. B-endorphin stimulates human polymorphonuclear leukocyte superoxide production via a stereoselective opiate receptor. J Pharmacol Exp Ther 1987;242:579–582.

450. Smith EM, Brosnan P, Meyer WJ III, Blalock JE. Medical intelligence. An ACTH receptor on human mononuclear leukocytes: relation to adrenal ACTH-receptor activity. N Engl J Med 1987;317:1266–1269.

451. Yahya MD, Watson RR. Minireview: immunomodulation by morphine and marijuana. Life Sci 1987;41:2503–2510.

452. Donahoe RM, Bueso-Ramos C, Falek A, McClure H, Nicholson JKA. Comparative effects of morphine on leukocytic antigenic markers of monkeys and humans. J Neurosci Res 1988; 19:157–165.

453. Donahoe RM, Falek A. Neuroimmunomodulation by opiates and other drugs of abuse: relationship to HIV infections and AIDS. Adv Biochem Psychopharmacology 1988;44:145–158.

454. Ochshorn M, Novick DM, Kreek MJ, Hahn EF. High concentrations of naloxone lower natural killer (NK) activity. NIDA Res Monogr 1988;81:338.

455. Sibinga NES, Goldstein A. Opioid peptides and opioid receptors in cells of the immune system. Ann Rev Immunol 1988;6:219.

456. Brenner BG, Dascal A, Margolese RG, Wainberg MA. Natural killer cell function in patients with acquired immunodeficiency syndrome and related diseases. J Leukocyte Biol 1989;46:75–83.

457. Kreek MJ. Immunological approaches to clinical issues in drug abuse. NIDA Res Monogr 1988;90:77–86.

458. Kreek MJ, Khuri E, Flomenberg N, Albeck H, Ochshorn M. Immune status of unselected methadone maintained former heroin addicts. In: Quirion R, Jhamandas K, Gianoulakis C, eds. International Narcotics research Conference 1989. New York: Alan R. Liss, 1989: 445–448.

459. Novick DM, Ochshorn M, Ghali V, Croxson TS, Mercer WD, Chiorazzi N, Kreek MJ. Natural killer cell activity and lymphocyte subsets in parenteral heroin abusers and long-term methadone maintenance patients. J Pharmacol Exp Ther 1989;250:606–610.

460. Ochshorn M, Kreek MJ, Khuri E, Fahey L, Craig J, Aldana MC, Albeck H. Normal and abnormal natural killer (NK) activity in methadone maintenance treatment patients. NIDA Res Monogr 1989;90:369.

461. Bodner G, Albeck H, Soda KM, Kreek MJ. Modulation of natural killer cell activity: possible role of hypothalamic-pituitary-adrenal axis hormones. In: Van Ree JM, Mulder AH, Wiegant VM, Van Wimersma Greulanus TB, eds. New leads in opioid research. Amsterdam: Excerpta Medica, 1990:330–331.

462. Kreek MJ. Immune function in heroin addicts and former heroin addicts in treatment: pre/post AIDS epidemic. NIDA Res Monogr 1990;96:192–219.

463. Ochshorn M, Novick DM, Kreek MJ. In vitro studies of the effect of methadone on natural killer (NK) cell activity. Isr J Med Sci 1990;26: 421–425.

464. Bodner G, Albeck H, Ochshorn M, Kreek MJ. Effect of ethanol on natural killer cell activity in vitro. Clin Res 1990;38:787A.

465. Bodner G, Soda KM, Kennedy J, Albeck H, Kreek MJ. Modulation of NK activity: role of neuroendocrine status. NIDA Res Monogr 1991;105:412–413.

466. Kreek MJ. Heroin, other opiates, and the immune function. Drug Abuse and Drug Abuse research, The Third Triennial report to Congress from the Secretary, U.S. Department of Health and Human Services. Alcohol, Drug Abuse, and Mental Health Administration, NIDA DHHS Publication No.(ADM) 1991:91–1704.

467. Kreek MJ. Immunological function in active heroin addicts and methadone maintained former addicts: observations and possible mechanisms. NIDA Res Monogr 1991;105:75–81.

468. Bodner G, Pinto S, Albeck H, Kreek MJ. Effects of dynorphin peptides on human natural killer cell activity in vitro. In: Harris LS, ed. Problems of drug dependence, 1991; Proceedings of the 53rd Annual Scientific Meeting of the Committee on Problems of Drug Dependence. Rockville, MD: U.S. Dept. of Health and Human Services, Public Health Service, Alcohol, Drug Abuse, and Mental Health Administration, 1992:331.

469. Novick DM, Ochshorn M, Kreek MJ. In vivo and in vitro studies of opiates and cellular immunity in narcotic addicts. In: Friedman H, Specter S, Klein TW, eds. Drugs of abuse, immunity and immunodeficiency. New York: Plenum Press, 1991:159–170.

470. Kreek MJ. Immune function in human IVDU's. NIDA Res Monogr 1993;132:72.

471. Siddiqui NS, Brown LS Jr, Makuch RW. Short-term declines in CD4 levels associated with cocaine use in HIV-1 seropositive, minority injecting drug users. J Natl Med Assoc 1993;85:293–296.

472. Eisenstein TK, Rogers TJ, Bussiere JL, Rojhavin M, Szabo I, Meissler JJ, et al. Drugs of abuse and immunosuppression. NIDA Res Monogr 1994;140:89–92.

473. Ochshorn-Adelson MO, Novick DM, Khuri E, Albeck H, Hahn EF, Kreek MJ. Effects of the opioid antagonist naloxone on human natural killer cell activity in vitro. Isr J Med Sci 1994; 30:679–684.

474. Ochshorn-Adelson M, Bodner G, Toraker P, Albeck P, Ho A, Kreek MJ. Effects of ethanol on human natural killer cell activity: in vitro and acute, low-dose in vivo studies. Alcohol Clin Exp Res 1994;18(6):1361–1367.

VI. PERSISTENT SEQUELAE DURING METHADONE TREATMENT OF MEDICAL COMPLICATIONS RELATED TO PARENTERAL DRUG ABUSE

A. Hepatitis A, B, C, Delta, Non-A, Non-B, and Alcoholic Liver Disease

475. Cherubin CE. The medical sequelae of narcotic addiction. Ann Intern Med 1967;67:23–33.

476. Sapira JD, Jasinski DR, Gorodetzky CW. Liver disease in narcotic addicts. II. The role of the needle. Clin Pharmacol Ther 1968;9:725–739.

477. Cherubin CE, Hargrove RL, Prince AM. The serum hepatitis related antigen (SH) in illicit drug users. Am J Epidemiol 1970;91:510–517.

478. Jersild T, Johansen C, Balslov JT, Hojgaard K, Johansen A, Ott C. Hepatitis in young drug users. Scand J Gastroenterol Suppl 1970;7:79.

479. Cherubin CE, Kane S, Weinberger DR, Wolfe E, Mcginn T. Persistence of transaminase abnormalities in former drug addicts. Ann Intern Med 1972;76:385–389.

480. Cherubin CE, Rosenthal WS, Stenger RE, Prince AM, Baden M, Strauss R, Mcginn TC. Chronic liver disease in asymptomatic narcotic addicts. Ann Intern Med 1972;76:391–395.

481. Kreek MJ, Dodes L, Kane S, Knobler J, Martin

R. Long-term methadone maintenance therapy: effects on liver function. Ann Intern Med 1972;77:598–602.

482. Stimmel B, Vernace S, Tobias H. Hepatic dysfunction in heroin addicts: the role of alcohol. JAMA 1972;222:811–812.

483. Stimmel B, Vernace S, Tobias H. Hepatic function in patients on methadone maintenance therapy. In: Proceedings of the Fourth National Conference on Methadone Treatment. New York: National Association for the Prevention of Addiction to Narcotics, 1972:419–420.

484. Stimmel B, Vernace S, Heller E, et al. Hepatitis B antigen and antibody in former heroin addicts on methadone maintenance: correlation with clinical and histological findings. In: Proceedings of the Fifth National Conference on Methadone Treatment. New York: National Association for the Prevention of Addiction to Narcotics, 1973:501–506.

485. Stimmel B, Vernace S, Schaffner F. Hepatitis B surface antigen and antibody: a prospective study in asymptomatic drug abusers. JAMA 1975;234:1135–1138.

486. Cherubin CE, Schaefer RA, Rosenthal WS, Mcginn T, Forte F, Purcell R, Walsnsley P. The natural history of liver disease in former drug users. Am J Med Sci 1976;272:244–253.

487. Berman M, Alter HJ, Ishak KG, Purcell RH, Jones EA. The chronic sequelae of non-A, non-B hepatitis. Ann Intern Med 1979;91:1–6.

488. Miller DJ, Kleber H, Bloomer JR. Chronic hepatitis associated with drug abuse: significance of hepatitis B virus. Yale J Biol Med 1979;52:135–140.

489. Novick DM, Gelb AM, Stenger RJ, Yancovitz SR, Adelsberg B, Chateau F, Kreek MJ. Hepatitis B serologic studies in narcotic users with chronic liver disease. Am J Gastroenterol 1981;75:111–115.

490. Stimmel B, Korts D, Jackson G. The relationship between hepatitis B surface antigen and antibody and continued drug use in narcotic dependency: a randomized controlled study. Drug Alcohol Depend 1982;10:251–256.

491. Shaw S, Korts D, Stimmel B. Abnormal liver function tests as biological markers for alcoholism in narcotic addicts. Am J Drug Alcohol Abuse 1982–1983;9:345–354.

492. Schalm SW, Heytink RA, Mannaerts H, et al. Immune response to hepatitis B vaccine in drug addicts. J Infect 1983;7:41–45.

493. Vandelli C, Piaggi V, Battilani R, Cariani E, Sirotti MA. Relationship between HBV markers and heroin as a cause of liver injury in drug addicts. Drug Alcohol Depend 1984–1985;14:129–133.

494. Alter MJ. Hepatic surveillance. MMWR Morb Mortal Wkly Rep 1985;34:1ss-10ss.

495. Novick DM, Enlow RW, Gelb AM, Stenger RJ, Fotino M, Winter JW, et al. Hepatic cirrhosis in young adults: association with adolescent onset of alcohol and parenteral heroin abuse. Gut 1985;26:8–13.

496. Novick DM, Farci P, Karayiannis P, Gelb AM, Stenger RJ, Kreek MJ, Thomas HC. Hepatitis D virus antibody in HBsAg-positive and HBsAg-negative substance abusers with chronic liver disease. J Med Virol 1985;15:351–356.

497. Kreek MJ, Khuri E, Fahey L, Miescher A, Arns P, Spagnoli D, et al. Long-term followup studies of the medical status of adolescent former heroin addicts in chronic methadone maintenance treatment: liver disease and immune status. NIDA Res Monogr 1986;67:307–309.

498. Novick DM, Stenger RJ, Gelb AM, Most J, Yancovitz SR, Kreek MJ. Chronic liver disease in abusers of alcohol and parenteral drugs: a report of 204 consecutive biopsy-proven cases. Alcohol Clin Exp Res 1986;10:500–505.

499. Girardi E, Zaccarelli M, Tossini G, Puro V, Narciso P, Visco G. Hepatitis C virus infection in intravenous drug users: prevalence and risk factors. Scand J Infect Dis 1990;22:751–752.

500. Kreek MJ, Khuri E, Melia D. Current patterns of hepatitis B and delta markers in former heroin addicts in methadone maintenance treatment: need for hepatitis B vaccination. In: Abstracts of International Association for Study of the Liver Meeting, Queensland, Australia, 1990.

501. Chetwynd J, Brunton C, Blank M, Plumridge E, Baldwin D. Hepatitis C seroprevalence amongst injecting drug users attending a methadone programme. N Z Med J 1995; 108:364–366.

502. Novick DM, Reagan KJ, Croxson TS, Gelb AM, Stenger RJ, Kreek MJ. Hepatitis C virus serology in parenteral drug users with chronic liver disease. NIDA Res Monogr 1995; 153:439.

503. Borg L, Khuri E, Wells A, Melia D, Sweeney J, Bergasa NV, et al. Hepatitis B vaccination of methadone maintained patients: a pilot study. NIDA Res Monogr 1996;162:191.

B. HIV-1 AIDS and Related Retroactive Infections

504. Des Jarlais DC, Marmor M, Cohen H, Yancovitz S, Garber J, Friedman S, et al. Antibodies to a retrovirus etiologically associated with Acquired Immunodeficiency Syndrome (AIDS) in populations with increased incidences of the syndrome. MMWR Morb Mortal Wkly Rep 1984;33:377–379.

505. Reddy MM, England A, Brown D, Buimovici-Klien E, Cirieco MH. Lymphoproliferative responses to human immunodeficiency virus antigen in asymptomatic intravenous drug abusers and in patients with lymphadenopathy or AIDS. J Infect Dis 1985;156:374–376.

506. Novick DM, Khan I, Kreek MJ. Acquired immunodeficiency syndrome and infection with hepatitis viruses in individuals abusing drugs by injection. United Nations Bulletin on Narcotics 1986;38:15–25.

507. Novick DM, Kreek MJ, Des Jarlais DC, Spira TJ, Khuri ET, Raghunath J, et al. Antibody to LAV, the putative agent of AIDS, in parenteral drug abusers and methadone-maintained patients: abstract of clinical research findings: therapeutic, historical, and ethical aspects. NIDA Res Monogr 1986;67:318–320.

508. Zolla-Pazner S, Des Jarlais DC, Friedman SR, Spira TJ, Marmor M, Holzman R, et al. Nonrandom development of immunologic abnormalities after infection with human immunodeficiency virus: implications for immunologic classification of the disease. Proc Natl Acad Sci U S A 1987;84:5404–5408.

509. Ball JC, Lange WR, Myers CP, Friedman SR. Reducing the risk of AIDS through methadone maintenance treatment. J Health Soc Behav 1988;29:214–226.

510. Blix O. AIDS and IV heroin addicts: the preventive effect of methadone maintenance in Sweden. Proceedings of the 4th International Conference on AIDS, Stockholm, 1988.

511. Novick DM, Des Jarlais DC, Kreek MJ, Spira TJ, Friedman SR, Gelb AM, et al. The specificity of antibody tests for human immunodeficiency virus in alcohol and parenteral drug abusers with chronic liver disease. Alcohol Clin Exp Res 1988;12:687–690.

512. Novick DM, Farci P, Croxson ST, Taylor MB, Schneebaum CW, Lai ME, et al. Hepatitis delta virus and human immunodeficiency virus antibodies in parenteral drug abusers who are hepatitis B surface antigen positive. J Infect Dis 1988;158:795–803.

513. Chaisson RE, Bacchetti P, Osmond D, Brodie B, Sande MA, Moss AR. Cocaine use and HIV infection in intravenous drug users in San Francisco. JAMA 1989;261:561–565.

514. Curtis JL, Crummey FC, Baker SN, Foster RE, Khanyile CS, Wilkins R. HIV screening and counseling for intravenous drug abuse patients. Staff and patient attitudes. JAMA 1989;261: 258–262.

515. Des Jarlais DC, Friedman SR, Novick DM, Sotheran JL, Thomas P, Yancovitz SR, et al. HIV-I Infection among intravenous drug users in Manhattan, New York City from 1977 to 1987. JAMA 1989:261:1008–1012.

516. Dole VP. Methadone treatment and the acquired immunodeficiency syndrome epidemic. JAMA 1989;262:1681–1682.

517. Magura S, Grossman JI, Lipton DS, Amann KR, Koger J, Gehan K. Correlates of participation in AIDS education and HIV antibody testing by methadone patients. Public Health Rep 1989;104:321–340.

518. Nathan JA, Karan LD. Substance abuse treatment modalities in the age of HIV spectrum disease. J Psychoactive Drugs 1989;21:423–429.

519. Novick DM, Trigg HL, Des Jarlais DC, Friedman SR, Vlahov D, Kreek MJ. Cocaine injection and ethnicity in parenteral drug users during the early years of the human immunodeficiency virus (HIV) epidemic in New York City. J Med Virol 1989;29:181–185.

520. Selwyn PA, Feingold AR, Iezza A, Satyadeo M, Colley J, Torres R, Shaw JFM. Primary care for patients with human immunodeficiency virus (HIV) infection in a methadone maintenance treatment program. Ann Intern Med 1989;110:761–763.

521. Brown LS, Kreek MJ, Trepo C, Chu A, Valdes M, Ajuluchukwu D, et al. Human immunodeficiency virus and viral hepatitis seroepidemiology in New York City intravenous drug abusers (IVDAs). NIDA Res Monogr 1989; 95:443–444.

522. Juber-Stemich R, Haas H. Prevention of HIV infection in the methadone program. A study of a drop-in clinic in Zurich. Schweiz rundsch Med Prax 1990;79:1017–1021.

523. Kreek MJ. HIV infection and parenteral drug abuse: ethical issues in diagnosis, treatment, research and the maintenance of confidentiality. In: Allebeck P, Jansson B, eds. Proceedings of the Third International Congress on Ethics in Medicine Nobel Conference Series. New York: Raven Press, 1990:181–187.

524. Kreek MJ, Des Jarlais DC, Trepo CL, Novick DM, Abdul-Quader A, Raghunath J. Contrasting prevalence of delta hepatitis markers in parenteral drug abusers with and without AIDS. J Infect Dis 1990;162:538–541.

525. McKegney FP, O'Dowd MA, Feiner C, Selwyn P, Drucker E, Friedland GH. A prospective comparison of neuropsychologic function in HIV-seropositive and seronegative methadone-maintained patients. AIDS (US) 1990;4:565–569.

526. Weber R, Ledergerber B, Opravil M, Siegenthaler W, Luthy R. Progression of HIV infection in misusers of injected drugs who stop injecting or follow a programme of maintenance treatment with methadone. Br J Med 1990; 301:1362–1365.

527. Banks SE, Brown LS Jr, Ajuluchukwu D. Sexual behaviors and HIV infection in intravenous drug users in New York City. J Addict Dis 1991;10(3):15–23.

528. Biggar RJ, Buskell-Bales Z, Yakshe PN, Caussy D, Grindley G, Seeff L. Antibody to human retroviruses among drug users in three east coast American cities 1972–1976. J Infect Dis 1991;163:57–63.

529. Ferrando SJ, Batki SL. HIV-infected intravenous drug users in methadone maintenance treatment: clinical problems and their management. J Psychoactive Drugs 1991;23:217–224.

530. Hofmeister-Wagner WD, Wiesner von Jagwitz E, Streidl C, Peters M. Development of lymphocyte subpopulations (CD4, CD8) in levomethadone treated HIV infected intravenous drug dependent patients. Offentl Gesundheitswes 1991;53(8–9):457–458.

531. Khabbaz RF, Hartel D, Lairmore M, Horsburgh CR, Schoenbaum EE, Roberts B, et al. Human T lymphotropic virus type II (HTLV-II) infection in a cohort of New York intravenous drug users: an old infection? J Infect Dis 1991;163:252–256.

532. Klimas NG, Blaney NT, Morgan RO, Chitwood D, Milles K, Lee H, Fletcher MA. Immune function and anti-HIV-I/II status in anti-HIV-1-negative intravenous drug users receiving methadone. Am J Med 1991;90(2):163–170.

533. Magura S, Siddiqi Q, Shapiro J, Grossman JI, Lipton DS, Marion IJ, et al. Outcomes of an AIDS prevention program for methadone patients. Int J Addict 1991;26(6):629–655.

534. DePhilippis D, Metzger DS, Woody GE, Navaline HA. Attitudes toward mandatory human immunodeficiency virus testing and contact tracing. A survey of intravenous drug users in treatment. J Subst Abuse Treat 1992;9(1):39–42.

535. Gachupin-Garcia A, Selwyn PA, Budner NS. Population-based study of malignancies and HIV infection among injecting drug users in a New York City methadone treatment program, 1985–1991. AIDS 1992;6(8):843–848.

536. Gill K, Nolimal D, Crowley TJ. Antisocial personality disorder, HIV risk behavior and retention in methadone maintenance therapy. Drug Alcohol Depend 1992;30(3):247–252.

537. Handelsman L, Horvath T, Aronson M, Schroeder M, Jacobson J, Wiener J, et al. Auditory event-related potentials in HIV-1 infection: a study in the drug-user risk group. J Neuropsychiatry Clin Neurosci 1992;4(3):294–302.

538. O'Connor PG, Molde S, Henry S, Shockhcor WT, Schottenfeld RS. Human immunodeficiency virus infection in intravenous drug users: a model for primary care. Am J Med 1992;93(4):382–386.

539. Selwyn PA, Alcabes P, Hartel D, Buono D, Schoenbaum EE, Klein RS, et al. Clinical manifestations and predictors of disease progression in drug users with human immunodeficiency virus infection. N Engl J Med 1992;327(24):1697–1703.

540. Zangerle R, Fuchs D, Rossler H, Reibnegger G, Riemer Y, Weiss SH, et al. Trends in HIV infection among intravenous drug users in Innsbruck, Austria. J Acquir Immune Defic Syndr 1992;5(9):365–371.

541. Ajuluchukwu DC, Brown LS Jr, Crummey FC, Foster KF Sr, Ismail YI, Siddiqui N. Demographic, medical history and sexual correlates of HIV seropositive methadone maintained women. J Addict Dis 1993;12(4):105–120.

542. Ferrando SJ, Batki SL. HIV-infected intravenous drug users in methadone maintenance treatment: clinical problems and their management. J Psychoactive Drugs 1993;23(2):217–224.

543. Gourevitch MN, Selwyn PA, Davenny K, Buono D, Schoenbaum EE, Klein RS, Friedland GH. Effects of HIV infection on the serologic manifestations and response to treatment of syphilis in intravenous drug users. Ann Intern Med 1993;118(5):350–355.

544. Handelsman L, Song IS, Losonczy M, Park S, Jacobson J, Wiener J, Aronson M. Magnetic resonance abnormalities in HIV infection: a study in the drug-user risk group. Psychiatry Res 1993;47(2):175–186.

545. Metzger DS, Woody GE, McLellan AT, O'Brien CP, Druley P, Navaline H, et al. Human immunodeficiency virus seroconversion among intravenous drug users in- and out-of-treatment: an 18-month prospective follow-up. J Acquir Immune Defic Syndr 1993;6:1049–1056.

546. Sawyer RC, Brown LS Jr, Bailey J, Hickson M, Lee P, McNair D, et al. Drug abuse treatment programs as centers for HIV-related research and treatment. J Addict Dis 1993;12(4):121–129.

547. Siddiqui NS, Brown LS Jr, Meyer TJ, Gonzalez V. Decline in HIV-1 seroprevalence and low seroconversion rate among injecting drug users at a methadone maintenance program in New York City. J Psychoactive Drugs 1993;25(3):245–250.

548. Siddiqui NS, Brown LS Jr, Phillips RY, Vargas O, Makuch RW. No seroconversions among steady sex partners of methadone-maintained HIV-1-seropositive injecting drug users in New York City. AIDS (US) 1992;6(12):1529–1533.

549. Rutherford MJ, Metzger DS, Alterman AI. Parental relationships and substance use among methadone patients. The impact on levels of psychological symptomatology. J Subst Abuse Treat 1994;11:415–423.

550. Shi JM, O'Connor PG, Kosten TR, Schottenfeld RS, Culpepper-Morgan J, Kreek MJ. Seroprevalence of viral hepatitis B, C, D in HIV-infected intravenous drug users. NIDA Res Monogr 1994;141:62.

551. Katz SM, Galanter M, Lifshutz H, Maslansky R. The impact on behavior of notifying methadone patients of their HIV serostatus. Am J Drug Alcohol Abuse 1995;21:37–45.

552. Wall TL, Sorensen JL, Batki SL, Delucchi KL, London JA, Chesney MA. Adherence to zidovudine (AZT) among HIV-infected methadone patients: a pilot study of supervised therapy and dispensing compared to usual care. Drug Alcohol Depend 1995;37:261–269.

553. Kreek MJ. Drugs of abuse and HIV-1: animal and clinical models (discussion). In: National Institute of Drug Abuse Special Monograph. 1997 (in press).

554. Rosen MI, McMahon TJ, Pearsall HR, Hameedi FA, Woods SW, Kosten TR, Kreek MJ. Correlations among measures of naloxone-precipitated opiate withdrawal. NIDA Res Monogr 1996;162:120.

555. Salomon MI, Poon TP, Goldblatt M, Tchertkoff V. Renal lesions in heroin addicts: a study based on kidney biopsies. Nephron 1972; 9:356–363.

556. Treser G, Cherubin C, Lonergan ET, Yoshizawa N, Viswanathan V, Tannenberg AM, et al. Renal lesions in narcotic addicts. Am J Med 1974;57:687–694.

557. Sreepada RTK, Nicastri AD, Friedman EA. renal consequences of narcotic abuse. Adv Nephrol 1978;7:261–290.

558. Novick DM, Yancovitz SR, Weinberg BA. Amyloidosis in parenteral drug abusers. Mt Sinai J Med 1979;46:163–167.

559. Scholes J, Derosena R, Appel GB, Jao W, Boyd MT, Pirani CL. Amyloidosis in chronic heroin addicts with the nephrotic syndrome. Ann Intern Med 1979;91:26–29.

C. Chronic Renal Diseases

D. Hematological Disorders

560. Sherwood GK, McGinniss MH, Katon RN, DuPont RL, Webster JB. Negative direct Coombs' tests in narcotic addicts receiving maintenance doses of methadone. Blood 1972; 40:902–904.

561. Burstein Y, Giardina PJV, Rausen AR, Kandall SR, Siljestrom K, Peterson CM. Thrombocytosis and increased circulating platelet aggregates in newborn infants of polydrug users. J Pediatr 1979;94:895–899.

VII. PSYCHONEUROLOGICAL STATUS OF METHADONE MAINTENANCE PATIENTS

A. Neurological Status

562. Gordon NB, Warner A, Henderson (Ho) A. Psychomotor and intellectual performance under methadone maintenance. Bull Probl Depend 1967:5136–5144.

563. Gordon NB. Reaction-times of methadone treated ex heroin addicts. Psychopharmacologia 1970;16:337–344.

564. Henderson (Ho) A, Nemes G, Gordon NB, Roos L. Sleep and narcotic tolerance [abstract]. Psychophysiology 1972;7:346–347.

565. Gordon NB, Appel PW. Performance effectiveness in relation to methadone maintenance. Proceedings, Fourth National Conference on Methadone Treatment. New York: National Association for the Prevention of Addiction to Narcotics, 1972:425–427.

566. Babst D, Newman S, Gordon NB, Warner A. Driving record of methadone maintenance patients in New York State. Albany, NY: NY State Addict Control Comm, 1973.

567. Gordon NB. The functional status of the methadone maintained person. In: Simmons LRS, Gold MB, eds. Discrimination and the addict. Beverly Hills, CA: Sage Publications, 1973:101–121.

568. Appel PW, Gordon NB. Attentional function and monitoring of performance of methadone-maintained ex heroin addicts. Paper presented at the American Psychological Association, New Orleans, 1974.

569. Appel PW, Gordon NB. Digit-symbol performance in methadone-treated ex-heroin addicts. Am J Psychiatry 1975–1976;133:1337–1340.

570. Gordon NB. Influence of narcotic drugs on highway safety. Accid Anal Prev 1976;8:3–7.

571. Lenn NJ, Senay EC, Renault PF, Devel RK. Neurological assessment of patients on prolonged methadone maintenance. Drug Alcohol Depend 1975–76;1:305–311.

572. Lombardo WK, Lombardo B, Goldstein A. Cognitive functioning under moderated and low dosage methadone maintenance. Int J Addict 1976;11:389–401.

573. Rubenstein RB, Spira I, Wolff WI. Management of surgical problems in patients on

methadone maintenance. Am J Surg 1976;131:566–569.

574. Grevert P, Masover B, Goldstein A. Failure of methadone and levomethadyl acetate (levo-alpha-acetylmethadol, LAAM) maintenance to affect memory. Arch Gen Psychiatry 1977;34:849–853.

575. Maddux JF, et al. Driving records before and during methadone maintenance. Am J Drug Alcohol Abuse 1977;4:91–100.

576. Ho A, Dole VP. Pain perception in drug-free and in methadone maintained human ex-addicts. Proc Soc Exp Biol Med 1979;162:392–395.

577. Silberstein CH, O'Dowd MA, Chartock P, Schoenbaum EE, Friedland G, Hartel D, McKegney FP. A prospective four-year follow-up of neuropsychological function in HIV seropositive and seronegative methadone-maintained patients. Gen Hosp Psychiatry 1993;15:351–359.

578. Rebeta JL, Kocsis JH, Baff R, Melia D, Sweeney J, Kreek MJ. Neuropsychological (NP) examination of methadone-maintained (MM) patients. NIDA Res Monogr 1996;162:163.

B. Psychiatric, Psychological, and Neuropsychological Status

579. Liebson I, Bigelow G. A behavioral-pharmacological treatment of dually addicted patients. Behav Res Ther 1972;10:403.

580. Gritz ER, Shiffman SM, Jarvik ME, Haber J, Dymond AM, Coger R, et al. Physiological and psychological effects of methadone in man. Arch Gen Psychiatry 1975;32:237–242.

581. Woody GE, O'Brien CP, Rickels K. Depression and anxiety in heroin addicts: a placebo-controlled study of doxepin in combination with methadone. Am J Psychiatry 1975;132:447–450.

582. Inwang EE, Primm BJ, Jones FL, et al. Metabolic disposition of 2 phenylethylamine and detoxified patients. Drug Alcohol Depend 1975–1976;1:295–303.

583. Weissman MM, Slobetz F, Prusoff B, Mezritz M, Howard P. Clinical depression among narcotic addicts maintained on methadone in the community. Am J Psychiatry 1976;133:1434–1438.

584. Crowley TJ, Jones RH, Hydinger-Macdonald MJ, Lingle JR, Wagner JE, Egan DJ. Every-other-day acetylmethadol disturbs circadian cycles of human motility. Psychopharmacology (Berlin) 1979;62:151–155.

585. Prusoff B, Thompson WD, Sholomskas D, Riordan C. Psychosocial stressors and depression among former heroin-dependent patients maintained on methadone. J Nerv Ment Dis 1977;165:57–63.

586. Kaufmann CA, Kreek MJ, Raghunath J, Arns P. Methadone, monoamine oxidase and depression: opioid distribution and acute effects on enzyme activity. Biol Psychiatry 1983;18:1007–1021.

587. Kaufmann CA, Kreek MJ, Karoum F, Chuang LW. Depression during methadone withdrawal: No role for beta-phenylethylamine. Drug Alcohol Depend 1984;13:21–29.

588. O'Brien CP, Woody GE, McLellan AT. Psychiatric disorders in opioid-dependent patients. J Clin Psychiatry 1984;45:9–13.

589. Okpaku SO. Psychoanalytically oriented psychotherapy of substance abuse (with observations on the Penn-VA study). Adv Alcohol Subst Abuse 1986;6:17–33.

590. Milby JB, Gurwitch RH, Hohmann AA, et al. Assessing pathological detoxification fear among methadone maintenance patients: the DFSS. J Clin Psychol 1987;43:528–538.

591. Corty E, Ball JC, Myers CP. Psychological symptoms in methadone maintenance patients: prevalence and change over treatment. J Consult Clin Psychol 1988;56(5):776–777.

592. Nunes EV, Quitkin FM, Brady R, Stewart JW. Imipramine treatment of methadone maintenance patients with affective disorder and illicit drug use. Am J Psychiatry 1991;148:667–669.

593. Gill K, Nolimal D, Crowley TJ. Antisocial personality disorder, HIV risk behavior and retention in methadone maintenance therapy. Drug Alcohol Depend 1992;30:247–252.

594. Mason B, Kreek MJ, Kocsis J, Melia D, Sweeney J. Psychiatric comorbidity in methadone maintained patients. NIDA Res Monogr 1992;132:392.

595. von Limbeek J, Wouters L, Kaplan CD, Geerlings PJ, von Alem V. Prevalence of psychopathology in drug-addicted Dutch. J Subst Abuse Treat 1992;9(1):43–52.

596. Kanof PD, Aronson MJ, Ness R. Organic mood syndrome associated with detoxification from methadone maintenance. Am J Psychiatry 1993;150(3):423–428.

597. Nunes E, Quitkin F, Brady R, Post-Koenig T. Antidepressant treatment in methadone maintenance patients. J Addict Dis 1994;13:13–24.

598. Joe GW, Brown BS, Simpson D. Psychological problems and client engagement in methadone treatment. J Nerv Ment Dis 1995;183:704–710.

VIII. ADDICTIONS AND CHEMICAL DEPENDENCY PROBLEMS COMPLICATING METHADONE MAINTENANCE TREATMENT

A. Alcohol Abuse and Alcoholism

599. Bihari B. Alcoholism in M.M.T. patients: etiological factors and treatment approaches. In: Proceedings of the Fifth National Conference on Methadone Treatment. New York: National Association for the Prevention of Addiction to Narcotics, 1973;1:288–295.

600. Brown SB, Kozel NJ, Meyers MB, Dupont RL. Use of alcohol by addict and nonaddict populations. Am J Psychiatry 1973;130:599–601.

601. Jackson GW, Richman A. Alcohol use among narcotic addicts. Alcohol Health Res World 1973;1:25.

602. Pascarelli EF, Eaton C. Disulfiram (Antabuse) in the treatment of methadone maintenance alcoholics. In: Proceedings of the Fifth National Conference on Methadone Treatment. New York: National Association for the Prevention of Addiction to Narcotics, 1973;1:316–322.

603. Richman A, Jackson G, Trigg H. Follow-up of methadone maintenance patients hospitalized for abuse of alcohol and barbiturates. In: Proceedings of the Fifth National Conference on Methadone Treatment. New York: National Association for the Prevention of Addiction to Narcotics, 1973;2:1484–1493.

604. Rosen A, Ottenberg DJ, Barr HL. Patterns of previous abuse of alcohol in a group of hospitalized drug addicts. In: Proceedings of the Fifth National Conference on Methadone Treatment. New York: National Association for the Prevention of Addiction to Narcotics, 1973;1:306–315.

605. Schut J, File K, Wohlmuth T. Alcohol use by narcotic addicts in methadone maintenance treatment. Q J Stud Alcohol 1973;34:1356.

606. Scott NR, Winslow WW, Gorman DG. Epidemiology of alcoholism in a methadone maintenance program. In Proceedings of the Fifth National Conference on Methadone Treatment. New York: National Association for the Prevention of Addiction to Narcotics, 1973;1:284–287.

607. Bihari B. Alcoholism and methadone maintenance. Am J Drug Alcohol Abuse 1974;1:79.

608. Maddux JF, Elliot B. Problem drinkers among patients on methadone. Am J Drug Alcohol Abuse 1975;2:245.

609. Pugliese A, Martinez M, Maselli A, Zalick DH. Treatment of alcoholic methadone-maintenance patients with disulfiram. J Stud Alcohol 1975;36:1584–1588.

610. Charuvastra CV, Panell J, Hopper M, Erhmann M, Blakis M, Ling W. The medical safety of the combined usage of disulfiram and methadone. Arch Gen Psychiatry 1976;33:391–393.

611. Riordan CE, Mezritz M, Slobetz F, Kleber HD. Successful detoxification from methadone maintenance: follow-up study of 38 patients. JAMA 1976;235:2604–2607.

612. Gordis E, Kreek MJ. Alcoholism and drug addiction in pregnancy. Curr Probl Obstet Gynecol 1977;1:1–48.

613. Cushman P, Kreek MJ, Gordis E. Ethanol and methadone in man: a possible drug interaction. Drug Alcohol Depend 1978;3:35–42.

614. Beverley CL, Kreek MJ, Wells AO, Cortis JL. Effects of alcohol abuse on progression of liver disease in methadone-maintained patients. NIDA Res Monogr 1979;27:399–401.

615. Marcovici M, McLellan AT, O'Brien CP, Rosenzweig J. Risk for alcoholism and methadone treatment. A longitudinal study. J Nerv Ment Dis 1980;168:556–558.

616. Jackson G, Korts D, Hanbury R, et al. Alcohol consumption in persons on methadone maintenance therapy. Am J Drug Alcohol Abuse 1982;9:69–76.

617. Nilsson MI, Anggard E, Holmstrand J, Gunne L-M. Pharmacokinetics of methadone during maintenance treatment: adaptive changes during the induction phase. Eur J Clin Pharmacol 1982;22:343–349.

618. Rounsaville BJ, Weissman MM, Kleber HD. The significance of alcoholism in treated opiate addicts. J Nerv Ment Dis 1982;170:479–488.

619. Hartman N, Kreek MJ, Ross A, Khuri E, Millman RB, Rodriguez R. Alcohol use in youthful methadone maintained former heroin addicts: liver impairment and treatment outcome. Alcohol Clin Exp Res 1983;7:316–320.

620. Khuri ET, Millman RB, Hartman N, Kreek MJ. Clinical issues concerning alcoholic youthful narcotic abusers. Adv Alcohol Subst Abuse 1984;3:69–86.

621. Kreek MJ, Stimmel B. Alcoholism and polydrug use: the need for the "basics." Adv Alcohol Subst Abuse 1984;3(4):1–6.

622. Kreek MJ. Opioid interactions with alcohol. Adv Alcohol Subst Abuse 1984;3(4):35–46.

623. Deleted in proof.

624. Novick DM. Major medical problems and detoxification treatment of parenteral drug-abusing alcoholics. Adv Alcohol Subst Abuse 1984;3:87.

625. Joseph H. Alcoholism and methadone treatment consequences for the patients and program. Am J Drug Alcohol Abuse 1985;11:37–53.

626. Cushman P Jr. Alcohol and opioids: possible interactions of clinical importance. Adv Alcohol Subst Abuse 1987;3:33–46.
627. Gordis E. Methadone maintenance patients in alcoholism treatment. Alcohol Alert 1988;1:1–5.

B. Cocaine Abuse and Cocaine Dependency (Coc)

628. Dipalma JR. Cocaine abuse and toxicity. Am Fam Physician 1981;24:236–238.
629. Fishbain DA, Wetli CV. Cocaine intoxication, delirium, and death in a body packer. Ann Emerg Med 1981;10:531–532.
630. Hunt DE, Lipton DS, Goldsmith D, Strug D. Street pharmacology: uses of cocaine and heroin in the treatment of addiction. Drug Alcohol Depend 1984;13:375–387.
631. Mittleman RE, Wetli CV. Death caused by recreational cocaine use: an update. JAMA 1984;252:1889–1893.
632. Chow MJ, Ambre JJ, Ruo TI, Atkinson AJ Jr, Bowsher DJ, Fischman MW. Kinetics of cocaine distribution, elimination, and chronotropic effects. Clin Pharmacol Ther 1985;38:318–324.
633. Fishel R, Hamamoto G, Barbul A, Jijl V, Efron G. Cocaine colitis: is this a new syndrome? Dis Colon Rectum 1985;28:264–266.
634. Welti C, Fishbain D. Cocaine-induced psychosis and sudden death in recreational cocaine users. J Forensic Sci 1985;30:873–880.
635. Cregler LL, Mark H. Cardiovascular dangers of cocaine abuse. Am J Cardiol 1986;57:1185–1186.
636. Madden JD, Payne TF, Miller S. Maternal cocaine abuse and effect on the newborn. Pediatrics 1986;77:209–211.
637. Hanbury R, Sturiano V, Cohen M, Stimmel B, Aguillaume C. Cocaine use in persons on methadone maintenance. Adv Alcohol Subst Abuse 1986;6:97–106.
638. Johanson CE, Fischman MW. The pharmacology of cocaine related to its abuse. Pharmacol Rev 1989;41:3–52.
639. Tabasco-Minguillan J, Novick DM, Kreek MJ. Liver function tests in non-parenteral cocaine users. Drug Alcohol Depend 1990;26:169–174.
640. Woody GE, McLellan AT, Luborsky L, O'Brien CP. Psychotherapy and counseling for methadone-maintained opiate addicts: results of research studies. NIDA Res Mongr 1990;104:9–23.
641. Kosten TR, Morgan CH, Schottenfeld RS. Amantadine and desipramine in the treatment of cocaine abusing methadone maintained pa-

tients. NIDA Res Monogr 1991;105:510–511.
642. Kothur R, Marsh F, Posner G. Liver function tests in nonparenteral cocaine users. Arch Intern Med 1991;151:1126–1128.
643. Magura S, Siddiqi Q, Freeman RC, Lipton DS. Changes in cocaine use after entry to methadone treatment. J Addict Dis 1991;10(4):31–45.
644. Pollack MH, Rosenbaum JF. Fluoxetine treatment of cocaine abuse in heroin addicts. J Clin Psychiatry 1991;52(1):31–33.
645. Tabasco-Minguillan J, Novick DM, Kreek MJ. Liver function tests in non-parenteral cocaine users. NIDA Res Monogr 1991;105:372.
646. Torrens M, San L, Peri JM, Olle JM. Cocaine abuse among heroin addicts in Spain. Drug Alcohol Depend 1991;27(1):29–34.
647. Ziedonis DM, Kosten TR. Pharmacotherapy improves treatment outcome in depressed cocaine addicts. J Psychoactive Drugs 1991;23(4):417–425.
648. Ziedonis DM, Kosten TR. Depression as a prognostic factor for pharmacological treatment of cocaine dependence. Psychopharmacol Bull 1991;27(3):337–343.
649. Amdt IO, Dorozynsky L, Woody GE, McLellan AT, O'Brien CP. Desipramine treatment of cocaine dependence in methadone-maintained patients. Arch Gen Psychiatry 1992;49(11):888–893.
650. Cambor R, Ho A, Bodner G, Lampert S, Kennedy J, Kreek MJ. Changes in clinical status of newly abstinent hospitalized cocaine users. NIDA Res Monogr 1992.
651. Des Jarlais DC, Wenston J, Friedman SR, Sotheran JL, Maslansky R, Marmor M. Crack cocaine use in a cohort of methadone maintenance patients. J Subst Abuse Treat 1992;9:319–325.
652. Gariti P, Auriacombe M, Incmikoski R, McLellan AT, Patterson L, Dhopesh V, et al. A randomized double-blind study of neuroelectric therapy in opiate and cocaine detoxification. J Subst Abuse 1992;4(3):299–308.
653. Ho A, Cambor R, Bodner G, Kreek MJ. Intensity of craving is independent of depression in newly abstinent chronic cocaine users. In: Harris LS, ed. Problems of drug dependence, 1991: proceedings of the 53rd Annual Scientific Meeting of the Committee on Problems of Drug Dependence. Rockville, MD: U.S. Dept. of Health and Human Services, Public Health Service, National Institutes of Health, National Institute of Drug Abuse, 1992.
654. Kosten TR, Morgan CM, Falcione J, Schottenfeld RS. Pharmacotherapy for cocaine-abusing

methadone-maintained patients using amantadine or desipramine. Arch Gen Psychiatry 1992;49(11):894–898.
655. Batki SL, Manfredi LB, Jacob P III, Jones RT. Fluoxetine for cocaine dependence in methadone maintenance: quantitative plasma and urine cocaine benzoylecgonine concentrations. J Clin Psychopharmacol 1993;13:243–250.
656. Magura S, Rosenblum A, Lovejoy M, Handelsman L, Foote J, Stimmel B. Neurobehavioral treatment for cocaine-using methadone patients: a preliminary report. J Addict Dis 1994;13:143–160.
657. Rawson RA, McCann MJ, Hasson AJ, Ling W. Cocaine abuse among methadone maintenance patients: are there effective treatment strategies? J Psychoactive Drugs 1994;26:129–136.
658. Stine SM, Kosten TR. Reduction of opiate withdrawal-like symptoms by cocaine abuse during methadone and buprenorphine maintenance. Am J Drug Alcohol Abuse 1994;20:445–458.
659. Avants SK, Margolin A, Kosten TR, Cooney NL. Differences between responders and nonresponders to cocaine cues in the laboratory. Addict Behav 1995;20:215–224.
660. Tennant F, Shannon J. Cocaine abuse in methadone maintenance patients is associated with low serum methadone concentrations. J Addict Dis 1995;14:67–74.
661. Kreek MJ. Cocaine, dopamine and the endogenous opioid system. J Addict Dis 1996;15(4):73–96.
662. Peters J, Chou J, Ho A, Reid K, Borg L, Kreek MJ. Simplified quantitation of urinary benzoylecgonine in cocaine addiction research and for related pharmacotherapeutic trials. Addiction 1996;91(11):1687–1697.

C. Other Drugs Abused During Maintenance Treatment

663. Stitzer ML, Griffiths RR, McLellan AT, Grabowski J, Hawthorne JW. Diazepam use among methadone maintenance patients. Patterns and dosages. Drug Alcohol Depend 1981;8:189–199.
664. Greenfield SF, Weiss RD, Griffin ML. Patients who use drugs during inpatient substance abuse treatment. Am J Psychiatry 1992;149(2):235–239.
665. Iguchi MY, Handelsman L, Bickel WK, Griffiths RR. Benzodiazepine and sedative use/abuse by methadone maintained clients. Drug Alcohol Depend 1993;32(3):257–266.

82 CLINICAL AND SOCIETAL IMPLICATIONS OF DRUG LEGALIZATION

Herbert D. Kleber, Joseph A. Califano, Jr., and John C. Demers

Promising everything from lower crime to fewer hospital visits, proponents of legalization and other radical changes in drug policy argue that the fight against drugs has been lost. They claim that drug prohibition, as opposed to the illegal drugs themselves, spawns increasing violence and crime and that drug abuse and addiction would not increase significantly after legalization. They ignore or scorn the view that drugs like heroin and cocaine are not dangerous because they are illegal; they are illegal because they are dangerous—that these drugs are not a threat to American society because they are illegal; they are illegal because they are a threat to American society. This chapter will explore the evidence for these various contentions.

HISTORICAL BACKGROUND AND TERMINOLOGY

In the last half of the nineteenth century, opiates and cocaine were widely and legally available both in their pure form and as ingredients in patent medicines promoted as remedies for ailments ranging from hay fever and sinusitis to arthritis and depression. Heroin and cocaine were touted as nonaddictive painkillers and as cures for morphine and alcohol addiction. But as the twentieth century began with hundreds of thousands of cocaine and opiate addicts (1), concern rose about the addictiveness and destructive nature of these drugs. President William H. Taft noted in a report to Congress in 1910 that "the misuse of cocaine is undoubtedly an American habit, the most threatening of the drug habits that has appeared in this country . . ." (2).

This concern over the effects of the legal use of drugs led to federal and state actions, which by 1920 had led to sharp decreases in the use of opiates and cocaine in patent medicines and the requirement of a physician's prescription to obtain them. By the 1930s cocaine and opiate use had markedly declined. Legislation in 1937 led to the illegality of marihuana and its subsequent decreased use (1).

While the same drugs are illegal in all 50 states and many have adopted schedules similar to those of the federal government, state penalties for possession and distribution vary widely, particularly with respect to marihuana. In a few states, possession of small amounts of marihuana is a civil violation punishable by fine rather than a criminal offense. Today, 32 states have mandatory minimum sentences; 14 distinguish between crack and powder cocaine (3). Like the federal government, states set higher penalties for selling drugs to minors and outlaw possession of drug paraphernalia and operation of premises where drugs are sold and used (4).

Terminology: Legalization, Decriminalization, Medicalization, Harm Reduction

The term "legalization" has been used to encompass a wide variety of policy options from the legal use of marihuana in private to free markets for all drugs. Four terms are commonly used: legalization, decriminalization, medicalization, and harm reduction—with much variation in each.

Legalization usually implies the most radical departure from current policy. Legalization proposals vary from making marihuana cigarettes as available as tobacco cigarettes to establishing an open and free market for all drugs. Variations on legalization include: making drugs legal for the adult population, but illegal for minors; having only the government produce and sell drugs; and/or allowing a private market in drugs, usually with restrictions on advertising, dosage, and place of consumption. Few proponents put forth detailed visions of a legalized market.

Decriminalization proposals retain laws that forbid manufacture, importation, and sale of illegal drugs, but remove criminal sanctions for possession of small amounts of drugs for personal use. Most commonly advocated for marihuana, such proposals suggest that possession of drugs for personal use be legal or subject only to civil penalties such as fines.

Medicalization refers to the prescription of currently illegal drugs by physicians to addicts already dependent on such drugs. The most frequently mentioned variation is heroin maintenance. Proponents argue that providing addicts with drugs prevents them from having to commit crimes to finance their habit and ensures that the drugs they ingest are pure.

Harm reduction generally implies that government policies should concentrate on lowering the harm to the individual associated with drug use, especially the risk of AIDS, rather than on reducing use itself or getting an addict off drugs. Beginning with the proposition that drug use is inevitable, harm reduction proposals can include the prescription of heroin and cocaine to addicts; removal of penalties for personal use of marihuana; advocating "responsible" drug use as opposed to no drug use; needle-exchange programs for injection drug users to prevent the spread of HIV infection; and "low threshold" methadone maintenance which does not require counseling or regular attendance.

Variations on these options are numerous. Some do not require any change in the legal status of these drugs. The government could, for instance, allow needle exchanges while maintaining current laws banning heroin, the most commonly injected drug. Others, however, represent a major shift from the current role of government and the goal of its policies with regard to drug use and availability. As has been pointed out, some advocates use the term "harm reduction" as a politically attractive cover for legalization (5).

WHERE WE ARE

Most arguments for legalization in all its different forms start with the contention that the fight against drugs has been lost and that prevailing criminal justice and social policies with respect to drug use have been a failure. Legalization advocates point to the 80 million Americans who have ever tried drugs during their lifetime, arguing that the laws have been futile and a liberal democracy should not ban what so many people do (6–8).

The majority of these individuals, however, have used only marihuana; generally their use was only brief experimentation. The size of this number especially reflects the large number of young people who tried marihuana and hallucinogenic drugs during the late 1960s and the 1970s when drug use was so widely tolerated that the 1972 Shafer Commission, established during the Nixon Administration, and, later, President Jimmy Carter called for decriminalization of marihuana (1, 9). It also reflects the period of the late 1970s when some physicians described cocaine as a relatively harmless drug even as related problems were escalating rapidly (10).

Since then, concerned public health and government leaders have mounted energetic efforts to denormalize drug use. As a result, current (past month) users of any illicit drugs, as measured by the National Household Survey on Drug Abuse, decreased from 24.8 million in 1979 to 13 million in 1994, a nearly 50% drop. Over the same time period, current marihuana users dropped from 23 million to 10 million and cocaine users from 4.4 million to 1.4 million (11). The drug-using segment of the population is also aging. In 1979, 10% of current drug users were older than 34; today almost 30% are (11). With these results and only 6% of the population over age 12 currently using drugs (11), it is difficult to say that drug reduction efforts have failed. This sharp decline in drug use occurred during a period of strict drug laws, societal disapproval, and increasing knowledge and awareness of the dangers and costs of illegal drug use.

Several factors, however, lead many to conclude that we have not made progress against drugs. This feeling of despair stems from the uneven nature of the success. While casual drug use and experimentation have declined substantially, certain neighborhoods and areas of the country remain infested with drugs and drug-related crime, and these continuing trouble spots draw media attention. At the same time, the number of drug addicts has not dropped significantly, and the spread of HIV among addicts has added a deadly new dimension to the problem.

The number of hard-core (at least weekly) cocaine users (as estimated by the Office of National Drug Control Policy based on a number of surveys including the Household Survey, Drug Use Forecasting and Drug Abuse Warning Network) has remained steady at roughly 2 million (12). (The accuracy of this figure may be called into doubt, however, because the drop in crime and murder rate in many cities across the country has been attributed to a decrease in cocaine, especially crack, addiction.) The overall number of illicit drug addicts has hovered between 5 and 6 million, a situation that many experts attribute both to a lack of treatment facilities (13) and the large numbers of drug-using individuals already in the pipeline to addiction, even though overall casual use has dropped. Further, after 13 years of sharp decline, teenage drug use increased from 1992 to 1995.

While strict drug laws and criminal sanctions are not likely to deter hard-core addicts, increased resources can be dedicated to prevention and treatment without changing the legal status of drugs. It is difficult to carry out effective prevention campaigns when drugs are available on every street corner and school corridor; witness the continued rise in teenage smoking in spite of major prevention efforts. The criminal justice system can be used to enhance treatment outcome by using such programs as an alternative to incarceration and by offering treatment in prisons. Though substantial problems remain, the significant progress in our struggle against drug abuse can be accelerated by improving the system rather than tearing it down.

WILL LEGALIZATION INCREASE DRUG USE?

Proponents of drug legalization claim that making drugs legally available would not significantly increase the number of addicts. They argue that drugs are already available to those who want them and that a policy of legalization could be combined with education and prevention programs to discourage drug use (6, 7, 14). Some contend that legalization might even reduce the number of users, arguing that there would be no pushers to lure new users and drugs would lose the "forbidden fruit" allure of illegality (7, 15). Proponents of legalization also play down the consequences of drug use, saying that most drug users can function normally (16). Some legalization advocates assert that a certain level of drug addiction is inevitable so that even if legalization increased the number of users, it would have little effect on the numbers of users who become addicts (17).

The effects of legalization on the numbers of users and addicts is an important question because the answer in large part determines whether legalization will reduce crime, improve public health, and lower economic, social, and health care costs or will have the opposite effects. The claimed benefits of legal change evaporate if the number of users and addicts, particularly among children, increases significantly.

Availability

An examination of this question begins with the issue of availability, which has three components:

- Physical, how convenient is access to drugs
- Psychological, the moral and social acceptability and perceived consequences of drug use
- Economic, the affordability of drugs

PHYSICAL

Despite assertions to the contrary, the evidence indicates that presently drugs are not accessible to all. Fewer than 50% of high school seniors and young adults under 22 believed they could obtain cocaine "fairly easily" or "very easily" (18, 19). Only 39% of the adult population reported they could get cocaine; and only 25% reported that they could obtain heroin, PCP, and LSD (20). Thus, only one quarter to one half of people can easily get illegal drugs (other than marihuana). After legalization, drugs would be more widely and easily available. Currently, only 11% of individuals reported seeing drugs available in the area where they lived (20); after legalization, there could be a place to purchase drugs in every neighborhood. Under such circumstances, it is logical to conclude that more individuals would use drugs.

PSYCHOLOGICAL

In arguing that legalization would not result in increased use, proponents of legalization often cite public opinion polls which indicate that the vast majority of Americans would not try drugs even if they were legally available (21, 22). They fail to take into account, however, that this strong public antagonism towards drugs has been formed during a period of strict prohibition, when government and institutions at every level made clear the health and criminal justice consequences of drug use. Furthermore, even if only 15% of the population would use drugs after legalization, this would be triple the current level of 5.6%.

Laws define what is acceptable conduct in a society and express the will of its citizens. Drug laws not only create a criminal sanction, they also serve as educational and normative statements that shape public attitudes (23). Criminal laws constitute a far stronger statement than civil laws, but even the latter can discourage individual consumption. Laws regulating smoking in public and workplaces, prohibiting certain types of tobacco advertising, and mandating warning labels are in part responsible for the decline in smoking prevalence among adults, which seems to be leveling off at the high rate of 48 million nicotine addicts.

The challenge of reducing drug abuse and addiction would be decidedly more difficult if society passed laws indicating that these substances are not sufficiently harmful to prohibit their use. Any move toward legalization would decrease the perception of risks and costs of drug use, which would lead to wider use (18). During the late 1960s and the 1970s, as society, laws, and law enforcement became more permissive about drug use, the number of individuals smoking marihuana and using heroin, hallucinogens, and other drugs rose sharply. During the 1980s, as society's attitude became more restrictive and antidrug laws stricter and more vigorously enforced, the perceived harmfulness of marihuana and other illicit drugs increased and use decreased.

Some legalization advocates point to the campaign against smoking as proof that reducing use is possible while substances are legally available (6, 8, 14). But it has taken smoking more than 30 years to decline as much as illegal drug use did in 10 years (12, 24). Moreover, reducing use of legal drugs among the young has proven especially difficult. While use of illegal drugs by high school seniors dropped 50% from 1979 to 1993, tobacco use remained virtually constant and is now increasing (18).

ECONOMIC

Unless one repeals the laws of economics, it is likely that reducing the price of drugs will increase consumption (23, 25, 26). Though interdiction and law enforcement have had limited success in reducing supply (seizing at best only 25–30% of cocaine imports, for example) (12) the illegality of drugs has increased their price (27). Prices of illegal drugs are roughly 6–10 times what they would cost to produce legally. Cocaine, for example, sells at $60–80 a gram today, but would cost only $10 a gram legally to produce and distribute. That would set the price of a dose at 50 cents, well within the reach of a schoolchild's lunch money (28). (For higher estimates of the differences between illegal and legal costs see references 8 and 23.)

Until the mid 1980s, cocaine was the drug of the middle and upper classes. Regular use was limited to those who had the money to purchase it or got the money through white collar crime or selling such assets as their car, house, or children's college funds. In the mid 1980s, the $5 crack cocaine vial made the drug inexpensive and more available to the poor and young. Use spread. Cocaine-exposed babies began to fill hospital neonatal wards, cocaine-related emergency room visits increased sharply, and cocaine-related crime and violence jumped (23).

Efforts to increase the price of legal drugs by taxing them heavily in order to discourage consumption would be accompanied by the black market, crime, violence, and corruption now associated with the illegal drug trade. Heroin addicts, who gradually build a tolerance to the drug, and cocaine addicts, who crave more of the drug as soon as its effects subside, would turn to a black market if an affordable and rising level of drugs were not made available to them legally.

Children

Drug use among children and adolescents is of particular concern since almost all individuals who use drugs begin before they are 21. Furthermore, adolescents rate drugs as the number one problem they face (19). Since we have been unable to keep legal drugs, like tobacco and alcohol, out of the hands of children, legalization of illegal drugs could cause a pediatric pandemic of drug abuse and addiction.

Most advocates of legalization support a regulated system in which access to presently illicit drugs would be illegal for minors (8). Such regulations would retain for children the "forbidden fruit" allure that many argue legalization would eliminate. Furthermore any such distinction between adults and minors could make drugs, like beer and cigarettes today, an attractive badge of adulthood.

The American experience with laws restricting access by children and adolescents to tobacco and alcohol makes it clear that keeping legal drugs away from minors would be a formidable, probably impossible, task. Today, 62% of high school seniors have smoked, 30% in the past month (18). Three million adolescents smoke cigarettes, an average of one half pack per day, a $1 billion a year market (29). Twelve million underage Americans drink beer and other alcohol, a market approaching $10 billion a year. Although alcohol use is illegal for all those under the age of 21, 87% of high school seniors report using alcohol, more than half in the past month (18). These rates of use persist despite school, community, and media activities that inform youths about the dangers of smoking and drinking and despite increasing public awareness of these risks.

Moreover, in contrast to these high rates of alcohol and tobacco use, only 18% of seniors use illicit drugs, which are illegal for the entire society (18). It is no accident that those substances which are mostly easily obtainable—alcohol, cigarettes, and inhalants such as those found in household cleaning fluids—are those most widely used by the youngest students (18, 30).

Supporters and opponents of legalization generally agree that education and prevention programs are an integral part of efforts to reduce drug use by children and adolescents. School programs, media campaigns such the Partnership for a Drug-Free America (PDFA), and news reports on the dangers of illegal drugs have helped reduce use by changing attitudes towards drugs.

Along with such educational programs, however, the stigma of illegality is especially important in preventing use among adolescents. From 1978 to 1993, current marihuana use among high school seniors dropped twice as fast as alcohol use (18). California started a $600 million antismoking campaign in 1989, and by 1995, the overall smoking rate had dropped 30%. But among teenagers the smoking rate remained constant—even though almost one quarter of the campaign targeted them (31).

In separate studies, 60–70% of New Jersey and California students reported that fear of getting in trouble with the authorities was a major reason why they did not use drugs (32, 33). Another study found that the greater the perceived likelihood of apprehension and swift punishment for using marihuana, the less likely adolescents are to smoke it (34). Because a legalized or decriminalized system would remove much, if not all, of this deterrent, drug use among teenagers could be expected to rise. Since most teens begin using drugs because their peers do (35)—not because of pressure from pushers (36)—and most drugs users initially exhibit few ill effects, more teenagers would be likely to try drugs (23, 36).

Hard-Core Addiction

A review of addiction in the past shows that the number of alcohol, heroin, and cocaine addicts, even when adjusted for changes in population, fluctuates widely over time, in response to changes in access, price, societal attitudes, and legal consequences. The fact that alcohol and tobacco, the most accepted and available legal drugs, are the most widely abused, demonstrates that behavior is influenced by opportunity, stigma, and price. Many soldiers who were regular heroin users in Vietnam stopped once they returned to the United States where heroin was much more difficult and dangerous to get (1). Studies have shown that even among chronic alcoholics, alcohol taxes lower consumption (37).

A systematic review of the relation between demand and criminal justice activities by Homer estimated that without retail-level drug arrests and seizures—which reduce availability, increase the danger of arrest for the drug user, and stigmatize use—the number of compulsive cocaine users would rise to between 10 and 32 million, a level 5–16 times the present one (38).

Not all new users become addicts. But few individuals foresee their addiction when they start using; most think they can control their consumption (28). Among the new users created by increased availability, many, including children, would find themselves unable to live without the drug, no longer able to work, go to school, or maintain personal relationships. In fact, as UCLA criminologist James Q. Wilson points out with regard to cocaine (39), the percentage of drug triers who become abusers when the drugs are illegal, socially unacceptable, and generally hard to get may be only a fraction of the users who become addicts when drugs are legal and easily available—physically, psychologically, and economically.

HARMING THY NEIGHBOR AND THYSELF: ADDICTION AND CASUAL DRUG USE

To offset any increased use as a result of legalization, many proponents contend that money presently spent on criminal justice and law enforcement could be used for treatment of addicts and prevention (6). In 1995, the federal government spent $13.2 billion to fight drug abuse, nearly two thirds of that on law enforcement; state and local governments are spending at least another $16 billion on drug control efforts, largely on law enforcement (12). Legalization proponents argue that most of this money could be used to fund treatment on demand for all addicts who want it and extensive public health campaigns to discourage new use.

With changes in the legal status of drugs, the number of new prisoners would initially decrease because many are currently there for drug law violations. As use increased, however, costs would quickly rise in health care, schools, and businesses. Soon, wider use and addiction would increase criminal activity related to the psychological and physical effects of drug use and criminal justice costs would rise again. The higher number of casual users and addicts would reduce worker productivity and students' ability and motivation to learn, cause more highway accidents and fatalities, and fill hospital beds with individuals suffering from ailments and injuries caused or aggravated by drug abuse.

Costs

It is doubtful whether legalization would produce any cost savings over time, even in the area of law enforcement. Indeed, the legal availability of alcohol has not eliminated law enforcement costs due to alcohol-related violence. A third of state prison inmates committed their crimes while under the influence of alcohol (40). Despite intense educational campaigns, the highest number of arrests—1.5 million in 1993—is for driving while intoxicated (41).

Like advocates of legalization today, opponents of alcohol prohibition claimed that taxes on the legal sale of alcohol would dramatically increase revenues and even help erase the federal deficit (42). The real-world result has been quite different. The more than $11 billion in 1995 state and federal revenues from alcohol taxes (43, 44) paid for less than half the $40 billion that alcohol abuse imposed in direct health care costs in 1995 (45), much less the costs laid on federal entitlement programs and the legal and criminal justice systems, to say nothing of lost economic productivity. The $13 billion in federal and state tobacco tax revenue (43, 44) was one sixth of the $75 billion in direct health care costs attributable to tobacco (45). This discrepancy between excise tax revenue and alcohol- and tobacco-related costs does decrease if one takes into account the "savings" from such programs as Social Security and Medicare due to premature death. The idea that a tobacco policy resulting in more than 400,000 deaths a year provides any kind of model for dealing with illegal drugs is hard to imagine.

Health care costs directly attributable to illegal drugs exceed $30 billion (45), an amount that would increase significantly if use spread after legalization. Experience renders it unrealistic to expect that taxes could be imposed on newly legalized drugs sufficient to cover the costs of increased use and abuse.

Public Health

Legalization proponents contend that prohibition has negative public health consequences such as the spread of HIV from addicts who share dirty needles, accidental poisoning, and overdoses from impure drugs of variable potency. Of those individuals who were newly diagnosed with AIDS between July, 1995, and June, 1996, more than one-third were among injection drug users who may have shared needles, cookers, cottons, rinse water, and other paraphernalia; many other individuals contracted AIDS by having sex with infected injection drug users (46).

Advocates of medicalization argue that while illicit drugs should not be freely available to all, doctors should be allowed to prescribe them (particularly heroin, but also cocaine) to addicts. They contend that giving addicts drugs assures purity and eliminates the need for addicts to steal in order to buy them (47).

Giving addicts drugs like heroin, however, poses many problems. Providing them by prescription raises the danger of diversion for sale on the black market. The alternative—insisting that addicts take drugs on the prescriber's premises—entails at least two visits a day, thus interfering with the stated goal of many maintenance programs to enable addicts to hold jobs. Early results from the Swiss heroin maintenance project show that a substantial number of enrolled individuals are unwilling to make such ongoing visits and are unwilling to do without the heroin or cocaine combination they like—leading the organizers to propose take-out heroin and the ability to use cocaine as well. Neither the Swiss project nor heroin maintenance in Liverpool, England, appear to have improved employment among addicts.

Heroin addicts require two to four shots each day in increasing doses as they build tolerance to its euphoric effect. On the other hand, methadone can be given at a constant dose since euphoria is not the objective. Addicts maintained on methadone need only a single oral dose each day, eliminating the need for injection (48–50). Because cocaine produces an intense but short euphoria and an immediate desire for more (51), addicts would have to be given the drug even more often than heroin in order to satisfy their craving sufficiently to prevent them from seeking additional cocaine on the street. The binge nature of cocaine use renders it unlikely that cocaine could be given on a "medicalization" basis. Because powder cocaine can be readily converted into crack, any proposal to expand availability of the former will increase the number of crack users and addicts.

Other less radical harm reduction proposals also have serious flaws. As compared to comprehensive methadone maintenance, "low threshold" methadone maintenance programs, when objectively studied, show sharply increased rates of illicit drug use and drug-related problems, and a failure to

reduce high-risk behaviors (52, 53). Distributing free needles does not ensure that addicts desperate for a high at inconvenient times would not continue to share them. But to the extent that needle exchange programs are effective in reducing the spread of the HIV virus, they can be adopted without legalizing drugs. Studies of whether needle exchange programs increase drug use, however, have generally focused on periods of no longer than 12 months (54). While use does not seem to increase in this period, data are lacking on the long-term effects of such programs and whether they prompt attitude shifts that in turn lead to increased drug use (55).

Some individuals do die as a result of drug impurities. But while drug purity could be assured in a government-regulated system (though not for those drugs sold on the black market), careful use could not. The increased numbers of users would probably produce a rising number of overdose deaths, similar to those caused by alcohol poisoning today. The deaths and costs due to unregulated drug quality pale in comparison to the negative impact that legalization would have on drug users, their families, and society. Casual drug use is dangerous, not simply because it can lead to addiction or accidental overdoses, but because it can be harmful per se, increasing worker accidents, highway fatalities, and children born with physical and psychological handicaps. Each year, roughly 500,000 newborns are exposed to illegal drugs in utero; many others are never born because of drug-induced spontaneous abortions (56, 57). Drug-exposed newborns are more likely to need intensive care and to suffer the numerous consequences of low birth weight and prematurity, including early death (56, 58). The additional costs just to raise drug-exposed infants would outweigh any potential savings of legalization in criminal justice expenditures (58).

Substance abuse both leads to and aggravates medical problems. Medicaid patients with a secondary diagnosis of substance abuse (including alcohol) remain in hospitals twice as long as patients with the same primary diagnosis but with no substance abuse problems. Girls and boys under age 15 remain in the hospital three and four times as long, respectively, when they have a secondary diagnosis of substance abuse (59). One third to one half of individuals with psychiatric problems are also substance abusers (60). Young people who use drugs are at higher risk of mental health problems including depression, suicide, and personality disorders (56) and are more likely to engage in risky behavior such as unprotected sex (61, 62). Such sexual behavior exposes these teens to increased risk of pregnancy as well as AIDS and other sexually transmitted diseases.

In schools and families, drug abuse can be devastating. Students who use drugs not only limit their own ability to learn, they also disrupt classrooms. Drug-using parents are more likely to provide inadequate or no economic support and put their children at greater risk of becoming substance abusers themselves (56). With the advent of crack cocaine in the mid 1980s, foster care cases soared over 50% nationwide in five years; more than 70% of these cases involved families in which at least one parent abused drugs (63).

Decreased coordination and impaired motor skills that result from drug use are dangerous not just to the individual but to society at large. A recent study in Tennessee found that 59% of reckless drivers, having been stopped by the police and tested negative for alcohol, test positive for marihuana and/or cocaine (64). Twenty percent of New York City drivers who die in automobile accidents test positive for cocaine use (65). The extent of driving while high on marihuana and other illegal drugs is still not well known because usually the police do not have the same capability for roadside drug testing as they do for alcohol testing.

The Workplace

Currently, three quarters of illegal drug users are employed full or part time (11); 15% of them admit to working under the influence of drugs (66). These workers impose costs on their employers and eventually society through their decreased productivity, health care needs, workplace accidents, and absenteeism. They drive buses and trucks, operate nuclear power plants, run the air traffic control system, perform surgery, deliver mail, and teach children.

Workers who use cocaine and marihuana are twice as likely to be absent from work and to be injured, and one and a half times more likely to be involved in an accident (56). Overall, workers who use drugs are three times likelier to be late for work, 10 times likelier to miss work, and three to six times likelier to injure themselves or others. Drug-using workers are responsible for 40% of industrial fatalities and experience more than 300% higher medical and benefits costs (67). In 1991, it is estimated that lost productivity due to illegal drugs totalled $35 billion (68, 68a).

CRIME AND VIOLENCE

Legalization advocates contend that *drug-related* violence is really *drug trade–related* violence, that antidrug laws spawn more violence and crime than the drugs themselves. Because illegality creates high prices for drugs and huge profits for dealers, advocates of legalization point out that users commit crimes to support their habit; drug pushers fight over turf; gangs and organized crime thrive; and users become criminals by coming into contact with the underworld (14, 16, 69, 70).

Researchers divide drug-related violence into three types: systemic, economically compulsive, and psychopharmacological (71):

- Systemic violence is that intrinsic to involvement with illegal drugs, including murders over drug turf, retribution for selling "bad" drugs, and fighting among users over drugs or drug paraphernalia.
- Economically compulsive violence results from addicts who engage in violent crime to support their addiction.
- Psychopharmacological violence is caused by the short-term or long-term use of certain drugs which lead to excitability, irrationality, and violence, such as a brutal murder committed under the influence of cocaine.

In a study of 130 drug-related 1984 homicides in New York State (but outside New York City), 60% resulted from the psychopharmacological effects of the drug (usually used with alcohol); only 20% were found to be related to the drug trade; 3.1% were committed for economic reasons. The remaining 17% either fell into more than one of these categories or were categorized as "other" (72). As the crack trade developed in New York City in the late 1980s and fighting over drug turf became prevalent, a later study by the authors found drug trade–related deaths to be the most common (73). As the crack trade has matured, the proportion of these types of homicides to the total number of drug-rated deaths has appeared to decrease, contributing to the decrease in the overall murder rate in the city.

U.S. Department of Justice statistics reveal that six times as many homicides, four times as many assaults, and almost one and a half times as many robberies are committed under the influence of drugs as are committed to get money to buy drugs (40). Given these facts, any decreases in violent acts committed because of the current high cost of drugs would be more than offset by increases in psychopharmacological violence, such as that caused by cocaine-related effects.

The threat of rising violence is particularly serious in the case of cocaine, crack, methamphetamine, and PCP. Unlike marihuana or heroin, which depress activity, these drugs are often associated with increased irritability and physical aggression. For instance, past increases in the New York City homicide rate have been tied to increases in cocaine use (74).

Because addicts engage in criminal behavior for different reasons, repeal of drug laws would not affect all addicts in the same way. A small proportion of addicts is responsible for a disproportionately high number of drug-related crimes and arrests. Virtually all of these addicts committed crimes before abusing drugs and use crime to support themselves as well as their habits. Their criminal activity and drug use are symptomatic of chronic antisocial behavior. Legally available drugs at lower prices would do little to discourage crime by this group (75, 76). Fagan, for example, found that the expanding crack markets attracted individuals with an extensive history of violence and drug selling rather than initiating individuals into such careers (77). For a second group, criminal activity is associated with the high cost of illegal drugs. For these addicts, lower prices would decrease drug-related crimes. For a third group, legally available drugs would mean an opportunity to create illegal diversion markets, as some addicts currently do with methadone (75, 76). (Under medicalization schemes, there would still be an illegal drug market for novice users and those unwilling to abide by program rules.)

Legalization advocates point to exploding prison populations and failure of drug laws to lower crime rates (78). From 1980 to 1993, arrests for drug offenses doubled from 470,000 to 1 million (41). Some 60% of the 95,000 federal inmates are in prison for drug law violations (41). Rising prison populations are generated in large part by stricter laws, tough enforcement, and mandatory minimum sentencing laws—policy choices of the public and Congress. But the growing number of prisoners is also a product of the high rate of recidivism—a phenomenon tied in good measure to the lack of treatment facilities, both in and out of prison. Eighty percent of state prisoners have prior convictions and 60% have served time before (40). Despite the fact that more than 60% of all state inmates have used illegal drugs regularly and 30% were under the influence of drugs at the time they committed the crime for which they were incarcerated (40), fewer than 20% of inmates with drug problems receive any treatment (79).

While strict laws and enforcement do not deter addicts from using drugs, the criminal justice system can be used to get them in treatment. Because of the nature of addiction, most drug abusers do not seek treatment voluntarily, but many respond to outside pressures including the threat of incarceration (76). Where the criminal justice system is used to encourage treatment participation, addicts are more likely to complete treatment and stay off drugs (80, 81).

THE LESSONS OF PROHIBITION

Legalization advocates often cite the era of national alcohol prohibition from 1920 to 1934 to support their case. As ratified in the 18th Amendment, Prohibition banned the "manufacture, sale, or transportation of intoxicating liquors within, the importation thereof into, or the exportation thereof from the United States. . . ." Proponents of legalization contend that the failure of the 18th Amendment supports their argument that prohibitions of this kind of individual behavior are not effective (21).

The alcohol prohibition–drug control law analogy is a false one. There are two important distinctions between Prohibition and current drug laws. First, Prohibition was in fact decriminalization because possession for personal consumption was not illegal. Second, alcohol, unlike illegal drugs, has a long history of widespread social acceptance and use in Western culture dating at least as far back as the Old Testament and Ancient Greece. Most Americans who drink do not get into trouble with alcohol. Thus, the public and political consensus favoring Prohibition was short-lived. By the early 1930s, most Americans no longer supported it. Today, on the other hand, the public overwhelmingly favors keeping illegal drugs illegal (19).

Despite these differences, which made alcohol prohibition more difficult to enforce than current drug laws, Prohibition reduced the amount of alcohol consumed, as well as the incidence of alcohol-related medical problems and violence. It is important not to confuse federal Prohibition with state laws restricting alcohol. Advocates of legalization point to the decline in consumption and cirrhosis pre-1919 to argue that consumption declined more before the 18th Amendment then after. Given the fact that by 1919, 36 of the 48 states had established some form of prohibition, this argument is true but disingenuous. At the beginning of the twentieth century, Americans consumed 2.6 gallons of alcohol per person. By 1919, this amount dropped to 1.96 gallons per person. In 1934, the first full year after repeal of national Prohibition, alcohol use stood at .97 gallons per person. From then on, consumption rose steadily to its present level, roughly three times as high as that immediately after Prohibition (82).

Death rates from cirrhosis of the liver corroborate available consumption statistics. Cirrhosis death rates fell from 12 per 100,000 in 1916 to 5 per 100,000 in 1920, and remained at that level throughout Prohibition before beginning to rise steadily again after repeal (83). Among men such rates declined even more sharply, from 29.5 per 100,000 in 1911 to 10.7 per 100,000 in 1929 (42).

The decrease in consumption had other positive health consequences. Admissions to mental health institutions for alcoholic psychosis dropped by more than 60% from 1919 to 1922. Arrests for drunkenness and disorderly conduct dropped 50% between 1916 and 1922, and welfare agencies reported dramatic declines in the number of cases due to alcohol-related family problems (42).

Nor is Hollywood's guns and gangsters depiction of Prohibition accurate. Homicide experienced a higher rate of increase between 1900 and 1910 than during Prohibition, and organized crime was well established in cities before 1920 (42).

Legalization proponents also argue that during Prohibition, an increased number of drinkers died from the consumption of dangerous wood and denatured alcohol, which were used as substitutes for commercial alcohol, just as today addicts die from impure drugs. The data do not bear this out. Through 1927, the rate of death from these substitutes remained nearly constant at its 1920 level (42).

The public may agree that the freedom to drink is worth the public health consequences. Worried by the high rate of alcohol-related disease and crime, the residents of Barrow, Alaska, the northernmost city in the United States, voted in 1994 to ban alcohol completely. Despite the 70% drop in crime and the immediate and persistent decline in alcohol-related emergency room visits from 118 in the month before the ban to 23 in the following month, residents voted to repeal the ban in 1995. In the two weeks after the ban was lifted, the detoxification center began to fill with patients and alcohol-related murders were on the rise (84).

These facts are presented to set the record straight and to dispel the exaggerated or false consequences often attributed to Prohibition. They are not an argument for the resumption of alcohol prohibition, which we oppose, but they do offer some lessons on the relevance of illegality to reducing drug use.

THE LESSONS OF LEGAL DRUGS

Legalization proponents point out that alcohol and tobacco cost society much more in lost productivity, increased health care, and criminal justice expenditures and lead to more deaths than all illegal drugs combined (7, 8, 14). From that, they conclude that we spend too much time and energy fighting illegal drugs, as compared to legal drugs. Alcohol and tobacco are indeed responsible for far more deaths and costs to society than illegal drugs, but this is precisely because alcohol and tobacco are legal and therefore widely available, used, and abused.

Illegal drug-related deaths are estimated at 20,000 annually. Tobacco is responsible for more than 400,000 deaths and alcohol for more than 100,000 deaths every year (85). Fetal alcohol syndrome is the leading known cause of mental retardation (86). Smoking by pregnant women kills up to 7,000 newborns annually and leads to as many as 141,000 miscarriages (87). Cigarettes are as addictive as heroin and spawn health problems ranging from lung cancer to emphysema and heart disease (88). Of the $66 billion that substance abuse cost federal health and disability entitlement programs in 1995, $56 billion were attributable to alcohol and tobacco (89). Of the $29 billion in Medicare costs attributable to substance abuse, 80% was related to smoking. Seventy percent of the $21 billion that Medicaid spent because of substance abuse is due to cigarettes and alcohol (45).

The high costs attributed to legal drugs do not indicate that we are concentrating prohibition on the wrong drugs, but rather that when drugs are legal, and therefore widely acceptable and available, they adversely affect more individuals and require more attention and resources. Indeed, the nation's experience with tobacco and alcohol send a warning about the dangers of making illegal drugs readily available. As drug policy expert Mark Kleiman has noted, "Until success is achieved in imposing reasonable controls on the currently licit killers, alcohol and nicotine, the case for adding a third or fourth recreational drug . . . will remain hopelessly speculative" (90).

Another argument made by legalization proponents is that the general decrease in consumption rates of both legal and illegal drugs in the past 15 years has nothing to do with law enforcement policy, but rather with education and increased societal concern with personal health (8). Yet despite widespread awareness of the risks of smoking and heavy media attention to tobacco-related problems, roughly 25% of Americans continue to smoke (24), and smoking is on the rise among young people (12). On the other hand, the number of illegal drug users has dropped by half over the last 15 years, to 6% of the population (11). Arguing that we should treat illicit drugs as we do tobacco, using education instead of prohibition, also implies a false dichotomy between education and prohibitive laws. In curbing illegal drug

use, when law enforcement and education complement and reinforce each other, they are most effective.

There are more than 48 million nicotine addicts, 12–18 million alcoholics and alcohol abusers and 5–6 million illegal drug addicts. Making illegal drugs more available would drive the number of marihuana, heroin, and cocaine users closer to the number of alcohol and tobacco users.

MARIHUANA

Marihuana is the most commonly used illegal drug in the United States and its use is particularly high among adolescents. Because relatively little street-level violence attends the marihuana trade, the legalization and decriminalization debate here centers on how harmful the drug is to the user, whether marihuana use leads to the use of harder drugs, whether marihuana use would increase, and whether any increase would translate into a decrease in alcohol use (21, 91, 92).

While clearly not as dangerous as snorting cocaine or shooting heroin, smoking marihuana is detrimental both physically and mentally, especially to adolescents. The effects of one marihuana joint on the lungs are equivalent to four cigarettes, placing the user at increased risk of bronchitis, emphysema and bronchial asthma. The active ingredient in marihuana, tetrahydrocannabinol (THC), is fat soluble and remains in the brain, lungs, and reproductive organs for weeks. Marihuana weakens the immune system, and regular use can disrupt the menstrual cycle and suppress ovarian function (93, 94). Regardless of socioeconomic status, prenatal use of marihuana by the mother appears to reduce significantly the IQs of babies (95). Marihuana impairs short-term memory and ability to concentrate (94) at a time when the main task of its young users is education. And marihuana use diminishes motor control functions, distorts perception, and impairs judgment, leading among other things to increased car accidents and vandalism. Marihuana toxicity, especially anxiety and panic attacks, is a frequently cited cause of emergency room visits, and treatment of marihuana dependence has become a common reason for seeking substance abuse treatment, treatment which is usually psychologic rather than pharmacologic. As Millman and Beeder note, stopping chronic cannabis use often results in "a marked and rapid improvement in mental clarity and energy levels" (96).

The link between the use of marihuana and the subsequent use of harder drugs has been the subject of much debate, with supporters of marihuana decriminalization and legalization arguing that many individuals who smoke marihuana never use hard drugs. While the latter is true, the statistical association between the teenage use of marihuana and the later use of other drugs such as cocaine is powerful. Even though the biomedical or other causal relationship for this has not yet been adequately explained, 12- to 17-year-olds who smoke marihuana are 85 times more likely to use cocaine than those who do not. Adults who as adolescents smoked marihuana are 17 times likelier to use cocaine regularly. Sixty percent of adolescents who use marihuana before age 15 will later use cocaine. These correlations are many times higher than the initial relationships found between smoking and lung cancer in the 1964 Surgeon General's report (9–10 times), high cholesterol and heart disease in the Framingham study (2–4 times), and asbestos and lung cancer in the Selikoff study (5 times) (97).

Marihuana use has been associated with many high-risk behaviors among young people. According to the U.S. Centers for Disease Control and Prevention, adolescents who smoke marihuana are twice as likely to attempt suicide and carry a weapon as those who do not. Adolescent marihuana smokers are three times as likely to have sex and far more likely to do so without a condom, putting themselves at much greater risk of teen pregnancy and sexually transmitted diseases (61).

Past experiences with marihuana decriminalization illustrate the consequences of more tolerant policies. During the 1970s, 11 states decriminalized personal possession of marihuana by making the offense a civil violation punishable by a fine. In 1975, the Alaska State Supreme Court decriminalized at-home personal use of small amounts of marihuana for individuals older than age 19. By 1988, 12- to 17-year-olds in Alaska were smoking joints at more than twice the national average. Marihuana use became part of the lifestyle of many teenagers and the age of initiation declined (98, 99). Because of this, in a 1990 referendum, Alaskans voted to recriminalize personal possession.

Proponents of legalization cite several surveys and studies which report that when Oregon, Maine, and California decriminalized marihuana, rates of use among teenagers did not increase significantly (100). These surveys, however, have severe shortcomings. They lack controls for other historical and demographic factors, such as sex, income, and education, and employ vaguely defined measurement criteria to estimate the prevalence of marihuana use (101, 102). They do not reflect the impact of legalization on long-term usage rates because they were conducted only 1–3 years after decriminalization laws were passed, and they fail to recognize that even minimal annual increases in use become significant when they accumulate over time. Though reported marihuana use increased only slightly following decriminalization, the time period surveyed was not long enough to allow the educational and attitude-forming aspects of the previous strict drug laws to dissipate.

Measurement problems also exist in trying to compare usage rates in states that decriminalized versus states that did not. The comparison is problematic because many states that did not decriminalize reduced penalties for marihuana use, and others chose not to enforce laws prohibiting personal use of marihuana. During the 1970s, many states and the federal government adopted more tolerant attitudes towards the drug. Nationwide, use rose significantly during this time, reaching almost 40% of high school seniors before beginning its long decline in 1979 (18).

Teenagers are not likely to stop using alcohol when they begin smoking marihuana. While on individual occasions teens may choose to get high on either marihuana or alcohol, these drugs are often used together. From 1975 to 1978, as the percentage of teens using marihuana increased from 27 to 37%, the percentage of teens who drank increased from 68 to 72%. Marihuana use then dropped to 12% of teens by 1992; alcohol use dropped to 51%. The recent rise in teenage marihuana use has been accompanied by little change in the percentage of students who drink (18).

Proponents of legalization argue that while smoking pot has detrimental health and social effects, so does use of our two legal drugs, alcohol and tobacco, and to be consistent, we should legalize marihuana. But legalizing marihuana would add a third drug that combines some of the most serious risks of the other two (94). Marihuana offers both the intoxicating effects of alcohol and the long-term lung damage of tobacco. It would be irresponsible to legalize or decriminalize marihuana and create a third legal drug, especially when we are still learning about its physical and psychological health effects as well as its relationship to other drugs and a variety of dangerous behaviors. One of the most serious drawbacks of marihuana legalization, Kleiman notes, is its "virtual irreversibility if it goes badly wrong" (103).

THE EUROPEAN EXPERIENCES

Many legalization advocates point to the policies of European countries as models for approaches to the American drug problem. They claim that some countries, notably the Netherlands and Great Britain, are more innovative because their aim is to minimize the harmful impact of drug use on the user and society, even if this requires legal change (104).

While the Netherlands' laws regarding illegal drugs remain unchanged, Dutch enforcement policy since 1976 has distinguished between "drugs presenting an unacceptable risk" (commonly termed "hard drugs," such as cocaine and heroin) and "cannabis products" (83). Special "coffee shops" were established where anyone age 18 can purchase marihuana. Legalization proponents claim that this policy has not increased drug use among young people or the population in general (16, 105, 106).

These claims are not supported by the facts. Though marihuana use did not explode immediately following decriminalization, it has recently been increasing, suggesting that the effects of decriminalization may only be fully realized in the longer term. Between 1984 and 1992, Dutch adolescent marihuana use increased nearly 200% (107); over the same period, marihuana use among American adolescents plummeted 66%. Since 1988, the Dutch have seen a 22% increase in the total number of registered addicts, and a 30% increase, from 1991 to 1993, in the number of registered cannabis addicts (108). From 1990 to 1995, the proportion of users who had smoked

cannabis for the previous five years increased from 2 to 9%, suggesting that increased availability will be associated with longer term use (109). The same study found that between 1990 and 1995, the percentage of 11- to 18-year-olds who had ever used marihuana more than doubled from 7 to 17% (109). Several marihuana "coffee shops" in Amsterdam have already been shut down for illegally selling hard drugs. Responding to pressure from other European countries and its own citizens, the Dutch Parliament passed restrictions in 1996 cutting the number of coffee houses in half and reducing the amount of marihuana an individual can buy from 30 to 5 grams (110).

The other country that legalization advocates cite favorably is Great Britain for its policy of allowing specially licensed doctors to prescribe drugs to addicts (111). Prescribing heroin to addicts, it is claimed, has lowered the rate of addiction and reduced crime (112); neither of these claims have been verified.

Nationwide, British doctors maintain 17,000 heroin addicts on methadone and less than 400 on heroin. Given the 150,000 heroin addicts in England, claims that maintaining a few hundred of them on heroin has driven drug dealers and drug-related crime from the streets are unfounded. There has been no movement among doctors in England to adopt heroin maintenance on a large scale (113).

In general, much confusion surrounds British policies. Until 1968, the government allowed all doctors to prescribe drugs to addicts in the context of their medical treatment, but this policy failed to contain the problem of addiction. Doctors carelessly or willfully abused their privilege and unlawfully supplied drugs to many individuals. Addicts diverted legally obtained drugs to the general population. In response to increasing rates of addiction, Britain mandated in 1968 that only doctors specially licensed by the Home Office could prescribe illegal drugs and that doctors must register all addicts with the Home Office (114). Over 100 doctors are currently licensed, of whom fewer than 20 prescribe such drugs (113).

The rate of increase in heroin addiction in England subsequently slowed until the late 1970s, when a large influx of black market heroin from southwest Asia fueled a sudden increase in new addicts that continued through the 1980s (115). This increase was not, as some legalization proponents claim, due to the fact that the British, following the American lead, adopted harsher drug laws. While on the national level, the government responded to this increase in addiction by emphasizing supply reduction, prevention, and criminal justice deterrents, at the local level officials emphasized harm reduction and loosely enforced antidrug laws. These conflicting national and local approaches persisted until the late 1980s, when concern over the spread of AIDS by injection drug users prompted national policy makers to shift towards such harm reduction programs as needle exchanges and condom distribution (116).

In short, the increasing number of addicts in Britain was not a result of strict national laws and "zero tolerance" policies. Rather, these policies were a response to the increased addiction. Moreover, strict national antidrug laws mean little if local enforcement is lax. One celebrated experiment in harm reduction and drug tolerance is less often mentioned now that it has been terminated. Beginning in 1987, Switzerland allowed all addicts and users to congregate in a park—the "Platzspitz," or "Needle Park," as it became known—in the center of downtown Zurich, where they could buy and use drugs freely. Strict enforcement of antidrug laws continued in the rest of the city and country. Like many proponents of harm reduction, Swiss policy makers believed that if drug dealing and use was going to happen anyway, it might as well occur in the open where the police and health officials could monitor it. In Needle Park, public health officials gave addicts free needles, condoms, medical care, counseling, and the opportunity for treatment (83).

This experiment in harm reduction had unintended consequences. The number of addicts in the park increased from a few hundred in 1987 to 20,000 in 1992. Twenty-five percent came from outside Switzerland, drawn to the park by its tolerant policies. Drug-related violence and crime rose rapidly in the area; 81 drug-related deaths were recorded in 1991, double the previous year. The city's chief medical officer reported that doctors were resuscitating an average of 12 people a day who had overdosed, and up to 40 on some days (117). Because of these high costs, the park was closed in 1992, but the fallout from this policy was damaging. The heroin-related death rate in Switzerland had become the highest in Europe and North America (118). Addicts wandered the city streets and open air markets proliferated. Three years after the experiment ended, Swiss police tried to disperse the continuing drug bazaar that had moved to an unused railroad station (119). To deal with their burgeoning heroin problem, Swiss authorities have since begun an experiment with heroin prescription for addicts. That Switzerland's tolerant policy has proved difficult to reverse even after its harmful consequences became apparent serves as a warning to those who claim that we can quickly reverse liberal drug policies if they have negative consequences.

Italy is infrequently mentioned by advocates of legalization despite its lenient drug laws. Personal possession of small amounts of drugs has not been a crime in Italy since 1975, other than for a brief period of "recriminalization" between 1990 and 1993 (though even then Italy permitted an individual to possess one daily dose of a drug). Under decriminalization, interpretation of the precise quantity allowed was left to individual judges, but generally, possession of two to three daily doses of drugs such as heroin was exempt from criminal sanction (120). Today, Italy has 300,000 heroin addicts (121), the highest rate of heroin addiction in Europe (118). Seventy percent of all AIDS cases in Italy are attributable to drug use (121).

In contrast, Sweden offers an example of a successful restrictive drug policy. Sweden has tried a variety of approaches to drugs (though none have involved legalization) since its first experiment with the prescription of drugs, particularly amphetamines, to addicts in 1965. This experiment ended two years later because eligible addicts diverted prescribed drugs to friends and acquaintances and, contrary to the expectation that freely available drugs would decrease crime among addicts, crimes committed by legal users increased.

In 1972, Swedish policy shifted towards harm reduction; enforcement became more lax, concentrating primarily on drug kingpins. Arrests for drug offenses dropped by half and police allowed possession of up to a week's supply of a drug. During this time drug use remained high and heroin use began on a large scale.

By 1980, increasing deaths from heroin use shifted public opinion and government policy toward a more restrictive approach to drugs. The aim of Swedish drug policy, like that of the United States, became a drug-free society. Possession of anything more than a single joint of marihuana was punished; drug arrests tripled in three years. In 1982, Sweden introduced mandatory treatment commitments. During the 1980s, drug use declined rapidly, particularly among the young. By 1988, the percentage of military conscripts using drugs fell by 75%; current use by 9th graders dropped 66%. The population of drug users aged considerably. In 1979, 37% of daily drug users were under age 25; in 1992, 10% were (122).

In short, the claim that permissive drug policies in some European nations stand as a success story is specious when measured against the facts and hardly an example for the United States to emulate.

CAN WE IMPROVE THE PRESENT SITUATION?

For all of the abovementioned reasons, particularly the increased numbers of users and addicts and the threat to our children, legalization would open a dangerous Pandora's box. The claimed panacea—change the legal status of drugs and the problems associated with them will disappear—is illusory. More questions and problems arise than are answered by proponents.

Legalization is a policy of despair, one that would write off millions of our citizens and lead to a terrible game of Russian roulette, particularly for children. It is not born of any new evidence regarding the nature of addiction or the pharmacological, public health, or criminal effects of drug use. At the beginning of the century, the visible results of widespread recreational opiate and cocaine use prompted the first antidrug laws. With so much more new knowledge about the devastating consequences of drug use, it would be foolhardy to turn back the clock.

To reject legal change, however, is not to accept all of current policy. We have not yet mounted an all-fronts assault on illegal drug use in America, a fact reflected in the recent increase in teenage drug use. We should provide equal protection in the enforcement of drug laws by ending the acceptance of open-air drug bazaars in Harlem, southeast Washington, DC, and south central Los Angeles, which would not be tolerated in Manhattan's Upper East Side, Georgetown, or Beverly Hills. This should be coupled with expanded opportunities for treatment (123), strengthened prevention campaigns, and increased research efforts to make treatment and prevention more effective.

Research on abuse and addiction has been woefully underfunded. The National Institutes of Health spend almost $5 billion in research on cancer ($2 billion), AIDS ($1.4 billion), and cardiovascular diseases ($1.3 billion), but only about 10% of that amount on research on addiction and abuse of illegal and legal drugs—the largest single cause and aggravator of all three of these killers (124). If a mainstream disease like diabetes or cancer affected as many individuals and families in this country as substance abuse and addiction do, this nation would mount an effort on the scale of the Manhattan project to deal with it.

Prevention is the least expensive way to reduce the burden of drugs on our society; a dollar spent on prevention saves up to $15 in health care, criminal justice, and other costs (125). An aggressive strategy of prevention should be aimed at the entire population, but with special attention to those currently at high risk of drug abuse (126). Prevention programs should target children and adolescents, because individuals who go from age 10–20 without trying illegal drugs are unlikely to use them. Community-wide organizations such as Fighting Back and Community Partnership Programs should be supported and expanded.

Treatment is both absolutely and relatively cost-effective. It pays for itself over time by saving $7 in criminal justice, health care, and welfare costs for every dollar invested (127). To reduce heavy cocaine use, an additional dollar spent on treatment is seven times more cost effective than an additional dollar spent on domestic enforcement and 20 times more cost effective than attempting to control supply in source countries (128). Still, more research is needed to raise treatment success rates, as well as to discern which types of treatment are most effective for which individuals.

Court-imposed treatment should be expanded and combined with programs that reintegrate the ex-offender into the community by providing continued substance abuse counseling and support groups, as well as education and job training. Treatment and aftercare can decrease recidivism by giving ex-offenders a new chance to become productive members of society. As many as 800,000 inmates have prior convictions. If treatment reduced recidivism by just 20%, there would be 160,000 fewer inmates; a 50% reduction would mean 400,000 fewer inmates.

Mandatory minimum sentencing laws need to be revisited to ensure that we are appropriately using and targeting the scarce commodity of prison cells. Alternatives to incarceration, especially those that coordinate the criminal justice and treatment systems, such as Drug Courts and Treatment Alternatives to Street Crime (TASC), should be expanded.

The objective of a drug-free America, derided by advocates of legalization (8), is a statement of hope that a generation of children can come of age less exposed to the life-destroying effects of illegal drugs. (For a similar statement from Sweden, see reference 122.) Our policies should aim to reduce drug use and addiction to a marginal phenomenon and to rehabilitate drug abusers. At its best, America strives to give all its citizens the chance to develop their talents. Cornering millions of individuals into drug addiction insults this fundamental value and demeans the dignity to which each is entitled.

References

1. Musto DF. The American disease: origins of narcotic control. New York: Oxford University Press, 1987.
2. Musto DF. Foreword. In: Erickson PG, Adlaf EM, Murray GF, Smart RG. The steel drug: cocaine in perspective. Toronto: Lexington Books, 1987.
3. U.S. Sentencing Commission. Cocaine and federal sentencing policy. Washington, DC: U.S. Government Printing Office, 1995.
4. Inciardi J, ed. Handbook of drug control in the United States. New York: Greenwood Press, 1990.
5. DuPont R, Voth E. Drug legalization, harm reduction, and drug policy. Ann Intern Med 1995;123(6):461–465.
6. Schmoke K. Decriminalizing drugs: it just might work—and nothing else does. In: Evans R, Berent I, eds. Drug legalization: for and against. La Salle, IL: Open Court Press, 1992:215–220.

7. Smith M. The drug problem: is there an answer? In: Evans R, Berent I, eds. Drug legalization: for and against. La Salle, IL: Open Court Press 1992:77–88.

8. Wisotsky S. Statement before the Select Committee on Narcotics Abuse and Control. In: Evans R, Berent I, eds. Drug legalization: for and against. La Salle, IL: Open Court Press, 1992:181–212.

9. National Commission on Marijuana and Drug Abuse. Marijuana: signal of misunderstanding. Washington, DC: U.S. Government Printing Office, 1972.

10. Grinspoon L, Bakalar JB. Drug dependence: non-narcotic agents. In: Kaplan HI, Sadock BJ, eds. Comprehensive textbook of psychiatry. Third edition. Baltimore: Williams & Wilkins, 1980.

11. Preliminary estimates from the 1994 National Household Survey on Drug Abuse. Rockville, MD: U.S. Department of Health and Human Services, 1995.

12. Office of National Drug Control Policy. National drug control strategy: strengthening communities' response to drugs and crime. Washington, DC: U.S. Government Printing Office, 1995.

13. Office of National Drug Control Policy. Breaking the cycle of drug abuse. Washington, DC: U.S. Government Printing Office, 1993.

14. Brenner TA. The legalization of drugs: why prolong the inevitable? In: Evans R, Berent I, eds. Drug legalization: for and against. La Salle, IL: Open Court Press 1992:157–180.

15. Zeese K. Drug war forever? In: Krauss M, Lazear E, eds. Searching for alternatives: drug-control policy in the United States. Stanford, CA: Hoover Institution Press, 1992:251–268.

16. Nadelmann E. The case for legalization. In: Inciardi J, ed. The drug legalization debate. Newbury Park, CA: Sage Publications, 1991:17–44.

17. Gazzaniga M. The opium of the people: crack in perspective. In: Evans R, Berent I, eds. Drug legalization: for and against. La Salle, IL: Open Court Press, 1992:231–246.

18. Johnston L, O'Malley P, Bachman J. National survey results on drug use from the Monitoring the Future Study, 1975–1993. Ann Arbor, MI: University of Michigan, 1994.

19. The National Center on Addiction and Substance Abuse at Columbia University. National survey of American attitudes on substance abuse. New York: CASA, 1995.

20. U.S. Department of Health and Human Services. Preliminary estimates from the 1993 National Household Survey: press release, 1994.

21. Grinspoon L, Bakalar J. The war on drugs—a peace proposal. N Engl J Med 1994;330: 357–360.

22. Trebach A. For legalization of drugs. In: Trebach A, Inciardi J. Legalize it? Debating American drug policy. Washington, DC: American University Press, 1993:7–138.

23. Moore M. Drugs: getting a fix on the problem and the solution. In: Evans R, Berent I, eds. Drug legalization: for and against. La Salle, IL: Open Court Press, 1992:123–156.

24. U.S. Centers for Disease Control and Prevention. MMWR Morbid Mortal Wkly Rep 1994;34(SS-3).

25. Moore M. Supply reduction and law enforcement. In: Tonry M, Wilson J, eds. Drugs and crime. Chicago: University of Chicago Press, 1990:109–158.

26. Grossman M, Becker G, Murphy K. Rational addiction and the effect of price on consumption. In: Krauss M, Lazear E, eds. Searching for alternatives: drug-control policy in the United States. Stanford, CA: Hoover Institution Press, 1992:77–86.

27. Farrell M, Strang J, Reuter P. The non-case for legalization. In: Stevenson RC, ed. Winning the war on drugs: to legalize or not. London: Institute of Economic Affairs, 1994.

28. Kleber HD. Our current approach to drug abuse—progress, problems, proposals. N Engl J Med 1994;330:361–364.

29. Cummings KM, Pechacek T, Shopland D. The illegal sale of cigarettes to US minors: estimates by state. Am J Public Health 1994;84:300–302.

30. Preliminary estimates from the 1996 Monitoring the Future study. Rockville, MD: U.S. Department of Health and Human Services, 1996.

31. Hooked on tobacco: the teen epidemic. Consumer Reports 1995;March:142–148.

32. Skager R, Austin G. Fourth biennial statewide survey of drug and alcohol use among California students in grades 7, 9 and 11. Sacramento, CA: Office of the Attorney General, 1993.

33. Fisher WS. Drug and alcohol use among New Jersey high school students. Trenton, NJ: Department of Law & Public Safety, 1993.

34. Peck D. Legal and social factors in the deterrence of adolescent marijuana use. J Alcohol Drug Educ 1983;28(3):58–74.

35. Dupre D. Initiation and progression of alcohol, marijuana and cocaine use among adolescent abusers. Am J Addict 1995;4:43–48.

36. Simmons R, Conger R, Whitbeck L. A multi-stage learning model of the influences of family and peers upon adolescent substance abuse. J Drug Issues 1988;18(3):293–315.

37. Cook P. The effect of liquor taxes on drinking, cirrhosis, and auto accidents. In: Moore M, Gerstein D, eds. Alcohol and public policy: beyond the shadow of prohibition. Washington, DC: National Academy Press, 1981:255–285.

38. Homer J. Projecting the impact of law enforcement on cocaine prevalence: a system dynamics approach. J Drug Issues 1993;23(2):281–295.

39. Wilson JQ. Against the legalization of drugs. Commentary 1990;February:21–28.

40. Bureau of Justice Statistics. Survey of state prison inmates, 1991. Washington, DC: U.S. Department of Justice, 1993.

41. Bureau of Justice Statistics. Prisoners in 1994. Washington, DC: U.S. Department of Justice, 1995.

42. Aaron P, Musto D. Temperance and prohibition in America: a historical overview. In: Moore M, Gerstein D, eds. Alcohol and public policy: beyond the shadow of prohibition. Washington, DC: National Academy Press, 1981:127–181.

43. Statistical release: alcohol, tobacco and firearms tax collections. Fiscal year 1995. Washington, DC: Department of the Treasury, Bureau of Alcohol, Tobacco and Firearms, 1995.

44. State government tax collections: 1995. Available at http://www.census.gov/govs/statetax/95 tax001.txt.

45. The National Center on Addiction, Substance Abuse at Columbia University. The cost of substance abuse to America's health care system, final report. New York: CASA, 1996.

46. U.S. Centers for Disease Control and Prevention. HIV/AIDS Surveillance Report 1996; 8(1):8.

47. Prescribing to addicts appears to work in Britain: interview with Dr. John Marks. Psychiatric News 1993;December 17.

48. Lowinson JH, Marion IJ, Joseph H, Dole VP. Methadone maintenance. In: Lowinson JH, Ruiz P, Millman R, eds. Substance abuse: a comprehensive textbook. 2nd edition. Baltimore: Williams & Wilkins, 1992:550–561.

49. Jaffe J. Opiates: clinical aspects. In: Lowinson JH, Ruiz P, Millman R, eds. Substance abuse: a comprehensive textbook. 2nd edition. Baltimore: Williams & Wilkins, 1992:186–194.

50. Simon E. Opiates: neurobiology. In: Lowinson JH, Ruiz P, Millman R, eds. Substance abuse: a comprehensive textbook. 2nd edition. Baltimore: Williams & Wilkins, 1992:195–204.

51. Gold M. Cocaine (and crack): clinical aspects. In: Lowinson JH, Ruiz P, Millman R, eds. Substance abuse: a comprehensive textbook. 2nd edition. Baltimore: Williams & Wilkins, 1992:205–221.

52. McLellan AT, et al. The effects of psychosocial services in substance abuse treatment. JAMA 1994;269:1953–1959.

53. Hartgers C, van den Hoek A, Krijnen P, Coutinho RA. HIV prevalence and risk behavior among injection drug users who participate in "low threshold" methadone programs in Amsterdam. Am J Public Health 1992;82:547–551.

54. Lurie P, Reingold A, et al. The public health impact of needle exchange programs in the United States and abroad. San Francisco: University of California, 1993.

55. Normand J, Vlahov D, Moses LA, eds. Panel on needle exchange and bleach distribution programs. Commission on Behavioral and Social Sciences and Education. National Research Council and Institute. Washington, DC: National Academy Press, 1995.

56. U.S. Department of Justice. Drugs, crime and the criminal justice system: a national report. Washington, DC: U.S. Government Printing Office, 1992.

57. Taubman P. Externalities and decriminalization of drugs. In: Krauss M, Lazear E, eds. Searching for alternatives: drug-control policy in the United States. Stanford, CA: Hoover Institution Press, 1992:90–111.

58. Hay J. The harm they do to others. In: Krauss M, Lazear E, eds. Searching for alternatives: drug-control policy in the United States. Stanford, CA: Hoover Institution Press, 1992:200–225.

59. The National Center on Addiction and Substance Abuse at Columbia University. The cost of substance abuse to America's health care system, report 1: Medicaid hospital costs. New York: CASA, 1993.

60. Kessler R, et al. Lifetime and 12-month prevalence of DSM-III-R psychiatric disorders in the United States: results from the National Comorbidity Study. Arch Gen Psychiatry 1994;51(1): 8–19.

61. U.S. Centers for Disease Control and Prevention. Youth Risk Behavior Survey, 1991. Rockville, MD: U.S. Department of Health and Human Services, 1991.

62. Cooper ML, Pierce R, Huselid RF. Substance abuse and sexual risk taking among black adolescents and white adolescents. Health Psychol 1994;13(3):251–262.

63. General Accounting Office. Foster care: parental drug abuse has alarming impact on young children. Washington, DC: U.S. Government Printing Office, 1994.

64. Brookoff B, et al. Testing reckless drivers for cocaine and marijuana. N Engl J Med 1994; 331(8):518–522.

65. Marzuk P, Tardiff K, et al. Prevalence of recent cocaine use among motor vehicle fatalities in New York City. JAMA 1990;263:250–256.

66. Institute of Health Policy, Brandeis University. Substance abuse: the nation's number one health problem. Princeton, NJ: The Robert Wood Johnson Foundation, 1993.

67. Drug Strategies. Keeping score. Washington, DC: Drug Strategies, 1995.
68. Rice D. Invest in treatment for alcohol and other drug problems: it pays. Washington, DC: National Association of State Alcohol and Drug Abuse Directors, 1990:7.
68a. Rice D. The economic costs of alcohol and drug abuse and mental illness: 1995. Washington, DC: U.S. Department of Health and Human Services, 1990:4–5.
69. Glasser I. Drug prohibition: an engine for crime. In: Krauss M, Lazear E, eds. Searching for alternatives: drug-control policy in the United States. Stanford, CA: Hoover Institution Press, 1992: 271–283.
70. Friedman M. The war we are losing. In: Krauss M, Lazear E, eds. Searching for alternatives: drug-control policy in the United States. Stanford, CA: Hoover Institution Press, 1992:53–67.
71. Goldstein PJ. The drugs/violence nexus: a tripartite conceptual framework. J Drug Issues 1985;Fall:493–516.
72. Brownstein H, Goldstein PJ. A typology of drug-related homicides. In: Weisheit R, ed. Drugs, crime and the criminal justice system. Cincinnati: Anderson Publishing Company, 1990:171–191.
73. Goldstein PJ, Brownstein HH, Ryan PJ, Bellucci PA. Crack and homicide in New York City, 1988: a conceptually based event analysis. Contemp Drug Probl 1989;16(4):651–687.
74. Tardiff K, et al. Homicide in New York City: cocaine use and firearms. JAMA 1994;272(1):43–46.
75. Chaiken J, Chaiken M. Varieties of criminal behavior. Santa Monica, CA: Rand, 1982.
76. De Leon G. Some problems with the anti-prohibitionist position on legalization of drugs. J Addict Dis 1994;13(2):35–57.
77. Fagan JA, Chin K. Social processes of initiation into crack cocaine. J Drug Issues 1991;21(2):432–466.
78. New York City Bar Association. A wiser course: ending drug prohibition. The Record 1994;49(5):523–577.
79. General Accounting Office. Drug treatment: state prisons face challenges in providing services. Washington, DC: U.S. Government Printing Office, 1991.
80. Anglin MD. The efficacy of civil commitment in treating narcotic addiction. NIDA Res Monogr 1988;86:8–34.
81. Hubbard R, et al. Drug abuse treatment: a national study of effectiveness. Chapel Hill, NC: University of North Carolina Press, 1989.
82. Lender ME, Martin JK. Drinking in America. a history. New York: Macmillan, 1982.
83. Goldstein A. Addiction: from biology to public policy. New York: WH Freeman, 1994.
84. McCoy C. Booze flows back into Barrow, Alaska after yearlong ban. Wall Street Journal 1995;November 15:A1.
85. McGinnis JM, Foege W. Actual causes of death in the United States. JAMA 1993;270(18):2207–2212.
86. Pytkowicz A, et al. Fetal alcohol syndrome in adolescents and adults. JAMA 1991;265(15):1961–1967.
87. DiFranza J, Lew R. Effect of maternal cigarette smoking on pregnancy complications and sudden infant death syndrome. J Fam Pract 1995;40(4):385–394.
88. Office of the Surgeon General. Nicotine addiction: the health consequences of smoking. Washington, DC: U.S. Government Printing Office, 1988.
89. The National Center on Addiction and Substance Abuse at Columbia University. Substance abuse and federal entitlement programs. New York: CASA, 1995.
90. Kleiman M. Legalizing drugs [letter]. Economist 1993; June 12–18:8.
91. Grinspoon L. Marijuana in a time of psychopharmacological McCarthyism. In: Krauss M, Lazear E, eds. Searching for alternatives: drug-control policy in the United States. Stanford, CA: Hoover Institution Press, 1992: 379–389.
92. Gettman J. Decriminalizing marijuana. Am Behav Sci 1989;32(3):243–248.
93. Munson A. Immunological effects of cannabis. In: Fehr KO, Kalant H, eds. Cannabis and health hazards. Toronto: Addiction Research Foundation, 1983:257–353.
94. Gold M. Marijuana. New York: Plenum, 1989.
95. Day NL, et al. Effect of prenatal marijuana exposure on the cognitive development of offspring at age three. Neurotoxicol Teratol 1994;16(2):169–175.
96. Millman R, Beeder AB. Cannabis. In: Galanter M, Kleber HD, eds. Textbook of substance abuse treatment. Washington, DC: American Psychiatric Press, 1994:91–109.
97. The National Center on Addiction and Substance Abuse at Columbia University. Cigarettes, alcohol, marijuana: gateways to illicit drug use. New York: CASA, 1994.
98. Segal B, et al. Patterns of drug use: school survey. Anchorage: Center for Alcohol and Addiction Studies, University of Alaska, 1983.
99. Segal B. Drug-taking behavior among Alaska youth—1988: a follow-up study. Anchorage: Center for Alcohol and Addiction Studies, University of Alaska, with the State Office of Alcoholism and Drug Abuse, August 1989.
100. Maloff D. A review of the effects of the decriminalization of marijuana. Contemp Drug Probl 1981;Fall:306–322.
101. Cuskey W, et al. The effects of marijuana decriminalization on drug use patterns: a literature review and research critique. Contemp Drug Probl 1978;Winter:491–532.
102. Cuskey W. Critique of marijuana decriminalization research. Contemp Drug Probl 1981;Fall:323–334.
103. Kleiman M. Against excess: drug policy for results. New York: Basic Books, 1992.
104. Nadelmann E. Europe's drug prescription. Rolling Stone 1995;January 26:38–39.
105. Karel R. A model legalization proposal. In: Inciardi J, ed. The drug legalization debate. Newbury Park, CA: Sage Publications, 1991:80–102.
106. McVay D. Marijuana legalization: the time is now. In: Inciardi J, ed. The drug legalization debate. Newbury Park, CA: Sage Publications, 1991:147–160.
107. de Zwart WM, Mensink C, Kuipers SBM. Key data: smoking, drinking, drug use and gambling among pupils aged 10 years and older.
Utrecht, Netherlands: Institute for Alcohol and Drugs, 1994.
108. Gunning KF, President, Dutch National Commission on Drug Prevention. Rotterdam, Holland, February 20, 1995.
109. Spanjer M. Dutch schoolchildren's drug-taking doubles. Lancet 1996;347(9000):534.
110. Kroon R. Interview with Dutch Prime Minister Kim Wok. International Herald Tribune 1996; April 9:5.
111. Zion S. Make them legal. New York Times 1993;December 15:op-ed page.
112. Interview with Dr. John Marks. Psychiatric News 1993;December 17:8, 14.
113. Glaze J, British Home Office. Letter to Michael Snell, Esq., British Embassy in Washington, DC, December 30, 1992.
114. Spear B. The early years of the 'British system' in practice. In: Strang J, Gossop M, eds. Heroin addiction and drug policy: the British system. New York: Oxford University Press, 1994:3–28.
115. Power R. Drug trends since 1968. In: Strang J, Gossop M, eds. Heroin addiction and drug policy: the British system. New York: Oxford University Press, 1994:29–41.
116. Turner D. Pragmatic incoherence: the changing face of British drug policy. In: Krauss M, Lazear E, eds. Searching for alternatives: drug-control policy in the United States. Stanford, CA: Hoover Institution Press, 1992:175–190.
117. Cohen R. Amid growing crime, Zurich closes a park it reserved for drug addicts. New York Times 1992;February 11:A10.
118. Reuter P, Falco M, MacCoun R. Comparing Western European and North American drug policies: an international conference report. Santa Monica, CA: Rand, 1993.
119. Cowell A. Zurich's open drug policy goes into withdrawal. New York Times 1995;March 12:A12.
120. Di Gennaro G. Antidrug legislation in Italy: historical background and present status. J Drug Issues 1994;24(4):673–678.
121. Mariani F, et al. An epidemiological overview of the situation of illicit drug abuse in Italy. J Drug Issues 1994;24(4):579–595.
122. A restrictive drug policy: the Swedish experience. Stockholm: Swedish National Institute of Public Health, 1993.
123. Greenwood P. Strategies for improving coordination between enforcement and treatment efforts in controlling illegal drug use. J Drug Issues 1995;25(1):73–89.
124. Office of Management and Budget. Budget of the United States government: appendix, fiscal year 1995. Washington, DC: U.S. Government Printing Office, 1994.
125. Kim S, et al. Benefit-cost analysis of drug abuse prevention programs: a macroscopic approach. J Drug Educ 1995;25(2):111–128.
126. Rosenthal M. Panacea or chaos: the legalization of drugs in America. J Subst Abuse Treat 1994;11(1):3–7.
127. State of California, Department of Alcohol and Drug Programs. Evaluating recovery services: the California drug and alcohol treatment assessment (CALDATA), 1994.
128. Rydell CP, Everingham S. Controlling cocaine: supply vs. demand programs. Santa Monica, CA: Rand, 1994.

83 ADVOCACY: THE VOICE OF THE CONSUMER

Joycelyn Sue Woods

Before the passing of the Harrison Narcotic Act the primary drug problem in the United States was alcohol, as it is today. In the nineteenth century drunkenness was considered a moral failing, a threat both to society and to the growth of the new country. While the imbibing of a bourbon by a wealthy man was considered quite acceptable, it was the poor drunkard from the lower classes that was looked upon as a problem for the community. Opiate addicts were either professionals, housewives, or Civil War veterans and were not perceived to be the menace that the drunkard was deemed to be (1, 2). Although addiction to morphine was undesirable, it was considered a vice like tobacco smoking. There were no restrictions on the purchase of opiates, which was a common medicine in most homes. Most opiate addicts were from the middle and upper classes and should they have needed treatment they simply went to a physician or sanitorium. The alcoholic was treated differently; drunkenness was considered a character flaw that could only be controlled through law enforcement (3–5). Thus, it is not surprising that the first advocacy movement came about through alcohol users searching for a means to stop their alcoholism. This movement grew into Alcoholics Anonymous (AA). The next group to organize on their behalf were heroin addicts, and like AA this group promoted drug treatment. This movement has become the abstinence-oriented modality, today known as therapeutic communities (TCs). It is unfortunate that both of these movements have only focused on treatment and never expanded their efforts to include all aspects of the alcoholic's or drug user's life. It was not until the expansion of methadone maintenance treatment that any group using licit or illicit substances advocated for issues other than treatment. This occurred as a response to the blatant stigmatization and prejudice towards methadone maintenance patients that harmed them and their families. Methadone patients faced discrimination in all areas of their lives, including employment and vocational opportunities, health insurance, housing, and health care.

Alcohol Advocacy

Prior to AA, treatment for alcoholism was not very successful. AA was founded in 1935 by Dr. Bob Smith (Dr. Bob) and Bill Wilson (Bill W.) who together were searching for a way to stay sober (6). The concepts of AA come from the idea that conversations between alcoholics can lead to chain reactions. Their ideas have evolved into a way of life for the members of AA who belong to the *Fellowship*. The AA program weaves spirituality and social psychology into a system called the Twelve Steps offering members a positive lifestyle that works for many. The success of AA may lay in its simplicity, but the fact remains that the program would have never grown to the size it is today had it not been for the tenacity of Bill W. and Dr. Bob. They knew they were on to something and they were determined to help others in the same way that they had been helped. Today the AA program is worldwide but even more important the program has been expanded by other groups to help with similar problems such as gambling and overeating. Today the Fellowship has affected the lives of possibly millions worldwide because of the insight of two men.

Therapeutic Communities

The first TC was established in 1958 when five addicts moved into a house in Santa Monica and "kicked cold turkey" together (7). The name it was given, Synanon, comes from an addict's mispronunciation of the word "seminar." Synanon and all TCs are based on the belief that addiction is symptomatic of a problem, an underlying character disorder that can be cured by removing the addict from their environment and placing them in a therapeutic one that involves reconditioning and reprogramming the learn-

ing process (8). Therapeutic communities were originally self-supporting and run entirely by former addicts with no professional staff because they were suspicious of individuals with degrees. Today that has changed drastically—TCs are big business, and many of the TCs that came after Synanon were started by professionals (7). This has had a converse effect on the original advocacy experienced at Synanon. The original Synanon group believed that there were enough addicts for everyone and that Synanon was not for every addict. But as the industry developed and depended more on government funding, the less these programs have focused on addict self-help and advocacy. Furthermore, their belief that heroin addiction is a character disorder has contributed to the continued stigmatization of heroin addicts and methadone patients, because they have promoted heroin addiction as a choice with no biological influences.

Therapeutic communities saw the new modality of methadone maintenance as a threat to their very existence (8–12). The philosophy of methadone maintenance and the very theory that it was based on—that addicts have a metabolic dysfunction—could possibly have signaled the demise of TCs. Therefore, it was under this self-imposed threat that TCs under the direction of former addicts themselves began their longstanding attack on methadone maintenance, which has spread misinformation, myths, and some outright falsehoods about methadone treatment (10–12). These attacks, which continue to the present, have been a major factor in the prejudice and stigma towards methadone patients. Thus, it was the assault of TCs upon methadone maintenance patients that initiated the first true advocacy movement amongst drug users of licit or illicit drugs.

Advocacy Comes of Age: A Voice for the Methadone Patient

The advocacy movement amongst methadone patients is better understood in context of the growth of the program itself. Prior to the early 1970s the program was small and patients in the program knew Drs. Dole and Nyswander and other esteemed clinicians who had come into the field because *they wanted to help addicts*. This period has been referred to as the "Golden Age" when clinicians and patients were proud of the program because it was the first time that any significant number of heroin addicts had been returned to mainstream society. It was as the program moved out of the research phase and into the treatment system in New York State that the overt attacks began.

Unfortunately, it was the methadone patients themselves who would bear the brunt of these vicious attacks. No feelings were spared and methadone patients were called everything from "mummy man" (13) to "losers" (S. Novick, personal communication, 1996); the literature inferred the most absurd things, including "methadone is a lie" (14) and " . . . permits the illusion of a solution" (15). But the most vicious assaults were publications intended for and distributed to methadone patients that promoted terrifying falsehoods such as "methadone deforms babies" (16). Although TCs cannot take credit for inventing many of the myths about methadone they were certainly responsible for advancing them and thus being a major contributor to continued misunderstandings about methadone maintenance and the stigma that methadone patients are forced to endure.

The First Methadone Advocacy Group: The Committee of Concerned Methadone Patients and Friends, Inc. (CCMP)

Thus it was against a background of offensive attacks that in the spring of 1973 a vanguard of patients met to explore the possibilities of organizing the first methadone advocacy group (9). Within the group were patients from the New York City methadone program, which treated well over 15,000 patients, and the Beth Israel program, which was the very first methadone program and treated about 8,000 patients (17–18). Previous attempts to organize, although short lived, demonstrated the need and ability of methadone patients to organize on their own behalf (19–20). Thus, when CCMP was organized methadone patients were wiser and more experienced; they did not want to repeat past failures. Within a few weeks of CCMP's first meeting a Board of Directors had been named, and an attorney set in motion the mechanisms necessary to obtain not-for-profit status. CCMP's first task was to build a strong organizational structure so that through consistent hard work methadone patients could hope to realize their long-range goals (21).

The Problem Stated

The mid 1970s in New York City were a period of increased community involvement, including the formation of neighborhood and block organizations; weekly community newspapers became an important source for local news. Up to the early 1970s methadone treatment had been praised as the solution for the heroin problem and welcomed by the community. Finding employment and vocational opportunities for patients was at first not a problem; however, as the number of patients increased in the early 1970s the opportunities for them decreased (9, 22).

Methadone patients—of which many were a minority within a minority—were one of the groups to suffer most during this period. A small number of patients unable to find something to do became visible troublemakers in the community. As community opposition grew patients became closeted in order to survive. The image of the methadone patient became that of the dysfunctional patient loitering on the corner. To contribute to the problem many communities in New York City were saturated with methadone programs while others had none. Methadone treatment had grown in two short years from only a few thousand to over 34,000 patients (18). The growing pains were felt most by the patients themselves who now found their lives regulated by rigid clinic rules initiated by legislators who knew nothing about addiction or drug treatment (23–25). Patients found it impossible to live a *normal life*—which after all should be the goal of drug treatment. Drug-free TCs seized the opportunity to proselytize their modality and propagate more misinformation about methadone treatment. "We are good junkies!" they told the community. Everyone seemed to agree: methadone was expendable since we don't have a drug problem in our community—anymore!

Methadone patients who should have been very proud of their accomplishments began to feel ashamed of their enrollment in methadone treatment. Methadone patients found themselves in a difficult position; paradoxically, the "monkey on their back" representing bondage to heroin addiction was replaced by a "methadone gorilla" of stigma and discrimination.

Making Change

Despite the fact that CCMP never attempted a large membership drive the organization was very successful in attracting members. CCMP brought patients into contact with other patients who were doing something about their dilemma. A small core group formed into the Public Relations Subcommittee (PRS), which became the heart of CCMP. One of the first tasks that the PRS undertook was the production of literature, including a brochure and a methadone fact sheet (25, 26). It was important to educate methadone patients about treatment and the issues that were affecting them.

This process of educating methadone patient would be called *socialization*. The PRS would be the first group socialized in order to provide leadership. The process would continue by breaking down the membership by zip code. This strategy gave patients the opportunity to meet other patients living in their community so these groups would continue to interact with the community. Socialization of CCMP members served another function since a significant number worked in the field as counselors, administrators, and researchers as now the patients that they came into contact with could also be socialized (27–29). But the most important function of the socialization groups was a support system, although the decision to reveal themselves as methadone patients was left up to each individual. Some who had already

gone public related good experiences; others experienced discrimination for themselves and their families.

Diffusing the Media's Antimethadone Propaganda

The media's critical view of methadone treatment was not new, as Dole and Nyswander had received sharp and acidic criticism from the beginning. Today, antimethadone sentiment has become acceptable in the media and it is not unusual to see methadone patients referred to in derogatory terms such as "methadonians" (30, 31). The media is a business that seeks stories that will sell newspapers or increase viewer ratings. Unfortunately, successful stories of methadone patients are not exciting; thus, the tendency has been to sensationalize and accentuate the negative.

The situation that confronted CCMP would have been difficult for experienced and seasoned public relations professionals, but there was no choice in the matter: the situation had to be challenged and changed. It was concluded that a response must be made to every negative or positive story about methadone. PRS began a project to monitor the media. PRS developed a strategy to personally meet with the editors of newspapers and producers of television shows. By meeting with methadone patients the media would be sensitized to the impact their negative stories had on patients. The results of these contacts produced positive results, including the publication of several articles and television programs that highlighted successful patients and the work of CCMP (32–35).

Civil Actions

One of the first cases of employment discrimination to come to the attention of CCMP was the famous *Beazer v. New York City Transit Authority* (72 Civ. 530). Beazer and three others were named in the original case and a fifth was later included (36). Their status as methadone patients was uncovered through physical examination and self-disclosure; none were ever suspected of being enrolled in methadone treatment. The Legal Action Center realized that here was the opportunity to challenge the existing discriminatory employment laws affecting methadone patients. The suit would be inclusive so that all former heroin addicts, even those from TCs who had done so much to harm methadone patients, would benefit from it. In a major breakthrough for *all* former heroin users the Honorable Judge Thomas Griesa ruled that, "A public entity such as the Transit Authority cannot bar persons from employment on the basis of criteria which have no rational relation to the demands of the job to be performed. To do so is a violation of both the due process and equal protection clause of the Fourteenth Amendment." Furthermore, Judge Griesa followed up the decision with a thorough nine-day investigation on methadone treatment that focused on the functionality and employability of methadone patients. This report remains the most complete work to date on this subject.

A second class action suit involved the Beth Israel methadone maintenance treatment program, which had been dispensing a new methadone formula in its Harlem Clinics (37). This new formula was very bitter, and to compensate a sweetener was added. The usual procedure involves readying medication weeks in advance; however, the sweetener caused the formula to spoil and grow mold. Patients started experiencing sweating, fever, and nausea, and as time went on they began to miss days at work and school. As it became clear that Beth Israel did not intend to remove the medication CCMP was forced into taking action. Several officers of the organization were Beth Israel employees, and they placed their jobs on the line. In July, 1975, a class action civil suit which would become known as the Harlem Medication Case was initialed by CCMP. The presiding judge, the Honorable Judge Motley, ruled that the continued use of the faulty formula was a blatant violation of the patients' civil rights. Beth Israel was ordered to return to the older proven formula immediately. The following day, after months of frustration and contention, patients at the Harlem Clinics were administered the older and proven formula.

CCMP's Heritage

CCMP was active for only about three or four years, yet the group made many important advances in promoting the rights of methadone patients

(38). Prior to CCMP there was no legislation to protect methadone patients from discrimination. Even though the Beazer case would be reversed by the Supreme Court in 1979, within months Congress would pass legislation that protected methadone patients (39). CCMP hoped to eventually bring together residents from TCs to join with methadone patients and form a coalition of former drug users. This concept paved the way for ADAPT.

CCMP meant different things for the many individuals involved with it. For professionals working in methadone treatment, CCMP was the vehicle to bring about effective changes in methadone treatment with the motto, "Let's bring treatment back to the patient." No doubt program administrators were somewhat uncertain about CCMP and yet they welcomed, in fact supported, many of the changes that CCMP encouraged. Forward thinking politicians and policy makers immediately saw the group as a friend to assist in changing rigid regulations. But patients envisioned CCMP as *theirs,* an organization for the *patients.*

ADAPT: Advocacy and the AIDS Epidemic

In 1979 the New York State Division of Substance Abuse Services (DSAS, now OASAS) sponsored a statewide conference. An important component of the conference was the formation of two organizations, one for providers of methadone treatment and the other for consumers of methadone maintenance and drug-free treatment. Former members of CCMP were invited to the conference as were a small number of former addicts from TCs. The name of the new consumers organization was the Association of Former Drug Abusers for Prevention and Treatment, or ADAPT. Everyone agreed that in order for the organization to have a chance of success it was necessary to put aside all previous animosities. It was agreed that as former addicts each member had basically the same concerns, i.e., employment discrimination. Unfortunately, leadership with the time and expertise to organize ADAPT never evolved and interest in the organization slowly dwindled. However, the providers group was successful in organizing the Committee of Methadone Program Administrators (COMPA). Through COMPA would evolve a national organization, the American Methadone Treatment Association (AMTA).

In 1986 the extent of the HIV epidemic amongst injection drug users in New York City was just being understood (33). DSAS realized the need for an organization similar to the Junkie Bonds or Unions in Holland, which had given birth to a movement of international self-organization among drug users (41, 42). Therefore, along with the assistance of DSAS the concept of ADAPT was revived to function as an AIDS advocacy organization for all drug users. The first director of ADAPT was Yolanda Serrano, whose drive and charisma immediately placed the organization in the spotlight (43).

During the early years ADAPT staff worked the streets *without pay* because the organization did not have funding. ADAPT volunteers went to the places where no one else would go or, if they did attempt to enter, would never be admitted. They worked in dangerous situations, in shooting galleries and vacant buildings, at all hours of the day and night. In one instance APAPT helpers were nearly caught in the cross fire of a street shootout. They helped the incorrigibles—the ones that society had given up on. In addition to working the streets ADAPT was very active voicing the needs of intravenous drug users. ADAPT's persistent criticism was instrumental in opening the first needle exchange in New York City (44).

The Rikers' Island Food Strike

Persons with AIDS faced extensive prejudice and fear in the early days of the AIDS epidemic. It was very difficult for individuals infected with the HIV virus; many were even ostracized by their close friends and family. Drug users who were often already disenfranchised from their families now faced the dual stigma of being a "junkie" and having AIDS. The public was still uneducated regarding the transmission of HIV and many harbored unrealistic fears of contracting it. The police and corrections departments were no different than the average citizen in their knowledge of how to handle HIV-infected persons. Many police or corrections officers were afraid—they wore rubber gloves or even refused to go near any prisoner even suspected of having AIDS.

Rikers' Island had set aside the old hospital building for inmates with HIV or AIDS. The building had not been used in several years, was old, and was in disrepair. It had a roof that leaked, no heat in winter, and no ventilation during the summer. On top of these indignities, the building was infested with roaches and mice, and inmates often went for days without receiving medication. The inmates began calling community organizations for help, including many well-known advocacy and AIDS prevention programs. Although many organizations expressed their sympathy, not a single one helped. Finally, the inmates contacted ADAPT, who responded immediately.

Together they decided on a food strike to get the attention of the press and the authorities who could do something about the situation (M. Bethea, personal communication, 1996). Frank Rizzo (unrelated to the late mayor of Philadelphia) emerged as the leader and articulated to reporters the inmates' demands to be treated as human beings. The publicity over the inhumane conditions prompted officials to respond quickly. The result was a newly renovated hospital building that today houses HIV infected inmates complete with medical personnel. Rizzo would go on to write a handbook for inmates infected with HIV. ADAPT still visits Rikers' Island providing assistance and support for injection drug users.

ADAPT's Contribution

ADAPT has grown into a large organization with offices throughout New York City providing user:friendly services to undeserved drug users. Their programs include a mobile needle exchange, primary medical care, treatment readiness and referral, to name a few. The staff of ADAPT must be commended for their untiring dedication in the early days of the HIV epidemic. They provided the only direct outreach to the addict community without financial support. ADAPT continues to go to the places that are avoided by other organizations. While other organizations now provide HIV prevention services to drug users now that funding is available, ADAPT was the only one serving injection drug users in New York City during the most critical years of the epidemic.

The National Alliance of Methadone Advocates: A Voice for Methadone Patients

In the fall of 1988 a group of current and former methadone patients and professionals in the field began meeting to discuss the possibility of organizing a methadone advocacy group. It was agreed methadone patients greatly needed a forum to voice their concerns. The National Alliance of Methadone Advocates (NAMA) was thus formed, with Stan Novick as the first president (see Appendix 83.A). Hector Maldonado, Luis Torres, and Joycelyn Woods, who were original members of the Organizing Committee, now serve as Vice Presidents. Although a membership drive has never been undertaken NAMA has grown by word of mouth to over 14,000 members. The membership represents not only the 50 states but also Puerto Rico and 14 countries; thus, it reflects the commonality of issues that methadone patients face worldwide. Through NAMA's support and encouragement many affiliated advocacy groups have formed in the United States, Canada, Australia, Sweden, Italy, England, and New Zealand (45, 46).

Methadone maintenance has saved the lives of thousands of intractable heroin addicts during its 30 years. In the United States there are approximately 120,000 patients receiving methadone maintenance treatment. From its beginning, methadone maintenance has been analyzed and consistently found to be the most effective treatment for narcotic addiction. No other medical procedure has received the scrutiny that methadone maintenance has, which gives methadone treatment the distinction of being the most evaluated medical procedure (8, 18, 47–55). Methadone maintenance should be held up as the "gold standard" to which other treatments for opiate addiction aspire, and, yet, despite the overwhelming positive evidence, methadone maintenance continues to be maligned. While negative attitudes affect the effectiveness of methadone treatment in a variety of ways, it is the patient who is harmed and bears the prejudice and stigma.

Methadone Advocacy: The Time Has Come

There are many approaches that a methadone advocacy organization can use to bring about change. NAMA's primary objective is the empowerment of patients. By confronting the negative stereotypes NAMA works to end the stigma and discrimination that has made recovery and reintegration back into society far more difficult for methadone patients. NAMA strives to improve treatment and to make recovery the positive experience that Drs. Dole and Nyswander intended it to be. By encouraging the organization of local and regional groups, NAMA is poised at realizing a network of methadone advocacy groups. By supporting one another NAMA affiliates have begun to make significant changes by targeting issues and working with program staff and community leaders. NAMA's affiliates have all made a strong commitment to methadone advocacy; they volunteer many hours each week in order to publish newsletters, register voters, visit politicians and policymakers, and assist individual patients. Methadone advocacy brings a sense of community and commitment to patients and staff. This is a very important aspect of recovery that has been missing from methadone treatment. The early methadone patients had the feeling of belonging to a community which engenders responsibility to self and others. They felt a sense of ownership towards the program and were proud to be a patient in it. But as methadone treatment expanded the sense of community was lost; now patients stood in line to be medicated, waited to see their counselor, and became something to be done to—not a person to work with. Through the accomplishments of NAMA and its affiliates methadone patients have begun to rebuild our community into a powerful national network.

The Greatest Barrier: Stigma

Stigma, prejudice, and discrimination have become the greatest barrier to recovery confronting methadone patients (56, 57). Securing employment and maintaining a stable, responsible lifestyle is an important aspect of treatment and recovery. But the working methadone patient lives with the constant fear that he or she will be discovered. Despite the fact that they are protected by the American with Disabilities Act (ADA) every year patients lose jobs merely for being enrolled in a methadone program (58). Many of these patients do not challenge their employer because they themselves do not realize that it is illegal and unconstitutional. Nor do they know how to proceed with such a case.

Not only are methadone patients confronted with employment discrimination but many schools, training opportunities, and service programs exclude them, thus making their road to recovery all the more difficult. Yet, the abstinence-oriented former addict from a TC who is cared for in a protective environment with all needs met receives all the accolades. Methadone patients from the day they enter treatment face opposition and oppression every step of the way. It is only because of their determination and strong character that the majority of methadone patients succeed as accomplished and productive taxpaying citizens of their community; they support themselves, their family, and very often pay $250–300 a month for their treatment (59). Methadone patients do not have the cheering squads or community support that recipients of abstinence-oriented treatment have; instead they make their contributions quietly, fearful that their secret will be discovered and that they and *their family* will lose everything (60).

Stigma is also a major barrier for dysfunctional methadone patients who need special services. Their enrollment in methadone treatment ensures that they will not be able to get the necessary help they need. The mental health community refuses methadone patients for treatment of depressive and affective disorders and typically tells patients that they must withdraw from methadone treatment in order to be considered for their services. Patients with a secondary drug problem, such as cocaine and alcoholism, are also refused services unless they too withdraw from methadone. Homeless methadone patients are denied housing or shown the street if it is discovered that they are enrolled in a methadone program.

A Special Case: Methaphobia and the Medical Profession

Obtaining health and medical care has become a serious problem for many methadone patients, especially since most methadone programs have been forced because of reductions in funding to eliminate the primary medical care that they provided in the past. Prejudice and hatred towards methadone treatment, methadone patients, and methadone itself has been given the name of *methaphobia*. Methaphobia has become critical during the past decade especially because of the large number of HIV-infected drug users admitted to methadone programs and the increasing number of former drug users being diagnosed with hepatitis C (61, 62).

The prejudice that methadone patients experience in health care is an extension of the medical profession's bias towards heroin addicts (63). With the passing of the Harrison Narcotic Act the problem of opiate addiction was removed from the medical profession and placed under the control of the criminal justice agencies. The first group to actually be persecuted under the Harrison Narcotic Act was the medical profession: approximately 38,000 physicians were arrested and over 5,000 were imprisoned (64). Medical schools began to advise their students to stay away from addicts because addiction was a law enforcement problem, a message which continues to this day. Given this background such prejudicial attitudes are understandable. The problem has been compounded by decades of ignorance: today the average medical student receives about one hour of training in addiction medicine. This includes alcohol use; thus, methadone is rarely mentioned except for its use in withdrawing addicts from opiates.

A recent study reported on the medical care received by methadone patients who were treated in their clinics compared to a group referred to mainstream medical clinics (65). While 92% of the patients treated on site received medical treatment, only 35% of the referred group received any medical care at all. The authors noted the difficulty they had in finding an off site medical clinic to participate in the study. A number of clinics refused to participate even though they would be paid for all appointments including those that the patients missed. The group stated that the behavior exhibited by the mainstream clinics reflects the stereotypical beliefs that the medical profession harbors toward methadone patients. Health care workers who are methadone patients themselves—and there are many—report consistent prejudices from their coworkers and teachers while they were in school. Very often they *must* stand by silent while another methadone patient is refused pain medication or even their prescribed methadone while hospitalized. A nurse who is a medical maintenance patient (a special program where functional patients are removed from the clinic system and treated by a physician in their office) described the following:

> About two years ago in a Manhattan hospital, I noted a patient that was tied in a restraint. It turned out that he was a methadone patient and was not given methadone for three days. I got very angry and when I spoke to the nurses they brushed the matter off stating that he was difficult to treat and they referred to him as an animal and that it was his fault that he was an addict. I told them that he should be medicated and when he was, he turned out to be a very cooperative patient. I then turned to the nurses and said, "Who is the animal now?" (8)

Another medical maintenance patient who revealed his methadone status to an examining physician in a hospital was faced with an abrupt change of attitude:

> I'll never forget this. I went to the local hospital because of pains in my chest. When I told the physician that I was on methadone, his attitude abruptly changed. He told me that "all I wanted was drugs" and "to get the hell out of here and if you don't leave immediately I'll call a cop." (8)

Many methadone patients have found that when they reveal their enrollment in a methadone program their chances of receiving adequate medical care, or even any care at all, becomes greatly reduced while the likelihood of being treated with disrespect is dramatically increased. This has resulted in many patients not informing doctors or other medical professionals that they are methadone patients. It is sad to say that is very unusual to find a methadone patient that has not experienced methaphobia from the medical profession—the healers who have taken an oath to help others and to do no harm.

Demanding Quality Methadone Treatment

Perhaps the greatest prejudice that methadone patients experience comes from the providers themselves (66). A number of studies have found that approximately half of the programs administer subtherapeutic doses and encourage patients to withdraw prematurely (54, 67–69). Several states set dose limits (i.e., Pennsylvania) but New Hampshire has the distinction of having outlawed methadone prescribing altogether, even for pain management (A. Diorio, personal communication, 1996). One would think that the medical profession and other organizations representing them would protest such interference—except for methadone. Thus, methadone treatment as experienced by the majority of patients is based on attitudes formed by the popular press, rather than scientific studies and evaluation research (70, 71).

Recent studies of staff attitudes have found a profound ambivalence regarding methadone treatment (72). This is not surprising considering that medical professionals, social workers, and addiction counselors receive absolutely no training at all to prepare them to work in methadone treatment. At its best methadone maintenance treatment is viewed as a tool to help addicts stay away from heroin, but long-term maintenance is not the desired result. As behaviorists are ignorant of the pharmacology of methadone, they do not believe or understand the concepts of narcotic blockade and even view the metabolic theory as negative because it gives patients an excuse to remain dependent on methadone (73, 74) (B. Kouny, personal communication, 1995). The behaviorist theory has been the predominant basis for setting policy in the majority of methadone programs despite the fact that there is no scientific evidence to back it up. In essence, physicians' ignorance has handed control over a medical procedure to social workers and other non-medical staff.

Unfortunately, because of ignorance the majority of programs have demeaning policies whose primary purpose is to control what they believe is a criminally inclined, manipulating, lying, antisocial patient population (75–78). Typically these programs place time limit on treatment, administer subtherapeutic doses, blind dose (i.e., don't tell the patient the dose of methadone they are receiving), raise or lower the dose without the patient's knowledge or input, refuse patients medication for punishment, discharge patients for drug use, supervise urine testing, bottle recall (i.e., when the clinic calls the patient must come in with the proper full and empty bottles), mandate counseling and groups, and use the medication as a behavioral tool (i.e., give a urine and then get medicated). Some programs have become so excessive with program policy that every humiliating tactic is used (79–83). For example, one program not only supervises urine testing with a female staff person for 300 patients of which the majority are male, but in addition has a camera in the bathroom and a two-way mirror so that a nurse in the dispensing room can keep an eye on the person supervising urines.

Influenced by demeaning regulations, some programs have removed the medical aspect of methadone treatment from the modality (84); they are easy to spot by the terminology they use. Instead of discharging a patient they "terminate" them, a criminal justice term and no doubt a Freudian slip. Or they call their patients "clients," removing any rights and self-respect that the patient may have had (85). There is no "Clients' Bill of Rights" as there is a Patients' Bill of Rights. Their policies infantilize and humiliate patients. The only intent of these policies can be to terrorize patients in order to keep them in line—never knowing how their behavior will be gauged or if they will be medicated that day or the next. No wonder patients feel disillusioned and ambivalent about methadone treatment when they experience demeaning treatment from the one place where they should feel comfortable and understood.

A large number of programs and state agencies bar or limit qualified methadone patients from working as counselors, in defiance of the American with Disabilities Act (D. Fleury-Seaman, personal communication, 1996; T. Daniel, personal communication, 1995). These policies do far more harm than discriminate against methadone patients; they send a subtle message to the staff that success is defined as abstinence and that methadone patients are not fully rehabilitated until they withdraw from methadone. Policies that besmirch the hard and difficult work of treatment professionals and undermine the philosophy of the program should be an affront to all professionals in the field.

Derogatory inferences and language have even reached the scientific literature. Typically researchers focus on dysfunctional patients (which is certainly important in understanding their problems and how they can be overcome), but rarely study functional patients. This would leave a reader to conclude that there are none. Objectivity seems to be forgotten when such papers are published resulting in stigmatizing titles like, "The Magic Fix . . ." and "It [Methadone] Takes Your Heart!" (86–87). No wonder professionals working in methadone also harbor biased attitudes when such publications exist in the scientific literature.

This is not to infer that there are not good programs operating. To the contrary, these programs consistently find themselves fighting a never-ending battle against an unbearable system that tolerates methadone maintenance treatment as a necessary evil. Unfortunately, there are more bad programs than good (67). Clearly, these situations will not change until patients know what is quality treatment and believe that they are worthy of it.

Creating a Positive Image

By the early 1970s the majority of the articles published about methadone were attacks upon the medication, the patients, and the work of Drs. Dole and Nyswander (88). These attacks have continued unabated and through the years have established the norm in the printed press. Successful stories about methadone patients are not interesting, resulting in the majority of media about methadone being negative (8, 20, 31). Therapeutic communities also took advantage of the situation to disparage methadone treatment and promote their program. The publication of negative media about methadone has become so acceptable that those who publish such slanted information do not even consider the impact that they have on the recovering methadone patient. It has become common for the print media to use stigmatizing labels throughout an article. Today methadone patients are made to feel ashamed of the one thing they should feel good about. As a disenfranchised group methadone patients do not feel a part of society—they feel alone and with nowhere to turn for support.

Through the building of a powerful network of affiliated groups NAMA has begun to respond to the negative media that has become the standard in newspapers, magazines and television. Sensational stories of methadone treatment that has become so painful to the psyche of methadone patients will no longer be tolerated (C. Pearman, S. Sweet, B. Francisco, personal communications, 1996). Local groups now respond and demand that the media portray methadone patients and the program accurately. And individual patients can also respond and demand accurate reporting with the knowledge that they are supported by a national network.

Working for Change Through Education and Advocacy

Stigma and social exclusion have hindered the self-organization of methadone patients (89–90). Because of the bias towards methadone treatment and its recipients methadone patients have been excluded and deprived of many aspects important to recovery. An important principle of self-help groups which prohibit the participation of methadone patients is the belief that "recovery becomes more valuable when you give it away" or, in other words, recovery includes helping your fellow addicts (D. Schoen, personal communication, 1975). Advocacy groups can bring this powerful phenomenon of sharing with others to methadone treatment, thus giving patients the chance to build self-esteem and confidence while experiencing altruism and humanity. Unlike these other groups and modalities methadone advocacy works for everyone. Very often the achievement of methadone advocacy groups not only protect methadone patients but all former addicts (i.e., a class action employment discrimination suit). There are other advantages that advocacy brings to the rehabilitation process. The results of treatment are all the more positive when patients become invested in their treatment and take responsibility for their recovery. Although not an intention of NAMA, advocacy engages patients in the treatment process (91).

Methadone advocacy is meant to comprise the entire methadone community, including professionals working in the field, families of those in treatment, policymakers, and concerned citizens. Even professionals who work in methadone treatment are stigmatized and find themselves ashamed to admit that they work in a methadone program—advocacy is for them too. Thus, the overall goal for methadone advocacy groups is to improve methadone treatment for patients, professionals, and the community.

As the national advocacy organization for methadone treatment, NAMA actively responds to the issues that affect the quality of treatment and affect the daily lives of methadone patients. NAMA's mission is to work towards the day when all methadone patients can publicly come forward to celebrate and state with pride their many achievements. Methadone patients should feel nothing but pride for their accomplishments. Only through the empowerment of patients and everyone working together—patients, professionals, and the community—will methadone treatment begin to gain the respect that it rightly deserves.

Dedication

This paper is dedicated to the work and spirit of Dr. Marie Nyswander whose dream was that some day addicts would be treated like any patient with a chronic disease.

Acknowledgments. *This author would like to acknowledge the inspiration and assistance of the following individuals: John Orraca, Stan Novick, Herman Joseph, Henry Blansfield, Ethan Nadelmann, Elizabeth Khouri, Tom Payte, Ernest Drucker, Robert Newman, Pat Rosenman, Alan Leshner, Richard Millstein, Charles Schuster, Joel Egertson, Jennifer McNeely, Jane Blansfield, Peter van der Kloot, Hector Maldonado, Luis Torres, NAMA's affiliates whose hard work and dedication have made methadone advocacy a reality, and Dr. Vincent Dole.*

References

1. Musto DF. The American disease: origins of narcotic control. New Haven, CT: Yale University Press, 1973.
2. Terry CE, Pellens M. The opium problem. New York: Bureau of Social Hygiene, 1928.
3. Sinclair A. Era of excess: a social history of the prohibition movement. New York: Harper and Row, 1962.
4. de Ropp RS. Drugs and the mind. New York: St. Martin's Press, 1957.
5. Lindesmith AR. Dope fiend mythology. J Am Inst Crim Law Criminol 1940;31:207–208.
6. Alcoholics Anonymous. New York: AA World Services, Inc., 1955.
7. Brecher EM and the editors of the Consumers Union. Licit and illicit drugs. The Consumers Union report on narcotics, stimulants, depressants, inhalants, hallucinogens, and marijuana. Boston: Little, Brown, 1972.
8. Joseph H. Medical methadone maintenance: the further concealment of a stigmatized condition [dissertation]. New York: City University of New York, 1995.
9. Woods JS. The Committee of Concerned Methadone Patients and Friends, Inc. [unpublished paper]. New York: City University of New York, 1980:223.
10. Velten E. Myths about methadone. NAMA Educ Ser 1992;3:1–7.
11. Goldsmith DS, Hunt DE, Lipton DS, Strug DL. Methadone folklore: beliefs about side effects and their impact on treatment. Human Org 1984;43(4):330–340.
12. Zweben JE, Sorensen JL. Misunderstandings about methadone. J Psychoactive Drugs 1988; 20(3):275–281.
13. Yablonsky L. Stoned on methadone. New Republic 1966 August;13:14–16.
14. Markam JM. Methadone therapy programs. New York Times 1973;April 17:30. Cited in Miller R. Towards a sociology of methadone maintenance. In: Winick C, ed. Sociological aspects of drug dependence. Cleveland: CRC Press, 1974.
15. Leonard H, Epstein IJ, Rosenthal MS. The methadone illusion. Science 1972;176:883.
16. The Truth about methadone [flyer]. New York: Project Return, 1974.
17. Joseph H, Woods JS. A point in time: the impact of expanded methadone treatment on citywide crime and public health in New York: City, 1971–1973. Arch Public Health 1995;53: 215–231.
18. Newman RG. A success story—waiting to be retold: methadone treatment in New York City. Bull N Y Acad Med 1993;Winter:135–195.
19. Zito F, Slutskin S, Ippolito M, Patterson D. Organizing methadone patients: problems and prospects. Paper presented at the Fifth National Conference on Methadone, Washington, DC, March, 1973.
20. Bayer R. Confronting discrimination against methadone patients: statement by the Methadone Coalition for Equal Opportunity. Paper presented at the Fifth National Conference on Methadone, Washington, DC, March, 1973.
21. Newman RG, Cates M. Methadone treatment in narcotic addiction: program management, findings and prospects for the future. New York: Academic Press, 1977.
22. Dole VP. Hazards of process regulations: the example of methadone maintenance. JAMA 1992;267(16):22–29.
23. Edelson E. Docs say methadone is failing. Daily News 1976 (May 10);20.
24. Nadelmann E, McNeely J. Doing methadone right. The Public Interest 1996;123:83–93.
25. What is CCMP? [brochure]. New York: Committee of Concerned Methadone Patients and Friends, Inc., 1975.
26. Methadone Facts [flyer]. New York: Committee of Concerned Methadone Patients and Friends, Inc., 1975.
27. Public Relations Subcommittee. Strategy session number 1 [minutes]. New York: Committee of Concerned Methadone Patients and Friends, Inc., September 1975:22.
28. Public Relations Subcommittee. Strategy session number 2 [minutes]. New York: Committee of Concerned Methadone Patients and Friends, Inc., October 1975:25.
29. Townley ACCMP's Work Board. CCMP Newsletter 1975;September:10.
30. Brown J. The methadonians. Our Town 1993 (September 23):18–20.
31. Joseph H, Woods JS, Beresky M, et al. Deviance and the labeling of methadone patients: the foundations of stigma. Unpublished report, 1996.
32. Torres J. The methadone users. New York Post 1975(October 25).
33. Figueroa ME. Group working to end discrimination against methadone patients. Our Town 1975(October 3):4.
34. Figueroa ME. Making methadone a household word people can live with. Soho Weekly News 1976(March 11);7:12.
35. NBC Six o'clock News (Local, New York). Special report on methadone maintenance treatment. Anchor: Tom Snyder. New York, September 8–12, 1975 (5 segments).
36. Legal Action Center. Beazer v. New York City Transit Authority: a landmark decision on methadone maintenance. New York: National Institute on Drug Abuse, 1975.
37. Novick S. How, why and what next? The Harlem medication case. CCMP Newsletter 1975(September);1:4.
38. Cordero A, Orraca J, Canton W, Contonzo C, Gutman J, Novick S, et al. The methadone patient's bill of rights. Paper presented at the National Methadone Conference, New York, 1975.
39. U.S. Supreme Court backs transit authority on refusal to hire ex-addicts. New York Times 1979(March 22).
40. Des Jarlais DC, Friedman SR, Novick DM, et al. HIV-1 infection among intravenous drug users in Manhattan. JAMA 1989;261:1008–1012.
41. van de Wijngaart GF. The Junkie League: promoting the interests of the Dutch hard drug user. Paper presented at the Fourteenth Institute on the Prevention and Treatment of Drug Dependence, Athens, 1984.
42. Dixon J. User self-organization in Australia. Newsletter of the International Working Group on AIDS and Drug Use 1989;4(2):5–7.
43. Woman of the year. Mademoiselle Magazine 1990(September).
44. ADAPT group to give out sterile needles. New York Times 1989(November 28).
45. Woods JS, Novick S, Maldonado HV, Millman J, van der Kloot P. Starting a methadone advocacy group. Journal of Maintenance in the Addictions (in press).
46. Martin BR. The need for patient advocacy. Kick, The Voice of Recovery 1994(August):1.
47. Ball JC, Ross A. The effectiveness of methadone maintenance treatment. New York: Springer-Verlag, 1991.
48. Blix O, Grondbladh L. AIDS and IV heroin addicts: the preventive effect of methadone maintenance in Sweden. Paper presented at the 4th International Conference on AIDS, Stockholm, Sweden, 1988;No. 8548.
49. Caplehorn JRM, McNeil DR, Kleinbaum DG. Clinic policy and retention in methadone maintenance. Int J Addict 1993;28:73–89.
50. Dole VP, Nyswander ME, Warner A. Successful treatment of 750 criminal addicts. JAMA 1968;206:2710–2711.
52. Dole VP, Nyswander ME. Methadone maintenance: a ten year perspective. JAMA 1976; 235(19):2117–2119.
53. Dole VP, Joseph H. Long term outcome of patients treated with methadone maintenance. Ann N Y Acad Sci 1978;311:181–189.
54. Gearing FR, Schweitzer MD. An epidemiologic evaluation of long-term methadone maintenance treatment for heroin addiction. Am J Epidemiol 1974;100:101–112.
55. General Accounting Office. Methadone maintenance: some treatment programs are not effective; greater federal oversight needed. GAO/HRD-90-104. Washington, DC: U.S. Government Printing Office, 1990.
56. Swan N. Research demonstrates long-term benefits of methadone treatment. NIDA Notes 1994;9(4):1:4.

57. Scro T. Let's stop the insanity! The Ombudsman 1995;3/4:1.
58. Joseph H, Woods J. Stigma. The invisible barrier. The Ombudsman 1995;3/4:5.
59. U.S. Congress. Americans with Disabilities Act. Washington, DC: U.S. Government Printing Office, 1992.
60. Joseph H. Methadone maintenance: profiles in success. OASAS Today 1994(Sept/Oct):7.
61. Murphy S, Irwin J. Living with the dirty secret: problems of disclosure for methadone maintenance clients. J Psychoactive Drugs 1992;24(3):257–264.
62. Sobel I. Doctors, discrimination and methadone: a matter of respect. The Ombudsman 1996:5;1, 8.
63. Remember Us! The Ombudsman 1996;5:6.
64. Blansfield HN. Addictophobia [editorial]. Conn Med 1991;55:361.
65. DeLong JV. Dealing with drug abuse: a report to the Ford Foundation. New York: Praeger Press, 1972. Cited in Miller R. Towards a sociology of methadone maintenance. In: Winick C, ed. Sociological aspects of drug dependence. Cleveland: CRC Press, 1974.
66. Umbricht-Schneiter A, Ginn DH, Pabst KM, Bigelow GE. Providing medical care to methadone clinic patients: referral vs on-site care. Am J Public Health 1994;84(2):208–210.
67. Novick S. Presidential notes. The Ombudsman 1995;3/4:2, 9–10.
68. D'Aunno T, Vaughn TE. Variations in methadone treatment practices. Results from a national study. JAMA 1992;267(2):253–258.
69. Schuster C. Methadone maintenance: an adequate dose is vital in checking the spread of AIDS (Director's Column). NIDA Notes 1989 Spring/Summer:3.
70. Cooper JR. Ineffective use of psychoactive drugs: Methadone treatment is no exception. JAMA 1992;67(2):281–282.
71. Blansfield HN. Medical mismanagement in public methadone programs. Conn Med 1994;58(3):161–164.
72. Payte JT. Methadone maintenance treatment: the first thirty years. Paper presented at the Second Summer Clinical Institute, La Jolla, CA, August 27–31, 1995.
73. Brown BS, Jansen DR, Bass UF. Staff attitudes and conflict regarding the use of methadone in the treatment of heroin addiction. Am J Psychiatry 1974;131:215–219.
74. Gordon GW. Methadone maintenance vs. treatment. Prof Coun 1994;August:41–42.
75. Bratter TE, Pennacchia MC. The negative self-fulfilling prophecy of methadone maintenance. In: Martin CV, ed. Basic readings in corrective and social psychiatry. Olathe, KS: Corrective and Social Psychiatry, 1976.
75a. Payte JT. The use of insulin in the treatment of diabetes: an analogy to methadone maintenance. J Psychoactive Drugs 1991;23(3):109–110.
76. Sobel I. Humiliations and abuse: Methaphobia in the 90s. Methadone Awareness 1995;2(8):1, 3.
77. Bolton K. Letter from the editor. Methadone Awareness 1995;2(11):1, 4.
78. Seaman D. Respect. MALTA Messenger 1995; 3(1):1, 6.
79. Blansfield HN. Methadone pogroms in the USA. The Seventh International Conference on Drug Policy Reform Medical Track Manual. Washington, DC: The Drug Policy Foundation, 1993.
80. Wurmser L, Flowers E, Weldon C. Methadone, discipline and revenge. Paper presented at the Fifth International Institute on the Prevention and Treatment of Drug Dependence, Copenhagen, 1972.
81. Discharging (methadone patients) from treatment for drug use. Policy Series. New York: National Alliance of Methadone Advocates, 1994.
82. On the issue of raising a patient's dose without their consultation. Policy Series. New York: National Alliance of Methadone Advocates, 1995.
83. The policy of blind dosing and patient dignity. Policy Series. New York: National Alliance of Methadone Advocates, 1994.
84. Rosenbaum M. The de-medicalization of methadone maintenance. J Psychoactive Drugs 1995;85(1):83–88.
85. Client v patient. Policy Series. New York: National Alliance of Methadone Advocates, 1994.
86. Kleinman PH, Lukoff IF, Kail BL. The magic fix: a critical analysis of methadone maintenance treatment. Paper presented at the annual meetings of the American Sociological Association, New York, 1976.
87. Hunt DE, Lipton DS, Goldsmith DS, Strug DL, Spunt B. It takes your heart: the image of methadone maintenance in the addict world and its effect on recruitment into treatment. Int J Addict 1985–1986;20(11–12):1751–1771.
88. Bayer R. Methadone under attack: an analysis of popular literature. Contemp Drug Probl 1978 Fall:367–399.
89. Friedman SR, Stepherson B, Woods J, Des Jarlais DC, Ward TP. Society, drug injectors and AIDS. J Health Care for Poor and Under Served 1992;3(1):73–89.
90. Stepherson BM. Mobilization of drug users to protect their welfare. The Ombudsman 1994; 1:1, 5.
91. Ford A. Methadone maintenance and patient self-advocacy. NAMA Educ Ser 1991;1:1. Reprinted from COMPA Newsletter 1989/1990; 8(2):6–8.

Appendix 83.A

National Alliance of Methadone Advocates
435 Second Avenue
New York, New York 10010
Voice/Message/Fax 212-595-NAMA
Email: nama@interport.net
Website: http://www.methadone.org

President:	Stan Novick, President
Executive Vice President:	Joycelyn Woods (Managing Editor, The Ombudsman)
Vice Presidents:	Hector Maldonado and Luis Torres
Webmaster:	Peter van der Kloot
Archivist:	Jeffrey Millman
General Counsel:	William Read (Chair, National Litigation Committee)

Advisory Board: Henry N. Blansfield, M.D., Bill Cohen (Publisher, Haworth Press), Vincent P. Dole, M.D., Edmund Drew, M.D., J.D., Charles Eaton, Samuel R. Friedman, Ph.D., Herman Joseph, Ph.D., Elizabeth Khuri, M.D., Joyce H. Lowinson, M.D., John J. McCarthy, M.D., Robert G. Newman, M.D., J. Thomas Payte, M.D., Nina Peskoe Peyser, Dave Purchase (NASEN), Charles Schuster, Ph.D., Alex Wodak, M.D.

Affiliates List*

Methadone A Legitimate Treatment Alternative Organization MALTA
  MALTA Chapters:

California (Statewide group)
Diane Fleury-Seaman and Don Seaman
Marysville (The Founding Chapter)
Oxnard Chapter, Vanessa York
Chico Chapter, Gino Wilson
Santa Rosa Chapter, Laurie Cole

MALTA Representatives Outside of California:

MALTA Sister Affiliates:

PEERS/CO Harm Reduction Coalition Methadone
Advocacy Group PEERS/CHRC MAG

Southern Colorado Affiliate of the National
Alliance of Methadone Advocates SCA-NAMA

The Washington DC Area Coalition of Methadone
Advocacy Groups WAMA

Methadone Awareness Advocacy Coalition MAAC
(ADAPT Clinic)

Patient Activity Group

The Methadone Advocacy Group of Gary T-MAG

Heartland Recovery Outreach & Information
Network He.R.O.I.N.

Clients Advisory Board CAB
Walter P. Carter Center MMTP

CSAC Patient Advisory Group

Detroit Organizational Needs in Treatment (DONT)
   DONT Chapters:

Advocates of Methadone Maintenance of Omaha AMMO

Atlantic City Methadone Awareness Patient
Advocacy Organization AC/MAPO

   MAPO Sister Affiliates:

Association for the Betterment of Addiction
Treatment & Education ABATE

St. Mary's Starter Group

Patient Advisory Board PAB BIMC/MMTP

Methadone Advocacy and Awareness Group MAAG
(Positive Health Project)

Patient Committee Long Island Jewish Medical
Center MMTP

Oceanside Chapter, Albert Woolfolk
Gardena Chapter, Craig Burazin
California Advocates for Methadone Patients
   CAMP (Sacramento Chapter), Eva Reynoso
Oregon Chapter, Richard H.
Detroit: Project Life, Jimmie Perkins
Houston: Gina Calmes
AMMO (Nebraska)

Denver, Colorado
Paul Simon and Wendy J. Ginsberg

Colorado Springs, Colorado
Mark Beresky

Washington, DC
David Monosson

Washington, DC
Hellene Allen

Washington, DC
Arnold Ford

Gary, Indiana
Carmen Pearman

Norwalk, Iowa
Tracy Gilmore and Cindy Bowers

Baltimore, Maryland
"Freddy" Washington, James Carey
and George Reed

Chicopee, Massachusetts
Deborah Worten, PAG
Evelyn Morales (newsletter)

Detroit (Citywide Group)
Pontiac, Beth Francisco and Jon Wilson
Roseville, Kenneth Thompson, William Jones
and Nancy Rose

Omaha, Nebraska
Renee Payne and Judith Ostergard

Ventnor, New Jersey
Katharine Bolton
Producer of Methadone Awareness Newsletter
Phila/MAPO (Pennsylvania)

New York (Statewide Group)
Anthony Scro and Frank Tardalo

Brooklyn, New York
Leslye Blackstock, Deborah Jackson
and Gwen Robinson

New York, New York
(Chair Vacant)

New York, New York
Jason Farrell and Thomas Burros

New Hyde Park, New York
Donna Schoen

Patient's Advocacy Council PAC	Raleigh, North Carolina Keith Dickens
Advantage Alliance 2A	Hulbert, Oklahoma Steve and Karen Phillips
Southern Oregon Methadone Advocacy Group SOMA	Medford, Oregon Ed Barrios and Susie Ellwood
Crozer-Chester SAS Clinic Methadone Patient Advocacy Group	Chester, Pennsylvania Linda Lunny
Philadelphia Methadone Advocacy Patient Organization Phila/MAPO (AMHA) 　MAPO Sister Affiliates:	Philadelphia, Pennsylvania Ellen Seidman (AMHA Liaison) AC/MAPO (New Jersey)
Methadone—An Alternative Treatment to Heroin Abuse Advocacy Group MATHAAG	Trexlertown, Pennsylvania Mary Louise Meixell-Moyer
Tennessee Methadone Advocates Coalition TMAC	Tennessee (Statewide Group) John Mack Draper
Client Advisory Committee CAC Tacoma-Pierce County Health Dept/MTP	Tacoma, Washington Jeri Neureuther
Wisconsin Chapter of the National Alliance of Methadone Advocates WI-NAMA	Wisconsin (Statewide Group) Greg Keller

International Affiliates

Australian IV League AIVL 　AIVL Chapters:	Australia Jude Byrne Northern Territory, Simon Stafford Queensland, Josie Walker New South Wales (NUAA), Annie Madden ACT, Jude Burne and Marion Watson Victoria, Sandra Fox Tasmania (Vacant) South Australia, Damon Brogan Western Australia, Ruth Wykes
NSW Users & AIDS Association NUAA	New South Wales, Australia Annie Madden
Sunshine Coast HIV/AIDS Awareness Project	Queensland, Australia Jenni Brzeski
Addiction Support and Prevention ASAP	Toronto, Canada Lynne M. Benson
International Alliance for Methadone Patients (Sverige) I*N*A*M*P (S)	Sweden Lars Gustafsson

NAMA is a member of the International Drug Users Network

*New affiliates are in the process of organizing in Texas, Chicago, Florida, Italy (2 groups), England, and New Zealand.

84 THE WORKPLACE

Paul F. Engelhart, Holly Robinson, and Hannah Kates

THE VALUE OF WORK IN THE RECOVERY PROCESS

Some of us may be uncomfortable with Thomas Carlyle's poetic assertion that "the whole soul of man is composed into a kind of harmony the instant he sets himself to work" (1). Still, we cannot deny the significant role that work can play both in the disease progression of alcohol and drug addiction as well as in the recovery process. Clients in substance abuse treatment programs realize the contribution that employment makes to their recovery. Research indicates that many recovering substance abusers express a need for greater vocational services than they are presently receiving (2).

Personality theorists from the early psychoanalysts to the more recent existential analysts have identified love and work, Freud's *liebe und arbeit,* as two of the most basic principles of human existence. Their absence can destroy a person's life and, just as powerfully, their presence can save it. Involvement in meaningful relationships and contribution to the tasks of society are crucial to the development of a healthy sense of self (3).

While not denying the equally important role which love plays, this chapter focuses on the role which work plays in the recovery process. In the first section of this chapter, the authors address problems recovering substance abusers face when returning to the workplace and the range of services for facilitating their success. The second section looks at the nature and extent of employee substance abuse problems and efforts in the workplace that effectively address these problems.

Work may be defined as purposeful effort expended to positively alter one's environment. Traditionally, work has been seen as a central component of one's identity. Standard adult social introductions usually begin with responses to two coupled questions. "What's your name?" "What do you do for a living?" Young children are repeatedly asked about their future worker identity: "What do you want to be when you grow up?" Older adults can find adjustment to retirement difficult not only because of a reduction in established activities but because of a loss of their specific occupational identity.

American culture extols the virtues of work and assigns a stigma to the unemployed. In our society employment is a sign of maturity and considered necessary for the independence associated with adulthood. Moreover, our society assigns degrees of respect to people based upon the type of work they do.

While there are different theories on how an individual determines a specific worker identity for himself or herself, most occupational psychologists agree that vocational identity is attained through a developmental process. If we agree with this perspective, then it is easy to see how a disability like substance abuse could deprive an individual of the experiences necessary for a transformation from a nonworking child into a working adult. Substance abuse is a disability which begins before or during early adulthood or removes a worker from employment for a significant period during later adulthood.

There are two basic groups of recovering substance abusers in the treatment setting: those who due to their abuse or other environmental or family factors have never worked, and those who have worked and been suspended from their jobs or fired due to substance abuse. The first group is looking to enter the work force for the first time and the second group is looking to return. Though there are similarities between the two, care must be taken to fully understand the unique dynamics influencing each group's movement toward work.

Recovering substance abusers entering the labor force for the first time may be confronted with poor, inadequate, or unrealistic concepts of what work is and who they are and can be as workers. Individuals who grew up in disadvantaged or unstable homes due to poverty, generational substance abuse, or family conflict may never have worked formally or been raised with close "worker" role models. Employment is seen by recovering substance abusers as foreign and unknown, creating feelings of inadequacy and

fear. Many of their lifestyle patterns and habits are maladaptive and not conducive to work. Adolescents and young adults whose lives have focused on drug or alcohol addiction have not experienced many of the stresses and fears which most people gradually confront in high school educational programs or their first part-time or summer jobs.

In addition to not experiencing these feelings early on, substance abusers have missed the opportunities to develop effective coping skills and strengths, to make mistakes in less significant vocational responsibilities, and to learn from these mistakes, integrating healthy social and personal management skills into their sense of self (4, 5). They lack concrete experiences in exploring specific occupational fields as well as the general expectations and unwritten rules associated with employment. As a result many have false and immature expectations of what to expect from a job or of the necessary elements to build a career. They may also lack awareness of their own values, interests, and abilities.

These individuals arrive at the job market overwhelmed by the enormity of the task of entering the "straight" world and meeting employers' expectations to have already completed the more basic vocational development tasks. Still, a position in the labor force is attractive, because it offers to place them into a recognized position in society for the first time in their lives.

Other individuals coming from the mainstream with an intact background may have come to accept their chemical addiction only when their substance abuse destroyed their ability to work. They were removed from the labor market for a period or periods of employment. Paradoxically, they may now question their ability to handle work demands sober and drugfree. They face discrimination due to employment gaps and poor previous work references. They may lack a career plan due to the unstable and interrupted patterns of their prior employment. Employment for these people is a sign of their restored health and a return to their place in society.

The current job market is characterized by keen competition and advanced skills requirements for even entry level jobs. Regretfully, both of these groups of recovering abusers are often further handicapped by a lack of marketable educational and occupational skills. Either they never developed these skills or they have been absent from the work force for so long that their developed skills are obsolete. Many of these individuals may also suffer additional discrimination due to a history of legal convictions.

Obviously, recovering men and women have many needs as they seek to enter or return to work and reestablish themselves in the community. Comprehensive, specialized services are needed to help them make this transition.

VOCATIONAL REHABILITATION

Rehabilitation can be simply defined as the series of steps taken by a disabled person to achieve fulfillment in life. The process that specifically addresses an individual's work fulfillment and remuneration is referred to as vocational rehabilitation. A further distinction in terms is important due to the specific needs of the recovering substance abusers. The process for many who are characterized by a late onset of substance abuse or who have worked before and are returning to competitive employment may appropriately be termed vocational "rehabilitation." These individuals are being restored to a former level of functioning. However, for those recovering people who have lived on the fringe of society, never having worked before, vocational "habilitation" provides a more accurate understanding of their need to learn what work is about and to establish for the first time effective work behaviors. Having made this distinction, the term "rehabilitation" is used in this chapter to refer to both concepts.

There are three basic vocational rehabilitation strategies (6). The first and most desirable strategy is to remedy the cause of the person's disability by restoring or developing functional ability. For example, a recovering person who is impaired by the lack of current marketable job skills may "cure" this handicap by completing an appropriate occupational skills training program. The second strategy is to enhance the individual's other vocational/educational attributes so that he or she can compensate for the disability. For example, a recovering substance abuser may need to outweigh a lack of past employment by obtaining significant positive references from volunteer positions he or she has held. The third strategy is to adapt the work environment so that the person's disability is not a functional impairment. This tactic is least feasible since the provision of specialized tools or techniques or making physical changes in a work station usually does not effectively rectify the consequences of a recovering substance abuser's disability. However, an example of this strategy might be the alteration of a regular work schedule to allow a recovering person to keep ongoing counseling support appointments.

The ultimate guideline for all rehabilitation and vocational rehabilitation is to provide help so that the recovering individual will become less dependent on external resources and more independent by making changes in himself or herself. With this as one of our guiding principles we can now examine the components of an effective vocational rehabilitation program for recovering substance abusers: assessment, counseling and referral, and placement and follow-up.

Assessment

The first and most crucial component of vocational rehabilitation for any disabled group is assessment. The fourth step of the Alcoholics Anonymous recovery program is a "searching and fearless moral inventory" (7). A similar vocational inventory needs to be undertaken by recovering individuals to develop their vocational plans. They must be evaluated in four key areas: Is the recovering substance abuser ready to enter or return to work? If so, for which specific employment position is the individual best suited? If not, what is the client lacking to effectively obtain and maintain a job? And finally, where and how can these needs be addressed?

The question of readiness for work is multifaceted. As a result the assessment must be ongoing in terms of evaluating the client initially in relation to work in general and then later in the process in relation to a specific job's demands. Obviously, a person's understanding of and attitude toward work must be evaluated. Often, due to their lack of exposure to healthy worker models and their own absence from the labor force, many substance abusers develop an inaccurate concept of what a job will require or provide. Frequently, recovering substance abusers see employment as a panacea. Obtaining a job, they believe, will solve all their problems, help them stay "straight" and move them into the mainstream. Their concept of employment is a fantasy: wearing a suit, having a secretary, going to lunch, and getting a paycheck.

Motivation is a crucial ingredient and unless properly assessed and addressed, will lead to resistance from the client and frustration for the counselor later in the process. If the client is not able to progress to a point where he or she is keeping appointments on time and demonstrating initiative and choice in selecting from available vocational options, then his or her motivation is questionable. Certainly, a criteria for evaluating motivation as well as overall work readiness is the client's chemical abuse status. If the individual is neither drug and alcohol free nor stabilized on a prescribed medication like methadone, then he or she is unable to be endorsed for employment. Moreover, a vocational/educational assessment battery would have little value if the client was abusing drugs or alcohol when involved in the testing.

If the recovering substance abuser has an accurate understanding of what employment involves, is expressing a desire to work, and showing some evidence of this motivation, the next issue is evaluating the client's ability to work. Specifically is the client physically, psychologically, occupationally, socially, and placement ready (8)?

First, is the client physically ready? Are there any medical problems which would either rule out employment or restrict job options? For example, a client affected by acquired immunodeficiency syndrome (AIDS) may be able to work full-time, part-time, or only on a temporary basis depending upon the status and progression of the disease. In some cases, health problems can be remedied. Still, care must be taken to allow adequate time and logical service provision so that the client is not expected to engage in vocational pursuits before stable health has been established. Further physical considerations include issues such as the possession of a stable residence, the availability of child-care if necessary, and realistic travel time to and from a job.

Second, is the client emotionally and psychologically ready? Has the client developed adequate coping skills to handle the frustration, rejection, and criticism associated with looking for, obtaining, and keeping a job? If clinical issues such as denial, transference, or projection are present, have they been adequately addressed? Is the client mature enough to appreciate the short-term benefits of a realistic vocational step as opposed to focusing on the long-term "ideal" job, which may be serving as a fantasized panacea? If further psychological support is necessary, does it preclude further vocational steps or can it be offered in conjunction with the progressive steps toward employment?

Third, is the client occupationally ready? Does the client have a job goal? Appropriate vocational interest assessment can be accomplished through a combination of psychometric testing and individual research. The combination of the two provides an opportunity for a client to be actively involved in the process with greater responsibility for the outcome. Based on John Holland's trait-factor theory of occupational choice, the Career Assessment Inventory, Strong Campbell Interest Inventory, and Self-Directed Search are some of the available standardized interest testing measures. Other tests such as the Minnesota Importance Questionnaire and the Gordon Occupational Checklist are available to help clients see the patterns of their values and preferences. There are even computerized programs such as the System of Interactive Guidance and Information to help clients obtain an integrated occupational profile of their interests and values. Many of these tests are available in Spanish and have forms for clients with lower reading levels.

Individualized research can be done in the Occupational Outlook Handbook (OOH) and the Dictionary of Occupational Titles (DOT), published by the United States Department of Labor. The OOH is a reference work describing the nature, qualifications, employment outlook, and promotional opportunities for general job groupings. The DOT is a specific classification system for the breakdown of general job groupings with descriptions of the exact efforts, techniques, and tools needed to accomplish the typical work tasks.

In addition to an interest focus, an occupationally ready client should possess the specific aptitudes, general intelligence, appropriate math, reading, and writing skills to adequately meet the job demands. General and specific assessment tools are available to help clients with limited awareness of their abilities to determine their strengths as well as to verify perceived abilities. Examples include: the Differential Aptitude test, the General Aptitude Test Battery, the Crawford Small Parts Dexterity Test, the Bennett Mechanical Comprehension Test, and Valpar International Corporation's MESA system.

A client's level of educational skills, particularly in the areas of reading and math, should also be assessed using measures such as the Adult Basic Learning Examination, the Test of Adult Basic Education, the California Achievement Tests, and the Wide Range Achievement Test. As with the interest tests, versions in Spanish and versions for different ages or skill levels are available to obtain a more accurate picture of an individual's functioning. Undiagnosed learning disabilities may be at the root of some clients' development of a substance abuse problem, and therefore, screening should be incorporated into all educational evaluation. Educational remediation services are available through the Literacy Volunteers of America, the Learning Disabilities Association of America, local school districts, and specialized diagnostic and tutorial agencies.

If the client possesses the basic aptitudes for an occupation, does he or she also possess sufficient, relevant experience, academic degrees, training certificates, or licenses to meet the hiring standards and compete in the job market? Does the client have any legal convictions that would be a bar to the desired employment goal? If the client has impairments in any of these areas, referrals for educational remediation, vocational, or legal assistance should be made.

A fourth area to evaluate is the client's social readiness. Remembering that a significant percentage of recovering substance abusers have been living in a "subculture" with little or no exposure to a work environment should help the reader appreciate the importance of this assessment. Can the client communicate effectively, talking as well as listening? Does the client know how to dress appropriately for a specific job environment, not underdressing or overdressing, not dressing to attract attention or make a statement? Has the client evidenced the ability to interact appropriately with coworkers and supervisors and employment authority figures? Observations of a client's interaction with his peers and treatment staff may provide excellent insight into this ability. Does the client possess sufficient self-management and planning skills to ask questions when unclear about instructions and to notify an employer when unable to meet a commitment? A supportive family and involvement in a 12-step program are important factors in determining social readiness.

Finally the client needs to be evaluated in terms of the ability to job hunt effectively. Can the client complete a job application or resume? Is the client capable of presenting marketable job qualities and a positive work attitude in a employment interview? Is the client able to address an employer's possible questions about work gaps and conviction history, or possibly past substance abuse, in a way that will relieve the employer's fears about hiring someone with negative elements in his or her background? Special attention must be paid to the level of work readiness skills in the counseling process.

It should therefore be clear that comprehensive vocational assessment of the recovering substance abuser may require a significant commitment of time and resources. It is essential that adequate time be allowed lest undiagnosed deficiencies surface later in the vocational rehabilitation process. Not only could this significantly delay or disrupt the progress which the client is making, it could also cause him or her to become discouraged and lose confidence in his or her abilities, thereby diminishing motivation. Proper assessment should determine the scope, timing, and logical sequence of the client's rehabilitation steps and services delivery.

An example of a comprehensive vocational assessment resource in New York State is the Work Evaluation & Resources Center (WERC), which is part of Nassau County's Department of Drug and Alcohol Addiction. WERC is a 5–6 week vocational assessment and work adjustment program. The agency serves clients from drug-free residential and outpatient programs, methadone maintenance clinics, and alcohol residential, half-way house, and outpatient modalities. Clients who participate in WERC are already working with a vocational rehabilitation counselor at their treatment program. Generally clients attend the WERC program to verify their aptitudes for specific occupational skills, to determine aptitudes and limitations so that an occupational goal can be developed, or to explore their abilities to complete a regimen of regularly scheduled employment-related assignments and tasks.

A referral to WERC is made by the counselor only after the client has achieved stability in terms of his or her substance abuse, demonstrated appropriate attendance and punctuality in treatment responsibilities, and given evidence of possessing the coping skills necessary to handle the stress associated with an evaluation program.

Based upon case background supplied by the referring counselor and the client's self-report, as well as reading and math testing, a weekly schedule of aptitude assessment, educational remediation, craft activities, and employment preparation workshops is designed. A client usually spends half of each day in the evaluation area where he or she completes work samples that are part of the Jewish Employment and Vocational Service (JEVS) assessment system. Aptitudes covered by the JEVS system include: color discrimination, counting ability, eye-hand-foot coordination, finger dexterity, manual dexterity, motor coordination, measuring ability, numerical ability, form perception, clerical perception, and spatial discrimination as well as the abilities to follow diagrammatic instructions, written instructions, and a model. Results of the testing are directly correlated to the Worker Trait Groups in the Dictionary of Occupational Titles. The Work Evaluator not only scores the completed task for speed and accuracy but also notes the manner in which the client approaches the task.

The remainder of a client's weekly schedule is divided among basic education, craft activities, and employability skills groups. In the educational

remediation program component a client's learning pace and retention rate regarding basic math and reading levels are charted. In the less structured craft activities area a client's socialization skills, creativity, artistic ability, and initiative are observed. Finally through the employability skills series a client's abilities to complete a job or training application, prepare a resume, interview for a job or training program, and communicate and behave appropriately with peers are further evaluated and remedied.

The results of the total evaluation are shared both with the client and counselor together in a feedback session. At this session plans are developed for employment or if necessary occupational training, additional educational assessment and remediation, further medical or psychiatric evaluation and more extensive clinical treatment. In 1988 and 1989 over 70% of the WERC program's participants entered employment or occupational skills training (9).

Counseling and Referral

The basic goal of counseling is accelerated learning. As a result of a proper assessment, a counselor should be able to depict what a client needs to know and clues for helping the client learn what he or she needs to know. A basic epistemological principle applies, helping a client understand the unknown by examining what he or she already knows.

Vocational counseling has four classic elements: developing a positive self-concept, obtaining occupational information, expressing the self in occupational terms, and learning job-seeking skills (10).

The starting point for all counseling is the client, and more specifically, the perception which the client has of himself or herself. A fundamental task for rehabilitation counselors is to help clients remove the stigma of disability that many have internalized. Vocational rehabilitation with recovering substance abusers must address this issue. Many of these clients believe the label that society has assigned them, more convinced of what they cannot do than confident of what they can do. Their histories of failures become a projection for the future, a self-fulfilling prophecy rooted in a negative self-concept or at best low self-esteem.

With histories of missed opportunities and nonsuccess, recovering substance abusers need to be reminded by their counselors of the obstacles which they overcame and the progress made in treatment. Vocational rehabilitation counselors can further boost their clients' self-concepts by extracting from their "street" experiences transferable job skills.

Recovering substance abusers in vocational counseling will generally present one of four major needs. The first group of clients possess no occupational goals and will therefore need assistance in establishing goals. The second group has inappropriate or unrealistic goals, and they will need help in developing more achievable goals. The third group has appropriate goals but needs support in planning the steps and obtaining the resources needed to achieve the goals. The fourth group sees no value in working. Values clarification activities must be the foundation of this group's vocational counseling (10).

Counselors need to help clients integrate their self-concepts, interest assessments, values clarifications, aptitude evaluations and the realities of the job market into a concrete employment goal. Additional assistance may be required by clients to locate the necessary resources and to plan the specific achievable steps to the desired goal. Empowering the client to choose is a central theme in the vocational counseling relationship. Clients will only invest energy in goals which they have had responsibility for selecting. Among the materials available to help clients achieve this integration and empowerment is the Adkins Life Skills Program: Career Development Series published by Columbia University's Institute for Life Coping Skills.

Referral to resource agencies for aptitude assessment, educational remediation, or occupational skills training may augment a client's strengths and may serve as a gradual step in the transition to employment. However, initially such referrals may also threaten a weakened self-concept. Returning to the classroom can rekindle the feelings of insecurity and self-doubt which a client experienced in school. Apprehensions about testing, competition, and acknowledgment of mistakes will need to be addressed by the counselor prior to and during a client's attendance at such programs. In light of these considerations it is important that a counselor develop a client's ability to evaluate not only the general efficacy of such a program but also the appropriateness of the program to the client's individual needs. Is a large or small program better for the client? Is a teaching approach with more hands-on lab experience more appropriate to the client's needs or is one with more classroom lecture?

Obtaining employment is a major challenge for even the most mentally, physically, and emotionally capable person. The basic skills necessary to look for and secure a job must either be learned or relearned by the recovering substance abuser. Moreover, due to their disability specialized techniques and strategies must be utilized for the job-hunting process to be successful. The importance of counseling support at this juncture cannot be overemphasized.

The seemingly simple task of completing a job application or resume can be overwhelming for clients. If they have never worked before, they may feel intimidated by the extensive questions about past employment and education. Even if they have worked before, many clients have poor memory and limited records of the training and job experiences during their periods of substance abuse. Moreover, some clients report that during the compilation of necessary work data they become overwhelmed by negative feelings associated with the failures and incomplete undertakings which were consequences of their abuse.

In general, job-hunting for clients with employment gaps and other stigmatized background elements is a very frustrating process. Equipping clients to handle the rejections and disappointments of a job search, offering them outlets to vent their feelings and providing them with coping strategies are necessary components of placement preparation.

Placement and Follow-up

The National Association on Drug Abuse Problems (NADAP) is a private nonprofit organization based in New York City that provides placement assistance to recovering substance abusers. NADAP has found that for many recovering persons it is necessary to augment the individual vocational rehabilitation counseling with specialized group workshops. These workshops have been designed as "groups" because, as has already been noted, work is public and requires socialization. As members of these groups, clients can be further assessed in terms of their ability to interact appropriately. The workshops also provide clients with opportunities to learn and practice job-related social skills.

The presence of other clients who are also job-searching helps each client realize that they are not alone in their rejections and frustrations. Also, they realize that they are not alone in their ignorance of aspects of the work world and job-hunting skills. They learn from others' mistakes and are encouraged by others' successes. The shared disability of the members allows for more direct peer critique of individual obstacles and assistance in breaking their goals into short-term concrete steps. The group often, very practically, serves as a networking resource for employment leads.

The skills-building exercises in the NADAP workshops incorporate role-playing, videotaping, and the involvement of employer representatives. Through role-playing and videotaping a client is able to see very clearly the strengths and weaknesses of his or her interviewing behaviors. The corporate personnel recruiters who participate in the role-plays provide an excellent "dress rehearsal" for the client's real interview, directly represent employers' expectations of job applicants, and offer clients suggestions on how they can better present their marketable traits and such negative elements in their background as legal convictions, job dismissals, and periods of unemployment.

Handling these elements of the application and in an interview is a major task for recovering substance abusers. Guidelines for the presentation of confidential information are also addressed in the workshops. Clients learn through group exercises that the way information is presented is as important as what the information is. First, clients are encouraged not to volunteer negative data unless it is specifically requested (11). Second, they are trained to couple their admittance of past negative experiences with at least one positive step or change that has occurred as a result of their substance abuse treatment.

Depending on the client's individual background and chosen employment direction, he or she may require consultations with agencies such as the Legal Action Center and the State Human Rights Office. Through such resources recovering substance abusers learn their employment rights, elimi-

nate unrealistic employment options, access bonding, licensure or certification alternatives, and challenge employment discrimination.

Participation in such workshops helps a client develop not only specific skills but also a self-evaluation ability that will help improve presentations on successive interviews and enhance their job performance. Research has demonstrated that recovering substance abusers who participate in job-hunting groups are more likely to secure and retain employment (12).

Faced with discrimination and impairments, clients looking for work have to try different strategies and use as many employment resources as possible: community, city, county, state, and federal agencies as well as specialized placement services for ex-offenders, such as the Fortune Society, and for recovering substance abusers, such as NADAP.

NADAP advocates with large and small employers and trade schools for competitive job and training opportunities for recovering substance abusers. In 1994 NADAP placed over 64% of the clients who entered the program as job-ready (13).

To enhance a client's success in employment NADAP provides follow-up services. A NADAP staff member is available to clients and their employers or trainers to resolve problems that might arise during the initial adjustment to a job or skills development course. Follow-up, aftercare, and ongoing support issues are important from a vocational rehabilitation as well as a clinical perspective.

Support services in the form of group or individual counseling should be available to employed clients. Issues of anxiety, self-confidence, socialization, communication, basic attendance, and punctuality are usually greater determinants of job terminations for recovering substance abusers than lack of adequate skills or inability to learn quickly enough. Clients may need continued opportunities to role-play problem situations on the job and concrete exercises addressing assertive as opposed to aggressive behaviors.

Being a "worker" puts a client in a new role with family and friends. These significant others may be threatened by the client's progress and attempt to sabotage job retention. Coupled with a new job, budgeting money, scheduling leisure pursuits, and attending to daily living needs may also create new stresses for a client who previously had never worked or had been unemployed for a long time. After securing an entry level position clients will need career planning assistance so that they can develop appropriate long-term goals, strategies, and timetables.

Given adequate rehabilitation time, comprehensive assessment, and appropriate services, recovering substance abusers can succeed in securing employment. The New York State Office of Vocational and Educational Services for Individuals with Disabilities (VESID) provides this proper climate and has established a history of helping disabled individuals achieve employment. During the 1994–95 service year VESID rehabilitated consumers with histories of substance abuse at about the same rate as consumers with other disabilities. VESID spends only slightly more money to help a recovering substance abuser secure employment than to rehabilitate most of the other disability groups it serves (14).

A final consideration in analyzing the placement of recovering substance abusers is how these individuals compare with other employees on the job. Two research studies indicate that there are no significant differences between recovering substance abusers and their peers on the job in terms of job retention, absenteeism, punctuality, performance, promotions, dismissals, and resignations (15, 16).

Illustrative Cases

JANE

Jane was a 34-year-old woman who had been raised in an alcoholic home and had a history of 11 years of heroin addiction. She had been stabilized on methadone for 18 months after four unsuccessful detoxification attempts. Recently divorced from her husband she was responsible for supporting herself and her 7-year-old son.

Jane was a high school graduate who had managed a retail business with her husband for six years. She had been unemployed for the past two years. Motivated by her desire to provide for her son, she entered into vocational rehabilitation counseling at her methadone clinic. Her counselor referred her to an employment exploration and skills development group and helped her complete some occupational research. As a result of these undertakings, Jane decided that she was interested in pursuing a career in computer programming. However, she lacked confidence in her academic skills and knew that her goal would require college-level training. She feared that with her existing child care responsibilities, therapy appointments, and necessary dental treatments she would not have sufficient time to devote to school. She was concerned that employment would reduce her welfare benefits for herself and her son. She also felt isolated from others due to her "addict" stigma and was afraid of entering into new social situations.

An initial educational assessment revealed basically strong reading and math skills though weak algebraic ability. As such ability would be needed for computer training, Jane was referred to a part-time tutoring program. She also decided to participate in a half-day vocational aptitude assessment program to address some of her other fears.

Jane made progress in her math tutoring and demonstrated the necessary aptitudes and work behaviors to consider a referral to the state office of vocational rehabilitation. This agency agreed to fund Jane for a two-year degree in computer programming at the local community college. Due to her age and child care responsibilities the college granted her special student status. This gave her priority in registering for courses and allowed her to design a class schedule which ensured that even though she was taking a full course load she could be home for most of the times when her son was not in school. For the other times she was able to barter housekeeping duties for her relatives in exchange for their provision of day care for her son.

Initially after starting college Jane maintained contact with her tutor for assistance with her first math classes. She also continued in primary therapy for support with her single-parenting issues and socialization needs. Jane graduated from college and was able to secure a job with a company that provided her with additional in-house programming training.

JOHN

John was a 24-year-old polydrug abuser. He had dropped out of high school and been living at home supporting himself on his earnings as a semi-professional athlete. The death of his girlfriend due to cancer was the catalyst for his involvement in counseling. His bereavement counselor noted John's need for substance abuse treatment. While attending outpatient treatment, John realized the need for vocational rehabilitation services.

Since John had no consistent work record, specific occupational interest, or sense of his abilities, his vocational counselor referred him to an aptitude assessment and work adjustment program. While there, John received occupational interest testing. The testing revealed John's preferences for manual and technical activities. Additional occupational exploration helped John focus on a position in electronic repair. The assessment indicated that he possessed the necessary aptitudes for such work but his math skills were not sufficient to pass the entrance exam for the appropriate training schools. Moreover, a high school diploma was required to meet the hiring standards of most of the employers in the computer repair field.

John investigated the three local trade schools offering electronic repair training. He decided to attend the longest and most advanced course because of the increased career opportunities it would afford him. John's counselor helped him see that this choice meant more homework than the other programs required and additional efforts on his part due to his math deficiencies. John rose to the challenge and enrolled in a part-time educational program offering preparation for the high school General Equivalency Diploma (GED) and math tutoring.

As a result he was able to raise his math skills sufficiently to pass the training program's entrance exam. He applied for and received government-sponsored financial aid to cover most of the tuition costs. Once in training he transferred the discipline he had developed as an athlete into his new endeavor. John established a specific study schedule and took advantage of every "extra help" session which his training instructors offered him. He secured a part-time, evening maintenance job to meet his general expenses and the tuition costs not covered by his financial aid. He continued his outpatient counseling to help him resolve his grief and relationship issues.

On his first attempt prior to the end of his electronics training, John passed the GED exam. He graduated from training and secured a position as a digital repair technician. After one year he left his first job for a more advanced position in the field. At the new firm he received specialized training on a unique piece of technology and became a troubleshooter and trainer of new staff.

IMPEDIMENTS TO VOCATIONAL REHABILITATION SERVICE DELIVERY

The federal government has joined with state and local governments in endorsing the connection between work and recovery. This is evident in their policy developments and antidiscrimination legislation. This extends to funding provisions for training and job opportunities for recovering substance abusers (17). Certainly the Rehabilitation Act of 1973 serves as a cornerstone for the legal rights and public opportunities available to individuals with disabilities (18).

However, it is naive to believe that this support alone guarantees vocational rehabilitation services to those who need and desire it. There are three major categories of hindrances to effective provision and utilization of these services by recovering substance abusers: the clients themselves, the programs that treat them, and the society to which they return (19).

Clients who have been addicted to drugs and/or alcohol typically suffer with multiple impairments: poor health, AIDS or AIDS-related complex (ARC), psychological limitations, educational deficits, vocational development deficiencies, conviction records, family problems, day care needs, and/or public assistance dependency. These factors affect the nature, pace, scope, and objectives of a client's vocational rehabilitation. As has already been outlined, careful, comprehensive assessment and appropriate remediation, compensation, or adaptation require significant commitments of time and energy to overcome these various problems. Some clients are too discouraged and alienated to persist in the process.

Treatment program obstacles can be examined in terms of the themes of philosophy and staffing. Historically, vocational rehabilitation, if considered at all by substance abuse treatment programs, has been seen as an adjunct, ancillary part of the recovery process. There is a significant lack of research addressing the vocational rehabilitation of substance abusers. This is indicative of the low priority and concern which treatment professionals in general have for this component of treatment (20). In most residential facilities the last few weeks or last few months at best are devoted to job placement referrals. In methadone and other outpatient treatment modalities there are usually no vocational rehabilitation services on site and only limited contact with educational/vocational resource agencies (21).

Many believe that the basic premise of most treatment programs is that if a client stops abusing drugs and alcohol then everything will fall into place and all things are possible. This principle is much too simplistic. Regretfully, clients accept this false expectation and find themselves returning to their communities without the knowledge and skills needed to function independently and achieve stability. Vocational rehabilitation is the treatment which helps these individuals develop much of this knowledge and many of these skills.

Unfortunately, a philosophical orientation toward vocational rehabilitation that downplays its contribution to the treatment process has translated into reduced staff resources available for such services. The drug and alcohol treatment field in general suffers from staff shortages and high turnover. The low pay, insufficient advancement opportunities, concerns about AIDS, and the frustrations and burnout associated with serving multidisabled clients have reduced the appeal of positions in substance abuse treatment (22). Faced with this reality treatment program administrators knowingly or unknowingly diminish the status of vocational rehabilitation services. If they can afford the time, effort, and funds to hire a vocational rehabilitation counselor, it is usually a last priority in their hiring hierarchy, offering lower salaries than most clinical positions, unrealistic caseloads, less than full-time opportunities, or combined responsibilities, e.g., general program intake and vocational counseling.

Due to these factors, personnel with limited vocational rehabilitation skills may be hired. Research has shown that less trained rehabilitation counselors provide less efficient, less cost-effective, and less successful delivery of vocational rehabilitation services (23). Certainly the multiple disabilities with which many recovering substance abusers suffer require highly trained counseling staff. Without such staff the integrity of the rehabilitation services provided to recovering substance abusers is compromised.

Societal obstacles are probably the most difficult to overcome because of the prevalent ignorance and fear which are at their roots. Recovering substance abusers suffer from the same degrees of employment discrimination as many other disabled individuals and ex-offenders. The fear about AIDS has been generalized to label all substance abusers and increase the stigma they already bear.

The discrimination which recovering substance abusers confront in the employment market is discouraging enough. Regretfully, they are also frequently faced with discrimination and misunderstanding by agencies in the social services system which supposedly exist to help them. This includes the disincentives to competitive employment imposed by public assistance guidelines as well as insensitive, illogical, and often contradictory eligibility criteria for counseling, educational remediation, training, and job placement assistance.

Is formal entry-level employment with limited or no fringe benefits attractive to a recovering substance abuser if it means surrendering the Medicaid which covers the cost of his or her treatment as well as the health insurance costs of his or her family? Substance abusers with psychiatric histories are often refused entry into substance abuse treatment programs because these programs do not provide psychiatric counseling and supervision. These same clients are refused entry into psychiatric facilities because of their substance abuse.

A similar, if not more extreme situation exists for physically disabled substance abusers who are often rejected by substance abuse treatment programs who cannot accommodate some of their special needs and are uneasy about how to treat these clients. Rehabilitation treatment programs for the physically disabled are just beginning to acknowledge that they may have clients with substance abuse problems and often cannot provide adequate substance abuse treatment for them.

Pregnant abusers are also ineligible for many programs because they are not designed to handle the needs of expectant mothers. Even clients who are functioning appropriately on monitored methadone dosages find it difficult to access many of the support services available to other substance abusers because they are not considered "drug free."

Against such obstacles even the most motivated client may lose hope that he or she can succeed in his or her employment recovery.

IMPROVING VOCATIONAL REHABILITATION SERVICES

The past three decades of providing vocational rehabilitation services to men and women recovering from drug and alcohol abuse point to three guidelines for improving these services: understanding, expansion, and coordination.

Regretfully, there will probably always be new drugs surfacing which carry with them certain unique vocational impairments. These impairments will need to be examined as they become evident and new rehabilitation strategies and resources developed to address them. However, we now have an understanding of the depth and scope which substance abuse has on an individual's vocational development and of the basic rehabilitation principles to apply. Most recovering substance abusers can make progress if they are allowed to do so in a slow, gradual manner with a full complement of support services. While it may be too strong to say that relapse is frequently part of the recovery process, we know that it is a reality for many clients. This is true in terms of a client's vocational development as well. It is not necessarily a neat progression but one that may be characterized by false starts and occasional steps backward. For some, due to the chronic nature of their substance abuse histories and the multiple handicaps they have, competitive or full-time employment may not be a realistic goal. For others it will only be appropriate as a very long-term goal.

In keeping with these characteristics we must adopt more of a mental health model of rehabilitation as opposed to a medical one. We must acknowledge this understanding in the design of vocational programs and in the expectations about working that we communicate to clients.

The second theme for future vocational rehabilitation is expansion. This means adding new services, but it also means expanding existing roles to involve more segments of society in the delivery of vocational rehabilitation services. If we acknowledge the need of recovering substance abusers for gradual movement from not working to working, then we must provide more work adjustment and transitional employment opportunities. These may include noncompetitive sheltered or semisheltered workshops that are available to other disability groups. Supported work programs for recovering substance abusers have been shown to increase levels of employment and income and to reduce arrests and jail time (24, 25). New programs alone, however, are not sufficient to meet the vocational rehabilitation needs of recovering substance abusers.

Employers in the United States are confronting a shrinking labor force of educated, skilled workers. Certainly the drug crisis is contributing to this deficit. Employers must respond with programs that offer alternatives to substance abuse and nourish the vocational development of recovering individuals who are looking for new positions or for a healthy return to their former jobs. Included must be nondiscriminatory hiring practices, business-sponsored training, transitional and noncompetitive work opportunities, and job maintenance and support services. At the very least, employers must be willing to abide by the current legislation addressing these issues. The Americans with Disabilities Act (ADA) specifically extends antidiscrimination treatment and employment policies to individuals with drug and alcohol problems and affected by the AIDS virus. While not protecting current users of illegal drugs, the ADA generally safeguards individuals with a history of substance abuse who have completed or are enrolled in treatment. For example, the ADA dictates that accommodations be made in the work schedule of a recovering individual to allow him or her to attend a treatment program, unless such an accommodation would create undue hardship for the employer (26).

Researchers, as well, must become more involved in examining the vocational rehabilitation of recovering substance abusers. They can help to better delineate specific needs of these individuals and enhance the design of effective interventions and strategies.

Finally, for there to be effective vocational rehabilitation of recovering substance abusers, there needs to be increased coordination of relevant services. Drug and alcohol prevention programs need to include career exploration, educational remediation, occupational skills training, and work adjustment experiences into their services. Treatment programs must integrate comprehensive educational/vocational services into the early, middle, and late stages of their clinical treatment. Staff of these programs should familiarize themselves with existing vocational rehabilitation resources and adapt their program procedures to allow clients to avail themselves of these services. Just as a placement specialist working with a recovering person must be aware of the client's clinical needs and progress so must a treatment counselor be aware of the client's vocational impairments and efforts at remedying or compensating for them. Treatment staff must be trained in the basic principles of vocational assessment so that while clients are in their care they can at least refer them to appropriate agencies which can prepare them for employment and independent living outside treatment.

In addition to the expected increases in employment, it appears from recent research that vocational rehabilitation programs are one of the psychosocial support services which can be effective in reducing drug use (27). Clearly such outcomes justify the costs associated with integrating these components into substance abuse treatment programs.

Work dignifies us as human beings. Unless we provide men and women recovering from substance abuse with support and opportunities to achieve this dignity, to earn a place in society, then we should not fault them for taxing our welfare system, straining our criminal justice system, and perpetuating a destructive subculture.

SUBSTANCE ABUSE AT THE WORKPLACE

This section addresses the scope and nature of substance abuse in the workplace and discusses efforts to effectively address the problem among employees.

While there is widespread agreement that employment is an ultimate goal in the vocational rehabilitation of the recovering substance abuser, it is also generally acknowledged that significant alcohol and drug abuse problems exist among employees at the workplace. The actual extent of substance abuse problems in the workplace and their cost to industry are difficult to measure and are probably underestimated. A variety of factors, some related to the very nature of alcoholism and addiction, contribute to difficulty in determining the scope of the problem.

For example, many problem drinkers and alcoholics are able to function adequately at their jobs. Problems may not be detected at least at the early stages of their disease. This is equally true of employees with other drug abuse and addiction problems. Unfortunately it is often at the late stages of alcoholism or other addiction, when control can no longer be sustained, that the problem becomes apparent at the workplace. The very nature of an employee's work may also contribute to difficulty in detecting a problem. For example, any kind of deviant behavior reflected by an employee would be hard to detect in a position which has low visibility and unclear production goals.

In addition, despite growing awareness and generally more constructive responses, there is still a stigma felt by many individuals attached to having a substance abuse problem. While undoubtedly felt less strongly in companies which have adopted nonpunitive drug and alcohol policies, this stigma and fear of job loss may nevertheless prevent a substance abuser from self-revealing or self-referring for help or even self-reporting in a survey where anonymity is assured.

Finally, contributing to the difficulty in determining the exact extent of the problem in the workplace are the supervisors and coworkers of the substance abusing employee. They may cover up for the worker's inadequate job performance even performing tasks themselves that are in fact the substance abuser's responsibility. In addition, many supervisors have difficulty confronting the employee whose job performance is unacceptable. While well intended, covering up and not confronting an employee feed into the employee's probably already well-developed denial that there is a problem. Such enabling behavior actually allows the alcoholism or addiction to progress further. These same supervisors probably underutilize existing company programs designed to help the substance-abusing employee. It is apparent that supervisors play a very critical role in implementing effective drug and alcohol abuse policy and programs.

Despite the difficulties inherent in acquiring accurate measures, surveys have been conducted and estimates of the extent of workplace substance abuse reflect the problem to be of alarming proportions. Data from the preliminary estimates from the 1994 National Household Survey on Drug Abuse states that 74% of all current illicit drug users aged 18 and older (8.0 million adults) were employed (28).

The 1993 National Household Survey on Drug Abuse states that the employed group reported higher levels of alcohol use than the unemployed group; these differences were significant only among 18–25 year olds in past year and past month use and among 26–34 year olds in lifetime (29). Research indicates that alcohol remains the primary drug of abuse in the workplace, adding that the problem is often one of polydrug abuse, i.e., employees taking a mixture of substances which include legal drugs including alcohol with illegal substances (30).

The Alcohol, Drug Abuse, and Mental Health Administration estimates that alcohol and drug abuse cost nearly $100 billion in lost productivity each year (31). In a survey of 273 human resource executives from Fortune 1000 companies and state governments, respondents indicated that employees with substance abuse problems are absent from two to six times as often as other employees. These same executives estimated that among substance abusers, absenteeism, worksite accidents, and disciplinary problems occurred from two to ten times the average for other employees. They also noted that the misuse of alcohol and drugs significantly affected their organizations as evidenced by increased absenteeism, decreased productivity, and increased medical benefit claims (32).

Other factors that may contribute to the direct and indirect costs of substance abuse in the workplace include increased disability and workers' compensation benefits; time to handle disciplinary and grievance proceedings; turnover, recruiting, and training costs; and lower employee morale.

JOB PERFORMANCE AND SUBSTANCE ABUSE

That there is a relationship between substance abuse and performance is unquestionable; it is the premise upon which many companies' successful Employee Assistance Programs (EAPs) have been established. However, the specific nature of the relationship between alcohol and other drugs and performance is complicated. The effects of drugs vary considerably from one individual to another and even within the same individual on different occasions. There are many variables that influence one's behavioral response to a particular drug. Physiological (age, weight, sex, disease state), pharmacological (type of drug, route and time of administration, tolerance, pharmacokinetics) and psychological (behavioral toxicity, emotional state, situational variables) factors all play a role in determining how an individual will respond to a drug.

However, despite the complexities involved in determining the effects of drugs on human performance there are some generalities that can be drawn. The effects of drugs on performance are dose dependent, i.e., the higher doses of drugs generally produce greater effects. Simple motor tasks (e.g., painting the hull of a ship) are less affected by drugs than complex, cognitive tasks (e.g., flying a jet aircraft).

Repetitive work is less affected than work requiring learning or coping skills. For example, driving a car is a fairly well-learned skill, and driving back and forth between work and home is generally a repetitive, fairly mechanical task involving little cognitive effort or concentration. However, the danger of driving under the influence involves those situations where suddenly coping skills, which are significantly impaired by minimal effects of drugs, are called upon as would happen when a child suddenly went in front of the car. Employees in jobs involving repetitive tasks with heavy equipment may encounter similar situations where suddenly coping skills need to be called into action. Finally, the duration of drug effects depends on the task being performed. Individuals resume normal functioning more quickly with simple tasks but cannot handle more complex cognitive tasks for much longer periods of time (33). For example, in a study on the effects of marihuana on pilots, Yesavage demonstrated that 24 hours after smoking a single 2% marihuana cigarette pilots were able to take off, level off, and perform various tasks in a simulator. However, they were unable to land the aircraft properly, a critical part of their job (34).

INDUSTRY'S RESPONSE TO SUBSTANCE ABUSE: A BRIEF HISTORY

Gradually industry has recognized and responded to the impact of substance abuse on the organization and its employees. The worksite has provided a unique opportunity to address these problems. Initially the focus of company policy and programs was on alcoholism. There is a long history of efforts by industry to address problems of alcoholism among employees. In the 1940s three developments precipitated alcohol abuse to surface as a major concern in the industrial sector. First was the founding and growth of Alcoholics Anonymous (AA). Second, respected and dedicated medical directors in companies came to initiate and support programs. Finally, World War II created a unique labor market. Lack of a better qualified work force forced employers to hire marginal, inexperienced workers during a time of unprecedented demand for mass production of war material. Consecutive work shifts exacerbated alcoholism and alcohol abuse already problematic for many of these marginal workers. Productivity and safety concerns precipitated interest in "occupational programming"; these alcohol-specific programs were the precursors of modern EAPs. To help integrate these marginal workers into the workplace the government funded hundreds of mental health and social service programs in industry. After the war the majority of these mental health programs shut down.

Of longer lasting impact were industrial alcoholism programs which also started during World War II. These programs used the prospect of job loss because of unsatisfactory job performance along with the offer of rehabilitation to motivate problem drinkers to change: to choose treatment, become sober, and improve their job performance. Early industrial alcoholism programs were informal arrangements generally involving teamwork between the company's "occupational physician" and dedicated members of AA who would approach employees suspected of having drinking problems. Gradually some companies developed this informal arrangement into a formal policy and program. The policy generally stated that alcoholism is a disease and emphasized the company's willingness to help alcoholics.

After the war, the Yale Center for Alcohol Studies promoted industrial alcoholism programs among business and labor leaders. By the mid 1950s about 50–60 such programs existed in American industry. In 1959, the National Council on Alcoholism (NCA) began marketing industrial alcoholism programs. Lewis F. Presnall, NCA's industrial consultant, began advocating broad-based programs to help alcoholic and other troubled employees and to train supervisors to observe deteriorating job performance and effectively use a strategy developed by Harrison M. Trice called the constructive confrontation. Effective interventions today are still largely based on observing and documenting deteriorating job performance and constructively confronting the employee.

The Hughes Act in 1970 and the subsequent establishment in 1971 of the National Institute on Alcohol Abuse and Alcoholism (NIAAA) contributed greatly to the advancement of EAPs. The Institute believed that alcoholism was the most prevalent personal problem among employees and that the workplace was the most effective place to identify, motivate, and provide for the treatment of alcoholics.

In 1972, to promote EAPs, NIAAA funded two occupational program consultants (OPCs) in each state. Many of the occupational program consultants were recruited from the mental health occupations, i.e., psychologists and social workers. Thus, the OPCs split into two groups, the alcoholism constituency and the mental health constituency. Both groups agreed that addressing an employee's problems would improve job performance but differed in their emphasis. The alcoholism constituency emphasized the importance of treating alcoholism and of supervisors' use of constructive confrontation to motivate the alcoholic employee. The mental health constituency emphasized the importance of treating all personal problems equally, de-emphasized the constructive confrontation strategy, and prompted employees to seek help from the EAP on their own initiative.

EAPs MULTIPLY

Despite the growing pains experienced by EAPs in developing a clear and distinctive identity, there has been tremendous growth of these programs in the past two decades. Between 1971 and 1980 OPC efforts contributed to increasing the number of programs in the United States from 350 to an estimated 5000. By 1981 the success of these programs spawned 200 private EAP consulting services (35, 36).

From 1980 to 1990 the estimated number of EAPs grew from 5,000 to 20,000. From 1980 to 1990 the estimated number of employees covered by EAPs grew from 12% to over 35%. A survey of Employer Anti-drug Programs released by the Bureau of Labor Statistics in January, 1989, reflects that the probability of an employee having access to an EAP increases as a function of establishment size ranging from 4.2% in the smallest to 86.8% in the largest companies. Another reflection of the significant growth in the EAP field is that from 1980 to 1990 the membership of the Employee Assistance Professionals Association (EAPA, formerly ALMACA, the Association of Labor-Management Administrators and Consultants on Alcoholism) grew from 1,500 to 6,000 (31, 37).

Why do employers adopt EAPs? According to research using both quantitative and qualitative methods the answer is that "programs are adopted because employers believe that helping employees to solve their personal problems is good business and demonstrates social responsibility" (35, p. 6).

In a more recent survey of 1238 EAPs, preliminary findings suggest that organizations adopt EAPs for the following reasons: a large majority want to help troubled employees; about 70% see EAPs as an employee benefit; over 50% want to relieve supervisors of dealing with employees' problems; over 40% see them as health care containment; and about 30% hope to avoid litigation (38).

The fact that a large majority of those surveyed want to help troubled employees may also be a reflection of the reduced stigma attached to substance abuse problems. The disease concept of alcoholism and other chemical dependencies has made a significant inroad in replacing the concept of the character flaw. Also, today very few business people have not been touched personally or by family members, friends, and business associates who have had to struggle with alcohol and other drug problems.

Another possible reason for companies adopting EAPs is because they work. For example, a comparison of more than 700 substance abuse patients who worked full time during the year before and the year after treatment showed a marked reduction in job absenteeism, performance problems such as making mistakes and incomplete work, and interpersonal problems (39).

Finally employers may adopt EAPs because they believe they work. Some employers adopted EAPs because they believed they were cost effective whether or not they had empirical data to support this. Conversely employers who have not adopted EAPs reject the idea that programs are cost effective. This difference appears to be largely in the underlying ideologies of employers (35).

Supporting this observation is the fact that in the earlier cited survey of Fortune 1000 companies, governors, and mayors 80% of the CEOs and government officials were satisfied with how their EAPs were addressing substance abuse among employees. They held this belief despite the fact that very few of their organizations systematically evaluated the effectiveness of their programs and therefore they had no information to support the notion that programs were working (32).

EFFECTIVE EAPs

EAPs Defined

Standards for Employee Assistance Programs, published in 1990 by the Employee Assistance Professionals Association, identifies the core ingredients of EAPs and professional standards for carrying them out. It defines EAPs as worksite-based programs which are designed to assist in the identification and resolution of productivity problems associated with employees impaired by personal concerns which may adversely affect employee job performance. Personal concerns may include but not be limited to: health, marital, family, financial, alcohol, drug, legal, emotional, stress, or other personal concerns (40). EAPs are worksite-based intervention programs designed to help employees identify and address personal concerns which may be affecting job performance.

Needs Assessment

These definitions reflect today's more popular broad-based EAP. However, there are no "cookie-cutters" for EAPs. Each program should take into account the unique milieu of each work organization and the needs of its employees. Balzer and Pargament describe the value of conducting a needs assessment and outline a manageable process for doing this. A good needs assessment maximizes the chances of successfully matching the needs of the organization and its employees with an EAP (41). Employers who need help in conducting a needs assessment and establishing an EAP should contact their local chapter of the EAPA. Another helpful resource is the National Institute on Drug Abuse's Drug-Free Workplace Helpline (1-800-967-5752).

EAP Objectives

In its program standards, EAPA describes three general EAP objectives. First, the EAP provides the company, its employees, and families with a broad range of services that may affect job performance. Second, it provides a resource to management and labor for interventions with employees whose personal problems are affecting their job performance. Third, it "effectively, efficiently and professionally provides assessment, referral and follow-up services for mental health, alcohol and other drug related problems in the workforce" (40, p. B).

Advisory Committee and Clear Policy

Critical to effective EAPs is the development and implementation of a clear policy. This policy should be developed by an advisory committee representing different levels of management and labor groups in the company. "Program acceptance and utilization is directly related to the amount of support from top management and involvement by employees, supervisors, management and unions" (40, p. C). The resulting policy statement defines the EAPs relationship to the organization and describes its confidential nature to both the organization and employees.

The policy statement should minimally cover the following concepts. It states that the company recognizes that mentally and physically well employees are an asset to the organization and that the availability of EAP services can benefit both labor and management. It also states that alcohol, drug abuse, emotional, marital, and other problems can adversely affect job performance. Employees with such problems may be unable to function efficiently, effectively, or safely on the job and, therefore, these problems are a legitimate concern of the employer. The policy statement points out that employees may voluntarily seek out EAP services or be referred by supervisors through constructive confrontation. Job security is assured as long as employees using the EAP maintain acceptable job performance standards. Finally, but most importantly, the policy statement assures employees that all records are kept in strict confidentiality (40).

Familiarity with Policy and Procedures Key

Familiarity with EAP policy and procedures is key to effective utilization of the program. The policy should be published in a clear, understandable manner and distributed to all employees on a periodic basis. In addition to publications, orientation or training sessions should be conducted to familiarize all employees with policy and procedures for using the EAP. The policy should be viewed by employees as nonpunitive, constructive, and totally confidential.

The procedures for using the EAPs should clarify the two categories of referrals. Self-referrals occur when the employee recognizes a possible need for assistance and consults with the EAP professional before job performance becomes problematic. Supervisory or administrative referrals happen when the supervisor recognizes, documents, and confronts the employee on job performance problems and refers for assistance to the EAP.

Supervisor's Key Role and the Constructive Confrontation

A supervisor's familiarity with EAP policy and procedure, as well as his or her comfort in confronting and referring troubled employees for help, are critical factors in the effective utilization of a company's EAP. Employers should consider integrating EAP training into their regular, standard supervisory training when such programs exist. Supervisory orientation to policy and procedures should be done in an atmosphere that allows for the expression and processing of questions and feelings.

EAP training and consultations should also be provided to supervisors to help them learn effective constructive confrontation strategies so that they can make successful interventions and EAP referrals with employees whose problems are affecting their job performance. Confronting employees on their poor job performance is a natural part of a supervisor's role but is a strategy with which many supervisors feel uncomfortable because of inadequate training.

Constructive confrontation is used to motivate employees to resolve their problems and to overcome denial. In the constructive confrontation supervisors document deteriorating job performance and confront the employee with the specific details of these performance problems. It clarifies what specific improvement is expected and what the consequences will be if improvement does not occur. It is suggested to the employee that if personal problems are affecting their job performance, help is available through referral to the company's EAP. Whether or not the offered assistance is accepted the supervisor demands that job performance return to acceptable levels within a specified period. "Constructive confrontation provides a powerful motivation for employees to solve their problems one way or the other because it demonstrates both the possible consequences of inaction and a way to help resolve the problems" (35). Training in effective confrontation techniques also helps supervisors learn skills that make them overall better supervisors.

Vague job descriptions or unclear minimum performance standards also contribute to supervisors' difficulties in making effective interventions with troubled employees. EAP consultations may facilitate correcting this problem. Effective EAPs nurture good relationships with company supervisors who are key staff to program utilization.

EAP Delivery Systems

EAP services may be provided through a variety of delivery systems. Some companies have internal programs where services are delivered by EAP professionals employed by the company. In external programs EAP services are delivered by EAP professionals under contract with the organization. Some companies combine a core internal EAP program with contracts with external EAP vendors for certain services. Consortia of smaller companies may contract with an independent EAP vendor to provide services.

Direct Services Provided by Qualified Staff

A primary responsibility of the EAP professional is to make accurate assessments to identify employee or family member problems and then make appropriate referrals to resources in the community that are most likely to resolve the problem. The EAP identifies, fosters, and evaluates community resources which provide the best quality care at the most reasonable cost. The EAP professional provides short-term counseling or problem resolution (as opposed to referral to community resources for long-term counseling) when this is assessed as the best response for timely and effective help. Crisis intervention is also within the purview of the EAP professional who is responsive with intervention services for employees, family members, or the organization when acute crises surface.

EAP staff need to be qualified to professionally and effectively deliver these services. They should show evidence of specialized understanding of alcohol and other drugs and have certification in employee assistance programming, i.e., be a Certified Employee Assistance Professional (CEAP). Since May, 1987, over 4,000 EAP practitioners have become CEAPs by passing the certification examination of the Employee Assistance Certification Commission of the EAPA (36). Many EAP professionals today have backgrounds as well in counseling and social work.

Evaluation

EAPs should measure the appropriateness, effectiveness, and efficiency of its operations. Programs should have measurable program objectives and data collection mechanisms. Data can be collected to look at the following program components: design effectiveness, implementation, management and administration, completeness of the program, direct services, program utilization, and linkages. An effective and well-run EAP also continually reassesses the needs of the organization (40).

MAXIMIZING EAP SUCCESS

Effective EAPs reflect a balance between enhancing employee well-being and organizational performance. They identify quality substance abuse services that are accessible to employees and their families and are a good fit between the substance abuser's needs and the services provided by the treatment program. Continuing post treatment care is critical for the recovering substance abuser.

Follow-up Services

Follow-up sessions with the EAP professional should supplement the individual's involvement in 12-step programs, e.g., AA or Narcotics Anonymous (NA), as well as other therapeutic groups. Twelve-step programs are strongly advocated by alcohol and drug rehabilitation programs; they support the recovery person's sobriety and abstinence in a manageable way — one day at a time. To reduce the chances of recidivism, EAP staff need to support an employee's involvement in the 12-step programs as well as in other needed relapse prevention and therapeutic follow-up services.

Healthy Work Environments and Performance

EAPs should also promote and support healthy work environments. It is sometimes job-related issues that may be causing or exacerbating poor job performance. Company reorganizations, particularly ones involving massive layoffs, will likely affect employees' job performance. Trice and Roman outline 12 risk factors which can aggravate and reinforce deviant behavior that may already have begun outside of the work setting. The two general types of risks which may occur in any business setting are absence of supervision and low visibility of job performance. Conversely, in a work environment in which there is adequate supervision and high visibility the chances are increased that supervisors will detect a troubled employee's deteriorating job performance early and make an effective intervention (42).

OTHER POLICIES AND PROGRAMS ADDRESSING SUBSTANCE ABUSE

The Drug-Free Workplace Act

A critical cornerstone for employment policies regarding drug abuse was laid by the federal government in 1988 with passage of the Federal Drug-Free Workplace Act, which mandates that publicly funded employers provide worker education about illegal drug abuse and monitor and discipline such activity.

The Act requires employers who have a contract with the federal government for at least $25,000 to maintain a drug-free workplace. First, these employers must establish a company substance abuse policy and inform all employees of its existence. They must also educate employees about drug abuse and the availability of drug counseling and treatment programs and specify the penalties for violating the company's substance abuse policy (43).

Union Programs

While joint labor-management programs are in operation and growing, there is a history of differing philosophies between labor and management; generally unions prefer to run their own programs. While both labor and management address deteriorating job performance and confront troubled employees, there is a distinction in their priorities. Unions have perceived the well-being of their members as coming first and have resisted management's last resort strategy of firing an employee whose job performance does not improve. Since World War II the AFL-CIO's Community Services Department has operated a peer counseling program for its members (35).

Drug Testing Programs

In recent years a variety of drug testing programs have developed including preemployment, random, incident, probable cause, and scheduled drug testing. Preemployment testing, in which urinalysis is used to screen job applicants for drug use, is increasingly being used by the nation's largest employers including major corporations, manufacturers, public utilities, transportation, and some smaller employers. Preemployment testing is primarily viewed as a deterrent for drug abusing job applicants. Interestingly the most abused drug, alcohol, is rarely included in these testing programs.

Post-employment drug testing programs have been implemented especially by federal employers and companies employing workers in safety sensitive positions. Some companies which have EAP capabilities view drug testing as a means of early identification and treatment of substance-abusing employees. While EAPs provide assistance to employees who have been identified as substance abusers through drug testing, they should never be involved in the actual testing. Testing programs belong in the medical department where fitness for employment can be determined. It appears that drug testing is becoming a more acceptable policy. A Gallop poll of 1007 American workers conducted in December, 1989, reflected an almost unanimous consensus (97%) that workplace drug testing is appropriate under certain circumstances. Eighty-five percent of those surveyed believed that drug testing deterred illicit drug use (28).

Wellness Programs

Wellness programs, as a part of or complementary to EAPs, are becoming more popular in the workplace. They are very diverse in the scope of services they provide which may range from health screening efforts to identify, for example, employees with high cholesterol to weight management or smoking cessation programs. Many wellness or health promotion programs provide training on stress management, fitness, and good nutrition. Programs which are most successful are accompanied by supportive company policies. For example, stress management programs are useless in a company where management's policies promote stress. Wellness programs seek to prevent problems and like EAPs are concerned with the well-being of employees (44). Wellness programs may contribute to reducing escalating health costs.

FUTURE CONCERNS

Managed health care has and will continue to have a strong impact on EAPs. Health maintenance and preferred provider organizations have flourished as employers have been forced to identify alternatives to rapidly increasing health insurance premiums. Catastrophic claims for ailments such as AIDS and substance abuse treatment expenses along with advanced medical technology and drug therapies have fueled increases in health costs. EAPs also will need to continue addressing concerns raised by the AIDS diagnosed employee. A challenge for today's EAP professional is identifying treatment resources that best meet the needs of the substance-abusing employee and at the same time are most cost effective. EAPs have an obligation and are entrusted to ensure that employees referred for treatment receive quality services. Many EAPs are now offering short-term counseling, which can also reduce health insurance costs for employers. The degreed professional who is also credentialed for EAP work is becoming the sought-after EAP worker.

The federal government employers and the general public as well are expressing growing concern to create drug-free work environments. While more EAPs in industry are broad brush programs addressing a wide range of employee problems, it is critical that they continue to recognize and target services to substance-abusing employees. EAPs will also need to address the growing concerns of employees who do not have drug problems themselves but have family members who do.

Research continues to be needed to evaluate and determine what are the most effective programs and strategies in addressing workplace substance abuse. EAP professionals will need to keep up with the demographic and technological changes that continue to have a tremendous impact on industry and its employees. EAP professionals will need to continue to strive to understand and service the needs of the employee balanced with the needs of the employer.

References

1. Carlyle T. Past and present. London: JM Dent & Sons, 1960:189.
2. Brewington V, Deren S, Arella L, Randell J. Obstacles to vocational rehabilitation: the client's perspective. J Appl Rehabil Counsel 1990; 21(2):27.
3. Stump W. Love, work and recovery. NADAP NewsReport 1973;14(4):3.
4. Neff WS. Work and human behavior. 2nd edition. Chicago: Aldine, 1977:264.
5. Adkins WR. Life skills education: a video-based counseling/learning delivery system. In: Larson D, ed. Teaching psychological skills: models for giving psychology away. Monterey, CA: Brooks/Cole, 1984:57.
6. Wright GN. Total rehabilitation. Boston: Little, Brown, 1980:5.
7. Twelve steps and twelve traditions. New York: Alcoholics Anonymous World Services, Inc., 1979.
8. Robinson H, Texeira M. Vocational rehabilitation. 2nd edition. New York: Narcotic & Drug Research, Inc., 1990:154–156.
9. Work Evaluation & Resources Center. Placement statistics 1988–1989. Nassau County (NY) Department of Drug and Alcohol Addiction, 1990.
10. Reichman W, Levy M, Herrington S. Vocational

counseling in early sobriety. Labor Management Alcoholism Journal 1979;8:193.

11. Beale AV. A replicable program for teaching job interview skills to recovering substance abusers. J Appl Rehabil Counsel 1988;19(1):5.

12. Hall S, Loeb P, Coyne K, Cooper J. Increasing employment in ex-heroin addicts II: methadone maintenance sample. Behav Ther 1981;12:443–460.

13. 1994 NADAP placement statistics. New York: National Association on Drug Abuse Problems, 1995.

14. New York State Education Department. The vocational and educational services for individuals with disabilities. Case Service Dollar Report, 4/1/94–3/31/95.

15. Graham R, Gottcent R. Restoration of drug abusers to useful employment. In: Smith D, Anderson S, Buton M, Gottieb N, Harvey W, Chung T, eds. A multicultural view of drug abuse. Cambridge: G.K. Hall/Schenkman, 1978:463.

16. Wijting JP. Employing, the recovering drug abuser—value? Personnel 1979:62.

17. Strategy Council on Drug Abuse. Federal strategy for drug abuse and drug traffic prevention. Washington, DC: U.S. Government Printing Office, 1979:24.

18. The Rehabilitation Act of 1973, Public Law 93–112, sections 503, 504.

19. Deren S, Randell J. The vocational rehabilitation of substance abusers. J Appl Rehabil Counsel 1990;21(2):5.

20. Rudner S. The role of vocational rehabilitation in the treatment of substance abusers. Nassau County (NY) Department of Drug and Alcohol Addiction, 1982:5–6.

21. Report to the Chairman, Select Committee on Narcotics Abuse and Control, House of Representatives. Methadone maintenance: some treatment programs are not effective: greater federal oversight needed. Washington, DC: U.S. General Accounting Office 1990:23–24.

22. Simeone RS, Kott A, Torrington W. Summary report on the DSAS personal services survey. New York State Division of Substance Abuse Services, 1989:3–10.

23. Szymanski EM, Parker RM. Relationship of rehabilitation client outcome to the level of rehabilitation counselor education. J Rehabil 1989; 10:35.

24. Friedman L. The Wildcat experiment: an early test of supported work. New York: Vera Institute of Justice, 1978.

25. Hollister RG Jr, Kemper P, Maynard RA, eds. The national supported work demonstration. Madison: University of Wisconsin Press, 1984.

26. The Americans with disabilities act: a summary of alcohol and drug and AIDS provisions. Legal Action Center's Action Watch 1990;10:2.

27. Millman R, Kleinman P. Comprehensive vocational enhancement program for MMTP's NIDA Grant DA 06153, 1995:25.

28. U.S. Department of Health and Human Services, Public Health Service, Substance Abuse and Mental Health Services Administration, Office of Applied Studies. Advance Report Number 10. September 1995:19–20.

29. U.S. Department of Health and Human Services, Public Health Service, Substance Abuse and Mental Health Services Administration. National Household Survey on Drug Abuse: main findings, 1993:97.

30. Walsh J, Gust S, eds. Workplace drug abuse policy, considerations and experience in the business community. Office of Workplace Initiatives. National Institute on Drug Abuse DHHS publication number (ADM) 1989;52:89–1610.

31. NIDA Capsules. Facts about drugs in the workplace. Rockville, MD: Press Office of the National Institute on Drug Abuse, 1986:1.

32. William M. Mercer-Meidinger-Hansen, Inc. Substance abuse in the workforce, A survey of employers conducted by Marsh & McLennan Companies, Inc., 1988:2–8.

33. Walsh J, Gust S. Drug abuse in the workplace: issues, policy decisions, and corporate response. Sem Occup Med 1986;1(4):237–239.

34. Yesavage JA, Leirer VO, Denari M, Hollister LE. Carry-over effects of marijuana intoxication on aircraft pilot performance: a preliminary report. Am J Psychiatry 1985;142:1325.

35. Sonnenstuhl W, Trice H. Strategies for employee assistance programs: the crucial balance. Ithaca, NY: ILR Press, New York State School of Industrial and Labor Relations, Cornell University, 1986:4–8.

36. Bickerton RL. Employee assistance: a history in progress. EAP Digest 1990;11(1):35–42, 82–84.

37. Watkins GT. In-House, a decade of change. EAP Digest 1990;11(1):6.

38. Kingman D Jr, ed. Why EAP's? Substance Abuse Issues 1990;1(2):1–2.

39. Kingman D Jr, ed. Treatment effectiveness. Substance Abuse Issues 1990;1(4):1.

40. The Employee Assistance Professionals Association, Inc. Standards for employee assistance programs. Exchange 1990;20(10):31–37.

41. Balzer WK, Pargament KI. The key to designing a successful EAP. EAP Digest 1988;1:55–59.

42. Trice HM, Roman PM. Spirits and demons at work: alcohol and other drugs on the job. Ithaca, NY: Publications Division, New York State School of Industrial and Labor Relations, Cornell University, 1978:101–102.

43. Complying with the drug-free workplace act of substance. New York: Legal Action Center, May/June 1989:1.

44. Franz JB. Promoting wellness and disease prevention in EAPs. The ALMACAN 1987; 17(11):8–9.

85 ETHICAL AND LEGAL ASPECTS OF CONFIDENTIALITY[a]

Margaret K. Brooks

Federal law and regulations guarantee the strict confidentiality of information about persons receiving alcohol or drug abuse assessment or treatment services. The legal citations for the law and regulations is 42 U.S.C. §290 dd-2 and 42 Code of Federal Regulations, Part 2. Originally passed by Congress in the early 1970s, the statute narrowly defines the circumstances in which information about patients in federally assisted or regulated substance abuse treatment may be disclosed. In 1975, a complex set of regulations was issued under the heading "Confidentiality of Alcohol and Drug Abuse Patient Records" (hereafter "the regulations"). These regulations, which were amended in 1987 and again in 1995, fill many gaps in the authorizing legislation. The federal statute and regulations supersede any state or local law less protective of the confidentiality of patient records. For most practical purposes the regulations constitute the universe of legal requirements in this area.

The regulations are more restrictive of communications in many instances than the physician-patient privilege. For example, the confidentiality regulations protect more than the information that a physician must obtain to provide treatment to a patient.[b] They also shield a patient's identity as a patient—information not generally protected in most states by the physician-patient privilege. As a consequence, compliance with the general ethical and legal standards that protect patient confidences in the field of medicine does not ensure compliance with the regulations protecting the confidentiality of information about patients in substance abuse treatment.

Familiarity with the confidentiality regulations is essential to anyone directly or indirectly involved with substance abuse treatment. Violation of the regulations is punishable by a fine of up to $500 for a first offense or up to

---

[a] This chapter provides an introduction to the legal requirements federal law and regulation impose on those providing alcohol or drug abuse assessment or treatment in the area of confidentiality of patient records. These requirements are subject to change. In fact, changes were made in the governing federal statutes and regulations in the mid 1980s and mid 1990s. Any understanding of the legal requirements in this area must be periodically updated. Moreover, although the chapter suggests methods for complying with the requirements in a variety of recurring problem areas, the chapter cannot be relied upon for a definitive answer in any particular situation, which may present its own unique circumstances. Finally, this chapter deals only with federal law and regulations. In the area of confidentiality and professional responsibility, state law also often applies. Anyone who needs legal advice should consult an attorney familiar with both state and federal law in these areas.

[b] On the scope of the privilege, see, e.g., New York C.P.L.R. §4504(a). On the scope of the regulations, see the definition of "records" on page 885.

$5000 for each subsequent offense (§2.4).[c] Moreover, federal, state, and local funding and regulatory authorities may require compliance with the regulations as a condition of grants to treatment programs. Violation may result in loss of funding.

Equally important, many of the nettlesome problems that may arise under the regulations can be avoided through foresight. Familiarity with the regulations' requirements will facilitate communication and reduce the confidentiality-related conflicts among program, patient, and outside agency to relatively few situations.

What follows is an overview of the regulations. This chapter will first examine the broad scope of the regulations and define the terms of their general prohibition on disclosures. It will then survey the rules governing disclosures with patient consent and the rules allowing for unconsented disclosures to third parties. Finally, it will discuss situations that frequently occur, including questions raised by programs' use of modern technology.

THE GENERAL RULE AGAINST DISCLOSURE: ITS BREADTH AND TERMS

Except under very limited circumstances, the regulations prohibit the disclosure of records or other information concerning any patient in a federally-assisted alcohol or drug abuse program (§§2.12, 2.13(a)). This prohibition on unauthorized disclosure applies whether or not the person seeking information already has the information, has other means of obtaining it, enjoys official status, has obtained a subpoena or warrant, or is authorized by state law (§§2.13(b), 2.20). Any state provision that would permit or require a disclosure prohibited by the federal rules is invalid. However, states may require greater confidentiality than the federal regulations (§2.20).

The general rule prohibiting disclosure applies to all who have access to patients' records—treatment program personnel, researchers, auditors, or others. It applies to them whether or not they are compensated for their activity, and it continues to apply to them after they have terminated their employment or relationship with the program.

The seriousness with which the regulations regard the nondisclosure rule is illustrated by the provisions concerning security. Programs must keep written records in a secure room, a locked file cabinet, a safe, or other similar container. They must also set up written procedures to regulate access to and use of patient records (§2.16).[d] To ensure compliance, programs should designate either the program director or a single member of the program staff to process inquiries and requests for patient information.

The definition section of the regulations underscores the broad reach of the general rule prohibiting disclosures:

A *patient* is any person who has applied or been assessed for, participated in, or received an interview, counseling, or any other service by a federally-assisted alcohol or drug abuse program, including someone who, after arrest on a criminal charge, is identified as a substance abuser during an evaluation of eligibility for treatment. Applicants are included, whether or not they are admitted to treatment. Former patients and deceased patients are also protected (§§2.11, 2.15(b)).

Patient-identifying information is any information that would identify a patient as a substance abuser, either directly or indirectly (§§2.11, 2.12(a)(1)(I)). It includes not only name and address, but also "social security number, fingerprints, photograph, or similar information by which the identity of a patient can be determined with reasonable accuracy and speed either directly or by reference to other publicly available information. . . ."

Records protected from unauthorized disclosure include any information acquired about a patient, whether or not it is in writing, including the patient's identity, address, medical or treatment information, and all communications made by him or her to program staff (§2.11).

The regulations prohibit any *disclosure* of information about an identified patient or information that would identify someone as a patient, including verification of information that is already known by the person making the inquiry (§2.11).

Implicit, as well as explicit, disclosures are prohibited (§2.13(c)). Thus, for example, one may not disclose that a particular individual is attending a program that is publicly identified as a place where only alcohol or drug abuse diagnosis, treatment, or referral is provided, unless the individual consents in accordance with the regulations or unless the disclosure fits within one of the narrow exceptions to the general rule. Accordingly, all requests for unauthorized disclosures about patients should be met with a noncommittal response such as, "Federal law prohibits the release of that information." The regulations permit giving the inquiring party a copy of the regulations, but prohibit any statement that the regulations restrict the disclosure of the records of an identified patient. Programs should avoid specific reference to the confidentiality regulations if the reference might identify the subject of the inquiry as a substance abuse patient.

A *program* covered by the regulations includes an individual or entity (other than a general medical care facility) that holds itself out as providing, and provides, alcohol or drug abuse diagnosis, treatment, or referral for treatment (§2.12). Application of the federal regulations does not depend on how a program characterizes its services. Calling itself a "prevention program" does not insulate a program from following the confidentiality rules. It is the kind of services, not the label, that will determine whether the program must comply with the federal law.[e]

In 1995, the U.S. Department of Health and Human Services (HHS) revised the definition of *program* to make clear the circumstances in which hospitals and other general medical care facilities are "programs" subject to the regulations.[f] With regard to hospitals and general medical care facilities, "programs" governed by the regulations are now limited to

- An identified unit . . . which holds itself out as providing, and provides, alcohol or drug abuse diagnosis, treatment or referral for treatment; or
- Medical personnel or other staff in a general medical care facility whose primary function is the provision of alcohol or drug abuse diagnosis, treatment or referral for treatment and who are identified as such providers.[g]

At the same time, HHS revised §2.12(e) (1), to further clarify its intentions:

However, these regulations would not apply, for example, to emergency room personnel who refer a patient to the intensive care unit for an apparent overdose, unless the primary function of such personnel is the provision of alcohol or drug abuse diagnosis, treatment or referral and they are identified as providing such services or the emergency room has promoted itself to the community as a provider of such services.[h]

A program is *federally assisted* and therefore covered by the regulations, if it:

1. Receives federal funds in any form, even if the funds do not directly pay for the alcohol or drug abuse services; *or*
2. Is assisted by the Internal Revenue Service through grant of tax exempt status or allowance of tax deductions for contributions; *or*
3. Is authorized to conduct business by the federal government (e.g., licensed to provide methadone or chemotherapy; certified as a Medicare provider); *or*

---

[c] Citations in the form " §2. . ." refer to specific sections of 42 C.F.R. Part 2.

[d] The security provisions of the regulations have implications for programs computerizing or networking their patient records. Section 2.16 also affects how programs deal with other instruments of modern technology. See the discussion in the later section "Confidentiality and Modern Technology."

[e] For example, some drug or alcohol abuse education programs are covered and some are not. A drug or alcohol abuse education program that admits students on the basis of involvement or suspected involvement in substance abuse would be covered by the regulations; a course in drug and alcohol abuse taught to all students at a junior high school would not.

[f] The revised definition of "program" was also intended to overturn *United States v. Eide,* 875 F.2d 1429 (9 Cir. 1989), a case in which the court held that, when a person is taken to the emergency room and diagnosed as a drug abuser, his records are protected by the federal confidentiality regulations.

[g] 60 Federal Register 22,297 (May 5, 1995).

[h] 60 Federal Register 22,297 (May 5, 1995).

4. Is conducted directly by the federal government (e.g., an employee assistance program in a federal agency) or by a state or local government that receives federal funds which could be (but are not necessarily) spent for alcohol or drug abuse programs (§2.12(b)).[i]

EXCEPTIONS TO THE GENERAL RULE PROHIBITING DISCLOSURE: A RULE OF THUMB

Although the general rule prohibiting disclosures of patient-identifying information is very broad, the regulations do permit programs to make limited disclosures when a patient consents and set out a number of circumstances in which programs may make disclosures whether or not the patient consents. Each condition permitting disclosure has its own peculiar requirements and limitations, all of practical significance. The welter of detail can pose a significant obstacle to one who, contemplating whether a particular inquiry into patient records is permissible, must locate and understand the regulations' answer.

However, nine simple questions will carry one a long way toward overcoming this hurdle. To determine whether a particular request for information about a patient falls within an exception to the general prohibition on disclosure, one should ask the following:

1. Is the proposed communication to be made pursuant to a valid written patient consent?
2. Is the proposed communication to be made to other staff of the program or to an entity with administrative control over the program having a need for the information in connection with duties that arise out of the provision of substance abuse services?
3. Can the proposed communication be made without revealing that the person the disclosure concerns is or was an alcohol or drug abuse patient?
4. Is the proposed communication related to a medical emergency?
5. Is the proposed communication authorized by a valid court order?
6. Does the proposed communication concern a crime or a threatened crime on the premises of the program or against program personnel?
7. Is the proposed communication for purposes of research or part of an audit or an examination of a program's activities?
8. Does the proposed communication involve the reporting of child abuse or neglect?
9. Is the proposed communication to be made pursuant to a qualified service organization agreement?

If the answer to all these questions is no, then the proposed communication *cannot* be made. If, on the other hand, the answer to one of the questions is yes, the situation may permit a disclosure. An examination of each of these nine exceptions follows.

A word of caution, first. The exceptions permitting disclosure present relatively complicated questions, not easily subject to generalized answers. One practical initial step toward minimizing confidentiality problems, therefore, is to inform program staff that, other than in such routine situations as the patient signing a valid consent form, only the program director or some designated individual versed in the confidentiality regulations may authorize disclosures. Even then, certain situations, particularly those involving court orders, may require the advice of counsel.

To avoid getting lost in the exceptions, one does well to keep the general rule uppermost in mind and to operate on the following principle: Do not disclose anything about a patient, at least without being able to state why the regulations permit the particular disclosure.

QUESTION 1: DISCLOSURES WITH PATIENT CONSENT

Most disclosures are permissible if a patient has signed a valid consent form that has not expired or been revoked by the patient (§2.31).[j] A proper consent form must be in writing and must contain *each* of the items contained in §2.31:

1. The name or general designation of the program(s) making the disclosure,
2. The name of the individual or organization that will receive the disclosure,
3. The name of the patient who is the subject of the disclosure,
4. The purpose or need for the disclosure,
5. How much and what kind of the information will be disclosed,
6. A statement that the patient may revoke the consent at any time, except to the extent that the program has already acted in reliance on it,
7. The date, event, or condition upon which the consent expires if not previously revoked,
8. The signature of the patient (and/or other authorized person), and
9. The date on which the consent is signed (§2.31(a)).

Understanding these requirements is important not only for those administering treatment programs, but also for anyone who would communicate with a program. Any form furnished to a program must meet these nine requirements, or the program is prohibited by the regulations from making the proposed disclosure (§2.31(c)).

The regulations explicitly preclude use of any general consent to the release of medical records. In most cases they contemplate a separate consent form for each type of disclosure and each different recipient. A single form may suffice for a series of disclosures of the same type to the same recipient, such as verifying to a particular funding source the occasions on which treatment was provided during the period of a patient's attendance at the program. But a disclosure of a different nature to the same organization or of the same nature to a different organization would require a new consent.

Understanding the Consent Requirements

Several of the items that must be included in a consent form merit further explanation.

PURPOSE OF THE DISCLOSURE AND HOW MUCH AND WHAT KIND OF INFORMATION WILL BE DISCLOSED

These two items are closely related. All disclosures must be limited to information that is necessary to accomplish the need or purpose for the disclosure (§2.13(a)). It would be improper to disclose everything in a patient's file if the recipient of the information only needs one specific piece of information.

REVOCABILITY AND DURATION OF CONSENT

The federal regulations permit patients to revoke consent at any time (orally or in writing), and the consent form must include a statement to this effect.[k] However, a program is not required to try to retrieve information it disclosed in reliance on a valid consent form prior to a patient's revocation of that consent.[l]

Since the regulations require that a consent be limited in duration to the period necessary to carry out the purpose of the disclosure, a valid consent form must also state a date, event, or condition on which it will expire if not previously revoked. For example, a consent for disclosures to a funding source to verify drug abuse treatment for purposes of reimbursement might properly be set to last throughout the patient's treatment at the program. Consent for disclosure of a methadone maintenance patient's dosage level to

---

[i] The regulations do not apply to records maintained by the Veterans Administration and, in certain cases, the Armed Forces (2.12(c)(1) and (2)).
[j] However, no information obtained from a program may be used in a criminal investigation or prosecution of a patient unless a court order has been issued under the special circumstances set forth in §2.65. 42 U.S.C. §290dd-2(c); 42 C.F.R. §2.12(a), (d).

[k] This is a key difference between the general §2.31 consent form and the criminal justice system consent form §2.35, discussed later, which does not permit revocation.
[l] The regulations state that "acting in reliance" includes providing services in reliance on a consent form permitting disclosures to a third-party payer. Thus, a program can bill the third-party payer for past services to the patient even after consent has been revoked. However, a program that continues to provide services after a patient has revoked a consent authorizing disclosure to a third-party payer cannot thereafter bill the third-party payer.

a physician treating the patient for an unrelated condition, on the other hand, should not be tied to the length of time the person is in methadone treatment. Rather, it should extend only through the period that the patient receives treatment for the other condition. Once that treatment ceases, further disclosures to the physician concerning the patient's methadone treatment would be unnecessary and violate the regulations.

As with the required statements of the need for disclosure and the nature of the information, the requirement that a consent form state when it expires rests on a simple rule for maintaining confidentiality: Disclose only what is necessary and only for so long as it is necessary.

THE SIGNATURE OF THE PATIENT

A *minor patient* must always sign the consent form in order for a program to release information, even to his or her parent.[m] The program must get the parent's signature in addition to the minor's signature only if the program is required by state law to obtain parental permission before providing treatment to the minor (§2.14).

In most states, a minor is a person under 18 years of age. Some states permit a minor to seek substance abuse treatment without consent or notification of parent or guardian; others do not. If a program is in a state that permits minors to seek treatment without parental consent, then the program need obtain only the minor's consent in making disclosures (§2.14(b)). Obtaining parental consent to a disclosure in these circumstances is not only unnecessary but would itself constitute an unauthorized disclosure.

On the other hand, in states that require parental consent for drug abuse treatment of minors, consent of both the minor patient and parent or guardian must be obtained prior to disclosures from the patient's records (§2.14(c)).

The regulations attempt to smooth one additional wrinkle presented by minors. As seen previously, applicants for treatment are considered "patients" whose records are protected by the confidentiality regulations. What should a program do with a minor applicant who does not want his or her parents notified in a state where parental consent is required for admission to treatment? The regulations' answer is that the program cannot notify the applicant's parents without the minor's approval. Of course, the program should explain to the applicant that it cannot provide treatment without contacting his or her parents, but the choice is left to the minor. If the individual refuses, the program cannot notify his or her parents of the application for treatment without violating the regulations (§2.14(c)).[n]

The only exception to this rule is the case of an applicant who in the program director's judgment "lacks the capacity because of extreme youth or mental or physical condition to make a rational choice" as to whether to give consent to make a disclosure to a parent and his or her situation poses a substantial threat to the life or well-being of the minor or any other person" (§2.14(d)). If the program director finds that both these conditions exist, he or she may contact the parent without the minor's consent. Note that §2.14(d) applies only to applicants for services. It does not apply to minors who are already patients. Thus, a program cannot contact the parents of a minor patient without consent, even if the program is concerned about his or her behavior.

There are special rules to deal with *incompetent and deceased* patients. Consent to disclosures of drug abuse treatment records of a patient who has been adjudicated incompetent to manage his or her affairs may be made by the individual's guardian or other person authorized by the state to act in his or her behalf. In such a situation, the patient's consent is not required (§2.15(a)(1)).

If the patient has not been adjudicated incompetent, but the program director determines that his or her medical condition prevents "knowing or effective action on his or her own behalf," the program director may authorize disclosures without patient consent for the sole purpose of obtaining payment for services from a third-party payer (§2.15(a)(2)).

Consent to the disclosure of records of deceased patients may be made by the executor, administrator, or other personal representative appointed under applicable state law. If no such appointment has been made, the patient's spouse or, if none, any responsible family member may give the required consent (§2.15(b)(2)). Even without consent, a program may make disclosures required by federal and state laws relating to the cause of death of a patient or other vital statistics.

WRITTEN PROHIBITION OF REDISCLOSURE

Once the consent form has been properly completed, there remains one formal prerequisite to a valid disclosure. The regulations require that any disclosure pursuant to written patient consent be accompanied by a written statement that the information disclosed is protected by federal law and that the recipient cannot make any further disclosure of it unless permitted by the regulations (§2.32). This statement, not the consent form itself, should be delivered and explained to the recipient at the time of disclosure or earlier. Section 2.32 of the regulations provides a model statement for this purpose.[o]

The regulations prohibit redisclosure by a third-party payer or an entity having direct administrative control over a program even if they have not received the written notice (§2.12(d)(2)). This provision means that records identifying individuals as recipients of substance abuse services that are maintained by third-party payers or funding sources are subject to the confidentiality regulations. In other words, once the state agency administering Medicaid, for example, has received patient-identifying information on individuals in drug abuse treatment, its records of those individuals become subject to the regulations and can only be redisclosed under the conditions explained throughout this chapter. The same would be true for third-party payers.

Although the regulations prohibit a third-party payer from redisclosing patient-identifying information even if it has not received the notice of prohibition on redisclosure, programs are still required to attach the notice to *all* disclosures made with patient consent, regardless of who is receiving the information.

Use of Consent Forms

The formal requirements for a valid consent may seem onerous or complicated at first blush. For the most part, however, they are easily met. One important step is the development of forms that eliminate the need to recall the formal requirements. The regulations contain a standard form, and programs can develop more specialized forms for disclosures that must be made for the same purpose to the same recipient for many patients, such as disclosures to funding sources or central registries.

The fact that a patient has signed a proper consent form authorizing the release of information does not *force* a program to make the proposed disclosure, unless the program has also received a subpoena or court order (§§2.3(b); 2.61(a), (b)). In most cases, then, the decision of whether or not to make a disclosure pursuant to a consent form is within the discretion of the program. What follows is some advice, based on experience, on how to handle some common situations involving patient consent. As a general proposition, a program or person can comply with the regulations by adhering to

---

[m] "Parent" here means the parent, guardian, or other person legally responsible for the minor. The confidentiality regulations leave the issue of who is a minor and whether a minor can obtain alcohol or drug abuse treatment without parental consent entirely to state laws.

[n] In states that do not require parental consent for treatment of minors, the regulations permit a program to withhold services if the minor will not authorize a disclosure that the program needs in order to obtain financial reimbursement for that minor's treatment. The regulations add a warning, however, that such action might violate a state or local law (§2.14(b)).

[o] The written statement must read substantially as follows:

This information has been disclosed to you from records whose confidentiality is protected by federal confidentiality rules (42 C.F.R. Part 2). The federal rules prohibit you from making any further disclosure of this information unless further disclosure is expressly permitted by the written consent of the person to whom it pertains or as otherwise permitted by 42 C.F.R. Part 2. A general authorization for the release of medical or other information is NOT sufficient for this purpose. The Federal rules restrict any use of the information to criminally investigate or prosecute any alcohol or drug abuse patient. (§2.23(a))

this rule: Disclose only what is necessary, for only as long as is necessary, in light of the purpose of the communication.

DISCLOSURES TO THIRD-PARTY PAYERS AND FUNDING SOURCES

Disclosures of patient records to third-party payers and funding sources raise a number of issues. Generally, programs prefer to document before admission that a patient is someone whose treatment is reimbursable (i.e., that the patient meets the eligibility criteria set by the funding source) and that the service to be provided is covered. The issue is how to accomplish this without violating the federal rules.

If a program calls an insurance carrier to ask whether Bob Smith's treatment for alcohol or drug abuse is reimbursable, it is making a disclosure that Bob Smith has applied for substance abuse treatment services. In order to make this call to verify coverage, the program must get the patient's written consent to disclose this information before it places the call.

A second issue is the kind and amount of information that third-party payers may require both before initial permission is granted and as treatment continues. Health maintenance organizations (HMOs) and managed care entities may request information in order to perform either "gatekeeping" functions or to coordinate a patient's care. In either case, they tend to take a more active role in treatment decisions than traditional insurance carriers. This more active role results in requests for greater amounts and kinds of information about patients. Programs that do not comply may well see continued treatment disallowed by the HMO, managed care entity or insurance company.

The demand for greater amounts of information has been accompanied by an increase in computerization and sharing of insurance and other third-party payment records, sometimes in violation of the regulations.

In these circumstances, how can programs best protect patients' privacy? Before a program discloses information to an insurance company, HMO, or managed care company, it should make sure that the consent form carefully defines the kind and amount of information it will be disclosing and that the patient has signed the form. (Of course, all disclosures should also be accompanied by the notice of prohibition on redisclosure (§2.32).[p]

If a patient refuses to consent and reporting eligibility data are prerequisite to the treatment program's receiving reimbursement or funding for its services, the program may have to deny that patient treatment. However, a program in those circumstances should consult with an attorney to ensure that state law permits it to refuse to treat someone in this situation.

DISCLOSURES TO CENTRAL REGISTRIES

The regulations permit disclosures to a "central registry" that collects patient data from narcotic maintenance treatment or detoxification treatment programs to enable the programs to prevent multiple patient enrollment.[q] Programs must obtain the patient's consent to make disclosures to the central registry before accepting the patient for treatment. The patient's consent to central registry disclosures remains effective as long as the patient is enrolled at the program that obtained the consent, and the consent form should state as much.

Subject to the limitations described later in this section, programs may disclose patient information to such central registries with the patient's consent. When an individual applies to a program for treatment, or the dosage is changed, or treatment ends or resumes, the program may contact the registry and ask whether the individual is currently enrolled in another maintenance or detoxification program. The consent must list the name and address of each central registry and program that will receive a disclosure (although programs within 200 miles need not be named specifically). It must also state

that the patient's consent covers all programs subsequently established within 200 miles and any registry serving them.

If the applicant for treatment is currently enrolled in another program, the registry may inform either program of the name, address, and phone number of the other program. The two programs involved may then communicate with one another to verify the multiple enrollment and to resolve the situation in accordance with sound clinical practice. No other disclosures are permitted (§2.34).

DISCLOSURES TO EMPLOYERS AND EMPLOYMENT AGENCIES

Programs may disclose records or other information to the patient's employer whenever the patient signs a consent form. Given the stigma that many employers attach to alcohol and drug abuse treatment, however, program staff may wish to withhold disclosures from employers they know will fire or refuse to hire anyone with a drug or alcohol abuse history.

Indeed, program staff should not assume that communications with a patient's employer will be beneficial to the patient. A patient who tells program staff that his or her employer will not be sympathetic about the decision to enter treatment may well have an accurate picture of the employer's attitude. Insistence by program staff on communicating with the employer may cost a patient his or her job.

If a program does decide to communicate with an employer (with the patient's consent), it should take care to limit any disclosures to information that is actually necessary. Often, disclosures to employers can be limited to a verification of treatment status or a general progress report. The program should disclose more detail only if the information is directly related to a particular employment situation and the patient has signed a consent form stating the kind and amount of detailed information that will be disclosed.

The regulations do permit a program to release adverse information, even with potentially harmful consequences. For example, a program may, with patient consent, provide a periodic progress report to an employer that contains negative information, including continued substance abuse, refusal to cooperate with the program, or other deleterious information. This is a matter for the program's own judgment. There is nothing wrong with a program disclosing negative evaluations to an employer if the program knows that the employer will attempt or is attempting to help the patient with an alcohol or drug abuse problem or will consider disciplinary steps only when an individual's substance abuse problem has reduced job performance to an unacceptable level.

Perhaps the most common example of this kind of disclosure occurs when an employee is referred for treatment by or to an employee assistance program as a condition of retaining a job, and the treating program provides periodic reports to the employer on the employee's progress (or lack of progress). Of course, any disclosure requires patient consent which, under the rules discussed earlier, is revocable at any time.

A program may also wish—or even be legally compelled—to disclose information to an employer when it knows the patient is continuing to use alcohol or other drugs and works in a job that directly affects public safety (e.g., a bus driver). Even then, the program must be sure to make the disclosure only in a manner permitted by the federal rules.

CRIMINAL JUSTICE SYSTEM REFERRALS

The confidentiality regulations set forth some special rules when a patient's participation in a treatment program is an official condition of probation or parole, sentence, dismissal of charges, release from imprisonment, or other disposition of a criminal proceeding. Under the regulations, a patient may consent to communication about himself or herself between the program and the agency or individual in the criminal justice system that is responsible for the referral or for supervising the individual, e.g., the court granting pretrial conditional release or a probation or parole officer.

The rules about patient consent to disclosures to a referring criminal justice agency differ in several respects from the rules governing other consented disclosures (compare §2.31 with §2.35). First, an individual whose release from confinement or whose probation or parole is conditioned upon

---

[p] For other ways to deal with the confidentiality issues created by managed care and HMOs see *Confidentiality: A Guide to the Federal Law and Regulations,* 1995 rev. edition, New York: Legal Action Center, pages 85–92.

[q] The regulations define detoxification treatment as "the dispensing of a narcotic drug in decreasing doses to an individual in order to reduce or eliminate adverse physiological or psychological effects incident to withdrawal from the sustained use of a narcotic drug" (§2.34(a)).

treatment may not revoke his or her consent to disclosures to the referral or supervisory agency. This is the only situation in which the regulations permit a program to require an irrevocable consent.

The regulations require that the following factors be considered in determining how long the consent will remain in effect: the anticipated length of treatment, the type of criminal proceeding, the need for treatment information in disposing of that proceeding, when the final disposition will occur, and anything else the patient, program, or criminal justice agency deems pertinent.

Experience shows that using the formulation required by the old regulations—"when there is a substantial change in the patient's criminal justice system status"—works well. A substantial change occurs when an individual moves from one stage of the criminal justice process to another. For example, an individual who, upon arrest, has been referred for treatment in lieu of prosecution and has consented to disclosures of this type would undergo a substantial change in status when the charges were dismissed or when formal criminal charges were filed. To cite another example, if a patient is on parole or probation, there would be a change in criminal justice system status when the parole or probation ends, either by successful completion or revocation. Thus, the program could provide periodic reports to the parole or probation officer monitoring the patient and could even testify at a parole or probation revocation hearing, since no change in criminal justice status would occur until after that hearing.

Of course, if a program or criminal justice agency wants to make use of these special rules, it must be sure that the consent form is correctly worded. The fact that a consent form could have been irrevocable will help little if the form actually signed by the patient says it can be revoked at any time.

The recipients of criminal justice system disclosures, it should be noted, may use the information only in connection with the subject patient and the criminal proceedings from which he or she was referred. The information may not be used in any other proceedings, for other purposes, or with respect to other individuals (§2.35(d)).

Whenever possible, it is best to have the judge or referring agency require that a proper criminal justice system consent form be signed before an individual is referred to the treatment program. If that is not possible, the program should obtain the patient's consent to the release of information to the appropriate agency at the very first meeting. This avoids the unfortunate problems that can arise if a patient referred by the justice system leaves before successfully completing treatment without ever having signed a consent form.[r]

One final note: If a person referred by the criminal justice system never applies for or receives services from the program, that fact may be communicated to a criminal justice agency without patient consent (§2.13(c)(2)). However, once a patient even makes an appointment to visit the program for assessment or treatment, consent or a court order is needed for any disclosures to criminal justice agencies.

DISCLOSURES TO PATIENTS' LEGAL COUNSEL

There are no special rules governing disclosure to a patient's attorney when the patient consents. Once the program determines that the attorney actually represents the patient, it may, upon consent, turn over all the patient's records.

A program does retain discretion to limit its response, and programs are sometimes nervous about turning records over to a lawyer representing a patient because they fear they may be sued. However, in most situations, it rarely pays to refuse to turn over records. The attorney will simply get a subpoena, which, with the patient's written consent, will compel the program to turn over the records. The process will antagonize the attorney, who will suspect that the program has something to hide. If the program has doubts about the wisdom of turning over records, it should consult its own counsel.

Records turned over to an attorney, like records turned over to anyone pursuant to consent, must be accompanied by the notice of prohibition on redisclosure. The attorney may not redisclose any information received from the program's records unless the patient consents or there is another authorization under the rules, such as a proper court order.

QUESTION 2: INTERNAL PROGRAM COMMUNICATIONS

The regulations permit some information to be disclosed to individual staff within the same program. The regulations' restrictions on disclosure do not apply to communications of information among staff (1) within a program or (2) between a program and "an entity that has direct administrative control over that program"—if the recipients need "the information in connection with their duties that arise out of the provision of diagnosis, treatment or referral for treatment of alcohol or drug abuse" (§2.12(c)(3)).

In other words, staff who have access to patient records because they work for or administratively direct the program (including full-time or part-time employees and unpaid volunteers) may consult among themselves or otherwise share information if their work so requires. And staff may communicate patient-identifying information to a person or entity having "direct administrative control" over a program if there is a need for the information "in connection with their [substance abuse services]."

Perhaps the most common example of making disclosures to an "entity having administrative control" over a program is where an alcohol or drug abuse unit is part of a general hospital, community mental health center, or other multiservice agency. The regulations permit disclosures to such an agency, including communications to central billing or record keeping departments, but only when necessary to provide the alcohol and drug abuse services. Communication of information outside the substance abuse unit that is not necessary to provide services to the unit's patients is prohibited.

Information that is communicated to an entity having administrative control over a program continues to be protected by the regulations. The administrative entity may not redisclose any patient-identifying information to the outside world.

QUESTION 3: COMMUNICATIONS THAT DO NOT DISCLOSE PATIENT-IDENTIFYING INFORMATION[s]

A communication is not a "disclosure" if it neither identifies an individual as an alcohol or drug abuser nor verifies someone else's identification of the patient (§§2.12(a)(1)(I), (e)(3)). The principal ways in which a program may make a "nonpatient identifying disclosure" are:

1. by reporting aggregate data about a program's population, or some portion of it; or
2. by communicating information about an individual in a manner that does not disclose the individual's status as a drug or alcohol abuse patient.

Three examples of communications of information about an individual that do not disclose that person's status as a substance abuse patient are:

- A disclosure of information by a hospital, community mental health center, employee assistance program, or other agency that provides services to people with other illnesses as well as to alcohol and drug abusers. Thus,

[r] If a program fails to obtain the consent of a patient who has been referred by the criminal justice system and that patient leaves before successfully completing treatment, the program has few options when faced with a request for information by the referring criminal justice agency. The program could attempt to locate the departed patient and have him or her sign a consent form, but that is unlikely to happen. And there is some question whether a court can issue an order to authorize the program to release information about a referred patient who has left the program in this type of case. This is because the regulations allow a court to order disclosure of treatment records for the purpose of investigating or prosecuting a patient for a crime only where the crime was "extremely serious." A failure to comply with a treatment referral may not be a criminal offense and a parole or probation violation generally will not meet the criterion of "extremely serious" either. Therefore, unless a program obtains consent at the very beginning of treatment it may find itself in a position where it is prevented from providing any information to the criminal justice agency that referred the patient for assessment or treatment.

[s] "Patient-identifying information" includes an individual's name, address, social security number, and any other information from which a patient's identity can be determined either directly or by reference to other public information.

a program may disclose that "John Doe is a patient at the Smithville General Hospital" as long as the fact that John has an alcohol or drug problem or is in substance abuse treatment is not revealed.

- An "anonymous" disclosure, by a program that only provides alcohol and/or drug services, of information about a patient without identifying the name of the program or otherwise revealing the individual's status as an alcohol or drug abuse patient.
- A report on an individual case history, provided the reader cannot piece together the subject's identity from the reported facts and other information.

QUESTION 4: MEDICAL EMERGENCIES

The regulations permit a program to make disclosures in a "medical emergency" to medical personnel "who have a need for information about a patient for the purpose of treating a condition which poses an immediate threat to the health of any individual and requires immediate medical intervention" (§2.51). Whenever a disclosure is made to cope with a medical emergency, the program must document in the patient's records the name and affiliation of the recipient of the information, the name of the individual making the disclosure, the date and time of the disclosure, and the nature of the emergency.

The "medical emergency" provision does not open a loophole for non-emergency disclosures; the situation must truly be one requiring immediate medical attention.

The medical emergency exception only permits disclosures to medical personnel. This means that this exception cannot be used as the basis for a disclosure to the police, parents, or other nonmedical personnel. Whenever a disclosure is made to cope with a medical emergency, the program must document in the patient's records the name and affiliation of the recipient of the information, the name of the individual making the disclosure, the date and time of the disclosure, and the nature of the emergency.

Finally, disclosures to the Food and Drug Administration (FDA) are permitted, even without patient consent, when the FDA determines that an error in packaging or manufacturing a drug that is used in substance abuse treatment may endanger the health of patients (§2.51(b)).

QUESTION 5: COURT-ORDERED DISCLOSURES

The regulations permit programs to disclose information without patient consent if a court issues an order authorizing disclosure. The regulations require the court to follow a particular procedure, limit the grounds upon which a court may authorize a program to make disclosures, and set out strict limits on the scope of such disclosures. More than any other situations covered by the confidentiality regulations, those involving court orders, subpoenas and search and arrest warrants are best handled by counsel.

Subject to this caveat on the advice of counsel, the regulations' approach to court orders may be briefly sketched. Under the regulations, a court may authorize a program to make disclosures of patient data that would otherwise be prohibited (§2.61) after it follows certain procedures and makes particular determinations specified by the regulations (§§2.63–2.67).

Procedure

Before a proper court order authorizing disclosure may be issued, the program and any patient whose records are sought must be given written notice that an order is sought and an opportunity to make an appearance or written statement to the court.[t] The application for the court order and the court order itself must use fictitious names for any known patient, and all court proceedings in connection with the application must be confidential unless the patient requests otherwise (§2.64).

Required Findings

Before authorizing a particular disclosure, a court must find that there is "good cause" for it. The court must find that the public interest and the need for disclosure outweigh any adverse effect that the disclosure will have on the patient, the doctor-patient relationship, and the effectiveness of the program's treatment services. If the information sought is available elsewhere, the court ordinarily should deny the application (§2.64(d)). The judge may examine the records before making a decision (§2.64(c)).

Limitations on the Scope of the Order

The regulations limit the scope of disclosure that a court may authorize, even when it finds good cause exists. Disclosure must be limited to the information essential to fulfill the purpose of the order and it must be restricted to those persons who need the information for that purpose. The court should also take any other steps that are necessary to protect the patient's confidentiality, including sealing court records from public scrutiny (§2.64).

A court may authorize disclosure of "confidential communications" by a patient to the program only if the disclosure (1) is necessary to protect against a threat to life or of serious bodily injury; (2) is necessary to investigate or prosecute an extremely serious crime; or (3) is in connection with a proceeding at which the patient has already presented evidence concerning confidential communications. In all other situations, not even a court can order disclosure of confidential communications (§2.63).

A program, investigative law enforcement, or prosecutorial agency seeking an order to authorize disclosures for purposes of investigating or prosecuting a patient for a crime must meet five additional, stringent criteria (§2.65).[u] Before issuing such an order, a court must find that:

1. The crime involved is extremely serious, such as an act causing or directly threatening to cause death or serious bodily injury, including homicide, rape, kidnaping, armed robbery, assault with a deadly weapon, and child abuse and neglect,
2. The records sought are likely to contain information of significance to the investigation or prosecution,
3. There is no other practical way to obtain the information,
4. The public interest in disclosure outweighs any actual or potential harm to the patient, the doctor-patient relationship, and the ability of the program to provide services to other patients, and
5. When law enforcement personnel seek an order, the program had an opportunity to be represented by independent counsel. (When the program is a governmental entity, it *must* be represented by counsel.) (§2.65(d))

The regulations require that a court follow the same special procedures that apply to court-ordered disclosures generally (except that the patient need not be given notice). In addition, court orders authorizing disclosure for the purpose of investigating or prosecuting patients are subject to the same limitations on scope that apply to court-ordered disclosures generally. Under no circumstances may a court authorize a program to turn over the entire patient record to a law enforcement, investigative, or prosecutorial agency.[v]

It bears repeating that the court orders contemplated by the regulations simply authorize a program to make a disclosure that would otherwise be prohibited. The regulations themselves do not give a court authority to compel disclosure. If, however, a court issues an order compelling disclosure under another source of judicial power and issues an order authorizing dis-

---

[t] However, no notice to the patient is required if an order is sought to authorize disclosure and use of records to criminally investigate or prosecute a patient (§2.65) and no notice at all is required if an order is sought to authorize disclosure and use of records to investigate or prosecute a program or the person holding records (§2.66).

---

[u] Note that the regulations do not permit courts to order researchers "who have obtained patient-identifying information without consent for the purpose of conducting research, audit or evaluation, to disclose that information or to use it to conduct any criminal investigation or prosecution of a patient" (§2.62).

[v] The regulations do contain special provisions regarding court orders authorizing disclosures for purposes of investigating or prosecuting a program or its employees (§2.66) and court orders authorizing a government agency to place an undercover agent or informant in a program to gather evidence of serious criminal conduct by the program or its employees (§2.67). The regulations set strict prerequisites for obtaining such orders and prohibit the use of information obtained through these means against patients.

closure under the regulations, or if an order authorizing disclosure is accompanied by a valid subpoena, the program is legally bound to make the disclosure that has been authorized. The variety of forms that these orders and processes may take reinforces the need for counsel in this area.

A final word about a positive use programs may make of court orders. On rare occasions, a program may feel constrained to disclose information over a patient's objection or to make a disclosure that will in some sense be against a patient's interests. Following the procedures discussed here, the program could place the problem before a court and allow it to resolve the competing claims of program, patient, and public.

QUESTION 5: PATIENT CRIMES ON PROGRAM PREMISES OR AGAINST PROGRAM PERSONNEL

When a patient has committed or threatened a crime on program premises or against program personnel, the regulations permit the program to report the crime to a law enforcement agency or to seek its assistance. In such a situation, the program can disclose the circumstances of the incident, including the suspect's name, address, last known whereabouts, and status as a patient at the program (§2.12(c)(5)).

QUESTION 6: DISCLOSURES FOR RESEARCH, AUDIT, OR EVALUATION PURPOSES

Scientific Research

The confidentiality regulations permit, but do not require, a program to disclose patient-identifying information to researchers without patient consent, providing certain safeguards are met.[w]

A program may only release data to researchers the program director finds qualified. This decision turns on the training and experience of the particular researcher in the area of research to be conducted. Researchers must also have a protocol that ensures that information will be securely stored and not redisclosed except as allowed by the regulations, and the protocol's confidentiality safeguards must be approved by an independent group of three or more individuals.

Researchers who do receive patient-identifying information are strictly prohibited from redisclosing any patient information to anyone except back to the program.[x] Research reports may not identify a patient, directly or indirectly. Finally, no patient-identifying information may be used to conduct any criminal investigation of a patient, even in response to a federal or state court order (§2.62).

Follow-up evaluations of former patients present a particular challenge under the confidentiality regulations. A program—or a researcher to whom it has disclosed patient data—may only attempt to contact a patient if it can do so without disclosing the patient's relationship with the treatment program to third persons. Accordingly, no inquiries—whether to relatives, friends, employers, or others—designed to locate a former patient may be

conducted unless they can be carried out in a way that will not reveal the individual's status as a former drug or alcohol abuse patient or unless the patient has signed a proper consent form under the regulations.[y]

Audits and Evaluations

Government agencies that fund or regulate a program, private agencies that provide financial assistance or third-party payments to a program, and peer review organizations that review utilization or quality control may have access to program records without patient consent to conduct an audit or evaluation. Any person or organization that conducts an audit or evaluation must agree in writing that it will redisclose patient-identifying information only (1) back to the program; (2) pursuant to a court order to investigate or prosecute the program (*not* a patient); or (3) to a government agency that is overseeing a Medicare or Medicaid audit or evaluation (§2.53(c), (d)).

The agencies listed in the first sentence of the preceding paragraph may also copy or remove records, but only if they promise in writing to safeguard the confidentiality of patient-identifying information in accordance with the regulations, to redisclose patients' identities only as permitted by the regulations, and to destroy all patient-identifying information when the audit or evaluation is completed (§2.53(b)).

Any other person or organization determined by the program director to be qualified, and that pledges in writing to observe the restrictions on redisclosure, may also inspect patient records for audit or evaluation purpose without consent, but only the agencies listed two paragraphs above can be permitted to copy or remove records.

QUESTION 7: CHILD ABUSE AND NEGLECT REPORTING

The federal law and regulations "do not apply to the reporting under state law of incidents of suspected child abuse and neglect to the appropriate state or local authorities" (§2.12(c)(6)). All treatment programs must strictly comply with the provisions of the mandatory reporting laws in their states.

However, the exemption for child abuse reporting applies only to *initial* reports of child abuse or neglect and not to requests or even subpoenas for additional information or records, even if the records are sought for use in civil or criminal proceedings resulting from the program's initial report. Thus, patient files must still be withheld from child protection agencies absent an appropriate court order or patient consent.

The legislative history of the amendment makes clear that reporting is permitted only when there is a danger of harm to the child and not merely because a parent has abused drugs or alcohol. The statute and regulations are thus carefully crafted to permit compliance with state laws mandating the reporting of child abuse and neglect while preserving confidentiality to the maximum extent possible.

QUESTION 8: QUALIFIED SERVICE ORGANIZATION

The regulations recognize that a program may need to communicate patient-identifying information in order to secure the services of outside agencies that offer urinalysis or data processing, accounting, or legal services, for example. To facilitate necessary communication, a program may enter into a "qualified service organization agreement" with the outside agency. Under this arrangement, which must be in writing, the outside organization (1) acknowledges that it is fully bound by the confidentiality regulations in handling all information about patients that it receives from the program and (2) promises that it will resist, if necessary in judicial proceedings, any attempt to obtain such information that is not permitted by the regulations (§2.12(c)(4)).

Once the program and the outside agency have entered an agreement of this kind, the program may freely communicate information from patient records to the "qualified service organization," but only that information needed by the organization to provide services to the program.

---

[w] The confidentiality regulations are concerned only with the release of patient-identifying data. Although they do not require patient consent for disclosures for research purposes, the regulations do not diminish the force of other laws that may require the informed consent of research subjects. When informed consent is required in human experimentation is beyond the scope of this chapter. The confidentiality regulations neither add to nor subtract from any such requirements.

Two additional federal laws permit the United States Attorney General and the Secretary of HHS to authorize researchers to withhold the names and identities of research subjects. Once such authorization is issued, the researcher "may not be compelled in any Federal, State or local civil, criminal, administrative, legislative or other proceeding to identify the subjects of research for which such authorization was obtained" (42 U.S.C. §241(d) (permits the Secretary of HHS to issue confidentiality certificates); 21 U.S.C. §872(c) (permits the Attorney General to issue confidentiality certificates)). The statute authorizing the Secretary of HHS to issue confidentiality certificates specifies that it applies to "persons engaged in biomedical, behavioral, clinical, or other research (including research on mental health, including research on the use and effect of alcohol and other psychoactive drugs). . . ."

[x] However, researchers who are required by state or local law to make child abuse reports based on information from patients' files may do so (§2.21(c)(6)).

---

[y] For a fuller discussion of ways in which follow-up research can be conducted, see *Developing State Outcomes Monitoring Systems for Alcohol and Other Drug Abuse Treatment: The Recommendations of a Consensus Panel,* The Center for Substance Abuse Treatment (Rockville, MD, 1995).

A qualified service organization agreement is not a substitute for individual consent in other situations. Disclosures under such an agreement must be limited to information that is needed by others so that the program can function effectively. It may not be used between programs providing substance abuse assessment or treatment services.

MISCELLANEOUS PROVISIONS

Patient Notice

The regulations require programs to notify patients of the existence of the federal confidentiality statute and regulations and to give them a written summary of their provisions. The notice and summary should be provided at admission or "as soon thereafter as the patient is capable of rational communication" (§2.22(a)).

The regulations specify five items that must be included in the written summary and a sample notice:

1. A list of the circumstances in which disclosures can be made without consent,
2. A statement that violation of the regulations is a reportable crime,
3. and 4. Specific mention that suspected child abuse or neglect and crimes on program premises or against program personnel can be reported, and
5. Citation to the law and regulations (§2.22(b)).

The regulations contain a sample notice at §2.22(d).

Patients' Access to Records

The revised regulations specify that they do not prohibit patients' access to their own records, and neither written consent or any other authorization is required to provide such access. Thus, programs have the discretion to decide when to permit patients to view or obtain copies of their records, unless they are governed by a state law that establishes circumstances in which patients have a right to such access. Information obtained by a patient from the program cannot be used to investigate or prosecute the patient in a criminal proceeding (§2.23).

REPRISE: THE GENERAL RULE

It is now time to return to the general rule. Except for disclosures made with written patient consent, internal program communications, communications that contain no patient-identifying information, disclosures to medical personnel in medical emergencies, disclosures pursuant to valid court orders, reports of patients crimes on program premises or against program personnel, disclosures made for research or audit purposes, initial child abuse and neglect reports, and communications with qualified service organizations, patient records simply may not be disclosed.

COMMONLY ARISING SITUATIONS

The discussion will now turn to applying the principles laid out here to situations programs confront most often. This discussion will also serve as a review, since solutions to the questions raised in this section require an understanding of the general rule prohibiting disclosure as well as the exceptions to the general rule.

Seeking Information from Collateral and Referral Sources

Making inquiries of relatives (including parents), doctors and other health care providers, employers, schools, or criminal justice agencies might seem at first glance to pose no risk to a patient's right to confidentiality, particularly if the person or entity approached for information referred the patient to treatment. But it does.

When a program that screens, assesses, or treats a patient asks someone to verify information it has obtained from the patient, it is making a patient-identifying disclosure that the patient has sought its services. In other words, when program staff seek information from other sources, they are letting these

sources know that the patient has asked for substance abuse services. The regulations generally prohibit this kind of disclosure unless the patient consents.

How then is a program to proceed? The easiest way is to get the patient's consent to contact the relative, doctor, employer, school, health care facility, etc.

As noted previously, when filling out the consent form, program staff should consider what the "purpose of the disclosure" is and "how much and what kind of information will be disclosed." For example, if a program is assessing a patient for treatment and seeks records from a mental health provider, the purpose of the disclosure would be "to obtain mental health treatment records to complete the assessment." The "kind of information disclosed" would then be limited to a statement that "James Jones (the patient) is being assessed by the XYZ Program." No other information about James Jones would be released to the mental health provider.

If the program seeks not only records, but needs to discuss with the mental health provider the treatment it provided the patient, the purpose of the disclosure would be "to discuss mental health treatment provided to James Jones by the mental health program." If the program merely seeks information, the kind of information disclosed would, as in the example here, be limited to a statement that "James Jones is being assessed by the XYZ Program." However, if the program needs to disclose information it gained in its assessment of James Jones to the mental health provider in order to further the discussion or coordinate care, the kind of information disclosed would be "assessment information about James Jones."

A program that routinely seeks collateral information from many sources could consider asking the patient to sign a consent form that permits it to make a disclosure for purposes of seeking information from collateral sources to any one of a number of entities or persons listed on the consent form. Note that this combination form must still include "the name or title of the individual or the name of the organization" for each collateral source the program may contact.

Programs should keep in mind that when they disclose information over the telephone with written patient consent, they are required to notify the recipients of the information of the prohibition on redisclosure. Mention should be made of this restriction during the conversation; for example, program staff could say, "I'll be sending you a written statement that the information I gave you about Mr. Jones cannot be redisclosed."

Handling Telephone Calls for Patients

If someone telephones a patient at a substance abuse program, the program cannot simply say that the patient is at the program, unless it has a written consent form signed by a patient to make a disclosure to that particular caller. How then should a program handle telephone calls to patients? There are a number of ways to deal with this issue:

1. The program can get the patient's consent to accept telephone calls from particular people and consult the patient's list when he or she receives a phone call.
2. If the patient has not consented to receive calls from a particular person, the program can put the caller on hold and ask the patient if he or she wants to speak to the caller. If the patient wants to accept the call, the patient (and not the program) is making the disclosure that he or she is at the substance abuse program. If the patient does not want to speak to the caller, the program must tell the caller, "I'm sorry, but I can't tell you whether Tommy Smith is here." At no time can the program reveal, even indirectly, that the person being inquired after is a patient at the program.
3. The program can uniformly take messages for patients, telling all callers, "I'm sorry, but I cannot tell you if Mr. Smith is here, but if he is I will give him this message." Again, this leaves it up to the patient whether to make a disclosure about being in treatment.
4. The program can set up a "patient phone" that is answered only by patients. Since only patients would be answering the telephone (and only patients would be giving the phone number to others if the number were unlisted), the program would be making no disclosures. Of course, the program should caution patients to act discreetly and thoughtfully when handling calls for others.

Dealing with Patients' Admissions of Planned, Past, or Current Criminal Activity

A patient confesses to a counselor that he has committed a serious crime. A patient reveals to a counselor that she plans to harm another person. In both these situations, the confidentiality regulations restrict the communications the program or its personnel may make to a law enforcement agency or a court. Both situations raise serious questions of treatment philosophy, community relations, and ethics. They tend to arouse strong emotions that may cloud decision making.

This chapter cannot solve those deeper questions or paint a bright line toward correct decisions. It can, however, describe the legal context in which these questions must be resolved and the limits imposed by the regulations.

Threatened Criminal Activity and the Duty to Warn

For most treatment professionals, the issue of reporting a patient's threat to commit a crime is a troubling one. Many people feel that they have an ethical, professional, or moral obligation to prevent a crime when they are in a position to do so; many are aware that when the crime is a serious one, they may have a legal duty to warn the intended victim.

Over the past 20 years, there has been a developing trend to require psychiatrists and other therapists to take "reasonable steps" to protect an intended victim when they learn that a patient presents a "serious danger of violence to another." This trend started with a case called *Tarasoff v. Regents of the University of California,* 17 Cal.3d 425 (1976), in which the California Supreme Court held a psychologist liable for money damages because he failed to warn a potential victim his patient threatened to—and then did—kill. The court ruled that if a psychologist knows that a patient poses a serious risk of violence to a particular person, the psychologist has a duty "to warn the intended victim or others likely to apprise the victim of the danger, to notify the police, or to take whatever other steps are reasonably necessary under the circumstances."

Although the *Tarasoff* case applied only in California, the courts and legislatures in a growing number of other states have adopted the rule and impose liability on therapists when they fail to warn someone threatened and then harmed by a patient. The statutes and cases tend to limit liability to situations where patients threaten a specific identifiable victim, and generally do not apply when a patient makes a threat without identifying an intended target.

Two and sometimes three legal questions must be asked in each situation:

1. Is there a legal duty to warn in this particular situation under state law?
2. Even if there is no state legal requirement that the program warn an intended victim or the police, does the program feel a moral obligation to warn someone?

The first question can only be answered by an attorney familiar with the law in the state in which the substance abuse program operates. If the answer to the first question is "no," it is advisable to discuss the second question with a knowledgeable lawyer too.

3. If the answer to questions 1 or 2 is "yes," can the program warn the victim or someone likely to be able to take action without violating the federal confidentiality regulations?

The problem is that there is an apparent conflict between the federal confidentiality requirements and the "duty to warn" imposed by states that have adopted the principles of the *Tarasoff* case. Simply put, the confidentiality law and regulations prohibit the type of disclosure that Tarasoff and similar cases require,[z] unless a program can use one of the regulations' narrow exceptions.

There are five ways a program can proceed when a patient makes a threat to harm himself or herself or another:

1. The program itself can make a disclosure to the potential victim or law enforcement officials if it does not identify the individual who threatens to commit the crime as a patient. This can be accomplished either by making an anonymous report or—for an program that is part of a larger non-drug/alcohol entity—by making the report in the larger entity's name. For example, a counselor employed by a program that is part of a mental health facility could phone the police or the potential target of an attack, identify herself as "a counselor at the Jackson City Mental Health Clinic" and explain the risk. This would convey the vital information without identifying the patient as an alcohol or drug abuser. Counselors at freestanding programs cannot give the name of the program.
2. The program can go to court and request a court order in accordance with §2.64 of the federal regulations, authorizing the disclosure to the intended victim, or in accordance with §2.65, authorizing disclosure to a law enforcement agency.[aa]
3. If the patient is participating in treatment as a condition of the disposition of a criminal charge, the program can make a report to the criminal justice agency that mandated the patient into treatment, so long as there is a criminal justice system consent form signed by the patient that is worded broadly enough to allow this sort of information to be disclosed. The criminal justice agency can then act on the information by warning the intended victim or notifying another law enforcement agency of the threat. However, in doing so, the criminal justice agency must be careful that no mention is made that the source of the tip was a program or that the patient is in alcohol or drug assessment or treatment. For example, if the prosecuting attorney is authorized by the consent form to receive the report, he or she can notify the police or the potential target of the attack, without mentioning that the individual threatening harm is a substance abuser or in treatment.[bb]
4. The program can make a report to medical personnel if the threat presents a medical emergency that poses an immediate threat to the health of any individual and requires immediate medical intervention (§2.51). For example, a program could notify a private physician about a suicidal patient so that medical intervention can be arranged.
5. The program can obtain the patient's consent. This may be unlikely, unless the patient is suicidal.[cc]

If none of these options is practical, what should a program do? It is, after all, confronted with conflicting moral and legal obligations. If a program believes there is clear and imminent danger to a patient or a particular other person, it is probably wiser to err on the side of making an effective report about the danger to the authorities or to the threatened individual. This is especially true in states that already follow the *Tarasoff* rule.

While each case presents different questions, it is doubtful that any pros-

---

[z] Moreover, the federal regulations make it clear that federal law overrides any state law that conflicts with the regulations (§2.20). In the only case, as of this writing, that addresses this conflict between federal and state law *(Hasenie v. United States,* 541 F. Supp. 999 (D. Md. 1982)), the court ruled that the federal confidentiality law prohibited any report.

[aa] As noted above, the regulations limit disclosures to law enforcement agencies for the purpose of investigating or prosecuting a patient to "extremely serious" crimes, "such as one which causes or directly threatens loss of life or serious bodily injury, including homicide, rape, kidnaping, armed robbery, assault with a deadly weapon, and child abuse and neglect" (§2.65).

[bb] As already noted, the federal regulations limit what the criminal justice agency can do with this information. Section 2.35(d) states that anyone receiving information pursuant to a criminal justice system consent "may redisclose and use it only to carry out that person's official duties with regard to the patient's conditional release or other action in connection with which the consent was given." Thus, the disclosure can be used by the criminal justice agency that permitted the patient to enter treatment to revoke his or her participation in treatment, but it most likely cannot be used to prosecute the patient for a separate crime (in other words, for making the threat). Only if a special court order is obtained pursuant to §2.65 of the regulations can information obtained from a program be used to investigate or prosecute a patient.

[cc] Note that the federal confidentiality statutes and regulations strictly prohibit any investigation or prosecution of a patient based on information obtained from records unless the court order exception is used (42 U.S.C.§§290 dd-2 and 42 C.F.R. §2.12(d)(1)).

ecution (or successful civil lawsuit) under the federal confidentiality regulations would be brought against a program or a counselor who warned about potential violence when the counselor believed in good faith that there was real danger to a particular individual. On the other hand, a civil lawsuit for failure to warn may well result if the threat is actually carried out. In any event, the program should at least try to make the warning in a manner that does not identify the individual as a alcohol or drug abuser.

As in other areas where the law is still developing, programs should find a lawyer familiar with the issues, who can provide advice on a case-by-case basis.

Reporting Past Criminal Activity

Does a program have a responsibility to call the police (or the criminal justice agency that mandated the patient into treatment) when a patient discloses to a counselor that he participated in a crime some time in the past—or during his participation in the treatment program?

Suppose, for example, that a patient admits during a counseling session that he killed someone during a robbery three years ago. Here the program is not warning anyone of a threat, but serious harm did come to another person. Does the program have a responsibility to report that?

The issue of reporting past criminal activity is one that arises frequently for treatment programs. When a patient tells a counselor that he or she committed a crime in the past, there are generally three questions the program needs to ask as it considers whether to make a report:

1. Is there a legal duty to report the past criminal activity to a law enforcement agency under state law? Generally, the answer to this question is no. In most states, there is no duty to report a crime committed in the past. Even those states that continue to make failure to report a crime rarely prosecute violations of the law.
2. Does state law permit a counselor to report the crime to law enforcement authorities if he or she wants to? Whether or not there is a legal obligation to imposed on citizens to report past crimes to the police, state law may protect conversations between counselors of alcohol and drug programs and their patients and exempt counselors from any requirement to report past criminal activity by patients. Such laws are important to patients in drug treatment, many of whom have committed offenses during their years of drug abuse. Part of the therapeutic process for patients is acknowledging the harm they have done others. If programs routinely reported patients' admissions of past criminal activity to the police, their ability to work with patients in the recovery process would be thwarted. Laws protecting conversations between counselors of alcohol and drug programs and their patients are designed to protect the special relationship drug and alcohol counselors have with their patients, as well as the treatment process.

State laws vary widely in the protection they accord communications between patients and counselors. In some states, admissions of past crimes may be considered privileged and counselors may be prohibited from reporting them; in others, admissions may not be privileged. Moreover, each state defines the kinds of relationships protected differently. Whether a communication about past criminal activity is privileged (and therefore cannot be reported) may depend upon the type of professional the counselor is and whether he or she is licensed or certified by the state.

Any program that is especially concerned about this issue should ask a local attorney for an opinion letter about whether there is a duty to report and whether any counselor-patient privilege exempts counselors from that duty.

3. If state law requires a report (or permits one and the program decides to make a report), how can the program comply with the confidentiality regulations and state law?

Any program that decides to make a report to law enforcement authorities about a patient's past criminal activity must do so without violating either the confidentiality regulations or state laws. A program that decides to report a patient's crime can comply with the federal regulations by following three of the five methods described above in the discussion of "Duty to Warn":[dd]

1. The program can obtain a court order under §2.65 of the regulations, permitting it to make a report if the crime is "extremely serious."
2. The program can make a report in a way that does not identify the individual as a patient in a substance abuse program.
3. If the patient is an offender participating in treatment as a condition of a criminal disposition, the program can make a report to the criminal justice agency that referred the patient, if it has a criminal justice system consent form signed by the patient that is worded broadly enough to allow this sort of information to be disclosed.

By using any one of these methods, the program will have discharged its reporting responsibility without violating the regulations. However, the law enforcement agency that receives the report is prohibited by the regulations from investigating or prosecuting a patient based on information obtained from a program unless the court order exception is used (42 U.S.C. §§290 dd-2(c) and 42 C.F.R. §2.12(d)(1)). Because of the complicated nature of this issue, any program considering reporting a patient's admission of criminal activity that occurred in the past should seek the advice of a lawyer familiar with local law as well as the federal regulations.

Reporting Current Criminal Activity

What should a program do when a patient tells a counselor that she has gotten, or intends to get, new clothes for her kids by shoplifting—a crime the counselor knows she has committed many times in the past? Does the program have a duty to tell the police? What should a program do if a patient admits she committed a crime during her time in treatment and that patient is in treatment as a condition of parole—or as a condition of any other criminal justice disposition? Should the program inform the parole department? Should the program report petty crime, like shoplifting, or should it limit its disclosures to more serious offenses?

By this time, the reader should know the answer to the first set of questions: A program generally does not have a duty to warn another person or the police about a patient's intended actions unless the patient presents a serious danger of violence to an identifiable individual. Shoplifting rarely involves violence, and it is unlikely that the counselor will know which stores are to be victimized. Petty crime like shoplifting is an important issue that should be dealt with therapeutically. It is not something a program should necessarily report to the police—either before or after the crime takes place.[ee]

Questions about what must be reported about patients in treatment as a condition of disposition of a criminal offense are somewhat different. Cooperation between a treatment program and a criminal justice agency referring patients requires trust and there is nothing more destructive of trust than misunderstanding and disagreement on this issue. At least two questions must be resolved before a program takes on the treatment of patients who will be participating as a condition of the disposition of criminal charges against them: (1) What kinds of offenses will the criminal justice partner expect the treatment agency to report and (2) how much discretion will the program retain. To ensure that no misunderstandings occur, the treatment program and criminal justice agency should enter into a written agreement outlining the parties' understanding.

In coming to an agreement on this issue, the program and the criminal justice agency must balance the goal of public safety with the goal of recovery. Those concerned with public safety will generally advocate drawing the line at a point that requires greater reporting of criminal activity by the treat-

---

[dd] Of course, if a patient has committed or threatens to commit a crime on program premises or against program personnel, §2.12(c) (5) permits the program to report the crime to a law enforcement agency or to seek its assistance. In such a situation, without any special authorization, the program can disclose the circumstances of the incident, including the suspect's name, address, last known whereabouts, and status as a patient at the program.

[ee] Moreover, state law may protect conversations between counselors of programs and their patients. See the discussion of this issue in the previous section.

ment program. Those concerned with the effectiveness of treatment programs may argue that reporting of criminal activity must be limited if patients are to continue to communicate freely about their deviant behavior as they struggle towards recovery.

Wherever the line is drawn, it is crucial that the patients participating in this kind of program be informed that their admissions of criminal activity committed during treatment will be reported. The criminal justice system consent form such patients sign should make clear that certain kinds of ongoing criminal activity will be reported promptly to the court and/or prosecutor.*ff*

How to Respond to Subpoenas

There are two kinds of subpoenas. One requires the person to whom it is addressed to appear to give testimony. The other, sometimes called "a subpoena duces tecum," requires a person to appear with documents and may also require testimony. A subpoena can be issued by a variety of people—a judge, a court clerk, a district attorney, the state attorney general, or even a private attorney. The following discussion applies to subpoenas of all kinds.

The federal law and regulations prohibit treatment programs from disclosing information concerning current or former patients in response to subpoenas. A program may not release any information (including both documents and verbal testimony) in response to a subpoena unless either:

1. The patient about whom information is sought signs a proper consent form authorizing the program to release the requested information; or
2. A court orders the program to release information or records after giving the program and the patient an opportunity to be heard and after making a good cause determination under the confidentiality law and regulations.

A subpoena, even one signed by a judge, is not the type of court order required by the confidentiality regulations; therefore, the program may not release information in response to a subpoena even if it is signed by a judge.

Except when the program itself is the subject of a criminal investigation, a valid court order may not be issued under the confidentiality law and regulations unless the program first received an opportunity to appear at a hearing. Therefore, unless the program was notified that a court order was being sought, no proper court order under the confidentiality law and regulations could be issued. Furthermore, a proper court order will usually state specifically that it is being issued pursuant to the federal confidentiality law and regulations (42 U.S.C. §290dd-2 and 42 C.F.R. Part 2). If the program has difficulty determining whether the document is a subpoena, a court order, or an application for a court order, it should consult an attorney without delay.

If the program has an attorney who handles these matters, then of course the first step should be to contact that person. In any event, three general principles apply to responding to a subpoena for programs covered by the federal confidentiality regulations:

1. No information should be released by a treatment program in response to a subpoena even if it is signed by a judge.
2. The subpoena should not be ignored. Failure to respond in some way may be grounds for a finding of contempt of court and can result in a fine or even a jail term.
3. The person (or the program) to whom the subpoena is addressed does not

automatically have to testify or turn over the requested materials. The person (or program) has the right to appear and object to the subpoena.

If the subpoena is signed by a lawyer representing the patient, the problem may be easily resolved: The program should inform the patient or the lawyer (after obtaining the patient's written consent) that the patient must sign a proper consent form authorizing the program to comply with the subpoena.

If the subpoena is served by someone other than the patient's lawyer, the patient will probably not sign a consent form permitting the program to turn over the information. The program should then inform the person who signed the subpoena that the federal confidentiality regulations prohibit the program from complying with the subpoena unless a court order is issued in accordance with the procedures and standards set forth in the regulations. The program could try to convince the person who signed the subpoena to withdraw it and apply for a court order.

If the subpoena does not require an immediate response, the program should write a letter (return receipt requested) to the person who signed it, explaining why the program cannot comply with the subpoena.*gg* If the subpoena requires a more immediate response, the program administrator could try to convey the same information over the telephone and then send a letter confirming its understanding of the conversation.

If the program's efforts to fend off the subpoena are unsuccessful, then the best course is to try once again to seek the assistance of a lawyer, preferably one who is familiar with the requirements of the confidentiality regulations. The advantages of having a lawyer represent the program are that in addition to explaining the requirements of the federal confidentiality regulations to the person, court, or administrative agency that issued the subpoena, the lawyer will also be familiar with other grounds upon which the program may object to a subpoena. For example, treatment records and information about patients may be protected from disclosure by a physician-patient, therapist-patient, or similar privilege created by state law. Or, an objection to a subpoena can be made if the information sought is irrelevant to the proceeding.*hh*

If the program cannot find a lawyer of its own, it can try to get help from the attorney for another party to the proceeding, that is, an attorney who did not issue the subpoena. This is because subpoenas may be attacked by either the person subpoenaed or by any other party to the proceeding, and there is often at least one party—usually the patient—who is interested in protecting the information his or her opponent is trying to obtain. Again, the program must be aware of the limitations that the confidentiality regulations place upon the kind and amount of information it can convey to the attorney from whom it is seeking help.

If all efforts to get help from an attorney fail, and the program is unsuccessful in its efforts to convince the person who issued the subpoena either to withdraw it or seek the required court order, the person or program subpoenaed should appear in court on the appropriate date. At that time, the program should request that the judge "quash" the subpoena. The program must explain to the judge the requirements of the federal confidentiality regulations, including the procedure and standards the judge must follow before he or she may issue an order authorizing the program to disclose information. It is a good idea to bring a copy of the regulations to show the judge, since the judge may be completely unfamiliar with them.

Once the program appears at the court hearing and asks the court to quash

---

ff As mentioned previously, the regulations strictly prohibit any investigation or prosecution of a patient based on information obtained from a substance abuse program unless the §2.65 court order exception is used (42 U.S.C. §§290 dd-2 and 42 C.F.R. §2.12(d)(1)). Thus, if the court or a prosecutor learns in any other way that a patient in treatment as a result of a criminal charge has committed a new crime during treatment, there is little either can do other than end the patient's participation in the diversion program. For this reason, programs with patients who are in treatment as a condition of the disposition of the criminal charges against them should consider developing the capacity to apply for a court order under §2.65 of the regulations in cases where patients commit serious crimes. All that is required is a model set of legal papers that the program can submit to the appropriate court on a moment's notice. This will permit prompt reporting of crimes that threaten public safety and call for separate investigation and prosecution.

---

gg See *Confidentiality: A Guide to the Federal Law and Regulations,* 1995 rev. edition, New York: Legal Action Center, 1995, which contains sample forms, including model letters for responding to subpoenas.

hh When a program seeks help from a lawyer, the lawyer is generally going to want to know the name of the patient whose records are at issue. This information is essential for the lawyer to be able to communicate with the attorney or judge who issued the subpoena. Technically, the program would be committing a breach of confidentiality if it divulged the name of the patient to the lawyer without the patient's consent. The best way to avoid this problem is to enter into a Qualified Service Organization Agreement (QSOA) with a lawyer that will permit the program to disclose information about patients to the attorney if the attorney needs the information to provide legal services to the program. The QSOA should be entered into *before* a legal problem arises.

the subpoena or issue a proper court order before requiring disclosure of any records, it has satisfied its obligations under the regulations. If the court decides not to issue any order, the program goes home a winner. If the court does issue an order—whether in writing or orally—the program can either turn over the records ordered disclosed or appeal, whichever it chooses. The regulations do not require a program to appeal a court's ruling, even if it appears to be wrong.

Dealing with Search and Arrest Warrants

If a police officer arrives at the door of a clinic with a search warrant authorizing him to seize all records about a particular patient, the program obviously has a problem. A search warrant is not the type of court order that authorizes a program to permit law enforcement officers onto its premises—an action that may well result in disclosure of patients' identities—or to release records. Yet, law enforcement officers are unlikely to know anything about the federal regulations and are likely to think that a search warrant entitles them to enter and obtain the records.

Like many legal problems, this one has no easy answer. If granting physical access to a program results in the officers' seeing either patients or any records identifying patients, then the program has made an unauthorized disclosure. Thus, the program should not just roll over and give in. Rather, a counselor or a program confronted by a law enforcement officer with a search warrant should:

1. Show the officer a copy of the regulations and explain that the program cannot allow access to patient records without an appropriate court order. It is a good idea to keep a copy of the confidentiality regulations at hand so that, when situations like this arise, the program can show them to the person seeking access to the program or its records.
2. Ask the officer to let the program call a lawyer who can attempt to resolve the situation with the officer.
3. Ask the officer to let the program contact the prosecuting attorney or commanding officer so that the program can repeat its arguments, stressing that a court order is required before any disclosure and that illegally seized records may not be admissible in court.
4. Allow the officer to enter if he or she insists. *A program should not forcibly resist.* Refusing to obey the orders of a law enforcement officer may constitute a crime, even though the officer's orders may later be shown to be erroneous or illegal. On the other hand, no one should be held liable under the regulations for permitting entry to an officer who insists on it.

As is often the case when a confidentiality problem arises, it is best to get help from a lawyer. Indeed, more than any other situations governed by the confidentiality regulations, those involving search warrants and court orders call for professional help. The best way to find a path through a morass created by conflicting federal and local demands in this area is with a lawyer's help.

Perhaps the most effective step that can be taken in this area is preventive. Whenever possible, programs should establish relationships with local law enforcement officials and familiarize them with the confidentiality regulations. If the police understand the steps they must take to obtain the limited information they may be entitled to get, traumatic confrontations may be avoidable.

An *arrest warrant,* unlike a search warrant, does give law enforcement officials the right to search the program. If the officers are in search of a particular patient who committed or threatened a crime on the premises of the program or against program personnel, the program may produce the individual, thereby minimizing disclosure of the identities of other patients as far as possible.

However, if the officers are in search of a particular patient because of a crime committed elsewhere, the program may not cooperate with the search, unless a court order has been issued under the regulations, which would permit the program to surrender the patient (and his identity) to the police.

Thus, a program faced with an arrest warrant not accompanied by a court order is placed in the worst of all possible worlds—the police can roam through the program, but the program cannot point out the patient to the po-

lice. It is best if the program can convince the police to obtain a proper court order before executing the arrest warrant. Alternatively, the program could, if it knows which patient is being sought by the police, try to convince that patient to surrender voluntarily. If the police are determined to execute the warrant, the patient will be arrested in any case. A voluntary surrender might make it easier for the patient's lawyer to apply for bail in the future.[ii]

Handling HIV/AIDS and Other Infectious Disease Information

Today, substance abuse programs treat patients with a variety of illnesses—tuberculosis (TB), sexually transmitted diseases (STDs), and HIV or AIDS. Each state has its own rules about how program staff must treat information about each of these diseases. Because the scope of each state's laws varies, programs that serve populations with these diseases must become familiar with the legal requirements in their states.

This chapter will discuss three issues relating to the disclosure of HIV-related information: releasing information from files containing both substance abuse and HIV/AIDS information; duty to warn issues; and making mandatory reports to public health authorities.

Releasing Information from Files Containing Both Substance Abuse and HIV/AIDS Information

Suppose that a patient signs a proper consent form permitting disclosure of information about his or her substance abuse problem, but the file also contains information about HIV/AIDS? Can the program release the information? The answer depends upon the law of the state in which the program is situated. Even if a patient has signed a consent form permitting release of information disclosing his connection to alcohol or drugs, the program may not release information related to the patient's HIV/AIDS status if state law prohibits it.

There are a number of ways to handle this problem:

1. If the patient wishes to have the program disclose information about both his HIV status and his substance abuse problem, the program can have the patient sign two consent forms—one complying with 42 C.F.R. Part 2 and the other complying with state consent laws regarding release of HIV information. Alternatively, the program can draft a single consent form that satisfies both the federal regulations and state law.
2. The consent form required by the federal regulations can be drafted in a way that includes all (or relevant parts) of the information related to substance abuse but excludes all HIV/AIDS information. Since the consent form must contain a statement of the purpose of the disclosure and how much and what kind of information will be disclosed, the program can restrict access to HIV/AIDS information in a patient's file by having the patient sign a consent form that has as its purpose, for example, "referral for inpatient substance abuse treatment." How much and what kind of information will be disclosed would then be "information about John Smith's alcohol problem that the program gained during screening and assessment."
3. The program can maintain a filing system that isolates drug and HIV-related information in two different "treatment" and "medical" files and discloses only information from the "treatment" file. This solution can be used whether or not state law protects HIV/AIDS information. Note, however, that some states may regulate the way in which HIV/AIDS information must be charted.
4. The program can send the patient's file *without the HIV/AIDS-related information* to the outside agency and put the following notice on the disclosure:

[ii] If law enforcement officers are in "hot pursuit" of a patient who is at the program, the program may have discretion under the regulations to point out the patient: If state law makes the patient's flight and presence at the program a crime, it is a crime committed on program premises and, therefore, reportable to law enforcement officers under §2.12(c) (5). If possible, an attorney should be consulted to determine whether a patient's presence at the program when the patient is sought by the police is considered to be a criminal act under state law.

This file does not contain any information protected by section [fill in applicable section] of the [state] law. The fact that this notice accompanies these records is *not* an indication that this client's file contains any information protected by section [fill in applicable section].

Duty to Warn Issues

Does a program have a "duty to warn" anyone when a patient is infected with HIV? Again, this is a matter of state law. Courts in some states have held that health care providers have a duty to warn third parties of potentially dangerous behavior of persons under their care.[jj]

Two behaviors of HIV-infected persons can put others at risk of infection: unprotected sex involving the exchange of bodily fluids and needle-sharing. In addition to court decisions that impose a "duty to warn," some states have enacted laws that either permit or require health care providers to warn certain third parties. These persons may include sex partners at risk or employees in certain occupations where there is a risk of exposure to infected blood or bodily fluids. Sometimes, these state laws prohibit disclosure of the infected person's identity, while allowing the health care provider to tell the person at risk that he or she may have been exposed. Finally, a program may be confronted with a situation where it *wants* to warn someone of a risk of HIV infection even if state law does not impose such a duty.

Thus, in a few situations, a program may be required or want to make a disclosure to warn an identifiable person who might be at significant risk of infection. Because the requirements of state laws vary, programs must learn the answers to these questions:

1. Does state law impose any duty to inform third parties about the HIV infection of a patient, and if so, when?
2. Does state law proscribe the ways in which the program can notify the person at risk? For example, is the program prohibited from disclosing the patient's name? Must the patient consent?
3. How can the program inform a third party at risk without violating the federal confidentiality regulations?

It is imperative that programs consult with an attorney familiar with state law to learn the answers to the first two questions. The answer to the third question should by now be clear:

1. The program can get the patient's consent to make the disclosure. Again, the consent form must comply with both the federal regulations and any state law requirements governing patient consent to release of HIV/AIDS information.
2. The program can make the disclosure in a way that does not identify the patient as a substance abuser. For example, a program that is part of a larger facility, such as a hospital or mental health facility, may be able to make a disclosure using that larger entity's name. However, any program that plans to disclose a patient's HIV status must be sure that this does not violate state law. The program may be able to make the disclosure without revealing the name of the infected person. A program should carefully document the efforts it makes to warn a third party in this way.
3. The program can obtain a court order under §2.64 authorizing it to make the disclosure. State law must be consulted to determine whether it imposes additional requirements when the information to be disclosed relates to HIV or AIDS.
4. The program may make a report to medical personnel under the medical emergency exception of the regulations. Since this exception requires that there be "an immediate threat to the health of any individual," it cannot to be used as the usual way of warning a third party of a patient's infection. In addition, the program must be sure that these methods would comply with any state HIV confidentiality law.

It is important to remember that any time a program warns someone of a threat a patient makes or presents without the patient's consent, the program

may be undermining the trust of other patients and thus its effectiveness. This may be particularly true for a program serving patients with HIV or AIDS that finds itself in a situation where it feels obligated to reveal HIV information without a patient's consent. Other patients may learn of the disclosure and the trust that the program worked so hard to build may be weakened. This is not to say that disclosures should not be made—particularly when the law requires that they be made. It is to say that they should not be made without careful thought.

Programs should consider developing a protocol about "duty to warn" cases, so that staff are not left to make decisions on their own about when and how to report threats.

Making Mandatory Reports to Public Health Authorities

All states require the reporting of AIDS cases to public health authorities, which use the information to report to the U.S. Centers for Disease Control and Prevention, and sometimes for other purposes. Some states also require the reporting of new cases of HIV infection or related diseases. States also require reporting of certain infectious diseases, such as TB and STDs. Often, reports of infectious diseases are used by the public health authority to engage in "contact tracing," that is, finding others to whom an infected person may have spread the disease.

In each state, what must be reported for which diseases, who must report, and the purposes to which the information is put varies. Therefore, programs must educate themselves about their state laws to discover (1) whether they or any of their staff is a mandated reporter; (2) when reporting is required; (3) what information must be reported (and does it include patient-identifying information); and (4) what will be done with the information reported.[kk]

If state law permits the use of a code rather than a patient's name, the program can make the report without the patient's consent, for no patient-identifying information is being revealed. If patient-identifying information must be reported, there are a number of ways programs can comply with state mandatory reporting laws without violating the confidentiality regulations:

1. *Consent.* The easiest way is comply with a state law that mandates reporting of patient-identifying information to a public health authority is to obtain the patient's consent. However, the information reported by the program cannot be redisclosed by the public health authority unless the consent form is drafted to permit redisclosure.
2. *Disclosing no patient-identifying information.* If the program is part of another health care facility—a general hospital or a mental health program—it can make reports including the patient's name if it does so under the name of the parent agency, so long as no information is released that would link the patient with drug or alcohol treatment.
3. *Qualified Service Organization Agreement.* A program that is required to report patients' names to a public health department can also enter into a Qualified Service Organization Agreement (QSOA) with a general medical care facility or a laboratory that conducts testing or other medical services for the program. The QSOA permits the program to report the names of patients to the medical care facility or laboratory, which can then report the information (including the patients' names) to the public

---

jj Since HIV is not transmitted by casual contact, the behaviors of those infected that actually put others at risk are limited.

kk If the state's reporting law is intended only to gather information for research purposes, programs can make reports including patients' names if the public health department complies with §2.52 of the federal regulations. That section permits release of patient-identifying information to researchers when three requirements are met. In most cases, a department of public health will easily satisfy the first requirement—that it be qualified to conduct the research. The U.S. Department of HHS has suggested in opinion letters that the second requirement of §2.52—that the researcher have a research protocol to protect patient-identifying information and a group of three or more individuals independent of the research project has reviewed the protocol and found it adequate—may not apply when the research is intended to track the incidence and causation of diseases. Thus, if the state is gathering information only for research purposes, the program can probably make reports including patients' names if the department agrees to meet the third requirement of §2.52 and not redisclose patients' names or identifying information except back to the program and not identify any patient in a report.

heath department, without any information that would link those names with drug or alcohol treatment.

4. *Audit and evaluation.* One of the exceptions to the general rule prohibiting disclosure without patient consent permits programs—under certain conditions—to disclose information to auditors and evaluators (§2.53). HHS has written two opinion letters that approve the use of the audit and evaluation exception to report HIV-related information to public health authorities.[ll] These two letters, read together, suggest that drug and alcohol programs may report patient-identifying information even if that information will be used by the public health department to conduct contact tracing, so long as the health department does not disclose the name of the patient to "contacts" it approaches. The letters also suggest that the public health authorities could use the information to contact the infected patient directly.

Some argue that using §2.53 to reveal information to public health authorities so that they can use the information to trace the spread of disease distorts the purpose of the audit and evaluation exception. As its name implies, §2.53 is intended to permit an outside entity such as a peer review organization or accountant to examine or copy a program's books or records in order to determine whether the program is operating properly (e.g., in accordance with regulations or funding requirements). Section 2.53 was not intended to permit an outside entity to gain information to perform other tasks or accomplish other social ends.

5. *Court order.* A program required to report names of patients with HIV or other reportable diseases can request a court order authorizing it to make the required disclosure.

6. *Medical emergency.* Under very limited circumstances, a program can disclose patient-identifying information to public or private medical personnel when such disclosure is necessary to deal with a real medical emergency affecting the patient or any other person. As noted earlier, the regulations define "medical emergency" rather stringently: a program must determine that the information is to be disclosed to medical personnel who need it "for the purpose of treating a condition which poses an immediate threat to the health of any individual and which requires immediate medical intervention" (§2.51(a)). Thus, reporting to public health authorities should occur under the medical emergency exception only when the patient's medical condition poses an immediate threat to his or her health or the health of another and when immediate medical intervention is required.

In a 1989 opinion letter, HHS' legal counsel suggested that sexually transmitted and other reportable diseases "should be assessed on an individual basis to determine whether they constitute a bona fide medical emergency" that would justify making a disclosure to a public health department under the medical emergency exception.[mm] While in certain circumstances, reporting the name of a patient with infectious TB would be justified under the medical emergency exception, it is probably not a good rationale to use to report a patient's HIV infection, since, in most circumstances, immediate medical intervention is unlikely to change the patient's or anyone else's health status.

Confidentiality and Modern Technology

COMPUTERS

Many programs have begun to computerize their patient records. Computerization is an attractive way of storing patient information; it is particularly attractive when substance abuse programs are coordinating care with other health or social welfare (or criminal justice) agencies. Computerization

permits a consortium of care-providers to gather information from patients once, rather than many times and to coordinate care more easily. It also facilitates program monitoring and research or outcome evaluation of programs or of entire social welfare systems.

Computerization, however, makes a key objective of the federal regulations—controlling the amount of information disclosed and the number of persons to whom information is disclosed—much more difficult. Computerization creates real risks that the limits on disclosure inherent in the federal rules' requirement that the patient sign a consent form before each new kind of disclosure to each new person or entity will become impossible to enforce. Several issues deserving consideration are discussed in this section.

Can Unauthorized Disclosures Be Prevented?

Computerization carries the distinct risk that treatment information entered by the alcohol or drug treatment provider can be accessed by (disclosed to) a person or entity not authorized to receive it. For example, at the simplest level (within a program), unless the computer system is designed to limit the amount of information that nonclinical staff can access, treatment information may be disclosed to clerical personnel who only have need for limited information to set up appointments or bill patients.

If a program is connected to other agencies via modem or computer network, the risk of unauthorized disclosure increases. Disclosure of protected information occurs each time someone accesses a file from a computer; therefore, the design of an integrated computer system must ensure that only those persons or agencies to whom the patient has consented to disclosing information receive information. Moreover, the design must limit the kind and amount of information that each person or agency receives in accordance with the patient's consent. For example, will the system enable a child welfare agency to access information about facts and issues A through F, while restricting a criminal justice agency to information about facts and issues C, D, and M?

Can Security of Information Stored in the Computer Be Ensured?

The regulations require that patient records be kept in a locked file or office (2.16), yet anyone with a disk and access to the computer containing patient files can instantly copy and carry away vast amounts of information without anyone's knowledge. In the time it takes to enter a few computer commands, it will be possible to copy large numbers of files that would have taken many hours to photocopy. Computer systems with telephone links between alcohol and drug programs and administrative offices or other social service agencies extend that possibility to anyone with a modem.

Will Rules about Consent Become Unenforceable?

Obtaining information from a computer file is often much easier—and much faster—than obtaining it from a paper file lodged in someone's office. How will programs enforce the rule that release occur only with written patient consent (or in accordance with one of the other limited exceptions)? If programs share networked systems with other social service agencies or the criminal justice system, how will the system fulfill the requirements of §2.31 regarding the identity of the recipient and the kind and amount of information to be disclosed? How will the program make a determination whether the information should be released to other agencies in the network? If a program is entering patient-identifying information in a management information system that other social service providers can access, it and the patient may well lose control over when and what information is released. They may also remain unaware of how often those outside agencies are obtaining information and exactly what information they have obtained.

Will Patients' Consents Ever Expire?

The regulations require that a patient's signed consent expire at some identifiable point in time. Computerization carries the risk that information entered into the system will not be deleted when the patient's consent

---

[ll] Letter to Oklahoma State Department of Health from the Legal Advisor to the U.S. Alcohol Drug Abuse and Mental Health Administration, dated September 2, 1988 and Letter to the New York State Department of Health from the Acting General Counsel of Health and Human Services, dated May 17, 1989.

[mm] Letter to the New York State Department of Health from the Acting General Counsel to the U.S. Department of Health and Human Services, dated May 17, 1989.

form expires. Systems should be designed to ensure that patient files be automatically deleted on their expiration date or that the system operators be reminded that the files should be deleted (or the consent form renewed).

Will Patients Be Able to Revoke Consent?

The regulations permit patients to revoke consent in most situations. Unless a mechanism is developed to delete information the patient previously consented to disclose, there is a danger that the patient will effectively be unable to revoke consent.

Can the Prohibition on Redisclosure Be Enforced?

The regulations require programs to notify recipients of information disclosed with patient consent that they may not redisclose that information. When a program's computer system is linked in a network with an intake unit or an administrative or funding agency or with other social service providers, it is unclear how the prohibition on redisclosure can be enforced. Can a computer system be structured to limit the dissemination of patient-identifying information to the first "tier" of persons or agencies to which disclosures are made?

CELLULAR PHONES

There is no mystery about the danger cellular telephones pose to confidentiality. Staff should be careful to be especially discrete if they are using a cellular telephone.

FAX MACHINES

Patient-identifying information can be sent via fax machine so long as the program is certain that it has the correct fax number. For example, if a patient who was receiving outpatient treatment has entered a hospital program, the hospital program may need information from the outpatient program. The hospital can fax the patient's consent form to the outpatient program in order to save time. However, it may be advisable for the hospital to fax a test sheet without any patient-identifying information to make sure it has the correct fax number for the outpatient treatment program. If the out-

patient program plans to fax its records back to the hospital, similar precautions should be taken.

VOICE MAIL

Telephone answering machines and voice mail have become common—some would argue indispensable. Before a program leaves a message that may disclose that the person it is trying to reach is a patient, however, it is important to consider the security of the telephone answering machine or voice mail system. Does the patient live alone, or does someone else listen to his or her messages? If voice mail is part of an employer's telephone system, can someone other than the patient access his messages? Unless the program is certain that its message will reach only the patient—or that its message reveals no connection with substance abuse treatment—it is better to leave no message at all.

E-MAIL

E-mail raises concerns similar to those discussed earlier with regard to fax machines and voice mail. An e-mail message may be accessible to someone other than the patient. It may also find its way into someone else's mailbox. A counselor treating a patient may find it convenient to communicate with her supervisor across town via e-mail; however, if any patient-identifying information is included in the message she sends, she runs the risk of its disclosure to others on the supervisor's e-mail account or to some unintended recipient.

CONCLUSION

At first blush, the federal confidentiality regulations may seem to be an indecipherable maze of legalese that diverts program resources from treatment to paperwork and that blocks people from communicating with the program on important matters. A basic understanding of the regulations, however, is not difficult to achieve. With it, compliance may be made routine with little drain on resources. However, compliance is not an end in itself. Rather, it is hoped that compliance will further the more important ends the regulations are designed to serve—encouraging those in need to seek alcohol and drug abuse treatment while protecting their privacy, consistent with the needs of the greater community.

86 PRIVATE AND PUBLIC INSURANCE
Jonathan W. Reader and Kathleen A. Sullivan

An estimated $7 billion is spent annually in the United States on the treatment of alcoholism and substance abuse (1). Private insurance underwrites nearly half this amount, while federal and state governments defray the other half of the treatment costs. Each mode of reimbursement is associated with a distinct treatment system. The private sector tends to use hospital-based programs, whereas the public sector uses community-based programs such as outpatient clinics and methadone maintenance clinics (2). Since 1970, with the rise in social awareness of addiction and the dramatic increase in insurance coverage, the treatment of alcoholism and drug addiction has become a billion dollar industry.

In the last half of the twentieth century, the diagnosis, treatment, and financing of addiction treatment has experienced prodigious growth. In effect, it has become institutionalized with some systematic coordination of diagnosis and treatment between various providers to become an emerging addiction care delivery system. Alcoholism and drug addictions are traditionally grouped under the category "behavioral health," which also includes psychiatric conditions. Benefit analysts, employers, and providers refer to

these conditions under this rubric, or by the acronym ADM for "alcohol, drug, and mental health." This chapter focuses upon the development and the current status of health insurance coverage for the treatment of the diseases of addiction.

The sheer magnitude of the private and public sectors' annual investment in the treatment of substance-abuse problems raises important questions: Are the various types of treatment effective? Do these therapies result in lasting recovery for a significant number of alcoholic and addicted patients? Are insurance companies, who underwrite the costs of treatment interventions, able to justify their investment in terms of either therapeutic gain, economic return, or both? Do the economic costs of treatment offset the economic and social costs of *not* treating these diseases? These questions have stimulated a host of empirical investigations and engendered numerous, albeit sometimes rancorous debates within both policy circles and the field of substance abuse research. However, neither research nor policy debates have produced definitive answers to these questions. Nonetheless, they have obvious heuristic value and will inform our discussion of the main themes and general trends with respect to public and private insurance for the treatment of alcoholism and drug addiction. In effect, these questions serve as poignant reminders that health insurance is not an end in itself but a means to an end—namely, making treatment more accessible and affordable for chemically addicted persons.

It should be noted that the treatment of alcoholism and drug addiction is still in its adolescence. Research has yet to discover definitive therapies for these pernicious afflictions. There is considerable disagreement among researchers as to the etiology of the family of diseases known as addiction. The main theoretical debate is between the biogenic and the psychogenic schools of thoughts. Chemical dependencies possess unique properties which make them difficult to treat. Two examples will suffice to illustrate this observation. First, unlike other diseases, the symptoms of alcoholism or drug addiction first become evident to the patient's family or employer and often much later to the patient. Because of the fear of being stigmatized and the attendant negative social sanctions, patients endure the discomfort of their symptoms rather than seek help. The pharmacodynamics of the chemicals themselves and the resultant toxicity confuse the patient, making rational decision making problematic. This state of confusion engenders in addicts anxiety and fear. For many of these individuals, the only recourse to this dreaded uncertainty is denial and continued substance use. Hence, addicts typically seek medical or psychological intervention only when their symptoms have become intolerable, often at an advanced stage of disease.

A second distinctive property of both alcoholism and drug addiction is that treatment is most often initiated by nonmedical personnel, such as the patient himself, family members, employers, or the court system. Moreover, a successful recovery depends more on the motivation and the cooperation of the patient than it does on either a particular medical technology or the expertise of a specific health care provider. In the treatment of addictions, there is no equivalent to a primary care physician who oversees the delivery of medical care. In fact, until recently, neither medicine nor psychiatry offered much help or hope to those suffering from addictions.

Evaluation research has demonstrated how difficult it is to associate lasting recovery with specific treatment factors. Most outcome studies in this area are hampered by flaws in research design. To cite a recurrent flaw, researchers find it more expedient to conduct retrospective studies than prospective ones, yet addicts' retrospective accounts of their journey from the premorbid state to chemical dependence are often unreliable. Another common problem in program evaluation research is that researchers encounter difficulty in assessing the separate effects of treatment and nontreatment factors on a patient's recovery. Hence, it is unclear which set of factors—treatment or nontreatment—is a better predictor of recovery. George Vaillant's oft-cited longitudinal study found that successful recovery was primarily linked with nonmedical factors, such as the peer support found in participation in Alcoholics Anonymous (AA) (3). By the same token, one inference which can be drawn from a number of empirical studies is that formal treatment has a positive but indeterminate effect on the disease. More importantly, to the well-organized, politically sophisticated advocates of addiction recovery, this unverified assumption is accepted as the first tenet of rehabilitation: Treatment works.

OVERVIEW

This chapter discusses the evolution of insurance benefits for alcohol and drug addiction treatment and the specific benefits provided by various commercial plans and public reimbursement mechanisms in the United States today. The authors describe and assess the therapeutic, economic, and social consequences of insurance coverage for these diseases. The chapter concludes by making some policy and programmatic recommendations and by citing issues whose resolution requires more research. This latter point is no casual observation. In the addiction treatment field, paradoxes, puzzles, and enigmas about addictions and the recovery process are rife. Neither politics nor moralizing can produce satisfactory answers. Only theoretically-grounded studies of addictions and their treatment can begin to resolve these issues.

This chapter has two hypotheses. First, health benefit coverage of chemical dependencies is influenced by four sets of factors: (a) the unique features

of these diseases; (b) the prevailing types of alcoholism and drug treatment; (c) political and economic decisions by key institutions; and (d) the assumptions of health care economics as they apply to insurance policies and plans.

A second hypothesis is that insurance coverage for chemical dependence has not only economic consequences but, more importantly, noneconomic consequences. As Mechanic has observed, health insurance policies can be usefully viewed as mechanisms for rationing the distribution of valued resources—health services (4). Moreover, rationing is not based solely on the ability to pay. Access to services is also predicated on an implicit contract between the insurer and the beneficiary that the latter will accept the former's prescriptions for remaining healthy. Health insurance policies, especially those that pertain to the coverage of behavioral conditions, seek to foster values and behaviors in their beneficiaries which are conducive to good health. To elaborate, health plans that cover addiction treatment do not simply defray the cost of an illness episode; they also provide incentives for the recovering addict to change his or her lifestyle, increasing the likelihood of enduring sobriety.

The Institutionalization of Alcoholism Treatment: A Sudden Birth, Short Childhood, but Protracted Adolescence

We will begin our analysis by providing a brief chronology of the emergence of each treatment field to show how certain historical events affected the development of insurance policies and plans. The treatment approach to alcoholism and addiction had to be institutionalized and legitimized before the insurance industry would provide benefits. The federal government, organized medicine, and corporations had to endorse the treatment concept before insurance companies would agree to invest in it as a viable approach to substance abuse. This sequence of events is readily comprehensible. The insurance industry was reluctant to provide benefits because the treatment field had not demonstrated persuasively that the rehabilitation of addicts, in a majority of cases, led to lasting recovery. Subsidizing unproven therapies for degenerative diseases—especially those which were characterized by brief remissions and lengthy relapses—flew in the face of conventional actuarial wisdom. More precisely, it violated a fundamental precept of insurance theory, limited liability (5). Thus the endorsement of the treatment concept by elite institutions signaled to the insurance industry that the federal government, corporations, and health care institutions were willing to share the risks associated with investing in these unproven treatment modalities.

The institutionalization of treatment as a new method for dealing with alcoholism began in the mid 1930s, preceding the development of drug addiction treatment by approximately 20 years. In 1935, in the wake of Prohibition, two alcoholics struggling to remain sober founded a grassroots organization, AA. An article by Jack Alexander in *The Saturday Evening Post* in 1940 gave national exposure to AA; groups began to form throughout the country. The publication of AA's "Big Book," a compilation of shared experiences in reaching sobriety, carried the message of recovery to thousands (6). Prior to the founding of AA, there was little or no humane care available for alcoholics; the popular perception was that the condition was untreatable and hopeless.

The relative lack of care is understandable, for policy makers and the public did not view alcoholism as a medical problem, but as a moral weakness resulting from a character defect. Hence, physicians were called upon to treat only the physical symptoms of alcoholism. Excessive, uncontrolled drinking was believed to be a symptom of an underlying psychopathology. There are many practitioners who still operate under this misguided assumption of the "psychogenic" causation of addiction. Given this assumption, social workers, ministers, psychiatrists, and the police attempted to treat the underlying problem, overlooking the possibility that alcoholism was the primary affliction. Hence, various social programs and legal measures were tried as remedies; none proved effective. The most conspicuously ineffective remedy was Prohibition, a policy which Congress enacted via the Eighteenth Amendment to the Constitution in 1919.

The establishment of AA marked the beginning of the move toward medicalization of alcoholism treatment, for in jurisdictional terms it initiated the gradual transfer of alcoholism from the judicial system to the health care system. In the early years of AA, compassionate recovering men and women took suffering alcoholics into their homes to help launch their recovery (6). Over the years, some of these "sober houses" evolved into more formal recovery facilities. They functioned as self-supporting communities—early examples of the social model of substance abuse treatment. More precisely, they were forerunners of today's therapeutic communities (TCs) and residential rehabilitation centers. Persons were referred to these recovery programs by fellow recovering alcoholics and a few enlightened members of the clergy and the medical profession. In the 1940s public opinion did not endorse the disease interpretation of alcoholism. Most physicians concurred with this view. Hence, not surprisingly, these recovery houses were operated by laymen, primarily recovering alcoholics. In fact, the medical profession had not given its official approval to this type of recovery support.

With respect to alcoholism, many doctors subscribed to a policy of benign neglect. They felt that the responsibility for dealing with this social problem should be delegated to people outside their profession. Private psychiatric hospitals were also available to those alcoholic patients who could afford to pay for their services directly; however, admission to these hospitals was predicated on the assumption that alcoholism was a symptom of a personality disorder or some other mental health problem.

Providing insurance coverage for the treatment of alcoholism by recovery houses, psychiatric hospitals, and other facilities would have been regarded as morally indulgent and fiscally imprudent in the 1940s and 1950s. The insurance industry was loath to offer benefits for the treatment of "moral," or self-induced problems such as alcoholism that were due to lapses in self-control. A basic axiom of insurance theory and policy was that benefits should be provided to individuals to offset losses caused by uncontrollable events such as car accidents, floods, or illnesses. The prevailing wisdom of the medical community and the insurance industry held that granting insurance benefits to alcoholics would reward a lack of self-control, thereby perpetuating a morally repugnant habit. In effect, such an act would change the public image of the alcoholic, for it would transform an irresponsible person into a victim whose plight deserved sympathy and financial assistance. More importantly, adhering to this manifestly generous policy would either reduce profits or incur substantial losses. After all, insurance companies are primarily concerned with making investment decisions that maximize profits and minimize risk.

Despite the prevailing moral interpretation of alcoholism, a number of farsighted physicians such as Howard W. Haggard, E. M. Jellinek, William Silkworth, and Harry Tiebout championed the disease interpretation. Their advocacy of this cause was not in vain. Through the tireless efforts of Jellinek, Selden Bacon, and other colleagues in the 1940s, the Yale University Center for Alcohol Studies and the National Committee for Education on Alcoholism were founded (6). (This committee subsequently changed its name to the National Council on Alcoholism. It now serves as both a public information clearinghouse and lobby organization.)

Establishing this research center signaled to the scientific community that alcoholism was an important social problem whose understanding could be enhanced through research. Concerning the institutionalization of the disease perspective, the Center's most significant contribution was the founding of a scientific journal, *The Quarterly Journal of Alcohol Studies* (7). By disseminating research findings, this journal lent considerable credibility to the view that alcoholism was a disease. It also served to legitimize research as a way of creating new knowledge which would help unravel the mysteries surrounding alcoholism's etiology and prognosis and uncover viable therapeutic remedies. This systematic production of scientific knowledge expedited the legitimization of the emergent field of alcoholism treatment, which was staffed primarily by laymen. The research conducted by the Yale Center, coupled with the public education campaign undertaken by the National Committee for Education on Alcoholism, helped win acceptance of the disease interpretation from skeptical opinion leaders, elite institutions, and the public.

This combined effort produced concrete results. In 1945 Connecticut became the first state to establish an alcohol treatment program within its public health department. In 1949 the Western Electric Corporation established the first company program to deal with alcoholism in the workplace, an early model of today's employee assistance programs (EAPs) (7). In 1951 the World Health Organization officially embraced the disease concept of alcoholism (8). In 1958 the House of Delegates of the American Medical Association took a similar position, unanimously adopting a resolution that alcoholism is a disease (8). These endorsements contributed to the diffusion of the therapeutic approach, making treatment programs more available and accessible to alcoholics. More importantly, the fact that representatives of the medical research community and the health care establishment adopted the disease concept made it more likely that the federal government would take a more active role in the crusade against alcoholism. Prior to 1960 federal involvement had been minimal. Lacking both a unified therapy and a significant commitment of resources by the federal government, the nascent recovery movement could not persuade insurance companies to defray the costs of rehabilitation.

Three inferences may be drawn from this synopsis of the evolution of the treatment of alcoholism. First, the definitions of a social problem by policy makers and elite institutions affect the solutions that are used to alleviate the problem. This variant of a sociological general axiom certainly applies to alcoholism, for initial definitions held that it was a moral problem which could be remedied by either social or legal solutions. Subsequently, labeling it a disease resulted in the application of health care solutions. Second, since advocates of the disease perspective lacked the requisite scientific evidence to champion their cause, they were obliged to blend research findings with ideological appeals. For example, AA's effective self-help peer advocacy of recovery is largely due to its strategic selection of the appropriate culture symbols from religion, science, and other secular traditions in American thought. Needless to say, if scientific research had produced a cure for alcoholism, such a discovery would have greatly accelerated the institutionalization of the disease concept. Third, greater government and corporate involvement are necessary before the insurance industry is willing to risk investing in an unproven therapy.

Drug Addiction, 1914-1958: The Legal Approach

The reader may ask why discuss drug addiction under a separate heading. After all, alcohol is a drug, and alcoholism is a type of addiction. The immediate answer to this question is that we are only reflecting the value judgments which American society has arbitrarily made and resolutely defended for most of the twentieth century—namely, that in social and moral terms, alcoholism is less offensive than addictions to other drugs. The criteria which society used to reach this conclusion are important. This distinction is not based on the fact that the physiological and psychological effects produced by excessive use of alcohol are less severe than those of other addictive drugs. In fact, empirical evidence suggests that the reverse is the case. Instead, the difference in society's reaction to alcoholism and drug addiction is attributable to four factors: (*a*) dominant cultural values; (*b*) the political and economic power of the upper middle and middle classes; (*c*) the perception and evaluation by these classes of the social characteristics of different types of drug users; and (*d*), most importantly, the widespread consumption of alcohol and, concomitantly, the prevalence of alcoholism within these classes. For these arbiters of taste and custom, alcoholism is a regrettable but understandable malady which has afflicted, at one time or another, a family member or a friend. However, drug addiction has been viewed as a plague which infects only strangers—a pathological condition associated with lower class status.

These perceptions and evaluations are consequential, for they shape public sector and private sector policies with respect to alcoholism and drug addiction. Two examples will illustrate this observation. First, for most of the twentieth century the sale and the consumption of alcohol has been legal; whereas, the purchase and use of other addictive drugs such as cocaine, marihuana, and the opiates have been and remain illegal. Second, for the first five decades of this century, the alcoholic was viewed as suffering from a moral problem and was either shunned or ostracized. In some cases, when the alcoholic's symptoms were offensive, he was found guilty of a misdemeanor and was given a short jail sentence. Since the mid-twentieth century, the public perception of alcoholism has been that it was either an illness or a mental health problem; thus, the alcoholic should not be punished but healed. By contrast, the prevailing cultural view for most of this century has been that drug addiction (or even the recreational use of an illegal drug) is a crime and that, therefore, the drug addict should be fined or incarcerated. As these examples attest, society's moral judgments about various types of drug addiction have greatly influenced how different addictions have been treated. The reluctance of society's leaders and institutions to label drug addiction a disease explains why the institutionalization of alcoholism occurred much sooner and more quickly than did the institutionalization of drug treatment. The criminal status of drug use explains why insurance companies have not, until the 1980s, underwritten the costs of treatment, even through they had begun to offer such benefits for the rehabilitation of persons with alcoholism (9).

In the mid 1950s and early 1960s drug addiction was still confined to inner-city youth, the marginally employed, and the unemployed. In an epidemiological sense, it was not prevalent in the workforce. Those segments of the workforce who had insurance—blue-collar and white-collar workers—seemed immune to this affliction. Hence, there was little economic incentive for employer-sponsored insurance to offer such coverage.

The Harrison Act of 1914 and the ensuing Supreme Court decisions changed the official interpretation of narcotics addiction from an illness to a crime. Prior to this legislation, cocaine, morphine, and other opiates could be purchased without a prescription at the local pharmacy or grocery. Drug addicts were viewed as patients and treated by physicians (10). The legacy of the Harrison Act has been an era of prohibition which has lasted until the present. This law has served as the prototype for subsequent drug addiction legislation. In fact, only recently when President Bush's much publicized policy initiative, the "War on Drugs," failed to produce dramatic results has there been discussion in policy circles and forums of public opinion of replacing this policy of prohibition with legalization. Even so, there is no widespread public support for legalization.

Drug Addiction Treatment, 1956–1970: The Reemergence of the Therapeutic Approach

Until the mid 1950s, the official view first established by the Harrison Act—that drug addiction was a crime and the drug addict a criminal—prevailed virtually unchallenged. Nonetheless, this view was not unanimously accepted. As Edward Brecher's historical account of drug addiction attests, law enforcement officials, physicians, and social scientists joined ex-addicts in their eloquent criticisms of the criminal view (11). The critics urged policy makers to view addictions as illnesses and addicts as patients. Addicts needed treatment, not imprisonment. Although this vocal opposition may have compelled skeptical policy makers to reconsider their position, it was two epidemiological events which primarily led to a major drug policy shift at the federal, state, and local levels in the 1960s. First, in the 1950s, heroin addiction became widespread in the ghettos of New York and other large cities in the United States. For two reasons, this epidemic proved particularly insidious. First, as the incidence of addiction in inner-city neighborhoods spread, the crime rate increased. Second, organized crime found the sale of heroin and other illegal drugs to be very lucrative; hence, it made a concerted effort to create a demand for these forbidden drugs, increasing the rate of addiction.

The second epidemiological event which altered public drug policy was that, in the early 1960s, middle-class youth, especially college students, resorted in significant numbers to the recreational use of a variety of drugs (amphetamines, heroin, hallucinogens, marihuana, and barbiturates). Suddenly, drug use had acquired a limited social legitimacy which, in American culture, only the middle classes can confer; therefore, the stigma associated with this habit, while not vanishing, began to fade. Behavior that once had been viewed as deviant had now become a leisure time diversion. Similarly, drug abuse, once construed as a sign of moral degeneracy, was perceived as a nasty habit, or, when harsher public judgments were evoked, as a chronic disease.

These two events produced three important changes in drug abuse policy and treatment. First, representatives of organized medicine, academia, the media, and most significantly, federal and state governments began to accept the view that drug addiction was an illness, even though, according to offi-

cial policy, the sale and the consumption of narcotics was still illegal. Thus, policy makers were content to view drug use and abuse alternately as criminal activities, health problems, or both. This change in the official definition ushered in an era of ambiguous government drug policies which has persisted until the present.

The second change is linked directly to the heroin epidemic which plagued New York City and other metropolitan areas in the late 1950s and early 1960s. In response to the growing recognition that heroin addicts could not be rehabilitated in jail, individuals in the private sector introduced two new, albeit very different, approaches to drug treatment on an experimental basis—TCs and methadone maintenance clinics. Both warrant brief description, for, to some degree, the type of treatment provided affects the type of benefits and the amount of coverage that health insurance companies will furnish.

In the late 1950s Charles Dederich, a recovering alcoholic, attempted to carry AA's message of recovery to heroin addicts. His lack of success brought the realization that these addicts required therapy which was more structured and confrontational than the group dynamics typically found at AA meetings. In 1958 Dederich used this insight to establish a new program called Synanon, in which addicts lived together in a community. Abstinence from drugs, self-reliance, and responsible behavior were emphasized in confrontive group encounter sessions. Synanon was the original TC (11). The early TCs were self-supporting groups, with the usual length of stay averaging between 1 and 2 years. The long length of stay limited the clientele. Addicts with jobs or family responsibilities could not afford such prolonged absences. Therefore, TCs—both then and now—tended to serve young or indigent addicts. The TC serves as the contemporary prototype of the social model approach to addiction.

In the mid 1960s two physicians affiliated with the Rockefeller Institute and Beth Israel Medical Center in New York, Vincent Dole and Marie Nyswander, pioneered a different therapy for heroin addicts. Their therapy substituted the long-acting synthetic opiate, methadone, for heroin. Dole and Nyswander advocated the use of methadone as a maintenance drug that would free addicts from the constant craving and need to search for heroin. Advocates of this therapy argued that its effectiveness in rehabilitating addicts depended on combining the drug component with psychological and vocational counseling (10). Indeed, the original methadone programs were funded as broad rehabilitation programs. The social model aspects of the programs lost state funding over time, leaving the dispensary function only (10).

Methadone maintenance gained acceptance as a promising, inexpensive, appropriate medical alternative to the TC (10). Many addicts cannot afford the prolonged confinement which TCs require. Methadone clinics were funded at the federal and state levels; private insurance coverage for methadone maintenance was not available because few heroin addicts were in the workforce in the 1960s.

The prevalence of heroin addiction in the urban lower classes and the ubiquitous recreational use of drugs by middle-class young contributed to a third major policy change, federal involvement in the treatment of drug addiction. Other factors figured prominently in this policy shift. In the early 1960s, the combined influence of peace, prosperity, and the Civil Rights movement led to an expansion of the welfare state. One manifestation of this expansion was the increased federal involvement in the financing and delivery of health care. In 1965 Congress enacted legislation establishing the Medicare and Medicaid programs. This legislation not only made medical care more accessible to the aged, indigent, and disabled and enhanced the opportunity for obtaining treatment for alcoholism and drug addiction. Admittedly, although not one of their main policy objectives, Medicare and Medicaid were the first large-scale insurance programs under which elderly and indigent alcoholics and addicts could be covered for treatment.

This observation warrants a qualification. In the mid 1960s treatment programs for drug addicts were not readily available. This was especially true for low-income addicts. TCs and methadone maintenance clinics only recently had been established. Thus only a modest amount of either Medicare or Medicaid money was expended on the treatment of addictions. A very significant change in federal drug policy occurred with the passage of the Narcotic Addict Rehabilitation Act in 1966 (10). For the first time, the federal government had made substantial funds available for the rehabilitation of addicts, thereby acknowledging that, for many addicts, treatment was a more effective solution than incarceration.

What effect did treatment innovations such as TCs and methadone maintenance programs and shifts in federal drug abuse policy have on the development of private and public insurance policies for addiction treatment? Several inferences can be drawn from the above discussion. First, the stigma associated with drug abuse was harder to remove than that associated with alcoholism. Government, business, organized medicine, and other influential social institutions had institutionalized the criminal view of drug abuse in the years since 1913. A second inference is that, unlike alcoholics who enjoyed the effective peer support of AA, drug addicts were unable to form a grassroots organization to champion the social and economic advantages of treatment. Indeed, many addicted individuals were prohibited by the terms of their status as former convicts from associating with each other in such peer groups (9). Nonetheless, the period of 1956–1970 witnessed an important modification in the definition of this problem. Neither the government nor the public was content to view addiction exclusively as a crime. Increasingly, they were also willing to label it a psychological problem or a mental illness. This change in the definition of addiction made both the institutionalization of treatment and changes in government policy possible. Although neither TCs nor methadone maintenance clinics could cure addiction, both offered interventions that were consistent with American values. TCs stress such dominant values as self-discipline and individual responsibility. Methadone maintenance, as Nelkin has noted, is congruent with the American belief that science and technology can be used to solve most problems (10). Each therapy's public acceptance was primarily based on its ideological compatibility with American culture.

Federal involvement, especially the provision of funds made available after the passage of the Narcotic Addict Rehabilitation Act (1966), accelerated the institutionalization of treatment which, in turn, enhanced its legitimacy as a method of dealing with drug addiction. These cultural changes, the redefinition of the problem, the emergence of therapeutic approaches, and government support for these approaches had to occur before private insurance companies would develop policies to underwrite the costs of drug rehabilitation. In the absence of a proven therapy such institutional acceptance must precede the development of substance abuse insurance.

Era of Rapid Institutionalization of the Disease Concept and Treatment: 1970–1990

The 1970s marked the beginning of a period of rapid institutionalization of alcoholism treatment programs. At the close of the twentieth century, there is an established alcohol treatment delivery system. To elaborate, nowadays treatment is more comprehensive, better integrated, and better financed. The federal government furnished the main impetus for this accelerated diffusion of alcoholism treatment programs by supplying funding, technical expertise, and legitimacy. In 1970 Congress passed the Hughes Act which established the National Institute for Alcohol Abuse and Alcoholism (NIAAA) symbolizing the high level of institutional legitimacy which alcoholism had attained. The new institute provided monies for research, prevention, and treatment of alcoholism. One of the first and most important programmatic initiatives undertaken by NIAAA was the training of 100 occupational alcoholism consultants, two from each state (12). These consultants helped corporations and labor unions set up occupational alcoholism intervention programs which, in turn, facilitated the widespread adoption of EAPs by both private sector and public sector organizations.

The decision of companies and unions to establish EAPs increased the demand for availability of treatment programs. Hospitals began to admit patients for detoxification; some established rehabilitation units. In response to the demand of their corporate clients, private insurance companies began to cover some levels of treatment for alcoholism, principally medical detoxification. By 1974, 75% of Blue Cross plans nationwide had some form of coverage for alcoholism detoxification in place (13).

Treatment of alcoholism became more formalized in the 1970s. The freestanding recovery facilities came under the jurisdiction of state accreditation authorities. By the end of the 1970s most states required that nonprofessional alcoholism counselors complete some training and credentialling process. Nowadays, state health officials, organized medicine, and representatives of the alcohol treatment field agree that counselors should receive formal training. The current debate concerns the content and the duration of training. Since the early 1980s, the freestanding recovery programs have sought accreditation by the Joint Commission on Accreditation of Hospitals (now the Joint Commission on Accreditation of Healthcare Organizations).

Acceptance and legitimization of the medical model of alcoholism was aided by the courageous leadership of many business and political figures. Notable among them were Senator Harold Hughes, former First Lady Betty Ford, and Congressman Wilbur Mills. Their willingness to share publicly the private agonies of their recovery experiences poignantly rebutted the prevailing public stereotype of alcoholics as derelicts. Such efforts gave credibility to the concept of alcoholism rehabilitation and recovery, as witnessed by the fact that, during the 1980s, the public confessional of substance abuse and the accompanying acknowledgment of the need for treatment have become accepted rites of atonement. The most popular forum for such confessionals has become the television talk show.

In 1970 Congress established the National Institute on Drug Abuse (NIDA) which funded research, education, prevention, and treatment of drug addiction (7). Federal monies went to the states in the form of block grants to stimulate the development of drug treatment and prevention programs within each state health department. The establishment of a national institute that advocated the treatment approach expedited institutionalization in both the public and the private sectors. Hospitals began to reserve a certain number of beds for the detoxification of addicts. Most coverage for treatment was provided by the public sector (Medicaid). Employer-sponsored (commercial and self insured) insurance plans did not offer coverage for drug addiction until the 1980s. Traditional public images of drug addicts as either moral degenerates or criminals still helped to impede the formulation of such plans.

The multifaceted federal involvement (research, prevention, treatment, and Medicaid) gave considerable legitimacy to an emergent treatment field whose outcomes were still unproven. A high level of federal commitment was a necessary prerequisite for private sector involvement. In effect, the federal government provided both legal and fiscal guarantees that the benefits of the treatment approach to drug addiction outweighed the costs. As a result, hospitals and insurance companies were more willing to participate. By establishing the research institutes for alcoholism and drug addiction simultaneously, the federal government challenged the ubiquitous but specious perception that alcoholism is a public health problem, whereas drug abuse is not. This policy decision did not immediately remove the stigma associated with drug abuse. Nonetheless, it has made the gradual elimination of this specious distinction possible. For most of the years since the establishment of NIDA, the public sector has continued to bear the cost of drug treatment. However, in the mid 1980s, a growing number of private institutions began to treat all types of chemical dependence. In part, this change is due to aggressive lobbying by treatment advocates and a vigorous public education campaign by government. However, the main impetus for the expansion of private treatment facilities was the increased use of cocaine by both white-collar and blue-collar workers. In the prosperous 1980s, corporations found it more cost effective to intervene with the addicted employee than to ignore or dismiss him or her. The inclusion of the diseases of addiction in the Americans with Disabilities Act (1990) added to employer incentives to offer intervention.

A notable development in addiction research came into high focus in the 1990s, namely the heated debate between advocates the biogenic and psychogenic paradigms of treatment. The authors have noted this debate throughout the historical sections of this chapter. In this decade, the prominence of health care reform on the national agenda in conjunction with a more competitive economy has limited both private and public dollars for the treatment of addictions. Employers were less tolerant of addicted employees, in spite of the aforementioned therapeutic initiatives. In the 1990s, the psychiatric field has aggressively advocated that the psychogenic model is the appropriate venue for the treatment of addictions, despite the dearth of legitimate research evidence attesting to the efficacy of this model (14, 15). The understanding of these two competing interpretations of addictive diseases (which other authors in this textbook discuss as well) is vital to the understanding of the issues surrounding health insurance coverage for these conditions.

HEALTH INSURANCE COVERAGE

Employer-sponsored group insurance is the most common form of health benefit coverage in the United States, followed by government sponsored plans, notably Medicare and Medicaid. By the mid 1990s, more than 210 million Americans, or 86% of the civilian noninstitutional population, were covered by one or more forms of health care coverage. More than 181 million persons were covered by private health insurance with commercial insurance companies, Blue Cross plans, self-funded employer plans, and prepaid plans such as health maintenance organizations (HMOs) (16). HMOs, with an enrollment of 60 million as of 1996, have become the dominant and fastest growing form of group health coverage. An estimated 41 million Americans are without any form of health insurance (16).

Group insurance is an economical way to cover a group of people under a single contract. The contract is between the insurer and the organization representing the group. The group must be associated with the organization for some purpose other than the purchase of insurance. The organization that underwrites the insurance policy is usually an employer, a labor union, or a trade association. Premium rates for each group are calculated by actuarial formulae that take into account such factors as the age and gender of the group members. By insuring groups of employed individuals, the risk to the insurance carrier is spread out among the members of the group, thereby minimizing loss by sharing the risk among a large number of insureds.

Group health insurance is a recent phenomenon. Congress had exempted health insurance coverage from the Social Security legislation in 1935. After World War II, labor unions gained power through collective bargaining agreements. In 1947, the Taft-Hartley Act restored the provisions concerning wages and conditions of employment which had been specified in the National Labor Relations Act of 1935. This legislation clarified for employers that health and welfare benefits were part of the wages and conditions of employment. Labor unions, through their welfare trust funds, entered the scene as purchasers of benefit coverage. By 1955, 12 million employees and 17 million dependents were covered under collectively bargained health care plans (5).

Most of the early employer-sponsored plans were indemnity plans that used a schedule of payments to reimburse doctors for services rendered. This means that the plan paid for whatever medical services were specified in the contract, at a set dollar amount for each procedure or diagnosis. Commercial indemnity plans expanded rapidly after World War II. By 1950 commercial insurance companies had more subscribers than Blue Cross (5). Employers, especially large companies with employees located in various parts of the country, favored indemnity plans because of their flexibility. In addition, commercial insurance companies were often able to grant a lower price for low-risk groups. In the prosperous economy of the 1950s and 1960s many employer-sponsored plans abandoned the schedule of payments in favor of "usual and customary" fee-for-service reimbursement. Concern about inflated costs was not evident during this period. However, in 1965, after years of public pressure and legislative wrangling, Congress enacted Medicare. Medicare provides hospital insurance under Social Security for persons over the age of 65 years and for younger persons with certain disabilities. Another section of this legislation, Medicaid, provided financial assistance to the states for delivering medical care to indigent persons (5). Medicare and Medicaid gave the elderly and the poor greater access to medical services. As noted earlier, the programs made it possible to pay the cost of rehabilitating elderly and indigent alcoholics and addicts. In effect, this legislation made the federal government and state governments major purchasers of health services, including those used to treat addictions. As a result of federal involvement in the financing of addiction treatment, insurance companies gradually began to offer health benefits for the rehabilitation of substance abusers.

Health benefit plans base their assumption of risk on the traditional medical models of disease treatment. For example, an important premise is the reliance on the physician and hospital as the hub of medical care; hence, insurance plans typically provide much better coverage for inpatient care than for outpatient care. Benefit plans generally do not provide coverage for un-

proven or experimental treatments, as their outcomes are unproven, and therefore the risk is incalculable. Because of the medical orientation of health insurance, coverage for mental and nervous disorders has always been less available than coverage for the treatment of physical disorders. Alcoholism and drug addiction are classified by insurance carriers as mental disorders. Most traditional plans emphasized acute hospital care and place limitations on the number of days allowed per year. Given the subjective nature of psychiatric diagnoses and the lack of consensus among practitioners about the appropriate level of care for alcoholic and addicted patients, it is no surprise that the insurance industry has been cautious in establishing direct benefits for these ailments. Chemically dependent patients have traditionally been treated in psychiatric institutions under a mental illness or neurological diagnosis. Until the 1970s, this was a generally accepted practice, for insurance carriers would reimburse for the treatment of a medical or psychiatric diagnosis, but not a diagnosis of alcoholism or drug addiction.

Indeed, many carriers resisted the trend to insure the treatment of addictions, until state law mandated such coverage under commercial group health plans in the 1980s. Listed in Table 86.1 are the states that, as of 1990, have mandated some level of group health coverage for the treatment of alcoholism, drug addiction, or both.

It is interesting to note that more states have mandated benefits for alcoholism and drug abuse treatment under group plans than have mandated psychiatric benefits. Increased public and corporate awareness of addiction and the availability of mandated benefit coverage for treatment have created a demand for treatment programs. As a result, medical hospitals established short-term residential rehabilitation programs. By the late 1970s the availability of health insurance for rehabilitation created a marketplace for entrepreneurs; and hence, the next decade witnessed the introduction and the growth of the for-profit rehabilitation center. The economics of health care

Table 86.1   States Mandating Benefit Coverage Under Group Plans for the Treatment of Alcoholism, Drug Addiction, or Both

Alabama
Arizona
Arkansas
California
Colorado
Connecticut
Florida
Indiana
Kansas
Kentucky
Louisiana
Maine
Maryland
Massachusetts
Michigan
Minnesota
Mississippi
Missouri
Montana
Nebraska
Nevada
New Jersey
New Mexico
New York
North Carolina
North Dakota
Ohio
Oregon
Pennsylvania
Rhode Island
South Dakota
Tennessee
Texas
Utah
Vermont
Virginia
Washington
West Virginia
Wisconsin

Table reprinted from Source book of health insurance data. Washington, DC: Health Insurance Association of America, 1989:7.

and greater public awareness of alcohol and drug problems increased the demand and the supply of treatment programs in the 1980s. This trend shifted into reverse in the more economically streamlined 1990s.

1980s: HOW MEDICAL COST CONTAINMENT EFFORTS CONTRIBUTED TO GROWTH IN THE PSYCHIATRIC AND SUBSTANCE ABUSE TREATMENT AREA

During the 1970s the United States economy entered a long period of inflation. General medical costs continued to rise faster than other economic indicators. The federal government was now a major purchaser of health services, and it began to intervene in an effort to regulate spiraling treatment costs. Prices in the medical marketplace were escalating faster than the Consumer Price Index, even in those years of high inflation.

A significant part of the problem lay in the fee-for-service reimbursement system. Medicare and Medicaid, Blue Cross, and most commercial insurance plans reimbursed hospitals on the basis of their costs. The payment system offered providers no incentive to lower costs. Such a system resulted in excessively expensive medical care. It also encouraged waste and fraud. This arrangement is called cost-based reimbursement.

By the late 1970s the federal government's Health Care Financing Administration (HCFA) had begun to study ways to institute a schedule of payments for those insured under Medicare. (Early indemnity plans had used payment schedules, but abandoned this system for the "usual and customary" fee arrangement). HCFA adapted Yale University research on medical resources and relative value scales in which medical illnesses were grouped into 470 diagnostic-related groups, or DRGs. HCFA devised reimbursement formulae calculated according to the patient's DRG. For each DRG, a fixed amount was paid to the hospital. Adjustments in this rate are made to take into account geographic differences and several other factors. The monetary reimbursement was tied to the DRG, regardless of how many days the patient remained in the hospital (17). This is a somewhat simplified explanation of the DRG system. The overall effect of returning to a schedule of payments is that hospitals no longer had an incentive to keep patients for lengthy or unneeded stays. This was the first insurance-based incentive that medical institutions had to decrease their costs. Its impact was prodigious.

The DRG payment system was enacted for Medicare in 1983. By 1986, all payers—Blue Cross and the commercial insurers—were calculating payments to hospitals for medical care under a variation of the DRG prospective payment system (5).

It is important to note that the DRG system applied to *medical* diagnoses only. Psychiatric and substance abuse services were exempt from DRG reimbursement schedules, primarily because it is difficult to categorize diagnoses and to estimate appropriate length of stay. The following provider institutions were exempt from the DRG reimbursement system (17):

1. Psychiatric units in general hospitals
2. Freestanding psychiatric hospitals
3. Alcohol or drug rehabilitation centers
4. Physical rehabilitation centers
5. Children's hospitals

As a result, the DRG system regulated the cost of providing medical care but left unregulated the cost of providing psychiatric care and addiction treatment. Hence, the consequence of such partial regulation was predictable. Beginning in 1983, the overall utilization of medical hospital days *decreased* markedly. At the same time, the number of psychiatric and substance abuse hospital days *rose* dramatically. Between 1985 and 1987 psychiatric and substance abuse services reported a 25% increase in number of inpatient days. The number of private, for-profit psychiatric and substance abuse treatment centers grew noticeably in the mid 1980s: in 1986, a 22% increase in the number of beds occurred (18). This era of "opportunity pricing" began to end in 1988, when the American economy shifted once again, and employers took a strong stance on premium costs.

This historical and economic perspective has set the stage for an examination of the costs of treating addiction and the availability of health insurance coverage for the various types of treatment.

COSTS OF ALCOHOL AND DRUG TREATMENT

Cost, as discussed in this section, refers to actual charges incurred for the delivery of varied levels of treatment. In other words, what does the payor, be that the individual patient, or the insurer, see on a claim? The actual charges for treatment varies according to the type of institution delivering the care and the type of care that is provided. Until the 1990s, fee-for-service reimbursement dominated American health care. This means that actual costs per "episode of illness" can be captured. Actual charges for treatment vary according to the venue in which treatment is delivered. Acute care medical hospitals and psychiatric units charge more for their services than do nonhospital (freestanding) rehabilitation centers ƒbecause their cost base is higher. Residential TCs are much less expensive and are largely supported by federal and state revenues, the setting is nontechnical, and the staff is mostly nonprofessionals. Outpatient counseling programs are understandably far less expensive than inpatient programs. As a result of their outpatient structure and inexpensive technology, methadone maintenance programs cost even less.

Between 1983 and 1988 total charges per person for inpatient substance abuse increased almost 25%; whereas, costs per person for mental disorders increased 18.8%. In 1988 the average charge per admission for *in-hospital detoxification and rehabilitation for substance abuse* was for employees, $8,164; for spouses $7,104; for dependents $12,364 (generally adolescent children) (David Renaldo, personal communication, Employer Health Care Data, Westport, CT, August, 1990).

The average cost per admission to a *special facility* (i.e., a *short-term residential rehabilitation center*) was slightly lower: for employees $6,394; for spouses $5,994; for dependents $8,832.

The average cost per admission to a *psychiatric hospital* was higher: for employees $9,430; for spouses $9,431; for dependents $18,160 (Note the enormous price differential for adolescent treatment) (David Renaldo, personal communication, Employer Health Care Data, Westport, CT, August, 1990).

1988 was the high water mark in the era of opportunity pricing in addiction treatment. Employer-sponsored managed behavioral plans began to reverse the upward trend of pricing in the 1990s, as we will document in the next section of this chapter.

Charges: Detoxification

For Medicare enrollees, in-hospital detoxification has been reimbursed under the DRG flat rate payment formula since the mid 1980s. The exact dollar amount for each DRG varies according to the location and type of hospital in which services are provided. The cost of detoxification from alcohol, which consists of a 3–5 day hospital stay, ranges from $850 to $2500. Opiate detoxification, lasting nine or more days, ranges in cost from $2800 to $4500.

For group health enrollees (non Medicare), hospitals charge a per diem fee, that ranges from $400 to $1200 per day.

Charges: Outpatient Treatment

In the 1980s, the outpatient treatment of alcoholism and drug addiction was established and institutionalized. In the 1990s, managed health plans and HMOs are demanding access to a wider range of more cost effective interventions, i.e., outpatient care. Greater public awareness coupled with the widespread adoption of EAPs by business and labor unions allowed for the identification of chemically dependent people at earlier stages of the problem. Many of those who were identified did not require detoxification or residential rehabilitation. They needed intervention, counseling, and health education.

Nearly all of the state-mandated insurance policies concerning alcoholism and drug addiction contained provisions for coverage of outpatient care. Hospital clinics, mental health centers, and private practices established outpatient rehabilitation programs. These are structured, intense coun-

Table 86.2   Net Mental Health Benefit Costs per Person per Year

Population	High Cost Sharing ($)	Low Cost Sharing ($)
Insured	53–76	92–122
Uninsured	120–171	207–276

Table adapted from Health Cost Guidelines. Seattle, WA: Milliman & Robertson, July, 1993.

seling programs in which patients attend four or more sessions per week for 3–6 months. Hospitals and clinics also offer less intensive recovery services such as individual, family, and group counseling sessions.

The cost of outpatient care varies with the customary charges for similar services in each area. Recovery programs in hospitals charge the rate for a clinic visit, which in some states is as high as $98 per visit. Private outpatient programs charge between $25 and $85 per visit. Some programs charge a comprehensive rate for an entire 3–6 month program. The authors' research indicated that these charges ranged from $2100 to $5000 for the entire course of treatment.

Charges: Insurance Premiums

Costs for ADM coverage should be no more than 5% of total premium. In the unmanaged market of the mid to late 1980s, some employer plan sponsors saw their group's premium costs exceed 20% of total premium. Rather than present a spreadsheet of representative premium pricing, the authors have elected to present a proposed ideal premium.

Table 86.2 shows the estimated premium costs for mental health benefits under the proposed Health Security Plan. Although this plan did not pass into law during the Clinton Administration, its content was the subject of intensive study and scrutiny. The plan's framers evaluated numerous pricing models, and offered projections for a High Cost Sharing Plan, and a Low Cost Sharing Plan. (Cost sharing refers to the portion of the plan that the covered individual contributes to the premium cost.) The figures shown project gross mental health premium costs for the existing insured population, and the current uninsured/underinsured population.

Coverage: Employer Sponsored Plans

In the United States, employers purchase health coverage from Blue Cross, commercial insurance carriers, and health maintenance organizations. Many corporations and union trust funds have chosen to self-insure all or part of their health plans. This means that the company or trust underwrites the costs of the plan, including reserves, becoming its own health plan sponsor. As of 1990, 138 million Americans are covered by some form of employer-sponsored group health insurance. According to the U.S. Bureau of Labor Statistics, alcoholism treatment benefits are provided for 80% of those covered under employer-sponsored benefit plans. Drug abuse treatment coverage is provided to 74% of those covered under such plans (13). Of all plan participants with alcohol abuse benefits, 95% were covered for inpatient detoxification and 78% for inpatient rehabilitation. Alcoholism withdrawal is considered to be medically emergent, so nearly all plans cover this level of treatment. Rehabilitation does not require acute or constant care; thus there is a greater tendency to exclude it from benefit packages. Outpatient treatment was available to 84% of the participants in those plans that offered alcoholism treatment coverage. Coverage patterns are similar for the diagnosis of drug addiction.

As noted earlier, health insurance plans have always been more restrictive in their coverage of ADM diagnoses than other (i.e., medical) diagnoses. Traditional indemnity health plans apply limitations for substance abuse treatment. A typical limitation on inpatient care has been a maximum of 30 days in patient coverage per year. Outpatient care has been usually limited to a maximum number of visits per year, sometimes as few as 20 visits or as many as 60 visits. Other plans apply a yearly dollar limitation on the amount that will be covered for these diagnoses. This can vary from a low of $3,000 to a high of $40,000. Most employer-sponsored plans have imposed "lifetime limitations" of a maximum of two in-hospital rehabilitations per lifetime of the insured.

In the 1990s, employers, elected officials and consumers moved the topic of health insurance costs into the public arena. President Clinton's first two years in office were dominated by the administration's and Congress' lengthy discussion of restructuring health insurance. Despite Congress' inability to formulate and pass legislation on the matter, the national debate had far-reaching repercussions. By 1994, providers, business leaders and consumers were far more aware of the costs and limitations of health insurance than they had been at the dawn of the decade. This widespread awareness, coupled with a leaner global economy, led employers of all sizes to examine less costly means of providing group health coverage.

Despite the failure of the Clinton Health Security Act to be enacted, the repercussions from this health insurance debate impelled businesses and medical institutions to make significant policy changes. The private sector, led by employer initiatives, has begun to transform the health care system by implementing these changes:

1. a shift from two levels of care (inpatient and outpatient) to a continuum of care, in which patient need determines the setting
2. a shift from a provider driven delivery system to a buyer driven system
3. a shift from a fee for service market to a capitated managed market
4. a shift from open ended freedom of choice to new restrictions on provider access and reimbursement (19).

The principal medical insurance vehicle for these shifts is the HMO.

Coverage: HMOs and Managed Behavioral Health Carve-Out Plans

HMOs, prepaid group plans that emphasize primary care, prevention, and utilization controls, presented employers and government plans with attractive premiums. HMOs have been a part of the American group health market since the 1940s. However, in the 1990s, for many employers, HMOs have become the preferred insurance mechanism because they are more effective at holding down premium costs.

In the majority of HMOs, the primary care physician (PCP) is the hub of access for all services received by the insured. HMOs build their provider networks selectively/only a portion of the doctors and hospitals in a geographic area are "in network," and therefore available to the insureds. Most HMOs "capitate" payments to the PCPs: the doctor receives a set amount per employee per month. The PCP is responsible for managing the care of that population within the "budget" created by the capitated payment. By 1996, nearly 60 million Americans received their health care through an HMO. Projections through the end of the century hold that 50% of the American population would be covered under an HMO.

HMOs emphasize primary medical care. Most cover acute treatment for the "behavioral" diagnoses, with the focus on stabilization of symptoms through the least invasive level of care, usually outpatient. Many employers have chosen to "carve out" the mental health portion of their benefit plan so as to offer enhanced, but managed, mental health care to their employees and dependents. The portion of the group premium, generally about 5% of total premium, is paid directly to specialty mental health managed care organizations (MCOs) such as Value Behavioral Health, GreenSpring Mental Health Services, or Managed Health Network.

These carve-out firms started up in the mid 1980s, in response to employer concern about the rapidly rising costs, and therefore premiums, for mental health care. The behavioral MCOs offered employers a credentialed panel of practitioners and centers, a range of treatment options, a comprehensive assessment for those seeking care, and the means of monitoring, reviewing, and reporting utilization and outcomes. Behavioral MCOs assume partial risk for managing the care of the population. Hence, the MCO is responsible for delivering and managing all aspects of care within the amount of premium paid. The MCO realizes profit if care is well managed and loss if its costs exceed the premium paid. By 1994, 80 million American employees and their dependents received their mental health services through some level of employer-sponsored mental health plan (20).

By the mid 1990s, the managed behavioral industry entered a time of maturation and consolidation. Consolidation of regional networks resulted in 12 national companies collectively covering the bulk of the market—the aforementioned 80 million lives. Two of the largest of these companies are owned or controlled largely by pharmaceutical firms, and most of the others are owned by insurance carriers.

The effects of managed behavioral health's consolidation on the provider sector were quickly visible. In 1994, the average length of stay for "behavioral" diagnoses, including addiction, fell to 11 days nationwide, having been nearly three times that a decade before. The decrease in length of stay and emphasis on outpatient interventions created a shift in the provider arena. Close to one third of all private psychiatric or chemical dependence facilities closed or changed venues between 1988 and 1995. Several of the more aggressive corporate psychiatric chains, such as National Medical Enterprises, faced legal action in several states for violation of patients' rights and insurance fraud. By the mid 1990s, the era of opportunity pricing in mental health had ceased through widespread cost containment efforts, a tighter economy, and heightened business and consumer awareness.

Coverage: Self-insured Plans

Managed behavioral health care is an accepted component of self insured and commercial insurance plans. It should be noted that the availability of benefit coverage for inpatient rehabilitation under self-insured plans is discretionary and not mandated by state insurance laws that govern commercial health plans. Self-insured plans are governed under the Federal Employee Income Retirement Security Act of 1974 and are, therefore, exempt from state-mandated benefited coverage. More employers have chosen to self-insure all or part of their benefit plans both to control costs and to avoid the many recent state mandates. One benefit consultant who advises self-insured plans said that nearly all of his companies' plans provide coverage for detoxification and some outpatient care; only about 45% provide coverage for inpatient rehabilitation (Edward Gluckmann, Consultant, Multiplan, Inc., personal communication, July, 1990). These tend to be the larger employers, with over 500 employees. Among those self-insured plans that do provide rehabilitation coverage, the use of behavioral managed care carve-out firms is the customary practice. Rehabilitation has been limited to one or two stays per lifetime in many plans.

Coverage: Medicare and Medicaid

At the close of the twentieth century, collaboration between the private and public sectors in health care is beginning to move forward. In the era of cost awareness, the greatest argument for an integrated public-private health system are the efficiencies that can be achieved through a universal managed care approach.

Historically, Medicare provided coverage for detoxification and rehabilitation in the general hospital setting under Part A for inpatient hospital care. The usual deductibles and copayments apply as with any other diagnosis. One general rule for services to be covered under either part of the Medicare program is that services must be reasonable and necessary for the diagnosis or treatment of the patient's condition. In addition, because alcoholism is classified as a mental disorder, the limitations that apply under Medicare to the use of mental health services apply also to alcoholism treatment services. Among these stipulations, the lifetime number of days of coverage available for inpatient care in a psychiatric hospital is limited to 190 days. Furthermore, coverage is allowed only for rehabilitation services that represent "active treatment" (i.e., services provided under an individualized treatment or diagnostic plan that are reasonably expected to improve the patient's condition and that are supervised and evaluated by a physician). Annual expenses covered in the treatment of mental disorders of persons who are not inpatients at hospitals are limited to $312.50 or 51.5% of the reasonable charges, whichever is less. The Medicare program then reimburses 80% of this amount, with a limitation of $250 per year. It has been reimbursing under the DRG flat-rate payment system since 1983. This reimbursement system has shortened the usual length of stay in rehabilitation to between 8 and 14 days (2).

Medicaid (Title XIX of the Social Security Act) is jointly financed by federal and state governments and is administered by the states with the as-

sistance of broad federal guidelines. As a state-administered program, Medicaid offers flexibility to each state in establishing its own package of covered services and in identifying eligible individuals. It does not provide specific benefits for alcoholism and drug addiction services; however, coverage is available for detoxification and rehabilitation, as well as for the treatment of medical conditions that may occur with or result from alcohol or drug addiction. Title XIX includes such benefits as inpatient and outpatient hospital services, physicians' services, rehabilitative services, and medical care provided by licensed practitioners, all of which are available for alcohol or drug abuse treatment.

All states impose specific limitations at all levels of care in terms of inpatient days used, type of treatment center, or practitioner credentials. Physician services are reimbursable under Medicaid regardless of the setting. States may also grant independent provider status to nonphysician professionals such as nurses, social workers, psychologists, and addiction counselors under "rehabilitative services." Five states reimburse for treatment of alcoholism at halfway houses. As a result of both the administrative complexity of the Medicaid program and the difficulty that states have in clearly identifying those services provided specifically for alcoholism and drug addiction, reliable Medicaid reimbursement data are not available.

In the mid 1990s, initiatives at the federal and state levels encourage the enrollment of Medicare and Medicaid enrollees in managed care plans, specifically HMOs. The shifts in the health delivery system started by the private sector are being adapted to the public sector. This effort is aimed at containing costs and enhancing access to rational care orchestrated by a PCP. Since the Health Security Act did not pass into law, state governments initiated their own behavioral health care reform programs at a rapid rate. HMOs established governmental departments to coordinate the challenge of network building, enrollee promotion, service, and outcome management. Some states are aggressively implementing programs statewide, while others are beginning to submit waiver requests to HCFA. Florida, Massachusetts, Iowa, Ohio, Pennsylvania, and Washington were in the forefront of implementing behavioral care reforms by 1995. The moving of large numbers of elderly and indigent persons into managed plans offers hope that sick alcoholic and addicted individuals will have access to appropriate levels of care in a timely, coordinated manner.

The reader will note that the levels of care discussed have not included residential TCs or halfway houses. Employer-sponsored plans as a rule do not cover services in such long-term residential settings. The use of state and federal funds supplemented by the client's welfare payments have been the usual means for paying the cost of rehabilitation in TCs. The authors discovered some self-insured plans that did provide some benefits for private TCs and halfway houses, particularly when such an arrangement is less expensive than other types of addiction care. The recent trend in all health benefit plans has been toward greater control over eligibility and cost. This trend has made its presence felt in the area of alcohol and drug abuse benefits by the application of managed care techniques by the insurance carriers. The recession economy of the early 1990s brought about changes in the role that third-party insurers play in the health care drama. These changes have been particularly consequential for those benefits that have been recently established—namely, for mental illness and chemical dependence care. The next section discusses the recent changes and trends in benefit administration pertaining to these diagnoses.

WHY THE ECONOMIC TIDE CHANGED

As noted in previous sections, the expansion of benefits for substance abuse treatment and the growing market in private sector treatment began to experience changes toward the end of the 1980s. Business and governmental concerns over escalating health care costs, coupled with a recession economy, raised serious questions about the costs of providing benefits for the treatment of addictions. Former director of the Federal Office of Management and Budget, James C. Miller III, identified health care costs, which represent 11% of the gross national product, as "the most significant" economic problem facing the Bush Administration (21). The issue of health insurance costs dominated the first two years of the Clinton administration.

In the "unmanaged" health system, costs for psychiatric and substance abuse treatment rose more rapidly than did the costs for any other type of health care*twice as fast as the medical component of the Consumer Price Index (18). According to a survey of companies offering psychiatric and substance abuse benefits, costs increased by 18% in 1989, after having increased by 27% in 1988 (22). In spite of the documented medical offset effects of providing addiction treatment (appropriate treatment of addiction yields lower utilization of medical care over time), any such benefit was canceled out by unmanaged care at high-cost settings (23).

This economic trend produced several ironic consequences. On the very day that President Bush announced his plan for achieving a drug-free nation, the *Wall Street Journal* published an article on firms curtailing benefit coverage for the treatment of addiction (24). At a time when public awareness of drug and alcohol problems was high, access to benefit coverage for treatment began to get more difficult.

Since the 1970s great changes have occurred in how decisions are made about a patient's medical care. Decisions that formerly only physicians and patients made are now subject to review by third parties who are accountable to whomever is underwriting the cost of care. Utilization management has been a component of medical practice since the mid 1970s, in the form of second opinions, prior authorization, and concurrent and prospective reviews. Its application in the areas of psychiatry and addictions is recent, but already it has made its impact felt.

Utilization management, also known as cost containment, is defined as "a set of techniques used by or on behalf of purchasers of health benefits to manage health care costs by influencing patient care decision making through case by case assessments of the appropriateness of care prior to its provision" (25). These efforts to control costs have focused on three general approaches:

1. Redesign of the benefit plan and its management
2. Increasing employee cost sharing through higher deductibles and copayments
3. Use of preferred provider panels, which limit the choice of practitioner, but allow greater cost saving and control

These activities may influence the quality of care (26).

However, mental illness and substance abuse do not lend themselves as readily as medical illnesses to diagnostic categorization. Insurers have effected savings in medical utilization by directing care toward outpatient or less intensive treatment. When applied to substance abuse or mental illness, such narrow cost containment criteria may be less effective in the long run. In the case of alcoholism and other addictions, the patient's denial, the degenerative nature of these diseases, and the lack of a universally accepted treatment model all prevent the effective application of traditional methods of utilization review and management. These factors contributed to the establishment of behavioral managed care organizations, which "carve out" the ADM diagnoses from the remainder of the benefit package.

The fact remains that hard cost-benefit analyses of treatment have been few. Nonetheless, there is some evidence to support the hypothesis that treatment of alcohol abuse is cost-effective. Holder and Hallan and Holder and Blose studied several large groups of individuals over several years (27). They compared total medical expenses of the patients in their samples both before and after alcoholism treatment. The researchers found an overall decrease in average total medical expenses in the experimental group. Over a 3-year period, the total cost of alcoholism treatment was offset by the reduction of the total cost of health care (28). Vaillant's longitudinal study of an adult male population over a 50-year span indicates that intervention and peer support contribute to improved physical and mental well-being (29). Similar studies on the cost efficiency of drug abuse treatment are not available.

High-quality care and effective cost management in addiction treatment are not inherently incompatible goals. As in medicine, providing high-quality care at a reasonable price is a desirable goal. If this goal is to be attained, the active support of both third-party payers and treatment providers is needed. The merging of payers and providers in managed care relationships underscores the importance of the integrity of decision making in assessment, referral, and treatment. It is vital that those performing case management be free from financial conflicts of interest and of therapeutic biases. The persistent view of addictive diseases as psychogenic, rather than biogenic, remains a significant bias that affects the provision of care (30). HMOs and some behavioral management firms have been criticized by providers for allowing crucial treatment decisions to be made by practitioners with no expertise in addiction medicine or psychological assessment. The utilization review companies defend their position by claiming that they only approve benefit coverage and do not render decisions about patient care.

Insurance decisions about the appropriateness and medical necessity of certain levels of care leave both patient and practitioner confused and at risk. Utilization management raises ethical dilemmas and questions about liability and confidentiality. Does the ability to pay for care determine access to treatment? To what risks do providers open themselves if they decline treatment to a sick or disturbed addict? Do providers alone bear the burden of liability in such cases?

The well-known case of *Wickline v. California* stated that "third party payers of health care services can be held legally accountable when medically inappropriate decisions result from defects in the design or implementation of cost containment mechanisms . . ." (31).

The *Wickline* case concerned a patient who was medically, not psychologically ill. She was able to assess her situation and pursue her grievance through the civil courts. Given the nature of alcoholism and drug dependence, few patients have the stamina and pride to pursue legal redress should their insurer decline claims for addiction treatment services. The denial and shame that accompany the disease leave the afflicted without the support of public advocacy groups that other diseases have.

The Institute of Medicine's Committee for the Study of Treatment and Rehabilitation Services for Alcoholism and Alcohol Abuse (1990) offers a set of comprehensive recommendations concerning the structure and financing of the ideal treatment system for alcoholism. The Committee recommends that public and private insurance should provide coverage for the following: (*a*) assessment, reassessment, and continuity assurance to facilitate matching to the appropriate level and intensity of treatment at each state; (*b*) brief interventions for alcohol problems, if coverage is needed to facilitate the use of the services; (*c*) detoxification and other forms of acute intervention in the lowest cost setting of appropriate quality; (*d*) rehabilitation in the lowest cost setting of appropriate quality; (*e*) maintenance in the lowest cost setting of appropriate quality; and (*f*) treatment for as long as is clinically necessary with no prespecified number of inpatient days and/or outpatient sessions as part of desired coverage (2).

The committee further recommends that coverage for detoxification and other forms of acute intervention, rehabilitation, and maintenance be provided in both social model and medical model programs. Another recommendation is that if nonmedical professionals are capable of providing high-quality care, medical supervision should not be required in order to be eligible for insurance benefits. The final recommendation is that a consensus activity be carried out to develop a common set of definitions and criteria for determining appropriate type and level of care placement at each stage of treatment, and that the criteria adopted be based on available research as well as the broadest range of shared clinical experience. Coverage for the treatment of alcohol problems should be subject to the same deductibles, coinsurance, limits, case management, and utilization review as are applied to coverage of treatment for other medical conditions (2).

The Institute of Medicine Committee's vision stresses the leadership opportunity for the federal government, state governments, employers, and insurers to formulate policies pertaining to the purchase of care and the containment of costs. Moreover, employers and insurers in the private sector can implement these policies on an experimental basis in their EAPs and managed care activities (2). In some respects, EAPs are similar in form and function to the kind of mechanism recommended in the Committee's report. EAPs, whether established by management or labor, have the resources needed to assess employee problems, to make referrals to treatment agencies, and to furnish both financial and clinical case management (9). EAPs, working in concert with their companies' top management and benefit administrators, are in a position to implement the committee's vision and to achieve a balance between cost containment and quality of care.

A study conducted by the benefits consulting firm of Alexander and Alexander demonstrated that such a balance is achievable. The study compared employees of the McDonnell Douglas Corporation who sought mental health and substance abuse care on their own with those who used their companies' EAP. Employee benefit coverage was essentially the same for both groups. The study found the EAP, which assesses and refers employees to appropriate levels of care, was much more cost effective. These data were examined for three years' prior to the initiation of treatment and for 4 years after treatment. Over four years, employees who used the EAP for chemical dependency problems missed 44% fewer work days, had 81% lower attrition, and filed $7,300 less in health care claims than did the control group. Savings were somewhat less in all categories for mental health problems (32). Evaluations of treatment programs typically produce unreliable results. They use unrepresentative samples and weak empirical indicators. By contrast, the research design employed in the McDonnell Douglas study deserves emulation. To cite just three of the methodological strengths of this research, the investigators used a prospective design, a large representative sample, and strong empirical measures of their outcome variables. For example, the findings in this study were based on the analysis of medical claims and work attendance records for more than 20,000 employees (32).

By the mid 1990s, the use of behavioral managed care and the application of core managed care technologies—selective network contracting and utilization review—effected greater cost efficiencies while preserving benefit coverage. Outcomes from the corporate sector are promising:

- Chrysler Corporation lowered the costs of their mental health benefits by nearly one third in 1990, the first year of the managed program. The program was instituted after a study showed that the company spent $45 million per year for ADM benefits, and had also lost $100 million due to absenteeism and lost productivity. The company utilized its EAP and concentrated on early intervention. In 1990, per employee mental health care costs fell by 31%, from $485 to $338. Second year benefit costs rose slightly to $349 per employee. The number of days per thousand of inpatient care dropped by 32% (33).
- BellSouth Corp (Atlanta) saw its mental health costs decline from 17% of total premium to 9.2% in 1993. This reduction was achieved through contracting directly with providers, insisting upon appropriate assessment, emphasizing partial hospitalization and outpatient care whenever appropriate, and utilization management for inpatient admissions. The company enhanced its outpatient mental health coverage, now covering 85% of outpatient visits up to 52 visits per year (34).

These two illustrations from the private sector provide encouraging evidence of economic outcomes. The question of evaluating therapeutic outcomes is more problematic. In the private sector, employers have such measurable outcomes as return to work rates and sick time usage. As the delivery of health care moves to an integrated public-private system, appropriate and measurable outcomes for the more chronically ill public sector clientele must be addressed.

Of interest is that the behavioral health carve-out programs are the prototypes of the "disease management" efforts of the late 1990s. Health plans are addressing other chronic relapsing conditions, such as diabetes mellitus, asthma, and cardiorespiratory conditions, in a systematic integrated manner. Afflicted individuals in the insured population are identified as early as possible through risk assessment algorithms and assisted through case management, patient education, and support along a defined care pathway. Health plans using disease management methods use sophisticated clinical data management systems to track patient progress and outcomes. This model of chronic/complex disease management was "beta tested" in the mental health field and adapted to the medical realm.

CONCLUSION

The diagnosis, treatment, and financing of care for alcoholism and drug addictions has evolved dramatically since 1970, and, given the current economic reform environment, continued change is assured. The first half of this chapter traced the institutionalization of two systems of treatment, one for alcoholism and the other for drug addiction. The discussion focused on the nature and the duration of each process, for both factors affected when the federal government, private employers, and insurance companies decided to insure the treatment of alcoholism and drug addiction. Institutionalization in conjunction with larger social and economic forces not only determined the availability of insurance plans but also influenced the amount and type of coverage they offered. As this abbreviated history affirmed, institutionalization of each treatment system was beset by many obstacles; hence, each system emerged very slowly. This historical account also indicated that each treatment system had to achieve a high degree of institutionalization before either public or private sector institutions offered insurance plans.

The founding of AA in 1935 signaled the beginning of the transfer of alcoholism from the field of law enforcement to the health care field. The therapeutic approach to alcoholism was fully institutionalized in the 1970s. The establishment of the first TC, Synanon, in the mid 1950s initiated the development of the modern treatment approach to drug addiction. (Prior to the prohibition era introduced by the Harrison Act in 1914, physicians treated drug addicts.) Approximately 30 years later, drug addiction treatment had finally attained a high level of institutionalization.

Why did each treatment system take such a long time to develop? Until the 1960s opinion leaders, elite institutions, and the public viewed alcoholism and drug addictions as moral problems. Hence, it was felt that the appropriate response to alcoholics and addicts was incarceration, ostracism, or avoidance. Unlike medicine, research on addictions did not produce any scientific breakthroughs which would have expedited the legitimization of addiction treatment. Specifically, researchers did not uncover a persuasive theoretical explanation of the causes of either alcoholism or addiction. There was no counterpart to medicine's germ theory. Moreover, this lack of a theory partially explains why researchers have failed to develop a treatment regimen or a technology which would make possible lasting recovery for the majority of addicts. Advocates of treatment could not base their case primarily on compelling scientific evidence; instead, they had to employ a wide array of communication and organizational skills to offer persuasive ideological arguments for the humanitarian and the therapeutic virtues of treatment. Ultimately, the institutionalization of treatment was a political triumph engineered by skillful, well-intended ideologues, not a scientific one wrought by diligent researchers.

With respect to alcoholism treatment, two factors are mainly responsible for institutionalization f effective lobbying by the National Council on Alcoholism, other grassroots organizations, and recovered individuals and the acceptance of the disease concept of alcoholism by the federal government. Federal involvement occurred in two ways. With the enactment of Medicare and Medicaid in 1965, the federal government became a major purchaser of addiction treatment services. In 1970 when the NIAAA was established, funding for research, prevention, and treatment helped expedite the institutional adoption and implementation of the treatment concept.

The following factors contributed to the institutionalization of drug addiction treatment: (a) the heroin epidemic of the late 1950s and early 1960s; (b) the widespread recreational use of drugs by high school and college students; (c) the establishment of NIDA in 1970; and (d) beginning in the mid 1970s, the dramatic increase in cocaine use by blue-collar and white-collar workers.

The federal research institutes for alcoholism and drug abuse have played a pivotal role in the institutionalization of treatment. These new institutes not only provided resources for research, prevention, and treatment, they also offered legitimacy, for their creation symbolized that alcoholism and drug addiction constituted sufficient threats to the public interest to warrant a high degree of federal intervention. Whenever Congress grants a social problem or an illness institute status as opposed to bureau or program status, it means that the problem in question, when compared to other problems, is entitled to a disproportionately large share of federal money. This gesture represents a positive self-fulfilling prophecy for it reinforces the public's perception that alcoholism and drug addiction are both widespread and severe, facilitating subsequent public and private efforts to fund treatment.

As a result, the period between 1970 and 1990 was characterized by the following developments with respect to substance abuse insurance. First, insurance coverage began to increase. Initially, there were more benefits available for alcoholism treatment than drug addiction. Then, states enacted legislation mandating insurance benefits for alcoholism and drug addiction. The expansion in insurance coverage led to an increase in the number of rehabilitation facilities. Moreover, treatment became a lucrative business venture as evidenced by the growth in the number of for-profit treatment centers. This interactive relationship between treatment and insurance drove up the cost of substance abuse care. In fact, the sizable increase in the cost of care occurred at the very time when public policy makers were devising strategies such as DRGs to contain other types of medical costs. As noted earlier, it is difficult to regulate the cost of substance abuse care because the relationship between treatment and recovery is not well understood. Nonetheless, insurers and EAPs have adopted utilization management procedures in an attempt to improve the quality of substance abuse care while reducing the cost. As the American economy enters a more turbulent period, corporations and the federal government have begun to significantly reduce the number and type of health insurance benefits. As a result, the availability of substance abuse insurance and treatment centers has begun to decline, responding to market forces rather than to the epidemiological dimensions of the problem.

In effect, similar to the established system of medical care, the emerging system of substance abuse care has had three tiers. In the first tier, there are alcoholics and addicts whose insurance coverage permits them access to the full range of inpatient and outpatient services. These patients are typically the fortunate beneficiaries of generous insurance plans provided by their employers. The second tier consists of substance abusers who are eligible for coverage in the public sector—Medicare, Medicaid, Veterans' Administration, or CHAMPUS. The individuals of the third tier are the uninsured—the working poor, young persons, the unemployed, self-employed, and the marginally employed. The number of persons without insurance is growing. Precise estimates are difficult to obtain. Waitzkin states, "More than 41 million people in the United States are uninsured for at least part of the year. Employed people and their dependents comprise more than three quarters of those in the United States who are uninsured" (35).

The questions posed at the outset of this chapter warrant a provisional reply. Since this is not a research paper, no definitive conclusions can be offered. The conventional wisdom holds that treatment is conducive to recovery. However, no study has conclusively demonstrated a causal relationship between treatment intervention and recovery. In fact, as Vaillant's research implied (3), the opposite may be true; namely, alcoholics may recover *in spite of* treatment. Nonetheless, powerful institutions such as organized medicine, commercial insurance companies, corporations, the federal government, and providers of health care accept, as a matter of faith, that treatment has some indeterminate therapeutic value. Depending on the frame of reference, this position has merit. Research and experience have demonstrated that neither moral censure nor imprisonment are viable solutions to alcoholism and drug addiction (10). Nonetheless, research has not unraveled the mysteries of the treatment process, such as which components are essential to recovery and which are merely the result of custom. For example, conventional wisdom has assumed that inpatient rehabilitation for alcoholism should last 28 or 30 days. Moreover, many insurance plans provided coverage for this phase of care. Why? The medical model is predicated on the assumption that effective treatment of disease begins with inpatient care. However, in the case of alcoholism, there is no scientific evidence suggesting that a month is an optimal time period. In fact, the concept of rehabilitation as customarily used may be challenged, for it may be a misnomer. The inpatient therapy which ensures detoxification is medical stabilization in preparation for rehabilitation which occurs during the outpatient phase of care. A similar problem is posed by treatment personnel. For example, in the field of alcoholism treatment, there is no consensus as to who is best qualified to deliver which type of care. In particular, who should counsel recovering addicts—nurses, social workers, psychiatrists, clinical psychologists, or certified alcohol counselors? What type of training is required to make a prospective counselor proficient in the delivery of substance abuse care? As these examples attest, neither commercial insurance companies nor the federal government can make compelling claims as to the quality of substance abuse care that they are purchasing. To underscore this point, the aphoristic wisdom of L. J. Henderson needs to be invoked. The renowned biochemist and social scientist (in spite of himself) observed "Somewhere between 1910 and 1912 a random patient with a random disease, consulting a doctor chosen at random had, for the first time in the history of mankind, a 50/50 chance of profiting from the encounter" (36).Henderson's observation still does not hold true for the interaction between the average alcoholic or addict and the average counselor.

Insurers and their corporate and public clients cope with the ambiguities of the treatment process in two ways. First, some degree of symbolic reassurance is afforded by the fact that the emerging system of substance abuse treatment resembles the established system of medical care. Moreover, the emulation is deliberate. Thus the technical language, therapeutic processes, and bureaucratic procedures have their equivalents in medicine. Second, insurers minimize economic risks through coinsurance mechanisms, eligibility requirements, managing utilization, and the number of beneficiaries. The basic assumption is that, in the insured population of employees, a "healthy" majority will pay for the addictions of the few. Thus, insurers justify their investment primarily on economic grounds. As the Institute of Medicine's report strongly recommends, only research can provide the necessary information by which to determine what constitutes the appropriate level of care in each stage of the treatment process. There is an urgent need for prospective evaluations of treatment programs if the precipitants of lasting recovery are to be systematically identified. More specifically, the relative contributions of treatment and nontreatment factors to recovery can only be determined through prospective studies; retrospective studies cannot furnish adequate answers (3). These observations are not intended to imply that the relationship between treatment and recovery is wholly enigmatic. By the same token, neither researchers nor providers of care can agree on what constitutes recovery or what determines quality of care. Regarding the latter, indirect measures such as the prestige of the treatment facility are used more often than direct measures reflecting the dynamics of the treatment process and its outcome (37).

Researchers know considerably more than they did in the 1960s, when evaluation research was in its infancy. The biogenic origins of alcoholism and other addictions have been amply demonstrated in numerous, though as yet unintegrated, studies. However, while research resolves these issues, insurers must rely on economic and cultural criteria in formulating policies, evaluating risk, and determining benefits. In many respects, the substance abuse treatment field is at the same stage of development as medicine was in the middle of the nineteenth century. It is waiting for a scientific discovery which will furnish the knowledge needed to develop effective cures. Thus far, research has not produced the equivalent of the germ theory, and hence there are no magic bullets. To carry this analogy further, after the crucial discovery occurs, research and treatment personnel need to conduct a systematic evaluation of the substance abuse field similar to Abraham Flexner's assessment of medicine. Until these events occur, decisions pertaining to substance abuse insurance will be governed primarily by political, economic, and cultural considerations. Similarly, until issues concerning the training of treatment personnel and the organization and the delivery of care are resolved, it will be difficult to make informed judgments as to the quality of care which various insurance plans purchase.

References

1. U.S. Department of Health and Human Services, Alcohol, Drug Abuse and Mental Health Services Administration, National Institute on Drug Abuse, National Institute on Alcohol Abuse and Alcoholism. National drug and alcoholism treatment unit survey. DHHS Publication No. (ADM) 89–1626. Rockville, MD: DHHS 1989;62.
2. Institute of Medicine. Broadening the base of treatment for alcoholism. Washington, DC: National Academy Press, 1990:1.
3. Vaillant G. The natural history of alcoholism. Cambridge, MA: Harvard University Press, 1983:185–186.
4. Mechanic D. Future issues in health care. New York: The Free Press, 1979:10–11.
5. Starr P. The social transformation of American

medicine. New York: Basic Books, 1982: 311.

6. Kurtz E. Not-God: a history of Alcoholics Anonymous. Center City, MN: Hazelden Press, 1979:101.

7. Hanlon JJ. Public health: administration and practice. St. Louis: CV Mosby, 1974:467.

8. Hingson R, Matthews D, Scotch NA. The use and abuse of psychoactive substances. In: Freeman HE, Levine S, Reeder LG, eds. Handbook of medical sociology. 3rd edition. Englewood Cliffs, NJ: Prentice-Hall, 1979:118.

9. Scanlon W. Alcoholism and drug abuse in the workplace: managing costs and care through employee assistance programs. Westport, CT: Praeger-Greenwood Press, 1991.

10. Nelkin D. Methadone maintenance: a technological fix. New York: George Braziller, 1973: 12–14.

11. Brecher EM, et al. Licit and illicit drugs. Boston: Little, Brown, 1972:52–55.

12. Sonnenstuhl WJ. Inside an emotional health program: a field study of workplace assistance for troubled employees. Ithaca, NY: Cornell University, ILR Press, 1986:22.

13. U.S. Department of Labor, Bureau of Labor Statistics. Employee benefits in medium and large firms, 1988. Bulletin 2336. Washington, DC: U.S. Government Printing Office, 1988:40.

14. Milam J. The alcoholism revolution. Professional Counselor 1992;August.

15. Milam J. The alcoholism revolution revisited. Professional Counselor 1993;October.

16. Hoechst Marion Roussel. Managed Care Digest, 1995.

17. Kasten B. The physicians' DRG handbook. Stow, OH: Lexi Company, 1987:14–16.

18. Weiner R, Seigel D. Managed mental health care: issues and strategies. Benefits Q 1989;5(3):21.

19. Monack DR. Medicaid and managed care. Behavioral Healthcare Tomorrow 1995; March/April.

20. TenHoor and Harbin. Legal and regulatory challenges in public-private managed behavioral healthcare program procurement. Behavioral Healthcare Tomorrow 1995;March/April.

21. Seay DJ. Annual report. Presented at the annual meeting of the New York Business Group on Health, November, 1989:16.

22. A. Foster Higgins Co. Benefits survey. New York, 1990.

23. Glazer W, Bell N. Mental health benefits. A purchaser's guide. Brookfield, WI: International Foundation of Employee Benefit Plans, 1993.

24. Pereira J. Firms cut drug treatment benefits. Wall Street Journal 1989(September 5).

25. Institute of Medicine. Controlling costs or changing patient care? The role of utilization management. Washington, DC: National Academy Press, 1989:3.

26. Warshaw L. The purchasers focus on quality. NY Bus Group Health Newslet 1990:July 1.

27. Holder HD, Hallan JB. Impact of alcoholism on total health care cost: a six year study. Adv Alcohol Subst Abuse 1986;6(1):1–15.

28. Holder HD, Blose JO. Alcoholism treatment and total health care utilization and costs. A four year longitudinal analysis of federal employees. JAMA 1986;256:1456–1460.

29. Vaillant G. The natural history of alcoholism revisited. Cambridge, MA: Harvard University Press, 1995.

30. Milam J. The alcoholism revolution revisited. Professional Counselor 1993 (October).

31. Wickline v. California, 228 Cal. Rptr., California Appeal, 1986.

32. Smith D, Mahoney J. McDonnell Douglas study produces hard data. ALMACAN 1989;November:8–14.

33. Gates M. Chrysler studying effect of managed mental health care. Managed Care Outlook 1992;Oct 9:7

34. Sardina C. BellSouth cuts MH costs through managed care. Managed Care Outlook 1993;Feb 12:3.

35. Waitzkin H. Health policy in the United States: problems and alternatives. In: Freeman HE, Levine S, eds. Handbook of medical sociology. 4th edition. Englewood Cliffs, NJ: Prentice-Hall, 1989:477.

36. Stoeckle JD. Introduction. In: Stoeckle JD, ed. Encounters between patients and doctors. Cambridge, MA: MIT Press, 1987:1–2.

37. Reader JW. Some theoretical dilemmas in the research on alcoholism and its treatment. Presented at the Public Health Symposium, Department of Public Health, Cornell Medical Center-New York Hospital, New York City, May, 1984:22.

87 MANAGED CARE

Gerard Armstrong

MANAGED CARE: WHY NOW? WHAT IS IT?

Managed care has hit America and everyone at every level of government is jumping on the bandwagon. Anyone associated with health care, whether a provider, a patient, or a payor is learning the jargon. But where is the emphasis: is it on management or is it on care? How governments decide to answer that question might reveal to future generations how America treated its poor, its sick, and its disadvantaged at the turn of the century. Did America manage or did America care?

Why Now?

Substance abuse treatment has come a long way in the last 30 years. The ultimate mission of treatment is to heal and restore the abuser to a healthier and more functional lifestyle. The acceptance of substance abuse as a disease entity which needs specialist attention is a premise which has come alive within both government and medicine in these last few decades. This premise became the foundation upon which treatment programs throughout the country were established. Substance abuse is a health problem, first and foremost, although mental dysfunction, criminality, homelessness, unemployment, and a whole host of other social problems may often accompany this disease.

Acknowledgment that substance abuse is a disease was good news for both the abuser and the treatment professional. Treatment of abuse became integrally tied to the treatment of other health and mental health disorders and the abuser began to be seen holistically. As this concept took hold and the premise that substance abuse was solely a criminal problem diminished,

what are now the traditional government funding streams began to take shape. Medicaid and federal disability funding became available for those patients who otherwise qualified because now there was acceptance that the treatment provider was dealing with a medical problem. Now, ironically, governments are going broke and substance abuse treatment is in trouble. Governments at all levels must find savings and priorities must be changed. Health care costs nationwide are breaking the bank and so, health care becomes a primary target for reshaping and for cost cutting. All health care, including substance abuse treatment, comes under scrutiny. Enter the world of managed care for governments to embrace as a new and different way of conducting business in the health care of patients who are uninsured, a world that has existed for insured patients since the early 1940s.

Commercial insurers had learned the lesson of managing care over 50 years ago; otherwise, never would they have survived. Government turned to the private sector and began to borrow its management principles in order bring health care costs under control. Governments all across the country wanted to get out of the liability business for the uninsured and began to shift the risk of being the payor to private for-profit and not-for-profit companies. What had made these companies so successful in managing the health care costs of the insured?

What Is It?

Managed care has many definitions but most contain the three fundamental elements of improved access to care, cost containment, and quality assurance. Hence, managed care is a health care delivery system wherein the patient has improved access to primary health care that is monitored on a continuous basis for quality assurance and where costs are contained precisely because there has been established an ongoing relationship between the patient and his or her primary care giver. Physicians and other health care givers see the patient for routine checkups, provide education and guidance about more healthy lifestyles by emphasizing prevention and early identification of health problems. Maintaining good health and living healthy lifestyles reduce health emergencies and costly acute care. Managed care is based on the assumption that good communication exists between primary care giver and patient. Where this communication is obscured by layers of administrative requirements or office staff, there is potential for failure of the entire system.

As managed care takes hold of the publicly funded health care system throughout the country and as substance abuse treatment is affected, another major force of change will occur. Just as the first appearances of the HIV virus changed substance abuse treatment in the early 1980s and just as the first appearances of crack cocaine changed treatment in the mid 1980s, so also will managed care change substance abuse treatment in the late 1990s and well beyond the year 2000. Patients will have to learn new habits of behavior, providers will have to focus not only on the patients but on the payors, and the new payors—the managed care and behavioral health care companies—will have to realize that substance abuse is chronic in nature with many forward and backward movements for the individual patient.

Change always brings anxiety and concern. A major change that affects patient, provider, and payor simultaneously necessarily brings resistance at all three levels. This is why government must move slowly and cautiously. Problems must be identified and addressed adequately so that the goals of managed care—improved access to primary health care, cost containment, and quality assurance—are achieved.

MANAGED CARE: A NATIONAL REMEDY?

One of the first national problems that President Bill Clinton attempted to tackle was health care for the uninsured. Three dimensions of health care were targeted systemwide: access to primary care, cost containment, and quality assurance. Far-reaching solutions were debated and ultimately discarded. Every citizen and citizen's group had an opinion to offer, frequently shaped by the relative public or private interest. Providers and payors differed on policy as well as need issues while the uninsured remained largely confused and frightened. In the end no unifying force prevailed and the Clinton attempt at reform became history.

The national plan to reform health care, however, did succeed in getting the issue on individual states' agendas for legislative change. After all, the fiscal problems that states were having because of health and welfare costs were only worsening. The states had no other choice but to plan for health care reform at the local level. Today there are as many different ways to implement health care change as there are states concerned about managing this problem into the future. What constitutes basic coverage for the uninsured in one state may be, and probably is, very different in another state, whether one has a cardiac problem or a substance abuse problem. Which patients receive what benefits and how remains very diversified nationwide. Why has this occurred?

States partially support the costs of health care for the indigent through federal reimbursement. Even though substance abuse treatment is not a federally mandated service (and therefore may or may not be included in an individual state's menu of Medicaid reimbursable treatment available to eligible patients), states realize that Medicaid costs for uninsured persons, including substance abusers, are breaking state treasuries. States, therefore, need to propose and impose cost containment measures on their own health care delivery systems. Furthermore, states can and do request various waivers from the U.S. Health Care Financing Administration (HCFA) based on an individual state's need and public health priorities which encourage differences in populations covered and services reimbursed through Medicaid. Since health care reform failed at the national level, states have been extremely busy in shaping and submitting plans to HCFA, and HCFA has been extremely busy in reviewing and approving states' waiver requests to implement Medicaid reform. The Clinton Administration has encouraged states to reform and reshape local health care through this process of submitting HCFA waivers. To date, some 12 states which have submitted Section 1115(a) statewide Medicaid demonstration project requests to HCFA have had such requests approved (1).[a]

In addition, HCFA has approved 128 of the more limited 1915(b) "freedom of choice" waivers (1). These waivers allow states to extend managed care coverage to Medicaid recipients.

What has developed nationwide is a desire to achieve health care reform through diverse local plans which affect the field of substance abuse treatment in myriad ways. New concepts as well as new language has been introduced to patients and practitioners alike and the learning curve is different among states and even within states. Managed care companies also are at various points along the learning curve depending upon their developing interest in substance abuse treatment directly or through their need to embrace patients with mental health problems within their covered Medicaid population. The changes are as stressful to the payors as they are to the providers and the patients. Like a young child learning a language, all three investors at the Medicaid managed care table may make mistakes and will, no doubt, misunderstand what the other investors are risking. Government has the responsibility to ensure such misunderstanding does not destroy the opportunity that the current fiscal conditions have presented.

SUBSTANCE ABUSE TREATMENT: "CARVE-IN" OR "CARVE-OUT"?

There is great difference of opinion whether or not substance abuse treatment should be included in managed care. This difference of opinion has roots in various assumptions about the disease itself. For some, substance abuse is a series of acute intermittent episodes which occur throughout a person's life and hence treatment should be limited to these episodic periods. Others recognize that substance abuse is a chronic relapsing condition which has no cure and which requires treatment that should not be constrained by artificial time limits. This latter belief holds that substance abuse treatment should be outside of, that is, "carved-out" of any Medicaid managed care plan and should be reimbursed based on individual client need. The former belief holds that substance abuse treatment is an acute need which should be included, that is, "carved-in" to any Medicaid managed care plan. The result of this divergence of beliefs is exemplified by some states "carving-in" substance abuse treatment and others "carving-out" treatment from the basic coverage of the Medicaid managed care plan. The bottom line is how the service gets paid, by the managed care company or by traditional government sources, but even more important is how very disruptive its impact on the client may be to the treatment process. In the "carve-in" case, the managed care company makes the treatment decisions because it is the payor. In the other case, the treatment provider makes the treatment decisions because substance abuse treatment has been "carved-out."

It probably is too early to judge which approach is more appropriate in terms of the goals of managed care. While the debate continues, however, it is important to remember why substance abuse treatment developed as a specialty treatment approach—substance abusers' needs generally were unmet in traditional medical care. The real question today is: has the health delivery system changed sufficiently so that history does not repeat itself?

The "carve-in/carve-out" issue also has financial differences which often dictate how states decide what to do with substance abuse treatment. In the "carve-in" approach, the managed care company usually receives a relatively small sum of money within its capitation rate in order to cover certain substance abuse treatment services which are usually limited in number of visits. For example, basic coverage for Medicaid patients may include a certain number of days for inpatient substance abuse treatment, a certain number of visits for outpatient treatment and detoxification services available on a medically needed basis. Once the client "maxes" out on the basic benefit,

---

[a]As of April 1996, these twelve states were Delaware, Florida, Hawaii, Kentucky, Massachusetts, Minnesota, Ohio, Oklahoma, Oregon, Rhode Island, Tennessee, and Vermont.

either a "stop-loss" insurance kicks in or government arranges to reimburse the managed care company for the additional treatment needed.

On the other hand, in the "carve-out" approach, substance abuse treatment is totally excluded from the coverage offered to Medicaid patients through managed care plans. Treatment is reimbursed by the federal and state government through the established Medicaid revenue system which is based on the eligibility of the client, eligibility of the provider, and eligibility of the service. This approach represents business as usual and thus is often the favorite of both providers and clients. Their argument is that clients consider the substance abuse treatment provider as the most responsive and trusted partner in their rehabilitative effort and oftentimes has the best understanding of the client's needs. Client satisfaction studies, especially in methadone maintenance programs, seem to bear this out (2).

HORIZONTAL AND VERTICAL INTEGRATION

Where does substance abuse treatment fit? When managed care companies begin to cover the lives of Medicaid clients, this question often presents itself immediately. Is substance abuse treatment just another part of mental health, or are there patients who have substance abuse alone, without clinical evidence of a mental health problem? Or is substance abuse just an external symptom of an underlying mental health problem? Whatever the real answer, it is being ignored more and more in the general trend nationwide to have substance abuse treatment managed through a behavioral health care company. At first glance, this may seem appropriate when one considers the high incidence of mental health problems among substance abusers and conversely, the high incidence of substance abuse problems among mental health patients (3, 4). It is the old chicken-and-the-egg problem: which came first?

This tendency to merge substance abuse treatment under the mental health umbrella is reflected in the organizational structure of governmental agencies, both at the federal and state levels. The U.S. Department of Health and Human Services (HHS), as well as Congress has opted to draw the agencies responsible for mental health and substance abuse closer together. Block grants accomplish the same goal. Furthermore, more than 40 states no longer have a separate governmental agency for substance abuse treatment.[b]

It is no wonder, then, that as states implement Medicaid managed care, the issue of the inclusion or exclusion of substance abuse under mental health presents itself for a decision from managed care companies.

This integration of mental health and substance abuse treatment is only one element of a continuum of care which needs to be available to Medicaid clients. Substance abuse treatment must address all the needs that the client has. In order to accomplish this, providers must offer comprehensive services onsite, or become part of a network of providers which together offer comprehensive services. Managed care demands this. Although this is a fairly straightforward and sound clinical approach, it shakes the structures upon which substance abuse treatment has been built during the last 25 years. Providers must stop thinking of themselves in terms of modality—that is, a methadone program, a therapeutic community, a halfway house, etc.— and begin thinking of themselves as agents of change, ensuring that clients are restored to a functioning, socially contributing status. Substance abuse programs must provide treatment, whatever it takes, to restore the individual patients to health. Therefore, the future will see the differences among and between modalities dissipate, and providers and/or networks of providers will make available comprehensive substance abuse treatment.

All this talk of comprehensive treatment with or without mental health treatment is a discussion about horizontal integration of services whose goal is improved management and coordination of the individual's care. But the discussion necessarily must be taken a step further. How does government bring substance abuse treatment into the mainstream in order to improve primary health care services, achieve Medicaid cost savings, and improve the quality of care by better coordination and management of the individual client? This question really has two parts: (a) how do managed care compa-

nies and other health care providers, including hospitals, identify, assess, and determine care levels for substance abusing patients; (b) how do substance abuse providers provide primary health care to their clients so that all their health needs can be met in a cost-efficient and coordinated manner?

These horizontal and vertical integrations are needed in order to achieve cost savings in other government supported services. Oftentimes, substance abusers left untreated create a revolving door which is costly to government and detrimental to the individual client. Whether the revolving door includes multiple inpatient hospitalizations for detoxification unconnected to treatment, multiple incarcerations, intermittent stays at homeless shelters, repeated emergency room visits because of trauma or illness related to substance abuse, or repeated episodes of domestic violence, nonetheless integrated treatment of substance abuse does effect cost savings in other systems of health, social service, and criminal justice (5).

So just where does substance abuse treatment fit? The answer is that it fits everywhere and unless and until this fact is accepted, the costs of Medicaid clients will continue to break the bank. Government has a responsibility to interrupt the revolving door cycle and to manage these clients who show up in the government-supported systems. To ignore or minimize substance abuse treatment while government attempts to cut health care costs or social service costs at the same time is destined to fail. Substance abuse treatment must be part of every health care, social service, and criminal justice initiative which is aimed at controlling costs.

"GATEKEEPING" ISSUES

A managed care company, as it takes on coverage of Medicaid patients either voluntarily or by governmental requirement, assumes the role of decision-maker regarding an individual's health care needs. Basic decisions such as who gets treatment, what kind of treatment, for how long and by what provider, all converge almost immediately on the managed care company. If the company is relatively unfamiliar with the Medicaid population, these basic decisions can cause not only delays in appropriate client treatment, but may also cause liability issues which ultimately can be very costly. Hence, it is extremely important that managed care companies are well prepared for this task. The simplest solution for the managed care company is to avail itself of the expertise available in substance abuse treatment through community-based providers. But the simplest solution is not always evident. What often happens is clients' substance abuse needs are missed entirely or are inappropriately assessed. This is not surprising given the history of the health care system not dealing with substance abusers and the usual lack of familiarity related to substance abuse treatment that is found in general medical practice.

This discussion brings to the fore a whole host of needs such as training of health care professionals in the area of substance abuse, standardized assessment tools, instruments to determine levels of care, credentialing of counselors, and standards of care. After all, the managed care company must identify how decisions for substance abuse treatment are to be made and by whom. In order that these decisions be guided by an up-to-date knowledge base and a firm belief that treatment works, these other issues must be met head-on. The need for training is obvious. Government must facilitate the utilization of standardized assessment tools so that substance abuse is not missed altogether. Similarly, government must guide managed care companies to utilize instruments that have been field tested and found to be satisfactory in terms of level of care determinations. The instruments chosen should reflect the kinds of treatment available in the local community. For example, if methadone maintenance treatment is available for opiate addiction, the instrument used in the initial assessment should lead the patient, where appropriate, to methadone maintenance treatment.

Government has an extremely active role to play in ensuring that the gatekeeping function is administered in an appropriate manner. The heart of the matter is that a client who presents for substance abuse treatment should be appropriately treated. Care must not be minimized nor postponed nor inappropriately directed. The more appropriate the match between the client's needs and the chosen treatment, the better will be the outcome in terms of recovery, cost savings, and social dysfunction.

Government must guard against the "creaming" of clients who need long-term treatment. Managed care companies and behavioral health companies which have short contract periods (usually two years or less) may have a temptation to delay long-term treatment in the hope that less expensive protocols may suffice. After all, a different contractor may have to endure the long-term treatment costs of the most dysfunctional clients. In addition, it is important that all managed care and behavioral health companies, as well as treatment providers, utilize the same criteria for admission which has been agreed upon when the contract is executed. This places all the managed care players on the same level field, and it seems appropriate that government should ensure that this occurs.

Health care costs are a combination of technological advancements, labor costs, and utilization of services. Managed care companies are hard pressed to affect either of the first two, and so, must control utilization of services in order to control costs. This is why the gatekeeping function is so critical, both to the managed care company and to the client. A professional balance between cost and need must be struck if both the need and the cost is not to explode. This is why government has a role as a facilitator and arbitrator in guarding against abuses in the gatekeeping function, especially where chronic conditions, such as substance abuse, are being addressed.

STAFFING REQUIREMENTS

The substance abuse treatment field has a long history of utilizing the talents and skills of recovering clients, so-called paraprofessionals, in the treatment process. Witness the documented success of Alcoholics Anonymous. Paraprofessionals have rightfully earned the respect of the treatment field and have contributed much to its development. This fact is rather unique in the health care field at large. Hence, with the advent of managed care for Medicaid clients, the question arises what is the role of the paraprofessional. If this issue is either ignored or minimized, an invaluable resource of human experience and proven skill will be lost both to the provider and the client. Not only will there be deep resentment directed at the payor, but the disruption of provider staffing patterns will affect client treatment.

No one can argue that treatment needs the most up-to-date and clinically proven knowledge base. Clients deserve nothing less. The demand for professional, credentialed staff is an appropriate and welcomed advance from managed care companies. Whether the managed care company sets as the standard a national credential or a state-issued certification, the bottom line is that an orderly transitional period must occur so that paraprofessionals can be given the opportunity to meet the standards set by the payor rather than be excluded as a matter of principle. It is important for managed care companies to understand the history of substance abuse treatment; on the other hand, it is also important for staff to realize that payors have every right to demand qualified, capable providers. When government rushes to implement managed care for the Medicaid population, such transitional periods are sometimes either too short or nonexistent. Is it any wonder, therefore, that resentment develops and ultimately the political process imposes its own delay or transitional period?

Another staffing issue is that managed care and behavioral health companies are accustomed to utilizing the expertise of mental health professionals, specifically psychiatrists, psychologists, and social workers. Frequently, the literature of behavioral health companies will use these words without ever mentioning such professional staff as "addiction specialists" or "credentialed counselors." The assumption that mental health professionals, or for that matter physicians and nurses, are professionally trained to deal with substance or alcohol abuse as a matter of course is erroneous. Addiction medicine is a specialized field, whether it is part of psychiatry or internal medicine. (That debate has never been resolved!) Although it may be convenient for the payor to use the services of a mental health professional on staff, that form of treatment may not be adequate for the substance abuser. On the other hand, a community-based substance abuse treatment provider may not be adequate to handle the client with an underlying psychosis. The point here is that no one profession has the key to treating substance abuse successfully. The complexity of the problem and the needs of the client dictate a team approach which includes adequately trained professionals representing various disciplines who are in constant communication with each other about this client and his or her progress or lack thereof in recovery. Turf wars should be avoided. Government must guard against the client being shuffled back and forth while professionals argue about which treatment protocol is most appropriate or which is the cheapest.

Payors must familiarize themselves with this new breed of clients and providers. Providers must familiarize themselves with the rights of the payors. Finally, clients must familiarize themselves with a new system where care is coordinated and managed by more than the provider.

STRENGTHS AND WEAKNESSES: PROVIDER AND PAYOR

Managed care and behavioral health companies have strengths and weaknesses which can be complimentary rather than detrimental to the strengths and weaknesses of community-based substance abuse treatment providers. Managed care companies offer financial expertise, capital, comfortable physical plants, professional management, opportunities for investment and a usually well-earned professional respect for success. In a similar vein, community-based treatment providers offer experience with the substance-abusing population, committed boards of directors, acceptance by the clients, and established roots in the community. Each side also has its own set of weaknesses. Managed care companies may be unknown in a local community, may lack experience with this population and may be directed by investors rather than committed community residents. Similarly, substance abuse treatment providers may lack financial expertise, usually have no capital, and often have less than desirable physical plants. Would it be too much to assume that by joining in a cooperative working relationship, the strengths of the payor and provider could overcome their respective weaknesses, for the greater good of the clients?

When managed care or behavioral health care companies come to the negotiating table with substance abuse treatment providers, each side must recognize its own strengths and weaknesses. Essentially, the payor brings infrastructure and financial strength; the provider brings the Medicaid client and the treatment process. If each side contributes its strength, it is a win-win situation for the three principals at the negotiating table: payor, provider, and patient. Once again, a period of transition is recommended so that this mutual understanding of each other is achieved. When Medicaid managed care is implemented too quickly, this understanding comes only after resentment has built and positions have become entrenched. This is certainly a role for government to assume: ensure a smooth and orderly transition for payor, provider, and patient.

Oftentimes, when substance abuse treatment providers come to the negotiating table with a behavioral health company, much of the discussion centers on the legal relationship that will dictate how each will operate as a business partner. The simplest relationship is that of a contractual one, wherein each party is obligated by a specific set of agreements. Generally, the provider must communicate clinical progress of the covered patient and must deliver the treatment agreed upon by the payor within a certain period. The contract usually specifies what financial arrangements will kick in after the approved time period or number of approved clinical visits is exhausted. Other joint ventures are certainly possible, but care must be taken to ensure that whatever relationship is established between the managed care company and the treatment entity complies with the requirements of federal and state antitrust laws. The bottom line is that both partners—the payor and the provider—must include reliable legal counsel from the onset of such business negotiations.

NETWORKING

Networks is a word with a variety of meanings. In fact, the term is so broad that it is probably not definable in law. When the managed care world talks about "networks," generally the term denotes a system of substance abuse care which forms a continuum capable of addressing the individual client's needs, from detoxification to relapse prevention. Oftentimes substance abuse providers are unable to offer such a comprehensive care continuum, and so these providers must join forces with other treatment providers that offer different services. In this context, a network becomes an identifiable entity which includes more than one treatment provider so that a continuum of care can be offered to the managed care market. One of the historical issues that substance abuse treatment providers must get beyond is a concentration on modality. Modality is the generic classification of services provided by programs, such as methadone, drug free, medically supervised, etc., usually with an accompanying environmental mode, such as ambulatory, residential, inpatient hospital, etc.

Over the last three decades, many federal and state funding streams were specifically directed to modalities of treatment. In a sense, this solidified providers' mission statements and so a methadone treatment program offered maintenance of opiate addicts on medication and that was the mission of this modality. To outsiders, these so-called modality classifications are confusing and, in many instances, lose their meaning. As a result, it is now necessary for substance abuse treatment providers to begin thinking about comprehensive services for clients and so, there is a market need to diminish the artificial boundaries created by the historical development of modalities. Thus, the concept of programs joining together to offer a continuum of comprehensive care for all substance-abusing clients has taken root in many states.

The network, as a single operating entity, takes on a corporate identity which is quite distinguishable from the treatment providers. The network negotiates reimbursement rates with the payors, provides the treatment entities with a unified management information system, may do the marketing, the training, the quality assurance for provider members, and so on. In addition, the network usually operates a central intake where clients are assessed and levels of care needed are determined. Once this intake process has been completed by experienced treatment professionals, the client is appropriately referred to the treatment agency which matches his or her needs.

It is easy to understand why networks are more attractive to managed care companies. The payors deal with a single entity which takes responsibility for the client's care and can more easily learn the client's progress in treatment by the tracking and management information system common to all treatment agencies which make up the network. However, the formation of networks is no small or easy task for treatment providers. Provider agencies have traditionally seen themselves as human service entities which serve their local community. Competition among and between treatment agencies has not been uncommon. Now the market is dictating that these same providers work together as business entities and share such organizational systems as administration, management information, and quality care. Invariably, questions begin to arise around the development of such networks. Should the network be for profit or not for profit? Should the network be licensed or certified by government? Should the network engage in unfamiliar functions, such as marketing or training or is it better for the network to contract out for such functions? Should the network itself be eligible for government funding in the area of vocational services or should providers only be eligible for such funding? There are more questions than answers, but the bottom line is that the payors find it more cost effective and time efficient to work with a network, rather than many individual treatment providers. (As networks developed, it is interesting to watch the costs savings that occur as multiple management information systems or administrative staff or training units are consolidated—the exercise of network development is the first step wherein managed care can bring about cost savings.)

Another issue that needs to be discussed relevant to networks is the so-called "wrap around services" so necessary for treatment to work. Managed care brings about changes in the way Medicaid services are delivered. However, drug treatment includes more than Medicaid (medical) services. Certainly, payors must be aware that substance abuse treatment is more inclusive than what traditional health care insurers pay for. Right from the beginning, treatment providers that form networks must identify how individual clients will receive such rehabilitative services that are not Medicaid reimbursable. Once again, states must decide how to fund such "wrap arounds." How the money flows to support these services must be clearly understood and accepted by all the managed care principals, the payor, the provider, and the patient. Such up-front understandings prevent unforeseen risks, both in terms of financial loss and client failure in treatment.

One often hears the term "vertical and horizontal" networks. As treatment programs develop business relationships with their fellow treatment providers, it is important not to forget what the market is calling for. To offer comprehensive drug treatment services together with mental health services is an example of a horizontal network. But the market wants more. Managed care companies want addiction services joined with not only mental health services, but with primary care services. The market wants a seamless continuum delivering comprehensive health care for each client. The more that health care services are integrated, the better for the client in terms of outcome, and the better for the system in terms of cost control. Once again, this may or may not be problematic for substance abuse treatment providers who have historically focused on specific modalities of addiction treatment. Substance abuse treatment providers have demonstrated that clients come to them because of trust and understanding. Using this notion of client trust and satisfaction, treatment agencies become sites of opportunity where "one stop shopping" can be delivered. Such an integrated network of care is the ultimate goal in any community because it forces the disciplines to work as a team on behalf of the patient and while doing that saves the payor money. For certain, the more services are integrated horizontally and vertically, the better chance of success for a managed care health delivery system.

THE ROLE OF PREVENTION

Traditionally, prevention services in the field of substance abuse are not reimbursable through Medicaid. Hence, it is not uncommon that the advent of Medicaid managed care creates an identity crisis for prevention programs. Such programs commonly ask: where do we fit, if at all? This seems ironic, in one sense, since one of the goals of a managed care system is to prevent health problems from becoming more serious for the patient and more costly for the payor. It has been demonstrated time and time again that the earlier a health problem is identified and addressed, the greater the chance of success for treatment. The same holds true in the area of substance abuse. Research has demonstrated that prevention programs work (6).

Prevention, like the term networks, has different meanings for different people. For some, prevention means education or the exchange of helpful information about lifestyles or peer pressure. This is not substance abuse prevention. Rather, substance abuse prevention is a holistic approach which addresses an individual's total life needs including intellectual, physical, psychological, and social skills. So what we are talking about is not the availability of literature on drugs or alcohol in a patient waiting room, but rather a very active and interactive relationship between health care provider and patient which assesses and identifies potential problems in the biopsychosocial dimensions of that patient's life, followed by a plan to address each of those potential problems.

If prevention is viewed in this more comprehensive way, it is easy to determine that there certainly is a role in a managed care system for substance abuse prevention services. Prevention programs have experience in assessing potential problems caused by family, peer groups, social settings, or repeated academic failures. Would it not then be appropriate for the payor to engage prevention providers with such experience so that early identification, assessment, and referral can be put in place expeditiously? The real issue here is exactly how much is the payor willing to pay for holistic substance abuse prevention. Basically, prevention is an investment and other issues, such as length of the managed care company's contract, the elements of basic health care coverage, the priority of substance abuse in the community, all influence the payor's decisions around prevention.

CRIMINAL JUSTICE ISSUES

It is well documented that the majority of inmates in prisons and jails nationwide are substance abusers (7). Despite the fact that numerous research initiatives have demonstrated the effectiveness of substance abuse treatment in prison, there continues to be a reluctance on the part of government to provide needed treatment services "within the walls" (8). Is it any wonder why recidivism remains so high for this population? Is it any wonder why government continues to build more jails and prisons without addressing the substance abuse treatment needs of offenders? One can only conclude that government either does not recognize the relationship between addiction and crime or that it prefers to spend limited resources on buildings rather than treatment. This issue bears relevance when one talks about the implementation of Medicaid managed care for substance abuse treatment.

Picture the following scenario: a first-time offender admits, in court, that his underlying problem is addiction. The judge decides that as an alternative to incarceration this offender needs substance abuse treatment. However, this offender has been out of work and, as a result, is on Medicaid in a state where managed care has become mandatory for Medicaid clients. The judge remands the offender to a treatment program. Immediately, the managed care company decides that admission to a particular treatment program is not clinically justified.

The offender is caught in the middle. On the one hand, the court has sentenced him to treatment as an alternative to incarceration; on the other hand, his managed care company indicates that this treatment is not appropriate, and, therefore, they will not reimburse the treatment provider for this client. This scenario presents in many different situations, but the common denominator is that more and more frequently managed care companies or behavioral health care companies seem to clash with court-mandated treatment referrals.

In these cases responsibility for the treatment of the client remains vague. The system has created an intolerable situation which cannot be blamed on the payor, the provider, or the patient. Government must ensure that the criminal justice system communicates with the treatment system. In the end, government as a payor must reimburse any health care provider, including a substance abuse treatment program, which gives care to an individual who is under a court mandate. Payors and providers must demand this policy as a matter of public health and safety.

Community-based substance abuse treatment programs, like the jails and prisons, are filled with patients who have had, or currently have, relationships with the criminal justice system. Just as the treatment provider must keep the various elements of the criminal justice system informed of the client's progress in treatment, always within the limits of federal confidentiality regulations (42 CFR 2) (9), so also the criminal justice system must bear the financial responsibility for the needs of clients remanded to treatment as a condition of probation, parole, or an alternative to incarceration. In many states, community-based treatment providers receive no funding for what amounts to a rather high volume of criminal justice clients. Does government expect that managed care companies or behavioral health companies should assume the financial responsibility of criminal justice clients in treatment when, in fact, their treatment needs have been ignored or inadequately addressed in the first place?

Providers and payors must guard against the "dumping" of criminal justice clients into treatment programs designed to meet the needs of a local community. Substance abuse treatment programs, especially as Medicaid managed care takes hold nationwide, should ensure equal access to treatment for all those who want or need services. Either government must fund treatment services for criminal justice clients inside jails and prisons, or fund these same services in community-based treatment programs outside of (carved-out) Medicaid managed care reimbursement. In other words, the implementation of Medicaid managed care has no real bearing on this common and familiar problem of inadequate treatment services availability to criminal justice clients. The problem remains that government must invest in treatment for criminal justice clients and not shift responsibility to either health care payors or health care providers.

TREATMENT: COST OFFSETS

The CalData study, as well as numerous other research efforts, including recent Califano studies, have demonstrated what a sound investment government makes in substance abuse treatment (5, 10, 11). For every dollar spent on substance abuse treatment, seven dollars is saved by government in other areas, such as health care, foster care, criminal justice, social service, etc. (5). The prevalence and incidence of substance abuse among the criminal justice population mentioned earlier is similarly found among the home-

less in shelters, families whose children are placed in foster care, individuals who suffer repeated trauma from injuries related to abuse, etc. Oftentimes, it is the same individuals who enter the hospital for detoxification, who get arrested, who find themselves homeless, and whose children are removed by social service for their protection. Until government interrupts "the vicious circle," taxpayers' dollars continue to be wasted because the addiction problem is not being adequately addressed. The more government invests in demand reduction by the funding of prevention and treatment substance abuse services, whether those services take place in prisons, shelters, or community-based providers, the better chance government has of interrupting "the vicious circle." Time and time again, based on public opinion, government will invest its resources on supply reduction through enforcement and interdiction as well as in the construction of new jails and prisons. Substance abuse treatment is an investment in both the individual's and the public's good. This same premise holds true in the world of Medicaid managed care.

Managed care companies and behavioral health companies want to provide appropriate health care treatment to Medicaid patients in a cost-efficient manner. Admitting a substance abuser to an inpatient detoxification unit, time and time again without connecting that individual to a substance abuse treatment program, is a disservice to the patient and the taxpayer. The health care payor quickly realizes what government often misses. The more invested up front, the more is returned down the line. Invest in treatment at the appropriate level of care and the payor may save money on more intense and more costly levels of treatment later on. Payors are smart, and one can be sure that the realization of investing in treatment hits home very quickly. Payors "connect the dots" and must do so to stay in business. Government, on the other hand, too often is slow to "connect the dots" and commonly shies away from investments in human services that may save taxpayers big money in the long run.

Unfortunately, the substance abuse field, in general, has not done an efficient job of educating both the public and the government of such cost offsets. It is exciting that the implementation of Medicaid managed care throughout the country has driven the field to concentrate on treatment outcomes with documented research that proves the case that treatment not only works, but also that treatment saves the taxpayers big money in other social service, criminal justice, and health care delivery systems. Providers have a responsibility to continue educating the decision-makers whether they be elected officials or managed care companies on the proven cost savings that investing in substance abuse treatment can yield.

CHANGING FINANCIAL ARRANGEMENTS

In addition to all of the programmatic and clinical changes, the implementation of Medicaid managed care in the substance abuse treatment system brings about major changes in how treatment programs are sustained financially and similarly how government monies flow to support substance abuse treatment. Whether a substance abuse program has been accustomed to receiving grants or contracts from the federal and/or state government or whether the program is supported through Medicaid and/or Social Security Disability Income and/or Home Relief and Aid to Families and Dependent Children or a combination of all of these sources of revenue, managed care introduces a different mechanism of financial support. In its new role as a business entity, the treatment program begins an ongoing relationship with payors and managed care companies from which the treatment program receives its primary financial support. The provider must learn new business skills, such as negotiating competitive reimbursement rates, cost control, utilization management, and marketing products. This new identity for the treatment provider demands acquisition of technical business and financial skill which, until this point in the historical development of substance abuse treatment, was unheard of. Traditionally, government was the provider's "big brother" who was always there to support the treatment program, not only with operational funds, but in some instances with capital funds to build or renovate physical plants. The relationship between the governmental agencies and the treatment provider community was direct and simple. Managed care alters these relationships and makes financial support of treatment a more complicated and competitive system.

In certain states, the combination of Medicaid funds and governmental funds for treatment formed what is known as a "net deficit financing" arrangement. The concept was that the provider was obligated to generate as much Medicaid and client entitlement revenues as possible, and then government would fund the difference between approved costs of the program and the revenue collected. In this system, Medicaid revenue was generated on a fee-for-service basis. In essence, the provider was reimbursed for every service that was eligible on behalf of any patient who was eligible. As long as the three "legs of the Medicaid stool" were present, Medicaid would pay—specifically, the client had to be eligible for Medicaid based on income and need, the provider had to be approved to offer a Medicaid reimbursable service, and the service itself had to be classified as a medical service defined by the Medicaid system which varies from state to state. (Some states offer a minimum array of Medicaid services, essentially those that the federal government mandates. Other states offer a rather generous array of services, at the discretion of the state government.)

The fee-for-service reimbursement system benefits the provider financially. It is a system driven by volume and so the more services the provider renders to the eligible clients, the more income accrues to the provider. Other than establishing the reimbursement rate, dictating client eligibility requirements and identifying service elements, the government has no control over expenditure ceilings. Such a financial system puts the payor at the mercy of the provider and essentially causes Medicaid spending to spin out of control. The fee-for-service system, obviously, is the most beneficial reimbursement system to the provider and may be the worst system for the payor.

States have gradually been getting away from Medicaid fee-for-service payment systems. So too has the federal government. The introduction of diagnostic related groups (DRG) is an example of how government has changed to a different financing system for health care providers. In the DRG system, a provider is reimbursed a fixed amount of money to treat specifically related diagnoses. If the provider is able to treat the individual patient in a shorter period, the provider usually gains because of the cost savings. On the other hand, if the provider treats the patient over a much longer period, the provider loses because of the additional costs. At least such a system offers an incentive to the treatment provider to save money. There is no such incentive within a fee-for-service system. Other reimbursement methodologies presently being used throughout the country are case reimbursement, episodic reimbursement, products of ambulatory care, pricing, and full or partial capitation. All methodologies provide unique incentives but have a common denominator—they are aimed at controlling health care costs.

As the substance abuse treatment field adjusts to the widespread implementation of Medicaid managed care, providers move away from the "big brother" relationship with government and the sense of security government provides. Providers now move toward new financial reimbursement systems which in the world of business take on competitive and product driven forces. Although such financial arrangements can be quite complex or relatively simple, the bottom line is that the new payor is the managed care and behavioral health care company rather than the traditional substance abuse governmental funding agencies. The check now comes from the XYZ managed care company and when billing errors or disputes arise, the business entities—payor and provider—must resolve the problems with government no longer an active participant. For example, in a capitation system, government negotiates with a managed care company a certain reimbursement rate per covered life for all health care needs. The government establishes the capitation rate based on past spending patterns for a particular segment of the Medicaid population in a certain community which is directly related to the experiential costs of health care treatment. The government then takes a percentage of savings up front, disperses the remaining available revenue to the managed care company, and establishes a "per capita rate," taking into account the number of Medicaid persons within that managed care company's responsibility. The government, therefore, has very clearly shifted the liability costs for this population to private payors thus ensuring that the payors assume the financial risk for these patients. The managed care company will then deliver the comprehensive health care services for each patient in their plan either directly or by subcontracting with community-based providers in what is called a "provider panel." These providers sign a contract with the

managed care company to treat patients with certain diagnoses for a certain fixed amount of money. Providers who are unable to negotiate a satisfactory reimbursement rate with the managed care company often are not able to get on a "provider panel."

In some cases, managed care companies close the panel for a variety of reasons or choose to eliminate a provider panel member after an initial contract period has expired. For example, the managed care company may find it too difficult to retrieve patient information from the provider in an expedient way, or the managed care company may determine that clients are not satisfied with the way the provider treats them. When this occurs, substance abuse treatment programs find themselves in trouble. With government out of the business relationship, the provider must find itself another managed care company panel if it is to survive financially. Substance abuse treatment programs over the next few years will have to hire skilled business administrators who can deal with payors on level ground, if they do not already have such skill in-house. Programs will have to learn negotiating skills, and to do this, they must have strong financial management information which gives them the basis for knowing what kind of rate to accept from the payors. Programs have another option—they can choose to purchase these necessary business skills from a management services organization, which takes on the responsibility of managing the business end of the programs' operations.

Another important element of the new financial arrangements that managed care brings to substance abuse treatment is utilization management. In essence, the payor must control the client's use of services, since this is the one way costs can be managed by the payor. Labor costs, technology costs, therapeutic costs, and so on, are not controllable by the payor. The one element under the payor's control in the health care delivery system is the client's utilization of the services—which kind of services, for how long, and how often. This element of utilization management, common to general health care, often presents unique problems for the substance abuse treatment system. Substance abuse, as has been mentioned, is a chronic biopsychosocial disease for which at the present time there is no known cure. Clients progress and regress throughout their lives and may need treatment interventions at very irregular rates. A utilization management system may or may not be appropriate for such long-term chronic conditions which, if left unaddressed when there is a need, will ultimately cost taxpayers by driving up other human service systems costs. Although utilization management is an important tool in the success that managed care companies have already achieved, it is too early to determine its ultimate effect in the substance abuse treatment field. If treatment is an investment as has been said, then to deny or minimize treatment is a bad investment.

If one is to add all of these financial changes onto the programmatic, clinical, philosophical, and administrative changes that managed care brings to substance abuse treatment, it is easy to understand why the implementation of a Medicaid managed care system must be done over an adequate period of transition. Patients must be protected and the investment that government has already spent over the last three decades in building treatment systems must not be wasted. In an effort to control Medicaid costs—which is clearly needed nationwide—government must strike a delicate balance between cost control and patient need. Just reviewing the health care costs without considering other human service need costs is a fiscal mistake.

PARITY ISSUES

At the current time, Congress continues to consider various bills which focus on whether or not insurance companies and private payors must offer the same free access to mental health and substance abuse services that such companies offer to primary health care services (12). This issue of making mental health and substance abuse treatment "equal to" the rest of one's basic benefit coverage is a controversial one. What action the Congress takes on this issue will, no doubt, spill over to managed care first, and then to Medicaid managed care shortly thereafter. On the one hand, insurance companies understand too well the chronic nature of mental illness and addiction. Such companies fear that if limitations on treatment episodes are not put in place, the fiscal risks are so great that companies could go out of business. On the other hand, patient advocates cry discrimination if the mental health and substance abuse treatment benefits are limited in any way which makes it appear that patient access is controlled and restricted, unlike any other health care benefit.

This parity issue has significant impact on a long-term treatment such as methadone maintenance. It is not infrequent that methadone patients who are stabilized and have returned to a socially acceptable functioning level need methadone for the rest of their lives. Such patients know through experience that detoxification only causes setbacks in their functionality. These patients make a deliberate decision to continue on methadone maintenance indefinitely in order to preserve family relationships, keep a job, stay healthy, and maintain a crime-free lifestyle. Much like a diabetic who must take insulin for the rest of his or her life, or like a hypertensive who must take blood pressure medication indefinitely, methadone maintenance is the only option for certain patients to remain stable and functioning with a socially acceptable lifestyle.

To introduce the concept of limiting reimbursement for a lifelong treatment is very threatening to such patients. Many arguments are put forth to support such limitations such as, the patient should pay for his treatment, the patient is a drain on the taxpayers, or the need for treatment is his or her own doing. In fact, many methadone patients already share the cost of their own treatment. If they are gainfully employed, they not only pay taxes but are also charged patient fees. Other methadone patients may be single parents who cannot work because of child care responsibilities or who work part time with no health benefits. These patients, at least as long as circumstances continue, cannot pay for their treatment and so, should treatment be limited and ultimately denied, the consequences for the individual patient, their families and dependents, and society at large are devastating. These patients cannot understand why payors dare to disturb successful treatment patterns which, in the end, will have such costly results.

This is not to say that all methadone maintenance patients should be on a program for their rest of their life. The ultimate choice is really the patient's in consultation with his or her treatment provider. It is important for payors to understand the notion of "different strokes for different folks." Certain patients, whether mental health or substance abuse patients, need lifelong treatment. Others need intensive treatment at frequent intervals, while others may do very well with shorter treatment episodes and longer periods between treatment. Payors need to recognize the nature of the disease entities which present and must be flexible enough to allow patient access when clinically indicated without placing artificial and ill-advised limitations on treatment.

Just think how consumers would react if a payor announced that treatment for ulcers would be limited to 30 days. Or imagine a consumer being told that his cancer treatment will be limited to 20 visits for chemotherapy. These sound unreal and probably are. What really happens is that the payor evaluates the patient's condition at certain intervals and if the condition has not been reversed, the payor and the provider collaborate on what course of treatment should follow. This same general principle is what mental health and substance abuse advocates argue for when it comes to parity. Providers and patients alike must accept the challenge of educating not only payors, but also legislators so that the dollars invested in treatment are well spent and bring successful outcomes, rather than limiting reimbursement for treatment based on a need for cost savings or a misunderstanding of the disease entity. As long as the substance abuse treatment field advocates for the patient and not for themselves, this issue of parity with other health care treatment will not go away.

OUTCOME, NOT PROCESS

A discussion of parity often leads to another one concerning patient outcome. Payors are very comfortable when patients' outcomes are clear and easily documented. But when patients do not get better, the question is often asked: "What are we paying for?" Whether the payor is a private insurance company or the taxpayer through Medicaid, current economic forces are driving everyone to ask this question.

This is particularly true of the substance abuse treatment field. As a relatively new medical specialty, treatment practices are more often than not subjected to excruciating scrutiny while providers are held to strict accountability. Methadone treatment, for example, while highly researched and with very well-documented successful outcomes, is probably the most regulated

field of medicine in the United States today. It is highly unlikely that changes in such scrutiny will occur. On the contrary, the implementation of Medicaid managed care to the substance abuse treatment field is already making accountability more important.

Managed care and behavioral health care companies need to know what they are paying for. Such payors need to know what happened as a result of a provider treating their patient. This emphasis on patient outcome on an individual basis adds a new layer of accountability on the provider. Client record keeping must change. To document that a client attended the clinic, participated in individual and group counseling, and has been seeing the physician will not suffice for the payors' needs. While all this process of participation may help the provider track the patient, it is inadequate documentation to answer the payor's fundamental question: "What are we paying for?"

Patient outcome in substance abuse treatment does have industry-accepted standards. Outcomes must be concrete and measurable over time. Such outcomes include getting a job, completing high school or gaining an equivalency diploma, maintaining or restoring stable family relationships, eliminating arrests, or entering a vocational training program. Unlike the rest of health care, such outcomes are not medical in nature. Hence, the payor is now requiring the provider to produce patient outcomes which are more socially and personally oriented. Such outcomes have always been the goals of substance abuse treatment; the difference that managed care brings is that unless these goals are achieved within a certain period, the provider may not be reimbursed for the treatment rendered.

Such a change dictates new emphasis not only on treatment success in general, but on individual success in particular. Research studies have, over the last two decades, documented that treatment works, but now the individual provider will have to document that this treatment works for this individual patient. Providers will have to put on a new evaluation headset, whereby patient tracking information clearly documents that individual patients are achieving treatment success. This kind of change supports the already discussed concept of networking. Treatment will necessitate moving an individual client through a comprehensive continuum of care with individual milestones of success being achieved along the way. Payors will need to see the documentation that the milestones achieved justify the progression to the next level of care. In addition, providers will need to dedicate staff to the evaluation of patient outcomes. Frequently, the smaller treatment program is unable to provide either the continuum of care or the resources to evaluate individual patient outcomes. The solution may be found in the smaller provider joining a network of other substance abuse and primary health care providers which can offer both comprehensive care and treatment evaluation.

The movement away from treatment process to treatment outcome also supports the concept that providers most assume the role of a business entity which has as a priority customer satisfaction. Products must be consumer friendly, and the need for such products must be carefully studied. The marketing efforts on behalf of a certain product are measured through customer feedback. Changes are often made based on this feedback. For a human service, community-based provider to think of treatment as a product that must meet the needs and satisfaction of customers demands a whole new, mostly unfamiliar way of thinking. How one measures customer satisfaction is a skill to be learned, but a skill that must be acquired rather quickly in a managed care atmosphere. Competition in the marketplace will demand this new emphasis on customer satisfaction in addition to the payors' demands. What a new and different way of thinking this brings to treatment where providers have historically been reimbursed for services rendered on a fee-for-service basis without regard to either treatment success or customer satisfaction. Government should not expect such a drastic change in thinking to occur overnight. Again, this is a change which added to all the other programmatic, fiscal as well as philosophical, changes managed care brings will require a transition period for all the managed care principals—payor, provider, and patient—to accept.

The integral link of clinical practice to individual patient outcome will drive providers to seek help from academic disciplines. Statistical analysis, research technology, adequate samplings, patient interviews, and longitudinal studies will all require a more intense relationship between clinicians and researchers. How one defines success for an individual patient and the methodology utilized to measure that success over longer periods will often reach beyond the resources of clinicians in a treatment program. One could say that this is long overdue in the substance abuse treatment field. Oftentimes, one of the criticisms of the field has been the lack of documentation on the treatment outcome of patients who complete treatment without any follow-up a year or two later, especially since it is widely accepted that addiction and substance abuse is a chronic biopsychosocial problem. True, providers may know that an individual patient has continued to participate in Narcotics Anonymous or Alcoholics Anonymous, but more complete documentation of how this patient fares in terms of successful rehabilitation is usually not a priority for most community-based providers. This is not a criticism of treatment programs, but rather an acknowledgment that such providers lack the necessary human and fiscal resources to attain such needed follow-up documentation.

SUMMARY

Given the tremendous fiscal burden that unmanaged health care places upon the taxpayers, the dissatisfaction in the quality of care rendered in many different parts of the United States, and the lack of access to primary health care experienced by underinsured and uninsured people, government at all levels finally undertook the very complex and controversial task of attempting to improve the health care delivery system. Substance abuse treatment as well as mental health treatment had to be a participant discipline in this government overhaul, not only because of the high health care costs of this population, but also because of the public safety issues and public health issues involved with this population.

Since efforts at national health care reform have thus far been unsuccessful, states have necessarily moved ahead with health care reform. How this is done varies from state to state, but it is a national trend that managed care must be extended to the public sector, following the example and success that managed care has had in private industry. The three essential elements of managed care, whether public or private, are increased access to primary health care, greater cost savings, and improved quality of health care through case management and integration of health care services. The role of federal and state governments is to drive the change and to ensure that patients who need treatment can access it more easily, more effectively, and more efficiently.

For the substance abuse treatment field, the implementation of Medicaid managed care is bringing dramatic philosophical, programmatic, and fiscal changes. Providers, payors, and patients—the three principals in the managed care system—all need a sufficiently adequate transition period to adjust to these changes. Providers must become business entities acquiring marketing skills. Differences in treatment modalities must begin to disappear as comprehensive care systems are developed through networking. Networking must reach beyond substance abuse and alcoholism treatment to include mental health as well as primary care, thus achieving both horizontal and vertical integration. Patients must change their health care behavior in a Medicaid managed care world. Patients must know the role of the primary care giver and understand that care is coordinated and managed through this primary care giver. Patients must understand that by establishing an ongoing relationship with a primary care giver, disease and dysfunction will be identified more quickly and addressed more cost efficiently. In this new system the emphasis is on maintaining good health and preventing health problems instead of incurring costly inpatient hospitalizations. The payor must get to know this new population of "covered lives." Substance abusers have a biopsychosocial disorder which is often complex in nature and chronic in duration. The goals of substance abuse treatment are not to cure, for there is no known cure to this disorder, but rather the acquisition or restoration of a stable, socially acceptable functioning individual who contributes to society. This is different from other health care treatment goals and is often difficult for payors to accept or to understand.

Fiscal changes bring even greater challenges to the substance abuse treatment field than do philosophical or programmatic changes. The very survival of long-established community-based treatment programs is at stake. Providers must understand that their "customer" is just as much the payor as

it is the client. If the payor is dissatisfied, the programs' fiscal support is threatened because government has shifted liability to the payor. Government as "big brother" will no longer supply net deficit financing. Government will no longer be there to bail out the programs' uncontrolled expenditures. Programs will have to join together and consolidate to establish centralized intake, user friendly management information systems, uniform record keeping systems, and around-the-clock accessibility for patients. These comprehensive care continua must agree to uniform reimbursement rates and must prioritize individual client success and treatment evaluation.

The new system of Medicaid managed care creates a great need for education and training among primary health care providers as horizontal and vertical integration takes hold. Substance-abusing patients under coverage in a managed care company must be identified, assessed, and referred to treatment promptly. For this to occur, clinicians in primary health care settings must learn the "tools of the trade" of addiction treatment. Level of care determinations will determine the ultimate cost and success or failure of treatment. The role of government is to ensure that as the systems integrate, all participants are knowledgeable about the roles and functions of this new Medicaid managed care approach. Most important of all, substance-abusing patients must receive adequate and appropriate treatment, not only for their own good but for the good of society. Treatment is an investment that affects governments' costs in other health, social service, and criminal justice systems. To the degree that government is willing to invest in treatment the more efficient delivery of services in these other health, social service, and criminal justice systems will result.

CONCLUSION

As government commits to imposing managed care on the Medicaid population, including mental health and substance abuse treatment, there are a number of issues which must be addressed. Without attention to these major issues, managed care for substance abuse treatment is threatened. First and foremost is the commitment of government to all the elements of a managed care system, rather than to just the goal of saving money. No one will deny that government followed the lead of private industry by assuming managed care systems to control unbridled costs. However, as this need to save taxpayer money is fundamental, the other elements of managed care need equal commitment from government. If there is not a commitment to improving the quality of patient care through case management, and if the new system does not improve the patient's access to primary as well as specialty care, then government has failed and the condition of health care in the United States will be worse rather than better. This is the most important principle which needs to govern implementation of Medicaid managed care.

The second principle to be embraced as government implements this new system is to protect the taxpayers' investment in substance abuse treatment over the last three decades. The new must build on the old rather than destroy the old. Accessibility to substance abuse treatment will not improve if experienced treatment programs are allowed to die. The substance abuse treatment workforce, both professional and paraprofessional, has a wealth of treatment experience which must benefit and enhance what is being developed as a system for the future. Shame on any government that wastes the investment of taxpayers over the years in a substance abuse treatment system which research has already documented to be successful.

The third principle to shape the new system should be the understanding that substance abuse treatment has on other taxpayer-supported human services. The cost offsets that treatment offers to criminal justice, social service, health care, and foster care, must be acknowledged and understood as government moves ahead with implementation. Elected officials must guard against analyzing human service systems in isolation from one another. Enforcement is complemented by a prevention and treatment system. Incarceration is affected by including treatment as a component of rehabilitation. Foster care is affected by addressing the addiction needs of abusive parents. Many substance abusers are regular consumers of these other government supported human service systems. To try solutions, whether they be aimed at cost savings or public safety, without considering substance abuse treatment becomes an exercise in futility.

One final word: Medicaid managed care is here to stay. Changes are occurring rapidly and this will continue. If government or the new payors or the providers are only interested in their own goals, changes will not be for the better. The patients are the primary focus of treatment and must continue to remain so. Managed care for this population will be a challenge which government and provider should not shrink from. Only time will tell whether government efforts in this area will achieve success. As is often said when change is so drastic, "The jury is still out." But while the jury is still out, government must not forget that everyday in America substance abuse takes a heavy toll in terms of human misery and high costs (13). Substance abusers must have adequate treatment available today and tomorrow, and that is one change government should bring about as it contemplates and evaluates the implementation steps of a Medicaid managed care system.

References

1. CCH State Pulse, The State Health Systems Report, pp. 7.
2. Umbricht-Schneiter A, Ginn DH, Pabst KM, Bigelow GE. Providing medical care to methadone clinic patients: referral vs. on-site care. Am J Public Health 1994;84:207–210.
3. Special populations. CSAT Technical Assistance Publication Series 1994;11:78–79.
4. Treatment of hardcore cocaine users. GAO/HEHS Report 95–179R, July 1995:4–6.
5. Gerstein DR, et al. Evaluating recovery services: the California Drug and Alcohol Treatment Assessment. CalData, July 1994.
6. Botvin GJ, Schinke S, Orlandi MA. Drug abuse prevention with multiethnic youth. Thousand Oaks, CA: Sage Publications, 1995: 182–184.
7. Massaro J, Pepper B. The relationship of addiction to crime, health and other social problems. CSAT Technical Assistance Publication Series 1994;11:11–15.
8. Lipton DS. The effectiveness of treatments for drug abusers under criminal justice supervision. Washington, DC: National Institute of Justice, 1995:5–6.
9. 42 CFR(Code of Federal Regulations) Part 2.
10. Finigan M. Societal outcomes and cost savings of drug and alcohol treatment in the State of Oregon. Salem, OR: Office of Alcohol and Drug Abuse Programs, Oregon Department of Human Resources and Governor's Council on Alcohol and Drug Abuse Programs, February 1996: 26–27.
11. Califano JA Jr. Substance abuse and urban America: its impact on an American city. New York: Center on Addiction and Substance Abuse, Columbia University, 1996:82.
12. Pear R. 800,000 may lose coverage if mental benefits are added. New York Times 1996(May 14).
13. Horgan CM. Costs of untreated substance abuse to society. Center for Substance Abuse Treatment Communique 1995;Spring:4–5.

Index

Page numbers in *italics* denote figures; those followed by "t" denote tables